First Published, May 2020

ISBN: 9798649735629

Email: haythum@haythum.com

Twitter: @haythumkhalid

Website: www.quotationz.com

The Book of
Famous Quotes

Volume I: Ability - Justice

Collected & Edited

by

Haythum Khalid

For the readers of this book, may the quotations within inspire and motivate you as much as they inspired me to publish it.

For my wife Dina, and our beautiful daughters
Nadine, Mariam and Talia

ABILITY

1. I have learnt that I am me, that I can do the things that, as one might put it, me can do, but I cannot do the things that me would like to do.
Agatha Christie (1891-1976, British Mystery Writer)

2. No amount of ability is of the slightest avail without honor.
Andrew Carnegie (1835-1919, American Industrialist, Philanthropist)

3. I thought he was a young man of promise, but it appears he is a young man of promises. [Speaking Of Winston Churchill]
Arthur James Balfour (1848-1930, British Conservative Politician, Prime Minister)

4. Natural abilities can almost compensate for the want of every kind of cultivation, but no cultivation of the mind can make up for the want of natural abilities.
Arthur Schopenhauer (1788-1860, German Philosopher)

5. The world cares very little about what a man or woman knows; it is what a man or woman is able to do that counts.
Booker T. Washington (1856-1915, American Black Leader and Educator)

6. To sentence a man of true genius, to the drudgery of a school is to put a racehorse on a treadmill.
Charles Caleb Colton (1780-1832, British Sportsman Writer)

7. Whatever women do they must do twice as well as men to be thought half as good. Luckily, this is not difficult.
Charlotte Whitton

8. Ability is sexless.
Christabel Pankhurst

9. Others have done it before me. I can, too.
Corporal John Faunce (American soldier)

10. The fox has many tricks. The hedgehog has but one. But that is the best of all.
Desiderius Erasmus (1466-1536, Dutch Humanist)

11. There are some people who live in a dream world, and there are some who face reality; and then there are those who turn one into the other.
Douglas Everett (American Hockey Player)

12. The boy was as useless as rubber lips on a woodpecker.
Earl Pitts

13. The winds and waves are always on the side of the ablest navigators.
Edward Gibbon (1737-1794, British Historian)

14. It is a fine thing to have ability, but the ability to discover ability in others is the true test.
Elbert Hubbard (1859-1915, American Author, Publisher)

15. Natural abilities are like natural plants; they need pruning by study.
Francis Bacon (1561-1626, British Philosopher, Essayist, Statesman)

16. To know how to hide one's ability is great skill.
François de La Rochefoucauld (1613-1680, French classical writer)

17. The height of ability consists in a thorough knowledge of the real value of things, and of the genius of the age in which we live.
François de La Rochefoucauld (1613-1680, French classical writer)

18. Every person is responsible for all the good within the scope of his abilities, and for no more, and none can tell whose sphere is the largest.
Gail Hamilton (1833-1896, American Writer, Humorist)

19. Martyrdom is the only way a man can become famous without ability.
George Bernard Shaw (1856-1950, Irish-born British Dramatist)

20. Analyzing what you haven't got as well as what you have is a necessary ingredient of a career.
Grace Moore

21. I know of no more encouraging fact than the unquestionable ability of man to elevate his life by conscious endeavor.
Henry David Thoreau (1817-1862, American Essayist, Poet, Naturalist)

22. He is the best sailor who can steer within fewest points of the wind, and exact a motive power out of the greatest obstacles.
Henry David Thoreau (1817-1862, American Essayist, Poet, Naturalist)

23. It is all one to me if a man comes from Sing Sing Prison or Harvard. We hire a man, not his history.
Henry Ford (1863-1947, American Industrialist, Founder of Ford Motor Company)

24. The question "Who ought to be boss?" is like as "Who ought to be the tenor in the quartet?" Obviously, the man who can sing tenor.
Henry Ford (1863-1947, American Industrialist, Founder of Ford Motor Company)

25. Whether you think you can or whether you think you can't, you're right!
Henry Ford (1863-1947, American Industrialist, Founder of Ford Motor Company)

26. As we advance in life we learn the limits of our abilities.
James A. Froude (1818-1894, British Historian)

27. I know I have the ability to do so much more than just stand in front of the camera the rest of my life.
Jennie Garth (Born 1972, American Actress)

28. The person born with a talent they are meant to use will find their greatest happiness in using it.
Johann Wolfgang Von Goethe (1749-1832, German Poet, Dramatist, Novelist)

29 People are so constituted that everybody would rather undertake what they see others do, whether they have an aptitude for it or not.
Johann Wolfgang Von Goethe (1749-1832, German Poet, Dramatist, Novelist)

30 Our work is the presentation of our capabilities.
Johann Wolfgang Von Goethe (1749-1832, German Poet, Dramatist, Novelist)

31 The really unhappy person is the one who leaves undone what they can do, and starts doing what they don't understand; no wonder they come to grief.
Johann Wolfgang Von Goethe (1749-1832, German Poet, Dramatist, Novelist)

32 Never tell a young person that anything cannot be done. God may have been waiting centuries for someone ignorant enough of the impossible to do that very thing.
John Andrew Holmes

33 Executive ability is deciding quickly and getting somebody else to do the work.
John G. Pollard

34 Ability hits the mark where presumption overshoots and diffidence falls short.
John Henry Newman (1801-1890, British Religious Leader, Prelate, Writer)

35 No great intellectual thing was ever done by great effort.
John Ruskin (1819-1900, British Critic, Social Theorist)

36 The principle of all successful effort is to try to do not what is absolutely the best, but what is easily within our power, and suited for our temperament and condition.
John Ruskin (1819-1900, British Critic, Social Theorist)

37 When love and skill work together, expect a masterpiece.
John Ruskin (1819-1900, British Critic, Social Theorist)

38 Ability may get you to the top, but it takes character to keep you there.
John Wooden (1910-, American Basketball Coach)

39 The extent of your consciousness is limited only by your ability to love and to embrace with your love the space around you, and all it contains
Ken Carey

40 It's pretty hard to be efficient without being obnoxious.
Kin Hubbard (1868-1930, American Humorist, Journalist)

41 Man cannot live by incompetence alone.
Laurence J. Peter

42 Knowing what you can not do is more important than knowing what you can do. In fact, that's good taste.
Lucille Ball (1911-1989, American Actress, Producer)

43 Ability is a poor man's wealth.
M. Wren

44 Ability will never catch up with the demand for it.
Malcolm S. Forbes (1919-1990, American Publisher, Businessman)

45 Ability without honor is useless.
Marcus T. Cicero (106-43 BC, Great Roman Orator, Politician)

46 I add this, that rational ability without education has more often raised a man to glory and virtue, than education without natural ability.
Marcus T. Cicero (106-43 BC, Great Roman Orator, Politician)

47 Certainly we're not satisfied with just winning games. We've been playing some pretty good hockey, but we think we can play much better.
Mario Lemieux (American Hockey Player)

48 Wicked people are always surprised to find ability in those that are good.
Marquis De Vauvenargues (1715-1747, French Moralist)

49 Ability is of little account without opportunity.
Napoleon Bonaparte (1769-1821, French General, Emperor)

50 Life has been compared to a race, but the allusion improves by observing, that the most swift are usually the least manageable and the most likely to stray from the course. Great abilities have always been less serviceable to the possessors than moderate ones.
Oliver Goldsmith (1728-1774, Anglo-Irish Author, Poet, Playwright)

51 As life is action and passion, it is required of a man that he should share the passion and action of his time, at the peril of being not to have lived.
Oliver Wendell Holmes (1809-1894, American Author, Wit, Poet)

52 The Creator has not given you a longing to do that which you have no ability to do.
Orison Swett Marden (1850-1924, American Author, Founder of Success Magazine)

53 When it is a question of God's almighty Spirit, never say, "I can't."
Oswald Chambers (1874-1917 Scottish Preacher, Author)

54 Big jobs usually go to the men who prove their ability to outgrow small ones.
Ralph Waldo Emerson (1803-1882, American Poet, Essayist)

55 People with great gifts are easy to find, but symmetrical and balanced ones never.
Ralph Waldo Emerson (1803-1882, American Poet, Essayist)

56 Just do what you do best.
Red Auerbach (1917-, American Basketball Coach)

57 There is something that is much more scarce, something rarer than ability. It is the ability to recognize ability.
Robert Half (American Businessman, Founder of Robert Half & Associates)

58 Aptitude found in the understanding and is often inherited. Genius coming from reason and imagination, rarely.
Samuel Taylor Coleridge (1772-1834, British Poet, Critic, Philosopher)

59 The abilities of man must fall short on one side or the other, like too scanty a blanket when you are abed. If you pull it upon your shoulders, your feet are left bare; if you thrust it down to your feet, your shoulders are uncovered.
Sir William Temple (1628-1699, British Diplomat, Essayist)

60 We all have ability. The difference is how we use it.
Stevie Wonder (1950-, American Musician, Singer, Songwriter, Producer)

61 The first requisite for success is the ability to apply your physical and mental energies to one problem incessantly without growing weary.
Thomas A. Edison (1847-1931, American Inventor, Entrepreneur, Founder of GE)

62 The king is the man who can.
Thomas Carlyle (1795-1881, Scottish Philosopher, Author)

63 What you see, but can't see over is as good as infinite.
Thomas Carlyle (1795-1881, Scottish Philosopher, Author)

64 A genius can't be forced; nor can you make an ape an alderman.
Thomas Somerville

65 Not many men have both good fortune and good sense.
Titus Livy (59 BC-17 AD, Roman Historian)

66 They are able because they think they are able.
Virgil (70-19 BC, Roman Poet)

67 When my horse is running good, I don't stop to give him sugar.
William Faulkner (1897-1962, American Novelist)

68 You are the only person on earth who can use your ability.
Zig Ziglar (American Sales Trainer, Author, Motivational Speaker)

ABORTION

1 The one regret I have about my own abortions is that they cost money that might otherwise have been spent on something more pleasurable, like taking the kids to movies and theme parks.
Barbara Ehrenreich (1941-, American Author, Columnist)

2 The cemetery of the victims of human cruelty in our century is extended to include yet another vast cemetery, that of the unborn.
John Paul II (1920, Polish-Born Italian Pope)

3 Dread not infanticide; the crime is imaginary: we are always mistress of what we carry in our womb, and we do no more harm in destroying this kind of matter than in evacuating another, by medicines, when we feel the need.
Marquis De Sade (1740-1814, French Author)

4 The greatest destroyer of peace is abortion because if a mother can kill her own child, what is left for me to kill you and you to kill me? There is nothing between.
Mother Teresa (1910-1997, Albanian-born Roman Catholic Missionary)

5 The emphasis must be not on the right to abortion but on the right to privacy and reproductive control.
Ruth Bader Ginsberg

6 The preservation of life seems to be rather a slogan than a genuine goal of the anti-abortion forces; what they want is control. Control over behavior: power over women. Women in the anti- choice movement want to share in male power over women, and do so by denying their own womanhood, their own rights and responsibilities.
Ursula K. Le Guin (1929-, American Author)

ABSENCE

1 Let me tell you I am better acquainted with you for a long absence, as men are with themselves for a long affliction: absence does but hold off a friend, to make one see him the truer.
Alexander Pope (1688-1744, British Poet, Critic, Translator)

2 Woman absent is woman dead.
Ambrose Bierce (1842-1914, American Author, Editor, Journalist, "The Devil's Dictionary")

3 The absent are never without fault. Nor the present without excuse.
Benjamin Franklin (1706-1790, American Scientist, Publisher, Diplomat)

4 I was court-martial in my absence, and sentenced to death in my absence, so I said they could shoot me in my absence.
Brendan F. Behan (1923-1964, Irish Writer)

5 Our hours in love have wings; in absence, crutches.
Colley Cibber (1671-1757, British Actor-Manager, Playwright)

6 Where you used to be, there is a hole in the world, which I find myself constantly walking around in the daytime, and falling in at night. I miss you like hell.
Edna St. Vincent Millay (1892-1950, American Poet)

7 Absence does not make the heart grow fonder, but it sure heats up the blood.
Elizabeth Ashley (American Actress)

8 The heart may think it knows better: the senses know that absence blots people out. We really have no absent friends. The friend becomes a traitor by breaking, however unwillingly or sadly, out of our own zone: a hard judgment is passed on him, for all the pleas of the heart.
Elizabeth Bowen (1899-1973, Anglo-Irish Novelist)

9 Absence blots people out. We really have no absent friends.
Elizabeth Bowen (1899-1973, Anglo-Irish Novelist)

10 Absence diminishes little passions and increases great ones, as wind extinguishes candles and fans a fire.
François de La Rochefoucauld (1613-1680, French classical writer)

11 Failing to be there when a man wants her is a woman's greatest sin, except to be there when he doesn't want her.
Helen Rowland (1875-1950, American Journalist)

12 Achilles absent was Achilles still!
Homer (850 BC, Greek Epic Poet)

13 No man is so perfect, so necessary to his friends, as to give them no cause to miss him less.
Jean De La Bruyere (1645-1696, French Writer)

14 The people who are absent are the ideal; those who are present seem to be quite commonplace.
Johann Wolfgang Von Goethe (1749-1832, German Poet, Dramatist, Novelist)

15 No more we meet in yonder bowers Absence has made me prone to roving; But older, firmer hearts than ours, Have found monotony in loving.
Lord Byron (1788-1824, British Poet)

16 Absence of proof is not proof of absence.
Michael Crichton (1942-, American Writer, Novelist, Screenwriter, Director, Producer)

17 Absence -- that common cure of love.
Miguel De Cervantes (1547-1616, Spanish Novelist, Dramatist, Poet)

18 The longest absence is less perilous to love than the terrible trials of incessant proximity.
Ouida (1838-1908, British Writer)

19 A short absence is the safest.
Ovid (43 BC-18 AD, Roman Poet)

20 Never find fault with the absent.
Proverb

21 Absence and a friendly neighbor washes away love.
Proverb

22 Greater things are believed of those who are absent.
Publius Cornelius Tacitus (55-117 AD, Roman Historian)

23 When delicate and feeling souls are separated, there is not a feature in the sky, not a movement of the elements, not an aspiration of the breeze, but hints some cause for a lover's apprehension.
Richard Brinsley Sheridan (1751-1816, Anglo-Irish Dramatist)

24 It takes time for the absent to assume their true shape in our thoughts. After death they take on a firmer outline and then cease to change.
Sidonie Gabrielle Colette (1873-1954, French Author)

25 Talk well of the absent whenever you have the opportunity.
Sir Matthew Hale (1609-1676, British Judge)

26 Absence sharpens love, presence strengthens it.
Thomas Fuller (1608-1661, British Clergyman, Author)

27 Absence makes the heart grow fonder.
Thomas Haynes Bayly (1791-1839, British Writer, Poet)

28 When a man is out of sight, it is not too long before he is out of mind.
Thomas p Kempis (1379-1471, German Monk, Mystic, Religious Writer)

29 Separated lovers cheat absence by a thousand fancies which have their own reality. They are prevented from seeing one another and they cannot write; nevertheless they find countless mysterious ways of corresponding, by sending each other the song of birds, the scent of flowers, the laughter of children, the light of the sun, the sighing of the wind, and the gleam of the stars --all the beauties of creation.
Victor Hugo (1802-1885, French Poet, Dramatist, Novelist)

30 Separation penetrates the disappearing person like a pigment and steeps him in gentle radiance.
Walter Benjamin (1982-1940, German Critic, Philosopher)

31 Absence and death are the same -- only that in death there is no suffering.
Walter Savage Landor (1775-1864, British Poet, Essayist)

32 Absence from whom we love is worse than death, and frustrates hope severer than despair.
William Cowper (1731-1800, British Poet)

33 Parting is such sweet sorrow.
William Shakespeare (1564-1616, British Poet, Playwright, Actor)

34 How like a winter hath my absence been. From thee, the pleasure of the fleeting year! What freezings have I felt, what dark days seen, What old December's bareness everywhere!
William Shakespeare (1564-1616, British Poet, Playwright, Actor)

ABSTINENCE

1 Abstainer. A weak man who yields to the temptation of denying himself a pleasure.
Ambrose Bierce (1842-1914, American Author, Editor, Journalist, "The Devil's Dictionary")

2 With renunciation life begins.
Amelia E. Barr (1831-1919, Anglo-American Novelist)

3 Subdue your appetites, my dears, and you've conquered human nature .
Charles Dickens (1812-1870, British Novelist)

4 The best thing to do with the best things in life is to give them up.
Dorothy Day (1897-1980, American Religious Leader)

5 All philosophy lies in two words, sustain and abstain.
Epictetus (50-120, Stoic Philosopher)

6 Renunciation remains sorrow, though a sorrow borne willingly.
George Eliot (1819-1880, British Novelist)

7 Abstaining is favorable both to the head and the pocket.
Horace Greeley (1811-1872, American Newspaper Editor)

8 Renouncement: the heroism of mediocrity.
Natalie Clifford Barney (1876-1972, American-born French Author)

9 Self-denial is the shining sore on the leprous body of Christianity.
Oscar Wilde (1856-1900, British Author, Wit)

10 The only way for a rich man to be healthy is by exercise and abstinence, to live as if he were poor.
Sir William Temple (1628-1699, British Diplomat, Essayist)

11 Complete abstinence is easier than perfect moderation.
St. Augustine (354-430, Numidian-born Bishop of Hippo, Theologian)

12 Once, during Prohibition, I was forced to live for days on nothing but food and water.
W. C. Fields (1879-1946, American Actor)

13 Always rise from the table with an appetite, and you will never sit down without one.
William Penn (1644-1718, British Religious Leader, Founder of Pennsylvania)

ABSURDITY

1 People who cannot recognize a palpable absurdity are very much in the way of civilization.
Agnes Repplier (1858-1950, American Author, Social Critic)

2 At any street corner the feeling of absurdity can strike any man in the face.
Albert Camus (1913-1960, French Existential Writer)

3 Absurdity. A statement or belief manifestly inconsistent with one's own opinion.
Ambrose Bierce (1842-1914, American Author, Editor, Journalist, "The Devil's Dictionary")

4 It is not in the world of ideas that life is lived. Life is lived for better or worse in life, and to a man in life, his life can be no more absurd than it can be the opposite of absurd, whatever that opposite may be.
Archibald Macleish (1892-1982, American Poet)

5 In the sphere of thought, absurdity and perversity remain the masters of the world, and their dominion is suspended only for brief periods.
Arthur Schopenhauer (1788-1860, German Philosopher)

6 The irrationality of a thing is no argument against its existence, rather a condition of it.
Friedrich Nietzsche (1844-1900, German Philosopher)

7 In the consciousness of the truth he has perceived, man now sees everywhere only the awfulness or the absurdity of existence and loathing seizes him.
Friedrich Nietzsche (1844-1900, German Philosopher)

8 It is not funny that anything else should fall down; only that a man should fall down. Why do we laugh? Because it is a gravely religious matter: it is the Fall of Man. Only man can be absurd: for only man can be dignified.
Gilbert K. Chesterton (1874-1936, British Author)

9 My turn of mind is so given to taking things in the absurd point of view, that it breaks out in spite of me every now and then.
Lord Byron (1788-1824, British Poet)

10 The privilege of absurdity; to which no living creature is subject, but man only.
Thomas Hobbes (1588-1679, British Philosopher)

11 Modern man must descend the spiral of his own absurdity to the lowest point; only then can he look beyond it. It is obviously impossible to get around it, jump over it, or simply avoid it.
Vaclav Havel (1936-, Czech Playwright, President)

ABUNDANCE

1 A man's life consisteth not in the abundance of the things which he possesseth. [Luke 12:15]
Bible (Sacred Scriptures of Christians and Judaism)

2 The universe is full of magical things patiently waiting for our wits to grow sharper.
Eden Phillpotts (1862-1960, Indian-born British Novelist)

3 Nothing is enough for the man to whom enough is to little.
Epicurus (341-270 BC, Greek Philosopher)

4 He who is plenteously provided for from within, needs but little from without.
Johann Wolfgang Von Goethe (1749-1832, German Poet, Dramatist, Novelist)

5 Not what we have But what we enjoy, constitutes our abundance.
John Petit-Senn (1792-1870, French Poet)

6 In my hut this spring, there is nothing -- there is everything!
Sodo

7 You can never get enough of what you don't want.
Wayne Dyer (1940-, American Psychotherapist, Author, Lecturer)

8 Abundance is not something we acquire. It is something we tune into.
Wayne Dyer (1940-, American Psychotherapist, Author, Lecturer)

9 Everything you need you already have. You are complete right now, you are a whole, total person, not an apprentice person on the way to someplace else. Your completeness must be understood by you and experienced in your thoughts as your own personal reality.
Wayne Dyer (1940-, American Psychotherapist, Author, Lecturer)

ABUSE

1   The only cure for contempt is counter-contempt.
    H. L. Mencken (1880-1956, American Editor, Author, Critic, Humorist)

2   People who treat other people as less than human must not be surprised when the bread they have cast on the waters comes floating back to them, poisoned.
    James Baldwin (1924-1987, American Author)

3   A fly may sting a stately horse and make him wince; but one is but an insect, and the other is a horse still.
    Samuel Johnson (1709-1784, British Author)

ACADEMIA

1   In universities and intellectual circles, academics can guarantee themselves popularity -- or, which is just as satisfying, unpopularity -- by being opinionated rather than by being learned.
    A. N. Wilson (Born 1950, English writer and newspaper columnist)

2   A serious problem in America is the gap between academe and the mass media, which is our culture. Professors of humanities, with all their leftist fantasies, have little direct knowledge of American life and no impact whatever on public policy.
    Camille Paglia (1947-, American Author, Critic, Educator)

3   I realized early on that the academy and the literary world alike -- and I don't think there really is a distinction between the two -- are always dominated by fools, knaves, charlatans and bureaucrats. And that being the case, any human being, male or female, of whatever status, who has a voice of her or his own, is not going to be liked.
    Harold Bloom (British Professor, Author)

4   If poetry is like an orgasm, an academic can be likened to someone who studies the passion- stains on the bedsheets.
    Irving Layton (1912-, Canadian Poet)

5   Art is not to be taught in Academies. It is what one looks at, not what one listens to, that makes the artist. The real schools should be the streets.
    Oscar Wilde (1856-1900, British Author, Wit)

6   There is but one step from the Academy to the Fad.
    Samuel Butler (1612-1680, British Poet, Satirist)

ACCEPTANCE

1   One must not attempt to justify them, but rather to sense their nature simply and clearly.
    Albert Einstein (1879-1955, German-born American Physicist)

2   Once we accept our limits, we go beyond them.
    Brendan Francis

3   Accept everything about yourself -- I mean everything, You are you and that is the beginning and the end -- no apologies, no regrets.
    Clark Moustakas (Humanistic Psychologist)

4   Happiness can exist only in acceptance.
    Denis De Rougamont

5   For the ordinary man is passive. Within a narrow circle (home life, and perhaps the trade unions or local politics) he feels himself master of his fate, but against major events he is as helpless as against the elements. So far from endeavoring to influence the future, he simply lies down and lets things happen to him.
    George Orwell (1903-1950, British Author, "Animal Farm")

6   Life has no other discipline to impose, if we would but realize it, than to accept life unquestioningly. Everything we shut our eyes to, everything we run away from, everything we deny, denigrate or despise, serves to defeat us in the end. What seems nasty, painful, evil, can become a source of beauty, joy and strength, if faced with an open mind. Every moment is a golden one for him who has the vision to recognize it as such.
    Henry Miller (1891-1980, American Author)

7   We must accept life for what it actually is -- a challenge to our quality without which we should never know of what stuff we are made, or grow to our full stature.
    Ida R. Wylie

8   We will have to repent in this generation not merely for the hateful words and actions of the bad people but for the appalling silence of the good people.
    Martin Luther King Jr. (1929-1968, American Black Leader, Nobel Prize Winner, 1964)

9   The minute you settle for less than you deserve, you get even less than you settled for.
    Maureen Dowd (American Newspaper Columnist)

10 The strongest and most effective force in guaranteeing the long-term maintenance of power is not violence in all the forms deployed by the dominant to control the dominated, but consent in all the forms in which the dominated acquiesce in their own domination.
    Maurice Godelier (1934-, French Anthropologist)

11 Accept the place the divine providence has found for you, the society of your contemporaries, the connection of events.
    Ralph Waldo Emerson (1803-1882, American Poet, Essayist)

12 Always fall in with what you're asked to accept. Take what is given, and make it over your way. My aim in life has always been to hold my own with whatever's going. Not against: with.
    Robert Frost (1875-1963, American Poet)

13 Ah, when to the heart of man was it ever less than a treason to go with the drift of things to yield with a grace to reason and bow and accept at the end of a love or a season.
    Robert Frost (1875-1963, American Poet)

14 Some people swallow the universe like a pill; they travel on through the world, like smiling images pushed from behind.
Robert Louis Stevenson (1850-1895, Scottish Essayist, Poet, Novelist)

15 The art of acceptance is the art of making someone who has just done you a small favor wish that he might have done you a greater one.
Russell Lynes (1910-, American Editor, Critic)

16 To make oneself an object, to make oneself passive, is a very different thing from being a passive object.
Simone De Beauvoir (1908-1986, French Novelist, Essayist)

ACCIDENTS

1 I don't believe in accidents. There are only encounters in history. There are no accidents.
Elie Wiesel (1928-, Rumanian-born American Writer)

2 A car crash harnesses elements of eroticism, aggression, desire, speed, drama, kinesthetic factors, the stylizing of motion, consumer goods, status -- all these in one event. I myself see the car crash as a tremendous sexual event really: a liberation of human and machine libido (if there is such a thing).
J. G. Ballard (1930-, British Author)

3 Accidents, try to change them -- it's impossible. The accidental reveals man.
Pablo Picasso (1881-1973, Spanish Artist)

ACCURACY

1 Accuracy is to a newspaper what virtue is to a lady, but a newspaper can always print a retraction.
Adlai E. Stevenson (1900-1965, American Lawyer, Politician)

2 Accuracy is the twin brother of honesty; inaccuracy, of dishonesty.
Charles Simmons

3 From principles is derived probability, but truth or certainty is obtained only from facts.
Nathaniel Hawthorne (1804-1864, American Novelist, Short Story Writer)

4 Accuracy of statement is one of the first elements of truth; inaccuracy is a near kin to falsehood.
Tryon Edwards (1809-1894, American Theologian)

5 Facts are God's arguments; we should be careful never to misunderstand or pervert them.
Tryon Edwards (1809-1894, American Theologian)

ACHIEVEMENT

1 If life were measured by accomplishments, most of us would die in infancy.
A. P. Gouthey

2 One of the secrets of getting more done is to make a TO DO List every day, keep it visible, and use it as a guide to action as you go through the day.
Alan Lakein (American Time Management Expert, Author, Trainer)

3 The greatest things are accomplished by individual people, not by committees or companies.
Alfred A. Montapert (American Author)

4 There is a woman at the beginning of all great things.
Alphonse De Lamartine (1790-1869, French Poet, Statesman, Historian)

5 The truth of the matter is that there's nothing you can't accomplish if: (1) You clearly decide what it is that you're absolutely committed to achieving, (2) You're willing to take massive action, (3) You notice what's working or not, and (4) You continue to change your approach until you achieve what you want, using whatever life gives you along the way.
Anthony Robbins (1960-, American Author, Speaker, Peak Performance Expert / Consultant)

6 For what is the best choice, for each individual is the highest it is possible for him to achieve.
Aristotle (384-322 BC, Greek Philosopher)

7 I was the kind nobody thought could make it. I had a funny Boston accent. I couldn't pronounce my R's. I wasn't a beauty.
Barbara Walters (1931-, American TV Personality)

8 The way to get things done is not to mind who gets the credit for doing them.
Benjamin Jowett (1817-1893, British Scholar)

9 Disciplining yourself to do what you know is right and important, although difficult, is the highroad to pride, self-esteem, and personal satisfaction.
Brian Tracy (American Trainer, Speaker, Author, Businessman)

10 I hope that my achievements in life shall be these -- that I will have fought for what was right and fair, that I will have risked for that which mattered, and that I will have given help to those who were in need that I will have left the earth a better place for what I've done and who I've been.
C. Hoppe

11 The achievements which society rewards are won at the cost of diminution of personality
Carl Jung (1875-1961, Swiss Psychiatrist)

12 Failures are finger posts on the road to achievement.
Charles F. Kettering (1876-1958, American Engineer, Inventor)

13 Said will be a little ahead, but done should follow at his heel.
Charles Haddon Spurgeon (1834-1892, British Baptist Preacher)

14 Great things are not accomplished by those who yield to trends and fads and popular opinion.
Charles Kuralt (American TV Commentator)

15 The journey is the reward.
Chinese Proverb

16 Do not be desirous of having things done quickly. Do not look at small advantages. Desire to have things done quickly prevents their being done thoroughly. Looking at small advantages prevents great affairs from being accomplished.
Confucius (551-479 BC, Chinese Ethical Teacher, Philosopher)

17 Nothing is as difficult as to achieve results in this world if one is filled full of great tolerance and the milk of human kindness. The person who achieves must generally be a one-idea individual, concentrated entirely on that one idea, and ruthless in his aspect toward other men and other ideas.
Corinne Roosevelt Robinson (1861-1933, American Poet, Sister of Theodore Roosevelt)

18 We live in deeds, not years: In thoughts not breaths; In feelings, not in figures on a dial. We should count time by heart throbs. He most lives Who thinks most, feels the noblest, acts the best.
David Bailey (1938-, British Photographer)

19 To get what you want, STOP doing what isn't working.
Dennis Weaver

20 I feel that the greatest reward for doing is the opportunity to do more.
Dr. Jonas Salk (1914-1995, Virologist, Discovered The First Vaccine Against Poliomyelitis)

21 The world is divided into people who do things and people who get the credit.
Dwight Whitney Morrow (1873-1931, American Lawyer, Banker, diplomat)

22 The sports page records people's accomplishments, the front page usually records nothing, but man's failures.
Earl Warren (1891-1974, American Politician, Judge)

23 The will to win, the desire to succeed, the urge to reach your full potential... these are the keys that will unlock the door to personal excellence.
Eddie Robinson (College Football Coach)

24 God will not look you over for medal, degrees or diplomas, but for scars.
Elbert Hubbard (1859-1915, American Author, Publisher)

25 It's not the having, it's the getting.
Elizabeth Taylor (1932-, British-born American Actress)

26 The greater the difficulty the more glory in surmounting it. Skillful pilots gain their reputation from storms and tempests.
Epictetus (50-120, Stoic Philosopher)

27 Our achievements speak for themselves. What we have to keep track of are our failures, discouragements and doubts. We tend to forget the past difficulties, the many false starts, and the painful groping. We see our past achievements as the end results of
Eric Hoffer (1902-1983, American Author, Philosopher)

28 One must marry one's feelings to one's beliefs and ideas. That is probably the only way to achieve a measure of harmony in one's life.
Etty Hilsum

29 Trust yourself. Create the kind of self that you will be happy to live with all your life. Make the most of yourself by fanning the tiny, inner sparks of possibility into flames of achievement.
Foster C. Mcclellan

30 Mere longevity is a good thing for those who watch Life from the side lines. For those who play the game, an hour may be a year, a single day's work an achievement for eternity.
Gabriel Heatter (1890-, American Journalist)

31 Man can acquire accomplishments or he can become an animal, whichever he wants. God makes the animals, man makes himself.
Georg C. Lichtenberg (1742-1799, German Physicist, Satirist)

32 Man can climb to the highest summits, but he cannot dwell there long.
George Bernard Shaw (1856-1950, Irish-born British Dramatist)

33 No great deed is done by falterers who ask for certainty.
George Eliot (1819-1880, British Novelist)

34 Death comes to all But great achievements build a monument which shall endure until the sun grows cold.
George Fabricius (1678-1707, Irish Dramatist)

35 Whoever is winning at the moment will always seem to be invincible.
George Orwell (1903-1950, British Author, "Animal Farm")

36 Where I was born and where and how I have lived is unimportant. It is what I have done with where I have been that should be of interest.
Georgia O'Keeffe (American painter)

37 Man is always more than he can know of himself; consequently, his accomplishments, time and again, will come as a surprise to him.
Golo Mann (1909-, German Historian, Son of Thomas Mann)

38 We will either find a way, or make one.
Hannibal (247-182 BC, Carthaginian General, Statesman)

39 There is nothing that war has ever achieved that we could not better achieve without it.
Havelock Ellis (1859-1939, British Psychologist)

40 My mother drew a distinction between achievement and success. She said that achievement is the knowledge that you have studied and worked hard and done the best that is in you. Success is being praised by others. That is nice but not as important or satisfying. Always aim for achievement and forget about success.
Helen Hayes (1900-1993, American Actress)

41 The man who is dissatisfied with himself, what can he do?
Henry David Thoreau (1817-1862, American Essayist, Poet, Naturalist)

42 Let us, then, be up and doing, with a heart for any fate; still achieving, still pursuing, learn to labor and to wait.
Henry Wadsworth Longfellow (1819-1892, American Poet)

43 High achievement always takes place in the framework of high expectation.
Jack Kinder

44 We always take credit for the good and attribute the bad to fortune.
Jean De La Fontaine (1621-1695, French Poet)

45 The average estimate themselves by what they do, the above average by what they are.
Johann Friedrich Von Schiller (1759-1805, German Dramatist, Poet, Historian)

46 Not the maker of plans and promises, but rather the one who offers faithful service in small matters. This is the person who is most likely to achieve what is good and lasting.
Johann Wolfgang Von Goethe (1749-1832, German Poet, Dramatist, Novelist)

47 For a man to achieve all that is demanded of him he must regard himself as greater than he is.
Johann Wolfgang Von Goethe (1749-1832, German Poet, Dramatist, Novelist)

48 For we must consider that we shall be a city upon a hill. The eyes of all people are upon us, so that if we shall deal falsely with our God in this work we have undertaken, and so cause Him to withdraw His present help from us, we shall be made a story and a byword through the world.
John Winthrop (1588-1649, Puritan, First Governor of Massachusetts)

49 Never mistake activity for achievement.
John Wooden (1910-, American Basketball Coach)

50 Don't mistake activity for achievement.
John Wooden (1910-, American Basketball Coach)

51 Out of the strain of doing and into the peace of the done.
Julia Woodruff

52 The whole point of getting things done is knowing what to leave undone.
Lady Stella Reading

53 So much to do, so little done, such things to be.
Lord Alfred Tennyson (1809-1892, British Poet)

54 You get whatever accomplishment you are willing to declare.
Mal Pancoast

55 Look at a day when you are supremely satisfied at the end. It's not a day when you lounge around doing nothing; it's when you've had everything to do, and you've done it.
Margaret Thatcher (1925-, British Stateswoman, Prime Minister (1979-90))

56 Dedicate yourself to the good you deserve and desire for yourself. Give yourself peace of mind. You deserve to be happy. You deserve delight.
Mark Victor Hansen (American Motivational Speaker, Author)

57 It is easy to hate and it is difficult to love. This is how the whole scheme of things works. All good things are difficult to achieve; and bad things are very easy to get.
Morarji Desai (1896-18, Indian Statesman, Prime Minister)

58 The best job goes to the person who can get it done without passing the buck or coming back with excuses.
Napoleon Hill (1883-1970, American Speaker, Motivational Writer, "Think and Grow Rich")

59 Empty pockets never held anyone back. Only empty heads and empty hearts can do that.
Norman Vincent Peale (1898-1993, American Christian Reformed Pastor, Speaker, Author)

60 A man may fulfill the object of his existence by asking a question he cannot answer, and attempting a task he cannot achieve.
Oliver Wendell Holmes (1809-1894, American Author, Wit, Poet)

61 The mode in which the inevitable comes to pass is through effort.
Oliver Wendell Holmes (1809-1894, American Author, Wit, Poet)

62 Success is not measured by what you accomplish, but by the opposition you have encountered, and the courage with which you have maintained the struggle against overwhelming odds.
Orison Swett Marden (1850-1924, American Author, Founder of Success Magazine)

63 In Switzerland they had brotherly love, five hundred years of democracy and peace, and what did they produce? The cuckoo clock!
Orson Welles (1915-1985, American Film Maker)

64 What we achieve inwardly will change outer reality.
Otto Rank (1884-1939, Vienna-born Psychoanalyst)

65 I attempt an arduous task; but there is no worth in that which is not a difficult achievement.
Ovid (43 BC-18 AD, Roman Poet)

66 I am always doing things I can't do, that's how I get to do them.
Pablo Picasso (1881-1973, Spanish Artist)

67 You will soon break the bow if you keep it always stretched.
Phaedrus (Macedonian Inventor and Writer)

68 The measure of a man is the way he bears up under misfortune.
Plutarch (46-120 AD, Greek Essayist, Biographer)

69 To be yourself in a world that is constantly trying to make you something else is the greatest accomplishment.
Ralph Waldo Emerson (1803-1882, American Poet, Essayist)

70 Finish each day and be done with it. You have done what you could. Some blunders and absurdities no doubt crept in; forget them as soon as you can. Tomorrow is a new day; begin it well and serenely and with too high a spirit to be encumbered with your old nonsense.
Ralph Waldo Emerson (1803-1882, American Poet, Essayist)

71 Every great achievement is the victory of a flaming heart.
Ralph Waldo Emerson (1803-1882, American Poet, Essayist)

72 The only way around is through.
Robert Frost (1875-1963, American Poet)

73 Nothing will ever be attempted if all possible objections must first be overcome.
Samuel Johnson (1709-1784, British Author)

74 Life affords no higher pleasure than that of surmounting difficulties, passing from one step of success to another, forming new wishes and seeing them gratified.
Samuel Johnson (1709-1784, British Author)

75 Where there is a will there is a way." is an old true saying. He who resolves upon doing a thing, by that very resolution often scales the barriers to it, and secures its achievement. To think we are able, is almost to be so -- to determine upon attainment is frequently attainment itself.
Samuel Smiles (1812-1904, Scottish Author)

76 When science, art, literature, and philosophy are simply the manifestation of personality they are on a level where glorious and dazzling achievements are possible, which can make a man's name live for thousands of years. But above this level, far above,
Simone Weil (1910-1943, French Philosopher, Mystic)

77 Every man who is high up loves to think that he has done it all himself; and the wife smiles, and lets it go at that.
Sir James M. Barrie (1860-1937, British Playwright)

78 I want to put a ding in the universe.
Steve Jobs (1955-, American Businessman, Founder of Apple Computers)

79 Having once decided to achieve a certain task, achieve it at all costs of tedium and distaste. The gain in self confidence of having accomplished a tiresome labor is immense.
Thomas A. Bennett

80 Great things are not done by impulse, but by a series of small things brought together.
Vincent Van Gogh (1853-1890, Dutch-born French Painter)

81 Somehow I can't believe that there are any heights that can't be scaled by a man who knows the secrets of making dreams come true. This special secret, it seems to me, can be summarized in four C s. They are curiosity, confidence, courage, and constancy, and the greatest of all is confidence. When you believe in a thing, believe in it all the way, implicitly and unquestionable.
Walt Disney (1901-1966, American Artist, Film Producer)

82 To spend life for something which outlasts it.
William James (1842-1910, American Psychologist, Professor, Author)

83 It's no use saying, "We are doing our best." You have got to succeed in doing what is necessary.
Winston Churchill (1874-1965, British Statesman, Prime Minister)

84 My most brilliant achievement was my ability to be able to persuade my wife to marry me.
Winston Churchill (1874-1965, British Statesman, Prime Minister)

85 It's your aptitude, not just your attitude that determines your ultimate altitude.
Zig Ziglar (American Sales Trainer, Author, Motivational Speaker)

ACQUAINTANCE

1 An acquaintance is someone we know well enough to borrow from, but not well enough to lend to.
Ambrose Bierce (1842-1914, American Author, Editor, Journalist, "The Devil's Dictionary")

2 Acquaintance. A person whom we know well enough to borrow from, but not well enough to lend to.
Ambrose Bierce (1842-1914, American Author, Editor, Journalist, "The Devil's Dictionary")

3 Acquaintance: a degree of friendship called slight when its object is poor or obscure, and intimate when he is rich or famous.
Ambrose Bierce (1842-1914, American Author, Editor, Journalist, "The Devil's Dictionary")

4 I believe we shall come to care about people less and less. The more people one knows the easier it becomes to replace them. It's one of the curses of London.
Edward M. Forster (1879-1970, British Novelist, Essayist)

5 The beginning of an acquaintance whether with persons or things is to get a definite outline of our ignorance.
George Eliot (1819-1880, British Novelist)

6 We need two kinds of acquaintances, one to complain to, while to the others we boast.
Logan Pearsall Smith (1865-1946, Anglo-American Essayist, Aphorist)

7 The mere process of growing old together will make the slightest acquaintance seem a bosom friend.
Logan Pearsall Smith (1865-1946, Anglo-American Essayist, Aphorist)

ACTING AND ACTORS

1 The actor becomes an emotional athlete. The process is painful -- my personal life suffers.
Al Pacino (1940-, American Actor, Director)

2 Abused as we abuse it at present, dramatic art is in no sense cathartic; it is merely a form of emotional masturbation. It is the rarest thing to find a player who has not had his character affected for the worse by the practice of his profession. Nobody can make a habit of self-exhibition, nobody can exploit his personality for the sake of exercising a kind of hypnotic power over others, and remain untouched by the process.
Aldous Huxley (1894-1963, British Author)

3 I don't get acting jobs because of my looks.
Alec Baldwin (1958-, American Actor)

4 Actors are one family over the entire world.
Alfre Woodard (1953-, American Actress)

5 I never said all actors are cattle, what I said was all actors should be treated like cattle.
Alfred Hitchcock (1899-1980, Anglo-American Filmmaker)

6 An agent is a person who is sore because an actor gets 90% of what they make.
Alva Johnson

7 I just stopped playing bitches on wheels and peoples' mothers. I have only a few more years to kick up my heels!
Angela Lansbury (1925-, British-born American Actress)

8 In Europe an actor is an artist. In Hollywood, if he isn't working, he's a bum.
Anthony Quinn (American Actor)

9 When an actor has money, he doesn't send letters, but telegrams.
Anton Chekhov (1860-1904, Russian Playwright, Short Story Writer)

10 A man who strains himself on the stage is bound, if he is any good, to strain all the people sitting in the stalls.
Bertolt Brecht (1898-1956, German Dramatist, Poet)

11 The real actor has a direct line to the collective heart.
Bette Davis (1908-1989, American Actress, Producer)

12 If a farmer fills his barn with grain, he gets mice. If he leaves it empty, he gets actors.
Bill Vaughan (1915-1977, American Author, Journalist)

13 The mug is a tool. My ace in the hole. To have looks is the bonus on top of what motivates me to be an actor. Not to realize they're an asset would be counterproductive to the cause; they serve the common good.
Billy Zane (1966-, American Actor)

14 If you have to be in a soap opera try not to get the worst role.
Boy George (British Rock Musician)

15 The hardest part has been maintaining a small head -- remaining down to earth. So many people try to make you more than you are. This business has changed a lot of good people and a lot of good families, and I don't want that to happen to me.
Brandy (Born 1979, American Actress)

16 Such is an actor's life. We must ride the waves of every film, barfing occasionally, yet maintain our dignity, even as the bulk of our Herculean efforts are keel-hauled before our very eyes. [On filming MacHale's Navy]
Bruce Campbell

17 Elizabeth Taylor is pre-feminist woman. This is the source of her continuing greatness and relevance. She wields the sexual power that feminism cannot explain and has tried to destroy. Through stars like Taylor, we sense the world-disordering impact of legendary women like Delilah, Salome, and Helen of Troy. Feminism has tried to dismiss the femme fatale as a misogynist libel, a hoary cliché. But the femme fatale expresses women's ancient and eternal control of the sexual realm. The specter of the femme fatale stalks all men's relations with women.
Camille Paglia (1947-, American Author, Critic, Educator)

18 The basic essential of a great actor is that he loves himself in acting.
Charlie Chaplin (1889-1977, British Comic Actor, Filmmaker)

19 Actors search for rejection. If they don't get it they reject themselves.
Chevy Chase (1943-, American Actor)

20 An actor is only merchandise.
Chow Yun-Fat (1955-, Hong Kong Actor)

21 The thing about performance, even if it's only an illusion, is that it is a celebration of the fact that we do contain within ourselves infinite possibilities.
Daniel Day Lewis (British-born American Actor)

22 You don't merely give over your creativity to making a film -- you give over your life! In theatre, by contrast, you live these two rather strange lives simultaneously; you have no option but to confront the mould on last night's washing-up.
Daniel Day Lewis (British-born American Actor)

23 A movie camera is like having someone you have a crush on watching you from afar -- you pretend it's not there.
Daryl Hannah (1960-, American Actress)

24 I have often seen an actor laugh off the stage, but I don't remember ever having seen one weep.
Denis Diderot (1713-1784, French Philosopher)

25 Actors ought to be larger than life. You come across quite enough ordinary, nondescript people in daily life and I don't see why you should be subjected to them on the stage too.
Donald Sinden (1923-, British Actor)

26 An actor who knows his business ought to be able to make the London telephone directory sound enthralling.
Donald Sinden (1923-, British Actor)

27 She runs the gamut of emotions from A to B.
Dorothy Parker (1893-1967, American Humorous Writer)

28 The actor's popularity is evanescent; applauded today, forgotten tomorrow.
Edwin Forrest

29 I mean, the question actors most often get asked is how they can bear saying the same things over and over again, night after night, but God knows the answer to that is, don't we all anyway; might as well get paid for it.
Elaine Dundy

30 If I wasn't an actor, I'd be a secret agent.
Elijah Wood (Born 1981, American Actor)

31 Acting is a matter of giving away secrets.
Ellen Barkin (1954-, American Actress)

32 Imagination, industry, and intelligence -- "the three I s" -- are all indispensable to the actress, but of these three the greatest is, without doubt, imagination.
Ellen Terry

33 I want to do a musical movie. Like Evita, but with good music.
Elton John (1947-, British Musician, Singer, Songwriter)

34 Ah just act the way ah feel.
Elvis Presley (1935-1977, American Singer, Actor)

35 For an actress to be a success, she must have the face of Venus, the brains of a Minerva, the grace of Terpsichore, the memory of a Macaulay, the figure of Juno, and the hide of a rhinoceros.
Ethel Barrymore (1879-1959, American Actress)

36 Mr. Clarke played the King all evening as though under constant fear that someone else was about to play the Ace.
Eugene Field (1850-1895, American Writer)

37 I'm an actor. And I guess I've done so many movies I've achieved some high visibility. But a star? I guess I still think of myself as kind of a worker ant.
Forest Whitaker (1961-, American Actor, Director)

38 After Blood Simple, everybody thought I was from Texas. After Mississippi Burning, everybody thought I was from Mississippi and uneducated. After Fargo, everybody's going to think I'm from Minnesota, pregnant, and have blonde hair. I don't think you can ever completely transform yourself on film, but if you do your job well, you can make people believe that you're the character you're trying to be.
Frances McDormand

39 Why, except as a means of livelihood, a man should desire to act on the stage when he has the whole world to act in, is not clear to me.
George Bernard Shaw (1856-1950, Irish-born British Dramatist)

40 An actor is a guy who, if you ain't talking about him, he ain't listening.
George Glass

41 There are no small parts. Only small actors.
Ginger Rogers (1911-1995, American Actress)

42 Acting provides the fulfillment of never being fulfilled. You're never as good as you'd like to be. So there's always something to hope for.
Glenda Jackson (1936-, British Actress and politician)

43 Acting is not about dressing up. Acting is about stripping bare. The whole essence of learning lines is to forget them so you can make them sound like you thought of them that instant.
Glenda Jackson (1936-, British Actress and politician)

44 I really think that effective acting has to do literally with the movement of molecules.
Glenn Close (1947-, American Actress)

45 I'm an assistant storyteller. It's like being a waiter or a gas-station attendant, but I'm waiting on six million people a week, if I'm lucky. [On being an actor]
Harrison Ford (1942-, American Actor)

46 We become actors without realizing it, and actors without wanting to.
Henri Frederic Amiel (1821-1881, Swiss Philosopher, Poet, Critic)

47 The best actors do not let the wheels show.
Henry Fonda (1905-1982, American Movie & Stage Actor)

48 Actors die so loud.
Henry Miller (1891-1980, American Author)

49 I have tried to be as eclectic as I possibly can with my professional life, and so far it's been pretty fun.
Holly Hunter (1958-, American Actress)

50 You spend all your life trying to do something they put people in asylums for.
Jane Fonda (1937-, American Screen Actor)

51 A good many dramatic situations begin with screaming.
Jane Fonda (1937-, American Screen Actor)

52 I am the Fred Astaire of karate.
Jean-Claude Van Damme (1960-, Belgian-born American Actor)

53 Some people are addicts. If they don't act, they don't exist.
Jeanne Moreau (1928-, French Actress and Director)

54 Acting deals with very delicate emotions. It is not putting up a mask. Each time an actor acts he does not hide; he exposes himself.
Jeanne Moreau (1928-, French Actress and Director)

55 Acting is nothing more or less than playing. The idea is to humanize life.
Jeff Goldblum (1952-, American Actor, Acting teacher)

56 Actors often behave like children, and so we're taken for children. I want to be grown up.
Jeremy Irons (1948-, British-born American Actor)

57 Until Ace Ventura, no actor had considered talking through his ass.
Jim Carrey (1962-, Canadian-born American Comedian, Actor)

58 Celebrity is death --- celebrity -- that's the worst thing that can happen to an actor.
John Cusack (1966-, American Actor, Playwright, Producer, Stage director)

59 Talk to them about things they don't know. Try to give them an inferiority complex. If the actress is beautiful, screw her. If she isn't, present her with a valuable painting she will not understand. If they insist on being boring, kick their asses or twist their noses. And that's about all there is to it.
John Huston (1906-1987, American Film Director)

60 It's not a field, I think, for people who need to have success every day: if you can't live with a nightly sort of disaster, you should get out. I wouldn't describe myself as lacking in confidence, but I would just say that the ghosts you chase you never catch.
John Malkovich

61 I can't tell you how many shows I've done with full-blown migraine headaches.
Jonathan Taylor Thomas (Born 1981, American Actor, Teen heartthrob)

62 I was born at the age of twelve on a Metro-Goldwyn-Mayer lot.
Judy Garland (1922-1969, American Actress, Singer)

63 People say I'm cocky, but am I supposed to sit here and be insecure and not know where my future's going or not realize that moviemaking is the greatest thing to happen to me?
Juliette Lewis (Born 1973, American Actress)

64 It's a business you go into because your an egocentric. It's a very embarrassing profession.
Katharine Hepburn (1907-, American Actress, Writer)

65 If you give an audience a chance they will do half your acting for you.
Katharine Hepburn (1907-, American Actress, Writer)

66 Acting is the perfect idiot's profession.
Katharine Hepburn (1907-, American Actress, Writer)

67 The most minor gifts and not a very high class way to earn a living. After all, Shirley Temple could do it at the age of four.
Katharine Hepburn (1907-, American Actress, Writer)

68 I think every American actor wants to be a movie star. But I never wanted to do stupid movies, I wanted to do films. I vowed I would never do a commercial, nor would I do a soap opera -- both of which I did as soon as I left the [Acting] Company and was starving.
Kevin Kline (1947-, American Actor, Stage director)

69 I think I am a much better actor than I have allowed myself to be.
Kevin Spacey (1959-, American Actor, Director, Producer)

70 You are not in business to be popular.
Kirstie Alley (1951-, American Actress)

71 The main factor in any form of creativeness is the life of a human spirit, that of the actor and his part, their joint feelings and subconscious creation.
Konstantin Stanislavisky (1863-1968, Russian Actor, Theatre director, Teacher)

72 Unless the theatre can ennoble you, make you a better person, you should flee from it.
Konstantin Stanislavisky (1863-1968, Russian Actor, Theatre director, Teacher)

73 Remember this practical piece of advice: Never come into the theatre with mud on your feet. Leave your dust and dirt outside. Check your little worries, squabbles, petty difficulties with your outside clothing -- all the things that ruin your life and draw your attention away from your art -- at the door.
Konstantin Stanislavisky (1863-1968, Russian Actor, Theatre director, Teacher)

74 Do not try to push your way through to the front ranks of your profession; do not run after distinctions and rewards; but do your utmost to find an entry into the world of beauty.
Konstantin Stanislavisky (1863-1968, Russian Actor, Theatre director, Teacher)

75 Stage charm guarantees in advance an actor's hold on the audience, it helps him to carry over to large numbers of people his creative purposes. It enhances his roles and his art. Yet it is of utmost importance that he use this precious gift with prudence, wisdom, and modesty. It is a great shame when he does not realize this and goes on to exploit, to play on his ability to charm.
Konstantin Stanislavisky (1863-1968, Russian Actor, Theatre director, Teacher)

76 A true priest is aware of the presence of the altar during every moment that he is conducting a service. It is exactly the same way that a true artist should react to the stage all the time he is in the theater. An actor who is incapable of this feeling will never be a true artist.
Konstantin Stanislavisky (1863-1968, Russian Actor, Theatre director, Teacher)

77 Remember: there are no small parts, only small actors.
Konstantin Stanislavisky (1863-1968, Russian Actor, Theatre director, Teacher)

78 Every time I get a script it's a matter of trying to know what I could do with it. I see colors, imagery. It has to have a smell. It's like falling in love. You can't give a reason why.
Lena Olin (1955-, Swedish-born American-born American Actress)

79 I am acquainted with no immaterial sensuality so delightful as good acting.
Lord Byron (1788-1824, British Poet)

80 I was sitting in the looping studio late one night, and I had this epiphany that they weren't paying me for my acting, for God's sake, but to own me. And from then on, it became clear and an awful lot easier to deal with.
Lucy Lawless (Born 1968, New Zealander Actress)

81 I have spent more than half a lifetime trying to express the tragic moment.
Marcel Marceau (1923-, French Mime Artist)

82 She represents the un-vowed aspiration of the male human being, his potential infidelity -- and infidelity of a very special kind, which would lead him to the opposite of his wife, to the "woman of wax" whom he could model at will, make and unmake in any way he wished, even unto death.
Marguerite Duras (1914-, French Author, Filmmaker)

83 Acting doesn't bring anything to a text. On the contrary, it detracts from it.
Marguerite Duras (1914-, French Author, Filmmaker)

84 Somebody told me I should put a pebble in my mouth to cure my stuttering. Well, I tried it, and during a scene I swallowed the pebble. That was the end of that.
Marion Davies (1897-1961, American Actress)

85 Acting is the expression of a neurotic impulse. It's a bum's life. The principal benefit acting has afforded me is the money to pay for my psychoanalysis.
Marlon Brando (1924-, American Actor, Director)

86 To grasp the full significance of life is the actor's duty, to interpret it is his problem, and to express it his dedication.
Marlon Brando (1924-, American Actor, Director)

87 I'm not an actress who can create a character. I play me.
Mary Tyler Moore (1936-, American Actress)

88 First of all, I choose the great [roles], and if none of these come, I choose the mediocre ones, and if they don't come, I choose the ones that pay the rent.
Michael Caine (1933-, British-born American Actor, Acting teacher)

89 We are born at the rise of the curtain and we die with its fall, and every night in the presence of our patrons we write our new creation, and every night it is blotted out forever; and of what use is it to say to audience or to critic, "Ah, but you should have seen me last Tuesday?"
Micheal Macliammoir

90 The most difficult character in comedy is that of the fool, and he must be no simpleton that plays that part.
Miguel De Cervantes (1547-1616, Spanish Novelist, Dramatist, Poet)

91 I'd prefer not to be the pretty thing in a film. It's such a bloody responsibility to look cute, because people know when you don't and they're like, "They're trying to pass her off as the cute girl and she's looking like a bedraggled sack of potatoes.
Minnie Driver (Born 1971, British-born American Actress, Guitarist, Singer)

92 The great actors are the luminous ones. They are the great conductors of the stage.
Minnie Fiske

93 You know how in high school you do these plays and people come up after the show and they're really excited for you? Well, that's what's happening to me right now.
Mira Sorvino (Born 1970, American Actress)

94 Insecurity, commonly regarded as a weakness in normal people, is the basic tool of the actor's trade.
Miranda Richardson

95 I don't think there's a punch-line scheduled, is there?
Monty Python

96 I must say that acting was good training for the political life that lay ahead of us.
Nancy Reagan (1923-, American First Lady, Wife of Former U.S. President, Ronald Reagan)

97 An actress must never lose her ego -- without it she has no talent.
Norma Shearer (1900-1983, Canadian-born American Actress)

98 Every actor in his heart believes everything bad that's printed about him.
Orson Welles (1915-1985, American Film Maker)

99 Man is least himself when he talks in his own person. Give him a mask, and he will tell you the truth.
Oscar Wilde (1856-1900, British Author, Wit)

100 I love acting. It is so much more real than life.
Oscar Wilde (1856-1900, British Author, Wit)

101 The mere mechanical technique of acting can be taught, but the spirit that is to give life to lifeless forms must be born in a man. No dramatic college can teach its pupils to think or to feel. It is Nature who makes our artists for us, though it may be Art who taught them their right mode of expression.
Oscar Wilde (1856-1900, British Author, Wit)

102 While we look to the dramatist to give romance to realism, we ask of the actor to give realism to romance.
Oscar Wilde (1856-1900, British Author, Wit)

103 Actors are loved because they are unoriginal. Actors stick to their script. The unoriginal man is loved by the mediocrity because this kind of "artistic" expression is something to which the merest five-eighth can climb.
Patrick Kavanagh (1905-1967, Irish Poet, Author)

104 Acting is a question of absorbing other people's personalities and adding some of your own experience.
Paul Newman (1925-, American Actor, Director, Philanthropist, Producer)

105 The actor searches vainly for the sound of a vanished tradition, and critic and audience follow suit. We have lost all sense of ritual and ceremony -- whether it be connected with Christmas, birthdays or funerals -- but the words remain with us and old impulses stir in the marrow. We feel we should have rituals, we should do something about getting them and we blame the artists for not finding them for us. So the artist sometimes attempts to find new rituals with only his imagination as his source: he imitates the outer form of ceremonies, pagan or baroque, unfortunately adding his own trapping -- the result is rarely convincing. And after the years and years of weaker and waterier imitations we now find ourselves rejecting the very notion of a holy stage. It is not the fault of the holy that it has become a middle-class weapon to keep the children good.
Peter (Stephen Paul) Brook (1925-, British Theatre and Film Director)

106 All men practice the actor's art.
Petron

107 From '86 until the summer of last year, wherever I went, people would say, "You would have made a great James Bond! Weren't you going to be James Bond? You should have been, you could have been, you may have been." Yes, yes, yes, yes, yes. It was like unfinished business in my life. I couldn't say no to it this time around.
Pierce Brosnan (1952-, Irish-born American Actor)

108 I find myself fascinating.
Richard Dryfus (American Actor)

109 One forgets too easily the difference between a man and his image, and that there is none between the sound of his voice on the screen and in real life.
Robert Bresson (1907-, French Film Director)

110 Acting on a good idea is better than just having a good idea.
Robert Half (American Businessman, Founder of Robert Half & Associates)

111 This is not a tough job. You read a script. If you like the part and the money is O.K., you do it. Then you remember your lines. You show up on time. You do what the director tells you to do. When you finish, you rest and then go on to the next part. That's it.
Robert Mitchum (1917-1997, American Actor)

112 A lot of what acting is paying attention.
Robert Redford (1937-, American Actor, Director, Producer)

113 Left eyebrow raised, right eyebrow raised.
Roger Moore (1927-, British-born American Actor)

114 The face of Garbo is an Idea, that of Hepburn an Event.
Roland Barthes (1915-1980, French Semiologist)

115 You reach a point where you say you're not going to do juveniles any longer.
Ron Howard (1954-, American Director, Actor, Producer)

116 You name it and I've done it. I'd like to say I did it my way. But that line, I'm afraid, belongs to someone else.
Sammy Davis Jr. (1925-1990, American Actor, Dancer, Singer)

117 Players, Sir! I look on them as no better than creatures set upon tables and joint stools to make faces and produce laughter, like dancing dogs.
Samuel Johnson (1709-1784, British Author)

118 To see him act is like reading Shakespeare by flashes of lightning.
Samuel Taylor Coleridge (1772-1834, British Poet, Critic, Philosopher)

119 For the theatre one needs long arms; it is better to have them too long than too short. An artiste with short arms can never, never make a fine gesture.
Sarah Bernhardt (1844-1923, French Actress)

120 You can't do four movies and be good to everybody and be flying all night and shooting all day with a different wig and then be going to sing on Broadway without feeling a little tired. You endlessly feel you're letting somebody down.
Sarah Jessica Parker (1965-, American Actress)

121 Acting is happy agony.
Sir Alec Guiness (1914-, British Actor)

122 I have to act to live.
Sir Lawrence Olivier (1907-1989, British Actor, Producer, Director)

123 I'm disappointed in acting as a craft. I want everything to go back to Orson Welles and fake noses and changing your voice. It's become so much about personality.
Skeet Ulrich (Born 1970, American Actor)

124 There were many times my pants were so thin I could sit on a dime and tell if it was heads or tails.
Spencer Tracy (1900-1967, American Film Actor)

125 When I was a fireman I was in a lot of burning buildings. It was a great job, the only job I ever had that compares with the thrill of acting. Before going into a fire, there's the same surge of adrenaline you get just before the camera rolls.
Steve Buscemi (1952-, American Actor, Director, Playwright, Producer, Screenwriter)

126 I'm not handsome in the classical sense. The eyes droop, the mouth is crooked, the teeth aren't straight, the voice sounds like a Mafioso pallbearer, but somehow it all works.
Sylvester Stallone (1946-, American Actor, Writer, Director, Producer)

127 The popularity of that baby-faced boy, who possessed not even the elements of a good actor, was a hallucination in the public mind, and a disgrace to our theatrical history.
Thomas Campbell (1777-1844, Scottish Poet)

128 Acting is not being emotional, but being able to express emotion.
Thomas Reid (1710-1769, Scottish Philosopher)

129 I regard the theatre as the greatest of all art forms, the most immediate way in which a human being can share with another the sense of what it is to be a human being.
Thornton Wilder (1897-1975, American Novelist, Playwright)

130 I was planning to go into architecture. But when I arrived, architecture was filled up. Acting was right next to it, so I signed up for acting instead. [On his college registration experience]
Tom Selleck (1945-, American Actor)

131 I don't do T & A very well because I haven't got much of either.
Téa Leoni (1966-, American Actress)

132 More than in any other performing arts the lack of respect for acting seems to spring from the fact that every layman considers himself a valid critic.
Uta Hagen

133 Some scenes you juggle two balls, some scenes you juggle three balls, some scenes you can juggle five balls. The key is always to speak in your own voice. Speak the truth. That's Acting 101. Then you start putting layers on top of that. [On his acting techniques]
Vincent D'Onofrio (1959-, American Actor, Producer)

134 I don't want to read about some of these actresses who are around today. They sound like my niece in Scarsdale. I love my niece in Scarsdale, but I won't buy tickets to see her act.
Vincent Price (1911-1993, American Actor and Writer)

135 Show me a great actor and I'll show you a lousy husband. Show me a great actress, and you've seen the devil.
W. C. Fields (1879-1946, American Actor)

136 The actors today really need the whip hand. They're so lazy. They haven't got the sense of pride in their profession that the less socially elevated musical comedy and music hall people or acrobats have. The theater has never been any good since the actors became gentlemen.
W. H. Auden (1907-1973, Anglo-American Poet)

137 In civilized life, where the happiness and indeed almost the existence of man, depends on the opinion of his fellow men. He is constantly acting a studied part.
Washington Irving (1783-1859, American Author)

138 They are the only honest hypocrites, their life is a voluntary dream, a studied madness.
William Hazlitt (1778-1830, British Essayist)

139 We must overact our part in some measure, in order to produce any effect at all.
William Hazlitt (1778-1830, British Essayist)

140 They are, as it were, train-bearers in the pageant of life, and hold a glass up to humanity, frailer than itself. We see ourselves at second-hand in them: they show us all that we are, all that we wish to be, and all that we dread to be. What brings the resemblance nearer is, that, as they imitate us, we, in our turn, imitate them. There is no class of society whom so many persons regard with affection as actors.
William Hazlitt (1778-1830, British Essayist)

141 Speak the speech, I pray you, as I pronounced it to you -- tripping on the tongue; but if you mouth it, as many of your players do, I had as Leif the town-crier spoke my lines. Nor do not saw the air too much with your hand, thus, but use all gently; for in the very torrent, tempest, and as I may say, the whirlwind of your passion, you must acquire and beget a temperance that may give it smoothness.
William Shakespeare (1564-1616, British Poet, Playwright, Actor)

142 Oh! it offends me to the soul to hear a robust periwig-pated fellow, tear a passion to tatters, to very rags, to split the ears of the groundlings.
William Shakespeare (1564-1616, British Poet, Playwright, Actor)

ACTION

1 Whatever fortune brings, don't be afraid of doing things.
A. A. Milne (1882-1956, British Born American Writer)

2 Actions are the seed of fate deeds grow into destiny.
A. L. Linall Jr. (Born 1947, American Editor)

3 I want it said of me by those who knew me best, that I always plucked a thistle and planted a flower where I thought a flower would grow.
Abraham Lincoln (1809-1865, Sixteenth President of the USA)

4 As our case is new, we must think and act anew.
Abraham Lincoln (1809-1865, Sixteenth President of the USA)

5 When deeds speak, words are nothing.
African Proverb

6 It is easy to sit up and take notice, What is difficult is getting up and taking action.
Al Batt

7 All such action would cease if those powerful elemental forces were to cease stirring within us.
Albert Einstein (1879-1955, German-born American Physicist)

8 The most important human endeavor is the striving for morality in our actions. Our inner balance and even our very existence depend on it. Only morality in our actions can give beauty and dignity to life. To make this a living force and bring it to clear consciousness is perhaps the foremost task of education. The foundation of morality should not be made dependent on myth nor tied to any authority lest doubt about the myth or about the legitimacy of the authority imperil the foundation of sound judgment and action.
Albert Einstein (1879-1955, German-born American Physicist)

9 All these primary impulses, not easily described in words, are the springs of man's actions.
Albert Einstein (1879-1955, German-born American Physicist)

10 Thought is the organizing factor in man, intersected between the causal primary instincts and the resulting actions.
Albert Einstein (1879-1955, German-born American Physicist)

11 But their intervention makes our acts to serve ever less merely the immediate claims of our instincts.
Albert Einstein (1879-1955, German-born American Physicist)

12 We are all ruled in what we do by impulses; and these impulses are so organized that our actions in general serve for our self preservation and that of the race.
Albert Einstein (1879-1955, German-born American Physicist)

13 Action is greater than writing. A good man is a nobler object of contemplation than a great author. There are but two things worth living for: to do what is worthy of being written; and to write what is worthy of being read; and the
Albert Pike (1809-1891, American Lawyer, Masonic Author, Historian)

14 Life leaps like a geyser for those who drill through the rock of inertia.
Alexis Carrel (1873-1944, French Biologist)

15 Ideas won't keep, something must be done about them.
Alfred North Whitehead (1861-1947, British Mathematician, Philosopher)

16 Periods of tranquillity are seldom prolific of creative achievement. Mankind has to be stirred up.
Alfred North Whitehead (1861-1947, British Mathematician, Philosopher)

17 Some will, some don't, so what!
American Proverb

18 After all is said and done, more is said than done.
American Proverb

19 From small beginnings come great things.
American Proverb

20 The early bird gets the worm.
American Proverb

21 And the day came when the risk to remain tight in a bud was more painful than the risk it took to blossom.
Anais Nin (1914-1977, French-born American Novelist, Dancer)

22 It is the function of art to renew our perception. What we are familiar with we cease to see. The writer shakes up the familiar scene, and, as if by magic, we see a new meaning in it.
Anais Nin (1914-1977, French-born American Novelist, Dancer)

23 Our life is composed greatly from dreams, from the unconscious, and they must be brought into connection with action. They must be woven together.
Anais Nin (1914-1977, French-born American Novelist, Dancer)

24 It is by acts and not by ideas that people live.
Anatole France (1844-1924, French Writer)

25 Man cannot discover new oceans unless he has the courage to lose sight of the shore.
Andre Gide (1869-1951, French Author)

26 Between eighteen and twenty, life is like an exchange where one buys stocks, not with money, but with actions. Most men buy nothing.
Andre Malraux (1901-1976, French Statesman, Novelist)

27 As I grow older, I pay less attention to what people say. I just watch what they do.
Andrew Carnegie (1835-1919, American Industrialist, Philanthropist)

28 Every action we take, everything we do, is either a victory or defeat in the struggle to become what we want to be.
Anne Byrhhe

29 Never forget that life can only be nobly inspired and rightly lived if you take it bravely and gallantly, as a splendid adventure in which you are setting out into an unknown country, to meet many a joy, to find many a comrade, to win and lose many a battle.
Annie Besant (1847-1933, British Theosophist)

30 We will act consistently with our view of who we truly are, whether that view is accurate or not.
Anthony Robbins (1960-, American Author, Speaker, Peak Performance Expert / Consultant)

31 Action is the foundational key to all success.
Anthony Robbins (1960-, American Author, Speaker, Peak Performance Expert / Consultant)

32 A real decision is measured by the fact that you've taken a new action. If there's no action, you haven't truly decided.
Anthony Robbins (1960-, American Author, Speaker, Peak Performance Expert / Consultant)

33 You see, in life, lots of people know what to do, but few people actually do what they know. Knowing is not enough! You must take action.
Anthony Robbins (1960-, American Author, Speaker, Peak Performance Expert / Consultant)

34 In essence, if we want to direct our lives, we must take control of our consistent actions. It's not what we do once in a while that shapes our lives, but what we do consistently.
Anthony Robbins (1960-, American Author, Speaker, Peak Performance Expert / Consultant)

35 What saves a man is to take a step. Then another step.
Antoine De Saint-Exupery (1900-1944, French Aviator, Writer)

36 If you think about it seriously, all the questions about the soul and the immortality of the soul and paradise and hell are at bottom only a way of seeing this very simple fact: that every action of ours is passed on to others according to its value, of good or evil, it passes from father to son, from one generation to the next, in a perpetual movement.
Antonio Gramsci (1891-1937, Italian Political Theorist)

37 Men acquire a particular quality by constantly acting a particular way. We become just by performing just actions, temperate by performing temperate actions, brave by performing brave actions.
Aristotle (384-322 BC, Greek Philosopher)

38 Well begun is half done.
Aristotle (384-322 BC, Greek Philosopher)

39 We become just by performing just action, temperate by performing temperate actions, brave by performing brave action.
Aristotle (384-322 BC, Greek Philosopher)

40 All human actions have one or more of these seven causes: chance, nature, compulsions, habit, reason, passion, desire.
Aristotle (384-322 BC, Greek Philosopher)

41 For the things we have to learn before we can do them, we learn by doing them.
Aristotle (384-322 BC, Greek Philosopher)

42 Where there is a will, there is a way. If there is a chance in a million that you can do something, anything, to keep what you want from ending, do it. Pry the door open or, if need be, wedge your foot in that door and keep it open.
Arthur Pine (American Publisher, Author)

43 In action a great heart is the chief qualification. In work, a great head.
Arthur Schopenhauer (1788-1860, German Philosopher)

44 The wise man does at once what the fool does finally.
Baltasar Gracian (1601-1658, Spanish Philosopher, Writer)

45 You don't have to get it right the first time.
Barbara Sher (American Author of "I Could Do Anything If I Only Knew What It Was")

46 Doing is a quantum leap from imagining. Thinking about swimming isn't much like actually getting in the water. Actually getting in the water can take your breath away. The defense force inside of us wants us to be cautious, to stay away from anything as intense as a new kind of action. Its job is to protect us, and it categorically avoids anything resembling danger. But it's often wrong. Anything worth doing is worth doing too soon.
Barbara Sher (American Author of "I Could Do Anything If I Only Knew What It Was")

47 What we need is to use what we have.
Basil S. Walsh

48 No one will do it for you.
Ben Stein (American Professor, Writer)

49 Unless a capacity for thinking be accompanied by a capacity for action, a superior mind exists in torture.
Benedetto Croce (1866-1952, Italian Philosopher, Historian, Critic)

50 Action may not always bring happiness; but there is no happiness without action.
Benjamin Disraeli (1804-1881, British Statesman, Prime Minister)

51 Words may show a man's wit but actions his meaning.
Benjamin Franklin (1706-1790, American Scientist, Publisher, Diplomat)

52 The secret of getting things done is to act!
Benjamin O. David (General, US Army)

53 Action is the product of the qualities inherent in nature.
Bhagavad Gita (400 BC, Sanskrit Poem Incorporated Into the Mahabharata)

54 All things whatsoever ye would that men should do to you, do ye even so to them. [Matthew 7:12]
Bible (Sacred Scriptures of Christians and Judaism)

55 But be doers of the word, and not hearers only, deceiving yourselves. [James 1:22]
Bible (Sacred Scriptures of Christians and Judaism)

56 Do unto others as you would have others do unto you. [Matthew 7:120]
Bible (Sacred Scriptures of Christians and Judaism)

57 All rivers run into the sea, yet the sea is not full.
Bible (Sacred Scriptures of Christians and Judaism)

58 Action is the highest perfection and drawing forth of the utmost power, vigor, and activity of man's nature.
Bishop Robert South (1634-1716, British Clergyman)

59 If there be any truer measure of a man than by what he does, it must be by what he gives.
Bishop Robert South (1634-1716, British Clergyman)

60 For every action there is an equal and opposite government program.
Bob Wells

61 Nothing wilts faster than laurels that have been rested upon.
Carl Rowan (1925-, American Journalist, 'The man')

62 The time for action is now. It's never too late to do something.
Carl Sandburg (1878-1967, American Poet)

63 Actions lie louder than words.
Carolyn Wells (1870-1942, American Author)

64 Action expresses priorities.
Charles A. Garfield (American Peak Performance Expert, Researcher, Trainer)

65 Every man of action has a strong dose of egoism, pride, hardness, and cunning. But all those things will be regarded as high qualities if he can make them the means to achieve great ends.
Charles De Gaulle (1890-1970, French President during World War II)

66 Deliberation is the work of many men. Action, of one alone.
Charles De Gaulle (1890-1970, French President during World War II)

67 Keep on going and the chances are you will stumble on something, perhaps when you are least expecting it. I have never heard of anyone stumbling on something sitting down.
Charles F. Kettering (1876-1958, American Engineer, Inventor)

68 In this country men seem to live for action as long as they can and sink into apathy when they retire.
Charles Francis Adams (1807 - 1886, American Statesman, Diplomat)

69 We are born to action; and whatever is capable of suggesting and guiding action has power over us from the first.
Charles Horton Cooley (1864-1929, American Sociologist)

70 It is vain to say human beings ought to be satisfied with tranquillity: they must have action; and they will make it if they cannot find it.
Charlotte Bronte (1816-1855, British Novelist)

71 To talk goodness is not good... only to do it is.
Chinese Proverb

72 I hear and I forget, I see and I remember. I do and I understand.
Chinese Proverb

73 The journey of a thousand miles must begin with a single step.
Chinese Proverb

74 Better do a good deed near at home than go far away to burn incense.
Chinese Proverb

75 Talk doesn't cook rice.
Chinese Proverb

76 Teachers open the door but you must walk through it yourself.
Chinese Proverb

77 It is not whether your words or actions are tough or gentle; it is the spirit behind your actions and words that announces your inner state.
Ching Ning Chu (Chinese-American Businesswoman, Lecturer, Author)

78 Good things happen to those who hustle.
Chuck Noll (American Football Coach)

79 My father didn't tell me how to live; he lived, and let me watch him do it.
Clarence Buddinton Kelland

80 Either move or be moved.
Colin Powell (1937-, American Army General)

81 The superior man acts before he speaks, and afterwards speaks according to his action.
Confucius (551-479 BC, Chinese Ethical Teacher, Philosopher)

82 The superior man is modest in his speech but exceeds in his actions.
Confucius (551-479 BC, Chinese Ethical Teacher, Philosopher)

83 The chief difference between words and deeds. is that words are always intended for men for their approbation, but deeds can be done only for God.
Count Leo Tolstoy (1828-1910, Russian Novelist, Philosopher)

84 In our era, the road to holiness necessarily passes through the world of action.
Dag Hammarskjold (1905-1961, Swedish Statesman, Secretary-general of U.N.)

85 The difficulties you meet will resolve themselves as you advance. Proceed, and light will dawn, and shine with increasing clearness on your path.
D'Alembert

86 Let us develop the resources of our land, call forth its powers, build up its institutions, promote all its great interests, and see whether we also, in our day and generation, may not perform something worthy to be remembered.
Daniel Webster (1782-1852, American Lawyer, Statesman)

87 Big words seldom accompany good deeds.
Danish Proverb

88 For what is liberty but the unhampered translation of will into act?
Dante (Alighieri) (1265-1321, Italian Philosopher, Poet)

89 A fair request should be followed by the deed in silence.
Dante (Alighieri) (1265-1321, Italian Philosopher, Poet)

90 Sometimes something worth doing is worth overdoing.
David Letterman (1947-, American TV Personality)

91 If you could get up the courage to begin, you have the courage to succeed.
David Viscott (American Author, Speaker, Trainer)

92 How to gain, how to keep, how to recover happiness is in fact for most men at all times the secret motive o all they do, and of all they are willing to endure.
Dean William R. Inge (1860-1954, Dean of St Paul's, London)

93 Begin -- to begin is half the work, let half still remain; again begin this, and thou wilt have finished.
Decimus Magnus Ausonius (310-395, Latin Poet, Man of Letters)

94 The secret to success is to start from scratch and keep on scratching.
Dennis Green (American Football Coach)

95 Just as a flower which seems beautiful and has color but no perfume, so are the fruitless words of the man who speaks them but does them not.
Dhammapada (300 BC, Buddhist Collection of Moral Aphorism)

96 Action springs not from thought, but from a readiness for responsibility.
Dietrich Bonhoeffer (1906-1945, German Lutheran Pastor and Theologian)

97 It is impossible to walk rapidly and be unhappy.
Dr. Howard Murphy

98 Existence was given us for action. Our worth is determined by the good deed we do, rather than by the fine emotions we feel,
Edgar F. Magnin

99 Resolved, never to do anything which I should be afraid to do, if it were my last of life.
Edward Edwards

100 A heart to resolve, a head to contrive, and a hand to execute.
Edward Gibbon (1737-1794, British Historian)

101 Every action of our lives touches on some chord that will vibrate in eternity.
Edwin Hubbel Chapin (1814-1880, American Author, Clergyman)

102 In activity we must find our joy as well as glory; and labor, like everything else that is good, is its own reward.
Edwin P. Whipple (1819-1886, American Essayist)

103 Dwell not on the past. Use it to illustrate a point, then leave it behind. Nothing really matters except what you do now in this instant of time. From this moment onwards you can be an entirely different person, filled with love and understanding, ready with an outstretched hand, uplifted and positive in every thought and deed.
Eileen Caddy (American Spiritual Writer)

104 Positive anything is better than negative nothing.
Elbert Hubbard (1859-1915, American Author, Publisher)

105 Allow motion to equal emotion.
Elbert Hubbard (1859-1915, American Author, Publisher)

106 Next in importance to having a good aim is to recognize when to pull the trigger.
Elmer G. Letterman

107 If you want a thing done, go. If not, send. The shortest answer is doing.
English Proverb

108 As you make your bed, so you must lie in it.
English Proverb

109 The link between ideas and action is rarely direct. There is almost always an intermediate step in which the idea is overcome. De Tocqueville points out that it is at times when passions start to govern human affairs that ideas are most obviously translated into political action. The translation of ideas into action is usually in the hands of people least likely to follow rational motives. Hence, it is that action is often the nemesis of ideas, and sometimes of the men who formulate them. One of the marks of the truly vigorous society is the ability to dispense with passion as a midwife of action the ability to pass directly from thought to action.
Eric Hoffer (1902-1983, American Author, Philosopher)

110 Action is at bottom a swinging and flailing of the arms to regain one's balance and keep afloat.
Eric Hoffer (1902-1983, American Author, Philosopher)

111 One of the marks of a truly vigorous society is the ability to dispense with passion as a midwife of action --the ability to pass directly from thought to action.
Eric Hoffer (1902-1983, American Author, Philosopher)

112 Never confuse motion with action.
Ernest Hemingway (1898-1961, American Writer)

113 The undertaking of a new action brings new strength.
Evenus (Ancient Greek Poet)

114 The curse of me and my nation is that we always think things can be bettered by immediate action of some sort, any sort rather than no sort.
Ezra Pound (1885-1972, American Poet, Critic)

115 It was prettily devised of Aesop, "The fly sat on the axle tree of the chariot wheel and said,   what dust do I raise! "
Francis Bacon (1561-1626, British Philosopher, Essayist, Statesman)

116 The action is best that secures the greatest happiness for the greatest number.
Francis Hutcheson

117 The act is unjustifiable that either begs for a blessing, or, having succeeded gives no thanksgiving.
Francis Quarles (1592-1644, British Poet)

118 Our actions are like the terminations of verses, which we rhyme as we please.
François de La Rochefoucauld (1613-1680, French classical writer)

119 We should be taught not to wait for inspiration to start a thing. Action always generates inspiration. Inspiration seldom generates action.
Frank Tibolt

120 When you see a rattlesnake poised to strike you, do not wait until he has struck before you crush him.
Franklin D. Roosevelt (1882-1945, Thirty-second President of the USA)

121 Do Something. If it works, do more of it. If it doesn't, do something else.
Franklin D. Roosevelt (1882-1945, Thirty-second President of the USA)

122 The words printed here are concepts. You must go through the experiences.
Frederick (Carl) Frieseke (1874-1939, American-Born French Painter)

123 It is better to be the hammer than the anvil.
French Proverb

124 An ounce of action is worth a ton of theory.
Friedrich Engels (1820-1895, German Social Philosopher)

125 He who would learn to fly one day must first learn to stand and walk and run and climb and dance; one cannot fly into flying.
Friedrich Nietzsche (1844-1900, German Philosopher)

126 Taking a new step, uttering a new word, is what people fear most.
Fyodor Dostoevski (1821-1881, Russian Novelist)

127 You can't aim a duck to death.
Gael Boardman (American Politician)

128 The sure conviction that we could if we wanted to is the reason so many good minds are idle.
Georg C. Lichtenberg (1742-1799, German Physicist, Satirist)

129 'Tis God gives skill, but not without men's hand: He could not make Antonio Stradivarius's violins without Antonio.
George Eliot (1819-1880, British Novelist)

130 Human beings must have action; and they will make it if they cannot find it.
George Eliot (1819-1880, British Novelist)

131 It will never rain roses: when we want to have more roses we must plant more trees.
George Eliot (1819-1880, British Novelist)

132 Do the things you know, and you shall learn the truth you need to know.
George Macdonald (1824-1905, Scottish Novelist)

133 It is better to rust out than wear out.
George Whitefield (1714-1970, British Methodist Evangelist)

134 When a man asks himself what is meant by action he proves that he isn't a man of action. Action is a lack of balance. In order to act you must be somewhat insane. A reasonably sensible man is satisfied with thinking.
Georges Clemenceau (1841-1929, French Statesman)

135 A man who waits to believe in action before acting is anything you like, but he's not a man of action.. You must act as you breathe.
Georges Clemenceau (1841-1929, French Statesman)

136 The greatest step is out the door.
German Proverb

137 God gives the nuts, but he does not crack them.
German Proverb

138 I do not believe in a fate that falls on men however they act; but I do believe in a fate that falls on them unless they act.
Gilbert K. Chesterton (1874-1936, British Author)

139 Give me the ready hand rather than the ready tongue.
Giuseppe Garibaldi (1807-1882, Italian Patriot, Soldier)

140 Dreams will get you nowhere, a good kick in the pants will take you a long way.
Graffiti

141 Act quickly, think slowly.
Greek Proverb

142 The dog that trots about finds a bone.
Gypsy Proverb

143 Let your performance do the thinking.
H. Jackson Brown Jr. (American Author of "Life's Little Instruction Book" Series)

144 I go on working for the same reason that a hen goes on laying eggs.
H. L. Mencken (1880-1956, American Editor, Author, Critic, Humorist)

145 The activist is not the man who says the river is dirty. The activist is the man who cleans up the river.
H. Ross Perot (1930-, American Businessman & Politician, Founder EDS)

146 Our deeds disguise us. People need endless time to try on their deeds, until each knows the proper deeds for him to do. But every day, every hour, rushes by. There is no time.
Haniel Long (1888-1956, American Author, Poet, Journalist)

147 What really distinguishes this generation in all countries from earlier generations... is its determination to act, its joy in action, the assurance of being able to change things by one's own efforts.
Hannah Arendt (1906-1975, German-born American Political Philosopher)

148 Action without a name, a "who" attached to it, is meaningless.
Hannah Arendt (1906-1975, German-born American Political Philosopher)

149 No steam or gas ever drives anything until it is confined. No Niagara is ever turned into light and power until it is tunneled. No life ever grows until it is focused, dedicated, disciplined.
Harry Emerson Fosdick (1878-1969, American Minister)

150 I am tomorrow, or some future day, what I establish today. I am today what I established yesterday or some previous day.
Harvey Spencer Lewis (American Author of "Mansions of the Soul")

151 Knowledge is of no value unless you put it into practice.
Heber J. Grant

152 Mark this well, you proud men of action! you are, after all, nothing but unconscious instruments of the men of thought.
Heinrich Heine (1797-1856, German Poet, Journalist)

153 I am only one, but still I am one. I cannot do everything, but still I can do something; And because I cannot do everything I will not refuse to do the something that I can do.
Helen Keller (1880-1968, American Blind/Deaf Author, Lecturer, Amorist)

154 Whoever wants to reach a distant goal must take small steps.
Helmut Schmidt

155 Action is coarsened thought; thought becomes concrete, obscure, and unconscious.
Henri Frederic Amiel (1821-1881, Swiss Philosopher, Poet, Critic)

156 Action and faith enslave thought, both of them in order not be troubled or inconvenienced by reflection, criticism, and doubt.
Henri Frederic Amiel (1821-1881, Swiss Philosopher, Poet, Critic)

157 For purposes of action nothing is more useful than narrowness of thought combined with energy of will.
Henri Frederic Amiel (1821-1881, Swiss Philosopher, Poet, Critic)

158 Think like a man of action, and act like a man of thought.
Henri L. Bergson (1859-1941, French Philosopher)

159 I did not wish to take a cabin passage, but rather to go before the mast and on the deck of the world, for there I could best see the moonlight amid the mountains. I do not wish to go below now.
Henry David Thoreau (1817-1862, American Essayist, Poet, Naturalist)

160 We do not learn by inference and deduction and the application of mathematics to philosophy, but by direct intercourse and sympathy.
Henry David Thoreau (1817-1862, American Essayist, Poet, Naturalist)

161 Build today, then strong and sure, With a firm and ample base; And ascending and secure. Shall tomorrow find its place.
Henry Wadsworth Longfellow (1819-1892, American Poet)

162 Each morning sees some task begun, each evening sees it close; Something attempted, something done, has earned a night's repose.
Henry Wadsworth Longfellow (1819-1892, American Poet)

163 We cannot live only for ourselves. A thousand fibers connect us with our fellow men; and among those fibers, as sympathetic threads, our actions run as courses, and they come back to us as effects.
Herman Melville (1819-1891, American Author)

164 Most people of action are inclined to fatalism and most of thought believe in providence.
Honore De Balzac (1799-1850, French Novelist)

165 He who has begun has half done. Dare to be wise; begin.
Horace (65-8 BC, Italian Poet)

166 He has half the deed done who has made a beginning
Horace (65-8 BC, Italian Poet)

167 I have never heard anything about the resolutions of the apostles, but a good deal about their acts.
Horace Mann (1796-1859, American Educator)

168 We will not know unless we begin.
Howard Zinn

169 What an elder sees sitting; the young can't see standing.
Ibo Proverb

170 Act as if the maxim of your action were to become through your will a be general natural law.
Immanuel Kant (1724-1804, German Philosopher)

171 Call on God, but row away from the rocks.
Indian Proverb

172 Being stuck is a position few of us like. We want something new but cannot let go of the old -- old ideas, beliefs, habits, even thoughts. We are out of contact with our own genius. Sometimes we know we are stuck; sometimes we don't. In both cases we have to DO something.
Inga Teekens (Dutch Instructor and Counselor)

173 The person who doesn't scatter the morning dew will not comb gray hairs
Irish Proverb

174 Between saying and doing, many a pair of shoes is worn out.
Italian Proverb

175 Everything you want is out there waiting for you to ask. Everything you want also wants you. But you have to take action to get it.
Jack Canfield (American Motivational Speaker, Author, Trainer)

176 The world can only be grasped by action, not by contemplation. The hand is the cutting edge of the mind.
Jacob Bronowski (1908-1974, British Scientist, Author)

177 He who believes is strong; he who doubts is weak. Strong convictions precede great actions.
James Freeman Clarke (1810-1888, American Minister, Theologian)

178 Follow effective action with quiet reflection. From the quiet reflection will come even more effective action.
James Levin (American educator)

179 One thought driven home is better than three left on base.
James Liter

180 Only the actions of the just smell sweet and blossom in the dust.
James Shirley (1596-1666, British Playwright)

181 Action to be effective must be directed to clearly conceived ends.
Jawaharlal Nehru (1889-1964, Indian Nationalist, Statesman)

182 Action itself, so long as I am convinced that it is right action, gives me satisfaction.
Jawaharlal Nehru (1889-1964, Indian Nationalist, Statesman)

183 Effective action is always unjust.
Jean Anouilh (1910-1987, French Playwright)

184 It's motive alone which gives character to the actions of men.
Jean De La Bruyere (1645-1696, French Writer)

185 Do not wait for extraordinary circumstances to do good action; try to use ordinary situations.
Jean Paul Richter (1763-1825, German Novelist)

186 All human actions are equivalent... and all are on principle doomed to failure.
Jean-Paul Sartre (1905-1980, French Writer, Philosopher)

187 The few who do are the envy of the many who only watch.
Jim Rohn (American Businessman, Author, Speaker, Philosopher)

188 Jump into the middle of things, get your hands dirty, fall flat on your face, and then reach for the stars.
Joan L. Curcio

189 Be wary of the man who urges an action in which he himself incurs no risk.
Joaquin Setanti

190 If you keep thinking about what you want to do or what you hope will happen, you don't do it, and it won't happen.
Joe Dimaggio (1914-, American baseball player)

191 You have to make it happen.
Joe Greene

192 Act like you expect to get into the end zone.
Joe Paterno (American Football Coach - Penn State)

193 He who considers too much will perform little.
Johann Friedrich Von Schiller (1759-1805, German Dramatist, Poet, Historian)

194 Your actions, and your action alone, determines your worth.
Johann G. Fichte (1762-1814, German Philosopher)

195 Act well at the moment, and you have performed a good action for all eternity.
Johann Kaspar Lavater (1741-1801, Swiss Theologian, Mystic)

196 He who has no taste for order, will be often wrong in his judgment, and seldom considerate or conscientious in his actions.
Johann Kaspar Lavater (1741-1801, Swiss Theologian, Mystic)

197 Before you can do something you must first be something.
Johann Wolfgang Von Goethe (1749-1832, German Poet, Dramatist, Novelist)

198 How shall we learn to know ourselves? By reflection? Never; but only through action. Strive to do thy duty; then you shall know what is in thee.
Johann Wolfgang Von Goethe (1749-1832, German Poet, Dramatist, Novelist)

199 Knowing is not enough; we must apply. Willing is not enough; we must do.
Johann Wolfgang Von Goethe (1749-1832, German Poet, Dramatist, Novelist)

200 Then indecision brings its own delays, And days are lost lamenting o'er lost days. Are you in earnest? Seize this very minute; What you can do, or dream you can, begin it.
Johann Wolfgang Von Goethe (1749-1832, German Poet, Dramatist, Novelist)

201 The deed is everything, the glory is naught.
Johann Wolfgang Von Goethe (1749-1832, German Poet, Dramatist, Novelist)

202 Thinking is easy, acting is difficult, and to put one's thoughts into action is the most difficult thing in the world.
Johann Wolfgang Von Goethe (1749-1832, German Poet, Dramatist, Novelist)

203 Fresh activity is the only means of overcoming adversity.
Johann Wolfgang Von Goethe (1749-1832, German Poet, Dramatist, Novelist)

204 When all is said the greatest action is to limit and isolate one's self.
Johann Wolfgang Von Goethe (1749-1832, German Poet, Dramatist, Novelist)

205 Are you in earnest? Seize this very minute! Boldness has genius, power, and magic in it. Only engage, and then the mind grows heated. Begin, and then the work will be completed.
John Anster

206 A dog barks when his master is attacked. I would be a coward if I saw that God's truth is attacked and yet would remain silent.
John Calvin (1509-1564, French Protestant Reformer)

207 We cannot seek or attain health, wealth, learning, justice or kindness in general. Action is always specific, concrete, individualized, unique.
John Dewey (1859-1952, American Philosopher, Educator)

208 The self is not something ready-made, but something in continuous formation through choice of action.
John Dewey (1859-1952, American Philosopher, Educator)

209 A man of action forced into a state of thought is unhappy until he can get out of it.
John Galsworthy (1867-1933, British Novelist, Playwright)

210 One mustn't allow acting to be like stockbroker -- you must not take it just as a means of earning a living, to go down every day to do a job of work. The big thing is to combine punctuality, efficiency, good nature, obedience, intelligence, and concentration with an unawareness of what is going to happen next, thus keeping yourself available for excitement.
John Gielgud

211 Speak out in acts; the time for words has passed, and only deeds will suffice.
John Greenleaf Whittier (1807-1892, American Poet, Reformer, Author)

212 You must get involved to have an impact. No one is impressed with the won-lost record of the referee.
John H. Holcomb

213 The actions of men are the best interpreters of their thoughts.
John Locke (1632-1704, British Philosopher)

214 If you act like you know what you're doing, you can do anything you want -- except neurosurgery.
John Lowenstein

215 You will be better advised to watch what we do instead of what we say.
John N. Mitchell (1913-1988, American Lawyer, Cabinet Member)

216 You can't pick cherries with your back to the tree.
John Pierpont Morgan (1837-1913, American Banker, Financier, Art Collector)

217 One of the greatest and simplest tools for learning more and growing is doing more.
John Roger (American Author of "Life 101")

218 One may walk over the highest mountain one step at a time.
John Wanamaker (1838-1922, American Merchant)

219 The successful men of action are not sufficiently self-observant to know exactly on what their success depends.
Joseph Jacobs

220 Leap, and the net will appear.
Julie Cameron (American Author of "The Artist's Way")

221 If you don't make things happen then things will happen to you.
Lanes Company

222 He who walks with the lame learns how to limp.
Latin Proverb

223 So what do we do? Anything. Something. So long as we just don't sit there. If we screw it up, start over. Try something else. If we wait until we've satisfied all the uncertainties, it may be too late.
Lee Iacocca (1924-, American Businessman, Former CEO of Chrysler)

224 People say to me, "You were a roaring success. How did you do it?" I go back to what my parents taught me. Apply yourself. Get all the education you can, but then, by God, do something. Don't just stand there, make something happen.
Lee Iacocca (1924-, American Businessman, Former CEO of Chrysler)

225 The discipline of writing something down is the first step toward making it happen.
Lee Iacocca (1924-, American Businessman, Former CEO of Chrysler)

226 Apply yourself. Get all the education you can, but then, by God, do something. Don't just stand there, make it happen.
Lee Iacocca (1924-, American Businessman, Former CEO of Chrysler)

227 You can tell more about a person by what he says about others than you can by what others say about him.
Leo Aikman

228 Now is the season for sailing; for already the chattering swallow is come and the pleasant west wind; the meadows bloom and the sea, tossed up with waves and rough blasts, has sunk to silence. Weigh thine anchors and unloose thy hawsers, O Mariner, and sail with all thy canvas set.
Leonidas of Tarentum

229 You must take action now that will move you towards your goals. Develop a sense of urgency in your life.
Les Brown (1945-, American Speaker, Author, Trainer, Motivator Lecturer)

230 Take action in order to move toward your goals.
Les Brown (1945-, American Speaker, Author, Trainer, Motivator Lecturer)

231 There is no use trying, said Alice; one can't believe impossible things. I dare say you haven't had much practice, said the Queen. When I was your age, I always did it for half an hour a day. Why, sometimes I've believed as many as six impossible things before breakfast.
Lewis Carroll (1832-1898, British Writer, Mathematician)

232 People may doubt what you say, but they will believe what you do.
Lewis Cass

233 Begin somewhere: you cannot build a reputation on what you intend to do.
Liz Smith (1923-, American Journalist, Gossip Columnist)

234 To strive, to seek, to find, and not to yield.
Lord Alfred Tennyson (1809-1892, British Poet)

235 I must lose myself in action, lest I wither in despair.
Lord Alfred Tennyson (1809-1892, British Poet)

236 You have to be fast on your feet and adaptive or else a strategy is useless.
Lou Gerstner (American Business Excessive, Chairman of IBM)

237 Don't be a spectator, don't let life pass you by.
Lou Holtz (1937-, American Football Coach)

238 When all is said and done, more is said than done.
Lou Holtz (1937-, American Football Coach)

239 The greatest potential for control tends to exist at the point where action takes place.
Louis A. Allen

240 As people are walking all the time, in the same spot, a path appears.
Lu Xun (1881-1936, Chinese Writer and Revolutionist)

241 Action makes more fortune than caution.
Luc De Clapiers

242 Whatever you do may seem insignificant, but it is most important that you do it.
Mahatma Gandhi (1869-1948, Indian Political, Spiritual Leader)

243 A man is the sum of his actions, of what he has done, of what he can do, Nothing else.
Mahatma Gandhi (1869-1948, Indian Political, Spiritual Leader)

244 The odds of hitting your target go up dramatically when you aim at it.
Mal Pancoast

245 Do every act of your life as if it were your last.
Marcus Aurelius (121-80 AD, Roman Emperor, Philosopher)

246 Thou wilt find rest from vain fancies if thou doest every act in life as though it were thy last.
Marcus Aurelius (121-80 AD, Roman Emperor, Philosopher)

247 Dig within. Within is the wellspring of Good; and it is always ready to bubble up, if you just dig.
Marcus Aurelius (121-80 AD, Roman Emperor, Philosopher)

248 We should not be so taken up in the search for truth, as to neglect the needful duties of active life; for it is only action that gives a true value and commendation to virtue.
Marcus T. Cicero (106-43 BC, Great Roman Orator, Politician)

249 Begin doing what you want to do now. We are not living in eternity. We have only this moment, sparkling like a star in our hand -- and melting like a snowflake.
Marie Beyon Ray

250 You don't always win your battles, but it's good to know you fought.
Marjorie Holmes

251 Twenty years from now you will be more disappointed by the things that you didn't do than by the ones you did do. So throw off the bowlines. Sail away from the safe harbor. Catch the trade winds in your sails. Explore. Dream. Discover.
Mark Twain (1835-1910, American Humorist, Writer)

252 Don't wait until everything is just right. It will never be perfect. There will always be challenges, obstacles and less than perfect conditions. So what. Get started now. With each step you take, you will grow stronger and stronger, more and more skilled, more and more self-confident and more and more successful.
Mark Victor Hansen (American Motivational Speaker, Author)

253 There is a vitality, a life force, a quickening that is translated through you into action, and there is only one of you in all time, this expression is unique, and if you block it, it will never exist through any other medium; and be lost. The world will not have it. It is not your business to determine how good it is, not how it compares with other expression. It is your business to keep it yours clearly and directly, to keep the channel open. You do not even have to believe in yourself or your work. You have to keep open and aware directly to the urges that motivate you. Keep the channel open. No artist is pleased. There is no satisfaction whatever at any time. There is on a queer, divine dissatisfaction, a blessed unrest that keeps us marching and makes us more alive than the others.
Martha Graham (1894-1991, American Dancer, Teacher, and Choreographer)

254 Let no one be deluded that a knowledge of the path can substitute for putting one foot in front of the other.
Mary Caroline Richards

255 Often the difference between a successful person and a failure is not one has better abilities or ideas, but the courage that one has to bet on one's ideas, to take a calculated risk -- and to act.
Maxwell Maltz (American Plastic Surgeon, Author of "Psycho-Cybernetics")

256 A bird doesn't sing because it has an answer, it sings because it has a song.
Maya Angelou (1928-, African-American poet, Writer, Performer)

257 He who strikes first, strikes twice.
Mexican Proverb

258 An ant on the move does more than a dozing ox.
Mexican Proverb

259 Somebody should tell us, right at the start of our lives, that we are dying. Then we might live life to the limit, every minute of every day. Do it! I say. Whatever you want to do, do it now! There are only so many tomorrows.
Michael Landon (1936-1991, American Actor, Director)

260 Good actions ennoble us, and we are the sons of our own deeds.
Miguel De Cervantes (1547-1616, Spanish Novelist, Dramatist, Poet)

261 There should be less talk; a preaching point is not a meeting point. What do you do then? Take a broom and clean someone's house. That says enough.
Mother Teresa (1910-1997, Albanian-born Roman Catholic Missionary)

262 Do not wait for leaders; do it alone, person to person.
Mother Teresa (1910-1997, Albanian-born Roman Catholic Missionary)

263 Let us be tried by our actions.
Motto

264 Do it now! can affect every phase of your life. It can help you do the things you should do but don't feel like doing. It can keep you from procrastinating when an unpleasant duty faces you. But it can also help you do those things that you want to do. It helps you seize those precious moments that, if lost, may never be retrieved.
Napoleon Hill (1883-1970, American Speaker, Motivational Writer, "Think and Grow Rich")

265 The world has the habit of making room for the man whose actions show that he knows where he is going.
Napoleon Hill (1883-1970, American Speaker, Motivational Writer, "Think and Grow Rich")

266 Action is the real measure of intelligence.
Napoleon Hill (1883-1970, American Speaker, Motivational Writer, "Think and Grow Rich")

267 Do not wait; the time will never be "just right." Start where you stand, and work with whatever tools you may have at your command, and better tools will be found as you go along.
Napoleon Hill (1883-1970, American Speaker, Motivational Writer, "Think and Grow Rich")

268 We will burn that bridge when we come to it.
Nick Gorski

269 Just do it.
Nike Corporation (American Shoe Company)

270 The shortest distance between two points is under construction.
Noelie Alito

271 The critical ingredient is getting off your butt and doing something. It's as simple as that. A lot of people have ideas, but there are few who decide to do something about them now. Not tomorrow. Not next week. But today. The true entrepreneur is a doer, not a dreamer.
Nolan Bushnell (American Businessman, Founder of Atari Computer)

272 The truth of the matter is that you always know the right thing to do. The hard part is doing it.
Norman Schwarzkopf (1934-, American General of the Gulf War)

273 Action is a great restorer and builder of confidence. Inaction is not only the result, but the cause, of fear. Perhaps the action you take will be successful; perhaps different action or adjustments will have to follow. But any action is better than no action at all.
Norman Vincent Peale (1898-1993, American Christian Reformed Pastor, Speaker, Author)

274 I will act now. I will act now. I will act now. Henceforth, I will repeat these words each hour, each day, everyday, until the words become as much a habit as my breathing, and the action which follows becomes as instinctive as the blinking of my eyelids. With these words I can condition my mind to perform every action necessary for my success. I will act now. I will repeat these words again and again and again. I will walk where failures fear to walk. I will work when failures seek rest. I will act now for now is all I have. Tomorrow is the day reserved for the labor of the lazy. I am not lazy. Tomorrow is the day when the failure will succeed. I am not a failure. I will act now. Success will not wait. If I delay, success will become wed to another and lost to me forever. This is the time. This is the place. I am the person.
Og Mandino (1923-1996, American Motivational Author, Speaker)

275 Let your actions always speak for you, but be forever on guard against the terrible traps of false pride and conceit that can halt your progress. The next time you are tempted to boast, just place your fist in a full pail of water, and when you remove it, the hole remaining will give you a correct measure of your importance.
Og Mandino (1923-1996, American Motivational Author, Speaker)

276 I find the great thing in this world is not so much where we stand, as in what direction we are moving: To reach the port of heaven, we must sail sometimes with the wind and sometimes against it, but we must sail, and not drift, nor lie at anchor.
Oliver Wendell Holmes (1809-1894, American Author, Wit, Poet)

277 To reach a port we must sail, sometimes with the wind, and sometimes against it. But we must not drift or lie at anchor.
Oliver Wendell Holmes (1809-1894, American Author, Wit, Poet)

278 Begin where you are; work where you are; the hour which you are now wasting, dreaming of some far off success may be crowded with grand possibilities.
Orison Swett Marden (1850-1924, American Author, Founder of Success Magazine)

279 Action is the last resource of those who know not how to dream.
Oscar Wilde (1856-1900, British Author, Wit)

280 No, Ernest, don't talk about action. It is the last resource of those who know not how to dream.
Oscar Wilde (1856-1900, British Author, Wit)

281 Men do not value a good deed unless it brings a reward.
Ovid (43 BC-18 AD, Roman Poet)

282 Let your hook always be cast. In the pool where you least expect it, will be a fish.
Ovid (43 BC-18 AD, Roman Poet)

283 Every act of creation is first of all an act of destruction.
Pablo Picasso (1881-1973, Spanish Artist)

284 You prove your worth with your actions, not with your mouth.
Pat Riley (1945, American Basketball Coach)

285 We have all the light we need, we just need to put it in practice.
Peace Pilgrim (1908-1981, American Peace Activist)

286 A good action is never lost; it is a treasure laid up and guarded for the doer's need.
Pedro Calderón de la Barca (1600-1681, Spanish Playwright)

287 Fertilizer does no good in a heap, but a little spread around works miracles all over.
Percy Ross (American Columnist)

288 Start with what is right rather than what is acceptable.
Peter F. Drucker (1909-, American Management Consultant, Author)

289 Sings. Hope in every sphere of life is a privilege that attaches to action. No action, no hope.
Peter Levi

290 Let us not be content to wait and see what will happen, but give us the determination to make the right things happen.
Peter Marshall (1902-1949, American Presbyterian Clergyman)

291 Your difficulty and my difficulty and the difficulty of every individual who ever desired to achieve something worthwhile, comes in the movement.
Peter Nivio Zarlenga (American Businessman, Founder of Blockbuster Videos)

292 To begin, begin.
Peter Nivio Zarlenga (American Businessman, Founder of Blockbuster Videos)

293 The chief condition on which, life, health and vigor depend on, is action. It is by action that an organism develops its faculties, increases its energy, and attains the fulfillment of its destiny.
Pierre Joseph Proudhon (1809-1865, French Socialist, Political Theorist)

294 It is not good enough for things to be planned -- they still have to be done; for the intention to become a reality, energy has to be launched into operation.
Pir Vilayat Khan (1916-, Western Philosopher Teacher, Master, Author)

295 A well begun is half ended.
Plato (427-347 BC, Greek Philosopher)

296 When Demosthenes was asked what were the three most important aspects of oratory, he answered, "Action, Action, Action."
Plutarch (46-120 AD, Greek Essayist, Biographer)

297 Try and trust will move mountains.
Proverb

298 Footprints on the sands of time are not made by sitting down.
Proverb

299 No sooner said than done -- so acts your man of worth.
Quintus Ennius

300 In the final analysis, the questions of why bad things happen to good people transmutes itself into some very different questions, no longer asking why something happened, but asking how we will respond, what we intend to do now that it happened.
Rabbi Harold S. Kushner

301 Men's actions are too strong for them. Show me a man who has acted, and who has not been the victim and slave of his action.
Ralph Waldo Emerson (1803-1882, American Poet, Essayist)

302 Real action is in silent moments.
Ralph Waldo Emerson (1803-1882, American Poet, Essayist)

303 The ancestor of every action is thought.
Ralph Waldo Emerson (1803-1882, American Poet, Essayist)

304 There is a tendency for things to right themselves.
Ralph Waldo Emerson (1803-1882, American Poet, Essayist)

305 We are always getting ready to live, but never living.
Ralph Waldo Emerson (1803-1882, American Poet, Essayist)

306 We are taught by great actions that the universe is the property of every individual in it.
Ralph Waldo Emerson (1803-1882, American Poet, Essayist)

307 Why should we be cowed by the name of Action?.
Ralph Waldo Emerson (1803-1882, American Poet, Essayist)

308 Act, if you like, but you do it at your peril. Men's actions are too strong for them. Show me a man who has acted and who has not been the victim and slave of his action.
Ralph Waldo Emerson (1803-1882, American Poet, Essayist)

309 A man's action is only a picture book of his creed.
Ralph Waldo Emerson (1803-1882, American Poet, Essayist)

310 The German intellect wants the French sprightliness, the fine practical understanding of the English, and the American adventure; but it has a certain probity, which never rests in a superficial performance, but asks steadily, To what end? A German public asks for a controlling sincerity.
Ralph Waldo Emerson (1803-1882, American Poet, Essayist)

311 Thought is the blossom; language the bud; action the fruit behind it.
Ralph Waldo Emerson (1803-1882, American Poet, Essayist)

312 Let us, if we must have great actions, make our own so. All action is of infinite elasticity, and the least admits of being inflated with celestial air, until it eclipses the sun and moon.
Ralph Waldo Emerson (1803-1882, American Poet, Essayist)

313 Do not be too timid and squeamish about your actions. All life is an experiment.
Ralph Waldo Emerson (1803-1882, American Poet, Essayist)

314 If you go on working with the light available, you will meet your Master, as he himself will be seeking you.
Ramana Maharshi

315 The only correct actions are those that demand no explanation and no apology.
Red Auerbach (1917-, American Basketball Coach)

316 Don't think, just do.
Reiko Horton

317 In action be primitive; in foresight, a strategist.
Rene Char

318 It isn't sufficient just to want -- you've got to ask yourself what you are going to do to get the things you want.
Richard D. Rosen

319 Everyone who got where he is had to begin where he was.
Richard L. Evans

320 Have a bias toward action -- let's see something happen now. You can break that big plan into small steps and take the first step right away.
Richard Thalheimer (American Business Executive, The Sharper Image)

321 It's easy to work for somebody else; all you have to do is show up.
Rita Warford

322 Let us do or die.
Robert Burns (1759-1796, Scottish Poet)

323 Take the first step, and your mind will mobilize all its forces to your aid. But the first essential is that you begin. Once the battle is startled, all that is within and without you will come to your assistance.
Robert Collier (American Writer, Publisher)

324 Begin to free yourself at once by doing all that is possible with the means you have, and as you proceed in this spirit the way will open for you to do more.
Robert Collier (American Writer, Publisher)

325 For as one star another far exceeds, So souls in heaven are placed by their deeds.
Robert Greene (1558-1592, British Author)

326 Better to do something imperfectly than to do nothing perfectly.
Robert H. Schuller (1926-, American Minister (Crystal Cathedral), Author, Social Leader)

327 I'd rather attempt to do something great and fail than to attempt to do nothing and succeed.
Robert H. Schuller (1926-, American Minister (Crystal Cathedral), Author, Social Leader)

328 Winning starts with beginning.
Robert H. Schuller (1926-, American Minister (Crystal Cathedral), Author, Social Leader)

329 You will never win if you never begin.
Robert H. Schuller (1926-, American Minister (Crystal Cathedral), Author, Social Leader)

330 The common conception is that motivation leads to action, but the reverse is true -- action precedes motivation. You have to "prime the pump" and get the juice flowing, which motivates you to work on your goals. Getting momentum going is the most difficult part of the job, and often taking the first step is enough to prompt you to make the best of your day.
Robert J. Mckain

331 The mark of a good action is that it appears inevitable in retrospect.
Robert Louis Stevenson (1850-1895, Scottish Essayist, Poet, Novelist)

332 Judge each day not by the harvest you reap but by the seeds you plant.
Robert Louis Stevenson (1850-1895, Scottish Essayist, Poet, Novelist)

333 It is the mark of a good action that it appears inevitable in retrospect.
Robert Louis Stevenson (1850-1895, Scottish Essayist, Poet, Novelist)

334 If you shoot for the stars and hit the moon, it's OK. But you've got to shoot for something. A lot of people don't even shoot.
Robert Townsend (American Businessman, President of Avis)

335 Let every man or woman here, if you never hear me again, remember this, that if you wish to be great at all, you must begin where you are and with what you are. He who would be great anywhere must first be great in his own Philadelphia.
Russel H. Conwell (1843-1925, American Lawyer, Baptist Minister, Lecturer)

336 I have been impressed with the urgency of doing. Knowing is not enough; we must apply. Being willing is not enough; we must do.
Russell C. Taylor

337 The secret of getting ahead is getting started.
Sally Berger

338 If you want to get along, go along.
Sam Rayburn (1882-1961, American Representative)

339 You can't start at the top.
Samuel Levenson

340 The reason why so little is done, is generally because so little is attempted.
Samuel Smiles (1812-1904, Scottish Author)

341 Only the guy who isn't rowing has time to rock the boat.
Saunders

342 The person of intellect is lost unless they unite with energy of character. When we have the lantern of Diogenes we must also have his staff.
Sebastien-Roch Nicolas De Chamfort (1741-1794, French Writer, Journalist, Playwright)

343 The view only changes for the lead dog.
Sergeant Preston of The Yukon (Fictional 1950's TV Character)

344 What really matters is what you do with what you have.
Shirley Lord (American Writer)

345 This body, full of faults, has yet one great quality: Whatever it encounters in this temporal life depends upon one's actions.
Siddha Nagarjuna (100-200 AD, Indian/Tibetan Father of Mahayan)

346 We must not sit still and look for miracles; up and doing, and the Lord will be with thee. Prayer and pains, through faith in Christ Jesus, will do anything.
Sir John Eliot (1592-1632, British Statesman)

347 Heaven never helps the men who will not act.
Sophocles (495-406 BC, Greek Tragic Poet)

348 You learn to speak by speaking, to study by studying, to run by running, to work by working; in just the same way, you learn to love by loving.
St. Francis De Sales (1567-1622, Roman Catholic Bishop, Writer)

349 Begin to be now what you will be hereafter.
St. Jerome (342-420, Croatian Christian Ascetic, Scholar)

350 Those who are more adapted to the active life can prepare themselves for contemplation in the practice of the active life, while those who are more adapted to the contemplative life can take upon themselves the works of the active life so as to become yet more apt for contemplation.
St. Thomas Aquinas (1225-1274, Italian Scholastic Philosopher and Theologian)

351 He who limps is still walking.
Stanislaw J. Lec (1909-, Polish Writer)

352 We are responsible for what we are, and whatever we wish ourselves to be, we have the power to make ourselves. If what we are now has been the result of our own past actions, it certainly follows that whatever we wish to be in future can be produced by our present actions; so we have to know how to act.
Swami Vivekananda

353 The greatest of all mistakes is to do nothing because you can only do a little. Do what you can.
Sydney Smith (1771-1845, British Writer, Clergyman)

354 Lead, follow, or get out of the way.
Ted Turner (1938-, American Businessman, Founder of CNN)

355 Get action. Seize the moment. Man was never intended to become an oyster.
Theodore Roosevelt (1858-1919, Twenty-sixth President of the USA)

356 Do what you can, with what you have, where you are.
Theodore Roosevelt (1858-1919, Twenty-sixth President of the USA)

357 What you are will show in what you do.
Thomas A. Edison (1847-1931, American Inventor, Entrepreneur, Founder of GE)

358 Action hangs, as it were, "dissolved" in speech, in thoughts whereof speech is the shadow; and precipitates itself therefrom. The kind of speech in a man betokens the kind of action you will get from him.
Thomas Carlyle (1795-1881, Scottish Philosopher, Author)

359 Our grand business is not to see what lies dimly at a distance, but to do what lies clearly at hand.
Thomas Carlyle (1795-1881, Scottish Philosopher, Author)

360 The end of man is action, and not thought, though it be of the noblest.
Thomas Carlyle (1795-1881, Scottish Philosopher, Author)

361 No man lives without jostling and being jostled; in all ways he has to elbow himself through the world, giving and receiving offence.
Thomas Carlyle (1795-1881, Scottish Philosopher, Author)

362 Narrative is linear, but action has breadth and depth as well as height and is solid.
Thomas Carlyle (1795-1881, Scottish Philosopher, Author)

363 Everywhere in life, the true question is not what we gain, but what we do.
Thomas Carlyle (1795-1881, Scottish Philosopher, Author)

364 The great end of life is not knowledge but action.
Thomas H. Huxley (1825-1895, British Biologist, Educator)

365 The soul is made for action, and cannot rest till it be employed. Idleness is its rust. Unless it will up and think and taste and see, all is in vain.
Thomas Traherne (1636-1674, British Clergyman, Poet, Mystic)

366 It is the direction and not the magnitude which is to be taken into consideration.
Thomas Troward

367 A human action becomes genuinely important when it springs from the soil of a clear-sighted awareness of the temporality and the ephemerally of everything human. It is only this awareness that can breathe any greatness into an action.
Vaclav Havel (1936-, Czech Playwright, President)

368 As one acts and conducts himself, so does he become. The doer of good becomes good. The doer of evil becomes evil. One becomes virtuous by virtuous action, bad by bad action.
Veda Upanishads (800 BC, Hindu Poetic Dialogues On Metaphysics)

369 When a man dies, what does not leave him? The voice of a dead man goes into fire, his breath into wind, his eyes into the sun, his mind into the moon, his hearing into the quarters of heaven, his body into the land cheerfully. earth, his spirit into space
Veda Upanishads (800 BC, Hindu Poetic Dialogues On Metaphysics)

370 Initiative is doing the right thing without being told.
Victor Hugo (1802-1885, French Poet, Dramatist, Novelist)

371 Our acts make or mar us, we are the children of our own deeds.
Victor Hugo (1802-1885, French Poet, Dramatist, Novelist)

372 Doing leads more surely to talking than talking to doing.
Vinet

373 It is no use trying to sum people up. One must follow hints, not exactly what is said, nor yet entirely what is done.
Virginia Woolf (1882-1941, British Novelist, Essayist)

374 Thinking will not overcome fear but action will.
W. Clement Stone (1902-, American Businessman, Author)

375 I think there is something, more important than believing: Action! The world is full of dreamers, there aren't enough who will move ahead and begin to take concrete steps to actualize their vision.
W. Clement Stone (1902-, American Businessman, Author)

376 So many fail because they don't get started -- they don't go. They don't overcome inertia. They don't begin.
W. Clement Stone (1902-, American Businessman, Author)

377 Every action is either strong or weak, and when every action is strong we are successful.
Wallace D. Wattles

378 We keep moving forward, opening new doors, and doing new things, because we're curious and curiosity keeps leading us down new paths.
Walt Disney (1901-1966, American Artist, Film Producer)

379 Now is the time for all good men to come to.
Walt Kelly (1913-1973, American Animator, Strip Cartoonist)

380 Someone's sitting in the shade today because someone planted a tree a long time ago.
Warren Buffett (1930-, American Investment Entrepreneur)

381 Everything is in motion. Everything flows. Everything is vibrating.
Wayne Dyer (1940-, American Psychotherapist, Author, Lecturer)

382 Go for it now. The future is promised to no one.
Wayne Dyer (1940-, American Psychotherapist, Author, Lecturer)

383 I didn't think; I experimented.
Wilhelm Roentgen

384 Even if you are on the right track, you will get run over if you just sit there.
Will Rogers (1879-1935, American Humorist, Actor)

385 An acre of performance is worth a whole world of promise.
William Dean Howells (1837-1920, American Novelist, Critic)

386 The man who removes a mountain begins by carrying away small stones.
William Faulkner (1897-1962, American Novelist)

387 You know more of a road by having traveled it than by all the conjectures and descriptions in the world.
William Hazlitt (1778-1830, British Essayist)

388 The more we do, the more we can do; the more busy we are, the more leisure we have.
William Hazlitt (1778-1830, British Essayist)

389 Never mind your happiness; do your duty.
William J. Durant (1885-1981, American Historian, Essayist)

390 Do something everyday for no other reason than you would rather not do it, so that when the hour of dire need draws nigh, it may find you not unnerved and untrained to stand the test.
William James (1842-1910, American Psychologist, Professor, Author)

391 Action seems to follow feeling, but really action and feeling go together; and by regulating the action, which is under the more direct control of the will, we can indirectly regulate the feeling, which is not.
William James (1842-1910, American Psychologist, Professor, Author)

392 If you want a trait, act as if you already have the trait.
William James (1842-1910, American Psychologist, Professor, Author)

393 I will act as if what I do makes a difference.
William James (1842-1910, American Psychologist, Professor, Author)

394 Act as if what you do makes a difference. It does.
William James (1842-1910, American Psychologist, Professor, Author)

395 Suit the action to the world, the world to the action, with this special observance, that you overstep not the modesty of nature.
William Shakespeare (1564-1616, British Poet, Playwright, Actor)

396 If it were done when 'tis done, then t'were well. It were done quickly.
William Shakespeare (1564-1616, British Poet, Playwright, Actor)

397 Be great in act, as you have been in thought.
William Shakespeare (1564-1616, British Poet, Playwright, Actor)

398 Things won are done, joy's soul lies in the doing.
William Shakespeare (1564-1616, British Poet, Playwright, Actor)

399 Action is eloquence.
William Shakespeare (1564-1616, British Poet, Playwright, Actor)

400 Thought and theory must precede all salutary action; yet action is nobler in itself than either thought or theory.
William Wordsworth (1770-1850, British Poet)

401 I never worry about action, but only inaction.
Winston Churchill (1874-1965, British Statesman, Prime Minister)

402 You have to "be" before you can "do," and do before you can "have."
Zig Ziglar (American Sales Trainer, Author, Motivational Speaker)

ADAPTABILITY

1 To the man who only has a hammer, everything he encounters begins to look like a nail.
Abraham H. Maslow (1908-1970, American Psychologist)

2 We must make the best of those ills which cannot be avoided.
Alexander Hamilton (1757-1804, American Statesman)

3 Singularity shows something wrong in the mind.
Clarissa

4 One learns to itch where one can scratch.
Ernest Bramah (American Writer)

5 They that will not apply new remedies must expect new evils.
Francis Bacon (1561-1626, British Philosopher, Essayist, Statesman)

6 Take the world as it is, not as it ought to be.
German Proverb

7 The weather-cock on the church spire, though made of iron, would soon be broken by the storm-wind if it did not understand the noble art of turning to every wind.
Heinrich Heine (1797-1856, German Poet, Journalist)

8 If you live in the river you should make friends with the crocodile.
Indian Proverb

9 A well adjusted person is one who makes the same mistake twice without getting nervous.
Jane Heard

10 Complete adaptation to environment means death. The essential point in all response is the desire to control environment.
John Dewey (1859-1952, American Philosopher, Educator)

11 As a rule, I am very careful to be shallow and conventional where depth and originality are wasted.
Lucy Maud Montgomery (1874-1942, Canadian Novelist)

12 Adaptability is not imitation. It means power of resistance and assimilation.
Mahatma Gandhi (1869-1948, Indian Political, Spiritual Leader)

13 I found out that if you are going to win games, you had better be ready to adapt.
Scotty Bowman (American Hockey Coach)

14 Learn to adjust yourself to the conditions you have to endure, but make a point of trying to alter or correct conditions so that they are most favorable to you.
William Frederick Book

15 In war as in life, it is often necessary when some cherished scheme has failed, to take up the best alternative open, and if so, it is folly not to work for it with all your might.
Winston Churchill (1874-1965, British Statesman, Prime Minister)

ADDICTION

1 In this country, don't forget, a habit is no damn private hell. There's no solitary confinement outside of jail. A habit is hell for those you love. And in this country it's the worst kind of hell for those who love you.
Billie Holiday (1915-1959, American Jazz Singer)

2 To possess your soul in patience, with all the skin and some of the flesh burnt off your face and hands, is a job for a boy compared with the pains of a man who has lived pretty long in the exhilarating world that drugs or strong waters seem to create and is trying to live now in the first bald desolation created by knocking them off.
C. E. Montague (1867-1928, British Author, Journalist)

3 Every form of addiction is bad, no matter whether the narcotic be alcohol or morphine or idealism.
Carl Jung (1875-1961, Swiss Psychiatrist)

4 It is not I who become addicted, it is my body.
Jean Cocteau (1889-1963, French Author, Filmmaker)

5 If an addict who has been completely cured starts smoking again he no longer experiences the discomfort of his first addiction. There exists, therefore, outside alkaloids and habit, a sense for opium, an intangible habit which lives on, despite the recasting of the organism. The dead drug leaves a ghost behind. At certain hours it haunts the house.
Jean Cocteau (1889-1963, French Author, Filmmaker)

6 My case is a species of madness, only that it is a derangement of the Volition, and not of the intellectual faculties.
Samuel Taylor Coleridge (1772-1834, British Poet, Critic, Philosopher)

7 It is not heroin or cocaine that makes one an addict, it is the need to escape from a harsh reality. There are more television addicts, more baseball and football addicts, more movie addicts, and certainly more alcohol addicts in this country than there are narcotics addicts.
Shirley Chisholm (1924-, American Social activist)

8 I feel that any form of so called psychotherapy is strongly contraindicated for addicts. The question "Why did you start using narcotics in the first place?" should never be asked. It is quite as irrelevant to treatment as it would be to ask a malarial patient why he went to a malarial area.
William S. Burroughs (1914-1997, American Writer)

ADMIRATION

1 Fools admire, but men of sense approve.
Alexander Pope (1688-1744, British Poet, Critic, Translator)

2 Admiration is the daughter of ignorance.
Benjamin Franklin (1706-1790, American Scientist, Publisher, Diplomat)

3 Animals do not admire each other. A horse does not admire its companion.
Blaise Pascal (1623-1662, French Scientist, Religious Philosopher)

4 When somebody gives you a sexy look, you know they're trying. It's terrible! But when you smile, it's so much sexier!
Carol Alt (1960-, American Model)

5 To cease to admire is a proof of deterioration.
Charles Horton Cooley (1864-1929, American Sociologist)

6 Distance is a great promoter of admiration!
Denis Diderot (1713-1784, French Philosopher)

7 You always admire what you really don't understand.
Eleanor Roosevelt (1884-1962, American First Lady, Columnist, Lecturer, Humanitarian)

8 The secret of happiness is to admire without desiring.
Francis H. Bradley (1846-1924, British Philosopher)

9 We always love those who admire us; we do not always love those whom we admire.
François de La Rochefoucauld (1613-1680, French classical writer)

10 The only things one can admire at length are those one admires without knowing why.
Jean Rostand (1894-1977, French Biologist, Writer)

11 Admiration is a very short-lived passion that immediately decays upon growing familiar with its object, unless it be still fed with fresh discoveries, and kept alive by a new perpetual succession of miracles rising up to its view.
Joseph Addison (1672-1719, British Essayist, Poet, Statesman)

12 Nothing is more admirable than the fortitude with which millionaires tolerate the disadvantages of their wealth.
Nero Wolfe

[13] Oh! death will find me long before I tire of watching you.
Rupert Brooke (1887-1915, British Poet)

[14] I have always been an admirer. I regard the gift of admiration as indispensable if one is to amount to something; I don't know where I would be without it.
Thomas Mann (1875-1955, German Author, Critic)

ADOLESCENCE

[1] They mustn't know my despair, I can't let them see the wounds which they have caused, I couldn't bear their sympathy and their kind-hearted jokes, it would only make me want to scream all the more. If I talk, everyone thinks I'm showing off; when I'm silent they think I'm ridiculous; rude if I answer, sly if I get a good idea, lazy if I'm tired, selfish if I eat a mouthful more than I should, stupid, cowardly, crafty, etc. etc.
Anne Frank (1929-1945, German Jewish Refugee, Diarist)

[2] Boys will be boys. And even that wouldn't matter if only we could prevent girls from being girls.
Anthony Hope (1863-1933, British Writer)

[3] In the life of children there are two very clear-cut phases, before and after puberty. Before puberty the child's personality has not yet formed and it is easier to guide its life and make it acquire specific habits of order, discipline, and work: after puberty the personality develops impetuously and all extraneous intervention becomes odious, tyrannical, insufferable. Now it so happens that parents feel the responsibility towards their children precisely during this second period, when it is too late: then of course the stick and violence enter the scene and yield very few results indeed. Why not instead take an interest in the child during the first period?
Antonio Gramsci (1891-1937, Italian Political Theorist)

[4] When you are seventeen you aren't really serious.
Arthur Rimbaud (1854-1891, French Poet)

[5] Teenage boys, goaded by their surging hormones run in packs like the primal horde. They have only a brief season of exhilarating liberty between control by their mothers and control by their wives.
Camille Paglia (1947-, American Author, Critic, Educator)

[6] Perhaps a modern society can remain stable only by eliminating adolescence, by giving its young, from the age of ten, the skills, responsibilities, and rewards of grownups, and opportunities for action in all spheres of life. Adolescence should be a time of useful action, while book learning and scholarship should be a preoccupation of adults.
Eric Hoffer (1902-1983, American Author, Philosopher)

[7] What a cunning mixture of sentiment, pity, tenderness, irony surrounds adolescence, what knowing watchfulness! Young birds on their first flight are hardly so hovered around.
Georges Bernanos (1888-1948, French Novelist, Political Writer)

[8] The imagination of a boy is healthy, and the mature imagination of a man is healthy; but there is a space of life between, in which the soul is in a ferment, the character undecided, the way of life uncertain, the ambition thick-sighted: thence proceeds mawkishness.
John Keats (1795-1821, British Poet)

[9] The big mistake that men make is that when they turn thirteen or fourteen and all of a sudden they've reached puberty, they believe that they like women. Actually, you're just horny. It doesn't mean you like women any more at twenty-one than you did at ten.
Jules Feiffer (1929-, American Cartoonist)

[10] So much alarmed that she is quite alarming, All Giggle, Blush, half Pertness, and half Pout.
Lord Byron (1788-1824, British Poet)

[11] Having a thirteen-year-old in the family is like having a general-admission ticket to the movies, radio and TV. You get to understand that the glittering new arts of our civilization are directed to the teen-agers, and by their suffrage they stand or fall.
Max Lerner (1902-, American Author, Columnist)

[12] I would there were no age between ten and three-and-twenty, or that youth would sleep out the rest; for there is nothing in the between but getting wenches with child, wronging the anciently, stealing, fighting.
William Shakespeare (1564-1616, British Poet, Playwright, Actor)

ADULTERY

[1] Adultery is the application of democracy to love.
H. L. Mencken (1880-1956, American Editor, Author, Critic, Humorist)

[2] One man's folly is often another man's wife.
Helen Rowland (1875-1950, American Journalist)

[3] I do not think that there are any men who are faithful to their wives.
Jacqueline Kennedy Onassis (1929-1994, American First Lady, Wife of John F. Kennedy & Aristotle Onassis)

[4] Adultery itself in its principle is many times nothing but a curious inquisition after, and envy of another man's enclosed pleasures: and there have been many who refused fairer objects that they might ravish an enclosed woman from her retirement and single possessor.
Jeremy Taylor (1613-1667, British Churchman, Writer)

[5] According to my sister, the expert novelist Jackie Collins, most men stray. And sex doesn't mean anything to most men. But I wouldn't date a man who slept around. Absolutely not. I've divorced people for that.
Joan Collins (1933-, British-born American Actress)

[6] It is not difficult to deceive the first time, for the deceived possesses no antibodies; unvaccinated by suspicion, she overlooks lateness, accepts absurd excuses, permits the flimsiest patching to repair great rents in the quotidian.
John Updike (1932-, American Novelist, Critic)

7 What men call gallantry, and gods adultery, is much more common where the climate's sultry.
Lord Byron (1788-1824, British Poet)

8 My attitude toward men who mess around is simple: If you find 'em, kill 'em.
Loretta Lynn (1935-, American Musician, Singer, Songwriter)

9 Husbands are chiefly good lovers when they are betraying their wives.
Marilyn Monroe (1926-, American Actress)

10 Life is a game in which the rules are constantly changing; nothing spoils a game more than those who take it seriously. Adultery? Phooey! You should never subjugate yourself to another nor seek the subjugation of someone else to yourself. If you follow that Crispian principle you will be able to say "Phooey," too, instead of reaching for your gun when you fancy yourself betrayed.
Quentin Crisp (1908-, British Author)

11 I never had but one intrigue yet: but I confess I long to have another. Pray heaven it end as the first did tho, that we may both grow weary at a time; for 'Tis a melancholy thing for lovers to outlive one another.
Sir John Vanbrugh (1664-1726, British Playwright and Baroque architect)

12 You know that the Tasmanians, who never committed adultery, are now extinct.
W. Somerset Maugham (1874-1965, British Novelist, Playwright)

13 O curse of marriage that we can call these delicate creatures ours and not their appetites!
William Shakespeare (1564-1616, British Poet, Playwright, Actor)

14 A mistress should be like a little country retreat near the town, not to dwell in constantly, but only for a night and away.
William Wycherley (1640-1716, British Dramatist)

ADULTHOOD

1 I believe a man is born first unto himself --for the happy developing of himself, while the world is a nursery, and the pretty things are to be snatched for, and pleasant things tasted; some people seem to exist thus right to the end. But most are born again on entering manhood; then they are born to humanity, to a consciousness of all the laughing, and the never-ceasing murmur of pain and sorrow that comes from the terrible multitudes of brothers.
D. H. Lawrence (1885-1930, British Author)

2 The distinction between children and adults, while probably useful for some purposes, is at bottom a specious one, I feel. There are only individual egos, crazy for love.
Don Barthelme (1931-1989, American Actor)

3 Part of the reason for the ugliness of adults, in a child's eyes, is that the child is usually looking upwards, and few faces are at their best when seen from below.
George Orwell (1903-1950, British Author, "Animal Farm")

4 In youth the human body drew me and was the object of my secret and natural dreams. But body after body has taken away from me that sensual phosphorescence which my youth delighted in. Within me is no disturbing interplay now, but only the steady currents of adaptation and of sympathy.
Haniel Long (1888-1956, American Author, Poet, Journalist)

5 We seem but to linger in manhood to tell the dreams of our childhood, and they vanish out of memory ere we learn the language.
Henry David Thoreau (1817-1862, American Essayist, Poet, Naturalist)

6 To be adult is to be alone.
Jean Rostand (1894-1977, French Biologist, Writer)

7 Men are but children of a larger growth, Our appetites as apt to change as theirs, And full as craving too, and full as vain.
John Dryden (1631-1700, British Poet, Dramatist, Critic)

8 A boy becomes an adult three years before his parents think he does, and about two years after he thinks he does.
Lewis B Hershey

9 In my case, adulthood itself was not an advance, although it was a useful waymark.
Nicholson Baker (1957-, American Author)

10 We have not passed that subtle line between childhood and adulthood until we move from the passive voice to the active voice -- that is, until we have stopped saying "It got lost," and say, "I lost it."
Sidney J. Harris (1917-, American Journalist)

11 What is an adult? A child blown up by age.
Simone De Beauvoir (1908-1986, French Novelist, Essayist)

12 Adulthood is the ever-shrinking period between childhood and old age. It is the apparent aim of modern industrial societies to reduce this period to a minimum.
Thomas Szasz (1920-, American Psychiatrist)

13 A child becomes an adult when he realizes that he has a right not only to be right but also to be wrong.
Thomas Szasz (1920-, American Psychiatrist)

14 One of the signs of passing youth is the birth of a sense of fellowship with other human beings as we take our place among them.
Virginia Woolf (1882-1941, British Novelist, Essayist)

ADVANTAGE

1 In life, as in chess, forethought wins.
Charles Buxton (1823-1871, British Author)

2   He who is in love with himself has at least this advantage -- he won't encounter many rivals.
Georg C. Lichtenberg (1742-1799, German Physicist, Satirist)

3   It is a great advantage for a system of philosophy to be substantially true.
George Santayana (1863-1952, American Philosopher, Poet)

4   If we do what is necessary, all the odds are in our favor.
Henry Kissinger (1923-, American Republican Politician, Secretary of State)

5   The two big advantages I had at birth were to have been born wise and to have been born in poverty.
Sophia Loren (1934-, Italian Film Actress)

6   If eighty percent of your sales come from twenty percent of all of your items, just carry those twenty percent.
Stew Leonard (American Businessman)

ADVENTURE

1   The little reed, bending to the force of the wind, soon stood upright again when the storm had passed over.
Aesop (620-560 BC, Greek Fabulist)

2   Without adventure civilization is in full decay.
Alfred North Whitehead (1861-1947, British Mathematician, Philosopher)

3   Adventure is worthwhile.
Amelia Earhart (1897-1937, American Aviator, Author)

4   Man needs difficulties; they are necessary for health.
Carl Jung (1875-1961, Swiss Psychiatrist)

5   Adventure is not outside man; it is within.
David Grayson (1870-1946, American Journalist and Writer)

6   We are the men of intrinsic value, who can strike our fortunes out of ourselves, whose worth is independent of accidents in life, or revolutions in government: we have heads to get money, and hearts to spend it.
George Farquhar (1677-1707, Irish Playwright)

7   An adventure is only an inconvenience rightly considered. An inconvenience is only an adventure wrongly considered.
Gilbert K. Chesterton (1874-1936, British Author)

8   We live in a wonderful world that is full of beauty, charm and adventure. There is no end to the adventures that we can have if only we seek them with our eyes open.
Jawaharlal Nehru (1889-1964, Indian Nationalist, Statesman)

9   Who dares nothing, need hope for nothing.
Johann Friedrich Von Schiller (1759-1805, German Dramatist, Poet, Historian)

10 A large volume of adventures may be grasped within this little span of life, by him who interests his heart in everything.
Laurence Sterne (1713-1768, British Author)

11 And yet a little tumult, now and then, is an agreeable quickener of sensation; such as a revolution, a battle, or an adventure of any lively description.
Lord Byron (1788-1824, British Poet)

12 You can't cross the sea merely by standing and staring at the water. Don't let yourself indulge in vain wishes.
Rabindranath Tagore (1861-1941, Indian Poet, Philosopher)

13 The thirst for adventure is the vent which Destiny offers; a war, a crusade, a gold mine, a new country, speak to the imagination and offer swing and play to the confined powers.
Ralph Waldo Emerson (1803-1882, American Poet, Essayist)

14 The test of an adventure is that when you're in the middle of it, you say to yourself, "Oh, now I've got myself into an awful mess; I wish I were sitting quietly at home." And the sign that something's wrong with you is when you sit quietly at home wish
Thornton Wilder (1897-1975, American Novelist, Playwright)

15 I am not an adventurer by choice but by fate.
Vincent Van Gogh (1853-1890, Dutch-born French Painter)

16 If we didn't live adventurously, plucking the wild goat by the beard, and trembling over precipices, we should never be depressed, I've no doubt; but already should be faded, fatalistic and aged.
Virginia Woolf (1882-1941, British Novelist, Essayist)

17 If we do not find anything very pleasant, at least we shall find something new.
Voltaire (1694-1778, French Historian, Writer)

18 There are two kinds of adventurers: those who go truly hoping to find adventure and those who go secretly hoping they won t.
William Trogdon (1939-, American Author)

ADVERSITY

1   The reward of suffering is experience.
Aeschylus (525-456 BC, Greek Dramatist)

2   Men often bear little grievances with less courage than they do large misfortunes.
Aesop (620-560 BC, Greek Fabulist)

3   That which causes us trials shall yield us triumph: and that which make our hearts ache shall fill us with gladness. The only true happiness is to learn, to advance, and to improve: which could not happen unless we had commence with error, ignorance, and imperfection. We must pass through the darkness, to reach the light.
Albert Pike (1809-1891, American Lawyer, Masonic Author, Historian)

4   One who gains strength by overcoming obstacles possesses the only strength which can overcome adversity.
Albert Schweitzer (1875-1965, German Born Medical Missionary, Theologian, Musician, and Philosopher)

5 Had there been no difficulties and no thorns in the way, then man would have been in his primitive state and no progress made in civilization and mental culture.
Anandabai Joshee (1865-1887, Indian Physician)

6 Suffering! We owe to it all that is good in us, all that gives value to life; we owe to it pity, we owe to it courage, we owe to it all the virtues.
Anatole France (1844-1924, French Writer)

7 Trouble is the common denominator of living. It is the great equalizer.
Ann Landers (1918-, American Advice Columnist)

8 If we had no winter, the spring would not be so pleasant: if we did not sometimes taste of adversity, prosperity would not be so welcome.
Anne Bradstreet (1612-1672, British Puritan Poet)

9 I have often been downcast, but never in despair; I regard our hiding as a dangerous adventure, romantic and interesting at the same time. In my diary I treat all the privations as amusing. I have made up my mind now to lead a different life from other girls and, later on, different from ordinary housewives. My start has been so very full of interest, and that is the sole reason why I have to laugh at the humorous side of the most dangerous moments.
Anne Frank (1929-1945, German Jewish Refugee, Diarist)

10 You never know what events are going to transpire to get you home.
Apollo 13 Movie

11 It's easier to go down a hill than up it but the view is much better at the top.
Arnold Bennett (1867-1931, British Novelist)

12 Nothing splendid was ever created in cold blood. Heat is required to forge anything. Every great accomplishment is the story of a flaming heart.
Arnold H. Glasgow

13 There is no doubt that life is given us, not to be enjoyed, but to be overcome --to be got over.
Arthur Schopenhauer (1788-1860, German Philosopher)

14 Every silver lining has a cloud.
Avon

15 You don't develop courage by being happy in your relationships everyday. You develop it by surviving difficult times and challenging adversity.
Barbara De Angelis (American Expert on Relationship & Love, Author)

16 He knows not his own strength that hath not met adversity
Ben Johnson (1573-1637, British Dramatist, Poet)

17 The proof of gold is fire...
Benjamin Franklin (1706-1790, American Scientist, Publisher, Diplomat)

18 If I traveled to the end of the rainbow as Dame Fortune did intend, Murphy would be there to tell me the pot's at the other end.
Bert Whitney

19 Therefore do not be anxious about tomorrow, for tomorrow will be anxious for itself. Let the day's own trouble be sufficient for the day.
Bible (Sacred Scriptures of Christians and Judaism)

20 They that sow in tears shall reap joy. [Psalms 126:5]
Bible (Sacred Scriptures of Christians and Judaism)

21 Behold, I have refined thee, but not with silver; I have chosen thee in the furnace of affliction. [Isaiah 48:10]
Bible (Sacred Scriptures of Christians and Judaism)

22 Enter through the narrow gate. The gate that leads to damnation is wide, the road is clear, and many choose to travel it. But how narrow is the gate that leads to life, how rough the road, and how few there are who find it. [Mathew 7:13-14]
Bible (Sacred Scriptures of Christians and Judaism)

23 I got in trouble with the police, and that was a rude awakening. That was it. I'd seen the bottom of the pit, and it was time to scrape myself out of it.
Bryan Adams (Born 1959, Canadian-born American Musician, Singer, Songwriter)

24 We deem those happy who from the experience of life have learnt to bear its ills without being overcome by them.
Carl Jung (1875-1961, Swiss Psychiatrist)

25 Duct tape is like the force. It has a light side, a dark side, and it holds the universe together.
Carl Zwanzig

26 If we study the lives of great men and women carefully and unemotionally we find that, invariably, greatness was developed, tested and revealed through the darker periods of their lives. One of the largest tributaries of the RIVER OF GREATNESS is always the STREAM OF ADVERSITY.
Cavett Robert

27 There are three modes of bearing the ills of life, by indifference, by philosophy, and by religion.
Charles Caleb Colton (1780-1832, British Sportsman Writer)

28 Constant success shows us but one side of the world; adversity brings out the reverse of the picture.
Charles Caleb Colton (1780-1832, British Sportsman Writer)

29 The hardest struggle of all is to be something different from what the average man is.
Charles M. Schwab (1862-1939, American Industrialist, Businessman)

30 Things don't go wrong and break your heart so you can become bitter and give up. They happen to break you down and build you up so you can be all that you were intended to be.
Charles "Tremendous" Jones (American Motivational Speaker, Author)

31 A gem cannot be polished without friction, nor a man perfected without trials.
Chinese Proverb

32 In order for the light to shine so brightly, the darkness must be present.
Danny Devito (1944-, American Actor, Comedian)

33 Trouble shared is trouble halved.
Dorothy L. Sayers (1893-1957, British Author)

34 They sicken at the calm that know the storm.
Dorothy Parker (1893-1967, American Humorous Writer)

35 The harder you fall, the higher you bounce.
Doug Horton

36 Gray skies are just clouds passing over.
Duke Ellington (American jazz musician)

37 In my room as a kid... I'd play a fighter and get knocked to the floor and come back to win.
Dustin Hoffman (1937-, American Actor)

38 Everything I did in my life that was worthwhile I caught hell for it.
Earl Warren (1891-1974, American Politician, Judge)

39 Abuse a man unjustly, and you will make friends for him.
Edgar Watson Howe (1853-1937, American Journalist, Author)

40 Never bear more than one kind of trouble at a time. Some people bear three kinds; all they have had, all they have now, and all they expect to have.
Edward Everett Hale (1822-1909, American Unitarian Clergyman, Writer)

41 Some people bear three kinds of trouble -- the ones they've had, the ones they have, and the ones they expect to have.
Edward Everett Hale (1822-1909, American Unitarian Clergyman, Writer)

42 A reasonable amount o fleas is good for a dog -- keeps him from brooding over being a dog, maybe.
Edward Noyes Westcott (1847-1898, American Author)

43 Tribulation will not hurt you, unless as it too often does; it hardens you and makes you sour, narrow and skeptical.
Edwin Hubbel Chapin (1814-1880, American Author, Clergyman)

44 Every hardship; every joy; every temptation is a challenge of the spirit; that the human soul may prove itself. The great chain of necessity wherewith we are bound has divine significance; and nothing happens which has not some service in working out the sublime destiny of the human soul.
Elias A. Ford

45 People are like stained -- glass windows. They sparkle and shine when the sun is out, but when the darkness sets in, their true beauty is revealed only if there is a light from within
Elizabeth Kubler Ross

46 It is easy enough to be pleasant, When life flows by like a song. But the man worth while is the one who can smile, when everything goes dead wrong. For the test of the heart is troubled, And it always comes with the years. And the smiles that is worth the praises of earth is the smile that shines through tears.
Ella Wheeler Wilcox (1855-1919, American Poet, Journalist)

47 Men stumble over pebbles, never over mountains
Emilie Cady

48 A wounded deer leaps the highest.
Emily Dickinson (1830-1886, American Poet)

49 A stumble may prevent a fall.
English Proverb

50 A smooth sea never made a skillful mariner.
English Proverb

51 To accuse others for one's own misfortunes is a sign of want of education. To accuse oneself shows that one's education has begun. To accuse neither oneself nor others shows that one's education is complete.
Epictetus (50-120, Stoic Philosopher)

52 Painful as it may be, a significant emotional event can be the catalyst for choosing a direction that serves us--and those around us -- more effectively. Look for the learning.
Eric Allenbaugh (American Author of "Wake-Up Calls")

53 The world breaks everyone and afterward many are stronger at the broken places.
Ernest Hemingway (1898-1961, American Writer)

54 Prosperity is not without many fears and distastes; adversity not without many comforts and hopes.
Francis Bacon (1561-1626, British Philosopher, Essayist, Statesman)

55 I bring to my life a certain amount of mess.
Francis Ford Coppola (1939-, American Director, Cinematographer, Magazine publisher,)

56 If you saw Atlas, the giant who holds the world on his shoulders, if you saw that he stood, blood running down his chest, his knees buckling, his arms trembling but still trying to hold the world aloft with the last of his strength, and the greater the effort the heavier the world bore down upon his shoulders -- what would you tell him to do? I don't know. What could he do? What would you tell him? To shrug.
Francisco D'Anconia

57 People need hard times and oppression to develop psychic muscles.
Frank Herbert, Dune

58 What doesn't kill us makes us stronger.
Friedrich Nietzsche (1844-1900, German Philosopher)

59 It is in the gift for employing all the vicissitudes of life to one's own advantage and to that of one's craft that a large part of genius consists.
Georg C. Lichtenberg (1742-1799, German Physicist, Satirist)

60 There is a great deal of unmapped country within us which would have to be taken into account in an explanation of our gusts and storms.
George Eliot (1819-1880, British Novelist)

61 In terms of the game theory, we might say the universe is so constituted as to maximize play. The best games are not those in which all goes smoothly and steadily toward a certain conclusion, but those in which the outcome is always in doubt. Similarly, the geometry of life is designed to keep us at the point of maximum tension between certainty and uncertainty, order and chaos. Every important call is a close one. We survive and evolve by the skin of our teeth. We really wouldn't want it any other way.
George Leonard

62 God left the world unfinished for man to work his skill upon. He left the electricity still in the cloud, the oil still in the earth. How often we look upon God as our last and feeblest resource! We go to Him because we have nowhere else to go. And then we learn that the storms of life have driven us, not upon the rocks, but into the desired haven.
George Macdonald (1824-1905, Scottish Novelist)

63 If you want to win anything -- a race, your self, your life -- you have to go a little berserk.
George Sheehan

64 Forget the times of your distress, but never forget what they taught you.
Gesser

65 One sees great things from the valley; only small things from the peak.
Gilbert K. Chesterton (1874-1936, British Author)

66 Do not free the camel of the burden of his hump; you may be freeing him from being a camel.
Gilbert K. Chesterton (1874-1936, British Author)

67 It is not good for all our wishes to be filled; through sickness we recognize the value of health; through evil, the value of good; through hunger, the value of food; through exertion, the value of rest.
Greek Saying

68 Humanity either makes, or breeds, or tolerates all its afflictions.
H.G. Wells (1866-1946, British-born American Author)

69 When walking through the "valley of shadows," remember, a shadow is cast by a Light.
H.K. Barclay

70 We must free ourselves of the hope that the sea will ever rest. We must learn to sail in high winds.
Hanmer Parsons Grant

71 Things were bad but now they are OK.
Harold J. Seymour

72 He who knows no hardships will know no hardihood. He who faces no calamity will need no courage. Mysterious though it is, the characteristics in human nature which we love best grow in a soil with a strong mixture of troubles.
Harry Emerson Fosdick (1878-1969, American Minister)

73 It takes a real storm in the average person's life to make him realize how much worrying he has done over the squalls.
Heartland Advisor

74 He that can heroically endure adversity will bear prosperity with equal greatest of the soul; for the mind that cannot be dejected by the former is not likely to be transported without the latter.
Henry Fielding (1707-1754, British Novelist, Dramatist)

75 Life is a series of experiences, each one of which makes us bigger, even though sometimes it is hard to realize this. For the world was built to develop character, and we must learn that the setbacks and grieves which we endure help us in our marching onward.
Henry Ford (1863-1947, American Industrialist, Founder of Ford Motor Company)

76 Each success only buys an admission ticket to a more difficult problem.
Henry Kissinger (1923-, American Republican Politician, Secretary of State)

77 We are always on the anvil; by trials God is shaping us for higher things.
Henry Ward Beecher (1813-1887, American Preacher, Orator, Writer)

78 Affliction comes to us, not to make us sad but sober; not to make us sorry but wise.
Henry Ward Beecher (1813-1887, American Preacher, Orator, Writer)

79 It would not be better if things happened to men just as they wish.
Heraclitus (535-475 BC, Greek Philosopher)

80 Be still my heart; thou hast known worse than this.
Homer (850 BC, Greek Epic Poet)

81 Adversity reveals genius, prosperity conceals it.
Horace (65-8 BC, Italian Poet)

82 The one who prosperity takes too much delight in will be the most shocked by reverses.
Horace (65-8 BC, Italian Poet)

83 As a rule, adversity reveals genius and prosperity hides it.
Horace (65-8 BC, Italian Poet)

84 A heart well prepared for adversity in bad times hopes, and in good times fears for a change in fortune.
Horace (65-8 BC, Italian Poet)

85 Adversity has the effect of eliciting talents, which in prosperous circumstances would have lain dormant.
Horace (65-8 BC, Italian Poet)

86 Not everything which is bad comes to hurt us.
Italian Proverb

87 I would never have amounted to anything were it not for adversity. I was forced to come up the hard way.
J. C. (James Cash) Penney (1875-1971, American Retailer, Philanthropist, Founder JC Penny's)

88 Trials, temptations, disappointments -- all these are helps instead of hindrances, if one uses them rightly. They not only test the fiber of character but strengthen it. Every conquering temptation represents a new fund of moral energy. Every trial endured and weathered in the right spirit makes a soul nobler and stronger than it was before.
James Buckham

89 Over every mountain there is a path, although it may not be seen from the valley.
James Rogers

90 Mishaps are like knives, that either serve us or cut us, as we grasp them by the blade or by the handle.
James Russell Lowell (1819-1891, American Poet, Critic, Editor)

91 I used to hurt so badly that I'd ask God why, what have I done to deserve any of this? I feel now He was preparing me for this, for the future. That's the way I see it.
Janet Jackson (1966-, American Musician, Actress)

92 The actual tragedies of life bear no relation to one's preconceived ideas. In the event, one is always bewildered by their simplicity, their grandeur of design, and by that element of the bizarre which seems inherent in them.
Jean Cocteau (1889-1963, French Author, Filmmaker)

93 To endure is the first thing that a child ought to learn, and that which he will have the most need to know.
Jean Jacques Rousseau (1712-1778, Swiss Political Philosopher, Educationist, Essayist)

94 Adversity is a great teacher, but this teacher makes us pay dearly for its instruction; and often the profit we derive, is not worth the price we paid.
Jean Jacques Rousseau (1712-1778, Swiss Political Philosopher, Educationist, Essayist)

95 If you can keep your head about you when all about you are losing theirs, its just possible you haven't grasped the situation.
Jean Kerr (1923-, American Author, Playwright)

96 Every man has a rainy corner of his life whence comes foul weather which follows him.
Jean Paul Richter (1763-1825, German Novelist)

97 And when it rains on your parade, look up rather than down. Without the rain, there would be no rainbow.
Jerry Chin

98 I have become my own version of an optimist. If I can't make it through one door, I'll go through another door -- or I'll make a door. Something terrific will come no matter how dark the present.
Joan Rivers (1933-, American Comedian, Talk Show Host, Actress)

99 The greatest difficulties lie where we are not looking for them.
Johann Wolfgang Von Goethe (1749-1832, German Poet, Dramatist, Novelist)

100 Do you not see how necessary a world of pains and troubles is to school an intelligence and make it a soul?
John Keats (1795-1821, British Poet)

101 A certain amount of opposition is a great help to a man. Kites rise against, not with, the wind.
John Neal

102 If the career you have chosen has some unexpected inconvenience, console yourself by reflecting that no career is without them.
Johnson

103 Adversity has the same effect on a man that severe training has on the pugilist -- it reduces him to his fighting weight.
Josh Billings (1815-1885, American Humorist, Lecturer)

104 March on. Do not tarry. To go forward is to move toward perfection. March on, and fear not the thorns, or the sharp stones on life's path.
Kahlil Gibran (1883-1931, Lebanese Poet, Novelist)

105 One may not reach the dawn save by the path of the night.
Kahlil Gibran (1883-1931, Lebanese Poet, Novelist)

106 What I am looking for is a blessing not in disguise.
Kitty O'neill Collins

107 The depth of darkness to which you can descend and still live is an exact measure of the height to which you can aspire to reach.
Laurens Van du Post

108 When it gets dark enough you can see the stars.
Lee Salk

109 Never let your head hang down. Never give up and sit down and grieve. Find another way. And don't pray when it rains if you don't pray when the sun shines.
Leroy "Satchel" Paige (1906?-1982, American Baseball Player)

110 Just because Fate doesn't deal you the right cards, it doesn't mean you should give up. It just means you have to play the cards you get to their maximum potential.
Les Brown (1945-, American Speaker, Author, Trainer, Motivator Lecturer)

111 Anytime you suffer a setback or disappointment, put your head down and plow ahead.
Les Brown (1945-, American Speaker, Author, Trainer, Motivator Lecturer)

112 Only entropy comes easy.
Lewis Mumford (1895-1990, American Social Philosopher)

113 Adversity is the first path to truth.
Lord Byron (1788-1824, British Poet)

114 It is odd but agitation or contest of any kind gives a rebound to my spirits and sets me up for a time.
Lord Byron (1788-1824, British Poet)

115 Show me someone who has done something worthwhile, and I'll show you someone who has overcome adversity.
Lou Holtz (1937-, American Football Coach)

116 I'm not afraid of storms, for I'm learning to sail my ship.
Louisa May Alcott (1832-1888, American Author)

117 Pain is inevitable, suffering is optional.
M Kathleen Casey

118 When things are bad, we take comfort in the thought that they could always get worse. And when they are, we find hope in the thought that things are so bad they have to get better.
Malcolm S. Forbes (1919-1990, American Publisher, Businessman)

119 Failure is success if we learn from it.
Malcolm S. Forbes (1919-1990, American Publisher, Businessman)

120 Usually when people are sad, they don't do anything. They just cry over their condition. But when they get angry, they bring about a change.
Malcolm X (1925-1965, American Black Leader, Activist)

121 Turn your face to the sun and the shadows fall behind you.
Maori Proverb

122 Here is the rule to remember in the future, When anything tempts you to be bitter: not, "This is a misfortune" but "To bear this worthily is good fortune."
Marcus Aurelius (121-80 AD, Roman Emperor, Philosopher)

123 Dust is a protective coating for fine furniture.
Mario Burata

124 By trying we can easily learn to endure adversity. Another man s, I mean.
Mark Twain (1835-1910, American Humorist, Writer)

125 It's a matter of ABC: When we encounter ADVERSITY, we react by thinking about it. Our thoughts rapidly congeal into BELIEFS. These beliefs may become so habitual we don't even realize we have them unless we stop to focus on them. And they don't just sit there idly; they have CONSEQUENCES. The beliefs are the direct cause of what we feel and what we do next. They can spell the difference between dejection and giving up, on the one hand, and well-being and constructive action on the other. The first step is to see the connection between adversity, belief, and consequence. The second step is to see how the ABCs operate every day in your own life.
Martin E. P. Seligman

126 The ultimate measure of a man is not where he stands in moments of comfort and convenience, but where he stands at times of challenge and controversy.
Martin Luther King Jr. (1929-1968, American Black Leader, Nobel Prize Winner, 1964)

127 Am I willing to give up what I have in order to be what I am not yet? Am I able to follow the spirit of love into the desert? It is a frightening and sacred moment. There is no return. One's life is charged forever. It is the fire that gives us our shape.
Mary Caroline Richards

128 No pressure, no diamonds.
Mary Case

129 When you come to a roadblock, take a detour.
Mary Kay Ash (American Businesswoman, Founder of Mary Kay Cosmetics)

130 You may live in an imperfect world but the frontiers are not closed and the doors are not all shut.
Maxwell Maltz (American Plastic Surgeon, Author of "Psycho-Cybernetics")

131 One often learns more from ten days of agony than from ten years of contentment.
Merle Shain

132 Every adversity, every failure, every heartache carries with it the seed of an equal or greater benefit.
Napoleon Hill (1883-1970, American Speaker, Motivational Writer, "Think and Grow Rich")

133 Cushion the painful effects of hard blows by keeping the enthusiasm going strong, even if doing so requires struggle.
Norman Vincent Peale (1898-1993, American Christian Reformed Pastor, Speaker, Author)

134 Part of the happiness of life consists not in fighting battles, but in avoiding them. A masterly retreat is in itself a victory.
Norman Vincent Peale (1898-1993, American Christian Reformed Pastor, Speaker, Author)

135 Always seek out the seed of triumph in every adversity.
Og Mandino (1923-1996, American Motivational Author, Speaker)

136 There is no better than adversity. Every defeat, every heartbreak, every loss, contains its own seed, its own lesson on how to improve your performance the next time.
Og Mandino (1923-1996, American Motivational Author, Speaker)

137 Search for the seed of good in every adversity. Master that principle and you will own a precious shield that will guard you well through all the darkest valleys you must traverse. Stars may be seen from the bottom of a deep well, when they cannot be discerned from the mountaintop. So will you learn things in adversity that you would never have discovered without trouble. There is always a seed of good. Find it and prosper.
Og Mandino (1923-1996, American Motivational Author, Speaker)

138 Always continue the climb. It is possible for you to do whatever you choose, if you first get to know who you are and are willing to work with a power that is greater than ourselves to do it.
Oprah Winfrey (1954-, American TV Personality, Producer, Actress, Author)

139 We say, sorrow, disaster, calamity. God says, chastening and it sounds sweet to him though it is a discord to our ears. Don't faint when you are rebuked, and don't despise the chastening of the Lord. "In your patience possess your souls."
Oswald Chambers (1874-1917 Scottish Preacher, Author)

140 When a man gets to despair he knows that all his thinking will never get him out. He will only get out by the sheer creative effort of God. Consequently he is in the right attitude to receive from God that which he cannot gain for himself.
Oswald Chambers (1874-1917 Scottish Preacher, Author)

141 The path of least resistance is the path of the loser.
Phil Weltman (American Business Executive, William Morris Agency)

142 Prosperity tries the fortunate, adversity the great.
Pliny The Elder (23-79, Roman Neophatonist)

143 Those who aim at great deeds must also suffer greatly.
Plutarch (46-120 AD, Greek Essayist, Biographer)

144 Prosperity is no just scale; adversity is the only balance to weigh friends.
Plutarch (46-120 AD, Greek Essayist, Biographer)

145 Stumbling is not falling.
Portuguese Proverb

146 We see many who are struggling against adversity who are happy, and more although abounding in wealth, who are wretched.
Publius Cornelius Tacitus (55-117 AD, Roman Historian)

147 Many who seem to be struggling with adversity are happy; many, amid great affluence, are utterly miserable.
Publius Cornelius Tacitus (55-117 AD, Roman Historian)

148 Do you think that you shall enter the Garden of Bliss without such trials as came to those who passed before you?
Qur'an (Holy Book)

149 Clouds come floating into my life, no longer to carry rain or usher storm, but to add color to my sunset sky.
Rabindranath Tagore (1861-1941, Indian Poet, Philosopher)

150 All life demands struggle. Those who have everything given to them become lazy, selfish, and insensitive to the real values of life. The very striving and hard work that we so constantly try to avoid is the major building block in the person we are today.
Ralph Ransom

151 A man is a god in ruins.
Ralph Waldo Emerson (1803-1882, American Poet, Essayist)

152 Out of love and hatred, out of earnings and borrowings and leadings and losses; out of sickness and pain; out of wooing and worshipping; out of traveling and voting and watching and caring; out of disgrace and contempt, comes our tuition in the serene and beautiful laws.
Ralph Waldo Emerson (1803-1882, American Poet, Essayist)

153 Most of the shadows of this life are caused by standing in one's own sunshine
Ralph Waldo Emerson (1803-1882, American Poet, Essayist)

154 The finest steel has to go through the hottest fire.
Richard M. Nixon (1913-1994, Thirty-seventh President of the USA)

155 Even if you fall on your face, you're still moving forward.
Robert C. Gallagher

156 In every adversity there lies the seed of an equivalent advantage. In every defeat is a lesson showing you how to win the victory next time.
Robert Collier (American Writer, Publisher)

157 Tough times never last, but tough people do.
Robert H. Schuller (1926-, American Minister (Crystal Cathedral), Author, Social Leader)

158 Every burden is a blessing.
Robert H. Schuller (1926-, American Minister (Crystal Cathedral), Author, Social Leader)

159 Adversity is the diamond dust Heaven polishes its jewels with.
Robert Leighton (1611-1684, British Clergyman)

160 When something an affliction happens to you, you either let it defeat you, or you defeat it.
Rosalind Russell

161 Birds sing after a storm; why shouldn't people feel as free to delight in whatever remains to them?
Rose F. Kennedy (1890-1995, Mother of President John F. Kennedy)

162 The racism, the sexism, I never let it be my problem, it's their problem. If I see a door comin' my way, I'm knockin' it down. And if I can't knock down the door, I'm sliding through the window. I'll never let it stop me from what I wanna do.
Rosie Perez (1963-, American Actress, Dancer, Choreographer)

163 Life is truly known only to those who suffer, lose, endure adversity and stumble from defeat to defeat.
Ryszard Kapuscinski (1932, Polish Report and Foreign Correspondent)

164 A man is insensible to the relish of prosperity until he has tasted adversity.
Saadi

165 I had to pick myself up and get on with it, do it all over again, only even better this time.
Sam Walton (1918-1992, American Businessman, Founder of Wal-Mart Stores)

166 Adversity is the state in which man mostly easily becomes acquainted with himself, being especially free of admirers then.
Samuel Johnson (1709-1784, British Author)

167 The battle of life is, in most cases, fought uphill; and to win it without a struggle were perhaps to win it without honor. If there were no difficulties there would be no success; if there were nothing to struggle for, there would be nothing to be achieved.
Samuel Smiles (1812-1904, Scottish Author)

168 Any port in a storm.
Scottish Proverb

169 The good things of prosperity are to be wished; but the good things that belong to adversity are to be admired.
Seneca (4 BC-65 AD, Spanish-born Roman Statesman, philosopher)

170 The bravest sight in the world is to see a great man struggling against adversity.
Seneca (4 BC-65 AD, Spanish-born Roman Statesman, philosopher)

171 Brave men rejoice in adversity, just as brave soldiers triumph in war.
Seneca (4 BC-65 AD, Spanish-born Roman Statesman, philosopher)

172 Fire is the test of gold; adversity, of strong men.
Seneca (4 BC-65 AD, Spanish-born Roman Statesman, philosopher)

173 No untroubled day has ever dawned for me.
Seneca (4 BC-65 AD, Spanish-born Roman Statesman, philosopher)

174 The seaman tells stories of winds, the ploughman of bulls; the soldier details his wounds, the shepherd his sheep.
Sextus Propertius (48-15 BC, Italian Latin Elegiac Poet)

175 Misfortunes leave wounds which bleed drop by drop even in sleep; thus little by little they train man by force and dispose him to wisdom in spite of himself. Man must learn to think of himself as a limited and dependent being; and only suffering teaches
Simone Weil (1910-1943, French Philosopher, Mystic)

176 The willow which bends to the tempest, often escapes better than the oak which resists it; and so in great calamities, it sometimes happens that light and frivolous spirits recover their elasticity and presence of mind sooner than those of a loftier character.
Sir Walter Scott (1771-1832, British Novelist, Poet)

177 Adversity is, to me at least, a tonic and a bracer.
Sir Walter Scott (1771-1832, British Novelist, Poet)

178 For gold is tried in the fire and acceptable men in the furnace of adversity.
Sirach

179 Adversity draws men together and produces beauty and harmony in life's relationships, just as the cold of winter produces ice-flowers on the window-panes, which vanish with the warmth.
Soren Kierkegaard (1813-1855, Danish Philosopher, Writer)

180 God had one son on earth without sin, but never one without suffering.
St. Augustine (354-430, Numidian-born Bishop of Hippo, Theologian)

181 Many miles away there's a shadow on the door of a cottage on the Shore of a dark Scottish lake.
Sting (1951-, British-born American Musician, Singer, Songwriter, Actor)

182 Life has meaning only in the struggle. Triumph or defeat is in the hands of the Gods. So let us celebrate the struggle!
Swahili Warrior Song

183 It is during our darkest moments that we must focus to see the light.
Taylor Benson

184 Every blade of grass has its angel that bends over it and whispers, grow, grow.
The Talmud (Jewish Archive of Oral Tradition)

185 In a dark time, the eye begins to see.
Theodore Roethke (1908-1963, American Poet)

186 Adversity is sometimes hard upon a man; but for one man who can stand prosperity, there are a hundred that will stand adversity.
Thomas Carlyle (1795-1881, Scottish Philosopher, Author)

187 There could be no honor in a sure success, but much might be wrested from a sure defeat.
Thomas E. Lawrence (1888-1935, British Soldier, Arabist, Writer)

188 Adversities do not make a man frail. They show what sort of man he is.
Thomas p Kempis (1379-1471, German Monk, Mystic, Religious Writer)

189 As iron put into the fire loseth its rust and becometh clearly red-hot, so he that wholly turneth himself unto God puts off all slothfulness, and is transformed into a new man.
Thomas p Kempis (1379-1471, German Monk, Mystic, Religious Writer)

190 I love those who can smile in trouble, who can gather strength from distress, and grow brave by reflection. 'Tis the business of little minds to shrink, but they whose heart is firm, and whose conscience approves their conduct, will pursue their principles unto death.
Thomas Paine (1737-1809, Anglo-American Political Theorist, Writer)

191 Sometimes your medicine bottle has on it, "Shake well before using." That is what God has to do with some of His people. He has to shake them well before they are ever usable.
Vance Havner

192 Adversity makes men, and prosperity makes monsters.
Victor Hugo (1802-1885, French Poet, Dramatist, Novelist)

193 What is to give light must endure the burning.
Viktor E. Frankl (1905-, Austrian Psychiatrist, Neurology, Writer, "Man's Search for Meaning")

194 You have endured worse things; God will grant an end even to these.
Virgil (70-19 BC, Roman Poet)

195 One likes people much better when they're battered down by a prodigious siege of misfortune than when they triumph.
Virginia Woolf (1882-1941, British Novelist, Essayist)

196 You'll never find a better sparring partner than adversity.
Walt Schmidt

197 There is in every woman's heart a spark of heavenly fire which lies dormant in the broad daylight of prosperity, but which kindles up and beams and blazes in the dark hour of adversity.
Washington Irving (1783-1859, American Author)

198 Little minds are tamed and subdued by misfortune; but great minds rise above them.
Washington Irving (1783-1859, American Author)

199 The worst thing that happens to you may be the best thing for you if you don't let it get the best of you.
Will Rogers (1879-1935, American Humorist, Actor)

200 Adversity causes some men to break, others to break records.
William A. Ward (1921-,)

201 Difficulty, my brethren, is the nurse of greatness --a harsh nurse, who roughly rocks her foster- children into strength and athletic proportion.
William C. Bryant (1794-1878, American Poet, Newspaper Editor)

202 Prosperity is a great teacher; adversity is a greater. Possession pampers the mind; privation trains and strengthens it.
William Hazlitt (1778-1830, British Essayist)

203 Acceptance of what has happened is the first step to overcoming the consequences of any misfortune.
William James (1842-1910, American Psychologist, Professor, Author)

204 Sweet are the uses of adversity which, like the toad, ugly and venomous, wears yet a precious jewel in his head.
William Shakespeare (1564-1616, British Poet, Playwright, Actor)

205 Through tattered clothes, small vices do appear. Robes and furred gowns hide all.
William Shakespeare (1564-1616, British Poet, Playwright, Actor)

206 Sometimes adversity is what you need to face in order to become successful.
Zig Ziglar (American Sales Trainer, Author, Motivational Speaker)

ADVERTISING

1 I have discovered the most exciting, the most arduous literary form of all, the most difficult to master, the most pregnant in curious possibilities. I mean the advertisement. It is far easier to write ten passably effective Sonnets, good enough to take in the not too inquiring critic, than one effective advertisement that will take in a few thousand of the uncritical buying public.
Aldous Huxley (1894-1963, British Author)

2 I do not read advertisements. I would spend all of my time wanting things.
Archibishop of Canterbury

3 The very first law in advertising is to avoid the concrete promise and cultivate the delightfully vague.
Bill Cosby (1937-, American Actor, Comedian, Producer)

4 Advertising is the very essence of democracy.
Bruce Barton (1886-1967, American Author, Advertising Executive)

5 The right name is an advertisement in itself.
Claude Hopkins

6 We read advertisements to discover and enlarge our desires. We are always ready -- even eager -- to discover, from the announcement of a new product, what we have all along wanted without really knowing it.
Daniel J. Boorstin (1914-, American Historian)

7 What you say in advertising is more important than how you say it.
David Ogilvy (1911-, American Businessman, Advertising Expert)

8 The more facts you tell, the more you sell. An advertisement's chance for success invariably increases as the number of pertinent merchandise facts included in the ad increases.
Dr. Charles Edwards

9 Advertisers are the interpreters of our dreams -- Joseph interpreting for Pharaoh. Like the movies, they infect the routine futility of our days with purposeful adventure. Their weapons are our weaknesses: fear, ambition, illness, pride, selfishness, desire, ignorance. And these weapons must be kept as bright as a sword.
E(lwyn) B(rooks) White (1899-1985, American Author, Editor)

10 An advertising agency is 85 percent confusion and 15 percent commission.
Fred A. Allen (1894-1957, American Radio Comic)

11 Advertising is the modern substitute for argument; its function is to make the worse appear the better.
George Santayana (1863-1952, American Philosopher, Poet)

12 Advertising is legalized lying.
H.G. Wells (1866-1946, British-born American Author)

13 How about this for a headline for tomorrow's paper? French fries.
James French

14 Advertising is the principal reason why the business person has come to inherit the earth.
James R. Adams

15 In order to sell a product or a service, a company must establish a relationship with the consumer. It must build trust and rapport. It must understand the customer's needs, and it must provide a product that delivers the promised benefits.
Jay Levinson (American Advertising Expert, Author)

16 If you don't believe in your product, of if you're not consistent and regular in the way you promote it, the odds of succeeding go way down. The primary function of the marketing plan is to ensure that you have the resources and the wherewithal to do what it takes to make your product work.
Jay Levinson (American Advertising Expert, Author)

17 Advertising is the most fun you can have with your clothes on.
Jerry Della Femina (American Advertising Executive)

18 Remove advertising, disable a person or firm from proclaiming its wares and their merits, and the whole of society and of the economy is transformed. The enemies of advertising are the enemies of freedom.
John Enoch Powell (1912-, British statesman,)

19 Society drives people crazy with lust and calls it advertising.
John Lahr

20 Early to bed, early to rise, work like hell, and advertise.
Laurence J. Peter

21 If you are writing about baloney, don't try and make it Cornish hen, because that's the worst kind of baloney there is. Just make it darn good baloney.
Leo Burnett (American Marketing Expert)

22 Make it simple. Make it memorable. Make it inviting to look at. Make it fun to read.
Leo Burnett (American Marketing Expert)

23 I've learned any fool can write a bad ad, but it takes a real genius to keep his hands off a good one.
Leo Burnett (American Marketing Expert)

24 'Be comfortable with who you are', reads the headline on the Hush Puppies poster. Are they mad? If people were comfortable with who they were, they'd never buy any products except the ones they needed, and then where would the advertising industry be?
Mark Edwards (British Journalist)

25 Advertising is the greatest art form of the twentieth century.
Marshall Mcluhan (1911-1980, Canadian Communications Theorist)

26 Ideally, advertising aims at the goal of a programmed harmony among all human impulses and aspirations and endeavors. Using handicraft methods, it stretches out toward the ultimate electronic goal of a collective consciousness.
Marshall Mcluhan (1911-1980, Canadian Communications Theorist)

27 The modern little red riding hood, reared on singing commercials, has no objections to being eaten by the wolf.
Marshall Mcluhan (1911-1980, Canadian Communications Theorist)

28 The headline is the most important element of an ad. It must offer a promise to the reader of a believable benefit. And it must be phrased in a way to make it memorable.
Morris Hite

29 No agency is better than its account executives.
Morris Hite

30 You can tell the ideals of a nation by its advertisements.
Norman Douglas (1868-1952, British Author)

31 Good wine needs no bush, and perhaps products that people really want need no hard-sell or soft-sell TV push. Why not? Look at pot.
Ogden Nash (1902-1971, American Humorous Poet)

32 Several years before birth, advertise for a couple of parents belonging to long-lived families.
Oliver Wendell Holmes (1809-1894, American Author, Wit, Poet)

33 The aim of marketing is to know and understand the customer so well the product or service fits him and sells itself.
Peter F. Drucker (1909-, American Management Consultant, Author)

34 It is pretty obvious that the debasement of the human mind caused by a constant flow of fraudulent advertising is no trivial thing. There is more than one way to conquer a country.
Raymond Chandler (1888-1959, American Author)

35 That's the kind of ad I like, facts, facts, facts.
Samuel Goldwyn (1882-1974, American Film Producer, Founder, MGM)

36 Promise, large promise, is the soul of an advertisement.
Samuel Johnson (1709-1784, British Author)

37 The trade of advertising is now so near perfection that it is not easy to propose any improvement. But as every art ought to be exercised in due subordination to the public good, I cannot but propose it as a moral question to these masters of the public ear, whether they do not sometimes play too wantonly with our passions.
Samuel Johnson (1709-1784, British Author)

38 Advertising is a valuable economic factor because it is the cheapest way of selling goods, particularly if the goods are worthless.
Sinclair Lewis (1885-1951, First American Novelist to win the Nobel Prize for literature)

39 Advertising may be described as the science of arresting the human intelligence long enough to get money from it.
Stephen B. Leacock (1869-1944, Canadian Humorist, Economist)

40 Watteau is no less an artist for having painted a fascia board while Sainsbury's is no less effective a business for producing advertisements which entertain and educate instead of condescending and exploiting.
Stephen Bayley (1951-, British Design Critic)

41 Sanely applied advertising could remake the world.
Stuart Chase (1888-1985, American Writer)

42 Telling lies does not work in advertising.
Tim Bell (British Publicity Expert)

43 One ad is worth more to a paper than forty editorials.
Will Rogers (1879-1935, American Humorist, Actor)

44 Advertising is the genie which is transforming America into a place of comfort, luxury and ease for millions.
William Allen White (1868-1944, American Editor, Writer)

45 In advertising, not to be different is virtual suicide.
William Bernbach (1911-1982, American Advertising Executive)

46 The art of advertisement, after the American manner, has introduced into all our life such a lavish use of superlatives, that no standard of value whatever is intact.
Wyndham Lewis (1882-1957, British Author, Painter)

47 We grew up founding our dreams on the infinite promise of American advertising. I still believe that one can learn to play the piano by mail and that mud will give you a perfect complexion.
Zelda Fitzgerald (1900-1948, American Writer)

ADVICE

1 It is easy when we are in prosperity to give advice to the afflicted.
Aeschylus (525-456 BC, Greek Dramatist)

2 Never trust the advice of a man in difficulties.
Aesop (620-560 BC, Greek Fabulist)

3 Consult. To seek another's approval of a course already decided on.
Ambrose Bierce (1842-1914, American Author, Editor, Journalist, "The Devil's Dictionary")

4 Never give advice in a crowd.
Arabian Proverb

5 No man is so foolish but he may sometimes give another good counsel, and no man so wise that he may not easily err if he takes no other counsel than his own. He that is taught only by himself has a fool for a master.
Ben Johnson (1573-1637, British Dramatist, Poet)

6 Wise men don't need advice. Fools won't take it.
Benjamin Franklin (1706-1790, American Scientist, Publisher, Diplomat)

7 They that will not be counseled, cannot be helped. If you do not hear reason she will rap you on the knuckles.
Benjamin Franklin (1706-1790, American Scientist, Publisher, Diplomat)

8 A fool think he needs no advice, but a wise man listens to others.
Bible (Sacred Scriptures of Christians and Judaism)

9 Where no counsel is, the people fall; but in the multitude of counselors there is safety.
Bible (Sacred Scriptures of Christians and Judaism)

10 A word to the wise isn't necessary, it is the stupid ones who need all the advice.
Bill Cosby (1937-, American Actor, Comedian, Producer)

11 We ask advice but we mean approbation.
Charles Caleb Colton (1780-1832, British Sportsman Writer)

12 If your strength is small, don't carry heavy burdens. If your words are worthless, don't give advice.
Chinese Proverb

13 Number one: Don't frisk me. Don't hurt me physically. Don't get anywhere near my neck. And don't call me Regis. [Advice to his guests]
David Letterman (1947-, American TV Personality)

14 Don't follow any advice, no matter how good, until you feel as deeply in your spirit as you think in your mind that the counsel is wise.
David Seabury (American Doctor, Author)

15 There is hardly a man on earth who will take advice unless he is certain that it is positively bad.
Edward Dahlberg (1900-1977, American Author, Critic)

16 Advice is what we ask for when we already know the answer but wish we didn't.
Erica Jong (1942-, American Author)

17 He that gives good advice, builds with one hand; he that gives good counsel and example, builds with both; but he that gives good admonition and bad example, builds with one hand and pulls down with the other.
Francis Bacon (1561-1626, British Philosopher, Essayist, Statesman)

18 There is as much difference between the counsel that a friend giveth, and that a man giveth himself, as there is between the counsel of a friend and of a flatterer. For there is no such flatterer as is a man's self.
Francis Bacon (1561-1626, British Philosopher, Essayist, Statesman)

19 We give advice, but we cannot give the wisdom to profit by it.
François de La Rochefoucauld (1613-1680, French classical writer)

20 Men give away nothing so liberally as their advice.
François de La Rochefoucauld (1613-1680, French classical writer)

21 The one thing people are the most liberal with, is their advice.
François de La Rochefoucauld (1613-1680, French classical writer)

22 We may give advice, but not the sense to use it.
François de La Rochefoucauld (1613-1680, French classical writer)

23 I am glad that I paid so little attention to good advice; had I abided by it I might have been saved from some of my most valuable mistakes.
Gene Fowler (1890-1960, American Journalist, Biographer)

24 I'm not a teacher: only a fellow-traveler of whom you asked the way. I pointed ahead -- ahead of myself as well as you.
George Bernard Shaw (1856-1950, Irish-born British Dramatist)

25 Let no man under value the price of a virtuous woman's counsel.
George Chapman (1557-1634, British Dramatist, Translator, Poet)

26 Never give advice unless asked.
German Proverb

27 To advise is not to compel.
German Proverb

28 To advise is easier than to help.
German Proverb

29 To listen to some devout people, one would imagine that God never laughs.
Ghose Aurobindo (1872-1950, Philosopher)

30 I owe my success to having listened respectfully to the very best advice, and then going away and doing the exact opposite.
Gilbert K. Chesterton (1874-1936, British Author)

31 The true secret of giving advice is, after you have honestly given it, to be perfectly indifferent whether it is taken or not, and never persist in trying to set people right.
Hannah Whitall Smith

32 These words dropped into my childish mind as if you should accidentally drop a ring into a deep well. I did not think of them much at the time, but there came a day in my life when the ring was fished up out of the well, good as new.
Harriet Beecher Stowe (1811-1896, American Novelist, Antislavery Campaigner)

33 I have lived some thirty-odd years on this planet, and I have yet to hear the first syllable of valuable or even earnest advice from my seniors.
Henry David Thoreau (1817-1862, American Essayist, Poet, Naturalist)

34 Aim above morality. Be not simply good, be good for something.
Henry David Thoreau (1817-1862, American Essayist, Poet, Naturalist)

35 We hate those who will not take our advice, and despise them who do.
Henry Wheeler Shaw (1818-1885, American Humorist)

36 A good scare is worth more than good advice.
Horace (65-8 BC, Italian Poet)

37 Whatever advice you give, be short.
Horace (65-8 BC, Italian Poet)

38 I wouldn't recommend sex, drugs or insanity for everyone, but they've always worked for me.
Hunter S. Thompson (1939-, American Journalist)

39 Great effort is required to arrest decay and restore vigor. One must exercise proper deliberation, plan carefully before making a move, and be alert in guarding against relapse following a renaissance.
I Ching (12th Century BC, Chinese Book of Changes)

40 Most of us ask for advice when we know the answer but we want a different one.
Ivern Ball

41 It takes a great man to give sound advice tactfully, but a greater to accept it graciously.
J. C. Macaulay

42 We all admire the wisdom of people who come to us for advice.
Jack Herbert

43 It is only too easy to make suggestions and later try to escape the consequences of what we say.
Jawaharlal Nehru (1889-1964, Indian Nationalist, Statesman)

44 Some of these people need ten years of therapy --ten sentences of mine do not equal ten years of therapy.
Jeff Zaslow (1925-, American Advice Columnist)

45 One can advise comfortably from a safe port.
Johann Friedrich Von Schiller (1759-1805, German Dramatist, Poet, Historian)

46 It is easy to give advice from a port of safety.
Johann Friedrich Von Schiller (1759-1805, German Dramatist, Poet, Historian)

47 Never claim as a right what you can ask as a favor.
John Churton Collins

48 To profit from good advice requires more wisdom than to give it.
John Churton Collins

49 Generally speaking, when a woman offers unsolicited advice or tries to help a man, she has no idea of how critical and unloving he may sound to him.
John Gray (American Relationship Expert, Author)

50 To offer a man unsolicited advice is to presume that he doesn't know what to do or that he can't do it on his own.
John Gray (American Relationship Expert, Author)

51 No one wants advice, only corroboration.
John Steinbeck (1902-1968, American Author)

52 Advice is like castor oil, easy to give, but dreadful to take.
Josh Billings (1815-1885, American Humorist, Lecturer)

53 Most people when they come to you for advice, come to have their own opinions strengthened, not corrected.
Josh Billings (1815-1885, American Humorist, Lecturer)

54 When we turn to one another for counsel we reduce the number of our enemies.
Kahlil Gibran (1883-1931, Lebanese Poet, Novelist)

55 He who can take advice is sometimes superior to him who can give it.
Karl Von Knebel

56 Most people who ask for advice from others have already resolved to act as it pleases them.
Knegge

57 I sometimes give myself admirable advice, but I am incapable of taking it.
Lady Mary Wortley Montagu (1689-1762, British Society Figure, Letter Writer)

58 Never give anyone the advice to buy or sell shares, because the most benevolent price of advice can turn out badly.
Lope de Vega (1562-1635, Spanish Playwright)

59 Advice is seldom welcome; and those who want it the most always like it the least.
Lord Chesterfield (1694-1773, British Statesman, Author)

60 In matters of religion and matrimony I never give any advice; because I will not have anybody's torments in this world or the next laid to my charge.
Lord Chesterfield (1694-1773, British Statesman, Author)

61 Always be nice to bankers. Always be nice to pension fund managers. Always be nice to the media. In that order.
Lord Hanson (British Executive)

62 Your friends praise your abilities to the skies, submit to you in argument, and seem to have the greatest deference for you; but, though they may ask it, you never find them following your advice upon their own affairs; nor allowing you to manage your own, without thinking that you should follow theirs. Thus, in fact, they all think themselves wiser than you, whatever they may say.
Lord Melbourne (1779-1848, British Statesman, Prime Minister)

63 When we ask for advice, we are usually looking for an accomplice.
Marquis de la Grange

64 Give help rather than advice.
Marquis De Vauvenargues (1715-1747, French Moralist)

65 Never play cards with a man called Doc. Never eat at a place called Mom s. Never sleep with a woman whose troubles are worse than your own.
Nelson Algren (1909-1981, American Author)

66 The advice of the elders to young men is very apt to be as unreal as a list of the hundred best books.
Oliver Wendell Holmes (1809-1894, American Author, Wit, Poet)

67 The only thing to do with good advice is to pass it on. It is never of any use to oneself.
Oscar Wilde (1856-1900, British Author, Wit)

68 The worst men often give the best advice.
Philip James Bailey (1816-1902, British Poet)

69 The best advisers, helpers and friends, always are not those who tell us how to act in special cases, but who give us, out of themselves, the ardent spirit and desire to act right, and leave us then, even through many blunders, to find out what our own form of right action is.
Phillips Brooks (1835-1893, American Minister, Poet)

70 Good advice is beyond all price.
Proverb

71 Write down the advice of him who loves you, though you like it not at present.
Proverb

72 Many receive advice, only the wise profit from it.
Publilius Syrus (1st Century BC, Roman Writer)

73 It is bad advice that cannot be changed.
Publilius Syrus (1st Century BC, Roman Writer)

74 The advice that is wanted is commonly not welcome and that which is not wanted, evidently an effrontery.
Samuel Johnson (1709-1784, British Author)

75 Advice is like snow; the softer it falls the longer it dwells upon, and the deeper it sinks into the mind.
Samuel Taylor Coleridge (1772-1834, British Poet, Critic, Philosopher)

76 When in doubt, don't.
Saul W. Gellerman (American Academic)

77 Consult your friend on all things, especially on those which respect yourself. His counsel may then be useful where your own self-love might impair your judgment.
Seneca (4 BC-65 AD, Spanish-born Roman Statesman, philosopher)

78 The rich are always advising the poor, but the poor seldom return the compliment.
Sir Arthur Helps (1813-1875, British Historian, Novelist, Essayist)

79 Never advise anyone to go to war or to get married. Write down the advice of him who loves you, though you like it not at present. He that has no children brings them up well.
Spanish Proverb

80 If one man says to thee, "Thou art a donkey," pay no heed. If two speak thus, purchase a saddle.
The Talmud (Jewish Archive of Oral Tradition)

81 Talk that does not end in any kind of action is better suppressed altogether.
Thomas Carlyle (1795-1881, Scottish Philosopher, Author)

82 Be yourself is about the worst advice you can give to some people.
Thomas L. Masson

83 Be smart, be intelligent and be informed.
Tony Alesandra (American Businessman, Author, Speaker)

84 Counsel woven into the fabric of real life is wisdom.
Walter Benjamin (1982-1940, German Critic, Philosopher)

85 We give advice by the bucket, but take it by the grain.
William R. Alger (1822-1905, American Writer)

86 I shall the effect of this good lesson keeps as watchman to my heart.
William Shakespeare (1564-1616, British Poet, Playwright, Actor)

87 In those days he was wiser than he is now -- he used frequently to take my advice.
Winston Churchill (1874-1965, British Statesman, Prime Minister)

AFFECTATION

1 Our greatest pretenses are built up not to hide the evil and the ugly in us, but our emptiness. The hardest thing to hide is something that is not there.
Eric Hoffer (1902-1983, American Author, Philosopher)

2 Let the world know you as you are, not as you think you should be, because sooner or later, if you are posing, you will forget the pose, and then where are you?
Fanny Brice (1891-1951, American Entertainer)

3 Affectation is a very good word when someone does not wish to confess to what he would none the less like to believe of himself.
Georg C. Lichtenberg (1742-1799, German Physicist, Satirist)

AFFECTION

1 One should never direct people towards happiness, because happiness too is an idol of the market-place. One should direct them towards mutual affection. A beast gnawing at its prey can be happy too, but only human beings can feel affection for each other, and this is the highest achievement they can aspire to.
Alexander Solzhenitsyn (1918-, Russian Novelist)

2 A mixture of admiration and pity is one of the surest recipes for affection.
Andre Maurois (1885-1967, French Writer)

3 Most people would rather give than get affection.
Aristotle (384-322 BC, Greek Philosopher)

4 The two qualities which chiefly inspire regard and affection [Are] that a thing is your own and that it is your only one.
Aristotle (384-322 BC, Greek Philosopher)

5 Set your affection on things above, not on things on the earth. [Colossians 3:2]
Bible (Sacred Scriptures of Christians and Judaism)

6 It's not till sex has died out between a man and a woman that they can really love. And now I mean affection. Now I mean to be fond of (as one is fond of oneself) --to hope, to be disappointed, to live inside the other heart. When I look back on the pain of sex, the love like a wild fox so ready to bite, the antagonism that sits like a twin beside love, and contrast it with affection, so deeply unrepeatable, of two people who have lived a life together (and of whom one must die) it's the affection I find richer. It's that I would have again. Not all those doubtful rainbow colors.
Enid Bagnold (1889-1981, British Novelist, Playwright)

7 If you value a man's regard, strive with him. As to liking, you like your newspaper -- and despise it.
George Bernard Shaw (1856-1950, Irish-born British Dramatist)

8 Talk not of wasted affection; affection never was wasted.
Henry Wadsworth Longfellow (1819-1892, American Poet)

9 In nine cases out of ten, a woman had better show more affection than she feels.
Jane Austen (1775-1817, British Novelist)

10 The affections are like lightning: you cannot tell where they will strike till they have fallen.
Jean Baptiste Lacordaire

11 Affection, like melancholy, magnifies trifles; but the magnifying of the one is like looking through a telescope at heavenly objects; that of the other, like enlarging monsters with a microscope.
Leigh Hunt (1784-1859, British Poet, Essayist)

12 A slight touch of friendly malice and amusement towards those we love keeps our affections for them from turning flat.
Logan Pearsall Smith (1865-1946, Anglo-American Essayist, Aphorist)

13 Caresses, expressions of one sort or another, are necessary to the life of the affections as leaves are to the life of a tree. If they are wholly restrained, love will die at the roots.
Nathaniel Hawthorne (1804-1864, American Novelist, Short Story Writer)

14 I love to hold people's hands when I visit hospitals, even though they are shocked because they haven't experienced anything like it before, but to me it is a normal thing to do.
Princess of Wales Diana (1961-1997, Wife of Charles, Prince of Wales)

15 Yes, I do touch. I believe that everyone needs that...
Princess of Wales Diana (1961-1997, Wife of Charles, Prince of Wales)

16 The moment we indulge our affections, the earth is metamorphosed, there is no winter and no night; all tragedies, all ennui s, vanish, all duties even.
Ralph Waldo Emerson (1803-1882, American Poet, Essayist)

17 Don't be afraid of showing affection. Be warm and tender, thoughtful and affectionate. Men are more helped by sympathy than by service. Love is more than money, and a kind word will give more pleasure than a present.
Sir John Lubbock (1834-1913, British Statesman, Banker, Naturalist)

18 A woman's life is a history of the affections.
Washington Irving (1783-1859, American Author)

19 I never met a man I didn't like.
Will Rogers (1879-1935, American Humorist, Actor)

AFFIRMATION

1 It's the repetition of affirmations that leads to belief. And once that belief becomes a deep conviction, things begin to happen.
Claude M. Bristol (1891-1951, American Author of "The Magic of Believing")

2 These repetitive words and phrases are merely methods of convincing the subconscious mind.
Claude M. Bristol (1891-1951, American Author of "The Magic of Believing")

3 You must begin to think of yourself as becoming the person you want to be.
David Viscott (American Author, Speaker, Trainer)

4 First say to yourself what you would be; and then do what you have to do.
Epictetus (50-120, Stoic Philosopher)

5 You will be a failure, until you impress the subconscious with the conviction you are a success. This is done by making an affirmation which "clicks."
Florence Scovel Shinn (American Artist, Metaphysics Teacher, Author)

6. We cannot always control our thoughts, but we can control our words, and repetition impresses the subconscious, and we are then master of the situation.
Florence Scovel Shinn (American Artist, Metaphysics Teacher, Author)

7. Only one thing registers on the subconscious mind: repetitive application -- practice. What you practice is what you manifest.
Grace Speare

8. When you affirm your own rightness in the universe, then you co-operate with others easily and automatically as part of your own nature. You, being yourself, helps others be themselves. Because you recognize your own uniqueness you will not need to dominate others, nor cringe before them
Jane Roberts

9. I figured that if I said it enough, I would convince the world that I really was the greatest.
Muhammad Ali (1942-, American Boxer)

10. Any thought that is passed on to the subconscious often enough and convincingly enough is finally accepted.
Robert Collier (American Writer, Publisher)

11. You must intensify and render continuous by repeatedly presenting with suggestive ideas and mental pictures of the feast of good things, and the flowing fountain, which awaits the successful achievement or attainment of the desires.
Robert Collier (American Writer, Publisher)

12. Constant repetition carries conviction.
Robert Collier (American Writer, Publisher)

13. One comes to believe whatever one repeats to oneself sufficiently often, whether the statement be true of false. It comes to be dominating thought in one's mind.
Robert Collier (American Writer, Publisher)

14. As long as you know what it is you desire, then by simply affirming that it is yours -- firmly and positively, with no ifs, buts, or maybes -- over and over again, from the minute you arise in the morning until the time you go to sleep at night, and as many times during the day as your work or activities permit, you will be drawn to those people, places, and events that will bring your desires to you.
Scott Reed

15. Our subconscious minds have no sense of humor, play no jokes and cannot tell the difference between reality and an imagined thought or image. What we continually think about eventually will manifest in our lives.
Sidney Madwed (American Speaker, Consultant, Author, Poet)

AFFLICTION

1. To bear other people's afflictions, everyone has courage and enough to spare.
Benjamin Franklin (1706-1790, American Scientist, Publisher, Diplomat)

2. Affliction, like the iron-smith, shapes as it smites.
Christian Nevell Bovee (1820-1904, American Author, Lawyer)

3. No one could be more happy than a man who has never known affliction
Demetrius Phalerens

4. Strength is born in the deep silence of long-suffering hearts; not amid joy.
Felicia D. Hemans (1794-1835, British Poet)

5. Though all afflictions are evils in themselves, yet they are good for us, because they discover to us our disease and tend to our cure.
John Tillotson (1630-1694, British Theologian - Archbishop of Canterbury)

6. As threshing separates the wheat from the chaff, so does affliction purify virtue.
Sir Richard Burton (1821-1890, Explorer, Born in Torquay)

AGE AND AGING

1. If you carry your childhood with you, you never become older.
Abraham Sutzkever

2. What a man knows at fifty that he did not know at twenty is for the most part incommunicable.
Adlai E. Stevenson (1900-1965, American Lawyer, Politician)

3. I married an archaeologist because the older I grow, the more he appreciates me.
Agatha Christie (1891-1976, British Mystery Writer)

4. An archaeologist is the best husband a woman can have; the older she gets the more interested he is in her.
Agatha Christie (1891-1976, British Mystery Writer)

5. I think when the full horror of being fifty hits you, you should stay home and have a good cry.
Alan Bleasdale (1946-, British Playwright, Novelist)

6. Perfection of means and confusion of goals seem -- in my opinion -- to characterize our age.
Albert Einstein (1879-1955, German-born American Physicist)

7 Every man who has lived for fifty years has buried a whole world or even two; he has grown used to its disappearance and accustomed to the new scenery of another act: but suddenly the names and faces of a time long dead appear more and more often on his way, calling up series of shades and pictures kept somewhere, "just in case," in the endless catacombs of the memory, making him smile or sigh, and sometimes almost weep.
Alexander Herzen (1812-1870, Russian Journalist, Political Thinker)

8 Some old men, continually praise the time of their youth. In fact, you would almost think that there were no fools in their days, but unluckily they themselves are left as an example.
Alexander Pope (1688-1744, British Poet, Critic, Translator)

9 Age. That period of life in which we compound for the vices that remain by reviling those we have no longer the vigor to commit.
Ambrose Bierce (1842-1914, American Author, Editor, Journalist, "The Devil's Dictionary")

10 Old age is the verdict of life.
Amelia E. Barr (1831-1919, Anglo-American Novelist)

11 While one finds company in himself and his pursuits, he cannot feel old, no matter what his years may be.
Amos Bronson Alcott (1799-1888, American Educator, Social Reformer)

12 The surest sign of age is loneliness.
Amos Bronson Alcott (1799-1888, American Educator, Social Reformer)

13 To me -- old age is always ten years older than I am.
Andre B. Buruch

14 Old age is far more than white hair, wrinkles, the feeling that it is too late and the game finished, that the stage belongs to the rising generations. The true evil is not the weakening of the body, but the indifference of the soul.
Andre Maurois (1885-1967, French Writer)

15 Growing old is no more than a bad habit which a busy man has no time to form.
Andre Maurois (1885-1967, French Writer)

16 She was a handsome woman of forty-five and would remain so for many years.
Anita Brookner (1938-, British Novelist, Art Historian)

17 You can only perceive real beauty in a person as they get older.
Anouk Aimee (1932-, French Actor)

18 Growing old is like being increasingly penalized for a crime you haven't committed.
Anthony Powell (1905-, British Novelist)

19 You know you're getting old when all the names in your black book have M. D. after them.
Arnold Palmer (1929-, American Golfer)

20 Preparation for old age should begin not later than one's teens. A life which is empty of purpose until 65 will not suddenly become filled on retirement.
Arthur E. Morgan (1878-1976, American Engineer, Educator)

21 The closing years of life are like the end of a masquerade party, when the masks are dropped.
Arthur Schopenhauer (1788-1860, German Philosopher)

22 At twenty a man is a peacock, at thirty a lion, at forty a camel, at fifty a serpent, at sixty a dog, at seventy an ape, at eighty a nothing at all.
Baltasar Gracian (1601-1658, Spanish Philosopher, Writer)

23 Talking is the disease of age.
Ben Johnson (1573-1637, British Dramatist, Poet)

24 Youth is a blunder, manhood is a struggle and old age a regret.
Benjamin Disraeli (1804-1881, British Statesman, Prime Minister)

25 The disappointment of manhood succeeds the delusion of youth.
Benjamin Disraeli (1804-1881, British Statesman, Prime Minister)

26 An old young man, will be a young old man.
Benjamin Franklin (1706-1790, American Scientist, Publisher, Diplomat)

27 Many foxes grow gray but few grow good.
Benjamin Franklin (1706-1790, American Scientist, Publisher, Diplomat)

28 At twenty years of age the will reigns; at thirty, the wit; and at forty, the judgment.
Benjamin Franklin (1706-1790, American Scientist, Publisher, Diplomat)

29 Those who love deeply never grow old; they may die of old age, but they die young.
Benjamin Franklin (1706-1790, American Scientist, Publisher, Diplomat)

30 If you wouldn't live long, live well; for folly and wickedness shorten life.
Benjamin Franklin (1706-1790, American Scientist, Publisher, Diplomat)

31 Men who have reached and passed forty-five, have a look as if waiting for the secret of the other world, and as if they were perfectly sure of having found out the secret of this.
Benjamin Haydon (1786-1846, British Artist)

32 I will never be an old man. To me, old age is always 15 years older than I am.
Bernard M. Baruch (1870-1965, American Financier)

33 With the ancient is wisdom; and in length of days understanding. [Job 12:12]
Bible (Sacred Scriptures of Christians and Judaism)

34 While we look not a that things which are seen, but at the things which are not seen; for the things which are seen are temporal; but the things which are not seen are eternal. [2 Corinthians 4:18]
Bible (Sacred Scriptures of Christians and Judaism)

35 Therefore we do not lose heart. Even though our outward man is perishing, yet the inward man is being renewed day by day. [2 Corinthians 4:16]
Bible (Sacred Scriptures of Christians and Judaism)

36 He is so old that his blood type was discontinued.
Bill Dana

37 Age doesn't matter, unless you're cheese.
Billie Burke

38 Age is something that doesn't matter, unless you are a cheese
Billie Burke

39 A woman past forty should make up her mind to be young; not her face.
Billie Burke

40 I don't generally feel anything until noon, then it's time for my nap.
Bob Hope (1903-, American Comedian, Actor)

41 Middle age is when your age starts to show around your middle.
Bob Hope (1903-, American Comedian, Actor)

42 You know you're getting old when the candles cost more than the cake.
Bob Hope (1903-, American Comedian, Actor)

43 To resist the frigidity of old age, one must combine the body, the mind, and the heart. And to keep these in parallel vigor one must exercise, study, and love.
Bonstettin

44 I am thirty-three -- the age of the good Sans-culotte Jesus; an age fatal to revolutionists.
Camille Desmoulins (1760-1794, French Journalist, Revolutionary Leader)

45 Old men should have more care to end life well than to live long.
Captain J. Brown

46 From the middle of life onward, only he remains vitally alive who is ready to die with life.
Carl Jung (1875-1961, Swiss Psychiatrist)

47 Age does not matter if the matter does not age.
Carlos Pena Romulo

48 The trick is growing up without growing old.
Casey Stengel (1889-1975, American Baseball Player and Manager)

49 Old age has deformities enough of its own. It should never add to them the deformity of vice.
Cato The Elder (234-149 BC, Roman Statesman, Orator)

50 There are people whose watch stops at a certain hour and who remain permanently at that age.
Charles Augustin Sainte-Beuve (1804-1869, French Critic)

51 The excess of our youth are checks written against our age and they are payable with interest thirty years later.
Charles Caleb Colton (1780-1832, British Sportsman Writer)

52 Old age is a shipwreck.
Charles De Gaulle (1890-1970, French President during World War II)

53 Father Time is not always a hard parent, and, though he tarries for none of his children, often lays his hand lightly upon those who have used him well; making them old men and women inexorably enough, but leaving their hearts and spirits young and in full vigor. With such people the gray head is but the impression of the old fellow's hand in giving them his blessing, and every wrinkle but a notch in the quiet calendar of a well-spent life.
Charles Dickens (1812-1870, British Novelist)

54 Just remember, once you're over the hill you begin to pick up speed.
Charles M. Schultz (1922-, American Cartoonist, Creator of "Peanuts")

55 The woman who tells her age is either too young to have anything to lose or too old to have anything to gain.
Chinese Proverb

56 At twenty a man is full of fight and hope. He wants to reform the world. When he is seventy he still wants to reform the world, but he know he can't.
Clarence Darrow (1857-1938, American Lawyer)

57 Age-based retirement arbitrarily severs productive persons from their livelihood, squanders their talents, scars their health, strains an already overburdened Social Security system, and drives many elderly people into poverty and despair. Ageism is as odious as racism and sexism.
Claude D. Pepper

58 Getting older is like riding a bicycle, if you don't keep peddling, you'll fall.
Claude D. Pepper

59 Ageism is as odious as racism and sexism.
Claude D. Pepper

60 A stockbroker urged me to buy a stock that would triple its value every year. I told him, "At my age, I don't even buy green bananas.
Claude D. Pepper

61 A woman would rather visit her own grave than the place where she has been young and beautiful after she is aged and ugly.
Corra May Harris (1869-1935, American Author)

62 Middle age is youth without levity, and age without decay.
Daniel Defoe (1661-1731, British Author)

63 Aging seems to be the only available way to live a long life.
Daniel François Esprit Auber (1782-1871, French Composer)

64 I think middle-age is the best time, if we can escape the fatty degeneration of the conscience which often sets in at about fifty.
Dean William R. Inge (1860-1954, Dean of St Paul's, London)

65 Most people think that aging is irreversible and we know that there are mechanisms even in the human machinery that allow for the reversal of aging, through correction of diet, through anti- oxidants, through removal of toxins from the body, through exercise, through yoga and breathing techniques, and through meditation.
Deepak Chopra (East-Indian- American M.D., New Age Author, Lecturer)

66 The way you think, the way you behave, the way you eat, can influence your life by 30 to 50 years.
Deepak Chopra (East-Indian- American M.D., New Age Author, Lecturer)

67 You can free yourself from aging by reinterpreting your body and by grasping the link between belief and biology.
Deepak Chopra (East-Indian- American M.D., New Age Author, Lecturer)

68 The nearer people approach old age the closer they return to a semblance of childhood, until the time comes for them to depart this life, again like children, neither tired of living nor aware of death.
Desiderius Erasmus (1466-1536, Dutch Humanist)

69 Middle age is the time when a man is always thinking that in a week or two he will feel as good as ever.
Don Marquis (1878-1937, American Humorist, Journalist)

70 The really frightening thing about middle age is that you know you'll grow out of it!"
Doris Day (1924-, American Singer, Film Actress)

71 The great secret that all old people share is that you really haven't changed in seventy or eighty years. Your body changes, but you don't change at all. And that, of course, causes great confusion.
Doris Lessing (1919-, British Novelist)

72 A man ninety years old was asked to what he attributed his longevity. I reckon, he said, with a twinkle in his eye, it because most nights I went to bed and slept when I should have sat up and worried.
Dorothea Kent

73 One of the many things nobody ever tells you about middle age is that it's such a nice change from being young.
Dorothy Canfield Fisher (1879-1958, American Writer)

74 For in all the world there are no people so piteous and forlorn as those who are forced to eat the bitter bread of dependency in their old age, and find how steep are the stairs of another man's house. Wherever they go they know themselves unwelcome. Wherever they are, they feel themselves a burden. There is no humiliation of the spirit they are not forced to endure. Their hearts are scarred all over with the stabs from cruel and callous speeches.
Dorothy Dix (1861-1951, American Columnist)

75 Time and trouble will tame an advanced young woman, but an advanced old woman is uncontrollable by any earthly force.
Dorothy L. Sayers (1893-1957, British Author)

76 Except ye become as little children, except you can wake on your fiftieth birthday with the same forward-looking excitement and interest in life that you enjoyed when you were five, "ye cannot enter the kingdom of God." One must not only die daily, but every day we must be born again.
Dorothy L. Sayers (1893-1957, British Author)

77 Growing old is not growing up.
Doug Horton

78 The aging process has you firmly in its grasp if you never get the urge to throw a snowball.
Doug Larson

79 I'm saving that rocker for the day when I feel as old as I really am.
Dwight D. Eisenhower (1890-1969, Thirty-fourth President of the USA)

80 Someday you will read in the papers that Moody is dead. Don't you believe a word of it. At that moment I shall be more alive than I am now. I was born of the flesh in 1837, I was born of the spirit in 1855. That which is born of the flesh may die. That which is born of the Spirit shall live forever.
Dwight L. Moody (1837-1899, American Evangelist)

81 In middle life, the human back is spoiling for a technical knockout and will use the flimsiest excuse, even a sneeze, to fall apart.
E(lwyn) B(rooks) White (1899-1985, American Author, Editor)

82 I think in twenty years I'll be looked at like Bob Hope. Doing those president jokes and golf shit. It scares me.
Eddie Murphy (1961-, American Actor, Comedian, Producer)

83 There's no such thing as old age, there is only sorrow.
Edith Wharton (1862-1937, American Author)

84 It is not by the gray of the hair that one knows the age of the heart.
Edward G. Bulwer-Lytton (1803-1873, British Novelist, Poet)

85 We should so provide for old age that it may have no urgent wants of this world to absorb it from meditation on the next. It is awful to see the lean hands of dotage making a coffer of the grave.
Edward G. Bulwer-Lytton (1803-1873, British Novelist, Poet)

86 Nobody expects to trust his body overmuch after the age of fifty.
Edward Hoagland (1932-, American Novelist, Essayist)

87 Be wise with speed; a fool at forty is a fool indeed.
Edward Young (1683-1765, British Poet, Dramatist)

88 An aged Christian, with the snow of time upon his head, may remind us that those points of earth are whitest which are nearest to heaven.
Edwin Hubbel Chapin (1814-1880, American Author, Clergyman)

89 Middle age is when a guy keeps turning off lights for economical rather than romantic reasons.
Eli Cass

90 I'm not interested in age. People who tell me their age are silly. You're as old as you feel.
Elizabeth Arden (1876-1966, Canadian-born American Beautician and Businesswoman)

91 A woman's always younger than a man at equal years.
Elizabeth Barrett Browning (1806-1861, British Poet)

92 At last now you can be what the old cannot recall and the young long for in dreams, yet still include them all.
Elizabeth Jennings (1926-, British Poet)

93 Minds ripen at very different ages.
Elizabeth Montagu

94 With care, and skill, and cunning art, She parried Time's malicious dart, And kept the years at bay, Till passion entered in her heart and aged her in a day!
Ella Wheeler Wilcox (1855-1919, American Poet, Journalist)

95 It is not all bad, this getting old, ripening. After the fruit has got its growth it should juice up and mellow. God forbid I should live long enough to ferment and rot and fall to the ground in a squash.
Emily Carr (1871-1945, Canadian Artist)

96 The older the fiddler, the sweeter the tune.
English Proverb

97 Old age equalizes -- we are aware that what is happening to us has happened to untold numbers from the beginning of time. When we are young we act as if we were the first young people in the world.
Eric Hoffer (1902-1983, American Author, Philosopher)

98 To grow old is to grow common. Old age equalizes -- we are aware that what is happening to us has happened to untold numbers from the beginning of time. When we are young we act as if we were the first young people in the world.
Eric Hoffer (1902-1983, American Author, Philosopher)

99 The end comes when we no longer talk with ourselves. It is the end of genuine thinking and the beginning of the final loneliness.
Eric Hoffer (1902-1983, American Author, Philosopher)

100 As you get older it is harder to have heroes, but it is sort of necessary.
Ernest Hemingway (1898-1961, American Writer)

101 Don't just count your years, make your years count.
Ernest Meyers

102 The old -- like children -- talk to themselves, for they have reached that hopeless wisdom of experience which knows that though one were to cry it in the streets to multitudes, or whisper it in the kiss to one's beloved, the only ears that can ever hear one's secrets are one's own!
Eugene O'Neill (1888-1953, American Dramatist)

103 You end up as you deserve. In old age you must put up with the face, the friends, the health, and the children you have earned.
Fay Weldon (1933-, British Novelist)

104 People of age object too much, consult too long, adventure too little, repent too soon and seldom drive business home to it's conclusion, but content themselves with a mediocrity of success.
Francis Bacon (1561-1626, British Philosopher, Essayist, Statesman)

105 Old wood best to burn, old wine to drink, old friends to trust, and old authors to read.
Francis Bacon (1561-1626, British Philosopher, Essayist, Statesman)

106 Men of age object too much, consult too long, adventure too little, repent too soon, and seldom drive business home to the full period, but content themselves with a mediocrity of success.
Francis Bacon (1561-1626, British Philosopher, Essayist, Statesman)

107 Discern of the coming on of years, and think not to do the same things still; for age will not be defied.
Francis Bacon (1561-1626, British Philosopher, Essayist, Statesman)

108 Age will not be defied.
Francis Bacon (1561-1626, British Philosopher, Essayist, Statesman)

109 As one grows older, one becomes wiser and more foolish.
François de La Rochefoucauld (1613-1680, French classical writer)

110 Old people love to give good advice to console themselves for no longer being able to set a bad example.
François de La Rochefoucauld (1613-1680, French classical writer)

111 Old age is a tyrant, who forbids, under pain of death, the pleasures of youth.
François de La Rochefoucauld (1613-1680, French classical writer)

112 Old men are fond of giving good advice to console themselves for their inability to give bad examples.
François de La Rochefoucauld (1613-1680, French classical writer)

113 Few people know how to be old.
François de La Rochefoucauld (1613-1680, French classical writer)

114 Old age is like everything else. To make a success of it, you've got to start young.
Fred Astaire (1899-1987, American Dancer, Singer, Actor)

115 How people keep correcting us when we are young! There is always some bad habit or other they tell us we ought to get over. Yet most bad habits are tools to help us through life.
Friedrich Nietzsche (1844-1900, German Philosopher)

116 Youth is the gift of nature, but age is a work of art.
Garson Kanin (1912-, American Playwright/Screenwriter, Stage/Movie Director)

117 It really costs me a lot emotionally to watch myself on-screen. I think of myself, and feel like I'm quite young, and then I look at this old man with the baggy chins and the tired eyes and the receding hairline and all that.
Gene Hackman (1930-, American Actor)

118 One is rarely an impulsive innovator after the age of sixty, but one can still be a very fine orderly and inventive thinker. One rarely procreates children at that age, but one is all the more skilled at educating those who have already been procreated, and education is procreation of another kind.
Georg C. Lichtenberg (1742-1799, German Physicist, Satirist)

119 He was then in his fifty-fourth year, when even in the case of poets reason and passion begin to discuss a peace treaty and usually conclude it not very long afterwards.
Georg C. Lichtenberg (1742-1799, German Physicist, Satirist)

120 Every man over forty is a scoundrel.
George Bernard Shaw (1856-1950, Irish-born British Dramatist)

121 Old men are dangerous: it doesn't matter to them what is going to happen to the world.
George Bernard Shaw (1856-1950, Irish-born British Dramatist)

122 How can I die? I'm booked.
George Burns (1896-1996, American Comedy Actor)

123 By the time you're eighty years old you've learned everything. You only have to remember it.
George Burns (1896-1996, American Comedy Actor)

124 You can't help getting older, but you don't have to get old.
George Burns (1896-1996, American Comedy Actor)

125 It's good to be here. At 98, it's good to be anywhere.
George Burns (1896-1996, American Comedy Actor)

126 Few women, I fear, have had such reason as I have to think the long sad years of youth were worth living for the sake of middle age.
George Eliot (1819-1880, British Novelist)

127 In the multitude of middle-aged men who go about their vocations in a daily course determined for them much in the same way as the tie of their cravats, there is always a good number who once meant to shape their own deeds and alter the world a little.
George Eliot (1819-1880, British Novelist)

128 He that is not handsome at 20, nor strong at 30, nor rich at 40, nor wise at 50, will never be handsome, strong, rich or wise.
George Herbert (1593-1632, British Metaphysical Poet)

129 When we are out of sympathy with the young, then I think our work in this world is over.
George Macdonald (1824-1905, Scottish Novelist)

130 Age is not all decay; it is the ripening, the swelling, of the fresh life within, that withers and bursts the husk.
George Macdonald (1824-1905, Scottish Novelist)

131 Not till the fire is dying in the grate, Look we for any kinship with the stars. Oh, wisdom never comes when it is gold, And the great price we paid for it full worth: We have it only when we are half earth. Little avails that coinage to the old!
George Meredith (1828-1909, British Author)

132 Age is a matter of feeling, not of years.
George William Curtis (1824-1892, American Journalist)

133 At twenty you have many desires which hide the truth, but beyond forty there are only real and fragile truths --your abilities and your failings.
Gerard Depardieu (1948-, French Screen Actor)

134 When a noble life has prepared old age, it is not decline that it reveals, but the first days of immortality.
Germaine De Stael (1766-1817, French-Swiss Novelist)

135 The misery of the middle-aged woman is a gray and hopeless thing, born of having nothing to live for, of disappointment and resentment at having been gypped by consumer society, and surviving merely to be the butt of its unthinking scorn.
Germaine Greer (1939-, Australian Feminist Writer)

136 Women over fifty already form one of the largest groups in the population structure of the western world. As long as they like themselves, they will not be an oppressed minority. In order to like themselves they must reject trivialization by others of who and what they are. A grown woman should not have to masquerade as a girl in order to remain in the land of the living.
Germaine Greer (1939-, Australian Feminist Writer)

137 The older woman's love is not love of herself, nor of herself mirrored in a lover's eyes, nor is it corrupted by need. It is a feeling of tenderness so still and deep and warm that it gilds every grass blade and blesses every fly. It includes the ones who have a claim on it, and a great deal else besides. I wouldn't have missed it for the world.
Germaine Greer (1939-, Australian Feminist Writer)

138 An old man loved is winter with flowers.
German Proverb

139 Youth is the period in which a man can be hopeless. The end of every episode is the end of the world. But the power of hoping through everything, the knowledge that the soul survives its adventures, that great inspiration comes to the middle-aged.
Gilbert K. Chesterton (1874-1936, British Author)

140 Old age is like flying through a storm. Once you're aboard, there's nothing you can do.
Golda Meir (1898-1978, Prime Minister of Israel, 1969-74)

141 Being seventy is not a sin.
Golda Meir (1898-1978, Prime Minister of Israel, 1969-74)

142 There are only three ages for women in Hollywood--Babe, District Attorney, and Driving Miss Daisy.
Goldie Hawn (1945-, American Actress)

143 Age is not a particularly interesting subject. Anyone can get old. All you have to do is live long enough.
Groucho Marx (1895-1977, American Comic Actor)

144 Getting older is no problem. You just have to live long enough.
Groucho Marx (1895-1977, American Comic Actor)

145 The older I grow the more I distrust the familiar doctrine that age brings wisdom.
H. L. Mencken (1880-1956, American Editor, Author, Critic, Humorist)

146 One of the most important phases of maturing is that of growth from self-centering to an understanding relationship to others. A person is not mature until he has both an ability and a willingness to see himself as one among others and to do unto those others as he would have them do to him.
Harry A. Overstreet (American Psychologist)

147 I wake up every morning at nine and grab for the morning paper. Then I look at the obituary page. If my name is not on it, I get up.
Harry Hershfield

148 Age is not important unless you're a cheese.
Helen Hayes (1900-1993, American Actress)

149 I have always felt that a woman has the right to treat the subject of her age with ambiguity until, perhaps, she passes into the realm of over ninety. Then it is better she be candid with herself and with the world.
Helena Rubinstein (1870-1965, Polish-born American Cosmetics Manufacturer)

150 If youth knew; if age could.
Henri Estienne (1531-1598, French Scholar, Publisher)

151 To know how to grow old is the master work of wisdom, and one of the most difficult chapters in the great art of living.
Henri Frederic Amiel (1821-1881, Swiss Philosopher, Poet, Critic)

152 None are so old as those who have outlived enthusiasm
Henry David Thoreau (1817-1862, American Essayist, Poet, Naturalist)

153 How earthy old people become --moldy as the grave! Their wisdom smacks of the earth. There is no foretaste of immortality in it. They remind me of earthworms and mole crickets.
Henry David Thoreau (1817-1862, American Essayist, Poet, Naturalist)

154 The youth gets together his materials to build a bridge to the moon, or, perchance, a palace or temple on the earth, and, at length, the middle-aged man concludes to build a woodshed with them.
Henry David Thoreau (1817-1862, American Essayist, Poet, Naturalist)

155 As for the pyramids, there is nothing to wonder at in them so much as the fact that so many men could be found degraded enough to spend their lives constructing a tomb for some ambitious booby, whom it would have been wiser and manlier to have drowned in the Nile, and then given his body to the dogs.
Henry David Thoreau (1817-1862, American Essayist, Poet, Naturalist)

156 They are all gone into the world of light, and I alone sit lingering here.
Henry Vaughan (1622-1695, Welsh Poet)

157 To be seventy years old is like climbing the Alps. You reach a snow-crowned summit, and see behind you the deep valley stretching miles and miles away, and before you other summits higher and whiter, which you may have strength to climb, or may not. Then you sit down and meditate and wonder which it will be.
Henry Wadsworth Longfellow (1819-1892, American Poet)

158 I venerate old age; and I love not the man who can look without emotion upon the sunset of life, when the dusk of evening begins to gather over the watery eye, and the shadows of twilight grow broader and deeper upon the understanding.
Henry Wadsworth Longfellow (1819-1892, American Poet)

159 For age is opportunity no less than youth itself, though in another dress, and as the evening twilight fades away, the sky is filled with stars, invisible by day.
Henry Wadsworth Longfellow (1819-1892, American Poet)

160 Whatever poet, orator, or sage may say of it, old age is still old age.
Henry Wadsworth Longfellow (1819-1892, American Poet)

161 Old age is always wakeful; as if, the longer linked with life, the less man has to do with aught that looks like death.
Herman Melville (1819-1891, American Author)

162 The only time you really live fully is from thirty to sixty. The young are slaves to dreams; the old servants of regrets. Only the middle-aged have all their five senses in the keeping of their wits.
Hervey Allen (1889-1949, American Author)

163 Those who search beyond the natural limits will retain good hearing and clear vision, their bodies will remain light and strong, and although they grow old in years they will remain able- bodied and flourishing; and those who are able-bodied can govern to
Huang Ti (2700-2600 BC, Chinese "Yellow Emperor")

164 When you are younger you get blamed for crimes you never committed and when you're older you begin to get credit for virtues you never possessed. It evens itself out.
I. F. Stone (1907-1989, American Author)

165 I hope I never get so old I get religious.
Ingmar Bergman (1918-, Swedish Stage, Film Writer, Director)

166 I'd like to grow very old as slowly as possible.
Irene Mayer Selznick

167 Twenty years a child; twenty years running wild; twenty years a mature man --and after that, praying.
Irish Proverb

168 One of the delights known to age, and beyond the grasp of youth, is that of Not Going.
J. B. Priestley (1894-1984, English Novelist, Playwright, Essayist)

169 The tendency of old age to the body, say the physiologists, is to form bone. It is as rare as it is pleasant to meet with an old man whose opinions are not ossified.
J. F. Boyse

170 Old age adds to the respect due to virtue, but it takes nothing from the contempt inspired by vice; it whitens only the hair.
J. P. Senn

171 The older you get the stronger the wind gets -- and it's always in your face.
Jack Nicklaus (1940-, American Golfer)

172 If wrinkles must be written upon our brows, let them not be written upon the heart. The spirit should never grow old.
James A. Garfield (1831-1881, Twentieth President of the USA)

173 As life runs on, the road grows strange with faces new -- and near the end. The milestones into headstones change, Neath every one a friend.
James Russell Lowell (1819-1891, American Poet, Critic, Editor)

174 With sixty staring me in the face, I have developed inflammation of the sentence structure and definite hardening of the paragraphs.
James Thurber (1894-1961, American Humorist, Illustrator)

175 I'm 65 and I guess that puts me in with the geriatrics. But if there were fifteen months in every year, I'd only be 48. That's the trouble with us. We number everything. Take women, for example. I think they deserve to have more than twelve years between the ages of 28 and 40.
James Thurber (1894-1961, American Humorist, Illustrator)

176 A man has every season while a woman only has the right to spring. That disgusts me.
Jane Fonda (1937-, American Screen Actor)

177 Old age, believe me, is a good and pleasant thing. It is true you are gently shouldered off the stage, but then you are given such a comfortable front stall as spectator.
Jane Harrison (1850-1928, British Classical Scholar, Writer)

178 The person who has lived the most is not the one with the most years but the one with the richest experiences.
Jean Jacques Rousseau (1712-1778, Swiss Political Philosopher, Educationist, Essayist)

179 The more sand has escaped from the hourglass of our life, the clearer we should see through it.
Jean Paul

180 As winter strips the leaves from around us, so that we may see the distant regions they formerly concealed, so old age takes away our enjoyments only to enlarge the prospect of the coming eternity.
Jean Paul Richter (1763-1825, German Novelist)

181 Gray hairs seem to my fancy like the soft light of the moon, silvering over the evening of life.
Jean Paul Richter (1763-1825, German Novelist)

182 Like a morning dream, life becomes more and more bright the longer we live, and the reason of everything appears more clear. What has puzzled us before seems less mysterious, and the crooked paths look straighter as we approach the end.
Jean Paul Richter (1763-1825, German Novelist)

183 A man is not old as long as he is seeking something.
Jean Rostand (1894-1977, French Biologist, Writer)

184 Age does not protect you from love but love to some extent protects you from age.
Jeanne Moreau (1928-, French Actress and Director)

185 Age does not make us childish, as some say; it finds us true children.
Johann Wolfgang Von Goethe (1749-1832, German Poet, Dramatist, Novelist)

186 We must not take the faults of our youth with us into old age, for age brings along its own defects.
Johann Wolfgang Von Goethe (1749-1832, German Poet, Dramatist, Novelist)

187 It is only necessary to grow old to become more charitable and even indulgent. I see no fault committed by others that I have not committed myself.
Johann Wolfgang Von Goethe (1749-1832, German Poet, Dramatist, Novelist)

188 Rejoice that you have still have a long time to live, before the thought comes to you that there is nothing more in the world to see.
Johann Wolfgang Von Goethe (1749-1832, German Poet, Dramatist, Novelist)

189 The older we get the more we must limit ourselves if we wish to be active.
Johann Wolfgang Von Goethe (1749-1832, German Poet, Dramatist, Novelist)

190 How beautifully leaves grow old. How full of light and color are their last days.
John Burroughs (1837-1921, American Naturalist, Author)

191 O Time and change! -- with hair as gray as was my sire's that winter day, how strange it seems, with so much gone of life and love, to still live on!
John Greenleaf Whittier (1807-1892, American Poet, Reformer, Author)

192 You're only young once, but you can be immature forever.
John Greier

193 An important antidote to American democracy is American gerontocracy. The positions of eminence and authority in Congress are allotted in accordance with length of service, regardless of quality. Superficial observers have long criticized the United States for making a fetish of youth. This is unfair. Uniquely among modern organs of public and private administration, its national legislature rewards senility.
John Kenneth Galbraith (1908-, American Economist)

194 How soon hath Time, the subtle thief of youth, stolen on his wing my three-and-twentieth year!
John Milton (1608-1674, British Poet)

195 When you get to my age life seems little more than one long march to and from the lavatory.
John Mortimer (1923-, British Barrister, Novelist)

196 You can judge your age by the amount of pain you feel when you come in contact with a new idea.
John Nuveen

197 Now that I am sixty, I see why the idea of elder wisdom has passed from currency.
John Updike (1932-, American Novelist, Critic)

198 One of the aged greatest miseries is that they cannot easily find a companion able to share the memories of the past.
Johnson

199 The latter part of a wise person's life is occupied with curing the follies, prejudices and false opinions they contracted earlier.
Jonathan Swift (1667-1745, Anglo-Irish Satirist)

200 Every one desires to live long, but no one would be old.
Jonathan Swift (1667-1745, Anglo-Irish Satirist)

201 No wise man ever wished to be younger.
Jonathan Swift (1667-1745, Anglo-Irish Satirist)

202 He who would pass his declining years with honor and comfort, should, when young, consider that he may one day become old, and remember when he is old, that he has once been young.
Joseph Addison (1672-1719, British Essayist, Poet, Statesman)

203 I have never known a person to live to be one hundred and be remarkable for anything else.
Josh Billings (1815-1885, American Humorist, Lecturer)

204 In youth we run into difficulties. In old age difficulties run into us.
Josh Billings (1815-1885, American Humorist, Lecturer)

205 A man of eighty has outlived probably three new schools of painting, two of architecture and poetry and a hundred in dress.
Joyce Carey

206 When you're 50 you start thinking about things you haven't thought about before. I used to think getting old was about vanity -- but actually it's about losing people you love. Getting wrinkles is trivial.
Joyce Carol Oates (1938-, American Author)

207 But it's hard to be hip over thirty when everyone else is nineteen, when the last dance we learned was the Lindy, and the last we heard, girls who looked like Barbara Streisand were trying to do something about it.
Judith Viorst (1935-, American Poet, Journalist)

208 Who soweth good seed shall surely reap; The year grows rich as it groweth old, And life's latest sands are its sands of gold!
Julia C. R. Dorr (1825-1913, American Poet, Novelist)

209 The short bloom of our brief and narrow life flies far away. While we are calling for flowers and wine and woman, old age is upon us.
Juvenal (Decimus Junius Juvenalis) (55-130, Roman Satirical Poet)

210 How incessant and great are the ills with which a prolonged old age is replete.
Juvenal (Decimus Junius Juvenalis) (55-130, Roman Satirical Poet)

211 Seek ye counsel of the aged for their eyes have looked on the faces of the years and their ears have hardened to the voices of Life. Even if their counsel is displeasing to you, pay heed to them.
Kahlil Gibran (1883-1931, Lebanese Poet, Novelist)

212 Getting old is a fascination thing. The older you get, the older you want to get.
Keith Richards (1943-, British-born American Musician, Survivor, Songwriter)

213 For the last third of life there remains only work. It alone is always stimulating, rejuvenating, exciting and satisfying.
KSThe Kollwitz (1867-1945, German Artist)

214 I refuse to admit that I am more than 52, even if that makes my children illegitimate.
Lady Nancy Astor (1897-1964, British Politician)

215 Old age is an insult. It's like being smacked.
Lawrence Durrell (1912-1990, British Author)

216 Old age is the most unexpected of all the things that can happen to a man.
Leon Trotsky (1879-1940, Russian Revolutionary)

217 Age is a question of mind over matter. If you don't mind, age don't matter.
Leroy "Satchel" Paige (1906?-1982, American Baseball Player)

218 How old would you be if you didn't know how old you are.
Leroy "Satchel" Paige (1906?-1982, American Baseball Player)

219 You are never too old to set another goal or to dream a new dream.
Les Brown (1945-, American Speaker, Author, Trainer, Motivator Lecturer)

220 Every time I think that I'm getting old, and gradually going to the grave, something else happens.
Lillian Carter

221 Like spring, but it is too young. I like summer, but it is too proud. So I like best of all autumn, because its tone is mellower, its colors are richer, and it is tinged with a little sorrow. Its golden richness speaks not of the innocence of spring, nor the power of summer, but of the mellowness and kindly wisdom of approaching age. It knows the limitations of life and its content.
Lin Yn-tang (1895-1976, Chinese Writer and Philologist)

222 Of all the barbarous middle ages, that which is most barbarous is the middle age of man! it is -- I really scarce know what; but when we hover between fool and sage, and don't know justly what we would be at -- a period something like a printed page, black letter upon foolscap, while our hair grows grizzled, and we are not what we were.
Lord Byron (1788-1824, British Poet)

223 I shall soon be six-and-twenty. Is there anything in the future that can possibly console us for not being always twenty-five?
Lord Byron (1788-1824, British Poet)

224 A lady of a "certain age," which means certainly aged.
Lord Byron (1788-1824, British Poet)

225 My time has been passed viciously and agreeably; at thirty-one so few years months days hours or minutes remain that "Carpe Diem" is not enough. I have been obliged to crop even the seconds -- for who can trust to tomorrow?
Lord Byron (1788-1824, British Poet)

226 What is the worst of woes that wait on age? What stamps the wrinkle deeper on the brow? To view each loved one blotted from life's page, And be alone on earth, as I am now.
Lord Byron (1788-1824, British Poet)

227 It was one of the deadliest and heaviest feelings of my life to feel that I was no longer a boy. From that moment I began to grow old in my own esteem --and in my esteem age is not estimable.
Lord Byron (1788-1824, British Poet)

228 I always looked to about thirty as the barrier of any real or fierce delight in the passions, and determined to work them out in the younger ore and better veins of the mine --and I flatter myself (perhaps) that I have pretty well done so --and now the dross is coming.
Lord Byron (1788-1824, British Poet)

229 The heart never grows better by age; I fear rather worse, always harder. A young liar will be an old one, and a young knave will only be a greater knave as he grows older.
Lord Chesterfield (1694-1773, British Statesman, Author)

230 The trouble with our age is that it is all signpost and no destination.
Louis Kronenberger

231 The secret to staying young is to live honestly, eat slowly, and lie about your age.
Lucille Ball (1911-1989, American Actress, Producer)

232 In the name of Hypocrites, doctors have invented the most exquisite form of torture ever known to man: survival.
Luis Bunuel (1900-1983, Spanish Film Director)

233 Childhood itself is scarcely more lovely than a cheerful, kindly, sunshiny old age.
Lydia M. Child (1802-1880, American Abolitionist, Writer, Editor)

234 A comfortable old age is the reward of a well-spent youth. Instead of its bringing sad and melancholy prospects of decay, it would give us hopes of eternal youth in a better world.
Lydia M. Child (1802-1880, American Abolitionist, Writer, Editor)

235 Old age is an excellent time for outrage. My goal is to say or do at least one outrageous thing every week.
Maggie Kuhn (1905-, American Civil Rights Activist, Author)

236 Old age is not a disease -- it is strength and survivorship, triumph over all kinds of vicissitudes and disappointments, trials and illnesses.
Maggie Kuhn (1905-, American Civil Rights Activist, Author)

237 You must become an old man in good time if you wish to be an old man long.
Marcus T. Cicero (106-43 BC, Great Roman Orator, Politician)

238 Every stage of human life, except the last, is marked out by certain and defined limits; old age alone has no precise and determinate boundary.
Marcus T. Cicero (106-43 BC, Great Roman Orator, Politician)

239 Old age, especially an honored old age, has so great authority, that this is of more value than all the pleasures of youth.
Marcus T. Cicero (106-43 BC, Great Roman Orator, Politician)

240 There is no one so old as to not think they may live a day longer.
Marcus T. Cicero (106-43 BC, Great Roman Orator, Politician)

241 The foolishness of old age does not characterize all who are old, but only the foolish.
Marcus T. Cicero (106-43 BC, Great Roman Orator, Politician)

242 No one is so old as to think he cannot live one more year.
Marcus T. Cicero (106-43 BC, Great Roman Orator, Politician)

243 Advice in old age is foolish; for what can be more absurd than to increase our provisions for the road the nearer we approach to our journey's end.
Marcus T. Cicero (106-43 BC, Great Roman Orator, Politician)

244 If you associate enough with older people who do enjoy their lives, who are not stored away in any golden ghettos, you will gain a sense of continuity and of the possibility for a full life.
Margaret Mead (1901-1978, American Anthropologist)

245 No one grows old by living. Only by losing interest in living.
Marie Beyon Ray

246 It is not how old you are, but how you are old.
Marie Dressler (1869-1934, Canadian Stage and Film Actor)

247 By the time we hit fifty, we have learned our hardest lessons. We have found out that only a few things are really important. We have learned to take life seriously, but never ourselves.
Marie Dressler (1869-1934, Canadian Stage and Film Actor)

248 Let us not be too particular; it is better to have old secondhand diamonds than none at all."
Mark Twain (1835-1910, American Humorist, Writer)

249 Life would be infinitely happier if we could only be born at the age of eighty and gradually approach eighteen.
Mark Twain (1835-1910, American Humorist, Writer)

250 Methuselah lived to be 969 years old . You boys and girls will see more in the next fifty years than Methuselah saw in his whole lifetime.
Mark Twain (1835-1910, American Humorist, Writer)

251 I am admonished in many ways that time is pushing me inexorably along. I am approaching the threshold of age; in 1977 I shall be 142. This is no time to be flitting about the earth. I must cease from the activities proper to youth and begin to take on the dignities and gravities and inertia proper to that season of honorable senility which is on its way.
Mark Twain (1835-1910, American Humorist, Writer)

252 The older we grow the greater becomes our wonder at how much ignorance one can contain without bursting one's clothes.
Mark Twain (1835-1910, American Humorist, Writer)

253 When your friends begin to flatter you on how young you look, it's a sure sign you're getting old.
Mark Twain (1835-1910, American Humorist, Writer)

254 The quality, not the longevity, of one's life is what is important.
Martin Luther King Jr. (1929-1968, American Black Leader, Nobel Prize Winner, 1964)

255 Thirty was so strange for me. I've really had to come to terms with the fact that I am now a walking and talking adult. [Reflecting on his former status as a teen idol]
Matt Dillon (1964-, American Actor)

256 Old age isn't so bad when you consider the alternatives.
Maurice Chevalier (1888-1972, French Singer, Actor)

257 The real sadness of fifty is not that you change so much but that you change so little.
Max Lerner (1902-, American Author, Columnist)

258 We grow neither better or worse as we get old, but more like ourselves.
May L. Becker

259 Age imprints more wrinkles in the mind than it does on the face.
Michel Eyquem De Montaigne (1533-1592, French Philosopher, Essayist)

260 Nature should have been pleased to have made this age miserable, without making it also ridiculous.
Michel Eyquem De Montaigne (1533-1592, French Philosopher, Essayist)

261 A man's as old as he's feeling. A woman as old as she looks.
Mortimer Collins (1827-1876, British Novelist, Poet)

262 Age is whatever you think it is. You are as old as you think you are.
Muhammad Ali (1942-, American Boxer)

263 Being over seventy is like being engaged in a war. All our friends are going or gone and we survive amongst the dead and the dying as on a battlefield.
Muriel Spark (1918-, British Novelist)

264 In youth the days are short and the years are long. In old age the years are short and day's long.
Nikita Ivanovich Panin (Indian Grammarian)

265 Live your life and forget your age.
Norman Vincent Peale (1898-1993, American Christian Reformed Pastor, Speaker, Author)

266 Middle age is when you've met so many people that every new person you meet reminds you of someone else.
Ogden Nash (1902-1971, American Humorous Poet)

267 A person is always startled when he hears himself called old for the first time.
Oliver Wendell Holmes (1809-1894, American Author, Wit, Poet)

268 Age, like distance lends a double charm.
Oliver Wendell Holmes (1809-1894, American Author, Wit, Poet)

269 To be seventy years young is sometimes far more cheerful and hopeful than to be forty years old.
Oliver Wendell Holmes (1809-1894, American Author, Wit, Poet)

270 Thirty-five is a very attractive age. London society is full of women of the highest birth who have, of their own free choice, remained thirty-five for years.
Oscar Wilde (1856-1900, British Author, Wit)

271 The tragedy of old age is not that one is old, but that one is young.
Oscar Wilde (1856-1900, British Author, Wit)

272 I delight in men over seventy. They always offer one the devotion of a lifetime.
Oscar Wilde (1856-1900, British Author, Wit)

273 No woman should ever be quite accurate about her age. It looks so calculating.
Oscar Wilde (1856-1900, British Author, Wit)

274 It takes a long time to become young.
Pablo Picasso (1881-1973, Spanish Artist)

275 In mid-life the man wants to see how irresistible he still is to younger women. How they turn their hearts to stone and more or less commit a murder of their marriage I just don't know, but they do.
Patricia Neal

276 Perhaps one has to be very old before one learns to be amused rather than shocked.
Pearl S. Buck (1892-1973, American Novelist)

277 My generation, faced as it grew with a choice between religious belief and existential despair, chose marijuana. Now we are in our Cabernet stage.
Peggy Noonan (1950-, American Author, Presidential Speechwriter)

278 I guess I don't so much mind being old, as I mind being fat and old.
Peter Gabriel (1950-, British Rock Musician)

279 Perhaps being old is having lighted rooms inside your head, and people in them, acting. People you know, yet can't quite name.
Philip Larkin (1922-1986, British Poet)

280 Gray hairs are signs of wisdom if you hold your tongue, speak and they are but hairs, as in the young.
Philo (2nd Century, Byzantine Scientist)

281 A graceful and honorable old age is the childhood of immortality.
Pindar (518-438 BC, Greek Poet)

282 He who is of a calm and happy nature will hardly feel the pressure of age, but to him who is of an opposite disposition youth and age are equally a burden.
Plato (427-347 BC, Greek Philosopher)

283 Old age has a great sense of calm and freedom. When the passions have relaxed their hold and have escaped, not from one master, but from many.
Plato (427-347 BC, Greek Philosopher)

284 If the young knew and the old could, there is nothing that couldn't be done.
Proverb

285 We pay when old for the excesses of youth.
Proverb

286 Old age though despised, is coveted by all.
Proverb

287 When you get to fifty-two food becomes more important than sex.
Prue Leith

288 Old things are always in good repute, present things in disfavor.
Publius Cornelius Tacitus (55-117 AD, Roman Historian)

289 It is a rare and difficult attainment to grow old gracefully and happily.
R. Palmer

290 Old age comes on suddenly, and not gradually as is thought.
Rahel

291 Age should not have its face lifted, but it should rather teach the world to admire wrinkles as the etchings of experience and the firm line of character.
Ralph B. Perry

292 We do not count a man's years until he has nothing else to count.
Ralph Waldo Emerson (1803-1882, American Poet, Essayist)

293 Nature is full of freaks, and now puts an old head on young shoulders, and then takes a young heart beating under fourscore winters.
Ralph Waldo Emerson (1803-1882, American Poet, Essayist)

294 Age considers; youth ventures.
Raupach

295 That old man dies prematurely whose memory records no benefits conferred. They only have lived long who have lived virtuously.
Richard Brinsley Sheridan (1751-1816, Anglo-Irish Dramatist)

296 I believe the true function of age is memory. I'm recording as fast as I can.
Rita Mae Brown (1944-, American Writer)

297 What's a man's age? He must hurry more, that's all; Cram in a day, what his youth took a year to hold.
Robert Browning (1812-1889, British Poet)

298 Grow old along with me! The best is yet to be, The last of life, for which the first was made.
Robert Browning (1812-1889, British Poet)

299 Grow old with me the best is yet to come.
Robert Browning (1812-1889, British Poet)

300 I'm at the age where food has taken the place of sex in my life. In fact, I've just had a mirror put over my kitchen table.
Rodney Dangerfield (American Comedian, Actor)

301 I'm like old wine. They don't bring me out very often, but I'm well preserved.
Rose F. Kennedy (1890-1995, Mother of President John F. Kennedy)

302 I have found it to be true that the older I've become the better my life has become.
Rush Limbaugh (1951-, American TV Personality)

303 To think, when one is no longer young, when one is not yet old, that one is no longer young, that one is not yet old, that is perhaps something.
Samuel Beckett (1906-1989, Irish Dramatist, Novelist)

304 We lose our hair, our teeth! Our bloom, our ideals.
Samuel Beckett (1906-1989, Irish Dramatist, Novelist)

305 At seventy-seven it is time to be in earnest.
Samuel Johnson (1709-1784, British Author)

306 When I was as you are now, towering in the confidence of twenty-one, little did I suspect that I should be at forty-nine, what I now am.
Samuel Johnson (1709-1784, British Author)

307 There are three classes into which all the women past seventy that ever I knew were to be divided: 1. That dear old soul; 2. That old woman; 3. That old witch.
Samuel Taylor Coleridge (1772-1834, British Poet, Critic, Philosopher)

308 Years may wrinkle the skin, but to give up enthusiasm wrinkles the soul. Worry, fear, self- distrust bows the heart and turns the spirit back to dust.
Samuel Ullman (1840-1924, German-born American Educator, Writer, Poet)

309 When the aerials are down, and your spirit is covered with snows of cynicism and the ice of pessimism, then you are grown old, even at twenty, but as long as your aerials are up, to catch the waves of optimism, there is hope you may die young at eighty.
Samuel Ullman (1840-1924, German-born American Educator, Writer, Poet)

310 Nobody grows old merely by living a number of years. We grow old by deserting our ideals.
Samuel Ullman (1840-1924, German-born American Educator, Writer, Poet)

311 Whether sixty or sixteen, there is in every human being's heart the lure of wonder, the unfailing child-like appetite of what's next, and the joy of the game of living. In the center of your heart and my heart there is a wireless station; so long as it receives messages of beauty, hope, cheer, courage and power from men and from the infinite, so long are you young.
Samuel Ullman (1840-1924, German-born American Educator, Writer, Poet)

312 Wrecked on the lee shore of age.
Sarah Orne Jewett (1849-1909, American Author)

313 Here, with whitened hair, desires failing, strength ebbing out of him, with the sun gone down and with only the serenity and the calm warning of the evening star left to him, he drank to Life, to all it had been, to what it was, to what it would be. Hurrah!
Sean O'Casey (1884-1964, Irish Dramatist)

314 There is nothing more despicable than an old man who has no other proof than his age to offer of his having lived long in the world.
Seneca (4 BC-65 AD, Spanish-born Roman Statesman, philosopher)

315 As for old age, embrace and love it. It abounds with pleasure if you know how to use it. The gradually declining years are among the sweetest in a man's life, and I maintain that, even when they have reached the extreme limit, they have their pleasure still.
Seneca (4 BC-65 AD, Spanish-born Roman Statesman, philosopher)

316 Middle Age is that perplexing time of life when we hear two voices calling us, one saying, "Why not?" and the other, "Why bother?"
Sidney J. Harris (1917-, American Journalist)

317 One keeps forgetting old age up to the very brink of the grave.
Sidonie Gabrielle Colette (1873-1954, French Author)

318 You must not pity me because my sixtieth year finds me still astonished. To be astonished is one of the surest ways of not growing old too quickly.
Sidonie Gabrielle Colette (1873-1954, French Author)

319 The age of a woman doesn't mean a thing. The best tunes are played on the oldest fiddles.
Sigmund Z. Engel

320 Since it is the Other within us who is old, it is natural that the revelation of our age should come to us from outside --from others. We do not accept it willingly.
Simone De Beauvoir (1908-1986, French Novelist, Essayist)

321 It is old age, rather than death, that is to be contrasted with life. Old age is life's parody, whereas death transforms life into a destiny: in a way it preserves it by giving it the absolute dimension. Death does away with time.
Simone De Beauvoir (1908-1986, French Novelist, Essayist)

322 A healthy old fellow, who is not a fool, is the happiest creature living.
Sir Richard Steele (1672-1729, British Dramatist, Essayist, Editor)

323 That man never grows old who keeps a child in his heart.
Sir Richard Steele (1672-1729, British Dramatist, Essayist, Editor)

324 Study until twenty five, investigate until forty, profession until sixty, at which age I would have him retired on a double allowance.
Sir William Osler (1849-1919, Canadian Physician)

325 There cannot live a more unhappy creature than an ill-natured old man, who is neither capable of receiving pleasures, nor sensible of conferring them on others.
Sir William Temple (1628-1699, British Diplomat, Essayist)

326 There is a fountain of youth: it is your mind, your talents, the creativity you bring to your life and the lives of the people you love. When you learn to tap into this source, you will truly have defeated age.
Sophia Loren (1934-, Italian Film Actress)

327 Old age realizes the dreams of youth: look at Dean Swift; in his youth he built an asylum for the insane, in his old age he was himself an inmate.
Soren Kierkegaard (1813-1855, Danish Philosopher, Writer)

328 The golden age is before us, not behind us.
St. Simon

329 In my twenties, my pleasures tended to be physical. In my thirties, my pleasures tended to be intellectual. I can't say which was more exquisite.
Steve Kangas

330 We are not limited by our old ages; we are liberate by it.
Stu Mittleman (American Health and Fitness Expert)

331 It is a bore, I admit, to be past seventy, for you are left for execution, and are daily expecting the death-warrant; but it is not anything very capital we quit. We are, at the close of life, only hurried away from stomach-aches, pains in the joints, from sleepless nights and unamusing days, from weakness, ugliness, and nervous tremors; but we shall all meet again in another planet, cured of all our defects.
Sydney Smith (1771-1845, British Writer, Clergyman)

332 I don't believe one grows older. I think that what happens early on in life is that at a certain age one stands still and stagnates.
T. S. Eliot (1888-1965, American-born British Poet, Critic)

333 The years between fifty and seventy are the hardest. You are always being asked to do things, and yet you are not decrepit enough to turn them down.
T. S. Eliot (1888-1965, American-born British Poet, Critic)

334 No man was ever so completely skilled in the conduct of life, as not to receive new information from age and experience.
Terence (185-159 BC, Roman Writer of Comedies)

335 Keep on raging -- to stop the aging.
The Delltones

336 There is not a more repulsive spectacle than on old man who will not forsake the world, which has already forsaken him.
Tholuck

337 Probably the happiest period in life most frequently is in middle age, when the eager passions of youth are cooled, and the infirmities of age not yet begun; as we see that the shadows, which are at morning and evening so large, almost entirely disappear at midday.
Thomas Arnold (1795-1842, British Educator, Scholar)

338 One's age should be tranquil, as childhood should be playful. Hard work at either extremity of life seems out of place. At midday the sun may burn, and men labor under it; but the morning and evening should be alike calm and cheerful.
Thomas Arnold (1795-1842, British Educator, Scholar)

339 To keep the heart unwrinkled, to be hopeful, kindly, cheerful, reverent that is to triumph over old age.
Thomas B. Aldrich (1836-1907, American Writer, Editor)

340 The outer passes away; the innermost is the same yesterday, today, and forever.
Thomas Carlyle (1795-1881, Scottish Philosopher, Author)

341 Old age is not a matter for sorrow. It is matter for thanks if we have left our work done behind us.
Thomas Carlyle (1795-1881, Scottish Philosopher, Author)

342 The value of old age depends upon the person who reaches it. To some men of early performance it is useless. To others, who are late to develop, it just enables them to finish the job.
Thomas Hardy (1840-1928, British Novelist, Poet)

343 My only fear is that I may live too long. This would be a subject of dread to me.
Thomas Jefferson (1743-1826, Third President of the USA)

344 For the first fourteen years for a rod they do while for the next as a pearl in the world they do shine. For the next trim beauty beginneth to swerve. For the next matrons or drudges they serve. For the next doth crave a staff for a stay. For the next a bier to fetch them away.
Thomas Tusser (1520-1580-, British Writer On Agriculture)

345 I will never give in to old age until I become old. And I'm not old yet!
Tina Turner (1938-, American Musician, Actress)

346 It is a sobering thought, that when Mozart was my age he had been dead for two years.
Tom Lehrer (1928-, American Musician, Song Writer)

347 Age is a high price to pay for maturity.
Tom Stoppard (1937-, Czech Playwright)

348 Men of my age live in a state of continual desperation.
Trevor Mcdonald

349 Age does not depend upon years, but upon temperament and health. Some men are born old, and some never grow up.
Tryon Edwards (1809-1894, American Theologian)

350 Some men are born old, and some men never seem so. If we keep well and cheerful, we are always young and at last die in youth even when in years would count as old.
Tryon Edwards (1809-1894, American Theologian)

351 Forty is the old age of youth, fifty is the youth of old age.
Victor Hugo (1802-1885, French Poet, Dramatist, Novelist)

352 When grace is joined with wrinkles, it is adorable. There is an unspeakable dawn in happy old age.
Victor Hugo (1802-1885, French Poet, Dramatist, Novelist)

353 Age carries all things away, even the mind.
Virgil (70-19 BC, Roman Poet)

354 Now, aged 50, I'm just poised to shoot forth quite free straight and undeflected my bolts whatever they are.
Virginia Woolf (1882-1941, British Novelist, Essayist)

355 These are the soul's changes. I don't believe in aging. I believe in forever altering one's aspect to the sun. Hence my optimism.
Virginia Woolf (1882-1941, British Novelist, Essayist)

356 At 46 one must be a miser; only have time for essentials.
Virginia Woolf (1882-1941, British Novelist, Essayist)

357 The older one grows, the more one likes indecency.
Virginia Woolf (1882-1941, British Novelist, Essayist)

358 No gray hairs streak my soul, no grandfatherly fondness there! I shake the world with the might of my voice, and walk --handsome, twenty-two year old.
Vladimir Mayakovsky (1893-1930, Russian Poet, Dramatist)

359 Every man is the creature of the age in which he lives; very few are able to raise themselves above the ideas of the time.
Voltaire (1694-1778, French Historian, Writer)

360 The class distinctions proper to a democratic society are not those of rank or money, still less, as is apt to happen when these are abandoned, of race, but of age.
W. H. Auden (1907-1973, Anglo-American Poet)

361 Old age is ready to undertake tasks that youth shirked because they would take too long.
W. Somerset Maugham (1874-1965, British Novelist, Playwright)

362 The complete life, the perfect pattern, includes old age as well as youth and maturity. The beauty of the morning and the radiance of noon are good, but it would be a very silly person who drew the curtains and turned on the light in order to shut out the tranquillity of the evening. Old age has its pleasures, which, though different, are not less than the pleasures of youth.
W. Somerset Maugham (1874-1965, British Novelist, Playwright)

363 When I was young I was amazed at Plutarch's statement that the elder Cato began at the age of eighty to learn Greek. I am amazed no longer. Old age is ready to undertake tasks that youth shirked because they would take too long.
W. Somerset Maugham (1874-1965, British Novelist, Playwright)

364 What makes old age hard to bear is not the failing of one's faculties, mental and physical, but the burden of one's memories.
W. Somerset Maugham (1874-1965, British Novelist, Playwright)

365 Old age has its pleasures, which, though different, are not less than the pleasures of youth.
W. Somerset Maugham (1874-1965, British Novelist, Playwright)

366 Old age, calm, expanded, broad with the haughty breadth of the universe, old age flowing free with the delicious near-by freedom of death.
Walt Whitman (1819-1892, American Poet)

367 O what a thing is age! Death without death's quiet.
Walter Savage Landor (1775-1864, British Poet, Essayist)

368 Whenever a man's friends begin to compliment him about looking young, he may be sure that they think he is growing old.
Washington Irving (1783-1859, American Author)

369 I'm aiming by the time I'm fifty to stop being an adolescent.
Wendy Cope (1945-, British Poet)

370 An aged man is but a paltry thing, a tattered coat upon a stick
William Butler Yeats (1865-1939, Irish Poet, Playwright.)

371 People between twenty and forty are not sympathetic. The child has the capacity to do but it can't know. It only knows when it is no longer able to do --after forty. Between twenty and forty the will of the child to do gets stronger, more dangerous, but it has not begun to learn to know yet. Since his capacity to do is forced into channels of evil through environment and pressures, man is strong before he is moral. The world's anguish is caused by people between twenty and forty.
William Faulkner (1897-1962, American Novelist)

372 Life begins at 40 -- but so do fallen arches, rheumatism, faulty eyesight, and the tendency to tell a story to the same person, three or four times.
William Feather (1888-18, American Writer, Businessman)

373 Among the virtues and vices that make up the British character, we have one vice, at least, that Americans ought to view with sympathy. For they appear to be the only people who share it with us. I mean our worship of the antique. I do not refer to beauty or even historical association. I refer to age, to a quantity of years.
William Golding (1911-1993, British Author)

374 The worst old age is that of the mind.
William Hazlitt (1778-1830, British Essayist)

375 To be happy, we must be true to nature, and carry our age along with us.
William Hazlitt (1778-1830, British Essayist)

376 How can the moribund old man reason back to himself the romance, the mystery, the imminence of great things with which our old earth tingled for him in the days when he was young and well?
William James (1842-1910, American Psychologist, Professor, Author)

377 I wasted time, and now time doth waste me.
William Shakespeare (1564-1616, British Poet, Playwright, Actor)

378 Have you not a moist eye, a dry hand, a yellow cheek, a white beard, a decreasing leg, an increasing belly? Is not your voice broken, your wind short, your chin double, your wit single, and every part about you blasted with antiquity?
William Shakespeare (1564-1616, British Poet, Playwright, Actor)

379 I have lived long enough. My way of life is to fall into the sere, the yellow leaf, and that which should accompany old age, as honor, love, obedience, troops of friends I must not look to have.
William Shakespeare (1564-1616, British Poet, Playwright, Actor)

380 Lord, Lord, how subject we old men are to this vice of lying!
William Shakespeare (1564-1616, British Poet, Playwright, Actor)

381 Youth is full of sport, age's breath is short; youth is nimble, age is lame; Youth is hot and bold, age is weak and cold; Youth is wild, and age is tame.
William Shakespeare (1564-1616, British Poet, Playwright, Actor)

382 My age is as a lusty winter, frosty but kindly.
William Shakespeare (1564-1616, British Poet, Playwright, Actor)

383 With mirth and laughter let old wrinkles come. [Merchant Of Venice]
William Shakespeare (1564-1616, British Poet, Playwright, Actor)

384 Though I look old, yet I am strong and lusty; for in my youth I never did apply hot and rebellious liquors in my blood; and did not, with unbashful forehead, woo the means of weakness and debility: therefore my age is as a lusty winter, frosty but kindly.
William Shakespeare (1564-1616, British Poet, Playwright, Actor)

385 The mind that is wise mourns less for what age takes away; than what it leaves behind.
William Wordsworth (1770-1850, British Poet)

386 But an old age serene and bright, and lovely as a Lapland night, shall lead thee to thy grave.
William Wordsworth (1770-1850, British Poet)

387 We are happier in many ways when we are old than when we were young. The young sow wild oats. The old grow sage.
Winston Churchill (1874-1965, British Statesman, Prime Minister)

388 The person of wisdom is the person of years.
Young

AGENTS

1 It is well-known what a middleman is: he is a man who bamboozles one party and plunders the other.
Benjamin Disraeli (1804-1881, British Statesman, Prime Minister)

2 If God had an agent, the world wouldn't be built yet. It'd only be about Thursday.
Jerry Reynolds

3 The agent never receipts his bill, puts his hat on and bows himself out. He stays around forever, not only for as long as you can write anything that anyone will buy, but as long as anyone will buy any portion of any right to anything that you ever did write. He just takes ten per cent of your life.
Raymond Chandler (1888-1959, American Author)

4 Throughout the history of commercial life nobody has ever quite liked the commission man. His function is too vague, his presence always seems one too many, his profit looks too easy, and even when you admit that he has a necessary function, you feel that this function is, as it were, a personification of something that in an ethical society would not need to exist. If people could deal with one another honestly, they would not need agents.
Raymond Chandler (1888-1959, American Author)

5 Let every eye negotiate for itself and trust no agent.
William Shakespeare (1564-1616, British Poet, Playwright, Actor)

6 O world, world! thus is the poor agent despised. O traitors and bawds, how earnestly are you set a-work, and how ill requited! Why should our endeavor be so loved, and the performance so loathed?
William Shakespeare (1564-1616, British Poet, Playwright, Actor)

AGGRESSION

1 Does our ferocity not derive from the fact that our instincts are all too interested in other people? If we attended more to ourselves and became the center, the object of our murderous inclinations, the sum of our intolerances would diminish.
E. M. Cioran (1911-, Rumanian-born French Philosopher)

2 To knock a thing down, especially if it is cocked at an arrogant angle, is a deep delight to the blood.
George Santayana (1863-1952, American Philosopher, Poet)

3 Wolves which batten upon lambs, lambs consumed by wolves, the strong who immolate the weak, the weak victims of the strong: there you have Nature, there you have her intentions, there you have her scheme: a perpetual action and reaction, a host of vices, a host of virtues, in one word, a perfect equilibrium resulting from the equality of good and evil on earth.
Marquis De Sade (1740-1814, French Author)

4 I love to see a young girl go out and grab the world by the lapels. Life's a bitch. You've got to go out and kick ass.
Maya Angelou (1928-, African-American poet, Writer, Performer)

5 Aggression, the writer's main source of energy.
Ted Solotaroff

6 We, the lineal representatives of the successful enactors of one scene of slaughter after another, must, whatever more pacific virtues we may also possess, still carry about with us, ready at any moment to burst into flame, the smoldering and sinister traits of character by means of which they lived through so many massacres, harming others, but themselves unharmed.
William James (1842-1910, American Psychologist, Professor, Author)

AGREEMENT

1 Man, an animal that makes bargains.
Adam Smith (1723-1790, Scottish Economist)

2 I trust that a graduate student some day will write a doctoral essay on the influence of the Munich analogy on the subsequent history of the twentieth century. Perhaps in the end he will conclude that the multitude of errors committed in the name of "Munich" may exceed the original error of 1938.
Arthur M. Schlesinger Jr. (1917-, American Historian)

3 My idea of an agreeable person is a person who agrees with me.
Benjamin Disraeli (1804-1881, British Statesman, Prime Minister)

4 Those who agree with us may not be right, but we admire their astuteness.
Cullen Hightower

5 I have never in my life learned anything from any man who agreed with me.
Dudley Field Malone

6 There is nothing more likely to start disagreement among people or countries than an agreement.
E(lwyn) B(rooks) White (1899-1985, American Author, Editor)

7 You may easily play a joke on a man who likes to argue -- agree with him.
Edgar Watson Howe (1853-1937, American Journalist, Author)

8 Too much agreement kills the chat.
Eldridge Cleaver (1935-, American Black Leader, Writer)

9 We seldom find any person of good sense, except those who share our opinions.
François de La Rochefoucauld (1613-1680, French classical writer)

10 The reason why so few people are agreeable in conversation is that each is thinking more about what he intends to say than others are saying.
François de La Rochefoucauld (1613-1680, French classical writer)

11 Minds do not act together in public; they simply stick together; and when their private activities are resumed, they fly apart again.
Frank Moore Colby (1865-1925, American Editor, Essayist)

12 There is no calamity which a great nation can invite which equals that which follows a supine submission to wrong and injustice and the consequent loss of national self-respect and honor, beneath which are shielded and defended a people's safety and greatness.
Grover Cleveland (1837-1908, Twenty-second & 24th President of the USA)

13 On one issue at least, men and women agree; they both distrust women.
H. L. Mencken (1880-1956, American Editor, Author, Critic, Humorist)

14 What usually comes first is the contract.
Ira Gershwin (American Songwriter)

15 One good analogy is worth three hours discussion.
James T. Mccay

16 It may offend us to hear our own thoughts expressed by others: we are not sure enough of their souls.
Jean Rostand (1894-1977, French Biologist, Writer)

17 If you wish to appear agreeable in society, you must consent to be taught many things which you know already.
Johann Kaspar Lavater (1741-1801, Swiss Theologian, Mystic)

18 One can be very happy without demanding that others agree with them.
Johann Wolfgang Von Goethe (1749-1832, German Poet, Dramatist, Novelist)

19 Three may keep counsel, if two are away.
John Heywood (1497-1580, British Dramatist, Proverb Collection)

20 You can get assent to almost any proposition so long as you are not going to do anything about it.
John Jay Chapman (1862-1933, American Author)

21 Thus Belial, with words clothed in reason's garb, counseled ignoble ease, and peaceful sloth, not peace.
John Milton (1608-1674, British Poet)

22 Even savage animals can agree among themselves.
Juvenal (Decimus Junius Juvenalis) (55-130, Roman Satirical Poet)

23 The fellow that agrees with everything you say is either a fool or he is getting ready to skin you.
Kin Hubbard (1868-1930, American Humorist, Journalist)

24 You can always tell when a man's well informed. His views are pretty much like your own.
Louie Morris

25 There's nothing is this world more instinctively abhorrent to me than finding myself in agreement with my fellow-humans.
Malcolm Muggeridge (1903-1990, British Broadcaster)

26 I seem to smell the stench of appeasement in the air.
Margaret Thatcher (1925-, British Stateswoman, Prime Minister (1979-90))

27 We should seek by all means in our power to avoid war, by analyzing possible causes, by trying to remove them, by discussion in a spirit of collaboration and good will. I cannot believe that such a program would be rejected by the people of this country, even if it does mean the establishment of personal contact with the dictators.
Neville Chamberlain

28 My opinion, my conviction, gains immensely in strength and sureness the minute a second mind as adopted it.
Novalis (1772-1801, German Poet, Novelist)

29 An alliance with a powerful person is never safe.
Phaedrus (Macedonian Inventor and Writer)

30 Better a lean agreement than a fat lawsuit.
Proverb

31 And that is called paying the Dane-geld; but we've proved it again and again, that if once you have paid him the Dane-geld you never get rid of the Dane.
Rudyard Kipling (1865-1936, British Author of Prose, Verse)

32 He that complies against his will is of his own opinion still.
Samuel Butler (1612-1680, British Poet, Satirist)

33 A verbal contract isn't worth the paper it's written on.
Samuel Goldwyn (1882-1974, American Film Producer, Founder, MGM)

34 Better a friendly refusal than an unwilling consent.
Spanish Proverb

35 No two on earth in all things can agree. All have some daring singularity.
Winston Churchill (1874-1965, British Statesman, Prime Minister)

AID AND ASSISTANCE

1 To give aid to every poor man is far beyond the reach and power of every man. Care of the poor is incumbent on society as a whole.
Baruch (Benedict de) Spinoza (1632-1677, Dutch Philosopher and Theologian)

2 It is not helpful to help a friend by putting coins in his pockets when he has got holes in his pockets.
Douglas Hurd (1930-, British Conservative Politician)

3 We can't help everyone, but everyone can help someone.
Dr. Loretta Scott (American Doctor)

4 When a person is down in the world, an ounce of help is better than a pound of preaching.
Edward G. Bulwer-Lytton (1803-1873, British Novelist, Poet)

5 Never reach out your hand unless you're willing to extend an arm.
Elizabeth Fuller

6 Almsgiving tends to perpetuate poverty; aid does away with it once and for all. Almsgiving leaves a man just where he was before. Aid restores him to society as an individual worthy of all respect and not as a man with a grievance. Almsgiving is the generosity of the rich; social aid levels up social inequalities. Charity separates the rich from the poor; aid raises the needy and sets him on the same level with the rich.
Eva Peran (1919-1952, Argentinean Government Official, Politician)

7 These unhappy times call for the building of plans that build from the bottom up and not from the top down, that put their faith once more in the forgotten man at the bottom of the economic pyramid.
Franklin D. Roosevelt (1882-1945, Thirty-second President of the USA)

8 For the cause that lacks assistance, The wrong that needs resistance, For the future in the distance, And the good that I can do.
George Linnaeus Banks

9 Nothing makes one feel so strong as a call for help.
George Macdonald (1824-1905, Scottish Novelist)

10 And who is any of us, that without starvation he can go through the kingdoms of starvation?
Haniel Long (1888-1956, American Author, Poet, Journalist)

11 There is something wrong about the man who wants help. There is somewhere a deep defect, a want, in brief, a need, a crying need, somewhere about that man.
Herman Melville (1819-1891, American Author)

12 Help a man against his will and you do the same as murder him.
Horace (65-8 BC, Italian Poet)

13 Fool that I was, upon my eagle's wings I bore this wren, till I was tired with soaring, and now he mounts above me.
John Dryden (1631-1700, British Poet, Dramatist, Critic)

14 To those people in the huts and villages of half the globe struggling to break the bonds of mass misery, we pledge our best efforts to help them help themselves, for whatever period is required, not because the Communists may be doing it, not because we seek their votes, but because it is right. If a free society cannot help the many who are poor, it cannot save the few who are rich.
John F. Kennedy (1917-1963, Thirty-fifth President of the USA)

15 Every great man is always being helped by everybody; for his gift is to get good out of all things and all persons.
John Ruskin (1819-1900, British Critic, Social Theorist)

16 If you're in trouble, or hurt or need -- go to the poor people. They're the only ones that'll help -- the only ones.
John Steinbeck (1902-1968, American Author)

17 No one will persist long in helping someone who will not help themselves.
Johnson

18 If my daughter, Liza, wants to become an actress, I'll do everything to help her.
Judy Garland (1922-1969, American Actress, Singer)

19 HELP = H(umor), E-go, edging God out, L-istening, P-urpose
Ken Blanchard (American Business Lecturer, Author)

20 We all need each other.
Leo Buscaglia (American Expert on Love, Lecturer, Author)

21 A man cannot be made comfortable without his own approval.
Mark Twain (1835-1910, American Humorist, Writer)

22 Never stand begging for that which you have the power to earn.
Miguel De Cervantes (1547-1616, Spanish Novelist, Dramatist, Poet)

23 To keep a lamp burning we have to keep putting oil in it.
Mother Teresa (1910-1997, Albanian-born Roman Catholic Missionary)

24 Let us more and more insist on raising funds of love, of kindness, of understanding, of peace. Money will come if we seek first the Kingdom of God --the rest will be given.
Mother Teresa (1910-1997, Albanian-born Roman Catholic Missionary)

25 It is a kingly act to assist the fallen.
Ovid (43 BC-18 AD, Roman Poet)

26 The truest help we can render an afflicted man is not to take his burden from him, but to call out his best energy, that he may be able to bear the burden.
Phillips Brooks (1835-1893, American Minister, Poet)

27 Mutual aid is as much a law of animal life as mutual struggle.
Prince Pyotr Kropotkin (1842-1921, Russian Revolutionary, Geographer)

28 So many people supported me through my public life and I will never forget them.
Princess of Wales Diana (1961-1997, Wife of Charles, Prince of Wales)

29 Anywhere I see suffering, that is where I want to be, doing what I can.
Princess of Wales Diana (1961-1997, Wife of Charles, Prince of Wales)

30 I've always though that people need to feel good about themselves and I see my role as offering support to them, to provide some light along the way.
Princess of Wales Diana (1961-1997, Wife of Charles, Prince of Wales)

31 Whoever is in the distress can call me. I will come running wherever they are.
Princess of Wales Diana (1961-1997, Wife of Charles, Prince of Wales)

32 Slow help is no help.
Proverb

33 We do not quite forgive a giver. The hand that feeds us is in some danger of being bitten.
Ralph Waldo Emerson (1803-1882, American Poet, Essayist)

34 He stands erect by bending over the fallen. He rises by lifting others.
Robert Green Ingersoll (1833-1899, American Orator, Lawyer)

35 We are for aiding our allies by sharing some of our material blessings with those nations which share in our fundamental beliefs, but we are against doling out money government to government, creating bureaucracy, if not socialism, all over the world. We set out to help 19 countries. We are helping 107 We spent $146 billion. With that money, we bought a 2-million-dollar yacht for Haile Selassie. We bought dress suits for Greek undertakers, extra wives for Kenya government officials. We bought a thousand TV sets for a place where they have no electricity.
Ronald Reagan (1911-, Fortieth President of the USA, Actor)

36 The needs of a human being are sacred. Their satisfaction cannot be subordinated either to reasons of state, or to any consideration of money, nationality, race, or color, or to the moral or other value attributed to the human being in question, or to any consideration whatsoever.
Simone Weil (1910-1943, French Philosopher, Mystic)

37 It is an eternal obligation toward the human being not to let him suffer from hunger when one has a chance of coming to his assistance.
Simone Weil (1910-1943, French Philosopher, Mystic)

38 The race of mankind would perish did they cease to aid each other. We cannot exist without mutual help. All therefore that need aid have a right to ask it from their fellow-men; and no one who has the power of granting can refuse it without guilt.
Sir Walter Scott (1771-1832, British Novelist, Poet)

39 The proverb warns; "Don't bite the hand that feeds you." But maybe you should, if it prevents you from feeding yourself.
Thomas Szasz (1920-, American Psychiatrist)

40 One does nothing who tries to console a despondent person with word. A friend is one who aids with deeds at a critical time when deeds are called for.
Titus Maccius Plautus (254-184 BC, Roman Comic Poet)

AIDS

1 Sometimes I have a terrible feeling that I am dying not from the virus, but from being untouchable.
Amanda Heggs

2 I have learned more about love, selflessness and human understanding in this great adventure in the world of AIDS than I ever did in the cut-throat, competitive world in which I spent my life.
Anthony Perkins

3 From the point of view of the pharmaceutical industry, the AIDS problem has already been solved. After all, we already have a drug which can be sold at the incredible price of $8, 000 an annual dose, and which has the added virtue of not diminishing the market by actually curing anyone.
Barbara Ehrenreich (1941-, American Author, Columnist)

4 The moral immune system of this country has been weakened and attacked, and the AIDS virus is the perfect metaphor for it. The malignant neglect of the last twelve years has led to breakdown of our country's immune system, environmentally, culturally, politically, spiritually and physically.
Barbara Streisand (1942-, American Singer, Actress, Director)

5 Both the Moral Majority, who are recycling medieval language to explain AIDS, and those ultra-leftists who attribute AIDS to some sort of conspiracy, have a clearly political analysis of the epidemic. But even if one attributes its cause to a microorganism rather than the wrath of God, or the workings of the CIA, it is clear that the way in which AIDS has been perceived, conceptualized, imagined, researched and financed makes this the most political of diseases.
Dennis Altman (American Author)

6 The slow-witted approach to the HIV epidemic was the result of a thousand years of Christian malpractice and the childlike approach of the church to sexuality. If any single man was responsible, it was Augustine of Hippo who murdered his way to sainthood spouting on about the sins located in his genitals.
Derek Jarman (1942-, British Filmmaker, Artist, Author)

7 We are all HIV-positive.
Diamanda Galas

8 The AIDS epidemic has rolled back a big rotting log and revealed all the squirming life underneath it, since it involves, all at once, the main themes of our existence: sex, death, power, money, love, hate, disease and panic. No American phenomenon has been so compelling since the Vietnam War.
Edmund White (1940-, American Writer)

9 Everywhere I go I see increasing evidence of people swirling about in a human cesspit of their own making.
James Anderton

10 Aim at the sun, and you may not reach it; but your arrow will fly far higher than if aimed at an object on a level with yourself.
Joel Hawes

11 We're all going to go crazy, living this epidemic every minute, while the rest of the world goes on out there, all around us, as if nothing is happening, going on with their own lives and not knowing what it's like, what we're going through. We're living through war, but where they're living it's peacetime, and we're all in the same country.
Larry Kramer

12 It could be said that the AIDS pandemic is a classic own-goal scored by the human race against itself.
Princess Anne Ireland (Princess Royal Of Great Britain)

13 AIDS obliges people to think of sex as having, possibly, the direst consequences: suicide. Or murder.
Susan Sontag (1933-, American Essayist)

14 AIDS occupies such a large part in our awareness because of what it has been taken to represent. It seems the very model of all the catastrophes privileged populations feel await them.
Susan Sontag (1933-, American Essayist)

15 My thoughts are crowded with death and it draws so oddly on the sexual that I am confused to be attracted by, in effect, my own annihilation.
Thom Gunn

16 High aims form high characters, and great objects bring out great minds.
Tryon Edwards (1809-1894, American Theologian)

AIRPLANE AND AVIATION

1 Lovers of air travel find it exhilarating to hang poised between the illusion of immortality and the fact of death.
Alexander Chase

2 Women must pay for everything. They do get more glory than men for comparable feats, But, they also get more notoriety when they crash.
Amelia Earhart (1897-1937, American Aviator, Author)

3 There are no signposts in the sky to show a man has passed that way before. There are no channels marked. The flier breaks each second into new uncharted seas.
Anne Morrow Lindbergh (1906-, American Author)

4 The aeroplane has unveiled for us the true face of the earth.
Antoine De Saint-Exupery (1900-1944, French Aviator, Writer)

5 Flying is learning how to throw yourself at the ground and miss.
Douglas Adams (Born 1952, British Science Fiction Writer)

6 Aviation is proof that given, the will, we have the capacity to achieve the impossible.
Edward Vernon Rickenbacker (1890-1973, American Aviator, World War I Ace)

7 I wish I could write well enough to write about aircraft. Faulkner did it very well in Pylon but you cannot do something someone else has done though you might have done it if they hadn't.
Ernest Hemingway (1898-1961, American Writer)

8 I like terra firma; the more firma, the less terra.
George S. Kaufman (1889-1961, American Playwright, Director)

9 Flying is hours and hours of boredom sprinkled with a few seconds of sheer terror.
Gregory "Pappy" Boyington (American Colonel During World War II)

10 I feel about airplanes the way I feel about diets. It seems to me that they are wonderful things for other people to go on.
Jean Kerr (1923-, American Author, Playwright)

11. Of all the inventions that have helped to unify China perhaps the airplane is the most outstanding. Its ability to annihilate distance has been in direct proportion to its achievements in assisting to annihilate suspicion and misunderstanding among provincial officials far removed from one another or from the officials at the seat of government.
Madame Chiang Kai-Shek (Chinese Revolutionary Leader)

12. Success four flights Thursday morning all against twenty one mile wind started from Level with engine power alone speed through air thirty one miles longest 57 second inform Press home Christmas.
Orville Wright (1871-1948, American Inventor, Aviation Pioneer)

13. Any landing you can walk away from is a good one.
Proverb

14. A plane is a bad place for an all-out sleep, but a good place to begin rest and recovery from the trip to the faraway places you've been, a decompression chamber between Here and There. Though a plane is not the ideal place really to think, to reassess or reevaluate things, it is a great place to have the illusion of doing so, and often the illusion will suffice.
Shana Alexander (1925-, American Writer, Editor)

ALCOHOL AND ALCOHOLISM

1. Ale, man, ale's the stuff to drink for fellows whom it hurts to think.
A. E. Housman (1859-1936, British Poet, Classical Scholar)

2. Malt does more than Milton can to justify God's ways to man.
A. E. Housman (1859-1936, British Poet, Classical Scholar)

3. I believe, if we take habitual drunkards as a class, their heads and their hearts will bear an advantageous comparison with those of any other class. There seems ever to have been a proneness in the brilliant and warm-blooded to fall into this vice.
Abraham Lincoln (1809-1865, Sixteenth President of the USA)

4. The best audience is one that is intelligent, well-educated, and a little drunk.
Alben W. Barkley (1877-1956, American Politician)

5. There is only one really safe, mild, harmless beverage and you can drink as much of that as you like without running the slightest risk, and what you say when you want it is, "Garcon! Un Pernod!"
Aleister Crowley (1875-1947, British Occultist)

6. An alcoholic has been lightly defined as a man who drinks more than his own doctor.
Alvan L. Barach

7. Drunkenness is temporary suicide.
Bertrand Russell (1872-1970, British Philosopher, Mathematician, Essayist)

8. Wine is a mocker, and strong drink is raging; and who is deceived by it is not wise.
Bible (Sacred Scriptures of Christians and Judaism)

9. There are two things that will be believed of any man whatsoever, and one of them is that he has taken to drink.
Booth Tarkington (1869-1946, American Writer)

10. One drink is too many for me and a thousand not enough.
Brendan F. Behan (1923-1964, Irish Writer)

11. Bring in the bottled lightning, a clean tumbler, and a corkscrew.
Charles Dickens (1812-1870, British Novelist)

12. Wine is a treacherous friend who you must always be on guard for.
Christian Nevell Bovee (1820-1904, American Author, Lawyer)

13. If you drink, don't drive. Don't even putt.
Dean Martin (1917-1995, French-born American-born American Actor, Singer, Lush)

14. I'd hate to be a teetotaler. Imagine getting up in the morning and knowing that's as good as you're going to feel all day.
Dean Martin (1917-1995, French-born American-born American Actor, Singer, Lush)

15. I made a commitment to completely cut out drinking and anything that might hamper me from getting my mind and body together. And the floodgates of goodness have opened upon me- spiritually and financially.
Denzel Washington (1954-, American Actor)

16. At the punch-bowl's brink, let the thirsty think, what they say in Japan: first the man takes a drink, then the drink takes a drink, then the drink takes the man!
Edward Rowland Sill

17. No power on earth or above the bottomless pit has such influence to terrorize and make cowards of men as the liquor power. Satan could not have fallen on a more potent instrument with which to thrall the world. Alcohol is king!
Eliza "Mother" Stewart

18. He is a drunkard who takes more than three glasses though he be not drunk.
Epictetus (50-120, Stoic Philosopher)

19. Never accept a drink from a Urologist.
Erma Bombeck (1927-, American Author, Humorist)

20 Don't you drink? I notice you speak slightingly of the bottle. I have drunk since I was fifteen and few things have given me more pleasure. When you work hard all day with your head and know you must work again the next day what else can change your ideas and make them run on a different plane like whisky? When you are cold and wet what else can warm you? Before an attack who can say anything that gives you the momentary well-being that rum does? The only time it isn't good for you is when you write or when you fight. You have to do that cold. But it always helps my shooting. Modern life, too, is often a mechanical oppression and liquor is the only mechanical relief.
Ernest Hemingway (1898-1961, American Writer)

21 Always do sober what you said you'd do drunk. That will teach you to keep your mouth shut.
Ernest Hemingway (1898-1961, American Writer)

22 Alcohol is necessary for a man so that he can have a good opinion of himself, undisturbed be the facts.
Finley Peter Dunne (1867-1936, American Journalist, Humorist)

23 You can't be a Real Country unless you have a BEER and an airline -- it helps if you have some kind of a football team, or some nuclear weapons, but at the very least you need a BEER.
Frank Zappa (1940-, American Rock Musician)

24 When I drink, I think; and when I think, I drink.
Frantois Rabelais (1495-1553, French Satirist, Physician, and Humanist)

25 For art to exist, for any sort of aesthetic activity or perception to exist, a certain physiological precondition is indispensable: intoxication.
Friedrich Nietzsche (1844-1900, German Philosopher)

26 Where does one not find that bland degeneration which beer produces in the spirit!
Friedrich Nietzsche (1844-1900, German Philosopher)

27 I'm only a beer teetotaler, not a champagne teetotaler.
George Bernard Shaw (1856-1950, Irish-born British Dramatist)

28 I have fed purely upon ale; I have eat my ale, drank my ale, and I always sleep upon ale.
George Farquhar (1677-1707, Irish Playwright)

29 Drink not the third glass, which thou canst not tame, when once it is within thee.
George Herbert (1593-1632, British Metaphysical Poet)

30 I only drink to make other people seem more interesting.
George Jean Nathan (1882-1958, American Critic)

31 Most Americans are born drunk, and really require a little wine or beer to sober them. They have a sort of permanent intoxication from within, a sort of invisible champagne. Americans do not need to drink to inspire them to do anything, though they do sometimes, I think, need a little for the deeper and more delicate purpose of teaching them how to do nothing.
Gilbert K. Chesterton (1874-1936, British Author)

32 A prohibitionist is the sort of man one couldn't care to drink with, even if he drank.
H. L. Mencken (1880-1956, American Editor, Author, Critic, Humorist)

33 If all be true that I do think, there are five reasons we should drink: Good wine -- a friend -- or being dry -- or lest we should be by and by -- or any other reason why.
Henry Aldrich (American Editor, Actor)

34 Water is the only drink for a wise man.
Henry David Thoreau (1817-1862, American Essayist, Poet, Naturalist)

35 Wine is a turncoat; first a friend and then an enemy.
Henry Fielding (1707-1754, British Novelist, Dramatist)

36 The whole world is about three drinks behind.
Humphrey Bogart (1899-1957, American Film Actor)

37 What whiskey will not cure, there is no cure for.
Irish Proverb

38 A sudden violent jolt of it has been known to stop the victim's watch, snap his suspenders and crack his glass eye right across.
Irvin S. Cobb

39 Old wine and friends improve with age.
Italian Proverb

40 It takes that je ne sais quoi which we call sophistication for a woman to be magnificent in a drawing-room when her faculties have departed but she herself has not yet gone home.
James Thurber (1894-1961, American Humorist, Illustrator)

41 Even though a number of people have tried, no one has ever found a way to drink for a living.
Jean Kerr (1923-, American Author, Playwright)

42 A man is never drunk if he can lay on the floor without holding on.
Joe E. Lewis (American Writer)

43 I always wake up at the crack of ice.
Joe E. Lewis (American Writer)

44 I drink to forget I drink.
Joe E. Lewis (American Writer)

45 I would take a bomb, but I can't stand the noise.
Joe E. Lewis (American Writer)

46 I don't drink any more than the man next to me, and the man next to me is Dean Martin.
Joe E. Lewis (American Writer)

47 It pays to get drunk with the best people.
Joe E. Lewis (American Writer)

48 Fill it up. I take as large draughts of liquor as I did of love. I hate a flincher in either.
John Gay (1688-1732, British Playwright, Poet)

49 A few years back I was more a candidate for skid row bum than an Emmy. If I hadn't stopped [drinking], I'd be playing handball with John Belushi right now.
John Larroquette (1947-, American Actor)

50 A torchlight procession marching down your throat.
John Louis O'Sullivan

51 And when night, darkens the streets, then wander forth the sons of Belial, flown with insolence and wine.
John Milton (1608-1674, British Poet)

52 It's not the drinking to be blamed, but the excess.
John Selden (1584-1654, British Jurist, Statesman)

53 I'm not so think as you drunk I am.
John Squire

54 Better belly burst than good liquor be lost.
Jonathan Swift (1667-1745, Anglo-Irish Satirist)

55 They make much of our drinking, but never think of our thirst.
L. Schefer

56 One reason I don't drink is that I want to know when I am having a good time.
Lady Nancy Astor (1897-1964, British Politician)

57 Let us have wine and women, mirth and laughter. Sermons and soda water the day after.
Lord Byron (1788-1824, British Poet)

58 Man, being reasonable, must get drunk; the best of life is but intoxication.
Lord Byron (1788-1824, British Poet)

59 The decline of the aperitif may well be one of the most depressing phenomena of our time.
Luis Bunuel (1900-1983, Spanish Film Director)

60 No other human being, no woman, no poem or music, book or painting can replace alcohol in its power to give man the illusion of real creation.
Marguerite Duras (1914-, French Author, Filmmaker)

61 Alcohol is barren. The words a man speaks in the night of drunkenness fade like the darkness itself at the coming of day.
Marguerite Duras (1914-, French Author, Filmmaker)

62 Alcohol doesn't console, it doesn't fill up anyone's psychological gaps, all it replaces is the lack of God. It doesn't comfort man. On the contrary, it encourages him in his folly, it transports him to the supreme regions where he is master of his own destiny.
Marguerite Duras (1914-, French Author, Filmmaker)

63 When a woman drinks it's as if an animal were drinking, or a child. Alcoholism is scandalous in a woman, and a female alcoholic is rare, a serious matter. It's a slur on the divine in our nature.
Marguerite Duras (1914-, French Author, Filmmaker)

64 Water, taken in moderation, cannot hurt anybody.
Mark Twain (1835-1910, American Humorist, Writer)

65 Sometimes too much drink is barely enough.
Mark Twain (1835-1910, American Humorist, Writer)

66 The Great Spirit, who made all things, made every thing for some use, and whatever use he designed anything for, that use it should always be put to. Now, when he made rum, he said "Let this be for the Indians to get drunk with," and it must be so.
Native American Elder

67 Candy, is dandy, but Liquor, is quicker.
Ogden Nash (1902-1971, American Humorous Poet)

68 I can't say whether we had more wit among us now than usual, but I am certain we had more laughing, which answered the end as well.
Oliver Goldsmith (1728-1774, Anglo-Irish Author, Poet, Playwright)

69 I do not live in the world of sobriety.
Oliver Reed

70 Drink! for you know not whence you came nor why: drink! for you know not why you go, nor where.
Omar Khayyam (1048-1131, Persian Astronomer, Poet)

71 If I remember right there are five excuses for drinking: the visit of a guest, present thirst, future thirst, the goodness of the wine, and any other excuse you choose!
Pete Sermond

72 There is this to be said in favor of drinking, that it takes the drunkard first out of society, then out of the world.
Ralph Waldo Emerson (1803-1882, American Poet, Essayist)

73 Alcohol is like love. The first kiss is magic, the second is intimate, the third is routine. After that you take the girl's clothes off.
Raymond Chandler (1888-1959, American Author)

74 I like whiskey. I always did, and that is why I never drink it.
Robert E. Lee (1807-1870, American Confederate Army Commander)

75 My experience through life has convinced me that, while moderation and temperance in all things are commendable and beneficial, abstinence from spirituous liquors is the best safeguard of morals and health.
Robert E. Lee (1807-1870, American Confederate Army Commander)

76 Wine is bottled poetry.
Robert Louis Stevenson (1850-1895, Scottish Essayist, Poet, Novelist)

77 Other countries drink to get drunk, and this is accepted by everyone; in France, drunkenness is a consequence, never an intention. A drink is felt as the spinning out of a pleasure, not as the necessary cause of an effect which is sought: wine is not only a philter, it is also the leisurely act of drinking.
Roland Barthes (1915-1980, French Semiologist)

78 It is immoral to get drunk because the headache comes after the drinking, but if the headache came first and the drunkenness afterwards, it would be moral to get drunk.
Samuel Butler (1612-1680, British Poet, Satirist)

79 A man who exposes himself when he is intoxicated, has not the art of getting drunk.
Samuel Johnson (1709-1784, British Author)

80 There are some sluggish men who are improved by drinking; as there are fruits that are not good until they are rotten.
Samuel Johnson (1709-1784, British Author)

81 There is nothing which has yet been contrived by man, by which so much happiness is produced as by a good tavern.
Samuel Johnson (1709-1784, British Author)

82 Thanks be to God. Since my leaving the drinking of wine, I do find myself much better, and do mind my business better, and do spend less money, and less time lost in idle company.
Samuel Pepys (1633-1703, British Diarist)

83 Some men are like musical glasses; to produce their finest tones you must keep them wet.
Samuel Taylor Coleridge (1772-1834, British Poet, Critic, Philosopher)

84 Drunkenness is nothing but voluntary madness.
Seneca (4 BC-65 AD, Spanish-born Roman Statesman, philosopher)

85 When I played drunks I had to remain sober because I didn't know how to play them when I was drunk.
Sir Richard Burton (1821-1890, Explorer, Born in Torquay)

86 Of all vices, drinking is the most incompatible with greatness.
Sir Walter Scott (1771-1832, British Novelist, Poet)

87 The first glass is for myself, the second for my friends, the third for good humor, and the forth for my enemies.
Sir William Temple (1628-1699, British Diplomat, Essayist)

88 And must I wholly banish hence these red and golden juices, and pay my vows to Abstinence, that pallidest of Muses?
Sir William Watson (1858-1935, British Poet)

89 Under a tattered cloak you will generally find a good drinker.
Spanish Proverb

90 There is a devil in every berry of the grape.
The Koran (500 AD, Islamic Religious Bible)

91 Wine hath drowned more men than the sea.
Thomas Fuller (1608-1661, British Clergyman, Author)

92 A drinker has a hole under his nose that all his money runs into.
Thomas Fuller (1608-1661, British Clergyman, Author)

93 Prohibition may be a disputed theory, but none can say that it doesn't hold water.
Thomas L. Masson

94 This is the great fault of wine; it first trips up the feet: it is a cunning wrestler.
Titus Maccius Plautus (254-184 BC, Roman Comic Poet)

95 The piano has been drinking, not me.
Tom Waits (1949-, American Musician, Singer, Songwriter, Composer, Actor)

96 I'm tied of hearing about temperance instead of abstinence, in order to please the cocktail crowd in church congregations.
Vance Havner

97 I'm tired of hearing sin called sickness and alcoholism a disease. It is the only disease I know of that we're spending hundreds of millions of dollars a year to spread.
Vance Havner

98 I never drink water. I'm afraid it will become habit-forming.
W. C. Fields (1879-1946, American Actor)

99 Somebody left the cork out of my lunch.
W. C. Fields (1879-1946, American Actor)

100 The cost of living has gone up another dollar a quart.
W. C. Fields (1879-1946, American Actor)

101 I never drink water; that is the stuff that rusts pipes.
W. C. Fields (1879-1946, American Actor)

102 You can't trust water: Even a straight stick turns crooked in it.
W. C. Fields (1879-1946, American Actor)

103 It was a woman who drove me to drink, and I never had the courtesy to thank her for it.
W. C. Fields (1879-1946, American Actor)

104 They who drink beer will think beer.
Washington Irving (1783-1859, American Author)

105 The worst thing about some men is that when they are not drunk they are sober.
William Butler Yeats (1865-1939, Irish Poet, Playwright.)

106 If merely "feeling good" could decide, drunkenness would be the supremely valid human experience.
William James (1842-1910, American Psychologist, Professor, Author)

107 The sway of alcohol over mankind is unquestionably due to its power to stimulate the mystical faculties of human nature, usually crushed to earth by the cold facts and dry criticisms of the sober hour. Sobriety diminishes, discriminates, and says no; drunkenness expands, unites, and says yes.
William James (1842-1910, American Psychologist, Professor, Author)

108 I told you, sir, they were red-hot with drinking; so full of valor that they smote the air, for breathing in their faces, beat the ground for kissing of their feet.
William Shakespeare (1564-1616, British Poet, Playwright, Actor)

109 It provokes the desire but it takes away the performance. Therefore much drink may be said to be an equivocator with lechery: it makes him and it mars him; it sets him on and it takes him off.
William Shakespeare (1564-1616, British Poet, Playwright, Actor)

110 O thou invisible spirit of wine, if thou hast no name to be known by, let us call thee devil.
William Shakespeare (1564-1616, British Poet, Playwright, Actor)

111 O God, that men should put an enemy in their mouths to steal away their brains! That we should with joy, pleasance, revel, and applause transform ourselves into beasts!
William Shakespeare (1564-1616, British Poet, Playwright, Actor)

112 Macduff: What three things does drink especially provoke? Porter: Marry, sir, nose-painting, sleep, and urine.
William Shakespeare (1564-1616, British Poet, Playwright, Actor)

113 I have been brought up and trained to have the utmost contempt for people who get drunk.
Winston Churchill (1874-1965, British Statesman, Prime Minister)

114 I have taken more out of alcohol than alcohol has taken out of me.
Winston Churchill (1874-1965, British Statesman, Prime Minister)

ALIENATION

1 Without alienation, there can be no politics.
Arthur Miller (1915-, American Dramatist)

2 Although the masters make the rules for the wise men and the fools got nothing, Ma, to live up to.
Bob Dylan (1941-, American Musician, Singer, Songwriter)

3 By alienation is meant a mode of experience in which the person experiences himself as an alien. He has become, one might say, estranged from himself. He does not experience himself as the center of his world, as the creator of his own acts -- but his acts and their consequences have become his masters, whom he obeys, or whom he may even worship. The alienated person is out of touch with himself as he is out of touch with any other person. He, like the others, is experienced as things are experienced; with the senses and with common sense, but at the same time without being related to oneself and to the world outside positively.
Erich Fromm (1900-1980, American Psychologist)

4 There is no religion in which everyday life is not considered a prison; there is no philosophy or ideology that does not think that we live in alienation.
Eugene Ionesco (1912-, Romanian-born French Playwright)

5 The most dangerous aspect of present-day life is the dissolution of the feeling of individual responsibility. Mass solitude has done away with any difference between the internal and the external, between the intellectual and the physical.
Eugenio Montale (1896-1981, Italian Poet)

6 We are bemused and crazed creatures, strangers to our true selves, to one another, and to the spiritual and material world -- mad, even, from an ideal standpoint we can glimpse but not adopt.
R. D. Laing (1927-1989, British Psychiatrist)

7 Alienation as our present destiny is achieved only by outrageous violence perpetrated by human beings on human beings.
R. D. Laing (1927-1989, British Psychiatrist)

8 There is only one way left to escape the alienation of present day society: to retreat ahead of it.
Roland Barthes (1915-1980, French Semiologist)

9 Human beings are compelled to live within a lie, but they can be compelled to do so only because they are in fact capable of living in this way. Therefore not only does the system alienate humanity, but at the same time alienated humanity supports this system as its own involuntary master plan, as a degenerate image of its own degeneration, as a record of people's own failure as individuals.
Vaclav Havel (1936-, Czech Playwright, President)

ALIMONY

1 Alimony is like buying oats for a dead horse.
Arthur Baer

2 Alimony -- the ransom that the happy pay to the devil.
H. L. Mencken (1880-1956, American Editor, Author, Critic, Humorist)

3 I've been involved in something which was chaotic and insane. All I can say now is that I am, and intend to stay, a single man.
Sylvester Stallone (1946-, American Actor, Writer, Director, Producer)

ALLIANCES

1 Alliance. In international politics, the union of two thieves who have their hands so deeply inserted in each other's pockets that they cannot separately plunder a third.
Ambrose Bierce (1842-1914, American Author, Editor, Journalist, "The Devil's Dictionary")

2 Coalitions though successful have always found this, that their triumph has been brief.
Benjamin Disraeli (1804-1881, British Statesman, Prime Minister)

3 I think that a young state, like a young virgin, should modestly stay at home, and wait the application of suitors for an alliance with her; and not run about offering her amity to all the world; and hazarding their refusal. Our virgin is a jolly one; and tho at present not very rich, will in time be a great fortune, and where she has a favorable predisposition, it seems to me well worth cultivating.
Benjamin Franklin (1706-1790, American Scientist, Publisher, Diplomat)

4 When bad men combine, the good must associate; else they will fall, one by one, an unpitied sacrifice in a contemptible struggle.
Edmund Burke (1729-1797, British Political Writer, Statesman)

5 'Tis our true policy to steer clear of permanent alliances with any portion of the foreign world.
George Washington (1732-1799, First President of the USA)

6 We cannot always assure the future of our friends; we have a better chance of assuring our future if we remember who our friends are.
Henry Kissinger (1923-, American Republican Politician, Secretary of State)

7 All who think cannot but see there is a sanction like that of religion which binds us in partnership in the serious work of the world.
John Hay (1838-1905, American Author, Statesman)

8 Union may be strength, but it is mere blind brute strength unless wisely directed.
Samuel Butler (1612-1680, British Poet, Satirist)

9 Peace, commerce and honest friendship with all nations; entangling alliances with none.
Thomas Jefferson (1743-1826, Third President of the USA)

10 An alliance is like a chain. It is not made stronger by adding weak links to it. A great power like the United States gains no advantage and it loses prestige by offering, indeed peddling, its alliances to all and sundry. An alliance should be hard diplomatic currency, valuable and hard to get, and not inflationary paper from the mimeograph machine in the State Department.
Walter Lippmann (1889-1974, American Journalist)

ALTRUISM

1 She is such a good friend that she would throw all her acquaintances into the water for the pleasure of fishing them out again.
Charles Maurice De Talleyrand (1754-1838, French Statesman)

2 The compulsion to do good is an innate American trait. Only North Americans seem to believe that they always should, may, and actually can choose somebody with whom to share their blessings. Ultimately this attitude leads to bombing people into the acceptance of gifts.
Ivan Illich (1926-, Austrian-born American Theologian, Author)

3 That man is good who does good to others; if he suffers on account of the good he does, he is very good; if he suffers at the hands of those to whom he has done good, then his goodness is so great that it could be enhanced only by greater sufferings; and if he should die at their hands, his virtue can go no further: it is heroic, it is perfect.
Jean De La Bruyere (1645-1696, French Writer)

4 No people do so much harm as those who go about doing good.
Mandell Creighton (1843-1901, British Historian, Bishop)

5 He who would do good to another must do it in Minute Particulars: general Good is the plea of the scoundrel, hypocrite, and flatterer, for Art and Science cannot exist but in minutely organized Particulars.
William Blake (1757-1827, British Poet, Painter)

AMBIGUITY

1 I fear explanations explanatory of things explained.
Abraham Lincoln (1809-1865, Sixteenth President of the USA)

2 Those who write clearly have readers, those who write obscurely have commentators.
Abraham Lincoln (1809-1865, Sixteenth President of the USA)

3 That must be wonderful; I have no idea of what it means.
Albert Camus (1913-1960, French Existential Writer)

4 Clearly spoken, Mr. Fogg; you explain English by Greek.
Benjamin Franklin (1706-1790, American Scientist, Publisher, Diplomat)

AMBITION

1 Keep your feet on the ground, but let your heart soar as high as it will. Refuse to be average or to surrender to the chill of your spiritual environment. [The Root Of The Righteous]
A. W. Tozer (Deceased 1963, American Preacher)

2 Every man is said to have his peculiar ambition.
Abraham Lincoln (1809-1865, Sixteenth President of the USA)

3 Men would be angels, angels would be gods.
Alexander Pope (1688-1744, British Poet, Critic, Translator)

4 Ambition. An overmastering desire to be vilified by enemies while living and made ridiculous by friends when dead.
Ambrose Bierce (1842-1914, American Author, Editor, Journalist, "The Devil's Dictionary")

5 I've got a great ambition to die of exhaustion rather than boredom.
Angus Grossart (American Business Executive)

6 There are glimpses of heaven to us in every act, or thought, or word, that raises us above ourselves.
Arthur P. Stanley

7 Ambition has its disappointments to sour us, but never the good fortune to satisfy us. Its appetite grows keener by indulgence and all we can gratify it with at present serves but the more to inflame its insatiable desires.
Benjamin Franklin (1706-1790, American Scientist, Publisher, Diplomat)

8 Intelligence without ambition is a bird without wings.
C. Archie Danielson

9 Ambition makes the same mistake concerning power that avarice makes concerning wealth. She begins by accumulating power as a means to happiness, and she finishes by continuing to accumulate it as an end.
Charles Caleb Colton (1780-1832, British Sportsman Writer)

10 The passion of self-aggrandizement is persistent but plastic; it will never disappear from a vigorous mind, but may become morally higher by attaching itself to a larger conception of what constitutes the self.
Charles Horton Cooley (1864-1929, American Sociologist)

11 Ambition is a poor excuse for not having sense enough to be lazy.
Charlie McCarthy

12 Nature that framed us of four elements, warring within our breasts for regiment, doth teach us all to have aspiring minds.
Christopher Marlowe (1564-1593, British Dramatist, Poet)

13 Where ambition can cover its enterprises, even to the person himself, under the appearance of principle, it is the most incurable and inflexible of passions.
David Hume (1711-1776, Scottish Philosopher, Historian)

14 Though ambition in itself is a vice, it often is also the parent of virtue.
Edgar Quinet (1803-1875, French Poet, Historian, Politician)

15 Ambition can creep as well as soar.
Edmund Burke (1729-1797, British Political Writer, Statesman)

16 Ambition is a Dead Sea fruit, and the greatest peril to the soul is that one is likely to get precisely what he is seeking.
Edward Dahlberg (1900-1977, American Author, Critic)

17 We grow small trying to be great.
Eli Stanley Jones (1884-1973, American Missionary)

18 Man is the only creature that strives to surpass himself, and yearns for the impossible.
Eric Hoffer (1902-1983, American Author, Philosopher)

19 It seems to me we can never give up longing and wishing while we are thoroughly alive. There are certain things we feel to be beautiful and good, and we must hunger after them.
George Eliot (1819-1880, British Novelist)

20 A life spent in constant labor is a life wasted, save a man be such a fool as to regard a fulsome obituary notice as ample reward.
George Jean Nathan (1882-1958, American Critic)

21 If men cease to believe that they will one day become gods then they will surely become worms.
Henry Miller (1891-1980, American Author)

22 Most people would succeed in small things if they were not troubled with great ambitions.
Henry Wadsworth Longfellow (1819-1892, American Poet)

23 All ambitions are lawful except those that climb upward on the miseries or credulities of mankind.
Henry Ward Beecher (1813-1887, American Preacher, Orator, Writer)

24 The men who succeed are the efficient few. They are the few who have the ambition and will power to develop themselves.
Herbert N. Casson (American Author)

25 Nothing is too high for the daring of mortals: we storm heaven itself in our folly.
Horace (65-8 BC, Italian Poet)

26 I shall strike the stars with my unlifted head.
Horace (65-8 BC, Italian Poet)

27 Oh that I were seated as high as my ambition, I'd place my naked foot on the necks of monarchs.
Horace Walpole (1717-1797, British Author)

28 When ambition ends, happiness begins.
Hungarian Proverb

29 Hasty climbers have sudden falls.
Italian Proverb

30 Big results require big ambitions.
James Champy (American Author and International Management Consultant)

31 I had ambition not only to go farther than any man had ever been before, but as far as it was possible for a man to go.
James R. Cook (1728-1779, British Navigator)

32 Greatly begin. Though thou have time, but for a line, be that sublime . Not failure, but low aim is crime.
James Russell Lowell (1819-1891, American Poet, Critic, Editor)

33 The slave has but one master, the ambitious man has as many as there are persons whose aid may contribute to the advancement of his fortunes.
Jean De La Bruyere (1645-1696, French Writer)

34 A slave has but one master. An ambition man, has as many as there are people who helped him get his fortune.
Jean De La Bruyere (1645-1696, French Writer)

35 The person who starts out simply with the idea of getting rich won't succeed; you must have a larger ambition. There is no mystery in business success. If you do each day's task successfully, and stay faithfully within these natural operations of commercial laws which I talk so much about, and keep your head clear, you will come out all right.
John D. Rockefeller (1839-1937, American Industrialist, Philanthropist, Founder Exxon)

36 I had no ambition to make a fortune. Mere money-making has never been my goal, I had an ambition to build.
John D. Rockefeller (1839-1937, American Industrialist, Philanthropist, Founder Exxon)

37 Ambition often puts Men upon doing the meanest offices; so climbing is performed in the same position with creeping.
Jonathan Swift (1667-1745, Anglo-Irish Satirist)

38 A noble man compares and estimates himself by an idea which is higher than himself; and a mean man, by one lower than himself. The one produces aspiration; the other ambition, which is the way in which a vulgar man aspires.
Joseph Conrad (1857-1924, Polish-born British Novelist)

39 Ambition is pitiless. Any merit that it cannot use it finds despicable.
Joseph Joubert (1754-1824, French Moralist)

40 Very few people are ambitious in the sense of having a specific image of what they want to achieve. Most people's sights are only toward the next run, the next increment of money.
Judith M. Bardwick (American Academic)

41 When you go in search of honey you must expect to be stung by bees.
Kenneth Kaunda (1924-, Zambian Politician, President)

42 Don't be afraid to give up the good to go for the great.
Kenny Rogers (American Country Singer, Actor)

43 He who tip-toes cannot stand; he who strides cannot walk.
Lao-Tzu (600 BC, Chinese Philosopher, Founder of Taoism, Author of the "Tao Te Ching")

44 I want to work with the top people, because only they have the courage and the confidence and the risk-seeking profile that you need.
Laurel Cutler (American Business Executive)

45 So many worlds, so much to do, so little done, such things to be.
Lord Alfred Tennyson (1809-1892, British Poet)

46 He who surpasses or subdues mankind, must look down on the hate of those below.
Lord Byron (1788-1824, British Poet)

47 As falls the dew on quenchless sands, blood only serves to wash ambition's hands.
Lord Byron (1788-1824, British Poet)

48 When you are aspiring to the highest place, it is honorable to reach the second or even the third rank.
Marcus T. Cicero (106-43 BC, Great Roman Orator, Politician)

49 The noblest spirit is most strongly attracted by the love of glory.
Marcus T. Cicero (106-43 BC, Great Roman Orator, Politician)

50 Keep away from small people who try to belittle your ambitions. Small people always do that, but the really great make you feel that you, too, can become great.
Mark Twain (1835-1910, American Humorist, Writer)

51 Ambition is not a vice of little people.
Michel Eyquem De Montaigne (1533-1592, French Philosopher, Essayist)

52 If you have a great ambition, take as big a step as possible in the direction of fulfilling it. The step may only be a tiny one, but trust that it may be the largest one possible for now.
Mildred Mcafee

53 Great ambition is the passion of a great character. Those endowed with it may perform very good or very bad acts. All depends on the principals which direct them.
Napoleon Bonaparte (1769-1821, French General, Emperor)

54 Ambition is so powerful a passion in the human breast, that however high we reach we are never satisfied.
Niccolo Machiavelli (1469-1527, Italian Author, Statesman)

55 The ambitious are forever followed by adulation for they receive the most pleasure from flattery.
Oliver Goldsmith (1728-1774, Anglo-Irish Author, Poet, Playwright)

56 Ambition is the last refuge of failure.
Oscar Wilde (1856-1900, British Author, Wit)

57 If you wish to reach the highest, begin at the lowest.
Publilius Syrus (1st Century BC, Roman Writer)

58 Without ambition one starts nothing. Without work one finishes nothing. The prize will not be sent to you. You have to win it. The man who knows how will always have a job. The man who also knows why will always be his boss. As to methods there may be a million and then some, but principles are few. The man who grasps principles can successfully select his own methods. The man who tries methods, ignoring principles, is sure to have trouble.
Ralph Waldo Emerson (1803-1882, American Poet, Essayist)

59 What I aspired to be and was not, comforts me.
Robert Browning (1812-1889, British Poet)

60 Ambition is not what man does... but what man would do.
Robert Browning (1812-1889, British Poet)

61 Ah, but a man's reach should exceed his grasp, or what's a heaven for?
Robert Browning (1812-1889, British Poet)

62 'Tis not what man does which exalts him, but what man Would do!
Robert Browning (1812-1889, British Poet)

63 Like dogs in a wheel, birds in a cage, or squirrels in a chain, ambitious men still climb and climb, with great labor, and incessant anxiety, but never reach the top.
Robert Burton (1576-1640, British Clergyman, Scholar)

64 Ambition is an idol, on whose wings great minds are carried only to extreme; to be sublimely great or to be nothing.
Robert Southey (1774-1843, British Author)

65 It is the nature of ambition to make men liars and cheats, to hide the truth in their breasts, and show, like jugglers, another thing in their mouths, to cut all friendships and enmities to the measure of their own interest, and to make a good countenance without the help of good will.
Sallust (86-34 BC, Roman Historian)

66 At the age of six I wanted to be a cook. At seven I wanted to be Napoleon. And my ambition has been growing steadily ever since.
Salvador Dali (1904-1989, Spanish Painter)

67 He that fails in his endeavors after wealth or power will not long retain either honesty or courage.
Samuel Johnson (1709-1784, British Author)

68 To be happy at home is the ultimate result of all ambition, the end to which every enterprise and labor tends, and of which every desire prompts the prosecution.
Samuel Johnson (1709-1784, British Author)

69 It is the constant fault and inseparable evil quality of ambition, that it never looks behind it.
Seneca (4 BC-65 AD, Spanish-born Roman Statesman, philosopher)

70 Every child has great ambitions. As he grows, he is bombarded by negative suggestions -- you can't do this; you can't do that; be careful; look for security, and so on. Year by year, he experiences the "realities" of life, and his ambitions fade away. Figuratively speaking, most children die by the time they reach their adulthood.
Shall Sinha

71 Where there are large powers with little ambition... nature may be said to have fallen short of her purposes.
Sir Henry Taylor (1800-1886, British Author)

72 Ambition -- it is the last infirmity of noble minds.
Sir James M. Barrie (1860-1937, British Playwright)

73 Ambition is like love, impatient both of delays and rivals.
Sir John Denham (1615-1668, British Poet, Dramatist)

74 Our ambition should be to rule ourselves, the true kingdom for each one of us; and true progress is to know more, and be more, and to do more.
Sir John Lubbock (1834-1913, British Statesman, Banker, Naturalist)

75 To be ambitious of true honor, of the true glory and perfection of our natures, is the very principle and incentive of virtue.
Sir Philip Sidney (1554-1586, British Author, Courtier)

76 Ambition breaks the ties of blood, and forgets the obligations of gratitude.
Sir Walter Scott (1771-1832, British Novelist, Poet)

77 Ambition if it feeds at all, does so on the ambition of others.
Susan Sontag (1933-, American Essayist)

78 Ambition is the germ from which all growth of nobleness proceeds.
Thomas Dunn English (1819-1902, American Physician, Lawyer)

79 Ambition is a lust that is never quenched, but grows more inflamed and madder by enjoyment.
Thomas Otway (1652-1685, British Dramatist)

80 I too must attempt a way by which I can raise myself above the ground, and soar triumphant through the lips of men.
Virgil (70-19 BC, Roman Poet)

81 Ambition has one heel nailed in well, though she stretch her fingers to touch the heavens.
William Lilly

82 The tallest trees are most in the power of the winds, and ambitious men of the blasts of fortune.
William Penn (1644-1718, British Religious Leader, Founder of Pennsylvania)

83 As he was valiant, I honor him. But as he was ambitious, I slew him.
William Shakespeare (1564-1616, British Poet, Playwright, Actor)

84 Ambition should be made of sterner stuff.
William Shakespeare (1564-1616, British Poet, Playwright, Actor)

85 The very substance of the ambitious is merely the shadow of a dream.
William Shakespeare (1564-1616, British Poet, Playwright, Actor)

86 Ambition never comes to an end.
Yoshida Kenko

AMERICA

1 In every American there is an air of incorrigible innocence, which seems to conceal a diabolical cunning.
A. E. Housman (1859-1936, British Poet, Classical Scholar)

2 The American lives even more for his goals, for the future, than the European. Life for him is always becoming, never being.
Albert Einstein (1879-1955, German-born American Physicist)

3 It is a noble land that God has given us: a land that can feed and clothe the world; a land whose coastlines would enclose half the countries of Europe; a land set like a sentinel between the two imperial oceans of the globe.
Albert J. Beveridge (American Senator)

4 We are not afraid to entrust the American people with unpleasant facts, foreign ideas, alien philosophies, and competitive values. For a nation that is afraid to let its people judge the truth and falsehood in an open market is a nation that is afraid of its people.
Alexander Pope (1688-1744, British Poet, Critic, Translator)

5 Two things in America are astonishing: the changeableness of most human behavior and the strange stability of certain principles. Men are constantly on the move, but the spirit of humanity seems almost unmoved.
Alexis De Tocqueville (1805-1859, French Social Philosopher)

6 The whole life of an American is passed like a game of chance, a revolutionary crisis, or a battle.
Alexis De Tocqueville (1805-1859, French Social Philosopher)

7 The spirit is at home, if not entirely satisfied, in America.
Allan Bloom (1930-1992, American Educator, Author)

8 It's the movies that have really been running things in America ever since they were invented. They show you what to do, how to do it, when to do it, how to feel about it, and how to look how you feel about it. Everybody has their own America, and then they have the pieces of a fantasy America that they think is out there but they can't see.
Andy Warhol (1930-, American Artist, Filmmaker)

9 America is promises to take! America is promises to us to take them.
Archibald Macleish (1892-1982, American Poet)

10 The American mood, perhaps even the American character, has changed. There are few manifestations any longer of the old American self-assurance which so irritated Dickens. Instead, there is a sense of frustration so perceptible that even our politicians have attempted to exploit it.
Archibald Macleish (1892-1982, American Poet)

11 America is a large, friendly dog in a very small room. Every time it wags its tail, it knocks over a chair.
Arnold Toynbee (1852-1883, British Economic Historian and Social Reformer)

12 America is an adorable woman chewing tobacco.
Auguste Bartholdi

13 We are more thoroughly an enlightened people, with respect to our political interests, than perhaps any other under heaven. Every man among us reads, and is so easy in his circumstances as to have leisure for conversations of improvement and for acquiring information.
Benjamin Franklin (1706-1790, American Scientist, Publisher, Diplomat)

14 I like America, just as everybody else does. I love America, I gotta say that. But America will be judged.
Bob Dylan (1941-, American Musician, Singer, Songwriter)

15 In America everything's about who's number one today.
Bruce Springsteen (1949-, American Musician, Singer, Songwriter)

16 The business of America is business and the chief ideal of the American people is idealism.
Calvin Coolidge (1872-1933, Thirtieth President of the USA)

17 It is capitalist America that produced the modern independent woman. Never in history have women had more freedom of choice in regard to dress, behavior, career, and sexual orientation.
Camille Paglia (1947-, American Author, Critic, Educator)

18 What the United States does best is to understand itself. What it does worst is understand others.
Carlos Fuentes (1928-, Mexican Novelist, Short-Story Writer)

19 If its individual citizens, to a man, are to be believed, it always is depressed, and always is stagnated, and always is at an alarming crisis, and never was otherwise; though as a body, they are ready to make oath upon the Evangelists, at any hour of the day or night, that it is the most thriving and prosperous of all countries on the habitable globe.
Charles Dickens (1812-1870, British Novelist)

20 I take space to be the central fact to man born in America. I spell it large because it comes large here. Large and without mercy.
Charles Olson

21 I have no further use for America. I wouldn't go back there if Jesus Christ was President.
Charlie Chaplin (1889-1977, British Comic Actor, Filmmaker)

22 America is like an unfaithful love who promises us more than we got.
Charlotte Bunch

23 We know that the white man does not understand our ways. One portion of land is the same to him as the next, for he is a stranger who comes in the night and takes from the land whatever he needs. The earth is not his brother, but his enemy, and when he has conquered it, he moves on.
Chief Seattle (1786-1866, American Indian Chief of the Suquamish)

24 The main thing that endears the United Nations to member governments, and so enables it to survive, is its proven capacity to fail. You can safely appeal to the United Nations in the comfortable certainty that it will let you down.
Conor Cruise O'Brien (1917-, Irish Historian, Critic, and Statesman)

25 America does to me what I knew it would do: it just bumps me. The people charge at you like trucks coming down on you -- no awareness. But one tries to dodge aside in time. Bump! bump! go the trucks. And that is human contact.
D. H. Lawrence (1885-1930, British Author)

26 America is neither free nor brave, but a land of tight, iron-clanking little wills, everybody trying to put it over everybody else, and a land of men absolutely devoid of the real courage of trust, trust in life's sacred spontaneity. They can't trust life until they can control it.
D. H. Lawrence (1885-1930, British Author)

27 Of all the nations in the world, the United States was built in nobody's image. It was the land of the unexpected, of unbounded hope, of ideals, of quest for an unknown perfection. It is all the more unfitting that we should offer ourselves in images. And all the more fitting that the images which we make wittingly or unwittingly to sell America to the world should come back to haunt and curse us.
Daniel J. Boorstin (1914-, American Historian)

28 The most important American addition to the World Experience was the simple surprising fact of America. We have helped prepare mankind for all its later surprises.
Daniel J. Boorstin (1914-, American Historian)

29 America is the world's living myth. There's no sense of wrong when you kill an American or blame America for some local disaster. This is our function, to be character types, to embody recurring themes that people can use to comfort themselves, justify themselves and so on. We're here to accommodate. Whatever people need, we provide. A myth is a useful thing.
Don Delillo (1926-, American Author)

30 Part of the American dream is to live long and die young. Only those Americans who are willing to die for their country are fit to live.
Douglas Macarthur (1880-1964, American Army General in WW II)

31 Whatever America hopes to bring to pass in the world must first come to pass in the heart of America.
Dwight D. Eisenhower (1890-1969, Thirty-fourth President of the USA)

32 Only Americans can hurt America.
Dwight D. Eisenhower (1890-1969, Thirty-fourth President of the USA)

33 I have only one yardstick by which I test every major problem -- and that yardstick is: Is it good for America?
Dwight D. Eisenhower (1890-1969, Thirty-fourth President of the USA)

34 There is nothing wrong with America that faith, love of freedom, intelligence, and energy of her citizens cannot cure.
Dwight D. Eisenhower (1890-1969, Thirty-fourth President of the USA)

35 Here in America we are descended in blood and in spirit from revolutionists and rebels -- men and women who dare to dissent from accepted doctrine. As their heirs, may we never confuse honest dissent with disloyal subversion.
Dwight D. Eisenhower (1890-1969, Thirty-fourth President of the USA)

36 A man is not expected to love his country, lest he make an ass of himself. Yet our country, seen through the mists of smog, is curiously lovable, in somewhat the way an individual who has got himself into an unconscionable scrape seems lovable -- or at least deserving of support.
E(lwyn) B(rooks) White (1899-1985, American Author, Editor)

37 America makes prodigious mistakes, America has colossal faults, but one thing cannot be denied: America is always on the move. She may be going to Hell, of course, but at least she isn't standing still.
E.E. (Edward. E.) Cummings (1894-1962, American Poet)

38 At least the Pilgrim Fathers used to shoot Indians: the Pilgrim Children merely punch time clocks.
E.E. (Edward. E.) Cummings (1894-1962, American Poet)

39 I despair of the Republic! Such dreariness, such whining sallow women, such utter absence of the amenities, such crass food, crass manners, crass landscape!! What a horror it is for a whole nation to be developing without the sense of beauty, and eating bananas for breakfast.
Edith Wharton (1862-1937, American Author)

40 Young man, there is America, which at this day serves for little more than to amuse you with stories of savage men and uncouth manners.
Edmund Burke (1729-1797, British Political Writer, Statesman)

41 A people who are still, as it were, but in the gristle, and not yet hardened into the bone of manhood.
Edmund Burke (1729-1797, British Political Writer, Statesman)

42 America -- rather, the United States -- seems to me to be the Jew among the nations. It is resourceful, adaptable, maligned, envied, feared, imposed upon. It is warm-hearted, over-friendly; quick-witted, lavish, colorful; given to extravagant speech and gestures; its people are travelers and wanderers by nature, moving, shifting, restless; swarming in Fords, in ocean liners; craving entertainment; volatile. The chuckle among the nations of the world.
Edna Ferber (1887-1968, American Author)

43 America is rather like life. You can usually find in it what you look for. It will probably be interesting, and it is sure to be large.
Edward M. Forster (1879-1970, British Novelist, Essayist)

44 A trait no other nation seems to possess in quite the same degree that we do -- namely, a feeling of almost childish injury and resentment unless the world as a whole recognizes how innocent we are of anything but the most generous and harmless intentions.
Eleanor Roosevelt (1884-1962, American First Lady, Columnist, Lecturer, Humanitarian)

45 The superficiality of the American is the result of his hustling. It needs leisure to think things out; it needs leisure to mature. People in a hurry cannot think, cannot grow, nor can they decay. They are preserved in a state of perpetual puerility.
Eric Hoffer (1902-1983, American Author, Philosopher)

46 Americans cannot realize how many chances for mental improvement they lose by their inveterate habit of keeping six conversations when there are twelve in the room.
Ernest Dimnet (1866-1954, French Clergyman)

47 America is not a democracy, it's an absolute monarchy ruled by King Kid. In a nation of immigrants, the child is automatically more of an American than his parents. Americans regard children as what Mr. Hudson in "Upstairs, Downstairs" called "betters." Aping their betters, American adults do their best to turn themselves into children. Puerility exercises droit de seigneur everywhere.
Florence King (1936-, American Author, Critic)

48 America has run the world for at least the past 50 years, and when you're at the top that long, you forget what it's like in the valley. There are 5+ billion people out there now who are willing to study harder, work harder for less money and be more industrious than we are. And we're linked to them by technology. With telecommunications, you can have your bookkeeping done in Madra, India, for less than it costs here. Today technology can replace whole new industries, so you have to stay flexible. To survive today, you have to be able to walk on quicksand and dance with electrons.
Frank Ogden

49 This generation of Americans has a rendezvous with destiny.
Franklin D. Roosevelt (1882-1945, Thirty-second President of the USA)

50 I sometimes think that the saving grace of America lies in the fact that the overwhelming majority of Americans are possessed of two great qualities- a sense of humor and a sense of proportion.
Franklin D. Roosevelt (1882-1945, Thirty-second President of the USA)

51 I have met charming people, lots who would be charming if they hadn't got a complex about the British and everyone has pleasant and cheerful manners and I like most of the American voices. On the other hand I don't believe they have any God and their hats are frightful. On balance I prefer the Arabs.
Freya Stark (1893-1993, British Travel Writer)

52 America is, therefore the land of the future, where, in the ages that lie before us, the burden of the World's history shall reveal itself. It is a land of desire for all those who are weary of the historical lumber-room of Old Europe.
Georg Hegel (1770-1831, German Philosopher)

53 The gap between ideals and actualities, between dreams and achievements, the gap that can spur strong men to increased exertions, but can break the spirit of others -- this gap is the most conspicuous, continuous land mark in American history. It is conspicuous and continuous not because Americans achieve little, but because they dream grandly. The gap is a standing reproach to Americans; but it marks them off as a special and singularly admirable community among the world's peoples.
George F. Will (1941-, American Political Columnist)

54 It is veneer, rouge, aestheticism, art museums, new theaters, etc. that make America impotent. The good things are football, kindness, and jazz bands.
George Santayana (1863-1952, American Philosopher, Poet)

55 America is a young country with an old mentality.
George Santayana (1863-1952, American Philosopher, Poet)

56 America is the only nation in history which, miraculously, has gone directly from barbarism to degeneration without the usual interval of civilization.
Georges Clemenceau (1841-1929, French Statesman)

57 One can not be an American by going about saying that one is an American. It is necessary to feel America, like America, love America and then work.
Georgia O'Keeffe (American painter)

58 Americans are very friendly and very suspicious, that is what Americans are and that is what always upsets the foreigner, who deals with them, they are so friendly how can they be so suspicious they are so suspicious how can they be so friendly but they just are.
Gertrude Stein (1874-1946, American Author)

59 The United States is just now the oldest country in the world, there always is an oldest country and she is it, it is she who is the mother of the twentieth century civilization. She began to feel herself as it just after the Civil War. And so it is a country the right age to have been born in and the wrong age to live in.
Gertrude Stein (1874-1946, American Author)

60 There is nothing the matter with Americans except their ideals. The real American is all right; it is the ideal American who is all wrong.
Gilbert K. Chesterton (1874-1936, British Author)

61 On 16 September 1985, when the Commerce Department announced that the United States had become a debtor nation, the American Empire died.
Gore Vidal (1925-, American Novelist, Critic)

62 The story of Americans is the story of arrested metamorphoses. Those who achieve success come to a halt and accept themselves as they are. Those who fail become resigned and accept themselves as they are.
Harold Rosenberg (1906-1978, American Art Critic, Author)

63 As for America, it is the ideal fruit of all your youthful hopes and reforms. Everybody is fairly decent, respectable, domestic, bourgeois, middle-class, and tiresome. There is absolutely nothing to revile except that it's a bore.
Henry Brooks Adams (1838 - 1918, American Historian)

64 No sovereign, no court, no personal loyalty, no aristocracy, no church, no clergy, no army, no diplomatic service, no country gentlemen, no palaces, no castles, nor manors, nor old country-houses, nor parsonages, nor thatched cottages nor ivied ruins; no cathedrals, nor abbeys, nor little Norman churches; no great Universities nor public schools -- no Oxford, nor Eton, nor Harrow; no literature, no novels, no museums, no pictures, no political society, no sporting class -- no Epsom nor Ascot! Some such list as that might be drawn up of the absent things in American life.
Henry James (1843-1916, American Author)

65 It is, I think, an indisputable fact that Americans are, as Americans, the most self-conscious people in the world, and the most addicted to the belief that the other nations of the earth are in a conspiracy to under value them.
Henry James (1843-1916, American Author)

66 The face of nature and civilization in this our country is to a certain point a very sufficient literary field. But it will yield its secrets only to a really grasping imagination. To write well and worthily of American things one need even more than elsewhere to be a master.
Henry James (1843-1916, American Author)

67 For other nations, utopia is a blessed past never to be recovered; for Americans it is just beyond the horizon.
Henry Kissinger (1923-, American Republican Politician, Secretary of State)

68 I see America spreading disaster. I see America as a black curse upon the world. I see a long night settling in and that mushroom which has poisoned the world withering at the roots.
Henry Miller (1891-1980, American Author)

69 Perhaps I am still very much of an American. That is to say, naive, optimistic, gullible. In the eyes of a European, what am I but an American to the core, an American who exposes his Americanism like a sore. Like it or not, I am a product of this land of plenty, a believer in superabundance, a believer in miracles.
Henry Miller (1891-1980, American Author)

70 Actually we are a vulgar, pushing mob whose passions are easily mobilized by demagogues, newspaper men, religious quacks, agitators and such like. To call this a society of free peoples is blasphemous. What have we to offer the world besides the superabundant loot which we recklessly plunder from the earth under the maniacal delusion that this insane activity represents progress and enlightenment?
Henry Miller (1891-1980, American Author)

71 I have never been able to look upon America as young and vital but rather as prematurely old, as a fruit which rotted before it had a chance to ripen.
Henry Miller (1891-1980, American Author)

72 The real democratic American idea is, not that every man shall be on a level with every other man, but that every man shall have liberty to be what God made him, without hindrance.
Henry Ward Beecher (1813-1887, American Preacher, Orator, Writer)

73 America is just a nation of two hundred million used car salesmen with all the money we need to buy guns and no qualms about killing anybody else in the world who tries to make us uncomfortable.
Hunter S. Thompson (1939-, American Journalist)

74 The biggest difference between ancient Rome and the USA is that in Rome the common man was treated like a dog. In America he sets the tone. This is the first country where the common man could stand erect.
I. F. Stone (1907-1989, American Author)

75 America's best buy is a telephone call to the right man.
Ilka Chase (1905-, American Author, Actor)

76 No... the real American has not yet arrived. He is only in the Crucible, I tell you -- he will be the fusion of all races, perhaps the coming superman.
Israel Zangwill (1864-1926, British Writer)

77 The American Dream has run out of gas. The car has stopped. It no longer supplies the world with its images, its dreams, its fantasies. No more. It's over. It supplies the world with its nightmares now: the Kennedy assassination, Watergate, Vietnam...
J. G. Ballard (1930-, British Author)

78 I don't see America as a mainland, but as a sea, a big ocean. Sometimes a storm arises, a formidable current develops, and it seems it will engulf everything. Wait a moment, another current will appear and bring the first one to naught.
Jacques Maritain (1882-1973, French Philosopher)

79 Americans, unhappily, have the most remarkable ability to alchemize all bitter truths into an innocuous but piquant confection and to transform their moral contradictions, or public discussion of such contradictions, into a proud decoration, such as are given for heroism on the battle field.
James Baldwin (1924-1987, American Author)

80 The rising power of the United States in world affairs requires, not a more compliant press, but a relentless barrage of facts and criticism. Our job in this age, as I see it, is not to serve as cheerleaders for our side in the present world struggle but to help the largest possible number of people to see the realities of the changing and convulsive world in which American policy must operate.
James Reston (1909-1995, Dutch Born American Journalist)

81 What you have to do is enter the fiction of America, enter America as fiction. It is, indeed, on this fictive basis that it dominates the world.
Jean Baudrillard (French Postmodern Philosopher, Writer)

82 Deep down, the US, with its space, its technological refinement, its bluff good conscience, even in those spaces which it opens up for simulation, is the only remaining primitive society.
Jean Baudrillard (French Postmodern Philosopher, Writer)

83 Thank God we're living in a country where the sky's the limit, the stores are open late and you can shop in bed thanks to television.
Joan Rivers (1933-, American Comedian, Talk Show Host, Actress)

84 I always consider the settlement of America with reverence and wonder, as the opening of a grand scene and design in providence, for the illumination of the ignorant and the emancipation of the slavish part of mankind all over the earth.
John Adams (1735-1826, Second President of the USA)

85 America is the country where you can buy a lifetime supply of aspirin For one dollar and use it up in two weeks.
John Barrymore (1882-1942, American Actor)

86 The Constitution gives every American the inalienable right to make a damn fool of himself.
John Ciardi (1916-1986, American Teacher, Poet, Writer)

87 Every American ought to have the right to be treated as he would wish to be treated, as one would wish his children to be treated. this is not the case.
John F. Kennedy (1917-1963, Thirty-fifth President of the USA)

88 Ours is the only country deliberately founded on a good idea.
John Gunther

89 America is a land where men govern, but women rule.
John Mason Brown (1800-1859, American Militant Abolitionist)

90 Americans are apt to be unduly interested in discovering what average opinion believes average opinion to be...
John Maynard Keynes (1883-1946, British Economist)

91 This monster of a land, this mightiest of nations, this spawn of the future, turns out to be the macrocosm of microcosm me.
John Steinbeck (1902-1968, American Author)

92 America is a vast conspiracy to make you happy.
John Updike (1932-, American Novelist, Critic)

93 America, America, God shed His grace on thee, and crown thy good with brotherhood, from sea to shining sea.
Katherine Lee Bates (1859-1921, American Author)

94 I can never suppose this country so far lost to all ideas of self-importance as to be willing to grant America independence; if that could ever be adopted I shall despair of this country being ever preserved from a state of inferiority and consequently falling into a very low class among the European States.
King George III (1738-1820, King of Great Britain and Ireland (1760--1820))

95 Knavery seems to be so much a the striking feature of its inhabitants that it may not in the end be an evil that they will become aliens to this kingdom.
King George III (1738-1820, King of Great Britain and Ireland (1760--1820))

96 Being American is to eat a lot of beef steak, and boy, we've got a lot more beef steak than any other country, and that's why you ought to be glad you're an American. And people have started looking at these big hunks of bloody meat on their plates, you know, and wondering what on earth they think they're doing.
Kurt Vonnegut Jr. (1922-, American Novelist)

97 Americans usually believe that nothing is impossible.
Lawrence S. Eagleburger

98 America and its demons, Europe and its ghost.
Le Monde

99 To be an American (unlike being English or French or whatever) is precisely to imagine a destiny rather than to inherit one; since we have always been, insofar as we are Americans at all, inhabitants of myth rather than history.
Leslie Fiedler (1917-, American Literary Critic, educator)

100 I would rather have a nod from an American, than a snuff-box from an emperor.
Lord Byron (1788-1824, British Poet)

101 America is a model of force and freedom and moderation -- with all the coarseness and rudeness of its people.
Lord Byron (1788-1824, British Poet)

102 It is impossible for a stranger traveling through the United States to tell from the appearance of the people or the country whether he is in Toledo, Ohio, or Portland, Oregon. Ninety million Americans cut their hair in the same way, eat each morning exactly the same breakfast, tie up the small girls curls with precisely the same kind of ribbon fashioned into bows exactly alike; and in every way all try to look and act as much like all the others as they can.
Lord Northcliffe

103 The trouble with us in America isn't that the poetry of life has turned to prose, but that it has turned to advertising copy.
Louis Kronenberger

104 I pray we are still a young and courageous nation, that we have not grown so old and so fat and so prosperous that all we can think about is to sit back with our arms around our money bags. If we choose to do that I have no doubt that the smoldering fires will burst into flame and consume us -- dollars and all.
Lyndon B. Johnson (1908-1973, Thirty-sixth President of the USA)

105 For this is what America is all about. It is the uncrossed desert and the unclimbed ridge. It is the star that is not reached and the harvest that is sleeping in the unplowed ground.
Lyndon B. Johnson (1908-1973, Thirty-sixth President of the USA)

106 Sitting at the table doesn't make you a diner, unless you eat some of what's on that plate. Being here in America doesn't make you an American. Being born here in America doesn't make you an American.
Malcolm X (1925-1965, American Black Leader, Activist)

107 People in America, of course, live in all sorts of fashions, because they are foreigners, or unlucky, or depraved, or without ambition; people live like that, but Americans live in white detached houses with green shutters. Rigidly, blindly, the dream takes precedence.
Margaret Mead (1901-1978, American Anthropologist)

108 Europe was created by history. America was created by philosophy.
Margaret Thatcher (1925-, British Stateswoman, Prime Minister (1979-90))

109 It is always dangerous to generalize, but the American people, while infinitely generous, are a hard and strong race and, but for the few cemeteries I have seen, I am inclined to think they never die.
Margot Asquith (1864-1945, British Socialite)

110 In Boston they ask, "How much does he know?" In New York, "How much is he worth?" In Philadelphia, "Who were his parents?"
Mark Twain (1835-1910, American Humorist, Writer)

111 It was wonderful to find America, but it would have been more wonderful to miss it.
Mark Twain (1835-1910, American Humorist, Writer)

112 There isn't a single human characteristic that can be safely labeled as "American."
Mark Twain (1835-1910, American Humorist, Writer)

113 America does not concern itself now with Impressionism. We own no involved philosophy. The psyche of the land is to be found in its movement. It is to be felt as a dramatic force of energy and vitality. We move; we do not stand still. We have not yet arrived at the stock-taking stage.
Martha Graham (1894-1991, American Dancer, Teacher, and Choreographer)

114 Being blunt with your feelings is very American. In this big country, I can be as brash as New York, as hedonistic as Los Angeles, as sensuous as San Francisco, as brainy as Boston, as proper as Philadelphia, as brawny as Chicago, as warm as Palm Springs, as friendly as my adopted home town of Dallas, Fort Worth, and as peaceful as the inland waterway that rubs up against my former home in Virginia Beach.
Martina Navratilova (1956-, American Tennis Player)

115 The American character looks always as if it had just had a rather bad haircut, which gives it, in our eyes at any rate, a greater humanity than the European, which even among its beggars has an all too professional air.
Mary Mccarthy (1912-1989, American Author, Critic)

116 Our society distributes itself into Barbarians, Philistines and Populace; and America is just ourselves with the Barbarians quite left out, and the Populace nearly.
Matthew Arnold (1822-1888, British Poet, Critic)

117 To me Americanism means an imperative duty to be nobler than the rest of the world.
Meyer London

118 I have a great fear for the moral will of Americans if it takes more than a week to achieve the results.
Michael S. Harper

119 No author, without a trial, can conceive of the difficulty of writing a romance about a country where there is no shadow, no antiquity, no mystery, no picturesque and gloomy wrong, nor anything but a commonplace prosperity, in broad and simple daylight, as is happily the case with my dear native land.
Nathaniel Hawthorne (1804-1864, American Novelist, Short Story Writer)

120 America is the best half-educated country in the world.
Nicholas Butler (1862-1947, American Educationist)

121 The history of the building of the American nation may justly be described as a laboratory experiment in understanding and in solving the problems that will confront the world tomorrow.
Nicholas Butler (1862-1947, American Educationist)

122 There is one expanding horror in American life. It is that our long odyssey toward liberty, democracy and freedom-for-all may be achieved in such a way that utopia remains forever closed, and we live in freedom and hell, debased of style, not individual from one another, void of courage, our fear rationalized away.
Norman Mailer (1923-, American Author)

123 To us Americans much has been given; of us much is required. With all our faults and mistakes, it is our strength in support of the freedom our forefathers loved which has saved mankind from subjection to totalitarian power.
Norman Thomas (1884-1968, American Socialist Leader)

124 The North American system only wants to consider the positive aspects of reality. Men and women are subjected from childhood to an inexorable process of adaptation; certain principles, contained in brief formulas are endlessly repeated by the Press, the radio, the churches, and the schools, and by those kindly, sinister beings, the North American mothers and wives. A person imprisoned by these schemes is like a plant in a flowerpot too small for it: he cannot grow or mature.
Octavio Paz (1914-, Mexican Poet, Essayist)

125 Good Americans when they die, go to Paris.
Oliver Wendell Holmes (1809-1894, American Author, Wit, Poet)

126 The ideal American type is perfectly expressed by the Protestant, individualist, anti- conformist, and this is the type that is in the process of disappearing. In reality there are few left.
Orson Welles (1915-1985, American Film Maker)

127 There is no country in the world where machinery is so lovely as in America.
Oscar Wilde (1856-1900, British Author, Wit)

128 America is the only country that went from barbarism to decadence without civilization in between.
Oscar Wilde (1856-1900, British Author, Wit)

129 The youth of America is their oldest tradition. It has been going on now for three hundred years.
Oscar Wilde (1856-1900, British Author, Wit)

130 America had often been discovered before Columbus, but it had always been hushed up.
Oscar Wilde (1856-1900, British Author, Wit)

131 Our democracy, our culture, our whole way of life is a spectacular triumph of the blah. Why not have a political convention without politics to nominate a leader who's out in front of nobody? Maybe our national mindlessness is the very thing that keeps us from turning into one of those smelly European countries full of pseudo-reds and crypto-fascists and greens who dress like forest elves.
P. J. O'Rourke (1947-, American Journalist)

132 The genius of the American system is that we have created extraordinary results from plain old ordinary people.
Phil Gramm

133 America, thou half-brother of the world; with something good and bad of every land.
Philip James Bailey (1816-1902, British Poet)

134 American dreams are strongest in the hearts of those who have seen America only in their dreams.
Pico Iyer (Travel Writer)

135 In America the geography is sublime, but the men are not; the inventions are excellent, but the inventors one is sometimes ashamed of.
Ralph Waldo Emerson (1803-1882, American Poet, Essayist)

136 We are a puny and fickle folk. Avarice, hesitation, and following are our diseases.
Ralph Waldo Emerson (1803-1882, American Poet, Essayist)

137 I hate this shallow Americanism which hopes to get rich by credit, to get knowledge by raps on midnight tables, to learn the economy of the mind by phrenology, or skill without study, or mastery without apprenticeship.
Ralph Waldo Emerson (1803-1882, American Poet, Essayist)

138 The keynote of American civilization is a sort of warm-hearted vulgarity. The Americans have none of the irony of the English, none of their cool poise, none of their manner. But they do have friendliness. Where an Englishman would give you his card, an American would very likely give you his shirt.
Raymond Chandler (1888-1959, American Author)

139 If you think the United States has stood still, who built The largest shopping center in the world?
Richard M. Nixon (1913-1994, Thirty-seventh President of the USA)

140 America: It's like Britain, only with buttons.
Ringo Starr (1940-, The Beatles Pop Group, on Drums)

141 If you don't know how great this country is, I know someone who does; Russia.
Robert Frost (1875-1963, American Poet)

142 America once had the clarity of the pioneer ax.
Robert Osborne

143 I think the greatest curse of American society has been the idea of an easy millennialism -- that some new drug, or the next election or the latest in social engineering will solve everything.
Robert Penn Warren (1905-1989, American Writer, Poet)

144 Double, no triple, our troubles and we'd still be better off than any other people on earth. It is time that we recognized that ours was, in truth, a noble cause.
Ronald Reagan (1911-, Fortieth President of the USA, Actor)

145 It's difficult to believe that people are still starving in this country because food isn't available.
Ronald Reagan (1911-, Fortieth President of the USA, Actor)

146 We must stop talking about the American dream and start listening to the dreams of the Americans.
Ruben Askew

147 By the definition accepted in the United States, any person with even a small amount of Negro Blood... is a Negro. Logically, it would be exactly as justifiable to say that any person with even a small amount of white blood is white. Why do they say one rather than the other? Because the former classification suits the convenience of those making the classification. Society, in short, regards as true those systems that produce the desired results. Science seeks only the most generally useful systems of classification; these it regards for the time being, until more useful classifications are invented, as true.
S. I. Hayakawa (1902-1992, Canadian Born American Senator, Educator)

148 I am willing to love all mankind, except an American.
Samuel Johnson (1709-1784, British Author)

149 Sir, they are a race of convicts, and ought to be thankful for anything we allow them short of hanging.
Samuel Johnson (1709-1784, British Author)

150 Is America a land of God where saints abide for ever? Where golden fields spread fair and broad, where flows the crystal river? Certainly not flush with saints, and a good thing, too, for the saints sent buzzing into man's ken now are but poor-mouthed ecclesiastical film stars and cliché- shouting publicity agents. Their little knowledge bringing them nearer to their ignorance, ignorance bringing them nearer to death, but nearness to death no nearer to God.
Sean O'Casey (1884-1964, Irish Dramatist)

151 America is the most grandiose experiment the world has seen, but, I am afraid, it is not going to be a success.
Sigmund Freud (1856-1939, Austrian Physician - Founder of Psychoanalysis)

152 America is a mistake, a giant mistake.
Sigmund Freud (1856-1939, Austrian Physician - Founder of Psychoanalysis)

153 The trouble with this country is that there are too many people going about saying, "The trouble with this country is..."
Sinclair Lewis (1885-1951, First American Novelist to win the Nobel Prize for literature)

154 American "energy" is the energy of violence, of free-floating resentment and anxiety unleashed by chronic cultural dislocations which must be, for the most part, ferociously sublimated. This energy has mainly been sublimated into crude materialism and acquisitiveness. Into hectic philanthropy. Into benighted moral crusades, the most spectacular of which was Prohibition. Into an awesome talent for uglifying countryside and cities. Into the loquacity and torment of a minority of gadflies: artists, prophets, muckrakers, cranks, and nuts. And into self-punishing neuroses. But the naked violence keeps breaking through, throwing everything into question.
Susan Sontag (1933-, American Essayist)

155 The quality of American life is an insult to the possibilities of human growth... the pollution of American space, with gadgetry and cars and TV and box architecture, brutalizes the senses, making gray neurotics of most of us, and perverse spiritual athletes and strident self-transcenders of the best of us.
Susan Sontag (1933-, American Essayist)

156 The things that will destroy America are prosperity-at-any-price, peace-at-any-price, safety- first instead of duty-first, the love of soft living, and the get-rich-quick theory of life.
Theodore Roosevelt (1858-1919, Twenty-sixth President of the USA)

157 The American people abhor a vacuum.
Theodore Roosevelt (1858-1919, Twenty-sixth President of the USA)

158 America is like one of those old-fashioned six-cylinder truck engines that can be missing two sparkplugs and have a broken flywheel and have a crankshaft that's 5000 millimeters off fitting properly, and two bad ball-bearings, and still runs. We're in that kind of situation. We can have substantial parts of the population committing suicide, and still run and look fairly good.
Thomas Mcguane

159 The ideology of this America wants to establish reassurance through Imitation. But profit defeats ideology, because the consumers want to be thrilled not only by the guarantee of the Good but also by the shudder of the Bad.
Umberto Eco (1929-, Italian Novelist and critic)

160 There is a constant in the average American imagination and taste, for which the past must be preserved and celebrated in full-scale authentic copy; a philosophy of immortality as duplication. It dominates the relation with the self, with the past, not infrequently with the present, always with History and, even, with the European tradition.
Umberto Eco (1929-, Italian Novelist and critic)

161 The voice of America has no undertones or overtones in it. It repeats its optimistic catchwords in a tireless monologue that has the slightly metallic sound of a gramophone.
Vance Palmer (1885-1959, Australian Author, Poet)

162 God bless the USA, so large, so friendly, and so rich.
W. H. Auden (1907-1973, Anglo-American Poet)

163 The Americans are violently oral. That's why in America the mother is all-important and the father has no position at all -- isn't respected in the least. Even the American passion for laxatives can be explained as an oral manifestation. They want to get rid of any unpleasantness taken in through the mouth.
W. H. Auden (1907-1973, Anglo-American Poet)

164 Their manners, speech, dress, friendships, -- the freshness and candor of their physiognomy -- the picturesque looseness of their carriage -- their deathless attachment to freedom -- their aversion to anything indecorous or soft or mean -- the practical acknowledgment of the citizens of one state by the citizens of all other states -- the fierceness of their roused resentment -- their curiosity and welcome of novelty -- their self-esteem and wonderful sympathy -- their susceptibility to a slight -- the air they have of persons who never knew how it felt to stand in the presence of superiors -- the fluency of their speech -- their delight in music, a sure symptom of manly tenderness and native elegance of soul -- their good temper and open-handedness -- the terrible significance of their elections, the President's taking off his hat to them, not they to him -- these too are unrhymed poetry. It awaits the gigantic and generous treatment worthy of it.
Walt Whitman (1819-1892, American Poet)

165 America fears the unshaven legs, the unshaven men's cheeks, the aroma of perspiration, and the limp prick. Above all it fears the limp prick.
Walter Abish (Born 1931, Austrian-born American Author)

166 America is a great country, but you can't live in it for nothing.
Will Rogers (1879-1935, American Humorist, Actor)

167 If we Americans are to survive it will have to be because we choose and elect and defend to be first of all Americans; to present to the world one homogeneous and unbroken front, whether of white Americans or black ones or purple or blue or green. If we in America have reached that point in our desperate culture when we must murder children, no matter for what reason or what color, we don't deserve to survive, and probably won t.
William Faulkner (1897-1962, American Novelist)

168 America is not so much a nightmare as a non-dream. The American non-dream is precisely a move to wipe the dream out of existence. The dream is a spontaneous happening and therefore dangerous to a control system set up by the non-dreamers.
William S. Burroughs (1914-1997, American Writer)

169 America is not a young land: it is old and dirty and evil before the settlers, before the Indians. The evil is there waiting.
William S. Burroughs (1914-1997, American Writer)

170 America lives in the heart of every man everywhere who wishes to find a region where he will be free to work out his destiny as he chooses.
Woodrow T. Wilson (1856-1924, Twenty-eighth President of the USA)

171 The interesting and inspiring thing about America is that she asks nothing for herself except what she has a right to ask for humanity itself.
Woodrow T. Wilson (1856-1924, Twenty-eighth President of the USA)

172 Sometimes people call me an idealist. Well, that is the way I know I am an American. America is the only idealistic nation in the world.
Woodrow T. Wilson (1856-1924, Twenty-eighth President of the USA)

173 No American worth his salt should go around looking for a root. I advance this in all modesty, as a not unreasonable opinion.
Wyndham Lewis (1882-1957, British Author, Painter)

174 I feel most at home in the United States, not because it is intrinsically a more interesting country, but because no one really belongs there any more than I do. We are all there together in its wholly excellent vacuum.
Wyndham Lewis (1882-1957, British Author, Painter)

175 Building a better you is the first step to building a better America.
Zig Ziglar (American Sales Trainer, Author, Motivational Speaker)

AMIABILITY

1 How easy to be amiable in the midst of happiness and success.
Anne Sophie Swetchine (1782-1857, Russian Author)

2 When the righteous man truth away from his righteousness that he hath committed and doeth that which is neither quite lawful nor quite right, he will generally be found to have gained in amiability what he has lost in holiness.
Samuel Butler (1612-1680, British Poet, Satirist)

3 Natural amiableness is too often seen in company with sloth, with uselessness, with the vanity of fashionable life.
William Ellery Channing (1780-1842, American Unitarian Minister, Author)

AMUSEMENT

1 Amusement to an observing mind is study.
Benjamin Disraeli (1804-1881, British Statesman, Prime Minister)

2 Cards were at first for benefits designed, sent to amuse, not to enslave the mind.
David Garrick (1717-1779, British Actor, Playwright, Theater Manager)

3 The only way to amuse some people is to slip and fall on an icy pavement.
Edgar Watson Howe (1853-1937, American Journalist, Author)

4 Life would be tolerable but for its amusements.
George Bernard Shaw (1856-1950, Irish-born British Dramatist)

5 You can't live on amusement. It is the froth on water -- an inch deep and then the mud.
George Macdonald (1824-1905, Scottish Novelist)

6 If those who are the enemies of innocent amusements had the direction of the world, they would take away the spring, and youth, the former from the year, the latter from human life.
Honore De Balzac (1799-1850, French Novelist)

7 To a man of pleasure every moment appears to be lost, which partakes not of the vivacity of amusement.
Joseph Addison (1672-1719, British Essayist, Poet, Statesman)

8 Nothing is so perfectly amusing as a total change of ideas.
Laurence Sterne (1713-1768, British Author)

9 When I play with my cat, who knows whether she is not amusing herself with me more than I with her.
Michel Eyquem De Montaigne (1533-1592, French Philosopher, Essayist)

10 The mind ought sometimes to be diverted, that it may return the better to thinking.
Phaedrus (Macedonian Inventor and Writer)

11 The intellectual man requires a fine bait; the sots are easily amused. But everybody is drugged with his own frenzy, and the pageant marches at all hours, with music and banner and badge.
Ralph Waldo Emerson (1803-1882, American Poet, Essayist)

ANALYSIS

1 Happiness never lays its finger on its pulse.
Adam Smith (1723-1790, Scottish Economist)

2 Observation more than books and experience more than persons, are the prime educators.
Amos Bronson Alcott (1799-1888, American Educator, Social Reformer)

3 When I was research head of General Motors and wanted a problem solved, I'd place a table outside the meeting room with a sign: LEAVE SLIDE RULES HERE! If I didn't do that, I'd find some engineer reaching for his slide rule. Then he'd be on his feet saying, "Boss you can't do that."
Charles F. Kettering (1876-1958, American Engineer, Inventor)

4 Psychoanalysis is confession without absolution.
Gilbert K. Chesterton (1874-1936, British Author)

5 Think as you work, for in the final analysis, your worth to your company comes not only in solving problems, but also in anticipating them.
Harold Wallace Ross (1892-1951, American Newspaper Editor)

6 Analysis kills spontaneity. The grain once ground into flour springs and germinates no more.
Henri Frederic Amiel (1821-1881, Swiss Philosopher, Poet, Critic)

7 He suffered from paralysis by analysis.
Saying

8   The unlived life is not worth examining.
    Tom Morris

ANARCHISM

1   My thinking tends to be libertarian. That is, I oppose intrusions of the state into the private realm -- as in abortion, sodomy, prostitution, pornography, drug use, or suicide, all of which I would strongly defend as matters of free choice in a representative democracy.
    Camille Paglia (1947-, American Author, Critic, Educator)

2   Anarchism is the only philosophy which brings to man the consciousness of himself; which maintains that God, the State, and society are non-existent, that their promises are null and void, since they can be fulfilled only through man's subordination. Anarchism is therefore the teacher of the unity of life; not merely in nature, but in man.
    Emma Goldman (1869-1940, American Anarchist)

3   The anarchist and the Christian have a common origin.
    Friedrich Nietzsche (1844-1900, German Philosopher)

4   The ordinary man is an anarchist. He wants to do as he likes. He may want his neighbor to be governed, but he himself doesn't want to be governed. He is mortally afraid of government officials and policemen.
    George Bernard Shaw (1856-1950, Irish-born British Dramatist)

5   The consistent anarchist should be a socialist, but a socialist of a particular sort. He will not only oppose alienated and specialized labor and look forward to the appropriation of capital by the whole body of workers, but he will also insist that this appropriation be direct, not exercised by some elite force acting in the name of the proletariat. Some sort of council communism is the natural form of revolutionary socialism in an industrial society. It reflects the intuitive understanding that democracy is largely a sham when the industrial system is controlled by any form of autocratic elite, whether of owners, managers, and technocrats, a "vanguard" party, or a State bureaucracy.
    Noam Chomsky (1928-, American Linguist, Political Activist)

6   People sometimes inquire what form of government is most suitable for an artist to live under. To this question there is only one answer. The form of government that is most suitable to the artist is no government at all.
    Oscar Wilde (1856-1900, British Author, Wit)

ANCESTRY

1   I don't know who my grandfather was; I am much more concerned to know what his grandson will be.
    Abraham Lincoln (1809-1865, Sixteenth President of the USA)

2   Genealogy. An account of one's descent from an ancestor who did not particularly care to trace his own.
    Ambrose Bierce (1842-1914, American Author, Editor, Journalist, "The Devil's Dictionary")

3   Unworthy offspring brag the most about their worthy descendants.
    Danish Proverb

4   None of us can boast about the morality of our ancestors. The record does not show that Adam and Eve were ever married.
    Edgar Watson Howe (1853-1937, American Journalist, Author)

5   Remember, remember always, that all of us, and you and I especially, are descended from immigrations and revolutionists.
    Franklin D. Roosevelt (1882-1945, Thirty-second President of the USA)

6   I don't have to look up my family tree, because I know that I'm the sap.
    Fred A. Allen (1894-1957, American Radio Comic)

7   Englishmen hate Liberty and Equality too much to understand them. But every Englishman loves a pedigree.
    George Bernard Shaw (1856-1950, Irish-born British Dramatist)

8   Breed is stronger than pasture.
    George Eliot (1819-1880, British Novelist)

9   Mules are always boasting that their ancestors were horses.
    German Proverb

10 The precise form of an individual's activity is determined, of course, by the equipment with which he came into the world. In other words, it is determined by his heredity.
    Henry Louis

11 Is anyone simply by birth to be applauded or punished?
    Hitopadesa (Sanskrit Fable From Panchatantra)

12 They talk about their Pilgrim blood, their birthright high and holy! a mountain-stream that ends in mud thinks is melancholy.
    James Russell Lowell (1819-1891, American Poet, Critic, Editor)

13 In church your grandsire cut his throat; to do the job too long he tarried: he should have had my hearty vote to cut his throat before he married.
    Jonathan Swift (1667-1745, Anglo-Irish Satirist)

14 We are linked by blood, and blood is memory without language.
    Joyce Carol Oates (1938-, American Author)

15 Good breeding is the result of good sense, some good nature, and a little self-denial for the sake of others.
    Lord Chesterfield (1694-1773, British Statesman, Author)

16 The scholar without good breeding is a nitpicker; the philosopher a cynic; the soldier a brute and everyone else disagreeable.
    Lord Chesterfield (1694-1773, British Statesman, Author)

17 Heredity is nothing, but stored environment.
Luther Burbank (1849-1926, American Horticulturist)

18 Good breeding consists in concealing how much we think of ourselves and how little we think of the other person.
Mark Twain (1835-1910, American Humorist, Writer)

19 If your descent is from heroic sires, show in your life a remnant of their fires.
Nicholas Boileau (1636-1711, French Literary Poet, Critic)

20 Stillness and steadiness of features are signal marks of good breeding. Vulgar persons can't sit still, or at least must always work their limbs and features.
Oliver Wendell Holmes (1809-1894, American Author, Wit, Poet)

21 Every man is an omnibus in which his ancestors ride.
Oliver Wendell Holmes (1809-1894, American Author, Wit, Poet)

22 The sharp thorn often produces delicate roses.
Ovid (43 BC-18 AD, Roman Poet)

23 High birth is an accident, not a virtue.
Pietro Metastasio (1698-1782, Italian Poet)

24 Hereditary honors are a noble and a splendid treasure to descendants.
Plato (427-347 BC, Greek Philosopher)

25 It is indeed a desirable thing to be well-descended, but the glory belongs to our ancestors.
Plutarch (46-120 AD, Greek Essayist, Biographer)

26 From our ancestors come our names from our virtues our honor.
Proverb

27 Good breeding, a union of kindness and independence.
Ralph Waldo Emerson (1803-1882, American Poet, Essayist)

28 Each has his own tree of ancestors, but at the top of all sits Probably Arboreal.
Robert Louis Stevenson (1850-1895, Scottish Essayist, Poet, Novelist)

29 Clever father, clever daughter; clever mother, clever son.
Russian Proverb

30 No one is better born than another, unless they are born with better abilities and a more amiable disposition.
Seneca (4 BC-65 AD, Spanish-born Roman Statesman, philosopher)

31 He who boasts of his descent, praises the deed of another.
Seneca (4 BC-65 AD, Spanish-born Roman Statesman, philosopher)

32 Those who boast of their decent, brag on what they owe to others.
Seneca (4 BC-65 AD, Spanish-born Roman Statesman, philosopher)

33 The person who has nothing to brag about but their ancestors is like a potato; the best part of them is underground.
Sir Thomas Overbore

34 Nothing is so soothing to our self esteem as to find our bad traits in our forebears. It seems to absolve us.
Van Wyck Brooks

35 Do well and you will have no need for ancestors.
Voltaire (1694-1778, French Historian, Writer)

36 I am, in point of fact, a particularly haughty and exclusive person, of pre-Adamite ancestral descent. You will understand this when I tell you that I can trace my ancestry back to a protoplasmal primordial atomic globule.
W. S. Gilbert (1836-1911, British Librettist)

37 There is a certain class of people who prefer to say that their fathers came down in the world through their own follies than to boast that they rose in the world through their own industry and talents. It is the same shabby-genteel sentiment, the same vanity of birth which makes men prefer to believe that they are degenerated angels rather than elevated apes.
W. Winwood Reade (1838-1875, American Writer)

38 My ancestors didn't come over on the Mayflower, but they were there to meet the boat.
Will Rogers (1879-1935, American Humorist, Actor)

ANECDOTES

1 When a man fell into his anecdotage it was a sign for him to retire from the world.
Benjamin Disraeli (1804-1881, British Statesman, Prime Minister)

2 It is not the voice that commands the story: it is the ear.
Italo Calvino (1923-1985, Cuban Writer, Essayist, Journalist)

3 Faith! he must make his stories shorter or change his comrades once a quarter.
Jonathan Swift (1667-1745, Anglo-Irish Satirist)

4 Life is too short for a long story.
Lady Mary Wortley Montagu (1689-1762, British Society Figure, Letter Writer)

5 The history of a soldier's wound beguiles the pain of it.
Laurence Sterne (1713-1768, British Author)

6 To have frequent recourse to narrative betrays great want of imagination.
Lord Chesterfield (1694-1773, British Statesman, Author)

7 With a tale, for sooth, he comet unto you; with a tale which holdeth children from play, and old men from the chimney corner.
Sir Philip Sidney (1554-1586, British Author, Courtier)

8 Twenty or thirty years ago, in the army, we had a lot of obscure adventures, and years later we tell them at parties, and suddenly we realize that those two very difficult years of our lives have become lumped together into a few episodes that have lodged in our memory in a standardized form, and are always told in a standardized way, in the same words. But in fact that lump of memories has nothing whatsoever to do with our experience of those two years in the army and what it has made of us.
Vaclav Havel (1936-, Czech Playwright, President)

9 Your tale, sir, would cure deafness.
William Shakespeare (1564-1616, British Poet, Playwright, Actor)

ANGELS

1 A man does not have to be an angel in order to be a saint.
Albert Schweitzer (1875-1965, German Born Medical Missionary, Theologian, Musician, and Philosopher)

2 Do not forget to entertain strangers, for by so doing some have unwittingly entertained angels. [Hebrews 13:2]
Bible (Sacred Scriptures of Christians and Judaism)

3 Christians should never fail to sense the operation of an angelic glory. It forever eclipses the world of demonic powers, as the sun does a candle's light.
Billy Graham (1918-, American Evangelist)

4 Were we as eloquent as angels we still would please people much more by listening rather than talking.
Charles Caleb Colton (1780-1832, British Sportsman Writer)

5 Tennessee Williams said if he got rid of his demons, he would lose his angels.
Dakin Williams

6 If an angel were ever to tell us anything of his philosophy I believe many propositions would sound like 2 times 2 equals 13.
Georg C. Lichtenberg (1742-1799, German Physicist, Satirist)

7 In Heaven an angel is nobody in particular.
George Bernard Shaw (1856-1950, Irish-born British Dramatist)

8 Angels fly because they take themselves lightly.
Gilbert K. Chesterton (1874-1936, British Author)

9 Make sure to send a lazy man the angel of death.
Jewish Proverb

10 We cannot pass our guardian angel's bounds, resigned or sullen, he will hear our sighs.
John Keble (1792-1866, British Anglican Clergyman, Poet)

11 Millions of spiritual creatures walk the earth unseen, both when we sleep and when we awake.
John Milton (1608-1674, British Poet)

12 Peace is the first thing the angels sang.
Leo The Great (390-461, Pope from 440-461)

13 The Angels were all singing out of tune, and hoarse with having little else to do, excepting to wind up the sun and moon or curb a runaway young star or two.
Lord Byron (1788-1824, British Poet)

14 An angel is a spiritual creature created by God without a body for the service of Christendom and the church.
Martin Luther (1483-1546, German Leader of the Protestant Reformation)

15 The angels are so enamoured of the language that is spoken in heaven, that they will not distort their lips with the hissing and unmusical dialects of men, but speak their own, whether there be any who understand it or not.
Ralph Waldo Emerson (1803-1882, American Poet, Essayist)

16 We are never like angels till our passion dies.
Sir John Denham (1615-1668, British Poet, Dramatist)

17 Make friends with the angels, who though invisible are always with you. Often invoke them, constantly praise them, and make good use of their help and assistance in all your temporal and spiritual affairs.
St. Francis De Sales (1567-1622, Roman Catholic Bishop, Writer)

18 There are nine orders of angels, to wit, angels, archangels, virtues, powers, principalities, dominations, thrones, cherubim, and seraphim.
St. Gregory The Great (540-604, Italian Pope)

19 It is not known precisely where angels dwell -- whether in the air, the void, or the planets. It has not been God's pleasure that we should be informed of their abode.
Voltaire (1694-1778, French Historian, Writer)

20 It is not because angels are holier than men or devils that makes them angels, but because they do not expect holiness from one another, but from God only.
William Blake (1757-1827, British Poet, Painter)

ANGER

1 Indulge not thyself in the passion of anger; it is whetting a sword to wound thine own breast, or murder thy friend.
Akhenaton (1375 BC, Egyptian King, Monotheist)

2 As the whirlwind in its fury teareth up trees, and deformeth the face of nature, or as an earthquake in its convulsions overturneth whole cities; so the rage of an angry man throweth mischief around him.
Akhenaton (1375 BC, Egyptian King, Monotheist)

3 To be angry about trifles is mean and childish; to rage and be furious is brutish; and to maintain perpetual wrath is akin to the practice and temper of devils; but to prevent and suppress rising resentment is wise and glorious, is manly and divine.
Alan W. Watts (1915-1973, British-born American Philosopher, Author)

4 Every time you get angry, you poison your own system.
Alfred A. Montapert (American Author)

5 Speak when you are angry and you will make the best speech you will ever regret.
Ambrose Bierce (1842-1914, American Author, Editor, Journalist, "The Devil's Dictionary")

6 Anyone can become angry -- that is easy. But to be angry with the right person, to the right degree, at the right time, for the right purpose, and in the right way -- this is not easy.
Aristotle (384-322 BC, Greek Philosopher)

7 We praise a man who feels angry on the right grounds and against the right persons and also in the right manner at the right moment and for the right length of time.
Aristotle (384-322 BC, Greek Philosopher)

8 All anger is not sinful, because some degree of it, and on some occasions, is inevitable. But it becomes sinful and contradicts the rule of Scripture when it is conceived upon slight and inadequate provocation, and when it continues long.
Babe Paley

9 Never do anything when you are in a temper, for you will do everything wrong.
Baltasar Gracian (1601-1658, Spanish Philosopher, Writer)

10 The more anger towards the past you carry in your heart, the less capable you are of loving in the present.
Barbara De Angelis (American Expert on Relationship & Love, Author)

11 Whatever is begun in anger, ends in shame.
Benjamin Franklin (1706-1790, American Scientist, Publisher, Diplomat)

12 Indignation is a submission of our thoughts, but not of our desires.
Bertrand Russell (1872-1970, British Philosopher, Mathematician, Essayist)

13 Be angry, and yet do not sin; do not let the sun go down on your anger. [Ephesians 4:26]
Bible (Sacred Scriptures of Christians and Judaism)

14 Be not hasty in thy spirit to be angry: for anger resteth in the bosom of fools. [Ecclesiastes 7:9]
Bible (Sacred Scriptures of Christians and Judaism)

15 He that is slow to anger is better than the mighty and he that ruleth his spirit than he that taketh a city.
Bible (Sacred Scriptures of Christians and Judaism)

16 It is better to dwell in the wilderness, than with a contentious and angry woman. [Proverbs 21:19]
Bible (Sacred Scriptures of Christians and Judaism)

17 Let not the sun go down upon your wrath. [Ephesians 4:26]
Bible (Sacred Scriptures of Christians and Judaism)

18 My dear brothers, take note of this: Everyone should be quick to listen, slow to speak and slow to become angry, for man's anger does not bring about the righteous life that God desires. [James 1:19-20]
Bible (Sacred Scriptures of Christians and Judaism)

19 Anger rest in the bosom of fools.
Bible (Sacred Scriptures of Christians and Judaism)

20 The words of the wicked are to lie in wait for blood, but the mouth of the upright shall deliver them. [Proverbs 12:6]
Bible (Sacred Scriptures of Christians and Judaism)

21 The discretion of a man deferreth his anger; and it is his glory to pass over a transgression. [Proverbs 19:11]
Bible (Sacred Scriptures of Christians and Judaism)

22 A soft answer truth away wrath, but grievous words stir up anger. [Proverbs 15:1]
Bible (Sacred Scriptures of Christians and Judaism)

23 Scornful men bring a city into a snare, but wise men turn away wrath. [Proverbs 29:8]
Bible (Sacred Scriptures of Christians and Judaism)

24 Always keep your composure. You can't score from the penalty box; and to win, you have to score.
Bobby Hull (American Hockey Player)

25 Anger will never disappear so long as thoughts of resentment are cherished in the mind. Anger will disappear just as soon as thoughts of resentment are forgotten.
Buddha (568-488 BC, Founder of Buddhism)

26 You will not be punished for your anger, you will be punished by your anger.
Buddha (568-488 BC, Founder of Buddhism)

27 Holding on to anger is like grasping a hot coal with the intent of throwing it at someone else; you are the one getting burned.
Buddha (568-488 BC, Founder of Buddhism)

28 No person is important enough to make me angry.
Carlos Castaneda (American Anthropologist, Author)

29 An angry man opens his mouth and shuts his eyes.
Cato The Elder (234-149 BC, Roman Statesman, Orator)

30 The intoxication of anger, like that of the grape, shows us to others, but hides us from ourselves.
Charles Caleb Colton (1780-1832, British Sportsman Writer)

31 When I am right, I get angry. Churchill gets angry when he is wrong. So we were often angry at each other.
Charles De Gaulle (1890-1970, French President during World War II)

32 A vigorous temper is not altogether an evil. Men who are easy as an old shoe are generally of little worth.
Charles Haddon Spurgeon (1834-1892, British Baptist Preacher)

33 If you are patient in one moment of anger, you will escape a hundred days of sorrow.
Chinese Proverb

34 Anger is the most impotent of passions. It effects nothing it goes about, and hurts the one who is possessed by it more than the one against whom it is directed.
Clarendon

35 Go ahead, make my day.
Clint Eastwood (1930-, American Actor, Director, Politician, Composer, Musician, Producer)

36 When anger rises, think of the consequences.
Confucius (551-479 BC, Chinese Ethical Teacher, Philosopher)

37 Keep cool; anger is not an argument.
Daniel Webster (1782-1852, American Lawyer, Statesman)

38 Anger itself does more harm than the condition which aroused anger.
David O. Mckay

39 He who holds back rising anger like a rolling chariot, him I call a real driver; other people are but holding the reins
Dhammapada (300 BC, Buddhist Collection of Moral Aphorism)

40 I am often mad, but I would hate to be nothing but mad: and I think I would lose what little value I may have as a writer if I were to refuse, as a matter of principle, to accept the warming rays of the sun, and to report them, whenever, and if ever, they
E(lwyn) B(rooks) White (1899-1985, American Author, Editor)

41 Most men's anger about religion is as if two men should quarrel for a lady they neither of them care for.
Edward F. Halifax (1881-1959, British Conservative Statesman)

42 Anger is never without an argument, but seldom with a good one.
Edward F. Halifax (1881-1959, British Conservative Statesman)

43 Anger ventilated often hurries towards forgiveness; anger concealed often hardens into revenge.
Edward G. Bulwer-Lytton (1803-1873, British Novelist, Poet)

44 Anger as soon as fed is dead; 'Tis starving makes it fat.
Emily Dickinson (1830-1886, American Poet)

45 Whenever you are angry, be assured that it is not only a present evil, but that you have increased a habit.
Epictetus (50-120, Stoic Philosopher)

46 Anger makes dull men witty -- but it keeps them poor.
Francis Bacon (1561-1626, British Philosopher, Essayist, Statesman)

47 Beware of him that is slow to anger; for when it is long coming, it is the stronger when it comes, and the longer kept. Abused patience turns to fury.
Francis Quarles (1592-1644, British Poet)

48 I know of no more disagreeable situation than to be left feeling generally angry without anybody in particular to be angry at.
Frank Moore Colby (1865-1925, American Editor, Essayist)

49 Anger may be kindled in the noblest breasts: but in these slow droppings of an unforgiving temper never takes the shape of consistency of enduring hatred.
G. S. Hillard

50 Anger cannot be dishonest.
George R. Bach

51 I lose my temper, but it's all over in a minute," said the student. "So is the hydrogen bomb," I replied. "But think of the damage it produces!
George Sweeting

52 Anger, even when it punishes the faults of delinquents, ought not to precede reason as its mistress, but attend as a handmaid at the back of reason, to come to the front when bidden. For once it begins to take control of the mind, it calls just what it does cruelly.
George William Curtis (1824-1892, American Journalist)

53 Anger begins with folly, and ends with repentance.
H. G. Bohn (British Publisher)

54 I used to store my anger and it affected my play. Now I get it out. I'm never rude to my playing partner. I'm very focused on the ball. Then it's over.
Helen Alfredsson (American Golfer)

55 The continuance and frequent fits of anger produce in the soul a propensity to be angry; which oftentimes ends in choler, bitterness, and moronity, when the mid becomes ulcerated, peevish, and querulous, and is wounded by the least occurrence.
Henry Ward Beecher (1813-1887, American Preacher, Orator, Writer)

56 If a man meets with injustice, it is not required that he shall not be roused to meet it; but if he is angry after he has had time to think upon it, that is sinful. The flame is not wring, but the coals are.
Henry Ward Beecher (1813-1887, American Preacher, Orator, Writer)

57 Never forget what a person says to you when they are angry.
Henry Ward Beecher (1813-1887, American Preacher, Orator, Writer)

58 Anger is short madness
Horace (65-8 BC, Italian Poet)

59 Anger is a brief lunacy.
Horace (65-8 BC, Italian Poet)

60 Anger is a momentary madness, so control your passion or it will control you.
Horace (65-8 BC, Italian Poet)

61 The one who cannot restrain their anger will wish undone, what their temper and irritation prompted them to do.
Horace (65-8 BC, Italian Poet)

62 My liver swells with bile difficult to repress.
Horace (65-8 BC, Italian Poet)

63 You cannot shake hands with a clenched fist.
Indira Gandhi (1917-1984, Indian Prime Minster)

64 Rage cannot be hidden, it can only be dissembled. This dissembling deludes the thoughtless, and strengthens rage and adds, to rage, contempt.
James Baldwin (1924-1987, American Author)

65 Let us not look back in anger or forward in fear, but around in awareness.
James Thurber (1894-1961, American Humorist, Illustrator)

66 It doesn't pay to say too much when you are mad enough to choke. For the word that stings the deepest is the word that is never spoke, Let the other fellow wrangle till the storm has blown away, then he'll do a heap of thinking about the things you didn't say.
James Whitcomb Riley (1849-1916, American Poet)

67 Violence in the voice is often only the death rattle of reason in the throat.
John F. Boyes

68 The anger of a person who is strong, can always bide its time.
John Ruskin (1819-1900, British Critic, Social Theorist)

69 There is not in nature, a thing that makes man so deformed, so beastly, as doth intemperate anger.
John Webster (1580-1625, British Dramatist)

70 The best remedy for a short temper is a long walk.
Joseph Joubert (1754-1824, French Moralist)

71 There are good and bad times, but our mood changes more often than our fortune.
Jules Renard (1864-1910, French Author, Dramatist)

72 It takes two flints to make a fire.
Louisa May Alcott (1832-1888, American Author)

73 Wise anger is like fire from a flint: there is great ado to get it out; and when it does come, it is out again immediately.
M. Henry

74 Anger and intolerance are the twin enemies of correct understanding.
Mahatma Gandhi (1869-1948, Indian Political, Spiritual Leader)

75 Anger is as a stone cast into a wasp's nest.
Malabar Proverb

76 Consider how much more you often suffer from your anger and grief, than from those very things for which you are angry and grieved.
Marcus Antonius (83-30 BC, Roman Triumvir, Related to Julius Caesar)

77 When thou art above measure angry, bethink thee how momentary is man's life.
Marcus Aurelius (121-80 AD, Roman Emperor, Philosopher)

78 How much more grievous are the consequences of anger than the causes of it.
Marcus Aurelius (121-80 AD, Roman Emperor, Philosopher)

79 When angry, count four; when very angry, swear.
Mark Twain (1835-1910, American Humorist, Writer)

80 When I am angry I can pray well and preach well.
Martin Luther (1483-1546, German Leader of the Protestant Reformation)

81 Anger is a noble infirmity; the generous failing of the just; the one degree that riseth above zeal, asserting the prerogative of virtue.
Martin Tupper (1810-1889, British Author, Poet, Inventor)

82 Bitterness is like cancer. It eats upon the host. But anger is like fire. It burns it all clean.
Maya Angelou (1928-, African-American poet, Writer, Performer)

83 A wave of anger washed over me, anger against myself, at my age at the time, that stupid lyrically age, when a man is too great a riddle to himself to be interested in the riddles outside himself and when other people are mere walking mirrors in which he is amazed to find his own emotions, his own worth.
Milan Kundera (1929-, Czech Author, Critic)

84 Depression is rage spread thin.
Paul Tillich (1886-1965, German Protestant Theologian, Philosopher)

85 Do not suppress it-that would hurt you inside. Do not express it-this would not only hurt you inside, it would cause ripples in your surroundings. What you do is transform it.
Peace Pilgrim (1908-1981, American Peace Activist)

86 Never go to bed angry, stay up and fight.
Phyllis Diller (1861-1951, American Columnist)

87 He best keeps from anger who remembers that God is always looking upon him.
Plato (427-347 BC, Greek Philosopher)

88 There are two things a person should never be angry at, what they can help, and what they cannot.
Proverb

89 He who is slow to anger has great understanding, but he who has a hasty temper exalts folly.
Proverb

90 No one is as angry as the person who is wrong.
Proverb

91 The wrath of brothers is fierce and devilish.
Proverb

92 An angry man is again angry with himself when he returns to reason.
Publilius Syrus (1st Century BC, Roman Writer)

93 A man makes inferiors his superiors by heat; self-control is the rule.
Ralph Waldo Emerson (1803-1882, American Poet, Essayist)

94 We boil at different degrees.
Ralph Waldo Emerson (1803-1882, American Poet, Essayist)

95 For every minute you are angry you lose sixty seconds of happiness.
Ralph Waldo Emerson (1803-1882, American Poet, Essayist)

96 Anger blows out the lamp of the mind. In the examination of a great and important question, everyone should be serene, slow-pulsed and calm.
Robert Green Ingersoll (1833-1899, American Orator, Lawyer)

97 Anger is a wind which blows out the lamp of the mind.
Robert Green Ingersoll (1833-1899, American Orator, Lawyer)

98 Doomed are the hotheads! Unhappy are they who lose their cool and are too proud to say, "I'm sorry."
Robert H. Schuller (1926-, American Minister (Crystal Cathedral), Author, Social Leader)

99 He took over anger to intimidate subordinates, and in time anger took over him.
Saint Albertus Magnus

100 The angry man will defeat himself in battle as well as in life.
Samurai Maxim

101 Anger: an acid that can do more harm to the vessel in which it is stored than to anything on which it is poured.
Seneca (4 BC-65 AD, Spanish-born Roman Statesman, philosopher)

102 Anger is like those ruins which smash themselves on what they fall.
Seneca (4 BC-65 AD, Spanish-born Roman Statesman, philosopher)

103 The deferring of anger is the best antidote to anger.
Seneca (4 BC-65 AD, Spanish-born Roman Statesman, philosopher)

104 The greatest remedy for anger is delay.
Seneca (4 BC-65 AD, Spanish-born Roman Statesman, philosopher)

105 If a small thing has the power to make you angry, does that not indicate something about your size?
Sidney J. Harris (1917-, American Journalist)

106 The tendency of aggression is an innate, independent, instinctual disposition in man... it constitutes the most powerful obstacle to culture.
Sigmund Freud (1856-1939, Austrian Physician - Founder of Psychoanalysis)

107 Temper is a weapon that we hold by the blade.
Sir James M. Barrie (1860-1937, British Playwright)

108 Anger is a great force. If you control it, it can be transmuted into a power which can move the whole world.
Sri Swami Sivananda (1887-, Indian Physician, Sage)

109 There was never an angry man that thought his anger unjust.
St. Francis De Sales (1567-1622, Roman Catholic Bishop, Writer)

110 Anger is an expensive luxury in which only men of a certain income can indulge.
St. Gregory The Great (540-604, Italian Pope)

111 In a controversy the instant we feel anger we have already ceased striving for the truth, and have begun striving for ourselves.
Thomas Carlyle (1795-1881, Scottish Philosopher, Author)

112 Man should forget his anger before he lies down to sleep.
Thomas De Quincey (1785-1859, British Author)

113 Act nothing in a furious passion. It's putting to sea in a storm.
Thomas Fuller (1608-1661, British Clergyman, Author)

114 Two things a man should never be angry at: what he can help, and what he cannot help.
Thomas Fuller (1608-1661, British Clergyman, Author)

115 Anger is one of the sinews of the soul; he that wants it hath a maimed mind.
Thomas Fuller (1608-1661, British Clergyman, Author)

116 When angry, count to ten before you speak. If very angry, count to one hundred.
Thomas Jefferson (1743-1826, Third President of the USA)

117 He that would be angry and sin not, must not be angry with anything but sin.
Thomas Secker

118 To rule one's anger is well; to prevent it is better.
Tryon Edwards (1809-1894, American Theologian)

119 The flame of anger, bright and brief, sharpens the barb of love.
Walter Savage Landor (1775-1864, British Poet, Essayist)

120 Temper never mellows with age, and a sharp tongue is the only edged tool that grows keener with constant use.
Washington Irving (1783-1859, American Author)

121 There's nothing wrong with anger provided you use it constructively.
Wayne Dyer (1940-, American Psychotherapist, Author, Lecturer)

122 When you squeeze an orange, orange juice comes out -- because that's what's inside. When you are squeezed, what comes out is what is inside.
Wayne Dyer (1940-, American Psychotherapist, Author, Lecturer)

123 What comes out of you when you are squeezed is what is inside of you.
Wayne Dyer (1940-, American Psychotherapist, Author, Lecturer)

124 Heaven has no rage like love to hatred turned, Nor hell a fury like a woman scorned.
William Congreve (1670-1729, British Dramatist)

125 Men often make up in wrath what they want in reason.
William R. Alger (1822-1905, American Writer)

126 Consider, when you are enraged at any one, what you would probably think if he should die during the dispute.
William Shenstone (1714-1763, British Poet)

127 The worst tempered people I have ever met were those who knew that they were wrong.
Wilson Mizner (1876-1933, American Author)

ANIMALS

1 Man is a clever animal who behaves like an imbecile.
Albert Schweitzer (1875-1965, German Born Medical Missionary, Theologian, Musician, and Philosopher)

2   Don't accept your dog's admiration as conclusive evidence that you are wonderful.
Ann Landers (1918-, American Advice Columnist)

3   At his best, man is the noblest of all animals; separated from law and justice he is the worst.
Aristotle (384-322 BC, Greek Philosopher)

4   No matter how eloquently a dog may bark, he cannot tell you that his parents were poor, but honest.
Bertrand Russell (1872-1970, British Philosopher, Mathematician, Essayist)

5   Happiness to a dog is what lies on the other side of a door.
Charleton Jr. Ogburn

6   What is man without the beasts? If all the beasts were gone, man would die from a great loneliness of spirit. For whatever happens to the beasts, soon happens to man. All things are connected.
Chief Seattle (1786-1866, American Indian Chief of the Suquamish)

7   Mankind differs from the animals only by a little and most people throw that away.
Confucius (551-479 BC, Chinese Ethical Teacher, Philosopher)

8   Be a good animal, true to your animal instincts.
D. H. Lawrence (1885-1930, British Author)

9   The following general definition of an animal: a system of different organic molecules that have combined with one another, under the impulsion of a sensation similar to an obtuse and muffled sense of touch given to them by the creator of matter as a whole, until each one of them has found the most suitable position for its shape and comfort.
Denis Diderot (1713-1784, French Philosopher)

10   There is something in the unselfish and self-sacrificing love of a brute, which goes directly to the heart of him who has had frequent occasion to test the paltry friendship and gossamer fidelity of mere Man.
Edgar Allan Poe (1809-1845, American Poet, Critic, short-story Writer)

11   Animals used to provide a lowlife way to kill and get away with it, as they do still, but, more intriguingly, for some people they are an aperture through which wounds drain. The scapegoat of olden times, driven off for the bystanders sins, has become a tender thing, a running injury. There, running away is me: hurt it and you are hurting me.
Edward Hoagland (1932-, American Novelist, Essayist)

12   Animals are stylized characters in a kind of old saga -- stylized because even the most acute of them have little leeway as they play out their parts.
Edward Hoagland (1932-, American Novelist, Essayist)

13   Those who wish to pet and baby wild animals, "love" them. But those who respect their natures and wish to let them live normal lives, love them more.
Edwin Way Teale (1899-1980, American Naturalist and Writer)

14   Animals often strike us as passionate machines.
Eric Hoffer (1902-1983, American Author, Philosopher)

15   I fear animals regard man as a creature of their own kind which has in a highly dangerous fashion lost its healthy animal reason -- as the mad animal, as the laughing animal, as the weeping animal, as the unhappy animal.
Friedrich Nietzsche (1844-1900, German Philosopher)

16   Animals are in possession of themselves; their soul is in possession of their body. But they have no right to their life, because they do not will it.
Georg Hegel (1770-1831, German Philosopher)

17   Animals are such agreeable friends, they ask no questions, they pass no criticisms.
George Eliot (1819-1880, British Novelist)

18   Four legs good, two legs bad.
George Orwell (1903-1950, British Author, "Animal Farm")

19   The fatter the flea the leaner the dog.
German Proverb

20   The keeping of bees is like the direction of sunbeams.
Henry David Thoreau (1817-1862, American Essayist, Poet, Naturalist)

21   What is a country without rabbits and partridges? They are among the most simple and indigenous animal products; ancient and venerable families known to antiquity as to modern times; of the very hue and substance of Nature, nearest allied to leaves and to the ground.
Henry David Thoreau (1817-1862, American Essayist, Poet, Naturalist)

22   Cats and monkeys; monkeys and cats; all human life is there.
Henry James (1843-1916, American Author)

23   The dog is the god of frolic.
Henry Ward Beecher (1813-1887, American Preacher, Orator, Writer)

24   I shoot the Hippopotamus with bullets made of platinum, because if I use the leaden one his hide is sure to flatten em.
Hilaire Belloc (1870-1953, British Author)

25   I distrust camels, and anyone else who can go a week without a drink.
Joe E. Lewis (American Writer)

26   A peasant becomes fond of his pig and is glad to salt away its pork. What is significant, and is so difficult for the urban stranger to understand, is that the two statements are connected by an and not by a but.
John Berger (1926-, British Actor, Critic)

27   Bats have no bankers and they do not drink and cannot be arrested and pay no tax and, in general, bats have it made.
John Berryman (1914-1972, American Poet)

28   Animals, in their generation, are wiser than the sons of men; but their wisdom is confined to a few particulars, and lies in a very narrow compass.
Joseph Addison (1672-1719, British Essayist, Poet, Statesman)

29 A dog is the only thing on earth that loves you more than you love yourself.
Josh Billings (1815-1885, American Humorist, Lecturer)

30 Who loves me loves my dog.
Latin Proverb

31 The poor dog, in life the firmest friend. The first to welcome, foremost to defend.
Lord Byron (1788-1824, British Poet)

32 Animals awaken, first facially, then bodily. Men's bodies wake before their faces do. The animal sleeps within its body, man sleeps with his body in his mind.
Malcolm De Chazal (1902-1981, French Writer)

33 What an ugly beast the ape, and how like us.
Marcus T. Cicero (106-43 BC, Great Roman Orator, Politician)

34 Mankind's true moral test, its fundamental test (which lies deeply buried from view), consists of its attitude towards those who are at its mercy: animals. And in this respect mankind has suffered a fundamental debacle, a debacle so fundamental that all others stem from it.
Milan Kundera (1929-, Czech Author, Critic)

35 Eagles do not beget Doves.
Motto

36 We know what the animals do, what are the needs of the beaver, the bear, the salmon, and other creatures, because long ago men married them and acquired this knowledge from their animal wives. Today the priests say we lie, but we know better.
Native Americans

37 The cow is of the bovine ilk: One end is moo, the other, milk.
Ogden Nash (1902-1971, American Humorous Poet)

38 In a few generations more, there will probably be no room at all allowed for animals on the earth: no need of them, no toleration of them. An immense agony will have then ceased, but with it there will also have passed away the last smile of the world's youth.
Ouida (1838-1908, British Writer)

39 Drinking, when we are not thirsty and making love all year round, madam; that is all there is to distinguish us from other animals.
Pierre De Beaumarchais (1732-1799, French Dramatist)

40 An eagle does not catch flies.
Proverb

41 The owl of ignorance lays the egg of pride.
Proverb

42 Who can guess how much industry and providence and affection we have caught from the pantomime of brutes?
Ralph Waldo Emerson (1803-1882, American Poet, Essayist)

43 Nothing to be done really about animals. Anything you do looks foolish. The answer isn't in us. It's almost as if we're put here on earth to show how silly they aren't.
Russell Hoban (1925-, American Author)

44 Man is the only animal that can remain on friendly terms with the victims he intends to eat until he eats them.
Samuel Butler (1612-1680, British Poet, Satirist)

45 A hen is only an egg's way of making another egg.
Samuel Butler (1612-1680, British Poet, Satirist)

46 Poor little Foal of an oppressed race! I love the languid patience of thy face.
Samuel Taylor Coleridge (1772-1834, British Poet, Critic, Philosopher)

47 Animals are considered as property only. To destroy or to abuse them, from malice to the proprietor, or with an intention injurious to his interest in them, is criminal. But the animals themselves are without protection. The law regards them not substantively. They have no RIGHTS!
Shirley Lord (American Writer)

48 Shall we never have done with that cliche, so stupid that it could only be human, about the sympathy of animals for man when he is unhappy? Animals love happiness almost as much as we do. A fit of crying disturbs them, they'll sometimes imitate sobbing, and for a moment they'll reflect our sadness. But they flee unhappiness as they flee fever, and I believe that in the long run they are capable of boycotting it.
Sidonie Gabrielle Colette (1873-1954, French Author)

49 The elephant, not only the largest but the most intelligent of animals, provides us with an excellent example. It is faithful and tenderly loving to the female of its choice, mating only every third year and then for no more than five days, and so secretly as never to be seen, until, on the sixth day, it appears and goes at once to wash its whole body in the river, unwilling to return to the herd until thus purified. Such good and modest habits are an example to husband and wife.
St. Francis De Sales (1567-1622, Roman Catholic Bishop, Writer)

50 Cows are amongst the gentlest of breathing creatures; none show more passionate tenderness to their young when deprived of them; and, in short, I am not ashamed to profess a deep love for these quiet creatures.
Thomas De Quincey (1785-1859, British Author)

51 Nothing can be more obvious than that all animals were created solely and exclusively for the use of man.
Thomas Love Peacock (1785-1866, British Author)

52 The best thing about animals is they don't talk much.
Thornton Wilder (1897-1975, American Novelist, Playwright)

53 From the oyster to the eagle, from the swine to the tiger, all animals are to be found in men and each of them exists in some man, sometimes several at the time. Animals are nothing but the portrayal of our virtues and vices made manifest to our eyes, the visible reflections of our souls. God displays them to us to give us food for thought.
Victor Hugo (1802-1885, French Poet, Dramatist, Novelist)

54 Be as a bird perched on a frail branch that she feels bending beneath her, still she sings away all the same, knowing she has wings.
Victor Hugo (1802-1885, French Poet, Dramatist, Novelist)

55 Animals have these advantages over man: They have no theologians to instruct them, their funerals cost them nothing, and no one starts lawsuits over their wills.
Voltaire (1694-1778, French Historian, Writer)

56 They do not sweat and whine about their condition, they do not lie awake in the dark and weep for their sins, they do not make me sick discussing their duty to God, not one is dissatisfied, not one is demented with the mania of owning things, not one kneels to another, nor to his kind that lived thousands of years ago.
Walt Whitman (1819-1892, American Poet)

57 Always remember, a cat looks down on man, a dog looks up to man, but a pig will look man right in the eye and see his equal.
Winston Churchill (1874-1965, British Statesman, Prime Minister)

58 Of all the wonders of nature, a tree in summer is perhaps the most remarkable; with the possible exception of a moose singing "Embraceable You" in spats.
Woody Allen (1935-, American Director, Screenwriter, Actor, Comedian)

ANNIVERSARIES

1 The secret anniversaries of the heart.
Henry Wadsworth Longfellow (1819-1892, American Poet)

2 Let us love nobly, and live, and add again years and years unto years, till we attain to write threescore: this is the second of our reign.
John Donne (1572-1632, British Metaphysical Poet)

3 We placed the wreaths upon the splendid granite sarcophagus, and at its feet, and felt that only the earthly robe we loved so much was there. The pure, tender, loving spirit which loved us so tenderly, is above us -- loving us, praying for us, and free from all suffering and woe -- yes, that is a comfort, and that first birthday in another world must have been a far brighter one than any in this poor world below!
Queen Victoria (1819-1901, Queen of Great Britain)

4 Are there memories left that are safe from the clutches of phony anniversaries?
W. J. Wetherby

5 The thought of our past years in me doth breed perpetual benedictions.
William Wordsworth (1770-1850, British Poet)

ANTICIPATION

1 A man's delight in looking forward to and hoping for some particular satisfaction is a part of the pleasure flowing out of it, enjoyed in advance. But this is afterward deducted, for the more we look forward to anything the less we enjoy it when it comes.
Arthur Schopenhauer (1788-1860, German Philosopher)

2 We usually get what we anticipate.
Claude M. Bristol (1891-1951, American Author of "The Magic of Believing")

3 If pleasures are greatest in anticipation, just remember that this is also true of trouble.
Elbert Hubbard (1859-1915, American Author, Publisher)

4 Our desires always disappoint us; for though we meet with something that gives us satisfaction, yet it never thoroughly answers our expectation.
François de La Rochefoucauld (1613-1680, French classical writer)

5 We love to expect, and when expectation is either disappointed or gratified, we want to be again expecting.
Samuel Johnson (1709-1784, British Author)

6 Few enterprises of great labor or hazard would be undertaken if we had not the power of magnifying the advantages we expect from them.
Samuel Johnson (1709-1784, British Author)

7 Nothing is so wretched or foolish as to anticipate misfortunes. What madness is it to be expecting evil before it comes.
Seneca (4 BC-65 AD, Spanish-born Roman Statesman, philosopher)

ANTIPATHY

1 Antipathy, dissimilarity of views, hate, contempt, can accompany true love.
J. August Strindberg (1849-1912, Swedish Dramatist, Novelist, Poet)

2 They exchanged the quick, brilliant smile of women who dislike each other on sight.
Marshall Pugh

3 Nothing is more common than mutual dislike, where mutual approbation is particularly expected.
Samuel Johnson (1709-1784, British Author)

4 Thou art all ice. Thy kindness freezes.
William Shakespeare (1564-1616, British Poet, Playwright, Actor)

5 Some men there are love not a gaping pig, some that are mad if they behold a cat, and others when the bagpipe sings I the nose cannot contain their urine.
William Shakespeare (1564-1616, British Poet, Playwright, Actor)

ANXIETY

1   Anxiety is a thin stream of fear trickling through the mind. If encouraged, it cuts a channel into which all other thoughts are drained.
Arthur Somers Roche

2   Cares that have entered once in the breast, will have whole possession of the rest.
Ben Johnson (1573-1637, British Dramatist, Poet)

3   Do not anticipate trouble, or worry about what may never happen. Keep in the sunlight.
Benjamin Franklin (1706-1790, American Scientist, Publisher, Diplomat)

4   It has been said that our anxiety does not empty tomorrow of its sorrow, but only empties today of its strength.
Charles Haddon Spurgeon (1834-1892, British Baptist Preacher)

5   Anxiety is the hand maiden of creativity
Chuck Jones

6   Where everything is bad it must be good to know the worst.
Francis H. Bradley (1846-1924, British Philosopher)

7   Neither comprehension nor learning can take place in an atmosphere of anxiety.
Frank Smith (American Author, Trainer)

8   The misfortunes hardest to bear are these which never came.
James Russell Lowell (1819-1891, American Poet, Critic, Editor)

9   Only man clogs his happiness with care, destroying what is, with thoughts of what may be.
John Dryden (1631-1700, British Poet, Dramatist, Critic)

10 The thinner the ice, the more anxious is everyone to see whether it will bear.
Josh Billings (1815-1885, American Humorist, Lecturer)

11 Cast your cares on God; that anchor holds.
Lord Alfred Tennyson (1809-1892, British Poet)

12 The suspense is terrible, I hope it will last.
Oscar Wilde (1856-1900, British Author, Wit)

13 There is no such thing as pure pleasure; some anxiety always goes with it.
Ovid (43 BC-18 AD, Roman Poet)

14 Love is full of anxious fears.
Ovid (43 BC-18 AD, Roman Poet)

15 If some great catastrophe is not announced every morning, we feel a certain void. nothing in the paper today , we sigh.
Paul Valery (1871-1945, French Poet, Essayist)

16 Who's not sat tense before his own heart's curtain.
Rainer Maria Rilke (1875-1926, German Poet)

17 Some of your grief you have cured, and lived to survive; but what torments of pain have you endured that haven't as yet arrived.
Ralph Waldo Emerson (1803-1882, American Poet, Essayist)

18 Suspense is worst than disappointment.
Robert Burns (1759-1796, Scottish Poet)

19 Anxiety about the future never profits; we feel no evil until it comes, and when we feel it, no counsel helps; wisdom is either too early or too late.
Ruckett

20 Borrow trouble for yourself, if that's your nature, but don't lend it to your neighbors.
Rudyard Kipling (1865-1936, British Author of Prose, Verse)

21 There are more things to alarm us than to harm us, and we suffer more often in apprehension than reality.
Seneca (4 BC-65 AD, Spanish-born Roman Statesman, philosopher)

22 The mind that is anxious about the future is miserable.
Seneca (4 BC-65 AD, Spanish-born Roman Statesman, philosopher)

23 Anxiety is the dizziness of freedom.
Soren Kierkegaard (1813-1855, Danish Philosopher, Writer)

24 God never built a Christian strong enough to carry today's duties and tomorrow's anxieties piled on the top of them.
Theodore L. Cuyler (1822-1909, American Pastor, Author)

25 Anxiety is the poison of human life; the parent of many sins and of more miseries. In a world where everything is doubtful, and where we may be disappointed, and be blessed in disappointment, why this restless stir and commotion of mind? Can it alter the cause, or unravel the mystery of human events?
Tryon Edwards (1809-1894, American Theologian)

26 We have a lot of anxieties, and one cancels out another very often.
Winston Churchill (1874-1965, British Statesman, Prime Minister)

APATHY

1   The world is a dangerous place to live; not because of the people who are evil, but because of the people who don't do anything about it.
Albert Einstein (1879-1955, German-born American Physicist)

2   Most human beings have an infinite capacity for taking things for granted.
Aldous Huxley (1894-1963, British Author)

3   You see few people here in America who really care very much about living a Christian life in a democratic world.
Clare Boothe Luce (1903-1987, American Diplomat, Writer)

4   The great menace to the life of an industry is industrial self-complacency.
David Sarnoff (1891-1971, Belarus-born American Entrepreneur)

5   I shall stay the way I am because I do not give a damn.
Dorothy Parker (1893-1967, American Humorous Writer)

6   Every difficulty slurred over will be a ghost to disturb your repose later on.
Frederic Chopin

7   If moderation is a fault, then indifference is a crime.
Georg C. Lichtenberg (1742-1799, German Physicist, Satirist)

8   We may have found a cure for most evils; but it has found no remedy for the worst of them all -- the apathy of human beings.
Helen Keller (1880-1968, American Blind/Deaf Author, Lecturer, Amorist)

9   I don't know, I don't care, and it doesn't make any difference!
Jack Kerouac (1922-1969, American Author)

10   The difference between our decadence and the Russians is that while theirs is brutal, ours is apathetic.
James Thurber (1894-1961, American Humorist, Illustrator)

11   There is nothing harder than the softness of indifference.
Juan Montalvo

12   I have a very strong feeling that the opposite of love is not hate -- it's apathy. It's not giving a damn.
Leo Buscaglia (American Expert on Love, Lecturer, Author)

13   Mourn not the dead that in the cool earth lie, but rather mourn the apathetic, throng the coward and the meek who see the world's great anguish and its wrong, and dare not speak.
Ralph Chaplin

14   Things have dropped from me. I have outlived certain desires; I have lost friends, some by death... others through sheer inability to cross the street.
Virginia Woolf (1882-1941, British Novelist, Essayist)

APHORISMS AND EPIGRAMS

1   Our live experiences, fixed in aphorisms, stiffen into cold epigrams. Our heart's blood, as we write it, turns to mere dull ink.
Francis H. Bradley (1846-1924, British Philosopher)

2   In the mountains the shortest route is from peak to peak, but for that you must have long legs. Aphorisms should be peaks: and those to whom they are spoken should be big and tall of stature.
Friedrich Nietzsche (1844-1900, German Philosopher)

3   The aphorism in which I am the first master among Germans, are the forms of "eternity"; my ambition is to say in ten sentences what everyone else says in a book -- what everyone else does not say in a book.
Friedrich Nietzsche (1844-1900, German Philosopher)

4   An aphorism ought to be entirely isolated from the surrounding world like a little work of art and complete in itself like a hedgehog.
Friedrich Schlegel (1772-1829, German Philosopher, Critic, Writer)

5   Certain brief sentences are peerless in their ability to give one the feeling that nothing remains to be said.
Jean Rostand (1894-1977, French Biologist, Writer)

6   They are the guiding oracles which man has found out for himself in that great business of ours, of learning how to be, to do, to do without, and to depart.
John Morley (1838-1923, British Journalist, Biographer, Statesman)

7   An aphorism can never be the whole truth; it is either a half-truth or a truth-and-a-half.
Karl Kraus (1874-1936, Austrian Satirist)

8   Most maxim-mongers have preferred the prettiness to the justness of a thought, and the turn to the truth; but I have refused myself to everything that my own experience did not justify and confirm.
Lord Chesterfield (1694-1773, British Statesman, Author)

9   An epigram is a flashlight of a truth; a witticism, truth laughing at itself.
Minna Antrim (1861-18?, American Epigrammist)

10   An epigram is only a wisecrack that's played at Carnegie Hall.
Oscar Levant (1906-1972, American Pianist, Actor)

11   He would stab his best friend for the sake of writing an epigram on his tombstone.
Oscar Wilde (1856-1900, British Author, Wit)

12   Epigrams succeed where epics fail.
Persian Proverb

13   Exclusively of the abstract sciences, the largest and worthiest portion of our knowledge consists of aphorisms: and the greatest and best of men is but an aphorism.
Samuel Taylor Coleridge (1772-1834, British Poet, Critic, Philosopher)

14   It is the nature of aphoristic thinking to be always in a state of concluding; a bid to have the final word is inherent in all powerful phrase-making.
Susan Sontag (1933-, American Essayist)

15   He had a wonderful talent for packing thought close, and rendering it portable.
Thomas B. Macaulay (1800-1859, American Essayist and Historian)

16   There are aphorisms that, like airplanes, stay up only while they are in motion.
Vladimir Nabokov (1899-1977, Russian-born American Novelist, Poet)

17   Anyone can tell the truth, but only very few of us can make epigrams.
W. Somerset Maugham (1874-1965, British Novelist, Playwright)

APOLOGIES

1. An apology? Bah! Disgusting! Cowardly! Beneath the dignity of any gentleman, however wrong he might be.
Baroness Orczy (1865-1947, Hungarian-born British Novelist, Playwright)

2. Never make a defense or apology before you are accused.
Charles I (1600-1649, King of England and Ireland)

3. A stiff apology is a second insult. The injured party does not want to be compensated because he has been wronged; he wants to be healed because he has been hurt.
Gilbert K. Chesterton (1874-1936, British Author)

4. Well, excuuuuuse me!!!!
Steve Martin (1945-, American Actor, Comedian, Screenwriter, Playwright, Writer)

APPEARANCE

1. Every person is responsible for his own looks after 40.
Abraham Lincoln (1809-1865, Sixteenth President of the USA)

2. The Lord prefers common looking people. That is why he made so many of them.
Abraham Lincoln (1809-1865, Sixteenth President of the USA)

3. Outside show is a poor substitute for inner worth.
Aesop (620-560 BC, Greek Fabulist)

4. Appearances are deceptive.
Aesop (620-560 BC, Greek Fabulist)

5. What I have to say is far more important than how long my eyelashes are.
Alanis Morissette (Canadian Singer)

6. Regardless of how you feel inside, always try to look like a winner. Even if you are behind, a sustained look of control and confidence can give you a mental edge that results in victory.
Arthur Ashe (1943-1993, African-American Tennis Player)

7. The non permanent appearance of happiness and distress, and their disappearance in due course, are like the appearance and disappearance of summer and winter seasons.
Bhagavad Gita (400 BC, Sanskrit Poem Incorporated Into the Mahabharata)

8. The beggar is the only person in the universe not obliged to study appearance.
Charles Lamb (1775-1834, British Essayist, Critic)

9. I tend to play mostly villains and twisted people. Unsavory guys. I think it's my face, the way I look.
Christopher Walken (1943-, American Actor)

10. Even I don't wake up looking like Cindy Crawford.
Cindy Crawford (1966-, American Model, Actress)

11. The world is governed more by appearances than by realities, so that it is fully as necessary to seem to know something as to know it.
Daniel Webster (1782-1852, American Lawyer, Statesman)

12. Everybody has that thing where they need to look one way but they come out looking another way and that's what people observe. You see someone on the street and essentially what you notice about them is the flaw. It's just extraordinary that we should have been given these peculiarities. Something is ironic in the world and it has to do with the fact that what you intend never comes out like you intend it.
Diane Arbus (1923-1971, American Photographer)

13. There's one thing about baldness, it's neat.
Don Herold

14. Do not judge from mere appearances; for the lift laughter that bubbles on the lip often mantles over the depths of sadness, and the serious look may be the sober veil that covers a divine peace and joy. The bosom can ache beneath diamond brooches; and many a blithe heart dances under coarse wool.
Edwin Hubbel Chapin (1814-1880, American Author, Clergyman)

15. Be not deceived with the first appearance of things, for show is not substance.
English Proverb

16. I do not think I had ever seen a nastier-looking man. Under the black hat, when I had first seen them, the eyes had been those of an unsuccessful rapist.
Ernest Hemingway (1898-1961, American Writer)

17. People that seem so glorious are all show; underneath they are like everyone else.
Euripides (480-406 BC, Greek Tragic Poet)

18. The most common error made in matters of appearance is the belief that one should disdain the superficial and let the true beauty of one's soul shine through. If there are places on your body where this is a possibility, you are not attractive -- you are leaking.
Fran Lebowitz (1951-, American Journalist)

19. To establish yourself in the world a person must do all they can to appear already established.
François de La Rochefoucauld (1613-1680, French classical writer)

20. Nothing so much prevents our being natural as the desire to seem so.
François de La Rochefoucauld (1613-1680, French classical writer)

21. A dimple on the chin, the devil within.
Gaelic Proverb

22. Great feelings will often take the aspect of error, and great faith the aspect of illusion.
George Eliot (1819-1880, British Novelist)

23 Woman cannot be content with health and agility: she must make exorbitant efforts to appear something that never could exist without a diligent perversion of nature. Is it too much to ask that women be spared the daily struggle for superhuman beauty in order to offer it to the caresses of a subhumanly ugly mate?
Germaine Greer (1939-, Australian Feminist Writer)

24 Clothes and manners do not make the man; but when he is made, they greatly improve his appearance
Henry Ward Beecher (1813-1887, American Preacher, Orator, Writer)

25 You and I do not see things as they are. We see things as we are.
Herb Cohen

26 A good man often appears gauche simply because he does not take advantage of the myriad mean little chances of making himself look stylish. Preferring truth to form, he is not constantly at work upon the fatade of his appearance.
Iris Murdoch (1919-, British Novelist, Philosopher)

27 A little man often cast a long shadow.
Italian Proverb

28 My breasts are beautiful, and I gotta tell you, they've gotten a lot of attention for what is relatively short screen time.
Jamie Lee Curtis (1958-, American Actress)

29 Beware, so long as you live, of judging men by their outward appearance.
Jean De La Fontaine (1621-1695, French Poet)

30 Appearance rules the world.
Johann Friedrich Von Schiller (1759-1805, German Dramatist, Poet, Historian)

31 No person who is well bred, kind and modest is ever offensively plain; all real deformity means want for manners or of heart.
John Ruskin (1819-1900, British Critic, Social Theorist)

32 Cleanliness is indeed next to godliness.
John Wesley (1703-1791, British Preacher, Founder of Methodism)

33 Getting talked about is one of the penalties for being pretty, while being above suspicion is about the only compensation for being homely.
Kin Hubbard (1868-1930, American Humorist, Journalist)

34 We are what we pretend to be, so we must be careful about what we pretend to be.
Kurt Vonnegut Jr. (1922-, American Novelist)

35 I've played a lot of bad guys, 'cause that was the only work I could get. People saw my face and went "Oooh."
Laurence Fishburne

36 We see things as we are, not as they are.
Leo Rosten (1908-1997, Polish Born American Political Scientist)

37 Think not I am what I appear.
Lord Byron (1788-1824, British Poet)

38 Barring that natural expression of villainy which we all have, the man looked honest enough.
Mark Twain (1835-1910, American Humorist, Writer)

39 If one wishes to become rich they must appear rich.
Oliver Goldsmith (1728-1774, Anglo-Irish Author, Poet, Playwright)

40 A hair in the head is worth two in the brush.
Oliver Herford (1863-1935, American Author, Illustrator)

41 It is only shallow people who do not judge by appearances. The true mystery of the world is the visible, not the invisible.
Oscar Wilde (1856-1900, British Author, Wit)

42 When disposition wins us, the features please.
Ovid (43 BC-18 AD, Roman Poet)

43 The time will come when it will disgust you to look in the mirror.
Ovid (43 BC-18 AD, Roman Poet)

44 Neglect of appearance becomes men.
Ovid (43 BC-18 AD, Roman Poet)

45 First appearance deceives many.
Phaedrus (Macedonian Inventor and Writer)

46 Things are not always what they seem; the first appearance deceives many; the intelligence of a few perceives what has been carefully hidden.
Phaedrus (Macedonian Inventor and Writer)

47 Wide will wear, but tight will tear.
Proverb

48 The best mirror is an old friend.
Proverb

49 All things are becoming to good people.
Proverb

50 'Tis very certain that each man carries in his eye the exact indication of his rank in the immense scale of men, and we are always learning to read it. A complete man should need no auxiliaries to his personal presence.
Ralph Waldo Emerson (1803-1882, American Poet, Essayist)

51 He looked about as inconspicuous as a tarantula on a slice of angel food.
Raymond Chandler (1888-1959, American Author)

52 When I see a bird that walks like a duck and swims like a duck and quacks like a duck, I call that bird a duck.
Richard C. Cushing (1895-1970, American Roman Catholic Cardinal)

53 You are only what you are when no one is looking.
Robert C. Edwards

54 People have been so busy relating to how I look, it's a miracle I didn't become a self-conscious blob of protoplasm.
Robert Redford (1937-, American Actor, Director, Producer)

55 I have told you of the Spaniard who always put on his spectacles when about to eat cherries, that they might look bigger and more attempting. In like manner I made the most of my enjoyment s: and through I do not cast my cares away, I pack them in as little compass as I can, and carry them as conveniently as I can for myself, and never let them annoy others.
Robert Southey (1774-1843, British Author)

56 How little do they see what is, who frame their hasty judgments upon that which seems.
Robert Southey (1774-1843, British Author)

57 I see myself as Rhoda, not Mary Tyler Moore.
Rosie O'Donnell (1962-, American Talk Show Host, TV Personality, Comedian, Actress,)

58 There are no greater wretches in the world than many of those whom people in general take to be happy.
Seneca (4 BC-65 AD, Spanish-born Roman Statesman, philosopher)

59 The most winning woman I ever knew was hanged for poisoning three little children for their insurance-money, and the most repellent man of my acquaintance is a philanthropist who has spent nearly a quarter of a million upon the London poor.
Sir Arthur Conan Doyle (1859-1930, British Author, "Sherlock Holmes")

60 You can lease the peace of mind You bought a mask, I put it on. You never thought to ask me If I wear it when you're gone
Sisters Of Mercy

61 Chins without beards deserve no honor.
Spanish Proverb

62 You're only has good as your last haircut.
Susan Lee

63 Nowadays those are rewarded who make right appear wrong.
Terence (185-159 BC, Roman Writer of Comedies)

64 God loveth the clean.
The Koran (500 AD, Islamic Religious Bible)

65 He that has a great nose, thinks everybody is speaking of it.
Thomas Fuller (1608-1661, British Clergyman, Author)

66 I don't consider myself bald, I'm just taller than my hair.
Tom Sharp

67 Trust not to much to appearances.
Virgil (70-19 BC, Roman Poet)

68 Things are seldom what they seem.
W. S. Gilbert (1836-1911, British Librettist)

69 First impressions are often the truest, as we find (not infrequently) to our cost, when we have been wheedled out of them by plausible professions or studied actions. A man's look is the work of years; it is stamped on his countenance by the events of his whole life, nay, more, by the hand of nature, and it is not to be got rid of easily.
William Hazlitt (1778-1830, British Essayist)

APPETITE

1 The most violent appetites in all creatures are lust and hunger; the first is a perpetual call upon them to propagate their kind, the latter to preserve themselves.
Joseph Addison (1672-1719, British Essayist, Poet, Statesman)

2 Appetite is essentially insatiable, and where it operates as a criterion of both action and enjoyment (that is, everywhere in the Western world since the sixteenth century) it will infallibly discover congenial agencies (mechanical and political) of expression.
Marshall Mcluhan (1911-1980, Canadian Communications Theorist)

APPLAUSE

1 We believe that the applause of silence is the only kind that counts.
Alfred Jarry (1873-1907, French Playwright, Author)

2 Applause is a receipt, not a bill.
Artur Schnabel (1882-1951, German-born American Pianist)

3 Applause is the spur of noble minds, the end and aim of weak ones.
Charles Caleb Colton (1780-1832, British Sportsman Writer)

4 Glorious bouquets and storms of applause are the trimmings which every artist naturally enjoys. But to move an audience in such a role, to hear in the applause that unmistakable note which breaks through good theatre manners and comes from the heart, is to feel that you have won through to life itself. Such pleasure does not vanish with the fall of the curtain, but becomes part of one's own life.
Dame Alice Markova

5 We must not always judge of the generality of the opinion by the noise of the acclamation.
Edmund Burke (1729-1797, British Political Writer, Statesman)

6 To receive applause for works which do not demand all our powers hinders our advance towards a perfecting of our spirit. It usually means that thereafter we stand still.
Georg C. Lichtenberg (1742-1799, German Physicist, Satirist)

7 Applause that comes thundering with such force you might think the audience merely suffers the music as an excuse for its ovations.
Greil Marcus (1945-, American Rock Journalist)

8 They named it Ovation from the Latin ovis [A Sheep].
Plutarch (46-120 AD, Greek Essayist, Biographer)

9 The silence that accepts merit as the most natural thing in the world is the highest applause.
Ralph Waldo Emerson (1803-1882, American Poet, Essayist)

10   O, popular applause! what heart of man is proof against thy sweet, seducing charms?
William Cowper (1731-1800, British Poet)

APPRAISAL

1   Appraisals are where you get together with your team leader and agree what an outstanding member of the team you are, how much your contribution has been valued, what massive potential you have and, in recognition of all this, would you mind having your salary halved.
Guy Browning (British Humorist)

2   Evaluate what you want -- because what gets measured, gets produced.
James A. Belasco (American Academic and Management Consultant)

3   How you measure the performance of your managers directly affects the way they act.
John Dearden (American Academic)

4   When your work speaks for itself, get out of the way.
Thomas 'Wayne' Brazell (American Army Material Command)

APPRECIATION

1   Like when I'm in the bathroom looking at my toilet paper, I'm like 'Wow! That's toilet paper?' I don't know if we appreciate how much we have.
Alicia Silverstone (Born 1976, American Actress, Producer)

2   One of the sanest, surest, and most generous joys of life comes from being happy over the good fortune of others.
Archibald Rutledge

3   Cherish your human connections: your relationships with friends and family.
Barbara Bush (1925-, American First Lady, Wife of President George Bush)

4   It is up to us to give ourselves recognition. If we wait for it to come from others, we feel resentful when it doesn't, and when it does, we may well reject it.
Bernard Berkowitz (American Psychoanalyst, Psychologist)

5   Whatever you do, make it an offering to me -- the food you eat, the sacrifices you make, the help you give, even your suffering.
Bhagavad Gita (400 BC, Sanskrit Poem Incorporated Into the Mahabharata)

6   Appreciation of life itself, becoming suddenly aware of the miracle of being alive, on this planet, can turn what we call ordinary life into a miracle. We come awake to such a realization when we recognize our connection to a spiritual dimension.
Dan Wakefield

7   Is there some principal of nature which states that we never know the quality of what we have until it is gone?
Elbert Hofstadter

8   I would rather be able to appreciate things I can not have than to have things I am not able to appreciate.
Elbert Hubbard (1859-1915, American Author, Publisher)

9   Prosperity depends more on wanting what you have than having what you want.
Geoffrey F. Abert

10   One we discover how to appreciate the timeless values in our daily experiences, we can enjoy the best things in life.
Harry Hepner

11   Thankfulness is the beginning of gratitude. Gratitude is the completion of thankfulness. Thankfulness may consist merely of words. Gratitude is shown in acts.
Henri Frederic Amiel (1821-1881, Swiss Philosopher, Poet, Critic)

12   When I'm not thanked at all, I'm thanked enough, I've done my duty, and I've done no more.
Henry Fielding (1707-1754, British Novelist, Dramatist)

13   The half is greater than the whole.
Hesiod (8th Century BC, Greek Poet)

14   Cherish your visions; cherish your ideals; cherish the music that stirs in your heart, the beauty that forms in your mind, the loveliness that drapes your purest thoughts, for out of them will grow delightful conditions, all heavenly environment; of these if you but remain true to them, your world will at last be built.
James Allen (1864-1912, British-born American Essayist, Author of "As a Man Thinketh")

15   Most of us, swimming against the tides of trouble the world knows nothing about, need only a bit of praise or encouragement -- and we will make the goal.
Jerome P. Fleishman

16   What sunshine is to flowers, smiles are to humanity. These are but trifles, to be sure; but, scattered along life's pathway, the good they do is inconceivable.
Joseph Addison (1672-1719, British Essayist, Poet, Statesman)

17   There is a serious defect in the thinking of someone who wants -- more than anything else -- to become rich. As long as they don't have the money, it'll seem like a worthwhile goal. Once they do, they'll understand how important other things are -- and have always been.
Joseph Brooks

18   Hay is more acceptable to an ass than gold.
Latin Proverb

19   To love one that is great, is almost to be great one's self.
Madame Neckar

20 Count your blessings. Once you realize how valuable you are and how much you have going for you, the smiles will return, the sun will break out, the music will play, and you will finally be able to move forward the life that God intended for you with grace, strength, courage, and confidence.
Og Mandino (1923-1996, American Motivational Author, Speaker)

21 Let us learn to appreciate there will be times when the trees will be bare, and look forward to the time when we may pick the fruit.
Peter Seller (British Actor)

22 If human beings are perceived as potentials rather than problems, as possessing strengths instead of weaknesses, as unlimited rather that dull and unresponsive, then they thrive and grow to their capabilities.
Robert Conklin (American Teacher, Author, Speaker)

23 There's a basic human weakness inherent in all people which tempts them to want what they can't have and not want what is readily available to them.
Robert J. Ringer (American Writer)

24 It is not the man who has too little, but the man who craves more, that is poor.
Seneca (4 BC-65 AD, Spanish-born Roman Statesman, philosopher)

25 Ignorant men don't know what good they hold in their hands until they've flung it away.
Sophocles (495-406 BC, Greek Tragic Poet)

26 No duty is more urgent than that of returning thanks.
St. Ambrose (340-397, Bishop of Milan)

27 He is not poor that hath not much, but he that craves much.
Thomas Fuller (1608-1661, British Clergyman, Author)

28 That which we obtain too easily, we esteem too lightly.
Thomas Paine (1737-1809, Anglo-American Political Theorist, Writer)

29 By appreciation, we make excellence in others our own property.
Voltaire (1694-1778, French Historian, Writer)

30 Let never day nor night unhallowed pass, but still remember what the Lord hath done.
William Shakespeare (1564-1616, British Poet, Playwright, Actor)

APPROVAL

1 Please all, and you will please none.
Aesop (620-560 BC, Greek Fabulist)

2 The best ballplayer's the one who doesn't think he made good. He keeps trying to convince you.
Casey Stengel (1889-1975, American Baseball Player and Manager)

3 The person who seeks all their applause from outside has their happiness in another's keeping .
Claudius Claudianus (340-410, Egyptian Latin Poet)

4 It is more noble to give yourself completely to one individual than to labor diligently for the salvation of the masses.
Dag Hammarskjold (1905-1961, Swedish Statesman, Secretary-general of U.N.)

5 Naturalness is the easiest thing in the world to acquire, if you will forget yourself-forget about the impression you are trying to make.
Dale Carnegie (1888-1955, American Author, Trainer)

6 I have no methods; all I do is accept people as they are.
Dr. Paul Tournier

7 It embarrasses me to think of all those years I was buying silk suits and alligator shoes that were hurting my feet; cars that I just parked, and the dust would just build up on them.
George Foreman (1949-, American Boxer)

8 There just isn't any pleasing some people. The trick is to stop trying.
Joel Rosenberg

9 At the heart of personality is the need to feel a sense of being lovable without having to qualify for that acceptance.
Maurice Wagner

10 Getting people to like you is merely the other side of liking them.
Norman Vincent Peale (1898-1993, American Christian Reformed Pastor, Speaker, Author)

11 Do not trust to the cheering, for those persons would shout as much if you and I were going to be hanged.
Oliver Cromwell (1599-1658, Parliamentarian General, Lord Protector of England)

12 He who trims himself to suit everyone will soon whittle himself away.
Raymond Hull

13 My advice to you concerning applause is this: enjoy it but never quite believe it.
Robert Montgomery (1807-1855, American Author)

14 Those whose approval you seek most give you the least.
Rozanne Weissman

15 The applause of a single human being is of great consequence.
Samuel Johnson (1709-1784, British Author)

16 Reproof on her lips, but a smile in her eyes.
Samuel Lover (1797-1868, American Author)

17 People who want the most approval get the least and people who need approval the least get the most.
Wayne Dyer (1940-, American Psychotherapist, Author, Lecturer)

[18] The deepest principle of human nature is the craving to be appreciated.
William James (1842-1910, American Psychologist, Professor, Author)

ARCHITECTURE

[1] Architect. One who drafts a plan of your house, and plans a draft of your money.
Ambrose Bierce (1842-1914, American Author, Editor, Journalist, "The Devil's Dictionary")

[2] The only legitimate artists in England are the architects.
Benjamin Haydon (1786-1846, British Artist)

[3] When it comes to getting things done, we need fewer architects and more bricklayers.
Colleen C. Barrett

[4] Architecture is inhabited sculpture.
Constantin Brancusi (1876-1957, Romanian Sculptor)

[5] In short, the building becomes a theatrical demonstration of its functional ideal. In this romanticism, high-tech architecture is, of course, no different in spirit -- if totally different in form -- from all the romantic architecture of the past.
Dan Cruickshank

[6] Heredity is a strong factor, even in architecture. Necessity first mothered invention. Now invention has little ones of her own, and they look just like grandma.
E(lwyn) B(rooks) White (1899-1985, American Author, Editor)

[7] Architecture is petrified music.
Felix E. Schelling (1858-1945, American Educator)

[8] All fine architectural values are human vales, else not valuable.
Frank Lloyd Wright (1869-1959, American Architect)

[9] A doctor can bury his mistakes, but an architect can only advise his clients to plant vines.
Frank Lloyd Wright (1869-1959, American Architect)

[10] The physician can bury his mistakes, but the architect can only advise his clients to plant vines.
Frank Lloyd Wright (1869-1959, American Architect)

[11] The architect represents neither a Dionysian nor an Apollinian condition: here it is the mighty act of will, the will which moves mountains, the intoxication of the strong will, which demands artistic expression. The most powerful men have always inspired the architects; the architect has always been influenced by power.
Friedrich Nietzsche (1844-1900, German Philosopher)

[12] A building is akin to dogma; it is insolent, like dogma. Whether or no it is permanent, it claims permanence, like a dogma. People ask why we have no typical architecture of the modern world, like impressionism in painting. Surely it is obviously because we have not enough dogmas; we cannot bear to see anything in the sky that is solid and enduring, anything in the sky that does not change like the clouds of the sky.
Gilbert K. Chesterton (1874-1936, British Author)

[13] All architecture is great architecture after sunset; perhaps architecture is really a nocturnal art, like the art of fireworks.
Gilbert K. Chesterton (1874-1936, British Author)

[14] A structure becomes architectural, and not sculptural, when its elements no longer have their justification in nature.
Guillaume Apollinaire (1880-1918, Italian-born French Poet, Critic)

[15] True, there are architects so called in this country, and I have heard of one at least possessed with the idea of making architectural ornaments have a core of truth, a necessity, and hence a beauty, as if it were a revelation to him. All very well perhaps from his point of view, but only a little better than the common dilettantism.
Henry David Thoreau (1817-1862, American Essayist, Poet, Naturalist)

[16] Ah, to build, to build! That is the noblest art of all the arts. Painting and sculpture are but images, are merely shadows cast by outward things on stone or canvas, having in themselves no separate existence. Architecture, existing in itself, and not in seeming a something it is not, surpasses them as substance shadow.
Henry Wadsworth Longfellow (1819-1892, American Poet)

[17] Nor aught availed him now to have built in heaven high towers; nor did he scrape by all his engines, but was headlong sent with his industrious crew to build in hell.
John Milton (1608-1674, British Poet)

[18] No person who is not a great sculptor or painter can be an architect. If he is not a sculptor or painter, he can only be a builder.
John Ruskin (1819-1900, British Critic, Social Theorist)

[19] When we build, let us think that we build for ever.
John Ruskin (1819-1900, British Critic, Social Theorist)

[20] No architecture is so haughty as that which is simple.
John Ruskin (1819-1900, British Critic, Social Theorist)

[21] We may live without her, and worship without her, but we cannot remember without her. How cold is all history, how lifeless all imagery, compared to that which the living nation writes, and the uncorrupted marble bears!
John Ruskin (1819-1900, British Critic, Social Theorist)

[22] An architect should live as little in cities as a painter. Send him to our hills, and let him study there what nature understands by a buttress, and what by a dome.
John Ruskin (1819-1900, British Critic, Social Theorist)

[23] Form ever follows function.
Louis Henry Sullivan

24 In my experience, if you have to keep the lavatory door shut by extending your left leg, it's modern architecture.
Nancy Banks-Smith

25 It is the Late city that first defies the land, contradicts Nature in the lines of its silhouette, denies all Nature. It wants to be something different from and higher than Nature. These high- pitched gables, these Baroque cupolas, spires, and pinnacles, neither are, nor desire to be, related with anything in Nature. And then begins the gigantic megalopolis, the city-as-world, which suffers nothing beside itself and sets about annihilating the country picture.
Oswald Spengler (1880-1936, German Philosopher)

26 All architects want to live beyond their deaths.
Philip Johnson (1906-, American Architect and Theorist)

27 Architecture is the art of how to waste space.
Philip Johnson (1906-, American Architect and Theorist)

28 You have to give this much to the Luftwaffe: when it knocked down our buildings it did not replace them with anything more offensive than rubble. We did that.
Prince Of Wales Charles (1948-, Duke of Edinburgh, Son of Queen Elizabeth II and Prince Philip)

29 Don't fight forces, use them.
R. Buckminster Fuller (1895-1983, American Inventor, Designer, Poet, Philosopher)

30 The job of buildings is to improve human relations: architecture must ease them, not make them worse.
Ralph Erskine

31 I don't think of form as a kind of architecture. The architecture is the result of the forming. It is the kinesthetic and visual sense of position and wholeness that puts the thing into the realm of art.
Roy Lichtenstein (1923, American Artist)

32 The terrifying and edible beauty of Art Nouveau architecture.
Salvador Dali (1904-1989, Spanish Painter)

33 The principle of the Gothic architecture is infinity made imaginable.
Samuel Taylor Coleridge (1772-1834, British Poet, Critic, Philosopher)

34 Believe me, that was a happy age, before the days of architects, before the days of builders.
Seneca (4 BC-65 AD, Spanish-born Roman Statesman, philosopher)

35 Architecture is to make us know and remember who we are.
Sir Geoffrey Jellicoe

36 Where do architects and designers get their ideas?" The answer, of course, is mainly from other architects and designers, so is it mere casuistry to distinguish between tradition and plagiarism?
Stephen Bayley (1951-, British Design Critic)

37 Light, God's eldest daughter, is a principal beauty in a building.
Thomas Fuller (1608-1661, British Clergyman, Author)

38 Le Corbusier was the sort of relentlessly rational intellectual that only France loves wholeheartedly, the logician who flies higher and higher in ever-decreasing circles until, with one last, utterly inevitable induction, he disappears up his own fundamental aperture and emerges in the fourth dimension as a needle-thin umber bird.
Thomas Wolfe (1931-, American Author, Journalist)

39 A modern, harmonic and lively architecture is the visible sign of an authentic democracy.
Walter Gropius (1883-1969, German Architect)

40 Architects, painters, and sculptors must recognize anew and learn to grasp the composite character of a building both as an entity and in its separate parts. Only then will their work be imbued with the architectonic spirit which it has lost as "salon art." Together let us desire, conceive, and create the new structure of the future, which will embrace architecture and sculpture and painting in one unity and which will one day rise toward heaven from the hands of a million workers like the crystal symbol of a new faith.
Walter Gropius (1883-1969, German Architect)

ARGUMENT

1 True disputants are like true sportsman: their whole delight is in the pursuit.
Alexander Pope (1688-1744, British Poet, Critic, Translator)

2 When much dispute has past, we find our tenets just the same as last.
Alexander Pope (1688-1744, British Poet, Critic, Translator)

3 Wise men argue cases, fools decide them.
Anacharsis (600 BC, Scythian Philosopher)

4 Most quarrels amplify a misunderstanding.
Andre Gide (1869-1951, French Author)

5 The difficult part in an argument is not to defend one's opinion, but rather to know it.
Andre Maurois (1885-1967, French Writer)

6 We must not contradict, but instruct him that contradicts us; for a madman is not cured by another running mad also.
Antisthenes (388-311 BC, Greek Dramatist)

7 Quarrels often arise in marriages when the bridal gifts are excessive.
Auson

8 He that blows the coals in quarrels that he has nothing to do with, has no right to complain if the sparks fly in his face.
Benjamin Franklin (1706-1790, American Scientist, Publisher, Diplomat)

9   Those disputing, contradicting, and confuting people are generally unfortunate in their affairs. They get victory, sometimes, but they never get good will, which would be of more use to them.
Benjamin Franklin (1706-1790, American Scientist, Publisher, Diplomat)

10 Men's arguments often prove nothing but their wishes.
Charles Caleb Colton (1780-1832, British Sportsman Writer)

11 It is the briefest yet wisest maxim which tells us to "meddle not".
Charles Caleb Colton (1780-1832, British Sportsman Writer)

12 There's nothing I like less than bad arguments for a view that I hold dear.
Daniel Dennett

13 The sounder your argument, the more satisfaction you get out of it.
Edgar Watson Howe (1853-1937, American Journalist, Author)

14 You punch me, I punch back. I do not believe it's good for ones self-respect to be a punching bag.
Edward Koch (1924-, American Politician)

15 Debate is the death of conversation.
Emil Ludwig (1881-1948, German Writer)

16 Use soft words and hard arguments.
English Proverb

17 Quarrels would not last so long if the fault lay only on one side.
François de La Rochefoucauld (1613-1680, French classical writer)

18 One often contradicts an opinion when what is uncongenial is really the tone in which it was conveyed.
Friedrich Nietzsche (1844-1900, German Philosopher)

19 People generally quarrel because they cannot argue.
Gilbert K. Chesterton (1874-1936, British Author)

20 But curb thou the high spirit in thy breast, for gentle ways are best, and keep aloof from sharp contentions.
Homer (850 BC, Greek Epic Poet)

21 When you argue with your inferiors, you convince them of only one thing: they are as clever as you.
Irving Layton (1912-, Canadian Poet)

22 There is no good in arguing with the inevitable. The only argument available with an east wind is to put on your overcoat.
James Russell Lowell (1819-1891, American Poet, Critic, Editor)

23 No matter what side of the argument you are on, you always find people on your side that you wish were on the other.
Jascha Heifetz (1901-1987, Lithuanian Violinist)

24 The purely agitation attitude is not good enough for a detailed consideration of a subject.
Jawaharlal Nehru (1889-1964, Indian Nationalist, Statesman)

25 The argument of the strongest is always the best.
Jean De La Fontaine (1621-1695, French Poet)

26 Argument, as usually managed, is the worst sort of conversation, as in books it is generally the worst sort of reading.
Jonathan Swift (1667-1745, Anglo-Irish Satirist)

27 Arguments out of a pretty mouth are unanswerable.
Joseph Addison (1672-1719, British Essayist, Poet, Statesman)

28 The aim of argument, or of discussion, should not be victory, but progress.
Joseph Joubert (1754-1824, French Moralist)

29 It is better to debate a question without settling it than to settle it without debate.
Joseph Joubert (1754-1824, French Moralist)

30 When all are wrong, everyone is right.
La Lehaussee

31 The long term versus the short term argument is one used by losers.
Larry Adler (American Founder of Fire & All Risk Insurances)

32 There are two things which cannot be attacked in front: ignorance and narrow-mindedness. They can only be shaken by the simple development of the contrary qualities. They will not bear discussion.
Lord Acton (1834 - 1902, British Historian)

33 The best way I know of to win an argument is to start by being in the right.
Lord Quintin Hogg Hailsham (1907-, British Statesman)

34 Behind every argument is someone's ignorance.
Louis D. Brandeis (1856-1941, American Judge)

35 When you have no basis for an argument, abuse the plaintiff.
Marcus T. Cicero (106-43 BC, Great Roman Orator, Politician)

36 Fear not those who argue but those who dodge.
Marie Ebner-Eschenbach

37 In argument similes are like songs in love; they describe much, but prove nothing.
Matthew Prior (1664-1721, British Diplomat, Poet)

38 It was completely fruitless to quarrel with the world, whereas the quarrel with oneself was occasionally fruitful and always, she had to admit, interesting.
May Sarton (1912-, American Poet, Novelist)

39 He who establishes his argument by noise and command shows that his reason is weak.
Michel Eyquem De Montaigne (1533-1592, French Philosopher, Essayist)

40 When a thing is said to be not worth refuting you may be sure that either it is flagrantly stupid -- in which case all comment is superfluous -- or it is something formidable, the very crux of the problem.
Miguel De Unamuno (1864-1936, Spanish Philosophical Writer)

41 I tell you Wellington is a bad general, the English are bad soldiers; we will settle this matter by lunch time.
Napoleon Bonaparte (1769-1821, French General, Emperor)

42 Any fact is better established by two or three good testimonies than by a thousand arguments.
Nathaniel Emmons

43 There is no arguing with him, for if his pistol misses fire, he knocks you down with the butt end of it.
Oliver Goldsmith (1728-1774, Anglo-Irish Author, Poet, Playwright)

44 Myself when young did eagerly frequent doctor and saint, and heard great argument about it and about: but evermore came out by the same door as in I went.
Omar Khayyam (1048-1131, Persian Astronomer, Poet)

45 Arguments are to be avoided; they are always vulgar and often convincing.
Oscar Wilde (1856-1900, British Author, Wit)

46 I dislike arguments of any kind. They are always vulgar, and often convincing.
Oscar Wilde (1856-1900, British Author, Wit)

47 Concerning God, freewill and destiny: Of all that earth has been or yet may be, all that vain men imagine or believe, or hope can paint or suffering may achieve, we descanted.
Percy Bysshe Shelley (1792-1822, British Poet)

48 It is not necessary to understand things in order to argue about them.
Pierre De Beaumarchais (1732-1799, French Dramatist)

49 Soft words win hard hearts.
Proverb

50 Two dogs strive for a bone and the third one runs off with it.
Proverb

51 Never argue at the dinner table, for the one who is not hungry always gets the best of the argument.
Richard Whately (1787-1863, British Prelate, Writer)

52 Weak arguments are often thrust before my path; but although they are most insubstantial, it is not easy to destroy them. There is not a more difficult feat known than to cut through a cushion with a sword.
Richard Whately (1787-1863, British Prelate, Writer)

53 Most of the arguments to which I am party fall somewhat short of being impressive, knowing to the fact that neither I nor my opponent knows what we are talking about
Robert Benchley (1889-1945, American Humorist, Critic, Parodist)

54 I had a lovers quarrel with the world.
Robert Frost (1875-1963, American Poet)

55 Argument is conclusive... but... it does not remove doubt, so that the mind may rest in the sure knowledge of the truth, unless it finds it by the method of experiment. For if any man who never saw fire proved by satisfactory arguments that fire burns. his hearer's mind would never be satisfied, nor would he avoid the fire until he put his hand in it that he might learn by experiment what argument taught.
Roger Bacon (1214-1294, British Philosopher, Scientist)

56 Neither irony or sarcasm is argument.
Rufus Choate (1799-1859, American Lawyer, Statesman)

57 Whenever you argue with another wiser than yourself in order that others may admire your wisdom, they will discover your ignorance.
Saadi

58 Arguments are like fire-arms which a man may keep at home but should not carry about with him.
Samuel Butler (1612-1680, British Poet, Satirist)

59 We are not won by arguments that we can analyze, but by tone and temper; by the manner, which is the man himself.
Samuel Butler (1612-1680, British Poet, Satirist)

60 The most important thing in an argument, next to being right, is to leave an escape hatch for your opponent, so that he can gracefully swing over to your side without too much apparent loss of face.
Sidney J. Harris (1917-, American Journalist)

61 It takes two to quarrel, but only one to end it.
Spanish Proverb

62 Hear one side and you will be in the dark. Hear both and all will be clear.
Thomas C. Haliburton (1796-1865, Canadian Jurist, Author)

63 A man lives by believing something: not by debating and arguing about many things.
Thomas Carlyle (1795-1881, Scottish Philosopher, Author)

64 Never contend with one that is foolish, proud, positive, testy, or with a superior, or a clown, in matter of argument.
Thomas Fuller (1608-1661, British Clergyman, Author)

65 Soft words are hard arguments.
Thomas Fuller (1608-1661, British Clergyman, Author)

66 When good people have a falling out, only one of them may be at fault at first; but if the strife continues long, usually both become guilty.
Thomas Fuller (1608-1661, British Clergyman, Author)

67 An association of men who will not quarrel with one another is a thing which has never yet existed, from the greatest confederacy of nations down to a town meeting or a vestry.
Thomas Jefferson (1743-1826, Third President of the USA)

68 Strong and bitter words indicate a weak cause.
Victor Hugo (1802-1885, French Poet, Dramatist, Novelist)

69 A long dispute means that both parties are wrong
Voltaire (1694-1778, French Historian, Writer)

70 Men argue, nature acts.
Voltaire (1694-1778, French Historian, Writer)

71 Weakness on both sides is, the motto of all quarrels.
Voltaire (1694-1778, French Historian, Writer)

72 How beggarly appear arguments before a defiant deed!
Walt Whitman (1819-1892, American Poet)

73 Heat and animosity, contest and conflict, may sharpen the wits, although they rarely do; they never strengthen the understanding, clear the perspicacity, guide the judgment, or improve the heart.
Walter Savage Landor (1775-1864, British Poet, Essayist)

74 I will name you the degrees. The first, the Retort Courteous; the second, the Quip Modest; the third, the Reply Churlish; the fourth, the Reproof Valiant; the fifth, the Countercheck Quarrelsome; the sixth, the Lie with Circumstance; the seventh, the Lie Direct.
William Shakespeare (1564-1616, British Poet, Playwright, Actor)

75 The devil can cite Scripture for his purpose.
William Shakespeare (1564-1616, British Poet, Playwright, Actor)

76 In a false quarrel there is no true valor.
William Shakespeare (1564-1616, British Poet, Playwright, Actor)

ARISTOCRACY

1 Real nobility is based on scorn, courage, and profound indifference.
Albert Camus (1913-1960, French Existential Writer)

2 Nothing is quite so wretchedly corrupt as an aristocracy which has lost its power but kept its wealth and which still has endless leisure to devote to nothing but banal enjoyments. All its great thoughts and passionate energy are things of the past, and nothing but a host of petty, gnawing vices now cling to it like worms to a corpse.
Alexis De Tocqueville (1805-1859, French Social Philosopher)

3 A fully equipped duke costs as much to keep up as two Dreadnoughts, and dukes are just as great a terror -- and they last longer.
David Lloyd George (1863-1945, British Statesman, Prime Minister)

4 Nobility is a graceful ornament to the civil order. It is the Corinthian capital of polished society.
Edmund Burke (1729-1797, British Political Writer, Statesman)

5 A degenerate nobleman is like a turnip. There is nothing good of him but that which is underground.
English Saying

6 Actual aristocracy cannot be abolished by any law: all the law can do is decree how it is to be imparted and who is to acquire it.
Georg C. Lichtenberg (1742-1799, German Physicist, Satirist)

7 All that is noble is in itself of a quiet nature, and appears to sleep until it is aroused and summoned forth by contrast.
Johann Wolfgang Von Goethe (1749-1832, German Poet, Dramatist, Novelist)

8 Lords are lordliest in their wine.
John Milton (1608-1674, British Poet)

9 What is the use of your pedigrees?
Juvenal (Decimus Junius Juvenalis) (55-130, Roman Satirical Poet)

10 I hate the noise and hurry inseparable from great Estates and Titles, and look upon both as blessings that ought only to be given to fools, for 'Tis only to them that they are blessings.
Lady Mary Wortley Montagu (1689-1762, British Society Figure, Letter Writer)

11 It is nobler to be good, and it is nobler to teach others to be good -- and less trouble!
Mark Twain (1835-1910, American Humorist, Writer)

12 An aristocracy in a republic is like a chicken whose head has been cut off: it may run about in a lively way, but in fact it is dead.
Nancy Mitford (1904-1973, British Writer)

13 I have known a German Prince with more titles than subjects, and a Spanish nobleman with more names than shirts.
Oliver Goldsmith (1728-1774, Anglo-Irish Author, Poet, Playwright)

14 You should study the Peerage, Gerald. It is the one book a young man about town should know thoroughly, and it is the best thing in fiction the English have ever done.
Oscar Wilde (1856-1900, British Author, Wit)

15 Put more trust in nobility of character than in an oath.
Solon (636-558 BC, Greek Statesman)

16 There is a natural aristocracy among men. The grounds of this are virtue and talents.
Thomas Jefferson (1743-1826, Third President of the USA)

17 Aristocracy has three successive ages. First superiority s, then privileges and finally vanities. Having passed from the first, it degenerates in the second and dies in the third.
Vicomte De Chateaubriand (1768-1848, French Politician, Writer)

18 Those comfortably padded lunatic asylums which are known, euphemistically, as the stately homes of England.
Virginia Woolf (1882-1941, British Novelist, Essayist)

19 Aristocracy is always cruel.
Wendell Phillips (1811-1884, American Reformer, Orator)

20 If, in looking at the lives of princes, courtiers, men of rank and fashion, we must perforce depict them as idle, profligate, and criminal, we must make allowances for the rich men's failings, and recollect that we, too, were very likely indolent and voluptuous, had we no motive for work, a mortal's natural taste for pleasure, and the daily temptation of a large income. What could a great peer, with a great castle and park, and a great fortune, do but be splendid and idle?
William M. Thackeray (1811-1863, Indian-born British Novelist)

ARMS RACE

1 Next week Reagan will probably announce that American scientists have discovered that the entire U.S. agricultural surplus can be compacted into a giant tomato one thousand miles across, which will be suspended above the Kremlin from a cluster of U.S. satellites flying in geosynchronous orbit. At the first sign of trouble the satellites will drop the tomato on the Kremlin, drowning the fractious Muscovites in ketchup.
Alexander Cockburn (1941-, Anglo-Irish Journalist)

2 At the rate science proceeds, rockets and missiles will one day seem like buffalo -- slow, endangered grazers in the black pasture of outer space.
Bernard Cooper

3 The superpowers often behave like two heavily armed blind men feeling their way around a room, each believing himself in mortal peril from the other, whom he assumes to have perfect vision.
Henry Kissinger (1923-, American Republican Politician, Secretary of State)

4 Guns will make us powerful; butter will only make us fat.
Hermann Goering (1893-1946, Nazi Politico-Military Leader)

5 If this phrase of the "balance of power" is to be always an argument for war, the pretext for war will never be wanting, and peace can never be secure.
John Bright (1811-1889, Radical British Statesman, Orator)

6 We dare not tempt them with weakness. For only when our arms are sufficient beyond doubt can we be certain beyond doubt that they will never be employed.
John F. Kennedy (1917-1963, Thirty-fifth President of the USA)

7 The ability to get to the verge without getting into the war is the necessary art. If you try to run away from it, if you are scared to go to the brink, you are lost.
John Foster Dulles (1888-1959, American Republican Secretary of State)

8 Weapons are like money; no one knows the meaning of enough.
Martin Amis (1949-, British Author)

9 I would die for my country, but I could never let my country die for me.
Neil Kinnock (1942-, British Labor Politician)

10 So in your discussions of the nuclear freeze proposals, I urge you to beware the temptation of pride -- the temptation blithely to declare yourselves above it all and label both sides equally at fault, to ignore the facts of history and the aggressive impulses of an evil empire, to simply call the arms race a giant misunderstanding and thereby remove yourself from the struggle between right and wrong, good and evil.
Ronald Reagan (1911-, Fortieth President of the USA, Actor)

11 The emotional security and political stability in this country entitle us to be a nuclear power.
Sir Ronald Mason

12 Let him who desires peace prepare for war.
Vegetius (375 BC, Roman Writer)

ARMY AND NAVY

1 Do you know what a soldier is, young man? He's the chap who makes it possible for civilized folk to despise war.
Allan Massie

2 Admiral. That part of a warship which does the talking while the figurehead does the thinking.
Ambrose Bierce (1842-1914, American Author, Editor, Journalist, "The Devil's Dictionary")

3 Valor, glory, firmness, skill, generosity, steadiness in battle and ability to rule -- these constitute the duty of a soldier. They flow from his own nature.
Bhagavad Gita (400 BC, Sanskrit Poem Incorporated Into the Mahabharata)

4 The nation which forgets its defenders will be itself forgotten.
Calvin Coolidge (1872-1933, Thirtieth President of the USA)

5 Come on, you sons of bitches! Do you want to live forever?
Daniel Daly

6 We have in the service the scum of the earth as common soldiers.
Duke of Wellington Arthur Wellesley (1769-1852, British Statesman, Military Leader)

7 I don't know what effect these men will have upon the enemy, but, by God, they terrify me.
Duke of Wellington Arthur Wellesley (1769-1852, British Statesman, Military Leader)

8 In the weakness of one kind of authority, and in the fluctuation of all, the officers of an army will remain for some time mutinous and full of faction, until some popular general, who understands the art of conciliating the soldiery, and who possesses the true spirit of command, shall draw the eyes of all men upon himself. Armies will obey him on his personal account. There is no other way of securing military obedience in this state of things.
Edmund Burke (1729-1797, British Political Writer, Statesman)

9 The courage of a soldier is found to be the cheapest and most common quality of human nature.
Edward Gibbon (1737-1794, British Historian)

10 Rogues, would you live forever?
Frederick The Great (Frederick II) (1712-1786, Born in Berlin, King of Prussia (1740-1786))

11 When we assumed the Soldier, we did not lay aside the Citizen.
George Washington (1732-1799, First President of the USA)

12 War is too important a matter to be left to the military.
Georges Clemenceau (1841-1929, French Statesman)

13 Now, you mummy's darlings, get a rift on them boots. Definitely shine em, my little curly- headed lambs, for in our mob, war or no war, you die with clean boots on.
Gerald Kersh

14 Soldiers have many faults, but they have one redeeming merit; they are never worshippers of force. Soldiers more than any other men are taught severely and systematically that might is not right. The fact is obvious. The might is in the hundred men who obey. The right (or what is held to be right) is in the one man who commands them.
Gilbert K. Chesterton (1874-1936, British Author)

15 Visit the Navy-Yard, and behold a marine, such a man as an American government can make, or such as it can make a man with its black arts -- a mere shadow and reminiscence of humanity, a man laid out alive and standing, and already, as one may say, buried under arms with funeral accompaniments.
Henry David Thoreau (1817-1862, American Essayist, Poet, Naturalist)

16 How happy is the sailor's life, from coast to coast to roam; in every port he finds a wife, in every land a home.
Isaac Bickerstaffe

17 Drinking is the soldier's pleasure.
John Dryden (1631-1700, British Poet, Dramatist, Critic)

18 There is nothing more enticing, disenchanting, and enslaving than the life at sea.
Joseph Conrad (1857-1924, Polish-born British Novelist)

19 History shows that there are no invincible armies.
Joseph Stalin (1879-1953, Georgian-born Soviet Leader)

20 Children play soldier. That makes sense. But why do soldiers play children?
Karl Kraus (1874-1936, Austrian Satirist)

21 The feeling about a soldier is, when all is said and done, he wasn't really going to do very much with his life anyway. The example usually is: "he wasn't going to compose Beethoven's Fifth."
Kurt Vonnegut Jr. (1922-, American Novelist)

22 The General Order is always to maneuver in a body and on the attack; to maintain strict but not pettifogging discipline; to keep the troops constantly at the ready; to employ the utmost vigilance on sentry go; to use the bayonet on every possible occasion; and to follow up the enemy remorselessly until he is utterly destroyed.
Lazare Carnot

23 What makes a regiment of soldiers a more noble object of view than the same mass of mob? Their arms, their dresses, their banners, and the art and artificial symmetry of their position and movements.
Lord Byron (1788-1824, British Poet)

24 An army without culture is a dull-witted army, and a dull-witted army cannot defeat the enemy.
Mao Zedong (1893-1976, Founder of Chinese Communist State)

25 That's what an army is -- a mob; they don't fight with courage that's born in them, but with courage that's borrowed from their mass, and from their officers.
Mark Twain (1835-1910, American Humorist, Writer)

26 There are few men more superstitious than soldiers. They are, after all, the men who live closest to death.
Mary Stewart

27 Standing armies can never consist of resolute robust men; they may be well-disciplined machines, but they will seldom contain men under the influence of strong passions, or with very vigorous faculties.
Mary Wollstonecraft (1759-1797, British Feminist Writer)

28 No profession or occupation is more pleasing than the military; a profession or exercise both noble in execution (for the strongest, most generous and proudest of all virtues is true valor) and noble in its cause. No utility either more just or universal than the protection of the repose or defense of the greatness of one's country. The company and daily conversation of so many noble, young and active men cannot but be well-pleasing to you.
Michel Eyquem De Montaigne (1533-1592, French Philosopher, Essayist)

29 The greatest general is he who makes the fewest mistakes.
Napoleon Bonaparte (1769-1821, French General, Emperor)

30 The army is the true nobility of our country.
Napoleon III (1808-1873, Third son of Louis Bonaparte, the President of the Second French Rep.)

31 I had rather have a plain, russet-coated Captain, that knows what he fights for, and loves what he knows, than that which you call a Gentle-man and is nothing else.
Oliver Cromwell (1599-1658, Parliamentarian General, Lord Protector of England)

32 There is something about going to sea. A little bit of discipline, self-discipline and humility are required.
Prince Andrew (British Prince)

33 The wonder is always new that any sane man can be a sailor.
Ralph Waldo Emerson (1803-1882, American Poet, Essayist)

34 The most advanced nations are always those who navigate the most.
Ralph Waldo Emerson (1803-1882, American Poet, Essayist)

35 When you're wounded and left on Afghanistan's plains, and the women come out to cut up what remains, jest roll to your rifle and blow out your brains and go to your gawd like a soldier.
Rudyard Kipling (1865-1936, British Author of Prose, Verse)

36 If I should die, think only this of me: that there's some corner of a foreign field that is for ever England.
Rupert Brooke (1887-1915, British Poet)

37 No man will be a sailor who has contrivance enough to get himself into a jail; for being in a ship is being in a jail, with the chance of being drowned. A man in a jail has more room, better food and commonly better company.
Samuel Johnson (1709-1784, British Author)

38 Every man thinks meanly of himself for not having been a soldier, or not having been at sea.
Samuel Johnson (1709-1784, British Author)

39 The military mind is indeed a menace. Old-fashioned futurity that sees only men fighting and dying in smoke and fire; hears nothing more civilized than a cannonade; scents nothing but the stink of battle-wounds and blood.
Sean O'Casey (1884-1964, Irish Dramatist)

40 I must have the gentleman to haul and draw with the mariner, and the mariner with the gentleman. I would know him, that would refuse to set his hand to a rope, but I know there is not any such here.
Sir Francis Drake (1540-1596, Elizabethan Seaman, Born in Crowndale, Devon)

41 We are as near to heaven by sea as by land.
Sir Humphrey Gilbert (1539-1583, British Navigator)

42 Conscription may have been good for the country, but it damn near killed the army.
Sir Richard Hull

43 The Royal Navy of England hath ever been its greatest defense and ornament; it is its ancient and natural strength; the floating bulwark of the island.
Sir William Blackstone (1723-1780, British Jurist)

44 If our soldiers are not overburdened with money, it is not because they have a distaste for riches; if their lives are not unduly long, it is not because they are disinclined to longevity.
Sun Tzu (400-430 BC, Chinese Military Strategist, Author of "Art of War")

45 There were gentlemen and there were seamen in the navy of Charles the Second. But the seamen were not gentlemen; and the gentlemen were not seamen.
Thomas B. Macaulay (1800-1859, American Essayist and Historian)

46 Making the world safe for hypocrisy.
Thomas Wolfe (1931-, American Author, Journalist)

47 In this country it's a good thing to kill an admiral now and then to encourage the others.
Voltaire (1694-1778, French Historian, Writer)

48 O the joy of the strong-brawn'd fighter, towering in the arena in perfect condition, conscious of power, thirsting to meet his opponent.
Walt Whitman (1819-1892, American Poet)

49 Those that I fight I do not hate, those that I guard I do not love.
William Butler Yeats (1865-1939, Irish Poet, Playwright.)

50 We few, we happy few, we band of brothers. For he today that sheds his blood with me shall be my brother; be never so vile. This day shall gentle his condition. And gentlemen in England now abed shall think themselves accursed they were not here, and hold their manhoods cheap whiles any speaks that fought with us upon Saint Crispin's day.
William Shakespeare (1564-1616, British Poet, Playwright, Actor)

51 'Tis the soldier's life to have their balmy slumbers waked with strife.
William Shakespeare (1564-1616, British Poet, Playwright, Actor)

52 Don't talk to me about naval tradition. It's nothing but rum, sodomy and the lash.
Winston Churchill (1874-1965, British Statesman, Prime Minister)

ARROGANCE

1 The need to be right is the sign of a vulgar mind.
Albert Camus (1913-1960, French Existential Writer)

2 Sure of their qualities and demanding praise, more go to ruined fortunes than are raised.
Alexander Pope (1688-1744, British Poet, Critic, Translator)

3 Nothing in the world is more haughty than a man of moderate capacity when once raised to power.
Baron Wessenberg

4 None are more unjust in their judgments of others than those who have a high opinion of themselves.
Charles Haddon Spurgeon (1834-1892, British Baptist Preacher)

5 Early in life, I had to choose between honest arrogance and hypocritical humility. I chose honest arrogance and have seen no occasions to change.
Frank Lloyd Wright (1869-1959, American Architect)

6 None are more haughty than a common place person raised to power.
French Proverb

ARTS AND ARTISTS

1 Twentieth-century art may start with nothing, but it flourishes by virtue of its belief in itself, in the possibility of control over what seems essentially uncontrollable, in the coherence of the inchoate, and in its ability to create its own values.
A. Alvarez (Born 1929, British Critic, Poet, Novelist)

2 Art is too serious to be taken seriously.
Ad Reinhardt (1913-1967, American Artist)

3 The art and science of asking questions is the source of all knowledge.
Adolf Berle (1937-1971, American Politician)

4 There is the falsely mystical view of art that assumes a kind of supernatural inspiration, a possession by universal forces unrelated to questions of power and privilege or the artist's relation to bread and blood. In this view, the channel of art can only become clogged and misdirected by the artist's concern with merely temporary and local disturbances. The song is higher than the struggle.
Adrienne Rich (1929-, American Poet)

5 Abstract Art: A product of the untalented, sold by the unprincipled to the utterly bewildered.
Al Capp (1909-1979, American Cartoonist)

6 To write is to become disinterested. There is a certain renunciation in art.
Albert Camus (1913-1960, French Existential Writer)

7 It is impossible to give a clear account of the world, but art can teach us to reproduce it --just as the world reproduces itself in the course of its eternal gyrations. The primordial sea indefatigably repeats the same words and casts up the same astonished beings on the same sea-shore.
Albert Camus (1913-1960, French Existential Writer)

8 The finest works of art are precious, among other reasons, because they make it possible for us to know, if only imperfectly and for a little while, what it actually feels like to think subtly and feel nobly.
Aldous Huxley (1894-1963, British Author)

9 The hidden harmony is better than the obvious.
Alexander Pope (1688-1744, British Poet, Critic, Translator)

10 Not everything has a name. Some things lead us into a realm beyond words.
Alexander Solzhenitsyn (1918-, Russian Novelist)

11 All great art, and today all great artlessness, must appear extreme to the mass of men, as we know them today. It springs from the anguish of great souls. From the souls of men not formed, but deformed in factories whose inspiration is pelf.
Alexander Trocchi (1925-1983, Italian-Scottish Novelist, Poet, Translator)

12 Art is the imposing of a pattern on experience, and our aesthetic enjoyment is recognition of the pattern.
Alfred North Whitehead (1861-1947, British Mathematician, Philosopher)

13 Fortunately art is a community effort --a small but select community living in a spiritualized world endeavoring to interpret the wars and the solitudes of the flesh.
Allen Ginsberg (1926-, American Poet)

14 In art as in love, instinct is enough.
Anatole France (1844-1924, French Writer)

15 The work of art, just like any fragment of human life considered in its deepest meaning, seems to me devoid of value if it does not offer the hardness, the rigidity, the regularity, the luster on every interior and exterior facet, of the crystal.
Andre Breton (1989-1966, French Surrealist)

16 The sole art that suits me is that which, rising from unrest, tends toward serenity.
Andre Gide (1869-1951, French Author)

17 Feminist art is not some tiny creek running off the great river of real art. It is not some crack in an otherwise flawless stone. It is, quite spectacularly I think, art which is not based on the subjugation of one half of the species. It is art which will take the great human themes --love, death, heroism, suffering, history itself --and render them fully human. It may also, though perhaps our imaginations are so mutilated now that we are incapable even of the ambition, introduce a new theme, one as great and as rich as those others --should we call it "joy"?
Andrea Dworkin (1946-, American Feminist Critic)

18 The art of creation is older than the art of killing.
Andrei Voznesensky

19 An artist is somebody who produces things that people don't need to have.
Andy Warhol (1930-, American Artist, Filmmaker)

20 Fine art, that exists for itself alone, is art in a final state of impotence. If nobody, including the artist, acknowledges art as a means of knowing the world, then art is relegated to a kind of rumpus room of the mind and the irresponsibility of the artist and the irrelevance of art to actual living becomes part and parcel of the practice of art.
Angela Carter (1940-1992, British Author)

21 Progressive art can assist people to learn not only about the objective forces at work in the society in which they live, but also about the intensely social character of their interior lives. Ultimately, it can propel people toward social emancipation.
Angela Y. Davis (1944-, American Political Activist)

22 Art is dangerous. It is one of the attractions: when it ceases to be dangerous you don't want it.
Anthony Burgess (1917-1993, British Writer, Critic)

23 I choose a block of marble and chop off whatever I don't need. [when asked how he managed to make his remarkable statues.]
Auguste Rodin (1840-1917, French Sculptor)

24 Art is a selective re-creation of reality according to an artist's metaphysical value-judgments. An artist recreates those aspects of reality which represent his fundamental view of man's nature.
Ayn Rand (1905-1982, Russian Writer, Philosopher)

25 I'm the artist formally known as Beck. I have a genius wig. When I put that wig on, then the true genius emerges. I don't have enough hair to be a genius. I think you have to have hair going everywhere.
Beck (1959-, American Musician, Singer, Songwriter)

26 Making social comment is an artificial place for an artist to start from. If an artist is touched by some social condition, what the artist creates will reflect that, but you can't force it.
Bella Lewitzky (1916-, American Dancer)

27 Art has an enemy called ignorance.
Ben Johnson (1573-1637, British Dramatist, Poet)

28 Art is a reality, not a definition; inasmuch as it approaches a reality, it approaches perfection, and inasmuch as it approaches a mere definition, it is imperfect and untrue.
Benjamin Haydon (1786-1846, British Artist)

29 Art is the signature of civilizations.
Beverly Sills (American Opera Singer)

30 There is no true expertise in the humanities without knowing all of the humanities. Art is a vast, ancient interconnected web-work, a fabricated tradition. Over-concentration on any one point is a distortion.
Camille Paglia (1947-, American Author, Critic, Educator)

31 I don't want life to imitate art. I want life to be art.
Carrie Fisher (1956-, American Actress, Novelist)

32 A frenzied passion for art is a canker that devours everything else.
Charles Baudelaire (1821-1867, French Poet)

33 The more a man cultivates the arts the less he fornicates. A more and more apparent cleavage occurs between the spirit and the brute.
Charles Baudelaire (1821-1867, French Poet)

34 Art is an absolute mistress; she will not be coquetted with or slighted; she requires the most entire self-devotion, and she repays with grand triumphs.
Charlotte Saunders Cushman (1816-1876, American Actor)

35 The great artist is a slave to his ideals.
Christian Nevell Bovee (1820-1904, American Author, Lawyer)

36 The function of art is to make that understood which in the form of argument would be incomprehensible.
Constantin Brancusi (1876-1957, Romanian Sculptor)

37 To say that a work of art is good, but incomprehensible to the majority of men, is the same as saying of some kind of food that it is very good but that most people can't eat it.
Count Leo Tolstoy (1828-1910, Russian Novelist, Philosopher)

38 The reward of art is not fame or success but intoxication: that is why so many bad artists are unable to give it up.
Cyril Connolly (1903-1974, British Critic)

39 The artist is a member of the leisured classes who cannot pay for his leisure.
Cyril Connolly (1903-1974, British Critic)

40 Every great work of art has two faces, one toward its own time and one toward the future, toward eternity.
Daniel Barenboim (1942-, Argentinean-born Israeli Pianist, Conductor)

41 If we are to change our world view, images have to change. The artist now has a very important job to do. He's not a little peripheral figure entertaining rich people, he's really needed.
David Hockney (1937-, British Artist)

42 Art is a form of catharsis.
Dorothy Parker (1893-1967, American Humorous Writer)

43 Of all the arts in which the wise excel, nature's chief masterpiece is writing well.
Duke of Buckingham (1628-1687, British Poet, Satirist, Dramatist)

44 Were I called on to define, very briefly, the term Art, I should call it "the reproduction of what the Senses perceive in Nature through the veil of the soul." The mere imitation, however accurate, of what is in Nature, entitles no man to the sacred name of "Artist."
Edgar Allan Poe (1809-1845, American Poet, Critic, short-story Writer)

45 The perfection of art is to conceal art.
Edgar Quinet (1803-1875, French Poet, Historian, Politician)

46 As a general truth, it is safe to say that any picture that produces a moral impression is a bad picture.
Edmond and Jules De Goncourt (1822-1896, French Writers)

47 A painting in a museum probably hears more foolish remarks than anything else in the world.
Edmond and Jules De Goncourt (1822-1896, French Writers)

48 Those who write for lucre or fame are grosser than the cartel robbers, for they steal the genius of the people, which is its will to resist evil.
Edward Dahlberg (1900-1977, American Author, Critic)

49 Art for art's sake? I should think so, and more so than ever at the present time. It is the one orderly product which our middling race has produced. It is the cry of a thousand sentinels, the echo from a thousand labyrinths, it is the lighthouse which cannot be hidden... it is the best evidence we can have of our dignity.
Edward M. Forster (1879-1970, British Novelist, Essayist)

50 Contrary to popular belief an artist is never ahead of his time, but most people are far behind theirs.
Edward Varese

51 Each of the arts whose office is to refine, purify, adorn, embellish and grace life is under the patronage of a muse, no god being found worthy to preside over them.
Eliza Farnham (American Author and Social Reformist)

52 What is art but life upon the larger scale, the higher. When, graduating up in a spiral line of still expanding and ascending gyres, it pushes toward the intense significance of all things, hungry for the infinite?
Elizabeth Barrett Browning (1806-1861, British Poet)

53 Art is the only thing that can go on mattering, once it has stopped hurting.
Elizabeth Bowen (1899-1973, Anglo-Irish Novelist)

54 Art, that great undogmatized church.
Ellen Key (1849-1926, Swedish Author, Feminist)

55 I am an artist... I am here to live out loud.
Emile Zola (1840-1902, French Novelist)

56 Art is skill, that is the first meaning of the word.
Eric Gill (1882-1940, British Sculptor, Engraver, Writer, Typographer)

57 In a decaying society, art, if it is truthful, must also reflect decay. And unless it wants to break faith with its social function, art must show the world as changeable. And help to change it.
Ernst Fischer (1899-1972, Austrian Editor, Poet, Critic)

58 A work of art is above all an adventure of the mind.
Eugene Ionesco (1912-, Romanian-born French Playwright)

59 Artists who seek perfection in everything are those who cannot attain it in anything.
EugFne Delacroix (1798-1863, French Artist)

60 An artist must be a reactionary. He has to stand out against the tenor of the age and not go flopping along.
Evelyn Waugh (1903-1966, British Novelist)

61 Humanity is the rich effluvium, it is the waste and the manure and the soil, and from it grows the tree of the arts.
Ezra Pound (1885-1972, American Poet, Critic)

62 But the one thing you should. not do is to suppose that when something is wrong with the arts, it is wrong with the arts ONLY.
Ezra Pound (1885-1972, American Poet, Critic)

63 Good art however "immoral" is wholly a thing of virtue. Good art can NOT be immoral. By good art I mean art that bears true witness, I mean the art that is most precise.
Ezra Pound (1885-1972, American Poet, Critic)

64 Wherever art appears, life disappears.
Francis Picabia (1878-1953, French Painter, Poet)

65 Pictures deface walls more often than they decorate them.
Frank Lloyd Wright (1869-1959, American Architect)

66 Art is not merely an imitation of the reality of nature, but in truth a metaphysical supplement to the reality of nature, placed alongside thereof for its conquest.
Friedrich Nietzsche (1844-1900, German Philosopher)

67 Art raises its head where creeds relax.
Friedrich Nietzsche (1844-1900, German Philosopher)

68 We have art in order not to die of the truth.
Friedrich Nietzsche (1844-1900, German Philosopher)

69 Great art is never produced for its own sake. It is too difficult to be worth the effort.
George Bernard Shaw (1856-1950, Irish-born British Dramatist)

70 It is not in life, but in art that self-fulfillment is to be found.
George E. Woodberry (1855-1930, American Literary Critic)

71 To speak of morals in art is to speak of legislature in sex. Art is the sex of the imagination.
George Jean Nathan (1882-1958, American Critic)

72 Caricature is rough truth.
George Meredith (1828-1909, British Author)

73 Art is not a study of positive reality, it is the seeking for ideal truth.
George Sand (1804-1876, French Novelist)

74 The effort of art is to keep what is interesting in existence, to recreate it in the eternal.
George Santayana (1863-1952, American Philosopher, Poet)

75 The contemporary thing in art and literature is the thing which doesn't make enough difference to the people of that generation so that they can accept it or reject it.
Gertrude Stein (1874-1946, American Author)

76 Art, like morality, consists in drawing the line somewhere.
Gilbert K. Chesterton (1874-1936, British Author)

77 The dignity of the artist lies in his duty of keeping awake the sense of wonder in the world. In this long vigil he often has to vary his methods of stimulation; but in this long vigil he is also himself striving against a continual tendency to sleep.
Gilbert K. Chesterton (1874-1936, British Author)

78 The artistic temperament is a disease that affects amateurs. Artists of a large and wholesome vitality get rid of their art easily, as they breathe easily or perspire easily. But in artists of less force, the thing becomes a pressure, and produces a definite pain, which is called the artistic temperament.
Gilbert K. Chesterton (1874-1936, British Author)

79 Art consists of limitation. The most beautiful part of every picture is the frame.
Gilbert K. Chesterton (1874-1936, British Author)

80 If I didn't start painting, I would have raised chickens.
Grandma Moses (1860-1961, American Artist)

81 Artists are, above all, men who want to become inhuman.
Guillaume Apollinaire (1880-1918, Italian-born French Poet, Critic)

82 Without poets, without artists, men would soon weary of nature's monotony. The sublime idea men have of the universe would collapse with dizzying speed. The order which we find in nature, and which is only an effect of art, would at once vanish. Everything would break up in chaos. There would be no seasons, no civilization, no thought, no humanity; even life would give way, and the impotent void would reign everywhere.
Guillaume Apollinaire (1880-1918, Italian-born French Poet, Critic)

83 Art is so wonderfully irrational, exuberantly pointless, but necessary all the same. Pointless and yet necessary, that's hard for a puritan to understand.
Gunther Grass (1927-, German Author)

84 Art need no longer be an account of past sensations. It can become the direct organization of more highly evolved sensations. It is a question of producing ourselves, not things that enslave us.
Guy Debord (1931-, French Philosopher)

85 Only conservatives believe that subversion is still being carried on in the arts and that society is being shaken by it. Advanced art today is no longer a cause --it contains no moral imperative. There is no virtue in clinging to principles and standards, no vice in selling or in selling out.
Harold Rosenberg (1906-1978, American Art Critic, Author)

86 What better way to prove that you understand a subject than to make money out of it?
Harold Rosenberg (1906-1978, American Art Critic, Author)

87 If that's art, I'm a Hottentot!
Harry S. Truman (1884-1972, Thirty-third President of the USA)

88 Every artist writes his own autobiography.
Havelock Ellis (1859-1939, British Psychologist)

89 There is nothing more difficult for a truly creative painter than to paint a rose, because before he can do so he has first to forget all the roses that were ever painted.
Henri Matisse (1869-1954, French Artist)

90 The history of modern art is also the history of the progressive loss of art's audience. Art has increasingly become the concern of the artist and the bafflement of the public.
Henry Geldzahler (1935-, Belgium-born American Curator, Art Critic)

91 It is art that makes life, makes interest, makes importance and I know of no substitute whatever for the force and beauty of its process.
Henry James (1843-1916, American Author)

92 Art teaches nothing, except the significance of life.
Henry Miller (1891-1980, American Author)

93 Art is only a means to life, to the life more abundant. It is not in itself the life more abundant. It merely points the way, something which is overlooked not only by the public, but very often by the artist himself. In becoming an end it defeats itself.
Henry Miller (1891-1980, American Author)

94 The artist is the opposite of the politically minded individual, the opposite of the reformer, the opposite of the idealist. The artist does not tinker with the universe; he recreates it out of his own experience and understanding of life.
Henry Miller (1891-1980, American Author)

95 Nature is a revelation of God; Art a revelation of man.
Henry Wadsworth Longfellow (1819-1892, American Poet)

96 Art is the child of Nature; yes, her darling child, in whom we trace the features of the mother's face, her aspect and her attitude.
Henry Wadsworth Longfellow (1819-1892, American Poet)

97 The more minimal the art, the more maximum the explanation.
Hilton Kramer

98 A picture is a poem without words.
Horace (65-8 BC, Italian Poet)

99 Art is the final cunning of the human soul which would rather do anything than face the gods.
Iris Murdoch (1919-, British Novelist, Philosopher)

100 Pop artists deal with the lowly trivia of possessions and equipment that the present generation is lugging along with it on its safari into the future.
J. G. Ballard (1930-, British Author)

101 Art distills sensations and embodies it with enhanced meaning.
Jacques Barzun (1907-, American Scholar)

102 Inside you there's an artist you don't know about. He's not interested in how things look different in moonlight.
Jalal-Uddin Rumi (1207-1273, Persian Sufi Mystic Poet)

103 The primary distinction of the artist is that he must actively cultivate that state which most men, necessarily, must avoid: the state of being alone.
James Baldwin (1924-1987, American Author)

104 Art is the human disposition of sensible or intelligible matter for an esthetic end.
James Joyce (1882-1941, Irish Author)

105 Art -- the one achievement of Man which has made the long trip up from all fours seem well advised.
James Thurber (1894-1961, American Humorist, Illustrator)

106 Art is a fruit that grows in man, like a fruit on a plant, or a child in its mother's womb.
Jean Arp (1887-1948, French-German Artist, Poet)

107 Art is science made clear.
Jean Cocteau (1889-1963, French Author, Filmmaker)

108 One must be a living man and a posthumous artist.
Jean Cocteau (1889-1963, French Author, Filmmaker)

109 Art is the most passionate orgy within man's grasp.
Jean Dubuffet (1901-1985, French Sculptor, Painter)

110 Art attracts us only by what it reveals of our most secret self.
Jean-Luc Godard (1930-, French Filmmaker, Author)

111 As noble Art has survived noble nature, so too she marches ahead of it, fashioning and awakening by her inspiration. Before Truth sends her triumphant light into the depths of the heart, imagination catches its rays, and the peaks of humanity will be glowing when humid night still lingers in the valleys.
Johann Friedrich Von Schiller (1759-1805, German Dramatist, Poet, Historian)

112 The artist is the child of his time; but woe to him if he is also its disciple, or even its favorite.
Johann Friedrich Von Schiller (1759-1805, German Dramatist, Poet, Historian)

113 One of the most striking signs of the decay of art is when we see its separate forms jumbled together.
Johann Wolfgang Von Goethe (1749-1832, German Poet, Dramatist, Novelist)

114 The biggest problem with every art is by the use of appearance to create a loftier reality.
Johann Wolfgang Von Goethe (1749-1832, German Poet, Dramatist, Novelist)

115 Personality is everything in art and poetry.
Johann Wolfgang Von Goethe (1749-1832, German Poet, Dramatist, Novelist)

116 Art is long, life short, judgment difficult, opportunity transient.
Johann Wolfgang Von Goethe (1749-1832, German Poet, Dramatist, Novelist)

117 The highest problem of any art is to cause by appearance the illusion of a higher reality.
Johann Wolfgang Von Goethe (1749-1832, German Poet, Dramatist, Novelist)

118 I can't tell you what art does and how it does it, but I know that often art has judged the judges, pleaded revenge to the innocent and shown to the future what the past suffered, so that it has never been forgotten. Art, when it functions like this, becomes a meeting-place of the invisible, the irreducible, the enduring, guts, and honor.
John Berger (1926-, British Actor, Critic)

119 The artist is extremely lucky who is presented with the worst possible ordeal which will not actually kill him. At that point, he's in business.
John Berryman (1914-1972, American Poet)

120 Modern art is what happens when painters stop looking at girls and persuade themselves they have a better idea.
John Ciardi (1916-1986, American Teacher, Poet, Writer)

121 The arts are not just instantaneous pleasure -- if you don't like it, the artist is wrong. I belong to the generation which says if you don't like it, you don't understand and you ought to find out.
John Drummond

122 If art is to nourish the roots of our culture, society must set the artist free to follow his vision wherever it takes him.
John F. Kennedy (1917-1963, Thirty-fifth President of the USA)

123 I see little of more importance to the future of our country and of civilization than full recognition of the place of the artist. If art is to nourish the roots of our culture, society must set the artist free to follow his vision wherever it takes him.
John F. Kennedy (1917-1963, Thirty-fifth President of the USA)

124 In free society art is not a weapon. Artists are not engineers of the soul.
John F. Kennedy (1917-1963, Thirty-fifth President of the USA)

125 What distinguishes a great artist from a weak one is first their sensibility and tenderness; second, their imagination, and third, their industry.
John Ruskin (1819-1900, British Critic, Social Theorist)

126 No art can be noble which is incapable of expressing thought, and no art is capable of expressing thought which does not change.
John Ruskin (1819-1900, British Critic, Social Theorist)

127 I have seen, and heard, much of Cockney impudence before now; but never expected to hear a coxcomb ask two hundred guineas for flinging a pot of paint in the public's face.
John Ruskin (1819-1900, British Critic, Social Theorist)

128 Art imitates Nature in this; not to dare is to dwindle.
John Updike (1932-, American Novelist, Critic)

129 Were art to redeem man, it could do so only by saving him from the seriousness of life and restoring him to an unexpected boyishness.
Jose Ortega Y Gasset (1883-1955, Spanish Essayist, Philosopher)

130 An artist is a man of action, whether he creates a personality, invents an expedient, or finds the issue of a complicated situation.
Joseph Conrad (1857-1924, Polish-born British Novelist)

131 Any work that aspires, however humbly, to the condition of art should carry its justification in every line.
Joseph Conrad (1857-1924, Polish-born British Novelist)

132 Art is parasitic on life, just as criticism is parasitic on art.
Kenneth Tynan (1927-1980, British Critic)

133 A good traveler has no fixed plans and is not intent upon arriving. A good artist lets his intuition lead him wherever it wants.
Lao-Tzu (600 BC, Chinese Philosopher, Founder of Taoism, Author of the "Tao Te Ching")

134 Art, whose honesty must work through artifice, cannot avoid cheating truth.
Laura Riding (1901-1991, American Poet)

135 For us artists there waits the joyous compromise through art with all that wounded or defeated us in daily life; in this way, not to evade destiny, as the ordinary people try to do, but to fulfil it in its true potential --the imagination.
Lawrence Durrell (1912-1990, British Author)

136 If the Revolution has the right to destroy bridges and art monuments whenever necessary, it will stop still less from laying its hand on any tendency in art which, no matter how great its achievement in form, threatens to disintegrate the revolutionary environment or to arouse the internal forces of the Revolution, that is, the proletariat, the peasantry and the intelligentsia, to a hostile opposition to one another. Our standard is, clearly, political, imperative and intolerant.
Leon Trotsky (1879-1940, Russian Revolutionary)

137 The first mistake of Art is to assume that it's serious.
Lester Bangs (1948-1982, American Rock Journalist)

[138] Art is an experience, not the formulation of a problem.
Lindsay Anderson (1923-, British Film Director)

[139] A primary function of art and thought is to liberate the individual from the tyranny of his culture in the environmental sense and to permit him to stand beyond it in an autonomy of perception and judgment.
Lionel Trilling (1905-1975, American Critic)

[140] The vitality of a new movement in Art must be gauged by the fury it arouses.
Logan Pearsall Smith (1865-1946, Anglo-American Essayist, Aphorist)

[141] In art there are tears that lie too deep for thought.
Louis Kronenberger

[142] Art! Who comprehends her? With whom can one consult concerning this great goddess?
Ludwig Van Beethoven (1770-1827, German Composer)

[143] No one should drive a hard bargain with an artist.
Ludwig Van Beethoven (1770-1827, German Composer)

[144] In any society, the artist has a responsibility. His effectiveness is certainly limited and a painter or writer cannot change the world. But they can keep an essential margin of non-conformity alive. Thanks to them the powerful can never affirm that everyone agrees with their acts. That small difference is important.
Luis Bunuel (1900-1983, Spanish Film Director)

[145] There is in fact no such thing as art for art's sake, art that stands above classes, art that is detached from or independent of politics. Proletarian literature and art are part of the whole proletarian revolutionary cause.
Mao Zedong (1893-1976, Founder of Chinese Communist State)

[146] When I am finishing a picture I hold some God-made object up to it -- a rock, a flower, the branch of a tree or my hand -- as a kind of final test. If the painting stands up beside a thing man cannot make, the painting is authentic. If there's a clash between the two, it is bad art.
Marc Chagall (1889-1985, French Artist)

[147] When I judge art, I take my painting and put it next to a God made object like a tree or flower. If it clashes, it is not art.
Marc Chagall (1889-1985, French Artist)

[148] A work of art that contains theories is like an object on which the price tag has been left.
Marcel Proust (1871-1922, French Novelist)

[149] One thing that makes art different from life is that in art things have a shape... it allows us to fix our emotions on events at the moment they occur, it permits a union of heart and mind and tongue and tear.
Marilyn French (1929-, American Author, Critic)

[150] Art at its most significant is a distant early warning system that can always be relied on to tell the old culture what is beginning to happen.
Marshall Mcluhan (1911-1980, Canadian Communications Theorist)

[151] Ads are the cave art of the twentieth century.
Marshall Mcluhan (1911-1980, Canadian Communications Theorist)

[152] As the unity of the modern world becomes increasingly a technological rather than a social affair, the techniques of the arts provide the most valuable means of insight into the real direction of our own collective purposes.
Marshall Mcluhan (1911-1980, Canadian Communications Theorist)

[153] The defining function of the artist is to cherish consciousness.
Max Eastman (American Commentator, Writer)

[154] The moment you cheat for the sake of beauty, you know you're an artist.
Max Jacob

[155] A man paints with his brains and not with his hands.
Michelangelo (1474-1564, Italian Renaissance Painter, Sculptor)

[156] The essence of all art is to have pleasure in giving pleasure
Mikhail Baryshnikov (1948-, Soviet Dancer, Actor)

[157] I'm still an artist. I'm never gonna do a shit movie, because I've got my modeling to support me.
Milla Jovovich (Born 1975, Soviet-born Actress, Model, Singer, Songwriter)

[158] Art is on the side of the oppressed. Think before you shudder at the simplistic dictum and its heretical definition of the freedom of art. For if art is freedom of the spirit, how can it exist within the oppressors?
Nadine Gordimer (1923-, South African Author)

[159] Art is good when it springs from necessity. This kind of origin is the guarantee of its value; there is no other.
Neal Cassady (1926-1968, American Beat Hero)

[160] The final purpose of art is to intensify, even, if necessary, to exacerbate, the moral consciousness of people.
Norman Mailer (1923-, American Author)

[161] Nature is inside art as its content, not outside as its model.
Northrop Frye (1912-1991, Canadian Literary Critic)

[162] The artist belongs to their work, not the work to the artist.
Novalis (1772-1801, German Poet, Novelist)

[163] Only an artist can interpret the meaning of life.
Novalis (1772-1801, German Poet, Novelist)

[164] What distinguishes modern art from the art of other ages is criticism.
Octavio Paz (1914-, Mexican Poet, Essayist)

[165] In a very ugly and sensible age, the arts borrow, not from life, but from each other.
Oscar Wilde (1856-1900, British Author, Wit)

[166] All art is quite useless.
Oscar Wilde (1856-1900, British Author, Wit)

167 Modern pictures are, no doubt, delightful to look at. At least, some of them are. But they are quite impossible to live with; they are too clever, too assertive, too intellectual. Their meaning is too obvious, and their method too clearly defined. One
Oscar Wilde (1856-1900, British Author, Wit)

168 No great artist ever sees things as they really are, if he did he would cease to be an artist.
Oscar Wilde (1856-1900, British Author, Wit)

169 Bad artists always admire each other's work. They call it being large-minded and free from prejudice. But a truly great artist cannot conceive of life being shown, or beauty fashioned, under any conditions other than those he has selected.
Oscar Wilde (1856-1900, British Author, Wit)

170 Art, like Nature, has her monsters, things of bestial shape and with hideous voices.
Oscar Wilde (1856-1900, British Author, Wit)

171 Bad art is a great deal worse than no art at all.
Oscar Wilde (1856-1900, British Author, Wit)

172 Art is a lie that makes us realize the truth.
Pablo Picasso (1881-1973, Spanish Artist)

173 The people who make art their business are mostly impostors.
Pablo Picasso (1881-1973, Spanish Artist)

174 Often while reading a book one feels that the author would have preferred to paint rather than write; one can sense the pleasure he derives from describing a landscape or a person, as if he were painting what he is saying, because deep in his heart he would have preferred to use brushes and colors.
Pablo Picasso (1881-1973, Spanish Artist)

175 Art washes away from the soul the dust of everyday life.
Pablo Picasso (1881-1973, Spanish Artist)

176 We all know that Art is not truth. Art is a lie that makes us realize truth, at least the truth that is given us to understand. The artist must know the manner whereby to convince others of the truthfulness of his lies.
Pablo Picasso (1881-1973, Spanish Artist)

177 Through art we express our conception of what nature is not.
Pablo Picasso (1881-1973, Spanish Artist)

178 If I spit, they will take my spit and frame it as great art.
Pablo Picasso (1881-1973, Spanish Artist)

179 With an apple I will astonish Paris.
Paul Cezanne (1839-1906. French Painter)

180 Art is either plagiarism or revolution.
Paul Gauguin (1848-1903, French Artist)

181 The more horrifying this world becomes, the more art becomes abstract.
Paul Klee (1879-1940, Swiss Artist)

182 Art does not reproduce the visible; rather, it makes visible.
Paul Klee (1879-1940, Swiss Artist)

183 Irresponsibility is part of the pleasure of all art; it is the part the schools cannot recognize.
Pauline Kael (1919-, American Film Critic)

184 He bores me. He ought to have stuck to his flying machine. [On Leonardo Da Vinci]
Pierre Auguste Renoir (1841-1919, French Impressionist Artist)

185 The highest art is always the most religious, and the greatest artist is always a devout person.
Professor Blackie

186 What is Art? It is the response of man's creative soul to the call of the Real.
Rabindranath Tagore (1861-1941, Indian Poet, Philosopher)

187 Surely all art is the result of one's having been in danger, of having gone through an experience all the way to the end, where no one can go any further.
Rainer Maria Rilke (1875-1926, German Poet)

188 The true poem is the poet's mind.
Ralph Waldo Emerson (1803-1882, American Poet, Essayist)

189 Classic art was the art of necessity: modern romantic art bears the stamp of caprice and chance.
Ralph Waldo Emerson (1803-1882, American Poet, Essayist)

190 The True Artist has the planet for his pedestal; the adventurer, after years of strife, has nothing broader than his shoes.
Ralph Waldo Emerson (1803-1882, American Poet, Essayist)

191 The arts and inventions of each period are only its costume, and do not invigorate men.
Ralph Waldo Emerson (1803-1882, American Poet, Essayist)

192 Sculpture and painting have the effect of teaching us manners and abolishing hurry.
Ralph Waldo Emerson (1803-1882, American Poet, Essayist)

193 Perpetual modernness is the measure of merit in every work of art.
Ralph Waldo Emerson (1803-1882, American Poet, Essayist)

194 New arts destroy the old.
Ralph Waldo Emerson (1803-1882, American Poet, Essayist)

195 Every artist was first an amateur.
Ralph Waldo Emerson (1803-1882, American Poet, Essayist)

196 Each work of art excludes the world, concentrates attention on itself. For the time it is the only thing worth doing --to do just that; be it a sonnet, a statue, a landscape, an outline head of Caesar, or an oration. Presently we return to the sight of another that globes itself into a whole as did the first, for example, a beautiful garden; and nothing seems worth doing in life but laying out a garden.
Ralph Waldo Emerson (1803-1882, American Poet, Essayist)

197 Artists must be sacrificed to their art.
Ralph Waldo Emerson (1803-1882, American Poet, Essayist)

198 Art is the path of the creator to his work.
Ralph Waldo Emerson (1803-1882, American Poet, Essayist)

199 Art is a jealous mistress; and if a man have a genius for painting, poetry, music, architecture or philosophy, he makes a bad husband and an ill provider.
Ralph Waldo Emerson (1803-1882, American Poet, Essayist)

200 The creative artist seems to be almost the only kind of man that you could never meet on neutral ground. You can only meet him as an artist. He sees nothing objectively because his own ego is always in the foreground of every picture.
Raymond Chandler (1888-1959, American Author)

201 Most works of art, like most wines, ought to be consumed in the district of their fabrication.
Rebecca West (1892-1983, British Author)

202 Experiment is necessary in establishing an academy, but certain principles must apply to this business of art as to any other business which affects the artistic tic sense of the community. Great art speaks a language which every intelligent person can understand. The people who call themselves modernists today speak a different language.
Robert Menzies (1894-1978, Australian Liberal Politician, Prime Minister)

203 The public history of modern art is the story of conventional people not knowing what they are dealing with.
Robert Motherwell (1915-1991, American Artist)

204 Nothing right can be accomplished in art without enthusiasm.
Robert Schumann (1810-1856, German Composer)

205 The artist vocation is to send light into the human heart.
Robert Schumann (1810-1856, German Composer)

206 The moment you think you understand a great work of art, it's dead for you.
Robert Wilson (1941-, American Theater Director, Designer)

207 And the first rude sketch that the world had seen was joy to his mighty heart, till the Devil whispered behind the leaves "It's pretty, but is it Art?"
Rudyard Kipling (1865-1936, British Author of Prose, Verse)

208 Not even the visionary or mystical experience ever lasts very long. It is for art to capture that experience, to offer it to, in the case of literature, its readers; to be, for a secular, materialist culture, some sort of replacement for what the love of god offers in the world of faith.
Salman Rushdie (1948-, Indian-born British Author)

209 This grandiose tragedy that we call modern art.
Salvador Dali (1904-1989, Spanish Painter)

210 It is either easy or impossible.
Salvador Dali (1904-1989, Spanish Painter)

211 There is only one difference between a madman and me. I am not mad.
Salvador Dali (1904-1989, Spanish Painter)

212 The youth of an art is, like the youth of anything else, its most interesting period. When it has come to the knowledge of good and evil it is stronger, but we care less about it.
Samuel Butler (1612-1680, British Poet, Satirist)

213 No man but a blockhead ever wrote, except for money.
Samuel Johnson (1709-1784, British Author)

214 As for types like my own, obscurely motivated by the conviction that our existence was worthless if we didn't make a turning point of it, we were assigned to the humanities, to poetry, philosophy, painting -- the nursery games of humankind, which had to be left behind when the age of science began. The humanities would be called upon to choose a wallpaper for the crypt, as the end drew near.
Saul Bellow (1915-, American Novelist)

215 Any artist should be grateful for a naive grace which puts him beyond the need to reason elaborately.
Saul Bellow (1915-, American Novelist)

216 All art is an imitation of nature.
Seneca (4 BC-65 AD, Spanish-born Roman Statesman, philosopher)

217 In order for the artist to have a world to express he must first be situated in this world, oppressed or oppressing, resigned or rebellious, a man among men.
Simone De Beauvoir (1908-1986, French Novelist, Essayist)

218 Art is the symbol of the two noblest human efforts: to construct and to refrain from destruction.
Simone Weil (1910-1943, French Philosopher, Mystic)

219 In other countries, art and literature are left to a lot of shabby bums living in attics and feeding on booze and spaghetti, but in America the successful writer or picture-painter is indistinguishable from any other decent businessman.
Sinclair Lewis (1885-1951, First American Novelist to win the Nobel Prize for literature)

220 As the twentieth century ends, commerce and culture are coming closer together. The distinction between life and art has been eroded by fifty years of enhanced communications, ever- improving reproduction technologies and increasing wealth.
Stephen Bayley (1951-, British Design Critic)

221 Much of modern art is devoted to lowering the threshold of what is terrible. By getting us used to what, formerly, we could not bear to see or hear, because it was too shocking, painful, or embarrassing, art changes morals.
Susan Sontag (1933-, American Essayist)

222 Art is the objectification of feeling.
Suzanne K. Langer (1895-1985, American Philosopher)

223 The progress of an artist is a continual self-sacrifice, a continual extinction of personality.
T. S. Eliot (1888-1965, American-born British Poet, Critic)

224 Art never improves, but the material of art is never quite the same.
T. S. Eliot (1888-1965, American-born British Poet, Critic)

225 Art is permitted to survive only if it renounces the right to be different, and integrates itself into the omnipotent realm of the profane.
Theodor W. Adorno (1903-1969, German Philosopher, Sociologist, Music Critic)

226 What is art but a way of seeing?
Thomas Berger

227 This is the artist, then, life's hungry man, the glutton of eternity, beauty's miser, glory's slave.
Thomas Wolfe (1931-, American Author, Journalist)

228 The notion that the public accepts or rejects anything in modern art is merely romantic fiction. The game is completed and the trophies distributed long before the public knows what has happened.
Thomas Wolfe (1931-, American Author, Journalist)

229 Art is a private thing, the artist makes it for himself; a comprehensible work is the product of a journalist. We need works that are strong, straight, precise, and forever beyond understanding.
Tristan Tzara (1896-1963, Rumanian-born French Dadaist)

230 There is only one art, whose sole criterion is the power, the authenticity, the revelatory insight, the courage and suggestiveness with which it seeks its truth. Thus, from the standpoint of the work and its worth it is irrelevant to which political ideas the artist as a citizen claims allegiance, which ideas he would like to serve with his work or whether he holds any such ideas at all.
Vaclav Havel (1936-, Czech Playwright, President)

231 It is not the language of painters but the language of nature which one should listen to, the feeling for the things themselves, for reality, is more important than the feeling for pictures.
Vincent Van Gogh (1853-1890, Dutch-born French Painter)

232 I can't work without a model. I won't say I turn my back on nature ruthlessly in order to turn a study into a picture, arranging the colors, enlarging and simplifying; but in the matter of form I am too afraid of departing from the possible and the true.
Vincent Van Gogh (1853-1890, Dutch-born French Painter)

233 The greater the decrease in the social significance of an art form, the sharper the distinction between criticism and enjoyment by the public. The conventional is uncritically enjoyed, and the truly new is criticized with aversion.
Walter Benjamin (1982-1940, German Critic, Philosopher)

234 Artistic growth is, more than it is anything else, a refining of the sense of truthfulness. The stupid believe that to be truthful is easy; only the artist, the great artist, knows how difficult it is.
Willa Cather (1876-1947, American Author)

235 Religion and art spring from the same root and are close kin. Economics and art are strangers.
Willa Cather (1876-1947, American Author)

236 An artist is forced by others to paint out of his own free will.
Willem De Kooning (1904-, Dutch-born American Artist)

237 Whatever an artist's personal feelings are, as soon as an artist fills a certain area on the canvas or circumscribes it, he becomes historical. He acts from or upon other artists.
Willem De Kooning (1904-, Dutch-born American Artist)

238 In art, one idea is as good as another. If one takes the idea of trembling, for instance, all of a sudden most art starts to tremble. Michelangelo starts to tremble. El Greco starts to tremble. All the Impressionists start to tremble.
Willem De Kooning (1904-, Dutch-born American Artist)

239 An artist is a creature driven by demons. He doesn't know why they choose him and he's usually too busy to wonder why.
William Faulkner (1897-1962, American Novelist)

240 The aim of every artist is to arrest motion, which is life, by artificial means and hold it fixed so that a hundred years later, when a stranger looks at it, it moves again since it is life. Since man is mortal, the only immortality possible for him is to leave something behind him that is immortal since it will always move. This is the artist's way of scribbling "Kilroy was here" on the wall of the final and irrevocable oblivion through which he must someday pass.
William Faulkner (1897-1962, American Novelist)

241 Art is man's expression of his joy in labor.
William Morris (1834-1896, British Artist, Writer, Printer)

242 Artists to my mind are the real architects of change, and not the political legislators who implement change after the fact.
William S. Burroughs (1914-1997, American Writer)

243 O, had I but followed the arts!
William Shakespeare (1564-1616, British Poet, Playwright, Actor)

244 The object of art is to give life a shape. [Midsummer Nights Dream]
William Shakespeare (1564-1616, British Poet, Playwright, Actor)

245 Is there not an art, a music, and a stream of words that shalt be life, the acknowledged voice of life?
William Wordsworth (1770-1850, British Poet)

246 The artist must conceive with warmth yet execute with coolness.
Winkelmann

247 Without tradition, art is a flock of sheep without a shepherd. Without innovation, it is a corpse.
Winston Churchill (1874-1965, British Statesman, Prime Minister)

248 Art for art's sake is a philosophy of the well-fed.
Yu Cao (1910-, Chinese Dramatist)

ASCETICISM

1 To attempt the destruction of our passions is the height of folly. What a noble aim is that of the zealot who tortures himself like a madman in order to desire nothing, love nothing, feel nothing, and who, if he succeeded, would end up a complete monster!
Denis Diderot (1713-1784, French Philosopher)

2 The ascetic makes a necessity of virtue.
Friedrich Nietzsche (1844-1900, German Philosopher)

3 In every ascetic morality man worships a part of himself as God and for that he needs to diabolize the other part.
Friedrich Nietzsche (1844-1900, German Philosopher)

4 The main motive for "nonattachment" is a desire to escape from the pain of living, and above all from love, which, sexual or non-sexual, is hard work.
George Orwell (1903-1950, British Author, "Animal Farm")

5 If a hermit lives in a state of ecstasy, his lack of comfort becomes the height of comfort. He must relinquish it.
Jean Cocteau (1889-1963, French Author, Filmmaker)

6 The principle of asceticism never was, nor ever can be, consistently pursued by any living creature. Let but one tenth part of the inhabitants of the earth pursue it consistently, and in a day's time they will have turned it into a Hell.
Jeremy Bentham (1748-1832, British Philosopher, Jurist, Political Theorist)

ASK

1 If one asks the whence derives the authority of fundamental ends, since they cannot be stated and justified merely by reason, one can only answer: they exist in a healthy society as powerful traditions, which act upon the conduct and aspirations and judgments of the individuals; they are there, that is, as something living, without its being necessary to find justification for their existence.
Albert Einstein (1879-1955, German-born American Physicist)

2 Ask with urgency and passion.
Arthur James Balfour (1848-1930, British Conservative Politician, Prime Minister)

3 You can't ask for what you want unless you know what it is. A lot of people don't know what they want or they want much less than they deserve. First you have figure out what you want. Second, you have to decide that you deserve it. Third, you have to believe you can get it. And, fourth, you have to have the guts to ask for it.
Barbara De Angelis (American Expert on Relationship & Love, Author)

4 Millions saw the apple fall, but Newton was the one who asked why.
Bernard M. Baruch (1870-1965, American Financier)

5 Ask, and it shall be given you; seek; and you shall find; knock and it shall be opened unto you. For every one that asketh receiveth; and he that seeketh findeth; and to him that knocketh it shall be opened. [Matthew 7:7-8]
Bible (Sacred Scriptures of Christians and Judaism)

6 Man who waits for roast duck to fly into mouth must wait very, very long time.
Chinese Proverb

7 Better to ask twice than to lose your way once.
Danish Proverb

8 You don't always get what you ask for, but you never get what you don't ask for... unless it's contagious!
Franklyn Broude

9 Asking is the beginning of receiving. Make sure you don't go to the ocean with a teaspoon. At least take a bucket so the kids won't laugh at you.
Jim Rohn (American Businessman, Author, Speaker, Philosopher)

10 I attribute the little I know to my not having been ashamed to ask for information, and to my rule of conversing with all descriptions of men on those topics that form their own peculiar professions and pursuits.
John Locke (1632-1704, British Philosopher)

11 Cats seem to go on the principle that it never does any harm to ask for what you want.
Joseph Wood Krutch (1893-1970, American Writer, Critic, Naturalist)

12 As long as men are free to ask what they must, free to say what they think, free to think what they will, freedom can never be lost and science can never regress.
Julius Robert Oppenheimer (1904-1967, American Nuclear Physicist)

13 Man, if you gotta ask you'll never know.
Louis Armstrong (1898/1900-1971, American Jazz Trumpeter, Singer)

14 If you don't ask, you don't get.
Mahatma Gandhi (1869-1948, Indian Political, Spiritual Leader)

15 What I point out to people is that it's silly to be afraid that you're not going to get what you want if you ask. Because you are already not getting what you want. They always laugh about that because they realize it's so true. Without asking you already have failed, you already have nothing. What are you afraid of? You're afraid of getting what you already have! It's ridiculous! Who cares if you don't get it when you ask for it, because, before you ask for it, you don't have it anyway. So there's really nothing to be afraid of.
Marcia Martin

16 You create your opportunities by asking for them.
Patty Hansen (American Author, Wife of Mark Victor Hansen)

17 The world is full of genies waiting to grant your wishes.
Percy Ross (American Columnist)

18 A clever, imagination, humorous request can open closed doors and closed minds.
Percy Ross (American Columnist)

19 You've got to ask! Asking is, in my opinion, the world's most powerful -- and neglected -- secret to success and happiness.
Percy Ross (American Columnist)

20 My greatest strength as a consultant is to be ignorant and ask a few questions.
Peter F. Drucker (1909-, American Management Consultant, Author)

21 Others have seen what is and asked why. I have seen what could be and asked why not.
Robert F. Kennedy (1925-1968, American Attorney General, Senator)

22 Asking the right questions takes as much skill as giving the right answers.
Robert Half (American Businessman, Founder of Robert Half & Associates)

23 We never reflect how pleasant it is to ask for nothing.
Seneca (4 BC-65 AD, Spanish-born Roman Statesman, philosopher)

24 Every moment of your life is infinitely creative and the universe is endlessly bountiful. Just put forth a clear enough request, and everything your heart desires must come to you.
Shakti Gawain (American Human Potential Teacher)

25 Remember you are just an extra in everyone else's play.
Stewart Emery

26 Great things are only possible with outrageous requests.
Thea Alexander (American Science Fiction Writer)

27 If there is something to gain and nothing to lose by asking, by all means ask!
W. Clement Stone (1902-, American Businessman, Author)

ASSASSINATION

1 If you wish to make a man look noble, your best course is to kill him. What superiority he may have inherited from his race, what superiority nature may have personally gifted him with, comes out in death.
Alexander Smith (1830-1867, Scottish Poet, Author)

2 Before I was shot, I always thought that I was more half-there than all-there -- I always suspected that I was watching TV instead of living life. Right when I was being shot and ever since, I knew that I was watching television.
Andy Warhol (1930-, American Artist, Filmmaker)

3 Assassination has never changed the history of the world.
Benjamin Disraeli (1804-1881, British Statesman, Prime Minister)

4 The figure of the gunman in the window was inextricable from the victim and his history. This sustained Oswald in his cell. It gave him what he needed to live. The more time he spent in a cell, the stronger he would get. Everybody knew who he was now.
Don Delillo (1926-, American Author)

5 My heart burnt within me with indignation and grief; we could think of nothing else. All night long we had only snatches of sleep, waking up perpetually to the sense of a great shock and grief. Every one is feeling the same. I never knew so universal a feeling.
Elizabeth Gaskell (1810-1865, British Novelist)

6 Assassination is the perquisite of princes.
European Court Cliche

7 Assassination is the extreme form of censorship.
George Bernard Shaw (1856-1950, Irish-born British Dramatist)

8 A desperate disease requires a dangerous remedy.
Guy Fawkes

9 I thought it was a wonderfully conceptual act actually, to fire a replica pistol at a figurehead -- the guy could have been working for Andy Warhol!
J. G. Ballard (1930-, British Author)

10 You never know what's hit you. A gunshot is the perfect way.
John F. Kennedy (1917-1963, Thirty-fifth President of the USA)

11 A shocking crime was committed on the unscrupulous initiative of few individuals, with the blessing of more, and amid the passive acquiescence of all.
Publius Cornelius Tacitus (55-117 AD, Roman Historian)

12 Honey, I forgot to duck.
Ronald Reagan (1911-, Fortieth President of the USA, Actor)

ASSERTIVENESS

1 Assertiveness is not what you do, it's who you are!
Cal Le Mon

2   Never allow a person to tell you no who doesn't have the power to say yes.
Eleanor Roosevelt (1884-1962, American First Lady, Columnist, Lecturer, Humanitarian)

3   Joint undertakings stand a better chance when they benefit both sides.
Euripides (480-406 BC, Greek Tragic Poet)

4   The basic difference between being assertive and being aggressive is how our words and behavior affect the rights and well being of others.
Sharon Anthony Bower (American Author)

ASSETS

1   Central banks don't have divine wisdom. They try to do the best analysis they can and must be prepared to stand or fall by the quality of that analysis.
Eddie George (Governor of The Bank of England)

2   I hate banks. They do nothing positive for anybody except take care of themselves. They're first in with their fees and first out when there's trouble.
Harvey Goldsmith (British Rock-Concert Promoter)

3   Most people...find a disorientating mismatch between the long-term nature of their liabilities and the increasingly short-term nature of their assets.
Howard Davies (Deputy Governor of The Bank of England)

4   Because bankers measure their self-worth in money, and pay themselves a lot of it, they think they're fine fellows and don't need to explain themselves.
James Buchan (British Journalist)

5   No one has a greater asset for his business than a man's pride in his work.
Mary Parker Follet (1868-1933, American Author)

ASSOCIATION

1   In all societies, it is advisable to associate if possible with the highest; not that the highest are always the best, but because, if disgusted there, we can descend at any time; but if we begin with the lowest, to ascend is impossible.
Charles Caleb Colton (1780-1832, British Sportsman Writer)

2   We gain nothing by being with such as ourselves. We encourage one another in mediocrity. I am always longing to be with men more excellent than myself.
Charles Lamb (1775-1834, British Essayist, Critic)

3   If you want to be a winner, hang around with winners
Christopher D. Furman

4   A king's son is no nobler than his company.
Gaelic Proverb

5   Associate yourself with men of good quality if you esteem your own reputation. It is better be alone than in bad company.
George Washington (1732-1799, First President of the USA)

6   I won't belong to any organization that would have me as a member.
Groucho Marx (1895-1977, American Comic Actor)

7   No one should form an acquaintance with one who has an evil character. A piece of coal, if it is hot burns, and if it's cold, blackens the hands.
Hitopadesa (Sanskrit Fable From Panchatantra)

8   You must constantly ask yourself these questions: Who am I around? What are they doing to me? What have they got me reading? What have they got me saying? Where do they have me going? What do they have me thinking? And most important, what do they have me becoming? Then ask yourself the big question: Is that okay? Your life does not get better by chance, it gets better by change.
Jim Rohn (American Businessman, Author, Speaker, Philosopher)

9   Like associates with like.
Marcus T. Cicero (106-43 BC, Great Roman Orator, Politician)

10   Surround yourself with only people who are going to lift you higher.
Oprah Winfrey (1954-, American TV Personality, Producer, Actress, Author)

11   Every man becomes, to a certain degree, what the people he generally converses with are.
Philip Dormer Stanhope

12   To take refuge with an inferior is to betray one's self.
Publilius Syrus (1st Century BC, Roman Writer)

13   Living with a saint is more grueling than being one.
Robert Neville

14   A rusty nail placed near a faithful compass, will sway it from the truth, and wreck the argosy.
Sir Walter Scott (1771-1832, British Novelist, Poet)

15   Show me the person you honor, for I know better by that the kind of person you are. For you show me what your idea of humanity is.
Thomas Carlyle (1795-1881, Scottish Philosopher, Author)

16   Sometimes a man hits upon a place to which he mysteriously feels that he belongs.
W. Somerset Maugham (1874-1965, British Novelist, Playwright)

ASTROLOGY

1   You stars that reigned at my nativity, whose influence hath allotted death and hell.
Christopher Marlowe (1564-1593, British Dramatist, Poet)

2　We need not feel ashamed of flirting with the zodiac. The zodiac is well worth flirting with.
D. H. Lawrence (1885-1930, British Author)

3　Look you, Doubloon, your zodiac here is the life of man in one round chapter. To begin: there's Aries, or the Ram -- lecherous dog, he begets us; then, Taurus, or the Bull -- he bumps us the first thing; then Gemini, or the Twins -- that is, Virtue and Vice; we try to reach Virtue, when lo! comes Cancer the Crab, and drags us back; and here, going from Virtue, Leo, a roaring Lion, lies in the path -- he gives a few fierce bites and surly dabs with his paw; we escape, and hail Virgo, the virgin! that's our first love; we marry and think to be happy for aye, when pop comes Libra, or the Scales -- happiness weighed and found wanting; and while we are very sad about that, Lord! how we suddenly jump, as Scorpio, or the Scorpion, stings us in rear; we are curing the wound, when come the arrows all round; Sagittarius, or the Archer, is amusing himself. As we pluck out the shafts, stand aside! here's the battering-ram, Capricornus, or the Goat; full tilt, he comes rushing, and headlong we are tossed; when Aquarius, or the Waterbearer, pours out his whole deluge and drowns us; and, to wind up, with Pisces, or the Fishes, we sleep.
Herman Melville (1819-1891, American Author)

4　About astrology and palmistry: they are good because they make people vivid and full of possibilities. They are communism at its best. Everybody has a birthday and almost everybody has a palm.
Kurt Vonnegut Jr. (1922-, American Novelist)

5　The stars which shone over Babylon and the stable in Bethlehem still shine as brightly over the Empire State Building and your front yard today. They perform their cycles with the same mathematical precision, and they will continue to affect each thing on earth, including man, as long as the earth exists.
Linda Goodman

6　Faithful horoscope-watching, practiced daily, provides just the sort of small but warm and infinitely reassuring fillip that gets matters off to a spirited start.
Shana Alexander (1925-, American Writer, Editor)

7　This is the excellent foppery of the world: that when we are sick in fortune -- often the surfeits of our own behavior -- we make guilty of our disasters the sun, the moon, and stars, as if we were villains on necessity, fools by heavenly compulsion, knaves, thieves, and treachers by spherical predominance, drunkards, liars, and adulterers by an enforced obedience of planetary influence. An admirable evasion of whoremaster man, to lay his goatish disposition on the charge of a star!
William Shakespeare (1564-1616, British Poet, Playwright, Actor)

ASTRONOMY

1　I try to forget what happiness was, and when that don't work, I study the stars.
Derek Walcott (1930-, Poet and Playwright, born in West Indies)

2　Astronomy is perhaps the science whose discoveries owe least to chance, in which human understanding appears in its whole magnitude, and through which man can best learn how small he is.
Georg C. Lichtenberg (1742-1799, German Physicist, Satirist)

3　Adam inquires concerning celestial motions, is doubtfully answered, and exhorted to search rather things more worthy of knowledge.
John Milton (1608-1674, British Poet)

4　It is clear to everyone that astronomy at all events compels the soul to look upwards, and draws it from the things of this world to the other.
Plato (427-347 BC, Greek Philosopher)

5　When I, sitting, heard the astronomer, where he lectured with such applause in the lecture room, how soon, unaccountable, I became tired and sick; Till rising and gliding out, I wandered off by myself, in the mystical moist night-air, and from time to time, looked up in perfect silence at the stars.
Walt Whitman (1819-1892, American Poet)

6　These earthly godfathers of Heaven's lights, that give a name to every fixed star, have no more profit of their shining nights than those that walk and know not what they are.
William Shakespeare (1564-1616, British Poet, Playwright, Actor)

ATHEISM

1　Irreligion. The principal one of the great faiths of the world.
Ambrose Bierce (1842-1914, American Author, Editor, Journalist, "The Devil's Dictionary")

2　What you don't understand is that it is possible to be an atheist, it is possible not to know if God exists or why He should, and yet to believe that man does not live in a state of nature but in history, and that history as we know it now began with Christ, it was founded by Him on the Gospels.
Boris Pasternak (1890-1960, Russian Poet, Novelist, Translator)

3　I am a daylight atheist.
Brendan F. Behan (1923-1964, Irish Writer)

4　During the crusades all were religious mad, and now all are mad for want of it.
Captain J. G. Stedman (1744-1797, British Soldier, Author, Artist)

5   An atheist is a man who watches a Notre Dame -- Southern Methodist University game and doesn't care who wins.
Dwight D. Eisenhower (1890-1969, Thirty-fourth President of the USA)

6   By night an atheist half believes in God.
Edward Young (1683-1765, British Poet, Dramatist)

7   Here lies an Atheist: All Dressed Up and No Place to Go.
Epitaph

8   I had rather believe all the Fables in the Legend, and the Talmud, and the Alcoran, than that this universal frame is without a Mind.
Francis Bacon (1561-1626, British Philosopher, Essayist, Statesman)

9   Atheism is rather in the lip than in the heart of man.
Francis Bacon (1561-1626, British Philosopher, Essayist, Statesman)

10 Small amounts of philosophy lead to atheism, but larger amounts bring us back to God.
Francis Bacon (1561-1626, British Philosopher, Essayist, Statesman)

11 It is true, that a little philosophy inclineth man's mind to atheism, but depth in philosophy bringeth men's minds about to religion.
Francis Bacon (1561-1626, British Philosopher, Essayist, Statesman)

12 An atheist is a man who believes himself an accident.
Francis Thompson (1859-1907, British Poet)

13 If there is no God, everything is permitted.
Fyodor Dostoevski (1821-1881, Russian Novelist)

14 I'm an atheist and I thank God for it.
George Bernard Shaw (1856-1950, Irish-born British Dramatist)

15 He was an embittered atheist (the sort of atheist who does not so much disbelieve in God as personally dislike Him).
George Orwell (1903-1950, British Author, "Animal Farm")

16 I can't believe in the God of my Fathers. If there is one Mind which understands all things, it will comprehend me in my unbelief. I don't know whose hand hung Hesperus in the sky, and fixed the Dog Star, and scattered the shining dust of Heaven, and fired the sun, and froze the darkness between the lonely worlds that spin in space.
Gerald Kersh

17 Those thinkers who cannot believe in any gods often assert that the love of humanity would be in itself sufficient for them; and so, perhaps, it would, if they had it.
Gilbert K. Chesterton (1874-1936, British Author)

18 If you don't believe in God, all you have to believe in is decency. Decency is very good. Better decent than indecent. But I don't think it's enough.
Harold Macmillan (1894-1986, British Conservative Politician, Prime Minister)

19 No one can be an unbeliever nowadays. The Christian Apologists have left one nothing to disbelieve.
Hector Hugh Munro (1870-1916, British Novelist, Writer)

20 Nobody talks so constantly about God as those who insist that there is no God.
Heywood Broun (1888-1939, American Journalist, Novelist)

21 If you can't believe in God, chances are your God is too small.
James Phillips

22 The divine is perhaps that quality in man which permits him to endure the lack of God.
Jean Rostand (1894-1977, French Biologist, Writer)

23 He must pull out his own eyes, and see no creature, before he can say, he sees no God; He must be no man, and quench his reasonable soul, before he can say to himself, there is no God.
John Donne (1572-1632, British Metaphysical Poet)

24 Here we are, we're alone in the universe, there's no God, it just seems that it all began by something as simple as sunlight striking on a piece of rock. And here we are. We've only got ourselves. Somehow, we've just got to make a go of it. We've only ourselves.
John Osborne (1929-, British Playwright)

25 Among the repulsions of atheism for me has been its drastic uninterestingness as an intellectual position. Where was the ingenuity, the ambiguity, the humanity (in the Harvard sense) of saying that the universe just happened to happen and that when we're dead we're dead?
John Updike (1932-, American Novelist, Critic)

26 First, whenever a man talks loudly against religion, always suspect that it is not his reason, but his passions, which have got the better of his creed. A bad life and a good belief are disagreeable and troublesome neighbors, and where they separate, depend upon it, 'Tis for no other cause but quietness sake.
Laurence Sterne (1713-1768, British Author)

27 When ever a person talks loudly against religion, always suspect that it is not their reason, but their passions, which have got the better of their beliefs. A bad life and a good belief are disagreeable and troublesome neighbors; and when they separate, depend on it that it is for the sake of peace and quiet.
Laurence Sterne (1713-1768, British Author)

28 If therefore my work is negative, irreligious, atheistic, let it be remembered that atheism -- at least in the sense of this work -- is the secret of religion itself; that religion itself, not indeed on the surface, but fundamentally, not in intention or according to its own supposition, but in its heart, in its essence, believes in nothing else than the truth and divinity of human nature.
Ludwig Feuerbach (1804-1872, German Philosopher)

29 There is no God, Nature sufficeth unto herself; in no wise hath she need of an author.
Marquis De Sade (1740-1814, French Author)

30 We find the most terrible form of atheism, not in the militant and passionate struggle against the idea of God himself, but in the practical atheism of everyday living, in indifference and torpor. We often encounter these forms of atheism among those who are formally Christians.
Nicolai A. Berdyaev

31 Now we have no God. We have had two: the old God that our fathers handed down to us, that we hated, and never liked; the new one that we made for ourselves, that we loved; but now he has flitted away from us, and we see what he was made of -- the shadow of our highest ideal, crowned and throned. Now we have no God.
Olive Schreiner

32 There are few people so stubborn in their atheism who when danger is pressing in will not acknowledge the divine power.
Plato (427-347 BC, Greek Philosopher)

33 When I told the people of Northern Ireland that I was an atheist, a woman in the audience stood up and said, yes, but is it the God of the Catholics or the God of the Protestants in whom you don't believe?"
Quentin Crisp (1908-, British Author)

34 And as for the unbelievers, their works are as a mirage in a spacious plain which the man athirst supposes to be water, till when he comes to it, he finds it is nothing; there indeed he finds God, and He pays him his account in full; (and God is swift at the reckoning).
Qur'an (Holy Book)

35 Atheism is easy in fair weather.
Ronald Dunn

36 Forth from his dark and lonely hiding-place, (Portentous sight!) the owlet Atheism, sailing on obscene wings athwart the noon, drops his blue-fringed lids, and holds them close, and hooting at the glorious sun in Heaven, cries out, "Where is it?"
Samuel Taylor Coleridge (1772-1834, British Poet, Critic, Philosopher)

37 An atheist may be simply one whose faith and love are concentrated on the impersonal aspects of God.
Simone Weil (1910-1943, French Philosopher, Mystic)

38 There are no atheists in foxholes.
William T. Cummings

ATHLETE

1 Durability is part of what makes a great athlete.
Bill Russell (1934-, American Basketball Player)

ATTACHMENT

1 Those who consciousness is unified abandon all attachment to the results of action and attain supreme peace. But those whose desires are fragmented, who are selfishly attached to the results of their work, are bound in everything they do.
Bhagavad Gita (400 BC, Sanskrit Poem Incorporated Into the Mahabharata)

2 By letting it go it all gets done. The world is won by those who let it go. But when you try and try. The world is beyond the winning.
Lao-Tzu (600 BC, Chinese Philosopher, Founder of Taoism, Author of the "Tao Te Ching")

3 Attachment is the great fabricator of illusions; reality can be attained only by someone who is detached.
Simone Weil (1910-1943, French Philosopher, Mystic)

4 Attachment to spiritual things is.. just as much an attachment as inordinate love of anything else.
Thomas Merton (1915-1968, American Religious Writer, Poet)

5 Softly and kindly remind yourself, "I cannot own anything." It is a valuable thought to keep in mind as you struggle to improve your financial picture, worry about investments, and plan how to acquire more and more. It is a universal principle which you are part of. You must release everything when you truly awaken. Are you letting your life go by in frustration and worry over not having enough? If so, relax and remember that you only get what you have for a short period of time. When you awaken you will see the folly of being attached to anything.
Wayne Dyer (1940-, American Psychotherapist, Author, Lecturer)

6 The tighter you squeeze, the less you have.
Zen Saying

ATTITUDE

1 Never elated when someone's oppressed, never dejected when another one's blessed.
Alexander Pope (1688-1744, British Poet, Critic, Translator)

2 If you can't change your fate, change your attitude.
Amy Tan (1952-, Chinese American Author, "The Joy Luck Club")

3 We don't see things as they are, we see things as we are.
Anais Nin (1914-1977, French-born American Novelist, Dancer)

4 My attitude is never to be satisfied, never enough, never.
Bela Karolyi (Gymnastic Coach)

5   Develop an attitude of gratitude, and give thanks for everything that happens to you, knowing that every step forward is a step toward achieving something bigger and better than your current situation.
Brian Tracy (American Trainer, Speaker, Author, Businessman)

6   There are things I can't force. I must adjust. There are times when the greatest change needed is a change of my viewpoint.
C. M. Ward

7   Always keep that happy attitude. Pretend that you are holding a beautiful fragrant bouquet.
Candice M. Pope

8   They say you can't do it, but sometimes it doesn't always work.
Casey Stengel (1889-1975, American Baseball Player and Manager)

9   An optimist is a driver who thinks that empty space at the curb won't have a hydrant beside it.
Changing Times (American Business Magazine)

10   Don't introduce me to that man! I want to go on hating him, and I can't hate a man whom I know.
Charles Lamb (1775-1834, British Essayist, Critic)

11   Eagles come in all shapes and sizes, but you will recognize them chiefly by their attitudes.
Charles Prestwich Scott (1846-1932, British Newspaper Editor)

12   Words can never adequately convey the incredible impact of our attitudes toward life. The longer I live the more convinced I become that life is 10 percent what happens to us and 90 percent how we respond to it.
Charles Swindoll (American Pastor, Author)

13   I believe the single most significant decision I can make on a day-to-day basis is my choice of attitude. It is more important than my past, my education, my bankroll, my successes or failures, fame or pain, what other people think of me or say about me, my circumstances, or my position. Attitude keeps me going or cripples my progress. It alone fuels my fire or assaults my hope. When my attitudes are right, there is no barrier too high, no valley too deep, no dream too extreme, no challenge too great for me.
Charles Swindoll (American Pastor, Author)

14   We cannot change our past. We can not change the fact that people act in a certain way. We can not change the inevitable. The only thing we can do is play on the one string we have, and that is our attitude.
Charles Swindoll (American Pastor, Author)

15   The remarkable thing is, we have a choice everyday regarding the attitude we will embrace for that day.
Charles Swindoll (American Pastor, Author)

16   The longer I live, the more I realize the impact of attitude on life. Attitude, to me, is more important than facts. It is more important than the past, the education, the money, than circumstances, than failure, than successes, than what other people think or say or do. It is more important than appearance, giftedness or skill. It will make or break a company... a church... a home. The remarkable thing is we have a choice everyday regarding the attitude we will embrace for that day. We cannot change our past... we cannot change the fact that people will act in a certain way. We cannot change the inevitable. The only thing we can do is play on the one string we have, and that is our attitude. I am convinced that life is 10% what happens to me and 90% of how I react to it. And so it is with you... we are in charge of our Attitudes.
Charles Swindoll (American Pastor, Author)

17   Attitude is more important than the past, than education, than money, than circumstances, than what people do or say. It is more important than appearance, giftedness, or skill.
Charles Swindoll (American Pastor, Author)

18   We would accomplish many more things if we did not think of them as impossible.
Chretien Malesherbes (1721-1794, French Statesman)

19   If you can react the same way to winning and losing, that's a big accomplishment. That quality is important because it stays with you the rest of your life, and there's going to be a life after tennis that's a lot longer than your tennis life.
Chris Evert (1954-, American Tennis Player)

20   You play the hand you're dealt. I think the game's worthwhile.
Christopher Reeve (1952-, American Actor, Director)

21   Don't be against things so much as for things.
Col. Harland Sanders (1890-1980, American Businessman, Founder of Kentucky Fried Chicken)

22   We lost because we told ourselves we lost.
Count Leo Tolstoy (1828-1910, Russian Novelist, Philosopher)

23   It's how you deal with failure that determines how you achieve success.
David Feherty

24   Life is the movie you see through your own eyes. It makes little difference what's happening out there. It's how you take it that counts.
Denis Waitley (1933-, American Author, Speaker, Trainer, Peak Performance Expert)

25   You are more likely to act yourself into feelings, than feel yourself into action.
Dr. Jerome Brunner

26   Don't spend time beating on a wall, hoping to transform it into a door.
Dr. Laura Schlessinger (American Family Therapist)

27 Success or failure depends more upon attitude than upon capacity successful men act as though they have accomplished or are enjoying something. Soon it becomes a reality. Act, look, feel successful, conduct yourself accordingly, and you will be amazed at the positive results.
Dupree Jordan

28 An attitude to life which seeks fulfillment in the single-minded pursuit of wealth -- in short, materialism -- does not fit into this world, because it contains within itself no limiting principle, while the environment in which it is placed is strictly limited.
E. F. Schumacher (1911-1977, German Economist)

29 A great attitude does much more than turn on the lights in our worlds; it seems to magically connect us to all sorts of serendipitous opportunities that were somehow absent before the change.
Earl Nightingale (1921-1989, American Radio Announcer, Author, Motivator, Speaker)

30 Our attitude toward life determines life's attitude towards us.
Earl Nightingale (1921-1989, American Radio Announcer, Author, Motivator, Speaker)

31 We awaken in others the same attitude of mind we hold toward them.
Elbert Hubbard (1859-1915, American Author, Publisher)

32 One ship drives east and other drives west by the same winds that blow. It's the set of the sails and not the gales that determines the way they go.
Ella Wheeler Wilcox (1855-1919, American Poet, Journalist)

33 Nothing in life is so hard that you can't make it easier by the way you take it.
Ellen Glasgow (1874-1945, American Novelist)

34 It's not what happens to you, but how you react to it that matters.
Epictetus (50-120, Stoic Philosopher)

35 Attitudes are the forerunners of conditions.
Eric Butterworth

36 Events will take their course, it is no good of being angry at them; he is happiest who wisely turns them to the best account.
Euripides (480-406 BC, Greek Tragic Poet)

37 Two men look out the same prison bars; one sees mud and the other stars.
Frederick Langbridge

38 Morale is a state of mind. It is steadfastness and courage and hope.
George Marshall (1880-1959, American Statesman)

39 If you wish to travel far and fast, travel light. Take off all your envies, jealousies, unforgiveness, selfishness and fears.
Glenn Clark

40 Win as if you were used to it, lose as if you enjoyed it for a change.
Golnik Eric

41 I never expect to lose. Even when I'm the underdog, I still prepare a victory speech.
H. Jackson Brown Jr. (American Author of "Life's Little Instruction Book" Series)

42 Adopting the right attitude can convert a negative stress into a positive one.
Hans Selye (1907-1982, Canadian Physician Born In Austria, Research On Stress)

43 Whenever a fellow tells me he is bipartisan, I know he's going to vote against me.
Harry S. Truman (1884-1972, Thirty-third President of the USA)

44 Keep your face to the sunshine and you cannot see the shadow.
Helen Keller (1880-1968, American Blind/Deaf Author, Lecturer, Amorist)

45 One's destination is never a place, but rather a new way of looking at things.
Henry Miller (1891-1980, American Author)

46 People Some people are like wheelbarrows; useful only when pushed, and very easily upset. The time to stop talking is when the other person nods his head affirmatively but says nothing.
Henry S. Haskins

47 Life would be a perpetual flea hunt if a man were obliged to run down all the innuendoes, inveracities, and insinuations and misrepresentations which are uttered against him.
Henry Ward Beecher (1813-1887, American Preacher, Orator, Writer)

48 Life is 10 percent what you make it and 90 percent how you take it.
Irving Berlin (1888-1989, Russian Composer)

49 Keep your heart right, even when it is sorely wounded.
J. C. Macaulay

50 It is not the position, but the disposition.
J. E. Dinger

51 We have unprecedented conditions to deal with and novel adjustments to make -- there can be no doubt of that. We also have a great stock of scientific knowledge unknown to our grandfathers with which to operate. So novel are the conditions, so copious the knowledge, that we must undertake the arduous task of reconsidering a great part of the opinions about man and his relations to his fellow men which have been handed down to us by previous generations who lived in far other conditions and possessed far less information about the world and themselves. We have, however, first to create an unprecedented attitude of mind to cope with unprecedented conditions, and to utilize unprecedented knowledge.
James H. Robinson (American Businessman, Chairman of American Express)

52 He was always leaning forward, pushing something invisible ahead of him.
James Thurber (1894-1961, American Humorist, Illustrator)

53 A pessimist and an optimist, so much the worse; so much the better.
Jean De La Fontaine (1621-1695, French Poet)

54 Attitude is your acceptance of the natural laws, or your rejection of the natural laws.
Jim Rohn (American Businessman, Author, Speaker, Philosopher)

55 It's easy to let life deteriorate into making a living instead of making a life. It's not the hours you put in, but what you out into the hours that count. Learn to express rather than impress. Expressing evokes a "me too" attitude while impressing evokes a "so what" attitude.
Jim Rohn (American Businessman, Author, Speaker, Philosopher)

56 Your living is determined not so much by what life brings to you as by the attitude you bring to life; not so much by what happens to you as by the way your mind looks at what happens.
John Homer Miller

57 If you will call your troubles experiences, and remember that every experience develops some latent force within you, you will grow vigorous and happy, however adverse your circumstances may seem to be.
John R. Miller

58 Things turn out best for the people who make the best of the way things turn out.
John Wooden (1910-, American Basketball Coach)

59 Nothing will work unless you do.
John Wooden (1910-, American Basketball Coach)

60 Good nature is more agreeable in conversation than wit and gives a certain air to the countenance which is more amiable than beauty.
Joseph Addison (1672-1719, British Essayist, Poet, Statesman)

61 It is better to know nothing than to know what ain't so.
Josh Billings (1815-1885, American Humorist, Lecturer)

62 Sometimes I'm so sweet even I can't stand it.
Julie Andrews (1935-, British Singer, Actress)

63 I would rather be first in a little Iberian village than second in Rome.
Julius Caesar (101-44 BC, Roman Emperor)

64 Attitudes are more important than facts.
Karl A. Menninger (1893-1990, American Psychiatrist)

65 It's not the load that breaks you down, it's the way you carry it.
Lena Horne (Singer)

66 There are two big forces at work, external and internal. We have very little control over external forces such as tornadoes, earthquakes, floods, disasters, illness and pain. What really matters is the internal force. How do I respond to those disasters? Over that I have complete control.
Leo Buscaglia (American Expert on Love, Lecturer, Author)

67 Ability is what you're capable of doing. Motivation determines what you do. Attitude determines how well you do it.
Lou Holtz (1937-, American Football Coach)

68 Life is ten percent what happens to you and ninety percent how you respond to it.
Lou Holtz (1937-, American Football Coach)

69 I got a simple rule about everybody. If you don't treat me right -- shame on you!
Louis Armstrong (1898/1900-1971, American Jazz Trumpeter, Singer)

70 What happens to a man is less significant than what happens within him.
Louis L. Mann

71 I've learned from experience that the greater part of our happiness or misery depends on our dispositions and not on our circumstances.
Martha Washington (1731-1802, American First Lady, Wife of President, George Washington)

72 We are injured and hurt emotionally, Not so much by other people or what they say and don't say, But by our own attitude and our own response.
Maxwell Maltz (American Plastic Surgeon, Author of "Psycho-Cybernetics")

73 Between the optimist and the pessimist, the difference is droll. The optimist sees the doughnut; the pessimist the hole!
Mclandburgh Wilson

74 An optimist may see a light where there is none, but why must the pessimist always run to blow it out?
Michel De Saint-Pierre

75 Life at any time can become difficult: life at any time can become easy. It all depends upon how one adjusts oneself to life.
Morarji Desai (1896-18, Indian Statesman, Prime Minister)

76 A man can believe a considerable deal of rubbish, and yet go about his daily work in a rational and cheerful manner.
Norman Douglas (1868-1952, British Author)

77 Any fact facing us is not as important as our attitude toward it, for that determines our success or failure. The way you think about a fact may defeat you before you ever do anything about it. You are overcome by the fact because you think you are.
Norman Vincent Peale (1898-1993, American Christian Reformed Pastor, Speaker, Author)

78 Take the attitude of a student, Never be too big to ask questions, Never know too much to learn something new.
Og Mandino (1923-1996, American Motivational Author, Speaker)

79 Seriousness is the only refuge of the shallow.
Oscar Wilde (1856-1900, British Author, Wit)

80 The basis of optimism is sheer terror.
Oscar Wilde (1856-1900, British Author, Wit)

81 Great effort springs naturally from a great attitude.
Pat Riley (1945, American Basketball Coach)

82 If you have a positive attitude and constantly strive to give your best effort, eventually you will overcome your immediate problems and find you are ready for greater challenges.
Pat Riley (1945, American Basketball Coach)

83 I don't wait for moods. You accomplish nothing if you do that. Your mind must know it has got to get down to earth.
Pearl S. Buck (1892-1973, American Novelist)

84 To different minds, the same world is a hell, and a heaven.
Ralph Waldo Emerson (1803-1882, American Poet, Essayist)

85 Each experience through which we pass operates ultimately for our good. This is a correct attitude to adopt and we must be able to see it in that light.
Raymond Holliwell

86 There are times when you just get down, you feel like nobody likes you. We're in high school forever. It's just what we do with it.
Rene Russo (1954-, American Actress)

87 It's not the situation. It's your reaction to the situation.
Robert Conklin (American Teacher, Author, Speaker)

88 This is the precept by which I have lived: Prepare for the worst; expect the best; and take what comes.
Robert E. Speer

89 There are only 3 colors, 10 digits, and 7 notes; its what we do with them that's important.
Ruth Ross

90 I've always believed that you can think positive just as well as you can think negative.
Sugar Ray Robinson (1920-1989, American Boxer)

91 You've got to sing like you don't need the money. You've got to love like you'll never get hurt. You've got to dance like there's nobody watching. You've got to come from the heart, if you want it to work.
Susanna Clark

92 I've never run into a guy who could win at the top level in anything today and didn't have the right attitude, didn't give it everything he had, at least while he was doing it; wasn't prepared and didn't have the whole program worked out.
Ted Turner (1938-, American Businessman, Founder of CNN)

93 What happens is not as important as how you react to what happens.
Thaddeus Golas

94 Nothing can stop the man with the right mental attitude from achieving his goal; nothing on earth can help the man with the wrong mental attitude.
Thomas Jefferson (1743-1826, Third President of the USA)

95 Whenever you're in conflict with someone, there is one factor that can make the difference between damaging your relationship and deepening it. That factor is attitude.
Timothy Bentley (Canadian Family Therapist)

96 Our attitudes control our lives. Attitudes are a secret power working twenty-four hours a day, for good or bad. It is of paramount importance that we know how to harness and control this great force.
Tom Blandi

97 Take everything easy and quit dreaming and brooding and you will be well guarded from a thousand evils.
Uhland

98 Let's not be narrow, nasty, and negative.
Vernon Grounds

99 Certain thoughts are prayers. There are moments when, whatever be the attitude of the body, the soul is on its knees.
Victor Hugo (1802-1885, French Poet, Dramatist, Novelist)

100 The Green Bay Packers never lost a football game. They just ran out of time.
Vince Lombardi (1913-1970, American Football Coach)

101 There is little difference in people, but that little difference makes a big difference. That little difference is attitude. The big difference is whether it is positive or negative.
W. Clement Stone (1902-, American Businessman, Author)

102 The greatest discovery of my generation is that human beings can alter their lives by altering their attitudes of mind.
William James (1842-1910, American Psychologist, Professor, Author)

103 It is our attitude at the beginning of a difficult task which, more than anything else, will affect its successful outcome.
William James (1842-1910, American Psychologist, Professor, Author)

104 There are no menial jobs, only menial attitudes.
William John Bennett (1943-, American Federal Official)

105 The world is a looking glass and gives back to every man the reflection of his own face.
William M. Thackeray (1811-1863, Indian-born British Novelist)

106 Some men have thousands of reasons why they cannot do what they want to, when all they need is one reason why they can.
Willis Whitney

107 In War: Resolution. In Defeat: Defiance. In Victory: Magnanimity. In Peace: Goodwill.
Winston Churchill (1874-1965, British Statesman, Prime Minister)

108 You cannot climb the ladder of success dressed in the costume of failure.
Zig Ziglar (American Sales Trainer, Author, Motivational Speaker)

109 Positive thinking will let you do everything better than negative thinking will.
Zig Ziglar (American Sales Trainer, Author, Motivational Speaker)

110 You cannot tailor make your situation in life, but you can tailor make your attitudes to fit those situations.
Zig Ziglar (American Sales Trainer, Author, Motivational Speaker)

111 A positive attitude can really make dreams come true -- it did for me.
Zina Garrison (1963-, American Tennis Player)

AUDIENCES

1 It is because the public are a mass -- inert, obtuse, and passive -- that they need to be shaken up from time to time so that we can tell from their bear-like grunts where they are -- and also where they stand. They are pretty harmless, in spite of their numbers, because they are fighting against intelligence.
Alfred Jarry (1873-1907, French Playwright, Author)

2 My conception of the audience is of a public each member of which is carrying about with him what he thinks is an anxiety, or a hope, or a preoccupation which is his alone and isolates him from mankind; and in this respect at least the function of a play is to reveal him to himself so that he may touch others by virtue of the revelation of his mutuality with them. If only for this reason I regard the theater as a serious business, one that makes or should make man more human, which is to say, less alone.
Arthur Miller (1915-, American Dramatist)

3 An audience is never wrong. An individual member of it may be an imbecile, but a thousand imbeciles together in the dark -- that is critical genius.
Billy Wilder (1906-, American Film Director)

4 It was a good thing to have a couple of thousand people all rigid and frozen together, in the palm of one's hand.
Charles Dickens (1812-1870, British Novelist)

5 It's easier to find a new audience than to write a new speech.
Dan Kennedy (American Businessman, Marketing Expert)

6 We respond to a drama to that extent to which it corresponds to our dream life.
David Mamet (1947-, American Playwright)

7 Discourse on virtue and they pass by in droves, whistle and dance the shimmy, and you've got an audience.
Diogenes of Sinope (410-320 BC, Cynic Philosopher)

8 I never let them cough. They wouldn't dare.
Ethel Barrymore (1879-1959, American Actress)

9 Your audience gives you everything you need. They tell you. There is no director who can direct you like an audience.
Fanny Brice (1891-1951, American Entertainer)

10 Some writers take to drink, others take to audiences.
Gore Vidal (1925-, American Novelist, Critic)

11 Never treat your audience as customers, always as partners.
Jimmy Stewart

12 I'm not here for your amusement. You're here for mine.
John Lydon Rotten (1957-, British Rock Musician)

13 Every crowd has a silver lining.
P.T. Barnum (1810-1891, American Showman, Entertainer, Circus Builder)

14 Many audiences all over the world will answer positively from their own experience that they have seen the face of the invisible through an experience on the stage that transcended their experience in life. They will maintain that Oedipus or Berenice or Hamlet or The Three Sisters performed with beauty and with love fires the spirit and gives them a reminder that daily drabness is not necessarily all.
Peter (Stephen Paul) Brook (1925-, British Theatre and Film Director)

15 When I'm talking to a large audience, I imagine that I'm talking to a single person.
Red Barber (1908-1992, American Baseball Broadcaster)

16 It's the admirer and the watcher who provoke us to all the inanities we commit.
Seneca (4 BC-65 AD, Spanish-born Roman Statesman, philosopher)

17 I never failed to convince an audience that the best thing they could do was to go away.
Thomas Love Peacock (1785-1866, British Author)

18 The audience is the most revered member of the theater. Without an audience there is no theater. Every technique learned by the actor, every curtain, every flat on the stage, every careful analysis by the director, every coordinated scene, is for the enjoyment of the audience. They are our guests, our evaluators, and the last spoke in the wheel which can then begin to roll. They make the performance meaningful.
Viola Spolin (1911-, American Theatrical Director, Producer)

19 To have great poets, there must be great audiences too.
Walt Whitman (1819-1892, American Poet)

AUTHORITY

1 Authority without wisdom is like a heavy ax without an edge, fitter to bruise than to polish.
Anne Bradstreet (1612-1672, British Puritan Poet)

2 Nothing strengthens authority so much as silence.
Charles De Gaulle (1890-1970, French President during World War II)

3   Authority is not a quality one person "has," in the sense that he has property or physical qualities. Authority refers to an interpersonal relation in which one person looks upon another as somebody superior to him.
Erich Fromm (1900-1980, American Psychologist)

4   To be free in an age like ours, one must be in a position of authority. That in itself would be enough to make me ambitious.
Ernest Renan (1823-1892, French Writer, Critic, Scholar)

5   Authority is never without hate.
Euripides (480-406 BC, Greek Tragic Poet)

6   However sugarcoated and ambiguous, every form of authoritarianism must start with a belief in some group's greater right to power, whether that right is justified by sex, race, class, religion or all four. However far it may expand, the progression inevitably rests on unequal power and airtight roles within the family.
Gloria Steinem (1934-, American Feminist Writer, Editor)

7   I grew up to always respect authority and respect those in charge.
Grant Hill (Basketball Player)

8   No statement should be believed because it is made by an authority.
Hans Reichenbach

9   No oppression is so heavy or lasting as that which is inflicted by the perversion and exorbitance of legal authority.
Joseph Addison (1672-1719, British Essayist, Poet, Statesman)

10 Anyone who in discussion relies upon authority uses, not his understanding, but rather his memory.
Leonardo Da Vinci (1452-1519, Italian Inventor, Architect, Painter, Scientist, Sculptor)

11 Does it follow that I reject all authority? Perish the thought. In the matter of boots, I defer to the authority of the boot-maker.
Mikhail Bakunin (1814-1876, Russian Political Theorist)

12 Authority has always attracted the lowest elements in the human race. All through history mankind has been bullied by scum. Those who lord it over their fellows and toss commands in every direction and would boss the grass in the meadow about which way to bend in the wind are the most depraved kind of prostitutes. They will submit to any indignity, perform any vile act, do anything to achieve power. The worst off-sloughings of the planet are the ingredients of sovereignty. Every government is a parliament of whores. The trouble is, in a democracy the whores are us.
P. J. O'Rourke (1947-, American Journalist)

13 Authority has every reason to fear the skeptic, for authority can rarely survive in the face of doubt.
Robert Lindner

14 To say that authority, whether secular or religious, supplies no ground for morality is not to deny the obvious fact that it supplies a sanction.
Sir Alfred Jules Ayer (1910-1989, British Philosopher)

15 Authority poisons everybody who takes authority on himself.
Vladimir Ilyich Lenin (1870-1924, Russian Revolutionary Leader)

AUTOBIOGRAPHY

1   Members rise from CMG (known sometimes in Whitehall as "Call Me God") to KCMG ("Kindly Call Me God") to GCMG ("God Calls Me God").
Anthony Sampson

2   Anyone who attempts to relate his life loses himself in the immediate. One can only speak of another.
Augusto Roa Bastos (1917-, Paraguayan Novelist)

3   My Turn is the distilled bathwater of Mrs. Reagan's life. It is for the most part sweetish, with a tart edge of rebuke, but disappointingly free of dirt or particulate matter of any kind.
Barbara Ehrenreich (1941-, American Author, Columnist)

4   That which resembles most living one's life over again, seems to be to recall all the circumstances of it; and, to render this remembrance more durable, to record them in writing.
Benjamin Franklin (1706-1790, American Scientist, Publisher, Diplomat)

5   All those writers who write about their childhood! Gentle God, if I wrote about mine you wouldn't sit in the same room with me.
Dorothy Parker (1893-1967, American Humorous Writer)

6   We can only write well about our sins because it is too difficult to recall a virtuous act or even whether it was the result of good or evil motives.
Edward Dahlberg (1900-1977, American Author, Critic)

7   Truth, naked, unblushing truth, the first virtue of all serious history, must be the sole recommendation of this personal narrative.
Edward Gibbon (1737-1794, British Historian)

8   When you write down your life, every page should contain something no one has ever heard about.
Elias Canetti (1905-, Austrian Novelist, Philosopher)

9   Autobiographies ought to begin with Chapter Two.
Ellery Sedgwick

10 The remarkable thing is that it is the crowded life that is most easily remembered. A life full of turns, achievements, disappointments, surprises, and crises is a life full of landmarks. The empty life has even its few details blurred, and cannot be remembered with certainty.
Eric Hoffer (1902-1983, American Author, Philosopher)

11 Don't give your opinions about Art and the Purpose of Life. They are of little interest and, anyway, you can't express them. Don't analyze yourself. Give the relevant facts and let your readers make their own judgments. Stick to your story. It is not the most important subject in history but it is one about which you are uniquely qualified to speak.
Evelyn Waugh (1903-1966, British Novelist)

12 A man's memory is bound to be a distortion of his past in accordance with his present interests, and the most faithful autobiography is likely to mirror less what a man was than what he has become.
Fawn M. Brodie (1915-1981, American Biographer)

13 Autobiography is only to be trusted when it reveals something disgraceful. A man who gives a good account of himself is probably lying, since any life when viewed from the inside is simply a series of defeats.
George Orwell (1903-1950, British Author, "Animal Farm")

14 The trouble with writing a book about yourself is that you can't fool around. If you write about someone else, you can stretch the truth from here to Finland. If you write about yourself the slightest deviation makes you realize instantly that there may be honor among thieves, but you are just a dirty liar.
Groucho Marx (1895-1977, American Comic Actor)

15 I am being frank about myself in this book. I tell of my first mistake on page 850.
Henry Kissinger (1923-, American Republican Politician, Secretary of State)

16 Biographical data, even those recorded in the public registers, are the most private things one has, and to declare them openly is rather like facing a psychoanalyst.
Italo Calvino (1923-1985, Cuban Writer, Essayist, Journalist)

17 Autobiography begins with a sense of being alone. It is an orphan form.
John Berger (1926-, British Actor, Critic)

18 Autobiography is now as common as adultery and hardly less reprehensible.
John Grigg

19 What pursuit is more elegant than that of collecting the ignominies of our nature and transfixing them for show, each on the bright pin of a polished phrase?
Logan Pearsall Smith (1865-1946, Anglo-American Essayist, Aphorist)

20 Such reproductions may not interest the reader; but after all, this is my autobiography, not his; he is under no obligation to read further in it; he was under none to begin. A modest or inhibited autobiography is written without entertainment to the writer and read with distrust by the reader.
Neville Cardus

21 I dislike modern memoirs. They are generally written by people who have either entirely lost their memories, or have never done anything worth remembering.
Oscar Wilde (1856-1900, British Author, Wit)

22 I write fiction and I'm told it's autobiography, I write autobiography and I'm told it's fiction, so since I'm so dim and they're so smart, let them decide what it is or it isn't.
Philip Roth (1933-, American Novelist)

23 It isn't that you subordinate your ideas to the force of the facts in autobiography but that you construct a sequence of stories to bind up the facts with a persuasive hypothesis that unravels your history's meaning.
Philip Roth (1933-, American Novelist)

24 An autobiography is an obituary in serial form with the last installment missing.
Quentin Crisp (1908-, British Author)

25 It is long ere we discover how rich we are. Our history, we are sure, is quite tame: we have nothing to write, nothing to infer. But our wiser years still run back to the despised recollections of childhood, and always we are fishing up some wonderful article out of that pond; until, by and by, we begin to suspect that the biography of the one foolish person we know is, in reality, nothing less than the miniature paraphrase of the hundred volumes of the Universal History.
Ralph Waldo Emerson (1803-1882, American Poet, Essayist)

26 There are people who can write their memoirs with a reasonable amount of honesty, and there are people who simply cannot take themselves seriously enough. I think I might be the first to admit that the sort of reticence which prevents a man from exploiting his own personality is really an inverted sort of egotism.
Raymond Chandler (1888-1959, American Author)

27 Democratic societies are unfit for the publication of such thunderous revelations as I am in the habit of making.
Salvador Dali (1904-1989, Spanish Painter)

28 I don't think anybody should write his autobiography until after he's dead.
Samuel Goldwyn (1882-1974, American Film Producer, Founder, MGM)

29 The record of one's life must needs prove more interesting to him who writes it than to him who reads what has been written.
Sister Elizabeth Kenny

30 Thus when I come to shape here at this table between my hands the story of my life and set it before you as a complete thing, I have to recall things gone far, gone deep, sunk into this life or that and become part of it; dreams, too, things surrounding me, and the inmates, those old half-articulate ghosts who keep up their hauntings by day and night... shadows of people one might have been; unborn selves.
Virginia Woolf (1882-1941, British Novelist, Essayist)

31 Every autobiography is concerned with two characters, a Don Quixote, the Ego, and a Sancho Panza, the Self.
W. H. Auden (1907-1973, Anglo-American Poet)

32 Reminiscences, even extensive ones, do not always amount to an autobiography. For autobiography has to do with time, with sequence and what makes up the continuous flow of life. Here, I am talking of a space, of moments and discontinuities. For even if months and years appear here, it is in the form they have in the moment of recollection. This strange form -- it may be called fleeting or eternal -- is in neither case the stuff that life is made of.
Walter Benjamin (1982-1940, German Critic, Philosopher)

33 When you put down the good things you ought to have done, and leave out the bad ones you did do -- well, that's Memoirs.
Will Rogers (1879-1935, American Humorist, Actor)

AUTOMOBILES

1 The improved American highway system isolated the American-in-transit. On his speedway he had no contact with the towns which he by-passed. If he stopped for food or gas, he was served no local fare or local fuel, but had one of Howard Johnson's nationally branded ice cream flavors, and so many gallons of Exxon. This vast ocean of superhighways was nearly as free of culture as the sea traversed by the Mayflower Pilgrims.
Daniel J. Boorstin (1914-, American Historian)

2 Everything in life is somewhere else, and you get there in a car.
E(lwyn) B(rooks) White (1899-1985, American Author, Editor)

3 What our children have to fear is not the cars on the highways of tomorrow but our own pleasure in calculating the most elegant parameters of their deaths.
J. G. Ballard (1930-, British Author)

4 The car as we know it is on the way out. To a large extent, I deplore its passing, for as a basically old-fashioned machine, it enshrines a basically old-fashioned idea: freedom. In terms of pollution, noise and human life, the price of that freedom may be high, but perhaps the car, by the very muddle and confusion it causes, may be holding back the remorseless spread of the regimented, electronic society.
J. G. Ballard (1930-, British Author)

5 Driving is a spectacular form of amnesia. Everything is to be discovered, everything to be obliterated.
Jean Baudrillard (French Postmodern Philosopher, Writer)

6 A car can massage organs which no masseur can reach. It is the one remedy for the disorders of the great sympathetic nervous system.
Jean Cocteau (1889-1963, French Author, Filmmaker)

7 The reason American cars don't sell anymore is that they have forgotten how to design the American Dream. What does it matter if you buy a car today or six months from now, because cars are not beautiful. That's why the American auto industry is in trouble: no design, no desire.
Karl Lagerfeld

8 Glorious, stirring sight! The poetry of motion! The real way to travel! The only way to travel! Here today -- in next week tomorrow! Villages skipped, towns and cities jumped -- always somebody else's horizons! O bliss! O poop-poop! O my! O my!
Kenneth Grahame (1859-1932, British Writer)

9 The car has become the carapace, the protective and aggressive shell, of urban and suburban man.
Marshall Mcluhan (1911-1980, Canadian Communications Theorist)

10 The car has become an article of dress without which we feel uncertain, unclad, and incomplete.
Marshall Mcluhan (1911-1980, Canadian Communications Theorist)

11 Automobiles are free of egotism, passion, prejudice and stupid ideas about where to have dinner. They are, literally, selfless. A world designed for automobiles instead of people would have wider streets, larger dining rooms, fewer stairs to climb and no smelly, dangerous subway stations.
P. J. O'Rourke (1947-, American Journalist)

12 I think that cars today are almost the exact equivalent of the great Gothic cathedrals: I mean the supreme creation of an era, conceived with passion by unknown artists, and consumed in image if not in usage by a whole population which appropriates them as a purely magical object.
Roland Barthes (1915-1980, French Semiologist)

13 No other man-made device since the shields and lances of the ancient knights fulfills a man's ego like an automobile.
Sir William

14 What I like, or one of the things I like, about motoring is the sense it gives one of lighting accidentally, like a voyager who touches another planet with the tip of his toe, upon scenes which would have gone on, have always gone on, will go on, unrecorded, save for this chance glimpse. Then it seems to me I am allowed to see the heart of the world uncovered for a moment.
Virginia Woolf (1882-1941, British Novelist, Essayist)

15 We are the first nation in the history of the world to go to the poorhouse in an automobile.
Will Rogers (1879-1935, American Humorist, Actor)

AUTONOMY

1 If sex and creativity are often seen by dictators as subversive activities, it's because they lead to the knowledge that you own your own body (and with it your own voice), and that's the most revolutionary insight of all.
Erica Jong (1942-, American Author)

2 Self-determination, the autonomy of the individual, asserts itself in the right to race his automobile, to handle his power tools, to buy a gun, to communicate to mass audiences his opinion, no matter how ignorant, how aggressive, it may be.
Herbert Marcuse (1898-1979, German Political Philosopher)

3 Self-determination has to mean that the leader is your individual gut, and heart, and mind or we're talking about power, again, and its rather well-known impurities. Who is really going to care whether you live or die and who is going to know the most intimate motivation for your laughter and your tears is the only person to be trusted to speak for you and to decide what you will or will not do.
June Jordan (1939-, American Poet, Civil Rights Activist)

4 We prefer self-government with danger to servitude in tranquility.
Kwame Nkrumah (Leader of Ghana's fight for Independence)

5 To be one's own master is to be the slave of self.
Natalie Clifford Barney (1876-1972, American-born French Author)

AUTUMN

1 O suns and skies and clouds of June, and flowers of June together. Ye cannot rival for one hour October's bright blue weather.
Helen Hunt Jackson (1830-1885, American Writer)

2 There is a harmony in autumn, and a luster in its sky, which through the summer is not heard or seen, as if it could not be, as if it had not been!
Percy Bysshe Shelley (1792-1822, British Poet)

3 Autumn wins you best by this its mute appeal to sympathy for its decay.
Robert Browning (1812-1889, British Poet)

4 My sorrow, when she's here with me, thinks these dark days of autumn rain are beautiful as days can be; she loves the bare, the withered tree; she walks the sodden pasture lane.
Robert Frost (1875-1963, American Poet)

5 The teeming Autumn big with rich increase, bearing the wanton burden of the prime like widowed wombs after their lords decease.
William Shakespeare (1564-1616, British Poet, Playwright, Actor)

AVERAGES

1 If you do it right 51 percent of the time you will end up a hero.
Alfred P. Sloan (American Business Executive, Former Chairman GM)

2 The average, healthy, well-adjusted adult gets up at seven-thirty in the morning feeling just plain terrible.
Jean Kerr (1923-, American Author, Playwright)

3 Ain't no man can avoid being born average, but there ain't no man got to be common.
Leroy "Satchel" Paige (1906?-1982, American Baseball Player)

4 I consider myself an average man, except in the fact that I consider myself an average man.
Michel Eyquem De Montaigne (1533-1592, French Philosopher, Essayist)

5 I am only an average man but, by George, I work harder at it than the average man.
Theodore Roosevelt (1858-1919, Twenty-sixth President of the USA)

AWARDS

1 The Oscars demonstrate the will of the people to control and judge those they have elected to stand above them (much, perhaps, as in bygone days, an election celebrated the same).
David Mamet (1947-, American Playwright)

2 Everyone in our culture wants to win a prize. Perhaps that is the grand lesson we have taken with us from kindergarten in the age of perversions of Dewey-style education: everyone gets a ribbon, and praise becomes a meaningless narcotic to soothe egoistic distemper.
Gerald Early (1952-, American Author)

3 Lots of people who complained about us receiving the MBE received theirs for heroism in the war --for killing people. We received ours for entertaining other people. I'd say we deserve ours more.
John Lennon (1940-1980, British Rock Musician)

4 Like Olympic medals and tennis trophies, all they signified was that the owner had done something of no benefit to anyone more capably than everyone else.
Joseph Heller (1923-, American Author)

5 The cross of the Legion of Honor has been conferred on me. However, few escape that distinction.
Mark Twain (1835-1910, American Humorist, Writer)

6 A new kind of award has been added -- the deathbed award. It is not an award of any kind. Either the recipient has not acted at all, or was not nominated, or did not win the award the last few times around. It is intended to relieve the guilty conscience of the Academy members and save face in front of the public. The Academy has the horrible taste to have a star, choking with emotion, present this deathbed award so that there can be no doubt in anybody's mind why the award is so hurriedly given. Lucky is the actor who is too sick to watch the proceedings on television.
Marlene Dietrich (1904-1992, German-born American Film Actor)

7 To refuse awards is another way of accepting them with more noise than is normal.
Peter Ustinov (1921-, British Actor, Writer, Director)

8 The award of a pure gold medal for poetry would flatter the recipient unduly: no poem ever attains such carat purity.
Robert Graves (1895-1985, British Poet, Novelist)

AWARENESS

1 To see, to hear, means nothing. To recognize (or not to recognize) means everything. Between what I do recognize and what I do not recognize there stands myself. And what I do not recognize I shall continue not to recognize.
Andre Breton (1989-1966, French Surrealist)

2 The aim of life is to live, and to live means to be aware, joyously, drunkenly, serenely, divinely aware.
Henry Miller (1891-1980, American Author)

3 Most people grow old within a small circle of ideas, which they have not discovered for themselves. There are perhaps less wrong-minded people than thoughtless.
Marquis De Vauvenargues (1715-1747, French Moralist)

4 Open-mindedness should not be fostered because, as Scripture teaches, Truth is great and will prevail, nor because, as Milton suggests, Truth will always win in a free and open encounter. It should be fostered for its own sake.
Richard Rorty (1931-, American Philosopher)

5 The man who is aware of himself is henceforward independent; and he is never bored, and life is only too short, and he is steeped through and through with a profound yet temperate happiness.
Virginia Woolf (1882-1941, British Novelist, Essayist)

6 To be happy is to be able to become aware of oneself without fright.
Walter Benjamin (1982-1940, German Critic, Philosopher)

BABIES

1 Since people are going to be living longer and getting older, they'll just have to learn how to be babies longer.
Andy Warhol (1930-, American Artist, Filmmaker)

2 A baby is God's opinion that life should go on.
Carl Sandburg (1878-1967, American Poet)

3 It is a pleasant thing to reflect upon, and furnishes a complete answer to those who contend for the gradual degeneration of the human species, that every baby born into the world is a finer one than the last.
Charles Dickens (1812-1870, British Novelist)

4 Everyone knows that by far the happiest and universally enjoyable age of man is the first. What is there about babies which makes us hug and kiss and fondle them, so that even an enemy would give them help at that age?
Desiderius Erasmus (1466-1536, Dutch Humanist)

5 Babies are necessary to grown-ups. A new baby is like the beginning of all things --wonder, hope, a dream of possibilities. In a world that is cutting down its trees to build highways, losing its earth to concrete... babies are almost the only remaining link with nature, with the natural world of living things from which we spring.
Eda J. Le Shan (1922-, American Educator, Author)

6 A baby is born with a need to be loved and never outgrows it.
Frank A. Clark

7 Except that right side up is best, there is not much to learn about holding a baby. There are one hundred and fifty-two distinctly different ways --and all are right! At least all will do.
Heywood Broun (1888-1939, American Journalist, Novelist)

8 If you desire to drain to the dregs the fullest cup of scorn and hatred that a fellow human being can pour out for you, let a young mother hear you call dear baby "it."
Jerome K. Jerome (1859-1927, British Humorous Writer, Novelist, Playwright)

9 Every new baby is a blind desperate vote for survival: people who find themselves unable to register an effective political protest against extermination do so by a biological act.
Lewis Mumford (1895-1990, American Social Philosopher)

10 We have not all had the good fortune to be ladies. We have not all been generals, or poets, or statesmen; but when the toast works down to the babies, we stand on common ground.
Mark Twain (1835-1910, American Humorist, Writer)

11 A soiled baby, with a neglected nose, cannot be conscientiously regarded as a thing of beauty.
Mark Twain (1835-1910, American Humorist, Writer)

12 Diaper backward spells repaid. Think about it.
Marshall Mcluhan (1911-1980, Canadian Communications Theorist)

13 I don't dislike babies, though I think very young ones rather disgusting.
Queen Victoria (1819-1901, Queen of Great Britain)

14 From the moment of birth, when the stone-age baby confronts the twentieth-century mother, the baby is subjected to these forces of violence, called love, as its mother and father have been, and their parents and their parents before them. These forces are mainly concerned with destroying most of its potentialities. This enterprise is on the whole successful.
R. D. Laing (1927-1989, British Psychiatrist)

15 Infancy conforms to nobody: all conform to it, so that one babe commonly makes four or five out of the adults who prattle and play to it.
Ralph Waldo Emerson (1803-1882, American Poet, Essayist)

16 A loud noise at one end and no sense of responsibility at the other.
Ronald Knox (1888-1957, British Scholar, Priest)

17 No one who has seen a baby sinking back satiated from the breast and falling asleep with flushed cheeks and a blissful smile can escape the reflection that this picture persists as a prototype of the expression of sexual satisfaction in later life.
Sigmund Freud (1856-1939, Austrian Physician - Founder of Psychoanalysis)

18 Moving between the legs of tables and of chairs, rising or falling, grasping at kisses and toys, advancing boldly, sudden to take alarm, retreating to the corner of arm and knee, eager to be reassured, taking pleasure in the fragrant brilliance of the Christmas tree.
T. S. Eliot (1888-1965, American-born British Poet, Critic)

19 The tiny madman in his padded cell.
Vladimir Nabokov (1899-1977, Russian-born American Novelist, Poet)

20 I have no name: I am but two days old. What shall I call thee? I happy am, Joy is my name. Sweet joy befall thee!
William Blake (1757-1827, British Poet, Painter)

21 I have no name:" I am but two days old. "What shall I call thee?" I happy am, "Joy is my name." sweet joy befall thee!
William Blake (1757-1827, British Poet, Painter)

22 Mark the babe not long accustomed to this breathing world; One that hath barely learned to shape a smile, though yet irrational of soul, to grasp with tiny finger -- to let fall a tear; And, as the heavy cloud of sleep dissolves, To stretch his limbs, becoming, as might seem. The outward functions of intelligent man.
William Wordsworth (1770-1850, British Poet)

BACHELOR

1 Let sinful bachelors their woes deplore; full well they merit all they feel, and more: unaw by precepts, human or divine, like birds and beasts, promiscuously they join.
Alexander Pope (1688-1744, British Poet, Critic, Translator)

2 A single man has not nearly the value he would have in a state of union. He is an incomplete animal. He resembles the odd half of a pair of scissors.
Benjamin Franklin (1706-1790, American Scientist, Publisher, Diplomat)

3 Show me a man who lives alone and has a perpetually clean kitchen, and 8 times out of 9 I'll show you a man with detestable spiritual qualities.
Charles Bukowski (1920-1994, German Poet, Short Stories Writer, Novelist)

4 The only good husbands stay bachelors: They're too considerate to get married.
Finley Peter Dunne (1867-1936, American Journalist, Humorist)

5 Certainly the best works, and of greatest merit for the public, have proceeded from the unmarried, or childless men.
Francis Bacon (1561-1626, British Philosopher, Essayist, Statesman)

6 The most threatened group in human societies as in animal societies is the unmated male: the unmated male is more likely to wind up in prison or in an asylum or dead than his mated counterpart. He is less likely to be promoted at work and he is considered a poor credit risk.
Germaine Greer (1939-, Australian Feminist Writer)

7 Bachelors know more about women than married men; if they didn't, they'd be married too.
H. L. Mencken (1880-1956, American Editor, Author, Critic, Humorist)

8 It is impossible to believe that the same God who permitted His own son to die a bachelor regards celibacy as an actual sin.
H. L. Mencken (1880-1956, American Editor, Author, Critic, Humorist)

9 Bachelors have consciences, married men have wives.
H. L. Mencken (1880-1956, American Editor, Author, Critic, Humorist)

10 Marrying an old bachelor is like buying second-hand furniture.
Helen Rowland (1875-1950, American Journalist)

11 A bachelor never quite gets over the idea that he is a thing of beauty and a boy forever.
Helen Rowland (1875-1950, American Journalist)

12 A Bachelor of Arts is one who makes love to a lot of women, and yet has the art to remain a bachelor.
Helen Rowland (1875-1950, American Journalist)

13 Somehow a bachelor never quite gets over the idea that he is a thing of beauty and a boy forever.
Helen Rowland (1875-1950, American Journalist)

14 It is a truth universally acknowledged, that a single man is in possession of a good fortune, must be in want of a wife.
Jane Austen (1775-1817, British Novelist)

15 A bachelor's life is a fine breakfast, a flat lunch, and a miserable dinner.
Jean De La Bruyere (1645-1696, French Writer)

16 Nowadays, all the married men live like bachelors, and all the bachelors like married men.
Oscar Wilde (1856-1900, British Author, Wit)

17 By persistently remaining single, a man converts himself into a permanent public temptation. Men should be more careful.
Oscar Wilde (1856-1900, British Author, Wit)

18 I would be married, but I'd have no wife, I would be married to a single life.
Richard Crashaw

19 They that have grown old in a single state are generally found to be morose, fretful and captious; tenacious of their own practices and maxims; soon offended by contradiction or negligence; and impatient of any association but with those that will watch their nod, and submit themselves to unlimited authority.
Samuel Johnson (1709-1784, British Author)

BALDNESS

1 The tenderest spot in a man's make-up is sometimes the bald spot on top of his head.
Helen Rowland (1875-1950, American Journalist)

2 There is more felicity on the far side of baldness than young men can possibly imagine.
Logan Pearsall Smith (1865-1946, Anglo-American Essayist, Aphorist)

3 Bald as the bare mountain tops are bald, with a baldness full of grandeur.
Matthew Arnold (1822-1888, British Poet, Critic)

4 I am not the archetypal leading man. This is mainly for one reason: as you may have noticed, I have no hair.
Patrick Stewart (1940-, British-born American Actor, Director, Playwright, Producer)

BANALITY

1 Banality is a terribly likely consequence of the underused of a good mind. That is why in particular it is a female affliction.
Cynthia Propper-Seton

2 Banality is a symptom of non-communication. Men hide behind their clichés.
Eugene Ionesco (1912-, Romanian-born French Playwright)

3 A mental disease has swept the planet: banalization presented with the alternative of love or a garbage disposal unit, young people of all countries have chosen the garbage disposal unit.
Ivan Chtcheglov

4 Men are seldom more commonplace than on supreme occasions.
Samuel Butler (1612-1680, British Poet, Satirist)

5 When the shriveled skin of the ordinary is stuffed out with meaning, it satisfies the senses amazingly.
Virginia Woolf (1882-1941, British Novelist, Essayist)

BANKERS AND BANKING

1 What's breaking into a bank compared with founding a bank?
Bertolt Brecht (1898-1956, German Dramatist, Poet)

2 It is easier to rob by setting up a bank than by holding up a bank clerk.
Bertolt Brecht (1898-1956, German Dramatist, Poet)

3 A bank is a place that will lend you money if you can prove you don't need it.
Bob Hope (1903-, American Comedian, Actor)

4 There is too much sour grapes for my taste in the present American attitude. The time to denounce the bankers was when we were all feeding off their gold plate; not now! At present they have not only my sympathy but my preference. They are the last representatives of our native industries.
Edith Wharton (1862-1937, American Author)

5 Good bankers, like good tea, can only be appreciated when they are in hot water.
Jaffar Hussein

6 I hesitate to deposit money in a bank. I am afraid I shall never dare to take it out again. When you go to confession and entrust your sins to the safe-keeping of the priest, do you ever come back for them?
Jean Baudrillard (French Postmodern Philosopher, Writer)

7 It is no accident that banks resemble temples, preferably Greek, and that the supplicants who come to perform the rites of deposit and withdrawal instinctively lower their voices into the registers of awe. Even the most junior tellers acquire within weeks of their employment the officiousness of hierophants tending an eternal flame. I don't know how they become so quickly inducted into the presiding mysteries, or who instructs them in the finely articulated inflections of contempt for the laity, but somehow they learn to think of themselves as suppliers of the monetarized DNA that is the breath of life.
Lewis H. Lapham (1935-, American Essayist, Editor)

8 With a group of bankers I always had the feeling that success was measured by the extent one gave nothing away.
Lord Longford

9 A banker is a fellow who lends his umbrella when the sun is shining and wants it back the minute it begins to rain.
Mark Twain (1835-1910, American Humorist, Writer)

10 I sincerely believe that banking establishments are more dangerous than standing armies, and that the principle of spending money to be paid by posterity, under the name of funding, is but swindling futurity on a large scale.
Thomas Jefferson (1743-1826, Third President of the USA)

11 Banking establishments are more dangerous than standing armies.
Thomas Jefferson (1743-1826, Third President of the USA)

BARGAINS

1 Sometimes one pays most for the things one gets for nothing.
Albert Einstein (1879-1955, German-born American Physicist)

2 There are very honest people who do not think that they have had a bargain unless they have cheated a merchant.
Anatole France (1844-1924, French Writer)

3 Here's the rule for bargains: "Do other men, for they would do you." That's the true business precept.
Charles Dickens (1812-1870, British Novelist)

4 Bargain... anything a customer thinks a store is losing money on.
Kin Hubbard (1868-1930, American Humorist, Journalist)

5 A bargain is in its very essence a hostile transaction do not all men try to abate the price of all they buy? I contend that a bargain even between brethren is a declaration of war.
Lord Byron (1788-1824, British Poet)

6   Nothing is cheap which is superfluous, for what one does not need, is dear at a penny.
    Plutarch (46-120 AD, Greek Essayist, Biographer)

BASEBALL

1   Most people miss the great part mental outlook plays in this game.
    Billy Martin (American Baseball Manager)

2   A full mind is an empty bat.
    Branch Rickey

3   Going to bed with a woman never hurt a ball player. It's staying up all night looking for them that does you in.
    Casey Stengel (1889-1975, American Baseball Player and Manager)

4   Managing is getting paid for home runs someone else hits.
    Casey Stengel (1889-1975, American Baseball Player and Manager)

5   Trying to get a fast ball past Hank Aaron is like trying to get the sun past a rooster.
    Curt Simmons

6   Whoever wants to know the heart and mind of America had better learn baseball, the rules and realities of the game.
    Jacques Barzun (1907-, American Scholar)

7   Back then, if you had a sore arm, the only people concerned were you and your wife. Now it's you, your wife, your agent, your investment counselor, your stockbroker, and your publisher.
    Jim Bouton (American Actor, Businessman, Baseball Player)

8   A ball player has got to be kept hungry be become a big leaguer. That is why no boy from a rich family ever made the big leagues.
    Joe Dimaggio (1914-, American baseball player)

9   Nolan Ryan is pitching much better now that he has his curve ball straightened out.
    Joe Garagiola

10 Baseball is like church. Many attend few understand.
    Leo Durocher (1905-1991, American Baseball Player/Manager)

11 You don't save a pitcher for tomorrow. Tomorrow, it may rain.
    Leo Durocher (1905-1991, American Baseball Player/Manager)

12 Give me some scratching, diving, hungry ballplayers who come to kill you.
    Leo Durocher (1905-1991, American Baseball Player/Manager)

13 A team of giants needs giant pitchers who throw good ideas but every pitcher needs an outstanding catcher. Without giant catchers, the ideas of the giant pitchers may eventually disappear.
    Max De Pree

14 See the ball; hit the ball.
    Pete Rose (1942-, American Baseball Player, Manager)

15 Cardinal rule for all hitters with two strikes on them: Never trust the umpire.
    Robert Smith

16 If I would be happy, I would be a very bad ball player. With me, when I get mad, it puts energy in my body.
    Roberto Clemente (1934 - 1972, American Baseball Player)

17 Being an umpire is like being a king. It prepares you for nothing.
    Ron Luciano

18 Catching a fly ball is a pleasure, but knowing what to do with it is a business.
    Tommy Henrich

19 Hit em where they ain't.
    Willie Keeler

20 You can't think and hit the ball at the same time.
    Yogi Berra (1925-, American Baseball Player)

21 Ninety percent of this game is half mental.
    Yogi Berra (1925-, American Baseball Player)

22 If the fans don't come out to the ball park, you can't stop them .
    Yogi Berra (1925-, American Baseball Player)

23 If people don't want to come out to the ball park, nobody's going to stop them.
    Yogi Berra (1925-, American Baseball Player)

24 Baseball is ninety percent mental. The other half if physical
    Yogi Berra (1925-, American Baseball Player)

BASKETBALL

1   You don't play against opponents, you play against the game of basketball.
    Bobby Knight (1940-, American Basketball Coach)

2   The only difference between a good shot and a bad shot is if it goes in or not.
    Charles Barkley (American Basketball Player)

3   If I weren't earning $3 million a year to dunk a basketball, most people on the street would run in the other direction if they saw me coming.
    Charles Barkley (American Basketball Player)

4   They said playing basketball would kill me. Well, not playing basketball was killing me.
    Earvin "Magic" Johnson (1959-, American Basketball Player)

5   I keep both eyes on my man. The basket hasn't moved on me yet.
    Julius Erving (1950-, American Basketball Player)

BATTLES

1 Dead battles, like dead generals, hold the military mind in their dead grip.
Barbara Tuchman (1912-1989, American Historian)

2 France has lost a battle. But France has not lost the war.
Charles De Gaulle (1890-1970, French President during World War II)

3 All quiet along the Potomac to-night, no sound save the rush of the river, while soft falls the dew on the face of the dead, the picket's off duty forever.
Ethel Lynn Beers (Poet)

4 A battle won is a battle which we will not acknowledge to be lost.
Ferdinand Foch (1851-1929, French Field Marshal)

5 My center is giving way, my right is in retreat; situation excellent. I shall attack.
Ferdinand Foch (1851-1929, French Field Marshal)

6 In a battle all you need to make you fight is a little hot blood and the knowledge that it's more dangerous to lose than to win.
George Bernard Shaw (1856-1950, Irish-born British Dramatist)

7 Any coward can fight a battle when he's sure of winning, but give me the man who has pluck to fight when he's sure of losing. That's my way, sir; and there are many victories worse than a defeat.
George Eliot (1819-1880, British Novelist)

8 After all the field of battle possesses many advantages over the drawing-room. There at least is no room for pretension or excessive ceremony, no shaking of hands or rubbing of noses, which make one doubt your sincerity, but hearty as well as hard hand-play. It at least exhibits one of the faces of humanity, the former only a mask.
Henry David Thoreau (1817-1862, American Essayist, Poet, Naturalist)

9 No battle is worth fighting except the last one.
John Enoch Powell (1912-, British statesman,)

10 Pick battles big enough to matter, but small enough to win.
Jonathan Kozol

11 There can be no reconciliation where there is no open warfare. There must be a battle, a brave boisterous battle, with pennants waving and cannon roaring, before there can be peaceful treaties and enthusiastic shaking of hands.
Mary Elizabeth Braddon (1837-1915, British Novelist, Playwright, Editor)

12 When soldiers have been baptized in the fire of a battle-field, they have all one rank in my eyes.
Napoleon Bonaparte (1769-1821, French General, Emperor)

13 The advantage of time and place in all practical actions is half a victory; which being lost is irrecoverable.
Sir Francis Drake (1540-1596, Elizabethan Seaman, Born in Crowndale, Devon)

14 War consisteth not in battle only, or the act of fighting; but in a tract of time, wherein the will to contend by battle is sufficiently known.
Thomas Hobbes (1588-1679, British Philosopher)

BEARDS

1 If you teach a poor young man to shave himself, and keep his razor in order, you may contribute more to the happiness of his life than in giving him a thousand guineas. This sum may be soon spent, the regret only remaining of having foolishly consumed it; but in the other case, he escapes the frequent vexation of waiting for barbers, and of their sometimes dirty fingers, offensive breaths, and dull razors.
Benjamin Franklin (1706-1790, American Scientist, Publisher, Diplomat)

2 A beard signifies lice, not brains.
Greek Proverb

3 There is always a period when a man with a beard shaves it off. This period does not last. He returns headlong to his beard.
Jean Cocteau (1889-1963, French Author, Filmmaker)

4 In England and America a beard usually means that its owner would rather be considered venerable than virile; on the continent of Europe it often means that its owner makes a special claim to virility.
Rebecca West (1892-1983, British Author)

5 He that hath a beard is more than a youth, and he that hath no beard is less than a man.
William Shakespeare (1564-1616, British Poet, Playwright, Actor)

BEAUTY

1 Beauty is in the heart of the beholder.
Al Bernstein

2 Beauty is unbearable, drives us to despair, offering us for a minute the glimpse of an eternity that we should like to stretch out over the whole of time.
Albert Camus (1913-1960, French Existential Writer)

3 At the heart of all beauty lies something inhuman, and these hills, the softness of the sky, the outline of these trees at this very minute lose the illusory meaning with which we had clothed them, henceforth more remote than a lost paradise... that denseness and that strangeness of the world is absurd.
Albert Camus (1913-1960, French Existential Writer)

4 Beauty for some provides escape, who gain a happiness in eyeing the gorgeous buttocks of the ape or Autumn sunsets exquisitely dying.
Aldous Huxley (1894-1963, British Author)

5   Where beauty is worshipped for beauty's sake as a goddess, independent of and superior to morality and philosophy, the most horrible putrefaction is apt to set in. The lives of the aesthetes are the far from edifying commentary on the religion of beauty.
Aldous Huxley (1894-1963, British Author)

6   Beauties in vain their pretty eyes may roll; charms strike the sight, but merit wins the soul.
Alexander Pope (1688-1744, British Poet, Critic, Translator)

7   Beauty. The power by which a woman charms a lover and terrifies a husband.
Ambrose Bierce (1842-1914, American Author, Editor, Journalist, "The Devil's Dictionary")

8   The flowers anew, returning seasons bring! But beauty faded has no second spring.
Ambrose Philips (1674-1749, British Poet, Politician)

9   Beauty will be convulsive or will not be at all.
Andre Breton (1989-1966, French Surrealist)

10 No; we have been as usual asking the wrong question. It does not matter a hoot what the mockingbird on the chimney is singing. The real and proper question is: Why is it beautiful?
Annie Dillard (1945-, American Author, Poet)

11 Personal beauty is a greater recommendation than any letter of reference.
Aristotle (384-322 BC, Greek Philosopher)

12 Beauty depends on size as well as symmetry. No very small animal can be beautiful, for looking at it takes so small a portion of time that the impression of it will be confused. Nor can any very large one, for a whole view of it cannot be had at once, and so there will be no unity and completeness.
Aristotle (384-322 BC, Greek Philosopher)

13 One evening I sat Beauty on my knees --And I found her bitter --And I reviled her.
Arthur Rimbaud (1854-1891, French Poet)

14 A beautiful woman should break her mirror early.
Baltasar Gracian (1601-1658, Spanish Philosopher, Writer)

15 I would warn you that I do not attribute to nature either beauty or deformity, order or confusion. Only in relation to our imagination can things be called beautiful or ugly, well-ordered or confused.
Baruch (Benedict de) Spinoza (1632-1677, Dutch Philosopher and Theologian)

16 Even with all my wrinkles! I am beautiful!
Bessie Delaney

17 Behold, thou art fair, my love; behold, thou art fair; thou hast doves eyes within thy locks: thy hair is as a flock of goats, that appear from mount Gilead. [Song Of Solomon 4:1]
Bible (Sacred Scriptures of Christians and Judaism)

18 Beauty is a harmonious relation between something in our nature and the quality of the object which delights us.
Blaise Pascal (1623-1662, French Scientist, Religious Philosopher)

19 Beauty is our weapon against nature; by it we make objects, giving them limit, symmetry, proportion. Beauty halts and freezes the melting flux of nature.
Camille Paglia (1947-, American Author, Critic, Educator)

20 There are as many kinds of beauty as there are habitual ways of seeking happiness.
Charles Baudelaire (1821-1867, French Poet)

21 All forms of beauty, like all possible phenomena, contain an element of the eternal and an element of the transitory -- of the absolute and of the particular. Absolute and eternal beauty does not exist, or rather it is only an abstraction creamed from the general surface of different beauties. The particular element in each manifestation comes from the emotions: and just as we have our own particular emotions, so we have our own beauty.
Charles Baudelaire (1821-1867, French Poet)

22 Beauty is power; a smile is its sword.
Charles Reade (1814-1884, British Novelist, Dramatist)

23 The beauty seen, is partly in him who sees it.
Christian Nevell Bovee (1820-1904, American Author, Lawyer)

24 Every trait of beauty may be referred to some virtue, as to innocence, candor, generosity, modesty, or heroism. St. Pierre To cultivate the sense of the beautiful, is one of the most effectual ways of cultivating an appreciation of the divine goodness.
Christian Nevell Bovee (1820-1904, American Author, Lawyer)

25 O, thou art fairer than the evening air clad in the beauty of a thousand stars.
Christopher Marlowe (1564-1593, British Dramatist, Poet)

26 Few girls are as well shaped as a good horse.
Christopher Morley (1890-1957, American Novelist, Journalist, Poet)

27 In every man's heart there is a secret nerve that answers to the vibrations of beauty.
Christopher Morley (1890-1957, American Novelist, Journalist, Poet)

28 Everything has beauty, but not everyone sees it.
Confucius (551-479 BC, Chinese Ethical Teacher, Philosopher)

29 It is amazing how complete is the delusion that beauty is goodness.
Count Leo Tolstoy (1828-1910, Russian Novelist, Philosopher)

30 Heat cannot be separated from fire, or beauty from the eternal.
Dante (Alighieri) (1265-1321, Italian Philosopher, Poet)

31 Beauty is variable, ugliness is constant.
Doug Horton

32 Beauty of whatever kind, in its supreme development, invariably excites the sensitive soul to tears.
Edgar Allan Poe (1809-1845, American Poet, Critic, short-story Writer)

33 There have been many definitions of beauty in art. What is it? Beauty is what the untrained eyes consider abominable.
Edmond and Jules De Goncourt (1822-1896, French Writers)

34 Beauty is the bait which with delight allures man to enlarge his kind.
Edmund Spenser (1552-1599, British Poet)

35 Walk on a rainbow trail; walk on a trail of song, and all about you will be beauty. There is a way out of every dark mist, over a rainbow trail.
Edward A. Navajo

36 The plainer the dress, the greater luster does beauty appear.
Edward F. Halifax (1881-1959, British Conservative Statesman)

37 In life, as in art, the beautiful moves in curves.
Edward G. Bulwer-Lytton (1803-1873, British Novelist, Poet)

38 Beauty is an outward gift, which is seldom despised, except by those to whom it has been refused.
Edward Gibbon (1737-1794, British Historian)

39 Beauty ought to look a little surprised: it is the emotion that best suits her face. The beauty who does not look surprised, who accepts her position as her due -- she reminds us too much of a prima donna.
Edward M. Forster (1879-1970, British Novelist, Essayist)

40 The difference between utility and utility plus beauty is the difference between telephone wires and the spider web.
Edwin Way Teale (1899-1980, American Naturalist and Writer)

41 The beautiful seems right by force of beauty, and the feeble wrong because of weakness.
Elizabeth Barrett Browning (1806-1861, British Poet)

42 Being pretty on the inside means you don't hit your brother and you eat all your peas -- that's what my grandma taught me.
Elizabeth Heller

43 Beauty is not caused. It is.
Emily Dickinson (1830-1886, American Poet)

44 Beauty is the still birth of suffering, every woman knows that.
Emily Prager (1948-, American Journalist, Author)

45 A poor beauty finds more lovers than husbands.
English Proverb

46 Beauty is a precious trace that eternity causes to appear to us and that it takes away from us. A manifestation of eternity, and a sign of death as well.
Eugene Ionesco (1912-, Romanian-born French Playwright)

47 What ever beauty may be, it has for its basis order, and for its essence unity.
Father Andre

48 There's beauty all around our paths, if but our watchful eyes can trace it midst familiar things, and through their lowly guise.
Felicia D. Hemans (1794-1835, British Poet)

49 The essence of the beautiful is unity in variety.
Felix Mendelssohn (1809-1847, German Composer)

50 All God's children are not beautiful. Most of God's children are, in fact, barely presentable.
Fran Lebowitz (1951-, American Journalist)

51 There is no excellent beauty that hath not some strangeness in the proportion.
Francis Bacon (1561-1626, British Philosopher, Essayist, Statesman)

52 The best part of beauty is that which no picture can express.
Francis Bacon (1561-1626, British Philosopher, Essayist, Statesman)

53 It is easy to be beautiful; it is difficult to appear so.
Frank O'Hara (1926-1966, American Poet, Art Critic)

54 Beauty, unaccompanied by virtue, is as a flower without perfume.
French Proverb

55 Nothing is beautiful, only man: on this piece of naivete rests all aesthetics, it is the first truth of aesthetics. Let us immediately add its second: nothing is ugly but degenerate man -- the domain of aesthetic judgment is therewith defined.
Friedrich Nietzsche (1844-1900, German Philosopher)

56 In the beautiful, man sets himself up as the standard of perfection; in select cases he worships himself in it. Man believes that the world itself is filled with beauty --he forgets that it is he who has created it. He alone has bestowed beauty upon the world --alas! only a very human, an all too human, beauty.
Friedrich Nietzsche (1844-1900, German Philosopher)

57 Beauty is the first present nature gives to women and the first it takes away.
George B. MTrT

58 Beauty is but the sensible image of the Infinite. Like truth and justice it lives within us; like virtue and the moral law it is a companion of the soul.
George Bancroft (1800-1891, American Historian)

59 Beauty itself is but the sensible image of the infinite.
George Bancroft (1800-1891, American Historian)

60 Beauty is all very well at first sight; but whoever looks at it when it has been in the house three days?
George Bernard Shaw (1856-1950, Irish-born British Dramatist)

61 It is generally a feminine eye that first detects the moral deficiencies hidden under the "dear deceit" of beauty.
George Eliot (1819-1880, British Novelist)

62 There are various orders of beauty, causing men to make fools of themselves in various styles... but there is one order of beauty which seems made to turn the heads not only of men, but of all intelligent mammals, even of women. It is a beauty like that of kittens, or very small downy ducks making gentle rippling noises with their soft bills, or babies just beginning to toddle and to engage in conscious mischief --a beauty with which you can never be angry, but that you feel ready to crush for inability to comprehend the state of mind into which it throws you.
George Eliot (1819-1880, British Novelist)

63 The beauty that addresses itself to the eyes is only the spell of the moment; the eye of the body is not always that of the soul.
George Sand (1804-1876, French Novelist)

64 Beauty as we feel it is something indescribable; what it is or what it means can never be said.
George Santayana (1863-1952, American Philosopher, Poet)

65 Beauty is desired in order that it may be befouled; not for its own sake, but for the joy brought by the certainty of profaning it.
Georges Bataille (1897-1962, French Novelist, Critic)

66 The fragrance always stays in the hand that gives the rose.
Hada Bejar

67 I spent a lot of time with a crown on my head. [On her beauty pageant days]
Halle Berry (Born 1968, American Actress)

68 How goodness heightens beauty!
Hannah More (1745-1833, British Writer, Reformer, Philanthropist)

69 Beauty can't amuse you, but brainwork -- reading, writing, thinking--can.
Helen Gurley Brown (American Businesswoman, Founder of Cosmopolitan Magazine)

70 Beauty is the promise of happiness.
Henri B. Stendhal (1783-1842, French Writer)

71 My work always tried to unite the true with the beautiful; but when I had to choose one or the other, I usually chose the beautiful.
Hermann Wey

72 Nothing's beautiful from every point of view.
Horace (65-8 BC, Italian Poet)

73 Beauty is whatever gives joy.
Hugh Nibley

74 Beauty is worse than wine, it intoxicates both the holder and beholder.
Immermann

75 Let the beauty we love be what we do.
Jalal-Uddin Rumi (1207-1273, Persian Sufi Mystic Poet)

76 Let there be nothing within thee that is not very beautiful and very gentle, and there will be nothing without thee that is not beautiful and softened by the spell of thy presence.
James Allen (1864-1912, British-born American Essayist, Author of "As a Man Thinketh")

77 Things are beautiful if you love them.
Jean Anouilh (1910-1987, French Playwright)

78 Beauty is one of the rare things that do not lead to doubt of God.
Jean Anouilh (1910-1987, French Playwright)

79 I'm tired of all this nonsense about beauty being only skin-deep. That's deep enough. What do you want --an adorable pancreas?
Jean Kerr (1923-, American Author, Playwright)

80 Beauty in art is often nothing but ugliness subdued.
Jean Rostand (1894-1977, French Biologist, Writer)

81 Beauty is composed of an eternal, invariable element whose quantity is extremely difficult to determine, and a relative element which might be, either by turns or all at once, period, fashion, moral, passion.
Jean-Luc Godard (1930-, French Filmmaker, Author)

82 If you have never seen beauty in a moment of suffering, you have never seen beauty at all. If you have never seen joy in a beautiful face, you have never seen joy at all.
Johann Friedrich Von Schiller (1759-1805, German Dramatist, Poet, Historian)

83 Truth exists for the wise, beauty for the feeling heart.
Johann Friedrich Von Schiller (1759-1805, German Dramatist, Poet, Historian)

84 Beauty is a manifestation of secret natural laws, which otherwise would have been hidden from us forever.
Johann Wolfgang Von Goethe (1749-1832, German Poet, Dramatist, Novelist)

85 Beauty is a primeval phenomenon, which itself never makes its appearance, but the reflection of which is visible in a thousand different utterances of the creative mind, and is as various as nature herself.
Johann Wolfgang Von Goethe (1749-1832, German Poet, Dramatist, Novelist)

86 Beauty is everywhere a welcome guest.
Johann Wolfgang Von Goethe (1749-1832, German Poet, Dramatist, Novelist)

87 Beauty seen is never lost, God's colors all are fast.
John Greenleaf Whittier (1807-1892, American Poet, Reformer, Author)

88 A thing of beauty is a joy for ever: Its loveliness increases; it will never pass into nothingness; but still will keep a bower quiet for us, and a sleep full of sweet dreams, and health, and quiet breathing...
John Keats (1795-1821, British Poet)

89 Beauty is truth, truth beauty -- that is all ye know on earth, and all ye need to know.
John Keats (1795-1821, British Poet)

90 There is certainly no absolute standard of beauty. That precisely is what makes its pursuit so interesting.
John Kenneth Galbraith (1908-, American Economist)

91 There are no better cosmetics than a severe temperance and purity, modesty and humility, a gracious temper and calmness of spirit; and there is no true beauty without the signatures of these graces in the very countenance.
John Ray (1627-1705, British Naturalist)

92 Remember that the most beautiful things in the world are the most useless; peacocks and lilies, for instance.
John Ruskin (1819-1900, British Critic, Social Theorist)

93 Nothing can be beautiful which is not true.
John Ruskin (1819-1900, British Critic, Social Theorist)

94 There is nothing that makes its way more directly to the soul than beauty.
Joseph Addison (1672-1719, British Essayist, Poet, Statesman)

95 Beauty is eternity gazing at itself in a mirror.
Kahlil Gibran (1883-1931, Lebanese Poet, Novelist)

96 Beauty in not in the face; beauty is a light in the heart.
Kahlil Gibran (1883-1931, Lebanese Poet, Novelist)

97 The esthete stands in the same relation to beauty as the pornographer stands to love, and the politician stands to life.
Karl Kraus (1874-1936, Austrian Satirist)

98 The real sin against life is to abuse and destroy beauty, even one's own --even more, one's own, for that has been put in our care and we are responsible for its well-being.
Katherine Anne Porter (1890-1980, American short-story Writer, Novelist)

99 Beauty is only skin deep, but it's a valuable asset if you're poor or haven't any sense.
Kin Hubbard (1868-1930, American Humorist, Journalist)

100 My heart that was rapt away by the wild cherry blossoms -- will it return to my body when they scatter?
Kotomichi

101 No woman can be handsome by the force of features alone, any more that she can be witty by only the help of speech.
Langston Hughes (1902-1967, American Poet, Short-story Writer, Playwright)

102 A day spent without the sight or sound of beauty, the contemplation of mystery, or the search of truth or perfection is a poverty-stricken day; and a succession of such days is fatal to human life.
Lewis Mumford (1895-1990, American Social Philosopher)

103 The criterion of true beauty is that it increases on examination; if false, that it lessens. There is therefore, something in true beauty that corresponds with right reason, and is not the mere creation of fancy.
Lord Greville (1554-1628, British Poet)

104 There is no cosmetic for beauty like happiness.
Marguerite Gardiner Blessington (1789-1849, Irish Writer and Socialite)

105 You can take no credit for beauty at sixteen. But if you are beautiful at sixty, it will be your soul's own doing.
Marie Carmichael Stopes (1880-1958, British Scientist, Pioneer of Birth Control)

106 The ideal beauty is a fugitive which is never found.
Marquise De STVignT

107 Strange that the vanity which accompanies beauty --excusable, perhaps, when there is such great beauty, or at any rate understandable --should persist after the beauty was gone.
Mary Arnim (1866-1941, Australian-born British Novelist)

108 Taught from infancy that beauty is woman's scepter, the mind shapes itself to the body, and roaming round its gilt cage, only seeks to adorn its prison.
Mary Wollstonecraft (1759-1797, British Feminist Writer)

109 The beauty of stature is the only beauty of men.
Michel Eyquem De Montaigne (1533-1592, French Philosopher, Essayist)

110 Beauty is the purgation of superfluities.
Michelangelo (1474-1564, Italian Renaissance Painter, Sculptor)

111 Too fair to worship, too divine to love.
Milman

112 The beauty myth moves for men as a mirage; its power lies in its ever-receding nature. When the gap is closed, the lover embraces only his own disillusion.
Naomi Wolf (1962-, American Author)

113 That which is striking and beautiful is not always good; but that which is good is always beautiful.
Ninon De L'Enclos (1620-1705, French Courtesan)

114 The pursuit of beauty is much more dangerous nonsense than the pursuit of truth or goodness, because it affords a stronger temptation to the ego.
Northrop Frye (1912-1991, Canadian Literary Critic)

115 Art is an invention of aesthetics, which in turn is an invention of philosophers. What we call art is a game.
Octavio Paz (1914-, Mexican Poet, Essayist)

116 Beauty is the index of a larger fact than wisdom.
Oliver Wendell Holmes (1809-1894, American Author, Wit, Poet)

117 It is better to be beautiful than to be good, but it is better to be good than to be ugly.
Oscar Wilde (1856-1900, British Author, Wit)

118 Beauty is a form of genius -- is higher, indeed, than genius, as it needs no explanation. It is of the great facts in the world like sunlight, or springtime, or the reflection in dark water of that silver shell we call the moon.
Oscar Wilde (1856-1900, British Author, Wit)

119 I have found that all ugly things are made by those who strive to make something beautiful, and that all beautiful things are made by those who strive to make something useful.
Oscar Wilde (1856-1900, British Author, Wit)

[120] I have a horror of people who speak about the beautiful. What is the beautiful? One must speak of problems in painting!
Pablo Picasso (1881-1973, Spanish Artist)

[121] To emphasize only the beautiful seems to me to be like a mathematical system that only concerns itself with positive numbers.
Paul Klee (1879-1940, Swiss Artist)

[122] Beauty is as relative as light and dark. Thus, there exists no beautiful woman, none at all, because you are never certain that a still far more beautiful woman will not appear and completely shame the supposed beauty of the first.
Paul Klee (1879-1940, Swiss Artist)

[123] The loveliest faces are to be seen by moonlight, when one sees half with the eye and half with the fancy.
Persian Proverb

[124] Whatever is beautiful is beautiful by necessity.
Pindar (518-438 BC, Greek Poet)

[125] Beauty of style and harmony and grace and good rhythm depends on simplicity.
Plato (427-347 BC, Greek Philosopher)

[126] Being is desirable because it is identical with Beauty, and Beauty is loved because it is Being. We ourselves possess Beauty when we are true to our own being; ugliness is in going over to another order; knowing ourselves, we are beautiful; in self-ignorance, we are ugly.
Plotinus

[127] Withdraw into yourself and look. And if you do not fine yourself beautiful yet, act as does the creator of a statue that is to be made beautiful: he cuts away here, he smoothes there, he makes this line lighter, this other purer, until a lovely face has grown his work. So do you also: cut away all that is excessive, straighten all that is crooked, bring light to all that is overcast, labor to make all one glow or beauty and never cease chiseling your statue, until there shall shine out on you from it the godlike splendor of virtue, until you see the perfect goodness surely established in the stainless shrine
Plotinus

[128] Beauty is a good letter of introduction.
Portuguese Proverb

[129] There is nothing in a caterpillar that tells you it's going to be a butterfly.
R. Buckminster Fuller (1895-1983, American Inventor, Designer, Poet, Philosopher)

[130] The line of beauty is the line of perfect economy.
Ralph Waldo Emerson (1803-1882, American Poet, Essayist)

[131] We ascribe beauty to that which is simple; which has no superfluous parts; which exactly answers its end; which stands related to all things; which is the mean of many extremes.
Ralph Waldo Emerson (1803-1882, American Poet, Essayist)

[132] A beautiful form is better than a beautiful face; it gives a higher pleasure than statues or pictures; it is the finest of the fine arts.
Ralph Waldo Emerson (1803-1882, American Poet, Essayist)

[133] As soon as beauty is sought not from religion and love, but for pleasure, it degrades the seeker.
Ralph Waldo Emerson (1803-1882, American Poet, Essayist)

[134] Beauty rests on necessities.
Ralph Waldo Emerson (1803-1882, American Poet, Essayist)

[135] Beauty is the pilot of the young soul.
Ralph Waldo Emerson (1803-1882, American Poet, Essayist)

[136] Beauty is the mark God sets on virtue. Every natural action is graceful; every heroic act is also decent, and causes the place and the bystanders to shine.
Ralph Waldo Emerson (1803-1882, American Poet, Essayist)

[137] Gather ye rose-buds while ye may, old Time is still a-flying: And this same flower that smiles today, tomorrow will be dying.
Robert Herrick (1591-1674, British Poet)

[138] Beauty is ever to the lonely mind a shadow fleeting; she is never plain. She is a visitor who leaves behind the gift of grief, the souvenir of pain.
Robert Nathan (1894-1985, American Novelist)

[139] Beauty when unadorned is adorned the most.
Roy Thompson (1894-1977, British Press Lord)

[140] What is beautiful is good, and who is good will soon be beautiful.
Sappho (600 BC, Greek Lyric Poet)

[141] Beauty always promises, but never gives anything.
Simone Weil (1910-1943, French Philosopher, Mystic)

[142] Sunsets are so beautiful that they almost seem as if we were looking through the gates of Heaven.
Sir John Lubbock (1834-1913, British Statesman, Banker, Naturalist)

[143] To give pain is the tyranny; to make happy, the true empire of beauty.
Sir Richard Steele (1672-1729, British Dramatist, Essayist, Editor)

[144] Remember if you marry for beauty, thou bindest thyself all thy life for that which perchance, will neither last nor please thee one year: and when thou hast it, it will be to thee of no price at all.
Sir Walter Raleigh (1552-1618, British Courtier, Navigator, Writer)

[145] Beauty is a short-lived tyranny.
Socrates (469-399 BC, Greek Philosopher of Athens)

[146] I have learnt to love you late, Beauty at once so ancient and so new!
St. Augustine (354-430, Numidian-born Bishop of Hippo, Theologian)

147 We know only that we are living in these bodies and have a vague idea, because we have heard it, and because our faith tells us so, that we possess souls. As to what good qualities there may be in our souls, or who dwells within them, or how precious they are, those are things which seldom consider and so we trouble little about carefully preserving the soul's beauty.
St. Teresa of Avila (1515-1582, Spanish Saint, Mystic)

148 What is most beautiful in virile men is sometimes feminine; what is most beautiful in feminine women is something masculine.
Susan Sontag (1933-, American Essayist)

149 Call for the grandest of all earthly spectacles, what is that? It is the sun going to his rest.
Thomas De Quincey (1785-1859, British Author)

150 Let us live for the beauty of our own reality.
Tim Robbins (1958-, American Actor, Director, Screenwriter, Producer, Writer)

151 I'm not ugly, but my beauty is a total creation.
Tyra Banks (Born 1973, American Model)

152 If either man or woman would realize that the full power of personal beauty, it must be by cherishing noble thoughts and hopes and purposes; by having something to do and something to live for that is worthy of humanity, and which, by expanding and symmetry to the body which contains it.
Upham

153 By cultivating the beautiful we scatter the seeds of heavenly flowers, as by doing good we cultivate those that belong to humanity.
Vernon Howard (19?-1992, American Author, Speaker)

154 Trust not too much to an enchanting face.
Virgil (70-19 BC, Roman Poet)

155 It is very necessary to have markers of beauty left in a world seemingly bent on making the most evil ugliness.
Vita Sackville-West (1892-1962, British Novelist, Poet)

156 Beauty is an ecstasy; it is as simple as hunger. There is really nothing to be said about it. It is like the perfume of a rose: you can smell it and that is all.
W. Somerset Maugham (1874-1965, British Novelist, Playwright)

157 The ideal has many names, and beauty is but one of them.
W. Somerset Maugham (1874-1965, British Novelist, Playwright)

158 The idea that happiness could have a share in beauty would be too much of a good thing.
Walter Benjamin (1982-1940, German Critic, Philosopher)

159 Exuberance is beauty.
William Blake (1757-1827, British Poet, Painter)

160 Beauty is but a vain and doubtful good; a shining gloss that fadeth suddenly; a flower that dies when it begins to bud; a doubtful good, a gloss, a glass, a flower, lost, faded, broken, dead within an hour. -
William Shakespeare (1564-1616, British Poet, Playwright, Actor)

161 To me, fair friend, you never can be old. For as you were when first your eye I eyed. Such seems your beauty still.
William Shakespeare (1564-1616, British Poet, Playwright, Actor)

BED

1 The bed is now as public as the dinner table and governed by the same rules of formal confrontation.
Angela Carter (1940-1992, British Author)

2 For I've been born and I've been wed -- all of man's peril comes of bed.
C. H. Webb

3 How it is I know not; but there is no place like a bed for confidential disclosures between friends. Man and wife, they say, there open the very bottom of their souls to each other; and some old couples often lie and chat over old times till nearly morning. Thus, then, in our hearts honeymoon, lay I and Queequeg -- a cozy, loving pair.
Herman Melville (1819-1891, American Author)

4 Bed is the poor man's opera.
Italian Proverb

5 It is comforting when one has a sorrow to lie in the warmth of one's bed and there, abandoning all effort and all resistance, to bury even one's head under the cover, giving one's self up to it completely, moaning like branches in the autumn wind. But there is still a better bed, full of divine odors. It is our sweet, our profound, our impenetrable friendship.
Marcel Proust (1871-1922, French Novelist)

6 Sleeping in a bed -- it is, apparently, of immense importance. Against those who sleep, from choice or necessity, elsewhere society feels righteously hostile. It is not done. It is disorderly, anarchical.
Rose Macaulay (1881-1958, British Novelist, Essayist)

7 The cool kindliness of sheets, that soon smooth away trouble; and the rough male kiss of blankets.
Rupert Brooke (1887-1915, British Poet)

8 The happiest part of a man's life is what he passes lying awake in bed in the morning.
Samuel Johnson (1709-1784, British Author)

9 I have thought of a pulley to raise me gradually; but that would give me pain, as it would counteract my natural inclination. I would have something that can dissipate the inertia and give elasticity to the muscles. We can heat the body, we can cool it; we can give it tension or relaxation; and surely it is possible to bring it into a state in which rising from bed will not be a pain.
Samuel Johnson (1709-1784, British Author)

10 What angel wakes me from my flowery bed?
William Shakespeare (1564-1616, British Poet, Playwright, Actor)

BEGGARS

1 Give a beggar a dime and he'll bless you. Give him a dollar and he'll curse you for withholding the rest of your fortune. Poverty is a bag with a hole at the bottom.
Anzia Yezierska (1885-1970, Polish Writer)

2 If begging should unfortunately be thy lot, knock at the large gates only.
Arabian Proverb

3 Beggars should be entirely abolished! Truly, it is annoying to give to them and annoying not to give to them.
Friedrich Nietzsche (1844-1900, German Philosopher)

4 God ordains that beggars should beg for greatness, as for all else, when greatness shines out of them, and they don't know it.
Georges Bernanos (1888-1948, French Novelist, Political Writer)

5 As for begging, it is safer to beg than to take, but it is finer to take than to beg.
Oscar Wilde (1856-1900, British Author, Wit)

6 All religions have honored the beggar. For he proves that in a matter at the same time as prosaic and holy, banal and regenerative as the giving of alms, intellect and morality, consistency and principles are miserably inadequate.
Walter Benjamin (1982-1940, German Critic, Philosopher)

BEGINNING

1 Though no one can go back and make a brand new start, anyone can start from now and make a brand new ending.
Carl Bard

2 A journey of a thousand miles begins with a single step.
Chinese Proverb

3 Whenever a thing is done for the first time, it releases a little demon.
Dave Sim

4 A good beginning makes a good end.
English Proverb

5 The beginning is the half of every action.
Greek Proverb

6 Great is the art of beginning, but greater is the art of ending.
Henry Wadsworth Longfellow (1819-1892, American Poet)

7 The world is round and the place which may seem like the end may also be only the beginning.
Ivy Baker

8 All this will not be finished in the first one hundred days. Nor will it be finished in the first thousand days, nor in the life of this administration, nor even perhaps in our lifetime on this planet. But let us begin.
John F. Kennedy (1917-1963, Thirty-fifth President of the USA)

9 A hard beginning maketh a good ending.
John Heywood (1497-1580, British Dramatist, Proverb Collection)

10 There will come a time when you believe everything is finished. That will be the beginning.
Louis L'Amour (1908-1988, American Western Author)

11 With the possible exception of the equator, everything begins somewhere.
Peter Robert Fleming (1907-1971, British Travel Writer, Journalist)

12 The great majority of men are bundles of beginnings.
Ralph Waldo Emerson (1803-1882, American Poet, Essayist)

13 In my beginning is my end.
T. S. Eliot (1888-1965, American-born British Poet, Critic)

14 In every phenomenon the beginning remains always the most notable moment.
Thomas Carlyle (1795-1881, Scottish Philosopher, Author)

15 Every exit is an entry somewhere else.
Tom Stoppard (1937-, Czech Playwright)

16 The truth is at the beginning of anything and its end are alike touching.
Yoshida Kenko

BEHAVIOR

1 Though our conduct seems so very different from that of the higher animals, the primary instincts are much alike in them and in us.
Albert Einstein (1879-1955, German-born American Physicist)

2 The test of one's behavior pattern; relationship to society, relationship to one's work, relationship to sex.
Alfred Adler (1870-1937, Austrian Psychiatrist)

3 Physics does not change the nature of the world it studies, and no science of behavior can change the essential nature of man, even though both sciences yield technologies with a vast power to manipulate the subject matters.
B. F. Skinner (1904-1990, American Psychologist)

4 Many people love in themselves what they hate in others.
Benzel Sternan

5 When new turns of behavior cease to appear in the life of the individual, its behavior ceases to be intelligent.
C. E. Coghill

6 Perfect behavior is born of complete indifference.
Cesare Pavese (1908-1950, Italian Poet, Novelist, Translator)

7 A mission could be defined as an image of a desired state that you want to get to. Once fully seen, it will inspire you to act, fuel your imagination and determine your behavior.
Charles A. Garfield (American Peak Performance Expert, Researcher, Trainer)

8   We are all serving a life sentence, and good behavior is our only hope for a pardon.
Doug Horton

9   When man learns to understand and control his own behavior as well as he is learning to understand and control the behavior of crop plants and domestic animals, he may be justified in believing that he has become civilized.
E. G. Stakman

10 I place a high moral value on the way people behave. I find it repellent to have a lot, and to behave with anything other than courtesy in the old sense of the word -- politeness of the heart, a gentleness of the spirit.
Emma Thompson (1959-, British-born American-born American Actress)

11 People don't change their behavior unless it makes a difference for them to do so.
Fran Tarkenton (American Football Player, Businessman, Corporate Consultant, Author)

12 Our natures are a lot like oil, mix us with anything else, and we strive to swim on top.
Francis Beaumont (1584-1616, British Dramatist)

13 We like to see others, but don't like others to see through us.
François de La Rochefoucauld (1613-1680, French classical writer)

14 Act the way you'd like to be and soon you'll be the way you act.
George W. Crane

15 It's no use growing older if you only learn new ways of misbehaving yourself.
Hector Hugh Munro (1870-1916, British Novelist, Writer)

16 If I repent of anything, it is very likely to be my good behavior.
Henry David Thoreau (1817-1862, American Essayist, Poet, Naturalist)

17 Behave so the aroma of your actions may enhance the general sweetness of the atmosphere.
Henry David Thoreau (1817-1862, American Essayist, Poet, Naturalist)

18 What ever is the natural propensity of a person is hard to overcome. If a dog were made a king, he would still gnaw at his shoes laces.
Hitopadesa (Sanskrit Fable From Panchatantra)

19 Still people are dangerous.
Jean De La Fontaine (1621-1695, French Poet)

20 The only normal people are the one's you don't know very well.
Joe Ancis

21 Behavior is the mirror in which everyone shows their image
Johann Wolfgang Von Goethe (1749-1832, German Poet, Dramatist, Novelist)

22 Live so that you can at least get the benefit of the doubt.
Kin Hubbard (1868-1930, American Humorist, Journalist)

23 No scoundrel is so stupid as to not find a reason for his vile conduct.
Korner

24 What is the appropriate behavior for a man or a woman in the midst of this world, where each person is clinging to his piece of debris? What's the proper salutation between people as they pass each other in this flood?
Leonard Cohen (1934-, Canadian-born American Musician, Songwriter, Singer)

25 Our humility rest upon a series of learned behaviors, woven together into patterns that are infinitely fragile and never directly inherited.
Margaret Mead (1901-1978, American Anthropologist)

26 Suppose that humans happen to be so constructed that they desire the opportunity for freely undertaken productive work. Suppose that they want to be free from the meddling of technocrats and commissars, bankers and tycoons, mad bombers who engage in psychological tests of will with peasants defending their homes, behavioral scientists who can't tell a pigeon from a poet, or anyone else who tries to wish freedom and dignity out of existence or beat them into oblivion.
Noam Chomsky (1928-, American Linguist, Political Activist)

27 I don't say we all ought to misbehave, but we ought to look as if we could.
Orson Welles (1915-1985, American Film Maker)

28 With a gentleman I am always a gentleman and a half, and with a fraud I try to be a fraud and a half.
Otto Von Bismarck (1815-1898, Prussian Statesman, Prime Minister)

29 Contraries are cured by contraries.
Proverb

30 The wolf changes his coat, but not his disposition.
Proverb

31 People who have little to do are excessive talkers.
Proverb

32 To know what people really think, pay regard to what they do, rather than what they say.
Rene Descartes (1596-1650, French Philosopher, Scientist)

33 If we ever do end up acting just like rats or Pavlov's dogs, it will be largely because behaviorism has conditioned us to do so.
Richard D. Rosen

34 At the time, my grandparents told my mom, "Lordy, what is Shannen doing?" Now I've calmed down. [on her reputation for bad behavior]
Shannen Doherty (Born 1971, American Actress)

35 We Barbie dolls are not supposed to behave the way I do.
Sharon Stone (1958-, American Actress)

36 It is the unseen and the spiritual in people that determines the outward and the actual.
Thomas Carlyle (1795-1881, Scottish Philosopher, Author)

37 Of course, behaviorism works. So does torture. Give me a no-nonsense, down-to-earth behaviorist, a few drugs, and simple electrical appliances, and in six months I will have him reciting the Athanasian Creed in public.
W. H. Auden (1907-1973, Anglo-American Poet)

38 Be nice to people on your way up because you'll meet them on your way down.
Wilson Mizner (1876-1933, American Author)

BELIEF

1 Every dogma has its day.
Abraham Rotstein

2 Some believe all that parents, tutors, and kindred believe. They take their principles by inheritance, and defend them as they would their estates, because they are born heirs to them.
Alan W. Watts (1915-1973, British-born American Philosopher, Author)

3 If you don't have solid beliefs you cannot build a stable life. Beliefs are like the foundation of a building, and they are the foundation to build your life upon.
Alfred A. Montapert (American Author)

4 To accomplish great things, we must not only act, but also dream; not only plan, but also believe.
Anatole France (1844-1924, French Writer)

5 Someone who thinks the world is always cheating him is right. He is missing that wonderful feeling of trust in someone or something.
Andrew V. Madson

6 If a horse has four legs, and I'm riding it, I think I can win.
Angel Cordero Jr.

7 What we can or cannot do, what we consider possible or impossible, is rarely a function of our true capability. It is more likely a function of our beliefs about who we are.
Anthony Robbins (1960-, American Author, Speaker, Peak Performance Expert / Consultant)

8 Beliefs have the power to create and the power to destroy. Human beings have the awesome ability to take any experience of their lives and create a meaning that disempowers them or one that can literally save their lives.
Anthony Robbins (1960-, American Author, Speaker, Peak Performance Expert / Consultant)

9 If you develop the absolute sense of certainty that powerful beliefs provide, then you can get yourself to accomplish virtually anything, including those things that other people are certain are impossible.
Anthony Robbins (1960-, American Author, Speaker, Peak Performance Expert / Consultant)

10 All personal breakthroughs being with a change in beliefs. So how do we change? The most effective way is to get your brain to associate massive pain to the old belief. You must feel deep in your gut that not only has this belief cost you pain in the past, but it's costing you in the present and, ultimately, can only bring you pain in the future. Then you must associate tremendous pleasure to the idea of adopting a new, empowering belief.
Anthony Robbins (1960-, American Author, Speaker, Peak Performance Expert / Consultant)

11 And above all things, never think that you're not good enough yourself. A man should never think that. My belief is that in life people will take you at your own reckoning
Anthony Trollope (1815-1882, British Novelist)

12 Of what worth are convictions that bring not suffering?
Antoine De Saint-Exupery (1900-1944, French Aviator, Writer)

13 I never quit trying. I never felt that I didn't have a chance to win.
Arnold Palmer (1929-, American Golfer)

14 The mind is the limit. As long as the mind can envision the fact that you can do something, you can do it, as long as you really believe 100 percent.
Arnold Schwarzenegger (1947-, Austrian-born American Actor, Author, Director, Restaurateur)

15 You can do what you think you can do and you cannot do what you think you cannot
Ben Stein (American Professor, Writer)

16 We are what we believe we are
Benjamin N. Cardozo (1870-1938, American Jurist, Supreme Court Justice)

17 What we need is not the will to believe, but the wish to find out.
Bertrand Russell (1872-1970, British Philosopher, Mathematician, Essayist)

18 When the intensity of emotional conviction subsides, a man who is in the habit of reasoning will search for logical grounds in favor of the belief which he finds in himself.
Bertrand Russell (1872-1970, British Philosopher, Mathematician, Essayist)

19 Everything is possible for him who believes.
Bible (Sacred Scriptures of Christians and Judaism)

20 If we let ourselves believe that man began with divine grace, that he forfeited this by sin, and that he can be redeemed only by divine grace through the crucified Christ, then we shall find peace of mind never granted to philosophers. He who cannot believe is cursed, for he reveals by his unbelief that God has not chosen to give him grace.
Blaise Pascal (1623-1662, French Scientist, Religious Philosopher)

21 Belief is a wise wager. Granted that faith cannot be proved, what harm will come to you if you gamble on its truth and it proves false? If you gain, you gain all; if you lose, you lose nothing. Wager, then, without hesitation, that He exists.
Blaise Pascal (1623-1662, French Scientist, Religious Philosopher)

22 Whatever you believe with feeling becomes your reality.
Brian Tracy (American Trainer, Speaker, Author, Businessman)

23 The essential element in personal magnetism is a consuming sincerity -- an overwhelming faith in the importance of the work one has to do.
Bruce Barton (1886-1967, American Author, Advertising Executive)

24 Believe nothing merely because you have been told it. Do not believe what your teacher tells you merely out of respect for the teacher. But whatsoever, after due examination and analysis, you find to be kind, conducive to the good, the benefit, the welfare of all beings -- that doctrine believe and cling to, and take it as your guide.
Buddha (568-488 BC, Founder of Buddhism)

25 Left to themselves, things tend to go from bad to worse. Murphy's First Corollary If you tell the boss you were late for work because you had a flat tire, the next morning you will have a flat tire.
Cannon's Law

26 The word "belief" is a difficult thing for me. I don't believe. I must have a reason for a certain hypothesis. Either I know a thing, and then I know it --I don't need to believe it.
Carl Jung (1875-1961, Swiss Psychiatrist)

27 He that will believe only what he can fully comprehend must have a long head or a very short creed.
Charles Caleb Colton (1780-1832, British Sportsman Writer)

28 Acquire the courage to believe in yourself. Many of the things that you have been taught were at one time the radical ideas of individuals who had the courage to believe what their own hearts and minds told them was true, rather than accept the common beliefs of their day.
Ching Ning Chu (Chinese-American Businesswoman, Lecturer, Author)

29 Every person is the creation of himself, the image of his own thinking and believing. As individuals think and believe, so they are.
Claude M. Bristol (1891-1951, American Author of "The Magic of Believing")

30 You've got to be success minded. You've got to feel that things are coming your way when you're out selling; otherwise, you won't be able to sell anything.
Curtis Carlson (American Businessman, Founder of Carlson Companies, Inc.)

31 The art of writing is the art of discovering what you believe.
David Hare (1947-, British Playwright, Director)

32 Believe Big. The size of your success is determined by the size of your belief. Think little goals and expect little achievements. Think big goals and win big success. Remember this, too! Big ideas and big plans are often easier -- certainly no more difficult -- than small ideas and small plans.
David J. Schwartz (American Trainer, Author of "The Magic of Thinking Big")

33 Remind yourself regularly that you are better than you think you are. Successful people are not superhuman. Success does not require a super-intellect. Nor is there anything mystical about success. And success doesn't based on luck. Successful people are just ordinary folks who have developed belief in themselves and what they do. Never -- yes, never -- sell yourself short.
David J. Schwartz (American Trainer, Author of "The Magic of Thinking Big")

34 Believe it can be done. When you believe something can be done, really believe, your mind will find the ways to do it. Believing a solution paves the way to solution.
David J. Schwartz (American Trainer, Author of "The Magic of Thinking Big")

35 As I get older I seem to believe less and less and yet to believe what I do believe more and more.
David Jenkins (1925-, British Ecclesiastic, Bishop of Durham)

36 Nothing is easier than self-deceit. For what each man wishes, that he also believes to be true.
Demosthenes (383-322 BC, Greek Orator)

37 If you believe you can, you probably can. If you believe you won t, you most assuredly won t. Belief is the ignition switch that gets you off the launching pad.
Denis Waitley (1933-, American Author, Speaker, Trainer, Peak Performance Expert)

38 You must understand that seeing is believing, but also know that believing is seeing.
Denis Waitley (1933-, American Author, Speaker, Trainer, Peak Performance Expert)

39 Believe only half of what you see and nothing that you hear.
Dinah Mulock Craik

40 If you don't change your beliefs, your life will be like this forever. Is that good news?
Dr. Robert Anthony (American educator)

41 It isn't enough to talk about peace. One must believe in it. And it isn't enough to believe in it. One must work at it.
Eleanor Roosevelt (1884-1962, American First Lady, Columnist, Lecturer, Humanitarian)

42 The abdication of belief makes the behavior small -- better an ignis fatuus than no illume at all.
Emily Dickinson (1830-1886, American Poet)

43 Men are disturbed not by things, but by the view which they take of them.
Epictetus (50-120, Stoic Philosopher)

44 If you think you can do it, you can.
Eric Lindros (Born 1973, Canadian Hockey Player)

45 Man makes holy what he believes.
Ernest Renan (1823-1892, French Writer, Critic, Scholar)

46 It is easier to believe than to doubt.
Everett D. Martin

47 Things that I felt absolutely sure of but a few years ago, I do not believe now. This thought makes me see more clearly how foolish it would be to expect all men to agree with me.
F. D. Van Amburgh

48 Magic is believing in yourself, if you can do that, you can make anything happen.
Foka Gomez

49 All beliefs are bald ideas.
Francis Picabia (1878-1953, French Painter, Poet)

50 Belief in oneself is one of the most important bricks in building any successful venture.
Frank Gifford (American sportscaster)

51 The barrier between success is not something which exists in the real world: it is composed purely and simply of doubts about ability.
Franklin D. Roosevelt (1882-1945, Thirty-second President of the USA)

52 A belief is like a guillotine, just as heavy, just as light.
Franz Kafka (1883-1924, German Novelist, Short-Story Writer)

53 To believe a thing is impossible is to make it so.
French Proverb

54 Any man worth his salt will stick up for what he believes right, but it takes a slightly better man to acknowledge instantly and without reservation that he is in error.
General Peyton C. March

55 With most people disbelief in a thing is founded on a blind belief in some other thing.
Georg C. Lichtenberg (1742-1799, German Physicist, Satirist)

56 With the majority of people unbelief in one thing is founded on the blind belief in another.
Georg C. Lichtenberg (1742-1799, German Physicist, Satirist)

57 First we have to believe, and then we believe.
Georg C. Lichtenberg (1742-1799, German Physicist, Satirist)

58 If one age believes too much it is natural that another believes too little.
George Earle Buckle (1854-1935, British Journalist)

59 Human beliefs, like all other natural growths, elude the barrier of systems.
George Eliot (1819-1880, British Novelist)

60 I am a winner each and every time I go into the ring.
George Foreman (1949-, American Boxer)

61 The world we see that seems so insane is the result of a belief system that is not working. To perceive the world differently, we must be willing to change our belief system, let the past slip away, expand our sense of now, and dissolve the fear in our minds.
Gerald G. Jampolsky (American Psychiatrist, Lecturer, Author)

62 Believing: it means believing in our own lies. And I can say that I am grateful that I got this lesson very early.
Gunther Grass (1927-, German Author)

63 People give us credit only for what we ourselves believe.
Gutzkow

64 Belief is a moral act for which the believer is to be held responsible.
H. A. Hodges

65 It is a sin to believe evil of others, but it is seldom a mistake.
H. L. Mencken (1880-1956, American Editor, Author, Critic, Humorist)

66 Our systems, perhaps, are nothing more than an unconscious apology for our faults --a gigantic scaffolding whose object is to hide from us our favorite sin.
Henri Frederic Amiel (1821-1881, Swiss Philosopher, Poet, Critic)

67 He can who thinks he can, and he can't who thinks he can't. This is an inexorable, indisputable law.
Henry Ford (1863-1947, American Industrialist, Founder of Ford Motor Company)

68 What distinguishes the majority of men from the few is their inability to act according to their beliefs.
Henry Miller (1891-1980, American Author)

69 I've always believed no matter how many shots I miss, I'm going to make the next one.
Isiah Thomas (American Basketball Player, Coach)

70 The practical effect of a belief is the real test of its soundness.
James A. Froude (1818-1894, British Historian)

71 The will to do springs from the knowledge that we can do.
James Allen (1864-1912, British-born American Essayist, Author of "As a Man Thinketh")

72 We have all had the experience of finding that our reactions and perhaps even our deeds have denied beliefs we thought were ours.
James Baldwin (1924-1987, American Author)

73 Confronted with the impossibility of remaining faithful to one's beliefs, and the equal impossibility of becoming free of them, one can be driven to the most inhuman excesses.
James Baldwin (1924-1987, American Author)

74 Everyone believes very easily whatever they fear or desire.
Jean De La Fontaine (1621-1695, French Poet)

75 The nobility of a human being is strictly independent of that of his convictions.
Jean Rostand (1894-1977, French Biologist, Writer)

76 To a very large extent men and women are a product of how they define themselves. As a result of a combination of innate ideas and the intimate influences of the culture and environment we grow up in, we come to have beliefs about the nature of being human. These beliefs penetrate to a very deep level of our psychosomatic systems, our minds and brains, our nervous systems, our endocrine systems, and even our blood and sinews. We act, speak, and think according to these deeply held beliefs and belief systems.
Jeremy W. Hayward

77 I started out by believing God for a newer car than the one I was driving. I started out believing God for a nicer apartment than I had. Then I moved up.
Jim Bakker (1940-, American Evangelist)

78 My father gave me the greatest gift anyone could give another person, he believed in me.
Jim Valvano (American College Basketball Coach)

79 Those who say it can't be done are usually interrupted by others doing it.
Joel A. Barker (American Businessman, Consultant, Author)

80 He is dead in this world who has no belief in another.
Johann Wolfgang Von Goethe (1749-1832, German Poet, Dramatist, Novelist)

81 If you must tell me your opinions, tell me what you believe in. I have plenty of doubts of my own.
Johann Wolfgang Von Goethe (1749-1832, German Poet, Dramatist, Novelist)

82 We are so constituted that we believe the most incredible things; and, once they are engraved upon the memory, woe to him who would endeavor to erase them.
Johann Wolfgang Von Goethe (1749-1832, German Poet, Dramatist, Novelist)

83 Oh how sweet it is to hear one's own convictions from another's lips.
Johann Wolfgang Von Goethe (1749-1832, German Poet, Dramatist, Novelist)

84 It is always easier to believe than to deny. Our minds are naturally affirmative.
John Burroughs (1837-1921, American Naturalist, Author)

85 In the province of the mind, what one believes to be true either is true or becomes true.
John C. Lilly (1915-, American Doctor, Author)

86 Whatever one believes to be true either is true or becomes true in one's mind.
John C. Lilly (1915-, American Doctor, Author)

87 One person with a belief is equal to a force of ninety-nine who have only interests.
John Stuart Mill (1806-1873, British Philosopher, Economist)

88 The lack of belief is a defect that ought to be concealed when it cannot be overcome.
Jonathan Swift (1667-1745, Anglo-Irish Satirist)

89 Men freely believe that which they desire.
Julius Caesar (101-44 BC, Roman Emperor)

90 Men willingly believe what they wish.
Julius Caesar (101-44 BC, Roman Emperor)

91 What we wish, we readily believe, and what we ourselves think, we imagine others think also.
Julius Caesar (101-44 BC, Roman Emperor)

92 I never cease being dumbfounded by the unbelievable things people believe.
Leo Rosten (1908-1997, Polish Born American Political Scientist)

93 Believe that you possess a basic goodness, which is the foundation for the greatness you can ultimately achieve.
Les Brown (1945-, American Speaker, Author, Trainer, Motivator Lecturer)

94 Your level of belief in yourself will inevitably manifest itself in whatever you do.
Les Brown (1945-, American Speaker, Author, Trainer, Motivator Lecturer)

95 One can't believe impossible things. I dare say you haven't had much practice," said the Queen. "When I was your age, I always did it for half-an-hour a day. Why, sometimes I've believed as many as six impossible things before breakfast."
Lewis Carroll (1832-1898, British Writer, Mathematician)

96 Sometimes I've believed as many as six possible things before breakfast.
Lewis Carroll (1832-1898, British Writer, Mathematician)

97 It's an indulgence to sit in a room and discuss your beliefs as if they were a juicy piece of gossip.
Lillian Hellman (1905-1984, American Playwright)

98 To believe in something not yet proved and to underwrite it with our lives: it is the only way we can leave the future open. Man, surrounded by facts, permitting himself no surmise, no intuitive flash, no great hypothesis, no risk, is in a locked cell. Ignorance cannot seal the mind and imagination more surely.
Lillian Smith (1897-1966, American Author)

99 All are inclined to believe what they covet, from a lottery-ticket up to a passport to Paradise.
Lord Byron (1788-1824, British Poet)

100 Men will not believe because they will not broaden their minds.
Lord Chesterfield (1694-1773, British Statesman, Author)

101 There seems to be a great misunderstanding on the part of a great many people to the effect that when you cease to believe you may cease to behave.
Louis Kronenberger

102 Some people will believe anything if you whisper it to them.
Louis Nizer (1902-1904, British Born American Lawyer, Writer)

103 Getting rid of a delusion makes us wiser than getting hold of a truth.
Ludwig Borne

104 A conservative believes nothing should be done for the first time.
Lynwood L. Giacomini

105 You can change your beliefs so they empower your dreams and desires. Create a strong belief in yourself and what you want.
Marcia Wieder (American Speaker, Trainer, Author)

106 If you don't believe in yourself, then who will believe in you? The next man's way of getting there might not necessarily work for me, so I have to create my own ways of getting there.
Martin Lawrence (1965-, German-born American Actor, Comedian, Director, Producer, Writer)

107 Even if I knew that tomorrow the world would go to pieces, I would still plant my apple tree.
Martin Luther (1483-1546, German Leader of the Protestant Reformation)

108 Learned helplessness is the giving-up reaction, the quitting response that follows from the belief that whatever you do doesn't matter.
Martin Seligan

109 In order to succeed, we must first believe that we can.
Michael Korda (1919-, American publisher)

110 As a first approximation, I define "belief" not as the object of believing (a dogma, a program, etc.) but as the subject's investment in a proposition, the act of saying it and considering it as true.
Michel De Certeau (French Writer)

111 Nothing is so firmly believed as that which we least know.
Michel Eyquem De Montaigne (1533-1592, French Philosopher, Essayist)

112 How many things served us but yesterday as articles of faith, which today we deem but fables?
Michel Eyquem De Montaigne (1533-1592, French Philosopher, Essayist)

113 I don't think anything is unrealistic if you believe you can do it.
Mike Ditka (American Football Player, Coach of Chicago Bears)

114 What you hear repeatedly you will eventually believe.
Mike Murdock

115 What ever the mind of man can conceive and believe, it can achieve.
Napoleon Hill (1883-1970, American Speaker, Motivational Writer, "Think and Grow Rich")

116 By believing passionately in something that still does not exist, we create it. The nonexistent is whatever we have not sufficiently desired.
Nikos Kazantzakis (1883-1957, Greek Writer)

117 Drugs are not always necessary, but belief in recovery always is.
Norman Cousins (1915-1990, American Editor, Humanitarian, Author)

118 First thing every morning before you arise say out loud, "I believe," three times.
Norman Vincent Peale (1898-1993, American Christian Reformed Pastor, Speaker, Author)

119 Believe in yourself! Have faith in your abilities! Without a humble but reasonable confidence in your own powers you cannot be successful or happy.
Norman Vincent Peale (1898-1993, American Christian Reformed Pastor, Speaker, Author)

120 To be absolutely certain about something, one must know everything or nothing about it.
Olin Miller

121 The man who believes he can do something is probably right, and so is the man who believes he can t. Anonymous I don't think of myself as a poor deprived ghetto girl who made good. I think of myself as someone who from an early age knew I was responsible for myself, and I had to make good.
Oprah Winfrey (1954-, American TV Personality, Producer, Actress, Author)

122 The old believe everything; the middle aged suspect everything, and the young know everything.
Oscar Wilde (1856-1900, British Author, Wit)

123 People are slow to believe that, which if believed would work them harm.
Ovid (43 BC-18 AD, Roman Poet)

124 We are slow to believe that which if believed would hurt our feelings.
Ovid (43 BC-18 AD, Roman Poet)

125 More persons, on the whole, are humbugged by believing in nothing than by believing in too much.
P.T. Barnum (1810-1891, American Showman, Entertainer, Circus Builder)

126 Everybody keeps telling me how surprised they are with what I've done. But I'm telling you honestly that it doesn't surprise me. I knew I could do it.
Patrick Ewing (1962-, American Basketball Player)

127 That which has been believed by everyone, always and everywhere, has every chance of being false.
Paul Valery (1871-1945, French Poet, Essayist)

128 Give to us clear vision that we may know where to stand and what to stand for -- because unless we stand for something, we shall fall for anything.
Peter Marshall (1902-1949, American Presbyterian Clergyman)

129 When we argue for our limitations, we get to keep them.
Peter Mcwilliams (American Author of "Life 101")

130 We have only to believe. And the more threatening and irreducible reality appears, the more firmly and desperately we must believe. Then, little by little, we shall see the universal horror unbend, and then smile upon us, and then take us in its more than human arms.
Pierre Teilhard De Chardin (1881-1955, French Christian Mystic, Author)

131 Men are most apt to believe what they least understand.
Pliny The Elder (23-79, Roman Neophatonist)

132 Belief consists in accepting the affirmations of the soul; unbelief, in denying them.
Ralph Waldo Emerson (1803-1882, American Poet, Essayist)

133 We are born believing. A man bears beliefs as a tree bears apples.
Ralph Waldo Emerson (1803-1882, American Poet, Essayist)

134 All the great ages have been ages of belief.
Ralph Waldo Emerson (1803-1882, American Poet, Essayist)

135 You must see first before you can believe.
Raymond Holliwell

136 Sooner or later, those who win are those who think they can.
Richard Bach (1936-, American Author)

137 The only thing that stands between a man and what he wants from life is often merely the will to try it and the faith to believe that it is possible.
Richard M. DeVos (1926-, American Businessman, Co-founder of Amway Corp.)

138 Belief gets in the way of learning.
Robert Heinlein (1907-1988, American Science Fiction Writer)

139 Belief is the death of intelligence. As soon as one believes a doctrine of any sort, or assumes certitude, one stops thinking about that aspect of existence.
Robert Wilson (1941-, American Theater Director, Designer)

140 Seeing is not always believing.
Rod Serling (1924-1975, American Television Script-writer)

141 We won't even attempt to achieve what we do not believe at a deep level we can have or deserve.
Ruth Ross

142 Once you begin to believe there is help "out there," you will know it to be true.
Saint Bartholomew

143 Belief like any other moving body follows the path of least resistance.
Samuel Butler (1612-1680, British Poet, Satirist)

144 Every man who attacks my belief, diminishes in some degree my confidence in it, and therefore makes me uneasy; and I am angry with him who makes me uneasy.
Samuel Johnson (1709-1784, British Author)

145 I stopped believing in Santa Claus when I was six. Mother took me to see him in a department store and he asked for my autograph.
Shirley Temple Black (1928-, American Film Child Star)

146 Devout believers are safeguarded in a high degree against the risk of certain neurotic illnesses; their acceptance of the universal neurosis spares them the task of constructing a personal one.
Sigmund Freud (1856-1939, Austrian Physician - Founder of Psychoanalysis)

147 Every time a child says, "I don't believe in fairies," there is a fairy somewhere that falls down dead.
Sir James M. Barrie (1860-1937, British Playwright)

148 It is so hard to believe because it is so hard to obey.
Soren Kierkegaard (1813-1855, Danish Philosopher, Writer)

149 If you believe what you like in the gospels, and reject what you don't like, it is not the gospel you believe, but yourself.
St. Augustine (354-430, Numidian-born Bishop of Hippo, Theologian)

150 To be a champ, you have to believe in yourself when nobody else will.
Sugar Ray Robinson (1920-1989, American Boxer)

151 I believe in using words, not fists... I believe in my outrage knowing people are living in boxes on the street. I believe in honesty. I believe in a good time. I believe in good food. I believe in sex.
Susan Sarandon (1946-, American Actress)

152 I believe because it is impossible.
Terence (185-159 BC, Roman Writer of Comedies)

153 You believe easily that which you hope for earnestly.
Terence (185-159 BC, Roman Writer of Comedies)

154 The battle that never ends is the battle of belief against unbelief.
Thomas Carlyle (1795-1881, Scottish Philosopher, Author)

155 No iron chain, or outward force of any kind, can ever compel the soul of a person to believe or to disbelieve.
Thomas Carlyle (1795-1881, Scottish Philosopher, Author)

156 Conviction never so excellent, is worthless until it coverts itself into conduct.
Thomas Carlyle (1795-1881, Scottish Philosopher, Author)

157 The most fearful unbelief is unbelief in your self.
Thomas Carlyle (1795-1881, Scottish Philosopher, Author)

158 He does not believe that does not live according to his belief .
Thomas Fuller (1608-1661, British Clergyman, Author)

159 Belief in a cruel God makes a cruel man.
Thomas Paine (1737-1809, Anglo-American Political Theorist, Writer)

160 What a person believes is not as important as how a person believes.
Timothy Virkkala

161 For those who believe, no proof is necessary. For those who don't believe, no proof is possible.
Traditional Saying

162 Loving is half of believing.
Victor Hugo (1802-1885, French Poet, Dramatist, Novelist)

163 They can because they think they can.
Virgil (70-19 BC, Roman Poet)

164 It doesn't matter how many say it cannot be done or how many people have tried it before; it's important to realize that whatever you're doing, it's your first attempt at it.
Wally Amos (American Businessman, Founder, Famous Amos Cookies)

165 Strong beliefs win strong men, and then make them stronger.
Walter Bagehot (1826-1877, British Economist, Critic)

166 Many a time I have wanted to stop talking and find out what I really believed.
Walter Lippmann (1889-1974, American Journalist)

167 We are all captives of the picture in our head -- our belief that the world we have experienced is the world that really exists.
Walter Lippmann (1889-1974, American Journalist)

168 I always knew I was going to be rich. I don't think I ever doubted it for a minute.
Warren Buffett (1930-, American Investment Entrepreneur)

169 You'll see it when you believe it.
Wayne Dyer (1940-, American Psychotherapist, Author, Lecturer)

170 You are always a valuable, worthwhile human being -- not because anybody says so, not because you're successful, not because you make a lot of money -- but because you decide to believe it and for no other reason.
Wayne Dyer (1940-, American Psychotherapist, Author, Lecturer)

171 Belief creates the actual fact.
William James (1842-1910, American Psychologist, Professor, Author)

172 Believe that life is worth living, and your belief will help create the fact.
William James (1842-1910, American Psychologist, Professor, Author)

173 As a rule we disbelieve all the facts and theories for which we have no use.
William James (1842-1910, American Psychologist, Professor, Author)

174 The Gateway to Christianity is not through an intricate labyrinth of dogma, but by a simple belief in the person of Christ.
William Lyon Phelps

175 My mother taught me very early to believe I could achieve any accomplishment I wanted to. The first was to walk without braces.
Wilma Rudolph (1940-1994, American Track Athlete)

BENEFACTORS

1 Nobody shoots at Santa Claus.
Alfred E. Smith (1873-1944, American Politician)

2 In your Salvation shelter I saw poverty, misery, cold and hunger. You gave them bread and treacle and dreams of heaven. I give from thirty shillings a week to twelve thousand a year. They find their own dreams; but I look after the drainage.
George Bernard Shaw (1856-1950, Irish-born British Dramatist)

3 With regard to donations always expect the most from prudent people, who keep their own accounts.
Joseph Addison (1672-1719, British Essayist, Poet, Statesman)

4 Because they did not see merit where they should have seen it, people, to express their regret, will go and leave a lot of money to the very people who will be the first to throw stones at the next person who has anything to say and finds a difficulty in getting a hearing.
Samuel Butler (1612-1680, British Poet, Satirist)

BEREAVEMENT

1 If, as I can't help suspecting, the dead also feel the pains of separation (and this may be one of their purgatorial sufferings), then for both lovers, and for all pairs of lovers without exception, bereavement is a universal and integral part of our experience of love.
C. S. Lewis (1898-1963, British Academic, Writer, Christian Apologist)

2 It is extraordinary how the house and the simplest possessions of someone who has been left become so quickly sordid. Even the stain on the coffee cup seems not coffee but the physical manifestation of one's inner stain, the fatal blot that from the beginning had marked one for ultimate aloneness.
Coleman Dowell (1925-1985, American Novelist, Dramatist, Lyricist)

3 Guilt is perhaps the most painful companion of death.
Elisabeth KnBler-Ross (1926-, Swiss-born American Psychiatrist)

4 Don't order any black things. Rejoice in his memory; and be radiant: leave grief to the children. Wear violet and purple. Be patient with the poor people who will snivel: they don't know; and they think they will live for ever, which makes death a division instead of a bond.
George Bernard Shaw (1856-1950, Irish-born British Dramatist)

5 On the death of a friend, we should consider that the fates through confidence have devolved on us the task of a double living, that we have henceforth to fulfill the promise of our friend's life also, in our own, to the world.
Henry David Thoreau (1817-1862, American Essayist, Poet, Naturalist)

6 We feel at first as if some opportunities of kindness and sympathy were lost, but learn afterward that any pure grief is ample recompense for all. That is, if we are faithful; -- for a spent grief is but sympathy with the soul that disposes events, and is as natural as the resin of Arabian trees. -- Only nature has a right to grieve perpetually, for she only is innocent. Soon the ice will melt, and the blackbirds sing along the river which he frequented, as pleasantly as ever. The same everlasting serenity will appear in this face of God, and we will not be sorrowful, if he is not.
Henry David Thoreau (1817-1862, American Essayist, Poet, Naturalist)

7 Bereavement is a darkness impenetrable to the imagination of the unbereaved.
Iris Murdoch (1919-, British Novelist, Philosopher)

8 Never does one feel oneself so utterly helpless as in trying to speak comfort for great bereavement. I will not try it. Time is the only comforter for the loss of a mother.
Jane Welsh Carlyle (1801-1866, British Diarist)

9 Grief that is dazed and speechless is out of fashion: the modern woman mourns her husband loudly and tells you the whole story of his death, which distresses her so much that she forgets not the slightest detail about it.
Jean De La Bruyere (1645-1696, French Writer)

10 They tell me, Lucy, thou art dead, that all of thee we loved and cherished has with thy summer roses perished; and left, as its young beauty fled, an ashen memory in its stead.
John Greenleaf Whittier (1807-1892, American Poet, Reformer, Author)

11 If we could know which of us, darling, would be the first to go, who would be first to breast the swelling tide and step alone upon the other side -- if we could know!
Julia Harris May

12 Tears are sometimes an inappropriate response to death. When a life has been lived completely honestly, completely successfully, or just completely, the correct response to death's perfect punctuation mark is a smile.
Julie Burchill (British Journalist, Writer)

13 A man's house burns down. The smoking wreckage represents only a ruined home that was dear through years of use and pleasant associations. By and by, as the days and weeks go on, first he misses this, then that, then the other thing. And when he casts about for it he finds that it was in that house. Always it is an essential -- there was but one of its kind. It cannot be replaced. It was in that house. It is irrevocably lost. It will be years before the tale of lost essentials is complete, and not till then can he truly know the magnitude of his disaster.
Mark Twain (1835-1910, American Humorist, Writer)

14 Peace, peace! he is not dead, he doth not sleep -- he hath awakened from the dream of life --   'Tis we, who lost in stormy visions, keep with phantoms an unprofitable strife.
Percy Bysshe Shelley (1792-1822, British Poet)

15 The death of a dear friend, wife, brother, lover, which seemed nothing but privation, somewhat later assumes the aspect of a guide or genius; for it commonly operates revolutions in our way of life, terminates an epoch of infancy or of youth which was waiting to be closed, breaks up a wonted occupation, or a household, or style of living, and allows the formation of new ones more friendly to the growth of character.
Ralph Waldo Emerson (1803-1882, American Poet, Essayist)

16 The sorrow for the dead is the only sorrow from which we refuse to be divorced. Every other wound we seek to heal -- every other affliction to forget: but this wound we consider it a duty to keep open -- this affliction we cherish and brood over in solitude.
Washington Irving (1783-1859, American Author)

17 For precious friends hid in death's dateless night.
William Shakespeare (1564-1616, British Poet, Playwright, Actor)

BETRAYAL

1 If I had to choose between betraying my country and betraying my friend, I hope I should have the guts to betray my country.
Edward M. Forster (1879-1970, British Novelist, Essayist)

2 To betray you must first belong.
Harold Philby

3 They talk of a man betraying his country, his friends, his sweetheart. There must be a moral bond first. All a man can betray is his conscience.
Joseph Conrad (1857-1924, Polish-born British Novelist)

4 It is all right to rat, but you can't re-rat.
Winston Churchill (1874-1965, British Statesman, Prime Minister)

BIBLE

1 The Word of God well understood and religiously obeyed is the shortest route to spiritual perfection. And we must not select a few favorite passages to the exclusion of others. Nothing less than a whole Bible can make a whole Christian.
A. W. Tozer (Deceased 1963, American Preacher)

2 The scripture in times of disputes is like an open town in times of war, which serves in differently the occasions of both parties.
Alexander Pope (1688-1744, British Poet, Critic, Translator)

3 A readiness to believe every promise implicitly, to obey every command unhesitatingly, to stand perfect and complete in all the will of God, is the only true spirit of Bible study.
Andrew Murray

4   The Good Book -- one of the most remarkable euphemisms ever copied.
    Ashley Montagu (1905-, British Anthropologist)

5   Fear is the denomination of the Old Testament; belief is the denomination of the New.
    Benjamin Whichcote (1609-1683, British Philosopher, Theologian)

6   There's a Bible on the shelf there. But I keep it next to Voltaire-poison and antidote.
    Bertrand Russell (1872-1970, British Philosopher, Mathematician, Essayist)

7   The law of Thy mouth is better to me than thousands of gold and silver pieces. [Psalm 119:72]
    Bible (Sacred Scriptures of Christians and Judaism)

8   We have used the Bible as if it were a mere special constable's handbook, an opium dose for keeping beasts of burden patient while they are overloaded.
    Charles Kingsley (1819-1875, British Author, Clergyman)

9   When the white man came, we had the land and they had the bibles. Now they have the land and we have the bibles.
    Chief Dan George (1899-1977, Native American Author)

10 The Bible will keep you from sin, or sin will keep you from the Bible.
    Dwight L. Moody (1837-1899, American Evangelist)

11 I know the Bible is inspired because it inspires me.
    Dwight L. Moody (1837-1899, American Evangelist)

12 There's no better book with which to defend the Bible than the Bible itself.
    Dwight L. Moody (1837-1899, American Evangelist)

13 light for every darkness, life in death, the promise of our Lord's return, and the assurance of everlasting glory.
    Dwight L. Moody (1837-1899, American Evangelist)

14 Well, Fitz, I looked all through that bible, it was in very fine print and stumbling on that great book Ecclesiastics, read it aloud to all who would listen. Soon I was alone and began cursing the bloody bible because there were no titles in it -- although I found the source of practically every good title you ever heard of. But the boys, principally Kipling, had been there before me and swiped all the good ones so I called the book Men Without Women hoping it would have a large sale among the fairies and old Vassar Girls.
    Ernest Hemingway (1898-1961, American Writer)

15 No one ever graduates from Bible study until he meets its Author face to face.
    Everett Harris

16 No one ever became, or can become truly eloquent without being a reader of the Bible, and an admirer of the purity and sublimity of its language.
    Fisher Ames (1758-1808, American Statesman)

17 The pencil of the Holy Ghost hath labored more in describing the afflictions of Job than the felicities of Solomon.
    Francis Bacon (1561-1626, British Philosopher, Essayist, Statesman)

18 Prosperity is the blessing of the Old Testament; adversity is the blessing of the New.
    Francis Bacon (1561-1626, British Philosopher, Essayist, Statesman)

19 The one book necessary to be understood by a divine, is the Bible; any others are to be read, chiefly, in order to understand that.
    Francis Lockier (1668-1740, British Prelate, Man of Letters)

20 In this one book are the two most interesting personalities in the whole world--God and yourself. The Bible is the story of God and man, a love story in which you and I must write our own ending, our unfinished autobiography of the creature and the Creator.
    Fulton Oursler

21 The Bible is the great family chronicle of the Jews.
    Heinrich Heine (1797-1856, German Poet, Journalist)

22 There is much in the Bible against which every instinct of my being rebels, so much that I regret the necessity which has compelled me to read it through from beginning to end. I do not think that the knowledge which I have gained of its history and sources compensates me for the unpleasant details it has forced upon my attention.
    Helen Keller (1880-1968, American Blind/Deaf Author, Lecturer, Amorist)

23 Unless we form the habit of going to the Bible in bright moments as well as in trouble, we cannot fully respond to its consolations because we lack equilibrium between light and darkness.
    Helen Keller (1880-1968, American Blind/Deaf Author, Lecturer, Amorist)

24 For eighteen hundred years, though perchance I have no right to say it, the New Testament has been written; yet where is the legislator who has wisdom and practical talent enough to avail himself of the light which it sheds on the science of legislation?
    Henry David Thoreau (1817-1862, American Essayist, Poet, Naturalist)

25 The Bible is God's chart for you to steer by, to keep you from the bottom of the sea, and to show you where the harbor is, and how to reach it without running on rocks or bars.
    Henry Ward Beecher (1813-1887, American Preacher, Orator, Writer)

26 Sink the Bible to the bottom of the sea, and man's obligation to God would be unchanged. He would have the same path to tread, only his lamp and his guide would be gone; he would have the same voyage to make, only his compass and chart would be overboard.
    Henry Ward Beecher (1813-1887, American Preacher, Orator, Writer)

27 The worth of a book is to be measured by what you can carry away from it.
    James Bryce

28 To me the greatest thing that has happened on this earth of ours is the rise of the human race to the vision of God. That story of the human rise to what I call the vision of God is the story which is told in the Bible.
Jan Christian Smuts (1870-1950, South African General, Statesman, and Prime Minister)

29 For this reason the Bible is a book of eternal and effective power; because, as long as the world lasts, no one will say: I comprehend it in the whole and understand it in the particular. Rather we must modestly say it on the whole it is venerable, and in the particular practical.
Johann Wolfgang Von Goethe (1749-1832, German Poet, Dramatist, Novelist)

30 The Bible among other books is as a diamond among precious stones.
John Stoughton

31 My ground is the Bible. Yea, I am a Bible-bigot. I follow it in all things, both great and small.
John Wesley (1703-1791, British Preacher, Founder of Methodism)

32 The Christian's Bible is a drug store. Its contents remain the same, but the medical practice changes.
Mark Twain (1835-1910, American Humorist, Writer)

33 It ain't those parts of the Bible that I can't understand that bother me, it is the parts that I do understand.
Mark Twain (1835-1910, American Humorist, Writer)

34 First I shake the whole [Apple] tree, that the ripest might fall. Then I climb the tree and shake each limb, and then each branch and then each twig, and then I look under each leaf.
Martin Luther (1483-1546, German Leader of the Protestant Reformation)

35 People cannot be well educated without the Bible.
Nott

36 The great, God-blessed churches in the world today have one common characteristic: an insistence upon an exposition of God's infallible Word.
O. S. Hawkins

37 Bible study is like eating peanuts. The more you eat, the more you want to eat.
Paul Little

38 To what greater inspiration and counsel can we turn than to the imperishable truth to be found in this treasure house, the Bible?
Queen Elizabeth (1926-, Current Queen of the United Kingdom)

39 God's Word is pure and sure, in spite of the devil, in spite of your fear, in spite of everything.
R. A. Torrey

40 In all my perplexities and distresses, the Bible has never failed to give me light and strength.
Robert E. Lee (1807-1870, American Confederate Army Commander)

41 More people are troubled by what is plain in Scripture than by what is obscure.
Roy L. Smith (American Clergyman)

42 There is no doubt that God has often brought a certain verse to the attention of one of His children in an unusual and almost miraculous manner, for a special need, but the Word was never intended to be consulted in a superstitious manner.
S. Maxwell Coder

43 Intense study of the Bible will keep any writer from being vulgar, in point of style.
Samuel Taylor Coleridge (1772-1834, British Poet, Critic, Philosopher)

44 The study of the Bible will keep anyone from being vulgar in style.
Samuel Taylor Coleridge (1772-1834, British Poet, Critic, Philosopher)

45 When you read God's Word, you must constantly be saying to yourself, "It is talking to me, and about me."
Soren Kierkegaard (1813-1855, Danish Philosopher, Writer)

46 Arguments about Scripture achieve nothing but a stomachache and a headache.
Tertullian (160-240, Roman Christian Author and Polemicist)

47 The English Bible -- a book which, if everything else in our language should perish, would alone suffice to show the whole extent of its beauty and power.
Thomas B. Macaulay (1800-1859, American Essayist and Historian)

48 I call the book of Job, apart from all theories about it, one of the grandest things ever written with the pen.
Thomas Carlyle (1795-1881, Scottish Philosopher, Author)

49 The Bible has been the Magna Carta of the poor and of the oppressed.
Thomas H. Huxley (1825-1895, British Biologist, Educator)

50 Either this is not the Gospel, or we are not Christians.
Thomas Linacre

51 Whenever we read the obscene stories, the voluptuous debaucheries, the cruel and torturous executions, the unrelenting vindictiveness, with which more than half the Bible is filled, it would be more consistent that we called it the word of a demon than the Word of God. It is a history of wickedness that has served to corrupt and brutalize mankind.
Thomas Paine (1737-1809, Anglo-American Political Theorist, Writer)

52 England has two books, one which she has made and one which has made her: Shakespeare and the Bible.
Victor Hugo (1802-1885, French Poet, Dramatist, Novelist)

53 W. C. Fields, a lifetime agnostic, was discovered reading a Bible on his deathbed. "I'm looking for a loop-hole," he explained.
W. C. Fields (1879-1946, American Actor)

54 Both read the Bible day and night, but thou read black where I read white.
William Blake (1757-1827, British Poet, Painter)

55 When you have read the Bible, you will know it is the word of God, because you have found it the key to your own heart, your own happiness and your own duty.
Woodrow T. Wilson (1856-1924, Twenty-eighth President of the USA)

BICYCLES

1 Cycle tracks will abound in Utopia.
H.G. Wells (1866-1946, British-born American Author)

2 Let a man find himself, in distinction from others, on top of two wheels with a chain -- at least in a poor country like Russia -- and his vanity begins to swell out like his tires. In America it takes an automobile to produce this effect.
Leon Trotsky (1879-1940, Russian Revolutionary)

3 If all feeling for grace and beauty were not extinguished in the mass of mankind at the actual moment, such a method of locomotion as cycling could never have found acceptance; no man or woman with the slightest aesthetic sense could assume the ludicrous position necessary for it.
Ouida (1838-1908, British Writer)

4 Consider a man riding a bicycle. Whoever he is, we can say three things about him. We know he got on the bicycle and started to move. We know that at some point he will stop and get off. Most important of all, we know that if at any point between the beginning and the end of his journey he stops moving and does not get off the bicycle he will fall off it. That is a metaphor for the journey through life of any living thing, and I think of any society of living things.
William Golding (1911-1993, British Author)

BIGOTRY

1 Bigot, one who is obstinately and zealously attached to an opinion that you do not entertain.
Ambrose Bierce (1842-1914, American Author, Editor, Journalist, "The Devil's Dictionary")

2 Bigotry murders religion to frighten fools with her ghost.
Charles Caleb Colton (1780-1832, British Sportsman Writer)

3 Those who believe in their truth -- the only ones whose imprint is retained by the memory of men -- leave the earth behind them strewn with corpses. Religions number in their ledgers more murders than the bloodiest tyrannies account for, and those whom humanity has called divine far surpass the most conscientious murderers in their thirst for slaughter.
E. M. Cioran (1911-, Rumanian-born French Philosopher)

4 Bigotry dwarfs the soul by shutting out the truth.
Edwin Hubbel Chapin (1814-1880, American Author, Clergyman)

5 When we believe ourselves in possession of the only truth, we are likely to be indifferent to common everyday truths.
Eric Hoffer (1902-1983, American Author, Philosopher)

6 We are least open to precise knowledge concerning the things we are most vehement about.
Eric Hoffer (1902-1983, American Author, Philosopher)

7 You are all fundamentalists with a top dressing of science. That is why you are the stupidest of conservatives and reactionists in politics and the most bigoted of obstructionists in science itself. When it comes to getting a move on you are all of the same opinion: stop it, flog it, hang it, dynamite it, stamp it out.
George Bernard Shaw (1856-1950, Irish-born British Dramatist)

8 We call a man a bigot or a slave of dogma because he is a thinker who has thought thoroughly and to a definite end.
Gilbert K. Chesterton (1874-1936, British Author)

9 Bigotry is the sacred disease.
Heraclitus (535-475 BC, Greek Philosopher)

10 There is no bigotry like that of "free thought" run to seed.
Horace Greeley (1811-1872, American Newspaper Editor)

11 A man must be both stupid and uncharitable who believes there is no virtue or truth but on his own side.
Joseph Addison (1672-1719, British Essayist, Poet, Statesman)

12 Wisdom has never made a bigot, but learning has.
Josh Billings (1815-1885, American Humorist, Lecturer)

13 How it infuriates a bigot, when he is forced to drag out his dark convictions!
Logan Pearsall Smith (1865-1946, Anglo-American Essayist, Aphorist)

14 Religion is as effectually destroyed by bigotry as by indifference.
Ralph Waldo Emerson (1803-1882, American Poet, Essayist)

15 Defoe says that there were a hundred thousand country fellows in his time ready to fight to the death against popery, without knowing whether popery was a man or a horse.
William Hazlitt (1778-1830, British Essayist)

BILLS

1 Dreading that climax of all human ills the inflammation of his weekly bills.
Lord Byron (1788-1824, British Poet)

2 It is only by not paying one's bills that one can hope to live in the memory of the commercial classes.
Oscar Wilde (1856-1900, British Author, Wit)

3 I did send to you for certain sums of gold, which you denied me.
William Shakespeare (1564-1616, British Poet, Playwright, Actor)

BIOGRAPHY

1 A great biography should, like the close of a great drama, leave behind it a feeling of serenity. We collect into a small bunch the flowers, the few flowers, which brought sweetness into a life, and present it as an offering to an accomplished destiny. It is the dying refrain of a completed song, the final verse of a finished poem.
Andre Maurois (1885-1967, French Writer)

2 Biography should be written by an acute enemy.
Arthur James Balfour (1848-1930, British Conservative Politician, Prime Minister)

3 An autobiography is a preemptive strike against biographers.
Barbara G. Harris

4 Read no history: nothing but biography, for that is life without theory.
Benjamin Disraeli (1804-1881, British Statesman, Prime Minister)

5 In writing biography, fact and fiction shouldn't be mixed. And if they are, the fictional points should be printed in red ink, the facts printed in black ink.
Catherine Drinker Bowen (1897-1973, American Author)

6 When my journal appears, many statues must come down.
Duke of Wellington Arthur Wellesley (1769-1852, British Statesman, Military Leader)

7 I am opposed to writing about the private lives of living authors and psychoanalyzing them while they are alive. Criticism is getting all mixed up with a combination of the Junior F.B.I. -men, discards from Freud and Jung and a sort of Columnist peep-hole and missing laundry list school. Every young English professor sees gold in them dirty sheets now. Imagine what they can do with the soiled sheets of four legal beds by the same writer and you can see why their tongues are slavering.
Ernest Hemingway (1898-1961, American Writer)

8 Only when one has lost all curiosity about the future has one reached the age to write an autobiography.
Evelyn Waugh (1903-1966, British Novelist)

9 Show me a character whose life arouses my curiosity, and my flesh begins crawling with suspense.
Fawn M. Brodie (1915-1981, American Biographer)

10 Memoirs are the backstairs of history.
George Meredith (1828-1909, British Author)

11 The immense majority of human biographies are a gray transit between domestic spasm and oblivion.
George Steiner (1929-, French-born American Critic, Novelist)

12 Just as there is nothing between the admirable omelet and the intolerable, so with autobiography.
Hilaire Belloc (1870-1953, British Author)

13 Many heroes lived before Agamemnon; but all are unknown and unwept, extinguished in everlasting night, because they have no spirited chronicler.
Horace (65-8 BC, Italian Poet)

14 Biography is one of the new terrors of death.
John Arbuthnot (1667-1735, Grampian-Born Physician and Writer)

15 If the reviewing of books be... "an ungentle craft," the making of them is, for the most part, a dishonest one -- and that department of literature which ought to be entrusted to those only who are distinguished for their moral qualities is, not infrequently, in the hands of authors totally devoid of good taste, good feeling, and generous sentiment. The writers of Lives have, in our time, assumed a license not enjoyed by their more scrupulous predecessors -- for they interweave the adventures of the living with the memoirs of the dead; and, pretending to portray the peculiarities which sometimes mark the man of genius, they invade the privacy and disturb the peace of his surviving associates.
John Cam Hobhouse

16 Anyone who profits from the experience of others probably writes biographies.
Jones

17 Biography is: a system in which the contradictions of a human life are unified.
Jose Ortega Y Gasset (1883-1955, Spanish Essayist, Philosopher)

18 I have not much interest in anyone's personal history after the tenth year, not even my own. Whatever one was going to be was all prepared before that.
Katherine Anne Porter (1890-1980, American short-story Writer, Novelist)

19 The secret of biography resides in finding the link between talent and achievement. A biography seems irrelevant if it doesn't discover the overlap between what the individual did and the life that made this possible. Without discovering that, you have shapeless happenings and gossip.
Leon Edel (1907-, American Biographer)

20 Biography is history seen through the prism of a person.
Louis Fischer

21 Biographies are but the clothes and buttons of the man. The biography of the man himself cannot be written.
Mark Twain (1835-1910, American Humorist, Writer)

22 There was never yet an uninteresting life. Such a thing is an impossibility. Inside of the dullest exterior there is a drama, a comedy, and a tragedy.
Mark Twain (1835-1910, American Humorist, Writer)

23 The facts of a person's life will, like murder, come out.
Norman Sherry

24 Formerly we used to canonize our heroes. The modern method is to vulgarize them. Cheap editions of great books may be delightful, but cheap editions of great men are absolutely detestable.
Oscar Wilde (1856-1900, British Author, Wit)

25 On the trail of another man, the biographer must put up with finding himself at every turn; any biography uneasily shelters an autobiography within it.
Paul Murray Kendall

26 Biography is a very definite region bounded on the north by history, on the south by fiction, on the east by obituary, and on the west by tedium.
Philip Guedalla (1889-1944, British Writer)

27 There is properly no history; only biography.
Ralph Waldo Emerson (1803-1882, American Poet, Essayist)

28 Great geniuses have the shortest biographies.
Ralph Waldo Emerson (1803-1882, American Poet, Essayist)

29 All good biography, as all good fiction, comes down to the study of original sin, of our inherent disposition to choose death when we ought to choose life.
Rebecca West (1892-1983, British Author)

30 Just how difficult it is to write biography can be reckoned by anybody who sits down and considers just how many people know the real truth about his or her love affairs.
Rebecca West (1892-1983, British Author)

31 A biography is like a handshake down the years, that can become an arm-wrestle.
Richard Holmes

32 For what is a poem, but a hazardous attempt at self-understanding. It is the deepest part of autobiography.
Robert Penn Warren (1905-1989, American Writer, Poet)

33 Biography is a higher gossip.
Robert Winder

34 Nobody can write the life of a man but those who have eat and drunk and lived in social intercourse with him.
Samuel Johnson (1709-1784, British Author)

35 The first thing to be done by a biographer in estimating character is to examine the stubs of his victim's check-books.
Silas Weir Mitchell (1829-1914, Physician, Writer, Poet)

36 To write the lives of the great in separating them from their works necessarily ends by above all stressing their pettiness, because it is in their work that they have put the best of themselves.
Simone Weil (1910-1943, French Philosopher, Mystic)

37 The surrounding that householders crave are glorified autobiographies.
T. H. Gibblings

38 History is the essence of innumerable biographies.
Thomas Carlyle (1795-1881, Scottish Philosopher, Author)

39 No sooner does a great man depart, and leave his character as public property, than a crowd of little men rushes towards it. There they are gathered together, blinking up to it with such vision as they have, scanning it from afar, hovering round it this way and that, each cunningly endeavoring, by all arts, to catch some reflex of it in the little mirror of himself.
Thomas Carlyle (1795-1881, Scottish Philosopher, Author)

40 A well-written life is almost as rare as a well-spent one.
Thomas Carlyle (1795-1881, Scottish Philosopher, Author)

41 If those gentlemen would let me alone I should be much obliged to them. I would say, as Shakespeare would say... "Sweet Friend, for Jesus sake forbear."
Thomas Carlyle (1795-1881, Scottish Philosopher, Author)

42 Almost any biographer, if he respects facts, can give us much more than another fact to add to our collection. He can give us the creative fact; the fertile fact; the fact that suggests and engenders.
Virginia Woolf (1882-1941, British Novelist, Essayist)

43 There ain't nothing that breaks up homes, country, and nations like somebody publishing their memoirs.
Will Rogers (1879-1935, American Humorist, Actor)

BIRDS

1 A turkey is more occult and awful than all the angels and archangels. In so far as God has partly revealed to us an angelic world, he has partly told us what an angel means. But God has never told us what a turkey means. And if you go and stare at a live turkey for an hour or two, you will find by the end of it that the enigma has rather increased than diminished.
Gilbert K. Chesterton (1874-1936, British Author)

2 To a man, ornithologists are tall, slender, and bearded so that they can stand motionless for hours, imitating kindly trees, as they watch for birds.
Gore Vidal (1925-, American Novelist, Critic)

3 O fret not after knowledge -- I have none, and yet my song comes native with the warmth. O fret not after knowledge -- I have none, and yet the Evening listens.
John Keats (1795-1821, British Poet)

4 She was not quite what you would call refined. She was not quite what you would call unrefined. She was the kind of person that keeps a parrot.
Mark Twain (1835-1910, American Humorist, Writer)

5 When thou seest an eagle, thou seest a portion of genius; lift up thy head!
William Blake (1757-1827, British Poet, Painter)

6 Happier of happy though I be, like them I cannot take possession of the sky, mount with a thoughtless impulse, and wheel there, one of a mighty multitude whose way and motion is a harmony and dance magnificent.
William Wordsworth (1770-1850, British Poet)

BIRTH

1 Being born is like being kidnapped. And then sold into slavery.
Andy Warhol (1930-, American Artist, Filmmaker)

2 And when our baby stirs and struggles to be born it compels humility: what we began is now its own.
Anne Ridler (1912-, British Poet)

3 I came to the place of my birth and cried, "The friends of my youth, where are they?" And echo answered, "Where are they?"
Arabian Proverb

4 We are brought nothing into this world, and it is certain we can carry nothing out.
Bible (Sacred Scriptures of Christians and Judaism)

5 Behold, I was shapened in iniquity; and in sin did my mother conceive me. [Psalms 51:5]
Bible (Sacred Scriptures of Christians and Judaism)

6 Abortion is a skillfully marketed product sold to women at a crisis time in their life. If the product is defective, she can't return it for a refund.
Carol Evertt

7 Every person is a God in embryo. Its only desire is to be born.
Deepak Chopra (East-Indian- American M.D., New Age Author, Lecturer)

8 Born to be wild -- live to outgrow it.
Doug Horton

9 Our birth is nothing but our death begun.
Edward Young (1683-1765, British Poet, Dramatist)

10 Man's main task in life is to give birth to himself, to become what he potentially is. The most important product of his effort is his own personality.
Erich Fromm (1900-1980, American Psychologist)

11 A man may be born, but in order to be born he must first die, and in order to die he must first awake.
George Gurdjieff (1873-1949, Russian Adept, Teacher, Writer)

12 Although it is generally known, I think it's about time to announce that I was born at a very early age.
Groucho Marx (1895-1977, American Comic Actor)

13 It is as painful perhaps to be awakened from a vision as to be born.
James Augustine (British Writer)

14 We are born, so to speak, twice over; born into existence, and born into life; born a human being, and born a man.
Jean Jacques Rousseau (1712-1778, Swiss Political Philosopher, Educationist, Essayist)

15 I like trying [to get pregnant]. I'm not so sure about childbirth.
Lauren Holly (American Actress)

16 The first thing which I can record concerning myself is, that I was born. These are wonderful words. This life, to which neither time nor eternity can bring diminution -- this everlasting living soul, began. My mind loses itself in these depths.
Margaret Oliphant (1828-1897, British Novelist, Historian)

17 We are celebrating the feast of the Eternal Birth which God the Father has borne and never ceases to bear in all eternity.... But if it takes not place in me, what avails it? Everything lies in this, that it should take place in me.
Meister Eckhart (1260-1326 AD, German Mystic)

18 Compassion and shame come over one who considers how precarious is the origin of the proudest of living beings: often the smell of a lately extinguished lamp is enough to cause a miscarriage. And to think that from such a frail beginning a tyrant or butcher may be born! You who trust in your physical strength, who embrace the gifts of fortune and consider yourself not their ward but their son, you who have a domineering spirit, you who consider yourself a god as soon as success swells your breast, think how little could have destroyed you!
Pliny The Elder (23-79, Roman Neophatonist)

19 Good birth is a fine thing, but the merit is our ancestors.
Plutarch (46-120 AD, Greek Essayist, Biographer)

20 What is this talked-of mystery of birth but being mounted bareback on the earth?
Robert Frost (1875-1963, American Poet)

21 Birth was the death of him.
Samuel Beckett (1906-1989, Irish Dramatist, Novelist)

22 Birth and death are so closely related that one could not destroy either without destroying the other at the same time. It is extinction that makes creation possible.
Samuel Butler (1612-1680, British Poet, Satirist)

23 The act of birth is the first experience of anxiety, and thus the source and prototype of the affect of anxiety.
Sigmund Freud (1856-1939, Austrian Physician - Founder of Psychoanalysis)

24 My mother groaned, my father wept, into the dangerous world I leapt; helpless, naked, piping loud, like a fiend hid in a cloud.
William Blake (1757-1827, British Poet, Painter)

25 When we are born we cry that we are come.. to this great stage of fools.
William Shakespeare (1564-1616, British Poet, Playwright, Actor)

26 Our birth is but a sleep and a forgetting. The soul that rises with us, our life's star, hath had elsewhere its setting, and comet from afar: not in entire forgetfulness, and not in utter nakedness, but trailing clouds of glory do we come from God, who is our home.
William Wordsworth (1770-1850, British Poet)

BIRTH CONTROL

1 The blind conviction that we have to do something about other people's reproductive behavior, and that we may have to do it whether they like it or not, derives from the assumption that the world belongs to us, who have so expertly depleted its resources, rather than to them, who have not.
Germaine Greer (1939-, Australian Feminist Writer)

2 It is now quite lawful for a Catholic woman to avoid pregnancy by a resort to mathematics, though she is still forbidden to resort to physics and chemistry.
H. L. Mencken (1880-1956, American Editor, Author, Critic, Humorist)

3   No woman can call herself free who does not own and control her body. No woman can call herself free until she can choose consciously whether she will or will not be a mother.
Margaret Sanger (1883-1966, American Social Reformer and Founder of the Birth Control Movement)

4   Contraceptives should be used on all conceivable occasions.
Spike Milligan (1918-, British Comedian, Humorous Writer)

5   If we can get that realistic feminine morality working for us, if we can trust ourselves and so let women think and feel that an unwanted child or an oversize family is wrong -- not ethically wrong, not against the rules, but morally wrong, all wrong, wrong like a thalidomide birth, wrong like taking a wrong step that will break your neck -- if we can get feminine and human morality out from under the yoke of a dead ethic, then maybe we'll begin to get somewhere on the road that leads to survival.
Ursula K. Le Guin (1929-, American Author)

BIRTHDAYS

1   I'm sorry you are wiser, I sorry you are taller; I liked you better foolish and I liked you better smaller.
Aline Murray Kilmer

2   To divide one's life by years is of course to tumble into a trap set by our own arithmetic. The calendar consents to carry on its dull wall-existence by the arbitrary timetables we have drawn up in consultation with those permanent commuters, Earth and Sun. But we, unlike trees, need grow no annual rings.
Cliff Fadiman (American Writer)

3   Our birthdays are feathers in the broad wing of time.
Jean Paul Richter (1763-1825, German Novelist)

4   Here lies interred in the eternity of the past, from whence there is no resurrection for the days - - whatever there may be for the dust -- the thirty-third year of an ill-spent life, which, after a lingering disease of many months sank into a lethargy, and expired, January 22d, 1821, A.D. leaving a successor inconsolable for the very loss which occasioned its existence.
Lord Byron (1788-1824, British Poet)

5   The return of my birthday, if I remember it, fills me with thoughts which it seems to be the general care of humanity to escape.
Samuel Johnson (1709-1784, British Author)

BLAME

1   There can be no doubt that the average man blames much more than he praises. His instinct is to blame. If he is satisfied he says nothing; if he is not, he most illogically kicks up a row.
Arnold Bennett (1867-1931, British Novelist)

2   I praise loudly, I blame softly.
Catherine II of Russia (1729-1796, Russian Empress)

3   Sometimes I lie awake at night and ask why me? Then a voice answers nothing personal, your name just happened to come up.
Charles M. Schultz (1922-, American Cartoonist, Creator of "Peanuts")

4   No one is a failure until they blame somebody else.
Charles "Tremendous" Jones (American Motivational Speaker, Author)

5   Better to light one small candle than to curse the darkness.
Chinese Proverb

6   Blame is a lazy man's wages.
Danish Proverb

7   It's easy to point when you can't heal it.
Don Walk (American Minister)

8   When you blame others, you give up your power to change.
Dr. Robert Anthony (American educator)

9   A man may fall many times but he won't be a failure until he says someone pushed him.
Elmer G. Letterman

10   Yes, there are times when something is legitimately not our fault. Blaming others, however, keeps us in a stuck state and is ultimately rough on our own self-esteem.
Eric Allenbaugh (American Author of "Wake-Up Calls")

11   Take your life in your own hands and what happens? A terrible thing: no one is to blame.
Erica Jong (1942-, American Author)

12   No one to blame! That was why most people led lives they hated, with people they hated. How wonderful to have someone to blame! How wonderful to live with one's nemesis! You may be miserable, but you feel forever in the right. You may be fragmented, but you feel absolved of all the blame for it. Take your life in your own hands, and what happens? A terrible thing: no one to blame.
Erica Jong (1942-, American Author)

13   Draw the curtain, the fraud is over.
Frantois Rabelais (1495-1553, French Satirist, Physician, and Humanist)

14   When we blame, we give away our power.
Greg Anderson (American Author of "The 22 Non-Negotiable Laws of Wellness")

15   A man can get discouraged many times but he is not a failure until he begins to blame somebody else and stops trying.
John Burroughs (1837-1921, American Naturalist, Author)

16   The easiest thing to do, whenever you fail, is to put yourself down by blaming your lack of ability for your misfortunes.
Kenneth Hildebrand (American Author)

17   In passing, also, I would like to say that the first time Adam had a chance he laid the blame on a woman.
Lady Nancy Astor (1897-1964, British Politician)

18 Whatever side I take, I know well that I will be blamed.
Louis XIV (1638-1715, King of France from 1643-1715)

19 There is luxury in self-reproach. When we blame ourselves, we feel no one else has a right to blame us.
Oscar Wilde (1856-1900, British Author, Wit)

20 To find a fault is easy; to do better may be difficult.
Plutarch (46-120 AD, Greek Essayist, Biographer)

21 The first mistake are theirs who commit them, the second are theirs that permit them.
Proverb

22 Neither blame or praise yourself.
Proverb

23 The search for someone to blame is always successful.
Robert Half (American Businessman, Founder of Robert Half & Associates)

24 Think how many blameless lives are brightened by the blazing indiscretions of other people.
Saki

25 There's man all over for you, blaming on his boots the fault of his feet.
Samuel Beckett (1906-1989, Irish Dramatist, Novelist)

26 We must remember not to judge any public servant by any one act, and especially should we beware of attacking the men who are merely the occasions and not the cause of disaster.
Theodore Roosevelt (1858-1919, Twenty-sixth President of the USA)

27 When you plant lettuce, if it does not grow well, you don't blame the lettuce. You look into the reasons it is not doing well. It may need fertilizer, or more water, or less sun. You never blame the lettuce. Yet if we have problems with our friends or our family, we blame the other person. But if we know how to take care of them, they will grow well, like lettuce. Blaming has no positive effect at all, nor does trying to persuade using reason and arguments. That is my experience. No blame, no reasoning, no argument, just understanding. If you understand, and you show that you understand, you can love, and the situation will change. -
Thich Nhat Hanh (Vietnamese Buddhist Monk, Teacher)

28 He has great tranquillity of heart who cares neither for the praises nor the fault-finding of men.
Thomas p Kempis (1379-1471, German Monk, Mystic, Religious Writer)

29 All blame is a waste of time. No matter how much fault you find with another, and regardless of how much you blame him, it will not change you. The only thing blame does is to keep the focus off you when you are looking for external reasons to explain your unhappiness or frustration. You may succeed in making another feel guilty about something by blaming him, but you won't succeed in changing whatever it is about you that is making you unhappy.
Wayne Dyer (1940-, American Psychotherapist, Author, Lecturer)

30 They have a right to censure that have a heart to help.
William Penn (1644-1718, British Religious Leader, Founder of Pennsylvania)

BLASPHEMY

1 I am very sorry to know and hear how unreverently that most precious jewel, the Word of God, is disputed, rhymed, sung and jangled in every ale-house and tavern, contrary to the true meaning and doctrine of the same.
Edward VIII

2 I don't think it is given to any of us to be impertinent to great religions with impunity.
John Le Carre

3 We cannot assume the injustice of any actions which only create offense, and especially as regards religion and morals. He who utters or does anything to wound the consciénce and moral sense of others, may indeed act immorally; but, so long as he is not guilty of being importunate, he violates no right.
Karl Wilhelm Von Humboldt (1767-1835, German Statesman, Philologist)

4 There is only one blasphemy, and that is the refusal to experience joy.
Paul Rudnick

5 Your blasphemy, Salman, can't be forgiven. To set your words against the Words of God.
Salman Rushdie (1948-, Indian-born British Author)

6 Where there is no belief, there is no blasphemy.
Salman Rushdie (1948-, Indian-born British Author)

BLINDNESS

1 A blind man will not thank you for a looking-glass.
English Proverb

2 My darkness has been filled with the light of intelligence, and behold, the outer day-lit world was stumbling and groping in social blindness.
Helen Keller (1880-1968, American Blind/Deaf Author, Lecturer, Amorist)

3 What a blind person needs is not a teacher but another self.
Helen Keller (1880-1968, American Blind/Deaf Author, Lecturer, Amorist)

4 O loss of sight, of thee I most complain! Blind among enemies, O worse than chains, dungeon or beggary, or decrepit age! Light, the prime work of God, to me is extinct, and all her various objects of delight annulled, which might in part my grief have eased. Inferior to the vilest now become of man or worm; the vilest here excel me, they creep, yet see; I, dark in light, exposed to daily fraud, contempt, abuse and wrong, within doors, or without, still as a fool, in power of others, never in my own; scarce half I seem to live, dead more than half.
John Milton (1608-1674, British Poet)

5   To be blind is not miserable; not to be able to bear blindness, that is miserable.
John Milton (1608-1674, British Poet)

6   There's none so blind as they that won't see.
Jonathan Swift (1667-1745, Anglo-Irish Satirist)

7   There is a condition worse than blindness, and that is, seeing something that isn't there.
L. Ron Hubbard (American Author, Philosopher, Founder of Scientology)

8   In the country of the blind, the one-eyed man is King.
Michael Apostolius

9   Sometimes, I feel I am really blessed to be blind because I probably would not last a minute if I were able to see things.
Stevie Wonder (1950-, American Musician, Singer, Songwriter, Producer)

10   Blindness hatred is blind, as well as love.
Thomas Fuller (1608-1661, British Clergyman, Author)

11   But who would rush at a benighted man, and give him two black eyes for being blind?
Thomas Hood (1799-1845, British Poet and Humorist)

12   We may remark in passing that to be blind and beloved may, in this world where nothing is perfect, be among the most strangely exquisite forms of happiness. The supreme happiness in life is the assurance of being loved; of being loved for oneself, even in spite of oneself; and this assurance the blind man possesses. In his affliction, to be served is to be caressed. Does he lack anything? no. Possessing love he is not deprived of light. A love, moreover, that is wholly pure. There can be no blindness where there is this certainty.
Victor Hugo (1802-1885, French Poet, Dramatist, Novelist)

BLOOD

1   Peace, above all things, is to be desired, but blood must sometimes be spilled to obtain it on equable and lasting terms.
Andrew Jackson (1767-1845, Seventh President of the USA)

2   The best blood will at some time get into a fool or a mosquito.
Austin O'Malley

3   Blood alone moves the wheels of history.
Benito Mussolini (1883-1945, Italian Prime Minister (1922--43) and Dictator)

4   The future can be anything we want it to be, providing we have the faith and that we realize that peace, no less than war, required "blood and sweat and tears."
Charles F. Kettering (1876-1958, American Engineer, Inventor)

5   Young blood must have its course, lad, and every dog its day.
Charles Kingsley (1819-1875, British Author, Clergyman)

6   Blood will tell, but often it tells too much.
Don Marquis (1878-1937, American Humorist, Journalist)

7   A pint of sweat will save a gallon of blood.
George S. Patton (1885-1945, American Army General during World War II)

8   No one need think that the world can be ruled without blood. The civil sword shall and must be red and bloody.
Martin Luther (1483-1546, German Leader of the Protestant Reformation)

9   Blood is a cleansing and sanctifying thing, and the nation that regards it as the final horror has lost its manhood... there are many things more horrible than bloodshed, and slavery is one of them!
Padraic Pearse

10   The blood of the martyrs is the seed of the church.
Tertullian (160-240, Roman Christian Author and Polemicist)

BLUSH

1   The man that blushes is not quite a brute.
Edward Young (1683-1765, British Poet, Dramatist)

2   As blushing will sometimes make a whore pass for a virtuous woman, so modesty may make a fool seem a man of sense.
Jonathan Swift (1667-1745, Anglo-Irish Satirist)

3   Man is the only animal that blushes -- or needs to.
Mark Twain (1835-1910, American Humorist, Writer)

4   When a girl ceases to blush, she has lost the most powerful charm of her beauty.
St. Gregory The Great (540-604, Italian Pope)

BODY

1   In order to live a fully human life we require not only control of our bodies (though control is a prerequisite); we must touch the unity and resonance of our physicality, our bond with the natural order, the corporeal grounds of our intelligence.
Adrienne Rich (1929-, American Poet)

2   What we feel and think and are is to a great extent determined by the state of our ductless glands and viscera.
Aldous Huxley (1894-1963, British Author)

3   Men renounce whatever they have in common with women so as to experience no commonality with women; and what is left, according to men, is one piece of flesh a few inches long, the penis. The penis is sensate; the penis is the man; the man is human; the penis signifies humanity.
Andrea Dworkin (1946-, American Feminist Critic)

4 What was my body to me? A kind of flunkey in my service. Let but my anger wax hot, my love grow exalted, my hatred collect in me, and that boasted solidarity between me and my body was gone.
Antoine De Saint-Exupery (1900-1944, French Aviator, Writer)

5 The brain may be regarded as a kind of parasite of the organism, a pensioner, as it were, who dwells with the body.
Arthur Schopenhauer (1788-1860, German Philosopher)

6 The body is mortal, but the person dwelling in the body is immortal and immeasurable.
Bhagavad Gita (400 BC, Sanskrit Poem Incorporated Into the Mahabharata)

7 Many people treat their bodies as if they were rented from Hertz-something they are using to get around in but nothing they genuinely care about understanding.
Chungliang Al Huang

8 Why am I so determined to put the shoulder where it belongs? Women have very round shoulders that push forward slightly; this touches me and I say: "One must not hide that!" Then someone tells you: "The shoulder is on the back." I've never seen women with shoulders on their backs.
Coco Chanel (1883-1971, French Couturier)

9 Wondrous hole! Magical hole! Dazzlingly influential hole! Noble and effulgent hole! From this hole everything follows logically: first the baby, then the placenta, then, for years and years and years until death, a way of life. It is all logic, and she who lives by the hole will live also by its logic. It is, appropriately, logic with a hole in it.
Cynthia Ozick (1928-, American Novelist, short-story Writer)

10 It is so much more difficult to live with one's body than with one's soul. One's body is so much more exacting: what it won't have it won't have, and nothing can make bitter into sweet.
D. H. Lawrence (1885-1930, British Author)

11 I don't think that the flesh is necessarily treacherous, evil, bad. It is cantankerous, and it is independent. The idea of independence is the key. It really is like colonialism. The colonies suddenly decide that they can and should exist with their own personality and should detach from the control of the mother country. At first the colony is perceived as being treacherous. It's a betrayal. Ultimately, it can be seen as the separation of a partner that could be very valuable as an equal rather than as something you dominate.
David Cronenberg (1943-, Canadian Filmmaker)

12 Man is a mind betrayed, not served, by his organs.
Edmond and Jules De Goncourt (1822-1896, French Writers)

13 Our own theological Church, as we know, has scorned and vilified the body till it has seemed almost a reproach and a shame to have one, yet at the same time has credited it with power to drag the soul to perdition.
Eliza Farnham (American Author and Social Reformist)

14 He had not an ounce of superfluous flesh on his bones, and leanness goes a great way towards gentility.
Elizabeth Gaskell (1810-1865, British Novelist)

15 It is a sign of a dull nature to occupy oneself deeply in matters that concern the body; for instance, to be over much occupied about exercise, about eating and drinking, about easing oneself, about sexual intercourse.
Epictetus (50-120, Stoic Philosopher)

16 I live in company with a body, a silent companion, exacting and eternal. He it is who notes that individuality which is the seal of the weakness of our race. My soul has wings, but the brutal jailer is strict.
EugFne Delacroix (1798-1863, French Artist)

17 Many things about our bodies would not seem to us so filthy and obscene if we did not have the idea of nobility in our heads.
Georg C. Lichtenberg (1742-1799, German Physicist, Satirist)

18 Who has not felt the beauty of a woman's arm? The unspeakable suggestions of tenderness that lie in the dimpled elbow, and all the varied gently-lessening curves, down to the delicate wrist, with its tiniest, almost imperceptible nicks in the firm softness.
George Eliot (1819-1880, British Novelist)

19 Of one thing I am certain, the body is not the measure of healing peace is the measure.
George Melton

20 The body is an instrument, the mind its function, the witness and reward of its operation.
George Santayana (1863-1952, American Philosopher, Poet)

21 The authority of any governing institution must stop at its citizen's skin.
Gloria Steinem (1934-, American Feminist Writer, Editor)

22 Every man is the builder of a temple, called his body, to the god he worships, after a style purely his own, nor can he get off by hammering marble instead. We are all sculptors and painters, and our material is our own flesh and blood and bones.
Henry David Thoreau (1817-1862, American Essayist, Poet, Naturalist)

23 Our own physical body possesses a wisdom which we who inhabit the body lack. We give it orders which make no sense.
Henry Miller (1891-1980, American Author)

24 My skull, my eyes, my nose three times, my jaw, my shoulder, my chest, two fingers, a knee, everything from the top of my head to the bottom of my feet. [Listing what body parts he has broken]
Jackie Chan (1954-, Hong Kong Actor, Director, Producer, Singer, Stun Choreographer)

25 For male and female alike, the bodies of the other sex are messages signaling what we must do -- they are glowing signifiers of our own necessities.
John Updike (1932-, American Novelist, Critic)

26 It takes more than just a good looking body. You've got to have the heart and soul to go with it.
Lee Haney (Bodybuilder)

27 A woman watches her body uneasily, as though it were an unreliable ally in the battle for love.
Leonard Cohen (1934-, Canadian-born American Musician, Songwriter, Singer)

28 The function of muscle is to pull and not to push, except in the case of the genitals and the tongue.
Leonardo Da Vinci (1452-1519, Italian Inventor, Architect, Painter, Scientist, Sculptor)

29 The basic Female body comes with the following accessories: garter belt, panty-girdle, crinoline, camisole, bustle, brassiere, stomacher, chemise, virgin zone, spike heels, nose ring, veil, kid gloves, fishnet stockings, fichu, bandeau, Merry Widow, weepers, chokers, barrettes, bangles, beads, lorgnette, feather boa, basic black, compact, Lycra stretch one-piece with modesty panel, designer peignoir, flannel nightie, lace teddy, bed, head.
Margaret Atwood (1939-, Canadian Novelist, Poet, Critic)

30 When human beings have been fascinated by the contemplation of their own hearts, the more intricate biological pattern of the female has become a model for the artist, the mystic, and the saint. When mankind turns instead to what can be done, altered, built, invented, in the outer world, all natural properties of men, animals, or metals become handicaps to be altered rather than clues to be followed.
Margaret Mead (1901-1978, American Anthropologist)

31 An impersonal and scientific knowledge of the structure of our bodies is the surest safeguard against prurient curiosity and lascivious gloating.
Marie Carmichael Stopes (1880-1958, British Scientist, Pioneer of Birth Control)

32 Your body is the church where Nature asks to be reverenced.
Marquis De Sade (1740-1814, French Author)

33 The human body is not a thing or substance, given, but a continuous creation. The human body is an energy system which is never a complete structure; never static; is in perpetual inner self- construction and self-destruction; we destroy in order to make it new.
Norman O. Brown (1913-, American Philosopher)

34 Our bodies are shaped to bear children, and our lives are a working out of the processes of creation. All our ambitions and intelligence are beside that great elemental point.
Phyllis Mcginley (1905-1978, American Poet, Author)

35 The human body has two ends on it: one to create with and one to sit on. Sometimes people get their ends reversed. When this happens they need a kick in the seat of the pants.
Roger Von Oech

36 The only bodily organ which is really regarded as inferior is the atrophied penis, a girl's clitoris.
Sigmund Freud (1856-1939, Austrian Physician - Founder of Psychoanalysis)

37 Let me look at the foulness and ugliness of my body. Let me see myself as an ulcerous sore running with every horrible and disgusting poison.
St. Ignatius Loyola (1495-1556, Spanish Theologian, Founder of the Jesuits)

38 The body is a community made up of its innumerable cells or inhabitants.
Thomas A. Edison (1847-1931, American Inventor, Entrepreneur, Founder of GE)

39 The more I work with the body, keeping my assumptions in a temporary state of reservation, the more I appreciate and sympathize with a given disease. The body no longer appears as a sick or irrational demon, but as a process with its own inner logic and wisdom.
Thomas Arnold Mindell

40 Addiction, obesity, starvation (anorexia nervosa) are political problems, not psychiatric: each condenses and expresses a contest between the individual and some other person or persons in his environment over the control of the individual's body.
Thomas Szasz (1920-, American Psychiatrist)

41 Man consists of two parts, his mind and his body, only the body has more fun.
Woody Allen (1935-, American Director, Screenwriter, Actor, Comedian)

42 Hide your body in the Big Dipper.
Zen Saying

BOHEMIA

1 Well, isn't Bohemia a place where everyone is as good as everyone else -- and must not a waiter be a little less than a waiter to be a good Bohemian?
Djuna Barnes (1892-1982, American Author, Poet, Columnist)

2 I could I trust starve like a gentleman. It's listed as part of the poetic training, you know.
Ezra Pound (1885-1972, American Poet, Critic)

3 It is not my fault that certain so-called bohemian elements have found in my writings something to hang their peculiar beatnik theories on.
Jack Kerouac (1922-1969, American Author)

4 Bohemia is nothing more than the little country in which you do not live. If you try to obtain citizenship in it, at once the court and retinue pack the royal archives and treasure and move away beyond the hills.
O. Henry Porter (1862-1910, American short-story Writer)

5 Bohemia has no banner. It survives by discretion.
Tennessee Williams (1914-1983, American Dramatist)

6 The modern picture of the artist began to form: The poor, but free spirit, plebeian but aspiring only to be classless, to cut himself forever free from the bonds of the greedy bourgeoisie, to be whatever the fat burghers feared most, to cross the line wherever they drew it, to look at the world in a way they couldn't see, to be high, live low, stay young forever -- in short, to be the bohemian.
Thomas Wolfe (1931-, American Author, Journalist)

BOLDNESS

1 Finite to fail, but infinite to venture.
Emily Dickinson (1830-1886, American Poet)

2 Boldness is a mask for fear, however great.
F. L. Lucan (39-65, Roman Epic Poet)

3 Boldness is ever blind, for it sees not dangers and inconveniences whence it is bad in council though good in execution.
Francis Bacon (1561-1626, British Philosopher, Essayist, Statesman)

4 Boldness is business is the first, second, and third thing.
H. G. Bohn (British Publisher)

5 Fortune befriends the bold.
John Dryden (1631-1700, British Poet, Dramatist, Critic)

6 The mind, ever the willing servant, will respond to boldness, for boldness, in effect, is a command to deliver mental resources.
Norman Vincent Peale (1898-1993, American Christian Reformed Pastor, Speaker, Author)

7 It is wonderful what strength of purpose and boldness and energy of will are roused by the assurance that we are doing our duty.
Sir Walter Scott (1771-1832, British Novelist, Poet)

8 In great straits and when hope is small, the boldest counsels are the safest.
Titus Livy (59 BC-17 AD, Roman Historian)

9 When you cannot make up your mind which of two evenly balanced courses of action you should take -- choose the bolder.
William Joseph Slim (1891-1970, British Field Marshall)

BOOKS AND READING

1 Very young children eat their books, literally devouring their contents. This is one reason for the scarcity of first editions of Alice in Wonderland and other favorites of the nursery.
A. S. W. Rosenbach (1876-1952, American collector, scholar, and seller of rare books and manuscripts)

2 The things I want to know are in books; my best friend is the man who'll get me a book I ain't read.
Abraham Lincoln (1809-1865, Sixteenth President of the USA)

3 A novel is never anything, but a philosophy put into images.
Albert Camus (1913-1960, French Existential Writer)

4 A bad book is as much of a labor to write as a good one; it comes as sincerely from the author's soul.
Aldous Huxley (1894-1963, British Author)

5 The failure to read good books both enfeebles the vision and strengthens our most fatal tendency --the belief that the here and now is all there is.
Allan Bloom (1930-1992, American Educator, Author)

6 The more sins you confess, the more books you will sell.
American Proverb

7 That is a good book which is opened with expectation, and closed with delight and profit.
Amos Bronson Alcott (1799-1888, American Educator, Social Reformer)

8 All books are either dreams or swords.
Amy Lowell (1874-1925, American Poet, Critic)

9 For books are more than books, they are the life, the very heart and core of ages past, the reason why men lived and worked and died, the essence and quintessence of their lives.
Amy Lowell (1874-1925, American Poet, Critic)

10 The books that everybody admires are those that nobody reads.
Anatole France (1844-1924, French Writer)

11 What is the most precious, the most exciting smell awaiting you in the house when you return to it after a dozen years or so? The smell of roses, you think? No, moldering books.
Andre Sinyavsky

12 I read the newspaper avidly. It is my one form of continuous fiction.
Aneurin Bevan (1897-1960, British Labor Politician)

13 Reading a book is like re-writing it for yourself. You bring to a novel, anything you read, all your experience of the world. You bring your history and you read it in your own terms.
Angela Carter (1940-1992, British Author)

14 The lessons taught in great books are misleading. The commerce in life is rarely so simple and never so just.
Anita Brookner (1938-, British Novelist, Art Historian)

15 Americans will listen, but they do not care to read. War and Peace must wait for the leisure of retirement, which never really comes: meanwhile it helps to furnish the living room. Blockbusting fiction is bought as furniture. Unread, it maintains its value. Read, it looks like money wasted. Cunningly, Americans know that books contain a person, and they want the person, not the book.
Anthony Burgess (1917-1993, British Writer, Critic)

16 A book might be written on the injustice of the just.
Anthony Hope (1863-1933, British Writer)

17 Once we have learned to read, meaning of words can somehow register without consciousness.
Anthony Marcel

18 Book love... is your pass to the greatest, the purest, and the most perfect pleasure that God has prepared for His creatures.
Anthony Trollope (1815-1882, British Novelist)

19 Does there, I wonder, exist a being who has read all, or approximately all, that the person of average culture is supposed to have read, and that not to have read is a social sin? If such a being does exist, surely he is an old, a very old man.
Arnold Bennett (1867-1931, British Novelist)

20 All the best stories in the world are but one story in reality -- the story of escape. It is the only thing which interests us all and at all times, how to escape.
Arthur Christopher Benson (1862-1925, British Author, Poet)

21 He has only half learned the art of reading who has not added to it the more refined art of skipping and skimming.
Arthur James Balfour (1848-1930, British Conservative Politician, Prime Minister)

22 Reading is equivalent to thinking with someone else's head instead of with one's own.
Arthur Schopenhauer (1788-1860, German Philosopher)

23 Buying books would be a good thing if one could also buy the time to read them in: but as a rule the purchase of books is mistaken for the appropriation of their contents.
Arthur Schopenhauer (1788-1860, German Philosopher)

24 To buy books would be a good thing if we also could buy the time to read them.
Arthur Schopenhauer (1788-1860, German Philosopher)

25 Without books the development of civilization would have been impossible. They are the engines of change, windows on the world, "Lighthouses" as the poet said "erected in the sea of time." They are companions, teachers, magicians, bankers of the treasures of the mind, Books are humanity in print.
Arthur Schopenhauer (1788-1860, German Philosopher)

26 Books are like a mirror. If an ass looks in, you can't expect an angel to look out.
Arthur Schopenhauer (1788-1860, German Philosopher)

27 No matter how busy you may think you are, you must find time for reading, or surrender yourself to self-chosen ignorance.
Atwood H. Townsend

28 Reading is not a duty, and has consequently no business to be made disagreeable.
Augustine Birrell (1850-1933, British Essayist, Liberal Politician)

29 I am what libraries and librarians have made me, with little assistance from a professor of Greek and poets.
B. K. Sandwell

30 He that loves a book will never want a faithful friend, a wholesome counselor, a cheerful companion, an effectual comforter. By study, by reading, by thinking, one may innocently divert and pleasantly entertain himself, as in all weathers, as in all fortunes.
Barrow

31 Books are fatal: they are the curse of the human race. Nine-tenths of existing books are nonsense, and the clever books are the refutation of that nonsense. The greatest misfortune that ever befell man was the invention of printing.
Benjamin Disraeli (1804-1881, British Statesman, Prime Minister)

32 Nine-tenths of the existing books are nonsense and the clever books are the refutation of that nonsense.
Benjamin Disraeli (1804-1881, British Statesman, Prime Minister)

33 Reading makes a full man, meditation a profound man, discourse a clear man.
Benjamin Franklin (1706-1790, American Scientist, Publisher, Diplomat)

34 Read much, but not many books.
Benjamin Franklin (1706-1790, American Scientist, Publisher, Diplomat)

35 One man is as good as another until he has written a book.
Benjamin Jowett (1817-1893, British Scholar)

36 Books had instant replay long before televised sports.
Bert Williams

37 The last thing one discovers in composing a work is what to put first.
Blaise Pascal (1623-1662, French Scientist, Religious Philosopher)

38 I don't think any good book is based on factual experience. Bad books are about things the writer already knew before he wrote them.
Carlos Fuentes (1928-, Mexican Novelist, Short-Story Writer)

39 For a good book has this quality, that it is not merely a petrifaction of its author, but that once it has been tossed behind, like Deucalion's little stone, it acquires a separate and vivid life of its own.
Caroline Lejeune (1897-1973, British Film Critic)

40 The books we think we ought to read are poky, dull, and dry; The books that we would like to read we are ashamed to buy; The books that people talk about we never can recall; And the books that people give us, oh, they're the worst of all.
Carolyn Wells (1870-1942, American Author)

41 Hypocrite reader -- my fellow -- my brother!
Charles Baudelaire (1821-1867, French Poet)

42 Books, like friends, should be few and well chosen. Like friends, too, we should return to them again and again for, like true friends, they will never fail us -- never cease to instruct -- never cloy.
Charles Caleb Colton (1780-1832, British Sportsman Writer)

43 Next to acquiring good friends, the best acquisition is that of good books.
Charles Caleb Colton (1780-1832, British Sportsman Writer)

44 I've never know any trouble than an hour's reading didn't assuage.
Charles de Secondat

45 There are books of which the backs and covers are by far the best parts.
Charles Dickens (1812-1870, British Novelist)

46 A person of mature years and ripe development, who is expecting nothing from literature but the corroboration and renewal of past ideas, may find satisfaction in a lucidity so complete as to occasion no imaginative excitement, but young and ambitious students are not content with it. They seek the excitement because they are capable of the growth that it accompanies.
Charles Horton Cooley (1864-1929, American Sociologist)

47 We ought to reverence books; to look on them as useful and mighty things. If they are good and true, whether they are about religion, politics, farming, trade, law, or medicine, they are the message of Christ, the maker of all things -- the teacher of all truth.
Charles Kingsley (1819-1875, British Author, Clergyman)

48 Except a living man there is nothing more wonderful than a book! a message to us from the dead -- from human souls we never saw, who lived, perhaps, thousands of miles away. And yet these, in those little sheets of paper, speak to us, arouse us, terrify us, teach us, comfort us, open their hearts to us as brothers.
Charles Kingsley (1819-1875, British Author, Clergyman)

49 He has left off reading altogether, to the great improvement of his originality.
Charles Lamb (1775-1834, British Essayist, Critic)

50 I love to lose myself in other men's minds. When I am not walking, I am reading. I cannot sit and think; books think for me.
Charles Lamb (1775-1834, British Essayist, Critic)

51 Borrowers of books --those mutilators of collections, spoilers of the symmetry of shelves, and creators of odd volumes.
Charles Lamb (1775-1834, British Essayist, Critic)

52 You will be the same person in five as you are today except for the people you meet and the books you read.
Charles "Tremendous" Jones (American Motivational Speaker, Author)

53 The man who is fond of books is usually a man of lofty thought, and of elevated opinions.
Christopher Dawson (1898-1970, Welsh Cultural Historian, Educational Theorist)

54 The world of books is the most remarkable creation of man nothing else that he builds ever lasts monuments fall; nations perish; civilization grow old and die out; new races build others. But in the world of books are volumes that have seen this happen again and again and yet live on. Still young, still as fresh as the day they were written, still telling men's hearts, of the hearts of men centuries dead.
Clarence Day (1874-1935, American Essayist)

55 Many books require no thought from those who read them, and for a very simple reason: they made no such demand upon those who wrote them. Those works, therefore, are the most valuable, that set our thinking faculties in the fullest operation. understand them.
Clarendon

56 When you reread a classic, you do not see more in the book than you did before; you see more in you than there was before.
Cliff Fadiman (American Writer)

57 I used to walk to school with my nose buried in a book.
Coolio (1963-, American Musician, Rapper, Actor, Singer, Songwriter)

58 The Brahmins say that in their books there are many predictions of times in which it will rain. But press those books as strongly as you can, you can not get out of them a drop of water. So you can not get out of all the books that contain the best precepts the smallest good deed.
Count Leo Tolstoy (1828-1910, Russian Novelist, Philosopher)

59 After all, the world is not a stage -- not to me: nor a theatre: nor a show-house of any sort. And art, especially novels, are not little theatres where the reader sits aloft and watches... and sighs, commiserates, condones and smiles. That's what you want a book to be: because it leaves you so safe and superior, with your two-dollar ticket to the show. And that's what my books are not and never will be. Whoever reads me will be in the thick of the scrimmage, and if he doesn't like it -- if he wants a safe seat in the audience -- let him read someone else.
D. H. Lawrence (1885-1930, British Author)

60 One sheds one's sicknesses in books -- repeats and presents again one's emotions, to be master of them.
D. H. Lawrence (1885-1930, British Author)

61 I can't bear art that you can walk round and admire. A book should be either a bandit or a rebel or a man in the crowd.
D. H. Lawrence (1885-1930, British Author)

62 Show me the books he loves and I shall know the man far better than through mortal friends.
Dawn Adams

63 When I get a little money, I buy books; and if any is left I buy food and clothes.
Desiderius Erasmus (1466-1536, Dutch Humanist)

64 This book is not to be tossed lightly aside, but to be hurled with great force.
Dorothy Parker (1893-1967, American Humorous Writer)

65 Read Homer once, and you can read no more. For all books else appear so mean, and so poor. Verse will seem prose; but still persist to read, and Homer will be all the books you need.
Duke of Buckingham (1628-1687, British Poet, Satirist, Dramatist)

66 A bad book is the worse that it cannot repent. It has not been the devil's policy to keep the masses of mankind in ignorance; but finding that they will read, he is doing all in his power to poison their books.
E.N. Kirk

67 Books are men of higher stature; the only men that speak aloud for future times to hear.
E.S. Barrett

68 A person who publishes a book appears willfully in public with his pants down.
Edna St. Vincent Millay (1892-1950, American Poet)

69 In science read the newest works, in literature read the oldest.
Edward G. Bulwer-Lytton (1803-1873, British Novelist, Poet)

70 Reading without purpose is sauntering not exercise.
Edward G. Bulwer-Lytton (1803-1873, British Novelist, Poet)

71 Books are those faithful mirrors that reflect to our mind the minds of sages and heroes.
Edward Gibbon (1737-1794, British Historian)

72 My early and invincible love of reading I would not exchange for all the riches of India.
Edward Gibbon (1737-1794, British Historian)

73 One always tends to overpraise a long book, because one has got through it.
Edward M. Forster (1879-1970, British Novelist, Essayist)

74 I suggest that the only books that influence us are those for which we are ready, and which have gone a little further down our particular path than we have yet got ourselves.
Edward M. Forster (1879-1970, British Novelist, Essayist)

75 The only books that influence us are those for which we are ready, and which have gone a little farther down our particular path than we have yet got ourselves.
Edward M. Forster (1879-1970, British Novelist, Essayist)

76 Books are lighthouses erected in the great sea of time.
Edwin P. Whipple (1819-1886, American Essayist)

77 This will never be a civilized country until we expend more money for books than we do for chewing gum.
Elbert Hubbard (1859-1915, American Author, Publisher)

78 The reason that fiction is more interesting than any other form of literature, to those who really like to study people, is that in fiction the author can really tell the truth without humiliating himself.
Eleanor Roosevelt (1884-1962, American First Lady, Columnist, Lecturer, Humanitarian)

79 Books, books, books had found the secret of a garret-room piled high with cases in my father's name; Piled high, packed large, --where, creeping in and out among the giant fossils of my past, like some small nimble mouse between the ribs of a mastodon, I nibbled here and there at this or that box, pulling through the gap, in heats of terror, haste, victorious joy, the first book first. And how I felt it beat under my pillow, in the morning's dark. An hour before the sun would let me read! My books!
Elizabeth Barrett Browning (1806-1861, British Poet)

80 Books succeed, and lives fail.
Elizabeth Barrett Browning (1806-1861, British Poet)

81 The greatest gift is the passion for reading. It is cheap, it consoles, it distracts, it excites, it gives you knowledge of the world and experience of a wide kind. It is a moral illumination.
Elizabeth Hardwick (1916-, American Novelist)

82 There is no Frigate like a book to take us lands away nor any coursers like a page of prancing Poetry.
Emily Dickinson (1830-1886, American Poet)

83 He ate and drank the precious Words, his Spirit grew robust; He knew no more that he was poor, nor that his frame was Dust.
Emily Dickinson (1830-1886, American Poet)

84 The good parts of a book may be only something a writer is lucky enough to overhear or it may be the wreck of his whole damn life --and one is as good as the other.
Ernest Hemingway (1898-1961, American Writer)

85 All good books are alike in that they are truer than if they had really happened and after you are finished reading one you will feel that all that happened to you and afterwards it all belongs to you; the good and the bad, the ecstasy, the remorse, and sorrow, the people and the places and how the weather was.
Ernest Hemingway (1898-1961, American Writer)

86 With one day's reading a man may have the key in his hands.
Ezra Pound (1885-1972, American Poet, Critic)

87 No man understands a deep book until he has seen and lived at least part of its contents.
Ezra Pound (1885-1972, American Poet, Critic)

88 Properly, we should read for power. Man reading should be man intensely alive. The book should be a ball of light in one's hand.
Ezra Pound (1885-1972, American Poet, Critic)

89 Some books are to be tasted; others to be swallowed; and some few to be chewed and digested.
Francis Bacon (1561-1626, British Philosopher, Essayist, Statesman)

90 Read not to contradict and confute; nor to believe and take for granted; nor to find talk and discourse; but to weigh and consider.
Francis Bacon (1561-1626, British Philosopher, Essayist, Statesman)

91 If the riches of the Indies, or the crowns of all the kingdom of Europe, were laid at my feet in exchange for my love of reading, I would spurn them all.
François Fénelon (1651-1715, French Roman Catholic archbishop, theologian, poet and writer)

92 The book salesman should be honored because he brings to our attention, as a rule, the very books we need most and neglect most.
Frank Crane (American Actor)

93 The great American novel has not only already been written, it has already been rejected.
Frank Dane

94 Why pay a dollar for a bookmark? Why not use the dollar for a bookmark?
Fred Stoller

95 The worst readers are those who behave like plundering troops: they take away a few things they can use, dirty and confound the remainder, and revile the whole.
Friedrich Nietzsche (1844-1900, German Philosopher)

96 Early in the morning, at break of day, in all the freshness and dawn of one's strength, to read a book --I call that vicious!
Friedrich Nietzsche (1844-1900, German Philosopher)

97 Education... has produced a vast population able to read but unable to distinguish what is worth reading, an easy prey to sensations and cheap appeals.
G. M. Trevelyan (1876-1962, British Historian)

98 To feel most beautifully alive means to be reading something beautiful, ready always to apprehend in the flow of language the sudden flash of poetry.
Gaston Bachelard (1884-1962, French Scientist, Philosopher, Literary Theorist)

99 A vacuum of ideas affects people differently than a vacuum of air, otherwise readers of books would be constantly collapsing.
Georg C. Lichtenberg (1742-1799, German Physicist, Satirist)

100 There are very many people who read simply to prevent themselves from thinking.
Georg C. Lichtenberg (1742-1799, German Physicist, Satirist)

101 Do we write books so that they shall merely be read? Don't we also write them for employment in the household? For one that is read from start to finish, thousands are leafed through, other thousands lie motionless, others are jammed against mouseholes, thrown at rats, others are stood on, sat on, drummed on, have gingerbread baked on them or are used to light pipes.
Georg C. Lichtenberg (1742-1799, German Physicist, Satirist)

102 A book is a mirror: If an ass peers into it, you can't expect an apostle to look out.
Georg C. Lichtenberg (1742-1799, German Physicist, Satirist)

103 How can you dare teach a man to read until you've taught him everything else first?
George Bernard Shaw (1856-1950, Irish-born British Dramatist)

104 No story is the same to us after a lapse of time; or rather we who read it are no longer the same interpreters.
George Eliot (1819-1880, British Novelist)

105 The newest books are those that never grow old.
George Holbrook Jackson (1874-1948, British Essayist, Literary Historian,)

106 The books one reads in childhood, and perhaps most of all the bad and good bad books, create in one's mind a sort of false map of the world, a series of fabulous countries into which one can retreat at odd moments throughout the rest of life, and which in some cases can survive a visit to the real countries which they are supposed to represent.
George Orwell (1903-1950, British Author, "Animal Farm")

107 I know every book of mine by its smell, and I have but to put my nose between the pages to be reminded of all sorts of things.
George Robert Gissing (1857-1903, British Novelist, Critic, Essayist)

108 The age of the book is almost gone.
George Steiner (1929-, French-born American Critic, Novelist)

109 I feel like I'm drowning. Every night, I'm carrying home loads of things to read but I'm too exhausted. I keep clipping things and Xeroxing them and planning to read them eventually, but I just end up throwing it all away and feeling guilty.
Ghita Levine

110 A good novel tells us the truth about it's hero; but a bad novel tells us the truth about its author.
Gilbert K. Chesterton (1874-1936, British Author)

111 The mere brute pleasure of reading --the sort of pleasure a cow must have in grazing.
Gilbert K. Chesterton (1874-1936, British Author)

112 Don't ask me who's influenced me. A lion is made up of the lambs he's digested, and I've been reading all my life.
Giorgos Seferis

113 From the moment I picked your book up until I laid it down I was convulsed with laughter. Some day I intend reading it.
Groucho Marx (1895-1977, American Comic Actor)

114 Read in order to live.
Gustave Flaubert (1821-1880, French Novelist)

115 There are people who read too much: bibliobibuli. I know some who are constantly drunk on books, as other men are drunk on whiskey or religion. They wander through this most diverting and stimulating of worlds in a haze, seeing nothing and hearing nothing.
H. L. Mencken (1880-1956, American Editor, Author, Critic, Humorist)

116 The chief knowledge that a man gets from reading books is the knowledge that very few of them are worth reading.
H. L. Mencken (1880-1956, American Editor, Author, Critic, Humorist)

117 There are two kinds of books. Those that no one reads and those that no one ought to read.
H. L. Mencken (1880-1956, American Editor, Author, Critic, Humorist)

118 This book fills a much-needed gap.
Hadas In A Review.

119 The constant habit of perusing devout books is so indispensable, that it has been termed the oil of the lamp of prayer. Too much reading, however, and too little meditation, may produce the effect of a lamp inverted; which is extinguished by the very excess of that ailment, whose property is to feed it.
Hannah More (1745-1833, British Writer, Reformer, Philanthropist)

120 When you have mastered numbers, you will in fact no longer be reading numbers, any more than you read words when reading books You will be reading meanings.
Harold S. Geneen (1910-, American Accountant, Industrialist, CEO, ITT)

121 Until I feared I would lose it, I never loved to read. One does not love breathing.
Harper Lee (1926-, American Author)

122 Readers are plentiful: thinkers are rare.
Harriet Martineau (1802-1876, British Writer, Social Critic)

123 Reading makes immigrants of us all. It takes us away from home, but more important, it finds homes for us everywhere.
Hazel Rochman

124 What is a diary as a rule? A document useful to the person who keeps it. Dull to the contemporary who reads it and invaluable to the student, centuries afterwards, who treasures it.
Helen Terry

125 A novel is a mirror carried along a main road.
Henri B. Stendhal (1783-1842, French Writer)

126 Upon books the collective education of the race depends; they are the sole instruments of registering, perpetuating and transmitting thought.
Henry C. Rogers

127 Books must be read as deliberately and reservedly as they were written.
Henry David Thoreau (1817-1862, American Essayist, Poet, Naturalist)

128 Read the best books first, or you may not have a chance to read them at all.
Henry David Thoreau (1817-1862, American Essayist, Poet, Naturalist)

129 How many a man has dated a new era in his life from the reading of a book! The book exists for us, perchance, that will explain our miracles and reveal new ones. The at present unutterable things we may find somewhere uttered.
Henry David Thoreau (1817-1862, American Essayist, Poet, Naturalist)

130 To read well, that is, to read true books in a true spirit, is a noble exercise, and one that will task the reader more than any other exercise which the customs of the day esteem. It requires a training such as the athletes underwent, the steady intention almost of the whole life to this object.
Henry David Thoreau (1817-1862, American Essayist, Poet, Naturalist)

131 Books, not which afford us a cowering enjoyment, but in which each thought is of unusual daring; such as an idle man cannot read, and a timid one would not be entertained by, which even make us dangerous to existing institution --such call I good books.
Henry David Thoreau (1817-1862, American Essayist, Poet, Naturalist)

132 We are as liable to be corrupted by books, as by companions.
Henry Fielding (1707-1754, British Novelist, Dramatist)

133 There is a set of religious, or rather moral, writings which teach that virtue is the certain road to happiness, and vice to misery in this world. A very wholesome and comfortable doctrine, and to which we have but one objection, namely, that it is not true.
Henry Fielding (1707-1754, British Novelist, Dramatist)

134 The only obligation to which in advance we may hold a novel, without incurring the accusation of being arbitrary, is that it be interesting.
Henry James (1843-1916, American Author)

135 All my good reading, you might say, was done in the toilet. There are passages in Ulysses which can be read only in the toilet -- if one wants to extract the full flavor of their content.
Henry Miller (1891-1980, American Author)

136 Until it is kindled by a spirit as flamingly alive as the one which gave it birth a book is dead to us. Words divested of their magic are but dead hieroglyphs.
Henry Miller (1891-1980, American Author)

137 This is not a book. This is libel, slander, defamation of character. This is not a book, in the ordinary sense of the word. No, this is a prolonged insult, a gob of spit in the face of Art, a kick in the pants to God, Man, Destiny, Time, Love, Beauty... what you will. I am going to sing for you, a little off key perhaps, but I will sing.
Henry Miller (1891-1980, American Author)

138 A book is a part of life, a manifestation of life, just as much as a tree or a horse or a star. It obeys its own rhythms, its own laws, whether it be a novel, a play, or a diary. The deep, hidden rhythm of life is always there -- that of the pulse, the heart beat.
Henry Miller (1891-1980, American Author)

139 Many readers judge of the power of a book by the shock it gives their feelings --as some savage tribes determine the power of muskets by their recoil; that being considered best which fairly prostrates the purchaser.
Henry Wadsworth Longfellow (1819-1892, American Poet)

140 I feel a kind of reverence for the first books of young authors. There is so much aspiration in them, so much audacious hope and trembling fear, so much of the heart's history, that all errors and shortcomings are for a while lost sight of in the amiable self assertion of youth.
Henry Wadsworth Longfellow (1819-1892, American Poet)

141 Where is human nature so weak as in the bookstore?
Henry Ward Beecher (1813-1887, American Preacher, Orator, Writer)

142 A book is a garden, an orchard, a storehouse, a party, a company by the way, a counselor, a multitude of counselors.
Henry Ward Beecher (1813-1887, American Preacher, Orator, Writer)

143 Books are not made for furniture, but there is nothing else that so beautifully furnishes a house.
Henry Ward Beecher (1813-1887, American Preacher, Orator, Writer)

144 A library is thought in cold storage.
Herbert Samuel (1870-1963, British Liberal Statesman, Philosophical Writer)

145 One half who graduate from college never read another book.
Herbert True

146 When I am dead, I hope it may be said: "His sins were scarlet, but his books were read."
Hilaire Belloc (1870-1953, British Author)

147 Read as you taste fruit or savor wine, or enjoy friendship, love or life.
Holbrook Jackson

148 A house without books is like a room without windows. No man has a right to bring up his children without surrounding them with books, if he has the means to buy them. It is a wrong to his family. Children learn to read by being in the presence of books. The love of knowledge comes with reading and grows upon it. And the love of knowledge, in a young mind, is almost always a warrant against the inferior excitement of passions and vices.
Horace Mann (1796-1859, American Educator)

149 A novel must be exceptionally good to live as long as the average cat.
Hugh Maclennan (1907-1990, Canadian Novelist, Essayist)

150 I am not a speed reader. I am a speed understander.
Isaac Asimov (1920-1992, Russian-born American Author)

151 There is an art of reading, as well as an art of thinking, and an art of writing.
Isaac Disraeli

152 There is no robber worse than a bad book.
Italian Proverb

153 Most books, like their authors, are born to die; of only a few books can it be said that death has no dominion over them; they live, and their influence lives forever.
J. Swartz

154 Never judge a book by its movie.
J. W. Eagan

155 Learning to read has been reduced to a process of mastering a series of narrow, specific, hierarchical skills. Where armed-forces recruits learn the components of a rifle or the intricacies of close order drill "by the numbers," recruits to reading learn its mechanics sound by sound and word by word.
Jacquelyn Gross

156 When the book comes out it may hurt you -- but in order for me to do it, it had to hurt me first. I can only tell you about yourself as much as I can face about myself.
James Baldwin (1924-1987, American Author)

157 What a sense of security in an old book which time has criticized for us.
James Russell Lowell (1819-1891, American Poet, Critic, Editor)

158 Books are the bees which carry the quickening pollen from one to another mind.
James Russell Lowell (1819-1891, American Poet, Critic, Editor)

159 What is important is not to be able to read rapidly, but to be able to decide what not to read.
James T. Mccay

160 I always begin at the left with the opening word of the sentence and read toward the right and I recommend this method.
James Thurber (1894-1961, American Humorist, Illustrator)

161 When a book raises your spirit, and inspires you with noble and manly thoughts, seek for no other test of its excellence. It is good, and made by a good workman.
Jean De La Bruyere (1645-1696, French Writer)

162 She could give herself up to the written word as naturally as a good dancer to music or a fine swimmer to water. The only difficulty was that after finishing the last sentence she was left with a feeling at once hollow and uncomfortably full. Exactly like indigestion.
Jean Rhys (1894-1979, British Author)

163 The books one has written in the past have two surprises in store: one couldn't write them again, and wouldn't want to.
Jean Rostand (1894-1977, French Biologist, Writer)

164 Prerequisite for rereadability in books: that they be forgettable.
Jean Rostand (1894-1977, French Biologist, Writer)

165 Books are but waste paper unless we spend in action the wisdom we get from thought -- asleep. When we are weary of the living, we may repair to the dead, who have nothing of peevishness, pride, or design in their conversation.
Jeremy Collier (1650-1726, British Clergyman, Conjuror)

166 Fiction reveals truth that reality obscures.
Jessamyn West (1903-1984, American Author)

167 You are wise, witty and wonderful, but you spend too much time reading this sort of stuff.
Jim Critchfield

168 Everything you need for better future and success has already been written. And guess what? All you have to do is go to the library.
Jim Rohn (American Businessman, Author, Speaker, Philosopher)

169 Miss a meal if you have to, but don't miss a book.
Jim Rohn (American Businessman, Author, Speaker, Philosopher)

170 The book you don't read won't help.
Jim Rohn (American Businessman, Author, Speaker, Philosopher)

171 Don't just read the easy stuff. You may be entertained by it, but you will never grow from it.
Jim Rohn (American Businessman, Author, Speaker, Philosopher)

172 Surviving and thriving as a professional today demands two new approaches to the written word. First, it requires a new approach to orchestrating information, by skillfully choosing what to read and what to ignore. Second, it requires a new approach to integrating information, by reading faster and with greater comprehension.
Jimmy Calano

173 He had read much, if one considers his long life; but his contemplation was much more than his reading. He was wont to say that if he had read as much as other men he should have known no more than other men.
John Aubrey (1626-1697, British Antiquarian, Writer)

174 When we read a story, we inhabit it. The covers of the book are like a roof and four walls. What is to happen next will take place within the four walls of the story. And this is possible because the story's voice makes everything its own.
John Berger (1926-, British Actor, Critic)

175 I heard his library burned down and both books were destroyed -- and one of them hadn't even been colored in yet.
John Dawkins

176 Books give not wisdom where none was before. But where some is, there reading makes it more.
John Harington

177 I am a part of everything that I have read.
John Kieran

178 Reading furnishes the mind only with material for knowledge; it is thinking that makes what we read ours.
John Locke (1632-1704, British Philosopher)

179 Deep versed in books and shallow in himself.
John Milton (1608-1674, British Poet)

180 For books are not absolutely dead things, but do contain a potency of life in them to be as active as that soul was whose progeny they are; nay, they do preserve as in a vial the purest efficacy and extraction of that living intellect that bred them. I know they are as lively, and as vigorously productive, as those fabulous dragon's teeth; and being sown up and down, may chance to spring up armed men.
John Milton (1608-1674, British Poet)

181 A good book is the precious life-blood of the master spirit, embalmed and treasured up on purpose for a life beyond.
John Milton (1608-1674, British Poet)

182 Who kills a man kills a reasonable creature, God's image, but thee who destroys a good book, kills reason itself.
John Milton (1608-1674, British Poet)

183 Books are not absolutely dead things, but do contain a certain potency of life in them, to be as active as the soul whose progeny they are; they preserve, as in a vial, the purest efficacy and extraction of the living intellect that bred them.
John Milton (1608-1674, British Poet)

184 You will find most books worth reading are worth reading twice.
John Morely

185 Some of the most famous books are the least worth reading. Their fame was due to their having done something that needed to be doing in their day. The work is done and the virtue of the book has expired.
John Morely

186 To use books rightly, is to go to them for help; to appeal to them when our own knowledge and power fail; to be led by them into wider sight and purer conception than our own, and to receive from them the united sentence of the judges and councils of all time, against our solitary and unstable opinions.
John Ruskin (1819-1900, British Critic, Social Theorist)

187 How long most people would look at the best book before they would give the price of a large turbot for it?
John Ruskin (1819-1900, British Critic, Social Theorist)

188 You should read books like you take medicine, by advice, and not by advertisement.
John Ruskin (1819-1900, British Critic, Social Theorist)

189 A book worth reading is worth buying.
John Ruskin (1819-1900, British Critic, Social Theorist)

190 Books are divided into two classes, the books of the hour and the books of all time.
John Ruskin (1819-1900, British Critic, Social Theorist)

191 Be sure that you go to the author to get at his meaning, not to find yours.
John Ruskin (1819-1900, British Critic, Social Theorist)

192 A book is like a man -- clever and dull, brave and cowardly, beautiful and ugly. For every flowering thought there will be a page like a wet and mangy mongrel, and for every looping flight a tap on the wing and a reminder that wax cannot hold the feathers firm too near the sun.
John Steinbeck (1902-1968, American Author)

193 Beware you be not swallowed up in books! An ounce of love is worth a pound of knowledge.
John Wesley (1703-1791, British Preacher, Founder of Methodism)

194 Tradition is but a meteor, which, if it once falls, cannot be rekindled. Memory, once interrupted, is not to be recalled. But written learning is a fixed luminary, which, after the cloud that had hidden it has passed away, is again bright in its proper station. So books are faithful repositories, which may be awhile neglected or forgotten, but when opened again, will again impart instruction.
Johnson

195 Books to judicious compilers, are useful; to particular arts and professions, they are absolutely necessary; to men of real science, they are tools: but more are tools to them.
Johnson

196 Books like friends, should be few and well-chosen.
Joineriana

197 Books are the legacies that a great genius leaves to mankind, which are delivered down from generation to generation as presents to the posterity of those who are yet unborn.
Joseph Addison (1672-1719, British Essayist, Poet, Statesman)

198 Of all the diversions of life, there is none so proper to fill up its empty spaces as the reading of useful and entertaining authors.
Joseph Addison (1672-1719, British Essayist, Poet, Statesman)

199 There are worse crimes than burning books. One of them is not reading them.
Joseph Brodsky (1940-, Russian-born American Poet, Critic)

200 The worst thing about new books is that they keep us from reading the old ones.
Joseph Joubert (1754-1824, French Moralist)

201 There was a time when the world acted on books; now books act on the world.
Joseph Joubert (1754-1824, French Moralist)

202 A novel points out that the world consists entirely of exceptions.
Joyce Carey

203 The pleasure of reading is doubled when one lives with another who shares the same books.
Katherine Mansfield (1888-1923, New Zealand-born British Author)

204 No entertainment is so cheap as reading, nor is any pleasure so lasting.
Lady Mary Wortley Montagu (1689-1762, British Society Figure, Letter Writer)

205 Digressions, incontestably, are the sunshine; they are the life, the soul of reading! Take them out of this book, for instance, --you might as well take the book along with them; --one cold external winter would reign in every page of it; restore them to the writer; --he steps forth like a bridegroom, - -bids All-hail; brings in variety, and forbids the appetite to fail.
Laurence Sterne (1713-1768, British Author)

206 One may as well be asleep as to read for anything but to improve his mind and morals, and regulate his conduct.
Laurence Sterne (1713-1768, British Author)

207 It is books that teach us to refine our pleasures when young, and to recall them with satisfaction when we are old.
Leigh Hunt (1784-1859, British Poet, Essayist)

208 In the dark colony of night, when I consider man's magnificent capacity for malice, madness, folly, envy, rage, and destructiveness, and I wonder whether we shall not end up as breakfast for newts and polyps, I seem to hear the muffled cries of all the words in all the books with covers closed.
Leo Rosten (1908-1997, Polish Born American Political Scientist)

209 Begin to read a book that will help you move toward your dream.
Les Brown (1945-, American Speaker, Author, Trainer, Motivator Lecturer)

210 Then I though of reading -- the nice and subtle happiness of reading ... this joy not dulled by age, this polite and unpunishable vice, this selfish, serene, lifelong intoxication.
Logan Pearsall Smith (1865-1946, Anglo-American Essayist, Aphorist)

211 People say that life is the thing, but I prefer reading.
Logan Pearsall Smith (1865-1946, Anglo-American Essayist, Aphorist)

212 Books in a large university library system: 2, 000,000. Books in an average large city library: 1 0,000. Average number of books in a chain bookstore: 30, 000. Books in an average neighborhood branch library: 20, 000.
Lois Horowitz (American Librarian)

213 'Tis pleasant, sure, to see one's name in print; A book's a book, although there's nothing in it.
Lord Byron (1788-1824, British Poet)

214 The reading or non-reading a book will never keep down a single petticoat.
Lord Byron (1788-1824, British Poet)

215 Let blockheads read what blockheads wrote.
Lord Chesterfield (1694-1773, British Statesman, Author)

216 Buy good books, and read them; the best books are the commonest, and the last editions are always the best, if the editors are not blockheads.
Lord Chesterfield (1694-1773, British Statesman, Author)

217 In science, read by preference the newest works. In literature, read the oldest. The classics are always modern.
Lord Edward Lytton (1803-1873, British Writer, Statesman)

218 It is well to read everything of something, and something of everything.
Lord Henry P. Brougham (1778-1868, Scottish Whig Politician)

219 The novel can't compete with cars, the movies, television, and liquor. A guy who's had a good feed and tanked up on good wine gives his old lady a kiss after supper and his day is over. Finished.
Louis-Ferdinand Celine (1894-1961, French Author)

220 A conventional good read is usually a bad read, a relaxing bath in what we know already. A true good read is surely an act of innovative creation in which we, the readers, become conspirators.
Malcolm Bradbury (1932-, British Author)

221 To read too many books is harmful.
Mao Zedong (1893-1976, Founder of Chinese Communist State)

222 A room without books is like a body without a soul.
Marcus T. Cicero (106-43 BC, Great Roman Orator, Politician)

223 It does not follow because many books are written by persons born in America that there exists an American literature. Books which imitate or represent the thoughts and life of Europe do not constitute an American literature. Before such can exist, an original idea must animate this nation and fresh currents of life must call into life fresh thoughts along the shore.
Margaret Fuller (1810-1850, American Writer, Lecturer)

224 A house is not a home unless it contains food and fire for the mind as well as the body.
Margaret Fuller (1810-1850, American Writer, Lecturer)

225 There are books so alive that you're always afraid that while you weren't reading, the book has gone and changed, has shifted like a river; while you went on living, it went on living too, and like a river moved on and moved away. No one has stepped twice into the same river. But did anyone ever step twice into the same book?
Marina Tsvetaeva (1892-1941, Russian Poet)

226 The man who does not read books has no advantage over the man that can not read them.
Mark Twain (1835-1910, American Humorist, Writer)

227 My books are water; those of the great geniuses are wine -- everybody drinks water.
Mark Twain (1835-1910, American Humorist, Writer)

228 A classic is something that everybody wants to have read and nobody wants to read.
Mark Twain (1835-1910, American Humorist, Writer)

229 A big leather-bound volume makes an ideal razor strap. A thin book is useful to stick under a table with a broken caster to steady it. A large, flat atlas can be used to cover a window with a broken pane. And a thick, old-fashioned heavy book with a clasp is the finest thing in the world to throw at a noisy cat.
Mark Twain (1835-1910, American Humorist, Writer)

230 People are much more willing to lend you books than bookcases.
Mark Twain (1835-1910, American Humorist, Writer)

231 A successful book cannot afford to be more than ten percent new.
Marshall Mcluhan (1911-1980, Canadian Communications Theorist)

232 The multitude of books is a great evil. There is no limit to this fever for writing.
Martin Luther (1483-1546, German Leader of the Protestant Reformation)

233 A good book is the best of friends, the same today and for ever.
Martin Tupper (1810-1889, British Author, Poet, Inventor)

234 The book to read is not the one which thinks for you, but the one which makes you think. No book in the world equals the Bible for that.
Mccosh

235 Every abridgement of a good book is a fool abridged.
Michel Eyquem De Montaigne (1533-1592, French Philosopher, Essayist)

236 Books and marriage go ill together.
MoliFre (1622-1673, French Playwright)

237 In the case of good books, the point is not how many of them you can get through, but rather how many can get through to you.
Mortimer J. Adler (1902-, American Educator, Philosopher)

238 Reading is a basic tool in the living of a good life.
Mortimer J. Adler (1902-, American Educator, Philosopher)

239 Thank you for sending me a copy of your book -- I'll waste no time reading it.
Moses Hadas (1900-1966, American Classicist and Translator)

240 I have read your book and much like it.
Moses Hadas (1900-1966, American Classicist and Translator)

241 Footnotes are the finer-suckered surfaces that allow testicular paragraphs to hold fast to the wider reality of the library.
Nicholson Baker (1957-, American Author)

242 No one can read with profit that which he cannot learn to read with pleasure.
Noah Porter

243 As writers become more numerous, it is natural for readers to become more indolent; whence must necessarily arise a desire of attaining knowledge with the greatest possible ease.
Oliver Goldsmith (1728-1774, Anglo-Irish Author, Poet, Playwright)

244 The best of a book is not the thought which it contains, but the thought which it suggests; just as the charm of music dwells not in the tones but in the echoes of our hearts.
Oliver Wendell Holmes (1809-1894, American Author, Wit, Poet)

245 The most foolish kind of a book is a kind of leaky boat on the sea of wisdom; some of the wisdom will get in anyhow.
Oliver Wendell Holmes (1809-1894, American Author, Wit, Poet)

246 Old books, you know well, are books of the world's youth, and new books are the fruits of its age.
Oliver Wendell Holmes (1809-1894, American Author, Wit, Poet)

247 The books that the world calls immoral are the books that show the world its own shame.
Oscar Wilde (1856-1900, British Author, Wit)

248 There is no such thing as a moral book or an immoral book. Books are well written or badly written. That is all.
Oscar Wilde (1856-1900, British Author, Wit)

249 Books are standing counselors and preachers, always at hand, and always disinterested; having this advantage over oral instructors, that they are ready to repeat their lesson as often as we please.
Oswald Chambers (1874-1917 Scottish Preacher, Author)

250 A good book, in the language of the book-sellers, is a salable one; in that of the curious, a scarce one; in that of men of sense, a useful and instructive one.
Oswald Chambers (1874-1917 Scottish Preacher, Author)

251 A bibliophile of little means is likely to suffer often. Books don't slip from his hands but fly past him through the air, high as birds, high as prices.
Pablo Neruda (1904-1973, Chilean Poet)

252 Next, in importance to books are their titles.
Paul Davies (1946-, British Physicist, Popularizer of Science)

253 The books we read should be chosen with great care, that they may be, as an Egyptian king wrote over his library, "The medicines of the soul."
Paxton Hood

254 Be as careful of the books you read, as of the company you keep; for your habits and character will be as much influenced by the former as by the latter.
Paxton Hood

255 Read good, big important things.
Peggy Noonan (1950-, American Author, Presidential Speechwriter)

256 You can either read something many times in order to be assured that you got it all, or else you can define your purpose and use techniques which will assure that you have met it and gotten what you need.
Peter Kump

257 Read nothing that you do not care to remember, and remember nothing you do not mean to use.
Professor Blackie

258 A wicked book cannot repent.
Proverb

259 Some books leave us free and some books make us free.
Ralph Waldo Emerson (1803-1882, American Poet, Essayist)

260 Our high respect for a well read person is praise enough for literature.
Ralph Waldo Emerson (1803-1882, American Poet, Essayist)

261 Never read any book that is not a year old.
Ralph Waldo Emerson (1803-1882, American Poet, Essayist)

262 If we encounter a man of rare intellect, we should ask him what books he reads.
Ralph Waldo Emerson (1803-1882, American Poet, Essayist)

263 There is creative reading as well as creative writing.
Ralph Waldo Emerson (1803-1882, American Poet, Essayist)

264 We are too civil to books. For a few golden sentences we will turn over and actually read a volume of four or five hundred pages.
Ralph Waldo Emerson (1803-1882, American Poet, Essayist)

265 'Tis the good reader that makes the good book; in every book he finds passages which seem to be confidences or sides hidden from all else and unmistakably meant for his ear; the profit of books is according to the sensibility of the reader; the profound thought or passion sleeps as in a mine, until it is discovered by an equal mind and heart.
Ralph Waldo Emerson (1803-1882, American Poet, Essayist)

266 Books are the best of things if well used; if abused, among the worst. They are good for nothing but to inspire. I had better never see a book than be warped by its attraction clean out of my own orbit, and made a satellite instead of a system.
Ralph Waldo Emerson (1803-1882, American Poet, Essayist)

267 Ideally a book would have no order to it, and the reader would have to discover his own.
Raoul Vaneigem (1934-, Belgian Situationist Philosopher)

268 You don't have to burn books to destroy a culture. Just get people to stop reading them.
Ray Bradbury (1920-, American Science Fiction Writer)

269 At least half the mystery novels published violate the law that the solution, once revealed, must seem to be inevitable.
Raymond Chandler (1888-1959, American Author)

270 A good title is the title of a successful book.
Raymond Chandler (1888-1959, American Author)

271 The reading of all good books is like a conversation with all the finest men of past centuries.
Rene Descartes (1596-1650, French Philosopher, Scientist)

272 Everything in this book may be wrong. [The Savior's Manual]
Richard Bach (1936-, American Author)

273 Here, my dear Lucy, hide these books. Quick, quick! Fling "Peregrine Pickle" under the toilette --throw "Roderick Random" into the closet --put "The Innocent Adultery" into "The Whole Duty of Man"; thrust "Lord Aimworth" under the sofa! cram "Ovid" behind the bolster; there --put "The Man of Feeling" into your pocket. Now for them.
Richard Brinsley Sheridan (1751-1816, Anglo-Irish Dramatist)

274 Books are masters who instruct us without rods or ferules, without words or anger, without bread or money. If you approach them, they are not asleep; if you seek them, they do not hide; if you blunder, they do not scold; if you are ignorant, they do not laugh at you.
Richard De Bury (1287-1345, British Chancellor)

275 Any book that helps a child to form a habit of reading, to make reading one of his deep and continuing needs, is good for him.
Richard McKenna

276 Books are the blessed chloroform of the mind.
Robert Chambers (1802-1871, Scottish Publisher, Writer)

277 No tears in the writer, no tears in the reader.
Robert Frost (1875-1963, American Poet)

278 Books are good enough in their own way, but they are a mighty bloodless substitute for life.
Robert Louis Stevenson (1850-1895, Scottish Essayist, Poet, Novelist)

279 If I had my way books would not be written in English, but in an exceedingly difficult secret language that only skilled professional readers and story-tellers could interpret. Then people like you would have to go to public halls and pay good prices to hear the professionals decode and read the books aloud for you. This plan would have the advantage of scaring off all amateur authors, retired politicians, country doctors and I-Married-a-Midget writers who would not have the patience to learn the secret language.
Robertson Davies (1913-, Canadian Novelist, Journalist)

280 A book is the only immortality.
Rufus Choate (1799-1859, American Lawyer, Statesman)

281 Happy is he who has laid up in his youth, and held fast in all fortune, a genuine and passionate love for reading.
Rufus Choate (1799-1859, American Lawyer, Statesman)

282 A book may be compared to your neighbor: if it be good, it cannot last too long; if bad, you cannot get rid of it too early.
Rupert Brooke (1887-1915, British Poet)

283 In a real sense, people who have read good literature have lived more than people who cannot or will not read. It is not true that we have only one life to live; if we can read, we can live as many more lives and as many kinds of lives as we wish.
S. I. Hayakawa (1902-1992, Canadian Born American Senator, Educator)

284 The real risks for any artist are taken in pushing the work to the limits of what is possible, in the attempt to increase the sum of what it is possible to think. Books become good when they go to this edge and risk falling over it --when they endanger the artist by reason of what he has, or has not, artistically dared.
Salman Rushdie (1948-, Indian-born British Author)

285 A book is a version of the world. If you do not like it, ignore it; or offer your own version in return.
Salman Rushdie (1948-, Indian-born British Author)

286 The oldest books are still only just out to those who have not read them.
Samuel Butler (1612-1680, British Poet, Satirist)

287 I read part of it all the way through.
Samuel Goldwyn (1882-1974, American Film Producer, Founder, MGM)

288 A man ought to read just as his inclination leads him; for what he reads as a task will do him little good.
Samuel Johnson (1709-1784, British Author)

289 What is written without effort is in general read without pleasure.
Samuel Johnson (1709-1784, British Author)

290 Books that you carry to the fire, and hold readily in your hand, are most useful after all.
Samuel Johnson (1709-1784, British Author)

291 Most books today seemed to have been written overnight from books read the day before.
Sebastien-Roch Nicolas De Chamfort (1741-1794, French Writer, Journalist, Playwright)

292 You will, I am sure, agree with me that... if page 534 only finds us in the second chapter, the length of the first one must have been really intolerable.
Sir Arthur Conan Doyle (1859-1930, British Author, "Sherlock Holmes")

293 The Bible remained for me a book of books, still divine -- but divine in the sense that all great books are divine which teach men how to live righteously.
Sir Arthur Keith

294 Choose an author as you choose a friend.
Sir Christopher Wren

295 The first time I read an excellent work, it is to me just as if I gained a new friend; and when I read over a book I have perused before, it resembles the meeting of an old one.
Sir James Goldsmith

296 The printing press is either the greatest blessing or the greatest curse of modern times, sometimes one forgets which it is.
Sir James M. Barrie (1860-1937, British Playwright)

297 Books should to one of these fours ends conduce, for wisdom, piety, delight, or use.
Sir John Denham (1615-1668, British Poet, Dramatist)

298 Old books that have ceased to be of service should no more be abandoned than should old friends who have ceased to give pleasure.
Sir Peregrine Worsthorne (1923-, British Journalist)

299 Reading is to the mind what exercise is to the body. It is wholesome and bracing for the mind to have its faculties kept on the stretch.
Sir Richard Steele (1672-1729, British Dramatist, Essayist, Editor)

300 Who ever converses among old books will be hard to please among the new.
Sir William Temple (1628-1699, British Diplomat, Essayist)

301 Books, like proverbs, receive their chief value from the stamp and esteem of the ages through which they have passed
Sir William Temple (1628-1699, British Diplomat, Essayist)

302 A multitude of books distracts the mind.
Socrates (469-399 BC, Greek Philosopher of Athens)

303 You've really got to start hitting the books because it's no joke out here.
Spike Lee (1956-, American Film director)

304 Beware of the person of one book.
St. Thomas Aquinas (1225-1274, Italian Scholastic Philosopher and Theologian)

305 The world may be full of fourth-rate writers but it's also full of fourth-rate readers.
Stan Barstow (1928-, British Novelist, Playwright)

306 Everything in the world exists to end up in a book.
Stephane Mallarme (1842-1898, French Symbolist Poet)

307 The classics are only primitive literature. They belong to the same class as primitive machinery and primitive music and primitive medicine.
Stephen B. Leacock (1869-1944, Canadian Humorist, Economist)

308 Books are not men and yet they stay alive.
Stephen Vincent Benet (1989-1943, American Novelist, Poet)

309 Only a generation of readers will span a generation of writers.
Steven Spielberg (1947-, American Director, Screenwriter)

310 Live always in the best company when you read.
Sydney Smith (1771-1845, British Writer, Clergyman)

311 No furniture is so charming as books.
Sydney Smith (1771-1845, British Writer, Clergyman)

312 Readers are less and less seen as mere non-writers, the subhuman "other" or flawed derivative of the author; the lack of a pen is no longer a shameful mark of secondary status but a positively enabling space, just as within every writer can be seen to lurk, as a repressed but contaminating antithesis, a reader.
Terry Eagleton (1943-, British Critic)

313 A good book is the very essence of a good man. His virtues survive in it, while the foibles and faults of his actual life are forgotten. All the goodly company of the excellent and great sit around my table, or look down on me from yonder shelves, waiting patiently to answer my questions and enrich me with their wisdom. A precious book is a foretaste of immortality.
Theodore L. Cuyler (1822-1909, American Pastor, Author)

314 The books that help you most are those which make you think that most. The hardest way of learning is that of easy reading; but a great book that comes from a great thinker is a ship of thought, deep freighted with truth and beauty.
Theodore Parker (1810-1860, American Minister)

315 The best effect of any book, is that it excites the reader to self-activity.
Thomas Carlyle (1795-1881, Scottish Philosopher, Author)

316 If a book comes from the heart it will contrive to reach other hearts. All art and author craft are of small account to that.
Thomas Carlyle (1795-1881, Scottish Philosopher, Author)

317 After all manner of professors have done their best for us, the place we are to get knowledge is in books. The true university of these days is a collection of books.
Thomas Carlyle (1795-1881, Scottish Philosopher, Author)

318 What we become depends on what we read after all the professors have finished with us. The greatest university of all is the collection of books.
Thomas Carlyle (1795-1881, Scottish Philosopher, Author)

319 A book that is shut is but a block.
Thomas Fuller (1608-1661, British Clergyman, Author)

320 Books are the money of Literature, but only the counters of Science.
Thomas H. Huxley (1825-1895, British Biologist, Educator)

321 My books kept me from the ring, the dog-pit, the tavern, and the saloon.
Thomas Hood (1799-1845, British Poet and Humorist)

322 Five daily newspapers arrive in my California driveway. The New York times and the Wall Street Journal are supplemented by three local papers. As for magazines, I read, or at least skim, Business Week, Forbes, The Economist, INC; Industry Week, Fortune. Other subscriptions include Sales and Marketing Management, Modern Health Care, Progressive Grocer, High Tech Business, and Slaon Management Review from MIT. I religiously read Business Tokyo, Asia Week, and Far Eastern Economic Review. I glance at Newsweek and Time ... but I devour the New Republic, Policy Review, Foreign Affairs, The Washington Monthly, and Public Interest. How about books? A dozen or more each month.
Thomas J. Peters (1942-, American Management Consultant, Author, Trainer)

323 Books constitute capital. A library book lasts as long as a house, for hundreds of years. It is not, then, an article of mere consumption but fairly of capital, and often in the case of professional men, setting out in life, it is their only capital.
Thomas Jefferson (1743-1826, Third President of the USA)

324 I cannot live without books.
Thomas Jefferson (1743-1826, Third President of the USA)

325 Everywhere I have sought rest and not found it, except sitting in a corner by myself with a little book.
Thomas p Kempis (1379-1471, German Monk, Mystic, Religious Writer)

326 An empty book is like an infant's soul, in which anything may be written. It is capable of all things, but containeth nothing. I have a mind to fill this with profitable wonders.
Thomas Traherne (1636-1674, British Clergyman, Poet, Mystic)

327 The reason a writer writes a book is to forget a book and the reason a reader reads one is to remember it.
Thomas Wolfe (1931-, American Author, Journalist)

328 We should be as careful of the books we read, as of the company we keep. The dead very often have more power than the living.
Tryon Edwards (1809-1894, American Theologian)

329 The good of a book lies in its being read. A book is made up of signs that speak of other signs, which in their turn speak of things. Without an eye to read them, a book contains signs that produce no concepts; therefore it is dumb.
Umberto Eco (1929-, Italian Novelist and critic)

330 The unread story is not a story; it is little black marks on wood pulp. The reader, reading it, makes it live: a live thing, a story.
Ursula K. Le Guin (1929-, American Author)

331 To learn to read is to light a fire; every syllable that is spelled out is a spark.
Victor Hugo (1802-1885, French Poet, Dramatist, Novelist)

332 It is from books that wise people derive consolation in the troubles of life.
Victor Hugo (1802-1885, French Poet, Dramatist, Novelist)

333 Somewhere, everywhere, now hidden, now apparent in what ever is written down, is the form of a human being. If we seek to know him, are we idly occupied?
Virginia Woolf (1882-1941, British Novelist, Essayist)

334 All the known world, excepting only savage nations, is governed by books.
Voltaire (1694-1778, French Historian, Writer)

335 It is far better to be silent than merely to increase the quantity of bad books.
Voltaire (1694-1778, French Historian, Writer)

336 Today a reader, tomorrow a leader.
W. Fusselman

337 Some books are undeservedly forgotten; none are undeservedly remembered.
W. H. Auden (1907-1973, Anglo-American Poet)

338 A real book is not one that we read, but one that reads us.
W. H. Auden (1907-1973, Anglo-American Poet)

339 I would sooner read a timetable or a catalog than nothing at all.
W. Somerset Maugham (1874-1965, British Novelist, Playwright)

340 The successful Accelerated Reader is able to read larger than normal "blocks" or "bites" of the printed page with each eye stop. He has accepted, without reservation, the philosophy that the most important benefit of reading is the gaining of information, ideas, mental "picture" and entertainment- not the fretting over words. He has come to the realization that words in and of themselves are for the most part insignificant.
Wade E. Cutler

341 There is more treasure in books than in all the pirates loot on Treasure Island and best of all, you can enjoy these riches every day of your life.
Walt Disney (1901-1966, American Artist, Film Producer)

342 I always like to look on the optimistic side of life, but I am realistic enough to know that life is a complex matter.
Walt Disney (1901-1966, American Artist, Film Producer)

343 Camerado! This is no book; who touches this touches a man.
Walt Whitman (1819-1892, American Poet)

344 The words of my book nothing, the drift of it everything.
Walt Whitman (1819-1892, American Poet)

345 The power of a text is different when it is read from when it is copied out. Only the copied text thus commands the soul of him who is occupied with it, whereas the mere reader never discovers the new aspects of his inner self that are opened by the text, that road cut through the interior jungle forever closing behind it: because the reader follows the movement of his mind in the free flight of day-dreaming, whereas the copier submits it to command.
Walter Benjamin (1982-1940, German Critic, Philosopher)

346 Of all the ways of acquiring books, writing them oneself is regarded as the most praiseworthy method. Writers are really people who write books not because they are poor, but because they are dissatisfied with the books which they could buy but do not like.
Walter Benjamin (1982-1940, German Critic, Philosopher)

347 What is reading, but silent conversation.
Walter Savage Landor (1775-1864, British Poet, Essayist)

348 The flood of print has turned reading into a process of gulping rather than savoring
Warren Chappell

349 What gunpowder did for war the printing press has done for the mind.
Wendell Phillips (1811-1884, American Reformer, Orator)

350 Perhaps there are none more lazy, or more truly ignorant, than your everlasting readers.
William Cobbett (1762-1835, British Journalist, Reformer)

351 The mortality of all inanimate things is terrible to me, but that of books most of all.
William Dean Howells (1837-1920, American Novelist, Critic)

352 It is chiefly through books that we enjoy intercourse with superior minds, and these invaluable means of communication are in the reach of all. In the best books, great men talk to us, give us their most precious thoughts, and pour their souls into ours.
William Ellery Channing (1780-1842, American Unitarian Minister, Author)

353 Every man is a volume if you know how to read him.
William Ellery Channing (1780-1842, American Unitarian Minister, Author)

354 God be thanked for books; they are the voices of the distant and the dead, and make us heirs of the spiritual life of past ages.
William Ellery Channing (1780-1842, American Unitarian Minister, Author)

355 The tools I need for my work are paper, tobacco, food, and a little whiskey.
William Faulkner (1897-1962, American Novelist)

356 Read, read, read. Read everything-- trash, classics, good and bad, and see how they do it. Just like a carpenter who works as an apprentice and studies the master. Read! You'll absorb it. Then write. If it is good, you'll find out. If it's not, throw it out the window.
William Faulkner (1897-1962, American Novelist)

357 If I have not read a book before, it is, for all intents and purposes, new to me whether it was printed yesterday or three hundred years ago.
William Hazlitt (1778-1830, British Essayist)

358 I divide all readers into two classes: those who read to remember and those who read to forget.
William Lyon Phelps

359 If a secret history of books could be written, and the author's private thoughts and meanings noted down alongside of his story, how many insipid volumes would become interesting, and dull tales excite the reader!
William M. Thackeray (1811-1863, Indian-born British Novelist)

360 A dose of poison can do its work but once. A bad book can go on poisoning minds for generations.
William Murray (1705-1793, American Judge)

361 Much reading is an oppression of the mind, and extinguishes the natural candle, which is the reason of so many senseless scholars in the world.
William Penn (1644-1718, British Religious Leader, Founder of Pennsylvania)

362 O, let my books be then the eloquence and dumb presages of my speaking breast.
William Shakespeare (1564-1616, British Poet, Playwright, Actor)

363 A great book should leave you with many experiences and slightly exhausted at the end. You should live several lives while reading it.
William Styron (1925-, American Novelist)

364 Thy books should, like thy friends, not many be, yet such wherein men may thy judgment see.
William Wycherley (1640-1716, British Dramatist)

365 Man ceased to be an ape, vanquished the ape, on the day the first book was written.
Yevgeny Zamyatin (1884-1937, Russian Writer)

366 To sit alone in the lamplight with a book spread out before you hold intimate converse with men of unseen generations -- such is pleasure beyond compare.
Yoshida Kenko

BOOKS: BESTSELLERS

1 A best-seller is the golden touch of mediocre talent.
Logan Pearsall Smith (1865-1946, Anglo-American Essayist, Aphorist)

2 The principle of procrastinated rape is said to be the ruling one in all the great bestsellers.
V. S. Pritchett (1900-, British Author, Critic)

3 No one can write a best seller by trying to. He must write with complete sincerity; the clichés that make you laugh, the hackneyed characters, the well-worn situations, the commonplace story that excites your derision, seem neither hackneyed, well worn nor commonplace to him. The conclusion is obvious: you cannot write anything that will convince unless you are yourself convinced. The best seller sells because he writes with his heart's blood.
W. Somerset Maugham (1874-1965, British Novelist, Playwright)

BOOKS: CLASSICS

1 Definition of a classic: a book everyone is assumed to have read and often thinks they have.
Alan Bennett (1934-, British Playwright)

2 A classic is a book that doesn't have to be written again.
Carl Van Doren (1885-1950, American Critic, Biographer)

3 A book is never a masterpiece: it becomes one. Genius is the talent of a dead man.
Edmond and Jules De Goncourt (1822-1896, French Writers)

4 A classic is classic not because it conforms to certain structural rules, or fits certain definitions (of which its author had quite probably never heard). It is classic because of a certain eternal and irrepressible freshness.
Ezra Pound (1885-1972, American Poet, Critic)

5 For what are the classics but the noblest thoughts of man? They are the only oracles which are not decayed, and there are such answers to the most modern inquiry in them as Delphi and Dodona never gave. We might as well omit to study Nature because she is old.
Henry David Thoreau (1817-1862, American Essayist, Poet, Naturalist)

6 Every man with a bellyful of the classics is an enemy to the human race.
Henry Miller (1891-1980, American Author)

7 A classic is a book that has never finished saying what it has to say.
Italo Calvino (1923-1985, Cuban Writer, Essayist, Journalist)

8 There is but one way left to save a classic: to give up revering him and use him for our own salvation.
Jose Ortega Y Gasset (1883-1955, Spanish Essayist, Philosopher)

9 The light that radiates from the great novels time can never dim, for human existence is perpetually being forgotten by man and thus the novelists discoveries, however old they may be, will never cease to astonish.
Milan Kundera (1929-, Czech Author, Critic)

10 The fact is, the public make use of the classics of a country as a means of checking the progress of Art. They degrade the classics into authorities. They use them as bludgeons for preventing the free expression of Beauty in new forms.
Oscar Wilde (1856-1900, British Author, Wit)

11 There are books which take rank in your life with parents and lovers and passionate experiences, so medicinal, so stringent, so revolutionary, so authoritative.
Ralph Waldo Emerson (1803-1882, American Poet, Essayist)

12 A truly great book should be read in youth, again in maturity and once more in old age, as a fine building should be seen by morning light, at noon and by moonlight.
Robertson Davies (1913-, Canadian Novelist, Journalist)

13 Books that have become classics -- books that have had their day and now get more praise than perusal -- always remind me of retired colonels and majors and captains who, having reached the age limit, find themselves retired on half pay.
Thomas B. Aldrich (1836-1907, American Writer, Editor)

14 The praise of ancient authors proceeds not from the reverence of the dead, but from the competition and mutual envy of the living.
Thomas Hobbes (1588-1679, British Philosopher)

15 There are certain books in the world which every searcher for truth must know: the Bible, the Critique of Pure Reason, the Origin of Species, and Karl Marx's Capital.
W. E. B. Du Bois (Civil Rights Activist)

BORES AND BOREDOM

1 Bore -- a person who talks when you wish him to listen.
Ambrose Bierce (1842-1914, American Author, Editor, Journalist, "The Devil's Dictionary")

2 People of Wealth and the so called upper class suffer the most from boredom.
Arthur Schopenhauer (1788-1860, German Philosopher)

3 One thing I can say about George... he may not be able to keep a job, but he's not boring.
Barbara Bush (1925-, American First Lady, Wife of President George Bush)

4 The age of chivalry is past. Bores have succeeded to dragons.
Benjamin Disraeli (1804-1881, British Statesman, Prime Minister)

5 A bore is a man who, when you ask him how he is, tells you.
Bert Leston Taylor

6 Boredom is a vital problem for the moralist, since at least half the sins of mankind are caused by the fear of it.
Bertrand Russell (1872-1970, British Philosopher, Mathematician, Essayist)

7 Unless one is taught what to do with success after getting it, achievement of it must inevitably leave him prey to boredom.
Bertrand Russell (1872-1970, British Philosopher, Mathematician, Essayist)

8 Only those who want everything done for them are bored.
Billy Graham (1918-, American Evangelist)

9 Man finds nothing so intolerable as to be in a state of complete rest, without passions, without occupation, without diversion, without effort. Then he feels his nullity, loneliness, inadequacy, dependence, helplessness, emptiness.
Blaise Pascal (1623-1662, French Scientist, Religious Philosopher)

10 Everything considered, work is less boring than amusing oneself.
Charles Baudelaire (1821-1867, French Poet)

11   I am quite serious when I say that I do not believe there are, on the whole earth besides, so many intensified bores as in these United States. No man can form an adequate idea of the real meaning of the word, without coming here.
Charles Dickens (1812-1870, British Novelist)

12   I have a fear of being boring.
Christian Bale (Born 1974, British-born American Actor)

13   Boredom: the desire for desires.
Count Leo Tolstoy (1828-1910, Russian Novelist, Philosopher)

14   Are you bored with life? Then throw yourself into some work you believe in with all your heart, live for it, die for it, and you will find happiness that you had thought could never be yours.
Dale Carnegie (1888-1955, American Author, Trainer)

15   Bores bore each other too; but it never seems to teach them anything.
Don Marquis (1878-1937, American Humorist, Journalist)

16   Boring people are a reflection of boring people.
Doug Horton

17   Somebody's boring me. I think it's me.
Dylan Thomas (1914-1953, Welsh Poet)

18   You'll find boredom where there is an absence of a good idea.
Earl Nightingale (1921-1989, American Radio Announcer, Author, Motivator, Speaker)

19   There are moments when, faced with our lack of success, I wonder whether we are failures, proud but impotent. One thing reassures me as to our value: the boredom that afflicts us. It is the hall-mark of quality in modern men.
Edmond and Jules De Goncourt (1822-1896, French Writers)

20   The cure for boredom is curiosity. There is no cure for curiosity.
Ellen Parr

21   When people are bored it is primarily with themselves.
Eric Hoffer (1902-1983, American Author, Philosopher)

22   Against boredom the gods themselves fight in vain.
Friedrich Nietzsche (1844-1900, German Philosopher)

23   Only the most acute and active animals are capable of boredom. -- A theme for a great poet would be God's boredom on the seventh day of creation.
Friedrich Nietzsche (1844-1900, German Philosopher)

24   What's wrong with being a boring kind of guy?
George Bush (1924-, Forty-first President of the USA)

25   Good-bye. I am leaving because I am bored.
George Sanders

26   The world is eaten up by boredom. You can't see it all at once. It is like dust. You go about and never notice, you breathe it in, you eat and drink it. It is sifted so fine, it doesn't even grit on your teeth. But stand still for an instant and there it is, coating your face and hands. To shake off this drizzle of ashes you must be for ever on the go. And so people are always "on the go."
Georges Bernanos (1888-1948, French Novelist, Political Writer)

27   Everyone is a bore to someone. That is unimportant. The things to avoid is being a bore to oneself.
Gerald Brenan (1894-1987, Maltan Travel Writer, Novelist)

28   A yawn is a silent shout.
Gilbert K. Chesterton (1874-1936, British Author)

29   Boredom is always counter-revolutionary. Always.
Guy Debord (1931-, French Philosopher)

30   A bore is a person who opens his mouth and puts his feats in it.
Henry Ford (1863-1947, American Industrialist, Founder of Ford Motor Company)

31   The nice thing about being a celebrity is that, if you bore people, they think it's their fault.
Henry Kissinger (1923-, American Republican Politician, Secretary of State)

32   The life of a creator is not the only life nor perhaps the most interesting which a man leads. There is a time for play and a time for work, a time for creation and a time for lying fallow. And there is a time, glorious too in its own way, when one scarcely exists, when one is a complete void. I mean -- when boredom seems the very stuff of life.
Henry Miller (1891-1980, American Author)

33   To do the same thing over and over again is not only boredom: it is to be controlled by rather than to control what you do.
Heraclitus (535-475 BC, Greek Philosopher)

34   Boredom is like a pitiless zooming in on the epidermis of time. Every instant is dilated and magnified like the pores of the face.
Jean Baudrillard (French Postmodern Philosopher, Writer)

35   The wise person often shuns society for fear of being bored.
Jean De La Bruyere (1645-1696, French Writer)

36   People who have nothing to do are quickly tired of their own company.
Jeremy Collier (1650-1726, British Clergyman, Conjuror)

37   Is boredom anything less than the sense of one's faculties slowly dying?
John Berger (1926-, British Actor, Critic)

38   Life, friends, is boring. We must not say so. After all, the sky flashes, the great sea yearns, we ourselves flash and yearn, and moreover my mother told me as a boy (repeatedly) "Ever to confess you're bored means you have no inner Resources." I conclude now I have no inner resources, because I am heavy bored.
John Berryman (1914-1972, American Poet)

39 A healthy male adult bore consumes each year one and a half times his own weight in other people's patience.
John Updike (1932-, American Novelist, Critic)

40 Never chain your dogs together with sausages. One must accustom one's self to be bored.
Lady Bloomfield

41 The penalty for success is to be bored by people who used to snub you.
Lady Nancy Astor (1897-1964, British Politician)

42 His shortcoming is his long staying.
Lewis L. Lewisohn

43 If you're bored with life -- you don't get up every morning with a burning desire to do things -- you don't have enough goals.
Lou Holtz (1937-, American Football Coach)

44 The most terrible thing about materialism, even more terrible than its proneness to violence, is its boredom, from which sex, alcohol, drugs, all devices for putting out the accusing light of reason and suppressing the unrealizable aspirations of love, offer a prospect of deliverance.
Malcolm Muggeridge (1903-1990, British Broadcaster)

45 And 'tis remarkable that they talk most who have the least to say.
Matthew Prior (1664-1721, British Diplomat, Poet)

46 The devil's name is dullness.
Robert E. Lee (1807-1870, American Confederate Army Commander)

47 The man who lets himself be bored is even more contemptible than the bore.
Samuel Butler (1612-1680, British Poet, Satirist)

48 Surely a long life must be somewhat tedious, since we are forced to call in so many trifling things to help rid us of our time, which will never return.
Samuel Johnson (1709-1784, British Author)

49 Sir, you have but two topics, yourself and me. I am sick of both.
Samuel Johnson (1709-1784, British Author)

50 The life of the creative man is lead, directed and controlled by boredom. Avoiding boredom is one of our most important purposes.
Saul Steinberg

51 My mind rebels at stagnation. Give me problems, give me work, give me the most abstruse cryptogram, or the most intricate analysis, and I am in my own proper atmosphere. I can dispense then with artificial stimulants. But I abhor the dull routine of existence. I crave for mental exaltation.
Sir Arthur Conan Doyle (1859-1930, British Author, "Sherlock Holmes")

52 Perhaps the world's second worst crime is boredom. The first is being a bore.
Sir Cecil Beaton (1904-1980, British-born American Photographer)

53 Since boredom advances and boredom is the root of all evil, no wonder, then, that the world goes backwards, that evil spreads. This can be traced back to the very beginning of the world. The gods were bored; therefore they created human beings.
Soren Kierkegaard (1813-1855, Danish Philosopher, Writer)

54 Boredom is the root of all evil--the despairing refusal to be oneself.
Soren Kierkegaard (1813-1855, Danish Philosopher, Writer)

55 I begin with the principle that all men are bores. Surely no one will prove himself so great a bore as to contradict me in this.
Soren Kierkegaard (1813-1855, Danish Philosopher, Writer)

56 Boredom is just the reverse side of fascination: both depend on being outside rather than inside a situation, and one leads to the other.
Susan Sontag (1933-, American Essayist)

57 The man who suspects his own tediousness is yet to be born.
Thomas B. Aldrich (1836-1907, American Writer, Editor)

58 Too many church services start at eleven sharp and end at twelve dull.
Vance Havner

59 All kinds are good except the kind that bores you.
Voltaire (1694-1778, French Historian, Writer)

60 Boredom is the dream bird that hatches the egg of experience. A rustling in the leaves drives him away.
Walter Benjamin (1982-1940, German Critic, Philosopher)

61 I spent a year in that town, one Sunday.
Warwick Deeping (1877-1950, British Novelist)

62 The concept of boredom entails an inability to use up present moments in a personally fulfilling way.
Wayne Dyer (1940-, American Psychotherapist, Author, Lecturer)

63 Life is never boring, but some people choose to be bored.
Wayne Dyer (1940-, American Psychotherapist, Author, Lecturer)

64 For I have neither wit, nor words, nor worth, action nor utterance, nor the power of speech, to stir men's blood. I only speak right on. I tell you that which you yourselves do know.
William Shakespeare (1564-1616, British Poet, Playwright, Actor)

BORROWING

1 Before borrowing money from a friend decide which you need most.
American Proverb

2 Let us all be happy, and live within our means, even if we have to borrow the money to do it with.
Artemus Ward

3 If you would know the value of money try to borrow some.
Benjamin Franklin (1706-1790, American Scientist, Publisher, Diplomat)

4 Borrowing is not much better than begging; just as lending with interest is not much better than stealing.
Doris Lessing (1919-, British Novelist)

5 People cannot live by lending money to one another.
John Ruskin (1819-1900, British Critic, Social Theorist)

6 Don't borrow money from a neighbor or a friend, but of a stranger where, paying for it you shall hear of it no more.
Lord Burleigh

7 When a person has no need to borrow they find multitudes willing to lend.
Oliver Goldsmith (1728-1774, Anglo-Irish Author, Poet, Playwright)

8 An empty purse and a new house make a man wise, but too late.
Portuguese Proverb

9 People lend only to the rich.
Proverb

10 Who goes a borrowing, goes a sorrowing.
Proverb

11 Quick to borrow is always slow to pay.
Proverb

12 Loans and debts make worry and frets.
Saying

BOSSES AND EMPLOYEES

1 If you think your boss is stupid, remember: you wouldn't have a job if he was any smarter.
Albert A. Grant (American Business Executive)

2 Being the boss anywhere is lonely. Being a female boss in a world of mostly men is especially so.
Alison Gomme (British Prison Governor)

3 By and large, mothers and housewives are the only workers who do not have regular time off. They are the great vacationless class.
Anne Morrow Lindbergh (1906-, American Author)

4 Reliable office staff come in the shape of mature married women working from 9.30 to 3.30 (inside school hours) during which they will do more than the 9-5ers.
Chris Brasher (British Sports and Business Executive)

5 The person who knows HOW will always have a job. The person who knows WHY will always be his boss.
Diane Ravitch

6 Most bosses know instinctively that their power depends more on employee's compliance than on threats or sanctions.
Fernanda Bartolme (French Business Academics)

7 The boss must first distinguish between action information and status information. He must discipline himself not to act on problems his managers can solve, and never to act on problems when he is explicitly reviewing status. I once knew a boss who invariably picked up the phone to give orders before the end of the first paragraph in a status report. That response is guaranteed to squelch full disclosure.
Frederick P. Brooks

8 I would be a billionaire if I was looking to be a selfish boss. That's not me.
John Gotti (American Mafia Boss)

9 It is your people who make the ultimate difference. You put the investment into training the people and then, when you get invited to the party with the big boys, that is a unique selling point.
Phil Dixon (Business Businessman, Founder of Newlife Cleaning Systems)

10 By working faithfully eight hours a day, you may eventually get to be a boss and work twelve hours a day.
Robert Frost (1875-1963, American Poet)

11 Most important for us is a good spiritual relationship between employees and management.
Tatsuhiko Andoh (Japanese Business Executive)

BOXING

1 It's the boxers who attract the real women, after all, with their raw primeval strength, beautifully toned bodies and just a touch of vulnerability.
Eamonn Mccabe

2 Boxing is just show business with blood.
Frank Bruno

3 I want to keep fighting because it is the only thing that keeps me out of the hamburger joints. If I don't fight, I'll eat this planet.
George Foreman (1949-, American Boxer)

4 That was always the difference between Muhammad Ali and the rest of us. He came, he saw, and if he didn't entirely conquer -- he came as close as anybody we are likely to see in the lifetime of this doomed generation.
Hunter S. Thompson (1939-, American Journalist)

5 All the time he's boxing, he's thinking. All the time he was thinking, I was hitting him.
Jack Dempsey (1895-1983, American Boxer)

6 All fighters are prostitutes and all promoters are pimps.
Larry Holmes (1949-, American Boxer)

7 Float like a butterfly, sting like a bee.
Muhammad Ali (1942-, American Boxer)

8 It's just a job. Grass grows, birds fly, waves pound the sand. I beat people up.
Muhammad Ali (1942-, American Boxer)

9 I have always adhered to two principles. The first one is to train hard and get in the best possible physical condition. The second is to forget all about the other fellow until you face him in the ring and the bell sounds for the fight.
Rocky Marciano (1923-1969, American Boxer)

BOYS

1 I never see any difference in boys. I only know two sorts of boys. Mealy boys and beef-faced boys.
Charles Dickens (1812-1870, British Novelist)

2 Boys are capital fellows in their own way, among their mates; but they are unwholesome companions for grown people.
Charles Lamb (1775-1834, British Essayist, Critic)

3 Boyhood is a most complex and incomprehensible thing. Even when one has been through it, one does not understand what it was. A man can never quite understand a boy, even when he has been the boy.
Gilbert K. Chesterton (1874-1936, British Author)

4 Every genuine boy is a rebel and an anarch. If he were allowed to develop according to his own instincts, his own inclinations, society would undergo such a radical transformation as to make the adult revolutionary cower and cringe.
Henry Miller (1891-1980, American Author)

5 A fairly bright boy is far more intelligent and far better company than the average adult.
John B. S. Haldane (1892-1964, British Scientist, Author)

6 Speak roughly to your little boy, and beat him when he sneezes: he only does it to annoy, because he knows it teases.
Lewis Carroll (1832-1898, British Writer, Mathematician)

7 There comes a time in every rightly constructed boy's life when he has a raging desire to go somewhere and dig for hidden treasure.
Mark Twain (1835-1910, American Humorist, Writer)

8 What money is better bestowed than that of a schoolboy's tip? How the kindness is recalled by the recipient in after days! It blesses him that gives and him that takes.
William M. Thackeray (1811-1863, Indian-born British Novelist)

BRAGGING

1 If I seem to boast more than is becoming, my excuse is that I brag for humanity rather than for myself.
Henry David Thoreau (1817-1862, American Essayist, Poet, Naturalist)

2 Mere flimflam stories, and nothing but shams and lies.
Miguel De Cervantes (1547-1616, Spanish Novelist, Dramatist, Poet)

3 If I cannot brag of knowing something, then I brag of not knowing it; at any rate, brag.
Ralph Waldo Emerson (1803-1882, American Poet, Essayist)

4 There is also this benefit in brag, that the speaker is unconsciously expressing his own ideal. Humor him by all means, draw it all out, and hold him to it.
Ralph Waldo Emerson (1803-1882, American Poet, Essayist)

5 Every other enjoyment malice may destroy; every other panegyric envy may withhold; but no human power can deprive the boaster of his own encomiums.
Samuel Johnson (1709-1784, British Author)

BREVITY

1 Good things, when short, are twice as good.
Baltasar Gracian (1601-1658, Spanish Philosopher, Writer)

2 I will be brief. Not nearly so brief as Salvador Dali, who gave the world's shortest speech. He said I will be so brief I have already finished, and he sat down.
Edward O. Wilson

3 It wasn't by accident that the Gettysburg address was so short. The laws of prose writing are as immutable as those of flight, of mathematics, of physics.
Ernest Hemingway (1898-1961, American Writer)

4 The more you say, the less people remember. The fewer the words, the greater the profit.
François Fénelon (1651-1715, French Roman Catholic archbishop, theologian, poet and writer)

5 It is my ambition to say in ten sentences; what others say in a whole book.
Friedrich Nietzsche (1844-1900, German Philosopher)

6 It is no great art to say something briefly when, like Tacitus, one has something to say; when one has nothing to say, however, and none the less writes a whole book and makes truth into a liar -- that I call an achievement.
Georg C. Lichtenberg (1742-1799, German Physicist, Satirist)

7 I strive to be brief, and I become obscure.
Horace (65-8 BC, Italian Poet)

8 Brevity and conciseness are the parents of correction.
Hosea Ballou (1771-1852, American Theologian, Founder of "Universalism")

9 There's a great power in words, if you don't hitch too many of them together.
Josh Billings (1815-1885, American Humorist, Lecturer)

10 Brevity is the best recommendation of speech, whether in a senator or an orator.
Marcus T. Cicero (106-43 BC, Great Roman Orator, Politician)

11   Brevity is a great charm of eloquence.
Marcus T. Cicero (106-43 BC, Great Roman Orator, Politician)

12   The fewer the words, the better the prayer.
Martin Luther (1483-1546, German Leader of the Protestant Reformation)

13   If you would be pungent, be brief; for it is with words as with sunbeams -- the more they are condensed, the deeper they burn.
Robert Southey (1774-1843, British Author)

14   The most valuable of all talents is that of never using two words when one will do.
Thomas Jefferson (1743-1826, Third President of the USA)

15   Never be so brief as to become obscure.
Tryon Edwards (1809-1894, American Theologian)

16   Brevity is the soul of wit, and tediousness the limbs and outward flourishes.
William Shakespeare (1564-1616, British Poet, Playwright, Actor)

BROADWAY

1   I'm the end of the line; absurd and appalling as it may seem, serious New York theater has died in my lifetime.
Arthur Miller (1915-, American Dramatist)

2   Broadway, such as I see it now and have seen it for twenty-five years, is a ramp that was conceived by St. Thomas Aquinas while he was yet in the womb. It was meant originally to be used only by snakes and lizards, by the horned toad and the red heron, but when the great Spanish Armada was sunk the human kind wriggled out of the ketch and slopped over, creating by a sort of foul, ignominious squirm and wiggle the cunt-like cleft that runs from the Battery south to the golf links north through the dead and wormy center of Manhattan Island.
Henry Miller (1891-1980, American Author)

3   We all know that the theater and every play that comes to Broadway have within themselves, like the human being, the seed of self-destruction and the certainty of death. The thing is to see how long the theater, the play, and the human being can last in spite of themselves.
James Thurber (1894-1961, American Humorist, Illustrator)

4   The wide wonder of Broadway is disconsolate in the daytime; but gaudily glorious at night, with a milling crowd filling sidewalk and roadway, silent, going up, going down, between upstanding banks of brilliant lights, each building braided and embossed with glowing, many-colored bulbs of man-rayed luminance. A glowing valley of the shadow of life. The strolling crowd went slowly by through the kinematically divine thoroughfare of New York.
Sean O'Casey (1884-1964, Irish Dramatist)

BROTHERHOOD

1   To correct the evils, great and small, which spring from want of sympathy and from positive enmity among strangers, as nations or as individuals, is one of the highest functions of civilization.
Abraham Lincoln (1809-1865, Sixteenth President of the USA)

2   On this shrunken globe, men can no longer live as strangers.
Adlai E. Stevenson (1900-1965, American Lawyer, Politician)

3   We cannot possibly let ourselves get frozen into regarding everyone we do not know as an absolute stranger.
Albert Schweitzer (1875-1965, German Born Medical Missionary, Theologian, Musician, and Philosopher)

4   The brotherhood of men does not imply their equality. Families have their fools and their men of genius, their black sheep and their saints, their worldly successes and their worldly failures. A man should treat his brothers lovingly and with justice, according to the deserts of each. But the deserts of every brother are not the same.
Aldous Huxley (1894-1963, British Author)

5   You can't hold a man down without staying down with him.
Booker T. Washington (1856-1915, American Black Leader and Educator)

6   Brotherhood is the very price and condition of man's survival.
Carlos Pena Romulo

7   There is a destiny that makes us brothers, No one goes his way alone; All that we send into the lives of others, Comes back into our own.
Edwin Markham (1852-1940, American Poet and Editor)

8   The crest and crowning of all good, Life's final star, is Brotherhood.
Edwin Markham (1852-1940, American Poet and Editor)

9   There is always a chance that he who sets himself up as his brother's keeper will end up by being his jail-keeper.
Eric Hoffer (1902-1983, American Author, Philosopher)

10   When man to man shall be friend and brother.
Gerald Massey

11   Brotherhood is not just a Bible word. Out of comradeship can come and will come the happy life for all.
Heywood Broun (1888-1939, American Journalist, Novelist)

12   I met a hundred men going to Delhi and everyone is my brother.
Indian Saying

13   We live in a world that has narrowed into a neighborhood before it has broadened into a brotherhood.
Lyndon B. Johnson (1908-1973, Thirty-sixth President of the USA)

14 I believe in the brotherhood of man, all men, but I don't believe in brotherhood with anybody who doesn't want brotherhood with me. I believe in treating people right, but I'm not going to waste my time trying to treat somebody right who doesn't know how to return the treatment.
Malcolm X (1925-1965, American Black Leader, Activist)

15 We must learn to live together as brothers or perish together as fools.
Martin Luther King Jr. (1929-1968, American Black Leader, Nobel Prize Winner, 1964)

16 You may call for peace as loudly as you wish, but where there is no brotherhood there can in the end be no peace.
Max Lerner (1902-, American Author, Columnist)

17 Speak not too well of one who scarce will know himself transfigured in its roseate glow; Say kindly of him what is, chiefly, true, remembering always he belongs to you; Deal with him as a truant, if you will, But claim him, keep him, call him brother still!
Oliver Wendell Holmes (1809-1894, American Author, Wit, Poet)

18 If you wish to be brothers, let the arms fall from your hands. One cannot love while holding offensive arms.
Pope Paul VI (1897-1978, Pope from 1963-1978)

19 The brotherhood of man is evoked by particular men according to their circumstances. But it seldom extends to all men. In the name of our freedom and our brotherhood we are prepared to blow up the other half of mankind and to be blown up in our turn.
R. D. Laing (1927-1989, British Psychiatrist)

20 The most dangerous word in any human tongue is the word for brother. It's inflammatory.
Tennessee Williams (1914-1983, American Dramatist)

BUDDHISM

1 Buddhism is not a creed, it is a doubt.
Gilbert K. Chesterton (1874-1936, British Author)

2 Our civilization, bequeathed to us by fierce adventurers, eaters of meat and hunters, is so full of hurry and combat, so busy about many things which perhaps are of no importance, that it cannot but see something feeble in a civilization which smiles as it refuses to make the battlefield the test of excellence.
James Joyce (1882-1941, Irish Author)

3 A religion so cheerless, a philosophy so sorrowful, could never have succeeded with the masses of mankind if presented only as a system of metaphysics. Buddhism owed its success to its catholic spirit and its beautiful morality.
W. Winwood Reade (1838-1875, American Writer)

BUDGETS

1 Budgets are for cutting, that's why you set them.
Dr. Laurence Buckman (British GP)

2 The budget evolved from a management tool into an obstacle to management.
Frank C. Carlucci (American Secretary of Defense)

3 We didn't actually overspend our budget. The health Commission allocation simply fell short of our expenditure.
Keith Davis (American Executive, Chairman of Wollongong Hospital)

4 Some couples go over their budgets very carefully every month. Others just go over them.
Sally Poplin

BURDENS

1 None knows the weight of another's burden.
George Herbert (1593-1632, British Metaphysical Poet)

2 Those who commit injustice bear the greatest burden.
Hosea Ballou (1771-1852, American Theologian, Founder of "Universalism")

3 I do not pray for a lighter load, but for a stronger back.
Phillips Brooks (1835-1893, American Minister, Poet)

4 It's easier traveling the road of life when I don't have so much to carry on my back.
Silas Weir Mitchell (1829-1914, Physician, Writer, Poet)

5 I have read in Plato and Cicero sayings that are wise and very beautiful; but I have never read in either of them: Come unto me all ye that labor and are heavy laden."
St. Augustine (354-430, Numidian-born Bishop of Hippo, Theologian)

6 God gave burdens, also shoulders.
Yiddish Proverb

BUREAUCRACY

1 If the copying machines that came along later had been here during the war, I'm not sure the allies would have won. We'd all have drowned in paper.
Alan Dickey (American World War II Pentagon Architect)

2 A bureaucrat is a Democrat who holds some office a Republican wants.
Alben W. Barkley (1877-1956, American Politician)

3 Official dignity tends to increase in inverse ratio to the importance of the country in which the office is held.
Aldous Huxley (1894-1963, British Author)

4 Poor fellow, he suffers from files.
Aneurin Bevan (1897-1960, British Labor Politician)

5 It seems to me that there must be an ecological limit to the number of paper pushers the earth can sustain, and that human civilization will collapse when the number of, say, tax lawyers exceeds the world's total population of farmers, weavers, fisherpersons, and pediatric nurses.
Barbara Ehrenreich (1941-, American Author, Columnist)

6 In the US we find the label requirements are crazy. It is almost as if we had to label a bookcase with the warning 'do not eat this bookcase -- it can be harmful to your health'.
Bjorn Bayley (Business Executive, President of Ikea US)

7 Those who can, do, those who can't teach; and those who can do neither, administer.
Calvin Calverley

8 The only thing that saves us from the bureaucracy is inefficiency. An efficient bureaucracy is the greatest threat to liberty.
Eugene J. Mccarthy (1916-, American Politician)

9 The longer the title, the less important the job.
George Mcgovern (1922-, American Democratic Politician)

10 There is something about a bureaucrat that does not like a poem.
Gore Vidal (1925-, American Novelist, Critic)

11 If we did not have such a thing as an airplane today, we would probably create something the size of N.A.S.A. to make one.
H. Ross Perot (1930-, American Businessman & Politician, Founder EDS)

12 If you're going to sin, sin against God, not the bureaucracy; God will forgive you but the bureaucracy won t.
Hyman G. Rickover (1900-1986, Naval Engineering Officer)

13 A bureaucrat is a person who cuts red tape sideways.
J. Mccabe

14 Endless meetings, sloppy communications and red tape steal the entrepreneur's time.
James L. Hayes (American Businessman, President, American Management Association)

15 The disease which inflicts bureaucracy and what they usually die from is routine.
John Stuart Mill (1806-1873, British Philosopher, Economist)

16 Bureaucracy is not an obstacle to democracy but an inevitable complement to it.
Joseph A. Schumpeter (1883-1950, Austrian-American Economist)

17 A multitude of little superfluous precautions engender here a population of deputies and sub- officials, each of whom acquits himself with an air of importance and a rigorous precision, which seemed to say, though everything is done with much silence, "Make way, I am one of the members of the grand machine of state."
Marquis De Custine (1790-1857, French Traveler, Author)

18 Bureaucracy, the rule of no one, has become the modern form of despotism.
Mary Mccarthy (1912-1989, American Author, Critic)

19 So many signatures for such a small heart.
Mother Teresa (1910-1997, Albanian-born Roman Catholic Missionary)

20 The inventor of the Xerox machine will, I am sure, find a special place reserved for him on one of the inner circles of Dante's Inferno.
Nicholas Goodison (British Business Executive, Chairman of London Stock Exchange)

21 Government proposes, bureaucracy disposes. And the bureaucracy must dispose of government proposals by dumping them on us.
P. J. O'Rourke (1947-, American Journalist)

22 No government ever voluntarily reduces itself in size. Government programs, once launched, never disappear. Actually, a government bureau is the nearest thing to eternal life we'll ever see on this earth!
Ronald Reagan (1911-, Fortieth President of the USA, Actor)

23 The white man knows how to make everything, but he does not know how to distribute it.
Sitting Bull (1834-1890, American Indian Warrior and chief of the Dakota Sioux)

24 A bureaucracy is sure to think that its duty is to augment official power, official business, or official members, rather than to leave free the energies of mankind; it overdoes the quantity of government, as well as impairs its quality. The truth is, that a skilled bureaucracy is, though it boasts of an appearance of science, quite inconsistent with the true principles of the art of business.
Walter Bagehot (1826-1877, British Economist, Critic)

25 I always get back to the question, is it really necessary that men should consume so much of their bodily and mental energies in the machinery of civilized life? The world seems to me to do much of its toil for that which is not in any sense bread. Again, does not the latent feeling that much of their striving is to no purpose tend to infuse large quantities of sham into men's work?"
William Allingham (1824-1889, Poet)

26 Nothing can be more contemptible than to suppose Public Records to be true.
William Blake (1757-1827, British Poet, Painter)

BURIAL

1 We therefore commit his body to the ground; earth to earth, ashes to ashes, dust to dust; in sure and certain hope of the Resurrection.
Book Of Common Prayer (Liturgy of the Anglican Church)

2 All places are alike, and every earth is fit for burial.
Christopher Marlowe (1564-1593, British Dramatist, Poet)

3 Corpses are more fit to be thrown out than is dung.
Heraclitus (535-475 BC, Greek Philosopher)

4   The dreariest spot in all the land to Death they set apart; with scanty grace from Nature's hand, and none from that of Art.
John Greenleaf Whittier (1807-1892, American Poet, Reformer, Author)

5   I could never bear to be buried with people to whom I had not been introduced.
Norman Parkinson

6   Just under the surface I shall be, all together at first, then separate and drift, through all the earth and perhaps in the end through a cliff into the sea, something of me. A ton of worms in an acre, that is a wonderful thought, a ton of worms, I believe it.
Samuel Beckett (1906-1989, Irish Dramatist, Novelist)

7   The beautiful uncut hair of graves.
Walt Whitman (1819-1892, American Poet)

BUSINESS

1   The propensity to truck, barter and exchange one thing for another is common to all men, and to be found in no other race of animals.
Adam Smith (1723-1790, Scottish Economist)

2   Doing well is the result of doing good. That's what capitalism is all about.
Adnan Kashoggi

3   Get me inside any boardroom and I'll get any decision I want.
Alan Bond (Australian Entrepreneur)

4   A generation which has passed through the shop has absorbed standards and ambitions which are not of those of spaciousness, and cannot get away from them. Everything with them is done as though for sale, and they naturally have in view the greatest possible benefit, profit and that end of the stuff that will make the best show.
Alexander Herzen (1812-1870, Russian Journalist, Political Thinker)

5   Business, that's easily defined; it's other people's money.
Alexandre Dumas (1802-1870, French Novelist, Dramatist)

6   Corporation. An ingenious device for obtaining individual profit without individual responsibility.
Ambrose Bierce (1842-1914, American Author, Editor, Journalist, "The Devil's Dictionary")

7   Don't steal; thou it never thus compete successfully in business. Cheat.
Ambrose Bierce (1842-1914, American Author, Editor, Journalist, "The Devil's Dictionary")

8   Cut your losses and let your profits run.
American Proverb

9   In business partnerships and marriage partnerships, oh, the cheating that goes on.
American Proverb

10 Markets change, tastes change, so the companies and the individuals who choose to compete in those markets must change.
An Wang (1920-1989, Chinese American Physicist, Founder of Wang Laboratories)

11 Business is a combination of war and sport.
Andre Maurois (1885-1967, French Writer)

12 Stressing output is the key to improving productivity, while looking to increase activity can result in just the opposite.
Andrew Grove (American, CEO of Intel)

13 Being good in business is the most fascinating kind of art. Making money is art and working is art and good business is the best art.
Andy Warhol (1930-, American Artist, Filmmaker)

14 One of the vices of the virtue of decentralization is that people don't share ideas.
Anthony J. F. O'Reilly (American Businessman, CEO of Heinz Foods)

15 Don't worry about your physical shortcomings. I am no Greek god. Don't get too much sleep and don 't tell anybody your troubles. Appearances count: Get a sun lamp to keep you looking as though you have just come back from somewhere expensive: maintain an elegant address even if you have to live in the attic. Never nickle when short of cash. Borrow big, but always repay promptly.
Aristotle Onassis (1906-1975, Turkish Born Shipping Magnate)

16 The secret of business is to know something that nobody else knows.
Aristotle Onassis (1906-1975, Turkish Born Shipping Magnate)

17 If you don't drive your business you will be driven out of business.
B. C. Forbes (1880-1954, American Publisher)

18 Don't forget until too late that the business of life is not business, but living.
B. C. Forbes (1880-1954, American Publisher)

19 Show me the business man or institution not guided by sentiment and service; by the idea that "he profits most who serves best" and I will show you a man or an outfit that is dead or dying.
B. F. Harris

20 Drive your business, let not you're business drive you.
Benjamin Franklin (1706-1790, American Scientist, Publisher, Diplomat)

21 So much for industry, my friends, and attention to one's own business; but to these we must add frugality if we would make our industry more certainly successful. A man may, if he knows not how to save as he gets, keep his nose all his life to the grindstone, and die not worth a grout at last.
Benjamin Franklin (1706-1790, American Scientist, Publisher, Diplomat)

22 If you can't pay for a thing, don't buy it. If you can't get paid for it, don't sell it. Do this, and you will have calm and drowsy nights, with all of the good business you have now and none of the bad. If you have time, don't wait for time.
Benjamin Franklin (1706-1790, American Scientist, Publisher, Diplomat)

23 Don't try to buy at the bottom and sell at the top. This can't be done, except by liars.
Bernard M. Baruch (1870-1965, American Financier)

24 Nobody ever lost money taking a profit.
Bernard M. Baruch (1870-1965, American Financier)

25 It's the economy, stupid.
Bill Clinton (1946-, Forty-second President of the USA)

26 Concentrate your strengths against your competitor's relative weaknesses.
Bruce Henderson (American Businessman, CEO of Boston Consulting Group)

27 The business of the country is business.
Calvin Coolidge (1872-1933, Thirtieth President of the USA)

28 Never say no when a client asks for something, even if it is the moon. You can always try, and anyhow there is plenty of time afterwards to explain that it was not possible.
Cesar Ritz

29 For the merchant, even honesty is a financial speculation.
Charles Baudelaire (1821-1867, French Poet)

30 Industry is the soul of business and the keystone of prosperity.
Charles Dickens (1812-1870, British Novelist)

31 What's good for the country is good for General Motors, and vice versa.
Charles E. Wilson (1886-1972, American Corporate Executive)

32 If a fellow wants to be a nobody in the business world, let him neglect sending the mail man to somebody on his behalf.
Charles F. Kettering (1876-1958, American Engineer, Inventor)

33 The morality of compromise' sounds contradictory. Compromise is usually a sign of weakness, or an admission of defeat. Strong men don't compromise, it is said, and principles should never be compromised. I shall argue that strong men, conversely, know when to compromise and that all principles can be compromised to serve a greater principle.
Charles Handy (American Business Executive and Writer)

34 Get the best people and train them well.
Charles Merrill (American Businessman, Founder of Merrill Lynch)

35 In our factory, we make lipstick. In our advertising, we sell hope.
Charles Revson (American Businessman, Chairman of Revlon)

36 Don't open a shop unless you like to smile.
Chinese Proverb

37 Formerly when great fortunes were only made in war, war was business; but now when great fortunes are only made by business: Business is war!
Christian Nevell Bovee (1820-1904, American Author, Lawyer)

38 Only as long as a company can produce a desired, worthwhile, and needed product or service, and can command the public, will it receive the public dollar and succeed
Curtis Carlson (American Businessman, Founder of Carlson Companies, Inc.)

39 You can close more business in two months by becoming interested in other people than you can in two years by trying to get people interested in you.
Dale Carnegie (1888-1955, American Author, Trainer)

40 Never write an advertisement which you wouldn't want your own family to read. You wouldn't tell lies to your own wife. Don't tell them to mine. Do as you would be done by. If you tell lies about a product, you will be found out -- either by the Government, which will prosecute you, or by the consumer, who will punish you by not buying your product a second time. Good products can be sold by honest advertising. If you don't think the product is good, you have no business to be advertising it.
David Ogilvy (1911-, American Businessman, Advertising Expert)

41 If each of us hires people smaller than we are, we shall become a company of dwarfs.
David Ogilvy (1911-, American Businessman, Advertising Expert)

42 The consumer isn't a moron. She is your wife.
David Ogilvy (1911-, American Businessman, Advertising Expert)

43 The most important word in the vocabulary of advertising is TEST. If you pretest your product with consumers, and pretest your advertising, you will do well in the marketplace.
David Ogilvy (1911-, American Businessman, Advertising Expert)

44 The business that considers itself immune to the necessity for advertising sooner or later finds itself immune to business.
Derby Brown

45 Deals are my art form. Other people paint beautifully on canvas or write wonderful poetry. I like making deals, preferably big deals. That's how I get my kicks.
Donald Trump (1946-, 45th President of the United States of America)

46 The commercial class has always mistrusted verbal brilliancy and wit, deeming such qualities, perhaps with some justice, frivolous and unprofitable.
Dorothy Nevill

47 Great is the hand that holds dominion over man by a scribbled name.
Dylan Thomas (1914-1953, Welsh Poet)

48 You generally hear that what a man doesn't know doesn't hurt him, but in business what a man doesn't know does hurt.
E. St. Elmo Lewis

49 It is the interest of the commercial world that wealth should be found everywhere.
Edmund Burke (1729-1797, British Political Writer, Statesman)

50 Utility is our national shibboleth: the savior of the American businessman is fact and his uterine half-brother, statistics.
Edward Dahlberg (1900-1977, American Author, Critic)

51 Men who do things without being told draw the most wages.
Edwin H. Stuart

52 The question is, then, do we try to make things easy on ourselves or do we try to make things easy on our customers, whoever they may be?
Erwin Frand

53 I am the world's worst salesman, therefore, I must make it easy for people to buy.
F. W. Woolworth (1852-1919, American Business, Founder of Woolworth's)

54 Blessed is he who talks in circles, for he shall become a big wheel.
Frank Dane

55 Treat employees like partners, and they act like partners.
Fred A. Allen (1894-1957, American Radio Comic)

56 We're going to see a lot more young people entering entrepreneurial ventures.
Fred Malek (American Businessman, President of Marriott Hotels)

57 Business is like war in one respect. If its grand strategy is correct, any number of tactical errors can be made and yet the enterprise proves successful.
General Robert E. Woods (President, Sears, Roebuck)

58 I'm not a driven businessman, but a driven artist. I never think about money. Beautiful things make money.
Geoffrey Beene (Fashion Designer)

59 Forty for you, sixty for me And equal partners we will be
Gerald Barzan

60 A man's success in business today turns upon his power of getting people to believe he has something that they want.
Gerald Stanley Lee

61 Business today consists in persuading crowds.
Gerald Stanley Lee

62 Work is our business; it's success is God s.
German Proverb

63 Business is not just doing deals; business is having great products, doing great engineering, and providing tremendous service to customers. Finally, business is a cobweb of human relationships.
H. Ross Perot (1930-, American Businessman & Politician, Founder EDS)

64 If we decide to take this level of business creating ability nationwide, we'll all be plucking chickens for a living.
H. Ross Perot (1930-, American Businessman & Politician, Founder EDS)

65 We are all manufacturers. Making good, making trouble, or making excuses.
H. V. Adolt

66 A consumer is a shopper who is sore about something.
Harold Coffin

67 You read a book from beginning to end. You run a business the opposite way. You start with the end, and then you do everything you must to reach it.
Harold Geneen Ceo

68 The five steps in teaching an employee new skills are preparation, explanation, showing, observation and supervision.
Harold Hook (American Businessman, CEO of American General)

69 It is much more difficult to measure non-performance than performance. Performance stands out like a ton of diamonds. Non-performance can almost always be explained away.
Harold S. Geneen (1910-, American Accountant, Industrialist, CEO, ITT)

70 The worst disease which can afflict executives in their work is not, as popularly supposed, alcoholism; it's egotism.
Harold S. Geneen (1910-, American Accountant, Industrialist, CEO, ITT)

71 In business, words are words; explanations are explanations, promises are promises, but only performance is reality.
Harold S. Geneen (1910-, American Accountant, Industrialist, CEO, ITT)

72 I think it is an immutable law in business that words are words, explanations are explanations, promises are promises -- but only performance is reality.
Harold S. Geneen (1910-, American Accountant, Industrialist, CEO, ITT)

73 You can't run a business or anything else on a theory.
Harold S. Geneen (1910-, American Accountant, Industrialist, CEO, ITT)

74 It's better to take over and build upon an existing business than to start a new one.
Harold S. Geneen (1910-, American Accountant, Industrialist, CEO, ITT)

75 A man with a surplus can control circumstances, but a man without a surplus is controlled by them, and often has no opportunity to exercise judgment.
Harvey S. Firestone (1868-1938, American Industrialist)

76 Business is never so healthy as when, like a chicken, it must do a certain amount of scratching around for what it gets.
Henry Ford (1863-1947, American Industrialist, Founder of Ford Motor Company)

77 It is not the employer who pays wages -- he only handles the money. It is the product who pays the wages.
Henry Ford (1863-1947, American Industrialist, Founder of Ford Motor Company)

78 A business that makes nothing but money is a poor kind of business.
Henry Ford (1863-1947, American Industrialist, Founder of Ford Motor Company)

79 I do not believe a man can ever leave his business. He ought to think of it by day and dream of it by night.
Henry Ford (1863-1947, American Industrialist, Founder of Ford Motor Company)

80 It doesn't matter to me if a man is from Harvard or Sing Sing. We hire the man, not his history.
Henry Ford (1863-1947, American Industrialist, Founder of Ford Motor Company)

81 Business, more than any other occupation, is a continual dealing with the future; it is a continual calculation, an instinctive exercise in foresight.
Henry Luce (American Businessman, Founder of Time Life)

82 If you did not look after today's business then you might as well forget about tomorrow.
Isaac Mophatlane

83 Every business is built on friendship.
J. C. (James Cash) Penney (1875-1971, American Retailer, Philanthropist, Founder JC Penny's)

84 I buy when other people are selling.
J. Paul Getty (1892-1976, American Oil Tycoon, Billionaire)

85 Executives are like joggers. If you stop a jogger, he goes on running on the spot. If you drag an executive away from his business, he goes on running on the spot, pawing the ground, talking business. He never stops hurtling onwards, making decisions and executing them.
Jean Baudrillard (French Postmodern Philosopher, Writer)

86 More business is lost every year through neglect than through any other cause.
Jim Cathcart (American Author, Lecturer)

87 Productivity is being able to do things that you were never able to do before.
Jim Manzi (American Businessman, President of Lotus Development)

88 Frankly, I don't want to see a rapid upturn. I want it to hold until some of these idiotic competitors go bust.
Joe Bamford (American Business Executive)

89 To succeed in business it is necessary to make others see things as you see them.
John H. Patterson (American Businessman, Founder of National Cash Register)

90 It is surprising, in the welter of questions that one gets at (AGMs), how few actually relate to the performance of the company, or the decisions taken by the board in particular areas.
John Harvey-Jones (Business Writer and Executive)

91 The great business of life is to be, to do, to do without and to depart.
John Morley (1838-1923, British Journalist, Biographer, Statesman)

92 Well, I don't know as I want a lawyer to tell me what I cannot do. I hire him to tell how to do what I want to do.
John Pierpont Morgan (1837-1913, American Banker, Financier, Art Collector)

93 Half the money I spend on advertising is wasted; the trouble is I don't know which half.
John Wanamaker (1838-1922, American Merchant)

94 Our planning system was dynamite when we first put it in. The thinking was fresh; the form mattered little. It was idea oriented. We then hired a head of planning, and he hired two vice presidents, and then he hired a planner; and the books got thicker, and the printing more sophisticated, and the covers got harder, and the drawings got better.
John Welch (1935-, American Businessman, Chairman of General Electric)

95 Good business leaders create a vision, articulate the vision, passionately own the vision, and relentlessly drive it to completion.
John Welch (1935-, American Businessman, Chairman of General Electric)

96 There is nothing more requisite in business than dispatch.
Joseph Addison (1672-1719, British Essayist, Poet, Statesman)

97 The happiest time in a man's life is when he is in the red hot pursuit of a dollar with a reasonable prospect of overtaking it.
Josh Billings (1815-1885, American Humorist, Lecturer)

98 Feedback is the breakfast of champions.
Ken Blanchard (American Business Lecturer, Author)

99 You make the best products you can, and you grow as fast as you deserve to.
Kenneth Olsen (American Businessman, Founder of Digital Equipment)

100 I work in a strange business, and trust is a word that's not even in the vocabulary.
Kim Basinger (1953-, American Actress)

101 No sale is really complete until the product is worn out, and the customer is satisfied.
L.L. Bean (American Businessman, Founder of L.L Bean's)

102 I don't want to do business with those who don't make a profit, because they can't give the best service.
Lee Bristol

103 When the product is right, you don't have to be a great marketer.
Lee Iacocca (1924-, American Businessman, Former CEO of Chrysler)

104 People want economy and they'll pay almost any price to get it.
Lee Iacocca (1924-, American Businessman, Former CEO of Chrysler)

105 What helps people, helps business.
Leo Burnett (American Marketing Expert)

106 We have yet to see the full impact of the open, global marketplace. By 1997 all raw materials and technology will be available everywhere in the world. The only differences between countries and markets will be skill levels, education, and the level of empowerment of the workplace.
Lew Pritchett (American Business Executive, VP Sales, Procter & Gamble)

107 Business is more exciting than any game.
Lord Beaverbrook (British Minister)

108 No man tastes pleasures truly, who does not earn them by previous business; and few people do business well, who do nothing else.
Lord Chesterfield (1694-1773, British Statesman, Author)

109 If when a businessman speaks of minority employment, or air pollution, or poverty, he speaks in the language of a certified public accountant analyzing a corporate balance sheet, who is to know that he understands the human problems behind the statistical ones? If the businessman would stop talking like a computer printout or a page from the corporate annual report, other people would stop thinking he had a cash register for a heart. It is as simple as that -- but that isn't simple.
Louis B. Lundborg

110 A compromise is the art of dividing a cake in such a way that everyone believes that he has got the biggest piece.
Ludwig Erhard (German Politician)

111 Conducting your business in a socially responsible way is good business. It means that you can attract better employees and that customers will know what you stand for and like you for it.
M. Anthony Burns (American Businessman, CEO of Ryder Systems)

112 Never hire someone who knows less than you do about what he's hired to do.
Malcolm S. Forbes (1919-1990, American Publisher, Businessman)

113 Goodwill is the one and only asset that competition cannot undersell or destroy.
Marshall Field (1834-1906, American Merchant)

114 Entrepreneurship is the last refuge of the trouble making individual.
Mason Cooley

115 The big will get bigger; the small will get wiped out.
Meshulam Riklis

116 The five essential entrepreneurial skills for success: Concentration, Discrimination, Organization, Innovation and Communication
Michael E. Gerber (American Businessman, Consultant, Author, Trainer)

117 You can't run a business without taking risks.
Millard Drexler (American Business Executive, President, The Gap)

118 The very best financial presentation is one that's well thought out and anticipates any questions... answering them in advance.
Nathan Collins (American Business Executive, VP of Valley National Bank)

119 What the customer demands is last year's model, cheaper. To find out what the customer needs you have to understand what the customer is doing as well as he understands it. Then you build what he needs and you educate him to the fact that he needs it.
Nicholas Dewolf (American Businessman, Founder, Teradyne, Inc.)

120 Women do not win formula one races, because they simply are not strong enough to resist the G-forces. In the boardroom, it is different. I believe women are better able to marshal their thoughts than men and because they are less egotistical they make fewer assumptions.
Nicola Foulston (American Business Executive)

121 When you are skinning your customers you should leave some skin on to grow again so that you can skin them again.
Nikita Khrushchev (1894-1971, Soviet Premier)

122 Unequal combinations are always disadvantageous to the weaker side.
Oliver Goldsmith (1728-1774, Anglo-Irish Author, Poet, Playwright)

123 Honor sinks where commerce long prevails.
Oliver Goldsmith (1728-1774, Anglo-Irish Author, Poet, Playwright)

124 It is very vulgar to talk about one's business. Only people like stockbrokers do that, and then merely at dinner parties.
Oscar Wilde (1856-1900, British Author, Wit)

125 Let love give way to business; give attention to business and you will be safe.
Ovid (43 BC-18 AD, Roman Poet)

126 In modern business it is not the crook who is to be feared most, it is the honest man who doesn't know what he is doing.
Owen D. Young (1874-1962, American Lawyer, Businessman, Public Official)

127 Anybody can cut prices, but it takes brains to produce a better article.
P. D. Armour

128 The City's reluctance to take a stand on an issue like the British Gas pay row makes a mockery of corporate governance and shareholders' ability to influence annual general meetings. Institutions should be obliged to make public how they vote at such events. They should be obliged to provide customers with a record of how they vote on every kind of issue.
Patrick Donovan (British Financial Journalist)

129 Few great men could pass personal.
Paul Goodman (1911-1972, American Author, Poet, Critic)

130 It is almost as difficult to keep a first class person in a fourth class job, as it is to keep a fourth class person in a first class job.
Paul H. Dunn

131 As a small businessperson, you have no greater leverage than the truth.
Paul Hawken (American Businessman, Founder of Smith & Hawken)

132 Business has only two functions -- marketing and innovation.
Peter F. Drucker (1909-, American Management Consultant, Author)

133 The purpose of a business is to create a customer.
Peter F. Drucker (1909-, American Management Consultant, Author)

134 Corporations are social organizations, the theater in which men and women realize or fail to realize purposeful and productive lives.
Peter Rena

135 When two friends have a common bank account, one sings and the other weeps.
Proverb

136 The right merchant is one who has the just average of faculties we call common sense; a man of a strong affinity for facts, who makes up his decision on what he has seen. He is thoroughly persuaded of the truths of arithmetic. There is always a reason, in the man, for his good or bad fortune in making money. Men talk as if there were some magic about this. He knows that all goes on the old road, pound for pound, cent for cent -- for every effect a perfect cause -- and that good luck is another name for tenacity of purpose.
Ralph Waldo Emerson (1803-1882, American Poet, Essayist)

137 Every man is a consumer and ought to be a producer.
Ralph Waldo Emerson (1803-1882, American Poet, Essayist)

138 There is no substitute for accurate knowledge. Know yourself, know your business, know your men.
Randall Jacobs

139 In business for yourself, not by yourself.
Ray Kroc (1902-1984, American businessman, Founder of McDonalds)

140 Such is the brutalization of commercial ethics in this country that no one can feel anything more delicate than the velvet touch of a soft buck.
Raymond Chandler (1888-1959, American Author)

141 It takes more than capital to swing business. You've got to have the A. I. D. degree to get by -- Advertising, Initiative, and Dynamics.
Ren Mulford Jr.

142 If you can run one business well, you can run any business well.
Richard Branson (American Businessman, Chairman of The Virgin Group)

143 If you train people properly, they won't be able to tell a drill from the real thing. If anything, the real thing will be easier.
Richard Marcinko (American Business Author)

144 You can employ men and hire hands to work for you, but you must win their hearts to have them work with you.
Riorio

145 Do not fear mistakes. You will know failure. Continue to reach out.
Robert Galvin

146 Perpetual devotion to what a man calls his business, is only to be sustained by perpetual neglect of many other things.
Robert Louis Stevenson (1850-1895, Scottish Essayist, Poet, Novelist)

147 Make every decision as if you owned the whole company.
Robert Townsend (American Businessman, President of Avis)

148 Compromise is usually bad. It should be a last resort. If two departments or divisions have a problem they can't solve and it comes up to you, listen to both sides and then pick one or the other. This places solid accountability on the winner to make it work. Condition your people to avoid compromise.
Robert Townsend (American Businessman, President of Avis)

149 If you don't do it with excellence, don't do it at all! Because if it's not excellent, it won't be profitable or fun, and if you're not in business for fun or profit, what the hell are you doing there?
Robert Townsend (American Businessman, President of Avis)

150 Anything that you do to increase job security automatically does work for you. It makes your employees a closer part of the unit.
Roger Smith (American Businessman, CEO of GM)

151 The best minds are not in government. If any were, business would hire them away.
Ronald Reagan (1911-, Fortieth President of the USA, Actor)

152 Never let an inventor run a company. You can never get him to stop tinkering and bring something to market.
Royal Little (American Businessman, Founder of Textron)

153 You don't want to get the same kind of advice from everyone on your board.
Ruben Cardenas (American Lawyer, Business Executive)

154 We let folks know we're interested in them and that they're vital to us. cause they are.
Sam Walton (1918-1992, American Businessman, Founder of Wal-Mart Stores)

155 There is only one boss. The customer. And he can fire everybody in the company from the chairman on down, simply by spending his money somewhere else.
Sam Walton (1918-1992, American Businessman, Founder of Wal-Mart Stores)

156 There's a lot more business out there in small town America than I ever dreamed of.
Sam Walton (1918-1992, American Businessman, Founder of Wal-Mart Stores)

157 In a start-up company, you basically throw out all assumptions every three weeks.
Scott Mcnealy (American Businessman, CEO of Sun Microsystems)

158 A client is to me a mere unit, a factor in a problem.
Sir Arthur Conan Doyle (1859-1930, British Author, "Sherlock Holmes")

159 Corporations cannot commit treason, or be outlawed or excommunicated, for they have no souls.
Sir Edward Coke (1552-1634, British Jurist)

160 The more business one has, the more you are able to accomplish, for you learn to economize your time.
Sir Matthew Hale (1609-1676, British Judge)

161 I've got to keep breathing. It'll be my worst business mistake if I don't.
Sir Nathan Rothschild (1910-, British Administrator)

162 Quality, service, cleanliness, and value.
Steven J. Ross (American Businessman, CEO of Time Warner)

163 Far too many executives have become more concerned with the "four P's" -- pay, perks, power and prestige -- rather than making profits for shareholders.
T. Boone Pickens (American Businessman, Chairman of Mesa Petroleum)

164 In a balanced organization, working towards a common objective, there is success.
T. L. Scrutton

165 The purpose of business is to create and keep a customer.
Theodore Leavitt

166 The magic formula that successful businesses have discovered is to treat customers like guests and employees like people.
Thomas J. Peters (1942-, American Management Consultant, Author, Trainer)

167 You have to have your heart in the business and the business in your heart.
Thomas J. Watson (18?-1956, American Businessman, Founder of IBM)

168 You don't hear things that are bad about your company unless you ask. It is easy to hear good tidings, but you have to scratch to get the bad news.
Thomas J. Watson (18?-1956, American Businessman, Founder of IBM)

169 The selfish spirit of commerce, which knows no country, and feels no passion or principle but that of gain.
Thomas Jefferson (1743-1826, Third President of the USA)

170 The poor man who enters into a partnership with one who is rich makes a risky venture.
Titus Maccius Plautus (254-184 BC, Roman Comic Poet)

171 I believe Mrs. Thatcher's emphasis on enterprise was right.
Tony Blair (1953-, British Prime Minister)

172 You can hype a questionable product for a little while, but you'll never build an enduring business.
Victor Kiam (American Businessman, CEO of Remington)

173 Entrepreneurs are simply those who understand that there is little difference between obstacle and opportunity and are able to turn both to their advantage.
Victor Kiam (American Businessman, CEO of Remington)

174 The employer generally gets the employees he deserves.
Walter Gilbey

175 The simple opposition between the people and big business has disappeared because the people themselves have become so deeply involved in big business.
Walter Lippmann (1889-1974, American Journalist)

176 If a business does well, the stock eventually follows.
Warren Buffett (1930-, American Investment Entrepreneur)

177 It's far better to buy a wonderful company at a fair price than a fair company at a wonderful price.
Warren Buffett (1930-, American Investment Entrepreneur)

178 If your advertising goes unnoticed, everything else is academic!
William Bernbach (1911-1982, American Advertising Executive)

179 Commerce is so far from being beneficial to arts, or to empire, that it is destructive of both, as all their history shows, for the above reason of individual merit being its great hatred. Empires flourish till they become commercial, and then they are scattered abroad to the four winds.
William Blake (1757-1827, British Poet, Painter)

180 Location, location, location.
William Dillard (American Businessman, Founder of Dillard's Department Store)

181 The most sensible people to be met with in society are men of business and of the world, who argue from what they see and know, instead of spinning cobweb distinctions of what things ought to be.
William Hazlitt (1778-1830, British Essayist)

182 In business, the competition will bite you if you keep running, if you stand still, they will swallow you.
William Knudsen (Jr., Chairman, Ford Motor Company)

183 If you have lower than a ten percent turnover, there is a problem. And if you have higher than, say 20%, there is a problem.
William Mcgovern (American Businessman, Founder of MCI)

184 Method goes far to prevent trouble in business: for it makes the task easy, hinders confusion, saves abundance of time, and instructs those that have business depending, both what to do and what to hope.
William Penn (1644-1718, British Religious Leader, Founder of Pennsylvania)

185 To business that we love we rise bedtime, and go to't with delight.
William Shakespeare (1564-1616, British Poet, Playwright, Actor)

186 When two men in business always agree, one of them is unnecessary.
William Wrigley Jr. (1861-1932, American Businessman, Founder of Wrigley & Co.)

187 Some people regard private enterprise as a predatory tiger to be shot. Others look on it as a cow they can milk. Not enough people see it as a healthy horse, pulling a sturdy wagon.
Winston Churchill (1874-1965, British Statesman, Prime Minister)

188 Most men are individuals no longer so far as their business, its activities, or its moralities are concerned. They are not units but fractions.
Woodrow T. Wilson (1856-1924, Twenty-eighth President of the USA)

BUSYNESS

1 The man who has nothing to do is always the busiest.
French Proverb

2 It is not enough to be busy. So are the ants. The question is: What are we busy about?
Henry David Thoreau (1817-1862, American Essayist, Poet, Naturalist)

3 A bee is never as busy as it seems; it's just that it can't buzz any slower.
Kin Hubbard (1868-1930, American Humorist, Journalist)

4 Some folks can look so busy doing nothing that they seem indispensable.
Kin Hubbard (1868-1930, American Humorist, Journalist)

5 The really idle man gets nowhere. The perpetually busy man does not get much further.
Sir Heneage Ogilvie

6 No thoroughly occupied person was ever found really miserable.
Walter Savage Landor (1775-1864, British Poet, Essayist)

CALAMITY

1 Calamities are of two kinds: misfortune to ourselves, and good fortune to others.
Ambrose Bierce (1842-1914, American Author, Editor, Journalist, "The Devil's Dictionary")

2 Calamity is man's true touchstone.
Beaumont and Fletcher

3 He who foresees calamities, suffers them twice over.
Bishop Porteous

4 It is only from the belief of the goodness and wisdom of a supreme being, that our calamities can be borne in the manner which becomes a man.
Henry Mackenzie

5 Every calamity is a spur and valuable hint.
Ralph Waldo Emerson (1803-1882, American Poet, Essayist)

6 Do not accustom yourself to consider debt only as an inconvenience. You will find it a calamity.
Samuel Johnson (1709-1784, British Author)

7 Calamity is the test of integrity.
Samuel Richardson

8 Calamity is virtue's opportunity.
Seneca (4 BC-65 AD, Spanish-born Roman Statesman, philosopher)

9 Calamity is the perfect glass wherein we truly see and know ourselves.
William Davenant

CANCER

1 I don't think makeup is rocket science or a cure for cancer.
Cindy Crawford (1966-, American Model, Actress)

2 We "need" cancer because, by the very fact of its insurability, it makes all other diseases, however virulent, not cancer.
Gilbert Adair (Born 1944, American Author)

3 I wish I had the voice of Homer to sing of rectal carcinoma.
John B. S. Haldane (1892-1964, British Scientist, Author)

4 My veins are filled, once a week with a Neapolitan carpet cleaner distilled from the Adriatic and I am as bald as an egg. However I still get around and am mean to cats.
John Cheever (1912-1982, American Author)

5 Cancer patients are lied to, not just because the disease is (or is thought to be) a death sentence, but because it is felt to be obscene -- in the original meaning of that word: ill-omened, abominable, repugnant to the senses.
Susan Sontag (1933-, American Essayist)

6 Nobody knows what the cause is, though some pretend they do; it like some hidden assassin waiting to strike at you. Childless women get it, and men when they retire; it as if there had to be some outlet for their foiled creative fire.
W. H. Auden (1907-1973, Anglo-American Poet)

CANDOR

1 Examine what is said, not him who speaks.
Arabian Proverb

2 There is no wisdom like frankness.
Benjamin Disraeli (1804-1881, British Statesman, Prime Minister)

3 Frank and explicit" -- that is the right line to take when you wish to conceal your own mind and to confuse the minds of others.
Benjamin Disraeli (1804-1881, British Statesman, Prime Minister)

4 Candor is the brightest gem of criticism.
Benjamin Disraeli (1804-1881, British Statesman, Prime Minister)

5 To be candid, in Middlemarch phraseology, meant, to use an early opportunity of letting your friends know that you did not take a cheerful view of their capacity, their conduct, or their position; and a robust candor never waited to be asked for its opinion.
George Eliot (1819-1880, British Novelist)

6 Friends, if we be honest with ourselves, we shall be honest with each other.
George Macdonald (1824-1905, Scottish Novelist)

7 Not to expose your true feelings to an adult seems to be instinctive from the age of seven or eight onwards.
George Orwell (1903-1950, British Author, "Animal Farm")

8 Candor is a proof of both a just frame of mind, and of a good tone of breeding. It is a quality that belongs equally to the honest man and to the gentleman.
James F. Cooper (1789-1851, American Novelist)

9 You may tell a man thou art a fiend, but not your nose wants blowing; to him alone who can bear a thing of that kind, you may tell all.
Johann Kaspar Lavater (1741-1801, Swiss Theologian, Mystic)

10 A "No" uttered from deepest conviction is better and greater than a "Yes" merely uttered to please, or what is worse, to avoid trouble.
Mahatma Gandhi (1869-1948, Indian Political, Spiritual Leader)

11 It is the weak and confused who worship the pseudosimplicities of brutal directness.
Marshall Mcluhan (1911-1980, Canadian Communications Theorist)

12 Let us not be ashamed to speak what we shame not to think.
Michel Eyquem De Montaigne (1533-1592, French Philosopher, Essayist)

13 Gracious to all, to none subservient, Without offense he spoke the word he meant.
Thomas B. Aldrich (1836-1907, American Writer, Editor)

14 If all hearts were open and all desires known -- as they would be if people showed their souls - - how many gapings, sighings, clenched fists, knotted brows, broad grins, and red eyes should we see in the market-place!
Thomas Hardy (1840-1928, British Novelist, Poet)

15 Always be ready to speak your mind, and a base man will avoid you.
William Blake (1757-1827, British Poet, Painter)

16 There is an unseemly exposure of the mind, as well as of the body.
William Hazlitt (1778-1830, British Essayist)

17 We want all our friends to tell us our bad qualities; it is only the particular ass that does so whom we can't tolerate.
William James (1842-1910, American Psychologist, Professor, Author)

CAPITALISM

1 These capitalists generally act harmoniously and in concert, to fleece the people.
Abraham Lincoln (1809-1865, Sixteenth President of the USA)

2 Labor is prior to, and independent of, capital. Capital is only the fruit of labor, and could never have existed if labor had not first existed. Labor is the superior of capital, and deserves much the higher consideration. Capital has its rights, which are as worthy of protection as any other rights.
Abraham Lincoln (1809-1865, Sixteenth President of the USA)

3 The most eloquent eulogy of capitalism was made by its greatest enemy. Marx is only anti- capitalist in so far as capitalism is out of date.
Albert Camus (1913-1960, French Existential Writer)

4 Advocates of capitalism are very apt to appeal to the sacred principles of liberty, which are embodied in one maxim: The fortunate must not be restrained in the exercise of tyranny over the unfortunate.
Bertrand Russell (1872-1970, British Philosopher, Mathematician, Essayist)

5 Capitalism is an art form, an Apollonian fabrication to rival nature. It is hypocritical for feminists and intellectuals to enjoy the pleasures and conveniences of capitalism while sneering at it. Everyone born into capitalism has incurred a debt to it. Give Caesar his due.
Camille Paglia (1947-, American Author, Critic, Educator)

6 Labor in this country is independent and proud. It has not to ask the patronage of capital, but capital solicits the aid of labor.
Daniel Webster (1782-1852, American Lawyer, Statesman)

7 The unpleasant and unacceptable face of capitalism.
Edward Heath (1916-, British Statesman and Prime Minister)

8 Capitalism is at its liberating best in a noncapitalist environment. The crypto-businessman is the true revolutionary in a Communist country.
Eric Hoffer (1902-1983, American Author, Philosopher)

9 Capitalism without bankruptcy is like Christianity without hell.
Frank Borman (American Astronaut, Business Executive)

10 Fact is Our Lord knew all about the power of money: He gave capitalism a tiny niche in His scheme of things, He gave it a chance, He even provided a first installment of funds. Can you beat that? It's so magnificent. God despises nothing. After all, if the deal had come off, Judas would probably have endowed sanatoriums, hospitals, public libraries or laboratories.
Georges Bernanos (1888-1948, French Novelist, Political Writer)

11 Capital is a result of labor, and is used by labor to assist it in further production. Labor is the active and initial force, and labor is therefore the employer of capital.
Henry George (1839-1897, American Social Reformer, Economist)

12 The decadent international but individualistic capitalism in the hands of which we found ourselves after the war is not a success. It is not intelligent. It is not beautiful. It is not just. It is not virtuous. And it doesn't deliver the goods.
John Maynard Keynes (1883-1946, British Economist)

13 The evolution of the capitalist style of life could be easily -- and perhaps most tellingly -- described in terms of the genesis of the modern Lounge Suit.
Joseph A. Schumpeter (1883-1950, Austrian-American Economist)

14 Capitalism inevitably and by virtue of the very logic of its civilization creates, educates and subsidizes a vested interest in social unrest.
Joseph A. Schumpeter (1883-1950, Austrian-American Economist)

15 Capital is money, capital is commodities. By virtue of it being value, it has acquired the occult ability to add value to itself. It brings forth living offspring, or, at the least, lays golden eggs.
Karl Marx (1818-1883, German Political Theorist, Social Philosopher)

16 Capital is dead labor, which, vampire-like, lives only by sucking living labor, and lives the more, the more labor it sucks.
Karl Marx (1818-1883, German Political Theorist, Social Philosopher)

17 The genius of capitalism consists precisely in its lack of morality. Unless he is rich enough to hire his own choir, a capitalist is a fellow who, by definition, can ill afford to believe in anything other than the doctrine of the bottom line. Deprive a capitalist of his God-given right to lie and cheat and steal, and the poor sap stands a better than even chance of becoming one of the abominable wards of the state from whose grimy fingers the Reagan Administration hopes to snatch the ark of democracy.
Lewis H. Lapham (1935-, American Essayist, Editor)

18 Capital as such is not evil; it is its wrong use that is evil. Capital in some form or other will always be needed.
Mahatma Gandhi (1869-1948, Indian Political, Spiritual Leader)

19 It is impossible for capitalism to survive, primarily because the system of capitalism needs some blood to suck. Capitalism used to be like an eagle, but now it's more like a vulture. It used to be strong enough to go and suck anybody's blood whether they were strong or not. But now it has become more cowardly, like the vulture, and it can only suck the blood of the helpless. As the nations of the world free themselves, the capitalism has less victims, less to suck, and it becomes weaker and weaker. It's only a matter of time in my opinion before it will collapse completely.
Malcolm X (1925-1965, American Black Leader, Activist)

20 History suggests that capitalism is a necessary condition for political freedom. Clearly it is not a sufficient condition.
Milton Friedman (1912-, American Economist)

21 Predatory capitalism created a complex industrial system and an advanced technology; it permitted a considerable extension of democratic practice and fostered certain liberal values, but within limits that are now being pressed and must be overcome. It is not a fit system for the mid-twentieth century.
Noam Chomsky (1928-, American Linguist, Political Activist)

22 What breaks capitalism, all that will ever break capitalism, is capitalists. The faster they run the more strain on their heart.
Raymond Williams (1921-1988, British Social Historian, Critic, Novelist)

23 The far right seeks to retain the material progress of American capitalism while removing some of its crucial causes and consequences -- as though a bridge could be made to change part of its function by blowing up part of its supports and part of its exit.
Ronald Segal

24 The first rule of venture capitalism should be Shoot the Inventor.
Sir Richard Storey

25 The ideology of capitalism makes us all into connoisseurs of liberty -- of the indefinite expansion of possibility.
Susan Sontag (1933-, American Essayist)

26 Making capitalism out of socialism is like making eggs out of an omelet.
Vadim Bakatin (Russian Politician)

27 Capitalists are no more capable of self-sacrifice than a man is capable of lifting himself up by his own bootstraps.
Vladimir Ilyich Lenin (1870-1924, Russian Revolutionary Leader)

28 The inherent vice of capitalism is the unequal sharing of blessings; the inherent vice of socialism is the equal sharing of miseries.
Winston Churchill (1874-1965, British Statesman, Prime Minister)

29 In the democratic western countries so-called capitalism leads a saturnalia of "freedom," like a bastard brother of reform.
Wyndham Lewis (1882-1957, British Author, Painter)

CAPRICE

1 "You gave me the key of your heart, my love; then why did you make me knock?" Oh that was yesterday, saints above! And last night -- I changed the lock!
John Boyle O'Reilly (1844-1890, Irish Author)

2 Never lose sight of the fact that all human felicity lies in man's imagination, and that he cannot think to attain it unless he heeds all his caprices. The most fortunate of persons is he who has the most means to satisfy his vagaries.
Marquis De Sade (1740-1814, French Author)

3 The only difference between a caprice and a life-long passion is that the caprice lasts a little longer.
Oscar Wilde (1856-1900, British Author, Wit)

4 We are the creatures of imagination, passion, and self-will, more than of reason or even of self- interest. Even in the common transactions and daily intercourse of life, we are governed by whim, caprice, prejudice, or accident. The falling of a teacup puts us out of temper for the day; and a quarrel that commenced about the pattern of a gown may end only with our lives.
William Hazlitt (1778-1830, British Essayist)

CARDS

1 Because people have no thoughts to deal in, they deal cards, and try and win one another's money. Idiots!
Arthur Schopenhauer (1788-1860, German Philosopher)

2 Cards are war, in disguise of a sport.
Charles Lamb (1775-1834, British Essayist, Critic)

3 The poker player learns that sometimes both science and common sense are wrong; that the bumblebee can fly; that, perhaps, one should never trust an expert; that there are more things in heaven and earth than are dreamt of by those with an academic bent.
David Mamet (1947-, American Playwright)

4 The best chess-player in Christendom may be little more than the best player of chess; but proficiency in whist implies capacity for success in all these more important undertakings where mind struggles with mind.
Edgar Allan Poe (1809-1845, American Poet, Critic, short-story Writer)

5 I am sorry I have not learnt to play at cards. It is very useful in life: it generates kindness, and consolidates society.
Samuel Johnson (1709-1784, British Author)

CAREERS

1 The life-fate of the modern individual depends not only upon the family into which he was born or which he enters by marriage, but increasingly upon the corporation in which he spends the most alert hours of his best years.
C. Wright Mills (1916-1962, American Sociologist)

2 The most successful career must show a waste of strength that might have removed mountains, and the most unsuccessful is not that of the man who is taken unprepared, but of him who has prepared and is never taken. On a tragedy of that kind our national morality is duly silent.
Edward M. Forster (1879-1970, British Novelist, Essayist)

3 He was at a starting point which makes many a man's career a fine subject for betting, if there were any gentlemen given to that amusement who could appreciate the complicated probabilities of an arduous purpose, with all the possible thwartings and furtherings of circumstance, all the niceties of inward balance, by which a man swings and makes his point or else is carried headlong.
George Eliot (1819-1880, British Novelist)

4 I have yet to hear a man ask for advice on how to combine marriage and a career.
Gloria Steinem (1934-, American Feminist Writer, Editor)

5 If I had my career over again? Maybe I'd say to myself, speed it up a little.
James Stewart (1908-1997, American Actor, Writer)

6 Sometimes you wonder how you got on this mountain. But sometimes you wonder, "How will I get off?"
Joan Manley

7 People don't choose their careers; they are engulfed by them.
John Dos Passos

8 Each of the professions means a prejudice. The necessity for a career forces every one to take sides. We live in the age of the overworked, and the under-educated; the age in which people are so industrious that they become absolutely stupid.
Oscar Wilde (1856-1900, British Author, Wit)

CARING

1 If you think nobody cares if you're alive, try missing a couple of car payments.
Flip Wilson (1933-, American Actor, Comedian)

2 Warm weather fosters growth: cold weather destroys it. Thus a man with an unsympathetic temperament has a scant joy: but a man with a warm and friendly heart overflowing blessings, and his beneficence will extend to posterity
Hung Tzu-Cheng

3 Caring is a powerful business advantage.
Scott Johnson

CATHOLICISM

1 All human life is here, but the Holy Ghost seems to be somewhere else.
Anthony Burgess (1917-1993, British Writer, Critic)

2 You can't run the Church on Hail Marys.
Archbishop Paul Marcinkus

3 Our religion is itself profoundly sad -- a religion of universal anguish, and one which, because of its very catholicity, grants full liberty to the individual and asks no better than to be celebrated in each man's own language -- so long as he knows anguish and is a painter.
Charles Baudelaire (1821-1867, French Poet)

4 Catholics are necessarily at war with this age. That we are not more conscious of the fact, that we so often endeavor to make an impossible peace with it -- that is the tragedy. You cannot serve God and Mammon.
Eric Gill (1882-1940, British Sculptor, Engraver, Writer, Typographer)

5 One cannot really be a Catholic and grown up.
George Orwell (1903-1950, British Author, "Animal Farm")

6 For support, I fall back on my heart. Has a man any fault a woman cannot weave with and try to change into something better, if the god her man prays to is a mother holding a baby?
Haniel Long (1888-1956, American Author, Poet, Journalist)

7 Here is everything which can lay hold of the eye, ear and imagination -- everything which can charm and bewitch the simple and ignorant. I wonder how Luther ever broke the spell.
John Adams (1735-1826, Second President of the USA)

8 The thing with Catholicism, the same as all religions, is that it teaches what should be, which seems rather incorrect. This is "what should be." Now, if you're taught to live up to a "what should be" that never existed -- only an occult superstition, no proof of this "should be" -- then you can sit on a jury and indict easily, you can cast the first stone, you can burn Adolf Eichmann, like that!
Lenny Bruce (1925-1966, American Comedian)

9 It is by far the most elegant worship, hardly excepting the Greek mythology. What with incense, pictures, statues, altars, shrines, relics, and the real presence, confession, absolution, -- there is something sensible to grasp at. Besides, it leaves no possibility of doubt; for those who swallow their Deity, really and truly, in transubstantiation, can hardly find any thing else otherwise than easy of digestion.
Lord Byron (1788-1824, British Poet)

10 It is a dogma of the Roman Church that the existence of God can be proved by natural reason. Now this dogma would make it impossible for me to be a Roman Catholic. If I thought of God as another being like myself, outside myself, only infinitely more powerful, then I would regard it as my duty to defy him.
Ludwig Wittgenstein (1889-1951, Austrian Philosopher)

11 Catholicism is not a soothing religion. It's a painful religion. We're all gluttons for punishment.
Madonna (1958-, American Musician, Singer, Actress,)

12 To care for the quarrels of the past, to identify oneself passionately with a cause that became, politically speaking, a losing cause with the birth of the modern world, is to experience a kind of straining against reality, a rebellious nonconformity that, again, is rare in America, where children are instructed in the virtues of the system they live under, as though history had achieved a happy ending in American civics.
Mary Mccarthy (1912-1989, American Author, Critic)

13 Today's Catholic church seems to reward authoritarian personalities who are clearly ill, violent, sexually obsessed and unable to remember the past.
Matthew Fox

14 If you're going to do a thing, you should do it thoroughly. If you're going to be a Christian, you may as well be a Catholic.
Muriel Spark (1918-, British Novelist)

15 Anti-Catholicism is the anti-Semitism of the intellectual.
Patrick Buchanan (1938-, American Statesman)

16 It is the custom of the Roman Church which I unworthily serve with the help of God, to tolerate some things, to turn a blind eye to some, following the spirit of discretion rather than the rigid letter of the law.
Pope Gregory VII

17 Good strong thick stupefying incense-smoke!
Robert Browning (1812-1889, British Poet)

18 Although every organized patriarchal religion works overtime to contribute its own brand of misogyny to the myth of woman-hate, woman-fear, and woman-evil, the Roman Catholic Church also carries the immense power of very directly affecting women's lives everywhere by its stand against birth control and abortion, and by its use of skillful and wealthy lobbies to prevent legislative change. It is an obscenity -- an all-male hierarchy, celibate or not, that presumes to rule on the lives and bodies of millions of women.
Robin Morgan (1941-, American Feminist Author, Poet)

19 Look through the whole history of countries professing the Romish religion, and you will uniformly find the leaven of this besetting and accursed principle of action -- that the end will sanction any means.
Samuel Taylor Coleridge (1772-1834, British Poet, Critic, Philosopher)

20 The Catholic Church has never really come to terms with women. What I object to is being treated either as Madonna's or Mary Magdalene's.
Shirley Williams (1930-, British Liberal-Democrat Politician)

21 She thoroughly understands what no other Church has ever understood, how to deal with enthusiasts.
Thomas B. Macaulay (1800-1859, American Essayist and Historian)

22 A little skill in antiquity inclines a man to Popery.
Thomas Fuller (1608-1661, British Clergyman, Author)

CATS

1 Cats always seem so very wise, when staring with their half-closed eyes. Can they be thinking, "I'll be nice, and maybe she will feed me twice?"
Bette Midler (American Singer, Entertainer, Actress)

2 Cats are autocrats of naked self-interest. They are both amoral and immoral, consciously breaking rules. Their "evil" look at such times is no human projection: the cat may be the only animal who savors the perverse or reflects upon it.
Camille Paglia (1947-, American Author, Critic, Educator)

3 Persian pussy from over the sea demure and lazy and smug and fat none of your ribbons and bells for me ours is the zest of the alley cat
Don Marquis (1878-1937, American Humorist, Journalist)

4 If a fish is the movement of water embodied, given shape, then cat is a diagram and pattern of subtle air.
Doris Lessing (1919-, British Novelist)

5 One cat in a house is a sign of loneliness, two of barrenness, and three of sodomy.
Edward Dahlberg (1900-1977, American Author, Critic)

6 Cats are smarter than dogs. You can not get eight cats to pull a sled through snow.
Jeff Valdez

7 Cats exercise... a magic influence upon highly developed men of intellect. This is why these long-tailed Graces of the animal kingdom, these adorable, scintillating electric batteries have been the favorite animal of a Mohammed, Cardinal Richlieu, Crebillon, Rousseau, Wieland.
Leopold Von Sacher-Masoch

8 Of all God's creatures there is only one that cannot be made the slave of the lash. That one is the cat. If man could be crossed with a cat it would improve man, but it would deteriorate the cat.
Mark Twain (1835-1910, American Humorist, Writer)

9 Dogs come when they are called; cats take a message and get back to you.
Mary Bly

10 I said something which gave you to think I hated cats. But gad, sir, I am one of the most fanatical cat lovers in the business. If you hate them, I may learn to hate you. If your allergies hate them, I will tolerate the situation to the best of my ability.
Raymond Chandler (1888-1959, American Author)

11 Your rat tail is all the fashion now. I prefer a bushy plume, carried straight up. You are Siamese and your ancestors lived in trees. Mine lived in palaces. It has been suggested to me that I am a bit of a snob. How true! I prefer to be.
Raymond Chandler (1888-1959, American Author)

12 Authors like cats because they are such quiet, lovable, wise creatures, and cats like authors for the same reasons.
Robertson Davies (1913-, Canadian Novelist, Journalist)

CAUSES

1 If you would win a man to your cause, first convince him that you are his sincere friend. Therein is a drop of honey that catches his heart, which, say what you will, is the great high-road to his reason, and which, when once gained, you will find but little trouble in convincing his judgment of the justice of your cause.
Abraham Lincoln (1809-1865, Sixteenth President of the USA)

2 The silent majority distrusts people who believe in causes.
Brian Moore (1921-, Irish Novelist)

3 The little trouble in the world that is not due to love is due to friendship.
Edgar Watson Howe (1853-1937, American Journalist, Author)

4 The history of progress is written in the blood of men and women who have dared to espouse an unpopular cause, as, for instance, the black man's right to his body, or woman's right to her soul.
Emma Goldman (1869-1940, American Anarchist)

5 A good cause can become bad if we fight for it with means that are indiscriminately murderous. A bad cause can become good if enough people fight for it in a spirit of comradeship and self-sacrifice. In the end it is how you fight, as much as why you fight, that makes your cause good or bad.
Freeman Dyson (1923-, British-born American Physicist, Author)

6 You say it is the good cause that hallows even war? I tell you: it is the good war that hallows every cause.
Friedrich Nietzsche (1844-1900, German Philosopher)

7 No cause is left but the most ancient of all, the one, in fact, that from the beginning of our history has determined the very existence of politics, the cause of freedom versus tyranny.
Hannah Arendt (1906-1975, German-born American Political Philosopher)

8 Men are blind in their own cause.
Heywood Broun (1888-1939, American Journalist, Novelist)

9 Perhaps misguided moral passion is better than confused indifference.
Iris Murdoch (1919-, British Novelist, Philosopher)

10 Great causes and little men go ill together.
Jawaharlal Nehru (1889-1964, Indian Nationalist, Statesman)

11 No cause is helpless if it is just. Errors, no matter how popular, carry the seeds of their own destruction.
John W. Scoville

12 In war, events of importance are the result of trivial causes.
Julius Caesar (101-44 BC, Roman Emperor)

13 Life is not an easy matter. You cannot live through it without falling into frustration and cynicism unless you have before you a great idea which raises you above personal misery, above weakness, above all kinds of perfidy and baseness.
Leon Trotsky (1879-1940, Russian Revolutionary)

14 It is only after an unknown number of unrecorded labors, after a host of noble hearts have succumbed in discouragement, convinced that ;their cause is lost; it is only then that cause triumphs.
Madame Guizot

15 Truth never damages a cause that is just.
Mahatma Gandhi (1869-1948, Indian Political, Spiritual Leader)

16 Take away the cause, and the effect ceases.
Miguel De Cervantes (1547-1616, Spanish Novelist, Dramatist, Poet)

17 A man who has never lost himself in a cause bigger than himself has missed one of life's mountaintop experiences. Only in losing himself does he find himself. Only then does he discover all the latent strengths he never knew he had and which otherwise would have remained dormant.
Richard M. Nixon (1913-1994, Thirty-seventh President of the USA)

18 It isn't until you begin to fight in your own cause that you (a) become really committed to winning, and (b) become a genuine ally of other people struggling for their freedom.
Robin Morgan (1941-, American Feminist Author, Poet)

19 The power of a movement lies in the fact that it can indeed change the habits of people. This change is not the result of force but of dedication, of moral persuasion.
Steven Biko (1946-1977, South African Political Activist)

20 No man is worth his salt who is not ready at all times to risk his well-being, to risk his body, to risk his life, in a great cause.
Theodore Roosevelt (1858-1919, Twenty-sixth President of the USA)

21 Ours is an abiding faith in the cause of human freedom. We know it is God's cause.
Thomas E. Dewey (1902-1971, American Politician)

22 A bad cause will never be supported by bad means and bad men.
Thomas Paine (1737-1809, Anglo-American Political Theorist, Writer)

23 It is not a field of a few acres of ground, but a cause, that we are defending, and whether we defeat the enemy in one battle, or by ;degrees, the consequences will be the same.
Thomas Paine (1737-1809, Anglo-American Political Theorist, Writer)

24 If you want to be an orator, first get your great cause.
Wendell Phillips (1811-1884, American Reformer, Orator)

25 We are all ready to be savage in some cause. The difference between a good man and a bad one is the choice of the cause.
William James (1842-1910, American Psychologist, Professor, Author)

26 The humblest citizen of all the land when clad in the armor of a righteous cause, is stronger than all the hosts of Error.
William Jennings Bryan (1860-1925, American Lawyer, Politician)

27 Respectable men and women content with good and easy living are missing some of the most important things in life. Unless you give ;yourself to some great cause you haven't even begun to live.
William P. Merrill

CAUTION

1 Half the failures in life arise from pulling in one's horse as he is leaping.
A. W. Hare

2 The chief danger in life is that you may take too many precautions.
Alfred Adler (1870-1937, Austrian Psychiatrist)

3 Always count the cost.
American Proverb

4 Beware the hobby that eats.
Benjamin Franklin (1706-1790, American Scientist, Publisher, Diplomat)

5 Of all forms of caution, caution in love is perhaps the most fatal to true happiness.
Bertrand Russell (1872-1970, British Philosopher, Mathematician, Essayist)

6 Take care that you do not despise one of these little ones; for I tell you, in heaven their angels continually see the face of my Father. [Matthew 18:10]
Bible (Sacred Scriptures of Christians and Judaism)

7 Vigilance is the virtue of vice.
C. J. Weber

8 Hasten slowly.
Caesar Augustus (63 BC-14 AD, Founder of Roman Empire)

9 Caution has its place, no doubt, but we cannot refuse our support to a serious venture which challenges the whole of the personality. If we oppose it, we are trying to suppress what is best in man --his daring and his aspirations. And should we succeed, we should only have stood in the way of that invaluable experience which might have given a meaning to life. What would have happened if Paul had allowed himself to be talked out of his journey to Damascus?
Carl Jung (1875-1961, Swiss Psychiatrist)

10 Look twice before you leap.
Charlotte Bronte (1816-1855, British Novelist)

11 Of all the thirty-six alternatives, running away is best.
Chinese Proverb

12 Whenever our neighbor's house is on fire, it cannot be amiss for the engines to play a little on our own.
Edmund Burke (1729-1797, British Political Writer, Statesman)

13 Set the foot down with distrust on the crust of the world -- it is thin.
Edna St. Vincent Millay (1892-1950, American Poet)

14 Those who prepared for all the emergencies of life beforehand may equip themselves at the expense of joy.
Edward M. Forster (1879-1970, British Novelist, Essayist)

15 Don't dance on a volcano.
French Proverb

16 Beware of all enterprises that require a new set of clothes.
Henry David Thoreau (1817-1862, American Essayist, Poet, Naturalist)

17 Beware of one who has nothing to lose.
Italian Proverb

18 He that is over -- cautious will accomplish little.
Johann Friedrich Von Schiller (1759-1805, German Dramatist, Poet, Historian)

19 Beware of the man who works hard to learn something, learns it, and finds himself no wiser than before, Bokonon tells us. He is full of murderous resentment of people who are ignorant without having come by their ignorance the hard way.
Kurt Vonnegut Jr. (1922-, American Novelist)

20 Every human being has, like Socrates, an attendant spirit; and wise are they who obey its signals. If it does not always tell us what to do, it always cautions us what not to do.
Lydia M. Child (1802-1880, American Abolitionist, Writer, Editor)

21 Put all your eggs in one basket and then watch that basket.
Mark Twain (1835-1910, American Humorist, Writer)

22 To withdraw is not to run away, and to stay is no wise action, when there's more reason to fear than to hope.
Miguel De Cervantes (1547-1616, Spanish Novelist, Dramatist, Poet)

23 Be slow of tongue and quick of eye.
Miguel De Cervantes (1547-1616, Spanish Novelist, Dramatist, Poet)

24 The torment of precautions often exceeds often exceeds the dangers to be avoided. It is sometimes better to abandon one's self to destiny.
Napoleon Bonaparte (1769-1821, French General, Emperor)

25 If one has to jump a stream and knows how wide it is, he will not jump. If he does not know how wide it is, he will jump, and six times out of ten he will make it.
Persian Proverb

26 Beware of silent dogs and still waters.
Portuguese Proverb

27 When a fox preaches, take care of your geese.
Proverb

28 Caution is the parent of safety.
Proverb

29 It is a good thing to learn caution from the misfortunes of others.
Publilius Syrus (1st Century BC, Roman Writer)

30 Don't throw away the old bucket until you know whether the new one holds water.
Swedish Proverb

31 Prudence is but experience, which equal time, equally bestows on all men, in those things they equally apply themselves unto.
Thomas Hobbes (1588-1679, British Philosopher)

32 To fear the worst oft cures the worse.
William Shakespeare (1564-1616, British Poet, Playwright, Actor)

33 It is the bright day that brings forth the adder, and that craves wary walking.
William Shakespeare (1564-1616, British Poet, Playwright, Actor)

34 Caution is the confidential agent of selfishness.
Woodrow T. Wilson (1856-1924, Twenty-eighth President of the USA)

CELEBRATION

1 The more you praise and celebrate your life, the more there is in life to celebrate.
Oprah Winfrey (1954-, American TV Personality, Producer, Actress, Author)

2 When you jump for joy, beware that no one moves the ground from beneath your feet.
Stanislaw J. Lec (1909-, Polish Writer)

CELIBACY

1 A celibate, like the fly in the heart of an apple, dwells in a perpetual sweetness, but sits alone, and is confined and dies in singularity.
Jeremy Taylor (1613-1667, British Churchman, Writer)

2   I think that one of the qualifications of artists should be a vow of celibacy. They should be confined to ruining only their own lives.
    Roger Lewis (Author)

3   How deep a wound to morals and social purity has that accursed article of the celibacy of the clergy been! Even the best and most enlightened men in Romanist countries attach a notion of impurity to the marriage of a clergyman. And can such a feeling be without its effect on the estimation of the wedded life in general? Impossible! and the morals of both sexes in Spain, Italy, France, and. prove it abundantly.
    Samuel Taylor Coleridge (1772-1834, British Poet, Critic, Philosopher)

4   Marriage may often be a stormy lake, but celibacy is almost always a muddy horse pond.
    Thomas Love Peacock (1785-1866, British Author)

5   Celibacy is not just a matter of not having sex. It is a way of admiring a person for their humanity, maybe even for their beauty.
    Timothy Radcliffe

CEMETERIES

1   The cemeteries are filled with people who thought the world couldn't get along without them.
    American Proverb

2   The fence around a cemetery is foolish, for those inside can't get out and those outside don't want to get in.
    Arthur Brisbane (American Editor, Columnist)

CENSORSHIP

1   Woe to that nation whose literature is cut short by the intrusion of force. This is not merely interference with freedom of the press but the sealing up of a nation's heart, the excision of its memory.
    Alexander Solzhenitsyn (1918-, Russian Novelist)

2   I am of course confident that I will fulfill my tasks as a writer in all circumstances -- from my grave even more successfully and more irrefutably than in my lifetime. No one can bar the road to truth, and to advance its cause I am prepared to accept even death. But may it be that repeated lessons will finally teach us not to stop the writer's pen during his lifetime? At no time has this ennobled our history.
    Alexander Solzhenitsyn (1918-, Russian Novelist)

3   No government ought to be without censors; and where the press is free, no one ever will. Chance is the pseudonym of God when he did not want to sign.
    Anatole France (1844-1924, French Writer)

4   Your own mind is a sacred enclosure into which nothing harmful can enter except by your permission.
    Arnold Bennett (1867-1931, British Novelist)

5   This film is apparently meaningless, but if it has any meaning it is doubtless objectionable.
    British Board of Film

6   They can't censor the gleam in my eye.
    Charles Laughton

7   The upshot was, my paintings must burn that English artists might finally learn.
    D. H. Lawrence (1885-1930, British Author)

8   Censors tend to do what only psychotics do: they confuse reality with illusion.
    David Cronenberg (1943-, Canadian Filmmaker)

9   We live in oppressive times. We have, as a nation, become our own thought police; but instead of calling the process by which we limit our expression of dissent and wonder "censorship," we call it "concern for commercial viability."
    David Mamet (1947-, American Playwright)

10 We do not fear censorship for we have no wish to offend with improprieties or obscenities, but we do demand, as a right, the liberty to show the dark side of wrong, that we may illuminate the bright side of virtue -- the same liberty that is conceded to the art of the written word, that art to which we owe the Bible and the works of Shakespeare.
    David Wark Griffiths (1875-1948, American Pioneer Film Director)

11 One of the curious things about censorship is that no one seems to want it for himself. We want censorship to protect someone else; the young, the unstable, the suggestible, the stupid. I have never heard of anyone who wanted a film banned because otherwise he might see it and be harmed.
    Edgar Dale

12 If we can't stamp out literature in the country, we can at least stop its being brought in from outside.
    Evelyn Waugh (1903-1966, British Novelist)

13 Censorship ends in logical completeness when nobody is allowed to read any books except the books nobody reads.
    George Bernard Shaw (1856-1950, Irish-born British Dramatist)

14 You can cage the singer but not the song.
    Harry Belafonte (1927-, American Actor and Singer)

15 Whenever books are burned men also in the end are burned.
    Heinrich Heine (1797-1856, German Poet, Journalist)

16 Instead of asking -- "How much damage will the work in question bring about?" why not ask -- "How much good? How much joy?"
    Henry Miller (1891-1980, American Author)

17 If some books are deemed most baneful and their sale forbid, how, then, with deadlier facts, not dreams of doting men? Those whom books will hurt will not be proof against events. Events, not books, should be forbid.
    Herman Melville (1819-1891, American Author)

18 When truth is no longer free, freedom is no longer real: the truths of the police are the truths of today.
    Jacques Prevert (1900-1977, French Poet)

19 As good almost kill a man as kill a good book; who kills a man kills a reasonable creature, God's image; but he who destroys a good book, kills reason itself, kills the image of God, as it were in the eye.
John Milton (1608-1674, British Poet)

20 It is useless to close the gates against ideas; they overlap them.
Klemens Von Metternich (1773-1859, Austrian Statesman)

21 Right now I think censorship is necessary; the things they're doing and saying in films right now just shouldn't be allowed. There's no dignity anymore and I think that's very important.
Mae West (1892-1980, American Actress)

22 The crime of book purging is that it involves a rejection of the word. For the word is never absolute truth, but only man's frail and human effort to approach the truth. To reject the word is to reject the human search.
Max Lerner (1902-, American Author, Columnist)

23 Would you approve of your young sons, young daughters -- because girls can read as well as boys -- reading this book? Is it a book that you would have lying around in your own house? Is it a book that you would even wish your wife or your servants to read?
Mervyn Griffith-Jones

24 Censorship is never over for those who have experienced it. It is a brand on the imagination that affects the individual who has suffered it, forever.
Nadine Gordimer (1923-, South African Author)

25 Art is never chaste. It ought to be forbidden to ignorant innocents, never allowed into contact with those not sufficiently prepared. Yes, art is dangerous. Where it is chaste, it is not art.
Pablo Picasso (1881-1973, Spanish Artist)

26 Every burned book or house enlightens the world; every suppressed or expunged word reverberates through the earth from side to side.
Ralph Waldo Emerson (1803-1882, American Poet, Essayist)

27 It seems not more reasonable to leave the right of printing unrestrained, because writers may be afterwards censured, than it would be to sleep with doors unbolted, because by our laws we can hang a thief.
Samuel Johnson (1709-1784, British Author)

28 No member of society has the right to teach any doctrine contrary to what society holds to be true.
Samuel Johnson (1709-1784, British Author)

29 Here we have bishops, priests, and deacons, a Censorship Board, vigilant librarians, confraternities and sodalities, Duce Maria, Legions of Mary, Knights of this Christian order and Knights of that one, all surrounding the sinner's free will in an embattled circle.
Sean O'Casey (1884-1964, Irish Dramatist)

30 Those expressions are omitted which can not with propriety be read aloud in the family.
Thomas Bowdler (1754-1825, British Physician, Editor)

31 The condition every art requires is, not so much freedom from restriction, as freedom from adulteration and from the intrusion of foreign matter.
Willa Cather (1876-1947, American Author)

32 I think you can leave the arts, superior or inferior, to the conscience of mankind.
William Butler Yeats (1865-1939, Irish Poet, Playwright.)

33 Art made tongue-tied by authority.
William Shakespeare (1564-1616, British Poet, Playwright, Actor)

CENSURE

1 The readiest and surest way to get rid of censure, is to correct ourselves.
Demosthenes (383-322 BC, Greek Orator)

2 Few persons have sufficient wisdom to prefer censure, which is useful, to praise which deceives them.
François de La Rochefoucauld (1613-1680, French classical writer)

3 Censure is the tax a man pays to the public for being eminent.
Jonathan Swift (1667-1745, Anglo-Irish Satirist)

4 A man's first care should be to avoid the reproaches of his own heart, and his next to escape the censures of the world.
Joseph Addison (1672-1719, British Essayist, Poet, Statesman)

5 It is folly for an eminent man to think of escaping censure, and a weakness to be affected with it. All the illustrious persons of ;antiquity, and indeed of every age in the world, have passed through this fiery persecution.
Joseph Addison (1672-1719, British Essayist, Poet, Statesman)

6 The censure of those who are opposed to us, is the highest commendation that can be given us.
Seigneur De Saint-Evremond (1610-1703, French Writer, Wit)

7 I find the pain of a little censure, even when it is unfounded, is more acute than the pleasure of much praise.
Thomas Jefferson (1743-1826, Third President of the USA)

8 He who would acquire fame must not show himself afraid of censure. The dread of censure is the death of genius.
William Gilmore Simms (1806-1870, American Author)

CEREMONY

1 We must learn which ceremonies may be breached occasionally at our convenience and which ones may never be if we are to live pleasantly with our fellow man.
Amy Vanderbilt (1908-1974, American Hostess, Author)

2 It is superstitious to put one's hopes in formalities, but arrogant to refuse to submit to them.
Blaise Pascal (1623-1662, French Scientist, Religious Philosopher)

3 Ceremony is the smoke of friendship.
Chinese Proverb

4 A funeral is not death, any more than baptism is birth or marriage union. All three are the clumsy devices, coming now too late, now too early, by which Society would register the quick motions of man.
Edward M. Forster (1879-1970, British Novelist, Essayist)

5 Ceremony and ritual spring from our heart of hearts: those who govern us know it well, for they would sooner deny us bread than dare alter the observance of tradition.
F. Gonzalez-Crussi

6 Every ceremony or rite has a value if it is performed without alteration. A ceremony is a book in which a great deal is written. Anyone who understands can read it. One rite often contains more than a hundred books.
George Gurdjieff (1873-1949, Russian Adept, Teacher, Writer)

7 Ceremony was but devised at first to set a gloss on faint deeds, hollow welcomes, recanting goodness, sorry ere 'Tis shown; but where there is true friendship, there needs none.
William Shakespeare (1564-1616, British Poet, Playwright, Actor)

CERTAINTY

1 We are not certain, we are never certain. If we were we could reach some conclusions, and we could, at last, make others take us seriously.
Albert Camus (1913-1960, French Existential Writer)

2 To be positive: to be mistaken at the top of one's voice.
Ambrose Bierce (1842-1914, American Author, Editor, Journalist, "The Devil's Dictionary")

3 Only one thing is certain -- that is, nothing is certain. If this statement is true, it is also false.
Ancient Paradox

4 Certainties are arrived at only on foot.
Antonio Porchia

5 The present is the only reality and the only certainty.
Arthur Schopenhauer (1788-1860, German Philosopher)

6 Certainty? In this world nothing is certain but death and taxes.
Benjamin Franklin (1706-1790, American Scientist, Publisher, Diplomat)

7 In this world nothing can be said to be certain, except death and taxes.
Benjamin Franklin (1706-1790, American Scientist, Publisher, Diplomat)

8 What men want is not knowledge, but certainty.
Bertrand Russell (1872-1970, British Philosopher, Mathematician, Essayist)

9 To be uncertain is to be uncomfortable, but to be certain is to be ridiculous.
Chinese Proverb

10 If we begin with certainties, we shall end in doubts; but if we begin with doubts, and are patient in them, we shall end in certainties.
Francis Bacon (1561-1626, British Philosopher, Essayist, Statesman)

11 If a man will begin with certainties, he shall end in doubts, but if he will be content to begin with doubts, he shall end in certainties.
Francis Bacon (1561-1626, British Philosopher, Essayist, Statesman)

12 There is nothing certain except the unforeseen.
Fraude

13 Convictions are more dangerous enemies of truth than lies.
Friedrich Nietzsche (1844-1900, German Philosopher)

14 Ah, what a dusty answer gets the soul when hot for certainties in this our life!
George Meredith (1828-1909, British Author)

15 We delight in one knowable thing, which comprehends all that is knowable; in one apprehensible, which draws together all that can be apprehended; in a single being that includes all, above all in the one which is itself the all.
Giordano Bruno (1548-1600, Italian Philosopher, Scientist)

16 When we are not sure, we are alive.
Graham Greene (1904-1991, British Novelist)

17 It is the dull man who is always sure, and the sure man who is always dull.
H. L. Mencken (1880-1956, American Editor, Author, Critic, Humorist)

18 The one unchangeable certainty is that nothing is unchangeable or certain.
John F. Kennedy (1917-1963, Thirty-fifth President of the USA)

19 I am certain of nothing but the holiness of the heart's affections, and the truth of imagination.
John Keats (1795-1821, British Poet)

20 The more I see the less I know for sure.
John Lennon (1940-1980, British Rock Musician)

21 I have lived in this world just long enough to look carefully the second time into things that I am the most certain of the first time.
Josh Billings (1815-1885, American Humorist, Lecturer)

22 Positiveness is an absurd foible. If you are in the right, it lessens your triumph; if in the wrong, it adds shame to your defeat.
Laurence Sterne (1713-1768, British Author)

23 If you do know that here is one hand, we'll grant you all the rest.
Ludwig Wittgenstein (1889-1951, Austrian Philosopher)

24 Education is the path from cocky ignorance to miserable uncertainty.
Mark Twain (1835-1910, American Humorist, Writer)

25 There is nothing certain in a man's life but that he must lose it.
Owen Meredith (1831-1891, British Politician, Poet)

26 The only certainty is that nothing is certain.
Pliny The Elder (23-79, Roman Neophatonist)

27 In these matters the only certainty is that there is nothing certain.
Pliny The Elder (23-79, Roman Neophatonist)

28 There is nothing certain, but the uncertain.
Proverb

29 There is no such uncertainty as a sure thing.
Robert Burns (1759-1796, Scottish Poet)

30 A woman's guess is much more accurate than a man's certainty.
Rudyard Kipling (1865-1936, British Author of Prose, Verse)

31 There is nothing so uncertain as a sure thing.
Scotty Bowman (American Hockey Coach)

32 I tore myself away from the safe comfort of certainties through my love for truth; and truth rewarded me.
Sylvia Ashton Warner

33 He who is certain he knows the ending of things when he is only beginning them is either extremely wise or extremely foolish; no matter which is true, he is certainly an unhappy man, for he has put a knife in the heart of wonder.
Tad Williams (American Author)

34 One must verify or expel his doubts, and convert them into the certainty of Yes or NO.
Thomas Carlyle (1795-1881, Scottish Philosopher, Author)

35 Doubt is not a pleasant mental state, but certainty is a ridiculous one.
Voltaire (1694-1778, French Historian, Writer)

36 The best lack all conviction, while the worst are full of passionate intensity.
William Butler Yeats (1865-1939, Irish Poet, Playwright.)

37 Inquiry is fatal to certainty.
William J. Durant (1885-1981, American Historian, Essayist)

CHALLENGES

1 There are only two problems in my life. The political ones are insoluble and the economic ones are incomprehensible.
Alexander Douglas Home

2 Life's challenges are not supposed to paralyze you, they're supposed to help you discover who you are.
Bernice Johnson Reagon

3 I wanted to be scared again... I wanted to feel unsure again. That's the only way I learn, the only way I feel challenged.
Connie Chung (1946-, Chinese-American TV Personality)

4 What to do if you find yourself stuck in a crack in the ground underneath a giant boulder you can't move, with no hope of rescue. Consider how lucky you are that life has been good to you so far. Alternatively, if life hasn't been good to you so far, which given your current circumstances seems more likely, consider how lucky you are that it won't be troubling you much longer.
Douglas Adams (Born 1952, British Science Fiction Writer)

5 To be tested is good. The challenged life may be the best therapist.
Gail Sheehy (1937-, American Journalist, Author)

6 Accept the challenges, so you may feel the exhilaration of victory.
George S. Patton (1885-1945, American Army General during World War II)

7 If you can't stand the heat, get out of the kitchen.
Harry S. Truman (1884-1972, Thirty-third President of the USA)

8 Mountains cannot be surmounted except by winding paths.
Johann Wolfgang Von Goethe (1749-1832, German Poet, Dramatist, Novelist)

9 The heights charm us, but the steps do not; with the mountain in our view we love to walk the plains.
Johann Wolfgang Von Goethe (1749-1832, German Poet, Dramatist, Novelist)

10 We only think when we are confronted with problems.
John Dewey (1859-1952, American Philosopher, Educator)

11 The New Frontier I speak of is not a set of promises -- it is a set of challenges. It sums up not what I intend to offer the American people, but what I intent to ask of them.
John F. Kennedy (1917-1963, Thirty-fifth President of the USA)

12 You have to erect a fence and say, "Okay, scale this."
Linda Ronstadt (American Entertainer, Singer)

13 When people keep telling you that you can't do a thing, you kind of like to try it.
Margaret Chase Smith

14 The real challenge (in life) is to choose, hold, and operate through intelligent, uplifting, and fully empowering beliefs.
Michael Sky

15 I love the challenge.
Nancy Lopez (1957-, American Golfer)

16 If we do not rise to the challenge of our unique capacity to shape our lives, to seek the kinds of growth that we find individually fulfilling, then we can have no security: we will live in a world of sham, in which our selves are determined by the will of others, in which we will be constantly buffeted and increasingly isolated by the changes round us.
Nena O'Neil (American Anthropologist, Author)

17 When someone tells me there is only one way to do things, it always lights a fire under my butt. My instant reaction is, "I'm going to prove you wrong!"
Picabo Street (Skier)

18 One must be aware that one is continually being tested in what one wishes most in order to make clear whether one's heart is on earth or in heaven.
Pir Vilayat Khan (1916-, Western Philosopher Teacher, Master, Author)

19 Never underestimate your problem or your ability to deal with it.
Robert H. Schuller (1926-, American Minister (Crystal Cathedral), Author, Social Leader)

20 It isn't the mountain ahead that wears you out; it's the grain of sand in your shoe.
Robert W. Service (1874-1958, British Poet)

21 When you've got something to prove, there's nothing greater than a challenge.
Terry Bradshaw (American Football Player, Sports Commentator)

22 Dreams can often become challenging, but challenges are what we live for.
Travis White

23 Great things are done when men and mountains meet. This is not done by jostling in the street.
William Blake (1757-1827, British Poet, Painter)

24 It's always the challenge of the future, this feeling of excitement, that drives me.
Yoshihisa Tabuchi (Japanese Business Executive, CEO of Nomura Securities)

CHANCE

1 Adventure upon all the tickets in the lottery, and you lose for certain; and the greater the number of your tickets the nearer your approach to this certainty.
Adam Smith (1723-1790, Scottish Economist)

2 Chance is the pseudonym God uses when He does not want to sign His name.
Anatole France (1844-1924, French Writer)

3 The pseudonym for God when He did not want to sign.
Anatole France (1844-1924, French Writer)

4 Chance can allow you to accomplish a goal every once in a while, but consistent achievement happens only if you love what you are doing.
Bart Conner (American Gymnast)

5 Do not always prove yourself to be the one in the right. The right will appear. You need only give it a chance.
C. H. Fowler

6 Chance favors only those who court her.
Charles Nicolle (1866-1936, French Physician, Bacteriologist)

7 He who leaves nothing to chance will do few things poorly, but he will do few things.
Edward F. Halifax (1881-1959, British Conservative Statesman)

8 Chance fights ever on the side of the prudent.
Euripides (480-406 BC, Greek Tragic Poet)

9 Sometimes I pause and sadly think of all the things that might have been. Of all the golden chances I let slip by, And which never returned again. It fills me with gloom when I ponder this, Till I look on the other side. How I might have been completely engulfed by misfortune's surging tide.
G.J. Russell

10 In practical life the wisest and soundest people avoid speculation.
George Earle Buckle (1854-1935, British Journalist)

11 Accident counts for as much in companionship as in marriage.
Henry Brooks Adams (1838 - 1918, American Historian)

12 Nobody owes anybody a living, but everybody is entitled to a chance.
Jack Dempsey (1895-1983, American Boxer)

13 Chance makes our parents, but choice makes our friends.
Jacques Delille (1738-1813, French Poet)

14 I didn't ask for it to be over. But then again I didn't ask for it to begin. For that's the way it is with life, as some of the most beautiful days come completely by chance. But even the most beautiful days eventually have their sunset
Javan

15 One chance is all you need.
Jesse Owens (1913-1980, American Olympic Track Athlete)

16 People who come up with "It may not work" or "What are we going to do if it fails?" do not have the credentials to be businessmen. If there is only a 1 percent chance of success, a true businessperson sees that 1 percent as the spark to light a fire.
Kim Woo-Choong (Business Executive)

17 Did you ever observe to whom the accidents happen? Chance favors only the prepared mind.
Louis Pasteur (1822-1895, French Scientist Who Developed "Pasteurization")

18 Many a happiness in life, as many a disaster, can be due to chance, but the peace within us can never be governed by chance.
Maurice Maeterlinck (1862-1949, Belgian Author)

19 Chance is the providence of adventurers.
Napoleon Bonaparte (1769-1821, French General, Emperor)

20 To get anywhere, or even live a long time, a man has to guess, and guess right, over and over again, without enough data for a logical answer.
Robert Heinlein (1907-1988, American Science Fiction Writer)

21 If you apply reason and logic to this career of mine, you're not going to get very far. You simply won't. The journey has been incredible from its beginning. So much of life, it seems to me, is determined by pure randomness.
Sidney Poitier (1924-, American Actor, Director, Producer, Ambassador)

22 I do not give money for just mere hopes.
Terence (185-159 BC, Roman Writer of Comedies)

23 How often things occur by mere chance which we dared not even hope for.
Terence (185-159 BC, Roman Writer of Comedies)

24 A wise man turns chance into good fortune.
Thomas Fuller (1608-1661, British Clergyman, Author)

25 A fool must now and then be right, by chance.
William Cowper (1731-1800, British Poet)

26 How come "fat chance" and "slim chance" mean the same thing?
Ziggy (Cartoon Character)

CHANGE

1 What is necessary to change a person is to change his awareness of himself.
Abraham H. Maslow (1908-1970, American Psychologist)

2 In pain is a new time born.
Adelbert Von Chamisso (1781-1838, French Poet, Biologist)

3 Change is inevitable. Change for the better is a full-time job.
Adlai E. Stevenson (1900-1965, American Lawyer, Politician)

4 The moment of change is the only poem.
Adrienne Rich (1929-, American Poet)

5 A rut is a grave with no ends.
Alan Lampkin

6 The only way to make sense out of change is to plunge into it, move with it, and join the dance.
Alan W. Watts (1915-1973, British-born American Philosopher, Author)

7 A photograph never grows old. You and I change, people change all through the months and years, but a photograph always remains the same. How nice to look at a photograph of mother or father taken many years ago. You see them as you remember them. But as people live on, they change completely. That is why I think a photograph can be kind.
Albert Einstein (1879-1955, German-born American Physicist)

8 All meaningful and lasting change starts first in your imagination and then works its way out. Imagination is more important than knowledge.
Albert Einstein (1879-1955, German-born American Physicist)

9 Nothing that I can do will change the structure of the universe. But maybe, by raising my voice I can help the greatest of all causes -- goodwill among men and peace on earth.
Albert Einstein (1879-1955, German-born American Physicist)

10 Be not the first by which a new thing is tried, or the last to lay the old aside.
Alexander Pope (1688-1744, British Poet, Critic, Translator)

11 The more things change, the more they remain the same.
Alphonse Karr

12 Man has a limited biological capacity for change. When this capacity is overwhelmed, the capacity is in future shock.
Alvin Toffler (1928-, American Author)

13 Never swap horses crossing a stream.
American Proverb

14 Don't change horses while crossing a stream.
American Proverb

15 In this world of change naught which comes stays and naught which goes is lost.
Anne Sophie Swetchine (1782-1857, Russian Author)

16 Don't fear change -- embrace it.
Anthony J. D'Angelo

17 Become a student of change. It is the only thing that will remain constant.
Anthony J. D'Angelo

18 For changes to be of any true value, they've got to be lasting and consistent.
Anthony Robbins (1960-, American Author, Speaker, Peak Performance Expert / Consultant)

19 I've continued to recognize the power individuals have to change virtually anything and everything in their lives in an instant. I've learned that the resources we need to turn our dreams into reality are within us, merely waiting for the day when we decide to wake up and claim our birthright.
Anthony Robbins (1960-, American Author, Speaker, Peak Performance Expert / Consultant)

20 Any time you sincerely want to make a change, the first thing you must do is to raise your standards. When people ask me what really changed my life eight years ago, I tell them that absolutely the most important thin was changing what I demanded of myself. I wrote down all the things I would no longer accept in my life, all the things I would no longer tolerate, and all the things that I aspired to becoming.
Anthony Robbins (1960-, American Author, Speaker, Peak Performance Expert / Consultant)

21 Any change, even for the better, is always accompanied by drawbacks and discomforts.
Arnold Bennett (1867-1931, British Novelist)

22 The longer you stay in one place, the greater your chances of disillusionment.
Art Spander

23 Change alone is eternal, perpetual, immortal.
Arthur Schopenhauer (1788-1860, German Philosopher)

24 The things that have come into being change continually. The man with a good memory remembers nothing because he forgets nothing.
Augusto Roa Bastos (1917-, Paraguayan Novelist)

25 Change is not only likely, it's inevitable.
Barbara Sher (American Author of "I Could Do Anything If I Only Knew What It Was")

26 Change is inevitable. Change is constant.
Benjamin Disraeli (1804-1881, British Statesman, Prime Minister)

27 When you're finished changing, you're finished.
Benjamin Franklin (1706-1790, American Scientist, Publisher, Diplomat)

28 All movements go too far.
Bertrand Russell (1872-1970, British Philosopher, Mathematician, Essayist)

29 There has never been a time when you and I have not existed, nor will there be a time when we will cease to exist. As the same person inhabits the body through childhood, youth, and old age, so too at the time of death he attains another body. The wise are not deluded by these changes.
Bhagavad Gita (400 BC, Sanskrit Poem Incorporated Into the Mahabharata)

30 There is no new thing under the sun. [Ecclesiastes 1:9]
Bible (Sacred Scriptures of Christians and Judaism)

31 Never change a winning game; always change a losing one.
Bill Tilden (1893-1953, American Tennis Player)

32 Music can't change the world.
Bob Geldof (1954-, Irish Rock Musician, Philanthropist)

33 Goals allow you to control the direction of change in your favor.
Brian Tracy (American Trainer, Speaker, Author, Businessman)

34 When you're through changing, you're through.
Bruce Barton (1886-1967, American Author, Advertising Executive)

35 Notice that the stiffest tree is most easily cracked, while the bamboo or willow survives by bending with the wind.
Bruce Lee (1940-1973, Chinese-American Actor, Director, Author, Martial Artist)

36 Everything changes, nothing remains without change.
Buddha (568-488 BC, Founder of Buddhism)

37 We emphasize that we believe in change because we were born of it, we have lived by it, we prospered and grew great by it. So the ;status quo has never been our god, and we ask no one else to bow down before it.
Carl Rowan (1925-, American Journalist, 'The man')

38 Only I can change my life. No one can do it for me.
Carol Burnett (American Television Comedian)

39 Some people change their ways when they see the light, others when they feel the heat.
Caroline Schoeder

40 Peak performers see the ability to manage change as a necessity in fulfilling their missions.
Charles A. Garfield (American Peak Performance Expert, Researcher, Trainer)

41 It is not the strongest of the species that survive, nor the most intelligent, but the one most responsive to change.
Charles Darwin (1809-1882, British Naturalist)

42 Change begets change. Nothing propagates so fast. If a man habituated to a narrow circle of cares and pleasures, out of which he seldom travels, step beyond it, though for never so brief a space, his departure from the monotonous scene on which he has been an actor of importance would seem to be the signal for instant confusion. The mine which Time has slowly dug beneath familiar objects is sprung in an instant; and what was rock before, becomes but sand and dust.
Charles Dickens (1812-1870, British Novelist)

43 Nature gives to every time and season some beauties of its own; and from morning to night, as from the cradle to the grave, it is but a succession of changes so gentle and easy that we can scarcely mark their progress.
Charles Dickens (1812-1870, British Novelist)

44 The world hates change, yet it is the only thing that has brought progress.
Charles F. Kettering (1876-1958, American Engineer, Inventor)

45 It is not well to make great changes in old age.
Charles Haddon Spurgeon (1834-1892, British Baptist Preacher)

46 The world goes up and the world goes down, the sunshine follows the rain; and yesterday's sneer and yesterday's frown can never come over again.
Charles Kingsley (1819-1875, British Author, Clergyman)

47 Only the wisest and the stupidest of men never change.
Confucius (551-479 BC, Chinese Ethical Teacher, Philosopher)

48 To put the world in order, we must first put the nation in order; to put the nation in order, we must put the family in order; to put the family in order, we must cultivate our personal life; and to cultivate our personal life, we must first set our hearts right.
Confucius (551-479 BC, Chinese Ethical Teacher, Philosopher)

49 They must change who would be constant in happiness and wisdom.
Confucius (551-479 BC, Chinese Ethical Teacher, Philosopher)

50 Everyone thinks of changing the world, but no one thinks of changing himself.
Count Leo Tolstoy (1828-1910, Russian Novelist, Philosopher)

51 The changes in our life must come from the impossibility to live otherwise than according to the demands of our conscience not from our mental resolution to try a new form of life.
Count Leo Tolstoy (1828-1910, Russian Novelist, Philosopher)

52 True life is lived when tiny changes occur.
Count Leo Tolstoy (1828-1910, Russian Novelist, Philosopher)

53 The customs and fashions of men change like leaves on the bough, some of which go and others come.
Dante (Alighieri) (1265-1321, Italian Philosopher, Poet)

54 With me a change of trouble is as good as a vacation.
David Lloyd George (1863-1945, British Statesman, Prime Minister)

55 There are two kinds of fools: One says, "This is old therefore it is good." The other one says, "This is new therefore it is better."
Dean William R. Inge (1860-1954, Dean of St Paul's, London)

56 You must welcome change as the rule but not as your ruler.
Denis Waitley (1933-, American Author, Speaker, Trainer, Peak Performance Expert)

57 Change the changeable, accept the unchangeable, and remove yourself from the unacceptable.
Denis Waitley (1933-, American Author, Speaker, Trainer, Peak Performance Expert)

58 We need to change so we can remain the same.
Dorothy Serrity

59 The powers in charge keep us in a perpetual state of fear keep us in a continuous stampede of patriotic fervor with the cry of grave national emergency. Always there has been some terrible evil to gobble us up if we did not blindly rally behind it by furnishing the exorbitant sums demanded. Yet, in retrospect, these disasters seem never to have happened, seem never to have been quite real.
Douglas Macarthur (1880-1964, American Army General in WW II)

60 Things have never been more like the way they are today in history.
Dwight D. Eisenhower (1890-1969, Thirty-fourth President of the USA)

61 We must all obey the great law of change. It is the most powerful law of nature.
Edmund Burke (1729-1797, British Political Writer, Statesman)

62 A state without the means of some change is without the means of its conservation.
Edmund Burke (1729-1797, British Political Writer, Statesman)

63 If a man like Malcolm X could change and repudiate racism, if I myself and other former Muslims can change, if young whites can change, then there is hope for America.
Eldridge Cleaver (1935-, American Black Leader, Writer)

64 Change is an easy panacea. It takes character to stay in one place and be happy there.
Elizabeth C. Dunn

65 All change is not growth; all movement is not forward.
Ellen Glasgow (1874-1945, American Novelist)

66 Only man is not content to leave things as they are but must always be changing them, and when he has done so, is seldom satisfied with the result.
Elspeth Huxley (1907-, British Author)

67 We don't change what we are, we change what we think what we are.
Eric Butterworth

68 To become different from what we are, we must have some awareness of what we are.
Eric Hoffer (1902-1983, American Author, Philosopher)

69 It is change; all yields its place and goes.
Euripides (480-406 BC, Greek Tragic Poet)

70 Chords that were broken will vibrate once more.
Fanny Crosby (1820-1915, American Hymn Writer)

71 That things are changed, and that nothing really perishes, and that the sum of matter remains exactly the same, is sufficiently certain.
Francis Bacon (1561-1626, British Philosopher, Essayist, Statesman)

72 There is such a thing as a general revolution which changes the taste of men as it changes the fortunes of the world.
François de La Rochefoucauld (1613-1680, French classical writer)

73 All changes, even the most longed for, have their melancholy; for what we leave behind is a part of ourselves; we must die to one life before we can enter into another!
Gail Sheehy (1937-, American Journalist, Author)

74 People don't change. Only their costumes do.
Gene Moorse

75 It seemed that each time we would become proficient at a given task there would be a change made for no apparent reason. It sometimes appeared that changes were made simply because sufficient time had elapsed since the last change. And then our efforts would begin again from the beginning.
General Adalphos

76 The reasonable man adapts himself to the world; the unreasonable man persists in trying to adapt the world to himself. Therefore, all progress depends on the unreasonable man.
George Bernard Shaw (1856-1950, Irish-born British Dramatist)

77 Progress is impossible without change, and those who cannot change their minds cannot change anything.
George Bernard Shaw (1856-1950, Irish-born British Dramatist)

78 It's hard for me to get used to these changing times. I can remember when the air was clean and sex was dirty.
George Burns (1896-1996, American Comedy Actor)

79 Life is measured by the rapidity of change, the succession of influences that modify the being.
George Eliot (1819-1880, British Novelist)

80 It is the greatest mistake to think that man is always one and the same. A man is never the same for long. He is continually changing. He seldom remains the same even for half an hour.
George Gurdjieff (1873-1949, Russian Adept, Teacher, Writer)

81 To change and change for the better are two different things
German Proverb

82 If one desires a change, one must be that change before that change can take place.
Gita Bellin

83 Slumber not in the tents of your fathers. The world is advancing.
Giuseppe Mazzini (1805-1872, Italian Patriot, Writer)

84 If we want everything to remain as it is, it will be necessary for everything to change.
Giuseppe Tomasi Di Lampedusa (1896-1957, Sicilian Author)

85 Adapt or perish, now as ever, is Nature's inexorable imperative.
H.G. Wells (1866-1946, British-born American Author)

86 The wind of change is blowing through the continent. Whether we like it or not, this growth of national consciousness is a political fact.
Harold Macmillan (1894-1986, British Conservative Politician, Prime Minister)

87 America is the civilization of people engaged in transforming themselves. In the past, the stars of the performance were the pioneer and the immigrant. Today, it is youth and the Black.
Harold Rosenberg (1906-1978, American Art Critic, Author)

88 He who rejects change is the architect of decay. The only human institution which rejects progress is the cemetery.
Harold Wilson (1916-1995, British Statesman, Prime Minister)

89 Christians are supposed not merely to endure change, nor even to profit by it, but to cause it.
Harry Emerson Fosdick (1878-1969, American Minister)

90 To act and act wisely when the time for action comes, to wait and wait patiently when it is time for repose, put man in accord with the rising and falling tides (of affairs), so that with nature and law at his back, and truth and beneficence as his beacon light, he may accomplish wonders. Ignorance of this law results in periods of unreasoning enthusiasm on the one hand, and depression on the other. Man thus becomes the victim of the tides when he should be their Master.
Helena Petrova Blavatsky (1831-1891, Russian Author, Translator, Theosophist)

91 So long as a person is capable of self-renewal they are a living being.
Henri Frederic Amiel (1821-1881, Swiss Philosopher, Poet, Critic)

92 To exist is to change, to change is to mature, to mature is to go on creating oneself endlessly
Henri L. Bergson (1859-1941, French Philosopher)

93 Things do not change, we do.
Henry David Thoreau (1817-1862, American Essayist, Poet, Naturalist)

94 Change does not necessarily assure progress, but progress implacably requires change. Education is essential to change, for education creates both new wants and the ability to satisfy them.
Henry S. Commager (American Writer)

95 All things must change to something new, to something strange.
Henry Wadsworth Longfellow (1819-1892, American Poet)

96 Everything flows and nothing abides, everything gives way and nothing stays fixed.
Heraclitus (535-475 BC, Greek Philosopher)

97 Change alone is unchanging.
Heraclitus (535-475 BC, Greek Philosopher)

98 There is nothing permanent except change.
Heraclitus (535-475 BC, Greek Philosopher)

99 You cannot step twice into the same river, for other waters are continually flowing on.
Heraclitus (535-475 BC, Greek Philosopher)

100 Change and growth take place when a person has risked himself and dares to become involved with experimenting with his own life.
Herbert A. Otto

101 A living thing is distinguished from a dead thing by the multiplicity of the changes at any moment taking place in it.
Herbert Spencer (1820-1903, British Philosopher)

102 Illness strikes men when they are exposed to change.
Herodotus (484-425 BC, Greek Historian)

103 Just when I think I have learned the way to live, life changes and I am left the same. The more things change the more I am the same. I am what I started with, and when it is all over I will be all that is left of me.
Hugh Prather

104 Change is certain. Peace is followed by disturbances; departure of evil men by their return. Such recurrences should not constitute occasions for sadness but realities for awareness, so that one may be happy in the interim.
I Ching (12th Century BC, Chinese Book of Changes)

105 The way of the creative works through change and transformation, so that each thing receives its true nature and destiny and comes into permanent accord with the great harmony: this is what furthers and what perseveres.
I Ching (12th Century BC, Chinese Book of Changes)

106 Just because everything's different doesn't mean anything's changed.
Irene Porter

107 It is change, continuing change, inevitable change, that is the dominant factor in society today. No sensible decision can be made any longer without taking into account not only the world as it is, but the world as it will be. This, in turn, means that our statesmen, our businessmen, our every man must take on a science fictional way of thinking.
Isaac Asimov (1920-1992, Russian-born American Author)

108 Everything changes but change.
Israel Zangwill (1864-1926, British Writer)

109 Familiarity may breed contempt in some areas of human behavior, but in the field of social ideas it is the touchstone of acceptability.
J. William Galbraith

110 Consider how hard it is to change yourself and you'll understand what little chance you have in trying to change others.
Jacob M. Braude (American Humor Author)

111 Most of us are about as eager to be changed as we were to be born, and go through our changes in a similar state of shock.
James Baldwin (1924-1987, American Author)

112 Not everything that is faced can be changed, but nothing can be changed until it is faced.
James Baldwin (1924-1987, American Author)

113 People can cry much easier than they can change.
James Baldwin (1924-1987, American Author)

114 Sometimes the answer to prayer is not that it changes life, but that it changes you.
James Dillet Freeman

115 The great person is ahead of their time, the smart make something out of it, and the blockhead, sets themselves against it.
Jean Baudrillard (French Postmodern Philosopher, Writer)

116 Strong character is brought out by change, weak ones by permanence.
Jean Paul

117 Change happens in the boiler room of our emotions... so find out how to light their fires.
Jeff Dewar

118 Both tears and sweat are salty, but they render a different result. Tears will get you sympathy; sweat will get you change.
Jesse Jackson (1941-, American Clergyman, Civil Rights Leader)

119 If you don't like how things are, change it! You're not a tree.
Jim Rohn (American Businessman, Author, Speaker, Philosopher)

120 I can't change the direction of the wind, but I can adjust my sails to always reach my destination.
Jimmy Dean (American Actor, Country Singer)

121 Nobody told me how hard and lonely change is.
Joan Gilbertson

122 Everybody wants to be somebody; nobody wants to grow.
Johann Wolfgang Von Goethe (1749-1832, German Poet, Dramatist, Novelist)

123 Human beings, by change, renew, rejuvenate ourselves; otherwise we harden.
Johann Wolfgang Von Goethe (1749-1832, German Poet, Dramatist, Novelist)

124 Life belongs to the living, and he who lives must be prepared for changes.
Johann Wolfgang Von Goethe (1749-1832, German Poet, Dramatist, Novelist)

125 What I possess I would gladly retain. Change amuses the mind, yet scarcely profits.
Johann Wolfgang Von Goethe (1749-1832, German Poet, Dramatist, Novelist)

126 Change is the law of life. And those who look only to the past or present are certain to miss the future.
John F. Kennedy (1917-1963, Thirty-fifth President of the USA)

127 Let us resolve to be masters, not the victims, of our history, controlling our own destiny without giving way to blind suspicions and emotions.
John F. Kennedy (1917-1963, Thirty-fifth President of the USA)

128 To live is to change, and to be perfect is to have changed often.
John Henry Newman (1801-1890, British Religious Leader, Prelate, Writer)

129 Fear of change perplexes monarchs.
John Milton (1608-1674, British Poet)

130 We are shifting from a managerial society to an entrepreneurial society.
John Naisbitt (American Trend Analyst, Futurist, Author)

131 I realized the problem was me and nobody could change me except myself.
John Petworth

132 They are the weakest-minded and the hardest-hearted men that most love change.
John Ruskin (1819-1900, British Critic, Social Theorist)

133 One of the prevailing sources of misery and crime is in the generally accepted assumption, that because things have been wrong a long time, it is impossible they will ever be right.
John Ruskin (1819-1900, British Critic, Social Theorist)

134 Of the events of life we may have some control. but over the law of its progress none.
John W. Draper (1811-1882, American Chemist)

135 The most serious charge that can be brought against New England is not Puritanism but February.
Joseph Wood Krutch (1893-1970, American Writer, Critic, Naturalist)

136 For good and evil, man is a free creative spirit. This produces the very queer world we live in, a world in continuous creation and therefore continuous change and insecurity.
Joyce Cary (1888-1957, British Author)

137 The atom, being for all practical purposes the stable unit of the physical plane, is a constantly changing vortex of reactions.
Kabbalah (Jewish Esoteric Doctrine)

138 Force never moves in a straight line, but always in a curve vast as the universe, and therefore eventually returns whence it issued forth, but upon a higher arc, for the universe has progressed since it started.
Kabbalah (Jewish Esoteric Doctrine)

139 Life is change. Growth is optional. Choose wisely.
Karen Kaiser Clark

140 For organizations and employees alike, the only real security is the ability to grow, change and adapt.
Kearney

141 Though I might travel afar, I will meet only what I carry with me, for every man is a mirror. We see only ourselves reflected in those around us. Their attitudes and actions are only a reflection of our own. The whole world and its condition has its counter parts within us all. Turn the gaze inward. Correct yourself and your world will change.
Kirsten Zambucka

142 The main dangers in this life are the people who want to change everything or nothing.
Lady Nancy Astor (1897-1964, British Politician)

143 Life is a series of natural and spontaneous changes. Don't resist them -- that only creates sorrow. Let reality be reality. Let things flow naturally forward in whatever way they like.
Lao-Tzu (600 BC, Chinese Philosopher, Founder of Taoism, Author of the "Tao Te Ching")

144 The problem is not whether business will survive in competition with business, but whether any business will survive at all in the ;face of social change.
Laurence J. Mcginley

145 The thing that lies at the foundation of positive change, the way I see it, is service to a fellow human being.
Lech Walesa (1943-, Polish Trade Union Leader, Politician)

146 Change is the end result of all true learning. Change involves three things: First, a dissatisfaction with self -- a felt void or need; second, a decision to change to fill the void or need; and third, a conscious dedication to the process of growth and change -- the willful act of making the change, doing something.
Leo Buscaglia (American Expert on Love, Lecturer, Author)

147 Change is difficult but often essential to survival.
Les Brown (1945-, American Speaker, Author, Trainer, Motivator Lecturer)

148 You cannot expect to achieve new goals or move beyond your present circumstances unless you change.
Les Brown (1945-, American Speaker, Author, Trainer, Motivator Lecturer)

149 You have the power to change.
Les Brown (1945-, American Speaker, Author, Trainer, Motivator Lecturer)

150 When you make a career change there has to be some kind of connection. I remember a Beverly Hills attorney who wanted to become a potato farmer in Oregon. Well, there's a guy who's born to lose.
Lew Richfield

151 That's the risk you take if you change: that people you've been involved with won't like the new you. But other people who do will come along.
Lisa Alther (1944-, American Author)

152 Let the great world spin for ever down the ringing grooves of change.
Lord Alfred Tennyson (1809-1892, British Poet)

153 The lapse of ages changes all things -- time, language, the earth, the bounds of the sea, the stars of the sky, and every thing "about, around, and underneath" man, except man himself.
Lord Byron (1788-1824, British Poet)

154 When it is not necessary to change, it is necessary not to change.
Lucius C. Falkland

155 Nothing is lasting but change; nothing perpetual but death.
Ludwig Borne

156 We are restless because of incessant change, but we would be frightened if change were stopped.
Lyman L. Bryson (American Writer, Director of the Commission Freedom of the Press)

157 We live in an era when rapid change breeds fear, and fear too often congeals us into a rigidity which we mistake for stability.
Lynn White

158 We must become the change we want to see.
Mahatma Gandhi (1869-1948, Indian Political, Spiritual Leader)

159 Be the change you want to see in the world.
Mahatma Gandhi (1869-1948, Indian Political, Spiritual Leader)

160 You must be the change you wish to see in the world.
Mahatma Gandhi (1869-1948, Indian Political, Spiritual Leader)

161 Things don't change, but by and by our wishes change.
Marcel Proust (1871-1922, French Novelist)

162 Observe constantly that all things take place by change, and accustom thyself to consider that the nature of the Universe loves nothing so much as to change the things which are, and to make new things like them.
Marcus Aurelius (121-80 AD, Roman Emperor, Philosopher)

163 No one can persuade another to change. Each of us guards a gate of change that can only be opened from the inside. We cannot open the gate of another, either by argument or emotional appeal.
Marilyn Ferguson (American Writer)

164 The primary and most beautiful of Nature's qualities is motion, which agitates her at all times, but this motion is simply a perpetual consequence of crimes, she conserves it by means of crimes only.
Marquis De Sade (1740-1814, French Author)

165 Change can either challenge or threaten us. Your beliefs pave your way to success or block you.
Marsha Sinetar (American Author of "To Build the Life You Want, Create the Work You Love")

166 Who we are never changes. Who we think we are does.
Mary S. Almanac

167 We cannot become what we need to be, remaining what we are.
Max Depree (1924-, American Furniture Manufacturing Company Executive)

168 The need for change bulldozed road down the center of my mind.
Maya Angelou (1928-, African-American poet, Writer, Performer)

169 Man must be prepared for every event of life, for there is nothing that is durable.
Menander of Athens (342-291 BC, Greek Dramatic Poet)

170 It's the most unhappy people who most fear change.
Mignon McLaughlin (1915?-, American Author, Editor)

171 You will never change your life until you change something you do daily.
Mike Murdock

172 The word change, so dear to our Europe, has been given a new meaning: it no longer means a new stage of coherent development (as it was understood by Vico, Hegel or Marx), but a shift from one side to another, from front to back, from the back to the left, from the left to the front (as understood by designers dreaming up the fashion for the next season).
Milan Kundera (1929-, Czech Author, Critic)

173 Any change or reform you make is going to have consequence you don't like.
Mo Udall

174 Believe, if thou wilt, that mountains change their place, but believe not that man changes his nature.
Mohammed (570-632, Prophet of Islam)

175 The first step toward change is awareness. The second step is acceptance.
Nathaniel Branden (American Expert on Self-esteem, Author, Psychologist)

176 I do not believe you can do today's job with yesterday's methods and be in business tomorrow.
Nelson Jackson

177 One change always leaves the way open for the establishment of others.
Niccolo Machiavelli (1469-1527, Italian Author, Statesman)

178 Enjoying success requires the ability to adapt. Only by being open to change will you have a true opportunity to get the most from your talent.
Nolan Ryan (1947-, American Baseball Player)

179 Every moment of one's existence one is growing into more or retreating into less. One is always living a little more or dying a little bit.
Norman Mailer (1923-, American Author)

180 Change your thoughts and you change your world.
Norman Vincent Peale (1898-1993, American Christian Reformed Pastor, Speaker, Author)

181 Change yourself and your work will seem different.
Norman Vincent Peale (1898-1993, American Christian Reformed Pastor, Speaker, Author)

182 Wisdom lies neither in fixity nor in change, but in the dialectic between the two.
Octavio Paz (1914-, Mexican Poet, Essayist)

183 A woman's mind is cleaner than a man s: She changes it more often.
Oliver Herford (1863-1935, American Author, Illustrator)

184 Grow we must, if we outgrow all that loves us.
Oliver Wendell Holmes (1809-1894, American Author, Wit, Poet)

185 It is a dangerous thing to reform anyone.
Oscar Wilde (1856-1900, British Author, Wit)

186 All things change, nothing is extinguished. There is nothing in the whole world which is permanent. Everything flows onward; all things are brought into being with a changing nature; the ages themselves glide by in constant movement.
Ovid (43 BC-18 AD, Roman Poet)

187 Perfection is immutable. But for things imperfect, change is the way to perfect them.
Owen Felltham (1602-1668, British Author)

188 People do no change with the times, they change the times.
P.K. Shaw

189 Being ready isn't enough; you have to be prepared for a promotion or any other significant change.
Pat Riley (1945, American Basketball Coach)

190 A single day is enough to make us a little larger or, another time, a little smaller.
Paul Klee (1879-1940, Swiss Artist)

191 Everybody wants to do something to help, but nobody wants to be the first.
Pearl Bailey (1918-1990, American Vocalist, Movie and Stage Actress)

192 Man's yesterday may never be like his morrow; Nought may endure but Mutability.
Percy Bysshe Shelley (1792-1822, British Poet)

193 Life may change, but it may fly not; Hope may vanish, but can die not; Truth be veiled, but still it burneth; Love repulsed, -- but it returneth.
Percy Bysshe Shelley (1792-1822, British Poet)

194 The entrepreneur always searches for change, responds to it, and exploits it as an opportunity.
Peter F. Drucker (1909-, American Management Consultant, Author)

195 We now accept the fact that learning is a lifelong process of keeping abreast of change. And the most pressing task is to teach people how to learn.
Peter F. Drucker (1909-, American Management Consultant, Author)

196 The only thing we know about the future is that it will be different.
Peter F. Drucker (1909-, American Management Consultant, Author)

197 If things change then they will be different, but if they don't then things will stay the same.
Peter Gilcrest

198 In human life there is constant change of fortune; and it is unreasonable to expect an exemption from the common fate. Life itself decays, and all things are daily changing.
Plutarch (46-120 AD, Greek Essayist, Biographer)

199 Change yourself, change your fortunes.
Portuguese Proverb

200 A rolling stone can gather no moss.
Publilius Syrus (1st Century BC, Roman Writer)

201 The industrial landscape is already littered with remains of once successful companies that could not adapt their strategic vision to altered conditions of competition.
Ralph D. Abernathy (1926 - 1990, Baptist Clergyman, Civil Rights Activist)

202 People wish to be settled. It is only as far as they are unsettled that there is any hope for them.
Ralph Waldo Emerson (1803-1882, American Poet, Essayist)

203 God grant me the serenity to accept the things I cannot change, the courage to change the things I can, and the wisdom to know the difference.
Reinhold Niebuhr (1892-1971, American Theologian, Historian)

204 A stop sign is a gift for you to learn that moving in the same direction won't take you any place new.
Rex Steven Sikes (Trainer, Peak Performance Expert)

205 Give wind and tide a chance to change.
Richard E. Byrd (1888-1957, American Aviator, Explorer, Rear-Admiral)

206 Change is not made without inconvenience, even from worse to better.
Richard Hooker (1554-1600, British Theologian)

207 Change hurts. It makes people insecure, confused, and angry. People want things to be the same as they've always been, because that makes life easier. But, if you're a leader, you can't let your people hang on to the past.
Richard Marcinko (American Business Author)

208 What we remember can always be changed, what we forget we are always.
Richard Shelton

209 Change is inevitable-except from a vending machine.
Robert C. Gallagher

210 Progress is a nice word, but change is its motivator and change has enemies.
Robert F. Kennedy (1925-1968, American Attorney General, Senator)

211 Most of the change we think we see in life is due to truths being in and out of favor.
Robert Frost (1875-1963, American Poet)

212 You will suddenly realize that the reason you never changed before was because you didn't want to.
Robert H. Schuller (1926-, American Minister (Crystal Cathedral), Author, Social Leader)

213 As the blessings of health and fortune have a beginning, so they must also find an end. Everything rises but to fall, and increases but to decay.
Sallust (86-34 BC, Roman Historian)

214 Such is the state of life, that none are happy but by the anticipation of change: the change itself is nothing; when we have made it, the next wish is to change again. The world is not yet exhausted; let me see something tomorrow which I never saw before.
Samuel Johnson (1709-1784, British Author)

215 Change means movement. Movement means friction. Only in the frictionless vacuum of a nonexistent abstract world can movement or change occur without that abrasive friction of conflict.
Saul Alinsky (1909-1972, American Radical Activist)

216 The world will change for the better when people decide they are sick and tired of being sick and tired of the way the world is, and decide to change themselves.
Sidney Madwed (American Speaker, Consultant, Author, Poet)

217 You do not notice changes in what is always before you.
Sidonie Gabrielle Colette (1873-1954, French Author)

218 Change your life today. Don't gamble on the future, act now, without delay.
Simone De Beauvoir (1908-1986, French Novelist, Essayist)

219 The most useless are those who never change through the years.
Sir James M. Barrie (1860-1937, British Playwright)

220 Today the world changes so quickly that in growing up we take leave not just of youth but of the world we were young in. Fear and resentment of what is new is really a lament for the memories of our childhood.
Sir Peter Medawar (1915-1987, British Immunologist)

221 There is nothing exempt from the peril of mutation; the earth, heavens, and whole world is thereunto subject.
Sir Walter Raleigh (1552-1618, British Courtier, Navigator, Writer)

222 Remember, no human condition is ever permanent. Then you will not be overjoyed in good fortune nor too scornful in misfortune.
Socrates (469-399 BC, Greek Philosopher of Athens)

223 A wise man changes his mind, a fool never will.
Spanish Proverb

224 People can't live with change if there's not a changeless core inside them. The key to the ability to change is a changeless sense of who you are, what you are about and what you value.
Stephen R. Covey (American Speaker, Trainer, Author of "The 7 Habits of Highly Effective People")

225 One person's constant is another person's variable.
Susan Gerhart

226 Anything in history or nature that can be described as changing steadily can be seen as heading toward catastrophe.
Susan Sontag (1933-, American Essayist)

227 When things come to the worse, they generally mend.
Susanna Moodie (1803-1885, Canadian Author)

228 I've always believed that it's important to show a new look periodically. Predictability can lead to failure.
T. Boone Pickens (American Businessman, Chairman of Mesa Petroleum)

229 There is a time for departure even when there's no certain place to go.
Tennessee Williams (1914-1983, American Dramatist)

230 In true dialogue, both sides are willing to change.
Thich Nhat Hanh (Vietnamese Buddhist Monk, Teacher)

231 The true past departs not, no truth or goodness realized by man ever dies, or can die; but all is still here, and, recognized or not, lives and works through endless change.
Thomas Carlyle (1795-1881, Scottish Philosopher, Author)

232 By nature man hates change; seldom will he quit his old home till it has actually fallen around his ears.
Thomas Carlyle (1795-1881, Scottish Philosopher, Author)

233 Today is not yesterday: we ourselves change; how can our works and thoughts, if they are always to be the fittest, continue always the same? Change, indeed is painful; yet ever needful; and if memory have its force and worth, so also has hope.
Thomas Carlyle (1795-1881, Scottish Philosopher, Author)

234 Being willing to change allows you to move from a point of view to a viewing point -- a higher, more expansive place, from which you can see both sides.
Thomas Crum

235 Winners must learn to relish change with the same enthusiasm and energy that we have resisted it in the past.
Thomas J. Peters (1942-, American Management Consultant, Author, Trainer)

236 Many deceive themselves, imagining they'll find happiness in change.
Thomas p Kempis (1379-1471, German Monk, Mystic, Religious Writer)

237 Life is made of millions of moments, but we live only one of these moments at a time. As we begin to change this moment, we begin to change our lives.
Trinidad Hunt (Author)

238 Thus all things are doomed to change for the worse and retrograde.
Virgil (70-19 BC, Roman Poet)

239 Let that which stood in front go behind, let that which was behind advance to the front, let bigots, fools, unclean persons, offer new propositions, let the old propositions be postponed.
Walt Whitman (1819-1892, American Poet)

240 If past history was all there was to the game, the richest people would be librarians.
Warren Buffett (1930-, American Investment Entrepreneur)

241 There is a certain relief in change, even though it be from bad to worse! As I have often found in traveling in a stagecoach, that ;it is often a comfort to shift one's position, and be bruised in a new place.
Washington Irving (1783-1859, American Author)

242 If all people are unique, and if they are constantly changing each and every day, then all one can say about any social research finding is that it applied to that group of people on that given day, and given the propensity of humans to be different and to change, then it is unlikely that one would get the same results if one were to repeat the study.
Wayne Dyer (1940-, American Psychotherapist, Author, Lecturer)

243 Everything is changing. People are taking the comedians seriously and the politicians as a joke.
Will Rogers (1879-1935, American Humorist, Actor)

244 Change, like sunshine, can be a friend or a foe, a blessing or a curse, a dawn or a dusk.
William A. Ward (1921-,)

245 It struck me while I was sitting here; everything changes but the sea.
William B. Davis

246 Weep not that the world changes -- did it keep a stable, changeless state, it were cause indeed to weep.
William C. Bryant (1794-1878, American Poet, Newspaper Editor)

247 Change starts when someone sees the next step.
William Drayton

248 Times change, and we change with them.
William Harrison (1773-1841, American Soldier, Statesman, President)

249 The only practice that's now constant is the practice of constantly accommodating to change.
William Mcgovern (American Businessman, Founder of MCI)

250 The search for static security -- in the law and elsewhere -- is misguided. The fact is security can only be achieved through constant change, adapting old ideas that have outlived their usefulness to current facts.
William O. Douglas (1898-1980, American Supreme Court Justice)

251 To improve is to change; to be perfect is to change often.
Winston Churchill (1874-1965, British Statesman, Prime Minister)

252 If you want to make enemies, try to change something.
Woodrow T. Wilson (1856-1924, Twenty-eighth President of the USA)

253 Life has got a habit of not standing hitched. You got to ride it like you find it. You got to change with it. If a day goes by that don't change some of your old notions for new ones, that is just about like trying to milk a dead cow.
Woody Guthrie (1912-1967, American Folksinger and Songwriter)

CHAOS

1 Lo! thy dread empire, Chaos! is restored; dies before thy uncreating word: thy hand, great Anarch! lets the curtain fall; and universal darkness buries all.
Alexander Pope (1688-1744, British Poet, Critic, Translator)

2 In all chaos there is a cosmos, in all disorder a secret order.
Carl Jung (1875-1961, Swiss Psychiatrist)

3 Chaos is a name for any order that produces confusion in our minds.
George Santayana (1863-1952, American Philosopher, Poet)

4 Chaos is the score upon which reality is written.
Henry Miller (1891-1980, American Author)

5 Pandemonium did not reign; it poured.
John Hendrick Bangs

6 In order to master the unruly torrent of life the learned man meditates, the poet quivers, and the political hero erects the fortress of his will.
Jose Ortega Y Gasset (1883-1955, Spanish Essayist, Philosopher)

7 Out of chaos God made a world, and out of high passions comes a people.
Lord Byron (1788-1824, British Poet)

8 We live in a rainbow of chaos.
Paul Cezanne (1839-1906. French Painter)

9 To find a form that accommodates the mess, that is the task of the artist now.
Samuel Beckett (1906-1989, Irish Dramatist, Novelist)

10 Mere anarchy is loosed upon the world, the blood-dimmed tide is loosed, and everywhere the ceremony of innocence is drowned.
William Butler Yeats (1865-1939, Irish Poet, Playwright.)

CHARACTER

1 Good character is like a rubber ball -- thrown down hard -- it bounces right back. Good reputation is like a crystal ball -- thrown for gain -- shattered and cracked.
A. L. Linall Jr. (Born 1947, American Editor)

2 The best index to a person's character is (a) how he treats people who can't do him any good, and (b) how he treats people who can't fight back.
Abigail Van Buren (American Journalist, Advice Columnist - "Dear Abby")

3 If I were to try to read, much less answer, all the attacks made on me, this shop might as well be closed for any other business. I do the very best I know how -- the very best I can. And I mean to keep on doing it to the end. If the end brings me out all right, what is said against me will not amount to anything. If the end brings me out all wrong, ten angels swearing I was right would make no difference.
Abraham Lincoln (1809-1865, Sixteenth President of the USA)

4 Character is like a tree and reputation like its shadow. The shadow is what we think of it; the tree is the real thing.
Abraham Lincoln (1809-1865, Sixteenth President of the USA)

5 We should be too big to take offense and too noble to give it.
Abraham Lincoln (1809-1865, Sixteenth President of the USA)

6 It is in the character of very few men to honor without envy a friend who has prospered.
Aeschylus (525-456 BC, Greek Dramatist)

7 Wherever man goes to dwell his character goes with him.
African Proverb

8 Be thou incapable of change in that which is right, and men will rely upon thee. Establish unto thyself principles of action; and see that thou ever act according to them. First know that thy principles are just, and then be thou
Akhenaton (1375 BC, Egyptian King, Monotheist)

9 Honor is the inner garment of the Soul; the first thing put on by it with the flesh, and the last it layeth down at its separation from it.
Akhenaton (1375 BC, Egyptian King, Monotheist)

10 Integrity has no need of rules.
Albert Camus (1913-1960, French Existential Writer)

11 Honor and shame from no condition rise; Act well your part, there all the honor lies.
Alexander Pope (1688-1744, British Poet, Critic, Translator)

12 Every man has three characters -- that which he exhibits, that which he has, and that which he thinks he has.
Alphonse Karr

13 Everyone has three characters, that which they exhibit, that which they have, and that which they think they have.
Alphonse Karr

14 If you create an act, you create a habit. If you create a habit, you create a character. If you create a character, you create a destiny.
Andre Maurois (1885-1967, French Writer)

15 Keep in mind that the true measure of an individual is how he treats a person who can do him absolutely no good.
Ann Landers (1918-, American Advice Columnist)

16 The final forming of a person's character lies in their own hands.
Anne Frank (1929-1945, German Jewish Refugee, Diarist)

17 Surmounting difficulty is the crucible that forms character.
Anthony Robbins (1960-, American Author, Speaker, Peak Performance Expert / Consultant)

18 Character is that which reveals moral purpose, exposing the class of things a man chooses or avoids.
Aristotle (384-322 BC, Greek Philosopher)

19 Dignity does not consist in possessing honors, but in deserving them.
Aristotle (384-322 BC, Greek Philosopher)

20 Look, we're all the same; a man is a fourteen-room house --in the bedroom he's asleep with his intelligent wife, in the living-room he's rolling around with some bareass girl, in the library he's paying his taxes, in the yard he's raising tomatoes, and in the cellar he's making a bomb to blow it all up.
Arthur Miller (1915-, American Dramatist)

21 It is with trifles and when he is off guard that a man best reveals his character.
Arthur Schopenhauer (1788-1860, German Philosopher)

22 Deep down, I'm pretty superficial.
Ava Gardner (1922-1990, American Actress)

23 Fame is what you have taken, character is what you give. When to this truth you awaken, then you begin to live.
Bayard Taylor (1825-1878, American Journalist, Traveler, Author)

24 There is no greater index of character so sure as the voice.
Benjamin Disraeli (1804-1881, British Statesman, Prime Minister)

25 Characters do not change. Opinions alter, but characters are only developed.
Benjamin Disraeli (1804-1881, British Statesman, Prime Minister)

26 During my eighty-seven years, I have witnessed a whole succession of technological revolutions. But none of them has done away with the need for character in the individual or the ability to think.
Bernard M. Baruch (1870-1965, American Financier)

27 As a man thinks in his heart, so is he. [Proverbs 23:7]
Bible (Sacred Scriptures of Christians and Judaism)

28 Character is power.
Booker T. Washington (1856-1915, American Black Leader and Educator)

29 Character, not circumstances, makes the man.
Booker T. Washington (1856-1915, American Black Leader and Educator)

30 Temperance is a tree which as for its root very little contentment, and for its fruit calm and peace.
Buddha (568-488 BC, Founder of Buddhism)

31 Faced with crisis, the man of character falls back on himself. He imposes his own stamp of action, takes responsibility for it, makes it his own.
Charles De Gaulle (1890-1970, French President during World War II)

32 Character is the impulse reined down into steady continuance.
Charles H. Parkhurst (1842-1933, American Clergyman, Reformer)

33 A good character is the best tombstone. Those who loved you, and were helped by you, will remember you when forget-me-nots are withered. Carve your name on hearts, and not on marble
Charles Haddon Spurgeon (1834-1892, British Baptist Preacher)

34 No artist work is so high, so noble, so grand, so enduring, so important for all time, as the making of character is a child.
Charlotte Saunders Cushman (1816-1876, American Actor)

35 If you stand straight, do not fear a crooked shadow.
Chinese Proverb

36 Clear conscience never fears midnight knocking.
Chinese Proverb

37 All men are alike in their lower natures; it is in their higher characters that they differ.
Christian Nevell Bovee (1820-1904, American Author, Lawyer)

38 You can buy a person's time; you can buy their physical presence at a given place; you can even buy a measured number of their skilled muscular motions per hour. But you can not buy enthusiasm... you can not buy loyalty. You can not buy the devotion of hearts, minds, or souls. You must earn these.
Clarence Francis

39 There's a fine line between character building and soul destroying.
Colin Hay

40 The superior man will watch over himself when he is alone. He examines his heart that there may be nothing wrong there, and that he may have no cause of dissatisfaction with himself.
Confucius (551-479 BC, Chinese Ethical Teacher, Philosopher)

41 When we see men of a contrary character, we should turn inwards and examine ourselves.
Confucius (551-479 BC, Chinese Ethical Teacher, Philosopher)

42 To be fond of learning is near to wisdom; to practice with vigor is near to benevolence; and to be conscious of shame is near to fortitude. He who knows these three things
Confucius (551-479 BC, Chinese Ethical Teacher, Philosopher)

43 Football doesn't build character. It eliminates weak ones.
Darrell Royal (College Football Coach)

44 Character is the result of a system of stereotyped principals.
David Hume (1711-1776, Scottish Philosopher, Historian)

45 When about to commit a base deed, respect thyself, though there is no witness.
Decimus Magnus Ausonius (310-395, Latin Poet, Man of Letters)

46 Character is what you are in the dark.
Dwight L. Moody (1837-1899, American Evangelist)

47 Few persons are made of such strong fiber that they will make a costly outlay when surface work will pass as well in the market.
E. M. Bounds

48 My father told me that if you saw a man in a Rolls Royce you could be sure he was not a gentleman unless he was the chauffeur.
Earl of Arran

49 I have only got down on to paper, really, three types of people: the person I think I am, the people who irritate me, and the people I'd like to be.
Edward M. Forster (1879-1970, British Novelist, Essayist)

50 The four cornerstones of character on which the structure of this nation was built are: initiative, imagination, individuality, and independence.
Edward Vernon Rickenbacker (1890-1973, American Aviator, World War I Ace)

51 The man that makes a character, makes foes.
Edward Young (1683-1765, British Poet, Dramatist)

52 Character is the result of two things: Mental attitude and the way we spend our time.
Elbert Hubbard (1859-1915, American Author, Publisher)

53 It is not fair to ask of others what you are not willing to do yourself.
Eleanor Roosevelt (1884-1962, American First Lady, Columnist, Lecturer, Humanitarian)

54 Too many lives are needed to make just one.
Eugenio Montale (1896-1981, Italian Poet)

55 Wealth stays with us a little moment if at all: only our characters are steadfast, not our gold.
Euripides (480-406 BC, Greek Tragic Poet)

56 Character builds slowly, but it can be torn down with incredible swiftness.
Faith Baldwin

57 Old age and sickness bring out the essential characteristics of a man.
Felix Frankfurter (1882-1965, Austrian-born American Law Teacher, Judge)

58 You can't go around hoping that most people have sterling moral characters. The most you can hope for is that people will pretend that they do.
Fran Lebowitz (1951-, American Journalist)

59 How difficult it is to save the bark of reputation from the rocks of ignorance.
Francesco Petrarch (1304-1374, Italian Poet, Humanist)

60 Weakness of character is the only defect which cannot be amended.
François de La Rochefoucauld (1613-1680, French classical writer)

61 The hardest job kids face today is learning good manners without seeing any.
Fred Astaire (1899-1987, American Dancer, Singer, Actor)

62 A person reveals his character by nothing so clearly as the joke he resents.
Georg C. Lichtenberg (1742-1799, German Physicist, Satirist)

63 Let us not say, every man is the architect of his own fortune; but let us say, every man is the architect of his own character.
George D. Boardman

64 For character too is a process and an unfolding... among our valued friends is there not someone or other who is a little too self confident and disdainful; whose distinguished mind is a little spotted with commonness; who is a little pinched here and protuberant there with native prejudices; or whose better energies are liable to lapse down the wrong channel under the influence of transient solicitations?
George Eliot (1819-1880, British Novelist)

65 Character is the basis of happiness and happiness the sanction of character.
George Santayana (1863-1952, American Philosopher, Poet)

66 By constant self-discipline and self-control you can develop greatness of character.
Grenville Kleiser (1868-1953, American Author)

67 When God measures man, He puts the tape around his heart -- not his head.
Guideposts

68 It isn't the size of the dog in the fight, but the size of the fight in the dog, that counts.
Harry Howell

69   A rich man has no need of character.
Hebrew Proverb

70   Character cannot be developed in ease and quiet. Only through experiences of trial and suffering can the soul be strengthened, vision cleared, ambition inspired and success achieved.
Helen Keller (1880-1968, American Blind/Deaf Author, Lecturer, Amorist)

71   It is not what he had, or even what he does which expresses the worth of a man, but what he is.
Henri Frederic Amiel (1821-1881, Swiss Philosopher, Poet, Critic)

72   Of all the properties which belong to honorable men, not one is so highly prized as that of character.
Henry Clay (1777-1852, American Statesman, Orator)

73   We know but a few men, a great many coats and breeches.
Henry David Thoreau (1817-1862, American Essayist, Poet, Naturalist)

74   Pity the man who has a character to support --it is worse than a large family -- he is silent poor indeed.
Henry David Thoreau (1817-1862, American Essayist, Poet, Naturalist)

75   The universe seems bankrupt as soon as we begin to discuss the characters of individuals.
Henry David Thoreau (1817-1862, American Essayist, Poet, Naturalist)

76   We falsely attribute to men a determined character -- putting together all their yesterdays -- and averaging them -- we presume we know them. Pity the man who has character to support -- it is worse than a large family -- he is the silent poor indeed.
Henry David Thoreau (1817-1862, American Essayist, Poet, Naturalist)

77   Therefore keep in the midst of life. Do not isolate yourself. Be among men and things, and among troubles, and difficulties, and obstacles.
Henry Drummond (1786-1860, British Banker, Politician, Religious Leader)

78   What is character but the determination of incident? What is incident but the illustration of character?
Henry James (1843-1916, American Author)

79   What you possess in the world will be found at the day of your death to belong to someone else. But what you are will be yours forever.
Henry Van Dyke (1852-1933, American Protestant Clergyman, Poet and Writer)

80   In this world a man must either be anvil or hammer.
Henry Wadsworth Longfellow (1819-1892, American Poet)

81   A man's character is the reality of himself; his reputation, the opinion others have formed about him; character resides in him, reputation in other people; that is the substance, this is the shadow.
Henry Ward Beecher (1813-1887, American Preacher, Orator, Writer)

82   Man's character is his fate.
Heraclitus (535-475 BC, Greek Philosopher)

83   Character is our destiny.
Heraclitus (535-475 BC, Greek Philosopher)

84   A man's character is his guardian divinity.
Heraclitus (535-475 BC, Greek Philosopher)

85   Those who cross the sea change only the climate, not their character.
Horace (65-8 BC, Italian Poet)

86   Fame is a vapor, popularity an accident, and riches take wings. Only one thing endures and that is character.
Horace Greeley (1811-1872, American Newspaper Editor)

87   It is well to think well. It is divine to act well.
Horace Mann (1796-1859, American Educator)

88   If all I'm remembered for is being a good basketball player, then I've done a bad job with the rest of my life.
Isiah Thomas (American Basketball Player, Coach)

89   A man with a so-called character is often a simple piece of mechanism; he has often only one point of view for the extremely complicated relationships of life.
J. August Strindberg (1849-1912, Swedish Dramatist, Novelist, Poet)

90   A man's reputation is what other people think of him; his character is what he really is.
Jack Miner

91   Character contributes to beauty. It fortifies a woman as her youth fades.
Jacqueline Bisset (1946-, American Screen Actor)

92   We don't love qualities, we love persons; sometimes by reason of their defects as well as of their qualities.
Jacques Maritain (1882-1973, French Philosopher)

93   Human improvement is from within outward.
James A. Froude (1818-1894, British Historian)

94   You cannot dream yourself into a character; you must hammer and forge yourself one.
James A. Froude (1818-1894, British Historian)

95   Character consists of what you do on the third and fourth tries.
James A. Michener (1907-, American Writer)

96   Reputation is only a candle, of wavering and uncertain flame, and easily blown out, but it is the light by which the world looks for and finds merit.
James Russell Lowell (1819-1891, American Poet, Critic, Editor)

97   They are slaves who fear to speak, for the fallen and the weak.
James Russell Lowell (1819-1891, American Poet, Critic, Editor)

98   While he was not as dumb as an ox, he was not any smarter either.
James Thurber (1894-1961, American Humorist, Illustrator)

99 It is fortunate to be of high birth, but it is no less so to be of such character that people do not care to know whether you are or are not.
Jean De La Bruyere (1645-1696, French Writer)

100 A man never discloses his own character so clearly as when he describes another s.
Jean Paul Richter (1763-1825, German Novelist)

101 Strong characters are brought out by change of situation, and gentle ones by permanence.
Jean Paul Richter (1763-1825, German Novelist)

102 Character isn't something you were born with and can't change, like your fingerprints. It's something you weren't born with and must take responsibility for forming.
Jim Rohn (American Businessman, Author, Speaker, Philosopher)

103 You are not very good if you are not better than your best friends imagine you to be.
Johann Kaspar Lavater (1741-1801, Swiss Theologian, Mystic)

104 Action, looks, words, steps, form the alphabet by which you may spell character.
Johann Kaspar Lavater (1741-1801, Swiss Theologian, Mystic)

105 Men show their character in nothing more clearly than what they think laughable.
Johann Wolfgang Von Goethe (1749-1832, German Poet, Dramatist, Novelist)

106 The formation of one's character ought to be everyone's chief aim.
Johann Wolfgang Von Goethe (1749-1832, German Poet, Dramatist, Novelist)

107 Character develops itself in the stream of life.
Johann Wolfgang Von Goethe (1749-1832, German Poet, Dramatist, Novelist)

108 Character is formed in the stormy billows of the world.
Johann Wolfgang Von Goethe (1749-1832, German Poet, Dramatist, Novelist)

109 Character, in great and little things, means carrying through what you feel able to do.
Johann Wolfgang Von Goethe (1749-1832, German Poet, Dramatist, Novelist)

110 Talents are best nurtured in solitude. Character is best formed in the stormy billows of the world.
Johann Wolfgang Von Goethe (1749-1832, German Poet, Dramatist, Novelist)

111 If you don't run your own life, somebody else will.
John Atkinson

112 Character is power; it makes friends, draws patronage and support and opens the way to wealth, honor and happiness.
John Howe

113 Good character is more to be praised than outstanding talent. Most talents are, to some extent, a gift. Good character, by contrast, is not given to us. We have to build it piece by piece-by thought, choice, courage and determination.
John Luther

114 You must regulate your life by the standards you admire when you are at your best.
John M. Thomas

115 While an original is always hard to find, he is easy to recognize.
John Mason

116 He that has light within his own clear breast may sit in the center, and enjoy bright day: But he that hides a dark soul and foul thoughts benighted walks under the mid-day sun;
John Milton (1608-1674, British Poet)

117 Be more concerned with your character than your reputation. Your character is what you really are while your reputation is merely what others think you are.
John Wooden (1910-, American Basketball Coach)

118 Few people can distinguish the genuinely good from the reverse.
Juvenal (Decimus Junius Juvenalis) (55-130, Roman Satirical Poet)

119 To keep your character intact you cannot stoop to filthy acts. It makes it easier to stoop the next time.
Katharine Hepburn (1907-, American Actress, Writer)

120 Another flaw in the human character is that everybody wants to build and nobody wants to do maintenance.
Kurt Vonnegut Jr. (1922-, American Novelist)

121 One stumble is enough to deface the character of an honorable life.
L. Estrange

122 The depth and strength of a human character are defined by its moral reserves. People reveal themselves completely only when they are thrown out of the customary conditions of their life, for only then do they have to fall back on their reserves.
Leon Trotsky (1879-1940, Russian Revolutionary)

123 You don't get in life what you want; you get in life what you are.
Les Brown (1945-, American Speaker, Author, Trainer, Motivator Lecturer)

124 Be your character what it will, it will be known; and nobody will take it upon your word.
Lord Chesterfield (1694-1773, British Statesman, Author)

125 Character must be kept bright as well as clean.
Lord Chesterfield (1694-1773, British Statesman, Author)

126 You must look into people, as well as at them.
Lord Chesterfield (1694-1773, British Statesman, Author)

127 The highest qualities of character... must be earned.
Lyman Abbott (1835 - 1922, American Congregational Clergyman and Editor)

128 A man without ethics is a wild beast loosed upon this world.
Manly Hall (1901-, American - Founder Philosophical Research Society)

129 As fire when thrown into water is cooled down and put out, so also a false accusation when brought against a man of the purest and holiest character, boils over and is at once dissipated, and vanishes and threats of heaven and sea, himself standing unmoved.
Marcus T. Cicero (106-43 BC, Great Roman Orator, Politician)

130 To succeed is nothing -- it's an accident. But to feel no doubts about oneself is something very different: it is character.
Marie Leneru

131 To arrive at a just estimate of a renowned man's character one must judge it by the standards of his time, not ours.
Mark Twain (1835-1910, American Humorist, Writer)

132 I look to a day when people will not be judged by the color of their skin, but by the content of their character.
Martin Luther King Jr. (1929-1968, American Black Leader, Nobel Prize Winner, 1964)

133 Character is what you know you are, not what others think you have.
Marva Collins (African-American educator)

134 To have character is to be big enough to take life on.
Mary Caroline Richards

135 The quality of strength lined with tenderness is an unbeatable combination, as are intelligence and necessity when unblunted by formal education.
Maya Angelou (1928-, African-American poet, Writer, Performer)

136 Instill the love of you into all the world, for a good character is what is remembered.
Merikare

137 If anyone tells you someone has changed their character; don't believe it.
Mohammed (570-632, Prophet of Islam)

138 If we have need of a strong will in order to do good, it is still more necessary for us in order not to do evil.
Mole

139 Character is victory organized.
Napoleon Bonaparte (1769-1821, French General, Emperor)

140 Character is to man what carbon is to steel.
Napoleon Hill (1883-1970, American Speaker, Motivational Writer, "Think and Grow Rich")

141 You can construct the character of a man and his age not only from what he does and says, but from what he fails to say and do.
Norman Douglas (1868-1952, British Author)

142 A character is a completely fashioned will.
Novalis (1772-1801, German Poet, Novelist)

143 Sound character provides the power with which a person may ride the emergencies of life instead of being overwhelmed by them. Failure is... the highway to success.
Og Mandino (1923-1996, American Motivational Author, Speaker)

144 You can preach a better sermon with your life than with your lips.
Oliver Goldsmith (1728-1774, Anglo-Irish Author, Poet, Playwright)

145 Character is the indelible mark that determines the only true value of all people and all their work.
Orison Swett Marden (1850-1924, American Author, Founder of Success Magazine)

146 Underneath this flabby exterior is an enormous lack of character.
Oscar Levant (1906-1972, American Pianist, Actor)

147 It is only the superficial qualities that last. Man's deeper nature is soon found out.
Oscar Wilde (1856-1900, British Author, Wit)

148 Character development is the aim of education.
O'Shea

149 Character in a saint means the disposition of Jesus Christ persistently manifested.
Oswald Chambers (1874-1917 Scottish Preacher, Author)

150 Character is the sum and total of a person's choices.
P. B. Fitzwater

151 I have conquered an empire but I have not been able to conquer myself.
Peter The Great (1672-1725, Tsar of Russia from1682-1721 and Emperor from 1721-5)

152 When men speak ill of thee, live so as nobody may believe them.
Plato (427-347 BC, Greek Philosopher)

153 Character is simply habit long continued.
Plutarch (46-120 AD, Greek Essayist, Biographer)

154 Some people are born hammers, others anvils.
Proverb

155 One can easily judge the character of a person by the way they treat people who can do nothing for them.
Proverb

156 If an ass goes traveling it will not come home a horse.
Proverb

157 Noble character is best appreciated in those ages in which it can most readily develop.
Publius Cornelius Tacitus (55-117 AD, Roman Historian)

158 Though intelligence is powerless to modify character, it is a dab hand at finding euphemisms for its weaknesses.
Quentin Crisp (1908-, British Author)

159 Character is the foundation stone upon which one must build to win respect. Just as no worthy building can be erected on a weak foundation, so no lasting reputation worthy of respect can be built on a weak character.
R. C. Samsel

160 That which we call character is a reserved force which acts directly by presence, and without means. It is conceived of as a certain undemonstrable force, a familiar or genius, by whose impulses the man is guided, but whose counsels he cannot impart.
Ralph Waldo Emerson (1803-1882, American Poet, Essayist)

161 People seem not to see that their opinion of the world is also a confession of character.
Ralph Waldo Emerson (1803-1882, American Poet, Essayist)

162 No change of circumstances can repair a defect of character.
Ralph Waldo Emerson (1803-1882, American Poet, Essayist)

163 Make the most of yourself, for that is all there is of you.
Ralph Waldo Emerson (1803-1882, American Poet, Essayist)

164 Judge of your natural character by what you do in dreams.
Ralph Waldo Emerson (1803-1882, American Poet, Essayist)

165 A character is like an acrostic or Alexandrian stanza; read it forward, backward, or across, it still spells the same thing.
Ralph Waldo Emerson (1803-1882, American Poet, Essayist)

166 Do what you know and perception is converted into character.
Ralph Waldo Emerson (1803-1882, American Poet, Essayist)

167 Gross and obscure natures, however decorated, seem impure shambles; but character gives splendor to youth, and awe to wrinkled skin and gray hairs.
Ralph Waldo Emerson (1803-1882, American Poet, Essayist)

168 Character is higher than intellect. A great soul will be strong to live as well as think.
Ralph Waldo Emerson (1803-1882, American Poet, Essayist)

169 Character is not made in a crisis -- it is only exhibited.
Robert Freeman

170 Property may be destroyed and money may lose its purchasing power; but, character, health, knowledge and good judgment will always be in demand under all conditions.
Roger Babson (1875-1967, American Statistician, Columnist)

171 You can tell a lot about a fellow's character by his way of eating jelly beans.
Ronald Reagan (1911-, Fortieth President of the USA, Actor)

172 The man who cannot believe in himself cannot believe in anything else. The basis of all integrity and character is whatever faith we have in our own integrity.
Roy L. Smith (American Clergyman)

173 Character matters; leadership descends from character.
Rush Limbaugh (1951-, American TV Personality)

174 An excellent man, like precious metal, is in every way invariable; A villain, like the beams of a balance, is always varying, upwards and downwards, himself his own dungeon.
Saskya Pandita (1182-1251, Tibetan Grand Lama of Saskya)

175 Not to be cheered by praise, not to be grieved by blame, but to know thoroughly ones own virtues or powers are the characteristics of an excellent man.
Saskya Pandita (1182-1251, Tibetan Grand Lama of Saskya)

176 Your character will be what you yourself choose to make it.
Sir John Lubbock (1834-1913, British Statesman, Banker, Naturalist)

177 The real character of a man is found out by his amusements.
Sir Joshua Reynolds (1723-1792, British Artist, Critic)

178 Good character is not formed in a week or a month. It is created little by little, day by day. Protracted and patient effort is needed to develop good character.
Sri Swami Sivananda (1887-, Indian Physician, Sage)

179 Temperance is simply a disposition of the mind which binds the passion.
St. Thomas Aquinas (1225-1274, Italian Scholastic Philosopher and Theologian)

180 Our character is basically a composite of our habits. Because they are consistent, often unconscious patterns, they constantly, daily, express our character...
Stephen R. Covey (American Speaker, Trainer, Author of "The 7 Habits of Highly Effective People")

181 It takes a great deal of character strength to apologize quickly out of one's heart rather than out of pity. A person must possess himself and have a deep sense of security in fundamental principles and values in order to genuinely apologize.
Stephen R. Covey (American Speaker, Trainer, Author of "The 7 Habits of Highly Effective People")

182 The measure of a man's real character is what he would do if he knew he would never be found out.
Thomas B. Macaulay (1800-1859, American Essayist and Historian)

183 The happiness of every country depends upon the character of its people, rather than the form of its government.
Thomas C. Haliburton (1796-1865, Canadian Jurist, Author)

184 Show me the man you honor, and I will know what kind of a man you are. It shows me what your ideal of manhood is, and what kind of a man you long to be.
Thomas Carlyle (1795-1881, Scottish Philosopher, Author)

185 It is part of the American character to consider nothing as desperate -- to surmount every difficulty by resolution and contrivance.
Thomas Jefferson (1743-1826, Third President of the USA)

186 Character is much easier kept than recovered.
Thomas Paine (1737-1809, Anglo-American Political Theorist, Writer)

187 Reputation is what men and women think of us. Character is what God and the angels know of us.
Thomas Paine (1737-1809, Anglo-American Political Theorist, Writer)

188 I would rather be adorned by beauty of character than jewels. Jewels are the gift of fortune, while character comes from within.
Titus Maccius Plautus (254-184 BC, Roman Comic Poet)

189 Success is always temporary. When all is said and one, the only thing you'll have left is your character.
Vince Gill (American Country Singer)

190 They attack the one man with their hate and their shower of weapons. But he is like some rock which stretches into the vast sea and which, exposed to the fury of the winds and beaten against by the waves, endures all the violence
Virgil (70-19 BC, Roman Poet)

191 The only way to compel men to speak good of us is to do it.
Voltaire (1694-1778, French Historian, Writer)

192 Nothing endures but personal qualities.
Walt Whitman (1819-1892, American Poet)

193 Between ourselves and our real natures we interpose that wax figure of idealizations and selections which we call our character.
Walter Lippmann (1889-1974, American Journalist)

194 Every human being is intended to have a character of his own; to be what no others are, and to do what no other can do.
William Ellery Channing (1780-1842, American Unitarian Minister, Author)

195 No matter how full a reservoir of maxims one may possess, and no matter how good one's sentiments may be, if one has not taken advantage of every concrete opportunity to act, one's character may remain entirely unaffected for the better.
William James (1842-1910, American Psychologist, Professor, Author)

196 It is well for the world that in most of us, by the age of thirty, the character has set like plaster, and will never soften again.
William James (1842-1910, American Psychologist, Professor, Author)

197 The hell to be endured hereafter, of which theology tells, is no worse than the hell we make for ourselves in this world by habitually fashioned our characters in the wrong way.
William James (1842-1910, American Psychologist, Professor, Author)

198 I have often thought the best way to define a man's character would be to seek out the particular mental or moral attitude in which, when it comes upon him, he felt himself most deeply and intensely active and alive. At such moments there is a voice inside which speaks and says: "This is the real me!".
William James (1842-1910, American Psychologist, Professor, Author)

199 There is never a better measure of what a person is than what he does when he is absolutely free to choose.
William M. Bulger (1934-, American Educator, Senator)

200 If a man character is to be abused there's nobody like a relative to do the business.
William M. Thackeray (1811-1863, Indian-born British Novelist)

201 The empty vessel makes the loudest sound.
William Shakespeare (1564-1616, British Poet, Playwright, Actor)

202 Life every man holds dear; but the dear man holds honor far more precious dear than life.
William Shakespeare (1564-1616, British Poet, Playwright, Actor)

203 Too often the strong, silent man is silent only because he does not know what to say, and is reputed strong only because he has remained silent.
Winston Churchill (1874-1965, British Statesman, Prime Minister)

204 If you will think about what you ought to do for other people, your character will take care of itself. Character is a by-product, and any man who devotes himself to its cultivation in his own case will become a selfish prig.
Woodrow T. Wilson (1856-1924, Twenty-eighth President of the USA)

205 Character is a by-product; it is produced in the great manufacture of daily duty.
Woodrow T. Wilson (1856-1924, Twenty-eighth President of the USA)

CHARITY

1 With malice toward none, with charity for all, with firmness in the right as God gives us to see the right, let us finish the work ;we are in.
Abraham Lincoln (1809-1865, Sixteenth President of the USA)

2 Charity never humiliated him who profited from it, nor ever bound him by the chains of gratitude, since it was not to him but to God that the gift was made.
Antoine De Saint-Exupery (1900-1944, French Aviator, Writer)

3 A man who sees another man on the street corner with only a stump for an arm will be so shocked the first time he'll give him sixpence. But the second time it'll only be a three penny bit. And if he sees him a third time, he'll have him cold-bloodedly handed over to the police.
Bertolt Brecht (1898-1956, German Dramatist, Poet)

4   And now abideth faith, hope and charity, these three, but the greatest of these is charity. [Corinthians]
Bible (Sacred Scriptures of Christians and Judaism)

5   Therefore when thou doest thine alms, do not sound a trumpet before thee, as the hypocrites do in the synagogues and in the streets, that they may have glory of men. Verily I say unto you, they have their reward. But when thou doest alms, let not thy left hand know what thy right hand doeth. [Mathew 6:2-3]
Bible (Sacred Scriptures of Christians and Judaism)

6   And though I bestow all my goods to feed the poor, and though I give my body to be burned, and have not charity, it profiteth me nothing. Charity suffereth long, and is kind; charity envieth not; charity vaunteth not itself, is not puffed up. [New Test.]
Bible (Sacred Scriptures of Christians and Judaism)

7   Though I speak with the tongues of men and angels and have not charity, I am become as sounding brass, or a tinkling cymbal.
Bible (Sacred Scriptures of Christians and Judaism)

8   God loveth a cheerful giver. [2 Corinthians 9:7]
Bible (Sacred Scriptures of Christians and Judaism)

9   If you haven't got any charity in your heart, you have the worst kind of heart trouble.
Bob Hope (1903-, American Comedian, Actor)

10 Posthumous charities are the very essence of selfishness, when bequeathed by those who. when alive, would not have contributed.
Charles Caleb Colton (1780-1832, British Sportsman Writer)

11 Did universal charity prevail, earth would be a heaven, and hell a fable.
Charles Caleb Colton (1780-1832, British Sportsman Writer)

12 Charity begins at home, and justice begins next door.
Charles Dickens (1812-1870, British Novelist)

13 Sometimes when I'm swimming, I think that maybe someday I'll put my red Speedo up for auction. Or maybe I'll donate it to the Smithsonian. They can stuff it with two plums and a gherkin and put it on display.
David Duchovny (1960-, American Actor)

14 Charity: a thing that begins at home, and usually stays there.
Elbert Hubbard (1859-1915, American Author, Publisher)

15 Having leveled my palace, don't erect a hovel and complacently admire your own charity in giving me that for a home.
Emily Bronte (1818-1848, British Novelist, Poet)

16 Not he who has much is rich, but he who gives much.
Erich Fromm (1900-1980, American Psychologist)

17 Should we grieve over a little misplaced charity, when an all knowing, all wise Being showers down every day his benefits on the unthankful and undeserving?
Francis Atterbury (1663-1732, British Anglican Clergyman, Controversialist)

18 In charity there is no excess.
Francis Bacon (1561-1626, British Philosopher, Essayist, Statesman)

19 The living need charity more than the dead.
George Arnold

20 Charity sees the need, not the cause.
German Proverb

21 If you give money, spend yourself with it.
Henry David Thoreau (1817-1862, American Essayist, Poet, Naturalist)

22 A rich man without charity is a rogue; and perhaps it would be no difficult matter to prove that he is also a fool.
Henry Fielding (1707-1754, British Novelist, Dramatist)

23 The truly generous is the truly wise, and he who loves not others, lives unblest.
Henry Home

24 Every charitable act is a stepping stone towards heaven.
Henry Ward Beecher (1813-1887, American Preacher, Orator, Writer)

25 To pity distress is but human; to relieve it is Godlike.
Horace Mann (1796-1859, American Educator)

26 The highest exercise of charity is charity towards the uncharitable.
J. S. Buckminster

27 A bone to the dog is not charity. Charity is the bone shared with the dog, when you are just as hungry as the dog.
Jack London (1876-1916, American Novelist)

28 Only great souls know the grandeur there is in charity.
Jacques BTNigne Bossuet (1627-1704, Catholic Churchman, Pulpit Orator)

29 The giving is the hardest part; what does it cost to add a smile?
Jean De La Bruyere (1645-1696, French Writer)

30 The organized charity, scrimped and iced, in the name of a cautious, statistical Christ.
John Boyle O'Reilly (1844-1890, Irish Author)

31 Charity is injurious unless it helps the recipient to become independent of it.
John D. Rockefeller (1839-1937, American Industrialist, Philanthropist, Founder Exxon)

32 The beginning and almost the end of all good law is that everyone shall work for their bread and receive good bread for their work.
John Ruskin (1819-1900, British Critic, Social Theorist)

33 As for charity, it is a matter in which the immediate effect on the persons directly concerned, and the ultimate consequence to the general good, are apt to be at complete war with one another.
John Stuart Mill (1806-1873, British Philosopher, Economist)

34 Nothing is so hard for those who abound in riches to conceive how others can be in want.
Jonathan Swift (1667-1745, Anglo-Irish Satirist)

35 Be charitable and indulge to everyone, but thyself.
Joseph Joubert (1754-1824, French Moralist)

36 The appalling thing is the degree of charity women are capable of. You see it all the time... love lavished on absolute fools. Love's a charity ward, you know.
Lawrence Durrell (1912-1990, British Author)

37 I have always heard, Sancho, that doing good to base fellows is like throwing water into the sea.
Miguel De Cervantes (1547-1616, Spanish Novelist, Dramatist, Poet)

38 We ourselves feel that what we are doing is just a drop in the ocean. But if that drop was not in the ocean, I think the ocean would be less because of that missing drop. I do not agree with the big way of doing things.
Mother Teresa (1910-1997, Albanian-born Roman Catholic Missionary)

39 They take the paper and they read the headlines. So they've heard of unemployment and they've heard of bread-lines. And they philanthropically cure them all by getting up a costume charity ball.
Ogden Nash (1902-1971, American Humorous Poet)

40 Charity creates a multitude of sins.
Oscar Wilde (1856-1900, British Author, Wit)

41 To give requires good sense.
Ovid (43 BC-18 AD, Roman Poet)

42 Charity should begin at home, but should not stay there.
Phillips Brooks (1835-1893, American Minister, Poet)

43 The charitable give out the door and God puts it back through the window.
Proverb

44 Do not tell me of my obligation to put all poor men in good situations. Are they my poor? I tell thee, thou foolish philanthropist, that I grudge the dollar, the dime, the cent, I give to such men as do not belong to me and to whom I do not belong.
Ralph Waldo Emerson (1803-1882, American Poet, Essayist)

45 Give no bounties: make equal laws: secure life and prosperity and you need not give alms.
Ralph Waldo Emerson (1803-1882, American Poet, Essayist)

46 The best loved by God are those that are rich, yet have the humility of the poor, and those that are poor and have the magnanimity of the rich.
Saadi

47 You are much surer that you are doing good when you pay money to those who work, as the recompense of their labor, than when you give money merely in charity.
Samuel Johnson (1709-1784, British Author)

48 He who waits to do a great deal of good at once, will never do anything.
Samuel Johnson (1709-1784, British Author)

49 Charity. To love human beings in so far as they are nothing. That is to love them as God does.
Simone Weil (1910-1943, French Philosopher, Mystic)

50 Be charitable before wealth makes you covetous.
Sir Thomas Browne (1605-1682, British Author, Physician,, Philosopher)

51 Charity But how shall we expect charity towards others, when we are uncharitable to ourselves? Charity begins at home, is the voice of the world; yet is every man his greatest enemy, and, as it were, his own executioner.
Sir Thomas Browne (1605-1682, British Author, Physician,, Philosopher)

52 Charity is no substitute for justice withheld.
St. Augustine (354-430, Numidian-born Bishop of Hippo, Theologian)

53 Teach us to give and not count the cost.
St. Ignatius Loyola (1495-1556, Spanish Theologian, Founder of the Jesuits)

54 Charity is the scope of all God's commands.
St. John Chrysosatom (345-407, Patriarch of Constantinople)

55 Prayer carries us half way to God, fasting brings us to the door of His palace, and alms-giving procures us admission.
The Koran (500 AD, Islamic Religious Bible)

56 Charity begins at home, but should not end there.
Thomas Fuller (1608-1661, British Clergyman, Author)

57 As the purse is emptied, the heart is filled.
Victor Hugo (1802-1885, French Poet, Dramatist, Novelist)

58 It is more agreeable to have the power to give than to receive.
Winston Churchill (1874-1965, British Statesman, Prime Minister)

CHARM

1 Charm is a way of getting the answer yes without having asked any clear question.
Albert Camus (1913-1960, French Existential Writer)

2 The charm of history and its enigmatic lesson consist in the fact that, from age to age, nothing changes and yet everything is completely different.
Aldous Huxley (1894-1963, British Author)

3 A man of such obvious and exemplary charm must be a liar.
Anita Brookner (1938-, British Novelist, Art Historian)

4 Marvelous is the power which can be exercised, almost unconsciously, over a company, or an individual, or even upon a crowd by one person gifted with good temper, good digestion, good intellects, and good looks.
Anthony Trollope (1815-1882, British Novelist)

5 All charming people have something to conceal, usually their total dependence on the appreciation of others.
Cyril Connolly (1903-1974, British Critic)

6 A plain woman is one who, however beautiful, neglects to charm.
Edgar Saltus

7 If most men and women were forced to rely upon physical charm to attract lovers, their sexual lives would be not only meager but in a youth-worshiping country like America painfully brief.
Gore Vidal (1925-, American Novelist, Critic)

8 Charm is the quality in others that makes us more satisfied with ourselves.
Henri Frederic Amiel (1821-1881, Swiss Philosopher, Poet, Critic)

9 There is no personal charm so great as the charm of a cheerful temperament.
Henry Van Dyke (1852-1933, American Protestant Clergyman, Poet and Writer)

10 Charm is a glow within a woman which casts a most becoming light on others.
John Mason Brown (1800-1859, American Militant Abolitionist)

11 Charm is a product of the unexpected.
Jose Marti (1853-1895, Cuban Patriot, National Hero)

12 Charming people live up to the very edge of their charm, and behave as outrageously as the world lets them.
Logan Pearsall Smith (1865-1946, Anglo-American Essayist, Aphorist)

13 The charms of the passing woman are generally in direct proportion to the swiftness of her passing.
Marcel Proust (1871-1922, French Novelist)

14 Rarity gives a charm; so early fruits and winter roses are the most prized; and coyness sets off an extravagant mistress, while the door always open tempts no suitor.
Marcus Valerius Martial (40-104, Latin poet and epigrammatist)

15 It's absurd to divide people into good and bad. People are either charming or tedious.
Oscar Wilde (1856-1900, British Author, Wit)

16 All charming people, I fancy, are spoiled. It is the secret of their attraction.
Oscar Wilde (1856-1900, British Author, Wit)

17 No one has it who isn't capable of genuinely liking others, at least at the actual moment of meeting and speaking. Charm is always genuine; it may be superficial but it isn't false.
P. D. James (1920-, British Mystery Writer)

18 Things forbidden have a secret charm.
Publius Cornelius Tacitus (55-117 AD, Roman Historian)

19 There are charms made only for distance admiration.
Samuel Johnson (1709-1784, British Author)

20 Faces that have charmed us the most escape us the soonest.
Sir Walter Scott (1771-1832, British Novelist, Poet)

21 I am bewitched with the rogue's company. If the rascal have not given me medicines to make me love him, I'll be hanged.
William Shakespeare (1564-1616, British Poet, Playwright, Actor)

22 Charm is more than beauty.
Yiddish Proverb

CHASTITY

1 How happy is the blameless vestal's lot? The world forgetting, by the world forgot.
Alexander Pope (1688-1744, British Poet, Critic, Translator)

2 Much of the modern resistance to chastity comes from men's belief that they "own" their bodies -- those vast and perilous estates, pulsating with the energy that made the worlds, in which they find themselves without their consent and from which they are ejected at the pleasure of Another!
C. S. Lewis (1898-1963, British Academic, Writer, Christian Apologist)

3 There are no chaste minds. Minds copulate wherever they meet.
Eric Hoffer (1902-1983, American Author, Philosopher)

4 There are few virtuous women who are not bored with their trade.
François de La Rochefoucauld (1613-1680, French classical writer)

5 These people abstain, it is true: but the bitch Sensuality glares enviously out of all they do.
Friedrich Nietzsche (1844-1900, German Philosopher)

6 It is fatally easy for Western folk, who have discarded chastity as a value for themselves, to suppose that it can have no value for anyone else. At the same time as Californians try to re-invent "celibacy," by which they seem to mean perverse restraint, the rest of us call societies which place a high value on chastity "backward."
Germaine Greer (1939-, Australian Feminist Writer)

7 Chastity does not mean abstention from sexual wrong; it means something flaming, like Joan of Arc.
Gilbert K. Chesterton (1874-1936, British Author)

8 The generative energy, which, when we are loose, dissipates and makes us unclean, when we are continent invigorates and inspires us. Chastity is the flowering of man; and what are called Genius, Heroism, Holiness, and the like, are but various fruits which succeed it.
Henry David Thoreau (1817-1862, American Essayist, Poet, Naturalist)

9 God hath prepared a little coronet or special reward (extraordinary and beside the great crown of all faithful souls) for those who have not defiled themselves with women.
Jeremy Taylor (1613-1667, British Churchman, Writer)

10   'Tis chastity, my brother, chastity. She that has that is clad in complete steel, and like a quivered nymph with arrows keen may trace huge forests and unharbored heaths, infamous hills and sandy perilous wilds, where through the sacred rays of chastity, no savage fierce, bandit, or mountaineer will dare to soil her virgin purity.
John Milton (1608-1674, British Poet)

11   Chastity is the cement of civilization and progress. Without it there is no stability in society, and without it one cannot attain the Science of Life.
Mary Baker Eddy (1821-1910, American Christian Writer, Founder of Christian Science Church)

12   An unattempted lady could not vaunt of her chastity.
Michel Eyquem De Montaigne (1533-1592, French Philosopher, Essayist)

13   A woman's chastity consists, like an onion, of a series of coats.
Nathaniel Hawthorne (1804-1864, American Novelist, Short Story Writer)

14   Chastity is a monkish and evangelical superstition, a greater foe to natural temperance even than unintellectual sensuality.
Percy Bysshe Shelley (1792-1822, British Poet)

15   Your old virginity is like one of our French withered pears: it looks ill, it eats dryly.
William Shakespeare (1564-1616, British Poet, Playwright, Actor)

CHEATING

1   Cheat me in the price, but not in the goods.
English Proverb

2   It was beautiful and simple as all truly great swindles are.
O. Henry Porter (1862-1910, American short-story Writer)

3   So cheat your landlord if you can and must, but do not try to shortchange the Muse. It cannot be done. You can't fake quality any more than you can fake a good meal.
William S. Burroughs (1914-1997, American Writer)

4   For nothing can seem foul to those that win.
William Shakespeare (1564-1616, British Poet, Playwright, Actor)

CHEERFULNESS

1   Developing a cheerful disposition can permit an atmosphere wherein one's spirit can be nurtured and encouraged to blossom and bear fruit. Being pessimistic and negative about our experiences will not enhance the quality of our lives. A determination to be of good cheer can help us and those around us to enjoy life more fully.
Barbara W. Winder

2   A cheerful face is nearly as good for an invalid as healthy weather.
Benjamin Franklin (1706-1790, American Scientist, Publisher, Diplomat)

3   I feel an earnest and humble desire, and shall till I die, to increase the stock of harmless cheerfulness.
Charles Dickens (1812-1870, British Novelist)

4   Cheerfulness and contentment are great beautifiers and are famous preservers of youthful looks.
Charles Dickens (1812-1870, British Novelist)

5   The cheerful live longest in years, and afterwards in our regards. Cheerfulness is the off-shoot of goodness.
Christian Nevell Bovee (1820-1904, American Author, Lawyer)

6   Cheerfulness in most cheerful people, is the rich and satisfying result of strenuous discipline.
Edwin P. Whipple (1819-1886, American Essayist)

7   The truest greatness lies in being kind, the truest wisdom in a happy mind.
Ella Wheeler Wilcox (1855-1919, American Poet, Journalist)

8   Delicate humor is the crowning virtue of the saints.
Evelyn Underhill

9   To be free minded and cheerfully disposed at hours of meat and sleep and of exercise is one of the best precepts of long lasting.
Francis Bacon (1561-1626, British Philosopher, Essayist, Statesman)

10   To watch the corn grow, or the blossoms set; to draw hard breath over the plough or spade; to read, to think, to love, to pray, are the things that make men happy.
John Ruskin (1819-1900, British Critic, Social Theorist)

11   Cheerfulness is the best promoter of health and is as friendly to the mind as to the body.
Joseph Addison (1672-1719, British Essayist, Poet, Statesman)

12   I always cheer up immensely if an attack is particularly wounding because I think, well, if they attack one personally, it means they have not a single political argument left.
Margaret Thatcher (1925-, British Stateswoman, Prime Minister (1979-90))

13   The best way to cheer yourself up is to try to cheer somebody else up.
Mark Twain (1835-1910, American Humorist, Writer)

14   In making up the character of God, the old theologians failed to mention that He is of infinite cheerfulness. The omission has caused the world much tribulation.
Michael Monahan

15   The most manifest sign of wisdom is a continual cheerfulness; her state is like that in the regions above the moon, always clear and serene.
Michel Eyquem De Montaigne (1533-1592, French Philosopher, Essayist)

16   The most certain sign of wisdom is cheerfulness.
Michel Eyquem De Montaigne (1533-1592, French Philosopher, Essayist)

17   The true source of cheerfulness is benevolence.
P. Godwin

18   Cheer up! The worst is yet to come!
Philander Johnson

19   So of cheerfulness, or a good temper, the more it is spent, the more it remains.
Ralph Waldo Emerson (1803-1882, American Poet, Essayist)

20   People are always good company when they are doing what they really enjoy.
Samuel Butler (1612-1680, British Poet, Satirist)

21   I went out to Charing Cross to see Major General Harrison hanged, drawn, and quartered; which was done there, he looking as cheerful as any man could in that condition.
Samuel Pepys (1633-1703, British Diarist)

22   A happy family is but an earlier heaven.
Sir John Bowring (1792-1872, British Statesman, Linguist)

23   O Holy Spirit, descend plentifully into my heart. Enlighten the dark corners of this neglected dwelling and scatter there Thy cheerful beams.
St. Augustine (354-430, Numidian-born Bishop of Hippo, Theologian)

24   It is not fitting, when one is in God's service, to have a gloomy face or a chilling look.
St. Francis of Assisi (1181-1226, Italian Preacher, Founder of the Franciscan Orde)

25   Wondrous is the strength of cheerfulness, and its power of endurance -- the cheerful man will do more in the same time, will do it ;better, will preserve it longer, than the sad or sullen.
Thomas Carlyle (1795-1881, Scottish Philosopher, Author)

26   Oh, give us the man who sings at his work.
Thomas Carlyle (1795-1881, Scottish Philosopher, Author)

27   An ounce of cheerfulness is worth a pound of sadness to serve God with.
Thomas Fuller (1608-1661, British Clergyman, Author)

28   Happiness is essentially a state of going somewhere wholeheartedly, one-directionally, without regret or reservation.
W. H. Sheldon

29   Thus the sovereign voluntary path to cheerfulness, if cheerfulness be lost, is to sit up cheerfully and to act and speak as if cheerfulness were already there.
William James (1842-1910, American Psychologist, Professor, Author)

30   The path to cheerfulness is to sit cheerfully and to act and speak as if cheerfulness were already there.
William James (1842-1910, American Psychologist, Professor, Author)

31   The voluntary path to cheerfulness, if our spontaneous be lost, is to sit up cheerfully, and act and speak as if cheerfulness wee already there. To feel brave, act as if we were brave, use all our will to that end, and courage will very likely replace fear. If we act as if from some better feeling, the bad feeling soon folds its tent like an Arab and silently steals away
William Shakespeare (1564-1616, British Poet, Playwright, Actor)

CHEMISTRY

1   There's nothing colder than chemistry.
Anita Loos (1893-1981, American Novelist, Screenwriter)

2   I feel like a white granular mass of amorphous crystals -- my formula appears to be isomeric with Spasmotoxin. My aurochloride precipitates into beautiful prismatic needles. My Platinochloride develops octahedron crystals, -- with a fine blue florescence. My physiological action is not indifferent. One millionth of a grain injected under the skin of a frog produced instantaneous death accompanied by an orange blossom odor.
Lafcadio Hearn (1850-1904 Greek Writer and Translator)

3   For me chemistry represented an indefinite cloud of future potentialities which enveloped my life to come in black volutes torn by fiery flashes, like those which had hidden Mount Sinai. Like Moses, from that cloud I expected my law, the principle of order in me, around me, and in the world. I would watch the buds swell in spring, the mica glint in the granite, my own hands, and I would say to myself: "I will understand this, too, I will understand everything."
Primo Levi (1919-1987, Italian Chemist, Author)

CHESS

1   Women, by their nature, are not exceptional chess players: they are not great fighters.
Gary Kasparov

2   Life's too short for chess.
Henry J. Byron

3   The chess pieces are the block alphabet which shapes thoughts; and these thoughts, although making a visual design on the chess-board, express their beauty abstractly, like a poem... I have come to the personal conclusion that while all artists are not chess players, all chess players are artists.
Marcel Duchamp (1887-1968, French Artist)

4   I am still a victim of chess. It has all the beauty of art -- and much more. It cannot be commercialized. Chess is much purer than art in its social position.
Marcel Duchamp (1887-1968, French Artist)

5   Chess is ruthless: you've got to be prepared to kill people.
Nigel Short

CHILDHOOD

1 Let a man turn to his own childhood -- no further -- if he will renew his sense of remoteness, and of the mystery of change.
Alice Meynell (1847-1922, British Poet, Essayist)

2 Heaven lies about us in our infancy and the world begins lying about us pretty soon afterward.
Ambrose Bierce (1842-1914, American Author, Editor, Journalist, "The Devil's Dictionary")

3 There is always one moment in childhood when the door opens and lets the future in.
Deepak Chopra (East-Indian- American M.D., New Age Author, Lecturer)

4 Childhood is the kingdom where nobody dies. Nobody that matters, that is.
Edna St. Vincent Millay (1892-1950, American Poet)

5 The stories of childhood leave an indelible impression, and their author always has a niche in the temple of memory from which the image is never cast out to be thrown on the rubbish heap of things that are outgrown and outlived.
Howard Pyle

6 The childhood shows the man, as morning shows the day.
John Milton (1608-1674, British Poet)

7 Seven to eleven is a huge chunk of life, full of dulling and forgetting. It is fabled that we slowly lose the gift of speech with animals, that birds no longer visit our windowsills to converse. As our eyes grow accustomed to sight they armor themselves against wonder.
Leonard Cohen (1934-, Canadian-born American Musician, Songwriter, Singer)

8 But childhood prolonged, cannot remain a fairyland. It becomes a hell.
Louise Bogan (1897-1970, American Poet, Critic)

9 There are perhaps no days of our childhood we lived so fully as those we spent with a favorite book.
Marcel Proust (1871-1922, French Novelist)

10 What a man takes in by contemplation, that he pours out in love.
Meister Eckhart (1260-1326 AD, German Mystic)

11 What might be taken for a precocious genius is the genius of childhood. When the child grows up, it disappears without a trace. It may happen that this boy will become a real painter some day, or even a great painter. But then he will have to begin everything again, from zero.
Pablo Picasso (1881-1973, Spanish Artist)

12 Is it not strange, that an infant should be heir of the whole world, and see those mysteries which the books of the learned never unfold?
Thomas Traherne (1636-1674, British Clergyman, Poet, Mystic)

13 I am convinced that, except in a few extraordinary cases, one form or another of an unhappy childhood is essential to the formation of exceptional gifts.
Thornton Wilder (1897-1975, American Novelist, Playwright)

14 That great Cathedral space which was childhood.
Virginia Woolf (1882-1941, British Novelist, Essayist)

15 Childhood is a disease -- a sickness that you grow out of.
William Golding (1911-1993, British Author)

16 Come children, let us shut up the box and the puppets, for our play is played out.
William M. Thackeray (1811-1863, Indian-born British Novelist)

17 Heaven lies about us in our infancy! Shades of the prison-house begin to close upon the growing boy.
William Wordsworth (1770-1850, British Poet)

CHILDREN

1 A little less worry over the child and a bit more concern about the world we make for the child to live in.
Adolph Meyer

2 My children cause me the most exquisite suffering of which I have any experience. It is the suffering of ambivalence: the murderous alternation between bitter resentment and raw-edged nerves, and blissful gratification and tenderness. Sometimes I seem to myself, in my feelings toward these tiny guiltless beings, a monster of selfishness and intolerance.
Adrienne Rich (1929-, American Poet)

3 Young people should be helped, sheltered, ignored, and clubbed of necessary.
Al Capp (1909-1979, American Cartoonist)

4 There are few successful adults who were not first successful children.
Alexander Chase

5 Behold the child, by nature's kindly law, pleased with a rattle, tickled with a straw.
Alexander Pope (1688-1744, British Poet, Critic, Translator)

6 It needs courage to let our children go, but we are trustees and stewards and have to hand them back to life--to God. As the old saying puts it: "What I gave I have." We have to love them and lose them.
Alfred Torrie

7 A child is beset with long traditions. And his infancy is so old, so old, that the mere adding of years in the life to follow will not seem to throw it further back -- it is already so far.
Alice Meynell (1847-1922, British Poet, Essayist)

8   What the vast majority of American children needs is to stop being pampered, stop being indulged, stop being chauffeured, stop being catered to. In the final analysis it is not what you do for your children but what you have taught them to do for themselves that will make them successful human beings.
Ann Landers (1918-, American Advice Columnist)

9   Childhood sometimes does pay a second visit to man; youth never.
Anna Jameson (1794-1860, British Essayist)

10 There is no sinner like a young saint.
Aphra Behn (1640-1689, British Playwright, Poet)

11 Before you beat a child, be sure yourself are not the cause of the offense.
Austin O'Malley

12 A child is not a salmon mousse. A child is a temporarily disabled and stunted version of a larger person, whom you will someday know. Your job is to help them overcome the disabilities associated with their size and inexperience so that they get on with being that larger person.
Barbara Ehrenreich (1941-, American Author, Columnist)

13 A society in which adults are estranged from the world of children, and often from their own childhood, tends to hear children's speech only as a foreign language, or as a lie. Children have been treated. as congenital fibbers, fakers and fantasisers.
Beatrix Campbell (1947-, British Journalist)

14 It is amazing how quickly the kids learn to drive a car, yet are unable to understand the lawnmower, snow-blower, or vacuum cleaner.
Ben Bergor

15 Let the child's first lesson be obedience, and the second will be what thou wilt.
Benjamin Franklin (1706-1790, American Scientist, Publisher, Diplomat)

16 The more people have studied different methods of bringing up children the more they have come to the conclusion that what good mother and fathers instinctively feel like doing for their babies is the best after all.
Benjamin Spock (1903-, American Pediatrician)

17 Discipline is a symbol of caring to a child. He needs guidance. If there is love, there is no such thing as being too tough with a child. A parent must also not be afraid to hang himself. If you have never been hated by your child, you have never been a parent.
Bette Davis (1908-1989, American Actress, Producer)

18 Strange new problems are being reported in the growing generations of children whose mothers were always there, driving them around, helping them with their homework --an inability to endure pain or discipline or pursue any self-sustained goal of any sort, a devastating boredom with life.
Betty Friedan (1921-, American Feminist Writer)

19 Wen I was a child, I spoke as a child, I thought as a child: but when I became a man I put away   my childish things. [I Corinthians]
Bible (Sacred Scriptures of Christians and Judaism)

20 It were better for him that a millstone were hanged about his neck, and he cast into the sea, than that he should offend one of these little ones. [Luke 17:2]
Bible (Sacred Scriptures of Christians and Judaism)

21 Foolishness is bound in the heart of a child; but the rod of correction shall drive it far from him. [Proverbs 22:15]
Bible (Sacred Scriptures of Christians and Judaism)

22 Even though your kids will consistently do the exact opposite of what you're telling them to do, you have to keep loving them just as much.
Bill Cosby (1937-, American Actor, Comedian, Producer)

23 A three year old child is a being who gets almost as much fun out of a fifty-six dollar set of swings as it does out of finding a small green worm.
Bill Vaughan (1915-1977, American Author, Journalist)

24 Grown men can learn from very little children for the hearts of little children are pure. Therefore, the Great Spirit may show to them many things which older people miss.
Black Elk (19th Century American Native Religious Leader)

25 Kids are wonderful, but I like mine barbecued.
Bob Hope (1903-, American Comedian, Actor)

26 It's fun being a kid.
Bradford Arthur Angier

27 If you raise your children to feel that they can accomplish any goal or task they decide upon, you will have succeeded as a parent and you will have given your children the greatest of all blessings.
Brian Tracy (American Trainer, Speaker, Author, Businessman)

28 Children have more need of models than of critics.
Carolyn Coats

29 The first duty to children is to make them happy, If you have not made them so, you have wronged them, No other good they may get can make up for that.
Charles Buxton (1823-1871, British Author)

30 When I consider how little of a rarity children are -- that every street and blind alley swarms with them -- that the poorest people commonly have them in most abundance -- that there are few marriages that are not blest with at least one of these bargains -- how often they turn out ill, and defeat the fond hopes of their parents, taking to vicious courses, which end in poverty, disgrace, the gallows, etc. -- I cannot for my life tell what cause for pride there can possibly be in having them.
Charles Lamb (1775-1834, British Essayist, Critic)

31 Do not confine your children to your own learning, for they were born in another time.
Chinese Proverb

32 Many children, many cares; no children, no felicity.
Christian Nevell Bovee (1820-1904, American Author, Lawyer)

33 We've had bad luck with our kids -- they've all grown up.
Christopher Morley (1890-1957, American Novelist, Journalist, Poet)

34 Viewing the child solely as an immature person is a way of escaping comforting him.
Clark Moustakas (Humanistic Psychologist)

35 It is dangerous to confuse children with angels.
David Fyfe (1900-1967, British Statesman, Jurist)

36 Children always turn to the light.
David Hare (1947-, British Playwright, Director)

37 The only moral lesson which is suited for a child, the most important lesson for every time of life, is this: "Never hurt anybody."
Denis Breeze

38 Listen to the desires of your children. Encourage them and then give them the autonomy to make their own decision.
Denis Waitley (1933-, American Author, Speaker, Trainer, Peak Performance Expert)

39 You should study not only that you become a mother when your child is born, but also that you become a child.
Dogen

40 The best way to keep children at home is to make the home a pleasant atmosphere and let the air out of the tires.
Dorothy Parker (1893-1967, American Humorous Writer)

41 Children are not casual guests in our home. They have been loaned to us temporarily for the purpose of loving them and instilling a foundation of values on which their future lives will be built.
Dr. James C. Dobson (American Psychologist, Author)

42 Don't throw away your friendship with your teenager over behavior that has no great moral significance. There will be plenty of real issues that require you to stand like a rock. Save your big guns for those crucial confrontations.
Dr. James C. Dobson (American Psychologist, Author)

43 We inevitably doom our children to failure and frustration when we try to set their goals for them.
Dr. Jess Lair (American Professor, Counselor)

44 Adults are obsolete children.
Dr. Seuss (1904-1991, American Writer and Illustrator of Children's Books)

45 There's no point in being grown up if you cant be childish sometimes.
Dr. Who

46 It takes three to make a child.
E.E. (Edward. E.) Cummings (1894-1962, American Poet)

47 In all our efforts to provide "advantages" we have actually produced the busiest, most competitive, highly pressured, and over-organized generation of youngsters in our history."
Eda J. Le Shan (1922-, American Educator, Author)

48 Families with babies and families without babies are sorry for each other.
Edgar Watson Howe (1853-1937, American Journalist, Author)

49 Adults find pleasure in deceiving a child. They consider it necessary, but they also enjoy it. The children very quickly figure it out and then practice deception themselves.
Elias Canetti (1905-, Austrian Novelist, Philosopher)

50 Once you bring life into the world, you must protect it. We must protect it by changing the world.
Elie Wiesel (1928-, Rumanian-born American Writer)

51 But the child's sob curses deeper in the silence than the strong man in his wrath!
Elizabeth Barrett Browning (1806-1861, British Poet)

52 For success in training children the first condition is to become as a child oneself, but this means no assumed childishness, no condescending baby-talk that the child immediately sees through and deeply abhors. What it does mean is to be as entirely and simply taken up with the child as the child himself is absorbed by his life.
Ellen Key (1849-1926, Swedish Author, Feminist)

53 Children suck the mother when they are young and the father when they are old.
English Proverb

54 Better a snotty child than his nose wiped off.
English Proverb

55 Who is not attracted by bright and pleasant children, to prattle, to creep, and to play with them?
Epictetus (50-120, Stoic Philosopher)

56 It goes without saying that you should never have more children than you have car windows.
Erma Bombeck (1927-, American Author, Humorist)

57 Never lend your car to anyone to whom you have given birth.
Erma Bombeck (1927-, American Author, Humorist)

58 Children are excellent observers, and will often perceive your slightest defects. In general, those who govern children, forgive nothing in them, but everything in themselves.
François Fénelon (1651-1715, French Roman Catholic archbishop, theologian, poet and writer)

59 You can learn many things from children. How much patience you have, for instance.
Franklin P. Jones

60 Children are unpredictable. You never know what inconsistency they're going to catch you in next.
Franklin P. Jones

61 She discovered with great delight that one does not love one's children just because they are one's children but because of the friendship formed while raising them.
Gabriel Garcia Marquez (1928-, Colombian Writer)

62 Nothing you do for children is ever wasted. They seem not to notice us, hovering, averting our eyes, and they seldom offer thanks, but what we do for them is never wasted.
Garrison Keillor (1942-, American Humorous Writer, Radio Performer)

63 Even a minor event in the life of a child is an event of that child's world and thus a world event.
Gaston Bachelard (1884-1962, French Scientist, Philosopher, Literary Theorist)

64 Ignorance... is a painless evil; so, I should think, is dirt, considering the merry faces that go along with it.
George Eliot (1819-1880, British Novelist)

65 We are given children to test us and make us more spiritual.
George F. Will (1941-, American Political Columnist)

66 One can love a child, perhaps, more deeply than one can love another adult, but it is rash to assume that the child feels any love in return.
George Orwell (1903-1950, British Author, "Animal Farm")

67 We in the West do not refrain from childbirth because we are concerned about the population explosion or because we feel we cannot afford children, but because we do not like children.
Germaine Greer (1939-, Australian Feminist Writer)

68 Never have children, only grand children.
Gore Vidal (1925-, American Novelist, Critic)

69 Unhappiness in a child accumulates because he sees no end to the dark tunnel. The thirteen weeks of a term might just as well be thirteen years.
Graham Greene (1904-1991, British Novelist)

70 My mother loved children -- she would have given anything if I had been one.
Groucho Marx (1895-1977, American Comic Actor)

71 You save an old man and you save a unit; but save a boy, and you save a multiplication table.
Gypsy Smith

72 Children need love, especially when they don't deserve it.
Harold Hulbert

73 We must teach our children to dream with their eyes open.
Harry Edwards

74 I have found the best way to give advice to your children is to find out what they want and then advise them to do it.
Harry S. Truman (1884-1972, Thirty-third President of the USA)

75 When children are doing nothing, they are doing mischief.
Henry Fielding (1707-1754, British Novelist, Dramatist)

76 Ah! what would the world be to us If the children were no more? We should dread the desert behind us Worse than the dark before.
Henry Wadsworth Longfellow (1819-1892, American Poet)

77 A torn jacket is soon mended; but hard words bruise the heart of a child.
Henry Wadsworth Longfellow (1819-1892, American Poet)

78 Children are our most valuable natural resource.
Herbert Clark Hoover (1874-1964, American - 31st American President)

79 Each child is an adventure into a better life --an opportunity to change the old pattern and make it new.
Hubert H. Humphrey (1911-1978, American Democratic Politician, Vice President)

80 Birds in their little nest agree; and 'Tis a shameful sight, when children of one family fall out, and chide, and fight.
Isaac Watts (1674-1748, British hymn-writer)

81 The finest inheritance you can give to a child is to allow it to make its own way, completely on its own feet.
Isadora Duncan (1878-1927, American Dancer)

82 So long as little children are allowed to suffer, there is no true love in this world.
Isadora Duncan (1878-1927, American Dancer)

83 I believe in making the world safe for our children, but not our children's children, because I don't think children should be having sex.
Jack Handey

84 Children have never been very good at listening to their elders, but they have never failed to imitate them.
James Baldwin (1924-1987, American Author)

85 There is a "sanctity" involved with bringing a child into this world: it is better than bombing one out of it.
James Baldwin (1924-1987, American Author)

86 A young and vital child knows no limit to his own will, and it is the only reality to him. It is not that he wants at the outset to fight other wills, but that they simply do not exist for him. Like the artist, he goes forth to the work of creation, gloriously alone.
Jane Harrison (1850-1928, British Classical Scholar, Writer)

87 Children enjoy the present because they have neither a past nor a future.
Jean De La Bruyere (1645-1696, French Writer)

88 Childhood is the sleep of reason.
Jean Jacques Rousseau (1712-1778, Swiss Political Philosopher, Educationist, Essayist)

89 The training of children is a profession, where we must know how to waste time in order to save it"
Jean Jacques Rousseau (1712-1778, Swiss Political Philosopher, Educationist, Essayist)

90 No man can tell but he that loves his children, how many delicious accents make a man's heart dance in the pretty conversation of those dear pledges; their childishness, their stammering, their little angers, their innocence, their imperfections, their necessities, are so many little emanations of joy and comfort to him that delights in their persons and society.
Jeremy Taylor (1613-1667, British Churchman, Writer)

91 Your children need your presence more than your presents.
Jesse Jackson (1941-, American Clergyman, Civil Rights Leader)

92 If children grew up according to early indications, we should have nothing but geniuses.
Johann Wolfgang Von Goethe (1749-1832, German Poet, Dramatist, Novelist)

93 We cannot fashion our children after our desires, we must have them and love them as God has given them to us.
Johann Wolfgang Von Goethe (1749-1832, German Poet, Dramatist, Novelist)

94 As much as I converse with sages and heroes, they have very little of my love and admiration. I long for rural and domestic scene, for the warbling of birds and the prattling of my children
John Adams (1735-1826, Second President of the USA)

95 Children are curious and are risk takers. They have lots of courage. They venture out into a world that is immense and dangerous. A child initially trusts life and the processes of life.
John Bradshaw (American Author, Lecturer, Leading Expert, Recovery & Dysfunctional Families)

96 A child miseducated is a child lost.
John F. Kennedy (1917-1963, Thirty-fifth President of the USA)

97 You know children are growing up when they start asking questions that have answers.
John Plomp

98 Children are poor men's riches.
John Ray (1627-1705, British Naturalist)

99 The distinctive character of a child is to always live in the tangible present.
John Ruskin (1819-1900, British Critic, Social Theorist)

100 Children see in their parents the past, their parents see in them the future; and if we find more love in the parents for their children than in children for their parents, this is sad but natural. Who does not entertain his hopes more than his recollections.
John Ruskin (1819-1900, British Critic, Social Theorist)

101 In great countries, children are always trying to remain children, and the parents want to make them into adults. In vile countries, the children are always wanting to be adults and the parents want to keep them children.
John Ruskin (1819-1900, British Critic, Social Theorist)

102 If men do not keep on speaking terms with children, they cease to be men, and become merely machines for eating and for earning money.
John Updike (1932-, American Novelist, Critic)

103 Before I got married, I had six theories about bringing up children. Now I have six children and no theories.
John Wilmot (1647-1680, British Courtier, Poet)

104 I have been assured by a very knowing American of my acquaintance in London, that a young healthy child, well nursed, is at a year old, a most delicious, nourishing, and wholesome food, whether stewed, roasted, baked, or boiled; and I make no doubt that it will equally serve in a fricassee, or a ragout.
Jonathan Swift (1667-1745, Anglo-Irish Satirist)

105 Children need models rather than critics.
Joseph Joubert (1754-1824, French Moralist)

106 To rescue our children we will have to let them save us from the power we embody: we will have to trust the very difference that they forever personify. And we will have to allow them the choice, without fear of death: that they may come and do likewise or that they may come and that we will follow them, that a little child will lead us back to the child we will always be, vulnerable and wanting and hurting for love and for beauty.
June Jordan (1939-, American Poet, Civil Rights Activist)

107 Our children will not survive our habits of thinking, our failures of the spirit, our wreck of the universe into which we bring new life as blithely as we do. Mostly, our children will resemble our own misery and spite and anger, because we give them no choice about it. In the name of motherhood and fatherhood and education and good manners, we threaten and suffocate and bind and ensnare and bribe and trick children into wholesale emulation of our ways.
June Jordan (1939-, American Poet, Civil Rights Activist)

108 You may give them your love but not your thoughts. For they have their own thoughts. You may house their bodies but not their souls, for their souls dwell in the house of tomorrow, which you cannot visit, not even in your dreams.
Kahlil Gibran (1883-1931, Lebanese Poet, Novelist)

109 What is done to children, they will do to society.
Karl A. Menninger (1893-1990, American Psychiatrist)

110 A child learns to discard his ideals, whereas a grown-up never wears out his short pants.
Karl Kraus (1874-1936, Austrian Satirist)

111 Americans, indeed, often seem to be so overwhelmed by their children that they'll do anything for them except stay married to the co-producer.
Katharine Whitehorn (1926-, British Journalist)

112 Children are apt to live up to what you believe of them.
Lady Bird Johnson

113 Do not handicap your children by making their lives easy.
Lazarus Long

114 Those who have lost an infant are never, in a way, without an infant.
Leigh Hunt (1784-1859, British Poet, Essayist)

115 Children's liberation is the next item on our civil rights shopping list.
Letty Cottin Pogrebin (1939-, American Journalist, Author)

116 What's more enchanting than the voices of young people, when you can't hear what they say?
Logan Pearsall Smith (1865-1946, Anglo-American Essayist, Aphorist)

117 Normally, children learn to gauge rather accurately from the tone of their parent's voice how seriously to take his threats. Of course, they sometimes misjudge and pay the penalty.
Louis Kaplan

118 You see much more of your children once they leave home.
Lucille Ball (1911-1989, American Actress, Producer)

119 If we had paid no more attention to our plants than we have to our children, we would now be living in a jungle of weed.
Luther Burbank (1849-1926, American Horticulturist)

120 A child is a beam of sunlight from the Infinite and Eternal, with possibilities of virtue and vice- but as yet unstained.
Lyman Abbott (1835 - 1922, American Congregational Clergyman and Editor)

121 All my life through, the new sights of Nature made me rejoice like a child.
Madame Marie Curie (1867-1934, Polish-born French Physicist)

122 Parents are often so busy with the physical rearing of children that they miss the glory of parenthood, just as the grandeur of the trees is lost when raking leaves.
Marcelene Cox (American Writer)

123 Children in a family are like flowers in a bouquet: there's always one determined to face in an opposite direction from the way the arranger desires.
Marcelene Cox (American Writer)

124 To be ignorant of what occurred before you were born is to remain always a child.
Marcus T. Cicero (106-43 BC, Great Roman Orator, Politician)

125 Instead of needing lots of children, we need high-quality children.
Margaret Mead (1901-1978, American Anthropologist)

126 If help and salvation are to come, they can only come from the children, for the children are the makers of men.
Maria Montessori (1870-1952, Italian Educator)

127 A child is fed with milk and praise.
Mary Lamb

128 Of all the needs (there are none imaginary) a lonely child has, the one that must be satisfied, if there is going to be hope and a hope of wholeness, is the unshaken need for an unshakable God.
Maya Angelou (1928-, African-American poet, Writer, Performer)

129 Children's talent to endure stems from their ignorance of alternatives.
Maya Angelou (1928-, African-American poet, Writer, Performer)

130 The secret of dealing successfully with a child is not to be its parent.
Mel Lazarus

131 For truly it is to be noted, that children's plays are not sports, and should be deemed as their most serious actions.
Michel Eyquem De Montaigne (1533-1592, French Philosopher, Essayist)

132 It might sound a paradoxical thing to say --for surely never has a generation of children occupied more sheer hours of parental time --but the truth is that we neglected you. We allowed you a charade of trivial freedoms in order to avoid making those impositions on you that are in the end both the training ground and proving ground for true independence. We pronounced you strong when you were still weak in order to avoid the struggles with you that would have fed your true strength. We proclaimed you sound when you were foolish in order to avoid taking part in the long, slow, slogging effort that is the only route to genuine maturity of mind and feeling. Thus, it was no small anomaly of your growing up that while you were the most indulged generation, you were also in many ways the most abandoned to your own meager devices by those into whose safe-keeping you had been given.
Midge Decter (1927-, American Author, Editor, Social Critic)

133 There are three ways to get something done: do it yourself, employ someone, or forbid your children to do it.
Monta Crane

134 Where children are, there is the golden age.
Novalis (1772-1801, German Poet, Novelist)

135 Children aren't happy with nothing to ignore, and that's what parents were created for.
Ogden Nash (1902-1971, American Humorous Poet)

136 Pretty much all the honest truth telling there is in the world is done by children.
Oliver Wendell Holmes (1809-1894, American Author, Wit, Poet)

137 A child's education should begin at least one hundred years before he is born.
Oliver Wendell Holmes (1809-1894, American Author, Wit, Poet)

138 Children begin by loving their parents. After a time they judge them. Rarely, if ever, do they forgive them.
Oscar Wilde (1856-1900, British Author, Wit)

139 Few parents nowadays pay any regard to what their children say to them. The old-fashioned respect for the young is fast dying out.
Oscar Wilde (1856-1900, British Author, Wit)

140 The best way to make children good is to make them happy.
Oscar Wilde (1856-1900, British Author, Wit)

141 How little is the promise of the child fulfilled in the man.
Ovid (43 BC-18 AD, Roman Poet)

142 Every child is an artist. The problem is to remain an artist once they grow up.
Pablo Picasso (1881-1973, Spanish Artist)

143 Children also have artistic ability, and there is wisdom in there having it! The more helpless they are, the more instructive are the examples they furnish us; and they must be preserved free of corruption from an early age.
Paul Klee (1879-1940, Swiss Artist)

144 What is a neglected child? He is a child not planned for, not wanted. Neglect begins, therefore, before he is born.
Pearl S. Buck (1892-1973, American Novelist)

145 Above all, though, children are linked to adults by the simple fact that they are in process of turning into them. For this they may be forgiven much. Children are bound to be inferior to adults, or there is no incentive to grow up.
Philip Larkin (1922-1986, British Poet)

146 Always be nice to your children because they are the ones who will choose your rest home.
Phyllis Diller (1861-1951, American Columnist)

147 The wildest colts make the best horses.
Plutarch (46-120 AD, Greek Essayist, Biographer)

148 Hugs can do great amounts of good -- especially for children.
Princess of Wales Diana (1961-1997, Wife of Charles, Prince of Wales)

149 There is not so much comfort in having children as there is sorrow in parting with them.
Proverb

150 A rich child often sits in a poor mothers lap.
Proverb

151 Children and drunks always speak the truth.
Proverb

152 The child with his sweet pranks, the fool of his senses, commanded by every sight and sound, without any power to compare and rank his sensations, abandoned to a whistle or a painted chip, to a lead dragoon, or a gingerbread dog, individualizing everything, generalizing nothing, delighted with every new thing, lies down at night overpowered by the fatigue, which this day of continual pretty madness has incurred. But Nature has answered her purpose with the curly, dimpled lunatic. She has tasked every faculty, and has secured the symmetrical growth of the bodily frame, by all these attitudes and exertions --an end of the first importance, which could not be trusted to any care less perfect than her own.
Ralph Waldo Emerson (1803-1882, American Poet, Essayist)

153 There never was a child so lovely, but his mother was glad to get him asleep.
Ralph Waldo Emerson (1803-1882, American Poet, Essayist)

154 One of the most obvious facts about grownups to a child is that they have forgotten what it is like to be a child.
Randall Jarrell (1914-1965, American Poet, Critic)

155 The potential possibilities of any child are the most intriguing and stimulating in all creation.
Ray L. Wilbur

156 Better to be driven out from among men than to be disliked of children.
Richard H. Dana (1815-1882, American Writer, Lawyer)

157 Children are the keys of paradise.
Richard Henry Stoddard (1825-1903, American Critic, Poet)

158 He continued to be an infant long after he ceased to be a prodigy.
Robert Moses

159 Children are living jewels dropped unsustained from heaven.
Robert Pollok (1798-1827, Scottish Religious Poet)

160 When I was a kid my parents moved a lot, but I always found them.
Rodney Dangerfield (American Comedian, Actor)

161 Too often when give children answers to remember rather than problems to solve.
Roger Lewin

162 If you have a great passion it seems that the logical thing is to see the fruit of it, and the fruit are children.
Roman Polanski (1933-, Polish Film, Director)

163 Often and often afterwards, the beloved Aunt would ask me why I had never told anyone how I was being treated. Children tell little more than animals, for what comes to them they accept as eternally established.
Rudyard Kipling (1865-1936, British Author of Prose, Verse)

164 Children are given to us to discourage our better emotions.
Saki

165 Let your children be as so many flowers, borrowed from God. If the flowers die or wither, thank God for a summer loan of them.
Samuel Rutherford (1600-1661, Scottish Pastor)

166 Children seldom have a proper sense of their own tragedy, discounting and keeping hidden the true horrors of their short lives, humbly imagining real calamity to be some prestigious drama of the grown-up world.
Shirley Hazzard (1931-, Australian-born American Author)

167 It is not a bad thing that children should occasionally, and politely, put parents in their place.
Sidonie Gabrielle Colette (1873-1954, French Author)

168 Children are completely egoistic; they feel their needs intensely and strive ruthlessly to satisfy them.
Sigmund Freud (1856-1939, Austrian Physician - Founder of Psychoanalysis)

169 Give me the children until they are seven and anyone may have them afterwards.
St.Francis Xavier (1506-1552, Roman Catholic Missionary)

170 We worry about what a child will be tomorrow, yet we forget that he is someone today.
Stacia Tauscher

171 For unflagging interest and enjoyment, a household of children, if things go reasonably well, certainly all other forms of success and achievement lose their importance by comparison.
Theodore Roosevelt (1858-1919, Twenty-sixth President of the USA)

172 Alas! regardless of their doom, the little victims play! No sense have they of ills to come nor care beyond today.
Thomas Gray (1716-1771, British Poet)

173 For many children, joy comes as the result of mining something unique and wondrous about themselves from some inner shaft.
Thomas J. Cottle

174 Winning children (who appear so guileless) are children who have discovered how effective charm and modesty and a delicately calculated spontaneity are in winning what they want.
Thornton Wilder (1897-1975, American Novelist, Playwright)

175 The planting of trees in the least self-centered of all that we can do. It is a purer act of faith than the procreation of children.
Thornton Wilder (1897-1975, American Novelist, Playwright)

176 There are few places outside his own play where a child can contribute to the world in which he finds himself. His world: dominated by adults who tell him what to do and when to do it -- benevolent tyrants who dispense gifts to their "good" subjects and punishment to their "bad" ones, who are amused at the "cleverness" of children and annoyed by their "stupidities."
Viola Spolin (1911-, American Theatrical Director, Producer)

177 Give me four years to teach the children and the seed I have sown will never be uprooted.
Vladimir Ilyich Lenin (1870-1924, Russian Revolutionary Leader)

178 The countenances of children, like those of animals, are masks, not faces, for they have not yet developed a significant profile of their own.
W. H. Auden (1907-1973, Anglo-American Poet)

179 Your children will see what you're all about by what you live rather than what you say.
Wayne Dyer (1940-, American Psychotherapist, Author, Lecturer)

180 Children wish fathers looked but with their eyes; fathers that children with their judgment looked; and either may be wrong.
William Shakespeare (1564-1616, British Poet, Playwright, Actor)

181 How sharper than a serpent's tooth it is to have a thankless child.
William Shakespeare (1564-1616, British Poet, Playwright, Actor)

182 The child is the father of the man.
William Wordsworth (1770-1850, British Poet)

183 There is no finer investment for any community than putting milk into babies.
Winston Churchill (1874-1965, British Statesman, Prime Minister)

184 When you put faith, hope and love together, you can raise positive kids in a negative world.
Zig Ziglar (American Sales Trainer, Author, Motivational Speaker)

CHOICE

1 I have been driven many times to my knees by the overwhelming conviction that I had nowhere to go. My own wisdom, and that of all about me, seemed insufficient for the day.
Abraham Lincoln (1809-1865, Sixteenth President of the USA)

2 Once in a while it really hits people that they don't have to experience the world in the way they have been told to.
Alan Keightley

3 Every person has free choice. Free to obey or disobey the Natural Laws. Your choice determines the consequences. Nobody ever did, or ever will, escape the consequences of his choices.
Alfred A. Montapert (American Author)

4 There is no shame in finding someone else to be attractive, or good company. Even if they don't like you, there is still no shame. If you happen to be fond of someone, and they're not fond of you, it's OK.. You don't have to wait and see if they'll love you back. You can announce it.. Joy in life comes from expressing ourselves, in taking risks and jumping in. Everyone is not going to like you. But you can like who you like.
Andrew Matthews (American Artist, Cartoonist, Author)

5 We are the only beings on the planet who lead such rich internal lives that it's not the events that matter most to us, but rather, it's how we interpret those events that will determine how we think about ourselves and how we will act in the future.
Anthony Robbins (1960-, American Author, Speaker, Peak Performance Expert / Consultant)

6 You see, it's never the environment; it's never the events of our lives, but the meaning we attach to the events -- how we interpret them -- that shapes who we are today and who we'll become tomorrow.
Anthony Robbins (1960-, American Author, Speaker, Peak Performance Expert / Consultant)

7 You are now at a crossroads. This is your opportunity to make the most important decision you will ever make. Forget your past. Who are you now? Who have you decided you really are now? Don't think about who you have been. Who are you now? Who have you decided to become? Make this decision consciously. Make it carefully. Make it powerfully.
Anthony Robbins (1960-, American Author, Speaker, Peak Performance Expert / Consultant)

8 We can change our lives. We can do, have, and be exactly what we wish.
Anthony Robbins (1960-, American Author, Speaker, Peak Performance Expert / Consultant)

9 Even as a tortoise draws in its limbs, the wise can draw in their senses at will.
Bhagavad Gita (400 BC, Sanskrit Poem Incorporated Into the Mahabharata)

10 Refuse the evil, and choose the good. [Isaiah 7:15]
Bible (Sacred Scriptures of Christians and Judaism)

11 I have set before you life and death, blessing and cursing: Therefore choose life. [Deuteronomy 30:19]
Bible (Sacred Scriptures of Christians and Judaism)

12 Our generation, like the one before us, must choose. Without the threat of the Cold War, without the pain of economic ruin, without the fresh memory of World War II's slaughter, it is tempting to pursue our private agendas -- to simply sit back and let history unfold. We must resist the temptation.
Bill Clinton (1946-, Forty-second President of the USA)

13 The highest order of mind is accused of folly, as well as the lowest. Nothing is thoroughly approved but mediocrity. The majority has established this, and it fixes its fangs on whatever gets beyond it either way.
Blaise Pascal (1623-1662, French Scientist, Religious Philosopher)

14 If you want to sing out, sing out, and if you want to be free, be free, cause there's a million ways to be, you know that there are...
Cat Stevens

15 It is the moment of evolutionary truth for the race, and what man does with that moment will be more important than the events of the previous millenium.
Charles Muses

16 There has never been another you. With no effort on your part you were born to be something very special and set apart. What you are going to do in appreciation of that gift is a decision only you can make.
Dan Zadra

17 Bright lights cast dark shadows when shone from only one direction.
David Kelley

18 You can do what you want to do. You can be what you want to be.
David Thomas (American Businessman, Founder of Wendy's Restaurants)

19 If there are things you don't like in the world you grew up in, make your own life different.
David Thomas (American Businessman, Founder of Wendy's Restaurants)

20 You and I are essentially infinite choice-makers. In every moment of our existence, we are in that field of all possibilities where we have access to an infinity of choices.
Deepak Chopra (East-Indian- American M.D., New Age Author, Lecturer)

21 There are two primary choices in life: to accept conditions as they exist, or accept the responsibility for changing them.
Denis Waitley (1933-, American Author, Speaker, Trainer, Peak Performance Expert)

22 Everything is something you decide to do, and there is nothing you have to do.
Denis Waitley (1933-, American Author, Speaker, Trainer, Peak Performance Expert)

23 Seeing the light is a choice, not seeing the light is no choice.
Doug Horton

24 People are where they are because that is exactly where they really want to be -- whether they will admit that or not.
Earl Nightingale (1921-1989, American Radio Announcer, Author, Motivator, Speaker)

25 You are the person who has to decide. Whether you'll do it or toss it aside; You are the person who makes up your mind. Whether you'll lead or will linger behind. Whether you'll try for the goal that's afar. Or just be contented to stay where you are.
Edgar A. Guest

26 The more equally attractive two alternatives seem, the harder it can be to choose between them -- no matter that, to the same degree, the choice can only matter less.
Edward Fredkin's Paradox

27 Every street has two sides, the shady side and the sunny. When two men shake hands and part, mark which of the two takes the sunny side; he will be the younger man of the two.
Edward G. Bulwer-Lytton (1803-1873, British Novelist, Poet)

28 You are either part of the solution or part of the problem.
Eldridge Cleaver (1935-, American Black Leader, Writer)

29 One's philosophy is not best expressed in words; it is expressed in the choices one makes. In the long run, we shape our lives and we shape ourselves. The process never ends until we die. And, the choices we make are ultimately our own responsibility.
Eleanor Roosevelt (1884-1962, American First Lady, Columnist, Lecturer, Humanitarian)

30 No life is so hard that you can't make it easier by the way you take it.
Ellen Glasgow (1874-1945, American Novelist)

31 It is your own convictions which compels you; that is, choice compels choice.
Epictetus (50-120, Stoic Philosopher)

32 Every choice moves us closer to or farther away from something. Where are your choices taking your life? What do your behaviors demonstrate that you are saying yes or no to in life?
Eric Allenbaugh (American Author of "Wake-Up Calls")

33 Each person designs his own life, freedom gives him the power to carry out his own designs, and power gives the freedom to interfere with the designs of others.
Eric Berne (1910-1970, Canadian Psychiatrist, Writer)

34 Choose the life that is most useful, and habit will make it the most agreeable.
Francis Bacon (1561-1626, British Philosopher, Essayist, Statesman)

35 The key to your universe is that you can choose.
Frederick (Carl) Frieseke (1874-1939, American-Born French Painter)

36 Man's power of choice enables him to think like an angel or a devil, a king or a slave. Whatever he chooses, mind will create and manifest.
Frederick Bailes

37 A man either lives life as it happens to him, meets it head-on and licks it, or he turns his back on it and starts to wither away.
Gene Roddenberry (American Producer, Director, Creator of Star Trek Series)

38 The difficulty in life is the choice.
George Moore (1852-1933, Irish Writer)

39 Watch what you choose to do. For instance, someone might want you to smoke. Never forget that I told you -- don't do it. Say no. That can of beer that somebody wants you to try, don't do it. Don't you ever do it. That drug that someone might want you to use, don't touch it. Stay away from it. It can destroy you.
Gordon B. Hinckley

40 I, not events, have the power to make me happy or unhappy today. I can choose which it shall be. Yesterday is dead, tomorrow hasn't arrived yet. I have just one day, today, and I'm going to be happy in it.
Groucho Marx (1895-1977, American Comic Actor)

41 Life is a constant oscillation between the sharp horns of dilemmas.
H. L. Mencken (1880-1956, American Editor, Author, Critic, Humorist)

42 You don't have to buy from anyone. You don't have to work at any particular job. You don't have to participate in any given relationship. You can choose
Harry Browne (1933-, American Financial Advisor, Writer)

43 He who chooses the beginning of a road chooses the place it leads to. It is the means that determine the end.
Harry Emerson Fosdick (1878-1969, American Minister)

44 A man is too apt to forget that in this world he cannot have everything. A choice is all that is left him.
Harry Mathews (1930-, American Novelist)

45 All my life, whenever it comes time to make a decision, I make it and forget about it.
Harry S. Truman (1884-1972, Thirty-third President of the USA)

46 No one ever went broke by saying no too often.
Harvey Mackay (American Businessman, Speaker, Author)

47 Nine-tenths of the people were created so you would want to be with the other tenth.
Horace Walpole (1717-1797, British Author)

48 Any person who recognizes this greatest power... the power to choose. Begins to realize that he is the one that is doing the choosing and that friends, although they mean well, cannot do his choosing for him, nor can his relatives. Consequently, he develops real self-confidence based upon his own ability, upon his own action, and upon his own initiative.
J. Martin Kohe (American Publisher, Author)

49 Let us choose to believe something good can happen.
J. Martin Kohe (American Publisher, Author)

50 The greatest power that a person possesses is the power to choose.
J. Martin Kohe (American Publisher, Author)

51 You can choose to be lazy or you can choose to be ambitious. Stop to think about it again. Don't you do your own choosing?
J. Martin Kohe (American Publisher, Author)

52 Man is made or unmade by himself. By the right choice he ascends. As a being of power, intelligence, and love, and the lord of his own thoughts, he holds the key to every situation.
James Allen (1864-1912, British-born American Essayist, Author of "As a Man Thinketh")

53 I have discovered that we may be in some degree whatever character we choose. Besides, practice forms a man to anything.
James Boswell (1740-1795, British Writer, Journalist)

54 It is not something I must do but something I want to do...
James Fixx

55 You can do one of two things; just shut up, which is something I don't find easy, or learn an awful lot very fast which is what I tried to do.
Jane Fonda (1937-, American Screen Actor)

56 Constantly choosing the lesser of two evils is still choosing evil.
Jerry Garcia (1945-1995, American Rock Musician, "Grateful Dead")

57 He that cannot decidedly say, "No," when tempted to evil, is on the highway to ruin. He loses the respect even of those who would tempt him, and becomes but the pliant tool and victim of their evil designs.
Joel Hawes

58 The path of least resistance and least trouble is a mental rut already made. It requires troublesome work to undertake the alternation of old beliefs. Self-conceit often regards it as a sign of weakness to admit that a belief to which we have once committed ourselves is wrong. We get so identified with an idea that it is literally a "pet" notion and we rise to its defense and stop our eyes and ears to anything different.
John Dewey (1859-1952, American Philosopher, Educator)

59 In the choice between changing one's mind and proving there's no need to do so, most people get busy on the proof.
John Kenneth Galbraith (1908-, American Economist)

60 To every man there openeth A way, and ways, and a way. And the high soul climbs the high way, And the low soul gropes the low: And in between, on the misty flats, The rest drift to and fro. But to every man there openeth A high way and a low, And every man decideth. The way his soul shall go.
John Oxenham

61 You can lay down and die, or you can get up and fight, but that's it -- there's no turning back.
Jon English

62 We cannot tell what may happen to us in the strange medley of life. But we can decide what happens in us -- how we can take it, what we do with it -- and that is what really counts in the end. How to take the raw stuff of life and make it a thing of worth and beauty -- that is the test of living.
Joseph Fort Newton

63 It is enough that we set out to mold the motley stuff of life into some form of our own choosing; when we do, the performance is itself the wage.
Learned Hand (American Judge)

64 What we call the secret of happiness is no more a secret than our willingness to choose life.
Leo Buscaglia (American Expert on Love, Lecturer, Author)

65 Other people's opinion of you does not have to become your reality.
Les Brown (1945-, American Speaker, Author, Trainer, Motivator Lecturer)

66 Instead of looking at life as a narrowing funnel, we can see it ever widening to choose the things we want to do, to take the wisdom we've learned and create something.
Liz Carpenter (American Writer)

67 Whenever I have to choose between two evils, I always like to try the one I haven't tried before.
Mae West (1892-1980, American Actress)

68 If I were going to convert to any religion I would probably choose Catholicism because it at least has female saints and the Virgin Mary.
Margaret Atwood (1939-, Canadian Novelist, Poet, Critic)

69 Most of life is choices, and the rest is pure dumb luck.
Marian Erickson

70 I am not a sound bite person. I prefer to run at the mouth.
Marina Sirtis (1964-, British-born American-born American Actress)

71 Inhabit ourselves that we may indeed do what we want to do.
Mary Caroline Richards

72 As simple as it sounds, we all must try to be the best person we can: by making the best choices, by making the most of the talents we've been given.
Mary Lou Retton (American Olympic Gymnast, Speaker)

73 I think there is a choice possible to us at any moment, as long as we live. But there is no sacrifice. There is a choice, and the rest falls away. Second choice does not exist. Beware of those who talk about sacrifice.
Muriel Rukeyser (1913-1980, American Writer)

74 It is always your next move.
Napoleon Hill (1883-1970, American Speaker, Motivational Writer, "Think and Grow Rich")

75 Choice strengthens all.
Neal Prescot

76 If you choose not to decide, you still have made a choice.
Neil Peart

77 That guy just cut right in front of me. But I'm not going to let it bother me. No. I'm on my way to work and I decided it doesn't matter who wants to cut in front of my lane today. I'm not going to let it bother me one bit. Once I get to work, find myself a parking space, if somebody wants to jump ahead of me and take it, I'm going to let them.
Oprah Winfrey (1954-, American TV Personality, Producer, Actress, Author)

78 When you can't have what you choose, you just choose what you have.
Owen Wister (1860-1938, American Writer)

79 Look for your choices, pick the best one, then go with it.
Pat Riley (1945, American Basketball Coach)

80 We do pretty much whatever we want to.
Philip Johnson (1906-, American Architect and Theorist)

81 I like to be a free spirit. Some don't like that, but that's the way I am.
Princess of Wales Diana (1961-1997, Wife of Charles, Prince of Wales)

82 Thus we see that the all important thing is not killing or giving life, drinking or not drinking, living in the town or the country, being unlucky or lucky, winning or losing. It is how we win, how we lose, how we live or die, finally, how we choose.
R. H. Blyth

83 We stand now where two roads diverge. But unlike the roads in Robert Frost's familiar poem, they are not equally fair. The road we have long been traveling is deceptively easy, a smooth superhighway on which we progress with great speed, but at its end lies disaster. The other fork of the road -- the one less traveled by -- offers our last, our only chance to reach a destination that assures the preservation of the earth.
Rachel Carson (1907-1964, American Marine Biologist, Author)

84 Trust your instinct to the end, though you can render no reason.
Ralph Waldo Emerson (1803-1882, American Poet, Essayist)

85 We are as much informed of a writer's genius by what he selects as by what he originates.
Ralph Waldo Emerson (1803-1882, American Poet, Essayist)

86 The world isn't interested in the storms you encountered, but whether or not you brought in the ship.
Raul Armesto

87 Every person, all the events of your life are there because you have drawn them there. What you choose to do with them is up to you.
Richard Bach (1936-, American Author)

88 The way to activate the seeds of your creation is by making choices about the results you want to create. When you make a choice, you activate vast human energies and resources, which otherwise go untapped. All too often people fail to focus their choices upon results and therefore their choices are ineffective. If you limit your choices only to what seems possible or reasonable, you disconnect yourself from what you truly want, and all that is left is compromise.
Robert Fritz

89 The first thing I do in the morning is to make my bed and while I am making up my bed I am making up my mind as to what kind of a day I am going to have.
Robert Frost (1875-1963, American Poet)

90 When we acknowledge that all of life is sacred and that each act is an act of choice and therefore sacred, then life is a sacred dance lived consciously each moment. When we live at this level, we participate in the creation of a better world. [The Circle is Sacred]
Scout Cloud Lee (American Author)

91 The Perfect Way is only difficult for those who pick and choose. Do not like, do not dislike; all will then be clear. Make a hairbreadth difference, and Heaven and Earth are set apart.
Seng-Ts'an

92 You are everything that is, your thoughts, your life, your dreams come true. You are everything you choose to be. You are as unlimited as the endless universe.
Shad Helmstetter (American Leading Behavioral Psychologist, Author)

93 Every single moment of your life you must choose from a number of alternatives. What you choose determines where you will end up.
Shall Sinha

94 On this narrow planet, we have only the choice between two unknown worlds. One of them tempts us --ah! what a dream, to live in that! --the other stifles us at the first breath.
Sidonie Gabrielle Colette (1873-1954, French Author)

95 You cannot be anything if you want to be everything.
Solomon Schechter

96 It's so hard when I have to, And so easy when I want to.
Sondra Anice Barnes

97 Choose your love, Love your choice.
Thomas S. Monson

98 For what human ill does dawn not seem to be alternative?
Thornton Wilder (1897-1975, American Novelist, Playwright)

99 When a defining moment comes along, you can do one of two things. Define the moment, or let the moment define you.
Tin Cup Movie

100 Between two evils, choose neither; between two goods, choose both.
Tryon Edwards (1809-1894, American Theologian)

101 A human being is a deciding being.
Viktor E. Frankl (1905-, Austrian Psychiatrist, Neurology, Writer, "Man's Search for Meaning")

102 Everything can be taken away from a man but one thing: the last of the human freedom -- to choose one's attitude in any given set of circumstances, to choose one's own way.
Viktor E. Frankl (1905-, Austrian Psychiatrist, Neurology, Writer, "Man's Search for Meaning")

103 Be careful the environment you choose for it will shape you; be careful the friends you choose for you will become like them.
W. Clement Stone (1902-, American Businessman, Author)

104 Before my accidents, there were ten thousands things I could do. I could spend the rest of my life dwelling on the things that I had lost, but instead I chose to focus on the nine thousand I still had left.
W. Mitchell (American Businessman, Mayor, Speaker)

105 I knew that I did not have to buy into society's notion that I had to be handsome and healthy to be happy. I was in charge of my "spaceship" and it was my up, my down. I could choose to see this situation as a setback or as a starting point. I chose to begin life again.
Warren Mitchell (1926-, British Actor)

106 Anything inside that immobilizes me, gets in my way, keeps me from my goals, is all mine.
Wayne Dyer (1940-, American Psychotherapist, Author, Lecturer)

107 You can't choose up sides on a round world.
Wayne Dyer (1940-, American Psychotherapist, Author, Lecturer)

108 Be miserable. Or motivate yourself. Whatever has to be done, it's always your choice.
Wayne Dyer (1940-, American Psychotherapist, Author, Lecturer)

109 When you have to make a choice and don't make it, that in itself is a choice.
William James (1842-1910, American Psychologist, Professor, Author)

110 If this life be not a real fight, in which something is eternally gained... it is no better than a game of private theatricals from which one may withdraw at will.
William James (1842-1910, American Psychologist, Professor, Author)

111 The Great Way is not difficult for those who have no preferences.
Zen Saying

112 Every choice you make has an end result.
Zig Ziglar (American Sales Trainer, Author, Motivational Speaker)

CHRISTIANS AND CHRISTIANITY

1 What the world requires of the Christians is that they should continue to be Christians.
Albert Camus (1913-1960, French Existential Writer)

2 Christianity is completed Judaism or it is nothing.
Benjamin Disraeli (1804-1881, British Statesman, Prime Minister)

3 Being a Christian is more than just an instantaneous conversion; it is like a daily process whereby you grow to be more and more like Christ.
Billy Graham (1918-, American Evangelist)

4 A real Christian is a person who can give his pet parrot to the town gossip.
Billy Graham (1918-, American Evangelist)

5 I believe in Christianity as I believe in the rising sun; not because I see it, but by it I can see all else.
C. S. Lewis (1898-1963, British Academic, Writer, Christian Apologist)

6 If Jesus Christ be God and died for me, then no sacrifice can be too great for me to make for Him.
C. T. Studd

7 Christianity, with its doctrine of humility, of forgiveness, of love, is incompatible with the state, with its haughtiness, its violence, its punishment and its wars.
Count Leo Tolstoy (1828-1910, Russian Novelist, Philosopher)

8 Christian means coming from Christ. Just as a Californian comes from California and a Bostonian is someone who comes from Boston, A Christian is one who comes from Christ.
Don Walk (American Minister)

9 Never think that Jesus commanded a trifle, nor dare to trifle with anything He has commanded.
Dwight L. Moody (1837-1899, American Evangelist)

10 I have had more trouble with myself than with any other man.
Dwight L. Moody (1837-1899, American Evangelist)

11 A good example is far better than a good precept.
Dwight L. Moody (1837-1899, American Evangelist)

12 There are many of us that are willing to do great things for the Lord, but few of us are willing to do little things.
Dwight L. Moody (1837-1899, American Evangelist)

13 A rule I have had for years is: to treat the Lord Jesus Christ as a personal friend. His is not a creed, a mere doctrine, but it is He Himself we have.
Dwight L. Moody (1837-1899, American Evangelist)

14 A strong argument for the religion of Christ is this -- that offences against Charity are about the only ones which men on their death-beds can be made -- not to understand -- but to feel -- as crime.
Edgar Allan Poe (1809-1845, American Poet, Critic, short-story Writer)

15 The fear of hell, or aiming to be blest, savors too much of private interest.
Edmund Waller (1606-1687, British Poet)

16 God doesn't have any grandchildren.
Eli Stanley Jones (1884-1973, American Missionary)

17 The Bible and the Church have been the greatest stumbling blocks in the way of women's emancipation.
Elizabeth Cady Stanton (1815-1902, American Social Reformer and Women's Suffrage Leader)

18 Any hope that America would finally grow up vanished with the rise of fundamentalist Christianity. Fundamentalism, with its born-again regression, its pink-and-gold concept of heaven, its literal-mindedness, its rambunctious good cheer... its anti-intellectualism... its puerile hymns... and its faith-healing... are made to order for King Kid America.
Florence King (1936-, American Author, Critic)

19 Christianity provides a unified answer for the whole of life.
Francis Schaeffer (1912-1984, American Author)

20 Most of us spend the first six days of each week sowing wild oats; then we go to church on Sunday and pray for a crop failure.
Fred A. Allen (1894-1957, American Radio Comic)

21 Two great European narcotics, alcohol and Christianity.
Friedrich Nietzsche (1844-1900, German Philosopher)

22 Wherever there are walls I shall inscribe this eternal accusation against Christianity upon them -- I can write in letters which make even the blind see. I call Christianity the one great curse, the one great intrinsic depravity, the one great instinct for revenge for which no expedient is sufficiently poisonous, secret, subterranean, petty -- I call it the one immortal blemish of mankind.
Friedrich Nietzsche (1844-1900, German Philosopher)

23 Christianity makes suffering contagious.
Friedrich Nietzsche (1844-1900, German Philosopher)

24 There were honest people long before there were Christians and there are, God be praised, still honest people where there are no Christians. It could therefore easily be possible that people are Christians because true Christianity corresponds to what they would have been even if Christianity did not exist.
Georg C. Lichtenberg (1742-1799, German Physicist, Satirist)

25 The early Christian rules of life were not made to last, because the early Christians did not believe that the world itself was going to last.
George Bernard Shaw (1856-1950, Irish-born British Dramatist)

26 The Christian ideal has not been tried and found wanting. It has been found difficult; and left untried.
Gilbert K. Chesterton (1874-1936, British Author)

27 Regardless of the day or the hour; whether in seeming good times or bad, the Christian lives in the world for the good of the world and for the sake of the world.
Harold Lindsell

28 He spends his life explaining from his pulpit that the glory of Christianity consists in the fact that though it is not true it has been found necessary to invent it.
Hector Hugh Munro (1870-1916, British Novelist, Writer)

29 The test of Christian character should be that a man is a joy-bearing agent to the world.
Henry Ward Beecher (1813-1887, American Preacher, Orator, Writer)

30 A Christian is nothing but a sinful man who has put himself to school for Christ for the honest purpose of becoming better.
Henry Ward Beecher (1813-1887, American Preacher, Orator, Writer)

31 The trouble with born-again Christians is that they are an even bigger pain the second time around.
Herb Caen

32 Scratch the Christian and you find the pagan -- spoiled.
Israel Zangwill (1864-1926, British Writer)

33 Christianity has operated with an unmitigated arrogance and cruelty -- necessarily, since a religion ordinarily imposes on those who have discovered the true faith the spiritual duty of liberating the infidels.
James Baldwin (1924-1987, American Author)

34 The great difference between present-day Christianity and that of which we read in these letters is that to us it is primarily a performance, to them it was a real experience. To these men it is quite plainly the invasion of their lives by a new quality of life altogether. They do not hesitate to describe this as Christ "living in" them.
James Phillips

35 The Christian religion, though scattered and abroad will in the end gather itself together at the foot of the cross.
Johann Wolfgang Von Goethe (1749-1832, German Poet, Dramatist, Novelist)

36 Christianity will go. It will vanish and shrink. I needn't argue with that; I'm right and I will be proved right. We're more popular than Jesus now; I don't know which will go first -- rock and roll or Christianity.
John Lennon (1940-1980, British Rock Musician)

37 Our brains are no longer conditioned for reverence and awe. We cannot imagine a Second Coming that would not be cut down to size by the televised evening news, or a Last Judgment not subject to pages of holier-than-thou second-guessing in The New York Review of Books.
John Updike (1932-, American Novelist, Critic)

38 The trouble with some of us is that we have been inoculated with small doses of Christianity which keep us from catching the real thing.
Leslie Weatherhead

39 I have a great mind to believe in Christianity for the mere pleasure of fancying I may be damned.
Lord Byron (1788-1824, British Poet)

40 With two thousand years of Christianity behind him... a man can't see a regiment of soldiers march past without going off the deep end. It starts off far too many ideas in his head.
Louis-Ferdinand Celine (1894-1961, French Author)

41 The Christianity which is shared is the Christianity which is convincing.
Lynn Harold Hough

42 It is only when all our Christian ancestors are allowed to become our contemporaries that the real splendor of the Christian faith and the Christian life begins to dawn upon us.
Lynn Harold Hough

43 If Christians would really live according to the teachings of Christ, as found in the Bible, all of India would be Christian today.
Mahatma Gandhi (1869-1948, Indian Political, Spiritual Leader)

44 Christian life consists of faith and charity.
Martin Luther (1483-1546, German Leader of the Protestant Reformation)

45 Christians are rare people on earth.
Martin Luther (1483-1546, German Leader of the Protestant Reformation)

46 Protestantism has the method of Jesus with His secret too much left out of mind; Catholicism has His secret with His method too much left out of mind; neither has His unerring balance, His intuition, His sweet reasonableness. But both have hold of a great truth, and get from it a great power.
Matthew Arnold (1822-1888, British Poet, Critic)

47 Do you wish to find out the really sublime? Repeat the Lord's Prayer.
Napoleon Bonaparte (1769-1821, French General, Emperor)

48 White people really deal more with God and black people with Jesus.
Nikki Giovanni (1943-, American Poet)

49 Christianity is the root of all democracy, the highest fact in the rights of men.
Novalis (1772-1801, German Poet, Novelist)

50 Real Christianity is lovely. There is a quality about a Spirit-filled, radiant Christian that draws and attracts others and causes them to "enjoy favor with all the people." The truth is that the gospel is not nearly as offensive as some of its proponents!
O. S. Hawkins

51 How natural that the errors of the ancient should be handed down and, mixing with the principles and system which Christ taught, give to us an adulterated Christianity.
Olympia Brown (1835-1926, American Women's Suffrage Leader)

52 I have now disposed of all my property to my family. There is one thing more I wish I could give them, and that is the Christian religion.
Patrick Henry (1736-1799, American Orator, Patriot)

53 Many people profess Christianity. Very few live it-almost none. And when you live it people may think you're crazy. It has been truthfully said that the world is equally shocked by one who repudiates Christianity as by one who practices it.
Peace Pilgrim (1908-1981, American Peace Activist)

54 Here I swear, and as I break my oath may eternity blast me, here I swear that never will I forgive Christianity! It is the only point on which I allow myself to encourage revenge. Oh, how I wish I were the Antichrist, that it were mine to crush the Demon; to hurl him to his native Hell never to rise again -- I expect to gratify some of this insatiable feeling in Poetry.
Percy Bysshe Shelley (1792-1822, British Poet)

55 If you make a great deal of Christ, He will make a great deal of you; But it you make but little of Christ, He will make but little of you.
R. A. Torrey

56 Christianity is either relevant all the time or useless anytime. It is not just a phase of life; it is life itself.
Richard Halverson

57 The question is not "How much may I indulge in and still be saved. God forbid! I must rather ask, "What about Christ's will and the example I set for my fellow Christians?"
Robert A. Cook

58 What if men take to following where He leads, weary of mumbling Athanasian creeds?
Roden Noel

59 The Three in One, the One in Three? Not so! To my own Gods I go. It may be they shall give me greater ease than your cold Christ and tangled Trinities.
Rudyard Kipling (1865-1936, British Author of Prose, Verse)

60 People in general are equally horrified at hearing the Christian religion doubted, and at seeing it practiced.
Samuel Butler (1612-1680, British Poet, Satirist)

61 If there is any moral in Christianity, if there is anything to be learned from it, if the whole story is not profitless from first to last, it comes to this: that a man should back his own opinion against the world s.
Samuel Butler (1612-1680, British Poet, Satirist)

62 Christianity is the highest perfection of humanity.
Samuel Johnson (1709-1784, British Author)

63 Is your Christianity ancient history--or current events?
Samuel M. Shoemaker

64 He who begins by loving Christianity better than truth, will proceed by loving his own sect or church better than Christianity, and end in loving himself better than all.
Samuel Taylor Coleridge (1772-1834, British Poet, Critic, Philosopher)

65 I am not a Catholic; but I consider the Christian idea, which has its roots in Greek thought and in the course of the centuries has nourished all of our European civilization, as something that one cannot renounce without becoming degraded.
Simone Weil (1910-1943, French Philosopher, Mystic)

66 The real security of Christianity is to be found in its benevolent morality, in its exquisite adaptation to the human heart, in the facility with which its scheme accommodates itself to the capacity of every human intellect, in the consolation which it bears to the house of mourning, in the light with which it brightens the great mystery of the grave.
Thomas B. Macaulay (1800-1859, American Essayist and Historian)

67 Bear the Cross cheerfully and it will bear you.
Thomas p Kempis (1379-1471, German Monk, Mystic, Religious Writer)

68 A Christian is a man who feels repentance on Sunday for what he did on Saturday and is going to do on Monday.
Thomas Ybarra

69 No egoism is so insufferable as that of the Christian with regard to his soul.
W. Somerset Maugham (1874-1965, British Novelist, Playwright)

70 Christianity is a battle not a dream.
Wendell Phillips (1811-1884, American Reformer, Orator)

71 The glory of Christianity is to conquer by forgiveness.
William Blake (1757-1827, British Poet, Painter)

72 Christianity is art and not money. Money is its curse.
William Blake (1757-1827, British Poet, Painter)

73 No one is without Christianity, if we agree on what we mean by that word. It is every individual's individual code of behavior by means of which he makes himself a better human being than his nature wants to be, if he followed his nature only. Whatever its symbol -- cross or crescent or whatever -- that symbol is man's reminder of his duty inside the human race.
William Faulkner (1897-1962, American Novelist)

74 To be like Christ is to be a Christian.
William Penn (1644-1718, British Religious Leader, Founder of Pennsylvania)

CHRISTMAS

1 Midnight, and the clock strikes. It is Christmas Day, the werewolves birthday, the door of the solstice still wide enough open to let them all slink through.
Angela Carter (1940-1992, British Author)

2 A lovely thing about Christmas is that it's compulsory, like a thunderstorm, and we all go through it together.
Garrison Keillor (1942-, American Humorous Writer, Radio Performer)

3 Christ was born in the first century, yet he belongs to all centuries. He was born a Jew, yet He belongs to all races. He was born in Bethlehem, yet He belongs to all countries.
George W. Truett

4 So stick up ivy and the bays, and then restore the heathen ways, green will remind you of the Spring, though this great day denies the thing, and mortifies the earth, and all, but your wild revels, and loose hall.
Henry Vaughan (1622-1695, Welsh Poet)

5 A woman spent all Christmas Day in a telephone box without ringing anyone. If someone comes to phone, she leaves the box, then resumes her place afterwards. No one calls her either, but from a window in the street, someone watched her all day, no doubt since they had nothing better to do. The Christmas syndrome.
Jean Baudrillard (French Postmodern Philosopher, Writer)

6 This is the month, and this the happy morn, wherein the Son of heaven's eternal King, of wedded Maid and Virgin Mother born, our great redemption from above did bring.
John Milton (1608-1674, British Poet)

7 From a commercial point of view, if Christmas did not exist it would be necessary to invent it.
Katharine Whitehorn (1926-, British Journalist)

8 Christmas waves a magic wand over this world, and behold, everything is softer and more beautiful.
Norman Vincent Peale (1898-1993, American Christian Reformed Pastor, Speaker, Author)

9 God walked down the stairs of heaven with a Baby in His arms.
Paul Scherer

10 The purpose and cause of the incarnation was that He might illuminate the world by His wisdom and excite it to the love of Himself.
Peter Abelard (1079-1142, French Philosopher, Priest)

11 Please to put a nickel, please to put a dime. How petitions trickle in at Christmas time!
Phyllis Mcginley (1905-1978, American Poet, Author)

12 There are some people who want to throw their arms round you simply because it is Christmas; there are other people who want to strangle you simply because it is Christmas.
Robert Lynd (1892-1970, American Sociology Author)

13 He who has not Christmas in his heart will never find it under a tree.
Roy L. Smith (American Clergyman)

14 Call a truce, then, to our labors -- let us feast with friends and neighbors, and be merry as the custom of our caste; for if "faint and forced the laughter," and if sadness follow after, we are richer by one mocking Christmas past.
Rudyard Kipling (1865-1936, British Author of Prose, Verse)

15 'Twas Christmas broach'd the mightiest ale; 'twas Christmas told the merriest tale; a Christmas gambol oft could cheer the poor man's heart through half the year.
Sir Walter Scott (1771-1832, British Novelist, Poet)

CHURCHES

1 One hundred religious persons knit into a unity by careful organizations do not constitute a church any more than eleven dead men make a football team. The first requisite is life, always.
A. W. Tozer (Deceased 1963, American Preacher)

2 But a priest's life is not supposed to be well-rounded; it is supposed to be one-pointed -- a compass, not a weathercock.
Aldous Huxley (1894-1963, British Author)

3 She say, Celie, tell the truth, have you ever found God in church? I never did. I just found a bunch of folks hoping for him to show. Any God I ever felt in church I brought in with me. And I think all the other folks did too. They come to church to share God, not find God.
Alice Walker (1944-, American Author, Critic)

4 Churchgoers are like coals in a fire. When they cling together, they keep the flame aglow; when they separate, they die out.
Billy Graham (1918-, American Evangelist)

5 I don't go to church. Kneeling bags my nylons.
Billy Wilder (1906-, American Film Director)

6 I have no objections to churches so long as they do not interfere with God's work.
Brooks Atkinson (1894-1984, American Journalist, Drama Critic)

7 Standards of conduct appropriate to civil society or the workings of a democracy cannot be purely and simply applied to the Church.
Cardinal Joseph Ratzinger

8 I'm a priest, not a priestess. "Priestess" implies mumbo jumbo and all sorts of pagan goings-on. Those who oppose us would love to call us priestesses. They can call us all the names in the world -- it's better than being invisible.
Carter Heyward

9 The Christian church is a society of sinners. It is the only society in the world, membership in which is based upon the single qualification that the candidate shall be unworthy of membership.
Charles C. Morrison

10 Church is the only place where someone speaks to me and I do not have to answer back.
Charles De Gaulle (1890-1970, French President during World War II)

11 The problem is not that the churches are filled with empty pews, but that the pews are filled with empty people.
Charlie Shedd

12　And of all plagues with which mankind are cursed, ecclesiastic tyranny's the worst.
Daniel Defoe (1661-1731, British Author)

13　The difference between listening to a radio sermon and going to church...is almost like the difference between calling your girl on the phone and spending an evening with her.
Dwight L. Moody (1837-1899, American Evangelist)

14　Church attendance is as vital to a disciple as a transfusion of rich, healthy blood to a sick man.
Dwight L. Moody (1837-1899, American Evangelist)

15　Many are called but few are chosen. There are sayings of Christ which suggest that the Church he came to establish will always be a minority affair.
Edward Norman

16　The act of bell ringing is symbolic of all proselytizing religions. It implies the pointless interference with the quiet of other people.
Ezra Pound (1885-1972, American Poet, Critic)

17　Mass ought to be in Latin, unless you could do it in Greek or Chinese. In fact, any abracadabra that no bloody member of the public or half-educated ape of a clargimint could think he understood.
Ezra Pound (1885-1972, American Poet, Critic)

18　The first time I sang in the church choir; two hundred people changed their religion.
Fred A. Allen (1894-1957, American Radio Comic)

19　He who is near the Church is often far from God.
French Proverb

20　We sing in a church, why can we not dance there?
George Bernard Shaw (1856-1950, Irish-born British Dramatist)

21　What is wrong with priests and popes is that instead of being apostles and saints, they are nothing but empirics who say "I know" instead of "I am learning," and pray for credulity and inertia as wise men pray for skepticism and activity.
George Bernard Shaw (1856-1950, Irish-born British Dramatist)

22　I believe with all my heart that the Church of Jesus Christ should be a Church of blurred edges.
George Carey (American Actor)

23　People have described me as a "management bishop" but I say to my critics, "Jesus was a management expert too."
George Carey (American Actor)

24　Those who marry God can become domesticated too -- it's just as hum-drum a marriage as all the others. The word "Love" means a formal touch of the lips as in the ceremony of the Mass, and "Ave Maria " like "dearest" is a phrase to open a letter. This marriage like the world's marriages was held together by habits and tastes shared in common between God and themselves -- it was God's taste to be worshipped and their taste to worship, but only at stated hours like a suburban embrace on a Saturday night.
Graham Greene (1904-1991, British Novelist)

25　Archbishop -- A Christian ecclesiastic of a rank superior to that attained by Christ.
H. L. Mencken (1880-1956, American Editor, Author, Critic, Humorist)

26　A church is a place in which gentlemen who have never been to heaven brag about it to persons who will never get there.
H. L. Mencken (1880-1956, American Editor, Author, Critic, Humorist)

27　A Church which has lost its memory is in a sad state of senility.
Henry Chadwick

28　There is not in the universe a more ridiculous, nor a more contemptible animal, than a proud clergyman.
Henry Fielding (1707-1754, British Novelist, Dramatist)

29　The Church is not a gallery for the exhibition of eminent Christians, but a school for the education of imperfect ones.
Henry Ward Beecher (1813-1887, American Preacher, Orator, Writer)

30　The priesthood is a marriage. People often start by falling in love, and they go on for years without realizing that love must change into some other love which is so unlike it that it can hardly be recognized as love at all.
Iris Murdoch (1919-, British Novelist, Philosopher)

31　Be neither intimate nor distant with the clergy.
Irish Proverb

32　There is no heresy or no philosophy which is so abhorrent to the church as a human being.
James Joyce (1882-1941, Irish Author)

33　I think a bishop who doesn't give offence to anyone is probably not a good bishop.
James Thomson (1700-1748, Scottish Poet)

34　A little, round, fat, oily man of God.
James Thomson (1700-1748, Scottish Poet)

35　It will, I believe, be everywhere found, that as the clergy are, or are not what they ought to be, so are the rest of the nation.
Jane Austen (1775-1817, British Novelist)

36　It is indolence... Indolence and love of ease; a want of all laudable ambition, of taste for good company, or of inclination to take the trouble of being agreeable, which make men clergymen. A clergyman has nothing to do but be slovenly and selfish; read the newspaper, watch the weather, and quarrel with his wife. His curate does all the work and the business of his own life is to dine.
Jane Austen (1775-1817, British Novelist)

37　Wherever we find the Word of God surely preached and heard, and the sacraments administered according to the institution of Christ, there, it is not to be doubted, is a church of God.
John Calvin (1509-1564, French Protestant Reformer)

38 We praise Him, we bless Him, we adore Him, we glorify Him, and we wonder who is that baritone across the aisle and that pretty woman on our right who smells of apple blossoms. Our bowels stir and our cod itches and we amend our prayers for the spiritual life with the hope that it will not be too spiritual.
John Cheever (1912-1982, American Author)

39 The question confronting the Church today is not any longer whether the man in the street can grasp a religious message, but how to employ the communications media so as to let him have the full impact of the Gospel message.
John Paul II (1920, Polish-Born Italian Pope)

40 The greatest hindrances to the evangelization of the world are those within the church.
John R. Mott

41 Nearly all the evils in the Church have arisen from bishops desiring power more than light. They want authority, not outlook.
John Ruskin (1819-1900, British Critic, Social Theorist)

42 The root of almost every schism and heresy from which the Christian Church has suffered, has been because of the effort of men to earn, rather than receive their salvation; and the reason preaching is so commonly ineffective is, that it often calls on people to work for God rather than letting God work through them.
John Ruskin (1819-1900, British Critic, Social Theorist)

43 A glorious Church is like a magnificent feast; there is all the variety that may be, but every one chooses out a dish or two that he likes, and lets the rest alone: how glorious soever the Church is, every one chooses out of it his own religion, by which he governs himself, and lets the rest alone.
John Selden (1584-1654, British Jurist, Statesman)

44 The priesthood in many ways is the ultimate closet in Western civilization, where gay people particularly have hidden for the past two thousand years.
John Spong (1931-, American Clergyman)

45 The Bible knows nothing of solitary religion.
John Wesley (1703-1791, British Preacher, Founder of Methodism)

46 I never saw, heard, nor read, that the clergy were beloved in any nation where Christianity was the religion of the country. Nothing can render them popular, but some degree of persecution.
Jonathan Swift (1667-1745, Anglo-Irish Satirist)

47 He was of the faith chiefly in the sense that the church he currently did not attend was Catholic.
Kingsley Amis (1922-1995, British Novelist)

48 A church is a hospital for sinners, not a museum for saints.
L. L. Nash

49 Once is orthodox, twice is puritanical.
Lord Melbourne (1779-1848, British Statesman, Prime Minister)

50 The separation of church and state is a source of strength, but the conscience of our nation does not call for separation between men of state and faith in the Supreme Being.
Lyndon B. Johnson (1908-1973, Thirty-sixth President of the USA)

51 Where God builds a church the devil builds a chapel.
Martin Luther (1483-1546, German Leader of the Protestant Reformation)

52 Yes, I see the Church as the body of Christ. But, oh! How we have blemished and scarred that body through social neglect and through fear of being nonconformists.
Martin Luther King Jr. (1929-1968, American Black Leader, Nobel Prize Winner, 1964)

53 A woman's asking for equality in the church would be comparable to a black person's demanding equality in the Ku Klux Klan.
Mary Daly (1928-, American Feminist and Theological Writer)

54 What makes a church great in the eyes of God? Participation, proclamation, preservation, and propagation. Every church ought to exhibit all four.
O. S. Hawkins

55 Too hot to go to Church? What about Hell?
Ohio, Poster In Dayton

56 The local church is the outcrop of the church universal.
Peter T. Forsyth

57 The Church has always been willing to swap off treasures in heaven for cash down.
Robert Green Ingersoll (1833-1899, American Orator, Lawyer)

58 I never weary of great churches. It is my favorite kind of mountain scenery. Mankind was never so happily inspired as when it made a cathedral.
Robert Louis Stevenson (1850-1895, Scottish Essayist, Poet, Novelist)

59 The Church cannot be content to live in its stained-glass house and throw stones through the picture window of modern culture.
Robert Mcafee Brown

60 This merriment of parsons is mighty offensive.
Samuel Johnson (1709-1784, British Author)

61 An instinctive taste teaches men to build their churches with spire steeples which point as with a silent finger to the sky and stars.
Samuel Taylor Coleridge (1772-1834, British Poet, Critic, Philosopher)

62 If church prelates, past or present, had even an inkling of physiology they'd realize that what they term this inner ugliness creates and nourishes the hearing ear, the seeing eye, the active mind, and energetic body of man and woman, in the same way that dirt and dung at the roots give the plant its delicate leaves and the full-blown rose.
Sean O'Casey (1884-1964, Irish Dramatist)

63 Here, the churches seemed to shrink away into eroding corners. They seem to have ceased to be essential parts of American life. They no longer give life. It is the huge buildings of commerce and trade which now align the people to attention. These in their massive manner of steel and stone say, Come unto me all ye who labor, and we will give you work.
Sean O'Casey (1884-1964, Irish Dramatist)

64 In the Church, considered as a social organism, the mysteries inevitably degenerate into beliefs.
Simone Weil (1910-1943, French Philosopher, Mystic)

65 His creed no parson ever knew, for this was still his "simple plan," to have with clergymen to do as little as a Christian can.
Sir Francis Doyle

66 The itch of disputing is the scab of the churches.
Sir Henry Wotton (1568-1639, British Diplomat, Traveler, Scholar, and Poet)

67 How can a bishop marry? How can he flirt? The most he can say is "I will see you in the vestry after service."
Sydney Smith (1771-1845, British Writer, Clergyman)

68 I have, alas, only one illusion left, and that is the Archbishop of Canterbury.
Sydney Smith (1771-1845, British Writer, Clergyman)

69 The old cathedrals are good, but the great blue dome that hangs over everything is better.
Thomas Carlyle (1795-1881, Scottish Philosopher, Author)

70 Many come to bring their clothes to church rather than themselves.
Thomas Fuller (1608-1661, British Clergyman, Author)

71 I do not believe in the creed professed by the Jewish Church, by the Roman Church, by the Greek Church, by the Turkish Church, by the Protestant Church, nor by any church that I know of. My own mind is my own church.
Thomas Paine (1737-1809, Anglo-American Political Theorist, Writer)

72 My own mind is my own church.
Thomas Paine (1737-1809, Anglo-American Political Theorist, Writer)

73 Many people are in a rut and a rut is nothing but a grave--with both ends kicked out.
Vance Havner

74 The church is so subnormal that if it ever got back to the New Testament normal it would seem to people to be abnormal.
Vance Havner

75 It is one of the ironies of the ministry that the very man who works in God's name is often hardest put to find time for God. The parents of Jesus lost Him at church, and they were not the last ones to lose Him there.
Vance Havner

76 It's about time we quit playing church in these services that start at eleven o clock sharp and end at twelve o clock dull.
Vance Havner

77 The Pope is an idol whose hands are tied and whose feet are kissed.
Voltaire (1694-1778, French Historian, Writer)

78 The church exists to train its member through the practice of the presence of God to be servants of others, to the end that Christlikeness may become common property.
William Adams Brown

79 The parson knows enough who knows a Duke.
William Cowper (1731-1800, British Poet)

80 A full-dressed ecclesiastic is a sort of go-cart of divinity; an ethical automaton. A clerical prig is, in general, a very dangerous as well as contemptible character. The utmost that those who thus habitually confound their opinions and sentiments with the outside coverings of their bodies can aspire to, is a negative and neutral character, like wax-work figures, where the dress is done as much to the life as the man, and where both are respectable pieces of pasteboard, or harmless compositions of fleecy hosiery.
William Hazlitt (1778-1830, British Essayist)

81 It would be far better to be of no church than to be bitter of any.
William Penn (1644-1718, British Religious Leader, Founder of Pennsylvania)

CINEMA

1 For me, the cinema is not a slice of life, but a piece of cake.
Alfred Hitchcock (1899-1980, Anglo-American Filmmaker)

2 Dialogue should simply be a sound among other sounds, just something that comes out of the mouths of people whose eyes tell the story in visual terms.
Alfred Hitchcock (1899-1980, Anglo-American Filmmaker)

3 People sometimes say that the way things happen in the movies is unreal, but actually it's the way things happen to you in life that's unreal. The movies make emotions look so strong and real, whereas when things really do happen to you, it's like watching television -- you don't feel anything.
Andy Warhol (1930-, American Artist, Filmmaker)

4 I discovered early in my movie work that a movie is never any better than the stupidest man connected with it. There are times when this distinction may be given to the writer or director. Most often it belongs to the producer.
Ben Hecht (1894-1964, American Newspaperman, Novelist, Playwright)

5 Movies are one of the bad habits that corrupted our century. Of their many sins, I offer as the worst their effect on the intellectual side of the nation. It is chiefly from that viewpoint I write of them -- as an eruption of trash that has lamed the American mind and retarded Americans from becoming a cultured people.
Ben Hecht (1894-1964, American Newspaperman, Novelist, Playwright)

6　Cinema is the culmination of the obsessive, mechanistic male drive in western culture. The movie projector is an Apollonian straight-shooter, demonstrating the link between aggression and art. Every pictorial framing is a ritual limitation, a barred precinct.
Camille Paglia (1947-, American Author, Critic, Educator)

7　The cinema, like the detective story, makes it possible to experience without danger all the excitement, passion and desirousness which must be repressed in a humanitarian ordering of life.
Carl Jung (1875-1961, Swiss Psychiatrist)

8　All television ever did was shrink the demand for ordinary movies. The demand for extraordinary movies increased. If any one thing is wrong with the movie industry today, it is the unrelenting effort to astonish.
Clive James (1939-, Australian-Born Writer, Satirist, Broadcaster, and Critic)

9　My belief is that no movie, nothing in life, leaves people neutral. You either leave them up or you leave them down.
David Puttnam

10　We have taken beauty and exchanged it for stilted voices.
David Wark Griffiths (1875-1948, American Pioneer Film Director)

11　The preserve of ambition and folly in pursuit of illusion, or delusion.
Derek Jarman (1942-, British Filmmaker, Artist, Author)

12　I guess I think that films have to be made totally by fascists -- there's no room for democracy in making film.
Don Alan Pennebaker (1930-, American Filmmaker)

13　Film is more than the twentieth-century art. It's another part of the twentieth-century mind. It's the world seen from inside. We've come to a certain point in the history of film. If a thing can be filmed, the film is implied in the thing itself. This is where we are. The twentieth century is on film. You have to ask yourself if there's anything about us more important than the fact that we're constantly on film, constantly watching ourselves.
Don Delillo (1926-, American Author)

14　All film directors, whether famous or obscure, regard themselves as misunderstood or underrated. Because of that, they all lie. They're obliged to overstate their own importance.
FrantOis Truffaut (1932-1984, French Film Critic and Director)

15　The movies today are too rich to have any room for genuine artists. They produce a few passable craftsmen, but no artists. Can you imagine a Beethoven making $100,000 a year?
H. L. Mencken (1880-1956, American Editor, Author, Critic, Humorist)

16　Curiosity doesn't matter any more. These days people don't want to be transported to emotional territories where they don't know how to react.
Hector Babenko

17　Film music should have the same relationship to the film drama that somebody's piano playing in my living room has to the book I am reading.
Igor Stravinsky (1882-1971, Russian Composer)

18　Film as dream, film as music. No art passes our conscience in the way film does, and goes directly to our feelings, deep down into the dark rooms of our souls.
Ingmar Bergman (1918-, Swedish Stage, Film Writer, Director)

19　The cinema is not an art which films life: the cinema is something between art and life. Unlike painting and literature, the cinema both gives to life and takes from it, and I try to render this concept in my films. Literature and painting both exist as art from the very start; the cinema doesn't.
Jean-Luc Godard (1930-, French Filmmaker, Author)

20　All you need for a movie is a gun and a girl.
Jean-Luc Godard (1930-, French Filmmaker, Author)

21　What is saved in the cinema when it achieves art is a spontaneous continuity with all mankind. It is not an art of the princes or the bourgeoisie. It is popular and vagrant. In the sky of the cinema people learn what they might have been and discover what belongs to them apart from their single lives.
John Berger (1926-, British Actor, Critic)

22　Does art reflect life? In movies, yes. Because more than any other art form, films have been a mirror held up to society's porous face.
Marjorie Rosen

23　It struck me that the movies had spent more than half a century saying, "They lived happily ever after" and the following quarter-century warning that they'll be lucky to make it through the weekend. Possibly now we are now entering a third era in which the movies will be sounding a note of cautious optimism: You know it just might work.
Nora Ephron (1941-, American Author, Journalist)

24　One of the joys of going to the movies was that it was trashy, and we should never lose that.
Oliver Stone (1946-, American Director, Writer, Producer)

25　The director is simply the audience. So the terrible burden of the director is to take the place of that yawning vacuum, to be the audience and to select from what happens during the day which movement shall be a disaster and which a gala night. His job is to preside over accidents.
Orson Welles (1915-1985, American Film Maker)

26　I rather think the cinema will die. Look at the energy being exerted to revive it -- yesterday it was color, today three dimensions. I don't give it forty years more. Witness the decline of conversation. Only the Irish have remained incomparable conversationalists, maybe because technical progress has passed them by.
Orson Welles (1915-1985, American Film Maker)

27 The words "Kiss Kiss Bang Bang," which I saw on an Italian movie poster, are perhaps the briefest statement imaginable of the basic appeal of movies. This appeal is what attracts us, and ultimately what makes us despair when we begin to understand how seldom movies are more than this.
Pauline Kael (1919-, American Film Critic)

28 The making of a picture ought surely to be a rather fascinating adventure. It is not; it is an endless contention of tawdry egos, some of them powerful, almost all of them vociferous, and almost none of them capable of anything much more creative than credit-stealing and self-promotion.
Raymond Chandler (1888-1959, American Author)

29 The motion picture is like a picture of a lady in a half-piece bathing suit. If she wore a few more clothes, you might be intrigued. If she wore no clothes at all, you might be shocked. But the way it is, you are occupied with noticing that her knees are too bony and that her toenails are too large. The modern film tries too hard to be real. Its techniques of illusion are so perfect that it requires no contribution form the audience but a mouthful of popcorn.
Raymond Chandler (1888-1959, American Author)

30 My movie is born first in my head, dies on paper; is resuscitated by the living persons and real objects I use, which are killed on film but, placed in a certain order and projected on to a screen, come to life again like flowers in water.
Robert Bresson (1907-, French Film Director)

31 Films can only be made by by-passing the will of those who appear in them, using not what they do, but what they are.
Robert Bresson (1907-, French Film Director)

32 Pictures are for entertainment, messages should be delivered by Western Union.
Samuel Goldwyn (1882-1974, American Film Producer, Founder, MGM)

33 If you can't believe a little in what you see on the screen, it's not worth wasting your time on cinema.
Serge Daney (1944-1992, French Film Critic)

34 In good films, there is always a directness that entirely frees us from the itch to interpret.
Susan Sontag (1933-, American Essayist)

35 A strange thing has happened -- while all the other arts were born naked, this, the youngest, has been born fully-clothed. It can say everything before it has anything to say. It is as if the savage tribe, instead of finding two bars of iron to play with, had found scattering the seashore fiddles, flutes, saxophones, trumpets, grand pianos by Erhard and Bechstein, and had begun with incredible energy, but without knowing a note of music, to hammer and thump upon them all at the same time.
Virginia Woolf (1882-1941, British Novelist, Essayist)

36 You should look straight at a film; that's the only way to see one. Film is not the art of scholars but of illiterates.
Werner Herzog (1942-, German Film Director)

37 There's only one thing that can kill the movies, and that's education.
Will Rogers (1879-1935, American Humorist, Actor)

38 As far as the filmmaking process is concerned, stars are essentially worthless -- and absolutely essential.
William Goldman (1931-, American Author)

CIRCUMSTANCE

1 In America nobody says you have to keep the circumstances somebody else gives you.
Amy Tan (1952-, Chinese American Author, "The Joy Luck Club")

2 It's not the events of our lives that shape us, but our beliefs as to what those events mean.
Anthony Robbins (1960-, American Author, Speaker, Peak Performance Expert / Consultant)

3 Man is not the creature of circumstances, circumstances are the creatures of men. We are free agents, and man is more powerful than matter.
Benjamin Disraeli (1804-1881, British Statesman, Prime Minister)

4 Man is more powerful than matter.
Benjamin Disraeli (1804-1881, British Statesman, Prime Minister)

5 Circumstances are beyond human control, but our conduct is in our own power.
Benjamin Disraeli (1804-1881, British Statesman, Prime Minister)

6 If all our happiness is bound up entirely in our personal circumstances it is difficult not to demand of life more than it has to give.
Bertrand Russell (1872-1970, British Philosopher, Mathematician, Essayist)

7 And as for you, you meant evil against me, but God meant it for good in order to bring about this present result, to preserve many people alive. [Genesis 50:20]
Bible (Sacred Scriptures of Christians and Judaism)

8 Circumstances hell! I make circumstances!
Bruce Lee (1940-1973, Chinese-American Actor, Director, Author, Martial Artist)

9 I am bigger than anything that can happen to me.
Charles F. Lummis

10 It is our relation to circumstances that determine their influence over us. The same wind that blows one ship into port may blow another off shore.
Christian Nevell Bovee (1820-1904, American Author, Lawyer)

11 Whether you're winning or losing, it is important to always be yourself. You can't change because of the circumstances around you.
Cotton Fitzsimmons (Basketball Coach)

12 He is happy whom circumstances suit his temper; but he Is more excellent who suits his temper to any circumstance.
David Hume (1711-1776, Scottish Philosopher, Historian)

13 How we think shows through in how we act. Attitudes are mirrors of the mind. They reflect thinking.
David J. Schwartz (American Trainer, Author of "The Magic of Thinking Big")

14 We can let circumstances rule us, or we can take charge and rule our lives from within.
Earl Nightingale (1921-1989, American Radio Announcer, Author, Motivator, Speaker)

15 It is not the situation that makes the man, but the man who makes the situation.
Frederick W. Robertson

16 People are always blaming their circumstances for what they are. I don't believe in circumstances. The people who get on in this world are the people who get up and look for the circumstances they want, and if they can't find them, make them.
George Bernard Shaw (1856-1950, Irish-born British Dramatist)

17 Although our inattention can contribute to our lack of total well-being, we also have the power to choose positive behaviors and responses. In that choice we change our every experience of life!
Greg Anderson (American Author of "The 22 Non-Negotiable Laws of Wellness")

18 You are where you are today because you've chosen to be there.
Harry Browne (1933-, American Financial Advisor, Writer)

19 Life is not a matter of holding good cards, but sometimes, playing a poor hand well.
Jack London (1876-1916, American Novelist)

20 Do not let circumstances control you. You change your circumstances.
Jackie Chan (1954-, Hong Kong Actor, Director, Producer, Singer, Stun Choreographer)

21 Circumstances do not make the man, they reveal him.
James Allen (1864-1912, British-born American Essayist, Author of "As a Man Thinketh")

22 You are an extremely valuable, worthwhile, significant person even though your present circumstances may have you felling otherwise.
James Newman

23 Tear man out of his outward circumstances; and what he then is; that only is he.
Johann G. Seume (1763-1810, German Theologist)

24 To see your drama clearly is to be liberated from it.
Ken Keyes Jr. (1921-1995, American Author)

25 We are no longer puppets being manipulated by outside powerful forces: we become the powerful force ourselves.
Leo Buscaglia (American Expert on Love, Lecturer, Author)

26 Men are the sport of circumstances when it seems circumstances are the sport of men.
Lord Byron (1788-1824, British Poet)

27 Circumstances may cause interruptions and delays, but never lose sight of your goal. Prepare yourself in every way you can by increasing your knowledge and adding to your experience, so that you can make the most of opportunity when it occurs.
Mario Andretti (1940-, Italian-born American Auto Racer)

28 I am determined to be cheerful and happy in whatever situation I may find myself. For I have learned that the greater part of our misery or unhappiness is determined not by our circumstance but by our disposition.
Martha Washington (1731-1802, American First Lady, Wife of President, George Washington)

29 Upright whether in prosperous or in critical circumstances.
Motto

30 It is a fact that you project what you are.
Norman Vincent Peale (1898-1993, American Christian Reformed Pastor, Speaker, Author)

31 How things look on the outside of us depends on how things are on the inside of us.
Parks Cousins

32 The circumstances of your life have uniquely qualified you to make a contribution. And if you don't make that contribution, nobody else can make it.
Rabbi Harold S. Kushner

33 Circumstances are the rulers of the weak; they are but the instruments of the wise.
Samuel Lover (1797-1868, American Author)

34 If you're proactive, you don't have to wait for circumstances or other people to create perspective expanding experiences. You can consciously create your own.
Stephen R. Covey (American Speaker, Trainer, Author of "The 7 Habits of Highly Effective People")

35 Events of great consequence often spring from trifling circumstances.
Titus Livy (59 BC-17 AD, Roman Historian)

36 We are exactly where we have chosen to be.
Vernon Howard (19?-1992, American Author, Speaker)

37 I thought how unpleasant it is to be locked out; and I thought how it is worse, perhaps, to be locked in.
Virginia Woolf (1882-1941, British Novelist, Essayist)

38 Men's activities are occupied into ways -- in grappling with external circumstances and in striving to set things at one in their own topsy-turvy mind.
William James (1842-1910, American Psychologist, Professor, Author)

CITIES AND CITY LIFE

1 Washington is an endless series of mock palaces clearly built for clerks.
Ada Louise Huxtable

2 As a remedy to life in society I would suggest the big city. Nowadays, it is the only desert within our means.
Albert Camus (1913-1960, French Existential Writer)

3 A large city cannot be experientially known; its life is too manifold for any individual to be able to participate in it.
Aldous Huxley (1894-1963, British Author)

4 Man's course begins in a garden, but it ends in a city.
Alexander Maclaren (1826-1910, British Preacher)

5 If one had but a single glance to give the world, one should gaze on Istanbul.
Alphonse De Lamartine (1790-1869, French Poet, Statesman, Historian)

6 When in Rome, do as Rome does.
Ambrose Bierce (1842-1914, American Author, Editor, Journalist, "The Devil's Dictionary")

7 A great city is not to be confounded with a populous one.
Aristotle (384-322 BC, Greek Philosopher)

8 A great city, whose image dwells in the memory of man, is the type of some great idea. Rome represents conquest; Faith hovers over the towers of Jerusalem; and Athens embodies the pre- eminent quality of the antique world, Art.
Benjamin Disraeli (1804-1881, British Statesman, Prime Minister)

9 America is a nation with no truly national city, no Paris, no Rome, no London, no city which is at once the social center, the political capital, and the financial hub.
C. Wright Mills (1916-1962, American Sociologist)

10 I found Rome brick, I left it marble.
Caesar Augustus (63 BC-14 AD, Founder of Roman Empire)

11 The life of our city is rich in poetic and marvelous subjects. We are enveloped and steeped as though in an atmosphere of the marvelous; but we do not notice it.
Charles Baudelaire (1821-1867, French Poet)

12 There is no quiet place in the white man's cities. No place to hear the unfurling of leaves in spring, or the rustle of an insect's wings. But perhaps it is because I am a savage and do not understand. The clatter only seems to insult the ears.
Chief Seattle (1786-1866, American Indian Chief of the Suquamish)

13 The City attaches an exaggerated importance to the healing power of lunch.
Christopher Fieldes (British Financial Journalist)

14 New York, the nation's thyroid gland.
Christopher Morley (1890-1957, American Novelist, Journalist, Poet)

15 What is a city, but the people; true the people are the city.
Coriolanus III

16 No city should be too large for a man to walk out of in a morning.
Cyril Connolly (1903-1974, British Critic)

17 Towns oftener swamp one than carry one out onto the big ocean of life.
D. H. Lawrence (1885-1930, British Author)

18 New York now leads the world's great cities in the number of people around whom you shouldn't make a sudden move.
David Letterman (1947-, American TV Personality)

19 The city is not a concrete jungle. It is a human zoo.
Desmond Morris (1928-, British Anthropologist)

20 There is more sophistication and less sense in New York than anywhere else on the globe.
Don Herold

21 There are a number of things wrong with Washington. One of them is that everyone is too far from home.
Dwight D. Eisenhower (1890-1969, Thirty-fourth President of the USA)

22 Either these [unsaved] people are to be evangelized, or the leaven of communism and infidelity will assume such enormous proportions that it will break you in a reign of terror such as this country has never known.
Dwight L. Moody (1837-1899, American Evangelist)

23 There is a time of life somewhere between the sullen fugues of adolescence and the retrenchments of middle age when human nature becomes so absolutely absorbing one wants to be in the city constantly, even at the height of summer.
Edward Hoagland (1932-, American Novelist, Essayist)

24 Towns are excrescences, gray fluxions, where men, hurrying to find one another, have lost themselves.
Edward M. Forster (1879-1970, British Novelist, Essayist)

25 If you are lucky enough to have lived in Paris as a young man, then wherever you go for the rest of your life, it stays with you, for Paris is a movable feast.
Ernest Hemingway (1898-1961, American Writer)

26 All great art is born of the metropolis.
Ezra Pound (1885-1972, American Poet, Critic)

27 The two elements the traveler first captures in the big city are extra human architecture and furious rhythm. Geometry and anguish. At first glance, the rhythm may be confused with gaiety, but when you look more closely at the mechanism of social life and the painful slavery of both men and machines, you see that it is nothing but a kind of typical, empty anguish that makes even crime and gangs forgivable means of escape.
Federico Garcia Lorca (1898-1936, Spanish Poet, Dramatist, Musician and Artist)

28 Paris is the café of Europe.
Ferdinando Galiani

29 Where the criminals cover their crimes by making them legal. [On Washington D. C.]
Frank Dane

30 To look at the cross-section of any plan of a big city is to look at something like the section of a fibrous tumor.
Frank Lloyd Wright (1869-1959, American Architect)

31 The screech and mechanical uproar of the big city turns the citified head, fills citified ears -- as the song of birds, wind in the trees, animal cries, or as the voices and songs of his loved ones once filled his heart. He is sidewalk-happy.
Frank Lloyd Wright (1869-1959, American Architect)

32 Washington is no place for a good actor. The competition from bad actors is too great.
Fred A. Allen (1894-1957, American Radio Comic)

33 The first thing that strikes a visitor to Paris is a taxi.
Fred A. Allen (1894-1957, American Radio Comic)

34 An artist has no home in Europe except in Paris.
Friedrich Nietzsche (1844-1900, German Philosopher)

35 Boston is a moral and intellectual nursery always busy applying first principals to trifles.
George Santayana (1863-1952, American Philosopher, Poet)

36 City life is millions of people being lonesome together.
Henry David Thoreau (1817-1862, American Essayist, Poet, Naturalist)

37 The city is loveliest when the sweet death racket begins. Her own life lived in defiance of nature, her electricity, her frigidaires, her soundproof walls, the glint of lacquered nails, the plumes that wave across the corrugated sky. Here in the coffin depths grow the everlasting flowers sent by telegraph.
Henry Miller (1891-1980, American Author)

38 A city is a large community where people are lonesome together.
Herbert Prochnow

39 We are in danger of making our cities places where business goes on but where life, in its real sense, is lost.
Hubert H. Humphrey (1911-1978, American Democratic Politician, Vice President)

40 Who goes to Rome a beast returns a beast.
Italian Proverb

41 The catalogue of forms is endless: until every shape has found its city, new cities will continue to be born. When the forms exhaust their variety and come apart, the end of cities begins.
Italo Calvino (1923-1985, Cuban Writer, Essayist, Journalist)

42 One has not great hopes from Birmingham. I always say there is something direful in the sound.
Jane Austen (1775-1817, British Novelist)

43 We do not look in our great cities for our best morality.
Jane Austen (1775-1817, British Novelist)

44 But look what we have built low-income projects that become worse centers of delinquency, vandalism and general social hopelessness than the slums they were supposed to replace. Cultural centers that are unable to support a good bookstore. Civic centers that are avoided by everyone but bums. Promenades that go from no place to nowhere and have no promenaders. Expressways that eviscerate great cities. This is not the rebuilding of cities. This is the sacking of cities.
Jane Jacobs (1916-, American Urban Theorist, Author)

45 The crime problem in New York is getting really serious. The other day the Statue of Liberty had both hands up.
Jay Leno (American TV Show Host)

46 Cities are distinguished by the catastrophic forms they presuppose and which are a vital part of their essential charm. New York is King Kong, or the blackout, or vertical bombardment: Towering Inferno. Los Angeles is the horizontal fault, California breaking off and sliding into the Pacific: Earthquake.
Jean Baudrillard (French Postmodern Philosopher, Writer)

47 The cities of the world are concentric, isomorphic, synchronic. Only one exists and you are always in the same one. It's the effect of their permanent revolution, their intense circulation, their instantaneous magnetism.
Jean Baudrillard (French Postmodern Philosopher, Writer)

48 Every city has a sex and an age which have nothing to do with demography. Rome is feminine. So is Odessa. London is a teenager, an urchin, and, in this, hasn't changed since the time of Dickens. Paris, I believe, is a man in his twenties in love with an older woman.
John Berger (1926-, British Actor, Critic)

49 A neighborhood is a residential area that is changing for the worse.
John Ciardi (1916-1986, American Teacher, Poet, Writer)

50 Washington is a city of Southern efficiency and Northern charm.
John F. Kennedy (1917-1963, Thirty-fifth President of the USA)

51 We will neglect our cities to our peril, for in neglecting them we neglect the nation.
John F. Kennedy (1917-1963, Thirty-fifth President of the USA)

52 Through this broad street, restless ever, ebbs and flows a human tide, wave on wave a living river; wealth and fashion side by side; Toiler, idler, slave and master, in the same quick current glide.
John Greenleaf Whittier (1807-1892, American Poet, Reformer, Author)

53 The Metropolis should have been aborted long before it became New York, London or Tokyo.
John Kenneth Galbraith (1908-, American Economist)

54 I look upon those pitiful concretions of lime and clay which spring up, in mildewed forwardness, out of the kneaded fields about our capital... not merely with the careless disgust of an offended eye, not merely with sorrow for a desecrated landscape, but with a painful foreboding that the roots of our national greatness must be deeply cankered when they are thus loosely struck in their native ground. The crowded tenements of a struggling and restless population differ only from the tents of the Arab or the Gipsy by their less healthy openness to the air of heaven, and less happy choice of their spot of earth; by their sacrifice of liberty without the gain of rest, and of stability without the luxury of change.
John Ruskin (1819-1900, British Critic, Social Theorist)

55 New York is an exciting town where something is happening all the time, most unsolved.
Johnny Carson (1925-, American TV Personality, Businessman)

56 Living in cities is an art, and we need the vocabulary of art, of style, to describe the peculiar relationship between man and material that exists in the continual creative play of urban living. The city as we imagine it, then, soft city of illusion, myth, aspiration, and nightmare, is as real, maybe more real, than the hard city one can locate on maps in statistics, in monographs on urban sociology and demography and architecture.
Jonathan Raban (1942-, British Author, Critic)

57 What I like about cities is that everything is king size, the beauty and the ugliness.
Joseph Brodsky (1940-, Russian-born American Poet, Critic)

58 All things may be bought in Rome with money.
Juvenal (Decimus Junius Juvenalis) (55-130, Roman Satirical Poet)

59 There is no solitude in the world like that of the big city.
Kathleen Norris (1880-1966, American Novelist)

60 The chief function of the city is to convert power into form, energy into culture, dead matter into the living symbols of art, biological reproduction into social creativity.
Lewis Mumford (1895-1990, American Social Philosopher)

61 The city is a fact in nature, like a cave, a run of mackerel or an ant-heap. But it is also a conscious work of art, and it holds within its communal framework many simpler and more personal forms of art. Mind takes form in the city; and in turn, urban forms condition mind.
Lewis Mumford (1895-1990, American Social Philosopher)

62 The city as a center where, any day in any year, there may be a fresh encounter with a new talent, a keen mind or a gifted specialist -- this is essential to the life of a country. To play this role in our lives a city must have a soul -- a university, a great art or music school, a cathedral or a great mosque or temple, a great laboratory or scientific center, as well as the libraries and museums and galleries that bring past and present together. A city must be a place where groups of women and men are seeking and developing the highest things they know.
Margaret Mead (1901-1978, American Anthropologist)

63 A city is a place where there is no need to wait for next week to get the answer to a question, to taste the food of any country, to find new voices to listen to and familiar ones to listen to again.
Margaret Mead (1901-1978, American Anthropologist)

64 Today's city is the most vulnerable social structure ever conceived by man.
Martin Oppenheimer

65 I'm impressed with the people from Chicago. Hollywood is hype, New York is talk, Chicago is work.
Michael Douglas (1944-, American Actor, Director, Producer)

66 I have never felt salvation in nature. I love cities above all.
Michelangelo (1474-1564, Italian Renaissance Painter, Sculptor)

67 The faces in New York remind me of people who played a game and lost.
Murray Kempton (1917-1997, American Author and Columnist)

68 New York is not Mecca. It just smells like it.
Neil Simon (1927-, American Playwright)

69 What else can you expect from a town that's shut off from the world by the ocean on one side and New Jersey on the other?
O. Henry (1862-1910, American Writer)

70 The cities of America are inexpressibly tedious. The Bostonians take their learning too sadly; culture with them is an accomplishment rather than an atmosphere; their "Hub," as they call it, is the paradise of prigs. Chicago is a sort of monster-shop, full of bustles and bores. Political life at Washington is like political life in a suburban vestry. Baltimore is amusing for a week, but Philadelphia is dreadfully provincial; and though one can dine in New York one could not dwell there.
Oscar Wilde (1856-1900, British Author, Wit)

71 In place of a world, there is a city, a point, in which the whole life of broad regions is collecting while the rest dries up. In place of a type-true people, born of and grown on the soil, there is a new sort of nomad, cohering unstably in fluid masses, the parasitical city dweller, traditionless, utterly matter-of-fact, religionless, clever, unfruitful, deeply contemptuous of the countryman and especially that highest form of countryman, the country gentleman.
Oswald Spengler (1880-1936, German Philosopher)

72 All that a city will ever allow you is an angle on it -- an oblique, indirect sample of what it contains, or what passes through it; a point of view.
Peter Conrad (1948-, Australian Critic, Author)

73 Any city however small, is in fact divided into two, one the city of the poor, the other of the rich. These are at war with one another.
Plato (427-347 BC, Greek Philosopher)

74 All things atrocious and shameless flock from all parts to Rome.
Publius Cornelius Tacitus (55-117 AD, Roman Historian)

75 Just as language has no longer anything in common with the thing it names, so the movements of most of the people who live in cities have lost their connection with the earth; they hang, as it were, in the air, hover in all directions, and find no place where they can settle.
Rainer Maria Rilke (1875-1926, German Poet)

76 Cities give us collision. 'Tis said, London and New York take the nonsense out of a man.
Ralph Waldo Emerson (1803-1882, American Poet, Essayist)

77 Cities force growth and make people talkative and entertaining, but they also make them artificial.
Ralph Waldo Emerson (1803-1882, American Poet, Essayist)

78 The city is recruited from the country.
Ralph Waldo Emerson (1803-1882, American Poet, Essayist)

79 Washington is a city of people doing badly what should not be done at all.
Robert Gurney

80 Washington is a place where politicians don't know which way is up and taxes don't know which way is down.
Robert Orben (1927-, American Editor, Writer, Humorist)

81 Cities, like cats, will reveal themselves at night.
Rupert Brooke (1887-1915, British Poet)

82 Prepare for death, if here at night you roam, and sign your will before you sup from home.
Samuel Johnson (1709-1784, British Author)

83 Paris, a city of gaieties and pleasures, where four-fifths of the inhabitants die of grief. [About Paris]
Sebastien-Roch Nicolas De Chamfort (1741-1794, French Writer, Journalist, Playwright)

84 In Washington, the first thing people tell you is what their job is. In Los Angeles you learn their star sign. In Houston you're told how rich they are. And in New York they tell you what their rent is.
Simon Hoggart

85 If you're not in New York, you're camping out.
Thomas E. Dewey (1902-1971, American Politician)

86 One belongs to New York instantly. One belongs to it as much in five minutes as in five years.
Thomas Wolfe (1931-, American Author, Journalist)

87 I once spent a year in Philadelphia, I think it was on a Sunday.
W. C. Fields (1879-1946, American Actor)

88 The great city is that which has the greatest man or woman: if it be a few ragged huts, it is still the greatest city in the whole world.
Walt Whitman (1819-1892, American Poet)

89 A great city is that which has the greatest men and women.
Walt Whitman (1819-1892, American Poet)

90 Not to find one's way in a city may well be uninteresting and banal. It requires ignorance -- nothing more. But to lose oneself in a city -- as one loses oneself in a forest -- that calls for a quite different schooling. Then, signboard and street names, passers-by, roofs, kiosks, or bars must speak to the wanderer like a cracking twig under his feet in the forest.
Walter Benjamin (1982-1940, German Critic, Philosopher)

91 This city now doth, like a garment, wear the beauty of the morning; silent bare, ships, towers, domes, theatres and temples lie open unto the fields and to the sky; All bright and glittering in the smokeless air.
William Wordsworth (1770-1850, British Poet)

CITIZENSHIP

1 Every good citizen makes his country's honor his own, and cherishes it not only as precious but as sacred. He is willing to risk his life in its defense and its conscious that he gains protection while he gives it.
Andrew Jackson (1767-1845, Seventh President of the USA)

2 Whatever makes men good Christians, makes them good citizens.
Daniel Webster (1782-1852, American Lawyer, Statesman)

3 The true courage of civilized nations is readiness for sacrifice in the service of the state, so that the individual counts as only one amongst many. The important thing here is not personal mettle but aligning oneself with the universal.
Georg Hegel (1770-1831, German Philosopher)

4 It is not the function of our Government to keep the citizen from falling into error; it is the function of the citizen to keep the Government from falling into error.
Robert H. Jackson (1892-1954, American Supreme Court Justice)

5 A strict observance of the written laws is doubtless one of the high virtues of a good citizen, but it is not the highest. The laws of necessity, of self-preservation, of saving our country when in danger, are of higher obligation.
Thomas Jefferson (1743-1826, Third President of the USA)

6 Our citizenship in the United States is our national character. Our citizenship in any particular state is only our local distinction. By the latter we are known at home, by the former to the world. Our great title is AMERICANS -- our inferior one varies with the place.
Thomas Paine (1737-1809, Anglo-American Political Theorist, Writer)

7 Without free, self-respecting, and autonomous citizens there can be no free and independent nations. Without internal peace, that is, peace among citizens and between the citizens and the state, there can be no guarantee of external peace.
Vaclav Havel (1936-, Czech Playwright, President)

CIVIL RIGHTS

1 The government of the United States is a device for maintaining in perpetuity the rights of the people, with the ultimate extinction of all privileged classes.
Calvin Coolidge (1872-1933, Thirtieth President of the USA)

2 Civil Rights: What black folks are given in the U.S. on the installment plan, as in civil-rights bills. Not to be confused with human rights, which are the dignity, stature, humanity, respect, and freedom belonging to all people by right of their birth.
Dick Gregory (American Comedian)

3 Men are qualified for civil liberty in exact proportion to their disposition to put moral chains upon their own appetites; in proportion as their love to justice is above their rapacity; in proportion as their soundness and sobriety of understanding is above their vanity and presumption; in proportion as they are more disposed to listen to the counsels of the wise and good, in preference to the flattery of knaves.
Edmund Burke (1729-1797, British Political Writer, Statesman)

4 Ignorance, forgetfulness, or contempt of the rights of man are the only causes of public misfortunes and of the corruption of governments.
French National Assembly

5 To exercise power costs effort and demands courage. That is why so many fail to assert rights to which they are perfectly entitled -- because a right is a kind of power but they are too lazy or too cowardly to exercise it. The virtues which cloak these faults are called patience and forbearance.
Friedrich Nietzsche (1844-1900, German Philosopher)

6 The modern state no longer has anything but rights; it does not recognize duties any more.
Georges Bernanos (1888-1948, French Novelist, Political Writer)

7 The theory of rights enables us to rise and overthrow obstacles, but not to found a strong and lasting accord between all the elements which compose the nation.
Giuseppe Mazzini (1805-1872, Italian Patriot, Writer)

8 There are those who say to you -- we are rushing this issue of civil rights. I say we are 172 years late.
Hubert H. Humphrey (1911-1978, American Democratic Politician, Vice President)

9 A state that denies its citizens their basic rights becomes a danger to its neighbors as well: internal arbitrary rule will be reflected in arbitrary external relations. The suppression of public opinion, the abolition of public competition for power and its public exercise opens the way for the state power to arm itself in any way it sees fit. A state that does not hesitate to lie to its own people will not hesitate to lie to other states.
Vaclav Havel (1936-, Czech Playwright, President)

10 Anglo-Saxon civilization has taught the individual to protect his own rights; American civilization will teach him to respect the rights of others.
William Jennings Bryan (1860-1925, American Lawyer, Politician)

CIVILIZATION

1 The human race has improved everything, but the human race.
Adlai E. Stevenson (1900-1965, American Lawyer, Politician)

2 A civilization is a heritage of beliefs, customs, and knowledge slowly accumulated in the course of centuries, elements difficult at times to justify by logic, but justifying themselves as paths when they lead somewhere, since they open up for man his inner distance.
Antoine De Saint-Exupery (1900-1944, French Aviator, Writer)

3 A civilization is built on what is required of men, not on that which is provided for them.
Antoine De Saint-Exupery (1900-1944, French Aviator, Writer)

4 Civilization is a movement and not a condition, a voyage and not a harbor.
Arnold Toynbee (1852-1883, British Economic Historian and Social Reformer)

5 To be able to fill leisure intelligently is the last product of civilization.
Arnold Toynbee (1852-1883, British Economic Historian and Social Reformer)

6 Civilizations die from suicide, not by murder.
Arnold Toynbee (1852-1883, British Economic Historian and Social Reformer)

7 Increased means and increased leisure are the two civilizers of man.
Benjamin Disraeli (1804-1881, British Statesman, Prime Minister)

8 The civilized savage is the worst of all savages.
C. J. Weber

9 Civilization is just a slow process of learning to be kind.
Charles L. Lucas

10 Civilization is an active deposit which is formed by the combustion of the present with the past. Neither in countries without a Present nor in those without a Past is it to be encountered. Proust in Venice, Matisse's birdcages overlooking the flower market at Nice, Gide on the seventeenth- century quais of Toulon, Lorca in Granada, Picasso by Saint-Germain-des-Prés: there lies civilization and for me it can exist only under those liberal regimes in which the Present is alive and therefore capable of assimilating the Past.
Cyril Connolly (1903-1974, British Critic)

11 The civilized are those who get more out of life than the uncivilized, and for this we are not likely to be forgiven.
Cyril Connolly (1903-1974, British Critic)

12 Every new stroke of civilization has cost the lives of countless brave men, who have fallen defeated by the "dragon," in their efforts to win the apples of the Hesperides, or the fleece of gold. Fallen in their efforts to overcome the old, half sordid savagery of the lower stages of creation, and win the next stage.
D. H. Lawrence (1885-1930, British Author)

13 The ultimate tendency of civilization is towards barbarism.
David Hare (1947-, British Playwright, Director)

14 Civilization...is a matter of imponderables, of delight in the thins of the mind, of love of beauty, of honor, grace, courtesy, delicate feeling. Where imponderables, are things of first importance, there is the height of civilization, and, if at the same time, the power of art exists unimpaired, human life has reached a level seldom attained and very seldom surpassed.
Edith Hamilton (1867-1963, American Classical Scholar, Translator)

15 The path of civilization is paved with tin cans.
Elbert Hubbard (1859-1915, American Author, Publisher)

16 We are born princes and the civilizing process makes us frogs.
Eric Berne (1910-1970, Canadian Psychiatrist, Writer)

17 A civilized man is one who will give a serious answer to a serious question. Civilization itself is a certain sane balance of values.
Ezra Pound (1885-1972, American Poet, Critic)

18 To accept civilization as it is practically means accepting decay.
George Orwell (1903-1950, British Author, "Animal Farm")

19 The test of civilization is its estimate of women.
George William Curtis (1824-1892, American Journalist)

20 I think there are only three things America will be known for 2, 000 years from now when they study this civilization: the Constitution, jazz music and baseball.
Gerald Early (1952-, American Author)

21 All civilization has from time to time become a thin crust over a volcano of revolution.
Havelock Ellis (1859-1939, British Psychologist)

22 One might enumerate the items of high civilization, as it exists in other countries, which are absent from the texture of American life, until it should become a wonder to know what was left.
Henry James (1843-1916, American Author)

23 The word "civilization" to my mind is coupled with death. When I use the word, I see civilization as a crippling, thwarting thing, a stultifying thing. For me it was always so. I don't believe in the golden ages, you see... civilization is the arteriosclerosis of culture.
Henry Miller (1891-1980, American Author)

24 Civilization is drugs, alcohol, engines of war, prostitution, machines and machine slaves, low wages, bad food, bad taste, prisons, reformatories, lunatic asylums, divorce, perversion, brutal sports, suicides, infanticide, cinema, quackery, demagogy, strikes, lockouts, revolutions, putsches, colonization, electric chairs, guillotines, sabotage, floods, famine, disease, gangsters, money barons, horse racing, fashion shows, poodle dogs, chow dogs, Siamese cats, condoms, peccaries, syphilis, gonorrhea, insanity, neuroses, etc., etc.
Henry Miller (1891-1980, American Author)

25 Each new generation is a fresh invasion of savages.
Hervey Allen (1889-1949, American Author)

26 The skylines lit up at dead of night, the air-conditioning systems· cooling empty hotels in the desert and artificial light in the middle of the day all have something both demented and admirable about them. The mindless luxury of a rich civilization, and yet of a civilization perhaps as scared to see the lights go out as was the hunter in his primitive night.
Jean Baudrillard (French Postmodern Philosopher, Writer)

27 Civilization is the making of civil persons.
John Ruskin (1819-1900, British Critic, Social Theorist)

28 People sometimes tell me that they prefer barbarism to civilization. I doubt if they have given it a long enough trial. Like the people of Alexandria, they are bored by civilization; but all the evidence suggests that the boredom of barbarism is infinitely greater.
Kenneth Clark

29 Civilization -- a heap of rubble scavenged by scrawny English Lit. vultures.
Malcolm Muggeridge (1903-1990, British Broadcaster)

30 Civilization is a limitless multiplication of unnecessary necessities.
Mark Twain (1835-1910, American Humorist, Writer)

31 Is civilization only a higher form of idolatry, that man should bow down to a flesh-brush, to flannels, to baths, diet, exercise, and air?
Mary Baker Eddy (1821-1910, American Christian Writer, Founder of Christian Science Church)

32 Civilization is not by any means an easy thing to attain to. There are only two ways by which man can reach it. One is by being cultured, the other by being corrupt.
Oscar Wilde (1856-1900, British Author, Wit)

33 As long as our civilization is essentially one of property, of fences, of exclusiveness, it will be mocked by delusions. Our riches will leave us sick; there will be bitterness in our laughter; and our wine will burn our mouth. Only that good profits, which we can taste with all doors open, and which serves all men.
Ralph Waldo Emerson (1803-1882, American Poet, Essayist)

34 Sunday is the core of our civilization, dedicated to thought and reverence.
Ralph Waldo Emerson (1803-1882, American Poet, Essayist)

35 Civilization depends on morality.
Ralph Waldo Emerson (1803-1882, American Poet, Essayist)

36 Civilization is a process in the service of Eros, whose purpose is to combine single human individuals, and after that families, then races, peoples and nations, into one great unity, the unity of mankind. Why this has to happen, we do not know; the work of Eros is precisely this.
Sigmund Freud (1856-1939, Austrian Physician - Founder of Psychoanalysis)

37 If Germany, thanks to Hitler and his successors, were to enslave the European nations and destroy most of the treasures of their past, future historians would certainly pronounce that she had civilized Europe.
Simone Weil (1910-1943, French Philosopher, Mystic)

38 Civilization is the lamb's skin in which barbarism masquerades.
Thomas B. Aldrich (1836-1907, American Writer, Editor)

39 The three great elements of modern civilization, Gun powder, Printing, and the Protestant religion.
Thomas Carlyle (1795-1881, Scottish Philosopher, Author)

40 Civilization today reminds me of an ape with a blowtorch playing in a room full of dynamite. It looks like the monkeys are about to operate the zoo, and the inmates are taking over the asylum.
Vance Havner

41 Civilization must be destroyed. The hairy saints of the North have earned this crumb by their complaints.
Wallace Stevens (1879-1955, American Poet)

42 Civilization is a stream with banks. The stream is sometimes filled with blood from people killing, stealing, shouting and doing the things historians usually record, while on the banks, unnoticed, people build homes, make love, raise children, sing songs, write poetry and even whittle statues. The story of civilization is the story of what happened on the banks. Historians are pessimists because they ignore the banks for the river.
William J. Durant (1885-1981, American Historian, Essayist)

43 Without winners, there wouldn't even be any civilization.
Woody Hayes (American College Football Coach)

CLASS

1 The distinctions separating the social classes are false; in the last analysis they rest on force.
Albert Einstein (1879-1955, German-born American Physicist)

2 I am his Highness dog at Kew; pray tell me, sir, whose dog are you?
Alexander Pope (1688-1744, British Poet, Critic, Translator)

3 The Americans never use the word peasant, because they have no idea of the class which that term denotes; the ignorance of more remote ages, the simplicity of rural life, and the rusticity of the villager have not been preserved among them; and they are alike unacquainted with the virtues, the vices, the coarse habits, and the simple graces of an early stage of civilization.
Alexis De Tocqueville (1805-1859, French Social Philosopher)

4 All mankind is divided into three classes: those that are immovable, those that are movable, and those that move.
Arabian Proverb

5 Between richer and poorer classes in a free country a mutually respecting antagonism is much healthier than pity on the one hand and dependence on the other, as is, perhaps, the next best thing to fraternal feeling.
Charles Horton Cooley (1864-1929, American Sociologist)

6 By bourgeoisie is meant the class of modern capitalists, owners of the means of social production and employers of wage labor. By proletariat, the class of modern wage laborers who, having no means of production of their own, are reduced to selling their labor power in order to live.
Friedrich Engels (1820-1895, German Social Philosopher)

7 Let the others have the charisma. I've got the class.
George Bush (1924-, Forty-first President of the USA)

8 Throughout recorded time... there have been three kinds of people in the world, the High, the Middle, and the Low. They have been subdivided in many ways, they have borne countless different names, and their relative numbers, as well as their attitude towards one another, have varied from age to age: but the essential structure of society has never altered. Even after enormous upheavals and seemingly irrevocable changes, the same pattern has always reasserted itself, just as a gyroscope will always return to equilibrium, however far it is pushed one way or the other. The aims of these three groups are entirely irreconcilable.
George Orwell (1903-1950, British Author, "Animal Farm")

9 The ignorant classes are the dangerous classes.
Henry Ward Beecher (1813-1887, American Preacher, Orator, Writer)

10 The traveler to the United States will do well to prepare himself for the class-consciousness of the natives. This differs from the already familiar English version in being more extreme and based more firmly on the conviction that the class to which the speaker belongs is inherently superior to all others.
John Kenneth Galbraith (1908-, American Economist)

11 For the duration of its collective life, or the time during which its identity may be assumed, each class resembles a hotel or an omnibus, always full, but always of different people.
Joseph A. Schumpeter (1883-1950, Austrian-American Economist)

12 Mankind is divided into rich and poor, into property owners and exploited; and to abstract oneself from this fundamental division ;and from the antagonism between poor and rich means abstracting oneself from fundamental facts.
Joseph Stalin (1879-1953, Georgian-born Soviet Leader)

13 Wearing overalls on weekdays, painting somebody else's house to earn money? You're working class. Wearing overalls at weekends, painting your own house to save money? You're middle class.
Lawrence Sutton

14 There is nothing to which men cling more tenaciously than the privileges of class.
Leonard Sidney Woolf (1880-1969, British Publisher, Writer)

15 Classes struggle, some classes triumph, others are eliminated. Such is history; such is the history of civilization for thousands of years.
Mao Zedong (1893-1976, Founder of Chinese Communist State)

16 If experience has established any one thing in this world, it has established this: that it is well for any great class and description of men in society to be able to say for itself what it wants, and not to have other classes, the so-called educated and intelligent classes, acting for it as its proctors, and supposed to understand its wants and to provide for them. A class of men may often itself not either fully understand its wants, or adequately express them; but it has a nearer interest and a more sure diligence in the matter than any of its proctors, and therefore a better chance of success.
Matthew Arnold (1822-1888, British Poet, Critic)

17 Really, if the lower orders don't set us a good example, what on earth is the use of them? They seem, as a class, to have absolutely no sense of moral responsibility.
Oscar Wilde (1856-1900, British Author, Wit)

18 Historically and politically, the petit-bourgeois is the key to the century. The bourgeois and proletariat classes have become abstractions: the petite-bourgeoisie, in contrast, is everywhere, you can see it everywhere, even in the areas of the bourgeois and the proletariat, what's left of them.
Roland Barthes (1915-1980, French Semiologist)

19 The want of education and moral training is the only real barrier that exists between the different classes of men. Nature, reason, and Christianity recognize no other. Pride may say Nay; but Pride was always a liar, and a great hater of the truth.
Susanna Moodie (1803-1885, Canadian Author)

20 Let him who expects one class of society to prosper in the highest degree, while the other is in distress, try whether one side ;of the face can smile while the other is pinched.
Thomas Fuller (1608-1661, British Clergyman, Author)

21 Lady Hodmarsh and the duchess immediately assumed the clinging affability that persons of rank assume with their inferiors in order to show them that they are not in the least conscious of any difference in station between them.
W. Somerset Maugham (1874-1965, British Novelist, Playwright)

22 Other lands have their vitality in a few, a class, but we have it in the bulk of our people.
Walt Whitman (1819-1892, American Poet)

23 All the world over, I will back the masses against the classes.
William E. Gladstone (1809-1888, British Liberal Prime Minister, Statesman)

24 When we say a woman is of a certain social class, we really mean her husband or father is.
Zoe Fairbairns

CLEVERNESS

1 Mother is far too clever to understand anything she does not like.
Arnold Bennett (1867-1931, British Novelist)

2 Cleverness is not wisdom.
Euripides (480-406 BC, Greek Tragic Poet)

3 It is great cleverness to know how to conceal our cleverness.
François de La Rochefoucauld (1613-1680, French classical writer)

4 The desire to seem clever often keeps us from being so.
François de La Rochefoucauld (1613-1680, French classical writer)

5 Find enough clever things to say, and you're a Prime Minister; write them down and you're a Shakespeare.
George Bernard Shaw (1856-1950, Irish-born British Dramatist)

6 The doctrine of human equality reposes on this: that there is no man really clever who has not found that he is stupid.
Gilbert K. Chesterton (1874-1936, British Author)

7 Cleverness is serviceable for everything, sufficient for nothing.
Henri Frederic Amiel (1821-1881, Swiss Philosopher, Poet, Critic)

8 A man likes his wife to be just clever enough to appreciate his cleverness, and just stupid enough to admire it.
Israel Zangwill (1864-1926, British Writer)

9 A cul-de-sac to which ideas are lured and then quietly strangled.
John A. Lincoln

10 Clever men are good, but they are not the best.
Thomas Carlyle (1795-1881, Scottish Philosopher, Author)

CLONING

1 The cloning of humans is on most of the lists of things to worry about from science, along with behavior control, genetic engineering, transplanted heads, computer poetry and the unrestrained growth of plastic flowers.
Lewis Thomas (1913-, American Physician, Educator)

CLUB

1 I'd never join a club that would allow a person like me to become a member.
Woody Allen (1935-, American Director, Screenwriter, Actor, Comedian)

COACHES AND COACHING

1 A good coach will make his players see what they can be rather than what they are.
Ara Parasheghian (American College Football Coach)

2 A good hitting instructor is able to mold his teaching to the individual. If a guy stands on his head, you perfect that.
Bill Robinson (American Baseball Manager)

3 One thing I never want to be accused of is not working.
Don Shula (American Football Coach)

4 Coaches have to watch for what they don't want to see and listen to what they don't want to hear.
John Madden (American Football Coach)

5 There are only two kinds of coaches -- those who have been fired, and those who will be fired.
Ken Loeffler (American College Basketball Coach)

6 Coaching is nothing more than eliminating mistakes before you get fired.
Lou Holtz (1937-, American Football Coach)

7 I have a lot of respect for tough coaches.
Reggie White

8 Coaches who can outline plays on a black board are a dime a dozen. The ones who win get inside their player and motivate.
Vince Lombardi (1913-1970, American Football Coach)

COLLEGES AND UNIVERSITIES

1 The most important function of the university in an age of reason is to protect reason from itself.
Allan Bloom (1930-1992, American Educator, Author)

2 The race of prophets is extinct. Europe is becoming set in its ways, slowly embalming itself beneath the wrappings of its borders, its factories, its law-courts and its universities. The frozen Mind cracks between the mineral staves which close upon it. The fault lies with your moldy systems, your logic of 2 + 2 = 4. The fault lies with you, Chancellors, caught in the net of syllogisms. You manufacture engineers, magistrates, doctors, who know nothing of the true mysteries of the body or the cosmic laws of existence. False scholars blind outside this world, philosophers who pretend to reconstruct the mind. The least act of spontaneous creation is a more complex and revealing world than any metaphysics.
Antonin Artaud (1896-1948, French Theater Producer, Actor, Theorist)

3 Our major universities are now stuck with an army of pedestrian, toadying careerists, Fifties types who wave around Sixties banners to conceal their record of ruthless, beaver-like tunneling to the top.
Camille Paglia (1947-, American Author, Critic, Educator)

4 American universities are organized on the principle of the nuclear rather than the extended family. Graduate students are grimly trained to be technicians rather than connoisseurs. The old German style of universal scholarship has gone.
Camille Paglia (1947-, American Author, Critic, Educator)

5 They were evidently small men, all wind and quibbles, flinging out their chuffy grain to us with far less interest than a farm-wife feels as she scatters corn to her fowls.
D. H. Lawrence (1885-1930, British Author)

6 In university they don't tell you that the greater part of the law is learning to tolerate fools.
Doris Lessing (1919-, British Novelist)

7 It is dangerous sending a young man who is beautiful to Oxford.
Dudley Ryder

8 I often think how much easier the world would have been to manage if Herr Hitler and Signor Mussolini had been at Oxford.
Edward F. Halifax (1881-1959, British Conservative Statesman)

9 Oxford is -- Oxford: not a mere receptacle for youth, like Cambridge. Perhaps it wants its inmates to love it rather than to love one another.
Edward M. Forster (1879-1970, British Novelist, Essayist)

10 Socrates gave no diplomas or degrees, and would have subjected any disciple who demanded one to a disconcerting catechism on the nature of true knowledge.
G. M. Trevelyan (1876-1962, British Historian)

11 Oxford, the paradise of dead philosophies.
George Santayana (1863-1952, American Philosopher, Poet)

12 Towery city and branching between towers; Cuckoo-echoing, bell-swarmed, lark-charmed, rook-racked, river-rounded.
Gerard Manley Hopkins (1844-1889, British Poet)

13   Let's not burn the universities yet. After all, the damage they do might be worse.
H. L. Mencken (1880-1956, American Editor, Author, Critic, Humorist)

14   To be sure, nothing is more important to the integrity of the universities than a rigorously enforced divorce from war-oriented research and all connected enterprises.
Hannah Arendt (1906-1975, German-born American Political Philosopher)

15   College isn't the place to go for ideas.
Helen Keller (1880-1968, American Blind/Deaf Author, Lecturer, Amorist)

16   Remote and ineffectual don.
Hilaire Belloc (1870-1953, British Author)

17   What poor education I have received has been gained in the University of Life.
Horatio Bottomley (American Politician)

18   Within the university... you can study without waiting for any efficient or immediate result. You may search, just for the sake of searching, and try for the sake of trying. So there is a possibility of what I would call playing. It's perhaps the only place within society where play is possible to such an extent.
Jacques Derrida

19   Master and Doctor are my titles; for ten years now, without repose, I held my erudite recitals and led my pupils by the nose.
Johann Wolfgang Von Goethe (1749-1832, German Poet, Dramatist, Novelist)

20   A university is what a college becomes when the faculty loses interest in students.
John Ciardi (1916-1986, American Teacher, Poet, Writer)

21   It might be said now that I have the best of both worlds: a Harvard education and a Yale degree.
John F. Kennedy (1917-1963, Thirty-fifth President of the USA)

22   This place is the Devil, or at least his principal residence, they call it the University, but any other appellation would have suited it much better, for study is the last pursuit of the society; the Master eats, drinks, and sleeps, the Fellows drink, dispute and pun, the employments of the undergraduates you will probably conjecture without my description.
Lord Byron (1788-1824, British Poet)

23   If the factory people outside the colleges live under the discipline of narrow means, the people inside live under almost every other kind of discipline except that of narrow means -- from the fruity austerities of learning, through the iron rations of English gentlemanhood, down to the modest disadvantages of occupying cold stone buildings without central heating and having to cross two or three quadrangles to take a bath.
Margaret Halsey (1910-, American Author)

24   Home of lost causes, and forsaken beliefs, and unpopular names, and impossible loyalties!
Matthew Arnold (1822-1888, British Poet, Critic)

25   They teach anything in universities today. You can major in mud pies.
Orson Welles (1915-1985, American Film Maker)

26   In spite of the roaring of the young lions at the Union, and the screaming of the rabbits in the home of the vivisect, in spite of Keble College, and the tramways, and the sporting prints, Oxford still remains the most beautiful thing in England, and nowhere else are life and art so exquisitely blended, so perfectly made one.
Oscar Wilde (1856-1900, British Author, Wit)

27   The exquisite art of idleness, one of the most important things that any University can teach.
Oscar Wilde (1856-1900, British Author, Wit)

28   I am not impressed by the Ivy League establishments. Of course they graduate the best -- it's all they'll take, leaving to others the problem of educating the country. They will give you an education the way the banks will give you money -- provided you can prove to their satisfaction that you don't need it.
Peter De Vries (1910-, American Author)

29   I had always imagined that Cliché was a suburb of Paris, until I discovered it to be a street in Oxford.
Philip Guedalla (1889-1944, British Writer)

30   One of the benefits of a college education is to show the boy its little avail.
Ralph Waldo Emerson (1803-1882, American Poet, Essayist)

31   Universities are of course hostile to geniuses, which, seeing and using ways of their own, discredit the routine: as churches and monasteries persecute youthful saints.
Ralph Waldo Emerson (1803-1882, American Poet, Essayist)

32   The colleges, while they provide us with libraries, furnish no professors of books; and I think no chair is so much needed.
Ralph Waldo Emerson (1803-1882, American Poet, Essayist)

33   While formal schooling is an important advantage, it is not a guarantee of success nor is its absence a fatal handicap.
Ray Kroc (1902-1984, American businessman, Founder of McDonalds)

34   Colleges are places where pebbles are polished and diamonds are dimmed.
Robert Green Ingersoll (1833-1899, American Orator, Lawyer)

35   The greatest gift that Oxford gives her sons is, I truly believe, a genial irreverence toward learning, and from that irreverence love may spring.
Robertson Davies (1913-, Canadian Novelist, Journalist)

36   I was a modest, good-humored boy. It is Oxford that has made me insufferable.
Sir Max Beerbohm (1872-1956, British Actor)

37   University degrees are a bit like adultery: you may not want to get involved with that sort of thing, but you don't want to be thought incapable.
Sir Peter Imbert

38 Apparently, the most difficult feat for a Cambridge male is to accept a woman not merely as feeling, not merely as thinking, but as managing a complex, vital interweaving of both.
Sylvia Plath (1932-1963, American Poet)

39 A thorough knowledge of the Bible is worth more than a college education.
Theodore Roosevelt (1858-1919, Twenty-sixth President of the USA)

40 A college education should equip one to entertain three things: a friend, an idea and oneself.
Thomas Ehrlich

41 The medieval university looked backwards; it professed to be a storehouse of old knowledge. The modern university looks forward, and is a factory of new knowledge.
Thomas H. Huxley (1825-1895, British Biologist, Educator)

42 I am willing to admit that some people might live there for years, or even a lifetime, so protected that they never sense the sweet stench of corruption that is all around them -- the keen, thin scent of decay that pervades everything and accuses with a terrible accusation the superficial youthfulness, the abounding undergraduate noise, that fills those ancient buildings.
Thomas Merton (1915-1968, American Religious Writer, Poet)

43 If we help an educated man's daughter to go to Cambridge are we not forcing her to think not about education but about war? -- not how she can learn, but how she can fight in order that she might win the same advantages as her brothers?
Virginia Woolf (1882-1941, British Novelist, Essayist)

44 I am told that today rather more than 60 per cent of the men who go to university go on a Government grant. This is a new class that has entered upon the scene. It is the white-collar proletariat. They do not go to university to acquire culture but to get a job, and when they have got one, scamp it. They have no manners and are woefully unable to deal with any social predicament. Their idea of a celebration is to go to a public house and drink six beers. They are mean, malicious and envious . They are scum.
W. Somerset Maugham (1874-1965, British Novelist, Playwright)

45 I wonder anybody does anything at Oxford but dream and remember, the place is so beautiful. One almost expects the people to sing instead of speaking. It is all like an opera.
William Butler Yeats (1865-1939, Irish Poet, Playwright.)

46 'Tis well enough for a servant to be bred at an University. But the education is a little too pedantic for a gentleman.
William Congreve (1670-1729, British Dramatist)

COLOR

1 The true color of life is the color of the body, the color of the covered red, the implicit and not explicit red of the living heart and the pulses. It is the modest color of the unpublished blood.
Alice Meynell (1847-1922, British Poet, Essayist)

2 Blueness doth express trueness.
Ben Johnson (1573-1637, British Dramatist, Poet)

3 Color is my day-long obsession, joy and torment. To such an extent indeed that one day, finding myself at the deathbed of a woman who had been and still was very dear to me, I caught myself in the act of focusing on her temples and automatically analyzing the succession of appropriately graded colors which death was imposing on her motionless face.
Claude Monet

4 Green how I want you green. Green wind. Green branches.
Federico Garcia Lorca (1898-1936, Spanish Poet, Dramatist, Musician and Artist)

5 White is not a mere absence of color; it is a shining and affirmative thing, as fierce as red, as definite as black. God paints in many colors; but He never paints so gorgeously, I had almost said so gaudily, as when He paints in white.
Gilbert K. Chesterton (1874-1936, British Author)

6 The purest and most thoughtful minds are those which love color the most.
John Ruskin (1819-1900, British Critic, Social Theorist)

7 Of all God's gifts to the sighted man, color is holiest, the most divine, the most solemn.
John Ruskin (1819-1900, British Critic, Social Theorist)

8 Colors answer feeling in man; shapes answer thought; and motion answers will.
John Sterling (American Sports Announcer)

9 Colors are the smiles of nature.
Leigh Hunt (1784-1859, British Poet, Essayist)

10 All colors are the friends of their neighbors and the lovers of their opposites.
Marc Chagall (1889-1985, French Artist)

11 He had that curious love of green, which in individuals is always the sign of a subtle artistic temperament, and in nations is said to denote a laxity, if not a decadence of morals.
Oscar Wilde (1856-1900, British Author, Wit)

12 Mere color, unspoiled by meaning, and unallied with definite form, can speak to the soul in a thousand different ways.
Oscar Wilde (1856-1900, British Author, Wit)

13 Why do two colors, put one next to the other, sing? Can one really explain this? no. Just as one can never learn how to paint.
Pablo Picasso (1881-1973, Spanish Artist)

14 Colors, like features, follow the changes of the emotions.
Pablo Picasso (1881-1973, Spanish Artist)

15 Color possesses me. I don't have to pursue it. It will possess me always, I know it. That is the meaning of this happy hour: Color and I are one. I am a painter.
Paul Klee (1879-1940, Swiss Artist)

16 Painting is something that takes place among the colors, and one has to leave them alone completely, so that they can settle the matter among themselves. Their intercourse: this is the whole of painting. Whoever meddles, arranges, injects his human deliberation, his wit, his advocacy, his intellectual agility in any way, is already disturbing and clouding their activity.
Rainer Maria Rilke (1875-1926, German Poet)

17 There is no blue without yellow and without orange.
Vincent Van Gogh (1853-1890, Dutch-born French Painter)

18 I cannot pretend to feel impartial about colors. I rejoice with the brilliant ones and am genuinely sorry for the poor browns.
Winston Churchill (1874-1965, British Statesman, Prime Minister)

COMEDY AND COMEDIANS

1 Comedy is tragedy that happens to other people.
Angela Carter (1940-1992, British Author)

2 Life is a tragedy when seen in close-up, but a comedy in long-shot.
Charlie Chaplin (1889-1977, British Comic Actor, Filmmaker)

3 All I need to make a comedy is a park, a policeman and a pretty girl.
Charlie Chaplin (1889-1977, British Comic Actor, Filmmaker)

4 Comedy is an escape, not from truth but from despair; a narrow escape into faith.
Christopher Fry (1907-, British Playwright)

5 In comedy, reconcilement with life comes at the point when to the tragic sense only an inalienable difference or dissension with life appears.
Constance Rourke (1885-1941, American Author)

6 I was doing stand-up at a restaurant and there was a chalkboard on the street out front. It said, "Soup of the Day: Cream of Asparagus. Ellen DeGeneres."
Ellen DeGeneres

7 Humorists can never start to take themselves seriously. It's literary suicide.
Erma Bombeck (1927-, American Author, Humorist)

8 A man's got to take a lot of punishment to write a really funny book.
Ernest Hemingway (1898-1961, American Writer)

9 When humor can be made to alternate with melancholy, one has a success, but when the same things are funny and melancholic at the same time, it's just wonderful.
FrantOis Truffaut (1932-1984, French Film Critic and Director)

10 We are living in the machine age. For the first time in history the comedian has been compelled to supply himself with jokes and comedy material to compete with the machine. Whether he knows it or not, the comedian is on a treadmill to oblivion.
Fred A. Allen (1894-1957, American Radio Comic)

11 The test of a real comedian is whether you laugh at him before he opens his mouth.
George Jean Nathan (1882-1958, American Critic)

12 We mustn't complain too much of being comedians -- it's an honorable profession. If only we could be good ones the world might gain at least a sense of style. We have failed -- that's all. We are bad comedians, we aren't bad men.
Graham Greene (1904-1991, British Novelist)

13 Comedy has to be done en clair. You can't blunt the edge of wit or the point of satire with obscurity. Try to imagine a famous witty saying that is not immediately clear.
James Thurber (1894-1961, American Humorist, Illustrator)

14 The only rules comedy can tolerate are those of taste, and the only limitations those of libel.
James Thurber (1894-1961, American Humorist, Illustrator)

15 My routines come out of total unhappiness. My audiences are my group therapy.
Joan Rivers (1933-, American Comedian, Talk Show Host, Actress)

16 There is not one female comic who was beautiful as a little girl.
Joan Rivers (1933-, American Comedian, Talk Show Host, Actress)

17 If I get a hard audience they are not going to get away until they laugh. Those seven laughs a minute -- I've got to have them.
Ken Dodd

18 Today's comedian has a cross to bear that he built himself. A comedian of the older generation did an "act" and he told the audience, "This is my act." Today's comic is not doing an act. The audience assumes he's telling the truth. What is truth today may be a damn lie next week.
Lenny Bruce (1925-1966, American Comedian)

19 The only honest art form is laughter, comedy. You can't fake it... try to fake three laughs in an hour -- ha ha ha ha ha -- they'll take you away, man. You can't.
Lenny Bruce (1925-1966, American Comedian)

20 Charlie Chaplin's genius was in comedy. He has no sense of humor, particularly about himself.
Lita Grey Chaplin

21 Comedy, like sodomy, is an unnatural act.
Marty Feldman

22 Comedy deflates the sense precisely so that the underlying lubricity and malice may bubble to the surface.
Paul Goodman (1911-1972, American Author, Poet, Critic)

23 I always loved comedy, but I never knew it was something you could learn to do. I always thought that some people are born comedians ... just like some people are born dentists.
Paul Reiser (1957-, American Actor, Comedian, Writer)

24 The perception of the comic is a tie of sympathy with other men, a pledge of sanity, and a protection from those perverse tendencies and gloomy insanities in which fine intellects sometimes lose themselves. A rogue alive to the ludicrous is still convertible. If that sense is lost, his fellow-men can do little for him.
Ralph Waldo Emerson (1803-1882, American Poet, Essayist)

25 The guy has baggy pants, flat feet, the most miserable, bedraggled-looking little bastard you ever saw; makes itchy gestures as though he's got crabs under his arms -- but he's funny.
Sterling Ford

26 The comic spirit is given to us in order that we may analyze, weigh, and clarify things in us which nettle us, or which we are outgrowing, or trying to reshape.
Thornton Wilder (1897-1975, American Novelist, Playwright)

27 While awaiting sentencing, I decided to give stand-up comedy a shot. The judge had suggested I get my act together, and I took him seriously.
Tim Allen (1953-, American Actor, Comedian, Author)

28 Comedy comes from conflict, from hatred.
Warren Mitchell (1926-, British Actor)

29 Comedy naturally wears itself out -- destroys the very food on which it lives; and by constantly and successfully exposing the follies and weaknesses of mankind to ridicule, in the end leaves itself nothing worth laughing at.
William Hazlitt (1778-1830, British Essayist)

30 And I did laugh sans intermission an hour by his dial. O noble fool, a worthy fool -- motley's the only wear.
William Shakespeare (1564-1616, British Poet, Playwright, Actor)

31 Though it make the unskillful laugh, cannot but make the judicious grieve.
William Shakespeare (1564-1616, British Poet, Playwright, Actor)

32 Comedy just pokes at problems, rarely confronts them squarely. Drama is like a plate of meat and potatoes, comedy is rather the dessert, a bit like meringue.
Woody Allen (1935-, American Director, Screenwriter, Actor, Comedian)

33 I think being funny is not anyone's first choice.
Woody Allen (1935-, American Director, Screenwriter, Actor, Comedian)

COMFORT

1 I'm comfortable being old... being black... being Jewish.
Billy Crystal (1947-, American Actor, Comedian, Director, Producer, Writer)

2 No woman has ever so comforted the distressed or distressed the comfortable. [On Eleanor Roosevelt]
Clare Boothe Luce (1903-1987, American Diplomat, Writer)

3 With the Supremes I made so much money so fast all I wanted to do was buy clothes and pretty things. Now I'm comfortable with money and it's comfortable with me.
Diana Ross (1944-, American Singer, Actress)

4 Oh the comfort, the inexpressible comfort of feeling safe with a person, having neither to weigh thoughts nor measure words, but pouring them all right out, just as they are -- chaff and grain together -- certain that a faithful hand will take and sift them, keep what is worth keeping, and with the breath of kindness blow the rest away...
Dinah Mulock

5 I think that there were only two people in my high school that were comfortable there, and I think they are both pumping gas now.
Grant Show (1962-, American Actor)

6 The lust for comfort, that stealthy thing that enters the house as a guest, and then becomes a host, and then a master.
Kahlil Gibran (1883-1931, Lebanese Poet, Novelist)

7 A scholar who cherishes the love of comfort is not fit to be deemed a scholar.
Lao-Tzu (600 BC, Chinese Philosopher, Founder of Taoism, Author of the "Tao Te Ching")

8 Do not assume that she who seeks to comfort you now, lives untroubled among the simple and quiet words that sometimes do you good. Her life may also have much sadness and difficulty, that remains far beyond yours. Were it otherwise, she would never have been able to find these words.
Rainer Maria Rilke (1875-1926, German Poet)

9 Of all created comforts, God is the lender; you are the borrower, not the owner.
Samuel Rutherford (1600-1661, Scottish Pastor)

COMMITMENT

1 There's always a way -- if you're committed.
Anthony Robbins (1960-, American Author, Speaker, Peak Performance Expert / Consultant)

2 There's no abiding success without commitment.
Anthony Robbins (1960-, American Author, Speaker, Peak Performance Expert / Consultant)

3   I believe life is constantly testing us for our level of commitment, and life's greatest rewards are reserved for those who demonstrate a never-ending commitment to act until they achieve. This level of resolve can move mountains, but it must be constant and consistent. As simplistic as this may sound, it is still the common denominator separating those who live their dreams from those who live in regret.
Anthony Robbins (1960-, American Author, Speaker, Peak Performance Expert / Consultant)

4   When you make a commitment to a relationship, you invest your attention and energy in it more profoundly because you now experience ownership of that relationship.
Barbara De Angelis (American Expert on Relationship & Love, Author)

5   Never let a day pass that you will have cause to say, I will do better tomorrow.
Brigham Young (1801-1877, American Mormon Leader)

6   If you want to take your mission in life to the next level, if you're stuck and you don't know how to rise, don't look outside yourself. Look inside. Don't let your fears keep you mired in the crowd. Abolish your fears and raise your commitment level to the point of no return, and I guarantee you that the Champion Within will burst forth to propel you toward victory.
Bruce Jenner (1949-, American Olympian, Actor, Speaker, Entrepreneur, Sports Commentator)

7   Carry on any enterprise as if all future success depended on it.
Cardinal De Richelieu (1585-1642, French Statesman)

8   Don't be afraid to take a big step if one is indicated. You can't cross a chasm in two small jumps.
David Lloyd George (1863-1945, British Statesman, Prime Minister)

9   You must stick to your conviction, but be ready to abandon your assumptions.
Denis Waitley (1933-, American Author, Speaker, Trainer, Peak Performance Expert)

10   If you don't invest very much, then defeat doesn't hurt very much and winning is not very exciting.
Dick Vermeil (American Football Coach, Sportscaster)

11   My satisfaction comes from my commitment to advancing a better world.
Faye Wattleton.

12   The resolved mind hath no cares.
George Herbert (1593-1632, British Metaphysical Poet)

13   The loftiest edifices need the deepest foundations.
George Santayana (1863-1952, American Philosopher, Poet)

14   It's no accident many accuse me of conducting public affairs with my heart instead of my head. Well, what if I do? Those who don't know how to weep with their whole heart don't know how to laugh either.
Golda Meir (1898-1978, Prime Minister of Israel, 1969-74)

15   Resolve and thou art free.
Henry Wadsworth Longfellow (1819-1892, American Poet)

16   We would rather have one man or woman working with us than three merely working for us.
J. Dabney Day

17   Until one is committed, there is hesitancy, the chance to draw back, always ineffectiveness. Concerning all acts of initiative and creation, there is one elementary truth the ignorance of which kills countless ideas and splendid plans: that the moment one definitely commits oneself, then providence moves too. All sorts of things occur to help one that would never otherwise have occurred. A whole stream of events issues from the decision, raising in one's favor all manner of unforeseen incidents, meetings and material assistance which no man could have dreamed would have come his way. Whatever you can do or dream you can, begin it. Boldness has genius, power and magic in it. Begin it now.
Johann Wolfgang Von Goethe (1749-1832, German Poet, Dramatist, Novelist)

18   Tolerance implies no lack of commitment to one's own beliefs. Rather it condemns the oppression or persecution of others.
John F. Kennedy (1917-1963, Thirty-fifth President of the USA)

19   One of the best kept secrets in America is that people are aching to make a commitment, if they only had the freedom and environment in which to do so.
John Naisbitt (American Trend Analyst, Futurist, Author)

20   You need to make a commitment, and once you make it, then life will give you some answers.
Les Brown (1945-, American Speaker, Author, Trainer, Motivator Lecturer)

21   The achievement of your goal is assured the moment you commit yourself to it.
Mack R. Douglas

22   What one has, one ought to use: and whatever he does he should do with all his might.
Marcus T. Cicero (106-43 BC, Great Roman Orator, Politician)

23   I don't like to commit myself about heaven and hell -- you see, I have friends in both places.
Mark Twain (1835-1910, American Humorist, Writer)

24   The uncommitted life isn't worth living.
Marshall Fishwick (1923-, American Writer)

25   The difference between involvement and commitment is like ham and eggs. The chicken is involved; the pig is committed.
Martina Navratilova (1956-, American Tennis Player)

26 You know from past experiences that whenever you have been driven to the wall, or thought you were, you have extricated yourself in a way which you never would have dreamed possible had you not been put to the test. The trouble is that in your everyday life you don't go deep enough to tap the divine mind within you.
Orison Swett Marden (1850-1924, American Author, Founder of Success Magazine)

27 The greatest trouble with most of us is that our demands upon ourselves are so feeble, the call upon the great within of us so weak and intermittent that it makes no impression upon the creative energies; it lacks the force that transmutes desires into realities.
Orison Swett Marden (1850-1924, American Author, Founder of Success Magazine)

28 Resolve that whatever you do, you will bring the whole man to it; that you will fling the whole weight of your being into it.
Orison Swett Marden (1850-1924, American Author, Founder of Success Magazine)

29 This force, which is the best thing in you, your highest self, will never respond to any ordinary half-hearted call, or any milk-and-water endeavor, It can only be reached by your supremest call, your supremest effort. It will respond only to the call that is backed up by the whole of you, not part of you; you must be all there in what you are trying to do. You must bring every particle of your energy, unanswerable resolution, your best efforts, your persistent industry to your task or the best will not come out of you. You must back up your ambition by your whole nature, by unbounded enthusiasm and a determination to win which knows no failure... Only a masterly call, a masterly will, a supreme effort, intense and persistent application, can unlock the door to your inner treasure and release your highest powers.
Orison Swett Marden (1850-1924, American Author, Founder of Success Magazine)

30 Unless commitment is made, there are only promises and hopes; but no plans.
Peter F. Drucker (1909-, American Management Consultant, Author)

31 All great masters are chiefly distinguished by the power of adding a second, a third, and perhaps a fourth step in a continuous line. Many a man had taken the first step. With every additional step you enhance immensely the value of your first.
Ralph Waldo Emerson (1803-1882, American Poet, Essayist)

32 It is only when you despair of all ordinary means, it is only when you convince it that it must help you or you perish, that the seed of life in you bestirs itself to provide a new resource.
Robert Collier (American Writer, Publisher)

33 If you make the unconditional commitment to reach your most important goals, if the strength of your decision is sufficient, you will find the way and the power to achieve your goals.
Robert Conklin (American Teacher, Author, Speaker)

34 Decide that you really want to achieve the goal...
Robert J. Mckain

35 Competing in sports has taught me that if I'm not willing to give 120 percent, somebody else will.
Ron Blomberg (American Baseball Player)

36 I like villains because there's something so attractive about a committed person -- they have a plan, an ideology, no matter how twisted. They're motivated.
Russell Crowe

37 Drink nothing with out seeing it; sign nothing without reading it.
Spanish Proverb

38 A person with half volition goes backwards and forwards, but makes no progress on even the smoothest of roads.
Thomas Carlyle (1795-1881, Scottish Philosopher, Author)

39 I remember committing myself to make it in the garbage business, "whatever it takes!"
Tom Fatjo (American Businessman, Founder of Browning-Ferris Industries)

40 A total commitment is paramount to reaching the ultimate in performance.
Tom Flores (American Football (NFL) Coach)

41 It's not whether you get knocked down, it's whether you get up.
Vince Lombardi (1913-1970, American Football Coach)

42 The quality of a person's life is in direct proportion to their commitment to excellence, regardless of their chosen field of endeavor.
Vince Lombardi (1913-1970, American Football Coach)

43 The difference between a successful person and others is not a lack of strength, not a lack of knowledge, but rather in a lack of will.
Vince Lombardi (1913-1970, American Football Coach)

44 You can do what you want to do, accomplish what you want to accomplish, attain any reasonable objective you may have in mind -- not all of a sudden, perhaps not in one swift and sweeping act of achievement -- but you can do it gradually, day by day and play by play, if you want to do it, if you work to do it, over a sufficiently long period of time.
William E. Holler

COMMITTEES AND MEETINGS

1 Muddle is the extra unknown personality in any committee.
Anthony Sampson

2 A committee is a cul-de-sac down which ideas are lured and then quietly strangled.
Barnett Cock (British Scientist)

3 A committee is organic rather than mechanical in its nature: it is not a structure but a plant. It takes root and grows, it flowers, wilts, and dies, scattering the seed from which other committees will bloom in their turn.
C. Northcote Parkinson (1909-1993, British Historian, Political Scientist)

4 The heaping together of paintings by Old Masters in museums is a catastrophe; likewise, a collection of a hundred Great Brains makes one big fathead.
Carl Jung (1875-1961, Swiss Psychiatrist)

5 A collection of a hundred Great brains makes one big fathead.
Carl Jung (1875-1961, Swiss Psychiatrist)

6 A committee is a thing which takes a week to do what one good man can do in an hour.
Elbert Hubbard (1859-1915, American Author, Publisher)

7 We always carry out by committee anything in which any one of us alone would be too reasonable to persist.
Frank Moore Colby (1865-1925, American Editor, Essayist)

8 A conference is a gathering of people who singly can do nothing, but together can decide that nothing can be done.
Fred A. Allen (1894-1957, American Radio Comic)

9 I've searched all the parks in all the cities and found no statues of committees.
Gilbert K. Chesterton (1874-1936, British Author)

10 One of the reasons why the Ten Commandments are so short and to the point is the fact they were given direct and did not come out of committees.
H. G. Hutcheson

11 A technical objection is the first refuge of a scoundrel.
Heywood Broun (1888-1939, American Journalist, Novelist)

12 A committee of one gets things done.
Joe Ryan

13 A committee is an animal with four back legs.
John Le Carre

14 Any committee that is the slightest use is composed of people who are too busy to want to sit on it for a second longer than they have to.
Katharine Whitehorn (1926-, British Journalist)

15 When committees gather, each member is necessarily an actor, uncontrollably acting out the part of himself, reading the lines that identify him, asserting his identity. We are designed, coded, it seems, to place the highest priority on being individuals, and we must do this first, at whatever cost, even if it means disability for the group.
Lewis Thomas (1913-, American Physician, Educator)

16 The ideal committee is one with me as the chairman, and two other members in bed with the flu.
Lord Milverton

17 Committee--a group of men who keep minutes and waste hours.
Milton Berle (1908-, American Actor, Entertainer)

18 A committee is a group that keeps minutes and loses hours.
Milton Berle (1908-, American Actor, Entertainer)

19 Meetings are a symptom of bad organization. The fewer meetings the better.
Peter F. Drucker (1909-, American Management Consultant, Author)

20 Committee: A group of the unwilling, picked from the unfit to do the unnecessary.
Richard Harkness

21 The real process of making decisions, of gathering support, of developing opinions, happens before the meeting or after.
Terrence Deal

22 The State, that craving rookery of committees and subcommittees.
V. S. Pritchett (1900-, British Author, Critic)

COMMON SENSE

1 When you have got an elephant by the hind legs and he is trying to run away, it's best to let him run.
Abraham Lincoln (1809-1865, Sixteenth President of the USA)

2 Common sense is the collection of prejudices acquired by age eighteen.
Albert Einstein (1879-1955, German-born American Physicist)

3 Simple solutions seldom are. It takes a very unusual mind to undertake analysis of the obvious.
Alfred North Whitehead (1861-1947, British Mathematician, Philosopher)

4 Common sense is genius in homespun.
Alfred North Whitehead (1861-1947, British Mathematician, Philosopher)

5 No one tests the depth of a river with both feet.
Ashanti Proverb

6 A person must have a certain amount of intelligent ignorance to get anywhere.
Charles F. Kettering (1876-1958, American Engineer, Inventor)

7 He was one of those men who possess almost every gift, except the gift of the power to use them.
Charles Kingsley (1819-1875, British Author, Clergyman)

8 Common sense is compelled to make its way without the enthusiasm of anyone.
Edgar Watson Howe (1853-1937, American Journalist, Author)

9 It makes sense that there is no sense without God.
Edith Schaeffer

10 Common sense is only a modification of talent. Genius is an exaltation of it. The difference is, therefore, in degree, not nature.
Edward G. Bulwer-Lytton (1803-1873, British Novelist, Poet)

11 The best prophet is common sense, our native wit.
Euripides (480-406 BC, Greek Tragic Poet)

12 The two World Wars came in part, like much modern literature and art, because men, whose nature is to tire of everything in turn, tired of common sense and civilization.
F. L. Lucan (39-65, Roman Epic Poet)

13 It is common sense to take a method and try it. If it fails, admit it frankly and try another, but above all try something.
Franklin D. Roosevelt (1882-1945, Thirty-second President of the USA)

14 Common sense hides shame.
Gaelic Proverb

15 The common people of America display a quality of good common sense which is heartening to anyone who believes in the democratic process.
George Gallup (1901-1984, American Public Opinion Expert)

16 That rarest gift to Beauty, Common Sense!
George Meredith (1828-1909, British Author)

17 To see what is in front of one's nose requires a constant struggle.
George Orwell (1903-1950, British Author, "Animal Farm")

18 Everybody gets so much common information all day long that they lose their common sense.
Gertrude Stein (1874-1946, American Author)

19 Common sense is judgment without reflection, shared by an entire class, an entire nation, or the entire human race.
Giambattista Vico (1688-1744, Italian Philosopher, Historian)

20 Common sense is calculation applied to life.
Henri Frederic Amiel (1821-1881, Swiss Philosopher, Poet, Critic)

21 Common sense is the measure of the possible; it is composed of experience and prevision; it is calculation applied to life.
Henri Frederic Amiel (1821-1881, Swiss Philosopher, Poet, Critic)

22 Why level downward to our dullest perception always, and praise that as common sense? The commonest sense is the sense of men asleep, which they express by snoring.
Henry David Thoreau (1817-1862, American Essayist, Poet, Naturalist)

23 There is nothing a man of good sense dreads in a wife so much as her having more sense than himself.
Henry Fielding (1707-1754, British Novelist, Dramatist)

24 The philosophy of one century is the common sense of the next.
Henry Ward Beecher (1813-1887, American Preacher, Orator, Writer)

25 Common Sense is instinct, and enough of it is genius.
Henry Wheeler Shaw (1818-1885, American Humorist)

26 Common Sense is very uncommon.
Horace Greeley (1811-1872, American Newspaper Editor)

27 The question of common sense is "what is it good for?" A question which would abolish the rose and be answered triumphantly by the cabbage.
James Russell Lowell (1819-1891, American Poet, Critic, Editor)

28 Who is the most sensible person? The one who finds what is to their own advantage in all that happens to them.
Johann Wolfgang Von Goethe (1749-1832, German Poet, Dramatist, Novelist)

29 Common sense is the genius of humanity.
Johann Wolfgang Von Goethe (1749-1832, German Poet, Dramatist, Novelist)

30 Common-sense is part of the home-made ideology of those who have been deprived of fundamental learning, of those who have been kept ignorant. This ideology is compounded from different sources: items that have survived from religion, items of empirical knowledge, items of protective skepticism, items culled for comfort from the superficial learning that is supplied. But the point is that common-sense can never teach itself, can never advance beyond its own limits, for as soon as the lack of fundamental learning has been made good, all items become questionable and the whole function of common-sense is destroyed. Common-sense can only exist as a category insofar as it can be distinguished from the spirit of inquiry, from philosophy.
John Berger (1926-, British Actor, Critic)

31 Common sense is the knack of seeing things as they are, and doing things as they ought to be done.
Josh Billings (1815-1885, American Humorist, Lecturer)

32 My greatest strength is... common sense. I'm really a standard brand -- like Campbell's tomato soup or Baker's chocolate.
Katharine Hepburn (1907-, American Actress, Writer)

33 Common Sense is that which judges the things given to it by other senses.
Leonardo Da Vinci (1452-1519, Italian Inventor, Architect, Painter, Scientist, Sculptor)

34 That's the way things come clear. All of a sudden. And then you realize how obvious they've been all along.
Madeleine L'Engle

35 When two men share an umbrella, both of them get wet.
Michael Isenberg

36 Science is a first-rate piece of furniture for a man's upper chamber, if it has common sense on the ground floor.
Oliver Wendell Holmes (1809-1894, American Author, Wit, Poet)

37 Nowadays most people die of a sort of creeping common sense, and discover when it is too late that the only things one never regrets are one's mistakes.
Oscar Wilde (1856-1900, British Author, Wit)

38 One pound of learning requires ten pounds of common sense to apply it.
Persian Proverb

39 Common Sense is in medicine the master workman.
Peter Latham

40 Nothing ventured, nothing gained -- but if everything is ventured, and still nothing gained, give up and venture elsewhere.
Peter Wastholm

41 He who does not have common sense at age thirty will never have it.
Proverb

42 Common sense is genius dressed in its working clothes.
Ralph Waldo Emerson (1803-1882, American Poet, Essayist)

43 Nothing astonishes people so much as common sense and plain dealing.
Ralph Waldo Emerson (1803-1882, American Poet, Essayist)

44 Common sense always speaks too late. Common sense is the guy who tells you ought to have had your brakes relined last week before you smashed a front end this week. Common sense is the Monday morning quarterback who could have won the ball game if he had been on the team. But he never is. He's high up in the stands with a flask on his hip. Common sense is the little man in a gray suit who never makes a mistake in addition. But it's always somebody else's money he's adding up.
Raymond Chandler (1888-1959, American Author)

45 Nothing is more fairly distributed than common sense: no one thinks he needs more of it than he already has.
Rene Descartes (1596-1650, French Philosopher, Scientist)

46 If a man has common sense, he has all the sense there is.
Sam Rayburn (1882-1961, American Representative)

47 The voice of the Lord is the voice of common sense, which is shared by all that is.
Samuel Butler (1612-1680, British Poet, Satirist)

48 What a grand thing it is to be clever and have common sense.
Terence (185-159 BC, Roman Writer of Comedies)

49 All truth, in the long run, is only common sense clarified.
Thomas H. Huxley (1825-1895, British Biologist, Educator)

50 Science is nothing, but trained and organized common sense.
Thomas H. Huxley (1825-1895, British Biologist, Educator)

51 Common sense is in spite of, not as the result of education.
Victor Hugo (1802-1885, French Poet, Dramatist, Novelist)

52 Common sense is not so common.
Voltaire (1694-1778, French Historian, Writer)

53 Common sense and nature will do a lot to make the pilgrimage of life not too difficult.
W. Somerset Maugham (1874-1965, British Novelist, Playwright)

54 Common-sense appears to be only another name for the thoughtlessness of the unthinking. It is made of the prejudices of childhood, the idiosyncrasies of individual character and the opinion of the newspapers.
W. Somerset Maugham (1874-1965, British Novelist, Playwright)

COMMONPLACE

1 Common looking people are the best in the world: that is the reason the Lord makes so many of them.
Abraham Lincoln (1809-1865, Sixteenth President of the USA)

2 Take a commonplace, clean it and polish it, light it so that it produces the same effect of youth and freshness and originality and spontaneity as it did originally, and you have done a poet's job. The rest is literature.
Jean Cocteau (1889-1963, French Author, Filmmaker)

3 The characteristic of the hour is that the commonplace mind, knowing itself to be commonplace, has the assurance to proclaim the rights of the commonplace and to impose them wherever it will.
Jose Ortega Y Gasset (1883-1955, Spanish Essayist, Philosopher)

4 If to be interesting is to be uncommonplace, it is becoming a question, with me, if there are any commonplace people.
Mark Twain (1835-1910, American Humorist, Writer)

5 Nothing is so commonplace has the wish to be remarkable.
Oliver Wendell Holmes (1809-1894, American Author, Wit, Poet)

6 We can escape the commonplace only by manipulating it, controlling it, thrusting it into our dreams or surrendering it to the free play of our subjectivity.
Raoul Vaneigem (1934-, Belgian Situationist Philosopher)

7 Thou unassuming common-place of Nature, with that homely face.
William Wordsworth (1770-1850, British Poet)

COMMUNICATION

1 He can compress the most words into the smallest idea of any man I ever met.
Abraham Lincoln (1809-1865, Sixteenth President of the USA)

2 Good communication is as stimulating as black coffee, and just as hard to sleep after.
Anne Morrow Lindbergh (1906-, American Author)

3 The way we communicate with others and with ourselves ultimately determines the quality of our lives.
Anthony Robbins (1960-, American Author, Speaker, Peak Performance Expert / Consultant)

4 To effectively communicate, we must realize that we are all different in the way we perceive the world and use this understanding as a guide to our communication with others.
Anthony Robbins (1960-, American Author, Speaker, Peak Performance Expert / Consultant)

5 Transport of the mails, transport of the human voice, transport of flickering pictures --in this century as in others our highest accomplishments still have the single aim of bringing men together.
Antoine De Saint-Exupery (1900-1944, French Aviator, Writer)

6 If you cry "Forward" you must be sure to make clear the direction in which to go. Don't you see that if you fail to do that and simply call out the word to a monk and a revolutionary, they will go in precisely opposite directions?
Anton Chekhov (1860-1904, Russian Playwright, Short Story Writer)

7 The art of conversation consist as much in listening politely, as in talking agreeably.
Atwell

8 The ability to express an idea is well nigh as important as the idea itself.
Bernard M. Baruch (1870-1965, American Financier)

9 Communication is a skill that you can learn. It's like riding a bicycle or typing. If you're willing to work at it, you can rapidly improve the quality of very part of your life.
Brian Tracy (American Trainer, Speaker, Author, Businessman)

10 For good or ill, your conversation is your advertisement. Every time you open your mouth you let men look into your mind. Do they see it well clothed, neat, businesswise?
Bruce Burton

11 Electric communication will never be a substitute for the face of someone who with their soul encourages another person to be brave and true.
Charles Dickens (1812-1870, British Novelist)

12 You people are telling me what you think I want to know. I want to know what is actually happening.
Creighton Williams Abrams, Jr. (1914 - 1974, American Commander of Forces in Vietnam)

13 There are four ways, and only four ways, in which we have contact with the world. We are evaluated and classified by these four contacts: what we do, how we look, what we say, and how we say it.
Dale Carnegie (1888-1955, American Author, Trainer)

14 The royal road to a man's heart is to talk to him about the things he treasures most.
Dale Carnegie (1888-1955, American Author, Trainer)

15 The higher you go, the wider spreads the network of communication that will make or break you. It extends not only to more people below, but to new levels above. And it extends all around, to endless other departments and interests interacting with yours.
Donald Walton

16 The whole problem is to establish communication with ones self.
E(lwyn) B(rooks) White (1899-1985, American Author, Editor)

17 The fantastic advances in the field of electronic communication constitute a greater danger to the privacy of the individual.
Earl Warren (1891-1974, American Politician, Judge)

18 Only connect! That was the whole of her sermon. Only connect the prose and the passion, and both will be exalted, and human love will be seen at its height. Live in fragments no longer. Only connect, and the beast and the monk, robbed of the isolation that is life to either, will die.
Edward M. Forster (1879-1970, British Novelist, Essayist)

19 There are men who would quickly love each other if once they were speak to each other; for when they spoke they would discover that their souls had only separated by phantoms and delusions.
Ernest Hello

20 Every improvement in communication makes the bore more terrible.
Frank Moore Colby (1865-1925, American Editor, Essayist)

21 You will get good attention and people will be more inclined to listen to you if you can make a statement whereby their response is, "No Shit!" or at least, "No kidding!"
Gael Boardman (American Politician)

22 To express the most difficult matters clearly and intelligently, is to strike coins out of pure gold.
Geibel

23 For parlor use, the vague generality is a life saver.
George Ade (1866-1944, American Humorist, Playwright)

24 We shall never be able to remove suspicion and fear as potential causes of war until communication is permitted to flow, free and open, across international boundaries.
Harry S. Truman (1884-1972, Thirty-third President of the USA)

25 Pure truth cannot be assimilated by the crowd; it must be communicated by contagion.
Henri Frederic Amiel (1821-1881, Swiss Philosopher, Poet, Critic)

26 The time to stop talking is when the other person nods his head affirmatively, but says nothing.
Henry S. Haskins

27 Of what does not concern you say nothing good or bad.
Italian Proverb

28 The art of communication is the language of leadership.
James Humes (American Lawyer, Speaker, Author)

29 Two monologues do not make a dialogue.
Jeff Daly

30 Take advantage of every opportunity to practice your communication skills so that when important occasions arise, you will have the gift, the style, the sharpness, the clarity, and the emotions to affect other people.
Jim Rohn (American Businessman, Author, Speaker, Philosopher)

31 Effective communication is 20% what you know and 80% how you feel about what you know.
Jim Rohn (American Businessman, Author, Speaker, Philosopher)

32 Don't hide your strategy under a bushel. Communicate it throughout your company. It's better today to disclose too much that too little.
Joel E. Ross

33 No one would talk much in society if they knew how often they misunderstood others.
Johann Wolfgang Von Goethe (1749-1832, German Poet, Dramatist, Novelist)

34 Communication is not only the essence of being human, but also a vital property of life.
John A. Piece

35 I've not got a first in philosophy without being able to muddy things pretty satisfactory.
John Banham (British Director General of Confederation of Industry)

36 I've noticed two things about men who get big salaries. They are almost invariably men who, in conversation or in conference, are adaptable. They quickly get the other fellow's view. They are more eager to do this than to express their own ideas. Also, they state their own point of view convincingly.
John Hallock

37 There cannot be greater rudeness than to interrupt another in the current of his discourse.
John Locke (1632-1704, British Philosopher)

38 Good, the more communicated, more abundant grows.
John Milton (1608-1674, British Poet)

39 Communication is a two-way street. And while we revel in the reality that we can always get through to heaven, our concern should be whether our Lord can always get through to us.
Joseph Stowell

40 Extremists think "communication" means agreeing with them.
Leo Rosten (1908-1997, Polish Born American Political Scientist)

41 Your ability to communicate is an important tool in your pursuit of your goals, whether it is with your family, your co-workers or your clients and customers.
Les Brown (1945-, American Speaker, Author, Trainer, Motivator Lecturer)

42 It must be that evil communications corrupt good dispositions.
Menander of Athens (342-291 BC, Greek Dramatic Poet)

43 It is good to rub and polish our brain against that of others.
Michel Eyquem De Montaigne (1533-1592, French Philosopher, Essayist)

44 There is no pleasure to me without communication: there is not so much as a sprightly thought comes into my mind that it does not grieve me to have produced alone, and that I have no one to tell it to.
Michel Eyquem De Montaigne (1533-1592, French Philosopher, Essayist)

45 We always speak well when we manage to be understood.
MoliFre (1622-1673, French Playwright)

46 Every absurdity has a champion to defend it; for error is always talkative.
Oliver Goldsmith (1728-1774, Anglo-Irish Author, Poet, Playwright)

47 The most important thing in communication is to hear what isn't being said.
Peter F. Drucker (1909-, American Management Consultant, Author)

48 The really important things are said over cocktails and are never done.
Peter F. Drucker (1909-, American Management Consultant, Author)

49 It's vital the monarchy keeps in touch with the people. It's what I try and do.
Princess of Wales Diana (1961-1997, Wife of Charles, Prince of Wales)

50 From listening comes wisdom and from speaking, repentance.
Proverb

51 When the eyes say one thing, and the tongue another, a practiced man relies on the language of the first.
Ralph Waldo Emerson (1803-1882, American Poet, Essayist)

52 Unless people can be kept in the dark, it is best for those who love the truth to give them the full light.
Richard Whately (1787-1863, British Prelate, Writer)

53 Half the world is composed of people who have something to say and can't, and the other half who have nothing to say and keep on saying it.
Robert Frost (1875-1963, American Poet)

54 Something there is that doesn't love a wall, and wants it down.
Robert Frost (1875-1963, American Poet)

55 Talk is by far the most accessible of pleasures. It costs nothing in money, it is all profit, it completes our education, founds and fosters our friendships, and can be enjoyed at any age and in almost any state of health.
Robert Louis Stevenson (1850-1895, Scottish Essayist, Poet, Novelist)

56 A world community can exist only with world communication, which means something more than extensive short-wave facilities scattered ;about the globe. It means common understanding, a common tradition, common ideas, and common ideals.
Robert M. Hutchins (1899-1977, American University President)

57 Two prisoners whose cells adjoin communicate with each other by knocking on the wall. The wall is the thing which separates them but is also their means of communication. It is the same with us and God. Every separation is a link.
Simone Weil (1910-1943, French Philosopher, Mystic)

58 Genuine poetry can communicate before it is understood.
T. S. Eliot (1888-1965, American-born British Poet, Critic)

59 Nothing is so simple that it cannot be misunderstood.
Teague, Jr.

60 Communication is everyone's panacea for everything.
Thomas J. Peters (1942-, American Management Consultant, Author, Trainer)

61 Communication across the revolutionary divide is inevitably partial.
Thomas S. Kuhn

62 I wish people that have trouble communicating would just shut up!
Tom Lehrer (1928-, American Musician, Song Writer)

63 I feel that if a person has problems communicating the very least he can do is to shut up.
Tom Lehrer (1928-, American Musician, Song Writer)

64 The tongue is the only instrument that gets sharper with use.
Washington Irving (1783-1859, American Author)

COMMUNISM AND SOCIALISM

1 The crusade against Communism was even more imaginary than the specter of Communism.
A. J. P. Taylor (1906-1990, British Historian)

2 Communism is the corruption of a dream of justice.
Adlai E. Stevenson (1900-1965, American Lawyer, Politician)

3 One strength of the communist system of the East is that it has some of the character of a religion and inspires the emotions of a religion.
Albert Einstein (1879-1955, German-born American Physicist)

4 For us in Russia communism is a dead dog. For many people in the West, it is still a living lion.
Alexander Solzhenitsyn (1918-, Russian Novelist)

5 I am a communist because I believe that the Communist idea is a state form of Christianity.
Alexander Zhuravlyov

6 Socialism is a vast machine for churning out piles of goods marked "Take it or leave it. "
Arthur Seldon

7 Let's not talk about Communism. Communism was just an idea, just pie in the sky.
Boris Yeltsin (1931-, Russian President)

8 Communism is the opiate of the intellectuals [With] no cure except as a guillotine might be called a cure for dandruff.
Clare Boothe Luce (1903-1987, American Diplomat, Writer)

9 Russian Communism is the illegitimate child of Karl Marx and Catherine the Great.
Clement Attlee (British Earl)

10 You'll see certain Pythagorean whose belief in communism of property goes to such lengths that they pick up anything lying about unguarded, and make off with it without a qualm of conscience as if it had come to them by law.
Desiderius Erasmus (1466-1536, Dutch Humanist)

11 Many people consider the things government does for them to be social progress, but they consider the things government does for others as socialism.
Earl Warren (1891-1974, American Politician, Judge)

12 What is a Communist? One who has yearnings for equal division of unequal earnings.
Ebenezer Elliot

13 Communism is in conflict with human nature.
Ernest Renan (1823-1892, French Writer, Critic, Scholar)

14 We are the party of all labor. The whole earth shall be ours to share. And every race and craft our neighbor. No idle class shall linger there like vultures on the wealth we render from field and factory, mill and mine. Tomorrow's sun will rise in splendor and light us till the end of time.
Eugene Pottier

15 Many people feel empty, a world that seemed so strong just collapsed. Forty years have been wasted on stupid strife for the sake of an unsuccessful experiment. The values gathered together have vanished, the strategies for survival have become ridiculous. And so forty years of our lives have become a story, a bad anecdote. But it may be possible to remember these adventures with a kind of irony.
George Konrad (1933-, Hungarian Writer, Politician)

16 As with the Christian religion, the worst advertisement for socialism is its adherents.
George Orwell (1903-1950, British Author, "Animal Farm")

17 The "Communism" of the English intellectual is something explicable enough. It is the patriotism of the deracinated.
George Orwell (1903-1950, British Author, "Animal Farm")

18 Communists are people who fancied that they had an unhappy childhood.
Gertrude Stein (1874-1946, American Author)

19 Communism, my friend, is more than Marxism, just as Catholicism is more than the Roman Curia. There is a mystique as well as a politick. Catholics and Communists have committed great crimes, but at least they have not stood aside, like an established society, and been indifferent. I would rather have blood on my hands than water like Pilate.
Graham Greene (1904-1991, British Novelist)

20 The final conflict will be between the Communists and the ex-Communists.
Ignazio Silone (1900-1978, Italian Novelist)

21 There are only two sorts of people in life you can trust -- good Christians and good Communists.
Joe Slovo

22 Communism has never come to power in a country that was not disrupted by war or corruption, or both.
John F. Kennedy (1917-1963, Thirty-fifth President of the USA)

23 When we hang the capitalists they will sell us the rope we use.
Joseph Stalin (1879-1953, Georgian-born Soviet Leader)

24 Socialism must come down from the brain and reach the heart.
Jules Renard (1864-1910, French Author, Dramatist)

25 The theory of the Communists may be summed up in the single sentence: Abolition of private property.
Karl Marx (1818-1883, German Political Theorist, Social Philosopher)

26 All I know is I'm not a Marxist.
Karl Marx (1818-1883, German Political Theorist, Social Philosopher)

27 In a higher phase of communist society... only then can the narrow horizon of bourgeois right be fully left behind and society inscribe on its banners: from each according to his ability, to each according to his needs.
Karl Marx (1818-1883, German Political Theorist, Social Philosopher)

28 A specter is haunting Europe -- the specter of communism.
Karl Marx (1818-1883, German Political Theorist, Social Philosopher)

29 Communism is like one big phone company.
Lenny Bruce (1925-1966, American Comedian)

30 Man will become immeasurably stronger, wiser, and subtler; his body will become more harmonious, his movements more rhythmic, his voice more musical. The forms of life will become dynamically dramatic. The average human type will rise to the heights of an Aristotle, a Goethe, or a Marx. And above these heights, new peaks will rise.
Leon Trotsky (1879-1940, Russian Revolutionary)

31 Communism is not love. Communism is a hammer which we use to crush the enemy.
Mao Zedong (1893-1976, Founder of Chinese Communist State)

32 I am a Communist, a convinced Communist! For some that may be a fantasy. But to me it is my main goal.
Mikhail Gorbachev (1931-, Soviet Statesman and President of USSR (1988-91))

33 The terrible thing is that one cannot be a Communist and not let oneself in for the shameful act of recantation. One cannot be a Communist and preserve an iota of one's personal integrity.
Milovan Djilas (1911-1995, Former Yugoslav Vice-president)

34 Communists have always played an active role in the fight by colonial countries for their freedom, because the short-term objects of Communism would always correspond with the long- term objects of freedom movements.
Nelson Mandela (1918-, South African President)

35 In the end we beat them with Levi 501 jeans. Seventy-two years of Communist indoctrination and propaganda was drowned out by a three-ounce Sony Walkman. A huge totalitarian system has been brought to its knees because nobody wants to wear Bulgarian shoes. Now they're lunch, and we're number one on the planet.
P. J. O'Rourke (1947-, American Journalist)

36 Communism is inequality, but not as property is. Property is exploitation of the weak by the strong. Communism is exploitation of the strong by the weak.
Pierre Joseph Proudhon (1809-1865, French Socialist, Political Theorist)

37 A common danger tends to concord. Communism is the exploitation of the strong by the weak. In Communism, inequality comes from placing mediocrity on a level with excellence.
Pierre Joseph Proudhon (1809-1865, French Socialist, Political Theorist)

38 We must conclude that it is not only a particular political ideology that has failed, but the idea that men and women could ever define themselves in terms that exclude their spiritual needs.
Salman Rushdie (1948-, Indian-born British Author)

39 I have no concern with any economic criticisms of the communist system; I cannot inquire into whether the abolition of private property is expedient or advantageous. But I am able to recognize that the psychological premisses on which the system is based are an untenable illusion. In abolishing private property we deprive the human love of aggression of one of its instruments... but we have in no way altered the differences in power and influence which are misused by aggressiveness.
Sigmund Freud (1856-1939, Austrian Physician - Founder of Psychoanalysis)

40 Communism is a cow of many; well milked and badly fed.
Spanish Proverb

41 Under socialism all will govern in turn and will soon become accustomed to no one governing.
Vladimir Ilyich Lenin (1870-1924, Russian Revolutionary Leader)

42 Communism is Soviet power plus the electrification of the whole country.
Vladimir Ilyich Lenin (1870-1924, Russian Revolutionary Leader)

43 Experience has taught me that the shallowest of communist platitudes contains more of a hierarchy of meaning than contemporary bourgeois profundity.
Walter Benjamin (1982-1940, German Critic, Philosopher)

44 Communism is like prohibition, it is a good idea, but it won't work.
Will Rogers (1879-1935, American Humorist, Actor)

45 Communism to me is one-third practice and two-thirds explanation.
Will Rogers (1879-1935, American Humorist, Actor)

46 There is nothing in socialism that a little age or a little money will not cure.
William J. Durant (1885-1981, American Historian, Essayist)

47 It is a socialist idea that making profits is a vice; I consider the real vice is making losses.
Winston Churchill (1874-1965, British Statesman, Prime Minister)

48 Socialists think profits are a vice; I consider losses the real vice.
Winston Churchill (1874-1965, British Statesman, Prime Minister)

49 Socialism is like a dream. Sooner or later you wake up to reality.
Winston Churchill (1874-1965, British Statesman, Prime Minister)

50 The substance of the eminent Socialist gentlemen's speech is that making a profit is a sin. It is my belief that the real sin is taking a loss!
Winston Churchill (1874-1965, British Statesman, Prime Minister)

51 Communists should be the first to be concerned about other people and country and the last to enjoy themselves.
Zhao Ziyang

COMMUNITIES

1 The community of living is the carriage of the Lord.
Hasidic Proverb

2 In communities where men build ships for their own sons to fish or fight from, quality is never a problem
J. A. Dever

3 In order to stand well in the eyes of the community, it is necessary to come up to a certain, somewhat indefinite, conventional standard of wealth.
Thorstein Veblen (1857-1929, American Social Scientist)

4 I grew up in dirt-poor hillbilly country. We lived this dry-below-the-waist kind of scene. If you were a sensual woman you were in league with that which is un-Christlike. Where I come from, a cockroach is a roach, and a cockerel is a rooster because they can't bring themselves to say cock.
Tori Amos (1963-, Canadian-born American Musician, Singer, Songwriter)

COMMUTERS

1 Commuter -- one who spends his life in riding to and from his wife; And man who shaves and takes a train, and then rides back to shave again.
E(lwyn) B(rooks) White (1899-1985, American Author, Editor)

2 Commuters give the city its tidal restlessness; natives give it solidity and continuity; but the settlers give it passion.
E(lwyn) B(rooks) White (1899-1985, American Author, Editor)

COMPANY

1 We've got a lemon factory and we're turning out 80-85 percent lemons.
Albert Shanker

2 Fan the sinking flame of hilarity with the wing of friendship; and pass the rosy wine.
Charles Dickens (1812-1870, British Novelist)

3 The ability to sign a check is the least reliable guide to a company's fitness.
David Plowright

4 If it were not for the company of fools, a witty man would often be greatly at a loss.
François de La Rochefoucauld (1613-1680, French classical writer)

5 We do not mind our not arriving anywhere nearly so much as our not having any company on the way.
Frank Moore Colby (1865-1925, American Editor, Essayist)

6 Man loves company, even if it is only that of a smoldering candle.
Georg C. Lichtenberg (1742-1799, German Physicist, Satirist)

7 I have a great deal of company in my house; especially in the morning, when nobody calls.
Henry David Thoreau (1817-1862, American Essayist, Poet, Naturalist)

8 A rich rogue nowadays is fit company for any gentleman; and the world, my dear, hath not such a contempt for roguery as you imagine.
John Gay (1688-1732, British Playwright, Poet)

9 For my own part, I would rather be in company with a dead man than with an absent one; for if the dead man gives me no pleasure, at least he shows me no contempt; whereas the absent one, silently indeed, but very plainly, tells me that he does not think me worth his attention.
Lord Chesterfield (1694-1773, British Statesman, Author)

10 Tell me thy company, and I'll tell thee what thou art.
Miguel De Cervantes (1547-1616, Spanish Novelist, Dramatist, Poet)

11 It contributes greatly towards a man's moral and intellectual health, to be brought into habits of companionship with individuals unlike himself, who care little for his pursuits, and whose sphere and abilities he must go out of himself to appreciate.
Nathaniel Hawthorne (1804-1864, American Novelist, Short Story Writer)

12 There is a fellowship more quiet even than solitude, and which, rightly understood, is solitude made perfect.
Robert Louis Stevenson (1850-1895, Scottish Essayist, Poet, Novelist)

13 You could read Kant by yourself, if you wanted; but you must share a joke with some one else.
Robert Louis Stevenson (1850-1895, Scottish Essayist, Poet, Novelist)

14 You can't operate a company by fear, because the way to eliminate fear is to avoid criticism. And the way to avoid criticism is to do nothing.
Steve Ross

15 If your company has a clean-desk policy, the company is nuts and you're nuts to stay there.
Thomas J. Peters (1942-, American Management Consultant, Author, Trainer)

16 More company increases happiness, but does not lighten or diminish misery.
Thomas Traherne (1636-1674, British Clergyman, Poet, Mystic)

17 A grave blockhead should always go about with a lively one -- they show one another off to the best advantage.
William Hazlitt (1778-1830, British Essayist)

18 Company, villainous company, hath been the spoil of me.
William Shakespeare (1564-1616, British Poet, Playwright, Actor)

COMPARISONS

1 Comparisons are odious.
Fourteenth Century Saying

COMPASSION

1 Until he extends his circle of compassion to include all living things, man will not himself find peace.
Albert Schweitzer (1875-1965, German Born Medical Missionary, Theologian, Musician, and Philosopher)

2 In democratic ages men rarely sacrifice themselves for another, but they show a general compassion for all the human race. One never sees them inflict pointless suffering, and they are glad to relieve the sorrows of others when they can do so without much trouble to themselves. They are not disinterested, but they are gentle.
Alexis De Tocqueville (1805-1859, French Social Philosopher)

3 In necessary things, unity; in doubtful things, liberty; in all things, charity.
Anne Baxter (1923-1985, American Actress)

4 The value of compassion cannot be over-emphasized. Anyone can criticize. It takes a true believer to be compassionate. No greater ;burden can be borne by an individual than to know no one cares or understands.
Arthur H. Stainback

5 Out of compassion I destroy the darkness of their ignorance. From within them I light the lamp of wisdom and dispel all darkness from their lives.
Bhagavad Gita (400 BC, Sanskrit Poem Incorporated Into the Mahabharata)

6 No deep and strong feeling, such as we may come across here and there in the world, is unmixed with compassion. The more we love, the more the object of our love seems to us to be a victim.
Boris Pasternak (1890-1960, Russian Poet, Novelist, Translator)

7 Minerva save us from the cloying syrup of coercive compassion!
Camille Paglia (1947-, American Author, Critic, Educator)

8 Compassion automatically invites you to relate with people because you no longer regard people as a drain on your energy.
Chogyam Trungpa

9 Compassion is the antitoxin of the soul: where there is compassion even the most poisonous impulses remain relatively harmless.
Eric Hoffer (1902-1983, American Author, Philosopher)

10 Christianity demands a level of caring that transcends human inclinations.
Erwin W. Lutzer (American Minister)

11 The mind is no match with the heart in persuasion; constitutionality is no match with compassion.
Everett M. Dirksen (1896-1969, American Representative, Senator)

12 Biblical orthodoxy without compassion is surely the ugliest thing in the world.
Francis Schaeffer (1912-1984, American Author)

13 We hand folks over to God's mercy, and show none ourselves.
George Eliot (1819-1880, British Novelist)

14 I know the compassion of others is a relief at first. I don't despise it. But it can't quench pain, it slips through your soul as through a sieve. And when our suffering has been dragged from one pity to another, as from one mouth to another, we can no longer respect or love it.
Georges Bernanos (1888-1948, French Novelist, Political Writer)

15 When an individual fear or apathy passes by the unfortunate, life is of no account.
Haniel Long (1888-1956, American Author, Poet, Journalist)

16 Compassion has no place in the natural order of the world which operates on the basis of necessity. Compassion opposes this order and is therefore best thought of as being in some way supernatural.
John Berger (1926-, British Actor, Critic)

17 Being part of an agenda beyond ourselves liberates us to complement each other rather than compete with each other.
Joseph Stowell

18 As we mature spiritually, we exhibit a growing capacity to care for and appreciate one another in the body of Christ, regardless of our differences.
Joseph Stowell

19 The dew of compassion is a tear.
Lord Byron (1788-1824, British Poet)

20 Get it into your head once and for all, my simple and very fainthearted fellow, that what fools call humanness is nothing but a weakness born of fear and egoism; that this chimerical virtue, enslaving only weak men, is unknown to those whose character is formed by stoicism, courage, and philosophy.
Marquis De Sade (1740-1814, French Author)

21 You may call God love, you may call God goodness. But the best name for God is compassion.
Meister Eckhart (1260-1326 AD, German Mystic)

22 There is nothing heavier than compassion. Not even one's own pain weighs so heavy as the pain one feels with someone, for someone, a pain intensified by the imagination and prolonged by a hundred echoes.
Milan Kundera (1929-, Czech Author, Critic)

23 Saving lives is not a top priority in the halls of power. Being compassionate and concerned about human life can cause a man to lose his job. It can cause a woman not to get the job to begin with.
Myriam Miedzian (American Actor)

24 The individual is capable of both great compassion and great indifference. He has it within his means to nourish the former and outgrow the latter.
Norman Cousins (1915-1990, American Editor, Humanitarian, Author)

25 I feel the capacity to care is the thing which gives life its deepest significance.
Pablo Casals (1876-1973, Spanish Cellist, Conductor, Composer)

26 Care is a state in which something does matter; it is the source of human tenderness.
Rollo May (American Psychologist)

27 Compassion is no substitute for justice.
Rush Limbaugh (1951-, American TV Personality)

28 The wretched have no compassion, they can do good only from strong principles of duty.
Samuel Johnson (1709-1784, British Author)

29 When we come into contact with the other person, our thoughts and actions should express our mind of compassion, even if that person says and does things that are not easy to accept. We practice in this way until we see clearly that our love is not contingent upon the other person being lovable.
Thich Nhat Hanh (Vietnamese Buddhist Monk, Teacher)

30 The whole idea of compassion is based on a keen awareness of the interdependence of all these living beings, which are all part of one another, and all involved in one another
Thomas Merton (1915-1968, American Religious Writer, Poet)

31 Man may dismiss compassion from his heart, but God never will.
William Cowper (1731-1800, British Poet)

32 Mercy but murders, pardoning those that kill.
William Shakespeare (1564-1616, British Poet, Playwright, Actor)

COMPATIBILITY

1 Love and sex can go together and sex and unlove can go together and love and unsex can go together. But personal love and personal sex is bad.
Andy Warhol (1930-, American Artist, Filmmaker)

2 I love her too, but our neuroses just don't match.
Arthur Miller (1915-, American Dramatist)

3 Her name was called Lady Helena Herring and her age was 25 and she mated well with the earl.
Daisy Ashford (American Author)

4 Madam your wife and I didn't hit it off the only time I ever saw her. I won't say she was silly, but I think one of us was silly, and it wasn't me.
Elizabeth Gaskell (1810-1865, British Novelist)

5 To be happy with a man you must understand him a lot and love him a little. To be happy with a woman you must love her a lot and not try to understand her at all.
Helen Rowland (1875-1950, American Journalist)

6 It's true love because if he said quit drinking martinis but I kept on drinking them and the next morning I couldn't get out of bed, he wouldn't tell me he told me.
Judith Viorst (1935-, American Poet, Journalist)

7 Her great merit is finding out mine -- there is nothing so amiable as discernment.
Lord Byron (1788-1824, British Poet)

8 If we reason, we would be understood; if we imagine, we would that the airy children of our brain were born anew within another s; if we feel, we would that another's nerves should vibrate to our own, that the beams of their eyes should kindle at once and mix and melt into our own, that lips of motionless ice should not reply to lips quivering and burning with the heart's best blood. This is Love.
Percy Bysshe Shelley (1792-1822, British Poet)

9 You can forgive people who do not follow you through a philosophical disquisition; but to find your wife laughing when you had tears in your eyes, or staring when you were in a fit of laughter, would go some way towards a dissolution of the marriage.
Robert Louis Stevenson (1850-1895, Scottish Essayist, Poet, Novelist)

10 Sometimes apparent resemblance of character will bring two men together and for a certain time unite them. But their mistake gradually becomes evident, and they are astonished to find themselves not only far apart, but even repelled, in some sort, at all their points of contact.
Sebastien-Roch Nicolas De Chamfort (1741-1794, French Writer, Journalist, Playwright)

11 Madam, I have been looking for a person who disliked gravy all my life; let us swear eternal friendship.
Sydney Smith (1771-1845, British Writer, Clergyman)

COMPENSATION

1 In certain situations we'd be down and the competitor in me would want to get it all back in one play. That impatience makes for bad plays, mistakes, and turnarounds.
Browning Nagle (American Football Player)

2 There is a good side to every situation.
David J. Schwartz (American Trainer, Author of "The Magic of Thinking Big")

3 For every force, there is a counter force. For every negative there is a positive. For every action there is a reaction. For every cause there is an effect.
Grace Speare

4 You cannot have the success without the failures.
H. G. Hasler

5 Managing directors are not paid to be busy, they are paid to think.
Kenneth Cork (American Business Executive)

6 You get paid to impact the world, not be impacted by it.
Mal Pancoast

7 For everything you have missed, you have gained something else; and for everything you gain, you lose something else.
Ralph Waldo Emerson (1803-1882, American Poet, Essayist)

8 Any experience can be transformed into something of value.
Vash Young

COMPETENCY

1 No letters after your name are ever going to be a total guarantee of competence any more than they are a guarantee against fraud. Improving competence involves continuing professional development ... That is the really crucial thing, not just passing an examination.
Colette Bowe (American Business Executive)

2 The differences between a competent person and an incompetent person are demonstrated in his environment (surroundings).
L. Ron Hubbard (American Author, Philosopher, Founder of Scientology)

3 Being competent means the ability to control and operate the things in the environment and the environment itself.
L. Ron Hubbard (American Author, Philosopher, Founder of Scientology)

4 People differ not only in their ability to do but also in their 'will to do'.
Paul Hersey (American Academics)

5 Competence, like truth, beauty and contact lenses, is in the eye of the beholder.
Raymond Hull

COMPETITION

1 You get out in front -- you stay out in front.
A. J. Foyt (Born 1935, American retired auto racing driver)

2 You have no control over what the other guy does. You only have control over what you do.
A. J. Kitt (Born 1968, American former World Cup alpine ski racer)

3 I don't compete with other discus throwers. I compete with my own history.
Al Oerter (1936-, American Athlete, Discus-thrower)

4 One cannot play chess if one becomes aware of the pieces as living souls and of the fact that the Whites and the Blacks have more in common with each other than with the players. Suddenly one loses all interest in who will be champion.
Anatol Rapoport

5 It has meant a lot to me to challenge the best players in the world and to beat them. And it means a lot to me to be out here and fighting for the title and, you know, it hurts not to win it.
Andre Agassi (Born 1970, American Tennis Player)

6 The price which society pays for the law of competition, like the price it pays for cheap comforts and luxuries, is great; but the advantages of this law are also greater still than its cost -- for it is to this law that we owe our wonderful material development, which brings improved conditions in its train. But, whether the law be benign or not, we must say of it: It is here; we cannot evade it; no substitutes for it have been found; and while the law may be sometimes hard for the individual, it is best for the race, because it ensures the survival of the fittest in every department.
Andrew Carnegie (1835-1919, American Industrialist, Philanthropist)

7 The ability to learn faster than your competitors may be only sustainable competitive advantage.
Arie de Geus (Dutch Business Strategist)

8 You must play boldly to win.
Arnold Palmer (1929-, American Golfer)

9 Thou shalt not covet; but tradition approves all forms of competition.
Arthur Hugh Clough (1819-1861, British Poet)

10 How can we hope to remain economically competitive in a world in which... 90% of Dutch high-school students take advanced math courses and 100% of teachers in Germany have double majors, while the best we can say about our pocket of excellence is that 75% of [American] students have learned to critique tactfully?
Barbara J. Alexander

11 Competitions are for horse, not artist.
Bela Bartok (1881-1945, Hungarian Composer)

12 I play [golf] with friends sometimes, but there are never friendly games.
Ben Hogan (1912-, American Golfer)

13 Running for money doesn't make you run fast. It makes you run first.
Ben Jipcho

14 It is better for a woman to compete impersonally in society, as men do, than to compete for dominance in her own home with her husband, compete with her neighbors for empty status, and so smother her son that he cannot compete at all.
Betty Friedan (1921-, American Feminist Writer)

15 Becoming number one is easier than remaining number one.
Bill Bradley (American Basketball Player)

16 We have a lot of players in their first year. Some of them are also in their last year.
Bill Walsh (American Football Coach)

17 I won it, at least five million times. Men who were stronger, bigger and faster than I was could have done it, but they never picked up a pole, and never made the feeble effort to pick their legs off the ground and get over the bar.
Bob Richards (American Olympic Pole Vaulting Champion)

18 Mental toughness is to physical as four is to one.
Bobby Knight (1940-, American Basketball Coach)

19 I love the winning, I can take the losing, but most of all I Love to play.
Boris Becker (Born 1967, German Tennis Player)

20 Most games are lost, not won.
Casey Stengel (1889-1975, American Baseball Player and Manager)

21 The general fact is that the most effective way of utilizing human energy is through an organized rivalry, which by specialization and social control is, at the same time, organized co- operation.
Charles Horton Cooley (1864-1929, American Sociologist)

22 Man is a gaming animal. He must always be trying to get the better in something or other.
Charles Lamb (1775-1834, British Essayist, Critic)

23 Playing safe is only playing.
Chuck Olson

24 Focus on competition has always been a formula for mediocrity.
Daniel Burrus (American Trend Predictor, Author of "Techo Trends")

25 And what is the greatest number? Number one.
David Hume (1711-1776, Scottish Philosopher, Historian)

26 If you make every game a life and death proposition, you're going to have problems. For one thing, you'll be dead a lot.
Dean Smith (American College Basketball Coach)

27 Every time you go out on the ice, there are slight flaws. You can always think of something you should have done better. These are the things you must work on.
Dorothy Hamill (American Figure Skater)

28 What counts is not necessarily the size of the dog in the fight; it's the size of the fight in the dog.
Dwight D. Eisenhower (1890-1969, Thirty-fourth President of the USA)

29 Somebody will always break your records. It is how you live that counts.
Earl Campbell (American Football Player)

30 Men often compete with one another until the day they die; comradeship consists of rubbing shoulders jocularly with a competitor.
Edward Hoagland (1932-, American Novelist, Essayist)

31 Do your work with your whole heart, and you will succeed -- there's so little competition.
Elbert Hubbard (1859-1915, American Author, Publisher)

32 World trade means competition from anywhere; advancing technology encourages cross- industry competition. Consequently, strategic planning must consider who our future competitors will be, not only who is here today.
Eric Allison (American Financial Writer)

33 If football taught me anything about business, it is that you win the game one play at a time.
Fran Tarkenton (American Football Player, Businessman, Corporate Consultant, Author)

34 When you step onto that field, you cannot concede a thing.
Gayle Sayers (American Football Player)

35 Competition is the spice of sports; but if you make spice the whole meal you'll be sick.
George Leonard

36 Thank God for competition. When our competitors upset our plans or outdo our designs, they open infinite possibilities of our own work to us.
Gil Atkinson

37 Hail Caesar, those who are about to die salute you.
Gladiator's Salute

38 You find that you have peace of mind and can enjoy yourself, get more sleep, and rest when you know that it was a one hundred percent effort that you gave -- win or lose.
Gordie Howe (1928-, Canadian Hockey Player)

39 For when the One Great Scorer comes to mark against your name, He writes -- not that you won or lost -- but how you played the Game.
Grantland Rice (1880-1954, American Sportswriter)

40 The Law of Win/Win says, "Let's not do it your way or my way; let's do it the best way.
Greg Anderson (American Author of "The 22 Non-Negotiable Laws of Wellness")

41 I don't care how good you play, you can find somebody who can beat you, and I don't care how bad you play, you can find somebody you can beat.
Harvey Penick (American Golfer)

42 There is nothing noble in being superior to some other person. The true nobility is in being superior to your previous self.
Indian Proverb

43 There are two kinds of people: Those who do the work and those who take the credit. Try to be in the first group because there is less competition there.
Indira Gandhi (1917-1984, Indian Prime Minster)

44 I ski to win. When the day comes that I can't get myself into a fighting mood anymore, I won't be able to win and I'll stop racing.
Ingemar Stenmark (Skier)

45 After the game the King and pawn go into the same box.
Italian Proverb

46 The medals don't mean anything and the glory doesn't last. It's all about your happiness. The rewards are going to come, but my happiness is just loving the sport and having fun performing.
Jackie Joyner Kersee (1962-, American Track Athlete)

47 Racing is a matter of spirit not strength.
Janet Guthrie (American Race Car Driver)

48 When the game is over it is really just beginning.
Jerry Kramer

49 When you have them by the balls, their hearts and minds will follow.
Jerry Martin (American Actor)

50 I worked very hard. I felt I could play the game. The only thing that could stop me was myself.
Jim Abbott (Born 1967, American Baseball Player)

51 You must sacrifice, train, do everything possible to put yourself in a position to win. But if you consider second or third a failure, I feel sorry for you.
Joe Falcon (American Athlete)

52 He can run but he can't hide.
Joe Louis (1914-1981, American Boxer)

53 No wise combatant underestimates their antagonist.
Johann Wolfgang Von Goethe (1749-1832, German Poet, Dramatist, Novelist)

54 We want to be first; not first if, not first but; but first!
John F. Kennedy (1917-1963, Thirty-fifth President of the USA)

55 You have to be able to center yourself, to let all of your emotions go... Don't ever forget that you play with your soul as well as your body.
Kareem Abdul-Jabbar (Born 1947, American Basketball Player)

56 When I go our on the ice, I just think about my skating. I forget it is a competition.
Katarina Witt (1955-, German Figure Skater)

57 Win or lose, do it fairly.
Knute Rockne (1888-1931, Norwegian-born American Football Coach)

58 How can they beat me? I've been struck by lightning, had two back operations, and been divorced twice.
Lee Trevino (1939-, American Golfer)

59 I believe in rules. Sure I do. If there weren't any rules, how could you break them?
Leo Durocher (1905-1991, American Baseball Player/Manager)

60 Don't look back. Something might be gaining on you.
Leroy "Satchel" Paige (1906?-1982, American Baseball Player)

61 Show me a guy who is afraid to look bad, and I'll show you a guy you can beat every time.
Lou Brock

62 How you respond to the challenge in the second half will determine what you become after the game, whether you are a winner or a loser.
Lou Holtz (1937-, American Football Coach)

63 I watch a man shoot pool for an hour. If he misses more than one shot I know I can beat him.
Luther Lassiter

64 To free the mind from the habit of competition, we must see in detail the process by which the mind is ensnared by competition.
Marguerite Beecher

65 The only competition worthy a wise man is with himself.
Mrs. Jamieson

66 A competitor will find a way to win. Competitors take bad breaks and use them to drive themselves just that much harder. Quitters take bad breaks and use them as reasons to give up. It's all a matter of pride.
Nancy Lopez (1957-, American Golfer)

67 You must not fight too often with one enemy, or you will teach him all your tricks of war.
Napoleon Bonaparte (1769-1821, French General, Emperor)

68 I consider myself one of a very small handful of drivers in the world that are top drivers. The best one? I don't think anybody can say they're the best one because, from one week to the next, you can be on form or off form a little bit.
Nigel Mansell (1953-, American Race Car Driver)

69 Surely the best way to meet the enemy is head on in the field and not wait till they plunder our very homes.
Oliver Goldsmith (1728-1774, Anglo-Irish Author, Poet, Playwright)

70 A horse never runs so fast as when he has other horses to catch up and outpace.
Ovid (43 BC-18 AD, Roman Poet)

71 You have to defeat a great players aura more than his game.
Pat Riley (1945, American Basketball Coach)

72 Once your physically capable of winning a gold medal, the rest is ninety percent mental.
Patti Johnson (American Athlete)

73 Enjoy the successes that you have, and don't be too hard on yourself when you don't do well. Too many times we beat up on ourselves. Just relax and enjoy it.
Patty Sheehan (1956, American Golfer)

74 The key to any game is to use your strengths and hide your weaknesses.
Paul Westphal

75 The difference of great players is at a certain point in a match they raise their level of play and maintain it. Lesser players play great for a set, but then less.
Pete Sampras (Born 1971, American Tennis Player)

76 It's amazing how much of this is mental. Everybody's in good shape. Everybody knows how to ski. Everybody has good equipment. When it really boils down to it, it's who wants it the most, and who's the most confident on his skis.
Reggie Crist (American Skier)

77 These are the days when it takes all you've got just to keep up with the losers.
Robert Orpen

78 The time your game is most vulnerable is when you're ahead, never let up.
Rod Laver (1938-, Australian Tennis Player)

79 In this game, by trying to win; you automatically lose.
Ruth Ross

80 The weakness of an enemy forms part of our own strength.
Saying

81 Competition is the whetstone of talent.
Saying

82 This is a tough game. There are times when you've got to play hurt, when you've got to block out the pain.
Shaquille O'Neal (Born 1971, American Basketball Player, Actor)

83 I don't psyche myself up. I psyche myself down. I think clearer when I'm not psyched up.
Steve Cauthen (American Jockey)

84 My hat's in the ring. The fight is on and I'm stripped to the buff.
Theodore Roosevelt (1858-1919, Twenty-sixth President of the USA)

85 Our life is not really a mutual helpfulness; but rather, it's fair competition cloaked under due laws of war; it's a mutual hostility.
Thomas Carlyle (1795-1881, Scottish Philosopher, Author)

86 When you want to win a game, you have to teach. When you lose a game, you have to learn.
Tom Landry (1924-, American Football Player, Coach)

87 What it comes down to is that anybody can win with the best horse. What makes you good is if you can take the second or third-best horse and win.
Vicky Aragon (American Jockey)

88 The person who figures out how to harness the collective genius of his or her organization is going to blow the competition away.
Walter Wriston

89 Competition is a process or variety of habitual behavior that grows out of a habit of mind.
Willard Beecher

90 So long as the system of competition in the production and exchange of the means of life goes on, the degradation of the arts will go on; and if that system is to last for ever, then art is doomed, and will surely die; that is to say, civilization will die.
William Morris (1834-1896, British Artist, Writer, Printer)

91 Every man in the world is better than someone else and not as good someone else.
William Saroyan (1908-1981, American Writer, Novelist,, Playwright)

92 When you fear a foe, fear crushes your strength; and this weakness gives strength to your opponents.
William Shakespeare (1564-1616, British Poet, Playwright, Actor)

93 Strive mightily, but eat and drink as friends.
William Shakespeare (1564-1616, British Poet, Playwright, Actor)

94 The biggest things are often the easiest to do because there is so little competition.
William Van Horne

95 When you're riding, only the race in which you're riding is important.
Willie Shoemaker (1931-, American Racing Jockey and Trainer)

96 Everybody pulls for David, nobody roots for Goliath.
Wilt Chamberlain (1936-, American Basketball Player)

97 The game isn't over until it's over.
Yogi Berra (1925-, American Baseball Player)

COMPLACENCY

1 I cannot help fearing that men may reach a point where they look on every new theory as a danger, every innovation as a toilsome trouble, every social advance as a first step toward revolution, and that they may absolutely refuse to move at all for fear of being carried off their feet. The prospect really does frighten me that they may finally become so engrossed in a cowardly love of immediate pleasures that their interest in their own future and in that of their descendants may vanish, and that they will prefer tamely to follow the course of their destiny rather than make a sudden energetic effort necessary to set things right.
Alexis De Tocqueville (1805-1859, French Social Philosopher)

2 A Frenchman is self-assured because he regards himself personally both in mind and body as irresistibly attractive to men and women. An Englishman is self-assured as being a citizen of the best- organized state in the world and therefore, as an Englishman, always knows what he should do and knows that all he does as an Englishman is undoubtedly correct. An Italian is self-assured because he is excitable and easily forgets himself and other people. A Russian is self-assured just because he knows nothing and does not want to know anything, since he does not believe that anything can be known. The German's self-assurance is worst of all, stronger and more repulsive than any other, because he imagines that he knows the truth -- science -- which he himself has invented but which is for him the absolute truth.
Count Leo Tolstoy (1828-1910, Russian Novelist, Philosopher)

3 Everybody in America is soft, and hates conflict. The cure for this, both in politics and social life, is the same -- hardihood. Give them raw truth.
John Jay Chapman (1862-1933, American Author)

4 In all life one should comfort the afflicted, but verily, also, one should afflict the comfortable, and especially when they are comfortably, contentedly, even happily wrong.
John Kenneth Galbraith (1908-, American Economist)

5 They act as if they supposed that to be very sanguine about the general improvement of mankind is a virtue that relieves them from taking trouble about any improvement in particular.
John Morley (1838-1923, British Journalist, Biographer, Statesman)

6 They believe that nothing will happen because they have closed their doors.
Maurice Maeterlinck (1862-1949, Belgian Author)

7 America is a hurricane, and the only people who do not hear the sound are those fortunate if incredibly stupid and smug White Protestants who live in the center, in the serene eye of the big wind.
Norman Mailer (1923-, American Author)

8 These are days when no one should rely unduly on his "competence." Strength lies in improvisation. All the decisive blows are struck left-handed.
Walter Benjamin (1982-1940, German Critic, Philosopher)

COMPLAINTS AND COMPLAINING

1 Realize that if you have time to whine and complain about something then you have the time to do something about it.
Anthony J. D'Angelo

2 If I were to say, "God, why me?" about the bad things, then I should have said, "God, why me?" about the good things that happened in my life.
Arthur Ashe (1943-1993, African-American Tennis Player)

3 Constant complaint is the poorest sort of pay for all the comforts we enjoy.
Benjamin Franklin (1706-1790, American Scientist, Publisher, Diplomat)

4 Just because nobody complains doesn't mean all parachutes are perfect.
Benny Hill (1925-1992, British Comedian)

5 One dog barks at something, the rest bark at him.
Chinese Proverb

6 It is the growling man who lives a dog's life.
Coleman Cox

7 Don't complain about the snow on your neighbor's roof when your own doorstep is unclean.
Confucius (551-479 BC, Chinese Ethical Teacher, Philosopher)

8 It is better to light one small candle than to curse the darkness.
Confucius (551-479 BC, Chinese Ethical Teacher, Philosopher)

9 The sun was shining in my eyes, and I could barely see to do the necessary task that was allotted me. Resentment of the vivid glow I started to complain. When all at once upon the air I heard the blind man's cane.
Earl Musselman

10 I believe in grumbling; it is the politest form of fighting known.
Edgar Watson Howe (1853-1937, American Journalist, Author)

11 It is a general popular error to suppose the loudest complainers for the public to be the most anxious for its welfare.
Edmund Burke (1729-1797, British Political Writer, Statesman)

12 When people complain of life, it is almost always because they have asked impossible things of it.
Ernest Renan (1823-1892, French Writer, Critic, Scholar)

13 Had we not faults of our own, we should take less pleasure in complaining of others.
François Fénelon (1651-1715, French Roman Catholic archbishop, theologian, poet and writer)

14 Never complain. Never explain.
Henry Ford (1863-1947, American Industrialist, Founder of Ford Motor Company)

15 The wheel that squeaks the loudest is the one that gets the grease.
Henry Wheeler Shaw (1818-1885, American Humorist)

16 What do sad complaints avail if the offense is not cut down by punishment.
Horace (65-8 BC, Italian Poet)

17 Those who do not complain are never pitied.
Jane Austen (1775-1817, British Novelist)

18 I personally think we developed language because of our deep inner need to complain.
Jane Wagner

19 I felt sorry for myself because I had no shoes -- until I met a man who had no feet.
Jewish Proverb

20 There are some people who knock the pyramids because they don't have elevators.
Jim Ferree

21 I can't complain, but sometimes I still do.
Joe Walsh

22 He cannot complain of a hard sentence, who is made master of his own fate.
Johann Friedrich Von Schiller (1759-1805, German Dramatist, Poet, Historian)

23 I will not be as those who spend the day in complaining of headache, and the night in drinking the wine that gives it.
Johann Wolfgang Von Goethe (1749-1832, German Poet, Dramatist, Novelist)

24 When complaints are freely heard, deeply considered and speedily reformed, then is the utmost bound of civil liberty attained that wise men look for.
John Milton (1608-1674, British Poet)

25 It is rare indeed that there is not ample occasion for grumbling.
John Wagstaff

26 To hear complaints is tiresome to the miserable and the happy.
Johnson

27 When any anxiety or gloom of the mind takes hold of you, make it a rule not to publish it by complaining; but exert yourselves to hide it, and by endeavoring to hide it you drive it away.
Johnson

28 When a person finds themselves predisposed to complaining about how little they are regarded by others, let them reflect how little they have contributed to the happiness of others.
Johnson

29 Complaint is the largest tribute Heaven receives.
Jonathan Swift (1667-1745, Anglo-Irish Satirist)

30 We have no more right to put our discordant states of mind into the lives of those around us and rob them of their sunshine and ;brighten possibilities.
Julia Moss Seton

31 We lose the right of complaining sometimes, by denying something, but this often triples its force.
Laurence Sterne (1713-1768, British Author)

32 Rich folks always talk hard times.
Lillian Smith (1897-1966, American Author)

33 The tendency to whining and complaining may be taken as the surest sign symptom of little souls and inferior intellects.
Lord Jeffrey

34 The man who complains about the way the ball bounces is likely the one who dropped it.
Lou Holtz (1937-, American Football Coach)

35 I think a compliment ought to always precede a complaint, where one is possible, because it softens resentment and insures for the complaint a courteous and gentle reception.
Mark Twain (1835-1910, American Humorist, Writer)

36 Noise proves nothing, Often a hen who has laid an egg cackles as if she had laid an asteroid.
Mark Twain (1835-1910, American Humorist, Writer)

37 What annoyances are more painful than those of which we cannot complain?
Marquis De Custine (1790-1857, French Traveler, Author)

38 Never excuse, never explain, never complain.
Motto

39 The world is sad enough without your woe.
Orison Swett Marden (1850-1924, American Author, Founder of Success Magazine)

40 Intelligence is nothing without delight.
Paul Claudel

41 I find it unusual that it is more socially acceptable to complain about what you have than it is to ask for what you want.
Phil Lout

42 There is one topic peremptorily forbidden to all well-bred, to all rational mortals, namely, their distempers. If you have not slept, or if you have slept, or if you have headache, or sciatica, or leprosy, or thunder-stroke, I beseech you, by all angels, to hold your peace, and not pollute the morning.
Ralph Waldo Emerson (1803-1882, American Poet, Essayist)

43 Say and do something positive that will help the situation; it doesn't take any brains to complain.
Robert A. Cook

44 The usual fortune of complaint is to excite contempt more than pity.
Samuel Johnson (1709-1784, British Author)

45 Depend upon it that if a man talks of his misfortunes there is something in them that is not disagreeable to him.
Samuel Johnson (1709-1784, British Author)

46 Our present time is indeed a criticizing and critical time, hovering between the wish, and the inability to believe. Our complaints are like arrows shot up into the air at no target: and with no purpose they only fall back upon our own heads and destroy ourselves.
Sir William Temple (1628-1699, British Diplomat, Essayist)

47 He that falls by himself never cries.
Turkish Proverb

48 One chops the wood, the other does the grunting.
Yiddish Proverb

COMPLEXITY

1 Man is an over-complicated organism. If he is doomed to extinction he will die out for want of simplicity.
Ezra Pound (1885-1972, American Poet, Critic)

2 The perplexity of life arises from there being too many interesting things in it for us to be interested properly in any of them.
Gilbert K. Chesterton (1874-1936, British Author)

3 I see mysteries and complications wherever I look, and I have never met a steadily logical person.
Martha Gellhorn (1908-, American Journalist, Author)

4 Everything is complicated; if that were not so, life and poetry and everything else would be a bore.
Wallace Stevens (1879-1955, American Poet)

COMPLIMENTS

1 Everybody likes a compliment.
Abraham Lincoln (1809-1865, Sixteenth President of the USA)

2 I really lack the words to compliment myself today.
Alberto Tomba

3 The best compliment to a child or a friend is the feeling you give him that he has been set free to make his own inquiries, to come to conclusions that are right for him, whether or not they coincide with your own.
Alistair Cooke (1908-, British Broadcaster, Journalist)

4 Nothing is so silly as the expression of a man who is being complimented.
Andre Gide (1869-1951, French Author)

5 Pleasant words are as an honeycomb, sweet to the soul, and health to the bones.
Bible (Sacred Scriptures of Christians and Judaism)

6 When millions applaud you seriously ask yourself what harm you have done; and when they disapprove you, what good.
Charles Caleb Colton (1780-1832, British Sportsman Writer)

7 After [my father had] seen me in five or six things, he said, "Son, your mother and I really enjoyed your recent film, and I must say that you're a lot like John Wayne." And I said, "How so?" And he said, "Well, you're exactly the same in all your roles." Now, as a modern American actor, that's not what you want to hear. But for a guy who watched John Wayne movies and grew up in Iowa, it's a sterling compliment.
Dermot Mulroney (1963-, American Actor, Musician, Producer)

8 Usually we praise only to be praised.
François de La Rochefoucauld (1613-1680, French classical writer)

9 There's nothing worse than someone coming up to me and going "Oh God, I really love your hair."
Gavin Rossdale (Born 1967, British-born American Musician, Singer, Songwriter)

10 No compliment can be eloquent, except as an expression of indifference.
George Eliot (1819-1880, British Novelist)

11 The greatest compliment that was ever paid me was when one asked what I thought, and attended to my answer.
Henry David Thoreau (1817-1862, American Essayist, Poet, Naturalist)

12 Don't tell a woman she's pretty; tell her there's no other woman like her, and all roads will open to you.
Jules Renard (1864-1910, French Author, Dramatist)

13 Nothing makes people so worthy of compliments as receiving them. One is more delightful for being told one is delightful -- just as one is more angry for being told one is angry.
Katherine F. Gerould

14 I can live for two months on a good compliment.
Mark Twain (1835-1910, American Humorist, Writer)

15 If you can't get a compliment any other way, pay yourself one.
Mark Twain (1835-1910, American Humorist, Writer)

16 When you cannot get a compliment in any other way pay yourself one.
Mark Twain (1835-1910, American Humorist, Writer)

17 There is nothing you can say in answer to a compliment. I have been complimented myself a great many times, and they always embarrass me --I always feel that they have not said enough.
Mark Twain (1835-1910, American Humorist, Writer)

18 I have been complimented many times and they always embarrass me; I always feel that they have not said enough.
Mark Twain (1835-1910, American Humorist, Writer)

19 If people did not compliment one another there would be little society.
Marquis De Vauvenargues (1715-1747, French Moralist)

20 Women are never disarmed by compliments. Men always are. That is the difference between the two sexes.
Oscar Wilde (1856-1900, British Author, Wit)

21 Hunger is never delicate; they who are seldom gorged to the full with praise may be safely fed with gross compliments, for the appetite must be satisfied before it is disgusted.
Samuel Johnson (1709-1784, British Author)

22 Compliments cost nothing, yet many pay dear for them.
Thomas Fuller (1608-1661, British Clergyman, Author)

23 A compliment is something like a kiss through a veil.
Victor Hugo (1802-1885, French Poet, Dramatist, Novelist)

COMPROMISE

1 Compromise. Such an adjustment of conflicting interests as gives each adversary the satisfaction of thinking he has got what he ought not to have, and is deprived of nothing except what was justly his due.
Ambrose Bierce (1842-1914, American Author, Editor, Journalist, "The Devil's Dictionary")

2 The compromise will always be more expensive than either of the suggestions it is compromising.
Arthur Bloch

3 If you are not very clever, you should be conciliatory.
Benjamin Disraeli (1804-1881, British Statesman, Prime Minister)

4 What are facts but compromises? A fact merely marks the point where we have agreed to let investigation cease.
Bliss Carman (1861-1929, Canadian Poet)

5 From the beginning of our history the country has been afflicted with compromise. It is by compromise that human rights have been ;abandoned.
Charles Sumner (1811-1874, American Statesman)

6 The swift wind of compromise is a lot more devastating than the sudden jolt of misfortune.
Charles Swindoll (American Pastor, Author)

7 All government, indeed every human benefit and enjoyment, every virtue, and every prudent act, is founded on compromise and barter.
Edmund Burke (1729-1797, British Political Writer, Statesman)

8 It is the weak man who urges compromise -- never the strong man.
Elbert Hubbard (1859-1915, American Author, Publisher)

9 A lean compromise is better than a fat lawsuit.
George Herbert (1593-1632, British Metaphysical Poet)

10 Compromise used to mean that half a loaf was better than no bread. Among modern statesmen it really seems to mean that half a loaf ;is better than a whole loaf.
Gilbert K. Chesterton (1874-1936, British Author)

11 Art is uncompromising and life is full of compromises.
Gunther Grass (1927-, German Author)

12 Once you consent to some concession, you can never cancel it and put things back the way they are.
Howard Hughes (1905-1976, American Businessman, Film Producer, Aviator)

13 Compromise makes a good umbrella, but a poor roof; it is temporary expedient, often wise in party politics, almost sure to be unwise ;in statesmanship.
James Russell Lowell (1819-1891, American Poet, Critic, Editor)

14 Gather in your resources, rally all your faculties, marshal all your energies, focus all your capacities upon mastery of at least one field of endeavor.
John Haggai

15 Your mind, which is yourself, can be likened to a house. The first necessary move then, is to rid that house of all but furnishings essential to success.
John Mcdonald

16 You can do only one thing at a time. I simply tackle one problem and concentrate all efforts on what I am doing at the moment.
Maxwell Maltz (American Plastic Surgeon, Author of "Psycho-Cybernetics")

17 If one cannot catch a bird of paradise, better take a wet hen.
Nikita Khrushchev (1894-1971, Soviet Premier)

18 Compromise is never anything but an ignoble truce between the duty of a man and the terror of a coward.
Reginald W. Kaufman

19 Life cannot subsist in society but by reciprocal concessions.
Samuel Johnson (1709-1784, British Author)

20 Better bend than break.
Scottish Proverb

21 Compromise is but the sacrifice of one right or good in the hope of retaining another -- too often ending in the loss of both.
Tryon Edwards (1809-1894, American Theologian)

22 An appeaser is one who feeds a crocodile -- hoping it will eat him last.
Winston Churchill (1874-1965, British Statesman, Prime Minister)

23 The English never draw a line without blurring it.
Winston Churchill (1874-1965, British Statesman, Prime Minister)

COMPUTERS

1 There is never finality in the display terminal's screen, but an irresponsible whimsicality, as words, sentences, and paragraphs are negated at the touch of a key. The significance of the past, as expressed in the manuscript by a deleted word or an inserted correction, is annulled in idle gusts of electronic massacre.
Alexander Cockburn (1941-, Anglo-Irish Journalist)

2 There will still be things that machines cannot do. They will not produce great art or great literature or great philosophy; they will not be able to discover the secret springs of happiness in the human heart; they will know nothing of love and friendship.
Bertrand Russell (1872-1970, British Philosopher, Mathematician, Essayist)

3 I have always wished for a computer that would be as easy to use as my telephone. My wish came true. I no longer know how to use my telephone.
Bjarne Stronstrup

4 Silicon Valley is like a person running around in front of a steamroller. You can outrun the steamroller on any given day. But if you ever sit down you get squashed.
Bob Boschert

5 Control over computing belongs with users.
Brandt Allen (American Academic)

6 The word user is the word used by the computer professional when they mean idiot.
Dave Barry (American Humorist, Author)

7 I am not the only person who uses his computer mainly for the purpose of diddling with his computer.
Dave Barry (American Humorist, Author)

8 To err is human, but to really foul things up requires a computer. Those who are serious in ridiculous matters will be ridiculous in serious matters.
Farmers Almanac

9 One of the best things to come out of the home computer revolution could be the general and widespread understanding of how severely limited logic really is.
Frank Herbert (1920-1986, American Writer)

10 It is hardly surprising that children should enthusiastically start their education at an early age with the Absolute Knowledge of computer science; while they are unable to read, for reading demands making judgments at every line. Conversation is almost dead, and soon so too will be those who knew how to speak.
Guy Debord (1931-, French Philosopher)

11 If builders built buildings the way programmers wrote programs, then the first woodpecker that came along would destroy civilization.
Harry Weinberger

12 Computers WORK, people THINK.
IBM Corporation Old Adage (American Computer Company)

13 I do not fear computers. I fear the lack of them.
Isaac Asimov (1920-1992, Russian-born American Author)

14 Electronic aids, particularly domestic computers, will help the inner migration, the opting out of reality. Reality is no longer going to be the stuff out there, but the stuff inside your head. It's going to be commercial and nasty at the same time.
J. G. Ballard (1930-, British Author)

15 The sad thing about artificial intelligence is that it lacks artifice and therefore intelligence.
Jean Baudrillard (French Postmodern Philosopher, Writer)

16 Computer science only indicates the retrospective omnipotence of our technologies. In other words, an infinite capacity to process data (but only data -- i.e. the already given) and in no sense a new vision. With that science, we are entering an era of exhaustivity, which is also an era of exhaustion.
Jean Baudrillard (French Postmodern Philosopher, Writer)

17 Man is still the most extraordinary computer of all.
John F. Kennedy (1917-1963, Thirty-fifth President of the USA)

18 I see no reason why anyone would want a computer in their home.
Kenneth Olsen (American Businessman, Founder of Digital Equipment)

19 A distributed system is one in which the failure of a computer you didn't even know existed can render your own computer unusable.
Leslie Lamport

20 The workers and professionals of the world will soon be divided into two distinct groups. Those who will control computers and those who will be controlled by computers. It would be best for you to be in the former group.
Lewis D. Eigen (American Executive VP of University Research Corp.)

21 A computer lets you make more mistakes faster than any invention in human history -- with the possible exceptions of hand guns and tequila.
Mitch Ratliffe

22 The most likely way for the world to be destroyed, most experts agree, is by accident. That's where we come in; we're computer professionals. We cause accidents.
Nathanie Borenstein (Author)

23 One of the most feared expressions in modern times is "The computer is down"
Norman Augustine (American Business Executive, CEO of Martin Marietta)

24 Computers are useless. They can only give you answers.
Pablo Picasso (1881-1973, Spanish Artist)

25 A computer won't clean up the errors in your manual of procedures.
Sheila M. Eby (American Business Executive)

26 The real danger is not that computers will begin to think like men, but that men will begin to think like computers.
Sidney J. Harris (1917-, American Journalist)

27 I think there is a world market for maybe five computers.
Thomas J. Watson (18?-1956, American Businessman, Founder of IBM)

28 As far as we know, our computer has never had an undetected error.
Weisert

29 I really don't care that I don't have what's current because whatever is at the moment, it will be infinitely better in a few months and even better months later.
William Fink (Superintendent with American Park Service)

30 Man is a slow, sloppy and brilliant thinker; the machine is fast, accurate and stupid.
William M. Kelly

CONCEIT

1 Whatever accomplishment you boast of in the world, there is someone better than you.
African Proverb

2 A national debt, if it is not excessive, will be to us a national blessing.
Alexander Hamilton (1757-1804, American Statesman)

3 See the man wise in his own conceit? There is more hope for a fool than for him. [Proverbs 26:7]
Bible (Sacred Scriptures of Christians and Judaism)

4 Conceit is incompatible with understanding.
Count Leo Tolstoy (1828-1910, Russian Novelist, Philosopher)

5 As individuals and as a nation, we now suffer from social narcissism. The beloved Echo of our ancestors, the virgin America, has been abandoned. We have fallen in love with our own image, with images of our making, which turn out to be images of ourselves.
Daniel J. Boorstin (1914-, American Historian)

6 Nobody can be kinder than the narcissist while you react to life in his own terms.
Elizabeth Bowen (1899-1973, Anglo-Irish Novelist)

7 Of great wealth there is no real use, except in its distribution, the rest is just conceit.
Francis Bacon (1561-1626, British Philosopher, Essayist, Statesman)

8 He who is enamored of himself will at least have the advantage of being inconvenienced by few rivals.
Georg C. Lichtenberg (1742-1799, German Physicist, Satirist)

9 I've never any pity for conceited people, because I think they carry their comfort about with them.
George Eliot (1819-1880, British Novelist)

10 It is possible to have a strong self-love without any self-satisfaction, rather with a self- discontent which is the more intense because one's own little core of egoistic sensibility is a supreme care.
George Eliot (1819-1880, British Novelist)

11 A person wrapped up in himself makes a small package.
Harry Emerson Fosdick (1878-1969, American Minister)

12 Conceit is God's gift to little men.
Harry S. Truman (1884-1972, Thirty-third President of the USA)

13 Whenever nature leaves a hole in a person's mind, she generally plasters it over with a thick coat of self-conceit.
Henry Wadsworth Longfellow (1819-1892, American Poet)

14 Conceit is bragging about yourself. Confidence means you believe you can get the job done.
Johnny Unitas (American Football Player)

15 Always hold your head up but be careful to keep your nose at a friendly level.
Max L. Forman

16 Some people are so heavenly minded that they are no earthly good.
Oliver Wendell Holmes (1809-1894, American Author, Wit, Poet)

17 Solvency is maintained by means of a national debt, on the principle, "If you will not lend me the money, how can I pay you?
Ralph Waldo Emerson (1803-1882, American Poet, Essayist)

18 Narcissist: psychoanalytic term for the person who loves himself more than his analyst; considered to be the manifestation of a dire mental disease whose successful treatment depends on the patient learning to love the analyst more and himself less.
Thomas Szasz (1920-, American Psychiatrist)

19 Had we not loved ourselves at all, we could never have been obliged to love anything. So that self-love is the basis of all love.
Thomas Traherne (1636-1674, British Clergyman, Poet, Mystic)

20 Narcissus does not fall in love with his reflection because it is beautiful, but because it is his. If it were his beauty that enthralled him, he would be set free in a few years by its fading.
W. H. Auden (1907-1973, Anglo-American Poet)

21 If you done it, it ain't bragging.
Walt Whitman (1819-1892, American Poet)

22 People who do not know how to laugh are always pompous and self-conceited.
William M. Thackeray (1811-1863, Indian-born British Novelist)

23 Conceit, more rich in matter than in words, brags of his substance: they are but beggars who can count their worth.
William Shakespeare (1564-1616, British Poet, Playwright, Actor)

24 Conceit in weakest bodies works the strongest.
William Shakespeare (1564-1616, British Poet, Playwright, Actor)

CONCENTRATION

1 It may be objected by some that I have concentrated too much on the dry bones, and too little on the flesh which clothes them, but I would ask such critics to concede at least that the bones have an austere beauty of their own.
A. B. Pippard (1920-2008, British physicist)

2 As long as I can concentrate and remain somewhat calm, I can normally do very well.
Al Oerter (1936-, American Athlete, Discus-thrower)

3 Concentrate, play your game, and don't be afraid to win.
Amy Alcott (American Golfer)

4 It's shocking how little there is to do with tennis when you're just thinking about nothing except winning every point.
Andre Agassi (Born 1970, American Tennis Player)

5 Concentrate; put all your eggs in one basket, and watch that basket...
Andrew Carnegie (1835-1919, American Industrialist, Philanthropist)

6 Concentration is my motto -- first honesty, then industry, then concentration.
Andrew Carnegie (1835-1919, American Industrialist, Philanthropist)

7 One reason so few of us achieve what we truly want is that we never direct our focus; we never concentrate our power. Most people dabble their way through life, never deciding to master anything in particular.
Anthony Robbins (1960-, American Author, Speaker, Peak Performance Expert / Consultant)

8 What do I mean by concentration? I mean focusing totally on the business at hand and commanding your body to do exactly what you want it to do.
Arnold Palmer (1929-, American Golfer)

9 Concentration and mental toughness are the margins of victory.
Bill Russell (1934-, American Basketball Player)

10 If you have to remind yourself to concentrate during competition, you've got no chance to concentrate.
Bobby Nichols (1936-, American Golfer)

11 I never could have done what I have done without the habits of punctuality, order, and diligence, without the determination to concentrate myself on one subject at a time...
Charles Dickens (1812-1870, British Novelist)

12 Ninety percent of my game is mental. It's my concentration that has gotten me this far.
Chris Evert (1954-, American Tennis Player)

13 The more intensely we feel about an idea or a goal, the more assuredly the idea, buried deep in our subconscious, will direct us along the path to its fulfillment.
Earl Nightingale (1921-1989, American Radio Announcer, Author, Motivator, Speaker)

14 Concentration is why some athletes are better than others. You develop that concentration in training. You can't be lackluster in training and concentrate in a meet.
Edwin Moses (1955-, American Track Athlete)

15 It is not the straining for great things that is most effective; it is the doing the little things, the common duties, a little better and better.
Elizabeth Stuart Phelps (1844-1911, American Writer)

16 Any individual can be, in time, what he earnestly desires to be, if he but set his face steadfastly in the direction of that one thing and bring all his powers to bear upon its attainment.
J. Herman Randall

17 My ability to concentrate and work toward that goal has been my greatest asset.
Jack Nicklaus (1940-, American Golfer)

18 Give whatever you are doing and whoever you are with the gift of your attention.
Jim Rohn (American Businessman, Author, Speaker, Philosopher)

19 Singleness of purpose is one of the chief essentials for success in life, no matter what may be one's aim.
John D. Rockefeller (1839-1937, American Industrialist, Philanthropist, Founder Exxon)

20 The ability to concentrate and to use time well is everything.
Lee Iacocca (1924-, American Businessman, Former CEO of Chrysler)

21 When you write down your ideas you automatically focus your full attention on them. Few if any of us can write one thought and think another at the same time. Thus a pencil and paper make excellent concentration tools.
Michael Leboeuf (American Researcher, Consultant, Author)

22 I'm trying not to look too far ahead. All I'm thinking is one shot at a time, one hole at a time, and that's what I want to keep doing.
Michelle Mcgann

23 The jack-of-all-trades seldom is good at any. Concentrate all of your efforts on one definite chief aim.
Napoleon Hill (1883-1970, American Speaker, Motivational Writer, "Think and Grow Rich")

24 Nothing can add more power to your life than concentrating all your energies on a limited set of targets.
Nido Qubein (American Businessman, Speaker, Consultant, Author)

25 When every physical and mental resources is focused, one's power to solve a problem multiplies tremendously.
Norman Vincent Peale (1898-1993, American Christian Reformed Pastor, Speaker, Author)

26 The weakest living creature, by concentrating his powers on a single object, can accomplish good results while the strongest, by dispersing his effort over many chores, may fail to accomplish anything. Drops of water, by continually falling, hone their passage through the hardest of rocks but the hasty torrent rushes over it with hideous uproar and leaves no trace behind.
Og Mandino (1923-1996, American Motivational Author, Speaker)

27 The master of a single trade can support a family. The master of seven trades cannot support himself. The wind is never for the sailor who knows not to what port he is bound.
Og Mandino (1923-1996, American Motivational Author, Speaker)

28 It is those who concentrates on but one thing at a time who advance in this world. The great man or woman is the one who never steps outside his or her specialty or foolishly dissipates his or her individuality.
Og Mandino (1923-1996, American Motivational Author, Speaker)

29 The great difference between those who succeed and those who fail does not consist in the amount of work done by each but in the amount of intelligent work. Many of those who fail most ignominiously do enough to achieve grand success but they labor haphazardly at whatever they are assigned, building up with one hand to tear down with the other. They do not grasp circumstances and change them into opportunities. They have no faculty for turning honest defeats into telling victories. With ability enough and ample time, the major ingredients of success, they are forever throwing back and forth an empty shuttle and the real web of their life is never woven.
Og Mandino (1923-1996, American Motivational Author, Speaker)

30 Concentration is the factor that causes the great discrepancy between men and the results they achieve... the difference in their power of calling together all the rays of their ability and concentrating on one point.
Orison Swett Marden (1850-1924, American Author, Founder of Success Magazine)

31 The giants of the race have been men of concentration, who have struck sledge-hammer blows in one place until they have accomplished their purpose. The successful men of today are men of one overmastering idea, one unwavering aim, men of single and intense purpose.
Orison Swett Marden (1850-1924, American Author, Founder of Success Magazine)

32 Enter every activity without giving mental recognition to the possibility of defeat. Concentrate on your strengths, instead of your weaknesses... on your powers, instead of your problems.
Paul J. Meyer (American Businessman, Author, Motivator)

33 Concentration is the key to economic results. No other principles of effectiveness is violated as constantly today as the basic principle of concentration.
Peter F. Drucker (1909-, American Management Consultant, Author)

34 It's tough trying to keep your feet on the ground, your head above the clouds, your nose to the grindstone, your shoulder to the wheel, your finger on the pulse, your eye on the ball and your ear to the ground.
Proverb

35 By concentrating our attention on the effect rather than the causes, we can avoid the laborious, nearly impossible task of trying to detect and deflect the many psychological influences on liking.
Robert Cialdini (American Professor of Psychology)

36 The next point -- that's all you must think about.
Rod Laver (1938-, Australian Tennis Player)

37 Those who attain to any excellence commonly spend life in some single pursuit, for excellence is not often gained upon easier terms.
Samuel Johnson (1709-1784, British Author)

38 It seems essential, in relationships and all tasks, that we concentrate only on what is most significant and important
Soren Kierkegaard (1813-1855, Danish Philosopher, Writer)

39 Put your heart, mind, intellect and soul even to your smallest acts. This is the secret of success.
Sri Swami Sivananda (1887-, Indian Physician, Sage)

40 Concentrating on the essentials. We will then be accomplishing the greatest possible results with the effort expended.
Ted W. Engstrom (American Religion and Social Leader)

41 Success is focusing the full power of all you are one what you have a burning desire to achieve.
Wilferd A. Peterson

CONCEPTS

1 On the other hand, the concept owes its meaning and its justification exclusively to the totality of the sense impressions which we associate with it.
Albert Einstein (1879-1955, German-born American Physicist)

CONDITIONING

1 Lord, with what care hast Thou begirt us round! Parents first season us; then schoolmasters deliver us to laws; they send us bound to rules of reason, holy messengers, pulpits and Sundays, sorrow dogging sin, afflictions sorted, anguish of all sizes, fine nets and stratagems to catch us in, bibles laid open, millions of surprises, blessings beforehand, ties of gratefulness, the sound of glory ringing in our ears: without, our shame; within, our consciences;" angels and grace, eternal hopes and fears. Yet all these fences and their whole array one cunning bosom-sin blows quite away.
George Herbert (1593-1632, British Metaphysical Poet)

2 Every time I say "sure" when I mean "no," every time I smile brightly when I'm exploding with rage, every time I imagine my man's achievement is my own, I know the cheerleader never really died. I feel her shaking her ass inside me and I hear her breathless, girlish voice mutter "T-E-A-M, Yea, Team."
Louise Bernikow (American Author)

3 All of childhood's unanswered questions must finally be passed back to the town and answered there. Heroes and bogey men, values and dislikes, are first encountered and labeled in that early environment. In later years they change faces, places and maybe races, tactics, intensities and goals, but beneath those penetrable masks they wear forever the stocking-capped faces of childhood.
Maya Angelou (1928-, African-American poet, Writer, Performer)

4 In schools all over the world, little boys learn that their country is the greatest in the world, and the highest honor that could befall them would be to defend it heroically someday. The fact that empathy has traditionally been conditioned out of boys facilitates their obedience to leaders who order them to kill strangers.
Myriam Miedzian (American Actor)

5 Hardly ever can a youth transferred to the society of his betters unlearn the nasality and other vices of speech bred in him by the associations of his growing years. Hardly ever, indeed, no matter how much money there be in his pocket, can he ever learn to dress like a gentleman-born. The merchants offer their wares as eagerly to him as to the veriest "swell," but he simply cannot buy the right things.
William James (1842-1910, American Psychologist, Professor, Author)

CONFESSION

1 No blame should attach to telling the truth. But it does, it does.
Anita Brookner (1938-, British Novelist, Art Historian)

2 We have left undone those things which we ought to have done; and we have done those things which we ought not to have done.
Book Of Common Prayer (Liturgy of the Anglican Church)

3 There is no refuge from confession but suicide; and suicide is confession.
Daniel Webster (1782-1852, American Lawyer, Statesman)

4 Confession is always weakness. The grave soul keeps its own secrets, and takes its own punishment in silence.
Dorothy Dix (1861-1951, American Columnist)

5 If any ambitious man have a fancy to revolutionize, at one effort, the universal world of human thought, human opinion, and human sentiment, the opportunity is his own -- the road to immortal renown lies straight, open, and unencumbered before him. All that he has to do is to write and publish a very little book. Its title should be simple -- a few plain words -- "My Heart Laid Bare." But -- this little book must be true to its title.
Edgar Allan Poe (1809-1845, American Poet, Critic, short-story Writer)

6 Forgiveness is always free. But that doesn't mean that confession is always easy. Sometimes it is hard. Incredibly hard. It is painful to admit our sins and entrust ourselves to God's care.
Erwin W. Lutzer (American Minister)

7 We only confess our little faults to persuade people that we have no big ones.
François de La Rochefoucauld (1613-1680, French classical writer)

8 He that jokes confesses.
Italian Proverb

9 I don't deserve this award, but I have arthritis, and I don't deserve that, either.
Jack Benny (1894-1974, American Comedian)

10 Let the trumpet of the day of judgment sound when it will, I shall appear with this book in my hand before the Sovereign Judge, and cry with a loud voice, This is my work, there were my thoughts, and thus was I. I have freely told both the good and the bad, have hid nothing wicked, added nothing good.
Jean Jacques Rousseau (1712-1778, Swiss Political Philosopher, Educationist, Essayist)

11 It is not the criminal things that are hardest to confess, but the ridiculous and the shameful.
Jean Jacques Rousseau (1712-1778, Swiss Political Philosopher, Educationist, Essayist)

12 There are things to confess that enrich the world, and things that need not be said.
Joni Mitchell (Canadian Folk Singer)

13 In confession... we open our lives to healing, reconciling, restoring, uplifting grace of him who loves us in spite of what we are.
Louis Cassels

14 A confession has to be part of your new life.
Ludwig Wittgenstein (1889-1951, Austrian Philosopher)

15 Teach thy tongue to say I do not know and thou shalt progress.
Maimonides (1135-1204, Spanish-born Jewish Philosopher)

16 The worst of my actions or conditions seem not so ugly unto me as I find it both ugly and base not to dare to avouch for them.
Michel Eyquem De Montaigne (1533-1592, French Philosopher, Essayist)

17 It is the confession, not the priest, that gives us absolution.
Oscar Wilde (1856-1900, British Author, Wit)

18 A man's very highest moment is, I have no doubt at all, when he kneels in the dust, and beats his breast, and tells all the sins of his life.
Oscar Wilde (1856-1900, British Author, Wit)

19 Confession is good for the soul only in the sense that a tweed coat is good for dandruff -- it is a palliative rather than a remedy.
Peter De Vries (1910-, American Author)

20 Confess you were wrong yesterday; it will show you are wise today.
Proverb

21 To confess a fault freely is the next thing to being innocent of it.
Publilius Syrus (1st Century BC, Roman Writer)

22 Confession, alas, is the new handshake.
Richard D. Rosen

23 I saved a girl from being attacked last night. I controlled myself.
Rodney Dangerfield (American Comedian, Actor)

24 Confessed faults are half-mended.
Scottish Proverb

25 Open confession is good for the soul.
Scottish Proverb

26 The confession of evil works is the first beginning of good works.
St. Augustine (354-430, Numidian-born Bishop of Hippo, Theologian)

27 Literary confessors are contemptible, like beggars who exhibit their sores for money, but not so contemptible as the public that buys their books.
W. H. Auden (1907-1973, Anglo-American Poet)

28 The confession of our failings is a thankless office. It savors less of sincerity or modesty than of ostentation. It seems as if we thought our weaknesses as good as other people's virtues.
William Hazlitt (1778-1830, British Essayist)

CONFIDENCE

1 If once you forfeit the confidence of your fellow-citizens, you can never regain their respect and esteem.
Abraham Lincoln (1809-1865, Sixteenth President of the USA)

2 Smile, for everyone lacks self-confidence and more than any other one thing a smile reassures them.
Andre Maurois (1885-1967, French Writer)

3 Class is an aura of confidence that is being sure without being cocky. Class has nothing to do with money. Class never runs scared. It is self-discipline and self-knowledge. It's the sure footedness that comes with having proved you can meet life.
Ann Landers (1918-, American Advice Columnist)

4 Bashfulness is an ornament to youth, but a reproach to old age.
Aristotle (384-322 BC, Greek Philosopher)

5 Watch my dust.
Babe Ruth (1895-1948, American Baseball Player)

6 One who has lost confidence can lose nothing more.
Boiste

7 When you engage in systematic, purposeful actin, using and stretching your abilities to the maximum, you cannot help but feel positive and confident abut yourself.
Brian Tracy (American Trainer, Speaker, Author, Businessman)

8 You've got to take the initiative and play your game. In a decisive set, confidence is the difference.
Chris Evert Lloyd (1954-, American Tennis Player)

9 Self-distrust is the cause of most of our failure. In the assurance of strength there is strength, and, they are the weakest, however strong, who have no faith in themselves or their powers.
Christian Nevell Bovee (1820-1904, American Author, Lawyer)

10 Confidence is courage at ease.
Daniel Maher

11 Have confidence that if you have done a little thing well, you can do a bigger thing well too.
David Storey (1933-, British Novelist, Playwright)

12 I don't feel any pressure. I just try to stay calm, follow my game plan and try not to overthrown.
Dwight Gooden

13 I never think that there's something I can't do, whether it's beating my opponent one on one or practicing another hour because something about my game is just not right.
Earvin "Magic" Johnson (1959-, American Basketball Player)

14 I've always had confidence. It came because I have lots of initiative. I wanted to make something of myself.
Eddie Murphy (1961-, American Actor, Comedian, Producer)

15 Silence is the safest course for any man to adopt who distrust himself.
François de La Rochefoucauld (1613-1680, French classical writer)

16 Ninety-two percent of the stuff told you in confidence you couldn't get anyone else to listen to.
Franklin Pierce Adams (1881 - 1960, American Journalist, Humorist)

17 Confidence awakens confidence.
Friedrich Von Sachsen

18 Assurance is two-thirds of success.
Gaelic Proverb

19 A decent boldness ever meets with friends.
Homer (850 BC, Greek Epic Poet)

20 Winning breeds confidence and confidence breeds winning.
Hubert Green (American Golfer)

21 If you have confidence you have patience. Confidence, that is everything.
Ilie Nastase (Romanian Tennis Player, Actor)

22 Never put much confidence in such, as put no confidence in others. A man prone to suspect evil is mostly looking in his neighbor for what he sees in himself. As to the pure all things are pure, even so to the impure all things are impure.
J. C. Hare

23 Confidence is the most important single factor in this game, and no matter how great your natural talent, there is only one way to obtain and sustain it: work.
Jack Nicklaus (1940-, American Golfer)

24 Confidence is a lot of this game or any game. If you don't think you can, you won't.
Jerry West

25 With confidence, you can reach truly amazing heights; without confidence, even the simplest accomplishments are beyond your grasp.
Jim Loehr (American Sports Psychologist)

26 I build confidence when I practice a variety of shots - hitting it high or low, working the ball. A lot of golfers go to the range and just hit full shots. That doesn't build on-course confidence, because you won't always hit full shots out there. My confidence is built on knowing I can effectively work the ball in any circumstance.
JoAnne Carner (1939-, American Golfer)

27 Confidence is a very fragile thing.
Joe Montana (1956-, American Football Player)

28 You need to play with supreme confidence, or else you'll lose again, and then losing becomes a habit.
Joe Paterno (American Football Coach - Penn State)

29 Besides pride, loyalty, discipline, heart, and mind, confidence is the key to all the locks.
Joe Paterno (American Football Coach - Penn State)

30 For they conquer who believe they can.
John Dryden (1631-1700, British Poet, Dramatist, Critic)

31 I think it's the mark of a great player to be confident in tough situations.
John McEnroe (1959-, American Tennis Player)

32 There is a difference between conceit and confidence. Conceit is bragging about yourself. Confidence means you believe you can get the job done.
Johnny Unitas (American Football Player)

33 I always thought I could play pro ball. I had confidence in my ability, You have to. If you don't who will?
Johnny Unitas (American Football Player)

34 Mere bashfulness without merit is awkwardness.
Joseph Addison (1672-1719, British Essayist, Poet, Statesman)

35 If you have no confidence in self, you are twice defeated in the race of life. With confidence, you have won even before you have started.
Marcus Garvey

36 Confidence is that feeling by which the mind embarks in great and honorable courses with a sure hope and trust in itself.
Marcus T. Cicero (106-43 BC, Great Roman Orator, Politician)

37 The mansion should not be graced by its master, the master should grace the mansion.
Marcus T. Cicero (106-43 BC, Great Roman Orator, Politician)

38 The human heart, at whatever age, opens only to the heart that opens in return.
Maria Edgeworth (1767-1849, British Writer)

39 Confidence is contagious. So is lack of confidence.
Michael O'Brien

40 Confidence in another person's virtue is no light evidence of your own.
Michel Eyquem De Montaigne (1533-1592, French Philosopher, Essayist)

41 The confidence in another man's virtue is no light evidence of a man's own, and God willingly favors such a confidence.
Michel Eyquem De Montaigne (1533-1592, French Philosopher, Essayist)

42 Show me a man with head held high and I'll show you a man who can't get used to bifocals.
Morse Telegraph Newsletter

43 It's lack of faith that makes people afraid of meeting challenges, and I believe in myself.
Muhammad Ali (1942-, American Boxer)

44 There can be no great courage where there is no confidence or assurance, and half the battle is in the conviction that we can do what we undertake.
Orison Swett Marden (1850-1924, American Author, Founder of Success Magazine)

45 People are slow to claim confidence in undertakings of magnitude.
Ovid (43 BC-18 AD, Roman Poet)

46 Self-confidence is either a petty pride in our own narrowness, or the realization of our duty and privilege as God's children.
Phillips Brooks (1835-1893, American Minister, Poet)

47 Danger breeds best on too much confidence.
Pierre Corneille (1606-1684, French Dramatist)

48 Who ever does not respect confidence will never find happiness in their path.
Proverb

49 Confidence is the bond of friendship.
Publilius Syrus (1st Century BC, Roman Writer)

50 He who believes in nobody knows that he himself is not to be trusted.
Red Auerbach (1917-, American Basketball Coach)

51 If you are prepared, then you are able to feel confident.
Robert J. Ringer (American Writer)

52 Confidence doesn't come out of nowhere. It's a result of something... hours and days and weeks and years of constant work and dedication.
Roger Staubach (American Football Player)

53 Confidence is the result of hours and days and weeks and years of constant work and dedication.
Roger Staubach (American Football Player)

54 Every failure made me more confident. Because I wanted even more to achieve as revenge. To show that I could.
Roman Polanski (1933-, Polish Film, Director)

55 It generally happens that assurance keeps an even pace with ability.
Samuel Johnson (1709-1784, British Author)

56 There can be no friendship without confidence, and no confidence without integrity.
Samuel Johnson (1709-1784, British Author)

57 Self-confidence is the first requisite to great undertakings.
Samuel Johnson (1709-1784, British Author)

58 In tribulation immediately draw near to God with confidence, and you will receive strength, enlightenment, and instruction.
St. John of the Cross (1542-1591, Spanish Christian Mystic and Poet)

59 Experience tells you what to do; confidence allows you to do it.
Stan Smith (American Tennis Player)

60 What's the worst thing that can happen to a quarterback? He loses his confidence.
Terry Bradshaw (American Football Player, Sports Commentator)

61 Life for both sexes is arduous, difficult, a perpetual struggle. More than anything... it calls for confidence in oneself...And how can we generate this imponderable quality most quickly? By thinking that other people are inferior to oneself.
Virginia Woolf (1882-1941, British Novelist, Essayist)

62 As is our confidence, so is our capacity.
William Hazlitt (1778-1830, British Essayist)

63 Only trust thyself, and another shall not betray thee.
William Penn (1644-1718, British Religious Leader, Founder of Pennsylvania)

64 Confidence is a plant of slow growth in an aged heart.
William Pitt (1759-1806, British Statesman)

CONFLICT

1 It is the eternal struggle between these two principles -- right and wrong. They are the two principles that have stood face to face from the beginning of time and will ever continue to struggle. It is the same spirit that says, "You work and toil and earn bread, and I'll eat it."
Abraham Lincoln (1809-1865, Sixteenth President of the USA)

2 You cannot simultaneously prevent and prepare for war.
Albert Einstein (1879-1955, German-born American Physicist)

3 Instead of suppressing conflicts, specific channels could be created to make this conflict explicit, and specific methods could be set up by which the conflict is resolved.
Albert Low (American Author)

4 I'm not a combative person. My long experience has taught me to resolve conflict by raising the issues before I or others burn their boats.
Alistair Grant (Business Executive, Chairman of Argyll Group)

5 A man can do what he wants, but not want what he wants.
Arthur Schopenhauer (1788-1860, German Philosopher)

6 If passion drives you, let reason hold the reins.
Benjamin Franklin (1706-1790, American Scientist, Publisher, Diplomat)

7 A man's own self is his friend. A man's own self is his foe.
Bhagavad Gita (400 BC, Sanskrit Poem Incorporated Into the Mahabharata)

8 For the good that I would I do not: but the evil which I would not, that I do. [(Romans 7:19]
Bible (Sacred Scriptures of Christians and Judaism)

9 Only by pride comes contention; but, with the well-advised is wisdom. [Proverbs 13:10]
Bible (Sacred Scriptures of Christians and Judaism)

10 The spirit indeed is willing, but the flesh is week. [Matthew 26:41]
Bible (Sacred Scriptures of Christians and Judaism)

11 I have fought a good fight. I have finished my course, I have kept the faith. [2 Timothy 4:7]
Bible (Sacred Scriptures of Christians and Judaism)

12 We are only falsehood, duplicity, contradiction; we both conceal and disguise ourselves from ourselves.
Blaise Pascal (1623-1662, French Scientist, Religious Philosopher)

13 The war existing between the senses and reason.
Blaise Pascal (1623-1662, French Scientist, Religious Philosopher)

14 The most intense conflicts, if overcome, leave behind a sense of security and calm that is not easily disturbed. It is just these intense conflicts and their conflagration which are needed to produce valuable and lasting results.
Carl Jung (1875-1961, Swiss Psychiatrist)

15 Those that are the loudest in their threats are the weakest in their actions.
Charles Caleb Colton (1780-1832, British Sportsman Writer)

16 Success has made failures of many men.
Cindy Adams

17 The most dramatic conflicts are perhaps, those that take place not between men but between a man and himself -- where the arena of conflict is a solitary mind.
Clark Moustakas (Humanistic Psychologist)

18 The most important of life's battles is the one we fight daily in the silent chambers of the soul.
David O. Mckay

19 Modern science knows much about such conflicts. We call the mental state that engenders it "ambivalence": a collision between thought and feeling.
David Seabury (American Doctor, Author)

20 No man is hurt but by himself
Diogenes of Sinope (410-320 BC, Cynic Philosopher)

21 What people need and what they want may be very different.
Elbert Hubbard (1859-1915, American Author, Publisher)

22 Don't jump on a man unless he is down.
Finley Peter Dunne (1867-1936, American Journalist, Humorist)

23 Have a dialogue between the two opposing parts and you will find that they always start out fighting each other until we come to an appreciation of difference, ... a oneness and integration of the two opposing forces. Then the civil war is finished, and your energies are ready for your struggle with the world.
Frederick Salomon Perls (1893-1970, German Psychiatrist)

24 A good swordsman is not given to quarrel.
French Proverb

25 Perhaps no mightier conflict of mind occurs ever again in a lifetime than that first decision to unseat one's own tooth.
Gene Fowler (1890-1960, American Journalist, Biographer)

26 Who digs a pit for others will fall in themselves.
German Proverb

27 I believe in getting into hot water. I think it keeps you clean.
Gilbert K. Chesterton (1874-1936, British Author)

28 I cannot divine how it happens that the man who knows the least is the most argumentative.
Giovani della Casa (1503-1556, Papal Secretary of State)

29 The fibers of all things have their tension and are strained like the strings of an instrument.
Henry David Thoreau (1817-1862, American Essayist, Poet, Naturalist)

30 You are at enmity with yourself.
Jacob Boehme (1575-1624, German Mystic)

31 We gain our ends only with the laws of nature; we control her only by understanding her laws.
Jacob Bronowski (1908-1974, British Scientist, Author)

32 Well, if I called the wrong number, why did you answer the phone?
James Thurber (1894-1961, American Humorist, Illustrator)

33 The split in you is clear. There is a part of you that knows what it should do, and a part that does what it feels like doing.
John Cantwell Kiley

34 If we cannot end our differences at least we can make the world safe for diversity.
John F. Kennedy (1917-1963, Thirty-fifth President of the USA)

35 Reason guides but a small part of man, and the rest obeys feeling, true or false, and passion, good or bad.
Joseph Roux (1834-1905, French Priest, Writer)

36 What a man knows is everywhere at war with what he wants.
Joseph Wood Krutch (1893-1970, American Writer, Critic, Naturalist)

37 What rights are those that dare not resist for them?
Lord Alfred Tennyson (1809-1892, British Poet)

38 No man ever did a designed injury to another, but at the same time he did a greater to himself.
Lord Kames

39 To believe in something, and not to live it, is dishonest.
Mahatma Gandhi (1869-1948, Indian Political, Spiritual Leader)

40 The days are too short even for love; how can there be enough time for quarreling?
Margaret Gatty

41 As long as you keep a person down, some part of you has to be down there to hold him down, so it means you cannot soar as you otherwise might.
Marian Anderson (1902-1993, American Contralto Concert and Opera Singer)

42 More will mean worse.
Martin Amis (1949-, British Author)

43 The people to fear are not those who disagree with you, but those who disagree with you and are too cowardly to let you know.
Napoleon Bonaparte (1769-1821, French General, Emperor)

44 Big pay and little responsibility are circumstances seldom found together.
Napoleon Hill (1883-1970, American Speaker, Motivational Writer, "Think and Grow Rich")

45 Reason and emotion are not antagonists. What seems like a struggle between two opposing ideas or values, one of which, automatic and unconscious, manifests itself in the form of a feeling.
Nathaniel Branden (American Expert on Self-esteem, Author, Psychologist)

46 There are always two forces warring against each other within us.
Paramahansa Yogananda (Spiritual Author, Lecturer)

47 I exhort you also to take part in the great combat, which is the combat of life, and greater than every other earthly conflict.
Plato (427-347 BC, Greek Philosopher)

48 You can't comfort the afflicted with afflicting the comfortable,
Princess of Wales Diana (1961-1997, Wife of Charles, Prince of Wales)

49 We know better than we do. We do not yet possess ourselves...
Ralph Waldo Emerson (1803-1882, American Poet, Essayist)

50 We are the prisoners of ideas.
Ralph Waldo Emerson (1803-1882, American Poet, Essayist)

51 Remember that when you meet your antagonist, to do everything in a mild agreeable manner. Let your courage be keen, but, at the same time, as polished as your sword.
Richard Brinsley Sheridan (1751-1816, Anglo-Irish Dramatist)

52 The easiest thing to find on God's green earth is someone to tell you all the things you cannot do.
Richard M. DeVos (1926-, American Businessman, Co-founder of Amway Corp.)

53 Let us move from the era of confrontation to the era of negotiation.
Richard M. Nixon (1913-1994, Thirty-seventh President of the USA)

54 One might as well try to ride two horses moving in different directions, as to try to maintain in equal force two opposing or contradictory sets of desires.
Robert Collier (American Writer, Publisher)

55 This duality has been reflected in classical as well as modern literature as reason versus passion, or mind versus intuition. The split between the "conscious" mind and the "unconscious." There are moments in each of our lives when our verbal-intellect suggests one course, and our "hearts," or intuition, another.
Robert E. Ornstein

56 Talk back to your internal critic. Train yourself to recognize and write down critical thoughts as they go through your mind. Learn why these thoughts are untrue and practice talking and writing back to them.
Robert J. Mckain

57 A quarrel is quickly settled when deserted by one party; there is no battle unless there be two.
Seneca (4 BC-65 AD, Spanish-born Roman Statesman, philosopher)

58 Commonly they must use their feet for defense whose only weapon is their tongue.
Sir Philip Sidney (1554-1586, British Author, Courtier)

59 The effect of violent dislike between groups has always created an indifference to the welfare and honor of the state.
Thomas B. Macaulay (1800-1859, American Essayist and Historian)

60 The archenemy is the arch stupid!
Thomas Carlyle (1795-1881, Scottish Philosopher, Author)

61 We cannot really think in one way and act in another...
Thomas Troward

62 It's when you're safe at home that you wish you were having an adventure. When you're having an adventure you wish you were safe at home.
Thornton Wilder (1897-1975, American Novelist, Playwright)

63 The term up has no meaning apart from the word down. The term fast has no meaning apart from the term slow. In addition such terms have no meaning even when used together, except when confined to a very particular situation... most of our language about the organization and objective's of government is made up of such polar terms. Justice and injustice are typical. A reformer who wants to abolish injustice and create a world in which nothing but justice prevails is like a man who wants to make everything up. Such a man might feel that if he took the lowest in the world and carried it up to the highest point and kept on doing this, everything would eventually become up. This would certainly move a great many objects and create an enormous amount of activity. It might or might not be useful, according to the standards which we apply. However it would never result in the abolishment of down.
Thurman W. Arnold

64 Why don't you want to do what you know you should do? The reason you don't is that you're in conflict with yourself.
Tom Hopkins (American Sales Trainer, Speaker, Author)

65 Insight into the two selves within a man clears up many confusions and contradictions. It was our understanding that preceded our victory.
Vernon Howard (19?-1992, American Author, Speaker)

66 We must become acquainted with our emotional household: we must see our feelings as they actually are, not as we assume they are. This breaks their hypnotic and damaging hold on us.
Vernon Howard (19?-1992, American Author, Speaker)

67 We are enslaved by anything we do not consciously see. We are freed by conscious perception.
Vernon Howard (19?-1992, American Author, Speaker)

68 When our knowing exceeds our sensing, we will no longer be deceived by the illusions of our senses.
Walter Russell

69 The subconscious part in us is called the subjective mind, because it does not decide and command. It is subject rather than a ruler. Its nature is to do what it is told, or what really in your heart of hearts you desire.
William T. Walsh

70 Like a ball bated back and forth, a human being is batted by two forces within.
Yogabindu Upanishad (Ancient Hindu Scripture)

71 You cannot perform in a manner inconsistent with the way you see yourself.
Zig Ziglar (American Sales Trainer, Author, Motivational Speaker)

CONFORMITY

1 It gives me great pleasure indeed to see the stubbornness of an incorrigible nonconformist warmly acclaimed.
Albert Einstein (1879-1955, German-born American Physicist)

2 I know of no country in which there is so little independence of mind and real freedom of discussion as in America.
Alexis De Tocqueville (1805-1859, French Social Philosopher)

3 Singularity in the right hath ruined many; happy those who are convinced of the general opinion.
Benjamin Franklin (1706-1790, American Scientist, Publisher, Diplomat)

4 The idea that men are created free and equal is both true and misleading: men are created different; they lose their social freedom and their individual autonomy in seeking to become like each other.
David Riesman (1909-, American Sociologist)

5 The opposite of bravery is not cowardice but conformity.
Dr. Robert Anthony (American educator)

6 I was part of that strange race of people aptly described as spending their lives doing things they detest to make money they don't want to buy things they don't need to impress people they dislike.
Emile Henry Gauvreau

7 To do exactly as your neighbors do is the only sensible rule.
Emily Post (1873-1960, American Hostess)

8 Nonconformists travel as a rule in bunches. You rarely find a nonconformist who goes it alone. And woe to him inside a nonconformist clique who does not conform with nonconformity.
Eric Hoffer (1902-1983, American Author, Philosopher)

9 The surest way to corrupt a youth is to instruct him to hold in higher esteem those who think alike than those who think differently.
Friedrich Nietzsche (1844-1900, German Philosopher)

10 As to conforming outwardly, and living your own life inwardly, I have not a very high opinion of that course.
Henry David Thoreau (1817-1862, American Essayist, Poet, Naturalist)

11 Most people can't understand how others can blow their noses differently than they do.
Ivan Turgenev (1818-1883, Russian Author)

12 Conform and be dull.
J. Frank Doble (1888-1964, American Author)

13 The American ideal, after all, is that everyone should be as much alike as possible.
James Baldwin (1924-1987, American Author)

14 Why do you have to a nonconformist like everybody else?
James Thurber (1894-1961, American Humorist, Illustrator)

15 We are citizens of an age, as well as of a State; and if it is held to be unseemly, or even inadmissible, for a man to cut himself off from the customs and manners of the circle in which he lives, why should it be less of a duty, in the choice of his activity, to submit his decision to the needs and the taste of his century?
Johann Friedrich Von Schiller (1759-1805, German Dramatist, Poet, Historian)

16 For all have not the gift of martyrdom.
John Dryden (1631-1700, British Poet, Dramatist, Critic)

17 Conformity is the jailer of freedom and the enemy of growth.
John F. Kennedy (1917-1963, Thirty-fifth President of the USA)

18 Take the tone of the company you are in.
Lord Chesterfield (1694-1773, British Statesman, Author)

19 We are discreet sheep; we wait to see how the drove is going, and then go with the drove.
Mark Twain (1835-1910, American Humorist, Writer)

20 The mark of our time is its revulsion against imposed patterns.
Marshall Mcluhan (1911-1980, Canadian Communications Theorist)

21 Every society honors its live conformists and its dead troublemakers.
Mignon McLaughlin (1915?-, American Author, Editor)

22 One lesson we learn early, that in spite of seeming difference, men are all of one pattern. We readily assume this with our mates, and are disappointed and angry if we find that we are premature, and that their watches are slower than ours. In fact, the only sin which we never forgive in each other is difference of opinion.
Ralph Waldo Emerson (1803-1882, American Poet, Essayist)

23 Conformity, humility, acceptance... with these coins we are to pay our fares to paradise.
Robert Lindner

24 Fear God, and offend not the Prince nor his laws, and keep thyself out of the magistrate's claws.
Thomas Tusser (1520-1580-, British Writer On Agriculture)

25 Once conform, once do what other people do because they do it, and a lethargy steals over all the finer nerves and faculties of the soul. She becomes all outer show and inward emptiness; dull, callous, and indifferent.
Virginia Woolf (1882-1941, British Novelist, Essayist)

26 Our wretched species is so made that those who walk on the well-trodden path always throw stones at those who are showing a new road.
Voltaire (1694-1778, French Historian, Writer)

CONFUSION

1 For I am a bear of very little brain and long words bother me.
A. A. Milne (1882-1956, British Born American Writer)

2 Confusion of goals and perfection of means seems, in my opinion, to characterize our age.
Albert Einstein (1879-1955, German-born American Physicist)

3 I have never been lost, but I will admit to being confused for several weeks.
Daniel Boone (1734-1820, American Pioneer, Frontiersman)

4 If you can't convince them; confuse them.
Harry S. Truman (1884-1972, Thirty-third President of the USA)

5 Confusion is a word we have invented for an order which is not yet understood.
Henry Miller (1891-1980, American Author)

6 If confusion is the first step to knowledge, I must be a genius.
Larry Leissner

7 I'm not confused, I'm just well mixed.
Robert Frost (1875-1963, American Poet)

CONGRESS

1 The debates of that great assembly are frequently vague and perplexed, seeming to be dragged rather than to march, to the intended goal. Something of this sort must, I think, always happen in public democratic assemblies.
Alexis De Tocqueville (1805-1859, French Social Philosopher)

2 The Senate is a body of old men charged with high duties and misdemeanors.
Ambrose Bierce (1842-1914, American Author, Editor, Journalist, "The Devil's Dictionary")

3 Sure the people are stupid: the human race is stupid. Sure Congress is an inefficient instrument of government. But the people are not stupid enough to abandon representative government for any other kind, including government by the guy who knows.
Bernard Devoto (1897-1955, American Writer, Critic, Historian)

4 This is a Senate of equals, of men of individual honor and personal character, and of absolute independence. We know no masters, we acknowledge no dictators. This is a hall for mutual consultation and discussion; not an arena for the exhibition of champions.
Daniel Webster (1782-1852, American Lawyer, Statesman)

5 The Few assume to be the deputies, but they are often only the despoilers of the Many.
Georg Hegel (1770-1831, German Philosopher)

6 If we were left solely to the wordy wit of legislators in Congress for our guidance, uncorrected by the seasonal experience and the effectual complaints of the people, America would not long retain her rank among the nations.
Henry David Thoreau (1817-1862, American Essayist, Poet, Naturalist)

7 I believe if we introduced the Lord's Prayer here, senators would propose a large number of amendments to it.
Henry Wilson

8 I have seen in the Halls of Congress more idealism, more humanness, more compassion, more profiles of courage than in any other institution that I have ever known.
Hubert H. Humphrey (1911-1978, American Democratic Politician, Vice President)

9 We have the power to do any damn fool thing we want to do, and we seem to do it about every ten minutes.
J. William Fulbright (1905-, American Democratic Politician)

10 Great is the power, great is the authority of a senate that is unanimous in its opinions.
Marcus T. Cicero (106-43 BC, Great Roman Orator, Politician)

11 Reader, suppose you were an idiot. And suppose you were a member of Congress. But I repeat myself.
Mark Twain (1835-1910, American Humorist, Writer)

12 The American, if he has a spark of national feeling, will be humiliated by the very prospect of a foreigner's visit to Congress -- these, for the most part, illiterate hacks whose fancy vests are spotted with gravy, and whose speeches, hypocritical, unctuous, and slovenly, are spotted also with the gravy of political patronage, these persons are a reflection on the democratic process rather than of it; they expose it in its process rather than of it; they expose it in its underwear.
Mary Mccarthy (1912-1989, American Author, Critic)

13 When buying and selling are controlled by legislation, the first things to be bought and sold are legislators.
P. J. O'Rourke (1947-, American Journalist)

14 I have been up to see the Congress and they do not seem to be able to do anything except to eat peanuts and chew tobacco, while my army is starving.
Robert E. Lee (1807-1870, American Confederate Army Commander)

15 With Congress, every time they make a joke it's a law, and every time they make a law it's a joke.
Will Rogers (1879-1935, American Humorist, Actor)

16 There should be one day when there is open season on senators.
Will Rogers (1879-1935, American Humorist, Actor)

17 This country has come to feel the same when Congress is in session as when the baby gets hold of a hammer.
Will Rogers (1879-1935, American Humorist, Actor)

CONQUEST

1 We are a conquering race. We must obey our blood and occupy new markets and if necessary new lands.
Albert J. Beveridge (American Senator)

2 If conquerors be regarded as the engine-drivers of History, then the conquerors of thought are perhaps the pointsmen who, less conspicuous to the traveler's eye, determine the direction of the journey.
Arthur Koestler (1905-1983, Hungarian Born British Writer)

3 Life yields only to the conqueror. Never accept what can be gained by giving in. You will be living off stolen goods, and your muscles will atrophy.
Dag Hammarskjold (1905-1961, Swedish Statesman, Secretary-general of U.N.)

4 I have tamed men of iron in my day, shall I not easily crush these men of butter?
Duke of Alba Ferdinand Alvarez De Toledo

5 The desire to conquer is itself a sort of subjection.
George Eliot (1819-1880, British Novelist)

6 Roused by the lash of his own stubborn tail our lion now will foreign foes assail.
John Dryden (1631-1700, British Poet, Dramatist, Critic)

7 In our own time we have seen domination spread over the social landscape to a point where it is beyond all human control. Compared to this stupendous mobilization of materials, of wealth, of human intellect, of human labor for the single goal of domination, all other recent human achievements pale to almost trivial significance. Our art, science, medicine, literature, music and "charitable" acts seem like mere droppings from a table on which gory feasts on the spoils of conquest have engaged the attention of a system whose appetite for rule is utterly unrestrained.
Murray Bookchin (1941-, American Ecologist)

8 It should be noted that when he seizes a state the new ruler ought to determine all the injuries that he will need to inflict. He should inflict them once and for all, and not have to renew them every day.
Niccolo Machiavelli (1469-1527, Italian Author, Statesman)

9 If there be one principle more deeply rooted than any other in the mind of every American, it is that we should have nothing to do with conquest.
Thomas Jefferson (1743-1826, Third President of the USA)

10 Conquest is the missionary of valor, and the hard impact of military virtues beats meanness out of the world.
Walter Bagehot (1826-1877, British Economist, Critic)

CONSCIENCE

1 Never do anything against conscience even if the state demands it.
Albert Einstein (1879-1955, German-born American Physicist)

2 My conscience aches but it's going to lose the fight.
Allanah Myles (Canadian Singer)

3 A conscience without God is like a court without a judge.
Alphonse De Lamartine (1790-1869, French Poet, Statesman, Historian)

4 Conscience has nothing to do as lawgiver or judge; but is a witness against me if I do wrong, and which approves if I do right. To act against conscience is to act against reason and God's Law.
Arthur Phelps

5 Men never do evil so fully and cheerfully as when we do it out of conscience.
Blaise Pascal (1623-1662, French Scientist, Religious Philosopher)

6 Conscience was the barmaid of the Victorian soul. Recognizing that human beings were fallible and that their failings, though regrettable, must be humored, conscience would permit, rather ungraciously perhaps, the indulgence of a number of carefully selected desires.
C. E. M. Joad (1891-1953, British Author, Academic)

7 He who sacrifices his conscience to ambition burns a picture to obtain the ashes.
Chinese Proverb

8 What we call conscience in many instances, is only a wholesome fear of the law.
Christian Nevell Bovee (1820-1904, American Author, Lawyer)

9 If you look into your own heart, you find nothing wrong there, what is there to fear?
Confucius (551-479 BC, Chinese Ethical Teacher, Philosopher)

10 When I contemplate the accumulation of guilt and remorse which, like a garbage-can, I carry through life, and which is fed not only by the lightest action but by the most harmless pleasure, I feel Man to be of all living things the most biologically incompetent and ill-organized. Why has he acquired a seventy years life-span only to poison it incurably by the mere being of himself? Why has he thrown Conscience, like a dead rat, to putrefy in the well?
Cyril Connolly (1903-1974, British Critic)

11 O conscience, upright and stainless, how bitter a sting to thee is a little fault!
Dante (Alighieri) (1265-1321, Italian Philosopher, Poet)

12 Honor is the moral conscience of the great.
D'Avenant (1606-1668, British Poet, Playwright)

13 Conscience is the window of our spirit, evil is the curtain.
Doug Horton

14 The conscience is the most flexible material in the world. Today you cannot stretch it over a mole hill; while tomorrow it can hide a mountain.
Edward G. Bulwer-Lytton (1803-1873, British Novelist, Poet)

15 There is one thing alone that stands the brunt of life throughout its length: a quite conscience.
Euripides (480-406 BC, Greek Tragic Poet)

16 A good conscience is a continual feast.
Francis Bacon (1561-1626, British Philosopher, Essayist, Statesman)

17 A man's conscience, like a warning line on the highway, tells him what he shouldn't do -- but it does not keep him from doing it.
Frank A. Clark

18 Again and again I am brought up against it, and again and again I resist it: I don't want to believe it, even though it is almost palpable: the vast majority lack an intellectual conscience; indeed, it often seems to me that to demand such a thing is to be in the most populous cities as solitary as in the desert.
Friedrich Nietzsche (1844-1900, German Philosopher)

19 Conscience is the mirror of our souls, which represents the errors of our lives in their full shape.
George Bancroft (1800-1891, American Historian)

20 The beginning of compunction is the beginning of a new life.
George Eliot (1819-1880, British Novelist)

21 Religions are the great fairy tales of conscience.
George Santayana (1863-1952, American Philosopher, Poet)

22 Labor to keep alive in your breast that little spark of celestial fire called conscience
George Washington (1732-1799, First President of the USA)

23 The voice of conscience is so delicate that it is easy to stifle it; but it is also so clear that it is impossible to mistake it.
Germaine De Stael (1766-1817, French-Swiss Novelist)

24 A clear conscience is a soft pillow.
German Proverb

25 Conscience is the inner voice which warns us that someone may be looking.
H. L. Mencken (1880-1956, American Editor, Author, Critic, Humorist)

26 Conscience is a mother-in-law whose visit never ends.
H. L. Mencken (1880-1956, American Editor, Author, Critic, Humorist)

27 The one thing that doesn't abide by majority rule is a person's conscience.
Harper Lee (1926-, American Author)

28 What a man calls his "conscience" is merely the mental action that follows a sentimental reaction after too much wine or love.
Helen Rowland (1875-1950, American Journalist)

29 Conscience -- the only incorruptible thing about us.
Henry Fielding (1707-1754, British Novelist, Dramatist)

30 People talk about the conscience, but it seems to me one must just bring it up to a certain point and leave it there. You can let your conscience alone if you're nice to the second housemaid.
Henry James (1843-1916, American Author)

31 Two things fill me with constantly increasing admiration and awe, the longer and more earnestly I reflect on them: the starry heavens without and the moral law within.
Immanuel Kant (1724-1804, German Philosopher)

32 Conscience: self-esteem with a halo.
Irving Layton (1912-, Canadian Poet)

33 The person that loses their conscience has nothing left worth keeping.
Izaak Walton (1593-1683, British Writer)

34 Conscience is the voice of the soul; the passions of the body.
Jean Jacques Rousseau (1712-1778, Swiss Political Philosopher, Educationist, Essayist)

35 Conscience in most men, is but the anticipation of the opinions of others.
Jeremy Taylor (1613-1667, British Churchman, Writer)

36 Conscience is the sentinel of virtue.
Johann Kaspar Lavater (1741-1801, Swiss Theologian, Mystic)

37 A good conscience is to the soul what health is to the body; it preserves constant ease and serenity within us; and more than countervails all the calamities and afflictions which can befall us from without.
Joseph Addison (1672-1719, British Essayist, Poet, Statesman)

38 Conscience is our magnetic compass; reason our chart.
Joseph Cook

39 Reason often makes mistakes, but conscience never does.
Josh Billings (1815-1885, American Humorist, Lecturer)

40 While conscience is our friend, all is at peace; however once it is offended, farewell to a tranquil mind.
Lady Mary Wortley Montagu (1689-1762, British Society Figure, Letter Writer)

41 I cannot and will not cut my conscience to fit this year's fashions.
Lillian Hellman (1905-1984, American Playwright)

42 We grow with years more fragile in body, but morally stutter, and can throw off the chill of a bad conscience almost at once.
Logan Pearsall Smith (1865-1946, Anglo-American Essayist, Aphorist)

43 No ear can hear nor tongue can tell the tortures of the inward hell!
Lord Byron (1788-1824, British Poet)

44 Though the dungeon, the scourge, and the executioner be absent, the guilty mind can apply the goad and scorch with blows.
Lucretius (95-55 BC, Roman poet and philosopher)

45 Rules of society are nothing; ones conscience is the umpire.
Madame Dudevant

46 The chief prerequisite for a escort is to have a flexible conscience and an inflexible politeness.
Marguerite Gardiner Blessington (1789-1849, Irish Writer and Socialite)

47 I feel bad that I don't feel worse.
Michael Frayn (1933-, British Playwright, Novelist, Journalist)

48 Freedom of conscience entails more dangers than authority and despotism.
Michel Foucault (1926-1984, French Essayist, Philosopher)

49 The conscience is the sacred haven of the liberty of man.
Napoleon Bonaparte (1769-1821, French General, Emperor)

50 In the depths of every heart, there is a tomb and a dungeon, though the lights, the music, and revelry above may cause us to forget their existence, and the buried ones, or prisoners whom they hide. But sometimes, and oftenest at midnight, those dark receptacles are flung wide open. In an hour like this, when the mind has a passive sensibility, but no active strength; when the imagination is a mirror, imparting vividness to all ideas, without the power of selecting or controlling them; then pray that your grieves may slumber, and the brotherhood of remorse not break their chain.
Nathaniel Hawthorne (1804-1864, American Novelist, Short Story Writer)

51 I think remorse ought to stop biting the consciences that feed it.
Ogden Nash (1902-1971, American Humorous Poet)

52 There is only one way to achieve happiness on this terrestrial ball, and that is to have either a clear conscience or none at all.
Ogden Nash (1902-1971, American Humorous Poet)

53 Conscience is the chamber of justice.
Origen (185-254, Egyptian Christian Biblical Scholar, Theologian)

54 Conscience is the dog that can't bite, but never stops barking.
Proverb

55 Conscience has no more to do with gallantry than it has with politics.
Richard Brinsley Sheridan (1751-1816, Anglo-Irish Dramatist)

56 A seared conscience is one whose warning voice has been suppressed and perverted habitually, so that eventually instead of serving as a guide, it only confirms the person in his premeditatedly evil course.
Robert J. Little

57 Conscience is thoroughly well-bred and soon leaves off talking to those who do not wish to hear it.
Samuel Butler (1612-1680, British Poet, Satirist)

58 Conscience is the internal perception of the rejection of a particular wish operating within us.
Sigmund Freud (1856-1939, Austrian Physician - Founder of Psychoanalysis)

59 The Non-Conformist Conscience makes cowards of us all.
Sir Max Beerbohm (1872-1956, British Actor)

60 There is no witness so terrible and no accuser so powerful as conscience which dwells within us.
Sophocles (495-406 BC, Greek Tragic Poet)

61 If a superior give any order to one who is under him which is against that man's conscience, although he do not obey it yet he shall not be dismissed.
St. Francis of Assisi (1181-1226, Italian Preacher, Founder of the Franciscan Orde)

62 In many walks of life, a conscience is a more expensive encumbrance than a wife or a carriage.
Thomas De Quincey (1785-1859, British Author)

63 A man's conscience and his judgment is the same thing; and as the judgment, so also the conscience, may be erroneous.
Thomas Hobbes (1588-1679, British Philosopher)

64 Conscience is a man's compass.
Vincent Van Gogh (1853-1890, Dutch-born French Painter)

65 Our conscience is not the vessel of eternal verities. It grows with our social life, and a new social condition means a radical change in conscience.
Walter Lippmann (1889-1974, American Journalist)

66 The innocent seldom find an uncomfortable pillow.
William Cowper (1731-1800, British Poet)

67 It is far more important to me to preserve an unblemished conscience than to compass any object however great.
William Ellery Channing (1780-1842, American Unitarian Minister, Author)

68 A man's moral conscience is the curse he had to accept from the gods in order to gain from them the right to dream.
William Faulkner (1897-1962, American Novelist)

69 Conscience does make cowards of us all.
William Shakespeare (1564-1616, British Poet, Playwright, Actor)

70 My conscience hath a thousand several tongues, and every tongue brings in a several tale, and every tale condemns me for a villain.
William Shakespeare (1564-1616, British Poet, Playwright, Actor)

71 There is only one duty, only one safe course, and that is to try to be right.
Winston Churchill (1874-1965, British Statesman, Prime Minister)

CONSCIOUSNESS

1 A sub-clerk in the post-office is the equal of a conqueror if consciousness is common to them.
Albert Camus (1913-1960, French Existential Writer)

2 But they for whom I am the supreme goal, who do all work renouncing self for me and meditate on me with single-hearted devotion, these I will swiftly rescue from death's vast sea, for their consciousness has entered into me.
Bhagavad Gita (400 BC, Sanskrit Poem Incorporated Into the Mahabharata)

3   The images of the unconscious place a great responsibility upon a man. Failure to understand them, or a shirking of ethical responsibility, deprives him of his wholeness and imposes a painful fragmentariness on his life.
Carl Jung (1875-1961, Swiss Psychiatrist)

4   The human consciousness is really homogeneous. There is no complete forgetting, even in death.
D. H. Lawrence (1885-1930, British Author)

5   Consciousness is a phase of mental life which arises in connection with the formation of new habits. When habit is formed, consciousness only interferes to spoil our performance.
Dean William R. Inge (1860-1954, Dean of St Paul's, London)

6   Consciousness is much more than the thorn, it is the dagger in the flesh.
E. M. Cioran (1911-, Rumanian-born French Philosopher)

7   Of Consciousness, her awful Mate. The Soul cannot be rid -- as easy the secreting her behind the Eyes of God.
Emily Dickinson (1830-1886, American Poet)

8   The unconscious is the ocean of the unsayable, of what has been expelled from the land of language, removed as a result of ancient prohibitions.
Italo Calvino (1923-1985, Cuban Writer, Essayist, Journalist)

9   The real history of consciousness starts with one's first lie.
Joseph Brodsky (1940-, Russian-born American Poet, Critic)

10   My unconscious knows more about the consciousness of the psychologist than his consciousness knows about my unconscious.
Karl Kraus (1874-1936, Austrian Satirist)

11   The only way to give finality to the world is to give it consciousness.
Miguel De Unamuno (1864-1936, Spanish Philosophical Writer)

12   It is our less conscious thoughts and our less conscious actions which mainly mould our lives and the lives of those who spring from us.
Samuel Butler (1612-1680, British Poet, Satirist)

13   The ego is not master in its own house.
Sigmund Freud (1856-1939, Austrian Physician - Founder of Psychoanalysis)

14   Our normal waking consciousness, rational consciousness as we call it, is but one special type of consciousness, whilst all about it, parted from it by the filmiest of screens, there lie potential forms of consciousness entirely different.
William James (1842-1910, American Psychologist, Professor, Author)

CONSENSUS

1   Consensus is what many people say in chorus but do not believe as individuals.
Abba Eban (1915-, Israeli Politician)

2   Uniform ideas originating among entire peoples unknown to each other must have a common ground of truth.
Giambattista Vico (1688-1744, Italian Philosopher, Historian)

3   A consensus politician is someone who does something that he doesn't believe is right because it keeps people quiet when he does it.
John Major (British Prime Minister)

4   Talk about the flag or drugs or crime (never about race or class or justice) and follow the yellow brick road to the wonderful land of "consensus." In place of honest argument among consenting adults the politicians substitute a lullaby for frightened children: the pretense that conflict doesn't really exist, that we have achieved the blessed state in which we no longer need politics.
Lewis H. Lapham (1935-, American Essayist, Editor)

5   It is not much matter which we say, but mind, we must all say the same.
Lord Melbourne (1779-1848, British Statesman, Prime Minister)

6   To me, consensus seems to be the process of abandoning all beliefs, principles, values and policies. So it is something in which no one believes and to which no one objects.
Margaret Thatcher (1925-, British Stateswoman, Prime Minister (1979-90))

CONSEQUENCES

1   The consequences of an act affect the probability of it's occurring again.
B. F. Skinner (1904-1990, American Psychologist)

2   There are no rewards or punishments -- only consequences.
Dean William R. Inge (1860-1954, Dean of St Paul's, London)

3   In history an additional result is commonly produced by human actions beyond that which they aim at and obtain -- that which they immediately recognize and desire. They gratify their own interest; but something further is thereby accomplished, latent in the actions in question, though not present to their consciousness, and not included in their design.
Georg Hegel (1770-1831, German Philosopher)

4   Nothing is worth doing unless the consequences may be serious.
George Bernard Shaw (1856-1950, Irish-born British Dramatist)

5   Perhaps his might be one of the natures where a wise estimate of consequences is fused in the fires of that passionate belief which determines the consequences it believes in.
George Eliot (1819-1880, British Novelist)

6 Everyone will experience the consequences of his own acts. If his act are right, he'll get good consequences; if they're not, he'll suffer for it.
Harry Browne (1933-, American Financial Advisor, Writer)

7 Every act of virtue is an ingredient unto reward.
Jeremy Taylor (1613-1667, British Churchman, Writer)

8 There is not any present moment that is unconnected with some future one. The life of every man is a continued chain of incidents, each link of which hangs upon the former. The transition from cause to effect, from event to event, is often carried on by secret steps, which our foresight cannot divine, and our sagacity is unable to trace. Evil may at some future period bring forth good; and good may bring forth evil, both equally unexpected.
Joseph Addison (1672-1719, British Essayist, Poet, Statesman)

9 Men must try and try again. They must suffer the consequences of their own mistakes and learn by their own failures and their own successes.
Lawson Purdy

10 The Devil beget darkness; darkness beget ignorance; ignorance beget error and his brethren; error beget free-will and presumption; free-will beget works; works beget forgetfulness of God; forgetfulness beget transgression; transgression beget superstition; superstition beget satisfaction; satisfaction beget the mass-offering; the mass-offering beget the priest; the priest beget unbelief; unbelief beget hypocrisy; hypocrisy beget traffic in offerings for gain; traffic in offerings for gain beget Purgatory; Purgatory beget the annual solemn vigils; the annual vigils beget church-livings; church-livings beget avarice; avarice beget swelling superfluity; swelling superfluity beget fulness; fulness beget rage; rage beget license; license beget empire and domination; domination beget pomp; pomp beget ambition; ambition beget simony; simony beget the pope and his brethren, about the time of the Babylonish captivity.
Martin Luther (1483-1546, German Leader of the Protestant Reformation)

11 I submit that an individual who breaks the law that conscience tells him is unjust and willingly accepts the penalty by staying in jail to arouse the conscience of the community over its injustice, is in reality expressing the very highest respect for law.
Martin Luther King Jr. (1929-1968, American Black Leader, Nobel Prize Winner, 1964)

12 A human being fashions his consequences as surely as he fashions his goods or his dwelling his goods or his dwelling. Nothing that he says, thinks or does is without consequences.
Norman Cousins (1915-1990, American Editor, Humanitarian, Author)

13 Whatever our creed, we feel that no good deed can by any possibility go unrewarded, no evil deed unpunished.
Orison Swett Marden (1850-1924, American Author, Founder of Success Magazine)

14 All successful men have agreed in one thing -- they were causationists. They believed that things went not by luck, but by law; that there was not a weak or a cracked link in the chain that joins the first and last of things.
Ralph Waldo Emerson (1803-1882, American Poet, Essayist)

15 In nature there are neither rewards nor punishments; there are only consequences.
Robert Green Ingersoll (1833-1899, American Orator, Lawyer)

16 Everybody, soon or late, sits down to a banquet of consequences.
Robert Louis Stevenson (1850-1895, Scottish Essayist, Poet, Novelist)

17 Sooner or later everyone sits down to a banquet of consequences.
Robert Louis Stevenson (1850-1895, Scottish Essayist, Poet, Novelist)

18 It is easy to dodge our responsibilities, but we cannot dodge the consequences of dodging our responsibilities.
Sir Josiah Stamp

19 For every life and every act consequence of good and evil can be shown and as in time results of many deeds are blended so good and evil in the end become confounded.
T. S. Eliot (1888-1965, American-born British Poet, Critic)

20 Logical consequences are the scarecrows of fools and the beacons of wise men.
Thomas H. Huxley (1825-1895, British Biologist, Educator)

21 It is an enduring truth, which can never be altered, that every infraction of the Law of nature must carry its punitive consequences with it. We can never get beyond that range of cause and effect.
Thomas Troward

22 You can do anything in this world if you are prepares to take the consequences.
W. Somerset Maugham (1874-1965, British Novelist, Playwright)

CONSERVATIVES

1 What is conservatism? It is not adherence to the old and tried, but against the new and untried?
Abraham Lincoln (1809-1865, Sixteenth President of the USA)

2 Conservative. A statesman who is enamored of existing evils, as distinguished from a Liberal, who wishes to replace them with others.
Ambrose Bierce (1842-1914, American Author, Editor, Journalist, "The Devil's Dictionary")

3 To be conservative requires no brains whatsoever. Cabbages, cows and conifers are conservatives, and are so stupid they don't even know it. All that is basically required is acceptance of what exists.
Colin Welch

4   A conservative is a fellow who thinks a rich man should have a square deal.
Frank Dane

5   A conservative is a man with two perfectly good legs, who has never learned to walk.
Franklin D. Roosevelt (1882-1945, Thirty-second President of the USA)

6   We hear the haunting presentiment of a dutiful middle age in the current reluctance of young people to select any option except the one they feel will impinge upon them the least.
Gail Sheehy (1937-, American Journalist, Author)

7   The appeal of the New Right is simply that it seems to promise that nothing will change in the domestic realm. People are terrified of change there, because it's the last humanizing force left in society, and they think, correctly, that it must be retained.
Gerda Lerner (1920-, American Educator, Author)

8   The values to which the conservative appeals are inevitably caricatured by the individuals designated to put them into practice.
Harold Rosenberg (1906-1978, American Art Critic, Author)

9   A little reflection will enable any person to detect in himself that setness in trifles which is the result of the unwatched instinct of self-will and to establish over himself a jealous guardianship.
Harriet Beecher Stowe (1811-1896, American Novelist, Antislavery Campaigner)

10 When a nation's young men are conservative, its funeral bell is already rung.
Henry Ward Beecher (1813-1887, American Preacher, Orator, Writer)

11 I do not know which makes a man more conservative -- to know nothing but the present, or nothing but the past.
John Maynard Keynes (1883-1946, British Economist)

12 Conservatives are not necessarily stupid, but most stupid people are conservatives.
John Stuart Mill (1806-1873, British Philosopher, Economist)

13 Some fellows get credit for being conservative when they are only stupid.
Kin Hubbard (1868-1930, American Humorist, Journalist)

14 That man's the true Conservative who lops the moldered branch away.
Lord Alfred Tennyson (1809-1892, British Poet)

15 All reactionaries are paper tigers.
Mao Zedong (1893-1976, Founder of Chinese Communist State)

16 The radical of one century is the conservative of the next. The radical invents the views. When he has worn them out, the conservative adopts them.
Mark Twain (1835-1910, American Humorist, Writer)

17 The radical invents the views. When he has worn them out, the conservative adopts them.
Mark Twain (1835-1910, American Humorist, Writer)

18 Loyalty to petrified opinions never yet broke a chain or freed a human soul in this world -- and never will.
Mark Twain (1835-1910, American Humorist, Writer)

19 The word "conservative" is used by the BBC as a portmanteau word of abuse for anyone whose views differ from the insufferable, smug, sanctimonious, naive, guilt-ridden, wet, pink orthodoxy of that sunset home of the third-rate minds of that third-rate decade, the nineteen-sixties.
Norman Tebbit (1931-, British Statesman)

20 All conservatives are such from personal defects. They have been effeminated by position or nature, born halt and blind, through luxury of their parents, and can only, like invalids, act on the defensive.
Ralph Waldo Emerson (1803-1882, American Poet, Essayist)

21 Men are conservatives when they are least vigorous, or when they are most luxurious. They are conservatives after dinner, or before taking their rest; when they are sick or aged. In the morning, or when their intellect or their conscience has been aroused, when they hear music, or when they read poetry, they are radicals.
Ralph Waldo Emerson (1803-1882, American Poet, Essayist)

22 The world is burdened with young fogies. Old men with ossified minds are easily dealt with. But men who look young, act young and everlastingly harp on the fact that they are young, but who nevertheless think and act with a degree of caution that would be excessive in their grandfathers, are the curse of the world. Their very conservatism is secondhand, and they don't know what they are conserving.
Robertson Davies (1913-, Canadian Novelist, Journalist)

23 There are no black conservatives. Oh, there are neoconservatives with black skin, but they lack any claim to blackness other than the biological. They have forgotten their roots.
Stephen Carter

24 All great peoples are conservative.
Thomas Carlyle (1795-1881, Scottish Philosopher, Author)

25 Almost always tradition is nothing but a record and a machine-made imitation of the habits that our ancestors created. The average conservative is a slave to the most incidental and trivial part of his forefathers glory -- to the archaic formula which happened to express their genius or the eighteenth-century contrivance by which for a time it was served.
Walter Lippmann (1889-1974, American Journalist)

CONSISTENCY

1   The only completely consistent people are the dead.
Aldous Huxley (1894-1963, British Author)

2 Consistency is contrary to nature, contrary to life. The only completely consistent people are the dead.
Aldous Huxley (1894-1963, British Author)

3 A consistent man believes in destiny, a capricious man in chance.
Benjamin Disraeli (1804-1881, British Statesman, Prime Minister)

4 Consistency requires you to be as ignorant today as you were a year ago.
Bernard Berenson (1865-1959, Lithuanian-born American Artist)

5 Consistency, madam, is the first of Christian duties.
Charlotte Bronte (1816-1855, British Novelist)

6 My goal in sailing isn't to be brilliant or flashy in individual races, just to be consistent over the long run.
Dennis Conner (American Yachtsman)

7 Look to make your course regular, that men may know beforehand what they may expect.
Francis Bacon (1561-1626, British Philosopher, Essayist, Statesman)

8 Consistency is the foundation of virtue.
Francis Bacon (1561-1626, British Philosopher, Essayist, Statesman)

9 Let your character be kept up the very end, just as it began, and so be consistent.
Horace (65-8 BC, Italian Poet)

10 Inconsistency is the only thing in which men are consistent.
Horatio Smith

11 You accuse a woman of wavering affections, but don't blame her; she is just looking for a consistent man.
Johann Wolfgang Von Goethe (1749-1832, German Poet, Dramatist, Novelist)

12 Constants aren't.
John Peers (American Businessman, President of Logical Machine)

13 Who ever has no fixed opinions has no constant feelings.
Joseph Joubert (1754-1824, French Moralist)

14 No well-informed person ever imputed inconsistency to another for changing his mind.
Marcus T. Cicero (106-43 BC, Great Roman Orator, Politician)

15 What, then, is the true Gospel of consistency? Change. Who is the really consistent man? The man who changes. Since change is the law of his being, he cannot be consistent if he stick in a rut.
Mark Twain (1835-1910, American Humorist, Writer)

16 Consistency is the last refuge of the unimaginative.
Oscar Wilde (1856-1900, British Author, Wit)

17 Without consistency there is no moral strength.
Owen

18 A foolish consistency is the hobgoblin of little minds, adored by little statesmen and philosophers and divines.
Ralph Waldo Emerson (1803-1882, American Poet, Essayist)

19 Consistency is a virtue for trains: what we want from a philosopher is insights, whether he comes by them consistently or not.
Stephen Vizinczey (1933-, Hungarian Novelist, Critic)

CONSPIRACY

1 In countries where associations are free, secret societies are unknown. In America there are factions, but no conspiracies.
Alexis De Tocqueville (1805-1859, French Social Philosopher)

2 The search for conspiracy only increases the elements of morbidity and paranoia and fantasy in this country. It romanticizes crimes that are terrible because of their lack of purpose. It obscures our necessary understanding, all of us, that in this life there is often tragedy without reason.
Anthony Lewis

3 If we are on the outside, we assume a conspiracy is the perfect working of a scheme. Silent nameless men with unadorned hearts. A conspiracy is everything that ordinary life is not. It's the inside game, cold, sure, undistracted, forever closed off to us. We are the flawed ones, the innocents, trying to make some rough sense of the daily jostle. Conspirators have a logic and a daring beyond our reach. All conspiracies are the same taut story of men who find coherence in some criminal act.
Don Delillo (1926-, American Author)

4 Civilization is a conspiracy. Modern life is the silent compact of comfortable folk to keep up pretences.
John Buchan (1875-1940, Scottish Writer, Statesman)

5 Who is that man over there? I don't know him. What is he doing? Is he a conspirator? Have you searched him? Give him till tomorrow to confess, then hang him! -- hang him!
Oscar Wilde (1856-1900, British Author, Wit)

CONSTITUTIONS

1 Constitutions should consist only of general provisions; the reason is that they must necessarily be permanent, and that they cannot calculate for the possible change of things.
Alexander Hamilton (1757-1804, American Statesman)

2 Our new Constitution is now established, and has an appearance that promises permanency; but in this world nothing can be said to be certain, except death and taxes.
Benjamin Franklin (1706-1790, American Scientist, Publisher, Diplomat)

3 The words of the Constitution are so unrestricted by their intrinsic meaning or by their history or by tradition or by prior decisions that they leave the individual Justice free, if indeed they do not compel him, to gather meaning not from reading the Constitution but from reading life.
Felix Frankfurter (1882-1965, Austrian-born American Law Teacher, Judge)

4 The United States Constitution has proved itself the most marvelously elastic compilation of rules of government ever written.
Franklin D. Roosevelt (1882-1945, Thirty-second President of the USA)

5 The American Constitution, one of the few modern political documents drawn up by men who were forced by the sternest circumstances to think out what they really had to face, instead of chopping logic in a university classroom.
George Bernard Shaw (1856-1950, Irish-born British Dramatist)

6 Our constitution works. Our great republic is a government of laws, not of men.
Gerald R. Ford (1913-, Thirty-eighth President of the USA)

7 The illegal we do immediately. The unconstitutional takes a little longer.
Henry Kissinger (1923-, American Republican Politician, Secretary of State)

8 The Constitution is a figment of your imagination, held up to make people believe they have rights. I don't believe anybody in this country has rights.
Ice-T (American Rap Musician)

9 There is a hearty Puritanism in the view of human nature which pervades the instrument of 1787 It is the work of men who believed in original sin, and were resolved to leave open for transgressors no door which they could possibly shut.
James Bryce

10 The proposed Constitution is, in strictness, neither a national nor a federal constitution; but a composition of both.
James Madison (1751-1836, American Statesman, President)

11 A constitution that is made for all nations is made for none.
Joseph De Maistre (1753-1821, French Diplomat, Philosopher)

12 It is the genius of our Constitution that under its shelter of enduring institutions and rooted principles there is ample room for the rich fertility of American political invention.
Lyndon B. Johnson (1908-1973, Thirty-sixth President of the USA)

13 A Constitution should be short and obscure.
Napoleon Bonaparte (1769-1821, French General, Emperor)

14 A good constitution is infinitely better than the best despot.
Thomas B. Macaulay (1800-1859, American Essayist and Historian)

15 Your Constitution is all sail and no anchor.
Thomas B. Macaulay (1800-1859, American Essayist and Historian)

16 The first principle of a civilized state is that the power is legitimate only when it is under contract.
Walter Lippmann (1889-1974, American Journalist)

17 There is a higher law than the Constitution.
William Seward (1801-1872, American Politician)

CONSULTANTS

1 A consultant is someone who saves his client almost enough to pay his fee.
Arnold H. Glasgow

2 While the doctors consult, the patient dies.
English Proverb

3 American couples have gone to such lengths to avoid the interference of in-laws that they have to pay marriage counselors to interfere between them.
Florence King (1936-, American Author, Critic)

4 In every society some men are born to rule, and some to advise.
Ralph Waldo Emerson (1803-1882, American Poet, Essayist)

5 The best servants of the people, like the best valets, must whisper unpleasant truths in the master's ear. It is the court fool, not the foolish courtier, whom the king can least afford to lose.
Walter Lippmann (1889-1974, American Journalist)

CONTEMPLATION

1 There exist certain individuals who are, by nature, given purely to contemplation and are utterly unsuited to action, and who, nevertheless, under a mysterious and unknown impulse, sometimes act with a speed which they themselves would have thought beyond them.
Charles Baudelaire (1821-1867, French Poet)

2 I admire people who are suited to the contemplative life. They can sit inside themselves like honey in a jar and just be. It's wonderful to have someone like that around, you always feel you can count on them. You can go away and come back, you can change your mind and your hairdo and your politics, and when you get through doing all these upsetting things, you look around and there they are, just the way they were, just being.
Elizabeth Janeway (1913-, American Author, Critic)

3 One cannot long remain so absorbed in contemplation of emptiness without being increasingly attracted to it. In vain one bestows on it the name of infinity; this does not change its nature. When one feels such pleasure in non-existence, one's inclination can be completely satisfied only by completely ceasing to exist.
Emile Durkheim (1858-1917, French Sociologist)

4   The national distrust of the contemplative temperament arises less from an innate Philistinism than from a suspicion of anything that cannot be counted, stuffed, framed or mounted over the fireplace in the den.
Lewis H. Lapham (1935-, American Essayist, Editor)

5   One is not idle because one is absorbed. There is both visible and invisible labor. To contemplate is to toil, to think is to do. The crossed arms work, the clasped hands act. The eyes upturned to Heaven are an act of creation.
Victor Hugo (1802-1885, French Poet, Dramatist, Novelist)

6   With an eye made quiet by the power of harmony, and the deep power of joy, we see into the life of things.
William Wordsworth (1770-1850, British Poet)

CONTENTMENT

1   Content makes poor men rich; discontentment makes rich men poor.
Benjamin Franklin (1706-1790, American Scientist, Publisher, Diplomat)

2   Who is wise? He that learns from everyone. Who is powerful? He that governs his passions. Who is rich? He who is content. Who is that? Nobody.
Benjamin Franklin (1706-1790, American Scientist, Publisher, Diplomat)

3   The most valuable things in life are not measured in monetary terms. The really important things are not houses and lands, stocks and bonds, automobiles and real state, but friendships, trust, confidence, empathy, mercy, love and faith.
Bertrand Russell (1872-1970, British Philosopher, Mathematician, Essayist)

4   I have learned in whatsoever state I am, therewith to be content. [Philippians 4:11]
Bible (Sacred Scriptures of Christians and Judaism)

5   For I have learned, in whatsoever state I am, therewith to be content. [St. Paul In Philippians 4:11]
Bible (Sacred Scriptures of Christians and Judaism)

6   Try to be like the turtle -- at ease in your own shell
Bill Copeland

7   My motto is: Contented with little, yet wishing for more.
Charles Lamb (1775-1834, British Essayist, Critic)

8   If the book is good, is about something that you know, and is truly written, and reading it over you see that this is so, you can let the boys yip and the noise will have that pleasant sound coyotes make on a very cold night when they are out in the snow and you are in your own cabin that you have built or paid for with your work.
Ernest Hemingway (1898-1961, American Writer)

9   One should either be sad or joyful. Contentment is a warm sty for eaters and sleepers.
Eugene O'Neill (1888-1953, American Dramatist)

10   Be always displeased at what thou art, if thou desire to attain to what thou art not; for where thou hast pleased thyself, there thou abidest.
Francis Quarles (1592-1644, British Poet)

11   When we cannot find contentment in ourselves, it is useless to seek it elsewhere.
François de La Rochefoucauld (1613-1680, French classical writer)

12   I don't want to own anything that won't fit into my coffin.
Fred A. Allen (1894-1957, American Radio Comic)

13   A man who is contented with what he has done will never become famous for what he will do.
Fred Estabrook

14   What makes us discontented with our condition is the absurdly exaggerated idea we have of the happiness of others.
French Proverb

15   To be content with life -- or to live merrily, rather --all that is required is that we bestow on all things only a fleeting, superficial glance; the more thoughtful we become the more earnest we grow.
Georg C. Lichtenberg (1742-1799, German Physicist, Satirist)

16   To feel that one has a place in life solves half the problems of contentment.
George E. Woodberry (1855-1930, American Literary Critic)

17   To have what we want is riches; but to be able to do without is power.
George Macdonald (1824-1905, Scottish Novelist)

18   True contentment is a thing as active as agriculture. It is the power of getting out of any situation all that there is in it. It is arduous and it is rare.
Gilbert K. Chesterton (1874-1936, British Author)

19   Being "contented" ought to mean in English, as it does in French, being pleased. Being content with an attic ought not to mean being unable to move from it and resigned to living in it; it ought to mean appreciating all there is in such a position.
Gilbert K. Chesterton (1874-1936, British Author)

20   There are two kinds of discontent in this world. The discontent that works, and the discontent that wrings its hands. The first gets what it wants. The second loses what it has. There's no cure for the first, but success and there's no cure at all for the second.
Gordon Graham

21   The contented man can be happy with what appears to be useless.
Hung Ko

22   It is right to be contented with what we have, but never with what we are.
James Mackintosh (1765-1832, British Author)

23 Contentment is a pearl of great price, and whoever procures it at the expense of ten thousand desires makes a wise and a happy purchase.
John Balguy (1686-1748, British Philosopher, Writer)

24 If we have not quiet in our minds, outward comfort will do no more for us than a golden slipper on a gouty foot.
John Bunyan (1628-1688, British Author)

25 Happy the man, and happy he alone, he who can call today his own; he who, secure within, can say, tomorrow do thy worst, for I have lived today.
John Dryden (1631-1700, British Poet, Dramatist, Critic)

26 Content is a word unknown to life; it is also a word unknown to man.
John Fowles (1926-, British Novelist)

27 A sound mind in a sound body, is a short, but full description of a happy state in this World: he that has these two, has little more to wish for; and he that wants either of them, will be little the better for anything else.
John Locke (1632-1704, British Philosopher)

28 It is invariable found that a content man is usually a weak one.
John Wagstaff

29 A contented mind is the greatest blessing a man can enjoy in this world.
Joseph Addison (1672-1719, British Essayist, Poet, Statesman)

30 Yes, there is a Nirvanah; it is leading your sheep to a green pasture, and in putting your child to sleep, and in writing the last line of your poem.
Kahlil Gibran (1883-1931, Lebanese Poet, Novelist)

31 The secret of contentment is knowing how to enjoy what you have, and to be able to lose all desire for things beyond your reach.
Lin Yn-tang (1895-1976, Chinese Writer and Philologist)

32 There's naught, no doubt, so much the spirit calms as rum and true religion.
Lord Byron (1788-1824, British Poet)

33 Nobody got anywhere in the world by simply being content.
Louis L'Amour (1908-1988, American Western Author)

34 The greatest wealth is to live content with little, for there is never want where the mind is satisfied.
Lucretius (95-55 BC, Roman poet and philosopher)

35 Riches are not from abundance of worldly goods, but from a contented mind.
Mohammed (570-632, Prophet of Islam)

36 People are never free of trying to be content.
Murray Bookchin (1941-, American Ecologist)

37 Learn to be pleased with everything; with wealth, so far as it makes us beneficial to others; with poverty, for not having much to care for; and with obscurity, for being unenvied.
Plutarch (46-120 AD, Greek Essayist, Biographer)

38 A Sunday well-spent brings a week of content.
Proverb

39 There are some days when I think I'm going to die from an overdose of satisfaction.
Salvador Dali (1904-1989, Spanish Painter)

40 Happy the man who can endure the highest and the lowest fortune. He, who has endured such vicissitudes with equanimity, has deprived misfortune of its power.
Seneca (4 BC-65 AD, Spanish-born Roman Statesman, philosopher)

41 Contentment is natural wealth, luxury is artificial poverty.
Socrates (469-399 BC, Greek Philosopher of Athens)

42 He is rich who is content with the least; for contentment is the wealth of nature.
Socrates (469-399 BC, Greek Philosopher of Athens)

43 Since we cannot get what we like, let us like what we can get.
Spanish Proverb

44 You can't have everything. Where would you put it?
Steven Wright (American Humorist)

45 To the right, books; to the left, a tea-cup. In front of me, the fireplace; behind me, the post. There is no greater happiness than this.
Teiga

46 Contentment is, after all, simply refined indolence.
Thomas C. Haliburton (1796-1865, Canadian Jurist, Author)

47 Contentment consist not in adding more fuel, but in taking away some fire.
Thomas Fuller (1608-1661, British Clergyman, Author)

48 If you are content, you have enough to live comfortably.
Titus Maccius Plautus (254-184 BC, Roman Comic Poet)

49 To rejoice in another's prosperity is to give content to your lot; to mitigate another's grief is to alleviate or dispel your own.
Tryon Edwards (1809-1894, American Theologian)

50 To accept what you are is to be content, and contentment is the greatest wealth. To work with patience is to gather power.
Vimalia Mcclure

51 Be happy with what you have and are, be generous with both, and you won't have to hunt for happiness.
William E. Gladstone (1809-1888, British Liberal Prime Minister, Statesman)

52 My crown is in my heart, not on my head, Nor decked with diamonds and Indian stones, Nor to be seen: My crown is called content: A crown it is, that seldom kings enjoy.
William Shakespeare (1564-1616, British Poet, Playwright, Actor)

53 He that is well paid is well satisfied.
William Shakespeare (1564-1616, British Poet, Playwright, Actor)

54 That blessed mood in which the burthen of the mystery, in which the heavy and the weary weight of all this unintelligible world is lightened.
William Wordsworth (1770-1850, British Poet)

CONTRADICTION

1 All concord's born of contraries.
Ben Johnson (1573-1637, British Dramatist, Poet)

2 Contradiction is not a sign of falsity, nor the lack of contradiction a sign of truth.
Blaise Pascal (1623-1662, French Scientist, Religious Philosopher)

3 How can what an Englishman believes be hearsay? It is a contradiction in terms.
George Bernard Shaw (1856-1950, Irish-born British Dramatist)

4 Everybody sets out to do something, and everybody does something, but no one does what he sets out to do.
George Moore (1852-1933, Irish Writer)

5 Doublethink means the power of holding two contradictory beliefs in one's mind simultaneously, and accepting both of them.
George Orwell (1903-1950, British Author, "Animal Farm")

6 I believe that truth has only one face: that of a violent contradiction.
Georges Bataille (1897-1962, French Novelist, Critic)

7 Even though I make those movies, I find myself wishing that more of those magic moments could happen in real life.
Jane Seymour

8 Einstein is an analytical mathematician seeking to give a physical interpretation to the conclusions of his mathematical process. In this he is hampered by a load of contradictory and absurd assumptions of the school that he follows, which throws him into all manner of difficulty. Einstein has such a faculty for embracing both sides of a contradiction that one would have to be of the same frame of mind to follow his thought, it is so peculiarly his own. The whole Relativity theory is as easy to follow as the path of a bat in the air at night.
Jeremiah Joseph

9 I happen to feel that the degree of a person's intelligence is directly reflected by the number of conflicting attitudes she can bring to bear on the same topic.
Lisa Alther (1944-, American Author)

10 What an antithetical mind! -- tenderness, roughness -- delicacy, coarseness -- sentiment, sensuality -- soaring and groveling, dirt and deity -- all mixed up in that one compound of inspired clay!
Lord Byron (1788-1824, British Poet)

11 I have forced myself to contradict myself in order to avoid conforming to my own taste.
Marcel Duchamp (1887-1968, French Artist)

12 People who honestly mean to be true really contradict themselves much more rarely than those who try to be "consistent."
Oliver Wendell Holmes (1809-1894, American Author, Wit, Poet)

13 The well-bred contradict other people. The wise contradict themselves.
Oscar Wilde (1856-1900, British Author, Wit)

14 Let me never fall into the vulgar mistake of dreaming that I am persecuted whenever I am contradicted.
Ralph Waldo Emerson (1803-1882, American Poet, Essayist)

15 Wise men are not wise at all hours, and will speak five times from their taste or their humor, to once from their reason.
Ralph Waldo Emerson (1803-1882, American Poet, Essayist)

16 Like the British Constitution, she owes her success in practice to her inconsistencies in principle.
Thomas Hardy (1840-1928, British Novelist, Poet)

17 Do I contradict myself? Very well then I contradict myself, (I am large, I contain multitudes).
Walt Whitman (1819-1892, American Poet)

18 The reserve of modern assertions is sometimes pushed to extremes, in which the fear of being contradicted leads the writer to strip himself of almost all sense and meaning.
Winston Churchill (1874-1965, British Statesman, Prime Minister)

CONTRAST

1 Where there is much light, the shadow is deep.
Johann Wolfgang Von Goethe (1749-1832, German Poet, Dramatist, Novelist)

2 Joy and grief are never far apart. In the same street the shutters of one house are closed while the curtains of the next are brushed by the shadows of the dance. A wedding party returns from the church; and a funeral winds to its door. The smiles and
Robert Eldridge Willmott

3 The rose and the thorn, and sorrow and gladness are linked together.
Saadi

4 The luster of diamonds is invigorated by the interposition of darker bodies; the lights of a picture are created by the shades; the highest pleasure which nature has indulged to sensitive perception is that of rest after fatigue.
Samuel Johnson (1709-1784, British Author)

CONTROL

1 Prohibition goes beyond the bounds of reason in that it attempts to control a man's appetite by legislation and makes crimes out of things that are not crimes.
Abraham Lincoln (1809-1865, Sixteenth President of the USA)

2 Be sure you put your feet in the right place, then stand firm.
Abraham Lincoln (1809-1865, Sixteenth President of the USA)

3 What I do say is that no man is good enough to govern another man without that other's consent.
Abraham Lincoln (1809-1865, Sixteenth President of the USA)

4 Question: Why are we Masters of our Fate, the captains of our souls? Because we have the power to control our thoughts, our attitudes. That is why many people live in the withering negative world. That is why many people live in the Positive Faith world.
Alfred A. Montapert (American Author)

5 The secret of success is learning how to use pain and pleasure instead of having pain and pleasure use you. If you do that, you're in control of your life. If you don't, life controls you.
Anthony Robbins (1960-, American Author, Speaker, Peak Performance Expert / Consultant)

6 Take control of your consistent emotions and begin to consciously and deliberately reshape your daily experience of life.
Anthony Robbins (1960-, American Author, Speaker, Peak Performance Expert / Consultant)

7 To decide to be at the level of choice, is to take responsibility for your life and to be in control of your life.
Arbie M. Dale

8 It's essential to distinguish between events that are really beyond your control and events you caused yourself.
Barbara Sher (American Author of "I Could Do Anything If I Only Knew What It Was")

9 While we may not be able to control all that happens to us, we can control what happens inside us.
Benjamin Franklin (1706-1790, American Scientist, Publisher, Diplomat)

10 Drive thy business or it will drive thee.
Benjamin Franklin (1706-1790, American Scientist, Publisher, Diplomat)

11 You cannot control what happens to you, but you can control your attitude toward what happens to you, and in that, you will be mastering change rather than allowing it to master you.
Brian Tracy (American Trainer, Speaker, Author, Businessman)

12 It is better to conquer yourself than to win a thousand battles. Then the victory is yours. It cannot be taken from you, not by angels or by demons, heaven or hell.
Buddha (568-488 BC, Founder of Buddhism)

13 If you are ruled by mind you are a king; if by body, a slave.
Cato The Elder (234-149 BC, Roman Statesman, Orator)

14 You brain shall be your servant instead of your master, You will rule it instead of allowing it to rule you.
Charles E. Popplestone

15 You cannot prevent the birds of sorrow from flying over your head, but you can prevent them from building nests in your hair.
Chinese Proverb

16 Flow with whatever is happening and let your mind be free. Stay centered by accepting whatever you are doing. This is the ultimate.
Chuang Tzu (369-286 BC, Chinese Philosopher)

17 Sometimes if you want to see a change for the better, you have to take things into your own hands.
Clint Eastwood (1930-, American Actor, Director, Politician, Composer, Musician, Producer)

18 The physical world, including our bodies, is a response of the observer. We create our bodies as we create the experience of our world.
Deepak Chopra (East-Indian- American M.D., New Age Author, Lecturer)

19 No one can drive us crazy unless we give them the keys.
Doug Horton

20 If you find a good solution and become attached to it, the solution may become your next problem.
Dr. Robert Anthony (American educator)

21 You are the one who can stretch your own horizon.
Edgar F. Magnin

22 I am not a glutton -- I am an explorer of food.
Erma Bombeck (1927-, American Author, Humorist)

23 He who has the pepper may season as he lists.
George Herbert (1593-1632, British Metaphysical Poet)

24 The best way to navigate through life is to give up all of our controls.
Gerald G. Jampolsky (American Psychiatrist, Lecturer, Author)

25 Let nothing come between you and the light.
Henry David Thoreau (1817-1862, American Essayist, Poet, Naturalist)

26 No temptation can gravitate to a man unless there is that is his heart which is capable of responding to it
James Allen (1864-1912, British-born American Essayist, Author of "As a Man Thinketh")

27 Never let the other fellow set the agenda.
James Baker

28 Every man wishes to rule the world. Unfortunately, the world rules every man.
Jeremy P. Johnson

29 You can't force anyone to love you or lend you money.
Jewish Proverb

30 Nature has placed mankind under the government of two sovereign masters, pain and pleasure... they govern us in all we do, in all we say, in all we think: every effort we can make to throw off our subjection, will serve but to demonstrate and confirm it.
John Bentham

31 The bird of paradise alights only on the hand that does not grasp.
John Berry

32 He is great enough that is his own master.
Joseph Hall (1574-1656, British Clergyman, Writer)

33 Don't take the bull by the horns, take him by the tail; then you can let go when you want to.
Josh Billings (1815-1885, American Humorist, Lecturer)

34 Getting your house in order and reducing the confusion gives you more control over your life. Personal organization some how releases or frees you to operate more effectively.
Larry King (1933-, American TV Personality, Prankster)

35 Don't let the negativity given to you by the world disempower you. Instead give to yourself that which empowers you.
Les Brown (1945-, American Speaker, Author, Trainer, Motivator Lecturer)

36 If you don't program yourself, life will program you!
Les Brown (1945-, American Speaker, Author, Trainer, Motivator Lecturer)

37 The control of the palate is a valuable aid for the control of the mind.
Mahatma Gandhi (1869-1948, Indian Political, Spiritual Leader)

38 You can chain me, you can torture me, you can even destroy this body, but you will never imprison my mind.
Mahatma Gandhi (1869-1948, Indian Political, Spiritual Leader)

39 If everything seems under control, you're just not going fast enough.
Mario Andretti (1940-, Italian-born American Auto Racer)

40 The drive to resist compulsion is more important in wild animals than sex, food, or water. He found that captive white-footed mice spent inordinate time and energy just resisting experimental manipulation. If the experimenters turned the lights up, the mouse spent his time turning them down. If the experimenter turned the lights down, the mouse turned them up. The drive for competence or to resist compulsion is a drive to avoid helplessness.
Martin E. P. Seligman

41 It's all happening too fast. I've got to put the brakes on or I'll smack into something.
Mel Gibson (1956-, American Actor, Director, Producer)

42 Your are in charge. You have the ability to master you destiny.
Michael J. Mccarthy (American Lawyer, Businessman)

43 Winners take chances. Like everyone else, they fear failing, but they refuse to let fear control them.
Nancy Simms

44 If you want a thing done well, do it yourself.
Napoleon Bonaparte (1769-1821, French General, Emperor)

45 I have only one counsel for you -- be master.
Napoleon Bonaparte (1769-1821, French General, Emperor)

46 The strong man is the one who is able to intercept at will the communication between the senses and the mind.
Napoleon Bonaparte (1769-1821, French General, Emperor)

47 If you do not conquer self, you will be conquered by self.
Napoleon Hill (1883-1970, American Speaker, Motivational Writer, "Think and Grow Rich")

48 No one can make you jealous, angry, vengeful, or greedy -- unless you let him.
Napoleon Hill (1883-1970, American Speaker, Motivational Writer, "Think and Grow Rich")

49 The word is control. That's my ultimate -- to have control.
Nick Faldo (American Golfer)

50 Never allow anyone to rain on your parade and thus cast a pall of gloom and defeat on the entire day. Remember that no talent, no self-denial, no brains, no character, are required to set up in the fault-finding business. Nothing external can have any power over you unless you permit it. Your time is too precious to be sacrificed in wasted days combating the menial forces of hate, jealously, and envy. Guard your fragile life carefully. Only God can shape a flower, but any foolish child can pull it to pieces.
Og Mandino (1923-1996, American Motivational Author, Speaker)

51 We fail to see that we can control our own destiny; make ourselves do whatever is possible; make ourselves become whatever we long to be.
Orison Swett Marden (1850-1924, American Author, Founder of Success Magazine)

52 Remain calm, serene, always in command of yourself. You will then find out how easy it is to get along.
Paramahansa Yogananda (Spiritual Author, Lecturer)

53 Don't let other people tell you what you want.
Pat Riley (1945, American Basketball Coach)

54 The one thing over which you have absolute control is your own thoughts. It is this that puts you in a position to control your own destiny.
Paul G. Thomas

55 The first and the best victory is to conquer self.
Plato (427-347 BC, Greek Philosopher)

56 The consuming desire of most human beings is deliberately to plant their whole life in the hands of some other person. I would describe this method of searching for happiness as immature. Development of character consists solely in moving toward self-sufficiency.
Quentin Crisp (1908-, British Author)

57 Nothing external to you has any power over you.
Ralph Waldo Emerson (1803-1882, American Poet, Essayist)

58 As the Sandwich Islander believes that the strength and valor of the enemy he kills passes into himself, so we gain the strength of the temptation we resist.
Ralph Waldo Emerson (1803-1882, American Poet, Essayist)

59 Are we controlled by our thoughts, or are we controlling our thoughts?
Raymond Holliwell

60 Your real self -- the "I am I" -- is master of this land, the ruler of this empire. You rightfully have power and dominion over it, all its inhabitants, and all contained in its realm.
Robert Collier (American Writer, Publisher)

61 To know is to control.
Scott Reed

62 Give me beauty in the inward soul; may the outward and the inward man be at one.
Socrates (469-399 BC, Greek Philosopher of Athens)

63 When I grip the wheel too tight, I find I lose control.
Steve Rapson (American writer)

64 What man's mind can create, man's character can control.
Thomas A. Edison (1847-1931, American Inventor, Entrepreneur, Founder of GE)

65 Slight small injuries, and they will become none at all.
Thomas Fuller (1608-1661, British Clergyman, Author)

66 Nothing gives a person so much advantage over another as to remain always cool and unruffled under all circumstances.
Thomas Jefferson (1743-1826, Third President of the USA)

67 I cannot make the universe obey me. I cannot make other people conform to my own whims and fancies. I cannot make even my own body obey me.
Thomas Merton (1915-1968, American Religious Writer, Poet)

68 There is no finer sensations in life that which comes with victory over one's self. Go forward to a goal of inward achievement, brushing aside all your old internal enemies as you advance.
Vash Young

69 When we direct our thoughts properly, we can control our emotions...
W. Clement Stone (1902-, American Businessman, Author)

70 When you do the wrong thing, knowing it is wrong, you do so because you haven't developed the habit of effectively controlling or neutralizing strong inner urges that tempt you, or because you have established the wrong habit and don't know how to eliminate them effectively.
W. Clement Stone (1902-, American Businessman, Author)

71 Oh while I live, to be the ruler of life, not a slave, to meet life as a powerful conqueror, and nothing exterior to me will ever take command of me.
Walt Whitman (1819-1892, American Poet)

72 You cannot always control what goes on outside. But you can always control what goes on inside.
Wayne Dyer (1940-, American Psychotherapist, Author, Lecturer)

73 No man is fit to command another that cannot command himself.
William Penn (1644-1718, British Religious Leader, Founder of Pennsylvania)

74 Are you a SNIOP? Someone who is Sensitive to the Negative Influence Of Others?
Zig Ziglar (American Sales Trainer, Author, Motivational Speaker)

CONTROVERSY

1 The most savage controversies are those about matters as to which there is no good evidence either way.
Bertrand Russell (1872-1970, British Philosopher, Mathematician, Essayist)

2 All great ideas are controversial, or have been at one time.
Gilbert Seldes

3 When people generally are aware of a problem, it can be said to have entered the public consciousness. When people get on their hind legs and holler, the problem has not only entered the public consciousness -- it has also become a part of the public conscience. At that point, things in our democracy begin to hum.
Hubert H. Humphrey (1911-1978, American Democratic Politician, Vice President)

4 No great advance has ever been made in science, politics, or religion, without controversy.
Lyman Beecher (1775-1863, American Presbyterian Minister, Revivalist)

5 I am continually fascinated at the difficulty intelligent people have in distinguishing what is controversial from what is merely offensive.
Nora Ephron (1941-, American Author, Journalist)

6 ... the hydrostatic paradox of controversy. Don't you know what that means? Well, I will tell you. You know that, if you had a bent tube, one arm of which was of the size of a pipe-stem, and the other big enough to hold the ocean, water would stand at the same height in one as in the other. Controversy equalizes fools and wise men in the same way. And the fools know it.
Oliver Wendell Holmes (1809-1894, American Author, Wit, Poet)

7 Every real thought on every real subject knocks the wind out of somebody or other.
Oliver Wendell Holmes (1809-1894, American Author, Wit, Poet)

8 The dust of controversy is merely the falsehood flying off.
Thomas Carlyle (1795-1881, Scottish Philosopher, Author)

9   When a subject is highly controversial... one cannot hope to tell the truth. One can only show how one came to hold whatever opinion one does hold. One can only give one's audience the chance of drawing their own conclusions as they observe the limitations, the prejudices, the idiosyncrasies of the speaker.
Virginia Woolf (1882-1941, British Novelist, Essayist)

10   When a thing ceases to be a subject of controversy, it ceases to be a subject of interest.
William Hazlitt (1778-1830, British Essayist)

CONVALESCENCE

1   One must not forget that recovery is brought about not by the physician, but by the sick man himself. He heals himself, by his own power, exactly as he walks by means of his own power, or eats, or thinks, breathes or sleeps.
Georg Groddeck

2   I enjoy convalescence. It is the part that makes the illness worth while.
George Bernard Shaw (1856-1950, Irish-born British Dramatist)

3   With any recovery from morbidity there must go a certain healthy humiliation.
Gilbert K. Chesterton (1874-1936, British Author)

4   Healing," Papa would tell me, "is not a science, but the intuitive art of wooing nature."
W. H. Auden (1907-1973, Anglo-American Poet)

CONVENTIONALITY

1   Conventional people are roused to fury by departures from convention, largely because they regard such departures as a criticism of themselves.
Bertrand Russell (1872-1970, British Philosopher, Mathematician, Essayist)

2   What greater reassurance can the weak have than that they are like anyone else?
Eric Hoffer (1902-1983, American Author, Philosopher)

3   Every generation laughs at the old fashions, but religiously follows the new.
Henry David Thoreau (1817-1862, American Essayist, Poet, Naturalist)

4   Why can't somebody give us a list of things that everybody thinks and nobody says, and another list of things that everybody says and nobody thinks.
Oliver Wendell Holmes (1809-1894, American Author, Wit, Poet)

5   He who would be a man must therefore be a non-conformist.
Ralph Waldo Emerson (1803-1882, American Poet, Essayist)

CONVERSATION

1   There is nothing so dangerous for anyone who has something to hide as conversation! A human being, Hastings, cannot resist the opportunity to reveal himself and express his personality which conversation gives him. Every time he will give himself away.
Agatha Christie (1891-1976, British Mystery Writer)

2   It is not what we learn in conversation that enriches us. It is the elation that comes of swift contact with tingling currents of thought.
Agnes Repplier (1858-1950, American Author, Social Critic)

3   An American cannot converse, but he can discuss, and his talk falls into a dissertation. He speaks to you as if he was addressing a meeting; and if he should chance to become warm in the discussion, he will say "Gentlemen" to the person with whom he is conversing.
Alexis De Tocqueville (1805-1859, French Social Philosopher)

4   Debate is masculine, conversation is feminine.
Amos Bronson Alcott (1799-1888, American Educator, Social Reformer)

5   Conversation would be vastly improved by the constant use of four simple words: I do not know.
Andre Maurois (1885-1967, French Writer)

6   No collection of people who are all waiting for the same thing are capable of holding a natural conversation. Even if the thing they are waiting for is only a taxi.
Ben Elton (1959-, British Author, Performer)

7   The great secret of succeeding in conversation is to admire little, to hear much; always to distrust our own reason, and sometimes that of our friends; never to pretend to wit, but to make that of others appear as much as possibly we can; to hearken to what is said and to answer to the purpose.
Benjamin Franklin (1706-1790, American Scientist, Publisher, Diplomat)

8   Repartee is perfect when it effects its purpose with a double edge. It is the highest order of wit, as it indicates the coolest yet quickest exercise of genius, at a moment when the passions are roused.
Charles Caleb Colton (1780-1832, British Sportsman Writer)

9   Reply to wit with gravity, and to gravity with wit.
Charles Caleb Colton (1780-1832, British Sportsman Writer)

10   Saying what we think gives a wider range of conversation than saying what we know.
Cullen Hightower

11   The real art of conversation is not only to say the right thing at the right place but to leave unsaid the wrong thing at the tempting moment.
Dorothy Nevill

12 A sudden silence in the middle of a conversation suddenly brings us back to essentials: it reveals how dearly we must pay for the invention of speech.
E. M. Cioran (1911-, Rumanian-born French Philosopher)

13 I would rather take hellebore than spend a conversation with a good, little man.
Edward Dahlberg (1900-1977, American Author, Critic)

14 The true spirit of conversation consists in building on another man's observation, not overturning it.
Edward G. Bulwer-Lytton (1803-1873, British Novelist, Poet)

15 Ideal conversation must be an exchange of thought, and not, as many of those who worry most about their shortcomings believe, an eloquent exhibition of wit or oratory.
Emily Post (1873-1960, American Hostess)

16 Mediocre people have an answer for everything and are astonished at nothing. They always want to have the air of knowing better than you what you are going to tell them; when, in their turn, they begin to speak, they repeat to you with the greatest confidence, as if dealing with their own property, the things that they have heard you say yourself at some other place. A capable and superior look is the natural accompaniment of this type of character.
EugFne Delacroix (1798-1863, French Artist)

17 The opposite of talking isn't listening. The opposite of talking is waiting.
Fran Lebowitz (1951-, American Journalist)

18 No one will ever shine in conversation, who thinks of saying fine things: to please, one must say many things indifferent, and many very bad.
Francis Lockier (1668-1740, British Prelate, Man of Letters)

19 Conceit causes more conversation than wit.
François de La Rochefoucauld (1613-1680, French classical writer)

20 We often forgive those who bore us, but we cannot forgive those whom we bore.
François de La Rochefoucauld (1613-1680, French classical writer)

21 Talk ought always to run obliquely, not nose to nose with no chance of mental escape.
Frank Moore Colby (1865-1925, American Editor, Essayist)

22 She has lost the art of conversation, but not, unfortunately, the power of speech.
George Bernard Shaw (1856-1950, Irish-born British Dramatist)

23 In conversation, humor is worth more than wit and easiness more than knowledge.
George Herbert (1593-1632, British Metaphysical Poet)

24 Not only to say the right thing in the right place, but far more difficult, to leave unsaid the wrong thing at the tempting moment.
George Sala

25 The primary use of conversation is to satisfy the impulse to talk.
George Santayana (1863-1952, American Philosopher, Poet)

26 Conversation. What is it? A Mystery! It's the art of never seeming bored, of touching everything with interest, of pleasing with trifles, of being fascinating with nothing at all. How do we define this lively darting about with words, of hitting them back and forth, this sort of brief smile of ideas which should be conversation?
Guy de Maupassant (1850-1893, French Writer)

27 We do not talk -- we bludgeon one another with facts and theories gleaned from cursory readings of newspapers, magazines and digests.
Henry Miller (1891-1980, American Author)

28 If other people are going to talk, conversation becomes impossible.
James Mcneill Whistler (1834-1903, American Artist)

29 The great gift of conversation lies less in displaying it ourselves than in drawing it out of others. He who leaves your company pleased with himself and his own cleverness is perfectly well pleased with you.
Jean De La Bruyere (1645-1696, French Writer)

30 Can we talk?
Joan Rivers (1933-, American Comedian, Talk Show Host, Actress)

31 A good conversationalist is not one who remembers what was said, but says what someone wants to remember.
John Mason Brown (1800-1859, American Militant Abolitionist)

32 With thee conversing I forget all time.
John Milton (1608-1674, British Poet)

33 The techniques of opening conversation are universal. I knew long ago and rediscovered that the best way to attract attention, help, and conversation is to be lost. A man who seeing his mother starving to death on a path kicks her in the stomach to clear the way, will cheerfully devote several hours of his time giving wrong directions to a total stranger who claims to be lost.
John Steinbeck (1902-1968, American Author)

34 There is nothing that exasperates people more than a display of superior ability or brilliance in conversation. They seem pleased at the time, but their envy makes them curse the conversationalist in their heart.
Johnson

35 One of the very best rules of conversation is to never, say anything which any of the company wish had been left unsaid.
Jonathan Swift (1667-1745, Anglo-Irish Satirist)

36 Say nothing good of yourself, you will be distrusted; say nothing bad of yourself, you will be taken at your word.
Joseph Roux (1834-1905, French Priest, Writer)

37 If you ever have to support a flagging conversation, introduce the topic of eating.
Leigh Hunt (1784-1859, British Poet, Essayist)

38 Never hold anyone by the button or the hand in order to be heard out; for if people are unwilling to hear you, you had better hold your tongue than them.
Lord Chesterfield (1694-1773, British Statesman, Author)

39 A good memory and a tongue tied in the middle is a combination which gives immortality to conversation.
Mark Twain (1835-1910, American Humorist, Writer)

40 There is no conversation more boring than the one where everybody agrees.
Michel Eyquem De Montaigne (1533-1592, French Philosopher, Essayist)

41 In my opinion, the most fruitful and natural play of the mind is in conversation. I find it sweeter than any other action in life; and if I were forced to choose, I think I would rather lose my sight than my hearing and voice. The study of books is a drowsy and feeble exercise which does not warm you up.
Michel Eyquem De Montaigne (1533-1592, French Philosopher, Essayist)

42 And when you stick on conversation's burrs, don't strew your pathway with those dreadful urs.
Oliver Wendell Holmes (1809-1894, American Author, Wit, Poet)

43 Talk to every woman as if you loved her, and to every man as if he bored you, and at the end of your first season you will have the reputation of possessing the most perfect social tact.
Oscar Wilde (1856-1900, British Author, Wit)

44 Conversation should touch everything, but should concentrate itself on nothing.
Oscar Wilde (1856-1900, British Author, Wit)

45 Things said for conversation are chalk eggs. Don't say things. What you are stands over you the while, and thunders so that I cannot hear what you say to the contrary.
Ralph Waldo Emerson (1803-1882, American Poet, Essayist)

46 Conversation is an art in which a man has all mankind for competitors.
Ralph Waldo Emerson (1803-1882, American Poet, Essayist)

47 In conversation the game is, to say something new with old words. And you shall observe a man of the people picking his way along, step by step, using every time an old boulder, yet never setting his foot on an old place.
Ralph Waldo Emerson (1803-1882, American Poet, Essayist)

48 There is no such thing as conversation. It is an illusion. There are intersecting monologues, that is all.
Rebecca West (1892-1983, British Author)

49 It is all right to hold a conversation but you should let go of it now and then.
Richard Armour (1906-1989, American Poet)

50 It's apparent that we can't proceed any further without a name for this institutionalized garrulousness, this psychological patter, this need to catalogue the ego's condition. Let's call it psychobabble, this spirit which now tyrannizes conversation in the seventies.
Richard D. Rosen

51 You guys are both saying the same thing. The only reason you're arguing is because you're using different words. Conversation in a dorm room quoted in Language in Thought and Action,
S. I. Hayakawa (1902-1992, Canadian Born American Senator, Educator)

52 The happiest conversation is that of which nothing is distinctly remembered but a general effect of pleasing impression.
Samuel Johnson (1709-1784, British Author)

53 I never desire to converse with a man who has written more than he has read.
Samuel Johnson (1709-1784, British Author)

54 Conversation has a kind of charm about it, an insinuating and insidious something that elicits secrets just like love or liquor.
Seneca (4 BC-65 AD, Spanish-born Roman Statesman, philosopher)

55 The first ingredient in conversation is truth, the next good sense, the third good humor, and the fourth wit.
Sir William Temple (1628-1699, British Diplomat, Essayist)

56 Nothing lowers the level on conversation more than raising the voice.
Stanley Horowitz

57 Never talk for half a minute without pausing and giving others a chance to join in.
Sydney Smith (1771-1845, British Writer, Clergyman)

58 No one is qualified to converse in public except those contented to do without such conversation.
Thomas p Kempis (1379-1471, German Monk, Mystic, Religious Writer)

59 I find we are growing serious, and then we are in great danger of being dull.
William Congreve (1670-1729, British Dramatist)

60 Conversation should be pleasant without scurrility, witty without affection, free without indecency, learned without conceitedness, novel without falsehood.
William Shakespeare (1564-1616, British Poet, Playwright, Actor)

CONVERSION

1 Jesus tapped me on the shoulder and said, Bob, why are you resisting me? I said, I'm not resisting you! He said, You gonna follow me? I said, I've never thought about that before! He said, When you're not following me, you're resisting me.
Bob Dylan (1941-, American Musician, Singer, Songwriter)

2   I believe that a man is converted when first he hears the low, vast murmur of life, of human life, troubling his hitherto unconscious self.
D. H. Lawrence (1885-1930, British Author)

3   The great danger of conversion in all ages has been that when the religion of the high mind is offered to the lower mind, the lower mind, feeling its fascination without understanding it, and being incapable of rising to it, drags it down to its level by degrading it.
George Bernard Shaw (1856-1950, Irish-born British Dramatist)

4   Once my heart was captured, reason was shown the door, deliberately and with a sort of frantic joy. I accepted everything, I believed everything, without struggle, without suffering, without regret, without false shame. How can one blush for what one adores?
George Sand (1804-1876, French Novelist)

5   I used to say: "there is a God-shaped hole in me." For a long time I stressed the absence, the hole. Now I find it is the shape which has become more important.
Salman Rushdie (1948-, Indian-born British Author)

CONVICTION

1   With the power of conviction, there is no sacrifice.
Pat Benatar (1953-, American Singer)

COOKING

1   To the old saying that man built the house but woman made of it a "home" might be added the modern supplement that woman accepted cooking as a chore but man has made of it a recreation.
Emily Post (1873-1960, American Hostess)

2   Kissing don't last: cookery do!
George Meredith (1828-1909, British Author)

3   I did toy with the idea of doing a cook-book. The recipes were to be the routine ones: how to make dry toast, instant coffee, hearts of lettuce and brownies. But as an added attraction, at no extra charge, my idea was to put a fried egg on the cover. I think a lot of people who hate literature but love fried eggs would buy it if the price was right.
Groucho Marx (1895-1977, American Comic Actor)

4   I don't even butter my bread; I consider that cooking.
Katherine Cebrian

5   To make a good salad is to be a brilliant diplomatist -- the problem is entirely the same in both cases. To know exactly how much oil one must put with one's vinegar.
Oscar Wilde (1856-1900, British Author, Wit)

6   Not on morality, but on cookery, let us build our stronghold: there brandishing our frying-pan, as censer, let us offer sweet incense to the Devil, and live at ease on the fat things he has provided for his elect!
Thomas Carlyle (1795-1881, Scottish Philosopher, Author)

7   There is no spectacle on earth more appealing than that of a beautiful woman in the act of cooking dinner for someone she loves.
Thomas Wolfe (1931-, American Author, Journalist)

8   If cooking becomes an art form rather than a means of providing a reasonable diet, then something is clearly wrong.
Tom Jaine

9   'Tis an ill cook that cannot lick his own fingers.
William Shakespeare (1564-1616, British Poet, Playwright, Actor)

COOPERATION

1   We travel together, passengers on a little spaceship, dependent on it's vulnerable reserves of air and soil, all committed, for our safety, to it's security and peace. Preserved from annihilation only by the care, the work and the love we give our fragile craft.
Adlai E. Stevenson (1900-1965, American Lawyer, Politician)

2   Union gives strength.
Aesop (620-560 BC, Greek Fabulist)

3   Affairs are easier of entrance than of exit; and it is but common prudence to see our way out before we venture in.
Aesop (620-560 BC, Greek Fabulist)

4   A hundred times every day I remind myself that my inner and outer life depend on the labors of other men, living and dead, and that I must exert myself in order to give in the same measure as I have received and am still receiving.
Albert Einstein (1879-1955, German-born American Physicist)

5   Each of us is here for a brief sojourn; for what purpose he knows not, though he senses it. But without deeper reflection one knows from daily life that one exists for other people.
Albert Einstein (1879-1955, German-born American Physicist)

6   How strange is the lot of us mortals! Each of us is here for a brief sojourn; for what purpose he knows not, though he senses it. But without deeper reflection one knows from daily life that one exists for other people.
Albert Einstein (1879-1955, German-born American Physicist)

7   In everyone's life, at some time, our inner fire goes out. It is then burst into flame by an encounter with another human being. We should all be thankful for those people who rekindle the inner spirit.
Albert Schweitzer (1875-1965, German Born Medical Missionary, Theologian, Musician, and Philosopher)

8   No matter what accomplishments you make, somebody helped you.
Althea Gibson (1927-, American Tennis Player)

9   Personal relationships are the fertile soil from which all advancement, all success, all achievement in real life grows.
Ben Stein (American Professor, Writer)

10 We must, indeed, all hang together or, most assuredly, we shall all hang separately.
Benjamin Franklin (1706-1790, American Scientist, Publisher, Diplomat)

11 If we do not hang together, we will all hang separately.
Benjamin Franklin (1706-1790, American Scientist, Publisher, Diplomat)

12 The only thing that will redeem mankind is cooperation.
Bertrand Russell (1872-1970, British Philosopher, Mathematician, Essayist)

13 Behold how good and how pleasant it is for brethren to dwell together in unity.
Bible (Sacred Scriptures of Christians and Judaism)

14 No one lives long enough to learn everything they need to learn starting from scratch. To be successful, we absolutely, positively have to find people who have already paid the price to learn the things that we need to learn to achieve our goals.
Brian Tracy (American Trainer, Speaker, Author, Businessman)

15 We are not going to be able to operate our Spaceship Earth successfully nor for much longer unless we see it as a whole spaceship and our fate as common. It has to be everybody or nobody.
Buckminster Fuller (American Engineer, Inventor, Designer, Architect "Geodesic Dome")

16 The meeting of two personalities is like the contact of two chemical substances. If there is any reaction, both are transformed.
Carl Jung (1875-1961, Swiss Psychiatrist)

17 It is one of the beautiful compensations of this life that no one can sincerely try to help another without helping himself.
Charles Dudley

18 Always try to do something for the other fellow and you will be agreeably surprised how things come your way -- how many pleasing things are done for you.
Claude M. Bristol (1891-1951, American Author of "The Magic of Believing")

19 Doing things for others always pays dividends...
Claude M. Bristol (1891-1951, American Author of "The Magic of Believing")

20 Live to learn, learn to live, then teach others.
Doug Horton

21 Only strength can cooperate. Weakness can only beg.
Dwight D. Eisenhower (1890-1969, Thirty-fourth President of the USA)

22 Everything in the world we want to do or get done, we must do with and through people.
Earl Nightingale (1921-1989, American Radio Announcer, Author, Motivator, Speaker)

23 If we would just support each other -- that's ninety percent of the problem.
Edward Gardner (American Businessman, Founder of Soft Sheen Products)

24 Put yourself in the other man's place and then you will know why he thinks certain things and does certain deeds.
Elbert Hubbard (1859-1915, American Author, Publisher)

25 Don't be afraid to let her into your heart and when your down, don't try to carry the whole world on your shoulders.
Elton John (1947-, British Musician, Singer, Songwriter)

26 There is the sky, which is all men's together.
Euripides (480-406 BC, Greek Tragic Poet)

27 It is probably not love that makes the world go around, but rather those mutually supportive alliances through which partners recognize their dependence on each other for the achievement of shared and private goals.
Fred A. Allen (1894-1957, American Radio Comic)

28 Now you can begin to see quite transparently that nothing purchased life is one of argument, If other people don't agree with you you're in big trouble. How far would you get in your work if nobody agreed that what you were doing had value?
Frederick (Carl) Frieseke (1874-1939, American-Born French Painter)

29 We are all dependent on one another, every soul of us on earth.
George Bernard Shaw (1856-1950, Irish-born British Dramatist)

30 There is no such thing as a self-made man. You will reach your goals only with the help of others.
George Shinn

31 Let's face it. In most of life we really are interdependent. We need each other. Staunch independence is an illusion, but heavy dependence isn't healthy, either. The only position of long- term strength is interdependence: win/win.
Greg Anderson (American Author of "The 22 Non-Negotiable Laws of Wellness")

32 It is in the shelter of each other that the people live.
Irish Proverb

33 We are not put on this earth for ourselves, but are placed here for each other. If you are there always for others, then in time of need, someone will be there for you.
Jeff Warner

34 We are so bound together that no man can labor for himself alone. Each blow he strikes in his own behalf helps to mold the universe.
Jerome K. Jerome (1859-1927, British Humorous Writer, Novelist, Playwright)

35 I'm not a self-made man. I cannot forget those who have sacrificed for me to get where I am today.
Jessie Hill (American Business Executive, CEO of Atlanta Life Insurance)

36 Let everyone sweep in front of his own door, and the whole world will be clean.
Johann Wolfgang Von Goethe (1749-1832, German Poet, Dramatist, Novelist)

37 No man is an island entire of itself; every man is a piece of the continent, a part of the main.
John Donne (1572-1632, British Metaphysical Poet)

38 Come all good people far and near, Oh, come and see what you can hear.
Julia A. Moore

39 In spite of my great admiration for individual splendid talents I do not accept the star system. Collective creative effort is the root of our kind of art. That requires ensemble acting and whoever mars that ensemble is committing a crime not only against his comrades but also against the very art of which he is the servant.
Konstantin Stanislavisky (1863-1968, Russian Actor, Theatre director, Teacher)

40 I have seen that in any great undertaking it is not enough for a man to depend simply upon himself.
Lone Man

41 Share our similarities, celebrate our differences.
M. Scott Peck (American Psychiatrist, Author)

42 Men exist for the sake of one another.
Marcus Aurelius (121-80 AD, Roman Emperor, Philosopher)

43 There is nothing wrong in using people. The success never uses people except to their advantage.
Mark Caine

44 There is nothing that puts a man more in your debt than that he owes you nothing.
Mark Caine

45 You are beginning to see that any man to whom you can do favor is your friend, and that you can do a favor to almost anyone.
Mark Caine

46 We may have all come on different ships, but we're in the same boat now.
Martin Luther King Jr. (1929-1968, American Black Leader, Nobel Prize Winner, 1964)

47 Pleasure usually takes the form of me and now; joy is us and always.
Marvin J. Ashton

48 Either men will learn to live like brothers, or they will die like beasts.
Max Lerner (1902-, American Author, Columnist)

49 Take the trouble to stop and think of the other person's feelings, his viewpoints, his desires and needs. Think more of what the other fellow wants, and how he must feel.
Maxwell Maltz (American Plastic Surgeon, Author of "Psycho-Cybernetics")

50 If your imagination leads you to understand how quickly people grant your requests when those requests appeal to their self-interest, you can have practically anything you go after.
Napoleon Hill (1883-1970, American Speaker, Motivational Writer, "Think and Grow Rich")

51 In walking, the will and the muscles are so accustomed to working together and performing their task with so little expenditure of force that the intellect is left comparatively free.
Oliver Wendell Holmes (1809-1894, American Author, Wit, Poet)

52 For everyone of us that succeeds, it's because there's somebody there to show you the way out.
Oprah Winfrey (1954-, American TV Personality, Producer, Actress, Author)

53 No employer today is independent of those about him. He cannot succeed alone, no matter how great his ability or capital. Business today is more than ever a question of cooperation.
Orison Swett Marden (1850-1924, American Author, Founder of Success Magazine)

54 I love to hear a choir. I love the humanity to see the faces of real people devoting themselves to a piece of music. I like the teamwork. It makes me feel optimistic about the human race when I see them cooperating like that.
Paul Mccartney (1942-, British Pop Star, Composer, Songwriter, Member of "Beatles")

55 No man has come to true greatness who has not felt that his life belongs to his race, and that which God gives to him, He gives him for mankind.
Phillips Brooks (1835-1893, American Minister, Poet)

56 The world basically and fundamentally is constituted on the basis of harmony. Everything works in co-operation with something else.
Preston Bradley

57 I felt compelled to perform -- to do my engagements and not let people down. And they supported me, although they weren't aware how much it carried me through.
Princess of Wales Diana (1961-1997, Wife of Charles, Prince of Wales)

58 We all end up in a single bed sooner or later.
Proverb

59 Imagine what a harmonious world it could be if every single person, both young and old shared a little of what he is good at doing.
Quincy Jones

60 It is through cooperation, rather than conflict, that your greatest successes will be derived...
Ralph Charell (American Author)

61 If one of us could ascend to the heavenly realm and for a few hours accompany the divine on His daily rounds, he would see below millions of his fellow humans busily hurling themselves into the passions, sports, and action of those around him. But if our observer had the power and omniscience of the Lord, he would also feel and sense, pulsing through and vibrating from every one of us here below, a desperate and unending plea, "Notice me! I want to be known admired, and loved by the whole world!" And it is this, this glorious weakness, this dependence of ours on each other, that makes some of us usually heroes and fools at the same time.
Rev. Michael Burry (American Minister)

62 We cannot learn from one another until we stop shouting at one another -- until we speak quietly enough so that our words can be heard as well as our voices.
Richard M. Nixon (1913-1994, Thirty-seventh President of the USA)

63 No two men can be half an hour together but one shall acquire an evident superiority over the other.
Samuel Johnson (1709-1784, British Author)

64 The duty of helping one's self in the highest sense involves the helping of one's neighbors.
Samuel Smiles (1812-1904, Scottish Author)

65 He that does good to another does good also to himself.
Seneca (4 BC-65 AD, Spanish-born Roman Statesman, philosopher)

66 God does notice us, and He watches over us. But it is usually through another person that he meets our needs.
Spencer W. Kimball

67 We do not exist for ourselves...
Thomas Merton (1915-1968, American Religious Writer, Poet)

68 People who work together will win, whether it be against complex football defenses, or the problems of modern society.
Vince Lombardi (1913-1970, American Football Coach)

69 Tell everyone what you want to do and someone will want to help you do it.
W. Clement Stone (1902-, American Businessman, Author)

70 We are all of us, more or less, the slaves of opinion.
William Hazlitt (1778-1830, British Essayist)

71 Now join your hands, and with your hands your hearts.
William Shakespeare (1564-1616, British Poet, Playwright, Actor)

CORRECTION

1 We reform others unconsciously when we walk uprightly.
Anne Sophie Swetchine (1782-1857, Russian Author)

2 To free a person from error is to give, and not to take away.
Arthur Schopenhauer (1788-1860, German Philosopher)

3 Sarcasm spoils reproof.
E. Wigglesworh

4 By continually scolding someone, they in time become accustomed to it and despise your reproof.
French Proverb

5 When a child can be brought to tears, and not from fear of punishment, but from repentance he needs no chastisement. When the tears begin to flow from the grief of their conduct you can be sure there is an angel nestling in their heart.
Horace Mann (1796-1859, American Educator)

6 With children use force with men reason; such is the natural order of things. The wise man requires no law.
Jean Jacques Rousseau (1712-1778, Swiss Political Philosopher, Educationist, Essayist)

7 The heart of every man lies open to the shafts of correction if the archer can take proper aim.
Oliver Goldsmith (1728-1774, Anglo-Irish Author, Poet, Playwright)

8 Rebuke with soft words and hard arguments.
Proverb

9 Private reproof is the best grave for private faults.
Proverb

10 Rebuke should have a grain more of salt than of sugar.
Proverb

11 Some who will not speak against another, in the end does them harm.
Proverb

12 Think not those faithful who praise all thy words and actions, but those who kindly reprove thy faults.
Socrates (469-399 BC, Greek Philosopher of Athens)

13 Find fault when you must find fault in private, and if possible sometime after the offense, rather than at the time.
Sydney Smith (1771-1845, British Writer, Clergyman)

14 What you dislike in another take care to correct in yourself.
Thomas Sprat

CORRUPTION

1 The accomplice to the crime of corruption is frequently our own indifference.
Bess Myerson

2 Among a people generally corrupt, liberty cannot long exist.
Edmund Burke (1729-1797, British Political Writer, Statesman)

3 I have often noticed that a bribe has that effect -- it changes a relation. The man who offers a bribe gives away a little of his own importance; the bribe once accepted, he becomes the inferior, like a man who has paid for a woman.
Graham Greene (1904-1991, British Novelist)

4 I am against government by crony.
Harold L. Ickes

5 There is no odor so bad as that which arises from goodness tainted.
Henry David Thoreau (1817-1862, American Essayist, Poet, Naturalist)

6 Wherever you see a man who gives someone else's corruption, someone else's prejudice as a reason for not taking action himself, you see a cog in The Machine that governs us.
John Jay Chapman (1862-1933, American Author)

7 The sun shineth upon the dunghill, and is not corrupted.
John Lyly (1554-1606, British Writer)

8 Corruption is worse than prostitution. The latter might endanger the morals of an individual, the former invariably endangers the morals of the entire country.
Karl Kraus (1874-1936, Austrian Satirist)

9 The jingling of the guinea helps the hurt that Honor feels.
Lord Alfred Tennyson (1809-1892, British Poet)

10 Life is a corrupting process from the time a child learns to play his mother off against his father in the politics of when to go to bed; he who fears corruption fears life.
Saul Alinsky (1909-1972, American Radical Activist)

11 Corrupt, stupid grasping functionaries will make at least as big a muddle of socialism as stupid, selfish and acquisitive employers can make of capitalism.
Walter Lippmann (1889-1974, American Journalist)

12 When rich villains have need of poor ones, poor ones may make what price they will.
William Shakespeare (1564-1616, British Poet, Playwright, Actor)

13 When I want to buy up any politician I always find the anti-monopolists the most purchasable -- they don't come so high.
William Vanderbilt

COSMETICS

1 Isn't that the problem? That women have been swindled for centuries into substituting adornment for love, fashion (as it were) for passion? All the cosmetics names seemed obscenely obvious to me in their promises of sexual bliss. They were all firming or uplifting or invigorating. They made you tingle. Or glow. Or feel young. They were prepared with hormones or placentas or royal jelly. All the juice and joy missing in the lives of these women were to be supplied by the contents of jars and bottles. No wonder they would spend twenty dollars for an ounce of face makeup or thirty for a half-ounce of hormone cream. What price bliss? What price sexual ecstasy?
Erica Jong (1942-, American Author)

2 Women have face-lifts in a society in which women without them appear to vanish from sight.
Naomi Wolf (1962-, American Author)

3 God hath given you one face, and you make yourselves another.
William Shakespeare (1564-1616, British Poet, Playwright, Actor)

COSMOS

1 Nothing puzzles me more than time and space; and yet nothing troubles me less, as I never think about them.
Charles Lamb (1775-1834, British Essayist, Critic)

2 How have I been able to live so long outside Nature without identifying myself with it? Everything lives, moves, everything corresponds; the magnetic rays, emanating either from myself or from others, cross the limitless chain of created things unimpeded; it is a transparent network that covers the world, and its slender threads communicate themselves by degrees to the planets and stars. Captive now upon earth, I commune with the chorus of the stars who share in my joys and sorrows.
Gerard De Nerval (1808-1855, French Novelist, Poet)

3 The cosmos is about the smallest hole that a man can hide his head in.
Gilbert K. Chesterton (1874-1936, British Author)

4 To sum up: 1. The cosmos is a gigantic fly-wheel making 10, 000 revolutions a minute. 2. Man is a sick fly taking a dizzy ride on it. 3. Religion is the theory that the wheel was designed and set spinning to give him the ride.
H. L. Mencken (1880-1956, American Editor, Author, Critic, Humorist)

5 Philosophy offers the rather cold consolation that perhaps we and our planet do not actually exist; religion presents the contradictory and scarcely more comforting thought that we exist but that we cannot hope to get anywhere until we cease to exist. Alcohol, in attempting to resolve the contradiction, produces vivid patterns of Truth which vanish like snow in the morning sun and cannot be recalled; the revelations of poetry are as wonderful as a comet in the skies -- and as mysterious. Love, which was once believed to contain the Answer, we now know to be nothing more than an inherited behavior pattern.
James Thurber (1894-1961, American Humorist, Illustrator)

6 Why I came here, I know not; where I shall go it is useless to inquire -- in the midst of myriads of the living and the dead worlds, stars, systems, infinity, why should I be anxious about an atom?
Lord Byron (1788-1824, British Poet)

COST

1 Expenditures rise to meet income.
C. Northcote Parkinson (1909-1993, British Historian, Political Scientist)

2 The gods sell to us all the goods which they give us.
Epicharmus

3 The cost of a thing is the amount of what I will call life which is required to be exchanged for it, immediately or in the long run.
Henry David Thoreau (1817-1862, American Essayist, Poet, Naturalist)

4 What you get free costs too much.
Jean Anouilh (1910-1987, French Playwright)

5 A thing is worth what it can do for you, not what you choose to pay for it.
John Ruskin (1819-1900, British Critic, Social Theorist)

6 The gods sell all things at a fair price.
Proverb

7 Something you don't want is dear at any price.
Proverb

8 Why so large a cost, having so short a lease, does thou upon your fading mansion spend?
William Shakespeare (1564-1616, British Poet, Playwright, Actor)

COUNSEL

1 Those that won't be counseled can't be helped.
Benjamin Franklin (1706-1790, American Scientist, Publisher, Diplomat)

2 Better Counsel comes overnight.
Doris Lessing (1919-, British Novelist)

3 Good council has no price.
Giuseppe Mazzini (1805-1872, Italian Patriot, Writer)

4 Good counsel rejected returns to enrich the givers bosom.
Oliver Goldsmith (1728-1774, Anglo-Irish Author, Poet, Playwright)

5 The counsel you would have another keep, first keep yourself.
Proverb

6 Give neither counsel or salt till you are asked for it.
Proverb

7 The best counselors are the dead.
Proverb

8 All who consult on doubtful matters, should be void of hatred, friendship, anger, and pity.
Sallust (86-34 BC, Roman Historian)

COUNTRY

1 Today the nations of the world may be divided into two classes -- the nations in which the government fears the people, and the nations in which the people fear the government.
Amos R. E. Pinochet

2 The common good of a collective -- a race, a class, a state -- was the claim and justification of every tyranny ever established over men. Every major horror of history was committed in the name of an altruistic motive. Has any act of selfishness ever equaled the carnage perpetrated by disciples of altruism? Does the fault lie in men's hypocrisy or in the nature of the principle? The most dreadful butchers were the most sincere. The believed in the perfect society reached through the guillotine and the firing squad. Nobody questioned their right to murder since they were murdering for an altruistic purpose. It was accepted that man must be sacrificed for other men. Actors change, but the course of the tragedy remains the same. A humanitarian who starts with the declarations of love for mankind and ends with a sea of blood. It goes on and will go on so long as men believe that an action is good if it is unselfish. That permits the altruist to act and forces his victims to bear it. The leaders of collectivist movements ask nothing of themselves. But observe the results.
Ayn Rand (1905-1982, Russian Writer, Philosopher)

3 Colonies do not cease to be colonies because they are independent.
Benjamin Disraeli (1804-1881, British Statesman, Prime Minister)

4 To read the papers and to listen to the news... one would think the country is in terrible trouble. You do not get that impression when you travel the back roads and the small towns do care about their country and wish it well.
Charles Kuralt (American TV Commentator)

5 It began in mystery, and it will end in mystery, but what a savage and beautiful country lies in between.
Diane Ackerman (Born 1948, American Poet, Writer, Naturalist)

6 My country owes me nothing. It gave me, as it gives every boy and girl, a chance. It gave me schooling, independence of action, opportunity for service and honor. In no other land could a boy from a country village, without inheritance or influential friends, look forward with unbounded hope.
Herbert Clark Hoover (1874-1964, American - 31st American President)

7 In any country there must be people who have to die. They are the Sacrifices any nation has to make to achieve law and order.
Idiamin

8 The greatness of a nation can be judged by the way its animals are treated.
Mahatma Gandhi (1869-1948, Indian Political, Spiritual Leader)

9 Shall we then judge a country by the majority, or by the minority? By the minority, surely. 'Tis pedantry to estimate nations by the census, or by square miles of land, or other than by their importance to the mind of the time.
Ralph Waldo Emerson (1803-1882, American Poet, Essayist)

10 The hand that rocks the cradle rules the nation and its destiny.
South African Proverb

11 It may be true that you can't fool all the people all the time, but you can fool enough of them to rule a large country.
William J. Durant (1885-1981, American Historian, Essayist)

12 My country is the world; my countrymen are mankind.
William Lloyd Garrison (1805-1879, American Abolitionist)

COURAGE

1 Courage is poorly housed that dwells in numbers; the lion never counts the herd that are about him, nor weighs how many flocks he has to scatter.
Aaron Hill (1685-1750, British Dramatist)

2 As a rock on the seashore he standeth firm, and the dashing of the waves disturbeth him not. He raiseth his head like a tower on a hill, and the arrows of fortune drop at his feet. In the instant of danger, the courage of his heart here, and scorn to fly.
Akhenaton (1375 BC, Egyptian King, Monotheist)

3 To put it boldly, it is the attempt at a posterior reconstruction of existence by the process of conceptualization.
Albert Einstein (1879-1955, German-born American Physicist)

4 The ideas that have lighted my way and, time after time, have given me new courage to face life cheerfully have been Kindness, Beauty, and Truth.
Albert Einstein (1879-1955, German-born American Physicist)

5 True courage is not the brutal force of vulgar heroes. Rather the firm resolve of virtue and reason.
Alfred North Whitehead (1861-1947, British Mathematician, Philosopher)

6 Courage is not the towering oak that sees storms come and go; it is the fragile blossom that opens in the snow.
Alice Mackenzie Swaim

7 If men knew all that women think, they would be twenty times more daring.
Alphonse Karr

8 Courage is not the absence of fear, but rather the judgment that something else is more important than fear.
Ambrose Redmoon

9 Courage is the price that life exacts for granting peace. The soul that knows it not, knows no release from little things; knows not the livid loneliness of fear.
Amelia Earhart (1897-1937, American Aviator, Author)

10 It takes courage to push yourself to places that you have never been before... to test your limits... to break through barriers. And the day came when the risk it took to remain tight inside the bud was more painful than the risk it took to blossom.
Anais Nin (1914-1977, French-born American Novelist, Dancer)

11 Life shrinks or expands in proportion to one's courage.
Anais Nin (1914-1977, French-born American Novelist, Dancer)

12 As for courage and will -- we cannot measure how much of each lies within us, we can only trust there will be sufficient to carry through trials which may lie ahead.
Andre Norton

13 One man with courage makes a majority.
Andrew Jackson (1767-1845, Seventh President of the USA)

14 The brave man inattentive to his duty, is worth little more to his country than the coward who deserts in the hour of danger.
Andrew Jackson (1767-1845, Seventh President of the USA)

15 The real acid test of courage is to be just your honest self when everybody is trying to be like somebody else.
Andrew Jensen

16 If I were asked to give what I consider the single most useful bit of advice for all humanity it would be this: Expect trouble as an inevitable part of life and when it comes, hold you head high, look it squarely in the eye and say, "I will be bigger than you. You cannot defeat me."
Ann Landers (1918-, American Advice Columnist)

17 It takes as much courage to have tried and failed as it does to have tried and succeeded.
Anne Morrow Lindbergh (1906-, American Author)

18 The ideal man bears the accidents of life with dignity and grace, making the best of circumstances.
Aristotle (384-322 BC, Greek Philosopher)

19 It is easy to fly into a passion... anybody can do that, but to be angry with the right person to the right extent and at the right time and in the right way... that is not easy.
Aristotle (384-322 BC, Greek Philosopher)

20 The beauty of the soul shines out when a man bears with composure one heavy mischance after another, not because he does not feel them, but because he is a man of high and heroic temper.
Aristotle (384-322 BC, Greek Philosopher)

21 What you have outside you counts less than what you have inside you.
B. C. Forbes (1880-1954, American Publisher)

22 We need to find the courage to say NO to the things and people that are not serving us if we want to rediscover ourselves and live our lives with authenticity.
Barbara De Angelis (American Expert on Relationship & Love, Author)

23 The most important thing in life is not the triumph but the struggle. The essential thing is not to have conquered but to have fought well.
Baron Pierre De Coubertin

24 Be bold-and mighty forces will come to your aid.
Basil King

25 The bravest are the most tender; the loving are the daring.
Bayard Taylor (1825-1878, American Journalist, Traveler, Author)

26 There's no substitute for guts.
Bear Bryant (1913-1983, American Football Coach)

27 We must have the courage to allow a little disorder in our lives.
Ben Weininger

28 Courage is fire, and bullying is smoke.
Benjamin Disraeli (1804-1881, British Statesman, Prime Minister)

29 Have I not commanded you? Be strong and courageous. Do not tremble or be dismayed, for the Lord your God is with you wherever you go. [Joshua 1:9]
Bible (Sacred Scriptures of Christians and Judaism)

30 But you be strong and do not lose courage, for there is reward for your work. [2 Chronicles 15:7]
Bible (Sacred Scriptures of Christians and Judaism)

31 I can do all things through him who strengthens me. [Philippians 4:13]
Bible (Sacred Scriptures of Christians and Judaism)

32 Do not fear, for those who are with us, are more than those who are with them. [2 Kings 6:16]
Bible (Sacred Scriptures of Christians and Judaism)

33 With your help I can advance against a troop; with my God I can scale a wall. [Psalms 18:29]
Bible (Sacred Scriptures of Christians and Judaism)

34 Finally, be strong in the Lord, and in the strength of His might. [Ephesians 6:10]
Bible (Sacred Scriptures of Christians and Judaism)

35 Like a boxer in a title fight, you have to walk in that ring alone.
Billy Joel (1949-, American Musician, Piano Man, Singer, Songwriter)

36 Nothing splendid has ever been achieved except by those who dared believe that something inside them was superior to circumstance.
Bruce Barton (1886-1967, American Author, Advertising Executive)

37 Courage is not simply one of the virtues but the form of every virtue at the testing point, which means at the point of highest reality.
C. S. Lewis (1898-1963, British Academic, Writer, Christian Apologist)

38 No man in the world has more courage than the man who can stop after eating one peanut.
Channing Pollock (American Actor)

39 Is he alone who has courage on his right hand and faith on his left hand?
Charles A. Lindbergh (1902-1974, American Pilot, Made The First Flight From New York To Paris)

40 Physical courage, which engages all danger, will make a person brave in one way; and moral courage, which defies all opinion, will make a person brave in another.
Charles Caleb Colton (1780-1832, British Sportsman Writer)

41 There are times to cultivate and create, when you nurture your world and give birth to new ideas and ventures. There are times of flourishing and abundance, when life feels in full bloom, energized and expanding. And there are times of fruition, when things come to an end. They have reached their climax and must be harvested before they begin to fade. And finally of course, there are times that are cold, and cutting and empty, times when the spring of new beginnings seems like a distant dream. Those rhythms in life are natural events. They weave into one another as day follows night, bringing, not messages of hope and fear, but messages of how things are.
Chogyam Trungpa

42 Courage enlarges, cowardice diminishes resources. In desperate straits the fears of the timid aggravate the dangers that imperil the brave.
Christian Nevell Bovee (1820-1904, American Author, Lawyer)

43 Courage is the ladder on which all the other virtues mount.
Clare Boothe Luce (1903-1987, American Diplomat, Writer)

44 The bravest thing you can do when you are not brave is to profess courage and act accordingly.
Corra May Harris (1869-1935, American Author)

45 All my life I knew that there was all the money you could want out there. All you have to do is go after it.
Curtis Carlson (American Businessman, Founder of Carlson Companies, Inc.)

46 The scars you acquire while exercising courage will never make you feel inferior.
D.A. Battista

47 Life only demands from you the strength that you possess. Only one feat is possible; not to run away.
Dag Hammarskjold (1905-1961, Swedish Statesman, Secretary-general of U.N.)

48 You are merely not feeling equal to the tasks before you.
Dale Carnegie (1888-1955, American Author, Trainer)

49 Most of us have far more courage than we ever dreamed we possessed.
Dale Carnegie (1888-1955, American Author, Trainer)

50 Courage is a special kind of knowledge: the knowledge of how to fear what ought to be feared and how not to fear what ought no to be feared.
David Ben-Gurion (1886-1973, Polish-born Israeli Statesman, Prime Minister)

51 No more turning away from the weak and the weary. No more turning away from the coldness inside. Just a world that we all must share. It's not enough just to stand and stare. Is it only a dream that there'll be no more turning away.
David Gilmore

52 Courage and conviction are powerful weapons against an enemy who depends only on fists or guns. Animals know when you are afraid; a coward knows when you are not.
David Seabury (American Doctor, Author)

53 Bravery and stupidity go hand in hand.
David Summers

54 Courage means to keep working a relationship, to continue seeking solutions to difficult problems, and to stay focused during stressful periods.
Denis Waitley (1933-, American Author, Speaker, Trainer, Peak Performance Expert)

55 Be strong and of a good courage, fear not, nor be afraid... for the Lord thy God, he it is that doth go with thee; he will not fail thee, nor forsake thee.
Deuteronomy

56 Screw up your courage, you screwed up everything else.
Donald Smith

57 Act boldly and unseen forces will come to your aid.
Dorothea Brande (American Success Writer)

58 Courage is fear that has said its prayers.
Dorothy Bernard

59 Last, but by no means least, courage-moral courage, the courage of one's convictions, the courage to see things through. The world ;is in a constant conspiracy against the brave. It's the age- old struggle-the roar of the crowd on one side and the voice of your ;conscience on the other.
Douglas Macarthur (1880-1964, American Army General in WW II)

60 It takes courage to grow up and turn out to be who you really are.
E.E. (Edward. E.) Cummings (1894-1962, American Poet)

61 Courage is the art of being the only one who knows you're scared to death.
Earl Wilson (1907-, American newspaper columnist)

62 I thought ten thousand swords must have leaped from their scabbards to avenge even a look that threatened her with insult. But the age of chivalry is gone. That of sophists, economists and calculators has succeeded; and the glory of Europe is gone forever.
Edmund Burke (1729-1797, British Political Writer, Statesman)

63 Courage is doing what you're afraid to do. There can be no courage unless you're scared.
Edward Vernon Rickenbacker (1890-1973, American Aviator, World War I Ace)

64 At the bottom of not a little of the bravery that appears in the world, there lurks a miserable cowardice. Men will face powder and steel because they have not the courage to face public opinion.
Edwin Hubbel Chapin (1814-1880, American Author, Clergyman)

65 Stride forward with a firm, steady step knowing with a deep, certain inner knowing that you will reach every goal you set yourselves, that you will achieve every aim .
Eileen Caddy (American Spiritual Writer)

66 The world's male chivalry has perished out, but women are knights-errant to the last; and, if Cervantes had been greater still, he had made his Don a Donna.
Elizabeth Barrett Browning (1806-1861, British Poet)

67 I've been through it all, baby. I'm Mother Courage.
Elizabeth Taylor (1932-, British-born American Actress)

68 'Tis easy enough to be pleasant, When life flows along like a song; But the man worth while is the one who will smile when everything goes dead wrong.
Ella Wheeler Wilcox (1855-1919, American Poet, Journalist)

69 Better to die on one's feet than to live on one's knees.
Emiliano Zapata (1883 - 1919, Mexican revolutionary)

70 It takes a lot of courage to show your dreams to someone else.
Erma Bombeck (1927-, American Author, Humorist)

71 Courage is grace under pressure.
Ernest Hemingway (1898-1961, American Writer)

72 Courage is sometimes frail as hope is frail: a fragile shoot between two stones that grows brave toward the sun though warmth and brightness fail, striving and faith the only strength it knows.
Frances Rodman

73 We can never be certain of our courage until we have faced danger.
François de La Rochefoucauld (1613-1680, French classical writer)

74 True bravery is shown by performing without witness what one might be capable of doing before all the world.
François de La Rochefoucauld (1613-1680, French classical writer)

75 Perfect courage is to do without witnesses what one would be capable of doing with the world looking on.
François de La Rochefoucauld (1613-1680, French classical writer)

76 Discoveries are often made by not following instructions, by going off the main road, by trying the untried.
Frank Tyger

77 There is another side to chivalry. If it dispenses leniency, it may with equal justification invoke control.
Freda Adler (1870-1937, Pioneer Psychiatrist, Born in Vienna)

78 I never thought much of the courage of a lion tamer. Inside the cage he is at least safe from people.
George Bernard Shaw (1856-1950, Irish-born British Dramatist)

79 You take a number of small steps which you believe are right, thinking maybe tomorrow somebody will treat this as a dangerous provocation. And then you wait. If there is no reaction, you take another step: courage is only an accumulation of small steps.
George Konrad (1933-, Hungarian Writer, Politician)

80 For the man sound of body and serene of mind there is no such thing as bad weather; every day has its beauty, and storms which whip the blood do but make it pulse more vigorously.
George Robert Gissing (1857-1903, British Novelist, Critic, Essayist)

81 Have the courage of your desire.
George Robert Gissing (1857-1903, British Novelist, Critic, Essayist)

82 Courage is fear holding on a minute longer.
George S. Patton (1885-1945, American Army General during World War II)

83 It is the perpetual dread of fear, the fear of fear, that shapes the face of a brave man.
Georges Bernanos (1888-1948, French Novelist, Political Writer)

84 Courage is almost a contradiction in terms. It means a strong desire to live taking the form of a readiness to die.
Gilbert K. Chesterton (1874-1936, British Author)

85 Brave men are all vertebrates; they have their softness on the surface and their toughness in the middle.
Gilbert K. Chesterton (1874-1936, British Author)

86 Courage is getting away from death by continually coming within an inch of it.
Gilbert K. Chesterton (1874-1936, British Author)

87 The most glorious moments in your life are not the so-called days of success, but rather those days when out of dejection and despair you feel rise in you a challenge to life, and the promise of future accomplishments.
Gustave Flaubert (1821-1880, French Novelist)

88 Real courage is when you know you're licked before you begin, but you begin anyway and see it through no matter what.
Harper Lee (1926-, American Author)

89 The more thou dost advance, the more thy feet pitfalls will meet. The Path that leadeth on is lighted by one fire -- the light of daring burning in the heart. The more one dares, the more he shall obtain. The more he fears, the more that light shall pale
Helena Petrova Blavatsky (1831-1891, Russian Author, Translator, Theosophist)

90 Write on your doors the saying wise and old. "Be bold!" and everywhere -- "Be bold; Be not too bold!" Yet better the excess Than the defect; better the more than less sustaineth him and the steadiness of his mind beareth him out.
Henry Wadsworth Longfellow (1819-1892, American Poet)

91 And what he greatly thought, he nobly dared.
Homer (850 BC, Greek Epic Poet)

92 Live as brave men and face adversity with stout hearts.
Horace (65-8 BC, Italian Poet)

93 The human race afraid of nothing, rushes on through every crime.
Horace (65-8 BC, Italian Poet)

94 Courage is acting in spite of fear.
Howard W. Hunter

95 I am convinced that one of the biggest factors in success is the courage to undertake something.
James A. Worsham

96 Whether you be man or woman you will never do anything in this world without courage. It is the greatest quality of the mind next to honor.
James Allen (1864-1912, British-born American Essayist, Author of "As a Man Thinketh")

97 Conscience is the root of all true courage; if a man would be brave let him obey his conscience.
James Freeman Clarke (1810-1888, American Minister, Theologian)

98 He either fears his fate too much, Or his deserts are small, That dares not put it to the touch, To gain or lose it all.
James Graham (1612-1650, Scottish General)

99 More firm and sure the hand of courage strikes, when it obeys the watchful eye of caution.
James Thomson (1700-1748, Scottish Poet)

100 Courage is the capacity to conduct oneself with restraint in times of prosperity and with courage and tenacity when things do not go well.
James V. Forrestal (1892-1949, American Statesman)

101 Until the day of his death, no man can be sure of his courage.
Jean Anouilh (1910-1987, French Playwright)

102 It takes a certain courage and a certain greatness to be truly base.
Jean Anouilh (1910-1987, French Playwright)

103 It is amidst great perils we see brave hearts.
Jean François Regnard (1655-1709, French Comic Dramatist)

104 It is in great dangers that we see great courage.
Jean François Regnard (1655-1709, French Comic Dramatist)

105 Woman and men of retiring timidity are cowardly only in dangers which affect themselves, but the first to rescue when others are in danger.
Jean Paul Richter (1763-1825, German Novelist)

106 A timid person is frightened before a danger, a coward during the time, and a courageous person afterwards.
Jean Paul Richter (1763-1825, German Novelist)

107 Courage consists not in blindly overlooking danger, but in seeing it, and conquering it.
Jean Paul Richter (1763-1825, German Novelist)

108 True courage is a result of reasoning. A brave mind is always impregnable.
Jeremy Collier (1650-1726, British Clergyman, Conjuror)

109 The brave man is not he who feels no fear, For that were stupid and irrational; But he, whose noble soul its fears subdues, And bravely dares the danger nature shrinks from.
Joanna Baillie (1762-1851, British Romantic Writer)

110 The brave person thinks of themselves last of all.
Johann Friedrich Von Schiller (1759-1805, German Dramatist, Poet, Historian)

111 Courage and modesty are the most unequivocal of virtues, for they are of a kind that hypocrisy cannot imitate; they too have this quality in common, that they are expressed by the same color.
Johann Wolfgang Von Goethe (1749-1832, German Poet, Dramatist, Novelist)

112 Rest not. Life is sweeping by; go and dare before you die. Something mighty and sublime, leave behind to conquer time.
Johann Wolfgang Von Goethe (1749-1832, German Poet, Dramatist, Novelist)

113 Wealth lost is something lost, honor lost is something lost: Courage lost all is lost.
Johann Wolfgang Von Goethe (1749-1832, German Poet, Dramatist, Novelist)

114 For without belittling the courage with which men have died, we should not forget those acts of courage with which men have lived.
John F. Kennedy (1917-1963, Thirty-fifth President of the USA)

115 The courage of life is often a less dramatic spectacle than the courage of the final moment; but it is no less a magnificent mixture of triumph and tragedy.
John F. Kennedy (1917-1963, Thirty-fifth President of the USA)

116 The brave love mercy, and delight to save.
John Gay (1688-1732, British Playwright, Poet)

117 I decided once and for all that I was going to make it or die.
John Johnson (American Businessman, Founder of Johnson Publishing)

118 True courage is like a kite; a contrary wind raises it higher.
John Petit-Senn (1792-1870, French Poet)

119 Courage and perseverance have a magical talisman, before which difficulties disappear and obstacles vanish into air.
John Quincy Adams (1767-1848, Sixth President of the USA)

120 Though the practice of chivalry fell even more sadly short of its theoretic standard than practice generally falls below theory, it remains one of the most precious monuments of the moral history of our race, as a remarkable instance of a concerted and organized attempt by a most disorganized and distracted society, to raise up and carry into practice a moral ideal greatly in advance of its social condition and institutions; so much so as to have been completely frustrated in the main object, yet never entirely inefficacious, and which has left a most sensible, and for the most part a highly valuable impress on the ideas and feelings of all subsequent times.
John Stuart Mill (1806-1873, British Philosopher, Economist)

121 I am more important than my problems.
Jose Ferrer (1912-1992, Puerto Rican Actor, Director, Producer)

122 Courage that grows from constitution often forsakes a man when he has occasion for it; courage which arises from a sense of duty acts ;in a uniform manner.
Joseph Addison (1672-1719, British Essayist, Poet, Statesman)

123 Facing it, always facing it, that's the way to get through. Face it.
Joseph Conrad (1857-1924, Polish-born British Novelist)

124 It takes far less courage to kill yourself than it takes to make yourself wake up one more time. It is harder to stay where you are than to get out.
Judith Rossner (1935-, American Author)

125 Success is never final and failure is never fatal. It's courage that counts.
Jules Ellinger

126 With courage you will dare to take risks, have the strength to be compassionate and the wisdom to be humble. Courage is the foundation of integrity.
Keshavan Nair

127 To love someone deeply gives you strength. Being loved by someone deeply gives you courage.
Lao-Tzu (600 BC, Chinese Philosopher, Founder of Taoism, Author of the "Tao Te Ching")

128 Because of a great love, one is courageous.
Lao-Tzu (600 BC, Chinese Philosopher, Founder of Taoism, Author of the "Tao Te Ching")

129 Courage is the capacity to confirm what can be imagined.
Leo Rosten (1908-1997, Polish Born American Political Scientist)

130 A lot of people do not muster the courage to live their dreams because they are afraid to die.
Les Brown (1945-, American Speaker, Author, Trainer, Motivator Lecturer)

131 I advise you to say your dream is possible and then overcome all inconveniences, ignore all the hassles and take a running leap through the hoop, even if it is in flames.
Les Brown (1945-, American Speaker, Author, Trainer, Motivator Lecturer)

132 I'm very brave generally, he went on in a low voice: only today I happen to have a headache.
Lewis Carroll (1832-1898, British Writer, Mathematician)

133 Stand upright, speak thy thoughts, declare the truth thou hast, that all may share; Be bold, proclaim it everywhere: They only live who dare.
Lewis Morris (1835-1907, Welsh Lawyer, Writer of British Verse)

134 Most men have more courage than even they themselves think they have.
Lord Greville (1554-1628, British Poet)

135 True courage is cool and calm. The bravest of men have the least of a brutal, bullying insolence, and in the very time of danger are found the most serene and free.
Lord Shaftesbury (1671-1713, British Statesman)

136 I'd rather give my life than be afraid to give it.
Lyndon B. Johnson (1908-1973, Thirty-sixth President of the USA)

137 Courage follows action.
Mack R. Douglas

138 A man of courage is also full of faith.
Marcus T. Cicero (106-43 BC, Great Roman Orator, Politician)

139 It shows a brave and resolute spirit not to be agitated in exciting circumstances.
Marcus T. Cicero (106-43 BC, Great Roman Orator, Politician)

140 No one can be brave who considers pain to be the greatest evil in life, or can they be temperate who considers pleasure to be the highest good.
Marcus T. Cicero (106-43 BC, Great Roman Orator, Politician)

141 In love, as in war, a fortress that parleys is half taken.
Margaret Valois

142 It is curious that physical courage should be so common in the world, and moral courage so rare.
Mark Twain (1835-1910, American Humorist, Writer)

143 Courage is resistance to fear, mastery of fear -- not absence of fear.
Mark Twain (1835-1910, American Humorist, Writer)

144 It's not the size of the dog in the fight, it's the size of the fight in the dog.
Mark Twain (1835-1910, American Humorist, Writer)

145 Here I stand; I can do no other. God help me. Amen!
Martin Luther (1483-1546, German Leader of the Protestant Reformation)

146 We must build dikes of courage to hold back the flood of fear.
Martin Luther King Jr. (1929-1968, American Black Leader, Nobel Prize Winner, 1964)

147 Courage is the power to let go of the familiar.
Mary Byrant

148 If we have the courage and tenacity of our forebears, who stood firmly like a rock against the lash of slavery, we shall find a way to do for our day what they did for theirs.
Mary Mcleod Bethune (1875-1955, American Educator, Consultant for the US Government)

149 Stand up to crises. Don't let them throw you! Fight to stay calm... even surmount the crisis completely and turn it into an opportunity. Refuse to renounce your self-image. No matter what happens, you must keep your good opinion of yourself. No matter what happens, you must hold your past successes in your imagination, ready for showing in the motion picture screen of your mind. No matter what happens, no matter what you lose, no matter what failures you must endure, you must keep faith in yourself. Then you can stand up to crises, with calm and courage, refusing to buckle; then you will not fall through the floor. You will be able to support yourself.
Maxwell Maltz (American Plastic Surgeon, Author of "Psycho-Cybernetics")

150 Never ask the Gods for life set free from grief, but ask for courage that endureth long.
Menander of Athens (342-291 BC, Greek Dramatic Poet)

151 The strangest, most generous, and proudest of all virtues is true courage.
Michel Eyquem De Montaigne (1533-1592, French Philosopher, Essayist)

152 He who loses wealth loses much; he who loses a friend loses more; but he that loses his courage loses all.
Miguel De Cervantes (1547-1616, Spanish Novelist, Dramatist, Poet)

153 You have to be tough.
Mike Ditka (American Football Player, Coach of Chicago Bears)

154 In fighting and in everyday life you should be determined though calm. Meet the situation without tenseness yet not recklessly, your spirit settled yet unbiased. An elevated spirit is weak and a low spirit is weak. Do not let the enemy see your spirit.
Miyamoto Musashi (1584-1645, Japanese Samurai Warrior, Strategist)

155 It requires more courage to suffer than to die.
Napoleon Bonaparte (1769-1821, French General, Emperor)

156 Courage is like love; it must have hope to nourish it.
Napoleon Bonaparte (1769-1821, French General, Emperor)

157 All brave men love; for he only is brave who has affections to fight for, whether in the daily battle of life, or in physical contests.
Nathaniel Hawthorne (1804-1864, American Novelist, Short Story Writer)

158 Courage brother, do not stumble, though thy path be dark as night: There is a star to guide the humble, Trust in God, and do the right. Let the road be dark and dreary and its end far out of sight. Face it bravely, strong or weary. Trust in God, and do the right.
Norman Macleod

159 To do anything truly worth doing, I must not stand back shivering and thinking of the cold and danger, but jump in with gusto and scramble through as well as I can.
Og Mandino (1923-1996, American Motivational Author, Speaker)

160 Give us the fortitude to endure the things which cannot be changed, and the courage to change the things which should be changed, ;and the wisdom to know one from the other.
Oliver J. Hart

161 Bravery is the capacity to perform properly even when scared half to death.
Omar Bradley (1893-1983, American General)

162 Be larger than your task.
Orison Swett Marden (1850-1924, American Author, Founder of Success Magazine)

163 This is the test of your manhood: How much is there left in you after you have lost everything outside of yourself?
Orison Swett Marden (1850-1924, American Author, Founder of Success Magazine)

164 Fortune and love favor the brave.
Ovid (43 BC-18 AD, Roman Poet)

165 The burden which is well borne becomes light.
Ovid (43 BC-18 AD, Roman Poet)

166 Courage conquers all things: it even gives strength to the body.
Ovid (43 BC-18 AD, Roman Poet)

167 It takes vision and courage to create -- it takes faith and courage to prove.
Owen D. Young (1874-1962, American Lawyer, Businessman, Public Official)

168 Part of courage is simple consistency.
Peggy Noonan (1950-, American Author, Presidential Speechwriter)

169 Good courage in a bad affair is half of the evil overcome.
Plaut

170 Courage consists not in hazarding without fear; but being resolutely minded in a just cause.
Plutarch (46-120 AD, Greek Essayist, Biographer)

171 Courage stands halfway between cowardice and rashness, one of which is a lack, the other an excess of courage.
Plutarch (46-120 AD, Greek Essayist, Biographer)

172 Some have been thought brave because they didn't have the courage to run away.
Proverb

173 No one reaches a high position without daring.
Publilius Syrus (1st Century BC, Roman Writer)

174 The brave and bold persist even against fortune; the timid and cowardly rush to despair though fear alone.
Publius Cornelius Tacitus (55-117 AD, Roman Historian)

175 If we must fall, we should boldly meet the danger.
Publius Cornelius Tacitus (55-117 AD, Roman Historian)

176 The test of tolerance comes when we are in a majority; the test of courage comes when we are in a minority.
Ralph W. Stockman

177 Half a man's wisdom goes with his courage.
Ralph Waldo Emerson (1803-1882, American Poet, Essayist)

178 Courage charms us, because it indicates that a man loves an idea better than all things in the world, that he is thinking neither of his bed, nor his dinner, nor his money, but will venture all to put in act the invisible thought of his mind.
Ralph Waldo Emerson (1803-1882, American Poet, Essayist)

179 A great part of courage is the courage of having done the thing before.
Ralph Waldo Emerson (1803-1882, American Poet, Essayist)

180 When a resolute young fellow steps up to the great bully, the world, and takes him boldly by the beard, he is often surprised to find it comes off in his hand, and that it was only tied on to scare away the timid adventurers.
Ralph Waldo Emerson (1803-1882, American Poet, Essayist)

181 Whatever you do, you need courage. Whatever course you decide upon, there is always someone to tell you that you are wrong. There are always difficulties arising that tempt you to believe your critics are right. To map out a course of action and follow it to an end requires some of the same courage that a soldier needs. Peace has its victories, but it takes brave men and women to win them.
Ralph Waldo Emerson (1803-1882, American Poet, Essayist)

182 What a new face courage puts on everything!
Ralph Waldo Emerson (1803-1882, American Poet, Essayist)

183 Courage consists in equality to the problem before us.
Ralph Waldo Emerson (1803-1882, American Poet, Essayist)

184 You've got to jump off cliffs and build your wings on the way down.
Ray Bradbury (1920-, American Science Fiction Writer)

185 Keep courage. Whatever you do, do not feel sorry for yourself. You will win in a great age of opportunity.
Richard L. Evans

186 It is impossible to win the race unless you venture to run, impossible to win the victory unless you dare to battle.
Richard M. DeVos (1926-, American Businessman, Co-founder of Amway Corp.)

187 A man not perfect, but of heart so high, of such heroic rage, That even his hopes became a part of earth's eternal heritage.
Richard Watson Gilder (1844-1909, American Editor, Poet)

188 One who never turned his back but marched breast forward, never doubted clouds would break, Never dreamed, though right were worsted, wrong would triumph,
Robert Browning (1812-1889, British Poet)

189 Have the courage to live. Anyone can die.
Robert Cody

190 Moral courage is a more rare commodity than bravery in battle or great intelligence.
Robert F. Kennedy (1925-1968, American Attorney General, Senator)

191 The greatest test of courage on earth is to bear defeat without losing heart.
Robert Green Ingersoll (1833-1899, American Orator, Lawyer)

192 Courage without conscience is a wild beast.
Robert Green Ingersoll (1833-1899, American Orator, Lawyer)

193 It is a blessed thing that in every age some one has had the individuality enough and courage enough to stand by his own convictions.
Robert Green Ingersoll (1833-1899, American Orator, Lawyer)

194 It takes guts to get out of the ruts.
Robert H. Schuller (1926-, American Minister (Crystal Cathedral), Author, Social Leader)

195 Courage is spelled I-N-T-E-G-R-I-T-Y.
Robert H. Schuller (1926-, American Minister (Crystal Cathedral), Author, Social Leader)

196 The acorn becomes an oak by means of automatic growth; no commitment is necessary. The kitten similarly becomes a cat on the basis of instinct. Nature and being are identical in creatures like them. But a man or woman becomes fully human only by his or her choices and his or her commitment to them. People attain worth and dignity by the multitude of decisions they make from day by day. These decisions require courage.
Rollo May (American Psychologist)

197 Bravery has no place where it can avail nothing.
Samuel Johnson (1709-1784, British Author)

198 He that would be superior to external influences must first become superior to his own passions.
Samuel Johnson (1709-1784, British Author)

199 Courage is a quality so necessary for maintaining virtue, that it is always respected, even when it is associated with vice.
Samuel Johnson (1709-1784, British Author)

200 Let us train our minds to desire what the situation demands.
Seneca (4 BC-65 AD, Spanish-born Roman Statesman, philosopher)

201 It is not because things are difficult that we do not dare; it is because we do not dare that they are difficult.
Seneca (4 BC-65 AD, Spanish-born Roman Statesman, philosopher)

202 Fortune can take away riches, but not courage.
Seneca (4 BC-65 AD, Spanish-born Roman Statesman, philosopher)

203 Courage leads to heaven; fear leads to death.
Seneca (4 BC-65 AD, Spanish-born Roman Statesman, philosopher)

204 There is nothing in the world so much admired as a man who knows how to bear unhappiness with courage.
Seneca (4 BC-65 AD, Spanish-born Roman Statesman, philosopher)

205 The pressure of adversity does not affect the mind of the brave man. It is more powerful than external circumstances.
Seneca (4 BC-65 AD, Spanish-born Roman Statesman, philosopher)

206 All of the significant battles are waged within the self.
Sheldon Kopp (1929-, American Psychologist)

207 Pugnacity is a form of courage, but a very bad form.
Sinclair Lewis (1885-1951, First American Novelist to win the Nobel Prize for literature)

208 Be daring, be different, be impractical, be anything that will assert integrity of purpose and imaginative vision against the play-it-safers, the creatures of the commonplace, the slaves of the ordinary.
Sir Cecil Beaton (1904-1980, British-born American Photographer)

209 A true knight is fuller of bravery in the midst, than in the beginning of danger.
Sir Philip Sidney (1554-1586, British Author, Courtier)

210 The will to do, the soul to dare.
Sir Walter Scott (1771-1832, British Novelist, Poet)

211 It's better to be a lion for a day, than a sheep all your life.
Sister Elizabeth Kenny

212 It requires courage not to surrender oneself to the ingenious or compassionate counsels of despair that would induce a man to eliminate himself from the ranks of the living; but it does not follow from this that every huckster who is fattened and nourished in self-confidence has more courage than the man who yielded to despair.
Soren Kierkegaard (1813-1855, Danish Philosopher, Writer)

213 Grant what thou commandest and then command what thou wilt.
St. Augustine (354-430, Numidian-born Bishop of Hippo, Theologian)

214 To have courage for whatever comes in life -- everything lies in that.
St. Teresa of Avila (1515-1582, Spanish Saint, Mystic)

215 To boldly go where no one has gone before.
Star Trek Movie

216 I think of those who were truly great. The names of those who in their lives fought for life, Who wore at their hearts the fire's center.
Stephen Spender

217 A great deal of talent is lost in the world for want of courage.
Sydney Smith (1771-1845, British Writer, Clergyman)

218 Don't foul, don't flinch. Hit the line hard.
Theodore Roosevelt (1858-1919, Twenty-sixth President of the USA)

219 Be courageous. I have seen many depressions in business. Always America has emerged from these stronger and more prosperous. Be brave as your fathers before you. Have faith! Go forward!
Thomas A. Edison (1847-1931, American Inventor, Entrepreneur, Founder of GE)

220 The courage we desire and prize is not the courage to die decently, but to live manfully.
Thomas Carlyle (1795-1881, Scottish Philosopher, Author)

221 The more wit the less courage.
Thomas Fuller (1608-1661, British Clergyman, Author)

222 Follow the path of the unsafe, independent thinker. Expose your ideas to the danger of controversy. Speak your mind and fear less the label of "crackpot" than the stigma of conformity.
Thomas J. Watson (18?-1956, American Businessman, Founder of IBM)

223 Courage, not compromise, brings the smile of God's approval.
Thomas S. Monson

224 The brave don't live forever, but the cautious don't live at all. Here's to the brave!
Timothy Luce

225 Courage in danger is half the battle.
Titus Maccius Plautus (254-184 BC, Roman Comic Poet)

226 Nothing gives a fearful man more courage than another's fear.
Umberto Eco (1929-, Italian Novelist and critic)

227 Quit thinking that you must halt before the barrier of inner negativity. You need not. You can crash through whatever we see a negative state, that is where we can destroy it.
Vernon Howard (19?-1992, American Author, Speaker)

228 There are obstinate and unknown braves who defend themselves inch by inch in the shadows against the fatal invasion of want and turpitude. There are noble and mysterious triumphs which no eye sees. No renown rewards, and no flourish of trumpets salutes. Life, misfortune, isolation, abandonment, and poverty and battlefields which have their heroes.
Victor Hugo (1802-1885, French Poet, Dramatist, Novelist)

229 Have courage for the great sorrows of life, and patience for the small ones. When you have laboriously accomplished your daily tasks, go to sleep in peace. God is awake.
Victor Hugo (1802-1885, French Poet, Dramatist, Novelist)

230 What would life be if we had no courage to attempt anything?
Vincent Van Gogh (1853-1890, Dutch-born French Painter)

231 Often the test of courage is not to die but to live.
Vittorio Alfieri (1749-1803, Italian Poet, Playwright)

232 He who dies before many witnesses always does so with courage.
Voltaire (1694-1778, French Historian, Writer)

233 Have the courage to say no. Have the courage to face the truth. Do the right thing because it is right. These are the magic keys to living your life with integrity.
W. Clement Stone (1902-, American Businessman, Author)

234 No matter how carefully you plan your goals they will never be more than pipe dreams unless you pursue them with gusto.
W. Clement Stone (1902-, American Businessman, Author)

235 All our dreams can come true, if we have the courage to pursue them.
Walt Disney (1901-1966, American Artist, Film Producer)

236 We are very much what others think of us. The reception our observations meet with gives us courage to proceed, or damps our efforts.
William Hazlitt (1778-1830, British Essayist)

237 Gallantry to women -- the sure road to their favor -- is nothing but the appearance of extreme devotion to all their wants and wishes, a delight in their satisfaction, and a confidence in yourself as being able to contribute toward it.
William Hazlitt (1778-1830, British Essayist)

238 You cannot fly like an eagle with wings of a wren.
William Henry Hudson

239 Much of what we call evil is due entirely to the way men take the phenomenon. It can so often be converted into a bracing and tonic good by a simple change of the sufferer's inner attitude from one of fear to one of fight; its string can so often depart and turn into a relish when, after vainly seeking to shun it, we agree to face about and bear it...
William James (1842-1910, American Psychologist, Professor, Author)

240 But screw your courage to the sticking-place and we'll not fail.
William Shakespeare (1564-1616, British Poet, Playwright, Actor)

241 I dare to do all that may become a man: who dares do more is none.
William Shakespeare (1564-1616, British Poet, Playwright, Actor)

242 That's a valiant flea that dares eat his breakfast on the lip of a lion.
William Shakespeare (1564-1616, British Poet, Playwright, Actor)

243 Courage -- a perfect sensibility of the measure of danger, and a mental willingness to endure it.
William T. Sherman (1820-1891, American Army Commander)

244 I would define true courage to be a perfect sensibility of the measure of danger, and a mental willingness to endure it.
William T. Sherman (1820-1891, American Army Commander)

245 Anybody with a little guts and the desire to apply himself can make it, he can make anything he wants to make of himself.
Willie Shoemaker (1931-, American Racing Jockey and Trainer)

246 This is no time for ease and comfort. It is the time to dare and endure.
Winston Churchill (1874-1965, British Statesman, Prime Minister)

247 I have nothing to offer but blood, toil, tears and sweat.
Winston Churchill (1874-1965, British Statesman, Prime Minister)

248 Courage is going from failure to failure without losing enthusiasm.
Winston Churchill (1874-1965, British Statesman, Prime Minister)

249 Here is the answer which I will give to President Roosevelt. Give us the tools, and we will finish the job.
Winston Churchill (1874-1965, British Statesman, Prime Minister)

250 Courage is the first of human qualities because it is the quality which guarantees all others.
Winston Churchill (1874-1965, British Statesman, Prime Minister)

251 Courage is rightly considered the foremost of the virtues, for upon it, all others depend.
Winston Churchill (1874-1965, British Statesman, Prime Minister)

COURT

1 Court... a place where they dispense with justice.
Arthur Train

2 The place of justice is a hallowed place.
Francis Bacon (1561-1626, British Philosopher, Essayist, Statesman)

3 Dictum is what a court thinks but is afraid to decide.
Henry Waldorf Francis

4 A court is a place where what was confused before becomes more unsettled than ever.
Henry Waldorf Francis

COURTESY

1 Politeness is the art of choosing among one's real thoughts.
Abel Stevens

2 True politeness consists in being easy one's self, and in making every one about one as easy as one can.
Alexander Pope (1688-1744, British Poet, Critic, Translator)

3 It is better to have too much courtesy than too little, provided you are not equally courteous to all, for that would be injustice.
Baltasar Gracian (1601-1658, Spanish Philosopher, Writer)

4 The small courtesies sweeten life; the greater ennoble it.
Christian Nevell Bovee (1820-1904, American Author, Lawyer)

5 There can be no defense like elaborate courtesy.
E. V. Lucas (1868-1938, British Journalist, Essayist)

6 Politeness is the slow poison of collaboration.
Edwin H. Land (1909-1991, American Scientist, Inventor of the Polaroid Camera & Co.)

7 Nothing is ever lost by courtesy. It is the cheapest of the pleasures; costs nothing and conveys much. It pleases him who gives and ;him who receives, and thus, like mercy, it is twice blessed.
Erastus Wiman

8 His courtesy was somewhat extravagant. He would write and thank people who wrote to thank him for wedding presents and when he encountered anyone as punctilious as himself the correspondence ended only with death.
Evelyn Waugh (1903-1966, British Novelist)

9 If a man be gracious and courteous to strangers, it shows he is a citizen of the world.
Francis Bacon (1561-1626, British Philosopher, Essayist, Statesman)

10 Courtesies of a small and trivial character are the ones which strike deepest in the grateful and appreciating heart.
Henry Clay (1777-1852, American Statesman, Orator)

11 Intelligence and courtesy not always are combined; Often in a wooden house a golden room we find.
Henry Wadsworth Longfellow (1819-1892, American Poet)

12 Men, like bullets, go farthest when they are smoothest.
Jean Paul Richter (1763-1825, German Novelist)

13 There is a courtesy of the heart; it is allied to love. From its springs the purest courtesy in the outward behavior.
Johann Wolfgang Von Goethe (1749-1832, German Poet, Dramatist, Novelist)

14 To speak kindly does not hurt the tongue.
Proverb

15 Courtesy Life be not so short but that there is always time for courtesy.
Ralph Waldo Emerson (1803-1882, American Poet, Essayist)

16 We must be as courteous to a man as we are to a picture, which we are willing to give the advantage of a good light.
Ralph Waldo Emerson (1803-1882, American Poet, Essayist)

17 Life is short, but there is always time for courtesy.
Ralph Waldo Emerson (1803-1882, American Poet, Essayist)

18 It is wise to apply the oil of refined politeness to the mechanism of friendship.
Sidonie Gabrielle Colette (1873-1954, French Author)

19 He who sows courtesy reaps friendship, and he who plants kindness gathers love.
St. Basil (329-379, Bishop of Caesarea)

20 All doors open to courtesy.
Thomas Fuller (1608-1661, British Clergyman, Author)

21 Really big people are, above everything else, courteous, considerate and generous -- not just to some people in some circumstances -- but to everyone all the time.
Thomas J. Watson (18?-1956, American Businessman, Founder of IBM)

22 To succeed in the world it is not enough to be stupid, you must also be well-mannered.
Voltaire (1694-1778, French Historian, Writer)

COWARD AND COWARDICE

1 A coward is one who in a perilous emergency thinks with his legs.
Ambrose Bierce (1842-1914, American Author, Editor, Journalist, "The Devil's Dictionary")

2 There is a level of cowardice lower than that of the conformist: the fashionable non-conformist.
Ayn Rand (1905-1982, Russian Writer, Philosopher)

3 Great occasions do not make heroes or cowards; they simply unveil them to the eyes of men.
Bishop Westcott

4 For cowards the road of desertion should be left open; they will carry over to the enemy nothing, but their fears.
Christian Nevell Bovee (1820-1904, American Author, Lawyer)

5 To know what is right and not do it is the worst cowardice.
Confucius (551-479 BC, Chinese Ethical Teacher, Philosopher)

6 It is better to be the widow of a hero than the wife of a coward.
Dolores Ibarruri (1895-1989, Spanish Politician, Orator)

7 All men would be cowards if they could.
Earl Rochester (1647-1680, British Courtier, Poet)

8 That man is not truly brave who is afraid either to seem or to be, when it suits him, a coward.
Edgar Allan Poe (1809-1845, American Poet, Critic, short-story Writer)

9 Covetousness like jealousy, when it has taken root, never leaves a person, but with their life. Cowardice is the dread of what will happen.
Epictetus (50-120, Stoic Philosopher)

10 When cowardice is made respectable, its followers are without number both from among the weak and the strong; it easily becomes a fashion.
Eric Hoffer (1902-1983, American Author, Philosopher)

11 Cowardice, as distinguished from panic, is almost always simply a lack of ability to suspend the functioning of the imagination.
Ernest Hemingway (1898-1961, American Writer)

12 Dishonesty, cowardice and duplicity are never impulsive.
George A. Knight

13 Man gives every reason for his conduct save one, every excuse for his crimes save one, every plea for his safety save one; and that one is his cowardice.
George Bernard Shaw (1856-1950, Irish-born British Dramatist)

14 When the adulation of life is gone, the coward sneaks to his death, but the brave live on.
George Sewell

15 It is better to be a coward for a minute than dead for the rest of your life.
Irish Proverb

16 The greatest braggarts are usually the biggest cowards.
Jean Jacques Rousseau (1712-1778, Swiss Political Philosopher, Educationist, Essayist)

17 How many feasible projects have miscarried through despondency, and been strangled in their birth by a cowardly imagination.
Jeremy Collier (1650-1726, British Clergyman, Conjuror)

18 The coward threatens when he is safe.
Johann Wolfgang Von Goethe (1749-1832, German Poet, Dramatist, Novelist)

19 Cowards are cruel, but the brave love mercy and delight to save.
John Gay (1688-1732, British Playwright, Poet)

20 It is the coward who fawns upon those above him. It is the coward who is insolent whenever he dares be so.
Junius (1769-1771, Anonymous British Letter Writer)

21 Fear has its use but cowardice has none.
Mahatma Gandhi (1869-1948, Indian Political, Spiritual Leader)

22 Cowards can never be moral.
Mahatma Gandhi (1869-1948, Indian Political, Spiritual Leader)

23 There are several good protections against temptation, but the surest is cowardice.
Mark Twain (1835-1910, American Humorist, Writer)

24 The human race is a race of cowards; and I am not only marching in that procession, but carrying a banner.
Mark Twain (1835-1910, American Humorist, Writer)

25 A coward is a hero with a wife, kids, and a mortgage.
Marvin Kitman

26 Faint heart never won fair lady.
Miguel De Cervantes (1547-1616, Spanish Novelist, Dramatist, Poet)

27 A light supper, a good night's sleep, and a fine morning have sometimes made a hero of the same man who, by an indigestion, a restless night, and a rainy morning would have proved a coward.
Philip Dormer Stanhope

28 Cowards falter, but danger is often overcome by those who nobly dare.
Queen's Mother Elizabeth (1900-, Mother of Current Queen of Great Britain)

29 A cowardly cur barks more fiercely than it bites.
Quintus Curtius Rufus (100 AD, Roman Historian)

30 My valor is certainly going, it is sneaking off! I feel it oozing out as it were, at the palms of my hands!
Richard Brinsley Sheridan (1751-1816, Anglo-Irish Dramatist)

31 It is better to be killed than frightened to death.
Robert S. Surtees

32 I hate a fellow whom pride, or cowardice, or laziness drives into a corner, and who does nothing when he is there but sit and growl; let him come out as I do, and bark.
Samuel Johnson (1709-1784, British Author)

33 I'm a hero with coward's legs.
Spike Milligan (1918-, British Comedian, Humorous Writer)

34 A coward is much more exposed to quarrels than a man of spirit.
Thomas Jefferson (1743-1826, Third President of the USA)

35 One of the chief misfortunes of honest people is that they are cowardly.
Voltaire (1694-1778, French Historian, Writer)

36 Cowards die many times before their deaths; The valiant never taste of death but once.
William Shakespeare (1564-1616, British Poet, Playwright, Actor)

37 Cowards die a thousand deaths. The valiant taste of death but once.
William Shakespeare (1564-1616, British Poet, Playwright, Actor)

CRAFTS

1 No man who is occupied in doing a very difficult thing, and doing it very well, ever loses his self-respect.
George Bernard Shaw (1856-1950, Irish-born British Dramatist)

2 The Artist is he who detects and applies the law from observation of the works of Genius, whether of man or Nature. The Artisan is he who merely applies the rules which others have detected.
Henry David Thoreau (1817-1862, American Essayist, Poet, Naturalist)

3 History repeats itself, but the special call of an art which has passed away is never reproduced. It is as utterly gone out of the world as the song of a destroyed wild bird.
Joseph Conrad (1857-1924, Polish-born British Novelist)

4 It is the privilege of any human work which is well done to invest the doer with a certain haughtiness. He can well afford not to conciliate, whose faithful work will answer for him.
Ralph Waldo Emerson (1803-1882, American Poet, Essayist)

5 A man cannot make a pair of shoes rightly unless he do it in a devout manner.
Thomas Carlyle (1795-1881, Scottish Philosopher, Author)

6 Let a human being throw the energies of his soul into the making of something, and the instinct of workmanship will take care of his honesty.
Walter Lippmann (1889-1974, American Journalist)

7 The irregular and intimate quality of things made entirely by the human hand.
Willa Cather (1876-1947, American Author)

CREATION

1 If the Lord Almighty had consulted me before embarking upon Creation, I should have recommended something simpler.
Alfonso X (1221-1284, Spanish King of León and Castile)

2 Imagine spending four billion years stocking the oceans with seafood, filling the ground with fossil fuels, and drilling the bees in honey production -- only to produce a race of bed-wetters!
Barbara Ehrenreich (1941-, American Author, Columnist)

3 God made man merely to hear some praise of what he'd done on those Five Days.
Christopher Morley (1890-1957, American Novelist, Journalist, Poet)

4 When god decided to invent everything he took one breath bigger than a circustent and everything began
E.E. (Edward. E.) Cummings (1894-1962, American Poet)

5 God's first creature, which was light.
Francis Bacon (1561-1626, British Philosopher, Essayist, Statesman)

6 Sometimes you gotta create what you want to be a part of.
Geri Weitzman

7 In the beginning was the Word. Man acts it out. He is the act, not the actor.
Henry Miller (1891-1980, American Author)

8 Man was created a little lower than the angels and has bin getting a little lower ever since.
Henry Wheeler Shaw (1818-1885, American Humorist)

9 What can be more foolish than to think that all this rare fabric of heaven and earth could come by chance, when all the skill of science is not able to make an oyster.
Jeremy Taylor (1613-1667, British Churchman, Writer)

10. We have seen when the earth had to be prepared for the habitation of man, a veil, as it were, of intermediate being was spread between him and its darkness, in which were joined in a subdued measure, the stability and insensibility of the earth, and the passion and perishing of mankind.
John Ruskin (1819-1900, British Critic, Social Theorist)

11. Either God is in the whole of nature, with no gaps, or He's not there at all.
L. A. Coulson

12. Why was the human race created? Or at least why wasn't something creditable created in place of it? God had His opportunity. He could have made a reputation. But no, He must commit this grotesque folly -- a lark which must have cost Him a regret or two when He came to think it over and observe effects.
Mark Twain (1835-1910, American Humorist, Writer)

13. Every man is as heaven made him, and sometimes a great deal worse.
Miguel De Cervantes (1547-1616, Spanish Novelist, Dramatist, Poet)

14. Have We not made the earth as a cradle and the mountains as pegs? And We created you in pairs, and We appointed your sleep for a rest; and We appointed night for a garment, and We appointed day for a livelihood. And We have built above you seven strong ones, and We appointed a blazing lamp and have sent down out of the rain-clouds water cascading that We may bring forth thereby grain and plants, and gardens luxuriant.
Qur'an (Holy Book)

15. There are innumerable questions to which the inquisitive mind can in this state receive no answer: Why do you and I exist? Why was this world created? Since it was to be created, why was it not created sooner?
Samuel Johnson (1709-1784, British Author)

16. It's a good thing that when God created the rainbow he didn't consult a decorator or he would still be picking colors.
Samuel Levenson

17. This most beautiful system [The Universe] could only proceed from the dominion of an intelligent and powerful Being.
Sir Isaac Newton (1642-1727, British Scientist, Mathematician)

18. Thou didst create the night, but I made the lamp. Thou didst create clay, but I made the cup. Thou didst create the deserts, mountains and forests, I produced the orchards, gardens and groves. It is I who made the glass out of stone, and it is I who turn a poison into an antidote.
Sir Muhammad Iqbal

19. I asked the whole frame of the world about my God; and he answered," I am not He, but He made me."
St. Augustine (354-430, Numidian-born Bishop of Hippo, Theologian)

20. Search not a wound too deep lest thou make a new one.
Thomas Fuller (1608-1661, British Clergyman, Author)

21. People often say that this or that person has not yet found himself. But the self is not something that one finds. It is something one creates.
Thomas Szasz (1920-, American Psychiatrist)

22. None merits the name of Creator but God and the poet.
Torquato Tasso (1544-1595, Italian Poet)

23. The world embarrasses me, and I cannot dream that this watch exists and has no watchmaker.
Voltaire (1694-1778, French Historian, Writer)

CREATIVITY

1. The creative urge is the demon that will not accept anything second rate.
Agnes De Mille (1905-1993, American Dancer, Choreographer, Writer)

2. The legs are the wheels of creativity.
Albert Einstein (1879-1955, German-born American Physicist)

3. The secret to creativity is knowing how to hide your sources.
Albert Einstein (1879-1955, German-born American Physicist)

4. Had I been present at the creation of the world I would have proposed some improvements.
Alfonso X (1221-1284, Spanish King of Le≤n and Castile)

5. Creative minds have always been known to survive any kind of bad training.
Anna Freud

6. No one has ever written, painted, sculpted, modeled, built, or invented except literally to get out of hell.
Antonin Artaud (1896-1948, French Theater Producer, Actor, Theorist)

7. Our current obsession with creativity is the result of our continued striving for immortality in an era when most people no longer believe in an after-life.
Arianna Stassinopoulos (1950-, Greek Author)

8. Much ingenuity with a little money is vastly more profitable and amusing than much money without ingenuity.
Arnold Bennett (1867-1931, British Novelist)

9. True creativity often starts where language ends.
Arthur Koestler (1905-1983, Hungarian Born British Writer)

10. Creative activity could be described as a type of learning process where teacher and pupil are located in the same individual.
Arthur Koestler (1905-1983, Hungarian Born British Writer)

11. Whatever creativity is, it is in part a solution to a problem.
Brian Aldiss (1925-, British Science Fiction Writer)

12 Man, the living creature, the creating individual, is always more important than any established style or system.
Bruce Lee (1940-1973, Chinese-American Actor, Director, Author, Martial Artist)

13 The creative person wants to be a know -it -all. He wants to know about all kinds of things: ancient history, nineteenth -century mathematics, current manufacturing techniques, flower arranging, and hog futures. Because he never knows when these ideas might come together to form a new idea. It may happen six minutes later or six months, or six years down the road. But he has faith that it will happen.
Carl Ally

14 Creative powers can just as easily turn out to be destructive. It rests solely with the moral personality whether they apply themselves to good things or to bad. And if this is lacking, no teacher can supply it or take its place.
Carl Jung (1875-1961, Swiss Psychiatrist)

15 One of the greatest necessities in America is to discover creative solitude.
Carl Sandburg (1878-1967, American Poet)

16 Creation is a drug I can't do without.
Cecil B. De Mille (1881-1959, American Film Producer and Director)

17 The good ideas are all hammered out in agony by individuals, not spewed out by groups.
Charles Browder

18 The whole difference between construction and creation is this; that a thing constructed can only be loved after it is constructed; but a thing created is loved before it exists.
Charles Dickens (1812-1870, British Novelist)

19 The person who can combine frames of reference and draw connections between ostensibly unrelated points of view is likely to be the one who makes the creative breakthrough.
Denise Shekerjian

20 It's like driving a car at night. You never see further than your headlights, but you can make the whole trip that way.
E. L. Doctorow (1931-, American Novelist)

21 The thing that makes a creative person is to be creative and that is all there is to it.
Edward Albee (1928-, American Playwright, Dramatist)

22 Creativity involves breaking out of established patterns in order to look at things in a different way.
Edward De Bono (Born 1933, Maltan-Born American Psychologist and Writer)

23 Creativity is the sudden cessation of stupidity.
Edwin H. Land (1909-1991, American Scientist, Inventor of the Polaroid Camera & Co.)

24 The essential part of creativity is not being afraid to fail.
Edwin H. Land (1909-1991, American Scientist, Inventor of the Polaroid Camera & Co.)

25 Creativity requires the courage to let go of certainties.
Erich Fromm (1900-1980, American Psychologist)

26 Most people die before they are fully born. Creativeness means to be born before one dies.
Erich Fromm (1900-1980, American Psychologist)

27 From things that have happened and from things as they exist and from all things that you know and all those you cannot know, you make something through your invention that is not a representation but a whole new thing truer than anything true and alive, and you make it alive, and if you make it well enough, you give it immortality. That is why you write and for no other reason that you know of. But what about all the reasons that no one knows?
Ernest Hemingway (1898-1961, American Writer)

28 Americans worship creativity the way they worship physical beauty -- as a way of enjoying elitism without guilt: God did it.
Florence King (1936-, American Author, Critic)

29 A hunch is creativity trying to tell you something.
Frank Capra (1897-1991, Italian Film Director)

30 Because of their courage, their lack of fear, they (creative people) are willing to make silly mistakes. The truly creative person is one who can think crazy; such a person knows full well that many of his great ideas will prove to be worthless. The creative person is flexible -- he is able to change as the situation changes, to break habits, to face indecision and changes in conditions without undue stress. He is not threatened by the unexpected as rigid, inflexible people are.
Frank Goble

31 The desire to create continually is vulgar and betrays jealousy, envy, ambition. If one is something one really does not need to make anything --and one nonetheless does very much. There exists above the "productive" man a yet higher species.
Friedrich Nietzsche (1844-1900, German Philosopher)

32 Genius is initiative on fire.
George Holbrook Jackson (1874-1948, British Essayist, Literary Historian,)

33 Creativity, as has been said, consists largely of rearranging what we know in order to find out what we do not know. Hence, to think creatively, we must be able to look afresh at what we normally take for granted.
George Kneller

34 Creativity can solve almost any problem. The creative act, the defeat of habit by originality, overcomes everything.
George Lois

35 The human mind cannot create anything. It produces nothing until after having been fertilized by experience and meditation; its acquisitions are the gems of its production.
Georges-Louis Leclerc Buffon (1707-1788, French Naturalist)

36 A truly creative person rids him or herself of all self-imposed limitations.
Gerald G. Jampolsky (American Psychiatrist, Lecturer, Author)

37 We try not to have ideas, preferring accidents. To create, you must empty yourself of every artistic thought.
Gilbert George (1943-, Italian-born British Artist)

38 Whoever undertakes to create soon finds himself engaged in creating himself. Self- transformation and the transformation of others have constituted the radical interest of our century, whether in painting, psychiatry, or political action.
Harold Rosenberg (1906-1978, American Art Critic, Author)

39 There is the happiness which comes from creative effort. The joy of dreaming, creating, building, whether in painting a picture, writing an epic, singing a song, composing a symphony, devising new invention, creating a vast industry.
Henry Miller (1891-1980, American Author)

40 All the lies and evasions by which man has nourished himself -- civilization, in a word is the fruits of the creative artist. It is the creative nature of man which has refused to let him lapse back into that unconscious unity with life which characterizes the animal world from which he made his escape.
Henry Miller (1891-1980, American Author)

41 Creativity comes from awakening and directing men's higher natures, which originate in the primal depths of the universe and are appointed by Heaven.
I Ching (12th Century BC, Chinese Book of Changes)

42 Our senses are indeed our doors and windows on this world, in a very real sense the key to the unlocking of meaning and the wellspring of creativity.
Jean Houston

43 To create something you must be something.
Johann Wolfgang Von Goethe (1749-1832, German Poet, Dramatist, Novelist)

44 A creation of importance can only be produced when its author isolates himself, it is a child of solitude.
Johann Wolfgang Von Goethe (1749-1832, German Poet, Dramatist, Novelist)

45 The power in which we must have faith if we would be well, is the creative and curative power which exists in every living thing.
John Kellogg

46 It is wise to learn; it is God-like to create.
John Saxe

47 We live at a time when man believes himself fabulously capable of creation, but he does not know what to create.
Jose Ortega Y Gasset (1883-1955, Spanish Essayist, Philosopher)

48 It is better to create than to learn! Creating is the essence of life.
Julius Caesar (101-44 BC, Roman Emperor)

49 Is not the tremendous strength in men of the impulse to creative work in every field precisely due to their feeling of playing a relatively small part in the creation of living beings, which constantly impels them to an overcompensation in achievement?
Karen Horney (1885-1952, American Psychiatrist)

50 Creativity is essentially a lonely art. An even lonelier struggle. To some a blessing. To others a curse. It is in reality the ability to reach inside yourself and drag forth from your very soul an idea.
Lou Dorfsman

51 An original is a creation motivated by desire. Any reproduction of an originals motivated be necessity. It is marvelous that we are the only species that creates gratuitous forms. To create is divine, to reproduce is human.
Man Ray (1890-1976, American Photographer)

52 All in all, the creative act is not performed by the artist alone; the spectator brings the work in contact with the external world by deciphering and interpreting its inner qualifications and thus adds his contribution to the creative act. This becomes even more obvious when posterity gives its final verdict and sometimes rehabilitates forgotten artists.
Marcel Duchamp (1887-1968, French Artist)

53 I understood that all the material of a literary work was in my past life, I understood that I had acquired it in the midst of frivolous amusements, in idleness, in tenderness and in pain, stored up by me without my divining its destination or even its survival, as the seed has in reserve all the ingredients which will nourish the plant.
Marcel Proust (1871-1922, French Novelist)

54 The things we fear most in organizations -- fluctuations, disturbances, imbalances -- are the primary sources of creativity.
Margaret J. Wheatley

55 When all is said and done, monotony may after all be the best condition for creation.
Margaret Sackville (1881-1963, British Poet)

56 Man was made at the end of the week's work when God was tired.
Mark Twain (1835-1910, American Humorist, Writer)

57 It seems safe to say that significant discovery, really creative thinking, does not occur with regard to problems about which the thinker is lukewarm.
Mary Henle

58 Creativity is inventing, experimenting, growing, taking risks, breaking rules, making mistakes, and having fun.
Mary Lou Cook

59 The creative person, the person who moves from an irrational source of power, has to face the fact that this power antagonizes. Under all the superficial praise of the "creative" is the desire to kill. It is the old war between the mystic and the nonmystic, a war to the death.
May Sarton (1912-, American Poet, Novelist)

60 There is in us a lyric germ or nucleus which deserves respect; it bids a man to ponder or create; and in this dim corner of himself he can take refuge and find consolations which the society of his fellow creatures does not provide.
Norman Douglas (1868-1952, British Author)

61 Creativity represents a miraculous coming together of the uninhibited energy of the child with its apparent opposite and enemy-the sense of order imposed on the disciplined adult intelligence.
Norman Podhoretz

62 I do not seek, I find.
Pablo Picasso (1881-1973, Spanish Artist)

63 The chief enemy of creativity is good taste.
Pablo Picasso (1881-1973, Spanish Artist)

64 Everything vanishes around me, and works are born as if out of the void. Ripe, graphic fruits fall off. My hand has become the obedient instrument of a remote will.
Paul Klee (1879-1940, Swiss Artist)

65 Serious people have few ideas. People with ideas are never serious.
Paul Valery (1871-1945, French Poet, Essayist)

66 Out of nothing can come, and nothing can become nothing.
Persius (34-62 AD, Satirical Poet)

67 Thoughts give birth to a creative force that is neither elemental nor sidereal. Thoughts create a new heaven, a new firmament, a new source of energy, from which new arts flow. When a man undertakes to create something, he establishes a new heaven.
Philipus A. Paracelsus (German Physician and Chemist)

68 Ideally a painter (and, generally, an artist) should not become conscious of his insights: without taking the detour through his reflective processes, and incomprehensibly to himself, all his progress should enter so swiftly into the work that he is unable to recognize them in the moment of transition. Alas, the artist who waits in ambush there, watching, detaining them, will find them transformed like the beautiful gold in the fairy tale which cannot remain gold because some small detail was not taken care of.
Rainer Maria Rilke (1875-1926, German Poet)

69 That which builds is better than that which is built.
Ralph Waldo Emerson (1803-1882, American Poet, Essayist)

70 Creativity is a highfalutin word for the work I have to do between now and Tuesday.
Ray Kroc (1902-1984, American businessman, Founder of McDonalds)

71 Make visible what, without you, might perhaps never have been seen.
Robert Bresson (1907-, French Film Director)

72 First, I do not sit down at my desk to put into verse something that is already clear in my mind. If it were clear in my mind, I should have no incentive or need to write about it. We do not write in order to be understood; we write in order to understand.
Robert Cecil Day-Lewis (1904-1972, Irish Poet)

73 Anyone can look for fashion in a boutique or history in a museum. The creative explorer looks for history in a hardware store and fashion in an airport.
Robert Wieder

74 The lash may force men to physical labor, it cannot force them to spiritual creativity.
Sholem Asch (1880-1957, Polish-born American Writer)

75 I do my best work when I am in pain and turmoil.
Sting (1951-, British-born American Musician, Singer, Songwriter, Actor)

76 It is almost as if you were frantically constructing another world while the world that you live in dissolves beneath your feet, and that your survival depends on completing this construction at least one second before the old habitation collapses.
Tennessee Williams (1914-1983, American Dramatist)

77 Creative power, is that receptive attitude of expectancy which makes a mold into which the plastic and as yet undifferentiated substance can flow and take the desired form.
Thomas Troward

78 Some collaboration has to take place in the mind between the woman and the man before the art of creation can be accomplished. Some marriage of opposites has to be consummated. The whole of the mind must lie wide open if we are to get the sense that the
Virginia Woolf (1882-1941, British Novelist, Essayist)

79 All works of art are commissioned in the sense that no artist can create one by a simple act of will but must wait until what he believes to be a good idea for a work "comes" to him.
W. H. Auden (1907-1973, Anglo-American Poet)

80 It seems that the creative faculty and the critical faculty cannot exist together in their highest perfection.
W. Somerset Maugham (1874-1965, British Novelist, Playwright)

81 I must create a system or be enslaved by another man s; I will not reason and compare: my business is to create.
William Blake (1757-1827, British Poet, Painter)

82 A line will take us hours maybe; Yet if it does not seem a moment's thought, our stitching and unstinting has been naught.
William Butler Yeats (1865-1939, Irish Poet, Playwright.)

CREDIT

1 Blest paper-credit! last and best supply! That lends corruption lighter wings to fly!
Alexander Pope (1688-1744, British Poet, Critic, Translator)

2 Creditor. One of a tribe of savages dwelling beyond the Financial Straits and dreaded for their desolating incursions.
Ambrose Bierce (1842-1914, American Author, Editor, Journalist, "The Devil's Dictionary")

3 Remember that credit is money.
Benjamin Franklin (1706-1790, American Scientist, Publisher, Diplomat)

4 A person who can't pay gets another person who can't pay to guarantee that he can pay. Like a person with two wooden legs getting another person with two wooden legs to guarantee that he has got two natural legs. It don't make either of them able to do a walking-match.
Charles Dickens (1812-1870, British Novelist)

5 Men are sent into the world with bills of credit, and seldom draw to their full extent.
Horace Walpole (1717-1797, British Author)

6 O Gold! I still prefer thee unto paper, which makes bank credit like a bark of vapor.
Lord Byron (1788-1824, British Poet)

7 Nothing so cements and holds together all the parts of a society as faith or credit, which can never be kept up unless men are under some force or necessity of honestly paying what they owe to one another.
Marcus T. Cicero (106-43 BC, Great Roman Orator, Politician)

8 Beautiful credit! The foundation of modern society. Who shall say that this is not the golden age of mutual trust, of unlimited reliance upon human promises? That is a peculiar condition of society which enables a whole nation to instantly recognize point and meaning in the familiar newspaper anecdote, which puts into the mouth of a distinguished speculator in lands and mines this remark: -- "I wasn't worth a cent two years ago, and now I owe two millions of dollars."
Mark Twain (1835-1910, American Humorist, Writer)

9 The surest way to establish your credit is to work yourself into the position of not needing any.
Maurice Switzer

10 There is no limit to what a man can do or how far he can go if he doesn't mind who gets the credit.
Robert Woodruff

11 Credit is like a looking-glass, which when once sullied by a breath, may be wiped clear again; but if once cracked can never be repaired.
Sir Walter Scott (1771-1832, British Novelist, Poet)

12 A pig bought on credit is forever grunting.
Spanish Proverb

13 The private control of credit is the modern form of slavery.
Upton Sinclair (1878-1968, American Novelist, Social Reformer)

14 Usually the greatest boasters are the smallest workers. The deep rivers pay a larger tribute to the sea than shallow brooks, and yet empty themselves with less noise.
W. Secker

CREDULITY

1 Man is a credulous animal, and must believe something; in the absence of good grounds for belief, he will be satisfied with bad ones.
Bertrand Russell (1872-1970, British Philosopher, Mathematician, Essayist)

2 When people are bewildered they tend to become credulous.
Calvin Coolidge (1872-1933, Thirtieth President of the USA)

3 A little credulity helps one on through life very smoothly.
Elizabeth Gaskell (1810-1865, British Novelist)

4 Our credulity is greatest concerning the things we know least about. And since we know least about ourselves, we are ready to believe all that is said about us. Hence the mysterious power of both flattery and calumny.
Eric Hoffer (1902-1983, American Author, Philosopher)

5 I cannot spare the luxury of believing that all things beautiful are what they seem.
Fitz-Greene Halleck

6 The fact that a believer is happier than a skeptic is no more to the point than the fact that a drunken man is happier than a sober one. The happiness of credulity is a cheap and dangerous quality.
George Bernard Shaw (1856-1950, Irish-born British Dramatist)

7 Let us believe neither half of the good people tell us of ourselves, nor half the evil they say of others.
John Petit-Senn (1792-1870, French Poet)

8 The most positive men are the most credulous.
Jonathan Swift (1667-1745, Anglo-Irish Satirist)

9 I have all my life been on my guard against the information conveyed by the sense of hearing - - it being one of my earliest observations, the universal inclination of humankind is to be led by the ears, and I am sometimes apt to imagine that they are given to men as they are to pitchers, purposely that they may be carried about by them.
Lady Mary Wortley Montagu (1689-1762, British Society Figure, Letter Writer)

10 We believe at once in evil, we only believe in good upon reflection. Is this not sad?
Madame DorothT Deluzy (1747-1830, French Actress)

11 One of the peculiar sins of the twentieth century which we've developed to a very high level is the sin of credulity. It has been said that when human beings stop believing in God they believe in nothing. The truth is much worse: they believe in anything.
Malcolm Muggeridge (1903-1990, British Broadcaster)

12 I believe we are still so innocent. The species are still so innocent that a person who is apt to be murdered believes that the murderer, just before he puts the final wrench on his throat, will have enough compassion to give him one sweet cup of water.
Maya Angelou (1928-, African-American poet, Writer, Performer)

13 I prefer credulity to skepticism and cynicism for there is more promise in almost anything than in nothing at all.
Ralph B. Perry

14 The only disadvantage of an honest heart is credulity.
Sir Philip Sidney (1554-1586, British Author, Courtier)

15 A certain portion of the human race has certainly a taste for being diddled.
Thomas Hood (1799-1845, British Poet and Humorist)

16 Credulity is belief in slight evidence, with no evidence, or against evidence.
Tryon Edwards (1809-1894, American Theologian)

CREEDS

1 I always divide people into two groups. Those who live by what they know to be a lie, and those who live by what they believe, falsely, to be the truth.
Christopher Hampton (1946-, British Playwright)

2 There lies at the back of every creed something terrible and hard for which the worshipper may one day be required to suffer.
Edward M. Forster (1879-1970, British Novelist, Essayist)

3 Vain are the thousand creeds that move men's hearts, unutterably vain; Worthless as withered weeds, or idlest froth amid the boundless main.
Emily Bronte (1818-1848, British Novelist, Poet)

4 I believe in Michelangelo, Velasquez, and Rembrandt; in the might of design, the mystery of color, the redemption of all things by Beauty everlasting, and the message of Art that has made these hands blessed. Amen. Amen.
George Bernard Shaw (1856-1950, Irish-born British Dramatist)

5 If you have embraced a creed which appears to be free from the ordinary dirtiness of politics -- a creed from which you yourself cannot expect to draw any material advantage --surely that proves that you are in the right?
George Orwell (1903-1950, British Author, "Animal Farm")

6 A man must not swallow more beliefs than he can digest.
Havelock Ellis (1859-1939, British Psychologist)

7 Light half-believers of our casual creeds, who never deeply felt, nor clearly will d, whose insight never has borne fruit in deeds, whose vague resolves never have been fulfilled.
Matthew Arnold (1822-1888, British Poet, Critic)

8 As men's prayers are a disease of the will, so are their creeds a disease of the intellect.
Ralph Waldo Emerson (1803-1882, American Poet, Essayist)

9 When suave politeness, tempering bigot zeal, corrected "I believe" to "One does feel."
Ronald Knox (1888-1957, British Scholar, Priest)

10 I believe in the equality of man; and I believe that religious duties consist in doing justice, loving mercy, and endeavoring to make our fellow-creatures happy.
Thomas Paine (1737-1809, Anglo-American Political Theorist, Writer)

CRIES AND CRYING

1 Only to have a grief equal to all these tears!
Adrienne Rich (1929-, American Poet)

2 It opens the lungs, washes the countenance, exercises the eyes, and softens down the temper; so cry away.
Charles Dickens (1812-1870, British Novelist)

3 I wept not, so to stone within I grew.
Dante (Alighieri) (1265-1321, Italian Philosopher, Poet)

4 Have a good cry, wash out your heart. If you keep it inside it'll tear you apart. Sometimes you lose, but you're gonna win if you just hang in.
Dr. Hook

5 Whatever tears one may shed, in the end one always blows one's nose.
Heinrich Heine (1797-1856, German Poet, Journalist)

6 There are people who laugh to show their fine teeth; and there are those who cry to show their good hearts.
Joseph Roux (1834-1905, French Priest, Writer)

7 Oh! too convincing -- dangerously dear -- In woman's eye the unanswerable tear!
Lord Byron (1788-1824, British Poet)

8 The drying up a single tear has more of honest fame, than shedding seas of gore.
Lord Byron (1788-1824, British Poet)

9 One weeps not save when one is afraid, and that is why kings are tyrants.
Marquis De Sade (1740-1814, French Author)

10 Crying is the refuge of plain women but the ruin of pretty ones.
Oscar Wilde (1856-1900, British Author, Wit)

11 I cry every chance I get.
Richard Gere (1949-, American Actor)

12 The tears of the world are a constant quality. For each one who begins to weep, somewhere else another stops. The same is true of the laugh.
Samuel Beckett (1906-1989, Irish Dramatist, Novelist)

13 It is only to the happy that tears are a luxury.
Thomas Moore (1779-1852, Irish Poet)

14 Shining through tears, like April suns in showers, that labor to overcome the cloud that loads em.
Thomas Otway (1652-1685, British Dramatist)

15 He does not weep who does not see.
Victor Hugo (1802-1885, French Poet, Dramatist, Novelist)

16 I have full cause of weeping, but this heart shall break into a hundred thousand flaws or ere I'll weep.
William Shakespeare (1564-1616, British Poet, Playwright, Actor)

CRIME AND CRIMINALS

1 He reminds me of the man who murdered both his parents, and then when the sentence was about to be pronounced, pleaded for mercy on the grounds that he was orphan.
Abraham Lincoln (1809-1865, Sixteenth President of the USA)

2 Crime is terribly revealing. Try and vary your methods as you will, your tastes, your habits, your attitude of mind, and your soul is revealed by your actions.
Agatha Christie (1891-1976, British Mystery Writer)

3 My rackets are run on strictly American lines and they're going to stay that way.
Al Capone (1899-1947, American Gangster)

4 For centuries the death penalty, often accompanied by barbarous refinements, has been trying to hold crime in check; yet crime persists. Why? Because the instincts that are warring in man are not, as the law claims, constant forces in a state of equilibrium.
Albert Camus (1913-1960, French Existential Writer)

5 Abscond. To "move" in a mysterious way, commonly with the property of another.
Ambrose Bierce (1842-1914, American Author, Editor, Journalist, "The Devil's Dictionary")

6 Every rascal is not a thief, but every thief is a rascal.
Aristotle (384-322 BC, Greek Philosopher)

7 Crime seems to change character when it crosses a bridge or a tunnel. In the city, crime is taken as emblematic of class and race. In the suburbs, though, it's intimate and psychological -- resistant to generalization, a mystery of the individual soul.
Barbara Ehrenreich (1941-, American Author, Columnist)

8 Crime expands according to our willingness to put up with it.
Barry J. Farber (American Trainer, Speaker, Author)

9 He threatens many that hath injured one.
Ben Johnson (1573-1637, British Dramatist, Poet)

10 Slums may well be breeding-grounds of crime, but middle-class suburbs are incubators of apathy and delirium.
Cyril Connolly (1903-1974, British Critic)

11 The world of crime is a last refuge of the authentic, uncorrupted, spontaneous event.
Daniel J. Boorstin (1914-, American Historian)

12 There is a new billboard outside Time Square. It keeps an up-to minute count of gun-related crimes in New York. Some goofball is going to shoot someone just to see the numbers move.
David Letterman (1947-, American TV Personality)

13 The wrongdoer is more unfortunate than the man wronged.
Democritus (460-370 BC, Greek Philosopher)

14 Like art and politics, gangsterism is a very important avenue of assimilation into society.
E. L. Doctorow (1931-, American Novelist)

15 Many a man is saved from being a thief by finding everything locked up.
Edgar Watson Howe (1853-1937, American Journalist, Author)

16 The fear of burglars is not only the fear of being robbed, but also the fear of a sudden and unexpected clutch out of the darkness.
Elias Canetti (1905-, Austrian Novelist, Philosopher)

17 There is no society known where a more or less developed criminality is not found under different forms. No people exists whose morality is not daily infringed upon. We must therefore call crime necessary and declare that it cannot be non-existent, that the fundamental conditions of social organization, as they are understood, logically imply it.
Emile Durkheim (1858-1917, French Sociologist)

18 Crime is naught but misdirected energy.
Emma Goldman (1869-1940, American Anarchist)

19 Almost all crime is due to the repressed desire for aesthetic expression.
Evelyn Waugh (1903-1966, British Novelist)

20 There are crimes which become innocent and even glorious through their splendor, number and excess.
François de La Rochefoucauld (1613-1680, French classical writer)

21 He 63 ways of getting money, the most common, most honorable ones being staling, thieving, and robbing.
Frantois Rabelais (1495-1553, French Satirist, Physician, and Humanist)

22 Stripped of ethical rationalizations and philosophical pretensions, a crime is anything that a group in power chooses to prohibit.
Freda Adler (1870-1937, Pioneer Psychiatrist, Born in Vienna)

23 Save a thief from the gallows and he will cut your throat.
French Proverb

24 Set a thief to catch a thief.
French Proverb

25 The faults of the burglar are the qualities of the financier.
George Bernard Shaw (1856-1950, Irish-born British Dramatist)

26 Today more Americans are imprisoned for drug offenses than for property crimes
George F. Will (1941-, American Political Columnist)

27 Crimes, like virtues, are their own rewards.
George Farquhar (1677-1707, Irish Playwright)

28 Crime is a fact of the human species, a fact of that species alone, but it is above all the secret aspect, impenetrable and hidden. Crime hides, and by far the most terrifying things are those which elude us.
Georges Bataille (1897-1962, French Novelist, Critic)

29 One usually dies because one is alone, or because one has got into something over one's head. One often dies because one does not have the right alliances, because one is not given support. In Sicily the Mafia kills the servants of the State that the State has not been able to protect.
Giovanni Falcone

30 The common argument that crime is caused by poverty is a kind of slander on the poor.
H. L. Mencken (1880-1956, American Editor, Author, Critic, Humorist)

31 Crime and bad lives are the measure of a State's failure, all crime in the end is the crime of the community.
H.G. Wells (1866-1946, British-born American Author)

32 No punishment has ever possessed enough power of deterrence to prevent the commission of crimes. On the contrary, whatever the punishment, once a specific crime has appeared for the first time, its reappearance is more likely than its initial emergence could ever have been.
Hannah Arendt (1906-1975, German-born American Political Philosopher)

33 We cannot be sure that we ought not to regard the most criminal country as that which in some aspects possesses the highest civilization.
Havelock Ellis (1859-1939, British Psychologist)

34 How vainly shall we endeavor to repress crime by our barbarous punishment of the poorer class of criminals so long as children are reared in the brutalizing influences of poverty, so long as the bite of want drives men to crime.
Henry George (1839-1897, American Social Reformer, Economist)

35 The study of crime begins with the knowledge of oneself. All that you despise, all that you loathe, all that you reject, all that you condemn and seek to convert by punishment springs from you.
Henry Miller (1891-1980, American Author)

36 We are often deterred from crime by the disgrace of others.
Horace (65-8 BC, Italian Poet)

37 A person with predatory instincts who has not sufficient capital to form a corporation.
Howard Scott

38 Not failure, but low aim, is crime.
James Russell Lowell (1819-1891, American Poet, Critic, Editor)

39 If poverty is the mother of crime, lack of good sense is the father.
Jean De La Bruyere (1645-1696, French Writer)

40 Crimes of which a people is ashamed constitute its real history. The same is true of man.
Jean Genet (1910-1986, French Playwright, Novelist)

41 Repudiating the virtues of your world, criminals hopelessly agree to organize a forbidden universe. They agree to live in it. The air there is nauseating: they can breathe it.
Jean Genet (1910-1986, French Playwright, Novelist)

42 Small crimes always precedes great ones.
Jean Racine (1639-1699, French Dramatist)

43 Locks keep out only the honest.
Jewish Proverb

44 It is because they took the easy way out that rivers, and people, go crooked.
Jill Peterson

45 There is no crime of which I do not deem myself capable.
Johann Wolfgang Von Goethe (1749-1832, German Poet, Dramatist, Novelist)

46 Successful crimes alone are justified.
John Dryden (1631-1700, British Poet, Dramatist, Critic)

47 Every society gets the kind of criminal it deserves. What is also true is that every community gets the kind of law enforcement it insists on.
John F. Kennedy (1917-1963, Thirty-fifth President of the USA)

48 After all, crime is only a left-handed form of human endeavor.
John Huston (1906-1987, American Film Director)

49 The man who is admired for the ingenuity of his larceny is almost always rediscovering some earlier form of fraud. The basic forms are all known, have all been practiced. The manners of capitalism improve. The morals may not.
John Kenneth Galbraith (1908-, American Economist)

50 Many commit the same crime with a different destiny; one bears a cross as the price of his villainy, another wears a crown.
Juvenal (Decimus Junius Juvenalis) (55-130, Roman Satirical Poet)

51 Squeeze human nature into the straitjacket of criminal justice and crime will appear.
Karl Kraus (1874-1936, Austrian Satirist)

52 One crime is everything, two is nothing.
Madame DorothT Deluzy (1747-1830, French Actress)

53 A crime persevered in a thousand centuries ceases to be a crime, and becomes a virtue. This is the law of custom, and custom supersedes all other forms of law.
Mark Twain (1835-1910, American Humorist, Writer)

54 All, all is theft, all is unceasing and rigorous competition in nature; the desire to make off with the substance of others is the foremost -- the most legitimate -- passion nature has bred into us and, without doubt, the most agreeable one.
Marquis De Sade (1740-1814, French Author)

55 It is certain that stealing nourishes courage, strength, skill, tact, in a word, all the virtues useful to a republican system and consequently to our own. Lay partiality aside, and answer me: is theft, whose effect is to distribute wealth more evenly, to be branded as a wrong in our day, under our government which aims at equality? Plainly, the answer is no.
Marquis De Sade (1740-1814, French Author)

56 The truth of the matter is that muggers are very interesting people.
Michael Winner

57 The lyricism of marginality may find inspiration in the image of the "outlaw," the great social nomad, who prowls on the confines of a docile, frightened order.
Michel Foucault (1926-1984, French Essayist, Philosopher)

58 The infectiousness of crime is like that of the plague.
Napoleon Bonaparte (1769-1821, French General, Emperor)

59 A burglar who respects his art always takes his time before taking anything else.
O. Henry Porter (1862-1910, American short-story Writer)

60 Crime generally punishes itself.
Oliver Goldsmith (1728-1774, Anglo-Irish Author, Poet, Playwright)

61 We may live without friends; we may live without books. But civilized men cannot live without cooks.
Owen Meredith (1831-1891, British Politician, Poet)

62 He who commits injustice is ever made more wretched than he who suffers it.
Plato (427-347 BC, Greek Philosopher)

63 Great thieves punish little ones.
Proverb

64 All criminals turn preachers under the gallows.
Proverb

65 In times of trouble leniency becomes crime.
Proverb

66 Commit a crime, and the earth is made of glass.
Ralph Waldo Emerson (1803-1882, American Poet, Essayist)

67 Crime and punishment grow out of one stem. Punishment is a fruit that, unsuspected, ripens with the flower of the pleasure that concealed it.
Ralph Waldo Emerson (1803-1882, American Poet, Essayist)

68 The greatest crime in the world is not developing your potential. When you do what you do best, you are helping not only yourself, but the world.
Roger Williams (1603-1683, American Founder of Rhode Island)

69 The thief. Once committed beyond a certain point he should not worry himself too much about not being a thief any more. Thieving is God's message to him. Let him try and be a good thief.
Samuel Butler (1612-1680, British Poet, Satirist)

70 One crime has to be concealed by another.
Seneca (4 BC-65 AD, Spanish-born Roman Statesman, philosopher)

71 He has committed the crime who profits by it.
Seneca (4 BC-65 AD, Spanish-born Roman Statesman, philosopher)

72 Crime when it succeeds is called virtue.
Seneca (4 BC-65 AD, Spanish-born Roman Statesman, philosopher)

73 From a single crime know the nation.
Virgil (70-19 BC, Roman Poet)

74 Want of money and the distress of a thief can never be alleged as the cause of his thieving, for many honest people endure greater hardships with fortitude. We must therefore seek the cause elsewhere than in want of money, for that is the miser's passion, not the thief s.
William Blake (1757-1827, British Poet, Painter)

75 There is a heroism in crime as well as in virtue. Vice and infamy have their altars and their religion.
William Hazlitt (1778-1830, British Essayist)

76 He that is robbed, not wanting what is stolen, him not know t, and he's not robbed at all.
William Shakespeare (1564-1616, British Poet, Playwright, Actor)

77 Organized crime in America takes in over forty billion dollars a year. This is quite a profitable sum, especially when one consider that the Mafia spends very little for office supplies.
Woody Allen (1935-, American Director, Screenwriter, Actor, Comedian)

CRISIS

1 I see in the near future a crisis approaching that unnerves me and causes me to tremble for the safety of my country. Corporations have been enthroned, an era of corruption in high places will follow, and the money-power of the country will endeavor to prolong it's reign by working upon the prejudices of the people until the wealth is aggregated in a few hands and the Republic is destroyed.
Abraham Lincoln (1809-1865, Sixteenth President of the USA)

2 Crises refine life. In them you discover what you are.
Allan K. Chalmers

3 The wise man does not expose himself needlessly to danger, since there are few things for which he cares sufficiently; but he is willing, in great crises, to give even his life -- knowing that under certain conditions it is not worthwhile to live.
Aristotle (384-322 BC, Greek Philosopher)

4   I think it's only in a crisis that Americans see other people. It has to be an American crisis, of course. If two countries fight that do not supply the Americans with some precious commodity, then the education of the public does not take place. But when the dictator falls, when the oil is threatened, then you turn on the television and they tell you where the country is, what the language is, how to pronounce the names of the leaders, what the religion is all about, and maybe you can cut out recipes in the newspaper of Persian dishes.
Don Delillo (1926-, American Author)

5   I believe that in the history of art and of thought there has always been at every living moment of culture a "will to renewal." This is not the prerogative of the last decade only. All history is nothing but a succession of "crises" -- of rupture, repudiation and resistance. When there is no "crisis," there is stagnation, petrifaction and death. All thought, all art is aggressive.
Eugene Ionesco (1912-, Romanian-born French Playwright)

6   Watch out for emergencies. They are your big chance.
Fritz Reiner

7   A crisis is a close encounter of the third kind.
Guy Finley

8   There can't be a crisis next week. My schedule is already full.
Henry Kissinger (1923-, American Republican Politician, Secretary of State)

9   Every little thing counts in a crisis.
Jawaharlal Nehru (1889-1964, Indian Nationalist, Statesman)

10 Crises and deadlocks when they occur have at least this advantage, that they force us to think.
Jawaharlal Nehru (1889-1964, Indian Nationalist, Statesman)

11 When written in Chinese, the word "crisis" is composed of two characters -- one represents danger, and the other represents opportunity.
John F. Kennedy (1917-1963, Thirty-fifth President of the USA)

12 I am walking over hot coals suspended over a deep pit at the bottom of which are a large number of vipers baring their fangs.
John Major (British Prime Minister)

13 Man is not imprisoned by habit. Great changes in him can be wrought by crisis -- once that crisis can be recognized and understood.
Norman Cousins (1915-1990, American Editor, Humanitarian, Author)

14 The easiest period in a crisis situation is actually the battle itself. The most difficult is the period of indecision -- whether to fight or run away. And the most dangerous period is the aftermath. It is then, with all his resources spent and his guard down, that an individual must watch out for dulled reactions and faulty judgment.
Richard M. Nixon (1913-1994, Thirty-seventh President of the USA)

15 Sooner or later comes a crisis in our affairs, and how we meet it determines our future happiness and success. Since the beginning of time, every form of life has been called upon to meet such crisis.
Robert Collier (American Writer, Publisher)

16 When is a crisis reached? When questions arise that can't be answered.
Ryszard Kapuscinski (1932, Polish Report and Foreign Correspondent)

17 We all live in a house on fire, no fire department to call; no way out, just the upstairs window to look out of while the fire burns the house down with us trapped, locked in it.
Tennessee Williams (1914-1983, American Dramatist)

18 These are the times that try men's souls.
Thomas Paine (1737-1809, Anglo-American Political Theorist, Writer)

19 Every crisis offers you extra desired power.
William Moulton Marston

20 The time is out of joint. O cursed spite that ever I was born to set it right!
William Shakespeare (1564-1616, British Poet, Playwright, Actor)

CRITICS AND CRITICISM

1   If the end brings me out all right, what is said against me won't amount to anything. If the end brings me out wrong, then ten angels swearing I was right would make no difference.
Abraham Lincoln (1809-1865, Sixteenth President of the USA)

2   If I care to listen to every criticism, let alone act on them, then this shop may as well be closed for all other businesses. I have learned to do my best, and if the end result is good then I do not care for any criticism, but if the end result is not good, then even the praise of ten angels would not make the difference.
Abraham Lincoln (1809-1865, Sixteenth President of the USA)

3   Did some more sober critics come abroad? If wrong, I smil'd; if right, I kiss'd the rod.
Alexander Pope (1688-1744, British Poet, Critic, Translator)

4   It is a barren kind of criticism which tells you what a thing is not.
Alfred Whitney Griswold (1906-1963, American President of Yale University)

5   It is healthier, in any case, to write for the adults one's children will become than for the children one's "mature" critics often are.
Alice Walker (1944-, American Author, Critic)

6   The covers of this book are too far apart.
Ambrose Bierce (1842-1914, American Author, Editor, Journalist, "The Devil's Dictionary")

7   Never criticize a man until you've walked a mile in his moccasins.
American Indian Proverb

8   The good critic is he who relates the adventures of his soul among masterpieces.
Anatole France (1844-1924, French Writer)

9   They will say you are on the wrong road, if it is your own.
Antonio Porchia

10   What we ask of him is, that he should find out for us more than we can find out for ourselves. He must have the passion of a lover.
Arthur Symons

11   Critics are those who have failed in literature and art.
Benjamin Disraeli (1804-1881, British Statesman, Prime Minister)

12   It is much easier to be critical than to be correct.
Benjamin Disraeli (1804-1881, British Statesman, Prime Minister)

13   If all printers were determined not to print anything till they were sure it would offend nobody, there would be very little printed.
Benjamin Franklin (1706-1790, American Scientist, Publisher, Diplomat)

14   A friend is a lot of things, but a critic isn't.
Bern Williams

15   Be swift to hear, slow to speak, and slow to wrath.
Bible (Sacred Scriptures of Christians and Judaism)

16   I remember when I was in college, people told me I couldn't play in the NBA. There's always somebody saying you can't do it, and those people have to be ignored.
Bill Cartwright (American Basketball Player)

17   I have found it advisable not to give too much heed to what people say when I am trying to accomplish something of consequence. Invariably they proclaim it can't be done. I deem that the very best time to make the effort.
Calvin Coolidge (1872-1933, Thirtieth President of the USA)

18   The greatest honor that can be paid to the work of art, on its pedestal of ritual display, is to describe it with sensory completeness. We need a science of description. Criticism is ceremonial revivification.
Camille Paglia (1947-, American Author, Critic, Educator)

19   Each generation produces its squad of "moderns" with peashooters to attack Gibraltar.
Channing Pollock (American Actor)

20   A critic is a legless man who teaches running.
Channing Pollock (American Actor)

21   I know I'm never as good or bad as one single performance. I've never believed in my critics or my worshippers, and I've always been able to leave the game at the arena.
Charles Barkley (American Basketball Player)

22   It is from the womb of art that criticism was born.
Charles Baudelaire (1821-1867, French Poet)

23   To be just, that is to say, to justify its existence, criticism should be partial, passionate and political, that is to say, written from an exclusive point of view, but a point of view that opens up the widest horizons.
Charles Baudelaire (1821-1867, French Poet)

24   Self-laudation abounds among the unpolished, but nothing can stamp a man more sharply as ill-bred.
Charles Buxton (1823-1871, British Author)

25   The rule in carving holds good as to criticism; never cut with a knife what you can cut with a spoon.
Charles Buxton (1823-1871, British Author)

26   Though by whim, envy, or resentment led, they damn those authors whom they never read.
Charles Churchill (1731-1764, British Poet, Satirist)

27   In judging others, folks will work overtime for no pay.
Charles Edwin Carruthers

28   In my wide association in life, meeting with many and great men in various parts of the world, I have yet to find the man, however great or exalted his station, who did not do better work and put forth greater effort under a spirit of approval than he would ever do under a spirit of criticism.
Charles M. Schwab (1862-1939, American Industrialist, Businessman)

29   Do not use a hatchet to remove a fly from your friend's forehead.
Chinese Proverb

30   Those who have free seats at a play hiss first.
Chinese Proverb

31   If I make a move, like raise my eyebrows, some critic says I'm doing Nicholson. What am I supposed to do, cut off my eyebrows?
Christian Slater (Born 1969, American Actor)

32   Asking a working writer what he thinks about critics is like asking a lamp-post what it feels about dogs.
Christopher Hampton (1946-, British Playwright)

33   Harsh counsels have no effect; they are like hammers which are always repulsed by the anvil.
Claude A. HelvTtius (1715-1771, French Philosopher)

34   As a work of art it has the same status as a long conversation between two not very bright drunks.
Clive James (1939-, Australian-Born Writer, Satirist, Broadcaster, and Critic)

35   Satire is often the reflection of a kind of moral nausea.
Crand Briton

36   I review novels to make money, because it is easier for a sluggard to write an article a fortnight than a book a year, because the writer is soothed by the opiate of action, the crank by posing as a good journalist, and having an air hole. I dislike it. I do it and I am always resolving to give it up.
Cyril Connolly (1903-1974, British Critic)

37   Never trust the artist. Trust the tale. The proper function of a critic is to save the tale from the artist who created it.
D. H. Lawrence (1885-1930, British Author)

38 Praise those of your critics for whom nothing is up to standard.
Dag Hammarskjold (1905-1961, Swedish Statesman, Secretary-general of U.N.)

39 If you believe in what you are doing, then let nothing hold you up in your work. Much of the best work of the world has been done against seeming impossibilities. The thing is to get the work done.
Dale Carnegie (1888-1955, American Author, Trainer)

40 Criticism of others is futile and if you indulge in it often you should be warned that it can be fatal to your career.
Dale Carnegie (1888-1955, American Author, Trainer)

41 A film is just like a muffin. You make it. You put it on the table. One person might say, "Oh, I don't like it." One might say it's the best muffin ever made. One might say it's an awful muffin. It's hard for me to say. It's for me to make the muffin.
Denzel Washington (1954-, American Actor)

42 Nothing is as peevish and pedantic as men's judgments of one another.
Desiderius Erasmus (1466-1536, Dutch Humanist)

43 This is not a novel to be tossed aside lightly. It should be thrown with great force.
Dorothy Parker (1893-1967, American Humorous Writer)

44 Criticism is an indirect form of self-boasting.
Dr. Emmit Fox

45 A good review from the critics is just another stay of execution.
Dustin Hoffman (1937-, American Actor)

46 Criticism is a misconception: we must read not to understand others but to understand ourselves.
E. M. Cioran (1911-, Rumanian-born French Philosopher)

47 In criticism I will be bold, and as sternly, absolutely just with friend and foe. From this purpose nothing shall turn me.
Edgar Allan Poe (1809-1845, American Poet, Critic, short-story Writer)

48 After all, one knows one's weak points so well, that it's rather bewildering to have the critics overlook them and invent others.
Edith Wharton (1862-1937, American Author)

49 Hardly a book of human worth, be it heaven's own secret, is honestly placed before the reader; it is either shunned, given a Periclean funeral oration in a hundred and fifty words, or interred in the potter's field of the newspapers back pages.
Edward Dahlberg (1900-1977, American Author, Critic)

50 Recognize the cunning man not by the corpses he pays homage to but by the living writers he conspires against with the most shameful weapon, Silence, or the briefest review.
Edward Dahlberg (1900-1977, American Author, Critic)

51 It is very perplexing how an intrepid frontier people, who fought a wilderness, floods, tornadoes, and the Rockies, cower before criticism, which is regarded as a malignant tumor in the imagination.
Edward Dahlberg (1900-1977, American Author, Critic)

52 The author himself is the best judge of his own performance; none has so deeply meditated on the subject; none is so sincerely interested in the event.
Edward Gibbon (1737-1794, British Historian)

53 To avoid criticism, do nothing, say nothing, be nothing.
Elbert Hubbard (1859-1915, American Author, Publisher)

54 Do what you feel in your heart to be right. You'll be criticized anyway.
Eleanor Roosevelt (1884-1962, American First Lady, Columnist, Lecturer, Humanitarian)

55 Writing about music is like dancing about architecture; it's a really stupid thing to want to do.
Elvis Costello (1955-, British-born American Musician, Singer, Songwriter)

56 If evil be spoken of you and it be true, correct yourself, if it be a lie, laugh at it.
Epictetus (50-120, Stoic Philosopher)

57 God knows people who are paid to have attitudes toward things, professional critics, make me sick; camp following eunuchs of literature. They won't even whore. They're all virtuous and sterile. And how well meaning and high minded. But they're all camp followers.
Ernest Hemingway (1898-1961, American Writer)

58 All the critics who could not make their reputations by discovering you are hoping to make them by predicting hopefully your approaching impotence, failure and general drying up of natural juices. Not a one will wish you luck or hope that you will keep on writing unless you have political affiliations in which case these will rally around and speak of you and Homer, Balzac, Zola and Link Steffens.
Ernest Hemingway (1898-1961, American Writer)

59 Critics are usually kinder to cheaper movies than to those they perceive to be big Hollywood releases. They cut you a lot more slack if you spend less money, which makes no sense.
Ethan Coen (1957-, American Director, Screenwriter, Editor, Producer)

60 I consider criticism merely a preliminary excitement, a statement of things a writer has to clear up in his own head sometime or other, probably antecedent to writing; of no value unless it come to fruit in the created work later.
Ezra Pound (1885-1972, American Poet, Critic)

61 Remember if people talk behind your back, it only means you're two steps ahead!
Fannie Flagg

62 Critical remarks are only made by people who love you.
Federico Mayor

63 Honest criticism is hard to take, especially from a relative, a friend, an acquaintance, or a stranger.
Franklin P. Jones

64 The television critic, whatever his pretensions, does not labor in the same vineyard as those he criticizes; his grapes are all sour.
Frederic Raphael (1931-, British Author, Critic)

65 A critic is a reader who ruminates. Thus, he should have more than one stomach.
Friedrich Schlegel (1772-1829, German Philosopher, Critic, Writer)

66 Prolonged, indiscriminate reviewing of books is a quite exceptionally thankless, irritating and exhausting job. It not only involves praising trash but constantly inventing reactions towards books about which one has no spontaneous feeling whatever.
George Orwell (1903-1950, British Author, "Animal Farm")

67 Even the lion has to defend himself against flies.
German Proverb

68 Let me tell you something that we Israelis have against Moses. He took us 40 years through the desert in order to bring us to the one spot in the Middle East that has no oil!
Golda Meir (1898-1978, Prime Minister of Israel, 1969-74)

69 All the world's a stage, and all the clergymen critics.
Gregory Nunn (1955-, American Golfer)

70 If what they are saying about you is true, mend your ways. If it isn't true, forget it, and go on and serve the Lord.
H. A. Ironside

71 It is impossible to think of a man of any actual force and originality, universally recognized as having those qualities, who spent his whole life appraising and describing the work of other men.
H. L. Mencken (1880-1956, American Editor, Author, Critic, Humorist)

72 Criticism is prejudice made plausible.
H. L. Mencken (1880-1956, American Editor, Author, Critic, Humorist)

73 As much as we thirst for approval we dread condemnation.
Hans Selye (1907-1982, Canadian Physician Born In Austria, Research On Stress)

74 Unlike other people, our reviewers are powerful because they believe in nothing.
Harold Clurman

75 One of the grotesqueries of present-day American life is the amount of reasoning that goes into displaying the wisdom secreted in bad movies while proving that modern art is meaningless. They have put into practice the notion that a bad art work cleverly interpreted according to some obscure Method is more rewarding than a masterpiece wrapped in silence.
Harold Rosenberg (1906-1978, American Art Critic, Author)

76 When a man spends his time giving his wife criticism and advice instead of compliments, he forgets that it was not his good judgment, but his charming manners, that won her heart.
Helen Rowland (1875-1950, American Journalist)

77 I am sorry to think that you do not get a man's most effective criticism until you provoke him. Severe truth is expressed with some bitterness.
Henry David Thoreau (1817-1862, American Essayist, Poet, Naturalist)

78 In reality, the world have paid too great a compliment to critics, and have imagined them men of much greater profundity than they really are.
Henry Fielding (1707-1754, British Novelist, Dramatist)

79 Of course you're always at liberty to judge the critic. Judge people as critics, however, and you'll condemn them all!
Henry James (1843-1916, American Author)

80 To criticize is to appreciate, to appropriate, to take intellectual possession, to establish in fine a relation with the criticized thing and to make it one's own.
Henry James (1843-1916, American Author)

81 Honest criticism means nothing: what one wants is unrestrained passion, fire for fire.
Henry Miller (1891-1980, American Author)

82 We have been educated to such a fine -- or dull -- point that we are incapable of enjoying something new, something different, until we are first told what it's all about. We don't trust our five senses; we rely on our critics and educators, all of whom are failures in the realm of creation. In short, the blind lead the blind. It's the democratic way.
Henry Miller (1891-1980, American Author)

83 Half of the secular unrest and dismal, profane sadness of modern society comes from the vain ideas that every man is bound to be a critic for life.
Henry Van Dyke (1852-1933, American Protestant Clergyman, Poet and Writer)

84 Doubtless criticism was originally benignant, pointing out the beauties of a work rather that its defects. The passions of men have made it malignant, as a bad heart of Procreates turned the bed, the symbol of repose, into an instrument of torture.
Henry Wadsworth Longfellow (1819-1892, American Poet)

85 Critics are sentinels in the grand army of letters, stationed at the corners of newspapers and reviews, to challenge every new author.
Henry Wadsworth Longfellow (1819-1892, American Poet)

86 The strength of criticism lies in the weakness of the thing criticized.
Henry Wadsworth Longfellow (1819-1892, American Poet)

87 We should not judge people by their peak of excellence; but by the distance they have traveled from the point where they started.
Henry Ward Beecher (1813-1887, American Preacher, Orator, Writer)

88 Ours is an age of criticism, to which everything must be subjected. The sacredness of religion, and the authority of legislation, are by many regarded as grounds for exemption from the examination by this tribunal, But, if they are exempted, and cannot lay claim to sincere respect, which reason accords only to that which has stood the test of a free and public examination.
Immanuel Kant (1724-1804, German Philosopher)

89 A bad review is even less important than whether it is raining in Patagonia.
Iris Murdoch (1919-, British Novelist, Philosopher)

90 David Lynch came out of it a genius, and I came out of it a fat girl. I'm sorry that the only comment I get about the part is the way I look. [Commenting on the critics' response to her performance in Blue Velvet]
Isabella Rossellini (1952-, Italian Actress, Model)

91 The biggest critics of my books are people who never read them.
Jackie Collins (American Author, Sister of Joan Collins)

92 You should not say it is not good. You should say you do not like it; and then, you know, you're perfectly safe.
James Mcneill Whistler (1834-1903, American Artist)

93 A sneer is the weapon of the weak.
James Russell Lowell (1819-1891, American Poet, Critic, Editor)

94 A wise skepticism is the first attribute of a good critic.
James Russell Lowell (1819-1891, American Poet, Critic, Editor)

95 A negative judgment gives you more satisfaction than praise, provided it smacks of jealousy.
Jean Baudrillard (French Postmodern Philosopher, Writer)

96 What the public criticizes in you, cultivate. It is you.
Jean Cocteau (1889-1963, French Author, Filmmaker)

97 Criticism is often not a science; it is a craft, requiring more good health than wit, more hard work than talent, more habit than native genius. In the hands of a man who has read widely but lacks judgment, applied to certain subjects it can corrupt both its readers and the writer himself.
Jean De La Bruyere (1645-1696, French Writer)

98 The pleasure we feel in criticizing robs us from being moved by very beautiful things.
Jean De La Bruyere (1645-1696, French Writer)

99 Take heed of critics even when they are not fair; resist them even when they are.
Jean Rostand (1894-1977, French Biologist, Writer)

100 A good writer is not necessarily a good book critic. No more so than a good drunk is automatically a good bartender.
Jim Bishop

101 Strike the dog dead, it's but a critic!
Johann Wolfgang Von Goethe (1749-1832, German Poet, Dramatist, Novelist)

102 The person of analytic or critical intellect finds something ridiculous in everything. The person of synthetic or constructive intellect, in almost nothing.
Johann Wolfgang Von Goethe (1749-1832, German Poet, Dramatist, Novelist)

103 Post-modernism has cut off the present from all futures. The daily media add to this by cutting off the past. Which means that critical opinion is often orphaned in the present.
John Berger (1926-, British Actor, Critic)

104 Praise or blame has but a momentary effect on the man whose love of beauty in the abstract makes him a severe critic on his own works.
John Keats (1795-1821, British Poet)

105 Never make the mistake of assuming the critters will beat a path to your door.
John P. Mascotte

106 Give a critic an inch, he'll write a play.
John Steinbeck (1902-1968, American Author)

107 Unless a reviewer has the courage to give you unqualified praise, I say ignore the bastard.
John Steinbeck (1902-1968, American Author)

108 Writing criticism is to writing fiction and poetry as hugging the shore is to sailing in the open sea.
John Updike (1932-, American Novelist, Critic)

109 We protest against unjust criticism but we accept unarmed applause.
Jose Narosky

110 Their is no defense against criticism except obscurity.
Joseph Addison (1672-1719, British Essayist, Poet, Statesman)

111 Criticism, that fine flower of personal expression in the garden of letters.
Joseph Conrad (1857-1924, Polish-born British Novelist)

112 Professional critics are incapable of distinguishing and appreciating either diamonds in the rough or gold in bars. They are traders, and in literature know only the coins that are current. Their critical lab has scales and weights, but neither crucible or touchstone.
Joseph Joubert (1754-1824, French Moralist)

113 A good drama critic is one who perceives what is happening in the theatre of his time. A great drama critic also perceives what is not happening.
Kenneth Tynan (1927-1980, British Critic)

114 A critic is a man who knows the way, but can't drive the car.
Kenneth Tynan (1927-1980, British Critic)

115 Of all the cants which are canted in this canting world -- though the cant of hypocrites may be the worst -- the cant of criticism is the most tormenting!
Laurence Sterne (1713-1768, British Author)

116 Most of us are umpires at heart; we like to call balls and strikes on somebody else.
Leo Aikman

117 People want you to be a crazy, out-of-control teen brat. They want you miserable, just like them. They don't want heroes; what they want is to see you fall.
Leonardo DiCaprio (Born 1974, American Actor)

118 A louse in the locks of literature.
Lord Alfred Tennyson (1809-1892, British Poet)

119 No man ever got very high by pulling other people down. The intelligent merchant does not knock his competitors. The sensible worker does not work those who work with him. Don't knock your friends. Don't knock your enemies. Don't knock yourself.
Lord Alfred Tennyson (1809-1892, British Poet)

120 Critics are already made.
Lord Byron (1788-1824, British Poet)

121 A man must serve his time to every trade save censure -- critics all are ready made.
Lord Byron (1788-1824, British Poet)

122 You should never assume contempt for that which it is not very manifest that you have it in your power to possess, nor does a wit ever make a more contemptible figure than when, in attempting satire, he shows that he does not understand that which he would make the subject of his ridicule.
Lord Melbourne (1779-1848, British Statesman, Prime Minister)

123 If you burn your neighbors house down, it doesn't make your house look any better.
Lou Holtz (1937-, American Football Coach)

124 You're never s good as everyone tells you when you win, and you're never as bad as they say when you lose.
Lou Holtz (1937-, American Football Coach)

125 The easiest thing a human being can do is to criticize another human being.
Lynn M. Little

126 They condemn what they do not understand.
Marcus T. Cicero (106-43 BC, Great Roman Orator, Politician)

127 He cannot be strict in judging, who does not wish others to be strict judges of himself.
Marcus T. Cicero (106-43 BC, Great Roman Orator, Politician)

128 There are two modes of criticism. One which crushes to earth without mercy all the humble buds of Phantasy, all the plants that, though green and fruitful, are also a prey to insects or have suffered by drought. It weeds well the garden, and cannot believe the weed in its native soil may be a pretty, graceful plant. There is another mode which enters into the natural history of every thing that breathes and lives, which believes no impulse to be entirely in vain, which scrutinizes circumstances, motive and object before it condemns, and believes there is a beauty in natural form, if its law and purpose be understood.
Margaret Fuller (1810-1850, American Writer, Lecturer)

129 Essays, entitled critical, are epistles addressed to the public, through which the mind of the recluse relieves itself of its impressions.
Margaret Fuller (1810-1850, American Writer, Lecturer)

130 We are suffering from too much sarcasm.
Marianne Moore (1887-1972, American Poet)

131 The public is the only critic whose opinion is worth anything at all.
Mark Twain (1835-1910, American Humorist, Writer)

132 It is critical vision alone which can mitigate the unimpeded operation of the automatic.
Marshall Mcluhan (1911-1980, Canadian Communications Theorist)

133 Since we cannot attain unto it, let us revenge ourselves with railing against it.
Michel Eyquem De Montaigne (1533-1592, French Philosopher, Essayist)

134 Without the meditative background that is criticism, works become isolated gestures, historical accidents, soon forgotten.
Milan Kundera (1929-, Czech Author, Critic)

135 Let us consider the critic, therefore, as a discoverer of discoveries.
Milan Kundera (1929-, Czech Author, Critic)

136 One ought to examine himself for a very long time before thinking of condemning others.
MoliFre (1622-1673, French Playwright)

137 If you must speak ill of another, do not speak it, write it in the sand near the water's edge"
Napoleon Hill (1883-1970, American Speaker, Motivational Writer, "Think and Grow Rich")

138 Never retract, never explain, never apologize; get things done and let them howl.
Nellie Mcclung (1873-1951, Canadian Suffragist, Writer, Speaker)

139 The avocation of assessing the failures of better men can be turned into a comfortable livelihood, providing you back it up with a Ph.D.
Nelson Algren (1909-1981, American Author)

140 Social criticism begins with grammar and the re-establishing of meanings.
Octavio Paz (1914-, Mexican Poet, Essayist)

141 Write how you want, the critic shall show the world you could have written better.
Oliver Goldsmith (1728-1774, Anglo-Irish Author, Poet, Playwright)

142 Nature, when she invented, manufactured, and patented her authors, contrived to make critics out of the chips that were left.
Oliver Wendell Holmes (1809-1894, American Author, Wit, Poet)

143 The critic has to educate the public; the artist has to educate the critic.
Oscar Wilde (1856-1900, British Author, Wit)

144 The true critic is he who bears within himself the dreams and ideas and feelings of myriad generations, and to whom no form of thought is alien, no emotional impulse obscure.
Oscar Wilde (1856-1900, British Author, Wit)

145 On an occasion of this kind it becomes more than a moral duty to speak one's mind. It becomes a pleasure.
Oscar Wilde (1856-1900, British Author, Wit)

146 Temperament is the primary requisite for the critic -- a temperament exquisitely susceptible to beauty, and to the various impressions that beauty gives us.
Oscar Wilde (1856-1900, British Author, Wit)

147 That is what the highest criticism really is, the record of one's own soul. It is more fascinating than history, as it is concerned simply with oneself. It is more delightful than philosophy, as its subject is concrete and not abstract, real and not vague. It is the only civilized form of autobiography.
Oscar Wilde (1856-1900, British Author, Wit)

148 Art is not the application of a canon of beauty but what the instinct and the brain can conceive beyond any canon. When we love a woman we don't start measuring her limbs.
Pablo Picasso (1881-1973, Spanish Artist)

149 One does not lash hat lies at a distance. The foibles that we ridicule must at least be a little bit our own. Only then will the work be a part of our own flesh. The garden must be weeded.
Paul Klee (1879-1940, Swiss Artist)

150 In the arts, the critic is the only independent source of information. The rest is advertising.
Pauline Kael (1919-, American Film Critic)

151 Reviewers, with some rare exceptions, are a most stupid and malignant race. As a bankrupt thief turns thief-taker in despair, so an unsuccessful author turns critic.
Percy Bysshe Shelley (1792-1822, British Poet)

152 Abuse if you slight it, will gradually die away; but if you show yourself irritated, you will be thought to have deserved it.
Publius Cornelius Tacitus (55-117 AD, Roman Historian)

153 Nothing would improve newspaper criticism so much as the knowledge that it was to be read by men too hardy to acquiesce in the authoritative statement of the reviewer.
R. H. Hutton

154 In an age of unscrupulous and shameless book-making, it is a duty to give notice of the rubbish that cumbers the ground. There is no credit, no real power required for this task. It is the work of an intellectual scavenger, and far from being specially honorable.
R. H. Hutton

155 Blame is safer than praise.
Ralph Waldo Emerson (1803-1882, American Poet, Essayist)

156 Criticism should not be querulous and wasting, all knife and root-puller, but guiding, instructive, inspiring.
Ralph Waldo Emerson (1803-1882, American Poet, Essayist)

157 Men over forty are no judges of a book written in a new spirit.
Ralph Waldo Emerson (1803-1882, American Poet, Essayist)

158 Most critical writing is drivel and half of it is dishonest. It is a short cut to oblivion, anyway. Thinking in terms of ideas destroys the power to think in terms of emotions and sensations.
Raymond Chandler (1888-1959, American Author)

159 It is wrong to be harsh with the New York critics, unless one admits in the same breath that it is a condition of their existence that they should write entertainingly about something which is rarely worth writing about at all.
Raymond Chandler (1888-1959, American Author)

160 Good critical writing is measured by the perception and evaluation of the subject; bad critical writing by the necessity of maintaining the professional standing of the critic.
Raymond Chandler (1888-1959, American Author)

161 Some people are always critical of vague statements. I tend rather to be critical of precise statements; they are the only ones which can correctly be labeled "wrong."
Raymond Smullyan

162 Any authentic work of art must start an argument between the artist and his audience.
Rebecca West (1892-1983, British Author)

163 The whole effort of a sincere man is to erect his personal impressions into laws.
Remy De Gourmont (1858-1915, French Novelist, Philosopher, Poet, Playwright)

164 For if there is anything to one's praise, it is foolish vanity to be gratified at it, and if it is abuse - - why one is always sure to hear of it from one damned good-natured friend or another!
Richard Brinsley Sheridan (1751-1816, Anglo-Irish Dramatist)

165 Critics! Those cut-throat bandits in the paths of fame.
Robert Burns (1759-1796, Scottish Poet)

166 Any jackass can kick a barn down, but it takes a carpenter to build it.
Sam Rayburn (1882-1961, American Representative)

167 Criticism is a study by which men grow important and formidable at very small expense. He whom nature has made weak, and idleness keeps ignorant, may yet support his vanity by the name of a critic.
Samuel Johnson (1709-1784, British Author)

168 I would rather be attacked than unnoticed. For the worst thing you can do to an author is to be silent as to his works. An assault upon a town is a bad thing; but starving it is still worse.
Samuel Johnson (1709-1784, British Author)

169 Criticism, as it was first instituted by Aristotle, was meant as a standard of judging well.
Samuel Johnson (1709-1784, British Author)

170 Reviewers are usually people who would have been, poets, historians, biographer, if they could. They have tried their talents at one thing or another and have failed; therefore they turn critic.
Samuel Taylor Coleridge (1772-1834, British Poet, Critic, Philosopher)

171 There's a fine line between participation and mockery.
Scott Adams (American Cartoonist, "Dilbert")

172 When subjected to the rain of criticism, let's not curse the rain. Let's accept it as a part of life. Let's remember that the more criticism we can successfully handle, the more zest we will experience in our lives.
Shall Sinha

173 There are two insults no human will endure. The assertion that he has no sense of humor and the doubly impertinent assertion that he has never known trouble.
Sinclair Lewis (1885-1951, First American Novelist to win the Nobel Prize for literature)

174 No matter how well you perform there's always somebody of intelligent opinion who thinks it's lousy.
Sir Lawrence Olivier (1907-1989, British Actor, Producer, Director)

175 Give me the critic bred in Nature's school, who neither talks by rote, nor thinks by rule; who feeling's honest dictates still obeys, and dares, without a precedent, to praise.
Sir Martin Archer Shee

176 When the critics come around it's always too late.
Sir Sidney Nolan

177 In most modern instances, interpretation amounts to the philistine refusal to leave the work of art alone. Real art has the capacity to make us nervous. By reducing the work of art to its content and then interpreting that, one tames the work of art. Interpretation makes art manageable, conformable.
Susan Sontag (1933-, American Essayist)

178 Any critic is entitled to wrong judgments, of course. But certain lapses of judgment indicate the radical failure of an entire sensibility.
Susan Sontag (1933-, American Essayist)

179 The aim of all commentary on art now should be to make works of art -- and, by analogy, our own experience -- more, rather than less, real to us. The function of criticism should be to show how it is what it is, even that it is what it is, rather than to show what it means.
Susan Sontag (1933-, American Essayist)

180 I never read a book before reviewing it; it prejudices a man so.
Sydney Smith (1771-1845, British Writer, Clergyman)

181 We might remind ourselves that criticism is as inevitable as breathing, and that we should be none the worse for articulating what passes in our minds when we read a book and feel an emotion about it, for criticizing our own minds in their work of criticism.
T. S. Eliot (1888-1965, American-born British Poet, Critic)

182 All my life people have said that I wasn't going to make it.
Ted Turner (1938-, American Businessman, Founder of CNN)

183 Culture is only true when implicitly critical, and the mind which forgets this revenges itself in the critics it breeds. Criticism is an indispensable element of culture.
Theodor W. Adorno (1903-1969, German Philosopher, Sociologist, Music Critic)

184 No sadder proof can be given of a person's own tiny stature, than their disbelief in great people.
Thomas Carlyle (1795-1881, Scottish Philosopher, Author)

185 Not even the most powerful organs of the press, including Time, Newsweek, and The New York Times, can discover a new artist or certify his work and make it stick. They can only bring you the scores.
Thomas Wolfe (1931-, American Author, Journalist)

186 Every writer is necessarily a critic -- that is, each sentence is a skeleton accompanied by enormous activity of rejection; and each selection is governed by general principles concerning truth, force, beauty, and so on. The critic that is in every fabulist is like the iceberg -- nine-tenths of him is under water.
Thornton Wilder (1897-1975, American Novelist, Playwright)

187 Most of our censure of others is only oblique praise of self, uttered to show the wisdom and superiority of the speaker. It has all the invidiousness of self-praise, and all the ill-desert of falsehood.
Tryon Edwards (1809-1894, American Theologian)

188 I'd rather be hissed at for a good verse, than applauded for a bad one.
Victor Hugo (1802-1885, French Poet, Dramatist, Novelist)

189 It is the nature of the artist to mind excessively what is said about him. Literature is strewn with the wreckage of men who have minded beyond reason the opinions of others.
Virginia Woolf (1882-1941, British Novelist, Essayist)

190 The critical opinions of a writer should always be taken with a large grain of salt. For the most part, they are manifestations of his debate with himself as to what he should do next and what he should avoid.
W. H. Auden (1907-1973, Anglo-American Poet)

191 Criticism should be a casual conversation.
W. H. Auden (1907-1973, Anglo-American Poet)

192 People who ask for your criticism want only praise.
W. Somerset Maugham (1874-1965, British Novelist, Playwright)

193 You know what the critics are. If you tell the truth they only say you're cynical and it does an author no good to get a reputation for cynicism.
W. Somerset Maugham (1874-1965, British Novelist, Playwright)

194 The art of the critic in a nutshell: to coin slogans without betraying ideas. The slogans of an inadequate criticism peddle ideas to fashion.
Walter Benjamin (1982-1940, German Critic, Philosopher)

195 Remember that nobody will ever get ahead of you as long as he is kicking you in the seat of the pants.
Walter Winchell (1897-1972, American Journalist)

196 In my conscience I believe the baggage loves me, for she never speaks well of me herself, nor suffers any body else to rail at me.
William Congreve (1670-1729, British Dramatist)

197 The artist doesn't have time to listen to the critics. The ones who want to be writers read the reviews, the ones who want to write don't have the time to read reviews.
William Faulkner (1897-1962, American Novelist)

198 Neither praise or blame is the object of true criticism. Justly to discriminate, firmly to establish, wisely to prescribe, and honestly to award. These are the true aims and duties of criticism.
William Gilmore Simms (1806-1870, American Author)

199 The dread of criticism is the death of genius.
William Gilmore Simms (1806-1870, American Author)

200 Writing prejudicial, off-putting reviews is a precise exercise in applied black magic. The reviewer can draw free-floating disagreeable associations to a book by implying that the book is completely unimportant without saying exactly why, and carefully avoiding any clear images that could capture the reader's full attention.
William S. Burroughs (1914-1997, American Writer)

201 A man generally has the good or ill qualities he attributes to mankind.
William Shenstone (1714-1763, British Poet)

202 A drama critic is a person who surprises the playwright by informing him what he meant.
Wilson Mizner (1876-1933, American Author)

203 When I am abroad, I always make it a rule to never criticize or attack the government of my own country. I make up for lost time when I come home.
Winston Churchill (1874-1965, British Statesman, Prime Minister)

204 It is just as hard to do your duty when men are sneering at you as when they are shouting at you.
Woodrow T. Wilson (1856-1924, Twenty-eighth President of the USA)

205 There has never been a statue erected to honor a critic.
Zig Ziglar (American Sales Trainer, Author, Motivational Speaker)

CROWDS

1 The man who follows the crowd will usually get no further than the crowd. The man who walks alone is likely to find himself in places no one has
Alan Ashley-Pitt

2 If there is a look of human eyes that tells of perpetual loneliness, so there is also the familiar look that is the sign of perpetual crowds.
Alice Meynell (1847-1922, British Poet, Essayist)

3 Look, when that crowd gets to cheering, when we know they're with us, when we know they like us, we play better. A hell of a lot better!
Bill Carlin

4 The crowd gives the leader new strength
Evenus (Ancient Greek Poet)

5 Crowds are somewhat like the sphinx of ancient fable: It is necessary to arrive at a solution of the problems offered by their psychology or to resign ourselves to being devoured by them.
Gustave Le Bon (1841-1931, French Author)

6 If it has to choose who is to be crucified, the crowd will always save Barabbas.
Jean Cocteau (1889-1963, French Author, Filmmaker)

7 Towns are full of people, houses full of tenants, hotels full of guests, trains full of travelers, cafés full of customers, parks full of promenaders, consulting-rooms of famous doctors full of patients, theatres full of spectators, and beaches full of bathers. What previously was, in general, no problem, now begins to be an everyday one, namely, to find room.
Jose Ortega Y Gasset (1883-1955, Spanish Essayist, Philosopher)

8 The only certainty about following the crowd is that you will all get there together.
Mychal Wynn (American Author)

9 Spiritual superiority only sees the individual. But alas, ordinarily we human beings are sensual and, therefore, as soon as it is a gathering, the impression changes -- we see something abstract, the crowd, and we become different. But in the eyes of God, the infinite spirit, all the millions that have lived and now live do not make a crowd, He only sees each individual.
Soren Kierkegaard (1813-1855, Danish Philosopher, Writer)

10 Great bodies of people are never responsible for what they do.
Virginia Woolf (1882-1941, British Novelist, Essayist)

11 Nobody goes there anymore. It's too crowded.
Yogi Berra (1925-, American Baseball Player)

CULT

1   What is a cult? It just means not enough people to make a minority.
    Robert Altman (American Filmmaker)

2   A cult is a religion with no political power.
    Thomas Wolfe (1931-, American Author, Journalist)

CULTURE

1   Culture: the cry of men in face of their destiny.
    Albert Camus (1913-1960, French Existential Writer)

2   Without culture, and the relative freedom it implies, society, even when perfect, is but a jungle. This is why any authentic creation is a gift to the future.
    Albert Camus (1913-1960, French Existential Writer)

3   We are like ignorant shepherds living on a site where great civilizations once flourished. The shepherds play with the fragments that pop up to the surface, having no notion of the beautiful structures of which they were once a part.
    Allan Bloom (1930-1992, American Educator, Author)

4   The manner of their living is very barbarous, because they do not eat at fixed times, but as often as they please.
    Amerigo Vespucci (1454-1512, Italian Explorer Who Discovered America)

5   All objects, all phases of culture are alive. They have voices. They speak of their history and interrelatedness. And they are all talking at once!
    Camille Paglia (1947-, American Author, Critic, Educator)

6   We are in the process of creating what deserves to be called the idiot culture. Not an idiot sub- culture, which every society has bubbling beneath the surface and which can provide harmless fun; but the culture itself. For the first time, the weird and the stupid and the coarse are becoming our cultural norm, even our cultural ideal.
    Carl Bernstein (1944-, American Journalist, writer)

7   Our attitude toward our own culture has recently been characterized by two qualities, braggadocio and petulance. Braggadocio -- empty boasting of American power, American virtue, American know-how -- has dominated our foreign relations now for some decades. Here at home -- within the family, so to speak -- our attitude to our culture expresses a superficially different spirit, the spirit of petulance. Never before, perhaps, has a culture been so fragmented into groups, each full of its own virtue, each annoyed and irritated at the others.
    Daniel J. Boorstin (1914-, American Historian)

8   Mrs. Ballinger is one of the ladies who pursue Culture in bands, as though it were dangerous to meet it alone.
    Edith Wharton (1862-1937, American Author)

9   Culture is a sham if it is only a sort of Gothic front put on an iron building -- like Tower Bridge -- or a classical front put on a steel frame -- like the Daily Telegraph building in Fleet Street. Culture, if it is to be a real thing and a holy thing, must be the product of what we actually do for a living -- not something added, like sugar on a pill.
    Eric Gill (1882-1940, British Sculptor, Engraver, Writer, Typographer)

10 The bourgeoisie and the petty bourgeoisie have armed themselves against the rising proletariat with, among other things, "culture." It's an old ploy of the bourgeoisie. They keep a standing "art" to defend their collapsing culture.
    George Grosz

11 We know that a man can read Goethe or Rilke in the evening, that he can play Bach and Schubert, and go to his day's work at Auschwitz in the morning.
    George Steiner (1929-, French-born American Critic, Novelist)

12 Men are not suffering from the lack of good literature, good art, good theatre, good music, but from that which has made it impossible for these to become manifest. In short, they are suffering from the silent shameful conspiracy (the more shameful since it is unacknowledged) which has bound them together as enemies of art and artists.
    Henry Miller (1891-1980, American Author)

13 Culture is the habit of being pleased with the best and knowing why.
    Henry Van Dyke (1852-1933, American Protestant Clergyman, Poet and Writer)

14 That is true culture which helps us to work for the social betterment of all.
    Henry Ward Beecher (1813-1887, American Preacher, Orator, Writer)

15 If mass communications blend together harmoniously, and often unnoticeably, art, politics, religion, and philosophy with commercials, they bring these realms of culture to their common denominator -- the commodity form. The music of the soul is also the music of salesmanship. Exchange value, not truth value, counts.
    Herbert Marcuse (1898-1979, German Political Philosopher)

16 Whenever I hear the word culture, I reach for my revolver.
    Hermann Goering (1893-1946, Nazi Politico-Military Leader)

17 Culture is the widening of the mind and of the spirit.
    Jawaharlal Nehru (1889-1964, Indian Nationalist, Statesman)

18 Here in the U.S., culture is not that delicious panacea which we Europeans consume in a sacramental mental space and which has its own special columns in the newspapers -- and in people's minds. Culture is space, speed, cinema, technology. This culture is authentic, if anything can be said to be authentic.
    Jean Baudrillard (French Postmodern Philosopher, Writer)

19 What culture lacks is the taste for anonymous, innumerable germination. Culture is smitten with counting and measuring; it feels out of place and uncomfortable with the innumerable; its efforts tend, on the contrary, to limit the numbers in all domains; it tries to count on its fingers.
Jean Dubuffet (1901-1985, French Sculptor, Painter)

20 Eclecticism is the degree zero of contemporary general culture: one listens to reggae, watches a western, eats McDonald's food for lunch and local cuisine for dinner, wears Paris perfume in Tokyo and "retro" clothes in Hong Kong; knowledge is a matter for TV games. It is easy to find a public for eclectic works.
Jean Frantois Lyotard (1924-, French Philosopher)

21 The acquiring of culture is the development of an avid hunger for knowledge and beauty.
Jesse Bennett (1769-1842, American Physician)

22 One ought, every day at least, to hear a little song, read a good poem, see a fine picture, and, if it were possible, to speak a few reasonable words.
Johann Wolfgang Von Goethe (1749-1832, German Poet, Dramatist, Novelist)

23 Every man's ability may be strengthened or increased by culture.
John Abbott (1905 - 1996, American Actor)

24 For the rest, whatever we have got has been by infinite labor, and search, and ranging through every corner of nature; the difference is that instead of dirt and poison, we have rather chosen to fill our hives with honey and wax, thus furnishing mankind with the two noblest of things, which are sweetness and light.
Jonathan Swift (1667-1745, Anglo-Irish Satirist)

25 Culture is the tacit agreement to let the means of subsistence disappear behind the purpose of existence. Civilization is the subordination of the latter to the former.
Karl Kraus (1874-1936, Austrian Satirist)

26 The ideas of the ruling class are in every epoch the ruling ideas, i.e., the class which is the ruling material force of society, is at the same time its ruling intellectual force.
Karl Marx (1818-1883, German Political Theorist, Social Philosopher)

27 Culture of the mind must be subservient to the heart.
Mahatma Gandhi (1869-1948, Indian Political, Spiritual Leader)

28 No culture can live if it attempts to be exclusive.
Mahatma Gandhi (1869-1948, Indian Political, Spiritual Leader)

29 Our culture has become something that is completely and utterly in love with its parent. It's become a notion of boredom that is bought and sold, where nothing will happen except that people will become more and more terrified of tomorrow, because the new continues to look old, and the old will always look cute.
Malcolm Mclaren

30 Letting a hundred flowers blossom and a hundred schools of thought contend is the policy for promoting the progress of the arts and the sciences and a flourishing culture in our land.
Mao Zedong (1893-1976, Founder of Chinese Communist State)

31 A society person who is enthusiastic about modern painting or Truman Capote is already half a traitor to his class. It is middle-class people who, quite mistakenly, imagine that a lively pursuit of the latest in reading and painting will advance their status in the world.
Mary Mccarthy (1912-1989, American Author, Critic)

32 Culture, then, is a study of perfection, and perfection which insists on becoming something rather than in having something, in an inward condition of the mind and spirit, not in an outward set of circumstances.
Matthew Arnold (1822-1888, British Poet, Critic)

33 Culture, the acquainting ourselves with the best that has been known and said in the world, and thus with the history of the human spirit.
Matthew Arnold (1822-1888, British Poet, Critic)

34 High culture is nothing but a child of that European perversion called history, the obsession we have with going forward, with considering the sequence of generations a relay race in which everyone surpasses his predecessor, only to be surpassed by his successor. Without this relay race called history there would be no European art and what characterizes it: a longing for originality, a longing for change. Robespierre, Napoleon, Beethoven, Stalin, Picasso, they're all runners in the relay race, they all belong to the same stadium.
Milan Kundera (1929-, Czech Author, Critic)

35 It is of the essence of imaginative culture that it transcends the limits both of the naturally possible and of the morally acceptable.
Northrop Frye (1912-1991, Canadian Literary Critic)

36 If everybody is looking for it, then nobody is finding it. If we were cultured, we would not be conscious of lacking culture. We would regard it as something natural and would not make so much fuss about it. And if we knew the real value of this word we would be cultured enough not to give it so much importance.
Pablo Picasso (1881-1973, Spanish Artist)

37 One of the surest signs of the Philistine is his reverence for the superior tastes of those who put him down.
Pauline Kael (1919-, American Film Critic)

38 Culture is one thing and varnish is another.
Ralph Waldo Emerson (1803-1882, American Poet, Essayist)

39 If you see in any given situation only what everybody else can see, you can be said to be so much a representative of your culture that you are a victim of it.
S. I. Hayakawa (1902-1992, Canadian Born American Senator, Educator)

40 A man should be just cultured enough to be able to look with suspicion upon culture at first, not second hand.
Samuel Butler (1612-1680, British Poet, Satirist)

41 Culture is an instrument wielded by teachers to manufacture teachers, who, in their turn, will manufacture still more teachers.
Simone Weil (1910-1943, French Philosopher, Mystic)

42 In the room the women come and go talking of Michelangelo.
T. S. Eliot (1888-1965, American-born British Poet, Critic)

43 Culture is the arts elevated to a set of beliefs.
Thomas Wolfe (1931-, American Author, Journalist)

44 Culture is the name for what people are interested in, their thoughts, their models, the books they read and the speeches they hear, their table-talk, gossip, controversies, historical sense and scientific training, the values they appreciate, the quality of life they admire. All communities have a culture. It is the climate of their civilization.
Walter Lippmann (1889-1974, American Journalist)

45 General jackdaw culture, very little more than a collection of charming miscomprehensions, untargeted enthusiasms, and a general habit of skimming.
William Bolitho (1890-1930, British Author)

CUNNING

1 The greatest cunning is to have none at all.
Carl Sandburg (1878-1967, American Poet)

2 The fly that does not want to be swatted is safest if it sits on the fly-swat.
Georg C. Lichtenberg (1742-1799, German Physicist, Satirist)

3 Simulated disorder postulates perfect discipline; simulated fear postulates courage; simulated weakness postulates strength.
Lao-Tzu (600 BC, Chinese Philosopher, Founder of Taoism, Author of the "Tao Te Ching")

4 With foxes we must play the fox.
Thomas Fuller (1608-1661, British Clergyman, Author)

5 The weak in courage is strong in cunning.
William Blake (1757-1827, British Poet, Painter)

CURIOSITY

1 The important thing is not to stop questioning. Curiosity has its own reason for existing. One cannot help but be in awe when he contemplates the mysteries of eternity, of life, of the marvelous structure of reality. It is enough if one tries merely to comprehend a little of this mystery everyday. Never lose a holy curiosity.
Albert Einstein (1879-1955, German-born American Physicist)

2 Never lose a holy curiosity.
Albert Einstein (1879-1955, German-born American Physicist)

3 A person who is too nice an observer of the business of the crowd, like one who is too curious in observing the labor of bees, will often be stung for his curiosity.
Alexander Pope (1688-1744, British Poet, Critic, Translator)

4 Curiosity ... endows the people who have it with a generosity in argument and a serenity in their own mode of life which springs from their cheerful willingness to let life take the form it will.
Alistair Cooke (1908-, British Broadcaster, Journalist)

5 The whole art of teaching is only the art of awakening the natural curiosity of young minds for the purpose of satisfying it afterwards.
Anatole France (1844-1924, French Writer)

6 The curiosity to know things has been given to man as a scourge.
Apocrypha

7 The alchemists in their search for gold discovered many other things of greater value.
Arthur Schopenhauer (1788-1860, German Philosopher)

8 Be not curious in unnecessary matters: for more things are shrewd unto thee than men understand.
Bible (Sacred Scriptures of Christians and Judaism)

9 Somewhere, something incredible is waiting to be known.
Carl Edward Sagan (1934-, American Astronomer, author)

10 I think most people are curious about what it would be like to be able to meet yourself -- it's eerie.
Christy Turlington (Born 1969, American Model)

11 Creatures whose mainspring is curiosity enjoy the accumulating of facts far more than the pausing at times to reflect on those facts.
Clarence Day (1874-1935, American Essayist)

12 We never stop investigating. We are never satisfied that we know enough to get by. Every question we answer leads on to another question. This has become the greatest survival trick of our species.
Desmond Morris (1928-, British Anthropologist)

13 The first and simplest emotion which we discover in the human mind, is curiosity.
Edmund Burke (1729-1797, British Political Writer, Statesman)

14 Curiosity is one of the lowest of the human faculties. You will have noticed in daily life that when people are inquisitive they nearly always have bad memories and are usually stupid at bottom.
Edward M. Forster (1879-1970, British Novelist, Essayist)

15 I think, at a child's birth, if a mother could ask a fairy godmother to endow it with the most useful gift, that gift would be curiosity.
Eleanor Roosevelt (1884-1962, American First Lady, Columnist, Lecturer, Humanitarian)

16 You must learn day by day, year by year, to broaden your horizon. The more things you love, the more you are interested in.
Ethel Barrymore (1879-1959, American Actress)

17 Disinterested intellectual curiosity is the life blood of real civilization.
G. M. Trevelyan (1876-1962, British Historian)

18 All that is really necessary for survival of the fittest, it seems, is an interest in life, good, bad or peculiar.
Grace Paley (1922-, American Short Story Writer)

19 Curiosity is the direct incontinence of the spirit.
Jeremy Taylor (1613-1667, British Churchman, Writer)

20 That low vice, curiosity!
Lord Byron (1788-1824, British Poet)

21 All my life I've been harassed by questions: Why is something this way and not another? How do you account for that? This rage to understand, to fill in the blanks, only makes life more banal. If we could only find the courage to leave our destiny to chance, to accept the fundamental mystery of our lives, then we might be closer to the sort of happiness that comes with innocence.
Luis Bunuel (1900-1983, Spanish Film Director)

22 It is a shameful thing to be weary of inquiry when what we search for is excellent.
Marcus T. Cicero (106-43 BC, Great Roman Orator, Politician)

23 Every age has a keyhole to which its eye is pasted.
Mary Mccarthy (1912-1989, American Author, Critic)

24 Curiosity is lying in wait for every secret.
Ralph Waldo Emerson (1803-1882, American Poet, Essayist)

25 Curiosity is as much the parent of attention, as attention is of memory.
Richard Whately (1787-1863, British Prelate, Writer)

26 Where the apple reddens never pry -- lest we lose our Edens, Eve and I.
Robert Browning (1812-1889, British Poet)

27 Curiosity is, in great and generous minds, the first passion and the last.
Samuel Johnson (1709-1784, British Author)

28 Curiosity is one of the permanent and certain characteristics of a vigorous mind.
Samuel Johnson (1709-1784, British Author)

29 The thirst to know and understand, a large and liberal discontent.
Sir William Watson (1858-1935, British Poet)

30 Desire to know why, and how -- curiosity, which is a lust of the mind, that a perseverance of delight in the continued and indefatigable generation of knowledge -- exceedeth the short vehemence of any carnal pleasure.
Thomas Hobbes (1588-1679, British Philosopher)

31 Curiosity is the lust of the mind.
Thomas Hobbes (1588-1679, British Philosopher)

32 Curiosity is one of the forms of feminine bravery.
Victor Hugo (1802-1885, French Poet, Dramatist, Novelist)

33 One of the secrets of life is to keep our intellectual curiosity acute.
William Lyon Phelps

34 A man should go on living -- if only to satisfy his curiosity.
Yiddish Proverb

CURSES

1 Vexed sailors cursed the rain, for which poor shepherds prayed in vain.
Edmund Waller (1606-1687, British Poet)

2 This is the curse of an evil deed, that it incites and must bring forth more evil.
Johann Friedrich Von Schiller (1759-1805, German Dramatist, Poet, Historian)

3 Cursing is invoking the assistance of a spirit to help you inflict suffering. Swearing on the other hand, is invoking, only the witness of a spirit to an statement you wish to make.
John Ruskin (1819-1900, British Critic, Social Theorist)

4 I wish my deadly foe, no worse than want of fiends, and empty purse.
Nicholas Breton (1545-1626, British Author, Poet)

5 Curses are like chickens, they always come home.
Proverb

6 Curses always recoil on the head of him who imprecates them. If you put a chain around the neck of a slave, the other end fastens itself around your own.
Ralph Waldo Emerson (1803-1882, American Poet, Essayist)

7 Many a man curses the rain that falls upon his head, and knows that it brings abundance to drive away hunger.
St. Basil (329-379, Bishop of Caesarea)

CUSTOM

1 Customs form us all, our thoughts, our morals, our most fixed beliefs; are consequences of our place of birth.
Aaron Hill (1685-1750, British Dramatist)

2 Custom, that unwritten law, By which the people keep even kings in awe.
Charles Davenport

3 Custom, then, is the great guide of human life.
David Hume (1711-1776, Scottish Philosopher, Historian)

4 Custom reconciles us to everything.
Edmund Burke (1729-1797, British Political Writer, Statesman)

5 People usually think according to their inclinations, speak according to their learning and ingrained opinions, but generally act according to custom.
Francis Bacon (1561-1626, British Philosopher, Essayist, Statesman)

6 The despotism of custom is everywhere the standing hindrance to human advancement.
John Stuart Mill (1806-1873, British Philosopher, Economist)

7 Customs and convictions change; respectable people are the last to know, or to admit, the change, and the ones most offended by fresh reflections of the facts in the mirror of art.
John Updike (1932-, American Novelist, Critic)

8 Nature is seldom in the wrong, custom always.
Lady Mary Wortley Montagu (1689-1762, British Society Figure, Letter Writer)

9 Often, the less there is to justify a traditional custom, the harder it is to get rid of it.
Mark Twain (1835-1910, American Humorist, Writer)

10 The way of the world is to make laws, but follow custom.
Michel Eyquem De Montaigne (1533-1592, French Philosopher, Essayist)

11 Nothing is more powerful than custom or habit.
Ovid (43 BC-18 AD, Roman Poet)

12 Custom is a tyrant.
Proverb

13 The empire of custom is most mighty.
Publilius Syrus (1st Century BC, Roman Writer)

14 Of course poets have morals and manners of their own, and custom is no argument with them.
Thomas Hardy (1840-1928, British Novelist, Poet)

15 Laws are subordinate to custom.
Titus Maccius Plautus (254-184 BC, Roman Comic Poet)

16 Without the aid of prejudice and custom, I should not be able to find my way across the room.
William Hazlitt (1778-1830, British Essayist)

CUSTOMERS

1 I don't build in order to have clients. I have clients in order to build.
Ayn Rand (1905-1982, Russian Writer, Philosopher)

2 The only way to know how customers see your business is to look at it through their eyes.
Daniel R. Scroggin (American Business Executive, CEO of TGI Friday's Inc.)

3 There are only two ways to get a new customer: 1. solicit a new customer any way you can. 2. Take good care of your present customers, so they don't become someone else's new customers.
Ed Zeitz

4 Worry about being better; bigger will take care of itself. Think one customer at a time and take care of each one the best way you can.
Gary Comer (American Businessman, Founder of Land's End)

5 Everything starts with the customer.
Gerstner, Jr. (American Business Executive, Chairman & CEO of IBM)

6 If you love your customer to death, you can't go wrong.
Graham Day (American Business Executive)

7 Revolve your world around the customer and more customers will revolve around you.
Heather Williams

8 Motivate them, train them, care about them and make winners out of them...we know that if we treat our employees correctly, they'll treat the customers right. And if customers are treated right, they'll come back.
J. Marriot Jr. (American Businessman)

9 If you're not serving the customer, you'd better be serving someone who is.
Karl Albrecht (American Management Consultant, Author)

10 Make a customer, not a sale.
Katherine Barchetti (American Clothing Retailer)

11 Above all, we wish to avoid having a dissatisfied customer. We consider our customers a part of our organization, and we want them to feel free to make any criticism they see fit in regard to our merchandise or service. Sell practical, tested merchandise at reasonable profit, treat your customers like human beings -- and they will always come back.
L.L. Bean (American Businessman, Founder of L.L Bean's)

12 We don't want to push our ideas on to customers, we simply want to make what they want.
Laura Ashley (Welsh Fabric Clothes Designer)

13 Sacred cows make the best hamburger.
Mark Twain (1835-1910, American Humorist, Writer)

14 If you don't care, your customer never will.
Marlene Blaszczyk

15 Look through your customer's eyes. Are you the solution provider or part of the problem?
Marlene Blaszczyk

16 Every company's greatest assets are its customers, because without customers there is no company.
Michael Leboeuf (American Researcher, Consultant, Author)

17 Treat your customers like lifetime partners.
Michael Leboeuf (American Researcher, Consultant, Author)

18 A satisfied customer is the best business strategy of all.
Michael Leboeuf (American Researcher, Consultant, Author)

19 Be it furniture, clothes, or health care, many industries today are marketing nothing more than commodities -- no more, no less. What will make the difference in the long run is the care and feeding of customers.
Micheal Mescon

20 Consumers are statistics. Customers are people.
Stanley Marcus (1905-, American Retail Merchant)

21 The 1990s customer expects service to be characterized by fast and efficient computer-based systems.
Steve Cuthbert (British Director General of the Chartered Institute of Marketing)

22 A customer who complains is my best friend.
Stew Leonard (American Businessman)

23 Always think of your customers as suppliers first. Work closely with them, so they can supply you with the information you need to supply them with the right products and services.
Susan Marthaller

24 Doing a great job and not meeting the customer's objectives is as useless as doing a poor job within the customer's objectives.
Thomas Faranda

CYCLES

1 Everything comes if a man will only wait.
Benjamin Disraeli (1804-1881, British Statesman, Prime Minister)

2 What has been will be again. What has been done will be done again... [Ecclesiastes 1:9]
Bible (Sacred Scriptures of Christians and Judaism)

3 That which the fountain sends forth returns again to the fountain.
Henry Wadsworth Longfellow (1819-1892, American Poet)

4 Each thing is of like form from everlasting and comes round again in its cycle.
Marcus Aurelius (121-80 AD, Roman Emperor, Philosopher)

5 By law of periodical repetition, everything which has happened once must happen again and again -- and not capriciously, but at regular periods, and each thing in its own period, not another's and each obeying its own law.
Mark Twain (1835-1910, American Humorist, Writer)

6 In all things there is a law of cycles.
Publius Cornelius Tacitus (55-117 AD, Roman Historian)

7 All motion is cyclic. It circulates to the limits of its possibilities and then returns to its starting point.
Robert Collier (American Writer, Publisher)

8 Events tend to recur in cycles...
W. Clement Stone (1902-, American Businessman, Author)

CYNICS AND CYNICISM

1 A cynic is a blackguard whose faulty vision sees things as they are, and not as they ought to be.
Ambrose Bierce (1842-1914, American Author, Editor, Journalist, "The Devil's Dictionary")

2 A cynic is a man who looks at the world with a monocle in his mind's eye.
Carolyn Wells (1870-1942, American Author)

3 The cynic never grows up, but commits intellectual suicide.
Dean Charles R. Brown

4 It takes a clever man to turn cynic and a wise man to be clever enough not to.
Fannie Hurst

5 The power of accurate observation is commonly called cynicism by those who have not got it.
George Bernard Shaw (1856-1950, Irish-born British Dramatist)

6 Cynicism is intellectual dandyism.
George Meredith (1828-1909, British Author)

7 Cynicism is cheap -- you can buy it at any Monoprix store -- it's built into all poor-quality goods.
Graham Greene (1904-1991, British Novelist)

8 The cynics are right nine times out of ten.
H. L. Mencken (1880-1956, American Editor, Author, Critic, Humorist)

9 A cynic is a man who, when he smells flowers, looks around for a coffin.
H. L. Mencken (1880-1956, American Editor, Author, Critic, Humorist)

10 Cynicism is humor in ill health.
H.G. Wells (1866-1946, British-born American Author)

11 The only deadly sin I know is cynicism.
Henry Lewis Stimson (1867-1930, American Statesman)

12 The cynic is one who never sees a good quality in a man, and never fails to see a bad one. He is the human owl, vigilant in darkness and blind to light, mousing for vermin, and never seeing noble game.
Henry Ward Beecher (1813-1887, American Preacher, Orator, Writer)

13 A cynic is just a man who found out when he was ten that there wasn't any Santa Claus, and he's still upset.
James G. Cozzens (1903-1978, American Novelist)

14 The cynic, a parasite of civilization, lives by denying it, for the very reason that he is convinced that it will not fail.
Jose Ortega Y Gasset (1883-1955, Spanish Essayist, Philosopher)

15 Cynicism is the only form in which base souls approach honesty.
Nietzche Evil

16 What is a cynic? A man who knows the price of everything and the value of nothing.
Oscar Wilde (1856-1900, British Author, Wit)

17 A cynic can chill and dishearten with a single word.
Ralph Waldo Emerson (1803-1882, American Poet, Essayist)

18 Don't be a cynic and disconsolate preacher. Don't bewail and moan. Omit the negative propositions. Challenge us with incessant affirmatives. Don't waste yourself in rejection, or bark against the bad, but chant the beauty of the good.
Ralph Waldo Emerson (1803-1882, American Poet, Essayist)

19 Cynicism is the intellectual cripple's substitute for intelligence.
Russell Lynes (1910-, American Editor, Critic)

20 A cynic is not merely one who reads bitter lessons from the past; he is one who is prematurely disappointed in the future.
Sidney J. Harris (1917-, American Journalist)

21 Cynicism is the humor of hatred.
Sir Herbert Beerbohm Tree (1853-1917, British actor-manager)

22 I'm a hopeful cynic.
Tracy Chapman (British Stage and Television Comedian)

DANCE AND DANCING

1 They seldom looked happy. They passed one another without a word in the elevator, like silent shades in hell, hell-bent on their next look from a handsome stranger. Their next rush from a popper. The next song that turned their bones to jelly and left them all on the dance floor with heads back, eyes nearly closed, in the ecstasy of saints receiving the stigmata.
Andrew Holleran

2 Dancing is a wonderful training for girls, it's the first way you learn to guess what a man is going to do before he does it.
Christopher Morley (1890-1957, American Novelist, Journalist, Poet)

3 To shake your rump is to be environmentally aware.
David Byrne

4 And we love to dance -- especially that new one called the Civil War Twist. The Northern part of you stands still while the Southern part tries to secede.
Dick Gregory (American Comedian)

5 The Twist was a guided missile, launched from the ghetto into the very heart of suburbia. The Twist succeeded, as politics, religion, and law could never do, in writing in the heart and soul what the Supreme Court could only write on the books.
Eldridge Cleaver (1935-, American Black Leader, Writer)

6 Remember, Ginger Rogers did everything Fred Astaire did, but she did it backwards and in high heels.
Faith Whittlesey

7 I just put my feet in the air and move them around.
Fred Astaire (1899-1987, American Dancer, Singer, Actor)

8 I do not know what the spirit of a philosopher could more wish to be than a good dancer. For the dance is his ideal, also his fine art, finally also the only kind of piety he knows, his "divine service."
Friedrich Nietzsche (1844-1900, German Philosopher)

9 We should consider every day lost in which we have not danced at least once.
Friedrich Nietzsche (1844-1900, German Philosopher)

10 A perpendicular expression of a horizontal desire.
George Bernard Shaw (1856-1950, Irish-born British Dramatist)

11 Dancing is the loftiest, the most moving, the most beautiful of the arts, because it is no mere translation or abstraction from life; it is life itself.
Havelock Ellis (1859-1939, British Psychologist)

12 Dancing begets warmth, which is the parent of wantonness. It is, Sir, the great grandfather of cuckoldom.
Henry Fielding (1707-1754, British Novelist, Dramatist)

13 The real American type can never be a ballet dancer. The legs are too long, the body too supple and the spirit too free for this school of affected grace and toe walking.
Isadora Duncan (1878-1927, American Dancer)

14 The only dance masters I could have were Jean-Jacques Rousseau, Walt Whitman and Nietzsche.
Isadora Duncan (1878-1927, American Dancer)

15 It may be possible to do without dancing entirely. Instances have been known of young people passing many, many months successively without being at any ball of any description, and no material injury accrue either to body or mind; but when a beginning is made -- when the felicities of rapid motion have once been, though slightly, felt -- it must be a very heavy set that does not ask for more.
Jane Austen (1775-1817, British Novelist)

16 When we were at school we were taught to sing the songs of the Europeans. How many of us were taught the songs of the Wanyamwezi or of the Wahehe? Many of us have learnt to dance the rumba, or the cha cha, to rock and roll and to twist and even to dance the waltz and foxtrot. But how many of us can dance, or have even heard of the gombe sugu, the mangala, nyang umumi, kiduo, or lele mama?
Julius Kambarge Nyerere (1922-, Tanzanian Statesman, President)

17 And let the winds of the heavens dance between you.
Kahlil Gibran (1883-1931, Lebanese Poet, Novelist)

18 There comes a pause, for human strength will not endure to dance without cessation; and everyone must reach the point at length of absolute prostration.
Lewis Carroll (1832-1898, British Writer, Mathematician)

19 Custom has made dancing sometimes necessary for a young man; therefore mind it while you learn it, that you may learn to do it well, and not be ridiculous, though in a ridiculous act.
Lord Chesterfield (1694-1773, British Statesman, Author)

20 On with dance, let joy be unconfined, is my motto; whether there's any dance to dance or any joy to unconfined.
Mark Twain (1835-1910, American Humorist, Writer)

21 Dancing with abandon, turning a tango into a fertility rite.
Marshall Pugh

22 We look at the dance to impart the sensation of living in an affirmation of life, to energize the spectator into keener awareness of the vigor, the mystery, the humor, the variety, and the wonder of life. This is the function of the American dance.
Martha Graham (1894-1991, American Dancer, Teacher, and Choreographer)

23 Great dancers are not great because of their technique; they are great because of their passion.
Martha Graham (1894-1991, American Dancer, Teacher, and Choreographer)

24 Nothing is more revealing than movement.
Martha Graham (1894-1991, American Dancer, Teacher, and Choreographer)

25 I am not the first straight dancer or the last.
Mikhail Baryshnikov (1948-, Soviet Dancer, Actor)

26 How inimitably graceful children are in general before they learn to dance!
Samuel Taylor Coleridge (1772-1834, British Poet, Critic, Philosopher)

DANGER

1 I destroy my enemy when I make him my friend.
Abraham Lincoln (1809-1865, Sixteenth President of the USA)

2 Beware lest you lose the substance by grasping at the shadow.
Aesop (620-560 BC, Greek Fabulist)

3 Every man is his own chief enemy.
Anacharsis (600 BC, Scythian Philosopher)

4 When danger approaches, sing to it.
Arabian Proverb

5 Many have had their greatness made for them by their enemies.
Baltasar Gracian (1601-1658, Spanish Philosopher, Writer)

6 It is better to do thine own duty, however lacking in merit, than to do that of another, even though efficiently. It is better to die doing one's own duty, for to do the duty of another is fraught with danger.
Bhagavad Gita (400 BC, Sanskrit Poem Incorporated Into the Mahabharata)

7 It is better to meet danger than to wait for it. He that is on a lee shore, and foresees a hurricane, stands out to sea and encounters a storm to avoid a shipwreck.
Charles Caleb Colton (1780-1832, British Sportsman Writer)

8 Biggest profits mean gravest risks.
Chinese Proverb

9 I may be compelled to face danger, but never fear it, and while our soldiers can stand and fight, I can stand and feed and nurse them.
Clara Barton (1821-1912, American Humanitarian)

10 The most dangerous thing in the world is to try to leap a chasm in two jumps.
David Lloyd George (1863-1945, British Statesman, Prime Minister)

11 We cannot banish dangers, but we can banish fears. We must not demean life by standing in awe of death.
David Sarnoff (1891-1971, Belarus-born American Entrepreneur)

12 The mere apprehension of a coming evil has put many into a situation of the utmost danger.
F. L. Lucan (39-65, Roman Epic Poet)

13 Let the fear of a danger be a spur to prevent it; he that fears not, gives advantage to the danger.
Francis Quarles (1592-1644, British Poet)

14 The secret of reaping the greatest fruitfulness and the greatest enjoyment from life is to liver dangerously.
Friedrich Nietzsche (1844-1900, German Philosopher)

15 In this world there is always danger for those who are afraid of it.
George Bernard Shaw (1856-1950, Irish-born British Dramatist)

16 Danger, the spur of all great minds.
George Chapman (1557-1634, British Dramatist, Translator, Poet)

17 Between the anvil and the hammer.
German Proverb

18 However well organized the foundations of life may be, life must always be full of risks.
Havelock Ellis (1859-1939, British Psychologist)

19 Avoiding danger is no safer in the long run than outright exposure. The fearful are caught as often as the bold.
Helen Keller (1880-1968, American Blind/Deaf Author, Lecturer, Amorist)

20 Would you learn the secret of the sea? Only those who brave its dangers, comprehend its mystery!
Henry Wadsworth Longfellow (1819-1892, American Poet)

21 The most dangerous people are the ignorant.
Henry Ward Beecher (1813-1887, American Preacher, Orator, Writer)

22 No one that encounters prosperity does not also encounter danger.
Heraclitus (535-475 BC, Greek Philosopher)

23 In time of danger it is proper to be alarmed until danger be near at hand; but when we perceive that danger is near, we should oppose it as if we were not afraid.
Hitopadesa (Sanskrit Fable From Panchatantra)

24 A person in danger should not try to escape at one stroke. He should first calmly hold his own, then be satisfied with small gains, which will come by creative adaptations.
I Ching (12th Century BC, Chinese Book of Changes)

25 The responses of human beings vary greatly under dangerous circumstances. The strong man advances boldly to meet them head on. The weak man grows agitated. But the superior man stands up to fate, endures resolutely in his inner certainty If ignorant both
I Ching (12th Century BC, Chinese Book of Changes)

26 When the danger is past God is cheated.
Italian Proverb

27 The person who runs away exposes himself to that very danger more than a person who sits quietly.
Jawaharlal Nehru (1889-1964, Indian Nationalist, Statesman)

28 Nothing is so dangerous as an ignorant friend.
Jean De La Fontaine (1621-1695, French Poet)

29 No one is worthy of a good home here or in heaven that is not willing to be in peril for a good cause.
John Mason Brown (1800-1859, American Militant Abolitionist)

30 Wise people say nothing in dangerous times.
John Selden (1584-1654, British Jurist, Statesman)

31 Being on the tightrope is living; everything else is waiting.
Karl Wallenda (Tightrope walker)

32 There is nobody who is not dangerous for someone.
Marquise De STVignT

33 Those who'll play with cats must expect to be scratched.
Miguel De Cervantes (1547-1616, Spanish Novelist, Dramatist, Poet)

34 Princes and governments are far more dangerous than other elements within society.
Niccolo Machiavelli (1469-1527, Italian Author, Statesman)

35 We triumph without glory when we conquer without danger.
Pierre Corneille (1606-1684, French Dramatist)

36 To conquer without danger is to conquer without glory.
Pierre Corneille (1606-1684, French Dramatist)

37 Stay out of the road, if you want to grow old.
Pink Floyd

38 Danger past, God forgotten.
Proverb

39 A wreck on shore is a beacon at sea.
Proverb

40 One is not exposed to danger who, even when in safety is always on their guard.
Publilius Syrus (1st Century BC, Roman Writer)

41 The wise man in the storm prays to God, not for safety from danger, but for deliverance from fear.
Ralph Waldo Emerson (1803-1882, American Poet, Essayist)

42 As soon as there is life there is danger.
Ralph Waldo Emerson (1803-1882, American Poet, Essayist)

43 One ought never to turn one's back on a threatened danger and try to run away from it. If you do that, you will double the danger. But if you meet it promptly and without flinching, you will reduce the danger by half. Never run away from anything. Never!
Ralph Waldo Emerson (1803-1882, American Poet, Essayist)

44 The most dangerous thing is illusion.
Ralph Waldo Emerson (1803-1882, American Poet, Essayist)

45 We are confronted by a first danger, the destructiveness of applied atomic energy. And then we are confronted by a second danger, that we do not enough appreciate the first danger.
Raymond G. Swing

46 If we survive danger it steels our courage more than anything else.
Reinhold Niebuhr (1892-1971, American Theologian, Historian)

47 Dangers bring fears, and fears more dangers bring.
Richard Baxter (1615-1691, British Nonconformist Theologian)

48 Danger and delight grow on one stalk.
Scottish Proverb

49 Constant exposure to dangers will breed contempt for them.
Seneca (4 BC-65 AD, Spanish-born Roman Statesman, philosopher)

50 Don't play for safety -- it's the most dangerous thing in the world.
Sir Hugh Walpole (1884-1941, New Zealand Writer)

51 If a little knowledge is dangerous, where is the man who has so much as to be out of danger?
Thomas H. Huxley (1825-1895, British Biologist, Educator)

52 Great perils have this beauty, that they bring to light the fraternity of strangers.
Victor Hugo (1802-1885, French Poet, Dramatist, Novelist)

53 Out of this nettle, danger, we pluck this flower, safety.
William Shakespeare (1564-1616, British Poet, Playwright, Actor)

54 Send danger from the east unto the west, so honor cross it from the north to south.
William Shakespeare (1564-1616, British Poet, Playwright, Actor)

55 Yond Cassius has a lean and hungry look; He thinks too much; such men are dangerous. [Julius Caesar]
William Shakespeare (1564-1616, British Poet, Playwright, Actor)

56 Danger -- if you meet it promptly and without flinching -- you will reduce the danger by half. Never run away from anything. Never!
Winston Churchill (1874-1965, British Statesman, Prime Minister)

57 Nothing is so exhilarating in life as to be shot at with no result.
Winston Churchill (1874-1965, British Statesman, Prime Minister)

DATING

1 The soundtrack to Indecent Exposure is a romantic mix of music that I know most women love to hear, so I never keep it far from me when women are nearby.
Fabio (1961-, Canadian-born American Model, Actor)

2 What's nice about my dating life is that I don't have to leave my house. All I have to do is read the paper: I'm marrying Richard Gere, dating Daniel Day-Lewis, parading around with John F. Kennedy, Jr., and even Robert De Niro was in there for a day.
Julia Roberts (Born 1967, American Actress)

3 When I had no work and all this time on my hands, I couldn't get a date. Now that I have women banging on my door, I have no time to answer it.
Scott Wolf (Born 1968, American Actor)

DAUGHTERS

1 A man is free to go up as high as he can reach up to; but I, with all my style and pep, can't get a man my equal because a girl is always judged by her mother.
Anzia Yezierska (1885-1970, Polish Writer)

2 Oh my son's my son till he gets him a wife, but my daughter's my daughter all her life.
Dinah Mulock Craik

3 How the mother is to be pitied who hath handsome daughters! Locks, bolts, bars, and lectures of morality are nothing to them: they break through them all. They have as much pleasure in cheating a father and mother, as in cheating at cards.
John Gay (1688-1732, British Playwright, Poet)

4 I only have two rules for my newly born daughter: she will dress well and never have sex.
John Malkovich

5 The ultimate end of your education was to make you a good wife.
Lady Mary Wortley Montagu (1689-1762, British Society Figure, Letter Writer)

6 As long as a woman can look ten years younger than her own daughter, she is perfectly satisfied.
Oscar Wilde (1856-1900, British Author, Wit)

7 You teach your daughters the diameters of the planets and wonder when you are done that they do not delight in your company.
Samuel Johnson (1709-1784, British Author)

DEATH AND DYING

1 Death is more universal than life; everyone dies but not everyone lives.
A. Sachs (1930-2016, German-born British actor and writer)

2 Die when I may, I want it said of me by those who knew me best, that I always plucked a thistle and planted a flower where I thought a flower would grow.
Abraham Lincoln (1809-1865, Sixteenth President of the USA)

3 I have a rendezvous with Death at some disputed barricade.
Alan Seeger (1888-1916, American Poet, Soldier)

4 There will be no lasting peace either in the heart of individuals or in social customs until death is outlawed.
Albert Camus (1913-1960, French Existential Writer)

5 Men are convinced of your arguments, your sincerity, and the seriousness of your efforts only by your death.
Albert Camus (1913-1960, French Existential Writer)

6 Men are never really willing to die except for the sake of freedom: therefore they do not believe in dying completely.
Albert Camus (1913-1960, French Existential Writer)

7 He who can no longer pause to wonder and stand rapt in awe is as good as dead; his eyes are closed.
Albert Einstein (1879-1955, German-born American Physicist)

8 A belief in hell and the knowledge that every ambition is doomed to frustration at the hands of a skeleton have never prevented the majority of human beings from behaving as though death were no more than an unfounded rumor.
Aldous Huxley (1894-1963, British Author)

9 Ignore death up to the last moment; then, when it can't be ignored any longer, have yourself squirted full of morphia and shuffle off in a coma. Thoroughly sensible, humane and scientific, eh?
Aldous Huxley (1894-1963, British Author)

10 Now, a corpse, poor thing, is an untouchable and the process of decay is, of all pieces of bad manners, the vulgarest imaginable. For a corpse is, by definition, a person absolutely devoid of savoir vivre.
Aldous Huxley (1894-1963, British Author)

11 Death is but a passage. It is not a house, it is only a vestibule. The grave has a door on its inner side.
Alexander Maclaren (1826-1910, British Preacher)

12 Good God! how often are we to die before we go quite off this stage? In every friend we lose a part of ourselves, and the best part.
Alexander Pope (1688-1744, British Poet, Critic, Translator)

13 The difficulty about all this dying, is that you can't tell a fellow anything about it, so where does the fun come in?
Alice James (1848-1892, American Diarist, Sister of Henry, William James)

14 Death is the last enemy: once we've got past that I think everything will be alright.
Alice Thomas Ellis (1932-, British Author)

15 If your time ain't come not even a doctor can kill you.
American Proverb

16 Death is not a period, but a comma in the story of life.
Amos Traver

17 Fish die belly upward, and rise to the surface. Its their way of falling.
Andre Gide (1869-1951, French Author)

18 The grave's a fine and private place, but none, I think, do there embrace.
Andrew Marvell (1621-1678, British Metaphysical Poet)

19 Death is a distant rumor to the young.
Andy Rooney (American Television News Personality)

20 Dying is the most embarrassing thing that can ever happen to you, because someone's got to take care of all your details.
Andy Warhol (1930-, American Artist, Filmmaker)

21 We need not fear life, because God is the Ruler of all and we need not fear death, because He shares immortality with us.
Ann Landers (1918-, American Advice Columnist)

22 When one by one our ties are torn, and friend from friend is snatched forlorn; When man is left alone to mourn, oh! then how sweet it is to die!
Anna Letitia Barbauld (1743-1825, British Author)

23 When the body sinks into death, the essence of man is revealed. Man is a knot, a web, a mesh into which relationships are tied. Only those relationships matter. The body is an old crock that nobody will miss. I have never known a man to think of himself when dying. Never.
Antoine De Saint-Exupery (1900-1944, French Aviator, Writer)

24 Death was afraid of him because he had the heart of a lion.
Arabian Proverb

25 Your lost friends are not dead, but gone before, advanced a stage or two upon that road which you must travel in the steps they trod.
Aristophanes (448-380 BC, Greek Comic Poet, Satirist)

26 The death of what's dead is the birth of what's living.
Arlo Guthrie (American Artist)

27 After your death you will be what you were before your birth.
Arthur Schopenhauer (1788-1860, German Philosopher)

28 Each day is a little life; every waking and rising a little birth; every fresh morning a little youth; every going to rest and sleep a little dearth.
Arthur Schopenhauer (1788-1860, German Philosopher)

29 There's a thing that keeps surprising you about stormy old friends after they die; their silence.
Ben Becht

30 I look upon death to be as necessary to our constitution as sleep. We shall rise refreshed in the morning.
Benjamin Franklin (1706-1790, American Scientist, Publisher, Diplomat)

31 Many people die at twenty five and aren't buried until they are seventy five.
Benjamin Franklin (1706-1790, American Scientist, Publisher, Diplomat)

32 To fear love is to fear life, and those who fear life are already three parts dead.
Bertrand Russell (1872-1970, British Philosopher, Mathematician, Essayist)

33 Most people would rather die than think: many do.
Bertrand Russell (1872-1970, British Philosopher, Mathematician, Essayist)

34 Death is as sure for that which is born, as birth is for that which is dead. Therefore grieve not for what is inevitable.
Bhagavad Gita (400 BC, Sanskrit Poem Incorporated Into the Mahabharata)

35 O death, where is thy sting? O grave, where is thy victory? [1 Corinthians 15:55]
Bible (Sacred Scriptures of Christians and Judaism)

36 As the waters fail from the sea, and the flood decayeth and drieth up: so man lieth down, and riseth not: till the heavens be no more, they shall not awake, nor be raised out of their sleep. [Job 14:11-12]
Bible (Sacred Scriptures of Christians and Judaism)

37 Yea, though I walk through the valley of the shadow of death, I will fear no evil: for thou art with me; thy rod and thy staff they comfort me. [Psalm 23:4]
Bible (Sacred Scriptures of Christians and Judaism)

38 The last enemy that shall be destroyed is death. [1 Corinthians 15:26]
Bible (Sacred Scriptures of Christians and Judaism)

39 And I looked, and behold a pale horse: and his name that sat on him was Death. [New Testament]
Bible (Sacred Scriptures of Christians and Judaism)

40 And fear not them which kill the body, but are not able to kill the soul: but rather fear him which is able to destroy both soul and body in hell. [Matthew 10:28]
Bible (Sacred Scriptures of Christians and Judaism)

41 Lord, make me to know mine end, and the measure of my days, what it is; that I may know how frail I am. [Psalms 39:4]
Bible (Sacred Scriptures of Christians and Judaism)

42 Precious in the sight of the Lord is the death of His godly ones. [Psalms 116:15]
Bible (Sacred Scriptures of Christians and Judaism)

43 For we brought nothing into this world, and it is certain we can carry nothing out. [1 Timothy 6:7]
Bible (Sacred Scriptures of Christians and Judaism)

44 I really wanted to die at certain periods in my life. Death was like love, a romantic escape. I took pills because I didn't want to throw myself off my balcony and know people would photograph me lying dead below.
Brigitte Bardot (1934-, French Film Actress)

45 If we really think that home is elsewhere and that this life is a "wandering to find home," why should we not look forward to the arrival?
C. S. Lewis (1898-1963, British Academic, Writer, Christian Apologist)

46 It is hard to have patience with people who say "There is no death" or "Death doesn't matter." There is death. And whatever is matters. And whatever happens has consequences, and it and they are irrevocable and irreversible. You might as well say that birth doesn't matter.
C. S. Lewis (1898-1963, British Academic, Writer, Christian Apologist)

47 So little done, so much to do.
Cecil Rhodes (1853-1902, British Imperialist, Business Magnate)

48 Death is the liberator of him whom freedom cannot release, the physician of him whom medicine cannot cure, and the comforter of him whom time cannot console.
Charles Caleb Colton (1780-1832, British Sportsman Writer)

49 I am not the least afraid to die.
Charles Darwin (1809-1882, British Naturalist)

50 We should weep for men at their birth, not at their death.
Charles De Montesquieu (1689-1755, French Jurist, Political Philosopher)

51 He would make a lovely corpse.
Charles Dickens (1812-1870, British Novelist)

52 Why fear death? It is the most beautiful adventure in life.
Charles Frohman

53 He had been, he said, an unconscionable time dying; but he hoped that they would excuse it.
Charles II (1630-1685, King of England and Ireland)

54 There is no such thing as death. In nature nothing dies. From each sad remnant of decay, some forms of life arise so shall his life be taken away before he knoweth that he hath it.
Charles Mackay (1814-1889, Scottish Poet, Song Writer)

55 God buries His workmen but carries on His work.
Charles Wesley

56 The white man's dead forget the country of their birth when they go to walk among the stars. Our dead never forget this beautiful earth, for it is the mother of the red man.
Chief Seattle (1786-1866, American Indian Chief of the Suquamish)

57 Life is a dream walking death is a going home.
Chinese Proverb

58 And all the winds go sighing, for sweet things dying.
Christina Rossetti (1830-1894, British Poet, Lyricist)

59 Be the green grass above me, with showers and dewdrops wet; and if thou wilt, remember, and if thou wilt, forget.
Christina Rossetti (1830-1894, British Poet, Lyricist)

60 No evil is honorable: but death is honorable; therefore death is not evil.
Citium Zeno (335-264 BC, Greek Philosopher)

61 I never wanted to see anybody die, but there are a few obituary notices I have read with pleasure.
Clarence Darrow (1857-1938, American Lawyer)

62 To you who have never died, may I say: Welcome to the world!
Clive Barker (American Author)

63 Life is a series of diminishments. Each cessation of an activity either from choice or some other variety of infirmity is a death, a putting to final rest. Each loss, of friend or precious enemy, can be equated with the closing off of a room containing blocks of nerves and soon after the closing off the nerves atrophy and that part of oneself, in essence, drops away. The self is lightened, is held on earth by a gram less of mass and will.
Coleman Dowell (1925-1985, American Novelist, Dramatist, Lyricist)

64 So that he seemed not to relinquish life, but to leave one home for another.
Cornelius Nepos (1st Century BC)

65 But the peasants -- how do the peasants die?
Count Leo Tolstoy (1828-1910, Russian Novelist, Philosopher)

66 Your body must become familiar with its death -- in all its possible forms and degrees -- as a self-evident, imminent, and emotionally neutral step on the way towards the goal you have found worthy of your life.
Dag Hammarskjold (1905-1961, Swedish Statesman, Secretary-general of U.N.)

67 In the last analysis it is our conception of death which decides our answers to all the questions life puts to us.
Dag Hammarskjold (1905-1961, Swedish Statesman, Secretary-general of U.N.)

68 If even dying is to be made a social function, then, grant me the favor of sneaking out on tiptoe without disturbing the party.
Dag Hammarskjold (1905-1961, Swedish Statesman, Secretary-general of U.N.)

69 These have not the hope to die.
Dante (Alighieri) (1265-1321, Italian Philosopher, Poet)

70 We all have to die some day, if we live long enough.
Dave Farber

71 If you treat every situation as a life and death matter, you'll die a lot of times.
Dean Smith (American College Basketball Coach)

72 We are not victims of aging, sickness and death. These are part of scenery, not the seer, who is immune to any form of change. This seer is the spirit, the expression of eternal being.
Deepak Chopra (East-Indian- American M.D., New Age Author, Lecturer)

73 The infant runs toward it with its eyes closed, the adult is stationary, the old man approaches it with his back turned.
Denis Diderot (1713-1784, French Philosopher)

74 I'm not afraid of death but I am afraid of dying. Pain can be alleviated by morphine but the pain of social ostracism cannot be taken away.
Derek Jarman (1942-, British Filmmaker, Artist, Author)

75 Few cross the river of time and are able to reach non-being. Most of them run up and down only on this side of the river. But those who when they know the law follow the path of the law, they shall reach the other shore and go beyond the realm of death.
Dhammapada (300 BC, Buddhist Collection of Moral Aphorism)

76 To awake from death is to die in peace.
Doug Horton

77 Death is feared as birth is forgotten.
Doug Horton

78 Death is the final wake-up call.
Doug Horton

79 Only those are fit to live who are not afraid to die.
Douglas Macarthur (1880-1964, American Army General in WW II)

80 Death may be the King of terrors... but Jesus is the King of kings!
Dwight L. Moody (1837-1899, American Evangelist)

81 Do not go gentle into the good night. Old age should burn and rage at close of day.
Dylan Thomas (1914-1953, Welsh Poet)

82 Though lovers be lost love shall not; And death shall have no dominion.
Dylan Thomas (1914-1953, Welsh Poet)

83 Thank Heaven! the crisis --The danger, is past, and the lingering illness, is over at last --, and the fever called "Living" is conquered at last.
Edgar Allan Poe (1809-1845, American Poet, Critic, short-story Writer)

84 To leave is to die a little... one leaves behind a little of oneself at any hour, at any place.
Edmond Haracourt

85 Death destroys a man, the idea of Death saves him.
Edward M. Forster (1879-1970, British Novelist, Essayist)

86 All men think that all men are mortal but themselves.
Edward Young (1683-1765, British Poet, Dramatist)

87 Virtue alone has majesty in death.
Edward Young (1683-1765, British Poet, Dramatist)

88 To stop sinning suddenly.
Elbert Hubbard (1859-1915, American Author, Publisher)

89 He who is obsessed by death is made guilty by it.
Elias Canetti (1905-, Austrian Novelist, Philosopher)

90 It is difficult to accept death in this society because it is unfamiliar. In spite of the fact that it happens all the time, we never see it.
Elisabeth KnBler-Ross (1926-, Swiss-born American Psychiatrist)

91 Dying is something we human beings do continuously, not just at the end of our physical lives on this earth.
Elisabeth KnBler-Ross (1926-, Swiss-born American Psychiatrist)

92 For 'Tis not in mere death that men die most.
Elizabeth Barrett Browning (1806-1861, British Poet)

93 Any relic of the dead is precious, if they were valued living.
Emily Bronte (1818-1848, British Novelist, Poet)

94 Death is a Dialogue between, the Spirit and the Dust.
Emily Dickinson (1830-1886, American Poet)

95 Let us go in; the fog is rising.
Emily Dickinson (1830-1886, American Poet)

96 Because I could not stop for death, He kindly stopped for me; The carriage held but just ourselves and immortality.
Emily Dickinson (1830-1886, American Poet)

97 Dying is a wild night and a new road.
Emily Dickinson (1830-1886, American Poet)

98 Death always comes too early or too late.
English Proverb

99 Death is a shadow that always follows the body.
English Proverb

100 As for death one gets used to it, even if it's only other people's death you get used to.
Enid Bagnold (1889-1981, British Novelist, Playwright)

101 Let death be daily before your eyes, and you will never entertain any abject thought, nor too eagerly covet anything.
Epictetus (50-120, Stoic Philosopher)

102 The art of living well and the art of dying well are one.
Epicurus (341-270 BC, Greek Philosopher)

103 It is possible to provide security against other ills, but as far as death is concerned, we men all live in a city without walls.
Epicurus (341-270 BC, Greek Philosopher)

104 Remember man as you walk by, as you are now so once was I, as I am now, so you will be, so prepare for death and follow me.
Epitaph

105 How frighteningly few are the persons whose death would spoil our appetite and make the world seem empty.
Eric Hoffer (1902-1983, American Author, Philosopher)

106 It is a sign of a creeping inner death when we no longer can praise the living.
Eric Hoffer (1902-1983, American Author, Philosopher)

107 Death has but one terror, that it has no tomorrow.
Eric Hoffer (1902-1983, American Author, Philosopher)

108 To die is poignantly bitter, but the idea of having to die without having lived is unbearable.
Erich Fromm (1900-1980, American Psychologist)

109 Nothing that is really good and God-like dies.
Ernest Moritz Arndt (1769-1860, Swedish-born German Poet, Patriot)

110 I can die when I wish to: that is my elixir of life.
Ernest Renan (1823-1892, French Writer, Critic, Scholar)

111 At death we cross from one territory to another, but we'll have no trouble with visas. Our representative is already there, preparing for our arrival. As citizens of heaven, our entrance is incontestable.
Erwin W. Lutzer (American Minister)

112 Since the death instinct exists in the heart of everything that lives, since we suffer from trying to repress it, since everything that lives longs for rest, let us unfasten the ties that bind us to life, let us cultivate our death wish, let us develop it, water it like a plant, let it grow unhindered. Suffering and fear are born from the repression of the death wish.
Eugene Ionesco (1912-, Romanian-born French Playwright)

113 We are all dead men on leave.
Eugene Levine (Russian Jew, Friend of Luxembourg's Lover, Jogiches)

114 But learn that to die is a debt we must all pay.
Euripides (480-406 BC, Greek Tragic Poet)

115 There are few things more difficult than to appraise the work of a man suddenly dead in his youth; to disentangle "promise" from achievement; to save him from that sentimentalizing which confuses the tragedy of the interruption with the merit of the work actually performed.
Ezra Pound (1885-1972, American Poet, Critic)

116 The gods conceal from men the happiness of death, that they may endure life.
F. L. Lucan (39-65, Roman Epic Poet)

117 It is natural to die as to be born.
Francis Bacon (1561-1626, British Philosopher, Essayist, Statesman)

118 I do not believe that any man fears to be dead, but only the stroke of death.
Francis Bacon (1561-1626, British Philosopher, Essayist, Statesman)

119 It is as natural to die as to be born; and to a little infant, perhaps, the one is as painful as the other.
Francis Bacon (1561-1626, British Philosopher, Essayist, Statesman)

120 Let no man fear to die, we love to sleep all, and death is but the sounder sleep.
Francis Beaumont (1584-1616, British Dramatist)

121 Between my head and my hand, there is always the face of death.
Francis Picabia (1878-1953, French Painter, Poet)

122 Neither the sun nor death can be looked at with a steady eye
François de La Rochefoucauld (1613-1680, French classical writer)

123 I am going to seek a great purpose, draw the curtain, the farce is played.
Frantois Rabelais (1495-1553, French Satirist, Physician, and Humanist)

124 One has to pay dearly for immortality; one has to die several times while one is still alive.
Friedrich Nietzsche (1844-1900, German Philosopher)

125 One should die proudly when it is no longer possible to live proudly.
Friedrich Nietzsche (1844-1900, German Philosopher)

126 A person doesn't die when he should but when he can.
Gabriel Garcia Marquez (1928-, Colombian Writer)

127 Death is the only inescapable, unavoidable, sure thing. We are sentenced to die the day we're born.
Gary Mark Gilmore

128 You just can't complain about being alive. It's self-indulgent to be unhappy. [When asked how she has coped since husband's death.]
Gena Rowland (American Actress)

129 Death is like an arrow that is already in flight, and your life lasts only until it reaches you.
Georg Hermes

130 I want to be all used up when I die.
George Bernard Shaw (1856-1950, Irish-born British Dramatist)

131 Dying is a troublesome business: there is pain to be suffered, and it wrings one's heart; but death is a splendid thing --a warfare accomplished, a beginning all over again, a triumph. You can always see that in their faces.
George Bernard Shaw (1856-1950, Irish-born British Dramatist)

132 Life levels all men. Death reveals the eminent.
George Bernard Shaw (1856-1950, Irish-born British Dramatist)

133 When death comes it is never our tenderness that we repent from, but our severity.
George Eliot (1819-1880, British Novelist)

134 Death is the king of this world: 'Tis his park where he breeds life to feed him. Cries of pain are music for his banquet
George Eliot (1819-1880, British Novelist)

135 Our dead are never dead to us, until we have forgotten them.
George Eliot (1819-1880, British Novelist)

136 A considerable percentage of the people we meet on the street are people who are empty inside, that is, they are actually already dead. It is fortunate for us that we do not see and do not know it. If we knew what a number of people are actually dead and what a number of these dead people govern our lives, we should go mad with horror.
George Gurdjieff (1873-1949, Russian Adept, Teacher, Writer)

137 Man has the possibility of existence after death. But possibility is one thing and the realization of the possibility is quite a different thing.
George Gurdjieff (1873-1949, Russian Adept, Teacher, Writer)

138 How strange this fear of death is! We are never frightened at a sunset.
George Macdonald (1824-1905, Scottish Novelist)

139 It is simply untrue that all our institutions are evil that all politicians are mere opportunists, that all aspects of university life are corrupt. Having discovered an illness, it's not terribly useful to prescribe death as a cure.
George Mcgovern (1922-, American Democratic Politician)

140 A human act once set in motion flows on forever to the great account. Our deathlessness is in what we do, not in what we are.
George Meredith (1828-1909, British Author)

141 One approaches the journey's end. But the end is a goal, not a catastrophe.
George Sand (1804-1876, French Novelist)

142 There is no cure for birth and death save to enjoy the interval. The dark background which death supplies brings out the tender colors of life in all their purity.
George Santayana (1863-1952, American Philosopher, Poet)

143 Take care of your of your life and the Lord will take of your death.
George Whitefield (1714-1970, British Methodist Evangelist)

144 We are all of us resigned to death: it's life we aren't resigned to.
Graham Greene (1904-1991, British Novelist)

145 How long after you are gone will ripples remain as evidence that you were cast into the pool of life?
Grant M. Bright (British-Born American Engineer)

146 Most of us die with much of our beautiful music still in us, un-sung, un-played.
Grant M. Bright (British-Born American Engineer)

147 Either he's dead or my watch has stopped.
Groucho Marx (1895-1977, American Comic Actor)

148 There are three kinds of death in this world. There's heart death, there's brain death, and there's being off the network.
Guy Almes

149 Oh you who have been removed from God in his solitude by the abyss of time, how can you expect to reach him without dying?
Hallaj (858-922 AD, Islamic Mystic)

150 Death not merely ends life, it also bestows upon it a silent completeness, snatched from the hazardous flux to which all things human are subject.
Hannah Arendt (1906-1975, German-born American Political Philosopher)

151 The Sea of Galilee and the Dead Sea are made of the same water. It flows down, clean and cool, from the heights of Herman and the roots of the cedars of Lebanon. the Sea of Galilee makes beauty of it, the Sea of Galilee has an outlet. It gets to give. It gathers in its riches that it may pour them out again to fertilize the Jordan plain. But the Dead Sea with the same water makes horror. For the Dead Sea has no outlet. It gets to keep.
Harry Emerson Fosdick (1878-1969, American Minister)

152 Live your life, do your work, then take your hat.
Henry David Thoreau (1817-1862, American Essayist, Poet, Naturalist)

153 It is not death, but dying, which is terrible.
Henry Fielding (1707-1754, British Novelist, Dramatist)

154 It hath often been said that it is not death but dying that is terrible.
Henry Fielding (1707-1754, British Novelist, Dramatist)

155 The world is the mirror of myself dying.
Henry Miller (1891-1980, American Author)

156 In the attempt to defeat death man has been inevitably obliged to defeat life, for the two are inextricably related. Life moves on to death, and to deny one is to deny the other.
Henry Miller (1891-1980, American Author)

157 Some people are so afraid to die that they never begin to live.
Henry Van Dyke (1852-1933, American Protestant Clergyman, Poet and Writer)

158 The course of my long life hath reached at last in fragile bark over a tempestuous sea the common harbor, where must rendered be account for all the actions of the past.
Henry Wadsworth Longfellow (1819-1892, American Poet)

159 When a great man dies, for years the light he leaves behind him, lies on the paths of men.
Henry Wadsworth Longfellow (1819-1892, American Poet)

160 I stay a little longer, as one stays, to cover up the embers that still burn.
Henry Wadsworth Longfellow (1819-1892, American Poet)

161 Living is death; dying is life. We are not what we appear to be. On this side of the grave we are exiles, on that citizens; on this side orphans, on that children;
Henry Ward Beecher (1813-1887, American Preacher, Orator, Writer)

162 Death is the dropping of the flower that the fruit may swell.
Henry Ward Beecher (1813-1887, American Preacher, Orator, Writer)

163 Some dying men are the most tyrannical; and certainly, since they will shortly trouble us so little for evermore, the poor fellows ought to be indulged.
Herman Melville (1819-1891, American Author)

164 No one's death comes to pass without making some impression, and those close to the deceased inherit part of the liberated soul and become richer in their humanness.
Hermann Broch (1886-1951, Austrian Novelist)

165 The call of death is a call of love. Death can be sweet if we answer it in the affirmative, if we accept it as one of the great eternal forms of life and transformation.
Hermann Hesse (1877-1962, German-born Swiss Novelist, Poet)

166 Death is a delightful hiding place for weary men.
Herodotus (484-425 BC, Greek Historian)

167 Loss and possession, Death and life are one. There falls no shadow where There shines no sun.
Hilaire Belloc (1870-1953, British Author)

168 I shall not wholly die, and a great part of me will escape the grave.
Horace (65-8 BC, Italian Poet)

169 Pale death with an impartial foot knocks at the hovels of the poor and the palaces of king.
Horace (65-8 BC, Italian Poet)

170 I never think he is quite ready for another world who is altogether weary of this.
Hugh Hamilton

171 Plan for this world as if you expect to live forever; but plan for the hereafter as if you expect to die tomorrow.
Ibn Gabirol

172 Once the game is over, the king and the pawn go back into the same box.
Italian Proverb

173 Our last garment is made without pockets.
Italian Proverb

174 When I die I want to decompose in a barrel of porter and have it served in all the pubs in Dublin.
J. P. Donleavy (1926-, American Writer)

175 I died a mineral, and became a plant. I died a plant and rose an animal. I died an animal and I was man. Why should I fear? When was I less by dying?
Jalal-Uddin Rumi (1207-1273, Persian Sufi Mystic Poet)

176 Perhaps the whole root of our trouble, the human trouble, is that we will sacrifice all the beauty of our lives, will imprison ourselves in totems, taboos, crosses, blood sacrifices, steeples, mosques, races, armies, flags, nations, in order to deny the fact of death, which is the only fact we have.
James Baldwin (1924-1987, American Author)

177 'Tis after death that we measure men.
James Barron Hope

178 A dead atheist is someone who is all dressed up with no place to go.
James Duffecy

179 Yet nightly pitch my moving tent, a day's march nearer home.
James Montgomery (1771-1854, British Poet)

180 But life is sweet, though all that makes it sweet. Lessen like sound of friends departing feet; And death is beautiful as feet of friend. Coming with welcome at our journey's end.
James Russell Lowell (1819-1891, American Poet, Critic, Editor)

181 Life is the jailer, death the angel sent to draw the unwilling bolts and set us free.
James Russell Lowell (1819-1891, American Poet, Critic, Editor)

182 But what is all this fear of and opposition to Oblivion? What is the matter with the soft Darkness, the Dreamless Sleep?
James Thurber (1894-1961, American Humorist, Illustrator)

183 Early to rise and early to bed makes a male healthy and wealthy and dead.
James Thurber (1894-1961, American Humorist, Illustrator)

184 Since the day of my birth, my death began its walk. It is walking toward me, without hurrying.
Jean Cocteau (1889-1963, French Author, Filmmaker)

185 I have a piece of great and sad news to tell you: I am dead.
Jean Cocteau (1889-1963, French Author, Filmmaker)

186 If some persons died, and others did not die, death would be a terrible affliction.
Jean De La Bruyere (1645-1696, French Writer)

187 Death never takes the wise man by surprise, he is always ready to go.
Jean De La Fontaine (1621-1695, French Poet)

188 The darkness of death is like the evening twilight; it makes all objects appear more lovely to the dying.
Jean Paul Richter (1763-1825, German Novelist)

189 Death gives us sleep, eternal youth, and immortality.
Jean Paul Richter (1763-1825, German Novelist)

190 At birth man is offered only one choice --the choice of his death. But if this choice is governed by distaste for his own existence, his life will never have been more than meaningless.
Jean-Pierre Melville (1917-1973, French Film Director)

191 When I die, I want people to play my music, go wild and freak out and do anything they want to do.
Jimi Hendrix (1942-1970, American Musician, Guitarist, Singer, Songwriter)

192 I'd rather die while I'm living then live while I'm dead.
Jimmy Buffet (American Songwriter, Singer)

193 Death is delightful. Death is dawn, the waking from a weary night of fevers unto truth and light.
Joaquin Miller (1839-1913, American Poet)

194 That which is so universal as death must be a benefit.
Johann Friedrich Von Schiller (1759-1805, German Dramatist, Poet, Historian)

195 What shall he fear that does not fear death.
Johann Friedrich Von Schiller (1759-1805, German Dramatist, Poet, Historian)

196 A useless life is an early death.
Johann Wolfgang Von Goethe (1749-1832, German Poet, Dramatist, Novelist)

197 Death is a commingling of eternity with time; in the death of a good man, eternity is seen looking through time.
Johann Wolfgang Von Goethe (1749-1832, German Poet, Dramatist, Novelist)

198 Die? I should say not, dear fellow. No Barrymore would allow such a conventional thing to happen to him.
John Barrymore (1882-1942, American Actor)

199 A man's death makes everything certain about him. Of course, secrets may die with him. And of course, a hundred years later somebody looking through some papers may discover a fact which throws a totally different light on his life and of which all the people who attended his funeral were ignorant. Death changes the facts qualitatively but not quantitatively. One does not know more facts about a man because he is dead. But what one already knows hardens and becomes definite. We cannot hope for ambiguities to be clarified, we cannot hope for further change, we cannot hope for more. We are now the protagonists and we have to make up our minds.
John Berger (1926-, British Actor, Critic)

200 As virtuous men pass mildly away, and whisper to their souls to go, whilst some of their sad friends do say, the breath goes now, and some say no.
John Donne (1572-1632, British Metaphysical Poet)

201 Death be not proud, though some have called thee Mighty and dreadful, for thou art not so. For, those, whom thou think'st thou dost overthrow. Die not, poor death, nor yet canst thou kill me.
John Donne (1572-1632, British Metaphysical Poet)

202 When one man dies, one chapter is not torn out of the book, but translated into a better language.
John Donne (1572-1632, British Metaphysical Poet)

203 I would not that death should take me asleep. I would not have him merely seize me, and only declare me to be dead, but win me, and overcome me. When I must shipwreck, I would do it in a sea, where mine impotency might have some excuse; not in a sullen weedy lake, where I could not have so much as exercise for my swimming.
John Donne (1572-1632, British Metaphysical Poet)

204 All human things are subject to decay, and when fate summons, monarchs must obey.
John Dryden (1631-1700, British Poet, Dramatist, Critic)

205 To die is landing on some distant shore.
John Dryden (1631-1700, British Poet, Dramatist, Critic)

206 Like pilgrims to the appointed place we tend; The world's an inn, and death the journey's end.
John Dryden (1631-1700, British Poet, Dramatist, Critic)

207 He was exhaled; his great Creator drew His spirit, as the sun the morning dew.
John Dryden (1631-1700, British Poet, Dramatist, Critic)

208 In the democracy of the dead all men at last are equal. There is neither rank nor station nor prerogative in the republic of the grave.
John J. Ingalls

209 When I have fears that I may cease to be, Before my pen has gleaned my teeming brain.
John Keats (1795-1821, British Poet)

210 Land and sea, weakness and decline are great separators, but death is the great divorcer for ever.
John Keats (1795-1821, British Poet)

211 There is no death. the stars go down to rise upon some other shore. And bright in Heaven's jeweled crown, they shine for ever more.
John Luckey Mccreery (1835-1906, American Journalist)

212 In the long run we are all dead.
John Maynard Keynes (1883-1946, British Economist)

213 How gladly would I meet mortality, my sentence, and be earth in sensible! how glad would lay me down, as in my mother's lap! There I should rest, and sleep secure.
John Milton (1608-1674, British Poet)

214 Death is the golden key that opens the palace of eternity.
John Milton (1608-1674, British Poet)

215 We all of us waited for him to die. The family sent him a check every month, and hoped he'd get on with it quietly, without too much vulgar fuss.
John Osborne (1929-, British Playwright)

216 One who does not know when to die, does not know how to live.
John Ruskin (1819-1900, British Critic, Social Theorist)

217 The pride of dying rich raises the loudest laugh in hell.
John W. Foster (1770-1843, British Clergyman, Essayist)

218 For days after death hair and fingernails continue to grow, but phone calls taper off.
Johnny Carson (1925-, American TV Personality, Businessman)

219 It is impossible that anything so natural, so necessary, and so universal as death, should ever have been designed by providence as an evil to mankind.
Jonathan Swift (1667-1745, Anglo-Irish Satirist)

220 See in what peace a Christian can die.
Joseph Addison (1672-1719, British Essayist, Poet, Statesman)

221 The fear of death often proves mortal, and sets people on methods to save their Lives, which infallibly destroy them.
Joseph Addison (1672-1719, British Essayist, Poet, Statesman)

222 Death always waits. The door of the hearse is never closed.
Joseph Bayly (American Author and Speaker on the Subject of Death.)

223 Death is the great adventure beside which moon landings and space trips pale into insignificance.
Joseph Bayly (American Author and Speaker on the Subject of Death.)

224 I have wrestled with death. It is the most unexciting contest you can imagine. It takes place in an impalpable grayness, with nothing underfoot, with nothing around, without spectators, without clamor, without glory, without the great desire of victory, without the great fear of defeat.
Joseph Conrad (1857-1924, Polish-born British Novelist)

225 You cannot live without lawyers, and certainly you cannot die without them.
Joseph H. Choate

226 We are but tenants and shortly the great landlord will give us notice that our lease has expired.
Joseph Jefferson (1829-1905, American Comic Actor)

227 I look upon life as a gift from God. I did nothing to earn it. Now that the time is coming to give it back, I have no right to complain.
Joyce Cary (1888-1957, British Author)

228 The Father is the Giver of Life; but the Mother is the Giver of Death, because her womb is the gate of ingress to matter, and through her life is ensouled to form, and no form can be either infinite or eternal. Death is implicit in birth.
Kabbalah (Jewish Esoteric Doctrine)

229 What is here is also there; what is there, is also here. Who sees multiplicity but not the one indivisible Self must wander on and on from death to death.
Katha Upanishad (Ancient Hindu Scripture)

230 My idea of walking into the jaws of death is marrying some woman who has lost three husbands.
Kin Hubbard (1868-1930, American Humorist, Journalist)

231 If only I could understand the reason for my crying. If only I could stop this fear of dreaming that I'm dying.
Laura Palmer

232 I'm trying to die correctly, but it's very difficult, you know.
Lawrence Durrell (1912-1990, British Author)

233 As a well-spent day brings happy sleep, so a life well spent brings happy death.
Leonardo Da Vinci (1452-1519, Italian Inventor, Architect, Painter, Scientist, Sculptor)

234 While I thought that I was learning how to live, I have been learning how to die.
Leonardo Da Vinci (1452-1519, Italian Inventor, Architect, Painter, Scientist, Sculptor)

235 Authority forgets a dying king.
Lord Alfred Tennyson (1809-1892, British Poet)

236 God's finger touched him and he slept.
Lord Alfred Tennyson (1809-1892, British Poet)

237 Death, so called, is a thing which makes men weep, and yet a third of life is passed in sleep.
Lord Byron (1788-1824, British Poet)

238 I have seen a thousand graves opened, and always perceived that whatever was gone, the teeth and hair remained of those who had died with them. Is not this odd? They go the very first things in youth and yet last the longest in the dust.
Lord Byron (1788-1824, British Poet)

239 For the sword outwears its sheath, and the soul wears out the breast. And the heart must pause to breathe, and love itself have rest.
Lord Byron (1788-1824, British Poet)

240 Die, my dear doctor! That's the last thing I shall do!
Lord Palmerston (1784-1865, British Politician, Prime Minister)

241 Death is not an event in life: we do not live to experience death. If we take eternity to mean not infinite temporal duration but timelessness, then eternal life belongs to those who live in the present.
Ludwig Wittgenstein (1889-1951, Austrian Philosopher)

242 We say that the hour of death cannot be forecast, but when we say this we imagine that hour as placed in an obscure and distant future. It never occurs to us that it has any connection with the day already begun or that death could arrive this same afternoon, this afternoon which is so certain and which has every hour filled in advance.
Marcel Proust (1871-1922, French Novelist)

243 Despise not death, but welcome it, for nature wills it like all else.
Marcus Aurelius (121-80 AD, Roman Emperor, Philosopher)

244 Death is a release from the impressions of the senses, and from desires that make us their puppets, and from the vagaries of the mind, and from the hard service of the flesh.
Marcus Aurelius (121-80 AD, Roman Emperor, Philosopher)

245 We begin to die as soon as we are born, and the end is linked to the beginning.
Marcus Manilius (100 AD, Latin Poet)

246 The life of the dead is placed in the memory of the living.
Marcus T. Cicero (106-43 BC, Great Roman Orator, Politician)

247 That last day does not bring extinction to us, but change of place.
Marcus T. Cicero (106-43 BC, Great Roman Orator, Politician)

248 All say, How hard it is that we have to die -- a strange complaint to come from the mouths of people who have had to live.
Mark Twain (1835-1910, American Humorist, Writer)

249 We owe a deep debt of gratitude to Adam, the first great benefactor of the human race: he brought death into the world.
Mark Twain (1835-1910, American Humorist, Writer)

250 We never become really and genuinely our entire and honest selves until we are dead -- and not then until we have been dead years and years. People ought to start dead and then they would be honest so much earlier.
Mark Twain (1835-1910, American Humorist, Writer)

251 Let us endeavor so to live that when we come to die even the undertaker will be sorry.
Mark Twain (1835-1910, American Humorist, Writer)

252 Whoever has lived long enough to find out what life is, knows how deep a debt of gratitude we owe to Adam, the first great benefactor of our race. He brought death into the world.
Mark Twain (1835-1910, American Humorist, Writer)

253 Why is it that we rejoice at birth and grieve at a funeral? It is because we are not the person involved.
Mark Twain (1835-1910, American Humorist, Writer)

254 Annihilation has no terrors for me, because I have already tried it before I was born --a hundred million years --and I have suffered more in an hour, in this life, than I remember to have suffered in the whole hundred million years put together. There was a peace, a serenity, an absence of all sense of responsibility, an absence of worry, an absence of care, grief, perplexity; and the presence of a deep content and unbroken satisfaction in that hundred million years of holiday which I look back upon with a tender longing and with a grateful desire to resume, when the opportunity comes.
Mark Twain (1835-1910, American Humorist, Writer)

255 If Nature denies eternity to beings, it follows that their destruction is one of her laws. Now, once we observe that destruction is so useful to her that she absolutely cannot dispense with it from this moment onward the idea of annihilation which we attach to death ceases to be real what we call the end of the living animal is no longer a true finish, but a simple transformation, a transmutation of matter. According to these irrefutable principles, death is hence no more than a change of form, an imperceptible passage from one existence into another.
Marquis De Sade (1740-1814, French Author)

256 Every man is born as many men and dies as a single one.
Martin Heidegger (1889-1976, German Philosopher)

257 Every man must do two things alone; he must do his own believing and his own dying.
Martin Luther (1483-1546, German Leader of the Protestant Reformation)

258 If a man hasn't discovered something that he will die for, he isn't fit to live.
Martin Luther King Jr. (1929-1968, American Black Leader, Nobel Prize Winner, 1964)

259 In my end is my beginning.
Mary Stuart (1916-, British Novelist)

260 Truth sits upon the lips of dying men.
Matthew Arnold (1822-1888, British Poet, Critic)

261 Unquiet souls. In the dark fermentation of earth, in the never idle workshop of nature, in the eternal movement, yea shall find yourselves again.
Matthew Arnold (1822-1888, British Poet, Critic)

262 Along with the lazy man... the dying man is the immoral man: the former, a subject that does not work; the latter, an object that no longer even makes itself available to be worked on by others.
Michel De Certeau (French Writer)

263 Death, they say, acquits us of all obligations.
Michel Eyquem De Montaigne (1533-1592, French Philosopher, Essayist)

264 I want death to find me planting my cabbage
Michel Eyquem De Montaigne (1533-1592, French Philosopher, Essayist)

265 It is not death that alarms me, but dying.
Michel Eyquem De Montaigne (1533-1592, French Philosopher, Essayist)

266 Dying is a very dull, dreary affair. My advice to you is to have nothing whatever to do with it.
Michel Eyquem De Montaigne (1533-1592, French Philosopher, Essayist)

267 If you don't know how to die, don't worry; Nature will tell you what to do on the spot, fully and adequately. She will do this job perfectly for you; don't bother your head about it.
Michel Eyquem De Montaigne (1533-1592, French Philosopher, Essayist)

268 Well, there's a remedy for all things but death, which will be sure to lay us flat one time or other.
Miguel De Cervantes (1547-1616, Spanish Novelist, Dramatist, Poet)

269 Death eats up all things, both the young lamb and old sheep; and I have heard our parson say, death values a prince no more than a clown; all's fish that comes to his net; he throws at all, and sweeps stakes; he's no mower that takes a nap at noon-day, but drives on, fair weather or foul, and cuts down the green grass as well as the ripe corn: he's neither squeamish nor queesy-stomach d, for he swallows without chewing, and crams down all things into his ungracious maw; and you can see no belly he has, he has a confounded dropsy, and thirsts after men's lives, which he gurgles down like mother's milk.
Miguel De Cervantes (1547-1616, Spanish Novelist, Dramatist, Poet)

270 'Tis the maddest trick a man can ever play in his whole life, to let his breath sneak out of his body without any more ado, and without so much as a rap o'er the pate, or a kick of the guts; to go out like the snuff of a farthing candle, and die merely of the mulligrubs, or the sullens.
Miguel De Cervantes (1547-1616, Spanish Novelist, Dramatist, Poet)

271 To be born free is an accident; To live free a responsibility; To die free is an obligation.
Mrs Hubbard Davis

272 If I had my life over again I should form the habit of nightly composing myself to thoughts of death. I would practice, as it were, the remembrance of death. There is no other practice which so intensifies life. Death, when it approaches, ought not to take one by surprise. It should be part of the full expectancy of life. Without an ever-present sense of death life is insipid. You might as well live on the whites of eggs.
Muriel Spark (1918-, British Novelist)

273 You must not fear death, my lads; defy him, and you drive him into the enemy's ranks.
Napoleon Bonaparte (1769-1821, French General, Emperor)

274 We sometimes congratulate ourselves at the moment of waking from a troubled dream; it may be so the moment after death.
Nathaniel Hawthorne (1804-1864, American Novelist, Short Story Writer)

275 The pomp of death is far more terrible than death itself.
Nathaniel Lee (1649-1692, British Playwright)

276 Only the young die good.
Oliver Herford (1863-1935, American Author, Illustrator)

277 A few can touch the magic string, and noisy fame is proud to win them: Alas for those that never sing, but die with all their music in them!
Oliver Wendell Holmes (1809-1894, American Author, Wit, Poet)

278 Our dead brothers still live for us and bid us think of life, not death -- of life to which in their youth they lent the passion and glory of Spring. As I listen, the great chorus of life and joy begins again, and amid the awful orchestra of seen and unseen powers and destinies of good and evil, our trumpets, sound once more a note of daring, hope, and will.
Oliver Wendell Holmes (1809-1894, American Author, Wit, Poet)

279 Alas, I am dying beyond my means.
Oscar Wilde (1856-1900, British Author, Wit)

280 For he who lives more lives than one: More deaths than one must die.
Oscar Wilde (1856-1900, British Author, Wit)

281 I am dying beyond my means.
Oscar Wilde (1856-1900, British Author, Wit)

282 Once can survive everything nowadays, except death.
Oscar Wilde (1856-1900, British Author, Wit)

283 An evil life is a kind of death.
Ovid (43 BC-18 AD, Roman Poet)

284 Death is a displaced name for a linguistic predicament.
Paul De Man (1919-1983, Belgian-born American Literary Critic)

285 Death is an endless night so awful to contemplate that it can make us love life and value it with such passion that it may be the ultimate cause of all joy and all art.
Paul Theroux (1941-, American Novelist, Travel Writer)

286 A man does not die of love or his liver or even of old age; he dies of being a man.
Percival Arland Ussher (1899-1980, Irish Author, Critic)

287 Death is the veil which those who live call life; They sleep, and it is lifted.
Percy Bysshe Shelley (1792-1822, British Poet)

288 How wonderful is death! Death and his brother sleep.
Percy Bysshe Shelley (1792-1822, British Poet)

289 He has outsoared the shadow of our night; envy and calumny and hate and pain, and that unrest which men miscall delight, can touch him not and torture not again; from the contagion of the world's slow stain, he is secure.
Percy Bysshe Shelley (1792-1822, British Poet)

290 Every man goes down to his death bearing in his hands only that which he has given away.
Persian Proverb

291 He has gone over to the majority.
Petronius (Roman Writer)

292 O how small a portion of earth will hold us when we are dead, who ambitiously seek after the whole world while we are living.
Philip II (382-336 BC, Macedonian King - Father of Alexander)

293 Just like those who are incurably ill, the aged know everything about their dying except exactly when.
Philip Roth (1933-, American Novelist)

294 The essential part of our being can only survive if the transient part dissolves. Death is a condition of survival. That which has been gained must be eternalized, and can only be eternalized by being transmuted, by passing through death they must return
Pir Vilayat Khan (1916-, Western Philosopher Teacher, Master, Author)

295 Must not all things at the last be swallowed up in death?
Plato (427-347 BC, Greek Philosopher)

296 Know one knows whether death, which people fear to be the greatest evil, may not be the greatest good.
Plato (427-347 BC, Greek Philosopher)

297 Not by lamentations and mournful chants ought we to celebrate the funeral of a good man, but by hymns, for in ceasing to be numbered with mortals he enters upon the heritage of a diviner life.
Plutarch (46-120 AD, Greek Essayist, Biographer)

298 There is a remedy for everything; it is called death.
Portuguese Proverb

299 Death doesn't frighten me.
Princess of Wales Diana (1961-1997, Wife of Charles, Prince of Wales)

300 Good men must die, but death cannot kill their names.
Proverb

301 We come and cry and that is life, we cry and go and that is death.
Proverb

302 I am ready to meet God face to face tonight and look into those eyes of infinite holiness, for all my sins are covered by the atoning blood.
R. A. Torrey

303 In the twentieth century, death terrifies men less than the absence of real life. All these dead, mechanized, specialized actions, stealing a little bit of life a thousand times a day until the mind and body are exhausted, until that death which is not the
Raoul Vaneigem (1934-, Belgian Situationist Philosopher)

304 Woe, woe, woe... in a little while we shall all be dead. Therefore let us behave as though we were dead already.
Raymond Chandler (1888-1959, American Author)

305 What did it matter where you lay once you were dead? In a dirty sump or in a marble tower on top of a high hill? You were dead, you were sleeping the big sleep, you were not bothered by things like that. Oil and water were the same as wind and air to you.
Raymond Chandler (1888-1959, American Author)

306 To a father, when a child dies, the future dies; to a child when a parent dies, the past dies.
Red Auerbach (1917-, American Basketball Coach)

307 The fear of death is worse than death.
Robert Burton (1576-1640, British Clergyman, Scholar)

308 When it comes to my own turn to lay my weapons down, I shall do so with thankfulness and fatigue, and whatever be my destiny afterward, I shall be glad to lie down with my fathers in honor. It is human at least, if not divine.
Robert Louis Stevenson (1850-1895, Scottish Essayist, Poet, Novelist)

309 I hate funerals and would not attend my own if it could be avoided, but it is well for every man to stop once in a while to think of what sort of a collection of mourners he is training for his final event.
Robert T. Morris

310 Death is nature's way of saying, Your table's ready.
Robin Williams (1952-, American Actor, Comedian)

311 Who is mightier than death? Those who can smile when death threatens.
Ruckett

312 A wooden bed is better than a golden coffin.
Russian Proverb

313 I've seen things you people wouldn't believe. Attack ships on fire off the shoulder of Orion. I watched C-beams glitter in the darkness at Tannhauser Gate. All those moments will be lost in time, like tears in rain. Time to die.
Rutger Hauer

314 Personally I have no bone to pick with graveyards, I take the air there willingly, perhaps more willingly than elsewhere, when take the air I must.
Samuel Beckett (1906-1989, Irish Dramatist, Novelist)

315 If life must not be taken too seriously -- then so neither must death.
Samuel Butler (1612-1680, British Poet, Satirist)

316 To die is but to leave off dying and do the thing once for all.
Samuel Butler (1612-1680, British Poet, Satirist)

317 There is nothing which at once affects a man so much and so little as his own death.
Samuel Butler (1612-1680, British Poet, Satirist)

318 The dead should be judged like criminals, impartially, but they should be allowed the benefit of the doubt.
Samuel Butler (1612-1680, British Poet, Satirist)

319 It matters not how a man dies, but how he lives. The act of dying is not of importance, it lasts so short a time.
Samuel Johnson (1709-1784, British Author)

320 I will be conquered; I will not capitulate.
Samuel Johnson (1709-1784, British Author)

321 An orphan's curse would drag to hell, a spirit from on high; but oh! more horrible than that, is a curse in a dead man's eye!
Samuel Taylor Coleridge (1772-1834, British Poet, Critic, Philosopher)

322 Death is the wish of some, the relief of many, and the end of all.
Seneca (4 BC-65 AD, Spanish-born Roman Statesman, philosopher)

323 A punishment to some, to some a gift, and to many a favor.
Seneca (4 BC-65 AD, Spanish-born Roman Statesman, philosopher)

324 The final hour when we cease to exist does not itself bring death; it merely of itself completes the death-process. We reach death at that moment, but we have been a long time on the way.
Seneca (4 BC-65 AD, Spanish-born Roman Statesman, philosopher)

325 The best place a person can die, is where they die for others.
Sir James M. Barrie (1860-1937, British Playwright)

326 To die will be an awfully big adventure.
Sir James M. Barrie (1860-1937, British Playwright)

327 Man is a noble animal, splendid in ashes, and pompous in the grave.
Sir Thomas Browne (1605-1682, British Author, Physician,, Philosopher)

328 We all labor against our own cure, for death is the cure of all diseases.
Sir Thomas Browne (1605-1682, British Author, Physician,, Philosopher)

329 Death is the cure for all diseases.
Sir Thomas Browne (1605-1682, British Author, Physician,, Philosopher)

330 Though it be in the power of the weakest arm to take away life, it is not in the strongest to deprive us of death.
Sir Thomas Browne (1605-1682, British Author, Physician,, Philosopher)

331 O eloquent, just, and mighty Death! whom none could advise, thou hast persuaded; what none hath dared, thou hast done; and whom all the world hath flattered, thou only hath cast out of the world and despised. Thou hast drawn together all the far-stretched greatness, all the pride, cruelty, and ambition of man, and covered it all over with these two narrow words, Hic jacet!
Sir Walter Raleigh (1552-1618, British Courtier, Navigator, Writer)

332 Death -- the last sleep? No, it is the final awakening.
Sir Walter Scott (1771-1832, British Novelist, Poet)

333 Come he slow or come he fast. It is but death who comes at last.
Sir Walter Scott (1771-1832, British Novelist, Poet)

334 Is death the last step? No, it is the final awakening.
Sir Walter Scott (1771-1832, British Novelist, Poet)

335 The hour of departure has arrived and we go our ways; I to die, and you to live. Which is better? Only God knows.
Socrates (469-399 BC, Greek Philosopher of Athens)

336 Death may be the greatest of all human blessings.
Socrates (469-399 BC, Greek Philosopher of Athens)

337 To fear death, my friends, is only to think ourselves wise, without being wise: for it is to think that we know what we do not know. For anything that men can tell, death may be the greatest good that can happen to them: but they fear it as if they knew quite well that it was the greatest of evils. And what is this but that shameful ignorance of thinking that we know what we do not know?
Socrates (469-399 BC, Greek Philosopher of Athens)

338 For the dead there are no more toils.
Sophocles (495-406 BC, Greek Tragic Poet)

339 Because of its tremendous solemnity death is the light in which great passions, both good and bad, become transparent, no longer limited by outward appearances.
Soren Kierkegaard (1813-1855, Danish Philosopher, Writer)

340 A dying man needs to die, as a sleepy man needs to sleep, and there comes a time when it is wrong, as well as useless, to resist.
Steward Alsop

341 For those who live neither with religious consolations about death nor with a sense of death (or of anything else) as natural, death is the obscene mystery, the ultimate affront, the thing that cannot be controlled. It can only be denied.
Susan Sontag (1933-, American Essayist)

342 A fiction about soft or easy deaths is part of the mythology of most diseases that are not considered shameful or demeaning.
Susan Sontag (1933-, American Essayist)

343 Fear of death has been the greatest ally of tyranny past and present.
Sydney Hook

344 dying is an art, like everything else. I do it exceptionally well. I do it so it feels like hell. I do it so it feels real. I guess you could say I've a call.
Sylvia Plath (1932-1963, American Poet)

345 And what the dead had no speech for, when living, they can tell you, being dead: the communication of the dead is tongued with fire beyond the language of the living.
T. S. Eliot (1888-1965, American-born British Poet, Critic)

346 Don't strew me with roses after I'm dead. When Death claims the light of my brow No flowers of life will cheer me: instead You may give me my roses now!
Thomas F. Healey

347 Each in his narrow cell for ever laid, the rude forefathers of the hamlet sleep.
Thomas Gray (1716-1771, British Poet)

348 Teach me to live that I may dread, the grave as little as my bed.
Thomas Ken (1637-1711, British Churchman, Hymn-Writer)

349 The only religious way to think of death is as part and parcel of life.
Thomas Mann (1875-1955, German Author, Critic)

350 Death is someone you see very clearly with eyes in the center of your heart: eyes that see not by reacting to light, but by reacting to a kind of a chill from within the marrow of your own life.
Thomas Merton (1915-1968, American Religious Writer, Poet)

351 Having seen and felt the end, you have willed the means to the realization of the end.
Thomas Troward

352 Death the last voyage, the longest, and the best.
Thomas Wolfe (1931-, American Author, Journalist)

353 At the moment of death there will appear to you, swifter than lightning, the luminous splendor of the colorless light of emptiness, and that will surround you on all sides. Terrified, you will flee from the radiance. Try to submerge it is an obstacle blocking the path of liberation. yourself in that light, giving up all belief in a separate self, all attachment to your illusory ego. Recognize that the boundless light of this true reality is your own true self, and you shall be saved!
Tibetan (780 AD, Tibetan Buddhist Esoteric Doctrine)

354 He whom the Gods love dies young, while he is in health, has his senses and his judgments sound.
Titus Maccius Plautus (254-184 BC, Roman Comic Poet)

355 You haven't lost anything when you know were it is. Death can hide but not divide.
Vance Havner

356 Dear me! I must be turning into a god.
Vespasian

357 Death twitches my ear. "Live," he says, "I am coming."
Virgil (70-19 BC, Roman Poet)

358 I have lived, and I have run the course which fortune allotted me; and now my shade shall descend illustrious to the grave.
Virgil (70-19 BC, Roman Poet)

359 Against you I will fling myself, unvanquished and unyielding, O Death!
Virginia Woolf (1882-1941, British Novelist, Essayist)

360 To the living we owe respect, but to the dead we owe only the truth.
Voltaire (1694-1778, French Historian, Writer)

361 The words of a dead man are modified in the guts of the living.
W. H. Auden (1907-1973, Anglo-American Poet)

362 Death is a very dull, dreary affair, and my advice to you is to have nothing whatever to do with it.
W. Somerset Maugham (1874-1965, British Novelist, Playwright)

363 Death doesn't affect the living because it has not happened yet. Death doesn't concern the dead because they have ceased to exist.
W. Somerset Maugham (1874-1965, British Novelist, Playwright)

364 Nothing can happen more beautiful than death.
Walt Whitman (1819-1892, American Poet)

365 To die is different from what any one supposed, and luckier.
Walt Whitman (1819-1892, American Poet)

366 I warmed both hands before the fire of life; It sinks, and I am ready to depart.
Walter Savage Landor (1775-1864, British Poet, Essayist)

367 The last suit that you wear, you don't need any pockets.
Wayne Dyer (1940-, American Psychotherapist, Author, Lecturer)

368 I balanced all, brought all to mind, the years to come seemed waste of breath, a waste of breath the years behind, in balance with this life, this death.
William Butler Yeats (1865-1939, Irish Poet, Playwright.)

369 All that tread, the globe are but a handful to the tribes, that slumber in its bosom.
William C. Bryant (1794-1878, American Poet, Newspaper Editor)

370 Madam, Life's a piece in bloom death goes dogging everywhere: She's the tenant of the room he's the ruffian on the stair.
William Ernest Henley (1849-1903, British Poet, Critic, Editor)

371 Death cancels everything but truth; and strips a man of everything but genius and virtue. It is a sort of natural canonization. It makes the meanest of us sacred --it installs the poet in his immortality, and lifts him to the skies. Death is the greatest assayer of the sterling ore of talent. At his touch the dropsy particles fall off, the irritable, the personal, the gross, and mingle with the dust -- the finer and more ethereal part mounts with winged spirit to watch over our latest memory, and protect our bones from insult. We consign the least worthy qualities to oblivion, and cherish the nobler and imperishable nature with double pride and fondness.
William Hazlitt (1778-1830, British Essayist)

372 Our repugnance to death increases in proportion to our consciousness of having lived in vain.
William Hazlitt (1778-1830, British Essayist)

373 Except for the young or very happy, I can't say I am sorry for anyone who dies.
William M. Thackeray (1811-1863, Indian-born British Novelist)

374 Men fear death, as if unquestionably the greatest evil, and yet no man knows that it may not be the greatest good.
William Mitford (1744-1827, British Historian, Writer)

375 He that lives to forever, never fears dying.
William Penn (1644-1718, British Religious Leader, Founder of Pennsylvania)

376 The undiscovered country form whose born no traveler returns. [Hamlet]
William Shakespeare (1564-1616, British Poet, Playwright, Actor)

377 The weariest and most loathed worldly life, that age, ache, penury and imprisonment can lay on nature is a paradise, to what we fear of death.
William Shakespeare (1564-1616, British Poet, Playwright, Actor)

378 All that live must die, passing through nature to eternity.
William Shakespeare (1564-1616, British Poet, Playwright, Actor)

379 Men must endure, their going hence even as their coming hither. Ripeness is all.
William Shakespeare (1564-1616, British Poet, Playwright, Actor)

380 I come to bury Caesar, not to praise him. The evil that men do lives after them; the good is oft interred with their bones.
William Shakespeare (1564-1616, British Poet, Playwright, Actor)

381 Our remedies oft in ourselves do lie, which we ascribe to heaven.
William Shakespeare (1564-1616, British Poet, Playwright, Actor)

382 But I will be a bridegroom in my death, and run into a lover's bed.
William Shakespeare (1564-1616, British Poet, Playwright, Actor)

383 Nothing in his life became him like the leaving it.
William Shakespeare (1564-1616, British Poet, Playwright, Actor)

384 I care not, a man can die but once; we owe God and death.
William Shakespeare (1564-1616, British Poet, Playwright, Actor)

385 After life's fitful fever he sleeps well. Treason has done his worst. Nor steel nor poison, malice domestic, foreign levy, nothing can touch him further.
William Shakespeare (1564-1616, British Poet, Playwright, Actor)

386 Every man dies. Not every man really lives. [In the movie Braveheart]
William Wallace (American Actor)

387 No motion has she now, no force; she neither hears nor sees; rolled around in earth's diurnal course, with rocks, and stones, and trees.
William Wordsworth (1770-1850, British Poet)

388 I am ready to meet my maker, but whether my maker is prepared for the great ordeal of meeting me is another matter.
Winston Churchill (1874-1965, British Statesman, Prime Minister)

389 As death, when we come to consider it closely, is the true goal of our existence, I have formed during the last few years such close relations with this best and truest friend of mankind, that his image is not only no longer terrifying to me, but is indeed very soothing and consoling! And I thank my God for graciously granting me the opportunity of learning that death is the key which unlocks the door to our true happiness.
Wolfgang Amadeus Mozart (1756-1791, Austrian Composer)

390 I'm not afraid to die, I just don't want to be there when it happens.
Woody Allen (1935-, American Director, Screenwriter, Actor, Comedian)

391 I don't believe in an after life, although I am bringing a change of underwear.
Woody Allen (1935-, American Director, Screenwriter, Actor, Comedian)

392 On the plus side, death is one of the few things that can be done just as easily as lying down.
Woody Allen (1935-, American Director, Screenwriter, Actor, Comedian)

393 In any man who dies there dies with him, his first snow and kiss and fight. Not people die but worlds die in them.
Yevgeny Yevtushenko (1933-, Russian Poet)

394 It's astonishing how important a man becomes when he dies.
Yiddish Proverb

395 Always go to other people's funerals, otherwise they won't come to yours.
Yogi Berra (1925-, American Baseball Player)

DEBATE

1 Information, usually seen as the precondition of debate, is better understood as its by-product.
Christopher Lasch (1932-, American Historian)

2 Freedom is hammered out on the anvil of discussion, dissent, and debate.
Hubert H. Humphrey (1911-1978, American Democratic Politician, Vice President)

3 A philosopher who is not taking part in discussions is like a boxer who never goes into the ring.
Ludwig Wittgenstein (1889-1951, Austrian Philosopher)

4 It is not he who gains the exact point in dispute who scores most in controversy -- but he who has shown the better temper.
Samuel Butler (1612-1680, British Poet, Satirist)

5 If I tell you that I would be disobeying the god and on that account it is impossible for me to keep quiet, you won't be persuaded by me, taking it that I am ionizing. And if I tell you that it is the greatest good for a human being to have discussions every day about virtue and the other things you hear me talking about, examining myself and others, and that the unexamined life is not livable for a human being, you will be even less persuaded.
Socrates (469-399 BC, Greek Philosopher of Athens)

6 Books and harlots have their quarrels in public.
Walter Benjamin (1982-1940, German Critic, Philosopher)

DEBT

1 Forgetfulness. A gift of God bestowed upon debtors in compensation for their destitution of conscience.
Ambrose Bierce (1842-1914, American Author, Editor, Journalist, "The Devil's Dictionary")

2 Rather go to bed with out dinner than to rise in debt.
Benjamin Franklin (1706-1790, American Scientist, Publisher, Diplomat)

3 Credit is a system whereby a person who can not pay gets another person who can not pay to guarantee that he can pay.
Charles Dickens (1812-1870, British Novelist)

4 Credit buying is much like being drunk. The buzz happens immediately, and it gives you a lift. The hangover comes the day after.
Dr. Joyce Brothers (1927-, American Psychologist, Television and Radio Personality)

5 Promises make debt, and debt makes promises.
Dutch Proverb

6 Modern man drives a mortgaged car over a bond-financed highway on credit-card gas.
Earl Wilson (1907-, American newspaper columnist)

7 Nowadays people can be divided into three classes -- the haves the have-nots and the have-not-paid-for-what-they-haves
Earl Wilson (1907-, American newspaper columnist)

8 Speak not of my debts unless you mean to pay them.
English Proverb

9 In the midst of life we are in debt.
Ethel Watts Mumford (1878-1940, American Novelist, Humor Writer)

10 Pay as you go is the philosopher's stone.
G. Randolf

11 One day Donald Trump will discover that he is owned by Lutheran Brotherhood and must re negotiate his debt load with a committee of silent Norwegians who don't understand why anyone would pay more than $120.00 for a suit.
Garrison Keillor (1942-, American Humorous Writer, Radio Performer)

12 The government who robs Peter to pay Paul can always depend on the support of Paul.
George Bernard Shaw (1856-1950, Irish-born British Dramatist)

13 Some people use one half their ingenuity to get into debt, and the other half to avoid paying it.
George D. Prentice (American Editor)

14 When I was born I owed twelve dollars.
George S. Kaufman (1889-1961, American Playwright, Director)

15 Interest works night and day in fair weather and in foul. It gnaws at a man's substance with invisible teeth.
Henry Ward Beecher (1813-1887, American Preacher, Orator, Writer)

16 God often pays debts without money.
Irish Proverb

17 A small debt makes a man your debtor, a large one your enemy.
Irish Proverb

18 A man isn't a man until he has to meet a payroll.
Ivan Shaffer

19 The 1980s are to debt what the 1960s were to sex. The 1960s left a hangover. So will the 1980s.
James Grant (American International Business Consultant)

20 The creditor hath a better memory than the debtor.
James Howell

21 If it isn't the sheriff, it's the finance company; I've got more attachments on me than a vacuum cleaner.
John Barrymore (1882-1942, American Actor)

22 Bankruptcy is a sacred state, a condition beyond conditions, as theologians might say, and attempts to investigate it are necessarily obscene, like spiritualism. One knows only that he has passed into it and lives beyond us, in a condition not ours.
John Updike (1932-, American Novelist, Critic)

23 Always live within your income, even if you have to borrow money to do so.
Josh Billings (1815-1885, American Humorist, Lecturer)

24 Never run into debt, not if you can find anything else to run into.
Josh Billings (1815-1885, American Humorist, Lecturer)

25 Energetic action on debt would make a radical difference to the prospects of many of the poorest countries in the world, at no practical cost to creditor countries.
Kenneth Clarke (British Chancellor of the Exchequer)

26 We at Chrysler borrow money the old fashion way. We pay it back.
Lee Iacocca (1924-, American Businessman, Former CEO of Chrysler)

27 It is very iniquitous to make me pay my debts -- you have no idea of the pain it gives one.
Lord Byron (1788-1824, British Poet)

28 Money is a poor man's credit card.
Marshall Mcluhan (1911-1980, Canadian Communications Theorist)

29 To John I owed great obligation; but John, unhappily, thought fit to publish it to all the nation: Sure John and I are more than quit.
Matthew Prior (1664-1721, British Diplomat, Poet)

30 You build on cost and you borrow on value.
Paul Reichmann (Canadian Businessman)

31 If you don't have some bad loans you are not in business.
Paul Volcker (American Chairman, Federal Reserve System)

32 Man was lost if he went to a usurer, for the interest ran faster than a tiger upon him.
Pearl S. Buck (1892-1973, American Novelist)

33 Better to go to bed hungry than to wake up in debt.
Proverb

34 Out of debt, out of danger.
Proverb

35 It is said that the world is in a state of bankruptcy, that the world owes the world more than the world can pay.
Ralph Waldo Emerson (1803-1882, American Poet, Essayist)

36 You know it is not my interest to pay the principal, or my principal to pay the interest.
Richard Brinsley Sheridan (1751-1816, Anglo-Irish Dramatist)

37 A man's indebtedness is not virtue; his repayment is. Virtue begins when he dedicates himself actively to the job of gratitude.
Ruth Benedict (1887-1948, American Anthropologist)

38 Small debts are like small gun shot; they are rattling around us on all sides and one can scarcely escape being wounded. Large debts are like canons, they produce a loud noise, but are of little danger.
Samuel Johnson (1709-1784, British Author)

[39] The payment of debts is necessary for social order. The non-payment is quite equally necessary for social order. For centuries humanity has oscillated, serenely unaware, between these two contradictory necessities.
Simone Weil (1910-1943, French Philosopher, Mystic)

[40] You can take a chance with any man who pays his bills on time.
Terence (185-159 BC, Roman Writer of Comedies)

[41] There are but two ways of paying debt: Increase of industry in raising income, increase of thrift in laying out.
Thomas Carlyle (1795-1881, Scottish Philosopher, Author)

[42] Debt is the worst poverty.
Thomas Fuller (1608-1661, British Clergyman, Author)

[43] The world is indebted for all triumphs which have been gained by reason and humanity over error and oppression.
Thomas Jefferson (1743-1826, Third President of the USA)

[44] A creditor is worse than a slave-owner; for the master owns only your person, but a creditor owns your dignity, and can command it.
Victor Hugo (1802-1885, French Poet, Dramatist, Novelist)

[45] The nation is prosperous on the whole, but how much prosperity is there in a hole?
Will Rogers (1879-1935, American Humorist, Actor)

[46] Words pay no debts.
William Shakespeare (1564-1616, British Poet, Playwright, Actor)

[47] I can get no remedy against this consumption of the purse: borrowing only lingers and lingers it out, but the disease is incurable.
William Shakespeare (1564-1616, British Poet, Playwright, Actor)

[48] He that dies pays all his debts.
William Shakespeare (1564-1616, British Poet, Playwright, Actor)

DECADENCE

[1] The goal of every culture is to decay through over-civilization; the factors of decadence, -- luxury, skepticism, weariness and superstition, -- are constant. The civilization of one epoch becomes the manure of the next.
Cyril Connolly (1903-1974, British Critic)

[2] Every civilization when it loses its inner vision and its cleaner energy, falls into a new sort of sordidness, more vast and more stupendous than the old savage sort. An Augean stable of metallic filth.
D. H. Lawrence (1885-1930, British Author)

[3] Decadence is a difficult word to use since it has become little more than a term of abuse applied by critics to anything they do not yet understand or which seems to differ from their moral concepts.
Ernest Hemingway (1898-1961, American Writer)

[4] Men first feel necessity, then look for utility, next attend to comfort, still later amuse themselves with pleasure, thence grow dissolute in luxury, and finally go mad and waste their substance.
Giambattista Vico (1688-1744, Italian Philosopher, Historian)

DECAY

[1] Show me one thing here on earth which has begun well and not ended badly. The proudest palpitations are engulfed in a sewer, where they cease throbbing, as though having reached their natural term: this downfall constitutes the heart's drama and the negative meaning of history.
E. M. Cioran (1911-, Rumanian-born French Philosopher)

[2] I have always looked upon decay as being just as wonderful and rich an expression of life as growth.
Henry Miller (1891-1980, American Author)

[3] There are people who, like houses, are beautiful in dilapidation.
Logan Pearsall Smith (1865-1946, Anglo-American Essayist, Aphorist)

[4] Thy decay's still impregnate with divinity.
Lord Byron (1788-1824, British Poet)

[5] Old age cannot be cured. An epoch or a civilization cannot be prevented from breathing its last. A natural process that happens to all flesh and all human manifestations cannot be arrested. You can only wring your hands and utter a beautiful swan song.
Renee Winegarten

[6] Just as the constant increase of entropy is the basic law of the universe, so it is the basic law of life to be ever more highly structured and to struggle against entropy.
Vaclav Havel (1936-, Czech Playwright, President)

[7] 'Tis but an hour ago since it was nine, and after one hour more twill be eleven. And so from hour to hour we ripe and ripe, and then from hour to hour we rot and rot. and thereby hangs a tale.
William Shakespeare (1564-1616, British Poet, Playwright, Actor)

DECEIT

[1] If you once forfeit the confidence of your fellow citizens, you can never regain their respect and esteem. You may fool all of the people some of the time; you can even fool some of the people all of the time; but you can't fool all of the people all of the time.
Abraham Lincoln (1809-1865, Sixteenth President of the USA)

[2] You can fool all the people all the time if the advertising budget is big enough.
Ed Rollins

3 The easiest person to deceive is one's own self.
Edward G. Bulwer-Lytton (1803-1873, British Novelist, Poet)

4 Deceive the rich and powerful if you will, but don't insult them.
Japanese Proverb

5 Oh, what a tangled web we weave, when first we practice to deceive.
Sir Walter Scott (1771-1832, British Novelist, Poet)

DECENCY

1 Decency is the least of all laws, but yet it is the law which is most strictly observed.
François de La Rochefoucauld (1613-1680, French classical writer)

2 Don't overestimate the decency of the human race.
H. L. Mencken (1880-1956, American Editor, Author, Critic, Humorist)

3 We are decent 99 percent of the time, when we could easily be vile.
R. W. Riis

4 No law reaches it, but all right-minded people observe it.
Sebastien-Roch Nicolas De Chamfort (1741-1794, French Writer, Journalist, Playwright)

DECEPTION

1 You can fool some of the people all the time, and all of the people some of the time, but you cannot fool all of the people all the time.
Abraham Lincoln (1809-1865, Sixteenth President of the USA)

2 Tricks and treachery are the practice of fools, that don't have brains enough to be honest.
Benjamin Franklin (1706-1790, American Scientist, Publisher, Diplomat)

3 Who had deceived thee so often as thyself?
Benjamin Franklin (1706-1790, American Scientist, Publisher, Diplomat)

4 We like to be deceived.
Blaise Pascal (1623-1662, French Scientist, Religious Philosopher)

5 To know how to disguise is the knowledge of kings.
Cardinal De Richelieu (1585-1642, French Statesman)

6 No man is happy without a delusion of some kind. Delusions are as necessary to our happiness as realities.
Christian Nevell Bovee (1820-1904, American Author, Lawyer)

7 I became a virtuoso of deceit. It wasn't pleasure I was after, it was knowledge. I consulted the strictest moralists to learn how to appear, philosophers to find out what to think and novelists to see what I could get away with. And, in the end, I distilled everything down to one wonderfully simple principle: win or die.
Christopher Hampton (1946-, British Playwright)

8 Man's mind is so formed that it is far more susceptible to falsehood than to truth.
Desiderius Erasmus (1466-1536, Dutch Humanist)

9 The great advantages of simulation and dissimulation are three. First to lay asleep opposition and to surprise. For where a man's intentions are published, it is an alarum to call up all that are against them. The second is to reserve a man's self a fair retreat: for if a man engage himself, by a manifest declaration, he must go through, or take a fall. The third is, the better to discover the mind of another. For to him that opens himself, men will hardly show themselves adverse; but will fair let him go on, and turn their freedom of speech to freedom of thought.
Francis Bacon (1561-1626, British Philosopher, Essayist, Statesman)

10 The sure way to be cheated is to think one's self more cunning than others.
François de La Rochefoucauld (1613-1680, French classical writer)

11 It seems to me that there are two kinds of trickery: the "fronts" people assume before one another's eyes, and the "front" a writer puts on the face of reality.
Françoise Sagan (1935-2004, French novelist, playwright)

12 The people of the world having once been deceived, suspect deceit in truth itself.
Hitopadesa (Sanskrit Fable From Panchatantra)

13 Hateful to me as the gates of Hades is that man who hides one thing in his heart and speaks another.
Homer (850 BC, Greek Epic Poet)

14 He who has made it a practice to lie and deceive his father, will be the most daring in deceiving others.
Horace (65-8 BC, Italian Poet)

15 It is twice the pleasure to deceive the deceiver.
Jean De La Fontaine (1621-1695, French Poet)

16 Nothing is more common on earth than to deceive and be deceived.
Johann G. Seume (1763-1810, German Theologist)

17 The craftiest trickery are too short and ragged a cloak to cover a bad heart.
Johann Kaspar Lavater (1741-1801, Swiss Theologian, Mystic)

18 We are never deceived; we deceive ourselves.
Johann Wolfgang Von Goethe (1749-1832, German Poet, Dramatist, Novelist)

19 Unlike grown ups, children have little need to deceive themselves.
Johann Wolfgang Von Goethe (1749-1832, German Poet, Dramatist, Novelist)

20 The art of using deceit and cunning grow continually weaker and less effective to the user.
John Tillotson (1630-1694, British Theologian - Archbishop of Canterbury)

21 The crafty person is always in danger; and when they think they walk in the dark, all their pretenses are transparent.
John Tillotson (1630-1694, British Theologian - Archbishop of Canterbury)

22 A deception that elevates us is dearer than a host of low truths.
Marina Tsvetaeva (1892-1941, Russian Poet)

23 Don't part with your illusions. When they are gone you may still exist, but you have ceased to live.
Mark Twain (1835-1910, American Humorist, Writer)

24 When a person cannot deceive himself the chances are against his being able to deceive other people.
Mark Twain (1835-1910, American Humorist, Writer)

25 The art of pleasing is the art of deception.
Marquis De Vauvenargues (1715-1747, French Moralist)

26 Everyone is born sincere and die deceivers.
Marquis De Vauvenargues (1715-1747, French Moralist)

27 Subtlety may deceive you; integrity never will.
Oliver Cromwell (1599-1658, Parliamentarian General, Lord Protector of England)

28 The easiest way to be cheated is to believe yourself to be more cunning than others.
Pierre Charron (1541-1603, French Philosopher)

29 Whatever deceives men seems to produce a magical enchantment.
Plato (427-347 BC, Greek Philosopher)

30 Every cloud has a silver lining.
Proverb

31 All deception in the course of life is indeed nothing else but a lie reduced to practice, and falsehood passing from words into things.
Robert Southey (1774-1843, British Author)

32 I have always considered it as treason against the great republic of human nature, to make any man's virtues the means of deceiving him.
Samuel Johnson (1709-1784, British Author)

33 Whenever, therefore, people are deceived and form opinions wide of the truth, it is clear that the error has slid into their minds through the medium of certain resemblances to that truth.
Socrates (469-399 BC, Greek Philosopher of Athens)

34 Cunning is the art of concealing our own defects, and discovering the weaknesses of others.
William Hazlitt (1778-1830, British Essayist)

35 Life is the art of being well deceived.
William Hazlitt (1778-1830, British Essayist)

36 To give up pretensions is as blessed a relief as to get them ratified.
William James (1842-1910, American Psychologist, Professor, Author)

37 For I have sworn thee fair, and thought thee bright, who art as black as hell, as dark as night.
William Shakespeare (1564-1616, British Poet, Playwright, Actor)

DECISIONS

1 Shelving hard decisions is the least ethical course.
Adrian Cadbury (American Business Executive)

2 In making our decisions, we must use the brains that God has given us. But we must also use our hearts which He also gave us. A man who has not learned to say, "No" --who is not resolved that he will take God's way, in spite of every dog that can bay or bark at him, in spite of every silvery choice that woos him aside--will be a weak and a wretched man till he dies.
Alexander Maclaren (1826-1910, British Preacher)

3 It is in your moments of decision that your destiny is shaped.
Anthony Robbins (1960-, American Author, Speaker, Peak Performance Expert / Consultant)

4 I also remember the moment my life changed, the moment I finally said, "I've had it! I know I'm much more than I'm demonstrating mentally, emotionally, and physically in my life." I made a decision in that moment which was to alter my life forever. I decided to change virtually every aspect of my life. I decided I would never again settle for less than I can be.
Anthony Robbins (1960-, American Author, Speaker, Peak Performance Expert / Consultant)

5 Your life changes the moment you make a new, congruent, and committed decision.
Anthony Robbins (1960-, American Author, Speaker, Peak Performance Expert / Consultant)

6 You must know that in any moment a decision you make can change the course of your life forever: the very next person stand behind in line or sit next to on an airplane, the very next phone call you make or receive, the very next movie you see or book you read or page you turn could be the one single thing that causes the floodgates to open, and all of the things that you've been waiting for to fall into place.
Anthony Robbins (1960-, American Author, Speaker, Peak Performance Expert / Consultant)

7 The indispensable first step to getting the things you want out of life is this: Decide what you want.
Ben Stein (American Professor, Writer)

8 I hate to see things done by halves. If it be right, do it boldly, if it be wrong leave it undone.
Bernard Gilpin

9 Where there is no counsel, the people perish; but in the multitude of counselors there is safety. [Proverbs 29:18; 11:14]
Bible (Sacred Scriptures of Christians and Judaism)

10 Decisiveness is a characteristic of high-performing men and women. Almost any decision is better than no decision at all.
Brian Tracy (American Trainer, Speaker, Author, Businessman)

11 Deliberate with caution, but act with decision; and yield with graciousness or oppose with firmness.
Charles Caleb Colton (1780-1832, British Sportsman Writer)

12 A wise man makes his own decisions, an ignorant man follows the public opinion.
Chinese Proverb

13 I determined never to stop until I had come to the end and achieved my purpose.
David Livingstone (1813-1873, British Missionary, Explorer)

14 Most of our executives make very sound decisions. The trouble is many of them have turned out not to have been right.
Donald Bullock (American Business Trainer)

15 The history of free men is never really written by chance but by choice; their choice!
Dwight D. Eisenhower (1890-1969, Thirty-fourth President of the USA)

16 When people ask for time, it's always for time to say no. Yes has one more letter in it, but it doesn't take half as long to say.
Edith Wharton (1862-1937, American Author)

17 Every decision you make is a mistake.
Edward Dahlberg (1900-1977, American Author, Critic)

18 It does not take much strength to do things, but it requires great strength to decide what to do.
Elbert Hubbard (1859-1915, American Author, Publisher)

19 Somewhere along the line of development we discover what we really are, and then we make our real decision for which we are responsible. Make that decision primarily for yourself because you can never really live anyone else's life, not even your own child's.
Eleanor Roosevelt (1884-1962, American First Lady, Columnist, Lecturer, Humanitarian)

20 Every decision is liberating, even if it leads to disaster. Otherwise, why do so many people walk upright and with open eyes into their misfortune?
Elias Canetti (1905-, Austrian Novelist, Philosopher)

21 Making a decision to have a child -- it's momentous. It is to decide forever to have your heart go walking around outside your body.
Elizabeth Stone

22 The difference is wide that sheets will not decide.
English Proverb

23 A decision without the pressure of consequence is hardly a decision at all.
Eric Langmuir.

24 The refusal to choose is a form of choice; disbelief is a form of belief.
Frank Barron

25 The roads we take are more important than the goals we announce. Decisions determine destiny.
Frederick Speakman

26 Indecision and delays are the parents of failure.
George Canning (1770-1827, British Statesman)

27 How could a man be satisfied with a decision between such alternatives and under such circumstances? No more than he can be satisfied with his hat, which he's chosen from among such shapes as the resources of the age offer him, wearing it at best with a resignation which is chiefly supported by comparison.
George Eliot (1819-1880, British Novelist)

28 No answer is also an answer.
German Proverb

29 Decision is a sharp knife that cuts or to do anything, never to turn back or to stop until the thing intended was clean and straight; indecision, a dull one that hacks and tears and leaves ragged edges behind it.
Gordon Graham

30 Whenever I make a bum decision, I go out and make another one.
Harry S. Truman (1884-1972, Thirty-third President of the USA)

31 Decisiveness is often the art of timely cruelty.
Henri Becquerel (1852-1908, French Physicist)

32 Some people, however long their experience or strong their intellect, are temperamentally incapable of reaching firm decisions.
James Callaghan (British Prime Minister)

33 Once to every person and nation come the moment to decide. In the conflict of truth with falsehood, for the good or evil side.
James Russell Lowell (1819-1891, American Poet, Critic, Editor)

34 It is only in our decisions that we are important.
Jean-Paul Sartre (1905-1980, French Writer, Philosopher)

35 It doesn't matter which side of the fence you get off on sometimes. What matters most is getting off. You cannot make progress without making decisions.
Jim Rohn (American Businessman, Author, Speaker, Philosopher)

36 The person who in shaky times also wavers only increases the evil, but the person of firm decision fashions the universe.
Johann Wolfgang Von Goethe (1749-1832, German Poet, Dramatist, Novelist)

37 Be slow to resolve, but quick in performance.
John Dryden (1631-1700, British Poet, Dramatist, Critic)

38 Once -- many, many years ago -- I thought I made a wrong decision. Of course, it turned out that I had been right all along. But I was wrong to have thought that I was wrong.
John Foster Dulles (1888-1959, American Republican Secretary of State)

39 A man without decision can never be said to belong to himself.
John W. Foster (1770-1843, British Clergyman, Essayist)

40 We have a choice: to plow new ground or let the weeds grow.
Jonathan Westover

41 The lives of the best of us are spent in choosing between evils.
Junius (1769-1771, Anonymous British Letter Writer)

42 You've got to know when to hold em, know when to fold em know when to walk away, know when to run.
Kenny Rogers (American Country Singer, Actor)

43 Decide promptly, but never give any reasons. Your decisions may be right, but your reasons are sure to be wrong.
Lord Mansfield (1867-1915, British Artist, Author)

44 Do not choose to be wrong for the sake of being different.
Lord Samuel

45 All our final decisions are made in a state of mind that is not going to last.
Marcel Proust (1871-1922, French Novelist)

46 Impelled by a state of mind which is destined not to last, we make our irrevocable decisions
Marcel Proust (1871-1922, French Novelist)

47 Nothing is more difficult, and therefore more precious, than to be able to decide.
Napoleon Bonaparte (1769-1821, French General, Emperor)

48 Indecision is the seedling of fear.
Napoleon Hill (1883-1970, American Speaker, Motivational Writer, "Think and Grow Rich")

49 Business leaders often get credit for the successful decisions that were forced on them.
Oliver A. Fick (American Environmental Service Manager)

50 We are given one life, and the decision is our whether to wait for circumstances to make up our mind, or whether to act, and in acting, to live.
Omar Nelson Bradley (1893-1981, American General)

51 Decision making is the specific executive task.
Peter F. Drucker (1909-, American Management Consultant, Author)

52 That should be considered long which can be decided but once.
Publilius Syrus (1st Century BC, Roman Writer)

53 Once you make a decision, the universe conspires to make it happen.
Ralph Waldo Emerson (1803-1882, American Poet, Essayist)

54 If you're already in a hole, it's no use to continue digging.
Roy W. Walters

55 People don't want to know that as a woman, I made my own decision as a woman to leave, It has to be I was so burnt out or in love. [On her decision to quit E.R.]
Sherry Stringfield (Born 1967, American Actress)

56 Make decisions from the heart and use your head to make it work out.
Sir Girad

57 In addition to self-awareness, imagination and conscience, it is the fourth human endowment- independent will-that really makes effective self-management possible. It is the ability to make decisions and choices and to act in accordance with them. It is the ability to act rather than to be acted upon, to proactively carry out the program we have developed through the other three endowments. Empowerment comes from learning how to use this great endowment in the decisions we make every day.
Stephen R. Covey (American Speaker, Trainer, Author of "The 7 Habits of Highly Effective People")

58 The quality of decision is like the well-timed swoop of a falcon which enables it to strike and destroy its victim.
Sun Tzu (400-430 BC, Chinese Military Strategist, Author of "Art of War")

59 Be willing to make decisions. That's the most important quality in a good leader. Don't fall victim to what I call the Ready- Aim-Aim-Aim Syndrome. You must be willing to fire.
T. Boone Pickens (American Businessman, Chairman of Mesa Petroleum)

60 In any moment of decision the best thing you can do is the right thing, the next best thing is the wrong thing, and the worst thing you can do is nothing.
Theodore Roosevelt (1858-1919, Twenty-sixth President of the USA)

61 The block of granite which was an obstacle in the pathway of the weak becomes a stepping- stone in the pathway of the strong.
Thomas Carlyle (1795-1881, Scottish Philosopher, Author)

62 Everything starts with yourself -- with you making up your mind about what you're going to do with your life. I tell kids that it's a cruel world, and that the world will bend them either left or right, and it's up to them to decide which way to bend.
Tony Dorsett (1954-, American Football Player)

63 Our lives are a sum total of the choices we have made.
Wayne Dyer (1940-, American Psychotherapist, Author, Lecturer)

64 When possible make the decisions now, even if action is in the future. A reviewed decision usually is better than one reached at the last moment.
William B. Given

65 They are decided only to be undecided, resolved to be irresolute, adamant for drift, solid for fluidity, all-powerful to be impotent.
Winston Churchill (1874-1965, British Statesman, Prime Minister)

66 When you come to a fork in the road, take it.
    Yogi Berra (1925-, American Baseball Player)

DEDICATION

1   The condition of an enlightened mind is a surrendered heart.
    Alan Redpath

2   There are two kinds of people: those who say to God, "Thy will be done," and those to whom God says, "All right, then, have it your way."
    C. S. Lewis (1898-1963, British Academic, Writer, Christian Apologist)

3   Obedience is the fruit of faith.
    Christina Rossetti (1830-1894, British Poet, Lyricist)

4   Nothing earthly will make me give up my work in despair.
    David Livingstone (1813-1873, British Missionary, Explorer)

5   I will place no value on anything I have or may possess except in relation to the kingdom of Christ.
    David Livingstone (1813-1873, British Missionary, Explorer)

6   God doesn't seek for golden vessels, and does not ask for silver ones, but He must have clean ones.
    Dwight L. Moody (1837-1899, American Evangelist)

7   By the grace of God, I'll be that man.
    Dwight L. Moody (1837-1899, American Evangelist)

8   Your powers are dead or dedicated. If they are dedicated, they are alive with God and tingle with surprising power. If they are saved up, taken care of for their own ends, they are dead.
    Eli Stanley Jones (1884-1973, American Missionary)

9   The world has yet to see what God will do with a man who is fully and wholly consecrated to the Holy Spirit.
    Henry Varley

10 It is a great deal easier to do that which God gives us to do, no matter how hard it is, than to face the responsibilities of not doing it.
    J. R. Miller (American Golfer)

11 The winning team has a dedication. It will have a core of veteran players who set the standards. They will not accept defeat.
    Merlin Olsen (American Football Player, Sports Broadcaster, Actor)

12 You will not be carried to Heaven lying at ease upon a feather bed.
    Samuel Rutherford (1600-1661, Scottish Pastor)

13 I wish to preach, not the doctrine of ignoble ease, but the doctrine of the strenuous life.
    Theodore Roosevelt (1858-1919, Twenty-sixth President of the USA)

14 The concentration and dedication- the intangibles are the deciding factors between who won and who lost.
    Tom Seaver

15 After the cheers have died down and the stadium is empty, after the headlines have been written and after you are back in the quiet of your room and the championship ring has been placed on the dresser and all the pomp and fanfare has faded, the enduring things that are left are: the dedication to excellence, the dedication to victory, and the dedication to doing with our lives the very best we can to make the world a better place in which to live.
    Vince Lombardi (1913-1970, American Football Coach)

16 In order to excel, you must be completely dedicated to your chosen sport. You must also be prepared to work hard and be willing to accept destructive criticism. Without 100 percent dedication, you won't be able to do this.
    Willie Mays (1931-, American Baseball Player)

DEEDS AND GOOD DEEDS

1   Anyone who proposes to do good must not expect people to roll stones out of his way, but must accept his lot calmly, even if they roll a few stones upon it.
    Albert Schweitzer (1875-1965, German Born Medical Missionary, Theologian, Musician, and Philosopher)

2   Ugly deeds are most estimable when hidden.
    Blaise Pascal (1623-1662, French Scientist, Religious Philosopher)

3   Fashion your life as a garland of beautiful deeds.
    Buddha (568-488 BC, Founder of Buddhism)

4   The greatest pleasure I know, is to do a good action by stealth, and to have it found out by accident.
    Charles Lamb (1775-1834, British Essayist, Critic)

5   Though it is possible to utter words only with the intention to fulfill the will of God, it is very difficult not to think about the impression which they will produce on men and not to form them accordingly. But deeds you can do quite unknown to men, only for God. And such deeds are the greatest joy that a man can experience.
    Count Leo Tolstoy (1828-1910, Russian Novelist, Philosopher)

6   Noble deeds and hot baths are the best cures for depression.
    Dodie Smith

7   The man who has accomplished all that he thinks worthwhile has begun to die.
    E. T. Trigg

8   Though language forms the preacher, 'Tis "good works" make the man.
    Eliza Cook (1818-1889, British Poet)

9   What monster have we here? A great Deed at this hour of day? A great just deed -- and not for pay? Absurd -- or insincere?
    Elizabeth Barrett Browning (1806-1861, British Poet)

10 How ever a brilliant an action, it should not be viewed as great unless it is the result of a great motive.
François de La Rochefoucauld (1613-1680, French classical writer)

11 Those who shine in the second rank, are eclipsed by the first.
French Proverb

12 Whatever is done for love always occurs beyond good and evil.
Friedrich Nietzsche (1844-1900, German Philosopher)

13 Our deeds still travel with us from afar, and what we have been makes us what we are.
George Eliot (1819-1880, British Novelist)

14 Our deeds determine us, as much as we determine our deeds.
George Eliot (1819-1880, British Novelist)

15 As for doing good; that is one of the professions which is full. Moreover I have tried it fairly and, strange as it may seem, am satisfied that it does not agree with my constitution.
Henry David Thoreau (1817-1862, American Essayist, Poet, Naturalist)

16 If I knew for a certainty that a man was coming to my house with the conscious design of doing me good, I should run for my life.
Henry David Thoreau (1817-1862, American Essayist, Poet, Naturalist)

17 Chop your own wood, and it will warm you twice.
Henry Ford (1863-1947, American Industrialist, Founder of Ford Motor Company)

18 Great deeds are usually wrought at great risks.
Herodotus (484-425 BC, Greek Historian)

19 Every man feels instinctively that all the beautiful sentiments in the world weigh less than a single lovely action.
James Russell Lowell (1819-1891, American Poet, Critic, Editor)

20 Ambition and love are the wings to great deeds.
Johann Wolfgang Von Goethe (1749-1832, German Poet, Dramatist, Novelist)

21 Verily the kindness that gazes upon itself in a mirror turns to stone, and a good deed that calls itself by tender names becomes the parent to a curse.
Kahlil Gibran (1883-1931, Lebanese Poet, Novelist)

22 In dreams the truth is learned that all good works are done in the absence of a caress.
Leonard Cohen (1934-, Canadian-born American Musician, Songwriter, Singer)

23 Happy is the man whose deeds are greater than his learning
Midrash (Early Jewish Biblical Commentary)

24 Mighty in deeds and not in words.
Motto

25 Men of real merit, whose noble and glorious deeds we are ready to acknowledge are not yet to be endured when they vaunt their own actions.
Schines

26 Real worth requires no interpreter: its everyday deeds form its emblem.
Sebastien-Roch Nicolas De Chamfort (1741-1794, French Writer, Journalist, Playwright)

27 Nothing can be made of nothing; he who has laid up no material can produce no combination.
Sir Joshua Reynolds (1723-1792, British Artist, Critic)

28 Talking much is a sign of vanity, for the one who is lavish with words is cheap in deeds.
Sir Walter Raleigh (1552-1618, British Courtier, Navigator, Writer)

29 To be doing good deeds is man's most glorious task.
Sophocles (495-406 BC, Greek Tragic Poet)

30 A good deed is never lost. He who sows courtesy, reaps friendship; he who plants kindness, gathers love; pleasure bestowed on a grateful mind was never sterile, but generally gratitude begets reward.
St. Basil (329-379, Bishop of Caesarea)

31 The last temptation is the greatest treason: To do the right deed for the wrong reason.
T. S. Eliot (1888-1965, American-born British Poet, Critic)

32 Everyone whose deeds are more than his wisdom, his wisdom endures; and everyone whose wisdom is more than his deeds, his wisdom does not endure.
The Talmud (Jewish Archive of Oral Tradition)

33 My country is the world, and my religion is to do good.
Thomas Paine (1737-1809, Anglo-American Political Theorist, Writer)

34 We are the children of our own deeds.
Victor Hugo (1802-1885, French Poet, Dramatist, Novelist)

35 A good picture is equivalent to a good deed.
Vincent Van Gogh (1853-1890, Dutch-born French Painter)

36 That best portion of a good man's life; His little, nameless, unremembered acts of kindness and of love.
William Wordsworth (1770-1850, British Poet)

DEFEAT

1 There are important cases in which the difference between half a heart and a whole heart makes just the difference between signal defeat and a splendid victory.
A. H. K. Boyd

2 The injustice of defeat lies in the fact that its most innocent victims are made to look like heartless accomplices. It is impossible to see behind defeat, the sacrifices, the austere performance of duty, the self-discipline and the vigilance that are there -- those things the god of battle does not take account of.
Antoine De Saint-Exupery (1900-1944, French Aviator, Writer)

3 Commonly, people believe that defeat is characterized by a general bustle and a feverish rush. Bustle and rush are the signs of victory, not of defeat. Victory is a thing of action. It is a house in the act of being built. Every participant in victory sweats and puffs, carrying the stones for the building of the house. But defeat is a thing of weariness, of incoherence, of boredom. And above all of futility.
Antoine De Saint-Exupery (1900-1944, French Aviator, Writer)

4 My lowest days as a Christian [and There Were Low Ones--Seven Months Worth Of Them In Prison, To Be Exact] have been more fulfilling and rewarding than all the days of glory in the White House.
Charles Caleb Colton (1780-1832, British Sportsman Writer)

5 When the frustration of my helplessness seemed greatest, I discovered God's grace was more than sufficient. And after my imprisonment, I could look back and see how God used my powerlessness for His purpose. What He has chosen for my most significant witness was not my triumphs or victories, but my defeat.
Charles Caleb Colton (1780-1832, British Sportsman Writer)

6 We are not retreating -- we are advancing in another direction.
Douglas Macarthur (1880-1964, American Army General in WW II)

7 A man can be destroyed but not defeated.
Ernest Hemingway (1898-1961, American Writer)

8 Defeat is not the worst of failures. Not to have tried is the true failure.
George E. Woodberry (1855-1930, American Literary Critic)

9 To walk through the ruined cities of Germany is to feel an actual doubt about the continuity of civilization.
George Orwell (1903-1950, British Author, "Animal Farm")

10 Making a comeback is one of the most difficult things to do with dignity.
Greg Lake

11 The man who wins may have been counted out several times but he didn't hear the referee.
H. E. Jansen

12 It is defeat that turns bone to flint; it is defeat that turns gristle to muscle; it is defeat that makes men invincible.
Henry Ward Beecher (1813-1887, American Preacher, Orator, Writer)

13 Defeat is a school in which truth always grows strong.
Henry Ward Beecher (1813-1887, American Preacher, Orator, Writer)

14 Most human organizations that fall short of their goals do so not because of stupidity or faulty doctrines, but because of internal decay and rigidification. They grow stiff in the joints. They get in a rut. They go to seed.
James A. Garfield (1831-1881, Twentieth President of the USA)

15 A man is not defeated by his opponents but by himself.
Jan Christian Smuts (1870-1950, South African General, Statesman, and Prime Minister)

16 Those who are prepared to die for any cause are seldom defeated.
Jawaharlal Nehru (1889-1964, Indian Nationalist, Statesman)

17 Defeat never comes to any man until he admits it.
Josephus Daniels (1862-1948, American Publisher, Editor)

18 I think everyone should experience defeat at least once during their career. You learn a lot from it.
Lou Holtz (1937-, American Football Coach)

19 We may encounter many defeats but we must not be defeated.
Maya Angelou (1928-, African-American poet, Writer, Performer)

20 There are some defeats more triumphant than victories.
Michel Eyquem De Montaigne (1533-1592, French Philosopher, Essayist)

21 Believe you are defeated, believe it long enough, and it is likely to become a fact.
Norman Vincent Peale (1898-1993, American Christian Reformed Pastor, Speaker, Author)

22 You can learn a line from a win and a book from a defeat.
Paul Brown (American Football Coach)

23 Defeat doesn't finish a man -- quit does. A man is not finished when he's defeated. He's finished when he quits.
Richard M. Nixon (1913-1994, Thirty-seventh President of the USA)

24 I give the fight up: let there be an end, a privacy, an obscure nook for me. I want to be forgotten even by God.
Robert Browning (1812-1889, British Poet)

25 The mark of a great player is in his ability to come back. The great champions have all come back from defeat.
Sam Snead (1912-, American Golfer)

26 I've learned that something constructive comes from every defeat.
Tom Landry (1924-, American Football Player, Coach)

27 Who asks whether the enemy were defeated by strategy or valor?
Virgil (70-19 BC, Roman Poet)

28 For by superior energies; more strict affiance in each other; faith more firm in their unhallowed principles, the bad have fairly earned a victory over the weak, the vacillating, inconsistent good.
William Wordsworth (1770-1850, British Poet)

29 The problems of victory are more agreeable than those of defeat, but they are no less difficult.
Winston Churchill (1874-1965, British Statesman, Prime Minister)

DEFENSE

1 They say that the best defense is offense, and I intend to start offending right now.
Captain James

2 Self-defense is Nature's eldest law.
John Dryden (1631-1700, British Poet, Dramatist, Critic)

3 Our capacity to retaliate must be, and is, massive in order to deter all forms of aggression.
John Foster Dulles (1888-1959, American Republican Secretary of State)

4 There's no telling what might have happened to our defense budget if Saddam Hussein hadn't invaded Kuwait that August and set everyone gearing up for World War II. Can we count on Saddam Hussein to come along every year and resolve our defense-policy debates? Given the history of the Middle East, it's possible.
P. J. O'Rourke (1947-, American Journalist)

5 Attack is the best form of defense.
Proverb

6 We're in greater danger today than we were the day after Pearl Harbor. Our military is absolutely incapable of defending this country.
Ronald Reagan (1911-, Fortieth President of the USA, Actor)

7 Harsh necessity, and the newness of my kingdom, force me to do such things and to guard my frontiers everywhere.
Virgil (70-19 BC, Roman Poet)

DEFINITION

1 Men have defined the parameters of every subject. All feminist arguments, however radical in intent or consequence, are with or against assertions or premises implicit in the male system, which is made credible or authentic by the power of men to name.
Andrea Dworkin (1946-, American Feminist Critic)

2 By speaking, by thinking, we undertake to clarify things, and that forces us to exacerbate them, dislocate them, schematize them. Every concept is in itself an exaggeration.
Jose Ortega Y Gasset (1883-1955, Spanish Essayist, Philosopher)

3 The human mind is so complex and things are so tangled up with each other that, to explain a blade of straw, one would have to take to pieces an entire universe. A definition is a sack of flour compressed into a thimble.
Remy De Gourmont (1858-1915, French Novelist, Philosopher, Poet, Playwright)

4 In the animal kingdom, the rule is, eat or be eaten; in the human kingdom, define or be defined.
Thomas Szasz (1920-, American Psychiatrist)

5 It is the business of thought to define things, to find the boundaries; thought, indeed, is a ceaseless process of definition. It is the business of Art to give things shape. Anyone who takes no delight in the firm outline of an object, or in its essential character, has no artistic sense. He cannot even be nourished by Art. Like Ephraim, he feeds upon the East wind, which has no boundaries.
Vance Palmer (1885-1959, Australian Author, Poet)

DELEGATION

1 No person will make a great business who wants to do it all himself or get all the credit.
Andrew Carnegie (1835-1919, American Industrialist, Philanthropist)

2 Give up control even if it means the employees have to make some mistakes.
Frank Flores (American Business Executive)

3 If you don't know what to do with many of the papers piled on your desk, stick a dozen colleagues initials on them and pass them along. When in doubt, route.
Malcolm S. Forbes (1919-1990, American Publisher, Businessman)

4 You have to do many things yourself. Things that you cannot delegate.
Nadine Gramling (American Business Executive)

5 You can delegate authority, but you can never delegate responsibility for delegating a task to someone else. If you picked the right man, fine, but if you picked the wrong man, the responsibility is yours -- not his.
Richard E Krafve

6 Delegating means letting others become the experts and hence the best.
Timothy Firnstahl (American Business Executive)

DELIBERATION

1 Deliberation. The act of examining one's bread to determine which side it is buttered on.
Ambrose Bierce (1842-1914, American Author, Editor, Journalist, "The Devil's Dictionary")

2 Nowadays not even a suicide kills himself in desperation. Before taking the step he deliberates so long and so carefully that he literally chokes with thought. It is even questionable whether he ought to be called a suicide, since it is really thought which takes his life. He does not die with deliberation but from deliberation.
Soren Kierkegaard (1813-1855, Danish Philosopher, Writer)

3 Reflection makes men cowards.
William Hazlitt (1778-1830, British Essayist)

DELINQUENCY

1   Violence among young people is an aspect of their desire to create. They don't know how to use their energy creatively so they do the opposite and destroy.
Anthony Burgess (1917-1993, British Writer, Critic)

2   There are souls that are incurable and lost to the rest of society. Deprive them of one means of folly, they will invent ten thousand others. They will create subtler, wilder methods, methods that are absolutely DESPERATE. Nature herself is fundamentally antisocial, it is only by a usurpation of powers that the organized body of society opposes the natural inclination of humanity.
Antonin Artaud (1896-1948, French Theater Producer, Actor, Theorist)

3   He that seeks trouble never misses.
English Proverb

4   We know that their adventures are childish. They themselves are fools. They are ready to kill or be killed over a card-game in which an opponent -- or they themselves -- was cheating. Yet, thanks to such fellows, tragedies are possible.
Jean Genet (1910-1986, French Playwright, Novelist)

5   Strange and predatory and truly dangerous, car thieves and muggers -- they seem to jeopardize all our cherished concepts, even our self-esteem, our property rights, our powers of love, our laws and pleasures. The only relationship we seem to have with them is scorn or bewilderment, but they belong somewhere on the dark prairies of a country that is in the throes of self-discovery.
John Cheever (1912-1982, American Author)

6   Gentleman-rankers out on the spree, damned from here to Eternity.
Rudyard Kipling (1865-1936, British Author of Prose, Verse)

7   Now, neighbor confines, purge you of your scum! Have you a ruffian that will swear, drink, dance, revel the night, rob, murder, and commit the oldest sins the newest kind of ways?
William Shakespeare (1564-1616, British Poet, Playwright, Actor)

DEMOCRACY

1   No man is good enough to govern another man without that other's consent.
Abraham Lincoln (1809-1865, Sixteenth President of the USA)

2   As I would not be a slave, so I would not be a master. This expresses my idea of democracy.
Abraham Lincoln (1809-1865, Sixteenth President of the USA)

3   All the ills of democracy can be cured by more democracy.
Alfred E. Smith (1873-1944, American Politician)

4   Democracy! Bah! When I hear that word I reach for my feather Boa!
Allen Ginsberg (1926-, American Poet)

5   The worst thing I can say about democracy is that it has tolerated the Right Honorable Gentleman for four and a half years.
Aneurin Bevan (1897-1960, British Labor Politician)

6   Democracy is never a thing done. Democracy is always something that a nation must be doing. What is necessary now is one thing and one thing only that democracy become again democracy in action, not democracy accomplished and piled up in goods and gold.
Archibald Macleish (1892-1982, American Poet)

7   Democracy don't rule the world, you better get that in your head; this world is ruled by violence, but I guess that's better left unsaid.
Bob Dylan (1941-, American Musician, Singer, Songwriter)

8   In a democracy everybody has a right to be represented, including the jerks.
Chris Patten (1944-, British Statesman, Governor of Hong Kong)

9   You must drop all your democracy. You must not believe in "the people." One class is no better than another. It must be a case of Wisdom, or Truth. Let the working classes be working classes. That is the truth. There must be an aristocracy of people who have wisdom, and there must be a Ruler: a Kaiser: no Presidents and democracies.
D. H. Lawrence (1885-1930, British Author)

10   The more I see of democracy the more I dislike it. It just brings everything down to the mere vulgar level of wages and prices, electric light and water closets, and nothing else.
D. H. Lawrence (1885-1930, British Author)

11   Democracy: In which you say what you like and do what you're told.
Dave Barry (American Humorist, Author)

12   Democracy is the recurrent suspicion that more than half of the people are right more than half of the time.
E(lwyn) B(rooks) White (1899-1985, American Author, Editor)

13   Freedom without obligation is anarchy. Freedom without obligation is democracy.
Earl Riney

14   Two cheers for Democracy: one because it admits variety and two because it permits criticism.
Edward M. Forster (1879-1970, British Novelist, Essayist)

15   When great changes occur in history, when great principles are involved, as a rule the majority are wrong.
Eugene V. Debs (1855-1926, American Socialist Leader)

16   Chinks in America's egalitarian armor are not hard to find. Democracy is the fig leaf of elitism.
Florence King (1936-, American Author, Critic)

17 Democracy substitutes election by the incompetent many for appointment by the corrupt few.
George Bernard Shaw (1856-1950, Irish-born British Dramatist)

18 I talk democracy to these men and women. I tell them that they have the vote, and that theirs is the kingdom and the power and the glory. I say to them "You are supreme: exercise your power." They say, "That's right: tell us what to do;" and I tell them. I say "Exercise our vote intelligently by voting for me." And they do. That's democracy; and a splendid thing it is too for putting the right men in the right place.
George Bernard Shaw (1856-1950, Irish-born British Dramatist)

19 Democracy means government by the uneducated, while aristocracy means government by the badly educated.
Gilbert K. Chesterton (1874-1936, British Author)

20 Apparently, a democracy is a place where numerous elections are held at great cost without issues and with interchangeable candidates.
Gore Vidal (1925-, American Novelist, Critic)

21 Democracy is supposed to give you the feeling of choice, like Painkiller X and Painkiller Y. But they're both just aspirin.
Gore Vidal (1925-, American Novelist, Critic)

22 The ship of Democracy, which has weathered all storms, may sink through the mutiny of those aboard.
Grover Cleveland (1837-1908, Twenty-second & 24th President of the USA)

23 I confess I enjoy democracy immensely. It is incomparably idiotic, and hence incomparably amusing.
H. L. Mencken (1880-1956, American Editor, Author, Critic, Humorist)

24 Democracy is also a form of religion. It is the worship of jackals by jackasses.
H. L. Mencken (1880-1956, American Editor, Author, Critic, Humorist)

25 Democracy is the theory that the common people know what They want, and deserve to get it good and hard.
H. L. Mencken (1880-1956, American Editor, Author, Critic, Humorist)

26 The cure for the evils of democracy is more democracy.
H. L. Mencken (1880-1956, American Editor, Author, Critic, Humorist)

27 Democracy is based upon the conviction that there are extraordinary possibilities in ordinary people.
Harry Emerson Fosdick (1878-1969, American Minister)

28 The majority is never right. Never, I tell you! That's one of these lies in society that no free and intelligent man can help rebelling against. Who are the people that make up the biggest proportion of the population -- the intelligent ones or the fools? I think we can agree it's the fools, no matter where you go in this world, it's the fools that form the overwhelming majority.
Henrik Ibsen (1828-1906, Norwegian Dramatist)

29 It is the American vice, the democratic disease which expresses its tyranny by reducing everything unique to the level of the herd.
Henry Miller (1891-1980, American Author)

30 It is not enough to merely defend democracy. To defend it may be to lose it; to extend it is to strengthen it. Democracy is not property; it is an idea.
Hubert H. Humphrey (1911-1978, American Democratic Politician, Vice President)

31 Democracy does not guarantee equality of conditions -- it only guarantees equality of opportunity.
Irving Kristol

32 Democracy without morality is impossible.
Jack Kemp (American Football Player)

33 The tendency of democracies is, in all things, to mediocrity.
James F. Cooper (1789-1851, American Novelist)

34 Democracy give every man the right to be his own oppressor.
James Russell Lowell (1819-1891, American Poet, Critic, Editor)

35 Democracy is the menopause of Western society, the Grand Climacteric of the body social. Fascism is its middle-aged lust.
Jean Baudrillard (French Postmodern Philosopher, Writer)

36 Remember, democracy never lasts long. It soon wastes, exhausts, and murders itself. There never was a democracy yet that did not commit suicide.
John Adams (1735-1826, Second President of the USA)

37 Nor is the people's judgment always true: the most may err as grossly as the few.
John Dryden (1631-1700, British Poet, Dramatist, Critic)

38 When people put their ballots in the boxes, they are, by that act, inoculated against the feeling that the government is not theirs. They then accept, in some measure, that its errors are their errors, its aberrations their aberrations, that any revolt will be against them. It's a remarkably shrewd and rather conservative arrangement when one thinks of it.
John Kenneth Galbraith (1908-, American Economist)

39 Democracy encourages the majority to decide things about which the majority is blissfully ignorant.
John Simon

40 Democracy is a political method, that is to say, a certain type of institutional arrangement for arriving at political -- legislative and administrative -- decisions and hence incapable of being an end in itself.
Joseph A. Schumpeter (1883-1950, Austrian-American Economist)

41 Democracy means the opportunity to be everyone's slave.
Karl Kraus (1874-1936, Austrian Satirist)

42 The best way of learning to be an independent sovereign state is to be an independent sovereign state.
Kwame Nkrumah (Leader of Ghana's fight for Independence)

43 I swear to the Lord, I still can't see, why Democracy means, everybody but me.
Langston Hughes (1902-1967, American Poet, Short-story Writer, Playwright)

44 Democracy is a process by which the people are free to choose the man who will get the blame.
Laurence J. Peter

45 There is a limit to the application of democratic methods. You can inquire of all the passengers as to what type of car they like to ride in, but it is impossible to question them as to whether to apply the brakes when the train is at full speed and accident threatens.
Leon Trotsky (1879-1940, Russian Revolutionary)

46 I am a democrat only on principle, not by instinct -- nobody is that. Doubtless some people say they are, but this world is grievously given to lying.
Mark Twain (1835-1910, American Humorist, Writer)

47 Everybody's for democracy in principle. It's only in practice that the thing gives rise to stiff objections.
Meg Greenfield

48 Democracy is the wholesome and pure air without which a socialist public organization cannot live a full-blooded life.
Mikhail Gorbachev (1931-, Soviet Statesman and President of USSR (1988-91))

49 The soviet people want full-blooded and unconditional democracy.
Mikhail Gorbachev (1931-, Soviet Statesman and President of USSR (1988-91))

50 A modern democracy is a tyranny whose borders are undefined; one discovers how far one can go only by traveling in a straight line until one is stopped.
Norman Mailer (1923-, American Author)

51 The freeman, casting with unpurchased hand the vote that shakes the turrets of the land.
Oliver Wendell Holmes (1809-1894, American Author, Wit, Poet)

52 Democracy means simply the bludgeoning of the people by the people for the people.
Oscar Wilde (1856-1900, British Author, Wit)

53 Democracy with its semi-civilization sincerely cherishes junk. The artist's power should be spiritual. But the power of the majority is material. When these worlds meet occasionally, it is pure coincidence.
Paul Klee (1879-1940, Swiss Artist)

54 These, then, will be some of the features of democracy... it will be, in all likelihood, an agreeable, lawless, parti-colored commonwealth, dealing with all alike on a footing of equality, whether they be really equal or not.
Plato (427-347 BC, Greek Philosopher)

55 Democracy is a charming form of government, full of variety and disorder, and dispensing a sort of equality to equals and unequal alike.
Plato (427-347 BC, Greek Philosopher)

56 There can be no daily democracy without daily citizenship.
Ralph Nader (1934-, American Lawyer, Consumer Activist)

57 Man's capacity for justice makes democracy possible, but man's inclination to injustice makes democracy necessary.
Reinhold Niebuhr (1892-1971, American Theologian, Historian)

58 We once worried that democracy could not survive if an undereducated populace knew too little. Now we worry if it can survive us knowing too much.
Robert Bianco (American Radio / TV Editor)

59 It is a strange fact that freedom and equality, the two basic ideas of democracy, are to some extent contradictory. Logically considered, freedom and equality are mutually exclusive, just as society and the individual are mutually exclusive.
Thomas Mann (1875-1955, German Author, Critic)

60 Everything that is right or natural pleads for separation. The blood of the slain, the weeping voice of nature cries, 'Tis time to part.
Thomas Paine (1737-1809, Anglo-American Political Theorist, Writer)

61 Unless democracy is to commit suicide by consenting to its own destruction, it will have to find some formidable answer to those who come to it saying: "I demand from you in the name of your principles the rights which I shall deny to you later in the name of my principles."
Walter Lippmann (1889-1974, American Journalist)

62 What we call a democratic society might be defined for certain purposes as one in which the majority is always prepared to put down a revolutionary minority.
Walter Lippmann (1889-1974, American Journalist)

63 This is one of the paradoxes of the democratic movement -- that it loves a crowd and fears the individuals who compose it -- that the religion of humanity should have no faith in human beings.
Walter Lippmann (1889-1974, American Journalist)

64 The best defense against usurpatory government is an assertive citizenry.
William F. Buckley (1925-, American Writer)

65 Let the people think they govern and they will be governed.
William Penn (1644-1718, British Religious Leader, Founder of Pennsylvania)

66 It has been said that Democracy is the worst form of government except all those other forms that have been tried from time to time.
Winston Churchill (1874-1965, British Statesman, Prime Minister)

67 Nothing can be more abhorrent to democracy than to imprison a person or keep him in prison because he is unpopular. This is really the test of civilization.
Winston Churchill (1874-1965, British Statesman, Prime Minister)

68 The world must be made safe for democracy.
Woodrow T. Wilson (1856-1924, Twenty-eighth President of the USA)

69 America is the place where you cannot kill your government by killing the men who conduct it.
Woodrow T. Wilson (1856-1924, Twenty-eighth President of the USA)

70 That a peasant may become king does not render the kingdom democratic.
Woodrow T. Wilson (1856-1924, Twenty-eighth President of the USA)

71 I believe in democracy, because it releases the energies of every human being.
Woodrow T. Wilson (1856-1924, Twenty-eighth President of the USA)

72 Democracy is not so much a form of government as a set of principles.
Woodrow T. Wilson (1856-1924, Twenty-eighth President of the USA)

DENIAL

1 Deny yourself! You must deny yourself! That is the song that never ends.
Johann Wolfgang Von Goethe (1749-1832, German Poet, Dramatist, Novelist)

2 Denial ain't just a river in Egypt.
Mark Twain (1835-1910, American Humorist, Writer)

DEPENDENCE

1 Depend on no man, on no friend but him who can depend on himself. He only who acts conscientiously toward himself, will act so toward others.
Johann Kaspar Lavater (1741-1801, Swiss Theologian, Mystic)

2 There is no dependence that can be sure but a dependence upon one's self.
John Gay (1688-1732, British Playwright, Poet)

3 There is no one subsists by himself alone.
Owen Felltham (1602-1668, British Author)

4 The ship of heaven guides itself and will not accept a wooden rudder.
Ralph Waldo Emerson (1803-1882, American Poet, Essayist)

5 Interdependency follows independence.
Stephen R. Covey (American Speaker, Trainer, Author of "The 7 Habits of Highly Effective People")

DEPRESSION

1 This is my depressed stance. When you're depressed, it makes a lot of difference how you stand. The worst thing you can do is straighten up and hold your head high because then you'll start to feel better. If you're going to get any joy out of being depressed, you've got to stand like this.
Charlie Brown (Peanuts Comic Strip Character)

2 The world leans on us. When we sag, the whole world seems to droop.
Eric Hoffer (1902-1983, American Author, Philosopher)

3 That terrible mood of depression of whether it's any good or not is what is known as The Artist's Reward.
Ernest Hemingway (1898-1961, American Writer)

4 It's a recession when your neighbor loses his job; it's a depression when you lose your own.
Harry S. Truman (1884-1972, Thirty-third President of the USA)

5 Depression moods lead, almost invariably, to accidents. But, when they occur, our mood changes again, since the accident shows we can draw the world in our wake, and that we still retain some degree of power even when our spirits are low. A series of accidents creates a positively light- hearted state, out of consideration for this strange power.
Jean Baudrillard (French Postmodern Philosopher, Writer)

6 I am in that temper that if I were under water I would scarcely kick to come to the top.
John Keats (1795-1821, British Poet)

7 Geez, if I could get through to you, kiddo, that depression is not sobbing and crying and giving vent, it is plain and simple reduction of feeling. Reduction, see? Of all feeling. People who keep stiff upper lips find that it's damn hard to smile.
Judith Guest

8 The term clinical depression finds its way into too many conversations these days. One has a sense that a catastrophe has occurred in the psychic landscape.
Leonard Cohen (1934-, Canadian-born American Musician, Songwriter, Singer)

9 In addition to my other numerous acquaintances, I have one more intimate confidant. My depression is the most faithful mistress I have known -- no wonder, then, that I return the love.
Soren Kierkegaard (1813-1855, Danish Philosopher, Writer)

10 Depression is melancholy minus its charms -- the animation, the fits.
Susan Sontag (1933-, American Essayist)

DESIGN

1 Design in art, is a recognition of the relation between various things, various elements in the creative flux. You can't invent a design. You recognize it, in the fourth dimension. That is, with your blood and your bones, as well as with your eyes.
D. H. Lawrence (1885-1930, British Author)

2 Art has to move you and design does not, unless it's a good design for a bus.
David Hockney (1937-, British Artist)

3 The complaint about modern steel furniture, modern glass houses, modern red bars and modern streamlined trains and cars is that all these objects modernize, while adequate and amusing in themselves, tend to make the people who use them look dated. It is an honest criticism. The human race has done nothing much about changing its own appearance to conform to the form and texture of its appurtenances.
E(lwyn) B(rooks) White (1899-1985, American Author, Editor)

4 Design is not for philosophy -- it's for life.
Issey Miyake

5 Retail is detail.
James Gulliver (American Business Executive, Chairman of Argyll Group)

6 Why kick the man downstream who can't put the parts together because the parts really weren't designed properly?
Philip Caldwell (American Business Executive, CEO of Ford Motor Co.)

7 Perhaps believing in good design is like believing in God, it makes you an optimist.
Sir Terence Conran (1931-, British Businessman, Designer)

8 Interior design is a travesty of the architectural process and a frightening condemnation of the credulity, helplessness and gullibility of the most formidable consumers -- the rich.
Stephen Bayley (1951-, British Design Critic)

9 Designs in connection with postage stamps and coinage may be described, I think, as the silent ambassadors on national taste.
William Butler Yeats (1865-1939, Irish Poet, Playwright.)

DESIRE

1 There are confessable agonies, sufferings of which one can positively be proud. Of bereavement, of parting, of the sense of sin and the fear of death the poets have eloquently spoken. They command the world's sympathy. But there are also discreditable anguishes, no less excruciating than the others, but of which the sufferer dare not, cannot speak. The anguish of thwarted desire, for example.
Aldous Huxley (1894-1963, British Author)

2 Every man's road in life is marked by the grave of his personal likings.
Alexander Smith (1830-1867, Scottish Poet, Author)

3 Limited in his nature, infinite in his desire, man is a fallen god who remembers heaven.
Alphonse De Lamartine (1790-1869, French Poet, Statesman, Historian)

4 If men could regard the events of their own lives with more open minds, they would frequently discover that they did not really desire the things they failed to obtain.
Andre Maurois (1885-1967, French Writer)

5 The man never feels the want of what it never occurs to him to ask for.
Arthur Schopenhauer (1788-1860, German Philosopher)

6 When desire dies, fear is born.
Baltasar Gracian (1601-1658, Spanish Philosopher, Writer)

7 Want is one only of five giants on the road of reconstruction; the others are Disease, Ignorance, Squalor, and Idleness.
Baron William Henry Beveridge (1879-1963, Indian Economist)

8 Desire is the essence of a man.
Baruch (Benedict de) Spinoza (1632-1677, Dutch Philosopher and Theologian)

9 From the desert I come to thee, On a stallion shod with fire; And the winds are left behind In the speed of my desire.
Bayard Taylor (1825-1878, American Journalist, Traveler, Author)

10 I desire not to desire, for my will is without value, since I am ignorant in any case. Therefore choose Thou for me what thou knowest to be best and do not put my perdition in what my autonomy and free choice prefer.
Bayazid Al-Bistami

11 It is much easier to suppress a first desire than to satisfy those that follow.
Benjamin Franklin (1706-1790, American Scientist, Publisher, Diplomat)

12 If you desire many things, many things will seem few.
Benjamin Franklin (1706-1790, American Scientist, Publisher, Diplomat)

13 All human activity is prompted by desire.
Bertrand Russell (1872-1970, British Philosopher, Mathematician, Essayist)

14 The desire of the lazy kill him; for his hands refuse to labor. [Proverbs 21:25]
Bible (Sacred Scriptures of Christians and Judaism)

15 And desire shall fail: because man goeth to his long home, and the mourners go about the streets. [Ecclesiastes 12:5]
Bible (Sacred Scriptures of Christians and Judaism)

16 The desire accomplished is sweet to the soul. [Proverbs 13:19]
Bible (Sacred Scriptures of Christians and Judaism)

17 The desire of our soul is to they name, and to the remembrance of thee. [Isaiah]
Bible (Sacred Scriptures of Christians and Judaism)

18 Desire and force between them are responsible for all our actions; desire causes our voluntary acts, force our involuntary.
Blaise Pascal (1623-1662, French Scientist, Religious Philosopher)

19 Desire! That's the one secret of every man's career. Not education. Not being born with hidden talents. Desire.
Bobby Unser (1934-, American Race Car Driver)

20 As an eagle, weary after soaring in the sky, folds its wings and flies down to rest in its nest, so does the shining Self enter the state of dreamless sleep, where one is freed from all desires.
Brihadaranyaka Upanishad (Ancient Hindu Scripture Expounding the Identity of the Real Self)

21 You are what your deep driving desire is.
Brihadaranyaka Upanishad (Ancient Hindu Scripture Expounding the Identity of the Real Self)

22 It's not who jumps the highest -- it's who wants it the most
Buck Williams (1960-, American Basketball Player)

23 You can really have everything you want, if you go after it, but you will have to want it. The desire for success must be so strong within you that it is the very breath of your life -- your first though when you awaken in the morning, your last thought when you go to bed at night...
Charles E. Popplestone

24 If you really want something you can figure out how to make it happen.
Cher (1946-, American Actress, Director, Singer)

25 We trifle when we assign limits to our desires, since nature hath set none.
Christian Nevell Bovee (1820-1904, American Author, Lawyer)

26 By annihilating the desires, you annihilate the mind. Every man without passions has within him no principle of action, nor motive to act.
Claude A. HelvTtius (1715-1771, French Philosopher)

27 One essential to success is that your desire be an all-obsessing one, your thoughts and aim be coordinated, and your energy be concentrated and applied without letup.
Claude M. Bristol (1891-1951, American Author of "The Magic of Believing")

28 The more wild and incredible your desire, the more willing and prompt God is in fulfilling it, if you will have it so."
Coventry Patmore (1823-1896, British Poet)

29 Know what you want. Become your real self.
David Harold Fink

30 Your desires and true beliefs have a way of playing blind man's bluff. You must corner the inner facts...
David Seabury (American Doctor, Author)

31 It is said that desire is a product of the will, but the converse is in fact true: will is a product of desire.
Denis Diderot (1713-1784, French Philosopher)

32 Out of need springs desire, and out of desire springs the energy and the will to win.
Denis Waitley (1933-, American Author, Speaker, Trainer, Peak Performance Expert)

33 Understand clearly that when a great need appears a great use appears also; when there is small need there is small use; it is obvious, then, that full use is made of all things at all times according to the necessity thereof.
Dogen Zenji

34 I can do whatever I want -- I'm rich, I'm famous, and I'm bigger than you.
Don Johnson (1949-, American Actor, Director, Producer, Singer)

35 There are no better masters than poverty and wants.
Dutch Proverb

36 Some people wanted champagne and caviar when they should have had beer and hot dogs.
Dwight D. Eisenhower (1890-1969, Thirty-fourth President of the USA)

37 The key that unlocks energy is "Desire." It's also the key to a long and interesting life. If we expect to create any drive, any real force within ourselves, we have to get excited.
Earl Nightingale (1921-1989, American Radio Announcer, Author, Motivator, Speaker)

38 Every human mind is a great slumbering power until awakened by a keen desire and by definite resolution to do.
Edgar F. Roberts

39 Desire is the thing you want in incipiency.
Emilie Cady

40 I never desired to please the rabble. What pleased them, I did not learn; and what I knew was far removed from their understanding.
Epicurus (341-270 BC, Greek Philosopher)

41 Nothing stops the man who desires to achieve. Every obstacle is simply a course to develop his achievement muscle. It's a strengthening of his powers of accomplishment.
Eric Butterworth

42 There is a supply for every demand.
Florence Scovel Shinn (American Artist, Metaphysics Teacher, Author)

43 The desire of excessive power caused the angels to fall; the desire of knowledge caused men to fall.
Francis Bacon (1561-1626, British Philosopher, Essayist, Statesman)

44 There are ways which lead to everything, and if we have sufficient will we should always have sufficient means.
François de La Rochefoucauld (1613-1680, French classical writer)

45 We never desire strongly, what we desire rationally.
François de La Rochefoucauld (1613-1680, French classical writer)

46 More than we use is more than we want.
Gaelic Proverb

47 Man is a creation of desire, not a creation of need.
Gaston Bachelard (1884-1962, French Scientist, Philosopher, Literary Theorist)

48 I learned that if you want to make it bad enough, no matter how bad it is, you can make it.
Gayle Sayers (American Football Player)

49 Our necessities are few, but our wants are endless.
George Bernard Shaw (1856-1950, Irish-born British Dramatist)

50 The desire of the man is for the woman, but the desire of the woman is for the desire of the man.
Germaine De Stael (1766-1817, French-Swiss Novelist)

51 I do want to get rich but I never want to do what there is to do to get rich.
Gertrude Stein (1874-1946, American Author)

52 You will live your life secure in that you are no longer manipulated by what other people want you to do and be, but are directed by your own inner desires.
H. Stanley Judd (American Author)

53 In all ranks of life the human heart yearns for the beautiful; and the beautiful things that God makes are his gift to all alike.
Harriet Beecher Stowe (1811-1896, American Novelist, Antislavery Campaigner)

54 One can never consent to creep when one feels an impulse to soar.
Helen Keller (1880-1968, American Blind/Deaf Author, Lecturer, Amorist)

55 If a man constantly aspires is he not elevated?
Henry David Thoreau (1817-1862, American Essayist, Poet, Naturalist)

56 It is not from nature, but from education and habits, that our wants are chiefly derived.
Henry Fielding (1707-1754, British Novelist, Dramatist)

57 You learnt that, whatever you are doing in life, obstacles don't matter very much. Pain or other circumstances can be there, but if you want to do a job bad enough, you'll find a way to get it done.
Jack Youngblood

58 To desire is to obtain; to aspire is to achieve.
James Allen (1864-1912, British-born American Essayist, Author of "As a Man Thinketh")

59 Be careful what you set your heart upon -- for it will surely be yours.
James Baldwin (1924-1987, American Author)

60 To educate the intelligence is to expand the horizon of its wants and desires.
James Russell Lowell (1819-1891, American Poet, Critic, Editor)

61 It (racing) is a matter of spirit, not strength. It is a matter of doing your best each little moment. There's never a break. You must have desire, a very intense desire to keep going.
Janet Guthrie (American Race Car Driver)

62 When you know what you want, and want it bad enough, you will find a way to get it.
Jim Rohn (American Businessman, Author, Speaker, Philosopher)

63 Without a sense of urgency, desire loses its value.
Jim Rohn (American Businessman, Author, Speaker, Philosopher)

64 I honestly believed I would make it. I had the desire. A lot of people have the ability, but they don't put forth the effort.
Joe Carter (1960-, American Baseball Player)

65 While man's desires and aspirations stir he cannot choose but err.
Johann Wolfgang Von Goethe (1749-1832, German Poet, Dramatist, Novelist)

66 A desire to be observed, considered, esteemed, praised, beloved, and admired by his fellows is one of the earliest as well as the keenest dispositions discovered in the heart of man.
John Adams (1735-1826, Second President of the USA)

67 No matter how old you get, if you can keep the desire to be creative, you're keeping the man- child alive.
John Cassavetes

68 The discipline of desire is the background of character.
John Locke (1632-1704, British Philosopher)

69 The intensity of your desire governs the power with which the force is directed.
John Mcdonald

70 Tell me what you like and I'll tell you what you are.
John Ruskin (1819-1900, British Critic, Social Theorist)

71 Just what you want to be, you will be in the end.
Justin Hayward (1946-, British songwriter, musician)

72 The significance of a man is not in what he attains, but rather what he longs to attain.
Kahlil Gibran (1883-1931, Lebanese Poet, Novelist)

73 Manifest plainness, embrace simplicity, reduce selfishness, have few desires.
Lao-Tzu (600 BC, Chinese Philosopher, Founder of Taoism, Author of the "Tao Te Ching")

74 You gotta be hungry!
Les Brown (1945-, American Speaker, Author, Trainer, Motivator Lecturer)

75 If you do not develop the hunger and courage to pursue your goal, you will lose your nerve and you will give up on your dream.
Les Brown (1945-, American Speaker, Author, Trainer, Motivator Lecturer)

76 Almost every desire a poor man has is a punishable offence.
Louis-Ferdinand Celine (1894-1961, French Author)

77 Desires are the pulses of the soul; as physicians judge by the appetite, so may you by desires.
Manton

78 We do not succeed in changing things according to our desire, but gradually our desire changes.
Marcel Proust (1871-1922, French Novelist)

79 There's nothing like desire to prevent the things one says from having any resemblance to the things in one's mind.
Marcel Proust (1871-1922, French Novelist)

80 Desire is a powerful force that can be used to make things happen.
Marcia Wieder (American Speaker, Trainer, Author)

81 Desire is the key to motivation, but it's the determination and commitment to an unrelenting pursuit of your goal -- a commitment to excellence -- that will enable you to attain the success you seek.
Mario Andretti (1940-, Italian-born American Auto Racer)

82 I can teach anybody how to get what they want out of life. The problem is that I can't find anybody who can tell me what they want.
Mark Twain (1835-1910, American Humorist, Writer)

83 Lord, grant that I may always desire more than I can accomplish.
Michelangelo (1474-1564, Italian Renaissance Painter, Sculptor)

84 Through some strange and powerful principle of "mental chemistry" which she has never divulged, nature wraps up in the impulse of strong desire, "that something" which recognizes no such word as "impossible," and accepts no such reality as failure.
Napoleon Hill (1883-1970, American Speaker, Motivational Writer, "Think and Grow Rich")

85 When your desires are strong enough you will appear to possess superhuman powers to achieve.
Napoleon Hill (1883-1970, American Speaker, Motivational Writer, "Think and Grow Rich")

86 The starting point of all achievement is desire. Keep this constantly in mind. Weak desires bring weak results, just as a small amount of fire makes a small amount of heat.
Napoleon Hill (1883-1970, American Speaker, Motivational Writer, "Think and Grow Rich")

87 Desire is the starting point of all achievement, not a hope, not a wish, but a keen pulsating desire which transcends everything.
Napoleon Hill (1883-1970, American Speaker, Motivational Writer, "Think and Grow Rich")

88 The battle is all over except the "shouting" when one knows what is wanted and has made up his mind to get it, whatever the price may be.
Napoleon Hill (1883-1970, American Speaker, Motivational Writer, "Think and Grow Rich")

89 The desire for success lubricates secret prostitution's in the soul.
Norman Mailer (1923-, American Author)

90 People seek within a short span of life to satisfy a thousand desires, each of which is insatiable.
Oliver Goldsmith (1728-1774, Anglo-Irish Author, Poet, Playwright)

91 We are ever striving after what is forbidden, and coveting what is denied us.
Ovid (43 BC-18 AD, Roman Poet)

92 Those who really desire to attain an independence, have only set their minds upon it, and adopt the proper means, as they do in regard to any other object which they wish to accomplish, and the thing is easily done.
P.T. Barnum (1810-1891, American Showman, Entertainer, Circus Builder)

93 A burning desire is the greatest motivator of every human action. The desire for success implants "success consciousness" which, in turn, creates a vigorous and ever-increasing "habit of success."
Paul J. Meyer (American Businessman, Author, Motivator)

94 Desire, like the atom, is explosive with creative force.
Paul Vernon Buser

95 Unbridled gratification produces unbridled desire.
Proverb

96 First deserve then desire.
Proverb

97 Whenever we confront an unbridled desire we are surely in the presence of a tragedy-in-the- making.
Quentin Crisp (1908-, British Author)

98 Can anything be so elegant as to have few wants, and to serve them one's self?
Ralph Waldo Emerson (1803-1882, American Poet, Essayist)

99 There is nothing capricious in nature and the implanting of a desire indicates that its gratification is in the constitution of the creature that feel it.
Ralph Waldo Emerson (1803-1882, American Poet, Essayist)

100 Desire creates the power.
Raymond Holliwell

101 Listen to what you know instead of what you fear.
Richard Bach (1936-, American Author)

102 This gift is from God and not of man's deserving. But certainly no one ever receives such a great grace without tremendous labor and burning desire.
Richard of Saint Victor

103 O lyric Love, half angel and half bird. And all a wonder and a wild desire.
Robert Browning (1812-1889, British Poet)

104 It sometimes seems that we have only to love a thing greatly to get it.
Robert Collier (American Writer, Publisher)

105 The first principle of success is desire -- knowing what you want. Desire is the planting of your seed.
Robert Collier (American Writer, Publisher)

106 First the stalk -- then the roots. First the need -- then the means to satisfy that need. First the nucleus -- then the elements needed for its growth.
Robert Collier (American Writer, Publisher)

107 Very few persons, comparatively, know how to Desire with sufficient intensity. They do not know what it is to feel and manifest that intense, eager, longing, craving, insistent, demanding, ravenous Desire which is akin to the persistent, insistent, ardent, overwhelming desire of the drowning man for a breath of air; of the shipwrecked or desert-lost man for a drink of water; of the famished man for bread and meat...
Robert Collier (American Writer, Publisher)

108 Supply always comes on the heels of demand.
Robert Collier (American Writer, Publisher)

109 Something must be done when you find an opposing set of desires of this kind well to the fore in your category of strong desires. You must set in operation a process of competition, from which one must emerge a victor and the other set be defeated.
Robert Collier (American Writer, Publisher)

110 Plant the seed of desire in your mind and it forms a nucleus with power to attract to itself everything needed for its fulfillment.
Robert Collier (American Writer, Publisher)

111 Desire is proof of the availability...
Robert Collier (American Writer, Publisher)

112 You can have anything you want -- if you want it badly enough. You can be anything you want to be, have anything you desire, accomplish anything you set out to accomplish -- if you will hold to that desire with singleness of purpose.
Robert Collier (American Writer, Publisher)

113 All through nature, you will find the same law. First the need, then the means.
Robert Collier (American Writer, Publisher)

114 To know what you prefer instead of humbly saying Amen to what the world tells you ought to prefer is to have kept your soul alive.
Robert Louis Stevenson (1850-1895, Scottish Essayist, Poet, Novelist)

115 Some desire is necessary to keep life in motion, and he whose real wants are supplied must admit those of fancy.
Samuel Johnson (1709-1784, British Author)

116 Life is a progress from want to want, not from enjoyment to enjoyment.
Samuel Johnson (1709-1784, British Author)

117 An intense anticipation itself transforms possibility into reality; our desires being often but precursors of the things which we are capable of performing.
Samuel Smiles (1812-1904, Scottish Author)

118 You can have anything you want if you want it desperately enough. You must want it with an inner exuberance that erupts through the skin and joins the energy that created the world.
Sheila Graham

119 Dreams do come true, if we only wish hard enough, You can have anything in life if you will sacrifice everything else for it.
Sir James M. Barrie (1860-1937, British Playwright)

120 The want of a thing is perplexing enough, but the possession of it, is intolerable.
Sir John Vanbrugh (1664-1726, British Playwright and Baroque architect)

121 The fewer our wants the more we resemble the Gods.
Socrates (469-399 BC, Greek Philosopher of Athens)

122 Life contains but two tragedies. One is not to get your heart's desire; the other is to get it.
Socrates (469-399 BC, Greek Philosopher of Athens)

123 It belongs to the imperfection of everything human that man can only attain his desire by passing through its opposite.
Soren Kierkegaard (1813-1855, Danish Philosopher, Writer)

124 A desire arises in the mind. It is satisfied immediately another comes. In the interval which separates two desires a perfect calm reigns in the mind. It is at this moment freed from all thought, love or hate. Complete peace equally reigns between two mental waves.
Sri Swami Sivananda (1887-, Indian Physician, Sage)

125 The desire is thy prayers; and if thy desire is without ceasing, thy prayer will also be without ceasing. The continuance of your longing is the continuance of your prayer.
St. Augustine (354-430, Numidian-born Bishop of Hippo, Theologian)

126 I was taught that everything is attainable if you are prepared to give up, to sacrifice, to get it. Whatever you want to do, you can do it, if you want it badly enough, and I do believe that. I believe that if I wanted to run a mile is four minutes I could do it. I would have to give up everything else in my life, but I could run a mile in four minutes. I believe that if a man wanted to walk on water and was prepared to give up everything else in life, he could do that.
Stirling Moss (1929-, British Motor Racing Driver)

127 Desire will in due time externalize itself as concrete fact.
Thomas Troward

128 Winning isn't everything, but wanting to win is.
Vince Lombardi (1913-1970, American Football Coach)

129 Where there is no power... there is never any desire to do a thing; and where there is strong desire to do a thing... the power to do it is strong.
Wallace D. Wattles

130 Ignore what a man desires and you ignore the very source of his power
Walter Lippmann (1889-1974, American Journalist)

131 Anything you really want, you can attain, if you really go after it.
Wayne Dyer (1940-, American Psychotherapist, Author, Lecturer)

132 He who desires but does not act, breeds pestilence.
William Blake (1757-1827, British Poet, Painter)

133 It is not the greatness of a man's means that makes him independent, so much as the smallness of his wants.
William Cobbett (1762-1835, British Journalist, Reformer)

134 A man must earnestly want.
William Frederick Book

135 A strong passion for any object will ensure success, for the desire of the end will point out the means.
William Hazlitt (1778-1830, British Essayist)

136 If you care enough for a result, you will most certainly attain it.
William James (1842-1910, American Psychologist, Professor, Author)

137 Events are influenced by our very great desires.
William James (1842-1910, American Psychologist, Professor, Author)

138 There is a vast difference in some instances between what we really need and that which we think we must have, and the realization of this truth will greatly lessen the seeming discomfort in doing without.
William M. Peck

139 Why not spend some time determining what is worthwhile for us, and then go after that?
William Ross

140 I have always believed that anybody with a little guts and the desire to apply himself can make it, can make anything he wants to make of himself.
Willie Shoemaker (1931-, American Racing Jockey and Trainer)

141 Desire is the most important factor in the success of any athlete.
Willie Shoemaker (1931-, American Racing Jockey and Trainer)

142 I know that if I ever go looking for my heart's desire, I'll never go any further than my own back yard. For if it isn't there, I never really lost it.
Wizard of Oz - Dorothy Movie

DESPAIR

1 Despair, in short, seeks its own environment as surely as water finds its own level.
A. Alvarez (Born 1929, British Critic, Poet, Novelist)

2 To those who despair of everything reason cannot provide a faith, but only passion, and in this case it must be the same passion that lay at the root of the despair, namely humiliation and hatred.
Albert Camus (1913-1960, French Existential Writer)

3 So long as we have failed to eliminate any of the causes of human despair, we do not have the right to try to eliminate those means by which man tries to cleanse himself of despair.
Antonin Artaud (1896-1948, French Theater Producer, Actor, Theorist)

4 To be thoroughly conversant with a man's heart, is to take our final lesson in the iron-clasped volume of despair.
Edgar Allan Poe (1809-1845, American Poet, Critic, short-story Writer)

5 Because I remember, I despair. Because I remember, I have the duty to reject despair.
Elie Wiesel (1928-, Rumanian-born American Writer)

6 All my life I believed I knew something. But then one strange day came when I realized that I knew nothing, yes, I knew nothing. And so words became void of meaning. I have arrived too late at ultimate uncertainty.
Ezra Pound (1885-1972, American Poet, Critic)

7 But what we call our despair is often only the painful eagerness of unfed hope.
George Eliot (1819-1880, British Novelist)

8 Intellectual despair results in neither weakness nor dreams, but in violence. It is only a matter of knowing how to give vent to one's rage; whether one only wants to wander like madmen around prisons, or whether one wants to overturn them.
Georges Bataille (1897-1962, French Novelist, Critic)

9 Despair is the price one pays for setting oneself an impossible aim. It is, one is told, the unforgivable sin, but it is a sin the corrupt or evil man never practices. He always has hope. He never reaches the freezing-point of knowing absolute failure. Only the man of goodwill carries always in his heart this capacity for damnation.
Graham Greene (1904-1991, British Novelist)

10 Melancholy has ceased to be an individual phenomenon, an exception. It has become the class privilege of the wage earner, a mass state of mind that finds its cause wherever life is governed by production quotas.
Gunther Grass (1927-, German Author)

11 The person who lives by hope will die by despair.
Italian Proverb

12 Despair is the only genuine atheism.
Jean Paul

13 Life begins on the other side of despair.
Jean-Paul Sartre (1905-1980, French Writer, Philosopher)

14 Action is the antidote to despair.
Joan Baez (1941-, American Singer, Songwriter)

15 The Christian's chief occupational hazards are depression and discouragement.
John R. Stott (1921-, British Anglican clergyman and writer)

16 I will indulge my sorrows, and give way to all the pangs and fury of despair.
Joseph Addison (1672-1719, British Essayist, Poet, Statesman)

17 Let judges secretly despair of justice: their verdicts will be more acute. Let generals secretly despair of triumph; killing will be defamed. Let priests secretly despair of faith: their compassion will be true.
Leonard Cohen (1934-, Canadian-born American Musician, Songwriter, Singer)

18 When I despair, I remember that all through history the way of truth and love has always won. There have been tyrants and murderers and for a time they seem invincible but in the end, they always fall -- think of it, ALWAYS.
Mahatma Gandhi (1869-1948, Indian Political, Spiritual Leader)

19 It is a time when one's spirit is subdued and sad, one knows not why; when the past seems a storm-swept desolation, life a vanity and a burden, and the future but a way to death.
Mark Twain (1835-1910, American Humorist, Writer)

20 Man dies of cold, not of darkness.
Miguel De Unamuno (1864-1936, Spanish Philosophical Writer)

21 Through our sunless lanes creeps Poverty with her hungry eyes, and Sin with his sodden face follows close behind her. Misery wakes us in the morning and Shame sits with us at night.
Oscar Wilde (1856-1900, British Author, Wit)

22 Depression is the inability to construct a future.
Rollo May (American Psychologist)

23 The depth of our despair measures what capability and height of claim we have to hope.
Thomas Carlyle (1795-1881, Scottish Philosopher, Author)

24 Despair gives courage to a coward.
Thomas Fuller (1608-1661, British Clergyman, Author)

25 Despair is typical of those who do not understand the causes of evil, see no way out, and are incapable of struggle. The modern industrial proletariat does not belong to the category of such classes.
Vladimir Ilyich Lenin (1870-1924, Russian Revolutionary Leader)

26 Then my verse I dishonor, my pictures despise, my person degrade and my temper chastise; and the pen is my terror, the pencil my shame; and my talents I bury, and dead is my fame.
William Blake (1757-1827, British Poet, Painter)

27 Despair is perfectly compatible with a good dinner, I promise you.
William M. Thackeray (1811-1863, Indian-born British Novelist)

28 O God, O God, how weary, stale, flat, and unprofitable seem to me all the uses of this world!
William Shakespeare (1564-1616, British Poet, Playwright, Actor)

29 Now, God be praised, that to believing souls gives light in darkness, comfort in despair.
William Shakespeare (1564-1616, British Poet, Playwright, Actor)

DESPERATION

1 Desperation is sometimes as powerful an inspirer as genius.
Benjamin Disraeli (1804-1881, British Statesman, Prime Minister)

2 Desperation is like stealing from the Mafia: you stand a good chance of attracting the wrong attention.
Doug Horton

3 The mass of men lead lives of quiet desperation.
Henry David Thoreau (1817-1862, American Essayist, Poet, Naturalist)

4 What is most original in a man's nature is often that which is most desperate. Thus new systems are forced on the world by men who simply cannot bear the pain of living with what is. Creators care nothing for their systems except that they be unique. If Hitler had been born in Nazi Germany he wouldn't have been content to enjoy the atmosphere.
Leonard Cohen (1934-, Canadian-born American Musician, Songwriter, Singer)

5 She wore far too much rouge last night and not quite enough clothes. That is always a sign of despair in a woman.
Oscar Wilde (1856-1900, British Author, Wit)

6 There exists, at the bottom of all abasement and misfortune, a last extreme which rebels and joins battle with the forces of law and respectability in a desperate struggle, waged partly by cunning and partly by violence, at once sick and ferocious, in which it attacks the prevailing social order with the pin-pricks of vice and the hammer-blows of crime.
Victor Hugo (1802-1885, French Poet, Dramatist, Novelist)

7 My interest in desperation lies only in that sometimes I find myself having become desperate. Very seldom do I start out that way. I can see of course that, in the abstract, thinking and all activity is rather desperate.
Willem De Kooning (1904-, Dutch-born American Artist)

8 Desperation is the raw material of drastic change. Only those who can leave behind everything they have ever believed in can hope to escape.
William S. Burroughs (1914-1997, American Writer)

DESPOTISM

1. The arbitrary rule of a just and enlightened prince is always bad. His virtues are the most dangerous and the surest form of seduction: they lull a people imperceptibly into the habit of loving, respecting, and serving his successor, whoever that successor may be, no matter how wicked or stupid.
Denis Diderot (1713-1784, French Philosopher)

2. Man is insatiable for power; he is infantile in his desires and, always discontented with what he has, loves only what he has not. People complain of the despotism of princes; they ought to complain of the despotism of man.
Joseph De Maistre (1753-1821, French Diplomat, Philosopher)

3. There are three kinds of despots. There is the despot who tyrannizes over the body. There is the despot who tyrannizes over the soul. There is the despot who tyrannizes over the soul and body alike. The first is called the Prince. The second is called the Pope. The third is called the People.
Oscar Wilde (1856-1900, British Author, Wit)

4. Despotism is unjust to everybody, including the despot, who was probably made for better things.
Oscar Wilde (1856-1900, British Author, Wit)

5. The real stumbling-block of totalitarian regimes is not the spiritual need of men for freedom of thought; it is men's inability to stand the physical and nervous strain of a permanent state of excitement, except during a few years of their youth.
Simone Weil (1910-1943, French Philosopher, Mystic)

6. Despots play their part in the works of thinkers. Fettered words are terrible words. The writer doubles and trebles the power of his writing when a ruler imposes silence on the people. Something emerges from that enforced silence, a mysterious fullness which filters through and becomes steely in the thought. Repression in history leads to conciseness in the historian, and the rocklike hardness of much celebrated prose is due to the tempering of the tyrant.
Victor Hugo (1802-1885, French Poet, Dramatist, Novelist)

7. So long as war is the main business of nations, temporary despotism -- despotism during the campaign -- is indispensable.
Walter Bagehot (1826-1877, British Economist, Critic)

DESTINY

1. And the high destiny of the individual is to serve rather than to rule, or to impose himself in any other way.
Albert Einstein (1879-1955, German-born American Physicist)

2. Destiny is an absolutely definite and inexorable ruler. Physical ability and moral determination count for nothing. It is impossible to perform the simplest act when the gods say "no." I have no idea how they bring pressure to bear on such occasions; I only know that it is irresistible.
Aleister Crowley (1875-1947, British Occultist)

3. Man's ultimate destiny is to become one with the Divine Power which governs and sustains the creation and its creatures.
Alfred A. Montapert (American Author)

4. But you can catch yourself entertaining habitually certain ideas and setting others aside; and that, I think, is where our personal destinies are largely decided.
Alfred North Whitehead (1861-1947, British Mathematician, Philosopher)

5. Destiny. A tyrant's authority for crime and a fool's excuse for failure.
Ambrose Bierce (1842-1914, American Author, Editor, Journalist, "The Devil's Dictionary")

6. More than anything else, I believe it's our decisions, not the conditions of our lives, that determine our destiny.
Anthony Robbins (1960-, American Author, Speaker, Peak Performance Expert / Consultant)

7. It's not what's happening to you now or what has happened in your past that determines who you become. Rather, it's your decisions about what to focus on, what things mean to you, and what you're going to do about them that will determine your ultimate destiny.
Anthony Robbins (1960-, American Author, Speaker, Peak Performance Expert / Consultant)

8. A consistent soul believes in destiny, a capricious one in chance.
Benjamin Disraeli (1804-1881, British Statesman, Prime Minister)

9. We are made for larger ends than Earth can encompass. Oh, let us be true to our exalted destiny.
Catherine Booth

10. I have a feeling this is destiny. [On the eve of her third marriage]
Christie Brinkley (1954-, American Model, Actress)

11. We are not permitted to choose the frame of our destiny. But what we put into it is ours.
Dag Hammarskjold (1905-1961, Swedish Statesman, Secretary-general of U.N.)

12. Nature is at work.. Character and destiny are her handiwork. She gives us love and hate, jealousy and reverence. All that is ours is the power to choose which impulse we shall follow.
David Seabury (American Doctor, Author)

13. Failure or success seem to have been allotted to men by their stars. But they retain the power of wriggling, of fighting with their star or against it, and in the whole universe the only really interesting movement is this wriggle.
Edward M. Forster (1879-1970, British Novelist, Essayist)

14 A strict belief, fate is the worst kind of slavery; on the other hand there is comfort in the thought that God will be moved by our prayers.
Epictetus (50-120, Stoic Philosopher)

15 Remember that you are an actor in a drama, of such a part as it may please the master to assign you, for a long time or for a little as he may choose. And if he will you to take the part of a poor man, or a cripple, or a ruler, or a private citizen, then may you act that part with grace! For to act well the part that is allotted to us, that indeed is ours to do, but to choose it is another s.
Epictetus (50-120, Stoic Philosopher)

16 No love, no friendship can cross the path of our destiny without leaving some mark on it forever.
François Mauriac (1885-1970, French novelist, dramatist, critic, poet, and journalist)

17 I must in the face of a storm, think, live and die as a king.
Frederick The Great (Frederick II) (1712-1786, Born in Berlin, King of Prussia (1740-1786))

18 He that is born to be hanged shall never be drowned.
French Proverb

19 One meets his destiny often in the road he takes to avoid it.
French Proverb

20 Destiny is something men select; women achieve it only by default or stupendous suffering.
Harriet Rosenstein (1932-, American Author)

21 No man is great enough or wise enough for any of us to surrender our destiny to. The only way in which anyone can lead us is to restore to us the belief in our own guidance.
Henry Miller (1891-1980, American Author)

22 The destiny of man is in his own soul
Herodotus (484-425 BC, Greek Historian)

23 The law of harvest is to reap more than you sow. Sow an act, and you reap a habit. Sow a habit and you reap a character. Sow a character and you reap a destiny.
James Allen (1864-1912, British-born American Essayist, Author of "As a Man Thinketh")

24 The real test of a man is not how well he plays the role he has invented for himself, but how well he plays the role that destiny assigned to him.
Jan Patocka (1907-1977, Czech Philosopher, Activist)

25 Not without a shudder may the human hand reach into the mysterious urn of destiny.
Johann Friedrich Von Schiller (1759-1805, German Dramatist, Poet, Historian)

26 There is no such thing as chance; and what seem to us merest accident springs from the deepest source of destiny.
Johann Friedrich Von Schiller (1759-1805, German Dramatist, Poet, Historian)

27 No cause has he to say his doom is harsh, who's made the master of his destiny.
Johann Friedrich Von Schiller (1759-1805, German Dramatist, Poet, Historian)

28 The destiny of any nation at any given time depends on the opinion of its young people, those under twenty-five.
Johann Wolfgang Von Goethe (1749-1832, German Poet, Dramatist, Novelist)

29 Only by joy and sorrow does a person know anything about themselves and their destiny. They learn what to do and what to avoid.
Johann Wolfgang Von Goethe (1749-1832, German Poet, Dramatist, Novelist)

30 Our problems are man-made, therefore they may be solved by man. No problem of human destiny is beyond human beings.
John F. Kennedy (1917-1963, Thirty-fifth President of the USA)

31 Men heap together the mistakes of their lives, and create a monster they call Destiny.
John Oliver Hobbes

32 Lots of folks confuse bad management with destiny.
Kin Hubbard (1868-1930, American Humorist, Journalist)

33 We are no more free agents than the queen of clubs when she victoriously takes prisoner the knave of hearts.
Lady Mary Wortley Montagu (1689-1762, British Society Figure, Letter Writer)

34 I believe that you control your destiny, that you can be what you want to be. You can also stop and say, No, I won't do it, I won't behave his way anymore. I'm lonely and I need people around me, maybe I have to change my methods of behaving and then you do it
Leo Buscaglia (American Expert on Love, Lecturer, Author)

35 We write our own destiny; we become what we do.
Madame Chiang Kai-Shek (Chinese Revolutionary Leader)

36 Our destiny changes with our thought; we shall become what we wish to become, do what we wish to do, when our habitual thought corresponds with our desire.
Orison Swett Marden (1850-1924, American Author, Founder of Success Magazine)

37 I knew what my job was; it was to go out and meet the people and love them.
Princess of Wales Diana (1961-1997, Wife of Charles, Prince of Wales)

38 Sow a thought and you reap an action; sow an act and you reap a habit; sow a habit and you reap a character; sow a character and you reap a destiny.
Ralph Waldo Emerson (1803-1882, American Poet, Essayist)

39 Fate, then, is a name for facts not yet passed under the fire of thought; for causes which are unpenetrated.
Ralph Waldo Emerson (1803-1882, American Poet, Essayist)

40 It appears I am destined for something; I will live.
Robert Clive

41 What do I know of man's destiny? I could tell you more about radishes.
Samuel Beckett (1906-1989, Irish Dramatist, Novelist)

42 Anatomy is destiny.
Sigmund Freud (1856-1939, Austrian Physician - Founder of Psychoanalysis)

43 Nothing can have as its destination anything other than its origin. The contrary idea, the idea of progress, is poison.
Simone Weil (1910-1943, French Philosopher, Mystic)

44 What God writes on your forehead you will become.
The Koran (500 AD, Islamic Religious Bible)

45 Thoughts lead on to purposes; purposes go forth in action; actions form habits; habits decide character; and character fixes our destiny.
Tryon Edwards (1809-1894, American Theologian)

46 Destiny is not a matter of chance, it is a matter of choice; it is not a thing to be waited for, it is a thing to be achieved.
William Jennings Bryan (1860-1925, American Lawyer, Politician)

47 Such as we are made of, such we be.
William Shakespeare (1564-1616, British Poet, Playwright, Actor)

48 If a man is destined to drown, he will drown even in a spoonful of water.
Yiddish Proverb

DESTRUCTIVENESS

1 We shall not have succeeded in demolishing everything unless we demolish the ruins as well. But the only way I can see of doing that is to use them to put up a lot of fine, well-designed buildings.
Alfred Jarry (1873-1907, French Playwright, Author)

2 Destruction, hence, like creation, is one of Nature's mandates.
Marquis De Sade (1740-1814, French Author)

3 The passion for destruction is also a creative passion.
Mikhail Bakunin (1814-1876, Russian Political Theorist)

4 The destructive character lives from the feeling, not that life is worth living, but that suicide is not worth the trouble.
Walter Benjamin (1982-1940, German Critic, Philosopher)

DETACHMENT

1 When you learn not to want things so badly, life comes to you.
Jessica Lange (1949-, American Actress)

2 He who would be serene and pure needs but one thing, detachment.
Meister Eckhart (1260-1326 AD, German Mystic)

3 The more you lose yourself in something bigger than yourself, the more energy you will have.
Norman Vincent Peale (1898-1993, American Christian Reformed Pastor, Speaker, Author)

4 When you become detached mentally from yourself and concentrate on helping other people with their difficulties, you will be able to cope with your own more effectively. Somehow, the act of self-giving is a personal power-releasing factor.
Norman Vincent Peale (1898-1993, American Christian Reformed Pastor, Speaker, Author)

DETAIL

1 It is in the treatment of trifles that a person shows what they are.
Arthur Schopenhauer (1788-1860, German Philosopher)

2 Although this may seem a paradox, all exact science is dominated by the idea of approximation. When a man tells you that he knows the exact truth about anything, you are safe in inferring that he is an inexact man.
Bertrand Russell (1872-1970, British Philosopher, Mathematician, Essayist)

3 Pedantry is the showy display of knowledge which crams our heads with learned lumber and then takes out our brains to make room for it.
Charles Caleb Colton (1780-1832, British Sportsman Writer)

4 The pathetic almost always consists in the detail of little events.
Edward Gibbon (1737-1794, British Historian)

5 The difference between failure and success is doing a thing nearly right and doing it exactly right.
Edward Simmons

6 Exactness and neatness in moderation is a virtue, but carried to extremes narrows the mind.
François Fénelon (1651-1715, French Roman Catholic archbishop, theologian, poet and writer)

7 Carelessness is worse than a thieve.
Gaelic Proverb

8 Men who wish to know about the world must learn about it in its particular details.
Heraclitus (535-475 BC, Greek Philosopher)

9 The fastidious are unfortunate; nothing satisfies them.
Jean De La Fontaine (1621-1695, French Poet)

10 I have always wanted to be somebody, but I see now I should have been more specific.
Lily Tomlin (1939-, American Comedienne)

11 Trifles make perfection, but perfection is no trifle.
Michelangelo (1474-1564, Italian Renaissance Painter, Sculptor)

12 One does a whole painting for one peach and people think just the opposite -- that particular peach is but a detail.
Pablo Picasso (1881-1973, Spanish Artist)

13 In a major matter no details are small.
Paul De Gondi

14 Many blunder in business through inability or an unwillingness to adopt new ideas. I have seen many a success turn to failure also, because the thought which should be trained on big things is cluttered up with the burdensome detail of little things.
Philip Delaney

15 Measure three times before you cut once.
Proverb

16 While I am busy with little things, I am not required to do greater things.
St. Francis De Sales (1567-1622, Roman Catholic Bishop, Writer)

17 Details often kill initiative, but there have been few successful men who weren't good at details. Don't ignore details. Lick them.
William B. Given

DETERMINATION

1 Determination that just won't quit -- that's what it takes.
A. J. Foyt (Born 1935, American retired auto racing driver)

2 Determine that the thing can and shall be done, and then we shall find the way.
Abraham Lincoln (1809-1865, Sixteenth President of the USA)

3 What this power is I cannot say; all I know is that it exists and it becomes available only when a man is in that state of mind in which he knows exactly what he wants and is fully determined not to quit until he finds it.
Alexander Graham Bell (1847-1922, British-born American Inventor of Telephone)

4 Determination is the wake-up call to the human will.
Anthony Robbins (1960-, American Author, Speaker, Peak Performance Expert / Consultant)

5 No man can fight his way to the top and stay at the top without exercising the fullest measure of grit, courage, determination, resolution. Every man who gets anywhere does so because he has first firmly resolved to progress in the world and then has enough stick-to-it-tiveness to transform his resolution into reality. Without resolution, no man can win any worthwhile place among his fellow men.
B. C. Forbes (1880-1954, American Publisher)

6 I have brought myself, by long meditation, to the conviction that a human being with a settled purpose must accomplish it, and that nothing can resist a will which will stake even existence upon its fulfillment.
Benjamin Disraeli (1804-1881, British Statesman, Prime Minister)

7 So we built the wall and the whole wall was joined together to half its height; for the people had a mind to work. [Nehemiah 4:6]
Bible (Sacred Scriptures of Christians and Judaism)

8 I am doing a great work and I cannot come down. Why should the work stop while I leave it and come down to you?
Bible (Sacred Scriptures of Christians and Judaism)

9 Your decision to be, have and do something out of ordinary entails facing difficulties that are out of the ordinary as well. Sometimes your greatest asset is simply your ability to stay with it longer than anyone else.
Brian Tracy (American Trainer, Speaker, Author, Businessman)

10 Nothing great will ever be achieved without great men, and men are great only if they are determined to be so.
Charles De Gaulle (1890-1970, French President during World War II)

11 The thing that contributes to anyone's reaching the goal he wants is simple wanting that goal badly enough.
Charles E. Wilson (1886-1972, American Corporate Executive)

12 I will go anywhere, provided it be forward.
David Livingstone (1813-1873, British Missionary, Explorer)

13 Determination gives you the resolve to keep going in spite of the roadblocks that lay before you.
Denis Waitley (1933-, American Author, Speaker, Trainer, Peak Performance Expert)

14 A man can do anything he wants to do in this world, at least if he wants to do it badly enough.
E(dward) W(yllis) Scripps (1854-1926, American Press Lord)

15 There is no chance, no destiny, no fate, that can hinder or control the firm resolve of a determined soul.
Ella Wheeler Wilcox (1855-1919, American Poet, Journalist)

16 There's no ceiling on effort!
Harvey C. Fruehauf

17 I put a piece of paper under my pillow, and when I could not sleep I wrote in the dark.
Henry David Thoreau (1817-1862, American Essayist, Poet, Naturalist)

18 To him who is determined it remains only to act.
Italian Proverb

19 The wayside of business is full of brilliant men who started out with a spurt, and lacked the stamina to finish. Their places were taken by patient and unshowy plodders who never knew when to quit.
J. R. Todd

20 In all human affairs there are efforts, and there are results, and the strength of effort is the measure of the results.
James Allen (1864-1912, British-born American Essayist, Author of "As a Man Thinketh")

21 We all have dreams. But in order to make dreams come into reality, it takes an awful lot of determination, dedication, self-discipline, and effort.
Jesse Owens (1913-1980, American Olympic Track Athlete)

22 You can do what you have to do, and sometimes you can do it even better than you think you can.
Jimmy Carter (1924-, American Statesman, 39th President)

23 Not an inch of our territory not a stone of our fortress.
Jules Favre

24 A thick skin is a gift from God.
Konrad Adenauer (1876-1967, German Statesman)

25 Be determined to handle any challenge in a way that will make you grow.
Les Brown (1945-, American Speaker, Author, Trainer, Motivator Lecturer)

26 Only a man who knows what it is like to be defeated can reach down to the bottom of his soul and come up with the extra ounce of power it takes to win when the match is even.
Muhammad Ali (1942-, American Boxer)

27 Earnestness is not by any means everything; it is very often a subtle form of pious pride because it is obsessed with the method and not with the Master.
Oswald Chambers (1874-1917 Scottish Preacher, Author)

28 Construct your Determination with Sustained Effort, Controlled Attention, and Concentrated Energy. opportunities never come to those who wait... they are captured by those who dare to attack.
Paul J. Meyer (American Businessman, Author, Motivator)

29 Firmness in enduring and exertion is a character I always wish to possess. I have always despised the whining yelp of complaint and cowardly resolve.
Robert Burns (1759-1796, Scottish Poet)

30 A determined soul will do more with a rusty monkey wrench than a loafer will accomplish with all the tools in a machine shop.
Robert Hughes (1938-, Australian Art Critic, Writer)

31 The man who can drive himself further once the effort gets painful is the man who will win.
Roger Bannister (1929-, British Athlete, First Sub 4 Minute Miler)

32 If your determination is fixed, I do not counsel you to despair. Few things are impossible to diligence and skill. Great works are performed not by strength, but perseverance.
Samuel Johnson (1709-1784, British Author)

33 The longer I live, the more I am certain that the great difference between the great and the insignificant, is energy -- invincible determination -- a purpose once fixed, and then death or victory.
Sir Thomas Fowell Buxton

34 An invincible determination can accomplish almost anything and in this lies the great distinction between great men and little men.
Thomas Fuller (1608-1661, British Clergyman, Author)

35 The difference between the impossible and the possible lies in a person's determination.
Tommy Lasorda (1927-, American Baseball Manager)

36 The price of success is hard work, dedication to the job at hand, and the determination that whether we win or lose, we have applied the best of ourselves to the task at hand.
Vince Lombardi (1913-1970, American Football Coach)

DEVIL

1 The devil is a better theologian than any of us and is a devil still.
A. W. Tozer (Deceased 1963, American Preacher)

2 Whenever science makes a discovery, the devil grabs it while the angels are debating the best way to use it.
Alan Valentine

3 Man can hardly even recognize the devils of his own creation.
Albert Schweitzer (1875-1965, German Born Medical Missionary, Theologian, Musician, and Philosopher)

4 Satan is wiser now than before, and tempts by making rich instead of poor.
Alexander Pope (1688-1744, British Poet, Critic, Translator)

5 The devil tempts all men, but idle men tempt the devil.
Arabian Proverb

6 The devil's most devilish when respectable.
Elizabeth Barrett Browning (1806-1861, British Poet)

7 The devil doesn't know how to sing, only how to howl.
Francis Thompson (1859-1907, British Poet)

8 Satan is neither omnipotent nor free to do everything he pleases. Prince of the world he may be, but the Prince of Peace has come and dealt him a death blow.
Harold Lindsell

9 Satan always finds some mischief for idle hands to do.
Isaac Watts (1674-1748, British hymn-writer)

10 Speak of the Devil and he appears.
Italian Proverb

11 I know nothing more mocking than a devil that despairs.
Johann Wolfgang Von Goethe (1749-1832, German Poet, Dramatist, Novelist)

12 The devil is God's ape!
Martin Luther (1483-1546, German Leader of the Protestant Reformation)

13 Speak the truth and shame the devil.
Proverb

14 Those who play with the devil's toys will be brought by degrees to wield his sword.
R. Buckminster Fuller (1895-1983, American Inventor, Designer, Poet, Philosopher)

15 The devil is the author of confusion.
Robert Burton (1576-1640, British Clergyman, Scholar)

16 Why should the devil have all the good tunes?
Rowland Hill

17 If the devil could be persuaded to write a bible, he would title it, "You Only Live Once."
Sidney J. Harris (1917-, American Journalist)

18 The devil helps his servants for a season; but when they get into a pinch; he leaves them in the lurch.
Sir Roger L'Estrange

19 At sometime in our lives a devil dwells within us, causes heartbreaks, confusion and troubles, then dies.
Theodore Roosevelt (1858-1919, Twenty-sixth President of the USA)

20 The devil has his elect.
Thomas Carlyle (1795-1881, Scottish Philosopher, Author)

21 The devil will let a preacher prepare a sermon if it will keep him from preparing himself.
Vance Havner

22 You must have the devil in you to succeed in the arts.
Voltaire (1694-1778, French Historian, Writer)

23 Satan trembles when he sees the weakest saint upon their knees.
William Cowper (1731-1800, British Poet)

24 The devil can site scripture for his own purpose! An evil soul producing holy witness is like a villain with a smiling cheek. [Merchant Of Venice]
William Shakespeare (1564-1616, British Poet, Playwright, Actor)

25 The devil has the power to assume a pleasing shape.
William Shakespeare (1564-1616, British Poet, Playwright, Actor)

DEVOTIONS

1 We are to be shut out from men, and shut in with God.
Andrew Murray

2 How rare it is to find a soul quiet enough to hear God speak.
François Fénelon (1651-1715, French Roman Catholic archbishop, theologian, poet and writer)

3 Whatever is your best time in the day, give that to communion with God.
Hudson Taylor

4 To be a Christian without prayer is no more possible than to be alive without breathing.
Martin Luther (1483-1546, German Leader of the Protestant Reformation)

5 An essential condition of listening to God is that the mind should not be distracted by thoughts of resentment, ill-temper, hatred or vengeance, all of which are comprised in the general term, the wrath of man.
R. V. G. Tasker

6 Cut your morning devotions into your personal grooming. You would not go out to work with a dirty face. Why start the day with the face of your soul unwashed?
Robert A. Cook

7 A devotee who can call on God while living a householder's life is a hero indeed. God thinks: 'He is blessed indeed who prays to me in the midst of his worldly duties. He is trying to find me, overcoming a great obstacle -- pushing away, as it were, a huge block of stone weighing a ton. Such a man is a real hero.'
Sri Ramakrishna (Indian Mystic)

DICTATORS AND DICTATORSHIP

1 Never permit a dichotomy to rule your life, a dichotomy in which you hate what you do so you can have pleasure in your spare time. Look for a situation in which your work will give you as much happiness as your spare time.
Edward L. Bernays (American Public Relations Expert)

2 One does not establish a dictatorship in order to safeguard a revolution; one makes a revolution in order to establish a dictatorship.
George Orwell (1903-1950, British Author, "Animal Farm")

3 In inner-party politics, these methods lead, as we shall yet see, to this: the party organization substitutes itself for the party, the central committee substitutes itself for the organization, and, finally, a "dictator" substitutes himself for the central committee.
Leon Trotsky (1879-1940, Russian Revolutionary)

4 The only tyrant I accept in this world is the still voice within.
Mahatma Gandhi (1869-1948, Indian Political, Spiritual Leader)

5 Disregard for human beings is the first qualification of a dictator.
Milton S. Eisenhower

6 Better the rule of One, whom all obey, than to let clamorous demagogues betray our freedom with the kiss of anarchy.
Oscar Wilde (1856-1900, British Author, Wit)

7 Dictatorship naturally arises out of democracy, and the most aggravated form of tyranny and slavery out of the most extreme liberty.
Plato (427-347 BC, Greek Philosopher)

8 Dictators never invent their own opportunities.
R. Buckminster Fuller (1895-1983, American Inventor, Designer, Poet, Philosopher)

9 A dictatorship is a country where they have taken the politics out of the politics.
Samuel Himmel

10 Dictators always look good until the last minutes.
Tomas G. Masaryk (1850-1937, Liberator of Czechoslovakia)

11 Dictators ride to and fro upon tigers which they dare not dismount.
Winston Churchill (1874-1965, British Statesman, Prime Minister)

DICTIONARIES

1 At painful times, when composition is impossible and reading is not enough, grammars and dictionaries are excellent for distraction.
Elizabeth Barrett Browning (1806-1861, British Poet)

2 Actually if a writer needs a dictionary he should not write. He should have read the dictionary at least three times from beginning to end and then have loaned it to someone who needs it. There are only certain words which are valid and similes (bring me my dictionary) are like defective ammunition (the lowest thing I can think of at this time).
Ernest Hemingway (1898-1961, American Writer)

3 Lexicographer: a writer of dictionaries, a harmless drudge, that busies himself in tracing the original, and detailing the signification of words.
Samuel Johnson (1709-1784, British Author)

4 Every other author may aspire to praise; the lexicographer can only hope to escape reproach, and even this negative recompense has been yet granted to very few.
Samuel Johnson (1709-1784, British Author)

5 Dictionaries are like watches; the worst is better than none, and the best cannot be expected to be quite true.
Samuel Johnson (1709-1784, British Author)

DIETS AND DIETING

1 The Diet Mentality has come about because there is agreement in our society that the only way to lose weight is by dieting. But dieting produces absolutely no permanent, positive results. In fact, it makes you feel worse about yourself and probably does more damage than good to your health.
Bob Schwartz (American Health Expert, Author)

2 Not only don't diets work, they're actually designed to fail. It's not you or your lack of will power that's the problem. It's that diets by their very nature simply don't work.
Bob Schwartz (American Health Expert, Author)

3 To safeguard one's health at the cost of too strict a diet is a tiresome illness indeed.
François de La Rochefoucauld (1613-1680, French classical writer)

4 Changing our diet is something we choose to do, not something we are forced to do. Instead of dreading it, try saying, "Here's another thing I get to do to help myself. Great!"
Greg Anderson (American Author of "The 22 Non-Negotiable Laws of Wellness")

5 To ask women to become unnaturally thin is to ask them to relinquish their sexuality.
Naomi Wolf (1962-, American Author)

6 'Tis a superstition to insist on a special diet. All is made at last of the same chemical atoms.
Ralph Waldo Emerson (1803-1882, American Poet, Essayist)

7 Probably nothing in the world arouses more false hopes Than the first four hours of a diet.
Samuel Beckett (1906-1989, Irish Dramatist, Novelist)

DIFFICULTIES

1 We have inherited new difficulties because we have inherited more privileges.
Abram Sacher

2 In the middle of difficulty lies opportunity.
Albert Einstein (1879-1955, German-born American Physicist)

3 Every life has dark tracts and long stretches of somber tint, and no representation is true to fact which dips its pencil only in light, and flings no shadows on the canvas.
Alexander Maclaren (1826-1910, British Preacher)

4 Difficulties should act as a tonic. They should spur us to greater exertion.
B. C. Forbes (1880-1954, American Publisher)

5 Difficult times always create opportunities for you to experience more love in your life.
Barbara De Angelis (American Expert on Relationship & Love, Author)

6 I don't like people who have never fallen or stumbled. Their virtue is lifeless and it isn't of much value. Life hasn't revealed its beauty to them.
Boris Pasternak (1890-1960, Russian Poet, Novelist, Translator)

7 We were promised sufferings. They were part of the program. We were even told, "Blessed are they that morn."
C. S. Lewis (1898-1963, British Academic, Writer, Christian Apologist)

8 Times of great calamity and confusion have been productive for the greatest minds. The purest ore is produced from the hottest furnace. The brightest thunder-bolt is elicited from the darkest storm.
Charles Caleb Colton (1780-1832, British Sportsman Writer)

9 Many men owe the grandeur of their lives to their tremendous difficulties.
Charles Haddon Spurgeon (1834-1892, British Baptist Preacher)

10 Stand still... and refuse to retreat. Look at it as God looks at it and draw upon His power to hold up under the blast.
Charles Swindoll (American Pastor, Author)

11 Hardship makes the world obscure.
Don Delillo (1926-, American Author)

12 Every cloud has its silver lining but it is sometimes a little difficult to get it to the mint
Don Marquis (1878-1937, American Humorist, Journalist)

13 Don't be crazy to do a lot of things you can't do .
Edgar Watson Howe (1853-1937, American Journalist, Author)

14 As a man handles his troubles during the day, so he goes to bed at night a General, Captain, or Private.
Edgar Watson Howe (1853-1937, American Journalist, Author)

15 It is a good rule to face difficulties at the time they arise and not allow them to increase unacknowledged.
Edward W. Ziegler

16 Difficulties are things that show a person what they are.
Epictetus (50-120, Stoic Philosopher)

17 Difficulties show men what they are. In case of any difficulty, God has pitted you against a rough antagonist that you may be a conqueror, and this cannot be without toil.
Epictetus (50-120, Stoic Philosopher)

18 Storms make the oak grow deeper roots.
George Herbert (1593-1632, British Metaphysical Poet)

19 The lowest ebb is the turn of the tide.
Henry Wadsworth Longfellow (1819-1892, American Poet)

20 Into each life some rain must fall, some days be dark and dreary.
Henry Wadsworth Longfellow (1819-1892, American Poet)

21 Trouble is the next best thing to enjoyment. There is no fate in the world so horrible as to have no share in either its joys or sorrows.
Henry Wadsworth Longfellow (1819-1892, American Poet)

22 Thy fate is the common fate of all; Into each life some rain must fall.
Henry Wadsworth Longfellow (1819-1892, American Poet)

23 Troubles are often the tools by which God fashions us for better things.
Henry Ward Beecher (1813-1887, American Preacher, Orator, Writer)

24 You never will be the person you can be if pressure, tension and discipline are taken out of your life.
James G. Bilkey

25 As favor and riches forsake a man, we discover in him the foolishness they concealed, and which no one perceived before.
Jean De La Bruyere (1645-1696, French Writer)

26 If you can't go over, you must go under.
Jewish Proverb

27 Hardship and opposition are the native soil of manhood and self-reliance.
John Neil

28 All things are difficult before they are easy.
John Norley

29 The difficulties which I meet with in order to realize my existence are precisely what awaken and mobilize my activities, my capacities.
Jose Ortega Y Gasset (1883-1955, Spanish Essayist, Philosopher)

30 In grave difficulties, and with little hope, the boldest measures are the safest. Livy Never make a defense or apology before you be accused.
King Charles I (1887-1922, Emperor of Austria, King of Hungary)

31 It is surmounting difficulties that makes heroes.
Louis Kossuth

32 Life's up and downs provide windows of opportunity to determine your values and goals. Think of using all obstacles as stepping stones to build the life you want.
Marsha Sinetar (American Author of "To Build the Life You Want, Create the Work You Love")

33 In every difficult situation is potential value. Believe this, then begin looking for it.
Norman Vincent Peale (1898-1993, American Christian Reformed Pastor, Speaker, Author)

34 Don't be afraid if things seem difficult in the beginning. That's only the initial impression. The important thing is not to retreat; you have to master yourself.
Olga Korbut (1955-, Soviet Gymnast)

35 When you are down and out something always turns up -- and it is usually the noses of your friends.
Orson Welles (1915-1985, American Film Maker)

36 There are two ways of meeting difficulties: you alter the difficulties or you alter yourself meeting them.
Phyllis Bottome (1884-1963, American Writer)

37 When difficulties are overcome they begin blessing.
Proverb

38 There is nothing so easy but that it becomes difficult when you do it reluctantly.
Publius Terentius Afer (185-159 B.C., Roman Dramatist)

39 There are always difficulties arising that tempt you to believe your critics are right.
Ralph Waldo Emerson (1803-1882, American Poet, Essayist)

40 When it is dark enough, you can see the stars.
Ralph Waldo Emerson (1803-1882, American Poet, Essayist)

41 Can anybody remember when the times were not hard, and money not scarce?
Ralph Waldo Emerson (1803-1882, American Poet, Essayist)

42 Bad times have a scientific value. These are occasions a good learner would not miss.
Ralph Waldo Emerson (1803-1882, American Poet, Essayist)

43 Life isn't meant to be easy. It's hard to take being on the top -- or on the bottom. I guess I'm something of a fatalist. You have to have a sense of history, I think, to survive some of these things. Life is one crisis after another.
Richard M. Nixon (1913-1994, Thirty-seventh President of the USA)

44 The best way out of a difficulty is through it.
Robert Frost (1875-1963, American Poet)

45 Undertake something that is difficult; it will do you good. Unless you try to do something beyond what you have already mastered, you will never grow.
Ronald E. Osborn

46 The very greatest things -- great thoughts, discoveries, inventions -- have usually been nurtured in hardship, often pondered over in sorrow, and at length established with difficulty.
Samuel Smiles (1812-1904, Scottish Author)

47 The apprenticeship of difficulty is one which the greatest of men have had to serve.
Samuel Smiles (1812-1904, Scottish Author)

48 The work of many of the greatest men, inspired by duty, has been done amidst suffering and trial and difficulty. They have struggled against the tide, and reached the shore exhausted.
Samuel Smiles (1812-1904, Scottish Author)

49 What is difficulty? Only a word indicating the degree of effort required to accomplish something! A mere notice of the necessity for exertion; a scarecrow to children and fools and a stimulus to real men.
Samuel Warren

50 Difficulties strengthen the mind, as labor does the body.
Seneca (4 BC-65 AD, Spanish-born Roman Statesman, philosopher)

51 No matter how bad things get you got to go on living, even if it kills you.
Sholom Aleichem (1859-1916, Ukraine-Born American Writer)

52 Bear the inevitable with dignity.
Streckfuss

53 People have a natural tendency to flee to the mountains when things get tough.
Stuart Briscoe

54 The eternal stars shine out as soon as it is dark enough.
Thomas Carlyle (1795-1881, Scottish Philosopher, Author)

55 As in nature, as in art, so in grace; it is rough treatment that gives souls, as well as stones, their luster. The more the diamond is cut the brighter it sparkles; and in what seems hard dealing, there God has no end in view but to perfect His people.
Thomas Guthrie

56 In really hard times the rules of the game are altered. The inchoate mass begins to stir. It becomes potent, and when it strikes, it strikes with incredible emphasis. Those are the rare occasions when a national will emerges from the scattered, specialized, or indifferent blocs of voters who ordinarily elect the politicians. Those are for good or evil the great occasions in a nation's history.
Walter Lippmann (1889-1974, American Journalist)

57 Bumps are the things we climb on.
Warren Wiersbe

58 Difficulties are meant to rouse, not discourage. The human spirit is to grow strong by conflict.
William Ellery Channing (1780-1842, American Unitarian Minister, Author)

59 It cannot be too often repeated that it is not helps, but obstacles, not facilities, but difficulties that make men.
William Mathews

60 Difficulties mastered are opportunities won.
Winston Churchill (1874-1965, British Statesman, Prime Minister)

DIGNITY

1 Dignity consists not in possessing honors, but in the consciousness that we deserve them.
Aristotle (384-322 BC, Greek Philosopher)

2 Every man has his dignity. I'm willing to forget mine, but at my own discretion and not when someone else tells me to.
Denis Diderot (1713-1784, French Philosopher)

3 At night, when the curtains are drawn and the fire flickers, my books attain a collective dignity.
Edward M. Forster (1879-1970, British Novelist, Essayist)

4 Dignity is a mask we wear to hide our ignorance.
Elbert Hubbard (1859-1915, American Author, Publisher)

5 The ultimate end of all revolutionary social change is to establish the sanctity of human life, the dignity of man, the right of every human being to liberty and well-being.
Emma Goldman (1869-1940, American Anarchist)

6 Perhaps the only true dignity of man is his capacity to despise himself.
George Santayana (1863-1952, American Philosopher, Poet)

7 Our dignity is not in what we do, but what we understand.
George Santayana (1863-1952, American Philosopher, Poet)

8 If a man happens to find himself, he has a mansion which he can inhabit with dignity all the days of his life.
James A. Michener (1907-, American Writer)

9 Human Dignity has gleamed only now and then and here and there, in lonely splendor, throughout the ages, a hope of the better men, never an achievement of the majority.
James Thurber (1894-1961, American Humorist, Illustrator)

10 Dignity belongs to the conquered.
Kenneth Burke (1897-1995, American Literary Critic)

11 Each of us, face to face with other men, is clothed with some sort of dignity, but we know only too well all the unspeakable things that go on in the heart.
Luigi Pirandello (1867-1936, Italian Author, Playwright)

12 True dignity is never gained by place, and never lost when honors are withdrawn.
Philip Massinger (1583-1640, British Dramatist)

13   Human rights rest on human dignity. The dignity of man is an ideal worth fighting for and worth dying for.
Robert Maynard

14   Only man has dignity; only man, therefore, can be funny.
Ronald Knox (1888-1957, British Scholar, Priest)

15   There is a healthful hardiness about real dignity that never dreads contact and communion with others however humble.
Washington Irving (1783-1859, American Author)

16   When boasting ends, there dignity begins.
Young

DILIGENCE

1   Diligence is the mother of good luck.
Benjamin Franklin (1706-1790, American Scientist, Publisher, Diplomat)

2   The expectations of life depend upon diligence; the mechanic that would perfect his work must first sharpen his tools.
Confucius (551-479 BC, Chinese Ethical Teacher, Philosopher)

3   He who labors diligently need never despair; for all things are accomplished by diligence and labor.
Menander of Athens (342-291 BC, Greek Dramatic Poet)

4   Diligence is the mother of good fortune, and idleness, its opposite, never brought a man to the goal of any of his best wishes.
Miguel De Cervantes (1547-1616, Spanish Novelist, Dramatist, Poet)

5   Few things are impossible to diligence and skill. Great works are performed not by strength, but perseverance.
Samuel Johnson (1709-1784, British Author)

6   That which ordinary men are fit for, I am qualified in. and the best of me is diligence.
William Shakespeare (1564-1616, British Poet, Playwright, Actor)

DIPLOMACY

1   Consul. In American politics, a person who having failed to secure an office from the people is given one by the Administration on condition that he leave the country.
Ambrose Bierce (1842-1914, American Author, Editor, Journalist, "The Devil's Dictionary")

2   Once the Xerox copier was invented, diplomacy died.
Andrew Young (1932-, Civil Rights Activist, Protestant Minister, Public Official)

3   Diplomacy means all the wicked devices of the Old World, spheres of influence, balances of power, secret treaties, triple alliances, and, during the interim period, appeasement of Fascism.
Barbara Tuchman (1912-1989, American Historian)

4   We have no commission from God to police the world.
Benjamin Harrison

5   My advice to any diplomat who wants to have a good press is to have two or three kids and a dog.
Carl Rowan (1925-, American Journalist, 'The man')

6   A diplomat is a person who can tell you to go to hell in such a way that you actually look forward to the trip.
Caskie Stinnett

7   Diplomats are useful only in fair weather. As soon as it rains, they drown in every drop.
Charles De Gaulle (1890-1970, French President during World War II)

8   Diplomacy is the art of letting someone have your way.
Daniele Vare

9   Diplomats were invented simply to waste time.
David Lloyd George (1863-1945, British Statesman, Prime Minister)

10   I have discovered the art of deceiving diplomats. I speak the truth, and they never believe me.
Di Cavour

11   To act with doubleness towards a man whose own conduct was double, was so near an approach to virtue that it deserved to be called by no meaner name than diplomacy.
George Eliot (1819-1880, British Novelist)

12   Diplomacy is to do and say the nastiest things in the nicest way.
Isaac Goldberg

13   There are few ironclad rules of diplomacy but to one there is no exception. When an official reports that talks were useful, it can safely be concluded that nothing was accomplished.
John Kenneth Galbraith (1908-, American Economist)

14   If you are to stand up for your Government you must be able to stand up to your Government.
Lord Harold Caccia

15   A diplomat these days in nothing, but a head waiter who is allowed to sit down occasionally.
Peter Ustinov (1921-, British Actor, Writer, Director)

16   A diplomat is a man who always remembers a woman's birthday but never remembers her age.
Robert Frost (1875-1963, American Poet)

17   Tell the truth, and so puzzle and confound your adversaries.
Sir Henry Wotton (1568-1639, British Diplomat, Traveler, Scholar, and Poet)

18   When envoys are sent with compliments in their mouths, it is a sign that the enemy wishes for a truce.
Sun Tzu (400-430 BC, Chinese Military Strategist, Author of "Art of War")

19   We are the greatest power in the world. If we behave like it.
Walt W. Rostow

20 An ambassador is not simply an agent; he is also a spectacle.
Walter Bagehot (1826-1877, British Economist, Critic)

21 Diplomacy is the art of saying "Nice doggie!" till you can find a rock.
Wynn Catlin

DIRECTION

1 Thy word is a lamp to my feet, and a light to my path. [Psalm 119:105]
Bible (Sacred Scriptures of Christians and Judaism)

2 Who then is the man who fears the Lord? He will instruct him in the way chosen for him. [Psalm 25:12]
Bible (Sacred Scriptures of Christians and Judaism)

3 I will instruct you and teach you in the way which you should go. I will counsel you with my eye upon you. [Psalm 25:12]
Bible (Sacred Scriptures of Christians and Judaism)

4 For such is God our God, forever and ever. He will guide us until death. [Psalm 48:14]
Bible (Sacred Scriptures of Christians and Judaism)

5 Ask for the old paths, where the way is good, and walk in it.
Bible (Sacred Scriptures of Christians and Judaism)

6 If we do not change our direction, we are likely to end up where we are headed.
Chinese Proverb

7 If you find a path with no obstacles, it probably doesn't lead anywhere.
Frank A. Clark

8 The best path through life is the highway.
Henri Frederic Amiel (1821-1881, Swiss Philosopher, Poet, Critic)

9 It is only in misery that we recognize the hand of God leading good men to good.
Johann Wolfgang Von Goethe (1749-1832, German Poet, Dramatist, Novelist)

10 Let the path be open to talent.
Napoleon Bonaparte (1769-1821, French General, Emperor)

11 It is better to run back than run the wrong way.
Proverb

12 Step by step one goes very far.
Proverb

13 You cannot be lost on a road that is straight.
Proverb

DISABILITY

1 The chief misery of the decline of the faculties, and a main cause of the irritability that often goes with it, is evidently the isolation, the lack of customary appreciation and influence, which only the rarest tact and thoughtfulness on the part of others can alleviate.
Charles Horton Cooley (1864-1929, American Sociologist)

2 The invalid is a parasite on society. In a certain state it is indecent to go on living. To vegetate on in cowardly dependence on physicians and medicaments after the meaning of life, the right to life, has been lost ought to entail the profound contempt of society.
Friedrich Nietzsche (1844-1900, German Philosopher)

3 The sense of an entailed disadvantage -- the deformed foot doubtfully hidden by the shoe, makes a restlessly active spiritual yeast, and easily turns a self-centered, unloving nature into an Ishmaelite. But in the rarer sort, who presently see their own frustrated claim as one among a myriad, the inexorable sorrow takes the form of fellowship and makes the imagination tender.
George Eliot (1819-1880, British Novelist)

4 I have often been asked, "Do not people bore you?" I do not understand quite what that means. I suppose the calls of the stupid and curious, especially of newspaper reporters, are always inopportune. I also dislike people who try to talk down to my understanding. They are like people who when walking with you try to shorten their steps to suit yours; the hypocrisy in both cases is equally exasperating.
Helen Keller (1880-1968, American Blind/Deaf Author, Lecturer, Amorist)

5 Disability is a matter of perception. If you can do just one thing well, you're needed by someone.
Martina Navratilova (1956-, American Tennis Player)

DISAGREEMENTS

1 If you have learned how to disagree without being disagreeable, then you have discovered the secrete of getting along -- whether it be business, family relations, or life itself.
Bernard Meltzer (1914-, American Law Professor)

2 When you run into someone who is disagreeable to others, you may be sure he is uncomfortable with himself; the amount of pain we inflict upon others is directly proportional to the amount we feel within us.
Sidney J. Harris (1917-, American Journalist)

DISAPPOINTMENTS

1 Blessed is the man who expects nothing, for he shall never be disappointed was the ninth beatitude.
Alexander Pope (1688-1744, British Poet, Critic, Translator)

2 Disappointment is a sort of bankruptcy -- the bankruptcy of a soul that expends too much in hope and expectation.
Eric Hoffer (1902-1983, American Author, Philosopher)

3 When you think of the huge uninterrupted success of a book like Don Quixote, you're bound to realize that if humankind have not yet finished being revenged, by sheer laughter, for being let down in their greatest hope, it is because that hope was cherished so long and lay so deep!
Georges Bernanos (1888-1948, French Novelist, Political Writer)

4 There can be no deep disappointment where there is not deep love.
Martin Luther King Jr. (1929-1968, American Black Leader, Nobel Prize Winner, 1964)

5 It's precisely the disappointing stories, which have no proper ending and therefore no proper meaning, that sound true to life.
Max Frisch (1911-1991, Swiss Playwright, Novelist)

6 The prompter the refusal, the less the disappointment.
Publilius Syrus (1st Century BC, Roman Writer)

7 Disappointment, when it involves neither shame nor loss, is as good as success; for it supplies as many images to the mind, and as many topics to the tongue.
Samuel Johnson (1709-1784, British Author)

DISAPPROVAL

1 No man likes to live under the eye of perpetual disapprobation.
Samuel Johnson (1709-1784, British Author)

DISASTERS

1 The popularity of disaster movies expresses a collective perception of a world threatened by irresistible and unforeseen forces which nevertheless are thwarted at the last moment. Their thinly veiled symbolic meaning might be translated thus: We are innocent of wrongdoing. We are attacked by unforeseeable forces come to harm us. We are, thus, innocent even of negligence. Though those forces are insuperable, chance will come to our aid and we shall emerge victorious.
David Mamet (1947-, American Playwright)

2 Our sympathy is cold to the relation of distant misery.
Edward Gibbon (1737-1794, British Historian)

3 The bosses of our mass media, press, radio, film and television, succeed in their aim of taking our minds off disaster. Thus, the distraction they offer demands the antidote of maximum concentration on disaster.
Ernst Fischer (1899-1972, Austrian Editor, Poet, Critic)

4 What quarrel, what harshness, what unbelief in each other can subsist in the presence of a great calamity, when all the artificial vesture of our life is gone, and we are all one with each other in primitive mortal needs?
George Eliot (1819-1880, British Novelist)

5 Perhaps catastrophe is the natural human environment, and even though we spend a good deal of energy trying to get away from it, we are programmed for survival amid catastrophe.
Germaine Greer (1939-, Australian Feminist Writer)

6 The earth is mankind's ultimate haven, our blessed terra firma. When it trembles and gives way beneath our feet, it's as though one of God's checks has bounced.
Gilbert Adair (Born 1944, American Author)

7 The stabbing horror of life is not contained in calamities and disasters, because these things wake one up and one gets very familiar and intimate with them and finally they become tame again. No, it is more like being in a hotel room in Hoboken let us say, and just enough money in one's pocket for another meal.
Henry Miller (1891-1980, American Author)

8 Man's extremity is God's opportunity.
John Flavel

9 A great calamity is as old as the trilobites an hour after it has happened.
Oliver Wendell Holmes (1809-1894, American Author, Wit, Poet)

10 The compensations of calamity are made apparent to the understanding also, after long intervals of time. A fever, a mutilation, a cruel disappointment, a loss of wealth, a loss of friends, seems at the moment unpaid loss, and unpayable. But the sure years reveal the deep remedial force that underlies all facts.
Ralph Waldo Emerson (1803-1882, American Poet, Essayist)

11 Down went the owners -- greedy men whom hope of gain allured: oh, dry the starting tear, for they were heavily insured.
W. S. Gilbert (1836-1911, British Librettist)

DISCIPLES

1 Once the good man was dead, one wore his hat and another his sword as he had worn them, a third had himself barbered as he had, a fourth walked as he did, but the honest man that he was -- nobody any longer wanted to be that.
Georg C. Lichtenberg (1742-1799, German Physicist, Satirist)

2 Every great man nowadays has his disciples, and it is usually Judas who writes the biography.
Oscar Wilde (1856-1900, British Author, Wit)

3 Disciples be damned. It's not interesting. It's only the masters that matter. Those who create.
Pablo Picasso (1881-1973, Spanish Artist)

DISCIPLINE

1 Self-respect is the root of discipline; the sense of dignity grows with the ability to say no to oneself.
Abraham J. Heschel (1907-1972, Polish educator, Author)

2 Blind and unwavering undisciplined at all times constitutes the real strength of all free men.
Alfred Jarry (1873-1907, French Playwright, Author)

3 What it lies in our power to do, it lies in our power not to do.
Aristotle (384-322 BC, Greek Philosopher)

4 Reasonable orders are easy enough to obey; it is capricious, bureaucratic or plain idiotic demands that form the habit of discipline.
Barbara Tuchman (1912-1989, American Historian)

5 The rod and reproof give wisdom: but a child left to himself bringeth his mother to shame. [Proverbs 29:15]
Bible (Sacred Scriptures of Christians and Judaism)

6 One of the great lessons I've learned in athletics is that you've got to discipline your life. No matter how good you may be, you've got to be willing to cut out of your life those things that keep you from going to the top.
Bob Richards (American Olympic Pole Vaulting Champion)

7 The only discipline that last is self discipline.
Bum Phillips (American Football Coach)

8 Temperance is a bridle of gold.
Burton

9 So far as discipline is concerned, freedom means not its absence but the use of higher and more rational forms as contrasted with those that are lower or less rational.
Charles Horton Cooley (1864-1929, American Sociologist)

10 No one is free who does not lord over himself.
Claudius (10 BC-54 AD, Roman Emperor)

11 If you will discipline yourself to make your mind self-sufficient you will thereby be least vulnerable to injury from the outside.
Critias of Athens

12 Practice yourself, for heaven's sake in little things, and then proceed to greater.
Epictetus (50-120, Stoic Philosopher)

13 Who loves well, chastises well.
French Proverb

14 Discipline is the soul of an army. It makes small numbers formidable; procures success to the weak, and esteem to all.
George Washington (1732-1799, First President of the USA)

15 Look upon your chastening as God's chariots sent to carry your soul into the high places of spiritual achievement.
Hannah Whitall Smith

16 Anybody who gets away with something will come back to get away with a little bit more.
Harold Schoenberg

17 What we do upon some great occasion will probably depend on what we already are. What we are will be the result of previous years of self-discipline.
Henry Parry Liddon (1829-1890, British Theologian)

18 No man is such a conqueror, as the one that has defeated himself.
Henry Ward Beecher (1813-1887, American Preacher, Orator, Writer)

19 When things are steep, remember to stay level-headed.
Horace (65-8 BC, Italian Poet)

20 He who lives without discipline dies without honor.
Icelandic Proverb

21 Where one person shapes their life by precept and example, there are a thousand who have shaped it by impulse and circumstances.
James Russell Lowell (1819-1891, American Poet, Critic, Editor)

22 To know how to dispense with things is to possess them.
Jean François Regnard (1655-1709, French Comic Dramatist)

23 Brave is the lion tamer, brave is the world subduer, but braver is the one who has subdued himself.
Johann Gottfried Von Herder (1744-1803, German Critic and Poet)

24 No man or woman has achieved an effective personality who is not self-disciplined. Such discipline must not be an end in itself, but must be directed to the development of resolute Christian character.
John S. Bonnell

25 Better to be pruned to grow than cut up to burn.
John Trapp

26 Some people regard discipline as a chore. For me, it is a kind of order that sets me free to fly.
Julie Andrews (1935-, British Singer, Actress)

27 He conquers twice who conquers himself in victory.
Jyrus

28 Without discipline, there is no life at all.
Katharine Hepburn (1907-, American Actress, Writer)

29 There is little that can withstand a man who can conquer himself.
Louis XIV (1638-1715, King of France from 1643-1715)

30 Discipline must come through liberty. We do not consider an individual disciplined only when he has been rendered as artificially silent as a mute and as immovable as a paralytic. He is an individual annihilated, not disciplined.
Maria Montessori (1870-1952, Italian Educator)

31 Lack of discipline leads to frustration and self-loathing.
Marie Chapian

32 Make your educational laws strict and your criminal ones can be gentle; but if you leave youth its liberty you will have to dig dungeons for ages.
Michel Eyquem De Montaigne (1533-1592, French Philosopher, Essayist)

33 No padlocks, bolts, or bars can secure a maiden better than her own reserve.
Miguel De Cervantes (1547-1616, Spanish Novelist, Dramatist, Poet)

34 Discipline is not a nasty word.
Pat Riley (1945, American Basketball Coach)

35 A colt is worth little if it does not break its halter.
Proverb

36 Self-command is the main discipline.
Ralph Waldo Emerson (1803-1882, American Poet, Essayist)

37 There is a certain combination of anarchy and discipline in the way I work.
Robert De Niro (1943-, American Actor, Director)

38 Discipline is the refining fire by which talent becomes ability.
Roy L. Smith (American Clergyman)

39 No evil propensity of the human heart is so powerful that it may mot be subdued by discipline.
Seneca (4 BC-65 AD, Spanish-born Roman Statesman, philosopher)

40 If you once turn on your side after the hour at which you ought to rise, it is all over. Bolt up at once.
Sir Walter Scott (1771-1832, British Novelist, Poet)

41 You can judge the quality of their faith from the way they behave. Discipline is an index to doctrine.
Tertullian (160-240, Roman Christian Author and Polemicist)

42 If we do not discipline ourselves the world will do it for us.
William Feather (1888-18, American Writer, Businessman)

43 Tired mothers find that spanking takes less time than reasoning and penetrates sooner to the seat of the memory.
William J. Durant (1885-1981, American Historian, Essayist)

44 If thou wouldn't conquer thy weakness thou must not gratify it.
William Penn (1644-1718, British Religious Leader, Founder of Pennsylvania)

45 It doesn't matter what you're trying to accomplish. It's all a matter of discipline. I was determined to discover what life held for me beyond the inner-city streets.
Wilma Rudolph (1940-1994, American Track Athlete)

DISCOMFORT

1 The only thing I can't stand is discomfort.
Gloria Steinem (1934-, American Feminist Writer, Editor)

DISCONTENT

1 He that is discontented in one place will seldom be content in another.
Aesop (620-560 BC, Greek Fabulist)

2 You will never be happy if you continue to search for what happiness consists of. You will never live if you are looking for the meaning of life.
Albert Camus (1913-1960, French Existential Writer)

3 All human situations have their inconveniences. We feel those of the present but neither see nor feel those of the future; and hence we often make troublesome changes without amendment, and frequently for the worse.
Benjamin Franklin (1706-1790, American Scientist, Publisher, Diplomat)

4 Let thy discontents be thy secrets.
Benjamin Franklin (1706-1790, American Scientist, Publisher, Diplomat)

5 The discontented man finds no easy chair.
Benjamin Franklin (1706-1790, American Scientist, Publisher, Diplomat)

6 Who is not satisfied with himself will grow; who is not sure of his own correctness will learn many things.
Chinese Proverb

7 If necessity is the mother of invention, discontent is the father of progress.
David Rockerfeller (American Businessman, Financier)

8 The splendid discontent of God With chaos made the world. And from the discontent of man The worlds best progress springs.
Ella Wheeler Wilcox (1855-1919, American Poet, Journalist)

9 The greatest weariness comes from work not done.
Eric Hoffer (1902-1983, American Author, Philosopher)

10 Discontent is something that follows ambition like a shadow.
Henry H. Haskins

11 Man hath still either toys or care: But hath no root, nor to one place is tied, but ever restless and irregular, about this earth doth run and ride. He knows he hath a home, but scarce knows where; He says it is so far, that he has quite forgot how to go there
Henry Vaughan (1622-1695, Welsh Poet)

12 That which makes people dissatisfied with their condition, is the chimerical idea they form of the happiness of others.
James Thomson (1700-1748, Scottish Poet)

13 The essence of man is, discontent, divine discontent; a sort of love without a beloved, the ache we feel in a member we no longer have.
Jose Ortega Y Gasset (1883-1955, Spanish Essayist, Philosopher)

14 Discontent is the first step in the progress of a man or a nation.
Oscar Wilde (1856-1900, British Author, Wit)

15 Who with a little cannot be content, endures an everlasting punishment.
Robert Herrick (1591-1674, British Poet)

16 Discontent is the first necessity of progress.
Thomas A. Edison (1847-1931, American Inventor, Entrepreneur, Founder of GE)

DISCOVERY

1 Discovery is seeing what everybody else has seen, and thinking what nobody else has thought.
Albert Szent-Gyorgyi (Hungarian Scientist)

2 A discovery is said to be an accident meeting a prepared mind.
Albert Szent-Gyorgyi (Hungarian Scientist)

3 What has become clear to you since we last met?
Benjamin Franklin (1706-1790, American Scientist, Publisher, Diplomat)

4 The way a child discovers the world constantly replicates the way science began. You start to notice what's around you, and you get very curious about how things work. How things interrelate. It's as simple as seeing a bug that intrigues you. You want to know where it goes at night; who its friends are; what it eats.
David Cronenberg (1943-, Canadian Filmmaker)

5 They are ill discoverers that think there is no land when they see nothing but sea.
Francis Bacon (1561-1626, British Philosopher, Essayist, Statesman)

6 If we make a couple of discoveries here and there we need not believe things will go on like this for ever. Just as we hit water when we dig in the earth, so we discover the incomprehensible sooner or later.
Georg C. Lichtenberg (1742-1799, German Physicist, Satirist)

7 The discovery of the North Pole is one of those realities which could not be avoided. It is the wages which human perseverance pays itself when it thinks that something is taking too long. The world needed a discoverer of the North Pole, and in all areas of social activity, merit was less important here than opportunity.
Karl Kraus (1874-1936, Austrian Satirist)

8 What is there that confers the noblest delight? What is that which swells a man's breast with pride above that which any other experience can bring to him? Discovery! To know that you are walking where none others have walked; that you are beholding what human eye has not seen before; that you are breathing a virgin atmosphere. To give birth to an idea, to discover a great thought -- an intellectual nugget, right under the dust of a field that many a brain-plough had gone over before. To find a new planet, to invent a new hinge, to find a way to make the lightning carry your messages. To be the first -- that is the idea.
Mark Twain (1835-1910, American Humorist, Writer)

9 If a man knew anything, he would sit in a corner and be modest; but he is such an ignorant peacock, that he goes bustling up and down, and hits on extraordinary discoveries.
Ralph Waldo Emerson (1803-1882, American Poet, Essayist)

DISCRETION

1 Never say "oops" in the operating room.
Dr. Leo Troy

2 Be discreet in all things, and so render it unnecessary to be mysterious.
Duke of Wellington Arthur Wellesley (1769-1852, British Statesman, Military Leader)

3 Discretion of speech is more than eloquence, and to speak agreeably to him with whom we deal is more than to speak in good words, or in good order.
Francis Bacon (1561-1626, British Philosopher, Essayist, Statesman)

4 Depart from discretion when it interferes with duty.
Hannah More (1745-1833, British Writer, Reformer, Philanthropist)

5 Nothing is more dangerous than a friend without discretion; even a prudent enemy is preferable.
Jean De La Fontaine (1621-1695, French Poet)

6 Notable talents are not necessarily connected with discretion.
Junius (1769-1771, Anonymous British Letter Writer)

7 Never wrestle with a strong man nor bring a rich man to court.
Latvian Proverb

8 Be wiser than other people, if you can; but do not tell them so.
Lord Chesterfield (1694-1773, British Statesman, Author)

9 For he that fights and runs away, may live to fight another day, but he, who is in battle slain, can never rise and fight again.
Oliver Goldsmith (1728-1774, Anglo-Irish Author, Poet, Playwright)

10 I cannot and do not live in the world of discretion, not as a writer, anyway. I would prefer to, I assure you -- it would make life easier. But discretion is, unfortunately, not for novelists.
Philip Roth (1933-, American Novelist)

11 Better a living dog than a dead lion.
Proverb

12 Be advised what thou dost discourse of, and what thou maintainest whether touching religion, state, or vanity; for if thou err in the first, thou shalt be accounted profane; if in the second, dangerous; if in the third, indiscreet and foolish.
Sir Walter Raleigh (1552-1618, British Courtier, Navigator, Writer)

DISEASE

1 It is with disease of the mind, as with those of the body; we are half dead before we understand our disorder, and half cured when we do.
Charles Caleb Colton (1780-1832, British Sportsman Writer)

2 A decadent civilization compromises with its disease, cherishes the virus infecting it, loses its self-respect.
E. M. Cioran (1911-, Rumanian-born French Philosopher)

3 The worst of all diseases is a nervous ability.
Edward Dyson

4 Disease is a vital expression of the human organism.
Georg Groddeck

5 The diseases which destroy a man are no less natural than the instincts which preserve him.
George Santayana (1863-1952, American Philosopher, Poet)

6 Is not disease the rule of existence? There is not a lily pad floating on the river but has been riddled by insects. Almost every shrub and tree has its gall, oftentimes esteemed its chief ornament and hardly to be distinguished from the fruit. If misery loves company, misery has company enough. Now, at midsummer, find me a perfect leaf or fruit.
Henry David Thoreau (1817-1862, American Essayist, Poet, Naturalist)

7 Natural forces within us are the true healers of disease
Hippocrates (Ancient Greek Physician)

8 He who considers disease results to be the disease itself, and expects to do away with these as diseases, is insane. It is an insanity in medicine, an insanity that has grown out of the milder forms of mental disorder in science, crazy whims.
James Tyler Kent (1849-1916, American Homeopathic Teacher, Physician)

9 Diseases are the tax on pleasures.
John Ray (1627-1705, British Naturalist)

10 We are so fond on one another because our ailments are the same.
Jonathan Swift (1667-1745, Anglo-Irish Satirist)

11 Misdirected life force is the activity in disease process. Disease has no energy save what it borrows from the life of the organism. It is by adjusting the life force that healing must be brought about, and it is the sun as transformer and distributor of primal spiritual energy that must be utilized in this process, for life and the sun are so intimately connected.
Kabbalah (Jewish Esoteric Doctrine)

12 Even diseases have lost their prestige, there aren't so many of them left. Think it over... no more syphilis, no more clap, no more typhoid... antibiotics have taken half the tragedy out of medicine.
Louis-Ferdinand Celine (1894-1961, French Author)

13 Disease is an experience of a so-called mortal mind. It is fear made manifest on the body.
Mary Baker Eddy (1821-1910, American Christian Writer, Founder of Christian Science Church)

14 The biggest disease today is not leprosy or tuberculosis, but rather the feeling of being unwanted.
Mother Teresa (1910-1997, Albanian-born Roman Catholic Missionary)

15 Once a disease has entered the body, all parts which are healthy must fight it: not one alone, but all. Because a disease might mean their common death. Nature knows this; and Nature attacks the disease with whatever help she can muster.
Philipus A. Paracelsus (German Physician and Chemist)

16 I think the biggest disease this world suffers from...is people feeling unloved.
Princess of Wales Diana (1961-1997, Wife of Charles, Prince of Wales)

17 All diseases run into one. Old age.
Ralph Waldo Emerson (1803-1882, American Poet, Essayist)

18 One might say, for example, that a patient has a kind of St Vitus's dance; a kind of dropsy; a kind of nerve fever; a kind of ague. One would never say, however (to end once and for all the confusion of these names) "He has St. Vitus's dance," "He has nerve fever," "He has dropsy," "He has ague," since there simply are not any fixed, unchanging diseases to be known by such names.
Samuel Hahnemann (1755-1843, German Physician, Founder of Homeopathy)

19 Disease generally begins that equality which death completes.
Samuel Johnson (1709-1784, British Author)

20 Disease an never be conquered, can never be quelled by emotion's willful screaming or faith's symbolic prayer. It can only be conquered by the energy of humanity and the cunning in the mind of man. In the patience of a Curie, in the enlightenment of a Faraday, a Rutherford, a Pasteur, a Nightingale, and all other apostles of light and cleanliness, rather than of a woebegone godliness, we shall find final deliverance from plague, pestilence, and famine.
Sean O'Casey (1884-1964, Irish Dramatist)

21 Disease is not of the body but of the place.
Seneca (4 BC-65 AD, Spanish-born Roman Statesman, philosopher)

22 Any important disease whose causality is murky, and for which treatment is ineffectual, tends to be awash in significance.
Susan Sontag (1933-, American Essayist)

23 With the modern diseases (once TB, now cancer) the romantic idea that the disease expresses the character is invariably extended to assert that the character causes the disease -- because it has not expressed itself. Passion moves inward, striking and blighting the deepest cellular recesses.
Susan Sontag (1933-, American Essayist)

24 He who cures a disease may be the skillfullest, but he that prevents it is the safest physician.
Thomas Fuller (1608-1661, British Clergyman, Author)

25 Everyone detected with AIDS should be tattooed in the upper forearm, to protect common needle users, and on the buttock, to prevent the victimization of other homosexuals.
William F. Buckley (1925-, American Writer)

26 Which came first the intestine or the tapeworm?
William S. Burroughs (1914-1997, American Writer)

DISGRACE

1 She is absolutely inadmissible into society. Many a woman has a past, but I am told that she has at least a dozen, and that they all fit.
Oscar Wilde (1856-1900, British Author, Wit)

2 Oh! no! we never mention her, her name is never heard; my lips are now forbid to speak, that once familiar word.
Thomas Haynes Bayly (1791-1839, British Writer, Poet)

DISHONESTY

1 Hope of ill gain is the beginning of loss.
Democritus (460-370 BC, Greek Philosopher)

2 If all mankind were suddenly to practice honesty, many thousands of people would be sure to starve.
Georg C. Lichtenberg (1742-1799, German Physicist, Satirist)

3 Dishonesty is so grasping it would deceive God himself, were it possible.
George Bancroft (1800-1891, American Historian)

4 Honesty pays, but it doesn't seem to pay enough to suit some people.
Kin Hubbard (1868-1930, American Humorist, Journalist)

5 Don't place too much confidence in the man who boasts of being as honest as the day is long. Wait until you meet him at night.
Robert C. Edwards

6 False words are not only evil in themselves, but they infect the soul with evil.
Socrates (469-399 BC, Greek Philosopher of Athens)

7 Men are able to trust one another, knowing the exact degree of dishonesty they are entitled to expect.
Stephen B. Leacock (1869-1944, Canadian Humorist, Economist)

DISILLUSION

1 We could hardly believe that after so many ordeals, after all the trials of modern skepticism, there was still so much left in our souls to destroy.
Alexander Herzen (1812-1870, Russian Journalist, Political Thinker)

2 I saw that all beings are fated to happiness: action is not life, but a way of wasting some force, an enervation. Morality is the weakness of the brain.
Arthur Rimbaud (1854-1891, French Poet)

3 The wise man, knowing how to enjoy achieved results without having constantly to replace them with others, finds in them an attachment to life in the hour of difficulty. But the man who has always pinned all his hopes on the future and lived with his eyes fixed upon it, has nothing in the past as a comfort against the present's afflictions, for the past was nothing to him but a series of hastily experienced stages. What blinded him to himself was his expectation always to find further on the happiness he had so far missed. Now he is stopped in his tracks; from now on nothing remains behind or ahead of him to fix his gaze upon.
Emile Durkheim (1858-1917, French Sociologist)

4 What if everything is an illusion and nothing exists? In that case, I definitely overpaid for my carpet.
Woody Allen (1935-, American Director, Screenwriter, Actor, Comedian)

DISSATISFACTION

1 Man is the only creature who refuses to be what he is.
Albert Camus (1913-1960, French Existential Writer)

2 The problem lay buried, unspoken for many years in the minds of American women. It was a strange stirring, a sense of dissatisfaction, a yearning that women suffered in the middle of the twentieth century in the United States. Each suburban housewife struggled with it alone. As she made the beds, shopped for groceries, matched slipcover material, ate peanut butter sandwiches with her children, chauffeured Cub Scouts and Brownies, lay beside her husband at night, she was afraid to ask even of herself the silent question: "Is this all?"
Betty Friedan (1921-, American Feminist Writer)

3 A fierce unrest seethes at the core, of all existing things:, it was the eager wish to soar, that gave the gods their wings.
Don Marquis (1878-1937, American Humorist, Journalist)

4 Change occurs in direct proportion to dissatisfaction, but dissatisfaction never changes.
Doug Horton

5 The chemistry of dissatisfaction is as the chemistry of some marvelously potent tar. In it are the building stones of explosives, stimulants, poisons, opiates, perfumes and stenches.
Eric Hoffer (1902-1983, American Author, Philosopher)

6 As long as I have a want, I have a reason for living. Satisfaction is death.
George Bernard Shaw (1856-1950, Irish-born British Dramatist)

7 If there is dissatisfaction with the status quo, good. If there is ferment, so much the better. If there is restlessness, I am pleased. Then let there be ideas, and hard thought, and hard work. If man feels small, let man make himself bigger.
Hubert H. Humphrey (1911-1978, American Democratic Politician, Vice President)

8 No, no, we are not satisfied, and we will not be satisfied until justice rolls down like waters and righteousness like a mighty stream.
Martin Luther King Jr. (1929-1968, American Black Leader, Nobel Prize Winner, 1964)

9 There are three wants which never can be satisfied: that of the rich, who wants something more; that of the sick, who wants something different; and that of the traveler, who says, "Anywhere but here."
Ralph Waldo Emerson (1803-1882, American Poet, Essayist)

10 If we are suffering illness, poverty, or misfortune, we think we shall be satisfied on the day it ceases. But there too, we know it is false; so soon as one has got used to not suffering one wants something else.
Simone Weil (1910-1943, French Philosopher, Mystic)

11 No sooner is your ocean filled, than he grumbles that it might have been of better vintage. Try him with half of a Universe, of an Omnipotence, he sets to quarrelling with the proprietor of the other half, and declares himself the most maltreated of men. Always there is a black spot in our sunshine: it is even as I said, the Shadow of Ourselves.
Thomas Carlyle (1795-1881, Scottish Philosopher, Author)

12 In a land which is fully settled, most men must accept their local environment or try to change it by political means; only the exceptionally gifted or adventurous can leave to seek his fortune elsewhere. In America, on the other hand, to move on and make a fresh start somewhere else is still the normal reaction to dissatisfaction and failure.
W. H. Auden (1907-1973, Anglo-American Poet)

13 The idiot who praises, with enthusiastic tone, All centuries but this, and every country but his own.
W. S. Gilbert (1836-1911, British Librettist)

DISSENT

1 The original "crime" of "niggers" and lesbians is that they prefer themselves.
Alice Walker (1944-, American Author, Critic)

2 Wild intelligence abhors any narrow world; and the world of women must stay narrow, or the woman is an outlaw. No woman could be Nietzsche or Rimbaud without ending up in a whorehouse or lobotomized.
Andrea Dworkin (1946-, American Feminist Critic)

3 I would like you to understand completely, also emotionally, that I'm a political detainee and will be a political prisoner, that I have nothing now or in the future to be ashamed of in this situation. That, at bottom, I myself have in a certain sense asked for this detention and this sentence, because I've always refused to change my opinion, for which I would be willing to give my life and not just remain in prison. That therefore I can only be tranquil and content with myself.
Antonio Gramsci (1891-1937, Italian Political Theorist)

4 The dissenter is every human being at those moments of his life when he resigns momentarily from the herd and thinks for himself.
Archibald Macleish (1892-1982, American Poet)

5 May we never confuse honest dissent with disloyal subversion.
Dwight D. Eisenhower (1890-1969, Thirty-fourth President of the USA)

6 Assent -- and you are sane -- , demur -- you're straightway dangerous -- , and handled with a Chain -- .
Emily Dickinson (1830-1886, American Poet)

7 The beginning of thought is in disagreement -- not only with others but also with ourselves.
Eric Hoffer (1902-1983, American Author, Philosopher)

8 Though dissenters seem to question everything in sight, they are actually bundles of dusty answers and never conceived a new question. What offends us most in the literature of dissent is the lack of hesitation and wonder.
Eric Hoffer (1902-1983, American Author, Philosopher)

9 To shoot a man because one disagrees with his interpretation of Darwin or Hegel is a sinister tribute to the supremacy of ideas in human affairs -- but a tribute nevertheless.
George Steiner (1929-, French-born American Critic, Novelist)

10 In a democracy dissent is an act of faith. Like medicine, the test of its value is not in its taste, but its effects.
J. William Fulbright (1905-, American Democratic Politician)

11 Has there ever been a society which has died of dissent? Several have died of conformity in our lifetime.
Jacob Bronowski (1908-1974, British Scientist, Author)

12 Discussion in America means dissent.
James Thurber (1894-1961, American Humorist, Illustrator)

13 If all mankind minus one, were of one opinion, and only one person were of the contrary opinion, mankind would be no more justified in silencing that one person, than he, if he had the power, would be justified in silencing mankind.
John Stuart Mill (1806-1873, British Philosopher, Economist)

14 I stood among them, but not of them; in a shroud of thoughts which were not their thoughts.
Lord Byron (1788-1824, British Poet)

15 The rule is perfect: in all matters of opinion our adversaries are insane.
Mark Twain (1835-1910, American Humorist, Writer)

16 You do not become a "dissident" just because you decide one day to take up this most unusual career. You are thrown into it by your personal sense of responsibility, combined with a complex set of external circumstances. You are cast out of the existing structures and placed in a position of conflict with them. It begins as an attempt to do your work well, and ends with being branded an enemy of society.
Vaclav Havel (1936-, Czech Playwright, President)

17 It is hard for any one to be an honest politician who is not born and bred a Dissenter.
William Hazlitt (1778-1830, British Essayist)

DISSIPATION

1 Dissipation is a form of self-sacrifice.
Eric Hoffer (1902-1983, American Author, Philosopher)

2 They had both noticed that a life of dissipation sometimes gave to a face the look of gaunt suffering spirituality that a life of asceticism was supposed to give and quite often did not.
Katherine Anne Porter (1890-1980, American short-story Writer, Novelist)

3 Voluptuaries, consumed by their senses, always begin by flinging themselves with a great display of frenzy into an abyss. But they survive, they come to the surface again. And they develop a routine of the abyss: "It's four o clock. At five I have my abyss... "
Sidonie Gabrielle Colette (1873-1954, French Author)

DISTRUST

1 Distrust any enterprise that requires new clothes.
Henry David Thoreau (1817-1862, American Essayist, Poet, Naturalist)

DIVERSITY

1 We cannot feel strongly toward the totally unlike because it is unimaginable, unrealizable; nor yet toward the wholly like because it is stale -- identity must always be dull company. The power of other natures over us lies in a stimulating difference which causes excitement and opens communication, in ideas similar to our own but not identical, in states of mind attainable but not actual.
Charles Horton Cooley (1864-1929, American Sociologist)

2 Since the 1960s, we have seen the failure of the melting pot ideology. This ideology suggested that different historical, cultural and socioeconomic backgrounds could be subordinated to a larger ideology or social amalgam which is "America." This concept obviously did not work, because paradoxically America encourages a politics of contestation.
Edward Said

3 The diversity in the faculties of men, from which the rights of property originate, is not less an insuperable obstacle to an uniformity of interests. The protection of these faculties is the first object of government.
James Madison (1751-1836, American Statesman, President)

4 The real death of America will come when everyone is alike.
James T. Ellison

5 Our flag is red, white and blue, but our nation is a rainbow -- red, yellow, brown, black and white -- and we're all precious in God's sight.
Jesse Jackson (1941-, American Clergyman, Civil Rights Leader)

6 America is not a blanket woven from one thread, one color, one cloth.
Jesse Jackson (1941-, American Clergyman, Civil Rights Leader)

7 You never realize how short a month is until you have to pay alimony.
John Barrymore (1882-1942, American Actor)

8 Diversity: the art of thinking independently together.
Malcolm S. Forbes (1919-1990, American Publisher, Businessman)

9 Ultimately, America's answer to the intolerant man is diversity, the very diversity which our heritage of religious freedom has inspired.
Robert F. Kennedy (1925-1968, American Attorney General, Senator)

DIVINITY

1 My appointed work is to awaken the divine nature that is within.
Peace Pilgrim (1908-1981, American Peace Activist)

2 We are Divine enough to ask and we are important enough to receive.
Wayne Dyer (1940-, American Psychotherapist, Author, Lecturer)

DIVORCE

1 Divorce. A resumption of diplomatic relations and rectification of boundaries.
Ambrose Bierce (1842-1914, American Author, Editor, Journalist, "The Devil's Dictionary")

2 Divorce is a game played by lawyers.
Cary Grant (1904-1986, British-born American Actor)

3 You know, that's the only good thing about divorce; you get to sleep with your mother.
Clare Boothe Luce (1903-1987, American Diplomat, Writer)

4 The possibility of divorce renders both marriage partners stricter in their observance of the duties they owe to each other. Divorces help to improve morals and to increase the population.
Denis Diderot (1713-1784, French Philosopher)

5 A New York divorce is in itself a diploma of virtue.
Edith Wharton (1862-1937, American Author)

6 Two lives that once part are as ships that divide.
Edward G. Bulwer-Lytton (1803-1873, British Novelist, Poet)

7 Many divorces are not really the result of irreparable injury but involve, instead, a desire on the part of the man or woman to shatter the setup, start out from scratch alone, and make life work for them all over again. They want the risk of disaster, want to touch bottom, see where bottom is, and, coming up, to breathe the air with relief and relish again.
Edward Hoagland (1932-, American Novelist, Essayist)

8 Divorce is the sacrament of adultery.
French Proverb

9 Divorce is a declaration of independence with only two signers.
Gerald F. Lieberman (American Writer)

10 France may claim the happiest marriages in the world, but the happiest divorces in the world are "made in America."
Helen Rowland (1875-1950, American Journalist)

11 When two people decide to get a divorce, it isn't a sign that they "don't understand" one another, but a sign that they have, at last, begun to.
Helen Rowland (1875-1950, American Journalist)

12 Love, the quest; marriage, the conquest; divorce, the inquest.
Helen Rowland (1875-1950, American Journalist)

13 Being divorced is like being hit by a Mack truck. If you live through it, you start looking very carefully to the right and to the left.
Jean Kerr (1923-, American Author, Playwright)

14 People named John and Mary never divorce. For better or for worse, in madness and in saneness, they seem bound together for eternity by their rudimentary nomenclature. They may loathe and despise one another, quarrel, weep, and commit mayhem, but they are not free to divorce. Tom, Dick, and Harry can go to Reno on a whim, but nothing short of death can separate John and Mary.
John Cheever (1912-1982, American Author)

15 My divorce came to me as a complete surprise. That's what happens when you haven't been home in eighteen years.
Lee Trevino (1939-, American Golfer)

16 The only solid and lasting peace between a man and his wife is, doubtless, a separation.
Lord Chesterfield (1694-1773, British Statesman, Author)

17 It takes two to destroy a marriage.
Margaret Trudeau (Wife of Former Canadian Prime Minister, Pierre Elliott Trudeau)

18 A lot of people have asked me how short I am. Since my last divorce, I think I'm about $100, 000 short.
Mickey Rooney (American Actor)

19 You can't stay married in a situation where you are afraid to go to sleep in case your wife might cut your throat.
Mike Tyson (1966-, American Boxer)

20 It is he who has broken the bond of marriage -- not I. I only break its bondage.
Oscar Wilde (1856-1900, British Author, Wit)

21 A Roman divorced from his wife, being highly blamed by his friends, who demanded, "Was she not chaste? Was she not fair? Was she not fruitful?" holding out his shoe, asked them whether it was not new and well made. "Yet," added he, "none of you can tell where it pinches me.
Plutarch (46-120 AD, Greek Essayist, Biographer)

22 Divorce is the one human tragedy that reduces everything to cash.
Rita Mae Brown (1944-, American Writer)

23 Every divorce is the result of selfishness on the part of one or the other or both parties to a marriage contract. Someone is thinking of self comforts, conveniences, freedoms, luxuries, or ease. Sometimes the ceaseless pin pricking of an unhappy, discontented, and selfish spouse can finally add up to serious physical violence. Sometimes people are goaded to the point where they erringly feel justified in doing the things that are so wrong. Nothing of course justifies sin.
Spencer W. Kimball

24 Like I said, I've got too much respect for women to marry them, but that doesn't mean you can't support them emotionally and financially.
Sylvester Stallone (1946-, American Actor, Writer, Director, Producer)

25 I know one husband and wife who, whatever the official reasons given to the court for the break up of their marriage, were really divorced because the husband believed that nobody ought to read while he was talking and the wife that nobody ought to talk while she was reading.
Vera Brittain (1893-1970, British Writer)

26 Divorce is probably of nearly the same date as marriage. I believe, however, that marriage is some weeks the more ancient.
Voltaire (1694-1778, French Historian, Writer)

27 You never really know a man until you have divorced him.
Zsa Zsa Gabor (1918-, Hungarian-born American Actress)

28 I am a marvelous housekeeper. Every time I leave a man I keep his house.
Zsa Zsa Gabor (1918-, Hungarian-born American Actress)

29 Getting divorced just because you don't love a man is almost as silly as getting married just because you do.
Zsa Zsa Gabor (1918-, Hungarian-born American Actress)

30 Conrad Hilton was very generous to me in the divorce settlement. He gave me 5, 000 Gideon Bibles.
Zsa Zsa Gabor (1918-, Hungarian-born American Actress)

DOCTORS

1 I suppose one has a greater sense of intellectual degradation after an interview with a doctor than from any human experience.
Alice James (1848-1892, American Diarist, Sister of Henry, William James)

2 Doctors are just the same as lawyers; the only difference is that lawyers merely rob you, whereas doctors rob you and kill you too.
Anton Chekhov (1860-1904, Russian Playwright, Short Story Writer)

3 God heals and the doctor takes the fee.
Benjamin Franklin (1706-1790, American Scientist, Publisher, Diplomat)

4 The superior doctor prevents sickness; The mediocre doctor attends to impending sickness; The inferior doctor treats actual sickness;
Chinese Proverb

5 Employment is nature's physician, and is essential to human happiness.
Claudius Galen (130-200, Physician born in Pergamus)

6 The best doctor is the one you run to and can't find.
Denis Diderot (1713-1784, French Philosopher)

7 The more ignorant, reckless and thoughtless a doctor is, the higher his reputation soars even amongst powerful princes.
Desiderius Erasmus (1466-1536, Dutch Humanist)

8 The majority of the diseases which the human family have been and still are suffering under, they have created by ignorance of their own organic health, and work perseveringly to tear themselves to pieces, and when broken down and debilitated in body and mind, send for the doctor and drug themselves to death.
Ellen Gould White (1827-1915, American Seventh-day Adventist Leader)

9 Surgeons must be very careful. When they take the knife!, underneath their fine incisions, stirs the Culprit -- Life!
Emily Dickinson (1830-1886, American Poet)

10 When a man goes through six years training to be a doctor he will never be the same. He knows too much.
Enid Bagnold (1889-1981, British Novelist, Playwright)

11 Never go to a doctor whose office plants have died.
Erma Bombeck (1927-, American Author, Humorist)

12 I have noticed that doctors who fail in the practice of medicine have a tendency to seek one another's company and aid in consultation. A doctor who cannot take out your appendix properly will recommend you to a doctor who will be unable to remove your tonsils with success.
Ernest Hemingway (1898-1961, American Writer)

13 Instead of wishing to see more doctors made by women joining what there are, I wish to see as few doctors, either male or female, as possible. For, mark you, the women have made no improvement -- they have only tried to be "men" and they have only succeeded in being third-rate men.
Florence Nightingale (1820-1910, British Nurse)

14 Cure the disease and kill the patient.
Francis Bacon (1561-1626, British Philosopher, Essayist, Statesman)

15 There are more old drunkards than old physicians.
Frantois Rabelais (1495-1553, French Satirist, Physician, and Humanist)

16 A surgeon should be young a physician old.
French Proverb

17 The doctor learns that if he gets ahead of the superstitions of his patients he is a ruined man; and the result is that he instinctively takes care not to get ahead of them.
George Bernard Shaw (1856-1950, Irish-born British Dramatist)

18 Every doctor will allow a colleague to decimate a whole countryside sooner than violate the bond of professional etiquette by giving him away.
George Bernard Shaw (1856-1950, Irish-born British Dramatist)

19 Deceive not thy physician, confessor, nor lawyer.
George Herbert (1593-1632, British Metaphysical Poet)

20 Nature, time and patience are the three great physicians.
H. G. Bohn (British Publisher)

21 Physician, heal thyself.
Hebrew Proverb

22 Whenever a doctor cannot do good, he must be kept from doing harm.
Hippocrates (Ancient Greek Physician)

23 Life is short, the art long, opportunity fleeting, experiment treacherous, judgment difficult.
Hippocrates (Ancient Greek Physician)

24 Every invalid is a physician.
Irish Proverb

25 Temperance and labor are the two real physicians of man.
Jean Jacques Rousseau (1712-1778, Swiss Political Philosopher, Educationist, Essayist)

26 One of the fundamental reasons why so many doctors become cynical and disillusioned is precisely because, when the abstract idealism has worn thin, they are uncertain about the value of the actual lives of the patients they are treating. This is not because they are callous or personally inhuman: it is because they live in and accept a society which is incapable of knowing what a human life is worth.
John Berger (1926-, British Actor, Critic)

27 I observe the physician with the same diligence as the disease.
John Donne (1572-1632, British Metaphysical Poet)

28 I wasn't driven into medicine by a social conscience but by rampant curiosity.
Jonathan Miller (1934-, British Actor, Director)

29 The best doctors in the world are Doctor Diet, Doctor Quiet, and Doctor Merryman.
Jonathan Swift (1667-1745, Anglo-Irish Satirist)

30 There are worse occupations in this world than feeling a woman's pulse.
Laurence Sterne (1713-1768, British Author)

31 For each illness that doctors cure with medicine, they provoke ten in healthy people by inoculating them with the virus that is a thousand times more powerful than any microbe: the idea that one is ill.
Marcel Proust (1871-1922, French Novelist)

32 He has been a doctor a year now and has had two patients, no, three, I think -- yes, it was three; I attended their funerals.
Mark Twain (1835-1910, American Humorist, Writer)

33 The practice of medicine is a thinker's art, the practice of surgery a plumber s.
Martin H. Fisher

34 Cured yesterday of my disease, I died last night of my physician.
Matthew Prior (1664-1721, British Diplomat, Poet)

35 Doctors will have more lives to answer for in the next world than even we generals.
Napoleon Bonaparte (1769-1821, French General, Emperor)

36 The doctor found, when she was dead, her last disorder mortal.
Oliver Goldsmith (1728-1774, Anglo-Irish Author, Poet, Playwright)

37 What I call a good patient is one who, having found a good physician, sticks to him till he dies.
Oliver Wendell Holmes (1809-1894, American Author, Wit, Poet)

38 Time is generally the best doctor.
Ovid (43 BC-18 AD, Roman Poet)

39 Is it not also true that no physician, in so far as he is a physician, considers or enjoins what is for the physician's interest, but that all seek the good of their patients? For we have agreed that a physician strictly so called, is a ruler of bodies, and not a maker of money, have we not?
Plato (427-347 BC, Greek Philosopher)

40 A skilful leech is better far, than half a hundred men of war.
Samuel Butler (1612-1680, British Poet, Satirist)

41 The physician's highest calling, his only calling, is to make sick people healthy -- to heal, as it is termed.
Samuel Hahnemann (1755-1843, German Physician, Founder of Homeopathy)

42 If the doctor cures, the sun sees it; if he kills, the earth hides it.
Scottish Proverb

43 The doctor should be opaque to his patients and, like a mirror, should show them nothing but what is shown to him.
Sigmund Freud (1856-1939, Austrian Physician - Founder of Psychoanalysis)

44 When a doctor does go wrong he is the first of criminals. He has nerve and he has knowledge.
Sir Arthur Conan Doyle (1859-1930, British Author, "Sherlock Holmes")

45 The first duties of the physician is to educate the masses not to take medicine.
Sir William Osler (1849-1919, Canadian Physician)

46 It is the duty of a doctor to prolong life and it is not his duty to prolong the act of dying.
Thomas Horder

47 For what Harley Street specialist has time to understand the body, let alone the mind or both in combination, when he is a slave to thirteen thousand a year?
Virginia Woolf (1882-1941, British Novelist, Essayist)

48 Doctors are men who prescribe medicines of which they know little, to cure diseases of which they know less, in human beings of whom they know nothing.
Voltaire (1694-1778, French Historian, Writer)

49 Men who are occupied in the restoration of health to other men, by the joint exertion of skill and humanity, are above all the great of the earth. They even partake of divinity, since to preserve and renew is almost as noble as to create.
Voltaire (1694-1778, French Historian, Writer)

50 I know of nothing more laughable than a doctor who does not die of old age.
Voltaire (1694-1778, French Historian, Writer)

51 A doctor, like anyone else who has to deal with human beings, each of them unique, cannot be a scientist; he is either, like the surgeon, a craftsman, or, like the physician and the psychologist, an artist. This means that in order to be a good doctor a man must also have a good character, that is to say, whatever weaknesses and foibles he may have, he must love his fellow human beings in the concrete and desire their good before his own.
W. H. Auden (1907-1973, Anglo-American Poet)

52 I asked [my doctors] if I'd be able to play singles tennis and they said I could. That made me very happy since I haven't played in five years.
Walter Cronkite (1916-, American Broadcast Journalist)

53 My doctor gave me six months to live but when I couldn't pay the bill, he gave me six months more.
Walter Matthau (1920-, American Actor)

54 Doctors don't know everything really. They understand matter, not spirit. And you and I live in spirit.
William Saroyan (1908-1981, American Writer, Novelist,, Playwright)

DOCTRINE

1   A striking feature of moral and political argument in the modern world is the extent to which it is innovators, radicals, and revolutionaries who revive old doctrines, while their conservative and reactionary opponents are the inventors of new ones.
Alasdair Chalmers Macintyre

2   The greatest horrors in the history of mankind are not due to the ambition of the Napoleons or the vengeance of the Agamemnons, but to the doctrinaire philosophers. The theories of the sentimentalist Rousseau inspired the integrity of the passionless Robespierre. The cold-blooded calculations of Karl Marx led to the judicial and business-like operations of the Cheka.
Aleister Crowley (1875-1947, British Occultist)

3   It was then that I began to look into the seams of your doctrine. I wanted only to pick at a single knot; but when I had got that undone, the whole thing raveled out. And then I understood that it was all machine-sewn.
Henrik Ibsen (1828-1906, Norwegian Dramatist)

4   The American doctrinaire is the converse of the American demagogue, and, in this way, is scarcely less injurious to the public. The first deals in poetry, the last in cant. He is as much a visionary on one side, as the extreme theoretical democrat is a visionary on the other.
James F. Cooper (1789-1851, American Novelist)

5   A doctrinaire is a fool but an honest man.
Lord Melbourne (1779-1848, British Statesman, Prime Minister)

6   A doctrine serves no purpose in itself, but it is indispensable to have one if only to avoid being deceived by false doctrines.
Simone Weil (1910-1943, French Philosopher, Mystic)

7   A faith is something you die for, a doctrine is something you kill for. There is all the difference in the world.
Tony Benn (1925-, British Labor Politician)

DOGS

1   How many legs does a dog have if you call the tail a leg? Four. Calling a tail a leg doesn't make it a leg.
Abraham Lincoln (1809-1865, Sixteenth President of the USA)

2   Dog. A kind of additional or subsidiary Deity designed to catch the overflow and surplus of the world's worship.
Ambrose Bierce (1842-1914, American Author, Editor, Journalist, "The Devil's Dictionary")

3   The more I see of men, the more I like dogs.
Clara Bow (1965-, American Actress)

4   In order to really enjoy a dog, one doesn't merely try to train him to be semi-human. The point of it is to open oneself to the possibility of becoming partly a dog.
Edward Hoagland (1932-, American Novelist, Essayist)

5   If a dog doesn't put you first where are you both? In what relation? A dog needs God. It lives by your glances, your wishes. It even shares your humor. This happens about the fifth year. If it doesn't happen you are only keeping an animal.
Enid Bagnold (1889-1981, British Novelist, Playwright)

6   If you are a dog and your owner suggests that you wear a sweater suggest that he wear a tail.
Fran Lebowitz (1951-, American Journalist)

7   I always disliked dogs, those protectors of cowards who lack the courage to fight an assailant themselves.
J. August Strindberg (1849-1912, Swedish Dramatist, Novelist, Poet)

8   You may drive a dog off the King's armchair, and it will climb into the preacher's pulpit; he views the world unmoved, unembarrassed, unabashed.
Jean De La Bruyere (1645-1696, French Writer)

9   Near this spot are deposited the remains of one who possessed Beauty without Vanity, Strength without Insolence, Courage without Ferocity, and all the Virtues of Man without his Vices. This praise, which would be unmeaning Flattery, if inscribed over human ashes, is but a just Tribute to the Memory of BOATSWAIN, a Dog.
John Cam Hobhouse

10   A door is what a dog is perpetually on the wrong side of.
Ogden Nash (1902-1971, American Humorous Poet)

11   A dog teaches a boy fidelity, perseverance, and to turn around three times before lying down.
Robert Benchley (1889-1945, American Humorist, Critic, Parodist)

12   The great pleasure of a dog is that you may make a fool of yourself with him and not only will he not scold you, but he will make a fool of himself too.
Samuel Butler (1612-1680, British Poet, Satirist)

13   His friends he loved. His direst earthly foes -- cats -- I believe he did but feign to hate. My hand will miss the insinuated nose, mine eyes the tail that wagg'd contempt at Fate.
Sir William Watson (1858-1935, British Poet)

14   Extraordinary creature! So close a friend, and yet so remote.
Thomas Mann (1875-1955, German Author, Critic)

15   The meeting in the open of two dogs, strangers to each other, is one of the most painful, thrilling, and pregnant of all conceivable encounters; it is surrounded by an atmosphere of the last canniness, presided over by a constraint for which I have no precise name; they simply cannot pass each other, their mutual embarrassment is frightful to behold.
Thomas Mann (1875-1955, German Author, Critic)

16   The nose of the bulldog has been slanted backwards so that he can breathe without letting go.
Winston Churchill (1874-1965, British Statesman, Prime Minister)

DOUBT

1 True wisdom is less presuming than folly. The wise man doubteth often, and changeth his mind; the fool is obstinate, and doubteth not; he knoweth all things but his own ignorance.
Akhenaton (1375 BC, Egyptian King, Monotheist)

2 Doubt, the essential preliminary of all improvement and discovery, must accompany the stages of man's onward progress. The faculty of doubting and questioning, without which those of comparison and judgment would be useless, is itself a divine prerogative of the reason.
Albert Pike (1809-1891, American Lawyer, Masonic Author, Historian)

3 A person who doubts himself is like a man who would enlist in the ranks of his enemies and bear arms against himself. He makes his failure certain by himself being the first person to be convinced of it.
Alexandre Dumas (1802-1870, French Novelist, Dramatist)

4 Despair is the conclusion of fools.
Benjamin Disraeli (1804-1881, British Statesman, Prime Minister)

5 In all affairs it's a healthy thing now and then to hang a question mark on the things you have long taken for granted.
Bertrand Russell (1872-1970, British Philosopher, Mathematician, Essayist)

6 The whole problem with the world is that fools and fanatics are always so certain of themselves, but wiser people so full of doubts.
Bertrand Russell (1872-1970, British Philosopher, Mathematician, Essayist)

7 Neither in this world nor elsewhere is there any happiness in store for him who always doubts.
Bhagavad Gita (400 BC, Sanskrit Poem Incorporated Into the Mahabharata)

8 Everybody in the world thought we couldn't do it. But we did, dammit. [After winning the America's Cup]
Bill Koch (1946-, American Skipper)

9 There is nothing more dreadful than the habit of doubt. Doubt separates people. It is a poison that disintegrates friendships and breaks up pleasant relations. It is a thorn that irritates and hurts; it is a sword that kills.
Buddha (568-488 BC, Founder of Buddhism)

10 Doubt is the vestibule through which all must pass before they can enter into the temple of wisdom.
Charles Caleb Colton (1780-1832, British Sportsman Writer)

11 Great doubts deep wisdom. Small doubts little wisdom.
Chinese Proverb

12 Doubt whom you will, but never yourself.
Christian Nevell Bovee (1820-1904, American Author, Lawyer)

13 Just think of the tragedy of teaching children not to doubt.
Clarence Darrow (1857-1938, American Lawyer)

14 Never despair, but if you do, work on in despair.
Edmund Burke (1729-1797, British Political Writer, Statesman)

15 Philosophy when superficially studied, excites doubt, when thoroughly explored, it dispels it.
Francis Bacon (1561-1626, British Philosopher, Essayist, Statesman)

16 Suspicion amongst thoughts are like bats amongst birds, they never fly by twilight.
Francis Bacon (1561-1626, British Philosopher, Essayist, Statesman)

17 Suspicions that the mind, of itself, gathers, are but buzzes; but suspicions that are artificially nourished and put into men's heads by the tales and whisperings of others, have stings.
Francis Bacon (1561-1626, British Philosopher, Essayist, Statesman)

18 In contemplation, if a man begins with certainties he shall end in doubts; but if he be content to begin with doubts, he shall end in certainties.
Francis Bacon (1561-1626, British Philosopher, Essayist, Statesman)

19 The road to perseverance lies by doubt.
Francis Quarles (1592-1644, British Poet)

20 Doubt is the father of invention.
Galileo Galilei (1564-1642, Italian Astronomer, Mathematician)

21 There is no despair so absolute as that which comes with the first moments of our first great sorrow, when we have not yet known what it is to have suffered and be healed, to have despaired and have recovered hope.
George Eliot (1819-1880, British Novelist)

22 He that knows nothing doubts nothing.
George Herbert (1593-1632, British Metaphysical Poet)

23 Doubt is the beginning, not the end, of wisdom.
George Iles

24 I wish I could be half as sure of anything as some people are of everything.
Gerald Barzan

25 Men become civilized, not in proportion to their willingness to believe, but in proportion to their readiness to doubt.
H. L. Mencken (1880-1956, American Editor, Author, Critic, Humorist)

26 There is no rule more invariable than that we are paid for our suspicions by finding what we suspect.
Henry David Thoreau (1817-1862, American Essayist, Poet, Naturalist)

27 Faith keeps many doubts in her pay. If I could not doubt, I should not believe.
Henry David Thoreau (1817-1862, American Essayist, Poet, Naturalist)

28 Doubt is the incentive to truth and inquiry leads the way.
Hosea Ballou (1771-1852, American Theologian, Founder of "Universalism")

29 Doubt can only be removed by action.
Johann Wolfgang Von Goethe (1749-1832, German Poet, Dramatist, Novelist)

30 We know accurately only when we know little, with knowledge doubt increases.
Johann Wolfgang Von Goethe (1749-1832, German Poet, Dramatist, Novelist)

31 I will listen to anyone's convictions, but pray keep your doubts to yourself.
Johann Wolfgang Von Goethe (1749-1832, German Poet, Dramatist, Novelist)

32 There was a castle called Doubting Castle, the owner whereof was Giant Despair.
John Bunyan (1628-1688, British Author)

33 Despair is the damp of hell, as joy is the serenity of heaven.
John Donne (1572-1632, British Metaphysical Poet)

34 Doubt is a pain too lonely to know that faith is his twin brother.
Kahlil Gibran (1883-1931, Lebanese Poet, Novelist)

35 There lives more faith in honest doubt, Believe me, than in half the creeds.
Lord Alfred Tennyson (1809-1892, British Poet)

36 There is no greater folly in the world than for a man to despair.
Miguel De Cervantes (1547-1616, Spanish Novelist, Dramatist, Poet)

37 Life is doubt, and faith without doubt is nothing but death.
Miguel De Unamuno (1864-1936, Spanish Philosophical Writer)

38 To have doubted one's own first principles is the mark of a civilized man.
Oliver Wendell Holmes (1809-1894, American Author, Wit, Poet)

39 Doubt is the key to knowledge.
Persian Proverb

40 Who never doubted, never half believed. Where doubt is, there truth is -- it is her shadow.
Philip James Bailey (1816-1902, British Poet)

41 To doubt is worse than to have lost; And to despair is but to antedate those miseries that must fall on us.
Philip Massinger (1583-1640, British Dramatist)

42 If you would be a real seeker after truth, it is necessary that at least once in your life you doubt, as far as possible, all things.
Rene Descartes (1596-1650, French Philosopher, Scientist)

43 Doubt, of whatever kind, can be ended by action alone.
Thomas Carlyle (1795-1881, Scottish Philosopher, Author)

44 The fearful unbelief is unbelief in yourself.
Thomas Carlyle (1795-1881, Scottish Philosopher, Author)

45 Doubt is to certainty as neurosis is to psychosis. The neurotic is in doubt and has fears about persons and things; the psychotic has convictions and makes claims about them. In short, the neurotic has problems, the psychotic has solutions.
Thomas Szasz (1920-, American Psychiatrist)

46 Doubt, indulged and cherished, is in danger of becoming denial; but if honest, and bent on thorough investigation, it may soon lead to full establishment of the truth.
Tryon Edwards (1809-1894, American Theologian)

47 An honest man can never surrender an honest doubt.
Walter Malone (1866-1915, American Jurist)

48 If the Sun and Moon should ever doubt, they'd immediately go out.
William Blake (1757-1827, British Poet, Painter)

49 Modest doubt is called the beacon of the wise.
William Shakespeare (1564-1616, British Poet, Playwright, Actor)

50 Our doubts are traitors and make us lose the good we might win, by fearing to attempt.[Measure For Measure]
William Shakespeare (1564-1616, British Poet, Playwright, Actor)

51 I respect faith, but doubt is what gets you an education.
Wilson Mizner (1876-1933, American Author)

52 When you doubt, abstain.
Zoroaster (628-551 BC, Persian Religious Leader-Founder of Zoroastrianism)

DRAFT

1 People have not been horrified by war to a sufficient extent... War will exist until that distant day when the conscientious objector enjoys the same reputation and prestige as the warrior does today.
John F. Kennedy (1917-1963, Thirty-fifth President of the USA)

2 A young man who does not have what it takes to perform military service is not likely to have what it takes to make a living.
John F. Kennedy (1917-1963, Thirty-fifth President of the USA)

3 Pressed into service means pressed out of shape.
Robert Frost (1875-1963, American Poet)

DRAWING

1 I could draw Bloom County with my nose and pay my cleaning lady to write it, and I'd bet I wouldn't lose 10 % of my papers over the next twenty years. Such is the nature of comic-strips. Once established, their half-life is usually more than nuclear waste.
Berke Breathed

2 My drawings have been described as pre-internationalist, meaning that they were finished before the ideas for them had occurred to me. I shall not argue the point.
James Thurber (1894-1961, American Humorist, Illustrator)

3 A drawing is always dragged down to the level of its caption.
James Thurber (1894-1961, American Humorist, Illustrator)

4 Matisse makes a drawing, then he makes a copy of it. He recopies it five times, ten times, always clarifying the line. He's convinced that the last, the most stripped down, is the best, the purest, the definitive one; and in fact, most of the time, it was the first. In drawing, nothing is better than the first attempt.
Pablo Picasso (1881-1973, Spanish Artist)

5 In the final analysis, a drawing simply is no longer a drawing, no matter how self-sufficient its execution may be. It is a symbol, and the more profoundly the imaginary lines of projection meet higher dimensions, the better.
Paul Klee (1879-1940, Swiss Artist)

6 There is a relationship between cartooning and people like Mir= and Picasso which may not be understood by the cartoonist, but it definitely is related even in the early Disney.
Roy Lichtenstein (1923, American Artist)

DREAMS

1 I dream of a place and a time where America will once again be seen as the last best hope of earth.
Abraham Lincoln (1809-1865, Sixteenth President of the USA)

2 Those who dream by day are cognizant of many things which escape those who dream only by night.
Alexander Pope (1688-1744, British Poet, Critic, Translator)

3 To accomplish great things we must first dream, then visualize, then plan... believe... act!
Alfred A. Montapert (American Author)

4 Our dreams drench us in senses, and senses steps us again in dreams.
Amos Bronson Alcott (1799-1888, American Educator, Social Reformer)

5 Dreams are necessary to life.
Anais Nin (1914-1977, French-born American Novelist, Dancer)

6 You're in the midst of a war: a battle between the limits of a crowd seeking the surrender of your dreams, and the power of your true vision to create and contribute. It is a fight between those who will tell you what you cannot do, and that part of you that knows -- and has always known -- that we are more than our environment; and that a dream, backed by an unrelenting will to attain it, is truly a reality with an imminent arrival.
Anthony Robbins (1960-, American Author, Speaker, Peak Performance Expert / Consultant)

7 There are those, I know, who will reply that the liberation of humanity, the freedom of man and mind, is nothing but a dream. They are right. It is. It is the American Dream.
Archibald Macleish (1892-1982, American Poet)

8 The smaller the head, the bigger the dream.
Austin O'Malley

9 Initially I wanted to be Muhammad Ali. But then I got into a fight and I got my butt kicked, so I figured I could choose something else.
Babyface (1959-, American Musician, Producer, Songwriter)

10 You must go after your wish. As soon as you start to pursue a dream, your life wakes up and everything has meaning.
Barbara Sher (American Author of "I Could Do Anything If I Only Knew What It Was")

11 And our dreams are who we are.
Barbara Sher (American Author of "I Could Do Anything If I Only Knew What It Was")

12 Don't be afraid of the space between your dreams and reality. If you can dream it, you can make it so.
Belva Davis

13 To dream anything that you want to dream, that is the beauty of the human mind. To do anything that you want to do, that is the strength of the human will. To trust yourself, to test your limits, that is the courage to succeed.
Bernard Edmonds (American Writer)

14 Who so regardeth dreams is like him that catcheth at a shadow, and followeth after the wind. [Ecclesiasticus 34:2]
Bible (Sacred Scriptures of Christians and Judaism)

15 Aim for your star, no matter how far, you must reach high above and touch your life with love, you must never look back, but charge on! Attack! See your goal your star of desire, see it red hot, feel it burning, you must be obsessed with it to make it your true yearning, be ready my friends for when you truly believe it, you will certainly achieve it and by all of God's universal laws you will always receive it!
Bob Smith (American Editor, Author, Founder of Orison Swett Marden Foundation)

16 It is on the whole probably that we continually dream, but that consciousness makes such a noise that we do not hear it.
Carl Jung (1875-1961, Swiss Psychiatrist)

17 Nothing happens unless first a dream.
Carl Sandburg (1878-1967, American Poet)

18 I dreamed a thousand new paths. I woke and walked my old one.
Chinese Proverb

19 I dream of you to wake; would that I might Dream of you and not wake but slumber on...
Christina Rossetti (1830-1894, British Poet, Lyricist)

20 Dreams are renewable. No matter what our age or condition, there are still untapped possibilities within us and new beauty waiting to be born.
Dale Turner

21 America has been a land of dreams. A land where the aspirations of people from countries cluttered with rich, cumbersome, aristocratic, ideological pasts can reach for what once seemed unattainable. Here they have tried to make dreams come true. Yet now... we are threatened by a new and particularly American menace. It is not the menace of class war, of ideology, of poverty, of disease, of illiteracy, or demagoguery, or of tyranny, though these now plague most of the world. It is the menace of unreality.
Daniel J. Boorstin (1914-, American Historian)

22 We've got to have a dream if we are going to make a dream come true.
Denis Waitley (1933-, American Author, Speaker, Trainer, Peak Performance Expert)

23 A dream is your creative vision for your life in the future. You must break out of your current comfort zone and become comfortable with the unfamiliar and the unknown.
Denis Waitley (1933-, American Author, Speaker, Trainer, Peak Performance Expert)

24 Don't ever let anyone steal your dreams.
Dexter Yager

25 You can't just sit there and wait for people to give you that golden dream. You've got to get out there and make it happen for yourself.
Diana Ross (1944-, American Singer, Actress)

26 Dreams have only the pigmentation of fact.
Djuna Barnes (1892-1982, American Author, Poet, Columnist)

27 If you're going to be thinking, you may as well think big.
Donald Trump (1946-, 45th President of the United States of America)

28 You have to think anyway, so why not think big?
Donald Trump (1946-, 45th President of the United States of America)

29 He felt that his whole life was some kind of dream and he sometimes wondered whose it was and whether they were enjoying it.
Douglas Adams (Born 1952, British Science Fiction Writer)

30 Before your dreams can come true, you have to have those dreams.
Dr. Joyce Brothers (1927-, American Psychologist, Television and Radio Personality)

31 You're the only one who can make the difference. Whatever your dream is, go for it.
Earvin "Magic" Johnson (1959-, American Basketball Player)

32 All that we see or seem, is but a dream within a dream.
Edgar Allan Poe (1809-1845, American Poet, Critic, short-story Writer)

33 Deep into that darkness peering, long I stood there, wondering, fearing, doubting, dreaming dreams no mortal ever dared to dream before.
Edgar Allan Poe (1809-1845, American Poet, Critic, short-story Writer)

34 Dream manfully and nobly, and thy dreams shall be prophets.
Edward G. Bulwer-Lytton (1803-1873, British Novelist, Poet)

35 Ah, great it is to believe the dream as we stand in youth by the starry stream; but a greater thing is to fight life through and say at the end, the dream is true!
Edwin Markham (1852-1940, American Poet and Editor)

36 The future belongs to those who believe in the beauty of their dreams.
Eleanor Roosevelt (1884-1962, American First Lady, Columnist, Lecturer, Humanitarian)

37 When I dream, I am ageless.
Elizabeth Coatsworth (1893-1986, American Writer, Poet)

38 I wanted so badly to study ballet, but it was really all about wearing the tutu. [On the subject of her early aspirations]
Elle Macpherson (1965-, Australian Model, Actress)

39 I have dreamed in my life, dreams that have stayed with me ever after, and changed my ideas; they have gone through and through me, like wine through water, and altered the color of my mind.
Emily Bronte (1818-1848, British Novelist, Poet)

40 You've got to create a dream. You've got to uphold the dream. If you can't, go back to the factory or go back to the desk.
Eric Burdon

41 We do not really feel grateful toward those who make our dreams come true; they ruin our dreams.
Eric Hoffer (1902-1983, American Author, Philosopher)

42 Ideologies separate us. Dreams and anguish bring us together.
Eugene Ionesco (1912-, Romanian-born French Playwright)

43 The main reason I wanted to be successful was to get out of the ghetto. My parents helped direct my path.
Florence Griffith-Joyner (1959-, American Track Athlete)

44 Dreaming is an act of pure imagination, attesting in all men a creative power, which, if it were available in waking, would make every man a Dante or Shakespeare.
Francis Herbert Hedge (1846-1924, British Philosopher)

45 He dreamed he was eating shredded wheat and woke up to find the mattress half gone.
Fred A. Allen (1894-1957, American Radio Comic)

46 I believe that any single dream contains the essential message about our existence.
Frederick Salomon Perls (1893-1970, German Psychiatrist)

47 Reverie is not a mind vacuum. It is rather the gift of an hour which knows the plenitude of the soul.
Gaston Bachelard (1884-1962, French Scientist, Philosopher, Literary Theorist)

48 It is never too late to be what you might have been.
George Eliot (1819-1880, British Novelist)

49 Our dreams are a second life. I have never been able to penetrate without a shudder those ivory or horned gates which separate us from the invisible world.
Gerard De Nerval (1808-1855, French Novelist, Poet)

50 When we can't dream any longer, we die.
Goldman Emma (Russian Writer)

51 I remember when I was in school, they would ask, "What are you going to be when you grow up?" and then you'd have to draw a picture of it. I drew a picture of myself as a bride.
Gwen Stefani (Born 1969, American Musician)

52 Dreams are real as long as they last. Can we say more of life?
Havelock Ellis (1859-1939, British Psychologist)

53 Dreams show you that you have the power...
Helen Schucman

54 Castles in the air - -they are so easy to take refuge in. And so easy to build as well.
Henrik Ibsen (1828-1906, Norwegian Dramatist)

55 If you have built castles in the air, your work need not be lost; that is where they should be. Now put the foundations under them.
Henry David Thoreau (1817-1862, American Essayist, Poet, Naturalist)

56 If one advances confidently in the directions of his dreams, and endeavors to live the life which he has imagined, he will meet with a success unexpected in common hours.
Henry David Thoreau (1817-1862, American Essayist, Poet, Naturalist)

57 Our truest life is when we are in our dreams awake.
Henry David Thoreau (1817-1862, American Essayist, Poet, Naturalist)

58 I always have to dream up there against the stars. If I don't dream I will make it, I won't even get close.
Henry J. Kaiser (1882-1967, American Industrialist)

59 The dreamer whose dreams are non-utilitarian has no place in this world. In this world the poet is anathema, the thinker a fool, the artist an escapist, the man of vision a criminal.
Henry Miller (1891-1980, American Author)

60 One half the world must sweat and groan that the other half may dream.
Henry Wadsworth Longfellow (1819-1892, American Poet)

61 Only things the dreamers make live on. They are the eternal conquerors.
Herbert Kaufman

62 When asked what he would do if he only had six months to live: Type faster.
Isaac Asimov (1920-1992, Russian-born American Author)

63 I dream, therefore I exist.
J. August Strindberg (1849-1912, Swedish Dramatist, Novelist, Poet)

64 Dream lofty dreams, and as you dream, so shall you become. Your vision is the promise of what you shall one day be; your ideal is the prophecy of what you shall at last unveil.
James Allen (1864-1912, British-born American Essayist, Author of "As a Man Thinketh")

65 Dream as if you'll live forever. Live as if you'll die tomorrow.
James Dean (1931-1955, American Actor)

66 All men of action are dreamers.
James G. Huneker (1860-1921, American Critic, Musician)

67 One of the characteristics of the dream is that nothing surprises us in it. With no regret, we agree to live in it with strangers, completely cut off from our habits and friends.
Jean Cocteau (1889-1963, French Author, Filmmaker)

68 We've removed the ceiling above our dreams. There are no more impossible dreams.
Jesse Jackson (1941-, American Clergyman, Civil Rights Leader)

69 Be a dreamer. If you don't know how to dream, you're dead.
Jim Valvano (American College Basketball Coach)

70 When your heart is in your dream, no request is too extreme.
Jiminy Cricket (Cartoon Character)

71 Keep true to the dreams of your youth.
Johann Friedrich Von Schiller (1759-1805, German Dramatist, Poet, Historian)

72 Dream no small dreams for they have no power to move the hearts of men.
Johann Wolfgang Von Goethe (1749-1832, German Poet, Dramatist, Novelist)

73 I have heard it said that the first ingredient of success -- the earliest spark in the dreaming youth -- if this; dream a great dream.
John A. Appleman

74 A man is not old until regrets take the place of dreams.
John Barrymore (1882-1942, American Actor)

75 Our heart oft times wakes when we sleep, and God can speak to that, either by words, by proverbs, by signs and similitudes, as well as if one was awake.
John Bunyan (1628-1688, British Author)

76 I do not understand the capricious lewdness of the sleeping mind.
John Cheever (1912-1982, American Author)

77 It's not what the dream is but what the dream does.
John Johnson (American Businessman, Founder of Johnson Publishing)

78 Know thyself, believe in God, and dare to dream.
John Salley (Basketball Player)

79 Toil, feel, think, hope; you will be sure to dream enough before you die, without arranging for it.
John Sterling (American Sports Announcer)

80 Dreams come true; without that possibility, nature would not incite us to have them.
John Updike (1932-, American Novelist, Critic)

81 Cutting the space budget really restores my faith in humanity. It eliminates dreams, goals, and ideals and lets us get straight to the business of hate, debauchery, and self-annihilation.
Johnny Hart

82 Follow your bliss.
Joseph Campbell (American Scholar, Writer, Teacher)

83 A man that is born falls into a dream like a man who falls into the sea. If he tries to climb out into the air as inexperienced people endeavor to do, he drowns.
Joseph Conrad (1857-1924, Polish-born British Novelist)

84 I want to keep my dreams, even bad ones, because without them, I might have nothing all night long.
Joseph Heller (1923-, American Author)

85 If your dream is a big dream, and if you want your life to work on the high level that you say you do, there's no way around doing the work it takes to get you there.
Joyce Chapman (American Author)

86 To understand the heart and mind of a person, look not at what he has already achieved, but at what he aspires to do.
Kahlil Gibran (1883-1931, Lebanese Poet, Novelist)

87 All human beings are also dream beings. Dreaming ties all mankind together.
Kerouac Jack (American writer)

88 Hold fast to dreams, for if dreams die, life is a broken winged bird that cannot fly.
Langston Hughes (1902-1967, American Poet, Short-story Writer, Playwright)

89 Everything starts as somebody's day dream.
Larry Niven

90 When you reach for the stars, you may not quite get one, but you won't come up with a handful of mud either.
Leo Burnett (American Marketing Expert)

91 You have the courage and power to live your dreams.
Les Brown (1945-, American Speaker, Author, Trainer, Motivator Lecturer)

92 Help others achieve their dreams and you will achieve yours.
Les Brown (1945-, American Speaker, Author, Trainer, Motivator Lecturer)

93 How many of our daydreams would darken into nightmares, were there a danger of their coming true!
Logan Pearsall Smith (1865-1946, Anglo-American Essayist, Aphorist)

94 Dreams have their place in managerial activity, but they need to be kept severely under control.
Lord Weinstock

95 In bed my real love has always been the sleep that rescued me by allowing me to dream.
Luigi Pirandello (1867-1936, Italian Author, Playwright)

96 When you cease to dream you cease to live.
Malcolm S. Forbes (1919-1990, American Publisher, Businessman)

97 It has never been my object to record my dreams, just the determination to realize them.
Man Ray (1890-1976, American Photographer)

98 If a little dreaming is dangerous, the cure for it is not to dream less but to dream more, to dream all the time.
Marcel Proust (1871-1922, French Novelist)

99 Focus more on your desire than on your doubt, and the dream will take care of itself. You may be surprised at how easily this happens. Your doubts are not as powerful as your desires, unless you make them so.
Marcia Wieder (American Speaker, Trainer, Author)

100 No person has the right to rain on your dreams.
Marian Wright Edelman (1939-, American Lobbyist on Behalf of Children)

101 I don't use drugs, my dreams are frightening enough.
Marie E. Eschenbach

102 You control your future, your destiny. What you think about comes about. By recording your dreams and goals on paper, you set in motion the process of becoming the person you most want to be. Put your future in good hands -- your own.
Mark Victor Hansen (American Motivational Speaker, Author)

103 I have a dream that my four little children will one day live in a nation when they will not be judged by the color of their skin, but by the content of their character.
Martin Luther King Jr. (1929-1968, American Black Leader, Nobel Prize Winner, 1964)

104 Now, I say to you today my friends, even though we face the difficulties of today and tomorrow, I still have a dream. It is a dream deeply rooted in the American dream. I have a dream that one day this nation will rise up and live out the true meaning of its creed: -- we hold these truths to be self-evident, that all men are created equal.
Martin Luther King Jr. (1929-1968, American Black Leader, Nobel Prize Winner, 1964)

105 Because thou must not dream, thou need not despair.
Matthew Arnold (1822-1888, British Poet, Critic)

106 The more you can dream, the more you can do.
Michael Korda (1919-, American publisher)

107 But sure there is need of other remedies than dreaming, a weak contention of art against nature.
Michel Eyquem De Montaigne (1533-1592, French Philosopher, Essayist)

108 Dream is not a revelation. If a dream affords the dreamer some light on himself, it is not the person with closed eyes who makes the discovery but the person with open eyes lucid enough to fit thoughts together. Dream --a scintillating mirage surrounded by shadows --is essentially poetry.
Michel Leiris (1901-1990, French Anthropologist, Author)

[109] Man, alone, has the power to transform his thoughts into physical reality; man, alone, can dream and make his dreams come true.
Napoleon Hill (1883-1970, American Speaker, Motivational Writer, "Think and Grow Rich")

[110] That's one small step for a man, one giant leap for mankind.
Neil Armstrong (1930-, American Astronaut, First Man Stepped on the Moon)

[111] Some people follow their dreams, others hunt them down and beat them mercilessly into submission.
Neil Kendall

[112] Dream big and dare to fail.
Norman D. Vaughan (American Colonel)

[113] We are near waking when we dream we are dreaming.
Novalis (1772-1801, German Poet, Novelist)

[114] You will achieve grand dream, a day at a time, so set goals for each day -- not long and difficult projects, but chores that will take you, step by step, toward your rainbow. Write them down, if you must, but limit your list so that you won't have to drag today's undone matters into tomorrow. Remember that you cannot build your pyramid in twenty-four hours. Be patient. Never allow your day to become so cluttered that you neglect your most important goal -- to do the best you can, enjoy this day, and rest satisfied with what you have accomplished.
Og Mandino (1923-1996, American Motivational Author, Speaker)

[115] If you don't have a dream, how are you going to make a dream come true?
Oscar Hammerstein (1846-1919, Theatrical Impresario; Born in Stettin, Germany)

[116] Society often forgives the criminal; it never forgives the dreamer.
Oscar Wilde (1856-1900, British Author, Wit)

[117] A dreamer is one who can only find his way by moonlight, and his punishment is that he sees the dawn before the rest of the world.
Oscar Wilde (1856-1900, British Author, Wit)

[118] It is a shame that when we have a good dream we are asleep at the time.
P.K. Shaw

[119] Unfortunately, the balance of nature decrees that a super-abundance of dreams is paid for by a growing potential for nightmares.
Peter Ustinov (1921-, British Actor, Writer, Director)

[120] In dream consciousness... we make things happen by wishing them, because we are not only the observer of what we experience but also the creator.
Pir Vilayat Khan (1916-, Western Philosopher Teacher, Master, Author)

[121] Did anyone ever have a boring dream?
Ralph Hodgson (1871-1962, British Poet)

[122] You are never given a dream without also being given the power to make it true. You may have to work for it, however.
Richard Bach (1936-, American Author)

[123] If you have a dream, give it a chance to happen.
Richard M. DeVos (1926-, American Businessman, Co-founder of Amway Corp.)

[124] Dreams get you into the future and add excitement to the present.
Robert Conklin (American Teacher, Author, Speaker)

[125] There are those that look at things the way they are, and ask why? I dream of things that never were, and ask why not.
Robert F. Kennedy (1925-1968, American Attorney General, Senator)

[126] You can often measure a person by the size of his dream.
Robert H. Schuller (1926-, American Minister (Crystal Cathedral), Author, Social Leader)

[127] Are you disappointed, discouraged and discontented with your present level of success? Are you secretly dissatisfied with your present status? Do you want to become a better and more beautiful person than you are today? Would you like to be able to really learn how to be proud of yourself and still not lose genuine humility? Then start dreaming! It's possible! You can become the person you have always wanted to be!
Robert H. Schuller (1926-, American Minister (Crystal Cathedral), Author, Social Leader)

[128] Build a dream and the dream will build you.
Robert H. Schuller (1926-, American Minister (Crystal Cathedral), Author, Social Leader)

[129] It is not for man to rest in absolute contentment. He is born to hopes and aspirations as the sparks fly upward, unless he has brutalized his nature and quenched the spirit of immortality which is his portion.
Robert Southey (1774-1843, British Author)

[130] Only in dreams does the happiness of the earth dwell.
Ruckett

[131] Maybe we are less than our dreams, but that less would make us more than some Gods would dream of.
Sister Corita Kent

[132] Let sleep itself be an exercise in piety, for such as our life and conduct have been, so also of necessity will be our dreams.
St. Basil (329-379, Bishop of Caesarea)

[133] It may be those who do most, dream most.
Stephen B. Leacock (1869-1944, Canadian Humorist, Economist)

[134] All men dream, but unequally. Those that dream at night in the dusty recesses of their minds awake the next day to find that their dreams were just vanity. But those who dream during the day with their eyes wide open are dangerous men; they act out their dreams to make them reality.
Thomas E. Lawrence (1888-1935, British Soldier, Arabist, Writer)

135 I like the dreams of the future better than the history of the past.
Thomas Jefferson (1743-1826, Third President of the USA)

136 If there were dreams to sell, what would you buy?
Thomas Lovell Beddoes (1803-1849, British Poet)

137 Nothing is as real as a dream. The world can change around you, but your dream will not. Responsibilities need not erase it. Duties need not obscure it. Because the dream is within you, no one can take it away.
Tom Clancy (1947-, American Author, "The Hunt for Red October")

138 I'll do my dreaming with my eyes wide open, and I'll do my looking back with my eyes closed.
Tony Arata (American Song Writer)

139 A dream is a scripture, and many scriptures are nothing but dreams.
Umberto Eco (1929-, Italian Novelist and critic)

140 The moment of enlightenment is when a person's dreams of possibilities become images of probabilities.
Vic Braden (American Tennis Coach)

141 A daydream is a meal at which images are eaten. Some of us are gourmets, some gourmands, and a good many take their images precooked out of a can and swallow them down whole, absent- mindedly and with little relish.
W. H. Auden (1907-1973, Anglo-American Poet)

142 If you can dream it, you can do it. Always remember this whole thing was started by a mouse.
Walt Disney (1901-1966, American Artist, Film Producer)

143 You can dream, create, design and build the most wonderful place in the world, but it requires people to make the dream a reality.
Walt Disney (1901-1966, American Artist, Film Producer)

144 Big thinking precedes great achievement.
Wilferd A. Peterson

145 But I, being poor, have only my dreams; I have spread my dreams under your feet; Tread softly because you tread on my dreams.
William Butler Yeats (1865-1939, Irish Poet, Playwright.)

146 Dreaming permits each and everyone of us to be quietly and safely insane every night of our lives.
William Dement

147 The end of wisdom is to dream high enough to lose the dream in the seeking of it.
William Faulkner (1897-1962, American Novelist)

148 There couldn't be a society of people who didn't dream. They'd be dead in two weeks.
William S. Burroughs (1914-1997, American Writer)

149 We are such stuff as dreams are made on, and our little life, is rounded with a sleep. [The Tempest]
William Shakespeare (1564-1616, British Poet, Playwright, Actor)

150 That, if then I had waked after a long sleep, will make me sleep again; and then, in dreaming, the clouds me thought would open and show riches ready to drop upon me; that, when I waked I cried to dream again.
William Shakespeare (1564-1616, British Poet, Playwright, Actor)

151 I have had a most rare vision. I have had a dream past the wit of man to say what dream it was. Man is but an ass if he go about to expound this dream.
William Shakespeare (1564-1616, British Poet, Playwright, Actor)

152 Thought are but dreams till their effects are tried.
William Shakespeare (1564-1616, British Poet, Playwright, Actor)

153 We grow by our dreams.
Woodrow T. Wilson (1856-1924, Twenty-eighth President of the USA)

154 We grow great by dreams. All big men are dreamers.
Woodrow T. Wilson (1856-1924, Twenty-eighth President of the USA)

155 What if nothing exists and we're all in somebody's dream? Or what's worse, what if only that fat guy in the third row exists?
Woody Allen (1935-, American Director, Screenwriter, Actor, Comedian)

156 If you want your dreams to come true, don't over sleep.
Yiddish Proverb

157 A man's dreams are an index to his greatness.
Zadoc Rabinowitz (1494-1553, French Satirist, Physician, Humanist)

DRESS

1 It is principally for the sake of the leg that a change in the dress of man is so much to be desired. The leg is the best part of the figure and the best leg is the man s. Man should no longer disguise the long lines, the strong forms, in those lengths of piping or tubing that are of all garments the most stupid.
Alice Meynell (1847-1922, British Poet, Essayist)

2 Women's sexy underwear is a minor but significant growth industry of late-twentieth-century Britain in the twilight of capitalism.
Angela Carter (1940-1992, British Author)

3 I dress for women and I undress for men.
Angie Dickenson

4 They are best dressed, whose dress no one observes.
Anthony Trollope (1815-1882, British Novelist)

5 I hold that gentleman to be the best-dressed whose dress no one observes.
Anthony Trollope (1815-1882, British Novelist)

6 If people turn to look at you on the street, you are not well dressed.
Beau Brummel

7 From the cradle to the coffin underwear comes first.
Bertolt Brecht (1898-1956, German Dramatist, Poet)

8 Great men are seldom over-scrupulous in the arrangement of their attire.
Charles Dickens (1812-1870, British Novelist)

9 Nothing goes out of fashion sooner than a long dress with a very low neck.
Coco Chanel (1883-1971, French Couturier)

10 You look rather rash my dear your colors don't quite match your face.
Daisy Ashford (American Author)

11 Where's the man could ease a heart, like a satin gown?
Dorothy Parker (1893-1967, American Humorous Writer)

12 Brevity is the soul of lingerie.
Dorothy Parker (1893-1967, American Humorous Writer)

13 A fine woman shows her charms to most advantage when she seems most to conceal them. The finest bosom in nature is not so fine as what imagination forms.
Dr. Gregory

14 Know first who you are; and then adorn yourself accordingly.
Euripides (480-406 BC, Greek Tragic Poet)

15 For women... bras, panties, bathing suits, and other stereotypical gear are visual reminders of a commercial, idealized feminine image that our real and diverse female bodies can't possibly fit. Without these visual references, each individual woman's body demands to be accepted on its own terms. We stop being comparatives. We begin to be unique.
Gloria Steinem (1934-, American Feminist Writer, Editor)

16 There is no such thing as a moral dress. It's people who are moral or immoral.
Jennie Jerome Churchill (1854-1921, Anglo-American Mother of Winston Churchill)

17 Where women are concerned, the rule is never to go out with anyone better dressed than you.
John Malkovich

18 So dress and conduct yourself so that people who have been in your company will not recall what you had on.
John Newton (1725-1807, British Poet, Wrote "Amazing Grace")

19 When a woman dresses up for an occasion, the man should become the black velvet pillow for the jewel.
John Weitz

20 She wears her clothes as if they were thrown on with a pitch folk.
Jonathan Swift (1667-1745, Anglo-Irish Satirist)

21 There is not so variable a thing in nature as a lady's head-dress.
Joseph Addison (1672-1719, British Essayist, Poet, Statesman)

22 They look quite promising in the shop; and not entirely without hope when I get them back into my wardrobe. But then, when I put them on they tend to deteriorate with a very strange rapidity and one feels so sorry for them.
Joyce Grenfell (1910-1979, British Entertainer)

23 The origins of clothing are not practical. They are mystical and erotic. The primitive man in the wolf-pelt was not keeping dry; he was saying: "Look what I killed. Aren't I the best?"
Katharine Hamnett

24 All women's dresses are merely variations on the eternal struggle between the admitted desire to dress and the unadmitted desire to undress.
Lin Yn-tang (1895-1976, Chinese Writer and Philologist)

25 If men can run the world, why can't they stop wearing neckties? How intelligent is it to start the day by tying a little noose around your neck?
Linda Ellerbee

26 The difference between a man of sense and a fop is that the fop values himself upon his dress; and the man of sense laughs at it, at the same time he knows he must not neglect it.
Lord Chesterfield (1694-1773, British Statesman, Author)

27 Any affectation whatsoever in dress implies, in my mind, a flaw in the understanding.
Lord Chesterfield (1694-1773, British Statesman, Author)

28 You can say what you like about long dresses, but they cover a multitude of shins.
Mae West (1892-1980, American Actress)

29 Be careless in your dress if you must, but keep a tidy soul.
Mark Twain (1835-1910, American Humorist, Writer)

30 Clothes make the poor invisible. America has the best-dressed poverty the world has ever known.
Michael Harrington

31 A modest woman, dressed out in all her finery, is the most tremendous object of the whole creation.
Oliver Goldsmith (1728-1774, Anglo-Irish Author, Poet, Playwright)

32 One should either be a work of art, or wear a work of art.
Oscar Wilde (1856-1900, British Author, Wit)

33 The beauty of the internal nature cannot be so far concealed by its accidental vesture, but that the spirit of its form shall communicate itself to the very disguise and indicate the shape it hides from the manner in which it is worn. A majestic form and graceful motions will express themselves through the most barbarous and tasteless costume.
Percy Bysshe Shelley (1792-1822, British Poet)

34 An accent mark, perhaps, instead of a whole western accent -- a point of punctuation rather than a uniform twang. That is how it should be worn: as a quiet point of character reference, an apt phrase of sartorial allusion -- macho, sotto voce.
Phil Patton

428

35 How to dress? When the money is going from you wear anything you like. When the money is coming to you, dress your best.
Proverb

36 I have heard with admiring submission the experience of the lady who declared that the sense of being perfectly well dressed gives a feeling of inward tranquility which religion is powerless to bestow.
Ralph Waldo Emerson (1803-1882, American Poet, Essayist)

37 Sir, a man who cannot get to heaven in a green coat, will not find his way thither the sooner in a gray one.
Samuel Johnson (1709-1784, British Author)

38 The best-dressed woman is one whose clothes wouldn't look too strange in the country.
Sir Hardy Amies (1909-, British Fashion Designer, Author)

39 He was a tubby little chap who looked as if he had been poured into his clothes and had forgotten to say "when!"
Sir P(elham) G(renville) Wodehouse (1881-1975, British Novelist)

40 No man is esteemed for colorful garments except by fools and women.
Sir Walter Raleigh (1552-1618, British Courtier, Navigator, Writer)

41 Good clothes open all doors.
Thomas Fuller (1608-1661, British Clergyman, Author)

42 Judge not a man by his clothes, but by his wife's clothes.
Thomas Robert Dewar

43 There is much to support the view that it is clothes that wear us, and not we, them; we may make them take the mould of arm or breast, but they mould our hearts, our brains, our tongues to their liking.
Virginia Woolf (1882-1941, British Novelist, Essayist)

44 Every time a woman leaves off something she looks better, but every time a man leaves off something he looks worse.
Will Rogers (1879-1935, American Humorist, Actor)

45 Those who make their dress a principal part of themselves will, in general, become of no more value than their dress.
William Hazlitt (1778-1830, British Essayist)

46 Costly thy habit as thy purse can buy, but not expressed in fancy; rich not gaudy; for the apparel oft proclaims the man.
William Shakespeare (1564-1616, British Poet, Playwright, Actor)

47 The apparel oft proclaims the man.
William Shakespeare (1564-1616, British Poet, Playwright, Actor)

48 I have often said that I wish I had invented blue jeans: the most spectacular, the most practical, the most relaxed and nonchalant. They have expression, modesty, sex appeal, simplicity -- all I hope for in my clothes.
Yves Saint-Laurent (1936-, Algerian-Born French Fashion Designer)

DRIVERS AND DRIVING

1 Fasten your seat belts, it's going to be a bum Margo Channing in All About Eve]
Bette Davis (1908-1989, American Actress, Producer)

2 Drive slow and enjoy the scenery -- drive fast and join the scenery.
Doug Horton

3 If it isn't a success, that still wouldn't be grounds for divorce. [On her film The Long Kiss Goodnight produced by husband Renny Harlin]
Geena Davis (1957-, American Actress)

4 A careful driver is one who honks his horn when he goes through a red light.
Henry Morgan (1635-1688, Buccaneer, Born in Llanrumney, South Glamorgan)

5 It seems to make an auto driver mad if he misses you.
Kin Hubbard (1868-1930, American Humorist, Journalist)

6 I'm the worst person to be stuck with in a traffic jam.
Larry King (1933-, American TV Personality, Prankster)

7 That she's the worst driver in the history of drivers. If I know she's going somewhere, I stay home. [When asked what time has taught him about Jennifer Aniston]
Matthew Perry

8 I don't like driving very much. That makes me very unhappy, because I scream a lot in the car, but other than that, life is actually pretty good.
Whoopi Goldberg (1949-, American Actress, Comedian)

DRUGS

1 Which is better: to have fun with fungi or to have Idiocy with ideology, to have wars because of words, to have tomorrow's misdeeds out of yesterday's miscreeds?
Aldous Huxley (1894-1963, British Author)

2 If we could sniff or swallow something that would, for five or six hours each day, abolish our solitude as individuals, atone us with our fellows in a glowing exaltation of affection and make life in all its aspects seem not only worth living, but divinely beautiful and significant, and if this heavenly, world-transfiguring drug were of such a kind that we could wake up next morning with a clear head and an undamaged constitution -- then, it seems to me, all our problems (and not merely the one small problem of discovering a novel pleasure) would be wholly solved and earth would become paradise.
Aldous Huxley (1894-1963, British Author)

3 No monster vibration, no snake universe hallucinations. Many tiny jeweled violet flowers along the path of a living brook that looked like Blake's illustration for a canal in grassy Eden: huge Pacific watery shore, Orlovsky dancing naked like Shiva long-haired before giant green waves, titanic cliffs that Wordsworth mentioned in his own Sublime, great yellow sun veiled with mist hanging over the planet's oceanic horizon. No harm.
Allen Ginsberg (1926-, American Poet)

4 Nobody saves America by sniffing cocaine, jiggling your knees blankly in the rain, when it snows in your nose you catch cold in your brain.
Allen Ginsberg (1926-, American Poet)

5 Opiate. An unlocked door in the prison of Identity. It leads into the jail yard.
Ambrose Bierce (1842-1914, American Author, Editor, Journalist, "The Devil's Dictionary")

6 Of course drugs were fun.
Anjelica Huston (1951-, American Actress)

7 It is in the interests of our society to promote those things that take the edge off, keep us busy with our fixes, and keep us slightly numbed out and zombie like. In this way our modern consumer society itself functions as an addict.
Anne W. Schaef

8 It is not opium which makes me work but its absence, and in order for me to feel its absence it must from time to time be present.
Antonin Artaud (1896-1948, French Theater Producer, Actor, Theorist)

9 There seems to be no stopping drug frenzy once it takes hold of a nation. What starts with an innocuous HUGS, NOT DRUGS bumper sticker soon leads to wild talk of shooting dealers and making urine tests a condition for employment -- anywhere.
Barbara Ehrenreich (1941-, American Author, Columnist)

10 In my day, we didn't have the cocaine, so we went out and knocked somebody over the head and took the money. But today, all this cocaine and crack, it doesn't give kids a chance.
Barry White

11 If you think dope is for kicks and for thrills, you're out of your mind. There are more kicks to be had in a good case of paralytic polio or by living in an iron lung. If you think you need stuff to play music or sing, you're crazy. It can fix you so you can't play nothing or sing nothing.
Billie Holiday (1915-1959, American Jazz Singer)

12 To punish drug takers is like a drunk striking the bleary face it sees in the mirror. Drugs will not be brought under control until society itself changes, enabling men to use them as primitive man did: welcoming the visions they provided not as fantasies, but as intimations of a different, and important, level of reality.
Brian Inglis

13 The whole LSD, STP, marijuana, heroin, hashish, prescription cough medicine crowd suffers from the "Watchtower" itch: you gotta be with us, man, or you're out, you're dead. This pitch is a continual and seeming MUST with those who use the stuff. It's no wonder they keep getting busted.
Charles Bukowski (1920-1994, German Poet, Short Stories Writer, Novelist)

14 Under the pressure of the cares and sorrows of our mortal condition, men have at all times, and in all countries, called in some physical aid to their moral consolations -- wine, beer, opium, brandy, or tobacco.
Edmund Burke (1729-1797, British Political Writer, Statesman)

15 A drug is neither moral nor immoral -- it's a chemical compound. The compound itself is not a menace to society until a human being treats it as if consumption bestowed a temporary license to act like an asshole.
Frank Zappa (1940-, American Rock Musician)

16 Only one thing is certain: if pot is legalized, it won't be for our benefit but for the authorities. To have it legalized will also be to lose control of it.
Germaine Greer (1939-, Australian Feminist Writer)

17 I learned why they're called wonder drugs -- you wonder what they'll do to you.
Harlan Miller

18 There is held to be no surer test of civilization than the increase per head of the consumption of alcohol and tobacco. Yet alcohol and tobacco are recognizable poisons, so that their consumption has only to be carried far enough to destroy civilization altogether.
Havelock Ellis (1859-1939, British Psychologist)

19 Everything one does in life, even love, occurs in an express train racing toward death. To smoke opium is to get out of the train while it is still moving. It is to concern oneself with something other than life or death.
Jean Cocteau (1889-1963, French Author, Filmmaker)

20 Drugs are reality's legal loopholes.
Jeremy P. Johnson

21 Nobody stopped thinking about those psychedelic experiences. Once you've been to some of those places, you think, "How can I get back there again but make it a little easier on myself?"
Jerry Garcia (1945-1995, American Rock Musician, "Grateful Dead")

22 Of all that Orient lands can vaunt, of marvels with our own competing, the strangest is the Haschish plant, and what will follow on its eating.
John Greenleaf Whittier (1807-1892, American Poet, Reformer, Author)

23 The worst drugs are as bad as anybody's told you. It's just a dumb trip, which I can't condemn people if they get into it, because one gets into it for one's own personal, social, emotional reasons. It's something to be avoided if one can help it.
John Lennon (1940-1980, British Rock Musician)

24 The basic thing nobody asks is why do people take drugs of any sort? Why do we have these accessories to normal living to live? I mean, is there something wrong with society that's making us so pressurized, that we cannot live without guarding ourselves against it?
John Lennon (1940-1980, British Rock Musician)

25 They shoulda called me Little Cocaine, I was sniffing so much of the stuff! My nose got big enough to back a diesel truck in, unload it, and drive it right out again.
Little Richard (American Entertainer)

26 I tried to give up drugs by drinking.
Lou Reed (1942-, American Musician, Guitarist, Singer, Songwriter)

27 I don't believe in playing hurt, in taking injections to cover the pain.
Monica Seles (Born 1973, Yugoslavian-born American Tennis Player)

28 One's condition on marijuana is always existential. One can feel the importance of each moment and how it is changing one. One feels one's being, one becomes aware of the enormous apparatus of nothingness -- the hum of a hi-fi set, the emptiness of a pointless interruption, one becomes aware of the war between each of us, how the nothingness in each of us seeks to attack the being of others, how our being in turn is attacked by the nothingness in others.
Norman Mailer (1923-, American Author)

29 Thou source of all my bliss and all my woe, that found me poor at first, and keep me so.
Oliver Goldsmith (1728-1774, Anglo-Irish Author, Poet, Playwright)

30 Anyway, no drug, not even alcohol, causes the fundamental ills of society. If we're looking for the source of our troubles, we shouldn't test people for drugs, we should test them for stupidity, ignorance, greed and love of power.
P. J. O'Rourke (1947-, American Journalist)

31 No drug, not even alcohol, causes the fundamental ills of society. If we're looking for the sources of our troubles, we shouldn't test people for drugs, we should test them for stupidity, ignorance, greed and love of power.
P. J. O'Rourke (1947-, American Journalist)

32 Marijuana is self-punishing. It makes you acutely sensitive, and in this world, what worse punishment could there be?
P. J. O'Rourke (1947-, American Journalist)

33 It's an ordinary day for Brian. Like, he died every day, you know.
Peter Townsend (British Singer, Songwriter)

34 Drug misuse is not a disease, it is a decision, like the decision to step out in front of a moving car. You would call that not a disease but an error of judgment.
Philip K. Dick (1928-1982, American Science Fiction Writer)

35 We're talking scum here. Air should be illegal if they breathe it.
Policeman

36 Tobacco and opium have broad backs, and will cheerfully carry the load of armies, if you choose to make them pay high for such joy as they give and such harm as they do.
Ralph Waldo Emerson (1803-1882, American Poet, Essayist)

37 Is marijuana addictive? Yes, in the sense that most of the really pleasant things in life are worth endlessly repeating.
Richard Neville

38 Cocaine is God's way of saying you're making too much money.
Robin Williams (1952-, American Actor, Comedian)

39 Let us not forget who we are. Drug abuse is a repudiation of everything America is.
Ronald Reagan (1911-, Fortieth President of the USA, Actor)

40 Words are the most powerful drugs used by mankind.
Rudyard Kipling (1865-1936, British Author of Prose, Verse)

41 Did you know that the White House drug test is multiple choice?
Rush Limbaugh (1951-, American TV Personality)

42 Take me, I am the drug; take me, I am hallucinogenic.
Salvador Dali (1904-1989, Spanish Painter)

43 Woe to you, my Princess, when I come... you shall see who is the stronger, a gentle little girl who doesn't eat enough or a big wild man who has cocaine in his body.
Sigmund Freud (1856-1939, Austrian Physician - Founder of Psychoanalysis)

44 Thou hast the keys of Paradise, oh just, subtle, and mighty opium!
Thomas De Quincey (1785-1859, British Author)

45 Junk is the ideal product... the ultimate merchandise. No sales talk necessary. The client will crawl through a sewer and beg to buy.
William S. Burroughs (1914-1997, American Writer)

46 The human mind is capable of excitement without the application of gross and violent stimulants; and he must have a very faint perception of its beauty and dignity who does not know this.
William Wordsworth (1770-1850, British Poet)

47 I don't respond well to mellow, you know what I mean, I have a tendency to... if I get too mellow, I ripen and then rot.
Woody Allen (1935-, American Director, Screenwriter, Actor, Comedian)

DULLNESS

1 Prudent dullness marked him for a mayor.
Charles Churchill (1731-1764, British Poet, Satirist)

2 There is no such thing on earth as an uninteresting subject; the only thing that can exist is an uninterested person.
Gilbert K. Chesterton (1874-1936, British Author)

3 Authors have established it as a kind of rule, that a man ought to be dull sometimes; as the most severe reader makes allowances for many rests and nodding-places in a voluminous writer.
Joseph Addison (1672-1719, British Essayist, Poet, Statesman)

4 What a comfort a dull but kindly person is, to be sure, at times! A ground-glass shade over a gas-lamp does not bring more solace to our dazzled eyes than such a one to our minds.
Oliver Wendell Holmes (1809-1894, American Author, Wit, Poet)

5 Dullness is the coming of age of seriousness.
Oscar Wilde (1856-1900, British Author, Wit)

6 What can he mean by coming among us? He is not only dull himself, but the cause of dullness in others.
Samuel Foote

7 Sir, he was dull in company, dull in his closet, dull everywhere. He was dull in a new way, and that made many people think him great.
Samuel Johnson (1709-1784, British Author)

8 It is to be noted that when any part of this paper appears dull there is a design in it.
Sir Richard Steele (1672-1729, British Dramatist, Essayist, Editor)

DUTY

1 The sense of obligation to continue is present in all of us. A duty to strive is the duty of us all. I felt a call to that duty.
Abraham Lincoln (1809-1865, Sixteenth President of the USA)

2 Duty. That which sternly impels us in the direction of profit, along the line of desire.
Ambrose Bierce (1842-1914, American Author, Editor, Journalist, "The Devil's Dictionary")

3 Oh! Duty is an icy shadow. It will freeze you. It cannot fill the heart's sanctuary.
Augusta Jane Evans (1835-1909, American Writer)

4 Duty cannot exist without faith.
Benjamin Disraeli (1804-1881, British Statesman, Prime Minister)

5 A sense of duty is useful in work but offensive in personal relations. People wish to be liked, not to be endured with patient resignation.
Bertrand Russell (1872-1970, British Philosopher, Mathematician, Essayist)

6 When we can say no not only to things that are wrong and sinful, but also to things pleasant, profitable, and good which would hinder and clog our grand duties and our chief work, we shall understand more fully what life is worth, and how to make the most of it.
Charles A. Stoddard

7 When one has come to accept a certain course as duty he has a pleasant sense of relief and of lifted responsibility, even if the course involves pain and renunciation. It is like obedience to some external authority; any clear way, though it lead to death, is mentally preferable to the tangle of uncertainty.
Charles Horton Cooley (1864-1929, American Sociologist)

8 I sighed as a lover, I obeyed as a son.
Edward Gibbon (1737-1794, British Historian)

9 I slept, and dreamed that life was beauty; I woke, and found that life was Duty.
Ellen Sturgis Hooper (1816-1841, American Poet)

10 Never step over one duty to perform another.
English Proverb

11 When a stupid man is doing something he is ashamed of, he always declares that it is his duty.
George Bernard Shaw (1856-1950, Irish-born British Dramatist)

12 The reward of one's duty is the power to fulfill another.
George Eliot (1819-1880, British Novelist)

13 Possession without obligation to the object possessed approaches felicity.
George Meredith (1828-1909, British Author)

14 Where there are no rights, there are no duties.
Henri Benjamin Rebecque (1767-1830, French Writer, Orator, Statesman)

15 For many years I was a self-appointed inspector of snowstorms and rainstorms and did my duty faithfully, though I never received payment for it.
Henry David Thoreau (1817-1862, American Essayist, Poet, Naturalist)

16 He who is false to present duty breaks a thread in the loom, and will find the flaw when he may have forgotten its cause.
Henry Ward Beecher (1813-1887, American Preacher, Orator, Writer)

17 The most beautiful things in the universe are the starry heavens above us and the feeling of duty within us.
Indian Proverb

18 Love can do much, but duty more.
Johann Wolfgang Von Goethe (1749-1832, German Poet, Dramatist, Novelist)

19 How can we know ourselves? Never by reflection, but only through action. Begin at once to do your duty and immediately you will know what is inside you.
Johann Wolfgang Von Goethe (1749-1832, German Poet, Dramatist, Novelist)

20 Every right implies a responsibility; Every opportunity, an obligation, Every possession, a duty.
John D. Rockefeller (1839-1937, American Industrialist, Philanthropist, Founder Exxon)

21 Duty largely consists of pretending that the trivial is critical.
John Fowles (1926-, British Novelist)

22 A duty dodged is like a debt unpaid; it is only deferred, and we must come back and settle the account at last.
Joseph Fort Newton

23 Without duty, life is sort of boneless; it cannot hold itself together.
Joseph Joubert (1754-1824, French Moralist)

24 Duties are not performed for duty's sake, but because their neglect would make the man uncomfortable. A man performs but one duty --the duty of contenting his spirit, the duty of making himself agreeable to himself.
Mark Twain (1835-1910, American Humorist, Writer)

25 Do something every day that you don't want to do. This is the golden rule for acquiring the habit of doing your duty without pain.
Mark Twain (1835-1910, American Humorist, Writer)

26 Rank imposes obligation.
Motto

27 But in his duty prompt at every call, he watched and wept, he prayed and felt for all.
Oliver Goldsmith (1728-1774, Anglo-Irish Author, Poet, Playwright)

28 The rule of joy and the law of duty seem to me all one.
Oliver Wendell Holmes Jr. (1841-1935, American Judge)

29 Oh, duty is what one expects from others, it is not what one does oneself.
Oscar Wilde (1856-1900, British Author, Wit)

30 The first duty of life is to be as artificial as possible. What the second duty is no one as yet discovered.
Oscar Wilde (1856-1900, British Author, Wit)

31 Do your duty and leave the rest to heaven.
Pierre Corneille (1606-1684, French Dramatist)

32 Our duty, as men and women, is to proceed as if limits to our ability did not exist. We are collaborators in creation.
Pierre Teilhard De Chardin (1881-1955, French Christian Mystic, Author)

33 Do that which is assigned to you and you cannot hope too much or dare too much.
Ralph Waldo Emerson (1803-1882, American Poet, Essayist)

34 Duty is the sublimest word in the language. You can never do more than your duty. You should never wish to do less.
Robert E. Lee (1807-1870, American Confederate Army Commander)

35 There is no duty we so much underrated as the duty of being happy.
Robert Louis Stevenson (1850-1895, Scottish Essayist, Poet, Novelist)

36 No eulogy is due to him who simply does his duty and nothing more.
St. Augustine (354-430, Numidian-born Bishop of Hippo, Theologian)

37 Sufficient to each day are the duties to be done and the trials to be endured. God never built a Christian strong enough to carry today's duties and tomorrow's anxieties piled on the top of them.
Theodore L. Cuyler (1822-1909, American Pastor, Author)

38 Let others laugh when you sacrifice desire to duty, if they will. You have time and eternity to rejoice in.
Theodore Parker (1810-1860, American Minister)

39 Let us do our duty, in our shop in our kitchen, in the market, the street, the office, the school, the home, just as faithfully as if we stood in the front rank of some great battle, and knew that victory for mankind depends on our bravery, strength, and skill. When we do that, the humblest of us will be serving in that great army which achieves the welfare of the world.
Theodore Parker (1810-1860, American Minister)

40 The first requisite of a good citizen in this republic of ours is that he shall be able and willing to pull his weight.
Theodore Roosevelt (1858-1919, Twenty-sixth President of the USA)

41 Do the duty which lies nearest to you, the second duty will then become clearer.
Thomas Carlyle (1795-1881, Scottish Philosopher, Author)

42 Activate yourself to duty by remembering your position, who you are, and what you have obliged yourself to be.
Thomas p Kempis (1379-1471, German Monk, Mystic, Religious Writer)

43 It is easier to do one's duty to others than to one's self. If you do your duty to others, you are considered reliable. If you do your duty to yourself, you are considered selfish.
Thomas Szasz (1920-, American Psychiatrist)

44 It is not enough for us to prostrate ourselves under the tree which is Creation, and to contemplate its tremendous branches filled with stars. We have a duty to perform, to work upon the human soul, to defend the mystery against the miracle, to worship the incomprehensible while rejecting the absurd; to accept, in the inexplicable, only what is necessary; to dispel the superstitions that surround religion --to rid God of His Maggots.
Victor Hugo (1802-1885, French Poet, Dramatist, Novelist)

45 Consult duty not events.
Walter Savage Landor (1775-1864, British Poet, Essayist)

46 What is possible is our highest duty.
William E. Mclaren

47 The line of life is a ragged diagonal between duty and desire.
William R. Alger (1822-1905, American Writer)

EARTH

1 The earth is like a spaceship that didn't come with an operating manual.
Buckminster Fuller (American Engineer, Inventor, Designer, Architect "Geodesic Dome")

ECCENTRICITY

1   Thou strange piece of wild nature!
Colley Cibber (1671-1757, British Actor-Manager, Playwright)

2   Eccentricity is not, as dull people would have us believe, a form of madness. It is often a kind of innocent pride, and the man of genius and the aristocrat are frequently regarded as eccentrics because genius and aristocrat are entirely unafraid of and uninfluenced by the opinions and vagaries of the crowd.
Dame Edith Sitwell (1887-1964, British Poet)

3   The world thinks eccentricity in great things is genius, but in small things, only crazy.
Edward G. Bulwer-Lytton (1803-1873, British Novelist, Poet)

4   The lunatic fringe wags the underdog.
H. L. Mencken (1880-1956, American Editor, Author, Critic, Humorist)

5   You must not blame me if I do talk to the clouds.
Henry David Thoreau (1817-1862, American Essayist, Poet, Naturalist)

6   People of uncommon abilities generally fall into eccentricities when their sphere of life is not adequate to their abilities.
Johann Wolfgang Von Goethe (1749-1832, German Poet, Dramatist, Novelist)

7   The amount of eccentricity in a society has generally been proportional to the amount of genius, mental vigor, and moral courage it contained. That so few now dare to be eccentric marks the chief danger of the time.
John Stuart Mill (1806-1873, British Philosopher, Economist)

8   Eccentricity has always abounded when and where strength of character has abounded; and the amount of eccentricity in a society has generally been proportional to the amount of genius, mental vigor, and moral courage which it contained.
John Stuart Mill (1806-1873, British Philosopher, Economist)

9   The English like eccentrics. They just don't like them living next door.
Julian Clary

10   The sound principle of a topsy-turvy lifestyle in the framework of an upside-down world order has stood every test.
Karl Kraus (1874-1936, Austrian Satirist)

11   So long as a man rides his Hobby-Horse peaceably and quietly along the King's highway, and neither compels you or me to get up behind him -- pray, Sir, what have either you or I to do with it?
Laurence Sterne (1713-1768, British Author)

12   Only the other day I was inquiring of an entire bed of old-fashioned roses, forced to listen to my ramblings on the meaning of the universe as I sat cross-legged in the lotus position in front of them.
Prince Of Wales Charles (1948-, Duke of Edinburgh, Son of Queen Elizabeth II and Prince Philip)

13   Cranks live by theory, not by pure desire. They want votes, peace, nuts, liberty, and spinning- looms not because they love these things, as a child loves jam, but because they think they ought to have them. That is one element which makes the crank.
Rose Macaulay (1881-1958, British Novelist, Essayist)

ECOLOGY

1   We abuse land because we regard it as a commodity belonging to us. When we see land as a community to which we belong, we may begin to use it with love and respect.
Aldo Leopold

2   Green politics at its worst amounts to a sort of Zen fascism; less extreme, it denounces growth and seeks to stop the world so that we can all get off.
Chris Patten (1944-, British Statesman, Governor of Hong Kong)

3   We cannot cheat on DNA. We cannot get round photosynthesis. We cannot say I am not going to give a damn about phytoplankton. All these tiny mechanisms provide the preconditions of our planetary life. To say we do not care is to say in the most literal sense that "we choose death."
Dame Barbara Ward (1914-1981, British Journalist, Economist, Conservationist)

4   How to be green? Many people have asked us this important question. It's really very simple and requires no expert knowledge or complex skills. Here's the answer. Consume less. Share more. Enjoy life.
Derek Wall

5   The question of whether it's God's green earth is not at center stage, except in the sense that if so, one is reminded with some regularity that He may be dying.
Edward Hoagland (1932-, American Novelist, Essayist)

6   The nation that destroys its soil destroys itself.
Franklin D. Roosevelt (1882-1945, Thirty-second President of the USA)

7   O if we but knew what we do when we delve or hew -- hack and rack the growing green! Since country is so tender to touch, her being so slender, that like this sleek and seeing ball but a prick will make no eye at all, where we, even where we mean to mend her we end her, when we hew or delve: after-comers cannot guess the beauty been.
Gerard Manley Hopkins (1844-1889, British Poet)

8 The sun, the moon and the stars would have disappeared long ago had they happened to be within the reach of predatory human hands.
Havelock Ellis (1859-1939, British Psychologist)

9 It's a morbid observation, but if every one on earth just stopped breathing for an hour, the greenhouse effect would no longer be a problem.
Jerry Adler (American Actor)

10 It is our task in our time and in our generation to hand down undiminished to those who come after us, as was handed down to us by those who went before, the natural wealth and beauty which is ours.
John F. Kennedy (1917-1963, Thirty-fifth President of the USA)

11 And he gave it for his opinion, that whoever could make two ears of corn, or two blades of grass, to grow upon a spot of ground where only one grew before, would deserve better of mankind, and do more essential service to his country, than the whole race of politicians put together.
Jonathan Swift (1667-1745, Anglo-Irish Satirist)

12 The development of civilization and industry in general has always shown itself so active in the destruction of forests that everything that has been done for their conservation and production is completely insignificant in comparison.
Karl Marx (1818-1883, German Political Theorist, Social Philosopher)

13 As soils are depleted, human health, vitality and intelligence go with them.
Louis Bromfield (1896-1956, American Author)

14 We won't have a society if we destroy the environment.
Margaret Mead (1901-1978, American Anthropologist)

15 Ecology is rather like sex -- every new generation likes to think they were the first to discover it.
Michael Allaby (American Actor)

16 The current collapse of industrial society may well be the planet's way of avoiding a larger death.
Morris Bergman

17 Humanity has passed through a long history of one-sidedness and of a social condition that has always contained the potential of destruction, despite its creative achievements in technology. The great project of our time must be to open the other eye: to see all-sidedly and wholly, to heal and transcend the cleavage between humanity and nature that came with early wisdom.
Murray Bookchin (1941-, American Ecologist)

18 We do not inherit the land from our ancestors, we borrow it form our children.
Native American Proverb

19 The universe is like a safe to which there is a combination. Bit the combination is locked up in the safe.
Peter De Vries (1910-, American Author)

20 We, the generation that faces the next century, can add the solemn injunction "If we don't do the impossible, we shall be faced with the unthinkable."
Petra Kelly

21 Obviously, the answer to oil spills is to paper-train the tankers.
Ralph Nader (1934-, American Lawyer, Consumer Activist)

22 Guns have metamorphosed into cameras in this earnest comedy, the ecology safari, because nature has ceased to be what it always had been -- what people needed protection from. Now nature tamed, endangered, mortal -- needs to be protected from people.
Susan Sontag (1933-, American Essayist)

23 A chain is no stronger than its weakest link, and life is after all a chain.
William James (1842-1910, American Psychologist, Professor, Author)

ECONOMY AND ECONOMICS

1 A nation is not in danger of financial disaster merely because it owes itself money.
Andrew William Mellon (1855-1937, American Financier, Philanthropist, Statesman)

2 Commerce is one of the daughters of Fortune, inconsistent and deceitful as her mother. she chooses her residence where she is least expected, and shifts her home when in appearance she seems firmly settled.
Ben Johnston

3 There can be economy only where there is efficiency.
Benjamin Disraeli (1804-1881, British Statesman, Prime Minister)

4 No nation was ever ruined by trade.
Benjamin Franklin (1706-1790, American Scientist, Publisher, Diplomat)

5 The notion that big business and big labor and big government can sit down around a table somewhere and work out the direction of the American economy is at complete variance with the reality of where the American economy is headed. I mean, it's like dinosaurs gathering to talk about the evolution of a new generation of mammals.
Bruce Babbit (American Politician)

6 Commerce flourishes by circumstances, precarious, transitory, contingent, almost as the winds and waves that bring it to our shores.
Charles Caleb Colton (1780-1832, British Sportsman Writer)

7 Profit is the ignition system of our economic engine.
Charles Sawyer

8 First rule of Economics 101: our desires are insatiable. Second rule: we can stomach only three Big Macs at a time.
Doug Horton

9 Call a thing immoral or ugly, soul-destroying or a degradation of man, a peril to the peace of the world or to the well-being of future generations; as long as you have not shown it to be "uneconomic" you have not really questioned its right to exist, grow, and prosper.
E. F. Schumacher (1911-1977, German Economist)

10 Ask five economists and you'll get five different explanations... six if one went to Harvard.
Edgar R. Fiedler

11 For economist the real world is often a special case.
Edgar R. Fiedler

12 Mere parsimony is not economy. Expense, and great expense, may be an essential part in true economy.
Edmund Burke (1729-1797, British Political Writer, Statesman)

13 Frugality is founded on the principal that all riches have limits.
Edmund Burke (1729-1797, British Political Writer, Statesman)

14 I am indeed rich, since my income is superior to my expenses, and my expense is equal to my wishes.
Edward Gibbon (1737-1794, British Historian)

15 The first panacea for a mismanaged nation is inflation of the currency; the second is war. Both bring a temporary prosperity; both bring a permanent ruin. But both are the refuge of political and economic opportunists.
Ernest Hemingway (1898-1961, American Writer)

16 In our time, the curse is monetary illiteracy, just as inability to read plain print was the curse of earlier centuries.
Ezra Pound (1885-1972, American Poet, Critic)

17 But while they prate of economic laws, men and women are starving. We must lay hold of the fact that economic laws are not made by nature. They are made by human beings.
Franklin D. Roosevelt (1882-1945, Thirty-second President of the USA)

18 If all the economists were laid end to end, they would not reach a conclusion.
George Bernard Shaw (1856-1950, Irish-born British Dramatist)

19 Be thrifty, but not covetous.
George Herbert (1593-1632, British Metaphysical Poet)

20 The science hangs like a gathering fog in a valley, a fog which begins nowhere and goes nowhere, an incidental, unmeaning inconvenience to passers-by.
H.G. Wells (1866-1946, British-born American Author)

21 Economic growth may one day turn out to be a curse rather than a good, and under no conditions can it either lead into freedom or constitute a proof for its existence.
Hannah Arendt (1906-1975, German-born American Political Philosopher)

22 According to the Bank of England the economy is growing too fast so interest rates must rise to counter the supposed inflationary threat. In lay terms, I interpret this to mean that people are working much harder, causing economic growth, and they're in danger of spending their money, which is what the recession-hit shops want them to do. But the Bank and the City seem to think this is wrong, and that if people work harder they should be punished by having their mortgages increased.
Harry Enfield (British Comedian)

23 Give me a one-handed economist! All my economics say, "On the one hand... on the other."
Harry S. Truman (1884-1972, Thirty-third President of the USA)

24 Economics is haunted by more fallacies than any other study known to man. This is no accident. The inherent difficulties of the subject would be great enough in any case, but they are multiplied a thousandfold by a factor that is insignificant in , say, physics, mathematics, or medicine -- the special pleading of selfish interests.
Henry Hazlitt

25 How great, my friends, is the virtue of living upon a little!
Horace (65-8 BC, Italian Poet)

26 I learned more about the economy from one South Dakota dust storm that I did in all my years of college.
Hubert H. Humphrey (1911-1978, American Democratic Politician, Vice President)

27 The rate of interest acts as a link between income-value and capital-value
Irving Fisher (American Mathematician and Economist)

28 The animals that depend on instinct have an inherent knowledge of the laws of economics and of how to apply them; Man, with his powers of reason, has reduced economics to the level of a farce which is at once funnier and more tragic than Tobacco Road.
James Thurber (1894-1961, American Humorist, Illustrator)

29 The economy depends about as much on economists as the weather does on weather forecasters.
Jean-Paul Kauffmann

30 Economic growth without social progress lets the great majority of people remain in poverty, while a privileged few reap the benefits of rising abundance.
John F. Kennedy (1917-1963, Thirty-fifth President of the USA)

31 There is much of economic theory which is pursued for no better reason than its intellectual attraction; it is a good game. We have no reason to be ashamed of that, since the same would hold for many branches of mathematics.
John Hicks (British Economist)

32 In the usual (though certainly not in every) public decision on economic policy, the choice is between courses that are almost equally good or equally bad. It is the narrowest decisions that are most ardently debated. If the world is lucky enough to enjoy peace, it may even one day make the discovery, to the horror of doctrinaire free-enterprisers and doctrinaire planners alike, that what is called capitalism and what is called socialism are both capable of working quite well.
John Kenneth Galbraith (1908-, American Economist)

33 In economics, hope and faith coexist with great scientific pretension and also a deep desire for respectability.
John Kenneth Galbraith (1908-, American Economist)

34 In economics the majority is always wrong.
John Kenneth Galbraith (1908-, American Economist)

35 The day is not far off when the economic problem will take the back seat where it belongs, and the arena of the heart and the head will be occupied or reoccupied, by our real problems -- the problems of life and of human relations, of creation and behavior and religion.
John Maynard Keynes (1883-1946, British Economist)

36 If economists could manage to get themselves thought of as humble, competent people on a level with dentists, that would be splendid.
John Maynard Keynes (1883-1946, British Economist)

37 Men cannot not live by exchanging articles, but producing them. They live by work not trade.
John Ruskin (1819-1900, British Critic, Social Theorist)

38 Few are sufficiently sensible of the importance of that economy in reading which selects, almost exclusively, the very first order of books. Why, except for some special reason, read an inferior book, at the very time you might be reading one of the highest order?
John W. Foster (1770-1843, British Clergyman, Essayist)

39 Economic progress, in capitalist society, means turmoil.
Joseph A. Schumpeter (1883-1950, Austrian-American Economist)

40 People do not understand what a great revenue economy is.
Marcus T. Cicero (106-43 BC, Great Roman Orator, Politician)

41 Much in little.
Motto

42 For the past 15 years or so, British governments have tried to persuade the rest of us that the best judges of the national interest are...businessmen. This may be a ridiculous statement, but -- ominously -- fewer and fewer people laugh at it.
Neil Ascherson (British Journalist)

43 Commerce has set the mark of selfishness, the signet of its all-enslaving power, upon a shining ore, and called it gold: before whose image bow the vulgar great, the vainly rich, the miserable proud, the mob of peasants, nobles, priests, and kings, and with blind feelings reverence the power that grinds them to the dust of misery.
Percy Bysshe Shelley (1792-1822, British Poet)

44 If all the economists in the world were laid end to end, it wouldn't be a bad thing.
Peter Lynch (American Businessman, Stock Trader)

45 Commerce is a game of skill which everyone cannot play and few can play well.
Ralph Waldo Emerson (1803-1882, American Poet, Essayist)

46 The government's view of the economy could be summed up in a few short phrases: If it moves, tax it. If it keeps moving, regulate it. And if it stops moving, subsidize it.
Ronald Reagan (1911-, Fortieth President of the USA, Actor)

47 We might come closer to balancing the Budget if all of us lived closer to the Commandments and the Golden Rule.
Ronald Reagan (1911-, Fortieth President of the USA, Actor)

48 It seems to be a law in American life that whatever enriches us anywhere except in the wallet inevitably becomes uneconomic.
Russell (Wayne) Baker (1925-, American Journalist)

49 If you laid ever economist in the country end to end you would still not reach a conclusion.
Salvador Nasello

50 Economy is too late when you are at the bottom of your purse.
Seneca (4 BC-65 AD, Spanish-born Roman Statesman, philosopher)

51 Everyone is always in favor of general economy and particular expenditure.
Sir Anthony Eden (1897-1977, British Statesman and Prime Minister (1955--7))

52 No one is rich whose expenditures exceed his means, and no one is poor whose incomings exceed his outgoings.
Thomas C. Haliburton (1796-1865, Canadian Jurist, Author)

53 Commerce changes the fate and genius of nations.
Thomas Gray (1716-1771, British Poet)

54 Never spend your money before you have earned it.
Thomas Jefferson (1743-1826, Third President of the USA)

55 An economist's guess is liable to be as good as anybody else s.
Will Rogers (1879-1935, American Humorist, Actor)

ECSTASY

1 Life has always taken place in a tumult without apparent cohesion, but it only finds its grandeur and its reality in ecstasy and in ecstatic love.
Georges Bataille (1897-1962, French Novelist, Critic)

2 Ecstasy is not really part of the scene we can do on celluloid.
Orson Welles (1915-1985, American Film Maker)

3   O my God, what must a soul be like when it is in this state!
It longs to be all one tongue with which to praise the Lord.
It utters a thousand pious follies, in a continuous endeavor
to please Him who thus possesses it.
St. Teresa of Avila (1515-1582, Spanish Saint, Mystic)

EDITING AND EDITORS

1   An editor is someone who separates the wheat from the
chaff and then prints the chaff.
*Adlai E. Stevenson (1900-1965, American Lawyer,
Politician)*

2   Words and sentences are subject to revision; paragraphs
and whole compositions are subjects of prevision.
Barrett Wendell

3   What I have crossed out I didn't like. What I haven't
crossed out I'm dissatisfied with.
*Cecil B. De Mille (1881-1959, American Film Producer and
Director)*

4   The work was like peeling an onion. The outer skin came
off with difficulty... but in no time you'd be down to its
innards, tears streaming from your eyes as more and more
beautiful reductions became possible.
Edward Blishen (1920-, British Actor)

5   There is a difference between a book of two hundred pages
from the very beginning, and a book of two hundred pages
which is the result of an original eight hundred pages. The
six hundred are there. Only you don't see them.
Elie Wiesel (1928-, Rumanian-born American Writer)

6   Will you tell me my fault, frankly as to yourself, for I had
rather wince, than die. Men do not call the surgeon to
commend the bone, but to set it, Sir.
Emily Dickinson (1830-1886, American Poet)

7   Editing is the same as quarreling with writers -- same thing
exactly.
*Harold Wallace Ross (1892-1951, American Newspaper
Editor)*

8   Whether the flower looks better in the nosegay than in the
meadow where it grew and we had to wet our feet to get
it! Is the scholastic air any advantage?
*Henry David Thoreau (1817-1862, American Essayist, Poet,
Naturalist)*

9   In art economy is always beauty.
Henry James (1843-1916, American Author)

10   The waste basket is a writer's best friend.
*Isaac Bashevis Singer (1904-1991, Polish-born American
Journalist, Writer)*

11   Editing should be, especially in the case of old writers, a
counseling rather than a collaborating task. The tendency
of the writer-editor to collaborate is natural, but he should
say to himself, "How can I help this writer to say it better
in his own style?" and avoid "How can I show him how I
would write it, if it were my piece?"
James Thurber (1894-1961, American Humorist, Illustrator)

12   Rides in the whirlwind and directs the storm.
*Joseph Addison (1672-1719, British Essayist, Poet,
Statesman)*

13   I trust it will not be giving away professional secrets to say
that many readers would be surprised, perhaps shocked, at
the questions which some newspaper editors will put to a
defenseless woman under the guise of flattery.
Kate Chopin (1851-1904, American Author)

14   If they have a popular thought they have to go into a
darkened room and lie down until it passes.
Kelvin Mackenzie

15   A writer is unfair to himself when he is unable to be hard
on himself.
Marianne Moore (1887-1972, American Poet)

16   Remember the waterfront shack with the sign FRESH FISH
SOLD HERE. Of course it's fresh, we're on the ocean. Of
course it's for sale, we're not giving it away. Of course it's
here, otherwise the sign would be someplace else. The final
sign: FISH.
*Peggy Noonan (1950-, American Author, Presidential
Speechwriter)*

17   When in doubt, delete it.
Philip Cosby

18   Would you convey my compliments to the purist who
reads your proofs and tell him or her that I write in a sort
of broken-down patois which is something like the way a
Swiss waiter talks, and that when I split an infinitive, God
damn it, I split it so it will stay split, and when I interrupt
the velvety smoothness of my more or less literate syntax
with a few sudden words of bar-room vernacular, that is
done with the eyes wide open and the mind relaxed but
attentive.
Raymond Chandler (1888-1959, American Author)

19   There is but one art, to omit.
*Robert Louis Stevenson (1850-1895, Scottish Essayist,
Poet, Novelist)*

20   Read your own compositions, and when you meet a
passage which you think is particularly fine, strike it out.
Samuel Johnson (1709-1784, British Author)

21   An editor should tell the author his writing is better than it
is. Not a lot better, a little better.
T. S. Eliot (1888-1965, American-born British Poet, Critic)

22   I suppose some editors are failed writers; but so are most
writers.
T. S. Eliot (1888-1965, American-born British Poet, Critic)

23   Art, it seems to me, should simplify finding what
conventions of form and what detail one can do without
and yet preserve the spirit of the whole -- so that all that
one has suppressed and cut away is there to the reader's
consciousness as much as if it were in type on the page.
Willa Cather (1876-1947, American Author)

EDUCATION

1 Upon the subject of education, not presuming to dictate any plan or system respecting it, I can only say that I view it as the most important subject which we as a people may be engaged in. That everyone may receive at least a moderate education appears to be an objective of vital importance.
Abraham Lincoln (1809-1865, Sixteenth President of the USA)

2 According to this conception, the sole function of education was to open the way to thinking and knowing, and the school, as the outstanding organ for the people's education, must serve that end exclusively.
Albert Einstein (1879-1955, German-born American Physicist)

3 It is our American habit if we find the foundations of our educational structure unsatisfactory to add another story or wing. We find it easier to add a new study or course or kind of school than to recognize existing conditions so as to meet the need. strangled the holy curious of inquiry. It is a very grave mistake to think that the enjoyment of seeing and searching can be promoted by means of coercion and a sense of duty.
Albert Einstein (1879-1955, German-born American Physicist)

4 It should be possible to explain the laws of physics to a barmaid.
Albert Einstein (1879-1955, German-born American Physicist)

5 Education is the progressive realization of our ignorance.
Albert Einstein (1879-1955, German-born American Physicist)

6 Every man who knows how to read has it in his power to magnify himself, to multiply the ways in which he exists, to make his life full, significant and interesting.
Aldous Huxley (1894-1963, British Author)

7 The most valuable of all education is the ability to make yourself do the thing you have to do, when it has to be done, whether you like it or not.
Aldous Huxley (1894-1963, British Author)

8 It is possible to store the mind with a million facts and still be entirely uneducated.
Alec Bourne

9 Education at school continues what has been done at home: it crystallizes the optical illusion, consolidates it with book learning, theoretically legitimizes the traditional trash and trains the children to know without understanding and to accept denominations for definitions. Astray in his conceptions, entangled in words, man loses the flair for truth, the taste for nature. What a powerful intellect must you possess, to be suspicious of this moral carbon dioxide and with your head swimming already, to hurl yourself out of it into the fresh air, with which, into the bargain, everyone round is trying to scare you!
Alexander Herzen (1812-1870, Russian Journalist, Political Thinker)

10 Education forms the common mind. Just as the twig is bent, the tree's inclined.
Alexander Pope (1688-1744, British Poet, Critic, Translator)

11 There is hardly a pioneer's hut which does not contain a few odd volumes of Shakespeare. I remember reading the feudal drama of Henry V for the first time in a log cabin.
Alexis De Tocqueville (1805-1859, French Social Philosopher)

12 It is among the commonplaces of education that we often first cut off the living root and then try to replace its natural functions by artificial means. Thus we suppress the child's curiosity and then when he lacks a natural interest in learning he is offered special coaching for his scholastic coaching for his scholastic difficulties.
Alice Duer Miller

13 I wonder whether if I had an education I should have been more or less a fool that I am.
Alice James (1848-1892, American Diarist, Sister of Henry, William James)

14 Education in our times must try to find whatever there is in students that might yearn for completion, and to reconstruct the learning that would enable them autonomously to seek that completion.
Allan Bloom (1930-1992, American Educator, Author)

15 The liberally educated person is one who is able to resist the easy and preferred answers, not because he is obstinate but because he knows others worthy of consideration.
Allan Bloom (1930-1992, American Educator, Author)

16 Education is that which discloses to the wise and disguises from the foolish their lack of understanding.
Ambrose Bierce (1842-1914, American Author, Editor, Journalist, "The Devil's Dictionary")

17 An education isn't how much you have committed to memory, or even how much you know. It's being able to differentiate between what you do know and what you don't.
Anatole France (1844-1924, French Writer)

18 Nine tenths of education is encouragement.
Anatole France (1844-1924, French Writer)

19 Moral education, as I understand it, is not about inculcating obedience to law or cultivating self-virtue, it is rather about finding within us an ever-increasing sense of the worth of creation. It is about how we can develop and deepen our intuitive sense of beauty and creativity.
Andrew Linzey

20 We are commanded to love God with all our minds, as well as with all our hearts, and we commit a great sin if we forbid or prevent that cultivation of the mind in others which would enable them to perform this duty.
Angelina Grimke (1805-1879, American Abolitionist, Feminist)

21 I am beginning to suspect all elaborate and special systems of education. They seem to me to be built up on the supposition that every child is a kind of idiot who must be taught to think.
Anne Sullivan (1866-1936, American Educator of the Deaf, Blind)

22 Education is an ornament in prosperity and a refuge in adversity.
Aristotle (384-322 BC, Greek Philosopher)

23 The educated differ from the uneducated as much as the living from the dead.
Aristotle (384-322 BC, Greek Philosopher)

24 Those who educate children well are more to be honored than they who produce them; for these only gave them life, those the art of living well.
Aristotle (384-322 BC, Greek Philosopher)

25 Education is the best provision for old age.
Aristotle (384-322 BC, Greek Philosopher)

26 The roots of education are bitter, but the fruit is sweet.
Aristotle (384-322 BC, Greek Philosopher)

27 The difficulty is to try and teach the multitude that something can be true and untrue at the same time.
Arthur Schopenhauer (1788-1860, German Philosopher)

28 Education is what survives when what has been learned has been forgotten.
B. F. Skinner (1904-1990, American Psychologist)

29 Education, we see, is not merely gaining knowledge or skills helpful toward productive work, though certainly that is a part of it. Rather it is a replenishment and an expansion of the natural thirst of the mind and soul. Learning is a gradual process of growth, each step building upon the other. It is a process whereby the learner organizes and integrates not only facts but attitudes and values. The Lord has told us that we must open our minds and our hearts to learn. There is a Chinese proverb: Wisdom is as the moon rises, perceptible not in progress but in result. As our knowledge is converted to wisdom, the door to opportunity is unlocked.
Barbara W. Winder

30 Both class and race survive education, and neither should. What is education then? If it doesn't help a human being to recognize that humanity is humanity, what is it for? So you can make a bigger salary than other people?
Beah Richards

31 On the education of the people of this country the fate of the country depends.
Benjamin Disraeli (1804-1881, British Statesman, Prime Minister)

32 Talk to a man about himself and he will listen for hours.
Benjamin Disraeli (1804-1881, British Statesman, Prime Minister)

33 There is no education like adversity.
Benjamin Disraeli (1804-1881, British Statesman, Prime Minister)

34 Upon the education of the people of this country the fate of this country depends.
Benjamin Disraeli (1804-1881, British Statesman, Prime Minister)

35 If a man empties his purse into his head, no man can take it away from him. An investment in knowledge always pays the best interest.
Benjamin Franklin (1706-1790, American Scientist, Publisher, Diplomat)

36 Train up a child in the way he should go; and when he is old he will not depart from it. [Proverbs 22:6]
Bible (Sacred Scriptures of Christians and Judaism)

37 America's founding fathers did not intend to take religion out of education. Many of the nation's greatest universities were founded by evangelists and religious leaders; but many of these have lost the founders concept and become secular institutions. Because of this attitude, secular education is stumbling and floundering.
Billy Graham (1918-, American Evangelist)

38 Education is the power to think clearly, the power to act well in the worlds work, and the power to appreciate life.
Brigham Young (1801-1877, American Mormon Leader)

39 The task of the modern educator is not to cut down jungles, but to irrigate deserts.
C. S. Lewis (1898-1963, British Academic, Writer, Christian Apologist)

40 Education has become a prisoner of contemporaneity. It is the past, not the dizzy present, that is the best door to the future.
Camille Paglia (1947-, American Author, Critic, Educator)

41 The only person who is educated is the one who has learned how to learn and change.
Carl Rogers (1902-1987, American Psychotherapist)

42 Rewards and punishment is the lowest form of education.
Chuang Tzu (369-286 BC, Chinese Philosopher)

43 If our education had included training to bear unpleasantness and to let the first shock pass until we could think more calmly, many an unbearable situation would become manageable, and many a nervous illness avoided. There is proverb expressing this. It says, trouble is a tunnel thorough which we pass and not a brick wall against which we must break our head.
Claire Weeks

44 We learn simply by the exposure of living. Much that passes for education is not education at all but ritual. The fact is that we are being educated when we know it least.
David P. Gardner

45 We are only now on the threshold of knowing the range of the educability of man-the perfectibility of man. We have never addressed ourselves to this problem before.
Dr. Jerome Brunner

46 Education is the ability to meet life's situations.
Dr. John G. Hibben

47 Educate people without religion and you make them but clever devils.
Duke of Wellington Arthur Wellesley (1769-1852, British Statesman, Military Leader)

48 An effeminate education weakens both the mind and the body.
Edgar Quinet (1803-1875, French Poet, Historian, Politician)

49 Education is not a discipline at all. Half vocational, half an emptiness dressed up in garments borrowed from philosophy, psychology, literature.
Edward Blishen (1920-, British Actor)

50 Education is a better safeguard of liberty than a standing army.
Edward Everett (1794-1865, American Statesman, Scholar)

51 Spoon feeding in the long run teaches us nothing but the shape of the spoon.
Edward M. Forster (1879-1970, British Novelist, Essayist)

52 You can lead a boy to college, but you cannot make him to think.
Elbert Hubbard (1859-1915, American Author, Publisher)

53 Better build schoolrooms for "the boy," than cells and gibbets for "the man."
Eliza Cook (1818-1889, British Poet)

54 The educator must above all understand how to wait; to reckon all effects in the light of the future, not of the present.
Ellen Key (1849-1926, Swedish Author, Feminist)

55 Since every effort in our educational life seems to be directed toward making of the child a being foreign to itself, it must of necessity produce individuals foreign to one another, and in everlasting antagonism with each other.
Emma Goldman (1869-1940, American Anarchist)

56 Only the educated are free.
Epictetus (50-120, Stoic Philosopher)

57 Real education must ultimately be limited to men who insist on knowing. The rest is mere sheep-herding.
Ezra Pound (1885-1972, American Poet, Critic)

58 True education makes for inequality; the inequality of individuality, the inequality of success, the glorious inequality of talent, of genius; for inequality, not mediocrity, individual superiority, not standardization, is the measure of the progress of the world.
Felix E. Schelling (1858-1945, American Educator)

59 It don't make much difference what you study, so long as you don't like it.
Finley Peter Dunne (1867-1936, American Journalist, Humorist)

60 Showing up at school already able to read is like showing up at the undertaker's already embalmed: people start worrying about being put out of their jobs.
Florence King (1936-, American Author, Critic)

61 Education is too important to be left solely to the educators.
Francis Keppel

62 Education is the fire-proofer of emotions.
Frank Crane (American Actor)

63 I can prove at any time that my education tried to make another person out of me than the one I became. It is for the harm, therefore, that my educators could have done me in accordance with their intentions that I reproach them; I demand from their hands the person I now am, and since they cannot give him to me, I make of my reproach and laughter a drumbeat sounding in the world beyond.
Franz Kafka (1883-1924, German Novelist, Short-Story Writer)

64 In large states public education will always be mediocre, for the same reason that in large kitchens the cooking is usually bad.
Friedrich Nietzsche (1844-1900, German Philosopher)

65 Every uneducated person is a caricature of himself.
Friedrich Schlegel (1772-1829, German Philosopher, Critic, Writer)

66 Education is the art of making man ethical.
Georg Hegel (1770-1831, German Philosopher)

67 What we call education and culture is for the most part nothing but the substitution of reading for experience, of literature for life, of the obsolete fictitious for the contemporary real.
George Bernard Shaw (1856-1950, Irish-born British Dramatist)

68 Those who trust us educate us.
George Eliot (1819-1880, British Novelist)

69 The great difficulty in education is to get experience out of ideas.
George Santayana (1863-1952, American Philosopher, Poet)

70 Education is the period during which you are being instructed by somebody you do not know, about something you do not want to know.
Gilbert K. Chesterton (1874-1936, British Author)

71 The wretch who digs the mine for bread, or ploughs, that others may be fed, feels less fatigued than that decreed to him who cannot think or read.
Hannah More (1745-1833, British Writer, Reformer, Philanthropist)

72 The purpose of education is to keep a culture from being drowned in senseless repetitions, each of which claims to offer a new insight.
Harold Rosenberg (1906-1978, American Art Critic, Author)

73 Now, if the principle of toleration were once admitted into classical education --if it were admitted that the great object is to read and enjoy a language, and the stress of the teaching were placed on the few things absolutely essential to this result, if the tortoise were allowed time to creep, and the bird permitted to fly, and the fish to swim, towards the enchanted and divine sources of Helicon --all might in their own way arrive there, and rejoice in its flowers, its beauty, and its coolness.
Harriet Beecher Stowe (1811-1896, American Novelist, Antislavery Campaigner)

74 They know enough who know how to learn.
Henry Brooks Adams (1838 - 1918, American Historian)

75 How could youths better learn to live than by at once trying the experiment of living?
Henry David Thoreau (1817-1862, American Essayist, Poet, Naturalist)

76 What does education often do? It makes a straight-cut ditch of a free, meandering brook.
Henry David Thoreau (1817-1862, American Essayist, Poet, Naturalist)

77 Public schools are the nurseries of all vice and immorality.
Henry Fielding (1707-1754, British Novelist, Dramatist)

78 Education is the knowledge of how to use the whole of oneself. Many men use but one or two faculties out of the score with which they are endowed. A man is educated who knows how to make a tool of every faculty--how to open it, how to keep it sharp, and how to apply it to all practical purposes.
Henry Ward Beecher (1813-1887, American Preacher, Orator, Writer)

79 Much learning does not teach understanding.
Heraclitus (535-475 BC, Greek Philosopher)

80 Education, then, beyond all other devices of human origin, is the great equalizer of the conditions of men -- the balance-wheel of the social machinery.
Horace Mann (1796-1859, American Educator)

81 A human being is not attaining his full heights until he is educated.
Horace Mann (1796-1859, American Educator)

82 Education is our only political safety. Outside of this ark all is deluge.
Horace Mann (1796-1859, American Educator)

83 The public school has become the established church of secular society.
Ivan Illich (1926-, Austrian-born American Theologian, Author)

84 The average Ph.D. thesis is nothing, but the transference of bones from one graveyard to another.
J. Frank Doble (1888-1964, American Author)

85 A liberally educated person meets new ideas with curiosity and fascination. An illiberally educated person meets new ideas with fear.
James B. Stockdale

86 The paradox of education is precisely this -- that as one begins to become conscious one begins to examine the society in which he is being educated.
James Baldwin (1924-1987, American Author)

87 It is very nearly impossible... to become an educated person in a country so distrustful of the independent mind.
James Baldwin (1924-1987, American Author)

88 A child cannot be taught by anyone who despises him, and a child cannot afford to be fooled.
James Baldwin (1924-1987, American Author)

89 Learned Institutions ought to be favorite objects with every free people. They throw that light over the public mind which is the best security against crafty and dangerous encroachments on the public liberty.
James Madison (1751-1836, American Statesman, President)

90 The regeneration of society is the regeneration of society by individual education.
Jean De La Bruyere (1645-1696, French Writer)

91 Education makes us more stupid than the brutes. A thousand voices call to us on every hand, but our ears are stopped with wisdom.
Jean Giraudoux (1882-1944, French Diplomat, Author)

92 We are born weak, we need strength; helpless, we need aid; foolish, we need reason. All that we lack at birth, all that we need when we come to man's estate, is the gift of education.
Jean Jacques Rousseau (1712-1778, Swiss Political Philosopher, Educationist, Essayist)

93 The principle goal of education is to create men who are capable of doing new things, not simply of repeating what other generations have done -- men who are creative, inventive and discoverers.
Jean Piaget (1896-1980, Swiss Experimenters and Theorists)

94 Formal education will make you a living; self-education will make you a fortune.
Jim Rohn (American Businessman, Author, Speaker, Philosopher)

95 They teach in academies far too many things, and far too much that is useless.
Johann Wolfgang Von Goethe (1749-1832, German Poet, Dramatist, Novelist)

96 Higher education must lead the march back to the fundamentals of human relationships, to the old discovery that is ever new, that man does not live by bread alone.
John A. Hannah

97 There are two educations. One should teach us how to make a living and the other how to live.
John Adams (1735-1826, Second President of the USA)

98 Education is a social process. Education is growth. Education is, not a preparation for life; education is life itself.
John Dewey (1859-1952, American Philosopher, Educator)

99 Let us think of education as the means of developing our greatest abilities, because in each of us there is a private hope and dream which, fulfilled, can be translated into benefit for everyone and greater strength for our nation.
John F. Kennedy (1917-1963, Thirty-fifth President of the USA)

100 Our progress as a nation can be no swifter than our progress in education. The human mind is our fundamental resource.
John F. Kennedy (1917-1963, Thirty-fifth President of the USA)

101 People should be free to find or make for themselves the kinds of educational experience they want their children to have.
John Holt (1908-1967, Australian Politician, Prime Minister)

102 The only fence against the world is a thorough knowledge of it.
John Locke (1632-1704, British Philosopher)

103 The aim of education should be to convert the mind into living fountain, and not a reservoir.
John Mason

104 The child who desires education will be bettered by it; the child who dislikes it disgraced.
John Ruskin (1819-1900, British Critic, Social Theorist)

105 The first condition of education is being able to put someone to wholesome and meaningful work.
John Ruskin (1819-1900, British Critic, Social Theorist)

106 Modern education has devoted itself to the teaching of impudence, and then we complain that we can no longer control our mobs.
John Ruskin (1819-1900, British Critic, Social Theorist)

107 The worst education which teaches self-denial, is better than the best which teaches everything else, and not that.
John Sterling (American Sports Announcer)

108 School is where you go between when your parents can't take you, and industry can't take you.
John Updike (1932-, American Novelist, Critic)

109 I am entirely certain that twenty years from now we will look back at education as it is practiced in most schools today and wonder that we could have tolerated anything so primitive.
John W. Gardner (1912-, American Educator, Social Activist)

110 America's greatness has been the greatness of a free people who shared certain moral commitments. Freedom without moral commitment is aimless and promptly self-destructive.
John W. Gardner (1912-, American Educator, Social Activist)

111 What sculpture is to a block of marble, education is to an human soul.
Joseph Addison (1672-1719, British Essayist, Poet, Statesman)

112 Education is a weapon, whose effect depends on who holds it in his hands and at whom it is aimed.
Joseph Stalin (1879-1953, Georgian-born Soviet Leader)

113 Adults who still derive childlike pleasure from hanging gifts of a ready-made education on the Christmas tree of a child waiting outside the door to life do not realize how unreceptive they are making the children to everything that constitutes the true surprise of life.
Karl Kraus (1874-1936, Austrian Satirist)

114 Education is a crutch with which the foolish attack the wise to prove that they are not idiots.
Karl Kraus (1874-1936, Austrian Satirist)

115 People commonly educate their children as they build their houses, according to some plan they think beautiful, without considering whether it is suited to the purposes for which they are designed.
Lady Mary Wortley Montagu (1689-1762, British Society Figure, Letter Writer)

116 Education is a method whereby one acquires a higher grade of prejudices.
Laurence J. Peter

117 We must do better or perish as the nation we know today.
Lauro Cavazos

118 No one wants a good education. Everyone wants a good degree.
Lee Rudolph

119 Education is a private matter between the person and the world of knowledge and experience, and has little to do with school or college.
Lillian Smith (1897-1966, American Author)

120 All my life, as down an abyss without a bottom. I have been pouring van loads of information into that vacancy of oblivion I call my mind.
Logan Pearsall Smith (1865-1946, Anglo-American Essayist, Aphorist)

121 Life is my college. May I graduate well, and earn some honors.
Louisa May Alcott (1832-1888, American Author)

122 The purpose of education is to replace an empty mind with an open one
Malcolm S. Forbes (1919-1990, American Publisher, Businessman)

123 Without education, you're not going anywhere in this world.
Malcolm X (1925-1965, American Black Leader, Activist)

124 The real object of education is to have a man in the condition of continually asking questions.
Mandell Creighton (1843-1901, British Historian, Bishop)

125 Our attitude towards ourselves should be "to be satiable in learning" and towards others "to be tireless in teaching."
Mao Zedong (1893-1976, Founder of Chinese Communist State)

126 If an educational act is to be efficacious, it will be only that one which tends to help toward the complete unfolding of life. To be thus helpful it is necessary rigorously to avoid the arrest of spontaneous movements and the imposition of arbitrary tasks.
Maria Montessori (1870-1952, Italian Educator)

127 If education is always to be conceived along the same antiquated lines of a mere transmission of knowledge, there is little to be hoped from it in the bettering of man's future. For what is the use of transmitting knowledge if the individual's total development lags behind?
Maria Montessori (1870-1952, Italian Educator)

128 Soap and education are not as sudden as a massacre, but they are more deadly in the long run. Training is everything. The peach was once a bitter almond; cauliflower is nothing but cabbage with a college education.
Mark Twain (1835-1910, American Humorist, Writer)

129 I have never let my schooling interfere with my education.
Mark Twain (1835-1910, American Humorist, Writer)

130 The school system, custodian of print culture, has no place for the rugged individual. It is, indeed, the homogenizing hopper into which we toss our integral tots for processing.
Marshall Mcluhan (1911-1980, Canadian Communications Theorist)

131 Education is the process of driving a set of prejudices down your throat.
Martin H. Fischer

132 I am afraid that the schools will prove the very gates of hell, unless they diligently labor in explaining the Holy Scriptures and engraving them in the heart of the youth.
Martin Luther (1483-1546, German Leader of the Protestant Reformation)

133 Education helps one case cease being intimidated by strange situations.
Maya Angelou (1928-, African-American poet, Writer, Performer)

134 The greatest education in the world is watching the masters at work.
Michael Jackson (1958-, American Musician, Songwriter)

135 We only labor to stuff the memory, and leave the conscience and the understanding unfurnished and void.
Michel Eyquem De Montaigne (1533-1592, French Philosopher, Essayist)

136 In true education, anything that comes to our hand is as good as a book: the prank of a page- boy, the blunder of a servant, a bit of table talk -- they are all part of the curriculum.
Michel Eyquem De Montaigne (1533-1592, French Philosopher, Essayist)

137 Most owners of small businesses openly state that they believe in the value of skills and operational training. However, they also admit that they themselves undertake very little training, or offer only limited training to their employees, because of time restraints.
Moshe Gerstenhaber (American Business Executive)

138 To me education is a leading out of what is already there in the pupil's soul. To Miss Mackay it is a putting in of something that is not there, and that is not what I call education, I call it intrusion.
Muriel Spark (1918-, British Novelist)

139 Education comes from within; you get it by struggle and effort and thought.
Napoleon Hill (1883-1970, American Speaker, Motivational Writer, "Think and Grow Rich")

140 The main part of intellectual education is not the acquisition of facts but learning how to make facts live.
Oliver Wendell Holmes Jr. (1841-1935, American Judge)

141 Education makes a people easy to lead, but difficult to drive; easy to govern, but impossible to enslave.
Omar Nelson Bradley (1893-1981, American General)

142 No pain that we suffer, no trial that we experience is wasted. It ministers to the development of such qualities as patience, faith, fortitude and humility. All that we suffer and all that we endure, especially when we endure it patiently, builds up our characters, purifies our hearts, expands our souls, and makes us more tender and charitable, more worthy to be called the children of God... and it is through sorrow and suffering, toil and tribulation, that we gain the education that we come here to acquire and which will make us more like our Father and Mother in heaven.
Orson F. Whitney

143 The whole theory of modern education is radically unsound. Fortunately in England, at any rate, education produces no effect whatsoever. If it did, it would prove a serious danger to the upper classes, and probably lead to acts of violence.
Oscar Wilde (1856-1900, British Author, Wit)

144 Education is an admirable thing, but it is well to remember from time to time that nothing that is worth knowing can be taught.
Oscar Wilde (1856-1900, British Author, Wit)

145 Parents have a right to insist that godless evolution not be taught to their children.
Patrick Buchanan (1938-, American Statesman)

146 Life at university, with its intellectual and inconclusive discussions at a postgraduate level is on the whole a bad training for the real world. Only men of very strong character surmount this handicap.
Paul Chambers (1904-1981, American Business Executive)

147 The most important outcome of education is to help students become independent of formal education.
Paul E. Gray

148 The best education consists in immunizing people against systematic attempts at education
Paul Karl Feyerabend

149 When a subject becomes totally obsolete we make it a required course.
Peter F. Drucker (1909-, American Management Consultant, Author)

150 Education can no longer be the sole property of the state.
Peter F. Drucker (1909-, American Management Consultant, Author)

151 The trouble with being educated is that it takes a long time; it uses up the better part of your life and when you are finished what you know is that you would have benefited more by going into banking.
Philip K. Dick (1928-1982, American Science Fiction Writer)

152 In my early life, and probably even today, it is not sufficiently understood that a child's education should include at least a rudimentary grasp of religion, sex, and money. Without a basic knowledge of these three primary facts in a normal human being's life --subjects which stir the emotions, create events and opportunities, and if they do not wholly decide must greatly influence an individual's personality --no human being's education can have a safe foundation.
Phyllis Bottome (1884-1963, American Writer)

153 The system -- the American one, at least -- is a vast and noble experiment. It has been polestar and exemplar for other nations. But from kindergarten until she graduates from college the girl is treated in it exactly like her brothers. She studies the same subjects, becomes proficient at the same sports. Oh, it is a magnificent lore she learns, education for the mind beyond anything Jane Austen or Saint Theresa or even Mrs. Pankhurst ever dreamed. It is truly Utopian. But Utopia was never meant to exist on this disheveled planet.
Phyllis Mcginley (1905-1978, American Poet, Author)

154 Let us describe the education of our men. What then is the education to be? Perhaps we could hardly find a better than that which the experience of the past has already discovered, which consists, I believe, in gymnastic, for the body, and music for the mind.
Plato (427-347 BC, Greek Philosopher)

155 Knowledge which is acquired under compulsion obtains no hold on the mind.
Plato (427-347 BC, Greek Philosopher)

156 The most important part of education is proper training in the nursery.
Plato (427-347 BC, Greek Philosopher)

157 It is only the ignorant who despise education.
Publilius Syrus (1st Century BC, Roman Writer)

158 Out of my general world-pattern-trend studies there now comes strong evidence that nothing is going to be quite so surprising and abrupt in the future history of man as the forward evolution in the educational process.
R. Buckminster Fuller (1895-1983, American Inventor, Designer, Poet, Philosopher)

159 What usually happens in the educational process is that the faculties are dulled, overloaded, stuffed and paralyzed so that by the time most people are mature they have lost their innate capabilities.
R. Buckminster Fuller (1895-1983, American Inventor, Designer, Poet, Philosopher)

160 Formal education is but an incident in the lifetime of an individual. Most of us who have given the subject any study have come to realize that education is a continuous process ending only when ambition comes to a halt.
R. I. Rees

161 Getting things done is not always what is most important. There is value in allowing others to learn, even if the task is not accomplished as quickly, efficiently or effectively.
R.D. Clyde

162 Respect the child. Be not too much his parent. Trespass not on his solitude.
Ralph Waldo Emerson (1803-1882, American Poet, Essayist)

163 We are shut up in schools and college recitation rooms for ten or fifteen years, and come out at last with a belly-full of words and do not know a thing. The things taught in schools and colleges are not an education, but the means of education.
Ralph Waldo Emerson (1803-1882, American Poet, Essayist)

164 The secret in education lies in respecting the student.
Ralph Waldo Emerson (1803-1882, American Poet, Essayist)

165 I pay the schoolmaster, but it is the school boys who educate my son.
Ralph Waldo Emerson (1803-1882, American Poet, Essayist)

166 There is a time in every man's education when he arrives at the conviction that envy is ignorance; that imitation is suicide.
Ralph Waldo Emerson (1803-1882, American Poet, Essayist)

167 It's fairly obvious that American education is a cultural flop. Americans are not a well- educated people culturally, and their vocational education often has to be learned all over again after they leave school and college. On the other hand, they have open quick minds and if their education has little sharp positive value, it has not the stultifying effects of a more rigid training.
Raymond Chandler (1888-1959, American Author)

168 We live less and less, and we learn more and more. Sensibility is surrendering to intelligence.
Remy De Gourmont (1858-1915, French Novelist, Philosopher, Poet, Playwright)

169 Mentoring is all about people -- it's about caring, about relationships and sensitivity. As it becomes increasingly in vogue it is becoming too formulated -- concerned with performance metrics, critical success factors, investment and spending. It'll be a disaster.
Rene Carayol (American Business Executive)

170 There's a new tribunal now higher than God's --The educated man s!
Robert Browning (1812-1889, British Poet)

171 The mark of a true MBA is that he is often wrong but seldom in doubt.
Robert Buzzell (American Professor, Harvard Business School)

172 Most people are willing to pay more to be amused than to be educated.
Robert C. Savage

173 The education of a man is never complete until he dies.
Robert E. Lee (1807-1870, American Confederate Army Commander)

174 Education is the ability to listen to almost anything without losing your temper or your self- confidence.
Robert Frost (1875-1963, American Poet)

175 Education is hanging around until you've caught on.
Robert Frost (1875-1963, American Poet)

176 Education is not to reform students or amuse them or to make them expert technicians. It is to unsettle their minds, widen their horizons, inflame their intellects, teach them to think straight, if possible.
Robert M. Hutchins (1899-1977, American University President)

177 The college graduate is presented with a sheepskin to cover his intellectual nakedness.
Robert M. Hutchins (1899-1977, American University President)

178 The three major administrative problems on a campus are sex for the students, athletics for the alumni, and parking for the faculty.
Robert M. Hutchins (1899-1977, American University President)

179 The benefits of education and of useful knowledge, generally diffused through a community, are essential to the preservation of a free government.
Sam Houston (1793-1863, American Soldier, Statesman)

180 Education must have two foundations --morality as a support for virtue, prudence as a defense for self against the vices of others. By letting the balance incline to the side of morality, you only make dupes or martyrs; by letting it incline to the other, you make calculating egoists.
Sebastien-Roch Nicolas De Chamfort (1741-1794, French Writer, Journalist, Playwright)

181 The most important part of teaching is to teach what it is to know.
Simone Weil (1910-1943, French Philosopher, Mystic)

182 Philosophy, astronomy, and politics were marked at zero, I remember. Botany variable, geology profound as regards the mud stains from any region within fifty miles of town, chemistry eccentric, anatomy unsystematic, sensational literature and crime records unique, violin player, boxer, swordsman, lawyer, and self-poisoner by cocaine and tobacco.
Sir Arthur Conan Doyle (1859-1930, British Author, "Sherlock Holmes")

183 Education costs money, but then so does ignorance.
Sir Claus Moser (1922-, German-born British Academic, Warden of Wadham College, Oxford)

184 A wise system of education will at last teach us how little man yet knows, how much he has still to learn.
Sir John Lubbock (1834-1913, British Statesman, Banker, Naturalist)

185 Education would be so much more effective if its purpose were to ensure that by the time they leave school every boy and girl should know how much they don't know, and be imbued with a lifelong desire to know it.
Sir William Haley

186 Whom do I call educated? First, those who manage well the circumstances they encounter day by day. Next, those who are decent and honorable in their intercourse with all men, bearing easily and good naturedly what is offensive in others and being as agreeable and reasonable to their associates as is humanly possible to be... those who hold their pleasures always under control and are not ultimately overcome by their misfortunes... those who are not spoiled by their successes, who do not desert their true selves but hold their ground steadfastly as wise and sober -- minded men.
Socrates (469-399 BC, Greek Philosopher of Athens)

187 An education obtained with money is worse than no education at all
Socrates (469-399 BC, Greek Philosopher of Athens)

188 Invest in yourself, in your education. There's nothing better.
Sylvia Porter

189 A man who has never gone to school may steal from a freight car; but if he has a university education, he may steal the whole railroad.
Theodore Roosevelt (1858-1919, Twenty-sixth President of the USA)

190 To educate a man in mind and not in morals is to educate a menace to society.
Theodore Roosevelt (1858-1919, Twenty-sixth President of the USA)

191 Perhaps the most valuable result of all education is the ability to make yourself do the things you have to do, when it ought to be done, whether you like it or not. It is the first lesson that ought to be learned and however early a person's training begins, it is probably the last lesson a person learns thoroughly.
Thomas H. Huxley (1825-1895, British Biologist, Educator)

192 It is because the body is a machine that education is possible. Education is the formation of habits, a superinducing of an artificial organization upon the natural organization of the body.
Thomas H. Huxley (1825-1895, British Biologist, Educator)

193 Enlighten the people generally, and tyranny and oppressions of body and mind will vanish like evil spirits at the dawn of day.
Thomas Jefferson (1743-1826, Third President of the USA)

194 Every act of conscious learning requires the willingness to suffer an injury to one's self-esteem. That is why young children, before they are aware of their own self-importance, learn so easily; and why older persons, especially if vain or important, cannot learn at all.
Thomas Szasz (1920-, American Psychiatrist)

195 Education ought everywhere to be religious education. Parents are bound to employ no instructors who will instruct their children religiously. To commit children to the care of irreligious persons is to commit lambs to the superintendency of wolves.
Timothy Dwight

196 We are dealing with the best-educated generation in history. But they've got a brain dressed up with nowhere to go.
Timothy Leary (1921-1996, American Actor)

197 He who opens a school door, closes a prison.
Victor Hugo (1802-1885, French Poet, Dramatist, Novelist)

198 Education is not merely a means for earning a living or an instrument for the acquisition of wealth. It is an initiation into life of spirit, a training of the human soul in the pursuit of truth and the practice of virtue.
Vijaya Lakshmi Pandit (1900-1990, Indian Diplomat)

199 There is that indescribable freshness and unconsciousness about an illiterate person that humbles and mocks the power of the noblest expressive genius.
Walt Whitman (1819-1892, American Poet)

200 No amount of charters, direct primaries, or short ballots will make a democracy out of an illiterate people.
Walter Lippmann (1889-1974, American Journalist)

201 The best education in the world is that got by struggling to get a living.
Wendell Phillips (1811-1884, American Reformer, Orator)

202 It is no small mischief to a boy, that many of the best years of his life should be devoted to the learning of what can never be of any real use to any human being. His mind is necessarily rendered frivolous and superficial by the long habit of attaching importance to words instead of things; to sound instead of sense.
William Cobbett (1762-1835, British Journalist, Reformer)

203 He is to be educated not because he's to make shoes, nails, and pins, but because he is a man.
William Ellery Channing (1780-1842, American Unitarian Minister, Author)

204 Anyone who has passed through the regular gradations of a classical education, and is not made a fool by it, may consider himself as having had a very narrow escape.
William Hazlitt (1778-1830, British Essayist)

205 Education is a progressive discovery of our ignorance.
William J. Durant (1885-1981, American Historian, Essayist)

206 Our schools should get five years to get back to where they were in 1963. If they're still bad maybe we should declare educational bankruptcy, give the people their money and let them educate themselves and start their own schools
William John Bennett (1943-, American Federal Official)

EFFICIENCY

1 Efficiency is intelligent laziness.
David Dunham

2 Efficiency is doing better what is already being done.
Peter F. Drucker (1909-, American Management Consultant, Author)

EFFORT

1 I don't believe people die from hard work. They die from stress and worry and fear -- the negative emotions. Those are the killers, not hard work. The fact is, in our society today, most people don't understand what hard work is all about.
A. L. Williams (Born 1942, American insurance executive)

2 If your efforts are sometimes greeted with indifference, don't lose heart. The sun puts on a wonderful show at daybreak, yet most of the people in the audience go on sleeping.
Ada Teixeira

3 Easy DOESN'T do it.
Al Bernstein

4 The bitter and the sweet come from the outside, the hard from within, from one's own efforts.
Albert Einstein (1879-1955, German-born American Physicist)

5 Infatuated, half through conceit, half through love of my art, I achieve the impossible working as no one else ever works.
Alexandre Dumas (1802-1870, French Novelist, Dramatist)

6 The one thing that matters is the effort.
Antoine De Saint-Exupery (1900-1944, French Aviator, Writer)

7 It is easier to go down a hill than up, but the view is from the top.
Arnold Bennett (1867-1931, British Novelist)

8 Always make a total effort, even when the odds are against you.
Arnold Palmer (1929-, American Golfer)

9 The secret of the truly successful, I believe, is that they learned very early in life how not to be busy. They saw through that adage, repeated to me so often in childhood, that anything worth doing is worth doing well. The truth is, many things are worth doing only in the most slovenly, halfhearted fashion possible, and many other things are not worth doing at all.
Barbara Ehrenreich (1941-, American Author, Columnist)

10 Doing your own thing" is a generous act. Being gifted creates obligations, which means you owe the world your best effort at the work you love. You too are a natural resource.
Barbara Sher (American Author of "I Could Do Anything If I Only Knew What It Was")

11 You may be disappointed if you fail, but you are doomed if you don't try.
Beverly Sills (American Opera Singer)

12 The race is not to the swift, nor the battle to the strong, neither yet bread to the wise, nor yet riches to men of understanding, nor yet favor to men of skill; but time and chance happeneth to them all. [Ecclesiastes 9:11]
Bible (Sacred Scriptures of Christians and Judaism)

13 The struggle alone pleases us, not the victory.
Blaise Pascal (1623-1662, French Scientist, Religious Philosopher)

14 Start early and begin raising the bar throughout the day.
Bruce Jenner (1949-, American Olympian, Actor, Speaker, Entrepreneur, Sports Commentator)

15 I learned that the only way you are going to get anywhere in life is to work hard at it. Whether you're a musician, a writer, an athlete or a businessman, there is no getting around it. If you do, you'll win -- if you don't you won t.
Bruce Jenner (1949-, American Olympian, Actor, Speaker, Entrepreneur, Sports Commentator)

16 The Buddhas do but tell the way; it is for you to swelter at the task.
Buddha (568-488 BC, Founder of Buddhism)

17 The smallest effort is not lost. Each wavelet on the ocean tost aids in the ebb-tide or the flow; each rain-drop makes some floweret blow; each struggle lessens human woe.
Charles Mackay (1814-1889, Scottish Poet, Song Writer)

18 The healthiest competition occurs when average people win by putting above average effort.
Colin Powell (1937-, American Army General)

19 But the effort, the effort! And as the marrow is eaten out of a man's bones and the soul out of his belly, contending with the strange rapacity of savage life, the lower stage of creation, he cannot make the effort any more.
D. H. Lawrence (1885-1930, British Author)

20 Do your duty, that is best; leave unto the Lord the rest.
David O. Mckay

21 The results you achieve will be in direct proportion to the effort you apply.
Denis Waitley (1933-, American Author, Speaker, Trainer, Peak Performance Expert)

22 Success is almost totally dependent upon drive and persistence. The extra energy required to make another effort or try another approach is the secret of winning.
Denis Waitley (1933-, American Author, Speaker, Trainer, Peak Performance Expert)

23 Swing hard, in case they throw the ball where you're swinging.
Duke Snider

24 You have to accept whatever comes and the only important thing is that you meet it with the best you have to give.
Eleanor Roosevelt (1884-1962, American First Lady, Columnist, Lecturer, Humanitarian)

25 Much effort, much prosperity.
Euripides (480-406 BC, Greek Tragic Poet)

26 Welcome the task that makes you go beyond yourself.
Frank Mcgee

27 One may go a long way after one is tired.
French Proverb

28 If a man has done his best, what else is there?
George S. Patton (1885-1945, American Army General during World War II)

29 If one has not given everything, one has given nothing.
Georges Guynemer

30 It is not the truth that a man possesses, or believes that he possesses, but the earnest effort which he puts forward to reach the truth, which constitutes the worth of a man. For it is not by the possession, but the search after truth that he enlarges his power, wherein alone consists his ever-increasing perfection.
Gotthold Lessing (1729-1781, German Dramatist, Critic)

31 People travel in the way of least resistance, by choosing one's environment, one will travel in a particular way.
H. Janicki

32 Be true to the best you know. This is your high ideal. If you do your best, you cannot do more.
H. W. Dresses

33 The human condition is such that pain and effort are not just symptoms which can be removed without changing life itself; they are the modes in which life itself, together with the necessity to which it is bound, makes itself felt. For mortals, the "easy life of the gods" would be a lifeless life.
Hannah Arendt (1906-1975, German-born American Political Philosopher)

34 Life does not require us to make good; it asks only that we give our best at each level of experience.
Harold Ruopp

35 Everyone confesses in the abstract that exertion which brings out all the powers of body and mind is the best thing for us all; but practically most people do all they can to get rid of it, and as a general rule nobody does much more than circumstances drive them to do.
Harriet Beecher Stowe (1811-1896, American Novelist, Antislavery Campaigner)

36 Whenever a man does the best he can, then that is all he can do.
Harry S. Truman (1884-1972, Thirty-third President of the USA)

37 When we do the best we can, we never know what miracle is wrought in our life, or in the life of another.
Helen Keller (1880-1968, American Blind/Deaf Author, Lecturer, Amorist)

38 Things don't turn up in this world until somebody turns them up.
James A. Garfield (1831-1881, Twentieth President of the USA)

39 Racing takes everything you've got -- intellectually, emotionally, physically -- and then you have to find about ten percent more and use that too.
Janet Guthrie (American Race Car Driver)

40 I've always tried to do my best on the ball field. I can't do any more than that. I always try to give one hundred percent; and if my team loses, I come back and give one hundred percent the next day.
Jesse Barfield (American Baseball Player)

41 For every disciplined effort there is a multiple reward.
Jim Rohn (American Businessman, Author, Speaker, Philosopher)

42 I would rather earn 1% off a 100 people's efforts than 100% of my own efforts.
John D. Rockefeller (1839-1937, American Industrialist, Philanthropist, Founder Exxon)

43 In the past, those who foolishly sought power by riding on the back of the tiger ended up inside.
John F. Kennedy (1917-1963, Thirty-fifth President of the USA)

44 Efforts and courage are not enough without purpose and direction.
John F. Kennedy (1917-1963, Thirty-fifth President of the USA)

45 The essence of our effort to see that every child has a chance must be to assure each an equal opportunity, not to become equal, but to become different- to realize whatever unique potential of body, mind and spirit he or she possesses.
John Fischer

46 Effort is only effort when it begins to hurt.
Jose Ortega Y Gasset (1883-1955, Spanish Essayist, Philosopher)

47 champions know there are no shortcuts to the top. They climb the mountain one step at a time. they have no use for helicopters!
Judi Adler

48 Push yourself again and again. Don't give an inch until the final buzzer sounds.
Larry Bird (1956-, American Basketball Player, Coach)

49 If you want something done, ask a busy person to do it. The more things you do, the more you can do.
Lucille Ball (1911-1989, American Actress, Producer)

50 Despite the success cult, men are most deeply moved not by the reaching of the goal but by the grandness of the effort involved in getting there -- or failing to get there.
Max Lerner (1902-, American Author, Columnist)

51 What you can't get out of, get into wholeheartedly.
Mignon McLaughlin (1915?-, American Author, Editor)

52 There's no taking trout with dry breeches.
Miguel De Cervantes (1547-1616, Spanish Novelist, Dramatist, Poet)

53 Effort only fully releases its reward after a person refuses to quit.
Napoleon Hill (1883-1970, American Speaker, Motivational Writer, "Think and Grow Rich")

54 God gives every bird his worm, but He does not throw it into the nest.
P. D. James (1920-, British Mystery Writer)

55 If someone had told me I would be pope one day, I would have studied harder.
Pope John I (Italian Pope)

56 If a job's worth doing, it's worth doing well.
Proverb

57 The only method by which people can be supported is out of the effort of those who are earning their own way. We must not create a deterrent to hard work.
Robert A. Taft (1889-1953, American Politician)

58 Inscribe all human effort with one word, artistry's haunting curse, the Incomplete!
Robert Browning (1812-1889, British Poet)

59 What we hope ever to do with ease, we must learn first to do with diligence.
Samuel Johnson (1709-1784, British Author)

60 When you do something, you should burn yourself up completely, like a good bonfire, leaving no trace of yourself.
Shunryu Suzuki (Japanese Zen Master)

61 Freedom from effort in the present merely means that there has been effort stored up in the past.
Theodore Roosevelt (1858-1919, Twenty-sixth President of the USA)

62 There has never yet been a man in our history who led a life of ease whose name is worth remembering.
Theodore Roosevelt (1858-1919, Twenty-sixth President of the USA)

63 I made up my mind long ago that life was too short to do anything for myself that I could pay others to do for me.
W. Somerset Maugham (1874-1965, British Novelist, Playwright)

64 I want to be remembered as the guy who gave his all whenever he was on the field.
Walter Payton (American Football Player)

65 I want you to start a crusade in you life -- to dare to be your best.
William Danforth (American Entrepreneur, Author)

66 We forget that every good that is worth possessing must be paid for in strokes of daily effort. We postpone and postpone, until those smiling possibilities are dead.
William James (1842-1910, American Psychologist, Professor, Author)

67 It is vain to do with more what can be done with less.
William Of Occam

68 Nothing can come of nothing.
William Shakespeare (1564-1616, British Poet, Playwright, Actor)

69 You have to give 100 percent in the first half of the game. If that isn't enough, in the second half, you have to give what is left.
Yogi Berra (1925-, American Baseball Player)

70 If you have enough push, you don't have to worry about the pull.
Zig Ziglar (American Sales Trainer, Author, Motivational Speaker)

EGOTISM

1 There is nothing in the world so enjoyable as a thorough-going monomania...
Agnes Repplier (1858-1950, American Author, Social Critic)

2 If the egotist is weak, his egotism is worthless. If the egotist is strong, acute, full of distinctive character, his egotism is precious, and remains a possession of the race.
Alexander Smith (1830-1867, Scottish Poet, Author)

3 An egotist is a person interested in himself than in me!
Ambrose Bierce (1842-1914, American Author, Editor, Journalist, "The Devil's Dictionary")

4 Egotist. A person of low taste, more interested in himself than me.
Ambrose Bierce (1842-1914, American Author, Editor, Journalist, "The Devil's Dictionary")

5 We reproach people for talking about themselves; but it is the subject they treat best.
Anatole France (1844-1924, French Writer)

6 If egotism means a terrific interest in one's self, egotism is absolutely essential to efficient living.
Arnold Bennett (1867-1931, British Novelist)

7 Egotism is the anesthetic given by a kindly nature to relieve the pain of being a damned fool.
Bellamy Brooks

8 An inflated consciousness is always egocentric and conscious of nothing but its own existence. It is incapable of learning from the past, incapable of understanding contemporary events, and incapable of drawing right conclusions about the future. It is hypnotized by itself and therefore cannot be argued with. It inevitably dooms itself to calamities that must strike it dead.
Carl Jung (1875-1961, Swiss Psychiatrist)

9 I" is a militant social tendency, working to hold and enlarge its place in the general current of tendencies. So far as it can it waxes, as all life does. To think of it as apart from society is a palpable absurdity of which no one could be guilty who really saw it as a fact of life.
Charles Horton Cooley (1864-1929, American Sociologist)

10 Sensitiveness is closely allied to egotism; and excessive sensibility is only another name for morbid self-consciousness. The cure for tender sensibilities is to make more of our objects and less of our selves.
Christian Nevell Bovee (1820-1904, American Author, Lawyer)

11 The one who overcomes egotism rids themselves of the most stubborn obstacle that blocks the way to all true greatness and all true happiness.
Coltvos

12 When Jerry Lewis and I were big, we used to go to parties, and everybody thought I was big- headed and stuck up, and I wasn't. It was because I didn't know how to speak good English, so I used to keep my mouth shut.
Dean Martin (1917-1995, French-born American-born American Actor, Singer, Lush)

13 Big egos are big shields for lots of empty space.
Diana Black

14 The source of our actions resides in an unconscious propensity to regard ourselves as the center, the cause, and the conclusion of time. Our reflexes and our pride transform into a planet the parcel of flesh and consciousness we are.
E. M. Cioran (1911-, Rumanian-born French Philosopher)

15 What will the world be quite overturned when you die?
Epictetus (50-120, Stoic Philosopher)

16 We would rather speak badly of ourselves than not talk about ourselves at all.
François de La Rochefoucauld (1613-1680, French classical writer)

17 Egotism is the anesthetic that dulls the pain of stupidity.
Frank Leahy

18 One must learn to love oneself with a wholesome and healthy love, so that one can bear to be with oneself and need not roam.
Friedrich Nietzsche (1844-1900, German Philosopher)

19 The egoism which enters into our theories does not affect their sincerity; rather, the more our egoism is satisfied, the more robust is our belief.
George Eliot (1819-1880, British Novelist)

20 Egotism is the art of seeing in yourself what others cannot see.
George V. Higgins (1939-, American Novelist)

21 There is nothing more natural than to consider everything as starting from oneself, chosen as the center of the world; one finds oneself thus capable of condemning the world without even wanting to hear its deceitful chatter.
Guy Debord (1931-, French Philosopher)

22 If someone is blessed as I am is not willing to clean out the barn, who will?
H. Ross Perot (1930-, American Businessman & Politician, Founder EDS)

23 I should not talk so much about myself if there were anybody else whom I knew as well.
Henry David Thoreau (1817-1862, American Essayist, Poet, Naturalist)

24 He who does not think much of himself is much more esteemed than he imagines.
Johann Wolfgang Von Goethe (1749-1832, German Poet, Dramatist, Novelist)

25 Mastery passes often for egotism.
Johann Wolfgang Von Goethe (1749-1832, German Poet, Dramatist, Novelist)

26 If being an egomaniac means I believe in what I do and in my art or my music, then in that respect you can call me that I believe in what I do, and I'll say it.
John Lennon (1940-1980, British Rock Musician)

27 When a man is wrapped up in himself he makes a pretty small package.
John Ruskin (1819-1900, British Critic, Social Theorist)

28 Our own self-love draws a thick veil between us and our faults.
Lord Chesterfield (1694-1773, British Statesman, Author)

29 The nice thing about egotists is that they don't talk about other people.
Lucille S. Harper

30 Egotism is usually subversive of sagacity.
Marianne Moore (1887-1972, American Poet)

31 The pest of society are the egotist, they are dull and bright, sacred and profane, course and fine. It is a disease that like the flu falls on all constitutions.
Ralph Waldo Emerson (1803-1882, American Poet, Essayist)

32 Loving is the only sure road out of darkness, the only serum known that cures self- centeredness.
Roger M'Ckuen

33 Egotism is the source and summary of all faults and miseries.
Thomas Carlyle (1795-1881, Scottish Philosopher, Author)

34 If some really acute observer made as much of egotism as Freud has made of sex, people would forget a good deal about sex and find the explanation for everything in egotism.
Wallace Stevens (1879-1955, American Poet)

35 Don't talk about yourself; it will be done when you leave.
Wilson Mizner (1876-1933, American Author)

ELECTIONS

1 If elected I shall be thankful; if not, it will be all the same.
Abraham Lincoln (1809-1865, Sixteenth President of the USA)

2 The idea that you can merchandise candidates for high office like breakfast cereal -- that you can gather votes like box tops -- is, I think, the ultimate indignity to the democratic process.
Adlai E. Stevenson (1900-1965, American Lawyer, Politician)

3 I'm not an old, experienced hand at politics. But I am now seasoned enough to have learned that the hardest thing about any political campaign is how to win without proving that you are unworthy of winning.
Adlai E. Stevenson (1900-1965, American Lawyer, Politician)

4 The only thing we learn from new elections is we learned nothing from the old.
American Proverb

5 Indeed, you won the elections, but I won the count.
Anastasio Somoza

6 Everyone was tired with the old style politicians and their flowery rhetoric. I just told them there are tough times ahead, but that they would be less tough with me in charge.
Anibal Cavaco Silva

7 We have a presidential election coming up. And I think the big problem, of course, is that someone will win.
Barry Crimmins

8 Everybody except us is running for governor.
Barry Gray

9 There is a sort of exotic preposterousness about a lot of elections, the way arguments are made even cruder.
Chris Patten (1944-, British Statesman, Governor of Hong Kong)

10 My opponent called me a cream puff. Well, I rushed out and got the baker's union to endorse me.
Claiborne Pell

11 In politics women type the letters, lick the stamps, distribute the pamphlets and get out the vote. Men get elected.
Clare Boothe Luce (1903-1987, American Diplomat, Writer)

12 When the leaders choose to make themselves bidders at an auction of popularity, their talents, in the construction of the state, will be of no service. They will become flatterers instead of legislators; the instruments, not the guides, of the people.
Edmund Burke (1729-1797, British Political Writer, Statesman)

13 Get the fools on your side and you can be elected to anything.
Frank Dane

14 An election cannot give a country a firm sense of direction if it has two or more national parties which merely have different names, but are as alike in their principals and aims as two peas in the same pod.
Franklin D. Roosevelt (1882-1945, Thirty-second President of the USA)

15 Elections are won by men and women chiefly because most people vote against somebody rather than for somebody.
Franklin Pierce Adams (1881 - 1960, American Journalist, Humorist)

16 Clever and attractive women do not want to vote; they are willing to let men govern as long as they govern men.
George Bernard Shaw (1856-1950, Irish-born British Dramatist)

17 An election is a moral horror, as bad as a battle except for the blood; a mud bath for every soul concerned in it.
George Bernard Shaw (1856-1950, Irish-born British Dramatist)

18 You don't have to fool all the people all of the time; you just have to fool enough to get elected.
Gerald Barzan

19 Elections are held to delude the populace into believing that they are participating in government.
Gerald F. Lieberman (American Writer)

20 Which one of the three candidates would you want your daughter to marry?
H. Ross Perot (1930-, American Businessman & Politician, Founder EDS)

21 If you want to get elected, shake hands with 25, 000 people between and November 7.
Harry S. Truman (1884-1972, Thirty-third President of the USA)

22 If God had wanted us to vote, he would have given us candidates.
Jay Leno (American TV Show Host)

23 The English people believes itself to be free; it is gravely mistaken; it is free only during election of members of parliament; as soon as the members are elected, the people is enslaved; it is nothing. In the brief moment of its freedom, the English people makes such a use of that freedom that it deserves to lose it.
Jean Jacques Rousseau (1712-1778, Swiss Political Philosopher, Educationist, Essayist)

24 Votes should be weighed not counted.
Johann Friedrich Von Schiller (1759-1805, German Dramatist, Poet, Historian)

25 I have just received the following wire from my generous Daddy. It says, "Dear Jack: Don't buy a single vote more than is necessary. I'll be damned if I am going to pay for a landslide."
John F. Kennedy (1917-1963, Thirty-fifth President of the USA)

26 anytime you see white men suppose to fight each other an you not white, well you know you got trouble, because they blah-blah loud about Democrat or Republican an they huffing an puff about democracy someplace else but relentless, see, the deal come down evil on somebody don have no shirt an tie, somebody don live in no whiteman house no whiteman country.
June Jordan (1939-, American Poet, Civil Rights Activist)

27 A new poll showed that if the election was held today, people would be confused because it is normally held in November.
Kevin Nealon

28 The election is not very far off when a candidate can recognize you across the street.
Kin Hubbard (1868-1930, American Humorist, Journalist)

29 You campaign in poetry. You govern in prose.
Mario Cuomo

30 American youth attributes much more importance to arriving at driver's license age than at voting age.
Marshall Mcluhan (1911-1980, Canadian Communications Theorist)

31 Reagan won because he ran against Jimmy Carter. If he ran unopposed he would have lost.
Mort Sahl

32 In every election in American history both parties have their clichés. The party that has the clichés that ring true wins.
Newt Gingrich (American Statesman)

33 Maybe a nation that consumes as much booze and dope as we do and has our kind of divorce statistics should pipe down about "character issues." Either that or just go ahead and determine the presidency with three-legged races and pie-eating contests. It would make better TV.
P. J. O'Rourke (1947-, American Journalist)

34 Defeat has its lessons as well as victory.
Patrick Buchanan (1938-, American Statesman)

35 Let's try winning and see what it feels like. If we don't like it, we can go back to our traditions.
Paul Tsongas

36 The advance planning and sense stimuli employed to capture a $10 million cigarette or soap market are nothing compared to the brainwashing and propaganda blitzes used to ensure control of the largest cash market in the world: the Executive Branch of the United States Government.
Phyllis Schlafly (1924-, American Author and Political Activist)

37 Finishing second in the Olympics gets you silver. Finishing second in politics gets you oblivion.
Richard M. Nixon (1913-1994, Thirty-seventh President of the USA)

38 Do not run a campaign that would embarrass your mother.
Robert C. Byrd

39 The universe is not rich enough to buy the vote of an honest man.
St. Gregory The Great (540-604, Italian Pope)

40 There is no excitement anywhere in the world, short of war, to match the excitement of the American presidential campaign.
Theodore White

41 I never vote for anyone. I always vote against.
W. C. Fields (1879-1946, American Actor)

⁴² I always voted at my party's call, and I never thought of thinking for myself at all.
W. S. Gilbert (1836-1911, British Librettist)

⁴³ Football strategy does not originate in a scrimmage: it is useless to expect solutions in a political campaign.
Walter Lippmann (1889-1974, American Journalist)

⁴⁴ The Republicans have their splits right after election and Democrats have theirs just before an election.
Will Rogers (1879-1935, American Humorist, Actor)

⁴⁵ There isn't any finer folks living than a Republican that votes the Democratic ticket.
Will Rogers (1879-1935, American Humorist, Actor)

⁴⁶ Vote early and vote often.
William Porcher Miles

⁴⁷ To win in this country these days you have got to campaign down to a thirteen year-old's level of mental development .
Willie Brown

ELEGANCE

¹ For me, elegance is not to pass unnoticed but to get to the very soul of what one is.
Christian Lacroix

² Elegance does not consist in putting on a new dress.
Coco Chanel (1883-1971, French Couturier)

³ Nothing is more elegant than ready money!
French Proverb

⁴ Even the wisest woman you talk to is ignorant of something you may know, but an elegant woman never forgets her elegance.
Oliver Wendell Holmes (1809-1894, American Author, Wit, Poet)

⁵ A high station in life is earned by the gallantry with which appalling experiences are survived with grace.
Tennessee Williams (1914-1983, American Dramatist)

⁶ It is not possible for a man to be elegant without a touch of femininity.
Vivienne Westwood (1941-, British Fashion Designer)

⁷ We must never confuse elegance with snobbery.
Yves Saint-Laurent (1936-, Algerian-Born French Fashion Designer)

ELOQUENCE

¹ To acquire immunity to eloquence is of the utmost importance to the citizens of a democracy.
Bertrand Russell (1872-1970, British Philosopher, Mathematician, Essayist)

² Eloquence, at its highest pitch, leaves little room for reason or reflection, but addresses itself entirely to the desires and affections, captivating the willing hearers, and subduing their understanding.
David Hume (1711-1776, Scottish Philosopher, Historian)

³ The finest eloquence is that which gets things done; the worst is that which delays them.
David Lloyd George (1863-1945, British Statesman, Prime Minister)

⁴ True eloquence consists in saying all that should be said, and that only.
François de La Rochefoucauld (1613-1680, French classical writer)

⁵ You have such strong words at command, that they make the smallest argument seem formidable.
George Eliot (1819-1880, British Novelist)

⁶ The longer I live, the more I have come to value the gift of eloquence. Every American youth, if he desires for any purpose to get influence over his countrymen in an honorable way, will seek to become a good public speaker.
George F. Hoar

⁷ When a man gets talking about himself, he seldom fails to be eloquent and often reaches the sublime.
Josh Billings (1815-1885, American Humorist, Lecturer)

⁸ They are eloquent who can speak low things acutely, and of great things with dignity, and of moderate things with temper.
Marcus T. Cicero (106-43 BC, Great Roman Orator, Politician)

⁹ Today it is not the classroom nor the classics which are the repositories of models of eloquence, but the ad agencies.
Marshall Mcluhan (1911-1980, Canadian Communications Theorist)

¹⁰ In an easy matter. Anybody can be eloquent.
Ovid (43 BC-18 AD, Roman Poet)

¹¹ The eloquent man is he who is no eloquent speaker, but who is inwardly drunk with a certain belief.
Ralph Waldo Emerson (1803-1882, American Poet, Essayist)

¹² There is no more sovereign eloquence than the truth in indignation.
Victor Hugo (1802-1885, French Poet, Dramatist, Novelist)

¹³ He talked on for ever; and you wished him to talk on for ever.
William Hazlitt (1778-1830, British Essayist)

EMBARRASSMENT

¹ Girls blush, sometimes, because they are alive, half wishing they were dead to save the shame. The sudden blush devours them, neck and brow; They have drawn too near the fire of life, like gnats, and flare up bodily, wings and all. What then? Who's sorry for a gnat or girl?
Elizabeth Barrett Browning (1806-1861, British Poet)

² We never forgive those who make us blush.
Jean-Frantois De La Harpe

³ There's a blush for won t, and a blush for shan't, and a blush for having done it: There's a blush for thought and a blush for naught, and a blush for just begun it.
John Keats (1795-1821, British Poet)

⁴ He scratched his ear, the infallible resource to which embarrassed people have recourse.
Lord Byron (1788-1824, British Poet)

⁵ Some people play very, very well just so they won't get embarrassed.
Lynn Swann (American Football Player, Sports Commentator)

⁶ The embarrassing thing is that the salad dressing is out-grossing my films.
Paul Newman (1925-, American Actor, Director, Philanthropist, Producer)

EMOTIONS

¹ We know too much and feel too little. At least, we feel too little of those creative emotions from which a good life springs.
Bertrand Russell (1872-1970, British Philosopher, Mathematician, Essayist)

² Each of us makes his own weather, determines the color of the skies in the emotional universe which he inhabits.
Bishop Fulton J. Sheen

³ There can be no transforming of darkness into light and of apathy into movement without emotion.
Carl Jung (1875-1961, Swiss Psychiatrist)

⁴ There are strings in the human heart that had better not be vibrated.
Charles Dickens (1812-1870, British Novelist)

⁵ Do not arouse disdainful mind when you prepare a broth of wild grasses; do not arouse joyful mind when you prepare a fine cream soup.
Dogen

⁶ It is not our exalted feelings, it is our sentiments that build the necessary home.
Elizabeth Bowen (1899-1973, Anglo-Irish Novelist)

⁷ One ought to hold on to one's heart; for if one lets it go, one soon loses control of the head too.
Friedrich Nietzsche (1844-1900, German Philosopher)

⁸ We find nothing easier than being wise, patient, superior. We drip with the oil of forbearance and sympathy, we are absurdly just, we forgive everything. For that very reason we ought to discipline ourselves a little; for that very reason we ought to cultivate a little emotion, a little emotional vice, from time to time. It may be hard for us; and among ourselves we may perhaps laugh at the appearance we thus present. But what of that! We no longer have any other mode of self- overcoming available to us: this is our asceticism, our penance.
Friedrich Nietzsche (1844-1900, German Philosopher)

⁹ The young man who has not wept is a savage, and the old man who will not laugh is a fool.
George Santayana (1863-1952, American Philosopher, Poet)

¹⁰ Emotion is primarily about nothing and much of it remains about nothing to the end.
George Santayana (1863-1952, American Philosopher, Poet)

¹¹ It is as healthy to enjoy sentiment as to enjoy jam.
Gilbert K. Chesterton (1874-1936, British Author)

¹² You can't expect to prevent negative feelings altogether. And you can't expect to experience positive feelings all the time. The Law of Emotional Choice directs us to acknowledge our feelings but also to refuse to get stuck in the negative ones.
Greg Anderson (American Author of "The 22 Non-Negotiable Laws of Wellness")

¹³ The heart is forever inexperienced.
Henry David Thoreau (1817-1862, American Essayist, Poet, Naturalist)

¹⁴ All humanity is passion; without passion, religion, history, novels, art would be ineffectual.
Honore De Balzac (1799-1850, French Novelist)

¹⁵ If you would have me weep, you must first of all feel grief yourself.
Horace (65-8 BC, Italian Poet)

¹⁶ All the knowledge I possess everyone else can acquire, but my heart is all my own.
Johann Wolfgang Von Goethe (1749-1832, German Poet, Dramatist, Novelist)

¹⁷ When I repress my emotion my stomach keeps score.
John Enoch Powell (1912-, British statesman,)

¹⁸ By starving emotions we become humorless, rigid and stereotyped; by repressing them we become literal, reformatory and holier-than-thou; encouraged, they perfume life; discouraged, they poison it.
Joseph Collins

¹⁹ It is very difficult to be wholly joyous or wholly sad on this earth. The comic, when it is human, soon takes upon itself a face of pain; and some of our grieves... have their source in weaknesses which must be recognized with smiling compassion as the common inheritance of us all.
Joseph Conrad (1857-1924, Polish-born British Novelist)

²⁰ Nothing vivifies, and nothing kills, like the emotions.
Joseph Roux (1834-1905, French Priest, Writer)

21 The only questions worth asking today are whether humans are going to have any emotions tomorrow, and what the quality of life will be if the answer is no.
Lester Bangs (1948-1982, American Rock Journalist)

22 You learn to put your emotional luggage where it will do some good, instead of using it to shit on other people, or blow up aeroplanes.
Margaret Drabble (1939-, British Novelist)

23 Emotions have taught mankind to reason.
Marquis De Vauvenargues (1715-1747, French Moralist)

24 Emotion is the surest arbiter of a poetic choice, and it is the priest of all supreme unions in the mind.
Max Eastman (American Commentator, Writer)

25 If I feel depressed I will sing. If I feel sad I will laugh. If I feel ill I will double my labor. If I feel fear I will plunge ahead. If I feel inferior I will wear new garments. If I feel uncertain I will raise my voice. If I feel poverty I will think of wealth to come. If I feel incompetent I will think of past success. If I feel insignificant I will remember my goals. Today I will be the master of my emotions.
Og Mandino (1923-1996, American Motivational Author, Speaker)

26 The advantage of the emotions is that they lead us astray.
Oscar Wilde (1856-1900, British Author, Wit)

27 All emotions are pure which gather you and lift you up; that emotion is impure which seizes only one side of your being and so distorts you.
Rainer Maria Rilke (1875-1926, German Poet)

28 Where the heart lies, let the brain lie also.
Robert Browning (1812-1889, British Poet)

29 Our emotions are only "incidents in the effort to keep day and night together.
T. S. Eliot (1888-1965, American-born British Poet, Critic)

30 He is not affected by the reality of distress touching his heart, but by the showy resemblance of it striking his imagination. He pities the plumage, but forgets the dying bird.
Thomas Paine (1737-1809, Anglo-American Political Theorist, Writer)

31 The heart is half a prophet.
Yiddish Proverb

EMPATHY

1 Are you then unable to recognize unless it has the same sound as yours?
Andre Gide (1869-1951, French Author)

2 Sometimes I'm asked by kids why I condemn marijuana when I haven't tried it. The greatest obstetricians in the world have never been pregnant.
Art Linkletter (Canadian-born American Radio and TV Personality, Actor)

3 When a good man is hurt all who would be called good must suffer with him.
Euripides (480-406 BC, Greek Tragic Poet)

4 Yet, taught by time, my heart has learned to glow for other's good, and melt at other's woe.
Homer (850 BC, Greek Epic Poet)

EMPIRE

1 To found a great empire for the sole purpose of raising up a people of customers, may at first sight appear a project fit only for a nation of shopkeepers. It is, however, a project altogether unfit for a nation of shopkeepers, but extremely fit for a nation that is governed by shopkeepers.
Adam Smith (1723-1790, Scottish Economist)

2 All who have meditated on the art of governing mankind have been convinced that the fate of empires depends on the education of youth.
Aristotle (384-322 BC, Greek Philosopher)

3 There is no human failure greater than to launch a profoundly important endeavor and then leave it half done. This is what the West has done with its colonial system. It shook all the societies in the world loose from their old moorings. But it seems indifferent whether or not they reach safe harbor in the end.
Dame Barbara Ward (1914-1981, British Journalist, Economist, Conservationist)

4 Great Britain has lost an Empire and has not yet found a role.
Dean Acheson (1893 - 1971, American Statesman, Lawyer)

5 Other nations use "force"; we Britons alone use "Might."
Evelyn Waugh (1903-1966, British Novelist)

6 Exploitation and oppression is not a matter of race. It is the system, the apparatus of world- wide brigandage called imperialism, which made the Powers behave the way they did. I have no illusions on this score, nor do I believe that any Asian nation or African nation, in the same state of dominance, and with the same system of colonial profit-amassing and plunder, would have behaved otherwise.
Han Suyin (1917-, Chinese Novelist and Doctor)

7 Keep our Empire undismembered guide our Forces by Thy Hand, gallant blacks from far Jamaica, Honduras and Togoland; protect them Lord in all their fights, and even more, protect the whites.
John Betjeman (1906-1984, British Poet)

8 The day of small nations has long passed away. The day of Empires has come.
Joseph Chamberlain

9 The conquest of the earth, which mostly means the taking it away from those who have a different complexion or slightly flatter noses than ourselves, is not a pretty thing when you look into it.
Joseph Conrad (1857-1924, Polish-born British Novelist)

10 Empires built on force will always be destroyed. Those built on trust in Christ will remain.
Joseph R. Sizoo

11 How is the Empire?
King George V (1865-1936, King of the United Kingdom (1910--36))

12 A thousand years may scare form a state. An hour may lay it in ruins.
Lord Byron (1788-1824, British Poet)

13 How marvelous it all is! Built not by saints and angels, but the work of men's hands; cemented with men's honest blood and with a world of tears, welded by the best brains of centuries past; not without the taint and reproach incidental to all human work, but constructed on the whole with pure and splendid purpose. Human, and yet not wholly human -- for the most heedless and the most cynical must see the finger of the Divine.
Lord Rosebery

14 Empire and liberty.
Marcus T. Cicero (106-43 BC, Great Roman Orator, Politician)

15 We must annex those people. We can afflict them with our wise and beneficent government. We can introduce the novelty of thieves, all the way up from street-car pickpockets to municipal robbers and Government defaulters, and show them how amusing it is to arrest them and try them and then turn them loose -- some for cash and some for "political influence." We can make them ashamed of their simple and primitive justice. We can make that little bunch of sleepy islands the hottest corner on earth, and array it in the moral splendor of our high and holy civilization. Annexation is what the poor islanders need. "Shall we to men benighted, the lamp of life deny?"
Mark Twain (1835-1910, American Humorist, Writer)

16 Man who man would be, must rule the empire of himself.
Percy Bysshe Shelley (1792-1822, British Poet)

17 To plunder, to slaughter, to steal, these things they misname empire; and where they make a wilderness, they call it peace.
Publius Cornelius Tacitus (55-117 AD, Roman Historian)

18 An empire is an immense egotism.
Ralph Waldo Emerson (1803-1882, American Poet, Essayist)

19 And the end of the fight is a tombstone white with the name of the late deceased, and the epitaph drear: "A Fool lies here who tried to hustle the East."
Rudyard Kipling (1865-1936, British Author of Prose, Verse)

20 Take up the White Man's burden -- send forth the best ye breed -- go, bind your sons to exile to serve your captives need.
Rudyard Kipling (1865-1936, British Author of Prose, Verse)

21 Sovereignty over any foreign land is insecure.
Seneca (4 BC-65 AD, Spanish-born Roman Statesman, philosopher)

22 We seem, as it were, to have conquered and peopled half the world in a fit of absence of mind.
Sir John Robert Seeley

23 The reluctant obedience of distant provinces generally costs more than it [The Territory] is worth. Empires which branch out widely are often more flourishing for a little timely pruning.
Thomas B. Macaulay (1800-1859, American Essayist and Historian)

24 Roman, remember that you shall rule the nations by your authority, for this is to be your skill, to make peace the custom, to spare the conquered, and to wage war until the haughty are brought low.
Virgil (70-19 BC, Roman Poet)

25 The foundation of empire is art and science. Remove them or degrade them, and the empire is no more. Empire follows art and not vice versa as Englishmen suppose.
William Blake (1757-1827, British Poet, Painter)

26 If Germany is to become a colonizing power, all I say is, "God speed her!" She becomes our ally and partner in the execution of the great purposes of Providence for the advantage of mankind.
William E. Gladstone (1809-1888, British Liberal Prime Minister, Statesman)

27 The mission of the United States is one of benevolent assimilation.
William Mckinley (1843-1901, US Statesman and 25th President)

28 Without the Empire we should be tossed like a cork in the cross current of world politics. It is at once our sword and our shield.
William Morris Hughes

ENCOURAGEMENT

1 I believe that any man's life will be filled with constant and unexpected encouragement, if he makes up his mind to do his level best each day, and as nearly as possible reaching the high water mark of pure and useful living.
Booker T. Washington (1856-1915, American Black Leader and Educator)

2 Those who are lifting the world upward and onward are those who encourage more than criticize.
Elizabeth Harrison

3 There are high spots in all of our lives and most of them have come about through encouragement from someone else. I don't care how great, how famous or successful a man or woman may be, each hungers for applause.
George M. Adams (1878 - 1962, American Author)

4 Correction does much, but encouragement does more. Encouragement after censure is as the sun after a shower.
Johann Wolfgang Von Goethe (1749-1832, German Poet, Dramatist, Novelist)

5 The spirited horse, which will try to win the race of its own accord, will run even faster if encouraged.
Ovid (43 BC-18 AD, Roman Poet)

6 The finest gift you can give anyone is encouragement. Yet, almost no one gets the encouragement they need to grow to their full potential. If everyone received the encouragement they need to grow, the genius in most everyone would blossom and the world would produce abundance beyond the wildest dreams. We would have more than one Einstein, Edison, Schweitzer, Mother Theresa, Dr. Salk and other great minds in a century.
Sidney Madwed (American Speaker, Consultant, Author, Poet)

7 Flatter me, and I may not believe you. Criticize me, and I may not like you. Ignore me, and I may not forgive you. Encourage me, and I may not forget you.
William Arthur

ENDING

1 Nothing ends nicely, that's why it ends.
Tom Cruise (1962-, American Actor)

ENDS AND MEANS

1 We have perhaps a natural fear of ends. We would rather be always on the way than arrive. Given the means, we hang on to them and often forget the ends.
Eric Hoffer (1902-1983, American Author, Philosopher)

2 The first sign of corruption in a society that is still alive is that the end justifies the means.
Georges Bernanos (1888-1948, French Novelist, Political Writer)

3 The end may justify the means as long as there is something that justifies the end.
Leon Trotsky (1879-1940, Russian Revolutionary)

ENDURANCE

1 I know quite certainly that I myself have no special talent; curiosity, obsession and dogged endurance, combined with self-criticism have brought me to my ideas.
Albert Einstein (1879-1955, German-born American Physicist)

2 People are too durable, that's their main trouble. They can do too much to themselves, they last too long.
Bertolt Brecht (1898-1956, German Dramatist, Poet)

3 Endurance is one of the most difficult disciplines, but it is to the one who endures that the final victory comes.
Buddha (568-488 BC, Founder of Buddhism)

4 The men who learn endurance, are they who call the whole world, brother.
Charles Dickens (1812-1870, British Novelist)

5 Brute force crushes many plants. Yet the plants rise again. The Pyramids will not last a moment compared with the daisy. And before Buddha or Jesus spoke the nightingale sang, and long after the words of Jesus and Buddha are gone into oblivion the nightingale still will sing. Because it is neither preaching nor commanding nor urging. It is just singing. And in the beginning was not a Word, but a chirrup.
D. H. Lawrence (1885-1930, British Author)

6 Hard pounding, gentlemen: but we shall see who can pound the longest.
Duke of Wellington Arthur Wellesley (1769-1852, British Statesman, Military Leader)

7 Not in achievement, but in endurance, of the human soul, does it show its divine grandeur and its alliance with the infinite.
Edwin Hubbel Chapin (1814-1880, American Author, Clergyman)

8 Know how sublime a thing it is to suffer and be strong.
Henry Wadsworth Longfellow (1819-1892, American Poet)

9 An arch never sleeps.
Indian Proverb

10 Endurance and to be able to endure is the first lesson a child should learn because it's the one they will most need to know.
Jean Jacques Rousseau (1712-1778, Swiss Political Philosopher, Educationist, Essayist)

11 Happy he who learns to bear what he cannot change.
Johann Friedrich Von Schiller (1759-1805, German Dramatist, Poet, Historian)

12 Since every man who lives is born to die, and none can boast sincere felicity, with equal mind, what happens, let us bear, nor joy nor grieve too much for things beyond our care.
John Dryden (1631-1700, British Poet, Dramatist, Critic)

13 Prolonged endurance tames the bold.
Lord Byron (1788-1824, British Poet)

14 Nothing happens to any man that he is not formed by nature to bear.
Marcus Aurelius (121-80 AD, Roman Emperor, Philosopher)

15 People have to learn sometimes not only how much the heart, but how much the head, can bear.
Maria Mitchell (1943-, Canadian Singer, Songwriter)

16 Those who can bear all can dare all.
Marquis De Vauvenargues (1715-1747, French Moralist)

17 Those who endure conquer.
Motto

18 It is the nature of the strong heart, that like the palm tree it strives ever upwards when it is most burdened.
Sir Philip Sidney (1554-1586, British Author, Courtier)

19 To bear is to conquer our fate.
Thomas Campbell (1777-1844, Scottish Poet)

20 What cannot be altered must be borne, not blamed.
Thomas Fuller (1608-1661, British Clergyman, Author)

21 Endurance is not just the ability to bear a hard thing, but to turn it into glory.
William Barclay (1907-1978, Scottish Theologian, Religious Writer, Broadcaster)

22 Many can brook the weather that love not the wind.
William Shakespeare (1564-1616, British Poet, Playwright, Actor)

ENEMIES

1 The best way to destroy your enemy is to make him your friend.
Abraham Lincoln (1809-1865, Sixteenth President of the USA)

2 We often give our enemies the means for our own destruction.
Aesop (620-560 BC, Greek Fabulist)

3 There once was a Bald Man who sat down after work on a hot summer's day. A Fly came up and kept buzzing about his bald pate, and stinging him from time to time. The Man aimed a blow at his little enemy, but - whack - his palm come on his own head instead; again the Fly tormented him, but this time the Man was wiser and said: "YOU WILL ONLY INJURE YOURSELF IF YOU TAKE NOTICE OF DISPICABLE ENEMIES."
Aesop (620-560 BC, Greek Fabulist)

4 Enemies promises were made to be broken.
Aesop (620-560 BC, Greek Fabulist)

5 When there is no enemy within, the enemies outside cannot hurt you.
African Proverb

6 One must be a somebody before they can have a enemy. One must be a force before he can be resisted by another force.
Anne Sophie Swetchine (1782-1857, Russian Author)

7 Observe your enemies, for they first find out your faults.
Antisthenes (388-311 BC, Greek Dramatist)

8 Pay attention to your enemies for they are the first to discover your mistakes.
Antisthenes (388-311 BC, Greek Dramatist)

9 Serve your enemies for they first find out your faults
Antisthenes (388-311 BC, Greek Dramatist)

10 Wise men learn many things from their enemies.
Aristophanes (448-380 BC, Greek Comic Poet, Satirist)

11 A wise man learns more from his enemies than a fool from his friends.
Baltasar Gracian (1601-1658, Spanish Philosopher, Writer)

12 Love your enemies, for they tell you your faults.
Benjamin Franklin (1706-1790, American Scientist, Publisher, Diplomat)

13 Promises may fit the friends, but non-performance will turn them into enemies.
Benjamin Franklin (1706-1790, American Scientist, Publisher, Diplomat)

14 I have met the enemy, and it is the eyes of other people.
Benjamin Franklin (1706-1790, American Scientist, Publisher, Diplomat)

15 Love your enemies, bless them that curse you, do good to them that hate you. [Matthew]
Bible (Sacred Scriptures of Christians and Judaism)

16 Take no thought of who is right or wrong or who is better than. Be not for or against.
Bruce Lee (1940-1973, Chinese-American Actor, Director, Author, Martial Artist)

17 Beware of no man more than of yourself; we carry our worst enemies within us.
Charles Haddon Spurgeon (1834-1892, British Baptist Preacher)

18 The fire you kindle for your enemy often burns yourself more than him.
Chinese Proverb

19 The enemies of the future are always the very nicest people.
Christopher Morley (1890-1957, American Novelist, Journalist, Poet)

20 I don't have a warm personal enemy left. They've all died off. I miss them terribly because they helped define me.
Clare Boothe Luce (1903-1987, American Diplomat, Writer)

21 Why do grandparents and grandchildren get along so well? They have the same enemy -- the mother.
Claudette Colbert

22 Was it a friend or foe that spread these lies? Nay, who but infants question in such wise, 'twas one of my most intimate enemies.
Dante Gabriel Rossetti (1828-1882, British Poet, Painter)

23 If it looks like shit, smells like shit, mail it to your enemy... he'll know what to do with it.
Doug Horton

24 The moment at which two people, approaching from opposite ends of a long passageway, recognize each other and immediately pretend they haven t. This is to avoid the ghastly embarrassment of having to continue recognizing each other the whole length of the corridor.
Douglas Adams (Born 1952, British Science Fiction Writer)

25 A strong foe is better than a weak friend.
Edward Dahlberg (1900-1977, American Author, Critic)

26 It is difficult to say who do you the most harm: enemies with the worst intentions or friends with the best.
Edward G. Bulwer-Lytton (1803-1873, British Novelist, Poet)

27 Man's chief enemy is his own unruly nature and the dark forces put up within him.
Ernest Jones (1879-1958, British Psychoanalyst)

28 There is nothing like the sight of an old enemy down on his luck.
Euripides (480-406 BC, Greek Tragic Poet)

29 Five enemies of peace inhabit with us -- avarice, ambition, envy, anger, and pride; if these were to be banished, we should infallibly enjoy perpetual peace.
Francesco Petrarch (1304-1374, Italian Poet, Humanist)

30 Man has no greater enemy than himself.
Francesco Petrarch (1304-1374, Italian Poet, Humanist)

31 Our enemies approach nearer to truth in their judgments of us than we do ourselves.
François de La Rochefoucauld (1613-1680, French classical writer)

32 Our enemies come nearer the truth in the opinions they form of us than we do in our opinion of ourselves.
François de La Rochefoucauld (1613-1680, French classical writer)

33 It is not necessary to have enemies if you go out of your way to make friends hate you.
Frank Dane

34 There is no stronger bond of friendship than a mutual enemy.
Frankfort Moore

35 He who lives by fighting with an enemy has an interest in the preservation of the enemy's life.
Friedrich Nietzsche (1844-1900, German Philosopher)

36 One enemy is too much.
George Herbert (1593-1632, British Metaphysical Poet)

37 I have had a lot of adversaries in my political life, but no enemies that I can remember.
Gerald R. Ford (1913-, Thirty-eighth President of the USA)

38 Convince an enemy, convince him that he's wrong. To win a bloodless battle, the victory is long. A simple act of faith, reason over might. To blow up his children would only prove him right.
Gordon Sumner

39 Even a paranoid can have enemies.
Henry Kissinger (1923-, American Republican Politician, Secretary of State)

40 The real enemy can always be met and conquered, or won over. Real antagonism is based on love, a love which has not recognized itself.
Henry Miller (1891-1980, American Author)

41 No man should ever display his bravery unless he is prepared for battle, nor bear the marks of defiance, until he has experienced the abilities of his enemy.
Hitopadesa (Sanskrit Fable From Panchatantra)

42 No prudent antagonist thinks light of his adversaries.
Johann Wolfgang Von Goethe (1749-1832, German Poet, Dramatist, Novelist)

43 Forgive your enemies, but never forget their names.
John F. Kennedy (1917-1963, Thirty-fifth President of the USA)

44 One enemy can do more hurt than ten friends can do good.
Jonathan Swift (1667-1745, Anglo-Irish Satirist)

45 You shall judge a man by his foes as well as by his friends.
Joseph Conrad (1857-1924, Polish-born British Novelist)

46 Enemies are so stimulating.
Katharine Hepburn (1907-, American Actress, Writer)

47 Let your enemies be disarmed by the gentleness of your manner, but at the same time let them feel, the steadiness of your resentment.
Lord Chesterfield (1694-1773, British Statesman, Author)

48 It pays to know the enemy -- not least because at some time you may have the opportunity to turn him into a friend.
Margaret Thatcher (1925-, British Stateswoman, Prime Minister (1979-90))

49 Who are enemies? Those who oppose each others will.
Mary Caroline Richards

50 Our greatest foes, and whom we must chiefly combat, are within.
Miguel De Cervantes (1547-1616, Spanish Novelist, Dramatist, Poet)

51 Remember, to them it is us who are the enemy.
N. F. Simpson

52 A man cannot be too careful in the choice of his enemies.
Oscar Wilde (1856-1900, British Author, Wit)

53 We look upon the enemy of our souls as a conquered foe, so he is, but only to God, not to us.
Oswald Chambers (1874-1917 Scottish Preacher, Author)

54 Bear patiently with a rival.
Ovid (43 BC-18 AD, Roman Poet)

55 Talk well of your friends and of your enemies say nothing.
Proverb

56 It is a pitiful fortune that is not without enemies.
Publilius Syrus (1st Century BC, Roman Writer)

57 Love your enemies just in case your friends turn out to be a bunch of bastards.
R A Dickson

58 Give us grace and strength to forbear and to persevere. Give us courage and gaiety and the quiet mind, spare to us our friends, soften to us our enemies.
Robert Louis Stevenson (1850-1895, Scottish Essayist, Poet, Novelist)

59 It is hard to fight an enemy who has outposts in your head.
Sally Kempton

60 False friends are worst than bitter enemies.
Scottish Proverb

61 Only enemies speak the truth. Friends and lovers lie endlessly, caught in the web of duty.
Stephen King (1947-, American Horror Writer, Actor)

62 If there be no enemy there's no fight. If no fight, no victory and if no victory there is no crown.
Thomas Carlyle (1795-1881, Scottish Philosopher, Author)

63 The enemy is more easily overcome if he be not suffered to enter the door of our hearts, but be resisted without the gate at his first knock.
Thomas p Kempis (1379-1471, German Monk, Mystic, Religious Writer)

64 In my life, I have prayed but one prayer: oh Lord, make my enemies ridiculous. And God granted it.
Voltaire (1694-1778, French Historian, Writer)

65 We have meet the enemy; and he is us.
Walt Kelly (1913-1973, American Animator, Strip Cartoonist)

66 I no doubt deserved my enemies, but I don't believe I deserved my friends.
Walt Whitman (1819-1892, American Poet)

67 I have no trouble with my enemies. I can take care of my enemies all right. But my damn friends. They're the ones that keep me walking the floor nights!
Warren Gamaliel Harding (1865-1923, American Republican Politician, President)

68 When a sinister person means to be your enemy, they always start by trying to become your friend.
William Blake (1757-1827, British Poet, Painter)

69 The worst tyrants are those which establish themselves in our own breasts.
William Ellery Channing (1780-1842, American Unitarian Minister, Author)

70 The person who builds a character makes foes.
Young

ENERGY

1 Energy and persistence alter all things.
Benjamin Franklin (1706-1790, American Scientist, Publisher, Diplomat)

2 If your energy is as boundless as your ambition, total commitment may be a way of life you should seriously consider.
Dr. Joyce Brothers (1927-, American Psychologist, Television and Radio Personality)

3 The energy produced by the breaking down of the atom is a very poor kind of thing. Anyone who expects a source of power from the transformation of these atoms is talking moonshine.
Ernest Rutherford

4 Controlled deep breathing helps the body to transform the air we breathe into energy. The stream of energized air produced by properly executed and controlled deep breathing produces a current of inner energy which radiates throughout the entire body and can be channeled to the body areas that need it the most, on demand.
Nancy Zi

5 Is it a fact -- or have I dreamt it -- that, by means of electricity, the world of matter has become a great nerve, vibrating thousands of miles in a breathless point of time?
Nathaniel Hawthorne (1804-1864, American Novelist, Short Story Writer)

6 Coal is a portable climate. It carries the heat of the tropics to Labrador and the polar circle; and it is the means of transporting itself whithersoever it is wanted. Watt and Stephenson whispered in the ear of mankind their secret, that a half-ounce of coal will draw two tons a mile, and coal carries coal, by rail and by boat, to make Canada as warm as Calcutta, and with its comfort brings its industrial power.
Ralph Waldo Emerson (1803-1882, American Poet, Essayist)

7 Energy is equal to desire and purpose.
Sheryl Adams

8 Energy is an eternal delight, and he who desires, but acts not, breeds pestilence.
William Blake (1757-1827, British Poet, Painter)

ENGAGEMENT

1 An engaged woman is always more agreeable than a disengaged. She is satisfied with herself. Her cares are over, and she feels that she may exert all her powers of pleasing without suspicion. All is safe with a lady engaged; no harm can be done.
Jane Austen (1775-1817, British Novelist)

2 Can you support the expense of a husband, hussy, in gaming, drinking and whoring? Have you money enough to carry on the daily quarrels of man and wife about who shall squander most?
John Gay (1688-1732, British Playwright, Poet)

3 I am about to be married, and am of course in all the misery of a man in pursuit of happiness.
Lord Byron (1788-1824, British Poet)

4 Pardon me, you are not engaged to any one. When you do become engaged to some one, I, or your father, should his health permit him, will inform you of the fact. An engagement should come on a young girl as a surprise, pleasant or unpleasant, as the case may be. It is hardly a matter that she could be allowed to arrange for herself.
Oscar Wilde (1856-1900, British Author, Wit)

5 No sooner met but they looked; no sooner looked but they loved; no sooner loved but they sighed; no sooner sighed but they asked one another the reason; no sooner knew the reason but they sought the remedy; and in these degrees have they made a pair of stairs to marriage, which they will climb incontinent, or else be incontinent before marriage.
William Shakespeare (1564-1616, British Poet, Playwright, Actor)

ENGINEERING

1 To define it rudely but not ineptly, engineering is the art of doing that well with one dollar, which any bungler can do with two after a fashion.
Duke of Wellington Arthur Wellesley (1769-1852, British Statesman, Military Leader)

2 A good scientist is a person with original ideas. A good engineer is a person who makes a design that works with as few original ideas as possible. There are no prima donnas in engineering.
Freeman Dyson (1923-, British-born American Physicist, Author)

3 My advice is to look out for engineers. They begin with sewing machines and end up with nuclear bombs.
Marcel Pagnol

4 Hedonic Engineering -- The human nervous system studying and improving itself: intelligence studying and improving intelligence. Why be depressed, dumb, and agitated when you can be happy, smart, and tranquil?
Robert Wilson (1941-, American Theater Director, Designer)

5 For 'Tis the sport to have the engineer hoisted with his own petard.
William Shakespeare (1564-1616, British Poet, Playwright, Actor)

ENJOYMENT

1 People who like this sort of thing will find this the sort of thing they like.
Abraham Lincoln (1809-1865, Sixteenth President of the USA)

2 Learn not only to find what you like, learn to like what you find.
Anthony J. D'Angelo

3 Chance can allow you to accomplish a goal every once in a while, but consistent achievement happens only if you love what you are doing.
Bart Conner (American Gymnast)

4 As you walk down the fairway of life you must smell the roses, for you only get to play one round.
Ben Hogan (1912-, American Golfer)

5 There is nothing better for a man, than that he should eat and drink, and that he should make his soul enjoy good in his labor. [Ecclesiastes 2:24]
Bible (Sacred Scriptures of Christians and Judaism)

6 If a man who enjoys a lesser happiness beholds a greater one, let him leave aside the lesser to gain the greater.
Buddha (568-488 BC, Founder of Buddhism)

7 The first essential in a boy's career is to find out what he's fitted for, what he's most capable of doing and doing with a relish.
Charles M. Schwab (1862-1939, American Industrialist, Businessman)

8 The enjoyment of life would be instantly gone if you removed the possibility of doing something.
Chauncey Depew (1834-1928, American Lawyer, Businessman, Public Official)

9 You never achieve real success unless you like what you are doing.
Dale Carnegie (1888-1955, American Author, Trainer)

10 You can't let one bad moment spoil a bunch of good ones.
Dale Earnhardt (1952-, American Race Car Driver)

11 Nobody can be successful if he doesn't love his work, love his job.
David Sarnoff (1891-1971, Belarus-born American Entrepreneur)

12 Winners take time to relish their work, knowing that scaling the mountain is what makes the view from the top so exhilarating.
Denis Waitley (1933-, American Author, Speaker, Trainer, Peak Performance Expert)

13 Learn to enjoy every minute of your life. Be happy now. Don't wait for something outside of yourself to make you happy in the future. Think how really precious is the time you have to spend, whether it's at work or with your family. Every minute should be enjoyed and savored.
Earl Nightingale (1921-1989, American Radio Announcer, Author, Motivator, Speaker)

14 We are at our very best, and we are happiest, when we are fully engaged in work we enjoy on the journey toward the goal we've established for ourselves. It gives meaning to our time off and comfort to our sleep. It makes everything else in life so wonderful, so worthwhile.
Earl Nightingale (1921-1989, American Radio Announcer, Author, Motivator, Speaker)

15 Live and work but do not forget to play, to have fun in life and really enjoy it.
Eileen Caddy (American Spiritual Writer)

16 No man is a success in business unless he loves his work.
Florence Scovel Shinn (American Artist, Metaphysics Teacher, Author)

17 Temper your enjoyments with prudence, lest there be written on your heart that fearful word "satiety."
Francis Quarles (1592-1644, British Poet)

18 Believe me! The secret of reaping the greatest fruitfulness and the greatest enjoyment from life is to live dangerously!
Friedrich Nietzsche (1844-1900, German Philosopher)

19 Be absolutely determined to enjoy what you do.
Gerry Sikorski

20 If your capacity to acquire has outstripped your capacity to enjoy, you are on the way to the scrap-heap.
Glen Buck

21 You've got to love what you're doing. If you love it, you can overcome any handicap or the soreness or all the aches and pains, and continue to play for a long, long time.
Gordie Howe (1928-, Canadian Hockey Player)

22 ... focus on the journey, not the destination. Joy is found not in finishing an activity but in doing it.
Greg Anderson (American Author of "The 22 Non-Negotiable Laws of Wellness")

23 Don't complain because you don't have. Enjoy what you've got.
H. Stanley Judd (American Author)

24 Don't set compensation as a goal. Find work you like, and the compensation will follow.
Harding Lawrence

25 Live your life each day as you would climb a mountain. An occasional glance toward the summit keeps the goal in mind, but many beautiful scenes are to be observed from each new vantage point. Climb slowly, steadily, enjoying each passing moment; and the view from the summit will serve as a fitting climax for the journey.
Harold V Melchert

26 Nothing is interesting if you are not interested.
Helen Macinness (Scottish author)

27 Only mediocrity of enjoyment is allowed to man.
Hugh Blair (British Poet)

28 The New England conscience doesn't keep you from doing what you shouldn't -- it just keeps you from enjoying it.
Isaac Bashevis Singer (1904-1991, Polish-born American Journalist, Writer).

29 I'm a firm believer that in the theory that people only do their best at things they truly enjoy. It is difficult to excel at something you don't enjoy.
Jack Nicklaus (1940-, American Golfer)

30 I have always said and felt that true enjoyment can not be described.
Jean Jacques Rousseau (1712-1778, Swiss Political Philosopher, Educationist, Essayist)

31 What you do is more important than how much you make, and how you feel about it is more important than what you do.
Jerry Gillies (American Author, Speaker)

32 The more you love what you are doing, the more successful it will be for you.
Jerry Gillies (American Author, Speaker)

33 I always loved running -- it was something you could do by yourself, and under your own power. You could go in any direction, fast or slow as you wanted, fighting the wind if you felt like it, seeking out new sights just on the strength of your feet and the courage of your lungs.
Jesse Owens (1913-1980, American Olympic Track Athlete)

34 People who enjoy what they are doing invariably do it well.
Joe Gibbs (American Football Coach)

35 He who enjoys doing and enjoys what he has done is happy.
Johann Wolfgang Von Goethe (1749-1832, German Poet, Dramatist, Novelist)

36 Enjoy what thou has inherited from thy sires if thou wouldn't really possess it. What we employ and use is never an oppressive burden; what the moment brings forth, that only can it profit by.
Johann Wolfgang Von Goethe (1749-1832, German Poet, Dramatist, Novelist)

37 Doing is the great thing, for if people resolutely do what is right, they come in time to like doing it.
John Ruskin (1819-1900, British Critic, Social Theorist)

38 People are going to be most creative and productive when they're doing something they're really interested in. So having fun isn't an outrageous idea at all. It's a very sensible one.
John Sculley (American Businessman, Former Chairman of Apple Computer)

39 True enjoyment comes from activity of the mind and exercise of the body; the two are ever united.
Karl Wilhelm Von Humboldt (1767-1835, German Statesman, Philologist)

40 If you always do what interests you, at least one person is pleased.
Katharine Hepburn (1907-, American Actress, Writer)

41 To love what you do and feel that it matters -- how could anything be more fun?
Katherine Graham

42 I always remember that I have everything I need to enjoy my here and now, unless I am letting my consciousness be dominated by demands and expectations based on the dead past or the imagined future.
Ken Keyes Jr. (1921-1995, American Author)

43 If you are going to do something wrong, at least enjoy it.
Leo Rosten (1908-1997, Polish Born American Political Scientist)

44 The love for work needs to be re-enthroned in our lives. Every family should have a plan for work that touches the life of each family member so that this eternal principle will be ingrained in their lives.
M. Russell Ballard (1928, American Missionary, Bishop,)

45 The biggest mistake people make in life is not trying to make a living at doing what they most enjoy.
Malcolm S. Forbes (1919-1990, American Publisher, Businessman)

46 Where a man can live, he can also live well.
Marcus Aurelius (121-80 AD, Roman Emperor, Philosopher)

47 The first half of life consists of the capacity to enjoy without the chance; the last half consists of the chance without the capacity.
Mark Twain (1835-1910, American Humorist, Writer)

48 Our works and our play. All our pleasures experienced as the pleasure of love. What could be better that? To feel in one's work the tender and flushed substance of one's dearest concern.
Mary Caroline Richards

49 Enjoy the journey, enjoy every moment, and quit worrying about winning and losing.
Matt Biondi (American Swimmer)

50 Inner work is finding joy in work. Our real work is heart work and soul work.
Matthew Fox

51 Just play. Have fun. Enjoy the game.
Michael Jordan (1963-, American Basketball Player, Actor)

52 Your chances of success are directly proportional to the degree of pleasure you desire from what you do. If you are in a job you hate, face the fact squarely and get out.
Michael Korda (1919-, American publisher)

53 The ultimate goal of a more effective and efficient life is to provide you with enough time to enjoy some of it.
Michael Leboeuf (American Researcher, Consultant, Author)

54 No man can succeed in a line of endeavor which he does not like.
Napoleon Hill (1883-1970, American Speaker, Motivational Writer, "Think and Grow Rich")

55 Everyone enjoys doing the kind of work for which he is best suited.
Napoleon Hill (1883-1970, American Speaker, Motivational Writer, "Think and Grow Rich")

56 Our Creator would never have made such lovely days, and have given us the deep hearts to enjoy them, above and beyond all thought, unless we were meant to be immortal.
Nathaniel Hawthorne (1804-1864, American Novelist, Short Story Writer)

57 The man who has no money is poor, but one who has nothing but money is poorer. He only is rich who can enjoy without owning; he is poor who though he has millions is covetous.
Orison Swett Marden (1850-1924, American Author, Founder of Success Magazine)

58 No man can be ideally successful until he has found his place. Like a locomotive he is strong on the track, but weak anywhere else.
Orison Swett Marden (1850-1924, American Author, Founder of Success Magazine)

59 You will never succeed while smarting under the drudgery of your occupation, if you are constantly haunted with the idea that you could succeed better in something else.
Orison Swett Marden (1850-1924, American Author, Founder of Success Magazine)

60 You have not found your place until all your faculties are roused, and your whole nature consents and approves of the work you are doing.
Orison Swett Marden (1850-1924, American Author, Founder of Success Magazine)

61 It is what we do easily and what we like to do that we do well.
Orison Swett Marden (1850-1924, American Author, Founder of Success Magazine)

62 To really enjoy the better things in life, one must first have experienced the things they are better than.
Oscar Homoka

63 Enjoyment is not a goal, it is a feeling that accompanies important ongoing activity.
Paul Goodman (1911-1972, American Author, Poet, Critic)

64 Like what you do, if you don't like it, do something else.
Paul Harvey (American Radio Broadcaster, Columnist, Author)

65 If you don't like what you're doing, then don't do it.
Ray Bradbury (1920-, American Science Fiction Writer)

66 The best way to pay for a lovely moment is to enjoy it.
Richard Bach (1936-, American Author)

67 He has spent his life best who has enjoyed it most. God will take care that we do not enjoy it any more than is good for us.
Samuel Butler (1612-1680, British Poet, Satirist)

68 If you don't get a kick out of the job you're doing you'd better hunt for another one.
Samuel Vauclain (1856-1940, American Engineer, Inventor)

69 Enjoy yourself -- it's later than you think.
Socrates (469-399 BC, Greek Philosopher of Athens)

70 Listen to the cry of a woman in labor at the hour of giving birth --look at the dying man's struggle at his last extremity, and then tell me whether something that begins and ends thus could be intended for enjoyment.
Soren Kierkegaard (1813-1855, Danish Philosopher, Writer)

71 The fact remains that the overwhelming majority of people who have become wealthy have become so thanks to work they found profoundly absorbing. The long term study of people who eventually become wealthy clearly reveals that their "Luck" arouse from the accidental dedication they had to an area they enjoyed.
Srully Blotnick (American Psychologist, Author)

72 As long as I can focus on enjoying what I'm doing, having fun, I know I'll play well.
Steffi Graf (Born 1969, German Tennis Player)

73 What we call creative work, ought not to be called work at all, because it isn't. I imagine that Thomas Edison never did a day's work in his last fifty years.
Stephen B. Leacock (1869-1944, Canadian Humorist, Economist)

74 A person will be called to account on Judgment Day for every permissible thing he might have enjoyed but did not.
The Talmud (Jewish Archive of Oral Tradition)

75 He enjoys much who is thankful for little.
Thomas Secker

76 My advice to you is not to inquire why or whither, but just enjoy your ice cream while it's on your plate -- that's my philosophy.
Thornton Wilder (1897-1975, American Novelist, Playwright)

77 I feel sorry for the person who can't get genuinely excited about his work. Not only will he never be satisfied, but he will never achieve anything worthwhile.
Walter Chrysler (American Businessman, Founder of Chrysler Motors)

78 It is essential to our well-being, and to our lives, that we play and enjoy life. Every single day do something that makes your heart sing.
Wieder Marcia (American Author, Speaker)

79 Fill your life with as many moments and experiences of joy and passion as you humanly can. Start with one experience and build on it.
Wieder Marcia (American Author, Speaker)

80 When you look at me, when you think of me, I am in paradise.
William M. Thackeray (1811-1863, Indian-born British Novelist)

ENLIGHTENMENT

1 No one who has lived even for a fleeting moment for something other than life in its conventional sense and has experienced the exaltation that this feeling produces can then renounce his new freedom so easily.
Andre Breton (1989-1966, French Surrealist)

2 The moment of truth, the sudden emergence of a new insight, is an act of intuition. Such intuitions give the appearance of miraculous flushes, or short-circuits of reasoning. In fact they may be likened to an immersed chain, of which only the beginning and the end are visible above the surface of consciousness. The diver vanishes at one end of the chain and comes up at the other end, guided by invisible links.
Arthur Koestler (1905-1983, Hungarian Born British Writer)

3 I don't know Who -- or what -- put the question, I don't know when it was put. I don't even remember answering. But at some moment I did answer Yes to Someone --or Something --and from that hour I was certain that existence is meaningful and that, therefore, my life, in self-surrender, had a goal.
Dag Hammarskjold (1905-1961, Swedish Statesman, Secretary-general of U.N.)

4 The light which puts out our eyes is darkness to us. Only that day dawns to which we are awake. There is more day to dawn. The sun is but a morning star.
Henry David Thoreau (1817-1862, American Essayist, Poet, Naturalist)

5 Enlightenment must come little by little-otherwise it would overwhelm.
Idries Shah

6 The real meaning of enlightenment is to gaze with undimmed eyes on all darkness.
Nikos Kazantzakis (1883-1957, Greek Writer)

7 A man whose mind feels that it is captive would prefer to blind himself to the fact. But if he hates falsehood, he will not do so; and in that case he will have to suffer a lot. He will beat his head against the wall until he faints. He will come to again
Simone Weil (1910-1943, French Philosopher, Mystic)

8 In this world, which is so plainly the antechamber of another, there are no happy men. The true division of humanity is between those who live in light and those who live in darkness. Our aim must be to diminish the number of the latter and increase the number of the former. That is why we demand education and knowledge.
Victor Hugo (1802-1885, French Poet, Dramatist, Novelist)

9 If I could define enlightenment briefly I would say it is "the quiet acceptance of what is."
Wayne Dyer (1940-, American Psychotherapist, Author, Lecturer)

ENTERTAINMENT

1 Every country gets the circus it deserves. Spain gets bullfights. Italy gets the Catholic Church. America gets Hollywood.
Erica Jong (1942-, American Author)

2 The Miss America contest is the most perfectly rendered theater in our culture, for it so perfectly captures what we yearn for: a low-class ritual, a polished restatement of vulgarity, that wants to open the door to high-class respectability by way of plain middle-class anxiety and ambition.
Gerald Early (1952-, American Author)

3 Compare the cinema with theatre. Both are dramatic arts. Theatre brings actors before a public and every night during the season they re-enact the same drama. Deep in the nature of theatre is a sense of ritual. The cinema, by contrast, transports its audience individually, singly, out of the theatre towards the unknown.
John Berger (1926-, British Actor, Critic)

4 The only way to entertain some folks is to listen to them.
Kin Hubbard (1868-1930, American Humorist, Journalist)

5 The reason I'm in this business, I assume all performers are -- it's "Look at me, Ma!" It's acceptance, you know -- "Look at me, Ma, look at me, Ma, look at me, Ma." And if your mother watches, you'll show off till you're exhausted; but if your mother goes, Ptshew!
Lenny Bruce (1925-1966, American Comedian)

6 The ultimate sin of any performer is contempt for the audience.
Lester Bangs (1948-1982, American Rock Journalist)

7 The essential is to excite the spectators. If that means playing Hamlet on a flying trapeze or in an aquarium, you do it.
Orson Welles (1915-1985, American Film Maker)

8 Fun can be the dessert of our lives but never its main course.
Rabbi Harold S. Kushner

9 A am a great friend of public amusements, they keep people from vice.
Samuel Johnson (1709-1784, British Author)

10 I believe entertainment can aspire to be art, and can become art, but if you set out to make art you're an idiot.
Steve Martin (1945-, American Actor, Comedian, Screenwriter, Playwright, Writer)

11 I would rather entertain and hope that people learned something than educate people and hope they were entertained.
Walt Disney (1901-1966, American Artist, Film Producer)

ENTHUSIASM

1 When I hear a man preach, I like to see him act as if he were fighting bees.
Abraham Lincoln (1809-1865, Sixteenth President of the USA)

2 The ambitious will always be first in the crowd; he presseth forward, he looketh not behind him. More anguish is it to his mind to see one before him, than joy to leave thousands at a distance.
Akhenaton (1375 BC, Egyptian King, Monotheist)

3 Enthusiasm. A distemper of youth, curable by small doses of repentance in connection with outward applications of experience.
Ambrose Bierce (1842-1914, American Author, Editor, Journalist, "The Devil's Dictionary")

4 I prefer the errors of enthusiasm to the indifference of wisdom.
Anatole France (1844-1924, French Writer)

5 Enthusiasm moves the world.
Arthur James Balfour (1848-1930, British Conservative Politician, Prime Minister)

6 Every production of genius must be the production of enthusiasm.
Benjamin Disraeli (1804-1881, British Statesman, Prime Minister)

7 The people of England are the most enthusiastic in the world.
Benjamin Disraeli (1804-1881, British Statesman, Prime Minister)

8 Earnestness is enthusiasm tempered by reason.
Blaise Pascal (1623-1662, French Scientist, Religious Philosopher)

9 If you can give your son or daughter only one gift, let it be enthusiasm.
Bruce Barton (1886-1967, American Author, Advertising Executive)

10 A man can succeed at almost anything for which he has unlimited enthusiasm.
Charles M. Schwab (1862-1939, American Industrialist, Businessman)

11 Enthusiasm is the inspiration of everything great. Without it no man is to be feared, and with it none despised.
Christian Nevell Bovee (1820-1904, American Author, Lawyer)

12 You can't sweep other people off their feet, if you can't be swept off your own.
Clarence Day (1874-1935, American Essayist)

13 Enthusiasm is a vital element toward the individual success of every man or woman.
Conrad Hilton (1887-1979, American Hotelier, Businessman, Founder, Hilton Hotels)

14 Flaming enthusiasm, backed up by horse sense and persistence, is the quality that most frequently makes for success.
Dale Carnegie (1888-1955, American Author, Trainer)

15 If you want to be enthusiastic, act enthusiastic.
Dale Carnegie (1888-1955, American Author, Trainer)

16 Enthusiasm is the best protection in any situation. Wholeheartedness is contagious. Give yourself, if you wish to get others.
David Seabury (American Doctor, Author)

17 Get excited and enthusiastic about you own dream. This excitement is like a forest fire -- you can smell it, taste it, and see it from a mile away.
Denis Waitley (1933-, American Author, Speaker, Trainer, Peak Performance Expert)

18 Great eagerness in the pursuit of wealth, pleasure, or honor, cannot exist without sin.
Desiderius Erasmus (1466-1536, Dutch Humanist)

19 Creativity is a natural extension of our enthusiasm.
Earl Nightingale (1921-1989, American Radio Announcer, Author, Motivator, Speaker)

20 One man has enthusiasm for 30 minutes, another for 30 days, but it is the man who has it for 30 years who makes a success of his life.
Edward B. Butler

21 The prudent person may direct a state, but it is the enthusiast who regenerates or ruins it.
Edward G. Bulwer-Lytton (1803-1873, British Novelist, Poet)

22 Enthusiasm is the genius of sincerity and truth accomplishes no victories without it.
Edward G. Bulwer-Lytton (1803-1873, British Novelist, Poet)

23 The sense of this word among the Greeks affords the noblest definition of it; enthusiasm signifies God in us.
Germaine De Stael (1766-1817, French-Swiss Novelist)

24 The worst bankruptcy in the world is the person who has lost his enthusiasm.
H. W. Arnold

25 Enthusiasm is the greatest asset in the world. It beats money, power and influence.
Henry Chester

26 Enthusiasm is the yeast that makes your hopes shine to the stars. Enthusiasm is the sparkle in your eyes, the swing in your gait. The grip of your hand, the irresistible surge of will and energy to execute your ideas.
Henry Ford (1863-1947, American Industrialist, Founder of Ford Motor Company)

27 In things pertaining to enthusiasm, no man is sane who does not know how to be insane on proper occasions.
Henry Ward Beecher (1813-1887, American Preacher, Orator, Writer)

28 He who possesses the source of enthusiasm will achieve great things. Doubt not. You will gather friends around you as a hair clasp gathers the hair.
I Ching (12th Century BC, Chinese Book of Changes)

29 No person is ever good for much, that hasn't been swept off their feet by enthusiasm between ages twenty and thirty.
James A. Froude (1818-1894, British Historian)

30 Fires can't be made with dead embers, nor can enthusiasm be stirred by spiritless men. Enthusiasm in our daily work lightens effort and turns even labor into pleasant tasks.
James Baldwin (1924-1987, American Author)

31 How poor a guide enthusiasm is when it is not informed with the mind and spirit of God.
James Stalker

32 No battle of any importance can be won without enthusiasm.
John Lord O'Brian

33 Catch on fire with enthusiasm and people will come for miles to watch you burn.
John Wesley (1703-1791, British Preacher, Founder of Methodism)

34 The figure of the enthusiast who has just discovered jogging or a new way to fix tofu can be said to stand or, more accurately, to tremble on the threshold of conversion, as the representative American.
Lewis H. Lapham (1935-, American Essayist, Editor)

35 People who never get carried away should be.
Malcolm S. Forbes (1919-1990, American Publisher, Businessman)

36 Enthusiasms, like stimulants, are often affected by people with small mental ballast.
Minna Antrim (1861-18?, American Epigrammist)

37 Your enthusiasm will be infectious, stimulating and attractive to others. They will love you for it. They will go for you and with you.
Norman Vincent Peale (1898-1993, American Christian Reformed Pastor, Speaker, Author)

38 Enthusiasm releases the drive to carry you over obstacles and adds significance to all you do.
Norman Vincent Peale (1898-1993, American Christian Reformed Pastor, Speaker, Author)

39 There is a real magic in enthusiasm. It spells the difference between mediocrity and accomplishment.
Norman Vincent Peale (1898-1993, American Christian Reformed Pastor, Speaker, Author)

40 Every memorable act in the history of the world is a triumph of enthusiasm. Nothing great was ever achieved without it because it gives any challenge or any occupation, no mater how frightening or difficult, a new meaning. Without enthusiasm you are doomed to a life of mediocrity but with it you can accomplish miracles.
Og Mandino (1923-1996, American Motivational Author, Speaker)

41 Enthusiasm is everything. It must be taut and vibrating like a guitar string.
Pele (Brazilian Soccer Star)

42 Charisma is the transference of enthusiasm.
Ralph Archbold (American Speaker, Entertainer, Performer, "Portrays Ben Franklin")

43 Every great and commanding movement in the annals of the world is due to the triumph of enthusiasm. Nothing great was ever achieved without it.
Ralph Waldo Emerson (1803-1882, American Poet, Essayist)

44 Enthusiasm is the mother of effort, and without it nothing great was ever achieved.
Ralph Waldo Emerson (1803-1882, American Poet, Essayist)

45 Nothing great was ever achieved without enthusiasm.
Ralph Waldo Emerson (1803-1882, American Poet, Essayist)

46 Enthusiasm is the leaping lightning, not to be measured by the horse-power of the understanding.
Ralph Waldo Emerson (1803-1882, American Poet, Essayist)

47 Success is not the result of spontaneous combustion, you must set yourself on fire first.
Reggie Leach (1950-, Canadian Hockey Player)

48 The love of life is necessary to the vigorous prosecution of any undertaking.
Samuel Johnson (1709-1784, British Author)

49 It is energy -- the central element of which is will -- that produces the miracle that is enthusiasm in all ages. Everywhere it is what is called force of character and the sustaining power of all great action.
Samuel Smiles (1812-1904, Scottish Author)

50 Enthusiasm... the sustaining power of all great action.
Samuel Smiles (1812-1904, Scottish Author)

51 Nothing is so contagious as enthusiasm.
Samuel Taylor Coleridge (1772-1834, British Poet, Critic, Philosopher)

52 You will do foolish things, but do them with enthusiasm.
Sidonie Gabrielle Colette (1873-1954, French Author)

53 No virtue is safe that is not enthusiastic.
Sir John Robert Seeley

54 The condition of the most passionate enthusiast is to be preferred over the individual who, because of the fear of making a mistake, won't in the end affirm or deny anything.
Thomas Carlyle (1795-1881, Scottish Philosopher, Author)

55 To waken interest and kindle enthusiasm is the sure way to teach easily and successfully.
Tryon Edwards (1809-1894, American Theologian)

56 National enthusiasm is the nursery of genius.
Tuckerman

57 If you aren't fired up with enthusiasm, you'll be fired with enthusiasm.
Vince Lombardi (1913-1970, American Football Coach)

58 The real secret to success is enthusiasm.
Walter Chrysler (American Businessman, Founder of Chrysler Motors)

59 No wild enthusiast could rest, till half the world like him was possessed.
William Cowper (1731-1800, British Poet)

60 All noble enthusiasms pass through a feverish stage, and grow wiser and more serene.
William Ellery Channing (1780-1842, American Unitarian Minister, Author)

61 The world belongs to the Enthusiast who keeps cool.
William Mcfee

ENVIRONMENT

1 We are the environment.
Charles Panati

2 It isn't pollution that's harming the environment. It's the impurities in our air and water that are doing it.
Dan Quayle (1947-, American Politician, Vice-President)

3 When we become a part of anything, it becomes a part of us.
David Harold Fink

4 Our environment, the world in which we live and work, is a mirror of our attitudes and expectations.
Earl Nightingale (1921-1989, American Radio Announcer, Author, Motivator, Speaker)

5 Every man is like the company he is wont to keep.
Euripides (480-406 BC, Greek Tragic Poet)

6 A man is not rightly conditioned until he is a happy, healthy, and prosperous being; and happiness, health, and prosperity are the result of a harmonious adjustment of the inner with the outer of the man with his surroundings.
James Allen (1864-1912, British-born American Essayist, Author of "As a Man Thinketh")

7 We live in a web of ideas, a fabric of our own making.
Joseph Chilton Pearce

8 We are shaped by each other. We adjust not to the reality of a world, but to the reality of other thinkers.
Joseph Chilton Pearce

9 A person is either the effect of his environment or is able to have an effect upon his environment.
L. Ron Hubbard (American Author, Philosopher, Founder of Scientology)

10 The first step toward success is taken when you refuse to be a captive of the environment in which you first find yourself.
Mark Caine

11 We begin to see, therefore, the importance of selecting our environment with the greatest of care, because environment is the mental feeding ground out of which the food that goes into our minds is extracted.
Napoleon Hill (1883-1970, American Speaker, Motivational Writer, "Think and Grow Rich")

12 Every experience in life, everything with which we have come in contact in life, is a chisel which has been cutting away at our life statue, molding, modifying, shaping it. We are part of all we have met. Everything we have seen, heard, felt or thought has had its hand in molding us, shaping us.
Orison Swett Marden (1850-1924, American Author, Founder of Success Magazine)

13 Your outlook upon life, your estimate of yourself, your estimate of your value are largely colored by your environment. Your whole career will be modified, shaped, molded by your surroundings, by the character of the people with whom you come in contact every day...
Orison Swett Marden (1850-1924, American Author, Founder of Success Magazine)

14 We make the world we live in and shape our own environment.
Orison Swett Marden (1850-1924, American Author, Founder of Success Magazine)

15 A strong, successful man is not the victim of his environment. He creates favorable conditions. His own inherent force and energy compel things to turn out as he desires.
Orison Swett Marden (1850-1924, American Author, Founder of Success Magazine)

16 Man shapes himself through decision that shape his environment.
Rene Dubos (1901-1982, French-born American Bacteriologist)

17 People blame their environment. There is only one person to blame -- and only one -- themselves.
Robert Collier (American Writer, Publisher)

18 We found that the most exciting environments, that treated people very well, are also tough as nails. There is no bureaucratic mumbo-jumbo... excellent companies provide two things simultaneously: tough environments and very supportive environments.
Thomas J. Peters (1942-, American Management Consultant, Author, Trainer)

19 You are a product of your environment. So choose the environment that will best develop you toward your objective. Analyze your life in terms of its environment. Are the things around you helping you toward success -- or are they holding you back?
W. Clement Stone (1902-, American Businessman, Author)

ENVIRONMENTALISM

1 Modern man's capacity for destruction is quixotic evidence of humanity's capacity for reconstruction. The powerful technological agents we have unleashed against the environment include many of the agents we require for its reconstruction.
George F. Will (1941-, American Political Columnist)

2 What have we achieved in mowing down mountain ranges, harnessing the energy of mighty rivers, or moving whole populations about like chess pieces, if we ourselves remain the same restless, miserable, frustrated creatures we were before? To call such activity progress is utter delusion. We may succeed in altering the face of the earth until it is unrecognizable even to the Creator, but if we are unaffected wherein lies the meaning?
Henry Miller (1891-1980, American Author)

3 I am I plus my surroundings and if I do not preserve the latter, I do not preserve myself.
Jose Ortega Y Gasset (1883-1955, Spanish Essayist, Philosopher)

4 It hurts the spirit, somehow, to read the word environments, when the plural means that there are so many alternatives there to be sorted through, as in a market, and voted on.
Lewis Thomas (1913-, American Physician, Educator)

5 That which is not good for the bee-hive cannot be good for the bees.
Marcus Aurelius (121-80 AD, Roman Emperor, Philosopher)

6 If the federal government had been around when the Creator was putting His hand to this state, Indiana wouldn't be here. It'd still be waiting for an environmental impact statement.
Ronald Reagan (1911-, Fortieth President of the USA, Actor)

ENVY

1 He who goes unenvied shall not be admired.
Aeschylus (525-456 BC, Greek Dramatist)

2 As iron is eaten away by rust, so the envious are consumed by their own passion.
Antisthenes (388-311 BC, Greek Dramatist)

3 The envious die not once, but as oft as the envied win applause.
Baltasar Gracian (1601-1658, Spanish Philosopher, Writer)

4 Envy and wrath shorten the life. [Ecclesiasticus]
Bible (Sacred Scriptures of Christians and Judaism)

5 Rust consumes iron and envy consumes itself.
Danish Proverb

6 None of the affections have been noted to fascinate and bewitch but envy.
Francis Bacon (1561-1626, British Philosopher, Essayist, Statesman)

7 Envy is more irreconcilable than hatred.
François de La Rochefoucauld (1613-1680, French classical writer)

8 The sure mark of one born with noble qualities is being born without envy.
François de La Rochefoucauld (1613-1680, French classical writer)

9 It is not enough to succeed, others must fail.
François de La Rochefoucauld (1613-1680, French classical writer)

10 Envy eats nothing, but its own heart.
German Proverb

11 Whenever a friend succeeds, a little something in me dies.
Gore Vidal (1925-, American Novelist, Critic)

12 There is no sweeter sound than the crumbling of ones fellow man.
Groucho Marx (1895-1977, American Comic Actor)

13 Some folks rail against other folks, because other folks have what some folks would be glad of.
Henry Fielding (1707-1754, British Novelist, Dramatist)

14 How much better a thing it is to be envied than to be pitied.
Herodotus (484-425 BC, Greek Historian)

15 He will be loved when dead, who was envied when he was living.
Horace (65-8 BC, Italian Poet)

16 Men are so constituted that every one undertakes what he sees another successful in, whether he has aptitude for it or not.
Johann Wolfgang Von Goethe (1749-1832, German Poet, Dramatist, Novelist)

17 The envied are like bureaucrats; the more impersonal they are, the greater the illusion (for themselves and for others) of their power.
John Berger (1926-, British Actor, Critic)

18 Fools may our scorn, not envy, raise. For envy is a kind of praise.
John Gay (1688-1732, British Playwright, Poet)

19   I never admire another's fortune so much that I became dissatisfied with my own.
Marcus T. Cicero (106-43 BC, Great Roman Orator, Politician)

20   Man will do many things to get himself loved; he will do all things to get himself envied.
Mark Twain (1835-1910, American Humorist, Writer)

21   Envy is honors foe.
Motto

22   Envy feeds on the living, after death it rests, then the honor of a man protects him.
Ovid (43 BC-18 AD, Roman Poet)

23   Envy aims very high.
Ovid (43 BC-18 AD, Roman Poet)

24   Helpless, unknown, and unremembered, most human beings, however sensitive, idealistic, intelligent, go through life as passengers rather than chauffeurs. Although we may pretend that it is the chauffeur who is the social inferior, most of us, like Toad of Toad Hall, would not mind a turn at the wheel ourselves.
Ralph Harper

25   Envy is the tax which all distinction must pay.
Ralph Waldo Emerson (1803-1882, American Poet, Essayist)

26   His scorn of the great is repeated too often to be real; no man thinks much of that which he despises.
Samuel Johnson (1709-1784, British Author)

27   They that envy others are their inferiors.
Saying

28   Let age, not envy, draw wrinkles on thy cheeks.
Sir Thomas Browne (1605-1682, British Author, Physician,, Philosopher)

29   The envious person grows lean with the fatness of their neighbor.
Socrates (469-399 BC, Greek Philosopher of Athens)

30   Nothing sharpens sight like envy.
Thomas Fuller (1608-1661, British Clergyman, Author)

31   Envy among other ingredients has a mixture of the love of justice in it. We are more angry at undeserved than at deserved good-fortune.
William Hazlitt (1778-1830, British Essayist)

32   All the world is competent to judge my pictures except those who are of my profession.
William Hogarth (1697-1764, British Painter, Engraver)

33   Oh, what a bitter thing it is to look into happiness through another man's eyes.
William Shakespeare (1564-1616, British Poet, Playwright, Actor)

EPITAPHS

1   If men could see the epitaphs their friends write they would believe they had gotten into the wrong grave.
American Proverb

2   Green leaves on a dead tree is our epitaph -- green leaves, dear reader, on a dead tree.
Cyril Connolly (1903-1974, British Critic)

3   When I die, my epitaph should read: She Paid the Bills. That's the story of my private life.
Gloria Swanson (1897-1983, American Actress)

4   The most touching epitaph I ever encountered was on the tombstone of the printer of Edinburgh. It said simply: "He kept down the cost and set the type right."
Gregory Nunn (1955-, American Golfer)

5   At last God caught his eye.
Harry Secombe

6   Oh, write of me, not "Died in bitter pains," but "Emigrated to another star!"
Helen Hunt Jackson (1830-1885, American Writer)

7   An epitaph is a belated advertisement for a line of goods that has been discontinued.
Irvin S. Cobb

8   Don't pity me now, don't pity me never; I'm going to do nothing for ever and ever.
James Agate (1877-1947) British Author, Critic)

9   Posterity will never survey a nobler grave than this: here lie the bones of Castlereagh: stop, traveler, and piss.
Lord Byron (1788-1824, British Poet)

10   Nor has his death the world deceiv'd than his wondrous life surprise d; if he like a madman liv'd least he like a wise one dy'd.
Miguel De Cervantes (1547-1616, Spanish Novelist, Dramatist, Poet)

11   The epitaphs on tombstones of a great many people should read: Died at thirty, and buried at sixty.
Nicholas Butler (1862-1947, American Educationist)

12   Reading the epitaphs, our only salvation lies in resurrecting the dead and burying the living.
Paul Eldridge

13   Let no man write my epitaph; for as no man who knows my motives dare now vindicate them, let not prejudice or ignorance asperse them. Let them rest in obscurity and peace! Let my memory be left in oblivion, my tomb remain uninscribed, until other times and other men can do justice to my character.
Robert Emmet (1778-1803 (hanged), Irish Rebel)

14   And were an epitaph to be my story I'd have a short one ready for my own. I would have written of me on my stone: I had a lover's quarrel with the world.
Robert Frost (1875-1963, American Poet)

15   In lapidary inscriptions a man is not upon oath.
Samuel Johnson (1709-1784, British Author)

EQUALITY

1 That all men are equal is a proposition to which, at ordinary times, no sane human being has ever given his assent.
Aldous Huxley (1894-1963, British Author)

2 The principle of equality does not destroy the imagination, but lowers its flight to the level of the earth.
Alexis De Tocqueville (1805-1859, French Social Philosopher)

3 You cannot have all chiefs; you gotta have Indians too.
American Proverb

4 A commitment to sexual equality with males is a commitment to becoming the rich instead of the poor, the rapist instead of the raped, the murderer instead of the murdered.
Andrea Dworkin (1946-, American Feminist Critic)

5 Equal opportunity is good, but special privilege is better.
Anna Chennault

6 She was not a women likely to settle for equality when sex gave her an advantage.
Anthony Delano

7 Equality consists in the same treatment of similar persons.
Aristotle (384-322 BC, Greek Philosopher)

8 The beginning of reform is not so much to equalize property as to train the noble sort of natures not to desire more, and to prevent the lower from getting more.
Aristotle (384-322 BC, Greek Philosopher)

9 The worst form of inequality is to try to make unequal things equal.
Aristotle (384-322 BC, Greek Philosopher)

10 In America everybody is of opinion that he has no social superiors, since all men are equal, but he does not admit that he has no social inferiors.
Bertrand Russell (1872-1970, British Philosopher, Mathematician, Essayist)

11 All this talk about equality. The only thing people really have in common is that they are all going to die.
Bob Dylan (1941-, American Musician, Singer, Songwriter)

12 The trauma of the Sixties persuaded me that my generation's egalitarianism was a sentimental error. I now see the hierarchical as both beautiful and necessary. Efficiency liberates; egalitarianism tangles, delays, blocks, deadens.
Camille Paglia (1947-, American Author, Critic, Educator)

13 The deadly Hydra now is the hydra of Equality. Liberty, Equality and Fraternity is the three- fanged serpent.
D. H. Lawrence (1885-1930, British Author)

14 Just as modern mass production requires the standardization of commodities, so the social process requires standardization of man, and this standardization is called equality.
Erich Fromm (1900-1980, American Psychologist)

15 When a bachelor of philosophy from the Antilles refuses to apply for certification as a teacher on the grounds of his color I say that philosophy has never saved anyone. When someone else strives and strains to prove to me that black men are as intelligent as white men I say that intelligence has never saved anyone: and that is true, for, if philosophy and intelligence are invoked to proclaim the equality of men, they have also been employed to justify the extermination of men.
Frantz Fanon (1925-1961, French Psychiatrist)

16 The doctrine of equality! There exists no more poisonous poison: for it seems to be preached by justice itself, while it is the end of justice.
Friedrich Nietzsche (1844-1900, German Philosopher)

17 Between persons of equal income there is no social distinction except the distinction of merit. Money is nothing: character, conduct, and capacity are everything. There would be great people and ordinary people and little people, but the great would always be those who had done great things, and never the idiots whose mothers had spoiled them and whose fathers had left them a hundred thousand a year; and the little would be persons of small minds and mean characters, and not poor persons who had never had a chance. That is why idiots are always in favor of inequality of income (their only chance of eminence), and the really great in favor of equality.
George Bernard Shaw (1856-1950, Irish-born British Dramatist)

18 No advance in wealth, no softening of manners, no reform or revolution has ever brought human equality a millimeter nearer.
George Orwell (1903-1950, British Author, "Animal Farm")

19 All animals are equal, but some animals are more equal than others.
George Orwell (1903-1950, British Author, "Animal Farm")

20 We've chosen the path to equality, don't let them turn us around.
Geraldine Ferraro

21 If the worker and his boss enjoy the same television program and visit the same resort places, if the typist is as attractively made up as the daughter of her employer, if the Negro owns a Cadillac, if they all read the same newspaper, then this assimilation indicates not the disappearance of classes, but the extent to which the needs and satisfactions that serve the preservation of the Establishment are shared by the underlying population.
Herbert Marcuse (1898-1979, German Political Philosopher)

22 Equality may perhaps be a right, but no power on earth can ever turn it into a fact.
Honore De Balzac (1799-1850, French Novelist)

23 Equality, in a social sense, may be divided into that of condition and that of rights. Equality of condition is incompatible with civilization, and is found only to exist in those communities that are but slightly removed from the savage state. In practice, it can only mean a common misery.
James F. Cooper (1789-1851, American Novelist)

24 The legacy of women's war work is our present post-industrial employment structure. It was the war that created the demand for a technologically advanced, de-skilled, low-paid, non-unionized female workforce and paved the way for making part-time work the norm for married women now. A generation later, it was the daughters of wartime women workers who completed their mothers' campaign for equal pay.
Linda Grant (British Journalist)

25 The battle for women's rights has been largely won.
Margaret Thatcher (1925-, British Stateswoman, Prime Minister (1979-90))

26 Prosperity or egalitarianism -- you have to choose. I favor freedom -- you never achieve real equality anyway: you simply sacrifice prosperity for an illusion.
Mario Vargas Llosa (1936-, Latin American Author)

27 We are all alike, on the inside.
Mark Twain (1835-1910, American Humorist, Writer)

28 An earthly kingdom cannot exist without inequality of persons. Some must be free, some serfs, some rulers, some subjects.
Martin Luther (1483-1546, German Leader of the Protestant Reformation)

29 I have a dream that one day this nation will rise up and live out the true meaning of its creed; We hold these truths to be self-evident: that all men are created equal...
Martin Luther King Jr. (1929-1968, American Black Leader, Nobel Prize Winner, 1964)

30 I will feel equality has arrived when we can elect to office women who are as unqualified as some of the men who are already there.
Maureen Reagan

31 We were equals once when we lay new-born babes on our nurse's knees. We will be equal again when they tie up our jaws for the last sleep.
Olive Schreiner

32 There has to be positive action that allows the most disadvantaged people to get their fair share of job opportunities.
Paul Burton (British Expert In Urban Studies)

33 What I am defending is the real rights of women. A woman should have the right to be in the home as a wife and mother.
Phyllis Schlafly (1924-, American Author and Political Activist)

34 Six feet of earth make all men equal.
Proverb

35 Some will always be above others. Destroy the inequality today, and it will appear again tomorrow.
Ralph Waldo Emerson (1803-1882, American Poet, Essayist)

36 Modern equalitarian societies whether democratic or authoritarian in their political forms, always base themselves on the claim that they are making life happier. Happiness thus becomes the chief political issue -- in a sense, the only political issue -- and for that reason it can never be treated as an issue at all.
Robert Warshow

37 Generally, employees who file complaints of discrimination do so as a last resort.
Rubye Fields (American President of Blacks in Government)

38 It is better that some should be unhappy than that none should be happy, which would be the case in a general state of equality.
Samuel Johnson (1709-1784, British Author)

39 Subordination tends greatly to human happiness. Were we all upon an equality, we should have no other enjoyment than mere animal pleasure.
Samuel Johnson (1709-1784, British Author)

40 It is not true that people are naturally equal for no two people can be together for even a half an hour without one acquiring an evident superiority over the other.
Samuel Johnson (1709-1784, British Author)

41 Perfect love cannot be without equality.
Scottish Proverb

42 The most mediocre of males feels himself a demigod as compared with women.
Simone De Beauvoir (1908-1986, French Novelist, Essayist)

43 Equality is the public recognition, effectively expressed in institutions and manners, of the principle that an equal degree of attention is due to the needs of all human beings.
Simone Weil (1910-1943, French Philosopher, Mystic)

44 A friend to everybody and to nobody is the same thing.
Spanish Proverb

45 By nature all men are equal in liberty, but not in other endowments.
St. Thomas Aquinas (1225-1274, Italian Scholastic Philosopher and Theologian)

46 No man is above the law, and no man is below it.
Theodore Roosevelt (1858-1919, Twenty-sixth President of the USA)

47 We hold these truths to be self-evident: that all men are created equal; that they are endowed by their Creator with certain unalienable rights; that among these are life, liberty, and the pursuit of happiness...
Thomas Jefferson (1743-1826, Third President of the USA)

48 The mandate for equal opportunity doesn't dictate disregard for the differences in candidates' qualities and skills. There is no constitutional right to play ball. All there is a right to compete for it on equal terms.
Tim III Ellis (American District Court Judge)

49 Equality of opportunity is an equal opportunity to prove unequal talents.
Viscount Samuel

50 All people are equal, it is not birth, it is virtue alone that makes the difference.
Voltaire (1694-1778, French Historian, Writer)

51 Nature has never read the Declaration of Independence. It continues to make us unequal.
William J. Durant (1885-1981, American Historian, Essayist)

52 The intelligence suffers today automatically in consequence of the attack on all authority, advantage, or privilege. These things are not done away with, it is needless to say, but numerous scapegoats are made of the less politically powerful, to satisfy the egalitarian rage awakened.
Wyndham Lewis (1882-1957, British Author, Painter)

EROTICISM

1 Erotica is simply high-class pornography; better produced, better conceived, better executed, better packaged, designed for a better class of consumer.
Andrea Dworkin (1946-, American Feminist Critic)

2 Eroticism is assenting to life even in death.
Georges Bataille (1897-1962, French Novelist, Critic)

3 In this loveless everyday life eroticism is a substitute for love.
Henri Lefebvre (1901-, French Philosopher)

4 A man's eroticism is a woman's sexuality.
Karl Kraus (1874-1936, Austrian Satirist)

5 Eroticism has its own moral justification because it says that pleasure is enough for me; it is a statement of the individual's sovereignty.
Mario Vargas Llosa (1936-, Latin American Author)

6 Eroticism is like a dance: one always leads the other.
Milan Kundera (1929-, Czech Author, Critic)

ESCAPISM

1 Leave everything. Leave Dada. Leave your wife. Leave your mistress. Leave your hopes and fears. Leave your children in the woods. Leave the substance for the shadow. Leave your easy life, leave what you are given for the future. Set off on the roads.
Andre Breton (1989-1966, French Surrealist)

2 There is a cheap literature that speaks to us of the need of escape. It is true that when we travel we are in search of distance. But distance is not to be found. It melts away. And escape has never led anywhere. The moment a man finds that he must play the races, go the Arctic, or make war in order to feel himself alive, that man has begin to spin the strands that bind him to other men and to the world. But what wretched strands! A civilization that is really strong fills man to the brim, though he never stir. What are we worth when motionless, is the question.
Antoine De Saint-Exupery (1900-1944, French Aviator, Writer)

3 Hell is of this world and there are men who are unhappy escapees from hell, escapees destined ETERNALLY to reenact their escape.
Antonin Artaud (1896-1948, French Theater Producer, Actor, Theorist)

4 Man staggers through life yapped at by his reason, pulled and shoved by his appetites, whispered to by fears, beckoned by hopes. Small wonder that what he craves most is self-forgetting.
Eric Hoffer (1902-1983, American Author, Philosopher)

5 What fugitive from his country can also escape from himself.
Horace (65-8 BC, Italian Poet)

6 Man seeks to escape himself in myth, and does so by any means at his disposal. Drugs, alcohol, or lies. Unable to withdraw into himself, he disguises himself. Lies and inaccuracy give him a few moments of comfort.
Jean Cocteau (1889-1963, French Author, Filmmaker)

7 The shortest way out of Manchester is notoriously a bottle of Gordon's gin; out of any businessman's life there is the mirage of Paris; out of Paris, or mediocrity of talent and imagination, there are all the drugs, from subtle, all-conquering opium to cheating, cozening cocaine.
William Bolitho (1890-1930, British Author)

ETERNITY

1 One never ends. It bears all things, believes all things, hopes all things, endures all things.
Bible (Sacred Scriptures of Christians and Judaism)

2 All that is not eternal is eternally out of date.
C. S. Lewis (1898-1963, British Academic, Writer, Christian Apologist)

3 Forever is a long bargain.
German Proverb

4 In eternity there is indeed something true and sublime. But all these times and places and occasions are now and here. God himself culminates in the present moment and will never be more divine in the lapse of the ages. Time is but a stream I go a-fishing in. I drink at it, but when I drink I see the sandy bottom and detect how shallow it is. Its thin current slides away but eternity remains.
Henry David Thoreau (1817-1862, American Essayist, Poet, Naturalist)

5 The Eternal looked upon me for a moment with His eye of power, and annihilated me in His being, and become manifest to me in His essence. I saw I existed through Him.
Jalal-Uddin Rumi (1207-1273, Persian Sufi Mystic Poet)

6 Every situation, every moment -- is of infinite worth; for it is the representative of a whole eternity.
Johann Wolfgang Von Goethe (1749-1832, German Poet, Dramatist, Novelist)

7 Our Lord has written the promise of resurrection, not in books alone, but in every leaf in springtime.
Martin Luther (1483-1546, German Leader of the Protestant Reformation)

8 Eternity -- waste of time.
Natalie Clifford Barney (1876-1972, American-born French Author)

9 Eternity is a terrible thought. I mean, where's it going to end?
Tom Stoppard (1937-, Czech Playwright)

10 Eternity is in love with the productions of time.
William Blake (1757-1827, British Poet, Painter)

11 To see the world in a grain of sand, and to see heaven in a wild flower, hold infinity in the palm of your hands, and eternity in an hour.
William Blake (1757-1827, British Poet, Painter)

ETHICS

1 I think it's unethical to take money for poor quality performance.
Alvin Burger (American Businessman, Founder of 'Bugs' Burger Bug Killers, Inc.)

2 Every aspect of Western culture needs a new code of ethics -- a rational ethics -- as a precondition of rebirth.
Ayn Rand (1905-1982, Russian Writer, Philosopher)

3 Ethics is in origin the art of recommending to others the sacrifices required for cooperation with oneself.
Bertrand Russell (1872-1970, British Philosopher, Mathematician, Essayist)

4 Those who cultivate moral confusion for profit should understand this: we will name their names and shame them as they deserve to be shamed.
Bob Dole (1923-, American Politician,)

5 Ethics and equity and the principles of justice do not change with the calendar.
D. H. Lawrence (1885-1930, British Author)

6 We're given a code to live our lives by. We don't always follow it, but it's still there.
Gary Oldman (1958-, British-born American Actor)

7 Actually, there is only one "first question" of government, and it is "How should we live?" or "What kind of people do we want our citizens to be?"
George F. Will (1941-, American Political Columnist)

8 I say statecraft is soulcraft. Just as all education is moral education because learning conditions conduct, most legislation is moral legislations because it conditions the action and the thought of the nation in broad and important spheres in life.
George F. Will (1941-, American Political Columnist)

9 Let us raise a standard to which the wise and honest can repair; the rest is in the hands of God.
George Washington (1732-1799, First President of the USA)

10 Everywhere, the ethical predicament of our time imposes itself with an urgency which suggests that even the question "Have we anything to eat?" will be answered not in material but in ethical terms.
Hugo Ball (1886-1927, German Dadaist Poet)

11 No artist has ethical sympathies. An ethical sympathy in an artist is an unpardonable mannerism of style.
Oscar Wilde (1856-1900, British Author, Wit)

12 It horrifies me that ethics is only an optional extra at Harvard Business School.
Sir John Harvey (1863-1944, British Actor-Manager)

13 The character ethic, which I believe to be the foundation of success, teaches that there are basic principles of effective living, and that people can only experience true success and enduring happiness as they learn and integrate these principles into their basic character.
Stephen R. Covey (American Speaker, Trainer, Author of "The 7 Habits of Highly Effective People")

14 Evangelical faith without Christian ethics is a travesty on the gospel.
V. Raymond Edman

15 Nothing that is morally wrong can be politically right.
William E. Gladstone (1809-1888, British Liberal Prime Minister, Statesman)

ETIQUETTE

1 Those who have mastered etiquette, who are entirely, impeccably right, would seem to arrive at a point of exquisite dullness.
Dorothy Parker (1893-1967, American Humorous Writer)

2 A commercial society whose members are essentially ascetic and indifferent in social ritual has to be provided with blueprints and specifications for evoking the right tone for every occasion.
Marshall Mcluhan (1911-1980, Canadian Communications Theorist)

3 Nothing more rapidly inclines a person to go into a monastery than reading a book on etiquette. There are so many trivial ways in which it is possible to commit some social sin.
Quentin Crisp (1908-, British Author)

4 He who observes etiquette but objects to lying is like someone who dresses fashionably but wears no vest.
Walter Benjamin (1982-1940, German Critic, Philosopher)

EVANGELISM

1 The salvation of a single soul is more important than the production or preservation of all the epics and tragedies in the world.
C. S. Lewis (1898-1963, British Academic, Writer, Christian Apologist)

2 In soliciting donations from his flock, a preacher may promise eternal life in a celestial city whose streets are paved with gold, and that's none of the law's business. But if he promises an annual free stay in a luxury hotel on Earth, he'd better have the rooms available.
Charlotte Observer

3 Evangelism is just one beggar telling another beggar where to find bread.
D. T. Niles

4 The world has more winnable people than ever before... but it is possible to come out of a ripe field empty-handed.
Donald H. Mcgannon

5 To call a man evangelical who is not evangelistic is an utter contradiction.
G. Campbell Morgan

6 Evangelism is selling a dream.
Guy Kawasaki

7 Our business is to present the Christian faith clothed in modern terms, not to propagate modern thought clothed in Christian terms. Confusion here is fatal.
J. I. Packer

8 Why should I apologize because God throws in crystal chandeliers, mahogany floors, and the best construction in the world?
Jim Bakker (1940-, American Evangelist)

9 God is definitely out of the closet.
Marianne Williamson (1952-, American Author, Lecturer on Spirituality)

10 Nothing makes one so vain as being told that one is a sinner.
Oscar Wilde (1856-1900, British Author, Wit)

11 Evangelism as the New Testament describes it is not child's play. Evangelism is work, often hard work. Yet it is not drudgery. It puts person in good humor, and makes him truly human.
Oswald C. Hoffman

12 The Holy Spirit can't save saints or seats. If we don't know any non-Christians, how can we introduce them to the Savior?
Paul Little

13 Being an extrovert isn't essential to evangelism--obedience and love are.
Rebecca M. Pippert

14 Evangelism is the spontaneous overflow of a glad and free heart in Jesus Christ.
Robert Munger

15 There is no arguing with the pretenders to a divine knowledge and to a divine mission. They are possessed with the sin of pride, they have yielded to the perennial temptation.
Walter Lippmann (1889-1974, American Journalist)

EVENTS

1 In the world we live in everything militates in favor of things that have not yet happened, of things that will never happen again.
Andre Breton (1989-1966, French Surrealist)

2 Like a kick in the butt, the force of events wakes slumberous talents.
Edward Hoagland (1932-, American Novelist, Essayist)

3 A society which allows an abominable event to burgeon from its dung heap and grow on its surface is like a man who lets a fly crawl unheeded across his face or saliva dribble from his mouth -- either epileptic or dead.
Jean Baudrillard (French Postmodern Philosopher, Writer)

4 The enemy of the conventional wisdom is not ideas but the march of events.
John Kenneth Galbraith (1908-, American Economist)

5 The great events of life often leave one unmoved; they pass out of consciousness, and, when one thinks of them, become unreal. Even the scarlet flowers of passion seem to grow in the same meadow as the poppies of oblivion.
Oscar Wilde (1856-1900, British Author, Wit)

6 One of the extraordinary things about human events is that the unthinkable becomes thinkable.
Salman Rushdie (1948-, Indian-born British Author)

EVIL

1 The pious pretence that evil does not exist only makes it vague, enormous and menacing.
Aleister Crowley (1875-1947, British Occultist)

2 Of two evils, it is always best to vote for the least hypocritical.
American Proverb

3 The love of evil is the root of all money.
American Proverb

4 Evil is always possible. Goodness is a difficulty.
Anne Rice (1941-, American Author, "Interview with the Vampire")

5 No notice is taken of a little evil, but when it increases it strikes the eye.
Aristotle (384-322 BC, Greek Philosopher)

6 Never open the door to a lesser evil, for other ones invariably slink in after it.
Baltasar Gracian (1601-1658, Spanish Philosopher, Writer)

7 They that know no evil will suspect none.
Ben Johnson (1573-1637, British Dramatist, Poet)

8   There surely is in human nature an inherent propensity to extract all the good out of all the evil.
Benjamin Haydon (1786-1846, British Artist)

9   Overcome evil with good. [St. Paul]]
Bible (Sacred Scriptures of Christians and Judaism)

10 No evil shall happen to the just.
Bible (Sacred Scriptures of Christians and Judaism)

11 Whoever rewards evil for good, evil will not depart from their house.
Bible (Sacred Scriptures of Christians and Judaism)

12 Those that are evil have not only the good against them, but also the bad.
Bischer

13 Evil is easy, and has infinite forms.
Blaise Pascal (1623-1662, French Scientist, Religious Philosopher)

14 I have discovered that all human evil comes from this, man's being unable to sit still and quiet in a room alone.
Blaise Pascal (1623-1662, French Scientist, Religious Philosopher)

15 Evil is something you recognize immediately you see it: it works through charm.
Brian Masters

16 There has to be evil so that good can prove its purity above it.
Buddha (568-488 BC, Founder of Buddhism)

17 What is worse than evil? The inability to bear it.
C. J. Weber

18 Evil is done without effort, naturally, it is the working of fate; good is always the product of an art.
Charles Baudelaire (1821-1867, French Poet)

19 It is a cursed evil to any man to become as absorbed in any subject as I am in mine.
Charles Darwin (1809-1882, British Naturalist)

20 Of two evils, choose neither.
Charles Haddon Spurgeon (1834-1892, British Baptist Preacher)

21 To do no evil is good, to intend none better.
Claudius (10 BC-54 AD, Roman Emperor)

22 This is the very worst wickedness, that we refuse to acknowledge the passionate evil that is in us. This makes us secret and rotten.
D. H. Lawrence (1885-1930, British Author)

23 Nature, more of a stepmother than a mother in several ways, has sown a seed of evil in the hearts of mortals, especially in the more thoughtful men, which makes them dissatisfied with their own lot and envious of another s.
Desiderius Erasmus (1466-1536, Dutch Humanist)

24 Man must vanquish himself, must do himself violence, in order to perform the slightest action untainted by evil.
E. M. Cioran (1911-, Rumanian-born French Philosopher)

25 The only thing necessary for the triumph of evil is for good men to do nothing.
Edmund Burke (1729-1797, British Political Writer, Statesman)

26 Evil be to him who evil thinks.
Edward II

27 Evil, and evil spirits, devils and devil possession, are the outgrowth of man's inadequate consciousness of God. We must avoid thinking of evil as a thing in itself-a force that works against man or, against God, if you will.
Eric Butterworth

28 It is by its promise of a sense of power that evil often attracts the weak.
Eric Hoffer (1902-1983, American Author, Philosopher)

29 Some people show evil as a great racehorse shows breeding. They have the dignity of a hard chancre.
Ernest Hemingway (1898-1961, American Writer)

30 Evil enters like a needle and spreads like an oak tree.
Ethiopian Proverb

31 Wickedness is its own punishment.
Francis Quarles (1592-1644, British Poet)

32 We often do good in order that we may do evil with impunity.
François de La Rochefoucauld (1613-1680, French classical writer)

33 There is hardly a man clever enough to recognize the full extent of the evil he does.
François de La Rochefoucauld (1613-1680, French classical writer)

34 Nothing baffles the schemes of evil people so much as the calm composure of great souls.
Gabriel Riqueti Mirabeau (1749-1791, French Revolutionary Politician, Orator)

35 I can forgive Alfred Nobel for having invented dynamite, but only a fiend in human form could have invented the Nobel Prize.
George Bernard Shaw (1856-1950, Irish-born British Dramatist)

36 May the forces of evil become confused on the way to your house.-
George Carlin (American Stage and Television Comedian)

37 No evil dooms us hopelessly except the evil we love, and desire to continue in, and make no effort to escape from.
George Eliot (1819-1880, British Novelist)

38 One soweth and another reapeth is a verity that applies to evil as well as good.
George Eliot (1819-1880, British Novelist)

39 The trouble with Eichmann was precisely that so many were like him, and that the many were neither perverted nor sadistic, that they were, and still are, terribly and terrifyingly normal. From the viewpoint of our legal institutions and of our moral standards of judgment, this normality was much more terrifying than all the atrocities put together.
Hannah Arendt (1906-1975, German-born American Political Philosopher)

40 It is a power stronger than will. Could a stone escape from the laws of gravity? Impossible. Impossible, for evil to form an alliance with good.
Isidore Ducasse Lautreamont (1846-1870, French Author, Poet)

41 Our greatest evils flow from ourselves.
Jean Jacques Rousseau (1712-1778, Swiss Political Philosopher, Educationist, Essayist)

42 Nothing in the nature around us is evil. This needs to be repeated since one of the human ways of talking oneself into inhuman acts is to cite the supposed cruelty of nature.
John Berger (1926-, British Actor, Critic)

43 Wicked is not much worse than indiscreet.
John Donne (1572-1632, British Metaphysical Poet)

44 What wisdom can there be to choose, what continence to forbear without the knowledge of evil? He that can apprehend and consider vice with all her baits and seeming pleasures, and yet abstain, and yet distinguish, and yet prefer that which is truly better, he is the true wayfaring Christian.
John Milton (1608-1674, British Poet)

45 The surest defense against Evil is extreme individualism, originality of thinking, whimsicality, even -- if you will -- eccentricity. That is, something that can't be feigned, faked, imitated; something even a seasoned imposter couldn't be happy with.
Joseph Brodsky (1940-, Russian-born American Poet, Critic)

46 The belief in a supernatural source of evil is not necessary; men alone are quite capable of every wickedness.
Joseph Conrad (1857-1924, Polish-born British Novelist)

47 We are tainted by modern philosophy which has taught us that all is good, whereas evil has polluted everything and in a very real sense all is evil, since nothing is in its proper place.
Joseph De Maistre (1753-1821, French Diplomat, Philosopher)

48 If there was no moral evil upon earth, there would be no physical evil.
Joseph De Maistre (1753-1821, French Diplomat, Philosopher)

49 I couldn't claim that I have never felt the urge to explore evil, but when you descend into hell you have to be very careful.
Kathleen Raine

50 Only among people who think no evil can Evil monstrously flourish.
Logan Pearsall Smith (1865-1946, Anglo-American Essayist, Aphorist)

51 I am one of those who think like Nobel, than humanity will draw more good than evil from new discoveries.
Madame Marie Curie (1867-1934, Polish-born French Physicist)

52 Between two evils, I always pick the one I never tried before.
Mae West (1892-1980, American Actress)

53 When choosing between two evils, I always like to try the one I've never tried before.
Mae West (1892-1980, American Actress)

54 Must I do all the evil I can before I learn to shun it? Is it not enough to know the evil to shun it? If not, we should be sincere enough to admit that we love evil too well to give it up.
Mahatma Gandhi (1869-1948, Indian Political, Spiritual Leader)

55 We may draw good out of evil; we must not do evil, that good may come.
Maria Weston Chapman

56 Evil is a moral entity and not a created one, an eternal and not a perishable entity: it existed before the world; it constituted the monstrous, the execrable being who was also to fashion such a hideous world. It will hence exist after the creatures which people this world.
Marquis De Sade (1740-1814, French Author)

57 He who passively accepts evil is as much involved in it as he who helps to perpetrate it.
Martin Luther King Jr. (1929-1968, American Black Leader, Nobel Prize Winner, 1964)

58 No man chooses evil because it is evil; he only mistakes it for happiness.
Mary Wollstonecraft (1759-1797, British Feminist Writer)

59 When you choose the lesser of two evils, always remember that it is still an evil.
Max Lerner (1902-, American Author, Columnist)

60 But what is the greatest evil? If you are going to epitomize evil, what is it? Is it the bomb? The greatest evil that one has to fight constantly, every minute of the day until one dies, is the worse part of oneself.
Patrick Mcgoohan

61 Submit to the present evil, lest a greater one befall you.
Phaedrus (Macedonian Inventor and Writer)

62 All evils are equal when they are extreme.
Pierre Corneille (1606-1684, French Dramatist)

63 There must always remain something that is antagonistic to good.
Plato (427-347 BC, Greek Philosopher)

64 By bravely enduring it, an evil which cannot be avoided is overcome
Proverb

65 Evil is like water, it abounds, is cheap, soon fouls, but runs itself clear of taint.
Samuel Butler (1612-1680, British Poet, Satirist)

66 There are evils that have the ability to survive identification and go on for ever... money, for instance, or war.
Saul Bellow (1915-, American Novelist)

67 No evil is without its compensation. The less money, the less trouble; the less favor, the less envy. Even in those cases which put us out of wits, it is not the loss itself, but the estimate of the loss that troubles us.
Seneca (4 BC-65 AD, Spanish-born Roman Statesman, philosopher)

68 Evil is neither suffering nor sin; it is both at the same time, it is something common to them both. For they are linked together; sin makes us suffer and suffering makes us evil, and this indissoluble complex of suffering and sin is the evil in which we are submerged against our will, and to our horror.
Simone Weil (1910-1943, French Philosopher, Mystic)

69 All histories do show, and wise politicians do hold it necessary that, for the well-governing of every Commonweal, it behoveth man to presuppose that all men are evil, and will declare themselves so to be when occasion is offered.
Sir Walter Raleigh (1552-1618, British Courtier, Navigator, Writer)

70 There is only one good -- knowledge; and only one evil -- ignorance.
Socrates (469-399 BC, Greek Philosopher of Athens)

71 So far as we are human, what we do must be either evil or good: so far as we do evil or good, we are human: and it is better, in a paradoxical way, to do evil than to do nothing: at least we exist.
T. S. Eliot (1888-1965, American-born British Poet, Critic)

72 All evil is like a nightmare; the instant you stir under it, the evil is gone.
Thomas Carlyle (1795-1881, Scottish Philosopher, Author)

73 But evil is wrought by want of thought as well as want of heart!
Thomas Hood (1799-1845, British Poet and Humorist)

74 My mother's obsession with the good scissors always scared me a bit. It implied that somewhere in the house there lurked: the evil scissors.
Tony Martin

75 Evil is nourished and grows by concealment.
Virgil (70-19 BC, Roman Poet)

76 As long as people believe in absurdities they will continue to commit atrocities.
Voltaire (1694-1778, French Historian, Writer)

77 Evil is unspectacular and always human, and shares our bed and eats at our own table.
W. H. Auden (1907-1973, Anglo-American Poet)

78 There is no explanation for evil. It must be looked upon as a necessary part of the order of the universe. To ignore it is childish, to bewail it senseless.
W. Somerset Maugham (1874-1965, British Novelist, Playwright)

79 There can be no existence of evil as a force to the healthy-minded individual.
William James (1842-1910, American Psychologist, Professor, Author)

80 The face of evil is always the face of total need.
William S. Burroughs (1914-1997, American Writer)

81 There's small choice in rotten apples.
William Shakespeare (1564-1616, British Poet, Playwright, Actor)

EVOLUTION

1 Natural selection, as it has operated in human history, favors not only the clever but the murderous.
Barbara Ehrenreich (1941-, American Author, Columnist)

2 The question is this -- Is man an ape or an angel? My Lord, I am on the side of the angels. I repudiate with indignation and abhorrence these new fanged theories.
Benjamin Disraeli (1804-1881, British Statesman, Prime Minister)

3 An extra-terrestrial philosopher, who had watched a single youth up to the age of twenty-one and had never come across any other human being, might conclude that it is the nature of human beings to grow continually taller and wiser in an indefinite progress towards perfection; and this generalization would be just as well founded as the generalization which evolutionists base upon the previous history of this planet.
Bertrand Russell (1872-1970, British Philosopher, Mathematician, Essayist)

4 Organic life, we are told, has developed gradually from the protozoon to the philosopher, and this development, we are assured, is indubitably an advance. Unfortunately it is the philosopher, not the protozoon, who gives us this assurance.
Bertrand Russell (1872-1970, British Philosopher, Mathematician, Essayist)

5 All the evolution we know of proceeds from the vague to the definite.
Charles Sanders Peirce (1839-1914, American Philosopher, Logician, Mathematician)

6 It is disturbing to discover in oneself these curious revelations of the validity of the Darwinian theory. If it is true that we have sprung from the ape, there are occasions when my own spring appears not to have been very far.
Cornelia Otis Skinner

7 The probability of life originating from accident is comparable to the probability of the unabridged dictionary resulting from an explosion in a printing shop.
Edward Conklin

8 The pre-human creature from which man evolved was unlike any other living thing in its malicious viciousness toward its own kind. Humanization was not a leap forward but a groping toward survival.
Eric Hoffer (1902-1983, American Author, Philosopher)

9 We are the products of editing, rather than of authorship.
George Wald (1906-, American Biochemist)

10 God created a number of possibilities in case some of his prototypes failed -- that is the meaning of evolution.
Graham Greene (1904-1991, British Novelist)

11 It is hard for the ape to believe he descended from man.
H. L. Mencken (1880-1956, American Editor, Author, Critic, Humorist)

12 Biologically the species is the accumulation of the experiments of all its successful individuals since the beginning.
H.G. Wells (1866-1946, British-born American Author)

13 It is curious how there seems to be an instinctive disgust in Man for his nearest ancestors and relations. If only Darwin could conscientiously have traced man back to the Elephant or the Lion or the Antelope, how much ridicule and prejudice would have been spared to the doctrine of Evolution.
Havelock Ellis (1859-1939, British Psychologist)

14 The more specific idea of Evolution now reached is -- a change from an indefinite, incoherent homogeneity to a definite, coherent heterogeneity, accompanying the dissipation of motion and integration of matter.
Herbert Spencer (1820-1903, British Philosopher)

15 Man has lost the basic skill of the ape, the ability to scratch its back. Which gave it extraordinary independence, and the liberty to associate for reasons other than the need for mutual back-scratching.
Jean Baudrillard (French Postmodern Philosopher, Writer)

16 Evolution is not a force but a process. Not a cause but a law.
John Morley (1838-1923, British Journalist, Biographer, Statesman)

17 Historians will have to face the fact that natural selection determined the evolution of cultures in the same manner as it did that of species.
Konrad Lorenz (1903-1989, Austrian Zoologist, Ethnologist)

18 The historic ascent of humanity, taken as a whole, may be summarized as a succession of victories of consciousness over blind forces -- in nature, in society, in man himself.
Leon Trotsky (1879-1940, Russian Revolutionary)

19 One of the stupidest theories of Western life.
Malcolm Muggeridge (1903-1990, British Broadcaster)

20 I believe that our Heavenly Father invented man because he was disappointed in the monkey.
Mark Twain (1835-1910, American Humorist, Writer)

21 Evolution is the law of policies: Darwin said it, Socrates endorsed it, Cuvier proved it and established it for all time in his paper on "The Survival of the Fittest." These are illustrious names, this is a mighty doctrine: nothing can ever remove it from its firm base, nothing dissolve it, but evolution.
Mark Twain (1835-1910, American Humorist, Writer)

22 Evolution is gaining the psychic zones of the world... life, being and ascent of consciousness, could not continue to advance indefinitely along its line without transforming itself in depth. The being who is the object of his own reflection, in consequence, of that very doubling back upon himself becomes in a flash able to raise himself to a new sphere.
Pierre Teilhard De Chardin (1881-1955, French Christian Mystic, Author)

23 Darwinian man, though well-behaved, at best is only a monkey shaved.
W. S. Gilbert (1836-1911, British Librettist)

24 We live between two worlds; we soar in the atmosphere; we creep upon the soil; we have the aspirations of creators and the propensities of quadrupeds. There can be but one explanation of this fact. We are passing from the animal into a higher form, and the drama of this planet is in its second act.
W. Winwood Reade (1838-1875, American Writer)

EXAGGERATION

1 Who breaks a butterfly on a wheel?
Alexander Pope (1688-1744, British Poet, Critic, Translator)

2 I never exaggerate. I just remember big.
Chi Chi Rodriguez (1935-, Golfer born in Puerto Rico)

3 It is only a short step from exaggerating what we can find in the world to exaggerating our power to remake the world. Expecting more novelty than there is, more greatness than there is, and more strangeness than there is, we imagine ourselves masters of a plastic universe. But a world we can shape to our will is a shapeless world.
Daniel J. Boorstin (1914-, American Historian)

4 Thought is a process of exaggeration. The refusal to exaggerate is not infrequently an alibi for the disinclination to think or praise.
Eric Hoffer (1902-1983, American Author, Philosopher)

5 Eschew the monumental. Shun the Epic. All the guys who can paint great big pictures can paint great small ones.
Ernest Hemingway (1898-1961, American Writer)

6 Love is a gross exaggeration of the difference between one person and everybody else.
George Bernard Shaw (1856-1950, Irish-born British Dramatist)

7 We exaggerate misfortune and happiness alike. We are never as bad off or as happy as we say we are.
Honore De Balzac (1799-1850, French Novelist)

8 Exaggeration is a blood relation to falsehood and nearly as blamable.
Hosea Ballou (1771-1852, American Theologian, Founder of "Universalism")

9 He's the type who makes mountains out of molehills and then sells climbing equipment.
Ivern Ball

10 I don't want to tell you how much insurance I carry with the Prudential, but all I can say is: when I go, they go too.
Jack Benny (1894-1974, American Comedian)

11 Pretense is the overrating of any kind of knowledge we pretend to.
Jonathan Swift (1667-1745, Anglo-Irish Satirist)

12 Danger lies in the writer becoming the victim of his own exaggeration, losing the exact notion of sincerity, and in the end coming to despise truth itself as something too cold, too blunt for his purpose -- as, in fact, not good enough for his insistent emotion. From laughter and tears the descent is easy to sniveling and giggles.
Joseph Conrad (1857-1924, Polish-born British Novelist)

13 There are some people so addicted to exaggeration that they can't tell the truth without lying.
Josh Billings (1815-1885, American Humorist, Lecturer)

14 An exaggeration is a truth that has lost its temper.
Kahlil Gibran (1883-1931, Lebanese Poet, Novelist)

15 We always weaken everything we exaggerate.
La Harpe

16 'Tis a rule of manners to avoid exaggeration.
Ralph Waldo Emerson (1803-1882, American Poet, Essayist)

17 There is no one who does not exaggerate!
Ralph Waldo Emerson (1803-1882, American Poet, Essayist)

18 Camp is a vision of the world in terms of style -- but a particular kind of style. It is love of the exaggerated.
Susan Sontag (1933-, American Essayist)

19 It is the essence of truth that it is never excessive. Why should it exaggerate? There is that which should be destroyed and that which should be simply illuminated and studied. How great is the force of benevolent and searching examination! We must not resort to the flame where only light is required.
Victor Hugo (1802-1885, French Poet, Dramatist, Novelist)

20 Exaggeration is the inseparable companion of greatness.
Voltaire (1694-1778, French Historian, Writer)

21 An element of exaggeration clings to the popular judgment: great vices are made greater, great virtues greater also; interesting incidents are made more interesting, softer legends more soft.
Walter Bagehot (1826-1877, British Economist, Critic)

EXAMINATIONS

1 As long as learning is connected with earning, as long as certain jobs can only be reached through exams, so long must we take this examination system seriously. If another ladder to employment was contrived, much so-called education would disappear, and no one would be a penny the stupider.
Edward M. Forster (1879-1970, British Novelist, Essayist)

2 Examinations, sir, are pure humbug from beginning to end. If a man is a gentleman, he knows quite enough, and if he is not a gentleman, whatever he knows is bad for him.
Oscar Wilde (1856-1900, British Author, Wit)

3 Do not on any account attempt to write on both sides of the paper at once.
W. C. Sellar

EXAMPLE

1 Example is the best precept.
Aesop (620-560 BC, Greek Fabulist)

2 Example is not the main thing in influencing others. It is the only thing.
Albert Schweitzer (1875-1965, German Born Medical Missionary, Theologian, Musician, and Philosopher)

3 Example is leadership.
Albert Schweitzer (1875-1965, German Born Medical Missionary, Theologian, Musician, and Philosopher)

4 No rules exist, and examples are simply life-savers answering the appeals of rules making vain attempts to exist.
Andre Breton (1989-1966, French Surrealist)

5 The greatest gift you and your partner can give your children is the example of an intimate, healthy, and loving relationship.
Barbara De Angelis (American Expert on Relationship & Love, Author)

6 Well done, is better than well said.
Benjamin Franklin (1706-1790, American Scientist, Publisher, Diplomat)

7 Nothing preaches better than the act.
Benjamin Franklin (1706-1790, American Scientist, Publisher, Diplomat)

8 We should never permit ourselves to do anything that we are not willing to see our children do.
Brigham Young (1801-1877, American Mormon Leader)

9 Example has more followers than reason. We unconsciously imitate what pleases us, and approximate to the characters we most admire.
Christian Nevell Bovee (1820-1904, American Author, Lawyer)

10 What you do not want others to do to you, do not do to others.
Confucius (551-479 BC, Chinese Ethical Teacher, Philosopher)

11 I don't know any other way to lead but by example.
Don Shula (American Football Coach)

12 Where one man reads the Bible, a hundred read you and me.
Dwight L. Moody (1837-1899, American Evangelist)

13 Example is the school of mankind, and they will learn at no other
Edmund Burke (1729-1797, British Political Writer, Statesman)

14 Illustrious examples engross, prejudice, and intimidate. They engross our attention, and so prevent a due inspection of ourselves; they prejudice our judgment in favor of their abilities, and so lessen the sense of our own; and they intimidate us with the
Edward Young (1683-1765, British Poet, Dramatist)

15 It is not so much the example of others we imitate as the reflection of ourselves in their eyes and the echo of ourselves in their words.
Eric Hoffer (1902-1983, American Author, Philosopher)

16 Nothing is so contagious as an example. We never do great good or evil without bringing about more of the same on the part of others.
François de La Rochefoucauld (1613-1680, French classical writer)

17 If you must hold yourself up to your children as an object lesson, hold yourself up as a warning and not an example.
George Bernard Shaw (1856-1950, Irish-born British Dramatist)

18 A young girl was asked: "Whose preaching brought you to Christ?" "It wasn't anybody's preaching; it was Aunt Mary's practicing," he replied. The beginning of anxiety is the end of faith, and the beginning of true faith is the end of anxiety.
George E. Mueller (1918-, American Engineer)

19 The presence of a noble nature, generous in its wishes, ardent in its charity, changes the lights for us: we begin to see things again in their larger, quieter masses, and to believe that we too can be seen and judged in the wholeness of our character.
George Eliot (1819-1880, British Novelist)

20 Folks don't like to have somebody around knowing more than they do. It aggravates em. You're not gonna change any of them by talking right, they've got to want to learn themselves, and when they don't want to learn there's nothing you can do but keep your mouth shut or talk their language.
Harper Lee (1926-, American Author)

21 Example moves the world more than doctrine. The great exemplars are the poets of action, and it makes little difference whether they be forces for good or forces for evil.
Henry Miller (1891-1980, American Author)

22 Education commences at the mother's knee, and every word spoken within hearsay of little children tends toward the formation of character.
Hosea Ballou (1771-1852, American Theologian, Founder of "Universalism")

23 This, then, is the test we must set for ourselves; not to march alone but to march in such a way that others will wish to join us.
Hubert H. Humphrey (1911-1978, American Democratic Politician, Vice President)

24 We are too quick to imitate depraved examples.
Juvenal (Decimus Junius Juvenalis) (55-130, Roman Satirical Poet)

25 Few things are harder to put up with than the annoyance of a good example.
Mark Twain (1835-1910, American Humorist, Writer)

26 There is nothing so annoying as a good example!!
Mark Twain (1835-1910, American Humorist, Writer)

27 You train people how to treat you by how you treat yourself.
Martin Rutte

28 Example is a bright looking-glass, universal and for all shapes to look into.
Michel Eyquem De Montaigne (1533-1592, French Philosopher, Essayist)

29 People seldom improve when they have no other model, but themselves to copy after.
Oliver Goldsmith (1728-1774, Anglo-Irish Author, Poet, Playwright)

30 The position of First Lady has no rules, just precedent, so its evolution has been at a virtual standstill for years. If Martha Washington didn't do it, then no one is sure it should be done.
Paula Poundstone

31 A man who lives right, and is right, has more power in his silence than another has by his words.
Phillips Brooks (1835-1893, American Minister, Poet)

32 An ounce of practice is worth a pound of preaching.
Proverb

33 Practice what you preach.
Proverb

34 Precept guides, but example draws.
Proverb

35 The world is upheld by the veracity of good men: they make the earth wholesome. They who lived with them found life glad and nutritious. Life is sweet and tolerable only in our belief in such society.
Ralph Waldo Emerson (1803-1882, American Poet, Essayist)

36 They teach the morals of a whore, and the manners of a dancing master.
Samuel Johnson (1709-1784, British Author)

37 I've always led by example and I'm not that vocal.
Scottie Pippen (American Basketball Player)

38 The road to learning by precept is long, but by example short and effective.
Seneca (4 BC-65 AD, Spanish-born Roman Statesman, philosopher)

39 You have to set the tone and the pace, define objectives and strategies, demonstrate through personal example what you expect from others.
Stanley C. Gault

40 It is easier to exemplify values than teach them.
Theodore M. Hesburgh (1917-, American Clergyman, University President)

41 He teaches me to be good that does me good.
Thomas Fuller (1608-1661, British Clergyman, Author)

42 The first great gift we can bestow on others is a good example.
Thomas Morell

43 Produce great men, the rest follows.
Walt Whitman (1819-1892, American Poet)

44 Be careful how you live; you will be the only Bible some people ever read.
William J. Toms

EXASPERATION

1 Your damned nonsense can I stand twice or once, but sometimes always, by God, never.
Hans Richter (1843-1916, German Conductor)

2 Sir, you have tasted two whole worms; you have hissed all my mystery lectures and been caught fighting a liar in the quad; you will leave by the next town drain.
Rev. W. A. Spooner (1844-1930, Warden of New College, Oxford)

3 Lord Ronald said nothing; he flung himself from the room, flung himself upon his horse and rode madly off in all directions.
Stephen B. Leacock (1869-1944, Canadian Humorist, Economist)

EXCELLENCE

1 Four short words sum up what has lifted most successful individuals above the crowd: a little bit more. They did all that was expected of them and a little bit more.
A. Lou Vickery (Former professional baseball player)

2 I never had a policy; I have just tried to do my very best each and every day.
Abraham Lincoln (1809-1865, Sixteenth President of the USA)

3 The quality of expectations determines the quality of our action.
Andre Godin

4 Do not look for approval except for the consciousness of doing your best.
Andrew Carnegie (1835-1919, American Industrialist, Philanthropist)

5 If you do things well, do them better. Be daring, be first, be different, be just.
Anita Roddick (British Entrepreneur, Founder of The Body Shop)

6 Excellence is an art won by training and habituation. We do not act rightly because we have virtue or excellence, but we rather have those because we have acted rightly. We are what we repeatedly do. Excellence, then, is not an act but a habit.
Aristotle (384-322 BC, Greek Philosopher)

7 It is the mark of an instructed mind to rest satisfied with the degree of precision which the nature of the subject admits and not to seek exactness when only an approximation of the truth is possible.
Aristotle (384-322 BC, Greek Philosopher)

8 Pleasure in the job puts perfection in the work.
Aristotle (384-322 BC, Greek Philosopher)

9 There is none who cannot teach somebody something, and there is none so excellent but he is excelled.
Baltasar Gracian (1601-1658, Spanish Philosopher, Writer)

10 Do more than you're supposed to do and you can have or be or do anything you want.
Bill Sands

11 Whatever you do, don't do it halfway.
Bob Beamon (1946, American Track Athlete, Long Jump)

12 Excellence is to do a common thing in an uncommon way.
Booker T. Washington (1856-1915, American Black Leader and Educator)

13 You can become an even more excellent person by constantly setting higher and higher standards for yourself and then by doing everything possible to live up to those standards.
Brian Tracy (American Trainer, Speaker, Author, Businessman)

14 No matter how small and unimportant what we are doing may seem, if we do it well, it may soon become the step that will lead us to better things.
Channing Pollock (American Actor)

15 The fact is, the difference between peak performers and everybody else are much smaller than everybody else thinks.
Charles A. Garfield (American Peak Performance Expert, Researcher, Trainer)

16 You must be resolutely determined that whatever you do shall always be the best of which you are capable.
Charles E. Popplestone

17 Being forced to work, and forced to do your best, will breed in you temperance and self- control, diligence and strength of will, cheerfulness and content, and a hundred virtues which the idle will never know.
Charles Kingsley (1819-1875, British Author, Clergyman)

18 Anybody who accepts mediocrity -- in school, on the job, in life -- is a person who compromises, and when the leader compromises, the whole organization compromises.
Charles Knight

19 All successful employers are stalking men who will do the unusual, men who think, men who attract attention by performing more than is expected of them.
Charles M. Schwab (1862-1939, American Industrialist, Businessman)

20 When you say you'll meet someone at 11:00 AM, be there at 10:45. When you promise a check on the 30th, send it on the 28th. Whatever you agree to do, do it a bit more. Start with your employees, then extend it to everyone you deal with. News will soon get around that you are a person of your word.
Charles Prestwich Scott (1846-1932, British Newspaper Editor)

21 True greatness consists in being great in little things.
Charles Simmons

22 I made a resolve then that I was going to amount to something if I could. And no hours, nor amount of labor, nor amount of money would deter me from giving the best that there was in me. And I have done that ever since, and I win by it. I know.
Col. Harland Sanders (1890-1980, American Businessman, Founder of Kentucky Fried Chicken)

23 The success combination in business is: Do what you do better... and: Do more of what you do...
David J. Schwartz (American Trainer, Author of "The Magic of Thinking Big")

24 Set exorbitant standards, and give your people hell when they don't live up to them. There is nothing so demoralizing as a boss who tolerates second rate work.
David Ogilvy (1911-, American Businessman, Advertising Expert)

25 Do your work; not just your work and no more, but a little more for the lavishing's sake -- that little more which is worth all the rest.
Dean Briggs (1965-, American Drummer, "Whitekaps")

26 Good enough never is.
Debbi Field (American Businesswoman, Founder of Mrs. Field's Cookies)

27 I use nothing but the best ingredients. My cookies are always baked fresh. I price cookies so that you cannot make them at home for any less. And I still give cookies away.
Debbie Fields (American Businesswoman, Founder, Mrs. Fields Cookies)

28 Winners have the ability to step back from the canvas of their lives like an artist gaining perspective. They make their lives a work of art -- an individual masterpiece.
Denis Waitley (1933-, American Author, Speaker, Trainer, Peak Performance Expert)

29 The most splendid achievement of all is the constant striving to surpass yourself and to be worthy of your own approval.
Denis Waitley (1933-, American Author, Speaker, Trainer, Peak Performance Expert)

30 You have to learn the rules of the game. And then you have to play better than anyone else.
Dianne Feinstein (American Senator)

31 Determine to become one of the best. Sufficient money will almost automatically follow if you get to be one of the "best" in your chosen field, whatever it is.
Don G. Mitchell

32 It isn't by size that you win or fail -- be the best of whatever you are.
Douglas Malloch

33 You always have to give 100 percent, because if you don't, someone, someplace, will give 100 percent and will beat you when you meet.
Ed Macauley

34 If something is exceptionally well done it has embedded in it's very existence the aim of lifting the common denominator rather than catering to it.
Edward Fischer

35 Much good work is lost for the lack of a little more.
Edward H. Harriman (1848-1909, American Financier, Railroad Executive)

36 We must do the best we can with what we have.
Edward Rowland Sill

37 It's enough for you to do it once for a few men to remember you. But if you do it year after year, then many people remember you and they tell it to their children, and their children and grandchildren remember and, if it concerns books, they can read them. And if it's good enough, it will last as long as there are human beings.
Ernest Hemingway (1898-1961, American Writer)

38 He who has put a good finish to his undertaking is said to have placed a golden crown to the whole.
Eustachius

39 I am a writer because writing is the thing I do best.
Flannery O'Connor (1925-1964, American Author)

40 There seems to be one quality of mind which seems to be of special and extreme advantage in leading him to make discoveries. It was the power of never letting exceptions go unnoticed.
Francis Darwin

41 To do great things is difficult, but to command great things is more difficult.
Friedrich Nietzsche (1844-1900, German Philosopher)

42 The real contest is always between what you've done and what you're capable of doing. You measure yourself against yourself and nobody else.
Geoffrey Gaberino

43 Excellence encourages one about life generally; it shows the spiritual wealth of the world.
George Eliot (1819-1880, British Novelist)

44 A racehorse that consistently runs just a second faster than another horse is worth millions of dollars more. Be willing to give that extra effort that separates the winner from the one in second place.
H. Jackson Brown Jr. (American Author of "Life's Little Instruction Book" Series)

45 To be really great in little things, to be truly noble and heroic in the insipid details of everyday life, is a virtue so rare as to be worthy of canonization.
Harriet Beecher Stowe (1811-1896, American Novelist, Antislavery Campaigner)

46 I always remember an epitaph which is in the cemetery at Tombstone, Arizona. It says: "Here lies Jack Williams. He done his damnedest." I think that is the greatest epitaph a man can have.
Harry S. Truman (1884-1972, Thirty-third President of the USA)

47 You get the best out of others when you get the best out of yourself.
Harvey S. Firestone (1868-1938, American Industrialist)

48 The best we can do is size up the chances, calculate the risks involved, estimate our ability to deal with them, and then make our plans with confidence.
Henry Ford (1863-1947, American Industrialist, Founder of Ford Motor Company)

49 Badness you can get easily, in quantity; the road is smooth, and it lies close by, But in front of excellence the immortal gods have put sweat, and long and steer is the way to it.
Hesiod (8th Century BC, Greek Poet)

50 People forget how fast you did a job, but they remember how well you did it.
Howard W. Newton

51 All you owe the public is a good performance.
Humphrey Bogart (1899-1957, American Film Actor)

52 It is a wretched taste to be gratified with mediocrity when the excellent lies before us.
Isaac Disraeli

53 Resolve to make each day the very best and don't let anyone get in your way. If they do, step on them.
Ivan Benson

54 The man who comes up with a means for doing or producing almost anything better, faster or more economically has his future and his fortune at his fingertips.
J. Paul Getty (1892-1976, American Oil Tycoon, Billionaire)

55 The master in the art of living makes little distinction between his work and his play, his labor and his leisure, his mind and his body, his information and his recreation, his love and his religion. He hardly knows which is which. He simply pursues his vision of excellence at whatever he does, leaving others to decide whether he is working or playing. To him he's always doing both.
James A. Michener (1907-, American Writer)

56 I can do small things in a great way.
James Freeman Clarke (1810-1888, American Minister, Theologian)

57 Our goal, simply stated, is to be the best.
James H. Robinson (American Businessman, Chairman of American Express)

58 You're probably not a member of a major league baseball team, your errors, unless they are truly spectacular, don't show up in the morning paper.
Jane Goodsell

59 There is no top. There are always further heights to reach.
Jascha Heifetz (1901-1987, Lithuanian Violinist)

60 From time to time there appear on the face of the earth men of rare and consummate excellence, who dazzle us by their virtue, and whose outstanding qualities shed a stupendous light. Like those extraordinary stars of whose origins we are ignorant, and of whose fate, once they have vanished, we know even less, such men have neither forebears nor descendants: they are the whole of their race.
Jean De La Bruyere (1645-1696, French Writer)

61 You do not merely want to be considered just the best of the best. You want to be considered the only ones who do what you do.
Jerry Garcia (1945-1995, American Rock Musician, "Grateful Dead")

62 People come out to see you perform and you've got to give them the best you have within you. The lives of most men are patchwork quilts. Or at best one matching outfit with a closet and laundry bag full of incongruous accumulations. A lifetime of training for just ten seconds.
Jesse Owens (1913-1980, American Olympic Track Athlete)

63 Excellence is rarely found, more rarely valued.
Johann Wolfgang Von Goethe (1749-1832, German Poet, Dramatist, Novelist)

64 The excellency of every art is its intensity, capable of making all disagreeable evaporate.
John Keats (1795-1821, British Poet)

65 To enjoy enduring success we should travel a little in advance of the world.
John Mcdonald

66 There is one plain rule of life. Try thyself unweariedly till thou findest the highest thing thou art capable of doing, faculties and outward circumstances being both duly considered, and then do it.
John Stuart Mill (1806-1873, British Philosopher, Economist)

67 Whoever I am, or whatever I am doing, some kind of excellence is within my reach.
John W. Gardner (1912-, American Educator, Social Activist)

68 The idea for which this nation stands will not survive if the highest goal free man can set themselves is an amiable mediocrity. Excellence implies striving for the highest standards in every phase of life.
John W. Gardner (1912-, American Educator, Social Activist)

69 Excellence is doing ordinary things extraordinarily well.
John W. Gardner (1912-, American Educator, Social Activist)

70 It isn't what you do, but how you do it.
John Wooden (1910-, American Basketball Coach)

71 We distinguish the excellent man from the common man by saying that the former is the one who makes great demands on himself, and the latter who makes no demands on himself.
Jose Ortega Y Gasset (1883-1955, Spanish Essayist, Philosopher)

72 Excellence means when a man or woman asks of himself more than others do.
Jose Ortega Y Gasset (1883-1955, Spanish Essayist, Philosopher)

73 We do not do well except when we know where the best is and when we are assured that we have touched it and hold its power within us.
Joseph Joubert (1754-1824, French Moralist)

74 I want to be all that I am capable of becoming.
Katherine Mansfield (1888-1923, New Zealand-born British Author)

75 People who produce good results feel good about themselves.
Ken Blanchard (American Business Lecturer, Author)

76 The kind of people I look for to fill top management spots are the eager beavers, the mavericks. These are the guys who try to do more than they're expected to do -- they always reach.
Lee Iacocca (1924-, American Businessman, Former CEO of Chrysler)

77 There is no such thing as natural touch. Touch is something you create by hitting millions of golf balls.
Lee Trevino (1939-, American Golfer)

78 I have offended God and mankind because my work didn't reach the quality it should have.
Leonardo Da Vinci (1452-1519, Italian Inventor, Architect, Painter, Scientist, Sculptor)

79 One of the most essential things you need to do for yourself is to choose a goal that is important to you. Perfection does not exist -- you can always do better and you can always grow.
Les Brown (1945-, American Speaker, Author, Trainer, Motivator Lecturer)

80 Shoot for the moon. Even if you miss it you will land among the stars.
Les Brown (1945-, American Speaker, Author, Trainer, Motivator Lecturer)

81 Do a little more each day than you think you possibly can.
Lowell Thomas (American Politician, Author)

82 The noblest search is the search for excellence.
Lyndon B. Johnson (1908-1973, Thirty-sixth President of the USA)

83 To do the right thing, at the right time, in the right way; to do some things better than they were ever done before; to eliminate errors; to know both sides of the question; to be courteous; to be an example; to work for the love of work; to anticipate requirements; to develop resources; to recognize no impediments; to master circumstances; to act from reason rather than rule; to be satisfied with nothing short of perfection.
Marshall Field & Company (American Company)

84 If a man is called to be a streetsweeper, he should sweep streets even as Michelangelo painted, or Beethoven composed music, or Shakespeare wrote poetry. He should sweep streets so well that all the hosts of heaven and earth will pause to say, here lived a great streetsweeper who did his job well.
Martin Luther King Jr. (1929-1968, American Black Leader, Nobel Prize Winner, 1964)

85 There is a canyon of difference between doing your best to glorify God and doing whatever it takes to glorify yourself. The quest for excellence is a mark of maturity. The quest for power is childish.
Max L. Lucado (American Author of "The Eye of the Storm")

86 The uncommon man is merely the common man thinking and dreaming of success in larger terms and in more fruitful areas.
Melvin Powers (American Businessman, Author)

87 It has always been my belief that a man should do his best, regardless of how much he receives for his services, or the number of people he may be serving or the class of people served.
Napoleon Hill (1883-1970, American Speaker, Motivational Writer, "Think and Grow Rich")

88 You can start right where you stand and apply the habit of going the extra mile by rendering more service and better service than you are now being paid for.
Napoleon Hill (1883-1970, American Speaker, Motivational Writer, "Think and Grow Rich")

89 If you cannot do great things, do small things in a great way.
Napoleon Hill (1883-1970, American Speaker, Motivational Writer, "Think and Grow Rich")

90 There is no finish line.
Nike Corporation (American Shoe Company)

91 Always do your best. What you plant now, you will harvest later.
Og Mandino (1923-1996, American Motivational Author, Speaker)

92 Today, and every day, deliver more than you are getting paid to do. The victory of success will be half won when you learn the secret of putting out more than is expected in all that you do. Make yourself so valuable in your work that eventually you will become indispensable. Exercise your privilege to go the extra mile, and enjoy all the rewards you receive. You deserve them!
Og Mandino (1923-1996, American Motivational Author, Speaker)

93 One of the great undiscovered joys of life comes from doing everything one attempts to the best of one's ability. There is a special sense of satisfaction, a pride in surveying such a work, a work which is rounded, full, exact, complete in its parts, which the superficial person who leaves his or her work in a slovenly, slipshod, half-finished condition, can never know. It is this conscientious completeness which turns any work into art. The smallest task, well done, becomes a miracle of achievement.
Og Mandino (1923-1996, American Motivational Author, Speaker)

94 Deliver more than you are getting paid to do. The victory of success will be half won when you learn the secret of putting out more than is expected in all that you do. Make yourself so valuable in your work that eventually you will become indispensable.
Og Mandino (1923-1996, American Motivational Author, Speaker)

95 The person who knows one thing and does it better than anyone else, even if it only be the art of raising lentils, receives the crown he merits. If he raises all his energy to that end, he is a benefactor of mankind and its rewarded as such.
Og Mandino (1923-1996, American Motivational Author, Speaker)

96 To aim at excellence, our reputation, and friends, and all must be ventured; to aim at the average we run no risk and provide little service.
Oliver Goldsmith (1728-1774, Anglo-Irish Author, Poet, Playwright)

97 My philosophy is that not only are you responsible for your life, but doing the best at this moment puts you in the best place for the next moment.
Oprah Winfrey (1954-, American TV Personality, Producer, Actress, Author)

98 I was raised to believe that excellence is the best deterrent to racism and sexism.
Oprah Winfrey (1954-, American TV Personality, Producer, Actress, Author)

99 Make it a life-rule to give your best to whatever passes through your hands. Stamp it with your manhood. Let superiority be your trademark...
Orison Swett Marden (1850-1924, American Author, Founder of Success Magazine)

100 Just make up your mind at the very outset that your work is going to stand for quality... that you are going to stamp a superior quality upon everything that goes out of your hands, that whatever you do shall bear the hall-mark of excellence.
Orison Swett Marden (1850-1924, American Author, Founder of Success Magazine)

101 Doing common things uncommonly well.
Orison Swett Marden (1850-1924, American Author, Founder of Success Magazine)

102 There is only one thing for us to do, and that is to do our level best right where we are every day of our lives; To use our best judgment, and then to trust the rest to that Power which holds the forces of the universe in his hands.
Orison Swett Marden (1850-1924, American Author, Founder of Success Magazine)

103 There is an infinite difference between a little wrong and just right, between fairly good and the best, between mediocrity and superiority...
Orison Swett Marden (1850-1924, American Author, Founder of Success Magazine)

104 It is just the little difference between the good and the best that makes the difference between the artist and the artisan. It is just the little touches after the average man would quit that makes the master's fame.
Orison Swett Marden (1850-1924, American Author, Founder of Success Magazine)

105 It is those who have this imperative demand for the best in their natures, and who will accept nothing short of it, that holds the banners of progress, that set the standards, the ideals, for others.
Orison Swett Marden (1850-1924, American Author, Founder of Success Magazine)

106 Superiority -- doing things a little better than anybody else can do them.
Orison Swett Marden (1850-1924, American Author, Founder of Success Magazine)

107 People who have accomplished work worthwhile have had a very high sense of the way to do things. They have not been content with mediocrity. They have not confined themselves to the beaten tracks; they have never been satisfied to do things just as others so them, but always a little better. They always pushed things that came to their hands a little higher up, this little farther on, that counts in the quality of life's work. It is constant effort to be first-class in everything one attempts that conquers the heights of excellence.
Orison Swett Marden (1850-1924, American Author, Founder of Success Magazine)

108 Put the uncommon effort into the common task... make it large by doing it in a great way.
Orison Swett Marden (1850-1924, American Author, Founder of Success Magazine)

109 The greatest thing a man can do in this world is to make the most possible out of the stuff that has been given him. This is success, and there is no other.
Orison Swett Marden (1850-1924, American Author, Founder of Success Magazine)

110 Great men are but common men more fully developed and ripened.
Orison Swett Marden (1850-1924, American Author, Founder of Success Magazine)

111 I have the simplest tastes. I am always satisfied with the best.
Oscar Wilde (1856-1900, British Author, Wit)

112 Excellence is the gradual result of always striving to do better.
Pat Riley (1945, American Basketball Coach)

113 Do a little bit more than average and from that point on our progress multiplies itself out of all proportion to the effort put in.
Paul J. Meyer (American Businessman, Author, Motivator)

114 There is always a best way of doing everything.
Ralph Waldo Emerson (1803-1882, American Poet, Essayist)

115 If I play my best, I can win anywhere in the world against anybody.
Ray Floyd (American Golfer)

116 Always strive to excel, but only on weekends.
Richard Rorty (1931-, American Philosopher)

117 Become all that you are capable of becoming!
Robert J. Mckain

118 It is quality rather than quantity that matters.
Seneca (4 BC-65 AD, Spanish-born Roman Statesman, philosopher)

119 The sad truth is that excellence makes people nervous.
Shana Alexander (1925-, American Writer, Editor)

120 If we want to make something really superb on this planet, there is nothing whatever that can stop us.
Shepherd Mead

121 When we have done our best, we should wait the result in peace.
Sir John Lubbock (1834-1913, British Statesman, Banker, Naturalist)

122 Don't waste your time striving for perfection, instead, strive for excellence -- doing your best.
Sir Lawrence Olivier (1907-1989, British Actor, Producer, Director)

123 There never will exist anything permanently noble and excellent in the character which is a stranger to resolute self-denial.
Sir Walter Scott (1771-1832, British Novelist, Poet)

124 The principle is competing against yourself. It's about self improvement, about being better than you were the day before.
Steve Young (American Football Player)

125 There's a way to do better... find it.
Thomas A. Edison (1847-1931, American Inventor, Entrepreneur, Founder of GE)

126 I start where the last man left off.
Thomas A. Edison (1847-1931, American Inventor, Entrepreneur, Founder of GE)

127 Let each become all that he was created capable of being.
Thomas Carlyle (1795-1881, Scottish Philosopher, Author)

128 Excellent firms don't believe in excellence -- only in constant improvement and constant change.
Thomas J. Peters (1942-, American Management Consultant, Author, Trainer)

129 If you want to achieve excellence, you can get there today. As of this second, quit doing less- than-excellent work.
Thomas J. Watson (18?-1956, American Businessman, Founder of IBM)

130 If you aren't playing well, the game isn't as much fun. When that happens I tell myself just to go out and play as I did when I was a kid.
Thomas J. Watson (18?-1956, American Businessman, Founder of IBM)

131 If you'll not settle for anything less than your best, you will be amazed at what you can accomplish in your lives.
Vince Lombardi (1913-1970, American Football Coach)

132 A masterpiece is something said once and for all, stated, finished, so that it's there complete in the mind, if only at the back.
Virginia Woolf (1882-1941, British Novelist, Essayist)

133 The best is the enemy of the good.
Voltaire (1694-1778, French Historian, Writer)

134 Only a mediocre person is always at his best.
W. Somerset Maugham (1874-1965, British Novelist, Playwright)

135 It is not from ourselves that we learn to be better than we are.
Wendell Berry (American Social Critic)

136 Great men are little men expanded; great lives are ordinary lives intensified.
Wilferd A. Peterson

137 One shining quality lends a luster to another, or hides some glaring defect.
William Hazlitt (1778-1830, British Essayist)

138 You have to create a track record of breaking your own mold, or at least other people's idea of that mold.
William Hurt (1950-, American Actor)

139 When workmen strive to do better than well, they do confound their skill in covetousness.
William Shakespeare (1564-1616, British Poet, Playwright, Actor)

140 Then to Silvia let us sing that Silvia is excelling. She excels each mortal thing upon the dull earth dwelling.
William Shakespeare (1564-1616, British Poet, Playwright, Actor)

141 Surely a man has come to himself only when he has found the best that is in him, and has satisfied his heart with the highest achievement he is fit for.
Woodrow T. Wilson (1856-1924, Twenty-eighth President of the USA)

EXCEPTION

1 How glorious it is -- and also how painful -- to be an exception.
Alfred De Musset

2 Never be the only one, except, possibly, in your own home.
Alice Walker (1944-, American Author, Critic)

EXCESS

1 To go too far is as bad as to fall short.
Confucius (551-479 BC, Chinese Ethical Teacher, Philosopher)

2 Riches are for spending.
Francis Bacon (1561-1626, British Philosopher, Essayist, Statesman)

3 Americans are overreaching; overreaching is the most admirable and most American of the many American excesses.
George F. Will (1941-, American Political Columnist)

4 We have almost succeeded in leveling all human activities to the common denominator of securing the necessities of life and providing for their abundance.
Hannah Arendt (1906-1975, German-born American Political Philosopher)

5 We are no longer in a state of growth; we are in a state of excess. We are living in a society of excrescence. The boil is growing out of control, recklessly at cross purposes with itself, its impacts multiplying as the causes disintegrate.
Jean Baudrillard (French Postmodern Philosopher, Writer)

6 Excess generally causes reaction, and produces a change in the opposite direction, whether it be in the seasons, or in individuals, or in governments.
Plato (427-347 BC, Greek Philosopher)

7 All progress is based upon a universal innate desire on the part of every organism to live beyond its income.
Samuel Butler (1612-1680, British Poet, Satirist)

8 Ours is a culture based on excess, on overproduction; the result is a steady loss of sharpness in our sensory experience. All the conditions of modern life -- its material plenitude, its sheer crowdedness -- conjoin to dull our sensory faculties.
Susan Sontag (1933-, American Essayist)

9 Let's not quibble! I'm the foe of moderation, the champion of excess. If I may lift a line from a die-hard whose identity is lost in the shuffle, "I'd rather be strongly wrong than weakly right."
Tallulah Bankhead (1903-1968, American Actress)

10 I hold this as a rule of life: Too much of anything is bad.
Terence (185-159 BC, Roman Writer of Comedies)

11 Excess on occasion is exhilarating. It prevents moderation from acquiring the deadening effect of a habit.
W. Somerset Maugham (1874-1965, British Novelist, Playwright)

12 The road to excess leads to the palace of wisdom.
William Blake (1757-1827, British Poet, Painter)

EXCUSES

1 No doubt Jack the Ripper excused himself on the grounds that it was human nature.
A. A. Milne (1882-1956, British Born American Writer)

2 An excuse is worse than a lie, for an excuse is a lie, guarded.
Alexander Pope (1688-1744, British Poet, Critic, Translator)

3 To offer the complexities of life as an excuse for not addressing oneself to the simpler, more manageable (trivial) aspects of daily existence is a perversity often indulged in by artists, husbands, intellectuals -- and critics of the Women's Movement.
Barbara Grizzuti Harrison (1941-, American Author, Publicist)

4 He that is good for making excuses is seldom good for anything else.
Benjamin Franklin (1706-1790, American Scientist, Publisher, Diplomat)

5 He who excuses himself, accuses himself.
Gabriel Meurier

6 Your letter of excuses has arrived. I receive the letter but do not admit the excuses except in courtesy, as when a man treads on your toes and begs your pardon -- the pardon is granted, but the joint aches, especially if there is a corn upon it.
Lord Byron (1788-1824, British Poet)

7 Apology is only egotism wrong side out.
Oliver Wendell Holmes (1809-1894, American Author, Wit, Poet)

8 We have forty million reasons for failure, but not a single excuse.
Rudyard Kipling (1865-1936, British Author of Prose, Verse)

9 It is good rule in life to never to apologize. The right sort of people do not want apologies, and the wrong sort take a mean advantage of them.
Sir P(elham) G(renville) Wodehouse (1881-1975, British Novelist)

10 Bad excuses are worse than none.
Thomas Fuller (1608-1661, British Clergyman, Author)

11 Two wrongs don't make a right, but they make a good excuse.
Thomas Szasz (1920-, American Psychiatrist)

12 And oftentimes excusing of a fault doth make the fault the worse by the excuse.
William Shakespeare (1564-1616, British Poet, Playwright, Actor)

13 The girl who can't dance says the band can't play.
Yiddish Proverb

14 If you don't want to do something, one excuse is as good as another.
Yiddish Proverb

EXECUTIVES

1 An executive is a man who can make quick decisions and is sometimes right.
Elbert Hubbard (1859-1915, American Author, Publisher)

2 An executive is a man who decides; sometimes he decides right, but always he decides.
John H. Patterson (American Businessman, Founder of National Cash Register)

3 The functions of an executive are to create and enforce policies rather than working out problems resulting from such policies.
Louis F. Musil

EXERCISE

1 I don't jog, if I die I want to be sick.
Abe Lemons

2 Exercise is the yuppie version of bulimia.
Barbara Ehrenreich (1941-, American Author, Columnist)

3 Modern bodybuilding is ritual, religion, sport, art, and science, awash in Western chemistry and mathematics. Defying nature, it surpasses it.
Camille Paglia (1947-, American Author, Critic, Educator)

4 I'm not into working out. My philosophy: No pain, no pain.
Carol Leifer

5 Jogging is very beneficial. It's good for your legs and your feet. It's also very good for the ground. If makes it feel needed.
Charles M. Schultz (1922-, American Cartoonist, Creator of "Peanuts")

6 I get my exercise acting as a pallbearer to my friends who exercise.
Chauncey Depew (1834-1928, American Lawyer, Businessman, Public Official)

7 Nothing lifts me out of a bad mood better than a hard workout on my treadmill. It never fails. To us, exercise is nothing short of a miracle.
Cher (1946-, American Actress, Director, Singer)

8 A pedestrian is a man in danger of his life. A walker is a man in possession of his soul.
David Mccord

9 The only athletic sport I ever mastered was backgammon.
Douglas William Jerrold (1803-1857, British Humorist, Playwright)

10 The only reason I would take up jogging is so that I could hear heaving breathing again.
Erma Bombeck (1927-, American Author, Humorist)

11 I can feel the wind go by when I run. It feels good. It feels fast.
Evelyn Ashford (American Track Athlete)

12 I like long walks, especially when they are taken by people who annoy me.
Fred A. Allen (1894-1957, American Radio Comic)

13 Athletes have studied how to leap and how to survive the leap some of the time and return to the ground. They don't always do it well. But they are our philosophers of actual moments and the body and soul in them, and of our maneuvers in our emergencies and longings.
Harold Brodkey

14 Exercise is bunk. If you are healthy you don't need it. If you are sick you shouldn't take it.
Henry Ford (1863-1947, American Industrialist, Founder of Ford Motor Company)

15 If we could give every individual the right amount of nourishment and exercise, not too little and not too much, we would have found the safest way to health.
Hippocrates (Ancient Greek Physician)

16 Other exercises develop single powers and muscles, but dancing embellishes, exercises, and equalizes all the muscles at once.
Jean Paul

17 Use it or lose it.
Jimmy Connors (1952-, American Tennis Player)

18 Our growing softness, our increasing lack of physical fitness, is a menace to our security.
John F. Kennedy (1917-1963, Thirty-fifth President of the USA)

19 We are under exercised as a nation. We look instead of play. We ride instead of walk. Our existence deprives us of the minimum of physical activity essential for healthy living.
John F. Kennedy (1917-1963, Thirty-fifth President of the USA)

20 The physically fit can enjoy their vices.
Lord Percival

21 Why do strong arms fatigue themselves with frivolous dumbbells? To dig a vineyard is worthier exercise for men.
Marcus Valerius Martial (40-104, Latin poet and epigrammatist)

22 I have never taken any exercise except sleeping and resting.
Mark Twain (1835-1910, American Humorist, Writer)

23 Few people know how to take a walk. The qualifications are endurance, plain clothes, old shoes, an eye for nature, good humor, vast curiosity, good speech, good silence and nothing too much.
Ralph Waldo Emerson (1803-1882, American Poet, Essayist)

24 Intellectual tasting of life will not supersede muscular activity.
Ralph Waldo Emerson (1803-1882, American Poet, Essayist)

25 Whenever I feel like exercise I lie down until the feeling passes.
Robert M. Hutchins (1899-1977, American University President)

26 Exercise is labor without weariness.
Samuel Johnson (1709-1784, British Author)

27 A fat stomach never breeds fine thoughts.
St. Jerome (342-420, Croatian Christian Ascetic, Scholar)

28 Walking is the best possible exercise. Habituate yourself to walk very fast.
Thomas Jefferson (1743-1826, Third President of the USA)

EXHILARATION

1 Exhilaration is that feeling you get just after a great idea hits you, and just before you realize what's wrong with it.
Rex Harrison

EXILE

1 It is a mistake to expect good work from expatriates for it is not what they do that matters but what they are not doing.
Cyril Connolly (1903-1974, British Critic)

2 We make a mistake forsaking England and moving out into the periphery of life. After all, Taormina, Ceylon, Africa, America -- as far as we go, they are only the negation of what we ourselves stand for and are: and we're rather like Jonahs running away from the place we belong.
D. H. Lawrence (1885-1930, British Author)

3 My first few weeks in America are always miserable, because the tastes I am cursed with are all of a kind that cannot be gratified here, and I am not enough in sympathy with our "gross public" to make up for the lack on the aesthetic side. One's friends are delightful; but we are none of us Americans, we don't think or feel as the Americans do, we are the wretched exotics produced in a European glass-house, the most displaced and useless class on earth!
Edith Wharton (1862-1937, American Author)

4 You're an expatriate. You've lost touch with the soil. You get precious. Fake European standards have ruined you. You drink yourself to death. You become obsessed by sex. You spend all your time talking, not working. You are an expatriate, see? You hang around cafés.
Ernest Hemingway (1898-1961, American Writer)

5 I dunno what my 23 infantile years in America signify. I left as soon as motion was autarchic -- I mean my motion.
Ezra Pound (1885-1972, American Poet, Critic)

6 If I were to live my life over again, I would be an American. I would steep myself in America, I would know no other land.
Henry James (1843-1916, American Author)

7 The ideal place for me is the one in which it is most natural to live as a foreigner.
Italo Calvino (1923-1985, Cuban Writer, Essayist, Journalist)

8 Voyagers discover that the world can never be larger than the person that is in the world; but it is impossible to foresee this, it is impossible to be warned.
James Baldwin (1924-1987, American Author)

9 When the Irishman is found outside of Ireland in another environment, he very often becomes a respected man. The economic and intellectual conditions that prevail in his own country do not permit the development of individuality. No one who has any self-respect stays in Ireland, but flees afar as though from a country that has undergone the visitation of an angered Jove.
James Joyce (1882-1941, Irish Author)

10 Excluded by my birth and tastes from the social order, I was not aware of its diversity. Nothing in the world was irrelevant: the stars on a general's sleeve, the stock-market quotations, the olive harvest, the style of the judiciary, the wheat exchange, flower-beds. Nothing. This order, fearful and feared, whose details were all inter-related, had a meaning: my exile.
Jean Genet (1910-1986, French Playwright, Novelist)

11 Let those who desire a secure homeland conquer it. Let those who do not conquer it live under the whip and in exile, watched over like wild animals, cast from one country to another, concealing the death of their souls with a beggar's smile from the scorn of free men.
Jose Marti (1853-1895, Cuban Patriot, National Hero)

12 It would be enough for me to have the system of a jury of twelve versus the system of one judge as a basis for preferring the U.S. to the Soviet Union. I would prefer the country you can leave to the country you cannot.
Joseph Brodsky (1940-, Russian-born American Poet, Critic)

13 Exile as a mode of genius no longer exists; in place of Joyce we have the fragments of work appearing in Index on Censorship.
Nadine Gordimer (1923-, South African Author)

14 The realization that he is white in a black country, and respected for it, is the turning point in the expatriate's career. He can either forget it, or capitalize on it. Most choose the latter.
Paul Theroux (1941-, American Novelist, Travel Writer)

15 I have loved justice and hated iniquity: therefore I die in exile.
Pope Gregory VII

16 Such is the miraculous nature of the future of exiles: what is first uttered in the impotence of an overheated apartment becomes the fate of nations.
Salman Rushdie (1948-, Indian-born British Author)

EXISTENCE

1 In order to exist just once in the world, it is necessary never again to exist.
Albert Camus (1913-1960, French Existential Writer)

2 It is living and ceasing to live that are imaginary solutions. Existence is elsewhere.
Andre Breton (1989-1966, French Surrealist)

3 There's nothing that makes you so aware of the improvisation of human existence as a song unfinished. Or an old address book.
Carson Mccullers (1917-1967, American Author)

4 Let us be moral. Let us contemplate existence.
Charles Dickens (1812-1870, British Novelist)

5 Being is a fiction invented by those who suffer from becoming.
Coleman Dowell (1925-1985, American Novelist, Dramatist, Lyricist)

6 To exist is equivalent to an act of faith, a protest against the truth, an interminable prayer. As soon as they consent to live, the unbeliever and the man of faith are fundamentally the same, since both have made the only decision that defines a being.
E. M. Cioran (1911-, Rumanian-born French Philosopher)

7 There is no means of proving it is preferable to be than not to be.
E. M. Cioran (1911-, Rumanian-born French Philosopher)

8 Every life is its own excuse for being.
Elbert Hubbard (1859-1915, American Author, Publisher)

9 The individual who has to justify his existence by his own efforts is in eternal bondage to himself.
Eric Hoffer (1902-1983, American Author, Philosopher)

10 Man is the only animal for whom his own existence is a problem which he has to solve.
Erich Fromm (1900-1980, American Psychologist)

11 Existence really is an imperfect tense that never becomes a present.
Friedrich Nietzsche (1844-1900, German Philosopher)

12 There's a time when you have to explain to your children why they're born, and it's a marvelous thing if you know the reason by then.
Hazel Scott (1920-1981, American Entertainer)

13 Being is the great explainer.
Henry David Thoreau (1817-1862, American Essayist, Poet, Naturalist)

14 One is still what one is going to cease to be and already what one is going to become. One lives one's death, one dies one's life.
Jean-Paul Sartre (1905-1980, French Writer, Philosopher)

15 Existence itself does not feel horrible; it feels like an ecstasy, rather, which we have only to be still to experience.
John Updike (1932-, American Novelist, Critic)

16 We spend our lives talking about this mystery. Our life.
Jules Renard (1864-1910, French Author, Dramatist)

17 Nothing exists except by virtue of a disequilibrium, an injustice. All existence is a theft paid for by other existences; no life flowers except on a cemetery.
Remy De Gourmont (1858-1915, French Novelist, Philosopher, Poet, Playwright)

18 I can, therefore I am.
Simone Weil (1910-1943, French Philosopher, Mystic)

19 I don't exist when you don't see me.
Sisters Of Mercy

20 I exist in a state of almost perpetual hysteria.
Sting (1951-, British-born American Musician, Singer, Songwriter, Actor)

21 Existence is no more than the precarious attainment of relevance in an intensely mobile flux of past, present, and future.
Susan Sontag (1933-, American Essayist)

22 The cradle rocks above an abyss, and common sense tells us that our existence is but a brief crack of light between two eternities of darkness.
Vladimir Nabokov (1899-1977, Russian-born American Novelist, Poet)

EXPECTATION

1 Don't count your chickens before they are hatched.
Aesop (620-560 BC, Greek Fabulist)

2 Expect nothing, live frugally on surprise.
Alice Walker (1944-, American Author, Critic)

3 You have to expect that if you cuss out the world, The world is going to cuss back.
Andrew Young (1932-, Civil Rights Activist, Protestant Minister, Public Official)

4 We expect everything and are prepared for nothing.
Anne Sophie Swetchine (1782-1857, Russian Author)

5 The world is full of abundance and opportunity, but far too many people come to the fountain of life with a sieve instead of a tank car... a teaspoon instead of a steam shovel. They expect little and as a result they get little.
Ben Sweetland

6 What we anticipate seldom occurs, what we least expected generally happens.
Benjamin Disraeli (1804-1881, British Statesman, Prime Minister)

7 Blessed is he who expects nothing, for he shall never be disappointed.
Benjamin Franklin (1706-1790, American Scientist, Publisher, Diplomat)

8 You can't expect a person to see eye to eye with you when you're looking down on him.
Best of Bits and Pieces

9   We will always tend to fulfill our own expectation of ourselves.
Brian Tracy (American Trainer, Speaker, Author, Businessman)

10   Whatever we expect with confidence becomes our own self-fulfilling prophecy.
Brian Tracy (American Trainer, Speaker, Author, Businessman)

11   I'm not in this world to live up to your expectations and you're not in this world to live up to mine.
Bruce Lee (1940-1973, Chinese-American Actor, Director, Author, Martial Artist)

12   Nothing sets a person up more than having something turn out just the way it's supposed to be, like falling into a Swiss snowdrift and seeing a big dog come up with a little cask of brandy round its neck.
Claud Cockburn (1904-1981, British Author, Journalist)

13   Our limitations and success will be based, most often, on your own expectations for ourselves. What the mind dwells upon, the body acts upon.
Denis Waitley (1933-, American Author, Speaker, Trainer, Peak Performance Expert)

14   Expect the best, plan for the worst, and prepare to be surprised.
Denis Waitley (1933-, American Author, Speaker, Trainer, Peak Performance Expert)

15   We tend to live up to our expectations.
Earl Nightingale (1921-1989, American Radio Announcer, Author, Motivator, Speaker)

16   Man's real life is happy, chiefly because he is ever expecting that it soon will be so.
Edgar Allan Poe (1809-1845, American Poet, Critic, short-story Writer)

17   For, he that expects nothing shall not be disappointed, but he that expects much -- if he lives and uses that in hand day by day -- shall be full to running over.
Edgar Cayce (1877-1945, American Psychic Medium)

18   Expect your every need to be met. Expect the answer to every problem, expect abundance on every level...
Eileen Caddy (American Spiritual Writer)

19   We find what we expect to find, and we receive what we ask for.
Elbert Hubbard (1859-1915, American Author, Publisher)

20   I have no expectation of making a hit every time I come to bat.
Franklin D. Roosevelt (1882-1945, Thirty-second President of the USA)

21   Men... are bettered and improved by trial, and refined out of broken hopes and blighted expectations.
Frederick W. Robertson

22   Nothing is so good as it seems beforehand.
George Eliot (1819-1880, British Novelist)

23   By asking for the impossible we obtain the best possible.
Giovanni Niccolini

24   Think and feel yourself there! To achieve any aim in life, you need to project the end-result. Think of the elation, the satisfaction, the joy! Carrying the ecstatic feeling will bring the desired goal into view.
Grace Speare

25   Let us be about setting high standards for life, love, creativity, and wisdom. If our expectations in these areas are low, we are not likely to experience wellness. Setting high standards makes every day and every decade worth looking forward to.
Greg Anderson (American Author of "The 22 Non-Negotiable Laws of Wellness")

26   If you do not the expect the unexpected you will not find it, for it is not to be reached by search or trail.
Heraclitus (535-475 BC, Greek Philosopher)

27   Life is largely a matter of expectation.
Horace (65-8 BC, Italian Poet)

28   Once you say you're going to settle for second, that's what happens to you in life.
John F. Kennedy (1917-1963, Thirty-fifth President of the USA)

29   When you expect things to happen -- strangely enough -- they do happen.
John Pierpont Morgan (1837-1913, American Banker, Financier, Art Collector)

30   I'm not out there just to be dancing around. I expect to win every time I tee up.
Lee Trevino (1939-, American Golfer)

31   If you expect nothing, you're apt to be surprised. You'll get it.
Malcolm S. Forbes (1919-1990, American Publisher, Businessman)

32   A cathedral, a wave of storm, a dancer's leap, never turn out to be as high as we had hoped.
Marcel Proust (1871-1922, French Novelist)

33   We should expect the best and the worst of mankind, as from the weather.
Marquis De Vauvenargues (1715-1747, French Moralist)

34   I've always got such high expectations for myself. I'm aware of them, but I can't relax them.
Mary Decker Slaney (American Track Athlete)

35   You have to expect things of yourself before you can do them.
Michael Jordan (1963-, American Basketball Player, Actor)

36   If something can go wrong it will.
Murphy's Law (Edward A. Murphy)

37   We tend to get what we expect.
Norman Vincent Peale (1898-1993, American Christian Reformed Pastor, Speaker, Author)

38   If you paint in your mind a picture of bright and happy expectations, you put yourself into a condition conducive to your goal.
Norman Vincent Peale (1898-1993, American Christian Reformed Pastor, Speaker, Author)

39 Most of the things we do, we do for no better reason than that our father's have done them or our neighbors do them, and the same is true of a large part than what we suspect of what we think.
Oliver Wendell Holmes Jr. (1841-1935, American Judge)

40 We advance on our journey only when we face our goal, when we are confident and believe we are going to win out.
Orison Swett Marden (1850-1924, American Author, Founder of Success Magazine)

41 Your expectations opens or closes the doors of your supply, If you expect grand things, and work honestly for them, they will come to you, your supply will correspond with your expectation.
Orison Swett Marden (1850-1924, American Author, Founder of Success Magazine)

42 A master can tell you what he expects of you. A teacher, though, awakens your own expectations.
Patricia Neal

43 Always expect the worst, and you will never be disappointed.
Peter Wastholm

44 Expect victory and you make victory.
Preston Bradley

45 Don't cross the bridge till you come to it.
Proverb

46 Nobody succeeds beyond his or her wildest expectations unless he or she begins with some wild expectations.
Ralph Charell (American Author)

47 How much of human life is lost in waiting.
Ralph Waldo Emerson (1803-1882, American Poet, Essayist)

48 In order to win, you must expect to win.
Richard Bach (1936-, American Author)

49 Life... It tends to respond to our outlook, to shape itself to meet our expectations.
Richard M. DeVos (1926-, American Businessman, Co-founder of Amway Corp.)

50 People expect a certain reaction from a business and when you pleasantly exceed those expectations, you've somehow passed an important psychological threshold.
Richard Thalheimer (American Business Executive, The Sharper Image)

51 High expectations are the key to everything.
Sam Walton (1918-1992, American Businessman, Founder of Wal-Mart Stores)

52 I know not anything more pleasant, or more instructive, than to compare experience with expectation, or to register from time to time the difference between idea and reality. It is by this kind of observation that we grow daily less liable to be disappointed.
Samuel Johnson (1709-1784, British Author)

53 Even if it is to be, what end do you serve by running to distress?
Seneca (4 BC-65 AD, Spanish-born Roman Statesman, philosopher)

54 Other people may not have had high expectations for me... but I had high expectations for myself.
Shannon Miller (American Olympic Gymnast)

55 You can't base your life on other people's expectations.
Stevie Wonder (1950-, American Musician, Singer, Songwriter, Producer)

56 Good is not good, when better is expected.
Thomas Fuller (1608-1661, British Clergyman, Author)

57 Prospect is often better than possession.
Thomas Fuller (1608-1661, British Clergyman, Author)

58 You begin by always expecting good things to happen
Tom Hopkins (American Sales Trainer, Speaker, Author)

59 One gift creates appreciation, many gifts create expectation.
Tony Bright

60 It's a funny thing about life: if you refuse to accept anything but the best, you very often get it.
W. Somerset Maugham (1874-1965, British Novelist, Playwright)

61 I skate to where the puck is going to be, not where it is.
Wayne Gretzky (1961-, Canadian Hockey Player)

62 The best part of our lives we pass in counting on what is to come.
William Hazlitt (1778-1830, British Essayist)

63 If you don't see yourself as a winner, then you cannot perform as a winner.
Zig Ziglar (American Sales Trainer, Author, Motivational Speaker)

64 You were born to win, but to be a winner, you must plan to win, prepare to win, and expect to win.
Zig Ziglar (American Sales Trainer, Author, Motivational Speaker)

EXPEDIENCY

1 Nobody is forgotten when it is convenient to remember him.
Benjamin Disraeli (1804-1881, British Statesman, Prime Minister)

2 The end justifies the means.
Proverb

3 Custom adapts itself to expediency.
Publius Cornelius Tacitus (55-117 AD, Roman Historian)

4 No man is justified in doing evil on the ground of expediency.
Theodore Roosevelt (1858-1919, Twenty-sixth President of the USA)

EXPENDITURE

1 Beware of little expenses. A small leak will sink a great ship.
Benjamin Franklin (1706-1790, American Scientist, Publisher, Diplomat)

2 Be at the pains of putting down every single item of expenditure whatsoever every day which could possibly be twisted into a professional expense and remember to lump in all the doubtfuls.
Hilaire Belloc (1870-1953, British Author)

3 You're biggest expense is the money you don't make.
Pante

EXPERIENCE

1 If we could sell our experience for what they cost us, we'd all be millionaires.
Abigail Van Buren (American Journalist, Advice Columnist - "Dear Abby")

2 We know nothing of what will happen in future, but by the analogy of experience.
Abraham Lincoln (1809-1865, Sixteenth President of the USA)

3 You can't create experience. You must undergo it.
Albert Camus (1913-1960, French Existential Writer)

4 Out of the multitude of our sense experiences we take, mentally and arbitrarily, certain repeatedly occurring complexes of sense impression (partly in conjunction with sense impressions which are interpreted as signs for sense experiences of others), and we attribute to them a meaning the meaning of the bodily object.
Albert Einstein (1879-1955, German-born American Physicist)

5 The only source of knowledge is experience.
Albert Einstein (1879-1955, German-born American Physicist)

6 Experience teaches only the teachable.
Aldous Huxley (1894-1963, British Author)

7 From their experience or from the recorded experience of others (history), men learn only what their passions and their metaphysical prejudices allow them to learn.
Aldous Huxley (1894-1963, British Author)

8 Experience is not what happens to a man; it is what a man does with what happens to him.
Aldous Huxley (1894-1963, British Author)

9 An enormous part of our mature experience cannot not be expressed in words.
Alfred North Whitehead (1861-1947, British Mathematician, Philosopher)

10 Experience is the only prophecy of wise men.
Alphonse De Lamartine (1790-1869, French Poet, Statesman, Historian)

11 Experience is a revelation in the light of which we renounce our errors of youth for those of age.
Ambrose Bierce (1842-1914, American Author, Editor, Journalist, "The Devil's Dictionary")

12 Experience. The wisdom that enables us to recognize in an undesirable old acquaintance the folly that we have already embraced.
Ambrose Bierce (1842-1914, American Author, Editor, Journalist, "The Devil's Dictionary")

13 Fooled once shame on you, fooled twice shame on me.
American Proverb

14 The notion of a universality of human experience is a confidence trick and the notion of a universality of female experience is a clever confidence trick.
Angela Carter (1940-1992, British Author)

15 You should make a point of trying every experience once, excepting incest and folk dancing.
Arnold Bax (1883-1953, British Composer)

16 Experience is the key to greatness.
Arthur Williams

17 I probably hold the distinction of being one movie star who, by all laws of logic, should never have made it. At each stage of my career, I lacked the experience.
Audrey Hepburn (1929-1993, American Actress, Dancer, Model)

18 Nothing is a waste of time if you use the experience wisely.
Auguste Rodin (1840-1917, French Sculptor)

19 Experience keeps a school, yet fools will learn in no other.
Benjamin Franklin (1706-1790, American Scientist, Publisher, Diplomat)

20 It is the experience of living that is important, not searching for meaning. We bring meaning by how we love the world
Bernie S. Siegel (American Doctor, Author, Lecturer)

21 In the revolt against idealism, the ambiguities of the word "experience" have been perceived, with the result that realists have more and more avoided the word.
Bertrand Russell (1872-1970, British Philosopher, Mathematician, Essayist)

22 Two things control men's nature, instinct and experience.
Blaise Pascal (1623-1662, French Scientist, Religious Philosopher)

23 You learn from a conglomeration of the incredible past -- whatever experience gotten in any way whatsoever.
Bob Dylan (1941-, American Musician, Singer, Songwriter)

24 Whatever you dwell on in the conscious grows in your experience.
Brian Tracy (American Trainer, Speaker, Author, Businessman)

25 My experience has taught me, and it has become a principle with me, that it is never any benefit to give out and out, to man or woman, money, food, clothing, or anything else, if they are able-bodied and can work and earn what they need, when there is anything on earth for them to do. This is my principle and I try to act upon it. To pursue a contrary course would ruin any community in the world and make them idlers.
Brigham Young Fun

26 I reached in experience the nirvana which is unborn, unrivalled, secure from attachment, undecaying and unstained. This condition is indeed reached by me which is deep, difficult to see, difficult to understand, tranquil, excellent, beyond the reach of mere logic, subtle, and to be realized only by the wise.
Buddha (568-488 BC, Founder of Buddhism)

27 A little experience often upsets a lot of theory.
Cadman

28 In a person who is open to experience each stimulus is freely relayed through the nervous system, without being distorted by any process of defensiveness.
Carl Rogers (1902-1987, American Psychotherapist)

29 Experience is a comb which nature gives to men when they are bald.
Chinese Proverb

30 Every creator painfully experiences the chasm between his inner vision and its ultimate expression.
Cleveland Amory (American Animal Rights Activist)

31 Good judgment comes from experience, and experience -- well, that comes from poor judgment.
Cousin Woodman

32 Experience taught me a few things. One is to listen to your gut, no matter how good something sounds on paper. The second is that you're generally better off sticking with what you know. And the third is that sometimes your best investments are the ones you don't make.
Donald Trump (1946-, 45th President of the United States of America)

33 I try to avoid experience if I can. Most experience is bad.
E. L. Doctorow (1931-, American Novelist)

34 Experience, like a pale musician, holds a dulcimer of patience in his hand.
Elizabeth Barrett Browning (1806-1861, British Poet)

35 Experience isn't interesting until it begins to repeat itself. In fact, till it does that, it hardly is experience.
Elizabeth Bowen (1899-1973, Anglo-Irish Novelist)

36 No matter how vital experience might be while you lived it, no sooner was it ended and dead than it became as lifeless as the piles of dry dust in a school history book.
Ellen Glasgow (1874-1945, American Novelist)

37 A burnt child dreads the fire.
English Proverb

38 Where you are in consciousness has everything to do with what you see in experience.
Eric Butterworth

39 In going where you have to go, and doing what you have to do, and seeing what you have to see, you dull and blunt the instrument you write with. But I would rather have it bent and dulled and know I had to put it on the grindstone again and hammer it into shape and put a whetstone to it, and know that I had something to write about, than to have it bright and shining and nothing to say, or smooth and well oiled in the closet, but unused.
Ernest Hemingway (1898-1961, American Writer)

40 Bad experience is a school that only fools keep going to.
Ezra Taft Benson (1899-1994, American Government Official and Religious Leader)

41 Experience is that marvelous thing that enables you to recognize a mistake when you make it again.
Franklin P. Jones

42 It is not necessary that you leave the house. Remain at your table and listen. Do not even listen, only wait. Do not even wait, be wholly still and alone. The world will present itself to you for its unmasking, it can do no other, in ecstasy it will writhe at your feet.
Franz Kafka (1883-1924, German Novelist, Short-Story Writer)

43 I know by my own pot how the others boil.
French Proverb

44 A strong and secure man digests his experiences (deeds and misdeeds alike) just as he digests his meat, even when he has some bits to swallow.
Friedrich Nietzsche (1844-1900, German Philosopher)

45 Experience, as a desire for experience, does not come off. We must not study ourselves while having an experience.
Friedrich Nietzsche (1844-1900, German Philosopher)

46 One is taught by experience to put a premium on those few people who can appreciate you for what you are.
Gail Godwin

47 What is the good of drawing conclusions from experience? I don't deny we sometimes draw the right conclusions, but don't we just as often draw the wrong ones?
Georg C. Lichtenberg (1742-1799, German Physicist, Satirist)

48 Everything happens to everybody sooner or later if there is time enough.
George Bernard Shaw (1856-1950, Irish-born British Dramatist)

49 Men are wise in proportion, not to their experience, but to their capacity for experience.
George Bernard Shaw (1856-1950, Irish-born British Dramatist)

50 If history repeats itself, and the unexpected always happens, how incapable must Man be of learning from experience!
George Bernard Shaw (1856-1950, Irish-born British Dramatist)

51 Is it not rather what we expect in men, that they should have numerous strands of experience lying side by side and never compare them with each other?
George Eliot (1819-1880, British Novelist)

52 But human experience is usually paradoxical, that means incongruous with the phrases of current talk or even current philosophy.
George Eliot (1819-1880, British Novelist)

53 I had a lot of experience with people smarter than I am.
Gerald R. Ford (1913-, Thirty-eighth President of the USA)

54 Experience which was once claimed by the aged is now claimed exclusively by the young.
Gilbert K. Chesterton (1874-1936, British Author)

55 When you have really exhausted an experience you always reverence and love it. The two things that nearly all of us have thoroughly and really been through are childhood and youth. And though we would not have them back again on any account, we feel that they are both beautiful, because we have drunk them dry.
Gilbert K. Chesterton (1874-1936, British Author)

56 Experience is determined by yourself -- not the circumstances of your life.
Gita Bellin

57 Perhaps the single most important element in mastering the techniques and tactics of racing is experience. But once you have the fundamentals, acquiring the experience is a matter of time.
Greg LeMond (1961-, American Cyclist, 3 Times Winner of the Tour de France)

58 In the business world, everyone is paid in two coins: cash and experience. Take the experience first; the cash will come later.
Harold S. Geneen (1910-, American Accountant, Industrialist, CEO, ITT)

59 Experience is a good school, but the fees are high.
Heinrich Heine (1797-1856, German Poet, Journalist)

60 Experience is in the fingers and head. The heart is inexperienced.
Henry David Thoreau (1817-1862, American Essayist, Poet, Naturalist)

61 If you take all the experience and judgment of men over fifty out of the world, there wouldn't be enough left to run it.
Henry Ford (1863-1947, American Industrialist, Founder of Ford Motor Company)

62 Experience is never limited, and it is never complete; it is an immense sensibility, a kind of huge spider-web of the finest silken threads suspended in the chamber of consciousness, and catching every air-borne particle in its tissue.
Henry James (1843-1916, American Author)

63 Deep experience is never peaceful.
Henry James (1843-1916, American Author)

64 The power to guess the unseen from the seen, to trace the implications of things, to judge the whole piece by the pattern, the condition of feeling life in general so completely that you are well on your way to knowing any particular corner of it --this cluster of gifts may almost be said to constitute experience.
Henry James (1843-1916, American Author)

65 The fool knows after he's suffered.
Hesiod (8th Century BC, Greek Poet)

66 If a man deceives me once, shame on him; if he deceives me twice, shame on me.
Italian Proverb

67 In times of rapid change, experience could be your worst enemy.
J. Paul Getty (1892-1976, American Oil Tycoon, Billionaire)

68 Experience that destroys innocents also leads one back to it.
James Baldwin (1924-1987, American Author)

69 Experience is a private, and a very largely speechless affair.
James Baldwin (1924-1987, American Author)

70 One thorn of experience is worth a whole wilderness of warning.
James Russell Lowell (1819-1891, American Poet, Critic, Editor)

71 Take time to gather up the past so that you will be able to draw from your experience and invest them in the future.
Jim Rohn (American Businessman, Author, Speaker, Philosopher)

72 Experience is a great advantage. The problem is that when you get the experience, you're too damned old to do anything about it.
Jimmy Connors (1952-, American Tennis Player)

73 Nothing ever becomes real till it is experienced -- even a proverb is no proverb to you till your life has illustrated it.
John Keats (1795-1821, British Poet)

74 No man's knowledge here can go beyond his experience.
John Locke (1632-1704, British Philosopher)

75 There are many truths of which the full meaning cannot be realized until personal experience has brought it home.
John Stuart Mill (1806-1873, British Philosopher, Economist)

76 If what happens does not make us richer, we must welcome it if it makes us wiser.
Johnson

77 I don't have to have faith, I have experience.
Joseph Campbell (American Scholar, Writer, Teacher)

78 Experience comprises illusions lost, rather than wisdom gained.
Joseph Roux (1834-1905, French Priest, Writer)

79 Experience increases our wisdom but doesn't reduce our follies.
Josh Billings (1815-1885, American Humorist, Lecturer)

80 Experience is a school where a man learns what a big fool he has been.
Josh Billings (1815-1885, American Humorist, Lecturer)

81 Experience is a comb that life gives you after you lose your hair.
Judith Stern

82 Experience praises the most happy the one who made the most people happy.
Karl Marx (1818-1883, German Political Theorist, Social Philosopher)

83 Experience does not err. Only your judgments err by expecting from her what is not in her power.
Leonardo Da Vinci (1452-1519, Italian Inventor, Architect, Painter, Scientist, Sculptor)

84 Men may rise on stepping-stones of their dead selves to higher things.
Lord Alfred Tennyson (1809-1892, British Poet)

85 There is a sort of veteran woman of condition, who, having lived always in the grand monde, and having possibly had some gallantries, together with the experience of five and twenty or thirty years, form a young fellow better than all the rules that can be given him. Wherever you go, make some of those women your friends; which a very little matter will do. Ask their advice, tell them your doubts or difficulties as to your behavior; but take great care not to drop one word of their experience; for experience implies age, and the suspicion of age, no woman, let her be ever so old, ever forgives.
Lord Chesterfield (1694-1773, British Statesman, Author)

86 Experience should teach us to be most on our guard to protect liberty when the Government's purposes are beneficent. Men born to freedom are naturally alert to repel invasion of their liberty by evil minded rulers. The greatest dangers to liberty lurk in insidious encroachment by men of zeal well meaning but without understanding.
Louis D. Brandeis (1856-1941, American Judge)

87 Experience is a dim lamp, which only lights the one who bears it.
Louis-Ferdinand Celine (1894-1961, French Author)

88 The cat, having sat upon a hot stove lid, will not sit upon a hot stove lid again. But he won't sit upon a cold stove lid, either.
Mark Twain (1835-1910, American Humorist, Writer)

89 We should be careful to get out of an experience only the wisdom that is in it -- and stop there; lest we be like the cat that sits down on a hot stove-lid. She will never sit down on a hot stove-lid again -- and that is well; but also she will never sit down on a cold one anymore.
Mark Twain (1835-1910, American Humorist, Writer)

90 Everybody experiences far more than he understands. Yet it is experience, rather than understanding, that influences behavior.
Marshall Mcluhan (1911-1980, Canadian Communications Theorist)

91 The school of hard knocks is an accelerated curriculum.
Menander of Athens (342-291 BC, Greek Dramatic Poet)

92 It is all right letting yourself go, as long as you can get yourself back.
Mick Jagger (1943-, British-born American-born American Musician, Singer)

93 Experience is a good teacher, but she sends in terrific bills.
Minna Antrim (1861-18?, American Epigrammist)

94 It takes half your life before you discover life is a do-it-yourself project.
Napoleon Hill (1883-1970, American Speaker, Motivational Writer, "Think and Grow Rich")

95 One of the greatest moments in anybody's developing experience is when he no longer tries to hide from himself but determines to get acquainted with himself as he really is.
Norman Vincent Peale (1898-1993, American Christian Reformed Pastor, Speaker, Author)

96 We can have in life but one great experience at best, and the secret of life is to reproduce that experience as often as possible.
Oscar Wilde (1856-1900, British Author, Wit)

97 Experience is one thing you can't get for nothing.
Oscar Wilde (1856-1900, British Author, Wit)

98 I have but one lamp by which my feet are guided; and that is the lamp of experience. I know of no way of judging the future but by the past.
Patrick Henry (1736-1799, American Orator, Patriot)

99 He who has been bitten by a snake fears a piece of string.
Persian Proverb

100 The rules which experience suggest are better than those which theorists elaborate in their libraries.
R. S. Storrs

101 The more experiments you make the better.
Ralph Waldo Emerson (1803-1882, American Poet, Essayist)

102 Our knowledge is the amassed thought and experience of innumerable minds.
Ralph Waldo Emerson (1803-1882, American Poet, Essayist)

103 There is no wider gulf in the universe than yawns between those on the hither and thither side of vital experience.
Rebecca West (1892-1983, British Author)

104 Common experience is the gold reserve which confers an exchange value on the currency which words are; without this reserve of shared experiences, all our pronouncements are checks drawn on insufficient funds.
Rene Daumal (1908-1944, French Poet, Critic)

105 Human beings hardly ever learn from the experience of others. They learn; when they do, which isn't often, on their own, the hard way.
Robert Heinlein (1907-1988, American Science Fiction Writer)

106 If you've seen one redwood, you've seen them all.
Ronald Reagan (1911-, Fortieth President of the USA, Actor)

107 Don't learn to do, but learn in doing. Let your falls not be on a prepared ground, but let them be bona fide falls in the rough and tumble of the world.
Samuel Butler (1612-1680, British Poet, Satirist)

108 To most men experience is like the stern lights of a ship, which illuminate only the track it has passed.
Samuel Taylor Coleridge (1772-1834, British Poet, Critic, Philosopher)

109 Man arrives as a novice at each age of his life.
Sebastien-Roch Nicolas De Chamfort (1741-1794, French Writer, Journalist, Playwright)

110 Experience is the extract of suffering.
Sir Arthur Helps (1813-1875, British Historian, Novelist, Essayist)

111 All is but lip-wisdom which wants experience.
Sir Philip Sidney (1554-1586, British Author, Courtier)

112 My mind withdrew its thoughts from experience, extracting itself from the contradictory throng of sensuous images, that it might find out what that light was wherein it was bathed.... And thus, with the flash of one hurried glance, it attained to the vision of That Which Is.
St. Augustine (354-430, Numidian-born Bishop of Hippo, Theologian)

113 To reach something good it is very useful to have gone astray, and thus acquire experience.
St. Teresa of Avila (1515-1582, Spanish Saint, Mystic)

114 Experience is what keeps a man who makes the same mistake twice from admitting it the third time around.
Terry Mccormick

115 Experience is the worst teacher; it gives the test before presenting the lesson.
Vernon S. Law

116 We learn through experience and experiencing, and no one teaches anyone anything. This is as true for the infant moving from kicking to crawling to walking as it is for the scientist with his equations. If the environment permits it, anyone can learn whatever he chooses to learn; and if the individual permits it, the environment will teach him everything it has to teach.
Viola Spolin (1911-, American Theatrical Director, Producer)

117 Only he who can view his own past as an abortion sprung from compulsion and need can use it to full advantage in the present. For what one has lived is at best comparable to a beautiful statue which has had all its limbs knocked off in transit, and now yields nothing but the precious block out of which the image of one's future must be hewn.
Walter Benjamin (1982-1940, German Critic, Philosopher)

118 Not the fruit of experience but experience itself, is the end.
Walter Pater (1839-1894, British Essayist, Critic)

119 Oh, how bitter it is to look into happiness through another man's eyes.
Wilfred T. Grenfell

120 Nothing which has entered into our experience is ever lost.
William Ellery Channing (1780-1842, American Unitarian Minister, Author)

EXPERTS

1 Brain surgeons earn 10 times that of a general practitioner... it pays to be an expert.
Alan Pease

2 Specialized meaninglessness has come to be regarded, in certain circles, as a kind of hall-mark of true science.
Aldous Huxley (1894-1963, British Author)

3 A professional; is someone who can do his best work when he doesn't feel like it.
Alistair Cooke (1908-, British Broadcaster, Journalist)

4 What is an expert? Someone who is twenty miles from home.
American Proverb

5 Even when the experts all agree, they may well be mistaken.
Bertrand Russell (1872-1970, British Philosopher, Mathematician, Essayist)

6 An expert is an ordinary fella away from home.
Bum Phillips (American Football Coach)

7 It is surely a matter of common observation that a man who knows no one thing intimately has no views worth hearing on things in general. The farmer philosophizes in terms of crops, soils, markets, and implements, the mechanic generalizes his experiences of wood and iron, the seaman reaches similar conclusions by his own special road; and if the scholar keeps pace with these it must be by an equally virile productivity.
Charles Horton Cooley (1864-1929, American Sociologist)

8 Experts often possess more data than judgment.
Colin Powell (1937-, American Army General)

9 This world is run by people who know how to do things. They know how things work. They are equipped. Up there, there's a layer of people who run everything. But we --we're just peasants. We don't understand what's going on, and we can't do anything.
Doris Lessing (1919-, British Novelist)

10 What a delightful thing is the conversation of specialists! One understands absolutely nothing and it's charming.
Edgar Degas (1834-1917, French Painter, Sculptor)

11 One who limits himself to his chosen mode of ignorance.
Elbert Hubbard (1859-1915, American Author, Publisher)

12 A lot of fellows nowadays have a B. A., M. D., or Ph. D. Unfortunately, they don't have a J. O. B.
Fats Domino (American Singer)

13 We do not need to be shoemakers to know if our shoes fit, and just as little have we any need to be professionals to acquire knowledge of matters of universal interest.
Georg Hegel (1770-1831, German Philosopher)

14 No man can be a pure specialist without being in the strict sense an idiot.
George Bernard Shaw (1856-1950, Irish-born British Dramatist)

15 We have not overthrown the divine right of kings to fall down for the divine right of experts.
Harold Macmillan (1894-1986, British Conservative Politician, Prime Minister)

16 It is, after all, the responsibility of the expert to operate the familiar and that of the leader to transcend it.
Henry Kissinger (1923-, American Republican Politician, Secretary of State)

17 There is nothing an economist should fear so much as applause.
Herbert Marshall (American Actor)

18 Make three correct guesses consecutively and you will establish a reputation as an expert.
Laurence J. Peter

19 Where there are two PhD's in a developing country, one is head of state and the other is in exile.
Lord Samuel

20 What's an expert? I read somewhere, that the more a man knows, the more he knows, he doesn't know. So I suppose one definition of an expert would be someone who doesn't admit out loud that he knows enough about a subject to know he doesn't really know how much.
Malcolm S. Forbes (1919-1990, American Publisher, Businessman)

21 The more the world is specialized the more it will be run by generalists.
Marcel Masse

22 A specialist is a person who fears the other subjects.
Martin H. Fisher

23 Only by strict specialization can the scientific worker become fully conscious, for once and perhaps never again in his lifetime, that he has achieved something that will endure. A really definitive and good accomplishment is today always a specialized ac
Max Weber (1864-1920, German Sociologist)

24 An expert is one who knows more and more about less and less.
Nicholas Butler (1862-1947, American Educationist)

25 An expert is someone who knows some of the worst mistakes, which can be made, in a very narrow field.
Niels Bohr (1885-1962, Danish Physicist)

26 Do not be bullied out of your common sense by the specialist; two to one, he is a pedant.
Oliver Wendell Holmes (1809-1894, American Author, Wit, Poet)

27 An ordinary man away from home giving advice.
Oscar Wilde (1856-1900, British Author, Wit)

28 My definition of an expert in any field is a person who knows enough about what's really going on to be scared.
P. J. Plauger

29 Always listen to experts. They'll tell you what can't be done and why. Then do it.
Robert Heinlein (1907-1988, American Science Fiction Writer)

30 Consultants are people who borrow your watch and tell you what time it is, and then walk off with the watch.
Robert Townsend (American Businessman, President of Avis)

31 A specialist is someone who does everything else worse.
Ruggiero Ricci (1918-, American Violinist)

32 The public do not know enough to be experts, but know enough to decide between them.
Samuel Butler (1612-1680, British Poet, Satirist)

33 An expert is a person who avoids the small errors while sweeping on to the grand fallacy.
Steven Weinberg (1933-, American Nuclear Physicist)

34 An expert is someone who knows a lot about the past.
Tom Hopkins (American Sales Trainer, Speaker, Author)

35 America has always been a country of amateurs where the professional, that is to say, the man who claims authority as a member of an Elite which knows the law in some field or other, is an object of distrust and resentment.
W. H. Auden (1907-1973, Anglo-American Poet)

36 There is nothing so stupid as an educated man, if you get him off the thing he was educated in.
Will Rogers (1879-1935, American Humorist, Actor)

37 How much a dunce that has been sent to roam, excels a dunce that has been kept at home.
William Cowper (1731-1800, British Poet)

38 Given one well-trained physician of the highest type he will do better work for a thousand people than ten specialists.
William James Mayo (1861-1939, American Surgeon, Founder of Mayo Clinic)

39 Good counselors lack no clients.
William Shakespeare (1564-1616, British Poet, Playwright, Actor)

EXPLANATIONS

1 The first forty years of life give us the text; the next thirty supply the commentary on it.
Arthur Schopenhauer (1788-1860, German Philosopher)

2 There is no waste of time in life like that of making explanations.
Benjamin Disraeli (1804-1881, British Statesman, Prime Minister)

3 Never explain -- your friends do not need it, and your enemies will not believe you anyway.
Elbert Hubbard (1859-1915, American Author, Publisher)

4 The simplest explanation is that it doesn't make sense.
Professor William Buechner

5 A little inaccuracy sometimes saves tons of explanations.
Saki

6   There is occasions and causes why and wherefore in all things.
William Shakespeare (1564-1616, British Poet, Playwright, Actor)

EXPLORATION

1   The American experience stirred mankind from discovery to exploration. From the cautious quest for what they knew (or thought they knew) was out there, into an enthusiastic reaching to the unknown. These are two substantially different kinds of human enterprise.
Daniel J. Boorstin (1914-, American Historian)

2   It is easier to sail many thousand miles through cold and storm and cannibals, in a government ship, with five hundred men and boys to assist one, than it is to explore the private sea, the Atlantic and Pacific Ocean of one's being alone. It is not worth the while to go round the world to count the cats in Zanzibar.
Henry David Thoreau (1817-1862, American Essayist, Poet, Naturalist)

3   We shall not cease from exploration and the end of all our exploring will be to arrive where we started... and know the place for the first time.
T. S. Eliot (1888-1965, American-born British Poet, Critic)

EXPRESSION

1   It is only by expressing all that is inside that purer and purer streams come.
Brenda Ueland (1891-1986, American Writer)

2   No comment is a splendid expression. I am using it again and again.
Winston Churchill (1874-1965, British Statesman, Prime Minister)

3   I have never accepted what many people have kindly said-namely that I inspired the nation. Their will was resolute and remorseless, and as it proved, unconquerable. It fell to me to express it.
Winston Churchill (1874-1965, British Statesman, Prime Minister)

EXTRA MILE

1   If someone takes your coat, give him your cloak as well; if he makes you go a mile with him, go with him two. [Mathew]
Bible (Sacred Scriptures of Christians and Judaism)

2   No one ever attains very eminent success by simply doing what is required of him; it is the amount and excellence of what is over and above the required, that determines the greatness of ultimate distinction.
Charles Francis Adams (1807 - 1886, American Statesman, Diplomat)

3   Give the world the best that you have, and the best will come back to you.
Madeline Bridges (American Professor)

4   The man who does more than he is paid for will soon be paid for more than he does.
Napoleon Hill (1883-1970, American Speaker, Motivational Writer, "Think and Grow Rich")

5   Here is the simple but powerful rule... always give people more than they expect to get.
Nelson Boswell

6   Always render more and better service than is expected of you, no matter what your task may be.
Og Mandino (1923-1996, American Motivational Author, Speaker)

7   I hate the giving of the hand unless the whole man accompanies it.
Ralph Waldo Emerson (1803-1882, American Poet, Essayist)

EXTRAVAGANCE

1   My candle burns at both ends; it will not last the night; but ah, my foes, and oh, my friends -- it gives a lovely light!
Edna St. Vincent Millay (1892-1950, American Poet)

2   I get so tired listening to one million dollars here, one million dollars there, it's so petty.
Imelda Marcos (1929-, Philippines First Lady)

3   Where there is no extravagance there is no love, and where there is no love there is no understanding.
Oscar Wilde (1856-1900, British Author, Wit)

4   As to the rout that is made about people who are ruined by extravagance, it is no matter to the nation that some individuals suffer. When so much general productive exertion is the consequence of luxury, the nation does not care though there are debtors; nay, they would not care though their creditors were there too.
Samuel Johnson (1709-1784, British Author)

EXTREMES AND EXTREMISTS

1   Nothing fools people as much as extreme passion.
Bishop Hall

2   The purest ore is produced from the hottest furnace, and the brightest thunderbolt is elicited from the darkest storm.
Charles Caleb Colton (1780-1832, British Sportsman Writer)

3   Extreme positions are not succeeded by moderate ones, but by contrary extreme positions.
Friedrich Nietzsche (1844-1900, German Philosopher)

4   Railing and praising were his usual themes; and both showed his judgment in extremes. Either over violent or over civil, so everyone to him was either god or devil.
John Dryden (1631-1700, British Poet, Dramatist, Critic)

5   So over violent, or over civil that every man with him was God or Devil.
    John Dryden (1631-1700, British Poet, Dramatist, Critic)

6   The question is not whether we will be extremists, but what kind of extremists we will be.
    Martin Luther King Jr. (1929-1968, American Black Leader, Nobel Prize Winner, 1964)

7   This woman did not fly to extremes; she lived there.
    Quentin Crisp (1908-, British Author)

8   Our age knows nothing but reaction, and leaps from one extreme to another.
    Reinhold Niebuhr (1892-1971, American Theologian, Historian)

9   What is objectionable, what is dangerous, about extremists is not that they are extreme, but that they are intolerant. The evil is not what they say about their cause, but what they say about their opponents.
    Robert F. Kennedy (1925-1968, American Attorney General, Senator)

10 It is the nature of men having escaped one extreme, which by force they were constrained long to endure, to run headlong into the other extreme, forgetting that virtue doth always consist in the mean.
    Sir Walter Raleigh (1552-1618, British Courtier, Navigator, Writer)

11 No violent extreme endures.
    Thomas Carlyle (1795-1881, Scottish Philosopher, Author)

EYES

1   Why has not man a microscopic eye? For the plain reason man is not a fly.
    Alexander Pope (1688-1744, British Poet, Critic, Translator)

2   The eye of the master will do more work than both his hands.
    Benjamin Franklin (1706-1790, American Scientist, Publisher, Diplomat)

3   It is the eye of other people that ruin us. If I were blind I would want, neither fine clothes, fine houses or fine furniture.
    Benjamin Franklin (1706-1790, American Scientist, Publisher, Diplomat)

4   The eyes of the lord are in every place seeing the evil and the good.
    Bible (Sacred Scriptures of Christians and Judaism)

5   He had but one eye and the pocket of prejudice runs in favor of two.
    Charles Dickens (1812-1870, British Novelist)

6   Tears are nature's lotion for the eyes. The eyes see better for being washed by them.
    Christian Nevell Bovee (1820-1904, American Author, Lawyer)

7   It is better to trust the eyes rather than the ears.
    German Proverb

8   An animal will always look for a person's intentions by looking them right in the eyes.
    H. Powers

9   Of all the senses, sight must be the most delightful.
    Helen Keller (1880-1968, American Blind/Deaf Author, Lecturer, Amorist)

10 The eye is the jewel of the body.
    Henry David Thoreau (1817-1862, American Essayist, Poet, Naturalist)

11 What we learn only through the ears makes less impression upon our minds than what is presented to the trustworthy eye.
    Horace (65-8 BC, Italian Poet)

12 Who has a daring eye tell downright truths and downright lies.
    Johann Kaspar Lavater (1741-1801, Swiss Theologian, Mystic)

13 One's eyes are what one is, one's mouth is what one becomes.
    John Galsworthy (1867-1933, British Novelist, Playwright)

14 It is not miserable to be blind; it is miserable to be incapable of enduring blindness.
    John Milton (1608-1674, British Poet)

15 Her eyes are homes of silent prayers.
    Lord Alfred Tennyson (1809-1892, British Poet)

16 The eyes like sentinel occupy the highest place in the body.
    Marcus T. Cicero (106-43 BC, Great Roman Orator, Politician)

17 The eye is the mirror of the soul.
    Proverb

18 What the eye does not admire the heart does not desire.
    Proverb

19 The eyes are not responsible when the mind does the seeing.
    Publilius Syrus (1st Century BC, Roman Writer)

20 The eye is easily frightened.
    Ralph Waldo Emerson (1803-1882, American Poet, Essayist)

21 The eyes indicate the antiquity of the soul.
    Ralph Waldo Emerson (1803-1882, American Poet, Essayist)

22 The eyes see only what the mind is prepared to comprehend.
    Robertson Davies (1913-, Canadian Novelist, Journalist)

23 Do everything as in the eye of another.
    Seneca (4 BC-65 AD, Spanish-born Roman Statesman, philosopher)

24 It is we that are blind, not fortune.
    Sir Thomas Browne (1605-1682, British Author, Physician,, Philosopher)

25 Eyes lie if you ever look into them for the character of the person.
Stevie Wonder (1950-, American Musician, Singer, Songwriter, Producer)

26 Weak eyes are fondest of glittering objects.
Thomas Carlyle (1795-1881, Scottish Philosopher, Author)

27 The ear tends to be lazy, craves the familiar and is shocked by the unexpected; the eye, on the other hand, tends to be impatient, craves the novel and is bored by repetition.
W. H. Auden (1907-1973, Anglo-American Poet)

FACES

1 As a beauty I'm not a great star. Others are handsomer far; but my face -- I don't mind it because I'm behind it; it the folks out in front that I jar.
A. H. Euwer (American poet and painter, published The Limeratomy in 1917)

2 If I were two-faced, would I be wearing this one?
Abraham Lincoln (1809-1865, Sixteenth President of the USA)

3 Every man over forty is responsible for his face.
Abraham Lincoln (1809-1865, Sixteenth President of the USA)

4 Alas after a certain age, every man is responsible for his own face.
Albert Camus (1913-1960, French Existential Writer)

5 A man's face as a rule says more, and more interesting things, than his mouth, for it is a compendium of everything his mouth will ever say, in that it is the monogram of all this man's thoughts and aspirations.
Arthur Schopenhauer (1788-1860, German Philosopher)

6 Wicked thoughts and worthless efforts gradually set their mark on the face, especially the eyes.
Arthur Schopenhauer (1788-1860, German Philosopher)

7 It is only at the first encounter that a face makes its full impression on us.
Arthur Schopenhauer (1788-1860, German Philosopher)

8 People remain what they are even if their faces fall apart.
Bertolt Brecht (1898-1956, German Dramatist, Poet)

9 Our masks, always in peril of smearing or cracking, in need of continuous check in the mirror or silverware, keep us in thrall to ourselves, concerned with our surfaces.
Carolyn Kizer

10 A strange and somewhat impassive physiognomy is often, perhaps, an advantage to an orator, or leader of any sort, because it helps to fix the eye and fascinate the mind.
Charles Horton Cooley (1864-1929, American Sociologist)

11 Was this the face that launched a thousand ships, and burnt the topless towers of Ileum?
Christopher Marlowe (1564-1593, British Dramatist, Poet)

12 After a certain number of years our faces become our biographies. We get to be responsible for our faces.
Cynthia Ozick (1928-, American Novelist, short-story Writer)

13 The human face is the organic seat of beauty. It is the register of value in development, a record of Experience, whose legitimate office is to perfect the life, a legible language to those who will study it, of the majestic mistress, the soul.
Eliza Farnham (American Author and Social Reformist)

14 We can see nothing whatever of the soul unless it is visible in the expression of the countenance; one might call the faces at a large assembly of people a history of the human soul written in a kind of Chinese ideograms.
Georg C. Lichtenberg (1742-1799, German Physicist, Satirist)

15 I never forget a face, but in your case I'll make an exception.
Groucho Marx (1895-1977, American Comic Actor)

16 A good face they say, is a letter of recommendation. O Nature, Nature, why art thou so dishonest, as ever to send men with these false recommendations into the World!
Henry Fielding (1707-1754, British Novelist, Dramatist)

17 The face of a child can say it all, especially the mouth part of the face.
Jack Handy

18 It has to be displayed, this face, on a more or less horizontal plane. Imagine a man wearing a mask, and imagine that the elastic which holds the mask on has just broken, so that the man (rather than let the mask slip off) has to tilt his head back and balance the mask on his real face. This is the kind of tyranny which Lawson's face exerts over the rest of his body as he cruises along the corridors. He doesn't look down his nose at you, he looks along his nose.
James Fenton (1949-, British Poet, Critic)

19 A blank helpless sort of face, rather like a rose just before you drench it with D.D.T.
John Carey

20 It has been said that a pretty face is a passport. But it's not, it's a visa, and it runs out fast.
Julie Burchill (British Journalist, Writer)

21 A face is too slight a foundation for happiness.
Lady Mary Wortley Montagu (1689-1762, British Society Figure, Letter Writer)

22 I think your whole life shows in your face and you should be proud of that.
Lauren Bacall (1924-, American Actress)

23 The features of our face are hardly more than gestures which force of habit made permanent. Nature, like the destruction of Pompeii, like the metamorphosis of a nymph into a tree, has arrested us in an accustomed movement.
Marcel Proust (1871-1922, French Novelist)

24   I have eyes like those of a dead pig.
Marlon Brando (1924-, American Actor, Director)

25   He had a face like a blessing.
Miguel De Cervantes (1547-1616, Spanish Novelist, Dramatist, Poet)

26   The eyes those silent tongues of love.
Miguel De Cervantes (1547-1616, Spanish Novelist, Dramatist, Poet)

27   The serial number of a human specimen is the face, that accidental and unrepeatable combination of features. It reflects neither character nor soul, nor what we call the self. The face is only the serial number of a specimen.
Milan Kundera (1929-, Czech Author, Critic)

28   Time engraves our faces with all the tears we have not shed.
Natalie Clifford Barney (1876-1972, American-born French Author)

29   What is your fortune, my pretty maid?" "My face is my fortune, Sir," she said.
Nursery Rhyme

30   A man's face is his autobiography. A woman's face is her work of fiction.
Oscar Wilde (1856-1900, British Author, Wit)

31   What is a face, really? Its own photo? Its make-up? Or is it a face as painted by such or such painter? That which is in front? Inside? Behind? And the rest? Doesn't everyone look at himself in his own particular way? Deformations simply do not exist.
Pablo Picasso (1881-1973, Spanish Artist)

32   That the public can grow accustomed to any face is proved by the increasing prevalence of Keith's ruined physiognomy on TV documentaries and chat shows, as familiar and homely a horror as Grandpa in The Munsters.
Philip Norman

33   The face is the index of the mind.
Proverb

34   A man finds room in the few square inches of the face for the traits of all his ancestors; for the expression of all his history, and his wants.
Ralph Waldo Emerson (1803-1882, American Poet, Essayist)

35   When matters are desperate we must put on a desperate face.
Robert Burn

36   Her face was her chaperone.
Rupert Hughes

37   It is the common wonder of all men, how among so many million faces, there should be none alike.
Sir Thomas Browne (1605-1682, British Author, Physician,, Philosopher)

38   The faces that have charmed us the most escape us the soonest.
Sir Walter Scott (1771-1832, British Novelist, Poet)

39   I am the family face; flesh perishes, I live on, projecting trait and trace through time to times anon, and leaping from place to place over oblivion.
Thomas Hardy (1840-1928, British Novelist, Poet)

40   Tom's great yellow bronze mask all draped upon an iron framework. An inhibited, nerve- drawn; dropped face -- as if hung on a scaffold of heavy private brooding; and thought.
Virginia Woolf (1882-1941, British Novelist, Essayist)

41   My face looks like a wedding-cake left out in the rain.
W. H. Auden (1907-1973, Anglo-American Poet)

42   Every European visitor to the United States is struck by the comparative rarity of what he would call a face, by the frequency of men and women who look like elderly babies. If he stays in the States for any length of time, he will learn that this cannot be put down to a lack of sensibility -- the American feels the joys and sufferings of human life as keenly as anybody else. The only plausible explanation I can find lies in his different attitude to the past. To have a face, in the European sense of the word, it would seem that one must not only enjoy and suffer but also desire to preserve the memory of even the most humiliating and unpleasant experiences of the past.
W. H. Auden (1907-1973, Anglo-American Poet)

43   This face is a dog's snout sniffing for garbage, snakes nest in that mouth, I hear the sibilant threat.
Walt Whitman (1819-1892, American Poet)

44   Thus is his cheek the map of days outworn.
William Shakespeare (1564-1616, British Poet, Playwright, Actor)

45   The tartness of his face sours ripe grapes.
William Shakespeare (1564-1616, British Poet, Playwright, Actor)

46   God had given you one face, and you make yourself another. [Hamlet]
William Shakespeare (1564-1616, British Poet, Playwright, Actor)

FACTS

1   The ultimate umpire of all things in life is -- fact.
Agnes C. Laut (1871-1936, Canadian Journalist, Author)

2   If the facts don't fit the theory, change the facts.
Albert Einstein (1879-1955, German-born American Physicist)

3   Facts are ventriloquists dummies. Sitting on a wise man's knee they may be made to utter words of wisdom; elsewhere, they say nothing, or talk nonsense, or indulge in sheer diabolism.
Aldous Huxley (1894-1963, British Author)

4   Facts don't cease to exist because they are ignored.
Aldous Huxley (1894-1963, British Author)

5 Facts can't be recounted; much less twice over, and far less still by different persons. I've already drummed that thoroughly into your head. What happens is that your wretched memory remembers the words and forgets what's behind them.
Augusto Roa Bastos (1917-, Paraguayan Novelist)

6 As a general rule, the most successful man in life is the man who has the best information.
Benjamin Disraeli (1804-1881, British Statesman, Prime Minister)

7 If you get all the facts, your judgment can be right; if you don't get all the facts, it can't be right.
Bernard M. Baruch (1870-1965, American Financier)

8 Those who forget good and evil and seek only to know the facts are more likely to achieve good than those who view the world through the distorting medium of their own desires.
Bertrand Russell (1872-1970, British Philosopher, Mathematician, Essayist)

9 The facts are always friendly, every bit of evidence one can acquire, in any area, leads one that much closer to what is true.
Carl Rogers (1902-1987, American Psychotherapist)

10 Now, what I want is, facts. Teach these boys and girls nothing but Facts. Facts alone are wanted in life. Plant nothing else, and root out everything else. You can only form the minds of reasoning animals upon Facts: nothing else will ever be of any service to them. This is the principle on which I bring up my own children, and this is the principle on which I bring up these children. Stick to Facts, sir!
Charles Dickens (1812-1870, British Novelist)

11 Comment is free but facts are sacred.
Charles Prestwich Scott (1846-1932, British Newspaper Editor)

12 A concept is stronger than a fact.
Charlotte P. Gillman (1860-1935, American Feminist and Writer)

13 I might show facts as plain as day: but, since your eyes are blind, you'd say, "Where? What?" and turn away.
Christina Rossetti (1830-1894, British Poet, Lyricist)

14 A fact in itself is nothing. It is valuable only for the idea attached to it, or for the proof which it furnishes.
Claude Bernard (1813-1878, French Physiologist)

15 I'm not afraid of facts, I welcome facts but a congeries of facts is not equivalent to an idea. This is the essential fallacy of the so-called "scientific" mind. People who mistake facts for ideas are incomplete thinkers; they are gossips.
Cynthia Ozick (1928-, American Novelist, short-story Writer)

16 I deal with the obvious. I present, reiterate and glorify the obvious -- because the obvious is what people need to be told.
Dale Carnegie (1888-1955, American Author, Trainer)

17 The sky is not less blue because the blind man does not see it.
Danish Proverb

18 She always says, my lord, that facts are like cows. If you look them in the face hard enough they generally run away.
Dorothy L. Sayers (1893-1957, British Author)

19 The facts: nothing matters but the facts: worship of the facts leads to everything, to happiness first of all and then to wealth.
Edmond and Jules De Goncourt (1822-1896, French Writers)

20 It is the nature of all greatness not to be exact.
Edmund Burke (1729-1797, British Political Writer, Statesman)

21 Facts are counterrevolutionary.
Eric Hoffer (1902-1983, American Author, Philosopher)

22 We should keep so close to facts that we never have to remember the second time what we said the first time.
F. Marion Smith

23 To some lawyers, all facts are created equal.
Felix Frankfurter (1882-1965, Austrian-born American Law Teacher, Judge)

24 Facts in books, statistics in encyclopedias, the ability to use them in men's heads.
Fogg Brackell

25 Men on their side must force themselves for a while to lay their notions by and begin to familiarize themselves with facts.
Francis Bacon (1561-1626, British Philosopher, Essayist, Statesman)

26 Facts are the most important thing in business. Study facts and do more than is expected of you.
Frederick Hudson Ecker (American Business Executive, Chairman of Metropolitan Life)

27 There are no eternal facts, as there are no absolute truths.
Friedrich Nietzsche (1844-1900, German Philosopher)

28 There are no facts, only interpretations.
Friedrich Nietzsche (1844-1900, German Philosopher)

29 Blessed is the man who, having nothing to say, abstains from giving us wordy evidence of the fact.
George Eliot (1819-1880, British Novelist)

30 It is the spirit of the age to believe that any fact, no matter how suspect, is superior to any imaginative exercise, no matter how true.
Gore Vidal (1925-, American Novelist, Critic)

31 Nothing in education is so astonishing as the amount of ignorance it accumulates in the form of inert facts.
Henry Brooks Adams (1838 - 1918, American Historian)

32 My facts shall be falsehoods to the common sense. I would so state facts that they shall be significant, shall be myths or mythologies. Facts which the mind perceived, thoughts which the body thought -- with these I deal.
Henry David Thoreau (1817-1862, American Essayist, Poet, Naturalist)

33 The fatal futility of Fact.
Henry James (1843-1916, American Author)

34 Remember son, many a good story has been ruined by over verification.
James Gordon Bennett (1795-1872, British-born American Journalist)

35 Facts are facts and will not disappear on account of your likes.
Jawaharlal Nehru (1889-1964, Indian Nationalist, Statesman)

36 Anyone who knows a strange fact shares in its singularity.
Jean Genet (1910-1986, French Playwright, Novelist)

37 Facts are stubborn things; and whatever may be our wishes, our inclinations, or the dictates of our passions, they cannot alter the state of facts and evidence.
John Adams (1735-1826, Second President of the USA)

38 Facts are generally overesteemed. For most practical purposes, a thing is what men think it is. When they judged the earth flat, it was flat. As long as men thought slavery tolerable, tolerable it was. We live down here among shadows, shadows among shadows.
John Updike (1932-, American Novelist, Critic)

39 One precedent creates another and they soon accumulate and constitute law. What yesterday was a fact, today is doctrine.
Junius (1769-1771, Anonymous British Letter Writer)

40 One of the most untruthful things possible, you know, is a collection of facts, because they can be made to appear so many different ways.
Karl A. Menninger (1893-1990, American Psychiatrist)

41 I have always found that if I move with seventy-five percent or more of the facts that I usually never regret it. It's the guys who wait to have everything perfect that drive you crazy.
Lee Iacocca (1924-, American Businessman, Former CEO of Chrysler)

42 A fact is like a sack -- it won't stand up if it's empty. To make it stand up, first you have to put in it all the reasons and feelings that caused it in the first place.
Luigi Pirandello (1867-1936, Italian Author, Playwright)

43 Get your facts first, and then you can distort them as much as you please.
Mark Twain (1835-1910, American Humorist, Writer)

44 It is not the facts which guide the conduct of men, but their opinions about facts; which may be entirely wrong. We can only make them right by discussion
Norman Angell (1872-1967, British Writer, Pacifist)

45 All generous minds have a horror of what are commonly called "facts." They are the brute beasts of the intellectual domain. Who does not know fellows that always have an ill-conditioned fact or two that they lead after them into decent company like so many bull-dogs, ready to let them slip at every ingenious suggestion, or convenient generalization, or pleasant fancy? I allow no "facts" at this table.
Oliver Wendell Holmes (1809-1894, American Author, Wit, Poet)

46 Obviously the facts are never just coming at you but are incorporated by an imagination that is formed by your previous experience. Memories of the past are not memories of facts but memories of your imaginings of the facts.
Philip Roth (1933-, American Novelist)

47 No facts are to me sacred; none are profane; I simply experiment, an endless seeker, with no past at my back.
Ralph Waldo Emerson (1803-1882, American Poet, Essayist)

48 If a man will kick a fact out of the window, when he comes back he finds it again in the chimney corner.
Ralph Waldo Emerson (1803-1882, American Poet, Essayist)

49 Every fact is related on one side to sensation, and, on the other, to morals. The game of thought is, on the appearance of one of these two sides, to find the other; given the upper, to find the under side.
Ralph Waldo Emerson (1803-1882, American Poet, Essayist)

50 Time dissipates to shining ether the solid angularity of facts.
Ralph Waldo Emerson (1803-1882, American Poet, Essayist)

51 The best current evidence is that media are mere vehicles that deliver instruction but do not influence student achievement any more than the truck that delivers groceries causes change in our nutrition.
Richard Clark

52 It may be said with a degree of assurance that not everything that meets the eye is as it appears.
Rod Serling (1924-1975, American Television Script-writer)

53 People can refute your facts, but never your feelings.
Sharon Anthony Bower (American Author)

54 There is nothing as deceptive as an obvious fact.
Sir Arthur Conan Doyle (1859-1930, British Author, "Sherlock Holmes")

55 Some facts should be suppressed, or, at least, a just sense of proportion should be observed in treating them.
Sir Arthur Conan Doyle (1859-1930, British Author, "Sherlock Holmes")

56 Oh, don't tell me of facts -- I never believe facts: you know Canning said nothing was so fallacious as facts, except figures.
Sydney Smith (1771-1845, British Writer, Clergyman)

57 I grow daily to honor facts more and more, and theory less and less. A fact, it seems to me, is a great thing -- a sentence printed, if not by God, then at least by the Devil.
Thomas Carlyle (1795-1881, Scottish Philosopher, Author)

58 What are your historical Facts; still more your biographical? Wilt thou know a man by stringing-together beadrolls of what thou namest Facts?
Thomas Carlyle (1795-1881, Scottish Philosopher, Author)

59 Conclusive facts are inseparable from inconclusive except by a head that already understands and knows.
Thomas Carlyle (1795-1881, Scottish Philosopher, Author)

60 Get the facts, or the facts will get you. And when you get em, get em right, or they will get you wrong.
Thomas Fuller (1608-1661, British Clergyman, Author)

61 A world of facts lies outside and beyond the world of words.
Thomas H. Huxley (1825-1895, British Biologist, Educator)

62 Sit down before fact like a little child, and be prepared to give up every preconceived notion. Follow humbly wherever and to whatever abyss Nature leads, or you shall learn nothing.
Thomas H. Huxley (1825-1895, British Biologist, Educator)

63 The construction of life is at present in the power of facts far more than convictions.
Walter Benjamin (1982-1940, German Critic, Philosopher)

64 Facts have a cruel way of substituting themselves for fancies. There is nothing more remorseless, just as there is nothing more helpful, than truth.
William C. Redfield

65 Facts and truth really don't have much to do with each other.
William Faulkner (1897-1962, American Novelist)

66 General principles are not the less true or important because from their nature they elude immediate observation; they are like the air, which is not the less necessary because we neither see nor feel it.
William Hazlitt (1778-1830, British Essayist)

67 Our esteem for facts has not neutralized in us all religiousness. It is itself almost religious. Our scientific temper is devout.
William James (1842-1910, American Psychologist, Professor, Author)

68 The god whom science recognizes must be a God of universal laws exclusively, a God who does a wholesale, not a retail business. He cannot accommodate his processes to the convenience of individuals.
William James (1842-1910, American Psychologist, Professor, Author)

FAD

1 Nobody creates a fad. It just happens. People love going along with the idea of a beautiful pig. It's like a conspiracy.
Jim Henson

FAILURE

1 You can give in to the failure messages and be a bitter deadbeat of excuses. Or you can choose to be happy and positive and excited about life.
A. L. Williams (Born 1942, American insurance executive)

2 My great concern is not whether you have failed, but whether you are content with your failure.
Abraham Lincoln (1809-1865, Sixteenth President of the USA)

3 Do not look where you fell, but where you slipped.
African Proverb

4 Everyone should fail in a big way at least once before reaching forty.
Al Neuharth (American publisher, Founder, USA Today)

5 No one ever won a chess game by betting on each move. Sometimes you have to move backward to get a step forward.
Amar Gopal Bose (Indian-Born American Engineer, MIT Professor, Founder of Bose Corporation)

6 It's best to have failure happen early in life. It wakes up the Phoenix bird in you so you rise from the ashes.
Anne Baxter (1923-1985, American Actress)

7 I wasn't afraid to fail. Something good always comes out of failure.
Anne Baxter (1923-1985, American Actress)

8 There is no such thing as failure. There are only results.
Anthony Robbins (1960-, American Author, Speaker, Peak Performance Expert / Consultant)

9 I've come to believe that all my past failure and frustration were actually laying the foundation for the understandings that have created the new level of living I now enjoy.
Anthony Robbins (1960-, American Author, Speaker, Peak Performance Expert / Consultant)

10 Most people fail in life because they major in minor things.
Anthony Robbins (1960-, American Author, Speaker, Peak Performance Expert / Consultant)

11 If we don't see a failure as a challenge to modify our approach, but rather as a problem with ourselves, as a personality defect, we will immediately feel overwhelmed.
Anthony Robbins (1960-, American Author, Speaker, Peak Performance Expert / Consultant)

12 Failure is not an option.
Apollo 13 Movie

13 A failure will not appear until a unit has passed final inspection.
Arthur Bloch

14 He's not the finest character that ever lived. But he's a human being, and a terrible thing is happening to him. So attention must be paid.
Arthur Miller (1915-, American Dramatist)

15 A failure is not always a mistake, it may simply be the best one can do under the circumstances. The real mistake is to stop trying.
B. F. Skinner (1904-1990, American Psychologist)

16 Every strike brings me closer to the next home run.
Babe Ruth (1895-1948, American Baseball Player)

17 It is inevitable that some defeat will enter even the most victorious life. The human spirit is never finished when it is defeated... it is finished when it surrenders.
Ben Stein (American Professor, Writer)

18 On this path effort never goes to waste, and there is no failure. Even a little effort toward spiritual awareness will protect you from the greatest fear.
Bhagavad Gita (400 BC, Sanskrit Poem Incorporated Into the Mahabharata)

19 Defeat should never be a source of discouragement, but rather a fresh stimulus.
Bishop Robert South (1634-1716, British Clergyman)

20 It doesn't matter where you are coming from. All that matters is where you are going.
Brian Tracy (American Trainer, Speaker, Author, Businessman)

21 We pay just as dearly for our triumphs as we do for our defeats. Go ahead and fail. But fail with wit, fail with grace, fail with style. A mediocre failure is as insufferable as a mediocre success. Embrace failure! Seek it out. Learn to love it. That may be the only way any of us will ever be free. Tom Robbins Before you give up hope, turn back and read the attacks that were made on Lincoln.
Bruce Barton (1886-1967, American Author, Advertising Executive)

22 In great attempts it is glorious even to fail.
Cassius Longinus

23 You will never stub your toe standing still. The faster you go, the more chance there is of stubbing your toe, but the more chance you have of getting somewhere.
Charles F. Kettering (1876-1958, American Engineer, Inventor)

24 Believe and act as if it were impossible to fail.
Charles F. Kettering (1876-1958, American Engineer, Inventor)

25 We often say that the biggest job we have is to teach a newly hired employee to fail intelligently... to experiment over and over again and to keep on trying and failing until he learns what will work.
Charles F. Kettering (1876-1958, American Engineer, Inventor)

26 We need to teach the highly educated man that it is not a disgrace to fail and that he must analyze every failure to find its cause. He must learn how to fail intelligently, for failing is one of the greatest arts in the world.
Charles F. Kettering (1876-1958, American Engineer, Inventor)

27 Use the losses and failures of the past as a reason for action, not inaction.
Charles J. Givens (American Businessman, Author, Trainer)

28 You can't be a winner and be afraid to lose.
Charles Lynch

29 Everyone pushes a falling fence.
Chinese Proverb

30 The great question is not whether you have failed, but whether you are content with failure.
Chinese Proverb

31 A failure establishes only this, that our determination to succeed was not strong enough.
Christian Nevell Bovee (1820-1904, American Author, Lawyer)

32 To win you've got to stay in the game.
Claude M. Bristol (1891-1951, American Author of "The Magic of Believing")

33 A man who has committed a mistake and doesn't correct it is committing another mistake.
Confucius (551-479 BC, Chinese Ethical Teacher, Philosopher)

34 Our greatest glory is not in never falling, but in rising every time we fall.
Confucius (551-479 BC, Chinese Ethical Teacher, Philosopher)

35 Remember your past mistakes just long enough to profit by them.
Dan Mckinnon

36 We fail far more often by timidity than by over-daring.
David Grayson (1870-1946, American Journalist and Writer)

37 In the end, the only people who fail are those who do not try.
David Viscott (American Author, Speaker, Trainer)

38 To fail is a natural consequence of trying, To succeed takes time and prolonged effort in the face of unfriendly odds. To think it will be any other way, no matter what you do, is to invite yourself to be hurt and to limit your enthusiasm for trying again.
David Viscott (American Author, Speaker, Trainer)

39 Failure should be our teacher, not our undertaker. Failure is delay, not defeat. It is a temporary detour, not a dead end. Failure is something we can avoid only by saying nothing, doing nothing, and being nothing.
Denis Waitley (1933-, American Author, Speaker, Trainer, Peak Performance Expert)

40 Forget about the consequences of failure. Failure is only a temporary change in direction to set you straight for your next success.
Denis Waitley (1933-, American Author, Speaker, Trainer, Peak Performance Expert)

41 There are no mistakes or failures, only lessons.
Denis Waitley (1933-, American Author, Speaker, Trainer, Peak Performance Expert)

42 Losing is a part of winning.
Dick Munro

43 Many men fail because they quit too soon. They lose faith when the signs are against them. They do not have the courage to hold on, to keep fighting in spite of that which seems insurmountable. If more of us would strike out and attempt the "impossible," we very soon would find the truth of that old saying that nothing is impossible... abolish fear and you can accomplish anything you wish.
Dr. C. E. Welch (American Businessman, Founder of Welch's Grape Juice)

44 If one does not fail at times, then one has not challenged himself.
Dr. Porsche

45 Anyone seen on a bus after age thirty has been a failure in life.
Duchess Loelia

46 You are beaten to earth? Well, well, what's that? Come up with a smiling face, It's nothing against you to fall down flat/ But to lie there-that's a disgrace.
E. V. Cooke

47 Everything ultimately fails, for we die, and that is either the penultimate failure or our most enigmatical achievement.
Edward Dahlberg (1900-1977, American Author, Critic)

48 Sometimes a noble failure serves the world as faithfully as a distinguished success.
Edward Dowden (1843-1913, Irish Critic)

49 You don't drown by falling in the water; you drown by staying there.
Edwin Louis Cole

50 There is no failure except in no longer trying. There is no defeat except from within, no insurmountable barrier except our own inherent weakness of purpose.
Elbert Hubbard (1859-1915, American Author, Publisher)

51 Failure -- The man who can tell others what to do and how to do it, but never does it himself.
Elbert Hubbard (1859-1915, American Author, Publisher)

52 A failure is a man who has blundered, but is not able to cash in on the experience.
Elbert Hubbard (1859-1915, American Author, Publisher)

53 All human beings have failings, all human beings have needs and temptations and stresses. Men and women who live together through long years get to know one another's failings; but they also come to know what is worthy of respect and admiration in those they live with and in themselves. If at the end one can say, This man used to the limit the powers that God granted him; he was worthy of love and respect and of the sacrifices of many people, made in order that he might achieve what he deemed to be his task, then that life has been lived well and there are no regrets.
Eleanor Roosevelt (1884-1962, American First Lady, Columnist, Lecturer, Humanitarian)

54 Men do not fail; they give up trying.
Elihu Root (1845-1937, American Statesman)

55 Just don't give up trying to do what you really want to do. Where there is love and inspiration, I don't think you can go wrong.
Ella Fitzgerald (American singer)

56 There is no loneliness greater than the loneliness of a failure. The failure is a stranger in his own house.
Eric Hoffer (1902-1983, American Author, Philosopher)

57 They who lack talent expect things to happen without effort. They ascribe failure to a lack of inspiration or ability, or to misfortune, rather than to insufficient application. At the core of every true talent there is an awareness of the difficulties inherent in any achievement, and the confidence that by persistence and patience something worthwhile will be realized. Thus talent is a species of vigor.
Eric Hoffer (1902-1983, American Author, Philosopher)

58 Those who have failed miserably are often the first to see God's formula for success.
Erwin W. Lutzer (American Minister)

59 A lost battle is a battle one thinks one has lost.
Ferdinand Foch (1851-1929, French Field Marshal)

60 To expect defeat is nine-tenths of defeat itself.
Francis Crawford

61 The world is divided into two categories: failures and unknowns.
Francis Picabia (1878-1953, French Painter, Poet)

62 It is for want of application, rather than of means that people fail,
François de La Rochefoucauld (1613-1680, French classical writer)

63 No persons are more frequently wrong, than those who will not admit they are wrong.
François de La Rochefoucauld (1613-1680, French classical writer)

64 If we were faultless we should not be so much annoyed by the defects of those with whom we associate.
François Fénelon (1651-1715, French Roman Catholic archbishop, theologian, poet and writer)

65 Failure does not count. If you accept this, you'll be successful. What causes most people to fail is that after one failure, they'll stop trying.
Frank Burford

66 The man who fails because he aims astray or because he does not aim at all is to be found everywhere.
Frank Swinnerton

67 If it fails, admit it frankly and try another. But above all, try something.
Franklin D. Roosevelt (1882-1945, Thirty-second President of the USA)

68 In God's world, for those who are in earnest, there is no failure. No work truly done, no word earnestly spoken, no sacrifice freely made, was ever made in vain.
Frederick W. Robertson

69 The only failure one should fear, is not hugging to the purpose they see as best.
George Eliot (1819-1880, British Novelist)

70 There is only one failure in life possible, and that is not to be true to the best one knows.
George Eliot (1819-1880, British Novelist)

71 Failure after long perseverance is much grander than never to have a striving good enough to be called a failure.
George Eliot (1819-1880, British Novelist)

72 Sometimes the best gain is to lose.
George Herbert (1593-1632, British Metaphysical Poet)

73 I don't measure a man's success by how high he climbs but how high he bounces when he hits bottom.
George S. Patton (1885-1945, American Army General during World War II)

74 Ninety-nine percent of the failures come from people who have the habit of making excuses.
George Washington Carver (1864-1943, American Scientist)

75 A man's life is interesting primarily when he has failed -- I well know. For it's a sign that he tried to surpass himself.
Georges Clemenceau (1841-1929, French Statesman)

76 The greatest failure is a person who never admits that he can be a failure.
Gerald. N. Weiskott

77 Who has never tasted what is bitter does not know what is sweet.
German Proverb

78 Failure too is a form of death...
Graham Greene (1904-1991, British Novelist)

79 No failure in America, whether of love or money, is ever simple; it is always a kind of betrayal, of a mass of shadowy, shared hopes.
Greil Marcus (1945-, American Rock Journalist)

80 Failures are like skinned knees, painful but superficial.
H. Ross Perot (1930-, American Businessman & Politician, Founder EDS)

81 I have always felt that although someone may defeat me, and I strike out in a ball game, the pitcher on the particular day was the best player. But I know when I see him again, I'm going to be ready for his curve ball. Failure is a part of success. There is no such thing as a bed of roses all your life. But failure will never stand in the way of success if you learn from it.
Hank Aaron (Born 1934, American Baseball Player)

82 The only true failure lies in failure to start.
Harold Blake Walker

83 Men are born to succeed, not to fail.
Henry David Thoreau (1817-1862, American Essayist, Poet, Naturalist)

84 Failure is only the opportunity to begin again more intelligently.
Henry Ford (1863-1947, American Industrialist, Founder of Ford Motor Company)

85 The world itself is pregnant with failure, is the perfect manifestation of imperfection, of the consciousness of failure.
Henry Miller (1891-1980, American Author)

86 However things may seem, no evil thing is success and no good thing is failure.
Henry Wadsworth Longfellow (1819-1892, American Poet)

87 Not in the clamor of the crowded street, not in the shouts and plaudits of the throng, but in ourselves, are triumph and defeat.
Henry Wadsworth Longfellow (1819-1892, American Poet)

88 I cannot give the formula for success, but I can give you the formula of failure -- which is try to please everybody.
Herbert B. Swope (1882-1958, American Journalist)

89 Failure is only postponed success as long as courage "coaches" ambition. The habit of persistence is the habit of victory.
Herbert Kaufman

90 He who has never failed somewhere, that man can not be great.
Herman Melville (1819-1891, American Author)

91 The only people who never fail are those who never try.
Ilka Chase (1905-, American Author, Actor)

92 Why is it so painful to watch a person sink? Because there is something unnatural in it, for nature demands personal progress, evolution, and every backward step means wasted energy.
J. August Strindberg (1849-1912, Swedish Dramatist, Novelist, Poet)

93 You cannot explain failure any more than you can argue with success.
J. Richard Clarke

94 Some defeats are only installments to victory.
Jacob Riis

95 To begin to think with purpose, is to enter the ranks of those strong ones who only recognize failure as one of the pathways to attainment.
James Allen (1864-1912, British-born American Essayist, Author of "As a Man Thinketh")

96 There are few things more dreadful than dealing with a man who knows he is going under, in his own eyes, and in the eyes of others. Nothing can help that man. What is left of that man flees from what is left of human attention.
James Baldwin (1924-1987, American Author)

97 Failure comes only when we forget our ideals and objectives and principles.
Jawaharlal Nehru (1889-1964, Indian Nationalist, Statesman)

98 It takes a lot more energy to fail than to succeed, since it takes a lot of concentrated energy to hold on to beliefs that don't work.
Jerry Gillies (American Author, Speaker)

99 Failure is simply a few errors in judgment, repeated every day.
Jim Rohn (American Businessman, Author, Speaker, Philosopher)

100 Failure is not a single, cataclysmic event. You don't fail overnight. Instead, failure is a few errors in judgment, repeated every day.
Jim Rohn (American Businessman, Author, Speaker, Philosopher)

101 All honor to him who shall win the prize. The world has cried for a thousand years. But to him who tries and fails and dies, I give great honor and glory and tears.
Joaquin Miller (1839-1913, American Poet)

102 Failures are divided into two classes -- those who thought and never did, and those who did and never thought.
John Charles Salak

103 Failure is in a sense the highway to success, as each discovery of what is false leads us to seek earnestly after what is true.
John Keats (1795-1821, British Poet)

104 There is not a fiercer hell than the failure in a great object.
John Keats (1795-1821, British Poet)

105 I would sooner fail than not be among the greatest.
John Keats (1795-1821, British Poet)

106 We pay a heavy price for our fear of failure. It is a powerful obstacle to growth. It assures the progressive narrowing of the personality and prevents exploration and experimentation. There is no learning without some difficulty and fumbling. If you want to keep on learning, you must keep on risking failure all your life.
John W. Gardner (1912-, American Educator, Social Activist)

107 Failure is not fatal, but failure to change might be.
John Wooden (1910-, American Basketball Coach)

108 He was a self-made man who owed his lack of success to nobody.
Joseph Heller (1923-, American Author)

109 Not many people are willing to give failure a second opportunity. They fail once and it's all over. The bitter pill of failure is often more than most people can handle. If you're willing to accept failure and learn from it, if you're willing to consider failure as a blessing in disguise and bounce back, you've got the potential of harnessing one of the most powerful success forces.
Joseph Sugarman (American Businessman)

110 The typical human life seems to be quite unplanned, undirected, unlived, and unsavored. Only those who consciously think about the adventure of living as a matter of making choices among options, which they have found for themselves, ever establish real self-control and live their lives fully.
Karl Albrecht (American Management Consultant, Author)

111 When we can begin to take our failures seriously, it means we are ceasing to be afraid of them. It is of immense importance to learn to laugh at ourselves.
Katherine Mansfield (1888-1923, New Zealand-born British Author)

112 Nothing fails like success because we don't learn from it. We learn only from failure.
Kenneth Boulding

113 Show me a good and gracious loser and I'll show you a failure.
Knute Rockne (1888-1931, Norwegian-born American Football Coach)

114 Thought is born of failure.
Lancelot Law Whyte (1896-1972, Scottish Physicist)

115 People in their handlings of affairs often fail when they are about to succeed. If one remains as careful at the end as he was at the beginning, there will be no failure.
Lao-Tzu (600 BC, Chinese Philosopher, Founder of Taoism, Author of the "Tao Te Ching")

116 You must think of failure and defeat as the springboards to new achievements or to the next level of accomplishment.
Les Brown (1945-, American Speaker, Author, Trainer, Motivator Lecturer)

117 Never give a man up until he has failed at something he likes.
Lewis E. Lawes

118 The man who tries to do something and fails is infinitely better than he who tries to do nothing and succeeds.
Lloyd Jones

119 Honest error is to be pitied, not ridiculed.
Lord Chesterfield (1694-1773, British Statesman, Author)

120 Our failings sometimes bind us to one another as closely as could virtue itself.
Marquis De Vauvenargues (1715-1747, French Moralist)

121 Never walk away from failure. On the contrary, study it carefully and imaginatively for its hidden assets.
Michael Korda (1919-, American publisher)

122 You always pass failure on the way to success.
Mickey Rooney (American Actor)

123 My downfall raises me to infinite heights.
Napoleon Bonaparte (1769-1821, French General, Emperor)

124 When defeat comes, accept it as a signal that your plans are not sound, rebuild those plans, and set sail once more toward your coveted goal.
Napoleon Hill (1883-1970, American Speaker, Motivational Writer, "Think and Grow Rich")

125 Failure is nature's plan to prepare you for great responsibilities.
Napoleon Hill (1883-1970, American Speaker, Motivational Writer, "Think and Grow Rich")

126 No man is ever whipped until he quits in his own mind.
Napoleon Hill (1883-1970, American Speaker, Motivational Writer, "Think and Grow Rich")

127 Edison failed 10, 000 times before he made the electric light. Do not be discouraged if you fail a few times.
Napoleon Hill (1883-1970, American Speaker, Motivational Writer, "Think and Grow Rich")

128 Many a man never fails because he never tries.
Norman Macewan

129 Failure will never overtake me if my determination to succeed is strong enough.
Og Mandino (1923-1996, American Motivational Author, Speaker)

130 If all this happened to you what paradigm might you develop? How might that paradigm affect you in terms of your life from that point on? What does this tell you about Abe? There are no failures, only lessons to be learned.
Oprah Winfrey (1954-, American TV Personality, Producer, Actress, Author)

131 Think like a queen. A queen is not afraid to fail. Failure is another steppingstone to greatness.
Oprah Winfrey (1954-, American TV Personality, Producer, Actress, Author)

132 Many a man has finally succeeded only because he has failed after repeated efforts. If he had never met defeat he would never have known any great victory.
Orison Swett Marden (1850-1924, American Author, Founder of Success Magazine)

133 There is no failure for the man who realizes his power, who never knows when he is beaten; there is no failure for the determined endeavor; the unconquerable will. There is no failure for the man who gets up every time he falls, who rebounds like a rubber ball, who persists when everyone else gives up, who pushes on when everyone else turns back.
Orison Swett Marden (1850-1924, American Author, Founder of Success Magazine)

134 You cannot measure a man by his failures. You must know what use he makes of them. What did they mean to him. What did he get out of them.
Orison Swett Marden (1850-1924, American Author, Founder of Success Magazine)

135 Misfortunes one can endure -- they come from outside, they are accidents. But to suffer for one's own faults -- Ah! there is the sting of life.
Oscar Wilde (1856-1900, British Author, Wit)

136 The season of failure is the best time for sowing the seeds of success.
Paramahansa Yogananda (Spiritual Author, Lecturer)

137 To make no mistakes is not in the power of man; but from their errors and mistakes the wise and good learn wisdom for the future.
Plutarch (46-120 AD, Greek Essayist, Biographer)

138 When someone is going downhill everyone likes to give them a kick.
Proverb

139 The surest way to fail is not to determine to succeed.
Richard Brinsley Sheridan (1751-1816, Anglo-Irish Dramatist)

140 Only if you have been in the deepest valley, can you ever know how magnificent it is to be on the highest mountain.
Richard M. Nixon (1913-1994, Thirty-seventh President of the USA)

141 If you have tried to do something and failed, you are vastly better off than if you had tried to do nothing and succeeded. You must never regret what might have been. The past that did not happen is as hidden from us as the future we cannot see.
Richard Martin Stern

142 He only is exempt from failures who makes no efforts.
Richard Whately (1787-1863, British Prelate, Writer)

143 Failure is good. It's fertilizer. Everything I've learned about coaching, I've learned from making mistakes.
Rick Pitino (American College Basketball Coach)

144 Those who dare to fail miserably can achieve greatly.
Robert F. Kennedy (1925-1968, American Attorney General, Senator)

145 And nothing to look backward to with pride, and nothing to look forward to with hope.
Robert Frost (1875-1963, American Poet)

146 Failure doesn't mean you are a failure... it just means you haven't succeeded yet.
Robert H. Schuller (1926-, American Minister (Crystal Cathedral), Author, Social Leader)

147 If there exists no possibility of failure, then victory is meaningless.
Robert H. Schuller (1926-, American Minister (Crystal Cathedral), Author, Social Leader)

148 Turn your scars into stars
Robert H. Schuller (1926-, American Minister (Crystal Cathedral), Author, Social Leader)

149 Our business in this world is not to succeed, but to continue to fail, in good spirits.
Robert Louis Stevenson (1850-1895, Scottish Essayist, Poet, Novelist)

150 If you are doing your best, you will not have to worry about failure.
Robert S. Hillyer

151 The moment avoiding failure becomes your motivation, you're down the path of inactivity. You stumble only if you're moving.
Roberto Goizueta (American Business Executive, CEO of Coca-Cola Company)

152 You win only if you aren't afraid to lose.
Rocky Aoki

153 Notice the difference between what happens when a man says to himself, I have failed three times, and what happens when he says, I am a failure.
S. I. Hayakawa (1902-1992, Canadian Born American Senator, Educator)

154 Ever tried. Ever failed. No matter. Try Again. Fail again. Fail better.
Samuel Beckett (1906-1989, Irish Dramatist, Novelist)

155 We learn from failure much more than from success; we often discover what we will do by finding our what we will not do; and probably he who never made a mistake never made a discovery.
Samuel Smiles (1812-1904, Scottish Author)

156 It is a mistake to suppose that men succeed through success; they much oftener succeed through failures. Precept, study, advice, and example could never have taught them so well as failure has done.
Samuel Smiles (1812-1904, Scottish Author)

157 If thou art a man, admire those who attempt great things, even though they fail.
Seneca (4 BC-65 AD, Spanish-born Roman Statesman, philosopher)

158 The most important of my discoveries has been suggested to me by my failures.
Sir Humphrey Davy (1778-1829, British Chemist)

159 We are all failures -- at least, all the best of us are.
Sir James M. Barrie (1860-1937, British Playwright)

160 There is much to be said for failure. It is more interesting than success.
Sir Max Beerbohm (1872-1956, British Actor)

161 Success is 99 percent failure.
Soichiro Honda (Japanese Industrialist, Founder of Honda Motor Corporation)

162 I would prefer even to fail with honor than win by cheating.
Sophocles (495-406 BC, Greek Tragic Poet)

163 Do not brood over your past mistakes and failures as this will only fill your mind with grief, regret and depression. Do not repeat them in the future.
Sri Swami Sivananda (1887-, Indian Physician, Sage)

164 There is something good in all seeming failures. You are not to see that now. Time will reveal it. Be patient.
Sri Swami Sivananda (1887-, Indian Physician, Sage)

165 If you don't stand for something, you'll fall for anything.
Steve Bartkowski (American Football Player)

166 We must expect to fail... but fail in a learning posture, determined no to repeat the mistakes, and to maximize the benefits from what is learned in the process.
Ted W. Engstrom (American Religion and Social Leader)

167 It is hard to fail, but it is worse never to have tried to succeed. In this life we get nothing save by effort.
Theodore Roosevelt (1858-1919, Twenty-sixth President of the USA)

168 The boy who is going to make a great man must not make up his mind merely to overcome a thousand obstacles, but to win in spite of a thousand repulses and defeats.
Theodore Roosevelt (1858-1919, Twenty-sixth President of the USA)

169 I am not discouraged, because every wrong attempt discarded is another step forward.
Thomas A. Edison (1847-1931, American Inventor, Entrepreneur, Founder of GE)

170 Just because something doesn't do what you planned it to do doesn't mean it's useless.
Thomas A. Edison (1847-1931, American Inventor, Entrepreneur, Founder of GE)

171 I have not failed. I've just found 10, 000 ways that won't work.
Thomas A. Edison (1847-1931, American Inventor, Entrepreneur, Founder of GE)

172 They fail, and they alone, who have not striven.
Thomas B. Aldrich (1836-1907, American Writer, Editor)

173 Failures to heroic minds are the stepping stones to success.
Thomas C. Haliburton (1796-1865, Canadian Jurist, Author)

174 There is the greatest practical benefit in making a few failures early in life.
Thomas H. Huxley (1825-1895, British Biologist, Educator)

175 We stumble and fall constantly even when we are most enlightened. But when we are in true spiritual darkness, we do not even know that we have fallen.
Thomas Merton (1915-1968, American Religious Writer, Poet)

176 Accept failure as a normal part of living. View it as part of the process of exploring your world; make a note of its lessons and move on.
Tom Hobson

177 I never see failure as failure, but only as the game I must play and win.
Tom Hopkins (American Sales Trainer, Speaker, Author)

178 I am not judged by the number of times I fail, but by the number of times I succeed; and the number of times I succeed is in direct proportion to the number of times I can fail and keep on trying.
Tom Hopkins (American Sales Trainer, Speaker, Author)

179 Failure is not fatal; victory is not success.
Tony Richardson (1928-1991, British Stage and Film Director)

180 No matter how far you have gone on a wrong road, turn back.
Turkish Proverb

181 You may not realize it when it happens, but a kick in the teeth may be the best thing in the world for you.
Walt Disney (1901-1966, American Artist, Film Producer)

182 Failure is the tuition you pay for success.
Walter Brunell

183 If you're not big enough to lose, you're not big enough to win
Walter Reuther

184 What is defeat? Nothing but education. Nothing but the first step to something better.
Wendell Phillips (1811-1884, American Reformer, Orator)

185 The wise man realistically accepts as part of life and builds a philosophy to meet them and make the most of them. He lives on the principle of "nothing attempted, nothing gained" and is resolved that if he fails he is going to fail while trying to succeed.
Wilferd A. Peterson

186 Failure is an event, never a person.
William D. Brown

187 No man ever became great or good except through many and great mistakes.
William E. Gladstone (1809-1888, British Liberal Prime Minister, Statesman)

188 All of us failed to match our dreams of perfection. So I rate us on the basis of our splendid failure to do the impossible.
William Faulkner (1897-1962, American Novelist)

189 No man is a failure who is enjoying life.
William Feather (1888-18, American Writer, Businessman)

190 I am often confronted by the necessity of standing by one of my empirical selves and relinquishing the rest. Not that I would not. If I could, be... a great athlete and make a million a year, be a wit, a born -- vivant and a lady killer, as well as a philosopher, a philanthropist ... and saint. But the thing is simply impossible. The millionaire's work would run counter to the saint s; the bon- vivant and the philanthropist would trip each other up; the philosopher and the lady killer could not well keep house in the same tenement of clay. Such different characters may conceivably, at the outset of life. Be alike possible for a man. But to make any one of them actual, the rest must more of less be suppressed. So the seeker of his truest, strongest, deepest self must review the list carefully and pick out on which to stake his salvation. All other selves thereupon become unreal, but the fortunes of this self are real. Its failure are real failures, its triumphs real triumphs carrying shame and gladness with them.
William James (1842-1910, American Psychologist, Professor, Author)

191 Failure, then, failure! so the world stamps us at every turn. We strew it with our blunders, our misdeeds, our lost opportunities, with all the memorials of our inadequacy to our vocation. And with what a damning emphasis does it then blot us out! No easy fine, no mere apology or formal expiation, will satisfy the world's demands, but every pound of flesh exacted is soaked with all its blood. The subtlest forms of suffering known to man are connected with the poisonous humiliations incidental to these results.
William James (1842-1910, American Psychologist, Professor, Author)

192 There is but one cause of human failure. And that is man's lack of faith in his true Self.
William James (1842-1910, American Psychologist, Professor, Author)

193 He's no failure. He's not dead yet.
William Lloyd George

194 The only time you don't fail is the last time you try anything -- and it works.
William Strong

195 Every failure is a step to success.
William Whewell (1794-1866, British Scholar)

196 Failure is a detour, not a dead-end street.
Zig Ziglar (American Sales Trainer, Author, Motivational Speaker)

FAITH

1 Faith, as Paul saw it, was a living, flaming thing leading to surrender and obedience to the commandments of Christ.
A. W. Tozer (Deceased 1963, American Preacher)

2 Let us have faith that right makes might, and in that faith let us dare to do our duty as we understand it.
Abraham Lincoln (1809-1865, Sixteenth President of the USA)

3 A faith that hasn't been tested can't be trusted.
Adrian Rogers

4 To know what is impenetrable to us really exists, manifesting itself as the highest wisdom and the most radiant beauty... this knowledge, this feeling is at the center of true religiousness.
Albert Einstein (1879-1955, German-born American Physicist)

5 I was not born for courts and great affairs, but I pay my debts, believe and say my prayers.
Alexander Pope (1688-1744, British Poet, Critic, Translator)

6 In faith and hope the world will disagree, But all mankind's concern is charity.
Alexander The Great (352-323 BC, Alexander III, Ancient Macedonian King)

7 Despotism may govern without faith, but liberty cannot. How is it possible that society should escape destruction if the moral tie is not strengthened in proportion as the political tie is relaxed? And what can be done with a people who are their own masters if they are not submissive to the Deity?
Alexis De Tocqueville (1805-1859, French Social Philosopher)

8 Faith. Belief without evidence in what is told by one who speaks without knowledge, of things without parallel.
Ambrose Bierce (1842-1914, American Author, Editor, Journalist, "The Devil's Dictionary")

9 It could be that our faithlessness is a cowering cowardice born of our very smallness, a massive failure of imagination. If we were to judge nature by common sense or likelihood, we wouldn't believe the world existed. .
Annie Dillard (1945-, American Author, Poet)

10 It is only with the heart that one can see rightly; what is essential is invisible to the eye.
Antoine De Saint-Exupery (1900-1944, French Aviator, Writer)

11 Faith is trust in what the spirit learned eons ago.
B. H. Roberts

12 The way to see by Faith is to shut the Eye of Reason.
Benjamin Franklin (1706-1790, American Scientist, Publisher, Diplomat)

13 In the affairs of this world, men are saved not by faith, but by the want of it.
Benjamin Franklin (1706-1790, American Scientist, Publisher, Diplomat)

14 According to your faith; be it done unto you.
Bible (Sacred Scriptures of Christians and Judaism)

15 If thou canst believe, all things are possible to him that believeth. [Mark 9:23]
Bible (Sacred Scriptures of Christians and Judaism)

16 All things are possible to him who believes. [Mark 9:23]
Bible (Sacred Scriptures of Christians and Judaism)

17 For verily I say unto you, that whosoever shall say unto this mountain, Be thou removed, and be thou cast into the sea; and shall not doubt in his heart, but shall believe that those things which he saith shall come to pass; he shall have whatsoever he saith.
Bible (Sacred Scriptures of Christians and Judaism)

18 Cast thy bread upon the waters: for thou shall find it after many days.
Bible (Sacred Scriptures of Christians and Judaism)

19 For the invisible things of him from the creation of the world are clearly seen, being understood by the things that are made... [Romans 1:20]
Bible (Sacred Scriptures of Christians and Judaism)

20 Now faith is the assurance of things hoped for, the conviction of things not seen. [Hebrews 11:1]
Bible (Sacred Scriptures of Christians and Judaism)

21 And without faith it is impossible to please him, for he who comes to God must believe that he is, and that he is a rewarder of those who seek him. [Hebrews 11:6]
Bible (Sacred Scriptures of Christians and Judaism)

22 Faith is the substance of things hoped for, the evidence of things not seen. [Hebrews 11:1]
Bible (Sacred Scriptures of Christians and Judaism)

23 Be ready always to give an answer to every man that asketh you a reason of the hope that is in you. [Peter 3:15]
Bible (Sacred Scriptures of Christians and Judaism)

24 Faith is different from proof; the latter is human, the former is a Gift from God.
Blaise Pascal (1623-1662, French Scientist, Religious Philosopher)

25 It is the heart which perceives God and not the reason. That is what faith is: God perceived by the heart, not by the reason.
Blaise Pascal (1623-1662, French Scientist, Religious Philosopher)

26 Faith certainly tells us what the senses do not, but not the contrary of what they see; it is above, not against them.
Blaise Pascal (1623-1662, French Scientist, Religious Philosopher)

27 Faith embraces many truths which seem to contradict each other.
Blaise Pascal (1623-1662, French Scientist, Religious Philosopher)

28 A faith to live by, a self to live with, and a purpose to live for.
Bob Harrington (American Minister of "Chaplain of Bourbon Street")

29 The ablest men in all walks of modern life are men of faith. Most of them have much more faith than they themselves realize.
Bruce Barton (1886-1967, American Author, Advertising Executive)

30 No Christian has ever been known to recant on his death bed.
C. M. Ward

31 Faith... is the art of holding on to things your reason once accepted, despite your changing moods.
C. S. Lewis (1898-1963, British Academic, Writer, Christian Apologist)

32 It is as absurd to argue men, as to torture them, into believing.
Cardinal J. Newman (1801-1890, British Preacher)

33 Faith is the heroism of the intellect.
Charles H. Parkhurst (1842-1933, American Clergyman, Reformer)

34 Faith is building on what you know is here, so you can reach what you know is there.
Cullen Hightower

35 Philosophic argument, especially that drawn from the vastness of the universe, in comparison with the apparent insignificance of this globe, has sometimes shaken my reason for the faith that is in me; but my heart has always assured and reassured me that
Daniel Webster (1782-1852, American Lawyer, Statesman)

36 Faith is the refusal to panic.
David Martyn Lloyd-Jones (1899-1981, British Preacher, Writer)

37 What we wish, that we readily believe.
Demosthenes (383-322 BC, Greek Orator)

38 Do you know how to digest your food? Do you know how to fill your lungs with air? Do you know how to establish, regulate and direct the metabolism of your body -- the assimilation of foodstuff so that it builds muscles, bones and flesh? No, you don't know how consciously, but there is a wisdom within you that does know.
Donald Curtis

39 Faith makes all things possible... love makes all things easy.
Dwight L. Moody (1837-1899, American Evangelist)

40 It is a masterpiece of the devil to make us believe that children cannot understand religion. Would Christ have made a child the standard of faith if He had known that it was not capable of understanding His words?
Dwight L. Moody (1837-1899, American Evangelist)

41 Faith, to my mind, is a stiffening process, a sort of mental starch, which ought to be applied as sparingly as possible.
Edward M. Forster (1879-1970, British Novelist, Essayist)

42 When you get to the end of all the light you know and it's time to step into the darkness of the unknown, faith is knowing that one of two things shall happen: either you will be given something solid to stand on, or you will be taught how to fly.
Edward Teller (American Physicist and Author)

43 The thing that is incredible is life itself. Why should we be here in this sun-illuminated universe? Why should there be green earth under our feet?
Edwin Markham (1852-1940, American Poet and Editor)

44 The supernatural is the natural not yet understood.
Elbert Hubbard (1859-1915, American Author, Publisher)

45 If you desire faith, then you have faith enough.
Elizabeth Barrett Browning (1806-1861, British Poet)

46 Talk unbelief, and you will have unbelief; but talk faith, and you will have faith. According to the seed sown will be the harvest.
Ellen Gould White (1827-1915, American Seventh-day Adventist Leader)

47 Faith is not belief without proof, but trust without reservation.
Elton Trueblood

48 I see heaven's glories shine and faith shines equal...
Emily Bronte (1818-1848, British Novelist, Poet)

49 There is no such thing as a lack of faith. We all have plenty of faith, it's just that we have faith in the wrong things. We have faith in what can't be done rather than what can be done. We have faith in lack rather than abundance but there is no lack of faith. Faith is a law.
Eric Butterworth

50 Absolute faith corrupts as absolutely as absolute power.
Eric Hoffer (1902-1983, American Author, Philosopher)

51 Only the person who has faith in himself is able to be faithful to others.
Erich Fromm (1900-1980, American Psychologist)

52 Faith without works is like a bird without wings; though she may hop with her companions on earth, yet she will never fly with them to heaven.
Francis Beaumont (1584-1616, British Dramatist)

53 The only limit to our realization of tomorrow will be our doubts of today. Let us move forward with strong and active faith.
Franklin D. Roosevelt (1882-1945, Thirty-second President of the USA)

54 In actual life every great enterprise begins with and takes its first forward step in faith.
Friedrich Schlegel (1772-1829, German Philosopher, Critic, Writer)

55 We have not lost faith, but we have transferred it from God to the medical profession.
George Bernard Shaw (1856-1950, Irish-born British Dramatist)

56 The beginning of anxiety is the end of faith, and the beginning of true faith is the end of anxiety.
George E. Mueller (1918-, American Engineer)

57 In properly organized groups no faith is required; what is required is simply a little trust and even that only for a little while, for the sooner a man begins to verify all he hears the better it is for him.
George Gurdjieff (1873-1949, Russian Adept, Teacher, Writer)

58 The principal part of faith is patience.
George Macdonald (1824-1905, Scottish Novelist)

59 Faith is an excitement and an enthusiasm: it is a condition of intellectual magnificence to which we must cling as to a treasure, and not squander on our way through life in the small coin of empty words, or in exact and priggish argument.
George Sand (1804-1876, French Novelist)

60 Faith in the ability of a leader is of slight service unless it be united with faith in his justice.
George W. Goethals

61 Faith is not a thing which one "loses," we merely cease to shape our lives by it.
Georges Bernanos (1888-1948, French Novelist, Political Writer)

62 Every Age has its own peculiar faith. Any attempt to translate into facts the mission of one Age with the machinery of another, can only end in an indefinite series of abortive efforts. Defeated by the utter want of proportion between the means and the end, such attempts might produce martyrs, but never lead to victory.
Giuseppe Mazzini (1805-1872, Italian Patriot, Writer)

63 If you have abandoned one faith, do not abandon all faith. There is always an alternative to the faith we lose. Or is it the same faith under another mask?
Graham Greene (1904-1991, British Novelist)

64 Faith may be defined briefly as an illogical belief in the occurrence of the improbable.
H. L. Mencken (1880-1956, American Editor, Author, Critic, Humorist)

65 If faith produce no works, I see That faith is not a living tree. Thus faith and works together grow, No separate life they never can know. They're soul and body, hand and heart, What God hath joined, let no man part.
Hannah More (1745-1833, British Writer, Reformer, Philanthropist)

66 Faith is a higher faculty than reason.
Henry Christopher Bailey

67 In order to be a realist you must believe in miracles.
Henry Christopher Bailey

68 The smallest seed of faith is better than the largest fruit of happiness.
Henry David Thoreau (1817-1862, American Essayist, Poet, Naturalist)

69 Through want of enterprise and faith men are where they are, buying and selling and spending their lives like servants.
Henry David Thoreau (1817-1862, American Essayist, Poet, Naturalist)

70 The words which express our faith and piety are not definite; yet they are significant and fragrant like frankincense to superior natures.
Henry David Thoreau (1817-1862, American Essayist, Poet, Naturalist)

71 We must have infinite faith in each other. If we have not, we must never let it leak out that we have not.
Henry David Thoreau (1817-1862, American Essayist, Poet, Naturalist)

72 Back of every creation, supporting it like an arch, is faith. Enthusiasm is nothing: it comes and goes. But if one believes, then miracles occur.
Henry Miller (1891-1980, American Author)

73 Faith, like a jackal, feeds among the tombs, and even from these dead doubts she gathers her most vital hope.
Herman Melville (1819-1891, American Author)

74 A person consists of his faith. Whatever is his faith, even so is he.
Indian Proverb

75 All the strength and force of man comes from his faith in things unseen. He who believes is strong; he who doubts is weak. Strong convictions precede great actions.
James Freeman Clarke (1810-1888, American Minister, Theologian)

76 All things are inconstant except the faith in the soul, which changes all things and fills their inconstancy with light, but though I seem to be driven out of my country as a misbeliever I have found no man yet with a faith like mine.
James Joyce (1882-1941, Irish Author)

77 The only faith that wears well and holds its color in all weathers is that which is woven of conviction and set with the sharp mordant of experience.
James Russell Lowell (1819-1891, American Poet, Critic, Editor)

78 Base souls have no faith in great individuals.
Jean Jacques Rousseau (1712-1778, Swiss Political Philosopher, Educationist, Essayist)

79 You don't decide to build a church because you have money in the bank. You build because God says this is what I should do. Faith is the supplier of things hoped for and the evidence of things not seen.
Jim Bakker (1940-, American Evangelist)

80 Reason is our soul's left hand, faith her right, by these we reach divinity.
John Donne (1572-1632, British Metaphysical Poet)

81 As he that fears God hears nothing else, so, he that sees God sees every thing else.
John Donne (1572-1632, British Metaphysical Poet)

82 When faith is lost, when honor dies, the man is dead.
John Greenleaf Whittier (1807-1892, American Poet, Reformer, Author)

83 Attempt something so impossible that unless God is in it, it's doomed to failure.
John Haggai

84 Your faith is what you believe, not what you know.
John Lancaster Spalding

85 Faith is a reasoning trust, a trust which reckons thoughtfully and confidently upon the trustworthiness of God.
John R. Stott (1921-, British Anglican clergyman and writer)

86 Out of suffering comes the serious mind; out of salvation, the grateful heart; out of endurance, fortitude; out of deliverance faith.
John Ruskin (1819-1900, British Critic, Social Theorist)

87 Justifying faith implies, not only a divine evidence or conviction that "God was in Christ, reconciling the world unto Himself," but a sure trust and confidence that Christ died for my sins, that He loved me and gave Himself for me.
John Wesley (1703-1791, British Preacher, Founder of Methodism)

88 There are many things that are essential to arriving at true peace of mind, and one of the most important is faith, which cannot be acquired without prayer.
John Wooden (1910-, American Basketball Coach)

89 If there was no faith there would be no living in this world. We could not even eat hash with any safety.
Josh Billings (1815-1885, American Humorist, Lecturer)

90 Faith is an oasis in the heart which will never be reached by the caravan of thinking.
Kahlil Gibran (1883-1931, Lebanese Poet, Novelist)

91 Faith lives in honest doubt.
Lord Alfred Tennyson (1809-1892, British Poet)

92 It is useless to tell one not to reason but to believe --you might as well tell a man not to wake but sleep.
Lord Byron (1788-1824, British Poet)

93 I claim to be an average man of less than average ability. I have not the shadow of a doubt that any man or woman can achieve what I have, if he or she would make the same effort and cultivate the same hope and faith.
Mahatma Gandhi (1869-1948, Indian Political, Spiritual Leader)

94 Faith must be enforced by reason. When faith becomes blind it dies.
Mahatma Gandhi (1869-1948, Indian Political, Spiritual Leader)

95 Faith is not something to grasp, it is a state to grow into.
Mahatma Gandhi (1869-1948, Indian Political, Spiritual Leader)

96 Non-violence is the article of faith.
Mahatma Gandhi (1869-1948, Indian Political, Spiritual Leader)

97 That's the thing about faith. If you don't have it you can't understand it. And if you do, no explanation is necessary
Major Kira Nerys

98 Faith is believing what you know ain't so.
Mark Twain (1835-1910, American Humorist, Writer)

99 It was the schoolboy who said, "Faith is believing what you know ain't so."
Mark Twain (1835-1910, American Humorist, Writer)

100 Faith must trample under foot all reason, sense, and understanding.
Martin Luther (1483-1546, German Leader of the Protestant Reformation)

101 Faith is a living, daring confidence in God's grace, so sure and certain that a man could stake his life on it a thousand times.
Martin Luther (1483-1546, German Leader of the Protestant Reformation)

102 You should not believe your conscience and your feelings more than the word which the Lord who receives sinners preaches to you.
Martin Luther (1483-1546, German Leader of the Protestant Reformation)

103 Reason is the enemy of faith.
Martin Luther (1483-1546, German Leader of the Protestant Reformation)

104 Be a sinner and sin strongly, but more strongly have faith and rejoice in Christ.
Martin Luther (1483-1546, German Leader of the Protestant Reformation)

105 Faith moves mountains, but you have to keep pushing while you are praying.
Mason Cooley

106 At the beginning of every act of faith, there is often a seed of fear. For great acts of faith are seldom born out of calm calculation.
Max L. Lucado (American Author of "The Eye of the Storm")

107 It's faith in something and enthusiasm for something that makes life worth living.
Oliver Wendell Holmes (1809-1894, American Author, Wit, Poet)

108 The greatest act of faith is when a man understands he is not God.
Oliver Wendell Holmes (1809-1894, American Author, Wit, Poet)

109 My faith is the grand drama of my life. I'm a believer, so I sing words of God to those who have no faith. I give bird songs to those who dwell in cities and have never heard them, make rhythms for those who know only military marches or jazz, and paint colors for those who see none.
Olivier Messiaen (1908-1992, French Composer, Organist)

110 I can believe anything provided it is incredible.
Oscar Wilde (1856-1900, British Author, Wit)

111 Faith is deliberate confidence in the character of God whose ways you may not understand at the time.
Oswald Chambers (1874-1917 Scottish Preacher, Author)

112 I feel no need for any other faith than my faith in the kindness of human beings. I am so absorbed in the wonder of earth and the life upon it that I cannot think of heaven and angels.
Pearl S. Buck (1892-1973, American Novelist)

113 We are twice armed if we fight with faith.
Plato (427-347 BC, Greek Philosopher)

114 Weave in faith and God will find the thread.
Proverb

115 Faith is much better than belief. Belief is when someone else does the thinking.
R. Buckminster Fuller (1895-1983, American Inventor, Designer, Poet, Philosopher)

116 Some things have to be believed to be seen.
Ralph Hodgson (1871-1962, British Poet)

117 All that I have seen teaches me to trust the Creator for all I have not seen.
Ralph Waldo Emerson (1803-1882, American Poet, Essayist)

118 The faith that stands on authority is not faith.
Ralph Waldo Emerson (1803-1882, American Poet, Essayist)

119 Our faith comes in moments... yet there is a depth in those brief moments which constrains us to ascribe more reality to them than to all other experiences.
Ralph Waldo Emerson (1803-1882, American Poet, Essayist)

120 The course of everything goes to teach us faith.
Ralph Waldo Emerson (1803-1882, American Poet, Essayist)

121 God does not require you to follow His leadings on blind trust. Behold the evidence of an invisible intelligence pervading everything, even your own mind and body.
Raymond Holliwell

122 Life is a battle between faith and reason in which each feeds upon the other, drawing sustenance from it and destroying it.
Reinhold Niebuhr (1892-1971, American Theologian, Historian)

123 The amplest knowledge has the largest faith. Ignorance is always incredulous.
Robert Eldridge Willmott

124 I always prefer to believe the best of everybody -- it saves so much trouble.
Rudyard Kipling (1865-1936, British Author of Prose, Verse)

125 There is no great future for any people whose faith has burned out.
Rufus M. Jones

126 Our faith in the present dies out long before our faith in the future.
Ruth Benedict (1887-1948, American Anthropologist)

127 Faith has to do with things that are not seen, and hope with things that are not in hand.
Saint Thomas Acquinas (1225-1274, Philosopher, Theologian, Doctor of the Church (Angelicus Doctor))

128 What is faith but a kind of betting or speculation after all? It should be, "I bet that my Redeemer liveth."
Samuel Butler (1612-1680, British Poet, Satirist)

129 You can do very little with faith, but you can do nothing without it.
Samuel Butler (1612-1680, British Poet, Satirist)

130 Eternal life does not begin with death; it begins with faith.
Samuel M. Shoemaker

131 My faith has no bed to sleep upon but omnipotence.
Samuel Rutherford (1600-1661, Scottish Pastor)

132 Faith is not contrary to reason...
Sherwood Eddy

133 The mysteries of faith are degraded if they are made into an object of affirmation and negation, when in reality they should be an object of contemplation.
Simone Weil (1910-1943, French Philosopher, Mystic)

134 Our duty is to believe that for which we have sufficient evidence, and to suspend our judgment when we have not.
Sir John Lubbock (1834-1913, British Statesman, Banker, Naturalist)

135 To believe only possibilities is not faith, but mere philosophy.
Sir Thomas Browne (1605-1682, British Author, Physician,, Philosopher)

136 Getting ahead in a difficult profession requires avid faith in yourself. You must be able to sustain yourself against staggering blows. There is no code of conduct to help beginners. That is why some people with mediocre talent, but with great inner drive, go much further than people with vastly superior talent.
Sophia Loren (1934-, Italian Film Actress)

137 Faith is the highest passion in a human being. Many in every generation may not come that far, but none comes further.
Soren Kierkegaard (1813-1855, Danish Philosopher, Writer)

138 Faith is to believe what we do not see; and the reward of this faith is to see what we believe.
St. Augustine (354-430, Numidian-born Bishop of Hippo, Theologian)

139 I believe though I do not comprehend, and I hold by faith what I cannot grasp with the mind.
St. Bernard (1090-1153, French Theologian and Reformer)

140 It is always right that a man should be able to render a reason for the faith that is within him.
Sydney Smith (1771-1845, British Writer, Clergyman)

141 To us also, through every star, through every blade of grass, is not God made visible if we will open our minds and our eyes.
Thomas Carlyle (1795-1881, Scottish Philosopher, Author)

142 The errors of faith are better than the best thoughts of unbelief.
Thomas Russell

143 Science has sometimes been said to be opposed to faith, and inconsistent with it. But all science, in fact, rests on a basis of faith, for it assumes the permanence and uniformity of natural laws -- a thing which can never be demonstrated.
Tryon Edwards (1809-1894, American Theologian)

144 The farther we go, the more the ultimate explanation recedes from us, and all we have left is faith.
Vaclav Hlavaty

145 Just as a small fire is extinguished by the storm whereas a large fire is enhanced by it-likewise a weak faith is weakened by predicament and catastrophes whereas a strong faith is strengthened by them.
Viktor E. Frankl (1905-, Austrian Psychiatrist, Neurology, Writer, "Man's Search for Meaning")

146 It's easy to have faith in yourself and have discipline when you're a winner, when you're number one. What you've got to have is faith and discipline when you're not yet a winner.
Vince Lombardi (1913-1970, American Football Coach)

147 May it not be that, just as we have to have faith in Him, God has to have faith in us and, considering the history of the human race so far, may it not be that "faith" is even more difficult for Him than it is for us?
W. H. Auden (1907-1973, Anglo-American Poet)

148 Faith is a continuation of reason.
William Adams (American Businessman)

149 Faith is love taking the form of aspiration.
William Ellery Channing (1780-1842, American Unitarian Minister, Author)

150 If you think you can win, you can win. Faith is necessary to victory.
William Hazlitt (1778-1830, British Essayist)

151 It is wrong always, everywhere, and for everyone, to believe anything upon insufficient evidence.
William James (1842-1910, American Psychologist, Professor, Author)

152 Our faith is faith in someone else's faith, and in the greatest matters this is most the case.
William James (1842-1910, American Psychologist, Professor, Author)

153 Faith means belief in something concerning which doubt is theoretically possible.
William James (1842-1910, American Psychologist, Professor, Author)

154 It is faith among men that holds the moral elements of society together, as it is faith in God that binds the world to his throne.
William M. Evarts (1818-1901, American Lawyer, Statesman)

155 'Tis not the dying for a faith that's so hard... 'Tis the living up to it that's difficult.
William M. Thackeray (1811-1863, Indian-born British Novelist)

156 It's not dying for faith that's so hard, it's living up to it.
William M. Thackeray (1811-1863, Indian-born British Novelist)

157 As the essence of courage is to stake one's life on a possibility, so the essence of faith is to believe that the possibility exists.
William Salter

158 Faith builds the bridge from this old world to the new.
Young

FAITHFULNESS

1 Some people say Liz and I are whores, but we are saints. We do not hide our loves hypocritically, and when in love, we are loyal and faithful to our men. [On the subject of her multiple marriages]
Ava Gardner (1922-1990, American Actress)

2 It is better to be unfaithful than faithful without wanting to be.
Brigitte Bardot (1934-, French Film Actress)

3 We must do our business faithfully, without trouble or disquiet, recalling our mind to God mildly, and with tranquility, as often as we find it wandering from him.
Brother Lawrence (17th Century Mystic of the Catholic Persuasion)

4 Faithfulness and sincerity are the highest things.
Confucius (551-479 BC, Chinese Ethical Teacher, Philosopher)

5 By faithfulness we are collected and wound up into unity within ourselves, whereas we had been scattered abroad in multiplicity.
St. Augustine (354-430, Numidian-born Bishop of Hippo, Theologian)

FALLIBILITY

1 In the stress of modern life, how little room is left for that most comfortable vanity that whispers in our ears that failures are not faults! Now we are taught from infancy that we must rise or fall upon our own merits; that vigilance wins success, and incapacity means ruin.
Agnes Repplier (1858-1950, American Author, Social Critic)

2 We all carry within us our places of exile, our crimes, and our ravages. But our task is not to unleash them on the world; it is to fight them in ourselves and in others.
Albert Camus (1913-1960, French Existential Writer)

3 If I have any justification for having lived it's simply, I'm nothing but faults, failures and so on, but I have tried to make a good pair of shoes. There's some value in that.
Arthur Miller (1915-, American Dramatist)

4 Both men and women are fallible. The difference is, women know it.
Eleanor Bron (British Actress)

5 The first faults are theirs that commit them, the second theirs that permit them.
English Proverb

6 It says nothing against the ripeness of a spirit that it has a few worms.
Friedrich Nietzsche (1844-1900, German Philosopher)

7 Once we know our weaknesses they cease to do us any harm.
Georg C. Lichtenberg (1742-1799, German Physicist, Satirist)

8 It is in our faults and failings, not in our virtues, that we touch each other, and find sympathy. It is in our follies that we are one.
Jerome K. Jerome (1859-1927, British Humorous Writer, Novelist, Playwright)

9 The organizations of men, like men themselves, seem subject to deafness, near-sightedness, lameness, and involuntary cruelty. We seem tragically unable to help one another, to understand one another.
John Cheever (1912-1982, American Author)

10 In the works of man, everything is as poor as its author; vision is confined, means are limited, scope is restricted, movements are labored, and results are humdrum.
Joseph De Maistre (1753-1821, French Diplomat, Philosopher)

11 It wounds a man less to confess that he has failed in any pursuit through idleness, neglect, the love of pleasure, etc., etc., which are his own faults, than through incapacity and unfitness, which are the faults of his nature.
Lord Melbourne (1779-1848, British Statesman, Prime Minister)

12 Fear of error which everything recalls to me at every moment of the flight of my ideas, this mania for control, makes men prefer reason's imagination to the imagination of the senses. And yet it is always the imagination alone which is at work.
Louis Aragon (1897-1982, French Poet)

FAME

1 It's too bad I'm not as wonderful a person as people say I am, because the world could use a few people like that.
Alan Alda (1936-, American Actor)

2 Those who have known the famous are publicly debriefed of their memories, knowing as their own dusk falls that they will only be remembered for remembering someone else.
Alan Bennett (1934-, British Playwright)

3 I'm afraid of losing my obscurity. Genuineness only thrives in the dark. Like celery.
Aldous Huxley (1894-1963, British Author)

4 What's fame? a fancy'd life in other's breath. A thing beyond us, even before our death.
Alexander Pope (1688-1744, British Poet, Critic, Translator)

5 How great are the dangers I face to win a good name in Athens.
Alexander The Great (352-323 BC, Alexander III, Ancient Macedonian King)

6 The day will come when everyone will be famous for fifteen minutes.
Andy Warhol (1930-, American Artist, Filmmaker)

7 Oblivion is the rule and fame the exception, of humanity.
Antoine Rivarol (1753-1801, French Journalist, Epigrammatist)

8 The longer a man's fame is likely to last, the longer it will be in coming.
Arthur Schopenhauer (1788-1860, German Philosopher)

9 Fame is something that must be won. Honor is something that must not be lost.
Arthur Schopenhauer (1788-1860, German Philosopher)

10 I was the only one there I never heard of.
Barry J. Farber (American Trainer, Speaker, Author)

11 Fame has also this great drawback, that if we pursue it, we must direct our lives so as to please the fancy of men.
Baruch (Benedict de) Spinoza (1632-1677, Dutch Philosopher and Theologian)

12 Fame and power are the objects of all men. Even their partial fruition is gained by very few; and that, too, at the expense of social pleasure, health, conscience, life.
Benjamin Disraeli (1804-1881, British Statesman, Prime Minister)

13 There have been as great souls unknown to fame as any of the most famous.
Benjamin Franklin (1706-1790, American Scientist, Publisher, Diplomat)

14 If you would not be forgotten as soon as you are dead, either write things worth reading or do things worth writing.
Benjamin Franklin (1706-1790, American Scientist, Publisher, Diplomat)

15 We movie stars all end up by ourselves. Who knows? Maybe we want to.
Bette Davis (1908-1989, American Actress, Producer)

16 Even those who write against fame wish for the fame of having written well, and those who read their works desire the fame of having read them.
Blaise Pascal (1623-1662, French Scientist, Religious Philosopher)

17 The charm of fame is so great that we like every object to which it is attached, even death.
Blaise Pascal (1623-1662, French Scientist, Religious Philosopher)

18 Heartthrobs are a dime a dozen.
Brad Pitt (1963-, American Actor)

19 The professional celebrity, male and female, is the crowning result of the star system of a society that makes a fetish of competition. In America, this system is carried to the point where a man who can knock a small white ball into a series of holes in the ground with more efficiency than anyone else thereby gains social access to the President of the United States.
C. Wright Mills (1916-1962, American Sociologist)

20 In the world of the celebrity, the hierarchy of publicity has replaced the hierarchy of descent and even of great wealth.
C. Wright Mills (1916-1962, American Sociologist)

21 I would much rather have men ask why I have no statue than why I have one.
Cato The Elder (234-149 BC, Roman Statesman, Orator)

22 After I'm dead I'd rather have people ask why I have no monument than why I have one.
Cato The Elder (234-149 BC, Roman Statesman, Orator)

23 It is better to be a has-been than a never-was.
Cecil Parkinson (1932-, British Conservative Politician)

24 Of present fame think little, and of future less; the praises that we receive after we are buried, like the flowers that are strewed over our grave, may be gratifying to the living, but they are nothing to the dead.
Charles Caleb Colton (1780-1832, British Sportsman Writer)

25 Riches: A dream in the night. Fame: A gull floating on water.
Chinese Proverb

26 Acquaintance lessens fame.
Claudius (10 BC-54 AD, Roman Emperor)

27 I am not concerned that I am not known, I seek to be worthy to be known.
Confucius (551-479 BC, Chinese Ethical Teacher, Philosopher)

28 Because I have conducted my own operas and love sheep-dogs; because I generally dress in tweeds, and sometimes, at winter afternoon concerts, have even conducted in them; because I was a militant suffragette and seized a chance of beating time to "The March of the Women" from the window of my cell in Holloway Prison with a tooth-brush; because I have written books, spoken speeches, broadcast, and don't always make sure that my hat is on straight; for these and other equally pertinent reasons, in a certain sense I am well known.
Dame Ethel Smyth (1858-1944, British Composer, Feminist)

29 Celebrity-worship and hero-worship should not be confused. Yet we confuse them every day, and by doing so we come dangerously close to depriving ourselves of all real models. We lose sight of the men and women who do not simply seem great because they are famous but are famous because they are great. We come closer and closer to degrading all fame into notoriety.
Daniel J. Boorstin (1914-, American Historian)

30 A sign of celebrity is often that their name is worth more than their services.
Daniel J. Boorstin (1914-, American Historian)

31 Worldly fame is but a breath of wind that blows now this way, and now that, and changes name as it changes direction.
Dante (Alighieri) (1265-1321, Italian Philosopher, Poet)

32 Fame is like a shaved pig with a greased tail, and it is only after it has slipped through the hands of some thousands, that some fellow, by mere chance, holds on to it!
Davy Crockett (1786-1836, American Backwoodsman)

33 What is popularly called fame is nothing but an empty name and a legacy from paganism.
Desiderius Erasmus (1466-1536, Dutch Humanist)

34 Once you become famous, there is nothing left to become but infamous.
Don Johnson (1949-, American Actor, Director, Producer, Singer)

35 Some people obtain fame, others deserve it.
Doris Lessing (1919-, British Novelist)

36 To want fame is to prefer dying scorned than forgotten.
E. M. Cioran (1911-, Rumanian-born French Philosopher)

37 Passion for fame: A passion which is the instinct of all great souls.
Edmund Burke (1729-1797, British Political Writer, Statesman)

38 I must say, I don't feel very qualified to be a pop star. I feel very awkward at times in the role.
Edward De Bono (Born 1933, Maltan-Born American Psychologist and Writer)

39 People should realize we're jerks just like them.
Edward De Bono (Born 1933, Maltan-Born American Psychologist and Writer)

40 Happy is the man who hath never known what it is to taste of fame --to have it is a purgatory, to want it is a Hell!
Edward G. Bulwer-Lytton (1803-1873, British Novelist, Poet)

41 Fame is a fickle food upon a shifting plate.
Emily Dickinson (1830-1886, American Poet)

42 'Tis the white stag, Fame, we're a-hunting, bid the world's hounds come to horn!
Ezra Pound (1885-1972, American Poet, Critic)

43 Good fame is like fire; when you have kindled you may easily preserve it; but if you extinguish it, you will not easily kindle it again.
Francis Bacon (1561-1626, British Philosopher, Essayist, Statesman)

44 Fame is like a river, that beareth up things light and swollen, and drowns things weighty and solid.
Francis Bacon (1561-1626, British Philosopher, Essayist, Statesman)

45 The fame of great men ought to be judged always by the means they used to acquire it.
François de La Rochefoucauld (1613-1680, French classical writer)

46 A celebrity is a person who works hard all of their life to become well known, and then wears dark glasses to avoid being recognized.
Fred A. Allen (1894-1957, American Radio Comic)

47 Few people rise to our esteem upon closer scrutiny.
French Proverb

48 The highest form of vanity is love of fame.
George Santayana (1863-1952, American Philosopher, Poet)

49 Men's fame is like their hair, which grows after they are dead, and with just as little use to them.
George Villiers (1628-1687, British Wit, Poet,, Statesman, Duke of Buckingham)

50 When you can do the common things in life in a uncommon way, you will command the attention of the world.
George Washington Carver (1864-1943, American Scientist)

51 The present condition of fame is merely fashion.
Gilbert K. Chesterton (1874-1936, British Author)

52 The fame you earn has a different taste from the fame that is forced upon you.
Gloria Vanderbilt

53 A celebrity is one who is known to many persons he is glad he doesn't know.
H. L. Mencken (1880-1956, American Editor, Author, Critic, Humorist)

54 Even the best things are not equal to their fame.
Henry David Thoreau (1817-1862, American Essayist, Poet, Naturalist)

55 Fame is an illusive thing -- here today, gone tomorrow. The fickle, shallow mob raises its heroes to the pinnacle of approval today and hurls them into oblivion tomorrow at the slightest whim; cheers today, hisses tomorrow; utter forgetfulness in a few months.
Henry Miller (1891-1980, American Author)

56 Fame comes only when deserved, and then is as inevitable as destiny, for it is destiny.
Henry Wadsworth Longfellow (1819-1892, American Poet)

57 Lives of great men all remind us we can make our lives sublime. And, departing, leave behind us footprints on the sands of time.
Henry Wadsworth Longfellow (1819-1892, American Poet)

58 How vain, without the merit, is the name.
Homer (850 BC, Greek Epic Poet)

59 Throughout my life, I have seen narrow-shouldered men, without a single exception, committing innumerable stupid acts, brutalizing their fellows and perverting souls by all means. They call the motive for their actions fame.
Isidore Ducasse Lautreamont (1846-1870, French Author, Poet)

60 A star on a movie set is like a time bomb. That bomb has got to be defused so people can approach it without fear.
Jack Nicholson (1937-, American Actor, Director, Producer, Screenwriter)

61 There is not in the world so toilsome a trade as the pursuit of fame; life concludes before you have so much as sketched your work.
Jean De La Bruyere (1645-1696, French Writer)

62 Fame is but the breath of people, and that often unwholesome.
Jean Jacques Rousseau (1712-1778, Swiss Political Philosopher, Educationist, Essayist)

63 Renown? I've already got more of it than those I respect, and will never have as much as those for whom I feel contempt..
Jean Rostand (1894-1977, French Biologist, Writer)

64 Of all the possessions of this life fame is the noblest; when the body has sunk into the dust the great name still lives.
Johann Friedrich Von Schiller (1759-1805, German Dramatist, Poet, Historian)

65 What life half gives a man, posterity gives entirely.
Johann Wolfgang Von Goethe (1749-1832, German Poet, Dramatist, Novelist)

66 If you modestly enjoy your fame you are not unworthy to rank with the holy.
Johann Wolfgang Von Goethe (1749-1832, German Poet, Dramatist, Novelist)

67 Wood burns because it has the proper stuff in it; and a man becomes famous because he has the proper stuff in him.
Johann Wolfgang Von Goethe (1749-1832, German Poet, Dramatist, Novelist)

68 Popular applause veers with the wind.
John Bright (1811-1889, Radical British Statesman, Orator)

69 Who would wish to be among the commonplace crowd of the little famous -- who are each individually lost in a throng made up of themselves?
John Keats (1795-1821, British Poet)

70 Fame is no plant that grows on mortal soil.
John Milton (1608-1674, British Poet)

71 Not to know me argues yourselves unknown.
John Milton (1608-1674, British Poet)

72 Celebrity is a mask that eats into the face. As soon as one is aware of being "somebody," to be watched and listened to with extra interest, input ceases, and the performer goes blind and deaf in his over-animation. One can either see or be seen.
John Updike (1932-, American Novelist, Critic)

73 What desire for fame attends both great and small; better be damned than mentioned not at all!
John Wolcot

74 If I'm such a legend, then why am I so lonely? Let me tell you, legends are all very well if you've got somebody around who loves you.
Judy Garland (1922-1969, American Actress, Singer)

75 There has never been a statue erected to the memory of someone who let well enough alone.
Jules Ellinger

76 Fame is a constant effort
Jules Renard (1864-1910, French Author, Dramatist)

77 It is a wretched thing to live on the fame of others.
Juvenal (Decimus Junius Juvenalis) (55-130, Roman Satirical Poet)

78 What is fame? The advantage of being known by people of whom you yourself know nothing, and for whom you care as little.
Leszczynski Stanislaus (1677-1766, Polish King)

79 It is a mark of many famous people that they cannot part with their brightest hour.
Lillian Hellman (1905-1984, American Playwright)

80 Fame is the thirst of youth.
Lord Byron (1788-1824, British Poet)

81 Folly loves the martyrdom of fame.
Lord Byron (1788-1824, British Poet)

82 My great comfort is, that the temporary celebrity I have wrung from the world has been in the very teeth of all opinions and prejudices. I have flattered no ruling powers; I have never concealed a single thought that tempted me.
Lord Byron (1788-1824, British Poet)

83 I awoke one morning and found myself famous.
Lord Byron (1788-1824, British Poet)

84 I want to be famous everywhere.
Luciano Pavarotti (1935-, Italian Musician, Opera singer)

85 To many fame comes too late.
Luis De Camoens (1524-1580, Portuguese Poet)

86 I won't be happy till I'm as famous as God.
Madonna (1958-, American Musician, Singer, Actress,)

87 True glory takes root, and even spreads; all false pretences, like flowers, fall to the ground; nor can any counterfeit last long.
Marcus T. Cicero (106-43 BC, Great Roman Orator, Politician)

88 Glory follows virtue as if it were its shadow.
Marcus T. Cicero (106-43 BC, Great Roman Orator, Politician)

89 I do not like the man who squanders life for fame; give me the man who living makes a name.
Marcus Valerius Martial (40-104, Latin poet and epigrammatist)

90 If fame is to come only after death, I am in no hurry for it.
Marcus Valerius Martial (40-104, Latin poet and epigrammatist)

91 A sex symbol becomes a thing. I hate being a thing.
Marilyn Monroe (1926-, American Actress)

92 Fame will go by and, so long, I've had you, fame. If it goes by, I've always known it was fickle. So at least it's something I experienced, but that's not where I live.
Marilyn Monroe (1926-, American Actress)

93 The majority of pop stars are complete idiots in every respect.
Marquis De Sade (1740-1814, French Author)

94 All the fame you should look for in life is to have lived it quietly.
Michel Eyquem De Montaigne (1533-1592, French Philosopher, Essayist)

95 I had it all and blew it.
Mickey Mantle (1931-1995, American Baseball Player)

96 If you are ambitious of climbing up to the difficult, and in a manner inaccessible, summit of the Temple of Fame, your surest way is to leave on one hand the narrow path of Poetry, and follow the narrower track of Knight-Errantry, which in a trice may raise you to an imperial throne.
Miguel De Cervantes (1547-1616, Spanish Novelist, Dramatist, Poet)

97 A legend is an old man with a cane known for what he used to do. I'm still doing it.
Miles Davis (1926-1991, American Jazz Musician)

98 It often happens that those of whom we speak least on earth are best known in heaven.
Nicolas Caussin

99 Fame usually comes to those who are thinking about something else.
Oliver Wendell Holmes (1809-1894, American Author, Wit, Poet)

100 The love of glory gives an immense stimulus.
Ovid (43 BC-18 AD, Roman Poet)

101 Now there is fame! Of all -- hunger, misery, the incomprehension by the public -- fame is by far the worst. It is the castigation of God by the artist. It is sad. It is true.
Pablo Picasso (1881-1973, Spanish Artist)

102 To become a celebrity is to become a brand name. There is Ivory Soap, Rice Krispies, and Philip Roth. Ivory is the soap that floats; Rice Krispies the breakfast cereal that goes snap-crackle- pop; Philip Roth the Jew who masturbates with a piece of liver.
Philip Roth (1933-, American Novelist)

103 True glory consists in doing what deserves to be written; in writing what deserves to be read; and in so living as to make the world happier and better for our living in it.
Pliny The Elder (23-79, Roman Neophatonist)

104 The love of fame is the last weakness which even the wise resign.
Publius Cornelius Tacitus (55-117 AD, Roman Historian)

105 Fame is proof that the people are gullible.
Ralph Waldo Emerson (1803-1882, American Poet, Essayist)

106 Being a sex symbol was rather like being a convict.
Raquel Welch (1940-, American Actress)

107 To get a name can happen but to few; it is one of the few things that cannot be brought. It is the free gift of mankind, which must be deserved before it will be granted, and is at last unwillingly bestowed.
Samuel Johnson (1709-1784, British Author)

108 He that pursues fame with just claims, trusts his happiness to the winds; but he that endeavors after it by false merit, has to fear, not only the violence of the storm, but the leaks of his vessel.
Samuel Johnson (1709-1784, British Author)

109 Celebrity is the advantage of being known to people who we don't know, and who don't know us.
Sebastien-Roch Nicolas De Chamfort (1741-1794, French Writer, Journalist, Playwright)

110 But the iniquity of oblivion blindly scattereth her poppy, and deals with the memory of men without distinction to merit of perpetuity.
Sir Thomas Browne (1605-1682, British Author, Physician,, Philosopher)

111 Fame is the perfume of heroic deeds.
Socrates (469-399 BC, Greek Philosopher of Athens)

112 The love of the famous, like all strong passions, is quite abstract. Its intensity can be measured mathematically, and it is independent of persons.
Susan Sontag (1933-, American Essayist)

113 Sometimes I wish I weren't famous.
Tammy Wynette (1942-, American Musician, Singer)

114 Fame, we may understand, is no sure test of merit, but only a probability of such; it is an accident, not a property of man.
Thomas Carlyle (1795-1881, Scottish Philosopher, Author)

115 Fame is the echo of actions, resounding them to the world, save that the echo repeats only the last art, but fame relates all, and often more than all.
Thomas Fuller (1608-1661, British Clergyman, Author)

116 We always hear about the haves and the have-nots. Why don't we hear about the doers and the do-nots.
Thomas Sewell

117 Fame is only good for one thing-they will cash your check in a small town.
Truman Capote (1942-, American Author)

118 Being famous was extremely disappointing for me. When I became famous it was a complete drag and it is still a complete drag.
Van Morrison (1945-, British-born American Singer, Songwriter, Musician)

119 Fame always brings loneliness. Success is as ice cold and lonely as the North Pole.
Vicki Baum (1888-1960, American Writer)

120 Let us not disdain glory too much; nothing is finer, except virtue. The height of happiness would be to unite both in this life.
Vicomte De Chateaubriand (1768-1848, French Politician, Writer)

121 Each man has his appointed day: short and irreparable in the brief life of all, but to extend our fame by our deeds, this is the work of mankind.
Virgil (70-19 BC, Roman Poet)

122 Fame hides her head among the clouds.
Virgil (70-19 BC, Roman Poet)

123 May the countryside and the gliding valley streams content me. Lost to fame, let me love river and woodland.
Virgil Publius Vergilius Maro

124 It is a short walk from the hallelujah to the hoot.
Vladimir Nabokov (1899-1977, Russian-born American Novelist, Poet)

125 What a heavy burden is a name that has become famous too soon.
Voltaire (1694-1778, French Historian, Writer)

126 Fame often makes a writer vain, but seldom makes him proud.
W. H. Auden (1907-1973, Anglo-American Poet)

127 It is dangerous to let the public behind the scenes. They are easily disillusioned and then they are angry with you, for it was the illusion they loved.
W. Somerset Maugham (1874-1965, British Novelist, Playwright)

128 The strongest poison ever known came from Caesar's laurel crown.
William Blake (1757-1827, British Poet, Painter)

129 There are names written in her immortal scroll at which Fame blushes!
William Hazlitt (1778-1830, British Essayist)

130 Fame is the inheritance not of the dead, but of the living. It is we who look back with lofty pride to the great names of antiquity.
William Hazlitt (1778-1830, British Essayist)

131 The love of fame is almost another name for the love of excellence; or it is the ambition to attain the highest excellence, sanctioned by the highest authority, that of time.
William Hazlitt (1778-1830, British Essayist)

132 Glory is like a circle in the water, which never ceaseth to enlarge itself, till, by broad spreading, it disperse to naught.
William Shakespeare (1564-1616, British Poet, Playwright, Actor)

133 Celebrity is never more admired than by the negligent.
William Shakespeare (1564-1616, British Poet, Playwright, Actor)

134 Death makes no conquest of this conqueror: For now he lives in fame, though not in life.
William Shakespeare (1564-1616, British Poet, Playwright, Actor)

135 Time hath a wallet at his back, wherein he puts. Alms for oblivion, a great-sized monster of ingratitudes.
William Shakespeare (1564-1616, British Poet, Playwright, Actor)

FAMILIARITY

1 A shocking occurrence ceases to be shocking when it occurs daily.
Alexander Chase

2 Familiar things happen, and mankind does not bother about them. It requires a very unusual mind to undertake the analysis of the obvious.
Alfred North Whitehead (1861-1947, British Mathematician, Philosopher)

3 Familiarity is the root of the closest friendships, as well as the interests hatreds.
Antoine Rivarol (1753-1801, French Journalist, Epigrammatist)

4 Nothing is wonderful when you get used to it.
Edgar Watson Howe (1853-1937, American Journalist, Author)

5 All objects lose by too familiar a view.
John Dryden (1631-1700, British Poet, Dramatist, Critic)

6 Familiarity breeds contempt; and children.
Mark Twain (1835-1910, American Humorist, Writer)

7 Familiarity is a magician that is cruel to beauty but kind to ugliness.
Ouida (1838-1908, British Writer)

8 Familiar acts are beautiful through love.
Percy Bysshe Shelley (1792-1822, British Poet)

9 Familiarity breeds contempt.
Publilius Syrus (1st Century BC, Roman Writer)

10 The hues of the opal, the light of the diamond, are not to be seen if the eye is too near.
Ralph Waldo Emerson (1803-1882, American Poet, Essayist)

11 Though familiarity may not breed contempt, it takes off the edge of admiration.
William Hazlitt (1778-1830, British Essayist)

12 Sweets grown common lose their dear delight.
William Shakespeare (1564-1616, British Poet, Playwright, Actor)

FAMILY

1 All I am, or can be, I owe to my angel mother.
Abraham Lincoln (1809-1865, Sixteenth President of the USA)

2 A farmer who had a quarrelsome family called his sons and told them to lay a bunch of sticks before him. Then, after laying the sticks parallel to one another and binding them, he challenged his sons, one after one, to pick up the bundle and break it. They all tried, but in vain. Then, untying the bundle, he gave them the sticks to break one by one. This they did with the greatest ease. Then said the father, Thus, my sons, as long as you remain united, you are a match for anything, but differ and separate, and you are undone.
Aesop (620-560 BC, Greek Fabulist)

3 Roots is not just a saga of my family. It is the symbolic saga of a people.
Alex Haley (1921-1992, American Writer)

4 Our notion of the perfect society embraces the family as its center and ornament, and this paradise is not secure until children appear to animate and complete the picture.
Amos Bronson Alcott (1799-1888, American Educator, Social Reformer)

5 You leave home to seek your fortune and, when you get it, you go home and share it with your family.
Anita Baker (American Singer, Entertainer)

6 Families are nothing other than the idolatry of duty.
Ann Oakley (1944-, British Sociologist, Author)

7 Other things may change us, but we start and end with family.
Anthony Brandt (American Composer, Editor)

8 None but a mule denies his family.
Arabian Proverb

9 Cruel is the strife of brothers.
Aristotle (384-322 BC, Greek Philosopher)

10 He that raises a large family does, indeed, while he lives to observe them, stand a broader mark for sorrow; but then he stands a broader mark for pleasure too.
Benjamin Franklin (1706-1790, American Scientist, Publisher, Diplomat)

11 A brother offended is harder to be won than a strong city: and their contentions are like the bars of a castle. [Proverbs 18:19]
Bible (Sacred Scriptures of Christians and Judaism)

12 A family is a place where minds come in contact with one another.
Buddha (568-488 BC, Founder of Buddhism)

13 The family is the most basic unit of government. As the first community to which a person is attached and the first authority under which a person learns to live, the family establishes society's most basic values.
Charles Caleb Colton (1780-1832, British Sportsman Writer)

14 Accidents will occur in the best-regulated families; and in families not regulated by that pervading influence which sanctifies while it enhances... in short, by the influence of Woman, in the lofty character of Wife, they may be expected with confidence, and must be borne with philosophy.
Charles Dickens (1812-1870, British Novelist)

15 A poor relation is the most irrelevant thing in nature, a piece of impertinent correspondence, an odious approximation, a haunting conscience, a preposterous shadow, lengthening in the noon- tide of our prosperity. He is known by his knock.
Charles Lamb (1775-1834, British Essayist, Critic)

16 Big sisters are the crab grass in the lawn of life.
Charles M. Schultz (1922-, American Cartoonist, Creator of "Peanuts")

17 A family is a place where principles are hammered and honed on the anvil of everyday living.
Charles Swindoll (American Pastor, Author)

18 All people are your relatives, therefore expect only trouble from them.
Chinese Proverb

19 Govern a family as you would cook a small fish -- very gently.
Chinese Proverb

20 Man is the head of the family, woman the neck that turns the head.
Chinese Proverb

21 In a broken nest there are few whole eggs.
Chinese Proverb

22 For there is no friend like a sister in calm or stormy weather; To cheer one on the tedious way, to fetch one if one goes astray, to lift one if one totters down, to strengthen whilst one stands.
Christina Rossetti (1830-1894, British Poet, Lyricist)

23 Women know what men have long forgotten. The ultimate economic and spiritual unit of any civilization is still the family.
Clare Boothe Luce (1903-1987, American Diplomat, Writer)

24 What a man sows, that shall he and his relations reap.
Clarissa Graves

25 The parents age must be remembered, both for joy and anxiety.
Confucius (551-479 BC, Chinese Ethical Teacher, Philosopher)

26 The strength of a nation derives from the integrity of the home.
Confucius (551-479 BC, Chinese Ethical Teacher, Philosopher)

27 It is not possible for one to teach others who cannot teach his own family.
Confucius (551-479 BC, Chinese Ethical Teacher, Philosopher)

28 All happy families resemble one another; every unhappy family is unhappy in its own way.
Count Leo Tolstoy (1828-1910, Russian Novelist, Philosopher)

29 I would rather start a family than finish one.
Don Marquis (1878-1937, American Humorist, Journalist)

30 When I do something in my family because I really enjoy it, then my duty has become my pleasure. And it is a pleasure for all the people around me.
Dr. Jess Lair (American Professor, Counselor)

31 A man ought to live so that everybody knows he is a Christian... and most of all, his family ought to know.
Dwight L. Moody (1837-1899, American Evangelist)

32 Growing up human is uniquely a matter of social relations rather than biology. What we learn from connections within the family takes the place of instincts that program the behavior of animals; which raises the question, how good are these connections?
Elizabeth Janeway (1913-, American Author, Critic)

33 A small family is soon provided for.
English Proverb

34 You hear a lot of dialogue on the death of the American family. Families aren't dying. They're merging into big conglomerates.
Erma Bombeck (1927-, American Author, Humorist)

35 The family is the school of duties... founded on love.
Felix Adler (1851-1933, American Educator, Social Critic)

36 The proliferation of support groups suggests to me that too many Americans are growing up in homes that do not contain a grandmother. A home without a grandmother is like an egg without salt and Helpists know it. They have jumped into the void left by the disappearance of morbid old ladies from the bosom of the American family.
Florence King (1936-, American Author, Critic)

37 He that hath wife and children hath given hostages to fortune; for they are impediments to great enterprises, either of virtue or mischief.
Francis Bacon (1561-1626, British Philosopher, Essayist, Statesman)

38 The family spirit has rendered man carnivorous.
Francis Picabia (1878-1953, French Painter, Poet)

39 Absence is one of the most useful ingredients of family life, and to dose it rightly is an art like any other.
Freya Stark (1893-1993, British Travel Writer)

40 A friend who is near and dear may in time become as useless as a relative.
George Ade (1866-1944, American Humorist, Playwright)

41 He didn't dare to, because his father had a weak heart and habitually threatened to drop dead if anybody hurt his feelings. You may have noticed that people with weak hearts are the tyrants of English married life.
George Bernard Shaw (1856-1950, Irish-born British Dramatist)

42 When our relatives are at home, we have to think of all their good points or it would be impossible to endure them. But when they are away, we console ourselves for their absence by dwelling on their vices.
George Bernard Shaw (1856-1950, Irish-born British Dramatist)

43 Happiness is having a large, loving, caring, close-knit family in another city.
George Burns (1896-1996, American Comedy Actor)

44 The family is one of nature's masterpieces.
George Santayana (1863-1952, American Philosopher, Poet)

45 The family is an early expedient and in many ways irrational. If the race had developed a special sexless class to be nurses, pedagogues, and slaves, like the workers among ants and bees, then the family would have been unnecessary. Such a division of labor would doubtless have involved evils of its own, but it would have obviated some drags and vexations proper to the family.
George Santayana (1863-1952, American Philosopher, Poet)

46 The only perfect love to be found on earth is not sexual love, which is riddled with hostility and insecurity, but the wordless commitment of families, which takes as its model mother-love. This is not to say that fathers have no place, for father-love, with its driving for self-improvement and discipline, is also essential to survival, but that uncorrected father-love, father-love as it were practiced by both parents, is a way to annihilation.
Germaine Greer (1939-, Australian Feminist Writer)

47 The family is the test of freedom; because the family is the only thing that the free man makes for himself and by himself.
Gilbert K. Chesterton (1874-1936, British Author)

48 The Family is the Country of the heart. There is an angel in the Family who, by the mysterious influence of grace, of sweetness, and of love, renders the fulfillment of duties less wearisome, sorrows less bitter. The only pure joys unmixed with sadness which it is given to man to taste upon earth are, thanks to this angel, the joys of the Family.
Giuseppe Mazzini (1805-1872, Italian Patriot, Writer)

49 The family is the basic cell of government: it is where we are trained to believe that we are human beings or that we are chattel, it is where we are trained to see the sex and race divisions and become callous to injustice even if it is done to ourselves, to accept as biological a full system of authoritarian government.
Gloria Steinem (1934-, American Feminist Writer, Editor)

525

50 Happy or unhappy, families are all mysterious. We have only to imagine how differently we would be described --and will be, after our deaths --by each of the family members who believe they know us.
Gloria Steinem (1934-, American Feminist Writer, Editor)

51 Every man sees in his relatives, and especially in his cousins, a series of grotesque caricatures of himself.
H. L. Mencken (1880-1956, American Editor, Author, Critic, Humorist)

52 So much of what is best in us is bound up in our love of family, that it remains the measure of our stability because it measures our sense of loyalty. All other pacts of love or fear derive from it and are modeled upon it.
Haniel Long (1888-1956, American Author, Poet, Journalist)

53 Love, by reason of its passion, destroys the in-between which relates us to and separates us from others. As long as its spell lasts, the only in-between which can insert itself between two lovers is the child, love's own product. The child, this in-between to which the lovers now are related and which they hold in common, is representative of the world in that it also separates them; it is an indication that they will insert a new world into the existing world. Through the child, it is as though the lovers return to the world from which their love had expelled them. But this new worldliness, the possible result and the only possibly happy ending of a love affair, is, in a sense, the end of love, which must either overcome the partners anew or be transformed into another mode of belonging together.
Hannah Arendt (1906-1975, German-born American Political Philosopher)

54 There is no friendship, no love, like that of the parent for the child.
Henry Ward Beecher (1813-1887, American Preacher, Orator, Writer)

55 The babe at first feeds upon the mother's bosom, but it is always on her heart.
Henry Ward Beecher (1813-1887, American Preacher, Orator, Writer)

56 My family begins with me, your family ends with you.
Iphicrates

57 In every dispute between parent and child, both cannot be right, but they may be, and usually are, both wrong. It is this situation which gives family life its peculiar hysterical charm.
Isaac Rosenfeld

58 Family... the home of all social evil, a charitable institution for comfortable women, an anchorage for house-fathers, and a hell for children.
J. August Strindberg (1849-1912, Swedish Dramatist, Novelist, Poet)

59 Lord, confound this surly sister, blight her brow with blotch and blister, cramp her larynx, lung and liver, in her guts a galling give her.
J. M. Synge (1871-1909, Irish Poet, Dramatist)

60 Our relatives are ours by chance, but we can choose our friends.
Jacques Delille (1738-1813, French Poet)

61 The awe and dread with which the untutored savage contemplates his mother-in-law are amongst the most familiar facts of anthropology.
James G. Frazer (1854-1941, Scottish Classicist, Anthropologist)

62 Call it a clan, call it a network, call it a tribe, call it a family: Whatever you call it, whoever you are, you need one.
Jane Howard

63 He that loves not his wife and children feeds a lioness at home, and broods a nest of sorrows.
Jeremy Taylor (1613-1667, British Churchman, Writer)

64 The government is becoming the family of last resort.
Jerry Brown

65 Look for the good, not the evil, in the conduct of members of the family.
Jewish Proverb

66 One of life's greatest mysteries is how the boy who wasn't good enough to marry your daughter can be the father of the smartest grandchild in the world.
Jewish Proverb

67 When a father gives to his son, both laugh; when a son gives to his father, both cry.
Jewish Proverb

68 Never did I think that I became family entertainment.
Jimmy Buffet (American Songwriter, Singer)

69 The roaring of the wind is my wife and the stars through the window pane are my children. The mighty abstract idea I have of beauty in all things stifles the more divided and minute domestic happiness.
John Keats (1795-1821, British Poet)

70 As the family goes, so goes the nation and so goes the whole world in which we live.
John Paul II (1920, Polish-Born Italian Pope)

71 One of the oddest features of western Christianized culture is its ready acceptance of the myth of the stable family and the happy marriage. We have been taught to accept the myth not as an heroic ideal, something good, brave, and nearly impossible to fulfil, but as the very fiber of normal life. Given most families and most marriages, the belief seems admirable but foolhardily.
Jonathan Raban (1942-, British Author, Critic)

72 Certain is it that there is no kind of affection so purely angelic as of a father to a daughter. In love to our wives there is desire; to our sons, ambition; but to our daughters there is something which there are no words to express.
Joseph Addison (1672-1719, British Essayist, Poet, Statesman)

73 Of all my wife's relations I like myself the best.
Joseph Cook

74 A brother is a friend provided by nature.
Legouve Pere

75 The striking point about our model family is not simply the compete-compete, consume- consume style of life it urges us to follow. The striking point, in the face of all the propaganda, is how few Americans actually live this way.
Louise Kapp Howe (1934-, American Author, Editor)

76 Nobody has ever before asked the nuclear family to live all by itself in a box the way we do. With no relatives, no support, we've put it in an impossible situation.
Margaret Mead (1901-1978, American Anthropologist)

77 We are always too busy for our children; we never give them the time or interest they deserve. We lavish gifts upon them; but the most precious gift, our personal association, which means so much to them, we give grudgingly.
Mark Twain (1835-1910, American Humorist, Writer)

78 Adam was the luckiest man; he had no mother-in-law.
Mark Twain (1835-1910, American Humorist, Writer)

79 Where can a person be better than in the bosom of their family.
Marmontel Gretry

80 Having a family is like having a bowling alley installed in your brain.
Martin Mull

81 Families are about love overcoming emotional torture.
Matt Groening (1954-, American Writer, Cartoonist, Animator, Producer, Screenwriter)

82 There is not much less vexation in the government of a private family than in the managing of an entire state.
Michel Eyquem De Montaigne (1533-1592, French Philosopher, Essayist)

83 There is little less trouble in governing a private family than a whole kingdom.
Michel Eyquem De Montaigne (1533-1592, French Philosopher, Essayist)

84 I can't help detesting my relations. I suppose it comes from the fact that none of us can stand other people having the same faults as ourselves.
Oscar Wilde (1856-1900, British Author, Wit)

85 Relations are simply a tedious pack of people, who haven't got the remotest knowledge of how to live, nor the smallest instinct about when to die.
Oscar Wilde (1856-1900, British Author, Wit)

86 The most socially subversive institution of our time is the one-parent family.
Paul Johnson (1928-, British Journalist)

87 Sisters are always drying their hair. Locked into rooms, alone, they pose at the mirror, shoulders bare, trying this way and that their hair, or fly importunate down the stair to answer the telephone.
Phyllis Mcginley (1905-1978, American Poet, Author)

88 Family is the most important thing in the world.
Princess of Wales Diana (1961-1997, Wife of Charles, Prince of Wales)

89 The hatred of relatives is the most violent.
Publius Cornelius Tacitus (55-117 AD, Roman Historian)

90 If Mr. Vincent Price were to be co-starred with Miss Bette Davis in a story by Mr. Edgar Allan Poe directed by Mr. Roger Corman, it could not fully express the pent-up violence and depravity of a single day in the life of the average family.
Quentin Crisp (1908-, British Author)

91 Women's liberationists spread the word that the only peaceful family is one in which either the wife is enslaved or the husband is androgynous.
R. Emmett Tyell

92 Family life is too intimate to be preserved by the spirit of justice. It can be sustained by a spirit of love which goes beyond justice.
Reinhold Niebuhr (1892-1971, American Theologian, Historian)

93 Rarely do members of the same family grow up under the same roof.
Richard Bach (1936-, American Author)

94 The family you come from isn't as important as the family you're going to have.
Ring Lardner (1885-1933, American Writer)

95 The greatest thing in family life is to take a hint when a hint is intended -- and not to take a hint when a hint isn't intended.
Robert Frost (1875-1963, American Poet)

96 As to the family, I have never understood how that fits in with the other ideals --or, indeed, why it should be an ideal at all. A group of closely related persons living under one roof; it is a convenience, often a necessity, sometimes a pleasure, sometimes the reverse; but who first exalted it as admirable, an almost religious ideal?
Rose Macaulay (1881-1958, British Novelist, Essayist)

97 Parents and children seldom act in concert: each child endeavors to appropriate the esteem or fondness of the parents, and the parents, with yet less temptation, betray each other to their children.
Samuel Johnson (1709-1784, British Author)

98 The family unit plays a critical role in our society and in the training of the generation to come.
Sandra Day O'connor (1930-, First American Woman Supreme Court Judge)

99 Nor need we power or splendor, wide hall or lordly dome; the good, the true, the tender- these form the wealth of home.
Sarah J. Hale (1788-1879, American Author)

100 Family jokes, though rightly cursed by strangers, are the bond that keeps most families alive.
Stella Benson (1892-1933, British Actor)

101 A family's photograph album is generally about the extended family and, often, is all that remains of it.
Susan Sontag (1933-, American Essayist)

102 Parents: persons who spend half their time worrying how a child will turn out, and the rest of the time wondering when a child will turn in.
Ted Cook

103 The happiest moments of my life have been the few which I have passed at home in the bosom of my family.
Thomas Jefferson (1743-1826, Third President of the USA)

104 In our family, as far as we are concerned, we were born and what happened before that is myth.
V. S. Pritchett (1900-, British Author, Critic)

105 I have known more men destroyed by the desire to have wife and child and to keep them in comfort than I have seen destroyed by drink and harlots.
William Butler Yeats (1865-1939, Irish Poet, Playwright.)

106 The family is the nucleus of civilization.
William J. Durant (1885-1981, American Historian, Essayist)

107 I think the ideal situation for a family is to be completely incestuous.
William S. Burroughs (1914-1997, American Writer)

108 The voice of parents is the voice of gods, for to their children they are heaven's lieutenants.
William Shakespeare (1564-1616, British Poet, Playwright, Actor)

109 With a new familiarity and a flesh-creeping "homeliness" entirely of this unreal, materialistic world, where all "sentiment" is coarsely manufactured and advertised in colossal sickly captions, disguised for the sweet tooth of a monstrous baby called "the Public," the family as it is, broken up on all hands by the agency of feminist and economic propaganda, reconstitutes itself in the image of the state.
Wyndham Lewis (1882-1957, British Author, Painter)

110 People who have good relationships at home are more effective in the marketplace.
Zig Ziglar (American Sales Trainer, Author, Motivational Speaker)

FAMINE

1 When the Somalians were merely another hungry third world people, we sent them guns. Now that they are falling down dead from starvation, we send them troops. Some may see in this a tidy metaphor for the entire relationship between north and south. But it would make a whole lot more sense nutritionally -- as well as providing infinitely more vivid viewing -- if the Somalians could be persuaded to eat the troops.
Barbara Ehrenreich (1941-, American Author, Columnist)

2 Half-starved spiders prey'd on half-starved flies.
Charles Churchill (1731-1764, British Poet, Satirist)

3 I will venture to affirm, that the three seasons wherein our corn has miscarried did no more contribute to our present misery, than one spoonful of water thrown upon a rat already drowned would contribute to his death; and that the present plentiful harvest, although it should be followed by a dozen ensuing, would no more restore us, than it would the rat aforesaid to put him near the fire, which might indeed warm his fur-coat, but never bring him back to life.
Jonathan Swift (1667-1745, Anglo-Irish Satirist)

4 There was no corn -- in the wide market-place all loathliest things, even human flesh, was sold; They weighed it in small scales -- and many a face was fixed in eager horror then; his gold the miser brought; the tender maid, grown bold through hunger, bared her scorned charms in vain.
Percy Bysshe Shelley (1792-1822, British Poet)

5 There are flood and drought over the eyes and in the mouth, dead water and dead sand contending for the upper hand. The parched eviscerate soil gapes at the vanity of toil, laughs without mirth. This is the death of the earth.
T. S. Eliot (1888-1965, American-born British Poet, Critic)

FAMOUS LAST WORDS

1 The fog is rising.
Emily Dickinson (1830-1886, American Poet)

2 My work is done why wait.
George Eastman

3 It is well, I die hard, but I am not afraid to go. [Dec. 14, 1977]
George Washington (1732-1799, First President of the USA)

4 What is the answer?... [Silence]... In that case, what is the question?
Gertrude Stein (1874-1946, American Author)

5 Go away...I'm alright.
H.G. Wells (1866-1946, British-born American Author)

6 Now comes the mystery.
Henry Ward Beecher (1813-1887, American Preacher, Orator, Writer)

7 More light!
Johann Wolfgang Von Goethe (1749-1832, German Poet, Dramatist, Novelist)

8 Thomas Jefferson -- still surv...
John Adams (1735-1826, Second President of the USA)

9 The best of it is, God is with us.
John Wesley (1703-1791, British Preacher, Founder of Methodism)

10 Friends applaud, the comedy is over.
Ludwig Van Beethoven (1770-1827, German Composer)

11 I don't fell good.
Luther Burbank (1849-1926, American Horticulturist)

12 Courage! I have shown it for years; think you I shall lose it at the moment when my sufferings are to end?
Marie Antoinette (1755-? Queen of France)

13 Turn up the lights. I don't want to go home in the dark.
O. Henry (1862-1910, American Writer)

14 And now, I am dying beyond my means. [Sipping champagne on his deathbed]
Oscar Wilde (1856-1900, British Author, Wit)

15 Drink to me.
Pablo Picasso (1881-1973, Spanish Artist)

16 Don't let it end like this. Tell them I said something. [Last words of Pancho Villa]
Pancho Villa (1877-1923, Mexican revolutionary)

17 Let the tent be struck.
Robert E. Lee (1807-1870, American Confederate Army Commander)

18 Crito, I owe a cock to Asclepius; will you remember to pay the debt?
Socrates (469-399 BC, Greek Philosopher of Athens)

19 Let us cross over the river and rest under the shade of the trees.
Stonewall Jackson

20 I am about to take my last voyage, a great leap in the dark.
Thomas Hobbes (1588-1679, British Philosopher)

21 This is the fourth?
Thomas Jefferson (1743-1826, Third President of the USA)

22 Lord, let me live until I die.
Will Rogers (1879-1935, American Humorist, Actor)

FANATICS AND FANATICISM

1 A fanatic is a man who consciously over compensates a secret doubt.
Aldous Huxley (1894-1963, British Author)

2 Defined in psychological terms, a fanatic is a man who consciously over-compensates a secret doubt.
Aldous Huxley (1894-1963, British Author)

3 The worst of madmen is a saint run mad.
Alexander Pope (1688-1744, British Poet, Critic, Translator)

4 The most dangerous madmen are those created by religion, and people whose aim is to disrupt society always know how to make good use of them on occasion.
Denis Diderot (1713-1784, French Philosopher)

5 The fanatic is incorruptible: if he kills for an idea, he can just as well get himself killed for one; in either case, tyrant or martyr, he is a monster.
E. M. Cioran (1911-, Rumanian-born French Philosopher)

6 Fanaticism obliterates the feelings of humanity.
Edward Gibbon (1737-1794, British Historian)

7 A fanatic is a man that does what he thinks the Lord would do if He knew the facts of the case.
Finley Peter Dunne (1867-1936, American Journalist, Humorist)

8 Fervor is the weapon of choice of the impotent.
Frantz Fanon (1925-1961, French Psychiatrist)

9 Fanatics are picturesque, mankind would rather see gestures than listen to reasons.
Friedrich Nietzsche (1844-1900, German Philosopher)

10 Fanaticism consists in redoubling your efforts when you have forgotten your aim.
George Santayana (1863-1952, American Philosopher, Poet)

11 Just as every conviction begins as a whim so does every emancipator serve his apprenticeship as a crank. A fanatic is a great leader who is just entering the room.
Heywood Broun (1888-1939, American Journalist, Novelist)

12 If you see one cold and vehement at the same time, set him down for a fanatic.
Johann Kaspar Lavater (1741-1801, Swiss Theologian, Mystic)

13 In the history of mankind, fanaticism has caused more harm than vice.
Louis Kronenberger

14 There is no place in a fanatic's head where reason can enter.
Napoleon Bonaparte (1769-1821, French General, Emperor)

15 Wisdom becomes nonsense in the mouth of a fanatic.
Otto Schuwdrmer

16 Throughout human history, the apostles of purity, those who have claimed to possess a total explanation, have wrought havoc among mere mixed-up human beings.
Salman Rushdie (1948-, Indian-born British Author)

17 Mere human beings can't afford to be fanatical about anything. Not even about justice or loyalty. The fanatic for justice ends by murdering a million helpless people to clear a space for his law-courts. If we are to survive on this planet, there must be compromises.
Storm Jameson (1891-1986, British Writer)

18 In the fevered state of our country, no good can ever result from any attempt to set one of these fiery zealots to rights, either in fact or principle. They are determined as to the facts they will believe, and the opinions on which they will act. Get by them, therefore, as you would by an angry bull; it is not for a man of sense to dispute the road with such an animal.
Thomas Jefferson (1743-1826, Third President of the USA)

19 I carry from my mother's womb a fanatic's heart.
William Butler Yeats (1865-1939, Irish Poet, Playwright.)

20 Fanaticism soberly defined, is the false fire of an over heated mind.
William Cowper (1731-1800, British Poet)

[21] A fanatic is one who can't change his mind and won't change the subject.
Winston Churchill (1874-1965, British Statesman, Prime Minister)

FANTASY

[1] Fantasies are more than substitutes for unpleasant reality; they are also dress rehearsals, plans. All acts performed in the world begin in the imagination.
Barbara Grizzuti Harrison (1941-, American Author, Publicist)

[2] I consider it useless and tedious to represent what exists, because nothing that exists satisfies me. Nature is ugly, and I prefer the monsters of my fancy to what is positively trivial.
Charles Baudelaire (1821-1867, French Poet)

[3] I like nonsense -- it wakes up the brain cells. Fantasy is a necessary ingredient in living. It's a way of looking at life through the wrong end of a telescope... and that enables you to laugh at all of life's realities.
Dr. Seuss (1904-1991, American Writer and Illustrator of Children's Books)

[4] The dream of reason produces monsters. Imagination deserted by reason creates impossible, useless thoughts. United with reason, imagination is the mother of all art and the source of all its beauty.
Francisco Jose De Goya Y Lucientes (1746-1828, Spanish Painter)

[5] The pleasures of the imagination are as it were only drawings and models which are played with by poor people who cannot afford the real thing.
Georg C. Lichtenberg (1742-1799, German Physicist, Satirist)

[6] But fantasy kills imagination, pornography is death to art.
Iris Murdoch (1919-, British Novelist, Philosopher)

[7] The mind can make substance, and people planets of its own with beings brighter than have been, and give a breath to forms which can outlive all flesh.
Lord Byron (1788-1824, British Poet)

[8] The whole fauna of human fantasies, their marine vegetation, drifts and luxuriates in the dimly lit zones of human activity, as though plaiting thick tresses of darkness. Here, too, appear the lighthouses of the mind, with their outward resemblance to less pure symbols. The gateway to mystery swings open at the touch of human weakness and we have entered the realms of darkness. One false step, one slurred syllable together reveal a man's thoughts.
Louis Aragon (1897-1982, French Poet)

[9] One's real life is so often the life that one does not lead.
Oscar Wilde (1856-1900, British Author, Wit)

[10] When a fantasy turns you on, you're obligated to God and nature to start doing it right away.
Stewart Brand (1938-, American Editor, Writer)

[11] We live under continual threat of two equally fearful, but seemingly opposed, destinies: unremitting banality and inconceivable terror. It is fantasy, served out in large rations by the popular arts, which allows most people to cope with these twin specters.
Susan Sontag (1933-, American Essayist)

FAREWELLS

[1] Every parting gives a foretaste of death; every coming together again a foretaste of the resurrection.
Arthur Schopenhauer (1788-1860, German Philosopher)

[2] Let us eat and drink; for tomorrow we shall die. [Isaiah 22:13]
Bible (Sacred Scriptures of Christians and Judaism)

[3] Parting is all we know of heaven and all we need of hell.
Emily Dickinson (1830-1886, American Poet)

[4] Partir, c'est mourir un peu. (To leave is to die a little.)
French Proverb

[5] Faithless is he that says farewell when the road darkens.
J. R. Tolkien (1892-1973, British Novelist, Scholar)

[6] When I died last, and, Dear, I die as often as from thee I go though it be but an hour ago and lovers hours be full eternity.
John Donne (1572-1632, British Metaphysical Poet)

[7] We only part to meet again.
John Gay (1688-1732, British Playwright, Poet)

[8] I always made an awkward bow.
John Keats (1795-1821, British Poet)

[9] All farewells should be sudden, when forever.
Lord Byron (1788-1824, British Poet)

[10] Don't be dismayed at good-byes. A farewell is necessary before you can meet again. And meeting again, after moments or lifetimes, is certain for those who are friends.
Richard Bach (1936-, American Author)

[11] Until we meet again, may the good Lord take a liking to you.
Roy Rogers (1912-, American Actor)

[12] Come, let's have one other gaudy night. Call to me. All my sad captains. Fill our bowls once more. Let's mock the midnight bell.
William Shakespeare (1564-1616, British Poet, Playwright, Actor)

FARMING AND FARMERS

1 There seem to be but three ways for a nation to acquire wealth. The first is by war, as the Romans did, in plundering their conquered neighbors. This is robbery. The second by commerce, which is generally cheating. The third by agriculture, the only honest way, wherein man receives a real increase of the seed thrown into the ground, in a kind of continual miracle, wrought by the hand of God in his favor, as a reward for his innocent life and his virtuous industry.
Benjamin Franklin (1706-1790, American Scientist, Publisher, Diplomat)

2 With the introduction of agriculture mankind entered upon a long period of meanness, misery, and madness, from which they are only now being freed by the beneficent operation of the machine.
Bertrand Russell (1872-1970, British Philosopher, Mathematician, Essayist)

3 There are only three things that can kill a farmer: lightning, rolling over in a tractor, and old age.
Bill Bryson (American Author)

4 It is thus with farming, if you do one thing late, you will be late in all your work.
Cato The Elder (234-149 BC, Roman Statesman, Orator)

5 When tillage begins, other arts follow. The farmers, therefore, are the founders of human civilization.
Daniel Webster (1782-1852, American Lawyer, Statesman)

6 Farming looks mighty easy when your plow is a pencil, and you're a thousand miles from the corn field.
Dwight D. Eisenhower (1890-1969, Thirty-fourth President of the USA)

7 A good farmer is nothing more nor less than a handy man with a sense of humus.
E(lwyn) B(rooks) White (1899-1985, American Author, Editor)

8 Farmers only worry during the growing season, but towns people worry all the time.
Edgar Watson Howe (1853-1937, American Journalist, Author)

9 Bowed by the weight of centuries he leans upon his hoe and gazes on the ground, the emptiness of ages in his face, and on his back the burden of the world.
Edwin Markham (1852-1940, American Poet and Editor)

10 He felt with the force of a revelation that to throw up the clods of earth manfully is as beneficent as to revolutionize the world. It was not the matter of the work, but the mind that went into it, that counted -- and the man who was not content to do small things well would leave great things undone.
Ellen Glasgow (1874-1945, American Novelist)

11 The farmer works the soil. The agriculturalist works the farmer.
Eugene F. Ware (American Lawyer, Poet)

12 There is, of course, a gold mine or a buried treasure on every mortgaged homestead. Whether the farmer ever digs for it or not, it is there, haunting his daydreams when the burden of debt is most unbearable.
Fawn M. Brodie (1915-1981, American Biographer)

13 Our farmers round, well pleased with constant gain, like other farmers, flourish and complain.
George Crabbe (1754-1832, British Clergyman, Poet)

14 It is sad, no doubt, to exhaust one's strength and one's days in cleaving the bosom of this jealous earth, which compels us to wring from it the treasures of its fertility, when a bit of the blackest and coarsest bread is, at the end of the day's work, the sole recompense and the sole profit attaching to so arduous a toil.
George Sand (1804-1876, French Novelist)

15 I see upon their noble brows the seal of the Lord, for they were born kings of the earth far more truly than those who possess it only from having bought it.
George Sand (1804-1876, French Novelist)

16 I know of no pursuit in which more real and important services can be rendered to any country than by improving its agriculture, its breed of useful animals, and other branches of a husbandman's cares.
George Washington (1732-1799, First President of the USA)

17 No one hates his job so heartily as a farmer.
H. L. Mencken (1880-1956, American Editor, Author, Critic, Humorist)

18 There is no gilding of setting sun or glamour of poetry to light up the ferocious and endless toil of the farmers wives.
Hamlin Garland

19 Life on a farm is a school of patience; you can't hurry the crops or make an ox in two days.
Henri Alain

20 Farmers are respectable and interesting to me in proportion as they are poor.
Henry David Thoreau (1817-1862, American Essayist, Poet, Naturalist)

21 By avarice and selfishness, and a groveling habit, from which none of us is free, of regarding the soil as property, or the means of acquiring property chiefly, the landscape is deformed, husbandry is degraded with us, and the farmer leads the meanest of lives. He knows Nature but as a robber.
Henry David Thoreau (1817-1862, American Essayist, Poet, Naturalist)

22 Sowing is not as difficult as reaping.
Johann Wolfgang Von Goethe (1749-1832, German Poet, Dramatist, Novelist)

23 The farmer is the only man in our economy who buys everything at retail, sells everything at wholesale, and pays the freight both ways.
John F. Kennedy (1917-1963, Thirty-fifth President of the USA)

24 Give fools their gold, and knaves their power; let fortune's bubbles rise and fall; who sows a field, or trains a flower, or plants a tree, is more than all.
John Greenleaf Whittier (1807-1892, American Poet, Reformer, Author)

25 Like a gardener I believe what goes down must come up.
Lynwood L. Giacomini

26 Farm policy, although it's complex, can be explained. What it can't be is believed. No cheating spouse, no teen with a wrecked family car, no mayor of Washington, D.C., videotaped in flagrant has ever come up with anything as farfetched as U.S. farm policy.
P. J. O'Rourke (1947-, American Journalist)

27 The master's eye is the best fertilizer.
Pliny The Elder (23-79, Roman Neophatonist)

28 The land too poor for any other crop, is best for raising men.
R. Pocock

29 The first farmer was the first man. All historic nobility rests on the possession and use of land.
Ralph Waldo Emerson (1803-1882, American Poet, Essayist)

30 Farmers are philosophical. They have learned that it is less wearing to shrug than to beat their breasts.
Ruth Stout

31 Whenever there are in any country uncultivated lands and unemployed poor, it is clear that the laws of property have been so far extended as to violate natural right. The earth is given as a common stock for man to labor and live on. The small landowners are the most precious part of a state.
Thomas Jefferson (1743-1826, Third President of the USA)

FASCISM

1 Fascism is not in itself a new order of society. It is the future refusing to be born.
Aneurin Bevan (1897-1960, British Labor Politician)

2 Fascism is a religion. The twentieth century will be known in history as the century of Fascism.
Benito Mussolini (1883-1945, Italian Prime Minister (1922--43) and Dictator)

3 Fascism, the more it considers and observes the future and the development of humanity, quite apart from political considerations of the moment, believes neither in the possibility nor the utility of perpetual peace.
Benito Mussolini (1883-1945, Italian Prime Minister (1922--43) and Dictator)

4 AS A MIND, who the hell else is there left for me to take an interest IN??
Ezra Pound (1885-1972, American Poet, Critic)

5 Our movement took a grip on cowardly Marxism and from it extracted the meaning of socialism. It also took from the cowardly middle-class parties their nationalism. Throwing both into the cauldron of our way of life there emerged, as clear as a crystal, the synthesis -- German National Socialism.
Hermann Goering (1893-1946, Nazi Politico-Military Leader)

6 Fascism was a counter-revolution against a revolution that never took place.
Ignazio Silone (1900-1978, Italian Novelist)

7 Fascism is a European inquietude. It is a way of knowing everything -- history, the State, the achievement of the proletarianization of public life, a new way of knowing the phenomena of our epoch.
J. A. Primo De Rivera (1903-1936, Spanish Falangist Politician)

8 Fascism is not defined by the number of its victims, but by the way it kills them.
Jean-Paul Sartre (1905-1980, French Writer, Philosopher)

9 Fascism is nothing but capitalist reaction.
Leon Trotsky (1879-1940, Russian Revolutionary)

10 The strategic adversary is fascism... the fascism in us all, in our heads and in our everyday behavior, the fascism that causes us to love power, to desire the very thing that dominates and exploits us.
Michel Foucault (1926-1984, French Essayist, Philosopher)

11 That which the Fascists hate above all else, is intelligence.
Miguel De Unamuno (1864-1936, Spanish Philosophical Writer)

12 I have often thought that if a rational Fascist dictatorship were to exist, then it would choose the American system.
Noam Chomsky (1928-, American Linguist, Political Activist)

13 We enter parliament in order to supply ourselves, in the arsenal of democracy, with its own weapons. If democracy is so stupid as to give us free tickets and salaries for this bear's work, that is its affair. We do not come as friends, nor even as neutrals. We come as enemies. As the wolf bursts into the flock, so we come.
Paul Joseph Goebbels (1897-1945, German Nazi Propaganda Minister)

14 Fascism is capitalism plus murder.
Upton Sinclair (1878-1968, American Novelist, Social Reformer)

FASHION

1 Only men who are not interested in women are interested in women's clothes. Men who like women never notice what they wear.
Anatole France (1844-1924, French Writer)

2 Women's fashion" is a euphemism for fashion created by men for women.
Andrea Dworkin (1946-, American Feminist Critic)

3 Eat to please thyself, but dress to please others.
Benjamin Franklin (1706-1790, American Scientist, Publisher, Diplomat)

4 Fashions are born and they die too quickly for anyone to learn to love them.
Bettina Ballard (American Writer)

5 When in doubt, wear red.
Bill Blass (1922-, American Fashion Designer)

6 All fashions are charming, or rather relatively charming, each one being a new striving, more or less well conceived, after beauty, an approximate statement of an ideal, the desire for which constantly teases the unsatisfied human mind.
Charles Baudelaire (1821-1867, French Poet)

7 You must be in fashion is the utterance of weak headed mortals.
Charles Haddon Spurgeon (1834-1892, British Baptist Preacher)

8 The beggar wears all colors fearing none.
Charles Lamb (1775-1834, British Essayist, Critic)

9 High heels were invented by a woman who had been kissed on the forehead.
Christopher Morley (1890-1957, American Novelist, Journalist, Poet)

10 Fashion is made to become unfashionable.
Coco Chanel (1883-1971, French Couturier)

11 Fashion is architecture: it is a matter of proportions.
Coco Chanel (1883-1971, French Couturier)

12 In olden days a glimpse of stocking was looked on as something shocking but now, God knows, anything goes.
Cole Porter (1893-1964, American Composer, Lyricist)

13 You know, one had as good be out of the world, as out of the fashion.
Colley Cibber (1671-1757, British Actor-Manager, Playwright)

14 He never chooses an opinion, he just wears whatever happens to be in style.
Count Leo Tolstoy (1828-1910, Russian Novelist, Philosopher)

15 I never cared for fashion much, amusing little seams and witty little pleats: it was the girls I liked.
David Bailey (1938-, British Photographer)

16 The pursuit of Fashion is the attempt of the middle class to co-opt tragedy. In adopting the clothing, speech, and personal habits of those in straitened, dangerous, or pitiful circumstances, the middle class seeks to have what it feels to be the exigent and nonequivocal experiences had by those it emulates.
David Mamet (1947-, American Playwright)

17 Fashion is born by small facts, trends, or even politics, never by trying to make little pleats and furbelows, by trinkets, by clothes easy to copy, or by the shortening or lengthening of a skirt.
Elsa Schiaparelli (1896-1973, Italian Fashion Designer)

18 Her hat is a creation that will never go out of style; it will just look ridiculous year after year.
Fred A. Allen (1894-1957, American Radio Comic)

19 Fashion is a tyrant from which there is no deliverance; all must conform to its whimsical.
French Proverb

20 If one considers how much reason every person has for anxiety and timid self-concealment, and how three-quarters of his energy and goodwill can be paralyzed and made unfruitful by it, one has to be very grateful to fashion, insofar as it sets that three-quarters free and communicates self- confidence and mutual cheerful agreeableness to those who know they are subject to its law.
Friedrich Nietzsche (1844-1900, German Philosopher)

21 Fashionabilty is a kind of elevated vulgarity.
G. Darley

22 Even truth needs to be clad in new garments if it is to appeal to a new age.
Georg C. Lichtenberg (1742-1799, German Physicist, Satirist)

23 Fashions, after all, are only induced epidemics.
George Bernard Shaw (1856-1950, Irish-born British Dramatist)

24 Fashion is something barbarous, for it produces innovation without reason and imitation without benefit.
George Santayana (1863-1952, American Philosopher, Poet)

25 I base most of my fashion taste on what doesn't itch.
Gilda Radner (1946-1989, American Comedienne)

26 Any girl can be glamorous. All you have to do is stand still and look stupid.
Hedy Lamarr

27 Nothing is so hideous as an obsolete fashion.
Henri B. Stendhal (1783-1842, French Writer)

28 We worship not the Graces, nor the Parcae, but Fashion. She spins and weaves and cuts with full authority. The head monkey at Paris puts on a traveler's cap, and all the monkeys in America do the same.
Henry David Thoreau (1817-1862, American Essayist, Poet, Naturalist)

29 Fashion is the science of appearance, and it inspires one with the desire to seem rather than to be.
Henry Fielding (1707-1754, British Novelist, Dramatist)

30 You couldn't tell if she was dressed for an opera or an operation.
Irvin S. Cobb

31 My weakness is wearing too much leopard print.
Jackie Collins (American Author, Sister of Joan Collins)

32 The same costume will be Indecent 10 years before its time, Shameless 5 years before its time, Outré (daring) 1 year before its time, Smart, Dowdy 1 year after its time, Hideous 20 years after its time, Ridiculous 20 years after its time, Amusing 30 years after its time, Quaint 50 years after its time, Charming 70 years after its time, Romantic 100 years after its time, Beautiful 150 years after its time.
James Laver

33 No doubt the artist is the child of his time; but woe to him if he is also its disciple, or even its favorite.
Johann Friedrich Von Schiller (1759-1805, German Dramatist, Poet, Historian)

34 Fashion for the most part is nothing but the ostentation of riches.
John Locke (1632-1704, British Philosopher)

35 Only the minute and the future are interesting in fashion -- it exists to be destroyed. If everybody did everything with respect, you'd go nowhere.
Karl Lagerfeld

36 I'd like to put on buckskins and a ponytail and go underwater with a reed, hiding from the Indians... To me, that's sexy!
Kevin Costner (1955-, American Actor, Director, Producer)

37 Fashion is more powerful than any tyrant.
Latin Proverb

38 He who goes against the fashion is himself its slave.
Logan Pearsall Smith (1865-1946, Anglo-American Essayist, Aphorist)

39 When a person is in fashion, all they do is right.
Lord Chesterfield (1694-1773, British Statesman, Author)

40 Fashions in bigotry come and go. The right thing lasts.
Mary Hays

41 Fashion is a form of ugliness so intolerable that we have to alter it every six months.
Oscar Wilde (1856-1900, British Author, Wit)

42 Woman's first duty in life is to her dressmaker. What the second duty is no one has yet discovered.
Oscar Wilde (1856-1900, British Author, Wit)

43 Fashion, by which what is really fantastic becomes for a moment the universal.
Oscar Wilde (1856-1900, British Author, Wit)

44 Nothing is so dangerous as being too modern; one is apt to grow old fashioned quite suddenly.
Oscar Wilde (1856-1900, British Author, Wit)

45 I who have been involved with all styles of painting can assure you that the only things that fluctuate are the waves of fashion which carry the snobs and speculators; the number of true connoisseurs remains more or less the same.
Pablo Picasso (1881-1973, Spanish Artist)

46 Fashion is like the ashes left behind by the uniquely shaped flames of the fire, the trace alone revealing that a fire actually took place.
Paul De Man (1919-1983, Belgian-born American Literary Critic)

47 Fashion exists for women with no taste, etiquette for people with no breeding.
Queen Maria

48 People ask how can a Jewish kid from the Bronx do preppy clothes? Does it have to do with class and money? It has to do with dreams.
Ralph Lauren (American Designer)

49 Change of fashion is the tax levied by the industry of the poor on the vanity of the rich.
Sebastien-Roch Nicolas De Chamfort (1741-1794, French Writer, Journalist, Playwright)

50 You don't learn style from watching people on a runway. Fashion happens every morning when you wake up.
Shalom Harlow (1961-, Canadian-born American Model, TV Personality)

51 Fashion is the most intense expression of the phenomenon of neomania, which has grown ever since the birth of capitalism. Neomania assumes that purchasing the new is the same as acquiring value. If the purchase of a new garment coincides with the wearing out of an old one, then obviously there is no fashion. If a garment is worn beyond the moment of its natural replacement, there is pauperization. Fashion flourishes on surplus, when someone buys more than he or she needs.
Stephen Bayley (1951-, British Design Critic)

52 The great attraction of fashion is that it diverted attention from the insoluble problems of beauty and provided an easy way -- which money could buy... to a simply stated, easily reproduced ideal of beauty, however temporary that ideal.
Theodore Zeldin

53 Society is founded upon cloth.
Thomas Carlyle (1795-1881, Scottish Philosopher, Author)

54 If the cut of the costume indicates intellect and talent, then the color indicates temper and heart.
Thomas Carlyle (1795-1881, Scottish Philosopher, Author)

55 It is fancy rather than taste which produces so many new fashions.
Voltaire (1694-1778, French Historian, Writer)

56 Fashion wears out more clothes than the man.
William Shakespeare (1564-1616, British Poet, Playwright, Actor)

57 It pains me physically to see a woman victimized, rendered pathetic, by fashion.
Yves Saint-Laurent (1936-, Algerian-Born French Fashion Designer)

FASTING

1 When the stomach is full, it is easy to talk of fasting.
St. Jerome (342-420, Croatian Christian Ascetic, Scholar)

FATE

1 Fate keeps on happening.
Anita Loos (1893-1981, American Novelist, Screenwriter)

2 Throw a lucky man into the sea, and he will come up with a fish in his mouth.
Arabian Proverb

3 It's the niceties that make the difference fate gives us the hand, and we play the cards.
Arthur Schopenhauer (1788-1860, German Philosopher)

4 We make our fortunes and we call them fate.
Benjamin Disraeli (1804-1881, British Statesman, Prime Minister)

5 But now our fate from unmomentous things, may rise like rivers out of little springs.
Campbell

6 When an inner situation is not made conscious, it appears outside as fate.
Carl Jung (1875-1961, Swiss Psychiatrist)

7 Fate is the endless chain of causation, whereby things are; the reason or formula by which the world goes on.
Citium Zeno (335-264 BC, Greek Philosopher)

8 Death and life have their determined appointments; riches and honors depend upon heaven.
Confucius (551-479 BC, Chinese Ethical Teacher, Philosopher)

9 The wheel of fortune turns round incessantly, and who can say to himself, "I shall today be uppermost."
Confucius (551-479 BC, Chinese Ethical Teacher, Philosopher)

10 Chance happens to all, but to turn chance to account is the gift of few.
Edward G. Bulwer-Lytton (1803-1873, British Novelist, Poet)

11 There is but one philosophy and its name is fortitude! To bear is to conquer our fate.
Edward G. Bulwer-Lytton (1803-1873, British Novelist, Poet)

12 Fate is not an eagle, it creeps like a rat.
Elizabeth Bowen (1899-1973, Anglo-Irish Novelist)

13 Fortune is like the market, where, many times, if you can stay a little, the price will fall.
Francis Bacon (1561-1626, British Philosopher, Essayist, Statesman)

14 Ill Fortune never crushed that man whom good fortune deceived not.
Francis Bacon (1561-1626, British Philosopher, Essayist, Statesman)

15 One must either be the hammer or the anvil.
German Proverb

16 Destiny has two ways of crushing us -- by refusing our wishes and by fulfilling them.
Henri Frederic Amiel (1821-1881, Swiss Philosopher, Poet, Critic)

17 Sail on ship of state, sail on, I union, strong and great! Humanity with all its fears, with all its hopes of future years, is hanging on thy fate!
Henry Wadsworth Longfellow (1819-1892, American Poet)

18 The lofty pine is oftenest shaken by the winds; High towers fall with a heavier crash; And the lightning strikes the highest mountain.
Horace (65-8 BC, Italian Poet)

19 There is no armor against fate.
James Shirley (1596-1666, British Playwright)

20 Full of wisdom are the ordinations of fate.
Johann Friedrich Von Schiller (1759-1805, German Dramatist, Poet, Historian)

21 Seek not to know what must not be reveal, for joy only flows where fate is most concealed. A busy person would find their sorrows much more; if future fortunes were known before!
John Dryden (1631-1700, British Poet, Dramatist, Critic)

22 All things are subject to decay and when fate summons, monarchs must obey.
John Dryden (1631-1700, British Poet, Dramatist, Critic)

23 The men and woman who make the best boon companions seem to have given up hope of doing something else...some defect of talent or opportunity has cut them off from their pet ambition and has thus left them with leisure to take an interest in their lives of others. Your ambition may be, it makes him keep his thoughts at home. But the heartbroken people -- if I may use the word in a mild, benevolent sense -- the people whose wills are subdued to fate, give us consolation, recognition, and welcome.
John Jay Chapman (1862-1933, American Author)

24 Chance generally favors the prudent.
Joseph Joubert (1754-1824, French Moralist)

25 The wheel goes round and round, some are up and some are on the down, and still the wheel goes round.
Josephine Pollard (1843-1892, American Poet)

26 Tempted fate will leave the loftiest star.
Lord Byron (1788-1824, British Poet)

27 Everything that exists is in a manner the seed of that which will be.
Marcus Aurelius (121-80 AD, Roman Emperor, Philosopher)

28 Whatever the universal nature assigns to any man at any time is for the good of that man at that time.
Marcus Aurelius (121-80 AD, Roman Emperor, Philosopher)

29 Every one is the architect of his own fortune.
Mathurin Regnier (1573-1613, French Poet)

30 The less we deserve good fortune, the more we hope for it.
MoliFre (1622-1673, French Playwright)

31 Chance is always powerful. Let your hook be always cast; in the pool where you least expect it, there will be a fish.
Ovid (43 BC-18 AD, Roman Poet)

32 Fate leads him who follows it, and drags him who resist.
Plutarch (46-120 AD, Greek Essayist, Biographer)

33 Whatever limits us we call fate.
Ralph Waldo Emerson (1803-1882, American Poet, Essayist)

34 Fate is nothing but the deeds committed in a prior state of existence.
Ralph Waldo Emerson (1803-1882, American Poet, Essayist)

35 If you believe in fate, believe in it, at least, for your good.
Ralph Waldo Emerson (1803-1882, American Poet, Essayist)

36 I do not know beneath what sky nor on what seas shall be thy fate; I only know it shall be high, I only know it shall be great.
Richard Hovey (1869-1900, American Poet)

37 The fates lead the willing, and drag the unwilling.
Seneca (4 BC-65 AD, Spanish-born Roman Statesman, philosopher)

38 Fate rules the affairs of men, with no recognizable order.
Seneca (4 BC-65 AD, Spanish-born Roman Statesman, philosopher)

39 Fate leads the willing, and drags along the reluctant.
Seneca (4 BC-65 AD, Spanish-born Roman Statesman, philosopher)

40 Human reason needs only to will more strongly than fate, and she is fate.
Thomas Mann (1875-1955, German Author, Critic)

41 Our fate, whatever it is to be, will be overcome by patience under it.
Virgil (70-19 BC, Roman Poet)

42 Wherever the fates lead us let us follow.
Virgil (70-19 BC, Roman Poet)

43 Chance is a word void of sense; nothing can exist without a cause.
Voltaire (1694-1778, French Historian, Writer)

44 There is tide in the affairs of men, which, taken at the flood, leads on to fortune; omitted, all the voyage of their life is bound in shallows and in miseries; on such a full sea we are now afloat; and we must take the current the clouds folding and unfolding beyond the horizon. when it serves, or lose our ventures.
William Shakespeare (1564-1616, British Poet, Playwright, Actor)

45 It is not in the stars to hold our destiny but in ourselves; we are underlings.
William Shakespeare (1564-1616, British Poet, Playwright, Actor)

46 Men at sometime are the masters of their fate.
William Shakespeare (1564-1616, British Poet, Playwright, Actor)

FATHERS

1 It no longer bothers me that I may be constantly searching for father figures; by this time, I have found several and dearly enjoyed knowing them all.
Alice Walker (1944-, American Author, Critic)

2 I stopped loving my father a long time ago. What remained was the slavery to a pattern.
Anais Nin (1914-1977, French-born American Novelist, Dancer)

3 It doesn't matter who my father was; it matters who I remember he was.
Anne Sexton (1928-1974, American Poet)

4 The worst misfortune that can happen to an ordinary man is to have an extraordinary father.
Austin O'Malley

5 The fundamental defect with fathers is that they want their children to be a credit to them.
Bertrand Russell (1872-1970, British Philosopher, Mathematician, Essayist)

6 Fathers do not exasperate your children; instead, bring them up in the training and instruction of the Lord. [Ephesians 6:4]
Bible (Sacred Scriptures of Christians and Judaism)

7 Call no man your father upon the earth, for one is your Father, which is in heaven.
Bible (Sacred Scriptures of Christians and Judaism)

8 If the new American father feels bewildered and even defeated, let him take comfort from the fact that whatever he does in any fathering situation has a fifty percent chance of being right.
Bill Cosby (1937-, American Actor, Comedian, Producer)

9 The father who does not teach his son his duties is equally guilty with the son who neglects them.
Confucius (551-479 BC, Chinese Ethical Teacher, Philosopher)

10 By profession I am a soldier and take pride in that fact. But I am prouder -- infinitely prouder -- to be a father. A soldier destroys in order to build; the father only builds, never destroys. The one has the potentiality of death; the other embodies creation and life. And while the hordes of death are mighty, the battalions of life are mightier still. It is my hope that my son, when I am gone, will remember me not from the battle field but in the home repeating with him our simple daily prayer, "Our Father Who Art in Heaven."
Douglas Macarthur (1880-1964, American Army General in WW II)

11 A father is always making his baby into a little woman. And when she is a woman he turns her back again.
Enid Bagnold (1889-1981, British Novelist, Playwright)

12 You know, fathers just have a way of putting everything together.
Erika Cosby

13 To be a successful father... there's one absolute rule: when you have a kid, don't look at it for the first two years.
Ernest Hemingway (1898-1961, American Writer)

14 To a father growing old nothing is dearer than a daughter.
Euripides (480-406 BC, Greek Tragic Poet)

15 Noble fathers have noble children.
Euripides (480-406 BC, Greek Tragic Poet)

16 A father is a banker provided by nature.
French Proverb

17 When one has not had a good father, one must create one.
Friedrich Nietzsche (1844-1900, German Philosopher)

18 A man knows when he is growing old because he begins to look like his father.
Gabriel Garcia Marquez (1928-, Colombian Writer)

19 My father must have had some elementary education for he could read and write and keep accounts inaccurately
George Bernard Shaw (1856-1950, Irish-born British Dramatist)

20 One father is more than a hundred schoolmasters.
George Herbert (1593-1632, British Metaphysical Poet)

21 That is the thankless position of the father in the family -- the provider for all, and the enemy of all.
J. August Strindberg (1849-1912, Swedish Dramatist, Novelist, Poet)

22 That he delights in the misery of others no man will confess, and yet what other motive can make a father cruel?
Joseph Addison (1672-1719, British Essayist, Poet, Statesman)

23 As fathers commonly go, it is seldom a misfortune to be fatherless; and considering the general run of sons, as seldom a misfortune to be childless.
Lord Chesterfield (1694-1773, British Statesman, Author)

24 Blessed indeed is the man who hears many gentle voices call him father!
Lydia M. Child (1802-1880, American Abolitionist, Writer, Editor)

25 Be kind to thy father, for when thou were young, who loved thee so fondly as he? He caught the first accents that fell from thy tongue, and joined in thy innocent glee.
Margaret Courtney

26 I watched a small man with thick calluses on both hands work fifteen and sixteen hours a day. I saw him once literally bleed from the bottoms of his feet, a man who came here uneducated, alone, unable to speak the language, who taught me all I needed to know about faith and hard work by the simple eloquence of his example.
Mario Cuomo

27 What a dreadful thing it must be to have a dull father.
Mary Mapes Dodge

28 Don't make a baby if you can't be a father.
National Urban League Slogan

29 The American father is never seen in London. He passes his life entirely in Wall Street and communicates with his family once a month by means of a telegram in cipher.
Oscar Wilde (1856-1900, British Author, Wit)

30 Fathers should be neither seen nor heard. That is the only proper basis for family life.
Oscar Wilde (1856-1900, British Author, Wit)

31 The thing to remember about fathers is, they're men. A girl has to keep it in mind: They are dragon-seekers, bent on improbable rescues. Scratch any father, you find someone chock-full of qualms and romantic terrors, believing change is a threat -- like your first shoes with heels on, like your first bicycle I it took such months to get.
Phyllis Mcginley (1905-1978, American Poet, Author)

32 An angry father is most cruel toward himself.
Publilius Syrus (1st Century BC, Roman Writer)

33 None of you can ever be proud enough of being the child of SUCH a Father who has not his equal in this world -- so great, so good, so faultless. Try, all of you, to follow in his footsteps and don't be discouraged, for to be really in everything like him none of you, I am sure, will ever be. Try, therefore, to be like him in some points, and you will have acquired a great deal.
Queen Victoria (1819-1901, Queen of Great Britain)

34 An unforgiving eye, and a damned disinheriting countenance!
Richard Brinsley Sheridan (1751-1816, Anglo-Irish Dramatist)

35 Those who have never had a father can at any rate never know the sweets of losing one. To most men the death of his father is a new lease of life.
Samuel Butler (1612-1680, British Poet, Satirist)

36 I cannot think of any need in childhood as strong as the need for a father's protection.
Sigmund Freud (1856-1939, Austrian Physician - Founder of Psychoanalysis)

37 What harsh judges fathers are to all young men!
Terence (185-159 BC, Roman Writer of Comedies)

38 The most important thing a father can do for his children is to love their mother.
Theodore M. Hesburgh (1917-, American Clergyman, University President)

39 There are fathers who do not love their children, but there is no grandfather who does not adore his grandson.
Victor Hugo (1802-1885, French Poet, Dramatist, Novelist)

40 He who is taught to live upon little owes more to his father's wisdom than he who has a great deal left him does to his father's care.
William Penn (1644-1718, British Religious Leader, Founder of Pennsylvania)

41 Men are generally more careful of the breed of their horses and dogs than of their children.
William Penn (1644-1718, British Religious Leader, Founder of Pennsylvania)

[42] It is a wise father that knows his own child.
William Shakespeare (1564-1616, British Poet, Playwright, Actor)

FATHERS AND SONS

[1] Sons have always a rebellious wish to be disillusioned by that which charmed their fathers.
Aldous Huxley (1894-1963, British Author)

[2] We think our fathers fools, so wise we grow. Our wiser sons, no doubt will think us so.
Alexander Pope (1688-1744, British Poet, Critic, Translator)

[3] By the time a man realizes that maybe his father was right, he usually has a son who thinks he's wrong.
Charles Wadworth

[4] In peace the sons bury their fathers, but in war the fathers bury their sons.
Croesus

[5] A man's desire for a son is usually nothing but the wish to duplicate himself in order that such a remarkable pattern may not be lost to the world.
Helen Rowland (1875-1950, American Journalist)

[6] If the relationship of father to son could really be reduced to biology, the whole earth would blaze with the glory of fathers and sons.
James Baldwin (1924-1987, American Author)

[7] Sir Walter, being strangely surprised and put out of his countenance at so great a table, gives his son a damned blow over the face. His son, as rude as he was, would not strike his father, but strikes over the face the gentleman that sat next to him and said "Box about: twill come to my father anon."
John Aubrey (1626-1697, British Antiquarian, Writer)

[8] His father watched him across the gulf of years and pathos which always must divide a father from his son.
John Marquand (1893-1960, American Author)

FATIGUE

[1] Never tire yourself more than necessary, even if you have to found a culture on the fatigue of your bones.
Antonin Artaud (1896-1948, French Theater Producer, Actor, Theorist)

[2] Fatigue dulls the pain, but awakes enticing thoughts of death. So! that is the way in which you are tempted to overcome your loneliness -- by making the ultimate escape from life. -- No! It may be that death is to be your ultimate gift to life: it must not be an act of treachery against it.
Dag Hammarskjold (1905-1961, Swedish Statesman, Secretary-general of U.N.)

[3] Our fatigue is often caused not by work, but by worry, frustration and resentment.
Dale Carnegie (1888-1955, American Author, Trainer)

[4] Men weary as much of not doing the things they want to do as of doing the things they do not want to do.
Eric Hoffer (1902-1983, American Author, Philosopher)

[5] Our greatest weariness comes from work not done.
Eric Hoffer (1902-1983, American Author, Philosopher)

[6] You've got to be in top physical condition. Fatigue makes cowards of us all.
Vince Lombardi (1913-1970, American Football Coach)

[7] Fatigue makes cowards of us all.
Vince Lombardi (1913-1970, American Football Coach)

[8] Nothing is so fatiguing as the eternal hanging on of an uncompleted task.
William James (1842-1910, American Psychologist, Professor, Author)

FAULTS

[1] Bad people excuse their faults; wise people leave them.
Ben Johnston

[2] He has not a single redeeming defect.
Benjamin Disraeli (1804-1881, British Statesman, Prime Minister)

[3] A benevolent man should allow a few faults in himself, to keep his friends in countenance.
Benjamin Franklin (1706-1790, American Scientist, Publisher, Diplomat)

[4] Rare is the person who can weigh the faults of others without putting his thumb on the scales.
Byron J. Langenfield

[5] Better a diamond with a flaw than a pebble without one.
Chinese Proverb

[6] Not to alter one's faults is to be faulty indeed.
Confucius (551-479 BC, Chinese Ethical Teacher, Philosopher)

[7] The real fault is to have faults and not amend them.
Confucius (551-479 BC, Chinese Ethical Teacher, Philosopher)

[8] When you have faults, do not fear to abandon them.
Confucius (551-479 BC, Chinese Ethical Teacher, Philosopher)

[9] The faults of a superior person are like the sun and moon. They have their faults, and everyone sees them; they change and everyone looks up to them.
Confucius (551-479 BC, Chinese Ethical Teacher, Philosopher)

[10] Trust no friend without faults, and love a woman, but no angel.
Doris Lessing (1919-, British Novelist)

[11] People may flatter themselves just as much by thinking that their faults are always present to other people's minds, as if they believe that the world is always contemplating their individual charms and virtues.
Elizabeth Gaskell (1810-1865, British Novelist)

12 The essence of a man is found in his faults.
Francis Picabia (1878-1953, French Painter, Poet)

13 If we had no faults of our own, we should not take so much pleasure in noticing those in others.
François de La Rochefoucauld (1613-1680, French classical writer)

14 Only the great can afford to have great defects.
François de La Rochefoucauld (1613-1680, French classical writer)

15 We forget our faults easily when they are known to ourselves alone.
François de La Rochefoucauld (1613-1680, French classical writer)

16 It is easier to discover a deficiency in individuals, in states, and in Providence, than to see their real import and value.
Georg Hegel (1770-1831, German Philosopher)

17 A man can become so accustomed to the thought of his own faults that he will begin to cherish them as charming little "personal characteristics."
Helen Rowland (1875-1950, American Journalist)

18 Don't find fault, find a remedy.
Henry Ford (1863-1947, American Industrialist, Founder of Ford Motor Company)

19 While fools shun one set of faults they run into the opposite one.
Horace (65-8 BC, Italian Poet)

20 Everyone has his faults which he continually repeats: neither fear nor shame can cure them.
Jean De La Fontaine (1621-1695, French Poet)

21 Humankind's chief fault is that they have so many small ones.
Jean Paul

22 I may have faults, but being wrong ain't one of them.
Jimmy Hoffa (1913-1975, Brazilian-born American Labor Leader)

23 Certain defects are necessary for the existence of individuality.
Johann Wolfgang Von Goethe (1749-1832, German Poet, Dramatist, Novelist)

24 Our friends don't see our faults, or conceal them, or soften them.
Joseph Addison (1672-1719, British Essayist, Poet, Statesman)

25 Fools can find fault, but they can't act anymore wisely.
Langbien

26 Conceal a flaw, and the world will imagine the worst.
Marcus Valerius Martial (40-104, Latin poet and epigrammatist)

27 Humility is not my forte, and whenever I dwell for any length of time on my own shortcomings, they gradually begin to seem mild, harmless, rather engaging little things, not at all like the staring defects in other people's characters.
Margaret Halsey (1910-, American Author)

28 The more defects a man may have, the older he is, the less lovable, the more resounding his success.
Marquis De Sade (1740-1814, French Author)

29 Why do we discover faults so much more readily than perfection.
Marquise De STVignT

30 Some faults are so closely allied to qualities that it is difficult to weed out the vice without eradicating the virtue.
Oliver Goldsmith (1728-1774, Anglo-Irish Author, Poet, Playwright)

31 There are some faults so nearly allied to excellence that we can scarce weed out the vice without eradicating the virtue.
Oliver Goldsmith (1728-1774, Anglo-Irish Author, Poet, Playwright)

32 None of us can stand other people having the same faults as ourselves.
Oscar Wilde (1856-1900, British Author, Wit)

33 Our faults irritate us most when we see them in others.
Pennsylvania Dutch Proverb

34 No one is worse, for knowing the worst of themselves.
Proverb

35 A man's personal defects will commonly have with the rest of the world precisely that importance which they have to himself. If he makes light of them, so will other men.
Ralph Waldo Emerson (1803-1882, American Poet, Essayist)

36 It is always well to accept your own shortcomings with candor but to regard those of your friends with polite incredulity.
Russell Lynes (1910-, American Editor, Critic)

37 Wink at small faults, for you have great ones yourself.
Scottish Proverb

38 Faults are beauties in a lovers eye.
Theocritus

39 The greatest of all faults, I should say, is to be conscious of none.
Thomas Carlyle (1795-1881, Scottish Philosopher, Author)

40 A good garden may have some weeds.
Thomas Fuller (1608-1661, British Clergyman, Author)

41 A fault is sooner found than mended.
Ulpian Fulwell

42 We are all full of weakness and errors; let us mutually pardon each other our follies it is the first law of nature.
Voltaire (1694-1778, French Historian, Writer)

43 It is well that there is no one without a fault; for he would not have a friend in the world.
William Hazlitt (1778-1830, British Essayist)

44 They say men are molded out of faults, and for the most, become much more the better; for being a little bad. [Measure For Measure]
William Shakespeare (1564-1616, British Poet, Playwright, Actor)

45 Love to faults is always blind, always is to joy inclined. Lawless, winged, and unconfined, and breaks all chains from every mind.
William Shakespeare (1564-1616, British Poet, Playwright, Actor)

46 Men's faults to themselves seldom appear.
William Shakespeare (1564-1616, British Poet, Playwright, Actor)

FAVORS

1 The pleasure we derive from doing favors is partly in the feeling it gives us that we are not altogether worthless. It is a pleasant surprise to ourselves.
Eric Hoffer (1902-1983, American Author, Philosopher)

2 To accept a favor is to forfeit liberty.
Laber

3 Benefits should be conferred gradually; and in that way they will taste better.
Niccolo Machiavelli (1469-1527, Italian Author, Statesman)

4 To a well deserving person God will show favor. To an ill deserving person He will simply be just.
Plaut

5 The person who receives the most favors is the one who knows how to return them.
Publilius Syrus (1st Century BC, Roman Writer)

6 To refuse graciously is to confer a favor.
Publilius Syrus (1st Century BC, Roman Writer)

7 When you confer a benefit on those worthy of it, you confer a favor on all.
Publilius Syrus (1st Century BC, Roman Writer)

8 How wretched is the person who hangs on by the favors of the powerful.
Robert Burns (1759-1796, Scottish Poet)

9 Never ask a favor of someone till they have had their dinner.
Saying

10 Our friends are generally ready to do everything for us, except the very thing we wish them to do.
William Hazlitt (1778-1830, British Essayist)

11 The person whose doors I enter with most pleasure, and quit with most regret, never did me the smallest favor.
William Hazlitt (1778-1830, British Essayist)

12 O how wretched is that poor man that hangs on princes favors! There is betwixt that smile we would aspire to, that sweet aspect of princes, and their ruin, more pangs and fears than wars or women have, and when he falls, he falls like Lucifer, never to hope again.
William Shakespeare (1564-1616, British Poet, Playwright, Actor)

FEAR

1 A woman is the only thing I am afraid of that I know will not hurt me.
Abraham Lincoln (1809-1865, Sixteenth President of the USA)

2 As the ostrich when pursued hideth his head, but forgetteth his body; so the fears of a coward expose him to danger.
Akhenaton (1375 BC, Egyptian King, Monotheist)

3 Only he who can say, "The Lord is my strength," can say, "Of whom shall I be afraid?"
Alexander Maclaren (1826-1910, British Preacher)

4 There is no terror in a bang, only in the anticipation of it.
Alfred Hitchcock (1899-1980, Anglo-American Filmmaker)

5 By the time we are women, fear is as familiar to us as air. It is our element. We live in it, we inhale it, we exhale it, and most of the time we do not even notice it. Instead of "I am afraid," we say, "I don't want to," or "I don't know how," or "I can't."
Andrea Dworkin (1946-, American Feminist Critic)

6 Never take counsel of your fears.
Andrew Jackson (1767-1845, Seventh President of the USA)

7 In morals what begins in fear usually ends in wickedness; in religion what begins in fear usually ends in fanaticism. Fear, either as a principle or a motive, is the beginning of all evil.
Anna Jameson (1794-1860, British Essayist)

8 Every time you win, it diminishes the fear a little bit. You never really cancel the fear of losing; you keep challenging it.
Arthur Ashe (1943-1993, African-American Tennis Player)

9 The worst sorrows in life are not in its losses and misfortune, but its fears.
Arthur Christopher Benson (1862-1925, British Author, Poet)

10 If hopes were dupes, fears may be liars.
Arthur Hugh Clough (1819-1861, British Poet)

11 I am deliberate and afraid of nothing.
Audre Lorde

12 I can say, I am terribly frightened and fear is terrible and awful and it makes me uncomfortable, so I won't do that because it makes me uncomfortable. Or I could say get used to being uncomfortable. It is uncomfortable doing something that's risky. But so what? Do you want to stagnate and just be comfortable?
Barbara Streisand (1942-, American Singer, Actress, Director)

13 Fear is the main source of superstition, and one of the main sources of cruelty. To conquer fear is the beginning of wisdom.
Bertrand Russell (1872-1970, British Philosopher, Mathematician, Essayist)

14 Anything I've ever done that ultimately was worthwhile... initially scared me to death.
Betty Bender

15 Take courage! It is I. Don't be afraid. [Matthew 14:27]
Bible (Sacred Scriptures of Christians and Judaism)

16 Fear is the biggest motivator.
Bill Dixon

17 A champion is afraid of losing. Everyone else is afraid of winning.
Billie Jean King (1943-, American Tennis Player)

18 Fear of the pain blinds us to the goal of healing. Only by seeing our problems clearly and experiencing them can we do something about them.
Bob Hoffman (American Peak Performance Consultant, Author)

19 The whole secret of existence is to have no fear. Never fear what will become of you, depend on no one. Only the moment you reject all help are you freed.
Buddha (568-488 BC, Founder of Buddhism)

20 When one has the feeling of dislike for evil, when one feels tranquil, one finds pleasure in listening to good teachings; when one has these feelings and appreciates them, one is free of fear.
Buddha (568-488 BC, Founder of Buddhism)

21 We often pretend to fear what we really despise, and more often despise what we really fear.
Charles Caleb Colton (1780-1832, British Sportsman Writer)

22 If you are not concerned about the outcome of a circumstance, you will experience no fear. Whatever the outcome will be, will be, whether you fear it or not.
Ching Ning Chu (Chinese-American Businesswoman, Lecturer, Author)

23 Good men have the fewest fears. He has but one great fear who fears to do wrong; he has a thousand who has overcome it.
Christian Nevell Bovee (1820-1904, American Author, Lawyer)

24 There is great beauty in going through life without anxiety or fear. Half our fears are baseless, and the other half discreditable.
Christian Nevell Bovee (1820-1904, American Author, Lawyer)

25 Panic is a sudden desertion of us, and a going over to the enemy of our imagination.
Christian Nevell Bovee (1820-1904, American Author, Lawyer)

26 He who strikes terror in others is himself continually in fear.
Claudius Claudianus (340-410, Egyptian Latin Poet)

27 The hero and the coward both feel the same thing, but the hero uses his fear, projects it onto his opponent, while the coward runs. It's the same thing, fear, but it's what you do with it that matters.
Cus D'Amato (American Boxing Trainer)

28 A fighter has to know fear.
Cus D'Amato (American Boxing Trainer)

29 Do the thing you fear to do and keep on doing it... that is the quickest and surest way ever yet discovered to conquer fear.
Dale Carnegie (1888-1955, American Author, Trainer)

30 Inaction breeds doubt and fear. Action breeds confidence and courage. If you want to conquer fear, do not sit home and think about it. Go out and get busy.
Dale Carnegie (1888-1955, American Author, Trainer)

31 You can conquer almost any fear if you will only make up your mind to do so. For remember, fear doesn't exist anywhere except in the mind.
Dale Carnegie (1888-1955, American Author, Trainer)

32 If you want to conquer fear, don't sit home and think about it. Go out and get busy
Dale Carnegie (1888-1955, American Author, Trainer)

33 Do what you fear and fear disappears.
David J. Schwartz (American Trainer, Author of "The Magic of Thinking Big")

34 Fear can be headier than whiskey, once man has acquired a taste for it.
Donald Downes

35 Only when we are no longer afraid do we begin to live...
Dorothy Thompson

36 Action cures fear, inaction creates terror.
Doug Horton

37 He without fear is king of the world.
E. E. Eddison

38 Fear can supplant our real problems only to the extent --unwilling either to assimilate or to exhaust it --we perpetuate it within ourselves like a temptation and enthrone it at the very heart of our solitude.
E. M. Cioran (1911-, Rumanian-born French Philosopher)

39 Whenever we're afraid, its because we don't know enough. If we understood enough, we would never be afraid.
Earl Nightingale (1921-1989, American Radio Announcer, Author, Motivator, Speaker)

40 Winners are those people who make a habit of doing the things losers are uncomfortable doing.
Ed Foreman (American Motivational Lecturer, Writer)

41 No passion so effectually robs the mind of all its powers of acting and reasoning as fear.
Edmund Burke (1729-1797, British Political Writer, Statesman)

42 To live with fear and not be afraid is the final test of maturity.
Edward Weeks

43 Less base the fear of death than fear of life.
Edward Young (1683-1765, British Poet, Dramatist)

44 You gain strength, courage, and confidence by each experience in which you really stop to look fear in the face. You are able to say to yourself, "I have lived through this horror. I can take the next thing that comes along." You must do the thing you think you cannot do.
Eleanor Roosevelt (1884-1962, American First Lady, Columnist, Lecturer, Humanitarian)

45 I believe that anyone can conquer fear by doing the things he fears to do, provided he keeps doing them until he gets a record of successful experience behind him.
Eleanor Roosevelt (1884-1962, American First Lady, Columnist, Lecturer, Humanitarian)

46 Fear is the sand in the machinery of life.
Eli Stanley Jones (1884-1973, American Missionary)

47 The first and great commandment is, "Don't let them scare you."
Elmer Davis

48 For it is not death or hardship that is a fearful thing, but the fear of death and hardship.
Epictetus (50-120, Stoic Philosopher)

49 Fear comes from uncertainty. When we are absolutely certain, whether of our worth or worthlessness, we are almost impervious to fear. Thus a feeling of utter unworthiness can be a source of courage.
Eric Hoffer (1902-1983, American Author, Philosopher)

50 Fear of becoming a has been keeps some people from becoming anything.
Eric Hoffer (1902-1983, American Author, Philosopher)

51 God incarnate is the end of fear; and the heart that realizes that He is in the midst... will be quiet in the middle of alarm.
F. B. Meyer

52 Great fear is concealed under daring.
F. L. Lucan (39-65, Roman Epic Poet)

53 How very little can be done under the spirit of fear.
Florence Nightingale (1820-1910, British Nurse)

54 Men fear death as children fear to go in the dark; and as that natural fear in children is increased with tales, so is the other.
Francis Bacon (1561-1626, British Philosopher, Essayist, Statesman)

55 It is a miserable state of mind to have few things to desire and many things to fear.
Francis Bacon (1561-1626, British Philosopher, Essayist, Statesman)

56 The man who has ceased to fear has ceased to care.
Francis H. Bradley (1846-1924, British Philosopher)

57 Fear is the mind killer
Frank Herbert (1920-1986, American Writer)

58 The only thing we have to fear is fear itself.
Franklin D. Roosevelt (1882-1945, Thirty-second President of the USA)

59 My "fear"... is my substance, and probably the best part of me.
Franz Kafka (1883-1924, German Novelist, Short-Story Writer)

60 Fear of failure must never be a reason not to try something.
Frederick Smith (American Businessman, Founder of Federal Express)

61 It's better to get mugged than to live a life of fear.
Freeman Dyson (1923-, British-born American Physicist, Author)

62 People always make the wolf more formidable than he is.
French Proverb

63 Fear is the mother of morality.
Friedrich Nietzsche (1844-1900, German Philosopher)

64 If we take the generally accepted definition of bravery as a quality which knows no fear, I have never seen a brave man. All men are frightened. The more intelligent they are, the more they are frightened.
George S. Patton (1885-1945, American Army General during World War II)

65 There is a time to take counsel of your fears, and there is a time to never listen to your fear.
George S. Patton (1885-1945, American Army General during World War II) ·

66 That fear first created the gods is perhaps as true as anything so brief could be on so great a subject.
George Santayana (1863-1952, American Philosopher, Poet)

67 At man's core there is a voice that wants him never to give in to fear. But if it is true that in general man cannot give in to fear, at the very least he postpones indefinitely the moment when he will have to confront himself with the object of his fear... when he will no longer have the assistance of reason as guaranteed by God, or when he will no longer have the assistance of God such as reason guaranteed. It is necessary to recoil, but it is necessary to leap, and perhaps one only recoils in order to leap better.
Georges Bataille (1897-1962, French Novelist, Critic)

68 The timidity of the child or the savage is entirely reasonable; they are alarmed at this world, because this world is a very alarming place. They dislike being alone because it is verily and indeed an awful idea to be alone. Barbarians fear the unknown for the same reason that Agnostics worship it --because it is a fact.
Gilbert K. Chesterton (1874-1936, British Author)

69 Depression, gloom, pessimism, despair, discouragement, these slay ten human beings to every one murdered by typhoid, influenza, diabetes or pneumonia. If tuberculosis is the great white plague, then fear is the great black plague.
Gilbert Murray (1866-1957, British Classical Scholar)

70 Don't be afraid your life will end; be afraid it will never begin.
Grace Hansen

71 A chicken doesn't stop scratching just because worms are scarce.
Grandma Axiom

72 Come to the edge," He said. They said, "We are afraid." "Come to the edge," He said. They cam. He pushed them... and they flew.
Guillaume Apollinaire (1880-1918, Italian-born French Poet, Critic)

73 Fear is the oldest and strongest emotion of mankind.
H. P. Lovecraft

74 To hate and to fear is the be psychologically ill... it is, in fact, the consuming illness of our time.
Harry A. Overstreet (American Psychologist)

75 Fear the man who fears you.
Hasidic Proverb

76 Fear only two: God, and the man who has no fear of God.
Hasidic Proverb

77 People die of fright and live of confidence.
Henry David Thoreau (1817-1862, American Essayist, Poet, Naturalist)

78 One of the greatest discoveries a man makes, one of his great surprises, is to find he can do what he was afraid he couldn't do.
Henry Ford (1863-1947, American Industrialist, Founder of Ford Motor Company)

79 There is nothing strange about fear: no matter in what guise it presents itself it is something with which we are all so familiar that when a man appears who is without it we are at once enslaved by him.
Henry Miller (1891-1980, American Author)

80 Fear secretes acids; but love and trust are sweet juices.
Henry Ward Beecher (1813-1887, American Preacher, Orator, Writer)

81 You are only afraid if you are not in harmony with yourself. People are afraid because they have never owned up to themselves.
Hermann Hesse (1877-1962, German-born Swiss Novelist, Poet)

82 I think over again my small adventures, my fears, These small ones that seemed so big. For all the vital things I had to get and to reach. And yet there is only one great thing, The only thing. To live to see the great day that dawns And the light that fills the world.
Inuit Song

83 Most fears cannot withstand the test of careful scrutiny and analysis. When we expose our fears to the light of thoughtful examination they usually just evaporate.
Jack Canfield (American Motivational Speaker, Author, Trainer)

84 Fear is met and destroyed with courage.
James F. Bell (American Educator)

85 Half the things that people do not succeed in are through fear of making the attempt.
James Northcote

86 Curiosity will conquer fear even more than bravery will.
James Stephens (1882-1950, Irish Poet, Author)

87 You mistake me, my dear. I have a high respect for your nerves. They are my old friends. I have heard you mention them with consideration these twenty years at least.
Jane Austen (1775-1817, British Novelist)

88 There is perhaps nothing so bad and so dangerous in life as fear.
Jawaharlal Nehru (1889-1964, Indian Nationalist, Statesman)

89 An ugly sight, a man who is afraid.
Jean Anouilh (1910-1987, French Playwright)

90 Terror is as much a part of the concept of truth as runniness is of the concept of jam. We wouldn't like jam if it didn't, by its very nature, ooze. We wouldn't like truth if it wasn't sticky, if, from time to time, it didn't ooze blood.
Jean Baudrillard (French Postmodern Philosopher, Writer)

91 The fear of being wrong is the prime inhibitor of the creative process.
Jean Bryant

92 The timid are afraid before the danger, the cowardly while in danger, and the courageous after danger.
Jean Paul

93 The truth is that there is no terror untempered by some great moral idea.
Jean-Luc Godard (1930-, French Filmmaker, Author)

94 Confront your fears, list them, get to know them, and only then will you be able to put them aside and move ahead.
Jerry Gillies (American Author, Speaker)

95 What is needed, rather than running away or controlling or suppressing or any other resistance, is understanding fear; that means, watch it, learn about it, come directly into contact with it. We are to learn about fear, not how to escape from it.
Jiddu Krishnamurti (1895-1986, Indian Theosophist)

96 Fear of success can also be tied into the idea that success means someone else's loss. Some people are unconsciously guilty because they believe their victories are coming at the expense of another.
Joan C. Harvey (American Clinical Psychologist, Lecturer, Author)

97 I have a fear of failure.
Joe Montana (1956-, American Football Player)

98 It is the strange fate of man, that even in the greatest of evils the fear of the worst continues to haunt him.
Johann Wolfgang Von Goethe (1749-1832, German Poet, Dramatist, Novelist)

99 We must travel in the direction of our fear.
John Berryman (1914-1972, American Poet)

100 He has not learned the first lesson of life who does not every day surmount a fear.
John Dryden (1631-1700, British Poet, Dramatist, Critic)

101 Let us never negotiate out of fear but let us never fear to negotiate.
John F. Kennedy (1917-1963, Thirty-fifth President of the USA)

102 Every day I run scared. That's the only way I can stay ahead.
John Johnson (American Businessman, Founder of Johnson Publishing)

103 Only with absolute fearlessness can we slay the dragons of mediocrity that invade our gardens.
John Maynard Keynes (1883-1946, British Economist)

104 Have no fear of moving into the unknown. Simply step out fearlessly knowing that I am with you, therefore no harm can befall you; all is very, very well. Do this in complete faith and confidence.
John Paul II (1920, Polish-Born Italian Pope)

105 How does one kill fear, I wonder? How do you shoot a specter through the heart, slash off its spectral head, take it by its spectral throat?
Joseph Conrad (1857-1924, Polish-born British Novelist)

106 There are moments when everything goes well, but don't be frightened.
Jules Renard (1864-1910, French Author, Dramatist)

107 If you're never scared or embarrassed or hurt, it means you never take any chances.
Julia Sorel

108 Become so wrapped up in something that you forget to be afraid.
Lady Bird Johnson

109 Favor and disgrace are like fear. Favor is in a higher place, and disgrace in a lower place. When you win them you are like being in fear, and when you lose them you are also like being in fear. So favor and disgrace are like fear.
Lao-Tzu (600 BC, Chinese Philosopher, Founder of Taoism, Author of the "Tao Te Ching")

110 Just as courage imperils life; fear protects it.
Leonardo Da Vinci (1452-1519, Italian Inventor, Architect, Painter, Scientist, Sculptor)

111 Too many of us are not living our dreams because we are living our fears.
Les Brown (1945-, American Speaker, Author, Trainer, Motivator Lecturer)

112 When you face your fear, most of the time you will discover that it was not really such a big threat after all. We all need some form of deeply rooted, powerful motivation -- it empowers us to overcome obstacles so we can live our dreams.
Les Brown (1945-, American Speaker, Author, Trainer, Motivator Lecturer)

113 Fear does not have any special power unless you empower it by submitting to it.
Les Brown (1945-, American Speaker, Author, Trainer, Motivator Lecturer)

114 Where fear is present, wisdom cannot be.
Lucius C. Lactantius (260-340, Latin Author, Apologist)

115 It is not death that a man should fear, but he should fear never beginning to live.
Marcus Aurelius (121-80 AD, Roman Emperor, Philosopher)

116 Fear is not a lasting teacher of duty.
Marcus T. Cicero (106-43 BC, Great Roman Orator, Politician)

117 Fear is a disease that eats away at logic and makes man inhuman.
Marian Anderson (1902-1993, American Contralto Concert and Opera Singer)

118 Our deepest fear is not that we are inadequate. Our deepest fear is that we are powerful beyond measure. It is our light, not our darkness, that most frightens us. We ask ourselves, who am I to be brilliant, gorgeous, talented, fabulous? Actually, who are you NOT to be? You are a child of God. Your playing small does not serve the world. There is nothing enlightened about shrinking so that other people won't feel insecure around you. We were born to make manifest the glory of God that is within us. It is not just in some of us, it is in everyone. And as we let our own light shine, we unconsciously give other people permission to do the same. As we are liberated from our own fear, our presence automatically liberates others.
Marianne Williamson (1952-, American Author, Lecturer on Spirituality)

119 Most fear stems from sin; to limit one's sins, one must assuredly limit one's fear, thereby bringing more peace to one's spirit.
Marvin Gaye (1939-1984, American Soul Singer)

120 It is an old psychological axiom that constant exposure to the object of fear immunizes against the fear.
Maxwell Maltz (American Plastic Surgeon, Author of "Psycho-Cybernetics")

121 Fear is that little darkroom where negatives are developed.
Michael Pritchard

122 The thing I fear most is fear.
Michel Eyquem De Montaigne (1533-1592, French Philosopher, Essayist)

123 There is no passion so contagious as that of fear.
Michel Eyquem De Montaigne (1533-1592, French Philosopher, Essayist)

124 I know what I am fleeing from, but not what I am in search of.
Michel Eyquem De Montaigne (1533-1592, French Philosopher, Essayist)

125 Fear has many eyes and can see things underground.
Miguel De Cervantes (1547-1616, Spanish Novelist, Dramatist, Poet)

126 He who is afraid of a thing gives it power over him.
Moorish Proverb

127 There are only two forces that unite men -- fear and interest.
Napoleon Bonaparte (1769-1821, French General, Emperor)

128 He who fears being conquered is sure of defeat.
Napoleon Bonaparte (1769-1821, French General, Emperor)

129 Men are Moved by two levers only: fear and self interest
Napoleon Bonaparte (1769-1821, French General, Emperor)

130 The most common cause of fear of old age is associated with the possibility of poverty.
Napoleon Hill (1883-1970, American Speaker, Motivational Writer, "Think and Grow Rich")

131 Fears are nothing more than states of mind.
Napoleon Hill (1883-1970, American Speaker, Motivational Writer, "Think and Grow Rich")

132 It is better to be feared than loved, if you cannot be both.
Niccolo Machiavelli (1469-1527, Italian Author, Statesman)

133 No Fear.
No Fear Company (American Clothing Company)

134 Fear guides more than gratitude.
Oliver Goldsmith (1728-1774, Anglo-Irish Author, Poet, Playwright)

135 The worst nightmare I ever had about Vietnam was that I had to go back. I woke up in a sweat, in total terror.
Oliver Stone (1946-, American Director, Writer, Producer)

136 Most of our obstacles would melt away if, instead of cowering before them, we should make up our minds to walk boldly through them.
Orison Swett Marden (1850-1924, American Author, Founder of Success Magazine)

137 An appeal to fear never finds an echo in German hearts.
Otto Von Bismarck (1815-1898, Prussian Statesman, Prime Minister)

138 You can't underestimate the power of fear.
Patricia Nixon

139 Humans, with the capacities of higher-order thinking, can overcome limiting behaviors and fears.
Paul R. Scheele (American NLP Expert and Human Potential, Author)

140 Action conquers fear.
Peter Nivio Zarlenga (American Businessman, Founder of Blockbuster Videos)

141 He who fears to suffer, suffers from fear.
Proverb

142 That fear may reach all, punish but few.
Proverb

143 A scalded cat dreads cold water.
Proverb

144 Valor grows by daring, fear by holding back.
Publilius Syrus (1st Century BC, Roman Writer)

145 Even the bravest men are frightened by sudden terrors.
Publius Cornelius Tacitus (55-117 AD, Roman Historian)

146 Fear makes men believe the worst.
Quintus Curtius Rufus (100 AD, Roman Historian)

147 Fear defeats more people than any other one thing in the world.
Ralph Waldo Emerson (1803-1882, American Poet, Essayist)

148 Do the thing we fear, and the death of fear is certain.
Ralph Waldo Emerson (1803-1882, American Poet, Essayist)

149 Fear always springs from ignorance.
Ralph Waldo Emerson (1803-1882, American Poet, Essayist)

150 Always do what you are afraid to do.
Ralph Waldo Emerson (1803-1882, American Poet, Essayist)

151 First you jump off the cliff and you build wings on the way down.
Ray Bradbury (1920-, American Science Fiction Writer)

152 My worst fear is that I'll end up living in some run-down duplex on Wilshire wearing pants hiked up to my nipples and muttering under my breath.
Richard Dreyfuss (1947-, American Actor)

153 People react to fear, not love --they don't teach that in Sunday School, but it's true.
Richard M. Nixon (1913-1994, Thirty-seventh President of the USA)

154 There is the fear that we shan't prove worthy in the eyes of someone who knows us at least as well as we know ourselves. That is the fear of God. And there is the fear of Man --fear that men won't understand us and we shall be cut of from them.
Robert Frost (1875-1963, American Poet)

155 When the will defies fear, when duty throws the gauntlet down to fate, when honor scorns to compromise with death -- that is heroism.
Robert Green Ingersoll (1833-1899, American Orator, Lawyer)

156 If you listen to your fears, you will die never knowing what a great person you might have been.
Robert H. Schuller (1926-, American Minister (Crystal Cathedral), Author, Social Leader)

157 Fear is excitement without breath.
Robert Heller (American Business Writer, Editor of Management Today)

158 Keep your fears to yourself, but share your courage with others.
Robert Louis Stevenson (1850-1895, Scottish Essayist, Poet, Novelist)

159 Fear can be conquered. I became a better person and a better football player when I learned that lesson.
Roger Craig (American Football Player)

160 Never fear shadows. They simply mean there's a light shining somewhere nearby.
Ruth E. Renkel

161 Fear is implanted in us as a preservative from evil; but its duty, like that of other passions, is not to overbear reason, but to assist it. It should not be suffered to tyrannize
Samuel Johnson (1709-1784, British Author)

162 Shame arises from the fear of men, conscience from the fear of God.
Samuel Johnson (1709-1784, British Author)

163 A person's fears are lighter when the danger is at hand.
Seneca (4 BC-65 AD, Spanish-born Roman Statesman, philosopher)

164 We are more often frightened than hurt; and we suffer more from imagination than from reality.
Seneca (4 BC-65 AD, Spanish-born Roman Statesman, philosopher)

165 Where the fear is, happiness is not.
Seneca (4 BC-65 AD, Spanish-born Roman Statesman, philosopher)

166 The more I traveled the more I realized that fear makes strangers of people who should be friends.
Shirley Maclaine (1934-, American Actress)

167 An anthill increases by accumulation. Medicine is consumed by distribution. That which is feared lessens by association. This is the thing to understand.
Siddha Nagarjuna (100-200 AD, Indian/Tibetan Father of Mahayan)

168 To him who is in fear everything rustles.
Sophocles (495-406 BC, Greek Tragic Poet)

169 There is nothing with which every man is so afraid as getting to know how enormously much he is capable of doing and becoming.
Soren Kierkegaard (1813-1855, Danish Philosopher, Writer)

170 Those who love to be feared fear to be loved, and they themselves are more afraid than anyone, for whereas other men fear only them, they fear everyone.
St. Francis De Sales (1567-1622, Roman Catholic Bishop, Writer)

171 It all changed when I realized I'm not the only one on the planet who's scared. Everyone else is, too. I started asking people, "Are you scared, too?" "You bet your sweet life I am." "Aha, so that's the way it is for you, too." We were all in the same boat. That's probably what is so effective at our workshops. When I ask, "Who else feels like this?" the whole room of hands goes up. People realize they are not the only one who feels that way.
Stan Dale (American Missionary)

172 Comfort zones are plush lined coffins. When you stay in your plush lined coffins, you die.
Stan Dale (American Missionary)

173 Feel the fear and do it anyway.
Susan Jeffers (American Author, Speaker)

174 Fear less, hope more; eat less, chew more; whine less breathe more; talk less, say more; hate less, love more; and all good things are yours.
Swedish Proverb

175 I will show you fear in a handful of dust.
T. S. Eliot (1888-1965, American-born British Poet, Critic)

176 The first duty of man is to conquer fear; he must get rid of it, he cannot act till then.
Thomas Carlyle (1795-1881, Scottish Philosopher, Author)

177 Scruples, temptations, and fears, and cutting perplexities of the heart, are often the lot of the most excellent persons.
Thomas p Kempis (1379-1471, German Monk, Mystic, Religious Writer)

178 We fear things in proportion to our ignorance of them.
Titus Livy (59 BC-17 AD, Roman Historian)

179 Do what you fear most and you control fear.
Tom Hopkins (American Sales Trainer, Speaker, Author)

180 He who knows self as the enjoyer of the honey from the flowers of the senses, ever present within, ruler of time, goes beyond fear. For this self is supreme!
Veda Upanishads (800 BC, Hindu Poetic Dialogues On Metaphysics)

181 Fear may come true that which one is afraid of.
Viktor E. Frankl (1905-, Austrian Psychiatrist, Neurology, Writer, "Man's Search for Meaning")

182 Fear is proof of a degenerate mind.
Virgil (70-19 BC, Roman Poet)

183 Fear is proof of a low born soul.
Virgil (70-19 BC, Roman Poet)

184 Try a thing you haven't done three times. Once, to get over the fear of doing it. Twice, to learn how to do it. And a third time to figure out whether you like it or not.
Virgil Thomson

185 You can get something done in a short time with fear, but in the long run it just doesn't pay off.
Wendell Parsons (American Businessman, CEO of Stamp-Rite)

186 Things done well and with a care, exempt themselves from fear.
William Shakespeare (1564-1616, British Poet, Playwright, Actor)

187 In time we hate that which we often fear.
William Shakespeare (1564-1616, British Poet, Playwright, Actor)

188 Of all base passions, fear is the most accursed.
William Shakespeare (1564-1616, British Poet, Playwright, Actor)

189 Fearless minds climb soonest into crowns.
William Shakespeare (1564-1616, British Poet, Playwright, Actor)

190 The best safety lies in fear.
William Shakespeare (1564-1616, British Poet, Playwright, Actor)

191 A man's doubts and fears are his worst enemies.
William Wrigley Jr. (1861-1932, American Businessman, Founder of Wrigley & Co.)

192 It is better to be frightened now than killed hereafter
Winston Churchill (1874-1965, British Statesman, Prime Minister)

193 Fear God and you need not fear anyone else.
Woodrow T. Wilson (1856-1924, Twenty-eighth President of the USA)

194 Grab the broom of anger and drive off the beast of fear.
Zora Neale Hurston (1903-1960, American Novelist)

FEELINGS

1 When I do good, I feel good. When I do bad, I feel bad. And that's my religion.
Abraham Lincoln (1809-1865, Sixteenth President of the USA)

2 When the senses contact sense objects, a person experiences cold or heat, pleasure or pain. These experiences are fleeting they come and go. Bear them patiently.
Bhagavad Gita (400 BC, Sanskrit Poem Incorporated Into the Mahabharata)

3 Feelings are like chemicals, the more you analyze them the worse they smell.
Charles Kingsley (1819-1875, British Author, Clergyman)

4 Feeling without judgment is a washy draught indeed; but judgment untempered by feeling is too bitter and husky a morsel for human deglutition.
Charlotte Bronte (1816-1855, British Novelist)

5 To have in general but little feeling, seems to be the only security against feeling too much on any particular occasion.
George Eliot (1819-1880, British Novelist)

6 See that each hour's feelings, and thoughts and actions are pure and true; then your life will be also.
Henry Ward Beecher (1813-1887, American Preacher, Orator, Writer)

7 Feelings are everywhere -- be gentle.
J. Masai

8 Cowardice and courage are never without a measure of affectation. Nor is love. Feelings are never true. They play with their mirrors.
Jean Baudrillard (French Postmodern Philosopher, Writer)

9 Do not give in too much to feelings. A overly sensitive heart is an unhappy possession on this shaky earth.
Johann Wolfgang Von Goethe (1749-1832, German Poet, Dramatist, Novelist)

10 He disliked emotion, not because he felt lightly, but because he felt deeply.
John Buchan (1875-1940, Scottish Writer, Statesman)

11 It's not sissy to show your feeling.
Princess of Wales Diana (1961-1997, Wife of Charles, Prince of Wales)

12 Our best evidence of what people truly feel and believe comes less from their words than from their deeds.
Robert Cialdini (American Professor of Psychology)

13 Lose/Win people bury a lot of feelings. And unexpressed feelings come forth later in uglier ways. Psychosomatic illnesses often are the reincarnation of cumulative resentment, deep disappointment and disillusionment repressed by the Lose/Win mentality. Disproportionate rage or anger, overreaction to minor provocation, and cynicism are other embodiments of suppressed emotion. People who are constantly repressing, not transcending feelings toward a higher meaning find that it affects the quality of their relationships with others.
Stephen R. Covey (American Speaker, Trainer, Author of "The 7 Habits of Highly Effective People")

14 Your emotions affect every cell in your body. Mind and body, mental and physical, are intertwined.
Thomas Tutko

15 Individuality is founded in feeling; and the recesses of feeling, the darker, blinder strata of character, are the only places in the world in which we catch real fact in the making, and directly perceive how events happen, and how work is actually done.
William James (1842-1910, American Psychologist, Professor, Author)

FELLOWSHIP

1 Fellowship with God means warfare with the world.
Charles E. Fuller

2 A gentleman is one who puts more into the world than he takes out.
George Bernard Shaw (1856-1950, Irish-born British Dramatist)

3 A habit of devout fellowship with God is the spring of all our life, and the strength of it.
Henry Edward Manning (1808-1892, British Cardinal)

FEMINISM

1 The modern woman is the curse of the universe. A disaster, that's what. She thinks that before her arrival on the scene no woman ever did anything worthwhile before, no woman was ever liberated until her time, no woman really ever amounted to anything.
Adela Rogers St. Johns

2 The connections between and among women are the most feared, the most problematic, and the most potentially transforming force on the planet.
Adrienne Rich (1929-, American Poet)

3 Women have been taught that, for us, the earth is flat, and that if we venture out, we will fall off the edge. Some of us have ventured out nevertheless, and so far we have not fallen off. It is my faith, my feminist faith, that we will not.
Andrea Dworkin (1946-, American Feminist Critic)

4 Men who want to support women in our struggle for freedom and justice should understand that it is not terrifically important to us that they learn to cry; it is important to us that they stop the crimes of violence against us.
Andrea Dworkin (1946-, American Feminist Critic)

5 Feminism is hated because women are hated. Anti-feminism is a direct expression of misogyny; it is the political defense of women hating.
Andrea Dworkin (1946-, American Feminist Critic)

6 Just because we're sisters under the skin doesn't mean we've got much in common.
Angela Carter (1940-1992, British Author)

7 Thou art blind to the danger of marrying a woman who feels and acts out the principle of equal rights.
Angelina Grimke (1805-1879, American Abolitionist, Feminist)

8 The people I'm furious with are the Women's Liberationists. They keep getting up on soapboxes and proclaiming women are brighter than men. That's true, but it should be kept quiet or it ruins the whole racket.
Anita Loos (1893-1981, American Novelist, Screenwriter)

9 Whether we regard the Women's Liberation movement as a serious threat, a passing convulsion, or a fashionable idiocy, it is a movement that mounts an attack on practically everything that women value today and introduces the language and sentiments of political confrontation into the area of personal relationships.
Arianna Stassinopoulos (1950-, Greek Author)

10 Liberation is an ever shifting horizon, a total ideology that can never fulfill its promises. It has the therapeutic quality of providing emotionally charged rituals of solidarity in hatred -- it is the amphetamine of its believers.
Arianna Stassinopoulos (1950-, Greek Author)

11 The feminist anti-pornography movement, no less than the feminist movement of a century ago, encourages the assumption that male and female sexuality, and possibly morality, are as unlike as yin and yang.
Barbara Ehrenreich (1941-, American Author, Columnist)

12 Women get more unhappy the more they try to liberate themselves.
Brigitte Bardot (1934-, French Film Actress)

13 We need a new kind of feminism, one that stresses personal responsibility and is open to art and sex in all their dark, unconsoling mysteries. The feminist of the fin de siècle will be bawdy, streetwise, and on-the-spot confrontational, in the prankish Sixties way.
Camille Paglia (1947-, American Author, Critic, Educator)

14 Feminism is an entire world view or gestalt, not just a laundry list of women's issues.
Charlotte Bunch

15 Male supremacy has kept woman down. It has not knocked her out.
Clare Boothe Luce (1903-1987, American Diplomat, Writer)

16 There must be a world revolution which puts an end to all materialistic conditions hindering woman from performing her natural role in life and driving her to carry out man's duties in order to be equal in rights.
Colonel Muhammar Qaddafi (1942-, Libyan Political and Military Leader)

17 If I were a woman, I would never trust men who say they are feminists. Either they are acting out of guilt, trying to establish credentials, or they think they might be able to pick up more girls. If I were a woman, I would say, go away and have your first period. Then come back and tell me you are a feminist.
David Thomas (American Businessman, Founder of Wendy's Restaurants)

18 I wanted to be the first woman to burn her bra, but it would have taken the fire department four days to put it out.
Dolly Parton (1946-, American Musician, Country singer, Actress, Songwriter)

19 The vote means nothing to women. We should be armed.
Edna O'Brien

20 The emancipation of women is practically the greatest egoistic movement of the nineteenth century, and the most intense affirmation of the right of the self that history has yet seen.
Ellen Key (1849-1926, Swedish Author, Feminist)

21 Merely external emancipation has made of the modern woman an artificial being. Now, woman is confronted with the necessity of emancipating herself from emancipation, if she really desires to be free.
Emma Goldman (1869-1940, American Anarchist)

22 Everything in woman hath a solution. It is called pregnancy.
Friedrich Nietzsche (1844-1900, German Philosopher)

23 Surely women's liberation is a most unpromising panacea. But the movement is working politically, because our sexuality is so confused, our masculinity so uncertain, and our families so beleaguered that no one knows what they are for or how they are sustained.
George Gilder (American Economist and Author)

24 The sight of women talking together has always made men uneasy; nowadays it means rank subversion.
Germaine Greer (1939-, Australian Feminist Writer)

25 I didn't fight to get women out from behind vacuum cleaners to get them onto the board of Hoover.
Germaine Greer (1939-, Australian Feminist Writer)

26 Women's liberation, if it abolishes the patriarchal family, will abolish a necessary substructure of the authoritarian state, and once that withers away Marx will have come true willy-nilly, so let's get on with it.
Germaine Greer (1939-, Australian Feminist Writer)

27 There has come into existence, chiefly in America, a breed of men who claim to be feminists. They imagine that they have understood "what women want" and that they are capable of giving it to them. They help with the dishes at home and make their own coffee in the office, basking the while in the refulgent consciousness of virtue. Such men are apt to think of the true male feminists as utterly chauvinistic.
Germaine Greer (1939-, Australian Feminist Writer)

28 Some of us are becoming the men we wanted to marry.
Gloria Steinem (1934-, American Feminist Writer, Editor)

29 A liberated woman is one who has sex before marriage and a job after.
Gloria Steinem (1934-, American Feminist Writer, Editor)

30 Women's Liberation is just a lot of foolishness. It's the men who are discriminated against. They can't bear children. And no one's likely to do anything about that.
Golda Meir (1898-1978, Prime Minister of Israel, 1969-74)

31 The embattled gates to equal rights indeed opened up for modern women, but I sometimes think to myself: "That is not what I meant by freedom -- it is only social progress. "
Helene Deutsch (1884-1982, American Psychiatrist)

32 Ah, I fancy it is just the same with most of what you call your "emancipation." You have read yourself into a number of new ideas and opinions. You have got a sort of smattering of recent discoveries in various fields -- discoveries that seem to overthrow certain principles which have hitherto been held impregnable and unassailable. But all this has only been a matter of intellect, Miss West -- superficial acquisition. It has not passed into your blood.
Henrik Ibsen (1828-1906, Norwegian Dramatist)

33 I am blackly bored when they are at large and at work; but somehow I am still more blackly bored when they are shut up in Holloway and we are deprived of them.
Henry James (1843-1916, American Author)

34 Movements born in hatred very quickly take on the characteristics of the thing they oppose.
J. S. Habgood (1927-, British Ecclesiastic, Archbishop of York)

35 The most important thing women have to do is to stir up the zeal of women themselves.
John Stuart Mill (1806-1873, British Philosopher, Economist)

36 A good part -- and definitely the most fun part -- of being a feminist is about frightening men.
Julie Burchill (British Journalist, Writer)

37 The freedom that women were supposed to have found in the Sixties largely boiled down to easy contraception and abortion; things to make life easier for men, in fact.
Julie Burchill (British Journalist, Writer)

38 I am a feminist, and what that means to me is much the same as the meaning of the fact that I am Black: it means that I must undertake to love myself and to respect myself as though my very life depends upon self-love and self-respect.
June Jordan (1939-, American Poet, Civil Rights Activist)

39 Men now monopolize the upper levels... depriving women of their rightful share of opportunities for incompetence.
Laurence J. Peter

40 The suffering of either sex -- of the male who is unable, because of the way in which he was reared, to take the strong initiating or patriarchal role that is still demanded of him, or of the female who has been given too much freedom of movement as a child to stay placidly within the house as an adult -- this suffering, this discrepancy, this sense of failure in an enjoined role, is the point of leverage for social change.
Margaret Mead (1901-1978, American Anthropologist)

41 I owe nothing to Women's Lib.
Margaret Thatcher (1925-, British Stateswoman, Prime Minister (1979-90))

42 Let us rise in the moral power of womanhood; and give utterance to the voice of outraged mercy, and insulted justice, and eternal truth, and mighty love and holy freedom.
Maria Weston Chapman

43 I hate discussions of feminism that end up with who does the dishes," she said. So do I. But at the end, there are always the damned dishes.
Marilyn French (1929-, American Author, Critic)

44 One of the things about equality is not just that you be treated equally to a man, but that you treat yourself equally to the way you treat a man.
Marlo Thomas

45 If the abstract rights of man will bear discussion and explanation, those of women, by a parity of reasoning, will not shrink from the same test: though a different opinion prevails in this country.
Mary Wollstonecraft (1759-1797, British Feminist Writer)

46 The sadness of the women's movement is that they don't allow the necessity of love. See, I don't personally trust any revolution where love is not allowed.
Maya Angelou (1928-, African-American poet, Writer, Performer)

47 The fundamental impulse of the movement is neither masturbatory nor concretely lesbian -- although it of course offers warm house to both these possibilities; it is an impulse to maidenhood -- to that condition in which a woman might pretend to a false fear or loathing of the penis in order to escape from any responsibility for the pleasure and well-being of the man who possesses it.
Midge Decter (1927-, American Author, Editor, Social Critic)

⁴⁸ Feminism is doomed to failure because it is based on an attempt to repeal and restructure human nature.
Phyllis Schlafly (1924-, American Author and Political Activist)

⁴⁹ The Queen is most anxious to enlist everyone who can speak or write to join in checking this mad, wicked folly of "Woman's Rights" with all its attendant horrors on which her poor, feeble sex is bent, forgetting every sense of womanly feeling and propriety.
Queen Victoria (1819-1901, Queen of Great Britain)

⁵⁰ People call me feminist whenever I express sentiments that differentiate me from a doormat or a prostitute.
Rebecca West (1892-1983, British Author)

⁵¹ One of the reasons for the failure of feminism to dislodge deeply held perceptions of male and female behavior was its insistence that women were victims, and men powerful patriarchs, which made a travesty of ordinary people's experience of the mutual interdependence of men and women.
Rosalind Coward

⁵² I became a feminist as an alternative to becoming a masochist.
Sally Kempton

⁵³ When an individual is kept in a situation of inferiority, the fact is that he does become inferior.
Simone De Beauvoir (1908-1986, French Novelist, Essayist)

⁵⁴ Women's liberation is the liberation of the feminine in the man and the masculine in the woman.
Sister Corita Kent

⁵⁵ Once made equal to man, woman becomes his superior.
Socrates (469-399 BC, Greek Philosopher of Athens)

⁵⁶ Men, their rights and nothing more; women, their rights and nothing less.
Susan B. Anthony (1820-1906, American Social Reformer and Women's Suffrage Leader)

⁵⁷ The true Republic: men, their rights and nothing more; women, their rights and nothing less.
Susan B. Anthony (1820-1906, American Social Reformer and Women's Suffrage Leader)

⁵⁸ The emancipation of today displays itself mainly in cigarettes and shorts. There is even a reaction from the ideal of an intellectual and emancipated womanhood, for which the pioneers toiled and suffered, to be seen in painted lips and nails, and the return of trailing skirts and other absurdities of dress which betoken the slave-woman's intelligent companionship.
Sylvia Pankhurst

⁵⁹ Women who seek to be equal with men lack ambition.
Timothy Leary (1921-1996, American Actor)

⁶⁰ Feminism is a political mistake. Feminism is a mistake made by women's intellect, a mistake which her instinct will recognize.
Valentine De Saint-Point

⁶¹ The history of men's opposition to women's emancipation is more interesting perhaps than the story of that emancipation itself.
Virginia Woolf (1882-1941, British Novelist, Essayist)

⁶² Feminism was recognized by the average man as a conflict in which it was impossible for a man, as a chivalrous gentleman, as a respecter of the rights of little nations (like little Belgium), as a highly evolved citizen of a highly civilized community, to refuse the claim of this better half to self-determination.
Wyndham Lewis (1882-1957, British Author, Painter)

⁶³ As a result of the feminist revolution, "feminine" becomes an abusive epithet.
Wyndham Lewis (1882-1957, British Author, Painter)

FERTILITY

¹ I don't know what it is about fecundity that so appalls. I suppose it is the teeming evidence that birth and growth, which we value, are ubiquitous and blind, that life itself is so astonishingly cheap, that nature is as careless as it is bountiful, and that with extravagance goes a crushing waste that will one day include our own cheap lives.
Annie Dillard (1945-, American Author, Poet)

² I'm hurt, hurt and humiliated beyond endurance, seeing the wheat ripening, the fountains never ceasing to give water, the sheep bearing hundreds of lambs, the she-dogs, until it seems the whole country rises to show me its tender sleeping young while I feel two hammer-blows here instead of the mouth of my child.
Federico Garcia Lorca (1898-1936, Spanish Poet, Dramatist, Musician and Artist)

³ The management of fertility is one of the most important functions of adulthood.
Germaine Greer (1939-, Australian Feminist Writer)

⁴ Virginity is now a mere preamble or waiting room to be got out of as soon as possible; it is without significance. Old age is similarly a waiting room, where you go after life's over and wait for cancer or a stroke. The years before and after the menstrual years are vestigial: the only meaningful condition left to women is that of fruitfulness.
Ursula K. Le Guin (1929-, American Author)

FESTIVALS

¹ Washington's birthday is as close to a secular Christmas as any Christian country dare come this side of blasphemy.
Alistair Cooke (1908-, British Broadcaster, Journalist)

² The red-letter days, now become, to all intents and purposes, dead-letter days.
Charles Lamb (1775-1834, British Essayist, Critic)

3   It is at a fair that man can be drunk forever on liquor, love, or fights; at a fair that your front pocket can be picked by a trotting horse looking for sugar, and your hind pocket by a thief looking for his fortune.
E(lwyn) B(rooks) White (1899-1985, American Author, Editor)

4   There is nothing funny about Halloween. This sarcastic festival reflects, rather, an infernal demand for revenge by children on the adult world.
Jean Baudrillard (French Postmodern Philosopher, Writer)

5   Seasons pursuing each other the indescribable crowd is gathered, it is the fourth of Seventh- month, (what salutes of cannon and small arms!)
Walt Whitman (1819-1892, American Poet)

FICTION

1   It's with bad sentiments that one makes good novels.
Aldous Huxley (1894-1963, British Author)

2   The really great novel tends to be the exact negative of its author's life.
Andre Maurois (1885-1967, French Writer)

3   Writing novels preserves you in a state of innocence -- a lot passes you by -- simply because your attention is otherwise diverted.
Anita Brookner (1938-, British Novelist, Art Historian)

4   If you write fiction you are, in a sense, corrupted. There's a tremendous corruptibility for the fiction writer because you're dealing mainly with sex and violence. These remain the basic themes, they're the basic themes of Shakespeare whether you like it or not.
Anthony Burgess (1917-1993, British Writer, Critic)

5   Novelists are perhaps the last people in the world to be entrusted with opinions. The nature of a novel is that it has no opinions, only the dialectic of contrary views, some of which, all of which, may be untenable and even silly. A novelist should not be too intelligent either, although he may be permitted to be an intellectual.
Anthony Burgess (1917-1993, British Writer, Critic)

6   By its very nature, the novel indicates that we are becoming. There is no final solution. There is no last word.
Carlos Fuentes (1928-, Mexican Novelist, Short-Story Writer)

7   The traditional novel form continues to enlarge our experience in those very areas where the wide-angle lens and the Cinema screen tend to narrow it.
Daniel J. Boorstin (1914-, American Historian)

8   If I were a writer, how I would enjoy being told the novel is dead. How liberating to work in the margins, outside a central perception. You are the ghoul of literature. Lovely.
Don Delillo (1926-, American Author)

9   Jesus of Nazareth could have chosen simply to express Himself in moral precepts; but like a great poet He chose the form of the parable, wonderful short stories that entertained and clothed the moral precept in an eternal form. It is not sufficient to catch man's mind, you must also catch the imaginative faculties of his mind.
Dudley Nichols (American Actor)

10   There is no longer any such thing as fiction or nonfiction; there's only narrative.
E. L. Doctorow (1931-, American Novelist)

11   The final test for a novel will be our affection for it, as it is the test of our friends, and of anything else which we cannot define.
Edward M. Forster (1879-1970, British Novelist, Essayist)

12   You know that fiction, prose rather, is possibly the roughest trade of all in writing. You do not have the reference, the old important reference. You have the sheet of blank paper, the pencil, and the obligation to invent truer than things can be true. You have to take what is not palpable and make it completely palpable and also have it seem normal and so that it can become a part of experience of the person who reads it.
Ernest Hemingway (1898-1961, American Writer)

13   When writing a novel a writer should create living people; people not characters. A character is a caricature.
Ernest Hemingway (1898-1961, American Writer)

14   It seems that the fiction writer has a revolting attachment to the poor, for even when he writes about the rich, he is more concerned with what they lack than with what they have.
Flannery O'Connor (1925-1964, American Author)

15   I at least have so much to do in unraveling certain human lots, and seeing how they were woven and interwoven, that all the light I can command must be concentrated on this particular web, and not dispersed over that tempting range of relevancies called the universe.
George Eliot (1819-1880, British Novelist)

16   I find in most novels no imagination at all. They seem to think the highest form of the novel is to write about marriage, because that's the most important thing there is for middle-class people.
Gore Vidal (1925-, American Novelist, Critic)

17   Writing fiction has become a priestly business in countries that have lost their faith.
Gore Vidal (1925-, American Novelist, Critic)

18   The time-honored bread-sauce of the happy ending.
Henry James (1843-1916, American Author)

19   The only reason for the existence of a novel is that it does attempt to represent life.
Henry James (1843-1916, American Author)

20   For a Jewish Puritan of the middle class, the novel is serious, the novel is work, the novel is conscientious application -- why, the novel is practically the retail business all over again.
Howard Nemerov (1920-1991, American Poet)

21 By measuring individual human worth, the novelist reveals the full enormity of the State's crime when it sets out to crush that individuality.
Ian Mcewan (1948-, British Author)

22 Novels as dull as dishwater, with the grease of random sentiments floating on top.
Italo Calvino (1923-1985, Cuban Writer, Essayist, Journalist)

23 We live in a world ruled by fictions of every kind -- mass merchandising, advertising, politics conducted as a branch of advertising, the instant translation of science and technology into popular imagery, the increasing blurring and intermingling of identities within the realm of consumer goods, the preempting of any free or original imaginative response to experience by the television screen. We live inside an enormous novel. For the writer in particular it is less and less necessary for him to invent the fictional content of his novel. The fiction is already there. The writer's task is to invent the reality.
J. G. Ballard (1930-, British Author)

24 When I heard the word "stream" uttered with such a revolting primness, what I think of is urine and not the contemporary novel. And besides, it isn't new, it is far from the dernier cri. Shakespeare used it continually, much too much in my opinion, and there's Tristram Shandy, not to mention the Agamemnon.
James Joyce (1882-1941, Irish Author)

25 Although our productions have afforded more extensive and unaffected pleasure than those of any other literary corporation in the world, no species of composition has been so much decried. "And what are you reading, Miss --?" "Oh! it is only a novel!" replies the young lady; while she lays down her book with affected indifference, or momentary shame. "It is only Cecilia, or Camilla, or Belinda "; or, in short, only some work in which the greatest powers of the mind are displayed, in which the most thorough knowledge of human nature, the happiest delineation of its varieties, the liveliest effusions of wit and humor, are conveyed to the world in the best chosen language.
Jane Austen (1775-1817, British Novelist)

26 Writing a novel is not merely going on a shopping expedition across the border to an unreal land: it is hours and years spent in the factories, the streets, the cathedrals of the imagination.
Janet Frame (1924-, New Zealand Novelist, Poet)

27 Fiction is not imagination. It is what anticipates imagination by giving it the form of reality. This is quite opposite to our own natural tendency which is to anticipate reality by imagining it, or to flee from it by idealizing it. That is why we shall never inhabit true fiction; we are condemned to the imaginary and nostalgia for the future.
Jean Baudrillard (French Postmodern Philosopher, Writer)

28 Writing a novel is actually searching for victims. As I write I keep looking for casualties. The stories uncover the casualties.
John Irving (1942-, American Author)

29 What is a novel if not a conviction of our fellow-men's existence strong enough to take upon itself a form of imagined life clearer than reality and whose accumulated verisimilitude of selected episodes puts to shame the pride of documentary history?
Joseph Conrad (1857-1924, Polish-born British Novelist)

30 Would you not like to try all sorts of lives -- one is so very small -- but that is the satisfaction of writing -- one can impersonate so many people.
Katherine Mansfield (1888-1923, New Zealand-born British Author)

31 Educating a son I should allow him no fairy tales and only a very few novels. This is to prevent him from having 1. the sense of romantic solitude (if he is worth anything he will develop a proper and useful solitude) which identification with the hero gives. 2. cant ideas of right and wrong, absurd systems of honor and morality which never will he be able completely to get rid of, 3. the attainment of "ideals," of a priori desires, of a priori emotions. He should amuse himself with fact only: he will then not learn that if the weak younger son do or do not the magical honorable thing he will win the princess with hair like flax.
Lionel Trilling (1905-1975, American Critic)

32 But I hate things all fiction... there should always be some foundation of fact for the most airy fabric -- and pure invention is but the talent of a liar.
Lord Byron (1788-1824, British Poet)

33 Romances I never read like those I have seen.
Lord Byron (1788-1824, British Poet)

34 When the characters are really alive before their author, the latter does nothing but follow them in their action, in their words, in the situations which they suggest to him.
Luigi Pirandello (1867-1936, Italian Author, Playwright)

35 No matter how ephemeral it is, a novel is something, while despair is nothing.
Mario Vargas Llosa (1936-, Latin American Author)

36 Persons attempting to find a motive in this narrative will be prosecuted; persons attempting to find a moral in it will be banished; persons attempting to find a plot in it will be shot.
Mark Twain (1835-1910, American Humorist, Writer)

37 The first sentence of every novel should be: "Trust me, this will take time but there is order here, very faint, very human." Meander if you want to get to town.
Michael Ondaatje

38 A novel that does not uncover a hitherto unknown segment of existence is immoral. Knowledge is the novel's only morality.
Milan Kundera (1929-, Czech Author, Critic)

39 All great novels, all true novels, are bisexual.
Milan Kundera (1929-, Czech Author, Critic)

40 Novels are longer than life.
Natalie Clifford Barney (1876-1972, American-born French Author)

41 One should not be too severe on English novels; they are the only relaxation of the intellectually unemployed.
Oscar Wilde (1856-1900, British Author, Wit)

42 The good ended happily, and the bad unhappily. That is what Fiction means.
Oscar Wilde (1856-1900, British Author, Wit)

43 Undermining experience, embellishing experience, rearranging and enlarging experience into a species of mythology.
Philip Roth (1933-, American Novelist)

44 All that non-fiction can do is answer questions. It's fiction's business to ask them.
Richard Hughes

45 Our interest's on the dangerous edge of things. The honest thief, the tender murderer, the superstitious atheist.
Robert Browning (1812-1889, British Poet)

46 The narrative impulse is always with us; we couldn't imagine ourselves through a day without it.
Robert Coover

47 The acceptance that all that is solid has melted into the air, that reality and morality are not givens but imperfect human constructs, is the point from which fiction begins.
Salman Rushdie (1948-, Indian-born British Author)

48 The novel does not seek to establish a privileged language but it insists upon the freedom to portray and analyze the struggle between the different contestants for such privileges.
Salman Rushdie (1948-, Indian-born British Author)

49 There is something else which has the power to awaken us to the truth. It is the works of writers of genius. They give us, in the guise of fiction, something equivalent to the actual density of the real, that density which life offers us every day but which we are unable to grasp because we are amusing ourselves with lies.
Simone Weil (1910-1943, French Philosopher, Mystic)

50 Fiction is the truth inside the lie.
Stephen King (1947-, American Horror Writer, Actor)

51 Novels so often provide an anodyne and not an antidote, glide one into torpid slumbers instead of rousing one with a burning brand.
Virginia Woolf (1882-1941, British Novelist, Essayist)

52 Fiction is like a spider's web, attached ever so lightly perhaps, but still attached to life at all four corners. Often the attachment is scarcely perceptible.
Virginia Woolf (1882-1941, British Novelist, Essayist)

53 A novelist is, like all mortals, more fully at home on the surface of the present than in the ooze of the past.
Vladimir Nabokov (1899-1977, Russian-born American Novelist, Poet)

54 For if the proper study of mankind is man, it is evidently more sensible to occupy yourself with the coherent, substantial and significant creatures of fiction than with the irrational and shadowy figures of real life.
W. Somerset Maugham (1874-1965, British Novelist, Playwright)

55 Democritus plucked his eye out because he could not look at a woman without thinking of her as a woman. If he had read a few of our novels, he would have torn himself to pieces.
Wallace Stevens (1879-1955, American Poet)

56 Novelists do not write as birds sing, by the push of nature. It is part of the job that there should be much routine and some daily stuff on the level of carpentry.
William Golding (1911-1993, British Author)

FIDELITY

1 Fidelity. A virtue peculiar to those who are about to be betrayed.
Ambrose Bierce (1842-1914, American Author, Editor, Journalist, "The Devil's Dictionary")

2 Not observation of a duty but liberty itself is the pledge that assures fidelity.
Ellen Key (1849-1926, Swedish Author, Feminist)

3 I have been faithful to thee, Cynara, in my fashion.
Ernest Dowson (1867-1900, British Poet)

4 Constancy is the complement of all other human virtues.
Giuseppe Mazzini (1805-1872, Italian Patriot, Writer)

5 Another of our highly prized virtues is fidelity. We are immensely pleased with ourselves when we are faithful.
Ida R. Wylie

6 Fidelity is seven-tenths of business success.
James Parton

7 Constancy... that small change of love, which people exact so rigidly, receive in such counterfeit coin, and repay in baser metal.
Lord Byron (1788-1824, British Poet)

8 Nothing is more noble, nothing more venerable than fidelity. Faithfulness and truth are the most sacred excellences and endowments of the human mind.
Marcus T. Cicero (106-43 BC, Great Roman Orator, Politician)

9 What a fuss people make about fidelity! Why, even in love it is purely a question for physiology. It has nothing to do with our own will. Young men want to be faithful, and are not; old men want to be faithless, and cannot: that is all one can say.
Oscar Wilde (1856-1900, British Author, Wit)

10 People who love only once in their lives are shallow people. What they call their loyalty, and their fidelity, I call either the lethargy of custom or their lack of imagination. Faithfulness is to the emotional life what consistency is to the life of the intellect -- simply a confession of failures.
Oscar Wilde (1856-1900, British Author, Wit)

11 Constancy has nothing virtuous in itself, independently of the pleasure it confers, and partakes of the temporizing spirit of vice in proportion as it endures tamely moral defects of magnitude in the object of its indiscreet choice.
Percy Bysshe Shelley (1792-1822, British Poet)

12 An ideal wife is one who remains faithful to you but tries to be just as charming as if she weren't.
Sacha Guitry (1885-1957, Actor and Playwright, Born in St Petersburg, Russia)

13 Matrimonial devotion doesn't seem to suit her notion.
W. S. Gilbert (1836-1911, British Librettist)

FIGHTS AND FIGHTING

1 People who fight fire with fire usually end up with ashes.
Abigail Van Buren (American Journalist, Advice Columnist - "Dear Abby")

2 No matter how much the cats fight, there always seem to be plenty of kittens.
Abraham Lincoln (1809-1865, Sixteenth President of the USA)

3 Never contend with a man who has nothing to lose.
Baltasar Gracian (1601-1658, Spanish Philosopher, Writer)

4 The underdog often starts the fight, and occasionally the upper dog deserves to win.
Edgar Watson Howe (1853-1937, American Journalist, Author)

5 I'm not going to get into the ring with Tolstoy.
Ernest Hemingway (1898-1961, American Writer)

6 He who fights with monsters might take care lest he thereby become a monster. And if you gaze for long into an abyss, the abyss gazes also into you.
Friedrich Nietzsche (1844-1900, German Philosopher)

7 That is the whole secret of successful fighting. Get your enemy at a disadvantage; and never, on any account, fight him on equal terms.
George Bernard Shaw (1856-1950, Irish-born British Dramatist)

8 The full value of this life can only be got by fighting; the violent take it by storm. And if we have accepted everything we have missed something -- war. This life of ours is a very enjoyable fight, but a very miserable truce.
Gilbert K. Chesterton (1874-1936, British Author)

9 You cannot love a thing without wanting to fight for it.
Gilbert K. Chesterton (1874-1936, British Author)

10 I have not yet begun to fight.
John Paul Jones

11 Fighting is like champagne. It goes to the heads of cowards as quickly as of heroes. Any fool can be brave on a battlefield when it's be brave or else be killed.
Margaret Mitchell (1900-1949, American Novelist)

12 He who attacks must vanquish. He who defends must merely survive.
Master Kahn

13 If you are losing a tug-of-war with a tiger, give him the rope before he gets to your arm. You can always buy a new rope.
Max Gunther (American Author)

14 My address is like my shoes. It travels with me. I abide where there is a fight against wrong.
Mother Jones

15 In the fight between you and the world, back the world.
Paul Dirac

16 I will fight for my children on any level so they can reach their potential as human beings and in their public duties.
Princess of Wales Diana (1961-1997, Wife of Charles, Prince of Wales)

17 Acts of kindness may soon be forgotten, but the memory of an offense remains.
Proverb

18 Let him that is without stone among you cast the first thing he can lay his hands on.
Robert Frost (1875-1963, American Poet)

19 There is such a thing as a man being too proud to fight.
Woodrow T. Wilson (1856-1924, Twenty-eighth President of the USA)

FINANCE

1 Of course I'm doing something about my overdraft: I'm seeing my accountant.
Barry Fantoni (British Cartoonist, Writer and Broadcaster)

2 The Law of Triviality... briefly stated, it means that the time spent on any item of the agenda will be in inverse proportion to the sum involved.
C. Northcote Parkinson (1909-1993, British Historian, Political Scientist)

3 The objects of a financier are, then, to secure an ample revenue; to impose it with judgment and equality; to employ it economically; and, when necessity obliges him to make use of credit, to secure its foundations in that instance, and for ever, by the clearness and candor of his proceedings, the exactness of his calculations, and the solidity of his funds.
Edmund Burke (1729-1797, British Political Writer, Statesman)

4 The system of book-keeping by double entry is, perhaps, the most beautiful one in the wide domain of literature or science. Were it less common, it would be the admiration of the learned world.
Edwin T. Freedley (1827-1904, British Business Writer)

5 I wake up every morning and thank God I'm not a chartered accountant any longer, but involved with property.
Godfrey Bradman (British Property Executive)

6 What is high finance? It's knowing the difference between one and ten, multiplying, subtracting and adding. You just add noughts. It's no more than that.
John Bentley (British Director of Wordnet PLC)

7 It is time that financial types developed a greater tolerance for imprecision, because that's the way the world is.
John C. Burton (American Writer)

8 The pen is mightier than the sword, but no match for the accountant.
Jonathan Glancey (British Journalist)

9 When it comes to finances, remember that there are no withholding taxes on the wages of sin.
Mae West (1892-1980, American Actress)

10 It sounds extraordinary but it's a fact that balance sheets can make fascinating reading.
Mary Archer (British Scientist and Business Executive)

11 You need to have enough immediate profits that you can finance the long-range growth without diluting the stock.
Paul Cook (Business Executive, CEO of Raychem Corp.)

12 Women's battle for financial equality has barely been joined, much less won. Society still traditionally assigns to woman the role of money-handler rather than money-maker, and our assigned specialty is far more likely to be home economics than financial economics.
Paula Nelson (1945-, American Business Executive)

13 We estimate the wisdom of nations by seeing what they did with their surplus capital.
Ralph Waldo Emerson (1803-1882, American Poet, Essayist)

14 What we now call "finance" is, I hold, an intellectual perversion of what began as warm human love.
Robert Graves (1895-1985, British Poet, Novelist)

15 Finance is the art of passing currency from hand to hand until it finally disappears.
Robert W. Sarnoff

16 The little I know of it has not served to raise my opinion of what is vulgarly called the "Monied Interest;" I mean, that blood-sucker, that muckworm, that calls itself "the friend of government."
William Pitt The Elder Chatham (1708 -1778, British Statesman)

FIRE

1 Fire is never a gentle master
Proverb

FIRMNESS

1 A wise man who stands firm is a statesman, a foolish man who stands firm is a catastrophe.
Adlai E. Stevenson (1900-1965, American Lawyer, Politician)

2 Real firmness is good for anything; strut is good for nothing.
Alexander Hamilton (1757-1804, American Statesman)

3 The purpose firm is equal to the deed.
Edward Young (1683-1765, British Poet, Dramatist)

4 It is only persons of firmness that can have real gentleness. Those who appear gentle are, in general, only a weak character, which easily changes into asperity.
François de La Rochefoucauld (1613-1680, French classical writer)

5 The greatest firmness is the greatest mercy.
Henry Wadsworth Longfellow (1819-1892, American Poet)

6 Steadfastness is a noble quality, but unguided by knowledge or humility it becomes rashness or obstinacy.
J. Swartz

7 Firmness of purpose is one of the most necessary sinews of character, and one of the best instruments of success. Without it genius wastes its efforts in a maze of inconsistencies.
Lord Chesterfield (1694-1773, British Statesman, Author)

FISHING

1 Fishing is a delusion entirely surrounded by liars in old clothes.
Don Marquis (1878-1937, American Humorist, Journalist)

2 Fishing seems to be the favorite form of loafing.
Edgar Watson Howe (1853-1937, American Journalist, Author)

3 Somebody just back of you while you are fishing is as bad as someone looking over your shoulder while you write a letter to your girl.
Ernest Hemingway (1898-1961, American Writer)

4 The perch swallows the grub-worm, the pickerel swallows the perch, and the fisherman swallows the pickerel; and so all the chinks in the scale of being are filled.
Henry David Thoreau (1817-1862, American Essayist, Poet, Naturalist)

5 All you need to be a fisherman is patience and a worm.
Herb Shriner

6 We may say of angling, as Dr. Boteler said of strawberries, "Doubtless God could have made a better berry, but doubtless God never did"; and so, if I might be judge, God never did make a more calm, quiet, innocent recreation than angling.
Izaak Walton (1593-1683, British Writer)

7 Angling may be said to be so like the mathematics that it can never be fully learned.
Izaak Walton (1593-1683, British Writer)

8 Some people are under the impression that all that is required to make a good fisherman is the ability to tell lies easily and without blushing; but this is a mistake. Mere bald fabrication is useless; the veriest tyro can manage that. It is in the circumstantial detail, the embellishing touches of probability, the general air of scrupulous -- almost of pedantic -- veracity, that the experienced angler is seen.
Jerome K. Jerome (1859-1927, British Humorous Writer, Novelist, Playwright)

9 No human being, however great, or powerful, was ever so free as a fish.
John Ruskin (1819-1900, British Critic, Social Theorist)

10 Fly fishing may be a very pleasant amusement; but angling or float fishing I can only compare to a stick and a string, with a worm at one end and a fool at the other.
Samuel Johnson (1709-1784, British Author)

11 If fishing is a religion, fly fishing is high church.
Tom Brokaw (1940-, American TV Personality, Editor)

FLATTERY

1 Flattery is all right if you don't inhale.
Adlai E. Stevenson (1900-1965, American Lawyer, Politician)

2 None are more taken in by flattery than the proud, who wish to be the first and are not.
Baruch (Benedict de) Spinoza (1632-1677, Dutch Philosopher and Theologian)

3 Flattery is a form of hatred.
Bible (Sacred Scriptures of Christians and Judaism)

4 We swallow with one gulp the lie that flatters us, and drink drop by drop the truth which is bitter to us.
Denis Diderot (1713-1784, French Philosopher)

5 For lack of a better term, they've labeled me a sex symbol. It's flattering and it should happen to every bald, overweight guy.
Dennis Franz (1944-, American Actor, Playwright)

6 Flattery corrupts both the receiver and the giver.
Edmund Burke (1729-1797, British Political Writer, Statesman)

7 A fool flatters himself, a wise man flatters the fool.
Edward G. Bulwer-Lytton (1803-1873, British Novelist, Poet)

8 Flatter not thyself in thy faith in God if thou hast not charity for thy neighbor.
Francis Quarles (1592-1644, British Poet)

9 Self-love is the greatest of all flatterers.
François de La Rochefoucauld (1613-1680, French classical writer)

10 Baloney is flattery laid on so thick it cannot be true, and blarney is flattery so thin we love it.
Fulton John Sheen (1895-1979, American Roman Catholic Clergyman, Broadcaster)

11 He who says he hates every kind of flattery, and says it in earnest, certainly does not yet know every kind of flattery.
Georg C. Lichtenberg (1742-1799, German Physicist, Satirist)

12 What really flatters a man is that you think him worth flattering.
George Bernard Shaw (1856-1950, Irish-born British Dramatist)

13 To make a man perfectly happy tell him he works too hard, that he spends too much money, that he is "misunderstood" or that he is "different"; none of this is necessarily complimentary, but it will flatter him infinitely more that merely telling him that he is brilliant, or noble, or wise, or good.
Helen Rowland (1875-1950, American Journalist)

14 He that flatters you more than you desire either has deceived you or wishes to deceive.
Italian Proverb

15 Every flatterer lives at the expense of him who listens to him.
Jean De La Fontaine (1621-1695, French Poet)

16 Look closely at those who patronize you. Half are unfeeling, half untaught.
Johann Wolfgang Von Goethe (1749-1832, German Poet, Dramatist, Novelist)

17 Flattery is like cologne water, to be smelt, not swallowed.
Josh Billings (1815-1885, American Humorist, Lecturer)

18 The reason that adulation is not displeasing is that, though untrue, it shows one to be of consequence enough, in one way or other, to induce people to lie.
Lord Byron (1788-1824, British Poet)

19 Women who are either indisputably beautiful, or indisputably ugly, are best flattered upon the score of their understandings; but those who are in a state of mediocrity are best flattered upon their beauty, or at least their graces: for every woman who is not absolutely ugly, thinks herself handsome.
Lord Chesterfield (1694-1773, British Statesman, Author)

20 Between flattery and admiration there often flows a river of contempt.
Minna Antrim (1861-18?, American Epigrammist)

21 The more we love our friends, the less we flatter them; it is by excusing nothing that pure love shows itself.
MoliFre (1622-1673, French Playwright)

22 Many lick before they bite.
Proverb

23 If we did not flatter ourselves the flattery from others would not harm us.
Proverb

24 Just praise is only a debt, but flattery is a present.
Samuel Johnson (1709-1784, British Author)

25 Nothing flatters a man as much as the happiness of his wife; he is always proud of himself as the source of it.
Samuel Johnson (1709-1784, British Author)

26 I cannot think of any character below the flatterer, except he who envies him.
Sir Richard Steele (1672-1729, British Dramatist, Essayist, Editor)

27 But it is hard to know them from friends, they are so obsequious and full of protestations; for a wolf resembles a dog, so doth a flatterer a friend.
Sir Walter Raleigh (1552-1618, British Courtier, Navigator, Writer)

28 Flattery makes friends and truth makes enemies.
Spanish Proverb

29 Don't flatter the rich, or appear to willing before the great.
Thomas p Kempis (1379-1471, German Monk, Mystic, Religious Writer)

30 I will praise any man that will praise me.
William Shakespeare (1564-1616, British Poet, Playwright, Actor)

31 He that loves to be flattered is worthy of the flatterer.
William Shakespeare (1564-1616, British Poet, Playwright, Actor)

FLAWS

1 Certain flaws are necessary for the whole. It would seem strange if old friends lacked certain quirks.
Johann Wolfgang Von Goethe (1749-1832, German Poet, Dramatist, Novelist)

2 I look at Liv Tyler and think "It's not fair," because I can't find a flaw on her. And on top of that she seems nice, so it's really not fair.
Tori Spelling (Born 1973, American Actress)

FLIRTING

1 Whoever loves above all the approach of love will never know the joy of attaining it.
Antoine De Saint-Exupery (1900-1944, French Aviator, Writer)

2 She learned to say things with her eyes that others waste time putting into words
Corey Ford

3 The pleasure of one's effect on other people still exists in age -- what's called making a hit. But the hit is much rarer and made of different stuff.
Enid Bagnold (1889-1981, British Novelist, Playwright)

4 All women are flirts, but some are restrained by shyness, and others by sense.
François de La Rochefoucauld (1613-1680, French classical writer)

5 No matter how happily a woman may be married, it always pleases her to discover that there is a nice man who wishes that she were not.
H. L. Mencken (1880-1956, American Editor, Author, Critic, Humorist)

6 Why does a man take it for granted that a girl who flirts with him wants him to kiss her -- when, nine times out of ten, she only wants him to want to kiss her?
Helen Rowland (1875-1950, American Journalist)

7 The hardest task of a girl's life, nowadays, is to prove to a man that his intentions are serious.
Helen Rowland (1875-1950, American Journalist)

8 Flirting is the gentle art of making a man feel pleased with himself.
Helen Rowland (1875-1950, American Journalist)

9 O Polly, you might have toyed and kissed, by keeping men off, you keep them on.
John Gay (1688-1732, British Playwright, Poet)

10 The pretty fellows you speak of, I own entertain me sometimes, but is it impossible to be diverted with what one despises? I can laugh at a puppet show, at the same time I know there is nothing in it worth my attention or regard.
Lady Mary Wortley Montagu (1689-1762, British Society Figure, Letter Writer)

11 We have progressively improved into a less spiritual species of tenderness -- but the seal is not yet fixed though the wax is preparing for the impression.
Lord Byron (1788-1824, British Poet)

12 To have a man who can flirt is next thing to indispensable to a leader of society.
Margaret Oliphant (1828-1897, British Novelist, Historian)

13 The amount of women in London who flirt with their own husbands is perfectly scandalous. It looks so bad. It is simply washing one's clean linen in public.
Oscar Wilde (1856-1900, British Author, Wit)

14 Is not the whole world a vast house of assignation of which the filing system has been lost?
Quentin Crisp (1908-, British Author)

15 There are few things that we so unwillingly give up, even in advanced age, as the supposition that we still have the power of ingratiating ourselves with the fair sex.
Samuel Johnson (1709-1784, British Author)

16 God created the flirt as soon as he made the fool.
Victor Hugo (1802-1885, French Poet, Dramatist, Novelist)

FLOWERS

1 Keep not your roses for my dead, cold brow the way is lonely, let me feel them now.
Arabella Smith

2 The fairest thing in nature, a flower, still has its roots in earth and manure.
D. H. Lawrence (1885-1930, British Author)

3 Roses fall, but the thorns remain.
Dutch Proverb

4 Today as in the time of Pliny and Columella, the hyacinth flourishes in Wales, the periwinkle in Illyria, the daisy on the ruins of Numantia; while around them cities have changed their masters and their names, collided and smashed, disappeared into nothingness, their peaceful generations have crossed down the ages as fresh and smiling as on the days of battle.
Edgar Quinet (1803-1875, French Poet, Historian, Politician)

5   I hate flowers -- I paint them because they're cheaper than models and they don't move.
Georgia O'Keeffe (American painter)

6   When you take a flower in your hand and really look at it, it's your world for the moment. I want to give that world to someone else. Most people in the city rush around so, they have no time to look at a flower. I want them to see it whether they want to or not.
Georgia O'Keeffe (American painter)

7   Every flower is a soul blossoming in Nature.
Gerard De Nerval (1808-1855, French Novelist, Poet)

8   Fair flowers are not left standing along the wayside long.
German Proverb

9   One of the most attractive things about the flowers is their beautiful reserve.
Henry David Thoreau (1817-1862, American Essayist, Poet, Naturalist)

10   The flower is the poetry of reproduction. It is the example of the eternal seductiveness of life.
Jean Giraudoux (1882-1944, French Diplomat, Author)

11   The silence of a flower: a kind of silence which we continually evade, of which we find only the shadow in dreams.
Lewis Thompson

12   Flowers always make people better, happier and more helpful; they are sunshine, food and medicine to the soul.
Luther Burbank (1849-1926, American Horticulturist)

13   Flowers have spoken to me more than I can tell in written words. They are the hieroglyphics of angels, loved by all men for the beauty of the character, though few can decipher even fragments of their meaning.
Lydia M. Child (1802-1880, American Abolitionist, Writer, Editor)

14   He does not care for flowers. Calls them rubbish, and cannot tell one from another, and thinks it is superior to feel like that.
Mark Twain (1835-1910, American Humorist, Writer)

15   The Amen of nature is always a flower.
Oliver Wendell Holmes (1809-1894, American Author, Wit, Poet)

16   Flowers are as common in the country as people are in London.
Oscar Wilde (1856-1900, British Author, Wit)

17   These flowers, which were splendid and sprightly, waking in the dawn of the morning, in the evening will be a pitiful frivolity, sleeping in the cold night's arms.
Pedro Calderón de la Barca (1600-1681, Spanish Playwright)

18   We trample grass, and prize the flowers of May; yet the grass is green when the flower fades away.
R. Southwell

19   Flowers are a proud assertion that a ray of beauty out-values all the utilities of the world.
Ralph Waldo Emerson (1803-1882, American Poet, Essayist)

20   Earth laughs in flowers.
Ralph Waldo Emerson (1803-1882, American Poet, Essayist)

21   Flowers are restful to look at. They have neither emotions nor conflicts.
Sigmund Freud (1856-1939, Austrian Physician - Founder of Psychoanalysis)

22   Flowers are happy things.
Sir P(elham) G(renville) Wodehouse (1881-1975, British Novelist)

23   Deep in their roots all flowers keep the light.
Theodore Roethke (1908-1963, American Poet)

24   Flowers that are so pathetic in their beauty, frail as the clouds, and in their coloring as gorgeous as the heavens, had through thousands of years been the heritage of children -- honored as the jewelry of God only by them -- when suddenly the voice of Christianity, counter-signing the voice of infancy, raised them to a grandeur transcending the Hebrew throne, although founded by God himself, and pronounced Solomon in all his glory not to be arrayed like one of these.
Thomas De Quincey (1785-1859, British Author)

25   'Tis the last rose of summer, left blooming alone; all her lovely companions are faded and gone.
Thomas Moore (1779-1852, Irish Poet)

26   A morning glory at my window satisfies me more than the metaphysics of books.
Walt Whitman (1819-1892, American Poet)

27   To create a little flower is the labor of ages.
William Blake (1757-1827, British Poet, Painter)

28   The flower that smells the sweetest is shy and lowly.
William Wordsworth (1770-1850, British Poet)

29   To me the meanest flower that blows can give thoughts that do often lie too deep for tears.
William Wordsworth (1770-1850, British Poet)

FOCUS

1   If you surrender completely to the moments as they pass, you live more richly those moments.
Anne Morrow Lindbergh (1906-, American Author)

2   Most people have no idea of the giant capacity we can immediately command when we focus all of our resources on mastering a single area of our lives.
Anthony Robbins (1960-, American Author, Speaker, Peak Performance Expert / Consultant)

3   Only when your consciousness is totally focused on the moment you are in can you receive whatever gift, lesson, or delight that moment has to offer.
Barbara De Angelis (American Expert on Relationship & Love, Author)

4 To me, the definition of focus is knowing exactly where you want to be today, next week, next month, next year, then never deviating from your plan. Once you can see, touch and feel your objective, all you have to do is pull back and put all your strength behind it, and you'll hit your target every time.
Bruce Jenner (1949-, American Olympian, Actor, Speaker, Entrepreneur, Sports Commentator)

5 Expansion means complexity and complexity decay.
C. Northcote Parkinson (1909-1993, British Historian, Political Scientist)

6 Get out of the blocks, run your race, stay relaxed. If you run your race, you'll win. Channel your energy. Focus.
Carol Lewis (American Athlete)

7 It is not good to have an oar in everyone's boat.
Earl Camden (1714-1794, British Chancellor)

8 In trying to defend everything he defended nothing.
Frederick The Great (Frederick II) (1712-1786, Born in Berlin, King of Prussia (1740-1786))

9 A matter that becomes clear ceases to concern us.
Friedrich Nietzsche (1844-1900, German Philosopher)

10 The human mind is not rich enough to drive many horses abreast and wants one general scheme, under which it strives to bring everything.
George Santayana (1863-1952, American Philosopher, Poet)

11 The immature mind hops from one thing to another; the mature mind seeks to follow through.
Harry A. Overstreet (American Psychologist)

12 Often he who does too much does too little.
Italian Proverb

13 If you focus on results, you will never change. If you focus on change, you will get results.
Jack Dixon

14 It is a process of diverting one's scattered forces into one powerful channel.
James Allen (1864-1912, British-born American Essayist, Author of "As a Man Thinketh")

15 You have to block everything out and be extremely focused and be relaxed and mellow too.
Jennifer Capriati (Born 1976, American Tennis Player)

16 Rather than viewing a brief relapse back to inactivity as a failure, treat it as a challenge and try to get back on track as soon as possible.
Jimmy Connors (1952-, American Tennis Player)

17 Lose not yourself in a far off time, seize the moment that is thine.
Johann Friedrich Von Schiller (1759-1805, German Dramatist, Poet, Historian)

18 Don't dissipate your powers; strive to concentrate them. Genius thinks it can do whatever it sees others doing, but it will surely repent of every ill-judged outlay.
Johann Wolfgang Von Goethe (1749-1832, German Poet, Dramatist, Novelist)

19 To succeed at the level I want to... you have to be focused and serious.
Kent Steffes (Born 1968, American Beach Volleyball Player)

20 You must remain focused on your journey to greatness.
Les Brown (1945-, American Speaker, Author, Trainer, Motivator Lecturer)

21 Our thoughts take the wildest flight: Even at the moment when they should arrange themselves in thoughtful order.
Lord Byron (1788-1824, British Poet)

22 Presence is more than just being there.
Malcolm S. Forbes (1919-1990, American Publisher, Businessman)

23 Every man's life lies within the present; for the past is spent and done with, and the future is uncertain.
Marcus Aurelius (121-80 AD, Roman Emperor, Philosopher)

24 Determine what specific goal you want to achieve. Then dedicate yourself to its attainment with unswerving singleness of purpose, the trenchant zeal of a crusader.
Paul J. Meyer (American Businessman, Author, Motivator)

25 All of us are watchers -- of television, of time clocks, of traffic on the freeway -- but few are observers. Everyone is looking, not many are seeing
Peter M. Leschak

26 It is better to excel in any single art than to arrive only at mediocrity in several, so moderate skill in several is to be preferred where one cannot attain to perfection in any.
Pliny The Younger (62-114, Roman Writer, Administrator)

27 Think of many things, do only one.
Proverb

28 The only prudence in life is concentration.
Ralph Waldo Emerson (1803-1882, American Poet, Essayist)

29 Concentration is the secret of strength in politics, in war, in trade, in short, in all the management of human affairs.
Ralph Waldo Emerson (1803-1882, American Poet, Essayist)

30 Concentration is the ability to think about absolutely nothing when it is absolutely necessary.
Ray Knight

31 Every year of my life I grow more convinced that it is wisest and best to fix our attention on the beautiful and the good, and dwell as little as possible on the evil and the false.
Richard Cecil (American Poet)

32 Extended empires are like expanded gold, exchanging solid strength for feeble splendor.
Samuel Johnson (1709-1784, British Author)

33 When a man knows he is to be hanged in a fortnight, it concentrates his mind wonderfully.
Samuel Johnson (1709-1784, British Author)

34 Keep your eye on the ball and your head in the game.
Saying

35   When you walk on a court, clear your mind of everything unrelated to the goal of playing the match as well as you can.
Stan Smith (American Tennis Player)

36   The shortest way to do many things is to do only one thing at a time.
Sydney Smiles

37   A well-aimed spear is worth three.
Tad Williams (American Author)

38   You're a wise person if you can easily direct your attention to what ever needs it.
Terence (185-159 BC, Roman Writer of Comedies)

39   A person who is gifted sees the essential point and leaves the rest as surplus.
Thomas Carlyle (1795-1881, Scottish Philosopher, Author)

40   My main focus is on my game.
Tiger Woods (Born 1975, American Golfer)

41   What I focus on in life is what I get. And if I concentrate on how bad I am or how wrong I am or how inadequate I am, if I concentrate on what I can't do and how there's not enough time in which to do it, isn't that what I get every time? And when I think about how powerful I am, and when I think about what I have left to contribute, and when I think about the difference I can make on this planet, then that's what I get. You see, I recognize that it's not what happens to you; it's what you do about it.
W. Mitchell (American Businessman, Mayor, Speaker)

42   Nothing focuses the mind better than the constant sight of a competitor who wants to wipe you off the map.
Wayne Calloway (American Businessman, CEO of PepsiCo)

FOOD AND EATING

1   Tomatoes and oregano make it Italian; wine and tarragon make it French. Sour cream makes it Russian; lemon and cinnamon make it Greek. Soy sauce makes it Chinese; garlic makes it good.
Alice May Brock

2   It has been an unchallengeable American doctrine that cranberry sauce, a pink goo with overtones of sugared tomatoes, is a delectable necessity of the Thanksgiving board and that turkey is uneatable without it. There are some things in every country that you must be born to endure; and another hundred years of general satisfaction with Americans and America could not reconcile this expatriate to cranberry sauce, peanut butter, and drum majorettes.
Alistair Cooke (1908-, British Broadcaster, Journalist)

3   Edible. Good to eat and wholesome to digest, as a worm to a toad, a toad to a snake, a snake to a pig, a pig to a man, and a man to a worm.
Ambrose Bierce (1842-1914, American Author, Editor, Journalist, "The Devil's Dictionary")

4   Want to learn to eat a lot? Here it is: Eat a little. That way, you will be around long enough to eat a lot.
Anthony Robbins (1960-, American Author, Speaker, Peak Performance Expert / Consultant)

5   He who eats alone chokes alone.
Arabian Proverb

6   My body is like breakfast, lunch, and dinner. I don't think about it, I just have it.
Arnold Schwarzenegger (1947-, Austrian-born American Actor, Author, Director, Restaurateur)

7   Although there is a great deal of controversy among scientists about the effects of ingested food on the brain, no one denies that you can change your cognition and mood by what you eat.
Arthur Winter

8   The right diet directs sexual energy into the parts that matter.
Barbara Cartland (1901-, British Novelist)

9   Upscale people are fixated with food simply because they are now able to eat so much of it without getting fat, and the reason they don't get fat is that they maintain a profligate level of calorie expenditure. The very same people whose evenings begin with melted goats cheese... get up at dawn to run, break for a mid-morning aerobics class, and watch the evening news while racing on a stationary bicycle.
Barbara Ehrenreich (1941-, American Author, Columnist)

10   One should eat to live, not live to eat.
Benjamin Franklin (1706-1790, American Scientist, Publisher, Diplomat)

11   Man shall not live by bread alone.
Bible (Sacred Scriptures of Christians and Judaism)

12   Put a knife to thy throat, if you're a man given to appetite.
Bible (Sacred Scriptures of Christians and Judaism)

13   Clearly, some time ago makers and consumers of American junk food passed jointly through some kind of sensibility barrier in the endless quest for new taste sensations. Now they are a little like those desperate junkies who have tried every known drug and are finally reduced to mainlining toilet bowl cleanser in an effort to get still higher.
Bill Bryson (American Author)

14   As a child my family's menu consisted of two choices: take it, or leave it.
Buddy Hackett

15   I judge a restaurant by the bread and by the coffee.
Burt Lancaster (1913-1994, American Actor)

16   Gluttony is the source of all our infirmities and the fountain of all our diseases. As fire extinguished by an excess of fuel, so is the natural health of the body destroyed by an intemperate diet.
Burton

17   It's better that it should make you sick than that you don't eat it at all.
Catalan Proverb

18 It is a difficult matter to argue with the belly since it has no ears.
Cato The Elder (234-149 BC, Roman Statesman, Orator)

19 Lunch kills half of Paris, supper the other half.
Charles De Montesquieu (1689-1755, French Jurist, Political Philosopher)

20 For its merit I will knight it, and then it will be Sir-Loin.
Charles II (1630-1685, King of England and Ireland)

21 To eat is human, to digest divine.
Charles T. Copeland

22 No man is lonely while eating spaghetti; it requires so much attention.
Christopher Morley (1890-1957, American Novelist, Journalist, Poet)

23 Cheese is milk's leap toward immortality.
Cliff Fadiman (American Writer)

24 That food has always been, and will continue to be, the basis for one of our greater snobbism does not explain the fact that the attitude toward the food choice of others is becoming more and more heatedly exclusive until it may well turn into one of those forms of bigotry against which gallant little committees are constantly planning campaigns in the cause of justice and decency.
Cornelia Otis Skinner

25 The one way to get thin is to re-establish a purpose in life.
Cyril Connolly (1903-1974, British Critic)

26 It ain't what you eat, but the way how you chew it.
Delbert Mcclinton

27 Square meals often make round people.
E. Joseph Cossman (American Businessman, Author, Lecturer)

28 Most of us are either too think to enjoy eating, or too fat to enjoy walking.
Edgar Watson Howe (1853-1937, American Journalist, Author)

29 Roast Beef, medium, is not only a food. It is a philosophy. Seated at Life's Dining Table, with the menu of Morals before you, your eye wanders a bit over the entrées, the hors d'oeuvres, and the things a la though you know that Roast Beef, medium, is safe and sane, and sure.
Edna Ferber (1887-1968, American Author)

30 Eating is not merely a material pleasure. Eating well gives a spectacular joy to life and contributes immensely to goodwill and happy companionship. It is of great importance to the morale.
Elsa Schiaparelli (1896-1973, Italian Fashion Designer)

31 Don't dig your grave with your knife and fork.
English Proverb

32 When a man's stomach is full it makes no difference whether he is rich or poor.
Euripides (480-406 BC, Greek Tragic Poet)

33 Ask your child what he wants for dinner only if he's buying.
Fran Lebowitz (1951-, American Journalist)

34 If you're going to America, bring your own food.
Fran Lebowitz (1951-, American Journalist)

35 Vegetables are interesting but lack a sense of purpose when unaccompanied by a good cut of meat.
Fran Lebowitz (1951-, American Journalist)

36 Food is an important part of a balanced diet.
Fran Lebowitz (1951-, American Journalist)

37 The act of putting into your mouth what the earth has grown is perhaps your most direct interaction with the earth.
Frances Moore Lappe

38 A good meal ought to begin with hunger.
French Proverb

39 Appetite comes with eating; the more one has, the more one would have.
French Proverb

40 If there were only turnips and potatoes in the world, someone would complain that plants grow the wrong way.
Georg C. Lichtenberg (1742-1799, German Physicist, Satirist)

41 Food probably has a very great influence on the condition of men. Wine exercises a more visible influence, food does it more slowly but perhaps just as surely. Who knows if a well-prepared soup was not responsible for the pneumatic pump or a poor one for a war?
Georg C. Lichtenberg (1742-1799, German Physicist, Satirist)

42 There is no love sincerer than the love of food.
George Bernard Shaw (1856-1950, Irish-born British Dramatist)

43 I do not like broccoli. And I haven't liked it since I was a little kid and my mother made me eat it. I am President of the United States, and I'm not going to eat any more broccoli.
George Bush (1924-, Forty-first President of the USA)

44 We may find in the long run that tinned food is a deadlier weapon than the machine-gun.
George Orwell (1903-1950, British Author, "Animal Farm")

45 There is nothing to which men, while they have food and drink, cannot reconcile themselves.
George Santayana (1863-1952, American Philosopher, Poet)

46 For much of the female half of the world, food is the first signal of our inferiority. It lets us know that our own families may consider female bodies to be less deserving, less needy, less valuable.
Gloria Steinem (1934-, American Feminist Writer, Editor)

47 Eat, drink, and be merry, for tomorrow we may diet.
Harry Kurnitz

48 He that eats till he is sick must fast till he is well.
Hebrew Proverb

49 You needn't tell me that a man who doesn't love oysters and asparagus and good wines has got a soul, or a stomach either. He's simply got the instinct for being unhappy highly developed.
Hector Hugh Munro (1870-1916, British Novelist, Writer)

50 Hors d'oeuvres have always a pathetic interest for me; they remind me of one's childhood that one goes through wondering what the next course is going to be like -- and during the rest of the menu one wishes one had eaten more of the hors d'oeuvres.
Hector Hugh Munro (1870-1916, British Novelist, Writer)

51 I have found it to be the most serious objection to coarse labors long continued, that they compelled me to eat and drink coarsely also.
Henry David Thoreau (1817-1862, American Essayist, Poet, Naturalist)

52 You can travel fifty thousand miles in America without once tasting a piece of good bread.
Henry Miller (1891-1980, American Author)

53 A store of grain, Oh king is the best of treasures. A gem put in your mouth will not support life.
Hitopadesa (Sanskrit Fable From Panchatantra)

54 A gourmet who thinks of calories is like a tart, who looks at her watch.
James Beard (Father of Modern American Cooking)

55 Sadder than destitution, sadder than a beggar is the man who eats alone in public. Nothing more contradicts the laws of man or beast, for animals always do each other the honor of sharing or disputing each other's food.
Jean Baudrillard (French Postmodern Philosopher, Writer)

56 To eat is to appropriate by destruction.
Jean-Paul Sartre (1905-1980, French Writer, Philosopher)

57 We live in an age when pizza gets to your home before the police.
Jeff Arder

58 I told my doctor I get very tired when I go on a diet, so he gave me pep pills. Know what happened? I ate faster.
Joe E. Lewis (American Writer)

59 I would like to find a stew that will give me heartburn immediately, instead of at three o clock in the morning.
John Barrymore (1882-1942, American Actor)

60 More die in the United States from too much food that from too little.
John Kenneth Galbraith (1908-, American Economist)

61 A lot of Thanksgiving days have been ruined by not carving the turkey in the kitchen.
Kin Hubbard (1868-1930, American Humorist, Journalist)

62 Avoid fresh meats, which angry up the blood. If your stomach disputes you, lie down and pacify it with cool thoughts. Keep the juices flowing by jangling around gently as you move. Go very light in the vices such as carrying on in society. The social ramble ain't restful. Don't look back. Someone might be gaining on you.
Leroy "Satchel" Paige (1906?-1982, American Baseball Player)

63 A woman should never be seen eating or drinking, unless it be lobster salad and Champagne, the only true feminine and becoming viands.
Lord Byron (1788-1824, British Poet)

64 Only the pure in heart can make a good soup.
Ludwig Van Beethoven (1770-1827, German Composer)

65 Sharing food with another human being is an intimate act that should not be indulged in lightly.
M. F. K. Fisher

66 God comes to the hungry in the form of food.
Mahatma Gandhi (1869-1948, Indian Political, Spiritual Leader)

67 Thou shouldst eat to live; not live to eat.
Marcus T. Cicero (106-43 BC, Great Roman Orator, Politician)

68 When one has tasted it [Watermelon] he knows what the angels eat.
Mark Twain (1835-1910, American Humorist, Writer)

69 Never eat more than you can lift.
Miss Piggy

70 Never eat anything you can't lift.
Miss Piggy

71 There is only one thing harder than looking for a dewdrop in the dew, and that is fishing for a clam in the clam chowder.
New England Proverb

72 He who cannot eat horsemeat need not do so. Let him eat pork. But he who cannot eat pork, let him eat horsemeat. It's simply a question of taste.
Nikita Khrushchev (1894-1971, Soviet Premier)

73 Lunch is for wimps.
Oliver Stone (1946-, American Director, Writer, Producer)

74 Only dull people are brilliant at breakfast.
Oscar Wilde (1856-1900, British Author, Wit)

75 There is such a thing as food and such a thing as poison. But the damage done by those who pass off poison as food is far less than that done by those who generation after generation convince people that food is poison.
Paul Goodman (1911-1972, American Author, Poet, Critic)

76 Make food a very incidental part of your life by filling your life so full of meaningful things that you'll hardly have time to think about food.
Peace Pilgrim (1908-1981, American Peace Activist)

77 Gluttony is an emotional escape, a sign something is eating us.
Peter De Vries (1910-, American Author)

78 A gourmet is just a glutton with brains.
Phillip H. Haberman Jr.

79 Abstain from beans.
Plutarch (46-120 AD, Greek Essayist, Biographer)

80 Hunger is a good cook.
Proverb

81 Much meat, much disease.
Proverb

82 Gluttony kills more than the sword.
Proverb

83 The most dangerous food to eat is a wedding cake.
Proverb

84 Seven's a banquet nine a brawl.
Proverb

85 Let the stoics say what they please, we do not eat for the good of living, but because the meat is savory and the appetite is keen.
Ralph Waldo Emerson (1803-1882, American Poet, Essayist)

86 I can reason down or deny everything, except this perpetual Belly: feed he must and will, and I cannot make him respectable.
Ralph Waldo Emerson (1803-1882, American Poet, Essayist)

87 The food here is so tasteless you could eat a meal of it and belch and it wouldn't remind you of anything.
Redd Foxx

88 I found there was only one way to look thin, hang out with fat people.
Rodney Dangerfield (American Comedian, Actor)

89 He who is a slave to his stomach seldom worships God.
Saadi

90 The healthy stomach is nothing if it is not conservative. Few radicals have good digestions.
Samuel Butler (1612-1680, British Poet, Satirist)

91 Eating is touch carried to the bitter end.
Samuel Butler (1612-1680, British Poet, Satirist)

92 A man seldom thinks with more earnestness of anything than he does of his dinner.
Samuel Johnson (1709-1784, British Author)

93 He who does not mind his belly, will hardly mind anything else.
Samuel Johnson (1709-1784, British Author)

94 Strange to see how a good dinner and feasting reconciles everybody.
Samuel Pepys (1633-1703, British Diarist)

95 Worthless people love only to eat and drink; people of worth eat and drink only to live.
Socrates (469-399 BC, Greek Philosopher of Athens)

96 Everything you see I owe to spaghetti.
Sophia Loren (1934-, Italian Film Actress)

97 It is the mark of a mean, vulgar and ignoble spirit to dwell on the thought of food before meal times or worse to dwell on it afterwards, to discuss it and wallow in the remembered pleasures of every mouthful. Those whose minds dwell before dinner on the spit, and after on the dishes, are fit only to be scullions.
St. Francis De Sales (1567-1622, Roman Catholic Bishop, Writer)

98 We know that ever woman wants to be thin. Our images of womanhood are almost synonymous with thinness.
Susie Orbach

99 The flesh endures the storms of the present alone; the mind, those of the past and future as well as the present. Gluttony is a lust of the mind.
Thomas Hobbes (1588-1679, British Philosopher)

100 We seldom report of having eaten too little.
Thomas Jefferson (1743-1826, Third President of the USA)

101 We are digging our graves with our teeth.
Thomas Moffett (American Physician)

102 I've been on a diet for two weeks and all I've lost is two weeks.
Totie Fields

103 Coffee should be black as Hell, strong as death, and sweet as love.
Turkish Proverb

104 Choose rather to punish your appetites than be punished by them.
Tyrius Maximus

105 One cannot think well, love well, sleep well, if one has not dined well.
Virginia Woolf (1882-1941, British Novelist, Essayist)

106 It isn't so much what's on the table that matters, as what's on the chairs.
W. S. Gilbert (1836-1911, British Librettist)

107 Taking food alone tends to make one hard and coarse. Those accustomed to it must lead a Spartan life if they are not to go downhill. Hermits have observed, if for only this reason, a frugal diet. For it is only in company that eating is done justice; food must be divided and distributed if it is to be well received.
Walter Benjamin (1982-1940, German Critic, Philosopher)

108 The soup is never hot enough if the waiter can keep his thumb in it.
William Collier

109 I will not eat oysters. I want my food dead -- not sick, not wounded -- dead.
Woody Allen (1935-, American Director, Screenwriter, Actor, Comedian)

110 Yogi ordered a pizza. The waitress asked How many pieces do you want your pie cut? Yogi responded, Four. I don't think I could eat eight.
Yogi Berra (1925-, American Baseball Player)

FOOLS AND FOOLISHNESS

1 Better to remain silent and be thought a fool, than to speak and remove all doubt.
Abraham Lincoln (1809-1865, Sixteenth President of the USA)

2 Only a fool tests the depth of the water with both feet.
African Proverb

3   Sometimes the fool who rushes in gets the job done.
Al Bernstein

4   A fool and his money get a lot of publicity.
Al Bernstein

5   Fools rush in where Angels fear to tread.
Alexander Pope (1688-1744, British Poet, Critic, Translator)

6   That's the penalty we have to pay for our acts of foolishness -- someone else always suffers for them.
Alfred Sutro

7   The person who writes for fools is always sure of a large audience.
Arthur Schopenhauer (1788-1860, German Philosopher)

8   The world is full of fools and faint hearts; and yet everyone has courage enough to bear the misfortunes, and wisdom enough to manage the affairs of his neighbor.
Benjamin Franklin (1706-1790, American Scientist, Publisher, Diplomat)

9   Spinoza Experience keeps a dear school, but fools will learn in no other.
Benjamin Franklin (1706-1790, American Scientist, Publisher, Diplomat)

10   Most fools think they are only ignorant.
Benjamin Franklin (1706-1790, American Scientist, Publisher, Diplomat)

11   If fifty million people say a foolish thing, it is still a foolish thing.
Bertrand Russell (1872-1970, British Philosopher, Mathematician, Essayist)

12   Folly is perennial, yet the human race has survived.
Bertrand Russell (1872-1970, British Philosopher, Mathematician, Essayist)

13   Every fool finds a greater one to admire them.
Bioleau

14   You ask whether I have ever been in love: fool as I am, I am not such a fool as that. But if one is only to talk from first-hand experience, conversation would be a very poor business. But though I have no personal experience of the things they call love, I have what is better -- the experience of Sappho, of Euripides, of Catallus, of Shakespeare, of Spenser, of Austen, of Bronte, of anyone else I have read.
C. S. Lewis (1898-1963, British Academic, Writer, Christian Apologist)

15   He who asks is a fool for five minutes, but he who does not ask remains a fool forever.
Chinese Proverb

16   If a man fools me once, shame on him. If he fools me twice, shame on me.
Chinese Proverb

17   A fool despises good counsel, but a wise man takes it to heart.
Confucius (551-479 BC, Chinese Ethical Teacher, Philosopher)

18   When in doubt, make a fool of yourself. There is a microscopically thin line between being brilliantly creative and acting like the most gigantic idiot on earth. So what the hell, leap.
Cynthia Heimel

19   Any fool can criticize, condemn, and complain -- and most fools do.
Dale Carnegie (1888-1955, American Author, Trainer)

20   No one but a fool is always right.
David Hare (1947-, British Playwright, Director)

21   The entire world is my temple, and a very fine one too, if I'm not mistaken, and I'll never lack priests to serve it as long as there are men.
Desiderius Erasmus (1466-1536, Dutch Humanist)

22   In short, no association or alliance can be happy or stable without me. People can't long tolerate a ruler, nor can a master his servant, a maid her mistress, a teacher his pupil, a friend his friend nor a wife her husband, a landlord his tenant, a soldier his comrade nor a party-goer his companion, unless they sometimes have illusions about each other, make use of flattery, and have the sense to turn a blind eye and sweeten life for themselves with the honey of folly.
Desiderius Erasmus (1466-1536, Dutch Humanist)

23   Fools are without number.
Desiderius Erasmus (1466-1536, Dutch Humanist)

24   Sometimes one likes foolish people for their folly, better than wise people for their wisdom.
Elizabeth Gaskell (1810-1865, British Novelist)

25   Fools build houses, and wise men buy them.
English Proverb

26   He is a fool that kisseth the maid when he may kiss the mistress.
English Proverb

27   He who lives without folly isn't so wise as he thinks.
François de La Rochefoucauld (1613-1680, French classical writer)

28   Foolproof systems do not take into account the ingenuity of fools.
Gene Brown

29   A clever child brought up with a foolish one can itself become foolish. Man is so perfectible and corruptible he can become a fool through good sense.
Georg C. Lichtenberg (1742-1799, German Physicist, Satirist)

30   Build a system that even a fool can use, and only a fool will want to use it.
George Bernard Shaw (1856-1950, Irish-born British Dramatist)

31   In the vain laughter of folly wisdom hears half its applause.
George Eliot (1819-1880, British Novelist)

32   While intelligent people can often simplify the complex, a fool is more likely to complicate the simple.
Gerald W. Grumet

33 Colleges don't make fools, they only develop them.
Geroge Lorimer

34 On Monday mornings I am dedicated to the proposition that all men are created jerks.
H. Allen Smith

35 It has been said that there is no fool like an old fool, except a young fool. But the young fool has first to grow up to be an old fool to realize what a damn fool he was when he was a young fool.
Harold Macmillan (1894-1986, British Conservative Politician, Prime Minister)

36 Men who know themselves are no longer fools. They stand on the threshold of the door of Wisdom.
Havelock Ellis (1859-1939, British Psychologist)

37 Commend a fool for his wit, or a rogue for his honesty and he will receive you into his favor.
Henry Fielding (1707-1754, British Novelist, Dramatist)

38 There are two fools in this world. One is the millionaire who thinks that by hoarding money he can somehow accumulate real power, and the other is the penniless reformer who thinks that if only he can take the money from one class and give it to another, all the world's ills will be cured.
Henry Ford (1863-1947, American Industrialist, Founder of Ford Motor Company)

39 The ultimate result of shielding men from the effects of folly, is to fill the world with fools.
Herbert Spencer (1820-1903, British Philosopher)

40 Why fools are endowed by nature with voices so much louder than sensible people possess is a mystery. It is a fact emphasized throughout history.
Hertzler

41 Nature makes only dumb animals. We owe the fools to society.
Honore De Balzac (1799-1850, French Novelist)

42 Mix a little foolishness with your serious plans. It is lovely to be silly at the right moment.
Horace (65-8 BC, Italian Poet)

43 There are four types of men in this world: 1. The man who knows, and knows that he knows; he is wise, so consult him. 2. The man who knows, but doesn't know that he knows; help him not forget what he knows. 3. The man who knows not, and knows that he knows not; teach him. 4. Finally, there is the man who knows not but pretends that he knows; he is a fool, so avoid him.
Ibn Gabirol

44 When he said we were trying to make a fool of him, I could only murmur that the Creator had beat us to it.
Ilka Chase (1905-, American Author, Actor)

45 The wise make proverbs, and fools repeat them.
Isaac Disraeli

46 The fool has to do at last what the wise did at first.
Italian Proverb

47 In days gone by, we were afraid of dying in dishonor or a state of sin. Nowadays, we are afraid of dying fools. Now the fact is that there is no Extreme Unction to absolve us of foolishness. We endure it here on earth as subjective eternity.
Jean Baudrillard (French Postmodern Philosopher, Writer)

48 Don't approach a goat from the front, a horse from the back, or a fool from any side.
Jewish Proverb

49 It seems to never occur to fools that merit and good fortune are closely united.
Johann Wolfgang Von Goethe (1749-1832, German Poet, Dramatist, Novelist)

50 A fool often fails because he thinks what is difficult is easy.
John Churton Collins

51 Looking foolish does the spirit good. The need not to look foolish is one of youth's many burdens; as we get older we are exempted from more and more, and float upward in our heedlessness, singing Gratia Dei sum quod sum.
John Updike (1932-, American Novelist, Critic)

52 Take all the fools out of this world and there wouldn't be any fun living in it, or profit.
Josh Billings (1815-1885, American Humorist, Lecturer)

53 There are two kinds of fools: those who can't change their opinions and those who won t.
Josh Billings (1815-1885, American Humorist, Lecturer)

54 The best way to convince a fool that he is wrong is to let him have his way.
Josh Billings (1815-1885, American Humorist, Lecturer)

55 The folly of all follies is to be love sick for a shadow.
Lord Alfred Tennyson (1809-1892, British Poet)

56 It is the peculiar quality of a fool to perceive the faults of others and to forget his own.
Marcus T. Cicero (106-43 BC, Great Roman Orator, Politician)

57 I was young and foolish then; now I am old and foolisher.
Mark Twain (1835-1910, American Humorist, Writer)

58 It is better to keep your mouth closed and let people think you are a fool than to open it and remove all doubt.
Mark Twain (1835-1910, American Humorist, Writer)

59 Who loves not women, wine and song remains a fool his whole life long.
Martin Luther (1483-1546, German Leader of the Protestant Reformation)

60 The great God endows His children variously. To some he gives intellect -- and they move the earth. To some he allots heart -- and the beating pulse of humanity is theirs. But to some He gives only a soul, without intelligence -- and these, who never grow up, but remain always His children, are God's fools, kindly, elemental, simple, as if from His palette the Artist of all had taken one color instead of many.
Mary Roberts Rinehart

61 Who is more foolish, the child afraid of the dark, or the man afraid of the light?
Maurice Freehill

62 The biggest fool in the world is he who merely does his work supremely well, without attending to appearance.
Michael Korda (1919-, American publisher)

63 Fortune, seeing that she could not make fools wise, has made them lucky.
Michel Eyquem De Montaigne (1533-1592, French Philosopher, Essayist)

64 He is mad past recovery, but yet he has lucid intervals.
Miguel De Cervantes (1547-1616, Spanish Novelist, Dramatist, Poet)

65 A learned fool is more foolish than an ignorant one.
MoliFre (1622-1673, French Playwright)

66 However big the fool, there is always a bigger fool to admire him.
Nicholas Boileau (1636-1711, French Literary Poet, Critic)

67 A fool always finds a greater fool to admire him.
Nicholas Boileau (1636-1711, French Literary Poet, Critic)

68 Greatest fools are the most often satisfied.
Nicholas Boileau (1636-1711, French Literary Poet, Critic)

69 The company of fools may first make us smile, but in the end we always feel melancholy.
Oliver Goldsmith (1728-1774, Anglo-Irish Author, Poet, Playwright)

70 No one but a fool would measure their satisfaction by what the world thinks of it.
Oliver Goldsmith (1728-1774, Anglo-Irish Author, Poet, Playwright)

71 He who knows he who knows not, and knows not that he knows not, is a fool, shun him; He who knows not, and knows that he knows not, is a child, teach him. He who knows, and knows not that he knows, is asleep, wake him. He who knows, and knows that he knows, is wise, follow him.
Persian Proverb

72 A fool and his money are soon parted.
Proverb

73 The fool is always beginning to live.
Proverb

74 A mother takes twenty years to make a man of her boy, and another woman makes a fool of him in twenty minutes.
Robert Frost (1875-1963, American Poet)

75 The fool needs company, the wise solitude.
Ruckett

76 There are more fools than knaves in the world, else the knaves would not have enough to live upon.
Samuel Butler (1612-1680, British Poet, Satirist)

77 How many fools does it take to make up a public?
Sebastien-Roch Nicolas De Chamfort (1741-1794, French Writer, Journalist, Playwright)

78 A foolishness is inflicted with a hatred of itself.
Seneca (4 BC-65 AD, Spanish-born Roman Statesman, philosopher)

79 The fool within himself is the object of pity, until he is flattered.
Sir Richard Steele (1672-1729, British Dramatist, Essayist, Editor)

80 What a fool does in the end, the wise do in the beginning.
Spanish Proverb

81 They never open their mouths without subtracting from the sum of human knowledge.
Thomas Brackett Reed (1839-1902, American Republican Politician)

82 The haste of a fool is the slowest thing in the world.
Thomas Shadwell (1642--1692, British Playwright)

83 A spoon does not know the taste of soup, nor a learned fool the taste of wisdom.
Welsh Proverb

84 Seek but provision of bread and wine, fools to flatter, and clothing fine; and nothing of God shall ever be thine.
Wes Smith

85 A fool sees not the same tree that a wise man sees.
William Blake (1757-1827, British Poet, Painter)

86 Lord, what fools these mortals be.
William Shakespeare (1564-1616, British Poet, Playwright, Actor)

87 The dullness of the fool is the whetstone of the wits.
William Shakespeare (1564-1616, British Poet, Playwright, Actor)

88 He uses his folly like a stalking-horse, and under the presentation of that he shoots his wit.
William Shakespeare (1564-1616, British Poet, Playwright, Actor)

89 The fool thinks himself to be wise, but the wise man knows himself to be a fool. [Measure For Measure]
William Shakespeare (1564-1616, British Poet, Playwright, Actor)

90 A fellow who is always declaring that he's no fool, usually has his suspicions.
Wilson Mizner (1876-1933, American Author)

91 In life, each of us must sometimes play the fool.
Yiddish Proverb

FOOTBALL

1 Conventional wisdom notwithstanding, there is no reason either in football or in poetry why the two should not meet in a man's life if he has the weight and cares about the words.
Archibald Macleish (1892-1982, American Poet)

2   People stress the violence. That's the smallest part of it. Football is brutal only from a distance. In the middle of it there's a calm, a tranquility. The players accept pain. There's a sense of order even at the end of a running play with bodies strewn everywhere. When the systems interlock, there's a satisfaction to the game that can't be duplicated. There's a harmony.
Don Delillo (1926-, American Author)

3   Sure, luck means a lot in football. Not having a good quarterback is bad luck.
Don Shula (American Football Coach)

4   Pro football is like nuclear warfare. There are no winners, only survivors.
Frank Gifford (American sportscaster)

5   Football combines the two worst features of American life. It is violence punctuated by committee meetings.
George F. Will (1941-, American Political Columnist)

6   There is a progression of understanding vis-a-vis pro football that varies drastically with the factor of distance -- physical, emotional, intellectual and every other way. Which is exactly the way it should be, in the eyes of the amazingly small number of people who own and control the game, because it is this finely managed distance factor that accounts for the high-profit mystique that blew the sacred institution of baseball off its "national pastime" pedestal in less than fifteen years.
Hunter S. Thompson (1939-, American Journalist)

7   When you win nothing hurts.
Joe Namath (1943-, American Football Player)

8   No star playing, just football.
Knute Rockne (1888-1931, Norwegian-born American Football Coach)

9   Let's win one for the Gipper.
Knute Rockne (1888-1931, Norwegian-born American Football Coach)

10   NFL owners should quit worrying about silly things like players celebrating in the end zone. They should give them something to really celebrate. Get rid of the artificial surfaces.
O. J. Simpson (1947-, American Football Player)

11   Football is a game of errors. The team that makes the fewest errors in a game usually wins.
Paul Brown (American Football Coach)

12   A school without football is in danger of deteriorating into a medieval study hall.
Vince Lombardi (1913-1970, American Football Coach)

13   Every time a football player goes to ply his trade he's got to play from the ground up -- from the soles of his feet right up to his head. Every inch of him has to play. Some guys play with their heads. That's OK You've got to be smart to be number one in any business. But more importantly, you've got to play with your heart, with every fiber of your body. If you're lucky enough to find a guy with a lot of head and a lot of heart, he's never going to come off the field second.
Vince Lombardi (1913-1970, American Football Coach)

14   Football is like life -- it requires perseverance, self-denial, hard work, sacrifice, dedication and respect for authority.
Vince Lombardi (1913-1970, American Football Coach)

15   Some people try to find things in this game that don't exist but football is only two things- blocking and tackling.
Vince Lombardi (1913-1970, American Football Coach)

FORCE

1   Force works on servile natures, not the free.
Ben Johnson (1573-1637, British Dramatist, Poet)

2   The direct use of force is such a poor solution to any problem, it is generally employed only by small children and large nations.
David Friedman

3   The use of force alone is but temporary. It may subdue for a moment; but it does not remove the necessity of subduing again: and a nation is not governed, which is perpetually to be conquered.
Edmund Burke (1729-1797, British Political Writer, Statesman)

4   Whatever needs to be maintained through force is doomed.
Henry Miller (1891-1980, American Author)

5   Force is not a remedy.
John Bright (1811-1889, Radical British Statesman, Orator)

6   Civilization is nothing more than the effort to reduce the use of force to the last resort.
Jose Ortega Y Gasset (1883-1955, Spanish Essayist, Philosopher)

7   Coercion may prevent many transgressions; but it robs even actions which are legal of a part of their beauty. Freedom may lead to many transgressions, but it lends even to vices a less ignoble form.
Karl Wilhelm Von Humboldt (1767-1835, German Statesman, Philologist)

8   Why slap them on the wrist with feather when you can belt them over the head with a sledgehammer.
Katharine Hepburn (1907-, American Actress, Writer)

9   Some people draw a comforting distinction between "force" and "violence." I refuse to cloud the issue by such word-play. The power which establishes a state is violence; the power which maintains it is violence; the power which eventually overthrows it is violence. Call an elephant a rabbit only if it gives you comfort to feel that you are about to be trampled to death by a rabbit.
Kenneth Kaunda (1924-, Zambian Politician, President)

10   Where force is necessary, there it must be applied boldly, decisively and completely. But one must know the limitations of force; one must know when to blend force with a maneuver, a blow with an agreement.
Leon Trotsky (1879-1940, Russian Revolutionary)

11 Not believing in force is the same as not believing in gravitation.
Leon Trotsky (1879-1940, Russian Revolutionary)

12 The great questions of the day will not be settled by means of speeches and majority decisions but by iron and blood.
Otto Von Bismarck (1815-1898, Prussian Statesman, Prime Minister)

13 Force is legitimate where gentleness avails not.
Pierre Corneille (1606-1684, French Dramatist)

14 Force without forecast is to little avail.
Proverb

15 Be careful: they have arms, and no alternatives.
Ryszard Kapuscinski (1932, Polish Report and Foreign Correspondent)

16 Force is that which rules the actions without regulating the will.
Saying

17 Force is as pitiless to the man who possesses it, or thinks he does, as it is to its victims; the second it crushes, the first it intoxicates. The truth is, nobody really possesses it.
Simone Weil (1910-1943, French Philosopher, Mystic)

18 Who were the fools who spread the story that brute force cannot kill ideas? Nothing is easier. And once they are dead they are no more than corpses.
Simone Weil (1910-1943, French Philosopher, Mystic)

FORGIVENESS

1 Absolute virtue is impossible and the republic of forgiveness leads, with implacable logic, to the republic of the guillotine.
Albert Camus (1913-1960, French Existential Writer)

2 The condition of being forgiven is self-abandonment. The proud man prefers self-reproach, however painful --because the reproached self isn't abandoned; it remains intact.
Aldous Huxley (1894-1963, British Author)

3 How shall I lose the sin, yet keep the sense, and love the offender, yet detest the offence?
Alexander Pope (1688-1744, British Poet, Critic, Translator)

4 To err is human, to forgive is divine.
Alexander Pope (1688-1744, British Poet, Critic, Translator)

5 To apologize is to lay the foundation for a future offense.
Ambrose Bierce (1842-1914, American Author, Editor, Journalist, "The Devil's Dictionary")

6 A man must learn to forgive himself.
Arthur Davison Ficke

7 I never forgive, but I always forget.
Arthur James Balfour (1848-1930, British Conservative Politician, Prime Minister)

8 The best thing to give to your enemy is forgiveness; to an opponent, tolerance; to a friend, your heart; to your child, a good example; to a father, deference; to your mother, conduct that will make her proud of you; to yourself, respect; to all men, charity.
Arthur James Balfour (1848-1930, British Conservative Politician, Prime Minister)

9 You should pardon many things in others, nothing in yourself.
Auson

10 In him we have redemption through his blood, the forgiveness of our trespasses, according to the riches of his grace. [Ephesians 1:7]
Bible (Sacred Scriptures of Christians and Judaism)

11 And be kind to one another, tender-hearted, forgiving each other, just as God in Christ also has forgiven you. [Ephesians 4:32]
Bible (Sacred Scriptures of Christians and Judaism)

12 My transgression is sealed up in a bag, and thou sewest up mine iniquity. [Job 14:17]
Bible (Sacred Scriptures of Christians and Judaism)

13 God has a big eraser.
Billy Zeoli

14 Love thy neighbor as thyself: Do not to others what thou wouldn't not wish be done to thyself: Forgive injuries. Forgive thy enemy, be reconciled to him, give him assistance, invoke God in his behalf.
Confucius (551-479 BC, Chinese Ethical Teacher, Philosopher)

15 To forgive oneself? No, that doesn't work: we have to be forgiven. But we can only believe this is possible if we ourselves can forgive.
Dag Hammarskjold (1905-1961, Swedish Statesman, Secretary-general of U.N.)

16 Forgive many things in others; nothing in yourself.
Decimus Magnus Ausonius (310-395, Latin Poet, Man of Letters)

17 A woman who can't forgive should never have more than a nodding acquaintance with a man.
Edgar Watson Howe (1853-1937, American Journalist, Author)

18 Never does the human soul appear so strong and noble as when it forgoes revenge and dares to forgive an injury.
Edwin Hubbel Chapin (1814-1880, American Author, Clergyman)

19 Forgive you? -- Oh, of course, dear, a dozen times a week! We women were created forgiveness but to speak.
Ella Higginson (1862-1940, American Writer, Journalist)

20 Forgive, son; men are men; they needs must err.
Euripides (480-406 BC, Greek Tragic Poet)

21 This is certain, that a man that studieth revenge keeps his wounds green, which otherwise would heal and do well.
Francis Bacon (1561-1626, British Philosopher, Essayist, Statesman)

22 We pardon to the extent that we love.
    François de La Rochefoucauld (1613-1680, French classical writer)

23 And if your friend does evil to you, say to him, "I forgive you for what you did to me, but how can I forgive you for what you did to yourself?"
    Friedrich Nietzsche (1844-1900, German Philosopher)

24 Forgive him, for he believes that the customs of his tribe are the laws of nature!
    George Bernard Shaw (1856-1950, Irish-born British Dramatist)

25 The secret of forgiving everything is to understand nothing.
    George Bernard Shaw (1856-1950, Irish-born British Dramatist)

26 Would not love see returning penitence afar off, and fall on its neck and kiss it?
    George Eliot (1819-1880, British Novelist)

27 He that cannot forgive others, breaks the bridge over which he himself must pass if he would ever reach heaven; for everyone has need to be forgiven.
    George Herbert (1593-1632, British Metaphysical Poet)

28 I can have peace of mind only when I forgive rather than judge.
    Gerald G. Jampolsky (American Psychiatrist, Lecturer, Author)

29 In contrast to revenge, which is the natural, automatic reaction to transgression and which, because of the irreversibility of the action process can be expected and even calculated, the act of forgiving can never be predicted; it is the only reaction that acts in an unexpected way and thus retains, though being a reaction, something of the original character of action.
    Hannah Arendt (1906-1975, German-born American Political Philosopher)

30 God will forgive me, that's his business.
    Heinrich Heine (1797-1856, German Poet, Journalist)

31 Of course God will forgive me; that's His job.
    Heinrich Heine (1797-1856, German Poet, Journalist)

32 If we could read the secret history of our enemies, we would find in each person's life sorrow and suffering enough to disarm all hostility.
    Henry Wadsworth Longfellow (1819-1892, American Poet)

33 God pardons like a mother, who kisses the offense into everlasting forgiveness.
    Henry Ward Beecher (1813-1887, American Preacher, Orator, Writer)

34 I can forgive, but I cannot forget," is only another way of saying, "I cannot forgive."
    Henry Ward Beecher (1813-1887, American Preacher, Orator, Writer)

35 Giving The best thing to give to your enemy is forgiveness; to an opponent, tolerance; to a friend, your heart; to your child, a good example; to a father, deference; to your mother, conduct that will make her proud of you; to yourself, respect; to all men.
    Henry Ward Beecher (1813-1887, American Preacher, Orator, Writer)

36 I can forgive, but I cannot forget, is only another way of saying, I will not forgive. Forgiveness ought to be like a canceled note -- torn in two, and burned up, so that it never can be shown against one.
    Henry Ward Beecher (1813-1887, American Preacher, Orator, Writer)

37 Every man should keep a fair-sized cemetery in which to bury the faults of his friends.
    Henry Ward Beecher (1813-1887, American Preacher, Orator, Writer)

38 It is a very delicate job to forgive a man, without lowering him in his own estimation, and yours too.
    Henry Wheeler Shaw (1818-1885, American Humorist)

39 The heart of a mother is a deep abyss at the bottom of which you will always find forgiveness.
    Honore De Balzac (1799-1850, French Novelist)

40 Forgiveness is a virtue of the brave.
    Indira Gandhi (1917-1984, Indian Prime Minster)

41 Humanity is never so beautiful as when praying for forgiveness, or else forgiving another.
    Jean Paul Richter (1763-1825, German Novelist)

42 Many have been ruined by their fortunes, and many have escaped ruin by the want of fortune. To obtain it the great have become little, and the little great.
    Johann Georg Zimmermann (1957-, German Physicist)

43 If a good person does you wrong, act as though you had not noticed it. They will make note of this and not remain in your debt long.
    Johann Wolfgang Von Goethe (1749-1832, German Poet, Dramatist, Novelist)

44 To be able to bear provocation is an argument of great reason, and to forgive it of a great mind."
    John Tillotson (1630-1694, British Theologian - Archbishop of Canterbury)

45 There is no revenge so complete as forgiveness.
    Josh Billings (1815-1885, American Humorist, Lecturer)

46 Forgiveness is the oil of relationships.
    Josh Mcdowell

47 They who forgive most shall be most forgiven.
    Josiah Bailey (1873-1946, American Senator)

48 We easily pardon an offense we had part in.
    Juoy

49 If the other person injures you, you may forget the injury; but if you injure him you will always remember.
    Kahlil Gibran (1883-1931, Lebanese Poet, Novelist)

50 Nobody ever forgets where he buried the hatchet.
    Kin Hubbard (1868-1930, American Humorist, Journalist)

51 He who forgiveth, and is reconciled unto his enemy, shall receive his reward from God; for he loveth not the unjust doers.
Koran Sura

52 Only the brave know how to forgive; it is the most refined and generous pitch of virtue human nature can arrive at.
Laurence Sterne (1713-1768, British Author)

53 He who has not forgiven an enemy has never yet tasted one of the most sublime enjoyments of life.
Lauter

54 Forgive yourself for your faults and your mistakes and move on.
Les Brown (1945-, American Speaker, Author, Trainer, Motivator Lecturer)

55 Forgive those who have hurt you.
Les Brown (1945-, American Speaker, Author, Trainer, Motivator Lecturer)

56 Forgive! How many will say, "forgive," and find a sort of absolution in the sound to hate a little longer!
Lord Alfred Tennyson (1809-1892, British Poet)

57 Wrongs are often forgiven, but contempt never is. Our pride remembers it forever. It implies a discovery of weakness, which we are more careful to conceal than a crime. Many a man will confess his crimes to a friend; but I never knew a man that would tell his silly weaknesses to his most intimate one.
Lord Chesterfield (1694-1773, British Statesman, Author)

58 Little, vicious minds abound with anger and revenge, and are incapable of feeling the pleasure of forgiving their enemies.
Lord Chesterfield (1694-1773, British Statesman, Author)

59 What is forgiven is usually well remembered.
Louis Dudek

60 One can't relive one's life. Forgiveness is not what's difficult; one's always too ready to forgive. And it does no good, that's obvious.
Louis-Ferdinand Celine (1894-1961, French Author)

61 It is easier to forgive an enemy than a friend.
Madame DorothT Deluzy (1747-1830, French Actress)

62 The weak can never forgive. Forgiveness is the attribute of the strong.
Mahatma Gandhi (1869-1948, Indian Political, Spiritual Leader)

63 The world can forgive practically anything except people who mind their own business.
Margaret Mitchell (1900-1949, American Novelist)

64 Forgiveness is the fragrance the violet sheds on the heel that has crushed it.
Mark Twain (1835-1910, American Humorist, Writer)

65 Forget and forgive. This is not difficult when properly understood. It means forget inconvenient duties, then forgive yourself for forgetting. By rigid practice and stern determination, it comes easy.
Mark Twain (1835-1910, American Humorist, Writer)

66 Once a woman has forgiven her man, she must not reheat his sins for breakfast.
Marlene Dietrich (1904-1992, German-born American Film Actor)

67 Forgiveness is God's command.
Martin Luther (1483-1546, German Leader of the Protestant Reformation)

68 Whoever approaches Me walking, I will come to him running; and he who meets Me with sins equivalent to the whole world, I will greet him with forgiveness equal to it.
Mishkat Al-massabaih

69 The best thing about giving of ourselves is that what we get is always better than what we give. The reaction is greater than the action.
Orison Swett Marden (1850-1924, American Author, Founder of Success Magazine)

70 Always forgive your enemies -- nothing annoys them so much.
Oscar Wilde (1856-1900, British Author, Wit)

71 Forgiveness does not change the past, but it does enlarge the future.
Paul Boese

72 Their errors have been weighed and found to have been dust in the balance; if their sins were as scarlet, they are now white as snow: they have been washed in the blood of the mediator and the redeemer, Time.
Percy Bysshe Shelley (1792-1822, British Poet)

73 Those who easily forgive invite offenses.
Pierre Corneille (1606-1684, French Dramatist)

74 We can easily forgive a child who is afraid of the dark; the real tragedy of life is when men are afraid of the light.
Plato (427-347 BC, Greek Philosopher)

75 When you are happy you can forgive a great deal.
Princess of Wales Diana (1961-1997, Wife of Charles, Prince of Wales)

76 Forgive and forget.
Proverb

77 A reconciled friend is a double enemy.
Proverb

78 Never repeat old grievances.
Proverb

79 Those that do you a very ill deed will never forgive you.
Proverb

80 A wise man will make haste to forgive, because he knows the full value of time and will not suffer it to pass away in unnecessary pain.
Rambler

81 If I owe Smith ten dollars and God forgives me, that doesn't pay Smith.
Robert Green Ingersoll (1833-1899, American Orator, Lawyer)

82 Forgive thyself little, and others much.
Robert Leighton (1611-1684, British Clergyman)

83 We all like to forgive, and love best not those who offend us least, nor who have done most for us, but those who make it most easy for us to forgive them.
Samuel Butler (1612-1680, British Poet, Satirist)

84 A winner rebukes and forgives; a loser is too timid to rebuke and too petty to forgive
Sidney J. Harris (1917-, American Journalist)

85 There is no sense in crying over spilt milk. Why bewail what is done and cannot be recalled?
Sophocles (495-406 BC, Greek Tragic Poet)

86 If I die, I forgive you. If I live we shall see.
Spanish Proverb

87 Forgiveness is the remission of sins. For it is by this that what has been lost, and was found, is saved from being lost again.
St. Augustine (354-430, Numidian-born Bishop of Hippo, Theologian)

88 Thou must be emptied of that wherewith thou art full, that thou mayest be filled with that whereof thou art empty.
St. Augustine (354-430, Numidian-born Bishop of Hippo, Theologian)

89 It is in pardoning that we are pardoned.
St. Francis of Assisi (1181-1226, Italian Preacher, Founder of the Franciscan Orde)

90 The stupid neither forgive nor forget; the naive forgive and forget; the wise forgive but do not forget.
Thomas Szasz (1920-, American Psychiatrist)

91 Right actions in the future are the best apologies for bad actions in the past.
Tryon Edwards (1809-1894, American Theologian)

FORTUNE

1 Every individual is the architect of his own fortune.
Appius Claudius (4th - 3rd Century BC, Aristocratic Roman Statesman, General)

2 He that waits upon fortune, is never sure of a dinner.
Benjamin Franklin (1706-1790, American Scientist, Publisher, Diplomat)

3 There is no one, says another, whom fortune does not visit once in his life; but when she does not find him ready to receive her, she walks in at the door, and flies out at the window.
Charles De Montesquieu (1689-1755, French Jurist, Political Philosopher)

4 Fortune has something of the nature of a woman. If she is too intensely wooed, she commonly goes the further away.
Charles V (1500-1558, King of Spain, Holy Roman Emperor.)

5 A great fortune depends on luck, a small one on diligence.
Chinese Proverb

6 I do have big tits. Always had 'em -- pushed 'em up, whacked 'em around. Why not make fun of 'em? I've made a fortune with 'em.
Dolly Parton (1946-, American Musician, Country singer, Actress, Songwriter)

7 Fortunes made in no time are like shirts made in no time; it's ten to one if they hang long together.
Douglas William Jerrold (1803-1857, British Humorist, Playwright)

8 Your fortune is not something to find but to unfold.
Eric Butterworth

9 Fortune truly helps those who are of good judgment.
Euripides (480-406 BC, Greek Tragic Poet)

10 Therefore if a man look sharply and attentively, he shall see Fortune; for though she be blind, yet she is not invisible.
Francis Bacon (1561-1626, British Philosopher, Essayist, Statesman)

11 Has fortune dealt you some bad cards. Then let wisdom make you a good gamester.
Francis Quarles (1592-1644, British Poet)

12 There is a kind of elevation which does not depend on fortune; it is a certain air which distinguishes us, and seems to destine us for great things; it is a price which we imperceptibly set upon ourselves.
François de La Rochefoucauld (1613-1680, French classical writer)

13 Against change of fortune set a brave heart.
French Proverb

14 In bad fortune hold out, in good hold in.
German Proverb

15 Behind every great fortune there is a crime.
Honore De Balzac (1799-1850, French Novelist)

16 Fortune makes a fool of those she favors too much.
Horace (65-8 BC, Italian Poet)

17 If a man's fortune does not fit him, it is like the shoe in the story; if too large it trips him up, if too small it pinches him.
Horace (65-8 BC, Italian Poet)

18 Fortune is the rod of the weak, and the staff of the brave.
James Russell Lowell (1819-1891, American Poet, Critic, Editor)

19 We do not know what is really good or bad fortune.
Jean Jacques Rousseau (1712-1778, Swiss Political Philosopher, Educationist, Essayist)

20 Only learn to seize good fortune, for good fortune's always here.
Johann Wolfgang Von Goethe (1749-1832, German Poet, Dramatist, Novelist)

21 It is madness to make fortune the mistress of events, because by herself she is nothing and is ruled by prudence.
John Dryden (1631-1700, British Poet, Dramatist, Critic)

22 Large fortunes are all founded either on the occupation of land, or lending or the taxation of labor.
John Ruskin (1819-1900, British Critic, Social Theorist)

23 Fortune favors the bold, but abandons the timid.
Latin Proverb

24 Fortune favors the prepared mind.
Louis Pasteur (1822-1895, French Scientist Who Developed "Pasteurization")

25 Fortune knocks at every man's door once in a life, but in a good many cases the man is in a neighboring saloon and does not hear her.
Mark Twain (1835-1910, American Humorist, Writer)

26 Good fortune and evil fortune come to all things alike in this world of time.
Moasi

27 Fortune is ever seen accompanying industry.
Oliver Goldsmith (1728-1774, Anglo-Irish Author, Poet, Playwright)

28 I am above being injured by fortune, though she steals away much, more will remain with me. The blessing I now enjoy transcend fear.
Ovid (43 BC-18 AD, Roman Poet)

29 Luck affects everything. Let your hook always be cast; in the stream where you least expect it there will be a fish.
Ovid (43 BC-18 AD, Roman Poet)

30 One's best fortune, or, their worst is their spouse.
Proverb

31 Speedy exception is the mother of good fortune.
Proverb

32 Fortune is like glass--the brighter the glitter, the more easily broken.
Publilius Syrus (1st Century BC, Roman Writer)

33 Nature magically suits a man to his fortunes, by making them the fruit of his character.
Ralph Waldo Emerson (1803-1882, American Poet, Essayist)

34 Fortune is a great deceiver. She sells very dear the things she seems to give us.
Vincent Voiture

35 Fortune sides with him who dares.
Virgil (70-19 BC, Roman Poet)

36 Fortune favors the brave.
Virgil (70-19 BC, Roman Poet)

37 Henceforth I ask not good fortune. I myself am good fortune.
Walt Whitman (1819-1892, American Poet)

38 There is a tide in the affairs of men, which taken at the flood, leads on to fortune; Omitted, all the voyage of their life is bound by shallows and in misery. [Julius Caesar]
William Shakespeare (1564-1616, British Poet, Playwright, Actor)

FRANKNESS

1 Frank and explicit--that is the right line to take when you wish to conceal your own mind and confuse the minds of others.
Benjamin Disraeli (1804-1881, British Statesman, Prime Minister)

2 We are franker towards others than towards ourselves.
Friedrich Nietzsche (1844-1900, German Philosopher)

3 All cruel people describe themselves as paragons of frankness.
Tennessee Williams (1914-1983, American Dramatist)

4 The great consolation in life is to say what one thinks.
Voltaire (1694-1778, French Historian, Writer)

5 All faults may be forgiven of him who has perfect candor.
Walt Whitman (1819-1892, American Poet)

FRAUD

1 There are some frauds so well conducted that it would be stupidity not to be deceived by them.
Charles Caleb Colton (1780-1832, British Sportsman Writer)

2 There is no greater fraud than a promise not kept.
Gaelic Proverb

3 A bad forgery's the ultimate insult.
Jonathan Gash (British Writer)

4 The first and worst of all frauds is to cheat one's self. All sin is easy after that.
Pearl Bailey (1918-1990, American Vocalist, Movie and Stage Actress)

5 It is a fraud to borrow what we are unable to pay.
Publilius Syrus (1st Century BC, Roman Writer)

FREE ENTERPRISE

1 A free-enterprise economy depends only on markets, and according to the most advanced mathematical macroeconomic theory, markets depend only on moods: specifically, the mood of the men in the pinstripes, also known as the Boys on the Street. When the Boys are in a good mood, the market thrives; when they get scared or sullen, it is time for each one of us to look into the retail apple business.
Barbara Ehrenreich (1941-, American Author, Columnist)

2 That's free enterprise, friends: freedom to gamble, freedom to lose. And the great thing -- the truly democratic thing about it -- is that you don't even have to be a player to lose.
Barbara Ehrenreich (1941-, American Author, Columnist)

3 In the long run, free trade benefits everyone; in the short run it is bound to produce much pain.
Henry Hobhouse (British Writer)

4   Freedom of enterprise was from the beginning not altogether a blessing. As the liberty to work or to starve, it spelled toil, insecurity, and fear for the vast majority of the population. If the individual were no longer compelled to prove himself on the market, as a free economic subject, the disappearance of this freedom would be one of the greatest achievements of civilization.
Herbert Marcuse (1898-1979, German Political Philosopher)

5   We Asians are the original Conservatives because for thousands of years we have believed in free enterprise... you have just stolen our philosophy.
Jayvantsinnji Gohel (1915-1995, Chairman of the Anglo-Asian Conservative Society)

6   The great dialectic in our time is not, as anciently and by some still supposed, between capital and labor; it is between economic enterprise and the state.
John Kenneth Galbraith (1908-, American Economist)

7   Entrepreneurial profit is the expression of the value of what the entrepreneur contributes to production.
Joseph A. Schumpeter (1883-1950, Austrian-American Economist)

8   The market came with the dawn of civilization and it is not an invention of capitalism. If it leads to improving the well-being of the people there is no contradiction with socialism.
Mikhail Gorbachev (1931-, Soviet Statesman and President of USSR (1988-91))

9   The basic rule of free enterprise: You must give in order to get.
Scott Alexander (American Author)

10 Agriculture, manufactures, commerce, and navigation, the four pillars of our prosperity, are then most thriving when left most free to individual enterprise. Protection from casual embarrassments, however, may sometimes be seasonably interposed.
Thomas Jefferson (1743-1826, Third President of the USA)

FREE WILL

1   Whereas the Greeks gave to will the boundaries of reason, we have come to put the will's impulse in the very center of reason, which has, as a result, become deadly.
Albert Camus (1913-1960, French Existential Writer)

2   A man may be a pessimistic determinist before lunch and an optimistic believer in the will's freedom after it.
Aldous Huxley (1894-1963, British Author)

3   Do what thou wilt shall be the whole of the law.
Aleister Crowley (1875-1947, British Occultist)

4   We human beings do have some genuine freedom of choice and therefore some effective control over our own destinies. I am not a determinist. But I also believe that the decisive choice is seldom the latest choice in the series. More often than not, it will turn out to be some choice made relatively far back in the past.
Arnold Toynbee (1852-1883, British Economic Historian and Social Reformer)

5   Will power is only the tensile strength of one's own disposition. One cannot increase it by a single ounce.
Cesare Pavese (1908-1950, Italian Poet, Novelist, Translator)

6   I assess the power of a will by how much resistance, pain, torture it endures and knows how to turn to its advantage.
Friedrich Nietzsche (1844-1900, German Philosopher)

7   The strongest knowledge (that of the total freedom of the human will) is nonetheless the poorest in successes: for it always has the strongest opponent, human vanity.
Friedrich Nietzsche (1844-1900, German Philosopher)

8   Man is a masterpiece of creation if for no other reason than that, all the weight of evidence for determinism notwithstanding, he believes he has free will.
Georg C. Lichtenberg (1742-1799, German Physicist, Satirist)

9   The liberated man is not the one who is freed in his ideal reality, his inner truth, or his transparency; he is the man who changes spaces, who circulates, who changes sex, clothes, and habits according to fashion, rather than morality, and who changes opinions not as his conscience dictates but in response to opinion polls.
Jean Baudrillard (French Postmodern Philosopher, Writer)

10 It can even come about that a created will cancels out, not perhaps the exertion, but the result of divine action; for in this sense, God himself has told us that God wishes things which do not happen because man does not wish them! Thus the rights of men are immense, and his greatest misfortune is to be unaware of them.
Joseph De Maistre (1753-1821, French Diplomat, Philosopher)

11 We are all bound to the throne of the Supreme Being by a flexible chain which restrains without enslaving us. The most wonderful aspect of the universal scheme of things is the action of free beings under divine guidance.
Joseph De Maistre (1753-1821, French Diplomat, Philosopher)

12 The will is never free -- it is always attached to an object, a purpose. It is simply the engine in the car -- it can't steer.
Joyce Cary (1888-1957, British Author)

13 One of the annoying things about believing in free will and individual responsibility is the difficulty of finding somebody to blame your problems on. And when you do find somebody, it's remarkable how often his picture turns up on your driver's license.
P. J. O'Rourke (1947-, American Journalist)

14 There are no galley-slaves in the royal vessel of divine love -- every man works his oar voluntarily!
St. Francis De Sales (1567-1622, Roman Catholic Bishop, Writer)

15 The most intellectual of men are moved quite as much by the circumstances which they are used to as by their own will. The active voluntary part of a man is very small, and if it were not economized by a sleepy kind of habit, its results would be null.
Walter Bagehot (1826-1877, British Economist, Critic)

16 Fatalism, whose solving word in all crises of behavior is "All striving is vain," will never reign supreme, for the impulse to take life strivingly is indestructible in the race. Moral creeds which speak to that impulse will be widely successful in spite of inconsistency, vagueness, and shadowy determination of expectancy. Man needs a rule for his will, and will invent one if one be not given him.
William James (1842-1910, American Psychologist, Professor, Author)

17 We defy augury. There's a special providence in the fall of a sparrow. If it be now, 'Tis not to come. If it be not to come, it will be now. If it not now, yet it will come. The readiness is all.
William Shakespeare (1564-1616, British Poet, Playwright, Actor)

FREEDOM

1 They want to be free and they do not know how to be just.
Abbe Sieyes

2 Those who deny freedom to others, deserve it not for themselves.
Abraham Lincoln (1809-1865, Sixteenth President of the USA)

3 Do not destroy that immortal emblem of humanity, the Declaration of Independence.
Abraham Lincoln (1809-1865, Sixteenth President of the USA)

4 Freedom is the last, best hope of earth.
Abraham Lincoln (1809-1865, Sixteenth President of the USA)

5 The shepherd drives the wolf from the sheep's throat, for which the sheep thanks the shepherd as his liberator, while the wolf denounces him for the same act as the destroyer of liberty.
Abraham Lincoln (1809-1865, Sixteenth President of the USA)

6 Freedom is not the right to do what we want, but what we ought. Let us have faith that right makes might and in that faith let us; to the end, dare to do our duty as we understand it.
Abraham Lincoln (1809-1865, Sixteenth President of the USA)

7 Freedom is an internal achievement rather than an external adjustment.
Adam Clayton Powell (African-American politician)

8 We have confused the free with the free and easy.
Adlai E. Stevenson (1900-1965, American Lawyer, Politician)

9 A hungry man is not a free man.
Adlai E. Stevenson (1900-1965, American Lawyer, Politician)

10 Freedom is not an ideal, it is not even a protection, if it means nothing more than freedom to stagnate, to live without dreams, to have no greater aim than a second car and another television set.
Adlai E. Stevenson (1900-1965, American Lawyer, Politician)

11 Freedom is just chaos with better lighting.
Alan Dean Foster

12 Freedom is nothing else but a chance to be better.
Albert Camus (1913-1960, French Existential Writer)

13 The only conception of freedom I can have is that of the prisoner or the individual in the midst of the State. The only one I know is freedom of thought and action.
Albert Camus (1913-1960, French Existential Writer)

14 Without freedom, no art; art lives only on the restraints it imposes on itself, and dies of all others. But without freedom, no socialism either, except the socialism of the gallows.
Albert Camus (1913-1960, French Existential Writer)

15 The sovereignty of one's self over one's self is called Liberty.
Albert Pike (1809-1891, American Lawyer, Masonic Author, Historian)

16 For in the end, freedom is a personal and lonely battle; and one faces down fears of today so that those of tomorrow might be engaged.
Alice Walker (1944-, American Author, Critic)

17 Freedom is the by-product of economic surplus.
Aneurin Bevan (1897-1960, British Labor Politician)

18 By the will art thou lost, by the will art thou found, by the will art thou free, captive, and bound.
Angelus Silesius

19 I know but one freedom and that is the freedom of the mind.
Antoine De Saint-Exupery (1900-1944, French Aviator, Writer)

20 What is freedom? Freedom is the right to choose: the right to create for oneself the alternatives of choice.
Archibald Macleish (1892-1982, American Poet)

21 Democracy arose from men's thinking that if they are equal in any respect, they are equal absolutely.
Aristotle (384-322 BC, Greek Philosopher)

22 Only that thing is free which exists by the necessities of its own nature, and is determined in its actions by itself alone.
Baruch (Benedict de) Spinoza (1632-1677, Dutch Philosopher and Theologian)

23 To be thrown upon one's own resources, is to be cast into the very lap of fortune; for our faculties then undergo a development and display an energy of which they were previously unsusceptible.
Benjamin Franklin (1706-1790, American Scientist, Publisher, Diplomat)

24 In the last analysis, our only freedom is the freedom to discipline ourselves.
Bernard M. Baruch (1870-1965, American Financier)

25 The greatest blessing of our democracy is freedom. But in the last analysis, our only freedom is the freedom to discipline ourselves.
Bernard M. Baruch (1870-1965, American Financier)

26 Freedom of opinion can only exist when the government thinks itself secure.
Bertrand Russell (1872-1970, British Philosopher, Mathematician, Essayist)

27 Governing sense, mind and intellect, intent on liberation, free from desire, fear and anger, the sage is forever free.
Bhagavad Gita (400 BC, Sanskrit Poem Incorporated Into the Mahabharata)

28 Just as war is freedom's cost, disagreement is freedom's privilege.
Bill Clinton (1946-, Forty-second President of the USA)

29 It is not good to be too free. It is not good to have everything one wants.
Blaise Pascal (1623-1662, French Scientist, Religious Philosopher)

30 It is especially important to encourage unorthodox thinking when the situation is critical: At such moments every new word and fresh thought is more precious than gold. Indeed, people must not be deprived of the right to think their own thoughts.
Boris Yeltsin (1931-, Russian President)

31 What a curious phenomenon it is that you can get men to die for the liberty of the world who will not make the little sacrifice that is needed to free themselves from their own individual bondage.
Bruce Barton (1886-1967, American Author, Advertising Executive)

32 Liberty will not descend to a people; a people must raise themselves to liberty; it is a blessing that must be earned before it can be enjoyed.
Charles Caleb Colton (1780-1832, British Sportsman Writer)

33 Tyrants have not yet discovered any chains that can fetter the mind.
Charles Caleb Colton (1780-1832, British Sportsman Writer)

34 Countries are well cultivated, not as they are fertile, but as they are free.
Charles De Montesquieu (1689-1755, French Jurist, Political Philosopher)

35 When we lose the right to be different, we lose the privilege to be free.
Charles Evans Hughes (1862-1948, American Jurist, Politician)

36 No matter what a man does, he is not fully sane or human unless there is a spirit of freedom in him, a soul unconfined by purpose and larger than the practicable world.
Charles Horton Cooley (1864-1929, American Sociologist)

37 Every general increase of freedom is accompanied by some degeneracy, attributable to the same causes as the freedom.
Charles Horton Cooley (1864-1929, American Sociologist)

38 There are two freedoms -- the false, where a man is free to do what he likes; the true, where he is free to do what he ought.
Charles Kingsley (1819-1875, British Author, Clergyman)

39 The saving man becomes the free man.
Chinese Proverb

40 Only very slowly and late have men come to realize that unless freedom is universal it is only extended privilege.
Christopher Hill (1912-, British Historian)

41 You can protect your liberties in this world only by protecting the other man's freedom. You can be free only if I am free.
Clarence Darrow (1857-1938, American Lawyer)

42 You can only be free if I am free.
Clarence Darrow (1857-1938, American Lawyer)

43 Men are free when they are in a living homeland, not when they are straying and breaking away. Men are free when they are obeying some deep, inward voice of religious belief. Obeying from within. Men are free when they belong to a living, organic, believing community, active in fulfilling some unfulfilled, perhaps unrealized purpose. Not when they are escaping to some wild west. The most unfree souls go west, and shout of freedom. Men are freest when they are most unconscious of freedom. The shout is a rattling of chains, always was.
D. H. Lawrence (1885-1930, British Author)

44 I believe we are on an irreversible trend toward more freedom and democracy -- but that could change.
Dan Quayle (1947-, American Politician, Vice-President)

45 Liberty has restraints but no frontiers.
David Lloyd George (1863-1945, British Statesman, Prime Minister)

46 Liberty is not merely a privilege to be conferred; it is a habit to be acquired.
David Lloyd George (1863-1945, British Statesman, Prime Minister)

47 No man has received from nature the right to give orders to others. Freedom is a gift from heaven, and every individual of the same species has the right to enjoy it as soon as he is in enjoyment of his reason.
Denis Diderot (1713-1784, French Philosopher)

48 In the light of his vision he has found his freedom: his thoughts are peace, his words are peace and his work is peace.
Dhammapada (300 BC, Buddhist Collection of Moral Aphorism)

49 The traveler has reached the end of the journey! In the freedom of the infinite he is free from all sorrows, the fetters that bound him are thrown away, and the burning fever of life is no more.
Dhammapada (300 BC, Buddhist Collection of Moral Aphorism)

50 No man is entitled to the blessings of freedom unless he be vigilant in its preservation.
Douglas Macarthur (1880-1964, American Army General in WW II)

51 History does not long entrust the care of freedom to the weak or the timid.
Dwight D. Eisenhower (1890-1969, Thirty-fourth President of the USA)

52 Only our individual faith in freedom can keep us free.
Dwight D. Eisenhower (1890-1969, Thirty-fourth President of the USA)

53 What we want is not freedom but its appearances. It is for these simulacra that man has always striven. And since freedom, as has been said, is no more than a sensation, what difference is there between being free and believing ourselves free?
E. M. Cioran (1911-, Rumanian-born French Philosopher)

54 American freedom consists largely in talking nonsense.
Edgar Watson Howe (1853-1937, American Journalist, Author)

55 When the freedom they wished for most was freedom from responsibility, then Athens ceased to be free and was never free again.
Edith Hamilton (1867-1963, American Classical Scholar, Translator)

56 When ever a separation is made between liberty and justice, neither is safe.
Edmund Burke (1729-1797, British Political Writer, Statesman)

57 Freedom is a condition of mind, and the best way to secure it is to breed it.
Elbert Hubbard (1859-1915, American Author, Publisher)

58 Freedom is the right to live as we wish.
Epictetus (50-120, Stoic Philosopher)

59 Is freedom anything else than the right to live as we wish? Nothing else.
Epictetus (50-120, Stoic Philosopher)

60 No man is free who is not a master of himself.
Epictetus (50-120, Stoic Philosopher)

61 There can be no real freedom without the freedom to fail.
Eric Hoffer (1902-1983, American Author, Philosopher)

62 The basic test of freedom is perhaps less in what we are free to do than in what we are free not to do.
Eric Hoffer (1902-1983, American Author, Philosopher)

63 The bigger the information media, the less courage and freedom they allow. Bigness means weakness.
Eric Sevareid (1912-1992, American Broadcast Journalist)

64 Liberty is being free from the things we don't like in order to be slaves of the things we do like.
Ernest Benn

65 No one is truly free, they are a slave to wealth, fortune, the law, or other people restraining them from acting according to their will.
Euripides (480-406 BC, Greek Tragic Poet)

66 No one who lives in error is free.
Euripides (480-406 BC, Greek Tragic Poet)

67 A slave is one who waits for someone to come and free him.
Ezra Pound (1885-1972, American Poet, Critic)

68 Seek freedom and become captive of your desires. Seek discipline and find your liberty.
Frank Herbert (1920-1986, American Writer)

69 True individual freedom cannot exist without economic security and independence. People who are hungry and out of a job are the stuff of which dictatorships are made.
Franklin D. Roosevelt (1882-1945, Thirty-second President of the USA)

70 Men are not prisoners of fate, but only prisoners of their own minds.
Franklin D. Roosevelt (1882-1945, Thirty-second President of the USA)

71 We look forward to a world founded upon four essential human freedoms. The first is freedom of speech and expression. The second is freedom of every person to worship God in his own way. The third is freedom from want.... The fourth is freedom from fear.
Franklin D. Roosevelt (1882-1945, Thirty-second President of the USA)

72 We, and all others who believe in freedom as deeply as we do, would rather die on our feet than live on our knees.
Franklin D. Roosevelt (1882-1945, Thirty-second President of the USA)

73 Freedom! Equality! Brotherhood!
French Revolution Motto

74 How is freedom measured, in individuals as in nations? By the resistance which has to be overcome, by the effort it costs to stay aloft. One would have to seek the highest type of free man where the greatest resistance is constantly being overcome: five steps from tyranny, near the threshold of the danger of servitude.
Friedrich Nietzsche (1844-1900, German Philosopher)

75 What most clearly characterizes true freedom and its true employment is its misemployment.
Georg C. Lichtenberg (1742-1799, German Physicist, Satirist)

76 The history of the world is none other than the progress of the consciousness of freedom.
Georg Hegel (1770-1831, German Philosopher)

77 The East knew and to the present day knows only that One is Free; the Greek and the Roman world, that some are free; the German World knows that All are free. The first political form therefore which we observe in History, is Despotism, the second Democracy and Aristocracy, the third, Monarchy.
Georg Hegel (1770-1831, German Philosopher)

78 Freedom is the freedom to say that two plus two make four. If that is granted, all else follows.
George Orwell (1903-1950, British Author, "Animal Farm")

79 I sometimes think that the price of liberty is not so much eternal vigilance as eternal dirt.
George Orwell (1903-1950, British Author, "Animal Farm")

80 A man is morally free when, in full possession of his living humanity, he judges the world, and judges other men, with uncompromising sincerity.
George Santayana (1863-1952, American Philosopher, Poet)

81 The time is near at hand which must determine whether Americans are to be free men or slaves.
George Washington (1732-1799, First President of the USA)

82 Liberty, when it begins to take root, is a plant of rapid growth.
George Washington (1732-1799, First President of the USA)

83 Freedom is fragile and must be protected. To sacrifice it, even as a temporary measure, is to betray it.
Germaine Greer (1939-, Australian Feminist Writer)

84 The fly that touches honey cannot use it's wings; so too the soul that clings to spiritual sweetness ruins it's freedom and hinders contemplation.
Ghose Aurobindo (1872-1950, Philosopher)

85 There are always risks in freedom. The only risk in bondage is breaking free.
Gita Bellin

86 We must be willing to pay a price for freedom.
H. L. Mencken (1880-1956, American Editor, Author, Critic, Humorist)

87 When we were told that by freedom we understood free enterprise, we did very little to dispel this monstrous falsehood. Wealth and economic well-being, we have asserted, are the fruits of freedom, while we should have been the first to know that this kind of "happiness" has been an unmixed blessing only in this country, and it is a minor blessing compared with the truly political freedoms, such as freedom of speech and thought, of assembly and association, even under the best conditions.
Hannah Arendt (1906-1975, German-born American Political Philosopher)

88 Whatever the price, identify it now. What will you have to go through to get where you want to be? There is a price you can pay to be free of the situation once and for all. It may be a fantastic price or a tiny one -- but there is a price.
Harry Browne (1933-, American Financial Advisor, Writer)

89 There's only one free person in this society, and he is white and male.
Hazel Scott (1920-1981, American Entertainer)

90 A forest bird never wants a cage.
Henrik Ibsen (1828-1906, Norwegian Dramatist)

91 Liberty is to the collective body, what health is to every individual body. Without health no pleasure can be tasted by man; without liberty, no happiness can be enjoyed by society.
Henry Bolingbroke (1678-1751, British Politician)

92 The law will never make men free, it is men that have to make the law free.
Henry David Thoreau (1817-1862, American Essayist, Poet, Naturalist)

93 True obedience is true freedom.
Henry Ward Beecher (1813-1887, American Preacher, Orator, Writer)

94 Freedom is the open window through which pours the sunlight of the human spirit and human dignity.
Herbert Clark Hoover (1874-1964, American - 31st American President)

95 Who then is free? The wise man who can govern himself.
Horace (65-8 BC, Italian Poet)

96 Who then is free? The one who wisely is lord of themselves, who neither poverty, death or captivity terrify, who is strong to resist his appetites and shun honors, and is complete in themselves smooth and round like a globe.
Horace (65-8 BC, Italian Poet)

97 We are free to yield to truth.
Horace (65-8 BC, Italian Poet)

98 The oppression of any people for opinion's sake has rarely had any other effect than to fix those opinions deeper, and render them more important.
Hosea Ballou (1771-1852, American Theologian, Founder of "Universalism")

99 Freedom is the most contagious virus known to man.
Hubert H. Humphrey (1911-1978, American Democratic Politician, Vice President)

100 Every emancipation has in it the seeds of a new slavery, and every truth easily becomes a lie.
I. F. Stone (1907-1989, American Author)

101 There is nothing more wonderful than freedom of speech.
Ilya G. Ehrenburg (1891-1967, Ukrainian Writer)

[102] Any honest examination of the national life proves how far we are from the standard of human freedom with which we began. The recovery of this standard demands of everyone who loves this country a hard look at himself, for the greatest achievements must begin somewhere, and they always begin with the person. If we are not capable of this examination, we may yet become one of the most distinguished and monumental failures in the history of nations.
James Baldwin (1924-1987, American Author)

[103] Freedom is the only law which genius knows.
James Russell Lowell (1819-1891, American Poet, Critic, Editor)

[104] As for freedom, it will soon cease to exist in any shape or form. Living will depend upon absolute obedience to a strict set of arrangements, which it will no longer be possible to transgress. The air traveler is not free. In the future, life's passengers will be even less so: they will travel through their lives fastened to their (corporate) seats.
Jean Baudrillard (French Postmodern Philosopher, Writer)

[105] Free people, remember this maxim: We may acquire liberty, but it is never recovered if it is once lost.
Jean Jacques Rousseau (1712-1778, Swiss Political Philosopher, Educationist, Essayist)

[106] A country cannot subsist well without liberty, nor liberty without virtue.
Jean Jacques Rousseau (1712-1778, Swiss Political Philosopher, Educationist, Essayist)

[107] Man is born free, yet he is everywhere in chains.
Jean Jacques Rousseau (1712-1778, Swiss Political Philosopher, Educationist, Essayist)

[108] The English think they are free. They are free only during the election of members of parliament.
Jean Jacques Rousseau (1712-1778, Swiss Political Philosopher, Educationist, Essayist)

[109] Freedom is what you do with what's been done to you.
Jean-Paul Sartre (1905-1980, French Writer, Philosopher)

[110] If we catch a glimpse of freedom, we wish to possess it; if we catch a glimpse of death, we want nothing to do with it. One we cannot have, the other we cannot avoid.
Jeremy P. Johnson

[111] Freedom and love go together. Love is not a reaction. If I love you because you love me, that is mere trade, a thing to be bought in the market; it is not love. To love is not to ask anything in return, not even to feel that you are giving something- and it is only such love that can know freedom.
Jiddu Krishnamurti (1895-1986, Indian Theosophist)

[112] Where there is much freedom there is much error.
Johann Friedrich Von Schiller (1759-1805, German Dramatist, Poet, Historian)

[113] Freedom exists only with power.
Johann Friedrich Von Schiller (1759-1805, German Dramatist, Poet, Historian)

[114] Only law can give us freedom.
Johann Wolfgang Von Goethe (1749-1832, German Poet, Dramatist, Novelist)

[115] Freedom consists not in refusing to recognize anything above us, but in respecting something which is above us; for by respecting it, we raise ourselves to it, and, by our very acknowledgment, prove that we bear within ourselves what is higher, and are worthy to be on a level with it
Johann Wolfgang Von Goethe (1749-1832, German Poet, Dramatist, Novelist)

[116] Yes! To this thought I hold with firm persistence; The last result of wisdom stamps it true; He only earns his freedom and existence Who daily conquers them anew.
Johann Wolfgang Von Goethe (1749-1832, German Poet, Dramatist, Novelist)

[117] Our Constitution was made only for a moral and religious people. It is wholly inadequate to the government of any other.
John Adams (1735-1826, Second President of the USA)

[118] Liberty, according to my metaphysics is a self-determining power in an intellectual agent. It implies thought and choice and power.
John Adams (1735-1826, Second President of the USA)

[119] Yesterday the greatest question was decided which ever was debated in America; and a greater perhaps never was, nor will be, decided among men. A resolution was passed without one dissenting colony, "that these United Colonies are, and of right ought to be, free and independent States."
John Adams (1735-1826, Second President of the USA)

[120] When people talk of the freedom of writing, speaking or thinking I cannot choose but laugh. No such thing ever existed. No such thing now exists; but I hope it will exist. But it must be hundreds of years after you and I shall write and speak no more.
John Adams (1735-1826, Second President of the USA)

[121] Freedom all solace to man gives: He lives at ease that freely lives.
John Barbour (1320-1395, Scottish Poet)

[122] The cost of freedom is always high, but Americans have always paid it. And one path we shall never choose, and that is the path of surrender, or submission.
John F. Kennedy (1917-1963, Thirty-fifth President of the USA)

[123] In the long history of the world, only a few generations have been granted the role of defending freedom in its hour of maximum danger. I do not shrink from this responsibility -- I welcome it.
John F. Kennedy (1917-1963, Thirty-fifth President of the USA)

[124] The unity of freedom has never relied on uniformity of opinion.
John F. Kennedy (1917-1963, Thirty-fifth President of the USA)

[125] None can love freedom heartily, but good men... the rest love not freedom, but license.
John Milton (1608-1674, British Poet)

126 Freedom is only granted us that obedience may be more perfect.
John Ruskin (1819-1900, British Critic, Social Theorist)

127 The only freedom which deserves the name is that of pursuing our own good, in our own way, so long as we do not attempt to deprive others of theirs, or impede their efforts to obtain it.
John Stuart Mill (1806-1873, British Philosopher, Economist)

128 Man in general, if reduced to himself, is too wicked to be free.
Joseph De Maistre (1753-1821, French Diplomat, Philosopher)

129 For me, the principal fact of life is the free mind. For good and evil, man is a free creative spirit. This produces the very queer world we live in, a world in continuous creation and therefore continuous change and insecurity. A perpetually new and lively world, but a dangerous one, full of tragedy and injustice. A world in everlasting conflict between the new idea and the old allegiances, new arts and new inventions against the old establishment.
Joyce Cary (1888-1957, British Author)

130 You can muffle the drum, and you can loosen the strings of the lyre, but who shall command the skylark not to sing?
Kahlil Gibran (1883-1931, Lebanese Poet, Novelist)

131 Freedom is but the possibility of a various and indefinite activity; while government, or the exercise of dominion, is a single, yet real activity. The longing for freedom, therefore, is at first only too frequently suggested by the deep-felt consciousness of its absence.
Karl Wilhelm Von Humboldt (1767-1835, German Statesman, Philologist)

132 A nation which makes the final sacrifice for life and freedom does not get beaten.
Kemal Atatnrk (1881-1938, Founder, President of Turkey)

133 Freedom is the opportunity to make decisions...
Kenneth Hildebrand (American Author)

134 Freedom's just another word for nothing left to lose.
Kris Kristofferson (1936-, American Singer, Songwriter)

135 The clash of ideas is the sound of freedom.
Lady Bird Johnson

136 If we wish to free ourselves from enslavement, we must choose freedom and the responsibility this entails.
Leo Buscaglia (American Expert on Love, Lecturer, Author)

137 It is easy to believe in freedom of speech for those with whom we agree.
Leo Mckern

138 The free man is he who does not fear to go to the end of his thought.
Leon Blum (1872-1950, French Statesman and Prime Minister)

139 Freedom is knowing who you really are.
Linda Thomson

140 If people have to choose between freedom and sandwiches, they will take sandwiches.
Lord Boyd Orr (1880-1971, Scottish Biologist)

141 Yet, Freedom! yet thy banner, torn, but flying, streams like the thunderstorm against the wind.
Lord Byron (1788-1824, British Poet)

142 I stand for freedom of expression, doing what you believe in, and going after your dreams.
Madonna (1958-, American Musician, Singer, Actress,)

143 The moment the slave resolves that he will no longer be a slave. His fetters fall... freedom and slavery are mental states.
Mahatma Gandhi (1869-1948, Indian Political, Spiritual Leader)

144 Freedom is not worth having if it does not connote freedom to err. It passes my comprehension how human beings, be they ever so experienced and able, can delight in depriving other human beings of that precious right.
Mahatma Gandhi (1869-1948, Indian Political, Spiritual Leader)

145 When a person places the proper value on freedom, there is nothing under the sun that he will not do to acquire that freedom. Whenever you hear a man saying he wants freedom, but in the next breath he is going to tell you what he won't do to get it, or what he doesn't believe in doing in order to get it, he doesn't believe in freedom. A man who believes in freedom will do anything under the sun to acquire... or preserve his freedom.
Malcolm X (1925-1965, American Black Leader, Activist)

146 The only way we'll get freedom for ourselves is to identify ourselves with every oppressed people in the world. We are blood brothers to the people of Brazil, Venezuela, Haiti, Cuba -- yes Cuba too.
Malcolm X (1925-1965, American Black Leader, Activist)

147 I believe in a religion that believes in freedom. Any time I have to accept a religion that won't let me fight a battle for my people, I say to hell with that religion.
Malcolm X (1925-1965, American Black Leader, Activist)

148 You can't separate peace from freedom because no one can be at peace unless he has his freedom.
Malcolm X (1925-1965, American Black Leader, Activist)

149 You don't have to be a man to fight for freedom. All you have to do is to be an intelligent human being.
Malcolm X (1925-1965, American Black Leader, Activist)

150 Nobody can give you freedom. Nobody can give you equality or justice or anything. If you're a man, you take it.
Malcolm X (1925-1965, American Black Leader, Activist)

151 If you're not ready to die for it, put the word "freedom" out of your vocabulary.
Malcolm X (1925-1965, American Black Leader, Activist)

152 Freedom suppressed and again regained bites with keener fangs than freedom never endangered.
Marcus T. Cicero (106-43 BC, Great Roman Orator, Politician)

153 Freedom is hunting, feeding, danger; that, that is freedom --that it is which makes the veins to swell, the breast to heave and glowaye, that is freedom, --that is pleasure --life!
Marie Lovell (1803-1877, British Actor, Playwright)

154 Ultimately we know deeply that the other side of fear is a freedom.
Marilyn Ferguson (American Writer)

155 It is by the goodness of God that in our country we have those three unspeakably precious things: freedom of speech, freedom of conscience, and the prudence never to practice either.
Mark Twain (1835-1910, American Humorist, Writer)

156 To be what no one ever was, to be what everyone has been: Freedom is the mean of those extremes that fence all effort in.
Mark Van Doren (1894-1972, American Poet, Critic)

157 Mankind has a free will; but it is free to milk cows and to build houses, nothing more.
Martin Luther (1483-1546, German Leader of the Protestant Reformation)

158 The Negro needs the white man to free him from his fears. The white man needs the Negro to free him from his guilt.
Martin Luther King Jr. (1929-1968, American Black Leader, Nobel Prize Winner, 1964)

159 Freedom is never voluntarily given by the oppressor; it must be demanded by the oppressed.
Martin Luther King Jr. (1929-1968, American Black Leader, Nobel Prize Winner, 1964)

160 When we let freedom ring, when we let it ring from every village and every hamlet, from every state and every city, we will be able to speed up that day when all of God's children, black men and white men, Jews and Gentiles, Protestants and Catholics, will be able to join hands and sing in the words of that old Negro spiritual, "Free at last! Free at last! Thank God Almighty, we are free at last!"
Martin Luther King Jr. (1929-1968, American Black Leader, Nobel Prize Winner, 1964)

161 It is for each of us freely to choose whom we shall serve, and find in that obedience our freedom.
Mary Caroline Richards

162 Liberty is one of the most precious gifts which heaven has bestowed on man; with it we cannot compare the treasures which the earth contains or the sea conceals; for liberty, as for honor, we can and ought to risk our lives; and, on for the other hand, captivity is the greatest evil that can befall man.
Miguel De Cervantes (1547-1616, Spanish Novelist, Dramatist, Poet)

163 A major source of objection to a free economy is precisely that group thinks they ought to want. Underlying most arguments against the free market is a lack of belief in freedom itself.
Milton Friedman (1912-, American Economist)

164 Freedom is the emancipation from the arbitrary rule of other men.
Mortimer J. Adler (1902-, American Educator, Philosopher)

165 Let freedom reign. The sun never set on so glorious a human achievement.
Nelson Mandela (1918-, South African President)

166 Freedom is poetry, taking liberties with words, breaking the rules of normal speech, violating common sense. Freedom is violence.
Norman O. Brown (1913-, American Philosopher)

167 Perfect freedom is as necessary to the health and vigor of commerce as it is to the health and vigor of citizenship.
Patrick Henry (1736-1799, American Orator, Patriot)

168 The higher one climbs on the spiritual ladder, the more they will grant others their own freedom, and give less interference to another's state of consciousness.
Paul Twitchell

169 None who have always been free can understand the terrible fascinating power of the hope of freedom to those who are not free.
Pearl S. Buck (1892-1973, American Novelist)

170 Freedom is the sure possession of those alone who have the courage to defend it.
Pericles (495-429 BC, Athenian Statesman)

171 Is any man free except the one who can pass his life as he pleases?
Persius (34-62 AD, Satirical Poet)

172 Emancipation from the bondage of the soil is no freedom for the tree.
Rabindranath Tagore (1861-1941, Indian Poet, Philosopher)

173 We gain freedom when we have paid the full price...
Rabindranath Tagore (1861-1941, Indian Poet, Philosopher)

174 Liberty is slow fruit. It is never cheap; it is made difficult because freedom is the accomplishment and perfectness of man.
Ralph Waldo Emerson (1803-1882, American Poet, Essayist)

175 For what avail the plough or sail, Or land or life, if freedom fail?
Ralph Waldo Emerson (1803-1882, American Poet, Essayist)

176 So far as a person thinks; they are free.
Ralph Waldo Emerson (1803-1882, American Poet, Essayist)

177 Nothing is more disgusting than the crowing about liberty by slaves, as most men are, and the flippant mistaking for freedom of some paper preamble like a Declaration of Independence, or the statute right to vote, by those who have never dared to think or to act.
Ralph Waldo Emerson (1803-1882, American Poet, Essayist)

178 If you think you're free, there's no escape possible.
Ram Dass (American Spiritual Author, Lecturer)

179 The progress of freedom depends more upon the maintenance of peace, the spread of commerce, and the diffusion of education, than upon the labors of cabinets and foreign offices.
Richard Cobden (1804-1865, British Radical Politician)

180 If I have freedom in my love, And in my soul am free, -- Angels alone that soar above, Enjoy such liberty.
Richard Lovelace (1618-1657, British Poet)

181 Yet we can maintain a free society only if we recognize that in a free society no one can win all the time. No one can have his own way all the time, and no one is right all the time.
Richard M. Nixon (1913-1994, Thirty-seventh President of the USA)

182 So free we seem, so fettered we are!
Robert Browning (1812-1889, British Poet)

183 This is America. You can do anything here.
Robert E. Turner (American Cable-TV Pioneer)

184 The free way of life proposes ends, but it does not prescribe means.
Robert F. Kennedy (1925-1968, American Attorney General, Senator)

185 The more internal freedom you achieve, the more you want: it is more fun to be happy than sad, more enjoyable to choose your own emotions than to have them inflicted on you by mechanical glandular processes, more pleasurable to solve your problems than to be stuck with them forever.
Robert Wilson (1941-, American Theater Director, Designer)

186 Perfect freedom is reserved for the man who lives by his own work and in that work does what he wants to do.
Robin G. Collingwood (1889-1943, British Historian, Philosopher)

187 There's something contagious about demanding freedom.
Robin Morgan (1941-, American Feminist Author, Poet)

188 It requires greater courage to preserve inner freedom, to move on in one's inward journey into new realms, than to stand defiantly for outer freedom. It is often easier to play the martyr, as it is to be rash in battle.
Rollo May (American Psychologist)

189 Freedom is man's capacity to take a hand in his own development. It is our capacity to mold ourselves.
Rollo May (American Psychologist)

190 Freedom prospers when religion is vibrant and the rule of law under God is acknowledged.
Ronald Reagan (1911-, Fortieth President of the USA, Actor)

191 Freedom is always and exclusively freedom for the one who thinks differently.
Rosa Luxemburg (1870-1919, German Revolutionary)

192 A hot bath! I cry, as I sit down in it! Again as I lie flat, a hot bath! How exquisite a pleasure, how luxurious, fervid and flagrant a consolation for the rigors, the austerities, the renunciation of the day.
Rose Macaulay (1881-1958, British Novelist, Essayist)

193 All we have of freedom -- all we use or know -- this our fathers bought for us, long and long ago.
Rudyard Kipling (1865-1936, British Author of Prose, Verse)

194 He is free... who knows how to keep in his own hands the power to decide.
Salvador De Madriaga (1886-1978, Spanish Writer, Scholar, Diplomat)

195 The cause of freedom is the cause of God.
Samuel Bowles (American Author)

196 All theory is against freedom of the will; all experience for it.
Samuel Johnson (1709-1784, British Author)

197 When I was a boy I used to do what my father wanted. Now I have to do what my boy wants. My problem is: When am I going to do what I want?
Samuel Levenson

198 It is quite possible for someone to choose incorrectly or to judge badly; but freedom must allow such mistakes.
Sang Kyu Shin (Chinese Activist)

199 Freedom is not being a slave to any circumstance, to any constraint, to any chance; it means compelling Fortune to enter the lists on equal terms.
Seneca (4 BC-65 AD, Spanish-born Roman Statesman, philosopher)

200 He who is brave is free.
Seneca (4 BC-65 AD, Spanish-born Roman Statesman, philosopher)

201 Within yourself deliverance must be searched for, because each man makes his own prison.
Sir Edwin Arnold (1832-1904, British Poet, Journalist)

202 Freedom, then, lies only in our innate human capacity to choose between different sorts of bondage, bondage to desire or self esteem, or bondage to the light that lightens all our olives.
Sri Madhava

203 He that is kind is free, though he is a slave; he that is evil is a slave, though he be a king.
St. Augustine (354-430, Numidian-born Bishop of Hippo, Theologian)

204 Our ultimate freedom is the right and power to decide how anybody or anything outside ourselves will affect us.
Stephen R. Covey (American Speaker, Trainer, Author of "The 7 Habits of Highly Effective People")

205 People who exercise their embryonic freedom day after day, little by little, expand that freedom. People who do not will find that it withers until they are literally "being lived." They are acting out scripts written by parents, associates and society.
Stephen R. Covey (American Speaker, Trainer, Author of "The 7 Habits of Highly Effective People")

206 Until economic freedom is attained for everybody, there can be no real freedom for anybody.
Suzanne La Follette

207 Liberty is a different kind of pain from prison.
T. S. Eliot (1888-1965, American-born British Poet, Critic)

208 We are all of us the worse for too much liberty.
Terence (185-159 BC, Roman Writer of Comedies)

209 There is no liberation without labor... and there is no freedom which is free.
The Siri Singh Sahib

210 The will of the people is the only legitimate foundation of any government, and to protect its free expression should be our first object.
Thomas Jefferson (1743-1826, Third President of the USA)

211 Set me free from evil passions, and heal my heart of all inordinate affections; that being inwardly cured and thoroughly cleansed, I may be made fit to love, courageous to suffer, steady to persevere.
Thomas p Kempis (1379-1471, German Monk, Mystic, Religious Writer)

212 Those who expect to reap the blessings of freedom must, like men, undergo the fatigue of supporting it.
Thomas Paine (1737-1809, Anglo-American Political Theorist, Writer)

213 We fight not to enslave, but to set a country free, and to make room upon the earth for honest men to live in.
Thomas Paine (1737-1809, Anglo-American Political Theorist, Writer)

214 The secret of freedom, courage.
Thucydides (460-400 BC, Greek Historian of Athens)

215 Freedom begins as we become conscious of it.
Vernon Howard (19?-1992, American Author, Speaker)

216 We clearly realize that freedom's inner kingdom cannot be touched by exterior attacks.
Vernon Howard (19?-1992, American Author, Speaker)

217 Liberation is not deliverance.
Victor Hugo (1802-1885, French Poet, Dramatist, Novelist)

218 We must determine whether we really want freedom -- whether we are willing to dare the perils of... rebirth... For we never take a step forward without surrendering something that we may have held dear, without dying to that which has been.
Virginia Hanson

219 Women, like men, ought to have their youth so glutted with freedom they hate the very idea of freedom.
Vita Sackville-West (1892-1962, British Novelist, Poet)

220 It is true that liberty is precious. So precious that it must be rationed.
Vladimir Ilyich Lenin (1870-1924, Russian Revolutionary Leader)

221 Freedom in capitalist society always remains about the same as it was in ancient Greek republics: Freedom for slave owners.
Vladimir Ilyich Lenin (1870-1924, Russian Revolutionary Leader)

222 It is hard to free fools from the chains they revere.
Voltaire (1694-1778, French Historian, Writer)

223 The true character of liberty is independence, maintained by force.
Voltaire (1694-1778, French Historian, Writer)

224 Liberty, then, about which so many volumes have been written is, when accurately defined, only the power of acting.
Voltaire (1694-1778, French Historian, Writer)

225 Bondage is... subjection to external influences and internal negative thoughts and attitudes.
W. Clement Stone (1902-, American Businessman, Author)

226 I gave my life for freedom --this I know: For those who bade me fight had told me so.
W. N. Ewer (1885-1976, British Journalist)

227 If a nation values anything more than freedom, it will lose its freedom: and the irony of it is that if it is comfort or money that it values more, it will lose that, too.
W. Somerset Maugham (1874-1965, British Novelist, Playwright)

228 There are two good things in life -- freedom of thought and freedom of action.
W. Somerset Maugham (1874-1965, British Novelist, Playwright)

229 Any nation that thinks more of its ease and comfort than its freedom will soon lose its freedom; and the ironical thing about it is that it will lose its ease and comfort too.
W. Somerset Maugham (1874-1965, British Novelist, Playwright)

230 Freedom -- to walk free and own no superior.
Walt Whitman (1819-1892, American Poet)

231 A useful definition of liberty is obtained only by seeking the principle of liberty in the main business of human life, that is to say, in the process by which men educate their responses and learn to control their environment.
Walter Lippmann (1889-1974, American Journalist)

232 Freedom means you are unobstructed in living your life as you choose. Anything less is a form of slavery.
Wayne Dyer (1940-, American Psychotherapist, Author, Lecturer)

233 It will free man from his remaining chains, the chains of gravity which still tie him to this planet. It will open to him the gates of heaven.
Wernher Von Braun (1912-1977, German Rocket Pioneer)

234 Freedom Know this, that every man is free To choose his life and what he'll be. For this eternal truth is given, God will force no man to heaven. He'll call, persuade, direct aright, Bless with wisdom, love, and light; In nameless ways be good and kind, But never force the human mind.
William C. Clegg

235 He who dares not (reason), is a slave.
William Drummond (1585-1649, Celtic Poet)

236 There should be a sympathy with freedom, a desire to give it scope, founded not upon visionary ideas, but upon the long experience of many generations within the shores of this happy isle, that in freedom you lay the firmest foundations both of loyalty and order.
William E. Gladstone (1809-1888, British Liberal Prime Minister, Statesman)

237 I am the master of my fate; I am the captain of my soul.
William Ernest Henley (1849-1903, British Poet, Critic, Editor)

238 The greatest Glory of a free-born People, Is to transmit that Freedom to their Children.
William Havard

239 We are living in the excesses of freedom. Just take a look at 42nd Street an Broadway.
William J. Durant (1885-1981, American Historian, Essayist)

240 Only necessity understood, and bondage to the highest is identical with true freedom.
William James (1842-1910, American Psychologist, Professor, Author)

241 How does the Meadow flower its bloom unfold? Because the lovely little flower is free down to its root, and in that freedom bold.
William Wordsworth (1770-1850, British Poet)

242 It is our belief that if people are set free to express themselves to the fullest, their accomplishments will be far beyond their dreams, and they will not only contribute to the growth of the company, but will also be more useful citizens and contribute to the society at large.
Wilton M. Blount (American Businessman, Founder of Blount, Inc.)

243 He who is conceived in a cage, yearns for the cage.
Yevgeny Yevtushenko (1933-, Russian Poet)

FREEDOM OF SPEECH

1 The first principle of a free society is an untrammeled flow of words in an open forum.
Adlai E. Stevenson (1900-1965, American Lawyer, Politician)

2 The sound of tireless voices is the price we pay for the right to hear the music of our own opinions.
Adlai E. Stevenson (1900-1965, American Lawyer, Politician)

3 In America the majority raises formidable barriers around the liberty of opinion; within these barriers an author may write what he pleases, but woe to him if he goes beyond them.
Alexis De Tocqueville (1805-1859, French Social Philosopher)

4 We who officially value freedom of speech above life itself seem to have nothing to talk about but the weather.
Barbara Ehrenreich (1941-, American Author, Columnist)

5 We are willing enough to praise freedom when she is safely tucked away in the past and cannot be a nuisance. In the present, amidst dangers whose outcome we cannot foresee, we get nervous about her, and admit censorship.
Edward M. Forster (1879-1970, British Novelist, Essayist)

6 The only way to make sure people you agree with can speak is to support the rights of people you don't agree with.
Eleanor Holmes Norton

7 We hear about constitutional rights, free speech and the free press. Every time I hear those words I say to myself, "That man is a Red, that man is a Communist." You never heard a real American talk in that manner.
Frank Hague

8 If the freedom of speech is taken away then dumb and silent we may be led, like sheep to the slaughter.
George Washington (1732-1799, First President of the USA)

9 Marks on paper are free -- free speech -- press -- pictures all go together I suppose.
Georgia O'Keeffe (American painter)

10 The freedom of the press works in such a way that there is not much freedom from it.
Grace (Patricia) Kelly (1929-82, American Actress and Princess of Monaco)

11 Give me the liberty to know, to utter, and to argue freely according to conscience, above all liberties.
John Milton (1608-1674, British Poet)

12 At no time is freedom of speech more precious than when a man hits his thumb with a hammer.
Marshall Lumsden

13 The primacy of the word, basis of the human psyche, that has in our age been used for mind- bending persuasion and brain-washing pulp, disgraced by Gobbles and debased by advertising copy, remains a force for freedom that flies out between all bars.
Nadine Gordimer (1923-, South African Author)

14 A people which is able to say everything becomes able to do everything.
Napoleon Bonaparte (1769-1821, French General, Emperor)

15 If we don't believe in freedom of expression for people we despise, we don't believe in it at all.
Noam Chomsky (1928-, American Linguist, Political Activist)

16 The very aim and end of our institutions is just this: that we may thing what we like and say what we think.
Oliver Wendell Holmes (1809-1894, American Author, Wit, Poet)

17 Free speech is the whole thing, the whole ball game. Free speech is life itself.
Salman Rushdie (1948-, Indian-born British Author)

18 Every man has a right to utter what he thinks truth, and every other man has a right to knock him down for it. Martyrdom is the test.
Samuel Johnson (1709-1784, British Author)

19 People demand freedom of speech to make up for the freedom of thought which they avoid.
Soren Kierkegaard (1813-1855, Danish Philosopher, Writer)

20 How absurd men are! They never use the liberties they have, they demand those they do not have. They have freedom of thought, they demand freedom of speech.
Soren Kierkegaard (1813-1855, Danish Philosopher, Writer)

21 When one makes a Revolution, one cannot mark time; one must always go forward -- or go back. He who now talks about the "freedom of the press" goes backward, and halts our headlong course towards Socialism.
Vladimir Ilyich Lenin (1870-1924, Russian Revolutionary Leader)

22 I disapprove of what you say, but I will defend to the death your right to say it.
Voltaire (1694-1778, French Historian, Writer)

FRIENDS AND FRIENDSHIP

1 The imaginary friends I had as a kid dropped me because their friends thought I didn't exist.
Aaron Machado

2 Am I not destroying my enemies when I make friends of them?
Abraham Lincoln (1809-1865, Sixteenth President of the USA)

3 I don't like that man. I'm going to have to get to know him better.
Abraham Lincoln (1809-1865, Sixteenth President of the USA)

4 I desire to so conduct the affairs of this administration that if at the end, when I come to lay down the reins of power, I have lost every other friend on earth, I shall at least have one friend left, and that friend shall be down inside of me.
Abraham Lincoln (1809-1865, Sixteenth President of the USA)

5 A drop of honey catches more flies than a gallon of gal." So with men. If you would win a man to your cause, first convince him that you are his sincere friend. Therein is a drop of honey which catches his heart, which, say what he will, is the highroad to his reason.
Abraham Lincoln (1809-1865, Sixteenth President of the USA)

6 Every murderer is probably somebody's old friend.
Agatha Christie (1891-1976, British Mystery Writer)

7 Don't walk in front of me, I may not follow; Don't walk behind me, I may not lead; Walk beside me, and just be my friend.
Albert Camus (1913-1960, French Existential Writer)

8 To act the part of a true friend requires more conscientious feeling than to fill with credit and complacency any other station or capacity in social life.
Albert Einstein (1879-1955, German-born American Physicist)

9 No person is your friend who demands your silence, or denies your right to grow.
Alice Walker (1944-, American Author, Critic)

10 Our friends interpret the world and ourselves to us, if we take them tenderly and truly.
Amos Bronson Alcott (1799-1888, American Educator, Social Reformer)

11 Each friend represents a world in us, a world possibly not born until they arrive, and it is only by this meeting that a new world is born.
Anais Nin (1914-1977, French-born American Novelist, Dancer)

12 There is an electricity about a friendship relationship. We are both more relaxed and more sensitive, more creative and more reflective, more energetic and more casual, more excited and more serene. It is as though when we come in contact with our friend we enter into a different environment. ANDREW M. GREELEY
Andrew M. Greeley

13 Accountability in friendship is the equivalent of love without strategy.
Anita Brookner (1938-, British Novelist, Art Historian)

14 Do not save your loving speeches for your friends till they are dead. Do not write them on their tombstones, speak them rather now instead.
Anna Cummins

15 The ideal friendship is to feel as one while remaining two.
Anne Sophie Swetchine (1782-1857, Russian Author)

16 A faithful friend is the medicine of life.
Apocrypha

17 Do not tell a friend anything you would conceal from an enemy.
Arabian Proverb

18 A friend is known when needed.
Arabian Proverb

19 The enemy of my enemy is my friend.
Arabian Proverb

20 The book is closed, the year is done, The pages full of tasks begun. A little joy, a little care, Along with dreams, are written there. This new day brings another year, Renewing hope, dispelling fear. And we may find before the end, A deep content, another friend.
Arch Ward

21 Without friends no one would choose to live.
Aristotle (384-322 BC, Greek Philosopher)

22 In poverty and other misfortunes of life, true friends are a sure refuge. The young they keep out of mischief; to the old they are a comfort and aid in their weakness, and those in the prime of life they incite to noble deeds.
Aristotle (384-322 BC, Greek Philosopher)

23 Friendship is essentially a partnership.
Aristotle (384-322 BC, Greek Philosopher)

24 What is a friend? A single soul dwelling in two bodies.
Aristotle (384-322 BC, Greek Philosopher)

25 To the query, "What is a friend?" his reply was "A single soul dwelling in two bodies."
Aristotle (384-322 BC, Greek Philosopher)

26 Without friends, no one would want to live, even if he had all other goods.
Aristotle (384-322 BC, Greek Philosopher)

27 Wishing to be friends is quick work, but friendship is a slow-ripening fruit.
Aristotle (384-322 BC, Greek Philosopher)

28 Friendship is composed of a single soul inhabiting two bodies.
Aristotle (384-322 BC, Greek Philosopher)

29 A true friend is one soul in two bodies.
Aristotle (384-322 BC, Greek Philosopher)

30 It is well, when judging a friend, to remember that he is judging you with the same godlike and superior impartiality.
Arnold Bennett (1867-1931, British Novelist)

31 A true friend never gets in your way unless you happen to be going down.
Arnold H. Glasgow

32 Friends come and go but enemies accumulate.
Arthur Bloch

33 Friends and acquaintances are the surest passport to fortune.
Arthur Schopenhauer (1788-1860, German Philosopher)

34 A home-made friend wears longer than one you buy in the market.
Austin O'Malley

35 Show me a genuine case of platonic friendship, and I shall show you two old or homely faces.
Austin O'Malley

36 Friendship multiplies the good of life and divides the evil.
Baltasar Gracian (1601-1658, Spanish Philosopher, Writer)

37 Never have a companion that casts you in the shade.
Baltasar Gracian (1601-1658, Spanish Philosopher, Writer)

38 Have friends. 'Tis a second existence.
Baltasar Gracian (1601-1658, Spanish Philosopher, Writer)

39 The greatest good you can do for another is not just to share your riches but to reveal to him his own.
Benjamin Disraeli (1804-1881, British Statesman, Prime Minister)

40 Friends and neighbors, the taxes are indeed very heavy, and if those laid on by the government were the only ones we had to pay, we might more easily discharge them; but we have many others, and much more grievous to some of us. We are taxed twice as much by our idleness, three times as much by our pride, and four times as much by our folly; and from these taxes the commissioners cannot ease or deliver us by allowing abatement.
Benjamin Franklin (1706-1790, American Scientist, Publisher, Diplomat)

41 There are three faithful friends, an old wife, an old dog, and ready money.
Benjamin Franklin (1706-1790, American Scientist, Publisher, Diplomat)

42 A true friend is someone who thinks that you are a good egg even though he knows that you are slightly cracked.
Bernard Meltzer (1914-, American Law Professor)

43 Some friends play at friendship, but a true friend sticks closer than one's nearest kin. [Proverbs 18:24]
Bible (Sacred Scriptures of Christians and Judaism)

44 Faithful are the wounds of a friend.
Bible (Sacred Scriptures of Christians and Judaism)

45 A mirror reflects a man's face, but what he is really like is shown by the kind of friends he chooses. [Proverbs 27:19]
Bible (Sacred Scriptures of Christians and Judaism)

46 Forsake not an old friend, for the new is not comparable unto him. A new friend is as new wine: when it is old thou shalt drink it with pleasure.
Bible (Sacred Scriptures of Christians and Judaism)

47 A faithful friend is a strong defense: and he that hath found one hath found a treasure.
Bible (Sacred Scriptures of Christians and Judaism)

48 A friend loveth at all times. [Proverbs 17:17]
Bible (Sacred Scriptures of Christians and Judaism)

49 In the adversity of our best friends we often find something that does not displease us.
Brigham Young (1801-1877, American Mormon Leader)

50 You can't eat your friends and have them too.
Budd Schulberg

51 The rule of friendship means there should be mutual sympathy between them, each supplying what the other lacks and trying to benefit the other, always using friendly and sincere words.
Buddha (568-488 BC, Founder of Buddhism)

52 A good friend who points out mistakes and imperfections and rebukes evil is to be respected as if he reveals a secret of hidden treasure.
Buddha (568-488 BC, Founder of Buddhism)

53 Love is only chatter, friends are all that matter.
Burgess (Frank) Gelett (1866-1951, American Writer, Humorist)

54 Friendship is unnecessary, like philosophy, like art. It has no survival value; rather it is one of those things that give value to survival.
C. S. Lewis (1898-1963, British Academic, Writer, Christian Apologist)

55 Friendship is held to be the severest test of character. It is easy, we think, to be loyal to a family and clan, whose blood is in your own veins. Love between a man and a woman is founded on the mating instinct and is not free from desire and self-seeking. But to have a friend and to be true under any and all trials is the mark of a man!
Charles Alexander Eastman

56 That is what friendship means. Sharing the prejudice of experience.
Charles Bukowski (1920-1994, German Poet, Short Stories Writer, Novelist)

57 Friendship, of itself a holy tie, is made more sacred by adversity.
Charles Caleb Colton (1780-1832, British Sportsman Writer)

58 True friendship is like sound health, the value of it is seldom known until it be lost.
Charles Caleb Colton (1780-1832, British Sportsman Writer)

59 A man's friendships are one of the best measures of his worth.
Charles Darwin (1809-1882, British Naturalist)

60 Friendship is an arrangement by which we undertake to exchange small favors for big ones.
Charles De Montesquieu (1689-1755, French Jurist, Political Philosopher)

61 Many merry Christmases, friendships, great accumulation of cheerful recollections, affection on earth, and Heaven at last for all of us.
Charles Dickens (1812-1870, British Novelist)

62 The wise man does not permit himself to set up even in his own mind any comparisons of his friends. His friendship is capable of going to extremes with many people, evoked as it is by many qualities.
Charles Dudley Warner (1829-1900, American Author)

63 Friendship is one of the sweetest joys of life. Many might have failed beneath the bitterness of their trial had they not found a friend.
Charles Haddon Spurgeon (1834-1892, British Baptist Preacher)

64 'Tis the privilege of friendship to talk nonsense, and have her nonsense respected.
Charles Lamb (1775-1834, British Essayist, Critic)

65 Separate from the pleasure of your company, I don't much care if I never see another mountain in my life.
Charles Lamb (1775-1834, British Essayist, Critic)

66 If we would build on a sure foundation in friendship, we must love friends for their sake rather than for our own.
Charlotte Bronte (1816-1855, British Novelist)

67 Be more prompt to go to a friend in adversity than in prosperity.
Chilo (560 BC, Greek Sage)

68 With true friends... even water drunk together is sweet enough.
Chinese Proverb

69 A man should choose a friend who is better than himself. There are plenty of acquaintances in the world; but very few real friends.
Chinese Proverb

70 False friends are like our shadow, keeping close to us while we walk in the sunshine, but leaving us the instant we cross into the shade.
Christian Nevell Bovee (1820-1904, American Author, Lawyer)

71 Remember, the greatest gift is not found in a store nor under a tree, but in the hearts of true friends.
Cindy Lew

72 Friends are like melons; shall I tell you why? To find one good you must one hundred try.
Claude Mermet

73 My friends, there are no friends.
Coco Chanel (1883-1971, French Couturier)

74 Have no friends not equal to yourself.
Confucius (551-479 BC, Chinese Ethical Teacher, Philosopher)

75 In America every woman has her set of girl-friends; some are cousins, the rest are gained at school. These form a permanent committee who sit on each other's affairs, who "come out" together, marry and divorce together, and who end as those groups of bustling, heartless well-informed club- women who govern society. Against them the Couple of Ehepaar is helpless and Man in their eyes but a biological interlude.
Cyril Connolly (1903-1974, British Critic)

76 Do not protect yourself by a fence, but rather by your friends.
Czech Proverb

77 Friendship needs no words...
Dag Hammarskjold (1905-1961, Swedish Statesman, Secretary-general of U.N.)

78 Every deed and every relationship is surrounded by an atmosphere of silence. Friendship needs no words -- it is solitude delivered from the anguish of loneliness.
Dag Hammarskjold (1905-1961, Swedish Statesman, Secretary-general of U.N.)

79 Old friends pass away, new friends appear. It is just like the days. An old day passes, a new day arrives. The important thing is to make it meaningful: a meaningful friend -- or a meaningful day.
Dalai Lama (1935-, Tibet Religious Leader Resides In India)

80 You can make more friends in two months by becoming interested in other people than you can in two years by trying to get other people interested in you.
Dale Carnegie (1888-1955, American Author, Trainer)

81 My mother used to say that there are no strangers, only friends you haven't met yet. She's now in a maximum security twilight home in Australia.
Dame Edna Everage

82 The road to a friend's house is never long.
Danish Proverb

83 Your friendship is your needs answered.
Danish Proverb

84 No one is rich enough to do without a neighbor.
Danish Proverb

85 Friendship is neither a formality nor a mode: it is rather a life.
David Grayson (1870-1946, American Journalist and Writer)

86 Friends will keep you sane, Love could fill your heart, A lover can warm your bed, But lonely is the soul without a mate.
David Pratt

87 The essence of true friendship is to make allowance for another's little lapses.
David Storey (1933-, British Novelist, Playwright)

88 True friendship comes when silence between two people is comfortable.
David Tyson Gentry

89 Do not have evil-doers for friends, do not have low people for friends: have virtuous people for friends, have for friends the best of men.
Dhammapada (300 BC, Buddhist Collection of Moral Aphorism)

90 A friend is one to whom one may pour out all the contents of one's heart, chaff and grain together, knowing that the gentlest of hands will take and sift it, keep what is worth keeping, and with a breath of kindness, blow the rest away.
Dinah Maria Mulock Craik

91 Friendship is the comfort, the inexpressible comfort of feeling safe with a person having neither to weigh thoughts or measure words, but pouring all right out just as they are, chaff and grain together, certain that a faithful friendly hand will take and sift them, keep what is worth keeping and, with a breath of comfort, blow the rest away.
Dinah Mulock Craik

92 Friendship is a very simple word, very commonly used. The word friend is almost used on a daily basis. Yet, the depth and meaning of friendship certainly go beyond the simple and the common. Throughout history friendship has been a favorite theme for many writers. The following passages highlight what others have said about friendship in the past.
Dorothy Riera

93 A true friend is one who overlooks your failures and tolerates your successes.
Doug Larson

94 ... I remember you and recall you without effort, without exercise of will; that is, by natural impulse, indicated by a sense of duty, or of obligation. And that, I take it, is the only sort of remembering worth the having. When we think of friends, and call their faces out of the shadows, and their voices out of the echoes that faint along the corridors of memory, and do it without knowing why save that we love to do it, we content ourselves that friendship is a Reality, and not a Fancy -- that it is built upon a rock, and not upon the sands that dissolve away with the ebbing tides and carry their monuments with them.
Douglas Fairbanks (1909-, American Film Actor, Writer, Producer)

95 Being taken for granted can be a compliment. It means you've become a comfortable, trusted element in another person's life.
Dr. Joyce Brothers (1927-, American Psychologist, Television and Radio Personality)

96 Everybody needs one essential friend.
Dr. William Glasser

97 Friendship consists in forgetting what one gives, and remembering what one receives.
Dumas The Younger

98 You have been my friends, replied Charlotte, that in itself is a tremendous thing...
E(lwyn) B(rooks) White (1899-1985, American Author, Editor)

99 Keep out of the suction caused by those who drift backwards.
E. K. Piper

100 Friendship is a horizon -- which expands whenever we approach it.
E.R. Hazlip

101 When you face a crisis, you know who your true friends are.
Earvin "Magic" Johnson (1959-, American Basketball Player)

102 Friendship is to have the latchkey of another's mind.
Edgar Godospeed

103 Instead of loving your enemies -- treat your friends a little better.
Edgar Watson Howe (1853-1937, American Journalist, Author)

104 When a friend is in trouble, don't annoy him by asking if there is anything you can do. Think up something appropriate and do it.
Edgar Watson Howe (1853-1937, American Journalist, Author)

105 It may be a cold, clammy thing to say, but those that treat friendship the same as any other selfishness seem to get the most out of it.
Edgar Watson Howe (1853-1937, American Journalist, Author)

106 Don't abuse your friends and expect them to consider it criticism.
Edgar Watson Howe (1853-1937, American Journalist, Author)

107 One of the surest evidences of friendship that one individual can display to another is telling him gently of a fault. If any other can excel it, it is listening to such a disclosure with gratitude, and amending the error.
Edward G. Bulwer-Lytton (1803-1873, British Novelist, Poet)

108 I would rather have a million friends than a million dollars.
Edward Vernon Rickenbacker (1890-1973, American Aviator, World War I Ace)

109 If you have no enemies you are apt to be in the same predicament in regard to friends.
Elbert Hubbard (1859-1915, American Author, Publisher)

110 Your friend is that man who knows all about you, and still likes you.
Elbert Hubbard (1859-1915, American Author, Publisher)

111 Friendship with oneself is all-important, because without it one cannot be friends with anyone else in the world.
Eleanor Roosevelt (1884-1962, American First Lady, Columnist, Lecturer, Humanitarian)

112 All love that has not friendship for its base, is like a mansion built upon the sand.
Ella Wheeler Wilcox (1855-1919, American Poet, Journalist)

113 Love is like the wild rose-briar; Friendship like the holly-tree. The holly is dark when the rose- briar blooms, but which will bloom most constantly?
Emily Bronte (1818-1848, British Novelist, Poet)

114 Friends are like fiddle strings, they must not be screwed too tight.
English Proverb

115 You may poke a man's fire after you've known him for seven years.
English Proverb

116 We do not so much need the help of our friends as the confidence of their help in need.
Epicurus (341-270 BC, Greek Philosopher)

117 Of all things which wisdom provides to make life entirely happy, much the greatest is the possession of friendship.
Epicurus (341-270 BC, Greek Philosopher)

118 Friendship Never explain -- your friends do not need it, and your enemies will not believe it anyway. A real friend never gets in your way, unless you happen to be on the way down. A friend is someone you can do nothing with and enjoy it. However much we guard ourselves against it, we tend to shape ourselves in the image others have of us. It is not so much the example of others we imitate, as the reflection of ourselves in their eyes and the echo of ourselves in their words.
Eric Hoffer (1902-1983, American Author, Philosopher)

119 However much we guard ourselves against it, we tend to shape ourselves in the image others have of us. It is not so much the example of others we imitate, as the reflection of ourselves in their eyes and the echo of ourselves in their words.
Eric Hoffer (1902-1983, American Author, Philosopher)

120 I have a friend who tells a tale With statements parenthetical; To start at the beginning must To her seem quite heretical; For her accounts of happenings Are full of disconnection s; She starts them in the middle, And proceeds in all directions.
Erica H. Stux

121 In a bad marriage, friends are the invisible glue. If we have enough friends, we may go on for years, intending to leave, talking about leaving --instead of actually getting up and leaving.
Erica Jong (1942-, American Author)

122 There is no friend as loyal as a book
Ernest Hemingway (1898-1961, American Writer)

123 Real friends are those who, when you've made a fool of yourself, don't feel that you've done a permanent job.
Erwin T. Randall

124 Give me one friend, just one, who meets The needs of all my varying moods.
Esther M. Clark (American Poet)

125 The best time to make friends is before you need them.
Ethel Barrymore (1879-1959, American Actress)

126 God gives us our relatives -- thank God we can choose our friends.
Ethel Watts Mumford (1878-1940, American Novelist, Humor Writer)

127 The real test of friendship is: Can you literally do nothing with the other person? Can you enjoy together those moments of life that are utterly simple? They are the moments people looks back on at the end of life and number as their most sacred experiences.
Eugene Kennedy

128 Friends show their love in times of trouble...
Euripides (480-406 BC, Greek Tragic Poet)

129 I hate it in friends when they come too late to help.
Euripides (480-406 BC, Greek Tragic Poet)

130 One loyal friend is worth ten thousand relatives.
Euripides (480-406 BC, Greek Tragic Poet)

131 Life has no blessing like a prudent friend.
Euripides (480-406 BC, Greek Tragic Poet)

132 Friendship is a strong and habitual inclination in two persons to promote the good and happiness of one another.
Eustace Budgell

133 We cherish our friends not for their ability to amuse us, but for our ability to amuse them.
Evelyn Waugh (1903-1966, British Novelist)

134 We shelter children for a time; we live side by side with men; and that is all. We owe them nothing, and are owed nothing. I think we owe our friends more, especially our female friends.
Fay Weldon (1933-, British Novelist)

135 A friend is one who knows us, but loves us anyway.
Fr. Jerome Cummings

136 The worst solitude is to have no real friendships.
Francis Bacon (1561-1626, British Philosopher, Essayist, Statesman)

137 Without friends the world is but a wilderness. There is no man that imparteth his joys to his friends, but he joyeth the more; and no man that imparteth his grieves to his friend, but he grieveth the less.
Francis Bacon (1561-1626, British Philosopher, Essayist, Statesman)

138 That friendship will not continue to the end which is begun for an end.
Francis Quarles (1592-1644, British Poet)

139 In the misfortunes of our best friends we always find something not altogether displeasing to us.
François de La Rochefoucauld (1613-1680, French classical writer)

140 However rare true love may be, it is less so than true friendship.
François de La Rochefoucauld (1613-1680, French classical writer)

141 A true friend is the greatest of all blessings, and that which we take the least care to acquire.
François de La Rochefoucauld (1613-1680, French classical writer)

142 What men have called friendship is only a social arrangement, a mutual adjustment of interests, an interchange of services given and received; it is, in sum, simply a business from which those involved propose to derive a steady profit for their own self-love.
François de La Rochefoucauld (1613-1680, French classical writer)

143 It is more shameful to distrust our friends than to be deceived by them.
François de La Rochefoucauld (1613-1680, French classical writer)

144 Do not make best friends with a melancholy sad soul. They always are heavily loaded, and you must bear half.
François Fénelon (1651-1715, French Roman Catholic archbishop, theologian, poet and writer)

145 What is a friend? I will tell you... it is someone with whom you dare to be yourself.
Frank Crane (American Actor)

146 A good motto is: Use friendliness but do not use your friends.
Frank Crane (American Actor)

147 A friend is someone with whom you dare to be yourself.
Frank Crane (American Actor)

148 The lonely one offers his hand too quickly to whomever he encounters.
Friedrich Nietzsche (1844-1900, German Philosopher)

149 A woman may very well form a friendship with a man, but for this to endure, it must be assisted by a little physical antipathy.
Friedrich Nietzsche (1844-1900, German Philosopher)

150 Truly great friends are hard to find, difficult to leave, and impossible to forget.
G. Randolf

151 But a lifetime of happiness! No man alive could bear it: it would be hell on earth.
George Bernard Shaw (1856-1950, Irish-born British Dramatist)

152 The only service a friend can really render is to keep up your courage by holding up to you a mirror in which you can see a noble image of yourself.
George Bernard Shaw (1856-1950, Irish-born British Dramatist)

153 Give me the avowed, the erect, the manly foe, bold I can meet, perhaps may turn his blow! But of all plagues, good Heavens, thy wrath can send, save, save, oh save me from the candid friend!
George Canning (1770-1827, British Statesman)

154 A friend you have to buy won't be worth what you pay for him.
George D. Prentice (American Editor)

155 Friendship is genuine when two friends can enjoy each others company without speaking a word to one another.
George Ebers

156 Friendships begin with liking or gratitude roots that can be pulled up.
George Eliot (1819-1880, British Novelist)

157 Best friend, my well-spring in the wilderness!
George Eliot (1819-1880, British Novelist)

158 Perhaps the most delightful friendships are those in which there is much agreement, much disputation, and yet more personal liking.
George Eliot (1819-1880, British Novelist)

159 Love demands infinitely less than friendship.
George Jean Nathan (1882-1958, American Critic)

160 Friendship is almost always the union of a part of one mind with the part of another; people are friends in spots.
George Santayana (1863-1952, American Philosopher, Poet)

161 Be courteous to all, but intimate with few, and let those few be well tried before you give them your confidence. True friendship is a plant of slow growth, and must undergo and withstand the shocks of adversity before it is entitled to the appellation.
George Washington (1732-1799, First President of the USA)

162 True friendship is a plant of slow growth, and must undergo and withstand the shocks of adversity, before it is entitled to the appellation.
George Washington (1732-1799, First President of the USA)

163 A slender acquaintance with the world must convince every man that actions, not words, are the true criterion of the attachment of friends.
George Washington (1732-1799, First President of the USA)

164 Thank You Friend I never came to you, my friend, and went away without some new enrichment of the heart; More faith and less of doubt, more courage in the days ahead. And often in great need coming to you, I went away comforted indeed. How can I find the shining word, the glowing phrase that tells all that your love has meant to me, all that your friendship spells? There is no word, no phrase for you on whom I so depend. All I can say to you is this, God bless you precious friend.
Grace Noll Crowell

165 Who ceases to be a friend never was one.
Greek Proverb

166 I am speaking now of the highest duty we owe our friends, the noblest, the most sacred --that of keeping their own nobleness, goodness, pure and incorrupt. If we let our friend become cold and selfish and exacting without a remonstrance, we are no true lover, no true friend.
Harriet Beecher Stowe (1811-1896, American Novelist, Antislavery Campaigner)

167 One who looks for a friend without faults will have none.
Hasidic Saying

168 The sacrifices of friendship were beautiful in her eyes as long as she was not asked to make them.
Hector Hugh Munro (1870-1916, British Novelist, Writer)

169 One friend in a lifetime is much, two are many, three are hardly possible. Friendship needs a certain parallelism of life, a community of thought, a rivalry of aim.
Henry Brooks Adams (1838 - 1918, American Historian)

170 One may discover a new side to his most intimate friend when for the first time he hears him speak in public. He will be stranger to him as he is more familiar to the audience. The longest intimacy could not foretell how he would behave then
Henry David Thoreau (1817-1862, American Essayist, Poet, Naturalist)

171 A man cannot be said to succeed in this life who does not satisfy one friend.
Henry David Thoreau (1817-1862, American Essayist, Poet, Naturalist)

172 A friend is one who incessantly pays us the compliment of expecting from us all the virtues, and who can appreciate them in us. The friend asks no return but that his friend will religiously accept and wear and not disgrace his apotheosis of him. They cherish each other's hopes. They are kind to each other's dreams.
Henry David Thoreau (1817-1862, American Essayist, Poet, Naturalist)

173 The most I can do for my friend is simply be his friend.
Henry David Thoreau (1817-1862, American Essayist, Poet, Naturalist)

174 To say that a man is your Friend, means commonly no more than this, that he is not your enemy. Most contemplate only what would be the accidental and trifling advantages of Friendship, as that the Friend can assist in time of need by his substance, or his influence, or his counsel. Even the utmost goodwill and harmony and practical kindness are not sufficient for Friendship, for Friends do not live in harmony merely, as some say, but in melody.
Henry David Thoreau (1817-1862, American Essayist, Poet, Naturalist)

175 We have not so good a right to hate any as our Friend.
Henry David Thoreau (1817-1862, American Essayist, Poet, Naturalist)

176 True friendship can afford true knowledge. It does not depend on darkness and ignorance.
Henry David Thoreau (1817-1862, American Essayist, Poet, Naturalist)

177 The language of friendship is not words but meanings.
Henry David Thoreau (1817-1862, American Essayist, Poet, Naturalist)

178 My best friend is the one who brings out the best in me.
Henry Ford (1863-1947, American Industrialist, Founder of Ford Motor Company)

179 The difficulty is not that great to die for a friend, the hard part is finding a friend worth dying for.
Henry Home

180 In the progress of personality, first comes a declaration of independence, then a recognition of interdependence.
Henry Van Dyke (1852-1933, American Protestant Clergyman, Poet and Writer)

181 Yes, we must ever be friends; and of all who offer you friendship Let me be ever the first, the truest, the nearest and dearest!
Henry Wadsworth Longfellow (1819-1892, American Poet)

182 I shot an arrow into the air, It fell to earth, I knew not where; For so swiftly it flew, the sight Could not follow it in its flight. I breathed a song into the air, It fell to earth, I knew not where; For, who has sight so keen and strong That it can follow the flight of song? Long, long afterward, in an oak I found the arrow, still unbroken; And the song, from beginning to end, I found again in the heart of a friend.
Henry Wadsworth Longfellow (1819-1892, American Poet)

183 Keep a fair-sized cemetery in your back yard, in which to bury the faults of your friends.
Henry Ward Beecher (1813-1887, American Preacher, Orator, Writer)

184 From quiet homes and first beginning, out to the undiscovered ends, there's nothing worth the wear of winning, but laughter and the love of friends.
Hilaire Belloc (1870-1953, British Author)

185 When friendship disappears then there is a space left open to that awful loneliness of the outside world which is like the cold space between the planets. It is an air in which men perish utterly.
Hilaire Belloc (1870-1953, British Author)

186 Never deceive a friend.
Hipparchus (2nd Century BC, Rhodian Astronomer)

187 The mind is lowered through association with inferiors. With equals it attains equality; and with superiors, superiority.
Hitopadesa (Sanskrit Fable From Panchatantra)

188 A sympathetic friend can be quite as dear as a brother.
Homer (850 BC, Greek Epic Poet)

189 Two friends, two bodies with one soul inspired.
Homer (850 BC, Greek Epic Poet)

190 Nothing so fortifies a friendship as a belief on the part of one friend that he is superior to the other.
Honore De Balzac (1799-1850, French Novelist)

191 Old friends are the great blessings of one's later years. Half a word conveys one's meaning. They have a memory of the same events, have the same mode of thinking. I have young relations that may grow upon me, for my nature is affectionate, but can they grow [To Be] old friends?
Horace Walpole (1717-1797, British Author)

192 The greatest healing therapy is friendship and love.
Hubert H. Humphrey (1911-1978, American Democratic Politician, Vice President)

193 My friend is he who will tell me my faults in private.
Ibn Gabirol

194 These can never be true friends: Hope, dice, a prostitute, a robber, a cheat, a goldsmith, a monkey, a doctor, a distiller.
Indian Proverb

195 For the friendship of two, the patience of one is required.
Indian Proverb

196 In the New Year, may your right hand always be stretched out in friendship, but never in want.
Irish Toast

197 Good friends are good for your health.
Irwin Sarason

198 In a friend you find a second self.
Isabelle Norton

199 Good company in a journey makes the way seem shorter.
Izaak Walton (1593-1683, British Writer)

200 Friendship can only exist between persons with similar interests and points of view. Man and woman by the conventions of society are born with different interests and different points of view.
J. August Strindberg (1849-1912, Swedish Dramatist, Novelist, Poet)

201 Fate chooses our relatives, we choose our friends.
Jacques Delille (1738-1813, French Poet)

202 We cannot tell the precise moment when friendship is formed. As in filling a vessel drop by drop, there is at last a drop which makes it run over. So in a series of kindness there is, at last, one which makes the heart run over.
James Boswell (1740-1795, British Writer, Journalist)

203 Friendship without self-interest is one of the rare and beautiful things of life.
James F. Byrnes (1879-1972, American Judge, Secretary of State)

204 The first day one is a guest, the second a burden, and the third a pest.
Jean De La Bruyere (1645-1696, French Writer)

205 Two persons cannot long be friends if they cannot forgive each other's little failings.
Jean De La Bruyere (1645-1696, French Writer)

206 Friendship is the shadow of the evening, which increases with the setting sun of life.
Jean De La Fontaine (1621-1695, French Poet)

207 Rare as is true love, true friendship is rarer.
Jean De La Fontaine (1621-1695, French Poet)

208 Every friend is to the other a sun, and a sunflower also. He attracts and follows.
Jean Paul Richter (1763-1825, German Novelist)

209 We learn our virtues from our friends who love us; our faults from the enemy who hates us. We cannot easily discover our real character from a friend. He is a mirror, on which the warmth of our breath impedes the clearness of the reflection.
Jean Paul Richter (1763-1825, German Novelist)

210 Treat your friends as you do your pictures, and place them in their best light.
Jennie Jerome Churchill (1854-1921, Anglo-American Mother of Winston Churchill)

211 We will win the world when we realize that fellowship, not evangelism, must be our primary emphasis. When we demonstrate the Big Miracle of Love, it won't be necessary for us to go out -- they will come in.
Jess Moody

212 Awards become corroded, friends gather no dust.
Jesse Owens (1913-1980, American Olympic Track Athlete)

213 A friend you have to buy; enemies you get for nothing.
Jewish Proverb

214 The good fellow to everyone is a good friend to no one.
Jewish Proverb

215 Who finds a faithful friend, finds a treasure.
Jewish Saying

216 Show me a friend in need and I'll show you a pest.
Joe E. Lewis (American Writer)

217 Friends show me what I can do, foes teach me what I should do.
Johann Friedrich Von Schiller (1759-1805, German Dramatist, Poet, Historian)

218 Be not the fourth friend of him who had three before and lost them.
Johann Kaspar Lavater (1741-1801, Swiss Theologian, Mystic)

219 In comradeship is danger countered best.
Johann Wolfgang Von Goethe (1749-1832, German Poet, Dramatist, Novelist)

220 If I cannot understand my friend's silence, I will never get to understand his words.
John Enoch Powell (1912-, British statesman,)

221 An open foe may prove a curse, but a pretended friend is worse.
John Gay (1688-1732, British Playwright, Poet)

222 Friends are the sunshine of life.
John Hay (1838-1905, American Author, Statesman)

223 The love of our private friends is the only preparatory exercise for the love of all men.
John Henry Newman (1801-1890, British Religious Leader, Prelate, Writer)

224 It takes a long time to grow an old friend.
John Leonard

225 Friendship should be a private pleasure, not a public boast. I loathe those braggarts who are forever trying to invest themselves with importance by calling important people by their first names in or out of print. Such first-naming for effect makes me cringe.
John Mason Brown (1800-1859, American Militant Abolitionist)

226 Men are more evanescent than pictures, yet one sorrows for lost friends, and pictures are my friends. I have none others. I am never long enough with men to attach myself to them; and whatever feelings of attachment I have are to material things.
John Ruskin (1819-1900, British Critic, Social Theorist)

227 Old friends are best. King James used to call for his old shoes; they were easiest for his feet.
John Selden (1584-1654, British Jurist, Statesman)

228 Two friendships in two breasts requires The same aversions and desires.
Jonathan Swift (1667-1745, Anglo-Irish Satirist)

229 Your notions of friendship are new to me; I believe every man is born with his quantum, and he cannot give to one without robbing another. I very well know to whom I would give the first place in my friendship, but they are not in the way, I am condemned to another scene, and therefore I distribute it in pennyworths to those about me, and who displease me least, and should do the same to my fellow prisoners if I were condemned to a jail.
Jonathan Swift (1667-1745, Anglo-Irish Satirist)

230 The friendships of the world are oft confederacies in vice, or leagues of pleasures.
Joseph Addison (1672-1719, British Essayist, Poet, Statesman)

231 Friendship improves happiness, and abates misery, by doubling our joys, and dividing our grief.
Joseph Addison (1672-1719, British Essayist, Poet, Statesman)

232 The greatest sweetener of human life is Friendship. To raise this to the highest pitch of enjoyment, is a secret which but few discover.
Joseph Addison (1672-1719, British Essayist, Poet, Statesman)

233 Friendships, in general, are suddenly contracted; and therefore it is no wonder they are easily dissolved.
Joseph Addison (1672-1719, British Essayist, Poet, Statesman)

234 How delightful to find a friend in everyone.
Joseph Brodsky (1940-, Russian-born American Poet, Critic)

235 He who has not the weakness of friendship has not the strength.
Joseph Joubert (1754-1824, French Moralist)

236 A puppy plays with every pup he meets, but an old dog has few associates.
Josh Billings (1815-1885, American Humorist, Lecturer)

237 The only way not to break a friendship is not to drop it.
Julie Holz

238 Let your best be for your friend...
Kahlil Gibran (1883-1931, Lebanese Poet, Novelist)

239 Friendship is always a sweet responsibility, never an opportunity.
Kahlil Gibran (1883-1931, Lebanese Poet, Novelist)

240 In the sweetness of friendship let there be laughter, and sharing of pleasures.
Kahlil Gibran (1883-1931, Lebanese Poet, Novelist)

241 Let there be no purpose in friendship save the deepening of the spirit.
Kahlil Gibran (1883-1931, Lebanese Poet, Novelist)

242 Your friend is your needs answered.
Kahlil Gibran (1883-1931, Lebanese Poet, Novelist)

243 Your friend is your field which you sow with love and reap with thanksgiving.
Kahlil Gibran (1883-1931, Lebanese Poet, Novelist)

244 There is nothing better than the encouragement of a good friend.
Katherine Hathaway

245 I always felt that the great high privilege, relief and comfort of friendship was that one had to explain nothing.
Katherine Mansfield (1888-1923, New Zealand-born British Author)

246 I'm treating you as a friend asking you to share my present minuses in the hope that I can ask you to share my future pluses
Katherine Mansfield (1888-1923, New Zealand-born British Author)

247 Friendship is one of the most tangible things in a world which offers fewer and fewer supports.
Kenneth Branagh (1960-, British-born American Actor, Director, Producer, Stage director)

248 You can always tell a real friend; when you've made a fool of yourself he doesn't feel you've done a permanent job.
Laurence J. Peter

249 My father always used to say that when you die, if you've got five real friends, then you've had a great life.
Lee Iacocca (1924-, American Businessman, Former CEO of Chrysler)

250 A true friend is someone who is there for you when he'd rather be anywhere else.
Len Wein

251 A single rose can be my garden... a single friend, my world.
Leo Buscaglia (American Expert on Love, Lecturer, Author)

252 Often we have no time for our friends but all the time in the world for our enemies.
Leon Uris (1924-, American Novelist)

253 He is a fine friend. He stabs you in the front.
Leonard Louis Levinson

254 If you want to make a dangerous man your friend, let him do you a favor.
Lewis E. Lawes

255 I can't forgive my friends for dying; I don't find these vanishing acts of theirs at all amusing.
Logan Pearsall Smith (1865-1946, Anglo-American Essayist, Aphorist)

256 Plant a seed of friendship; reap a bouquet of happiness.
Lois L. Kaufman

257 He makes no friends who never made a foe.
Lord Alfred Tennyson (1809-1892, British Poet)

258 Win hearts, and you have hands and purses.
Lord Burleigh

259 Friendship is Love without his wings!
Lord Byron (1788-1824, British Poet)

260 A mistress never is nor can be a friend. While you agree, you are lovers; and when it is over, anything but friends.
Lord Byron (1788-1824, British Poet)

261 I have always laid it down as a maxim --and found it justified by experience --that a man and a woman make far better friendships than can exist between two of the same sex --but then with the condition that they never have made or are to make love to each other.
Lord Byron (1788-1824, British Poet)

262 I have had, and may have still, a thousand friends, as they are called, in life, who are like one's partners in the waltz of this world --not much remembered when the ball is over.
Lord Byron (1788-1824, British Poet)

263 Most people enjoy the inferiority of their best friends.
Lord Chesterfield (1694-1773, British Statesman, Author)

264 Stay is a charming word in a friend's vocabulary.
Louisa May Alcott (1832-1888, American Author)

265 Never shall I forget the time I spent with you. Please continue to be my friend, as you will always find me yours.
Ludwig Van Beethoven (1770-1827, German Composer)

266 It is easy enough to be friendly to one's friends. But to befriend the one who regards himself as your enemy is the quintessence of true religion. The other is mere business.
Mahatma Gandhi (1869-1948, Indian Political, Spiritual Leader)

267 The good man is the friend of all living things.
Mahatma Gandhi (1869-1948, Indian Political, Spiritual Leader)

268 The richer your friends, the more they will cost you.
Marbury

269 What sweetness is left in life, if you take away friendship? Robbing life of friendship is like robbing the world of the sun. A true friend is more to be esteemed than kinsfolk.
Marcus T. Cicero (106-43 BC, Great Roman Orator, Politician)

270 Friendship makes prosperity brighter, while it lightens adversity by sharing its grieves and anxieties.
Marcus T. Cicero (106-43 BC, Great Roman Orator, Politician)

271 Friends are proved by adversity.
Marcus T. Cicero (106-43 BC, Great Roman Orator, Politician)

272 Friendship is the only thing in the world concerning the usefulness of which all mankind are agreed.
Marcus T. Cicero (106-43 BC, Great Roman Orator, Politician)

273 Life is nothing without friendship.
Marcus T. Cicero (106-43 BC, Great Roman Orator, Politician)

274 Every man can tell how many goats or sheep he possesses, but not how many friends.
Marcus T. Cicero (106-43 BC, Great Roman Orator, Politician)

275 A friend is, as it were, a second self.
Marcus T. Cicero (106-43 BC, Great Roman Orator, Politician)

276 True friendship is never serene.
Marie De Rabutin-Chantal

277 All things being equal, people will do business with a friend; all things being unequal, people will still do business with a friend.
Mark Mccormack (1930-, America Sports Agent, Promoter, Businessman)

278 Good friends, good books and a sleepy conscience: this is the ideal life. The conviction of the rich that the poor are happier is no more foolish than the conviction of the poor that the rich are.
Mark Twain (1835-1910, American Humorist, Writer)

279 Grief can take care of itself; but to get the full value of a joy you must have somebody to divide it with.
Mark Twain (1835-1910, American Humorist, Writer)

280 The holy passion of friendship is of so sweet and steady and loyal and enduring a nature that it will last through a whole lifetime, if not asked to lend money.
Mark Twain (1835-1910, American Humorist, Writer)

281 To gather with God's people in united adoration of the Father is as necessary to the Christian life as prayer.
Martin Luther (1483-1546, German Leader of the Protestant Reformation)

282 It is not what you give your friend, but what you are willing to give him that determines the quality of friendship.
Mary Dixon Thayer

283 Do not choose for your friends and familiar acquaintance those that are of an estate or quality too much above yours...You will hereby accustom yourselves to live after their rate in clothes, in habit, and in expenses, whereby you will learn a fashion and rank of life above your degree and estate, which will in the end be your undoing.
Matthew Hale

284 Friendship is one mind in two bodies.
Mencius (Mengzi Meng-tse) (370-300 BC, Chinese Philosopher)

285 If a man urge me to tell wherefore I loved him, I feel it cannot be expressed but by answering: Because it was he, because it was myself.
Michel Eyquem De Montaigne (1533-1592, French Philosopher, Essayist)

286 It is important to our friends to believe that we are unreservedly frank with them, and important to friendship that we are not.
Mignon McLaughlin (1915?-, American Author, Editor)

287 A man must eat a peck of salt with his friend, before he knows him.
Miguel De Cervantes (1547-1616, Spanish Novelist, Dramatist, Poet)

288 When all is said and done, friendship is the only trustworthy fabric of the affections. So-called love is a delirious inhuman state of mind: when hot it substitutes indulgence for fair play; when cold it is cruel, but friendship is warmth in cold, firm ground in a bog.
Miles Franklin (1879-1954, Australian Author)

289 It's funny, isn't it? How your best friend can just blow up like that?
Monty Python

290 Friendship's the privilege of private men; for wretched greatness knows no blessing so substantial.
Nahum Tate (1652-1715, British Poet, Dramatist)

291 Our most intimate friend is not he to whom we show the worst, but the best of our nature.
Nathaniel Hawthorne (1804-1864, American Novelist, Short Story Writer)

292 Thus much for thy assurance know; a hollow friend is but a hellish foe.
Nicholas Breton (1545-1626, British Author, Poet)

293 Friends, both the imaginary ones you build for yourself out of phrases taken from a living writer, or real ones from college, and relatives, despite all the waste of ceremony and fakery and the fact that out of an hour of conversation you may have only five minutes in which the old entente reappears, are the only real means for foreign ideas to enter your brain.
Nicholson Baker (1957-, American Author)

294 Hold a true friend with both your hands.
Nigerian Proverb

295 To find a friend one must close one eye -- to keep him, two.
Norman Douglas (1868-1952, British Author)

296 The proper office of a friend is to side with you when you are in the wrong. Nearly anybody will side with you when you are in the right.
Notebook

297 Friendship is a disinterested commerce between equals; love, an abject intercourse between tyrants and slaves.
Oliver Goldsmith (1728-1774, Anglo-Irish Author, Poet, Playwright)

298 Don't flatter yourself that friendship authorizes you to say disagreeable things to your intimates. The nearer you come into relation with a person, the more necessary do tact and courtesy become.
Oliver Wendell Holmes (1809-1894, American Author, Wit, Poet)

299 Lots of people want to ride with you in the limo, but what you want is someone who will take the bus with you when the limo breaks down.
Oprah Winfrey (1954-, American TV Personality, Producer, Actress, Author)

300 No young man starting in life could have better capital than plenty of friends. They will strengthen his credit, support him in every great effort, and make him what, unaided, he could never be. Friends of the right sort will help him more -- to be happy and successful -- than much money...
Orison Swett Marden (1850-1924, American Author, Founder of Success Magazine)

301 Laughter is not at all a bad beginning for a friendship, and it is far the best ending for one.
Oscar Wilde (1856-1900, British Author, Wit)

302 An acquaintance that begins with a compliment is sure to develop into a real friendship.
Oscar Wilde (1856-1900, British Author, Wit)

303 The dearest friend on earth is a mere shadow compared to Jesus Christ.
Oswald Chambers (1874-1917 Scottish Preacher, Author)

304 As the yellow gold is tried in fire, so the faith of friendship must be seen in adversity.
Ovid (43 BC-18 AD, Roman Poet)

305 A friendship can weather most things and thrive in thin soil -- but it needs a little mulch of letters and phone calls and small silly presents every so often -- just to save it from drying out completely
Pam Brown

306 There is a magnet in your heart that will attract true friends. That magnet is unselfishness, thinking of others first... when you learn to live for others, they will live for you.
Paramahansa Yogananda (Spiritual Author, Lecturer)

307 I do not believe that friends are necessarily the people you like best, they are merely the people who got there first.
Peter Ustinov (1921-, British Actor, Writer, Director)

308 The world is round so that friendship may encircle it.
Pierre Teilhard De Chardin (1881-1955, French Christian Mystic, Author)

309 I keep my friends as misers do their treasure, because, of all the things granted us by wisdom, none is greater or better than friendship.
Pietro Aretino (1492-1556, Italian Writer)

310 Be slow in choosing a friend, but slower in changing him.
Proverb

311 Broken friendships can be soldered, but never sound.
Proverb

312 A friend is someone who doesn't like the same people you do.
Proverb

313 Short judgments make long friends.
Proverb

314 The time to make friends is before you need them.
Proverb

315 It is prosperity that gives us friends, adversity that proves them.
Proverb

316 We die as often as we lose a friend.
Publilius Syrus (1st Century BC, Roman Writer)

317 Reprove your friends in secret, praise them openly.
Publilius Syrus (1st Century BC, Roman Writer)

318 Treat your friend as if he might become an enemy.
Publilius Syrus (1st Century BC, Roman Writer)

319 Friends are as companions on a journey, who ought to aid each other to persevere in the road to a happier life.
Pythagoras (582-507 BC, Greek Philosopher, Mathematician)

320 Wherever you are it is your own friends who make your world.
Ralph B. Perry

321 A friend is a person with whom I may be sincere. Before him, I may think aloud.
Ralph Waldo Emerson (1803-1882, American Poet, Essayist)

322 A friend may well be reckoned the masterpiece of nature.
Ralph Waldo Emerson (1803-1882, American Poet, Essayist)

323 Friends, such as we desire, are dreams and fables.
Ralph Waldo Emerson (1803-1882, American Poet, Essayist)

324 The glory of friendship is not in the outstretched hand, nor the kindly smile, nor the joy of companionship; it is in the spiritual inspiration that comes to one when he discovers that someone else believes in him and is willing to trust him.
Ralph Waldo Emerson (1803-1882, American Poet, Essayist)

325 Every man passes his life in the search after friendship.
Ralph Waldo Emerson (1803-1882, American Poet, Essayist)

326 We talk of choosing our friends, but friends are self-elected
Ralph Waldo Emerson (1803-1882, American Poet, Essayist)

327 It is one of the blessings of old friends that you can afford to be stupid with them.
Ralph Waldo Emerson (1803-1882, American Poet, Essayist)

328 I do then with my friends as I do with my books. I would have them where I can find them, but I seldom use them.
Ralph Waldo Emerson (1803-1882, American Poet, Essayist)

329 I didn't find my friends; the good Lord gave them to me.
Ralph Waldo Emerson (1803-1882, American Poet, Essayist)

330 The only way to have a friend is to be one.
Ralph Waldo Emerson (1803-1882, American Poet, Essayist)

331 Go oft to the house of thy friend, for weeds choke the unused path.
Ralph Waldo Emerson (1803-1882, American Poet, Essayist)

332 He who has a thousand friends has not a friend to spare, And he who has one enemy will meet him everywhere.
Ralph Waldo Emerson (1803-1882, American Poet, Essayist)

333 A true friend is somebody who can make us do what we can.
Ralph Waldo Emerson (1803-1882, American Poet, Essayist)

334 The ornament of a house is the friends who frequent it.
Ralph Waldo Emerson (1803-1882, American Poet, Essayist)

335 A day for toil, an hour for sport, but for a friend is life too short.
Ralph Waldo Emerson (1803-1882, American Poet, Essayist)

336 Friendships are fragile things and require as much care in handling as any other fragile and precious thing.
Randolph S. Bourne (1886-1918, American Writer)

337 A friend hears the song in my heart and sings it to me when my memory fails.
Readers Digest

338 Can miles truly separate us from friends? If we want to be with someone we love, aren't we already there?
Richard Bach (1936-, American Author)

339 Your friends will know you better in the first minute they meet you than your acquaintances will know you in a thousand years.
Richard Bach (1936-, American Author)

340 Every gift from a friend is a wish for your happiness...
Richard Bach (1936-, American Author)

341 I value the friend who for me finds time on his calendar, but I cherish the friend who for me does not consult his calendar.
Robert Brault

342 Never exaggerate your faults, your friends will attend to that.
Robert C. Edwards

343 Never do a wrong thing to make a friend or to keep one.
Robert E. Lee (1807-1870, American Confederate Army Commander)

344 Friends make pretence of following to the grave but before one is in it, their minds are turned and making the best of their way back to life and living people and things they understand.
Robert Frost (1875-1963, American Poet)

345 A friend should be one in whose understanding and virtue we can equally confide, and whose opinion we can value at once for its justness and its sincerity.
Robert Hall

346 No man is useless while he has a friend.
Robert Louis Stevenson (1850-1895, Scottish Essayist, Poet, Novelist)

347 The very flexibility and ease which make men's friendships so agreeable while they endure, make them the easier to destroy and forget. And a man who has a few friends, or one who has a dozen (if there be any one so wealthy on this earth), cannot forget on how precarious a base his happiness reposes; and how by a stroke or two of fate --a death, a few light words, a piece of stamped paper, a woman's bright eyes --he may be left, in a month, destitute of all.
Robert Louis Stevenson (1850-1895, Scottish Essayist, Poet, Novelist)

348 A friend is a present you give to yourself.
Robert Louis Stevenson (1850-1895, Scottish Essayist, Poet, Novelist)

349 So long as we are loved by others I should say that we are almost indispensable; and no man is useless while he has a friend.
Robert Louis Stevenson (1850-1895, Scottish Essayist, Poet, Novelist)

350 Friendship will not stand the strain of very much good advice for very long.
Robert Lynd (1892-1970, American Sociology Author)

351 No distance of place or lapse of time can lessen the friendship of those who are thoroughly persuaded of each other's worth.
Robert Southey (1774-1843, British Author)

352 Tell me who's your friend and I'll tell you who you are.
Russian Proverb

353 To keep a new friend, never break with the old.
Russian Proverb

354 Give me work to do, Give me health, Give me joy in simple things, Give me an eye for beauty, A tongue for truth, A heart that loves, A mind that reasons, A sympathy that understands. Give me neither malice nor envy, But a true kindness And a noble common sense. At the close of each day Give me a book And a friend with whom I can be silent.
S. M. Frazier

355 To like and dislike the same things, this is what makes a solid friendship.
Sallust (86-34 BC, Roman Historian)

356 Let me live in a house by the side of the road and be a friend to man.
Sam Walter Foss

357 A friend who cannot at a pinch remember a thing or two that never happened is as bad as one who does not know how to forget.
Samuel Butler (1612-1680, British Poet, Satirist)

358 A man's friendships are, like his will, invalidated by marriage -- but they are also no less invalidated by the marriage of his friends.
Samuel Butler (1612-1680, British Poet, Satirist)

359 Friendship is like money, easier made than kept.
Samuel Butler (1612-1680, British Poet, Satirist)

360 I look upon every day to be lost, in which I do not make a new acquaintance.
Samuel Johnson (1709-1784, British Author)

361 Never, my dear Sir, do you take it into your head that I do not love you; you may settle yourself in full confidence both of my love and my esteem; I love you as a kind man, I value you as a worthy man, and hope in time to reverence you as a man of exemplary piety.
Samuel Johnson (1709-1784, British Author)

362 The endearing elegance of female friendship.
Samuel Johnson (1709-1784, British Author)

363 The most fatal disease of friendship is gradual decay, or dislike hourly increased by causes too slender for complaint, and too numerous for removal.
Samuel Johnson (1709-1784, British Author)

364 To let friendship die away by negligence and silence is certainly not wise. It is voluntarily to throw away one of the greatest comforts of the weary pilgrimage.
Samuel Johnson (1709-1784, British Author)

365 If a man does not make new acquaintances as he advances through life, he will soon find himself left alone; one should keep his friendships in constant repair.
Samuel Johnson (1709-1784, British Author)

366 Friends are needed both for joy and for sorrow.
Samuel Paterson

367 Mighty proud I am that I am able to have a spare bed for my friends.
Samuel Pepys (1633-1703, British Diarist)

368 And though thou notest from thy safe recess old friends burn dim, like lamps in noisome air love them for what they are; nor love them less, because to thee they are not what they were.
Samuel Taylor Coleridge (1772-1834, British Poet, Critic, Philosopher)

369 Friendship is a sheltering tree.
Samuel Taylor Coleridge (1772-1834, British Poet, Critic, Philosopher)

370 I have three kinds of friends: those who love me, those who pay no attention to me, and those who detest me.
Sebastien-Roch Nicolas De Chamfort (1741-1794, French Writer, Journalist, Playwright)

371 Friendship always benefits; love sometimes injures.
Seneca (4 BC-65 AD, Spanish-born Roman Statesman, philosopher)

372 Those that are a friend to themselves are sure to be a friend to all.
Seneca (4 BC-65 AD, Spanish-born Roman Statesman, philosopher)

373 A friend is someone you can be alone with and have nothing to do and not be able to think of anything to say and be comfortable in the silence.
Sheryl Condie

374 Only your real friends will tell you when your face is dirty.
Sicilian Proverb

375 But just as delicate fare does not stop you from craving for saveloys, so tried and exquisite friendship does not take away your taste for something new and dubious.
Sidonie Gabrielle Colette (1873-1954, French Author)

376 My true friends have always given me that supreme proof of devotion, a spontaneous aversion for the man I loved.
Sidonie Gabrielle Colette (1873-1954, French Author)

377 And what a delight it is to make friends with someone you have despised.
Sidonie Gabrielle Colette (1873-1954, French Author)

378 Then come the wild weather, come sleet or come snow, we will stand by each other, however it blow.
Simon Dach (1605-1659, German Lyric Poet)

379 Learn to reject friendship, or rather the dream of friendship. To want friendship is a great fault. Friendship ought to be a gratuitous joy, like the joys afforded by art, or life (like aesthetic joys). I must refuse it in order to be worthy to receive it
Simone Weil (1910-1943, French Philosopher, Mystic)

380 For when two beings who are not friends are near each other there is no meeting, and when friends are far apart there is no separation.
Simone Weil (1910-1943, French Philosopher, Mystic)

381 False friendship, like the ivy, decays and ruins the walls it embraces; but true friendship gives new life and animation to the object it supports.
Sir Richard Burton (1821-1890, Explorer, Born in Torquay)

382 If you have no friends to share or rejoice in your success in life -- if you cannot look back to those whom you owe gratitude, or forward to those to whom you ought to afford protection, still it is no less incumbent on you to move steadily in the path of duty; for your active excretions are due not only to society; but in humble gratitude to the Being who made you a member of it, with powers to save yourself and others.
Sir Walter Scott (1771-1832, British Novelist, Poet)

383 Be slow to fall into friendship; but when thou art in, continue firm and constant.
Socrates (469-399 BC, Greek Philosopher of Athens)

384 Money can't buy you friends; but you do get a better class of enemies.
Somers White (American Banker, Speaker)

385 An ounce of blood is worth more than a pound of friendship.
Spanish Proverb

386 I want my friend to miss me as long as I miss him.
St. Augustine (354-430, Numidian-born Bishop of Hippo, Theologian)

387 If two friends ask you to judge a dispute, don't accept, because you will lose one friend; on the other hand, if two strangers come with the same request, accept because you will gain one friend.
St. Augustine (354-430, Numidian-born Bishop of Hippo, Theologian)

388 Friendships begun in this world will be taken up again, never to be broken off.
St. Francis De Sales (1567-1622, Roman Catholic Bishop, Writer)

389 The friendship that can cease has never been real.
St. Jerome (342-420, Croatian Christian Ascetic, Scholar)

390 True friendship ought never to conceal what it thinks.
St. Jerome (342-420, Croatian Christian Ascetic, Scholar)

391 A friend is long sought, hardly found, and with difficulty kept.
St. Jerome (342-420, Croatian Christian Ascetic, Scholar)

392 Friendship is the source of the greatest pleasures, and without friends even the most agreeable pursuits become tedious.
St. Thomas Aquinas (1225-1274, Italian Scholastic Philosopher and Theologian)

393 Life is to be fortified by many friendships. To love and to be loved is the greatest happiness of existence.
Sydney Smith (1771-1845, British Writer, Clergyman)

394 Friendship should be more than biting time can sever.
T. S. Eliot (1888-1965, American-born British Poet, Critic)

395 Life is partly what we make it, and partly what it is made by the friends we choose.
Tehyi Hsieh

396 Many a time from a bad beginning great friendships have sprung up.
Terence (185-159 BC, Roman Writer of Comedies)

397 Join the company of lions rather than assume the lead among foxes.
The Talmud (Jewish Archive of Oral Tradition)

398 Man has three friends on whose company he relies. First, wealth which goes with him only while good fortune lasts. Second, his relatives; they go only as far as the grave, leave him there. The third friend, his good deeds, go with him beyond the grave.
The Talmud (Jewish Archive of Oral Tradition)

399 Your friendship is a glowing ember Through the year; and each December From its warm and living spark We kindle flame against the dark And with its shining radiance light Our tree of faith on Christmas night.
Thelma J. Lund

400 Verily, great grace may go with a little gift; and precious are all things that come from a friend.
Theocritus

401 There is a scarcity of friendship, but not of friends.
Thomas Fuller (1608-1661, British Clergyman, Author)

402 A good friend is my nearest relation.
Thomas Fuller (1608-1661, British Clergyman, Author)

403 If you have one true friend you have more than your share.
Thomas Fuller (1608-1661, British Clergyman, Author)

404 Purchase not friends by gifts; when thou ceasest to give, such will cease to love.
Thomas Fuller (1608-1661, British Clergyman, Author)

405 Don't make friends who are comfortable to be with. Make friends who will force you to lever yourself up.
Thomas J. Watson (18?-1956, American Businessman, Founder of IBM)

406 But friendship is precious, not only in the shade, but in the sunshine of life; and thanks to a benevolent arrangement of things, the greater part of life is sunshine.
Thomas Jefferson (1743-1826, Third President of the USA)

407 To myself, personally, it brings nothing but increasing drudgery and daily loss of friends.
Thomas Jefferson (1743-1826, Third President of the USA)

408 Friendship is but another name for an alliance with the follies and the misfortunes of others. Our own share of miseries is sufficient: why enter then as volunteers into those of another?
Thomas Jefferson (1743-1826, Third President of the USA)

409 Friends may come and go, but enemies accumulate.
Thomas Jones

410 Love Him, and keep Him for thy Friend, who, when all go away, will not forsake thee, nor suffer thee to perish at the last.
Thomas p Kempis (1379-1471, German Monk, Mystic, Religious Writer)

411 Friendship is to be purchased only by friendship. A man may have authority over others, but he can never have their hearts but by giving his own.
Thomas Wilson

412 Every man, however wise, needs the advice of some sagacious friend in the affairs of life.
Titus Maccius Plautus (254-184 BC, Roman Comic Poet)

413 Nothing is there more friendly to a man than a friend in need.
Titus Maccius Plautus (254-184 BC, Roman Comic Poet)

414 What is thine is mine, and all mine is thine.
Titus Maccius Plautus (254-184 BC, Roman Comic Poet)

415 Ones oldest friend is the best.
Titus Maccius Plautus (254-184 BC, Roman Comic Poet)

416 Friendship is a pretty full-time occupation if you really are friendly with somebody. You can't have too many friends because then you're just not really friends.
Truman Capote (1942-, American Author)

417 Who seeks a faultless friend remains friendless.
Turkish Proverb

418 The friend in my adversity I shall always cherish most. I can better trust those who helped to relieve the gloom of my dark hours than those who are so ready to enjoy with me the sunshine of my prosperity.
Ulysses S. Grant (1822-1885, American General, President)

419 Some people go to priests; others to poetry; I to my friends.
Virginia Woolf (1882-1941, British Novelist, Essayist)

420 May God defend me from my friends; I can defend myself from my enemies.
Voltaire (1694-1778, French Historian, Writer)

421 Between friends differences in taste or opinion are irritating in direct proportion to their triviality.
W. H. Auden (1907-1973, Anglo-American Poet)

422 We know our friends by their defects rather than their merits.
W. Somerset Maugham (1874-1965, British Novelist, Playwright)

423 Camerado, I give you my hand, I give you my love more precious than money, I give you myself before preaching or law; Will you give me yourself?
Walt Whitman (1819-1892, American Poet)

424 A real friend is one who walks in when the rest of the world walks out.
Walter Winchell (1897-1972, American Journalist)

425 Strangers are just friends I haven't met yet.
Will Rogers (1879-1935, American Humorist, Actor)

426 Only solitary men know the full joys of friendship. Others have their family --but to a solitary and an exile his friends are everything.
Willa Cather (1876-1947, American Author)

427 Thy friendship oft has made my heart to ache; do be my enemy for friendship's sake.
William Blake (1757-1827, British Poet, Painter)

428 Think where man's glory most begins and ends, And say my glory was I had such friends.
William Butler Yeats (1865-1939, Irish Poet, Playwright.)

429 And say my glory was I had such friends.
William Butler Yeats (1865-1939, Irish Poet, Playwright.)

430 The man that hails you Tom or Jack, and proves by thumps upon your back how he esteems your merit, is such a friend, that one had need be very much his friend indeed to pardon or to bear it.
William Cowper (1731-1800, British Poet)

431 How rare and wonderful is that flash of a moment when we realize we have discovered a friend.
William E. Rothschild

432 There are persons who cannot make friends. Who are they? Those who cannot be friends. It is not the want of understanding or good nature, of entertaining or useful qualities, that you complain of: on the contrary, they have probably many points of attraction; but they have one that neutralizes all these --they care nothing about you, and are neither the better nor worse for what you think of them. They manifest no joy at your approach; and when you leave them, it is with a feeling that they can do just as well without you. This is not sullenness, nor indifference, nor absence of mind; but they are intent solely on their own thoughts, and you are merely one of the subjects they exercise them upon. They live in society as in a solitude.
William Hazlitt (1778-1830, British Essayist)

433 I like a friend the better for having faults that one can talk about.
William Hazlitt (1778-1830, British Essayist)

434 There are no rules for friendship. It must be left to itself. We cannot force it any more than love.
William Hazlitt (1778-1830, British Essayist)

435 The most violent friendships soonest wear themselves out.
William Hazlitt (1778-1830, British Essayist)

436 Old friendships are like meats served up repeatedly, cold, comfortless, and distasteful. The stomach turns against them.
William Hazlitt (1778-1830, British Essayist)

437 There are few things in which we deceive ourselves more than in the esteem we profess to entertain for our friends. It is little better than a piece of quackery. The truth is, we think of them as we please --that is, as they please or displease us.
William Hazlitt (1778-1830, British Essayist)

438 Human beings are born into this little span of life of which the best thing is its friendship and intimacies, and soon their places will know them no more, and yet they leave their friendships and intimacies with no cultivation, to grow as they will by the roadside, expecting them to keep by force of inertia.
William James (1842-1910, American Psychologist, Professor, Author)

439 Those who forgets their friends to follow those of a higher status are truly snobs.
William M. Thackeray (1811-1863, Indian-born British Novelist)

440 A true friend unbosoms freely, advises justly, assists readily, adventures boldly, takes all patiently, defends courageously, and continues a friend unchangeably.
William Penn (1644-1718, British Religious Leader, Founder of Pennsylvania)

441 There can be no friendship where there is no freedom. Friendship loves a free air, and will not be fenced up in straight and narrow enclosures.
William Penn (1644-1718, British Religious Leader, Founder of Pennsylvania)

442 A friend is one that knows you as you are, understands where you have been, accepts what you have become, and still, gently allows you to grow.
William Shakespeare (1564-1616, British Poet, Playwright, Actor)

443 Words are easy, like the wind; Faithful friends are hard to find.
William Shakespeare (1564-1616, British Poet, Playwright, Actor)

444 A friend should bear a friend's infirmities, But Brutus makes mine greater than they are.
William Shakespeare (1564-1616, British Poet, Playwright, Actor)

445 Friendship is constant in all other things, Save in the office and affairs of love.
William Shakespeare (1564-1616, British Poet, Playwright, Actor)

446 The friends thou hast, and their adoption tried, grapple them to thy soul with hoops of steel, but do not dull thy palm with entertainment of each new-hatched unfledged comrade.
William Shakespeare (1564-1616, British Poet, Playwright, Actor)

447 I am already kindly disposed towards you. My friendship it is not in my power to give: this is a gift which no man can make, it is not in our own power: a sound and healthy friendship is the growth of time and circumstance, it will spring up and thrive li
William Wordsworth (1770-1850, British Poet)

448 Good fellowship and friendship are lasting, rational and manly pleasures.
William Wycherley (1640-1716, British Dramatist)

449 The best way to keep your friends is not to give them away.
Wilson Mizner (1876-1933, American Author)

450 You cannot be friends upon any other terms than upon the terms of equality.
Woodrow T. Wilson (1856-1924, Twenty-eighth President of the USA)

451 Friendship is the only cement that will ever hold the world together.
Woodrow T. Wilson (1856-1924, Twenty-eighth President of the USA)

452 If you go looking for a friend, you're going to find they're very scarce. If you go out to be a friend, you'll find them everywhere.
Zig Ziglar (American Sales Trainer, Author, Motivational Speaker)

FRIGIDITY

1 Men always fall for frigid women because they put on the best show.
Fanny Brice (1891-1951, American Entertainer)

2 Show me a frigid women and, nine times out of ten, I'll show you a little man.
Julie Burchill (British Journalist, Writer)

3 Frigidity is desire imagined by a woman who doesn't desire the man offering himself to her. It's the desire of a woman for a man who hasn't yet come to her, whom she doesn't yet know. She's faithful to this stranger even before she belongs to him. Frigidity is the non-desire for whatever is not him.
Marguerite Duras (1914-, French Author, Filmmaker)

4 Frigidity is largely nonsense. It is this generation's catchword, one only vaguely understood and constantly misused. Frigid women are few. There is a host of diffident and slow-ripening ones.
Phyllis Mcginley (1905-1978, American Poet, Author)

FRUSTRATION

1 I am as frustrated with society as a pyromaniac in a petrified forest.
A. Whitney Brown

2 Every thought derives from a thwarted sensation.
E. M. Cioran (1911-, Rumanian-born French Philosopher)

3 The torment of human frustration, whatever its immediate cause, is the knowledge that the self is in prison, its vital force and "mangled mind" leaking away in lonely, wasteful self-conflict.
Elizabeth Drew (1887-1965, Anglo-American Author, Critic)

4 It is the awareness of unfulfilled desires which gives a nation the feeling that it has a mission and a destiny.
Eric Hoffer (1902-1983, American Author, Philosopher)

5 It is misery, you know, unspeakable misery for the man who lives alone and who detests sordid, casual affairs; not old enough to do without women, but not young enough to be able to go and look for one without shame!
Luigi Pirandello (1867-1936, Italian Author, Playwright)

6 I feel as if I were a piece in a game of chess, when my opponent says of it: That piece cannot be moved.
Soren Kierkegaard (1813-1855, Danish Philosopher, Writer)

FULFILLMENT

1 Only those who have learned the power of sincere and selfless contribution experience life's deepest joy: true fulfillment.
Anthony Robbins (1960-, American Author, Speaker, Peak Performance Expert / Consultant)

2 Personal satisfaction is the most important ingredient of success.
Denis Waitley (1933-, American Author, Speaker, Trainer, Peak Performance Expert)

3 My riches consist not in the extent of my possessions but in the fewness of my wants.
J. Brotherton

4 I love being in therapy. It's just constantly fulfilling for me.
Jennifer Jason Leigh (1962-, American Actress)

5 You can't live a perfect day without doing something for someone who will never be able to repay you.
John Wooden (1910-, American Basketball Coach)

6 A man should always consider how much he has more than he wants...
Joseph Addison (1672-1719, British Essayist, Poet, Statesman)

7 Let not your mind run on what you lack as much as on what you have already.
Marcus Aurelius (121-80 AD, Roman Emperor, Philosopher)

8 People think that at the end of the day a man is the only answer. Actually, a fulfilling job is better for me.
Princess of Wales Diana (1961-1997, Wife of Charles, Prince of Wales)

9 People want riches; they need fulfillment.
Robert Conklin (American Teacher, Author, Speaker)

10 I firmly believe that any man's finest hour, the greatest fulfillment of all that he holds dear, is that moment when he has worked his heart out in a good cause and lies exhausted on the field of battle -- victorious.
Vince Lombardi (1913-1970, American Football Coach)

11 The fact that it had never been done before made it even more irresistible.
William Mcgovern (American Businessman, Founder of MCI)

FUN

1 People must not do things for fun. We are not here for fun. There is no reference to fun in any act of Parliament.
A. P. Herbert (1890-1971, British Author, Politician)

2 Oh! The good times when we were so unhappy.
Alexandre Dumas (1802-1870, French Novelist, Dramatist)

3 You got to like your work. You have got to like what you are doing, you have got to be doing something worthwhile so you can like it -- because it is worthwhile, that it makes a difference, don't you see?
Col. Harland Sanders (1890-1980, American Businessman, Founder of Kentucky Fried Chicken)

4 People rarely succeed unless they have fun in what they are doing.
Dale Carnegie (1888-1955, American Author, Trainer)

5 You go for it. All the stops are out. Caution is to the wind, and you're battling with everything you have. That's the real fun of the game.
Dan Dierdorf (American Football Player)

6 Fun is a good thing but only when it spoils nothing better.
George Santayana (1863-1952, American Philosopher, Poet)

7 Blessed is the man who has some congenial work, some occupation in which he can put his heart, and which affords a complete outlet to all the forces there are in him.
John Burroughs (1837-1921, American Naturalist, Author)

8 If you cannot work with love but only with distaste, it is better that you should leave your work.
Kahlil Gibran (1883-1931, Lebanese Poet, Novelist)

9 She concedes that she's the one she pleases.
Kim Carnes (American Singer)

10 Horse-play, romping, frequent and loud fits of laughter, jokes, and indiscriminate familiarity, will sink both merit and knowledge into a degree of contempt. They compose at most a merry fellow; and a merry fellow was never yet a respectable man.
Lord Chesterfield (1694-1773, British Statesman, Author)

11 A joke is not a thing but a process, a trick you play on the listener's mind. You start him off toward a plausible goal, and then by a sudden twist you land him nowhere at all or just where he didn't expect to go.
Max Eastman (American Commentator, Writer)

12 If you do not feel yourself growing in your work and your life broadening and deepening, if your task is not a perpetual tonic to you, you have not found your place.
Orison Swett Marden (1850-1924, American Author, Founder of Success Magazine)

13 All animals, except man, know that the principal business of life is to enjoy it.
Samuel Butler (1612-1680, British Poet, Satirist)

14 Every time I hear that word, I cringe. Fun! I think it's disgusting; it's just running around. It's not my idea of pleasure.
Vivienne Westwood (1941-, British Fashion Designer)

15 Fun I love, but too much fun is of all things the most loathsome. Mirth is better than fun, and happiness is better than mirth.
William Blake (1757-1827, British Poet, Painter)

16 Innocent amusements are such as excite moderately, and such as produce a cheerful frame of mind, not boisterous mirth; such as refresh, instead of exhausting, the system; such as recur frequently, rather than continue long; such as send us back to our daily duties invigorated in body and spirit; such as we can partake of in the presence and society of respectable friends; such as consist with and are favorable to a grateful piety; such as are chastened by self-respect, and are accompanied with the consciousness that life has a higher end than to be amused.
William Ellery Channing (1780-1842, American Unitarian Minister, Author)

FUNCTION

1 He gains everyone's approval who mixes the pleasant with the useful.
Horace (65-8 BC, Italian Poet)

2 Form and function are a unity, two sides of one coin. In order to enhance function, appropriate form must exist or be created.
Ida P. Rolf (1896-1979, American Biochemist, Physical Therapist)

3 Utility is the great idol of the age, to which all powers must do service and all talents swear allegiance.
Johann Friedrich Von Schiller (1759-1805, German Dramatist, Poet, Historian)

4 We can forgive a man for making a useful thing as long as he does not admire it. The only excuse for making a useless thing is that one admires it intensely.
Oscar Wilde (1856-1900, British Author, Wit)

FUNERALS

1 A funeral is a pageant whereby we attest our respect for the dead by enriching the undertaker.
Ambrose Bierce (1842-1914, American Author, Editor, Journalist, "The Devil's Dictionary")

2   On a day of burial there is no perspective -- for space itself is annihilated. Your dead friend is still a fragmentary being. The day you bury him is a day of chores and crowds, of hands false or true to be shaken, of the immediate cares of mourning. The dead friend will not really die until tomorrow, when silence is round you again. Then he will show himself complete, as he was -- to tear himself away, as he was, from the substantial you. Only then will you cry out because of him who is leaving and whom you cannot detain.
Antoine De Saint-Exupery (1900-1944, French Aviator, Writer)

3   Funeral pomp is more for the vanity of the living than for the honor of the dead.
François de La Rochefoucauld (1613-1680, French classical writer)

4   In the city a funeral is just an interruption of traffic; in the country it is a form of popular entertainment.
George Ade (1866-1944, American Humorist, Playwright)

5   Worldly faces never look so worldly as at a funeral. They have the same effect of grating incongruity as the sound of a coarse voice breaking the solemn silence of night.
George Eliot (1819-1880, British Novelist)

6   Memorial services are the cocktail parties of the geriatric set.
Harold Macmillan (1894-1986, British Conservative Politician, Prime Minister)

7   A funeral eulogy is a belated plea for the defense delivered after the evidence is all in.
Irvin S. Cobb

8   Even the best of friends cannot attend each other's funeral.
Kehlog Albran (1933-?, Author born in Brest-Litovsk)

9   I did not attend his funeral; but I wrote a nice letter saying I approved of it. [About a politician who had recently died]
Mark Twain (1835-1910, American Humorist, Writer)

10   Where a blood relation sobs, an intimate friend should choke up, a distant acquaintance should sigh, a stranger should merely fumble sympathetically with his handkerchief.
Mark Twain (1835-1910, American Humorist, Writer)

11   The chief mourner does not always attend the funeral.
Ralph Waldo Emerson (1803-1882, American Poet, Essayist)

12   As grand and griefless as a rich man's funeral.
Sidney Thompson Dobell

FUTILITY

1   The gods had condemned Sisyphus to ceaselessly rolling a rock to the top of a mountain, whence the stone would fall back of its own weight. They had thought with some reason that there is no more dreadful punishment than futile and hopeless labor.
Albert Camus (1913-1960, French Existential Writer)

2   Life is indeed darkness save when there is urge, and all urge is blind save when there is knowledge, and all knowledge is vain save when there is work, and all work is empty save when there is love.
Kahlil Gibran (1883-1931, Lebanese Poet, Novelist)

3   A constant smirk upon the face, and a whiffing activity of the body, are strong indications of futility.
Lord Chesterfield (1694-1773, British Statesman, Author)

4   He is useless on top of the ground; he ought to be under it, inspiring the cabbages.
Mark Twain (1835-1910, American Humorist, Writer)

5   It is the superfluous things for which men sweat.
Seneca (4 BC-65 AD, Spanish-born Roman Statesman, philosopher)

6   I have measured out my life with coffee spoons.
T. S. Eliot (1888-1965, American-born British Poet, Critic)

7   No! I am not Prince Hamlet, nor was meant to be: am an attendant lord, one that will do to swell a progress, start a scene or two, advise the prince.
T. S. Eliot (1888-1965, American-born British Poet, Critic)

8   A walking shadow, a poor player, that struts and frets his hour upon the stage, and then is heard no more.
William Shakespeare (1564-1616, British Poet, Playwright, Actor)

FUTURE

1   The best thing about the future is that it comes only one day at a time.
Abraham Lincoln (1809-1865, Sixteenth President of the USA)

2   I never think of the future. It comes soon enough.
Albert Einstein (1879-1955, German-born American Physicist)

3   Future: That period of time in which our affairs prosper, our friends are true and our happiness is assured.
Ambrose Bierce (1842-1914, American Author, Editor, Journalist, "The Devil's Dictionary")

4   That man is prudent who neither hopes nor fears anything from the uncertain events of the future.
Anatole France (1844-1924, French Writer)

5   America, which has the most glorious present still existing in the world today, hardly stops to enjoy it, in her insatiable appetite for the future.
Anne Morrow Lindbergh (1906-, American Author)

6   The wave of the future is coming and there is no fighting it.
Anne Morrow Lindbergh (1906-, American Author)

7   Those who foretell the future lies, even if he tells the truth.
Arabian Proverb

8   The trouble with the future is that is usually arrives before we're ready for it.
Arnold H. Glasgow

9 Upper classes are a nation's past, the middle class its future.
Ayn Rand (1905-1982, Russian Writer, Philosopher)

10 Take no thought for tomorrow; for tomorrow shall take thought for the things of itself. [Matthew 6:34]
Bible (Sacred Scriptures of Christians and Judaism)

11 I've read the last page of the Bible. It's all going to turn out all right.
Billy Graham (1918-, American Evangelist)

12 The good days weren't really so good, and tomorrow ain't as bad as it seems.
Billy Joel (1949-, American Musician, Piano Man, Singer, Songwriter)

13 The future looks extremely bright indeed, with lots of possibilities ahead -- big possibilities. Like the song says, "We've just begun."
Bruce Lee (1940-1973, Chinese-American Actor, Director, Author, Martial Artist)

14 We should all be concerned about the future because we will have to spend the rest of our lives there.
Charles F. Kettering (1876-1958, American Engineer, Inventor)

15 My interest is in the future because I am going to spend the rest of my life there.
Charles F. Kettering (1876-1958, American Engineer, Inventor)

16 Failure is unimportant. It takes courage to make a fool of yourself.
Charlie Chaplin (1889-1977, British Comic Actor, Filmmaker)

17 When men speak of the future, the Gods laugh.
Chinese Proverb

18 When all else is lost, the future still remains.
Christian Nevell Bovee (1820-1904, American Author, Lawyer)

19 Never be afraid to trust an unknown future to a known God.
Corrie Ten Boom (Dutch Evangelist)

20 The future comes one day at a time.
Dean Acheson (1893 - 1971, American Statesman, Lawyer)

21 The future? Like unwritten books and unborn children, you don't talk about it.
Dietrich Fischer-Dieskau (1925-, German Baritone Singer)

22 The danger of the past was that men became slaves. The danger of the future is that men may become robots. True enough, robots do not rebel. But given man's nature, robots cannot live and remain sane, they become "Golems," they will destroy their world and themselves because they cannot stand any longer the boredom of a meaningless life.
Erich Fromm (1900-1980, American Psychologist)

23 We have always held to the hope, the belief, the conviction that there is a better life, a better world, beyond the horizon.
Franklin D. Roosevelt (1882-1945, Thirty-second President of the USA)

24 The cradle of the future is the grave of the past.
Franz Grillparzer (1791-1872, Austrian Dramatic Poet)

25 The future influences the present just as much as the past.
Friedrich Nietzsche (1844-1900, German Philosopher)

26 Predicting the future is easy. It's trying to figure out what's going on now that's hard.
Fritz R. S. Dressler (American President of FRS Dressler Associates)

27 We are made wise not by the recollection of our past, but by the responsibility for our future.
George Bernard Shaw (1856-1950, Irish-born British Dramatist)

28 I desire no future that will break the ties with the past.
George Eliot (1819-1880, British Novelist)

29 It is not the cares of today, but the cares of tomorrow that weigh a man down. For the needs of today we have corresponding strength given. For the morrow we are told to trust. It is not ours yet.
George Macdonald (1824-1905, Scottish Novelist)

30 It is extraordinary that whole populations have no projects for the future, none at all. It certainly is extraordinary, but it is certainly true.
Gertrude Stein (1874-1946, American Author)

31 We already have the statistics for the future: the growth percentages of pollution, overpopulation, desertification. The future is already in place.
Gunther Grass (1927-, German Author)

32 It is possible to believe that all the past is but the beginning of a beginning, and that all that is and has been is but the twilight of the dawn. It is possible to believe that all the human mind has ever accomplished is but the dream before the awakening.
H.G. Wells (1866-1946, British-born American Author)

33 I have always been delighted at the prospect of a new day, a fresh try, one more start, with perhaps a bit of magic waiting somewhere behind the morning...
J. B. Priestley (1894-1984, English Novelist, Playwright, Essayist)

34 I would sum up my fear about the future in one word: boring. And that's my one fear: that everything has happened; nothing exciting or new or interesting is ever going to happen again... the future is just going to be a vast, conforming suburb of the soul.
J. G. Ballard (1930-, British Author)

35 The future is... black.
James Baldwin (1924-1987, American Author)

36 Tomorrow, you promise yourself, will be different, yet, tomorrow is too often a repetition of today.
James T. Mccay

37 The child is not to be educated for the present, but for the remote future, and often is opposition to the immediate future.
Jean Paul

38 There are certain moments when we might wish the future were built by men of the past.
Jean Rostand (1894-1977, French Biologist, Writer)

39 The future comes slowly, the present flies and the past stands still forever.
Johann Friedrich Von Schiller (1759-1805, German Dramatist, Poet, Historian)

40 I have a Vision of the Future, chum. The workers flats in fields of soya beans tower up like silver pencils, score on score.
John Betjeman (1906-1984, British Poet)

41 If you do not think about your future, you cannot have one.
John Galsworthy (1867-1933, British Novelist, Playwright)

42 A fixed image of the future is in the worst sense a historical.
Juliet Mitchell (1940-, New Zealand Author)

43 Yesterday is but today's memory, and tomorrow is today's dream.
Kahlil Gibran (1883-1931, Lebanese Poet, Novelist)

44 Ignorance of God's prophetic outline, failure to know God's program for the Church, the nations, and Israel, is the cause of the overwhelming amount of error and misunderstanding of the events of the future.
M. R. Dehaan

45 The past cannot be changed. The future is yet in your power.
Mary Pickford (1893-1979, Canadian-born American Actress)

46 our day will come is another way of saying you get yours.
Merelene Cornish

47 By the street of by-and-by, one arrives at the house of never.
Miguel De Cervantes (1547-1616, Spanish Novelist, Dramatist, Poet)

48 People are always shouting they want to create a better future. It's not true. The future is an apathetic void of no interest to anyone. The past is full of life, eager to irritate us, provoke and insult us, tempt us to destroy or repaint it. The only reason people want to be masters of the future is to change the past.
Milan Kundera (1929-, Czech Author, Critic)

49 The future destiny of the child is always the work of the mother.
Napoleon Bonaparte (1769-1821, French General, Emperor)

50 There was a door to which I found no key: There was the veil through which I might not see.
Omar Khayyam (1048-1131, Persian Astronomer, Poet)

51 When I look into the future, it is so bright it burns my eyes.
Oprah Winfrey (1954-, American TV Personality, Producer, Actress, Author)

52 The past is of no importance. The present is of no importance. It is with the future that we have to deal. For the past is what man should not have been. The present is what man ought not to be. The future is what artists are.
Oscar Wilde (1856-1900, British Author, Wit)

53 I know of know way of judging the future but by the past.
Patrick Henry (1736-1799, American Orator, Patriot)

54 The trouble with our times is that the future is not what it used to be.
Paul Valery (1871-1945, French Poet, Essayist)

55 The gigantic shadows which futurity casts upon the present.
Percy Bysshe Shelley (1792-1822, British Poet)

56 The best way to predict the future is to create it.
Peter F. Drucker (1909-, American Management Consultant, Author)

57 Tomorrow never comes.
Proverb

58 I don't try to describe the future. I try to prevent it.
Ray Bradbury (1920-, American Science Fiction Writer)

59 They gave each other a smile with a future in it.
Ring Lardner (1885-1933, American Writer)

60 You don't just stumble into the future. You create your own future.
Roger Smith (American Businessman, CEO of GM)

61 Tomorrow is an old deceiver, and his cheat never grows stale.
Samuel Johnson (1709-1784, British Author)

62 The future is purchased by the present.
Samuel Johnson (1709-1784, British Author)

63 The future is made of the same stuff as the present.
Simone Weil (1910-1943, French Philosopher, Mystic)

64 I don't ever look back. I look forward.
Steffi Graf (Born 1969, German Tennis Player)

65 The more unpredictable the world is the more we rely on predictions.
Steve Rivkin

66 The future will one day be the present and will seem as unimportant as the present does now.
W. Somerset Maugham (1874-1965, British Novelist, Playwright)

67 Everything that looks to the future elevates human nature. Never is life so low or so little as when occupied with the present.
Walter Savage Landor (1775-1864, British Poet, Essayist)

68 Create your future from your future not your past.
Werner Erhard (American Entrepreneur, Scientologist)

69 I am not afraid of tomorrow, for I have seen yesterday and I love today.
William Allen White (1868-1944, American Editor, Writer)

70 All futurity seems teeming with endless destruction never to be repelled; Desperate remorse swallows the present in a quenchless rage.
William Blake (1757-1827, British Poet, Painter)

71 The future is as bright as the promises of God.
William Carey (1761-1834, British Missionary, Orientalist)

72 We know what we are, but know not what we may be.
William Shakespeare (1564-1616, British Poet, Playwright, Actor)

73 It's tough to make predictions, especially about the future.
Yogi Berra (1925-, American Baseball Player)

GAIN

1 The true way to gain much, is never to desire to gain too much.
Francis Beaumont (1584-1616, British Dramatist)

2 No gain is so certain as that which proceeds from the economical use of what you already have.
Latin Proverb

3 And gain is gain, however small.
Robert Browning (1812-1889, British Poet)

4 It is always sound business to take any obtainable net gain, at any cost and at any risk to the rest of the community.
Thorstein Veblen (1857-1929, American Social Scientist)

GAMBLING

1 I can't believe that God plays dice with the universe.
Albert Einstein (1879-1955, German-born American Physicist)

2 The gambling known as business looks with severe disfavor on the business known as gambling.
Ambrose Bierce (1842-1914, American Author, Editor, Journalist, "The Devil's Dictionary")

3 Nobody has ever bet enough on a winning horse.
American Proverb

4 Smith and Wesson or a Colt always beat four aces.
American Proverb

5 Nothing is sacred to a gamester.
Bernard Joseph Saurin (1706-1781, French Dramatist)

6 I have to confess that I had gambled on my soul and lost it with heroic insouciance and lightness of touch. The soul is so impalpable, so often useless, and sometimes such a nuisance, that I felt no more emotion on losing it than if, on a stroll, I had mislaid my visiting card.
Charles Baudelaire (1821-1867, French Poet)

7 I came to the conclusion long ago that all life is six to five against.
Damon Runyon (1884-1946, American Writer, Journalist)

8 The race is not always to the swift, nor the battle to the strong, but that is the way to bet.
Damon Runyon (1884-1946, American Writer, Journalist)

9 One of the worst things that can happen to you in life is to win a bet on a horse at an early age.
Danny Mcgoorty

10 The world is the house of the strong. I shall not know until the end what I have lost or won in this place, in this vast gambling den where I have spent more than sixty years, dicebox in hand, shaking the dice.
Denis Diderot (1713-1784, French Philosopher)

11 The only man who makes money following the races is one who does it with a broom and shovel.
Elbert Hubbard (1859-1915, American Author, Publisher)

12 The best throw of the dice is to throw them away.
English Proverb

13 Gambling is the son of avarice and the father of despair.
French Proverb

14 There are two great pleasures in gambling: that of winning and that of losing.
French Proverb

15 Gambling promises the poor what property performs for the rich, something for nothing.
George Bernard Shaw (1856-1950, Irish-born British Dramatist)

16 It is the child of avarice, the brother of iniquity, and the father of mischief.
George Washington (1732-1799, First President of the USA)

17 Someone once asked me why women don't gamble as much as men do, and I gave the common-sensical reply that we don't have as much money. That was a true but incomplete answer. In fact, women's total instinct for gambling is satisfied by marriage.
Gloria Steinem (1934-, American Feminist Writer, Editor)

18 The urge to gamble is so universal and its practice so pleasurable that I assume it must be evil.
Heywood Broun (1888-1939, American Journalist, Novelist)

19 I've been on such a losing streak that if I had been around I would have taken General Custer and given points.
Joe E. Lewis (American Writer)

20 If you play bridge badly you make your partner suffer, but if you play poker badly you make everybody happy.
Joe Laurie Jr.

21 Of all mechanics, of all servile handycrafts-men, a gamester is the vilest. But yet, as many of the quality are of the profession, he is admitted amongst the politest company.
John Gay (1688-1732, British Playwright, Poet)

22 You cannot get anything out of nature or from God by gambling; only out of your neighbor.
John Ruskin (1819-1900, British Critic, Social Theorist)

23 The losses as well as the prizes must be drawn from the cheating lottery of life.
Le Sage

24 I have a notion that gamblers are as happy as most people, being always excited; women, wine, fame, the table, even ambition, sate now and then, but every turn of the card and cast of the dice keeps the gambler alive -- besides one can game ten times longer than one can do any thing else.
Lord Byron (1788-1824, British Poet)

25 He was a degenerate gambler. That is, a man who gambled simply to gamble and must lose. As a hero who goes to war must die. Show me a gambler and I'll show you a loser, show me a hero and I'll show you a corpse.
Mario Puzo (1920-, American Novelist)

26 Whenever you see a gaming table be sure to know fortune is not there. Rather she is always in the company of industry.
Oliver Goldsmith (1728-1774, Anglo-Irish Author, Poet, Playwright)

27 One should always play fair when one has the winning cards.
Oscar Wilde (1856-1900, British Author, Wit)

28 Never bet on baseball.
Pete Rose (1942-, American Baseball Player, Manager)

29 Rule: Never perform card tricks for the people you play poker with.
Proverb

30 Sir, I do not call a gamester a dishonest man; but I call him an unsociable man, an unprofitable man. Gaming is a mode of transferring property without producing any intermediate good.
Samuel Johnson (1709-1784, British Author)

31 The dice of Zeus always fall luckily.
Sophocles (495-406 BC, Greek Tragic Poet)

32 No wife can endure a gambling husband; unless he is a steady winner.
Thomas Robert Dewar

33 Don't gamble; take all your savings and buy some good stock and hold it till it goes up. If it don't go up, don't buy it.
Will Rogers (1879-1935, American Humorist, Actor)

GAMES

1 One of life's primal situations; the game of hide and seek. Oh, the delicious thrill of hiding while the others come looking for you, the delicious terror of being discovered, but what panic when, after a long search, the others abandon you! You mustn't hide too well. You mustn't be too good at the game. The player must never be bigger than the game itself.
Jean Baudrillard (French Postmodern Philosopher, Writer)

2 I recently learned something quite interesting about video games. Many young people have developed incredible hand, eye, and brain coordination in playing these games. The air force believes these kids will be our outstanding pilots should they fly our jets.
Ronald Reagan (1911-, Fortieth President of the USA, Actor)

3 No human being is innocent, but there is a class of innocent human actions called Games.
W. H. Auden (1907-1973, Anglo-American Poet)

4 Intelligence and war are games, perhaps the only meaningful games left. If any player becomes too proficient, the game is threatened with termination.
William S. Burroughs (1914-1997, American Writer)

GARDENING AND GARDENS

1 God almighty first planted a garden: and, indeed, it is the purest of human pleasure.
Francis Bacon (1561-1626, British Philosopher, Essayist, Statesman)

2 The best place to seek God is in a garden. You can dig for him there.
George Bernard Shaw (1856-1950, Irish-born British Dramatist)

3 A garden must be looked into, and dressed as the body.
George Herbert (1593-1632, British Metaphysical Poet)

4 It is a golden maxim to cultivate the garden for the nose, and the eyes will take care of themselves.
Robert Louis Stevenson (1850-1895, Scottish Essayist, Poet, Novelist)

5 No occupation is so delightful to me as the culture of the earth, and no culture comparable to that of the garden.
Thomas Jefferson (1743-1826, Third President of the USA)

GENDER

1 It would be futile to attempt to fit women into a masculine pattern of attitudes, skills and abilities and disastrous to force them to suppress their specifically female characteristics and abilities by keeping up the pretense that there are no differences between the sexes.
Arianna Stassinopoulos (1950-, Greek Author)

2 The multitude will hardly believe the excessive force of education, and in the difference of modesty between men and women, ascribe that to nature, which is altogether owing to early instruction: Miss is scarce three years old, but she's spoke to every day to hide her leg, and rebuked in good earnest if she shows it; whilst little Master at the same age is bid to take up his coats, and piss like a man.
Bernard Mandeville (1670-1733, Dutch-born British Author, Physician)

3 In the theory of gender I began from zero. There is no masculine power or privilege I did not covet. But slowly, step by step, decade by decade, I was forced to acknowledge that even a woman of abnormal will cannot escape her hormonal identity.
Camille Paglia (1947-, American Author, Critic, Educator)

4 After centuries of conditioning of the female into the condition of perpetual girlishness called femininity, we cannot remember what femaleness is. Though feminists have been arguing for years that there is a self-defining female energy, and a female libido that is not expressed merely in response to demands by the male, and a female way of being and of experiencing the world, we are still not close to understanding what it might be. Yet every mother who has held a girl child in her arms has known that she was different from a boy child and that she would approach the reality around her in a different way. She is a female and she will die female, and though many centuries should pass, archaeologists would identify her skeleton as the remains of a female creature.
Germaine Greer (1939-, Australian Feminist Writer)

5 The loss of sex polarity is part and parcel of the larger disintegration, the reflex of the soul's death, and coincident with the disappearance of great men, great deeds, great causes, great wars, etc.
Henry Miller (1891-1980, American Author)

6 We are all androgynous, not only because we are all born of a woman impregnated by the seed of a man but because each of us, helplessly and forever, contains the other -- male in female, female in male, white in black and black in white. We are a part of each other. Many of my countrymen appear to find this fact exceedingly inconvenient and even unfair, and so, very often, do I. But none of us can do anything about it.
James Baldwin (1924-1987, American Author)

7 Perhaps nothing is so depressing an index of the inhumanity of the male-supremacist mentality as the fact that the more genial human traits are assigned to the underclass: affection, response to sympathy, kindness, cheerfulness.
Kate Millet (1934-, American Feminist Author)

8 Except for their genitals, I don't know what immutable differences exist between men and women. Perhaps there are some other unchangeable differences; probably there are a number of irrelevant differences. But it is clear that until social expectations for men and women are equal, until we provide equal respect for both sexes, answers to this question will simply reflect our prejudices.
Naomi Weisstein

9 In sex we have the source of man's true connection with the cosmos and of his servile dependence. The categories of sex, male and female, are cosmic categories, not merely anthropological categories.
Nicolai A. Berdyaev

10 To be sure he's a "Man," the male must see to it that the female be clearly a "Woman," the opposite of a "Man," that is, the female must act like a faggot.
Valerie Solanis

11 Different though the sexes are, they inter-mix. In every human being a vacillation from one sex to the other takes place, and often it is only the clothes that keep the male or female likeness, while underneath the sex is very opposite of what it is above.
Virginia Woolf (1882-1941, British Novelist, Essayist)

12 It would be a thousand pities if women wrote like men, or lived like men, or looked like men, for if two sexes are quite inadequate, considering the vastness and variety of the world, how should we manage with one only? Ought not education to bring out and fortify the differences rather than the similarities? For we have too much likeness as it is, and if an explorer should come back and bring word of other sexes looking through the branches of other trees at other skies, nothing would be of greater service to humanity; and we should have the immense pleasure into the bargain of watching Professor X rush for his measuring-rods to prove himself "superior."
Virginia Woolf (1882-1941, British Novelist, Essayist)

GENERALIZATIONS

1 We are more prone to generalize the bad than the good. We assume that the bad is more potent and contagious.
Eric Hoffer (1902-1983, American Author, Philosopher)

2 Any general statement is like a check drawn on a bank. Its value depends on what is there to meet it.
Ezra Pound (1885-1972, American Poet, Critic)

3 An idea is always a generalization, and generalization is a property of thinking. To generalize means to think.
Georg Hegel (1770-1831, German Philosopher)

4 Obvious enough that generalities work to protect the mind from the great outdoors; is it possible that this was in fact their first purpose?
Howard Nemerov (1920-1991, American Poet)

5 A sweeping statement is the only statement worth listening to. The critic without faith gives balanced opinions, usually about second-rate writers.
Patrick Kavanagh (1905-1967, Irish Poet, Author)

6 Generalization is necessary to the advancement of knowledge; but particularly is indispensable to the creations of the imagination. In proportion as men know more and think more they look less at individuals and more at classes. They therefore make better theories and worse poems.
Thomas B. Macaulay (1800-1859, American Essayist and Historian)

7 To generalize is to be an idiot. To particularize is the alone distinction of merit. General knowledge are those knowledge that idiots possess.
William Blake (1757-1827, British Poet, Painter)

GENERALS

1 Perfect soldier, perfect gentleman never gave offence to anyone not even the enemy.
A. J. P. Taylor (1906-1990, British Historian)

2 Tell me what brand of whiskey that Grant drinks. I would like to send a barrel of it to my other generals.
Abraham Lincoln (1809-1865, Sixteenth President of the USA)

3 The nearest the modern general or admiral comes to a small-arms encounter of any sort is at a duck hunt in the company of corporation executives at the retreat of Continental Motors, Inc.
C. Wright Mills (1916-1962, American Sociologist)

4 The best generals I have known were... stupid or absent-minded men. Not only does a good army commander not need any special qualities, on the contrary he needs the absence of the highest and best human attributes -- love, poetry, tenderness, and philosophic inquiring doubt. He should be limited, firmly convinced that what he is doing is very important (otherwise he will not have sufficient patience), and only then will he be a brave leader. God forbid that he should be humane, should love, or pity, or think of what is just and unjust.
Count Leo Tolstoy (1828-1910, Russian Novelist, Philosopher)

5 A general is just as good or just as bad as the troops under his command make him.
Douglas Macarthur (1880-1964, American Army General in WW II)

6 Like the old soldier of the ballad, I now close my military career and just fade away, an old soldier who tried to do his duty as God gave him the light to see that duty. Goodbye.
Douglas Macarthur (1880-1964, American Army General in WW II)

7 Humility must always be the portion of any man who receives acclaim earned in the blood of his followers and the sacrifices of his friends.
Dwight D. Eisenhower (1890-1969, Thirty-fourth President of the USA)

8 To a surprising extent the war-lords in shining armor, the apostles of the martial virtues, tend not to die fighting when the time comes. History is full of ignominious getaways by the great and famous.
George Orwell (1903-1950, British Author, "Animal Farm")

9 I made all my generals out of mud.
Napoleon Bonaparte (1769-1821, French General, Emperor)

10 I am convinced that the best service a retired general can perform is to turn in his tongue along with his suit, and to mothball his opinions.
Omar Nelson Bradley (1893-1981, American General)

11 The Creator has not thought proper to mark those in the forehead who are of stuff to make good generals. We are first, therefore, to seek them blindfold, and then let them learn the trade at the expense of great losses.
Thomas Jefferson (1743-1826, Third President of the USA)

12 I think with the Romans, that the general of today should be a soldier tomorrow if necessary.
Thomas Jefferson (1743-1826, Third President of the USA)

13 In enterprise of martial kind, when there was any fighting, he led his regiment from behind -- he found it less exciting.
W. S. Gilbert (1836-1911, British Librettist)

GENERATIONS

1 Nothing so dates a man as to decry the younger generation.
Adlai E. Stevenson (1900-1965, American Lawyer, Politician)

2 What one generation sees as a luxury, the next sees as a necessity.
Anthony Crosland

3 It is fortunate that each generation does not comprehend its own ignorance. We are thus enabled to call our ancestors barbarous.
Charles Dudley Warner (1829-1900, American Author)

4 We have to hate our immediate predecessors to get free of their authority.
D. H. Lawrence (1885-1930, British Author)

5 A man's liberal and conservative phases seem to follow each other in a succession of waves from the time he is born. Children are radicals. Youths are conservatives, with a dash of criminal negligence. Men in their prime are liberals (as long as their digestion keeps pace with their intellect). The middle aged run to shelter: they insure their life, draft a will, accumulate mementos and occasional tables, and hope for security. And then comes old age, which repeats childhood -- a time full of humors and sadness, but often full of courage and even prophecy.
E(lwyn) B(rooks) White (1899-1985, American Author, Editor)

6 Twenty can't be expected to tolerate sixty in all things, and sixty gets bored stiff with twenty's eternal love affairs.
Emily Carr (1871-1945, Canadian Artist)

7 It's all that the young can do for the old, to shock them and keep them up to date.
George Bernard Shaw (1856-1950, Irish-born British Dramatist)

8 I suppose you think that persons who are as old as your father and myself are always thinking about very grave things, but I know that we are meditating the same old themes that we did when we were ten years old, only we go more gravely about it.
Henry David Thoreau (1817-1862, American Essayist, Poet, Naturalist)

9 I avoid talking before the youth of the age as I would dancing before them: for if one's tongue don't move in the steps of the day, and thinks to please by its old graces, it is only an object of ridicule.
Horace Walpole (1717-1797, British Author)

10 The old know what they want; the young are sad and bewildered.
Logan Pearsall Smith (1865-1946, Anglo-American Essayist, Aphorist)

11 The longer I live the more keenly I feel that whatever was good enough for our fathers is not good enough for us.
Oscar Wilde (1856-1900, British Author, Wit)

12 Our tastes greatly alter. The lad does not care for the child's rattle, and the old man does not care for the young man's whore.
Samuel Johnson (1709-1784, British Author)

13 We may consider each generation as a distinct nation, with a right, by the will of its majority, to bind themselves, but none to bind the succeeding generation, more than the inhabitants of another country.
Thomas Jefferson (1743-1826, Third President of the USA)

14 From the earliest times the old have rubbed it into the young that they are wiser than they, and before the young had discovered what nonsense this was they were old too, and it profited them to carry on the imposture.
W. Somerset Maugham (1874-1965, British Novelist, Playwright)

15 The dead might as well try to speak to the living as the old to the young.
Willa Cather (1876-1947, American Author)

16 The generations of men run on in the tide of time, but leave their destined lineaments permanent for ever and ever.
William Blake (1757-1827, British Poet, Painter)

GENEROSITY

1 Many people are capable of doing a wise thing, more a cunning thing, but very few a generous thing.
Alexander Pope (1688-1744, British Poet, Critic, Translator)

2 All my experience of the world teaches me that in ninety-nine cases out of a hundred, the safe and just side of a question is the generous and merciful side.
Anna Jameson (1794-1860, British Essayist)

3 Men of the noblest dispositions think themselves happiest when others share their happiness with them.
Barry Duncan

4 There is sublime thieving in all giving. Someone gives us all he has and we are his.
Eric Hoffer (1902-1983, American Author, Philosopher)

5 To generous souls every task is noble.
Euripides (480-406 BC, Greek Tragic Poet)

6 What is called generosity is usually only the vanity of giving; we enjoy the vanity more than the thing given.
François de La Rochefoucauld (1613-1680, French classical writer)

7 What seems to be generosity is often no more than disguised ambition, which overlooks a small interest in order to secure a great one.
François de La Rochefoucauld (1613-1680, French classical writer)

8 I take as my guide the hope of a saint: in crucial things, unity... in important things, diversity... in all things, generosity.
George Bush (1924-, Forty-first President of the USA)

9 Generosity during life is a very different thing from generosity in the hour of death; one proceeds from genuine liberality and benevolence, the other from pride or fear.
Horace Mann (1796-1859, American Educator)

10 Liberality consists less in giving a great deal than in gifts well-timed.
Jean De La Bruyere (1645-1696, French Writer)

11 Generosity lies less in giving much than in giving at the right moment.
Jean De La Bruyere (1645-1696, French Writer)

12 Generosity is nothing else than a craze to possess. All which I abandon, all which I give, I enjoy in a higher manner through the fact that I give it away. To give is to enjoy possessively the object which one gives.
Jean-Paul Sartre (1905-1980, French Writer, Philosopher)

13 The poor don't know that their function in life is to exercise our generosity.
Jean-Paul Sartre (1905-1980, French Writer, Philosopher)

14 Giving is the business of the rich.
Johann Wolfgang Von Goethe (1749-1832, German Poet, Dramatist, Novelist)

15 The more he cast away the more he had.
John Bunyan (1628-1688, British Author)

16 Generosity is another quality which, like patience, letting go, non-judging, and trust, provides a solid foundation for mindfulness practice. You might experiment with using the cultivation of generosity as a vehicle for deep self-observation and inquiry as well as an exercise in giving. A good place to start is with yourself. See if you can give yourself gifts that may be true blessings, such as self-acceptance, or some time each day with no purpose. Practice feeling deserving enough to accept these gifts without obligation-to simply receive from yourself, and from the universe.
Jon Kabat Zinn

17 How much easier is it to be generous than just.
Junius (1769-1771, Anonymous British Letter Writer)

18 Generosity is giving more than you can, and pride is taking less than you need.
Kahlil Gibran (1883-1931, Lebanese Poet, Novelist)

19 A generous man places the benefits he confers beneath his feet; those he receives, nearest his heart.
Lord Greville (1554-1628, British Poet)

20 Generosity is the flower of justice.
Nathaniel Hawthorne (1804-1864, American Novelist, Short Story Writer)

21 Is it not odd that the only generous person I ever knew, who had money to be generous with, should be a stockbroker.
Percy Bysshe Shelley (1792-1822, British Poet)

22 It is always so pleasant to be generous, though very vexatious to pay debts.
Ralph Waldo Emerson (1803-1882, American Poet, Essayist)

23 What I gave I have, what I spent I had; and what I left I lost.
Robert of Doncaste

24 Sir, he throws away his money without thought and without merit. I do not call a tree generous that sheds its fruit at every breeze.
Samuel Johnson (1709-1784, British Author)

25 People who think they're generous to a fault usually think that's their only fault.
Sidney J. Harris (1917-, American Journalist)

26 He who gives what he would as readily throw away, gives without generosity; for the essence of generosity is in self sacrifice.
Sir Henry Taylor (1800-1886, British Author)

27 Lavishness is not generosity.
Thomas Fuller (1608-1661, British Clergyman, Author)

28 Give all thou canst; high Heaven rejects the lore of nicely-calculated less or more.
William Wordsworth (1770-1850, British Poet)

GENIUS

1 Towering genius disdains a beaten path.
Abraham Lincoln (1809-1865, Sixteenth President of the USA)

2 We are all geniuses up to the age of ten.
Aldous Huxley (1894-1963, British Author)

3 Men give me credit for some genius. All the genius I have is this. When I have a subject in mind. I study it profoundly. Day and night it is before me. My mind becomes pervaded with it... the effort which I have made is what people are pleased to call the fruit of genius. It is the fruit of labor and thought.
Alexander Hamilton (1757-1804, American Statesman)

4 There is no great genius without a mixture of madness.
Aristotle (384-322 BC, Greek Philosopher)

5 The principal mark of genius is not perfection but originality, the opening of new frontiers.
Arthur Koestler (1905-1983, Hungarian Born British Writer)

6 Great minds are related to the brief span of time during which they live as great buildings are to a little square in which they stand: you cannot see them in all their magnitude because you are standing too close to them.
Arthur Schopenhauer (1788-1860, German Philosopher)

7 Nothing is so envied as genius, nothing so hopeless of attainment by labor alone. Though labor always accompanies the greatest genius, without the intellectual gift labor alone will do little.
B. R. Hayden (1913-1980, American Poet)

8 Patience is a necessary ingredient of genius.
Benjamin Disraeli (1804-1881, British Statesman, Prime Minister)

9 Genius, when young, is divine.
Benjamin Disraeli (1804-1881, British Statesman, Prime Minister)

10 Genius without education is like silver in the mine.
Benjamin Franklin (1706-1790, American Scientist, Publisher, Diplomat)

11 Hide not your talents. They for use were made. What's a sundial in the shade.
Benjamin Franklin (1706-1790, American Scientist, Publisher, Diplomat)

12 Talent is a flame. Genius is a fire.
Bern Williams

13 I'm not a genius. I'm just a tremendous bundle of experience.
Buckminster Fuller (American Engineer, Inventor, Designer, Architect "Geodesic Dome")

14 Genius is the ability to reduce the complicated to the simple.
C. W. Ceran

15 Sometimes, indeed, there is such a discrepancy between the genius and his human qualities that one has to ask oneself whether a little less talent might not have been better.
Carl Jung (1875-1961, Swiss Psychiatrist)

16 Passion holds up the bottom of the universe and genius paints up its roof.
Chao Chang

17 Genius is no more than childhood recaptured at will, childhood equipped now with man's physical means to express itself, and with the analytical mind that enables it to bring order into the sum of experience, involuntarily amassed.
Charles Baudelaire (1821-1867, French Poet)

18 The drafts which true genius draws upon posterity, although they may not always be honored so soon as they are due, are sure to be paid with compound interest in the end.
Charles Caleb Colton (1780-1832, British Sportsman Writer)

19 Genius is independent of situation.
Charles Churchill (1731-1764, British Poet, Satirist)

20 Genius makes its observations in short-hand; talent writes them out at length.
Christian Nevell Bovee (1820-1904, American Author, Lawyer)

21 The richest genius, like the most fertile soil, when uncultivated, shoots up into the rankest weeds.
David Hume (1711-1776, Scottish Philosopher, Historian)

22 Genius is present in every age, but the men carrying it within them remain benumbed unless extraordinary events occur to heat up and melt the mass so that it flows forth.
Denis Diderot (1713-1784, French Philosopher)

23 Everybody hates a prodigy, detests an old head on young shoulders.
Desiderius Erasmus (1466-1536, Dutch Humanist)

24 There is no genius in life like the genius of energy and industry.
Don G. Mitchell

25 Genius, like truth, has a shabby and neglected mien.
Edward Dahlberg (1900-1977, American Author, Critic)

26 Every man who observes vigilantly and resolves steadfastly grows unconsciously into genius.
Edward G. Bulwer-Lytton (1803-1873, British Novelist, Poet)

27 Genius is the ability to act rightly without precedent -- the power to do the right thing the first time.
Elbert Hubbard (1859-1915, American Author, Publisher)

28 What is genius but the power of expressing a new individuality?
Elizabeth Barrett Browning (1806-1861, British Poet)

29 Since when was genius found respectable?
Elizabeth Barrett Browning (1806-1861, British Poet)

30 What makes men of genius, or rather, what they make, is not new ideas, it is that idea -- possessing them -- that what has been said has still not been said enough.
EugFne Delacroix (1798-1863, French Artist)

31 A man of genius has a right to any mode of expression.
Ezra Pound (1885-1972, American Poet, Critic)

32 Talent is a faculty that is highly developed, but genius commands all the faculties.
Francis Herbert Hedge (1846-1924, British Philosopher)

33 Genius is, to be sure, not a matter of arbitrariness, but rather of freedom, just as wit, love, and faith, which once shall become arts and disciplines. We should demand genius from everybody, without, however, expecting it.
Friedrich Schlegel (1772-1829, German Philosopher, Critic, Writer)

34 What I do not like about our definitions of genius is that there is in them nothing of the day of judgment, nothing of resounding through eternity and nothing of the footsteps of the Almighty.
Georg C. Lichtenberg (1742-1799, German Physicist, Satirist)

35 Everyone is a genius at least once a year; a real genius has his original ideas closer together.
Georg C. Lichtenberg (1742-1799, German Physicist, Satirist)

36 Genius at first is little more than a great capacity for receiving discipline.
George Eliot (1819-1880, British Novelist)

37 The real people of genius were resolute workers not idle dreamers.
George Henry Lewes (1817-1878, British Writer)

38 Genius is nothing but a great capacity for patience.
Georges-Louis Leclerc Buffon (1707-1788, French Naturalist)

39 Genius is essentially creative; it bears the stamp of the individual who possesses it.
Germaine De Stael (1766-1817, French-Swiss Novelist)

40 It takes a lot of time to be a genius. You have to sit around so much doing nothing, really doing nothing.
Gertrude Stein (1874-1946, American Author)

41 The function of genius is not to give new answers, but to pose new questions which time and mediocrity can resolve.
H. R. Trevor-Roper

42 Genius without religion is only a lamp on the outer gate of a palace; it may serve to cast a gleam of light on those that are without, while the inhabitant sits in darkness.
Hannah More (1745-1833, British Writer, Reformer, Philanthropist)

43 Great genius takes shape by contact with another great genius, but, less by assimilation than by fiction.
Heinrich Heine (1797-1856, German Poet, Journalist)

44 To do easily what is difficult for others is the mark of talent. To do what is impossible for talent is the mark of genius.
Henri Frederic Amiel (1821-1881, Swiss Philosopher, Poet, Critic)

45 Doing easily what others find difficult is talent; doing what is impossible for talent is genius.
Henri Frederic Amiel (1821-1881, Swiss Philosopher, Poet, Critic)

46 All the means of action -- the shapeless masses -- the materials -- lie everywhere about us. What we need is the celestial fire to change the flint into the transparent crystal, bright and clear. That fire is genius."
Henry Wadsworth Longfellow (1819-1892, American Poet)

47 Genius unexerted is no more genius than a bushel of acorns is a forest of oaks.
Henry Ward Beecher (1813-1887, American Preacher, Orator, Writer)

48 Fortune has rarely condescended to be the companion of genius.
Isaac D'Israeli (1766-1848, British Critic, Historian)

49 What Romantic terminology called genius or talent or inspiration is nothing other than finding the right road empirically, following one's nose, taking shortcuts.
Italo Calvino (1923-1985, Cuban Writer, Essayist, Journalist)

50 Geniuses themselves don't talk about the gift of genius, they just talk about hard work and long hours.
J. C. (James Cash) Penney (1875-1971, American Retailer, Philanthropist, Founder JC Penny's)

51 Saying that a great genius is mad, while at the same time recognizing his artistic worth, is like saying that he had rheumatism or suffered from diabetes. Madness, in fact, is a medical term that can claim no more notice from the objective critic than he grants the charge of heresy raised by the theologian, or the charge of immorality raised by the police.
James Joyce (1882-1941, Irish Author)

52 It is the privilege of genius that life never grows common place, as it does for the rest of us.
James Russell Lowell (1819-1891, American Poet, Critic, Editor)

53 Genius is childhood recaptured.
Jean Baudrillard (French Postmodern Philosopher, Writer)

54 A genius is one who can do anything except make a living.
Joey Lauren Adams (Born 1971, American Actress)

55 The lamp of genius burns quicker than the lamp of life.
Johann Friedrich Von Schiller (1759-1805, German Dramatist, Poet, Historian)

56 Genius always gives its best at first; prudence, at last.
Johann Kaspar Lavater (1741-1801, Swiss Theologian, Mystic)

57 Who in the same given time can produce more than others has vigor; who can produce more and better, has talents; who can produce what none else can, has genius.
Johann Kaspar Lavater (1741-1801, Swiss Theologian, Mystic)

58 The greatest genius will never be worth much if he pretends to draw exclusively from his own resources.
Johann Wolfgang Von Goethe (1749-1832, German Poet, Dramatist, Novelist)

59 The first and last thing required of genius is, love of the truth.
Johann Wolfgang Von Goethe (1749-1832, German Poet, Dramatist, Novelist)

60 Genius is sorrow's child.
John Adams (1735-1826, Second President of the USA)

61 Time, place, and action may with pains be wrought, but genius must be born; and never can be taught.
John Dryden (1631-1700, British Poet, Dramatist, Critic)

62 Genius must be born, and never can be taught.
John Dryden (1631-1700, British Poet, Dramatist, Critic)

63 Great wits are sure to madness near allied, and thin partitions do their bounds divide.
John Dryden (1631-1700, British Poet, Dramatist, Critic)

64 When a true genius appears in this world, you may know him by this sign, that the dunces are all in confederacy against him.
Jonathan Swift (1667-1745, Anglo-Irish Satirist)

65 Better beware of notions like genius and inspiration; they are a sort of magic wand and should be used sparingly by anybody who wants to see things clearly.
Jose Ortega Y Gasset (1883-1955, Spanish Essayist, Philosopher)

66 Nature is the master of talents; genius is the master of nature.
Josiah Gilbert Holland (1819-1881, American Author)

67 To see things in the seed is genius.
Lao-Tzu (600 BC, Chinese Philosopher, Founder of Taoism, Author of the "Tao Te Ching")

68 Men of lofty genius when they are doing the least work are most active.
Leonardo Da Vinci (1452-1519, Italian Inventor, Architect, Painter, Scientist, Sculptor)

69 I really cannot know whether I am or am not the Genius you are pleased to call me, but I am very willing to put up with the mistake, if it be one. It is a title dearly enough bought by most men, to render it endurable, even when not quite clearly made out, which it never can be till the Posterity, whose decisions are merely dreams to ourselves, has sanctioned or denied it, while it can touch us no further.
Lord Byron (1788-1824, British Poet)

70 Genius is entitled to respect only when it promotes the peace and improves the happiness of mankind.
Lord Essex

71 We know that the nature of genius is to provide idiots with ideas twenty years later.
Louis Aragon (1897-1982, French Poet)

72 It takes people a long time to learn the difference between talent and genius, especially ambitious young men and women.
Louisa May Alcott (1832-1888, American Author)

73 The eye of genius has always a plaintive expression, and its natural language is pathos.
Lydia M. Child (1802-1880, American Abolitionist, Writer, Editor)

74 One of the satisfactions of a genius is his will-power and obstinacy.
Man Ray (1890-1976, American Photographer)

75 It is not because the touch of genius has roused genius to production, but because the admiration of genius has made talent ambitious, that the harvest is still so abundant.
Margaret Fuller (1810-1850, American Writer, Lecturer)

76 There are big men, men of intellect, intellectual men, men of talent and men of action; but the great man is difficult to find, and it needs --apart from discernment --a certain greatness to find him.
Margot Asquith (1864-1945, British Socialite)

77 Genius is the gold in the mine; talent is the miner who works and brings it out.
Marguerite Gardiner Blessington (1789-1849, Irish Writer and Socialite)

78 Thousands of geniuses live and die undiscovered -- either by themselves or by others.
Mark Twain (1835-1910, American Humorist, Writer)

79 The divine egoism hat is genius.
Mary Webb (1881-1927, British Novelist)

80 Genius is eternal patience.
Michelangelo (1474-1564, Italian Renaissance Painter, Sculptor)

81 The world is always ready to receive talent with open arms. Very often it does not know what to do with genius.
Oliver Wendell Holmes (1809-1894, American Author, Wit, Poet)

82 Unpretending mediocrity is good, and genius is glorious; but a weak flavor of genius in an essentially common person is detestable. It spoils the grand neutrality of a commonplace character, as the rinsings of an unwashed wine-glass spoil a draught of fair water.
Oliver Wendell Holmes (1809-1894, American Author, Wit, Poet)

83 Everybody denies I am a genius --but nobody ever called me one!
Orson Welles (1915-1985, American Film Maker)

84 Genius lasts longer than Beauty. That accounts for the fact that we all take such pains to over- educate ourselves.
Oscar Wilde (1856-1900, British Author, Wit)

85 I have nothing to declare except my genius.
Oscar Wilde (1856-1900, British Author, Wit)

86 I put all my genius into my life; I put only my talent into my works.
Oscar Wilde (1856-1900, British Author, Wit)

87 The public is wonderfully tolerant. It forgives everything except genius.
Oscar Wilde (1856-1900, British Author, Wit)

88 The genius of Einstein leads to Hiroshima.
Pablo Picasso (1881-1973, Spanish Artist)

89 It is personality with a penny's worth of talent. Error which chances to rise above the commonplace.
Pablo Picasso (1881-1973, Spanish Artist)

90 Genius sits in a glass house -- but in an unbreakable one --conceiving ideas. After giving birth, it falls into madness. Stretches out its hand through the window toward the first person happening by. The demon's claw rips, the iron fist grips. Before, you were a model, mocks the ironic voice between serrated teeth, for me, you are raw material to work on. I throw you against the glass wall, so that you remain stuck there, projected and stuck. (Then come the lovers of art and contemplate the bleeding work from outside. Then come the photographers. "New art," it says in the newspaper the following day. The learned journals give it a name that ends in "ism.")
Paul Klee (1879-1940, Swiss Artist)

91 All of us, you, your children, your neighbors and their children are everyday geniuses, even though the fact is unnoticed and unremembered by everyone. That's probably because school hasn't encouraged us to notice what's hidden inside us waiting for the right environment to express itself.
Peter Kline (American Peak Performance Expert)

92 True genius sees with the eyes of a child and thinks with the brain of a genius.
Puzant Kevork Thomajan

93 To believe your own thought, to believe that what is true for you in your private heart is true for all men -- that is genius.
Ralph Waldo Emerson (1803-1882, American Poet, Essayist)

94 Only an inventor knows how to borrow, and every man is or should be an inventor.
Ralph Waldo Emerson (1803-1882, American Poet, Essayist)

95 The hearing ear is always found close to the speaking tongue; and no genius can long or often utter anything which is not invited and gladly entertained by men around him.
Ralph Waldo Emerson (1803-1882, American Poet, Essayist)

96 When Nature has work to be done, she creates a genius to do it.
Ralph Waldo Emerson (1803-1882, American Poet, Essayist)

97 The greatest genius is the most indebted person.
Ralph Waldo Emerson (1803-1882, American Poet, Essayist)

98 Coffee is good for talent, but genius wants prayer.
Ralph Waldo Emerson (1803-1882, American Poet, Essayist)

99 Accept your genius and say what you think.
Ralph Waldo Emerson (1803-1882, American Poet, Essayist)

100 A man of genius is privileged only as far as he is genius. His dullness is as insupportable as any other dullness.
Ralph Waldo Emerson (1803-1882, American Poet, Essayist)

101 In every work of genius we recognize our own rejected thoughts; they come back to us with a certain alienated majesty.
Ralph Waldo Emerson (1803-1882, American Poet, Essayist)

102 Every person of genius is considerably helped by being dead.
Robert S. Lund

103 Few people can see genius in someone who has offended them.
Robertson Davies (1913-, Canadian Novelist, Journalist)

104 A genius can never expect to have a good time anywhere, if he is a genuine article, but America is about the last place in which life will be endurable at all for an inspired writer of any kind.
Samuel Butler (1612-1680, British Poet, Satirist)

105 As it must not, so genius cannot be lawless; for it is even that constitutes its genius -- the power of acting creatively under laws of its own origination.
Samuel Taylor Coleridge (1772-1834, British Poet, Critic, Philosopher)

106 One is not born a genius, one becomes a genius.
Simone De Beauvoir (1908-1986, French Novelist, Essayist)

107 Real genius is nothing else but the supernatural virtue of humility in the domain of thought.
Simone Weil (1910-1943, French Philosopher, Mystic)

108 Every man is a potential genius until he does something.
Sir Herbert Beerbohm Tree (1853-1917, British actor-manager)

109 Men of genius are not quick judges of character. Deep thinking and high imagining blunt that trivial instinct by which you and I size people up.
Sir Max Beerbohm (1872-1956, British Actor)

110 Genius is one percent inspiration and ninety-nine percent perspiration.
Thomas A. Edison (1847-1931, American Inventor, Entrepreneur, Founder of GE)

111 His genius he was quite content in one brief sentence to define; Of inspiration one percent, of perspiration, ninety nine.
Thomas A. Edison (1847-1931, American Inventor, Entrepreneur, Founder of GE)

112 Genius is an infinite capacity for taking pains.
Thomas Carlyle (1795-1881, Scottish Philosopher, Author)

113 Genius is a promontory jutting out into the infinite.
Victor Hugo (1802-1885, French Poet, Dramatist, Novelist)

114 Masterpieces are not single and solitary births; they are the outcome of many years of thinking in common, of thinking by the body of the people, so that the experience of the mass is behind the single voice.
Virginia Woolf (1882-1941, British Novelist, Essayist)

115 Genius is an African who dreams up snow.
Vladimir Nabokov (1899-1977, Russian-born American Novelist, Poet)

116 Geniuses are the luckiest of mortals because what they must do is the same as what they most want to do.
W. H. Auden (1907-1973, Anglo-American Poet)

117 Rising genius always shoots out its rays from among the clouds, but these will gradually roll away and disappear as it ascends to its steady luster.
Washington Irving (1783-1859, American Author)

118 When human power becomes so great and original that we can account for it only as a kind of divine imagination, we call it genius.
William Crashaw

119 The definition of genius is that it acts unconsciously; and those who have produced immortal works, have done so without knowing how or why. The greatest power operates unseen.
William Hazlitt (1778-1830, British Essayist)

120 Genius... means little more than the faculty of perceiving in an unhabitual way.
William James (1842-1910, American Psychologist, Professor, Author)

121 True genius resides in the capacity for evaluation of uncertain, hazardous, and conflicting information.
Winston Churchill (1874-1965, British Statesman, Prime Minister)

GENTLEMEN

1 Gentlemen prefer bonds.
Andrew William Mellon (1855-1937, American Financier, Philanthropist, Statesman)

2 It is almost the definition of a gentleman to say that he is one who never inflicts pain.
Cardinal J. Newman (1801-1890, British Preacher)

3 I do not know the American gentleman, God forgive me for putting two such words together.
Charles Dickens (1812-1870, British Novelist)

4 The word of a gentleman is as good as his bond; and sometimes better.
Charles Dickens (1812-1870, British Novelist)

5 Women do not find it difficult nowadays to behave like men, but they often find it extremely difficult to behave like gentlemen.
Compton Mackenzie (1883-1972, British Writer)

6 I am partial to ladies if they are nice. I suppose it is my nature. I am not quite a gentleman but you would hardly notice it.
Daisy Ashford (American Author)

7 Believe me, there exists no such dilemma as that in which a gentleman is placed when he is forced to reply to a blackguard.
Edgar Allan Poe (1809-1845, American Poet, Critic, short-story Writer)

8 Being a gentleman is the number one priority, the chief question integral to our national life.
Edward Fox

9 Education begins a gentleman, conversation completes him.
English Proverb

10 A gentleman is any man who wouldn't hit a woman with his hat on.
Fred A. Allen (1894-1957, American Radio Comic)

11 A gentleman will not insult me, and no man not a gentleman can insult me.
Frederick Douglass (1817-1895, American Abolitionist, Journalist)

12 A gentlemen is one who never strikes a woman without provocation.
H. L. Mencken (1880-1956, American Editor, Author, Critic, Humorist)

13 He was the product of an English public school and university. He was, moreover, a modern product of those seats of athletic exercise. He had little education and highly developed muscles -- that is to say, he was no scholar, but essentially a gentleman.
H. Seton Merriman

14 Anyone can be heroic from time to time, but a gentleman is something you have to be all the time.
Luigi Pirandello (1867-1936, Italian Author, Playwright)

15 For everybody knows that it requires very little to satisfy the gentlemen, if a woman will only give her mind to it.
Margaret Oliphant (1828-1897, British Novelist, Historian)

16 Gentleman. A man who buys two of the same morning paper from the doorman of his favorite nightclub when he leaves with his girl.
Marlene Dietrich (1904-1992, German-born American Film Actor)

17 A true gentleman is one who is never unintentionally rude.
Oscar Wilde (1856-1900, British Author, Wit)

18 Repose and cheerfulness are the badge of the gentleman -- repose in energy.
Ralph Waldo Emerson (1803-1882, American Poet, Essayist)

19 He is every other inch a gentleman.
Rebecca West (1892-1983, British Author)

20 The final test of a gentleman is his respect for those who can be of no possible service to him.
William Lyon Phelps

GENTLENESS

1 There is nothing stronger in the world than gentleness.
Han Suyin (1917-, Chinese Novelist and Doctor)

GETTING AHEAD

1 It's them as take advantage that get advantage I this world.
George Eliot (1819-1880, British Novelist)

2 The path of social advancement is, and must be, strewn with broken friendships.
H.G. Wells (1866-1946, British-born American Author)

3 There are only two ways of getting on in the world: by one's own industry, or by the stupidity of others.
Jean De La Bruyere (1645-1696, French Writer)

4 You have to be a bastard to make it, and that's a fact. And the Beatles are the biggest bastards on earth.
John Lennon (1940-1980, British Rock Musician)

5 No man rises so high as he knows not whither he goes.
Oliver Cromwell (1599-1658, Parliamentarian General, Lord Protector of England)

6 To get it right, be born with luck or else make it. Never give up. Get the knack of getting people to help you and also pitch in yourself. A little money helps, but what really gets it right is to never -- I repeat -- never under any conditions face the facts.
Ruth Gordon

7 It is commonly supposed that the art of pleasing is a wonderful aid in the pursuit of fortune; but the art of being bored is infinitely more successful.
Sebastien-Roch Nicolas De Chamfort (1741-1794, French Writer, Journalist, Playwright)

GIFTS

1 A gift blinds the wise and perverts the words of the righteous.
Bible (Sacred Scriptures of Christians and Judaism)

2 Presents, I often say, endear absents.
Charles Lamb (1775-1834, British Essayist, Critic)

3 What we share with another ceases to be our own.
Edgar Quinet (1803-1875, French Poet, Historian, Politician)

4 He that parts with his property before his death prepares himself for much suffering.
French Proverb

5 Take all that is given whether wealth, love or language, nothing comes by mistake and with good digestion all can be turned to health.
George Herbert (1593-1632, British Metaphysical Poet)

6 Money is good for bribing yourself through the inconveniences of life.
Gottfried Reinhardt

7 Nothing is so strongly fortified that it cannot be taken by money.
Marcus T. Cicero (106-43 BC, Great Roman Orator, Politician)

8 What gift has providence bestowed on man that is so dear to him as his children?
Marcus T. Cicero (106-43 BC, Great Roman Orator, Politician)

9 Gifts, believe me, captivate both men and Gods, Jupiter himself was won over and appeased by gifts.
Ovid (43 BC-18 AD, Roman Poet)

10 It takes all the fun out of a bracelet if you have to buy it yourself.
Peggy Joyce

11 Gifts dissolve rocks.
Proverb

12 Gifts make their way through stone walls.
Proverb

13 The only gift is a portion of thyself.
Ralph Waldo Emerson (1803-1882, American Poet, Essayist)

14 Men are more often bribed by their loyalties and ambitions than by money.
Robert H. Jackson (1892-1954, American Supreme Court Justice)

15 To receive gifts is to lose freedom.
Sandi

16 A gift consists not in what is done or given, but in the intention of the giver or doer.
Seneca (4 BC-65 AD, Spanish-born Roman Statesman, philosopher)

17 Every day is a gift- even if it sucks.
Sherry Hochman

18 One rose says more than the dozen
Wendy Craig

19 In suggesting gifts: Money is appropriate, and one size fits all.
William Randolph Hearst (1863-1951, American Newspaper Publisher)

20 Rich gifts wax poor when givers prove unkind.
William Shakespeare (1564-1616, British Poet, Playwright, Actor)

GIRLS

1 It is easy to see that, even in the freedom of early youth, an American girl never quite loses control of herself; she enjoys all permitted pleasures without losing her head about any of them, and her reason never lets the reins go, though it may often seem to let them flap.
Alexis De Tocqueville (1805-1859, French Social Philosopher)

2 We say that a girl with her doll anticipates the mother. It is more true, perhaps, that most mothers are still but children with playthings.
Francis H. Bradley (1846-1924, British Philosopher)

3 A toddling little girl is a center of common feeling which makes the most dissimilar people understand each other.
George Eliot (1819-1880, British Novelist)

4 What we ought to see in the agonies of puberty is the result of the conditioning that maims the female personality in creating the feminine.
Germaine Greer (1939-, Australian Feminist Writer)

5 You may chisel a boy into shape, as you would a rock, or hammer him into it, if he be of a better kind, as you would a piece of bronze. But you cannot hammer a girl into anything. She grows as a flower does.
John Ruskin (1819-1900, British Critic, Social Theorist)

6 Girls are so queer you never know what they mean. They say No when they mean Yes, and drive a man out of his wits for the fun of it.
Louisa May Alcott (1832-1888, American Author)

7 Even from their infancy we frame them to the sports of love: their instruction, behavior, attire, grace, learning and all their words azimuth only at love, respects only affection. Their nurses and their keepers imprint no other thing in them.
Michel Eyquem De Montaigne (1533-1592, French Philosopher, Essayist)

8 Girls like to be played with, and rumpled a little too, sometimes.
Oliver Goldsmith (1728-1774, Anglo-Irish Author, Poet, Playwright)

9 The knowingness of little girls hidden underneath their curls.
Phyllis Mcginley (1905-1978, American Poet, Author)

10 The restlessness that comes upon girls upon summer evenings results in lasting trouble unless it is speedily controlled. The right kind of man does not look for a wife on the streets, and the right kind of girl waits till the man comes to her home for her.
Sedalia Times

11 There is no need to waste pity on young girls who are having their moments of disillusionment, for in another moment they will recover their illusion.
Sidonie Gabrielle Colette (1873-1954, French Author)

12 We know less about the sexual life of little girls than of boys. But we need not feel ashamed of this distinction; after all, the sexual life of adult women is a "dark continent" for psychology.
Sigmund Freud (1856-1939, Austrian Physician - Founder of Psychoanalysis)

13 Between the age limits of nine and fourteen there occur maidens who, to certain bewitched travelers, twice or many times older than they, reveal their true nature which is not human, but nymphic (that is, demoniac); and these chosen creatures I propose to designate as "nymphets."
Vladimir Nabokov (1899-1977, Russian-born American Novelist, Poet)

GIVING

1 Before he left, Aunt William pressed a sovereign into his hand guiltily, as if it were conscience money. He, on his side, took it as though it were a doctor's fee, and both ignored the transaction.
Ada Leverson

2 It is normal to give away a little of one's life in order not to lose it all.
Albert Camus (1913-1960, French Existential Writer)

3 All that this world knows of living lies in giving -- and more giving; He that keeps, be sure he loses -Friendship grows by what it uses.
Alexander Maclaren (1826-1910, British Preacher)

4 Complete possession is proved only by giving. All you are unable to give possesses you.
Andre Gide (1869-1951, French Author)

5   To give without any reward, or any notice, has a special quality of its own.
Anne Morrow Lindbergh (1906-, American Author)

6   We are rich only through what we give; and poor only through we refuse and keep.
Anne Sophie Swetchine (1782-1857, Russian Author)

7   Plant a kernel of wheat and you reap a pint; plant a pint and you reap a bushel. Always the law works to give you back more than you give.
Anthony Norvell

8   It is not what we get. But who we become, what we contribute... that gives meaning to our lives.
Anthony Robbins (1960-, American Author, Speaker, Peak Performance Expert / Consultant)

9   When you give yourself, you receive more than you give.
Antoine De Saint-Exupery (1900-1944, French Aviator, Writer)

10   For true love is inexhaustible; the more you give, the more you have. And if you go to draw at the true fountainhead, the more water you draw, the more abundant is its flow.
Antoine De Saint-Exupery (1900-1944, French Aviator, Writer)

11   From what we get, we can make a living; what we give, however, makes a life.
Arthur Ashe (1943-1993, African-American Tennis Player)

12   What you keep to yourself you lose, what you give away, you keep forever.
Axel Munthe

13   No matter what age you are, or what your circumstances might be, you are special, and you still have something unique to offer. Your life, because of who you are, has meaning.
Barbara De Angelis (American Expert on Relationship & Love, Author)

14   Blessed are those who give without remembering. And blessed are those who take without forgetting.
Bernard Meltzer (1914-, American Law Professor)

15   We may give without loving, but we cannot love without giving
Bernard Meltzer (1914-, American Law Professor)

16   It is more blessed to give than to receive. [Acts 20:35]
Bible (Sacred Scriptures of Christians and Judaism)

17   Let each one do just as he has purposed in his heart; not grudgingly or under compulsion; for God loves a cheerful giver. [2 Corinthians 9:7]
Bible (Sacred Scriptures of Christians and Judaism)

18   Give and it shall be given unto you: good measure, pressed down, and shaken together, and running over... [Luke 6:38]
Bible (Sacred Scriptures of Christians and Judaism)

19   Give, and it shall be given to you. For whatever measure you deal out to others, it will be dealt to you in return.
Bible (Sacred Scriptures of Christians and Judaism)

20   One man gives freely, yet grows all the richer; another withholds what he should give, and only suffers want. [Proverbs 11-24]
Bible (Sacred Scriptures of Christians and Judaism)

21   The Liberal soul shall be made fat: and he that watereth shall be watered also himself. [Proverbs 11.25]
Bible (Sacred Scriptures of Christians and Judaism)

22   God has given us two hands, one to receive with and the other to give with.
Billy Graham (1918-, American Evangelist)

23   To get, give.
Bob Roth

24   The more credit you give away, the more will come back to you. The more you help others, the more they will want to help you.
Brian Tracy (American Trainer, Speaker, Author, Businessman)

25   Nothing that you have not given away will ever be really yours.
C. S. Lewis (1898-1963, British Academic, Writer, Christian Apologist)

26   I do not believe one can settle how much we ought to give. I am afraid the only safe rule is to give more than we can spare.
C. S. Lewis (1898-1963, British Academic, Writer, Christian Apologist)

27   Giving is true having.
Charles Haddon Spurgeon (1834-1892, British Baptist Preacher)

28   Sow much, reap much; sow little, reap little.
Chinese Proverb

29   Giving half answers won't make the conversation half as long.
Dave Johnson

30   Why is it no one ever sent me yet one perfect limousine, do you suppose? Ah no, it's always just my luck to get one perfect rose.
Dorothy Parker (1893-1967, American Humorous Writer)

31   Any person who contributes to prosperity must prosper in turn.
Earl Nightingale (1921-1989, American Radio Announcer, Author, Motivator, Speaker)

32   There are two ways of spreading light: to be the candle or the mirror that reflects it.
Edith Wharton (1862-1937, American Author)

33   Do unto the other feller the way he'd like to do unto you, and do it fast.
Edward Noyes Westcott (1847-1898, American Author)

34   Men are rich only as they give. He who gives great service gets great rewards.
Elbert Hubbard (1859-1915, American Author, Publisher)

35 The human contribution is the essential ingredient. It is only in the giving of oneself to others that we truly live.
Ethel Percy Andrus (American Educator, Founder of the National Retired Teachers)

36 Getters don't get -- givers get.
Eugene Benge

37 A handful of pine-seed will cover mountains with the green majesty of forests. I too will set my face to the wind and throw my handful of seed on high.
Fiona Macleod

38 In helping others, we shall help ourselves, for whatever good we give out completes the circle and comes back to us.
Flora Edwards

39 Giving opens the way for receiving.
Florence Scovel Shinn (American Artist, Metaphysics Teacher, Author)

40 The test of our progress is not whether we add more to the abundance of those who have much; it is whether we provide enough for those who have too little.
Franklin D. Roosevelt (1882-1945, Thirty-second President of the USA)

41 The big print giveth, and the fine print taketh away.
Fulton John Sheen (1895-1979, American Roman Catholic Clergyman, Broadcaster)

42 Do not do unto others as you would that they should do unto you. Their tastes may not be the same.
George Bernard Shaw (1856-1950, Irish-born British Dramatist)

43 One must be poor to know the luxury of giving.
George Eliot (1819-1880, British Novelist)

44 In Giving, a man receives more than he gives; and the more is in proportion to the worth of the thing given.
George Mcdonald

45 To give is to receive...
Gerald G. Jampolsky (American Psychiatrist, Lecturer, Author)

46 The more we give of anything, the more we shall get back.
Grace Speare

47 When people grow gradually rich their requirements and standard of living expand in proportion, while their present-giving instincts often remain in the undeveloped condition of their earlier days. Something showy and not-too-expensive in a shop is their only conception of the ideal gift.
Hector Hugh Munro (1870-1916, British Novelist, Writer)

48 It is by teaching that we teach ourselves, by relating that we observe, by affirming that we examine, by showing that we look, by writing that we think, by pumping that we draw water into the well.
Henri Frederic Amiel (1821-1881, Swiss Philosopher, Poet, Critic)

49 The man who will use his skill and constructive imagination to see how much he can give for a dollar, instead of how little he can give for a dollar, is bound to succeed.
Henry Ford (1863-1947, American Industrialist, Founder of Ford Motor Company)

50 Look around for a place to sow a few seeds.
Henry Van Dyke (1852-1933, American Protestant Clergyman, Poet and Writer)

51 There never was a person who did anything worth doing, who did not receive more than he gave.
Henry Ward Beecher (1813-1887, American Preacher, Orator, Writer)

52 The nine-tenths prove man's love, but the one-tenth tests man's legal obedience.
Herschel Hobbs

53 When you're nice to people, they want to be nice back to you.
Jack Canfield (American Motivational Speaker, Author, Trainer)

54 It is rare indeed that people give. Most people guard and keep; they suppose that it is they themselves and what they identify with themselves that they are guarding and keeping, whereas what they are actually guarding and keeping is their system of reality and what they assume themselves to be.
James Baldwin (1924-1987, American Author)

55 While you have a thing it can be taken from you... but when you give it, you have given it. No robber can take it from you. It is yours then for ever when you have given it. It will be yours always. That is to give.
James Joyce (1882-1941, Irish Author)

56 Always think in terms of what the other person wants.
James Van Fleet (American Author, Lecturer)

57 We read on the foreheads of those who are surrounded by a foolish luxury, that fortune sells what she is thought to give.
Jean De La Fontaine (1621-1695, French Poet)

58 A check or credit card, a Gucci bag strap, anything of value will do. Give as you live.
Jesse Jackson (1941-, American Clergyman, Civil Rights Leader)

59 Giving is better than receiving because giving starts the receiving process.
Jim Rohn (American Businessman, Author, Speaker, Philosopher)

60 He who bestows his goods upon the poor shall have as much again, and ten times more.
John Bunyan (1628-1688, British Author)

61 For of those to whom much is given, much is required.
John F. Kennedy (1917-1963, Thirty-fifth President of the USA)

62 Give little love to a child, and you get a great deal back.
John Ruskin (1819-1900, British Critic, Social Theorist)

63 I have somewhere met with the epitaph on a charitable man which has pleased me very much. I cannot recollect the words, but here is the sense of it: "What I spent I lost; what I possessed is left to others; what I gave away remains with me."
Joseph Addison (1672-1719, British Essayist, Poet, Statesman)

64 You give but little when you give of your possessions. It is when you give of yourself that you truly give.
Kahlil Gibran (1883-1931, Lebanese Poet, Novelist)

65 He who obtains has little. He who scatters has much.
Lao-Tzu (600 BC, Chinese Philosopher, Founder of Taoism, Author of the "Tao Te Ching")

66 If you would take, you must first give, this is the beginning of intelligence.
Lao-Tzu (600 BC, Chinese Philosopher, Founder of Taoism, Author of the "Tao Te Ching")

67 I do detest everything which is not perfectly mutual.
Lord Byron (1788-1824, British Poet)

68 All who joy would win must share it. Happiness was born a Twin.
Lord Byron (1788-1824, British Poet)

69 The more sympathy you give, the less you need.
Malcolm S. Forbes (1919-1990, American Publisher, Businessman)

70 If I choose to bless another person, I will always end up feeling more blessed.
Marianne Williamson (1952-, American Author, Lecturer on Spirituality)

71 Sharing is sometimes more demanding than giving.
Mary Bateson (American Author)

72 There is only one real deprivation... and that is not to be able to give one's gifts to those one loves most.
May Sarton (1912-, American Poet, Novelist)

73 It's not how much we give but how much love we put into giving.
Mother Teresa (1910-1997, Albanian-born Roman Catholic Missionary)

74 You give before you get.
Napoleon Hill (1883-1970, American Speaker, Motivational Writer, "Think and Grow Rich")

75 There would be no advantage to be gained by sowing a field of wheat if the harvest did not return more than was sown.
Napoleon Hill (1883-1970, American Speaker, Motivational Writer, "Think and Grow Rich")

76 we make a living by what we get, but we make a life by what we give.
Norman Macewan

77 It is like the seed put in the soil -- the more one sows, the greater the harvest.
Orison Swett Marden (1850-1924, American Author, Founder of Success Magazine)

78 We must give more in order to get more, It is the generous giving of ourselves that produce the generous harvest.
Orison Swett Marden (1850-1924, American Author, Founder of Success Magazine)

79 Giving presents is a talent; to know what a person wants, to know when and how to get it, to give it lovingly and well. Unless a character possesses this talent there is no moment more annihilating to ease than that in which a present is received and given.
Pamela Glenconner

80 He who gives while he lives, get to know where it goes.
Percy Ross (American Columnist)

81 It is better to give than to lend, and it costs about the same.
Philip Gibbs

82 The manner of giving is worth more than the gift.
Pierre Corneille (1606-1684, French Dramatist)

83 The most satisfying thing in life is to have been able to give a large part of oneself to others.
Pierre Teilhard De Chardin (1881-1955, French Christian Mystic, Author)

84 A bit of fragrance always clings to the hand that gives you roses.
Proverb

85 Nature does not give to those who will not spend...
R.J. Baughan

86 EARN as much as you can. SAVE as much as you can. INVEST as much as you can. GIVE as much as you can.
Rev. John Wellesly (American Minister)

87 It is possible to give without loving, but it is impossible to love without giving.
Richard Braunstein

88 You have to sow before you can reap. You have to give before you can get.
Robert Collier (American Writer, Publisher)

89 You cannot hold on to anything good. You must be continually giving -- and getting. You cannot hold on to your seed. You must sow it -- and reap anew. You cannot hold on to riches. You must use them and get other riches in return.
Robert Collier (American Writer, Publisher)

90 The gifts that one receives for giving are so immeasurable that it is almost an injustice to accept them.
Rod Mckeun

91 You must give to get, You must sow the seed, before you can reap the harvest.
Scott Reed

92 There is no delight in owning anything unshared.
Seneca (4 BC-65 AD, Spanish-born Roman Statesman, philosopher)

93 We should give as we would receive, cheerfully, quickly, and without hesitation; for there is no grace in a benefit that sticks to the fingers.
Seneca (4 BC-65 AD, Spanish-born Roman Statesman, philosopher)

94 You only get to keep what you give away.
Sheldon Kopp (1929-, American Psychologist)

95 In the long run, we get no more than we have been willing to risk giving.
Sheldon Kopp (1929-, American Psychologist)

96 The trick is to realize that after giving your best, there's nothing more to give.
Sparky Anderson (American Baseball Manager)

97 For it is in giving that we receive.
St. Francis of Assisi (1181-1226, Italian Preacher, Founder of the Franciscan Orde)

98 He that bringeth a present findeth the door open.
Thomas Fuller (1608-1661, British Clergyman, Author)

99 Give a lot, expect a lot, and if you don't get it, prune.
Thomas J. Peters (1942-, American Management Consultant, Author, Trainer)

100 He that loveth, flieth, runneth, and rejoiceth. He is free, and cannot be held in. He giveth all for all, and hath all in all, because he resteth in one highest above all things, from whom all that is good flows and proceeds.
Thomas p Kempis (1379-1471, German Monk, Mystic, Religious Writer)

101 What we gave, we have; What we spent, we had; What we left, we lost.
Tryon Edwards (1809-1894, American Theologian)

102 I have always noticed that a man who gives the most for the money, gets the most business.
Vash Young

103 There is only one way to succeed in anything and that is to give everything. I do and I demand that my players do. Any man's finest hour is when he has worked his heart out in a good cause and lies exhausted on the field of battle... victorious.
Vince Lombardi (1913-1970, American Football Coach)

104 Trust not the horse, O Trojans. Be it what it may, I fear the Grecians even when they offer gifts.
Virgil (70-19 BC, Roman Poet)

105 When I give I give myself.
Walt Whitman (1819-1892, American Poet)

106 Gifts must affect the receiver to the point of shock.
Walter Benjamin (1982-1940, German Critic, Philosopher)

107 I wonder if it isn't just cowardice instead of generosity that makes us give tips.
Will Rogers (1879-1935, American Humorist, Actor)

108 What we are doing is satisfying the American public. That's our job. I always say we have to give most of the people what they want most of the time. That's what they expect from us.
William S. Paley (American Businessman, Chairman of CBS)

GLAMOUR

1 Glamour cannot exist without personal social envy being a common and widespread emotion.
John Berger (1926-, British Actor, Critic)

2 It was a blonde. A blonde to make a bishop kick a hole in a stained-glass window.
Raymond Chandler (1888-1959, American Author)

3 A blond in a red dress can do without introductions -- but not without a bodyguard.
Rona Jaffe

GLORY

1 Military glory --the attractive rainbow that rises in showers of blood.
Abraham Lincoln (1809-1865, Sixteenth President of the USA)

2 The glory of a nation and an age is always the work of a few great persons, and it disappears with them.
Baron Grimm

3 The glory of young men is their strength, and the beauty of old men is their gray head.
Bible (Sacred Scriptures of Christians and Judaism)

4 For glory gives herself only to those who have always dreamed of her.
Charles De Gaulle (1890-1970, French President during World War II)

5 Love of glory can only create a great hero; contempt of glory creates a great man.
Charles Maurice De Talleyrand (1754-1838, French Statesman)

6 Is it not passing brave to be a King and ride in triumph through Persepolis?
Christopher Marlowe (1564-1593, British Dramatist, Poet)

7 No statement about God is simply, literally true. God is far more than can be measured, described, defined in ordinary language, or pinned down to any particular happening.
David Jenkins (1925-, British Ecclesiastic, Bishop of Durham)

8 Glory is largely a theatrical concept. There is no striving for glory without a vivid awareness of an audience.
Eric Hoffer (1902-1983, American Author, Philosopher)

9 All glory comes from daring to begin.
Eugene F. Ware (American Lawyer, Poet)

10 Real glory springs from the silent conquest of ourselves.
Joseph P. Thompson

11 Glory is the shadow of virtue.
Latin Proverb

12 There is no greater glory than love, nor any great punishment than jealously.
Lope de Vega (1562-1635, Spanish Playwright)

13 There's no glory like those who save their country.
Lord Alfred Tennyson (1809-1892, British Poet)

14 Who tracks the steps of glory to the grave?
Lord Byron (1788-1824, British Poet)

15 The greater the difficulty, the greater the glory.
Marcus T. Cicero (106-43 BC, Great Roman Orator, Politician)

16 Glory comes too late, after one as been reduced to ashes.
Marcus Valerius Martial (40-104, Latin poet and epigrammatist)

17 Glory paid to our ashes comes too late.
Marcus Valerius Martial (40-104, Latin poet and epigrammatist)

18 Glory is fleeting, but obscurity is forever.
Napoleon Bonaparte (1769-1821, French General, Emperor)

19 The chief glory of every people arises from its authors.
Samuel Johnson (1709-1784, British Author)

20 The nearest way to glory is to strive to be what you wish to be thought to be.
Socrates (469-399 BC, Greek Philosopher of Athens)

21 Avoid shame but do not seek glory --nothing so expensive as glory.
Sydney Smith (1771-1845, British Writer, Clergyman)

22 The paths of glory lead but to the grave.
Thomas Gray (1716-1771, British Poet)

23 Sudden glory is the passion which makes those grimaces called laughter.
Thomas Hobbes (1588-1679, British Philosopher)

24 The final event to himself has been, that as he rose like a rocket, he fell like the stick.
Thomas Paine (1737-1809, Anglo-American Political Theorist, Writer)

25 I will not by the noise of bloody wars and the dethroning of kings advance you to glory: but by the gentle ways of peace and love.
Thomas Traherne (1636-1674, British Clergyman, Poet, Mystic)

26 Glory is the child of peril.
Tobias G. Smollett (1721-1771, Scottish Novelist, Surgeon)

27 Glory, built on selfish principles, is shame and guilt.
William Cowper (1731-1800, British Poet)

28 I have touched the highest point of all my greatness, and from that full meridian of my glory I haste now to my setting.
William Shakespeare (1564-1616, British Poet, Playwright, Actor)

29 There is many a boy here today who looks on war as all glory, but boys it is all hell.
William T. Sherman (1820-1891, American Army Commander)

GLUTTON

1 In general, mankind, since the improvement of cookery, eats twice as much as nature requires.
Benjamin Franklin (1706-1790, American Scientist, Publisher, Diplomat)

2 Their kitchen is their shrine, the cook their priest, the table their altar, and their belly their god.
Charles Buck

3 A poor man who eats too much, as contradistinguished from a gourmand, who is a rich man who "lives well."
Elbert Hubbard (1859-1915, American Author, Publisher)

4 Glutton: one who digs his grave with his teeth.
French Proverb

5 One meal a day is enough for a lion, and it ought to be for a man.
George Fordyce

6 The fool that eats till he is sick must fast till he is well.
George W. Thornbury

7 The miser and the glutton are two facetious buzzards: one hides his store, and the other stores his hide.
Josh Billings (1815-1885, American Humorist, Lecturer)

8 They whose sole bliss is eating can give but that one brutish reason why they live.
Juvenal (Decimus Junius Juvenalis) (55-130, Roman Satirical Poet)

9 The pleasures of the palate deal with us like the Egyptian thieves, who strangle those whom they embrace.
Seneca (4 BC-65 AD, Spanish-born Roman Statesman, philosopher)

GOALS

1 You cannot do a goal. Long-term planning and goal-setting must therefore be complemented by short-term planning. This kind of planning requires specifying activities. You can do an activity. Activities are steps along the way to a goal. Let's say you desire security. Putting $10.00 in the bank or talking to your stockbroker about your investment plans are activities that will move you toward your goal.
Alan Lakein (American Time Management Expert, Author, Trainer)

2 If one were to take that goal out of out of its religious form and look merely at its purely human side, one might state it perhaps thus: free and responsible development of the individual, so that he may place his powers freely and gladly in the service of all mankind.
Albert Einstein (1879-1955, German-born American Physicist)

3 It is a very high goal which, with our weak powers, we can reach only very inadequately, but which gives a sure foundation to our aspirations and valuations.
Albert Einstein (1879-1955, German-born American Physicist)

4   Let us watch well our beginnings, and results will manage themselves.
Alexander Clark

5   In life, the first thing you must do is decide what you really want. Weigh the costs and the results. Are the results worthy of the costs? Then make up your mind completely and go after your goal with all your might.
Alfred A. Montapert (American Author)

6   A straight path never leads anywhere except to the objective.
Andre Gide (1869-1951, French Author)

7   Your goal should be out of reach but not out of sight.
Anita DeFrantz (American Lawyer, Olympic Rower)

8   You can plant a dream.
Anne Campbell

9   There are two ways of attaining an important end, force and perseverance; the silent power of the latter grows irresistible with time.
Anne Sophie Swetchine (1782-1857, Russian Author)

10 Goals are a means to an end, not the ultimate purpose of our lives. They are simply a tool to concentrate our focus and move us in a direction. The only reason we really pursue goals is to cause ourselves to expand and grow. Achieving goals by themselves will never make us happy in the long term; it's who you become, as you overcome the obstacles necessary to achieve your goals, that can give you the deepest and most long-lasting sense of fulfillment.
Anthony Robbins (1960-, American Author, Speaker, Peak Performance Expert / Consultant)

11 The most important thing you can do to achieve your goals is to make sure that as soon as you set them, you immediately begin to create momentum. The most important rules that I ever adopted to help me in achieving my goals were those I learned from a very successful man who taught me to first write down the goal, and then to never leave the site of setting a goal without firs taking some form of positive action toward its attainment.
Anthony Robbins (1960-, American Author, Speaker, Peak Performance Expert / Consultant)

12 Setting goals is the first step in turning the invisible into the visible.
Anthony Robbins (1960-, American Author, Speaker, Peak Performance Expert / Consultant)

13 People are not lazy. They simply have impotent goals -- that is, goals that do not inspire them.
Anthony Robbins (1960-, American Author, Speaker, Peak Performance Expert / Consultant)

14 Man is a goal seeking animal. His life only has meaning if he is reaching out and striving for his goals.
Aristotle (384-322 BC, Greek Philosopher)

15 First, have a definite, clear practical ideal; a goal, an objective. Second, have the necessary means to achieve your ends; wisdom, money, materials, and methods. Third, adjust all your means to that end.
Aristotle (384-322 BC, Greek Philosopher)

16 In life, as in football, you won't go far unless you know where the goalposts are.
Arnold H. Glasgow

17 Before I was ever in my teens, I knew exactly what I wanted to be when I grew up. My goal was to be the greatest athlete that ever lived.
Babe Didrikson Zaharias (1924-1956, American Sportswoman -- Basketball, Golf, Track & Field)

18 If you don't know where you are going. How can you expect to get there?
Basil S. Walsh

19 There is no sudden leap into the stratosphere. There is only advancing step by step, slowly and tortuously, up the pyramid towards your goals.
Ben Stein (American Professor, Writer)

20 It must be borne in mind that the tragedy of life doesn't lie in not reaching your goal. The tragedy lies in having no goal to reach. It isn't a calamity to die with dreams unfulfilled, but it is a calamity not to dream. It is not a disaster to be unable to capture your ideal, but it is a disaster to have no ideal to capture. It is not a disgrace not to reach the stars, but it is a disgrace to have no stars to reach for. Not failure, but low aim is a sin
Benjamin E. Mayes

21 Set your goals high and don't stop until you get there.
Bo Jackson (American Baseball and Football Player)

22 Every single life only becomes great when the individual sets upon a goal or goals which they really believe in, which they can really commit themselves to, which they can put their whole heart and soul into.
Brian Tracy (American Trainer, Speaker, Author, Businessman)

23 You just wait. I'm going to be the biggest Chinese Star in the world.
Bruce Lee (1940-1973, Chinese-American Actor, Director, Author, Martial Artist)

24 Becoming a star may not be your destiny, but being the best that you can be is a goal that you can set for yourselves.
Bryan Lindsay

25 The person who makes a success of living is the one who sees his goal steadily and aims for it unswervingly. That is dedication.
Cecil B. De Mille (1881-1959, American Film Producer and Director)

26 You must have long term goals to keep you from being frustrated by short term failures.
Charles C. Noble

27 The goals you set for yourself and the strategies you choose become your blueprint or plan. Strategies are like recipes: choose the right ingredients, mix them in the correct proportions, and you will always produce the same predictable results: in this case financial success. The success strategies for managing money and building wealth are called Money Strategies. By learning to use money strategies as a part of your day-to-day life, financial frustration and failure will become a thing of the past.
Charles J. Givens (American Businessman, Author, Trainer)

28 The more specific and measurable your goal, the more quickly you will be able to identify, locate, create, and implement the use of the necessary resources for its achievement.
Charles J. Givens (American Businessman, Author, Trainer)

29 Everyone has a success mechanism and a failure mechanism. The failure mechanism goes off by itself. The success mechanism only goes off with a goal. Every time we write down and talk about a goal we push the button to start the success mechanism.
Charles "Tremendous" Jones (American Motivational Speaker, Author)

30 The person with a fixed goal, a clear picture of his desire, or an ideal always before him, causes it, through repetition, to be buried deeply in his subconscious mind and is thus enabled, thanks to its generative and sustaining power, to realize his goal in a minimum of time and with a minimum of physical effort. Just pursue the thought unceasingly. Step by step you will achieve realization, for all your faculties and powers become directed to that end.
Claude M. Bristol (1891-1951, American Author of "The Magic of Believing")

31 I consider a goal as a journey rather than a destination. And each year I set a new goal.
Curtis Carlson (American Businessman, Founder of Carlson Companies, Inc.)

32 A salesman must also have flexible goals. You may say, "I want to sell 10 accounts this week," and you sell five. You're ready to die. But, you tell yourself, "Five isn't too bad. You know, next week maybe I'll sell 10.
Curtis Carlson (American Businessman, Founder of Carlson Companies, Inc.)

33 Never look down to test the ground before taking your next step; only those who keep their eye fixed on the far horizon will find their right road.
Dag Hammarskjold (1905-1961, Swedish Statesman, Secretary-general of U.N.)

34 If I've got correct goals, and if I keep pursuing them the best way I know how, everything else falls into line. If I do the right thing right, I'm going to succeed.
Dan Dierdorf (American Football Player)

35 Think little goals and expect little achievements. Think big goals and win big success.
David J. Schwartz (American Trainer, Author of "The Magic of Thinking Big")

36 The world turns aside to let any man pass who knows whither he is going.
David Starr Jordan (1851-1931, American Biologist, Educator)

37 Goals provide the energy source that powers our lives. One of the best ways we can get the most from the energy we have is to focus it. That is what goals can do for us; concentrate our energy.
Denis Waitley (1933-, American Author, Speaker, Trainer, Peak Performance Expert)

38 Instead of looking at the past, I put myself ahead twenty years and try to look at what I need to do now in order to get there then.
Diana Ross (1944-, American Singer, Actress)

39 Goals are dreams with deadlines.
Diana Scharf Hunt

40 When you determined what you want, you have made the most important decision of your life. You have to know what you want in order to attain it.
Douglas Lurtan

41 Often the search proves more profitable than the goal.
E. L. Konigsburg

42 Picture yourself in your minds eye as having already achieved this goal. See yourself doing the things you'll be doing when you've reached your goal.
Earl Nightingale (1921-1989, American Radio Announcer, Author, Motivator, Speaker)

43 People with goals succeed because they know where they're going.
Earl Nightingale (1921-1989, American Radio Announcer, Author, Motivator, Speaker)

44 All you have to do is know where you're going. The answers will come to you of their own accord.
Earl Nightingale (1921-1989, American Radio Announcer, Author, Motivator, Speaker)

45 The big thing is that you know what you want.
Earl Nightingale (1921-1989, American Radio Announcer, Author, Motivator, Speaker)

46 Some people drift along like a cork on a river, feeling that they cannot do anything except drift, moment to moment. This is an attitude of mind. Everyone can be constructive even in tiny ways.
Edward De Bono (Born 1933, Maltan-Born American Psychologist and Writer)

47 Those who build beneath the stars build too low.
Edward Young (1683-1765, British Poet, Dramatist)

48 A soul without a high aim is like a ship without a rudder.
Eileen Caddy (American Spiritual Writer)

49 What an immense power over the life is the power of possessing distinct aims. The voice, the dress, the look, the very motion of a person, define and alter when he or she begins to live for a reason.
Elizabeth Stuart Phelps (1844-1911, American Writer)

50 Take heed you do not find what you do not seek.
English Proverb

51 Slight not what's near through aiming at what's far.
Euripides (480-406 BC, Greek Tragic Poet)

52 In whatever position you find yourself determine first your objective.
Ferdinand Foch (1851-1929, French Field Marshal)

53 Without goals, and plans to reach them, you are like a ship that has set sail with no destination.
Fitzhugh Dodson

54 Great souls are not those who have fewer passions and more virtues than others, but only those who have greater designs.
François de La Rochefoucauld (1613-1680, French classical writer)

55 From a certain point onward there is no longer any turning back. That is the point that must be reached.
Franz Kafka (1883-1924, German Novelist, Short-Story Writer)

56 Knowing where you're going is all you need to get there.
Frederick (Carl) Frieseke (1874-1939, American-Born French Painter)

57 No wind is of service to him that is bound for nowhere.
French Proverb

58 Arriving at one goal is the starting point to another.
Fyodor Dostoevski (1821-1881, Russian Novelist)

59 The most important thing about goals is having one.
Geoffrey F. Abert

60 You need to overcome the tug of people against you as you reach for high goals.
George S. Patton (1885-1945, American Army General during World War II)

61 When we are motivated by goals that have deep meaning, by dreams that need completion, by pure love that needs expressing, then we truly live life.
Greg Anderson (American Author of "The 22 Non-Negotiable Laws of Wellness")

62 Setting goals for your game is an art. The trick is in setting them at the right level neither too low nor too high.
Greg Norman (1955-, Australian Golfer)

63 Decide what you want, decide what you are willing to exchange for it. Establish your priorities and go to work.
H. L. Hunt (American Oil Magnate)

64 You will now have a starting place and a destination, and you will be able to determine what it will cost you to get there. You will be going someplace.
H. Stanley Judd (American Author)

65 In the long run you hit only what you aim at. Therefore, though you should fail immediately, you had better aim at something high.
Henry David Thoreau (1817-1862, American Essayist, Poet, Naturalist)

66 If you don't know where you are going, every road will get you nowhere.
Henry Kissinger (1923-, American Republican Politician, Secretary of State)

67 To be come fully alive a person must have goals and aims that transcend himself.
Herbert A. Otto

68 Begin, be bold and venture to be wise.
Horace (65-8 BC, Italian Poet)

69 Give me a stock clerk with a goal and I'll give you a man who will make history. Give me a man with no goals and I'll give you a stock clerk.
J. C. (James Cash) Penney (1875-1971, American Retailer, Philanthropist, Founder JC Penny's)

70 I learned that, before you reach an objective, you must be ready with a new one, and you must start to communicate it to the organization. But it is not the goal itself that is important.
Jan Carlzon (Business Executive, CEO of SAS)

71 Make measurable progress in reasonable time.
Jim Rohn (American Businessman, Author, Speaker, Philosopher)

72 The major reason for setting a goal is for what it makes of you to accomplish it. What it makes of you will always be the far greater value than what you get.
Jim Rohn (American Businessman, Author, Speaker, Philosopher)

73 Difficulties increase the nearer we approach the goal.
Johann Wolfgang Von Goethe (1749-1832, German Poet, Dramatist, Novelist)

74 A distracted existence leads us to no goal.
Johann Wolfgang Von Goethe (1749-1832, German Poet, Dramatist, Novelist)

75 Their is nothing so terrible as activity without insight.
Johann Wolfgang Von Goethe (1749-1832, German Poet, Dramatist, Novelist)

76 What by a straight path cannot be reached by crooked ways is never won.
Johann Wolfgang Von Goethe (1749-1832, German Poet, Dramatist, Novelist)

77 One never goes further than when they do not know where they are going.
Johann Wolfgang Von Goethe (1749-1832, German Poet, Dramatist, Novelist)

78 If your only goal is to become rich, you will never achieve it.
John D. Rockefeller (1839-1937, American Industrialist, Philanthropist, Founder Exxon)

79 Without some goals and some efforts to reach it, no man can live.
John Dewey (1859-1952, American Philosopher, Educator)

80 Unless you have some goals, I don't think there's any way to get above the pack. My vision was always well beyond what I had any reason to expect.
John Fuqua (Founder of Fuqua Industries)

81 You get what you set out to do.
John Hanson (American Businessman, Founder of Winnebago Industries)

82 A set definite objective must be established if we are to accomplish anything in a big way.
John Mcdonald

83 You return and again take the proper course, guided by what? -- By the picture in mind of the place you are headed for...
John Mcdonald

84 The first step towards getting somewhere is to decide that you are not going to stay where you are.
John Pierpont Morgan (1837-1913, American Banker, Financier, Art Collector)

85 It is far better to give work that is above a person, than to educate the person to be above their work.
John Ruskin (1819-1900, British Critic, Social Theorist)

86 The mind's direction is more important than its progress.
Joseph Joubert (1754-1824, French Moralist)

87 You have to set new goals every day.
Julie Krone (Jockey)

88 Goals determine what you're going to be.
Julius Erving (1950-, American Basketball Player)

89 I feel that the most important step in any major accomplishment is setting a specific goal. This enables you to keep your mind focused on your goal and off the many obstacles that will arise when you're striving to do your best.
Kurt Thomas (American Gymnast)

90 As you reach your goals, set new ones. That is how you grow and become a more powerful person.
Les Brown (1945-, American Speaker, Author, Trainer, Motivator Lecturer)

91 If you set goals and go after them with all the determination you can muster, your gifts will take you places that will amaze you.
Les Brown (1945-, American Speaker, Author, Trainer, Motivator Lecturer)

92 Choosing goals that are important to you is one of the most essential things you can do in order to live your dreams.
Les Brown (1945-, American Speaker, Author, Trainer, Motivator Lecturer)

93 Goals are not dreamy, pie-in-the-sky ideals. They have every day practical applications and they should be practical.
Les Brown (1945-, American Speaker, Author, Trainer, Motivator Lecturer)

94 Review your goals twice every day in order to be focused on achieving them.
Les Brown (1945-, American Speaker, Author, Trainer, Motivator Lecturer)

95 You may not accomplish every goal you set -- no one does -- but what really matters is having goals and going after them wholeheartedly.
Les Brown (1945-, American Speaker, Author, Trainer, Motivator Lecturer)

96 Your goals are the road maps that guide you and show you what is possible for your life.
Les Brown (1945-, American Speaker, Author, Trainer, Motivator Lecturer)

97 Goals help you channel your energy into action.
Les Brown (1945-, American Speaker, Author, Trainer, Motivator Lecturer)

98 One day Alice came to a fork in the road and saw a Cheshire cat in a tree. Which road do I take? she asked. Where do you want to go? was his response. I don't know, Alice answered. Then, said the cat, it doesn't matter.
Lewis Carroll (1832-1898, British Writer, Mathematician)

99 Would you tell me, please, which way I ought to go from here? "That depends a good deal on where you want to get to." Said the Cat. I don't much care where -- Said Alice. Then it doesn't matter which way you go, said the Cat.
Lewis Carroll (1832-1898, British Writer, Mathematician)

100 If you don't know where you are going, any road will get you there.
Lewis Carroll (1832-1898, British Writer, Mathematician)

101 Always have some project underway... an ongoing project that goes over from day to day and thus makes each day a small unit of time.
Lillian Troll (American Doctor)

102 There are two things to aim at in life: first, to get what you want; and, after that, to enjoy it. Only the wisest of mankind achieve the second.
Logan Pearsall Smith (1865-1946, Anglo-American Essayist, Aphorist)

103 Let me tell you the secret that has led me to my goal, My strength lies solely in my tenacity.
Louis Pasteur (1822-1895, French Scientist Who Developed "Pasteurization")

104 There must be a goal at every stage of life! There must be a goal!
Maggie Kuhn (1905-, American Civil Rights Activist, Author)

105 There are those who travel and those who are going somewhere. They are different and yet they are the same. The success has this over his rivals: He knows where he is going.
Mark Caine

106 Give yourself something to work toward -- constantly.
Mary Kay Ash (American Businesswoman, Founder of Mary Kay Cosmetics)

107 Who walks the fastest, but walks astray, is only furthest from his way.
Matthew Prior (1664-1721, British Diplomat, Poet)

108 People who say that life is not worthwhile are really saying that they themselves have no personal goals which are worthwhile. Get yourself a goal worth working for. Better still, get yourself a project. Always have something ahead of you to "look forward to" -- to work for and hope for.
Maxwell Maltz (American Plastic Surgeon, Author of "Psycho-Cybernetics")

625

[109] The person who has the will to undergo all labor may win any goal.
Menander of Athens (342-291 BC, Greek Dramatic Poet)

[110] Concentrate on finding your goal, then concentrate on reaching it.
Michael Friedsam

[111] To will is to select a goal, determine a course of action that will bring one to that goal, and then hold to that action until the goal is reached. The key is action.
Michael Hanson

[112] The capabilities of the human mind are enormous. There is usually no inherent reason you cannot accomplish whatever goal you set for yourself.
Michael J. Mccarthy (American Lawyer, Businessman)

[113] No wind favors him who has no destined port.
Michel Eyquem De Montaigne (1533-1592, French Philosopher, Essayist)

[114] No wind serves him who addresses his voyage to no certain port.
Michel Eyquem De Montaigne (1533-1592, French Philosopher, Essayist)

[115] What we truly and earnestly aspire to be, in some sense we are. The mere aspiration, changes one frame of mind and for the moment realizes itself.
Mrs. Jamieson

[116] A goal is a dream with a deadline.
Napoleon Hill (1883-1970, American Speaker, Motivational Writer, "Think and Grow Rich")

[117] There is one quality which one must possess to win, and that is definiteness of purpose, the knowledge of what one wants, and a burning desire to possess it.
Napoleon Hill (1883-1970, American Speaker, Motivational Writer, "Think and Grow Rich")

[118] Without a goal to work toward, we will not get there.
Natasha Josefowitz

[119] We're all pilgrims on the same journey-but some pilgrims have better road maps.
Nelson Demille

[120] If you want to accomplish the goals of your life, you have to begin with the Spirit.
Oprah Winfrey (1954-, American TV Personality, Producer, Actress, Author)

[121] We are all in the gutter, but some of us are looking at the stars.
Oscar Wilde (1856-1900, British Author, Wit)

[122] Until input thought is linked to a goal purpose there can be no intelligent accomplishment.
Paul G. Thomas

[123] You are not likely to get anywhere in particular if you don't know where you want to go.
Percy H. Johnson

[124] Objectives are not fate; they are direction. They are not commands; they are commitments. They do not determine the future; they are means to mobilize the resources and energies of the business for the making of the future.
Peter F. Drucker (1909-, American Management Consultant, Author)

[125] If you're not sure where you're going, you'll probably end up somewhere else.
Peter Laurence

[126] It is hard to begin to move when you don't know where you are moving, how to move, or if you are going to get there.
Peter Nivio Zarlenga (American Businessman, Founder of Blockbuster Videos)

[127] It is better to finish something than begin.
Proverb

[128] It is necessary to try to surpass one's self always; this occupation ought to last as long as life.
Queen Christina (1626-1689, Queen of Sweden)

[129] Those who cannot tell what they desire or expect, still sigh and struggle with indefinite thoughts and vast wishes.
Ralph Waldo Emerson (1803-1882, American Poet, Essayist)

[130] We aim above the mark to hit the mark.
Ralph Waldo Emerson (1803-1882, American Poet, Essayist)

[131] We didn't get great goals. We just scored no-fear goals. Heart goals.
Rich Pilon (American Hockey Player)

[132] The goal you set must be challenging. At the same time, it should be realistic and attainable, not impossible to reach. It should be challenging enough to make you stretch, but not so far that you break.
Rick Hansen (Canadian Wheelchair Athlete, Speaker, Founder of Man in Motion World Tour)

[133] I've surpassed any goal I set for myself as far as my body, my career, and getting married.
Ricki Lake (Born 1968, American Actress, Animal rights activist)

[134] Many a person who started out to conquer the world in shining army has ended up just getting along. The horse got tired, the army rusty. The goal was removed and unsure.
Robert A. Cook

[135] A man's reach should exceed his grasp, or what's heaven for?
Robert Browning (1812-1889, British Poet)

[136] The first essentials, of course, is to know what you want.
Robert Collier (American Writer, Publisher)

[137] Goals must never be from your ego, but problems that cry for a solution.
Robert H. Schuller (1926-, American Minister (Crystal Cathedral), Author, Social Leader)

[138] There is no achievement without goals.
Robert J. Mckain

139 An aim in life is the only fortune worth finding.
Robert Louis Stevenson (1850-1895, Scottish Essayist, Poet, Novelist)

140 Whether or not you reach your goals in life depends entirely on how well you prepare for them and how badly you want them. You're eagles! Stretch your wings and fly to the sky.
Ronald McNair

141 My philosophy of life is that if we make up our mind what we are going to make of our lives, then work hard toward that goal, we never lose -- somehow we win out
Ronald Reagan (1911-, Fortieth President of the USA, Actor)

142 The goal of all inanimate objects is to resist man and ultimately defeat him.
Russell (Wayne) Baker (1925-, American Journalist)

143 Aim for the top. There is plenty of room there. There are so few at the top it is almost lonely there.
Samuel Insull

144 This one step -- choosing a goal and sticking to it -- changes everything.
Scott Reed

145 Our plans miscarry because they have no aim. When a man does not know what harbor he is making for, no wind is the right wind.
Seneca (4 BC-65 AD, Spanish-born Roman Statesman, philosopher)

146 If a man knows not what harbor he seeks, any wind is the right wind.
Seneca (4 BC-65 AD, Spanish-born Roman Statesman, philosopher)

147 If a man does not know what port he is steering for, no wind is favorable to him.
Seneca (4 BC-65 AD, Spanish-born Roman Statesman, philosopher)

148 You don't have to be a fantastic hero to do certain things -- to compete. You can be just an ordinary chap, sufficiently motivated to reach challenging goals.
Sir Edmund Hillary (1919-, New Zealand Mountaineer)

149 Our goals can only be reached through a vehicle of a plan, in which we must fervently believe, and upon which we must vigorously act. There is no other route to success.
Stephen A. Brennan (American Basketball Coach)

150 A man has to have goals- for a day, for a lifetime- that was mine, to have people say, "There goes Ted Williams, the greatest hitter who ever lived."
Ted Williams (1918-, American Baseball Player)

151 A man without a goal is like a ship without a rudder.
Thomas Carlyle (1795-1881, Scottish Philosopher, Author)

152 Whatever you do, do it with intelligence, and keep the end in view.
Thomas p Kempis (1379-1471, German Monk, Mystic, Religious Writer)

153 When a man has not a good reason for doing a thing, he has one good reason for letting it alone.
Thomas Scott

154 Providence has nothing good or high in store for one who does not resolutely aim at something high or good. A purpose is the eternal condition of success.
Thornton T. Munger (American Scientist)

155 To meet my goals, I couldn't let up when I was playing tennis.
Tracy Austin (American Tennis Player)

156 To solve a problem or to reach a goal, you don't need to know all the answers in advance. But you must have a clear idea of the problem or the goal you want to reach.
W. Clement Stone (1902-, American Businessman, Author)

157 You. too, can determine what you want. You can decide on your major objectives, targets, aims, and destination.
W. Clement Stone (1902-, American Businessman, Author)

158 People, like nails, lose their effectiveness when they lose direction and begin to bend.
Walter Savage Landor (1775-1864, British Poet, Essayist)

159 If you don't know where you are going, you might wind up someplace else.
Yogi Berra (1925-, American Baseball Player)

160 You cannot make it as a wandering generality. You must become a meaningful specific.
Zig Ziglar (American Sales Trainer, Author, Motivational Speaker)

161 A goal properly set is halfway reached.
Zig Ziglar (American Sales Trainer, Author, Motivational Speaker)

162 Famous archer, Howard Hill won all of the 267 archery contests he entered. He could hit a bullseye at 50 feet, then split first arrow with the second. Would it be possible for you to shoot better than him? YES, if he were blindfolded! How can you hit a target you can't see? Even worse, how can you hit a target you don't even have!? You need to have GOALS in your life!
Zig Ziglar (American Sales Trainer, Author, Motivational Speaker)

163 What you get by achieving your goals is not as important as what you become by achieving your goals.
Zig Ziglar (American Sales Trainer, Author, Motivational Speaker)

GOD

1 I like to interpose in all of my appointments, if the Lord wills.
A. B. Simpson (1843-1919, Canadian preacher, theologian, author, and founder of the Christian and Missionary Alliance)

2 The man or woman who is wholly or joyously surrendered to Christ can't make a wrong choice--any choice will be the right one.
A. W. Tozer (Deceased 1963, American Preacher)

3   In almost everything that touches our everyday life on earth, God is pleased when we're pleased. He wills that we be as free as birds to soar and sing our maker's praise without anxiety.
A. W. Tozer (Deceased 1963, American Preacher)

4   What I believe about God is the most important thing about me.
A. W. Tozer (Deceased 1963, American Preacher)

5   An infinite God can give all of Himself to each of His children. He does not distribute Himself that each may have a part, but to each one He gives all of Himself as fully as if there were no others.
A. W. Tozer (Deceased 1963, American Preacher)

6   If God gives you a watch, are you honoring Him more by asking Him what time it is or by simply consulting the watch?
A. W. Tozer (Deceased 1963, American Preacher)

7   It is difficult to make a man miserable while he feels he is worthy of himself and claims kindred to the great God who made him.
Abraham Lincoln (1809-1865, Sixteenth President of the USA)

8   And even in our sleep pain that cannot forget falls drop by drop upon the heart, and in our own despair, against our will, comes wisdom to us by the awful grace of God.
Aeschylus (525-456 BC, Greek Dramatist)

9   God does not play dice with the universe.
Albert Einstein (1879-1955, German-born American Physicist)

10 God is subtle, but He is not malicious. I cannot believe that God plays dice with the world.
Albert Einstein (1879-1955, German-born American Physicist)

11 God is clever, but not dishonest.
Albert Einstein (1879-1955, German-born American Physicist)

12 Seek to cultivate a buoyant, joyous sense of the crowded kindnesses of God in your daily life.
Alexander Maclaren (1826-1910, British Preacher)

13 God is the tangential point between zero and infinity.
Alfred Jarry (1873-1907, French Playwright, Author)

14 The experience of God, or in any case the possibility of experiencing God, is innate.
Alice Walker (1944-, American Author, Critic)

15 To speak of God, to think of God, is in every respect to show what one is made of. I have always wagered against God and I regard the little that I have won in this world as simply the outcome of this bet. However paltry may have been the stake (my life) I am conscious of having won to the full. Everything that is doddering, squint-eyed, vile, polluted and grotesque is summoned up for me in that one word: God!
Andre Breton (1989-1966, French Surrealist)

16 Man is a dog's ideal of what God should be.
Andre Malraux (1901-1976, French Statesman, Novelist)

17 Mother goddesses are just as silly a notion as father gods. If a revival of the myths of these cults gives woman emotional satisfaction, it does so at the price of obscuring the real conditions of life. This is why they were invented in the first place.
Angela Carter (1940-1992, British Author)

18 All good fortune is a gift of the gods, and you don't win the favor of the ancient gods by being good, but by being bold.
Anita Brookner (1938-, British Novelist, Art Historian)

19 And again: No more gods! no more gods! Man is King, Man is God! -- But the great Faith is Love!
Arthur Rimbaud (1854-1891, French Poet)

20 Oh the depth of both the wisdom and riches of God! How unsearchable are his judgments, and his ways beyond understanding.
Bible (Sacred Scriptures of Christians and Judaism)

21 God is not a man, that he should lie, nor a son of man, that he should repent; has he not said, and will he not do it? Or has he spoken, and will he not make it good? [Numbers 23:19]
Bible (Sacred Scriptures of Christians and Judaism)

22 For now we see through a glass darkly, but then face to face; now I know in part, but then shall I know even as also I am known. [I Corinthians]
Bible (Sacred Scriptures of Christians and Judaism)

23 And now Israel, what does the Lord your God require from you, but to fear the Lord your God, to walk in all His ways and love Him, and to serve the Lord your God with all your heart and all your soul. [Deuteronomy 10:12]
Bible (Sacred Scriptures of Christians and Judaism)

24 But from there you will seek the Lord you God and you will find Him if you search for Him with all your heart and all your soul. [Deuteronomy 4:29]
Bible (Sacred Scriptures of Christians and Judaism)

25 If you gain, you gain all; if you lose, you lose nothing. Wager then without hesitation, that He exists.
Blaise Pascal (1623-1662, French Scientist, Religious Philosopher)

26 God is a verb.
Buckminster Fuller (American Engineer, Inventor, Designer, Architect "Geodesic Dome")

27 Can a mortal ask questions which God finds unanswerable? Quite easily, I should think. All nonsense questions are unanswerable.
C. S. Lewis (1898-1963, British Academic, Writer, Christian Apologist)

28 If triangles made a god, they would give him three sides.
Charles De Montesquieu (1689-1755, French Jurist, Political Philosopher)

29 As you know, God is generally on the side of the big squadrons against the small ones.
Comte De Bussy-Rabutin

30 We may seek God by our intellect, but we only can find him with our heart.
Cotvos

31 There cannot be a personal God without a pessimistic religion. As soon as there is a personal God he is a disappointing God.
Cyril Connolly (1903-1974, British Critic)

32 God is only a great imaginative experience.
D. H. Lawrence (1885-1930, British Author)

33 I cannot be a materialist -- but Oh, how is it possible that a God who speaks to all hearts can let Belgravia go laughing to a vicious luxury, and Whitechapel cursing to a filthy debauchery -- such suffering, such dreadful suffering -- and shall the short years of Christ's mission atone for it all?
D. H. Lawrence (1885-1930, British Author)

34 What preoccupies us, then, is not God as a fact of nature, but as a fabrication useful for a God- fearing society. God himself becomes not a power but an image.
Daniel J. Boorstin (1914-, American Historian)

35 The most important thought that ever occupied my mind is that of my individual responsibility to God.
Daniel Webster (1782-1852, American Lawyer, Statesman)

36 In His will is our peace.
Dante (Alighieri) (1265-1321, Italian Philosopher, Poet)

37 A god who let us prove his existence would be an idol.
Dietrich Bonhoeffer (1906-1945, German Lutheran Pastor and Theologian)

38 God: a disease we imagine we are cured of because no one dies of it nowadays.
E. M. Cioran (1911-, Rumanian-born French Philosopher)

39 A civilization is destroyed only when its gods are destroyed.
E. M. Cioran (1911-, Rumanian-born French Philosopher)

40 God, I can push the grass apart and lay my finger on Thy heart.
Edna St. Vincent Millay (1892-1950, American Poet)

41 All the gods are dead except the god of war.
Eldridge Cleaver (1935-, American Black Leader, Writer)

42 Whether or not God is dead: it is impossible to keep silent about him who was there for so long.
Elias Canetti (1905-, Austrian Novelist, Philosopher)

43 I rarely speak about God. To God, yes. I protest against Him. I shout at Him. But to open a discourse about the qualities of God, about the problems that God imposes, theodicy, no. And yet He is there, in silence, in filigree.
Elie Wiesel (1928-, Rumanian-born American Writer)

44 God hath entrusted me with myself.
Epictetus (50-120, Stoic Philosopher)

45 The one thing that a fish can never find is water; and the one thing that man can never find is God.
Eric Butterworth

46 God can only do for you what He can do through you.
Eric Butterworth

47 Fundamentalists believe Jesus was God becoming man. I believe that Jesus was man becoming God.
Eric Butterworth

48 To the excessively fearful the chief characteristic of power is its arbitrariness. Man had to gain enormously in confidence before he could conceive an all-powerful God who obeys his own laws.
Eric Hoffer (1902-1983, American Author, Philosopher)

49 When men make gods, there is no God!
Eugene O'Neill (1888-1953, American Dramatist)

50 When we want to know God's will, there are three things which always concur: the inward impulse, the Word of God and the trend of circumstances. Never act until these three things agree.
F. B. Meyer

51 Men have always need of god! A god to defend them against other men..
Francis Picabia (1878-1953, French Painter, Poet)

52 One and God make a majority.
Frederick Douglass (1817-1895, American Abolitionist, Journalist)

53 I fear we are not getting rid of God because we still believe in grammar.
Friedrich Nietzsche (1844-1900, German Philosopher)

54 Is man one of God's blunders or is God one of man's blunders?
Friedrich Nietzsche (1844-1900, German Philosopher)

55 There is in general good reason to suppose that in several respects the gods could all benefit from instruction by us human beings. We humans are -- more humane.
Friedrich Nietzsche (1844-1900, German Philosopher)

56 It is an insult to God to believe in God. For on the one hand it is to suppose that he has perpetrated acts of incalculable cruelty. On the other hand, it is to suppose that he has perversely given his human creatures an instrument -- their intellect -- which must inevitably lead them, if they are dispassionate and honest, to deny his existence. It is tempting to conclude that if he exists, it is the atheists and agnostics that he loves best, among those with any pretensions to education. For they are the ones who have taken him most seriously.
Galen Strawson

57 God is more concerned about who you are than what you do, and He is more concerned about what you do than where you do it.
Gary Gulbranson

58 To me the sole hope of human salvation lies in teaching Man to regard himself as an experiment in the realization of God, to regard his hands as God's hand, his brain as God's brain, his purpose as God's purpose. He must regard God as a helpless Longing, which longed him into existence by its desperate need for an executive organ.
George Bernard Shaw (1856-1950, Irish-born British Dramatist)

59 Throw away thy rod, throw away thy wrath; O my God, take the gentle path.
George Herbert (1593-1632, British Metaphysical Poet)

60 I find that doing of the will of God leaves me no time for disputing about His plans.
George Macdonald (1824-1905, Scottish Novelist)

61 To know the will of God is the greatest knowledge! To do the will of God is the greatest achievement.
George W. Truett

62 When I was young, I said to God, god, tell me the mystery of the universe. But God answered,   that knowledge is for me alone. So I said, god, tell me the mystery of the peanut. Then God said,   well, George, that's more nearly your size.
George Washington Carver (1864-1943, American Scientist)

63 To place oneself in the position of God is painful: being God is equivalent to being tortured. For being God means that one is in harmony with all that is, including the worst. The existence of the worst evils is unimaginable unless God willed them.
Georges Bataille (1897-1962, French Novelist, Critic)

64 By the year 2000 we will, I hope, raise our children to believe in human potential, not God.
Gloria Steinem (1934-, American Feminist Writer, Editor)

65 God is the immemorial refuge of the incompetent, the helpless, the miserable. They find not only sanctuary in His arms, but also a kind of superiority, soothing to their macerated egos: He will set them above their betters.
H. L. Mencken (1880-1956, American Editor, Author, Critic, Humorist)

66 Give God the margin of eternity to justify himself.
H. R. Haweis

67 It seems to me that the god that is commonly worshipped in civilized countries is not at all divine, though he bears a divine name, but is the overwhelming authority and respectability of mankind combined. Men reverence one another, not yet God.
Henry David Thoreau (1817-1862, American Essayist, Poet, Naturalist)

68 I believe God is managing affairs and that He doesn't need any advice from me. With God in charge, I believe everything will work out for the best in the end. So what is there to worry about.
Henry Ford (1863-1947, American Industrialist, Founder of Ford Motor Company)

69 God is day and night, winter and summer, war and peace, surfeit and hunger.
Heraclitus (535-475 BC, Greek Philosopher)

70 You have to believe in gods to see them.
Hopi Indian saying

71 God is indeed dead. He died of self-horror when He saw the creature He had made in His own image.
Irving Layton (1912-, Canadian Poet)

72 Fear God, yes, but don't be afraid of Him.
J. A. Spender

73 And some to Meccah turn to pray, and I toward thy bed, Yasmin.
James Elroy Flecker (1884-1915, British Poet)

74 With God, what is terrible is that one never knows whether it's not just a trick of the devil.
Jean Anouilh (1910-1987, French Playwright)

75 I would not like to see a person who is sober, moderate, chaste and just say that there is no God. They would speak disinterestedly at least, but such a person is not to be found.
Jean De La Bruyere (1645-1696, French Writer)

76 Without God there is for mankind no purpose, no goal, no hope, only a wavering future, an eternal dread of every darkness.
Jean Paul

77 God, that checkroom of our dreams.
Jean Rostand (1894-1977, French Biologist, Writer)

78 God, that dumping ground of our dreams.
Jean Rostand (1894-1977, French Biologist, Writer)

79 God is closest to those with broken hearts.
Jewish Proverb

80 If God lived on earth, people would break his windows.
Jewish Proverb

81 While the womanly god demands our veneration, the godlike woman kindles our love; but while we allow ourselves to melt in the celestial loveliness, the celestial self-sufficiency holds us back in awe.
Johann Friedrich Von Schiller (1759-1805, German Dramatist, Poet, Historian)

82 Let none turn over books, or roam the stars in quest of God, who sees him not in man.
Johann Kaspar Lavater (1741-1801, Swiss Theologian, Mystic)

83 God is infinite and without end, but the soul's desire is an abyss which cannot be filled except by a Good which is infinite; and the more ardently the soul longeth after God, the more she wills to long after him; for God is a Good without drawback, and a well of living water without bottom, and the soul is made in the image of God, and therefore it is created to know and love God.
Johannes Tauler

84 God brings men into deep waters not to drown them, but to cleanse them.
John H. Aughey (American Scientist)

85 The only way God could impose peace on the world would be to robotize our wills and rob every human being of the power of choice. He has not chosen to do that. He has given every person a free will.
John Haggai

86 God is concerned with nations, but nations also need to be concerned with God. No nation can have a monopoly on God, but God will bless any nation whose people seek and honor His will as revealed by Christ and declared through the Holy Spirit.
John Haggai

87 God is a concept by which we measure our pain.
John Lennon (1940-1980, British Rock Musician)

88 If the Lord be with us, we have no cause of fear. His eye is upon us, His arm over us, His ear open to our prayer--His grace sufficient, His promises unchangeable.
John Newton (1725-1807, British Poet, Wrote "Amazing Grace")

89 The guarantee that our self enjoys an intended relation to the outer world is most, if not all, we ask from religion. God is the self projected onto reality by our natural and necessary optimism. He is the not-me personified.
John Updike (1932-, American Novelist, Critic)

90 Without doubt God is the universal moving force, but each being is moved according to the nature that God has given it. He directs angels, man, animals, brute matter, in sum all created things, but each according to its nature, and man having been created free, he is freely led. This rule is truly the eternal law and in it we must believe.
Joseph De Maistre (1753-1821, French Diplomat, Philosopher)

91 We always believe God is like ourselves, the indulgent think him indulgent and the stern, terrible.
Joseph Joubert (1754-1824, French Moralist)

92 God has marvelous ways of taking our worst tragedies and turning them into His most glorious triumphs.
Joseph Stowell

93 Suddenly is the soul oned to God when it is truly peaced in itself: for in Him is found no wrath. And thus I saw when we are all in peace and in love, we find no contrariness, nor no manner of letting through that contrariness which is now in us.
Julian of Norwich

94 Providence certainly does not favor just certain individuals, but the deep wisdom of its counsel, instruction and ennoblement extends to all.
Karl Wilhelm Von Humboldt (1767-1835, German Statesman, Philologist)

95 Every day people are straying away from the church and going back to God.
Lenny Bruce (1925-1966, American Comedian)

96 Those who set out to serve both God and Mammon soon discover that there isn't a God.
Logan Pearsall Smith (1865-1946, Anglo-American Essayist, Aphorist)

97 I know not what you believe of God, but I believe He gave yearnings and longings to be filled, and that He did not mean all our time should be devoted to feeding and clothing the body.
Lucy Stone

98 If someone were to prove to me -- right this minute -- that God, in all his luminousness, exists, it wouldn't change a single aspect of my behavior.
Luis Bunuel (1900-1983, Spanish Film Director)

99 God always has another custard pie up his sleeve.
Lynn Redgrave

100 The mantram becomes one's staff of life and carries one through every ordeal. Each repetition has a new meaning, carrying you nearer and nearer to God.
Mahatma Gandhi (1869-1948, Indian Political, Spiritual Leader)

101 The God of this world is riches, pleasure and pride.
Martin Luther (1483-1546, German Leader of the Protestant Reformation)

102 I'm one of those cliff-hanging Catholics. I don't believe in God, but I do believe that Mary was his mother.
Martin Sheen (1940-, American Actor)

103 If God is male, then male is God. The divine patriarch castrates women as long as he is allowed to live on in the human imagination.
Mary Daly (1928-, American Feminist and Theological Writer)

104 Why indeed must "God" be a noun? Why not a verb -- the most active and dynamic of all.
Mary Daly (1928-, American Feminist and Theological Writer)

105 I find it interesting that the meanest life, the poorest existence, is attributed to God's will, but as human beings become more affluent, as their living standard and style begin to ascend the material scale, God descends the scale of responsibility at a commensurate speed.
Maya Angelou (1928-, African-American poet, Writer, Performer)

106 Jesus might have said, "I became man for you. If you do not become God for me, you wrong me."
Meister Eckhart (1260-1326 AD, German Mystic)

107 God is at home, it's we who have gone out for a walk.
Meister Eckhart (1260-1326 AD, German Mystic)

108 To be full of things is to be empty of God. To be empty of things is to be full of God.
Meister Eckhart (1260-1326 AD, German Mystic)

109 Man goes far away or near but God never goes far-off; he is always standing close at hand, and even if he cannot stay within he goes no further than the door.
Meister Eckhart (1260-1326 AD, German Mystic)

110 The seed of God is in us. Given an intelligent and hard-working farmer, it will thrive and grow up to God, whose seed it is; and accordingly its fruits will be God-nature. Pear seeds grow into pear trees, nut seeds into nut trees, and God-seed into God.
Meister Eckhart (1260-1326 AD, German Mystic)

111 To honor him whom we have made is far from honoring him that hath made us..
Michel Eyquem De Montaigne (1533-1592, French Philosopher, Essayist)

112 Though God's attributes are equal, yet his mercy is more attractive and pleasing in our eyes than his justice.
Miguel De Cervantes (1547-1616, Spanish Novelist, Dramatist, Poet)

113 Man appoints, and God disappoints.
Miguel De Cervantes (1547-1616, Spanish Novelist, Dramatist, Poet)

114 Among the attributes of God, although they are equal, mercy shines with even more brilliance than justice.
Miguel de Cervantes Saavadra

115 We need God, not in order to understand the why, but in order to feel and sustain the ultimate wherefore, to give a meaning to the universe.
Miguel De Unamuno (1864-1936, Spanish Philosophical Writer)

116 I went to the root of things, and found nothing but Him alone.
Mira Bai (1498-1547, Hindi Poet)

117 I know God will not give me anything I can't handle. I just wish that He didn't trust me so much.
Mother Teresa (1910-1997, Albanian-born Roman Catholic Missionary)

118 God is the name we give our conscience.
Nader Shureih

119 We know all their gods; they ignore ours. What they call our sins are our gods, and what they call their gods, we name otherwise.
Natalie Clifford Barney (1876-1972, American-born French Author)

120 Two men please God -- who serves Him with all his heart because he knows Him; who seeks Him with all his heart because he knows Him not.
Nikita Ivanovich Panin (Indian Grammarian)

121 Having given us the package, do you think God will deny us the ribbon?
Oswald C. Hoffman

122 God is really only another artist. He invented the giraffe, the elephant, and the cat. He has no real style. He just keeps on trying other things.
Pablo Picasso (1881-1973, Spanish Artist)

123 Has it ever struck you that the vast majority of the will of God for your life has already been revealed in the Bible? That is a crucial thing to grasp.
Paul Little

124 I was frustrated out of my mind, trying to figure out the will of God. I was doing everything but getting into the presence of God and asking Him to show me.
Paul Little

125 Others think it's a choice between doing what we want to do and being happy, and doing what God wants us to do and being miserable.
Paul Little

126 Some people think that God peers over the balcony of heaven trying to find anybody who is enjoying life. And when He spots a happy person, He yells, "Now cut that out!" That concept of God should make us shudder because it's blasphemous!
Paul Little

127 I hope for the day when everyone can speak again of God without embarrassment.
Paul Tillich (1886-1965, German Protestant Theologian, Philosopher)

128 You are within God. God is within you.
Peace Pilgrim (1908-1981, American Peace Activist)

129 People see God every day; they just don't recognize Him.
Pearl Bailey (1918-1990, American Vocalist, Movie and Stage Actress)

130 It is fear that first brought gods into the world.
Petronius (Roman Writer)

131 God is not external to anyone, but is present with all things, though they are ignorant that he is so.
Plotinus

132 Man does what he can, God does what he will.
Proverb

133 If the sea were ink for the words of my Lord, the sea would be spent before the Words of my lord are spent.
Qur'an (Holy Book)

134 Here is God's purpose -- for God, to me, it seems, is a verb not a noun, proper or improper.
R. Buckminster Fuller (1895-1983, American Inventor, Designer, Poet, Philosopher)

135 I admit that the generation which produced Stalin, Auschwitz and Hiroshima will take some beating; but the radical and universal consciousness of the death of God is still ahead of us; perhaps we shall have to colonize the stars before it is finally borne in upon us that God is not out there.
R. J. Hollingdale

136 Your idol is shattered in the dust to prove that God's dust is greater than your idol.
Rabindranath Tagore (1861-1941, Indian Poet, Philosopher)

137 'Tis the old secret of the gods that they come in low disguises.
Ralph Waldo Emerson (1803-1882, American Poet, Essayist)

138 There is a crack in everything God has made.
Ralph Waldo Emerson (1803-1882, American Poet, Essayist)

139 The dice of God are always loaded.
Ralph Waldo Emerson (1803-1882, American Poet, Essayist)

140 The history of all the great characters of the Bible is summed up in this one sentence: They acquainted themselves with God, and acquiesced His will in all things.
Richard Cecil (American Poet)

141 Forgive, O Lord, my little jokes on Thee and I'll forgive Thy great big one on me.
Robert Frost (1875-1963, American Poet)

142 What men usually ask for when they pray to God is, that two and two may not make four.
Russian Proverb

143 It is not a difficult matter to learn what it means to delight ourselves in the Lord. It is to live so as to please Him, to honor everything we find in His Word, to do everything the way He would like to have it done, and for Him.
S. Maxwell Coder

144 I fear God and next to God I mostly fear them that fear him not.
Saadi

145 If we really think about it, God exists for any single individual who puts his trust in Him, not for the whole of humanity, with its laws, its organizations, and its violence. Humanity is the demon which God does not succeed in destroying.
Salvatore Satta (1902-1975, Italian Jurist, Novelist)

146 The bastard! He doesn't exist!
Samuel Beckett (1906-1989, Irish Dramatist, Novelist)

147 How can one better magnify the Almighty than by sniggering with him at his little jokes, particularly the poorer ones.
Samuel Beckett (1906-1989, Irish Dramatist, Novelist)

148 If God wants us to do a thing, he should make his wishes sufficiently clear. Sensible people will wait till he has done this before paying much attention to him.
Samuel Butler (1612-1680, British Poet, Satirist)

149 Forsake not God till you find a better master.
Scottish Proverb

150 Nothing is void of God, his work is everywhere his full of himself.
Seneca (4 BC-65 AD, Spanish-born Roman Statesman, philosopher)

151 The psychoanalysis of individual human beings, however, teaches us with quite special insistence that the god of each of them is formed in the likeness of his father, that his personal relation to God depends on his relation to his father in the flesh and oscillates and changes along with that relation, and that at bottom God is nothing other than an exalted father.
Sigmund Freud (1856-1939, Austrian Physician - Founder of Psychoanalysis)

152 In relation to God, we are like a thief who has burgled the house of a kindly householder and been allowed to keep some of the gold. From the point of view of the lawful owner this gold is a gift; Form the point of view of the burglar it is a theft. He must go and give it back. It is the same with our existence. We have stolen a little of God's being to make it ours. God has made us a gift of it. But we have stolen it. We must return it.
Simone Weil (1910-1943, French Philosopher, Mystic)

153 It is only the impossible that is possible for God. He has given over the possible to the mechanics of matter and the autonomy of his creatures.
Simone Weil (1910-1943, French Philosopher, Mystic)

154 We can only know one thing about God -- that he is what we are not. Our wretchedness alone is an image of this. The more we contemplate it, the more we contemplate him.
Simone Weil (1910-1943, French Philosopher, Mystic)

155 People are too apt to treat God as if he were a minor royalty.
Sir Herbert Beerbohm Tree (1853-1917, British actor-manager)

156 Every man for himself and God for us all.
Spanish Proverb

157 The grace of God is a wind which is always blowing.
Sri Ramakrishna (Indian Mystic)

158 I found thee not, O Lord, without, because I erred in seeking thee without that wert within.
St. Augustine (354-430, Numidian-born Bishop of Hippo, Theologian)

159 Abide in peace, banish cares, take no account of all that happens, and you will serve God according to his good pleasure and rest in him.
St. John of the Cross (1542-1591, Spanish Christian Mystic and Poet)

160 People do not know what the Name of God can do. Those who repeat it constantly alone know its power. It can purify our mind completely... The Name can take us to the summit of spiritual experience.
Swami Ramdas

161 Place yourself as an instrument in the hands of God, who does his own work in his own way.
Swami Ramdas

162 God gets you to the plate, but once your there your on your own.
Ted Williams (1918-, American Baseball Player)

163 All your Western theologies, the whole mythology of them, are based on the concept of God as a senile delinquent.
Tennessee Williams (1914-1983, American Dramatist)

164 There is no God but God.
The Koran (500 AD, Islamic Religious Bible)

165 God hears no more than the heart speaks; and if the heart be dumb, God will certainly be deaf.
Thomas Brooks

166 Don't think so much about who is for or against you, rather give all your care, that God be with you in everything you do.
Thomas p Kempis (1379-1471, German Monk, Mystic, Religious Writer)

167 Man proposes, but God disposes.
Thomas p Kempis (1379-1471, German Monk, Mystic, Religious Writer)

168 He does much who loves God much, and he does much who does his deed well, and he does his deed well who does it rather for the common good than for his own will.
Thomas p Kempis (1379-1471, German Monk, Mystic, Religious Writer)

169 The intention which is fixed on God as its only end will keep people steady in their purposes, and deliver them from being the joke and scorn of fortune.
Thomas p Kempis (1379-1471, German Monk, Mystic, Religious Writer)

170 Each person, makes their own terrible passion their God.
Virgil (70-19 BC, Roman Poet)

171 God is always on the side of the heaviest battalions.
Voltaire (1694-1778, French Historian, Writer)

172 God is not on the side of the big battalions, but on the side of those who shoot best.
Voltaire (1694-1778, French Historian, Writer)

173 God is a circle whose center is everywhere and circumference nowhere.
Voltaire (1694-1778, French Historian, Writer)

174 If God did not exist, it would be necessary to invent Him.
Voltaire (1694-1778, French Historian, Writer)

175 God is Love," we are taught as children to believe. But when we first begin to get some inkling of how He loves us, we are repelled; it seems so cold, indeed, not love at all as we understand the word.
W. H. Auden (1907-1973, Anglo-American Poet)

176 In the faces of men and women I see God, and in my own face in the glass, I find letters from God dropped in the street, and every one is signed by God's name. And I leave them where they are, for I know that wherever I go, others will punctually come for ever and ever.
Walt Whitman (1819-1892, American Poet)

177 One on God's side is a majority.
Wendell Phillips (1811-1884, American Reformer, Orator)

178 God has been so lavish in his gifts that you can lose some priceless ones, the equivalent of whole kingdoms, and still be indecently rich,
Wilfrid Heed

179 Smitten as we are with the vision of social righteousness, a God indifferent to everything but adulation, and full of partiality for his individual favorites, lacks an essential element of largeness.
William James (1842-1910, American Psychologist, Professor, Author)

180 Nothing hath separated us from God but our own will, or rather our own will is our separation from God.
William Law (American Merchant)

181 There will be no peace so long as God remains unseated at the conference table.
William M. Peck

182 God has been pleased to prescribe limits to his power and to work out his ends within these limits.
William Paley (1743-1805, British Philosopher)

183 Men must be governed by God, or they will be ruled by tyrants.
William Penn (1644-1718, British Religious Leader, Founder of Pennsylvania)

184 I think there are innumerable gods. What we on earth call God is a little tribal God who has made an awful mess. Certainly forces operating through human consciousness control events.
William S. Burroughs (1914-1997, American Writer)

185 If the Almighty were to rebuild the world and asked me for advice, I would have English Channels round every country. And the atmosphere would be such that anything which attempted to fly would be set on fire.
Winston Churchill (1874-1965, British Statesman, Prime Minister)

186 God will provide -- ah, if only He would till He does!
Yiddish Proverb

187 If God would have wanted us to live in a permissive society He would have given us Ten Suggestions and not Ten Commandments.
Zig Ziglar (American Sales Trainer, Author, Motivational Speaker)

GOLD

1 Gold like the sun, which melts wax, but hardens clay, expands great souls.
Antoine Rivarol (1753-1801, French Journalist, Epigrammatist)

2 Gold has worked down from Alexander's time... When something holds good for two thousand years I do not believe it can be so because of prejudice or mistaken theory.
Bernard M. Baruch (1870-1965, American Financier)

3 The golden age only comes to men when they have forgotten gold.
Gilbert K. Chesterton (1874-1936, British Author)

4 Gold will be slave or master.
Horace (65-8 BC, Italian Poet)

5 To have gold is to be in fear, and to want it to be sorrow.
Johnson

6 The man who works for the gold in the job rather than for the money in the pay envelope, is the fellow who gets on.
Joseph French Johnson

7 Gold makes the ugly beautiful.
MoliFre (1622-1673, French Playwright)

8 Gold and silver from the dead turn often into lead.
R. Buckminster Fuller (1895-1983, American Inventor, Designer, Poet, Philosopher)

9 A mask of gold hides all deformities.
Thomas Dekker (1572-1632, British Playwright)

10 It is much better to have your gold in the hand than in the heart.
Thomas Fuller (1608-1661, British Clergyman, Author)

11 Gold! Gold! Gold! Bright and yellow, hard and cold.
Thomas Hood (1799-1845, British Poet and Humorist)

12 Curst greed of gold, what crimes thy tyrant power has caused.
Virgil (70-19 BC, Roman Poet)

13 Gold's father is dirt, yet it regards itself as noble.
Yiddish Proverb

GOLF

1 Elderly gentlemen, gentle in all respects, kind to animals, beloved by children, and fond of music, are found in lonely corners of the downs, hacking at sandpits or tussocks of grass, and muttering in a blind, ungovernable fury elaborate maledictions which could not be extracted from them by robbery or murder. Men who would face torture without a word become blasphemous at the short fourteenth. It is clear that the game of golf may well be included in that category of intolerable provocations which may legally excuse or mitigate behavior not otherwise excusable.
A. P. Herbert (1890-1971, British Author, Politician)

2 Golf is a fine relief from the tensions of office, but we are a little tired of holding the bag.
Adlai E. Stevenson (1900-1965, American Lawyer, Politician)

3 Have you ever noticed what golf spells backwards?
Al Boliska

4 All is fair in love and golf.
American Proverb

5 Anyone who lies golf on television would enjoy watching the grass grow on the greens.
Andy Rooney (American Television News Personality)

6 A typical day in the life of a heavy metal musician consists of a round of golf and an AA meeting.
Billy Joel (1949-, American Musician, Piano Man, Singer, Songwriter)

7 If you watch a game, it's fun. If you play it, it's recreation. If you work at it, it's golf.
Bob Hope (1903-, American Comedian, Actor)

8 When I joined the Tour I studied the best players to see what they did that I didn't do. I came to the conclusion that the successful players had the Three Cs: Confidence, Composure, Concentration.
Bob Toski (1926-, American Golfer)

9 Drive for show, but putt for dough.
Bobby Locke

10 Although Golf was originally restricted to wealthy Protestants, today its open to anybody who owns hideous clothing.
Dave Barry (American Humorist, Author)

11 I used to get out there and have a thousand swing thoughts. Now I try not to have any.
Davis III Love (1964-, American Golfer)

12 Aggressive play is a vital asset of the world's greatest golfers. However, it's even more important to the average player. Attack this game in a bold, confident, and determined way, and you'll make a giant leap toward realizing your full potential as a player.
Greg Norman (1955-, Australian Golfer)

13 It took me seventeen years to get three thousand hits in baseball. I did it in one afternoon on the golf course.
Hank Aaron (Born 1934, American Baseball Player)

14 If you think it's hard to meet new people, try picking up the wrong golf ball.
Jack Lemmon (1925-, American Actor)

15 I go into the locker room and find a corner and just sit there. I try to achieve a peaceful state of nothingness that will carry over onto the golf course. If I can get that feeling of quiet and obliviousness within myself, I feel I can't lose.
Jane Blalock (1945-, American golfer)

16 I throw a ball and get paid for it. Others do it by throwing the bull.
Jerome Dean

17 Golf is the pursuit of the infinite.
Jim Murray (American Author)

18 Magellan went around the world in 1521, which is not too many strokes when you consider the distance.
Joe Laurie Jr.

19 Golf is a good walk spoiled.
Mark Twain (1835-1910, American Humorist, Writer)

20 The pressure makes me more intent about each shot. Pressure on the last few holes makes me play better.
Nancy Lopez (1957-, American Golfer)

21 If there is any larceny in a man, golf will bring it out.
Paul Gallico

22 A day spent in a round of strenuous idleness.
William Wordsworth (1770-1850, British Poet)

23 Golf is a game whose aim is to hit a very small ball into an even smaller hole, with weapons singularly ill-designed for the purpose.
Winston Churchill (1874-1965, British Statesman, Prime Minister)

GOOD AND EVIL

1 Before man is life and death, good and evil; that which he shall choose shall be given him. [Ecclesiasticus]
Bible (Sacred Scriptures of Christians and Judaism)

2 There is no bad in good.
Doug Horton

3 Remember only the good, the bad will never forget you.
Doug Horton

4 Evil comes at leisure like the disease. Good comes in a hurry like the doctor.
Gilbert K. Chesterton (1874-1936, British Author)

5   To rid ourselves of our shadows -- who we are -- we must step into either total light or total darkness. Goodness and evil.
Jeremy P. Johnson

6   Non-cooperation with evil is as much a duty as is cooperation with good.
Mahatma Gandhi (1869-1948, Indian Political, Spiritual Leader)

7   Life is neither good or evil, but only a place for good and evil.
Marcus Aurelius (121-80 AD, Roman Emperor, Philosopher)

8   Them meaning of good and bad, of better and worse, is simply helping or hurting.
Ralph Waldo Emerson (1803-1882, American Poet, Essayist)

9   The Supreme end of education is expert discernment in all things -- the power to tell the good from the bad, the genuine from the counterfeit, and to prefer the good and the genuine to the bad and the counterfeit.
Samuel Johnson (1709-1784, British Author)

10 The only good is knowledge and the only evil is ignorance.
Socrates (469-399 BC, Greek Philosopher of Athens)

11 The web of our life is of a mingled yarn, good and ill together.
William Shakespeare (1564-1616, British Poet, Playwright, Actor)

GOODNESS

1   Good is a product of the ethical and spiritual artistry of individuals; it cannot be mass- produced.
Aldous Huxley (1894-1963, British Author)

2   To make one good action succeed another, is the perfection of goodness.
Ali Ibn-Abi-Talib

3   How sick one gets of being "good," how much I should respect myself if I could burst out and make everyone wretched for twenty-four hours; embody selfishness.
Alice James (1848-1892, American Diarist, Sister of Henry, William James)

4   It is easy to perform a good action, but not easy to acquire a settled habit of performing such actions.
Aristotle (384-322 BC, Greek Philosopher)

5   No one can be good for long if goodness is not in demand.
Bertolt Brecht (1898-1956, German Dramatist, Poet)

6   There are two perfectly good men, one dead, and the other unborn.
Chinese Proverb

7   Goodness is uneventful. It does not flash, it glows.
David Grayson (1870-1946, American Journalist and Writer)

8   As if one could know the good a person is capable of, when one doesn't know the bad he might do.
Elias Canetti (1905-, Austrian Novelist, Philosopher)

9   We all have known good critics, who have stamped out poet's hopes; Good statesmen, who pulled ruin on the state; Good patriots, who, for a theory, risked a cause; Good kings, who disemboweled for a tax; Good Popes, who brought all good to jeopardy; Good Christians, who sat still in easy-chairs; And damned the general world for standing up. Now, may the good God pardon all good men!
Elizabeth Barrett Browning (1806-1861, British Poet)

10 A good heart will help you to a bonny face, my lad and a bad one will turn the bonniest into something worse than ugly.
Emily Bronte (1818-1848, British Novelist, Poet)

11 To conceive the good, in fact, is not sufficient; it must be made to succeed among men. To accomplish this less pure paths must be followed.
Ernest Renan (1823-1892, French Writer, Critic, Scholar)

12 In goodness there are all kinds of wisdom.
Euripides (480-406 BC, Greek Tragic Poet)

13 There are few good women who do not tire of their role.
François de La Rochefoucauld (1613-1680, French classical writer)

14 What is good? All that heightens the feeling of power, the will to power, power itself in man.
Friedrich Nietzsche (1844-1900, German Philosopher)

15 Mere goodness can achieve little against the power of nature.
Georg Hegel (1770-1831, German Philosopher)

16 On the whole, human beings want to be good, but not too good, and not quite all the time.
George Orwell (1903-1950, British Author, "Animal Farm")

17 One of the darkest evils of our world is surely the unteachable wildness of the Good.
H.G. Wells (1866-1946, British-born American Author)

18 Goodness is the only investment which never fails.
Henry David Thoreau (1817-1862, American Essayist, Poet, Naturalist)

19 Being good is just a matter of temperament in the end.
Iris Murdoch (1919-, British Novelist, Philosopher)

20 The measure of your holiness is proportionate to the goodness of your will.
Jan Van Ruysbroeck

21 Our will is always for our own good, but we do not always see what that is.
Jean Jacques Rousseau (1712-1778, Swiss Political Philosopher, Educationist, Essayist)

22 Nothing leads to good that is not natural.
Johann Friedrich Von Schiller (1759-1805, German Dramatist, Poet, Historian)

23 The good is, like nature, an immense landscape in which man advances through centuries of exploration.
Jose Ortega Y Gasset (1883-1955, Spanish Essayist, Philosopher)

24 Live not as though there were a thousand years ahead of you. Fate is at your elbow; make yourself good while life and power are still yours.
Marcus Aurelius (121-80 AD, Roman Emperor, Philosopher)

25 The Crucifixion and other historical precedents notwithstanding, many of us still believe that outstanding goodness is a kind of armor, that virtue, seen plain and bare, gives pause to criminality. But perhaps it is the other way around.
Mary Mccarthy (1912-1989, American Author, Critic)

26 Freedom, morality, and the human dignity of the individual consists precisely in this; that he does good not because he is forced to do so, but because he freely conceives it, wants it, and loves it.
Mikhail Bakunin (1814-1876, Russian Political Theorist)

27 True human goodness, in all its purity and freedom, can come to the fore only when its recipient has no power.
Milan Kundera (1929-, Czech Author, Critic)

28 If you pretend to be good, the world takes you very seriously. If you pretend to be bad, it doesn't. Such is the astounding stupidity of optimism.
Oscar Wilde (1856-1900, British Author, Wit)

29 To be good, according to the vulgar standard of goodness, is obviously quite easy. It merely requires a certain amount of sordid terror, a certain lack of imaginative thought, and a certain low passion for middle-class respectability.
Oscar Wilde (1856-1900, British Author, Wit)

30 Each person has inside a basic decency and goodness. If he listens to it and acts on it, he is giving a great deal of what it is the world needs most. It is not complicated but it takes courage. It takes courage for a person to listen to his own goodness and act on it.
Pablo Casals (1876-1973, Spanish Cellist, Conductor, Composer)

31 A man, to be greatly good, must imagine intensely and comprehensively; he must put himself in the place of another and of many others; the pains and pleasures of his species must become his own.
Percy Bysshe Shelley (1792-1822, British Poet)

32 No man or woman can be strong, gentle, pure, and good, without the world being better for it and without someone being helped and comforted by the very existence of that goodness.
Phillips Brooks (1835-1893, American Minister, Poet)

33 In the world of knowledge, the essential Form of Good is the limit of our inquiries, and can barely be perceived; but, when perceived, we cannot help concluding that it is in every case the source of all that is bright and beautiful --in the visible world giving birth to light and its master, and in the intellectual world dispensing, immediately and with full authority, truth and reason --and that whosoever would act wisely, either in private or in public, must set this Form of Good before his eyes.
Plato (427-347 BC, Greek Philosopher)

34 It is very hard to be simple enough to be good.
Ralph Waldo Emerson (1803-1882, American Poet, Essayist)

35 Good and bad men are less than they seem.
Samuel Taylor Coleridge (1772-1834, British Poet, Critic, Philosopher)

36 Beauty endures only for as long as it can be seen; goodness, beautiful today, will remain so tomorrow.
Sappho (600 BC, Greek Lyric Poet)

37 Goodness is achieved not in a vacuum, but in the company of other men, attended by love.
Saul Bellow (1915-, American Novelist)

38 At the bottom of the heart of every human being, from earliest infancy until the tomb, there is something that goes on indomitably expecting, in the teeth of all experience of crimes committed, suffered, and witnessed, that good and not evil will be done
Simone Weil (1910-1943, French Philosopher, Mystic)

39 Nothing that was worthy in the past departs; no truth or goodness realized by man ever dies, or can die.
Thomas Carlyle (1795-1881, Scottish Philosopher, Author)

40 The devil himself is good when he is pleased.
Thomas Fuller (1608-1661, British Clergyman, Author)

41 Goodness speaks in a whisper, evil shouts
Tibetan Proverb

42 If goodness were only a theory, it were a pity it should be lost to the world. There are a number of things, the idea of which is a clear gain to the mind. Let people, for instance, rail at friendship, genius, freedom, as long as they will --the very names of these despised qualities are better than anything else that could be substituted for them, and embalm even the most envenomed satire against them.
William Hazlitt (1778-1830, British Essayist)

43 How far that little candle throws its beams! So shines a good dead in a naughty world.
William Shakespeare (1564-1616, British Poet, Playwright, Actor)

GOSPEL

1 The gospel to me is simply irresistible.
Blaise Pascal (1623-1662, French Scientist, Religious Philosopher)

2 Philosophical argument has sometimes shaken my reason for the faith that was in me; but my heart has always assured me that the Gospel of Jesus Christ must be reality.
Daniel Webster (1782-1852, American Lawyer, Statesman)

3 The glory of the gospel is that when the church is absolutely different from the world, she invariably attracts it.
David Martyn Lloyd-Jones (1899-1981, British Preacher, Writer)

4 Men may not read the gospel in sealskin, or the gospel in morocco, or the gospel in cloth covers, but they can't get away from the gospel in shoe leather.
Donald Grey Barnhouse (Christian Author)

5 Each generation of the church in each setting has the responsibility of communicating the gospel in understandable terms, considering the language and thought-forms of that setting.
Francis Schaeffer (1912-1984, American Author)

6 The gospel is neither a discussion or a debate. It is an announcement.
Paul S. Rees

7 The real truth is that while He came to preach the gospel, His chief object in coming was that there might be a gospel to preach.
R. W. Dale (Late 19th Century British Reverend)

8 If they had a social gospel in the days of the prodigal son, somebody would have given him a bed and a sandwich and he never would have gone home.
Vance Havner

GOSSIP

1 And all who told it added something new, and all who heard it, made enlargements too.
Alexander Pope (1688-1744, British Poet, Critic, Translator)

2 At every word a reputation dies.
Alexander Pope (1688-1744, British Poet, Critic, Translator)

3 If you haven't got anything nice to say about anybody, come sit next to me.
Alice Roosevelt Longworth (1884-1980, American Author, Daughter of Theodore Roosevelt)

4 Confidante. One entrusted by A with the secrets of B confided to herself by C.
Ambrose Bierce (1842-1914, American Author, Editor, Journalist, "The Devil's Dictionary")

5 A malignant sore throat is a danger, a malignant throat not sore is worse.
American Proverb

6 While gossip among women is universally ridiculed as low and trivial, gossip among men, especially if it is about women, is called theory, or idea, or fact.
Andrea Dworkin (1946-, American Feminist Critic)

7 Show me someone who never gossips, and I will show you someone who is not interested in people.
Barbara Walters (1931-, American TV Personality)

8 No one gossips about other people's secret virtues.
Bertrand Russell (1872-1970, British Philosopher, Mathematician, Essayist)

9 With well doing you may put to silence foolish men.
Bible (Sacred Scriptures of Christians and Judaism)

10 Where no wood is, the fire goes out; so where there is no tale bearer, the strife ceaseth.
Bible (Sacred Scriptures of Christians and Judaism)

11 I maintain that, if everyone knew what others said about him, there would not be four friends in the world.
Blaise Pascal (1623-1662, French Scientist, Religious Philosopher)

12 If all men knew what each said of the other, there would not be four friends in the world.
Blaise Pascal (1623-1662, French Scientist, Religious Philosopher)

13 None are so fond of secrets as those who do not mean to keep them.
Charles Caleb Colton (1780-1832, British Sportsman Writer)

14 Speak no evil of the dead.
Chilo (560 BC, Greek Sage)

15 Your friend has a friend; don't tell him.
Chinese Proverb

16 Never trust the teller, trust the tale.
D. H. Lawrence (1885-1930, British Author)

17 Sight before hearsay.
Danish Proverb

18 I don't care what anybody says about me as long as it isn't true.
Dorothy Parker (1893-1967, American Humorous Writer)

19 Gossip is when you hear something you like about someone, you don't.
Earl Wilson (1907-, American newspaper columnist)

20 Remember, every time you open your mouth to talk, your mind walks out and parades up and down the words.
Edwin H. Stuart

21 Gossip is only the lack of a worthy memory.
Elbert Hubbard (1859-1915, American Author, Publisher)

22 The inspired scribbler always has the gift for gossip in our common usage he or she can always inspire the commonplace with an uncommon flavor, and transform trivialities by some original grace or sympathy or humor or affection.
Elizabeth Drew (1887-1965, Anglo-American Author, Critic)

23 Gossip is the opiate of the oppressed.
Erica Jong (1942-, American Author)

24 Men have always detested women's gossip because they suspect the truth: their measurements are being taken and compared.
Erica Jong (1942-, American Author)

25 My ass contemplates those who talk behind my back.
Francis Picabia (1878-1953, French Painter, Poet)

26 The things most people want to know about are usually none of their business.
George Bernard Shaw (1856-1950, Irish-born British Dramatist)

27 Gossip is a sort of smoke that comes from the dirty tobacco-pipes of those who diffuse it: it proves nothing but the bad taste of the smoker.
George Eliot (1819-1880, British Novelist)

28 She poured a little social sewage into his ears.
George Meredith (1828-1909, British Author)

29 Language is the apparel in which your thoughts parade before the public. Never clothe them in vulgar or shoddy attire.
George W. Crane

30 The objection of the scandalmonger is not that she tells of racy doings, but that she pretends to be indignant about them.
H. L. Mencken (1880-1956, American Editor, Author, Critic, Humorist)

31 Nobody's interested in sweetness and light.
Hedda Hopper

32 Love and scandal are the best sweeteners of tea.
Henry Fielding (1707-1754, British Novelist, Dramatist)

33 There are two good rules which ought to be written on every heart; never to believe anything bad about anybody unless you positively know it to be true; and never to tell that unless you feel that it is absolutely necessary, and that God is listening while you tell it.
Henry Van Dyke (1852-1933, American Protestant Clergyman, Poet and Writer)

34 He who hunts for flowers will finds flowers; and he who loves weeds will find weeds.
Henry Ward Beecher (1813-1887, American Preacher, Orator, Writer)

35 Conversation is three women stand on the corner talking. Gossip is when one of them leaves.
Herb Shriner

36 Avoid inquisitive persons, for they are sure to be gossips, their ears are open to hear, but they will not keep what is entrusted to them.
Horace (65-8 BC, Italian Poet)

37 There is so much good in the worst of us, and so much bad in the best of us, that it ill behaves any of us to find fault with the rest of us.
James Truslow Adams (American Statesman)

38 What you don't see with your eyes, don't witness with your mouth.
Jewish Proverb

39 Loose tongues are worse than wicked han/
Jewish Proverb

40 Don't speak evil of someone if you don'
and if you do know ask yourself, why am I te..
Johann Kaspar Lavater (1741-1801, Swiss Theologian, Mystic)

41 Gossip is what no one claims to like, but everybody enjoys.
Joseph Conrad (1857-1924, Polish-born British Novelist)

42 A gossip is one who talks to you about others; a bore is one who talks to you about himself; and a brilliant conversationalist is one who talks to you about yourself.
Lisa Kirk

43 Gossip is news running ahead of itself in a red satin dress.
Liz Smith (1923-, American Journalist, Gossip Columnist)

44 How awful to reflect that what people say of us is true!
Logan Pearsall Smith (1865-1946, Anglo-American Essayist, Aphorist)

45 The idea of strictly minding our own business is moldy rubbish. Who could be so selfish?
Myrtle Barker

46 There is only one thing in the world worse than being talked about, and that is not being talked about.
Oscar Wilde (1856-1900, British Author, Wit)

47 It is perfectly monstrous the way people go about nowadays saying things against one, behind one's back, that are absolutely and entirely true.
Oscar Wilde (1856-1900, British Author, Wit)

48 A cruel story runs on wheels, and every hand oils the wheels as they run.
Ouida (1838-1908, British Writer)

49 Ah, well, the truth is always one thing, but in a way it's the other thing, the gossip, that counts. It shows where people's hearts lie.
Paul Scott

50 Of course we women gossip on occasion. But our appetite for it is not as avid as a man s. It is in the boys gyms, the college fraternity houses, the club locker rooms, the paneled offices of business that gossip reaches its luxuriant flower.
Phyllis Mcginley (1905-1978, American Poet, Author)

51 Gossip isn't scandal and it's not merely malicious. It's chatter about the human race by lovers of the same. Gossip is the tool of the poet, the shop-talk of the scientist, and the consolation of the housewife, wit, tycoon and intellectual. It begins in the nursery and ends when speech is past.
Phyllis Mcginley (1905-1978, American Poet, Author)

52 Vilify, Vilify, some of it will always stick.
Pierre De Beaumarchais (1732-1799, French Dramatist)

53 Anyone who has obeyed nature by transmitting a piece of gossip experiences the explosive relief that accompanies the satisfying of a primary need.
Primo Levi (1919-1987, Italian Chemist, Author)

54 Gossiping and lying go hand in hand.
Proverb

Count not him among your friends who will retail your privacies to the world.
Publilius Syrus (1st Century BC, Roman Writer)

56 Rest satisfied with doing well, and leave others to talk of you as they will.
Pythagoras (582-507 BC, Greek Philosopher, Mathematician)

57 Everyone realizes that one can believe little of what people say about each other. But it is not so widely realized that even less can one trust what people say about themselves.
Rebecca West (1892-1983, British Author)

58 When of a gossiping circle it was asked, What are they doing? The answer was, Swapping lies.
Richard Brinsley Sheridan (1751-1816, Anglo-Irish Dramatist)

59 Alas! they had been friends in youth; but whispering tongues can poison truth.
Samuel Taylor Coleridge (1772-1834, British Poet, Critic, Philosopher)

60 Gossip is nature's telephone.
Sholom Aleichem (1859-1916, Ukraine-Born American Writer)

61 Fire and swords are slow engines of destruction, compared to the tongue of a Gossip.
Sir Richard Steele (1672-1729, British Dramatist, Essayist, Editor)

62 Whoever gossips to you will gossip about you.
Spanish Proverb

63 Thy friend has a friend, and thy friend's friend has a friend; be discreet.
The Talmud (Jewish Archive of Oral Tradition)

64 A lie has no leg, but a scandal has wings.
Thomas Fuller (1608-1661, British Clergyman, Author)

65 One eye witness is better than ten hear sayers.
Titus Maccius Plautus (254-184 BC, Roman Comic Poet)

66 For prying into any human affairs, non are equal to those whom it does not concern.
Victor Hugo (1802-1885, French Poet, Dramatist, Novelist)

67 Rumor grows as it goes.
Virgil (70-19 BC, Roman Poet)

68 Gossip is the art of saying nothing in a way that leaves practically nothing unsaid.
Walter Winchell (1897-1972, American Journalist)

69 The only time people dislike gossip is when you gossip about them.
Will Rogers (1879-1935, American Humorist, Actor)

70 So live that you wouldn't be ashamed to sell the family parrot to the town gossip.
Will Rogers (1879-1935, American Humorist, Actor)

71 They come together like the Coroner's Inquest, to sit upon the murdered reputations of the week.
William Congreve (1670-1729, British Dramatist)

72 There is a lust in man no charm can tame: Of loudly publishing his neighbor's shame: On eagles wings immortal scandals fly, while virtuous actions are born and die.
William Harvey (1578-1657, British Physician)

GOVERNMENT

1 Well, fancy giving money to the Government! Might as well have put it down the drain.
A. P. Herbert (1890-1971, British Author, Politician)

2 A Government of the people, by the people and for the people, shall not perish from the earth.
Abraham Lincoln (1809-1865, Sixteenth President of the USA)

3 By definition, a government has no conscience. Sometimes it has a policy, but nothing more.
Albert Camus (1913-1960, French Existential Writer)

4 In a healthy nation there is a kind of dramatic balance between the will of the people and the government, which prevents its degeneration into tyranny.
Albert Einstein (1879-1955, German-born American Physicist)

5 Nothing is more destructive of respect for the government and the law of the land than passing laws which cannot be enforced.
Albert Einstein (1879-1955, German-born American Physicist)

6 Even to observe neutrality you must have a strong government.
Alexander Hamilton (1757-1804, American Statesman)

7 For Forms of Government let fools contest; whatever is best administered is best.
Alexander Pope (1688-1744, British Poet, Critic, Translator)

8 A government, for protecting business only, is but a carcass, and soon falls by its own corruption and decay.
Amos Bronson Alcott (1799-1888, American Educator, Social Reformer)

9 There are no necessary evils in government. Its evils exist only in its abuses.
Andrew Jackson (1767-1845, Seventh President of the USA)

10 As long as our government is administered for the good of the people, and is regulated by their will; as long as it secures to us the rights of persons and of property, liberty of conscience and of the press, it will be worth defending.
Andrew Jackson (1767-1845, Seventh President of the USA)

11 Government can be bigger than any of the players on the field as a referee, but it has no right to become one of the players.
Austin Igleheart

12 No more distressing moment can ever face a British government than that which requires it to come to a hard, fast and specific decision.
Barbara Tuchman (1912-1989, American Historian)

13 The object of government in peace and in war is not the glory of rulers or of races, but the happiness of the common man.
Baron William Henry Beveridge (1879-1963, Indian Economist)

14 A government that is big enough to give you all you want is big enough to take it all away.
Barry Goldwater (1909-, American Politician and Writer)

15 But their determination to banish fools foundered ultimately in the installation of absolute idiots.
Basil Bunting (1900-1985, British Poet)

16 Those who govern, having much business on their hands, do not generally like to take the trouble of considering and carrying into execution new projects. The best public measures are therefore seldom adopted from previous wisdom, but forced by the occasion.
Benjamin Franklin (1706-1790, American Scientist, Publisher, Diplomat)

17 There is no nonsense so arrant that it cannot be made the creed of the vast majority by adequate government action.
Bertrand Russell (1872-1970, British Philosopher, Mathematician, Essayist)

18 Beaverbrook is so pleased to be in the government that he is like the town tart who finally married the Mayor.
Beverley Baxter

19 The government can destroy wealth but it cannot create wealth, which is the product of labor and management working with creation.
Bill Murray (1950-, American Comedian, Actor, Writer)

20 Congress is so strange. A man gets up to speak and says nothing. Nobody listens, then everybody disagrees.
Boris Marshalov

21 Not wishing to be disturbed over moral issues of the political economy, Americans cling to the notion that the government is a sort of automatic machine, regulated by the balancing of competing interests.
C. Wright Mills (1916-1962, American Sociologist)

22 To administer is to govern: to govern is to reign. That is the essence of the problem.
Comte De Mirabeau (1749-1791, French Revolutionary Politician and Orator)

23 No government is safe unless fortified by goodwill.
Cornelius Nepos (1st Century BC)

24 The government must always be a step ahead of the popular movement.
Count Boytzwnburg

25 In quiet and untroubled times it seems to every administrator that it is only by his efforts that the whole population under his rule is kept going, and in this consciousness of being indispensable every administrator finds the chief reward of his labor and efforts. While the sea of history remains calm the ruler-administrator in his frail bark, holding on with a boat hook to the ship of the people and himself moving, naturally imagines that his efforts move the ship he is holding on to. But as soon as a storm arises and the sea begins to heave and the ship to move, such a delusion is no longer possible. The ship moves independently with its own enormous motion, the boat hook no longer reaches the moving vessel, and suddenly the administrator, instead of appearing a ruler and a source of power, becomes an insignificant, useless, feeble man.
Count Leo Tolstoy (1828-1910, Russian Novelist, Philosopher)

26 Nothing is more surprising than the easiness with which the many are governed by the few.
David Hume (1711-1776, Scottish Philosopher, Historian)

27 Remember that a government big enough to give you everything you want is also big enough to take away everything you have.
Davy Crockett (1786-1836, American Backwoodsman)

28 Any party which takes credit for the rain must not be surprised if its opponents blame it for the drought.
Dwight Whitney Morrow (1873-1931, American Lawyer, Banker, diplomat)

29 Nothing turns out to be so oppressive and unjust as a feeble government.
Edmund Burke (1729-1797, British Political Writer, Statesman)

30 It is the duty of the President to propose and it is the privilege of the Congress to dispose.
Franklin D. Roosevelt (1882-1945, Thirty-second President of the USA)

31 Government is the great fiction, through which everybody endeavors to live at the expense of everybody else.
Frederic Bastiat (1801-1850, French Legislator)

32 An educated people can be easily governed.
Frederick The Great (Frederick II) (1712-1786, Born in Berlin, King of Prussia (1740-1786))

33 In the councils of a state, the question is not so much, what ought to be done? As, what can be done?
French Proverb

34 Men are not governed by justice, but by law or persuasion. When they refuse to be governed by law or persuasion, they have to be governed by force or fraud, or both.
George Bernard Shaw (1856-1950, Irish-born British Dramatist)

35 The art of government is the organization of idolatry. The bureaucracy consists of functionaries; the aristocracy, of idols; the democracy, of idolaters. The populace cannot understand the bureaucracy: it can only worship the national idols.
George Bernard Shaw (1856-1950, Irish-born British Dramatist)

36 Too bad that all the people who know how to run the country are busy driving taxicabs and cutting hair.
George Burns (1896-1996, American Comedy Actor)

37 Mankind, when left to themselves, are unfit for their own government.
George Washington (1732-1799, First President of the USA)

38 Government is not reason and it is not eloquence. It is force! Like fire it is a dangerous servant and a fearful master. Never for a moment should it be left to irresponsible action.
George Washington (1732-1799, First President of the USA)

39 Truth is the glue that holds government together.
Gerald R. Ford (1913-, Thirty-eighth President of the USA)

40 Office without pay makes thieves.
German Proverb

41 Though the people support the government; the government should not support the people.
Grover Cleveland (1837-1908, Twenty-second & 24th President of the USA)

42 Government is actually the worst failure of civilized man. There has never been a really good one, and even those that are most tolerable are arbitrary, cruel, grasping and unintelligent.
H. L. Mencken (1880-1956, American Editor, Author, Critic, Humorist)

43 All good government must begin at home.
H. R. Haweis

44 The monarchy is a labor intensive industry.
Harold Wilson (1916-1995, British Statesman, Prime Minister)

45 Whenever you have an efficient government, you have a dictatorship.
Harry S. Truman (1884-1972, Thirty-third President of the USA)

46 Government is at best but an expedient; but most governments are usually, and all governments are sometimes, inexpedient. The objections which have been brought against a standing army, and they are many and weighty, and deserve to prevail, may also at last be brought against a standing government.
Henry David Thoreau (1817-1862, American Essayist, Poet, Naturalist)

47 That government is best which governs least.
Henry David Thoreau (1817-1862, American Essayist, Poet, Naturalist)

48 The government of the world I live in was not framed, like that of Britain, in after-dinner conversations over the wine.
Henry David Thoreau (1817-1862, American Essayist, Poet, Naturalist)

49 This American government -- what is it but a tradition, though a recent one, endeavoring to transmit itself unimpaired to posterity, but each instant losing some of its integrity? It has not the vitality and force of a single living man; for a single man can bend it to his will.
Henry David Thoreau (1817-1862, American Essayist, Poet, Naturalist)

50 The worst thing in the world next to anarchy, is government.
Henry Ward Beecher (1813-1887, American Preacher, Orator, Writer)

51 Neither snow, nor rain, nor heat, nor gloom of night stays these couriers from the swift completion of their appointed rounds. [The Motto Of The U.S. Postal Service]
Herodotus (484-425 BC, Greek Historian)

52 Bureaucracy is a giant mechanism operated by pygmies.
Honore De Balzac (1799-1850, French Novelist)

53 What is government itself but the greatest of all reflections on human nature? If men were angels, no government would be necessary. If angels were to govern men, neither external nor internal controls on government would be necessary.
James Madison (1751-1836, American Statesman, President)

54 A government is the only vessel that leaks from the top.
James Reston (1909-1995, Dutch Born American Journalist)

55 The ship of state is the only known vessel that leaks from the top.
James Reston (1909-1995, Dutch Born American Journalist)

56 In our consumer confidence surveys, we ask people whether they think government economic policy is good, fair, or poor. Increasingly, the answer we get is just plain laughter.
Jay Schmiedeskamp

57 Governing today means giving acceptable signs of credibility. It is like advertising and it is the same effect that is achieved -- commitment to a scenario.
Jean Baudrillard (French Postmodern Philosopher, Writer)

58 The body politic, as well as the human body, begins to die as soon as it is born, and carries itself the causes of its destruction.
Jean Jacques Rousseau (1712-1778, Swiss Political Philosopher, Educationist, Essayist)

59 I don't judge a regime by the damning criticism of the opposition, but by the ingenuous praise of the partisan.
Jean Rostand (1894-1977, French Biologist, Writer)

60 The best government is that which teaches us to govern ourselves.
Johann Wolfgang Von Goethe (1749-1832, German Poet, Dramatist, Novelist)

61 Fear is the foundation of most government.
John Adams (1735-1826, Second President of the USA)

62 The basis of effective government if public confidence.
John F. Kennedy (1917-1963, Thirty-fifth President of the USA)

63 Of all tasks of government the most basic is to protect its citizens against violence.
John Foster Dulles (1888-1959, American Republican Secretary of State)

64 The greater the hold of government upon the life of the individual citizen, the greater the risk of war.
John Hospers

65 Good government is the outcome of private virtue.
John Jay Chapman (1862-1933, American Author)

66 It would be foolish to suggest that government is a good custodian of aesthetic goals. But, there is no alternative to the state.
John Kenneth Galbraith (1908-, American Economist)

67 The contented and economically comfortable have a very discriminating view of government. Nobody is ever indignant about bailing out failed banks and failed savings and loans associations. But when taxes must be paid for the lower middle class and poor, the government assumes an aspect of wickedness.
John Kenneth Galbraith (1908-, American Economist)

68 Freedom of men under government is to have a standing rule to live by, common to every one of that society, and made by the legislative power vested in it; a liberty to follow my own will in all things, when the rule prescribes not, and not to be subject to the inconstant, unknown, arbitrary will of another man.
John Locke (1632-1704, British Philosopher)

69 Government has no other end, but the preservation of property.
John Locke (1632-1704, British Philosopher)

70 The point to remember is what government gives it must first take away
John S. Caldwell

71 I love my government not least for the extent to which it leaves me alone.
John Updike (1932-, American Novelist, Critic)

72 Government is either organized benevolence or organized madness; its peculiar magnitude permits no shading.
John Updike (1932-, American Novelist, Critic)

73 It is hard to feel individually responsible with respect to the invisible processes of a huge and distant government.
John W. Gardner (1912-, American Educator, Social Activist)

74 To rule is not so much a question of the heavy hand as the firm seat.
Jose Ortega Y Gasset (1883-1955, Spanish Essayist, Philosopher)

75 Nations it may be have fashioned their Governments, but the Governments have paid them back in the same coin.
Joseph Conrad (1857-1924, Polish-born British Novelist)

76 Every country has the government it deserves.
Joseph De Maistre (1753-1821, French Diplomat, Philosopher)

77 Being nice to governments doesn't work, they are such lying bastards.
Joy Baluch

78 Safety of the state is the highest law.
Justinian (482-565, Roman Emperor)

79 The government is best which makes itself unnecessary.
Karl Wilhelm Von Humboldt (1767-1835, German Statesman, Philologist)

80 Of the best rulers, The people only know that they exist; the next best they love and praise the next they fear; and the next they revile. When they do not command the people's faith, some will lose faith in them, and then they resort to oaths! But of the best when their task is accomplished, their work done, the people all remark, "We have done it ourselves."
Lao-Tzu (600 BC, Chinese Philosopher, Founder of Taoism, Author of the "Tao Te Ching")

81 Generosity is a part of my character, and I therefore hasten to assure this Government that I will never make an allegation of dishonesty against it wherever a simple explanation of stupidity will suffice.
Leslie Baron Lever

82 The supply of government exceeds demand.
Lewis H. Lapham (1935-, American Essayist, Editor)

83 The auditor is a watchdog and not a bloodhound.
Lord Justice Topes

84 The whole duty of government is to prevent crime and to preserve contracts.
Lord Melbourne (1779-1848, British Statesman, Prime Minister)

85 A man without a vote is man without protection.
Lyndon B. Johnson (1908-1973, Thirty-sixth President of the USA)

86 It could probably be shown by facts and figures that there is no distinctly native American criminal class except Congress.
Mark Twain (1835-1910, American Humorist, Writer)

87 We have the best government that money can buy.
Mark Twain (1835-1910, American Humorist, Writer)

88 The mechanism that directs government cannot be virtuous, because it is impossible to thwart every crime, to protect oneself from every criminal without being criminal too; that which directs corrupt mankind must be corrupt itself; and it will never be by means of virtue, virtue being inert and passive, that you will maintain control over vice, which is ever active: the governor must be more energetic than the governed.
Marquis De Sade (1740-1814, French Author)

89 Our Congress is the finest body of men money can buy.
Maury Amsterdam

90 It is very easy to accuse a government of imperfection, for all mortal things are full of it.
Michel Eyquem De Montaigne (1533-1592, French Philosopher, Essayist)

91 Thou camest out of thy mother's belly without government, thou hast liv'd hitherto without government, and thou mayst be carried to thy long home without government, when it shall please the Lord. How many people in this world live without government, yet do well enough, and are well look'd upon?
Miguel De Cervantes (1547-1616, Spanish Novelist, Dramatist, Poet)

92 Many people want the government to protect the consumer. A much more urgent problem is to protect the consumer from the government.
Milton Friedman (1912-, American Economist)

93 Governments never learn. Only people learn.
Milton Friedman (1912-, American Economist)

94 The government solution to a problem is usually as bad as the problem.
Milton Friedman (1912-, American Economist)

95 It is function of government to invent philosophies to explain the demands of its own convenience.
Murray Kempton (1917-1997, American Author and Columnist)

96 The art of government is not to let me grow stale.
Napoleon Bonaparte (1769-1821, French General, Emperor)

97 Large legislative bodies resolve themselves into coteries, and coteries into jealousies.
Napoleon Bonaparte (1769-1821, French General, Emperor)

98 Public instruction should be the first object of government.
Napoleon Bonaparte (1769-1821, French General, Emperor)

99 To govern is to choose. To appear to be unable to choose is to appear to be unable to govern.
Nigel Lawson

100 A government must not waiver once it has chosen it's course. It must not look to the left or right but go forward.
Otto Von Bismarck (1815-1898, Prussian Statesman, Prime Minister)

101 The government is huge, stupid, greedy and makes nosy, officious and dangerous intrusions into the smallest corners of life -- this much we can stand. But the real problem is that government is boring. We could cure or mitigate the other ills Washington visits on us if we could only bring ourselves to pay attention to Washington itself. But we cannot.
P. J. O'Rourke (1947-, American Journalist)

102 Giving money and power to government is like giving whiskey and car keys to teenage boys.
P. J. O'Rourke (1947-, American Journalist)

103 If you join government, calmly make your contribution and move on. Don't go along to get along; do your best and when you have to -- and you will -- leave, and be something else.
Peggy Noonan (1950-, American Author, Presidential Speechwriter)

104 Government is an evil; it is only the thoughtlessness and vices of men that make it a necessary evil. When all men are good and wise, government will of itself decay.
Percy Bysshe Shelley (1792-1822, British Poet)

105 That state is best ordered when the wicked have no command, and the good have.
Pittacus (650-570 BC, Statesman from Ancient Greece)

106 The punishment which the wise suffer who refuse to take part in the government, is to live under the government of worse men.
Plato (427-347 BC, Greek Philosopher)

107 The less government we have the better.
Ralph Waldo Emerson (1803-1882, American Poet, Essayist)

108 I say to myself that I mustn't let myself be cut off in there, and yet the moment I enter my bag is taken out of my hand, I'm pushed in, shepherded, nursed and above all cut off, alone. Whitehall envelops me.
Richard Crossman (1907-1974, British Writer, Editor, Socialist)

109 For its part, Government will listen. We will strive to listen in new ways -- to the voices of quiet anguish, to voices that speak without words, the voices of the heart, to the injured voices, and the anxious voices, and the voices that have despaired of being heard.
Richard M. Nixon (1913-1994, Thirty-seventh President of the USA)

110 When any government, or church for that matter, undertakes to say to it's subjects, this you may not read, this you must not see, this you are forbidden to know the end result is tyranny and oppression, no matter how holy the motive.
Robert Heinlein (1907-1988, American Science Fiction Writer)

111 The whole country is one vast insane asylum and they're letting the worst patients run the place.
Robert Welch

112 Government does not solve problems; it subsidizes them.
Ronald Reagan (1911-, Fortieth President of the USA, Actor)

113 Government is like a baby. An alimentary canal with a big appetite at one end and no sense of responsibility at the other.
Ronald Reagan (1911-, Fortieth President of the USA, Actor)

114 Today, if you invent a better mousetrap, the government comes along with a better mouse.
Ronald Reagan (1911-, Fortieth President of the USA, Actor)

115 Governments tend not to solve problems, only to rearrange them.
Ronald Reagan (1911-, Fortieth President of the USA, Actor)

116 You could afford your house without the government if it weren't for the government.
Rush Limbaugh (1951-, American TV Personality)

117 I would not give half a guinea to live under one form of government rather than another. It is of no moment to the happiness of an individual.
Samuel Johnson (1709-1784, British Author)

118 The three great ends which a statesman ought to propose to himself in the government of a nation, are -- 1. Security to possessors; 2. Facility to acquirers; and, 3. Hope to all.
Samuel Taylor Coleridge (1772-1834, British Poet, Critic, Philosopher)

119 An ambassador is an honest person sent to lie abroad for their country.
Sir Henry Wotton (1568-1639, British Diplomat, Traveler, Scholar, and Poet)

120 Who so taketh in hand to frame any state or government ought to presuppose that all men are evil, and at occasions will show themselves so to be.
Sir Walter Raleigh (1552-1618, British Courtier, Navigator, Writer)

121 No man undertakes a trade he has not learned, even the meanest; yet everyone thinks himself sufficiently qualified for the hardest of all trades, that of government.
Socrates (469-399 BC, Greek Philosopher of Athens)

122 Society is well governed when its people obey the magistrates, and the magistrates obey the law.
Solon (636-558 BC, Greek Statesman)

123 The Athenians govern the Greeks; I govern the Athenians; you, my wife, govern me; your son governs you.
Themistocles (528-462 BC, Greek Statesman, Soldier)

124 The government is us; we are the government, you and I.
Theodore Roosevelt (1858-1919, Twenty-sixth President of the USA)

125 There is something to be said for government by a great aristocracy which has furnished leaders to the nation in peace and war for generations; even a democrat like myself must admit this. But there is absolutely nothing to be said for government by a plutocracy, for government by men very powerful in certain lines and gifted with the "money touch," but with ideals which in their essence are merely those of so many glorified pawnbrokers.
Theodore Roosevelt (1858-1919, Twenty-sixth President of the USA)

126 We must judge a government by its general tendencies and not by its happy accidents.
Thomas B. Macaulay (1800-1859, American Essayist and Historian)

127 Nothing is so galling to a people not broken in from the birth as a paternal, or in other words a meddling government, a government which tells them what to read and say and eat and drink and wear.
Thomas B. Macaulay (1800-1859, American Essayist and Historian)

128 In the long-run every Government is the exact symbol of its People, with their wisdom and unwisdom; we have to say, Like People like Government.
Thomas Carlyle (1795-1881, Scottish Philosopher, Author)

129 Men are to be guided only by their self-interests. Good government is a good balancing of these; and, except a keen eye and appetite for self-interest, requires no virtue in any quarter. To both parties it is emphatically a machine: to the discontented, a "taxing-machine;" to the contented, a "machine for securing property." Its duties and its faults are not those of a father, but of an active parish-constable.
Thomas Carlyle (1795-1881, Scottish Philosopher, Author)

130 I have no ambition to govern men. It is a painful and thankless office
Thomas Jefferson (1743-1826, Third President of the USA)

131 Whenever the people are well informed, they can be trusted with their own government; that whenever things get so far wrong as to attract their notice, they may be relied on to set them to rights.
Thomas Jefferson (1743-1826, Third President of the USA)

132 The care of human life and happiness, and not their destruction, is the first and only legitimate object of good government.
Thomas Jefferson (1743-1826, Third President of the USA)

133 That government is the strongest of which every man feels himself a part.
Thomas Jefferson (1743-1826, Third President of the USA)

134 My reading of history convinces me that most bad government results from too much government.
Thomas Jefferson (1743-1826, Third President of the USA)

135 Society in every state is a blessing, but Government, even in its best state, is but a necessary evil; in its worst state, an intolerable one.
Thomas Paine (1737-1809, Anglo-American Political Theorist, Writer)

136 It is easy to rule over the good.
Titus Maccius Plautus (254-184 BC, Roman Comic Poet)

137 You can only govern men by serving them. The rule is without exception.
Victor Cousin (1792-1867, French Philosopher)

138 Any cook should be able to run the country.
Vladimir Ilyich Lenin (1870-1924, Russian Revolutionary Leader)

139 It is dangerous to be right when the government is wrong.
Voltaire (1694-1778, French Historian, Writer)

140 The best government is a benevolent tyranny tempered by an occasional assassination.
Voltaire (1694-1778, French Historian, Writer)

141 Governments need to have both shepherds and butchers.
Voltaire (1694-1778, French Historian, Writer)

142 It is doubtful that the government knows much more than the public does about how government [Economic] policies will work.
W. Allen Wallis

143 It is often said that men are ruled by their imaginations; but it would be truer to say they are governed by the weakness of their imaginations.
Walter Bagehot (1826-1877, British Economist, Critic)

144 It is perfectly true that that government is best which governs least. It is equally true that that government is best which provides most.
Walter Lippmann (1889-1974, American Journalist)

145 Be thankful we're not getting all the government we're paying for.
Will Rogers (1879-1935, American Humorist, Actor)

146 I don't make jokes. I just watch the government and report the facts.
Will Rogers (1879-1935, American Humorist, Actor)

147 It is the duty of government to make it difficult for people to do wrong, easy to do right.
William E. Gladstone (1809-1888, British Liberal Prime Minister, Statesman)

148 Every form of government tends to perish by excess of its basic principles.
William J. Durant (1885-1981, American Historian, Essayist)

149 The constitution is not neutral. It was designed to take the government off the backs of people.
William O. Douglas (1898-1980, American Supreme Court Justice)

150 Many forms of Government have been tried, and will be tried in this world of sin and woe. No one pretends that democracy is perfect or all-wise. Indeed, it has been said that democracy is the worst form of Government except all those others that have been tried from time to time.
Winston Churchill (1874-1965, British Statesman, Prime Minister)

GRACE

1 Salvation is from our side a choice, from the divine side it is a seizing upon, an apprehending, a conquest by the Most High God. Our "accepting" and "willing" are reactions rather than actions. The right of determination must always remain with God.
A. W. Tozer (Deceased 1963, American Preacher)

2 The grace of God," says Luther, "is like a flying summer shower." It has fallen upon more than one land, and passed on. Judea had it, and lies barren and dry. These Asiatic coasts had it, and flung it away.
Alexander Maclaren (1826-1910, British Preacher)

3 Grace is free sovereign favor to the ill-deserving.
Benjamin B. Warfield

4 We're all stumbling towards the light with varying degrees of grace at any given moment.
Bo Lozoff

5 Grace is savage and must be savage in order to be perfect.
Charles A. Stoddard

6 To hit bottom is to fall from grace.
Doug Horton

7 A graceful and pleasing figure is a perpetual letter of recommendation.
Francis Bacon (1561-1626, British Philosopher, Essayist, Statesman)

8 Gracefulness is to the body what understanding is to the mind.
François de La Rochefoucauld (1613-1680, French classical writer)

9 Without grace beauty is an unabated hook.
French Proverb

10 Do you know that the ready concession of minor points is a part of the grace of life?
Henry Harland

11 God appoints our graces to be nurses to other men's weaknesses.
Henry Ward Beecher (1813-1887, American Preacher, Orator, Writer)

12 Grace is the beauty of form under the influence of freedom.
Johann Friedrich Von Schiller (1759-1805, German Dramatist, Poet, Historian)

13 There, but for the grace of God, goes John Bradford.
John Braford

14 Grace is but glory begun, and glory is but grace perfected.
Jonathan Edwards (1703-1758, British Theologian, Metaphysician)

15 Grace is in garments, in movements, in manners; beauty in the nude, and in forms. This is true of bodies; but when we speak of feelings, beauty is in their spirituality, and grace in their moderation.
Joseph Joubert (1754-1824, French Moralist)

16 Always accept good fortune with grace and humility.
Mark L. Mika

17 Grace is always natural, though that does not prevent its being often used to hide a lie. The rude shocks and uncomfortably constraining influences of life disappear among graceful women and poetical men; they are the most deceptive beings in creation; distrust and doubt cannot stand before them; they create what they imagine; if they do not lie to others, they do to their own hearts; for illusion is their element, fiction their vocation, and pleasures in appearance their happiness. Beware of grace in woman, and poetry in man -- weapons the more dangerous because the least dreaded!
Marquis De Custine (1790-1857, French Traveler, Author)

18 Beauty and grace command the world.
Park Benjamin (1809-1864, American Poet, Writer)

19 There can be a fundamental gulf of gracelessness in a human heart which neither our love nor our courage can bridge.
Patrick Campbell (1913-1980, Irish Humorist)

20 Grace means the free, unmerited, unexpected love of God, and all the benefits, delights, and comforts which flow from it. It means that while we were sinners and enemies we have been treated as sons and heirs.
R. P. C. Hanson

21 Their sighing , canting , grace-proud faces, their three-mile prayers, and half-mile graces.
Robert Burns (1759-1796, Scottish Poet)

22 Grace in women has more effect than beauty.
William Hazlitt (1778-1830, British Essayist)

23 Grace is the absence of everything that indicates pain or difficulty, hesitation or incongruity.
William Hazlitt (1778-1830, British Essayist)

24 Grace has been defined as the outward expression of the inward harmony of the soul.
William Hazlitt (1778-1830, British Essayist)

GRAFFITI

1 Gray hair is God's graffiti.
Bill Cosby (1937-, American Actor, Comedian, Producer)

2 In the dime stores and bus stations, people talk of situations, read books, repeat quotations, draw conclusions on the wall.
Bob Dylan (1941-, American Musician, Singer, Songwriter)

3 In New York -- whose subway trains in particular have been "tattooed" with an energy to put our own rude practitioners to shame -- not an inch of free space is spared except that of advertisements . Even the most chronically dispossessed appear prepared to endorse the legitimacy of the "haves."
Gilbert Adair (Born 1944, American Author)

4 What harm cause not those huge draughts or pictures which wanton youth with chalk or coals draw in each passage, wall or stairs of our great houses, whence a cruel contempt of our natural store is bred in them?
Michel Eyquem De Montaigne (1533-1592, French Philosopher, Essayist)

GRAMMAR

1 Spel chekers, hoo neeeds em?
Alan James Bean

2 I never made a mistake in grammar but one in my life and as soon as I done it I seen it.
Carl Sandburg (1878-1967, American Poet)

3 Commas in The New Yorker fall with the precision of knives in a circus act, outlining the victim.
E(lwyn) B(rooks) White (1899-1985, American Author, Editor)

4 The writer who neglects punctuation, or mispunctuates, is liable to be misunderstood for the want of merely a comma, it often occurs that an axiom appears a paradox, or that a sarcasm is converted into a sermonoid.
Edgar Allan Poe (1809-1845, American Poet, Critic, short-story Writer)

5 Grammar is the grave of letters.
Elbert Hubbard (1859-1915, American Author, Publisher)

6 My attitude toward punctuation is that it ought to be as conventional as possible. The game of golf would lose a good deal if croquet mallets and billiard cues were allowed on the putting green. You ought to be able to show that you can do it a good deal better than anyone else with the regular tools before you have a license to bring in your own improvements.
Ernest Hemingway (1898-1961, American Writer)

7 When I hear the hypercritical quarreling about grammar and style, the position of the particles, etc., etc., stretching or contracting every speaker to certain rules of theirs. I see that they forget that the first requisite and rule is that expression shall be vital and natural, as much as the voice of a brute or an interjection: first of all, mother tongue; and last of all, artificial or father tongue. Essentially your truest poetic sentence is as free and lawless as a lamb's bleat.
Henry David Thoreau (1817-1862, American Essayist, Poet, Naturalist)

8 No iron can pierce the heart with such force as a period put just at the right place.
Isaac Babel (1894-1941, Jewish Writer)

9 From one casual of mine he picked this sentence. "After dinner, the men moved into the living room." I explained to the professor that this was Rose' way of giving the men time to push back their chairs and stand up. There must, as we know, be a comma after every move, made by men, on this earth.
James Thurber (1894-1961, American Humorist, Illustrator)

10 Grammar is a piano I play by ear. All I know about grammar is its power.
Joan Didion (1934-, American Essayist)

11 Sometimes you get a glimpse of a semicolon coming, a few lines farther on, and it is like climbing a steep path through woods and seeing a wooden bench just at a bend in the road ahead, a place where you can expect to sit for a moment, catching your breath.
Lewis Thomas (1913-, American Physician, Educator)

12 Like everything metaphysical the harmony between thought and reality is to be found in the grammar of the language.
Ludwig Wittgenstein (1889-1951, Austrian Philosopher)

13 Damn the subjunctive. It brings all our writers to shame.
Mark Twain (1835-1910, American Humorist, Writer)

14 Grammar, which can govern even Kings.
MoliFre (1622-1673, French Playwright)

15 You can be a little ungrammatical if you come from the right part of the country.
Robert Frost (1875-1963, American Poet)

16 From now on, ending a sentence with a preposition is something up with which I will not put.
Winston Churchill (1874-1965, British Statesman, Prime Minister)

GRATITUDE

1 Many times a day I realize how much my own life is built on the labors of my fellowmen, and how earnestly I must exert myself in order to give in return as much as I have received.
Albert Einstein (1879-1955, German-born American Physicist)

2 One can never pay in gratitude; one can only pay "in kind" somewhere else in life.
Anne Morrow Lindbergh (1906-, American Author)

3 He that has satisfied his thirst turns his back on the well.
Baltasar Gracian (1601-1658, Spanish Philosopher, Writer)

4 Hope has a good memory, gratitude a bad one.
Baltasar Gracian (1601-1658, Spanish Philosopher, Writer)

5 Most people return small favors, acknowledge medium ones and repay greater ones -- with ingratitude.
Benjamin Franklin (1706-1790, American Scientist, Publisher, Diplomat)

6 When befriended, remember it; when you befriend, forget it.
Benjamin Franklin (1706-1790, American Scientist, Publisher, Diplomat)

7 Whatever I am offered in devotion with a pure heart -- a leaf, a flower, fruit, or water -- I accept with joy.
Bhagavad Gita (400 BC, Sanskrit Poem Incorporated Into the Mahabharata)

8 Unto every one that hath shall be given, and he shall have abundance: but from him that hath not shall be taken away even that which he hath. [Matthew]
Bible (Sacred Scriptures of Christians and Judaism)

9 When the insects take over the world we hope they will remember, with gratitude, how we took them along on all our picnics.
Bill Vaughan (1915-1977, American Author, Journalist)

10 Just because you like my stuff doesn't mean I owe you anything.
Bob Dylan (1941-, American Musician, Singer, Songwriter)

11 Every professional athlete owes a debt of gratitude to the fans and management, and pays an installment every time he plays. He should never miss a payment.
Bobby Hull (American Hockey Player)

12 Reflect upon your present blessings, of which every man has plenty; not on your past misfortunes, of which all men have some.
Charles Dickens (1812-1870, British Novelist)

13 Do you realize what this means? The fact of being alive... I still find it staggering that I am here at all.
Christopher Leach (American Poet)

14 For today and its blessings, I owe the world an attitude of gratitude.
Clarence E. Hodges

15 Nothing purchased can come close to the renewed sense of gratitude for having family and friends.
Courtland Milloy

16 To remind a man of the good turns you have done him is very much like a reproach.
Demosthenes (383-322 BC, Greek Orator)

17 Gratitude -- the meanest and most sniveling attribute in the world.
Dorothy Parker (1893-1967, American Humorous Writer)

18 Gratitude is one of those things that cannot be bought. It must be born with men, or else all the obligations in the world will not create it.
Edward F. Halifax (1881-1959, British Conservative Statesman)

19 Revenge is profitable, gratitude is expensive.
Edward Gibbon (1737-1794, British Historian)

20 Two kinds of gratitude: The sudden kind we feel for what we take; the larger kind we feel for what we give.
Edwin Arlington Robinson (1869-1935, American Poet)

21 Gratitude helps you to grow and expands; gratitude brings you and laughter into your life and into the lives of all those around you.
Eileen Caddy (American Spiritual Writer)

22 This race is never grateful: from the first, One fills their cup at supper with pure wine, Which back they give at cross-time on a sponge, In bitter vinegar.
Elizabeth Barrett Browning (1806-1861, British Poet)

23 Remember that not to be happy is not to be grateful.
Elizabeth Carter

24 Do not spoil what you have by desiring what you have not; but remember that what you now have was once among the things you only hoped for.
Epicurus (341-270 BC, Greek Philosopher)

25 Gratitude is one of the least articulate of the emotions, especially when it is deep.
Felix Frankfurter (1882-1965, Austrian-born American Law Teacher, Judge)

26 In most of mankind gratitude is merely a secret hope of further favors.
François de La Rochefoucauld (1613-1680, French classical writer)

27 We seldom find people ungrateful so long as it is thought we can serve them.
François de La Rochefoucauld (1613-1680, French classical writer)

28 If a fellow isn't thankful for what he's got, he isn't likely to be thankful for what he's going to get.
Frank A. Clark

29 Gratitude is the heart's memory.
French Proverb

30 It is not possible to eat me without insisting that I sing praises of my devourer?
Fyodor Dostoevski (1821-1881, Russian Novelist)

31 True thanksgiving means that we need to thank God for what He has done for us, and not to tell Him what we have done for Him. -
George R. Hendrick

32 Gratitude is a twofold love -- love coming to visit us, and love running out to greet a welcome guest.
Henry Van Dyke (1852-1933, American Protestant Clergyman, Poet and Writer)

33 Gratitude is the inward feeling of kindness received. Thankfulness is the natural impulse to express that feeling. Thanksgiving is the following of that impulse.
Henry Van Dyke (1852-1933, American Protestant Clergyman, Poet and Writer)

34 A proud man is seldom a grateful man, for he never thinks he gets as much as he deserves.
Henry Ward Beecher (1813-1887, American Preacher, Orator, Writer)

35 Gratitude is the fairest blossom which springs from the soul.
Henry Ward Beecher (1813-1887, American Preacher, Orator, Writer)

36 Next to ingratitude the most painful thing to bear is gratitude.
Henry Ward Beecher (1813-1887, American Preacher, Orator, Writer)

37 God has two dwellings; one in heaven, and the other in a meek and thankful heart.
Izaak Walton (1593-1683, British Writer)

38 Gratitude is the most exquisite form of courtesy.
Jacques Maritain (1882-1973, French Philosopher)

39 Thank God every morning when you get up that you have something to do that day, which must be done, whether you like it or not.
James Russell Lowell (1819-1891, American Poet, Critic, Editor)

40 Gratitude is a duty which ought to be paid, but which none have a right to expect.
Jean Jacques Rousseau (1712-1778, Swiss Political Philosopher, Educationist, Essayist)

41 Because gratification of a desire leads to the temporary stilling of the mind and the experience of the peaceful, joyful Self it's no wonder that we get hooked on thinking that happiness comes from the satisfaction of desires. This is the meaning of the old adage, "Joy is not in things, it is in us."
Joan Borysenko (American Clinical Psychologist, Author)

42 To speak gratitude is courteous and pleasant, to enact gratitude is generous and noble, but to live gratitude is to touch Heaven.
Johannes A. Gaertner

43 Gratitude is a sickness suffered by dogs.
Joseph Stalin (1879-1953, Georgian-born Soviet Leader)

44 Gratitude is not only the greatest of virtues, but the parent of all the others.
Marcus T. Cicero (106-43 BC, Great Roman Orator, Politician)

45 If you pick up a starving dog and make him prosperous, he will not bite you; that is the principal difference between a dog and a man.
Mark Twain (1835-1910, American Humorist, Writer)

46 Gratitude unlocks the fullness of life. It turns what we have into enough, and more. It turns denial into acceptance, chaos to order, confusion to clarity. It can turn a meal into a feast, a house into a home, a stranger into a friend. Gratitude makes sense of our past, brings peace for today, and creates a vision for tomorrow.
Melody Beattie (American Author)

47 Gratitude is not only the memory but the homage of the heart rendered to God for his goodness.
Nathaniel P. Willis (1806-1867, Polish American Poet, writer, editor)

48 I don't like it when people on the street say "smile" or "cheer up." It's a real cheap line. I'm feeling good. I'm feeling real grateful for everything. It's a solid time in my life. When people say I look sad, they're wrong.
Nicolas Cage (1964-, American Actor)

49 Feeling grateful or appreciative of someone or something in your life actually attracts more of the things that you appreciate and value into your life.
Northrup Christiane (American Medical Doctor)

50 One ungrateful person, does an injury to all needy people.
Publilius Syrus (1st Century BC, Roman Writer)

51 There is a calmness to a life lived in Gratitude, a quiet joy.
Ralph H. Blum (American Author)

52 I awoke this morning with devout thanksgiving for my friends, the old and new.
Ralph Waldo Emerson (1803-1882, American Poet, Essayist)

53 There are minds so impatient of inferiority that their gratitude is a species of revenge, and they return benefits, not because recompense is a pleasure, but because obligation is a pain.
Samuel Johnson (1709-1784, British Author)

54 Let's choose today to quench our thirst for the "good life" we thinks others lead by acknowledging the good that already exists in our lives. We can then offer the universe the gift of our grateful hearts.
Sarah Ban Breathnach (American Author)

55 Grace is available for each of us every day -- our spiritual daily bread -- but we've got to remember to ask for it with a grateful heart and not worry about whether there will be enough for tomorrow.
Sarah Ban Breathnach (American Author)

56 Both abundance and lack exist simultaneously in our lives, as parallel realities. It is always our conscious choice which secret garden we will tend... when we choose not to focus on what is missing from our lives but are grateful for the abundance that's present -- love, health, family, friends, work, the joys of nature and personal pursuits that bring us pleasure -- the wasteland of illusion falls away and we experience Heaven on earth.
Sarah Ban Breathnach (American Author)

57 Whatever we are waiting for -- peace of mind, contentment, grace, the inner awareness of simple abundance -- it will surely come to us, but only when we are ready to receive it with an open and grateful heart.
Sarah Ban Breathnach (American Author)

58 It is another's fault if he be ungrateful, but it is mine if I do not give. To find one thankful man, I will oblige a great many that are not so.
Seneca (4 BC-65 AD, Spanish-born Roman Statesman, philosopher)

59 See how many are better off than you are, but consider how many are worse.
Seneca (4 BC-65 AD, Spanish-born Roman Statesman, philosopher)

60 There is as much greatness of mind in acknowledging a good turn, as in doing it.
Seneca (4 BC-65 AD, Spanish-born Roman Statesman, philosopher)

61 Gratitude is our most direct line to God and the angels. If we take the time, no matter how crazy and troubled we feel, we can find something to be thankful for. The more we seek gratitude, the more reason the angels will give us for gratitude and joy to exist in our lives.
Terry Lynn Taylor

62 Eaten bread is soon forgotten.
Thomas Fuller (1608-1661, British Clergyman, Author)

63 Love is the true means by which the world is enjoyed: our love to others, and others love to us.
Thomas Traherne (1636-1674, British Clergyman, Poet, Mystic)

64 Deficiency motivation doesn't work. It will lead to a life-long pursuit of try to fix me. Learn to appreciate what you have and where and who you are.
Wayne Dyer (1940-, American Psychotherapist, Author, Lecturer)

65 Maybe the only thing worse than having to give gratitude constantly is having to accept it.
William Faulkner (1897-1962, American Novelist)

66 The public have neither shame or gratitude.
William Hazlitt (1778-1830, British Essayist)

67 Sometimes we need to remind ourselves that thankfulness is indeed a virtue.
William John Bennett (1943-, American Federal Official)

68 He receives comfort like cold porridge.
William Shakespeare (1564-1616, British Poet, Playwright, Actor)

69 I hate ingratitude more in a person; than lying, vainness, babbling, drunkenness, or, any taint of vice whose strong corruption inhabits our frail blood. [Twelfth Night]
William Shakespeare (1564-1616, British Poet, Playwright, Actor)

GRAVE

1 Under the wide and starry sky. Dig the grave and let me lie.
Adlai E. Stevenson (1900-1965, American Lawyer, Politician)

2 A tomb now suffices him for whom the whole world was not sufficient.
Alexander The Great (352-323 BC, Alexander III, Ancient Macedonian King)

3 The house appointed for all the living.
Bible (Sacred Scriptures of Christians and Judaism)

4 Tombs are the clothes of the dead and a grave is a plain suit; while an expensive monument is one with embroidery.
R. Buckminster Fuller (1895-1983, American Inventor, Designer, Poet, Philosopher)

5 There is little much beyond the grave, but the strong are saying nothing until they see.
Robert Frost (1875-1963, American Poet)

GRAVITY

1 We can lick gravity but sometimes the paperwork is overwhelming.
Wernher Von Braun (1912-1977, German Rocket Pioneer)

GREATNESS

1 In my opinion, most of the great men of the past were only there for the beer --the wealth, prestige and grandeur that went with the power.
A. J. P. Taylor (1906-1990, British Historian)

2   Whatever you are, be a good one.
Abraham Lincoln (1809-1865, Sixteenth President of the USA)

3   I can write good songs. I can sing 'em, and I mean it, I mean it deeply, and I pour everything into that. Other than that, I suck.
Adam Duritz (1965-, American Musician, Singer, Songwriter)

4   All great deeds and all great thoughts have a ridiculous beginning.
Albert Camus (1913-1960, French Existential Writer)

5   All great men are gifted with intuition. They know without reasoning or analysis, what they need to know.
Alexis Carrel (1873-1944, French Biologist)

6   Great men are like eagles, and build their nest on some lofty solitude.
Arthur Schopenhauer (1788-1860, German Philosopher)

7   Man is only truly great when he acts from his passions.
Benjamin Disraeli (1804-1881, British Statesman, Prime Minister)

8   A great person is one who affects the mind of their generation.
Benjamin Disraeli (1804-1881, British Statesman, Prime Minister)

9   There never was a truly great man that was not at the same time truly virtuous.
Benjamin Franklin (1706-1790, American Scientist, Publisher, Diplomat)

10 Great men are not always wise.
Bible (Sacred Scriptures of Christians and Judaism)

11 Despite everybody who has been born and has died, the world has just gone on. I mean, look at Napoleon --but we went right on. Look at Harpo Marx --the world went around, it didn't stop for a second. It's sad but true. John Kennedy, right?
Bob Dylan (1941-, American Musician, Singer, Songwriter)

12 A good man, is a good man, whether in this church, or out of it.
Brigham Young (1801-1877, American Mormon Leader)

13 It is always the adventurers who do great things, not the sovereigns of great empires.
Charles De Montesquieu (1689-1755, French Jurist, Political Philosopher)

14 It is a melancholy truth that even great men have their poor relations.
Charles Dickens (1812-1870, British Novelist)

15 He's the greatest man who ever came out of Plymouth, Vermont. [On Calvin Coolidge]
Clarence Darrow (1857-1938, American Lawyer)

16 There is no greatness where there is not simplicity, goodness and truth.
Count Leo Tolstoy (1828-1910, Russian Novelist, Philosopher)

17 In historic events, the so-called great men are labels giving names to events, and like labels they have but the smallest connection with the event itself. Every act of theirs, which appears to them an act of their own will, is in an historical sense involuntary and is related to the whole course of history and predestined from eternity.
Count Leo Tolstoy (1828-1910, Russian Novelist, Philosopher)

18 Great men are the guideposts and landmarks in the state.
Edmund Burke (1729-1797, British Political Writer, Statesman)

19 The great must submit to the dominion of prudence and of virtue, or none will long submit to the dominion of the great.
Edmund Burke (1729-1797, British Political Writer, Statesman)

20 It's not what you take but what you leave behind that defines greatness.
Edward Gardner (American Businessman, Founder of Soft Sheen Products)

21 I distrust Great Men. They produce a desert of uniformity around them and often a pool of blood too, and I always feel a little man's pleasure when they come a cropper.
Edward M. Forster (1879-1970, British Novelist, Essayist)

22 None think the great unhappy, but the great.
Edward Young (1683-1765, British Poet, Dramatist)

23 All your youth you want to have your greatness taken for granted; when you find it taken for granted, you are unnerved.
Elizabeth Bowen (1899-1973, Anglo-Irish Novelist)

24 No great thing is created suddenly.
Epictetus (50-120, Stoic Philosopher)

25 A great man's greatest good luck is to die at the right time.
Eric Hoffer (1902-1983, American Author, Philosopher)

26 The greatest men of a nation are those it puts to death.
Ernest Renan (1823-1892, French Writer, Critic, Scholar)

27 Let us never forget that the greatest man is never more than an animal disguised as a god.
Francis Picabia (1878-1953, French Painter, Poet)

28 To achieve greatness one should live as if they will never die.
François de La Rochefoucauld (1613-1680, French classical writer)

29 Some have greatness thrust upon them, but not lately.
Frank Dane

30 There are people who possess not so much genius as a certain talent for perceiving the desires of the century, or even of the decade, before it has done so itself.
Georg C. Lichtenberg (1742-1799, German Physicist, Satirist)

31 There would be no great men if there were no little ones.
George Herbert (1593-1632, British Metaphysical Poet)

32 You know, sometimes, when they say you're ahead of your time, it's just a polite way of saying you have a real bad sense of timing.
George Mcgovern (1922-, American Democratic Politician)

33 Traditionally the great men of our country have sprung from poor environments; that being so, it would appear we have long suffered from a severe lack of poverty.
Gerald F. Lieberman (American Writer)

34 There is a great man who makes every man feel small. But the real great man is the man who makes every man feel great.
Gilbert K. Chesterton (1874-1936, British Author)

35 Being too good is apt to be uninteresting.
Harry S. Truman (1884-1972, Thirty-third President of the USA)

36 Well, I wouldn't say that I was in the great class, but I had a great time while I was trying to be great.
Harry S. Truman (1884-1972, Thirty-third President of the USA)

37 Great men are true men, the men in whom nature has succeeded. They are not extraordinary -- they are in the true order. It is the other species of men who are not what they ought to be.
Henri Frederic Amiel (1821-1881, Swiss Philosopher, Poet, Critic)

38 The world isn't kept running because it's a paying proposition. (God doesn't make a cent on the deal.) The world goes on because a few men in every generation believe in it utterly, accept it unquestioningly; they underwrite it with their lives.
Henry Miller (1891-1980, American Author)

39 Greatness does not approach him who is forever looking down.
Hitopadesa (Sanskrit Fable From Panchatantra)

40 To have a great man for a friend seems pleasant to those who have never tried it; those who have, fear it.
Horace (65-8 BC, Italian Poet)

41 The essence of greatness is neglect of the self.
James A. Froude (1818-1894, British Historian)

42 You will become as small as your controlling desire; as great as your dominant aspiration.
James Allen (1864-1912, British-born American Essayist, Author of "As a Man Thinketh")

43 It is necessary to be slightly under employed if you are to do something significant.
James Watson (1928-, American Geneticist)

44 We shall never resolve the enigma of the relation between the negative foundations of greatness and that greatness itself.
Jean Baudrillard (French Postmodern Philosopher, Writer)

45 False greatness is unsociable and remote: conscious of its own frailty, it hides, or at least averts its face, and reveals itself only enough to create an illusion and not be recognized as the meanness that it really is. True greatness is free, kind, familiar and popular; it lets itself be touched and handled, it loses nothing by being seen at close quarters; the better one knows it, the more one admires it.
Jean De La Bruyere (1645-1696, French Writer)

46 A position of eminence makes a great person greater and a small person less.
Jean De La Bruyere (1645-1696, French Writer)

47 Neither wealth or greatness render us happy.
Jean De La Fontaine (1621-1695, French Poet)

48 Great men never make bad use of their superiority. They see it and feel it and are not less modest. The more they have, the more they know their own deficiencies.
Jean Jacques Rousseau (1712-1778, Swiss Political Philosopher, Educationist, Essayist)

49 Greatness, in order to gain recognition, must all too often consent to ape greatness.
Jean Rostand (1894-1977, French Biologist, Writer)

50 At most, the greatest persons are but great wens, and excrescences; men of wit and delightful conversation, but as morals for ornament, except they be so incorporated into the body of the world that they contribute something to the sustentation of the whole.
John Donne (1572-1632, British Metaphysical Poet)

51 A great thing can only be done by a great person; and they do it without effort.
John Ruskin (1819-1900, British Critic, Social Theorist)

52 I never knew a man come to greatness or eminence who lay abed late in the morning.
Jonathan Swift (1667-1745, Anglo-Irish Satirist)

53 What millions died that Caesar might be great?
Joseph Campell

54 The lights of stars that were extinguished ages ago still reaches us. So it is with great men who died centuries ago, but still reach us with the radiations of their personalities.
Kahlil Gibran (1883-1931, Lebanese Poet, Novelist)

55 After a fellow gets famous it does not take long for someone to bob up that used to sit next to him in school.
Kin Hubbard (1868-1930, American Humorist, Journalist)

56 Great woman belong to history and to self sacrifice.
Leigh Hunt (1784-1859, British Poet, Essayist)

57 Sighing that Nature formed but one such man, and broke the die.
Lord Byron (1788-1824, British Poet)

58 Great merit, or great failings, will make you respected or despised; but trifles, little attentions, mere nothings, either done or neglected, will make you either liked or disliked in the general run of the world.
Lord Chesterfield (1694-1773, British Statesman, Author)

59 Nobody's ever the greatest anything.
Maralyn Polak

60 The first element of greatness is fundamental humbleness (this should not be confused with servility); the second is freedom from self; the third is intrepid courage, which, taken in its widest interpretation, generally goes with truth; and the fourth --the power to love --although I have put it last, is the rarest.
Margot Asquith (1864-1945, British Socialite)

61 Everybody can be great... because anybody can serve. You don't have to have a college degree to serve. You don't have to make your subject and verb agree to serve. you only need a heart full of grace. a soul generated by love.
Martin Luther King Jr. (1929-1968, American Black Leader, Nobel Prize Winner, 1964)

62 In our society those who are in reality superior in intelligence can be accepted by their fellows only if they pretend they are not.
Marya Mannes (1904-1990, American Writer)

63 Greatness is a spiritual condition.
Matthew Arnold (1822-1888, British Poet, Critic)

64 Great people are meteors designed to burn so that the earth may be lighted.
Napoleon Bonaparte (1769-1821, French General, Emperor)

65 Greatness be nothing unless it be lasting.
Napoleon Bonaparte (1769-1821, French General, Emperor)

66 The herd seek out the great, not for their sake but for their influence; and the great welcome them out of vanity or need.
Napoleon Bonaparte (1769-1821, French General, Emperor)

67 All my life I have always known I was born to greatness.
Oprah Winfrey (1954-, American TV Personality, Producer, Actress, Author)

68 No one who has come to true greatness has not felt in some degree that his life belongs to the people, and what God has given them he gives it for mankind.
Phillips Brooks (1835-1893, American Minister, Poet)

69 Because you are a great lord, you believe yourself to be a great genius. You took the trouble to be born, but no more.
Pierre De Beaumarchais (1732-1799, French Dramatist)

70 Those who intend on becoming great should love neither themselves or their own things, but only what is just, whether it happens to be done by themselves or others.
Plato (427-347 BC, Greek Philosopher)

71 The first step toward greatness is to be honest.
Proverb

72 Do not despise the bottom rungs in the ascent to greatness.
Publilius Syrus (1st Century BC, Roman Writer)

73 He is great who is what he is from nature, and who never reminds us of others.
Ralph Waldo Emerson (1803-1882, American Poet, Essayist)

74 To be great is to be misunderstood.
Ralph Waldo Emerson (1803-1882, American Poet, Essayist)

75 Great people are they who see that spiritual is stronger than any material force, that thoughts rule the world.
Ralph Waldo Emerson (1803-1882, American Poet, Essayist)

76 A great man stands on God. A small man on a great man.
Ralph Waldo Emerson (1803-1882, American Poet, Essayist)

77 Not he is great who can alter matter, but he who can alter my state of mind.
Ralph Waldo Emerson (1803-1882, American Poet, Essayist)

78 No great man ever complains of want of opportunity.
Ralph Waldo Emerson (1803-1882, American Poet, Essayist)

79 The essence of greatness is the perception that virtue is enough.
Ralph Waldo Emerson (1803-1882, American Poet, Essayist)

80 The search after the great men is the dream of youth, and the most serious occupation of manhood.
Ralph Waldo Emerson (1803-1882, American Poet, Essayist)

81 The measure of a master is his success in bringing all men around to his opinion twenty years later.
Ralph Waldo Emerson (1803-1882, American Poet, Essayist)

82 I never wanted to be famous. I only wanted to be great.
Ray Charles (1930-, American Musician, Singer, Songwriter)

83 No one ever became great by imitation.
Samuel Johnson (1709-1784, British Author)

84 The superiority of some men is merely local. They are great because their associates are little.
Samuel Johnson (1709-1784, British Author)

85 He was dull in a new way, and that made many think him great.
Samuel Johnson (1709-1784, British Author)

86 Greatness and goodness are not means, but ends.
Samuel Taylor Coleridge (1772-1834, British Poet, Critic, Philosopher)

87 It is true greatness to have in one the frailty of a man and the security of a god.
Seneca (4 BC-65 AD, Spanish-born Roman Statesman, philosopher)

88 The dullard's envy of brilliant men is always assuaged by the suspicion that they will come to a bad end.
Sir Max Beerbohm (1872-1956, British Actor)

89 I want to be great, something special.
Sugar Ray Leonard (1956-, American Boxer)

90 Great men hallow a whole people, and lift up all who live in their time.
Sydney Smith (1771-1845, British Writer, Clergyman)

91 No great man lives in vain. The history of the world is but the biography of great men.
Thomas Carlyle (1795-1881, Scottish Philosopher, Author)

92 The difference between Socrates and Jesus? The great conscious and the immeasurably great unconscious.
Thomas Carlyle (1795-1881, Scottish Philosopher, Author)

93 Great men are rarely isolated mountain-peaks; they are the summits of ranges.
Thomas Wentworth Higginson (1823-1911, American Clergyman, Writer)

94 There is a sacred horror about everything grand. It is easy to admire mediocrity and hills; but whatever is too lofty, a genius as well as a mountain, an assembly as well as a masterpiece, seen too near, is appalling.
Victor Hugo (1802-1885, French Poet, Dramatist, Novelist)

95 Great men always pay deference to greater.
Walter Savage Landor (1775-1864, British Poet, Essayist)

96 The greatness of a man's power is the measure of his surrender.
William Booth (1829-1912, British Religious Leader, Salvation Army Founder)

97 There are no great men, only great challenges that ordinary men are forced by circumstances to meet.
William F. Halsey (American Admiral)

98 No man is truly great who is great only in his lifetime. The test of greatness is the page of history.
William Hazlitt (1778-1830, British Essayist)

99 Th abuse of greatness is when it disjoins remorse from power.
William Shakespeare (1564-1616, British Poet, Playwright, Actor)

100 In my stars I am above thee, but be not afraid of greatness. Some are born great, some achieve greatness, and some have greatness ;thrust upon em.
William Shakespeare (1564-1616, British Poet, Playwright, Actor)

101 He is not great who is not greatly good.
William Shakespeare (1564-1616, British Poet, Playwright, Actor)

102 Some are born great, some achieve greatness, and others have greatness thrust upon them. [Twelfth Night]
William Shakespeare (1564-1616, British Poet, Playwright, Actor)

103 Be not afraid of greatness; some are born great, some achieve greatness, and others have greatness thrust upon them.
William Shakespeare (1564-1616, British Poet, Playwright, Actor)

104 Great and good are seldom the same man.
Winston Churchill (1874-1965, British Statesman, Prime Minister)

105 The price of greatness is responsibility.
Winston Churchill (1874-1965, British Statesman, Prime Minister)

654

GREED

1 The average man does not know what to do with this life, yet wants another one which will last forever.
Anatole France (1844-1924, French Writer)

2 Nothing retains less of desire in art, in science, than this will to industry, booty, possession.
Andre Breton (1989-1966, French Surrealist)

3 Wealth is like sea-water; the more we drink, the thirstier we become; and the same is true of fame.
Arthur Schopenhauer (1788-1860, German Philosopher)

4 I have news for the forces of greed and the defenders of the status quo; your time has come and gone. It's time for change in America.
Bill Clinton (1946-, Forty-second President of the USA)

5 God forgives the sin of gluttony.
Catalan Proverb

6 Avarice has ruined more souls than extravagance.
Charles Caleb Colton (1780-1832, British Sportsman Writer)

7 Greed, like the love of comfort, is a kind of fear.
Cyril Connolly (1903-1974, British Critic)

8 Avarice, the spur of industry.
David Hume (1711-1776, Scottish Philosopher, Historian)

9 The point is that you can't be too greedy.
Donald Trump (1946-, 45th President of the United States of America)

10 From top to bottom of the ladder, greed is aroused without knowing where to find ultimate foothold. Nothing can calm it, since its goal is far beyond all it can attain. Reality seems valueless by comparison with the dreams of fevered imaginations; reality is therefore abandoned.
Emile Durkheim (1858-1917, French Sociologist)

11 Greed is a bottomless pit which exhausts the person in an endless effort to satisfy the need without ever reaching satisfaction.
Erich Fromm (1900-1980, American Psychologist)

12 Avarice is the vice of declining years.
George Bancroft (1800-1891, American Historian)

13 He who distinguishes the true savor of his food can never be a glutton; he who does not cannot be otherwise.
Henry David Thoreau (1817-1862, American Essayist, Poet, Naturalist)

14 The avarice person is ever in want; let your desired aim have a fixed limit.
Horace (65-8 BC, Italian Poet)

15 Big mouthfuls often choke.
Italian Proverb

16 Greed is all right, by the way I think greed is healthy. You can be greedy and still feel good about yourself.
Ivan F. Boesky

17 For at least another hundred years we must pretend to ourselves and to every one that fair is foul and foul is fair; for foul is useful and fair is not. Avarice and usury and precaution must be our gods for a little longer still.
John Maynard Keynes (1883-1946, British Economist)

18 So for a good old-gentlemanly vice, I think I must take up with avarice.
Lord Byron (1788-1824, British Poet)

19 You show me a capitalist, and I'll show you a bloodsucker.
Malcolm X (1925-1965, American Black Leader, Activist)

20 Avarice is the sphincter of the heart.
Matthew Green

21 It is not the want, but rather abundance that creates avarice.
Michel Eyquem De Montaigne (1533-1592, French Philosopher, Essayist)

22 The problem of social organization is how to set up an arrangement under which greed will do the least harm, capitalism is that kind of a system.
Milton Friedman (1912-, American Economist)

23 Satiety is a mongrel that barks at the heels of plenty.
Minna Antrim (1861-18?, American Epigrammist)

24 The wish to acquire more is admittedly a very natural and common thing; and when men succeed in this they are always praised rather than condemned. But when they lack the ability to do so and yet want to acquire more at all costs, they deserve condemnation for their mistakes.
Niccolo Machiavelli (1469-1527, Italian Author, Statesman)

25 Avarice is generally the last passion of those lives of which the first part has been squandered in pleasure, and the second devoted to ambition. He that sinks under the fatigue of getting wealth, lulls his age with the milder business of saving it.
Samuel Johnson (1709-1784, British Author)

26 For greed all nature is too little.
Seneca (4 BC-65 AD, Spanish-born Roman Statesman, philosopher)

27 Wars and revolutions and battles are due simply and solely to the body and its desires. All wars are undertaken for the acquisition of wealth; and the reason why we have to acquire wealth is the body, because we are slaves in its service.
Socrates (469-399 BC, Greek Philosopher of Athens)

28 If your desires be endless, your cares and fears will be so too.
Thomas Fuller (1608-1661, British Clergyman, Author)

29 Experience demands that man is the only animal which devours his own kind, for I can apply no milder term to the general prey of the rich on the poor.
Thomas Jefferson (1743-1826, Third President of the USA)

30 It is of the nobility of man's soul that he is insatiable: for he hath a benefactor so prone to give, that he delighteth in us for asking. Do not your inclinations tell you that the WORLD is yours? Do you not covet all? Do you not long to have it; to enjoy it; to overcome it? To what end do men gather riches, but to multiply more? Do they not like Pyrrhus the King of Epire, add house to house and lands to lands, that they may get it all?
Thomas Traherne (1636-1674, British Clergyman, Poet, Mystic)

31 Men hate the individual whom they call avaricious only because nothing can be gained from him.
Voltaire (1694-1778, French Historian, Writer)

32 To hazard much to get much has more of avarice than wisdom.
William Penn (1644-1718, British Religious Leader, Founder of Pennsylvania)

33 Let me tell you, Cassius, you yourself are much condemned to have an itching palm.
William Shakespeare (1564-1616, British Poet, Playwright, Actor)

GRIEF

1 Grief knits two hearts in closer bonds than happiness ever can; and common sufferings are far stronger links than common joys.
Alphonse De Lamartine (1790-1869, French Poet, Statesman, Historian)

2 Grief can't be shared. Everyone carries it alone. His own burden in his own way.
Anne Morrow Lindbergh (1906-, American Author)

3 Pain hardens, and great pain hardens greatly, whatever the comforters say, and suffering does not ennoble, though it may occasionally lend a certain rigid dignity of manner to the suffering frame.
Antonia S. Byatt (1936-, British Writer, Critic)

4 Grief is the agony of an instant. The indulgence of grief the blunder of a life.
Benjamin Disraeli (1804-1881, British Statesman, Prime Minister)

5 Weeping may endure for a night, but joy comet in the morning. [Psalms 30:5]
Bible (Sacred Scriptures of Christians and Judaism)

6 No one ever told me that grief felt so like fear.
C. S. Lewis (1898-1963, British Academic, Writer, Christian Apologist)

7 There is immunity in reading, immunity in formal society, in office routine, in the company of old friends and in the giving of officious help to strangers, but there is no sanctuary in one bed from the memory of another. The past with its anguish will break through every defense-line of custom and habit; we must sleep and therefore we must dream.
Cyril Connolly (1903-1974, British Critic)

8   Time takes away the grief of men.
Desiderius Erasmus (1466-1536, Dutch Humanist)

9   No one can keep his grieves in their prime; they use themselves up.
E. M. Cioran (1911-, Rumanian-born French Philosopher)

10   I tell you, hopeless grief is passionless.
Elizabeth Barrett Browning (1806-1861, British Poet)

11   Who originated that most exquisite of inquisitions, the condolence system?
Elizabeth Stuart Phelps (1844-1911, American Writer)

12   She was no longer wrestling with the grief, but could sit down with it as a lasting companion and make it a sharer in her thoughts.
George Eliot (1819-1880, British Novelist)

13   The only cure for grief is action.
George Henry Lewis

14   Those who don't know how to weep with their whole heart don't know how to laugh either.
Golda Meir (1898-1978, Prime Minister of Israel, 1969-74)

15   In private grief with careless scorn. In public seem to triumph and not to mourn.
Grannville

16   Grief, and an estate, is joy understood,
Gregory Nunn (1955-, American Golfer)

17   Time heals old pain, while it creates new ones.
Hebrew Proverb

18   What right have I to grieve, who have not ceased to wonder?
Henry David Thoreau (1817-1862, American Essayist, Poet, Naturalist)

19   Well has it been said that there is no grief like the grief which does not speak.
Henry Wadsworth Longfellow (1819-1892, American Poet)

20   There is not grief that does not speak.
Henry Wadsworth Longfellow (1819-1892, American Poet)

21   The grief of the keen is no personal complaint for the death of one woman over eighty years, but seems to contain the whole passionate rage that lurks somewhere in every native of the island. In this cry of pain the inner consciousness of the people seems to lay itself bare for an instant, and to reveal the mood of beings who feel their isolation in the face of a universe that wars on them with winds and seas.
J. M. Synge (1871-1909, Irish Poet, Dramatist)

22   Grief is only the memory of widowed affections.
James Martineau

23   Sorrow is the great idealizer.
James Russell Lowell (1819-1891, American Poet, Critic, Editor)

24   Grief at the absence of a loved one is happiness compared to life with a person one hates.
Jean De La Bruyere (1645-1696, French Writer)

25   All things grow with time -- except grief.
Jewish Proverb

26   When we suffer anguish we return to early childhood because that is the period in which we first learnt to suffer the experience of total loss. It was more than that. It was the period in which we suffered more total losses than in all the rest of our life put together.
John Berger (1926-, British Actor, Critic)

27   The human heart dares not stay away too long from that which hurt it most. There is a return journey to anguish that few of us are released from making.
Lillian Smith (1897-1966, American Author)

28   No matter how deep and dark your pit, how dank your shroud, their heads are heroically unbloody and unbowed.
Ogden Nash (1902-1971, American Humorous Poet)

29   In all the silent manliness of grief.
Oliver Goldsmith (1728-1774, Anglo-Irish Author, Poet, Playwright)

30   Our trials, our sorrows, and our grieves develop us...
Orison Swett Marden (1850-1924, American Author, Founder of Success Magazine)

31   One often calms one's grief by recounting it.
Pierre Corneille (1606-1684, French Dramatist)

32   Grief is light that is capable of counsel.
Proverb

33   But there are other things than dissipation that thicken the features. Tears, for example.
Rebecca West (1892-1983, British Author)

34   While grief is fresh, every attempt to divert only irritates. You must wait till grief be digested, and then amusement will dissipate the remains of it.
Samuel Johnson (1709-1784, British Author)

35   Where grief is fresh, any attempt to divert it only irritates.
Samuel Johnson (1709-1784, British Author)

36   Nothing becomes so offensive so quickly as grief. When fresh it finds someone to console it, but when it becomes chronic, it is ridiculed, and rightly.
Seneca (4 BC-65 AD, Spanish-born Roman Statesman, philosopher)

37   The display of grief makes more demands than grief itself. How few men are sad in their own company.
Seneca (4 BC-65 AD, Spanish-born Roman Statesman, philosopher)

38   In struggling against anguish one never produces serenity; the struggle against anguish only produces new forms of anguish.
Simone Weil (1910-1943, French Philosopher, Mystic)

39   When the heart grieves over what is has lost, the spirit rejoices over what it has left.
Sufi Epigram

40   Since grief only aggravates your loss, grieve not for what is past.
Walker Percy (1916-1990, American Novelist)

41 In deep sadness there is no place for sentimentality.
William S. Burroughs (1914-1997, American Writer)

42 Patch grief with proverbs.
William Shakespeare (1564-1616, British Poet, Playwright, Actor)

43 Grief fills the room up of my absent child, lies in his bed, walks up and down with me, puts on his pretty looks, repeats his words.
William Shakespeare (1564-1616, British Poet, Playwright, Actor)

GROWTH

1 If we don't change, we don't grow. If we don't grow, we aren't really living.
Anatole France (1844-1924, French Writer)

2 I am a frayed and nibbled survivor in a fallen world, and I am getting along. I am aging and eaten and have done my share of eating too. I am not washed and beautiful, in control of a shining world in which everything fits, but instead am wondering awed about on a splintered wreck I've come to care for, whose gnawed trees breathe a delicate air, whose bloodied and scarred creatures are my dearest companions, and whose beauty bats and shines not in its imperfections but overwhelmingly in spite of them...
Annie Dillard (1945-, American Author, Poet)

3 We grow a little every time we do not take advantage of somebody's weakness.
Bern Williams

4 Only by contending with challenges that seem to be beyond your strength to handle at the moment you can grow more surely toward the stars.
Brian Tracy (American Trainer, Speaker, Author, Businessman)

5 Ever since I was a child I have had this instinctive urge for expansion and growth. To me, the function and duty of a quality human being is the sincere and honest development of one's potential.
Bruce Lee (1940-1973, Chinese-American Actor, Director, Author, Martial Artist)

6 Unless you try to do something beyond what you have mastered, you will never grow.
C.R. Lawton

7 All growth depends upon activity. There is no development physically or intellectually without effort, and effort means work.
Calvin Coolidge (1872-1933, Thirtieth President of the USA)

8 I am convinced that the world is not a mere bog in which men and woman trample themselves in the mire and die. Something magnificent is taking place here amid the cruelties and tragedies, and the supreme challenge to intelligence is that of making the noblest and best in our curious heritage prevail.
Charles A. Beard (American Writer)

9 Climb mountains to see lowlands.
Chinese Proverb

10 Enough shovels of earth -- a mountain. Enough pails of water -- a river.
Chinese Proverb

11 The perfecting of one's self is the fundamental base of all progress and all moral development.
Confucius (551-479 BC, Chinese Ethical Teacher, Philosopher)

12 Those who have high thoughts are ever striving; they are not happy to remain in the same place. Like swans that leave their lake and rise into the air, they leave their home and fly for a higher home.
Dhammapada (300 BC, Buddhist Collection of Moral Aphorism)

13 Growth for the sake of growth is the ideology of the cancer cell.
Edward Abbey (1927 - 1989, American Writer)

14 All that is human must retrograde if it does not advance.
Edward Gibbon (1737-1794, British Historian)

15 Some people are molded by their admirations, others by their hostilities.
Elizabeth Bowen (1899-1973, Anglo-Irish Novelist)

16 Don't go through life, grow through life.
Eric Butterworth

17 We find comfort among those who agree with us-growth among those who don't.
Frank A. Clark

18 You don't learn to hold your own in the world by standing on guard, but by attacking and getting well hammered yourself.
George Bernard Shaw (1856-1950, Irish-born British Dramatist)

19 The strongest principle of growth lies in human choice.
George Eliot (1819-1880, British Novelist)

20 Growth means change and change involves risk, stepping from the known to the unknown.
George Shinn

21 The fatal metaphor of progress, which means leaving things behind us, has utterly obscured the real idea of growth, which means leaving things inside us.
Gilbert K. Chesterton (1874-1936, British Author)

22 Unless a tree has borne blossoms in spring, you will vainly look for fruit on it in autumn.
Hare Charles

23 All growth is a leap in the dark, a spontaneous, unpremeditated act without benefit of experience.
Henry Miller (1891-1980, American Author)

24 Every winner has scars.
Herbert N. Casson (American Author)

25 I have always believed, and I still believe, that whatever good or bad fortune may come our way we can always give it meaning and transform it into something of value.
Hermann Hesse (1877-1962, German-born Swiss Novelist, Poet)

26 All men's gains are the fruit of venturing.
Herodotus (484-425 BC, Greek Historian)

27 Some people grow under responsibility, others merely swell.
Hubbell

28 Good timber does not grow with ease. The stronger the wind the stronger the trees.
J. Willard Marriott (American Businessman, Founder of Marriott Hotels)

29 Progress has not followed a straight ascending line, but a spiral with rhythms of progress and retrogression, of evolution and dissolution.
Johann Wolfgang Von Goethe (1749-1832, German Poet, Dramatist, Novelist)

30 Growth is the only evidence of life.
John Henry Newman (1801-1890, British Religious Leader, Prelate, Writer)

31 The key to success is to keep growing in all areas of life -- mental, emotional, spiritual, as well as physical.
Julius Erving (1950-, American Basketball Player)

32 Every phase of evolution commences by being in a state of unstable force and proceeds through organization to equilibrium. Equilibrium having been achieved, no further development is possible without once more oversetting the A journey of a thousand miles starts in front of your feet. Whosoever acts spoils it. Whosoever keeps loses it.
Kabbalah (Jewish Esoteric Doctrine)

33 Today I have grown taller from walking with the trees.
Karl Baker

34 A tree trunk the size of a man grows from a blade as thin as a hair. A tower nine stories high is built from a small heap of earth.
Lao-Tzu (600 BC, Chinese Philosopher, Founder of Taoism, Author of the "Tao Te Ching")

35 The growth of affluence, the growth of education, has led to a shortage of morons.
Leonard Neal

36 In the end, it is the person you become, not the things you have achieved, that is the most important.
Les Brown (1945-, American Speaker, Author, Trainer, Motivator Lecturer)

37 All of us need to grow continuously in our lives.
Les Brown (1945-, American Speaker, Author, Trainer, Motivator Lecturer)

38 The entrepreneurial approach is not a sideline at 3M. It is the heart of our design for growth.
Lewis Lehr (American Businessman, President of 3M Company)

39 I don't know what it's like for a book writer or a doctor or a teacher as they work to get established in their jobs. But for a singer, you've got to continue to grow or else you're just like last night's cornbread -- stale and dry.
Loretta Lynn (1935-, American Musician, Singer, Songwriter)

40 Nirvana or lasting enlightenment or true spiritual growth can be achieved only through persistent exercise of real love.
M. Scott Peck (American Psychiatrist, Author)

41 The harvest of old age is the recollection and abundance of blessing previously secured.
Marcus T. Cicero (106-43 BC, Great Roman Orator, Politician)

42 What is the most rigorous law of our being? Growth. No smallest atom of our moral, mental, or physical structure can stand still a year. It grows -- it must grow; nothing can prevent it.
Mark Twain (1835-1910, American Humorist, Writer)

43 The need of expansion is as genuine an instinct in man as the need in a plant for the light, or the need in man himself for going upright. The love of liberty is simply the instinct in man for expansion.
Matthew Arnold (1822-1888, British Poet, Critic)

44 Close scrutiny will show that most "crisis situations" are opportunities to either advance, or stay where you are.
Maxwell Maltz (American Plastic Surgeon, Author of "Psycho-Cybernetics")

45 If it's not growing, it's going to die.
Michael Eisner (American Business Executive, CEO of Walt Disney Productions)

46 Strength and growth come only through continuous effort and struggle...
Napoleon Hill (1883-1970, American Speaker, Motivational Writer, "Think and Grow Rich")

47 Unlimited economic growth has the marvelous quality of stilling discontent while maintaining privilege, a fact that has not gone unnoticed among liberal economists.
Noam Chomsky (1928-, American Linguist, Political Activist)

48 The sculptor will chip off all unnecessary material to set free the angel. Nature will chip and pound us remorselessly to bring out our possibilities. She will strip us of wealth, humble our pride, humiliate our ambition, let us down from the ladder of fame, will discipline us in a thousand ways, if she can develop a little character, Everything must give way to that. Wealth is nothing, position is nothing, fame is nothing, manhood is everything.
Orison Swett Marden (1850-1924, American Author, Founder of Success Magazine)

49 Growth itself contains the germ of happiness.
Pearl S. Buck (1892-1973, American Novelist)

50 Love dies only when growth stops.
Pearl S. Buck (1892-1973, American Novelist)

51 The key to growth is the introduction of higher dimensions of consciousness into our awareness.
Pir Vilayat Khan (1916-, Western Philosopher Teacher, Master, Author)

52 Thou mayest as well expect to grow stronger by always eating as wiser by always reading. Too much overcharges Nature, and turns more into disease than nourishment. 'Tis thought and digestion which makes books serviceable, and give health and vigor to the mind.
R. Buckminster Fuller (1895-1983, American Inventor, Designer, Poet, Philosopher)

53 We grow because we struggle, we learn and overcome.
R. C. Allen

54 Are you green and growing or ripe and rotting?
Ray Kroc (1902-1984, American businessman, Founder of McDonalds)

55 When I am grown to man's estate I shall be very proud and great. And tell the other girls and boys Not to meddle with my toys.
Robert Louis Stevenson (1850-1895, Scottish Essayist, Poet, Novelist)

56 By depending on the great, The small may rise high. See: the little plant ascending the tall tree Has climbed to the top.
Saskya Pandita (1182-1251, Tibetan Grand Lama of Saskya)

57 The unexamined life is not worth living.
Socrates (469-399 BC, Greek Philosopher of Athens)

58 Slow buds the pink dawn like a rose From out night's gray and cloudy sheath; Softly and still it grows and grows, Petal by petal, leaf by leaf.
Susan Coolidge (1845-1905, American Writer)

59 We need 4 hugs a day for survival. We need 8 hugs a day for maintenance. We need 12 hugs a day for growth.
Virginia Satir (American Family Therapist, Lecturer, Trainer, Author)

60 I will grow. I will become something new and grand, but no grander than I now am. Just as the sky will be different in a few hours, its present perfection and completeness is not deficient, so am I presently perfect and not deficient because I will be different tomorrow. I will grow and I am not deficient.
Wayne Dyer (1940-, American Psychotherapist, Author, Lecturer)

61 The minute a man ceases to grow, no matter what his years, that minute he begins to be old.
William James (1842-1910, American Psychologist, Professor, Author)

GRUDGE

1 I've had a few arguments with people, but I never carry a grudge. You know why? While you're carrying a grudge, they're out dancing.
Buddy Hackett

GUESTS

1 Every guest hates the others, and the host hates them all.
Albanian Proverb

2 Guests, like fish, begin to smell after three days.
Benjamin Franklin (1706-1790, American Scientist, Publisher, Diplomat)

3 Fish and guests smell at three days old.
Danish Proverb

4 To be an ideal guest, stay at home.
Edgar Watson Howe (1853-1937, American Journalist, Author)

5 The first day, a guest; the second, a burden; the third, a pest.
Edouard R. Laboulaye

6 A civil guest will no more talk all, than eat all the feast.
George Herheri

7 A guest never forgets the host who had treated him kindly.
Homer (850 BC, Greek Epic Poet)

8 Making a long stay short is a great aid to popularity.
Kin Hubbard (1868-1930, American Humorist, Journalist)

9 Nobody can be as agreeable as an uninvited guest.
Kin Hubbard (1868-1930, American Humorist, Journalist)

10 Whoever is admitted or sought for, in company, upon any other account than that of his merit and manners, is never respected there, but only made use of. We will have such-a-one, for he sings prettily; we will invite such-a-one to a ball, for he dances well; we will have such-a-one at supper, for he is always joking and laughing; we will ask another because he plays deep at all games, or because he can drink a great deal. These are all vilifying distinctions, mortifying preferences, and exclude all ideas of esteem and regard. Whoever is had (as it is called) in company for the sake of any one thing singly, is singly that thing, and will never be considered in any other light; consequently never respected, let his merits be what they will.
Lord Chesterfield (1694-1773, British Statesman, Author)

11 Superior people never make long visits.
Marianne Moore (1887-1972, American Poet)

12 When any one of our relations was found to be a person of a very bad character, a troublesome guest, or one we desired to get rid of, upon his leaving my house I ever took care to lend him a riding-coat, or a pair of boots, or sometimes a horse of small value, and I always had the satisfaction of finding he never came back to return them.
Oliver Goldsmith (1728-1774, Anglo-Irish Author, Poet, Playwright)

13 Frank Harris has been received in all the great houses -- once!
Oscar Wilde (1856-1900, British Author, Wit)

14 My evening visitors, if they cannot see the clock should find the time in my face.
Ralph Waldo Emerson (1803-1882, American Poet, Essayist)

15 Quite a nasty piece of work. Not the sort of person you'd want to have dinner with. [On the subject of Mr. Bean]
Rowan Atkinson (1955-, British-born American Actor, Comedian, Writer)

16 One might well say that mankind is divisible into two great classes: hosts and guests.
Sir Max Beerbohm (1872-1956, British Actor)

17 No one can be so welcome a guest that he will not annoy his host after three days.
Titus Maccius Plautus (254-184 BC, Roman Comic Poet)

18 Visitors are insatiable devourers of time, and fit only for those who, if they did not visit, would do nothing.
William Cowper (1731-1800, British Poet)

GUIDANCE

1 As you walk through the valley of the unknown, you will find the footprints of Jesus both in front of you and beside you.
Charles Stanley

2 It is difficult to steer a parked car, so get moving.
Henrietta Mears

3 So act that your principle of action might safely be made a law for the whole world.
Immanuel Kant (1724-1804, German Philosopher)

4 The conscience of children is formed by the influences that surround them; their notions of good and evil are the result of the moral atmosphere they breathe.
Jean Paul Richter (1763-1825, German Novelist)

5 The speed of the boss is the speed of the team.
Lee Iacocca (1924-, American Businessman, Former CEO of Chrysler)

6 Men give advice; God gives guidance.
Leonard Ravenhill

7 Examples is more forcible than precept. People look at my six days in the week to see what I mean on the seventh.
Robert Cecil (1830-1903, British Conservative Politician, Prime Minister)

8 You can't drive straight on a twisting lane.
Russian Proverb

9 Alexander received more bravery of mind by the pattern of Achilles, than by hearing the definition of fortitude.
Sir Philip Sidney (1554-1586, British Author, Courtier)

10 It is no use walking anywhere to preach unless our walking is our preaching.
St. Francis of Assisi (1181-1226, Italian Preacher, Founder of the Franciscan Orde)

GUILT

1 Guilt upon the conscience, like rust upon iron, both defiles and consumes it, gnawing and creeping into it, as that does which at last eats out the very heart and substance of the metal.
Bishop Robert South (1634-1716, British Clergyman)

2 He that is conscious of guilt cannot bear the innocence of others: So they will try to reduce all others to their own level.
Charles James Fox (1749-1806, British Statesman, Foreign Secretary)

3 I am having so much fun performing, I feel almost guilty. I think, my God, I hope no one comes and busts me for this.
David Crosby (American Rock Musician)

4 The more sinful and guilty a person tends to feel, the less chance there is that he will be a happy, healthy, or law-abiding citizen. He will become a compulsive wrong-doer.
Dr. Albert Ellis (1913-, American Psychotherapist)

5 Whoever blushes confesses guilt, true innocence never feels shame.
Jean Jacques Rousseau (1712-1778, Swiss Political Philosopher, Educationist, Essayist)

6 It is criminal to steal a purse, daring to steal a fortune, a mark of greatness to steal a crown. The blame diminishes as the guilt increases.
Johann Friedrich Von Schiller (1759-1805, German Dramatist, Poet, Historian)

7 Life without industry is guilt. Industry without Art is Brutality.
John Ruskin (1819-1900, British Critic, Social Theorist)

8 Guilt is the source of sorrows, the avenging fiend that follows us behind with whips and stings.
Nicholas Rowe

9 Forbear to lay the guilt of a few on the many.
Ovid (43 BC-18 AD, Roman Poet)

10 Seek to make a person blush for their guilt rather than shed their blood.
Publius Cornelius Tacitus (55-117 AD, Roman Historian)

11 If you commit a crime, you're guilty.
Rush Limbaugh (1951-, American TV Personality)

12 Defending the truth is not something one does out of a sense of duty or to allay guilt complexes, but is a reward in itself.
Simone De Beauvoir (1908-1986, French Novelist, Essayist)

13 It is more dangerous that even a guilty person should be punished without the forms of law than that he should escape.
Thomas Jefferson (1743-1826, Third President of the USA)

14 Suspicion always haunts the guilty mind; the thief doth fear each bush an officer.
William Shakespeare (1564-1616, British Poet, Playwright, Actor)

GULLIBILITY

1   A man is his own easiest dupe, for what he wishes to be true he generally believes to be true.
Demosthenes (383-322 BC, Greek Orator)

2   We are inclined to believe those whom we don not know because they have never deceived us.
Samuel Johnson (1709-1784, British Author)

HABIT

1   Laws are never as effective as habits.
Adlai E. Stevenson (1900-1965, American Lawyer, Politician)

2   Curious things, habits. People themselves never knew they had them.
Agatha Christie (1891-1976, British Mystery Writer)

3   In every age of well-marked transition, there is the pattern of habitual dumb practice and emotion which is passing and there is oncoming a new complex of habit.
Alfred North Whitehead (1861-1947, British Mathematician, Philosopher)

4   Habit with it's iron sinews, clasps us and leads us day by day.
Alphonse De Lamartine (1790-1869, French Poet, Statesman, Historian)

5   Habit is a shackle for the free.
Ambrose Bierce (1842-1914, American Author, Editor, Journalist, "The Devil's Dictionary")

6   Tell me what you eat, and I will tell you what you are.
Anthelme Brillat-Savarin

7   It is well to be up before daybreak, for such habits contribute to health, wealth, and wisdom.
Aristotle (384-322 BC, Greek Philosopher)

8   We are what we repeatedly do. Excellence, then, is not an act, but a habit.
Aristotle (384-322 BC, Greek Philosopher)

9   Your net worth to the world is usually determined by what remains after your bad habits are subtracted from your good ones.
Benjamin Franklin (1706-1790, American Scientist, Publisher, Diplomat)

10   Each year one vicious habit discarded, in time might make the worst of us good.
Benjamin Franklin (1706-1790, American Scientist, Publisher, Diplomat)

11   It is easier to prevent bad habits than to break them.
Benjamin Franklin (1706-1790, American Scientist, Publisher, Diplomat)

12   Habit is the second nature which destroys the first.
Blaise Pascal (1623-1662, French Scientist, Religious Philosopher)

13   Habit is a second nature that destroys the first. But what is nature? Why is habit not natural? I am very much afraid that nature itself is only a first habit, just as habit is a second nature.
Blaise Pascal (1623-1662, French Scientist, Religious Philosopher)

14   Successful people are simply those with success habits.
Brian Tracy (American Trainer, Speaker, Author, Businessman)

15   Achieve success in any area of life by identifying the optimum strategies and repeating them until they become habits.
Charles J. Givens (American Businessman, Author, Trainer)

16   Habits are cobwebs at first; cables at last.
Chinese Proverb

17   Feeling sorry for yourself, and you present condition, is not only a waste of energy but the worst habit you could possibly have.
Dale Carnegie (1888-1955, American Author, Trainer)

18   A nail is driven out by another nail. Habit is overcome by habit.
Desiderius Erasmus (1466-1536, Dutch Humanist)

19   First we form habits, then they form us. Conquer your bad habits, or they'll eventually conquer you.
Dr. Rob Gilbert

20   Habit is ten times nature.
Duke of Wellington Arthur Wellesley (1769-1852, British Statesman, Military Leader)

21   To exist is a habit I do not despair of acquiring.
E. M. Cioran (1911-, Rumanian-born French Philosopher)

22   Habit is a form of exercise
Elbert Hubbard (1859-1915, American Author, Publisher)

23   Cultivate only the habits that you are willing should master you.
Elbert Hubbard (1859-1915, American Author, Publisher)

24   The easier it is to do, the harder it is to change.
Eng's Principle

25   Wise living consists perhaps less in acquiring good habits than in acquiring as few habits as possible.
Eric Hoffer (1902-1983, American Author, Philosopher)

26   My problem lies in reconciling my gross habits with my net income.
Errol Flynn (1909-1959, Tasmanian Actor)

27   Habit, my friend, is practice long pursued, that at last becomes man himself.
Evenus (Ancient Greek Poet)

28   It seems, in fact, as though the second half of a man's life is made up of nothing, but the habits he has accumulated during the first half.
Fyodor Dostoevski (1821-1881, Russian Novelist)

29 Certes, they been lye to hounds, for an hound when he cometh by the roses, or by other bushes, though he may nat pisse, yet wole he heve up his leg and make a countenance to pisse.
Geoffrey Chaucer (1340-1400, British Poet)

30 One might call habit a moral friction: something that prevents the mind from gliding over things but connects it with them and makes it hard for it to free itself from them.
Georg C. Lichtenberg (1742-1799, German Physicist, Satirist)

31 Habit with him was all the test of truth, it must be right: I've done it from my youth.
George Crabbe (1754-1832, British Clergyman, Poet)

32 Habit is stronger than reason.
George Santayana (1863-1952, American Philosopher, Poet)

33 Habits are to the soul what the veins and arteries are to the blood, the courses in which it moves.
Horace Bushnell (1802-1876, American Congregational Minister, Theologian)

34 Habit is a cable; we weave a thread of it each day, and at last we cannot break it.
Horace Mann (1796-1859, American Educator)

35 If an idiot were to tell you the same story every day for a year, you would end by believing it.
Horace Mann (1796-1859, American Educator)

36 A single bad habit will mar an otherwise faultless character, as an ink-drop soileth the pure white page.
Hosea Ballou (1771-1852, American Theologian, Founder of "Universalism")

37 The individual who wants to reach the top in business must appreciate the might of the force of habit and must understand that practices are what create habits. He must be quick to break those habits that can break him and hasten to adopt those practices that will become the habits that help him achieve the success he desires.
J. Paul Getty (1892-1976, American Oil Tycoon, Billionaire)

38 The greatest people will be those who possess the best capacities, cultivated with the best habits.
James Harris

39 There is an invisible garment woven around us from our earliest years; it is made of the way we eat, the way we walk, the way we greet people...
Jean Giraudoux (1882-1944, French Diplomat, Author)

40 Habits are the daughters of action, but then they nurse their mother, and produce daughters after her image, but far more beautiful and prosperous.
Jeremy Taylor (1613-1667, British Churchman, Writer)

41 The more deeply the path is etched, the more it is used, and the more it is used, the more deeply it etched.
Jo Coudert (American Author)

42 The phrases that men hear or repeat continually, end by becoming convictions and ossify the organs of intelligence.
Johann Wolfgang Von Goethe (1749-1832, German Poet, Dramatist, Novelist)

43 Ill habits gather unseen degrees, as brooks make rivers, rivers run to seas.
John Dryden (1631-1700, British Poet, Dramatist, Critic)

44 We first make our habits, and then our habits make us. ·
John Dryden (1631-1700, British Poet, Dramatist, Critic)

45 Practice conquers the habit of doing, without reflecting on the rule.
John Locke (1632-1704, British Philosopher)

46 Habits... the only reason they persist is that they are offering some satisfaction. You allow them to persist by not seeking any other, better form of satisfying the same needs. Every habit, good or bad, is acquired and learned in the same way -- by finding that it is a means of satisfaction.
Juliene Berk

47 Every once in a while someone without a single bad habit gets caught.
Kin Hubbard (1868-1930, American Humorist, Journalist)

48 In early childhood you may lay the foundation of poverty or riches, industry of idleness, good or evil, by the habits to which you train your children. Teach them right habits then, and their future life is safe.
Lydia Sigourney (1791-1865, American Poet)

49 The regularity of a habit is generally in proportion to its absurdity.
Marcel Proust (1871-1922, French Novelist)

50 Great is the power of habit. It teaches us to bear fatigue and to despise wounds and pain.
Marcus T. Cicero (106-43 BC, Great Roman Orator, Politician)

51 The power of habit and the charm of novelty are the two adverse forces which explain the follies of mankind.
Maria De Beausacq

52 A habit cannot be tossed out the window; it must be coaxed down the stairs a step at a time.
Mark Twain (1835-1910, American Humorist, Writer)

53 Habit is habit, and not to be flung out of the window by any man, but coaxed downstairs a step at a time.
Mark Twain (1835-1910, American Humorist, Writer)

54 To stop smoking is the easiest thing I ever did. I ought to know; I've done it a thousand times.
Mark Twain (1835-1910, American Humorist, Writer)

55 Stop the habit of wishful thinking and start the habit of thoughtful wishes.
Mary Martin

56 To change a habit, make a conscious decision, then act out the new behavior.
Maxwell Maltz (American Plastic Surgeon, Author of "Psycho-Cybernetics")

57 Habit is second nature.
Michel Eyquem De Montaigne (1533-1592, French Philosopher, Essayist)

58 To fall into a habit is to begin to cease to be.
Miguel De Unamuno (1864-1936, Spanish Philosophical Writer)

59 Habits are formed by the repetition of particular acts. They are strengthened by an increase in the number of repeated acts. Habits are also weakened or broken, and contrary habits are formed by the repetition of contrary acts.
Mortimer J. Adler (1902-, American Educator, Philosopher)

60 Habit is either the best of servants or the worst of masters.
Nathaniel Emmons

61 The beginning of a habit is like an invisible thread, but every time we repeat the act we strengthen the strand, add to it another filament, until it becomes a great cable and binds us irrevocably thought and act.
Orison Swett Marden (1850-1924, American Author, Founder of Success Magazine)

62 Man becomes a slave to his constantly repeated acts. What he at first chooses, at last compels.
Orison Swett Marden (1850-1924, American Author, Founder of Success Magazine)

63 Habits change into character.
Ovid (43 BC-18 AD, Roman Poet)

64 Make good habits and they will make you.
Parks Cousins

65 You were not born with the habit of brushing your teeth. With persistent action, over a period of time, you developed the habit. Now, I'll bet you would never consider going a week without brushing.
Paul R. Scheele (American NLP Expert and Human Potential, Author)

66 Good habits result from resisting temptation.
Proverb

67 Good habits, which bring our lower passions and appetites under automatic control, leave our natures free to explore the larger experiences of life. Too many of us divide and dissipate our energies in debating actions which should be taken for granted.
Ralph W. Sockman

68 A man who gives his children habits of industry provides for them better than by giving them a fortune.
Richard Whately (1787-1863, British Prelate, Writer)

69 Habit is a great deadener.
Samuel Beckett (1906-1989, Irish Dramatist, Novelist)

70 The chains of habit are generally too week to be felt, until they are too strong to be broken.
Samuel Johnson (1709-1784, British Author)

71 The habit of looking on the best side of every event is worth more than a thousand pounds a years.
Samuel Johnson (1709-1784, British Author)

72 Habit, if not resisted, soon becomes necessity.
St. Augustine (354-430, Numidian-born Bishop of Hippo, Theologian)

73 Our repeated failure to fully act as we would wish must not discourage us. It is the sincere intention that is the essential thing, and this will in time release us from the bondage of habits which at present seem almost insuperable.
Thomas Troward

74 Good habits are as easy to form as bad ones.
Tim Mccarver

75 Incredibly, many people continue their old life-style, their habits even if they feel miserable, lonely, bored, inadequate, or abused. Why? Of course... because habit is an easy place to hide.
Tom Rusk

76 Any act often repeated soon forms a habit; and habit allowed, steady gains in strength, At first it may be but as a spider's web, easily broken through, but if not resisted it soon binds us with chains of steel.
Tryon Edwards (1809-1894, American Theologian)

77 Once you learn to quit, it becomes a habit.
Vince Lombardi (1913-1970, American Football Coach)

78 As a twig is bent the tree inclines.
Virgil (70-19 BC, Roman Poet)

79 Rigid, the skeleton of habit alone upholds the human frame.
Virginia Woolf (1882-1941, British Novelist, Essayist)

80 The unfortunate thing about this world is that the good habits are much easier to give up than the bad ones.
W. Somerset Maugham (1874-1965, British Novelist, Playwright)

81 Never permit failure to become a habit.
William Frederick Book

82 We must make automatic and habitual, as early as possible, as many useful actions as we can...in the acquisition of a new habit, we must take car to launch ourselves with as strong and decided initiative as possible. Never suffer an exception to occur till the new habit is securely rooted in your life.
William James (1842-1910, American Psychologist, Professor, Author)

83 Habit is thus the enormous fly-wheel of society, its most precious conservative agent. It alone is what keeps us all within the bounds of ordinance, and saves the children of fortune from the envious uprisings of the poor.
William James (1842-1910, American Psychologist, Professor, Author)

84 How use doth breed a habit in man!
William Shakespeare (1564-1616, British Poet, Playwright, Actor)

HAIR

1. Gray hairs are death's blossoms.
   English Proverb

2. It's not the hair on your head that matters. It's the kind of hair you have inside.
   Garry Shandling (1949-, American Comedian, Talk Show Host, Actor)

3. By common consent gray hairs are a crown of glory; the only object of respect that can never excite envy.
   George Bancroft (1800-1891, American Historian)

4. Gray hair is a sign of age, not of wisdom.
   Greek Proverb

5. The hair is the richest ornament of women.
   Martin Luther (1483-1546, German Leader of the Protestant Reformation)

6. Babies haven't any hair; Old men's heads are just as bare; between the cradle and the grave lie a haircut and a shave
   Samuel Hoffenstein

HAPPINESS

1. Happiness adds and multiplies, as we divide it with others.
   A. Nielsen (1897-1980, American Businessman, Market Researcher)

2. No man should desire to be happy who is not at the same time holy. He should spend his efforts in seeking to know and do the will of God, leaving to Christ the matter of how happy he should be.
   A. W. Tozer (Deceased 1963, American Preacher)

3. A person will be just about as happy as they make up their minds to be.
   Abraham Lincoln (1809-1865, Sixteenth President of the USA)

4. What can be added to the happiness of a man who is in health, out of debt, and has a clear conscience?
   Adam Smith (1723-1790, Scottish Economist)

5. People who never achieve happiness are the ones who complain whenever they're awake, and whenever they're asleep, they are thinking about what to complain about tomorrow.
   Adam Zimbler

6. Call no man happy till he is dead.
   Aeschylus (525-456 BC, Greek Dramatist)

7. It is not easy to find happiness in ourselves, and it is not possible to find it elsewhere.
   Agnes Repplier (1858-1950, American Author, Social Critic)

8. It isn't necessary to be rich and famous to be happy. It's only necessary to be rich.
   Alan Alda (1936-, American Actor)

9. To be happy we must not be too concerned with others.
   Albert Camus (1913-1960, French Existential Writer)

10. But what is happiness except the simple harmony between a person and life they lead.
    Albert Camus (1913-1960, French Existential Writer)

11. When you have once seen the glow of happiness on the face of a beloved person, you know that a man can have no vocation but to awaken that light on the faces surrounding him; and you are torn by the thought of the unhappiness and night you cast, by the mere fact of living, in the hearts you encounter.
    Albert Camus (1913-1960, French Existential Writer)

12. The only ones among you who will be really happy are those who will have sought and found how to serve.
    Albert Schweitzer (1875-1965, German Born Medical Missionary, Theologian, Musician, and Philosopher)

13. I can sympathize with people's pains, but not with their pleasures. There is something curiously boring about somebody else's happiness.
    Aldous Huxley (1894-1963, British Author)

14. Know then this truth, enough for man to know virtue alone is happiness below.
    Alexander Pope (1688-1744, British Poet, Critic, Translator)

15. Happy the man whose wish and care a few paternal acres bound, content to breathe his native air in his own ground.
    Alexander Pope (1688-1744, British Poet, Critic, Translator)

16. We are never happy; we can only remember that we were so once.
    Alexander Smith (1830-1867, Scottish Poet, Author)

17. A man is happy so long as he chooses to be happy and nothing can stop him.
    Alexander Solzhenitsyn (1918-, Russian Novelist)

18. Happiness is like those palaces in fairy tales whose gates are guarded by dragons: we must fight in order to conquer it.
    Alexandre Dumas (1802-1870, French Novelist, Dramatist)

19. Happiness is not a matter of events; it depends upon the tides of the mind.
    Alice Meynell (1847-1922, British Poet, Essayist)

20. They say a person needs just three things to be truly happy in this world. Someone to love, something to do, and something to hope for.
    Allan K. Chalmers

21. Celebrate the happiness that friends are always giving, make every day a holiday and celebrate just living!
    Amanda Bradley

22. Happiness is an agreeable sensation, arising from contemplating the misery of others.
    Ambrose Bierce (1842-1914, American Author, Editor, Journalist, "The Devil's Dictionary")

23. Happiness depends more on how life strikes you than on what happens.
    Andy Rooney (American Television News Personality)

24 Whoever is happy will make others happy too.
Anne Frank (1929-1945, German Jewish Refugee, Diarist)

25 The best advice on the art of being happy is about as easy to follow as advice to be well when one is sick.
Anne Sophie Swetchine (1782-1857, Russian Author)

26 It is in the compelling zest of high adventure and of victory, and in creative action, that man finds his supreme joys.
Antoine De Saint-Exupery (1900-1944, French Aviator, Writer)

27 True happiness comes from the joy of deeds well done, the zest of creating things new.
Antoine De Saint-Exupery (1900-1944, French Aviator, Writer)

28 If happiness is activity in accordance with excellence, it is reasonable that it should be in accordance with the highest excellence.
Aristotle (384-322 BC, Greek Philosopher)

29 Happiness is activity.
Aristotle (384-322 BC, Greek Philosopher)

30 Happiness depends upon ourselves.
Aristotle (384-322 BC, Greek Philosopher)

31 Happiness is a sort of action.
Aristotle (384-322 BC, Greek Philosopher)

32 Happiness includes chiefly the idea of satisfaction after full honest effort. No one can possibly be satisfied and no one can be happy who feels that in some paramount affairs he failed to take up the challenge of life.
Arnold Bennett (1867-1931, British Novelist)

33 Most people ask for happiness on condition. Happiness can only be felt if you don't set any condition.
Arthur Rubenstein (1887-1982, Polish-born American Pianist-artist)

34 The two enemies of human happiness are pain and boredom.
Arthur Schopenhauer (1788-1860, German Philosopher)

35 Happiness is the harvest of a quiet eye.
Austin O'Malley

36 No one is in control of your happiness but you; therefore, you have the power to change anything about yourself or your life that you want to change.
Barbara De Angelis (American Expert on Relationship & Love, Author)

37 True happiness consists not in the multitude of friends, but in the worth and choice.
Ben Johnson (1573-1637, British Dramatist, Poet)

38 The human spirit needs to accomplish, to achieve, to triumph to be happy.
Ben Stein (American Professor, Writer)

39 Happiness is a journey... not a destination.
Ben Sweetland

40 There are two ways of being happy: We must either diminish our wants or augment our means -- either may do -- the result is the same and it is for each man to decide for himself and to do that which happens to be easier.
Benjamin Franklin (1706-1790, American Scientist, Publisher, Diplomat)

41 Happiness consists more in small conveniences of pleasures that occur every day, than in great pieces of good fortune that happen but seldom to a man in the course of his life.
Benjamin Franklin (1706-1790, American Scientist, Publisher, Diplomat)

42 A great obstacle to happiness is to expect too much happiness.
Bernard Le Bovier Fontenelle (1657-1757, Scientist, Man of Letter)

43 Success is getting and achieving what you want. Happiness is wanting and being content with what you get.
Bernard Meltzer (1914-, American Law Professor)

44 The good life, as I conceive it, is a happy life. I do not mean that if you are good you will be happy; I mean that if you are happy you will be good.
Bertrand Russell (1872-1970, British Philosopher, Mathematician, Essayist)

45 To be happy in this world, especially when youth is past, it is necessary to feel oneself not merely an isolated individual whose day will soon be over, but part of the stream of life slowing on from the first germ to the remote and unknown future.
Bertrand Russell (1872-1970, British Philosopher, Mathematician, Essayist)

46 Men who are unhappy, like men who sleep badly, are always proud of the fact.
Bertrand Russell (1872-1970, British Philosopher, Mathematician, Essayist)

47 If there were in the world today any large number of people who desired their own happiness more than they desired the unhappiness of others, we could have paradise in a few years.
Bertrand Russell (1872-1970, British Philosopher, Mathematician, Essayist)

48 Few people can be happy unless they hate some other person, nation, or creed.
Bertrand Russell (1872-1970, British Philosopher, Mathematician, Essayist)

49 The secret of happiness is this: let your interests be as wide as possible, and let your reactions to the things and persons that interest you be as far as possible friendly rather than hostile.
Bertrand Russell (1872-1970, British Philosopher, Mathematician, Essayist)

50 Happiness is not best achieved by those who seek it directly.
Bertrand Russell (1872-1970, British Philosopher, Mathematician, Essayist)

51 Anything you're good at contributes to happiness.
Bertrand Russell (1872-1970, British Philosopher, Mathematician, Essayist)

52 To be without some of the things you want is an indispensable part of happiness.
Bertrand Russell (1872-1970, British Philosopher, Mathematician, Essayist)

53 When we recall the past, we usually find that it is the simplest things -- not the great occasions -- that in retrospect give off the greatest glow of happiness.
Bob Hope (1903-, American Comedian, Actor)

54 Like swimming, riding, writing, or playing golf, happiness can be learned.
Boris Sokoloff

55 I am learning to understand rather than immediately judge or to be judged. I cannot blindly follow the crowd and accept their approach. I will not allow myself to indulge in the usual manipulating game of role creation. Fortunately for me, my self-knowledge has transcended that and I have come to understand that life is best to be lived and not to be conceptualized. I am happy because I am growing daily and I am honestly not knowing where the limit lies. To be certain, every day there can be a revelation or a new discovery. I treasure the memory of the past misfortunes. It has added more to my bank of fortitude.
Bruce Lee (1940-1973, Chinese-American Actor, Director, Author, Martial Artist)

56 Thousands of candles can be lighted from a single candle, and the life of the candle will not be shortened. Happiness never decreases by being shared.
Buddha (568-488 BC, Founder of Buddhism)

57 Happiness is not a destination. It is a method of life.
Burton Hills

58 The pursuit of happiness is a most ridiculous phrase; if you pursue happiness you'll never find it.
C(harles) P(ercy) Snow (1905-1980, British Novelist, Physicist)

59 If you pursue happiness you never find it.
C(harles) P(ercy) Snow (1905-1980, British Novelist, Physicist)

60 God cannot give us a happiness and peace apart from Himself, because it is not there. There is no such thing.
C. S. Lewis (1898-1963, British Academic, Writer, Christian Apologist)

61 Even a happy life cannot be without a measure of darkness, and the word happy would lose its meaning if it were not balanced by sadness. It is far better take things as they come along with patience and equanimity.
Carl Jung (1875-1961, Swiss Psychiatrist)

62 Happiness, that grand mistress of the ceremonies in the dance of life, impels us through all its mazes and meandering, but leads none of us by the same route
Charles Caleb Colton (1780-1832, British Sportsman Writer)

63 There is this difference between happiness and wisdom, that he that thinks himself the happiest man, really is so; but he who thinks himself the wisest, is generally the greatest fool.
Charles Caleb Colton (1780-1832, British Sportsman Writer)

64 We wish to be happier than other people; and this is difficult, for we believe others to be happier than they are.
Charles De Montesquieu (1689-1755, French Jurist, Political Philosopher)

65 False happiness renders men stern and proud, and that happiness is never communicated. True happiness renders them kind and sensible, and that happiness is always shared.
Charles De Montesquieu (1689-1755, French Jurist, Political Philosopher)

66 If one only wished to be happy, this could be easily accomplished; but we wish to be happier that other people, and this is always difficult, for we believe others to be happier than they are.
Charles De Montesquieu (1689-1755, French Jurist, Political Philosopher)

67 It is not how much we have, but how much we enjoy, that makes happiness.
Charles Haddon Spurgeon (1834-1892, British Baptist Preacher)

68 We act as though comfort and luxury were the chief requirements of life, when all that we need to make us really happy is something to be enthusiastic about.
Charles Kingsley (1819-1875, British Author, Clergyman)

69 Lead the life that will make you kindly and friendly to everyone about you, and you will be surprised what a happy life you will lead.
Charles M. Schwab (1862-1939, American Industrialist, Businessman)

70 If you can't be happy where you are, it's a cinch you can't be happy where you ain't.
Charles "Tremendous" Jones (American Motivational Speaker, Author)

71 Happiness is like a sunbeam, which the least shadow intercepts, while adversity is often as the rain of spring.
Chinese Proverb

72 If you want happiness for an hour -- take a nap. If you want happiness for a day -- go fishing. If you want happiness for a month -- get married. If you want happiness for a year -- inherit a fortune. If you want happiness for a lifetime -- help someone else.
Chinese Proverb

73 Happiness is the absence of the striving for happiness.
Chuang Tzu (369-286 BC, Chinese Philosopher)

74 We take greater pains to persuade others we are happy than in trying to think so ourselves.
Confucius (551-479 BC, Chinese Ethical Teacher, Philosopher)

75 I'm fulfilled in what I do... I never thought that a lot of money or fine clothes -- the finer things of life -- would make you happy. My concept of happiness is to be filled in a spiritual sense.
Coretta Scott King

76 If you want others to be happy, practice compassion. If you want to be happy, practice compassion.
Dalai Lama (1935-, Tibet Religious Leader Resides In India)

77 Happiness is not something ready made. It comes from your own actions.
Dalai Lama (1935-, Tibet Religious Leader Resides In India)

78 Many people think that if they were only in some other place, or had some other job, they would be happy. Well, that is doubtful. So get as much happiness out of what you are doing as you can and don't put off being happy until some future date.
Dale Carnegie (1888-1955, American Author, Trainer)

79 Did you ever see an unhappy horse? Did you ever see bird that had the blues? One reason why birds and horses are not unhappy is because they are not trying to impress other birds and horses.
Dale Carnegie (1888-1955, American Author, Trainer)

80 Remember, happiness doesn't depend upon who you are or what you have, it depends solely upon what you think.
Dale Carnegie (1888-1955, American Author, Trainer)

81 Act happy, feel happy, be happy, without a reason in the world. Then you can love, and do what you will.
Dan Millman

82 All you need for happiness is a good gun, a good horse, and a good wife.
Daniel Boone (1734-1820, American Pioneer, Frontiersman)

83 Happiness is not a possession to be prized. It is a quality of thought, a state of mind.
Daphne Du Maurier

84 Happiness... she loves, to see men at work. She loves sweat, weariness, self sacrifice. She will be found not in places but lurking in cornfields and factories; and hovering over littered desks; she crowns the unconscious head of the busy child.
David Grayson (1870-1946, American Journalist and Writer)

85 The great end of all human industry is the attainment of happiness. For this were arts invented, sciences cultivated, laws ordained, and societies modeled, by the most profound wisdom of patriots and legislators. Even the lonely savage, who lies exposed to the inclemency of the elements and the fury of wild beasts, forgets not, for a moment, this grand object of his being.
David Hume (1711-1776, Scottish Philosopher, Historian)

86 Human happiness seems to consist in three ingredients; action, pleasure and indolence. And though these ingredients ought to be mixed in different proportions, according to the disposition of the person, yet no one ingredient can be entirely wanting without destroying in some measure the relish of the whole composition. composition.
David Hume (1711-1776, Scottish Philosopher, Historian)

87 Work and live to serve others, to leave the world a little better than you found it and garner for yourself as much peace of mind as you can. This is happiness.
David Sarnoff (1891-1971, Belarus-born American Entrepreneur)

88 Happiness is a continuation of happenings which are not resisted.
Deepak Chopra (East-Indian- American M.D., New Age Author, Lecturer)

89 Happiness resides not in possessions, and not in gold, happiness dwells in the soul.
Democritus (460-370 BC, Greek Philosopher)

90 Gaiety --a quality of ordinary men. Genius always presupposes some disorder in the machine.
Denis Diderot (1713-1784, French Philosopher)

91 Happiness cannot be traveled to, owned, earned, worn or consumed. Happiness is the spiritual experience of living every minute with love, grace, and gratitude.
Denis Waitley (1933-, American Author, Speaker, Trainer, Peak Performance Expert)

92 It is not in the pursuit of happiness that we find fulfillment, it is in the happiness of pursuit.
Denis Waitley (1933-, American Author, Speaker, Trainer, Peak Performance Expert)

93 That which you create in beauty and goodness and truth lives on for all time to come. Don't spend your life accumulating material objects that will only turn to dust and ashes.
Denis Waitley (1933-, American Author, Speaker, Trainer, Peak Performance Expert)

94 It is the chiefest point of happiness that a man is willing to be what he is.
Desiderius Erasmus (1466-1536, Dutch Humanist)

95 Happiness is the interval between periods of unhappiness.
Don Marquis (1878-1937, American Humorist, Journalist)

96 To buy happiness is to sell soul.
Doug Horton

97 Happiness in the present is only shattered by comparison with the past.
Doug Horton

98 It's not a question of happiness, it's a requirement. Consider the alternative.
Doug Horton

99 Happiness grows at our own firesides, and is not to be picked in stranger's gardens.
Douglas William Jerrold (1803-1857, British Humorist, Playwright)

100 Our happiness in this world depends on the affections we are able to inspire.
Duchess Prazlin

101 Suspicion of happiness is in our blood.
E. V. Lucas (1868-1938, British Journalist, Essayist)

102 If only we'd stop trying to be happy we could have a pretty good time.
Edith Wharton (1862-1937, American Author)

103 When one is happy there is no time to be fatigued; being happy engrosses the whole attention.
Edward Frederic Benson (1867-1940, American Author)

104 Happiness and virtue rest upon each other; the best are not only the happiest, but the happiest are usually the best.
Edward G. Bulwer-Lytton (1803-1873, British Novelist, Poet)

105 What ever our wandering our happiness will always be found within a narrow compass, and in the middle of the objects more immediately within our reach.
Edward G. Bulwer-Lytton (1803-1873, British Novelist, Poet)

106 The creed of a true saint is to make the best of life, and to make the most of it.
Edwin Hubbel Chapin (1814-1880, American Author, Clergyman)

107 The mintage of wisdom is to know that rest is rust, and that real life is love, laughter, and work.
Elbert Hubbard (1859-1915, American Author, Publisher)

108 Happiness is not a goal, it is a by-product.
Eleanor Roosevelt (1884-1962, American First Lady, Columnist, Lecturer, Humanitarian)

109 The Greeks said grandly in their tragic phrase, "Let no one be called happy till his death;" to which I would add, "Let no one, till his death be called unhappy."
Elizabeth Barrett Browning (1806-1861, British Poet)

110 Happiness must be cultivated. It is like character. It is not a thing to be safely let alone for a moment, or it will run to weeds.
Elizabeth Stuart Phelps (1844-1911, American Writer)

111 If you want to be happy for a year, plant a garden; If you want to be happy for life, plant a tree.
English Proverb

112 There is only one way to happiness and that is to cease worrying about things which are beyond the power of our will.
Epictetus (50-120, Stoic Philosopher)

113 Whoever does not regard what he has as most ample wealth, is unhappy, though he be master of the world.
Epictetus (50-120, Stoic Philosopher)

114 It is impossible to live a pleasant life without living wisely and well and justly. And it is impossible to live wisely and well and justly without living a pleasant life.
Epicurus (341-270 BC, Greek Philosopher)

115 If thou wilt make a man happy, add not unto his riches but take away from his desires.
Epicurus (341-270 BC, Greek Philosopher)

116 The search for happiness is one of the chief sources of unhappiness.
Eric Hoffer (1902-1983, American Author, Philosopher)

117 Farms and in castles, in homes, studies, and cloisters -- where sensible people manage to live relatively lusty and decent lives, as moral as they must be, as free as they may be, and as masterly as they can be. If we only knew it, this elusive arrangement is happiness.
Erik H. Erikson (Austrian Developmental Psychologist)

118 The happiness of most people we know is not ruined by great catastrophes or fatal errors, but by the repetition of slowly destructive little things.
Ernest Dimnet (1866-1954, French Clergyman)

119 What a man really wants is creative challenge with sufficient skills to bring him within the reach of success so that he may have the expanding joy of achievement.
Fay B. Nash

120 We are more interested in making others believe we are happy than in trying to be happy ourselves.
François de La Rochefoucauld (1613-1680, French classical writer)

121 We are never so happy nor so unhappy as we imagine.
François de La Rochefoucauld (1613-1680, French classical writer)

122 Happiness lies in the joy of achievement and the thrill of creative effort.
Franklin D. Roosevelt (1882-1945, Thirty-second President of the USA)

123 In theory there is a possibility of perfect happiness: To believe in the indestructible element within one, and not to strive towards it.
Franz Kafka (1883-1924, German Novelist, Short-Story Writer)

124 Happiness is a positive cash flow.
Fred Adler

125 We tend to forget that happiness doesn't come as a result of getting something we don't have, but rather of recognizing and appreciating what we do have.
Frederick Koenig

126 There can be no happiness if the things we believe in are different from the things we do.
Freya Stark (1893-1993, British Travel Writer)

127 Happiness does not lie in happiness, but in the achievement of it.
Fyodor Dostoevski (1821-1881, Russian Novelist)

128 The greatest happiness is to know the source of unhappiness.
Fyodor Dostoevski (1821-1881, Russian Novelist)

129 If you were happy every day of your life you wouldn't be a human being, you'd be a game show host.
Gabriel Heatter (1890-, American Journalist)

130 A lifetime of happiness? No man alive could bear it; it would be hell on earth.
George Bernard Shaw (1856-1950, Irish-born British Dramatist)

131 Give a man health and a course to steer; and he'll never stop to trouble about whether he's happy or not.
George Bernard Shaw (1856-1950, Irish-born British Dramatist)

132 Life at its noblest leaves mere happiness far behind; and indeed cannot endure it. Happiness is not the object of life: life has no object: it is an end in itself; and courage consists in the readiness to sacrifice happiness for an intenser quality of life.
George Bernard Shaw (1856-1950, Irish-born British Dramatist)

133 We have no more right to consume happiness without producing it than to consume wealth without producing it.
George Bernard Shaw (1856-1950, Irish-born British Dramatist)

134 Men can only be happy when they do not assume that the object of life is happiness
George Orwell (1903-1950, British Author, "Animal Farm")

135 Happiness is the only sanction of life; where happiness fails, existence remains a mad and lamentable experience.
George Santayana (1863-1952, American Philosopher, Poet)

136 Knowledge of what is possible is the beginning of happiness.
George Santayana (1863-1952, American Philosopher, Poet)

137 Happiness lies first of all in health.
George William Curtis (1824-1892, American Journalist)

138 Happiness is a mystery, like religion, and should never be rationalized.
Gilbert K. Chesterton (1874-1936, British Author)

139 Point me out the happy man and I will point you out either egotism, selfishness, evil --or else an absolute ignorance.
Graham Greene (1904-1991, British Novelist)

140 Only one thing has to change for us to know happiness in our lives: where we focus our attention.
Greg Anderson (American Author of "The 22 Non-Negotiable Laws of Wellness")

141 Happiness is a by product of an effort to make someone else happy.
Gretta Brooker Palmer

142 Now and then it's good to pause in our pursuit of happiness and just be happy.
Guillaume Apollinaire (1880-1918, Italian-born French Poet, Critic)

143 Happiness requires problems...
H. L. Hollingworth

144 Happiness... is not a destination: it is a manner of traveling. Happiness is not an end in itself. It is a by-product of working, playing, loving and living.
Haim Ginott

145 Do you want my one-word secret of happiness -- It's growth -- mental, financial, you name it.
Harold S. Geneen (1910-, American Accountant, Industrialist, CEO, ITT)

146 While we pursue happiness, we flee from contentment.
Hasidic Proverb

147 He's simply got the instinct for being unhappy highly developed.
Hector Hugh Munro (1870-1916, British Novelist, Writer)

148 Many people have the wrong idea of what constitutes true happiness. It is not attained through self-gratification, but through fidelity to a worthy purpose.
Helen Keller (1880-1968, American Blind/Deaf Author, Lecturer, Amorist)

149 To describe happiness is to diminish it.
Henri B. Stendhal (1783-1842, French Writer)

150 To live we must conquer incessantly, we must have the courage to be happy.
Henri Frederic Amiel (1821-1881, Swiss Philosopher, Poet, Critic)

151 There is no greater joy than that of feeling oneself a creator. The triumph of life is expressed by creation.
Henri L. Bergson (1859-1941, French Philosopher)

152 Man is the artificer of his own happiness.
Henry David Thoreau (1817-1862, American Essayist, Poet, Naturalist)

153 We are made happy when reason can discover no occasion for it. The memory of some past moments is more persuasive than the experience of present ones. There have been visions of such breadth and brightness that these motes were invisible in their light.
Henry David Thoreau (1817-1862, American Essayist, Poet, Naturalist)

154 Scarcely one person in a thousand is capable of tasting the happiness of others.
Henry Fielding (1707-1754, British Novelist, Dramatist)

155 Objects we ardently pursue bring little happiness when gained; most of our pleasures come from unexpected sources.
Herbert Spencer (1820-1903, British Philosopher)

156 Happiness is a how, not a what: a talent, not an object
Hermann Hesse (1877-1962, German-born Swiss Novelist, Poet)

157 Those who seek happiness miss it, and those who discuss it, lack it.
Holbrook Jackson

158 My happiness derives from knowing the people I love are happy.
Holly Ketchel

159 You traverse the world in search of happiness, which is within the reach of every man. A contented mind confers it on all.
Horace (65-8 BC, Italian Poet)

160 Real happiness is cheap enough, yet how dearly we pay for its counterfeit.
Hosea Ballou (1771-1852, American Theologian, Founder of "Universalism")

161 A happy person is not a person in a certain set of circumstances, but rather a person with a certain set of attitudes.
Hugh Downs (American Television Host)

162 It is the paradox of life that the way to miss pleasure is to seek it first. The very first condition of lasting happiness is that a life should be full of purpose, aiming at something outside self.
Hugo Black (1886-1971, American Supreme Court Judge)

163 He is rich who owes nothing.
Hungarian Proverb

164 It is not God's will merely that we should be happy, but that we should make ourselves happy
Immanuel Kant (1724-1804, German Philosopher)

165 Happiness is good health and a bad memory.
Ingrid Bergman (1915-1982, Swedish-born American Screen, Stage Actress)

166 Happiness is a matter of one's most ordinary everyday mode of consciousness being busy and lively and unconcerned with self. To be damned is for one's ordinary everyday mode of consciousness to be unremitting agonizing preoccupation with self.
Iris Murdoch (1919-, British Novelist, Philosopher)

167 Happiness consumes itself like a flame. It cannot burn for ever, it must go out, and the presentiment of its end destroys it at its very peak.
J. August Strindberg (1849-1912, Swedish Dramatist, Novelist, Poet)

168 Happiness is not a brilliant climax to years of grim struggle and anxiety. It is a long succession of little decisions simply to be happy in the moment.
J. Donald Walters (American Author, Lecturer, Playwright)

169 Happiness is understanding that friendship is more precious than mere things, more precious than getting your own way, more precious than being in situations where true principles are not at stake.
J. Donald Walters (American Author, Lecturer, Playwright)

170 The secret of happiness and prosperity in this world, as in the world to come, lies in thinking of the welfare of others first, and not taking one's self too seriously.
J. Kindleberger

171 Happiness comes more from loving than being loved; and often when our affection seems wounded it is only our vanity bleeding. To love, and to be hurt often, and to love again -- this is the brave and happy life.
J.E Buckrose

172 Even if happiness forgets you a little bit, never completely forget about it.
Jacques Prevert (1900-1977, French Poet)

173 Most of us experience happiness when we are enjoying life and feeling free, enjoying the process and products of our creative and intellectual processes, enjoying the ecstasy of transcendent oneness with the universe.
James Muriel (American Author, Lecturer)

174 Happiness is perfume, you can't pour it on somebody else without getting a few drops on yourself
James Van Der Zee

175 Happiness is a sunbeam which may pass through a thousand bosoms without losing a particle of its original ray; nay, when it strikes on a kindred heart, like the converged light on a mirror, it reflects itself with redoubled brightness. It is not perfected till it is shared.
Jane Porter (1776-1850, British Novelist)

176 The thirst after happiness is never extinguished in the heart of man.
Jean Jacques Rousseau (1712-1778, Swiss Political Philosopher, Educationist, Essayist)

177 Joy descends gently upon us like the evening dew, and does not patter down like a hailstorm.
Jean Paul Richter (1763-1825, German Novelist)

178 The said truth is that it is the greatest happiness of the greatest number that is the measure of right and wrong.
Jeremy Bentham (1748-1832, British Philosopher, Jurist, Political Theorist)

179 Happiness is not something you postpone for the future; it is something you design for the present.
Jim Rohn (American Businessman, Author, Speaker, Philosopher)

180 To be happy is not the purpose of our being rather it is to deserve happiness.
Johann G. Fichte (1762-1814, German Philosopher)

181 If we cannot live so as to be happy, let us so live as to deserve happiness.
Johann G. Fichte (1762-1814, German Philosopher)

182 What makes people happy is activity; changing evil itself into good by power, working in a God like manner.
Johann Wolfgang Von Goethe (1749-1832, German Poet, Dramatist, Novelist)

183 A person is never happy till their vague strivings has itself marked out its proper limitations.
Johann Wolfgang Von Goethe (1749-1832, German Poet, Dramatist, Novelist)

184 The highest happiness of man is to have probed what is knowable and quietly to revere what is unknowable.
Johann Wolfgang Von Goethe (1749-1832, German Poet, Dramatist, Novelist)

185 The man who is born with a talent which he was meant to use finds his greatest happiness in using it.
Johann Wolfgang Von Goethe (1749-1832, German Poet, Dramatist, Novelist)

186 The most happy man is he who knows how to bring into relation the end and beginning of his life.
Johann Wolfgang Von Goethe (1749-1832, German Poet, Dramatist, Novelist)

187 Happiness is a ball after which we run wherever it rolls, and we push it with our feet when it stops.
Johann Wolfgang Von Goethe (1749-1832, German Poet, Dramatist, Novelist)

188 What would you call the highest happiness? Wratislaw was ask. The sense of competence, was the answer, given without hesitation.
John Buchan (1875-1940, Scottish Writer, Statesman)

189 The secret of happiness is something to do.
John Burroughs (1837-1921, American Naturalist, Author)

190 It is wrong to assume that men of immense wealth are always happy.
John D. Rockefeller (1839-1937, American Industrialist, Philanthropist, Founder Exxon)

191 Such happiness as life is capable of comes from the full participation of all our powers in the endeavor to wrest from each changing situations of experience its own full and unique meaning.
John Dewey (1859-1952, American Philosopher, Educator)

192 True happiness is the full use of your powers along lines of excellence in a life affording scope.
John F. Kennedy (1917-1963, Thirty-fifth President of the USA)

193 Happy were men if they but understood There is no safety but in doing good
John Fountain.

194 Happiness held is the seed; Happiness shared is the flower-Author Unknown People need your love the most when they appear to deserve it the least.
John Harrigan

195 The loss of wealth is loss of dirt, as sages in all times assert; The happy man's without a shirt.
John Heywood (1497-1580, British Dramatist, Proverb Collection)

196 Be open to your happiness and sadness as they arise.
John M. Thomas

197 Happiness consists in activity -- it is a running stream, not a stagnant pool.
John Mason

198 Not only is there a right to be happy, there is a duty to be happy. So much sadness exists in the world that we are all under obligation to contribute as much joy as lies within our powers.
John S. Bonnell

199 Happiness comes when we test our skills towards some meaningful purpose.
John Stossel

200 Ask yourself whether you are happy, and you cease to be so.
John Stuart Mill (1806-1873, British Philosopher, Economist)

201 I have learned to seek my happiness by limiting my desires, rather than in attempting to satisfy them.
John Stuart Mill (1806-1873, British Philosopher, Economist)

202 Men expect that religion should cost them no pains, that happiness should drop into their laps without any design and endeavor on their part, and that, after they have done what they please while they live, God should snatch them up to heaven when they die. But though the commandments of God be not grievous, yet it is fit to let men know that they are not thus easy.
John Tillotson (1630-1694, British Theologian - Archbishop of Canterbury)

203 True happiness involves the full use of one's power and talents.
John W. Gardner (1912-, American Educator, Social Activist)

204 Happiness is a perpetual possession of being well deceived.
Jonathan Swift (1667-1745, Anglo-Irish Satirist)

205 True happiness arises, in the first place, from the enjoyment of one's self, and in the next, from the friendship and conversation of a few select companions.
Joseph Addison (1672-1719, British Essayist, Poet, Statesman)

206 Many persons have a wrong idea of what constitutes true happiness. It is not attained through self-gratification but through fidelity to a worthy purpose.
Joseph Addison (1672-1719, British Essayist, Poet, Statesman)

207 Three grand essentials to happiness in this life are something to do, something to love, and something to hope for.
Joseph Addison (1672-1719, British Essayist, Poet, Statesman)

208 Enjoy your happiness while you have it, and while, you have it do not too closely scrutinize its foundation.
Joseph Farrall

209 If you ever find happiness by hunting for it, you will find it as the old woman did her lost spectacles. Safe on her own nose all the time.
Josh Billings (1815-1885, American Humorist, Lecturer)

210 A good way I know to find happiness, is to not bore a hole to fit the plug.
Josh Billings (1815-1885, American Humorist, Lecturer)

211 The foolish man seeks happiness in the distance; The wise grows it under his feet.
Julius Robert Oppenheimer (1904-1967, American Nuclear Physicist)

212 I am more and more convinced that our happiness or our unhappiness depends far more on the way we meet the events of life than on the nature of those events themselves.
Karl Wilhelm Von Humboldt (1767-1835, German Statesman, Philologist)

213 Happiness is experienced when your life gives you what you are willing to accept.
Ken Keyes Jr. (1921-1995, American Author)

214 It is pretty hard to tell what does bring happiness; poverty and wealth have both failed.
Kin Hubbard (1868-1930, American Humorist, Journalist)

215 Seek not happiness too greedily, and be not fearful of unhappiness.
Lao-Tzu (600 BC, Chinese Philosopher, Founder of Taoism, Author of the "Tao Te Ching")

216 In order to have great happiness, you have to have great pain and unhappiness-otherwise how would you know when you're happy?
Leslie Caron

217 No thoroughly occupied man was ever yet very miserable.
Letitia Elizabeth Landon

218 Happiness is not in having being; it is in doing.
Lilian Eichler Watson

219 Happiness is a wine of the rarest vintage, and seems insipid to a vulgar taste.
Logan Pearsall Smith (1865-1946, Anglo-American Essayist, Aphorist)

220 To have joy one must share it. Happiness was born a twin.
Lord Byron (1788-1824, British Poet)

221 The world's literature and folklore are full of stories that point out how futile it can be to seek happiness. Rather, happiness is a blessing that comes to you as you go along; a treasure that you incidentally find.
Louis Binstock (American Minister)

222 Happy is the son whose faith in his mother remains unchallenged.
Louisa May Alcott (1832-1888, American Author)

223 The happy think a lifetime short, but to the unhappy one night can be an eternity.
Lucian (117-180, Syrian Rhetorician)

224 Happiness radiates like the fragrance from a flower, and draws all good things toward you. Allow your love to nourish yourself as well as others. Do not strain after the needs of life. It is sufficient to be quietly alert and aware of them. In this way life proceeds more naturally and effortlessly. Life is here to Enjoy!
Maharishi Mahesh Yogi (Indian Spiritual Teacher, Founder of Transcendental Meditation)

225 Happiness is when what you think, what you say, and what you do are in harmony.
Mahatma Gandhi (1869-1948, Indian Political, Spiritual Leader)

226 I can say that I never knew what joy was like until I gave up pursuing happiness, or cared to live until I chose to die. For these two discoveries I am beholden to Jesus.
Malcolm Muggeridge (1903-1990, British Broadcaster)

227 There is something ridiculous and even quite indecent in an individual claiming to be happy. Still more a people or a nation making such a claim. The pursuit of happiness... is without any question the most fatuous which could possibly be undertaken. This lamentable phrase "the pursuit of happiness" is responsible for a good part of the ills and miseries of the modern world.
Malcolm Muggeridge (1903-1990, British Broadcaster)

228 When what we are is what we want to be, that's happiness.
Malcolm S. Forbes (1919-1990, American Publisher, Businessman)

229 Let us be grateful to people who make us happy; they are the charming gardeners who make our souls blossom.
Marcel Proust (1871-1922, French Novelist)

230 Happiness serves hardly any other purpose than to make unhappiness possible.
Marcel Proust (1871-1922, French Novelist)

231 Remember that very little is needed to make a happy life.
Marcus Aurelius (121-80 AD, Roman Emperor, Philosopher)

232 The happiness of your life depends upon the quality of your thoughts: therefore, guard accordingly, and take care that you entertain no notions unsuitable to virtue and reasonable nature.
Marcus Aurelius (121-80 AD, Roman Emperor, Philosopher)

233 We think a happy life consists in tranquility of mind.
Marcus T. Cicero (106-43 BC, Great Roman Orator, Politician)

234 What happiness is there which is not purchased with more or less of pain?
Margaret Oliphant (1828-1897, British Novelist, Historian)

235 Often people attempt to live their lives backwards; they try to have more things, or more money, in order to do more of what they want, so they will be happier.
Margaret Young (American Author)

236 There are people who can do all fine and heroic things but one: keep from telling their happiness to the unhappy.
Mark Twain (1835-1910, American Humorist, Writer)

237 Happiness ain't a thing in itself --it's only a contrast with something that ain't pleasant. And so, as soon as the novelty is over and the force of the contrast dulled, it ain't happiness any longer, and you have to get something fresh.
Mark Twain (1835-1910, American Humorist, Writer)

238 Happiness lies neither in vice nor in virtue; but in the manner we appreciate the one and the other, and the choice we make pursuant to our individual organization.
Marquis De Sade (1740-1814, French Author)

239 Remember that happiness is as contagious as gloom. It should be the first duty of those who are happy to let others know of their gladness.
Maurice Maeterlinck (1862-1949, Belgian Author)

240 No burden is so heavy for a man to bear as a succession of happy days.
Max Muller (1823-1900, British Philosopher, Philologist)

241 The smallest annoyances, disturb us the most.
Michel Eyquem De Montaigne (1533-1592, French Philosopher, Essayist)

242 It seldom happens that any felicity comes so pure as not to be tempered and allayed by some mixture of sorrow.
Miguel De Cervantes (1547-1616, Spanish Novelist, Dramatist, Poet)

243 Happiness is the longing for repetition.
Milan Kundera (1929-, Czech Author, Critic)

244 Happiness is a conscious choice, not an automatic response.
Mildred Barthel

245 Happiness is a butterfly, which, when pursued, is always just beyond your grasp, but which, if you will sit down quietly, may alight upon you.
Nathaniel Hawthorne (1804-1864, American Novelist, Short Story Writer)

246 Happiness in this world, when it comes, comes incidentally. Make it the object of pursuit, and it leads us a wild-goose chase, and is never attained.
Nathaniel Hawthorne (1804-1864, American Novelist, Short Story Writer)

247 Many search for happiness as we look for a hat we wear on our heads.
Nikolaus Lenus

248 Shall I give you my recipe for happiness? I find everything useful and nothing indispensable. I find everything wonderful and nothing miraculous. I reverence the body. I avoid first causes like the plague.
Norman Douglas (1868-1952, British Author)

249 Happiness is not so much in having or sharing. We make a living by what we get, but we make a life by what we give.
Norman Macewan

250 Our happiness depends on the habit of mind we cultivate. So practice happy thinking every day. Cultivate the merry heart, develop the happiness habit, and life will become a continual feast.
Norman Vincent Peale (1898-1993, American Christian Reformed Pastor, Speaker, Author)

251 Realize that true happiness lies within you. Waste no time and effort searching for peace and contentment and joy in the world outside. Remember that there is no happiness in having or in getting, but only in giving. Reach out. Share. Smile. Hug. Happiness is a perfume you cannot pour on others without getting a few drops on yourself.
Og Mandino (1923-1996, American Motivational Author, Speaker)

252 The most exciting happiness is the happiness generated by forces beyond your control.
Ogden Nash (1902-1971, American Humorous Poet)

253 If frugality were established in the state, and if our expenses were laid out to meet needs rather than superfluities of life, there might be fewer wants, and even fewer pleasures, but infinitely more happiness.
Oliver Goldsmith (1728-1774, Anglo-Irish Author, Poet, Playwright)

254 The glow of satisfaction which follows the consciousness of doing our level best never comes to a human being from any other experience.
Orison Swett Marden (1850-1924, American Author, Founder of Success Magazine)

255 Talk happiness. The world is sad enough without your woe.
Orison Swett Marden (1850-1924, American Author, Founder of Success Magazine)

256 Happiness isn't something you experience; it's something you remember.
Oscar Levant (1906-1972, American Pianist, Actor)

257 When we are happy we are always good, but when we are good we are not always happy.
Oscar Wilde (1856-1900, British Author, Wit)

258 Some cause happiness wherever they go; others whenever they go.
Oscar Wilde (1856-1900, British Author, Wit)

259 Holiness, not happiness, is the chief end of man.
Oswald Chambers (1874-1917 Scottish Preacher, Author)

260 Be it jewel or toy, not the prize gives the joy, but the striving to win the prize.
Owen Meredith (1831-1891, British Politician, Poet)

261 Happiness is never stopping to think if you are.
Palmer Sondreal

262 The soul's joy lies in doing.
Percy Bysshe Shelley (1792-1822, British Poet)

263 Happiness seems made to be shared.
Pierre Corneille (1606-1684, French Dramatist)

264 The happier the moment the shorter.
Pliny The Elder (23-79, Roman Neophatonist)

265 Do not speak of your happiness to one less fortunate than yourself.
Plutarch (46-120 AD, Greek Essayist, Biographer)

266 The really happy man never laughs -- seldom -- though he may smile. He does not need to laugh, for laughter, like weeping is a relief of mental tension -- and the happy are not over strung.
Prof. F. A. P. Aveling (American Professor)

267 Where one is wise two are happy.
Proverb

268 If you cannot renounce the world the genius of happiness will never salute you.
Prutz

269 The greatest joy of life is to love and be loved.
R.D. Clyde

270 We find greatest joy, not in getting, but in expressing what we are. Men do not really live for honors or for pay; their gladness is not the taking and holding, but in doing, the striving, the building, the living. It is a higher joy to teach than to be taught. It is good to get justice, but better to do it; fun to have things but more to make them. The happy man is he who lives the life of love, not for the honors it may bring, but for the life itself.
R.J. Baughan

271 Happiness is not having what you want, but wanting what you have.
Rabbi H. Schachtel

272 I look on that man as happy, who, when there is question of success, looks into his work for a reply.
Ralph Waldo Emerson (1803-1882, American Poet, Essayist)

273 To fill the hour -- that is happiness.
Ralph Waldo Emerson (1803-1882, American Poet, Essayist)

274 Happiness is a perfume which you cannot pour on someone without getting some on yourself.
Ralph Waldo Emerson (1803-1882, American Poet, Essayist)

275 The journey to happiness involves finding the courage to go down into ourselves and take responsibility for what's there: all of it.
Richard Rohr

276 Be happy or die.
Rob Cohen

277 Happiness makes up in height for what it lacks in length.
Robert Frost (1875-1963, American Poet)

278 There's a hope for every woe, and a balm for every pain, but the first joys of our heart come never back again!
Robert Gilfillan (1798-1850, Scottish Poet)

279 Happiness is not a reward -- it is a consequence. Suffering is not a punishment -- it is a result.
Robert Green Ingersoll (1833-1899, American Orator, Lawyer)

280 Happiness is the only good. The time to be happy is now. The place to be happy is here. The way to be happy is to make others so.
Robert Green Ingersoll (1833-1899, American Orator, Lawyer)

281 Happiness lies in being privileged to work hard for long hours in doing whatever you think is worth doing. One man may find happiness in supporting a wife and children. Another may find it in robbing banks. Still another may labor mightily for years in pursuing pure research with no discernible result. Note the individual and subjective nature of each case. No two are alike and there is no reason to expect them to be. Each man or woman must find for himself or herself that occupation in which hard work and long hours make him or her happy. Contrariwise, if you are looking for shorter hours and longer vacations and early retirement, you are in the wrong job. Perhaps you need to take up bank robbing. Or geeking in a sideshow. Or even politics.
Robert Heinlein (1907-1988, American Science Fiction Writer)

282 Happiness is always a by-product. It is probably a matter of temperament, and for anything I know it may be glandular. But it is not something that can be demanded from life, and if you are not happy you had better stop worrying about it and see what treasures you can pluck from your own brand of unhappiness.
Robertson Davies (1913-, Canadian Novelist, Journalist)

283 Happiness is something that comes into our lives through doors we don't even remember leaving open.
Rose Wilder Lane (1886-1968, American Author and Journalist)

284 Remember that happiness is a way of travel, not a destination.
Roy Goodman

285 Happiness is a small and unworthy goal for something as big and fancy as a whole lifetime, and should be taken in small doses.
Russell (Wayne) Baker (1925-, American Journalist)

286 Happiness is not a horse, you cannot harness it.
Russian Proverb

287 Sir, that all who are happy, are equally happy, is not true. A peasant and a philosopher may be equally satisfied, but not equally happy. Happiness consists in the multiplicity of agreeable consciousness.
Samuel Johnson (1709-1784, British Author)

288 Happiness is not a state to arrive at, rather, a manner of traveling.
Samuel Johnson (1709-1784, British Author)

289 For who is pleased with himself.
Samuel Johnson (1709-1784, British Author)

290 To strive with difficulties, and to conquer them, is the highest human felicity.
Samuel Johnson (1709-1784, British Author)

291 We are long before we are convinced that happiness is never to be found; and each believes it possessed by others, to keep alive the hope of obtaining it for himself.
Samuel Johnson (1709-1784, British Author)

292 Happiness is a by-product. You cannot pursue it by itself.
Samuel Levenson

293 As happy a man as any in the world, for the whole world seems to smile upon me!
Samuel Pepys (1633-1703, British Diarist)

294 Be happy while you're living, for you're a long time dead.
Scottish Proverb

295 True happiness is to enjoy the present, without anxious dependence upon the future, not to amuse ourselves with either hopes or fears but to rest satisfied with what we have, which is sufficient, for he that is so wants nothing. The great blessings of mankind are within us and within our reach. A wise man is content with his lot, whatever it may be, without wishing for what he has not.
Seneca (4 BC-65 AD, Spanish-born Roman Statesman, philosopher)

296 One feels inclined to say that the intention that man should be "happy" is not included in the plan of "Creation."
Sigmund Freud (1856-1939, Austrian Physician - Founder of Psychoanalysis)

297 Happiness comes from... some curious adjustment to life.
Sir Hugh Walpole (1884-1941, New Zealand Writer)

298 The really happy person is the one who can enjoy the scenery, even when they have to take a detour.
Sir James Jeans (1877-1946, British Scientist, Astronomer Royal)

299 The secret of happiness is not in doing what one likes, but in liking what one does.
Sir James M. Barrie (1860-1937, British Playwright)

300 Happiness is a thing to be practiced, like the violin.
Sir John Lubbock (1834-1913, British Statesman, Banker, Naturalist)

301 It is not the place, nor the condition, but the mind alone that can make anyone happy or miserable."
Sir Roger L'Estrange

302 The truth is that all of us attain the greatest success and happiness possible in this life whenever we use our native capacities to their greatest extent.
Smiley Blanton (1882-?, American Author)

303 Call no man unhappy until he is married.
Socrates (469-399 BC, Greek Philosopher of Athens)

304 Happiness is unrepentant pleasure.
Socrates (469-399 BC, Greek Philosopher of Athens)

305 No man is happy; he is at best fortunate.
Solon (636-558 BC, Greek Statesman)

306 Let no man be called happy before his death. Till then, he is not happy, only lucky.
Solon (636-558 BC, Greek Statesman)

307 There is no happiness; there are only moments of happiness.
Spanish Proverb

308 There is no end of craving. Hence contentment alone is the best way to happiness. Therefore, acquire contentment.
Sri Swami Sivananda (1887-, Indian Physician, Sage)

309 Happiness is a hard thing because it is achieved only by making others happy.
Stuart Cloete

310 Happiness does not come from doing easy work but from the afterglow of satisfaction that comes after the achievement of a difficult task that demanded our best.
Theodore I. Rubin

311 The hardest habit of all to break is the terrible habit of happiness.
Theodosia Garrison (1874-1944, American Poet, Author)

312 But the whim we have of happiness is somewhat thus. By certain valuations, and averages, of our own striking, we come upon some sort of average terrestrial lot; this we fancy belongs to us by nature, and of indefeasible rights. It is simple payment of our wages, of our deserts; requires neither thanks nor complaint. Foolish soul! What act of legislature was there that thou shouldst be happy? A little while ago thou hadst no right to be at all.
Thomas Carlyle (1795-1881, Scottish Philosopher, Author)

313 The only happiness a brave person ever troubles themselves in asking about, is happiness enough to get their work done.
Thomas Carlyle (1795-1881, Scottish Philosopher, Author)

314 Happiness is not being pained in body or troubled in mind.
Thomas Jefferson (1743-1826, Third President of the USA)

315 A mind always employed is always happy. This is the true secret, the grand recipe, for felicity.
Thomas Jefferson (1743-1826, Third President of the USA)

316 Our greatest happiness does not depend on the condition of life in which chance has placed us, but is always the result of a good conscience, good health, occupation, and freedom in all just pursuits.
Thomas Jefferson (1743-1826, Third President of the USA)

317 Happiness is an imaginary condition, formerly often attributed by the living to the dead, now usually attributed by adults to children, and by children to adults.
Thomas Szasz (1920-, American Psychiatrist)

318 Happiness was not made to be boasted, but enjoyed. Therefore tho others count me miserable, I will not believe them if I know and feel myself to be happy; nor fear them.
Thomas Traherne (1636-1674, British Clergyman, Poet, Mystic)

319 You never enjoy the world aright, till the sea itself floweth in your veins, till you are clothed with the heavens and crowned with the stars.
Thomas Traherne (1636-1674, British Clergyman, Poet, Mystic)

320 The secret of Happiness is Freedom, and the secret of Freedom, Courage.
Thucydides (460-400 BC, Greek Historian of Athens)

321 Happiness is like manna; it is to be gathered in grains, and enjoyed every day. It will not keep; it cannot be accumulated; nor have we got to go out of ourselves or into remote places to gather it, since it has rained down from a Heaven, at our very door
Tryon Edwards (1809-1894, American Theologian)

322 Where there is joy there is creation. Where there is no joy there is no creation: know the nature of joy.
Veda Upanishads (800 BC, Hindu Poetic Dialogues On Metaphysics)

323 You have succeeded in life when all you really want is only what you really need.
Vernon Howard (19?-1992, American Author, Speaker)

324 Life's greatest happiness is to be convinced we are loved.
Victor Hugo (1802-1885, French Poet, Dramatist, Novelist)

325 If you observe a really happy man you will find him building a boat, writing a symphony, educating his son, growing Double Dahlias in his garden.
W Wolfe

326 We are no longer happy as soon as we wish to be happier.
Walter Savage Landor (1775-1864, British Poet, Essayist)

327 We cannot be contented because we are happy, and we cannot be happy because we are contented.
Walter Savage Landor (1775-1864, British Poet, Essayist)

328 There is no way to happiness. Happiness is the way.
Wayne Dyer (1940-, American Psychotherapist, Author, Lecturer)

329 It's never too late to have a happy childhood.
Wayne Dyer (1940-, American Psychotherapist, Author, Lecturer)

330 Happiness doesn't come from doing what we like to do but from liking what we have to do.
Wilferd A. Peterson

331 Joy comes from using your potential.
Will Schultz

332 That is happiness: to be dissolved into something complete and great.
Willa Cather (1876-1947, American Author)

333 We all want to be happy, and we're all going to die. You might say those are the only two unchallengeably true facts that apply to every human being on this planet.
William Boyd (1952-, British Novelist)

334 Happiness is neither virtue nor pleasure nor this thing nor that but simply growth, We are happy when we are growing.
William Butler Yeats (1865-1939, Irish Poet, Playwright.)

335 We are happy when for everything inside us there is a corresponding something outside us.
William Butler Yeats (1865-1939, Irish Poet, Playwright.)

336 Happiness, or misery, is in the mind. It is the mind that lives.
William Cobbett (1762-1835, British Journalist, Reformer)

337 One of the indictments of civilizations is that happiness and intelligence are so rarely found in the same person.
William Feather (1888-18, American Writer, Businessman)

338 Some of us might find happiness if we quit struggling so desperately for it.
William Feather (1888-18, American Writer, Businessman)

339 Look up, laugh loud, talk big, keep the color in your cheek and the fire in your eye, adorn your person, maintain your health, your beauty and your animal spirits.
William Hazlitt (1778-1830, British Essayist)

340 Happiness comes of the capacity to feel deeply, to enjoy simply, to think freely, to risk life, to be needed. which give happiness. Thomas Jefferson We never enjoy perfect happiness; our most fortunate successes are mingled with sadness; some anxieties always perplex the reality of our satisfaction.
William James (1842-1910, American Psychologist, Professor, Author)

341 Happiness is like a cat, If you try to coax it or call it, it will avoid you; it will never come. But if you pay not attention to it and go about your business, you'll find it rubbing against your legs and jumping into your lap.
William John Bennett (1943-, American Federal Official)

342 The happiest people are those who think the most interesting thoughts. Those who decide to use leisure as a means of mental development, who love good music, good books, good pictures, good company, good conversation, are the happiest people in the world. And they are not only happy in themselves, they are the cause of happiness in others.
William Lyon Phelps

343 Happiness is the light on the water. The water is cold and dark and deep.
William Maxwell (1676-1744, British - 5th Earl of Nithsdale)

344 The greatest happiness you can have is knowing that you do not necessarily require happiness.
William Saroyan (1908-1981, American Writer, Novelist,, Playwright)

345 But O, how bitter a thing it is to look into happiness through another man's eyes.
William Shakespeare (1564-1616, British Poet, Playwright, Actor)

346 I had rather have a fool make me merry, than experience make me sad.
William Shakespeare (1564-1616, British Poet, Playwright, Actor)

347 Happiness is not pleasure, it is victory.
Zig Ziglar (American Sales Trainer, Author, Motivational Speaker)

HARMONY

1 You don't get harmony when everybody sings the same note.
Doug Floyd

2 He who lives in harmony with himself lives in harmony with the universe.
Marcus Aurelius (121-80 AD, Roman Emperor, Philosopher)

HASTE

1 Rapidity does not always mean progress, and hurry is akin to waste. The old fable of the hare and the tortoise is just as good now, and just as true, as when it was first written.
Charles A. Stoddard

2 Though I am always in haste, I am never in a hurry.
John Wesley (1703-1791, British Preacher, Founder of Methodism)

3 Make haste slowly.
Latin Proverb

4 Hasten slowly and ye shall soon arrive.
Milarepa

5 Haste and rashness are storms and tempests, breaking and wrecking business; but nimbleness is a full, fair wind, blowing it with speed to the heaven.
Thomas Fuller (1608-1661, British Clergyman, Author)

6 No man who is in a hurry is quite civilized.
William J. Durant (1885-1981, American Historian, Essayist)

HATRED

1 Resentment seems to have been given us by nature for a defense, and for a defense only! It is the safeguard of justice and the security of innocence.
Adam Smith (1723-1790, Scottish Economist)

2 Chivalry is the most delicate form of contempt.
Albert Guerard

3 To be angry is to revenge the faults of others on ourselves.
Alexander Pope (1688-1744, British Poet, Critic, Translator)

4 Hatred -- The anger of the weak.
Alphonse Daudet (1840-1897, French Writer)

5 Hate is ravening vulture beaks descending on a place of skulls.
Amy Lowell (1874-1925, American Poet, Critic)

6 It is better to be hated for what you are than to be loved for what you are not.
Andre Gide (1869-1951, French Author)

7 A man who lives, not by what he loves but what he hates, is a sick man.
Archibald Macleish (1892-1982, American Poet)

8 We never get to love by hate, least of all by self-hatred.
Basil W. Maturin

9 Take time for all things; great haste makes great waste.
Benjamin Franklin (1706-1790, American Scientist, Publisher, Diplomat)

10 Hatred of enemies is easier and more intense than love of friends. But from men who are more anxious to injure opponents than to benefit the world at large no great good is to be expected.
Bertrand Russell (1872-1970, British Philosopher, Mathematician, Essayist)

11 That one I love who is incapable of ill will, and returns love for hatred. Living beyond the reach of I and mind, and of pain and pleasure, full of mercy, contented, self-controlled, with all his heart and all his mind given to Me -- with such a one I am in love.
Bhagavad Gita (400 BC, Sanskrit Poem Incorporated Into the Mahabharata)

12 Hate is such a luxurious emotion, it can only be spent on one we love.
Bob Udkoff

13 I will not permit any man to narrow and degrade my soul by making me hate him.
Booker T. Washington (1856-1915, American Black Leader and Educator)

14 Hatred does not cease through hatred at any time. Hatred ceases through love. This is an unalterable law.
Buddha (568-488 BC, Founder of Buddhism)

15 Never in this world can hatred be stilled by hatred; it will be stilled only by non-hatred -- this is the law of eternal.
Buddha (568-488 BC, Founder of Buddhism)

16 Hatred does not cease by hatred, but only by love; this is the eternal rule.
Buddha (568-488 BC, Founder of Buddhism)

17 Hate is always a clash between our spirit and someone else's body.
Cesare Pavese (1908-1950, Italian Poet, Novelist, Translator)

18 Passionate hatred can give meaning and purpose to an empty life.
Eric Hoffer (1902-1983, American Author, Philosopher)

19 Anger may repast with thee for an hour, but not repose for a night; the continuance of anger is hatred, the continuance of hatred turns malice.
Francis Quarles (1592-1644, British Poet)

20 When our hatred is violent, it sinks us even beneath those we hate.
François de La Rochefoucauld (1613-1680, French classical writer)

21 Hatred is the coward's revenge for being intimidated.
George Bernard Shaw (1856-1950, Irish-born British Dramatist)

22 One of the great disadvantages of hurry is that it takes such a long time.
Gilbert K. Chesterton (1874-1936, British Author)

23 Hating people is like burning down your own house to get rid of a rat.
Harry Emerson Fosdick (1878-1969, American Minister)

24 There is no faculty of the human soul so persistent and universal as that of hatred.
Henry Ward Beecher (1813-1887, American Preacher, Orator, Writer)

25 If you hate a person, you hate something in him that is part of yourself. What isn't part of ourselves doesn't disturb us.
Hermann Hesse (1877-1962, German-born Swiss Novelist, Poet)

26 Hatred is the vice of narrow souls; they feed it with all their littleness, and make it the pretext of base tyrannies.
Honore De Balzac (1799-1850, French Novelist)

27 Hatred is self-punishment. Hatred it the coward's revenge for being intimidated.
Hosea Ballou (1771-1852, American Theologian, Founder of "Universalism")

28 Love blinds us to faults, but hatred blinds us to virtues.
Iba Ezra

29 The passion of hatred is so long lived and so obstinate a malady that the surest sign of death in a sick person is their desire for reconciliation.
Jean De La Bruyere (1645-1696, French Writer)

30 To hate fatigues.
Jean Rostand (1894-1977, French Biologist, Writer)

31 People hate me because I am a multifaceted, talented, wealthy, internationally famous genius.
Jerry Lewis (1926-, American Comedian, Actor, Screenwriter, Director, Producer)

32 One drop of hatred left in the cup of joy turns the most blissful draught into poison.
Johann Friedrich Von Schiller (1759-1805, German Dramatist, Poet, Historian)

33 Hatred is active, and envy passive dislike; there is but one step from envy to hate.
Johann Wolfgang Von Goethe (1749-1832, German Poet, Dramatist, Novelist)

34 Hatred is something peculiar. You will always find it strongest and most violent where there is the lowest degree of culture.
Johann Wolfgang Von Goethe (1749-1832, German Poet, Dramatist, Novelist)

35 Anyone can hate. It costs to love.
John Williamson

36 You know that when I hate you, it is because I love you to a point of passion that unhinges my soul.
Julie De Lespinasse

37 Hatred is the madness of the heart.
Lord Byron (1788-1824, British Poet)

38 Hatred can be overcome only by love.
Mahatma Gandhi (1869-1948, Indian Political, Spiritual Leader)

39 Hatreds not vowed and concealed are to be feared more than those openly declared.
Marcus T. Cicero (106-43 BC, Great Roman Orator, Politician)

40 Hatred is inveterate anger.
Marcus T. Cicero (106-43 BC, Great Roman Orator, Politician)

41 We are almost always guilty of the hate we encounter.
Marquis De Vauvenargues (1715-1747, French Moralist)

42 Hatred paralyzes life; love releases it. Hatred confuses life; love harmonizes it. Hatred darkens life; love illuminates it.
Martin Luther King Jr. (1929-1968, American Black Leader, Nobel Prize Winner, 1964)

43 Reject hatred without hating.
Mary Baker Eddy (1821-1910, American Christian Writer, Founder of Christian Science Church)

44 Hatred is gained as much by good works as by evil.
Niccolo Machiavelli (1469-1527, Italian Author, Statesman)

45 Like fragile ice anger passes away in time.
Ovid (43 BC-18 AD, Roman Poet)

46 There is something to that old saying that hate injures the hater, not the hated.
Peace Pilgrim (1908-1981, American Peace Activist)

47 Some evils are cured by contempt.
Proverb

48 Many can bear adversity, but few contempt.
Proverb

49 There is no medicine to cure hatred.
Publilius Syrus (1st Century BC, Roman Writer)

50 Take care that no one hates you justly.
Publilius Syrus (1st Century BC, Roman Writer)

51 It is a weakness of your human nature to hate those whom you have wronged.
Publius Cornelius Tacitus (55-117 AD, Roman Historian)

52 Always remember, others may hate you, but those who hate you don't win unless you hate them-and then you destroy yourself.
Richard M. Nixon (1913-1994, Thirty-seventh President of the USA)

53 Those who hate you don't win unless you hate them; and then you destroy yourself.
Richard M. Nixon (1913-1994, Thirty-seventh President of the USA)

54 I have tried -- not always successful -- to remember this lesson: Even people I dislike have a piece of God. My task is to move the junk out of the way so that I can find it.
Robert P. O'Brien

55 Hate is not the opposite of love; apathy is.
Rollo May (American Psychologist)

56 He that will be angry for anything will be angry for nothing.
Sallust (86-34 BC, Roman Historian)

57 I have always hated that damn James Bond. I'd like to kill him.
Sean Connery (1930-, Scottish-born American Actor)

58 No one can be despised by another until he has learned to despise himself.
Seneca (4 BC-65 AD, Spanish-born Roman Statesman, philosopher)

59 Anger, if not restrained, is frequently more hurtful to us than the injury that provokes it.
Seneca (4 BC-65 AD, Spanish-born Roman Statesman, philosopher)

60 Although you may spend your life killing, You will not exhaust all your foes. But if you quell your own anger, your real enemy will be slain.
Siddha Nagarjuna (100-200 AD, Indian/Tibetan Father of Mahayan)

61 Forcible ways make not an end of evil, but leave hatred and malice behind them.
Sir Thomas Browne (1605-1682, British Author, Physician,, Philosopher)

62 Hatreds are the cinders of affection.
Sir Walter Raleigh (1552-1618, British Courtier, Navigator, Writer)

63 From the deepest desires often come the deadliest hate.
Socrates (469-399 BC, Greek Philosopher of Athens)

64 Do nothing hastily but catching of fleas.
Thomas Fuller (1608-1661, British Clergyman, Author)

65 Press no further with hate.
Virgil (70-19 BC, Roman Poet)

66 Hate can only flourish where love is absent.
William C. Menninger

67 We can scarcely hate anyone that we know.
William Hazlitt (1778-1830, British Essayist)

68 People hate as they love, unreasonably.
William M. Thackeray (1811-1863, Indian-born British Novelist)

69 Oppose not rage while rage is in its force, but give it way a while and let it waste.
William Shakespeare (1564-1616, British Poet, Playwright, Actor)

70 Wisely, and slow. They stumble that run fast.
William Shakespeare (1564-1616, British Poet, Playwright, Actor)

HEALTH

1 Health consists with temperance alone.
Alexander Pope (1688-1744, British Poet, Critic, Translator)

2 The quality of your life is dependent upon the quality of the life of your cells. If the bloodstream is filled with waste products, the resulting environment does not promote a strong, vibrant, healthy cell life-nor a biochemistry capable of creating a balanced emotional life for an individual.
Anthony Robbins (1960-, American Author, Speaker, Peak Performance Expert / Consultant)

3 The higher your energy level, the more efficient your body. The more efficient your body, the better you feel and the more you will use your talent to produce outstanding results.
Anthony Robbins (1960-, American Author, Speaker, Peak Performance Expert / Consultant)

4 Any idiot can face a crisis, it's the day to day living that wears you out.
Anton Chekhov (1860-1904, Russian Playwright, Short Story Writer)

5 I know a lot of athletes and models are written off as just bodies. I never felt used for my body.
Arnold Schwarzenegger (1947-, Austrian-born American Actor, Author, Director, Restaurateur)

6 Cheerfulness, sir, is the principle ingredient in the composition of health.
Arthur Murphy

7 I believe you can have whatever you really want in this life, in one form or another, sooner or later. All you have to do is take care of your health and be lucky enough to live for a while. But you can't have it all at once and you can't have it forever. No life has the room for everything in it, not on the same day.
Barbara Sher (American Author of "I Could Do Anything If I Only Knew What It Was")

8 The health of the people is really the foundation upon which all their happiness and all their powers as a state depend.
Benjamin Disraeli (1804-1881, British Statesman, Prime Minister)

9 To lengthen thy Life, lessen thy meals.
Benjamin Franklin (1706-1790, American Scientist, Publisher, Diplomat)

10 Nothing is more fatal to health than an over care of it.
Benjamin Franklin (1706-1790, American Scientist, Publisher, Diplomat)

11 One of the signs of an approaching nervous breakdown is the belief that one's work is terribly important.
Bertrand Russell (1872-1970, British Philosopher, Mathematician, Essayist)

12 Is not that a great principle for all of living? The people who will really accomplish great things in life are those who are willing to discipline their lives, who maintain their health, their vitality, their efficiency through this process of rigorous disciplining of what they take into their bodies and what they do in life. It's a very important thing in terms of championship living.
Bob Richards (American Olympic Pole Vaulting Champion)

13 Just as your car runs more smoothly and requires less energy to go faster and farther when the wheels are in perfect alignment, you perform better when your thoughts, feelings, emotions, goals, and values are in balance.
Brian Tracy (American Trainer, Speaker, Author, Businessman)

14 Health is the greatest gift, contentment the greatest wealth, faithfulness the best relationship.
Buddha (568-488 BC, Founder of Buddhism)

15 As a remedy against all ills; poverty, sickness, and melancholy only one thing is absolutely necessary; a liking for work.
Charles Baudelaire (1821-1867, French Poet)

16 Money is the most envied, but the least enjoyed. Health is the most enjoyed, but the least envied.
Charles Caleb Colton (1780-1832, British Sportsman Writer)

17 The winners in life treat their body as if it were a magnificent spacecraft that gives them the finest transportation and endurance for their lives.
Denis Waitley (1933-, American Author, Speaker, Trainer, Peak Performance Expert)

18 Time And health are two precious assets that we don't recognize and appreciate until they have been depleted.
Denis Waitley (1933-, American Author, Speaker, Trainer, Peak Performance Expert)

19 The building of a perfect body crowned by a perfect brain, is at once the greatest earthly problem and grandest hope of the race.
Dio Lewis

20 Some people think that doctors and nurses can put scrambled eggs back into the shell.
Dorothy Canfield Fisher (1879-1958, American Writer)

21 I've never felt better.
Douglas Fairbanks (1909-, American Film Actor, Writer, Producer)

22 Refuse to be ill. Never tell people you are ill; never own it to yourself. Illness is one of those things which a man should resist on principle at the onset.
Edward G. Bulwer-Lytton (1803-1873, British Novelist, Poet)

23 I am always busy, which is perhaps the chief reason why I am always well.
Elizabeth Cady Stanton (1815-1902, American Social Reformer and Women's Suffrage Leader)

24 You have to stay in shape. My grandmother, she started walking five miles a day when she was 60. She's 97 today and we don't know where the hell she is.
Ellen DeGeneres

25 We are usually the best men when in the worst health.
English Proverb

26 If I'd known I was gonna live this long. I'd have taken better care of myself. [Eubie Blake At Age 100]
Eubie Blake (1883-1983, American Song Writer, Composer)

27 The vitamin has been reified. A chemical intangible originally defined as a unit of nutritive value, it was long ago reified into a pill. Now it is a pill; no one except a few precise scientists define it as anything else. Once the vitamin became a pill, it became "real" according to the precepts of American Cartesianism: "I swallow it, therefore it is."
Florence King (1936-, American Author, Critic)

28 To become a thoroughly good man is the best prescription for keeping a sound mind and a sound body.
Francis Bowen (American Writer)

29 It is a wearisome disease to preserve health by too strict a regimen.
François de La Rochefoucauld (1613-1680, French classical writer)

30 Health is the thing that makes you feel that now is the best time of the year.
Franklin Pierce Adams (1881 - 1960, American Journalist, Humorist)

31 As we free our breath (through diaphragmatic breathing) we relax our emotions and let go our body tensions.
Gay Hendricks (American Psychologist, Lecturer, Author)

32 Of all the anti-social vested interests the worst is the vested interest in ill-health.
George Bernard Shaw (1856-1950, Irish-born British Dramatist)

33 The concept of total wellness recognizes that our every thought, word, and behavior affects our greater health and well-being. And we, in turn, are affected not only emotionally but also physically and spiritually.
Greg Anderson (American Author of "The 22 Non-Negotiable Laws of Wellness")

34 The human body has been designed to resist an infinite number of changes and attacks brought about by its environment. The secret of god health lies in successful adjustment to changing stresses on the body.
Harry J. Johnson (American Medical Doctor)

35 Health is a state of complete physical, mental and social well-being, and not merely the absence of disease or infirmity.
Heave

36 People who don't know how to keep themselves healthy ought to have the decency to get themselves buried, and not waste time about it.
Henrik Ibsen (1828-1906, Norwegian Dramatist)

37 Measure your health by your sympathy with morning and spring. If there is no response in you to the awakening of nature --if the prospect of an early morning walk does not banish sleep, if the warble of the first bluebird does not thrill you --know that the morning and spring of your life are past. Thus may you feel your pulse.
Henry David Thoreau (1817-1862, American Essayist, Poet, Naturalist)

38 Must be out-of-doors enough to get experience of wholesome reality, as a ballast to thought and sentiment. Health requires this relaxation, this aimless life.
Henry David Thoreau (1817-1862, American Essayist, Poet, Naturalist)

39 Joy, temperance, and repose, slam the door on the doctor's nose.
Henry Wadsworth Longfellow (1819-1892, American Poet)

40 It's not the work which kills people, it's the worry. It's not the revolution that destroys machinery it's the friction.
Henry Ward Beecher (1813-1887, American Preacher, Orator, Writer)

41 The preservation of health is a duty. Few seem conscious that there is such a thing as physical morality.
Herbert Spencer (1820-1903, British Philosopher)

42 It is the false shame of fools to try to conceal wounds that have not healed.
Horace (65-8 BC, Italian Poet)

43 The healthy die first.
Italian Proverb

44 He who enjoys good health is rich, though he knows it not.
Italian Proverb

45 Look to your health; and if you have it, praise God and value it next to a good conscience; for health is the second blessing that money cannot buy; therefore value it, and be thankful for it.
Izaak Walton (1593-1683, British Writer)

46 Never hurry. Take plenty of exercise. Always be cheerful. Take all the sleep you need. You may expect to be well.
James Freeman Clarke (1810-1888, American Minister, Theologian)

47 Drinking freshly made juices and eating enough whole foods to provide adequate fiber is a sensible approach to a healthful diet.
Jay Kordich (American Health Expert, Author, Lecturer)

48 A feeble body weakens the mind.
Jean Jacques Rousseau (1712-1778, Swiss Political Philosopher, Educationist, Essayist)

49 Take care of your body. It's the only place you have to live.
Jim Rohn (American Businessman, Author, Speaker, Philosopher)

50 A man's health can be judged by which he takes two at a time -- pills or stairs.
Joan Welsh

51 Take care of your body with steadfast fidelity. The soul must see through these eyes alone, and if they are dim, the whole world is clouded.
Johann Wolfgang Von Goethe (1749-1832, German Poet, Dramatist, Novelist)

52 I have never yet met a healthy person who worried very much about his health, or a really good person who worried much about his own soul.
John B. S. Haldane (1892-1964, British Scientist, Author)

53 Health is my expected heaven.
John Keats (1795-1821, British Poet)

54 There's lots of people who spend so much time watching their health, they haven't got time to enjoy it.
Josh Billings (1815-1885, American Humorist, Lecturer)

55 If you don't do what's best for your body, you're the one who comes up on the short end.
Julius Erving (1950-, American Basketball Player)

56 People who overly take care of their health are like misers. They hoard up a treasure which they never enjoy.
Laurence Sterne (1713-1768, British Author)

57 The groundwork of all happiness is health.
Leigh Hunt (1784-1859, British Poet, Essayist)

58 The human body is the best picture of the human soul.
Ludwig Wittgenstein (1889-1951, Austrian Philosopher)

59 By the time we've made it, we've had it.
Malcolm S. Forbes (1919-1990, American Publisher, Businessman)

60 Be careful about reading health books. You may die of a misprint.
Mark Twain (1835-1910, American Humorist, Writer)

61 The way to keep your health is to eat what you don't want, drink what you don't like, and do what you'd rather not.
Mark Twain (1835-1910, American Humorist, Writer)

62 From labor health, from health contentment springs.
Melody Beattie (American Author)

63 A bodily disease which we look upon as whole and entire within itself, may, after all, be but a symptom of some ailment in the spiritual part.
Nathaniel Hawthorne (1804-1864, American Novelist, Short Story Writer)

64 I don't eat junk foods and I don't think junk thoughts.
Peace Pilgrim (1908-1981, American Peace Activist)

65 Attention to health is life greatest hindrance.
Plato (427-347 BC, Greek Philosopher)

66 All bodies are slow in growth but rapid in decay.
Publius Cornelius Tacitus (55-117 AD, Roman Historian)

67 Health is the condition of wisdom, and the sign is cheerfulness -- an open and noble temper.
Ralph Waldo Emerson (1803-1882, American Poet, Essayist)

68 Give me health and a day, and I will make the pomp of emperors ridiculous.
Ralph Waldo Emerson (1803-1882, American Poet, Essayist)

69 To get rich never risk your health. For it is the truth that health is the wealth of wealth.
Richard Baker

70 Quit worrying about your health. It'll go away.
Robert Orben (1927-, American Editor, Writer, Humorist)

71 Older people shouldn't eat health food, they need all the preservatives they can get.
Robert Orben (1927-, American Editor, Writer, Humorist)

72 The healthy, the strong individual, is the one who asks for help when he needs it. Whether he has an abscess on his knee or in his soul.
Rona Barrett (American Actress)

73 If you need medical advice, let these three things be your physicians; a cheerful mind, relaxation from business, and a moderate diet.
Schola Salern

74 The ingredients of health and long life, are great temperance, open air, easy labor, and little care.
Sir Philip Sidney (1554-1586, British Author, Courtier)

75 A man too busy to take care of his health is like a mechanic too busy to take care of his tools.
Spanish Proverb

76 Ill-health, of body or of mind, is defeat. Health alone is victory. Let all men, if they can manage it, contrive to be healthy!
Thomas Carlyle (1795-1881, Scottish Philosopher, Author)

77 The sovereign invigorator of the body is exercise, and of all the exercises walking is the best.
Thomas Jefferson (1743-1826, Third President of the USA)

78 To be or not to be isn't the question. The question is how to prolong being.
Tom Robbins (American Author)

79 You can set yourself up to be sick, or you can choose to stay well.
Wayne Dyer (1940-, American Psychotherapist, Author, Lecturer)

80 Energy is eternal delight.
William Blake (1757-1827, British Poet, Painter)

81 To insure good health: Eat lightly, breathe deeply, live moderately, cultivate cheerfulness, and maintain an interest in life.
William Londen

82 All excess is ill, but drunkenness is of the worst sort. It spoils health, dismounts the mind, and unmans men. It reveals secrets, is quarrelsome, lascivious, impudent, dangerous and bad.
William Penn (1644-1718, British Religious Leader, Founder of Pennsylvania)

83 Doing good to others is not a duty, it is a joy, for it increases our own health and happiness.
Zoroaster (628-551 BC, Persian Religious Leader-Founder of Zoroastrianism)

HEART

1 Few are those who see with their own eyes and feel with their own hearts.
Albert Einstein (1879-1955, German-born American Physicist)

2 In a full heart there is room for everything, and in an empty heart there is room for nothing.
Antonio Porchia

3 The heart of a fool is in his mouth, but the mouth of a wise man is in his heart.
Benjamin Franklin (1706-1790, American Scientist, Publisher, Diplomat)

4 Two things are bad for the heart -- running up stairs and running down people.
Bernard M. Baruch (1870-1965, American Financier)

5 Seek not good from without: seek it within yourselves, or you will never find it.
Bertha Von Suttner

6 It's the heart afraid of breaking that never learns to dance.
Bette Midler (American Singer, Entertainer, Actress)

7 The heart is deceitful above all things, and desperately wicked; who can know it?
Bible (Sacred Scriptures of Christians and Judaism)

8 The heart of the wise is in the house of mourning, while the heart of the fool is in the house of entertainment.
Bible (Sacred Scriptures of Christians and Judaism)

9 The heart has its reasons of which reason knows nothing: we know this in countless ways.
Blaise Pascal (1623-1662, French Scientist, Religious Philosopher)

10 To live in hearts we leave behind is not to die.
Campbell

11 Look at every path closely and deliberately, then ask ourselves this crucial question: Does this path have a heart? If it does, then the path is good. If it doesn't, it is of no use.
Carlos Castaneda (American Anthropologist, Author)

12 All paths are the same, leading nowhere. Therefore, pick a path with heart!
Carlos Castaneda (American Anthropologist, Author)

13 I know the answer! The answer lies within the heart of all mankind! The answer is twelve? I think I'm in the wrong building.
Charles Shulz

14 If I keep a green bough in my heart, the singing bird will come.
Chinese Proverb

15 Faint hearts never win fair ladies.
Danish Proverb

16 Some people carry their heart in their head and some carry their head in their heart. The trick is to keep them apart yet working together.
David Hare (1947-, British Playwright, Director)

17 The less you open your heart to others, the more your heart suffers.
Deepak Chopra (East-Indian- American M.D., New Age Author, Lecturer)

18 The surest way to hit a woman's heart is to take aim kneeling.
Douglas William Jerrold (1803-1857, British Humorist, Playwright)

19　A good heart is better than all the heads in the world.
Edward G. Bulwer-Lytton (1803-1873, British Novelist, Poet)

20　If I can stop one heart from breaking, I shall not live in vain.
Emily Dickinson (1830-1886, American Poet)

21　It is not the size of a man but the size of his heart that matters.
Evander Holyfield (1962-, American World Boxing Champion)

22　Their is a road from the eye to heart that does not go through the intellect.
Gilbert K. Chesterton (1874-1936, British Author)

23　There must be hearts which know the depths of our being, and swear by us, even when the whole world forsakes us.
Gutzkow

24　As the arteries grow hard, the heart grows soft.
H. L. Mencken (1880-1956, American Editor, Author, Critic, Humorist)

25　The best and most beautiful things in the world cannot be seen or even touched. They must be felt with the heart.
Helen Keller (1880-1968, American Blind/Deaf Author, Lecturer, Amorist)

26　The head learns new things, but the heart forever practices old experiences.
Henry Ward Beecher (1813-1887, American Preacher, Orator, Writer)

27　In our own hearts, we mold the whole world's hereafters; and in our own hearts we fashion our own gods.
Herman Melville (1819-1891, American Author)

28　What ever purifies the heart also fortifies it.
Hugh Blair (British Poet)

29　I have joined my heart to thee: all that exists are thou. O Lord, beloved of my heart, thou art the home of all; where indeed is the heart in which thou dost not dwell?
Jafar

30　Everyone sees the unseen in proportion to the clarity of his heart, and that depends upon how much he has polished it. Whoever has polished it more sees more -- more unseen forms become manifest to him.
Jalal-Uddin Rumi (1207-1273, Persian Sufi Mystic Poet)

31　The brain can be easy to buy, but the heart never comes to market.
James Russell Lowell (1819-1891, American Poet, Critic, Editor)

32　In every veil you see, the Divine Beauty is concealed, making every heart a slave to him. In love to him the heart finds its life; in desire for him the soul finds its happiness. The heart which loves a fair one here, though it knows it not, is really his lover.
Jami

33　Nothing is less in our power than the heart, and far from commanding we are forced to obey it.
Jean Jacques Rousseau (1712-1778, Swiss Political Philosopher, Educationist, Essayist)

34　It is not flesh and blood, but heart which makes us fathers and sons.
Johann Friedrich Von Schiller (1759-1805, German Dramatist, Poet, Historian)

35　What of us lies in the hearts of others is our truest and deepest self.
Johann Gottfried Von Herder (1744-1803, German Critic and Poet)

36　I do not know what the heart of a rascal may be, but I know what is in the heart of an honest man; it is horrible.
Joseph De Maistre (1753-1821, French Diplomat, Philosopher)

37　There is nothing enduring in life for a women except what she builds in a man's heart.
Judith Anderson (1898-1992, Australian Actress)

38　Where are you searching for me, friend? Look! Here am I right within you. Not in temple, nor in mosque, not in Kaaba nor Kailas, but here right within you am I.
Kabir (1400-1499, Hindu Philosopher, Reformer)

39　The heart will break, but broken live on.
Lord Byron (1788-1824, British Poet)

40　Men, as well as women, are much oftener led by their hearts than by their understandings.
Lord Chesterfield (1694-1773, British Statesman, Author)

41　Within your heart, keep one still, secret spot where dreams may go.
Louise Driscoll

42　To wear your heart on your sleeve isn't a very good plan; you should wear it inside, where it functions best.
Margaret Thatcher (1925-, British Stateswoman, Prime Minister (1979-90))

43　I am more afraid of my own heart than the Pope and all his cardinals. I have within me the great Pope, Self.
Martin Luther (1483-1546, German Leader of the Protestant Reformation)

44　My heart, which is so full to overflowing, has often been solaced and refreshed by music when sick and weary.
Martin Luther (1483-1546, German Leader of the Protestant Reformation)

45　All God wants of man is a peaceful heart.
Meister Eckhart (1260-1326 AD, German Mystic)

46　A Great man is he who does not lose his childlike heart.
Mencius (Mengzi Meng-tse) (370-300 BC, Chinese Philosopher)

47　Charity is in the heart of man, and righteousness in the path of men. Pity the man who has lost his path and does not follow it and who has lost his heart and does not know how to recover it. When people's dogs and chicks are lost they go out and look for them and yet the people who have lost their hearts do not go out and look for them. The principle of self-cultivation consists in nothing but trying to look for the lost heart.
Mencius (Mengzi Meng-tse) (370-300 BC, Chinese Philosopher)

48 A good head and a good heart are always a formidable combination.
Nelson Mandela (1918-, South African President)

49 I will greet this day with love in my heart. For this is the greatest secret of success in all ventures. Muscles can split a shield and even destroy life itself but only the unseen power of love can open the hearts of man. And until I master this act I will remain no more than a peddler in the marketplace. I will make love my greatest weapon and none on who I call can defend upon its force... my love will melt all hearts liken to the sun whose rays soften the coldest day.
Og Mandino (1923-1996, American Motivational Author, Speaker)

50 Whether you call my heart affectionate, or you call it womanish: I confess, that to my misfortune, it is soft.
Ovid (43 BC-18 AD, Roman Poet)

51 Why should I go into details, we have nothing that is not perishable except what our hearts and our intellects endows us with.
Ovid (43 BC-18 AD, Roman Poet)

52 It is a weakness that I lead from my heart, and not my head?
Princess of Wales Diana (1961-1997, Wife of Charles, Prince of Wales)

53 I wear my heart on my sleeve.
Princess of Wales Diana (1961-1997, Wife of Charles, Prince of Wales)

54 The heart that truly loves never forgets.
Proverb

55 No sheath shall hold what finds its home in flesh.
Proverb

56 Not the glittering weapon fights the fight, but rather the hero's heart.
Proverb

57 Great hearts steadily send forth the secret forces that incessantly draw great events.
Ralph Waldo Emerson (1803-1882, American Poet, Essayist)

58 His heart was as great as the world, but there was no room in it to hold the memory of a wrong.
Ralph Waldo Emerson (1803-1882, American Poet, Essayist)

59 For the outer sense alone perceives visible things and the eye of the heart alone seeds the invisible.
Richard of Saint-Victor

60 There never was any heart truly great and generous, that was not also tender and compassionate.
Robert Frost (1875-1963, American Poet)

61 Whether joy or sorrowful, the heart needs a double, because a joy shared is doubled and a pain that is shared is divided.
Ruckett

62 There is in every human heart Some not completely barren part, Where seeds of truth and love might grow, And flowers of generous virtue flow; To plant, to watch, to water there, This be our duty, be our care.
Sir John Bowring (1792-1872, British Statesman, Linguist)

63 If the heart wanders or is distracted, bring it back to the point quite gently and replace it tenderly in its Master's presence. And even if you did nothing during the whole of your hour but bring your heart back and place it again in Our Lord's presence, though it went away every time you brought it back, your hour would be very well employed.
St. Francis De Sales (1567-1622, Roman Catholic Bishop, Writer)

64 Let your heart guide you. It whispers, so listen closely.
The Land Before Time

65 Wealth and want equally harden the human heart, like frost and fire both are alien to human flesh.
Theodore Parker (1810-1860, American Minister)

66 I think there is only one quality worse than hardness of heart and that is softness of head.
Theodore Roosevelt (1858-1919, Twenty-sixth President of the USA)

67 The heart always sees before than the head can see.
Thomas Carlyle (1795-1881, Scottish Philosopher, Author)

68 If your heart were sincere and upright, every creature would be unto you a looking-glass of life and a book of holy doctrine.
Thomas p Kempis (1379-1471, German Monk, Mystic, Religious Writer)

69 Thou art my glory and the exultation of y heart: thou art my hope and refuge in the day of my trouble.
Thomas p Kempis (1379-1471, German Monk, Mystic, Religious Writer)

70 Have thy heart in heaven and thy hands upon the earth. Ascend in piety and descend in charity. For this is the Nature of Light and the way of the children.
Thomas Vaughan

71 A heart in love with beauty never grows old.
Turkish Proverb

72 The eyes see what the heart loves. If the heart loves God and is single in this devotion, then the eyes will see God whether others see Him or not.
Warren Wiersbe

73 The heart is the best reflective thinker.
Wendell Phillips (1811-1884, American Reformer, Orator)

74 What stronger breastplate than a heart untainted. [Henry Iv]
William Shakespeare (1564-1616, British Poet, Playwright, Actor)

HEARTBREAK

1   It isn't enough for your heart to break because everybody's heart is broken now.
Allen Ginsberg (1926-, American Poet)

2   A broken heart is a very pleasant complaint for a man in London if he has a comfortable income.
George Bernard Shaw (1856-1950, Irish-born British Dramatist)

3   It is a curious sensation: the sort of pain that goes mercifully beyond our powers of feeling. When your heart is broken, your boats are burned: nothing matters any more. It is the end of happiness and the beginning of peace.
George Bernard Shaw (1856-1950, Irish-born British Dramatist)

4   Don't waste time trying to break a man's heart; be satisfied if you can just manage to chip it in a brand new place.
Helen Rowland (1875-1950, American Journalist)

5   How else but through a broken heart may Lord Christ enter in?
Oscar Wilde (1856-1900, British Author, Wit)

6   Had we never lov'd sae kindly, Had we never lov'd sae blindly, Never met -- or never parted -- we had never been broken-hearted.
Robert Burns (1759-1796, Scottish Poet)

HEAVEN

1   Christ's grave was the birthplace of an indestructible belief that death is vanquished and there is life eternal.
Adolph Harnack

2   In heaven after "ages of ages" of growing glory, we shall have to say, as each new wave of the shoreless, sunlit sea bears us onward, "It doth not yet appear what we shall be."
Alexander Maclaren (1826-1910, British Preacher)

3   Can you tell a plain man the road to heaven? Certainly, turn at once to the right, then go straight forward.
B. Wilberforce

4   The heavens declare the glory of God, and the earth is shows his handiwork.
Bible (Sacred Scriptures of Christians and Judaism)

5   Except ye be converted, and become as little children, ye shall not enter into the kingdom of heaven. [Mathew]
Bible (Sacred Scriptures of Christians and Judaism)

6   It is easier for a camel to pass through they eye of the needle than for a rich man to enter the Kingdom of God.
Bible (Sacred Scriptures of Christians and Judaism)

7   Seek ye first the kingdom of heaven, and all else shall be added unto you. [Mathew]
Bible (Sacred Scriptures of Christians and Judaism)

8   Well, I don't know, but I've been told the streets in heaven are lined with gold. I ask you how things could get much worse if the Russians happen to get up there first; Wowee! pretty scary!
Bob Dylan (1941-, American Musician, Singer, Songwriter)

9   Aim at heaven, and you will get earth thrown in; aim at earth, and you will get neither.
C. S. Lewis (1898-1963, British Academic, Writer, Christian Apologist)

10   If you read history you will find that the Christians who did most for the present world were precisely those who thought most of the next. It is since Christians have largely ceased to think of the other world that they have become so ineffective in this.
C. S. Lewis (1898-1963, British Academic, Writer, Christian Apologist)

11   Has this world been so kind to you that you should leave with regret? There are better things ahead than any we leave behind.
C. S. Lewis (1898-1963, British Academic, Writer, Christian Apologist)

12   I had a million questions to ask God: but when I met Him, they all fled my mind; and it didn't seem to matter.
Christopher Morley (1890-1957, American Novelist, Journalist, Poet)

13   To be with God.
Confucius (551-479 BC, Chinese Ethical Teacher, Philosopher)

14   Nothing is further than earth from heaven, and nothing is nearer than heaven to earth.
David Hare (1947-, British Playwright, Director)

15   As the fly bangs against the window attempting freedom while the door stands open, so we bang against death ignoring heaven.
Doug Horton

16   If the destination is heaven, why do we scramble to be first in line for hell?
Doug Horton

17   The key to heaven's gate cannot be duplicated.
Doug Horton

18   It is not the fact that a person has riches that keeps them from heaven, but the fact that riches have them.
Dr. Caird

19   We talk about heaven being so far away. It is within speaking distance to those who belong there. Heaven is a prepared place for a prepared people.
Dwight L. Moody (1837-1899, American Evangelist)

20   No man can resolve himself into Heaven.
Dwight L. Moody (1837-1899, American Evangelist)

21   Heaven is so far of the mind that were the mind dissolved -- the site of it by architect could not again be proved.
Emily Dickinson (1830-1886, American Poet)

22   Heaven must be an awfully dull place if the poor in spirit live there.
Emma Goldman (1869-1940, American Anarchist)

23 To me heaven would be a big bull ring with me holding two barrera seats and a trout stream outside that no one else was allowed to fish in and two lovely houses in the town; one where I would have my wife and children and be monogamous and love them truly and well and the other where I would have my nine beautiful mistresses on nine different floors.
Ernest Hemingway (1898-1961, American Writer)

24 The human mind is inspired enough when it comes to inventing horrors; it is when it tries to invent a Heaven that it shows itself cloddish.
Evelyn Waugh (1903-1966, British Novelist)

25 Heaven finds an ear when sinners find a tongue.
Francis Quarles (1592-1644, British Poet)

26 Look for me in the nurseries of Heaven.
Francis Thompson (1859-1907, British Poet)

27 The "kingdom of Heaven" is a condition of the heart --not something that comes "upon the earth" or "after death."
Friedrich Nietzsche (1844-1900, German Philosopher)

28 In Heaven all the interesting people are missing.
Friedrich Nietzsche (1844-1900, German Philosopher)

29 Of all the inventions of man I doubt whether any was more easily accomplished than that of a Heaven.
Georg C. Lichtenberg (1742-1799, German Physicist, Satirist)

30 The doctrine of the Kingdom of Heaven, which was the main teaching of Jesus, is certainly one of the most revolutionary doctrines that ever stirred and changed human thought.
H.G. Wells (1866-1946, British-born American Author)

31 Heaven will be inherited by every man who has heaven in his soul.
Henry Ward Beecher (1813-1887, American Preacher, Orator, Writer)

32 You forget that the kingdom of heaven suffers violence: and the kingdom of heaven is like a woman.
James Joyce (1882-1941, Irish Author)

33 I hope with all my heart there will be painting in heaven.
Jean-Baptiste Corot (1796-1875, French Landscape Painter)

34 Everybody wants to go heaven, but nobody wants to die.
Joe Louis (1914-1981, American Boxer)

35 Those are dead even for this life who hope for no other.
Johann Wolfgang Von Goethe (1749-1832, German Poet, Dramatist, Novelist)

36 What they do in heaven we are ignorant of; what they do not do we are told expressly.
Jonathan Swift (1667-1745, Anglo-Irish Satirist)

37 On earth there is no heaven, but there are pieces of it.
Jules Renard (1864-1910, French Author, Dramatist)

38 Celestial navigation is based on the premise that the Earth is the center of the universe. The premise is wrong, but the navigation works. An incorrect model can be a useful tool.
Kelvin Throop III

39 Men long for an afterlife in which there apparently is nothing to do but delight in heaven's wonders.
Louis D. Brandeis (1856-1941, American Judge)

40 The trouble with kingdoms of heaven on earth is that they're liable to come to pass, and then their fraudulence is apparent for all to see. We need a kingdom of heaven in Heaven, if only because it can't be realized.
Malcolm Muggeridge (1903-1990, British Broadcaster)

41 Heaven goes by favor; if it went by merit, you would stay out and your dog would go in.
Mark Twain (1835-1910, American Humorist, Writer)

42 All things come from above.
Motto

43 If people would forget about utopia! When rationalism destroyed heaven and decided to set it up here on earth, that most terrible of all goals entered human ambition. It was clear there'd be no end to what people would be made to suffer for it.
Nadine Gordimer (1923-, South African Author)

44 We send missionaries to China so the Chinese can get to heaven, but we won't let them into our country.
Pearl S. Buck (1892-1973, American Novelist)

45 We ought to fly away from earth to heaven as quickly as we can; and to fly away is to become like God, as far as this is possible; and to become like him is to become holy, just, and wise.
Plato (427-347 BC, Greek Philosopher)

46 As for evildoers, for them awaits a painful chastisement; but for those who believe, and do deeds of righteousness, they shall be admitted to gardens underneath which rivers flow, therein dwelling forever, by the leave of their Lord, their greeting therein: "Peace!"
Qur'an (Holy Book)

47 I would rather go to heaven alone than go to hell in company.
R. A. Torrey

48 Many might go to Heaven with half the labor they go to hell.
Ralph Waldo Emerson (1803-1882, American Poet, Essayist)

49 Heaven gives its glimpses only to those not in position to look too close.
Robert Frost (1875-1963, American Poet)

50 But somewhere, beyond Space and Time, is wetter water, slimier slime! And there (they trust) there swimmeth one who swam ere rivers were begun, immense of fishy form and mind, squamous omnipotent, and kind.
Rupert Brooke (1887-1915, British Poet)

51 Heaven for climate, Hell for company.
Sir James M. Barrie (1860-1937, British Playwright)

52 The heavens and the earth and all that is between them, do you think they were created in jest?
The Koran (500 AD, Islamic Religious Bible)

53 The ink of the scholar and the blood of a martyr are of equal value in heaven.
The Koran (500 AD, Islamic Religious Bible)

54 The main object of religion is not to get a man into heaven, but to get heaven into him.
Thomas Hardy (1840-1928, British Novelist, Poet)

55 Men are admitted into Heaven not because they have curbed and governed their passions or have no passions, but because they have cultivated their understandings. The treasures of Heaven are not negations of passion, but realities of intellect, from which all the passions emanate uncurbed in their eternal glory. The fool shall not enter into Heaven let him be ever so holy.
William Blake (1757-1827, British Poet, Painter)

56 If you have not chosen the Kingdom of God first, it will in the end make no difference what you have chosen instead.
William Law (American Merchant)

HELL

1 The vague and tenuous hope that God is too kind to punish the ungodly has become a deadly opiate for the consciences of millions.
A. W. Tozer (Deceased 1963, American Preacher)

2 Of all the inhabitants of the inferno, none but Lucifer knows that hell is hell, and the secret function of purgatory is to make of heaven an effective reality.
Arnold Bennett (1867-1931, British Novelist)

3 I believe that I am in hell, therefore I am there.
Arthur Rimbaud (1854-1891, French Poet)

4 There is no greater hell than to be a prisoner of fear.
Ben Johnson (1573-1637, British Dramatist, Poet)

5 Hell is the highest reward that the devil can offer you for being a servant of his.
Billy Sunday

6 The safest road to hell is the gradual one -- the gentle slope, soft underfoot, without sudden turnings, without milestones, without signposts.
C. S. Lewis (1898-1963, British Academic, Writer, Christian Apologist)

7 Hell hath no limits, nor is circumscrib'd one self place; for where we are is Hell, and where Hell is, there must we ever be.
Christopher Marlowe (1564-1593, British Dramatist, Poet)

8 There sighs, lamentations and loud wailings resounded through the starless air, so that at first it made me weep; strange tongues, horrible language, words of pain, tones of anger, voices loud and hoarse, and with these the sound of hands, made a tumult which is whirling through that air forever dark, and sand eddies in a whirlwind.
Dante (Alighieri) (1265-1321, Italian Philosopher, Poet)

9 Abandon all hope, you who enter here!
Dante (Alighieri) (1265-1321, Italian Philosopher, Poet)

10 Hell hath no fury like a liberal scorned.
Dick Gregory (American Comedian)

11 A perpetual holiday is a good working definition of hell.
George Bernard Shaw (1856-1950, Irish-born British Dramatist)

12 Here there is no hope, and consequently no duty, no work, nothing to be gained by praying, nothing to be lost by doing what you like. Hell, in short, is a place where you have nothing to do but amuse yourself.
George Bernard Shaw (1856-1950, Irish-born British Dramatist)

13 And what have you laymen made of hell? A kind of penal servitude for eternity, on the lines of your convict prisons on earth, to which you condemn in advance all the wretched felons your police have hunted from the beginning -- "enemies of society," as you call them. You're kind enough to include the blasphemers and the profane. What proud or reasonable man could stomach such a notion of God's justice? And when you find that notion inconvenient it's easy enough for you to put it on one side. Hell is not to love any more, Madame. Not to love any more!
Georges Bernanos (1888-1948, French Novelist, Political Writer)

14 Hell is paved with great granite blocks hewn from the hearts of those who said, "I can do no other."
Heywood Broun (1888-1939, American Journalist, Novelist)

15 Hell is out of fashion -- institutional hells at any rate. The populated infernos of the 20th century are more private affairs, the gaps between the bars are the sutures of one's own skull. A valid hell is one from which there is a possibility of redemption, even if this is never achieved, the dungeons of an architecture of grace whose spires point to some kind of heaven. The institutional hells of the present century are reached with one-way tickets, marked Nagasaki and Buchenwald, worlds of terminal horror even more final than the grave.
J. G. Ballard (1930-, British Author)

16 Hell is other people.
Jean-Paul Sartre (1905-1980, French Writer, Philosopher)

17 If I'm going to Hell, I'm going there playing the piano.
Jerry Lee Lewis (1935-, American Rock Singer, Country Singer, and Pianist)

18 When I go to hell, I mean to carry a bribe: for look you, good gifts evermore make way for the worst persons.
John Webster (1580-1625, British Dramatist)

19 Those who promise us paradise on earth never produced anything but a hell.
Karl Popper (1902-1994, Australian Philosopher)

20 I cannot help thinking that the menace of Hell makes as many devils as the severe penal codes of inhuman humanity make villains.
Lord Byron (1788-1824, British Poet)

21 It is an open question whether any behavior based on fear of eternal punishment can be regarded as ethical or should be regarded as merely cowardly.
Margaret Mead (1901-1978, American Anthropologist)

22 The trouble with you Chicago people is that you think you are the best people down here, whereas you are merely the most numerous.
Mark Twain (1835-1910, American Humorist, Writer)

23 For mortal men there is but one hell, and that is the folly and wickedness and spite of his fellows; but once his life is over, there's an end to it: his annihilation is final and entire, of him nothing survives.
Marquis De Sade (1740-1814, French Author)

24 The hottest place in Hell is reserved for those who remain neutral in times of great moral conflict.
Martin Luther King Jr. (1929-1968, American Black Leader, Nobel Prize Winner, 1964)

25 O Lord, wandering with thee, even hell itself would be to me a heaven of bliss.
Ramayana

26 I hold it to be the inalienable right of anybody to go to hell in his own way.
Robert Frost (1875-1963, American Poet)

27 Hell is a half-filled auditorium.
Robert Frost (1875-1963, American Poet)

28 Hell is oneself, hell is alone, the other figures in it merely projections. There is nothing to escape from and nothing to escape to. One is always alone.
T. S. Eliot (1888-1965, American-born British Poet, Critic)

29 The hell of these days is the fear of not getting along, especially of not making money.
Thomas Carlyle (1795-1881, Scottish Philosopher, Author)

30 Hell is where everyone is doing his own thing. Paradise is where everyone is doing God's thing.
Thomas Howard

31 When I pastored a country church, a farmer didn't like the sermons I preached on hell. He said, "Preach about the meek and lowly Jesus." I said, "That's where I got my information about hell."
Vance Havner

32 The gates of Hell are open night and day; smooth the descent, and easy is the way: but, to return, and view the cheerful skies; in this, the task and mighty labor lies.
Virgil (70-19 BC, Roman Poet)

33 One cannot walk through an assembly factory and not feel that one is in Hell.
W. H. Auden (1907-1973, Anglo-American Poet)

34 To appreciate heaven well, it's good for a person to have some fifteen minutes of hell.
Will Carleton

35 If there is no Hell a good many preachers are obtaining money under false pretenses.
William A. Sunday (1862-1935, American Evangelist)

36 To be in a world which is a hell, to be of that world and neither to believe in or guess at anything but that world is not merely hell but the only possible damnation: the act of a man damning himself. It may be -- I hope it is -- redemption to guess and perhaps perceive that the universe, the hell which we see for all its beauty, vastness, majesty, is only part of a whole which is quite unimaginable.
William Golding (1911-1993, British Author)

37 Hell is paved with good Samaritans.
William M. Holden

HERESY

1 The conscience of the world is so guilty that it always assumes that people who investigate heresies must be heretics; just as if a doctor who studies leprosy must be a leper. Indeed, it is only recently that science has been allowed to study anything without reproach.
Aleister Crowley (1875-1947, British Occultist)

2 A heresy can spring only from a system that is in full vigor.
Eric Hoffer (1902-1983, American Author, Philosopher)

3 If the individual, or heretic, gets hold of some essential truth, or sees some error in the system being practiced, he commits so many marginal errors himself that he is worn out before he can establish his point.
Ezra Pound (1885-1972, American Poet, Critic)

4 For my name and memory I leave to men's charitable speeches, and to foreign nations and the next ages.
Francis Bacon (1561-1626, British Philosopher, Essayist, Statesman)

5 It may be you fear more to deliver judgment upon me than I fear judgment.
Giordano Bruno (1548-1600, Italian Philosopher, Scientist)

6 The difference between heresy and prophecy is often one of sequence. Heresy often turns out to have been prophecy -- when properly aged.
Hubert H. Humphrey (1911-1978, American Democratic Politician, Vice President)

7 A man may be a heretic in the truth; and if he believe things only because his pastor says so, or the assembly so determines, without knowing other reason, though his belief be true, yet the very truth he holds becomes his heresy.
John Milton (1608-1674, British Poet)

8 I shall never be a heretic; I may err in dispute, but I do not wish to decide anything finally; on the other hand, I am not bound by the opinions of men.
Martin Luther (1483-1546, German Leader of the Protestant Reformation)

HERITAGE

1 It is impossible, as impossible as to raise the dead, to restore anything that has ever been great or beautiful in architecture. That which I have... insisted upon as the life of the whole, that spirit which is given only by the hand and eye of the workman, can never be recalled.
John Ruskin (1819-1900, British Critic, Social Theorist)

2 Stands the Church clock at ten to three? And is there honey still for tea?
Rupert Brooke (1887-1915, British Poet)

3 I love art, and I love history, but it is living art and living history that I love. It is in the interest of living art and living history that I oppose so-called restoration. What history can there be in a building bedaubed with ornament, which cannot at the best be anything but a hopeless and lifeless imitation of the hope and vigor of the earlier world?
William Morris (1834-1896, British Artist, Writer, Printer)

HEROES AND HEROISM

1 What with making their way and enjoying what they have won, heroes have no time to think. But the sons of heroes --ah, they have all the necessary leisure.
Aldous Huxley (1894-1963, British Author)

2 Sometimes, when one person is missing, the whole world seems depopulated.
Alphonse De Lamartine (1790-1869, French Poet, Statesman, Historian)

3 A man can be a hero if he is a scientist, or a soldier, or a drug addict, or a disc jockey, or a crummy mediocre politician. A man can be a hero because he suffers and despairs; or because he thinks logically and analytically; or because he is "sensitive;" or because he is cruel. Wealth establishes a man as a hero, and so does poverty. Virtually any circumstance in a man's life will make him a hero to some group of people and has a mythic rendering in the culture -- in literature, art, theater, or the daily newspapers.
Andrea Dworkin (1946-, American Feminist Critic)

4 The opportunities for heroism are limited in this kind of world: the most people can do is sometimes not to be as weak as they've been at other times.
Angus Wilson (1913-1991, British Author)

5 Aspire rather to be a hero than merely appear one.
Baltasar Gracian (1601-1658, Spanish Philosopher, Writer)

6 The legacy of heroes is the memory of a great name and the inheritance of a great example.
Benjamin Disraeli (1804-1881, British Statesman, Prime Minister)

7 Unhappy the land that is in need of heroes.
Bertolt Brecht (1898-1956, German Dramatist, Poet)

8 One murder makes a villain, millions often a hero.
Bishop Porteous

9 I think of a hero as someone who understands the degree of responsibility that comes with his freedom.
Bob Dylan (1941-, American Musician, Singer, Songwriter)

10 You lived too long, we have supped full with heroes, they waste their deaths on us.
C. D. Andrews (1913-1992, British Poet, Scholar)

11 Heroism is not only in the man, but in the occasion.
Calvin Coolidge (1872-1933, Thirtieth President of the USA)

12 To have no heroes is to have no aspiration, to live on the momentum of the past, to be thrown back upon routine, sensuality, and the narrow self.
Charles Horton Cooley (1864-1929, American Sociologist)

13 Bardot, Byron, Hitler, Hemingway, Monroe, Sade: we do not require our heroes to be subtle, just to be big. Then we can depend on someone to make them subtle.
D. J. Enright (1920-, British Poet, Critic)

14 In our world of big names, curiously, our true heroes tend to be anonymous. In this life of illusion and quasi-illusion, the person of solid virtues who can be admired for something more substantial than his well-knownness often proves to be the unsung hero: the teacher, the nurse, the mother, the honest cop, the hard worker at lonely, underpaid, unglamorous, unpublicized jobs.
Daniel J. Boorstin (1914-, American Historian)

15 What is our task? To make Britain a fit country for heroes to live in.
David Lloyd George (1863-1945, British Statesman, Prime Minister)

16 What is a hero without love for mankind.
Doris Lessing (1919-, British Novelist)

17 Be your own hero, it's cheaper than a movie ticket.
Doug Horton

18 A boy doesn't have to go to war to be a hero; he can say he doesn't like pie when he sees there isn't enough to go around.
Edgar Watson Howe (1853-1937, American Journalist, Author)

19 The "paper tiger" hero, James Bond, offering the whites a triumphant image of themselves, is saying what many whites want desperately to hear reaffirmed: I am still the White Man, lord of the land, licensed to kill, and the world is still an empire at my feet.
Eldridge Cleaver (1935-, American Black Leader, Writer)

20 A hero is a man who is afraid to run away.
English Proverb

21 As a rule, all heroism is due to a lack of reflection, and thus it is necessary to maintain a mass of imbeciles. If they once understand themselves the ruling men will be lost.
Ernest Renan (1823-1892, French Writer, Critic, Scholar)

22 The hero is one who kindles a great light in the world, who sets up blazing torches in the dark streets of life for men to see by.
Felix Adler (1851-1933, American Educator, Social Critic)

23 There are heroes in evil as well as in good.
François de La Rochefoucauld (1613-1680, French classical writer)

24 Once the state has been founded, there can no longer be any heroes. They come on the scene only in uncivilized conditions.
Georg Hegel (1770-1831, German Philosopher)

25 No man is a hero to his valet. This is not because the hero is no hero, but because the valet is a valet.
Georg Hegel (1770-1831, German Philosopher)

26 You cannot be a hero without being a coward.
George Bernard Shaw (1856-1950, Irish-born British Dramatist)

27 Children demand that their heroes should be freckleless, and easily believe them so: perhaps a first discovery to the contrary is less revolutionary shock to a passionate child than the threatened downfall of habitual beliefs which makes the world seem to totter for us in maturer life.
George Eliot (1819-1880, British Novelist)

28 A hero is someone right who doesn't change.
George Foreman (1949-, American Boxer)

29 Heroes are created by popular demand, sometimes out of the scantiest materials.
Gerald W. Johnson (1890-1980, American Author)

30 I offer neither pay, nor quarters, nor food; I offer only hunger, thirst, forced marches, battles and death. Let him who loves his country with his heart, and not merely with his lips, follow me.
Giuseppe Garibaldi (1807-1882, Italian Patriot, Soldier)

31 In war the heroes always outnumber the soldiers ten to one.
H. L. Mencken (1880-1956, American Editor, Author, Critic, Humorist)

32 We relish news of our heroes, forgetting that we are extraordinary to somebody too.
Helen Hayes (1900-1993, American Actress)

33 The ordinary man is involved in action, the hero acts. An immense difference.
Henry Miller (1891-1980, American Author)

34 The world's battlefields have been in the heart chiefly; more heroism has been displayed in the household and the closet, than on the most memorable battlefields in history.
Henry Ward Beecher (1813-1887, American Preacher, Orator, Writer)

35 Listen, my friend, there are two races of beings. The masses teeming and happy --common clay, if you like --eating, breeding, working, counting their pennies; people who just live; ordinary people; people you can't imagine dead. And then there are the others --the noble ones, the heroes. The ones you can quite well imagine lying shot, pale and tragic; one minute triumphant with a guard of honor, and the next being marched away between two gendarmes.
Jean Anouilh (1910-1987, French Playwright)

36 What is a society without a heroic dimension?
Jean Baudrillard (French Postmodern Philosopher, Writer)

37 The fame of heroes owes little to the extent of their conquests and all to the success of the tributes paid to them.
Jean Genet (1910-1986, French Playwright, Novelist)

38 Heroes are not known by the loftiness of their carriage; the greatest braggarts are generally the merest cowards.
Jean Jacques Rousseau (1712-1778, Swiss Political Philosopher, Educationist, Essayist)

39 How many famous and high-spirited heroes have lived a day too long?
Jean Jacques Rousseau (1712-1778, Swiss Political Philosopher, Educationist, Essayist)

40 No heroine can create a hero through love of one, but she can give birth to one.
Jean Paul

41 It's true that heroes are inspiring, but mustn't they also do some rescuing if they are to be worthy of their name? Would Wonder Woman matter if she only sent commiserating telegrams to the distressed?
Jeanette Winterson (1959-, British Author)

42 The prudent see only the difficulties, the bold only the advantages, of a great enterprise; the hero sees both; diminishes the former and makes the latter preponderate, and so conquers.
Johann Kaspar Lavater (1741-1801, Swiss Theologian, Mystic)

43 The hero draws inspiration from the virtue of his ancestors.
Johann Wolfgang Von Goethe (1749-1832, German Poet, Dramatist, Novelist)

44 It is said, that no one is a hero to their butler. The reason is, that it requires a hero to recognize a hero. The butler, however, will probably know well how to estimate his equals.
Johann Wolfgang Von Goethe (1749-1832, German Poet, Dramatist, Novelist)

45 Everyone is necessarily the hero of his own life story.
John Barth (1930-, American Novelist, Short Story Writer)

46 One brave deed makes no hero.
John Greenleaf Whittier (1807-1892, American Poet, Reformer, Author)

47 Calculation never made a hero.
John Henry Newman (1801-1890, British Religious Leader, Prelate, Writer)

48 A hero is someone we can admire without apology.
Kitty Kelley

49 Now stiff on a pillar with a phallic air nelson stylites in Trafalgar square reminds the British what once they were.
Lawrence Durrell (1912-1990, British Author)

50 They wouldn't be heroes if they were infallible, in fact they wouldn't be heroes if they weren't miserable wretched dogs, the pariahs of the earth, besides which the only reason to build up an idol is to tear it down again.
Lester Bangs (1948-1982, American Rock Journalist)

51 I am convinced that a light supper, a good night's sleep, and a fine morning, have sometimes made a hero of the same man, who, by an indigestion, a restless night, and rainy morning, would have proved a coward.
Lord Chesterfield (1694-1773, British Statesman, Author)

52 The poetry of heroism appeals irresistibly to those who don't go to a war, and even more to those whom the war is making enormously wealthy. It's always so.
Louis-Ferdinand Celine (1894-1961, French Author)

53 The more characteristic American hero in the earlier day, and the more beloved type at all times, was not the hustler but the whittler.
Mark Sullivan (1874-1952, American Journalist, Historian)

54 One must think like a hero to behave like a merely decent human being.
May Sarton (1912-, American Poet, Novelist)

55 My heroes are and were my parents. I can't see having anyone else as my heroes.
Michael Jordan (1963-, American Basketball Player, Actor)

56 True heroism consists in being superior to the ills of life, in whatever shape they may challenge us to combat.
Napoleon Bonaparte (1769-1821, French General, Emperor)

57 The greatest obstacle to being heroic is the doubt whether one may not be going to prove one's self a fool; the truest heroism is to resist the doubt; and the profoundest wisdom, to know when it ought to be resisted, and when it be obeyed.
Nathaniel Hawthorne (1804-1864, American Novelist, Short Story Writer)

58 Ultimately a hero is a man who would argue with the gods, and so awakens devils to contest his vision. The more a man can achieve, the more he may be certain that the devil will inhabit a part of his creation.
Norman Mailer (1923-, American Author)

59 It doesn't take a hero to order men into battle. It takes a hero to be one of those men who goes into battle.
Norman Schwarzkopf (1934-, American General of the Gulf War)

60 Most people aren't appreciated enough, and the bravest things we do in our lives are usually known only to ourselves. No one throws ticker tape on the man who chose to be faithful to his wife, on the lawyer who didn't take the drug money, or the daughter who held her tongue again and again. All this anonymous heroism.
Peggy Noonan (1950-, American Author, Presidential Speechwriter)

61 Every hero becomes a bore at last.
Ralph Waldo Emerson (1803-1882, American Poet, Essayist)

62 A hero is no braver than an ordinary man, but he is braver five minutes longer.
Ralph Waldo Emerson (1803-1882, American Poet, Essayist)

63 The characteristic of genuine heroism is its persistency. All men have wandering impulses, fits and starts of generosity. But when you have resolved to be great, abide by yourself, and do not weakly try to reconcile yourself with the world. The heroic cannot be the common, nor the common the heroic.
Ralph Waldo Emerson (1803-1882, American Poet, Essayist)

64 Heroism feels and never reasons, and therefore is always right.
Ralph Waldo Emerson (1803-1882, American Poet, Essayist)

65 Down these mean streets a man must go who is not himself mean, who is neither tarnished nor afraid... He is the hero, he is everything. He must be a complete man and a common man and yet an unusual man. He must be, to use a rather weathered phrase, a man of honor, by instinct, by inevitability, without thought of it, and certainly without saying it. He must be the best man in his world and a good enough man for any world.
Raymond Chandler (1888-1959, American Author)

66 Had we lived I should have had a tale to tell of the hardihood, endurance and courage of my companions which would have stirred the heart of every Englishman. These rough notes and our dead bodies must tell the tale.
Robert Falcon Scott (1863-1912, British Antarctic Explorer)

67 What makes a hero truly great is that they never despair.
Roy Thompson (1894-1977, British Press Lord)

68 Claret is the liquor for boys; port for men; but he who aspires to be a hero must drink brandy.
Samuel Johnson (1709-1784, British Author)

69 And how can man die better than facing fearful odds, for the ashes of his fathers, and the temples of his Gods?
Thomas B. Macaulay (1800-1859, American Essayist and Historian)

70 Heroism is the divine relation which, in all times, unites a great man to other men.
Thomas Carlyle (1795-1881, Scottish Philosopher, Author)

71 All our lives we fought against exalting the individual, against the elevation of the single person, and long ago we were over and done with the business of a hero, and here it comes up again: the glorification of one personality. This is not good at all. I am just like everybody else.
Vladimir Ilyich Lenin (1870-1924, Russian Revolutionary Leader)

72 The idol of today pushes the hero of yesterday out of our recollection; and will, in turn, be supplanted by his successor of tomorrow.
Washington Irving (1783-1859, American Author)

73 Being a hero is about the shortest lived profession on earth.
Will Rogers (1879-1935, American Humorist, Actor)

74 The main thing about being a hero is to know when to die.
Will Rogers (1879-1935, American Humorist, Actor)

75 We can't all be heroes, because somebody has to sit on the curb and clap as they go by.
Will Rogers (1879-1935, American Humorist, Actor)

76 Mankind's common instinct for reality has always held the world to be essentially a theatre for heroism. In heroism, we feel, life's supreme mystery is hidden. We tolerate no one who has no capacity whatever for it in any direction. On the other hand, no matter what a man's frailties otherwise may be, if he be willing to risk death, and still more if he suffer it heroically, in the service he has chosen, the fact consecrates him forever. .
William James (1842-1910, American Psychologist, Professor, Author)

77 If we are marked to die, we are enough to do our country loss; and if to live, the fewer men, the greater share of honor.
William Shakespeare (1564-1616, British Poet, Playwright, Actor)

78 Never in the field of human conflict was so much owed by so many to so few.
Winston Churchill (1874-1965, British Statesman, Prime Minister)

79 Let us therefore brace ourselves to our duty, and so bear ourselves that if the British Empire and its Commonwealth last for a thousand years, men will still say, "This was their finest hour."
Winston Churchill (1874-1965, British Statesman, Prime Minister)

HIRING

1 If you suspect a man, don't employ him, and if you employ him, don't suspect him.
Chinese Proverb

2 Do not employ handsome servants.
Chinese Proverb

3 If he's got golf clubs in his truck or a camper in his driveway, I don't hire him.
Lou Holtz (1937-, American Football Coach)

4 After finding no qualified candidates for the position of principal, the school board is extremely pleased to announce the appointment of David Steele to the post.
Philip Streifer

5 When you hire people that are smarter than you are, you prove you are smarter than they are.
R. H. Grant

HISTORY AND HISTORIANS

1 Fellow citizens, we cannot escape history.
Abraham Lincoln (1809-1865, Sixteenth President of the USA)

2 A land without ruins is a land without memories -- a land without memories is a land without history.
Abram Joseph Ryan

3 Until the lions have their historians, tales of the hunt shall always glorify the hunter.
African Proverb

4 In our wildest aberrations we dream of an equilibrium we have left behind and which we naively expect to find at the end of our errors. Childish presumption which justifies the fact that child-nations, inheriting our follies, are now directing our history.
Albert Camus (1913-1960, French Existential Writer)

5 Providence conceals itself in the details of human affairs, but becomes unveiled in the generalities of history.
Alphonse De Lamartine (1790-1869, French Poet, Statesman, Historian)

6 Historian. A broad -- gauge gossip.
Ambrose Bierce (1842-1914, American Author, Editor, Journalist, "The Devil's Dictionary")

7 An account, mostly false, of events, mostly unimportant, which are brought about by rulers, mostly knaves, and soldiers, mostly fools.
Ambrose Bierce (1842-1914, American Author, Editor, Journalist, "The Devil's Dictionary")

8 History books that contain no lies are extremely dull.
Anatole France (1844-1924, French Writer)

9 It is humiliating to remain with our hands folded while others write history. It matters little who wins. To make a people great it is necessary to send them to battle even if you have to kick them in the pants. That is what I shall do.
Benito Mussolini (1883-1945, Italian Prime Minister (1922--43) and Dictator)

10 History repeats itself. That's one of the things wrong with history.
Clarence Darrow (1857-1938, American Lawyer)

11 People will not look forward to posterity who will not look backward to their ancestors.
Edmund Burke (1729-1797, British Political Writer, Statesman)

12 History is little more than the register of the crimes, follies and misfortunes of mankind.
Edward Gibbon (1737-1794, British Historian)

13 The historian must have some conception of how men who are not historians behave. Otherwise he will move in a world of the dead. He can only gain that conception through personal experience, and he can only use his personal experiences when he is a genius.
Edward M. Forster (1879-1970, British Novelist, Essayist)

14 The game of history is usually played by the best and the worst over the heads of the majority in the middle.
Eric Hoffer (1902-1983, American Author, Philosopher)

15 The history of the past interests us only in so far as it illuminates the history of the present.
Ernest Dimnet (1866-1954, French Clergyman)

16 Histories make men wise; poets, witty; the mathematics, subtle; natural philosophy, deep; moral, grave; logic and rhetoric, able to contend.
Francis Bacon (1561-1626, British Philosopher, Essayist, Statesman)

17 It is the true office of history to represent the events themselves, together with the counsels, and to leave the observations and conclusions thereupon to the liberty and faculty of every man's judgment.
Francis Bacon (1561-1626, British Philosopher, Essayist, Statesman)

18 The only thing we learn from history is that we learn nothing from history.
Friedrich Hegel

19 History tells us more than we want to know about what is wrong with man, and we can hardly turn a page in the daily press without learning the specific time, place, and name of evil. But perhaps the most pervasive evil of all rarely appears in the news. This evil, the waste of human potential, is particularly painful to recognize for it strikes our parents and children, our friends and brothers, ourselves.
George Leonard

20 History is always written wrong, and so always needs to be rewritten.
George Santayana (1863-1952, American Philosopher, Poet)

21 We should not look back unless it is to derive useful lessons from past errors, and for the purpose of profiting by dearly bought experience.
George Washington (1732-1799, First President of the USA)

22 While we read history we make history.
George William Curtis (1824-1892, American Journalist)

23 Fable is more historical than fact, because fact tells us about one man and fable tells us about a million men.
Gilbert K. Chesterton (1874-1936, British Author)

24 Our ignorance of history causes us to slander our own times.
Gustave Flaubert (1821-1880, French Novelist)

25 I can see only one safe rule for the historian: that he should recognize in the development of human destinies the play of the contingent and the unforeseen.
H(erbert) A(lbert) L(aurens) Fisher (1865-1940, British Writer)

26 Historian -- an unsuccessful novelist.
H. L. Mencken (1880-1956, American Editor, Author, Critic, Humorist)

27 Human history in essence is the history of ideas.
H.G. Wells (1866-1946, British-born American Author)

28 History is a race between education and catastrophe.
H.G. Wells (1866-1946, British-born American Author)

29 Human history becomes more and more a race between education and catastrophe.
H.G. Wells (1866-1946, British-born American Author)

30 Study men, not historians.
Harry S. Truman (1884-1972, Thirty-third President of the USA)

31 History is more or less bunk.
Henry Ford (1863-1947, American Industrialist, Founder of Ford Motor Company)

32 Caesar had perished from the world of men, had not his sword been rescued by his pen.
Henry Vaughan (1622-1695, Welsh Poet)

33 You treat world history as a mathematician does mathematics, in which nothing but laws and formulas exist, no reality, no good and evil, no time, no yesterday, no tomorrow, nothing but an eternal, shallow, mathematical present.
Hermann Hesse (1877-1962, German-born Swiss Novelist, Poet)

34 The first duty of an historian is to be on guard against his own sympathies.
James A. Froude (1818-1894, British Historian)

35 History is a better guide than good intentions.
Jeane Kirkpatrick (1926-, American Stateswoman, Academic)

36 Might does not make right, it only makes history.
Jim Fiebig

37 Historians are prophets with their face turned backward.
Johann Friedrich Von Schiller (1759-1805, German Dramatist, Poet, Historian)

38 The history of mankind is his character.
Johann Wolfgang Von Goethe (1749-1832, German Poet, Dramatist, Novelist)

39 The Thames is liquid history.
John Burns

40 The history of all hitherto existing society is the history of class struggles.
Karl Marx (1818-1883, German Political Theorist, Social Philosopher)

41 The men who make history have not time to write it.
Klemens Von Metternich (1773-1859, Austrian Statesman)

42 History is the devil's scripture.
Lord Byron (1788-1824, British Poet)

43 And having wisdom with each studious year, in meditation dwelt, with learning wrought, and shaped his weapon with an edge severe, sapping a solemn creed with solemn sneer.
Lord Byron (1788-1824, British Poet)

44 History is but a confused heap of facts.
Lord Chesterfield (1694-1773, British Statesman, Author)

45 Ignorance is the first requisite of the historian -- ignorance, which simplifies and clarifies, which selects and omits, with a placid perfection unattainable by the highest art.
Lytton Strachey

46 To believe what has not occurred in history will not occur at all, is to argue disbelief in the dignity of man.
Mahatma Gandhi (1869-1948, Indian Political, Spiritual Leader)

47 Not to know what has been transacted in former times is to be always a child. If no use is made of the labors of past ages, the world must remain always in the infancy of knowledge.
Marcus T. Cicero (106-43 BC, Great Roman Orator, Politician)

48 The causes of events are ever more interesting than the events themselves.
Marcus T. Cicero (106-43 BC, Great Roman Orator, Politician)

49 History is strewn thick with evidence that a truth is not hard to kill, but a lie, well told, is immortal.
Mark Twain (1835-1910, American Humorist, Writer)

50 I love those historians that are either very simple or most excellent. Such as are between both (which is the most common fashion), it is they that spoil all; they will needs chew our meat for us and take upon them a law to judge, and by consequence to square and incline the story according to their fantasy.
Michel Eyquem De Montaigne (1533-1592, French Philosopher, Essayist)

51 For historians ought to be precise, truthful, and quite unprejudiced, and neither interest nor fear, hatred nor affection, should cause them to swerve from the path of truth, whose mother is history, the rival of time, the depository of great actions, the witness of what is past, the example and instruction of the present, the monitor of the future.
Miguel De Cervantes (1547-1616, Spanish Novelist, Dramatist, Poet)

52 From the heights of these pyramids, forty centuries look down on us.
Napoleon Bonaparte (1769-1821, French General, Emperor)

53 What is all our histories, but God showing himself, shaking and trampling on everything that he has not planted.
Oliver Cromwell (1599-1658, Parliamentarian General, Lord Protector of England)

54 A page of history is worth a pound of logic.
Oliver Wendell Holmes (1809-1894, American Author, Wit, Poet)

55 Every library should try to be complete on something, if it were only the history of pinheads.
Oliver Wendell Holmes (1809-1894, American Author, Wit, Poet)

56 Anybody can make history. Only a great man can write it.
Oscar Wilde (1856-1900, British Author, Wit)

57 To give an accurate description of what has never occurred is not merely the proper occupation of the historian, but the inalienable privilege of any man of parts and culture.
Oscar Wilde (1856-1900, British Author, Wit)

58 The main thing is to make history, not to write it.
Otto Von Bismarck (1815-1898, Prussian Statesman, Prime Minister)

59 The historian's job is to aggrandize, promoting accident to inevitability and innocuous circumstance to portent.
Peter Conrad (1948-, Australian Critic, Author)

60 However gradual the course of history, there must always be the day, even an hour and minute, when some significant action is performed for the first or last time.
Peter Quennell

61 History repeats itself. Historians repeat each other.
Philip Guedalla (1889-1944, British Writer)

62 To be ignorant of the lives of the most celebrated men of antiquity is to continue in a state of childhood all our days.
Plutarch (46-120 AD, Greek Essayist, Biographer)

63 The pyramids, attached with age, have forgotten the names of their founders.
R. Buckminster Fuller (1895-1983, American Inventor, Designer, Poet, Philosopher)

64 Our best history is still poetry.
Ralph Waldo Emerson (1803-1882, American Poet, Essayist)

65 Few will have the greatness to bend history itself; but each of us can work to change a small portion of events, and in the total; of all those acts will be written the history of this generation.
Robert F. Kennedy (1925-1968, American Attorney General, Senator)

66 A generation which ignores history has no past and no future.
Robert Heinlein (1907-1988, American Science Fiction Writer)

67 God cannot alter the past, but historians can.
Samuel Butler (1612-1680, British Poet, Satirist)

68 Great abilities are not requisite for an Historian; for in historical composition, all the greatest powers of the human mind are quiescent. He has facts ready to his hand; so there is no exercise of invention. Imagination is not required in any degree; only about as much as is used in the lowest kinds of poetry. Some penetration, accuracy, and coloring, will fit a man for the task, if he can give the application which is necessary.
Samuel Johnson (1709-1784, British Author)

69 It does seem so pleasant to talk with an old acquaintance who knows what you know. I see so many new folks nowadays who seem to have neither past nor future. Conversation has got to have some root in the past, or else you have got to explain every remark you make, and it wears a person out.
Sarah Orne Jewett (1849-1909, American Author)

70 Historians are left forever chasing shadows, painfully aware of their inability ever to reconstruct a dead world in its completeness however thorough or revealing their documentation. We are doomed to be forever hailing someone who has just gone around the corner and out of earshot.
Simon Schama

71 To give an accurate and exhaustive account of that period would need a far less brilliant pen than mine.
Sir Max Beerbohm (1872-1956, British Actor)

72 Historians desiring to write the actions of men, ought to set down the simple truth, and not say anything for love or hatred; also to choose such an opportunity for writing as it may be lawful to think what they will, and write what they think, which is a rare happiness of the time.
Sir Walter Raleigh (1552-1618, British Courtier, Navigator, Writer)

73 History, is made up of the bad actions of extraordinary men and woman. All the most noted destroyers and deceivers of our species, all the founders of arbitrary governments and false religions have been extraordinary people; and nine tenths of the calamities that have befallen the human race had no other origin than the union of high intelligence with low desires.
Thomas B. Macaulay (1800-1859, American Essayist and Historian)

74 History is the distillation of rumor.
Thomas Carlyle (1795-1881, Scottish Philosopher, Author)

75 Stern accuracy in inquiring, bold imagination in describing, these are the cogs on which history soars or flutters and wobbles.
Thomas Carlyle (1795-1881, Scottish Philosopher, Author)

76 The whole past is the procession of the present.
Thomas Carlyle (1795-1881, Scottish Philosopher, Author)

77 The history of the world is but the biography of great men.
Thomas Carlyle (1795-1881, Scottish Philosopher, Author)

78 One cannot be a good historian of the outward, visible world without giving some thought to the hidden, private life of ordinary people; and on the other hand one cannot be a good historian of this inner life without taking into account outward events where these are relevant. They are two orders of fact which reflect each other, which are always linked and which sometimes provoke each other.
Victor Hugo (1802-1885, French Poet, Dramatist, Novelist)

79 History is nothing but a pack of tricks that we play upon the dead.
Voltaire (1694-1778, French Historian, Writer)

80 History is just the portrayal of crimes and misfortunes.
Voltaire (1694-1778, French Historian, Writer)

81 He is the purest figure in history. [About George Washington]
William E. Gladstone (1809-1888, British Liberal Prime Minister, Statesman)

82 One of the lessons of history is that nothing is often a good thing to do and always a clever thing to say.
William J. Durant (1885-1981, American Historian, Essayist)

83 There is a history in all men's lives.
William Shakespeare (1564-1616, British Poet, Playwright, Actor)

84 For my part, I consider that it will be found much better by all parties to leave the past to history, especially as I propose to write that history myself.
Winston Churchill (1874-1965, British Statesman, Prime Minister)

85 More than any time in history mankind faces a crossroads. One path leads to despair and utter hopelessness, the other to total extinction. Let us pray that we have the wisdom to choose correctly.
Woody Allen (1935-, American Director, Screenwriter, Actor, Comedian)

HOBOS

1 Those colorful denizens of male despair, the Bowery bum and the rail-riding hobo, have been replaced by the bag lady and the welfare mother. Women have even taken over Skid Row.
Florence King (1936-, American Author, Critic)

2 Bums are the well-to-do of this day. They didn't have as far to fall.
Jackson Pollock

3 Like two doomed ships that pass in storm we had crossed each other's way: but we made no sign, we said no word, we had no word to say.
Oscar Wilde (1856-1900, British Author, Wit)

HOCKEY

1 How would you like a job where when you made a mistake, a big red light goes on and 18,000 people boo?
Jacques Plante (Hockey Player)

HOLLYWOOD

1 If we have to tell Hollywood good-by, it may be with one of those tender, old-fashioned, seven- second kisses exchanged between two people of the opposite sex, with all their clothes on.
Anita Loos (1893-1981, American Novelist, Screenwriter)

2 Just like those other black holes from outer space, Hollywood is postmodern to this extent: it has no center, only a spreading dead zone of exhaustion, inertia, and brilliant decay.
Arthur Kroker

3 In the court of the movie Owner, none criticized, none doubted. And none dared speak of art. In the Owner's mind art was a synonym for bankruptcy. The movie Owners are the only troupe in the history of entertainment that has never been seduced by the adventure of the entertainment world.
Ben Hecht (1894-1964, American Newspaperman, Novelist, Playwright)

4 Hollywood held this double lure for me, tremendous sums of money for work that required no more effort than a game of pinochle.
Ben Hecht (1894-1964, American Newspaperman, Novelist, Playwright)

5 If New York is the Big Apple, tonight Hollywood is the Big Nipple.
Bernardo Bertolucci (Italian Actor)

6 To survive there, you need the ambition of a Latin-American revolutionary, the ego of a grand opera tenor, and the physical stamina of a cow pony.
Billie Burke

7 Bankers, nepotists, contracts and talkies: on four fingers one may count the leeches which have sucked a young and vigorous industry into paresis.
Dalton Trumbo

8 We Americans have always considered Hollywood, at best, a sinkhole of depraved venality. And, of course, it is. It is not a Protective Monastery of Aesthetic Truth. It is a place where everything is incredibly expensive.
David Mamet (1947-, American Playwright)

9 Hollywood's like Egypt, full of crumbled pyramids. It'll never come back. It'll just keep on crumbling until finally the wind blows the last studio prop across the sands.
David O. Selznick

10 You don't resign from these jobs, you escape from them.
Dawn Steel

11 Hollywood's a very weird place. I think there's less of everything except for attitude.
Dean Cain (1966-, American Actor, Writer)

12 Hollywood money isn't money. It's congealed snow, melts in your hand, and there you are.
Dorothy Parker (1893-1967, American Humorous Writer)

13 I can't talk about Hollywood. It was a horror to me when I was there and it's a horror to look back on. I can't imagine how I did it. When I got away from it I couldn't even refer to the place by name. "Out there," I called it.
Dorothy Parker (1893-1967, American Humorous Writer)

14 I devoutly believe it is the writer who has matured the film medium more than anyone else in Hollywood. Even when he knew nothing about his work, he brought at least knowledge of life and a more grown-up mind, a maturer feeling about the human being.
Dudley Nichols (American Actor)

15 Where is Hollywood located? Chiefly between the ears. In that part of the American brain lately vacated by God.
Erica Jong (1942-, American Author)

16 You write a book like that you're fond of over the years, then you see that happen to it, it's like pissing in your father's beer.
Ernest Hemingway (1898-1961, American Writer)

17 An associate producer is the only guy in Hollywood who will associate with a producer.
Fred A. Allen (1894-1957, American Radio Comic)

18 Hollywood is a place where people from Iowa mistake each other for stars.
Fred A. Allen (1894-1957, American Radio Comic)

19 If it's a good script I'll do it. And if it's a bad script, and they pay me enough, I'll do it.
George Burns (1896-1996, American Comedy Actor)

20 My attitude about Hollywood is that I wouldn't walk across the street to pull one of those executives out of the snow if he was bleeding to death. Not unless I was paid for it. None of them ever did me any favors.
James Woods (1947-, American Actor)

21 The sumptuous age of stars and images is reduced to a few artificial tornado effects, pathetic fake buildings, and childish tricks which the crowd pretends to be taken in by to avoid feeling too disappointed. Ghost towns, ghost people. The whole place has the same air of obsolescence about it as Sunset or Hollywood Boulevard.
Jean Baudrillard (French Postmodern Philosopher, Writer)

22 There is in Hollywood, as in all cultures in which gambling is the central activity, a lowered sexual energy, an inability to devote more than token attention to the preoccupations of the society outside. The action is everything, more consuming than sex, more immediate than politics; more important always than the acquisition of money, which is never, for the gambler, the true point of the exercise.
Joan Didion (1934-, American Essayist)

23 Hollywood has always been a cage... a cage to catch our dreams.
John Huston (1906-1987, American Film Director)

24 Hollywood is a place that attracts people with massive holes in their souls.
Julia Phillips

25 Fame is no sanctuary from the passing of youth... suicide is much easier and more acceptable in Hollywood than growing old gracefully.
Julie Burchill (British Journalist, Writer)

26 The average Hollywood film star's ambition is to be admired by an American, courted by an Italian, married to an Englishman and have a French boyfriend.
Katharine Hepburn (1907-, American Actress, Writer)

27 Hollywood's a place where they'll pay you a thousand dollars for a kiss, and fifty cents for your soul. I know, because I turned down the first offer often enough and held out for the fifty cents.
Marilyn Monroe (1926-, American Actress)

28 It feels like a barbell. [When asked what she thought of her newly acquired Oscar statuette]
Marisa Tomei (1964-, American Actress)

29 The only reason I'm in Hollywood is that I don't have the moral courage to refuse the money.
Marlon Brando (1924-, American Actor, Director)

30 I went out there for a thousand a week, and I worked Monday, and I got fired Wednesday. The guy that hired me was out of town Tuesday.
Nelson Algren (1909-1981, American Author)

31 Hollywood is the only industry, even taking in soup companies, which does not have laboratories for the purpose of experimentation.
Orson Welles (1915-1985, American Film Maker)

32 Strip away the phony tinsel of Hollywood and you will find the real tinsel underneath.
Oscar Levant (1906-1972, American Pianist, Actor)

33 Hollywood has gone from Pola to Polaroid.
Pola Negri (1897-1987, Polish Actress)

34 If my books had been any worse, I should not have been invited to Hollywood, and if they had been any better, I should not have come.
Raymond Chandler (1888-1959, American Author)

35 That's one thing I like about Hollywood. The writer is there revealed in his ultimate corruption. He asks no praise, because his praise comes to him in the form of a salary check. In Hollywood the average writer is not young, not honest, not brave, and a bit overdressed. But he is darn good company, which book writers as a rule are not. He is better than what he writes. Most book writers are not as good.
Raymond Chandler (1888-1959, American Author)

36 The motion picture made in Hollywood, if it is to create art at all, must do so within such strangling limitations of subject and treatment that it is a blind wonder it ever achieves any distinction beyond the purely mechanical slickness of a glass and chromium bathroom.
Raymond Chandler (1888-1959, American Author)

37 The overall picture, as the boys say, is of a degraded community whose idealism even is largely fake. The pretentiousness, the bogus enthusiasm, the constant drinking, the incessant squabbling over money, the all-pervasive agent, the strutting of the big shots (and their usually utter incompetence to achieve anything they start out to do), the constant fear of losing all this fairy gold and being the nothing they have never ceased to be, the snide tricks, the whole damn mess is out of this world.
Raymond Chandler (1888-1959, American Author)

38 They don't want you until you have made a name, and by the time you have made a name, you have developed some kind of talent they can't use. All they will do is spoil it, if you let them.
Raymond Chandler (1888-1959, American Author)

39 Its idea of "production value" is spending a million dollars dressing up a story that any good writer would throw away. Its vision of the rewarding movie is a vehicle for some glamour-puss with two expressions and eighteen changes of costume, or for some male idol of the muddled millions with a permanent hangover, six worn-out acting tricks, the build of a lifeguard, and the mentality of a chicken-strangler.
Raymond Chandler (1888-1959, American Author)

40 Some are able and humane men and some are low-grade individuals with the morals of a goat, the artistic integrity of a slot machine, and the manners of a floorwalker with delusions of grandeur.
Raymond Chandler (1888-1959, American Author)

41 In Hollywood if you don't have happiness you send out for it.
Rex Reed

42 There rise her timeless capitals of empires daily born, whose plinths are laid at midnight and whose streets are packed at morn; and here come tired youths and maids that feign to love or sin in tones like rusty razor blades to tunes like smitten tin.
Rudyard Kipling (1865-1936, British Author of Prose, Verse)

43 I hate a man who always says "yes" to me. When I say "no" I like a man who also says "no."
Samuel Goldwyn (1882-1974, American Film Producer, Founder, MGM)

44 If you have a vagina and an attitude in this town, then that's a lethal combination.
Sharon Stone (1958-, American Actress)

45 Hollywood gives a young girl the aura of one giant, self-contained orgy farm, its inhabitants dedicated to crawling into every pair of pants they can find.
Veronica Lake (1919-1973, American Actress)

46 Studio executives are intelligent, brutally overworked men and women who share one thing in common with baseball managers: they wake up every morning of the world with the knowledge that sooner or later they're going to get fired.
William Goldman (1931-, American Author)

47 In Beverly Hills... they don't throw their garbage away. They make it into television shows.
Woody Allen (1935-, American Director, Screenwriter, Actor, Comedian)

HOME

1 What the Nation must realize is that the home, when both parents work, is non-existent. Once we have honestly faced that fact, we must act accordingly.
Agnes Meyer

2 A man's home is his wife's castle.
Alexander Chase

3   Woman, the more careful she is about her face, the more careless about her house.
Ben Johnson (1573-1637, British Dramatist, Poet)

4   There are things you just can't do in life. You can't beat the phone company, you can't make a waiter see you until he's ready to see you, and you can't go home again.
Bill Bryson (American Author)

5   Home is the most popular, and will be the most enduring of all earthly establishments.
Channing Pollock (American Actor)

6   Home is a name, a word, it is a strong one; stronger than magician ever spoke, or spirit ever answered to, in the strongest conjuration.
Charles Dickens (1812-1870, British Novelist)

7   Home interprets heaven. Home is heaven for beginners.
Charles H. Parkhurst (1842-1933, American Clergyman, Reformer)

8   Were I Diogenes, I would not move out of a kilderkin into a hogshead, though the first had had nothing but small beer in it, and the second reeked claret.
Charles Lamb (1775-1834, British Essayist, Critic)

9   Home is where there's one to love us.
Charles Swain

10   A hundred men may make an encampment, but it takes a woman to make a home.
Chinese Proverb

11   A man's home may seem to be his castle on the outside; inside, it is more often his nursery.
Clare Boothe Luce (1903-1987, American Diplomat, Writer)

12   The worst feeling in the world is the homesickness that comes over a man occasionally when he is at home.
Edgar Watson Howe (1853-1937, American Journalist, Author)

13   There is no sanctuary of virtue like home.
Edward Everett (1794-1865, American Statesman, Scholar)

14   I have been photographing our toilet, that glossy enameled receptacle of extraordinary beauty. Here was every sensuous curve of the "human figure divine" but minus the imperfections. Never did the Greeks reach a more significant consummation to their culture, and it somehow reminded me, in the glory of its chaste convulsions and in its swelling, sweeping, forward movement of finely progressing contours, of the Victory of Samothrace.
Edward Weston (1886-1958, American Photographer)

15   It is the personality of the mistress that the home expresses. Men are forever guests in our homes, no matter how much happiness they may find there.
Elsie De Wolfe

16   Where thou art, that is home.
Emily Dickinson (1830-1886, American Poet)

17   Drab Habitation of Whom? Tabernacle or Tomb -- or Dome of Worm -- or Porch of Gnome -- or some Elf's Catacomb?
Emily Dickinson (1830-1886, American Poet)

18   Housework is what a woman does that nobody notices unless she hasn't done it.
Evan Esar

19   Owning your own home is America's unique recipe for avoiding revolution and promoting pseudo-equality at the same time. To keep citizens puttering in their yards instead of sputtering on the barricades, the government has gladly deprived itself of billions in tax revenues by letting home "owners" deduct mortgage interest payments.
Florence King (1936-, American Author, Critic)

20   Houses are built to live in, and not to look on: therefore let use be preferred before uniformity.
Francis Bacon (1561-1626, British Philosopher, Essayist, Statesman)

21   Nothing annoys a woman more than to have company drop in unexpectedly and find the house looking as it usually does.
Frank Dane

22   If I were asked to name the chief benefit of the house, I should say: the house shelters day- dreaming, the house protects the dreamer, the house allows one to dream in peace.
Gaston Bachelard (1884-1962, French Scientist, Philosopher, Literary Theorist)

23   Home is a place not only of strong affections, but of entire unreserved; it is life's undress rehearsal, its backroom, its dressing room, from which we go forth to more careful and guarded intercourse, leaving behind us much debris of cast-off and everyday clothing.
Harriet Beecher Stowe (1811-1896, American Novelist, Antislavery Campaigner)

24   Home" is any four walls that enclose the right person.
Helen Rowland (1875-1950, American Journalist)

25   We should come home from adventures, and perils, and discoveries every day with new experience and character.
Henry David Thoreau (1817-1862, American Essayist, Poet, Naturalist)

26   Should not every apartment in which man dwells be lofty enough to create some obscurity overhead, where flickering shadows may play at evening about the rafters?
Henry David Thoreau (1817-1862, American Essayist, Poet, Naturalist)

27   I had three chairs in my house; one for solitude, two for friendship, three for society.
Henry David Thoreau (1817-1862, American Essayist, Poet, Naturalist)

28   One never reaches home, but wherever friendly paths intersect the whole world looks like home for a time.
Hermann Hesse (1877-1962, German-born Swiss Novelist, Poet)

29   One returns to the place one came from.
Jean De La Fontaine (1621-1695, French Poet)

30 I want a house that has got over all its troubles; I don't want to spend the rest of my life bringing up a young and inexperienced house.
Jerome K. Jerome (1859-1927, British Humorous Writer, Novelist, Playwright)

31 There is room in the smallest cottage for a happy loving pair.
Johann Friedrich Von Schiller (1759-1805, German Dramatist, Poet, Historian)

32 Be he a king or a peasant, he is happiest who finds peace at home.
Johann Wolfgang Von Goethe (1749-1832, German Poet, Dramatist, Novelist)

33 He is the happiest, be he king or peasant, who finds peace in his home.
Johann Wolfgang Von Goethe (1749-1832, German Poet, Dramatist, Novelist)

34 People's backyards are much more interesting than their front gardens, and houses that back on to railways are public benefactors.
John Betjeman (1906-1984, British Poet)

35 Our country is where ever we are well off.
John Milton (1608-1674, British Poet)

36 If men lived like men indeed, their houses would be temples -- temples which we should hardly dare to injure, and in which it would make us holy to be permitted to live; and there must be a strange dissolution of natural affection, a strange unthankfulness for all that homes have given and parents taught, a strange consciousness that we have been unfaithful to our fathers honor, or that our own lives are not such as would make our dwellings sacred to our children, when each man would fain build to himself, and build for the little revolution of his own life only.
John Ruskin (1819-1900, British Critic, Social Theorist)

37 Going home must be like going to render an account.
Joseph Conrad (1857-1924, Polish-born British Novelist)

38 The examples of vice at home corrupt us more quickly and easily than others, since they steal into our minds under the highest authority.
Juvenal (Decimus Junius Juvenalis) (55-130, Roman Satirical Poet)

39 The fellow that owns his own home is always just coming out of a hardware store.
Kin Hubbard (1868-1930, American Humorist, Journalist)

40 The worst thing about work in the house or home is that whatever you do is destroyed, laid waste or eaten within twenty four hours.
Lady Kasluck

41 He makes his home where the living is best.
Latin Proverb

42 A house is a machine for living in.
Le Corbusier

43 The place is very well and quiet and the children only scream in a low voice.
Lord Byron (1788-1824, British Poet)

44 Home -- that blessed word, which opens to the human heart the most perfect glimpse of Heaven, and helps to carry it thither, as on an angel's wings.
Lydia M. Child (1802-1880, American Abolitionist, Writer, Editor)

45 There is no place more delightful than one's own fireplace.
Marcus T. Cicero (106-43 BC, Great Roman Orator, Politician)

46 Any woman who understands the problems of running a home will be nearer to understanding the problems of running a country.
Margaret Thatcher (1925-, British Stateswoman, Prime Minister (1979-90))

47 A house means a family house, a place specially meant for putting children and men in so as to restrict their waywardness and distract them from the longing for adventure and escape they've had since time began.
Marguerite Duras (1914-, French Author, Filmmaker)

48 The house a woman creates is a Utopia. She can't help it -- can't help trying to interest her nearest and dearest not in happiness itself but in the search for it.
Marguerite Duras (1914-, French Author, Filmmaker)

49 One may make their house a palace of sham, or they can make it a home, a refuge.
Mark Twain (1835-1910, American Humorist, Writer)

50 My home...It is my retreat and resting place from wars, I try to keep this corner as a haven against the tempest outside, as I do another corner in my soul.
Michel Eyquem De Montaigne (1533-1592, French Philosopher, Essayist)

51 You are a king by your own fireside, as much as any monarch in his throne.
Miguel De Cervantes (1547-1616, Spanish Novelist, Dramatist, Poet)

52 Many a man who thinks to found a home discovers that he has merely opened a tavern for his friends.
Norman Douglas (1868-1952, British Author)

53 You can't appreciate home till you've left it, money till it's spent, your wife till she's joined a woman's club, nor Old Glory till you see it hanging on a broomstick on the shanty of a consul in a foreign town.
O. Henry Porter (1862-1910, American short-story Writer)

54 When I can no longer bear to think of the victims of broken homes, I begin to think of the victims of intact ones.
Peter De Vries (1910-, American Author)

55 Home is where the heart is.
Pliny The Elder (23-79, Roman Neophatonist)

56 I live in my house as I live inside my skin: I know more beautiful, more ample, more sturdy and more picturesque skins: but it would seem to me unnatural to exchange them for mine.
Primo Levi (1919-1987, Italian Chemist, Author)

57 Construed as turf, home just seems a provisional claim, a designation you make upon a place, not one it makes on you. A certain set of buildings, a glimpsed, smudged window-view across a schoolyard, a musty aroma sniffed behind a garage when you were a child, all of which come crowding in upon your latter-day senses -- those are pungent things and vivid, even consoling. But to me they are also inert and nostalgic and unlikely to connect you to the real, to that essence art can sometimes achieve, which is permanence.
Richard Ford (1944-, American Author)

58 Home is the place where, when you have to go there, They have to take you in.
Robert Frost (1875-1963, American Poet)

59 Home, the spot of earth supremely blest, A dearer, sweeter spot than all the rest.
Robert Montgomery (1807-1855, American Author)

60 An empty house is like a stray dog or a body from which life has departed.
Samuel Butler (1612-1680, British Poet, Satirist)

61 No money is better spent than what is laid out for domestic satisfaction.
Samuel Johnson (1709-1784, British Author)

62 It is, indeed, at home that every man must be known by those who would make a just estimate either of his virtue or felicity; for smiles and embroidery are alike occasional, and the mind is often dressed for show in painted honor, and fictitious benevolence.
Samuel Johnson (1709-1784, British Author)

63 Be grateful for the home you have, knowing that at this moment, all you have is all you need.
Sarah Ban Breathnach (American Author)

64 In the matter of furnishing, I find a certain absence of ugliness far worse than ugliness.
Sidonie Gabrielle Colette (1873-1954, French Author)

65 Estate agents. You can't live with them, you can't live with them. The first sign of these nasty purulent sores appeared round about 1894. With their jangling keys, nasty suits, revolting beards, moustaches and tinted spectacles, estate agents roam the land causing perturbation and despair. If you try and kill them, you're put in prison: if you try and talk to them, you vomit. There's only one thing worse than an estate agent but at least that can be safely lanced, drained and surgically dressed. Estate agents. Love them or loathe them, you'd be mad not to loathe them.
Stephen Fry

66 A comfortable house is a great source of happiness. It ranks immediately after health and a good conscience.
Sydney Smith (1771-1845, British Writer, Clergyman)

67 Never weather-beaten sail more willing bent to shore.
Thomas Campion

68 The ordinary acts we practice every day at home are of more importance to the soul than their simplicity might suggest.
Thomas Moore (1779-1852, Irish Poet)

69 It matters less to a person where they are born than where they can live.
Turkish Proverb

70 If you want a golden rule that will fit everything, this is it: Have nothing in your houses that you do not know to be useful or believe to be beautiful.
William Morris (1834-1896, British Artist, Writer, Printer)

71 Have nothing in your house that you do not know to be useful, or believe to be beautiful.
William Morris (1834-1896, British Artist, Writer, Printer)

72 The poorest man may in his cottage bid defiance to all the forces of the Crown. It may be frail -- its roof may shake -- the wind may blow through it -- the storm may enter -- the rain may enter -- but the King of England cannot enter! -- all his forces dare not cross the threshold of the ruined tenement!
William Pitt The Elder Chatham (1708 -1778, British Statesman)

73 People usually are the happiest at home.
William Shakespeare (1564-1616, British Poet, Playwright, Actor)

74 We shape our dwellings, and afterwards our dwellings shape us.
Winston Churchill (1874-1965, British Statesman, Prime Minister)

HONESTY

1 There are two great forces in this world -- good and evil; and no man is worth his salt unless he has lost and won battle for a principle.
A. P. Gouthey

2 An honest man's the noblest work of God.
Alexander Pope (1688-1744, British Poet, Critic, Translator)

3 Honesty is the best policy.
Benjamin Franklin (1706-1790, American Scientist, Publisher, Diplomat)

4 You shall not steal, nor deal falsely, nor lie to one another. [Leviticus 19:11]
Bible (Sacred Scriptures of Christians and Judaism)

5 Everybody has a little bit of Watergate in him.
Billy Graham (1918-, American Evangelist)

6 To live outside the law, you must be honest.
Bob Dylan (1941-, American Musician, Singer, Songwriter)

7 Honest hearts produce honest actions.
Brigham Young (1801-1877, American Mormon Leader)

8 If you give me six lines written by the hand of the most honest of men, I will find something in them which will hang him.
Cardinal De Richelieu (1585-1642, French Statesman)

9 The honest man must be a perpetual renegade, the life of an honest man a perpetual infidelity. For the man who wishes to remain faithful must take himself perpetually unfaithful to all the continual, successive, indefatigable, renascent errors.
Charles Peguy (1873-1914, French Poet, Philosopher)

10 Prefer a loss to dishonest gain; the one brings pain at the moment, the other for all time.
Chilo (560 BC, Greek Sage)

11 Dishonest people conceal their faults from themselves as well as others, honest people know and confess them.
Christian Nevell Bovee (1820-1904, American Author, Lawyer)

12 When we are not honest, we are cut off from a significant resource of ourselves, a vital dimension that is necessary for unity and wholeness.
Clark Moustakas (Humanistic Psychologist)

13 Successful people have cultivated the habit of never denying to themselves their true feelings and attitudes. They have no need for pretenses.
David Harold Fink

14 People may or may not say what they mean... but they always say something designed to get what they want.
David Mamet (1947-, American Playwright)

15 Some persons are likable in spite of their unswerving integrity.
Don Marquis (1878-1937, American Humorist, Journalist)

16 Honesty is a good thing, but it is not profitable to its possessor unless it is kept under control.
Don Marquis (1878-1937, American Humorist, Journalist)

17 Honesty is the most single most important factor having a direct bearing on the final success of an individual, corporation, or product.
Ed Mcmahon (American TV Host)

18 You can never lose anything that really belongs to you, and you can't keep that which belongs to someone else.
Edgar Cayce (1877-1945, American Psychic Medium)

19 How desperately difficult it is to be honest with oneself. It is much easier to be honest with other people.
Edward Frederic Benson (1867-1940, American Author)

20 No such thing as a man willing to be honest --that would be like a blind man willing to see.
F. Scott Fitzgerald (1896-1940, American Writer)

21 Nothing resembles an honest man more than a cheat.
French Proverb

22 If honesty did not exist, we ought to invent it as the best means of getting rich.
Gabriel Riqueti Mirabeau (1749-1791, French Revolutionary Politician, Orator)

23 We must make the world honest before we can honestly say to our children that honesty is the best policy.
George Bernard Shaw (1856-1950, Irish-born British Dramatist)

24 You've got to be honest; if you can fake that, you've got it made.
George Burns (1896-1996, American Comedy Actor)

25 They're only truly great who are truly good.
George Chapman (1557-1634, British Dramatist, Translator, Poet)

26 I hope I shall possess firmness and virtue enough to maintain what I consider the most enviable of all titles, the character of an honest man.
George Washington (1732-1799, First President of the USA)

27 You can't make wrong work.
Gerald Waterhouse

28 There is one way to find out if a man is honest; ask him! If he says yes you know he's crooked.
Groucho Marx (1895-1977, American Comic Actor)

29 When we honestly ask ourselves which person in our lives mean the most to us, we often find that it is those who, instead of giving advice, solutions, or cures, have chosen rather to share our pain and touch our wounds with a warm and tender hand. The friend who can be silent with us in a moment of despair or confusion, who can stay with us in an hour of grief and bereavement, who can tolerate now knowing, not curing, not healing and face with us the reality of our powerlessness, that is a friend who cares.
Henri Nouwen (Christian Author)

30 Be true to your work, your word, and your friend.
Henry David Thoreau (1817-1862, American Essayist, Poet, Naturalist)

31 Without adversity a person hardly knows whether they are honest or not.
Henry Fielding (1707-1754, British Novelist, Dramatist)

32 From such crooked wood as that which man is made of, nothing straight can be fashioned.
Immanuel Kant (1724-1804, German Philosopher)

33 Good thoughts bear good fruit, bad thoughts bear bad fruit.
James Allen (1864-1912, British-born American Essayist, Author of "As a Man Thinketh")

34 Honesty prospers in every condition of life.
Johann Friedrich Von Schiller (1759-1805, German Dramatist, Poet, Historian)

35 Where is the man who has the strength to be true, and to show himself as he is?
Johann Wolfgang Von Goethe (1749-1832, German Poet, Dramatist, Novelist)

36 There is no twilight zone of honesty in business. A thing is right or it's wrong. It's black or it's white.
John F. Dodge

37 The true measure of life is not length, but honesty.
John Lyly (1554-1606, British Writer)

38 To make your children capable of honesty is the beginning of education.
John Ruskin (1819-1900, British Critic, Social Theorist)

39 Be prepared and be honest.
John Wooden (1910-, American Basketball Coach)

40 Each time you are honest and conduct yourself with honesty, a success force will drive you toward greater success. Each time you lie, even with a little white lie, there are strong forces pushing you toward failure.
Joseph Sugarman (American Businessman)

41 Honesty is the rarest wealth anyone can possess, and yet all the honesty in the world ain't lawful tender for a loaf of bread.
Josh Billings (1815-1885, American Humorist, Lecturer)

42 When you accept yourself completely you do not have to maintain a phony front, drive yourself to "achieve" or feel insecure if people tune-in to you and what you are doing.
Ken Keyes Jr. (1921-1995, American Author)

43 Do not do what you would undo if caught.
Leah Arendt

44 I have found that being honest is the best technique I can use. Right up front, tell people what you're trying to accomplish and what you're willing to sacrifice to accomplish it.
Lee Iacocca (1924-, American Businessman, Former CEO of Chrysler)

45 The easiest thing to be in the world is you. The most difficult thing to be is what other people want you to be. Don't let them put you in that position.
Leo Buscaglia (American Expert on Love, Lecturer, Author)

46 Morality may consist solely in the courage of making a choice.
Leon Blum (1872-1950, French Statesman and Prime Minister)

47 Every man who says frankly and fully what he thinks is doing a public service.
Leslie Stephen

48 Oh for someone with a heart, head and hand. Whatever they call them, what do I care, aristocrat, democrat, autocrat, just be it one that can rule and dare not lie.
Lord Alfred Tennyson (1809-1892, British Poet)

49 That which is won ill, will never wear well, for there is a curse attends it which will waste it. The same corrupt dispositions which incline men to sinful ways of getting, will incline them to the like sinful ways of spending.
M. Henry

50 Honesty is the best policy -- when there is money in it.
Mark Twain (1835-1910, American Humorist, Writer)

51 Honesty is the cornerstone of all success, without which confidence and ability to perform shall cease to exist.
Mary Kay Ash (American Businesswoman, Founder of Mary Kay Cosmetics)

52 The elegance of honesty needs no adornment.
Merry Browne

53 No man is so exquisitely honest or upright in living, but that ten times in his life he might not lawfully be hanged.
Michel Eyquem De Montaigne (1533-1592, French Philosopher, Essayist)

54 Understand this law and you will then know, beyond room for the slightest doubt, that you are constantly punishing yourself for every wrong you commit and rewarding yourself for every act of constructive conduct in which you indulge.
Napoleon Hill (1883-1970, American Speaker, Motivational Writer, "Think and Grow Rich")

55 No man, for any considerable period, can wear one face to himself, and another to the multitude, without finally getting bewildered as to which may be true.
Nathaniel Hawthorne (1804-1864, American Novelist, Short Story Writer)

56 A few honest men are better than numbers.
Oliver Cromwell (1599-1658, Parliamentarian General, Lord Protector of England)

57 To many a man, and sometimes to a youth, there comes the opportunity to choose between honorable competence and tainted wealth. The young man who starts out to be poor and honorable, holds in his hand one of the strongest elements of success.
Orison Swett Marden (1850-1924, American Author, Founder of Success Magazine)

58 If we put the emphasis upon the right things, if we live the life that is worth while and then fail, we will survive all disasters, we will out-live all misfortune. We should be so well balanced and symmetrical, that nothing which could ever happen could throw us off our center, so that no matter what misfortune should overtake us, there would still be a whole magnificent man or woman left after being stripped of everything else.
Orison Swett Marden (1850-1924, American Author, Founder of Success Magazine)

59 There is something greater than wealth, grander even than fame -- manhood, character, stand for success... nothing else really does.
Orison Swett Marden (1850-1924, American Author, Founder of Success Magazine)

60 A man is sorry to be honest for nothing.
Ovid (43 BC-18 AD, Roman Poet)

61 It is annoying to be honest to no purpose.
Ovid (43 BC-18 AD, Roman Poet)

62 Honesty is for the most par less profitable than dishonesty.
Plato (427-347 BC, Greek Philosopher)

63 Be true to your own act and congratulate yourself if you have done something strange and extravagant to break the monotony of a decorous age.
Ralph Waldo Emerson (1803-1882, American Poet, Essayist)

64 It is impossible for a man to be cheated by anyone but himself.
Ralph Waldo Emerson (1803-1882, American Poet, Essayist)

65 People who are brutally honest get more satisfaction out of the brutality than out of the honesty.
Richard J. Needham

66 Honesty is the best policy; but he who is governed by that maxim is not an honest man.
Richard Whately (1787-1863, British Prelate, Writer)

67 Dare to be honest and fear no labor.
Robert Burns (1759-1796, Scottish Poet)

68 I would give no thought of what the world might say of me, if I could only transmit to posterity the reputation of an honest man.
Sam Houston (1793-1863, American Soldier, Statesman)

69 A thread will tie an honest man better than a chain a rogue.
Scottish Proverb

70 Would you want to do business with a person who was 99% honest?
Sidney Madwed (American Speaker, Consultant, Author, Poet)

71 Being entirely honest with oneself is a good exercise.
Sigmund Freud (1856-1939, Austrian Physician - Founder of Psychoanalysis)

72 No one is wise or safe, but they that are honest.
Sir Walter Raleigh (1552-1618, British Courtier, Navigator, Writer)

73 Rather fail with honor than succeed by fraud.
Sophocles (495-406 BC, Greek Tragic Poet)

74 Honesty is as rare as a man without self-pity.
Stephen Vincent Benet (1989-1943, American Novelist, Poet)

75 Honesty is the best policy, but insanity is a better defense.
Steve Landesberg

76 Make yourself an honest man, and then you may be sure there is one less rascal in the world.
Thomas Carlyle (1795-1881, Scottish Philosopher, Author)

77 Honesty is the first chapter of the book of wisdom.
Thomas Jefferson (1743-1826, Third President of the USA)

78 Honest men are the soft easy cushions on which knaves repose and fatten.
Thomas Otway (1652-1685, British Dramatist)

79 I grew up in New York, and I have that in me, that be-honest-at-all-costs, don't b.s. me attitude. I say, "If you've got something to say about me, say it to my face. And then we'll either talk about it or fight about it."
Tim Robbins (1958-, American Actor, Director, Screenwriter, Producer, Writer)

80 Just be honest with yourself. That opens the door.
Vernon Howard (19?-1992, American Author, Speaker)

81 Act in earnest and you will become earnest in all you do.
William James (1842-1910, American Psychologist, Professor, Author)

82 No one can earn a million dollars honestly.
William Jennings Bryan (1860-1925, American Lawyer, Politician)

83 Though I am not naturally honest, I am so sometimes by chance.
William Shakespeare (1564-1616, British Poet, Playwright, Actor)

84 Honesty is the best policy. If I lose mine honor, I lose myself.
William Shakespeare (1564-1616, British Poet, Playwright, Actor)

85 It is a fine thing to be honest, but it is also very important to be right.
Winston Churchill (1874-1965, British Statesman, Prime Minister)

HONOR

1 The fiery trials through which we pass will light us down in honor or dishonor to the latest generation.
Abraham Lincoln (1809-1865, Sixteenth President of the USA)

2 Say not that honor is the child of boldness, nor believe thou that the hazard of life alone can pay the price of it: it is not to the action that it is due, but to the manner of performing it.
Akhenaton (1375 BC, Egyptian King, Monotheist)

3 Act well your part; there all honor lies.
Alexander Pope (1688-1744, British Poet, Critic, Translator)

4 It is the dissimilarities and inequalities among men which give rise to the notion of honor; as such differences become less, it grows feeble; and when they disappear, it will vanish too.
Alexis De Tocqueville (1805-1859, French Social Philosopher)

5 All honor's wounds are self-inflicted.
Andrew Carnegie (1835-1919, American Industrialist, Philanthropist)

6 Honor has not to be won; it must only not be lost.
Arthur Schopenhauer (1788-1860, German Philosopher)

7 When a virtuous man is raised, it brings gladness to his friends, grief to his enemies, and glory to his posterity.
Ben Johnson (1573-1637, British Dramatist, Poet)

8 The only thing of weight that can be said against modern honor is that it is directly opposite to religion. The one bids you bear injuries with patience, the other tells you if you don't resent them, you are not fit to live.
Bernard Mandeville (1670-1733, Dutch-born British Author, Physician)

9 For one who has been honored, dishonor is worse than death.
Bhagavad Gita (400 BC, Sanskrit Poem Incorporated Into the Mahabharata)

10 A prophet is not without honor, save in his own country.
Bible (Sacred Scriptures of Christians and Judaism)

11   A Code of Honor-never approach a friend's girlfriend or wife with mischief as your goal. There are just too many women in the world to justify that sort of dishonorable behavior. Unless she's really attractive.
Bruce J Freidmen

12   No person was ever honored for what he received. Honor has been the reward for what he gave.
Calvin Coolidge (1872-1933, Thirtieth President of the USA)

13   Honor is unstable and seldom the same; for she feeds upon opinion, and is as fickle as her food.
Charles Caleb Colton (1780-1832, British Sportsman Writer)

14   To those whose God is honor; only disgrace is a sin.
David Hare (1947-, British Playwright, Director)

15   The person is a poor judge who by an action can be disgraced more in failing than they can be honored in succeeding.
Francis Bacon (1561-1626, British Philosopher, Essayist, Statesman)

16   Honor lies in honest toil.
Grover Cleveland (1837-1908, Twenty-second & 24th President of the USA)

17   Honor is simply the morality of superior men.
H. L. Mencken (1880-1956, American Editor, Author, Critic, Humorist)

18   You will never do anything in this world without courage. It is the greatest quality of the mind next to honor.
James Allen (1864-1912, British-born American Essayist, Author of "As a Man Thinketh")

19   Without money honor is merely a disease.
Jean Racine (1639-1699, French Dramatist)

20   Worthless is the nation that does not gladly stake its all on its honor.
Johann Friedrich Von Schiller (1759-1805, German Dramatist, Poet, Historian)

21   Woman's honor is nice as ermine; it will not bear a soil.
John Dryden (1631-1700, British Poet, Dramatist, Critic)

22   The post of honor is a private station.
Joseph Addison (1672-1719, British Essayist, Poet, Statesman)

23   Better to die ten thousand deaths than wound my honor.
Joseph Addison (1672-1719, British Essayist, Poet, Statesman)

24   As to honor -- you know -- it's a very fine mediaeval inheritance which women never got hold of. It wasn't theirs.
Joseph Conrad (1857-1924, Polish-born British Novelist)

25   I love the name of honor, more than I fear death.
Julius Caesar (101-44 BC, Roman Emperor)

26   Better not be at all than not be noble.
Lord Alfred Tennyson (1809-1892, British Poet)

27   Honor is the reward of virtue.
Marcus T. Cicero (106-43 BC, Great Roman Orator, Politician)

28   Since an intelligence common to us all makes things known to us and formulates them in our minds, honorable actions are ascribed by us to virtue, and dishonorable actions to vice; and only a madman would conclude that these judgments are matters of opinion, and not fixed by nature.
Marcus T. Cicero (106-43 BC, Great Roman Orator, Politician)

29   It is better to deserve honors and not have them than to have them and not deserve them.
Mark Twain (1835-1910, American Humorist, Writer)

30   Honor isn't about making the right choices. It's about dealing with the consequences.
Midori Koto

31   A person dishonored is worst than dead.
Miguel De Cervantes (1547-1616, Spanish Novelist, Dramatist, Poet)

32   Death rather than disgrace.
Motto

33   Let my honor be without stain.
Motto

34   Honor is like an island, rugged and without a beach; once we have left it, we can never return.
Nicholas Boileau (1636-1711, French Literary Poet, Critic)

35   Because there is very little honor left in American life, there is a certain built-in tendency to destroy masculinity in American men.
Norman Mailer (1923-, American Author)

36   It was just him and me. He fought with honor. If it weren't for his honor, he and the others would have beaten me together. They might have killed me, then. His sense of honor saved my life. I didn't fight with honor... I fought to win.
Orson Scott Card (American Author)

37   I have deserved neither so much honor or so much disgrace.
Pierre Corneille (1606-1684, French Dramatist)

38   Let honor be to us as strong an obligation as necessity is to others.
Pliny The Elder (23-79, Roman Neophatonist)

39   A hundred years cannot repair a moment's loss of honor.
Proverb

40   Ease and honor are seldom bedfellows.
Proverb

41   He who has lost honor can lose nothing more.
Publilius Syrus (1st Century BC, Roman Writer)

42   No one ever lost his honor, except he who had it not.
Publilius Syrus (1st Century BC, Roman Writer)

43 The louder he talked of his honor, the faster we counted our spoons.
Ralph Waldo Emerson (1803-1882, American Poet, Essayist)

44 The higher the culture the more honorable the work.
Roucher

45 Our own heart, and not other men's opinion, forms our true honor.
Samuel Taylor Coleridge (1772-1834, British Poet, Critic, Philosopher)

46 It wasn't the reward that mattered or the recognition you might harvest. It was your depth of commitment, your quality of service, the product of your devotion -- these were the things that counted in a life. When you gave purely, the honor came in the giving, and that was honor enough.
Scott O'Grady

47 One may survive distress, but not disgrace.
Scottish Proverb

48 Why should honor outlive honestly? [Orthello]
William Shakespeare (1564-1616, British Poet, Playwright, Actor)

49 There is no question what the roll of honor in America is. The roll of honor consists of the names of men who have squared their conduct by ideals of duty.
Woodrow T. Wilson (1856-1924, Twenty-eighth President of the USA)

50 The nation's honor is dearer than the nation's comfort; yes, than the nation's life itself.
Woodrow T. Wilson (1856-1924, Twenty-eighth President of the USA)

HOPE

1 Of all ills that one endures, hope is a cheap and universal cure.
Abraham Cowley (1618-1667, British Poet)

2 With high hope for the future, no prediction is ventured.
Abraham Lincoln (1809-1865, Sixteenth President of the USA)

3 Hope is nature's veil for hiding truth's nakedness.
Alfred Nobel (1833-1886, Swedish-Russian Chemist, Industrialist, Founder of the Nobel Prizes)

4 He who has health, has hope. And he who has hope, has everything.
Arabian Proverb

5 Hope is a waking dream.
Aristotle (384-322 BC, Greek Philosopher)

6 Hope is the dream of a waking man.
Aristotle (384-322 BC, Greek Philosopher)

7 The very least you can do in your life is to figure out what you hope for. And the most you can do is live inside that hope. Not admire it from a distance but live right in it, under its roof.
Barbara Kingsolver

8 Fear cannot be without hope nor hope without fear.
Baruch (Benedict de) Spinoza (1632-1677, Dutch Philosopher and Theologian)

9 He that lives upon hope will die fasting.
Benjamin Franklin (1706-1790, American Scientist, Publisher, Diplomat)

10 Extreme hopes are born from extreme misery.
Bertrand Russell (1872-1970, British Philosopher, Mathematician, Essayist)

11 Before you give up hope, turn back and read the attacks that were made on Lincoln.
Bruce Barton (1886-1967, American Author, Advertising Executive)

12 Such is hope, heaven's own gift to struggling mortals, pervading, like some subtle essence from the skies, all things both good and bad.
Charles Dickens (1812-1870, British Novelist)

13 The men whom I have seen succeed best in life always have been cheerful and hopeful men; who went about their business with a smile on their faces; and took the changes and chances of this mortal life like men; facing rough and smooth alike as it came.
Charles Kingsley (1819-1875, British Author, Clergyman)

14 In the factory we make cosmetics; in the store we sell hope.
Charles Revson (American Businessman, Chairman of Revlon)

15 Of all the forces that make for a better world, none is so indispensable, none so powerful, as hope. Without hope men are only half alive. With hope they dream and think and work.
Charles Sawyer

16 Hope is the best part of our riches.
Christian Nevell Bovee (1820-1904, American Author, Lawyer)

17 Hope is like a hairball trembling from its birth...
Christina Rossetti (1830-1894, British Poet, Lyricist)

18 Hope is the parent of faith.
Cyrus A. Bartol

19 Let hope inspire you, but let not idealism blind you. Proverb Don't look back, you can never look back.
Don Henley (American Musician)

20 Hope is the expectation that something outside of ourselves, something or someone external, is going to come to our rescue and we will live happily ever after.
Dr. Robert Anthony (American educator)

21 Just as despair can come to one only from other human beings, hope, too, can be given to one only by other human beings.
Elie Wiesel (1928-, Rumanian-born American Writer)

22 Hope is the thing with feathers that perches in the soul --
and sings the tunes without the words -- and never stops at
all.
Emily Dickinson (1830-1886, American Poet)

23 Hope for the best, but prepare for the worst.
English Proverb

24 Neither should a ship rely on one small anchor, nor should
life rest on a single hope.
Epictetus (50-120, Stoic Philosopher)

25 Hope is both the earliest and the most indispensable virtue
inherent in the state of being alive. If life is to be sustained
hope must remain, even where confidence is wounded,
trust impaired.
Erik H. Erikson (Austrian Developmental Psychologist)

26 That glittering hope is immemorial and beckons many men
to their undoing.
Euripides (480-406 BC, Greek Tragic Poet)

27 One measure of a civilization, either of an age or of a single
individual, is what that age or person really wishes to do.
A man's hope measures his civilization. The attainability of
the hope measures, or may measure, the civilization of his
nation and time.
Ezra Pound (1885-1972, American Poet, Critic)

28 Hope is a good breakfast but a bad supper.
*Francis Bacon (1561-1626, British Philosopher, Essayist,
Statesman)*

29 Hope is the last thing that dies in man; and though it be
exceedingly deceitful, yet it is of this good use to us, that
while we are traveling through life it conducts us in an
easier and more pleasant way to our journey's end.
*François de La Rochefoucauld (1613-1680, French classical
writer)*

30 Hope and fear are inseparable.
*François de La Rochefoucauld (1613-1680, French classical
writer)*

31 Hope is the dream of a soul awake.
French Proverb

32 He that waits for a dead man's shoes may long go barefoot.
French Proverb

33 To live without Hope is to Cease to live.
Fyodor Dostoevski (1821-1881, Russian Novelist)

34 Amateurs hope, professionals work.
*Garson Kanin (1912-, American Playwright/Screenwriter,
Stage/Movie Director)*

35 He who has never hoped can never despair.
*George Bernard Shaw (1856-1950, Irish-born British
Dramatist)*

36 Honest winter, snow clad and with the frosted beard, I can
welcome not uncordially; but that long deferment of the
calendar's promise, that weeping loom of March and April,
that bitter blast outraging the honor of May -- how often
has it robbed me of heart and hope.
*George Robert Gissing (1857-1903, British Novelist, Critic,
Essayist)*

37 Where there is no vision, there is no hope.
*George Washington Carver (1864-1943, American
Scientist)*

38 To love means loving the unlovable. To forgive means
pardoning the unpardonable. Faith means believing the
unbelievable. Hope means hoping when everything seems
hopeless.
Gilbert K. Chesterton (1874-1936, British Author)

39 No winter lasts forever; no spring skips it's turn.
Hal Borland (1900-1978, American Writer)

40 Hope is a bad thing. It means that you are not what you
want to be. It means that part of you is dead, if not all of
you. It means that you entertain illusions. It's a sort of
spiritual clap, I should say.
Henry Miller (1891-1980, American Author)

41 Hope is the struggle of the soul, breaking loose from what
is perishable, and attesting her eternity.
Herman Melville (1819-1891, American Author)

42 What can I know? What ought I to do? What can I hope?
Immanuel Kant (1724-1804, German Philosopher)

43 He gains a great deal who loses a vain hope.
Italian Proverb

44 Hope is the last to abandon the unhappy.
Italian Proverb

45 Hope is the feeling you have that the feeling you have isn't
permanent.
Jean Kerr (1923-, American Author, Playwright)

46 My only hope lies in my despair.
Jean Racine (1639-1699, French Dramatist)

47 Hold your head high, stick your chest out. You can make it.
It gets dark sometimes, but morning comes. Keep hope
alive.
*Jesse Jackson (1941-, American Clergyman, Civil Rights
Leader)*

48 Don't wish it were easier, wish you were better.
*Jim Rohn (American Businessman, Author, Speaker,
Philosopher)*

49 Those who hope for no other life are dead even for this.
*Johann Wolfgang Von Goethe (1749-1832, German Poet,
Dramatist, Novelist)*

50 In all things it is better to hope than to despair.
*Johann Wolfgang Von Goethe (1749-1832, German Poet,
Dramatist, Novelist)*

51 Every parent is at some time the father of the unreturned
prodigal, with nothing to do but keep his house open to
hope.
John Ciardi (1916-1986, American Teacher, Poet, Writer)

52 Men and women are limited not by the place of their birth,
not by the color of their skin, but by the size of their hope.
*John Johnson (American Businessman, Founder of Johnson
Publishing)*

53 Where no hope is left, is left no fear.
John Milton (1608-1674, British Poet)

54 He who does not hope to win has already lost.
Jose Joaquin Olmedo

55 If we hope for what we are not likely to possess, we act and think in vain, and make life a greater dream and shadow than it really is.
Joseph Addison (1672-1719, British Essayist, Poet, Statesman)

56 There is a crack in everything, that's how the light gets in.
Leonard Cohen (1934-, Canadian-born American Musician, Songwriter, Singer)

57 But what is Hope? Nothing but the paint on the face of Existence; the least touch of truth rubs it off, and then we see what a hollow-cheeked harlot we have got hold of.
Lord Byron (1788-1824, British Poet)

58 To the sick, while there is life there is hope.
Marcus T. Cicero (106-43 BC, Great Roman Orator, Politician)

59 Hope is the most sensitive part of a poor wretch's soul; whoever raises it only to torment him is behaving like the executioners in Hell who, they say, incessantly renew old wounds and concentrate their attention on that area of it that is already lacerated.
Marquis De Sade (1740-1814, French Author)

60 In our sad condition our only consolation is the expectancy of another life. Here below all is incomprehensible.
Martin Luther (1483-1546, German Leader of the Protestant Reformation)

61 We must accept finite disappointment, but never lose infinite hope.
Martin Luther King Jr. (1929-1968, American Black Leader, Nobel Prize Winner, 1964)

62 Still bent to make some port he knows not where, still standing for some false impossible shore.
Matthew Arnold (1822-1888, British Poet, Critic)

63 Hopes are but the dreams of those that wake.
Matthew Prior (1664-1721, British Diplomat, Poet)

64 There is hope for all of us. Well, anyway, if you don't die you live through it, day in, day out.
May L. Becker

65 My great hope is to laugh as much as I cry; to get my work done and try to love somebody and have the courage to accept the love in return.
Maya Angelou (1928-, African-American poet, Writer, Performer)

66 The phoenix hope, can wing her way through the desert skies, and still defying fortune's spite; revive from ashes and rise.
Miguel De Cervantes (1547-1616, Spanish Novelist, Dramatist, Poet)

67 The safest hope is in heaven.
Motto

68 Man is a victim of dope in the incurable form of hope.
Ogden Nash (1902-1971, American Humorous Poet)

69 The hours that we pass with happy prospects in view are more pleasing than those crowned with success.
Oliver Goldsmith (1728-1774, Anglo-Irish Author, Poet, Playwright)

70 There is no medicine like hope, no incentive so great, and no tonic so powerful as expectation of something tomorrow.
Orison Swett Marden (1850-1924, American Author, Founder of Success Magazine)

71 Take hope from the heart of man and you make him a beast of prey.
Ouida (1838-1908, British Writer)

72 My hopes are not always realized, but I always hope.
Ovid (43 BC-18 AD, Roman Poet)

73 Cold hopes swarm like worms within our living clay.
Percy Bysshe Shelley (1792-1822, British Poet)

74 I've found that the chief difficulty for most people was to realize that they had really heard new things: that is things that they had never heard before. They kept translating what they heard into their habitual language. They had ceased to hope and believe there might be anything new.
Peter Demianovich Ouspensky (1878-1947, Russian Philosopher)

75 A misty morning does not signify a cloudy day.
Proverb

76 Quit not certainty for hope.
Proverb

77 Man partly is and wholly hopes to be.
Robert Browning (1812-1889, British Poet)

78 Hope is the only universal liar who never loses his reputation for veracity.
Robert Green Ingersoll (1833-1899, American Orator, Lawyer)

79 Let your hopes, not your hurts, shape your future.
Robert H. Schuller (1926-, American Minister (Crystal Cathedral), Author, Social Leader)

80 Though you are disappointed is hope; never let hope fail you! Though one door is shut, there are thousands still open to you.
Ruckett

81 Hope is itself a species of happiness, and, perhaps, the chief happiness which this world affords: but, like all other pleasures immoderately enjoyed, the excesses of hope must be expiated by pain; and expectations improperly indulged must end in disappointment.
Samuel Johnson (1709-1784, British Author)

82 The natural flights of the human mind are not from pleasure to pleasure, but from hope to hope.
Samuel Johnson (1709-1784, British Author)

83 Nothing is more hopeless than a scheme of merriment.
Samuel Johnson (1709-1784, British Author)

84 Hope is the companion of power, and mother of success; for who so hopes strongly has within him the gift of miracles.
Samuel Smiles (1812-1904, Scottish Author)

85 Were it not for hope the heart would break.
Scottish Proverb

86 Who can hope for nothing, should despair for nothing.
Seneca (4 BC-65 AD, Spanish-born Roman Statesman, philosopher)

87 The secret of the true love of work is the hope of success in that work. It is not for the money reward, for the time spent, or for the skill exercised, but for the successful result in the accomplishment of the work itself.
Sidney A. Weltmer

88 Ah, Hope! what would life be, stripped of thy encouraging smiles, that teach us to look behind the dark clouds of to-day, for the golden beams that are to gild the morrow.
Susanna Moodie (1803-1885, Canadian Author)

89 Hope is the poor man's bread.
Thales of Miletus (640-546 BC, Semitic Founder of Greek Philosophy, Sciences)

90 Hope is a pleasant acquaintance, but an unsafe friend.
Thomas C. Haliburton (1796-1865, Canadian Jurist, Author)

91 If it were not for hopes, the heart would break.
Thomas Fuller (1608-1661, British Clergyman, Author)

92 Hope is definitely not the same thing as optimism. It is not the conviction that something will turn out well, but the certainty that something makes sense, regardless of how it turns out.
Vaclav Havel (1936-, Czech Playwright, President)

93 Hope on, and save yourself for prosperous times.
Virgil (70-19 BC, Roman Poet)

94 Hope, the patent medicine for disease, disaster, sin.
Wallace Rice (1859-1939, American Poet, Editor)

95 The darkest day, If you live till tomorrow will have past away.
William Cowper (1731-1800, British Poet)

96 To give a generous hope to a man of his own nature, is to enrich him immeasurably.
William Ellery Channing (1780-1842, American Unitarian Minister, Author)

97 Hope is the best possession. None are completely wretched but those who are without hope. Few are reduced so low as that.
William Hazlitt (1778-1830, British Essayist)

98 The miserable have no other medicine but only hope.
William Shakespeare (1564-1616, British Poet, Playwright, Actor)

HORROR

1 I think of horror films as art, as films of confrontation. Films that make you confront aspects of your own life that are difficult to face. Just because you're making a horror film doesn't mean you can't make an artful film.
David Cronenberg (1943-, Canadian Filmmaker)

2 I don't believe in evil, I believe only in horror. In nature there is no evil, only an abundance of horror: the plagues and the blights and the ants and the maggots.
Isak Dinesen (American Author)

3 One might say that the true subject of the horror genre is the struggle for recognition of all that our civilization represses and oppresses.
Robin Wood

4 Where there is no imagination there is no horror.
Sir Arthur Conan Doyle (1859-1930, British Author, "Sherlock Holmes")

HORSES

1 I can make a General in five minutes but a good horse is hard to replace.
Abraham Lincoln (1809-1865, Sixteenth President of the USA)

2 They say Princes learn no art truly, but the art of horsemanship. The reason is, the brave beast is no flatterer. He will throw a prince as soon as his groom.
Ben Johnson (1573-1637, British Dramatist, Poet)

3 My beautiful, my beautiful! That standest meekly by, with thy proudly-arched and glossy neck, and dark and fiery eye!
Caroline Sheridan Norton

4 The horse, the horse! The symbol of surging potency and power of movement, of action, in man.
D. H. Lawrence (1885-1930, British Author)

5 Go anywhere in England where there are natural, wholesome, contented, and really nice English people; and what do you always find? That the stables are the real center of the household.
George Bernard Shaw (1856-1950, Irish-born British Dramatist)

6 A horse is dangerous at both ends and uncomfortable in the middle.
Ian Fleming (1908-1964, British Writer and Journalist, "James Bond")

7 I've often said there's nothing better for the inside of a man than the outside of a horse.
Ronald Reagan (1911-, Fortieth President of the USA, Actor)

8   It takes a good deal of physical courage to ride a horse. This, however, I have. I get it at about forty cents a flask, and take it as required.
Stephen B. Leacock (1869-1944, Canadian Humorist, Economist)

HOSPITALITY

1   Nowadays the host does not admit you to his hearth, but has got the mason to build one for yourself somewhere in his alley, and hospitality is the art of keeping you at the greatest distance.
Henry David Thoreau (1817-1862, American Essayist, Poet, Naturalist)

2   I'm sure I don't know half the people who come to my house. Indeed, from all I hear, I shouldn't like to.
Oscar Wilde (1856-1900, British Author, Wit)

3   We'll teach you to drink deep ere you depart.
William Shakespeare (1564-1616, British Poet, Playwright, Actor)

4   I have heard people eat most heartily of another man's meat, that is, what they do not pay for.
William Wycherley (1640-1716, British Dramatist)

HOSPITALS

1   I would rather be kept alive in the efficient if cold altruism of a large hospital than expire in a gush of warm sympathy in a small one.
Aneurin Bevan (1897-1960, British Labor Politician)

2   How many desolate creatures on the earth have learnt the simple dues of fellowship and social comfort, in a hospital.
Elizabeth Barrett Browning (1806-1861, British Poet)

3   The sick man must follow his illness to the place where it is treated. He is set aside in one of the technical and secret zones (hospitals, prisons, refuse dumps) which relieve the living of everything that might hinder the chain of production and consumption, and which repair and select what can be sent back up to the surface of progress.
Michel De Certeau (French Writer)

4   A Hospital is no place to be sick.
Samuel Goldwyn (1882-1974, American Film Producer, Founder, MGM)

5   We achieve "active" mastery over illness and death by delegating all responsibility for their management to physicians, and by exiling the sick and the dying to hospitals. But hospitals serve the convenience of staff not patients: we cannot be properly ill in a hospital, nor die in one decently; we can do so only among those who love and value us. The result is the institutionalized dehumanization of the ill, characteristic of our age.
Thomas Szasz (1920-, American Psychiatrist)

HOSTAGES

1   Hostage is a crucifying aloneness. It is a silent, screaming slide into the bowels of ultimate despair. Hostage is a man hanging by his fingernails over the edge of chaos, feeling his fingers slowly straightening. Hostage is the humiliating stripping away of every sense and fiber of body and mind and spirit that make us what we are. Hostage is a mutant creation filled with fear, self-loathing, guilt and death-wishing. But he is a man, a rare, unique and beautiful creation of which these things are no part.
Brian Keenan

2   Neither dead nor alive, the hostage is suspended by an incalculable outcome. It is not his destiny that awaits for him, nor his own death, but anonymous chance, which can only seem to him something absolutely arbitrary. He is in a state of radical emergency, of virtual extermination.
Jean Baudrillard (French Postmodern Philosopher, Writer)

3   We are all hostages, and we are all terrorists. This circuit has replaced that other one of masters and slaves, the dominating and the dominated, the exploiters and the exploited. It is worse than the one it replaces, but at least it liberates us from liberal nostalgia and the ruses of history.
Jean Baudrillard (French Postmodern Philosopher, Writer)

4   If I were to be taken hostage, I would not plead for release nor would I want my government to be blackmailed. I think certain government officials, industrialists and celebrated persons should make it clear they are prepared to be sacrificed if taken hostage. If that were done, what gain would there be for terrorists in taking hostages?
Margaret Mead (1901-1978, American Anthropologist)

5   People are capable of doing an awful lot when they have no choice and I had no choice. Courage is when you have choices.
Terry Anderson

6   Freeing hostages is like putting up a stage set, which you do with the captors, agreeing on each piece as you slowly put it together; then you leave an exit through which both the captor and the captive can walk with sincerity and dignity.
Terry Waite (1939-, Consultant and Former Hostage, Born in Bollington, Cheshire)

HOTELS

1   I've always thought a hotel ought to offer optional small animals. I mean a cat to sleep on your bed at night, or a dog of some kind to act pleased when you come in. You ever notice how a hotel room feels so lifeless?
Anne Tyler

2   A writer is in danger of allowing his talent to dull who lets more than a year go past without finding himself in his rightful place of composition, the small single unluxurious "retreat" of the twentieth century, the hotel bedroom.
Cyril Connolly (1903-1974, British Critic)

3 Doorman -- a genius who can open the door of your car with one hand, help you in with the other, and still have one left for the tip.
Dorothy Kilgallen

4 Of course great hotels have always been social ideas, flawless mirrors to the particular societies they service.
Joan Didion (1934-, American Essayist)

5 The hotel was once where things coalesced, where you could meet both townspeople and travelers. Not so in a motel. No matter how you build it, the motel remains the haunt of the quick and dirty, where the only locals are Chamber of Commerce boys every fourth Thursday. Who ever heard the returning traveler exclaim over one of the great motels of the world he stayed in? Motels can be big, but never grand.
William Trogdon (1939-, American Author)

HOUSEWORK

1 Housework is work directly opposed to the possibility of human self-actualization.
Ann Oakley (1944-, British Sociologist, Author)

2 The suburban housewife -- she was the dream image of the young American women and the envy, it was said, of women all over the world. The American housewife -- freed by science and labor-saving appliances from the drudgery, the dangers of childbirth, and the illnesses of her grandmother had found true feminine fulfillment.
Betty Friedan (1921-, American Feminist Writer)

3 Now, as always, the most automated appliance in a household is the mother.
Beverly Jones (1927-, American Feminist Writer)

4 The labor of women in the house, certainly, enables men to produce more wealth than they otherwise could; and in this way women are economic factors in society. But so are horses.
Charlotte P. Gillman (1860-1935, American Feminist and Writer)

5 For a woman to get a rewarding sense of total creation by way of the multiple monotonous chores that are her daily lot would be as irrational as for an assembly line worker to rejoice that he had created an automobile because he tightened a bolt.
Edith Mendel Stern

6 The works of women are symbolical. We sew, sew, prick our fingers, dull our sight, producing what? A pair of slippers, sir, to put on when you're weary -- or a stool. To stumble over and vex you... "curse that stool!" Or else at best, a cushion, where you lean and sleep, and dream of something we are not, but would be for your sake. Alas, alas! This hurts most, this... that, after all, we are paid the worth of our work, perhaps.
Elizabeth Barrett Browning (1806-1861, British Poet)

7 Perhaps all artists were, in a sense, housewives: tenders of the earth household.
Erica Jong (1942-, American Author)

8 I hate housework! You make the beds, you do the dishes -- and six months later you have to start all over again.
Joan Rivers (1933-, American Comedian, Talk Show Host, Actress)

9 When it comes to housework the one thing no book of household management can ever tell you is how to begin. Or maybe I mean why.
Katharine Whitehorn (1926-, British Journalist)

10 Housekeeping ain't no joke.
Louisa May Alcott (1832-1888, American Author)

11 Each home has been reduced to the bare essentials -- to barer essentials than most primitive people would consider possible. Only one woman's hands to feed the baby, answer the telephone, turn off the gas under the pot that is boiling over, soothe the older child who has broken a toy, and open both doors at once. She is a nutritionist, a child psychologist, an engineer, a production manager, an expert buyer, all in one. Her husband sees her as free to plan her own time, and envies her; she sees him as having regular hours and envies him.
Margaret Mead (1901-1978, American Anthropologist)

12 The labor of keeping house is labor in its most naked state, for labor is toil that never finishes, toil that has to be begun again the moment it is completed, toil that is destroyed and consumed by the life process.
Mary Mccarthy (1912-1989, American Author, Critic)

13 Man is made for something better than disturbing dirt.
Oscar Wilde (1856-1900, British Author, Wit)

14 Cleaning your house while your kids are still growing is like shoveling the walk before it stops snowing.
Phyllis Diller (1861-1951, American Columnist)

15 I make no secret of the fact that I would rather lie on a sofa than sweep beneath it. But you have to be efficient if you're going to be lazy.
Shirley Conran (1932-, British Designer, Journalist)

16 You all know that even when women have full rights, they still remain fatally downtrodden because all housework is left to them. In most cases housework is the most unproductive, the most barbarous and the most arduous work a woman can do. It is exceptionally petty and does not include anything that would in any way promote the development of the woman.
Vladimir Ilyich Lenin (1870-1924, Russian Revolutionary Leader)

HUMAN FELLOWSHIP

1 The common erotic project of destroying women makes it possible for men to unite into a brotherhood; this project is the only firm and trustworthy groundwork for cooperation among males and all male bonding is based on it.
Andrea Dworkin (1946-, American Feminist Critic)

2   One can be a brother only in something. Where there is no tie that binds men, men are not united but merely lined up.
Antoine De Saint-Exupery (1900-1944, French Aviator, Writer)

3   The principle of the brotherhood of man is narcissistic... for the grounds for that love have always been the assumption that we ought to realize that we are the same the whole world over.
Germaine Greer (1939-, Australian Feminist Writer)

4   I feel that the Godhead is broken up like the bread at the Supper, and that we are the pieces. Hence this infinite fraternity of feeling.
Herman Melville (1819-1891, American Author)

5   The great universal family of men is a utopia worthy of the most mediocre logic.
Isidore Ducasse Lautreamont (1846-1870, French Author, Poet)

6   The ideal of brotherhood of man, the building of the Just City, is one that cannot be discarded without lifelong feelings of disappointment and loss. But, if we are to live in the real world, discard it we must. Its very nobility makes the results of its breakdown doubly horrifying, and it breaks down, as it always will, not by some external agency but because it cannot work.
Kingsley Amis (1922-1995, British Novelist)

7   I have a dream that one day on the red hills of Georgia the sons of former slaves and the sons of former slave owners will be able to sit down together at the table of brotherhood.
Martin Luther King Jr. (1929-1968, American Black Leader, Nobel Prize Winner, 1964)

8   Nothing is more repugnant to me than brotherly feelings grounded in the common baseness people see in one another.
Milan Kundera (1929-, Czech Author, Critic)

9   We must love one another, yes, yes, that's all true enough, but nothing says we have to like each other. It may be the very recognition of all men as our brothers that accounts for the sibling rivalry, and even enmity, we have toward so many of them.
Peter De Vries (1910-, American Author)

HUMAN NATURE

1   Two things are infinite: the universe and human stupidity; and I'm not sure about the universe.
Albert Einstein (1879-1955, German-born American Physicist)

2   It is human nature to think wisely and act foolishly.
Anatole France (1844-1924, French Writer)

3   It is not human nature we should accuse but the despicable conventions that pervert it.
Denis Diderot (1713-1784, French Philosopher)

4   Now I believe I can hear the philosophers protesting that it can only be misery to live in folly, illusion, deception and ignorance, but it isn't --it's human.
Desiderius Erasmus (1466-1536, Dutch Humanist)

5   Poor human nature, what horrible crimes have been committed in thy name!
Emma Goldman (1869-1940, American Anarchist)

6   What is called an acute knowledge of human nature is mostly nothing but the observer's own weaknesses reflected back from others.
Georg C. Lichtenberg (1742-1799, German Physicist, Satirist)

7   There is nothing that can be changed more completely than human nature when the job is taken in hand early enough.
George Bernard Shaw (1856-1950, Irish-born British Dramatist)

8   The nature of peoples is first crude, then severe, then benign, then delicate, finally dissolute.
Giambattista Vico (1688-1744, Italian Philosopher, Historian)

9   Man has demonstrated that he is master of everything -- except his own nature.
Henry Miller (1891-1980, American Author)

10   The man of power is ruined by power, the man of money by money, the submissive man by subservience, the pleasure seeker by pleasure.
Hermann Hesse (1877-1962, German-born Swiss Novelist, Poet)

11   There is an electric fire in human nature tending to purify -- so that among these human creatures there is continually some birth of new heroism. The pity is that we must wonder at it, as we should at finding a pearl in rubbish.
John Keats (1795-1821, British Poet)

12   Give a small boy a hammer and he will find that everything he encounters needs pounding.
Kalan

13   I have never, in all my various travels, seen but two sorts of people I mean men and women, who always have been, and ever will be, the same. The same vices and the same follies have been the fruit of all ages, though sometimes under different names.
Lady Mary Wortley Montagu (1689-1762, British Society Figure, Letter Writer)

14   There is a great deal of human nature in people.
Mark Twain (1835-1910, American Humorist, Writer)

15   The principle that human nature, in its psychological aspects, is nothing more than a product of history and given social relations removes all barriers to coercion and manipulation by the powerful.
Noam Chomsky (1928-, American Linguist, Political Activist)

711

16 The only thing that one really knows about human nature is that it changes. Change is the one quality we can predicate of it. The systems that fail are those that rely on the permanency of human nature, and not on its growth and development. The error of Louis XIV was that he thought human nature would always be the same. The result of his error was the French Revolution. It was an admirable result.
Oscar Wilde (1856-1900, British Author, Wit)

17 Nature is trying very hard to make us succeed, but nature does not depend on us. We are not the only experiment.
R. Buckminster Fuller (1895-1983, American Inventor, Designer, Poet, Philosopher)

18 We are all murderers and prostitutes --no matter to what culture, society, class, nation one belongs, no matter how normal, moral, or mature, one takes oneself to be.
R. D. Laing (1927-1989, British Psychiatrist)

19 Human nature is not of itself vicious.
Thomas Paine (1737-1809, Anglo-American Political Theorist, Writer)

20 Really I don't like human nature unless all candied over with art.
Virginia Woolf (1882-1941, British Novelist, Essayist)

21 There seems to be some perverse human characteristic that likes to make easy things difficult.
Warren Buffett (1930-, American Investment Entrepreneur)

22 My nature is subdued to what it works in, like the dyer's hand.
William Shakespeare (1564-1616, British Poet, Playwright, Actor)

HUMAN RIGHTS

1 The demand for equal rights in every vocation of life is just and fair; but, after all, the most vital right is the right to love and be loved.
Emma Goldman (1869-1940, American Anarchist)

2 Words like "freedom," "justice," "democracy" are not common concepts; on the contrary, they are rare. People are not born knowing what these are. It takes enormous and, above all, individual effort to arrive at the respect for other people that these words imply.
James Baldwin (1924-1987, American Author)

3 America did not invent human rights. In a very real sense... human rights invented America.
Jimmy Carter (1924-, American Statesman, 39th President)

4 In the old times men carried out their rights for themselves as they lived, but nowadays every baby seems born with a social manifesto in its mouth much bigger than itself.
Oscar Wilde (1856-1900, British Author, Wit)

5 Most people, no doubt, when they espouse human rights, make their own mental reservations about the proper application of the word "human."
Suzanne Lafollette (1893-1983, American Feminist, Writer)

6 Close by the Rights of Man, at the least set beside them, are the Rights of the Spirit.
Victor Hugo (1802-1885, French Poet, Dramatist, Novelist)

HUMAN SPIRIT

1 Man never made any material as resilient as the human spirit.
Bern Williams

2 There are incalculable resources in the human spirit, once it has been set free.
Hubert H. Humphrey (1911-1978, American Democratic Politician, Vice President)

3 I am certain that after the dust of centuries has passed over our cities, we, too, will be remembered not for victories or defeats in battle or in politics, but for our contribution to the human spirit.
John F. Kennedy (1917-1963, Thirty-fifth President of the USA)

4 The human spirit is your specifically human dimension and contains abilities other creatures do not have. Every human is spiritual; in fact, spirit is the essence of being human. You have a body that may become ill; you have a psyche that may become disturbed. But the spirit is what you are. It is your healthy core.
Joseph Fabry (1909 - ? Austrian Born American Professor, Lecturer, Author)

5 The human spirit is so great a thing that no man can express it; could we rightly comprehend the mind of man nothing would be impossible to us upon the earth.
Philipus A. Paracelsus (German Physician and Chemist)

HUMANISM

1 Humanism, it seems, is almost impossible in America where material progress is part of the national romance whereas in Europe such progress is relished because it feels nice.
Paul West

2 Humanism was not wrong in thinking that truth, beauty, liberty, and equality are of infinite value, but in thinking that man can get them for himself without grace.
Simone Weil (1910-1943, French Philosopher, Mystic)

3 When men can no longer be theists, they must, if they are civilized, become humanists.
Walter Lippmann (1889-1974, American Journalist)

HUMANKIND

1 God must love the common man, he made so many of them.
Abraham Lincoln (1809-1865, Sixteenth President of the USA)

2 Humanity is the virtue of a woman, generosity that of a man.
Adam Smith (1723-1790, Scottish Economist)

3 Man is an animal that makes bargains; no other animal does this--one dog does not change a bone with another.
Adam Smith (1723-1790, Scottish Economist)

4 Mankind are animals that makes bargains, no other animal does this.
Adam Smith (1723-1790, Scottish Economist)

5 How is it possible that a being with such sensitive jewels as the eyes, such enchanted musical instruments as the ears, and such fabulous arabesque of nerves as the brain can experience itself anything less than a god.
Alan W. Watts (1915-1973, British-born American Philosopher, Author)

6 Considered logically this concept is not identical with the totality of sense impressions referred to; but it is an arbitrary creation of the human (or animal) mind.
Albert Einstein (1879-1955, German-born American Physicist)

7 We cannot despair of humanity, since we ourselves are human beings.
Albert Einstein (1879-1955, German-born American Physicist)

8 A human being is part of the whole, called by us 'universe,' a part limited in time and space. He experiences himself, his thoughts and feelings, as something separate from the rest -- a kind of optical delusion of consciousness. This delusion is a kind of prison for us, restricting us to our personal desires and to affection for a few persons nearest to us. Our task must be to free ourselves from this prison by widening our circle of compassion to embrace all living creatures and the whole of nature in its beauty.
Albert Einstein (1879-1955, German-born American Physicist)

9 To the eyes of a god, mankind must appear as a species of bacteria which multiply and become progressively virulent whenever they find themselves in a congenial culture, and whose activity diminishes until they disappear completely as soon as proper measures are taken to sterilize them.
Aleister Crowley (1875-1947, British Occultist)

10 If, presume not to God to scan; The proper study of Mankind is Man. Plac'd on this isthmus of a middle state, a being darkly wise, and rudely great.
Alexander Pope (1688-1744, British Poet, Critic, Translator)

11 Of all the ways of defining man, the worst is the one which makes him out to be a rational animal.
Anatole France (1844-1924, French Writer)

12 Man is more interesting than men. God made him and not them in his image. Each one is more precious than all.
Andre Gide (1869-1951, French Author)

13 We say nothing essential about the cathedral when we speak of its stones. We say nothing essential about Man when we seek to define him by the qualities of men.
Antoine De Saint-Exupery (1900-1944, French Aviator, Writer)

14 Man is by nature a political animal.
Aristotle (384-322 BC, Greek Philosopher)

15 Either a beast or a god.
Aristotle (384-322 BC, Greek Philosopher)

16 The best security for civilization is the dwelling, and upon properly appointed and becoming dwellings depends, more than anything else, the improvement of mankind.
Benjamin Disraeli (1804-1881, British Statesman, Prime Minister)

17 Ye shall be as gods, knowing good and evil. [Genesis 3:5]
Bible (Sacred Scriptures of Christians and Judaism)

18 We are called to be architects of the future, not its victims.
Buckminster Fuller (American Engineer, Inventor, Designer, Architect "Geodesic Dome")

19 Humans are amphibians -- half spirit and half animal. As spirits they belong to the eternal world, but as animals they inhabit time.
C. S. Lewis (1898-1963, British Academic, Writer, Christian Apologist)

20 The race of man, while sheep in credulity, are wolves for conformity.
Carl Van Doren (1885-1950, American Critic, Biographer)

21 I love mankind; it's people I can't stand.
Charles M. Schultz (1922-, American Cartoonist, Creator of "Peanuts")

22 The true grandeur of humanity is in moral elevation, sustained, enlightened and decorated by the intellect of man.
Charles Sumner (1811-1874, American Statesman)

23 The age of chivalry has gone; the age of humanity has come.
Charles Sumner (1811-1874, American Statesman)

24 Man lives consciously for himself, but is an unconscious instrument in the attainment of the historic, universal, aims of humanity.
Count Leo Tolstoy (1828-1910, Russian Novelist, Philosopher)

25 There are two kinds of men who never amount to much -- those who cannot do what they are told and those who can do nothing else.
Cyrus H. K Curtis

26 The world of men is dreaming, it has gone mad in its sleep, and a snake is strangling it, but it can't wake up.
D. H. Lawrence (1885-1930, British Author)

27 Consider your breed; you were not made to live like beasts, but to follow virtue and knowledge.
Dante (Alighieri) (1265-1321, Italian Philosopher, Poet)

28 There are two distinctive classes of people today, those who have personal computers, and those who have several thousand extra dollars apiece.
Dave Barry (American Humorist, Author)

29 We are, to put it mildly, in a mess, and there is a strong chance that we shall have exterminated ourselves by the end of the century. Our only consolation will have to be that, as a species, we have had an exciting term of office.
Desmond Morris (1928-, British Anthropologist)

30 Man who is he? Too bad, to be the work of God: Too good for the work of chance!
Doris Lessing (1919-, British Novelist)

31 In the beginning the Universe was created. This has made a lot of people very angry and has been widely regarded as a bad move.
Douglas Adams (Born 1952, British Science Fiction Writer)

32 What is the use of this fuss about morality when the issue only involves a horse? The first and most difficult teaching of civilization concerns man's behavior to his inferiors. Make humanity gentle or reasonable toward animals, and strife or injustice between human beings would speedily terminate.
Dr Edward Mayhew

33 Humanity I love you because when you're hard up you pawn your intelligence to buy a drink
E.E. (Edward. E.) Cummings (1894-1962, American Poet)

34 The law of humanity ought to be composed of the past, the present, and the future, that we bear within us; whoever possesses but one of these terms, has but a fragment of the law of the moral world.
Edgar Quinet (1803-1875, French Poet, Historian, Politician)

35 Mind and spirit together make up that which separates us from the rest of the animal world, that which enables a man to know the truth and that which enables him to die for the truth.
Edith Hamilton (1867-1963, American Classical Scholar, Translator)

36 Though man is the only beast that can write, he has small reason to be proud of it. When he utters something that is wise it is nothing that the river horse does not know, and most of his creations are the result of accident.
Edward Dahlberg (1900-1977, American Author, Critic)

37 A human being is a single being. Unique and unrepeatable.
Eileen Caddy (American Spiritual Writer)

38 One machine can do the work of fifty ordinary men. No machine can do the work of one extraordinary man.
Elbert Hubbard (1859-1915, American Author, Publisher)

39 There is no doubt: the study of man is just beginning, at the same time that his end is in sight.
Elias Canetti (1905-, Austrian Novelist, Philosopher)

40 The Goddamn human race deserves itself, and as far as I'm concerned it can have it.
Elizabeth Janeway (1913-, American Author, Critic)

41 Man was nature's mistake --she neglected to finish him -- and she has never ceased paying for her mistake.
Eric Hoffer (1902-1983, American Author, Philosopher)

42 Man, became man through work, who stepped out of the animal kingdom as transformer of the natural into the artificial, who became therefore the magician, man the creator of social reality, will always stay the great magician, will always be Prometheus bringing fire from heaven to earth, will always be Orpheus enthralling nature with his music. Not until humanity itself dies will art die.
Ernst Fischer (1899-1972, Austrian Editor, Poet, Critic)

43 Our humanity is a poor thing, except for the divinity that stirs within us.
Francis Bacon (1561-1626, British Philosopher, Essayist, Statesman)

44 I teach you the Superman. Man is something that should be overcome.
Friedrich Nietzsche (1844-1900, German Philosopher)

45 Man is no longer an artist, he has become a work of art.
Friedrich Nietzsche (1844-1900, German Philosopher)

46 It is peculiar to mankind to transcend mankind.
Friedrich Schlegel (1772-1829, German Philosopher, Critic, Writer)

47 To be human is to keep rattling the bars of the cage of existence hollering, "What's it for?"
Fulghum Robert (American Author)

48 Man only likes to count his troubles, but he does not count his joys.
Fyodor Dostoevski (1821-1881, Russian Novelist)

49 That man is the noblest creature may also be inferred from the fact that no other creature has yet contested this claim.
Georg C. Lichtenberg (1742-1799, German Physicist, Satirist)

50 Physically there is nothing to distinguish human society from the farm-yard except that children are more troublesome and costly than chickens and calves and that men and women are not so completely enslaved as farm stock.
George Bernard Shaw (1856-1950, Irish-born British Dramatist)

51 Human beings are the only animals of which I am thoroughly and cravenly afraid.
George Bernard Shaw (1856-1950, Irish-born British Dramatist)

52 The simplest single-celled organism oscillates to a number of different frequencies, at the atomic, molecular, sub-cellular, and cellular levels. Microscopic movies of these organisms are striking for the ceaseless, rhythmic pulsation that is revealed. In an organism as complex as a human being, the frequencies of oscillation and the interactions between those frequencies are multitudinous.
George Leonard

53 After all there is but one race -- humanity.
George Moore (1852-1933, Irish Writer)

54 Man is an exception, whatever else he is. If he is not the image of God, then he is a disease of the dust. If it is not true that a divine being fell, then we can only say that one of the animals went entirely off its head.
Gilbert K. Chesterton (1874-1936, British Author)

55 I love men, not for what unites them, but for what divides them, and I want to know most of all what gnaws at their hearts.
Guillaume Apollinaire (1880-1918, Italian-born French Poet, Critic)

56 Have you ever watched a crab on the shore crawling backward in search of the Atlantic Ocean, and missing? That's the way the mind of man operates.
H. L. Mencken (1880-1956, American Editor, Author, Critic, Humorist)

57 Man is a beautiful machine that works very badly.
H. L. Mencken (1880-1956, American Editor, Author, Critic, Humorist)

58 The basic fact about human existence is not that it is a tragedy, but that it is a bore. It is not so much a war as an endless standing in line.
H. L. Mencken (1880-1956, American Editor, Author, Critic, Humorist)

59 Man is the unnatural animal, the rebel child of nature, and more and more does he turn himself against the harsh and fitful hand that reared him.
H.G. Wells (1866-1946, British-born American Author)

60 The proper study of mankind is woman.
Henry Brooks Adams (1838 - 1918, American Historian)

61 The man who is forever disturbed about the condition of humanity either has no problems of his own or has refused to face them.
Henry Miller (1891-1980, American Author)

62 The real man is one who always finds excuses for others, but never excuses himself.
Henry Ward Beecher (1813-1887, American Preacher, Orator, Writer)

63 Let me look into a human eye; it is better than to gaze into sea or sky; better than to gaze upon God.
Herman Melville (1819-1891, American Author)

64 What constitutes a real, live human being is more of a mystery than ever these days, and men - - each one of whom is a valuable, unique experiment on the part of nature -- are shot down wholesale.
Hermann Hesse (1877-1962, German-born Swiss Novelist, Poet)

65 It's funny. All you have to do is say something nobody understands and they'll do practically anything you want them to.
Holden Caulfield

66 An effective human being is a whole that is greater than the sum of its parts.
Ida P. Rolf (1896-1979, American Biochemist, Physical Therapist)

67 Out of timber so crooked as that from which man is made nothing entirely straight can be carved.
Immanuel Kant (1724-1804, German Philosopher)

68 Human affairs are not serious, but they have to be taken seriously.
Iris Murdoch (1919-, British Novelist, Philosopher)

69 The human race is a zone of living things that should be defined by tracing its confines.
Italo Calvino (1923-1985, Cuban Writer, Essayist, Journalist)

70 There are realities we all share, regardless of our nationality, language, or individual tastes. As we need food, so do we need emotional nourishment: love, kindness, appreciation, and support from others. We need to understand our environment and our relationship to it. We need to fulfill certain inner hungers: the need for happiness, for peace of mind for wisdom.
J. Donald Walters (American Author, Lecturer, Playwright)

71 The secret of a person's nature lies in their religion and what they really believes about the world and their place in it.
James A. Froude (1818-1894, British Historian)

72 Wild animals never kill for sport. Man is the only one to whom the torture and death of his fellow creatures is amusing in itself.
James A. Froude (1818-1894, British Historian)

73 One has but to observe a community of beavers at work in a stream to understand the loss in his sagacity, balance, co-operation, competence, and purpose which Man has suffered since he rose up on his hind legs. He began to chatter and he developed Reason, Thought, and Imagination, qualities which would get the smartest group of rabbits or orioles in the world into inextricable trouble overnight.
James Thurber (1894-1961, American Humorist, Illustrator)

74 If we consider the superiority of the human species, the size of its brain, its powers of thinking, language and organization, we can say this: were there the slightest possibility that another rival or superior species might appear, on earth or elsewhere, man would use every means at his disposal to destroy it.
Jean Baudrillard (French Postmodern Philosopher, Writer)

75 Man is a useless passion.
Jean-Paul Sartre (1905-1980, French Writer, Philosopher)

76 Mankind is made great or little by its own will.
Johann Friedrich Von Schiller (1759-1805, German Dramatist, Poet, Historian)

77 Man... knows only when he is satisfied and when he suffers, and only his sufferings and his satisfactions instruct him concerning himself, teach him what to seek and what to avoid. For the rest, man is a confused creature; he knows not whence he comes or whither he goes, he knows little of the world, and above all, he knows little of himself.
Johann Wolfgang Von Goethe (1749-1832, German Poet, Dramatist, Novelist)

78 It is well to remember that the entire population of the universe, with one trifling exception, is composed of others.
John Andrew Holmes

79 Man is not only a contributory creature, but a total creature; he does not only make one, but he is all; he is not a piece of the world, but the world itself; and next to the glory of God, the reason why there is a world.
John Donne (1572-1632, British Metaphysical Poet)

80 Our most basic common link is that we all inhabit this planet. We all breathe the same air. We all cherish our children's future. And we are all mortal.
John F. Kennedy (1917-1963, Thirty-fifth President of the USA)

81 Good and evil, reward and punishment, are the only motives to a rational creature: these are the spur and reins whereby all mankind are set on work, and guided.
John Locke (1632-1704, British Philosopher)

82 Man's only true happiness is to live in hope of something to be won by him. Reverence something to be worshipped by him, and love something to be cherished by him, forever.
John Ruskin (1819-1900, British Critic, Social Theorist)

83 No man really knows about other human beings. The best he can do is to suppose that they are like himself.
John Steinbeck (1902-1968, American Author)

84 Man is a substance clad in shadows.
John Sterling (American Sports Announcer)

85 Being reproached for giving to an unworthy person, Aristotle said, "I did not give it to the man, but to humanity.
Johnson

86 As far as many statistical series that are related to activities of mankind are concerned, the date that divides human history into two equal parts is well within living memory. The world of today is as different from the world I was born in as that world was from Julius Caesar s. I was born in the middle of human history, to date, roughly. Almost as much has happened since I was born as happened before.
Kenneth Boulding

87 We all live under the same sky, but we don't all have the same horizon.
Konrad Adenauer (1876-1967, German Statesman)

88 [Three classes of people]: Those who see. Those who see when they are shown. Those who do not see.
Leonardo Da Vinci (1452-1519, Italian Inventor, Architect, Painter, Scientist, Sculptor)

89 Man is born passionate of body, but with an innate though secret tendency to the love of Good in his main-spring of Mind. But God help us all! It is at present a sad jar of atoms.
Lord Byron (1788-1824, British Poet)

90 The history of mankind is the history of ideas.
Ludwig Von Mises

91 As human beings, our greatness lies not so much in being able to remake the world -- that is the myth of the atomic age -- as in being able to remake ourselves.
Mahatma Gandhi (1869-1948, Indian Political, Spiritual Leader)

92 You must not lose faith in humanity. Humanity is an ocean; if a few drops of the ocean are dirty, the ocean does not become dirty.
Mahatma Gandhi (1869-1948, Indian Political, Spiritual Leader)

93 Mark how fleeting and paltry is the estate of man--yesterday in embryo, tomorrow a mummy or ashes. So for the hairsbreadth of time assigned to thee, live rationally, and part with life cheerfully, as drops the ripe olive, extolling the season that bore it and the tree that matured it.
Marcus Antonius (83-30 BC, Roman Triumvir, Related to Julius Caesar)

94 Always observe how ephemeral and worthless human things are. Pass then through this little space of time conformably to nature, and end thy journey in content, just as an olive falls off when it is ripe, blessing nature who produced it, and thanking the tree on which it grew.
Marcus Aurelius (121-80 AD, Roman Emperor, Philosopher)

95 One of the oldest human needs is having someone wonder where you are when you don't come home at night.
Margaret Mead (1901-1978, American Anthropologist)

96 The human race was always interesting and we know by its past that it will always continue so, monotonously.
Mark Twain (1835-1910, American Humorist, Writer)

97 Man is a creature made at the end of the week's work when God was tired.
Mark Twain (1835-1910, American Humorist, Writer)

98 Such is the human race. Often it does seem such a pity that Noah and his party did not miss the boat.
Mark Twain (1835-1910, American Humorist, Writer)

99 If man had created man, he would be ashamed of his performance.
Mark Twain (1835-1910, American Humorist, Writer)

100 There are times when one would like to hang the whole human race, and finish the farce.
Mark Twain (1835-1910, American Humorist, Writer)

101 Mankind must evolve for all human conflict a method which rejects revenge, aggression, and retaliation. The foundation of such a method is love.
Martin Luther King Jr. (1929-1968, American Black Leader, Nobel Prize Winner, 1964)

102 Man is stark mad; he cannot make a flea, and yet he will be making gods by the dozens.
Michel Eyquem De Montaigne (1533-1592, French Philosopher, Essayist)

103 As the archeology of our thought easily shows, man is an invention of recent date. And one perhaps nearing its end.
Michel Foucault (1926-1984, French Essayist, Philosopher)

104 Everyone is as God made him, and often a great deal worse.
Miguel De Cervantes (1547-1616, Spanish Novelist, Dramatist, Poet)

105 Those who live in a world of human beings can only retrace their steps.
Nathalie Sarraute (1902-, Russian Writer)

106 Mankind are earthen jugs with spirits in them.
Nathaniel Hawthorne (1804-1864, American Novelist, Short Story Writer)

107 Of mankind we may say in general they are fickle, hypocritical, and greedy of gain.
Niccolo Machiavelli (1469-1527, Italian Author, Statesman)

108 People can be divided into two classes: those who go ahead and do something, and those who sit still and inquire, why wasn't it done the other way?
Oliver Wendell Holmes (1809-1894, American Author, Wit, Poet)

109 I sometimes think that God in creating man somewhat overestimated his ability.
Oscar Wilde (1856-1900, British Author, Wit)

110 It is because Humanity has never known where it was going that it has been able to find its way.
Oscar Wilde (1856-1900, British Author, Wit)

111 The brotherhood of man is not a mere poet's dream: it is a most depressing and humiliating reality.
Oscar Wilde (1856-1900, British Author, Wit)

112 We ought to think that we are one of the leaves of a tree, and the tree is all humanity. We cannot live without the others, without the tree.
Pablo Casals (1876-1973, Spanish Cellist, Conductor, Composer)

113 We are all cells in the same body of humanity.
Peace Pilgrim (1908-1981, American Peace Activist)

114 Man is a being in search of meaning.
Plato (427-347 BC, Greek Philosopher)

115 Man is a two-legged animal without feathers.
Plato (427-347 BC, Greek Philosopher)

116 All people are a single nation.
Qur'an (Holy Book)

117 Man must realize his own unimportance before he can appreciate his importance.
R. M. Baumgardy

118 The end of the human race will be that it will eventually die of civilization.
Ralph Waldo Emerson (1803-1882, American Poet, Essayist)

119 Man is head, chest and stomach. Each of these animals operates, more often than not, individually. I eat, I feel, I even, although rarely, think. This jungle crawls and teems, is hungry, roars, gets angry, devours itself, and its cacophonic concert does not even stop when you are asleep.
Rene Daumal (1908-1944, French Poet, Critic)

120 A human being should be able to change a diaper, plan an invasion, butcher a hog, cone a ship, design a building, write a sonnet, balance accounts, build a wall, set a bone, comfort the dying, take orders, give orders, cooperate, act alone, solve equations, analyze a new problem, pitch manure, program a computer, cook a tasty meal, fight efficiently, die gallantly.
Robert Heinlein (1907-1988, American Science Fiction Writer)

121 Every man has a sane spot somewhere.
Robert Louis Stevenson (1850-1895, Scottish Essayist, Poet, Novelist)

122 Let us ask ourselves; "What kind of people do we think we are?"
Ronald Reagan (1911-, Fortieth President of the USA, Actor)

123 Man is an ape with possibilities.
Roy Chapman Andrews (1884-1960, American Adventurer, Administrator, Museum Promoter)

124 But remember please, the Law by which we live, we are not built to comprehend a lie, we can neither love nor pity nor forgive. If you make a slip in handling us you die.
Rudyard Kipling (1865-1936, British Author of Prose, Verse)

125 Man is God's highest present development. He is the latest thing in God.
Samuel Butler (1612-1680, British Poet, Satirist)

126 I hate mankind, for I think of myself as one of the best of them, and I know how bad I am.
Samuel Johnson (1709-1784, British Author)

127 Man has, as it were, become a kind of prosthetic God. When he puts on all his auxiliary organs, he is truly magnificent; but those organs have not grown on him and they still give him much trouble at times.
Sigmund Freud (1856-1939, Austrian Physician - Founder of Psychoanalysis)

128 I have found little that is "good" about human beings on the whole. In my experience most of them are trash, no matter whether they publicly subscribe to this or that ethical doctrine or to none at all. That is something that you cannot say aloud, or perhaps even think.
Sigmund Freud (1856-1939, Austrian Physician - Founder of Psychoanalysis)

129 I would suggest that barbarism be considered as a permanent and universal human characteristic which becomes more or less pronounced according to the play of circumstances.
Simone Weil (1910-1943, French Philosopher, Mystic)

130 The course of human history is determined, not by what happens in the skies, but by what takes place in our hearts.
Sir Arthur Kent

131 I wish I loved the Human Race; I wish I loved its silly face; I wish I liked the way it walks; I wish I liked the way it talks; And when I'm introduced to one I wish I thought What Jolly Fun!
Sir Walter Raleigh (1552-1618, British Courtier, Navigator, Writer)

132 On earth there is nothing great but man; in man there is nothing great but mind.
Sir William Hamilton (1730-1803, Scottish Diplomat, Antiquary)

133 When all is done, human life is, at the greatest and the best, but like a froward child, that must be played with and humored a little to keep it quiet till it falls asleep, and then the care is over.
Sir William Temple (1628-1699, British Diplomat, Essayist)

134 I am not an Athenian, nor a Greek, but a citizen of the world.
Socrates (469-399 BC, Greek Philosopher of Athens)

135 Those are the same stars, and that is the same moon, that look down upon your brothers and sisters, and which they see as they look up to them, though they are ever so far away from us, and each other.
Sojourner Truth (1797-1883, American Feminist, Anti-slavery Advocate)

136 We are not human beings on a spiritual journey. We are spiritual beings on a human journey.
Stephen R. Covey (American Speaker, Trainer, Author of "The 7 Habits of Highly Effective People")

137 We're all of us guinea pigs in the laboratory of God. Humanity is just a work in progress.
Tennessee Williams (1914-1983, American Dramatist)

138 I am human and let nothing human be alien to me.
Terence (185-159 BC, Roman Writer of Comedies)

139 In our civilization, men are afraid that they will not be men enough and women are afraid that they might be considered only women.
Theodor Reik (1888-1969, Austrian Psychoanalyst)

140 Man is emphatically a proselytizing creature.
Thomas Carlyle (1795-1881, Scottish Philosopher, Author)

141 In recognizing the humanity of our fellow beings, we pay ourselves the highest tribute.
Thurgood Marshall (1908-1993, American Judge)

142 Humanity has advanced, when it has advanced, not because it has been sober, responsible, and cautious, but because it has been playful, rebellious, and immature.
Tom Robbins (American Author)

143 Man is harder than iron, stronger than stone and more fragile than a rose.
Turkish Proverb

144 Mankind is not a circle with a single center but an ellipse with two focal points of which facts are one and ideas the other.
Victor Hugo (1802-1885, French Poet, Dramatist, Novelist)

145 Human beings, for all their pretensions, have a remarkable propensity for lending themselves to classification somewhere within neatly labeled categories. Even the outrageous exceptions may be classified as outrageous exceptions!
W.J. Reichmann

146 The whole theory of the universe is directed unerringly to one single individual.
Walt Whitman (1819-1892, American Poet)

147 The decay of decency in the modern age, the rebellion against law and good faith, the treatment of human beings as things, as the mere instruments of power and ambition, is without a doubt the consequence of the decay of the belief in man as something more than an animal animated by highly conditioned reflexes and chemical reactions. For, unless man is something more than that, he has no rights that anyone is bound to respect, and there are no limitations upon his conduct which he is bound to obey.
Walter Lippmann (1889-1974, American Journalist)

148 There is nothing on earth divine except humanity.
Walter Savage Landor (1775-1864, British Poet, Essayist)

149 I am a member of the rabble in good standing.
Westbrook Pegler

150 It's great to be great, but it's greater to be human.
Will Rogers (1879-1935, American Humorist, Actor)

151 Cruelty has a Human Heart, And jealousy a Human Face; Terror the Human Form Divine, And secrecy the Human Dress. The Human Dress is forged Iron, The Human Form a Fiery Forge, The Human Face a Furnace seal d, The Human Heart its hungry gorge.
William Blake (1757-1827, British Poet, Painter)

152 What a piece of work is a man! How noble in reason, how infinite in faculty, in form and moving how express and admirable, in action how like an angel, in apprehension how like a god -- the beauty of the world, the paragon of animals!
William Shakespeare (1564-1616, British Poet, Playwright, Actor)

153 Man will occasionally stumble over the truth, but most of the time he will pick himself up and continue on.
Winston Churchill (1874-1965, British Statesman, Prime Minister)

154 If the human race wishes to have a prolonged and indefinite period of material prosperity, they have only got to behave in a peaceful and helpful way toward one another
Winston Churchill (1874-1965, British Statesman, Prime Minister)

HUMILITY

1 No one should be ashamed to admit they are wrong, which is but saying, in other words, that they are wiser today than they were yesterday.
Alexander Pope (1688-1744, British Poet, Critic, Translator)

2 Those who are believed to be most abject and humble are usually most ambitious and envious.
Baruch (Benedict de) Spinoza (1632-1677, Dutch Philosopher and Theologian)

3 Before honor is humility.
Bible (Sacred Scriptures of Christians and Judaism)

4 Do nothing out of selfish ambition or vain conceit, but in humility consider others better than yourselves. [Philippians 2:3]
Bible (Sacred Scriptures of Christians and Judaism)

5 If you would have people speak well of you, then do not speak well of yourself.
Blaise Pascal (1623-1662, French Scientist, Religious Philosopher)

6 The graveyards are full of indispensable men.
Charles De Gaulle (1890-1970, French President during World War II)

7 A modest man is usually admired, if people ever hear of him.
Edgar Watson Howe (1853-1937, American Journalist, Author)

8 The cross is the invincible sanctuary of the humble.
Eli Cass

9 Only those who feel little in the eyes of God, can hope to be mighty in the eyes of men.
Ernest Moritz Arndt (1769-1860, Swedish-born German Poet, Patriot)

10 Humility is no substitute for a good personality.
Fran Lebowitz (1951-, American Journalist)

11 If thou desire the love of God and man, be humble, for the proud heart, as it loves none but itself, is beloved of none but itself. Humility enforces where neither virtue, nor strength, nor reason can prevail.
Francis Quarles (1592-1644, British Poet)

12 Humility is often a false front we employ to gain power over others.
François de La Rochefoucauld (1613-1680, French classical writer)

13 He that humbleth himself wishes to be exalted.
Friedrich Nietzsche (1844-1900, German Philosopher)

14 The proud man counts his newspaper clippings, the humble man his blessings.
Fulton John Sheen (1895-1979, American Roman Catholic Clergyman, Broadcaster)

15 Humility is the only true wisdom by which we prepare our minds for all the possible changes of life.
George Arliss (1868-1946, British Actor)

16 Too much humility is pride.
German Proverb

17 Don't be humble, you're not that great.
Golda Meir (1898-1978, Prime Minister of Israel, 1969-74)

18 Nothing is more humiliating than to see idiots succeed in enterprises we have failed in.
Gustave Flaubert (1821-1880, French Novelist)

19 Humility is like underwear; essential, but indecent if it shows.
Helen Nielsen

20 Humility like the darkness, reveals the heavenly lights.
Henry David Thoreau (1817-1862, American Essayist, Poet, Naturalist)

21 Study the best and highest things that are; but of yourself humble thoughts retain.
Joe Davis (1901-1978, British Billiards and Snooker Champion)

22 The humble and meek are thirsting for blood.
Joe Orton (1933-1967, British Playwright, Actor)

23 One that does not think to highly of himself is more than he thinks.
Johann Wolfgang Von Goethe (1749-1832, German Poet, Dramatist, Novelist)

24 Humility leads to strength and not to weakness. It is the highest form of self-respect to admit mistakes and to make amends for them.
John (Jay) Mccloy (1895-1989, American Lawyer, Government Official)

25 Without humility there can be no humanity.
John Buchan (1875-1940, Scottish Writer, Statesman)

26 The first test of a truly great man is his humility. By humility I don't mean doubt of his powers or hesitation in speaking his opinion, but merely an understanding of the relationship of what he can say and what he can do.
John Ruskin (1819-1900, British Critic, Social Theorist)

27 A man who is at the top is a man who has the habit of getting to the bottom.
Joseph E. Rogers

28 The more humble a man is before God the more he will be exalted; the more humble he is before man, the more he will get rode roughshod.
Josh Billings (1815-1885, American Humorist, Lecturer)

29 Nothing is more intolerable than to have to admit to yourself your own errors.
Ludwig Van Beethoven (1770-1827, German Composer)

30 What makes humility so desirable is the marvelous thing it does to us; it creates in us a capacity for the closest possible intimacy with God.
Monica Baldwin

31 I am the greatest, I said that even before I knew I was.
Muhammad Ali (1942-, American Boxer)

32 When you are as great as I am it is hard to be humble.
Muhammad Ali (1942-, American Boxer)

33 I confess that altruistic and cynically selfish talk seem to me about equally unreal. With all humility, I think whatsoever thy hand findeth to do, do it with thy might, infinitely more important than the vain attempt to love one's neighbor as one's self. If you want to hit a bird on the wing you must have all your will in focus, you must not be thinking about yourself, and equally, you must not be thinking about your neighbor; you must be living with your eye on that bird. Every achievement is a bird on the wing.
Oliver Wendell Holmes Jr. (1841-1935, American Judge)

34 With all humility, I think, "Whatsoever thy hand findeth to do, do it with thy might." Infinitely more important than the vain attempt to love one's neighbor as one's self. If you want to hit a bird on the wing, you must have all your will in focus, you must not be thinking about yourself, and equally, you must not be thinking about your neighbor: you must be living in your eye on that bird. Every achievement is a bird on the wing.
Oliver Wendell Holmes Jr. (1841-1935, American Judge)

35 The humble are in danger when those in power disagree.
Phaedrus (Macedonian Inventor and Writer)

36 We come nearest to the great when we are great in humility.
Rabindranath Tagore (1861-1941, Indian Poet, Philosopher)

37 Many people believe that humility is the opposite of pride, when, in fact, it is a point of equilibrium. The opposite of pride is actually a lack of self esteem. A humble person is totally different from a person who cannot recognize and appreciate himself as part of this worlds marvels
Rabino Nilton Bonder

38 They are proud in humility, proud that they are not proud.
Robert Burton (1576-1640, British Clergyman, Scholar)

39 A vulgar mind is proud in prosperity and humble in adversity. A noble mind is humble in prosperity and proud in adversity.
Ruckett

40 It was pride that changed angels into devils; it is humility that makes men as angels.
St. Augustine (354-430, Numidian-born Bishop of Hippo, Theologian)

41 It is no great thing to be humble when you are brought low; but to be humble when you are praised is a great and rare attainment.
St. Bernard (1090-1153, French Theologian and Reformer)

42 Painful for a person is rebellious independence, only in loving companionship with his associates does a person feel safe: Only in reverently bowing down before the higher does a person feel exalted.
Thomas Carlyle (1795-1881, Scottish Philosopher, Author)

43 Mental toughness is many things. It is humility because it behooves all of us to remember that simplicity is the sign of greatness and meekness is the sign of true strength. Mental toughness is spartanism with qualities of sacrifice, self-denial, dedication. It is fearlessness, and it is love.
Vince Lombardi (1913-1970, American Football Coach)

44 Humility is indeed beatness, a compulsory virtue that no one exhibits unless he has to.
William S. Burroughs (1914-1997, American Writer)

45 Too humble is half proud.
Yiddish Proverb

HUMOR

1 If this is coffee, please bring me some tea; but if this is tea, please bring me some coffee.
Abraham Lincoln (1809-1865, Sixteenth President of the USA)

2 Be simple in words, manners, and gestures. Amuse as well as instruct. If you can make a man laugh, you can make him think and make him like and believe you.
Alfred E. Smith (1873-1944, American Politician)

3 I used to think that everything was just being funny but now I don't know. I mean, how can you tell?
Andy Warhol (1930-, American Artist, Filmmaker)

4 The secret to humor is surprise.
Aristotle (384-322 BC, Greek Philosopher)

5 The absolute truth is the thing that makes people laugh
Carl Reiner (American Director, Actor)

6 Comedy is a tragedy plus time.
Carol Burnett (American Television Comedian)

7 Levity is often less foolish and gravity less wise than each of them appears.
Charles Caleb Colton (1780-1832, British Sportsman Writer)

8 In the end, everything is a gag.
Charlie Chaplin (1889-1977, British Comic Actor, Filmmaker)

9 One never needs their humor as much a when they argue with a fool.
Chinese Proverb

10 Humor has been a fashioning instrument in America, cleaving its way through the national life, holding tenaciously to the spread elements of that life. Its mode has often been swift and coarse and ruthless, beyond art and beyond established civilization. It has engaged in warfare against the established heritage, against the bonds of pioneer existence. Its objective --the unconscious objective of a disunited people --has seemed to be that of creating fresh bonds, a new unity, the semblance of a society and the rounded completion of an American type.
Constance Rourke (1885-1941, American Author)

11 Good humor isn't a trait of character, it is an art which requires practice.
David Seabury (American Doctor, Author)

12 Humor is always based on a modicum of truth. Have you ever heard a joke about a father-in- law.
Dick Clark (American Entertainer, Television Personality)

13 A humorist is a person who feels bad, but who feels good about it.
Don Herold

14 I have a fine sense of the ridiculous, but no sense of humor.
Edward Albee (1928-, American Playwright, Dramatist)

15 Humor is by far the most significant activity of the human brain.
Edward De Bono (Born 1933, Maltan-Born American Psychologist and Writer)

16 Where ever you find humor, you find pathos close by it side.
Edwin P. Whipple (1819-1886, American Essayist)

17 WARNING: Humor may be hazardous to your illness.
Ellie Katz

18 Get well cards have become so humorous that if you don't get sick you're missing half the fun.
Flip Wilson (1933-, American Actor, Comedian)

19 Any discussion of the problems of being funny in America will not make sense unless we substitute the word wit for humor. Humor inspires sympathetic good-natured laughter and is favored by the "healing-power" gang. Wit goes for the jugular, not the jocular, and it's the opposite of football; instead of building character, it tears it down.
Florence King (1936-, American Author, Critic)

20 Imagination was given man to compensate for what he is not, and a sense of humor to console him for what he is.
Francis Bacon (1561-1626, British Philosopher, Essayist, Statesman)

21 Fortune and humor govern the world.
François de La Rochefoucauld (1613-1680, French classical writer)

22 The happiness or unhappiness of men depends as much on their humors as on fortune.
François de La Rochefoucauld (1613-1680, French classical writer)

23 Wit is a weapon. Jokes are a masculine way of inflicting superiority. But humor is the pursuit of a gentle grin, usually in solitude.
Frank Muir (1920-, British Humorist, Writer)

24 A joke is an epigram on the death of a feeling.
Fredrich

25 Humor, a good sense of it, is to Americans what manhood is to Spaniards and we will go to great lengths to prove it. Experiments with laboratory rats have shown that, if one psychologist in the room laughs at something a rat does, all of the other psychologists in the room will laugh equally. Nobody wants to be left holding the joke.
Garrison Keillor (1942-, American Humorous Writer, Radio Performer)

26 A difference of taste in jokes is a great strain on the affections.
George Eliot (1819-1880, British Novelist)

27 Comedy is the last refuge of the nonconformist mind.
Gilbert Seldes

28 Good humor is a tonic for mind and body. It is the best antidote for anxiety and depression. It is a business asset. It attracts and keeps friends. It lightens human burdens. It is the direct route to serenity and contentment.
Grenville Kleiser (1868-1953, American Author)

29 Any man who has had the job I've had and didn't have a sense of humor wouldn't still be here.
Harry S. Truman (1884-1972, Thirty-third President of the USA)

30 A person without a sense of humor is like a wagon without springs-jolted by every pebble in the road.
Henry Ward Beecher (1813-1887, American Preacher, Orator, Writer)

31 A jest often decides matters of importance more effectual and happily than seriousness.
Horace (65-8 BC, Italian Poet)

32 There are things of deadly earnest that can only be mentioned under the cover of a joke.
J. J. Procter (American Businessman)

33 Humor is emotional chaos remembered in tranquility.
James Thurber (1894-1961, American Humorist, Illustrator)

34 The wit makes fun of other persons; the satirist makes fun of the world; the humorist makes fun of himself, but in so doing, he identifies himself with people --that is, people everywhere, not for the purpose of taking them apart, but simply revealing their true nature.
James Thurber (1894-1961, American Humorist, Illustrator)

35 One should never risk a joke, even of the mildest and most unexceptional charters, except among people of culture and wit.
Jean De La Bruyere (1645-1696, French Writer)

36 Comedians are not usually actors, but imitations of actors.
Johann Georg Zimmermann (1957-, German Physicist)

37 What some people invent the rest enlarge.
Jonathan Swift (1667-1745, Anglo-Irish Satirist)

38 Mirth is like a flash of lightning, that breaks through a gloom of clouds, and glitters for a moment; cheerfulness keeps up a kind of daylight in the mind, and fills it with a steady and perpetual serenity.
Joseph Addison (1672-1719, British Essayist, Poet, Statesman)

39 A caricature is putting the face of a joke on the body of a truth.
Joseph Conrad (1857-1924, Polish-born British Novelist)

40 There is always some frivolity in excellent minds; they have wings to rise, but also stray.
Joseph Joubert (1754-1824, French Moralist)

41 Humor is laughing at what you haven't got when you ought to have it.
Langston Hughes (1902-1967, American Poet, Short-story Writer, Playwright)

42 A poor joke must invent its own laughter.
Latin Proverb

43 For every ten jokes you acquire a hundred enemies.
Laurence Sterne (1713-1768, British Author)

44 All my humor is based upon destruction and despair. If the whole world were tranquil, without disease and violence, I'd be standing on the breadline right in back of J. Edgar Hoover.
Lenny Bruce (1925-1966, American Comedian)

45 The role of a comedian is to make the audience laugh, at a minimum of once every fifteen seconds.
Lenny Bruce (1925-1966, American Comedian)

46 Humor is, I think, the sublets and chanciest of literary forms. It is surely not accidental that there are a thousand novelists, essayists, poets or journalists for each humorist. It is a long, long time between James Thurbers
Leo Rosten (1908-1997, Polish Born American Political Scientist)

47 Humor is the affectionate communication of insight.
Leo Rosten (1908-1997, Polish Born American Political Scientist)

48 A brilliant epigram is a solemn platitude gone to a masquerade ball.
Lionel Strachey

49 Probably it is impossible for humor to be ever a revolutionary weapon. Candide can do little more than generate irony.
Lionel Trilling (1905-1975, American Critic)

50 By blood a king, in heart a clown.
Lord Alfred Tennyson (1809-1892, British Poet)

51 I could not tread these perilous paths in safety, if I did not keep a saving sense of humor.
Lord Nelson

52 It is the saying of an ancient sage that humor was the only test of gravity, and gravity of humor.
Lord Shaftesbury (1671-1713, British Statesman)

53 Humor is not a mood but a way of looking at the world. So if it is correct to say that humor was stamped out in Nazi Germany, that does not mean that people were not in good spirits, or anything of that sort, but something much deeper and more important.
Ludwig Wittgenstein (1889-1951, Austrian Philosopher)

54 It's hard to be funny when you have to be clean.
Mae West (1892-1980, American Actress)

55 If I had no sense of humor, I would long ago have committed suicide.
Mahatma Gandhi (1869-1948, Indian Political, Spiritual Leader)

56 Good taste and humor are a contradiction in terms, like a chaste whore.
Malcolm Muggeridge (1903-1990, British Broadcaster)

57 We never respect those who amuse us, however we may smile at their comic powers.
Marguerite Gardiner Blessington (1789-1849, Irish Writer and Socialite)

58 Humor must not professedly teach and it must not professedly preach, but it must do both if it would live forever.
Mark Twain (1835-1910, American Humorist, Writer)

59 The secret source of humor itself is not joy but sorrow. There is no humor in heaven.
Mark Twain (1835-1910, American Humorist, Writer)

60 Humor is just another defense against the universe.
Mel Brooks (1926-, American Actor, Director)

61 We must laugh at man to avoid crying for him.
Napoleon Bonaparte (1769-1821, French General, Emperor)

62 If you can make a woman laugh you can do anything with her.
Nicol Williamson

63 Comedy is simply a funny way of being serious.
Peter Ustinov (1921-, British Actor, Writer, Director)

64 Burt Reynolds once asked me out. I was in his room.
Phyllis Diller (1861-1951, American Columnist)

65 Even the gods love jokes.
Plato (427-347 BC, Greek Philosopher)

66 There is this benefit in brag, that the speaker is unconsciously expressing his own ideal. Humor him by all means; draw it all out, and hold him to it.
Ralph Waldo Emerson (1803-1882, American Poet, Essayist)

67 The right honorable gentlemen is indebted to his memory for his jokes and his imagination for his facts.
Richard Brinsley Sheridan (1751-1816, Anglo-Irish Dramatist)

68 Humor is an affirmation of dignity, a declaration of man's superiority to all that befalls him.
Roman Gary

69 The hall-mark of American humor is its pose of illiteracy.
Ronald Knox (1888-1957, British Scholar, Priest)

70 I am a great friend to public amusements, for they keep the people from vice.
Samuel Johnson (1709-1784, British Author)

71 People of humor are always in some degree people of genius.
Samuel Taylor Coleridge (1772-1834, British Poet, Critic, Philosopher)

72 A person who knows how to laugh at himself will never ceased to be amused.
Shirley Maclaine (1934-, American Actress)

73 Never say a humorous thing to a man who does not possess humor. He will always use it in evidence against you.
Sir Herbert Beerbohm Tree (1853-1917, British actor-manager)

74 The comic and the tragic lie inseparably close, like light and shadow.
Socrates (469-399 BC, Greek Philosopher of Athens)

75 Musical comedies aren't written, they are rewritten.
Stephen Sondheim (1930-, American Composer, Lyricist)

76 Comedy may be big business but it isn't pretty.
Steve Martin (1945-, American Actor, Comedian, Screenwriter, Playwright, Writer)

77 Chaos in the midst of chaos isn't funny, but chaos in the midst of order is.
Steve Martin (1945-, American Actor, Comedian, Screenwriter, Playwright, Writer)

78 As a person is so must you humor them.
Terence (185-159 BC, Roman Writer of Comedies)

79 True humor springs not more from the head than from the heart. It is not contempt; its essence is love. It issues not in laughter, but in still smiles, which lie far deeper.
Thomas Carlyle (1795-1881, Scottish Philosopher, Author)

80 A rich man's joke is always funny.
Thomas Edward Brown

81 The comic is the perception of the opposite; humor is the feeling of it.
Umberto Eco (1929-, Italian Novelist and critic)

82 Humor is something that thrives between man's aspirations and his limitations. There is more logic in humor than in anything else. Because, you see, humor is truth.
Victor Borge (1909-, Danish Entertainer, Pianist)

83 Among those whom I like or admire, I can find no common denominator, but among those whom I love, I can: all of them make me laugh.
W. H. Auden (1907-1973, Anglo-American Poet)

84 It is well known that Beauty does not look with a good grace on the timid advances of Humor.
W. Somerset Maugham (1874-1965, British Novelist, Playwright)

85 An inexhaustible good nature is one of the most precious gifts of heaven, spreading itself like oil over the troubled sea of thought, and keeping the mind smooth and equable in the roughest weather.
Washington Irving (1783-1859, American Author)

86 Everything is funny as long as it is happening to somebody else.
Will Rogers (1879-1935, American Humorist, Actor)

87 Anyone without a sense of humor is at the mercy of everyone else.
William E. Rothschild

88 Good humor is one of the best articles of dress one can wear in society.
William M. Thackeray (1811-1863, Indian-born British Novelist)

HUNGER

1 Hunger is the best sauce.
Italian Proverb

2 Wanting something is not enough. You must hunger for it. Your motivation must be absolutely compelling in order to overcome the obstacles that will invariably come your way.
Les Brown (1945-, American Speaker, Author, Trainer, Motivator Lecturer)

3 There is hunger for ordinary bread, and there is hunger for love, for kindness, for thoughtfulness; and this is the great poverty that makes people suffer so much.
Mother Teresa (1910-1997, Albanian-born Roman Catholic Missionary)

HUNTING

1 Though I am an old horse, and have seen and heard a great deal, I never yet could make out why men are so fond of this sport; they often hurt themselves, often spoil good horses, and tear up the fields, and all for a hare, or a fox, or a stag, that they could get more easily some other way; but we are only horses, and don't know.
Anna Sewell

2 There is a passion for hunting something deeply implanted in the human breast.
Charles Dickens (1812-1870, British Novelist)

3 They take unbelievable pleasure in the hideous blast of the hunting horn and baying of the hounds. Dogs dung smells sweet as cinnamon to them.
Desiderius Erasmus (1466-1536, Dutch Humanist)

4 When you have shot one bird flying you have shot all birds flying. They are all different and they fly in different ways but the sensation is the same and the last one is as good as the first.
Ernest Hemingway (1898-1961, American Writer)

5   When a man wants to murder a tiger he calls it sport; when a tiger wants to murder him he calls it ferocity.
George Bernard Shaw (1856-1950, Irish-born British Dramatist)

6   Courage and grace is a formidable mixture. The only place to see it is the bullring.
Marlene Dietrich (1904-1992, German-born American Film Actor)

7   One knows so well the popular idea of health. The English country gentleman galloping after a fox -- the unspeakable in full pursuit of the uneatable.
Oscar Wilde (1856-1900, British Author, Wit)

8   It is very strange, and very melancholy, that the paucity of human pleasures should persuade us ever to call hunting one of them.
Samuel Johnson (1709-1784, British Author)

HUSBANDS

1   I think every woman's entitled to a middle husband she can forget.
Adela Rogers St. Johns

2   Personally, I can't see why it would be any less romantic to find a husband in a nice four-color catalogue than in the average downtown bar at happy hour.
Barbara Ehrenreich (1941-, American Author, Columnist)

3   I revere the memory of Mr. F. as an estimable man and most indulgent husband, only necessary to mention Asparagus and it appeared or to hint at any little delicate thing to drink and it came like magic in a pint bottle; it was not ecstasy but it was comfort.
Charles Dickens (1812-1870, British Novelist)

4   You -- poor and obscure, and small and plain as you are -- I entreat to accept me as a husband.
Charlotte Bronte (1816-1855, British Novelist)

5   I think there's something degrading about having a husband for a rival. It's humiliating if you fail and commonplace if you succeed.
Christopher Hampton (1946-, British Playwright)

6   The calmest husbands make the stormiest wives.
English Proverb

7   An early-rising man... a good spouse but a bad husband.
Gabriel Garcia Marquez (1928-, Colombian Writer)

8   Husbands never become good; they merely become proficient.
H. L. Mencken (1880-1956, American Editor, Author, Critic, Humorist)

9   Strike an average between what a woman thinks of her husband a month before she marries him and what she thinks of him a year afterward, and you will have the truth about him.
H. L. Mencken (1880-1956, American Editor, Author, Critic, Humorist)

10   A husband is what's left of the lover after the nerve has been extracted.
Helen Rowland (1875-1950, American Journalist)

11   When you see what some girls marry, you realize how they must hate to work for a living.
Helen Rowland (1875-1950, American Journalist)

12   A good husband is healthy and absent.
Japanese Proverb

13   I've never yet met a man who could look after me. I don't need a husband. What I need is a wife.
Joan Collins (1933-, British-born American Actress)

14   A good husband makes a good wife.
John Florio (1553-1625, British Author, Translator)

15   I've had the boyhood thing of being Elvis. Now I want to be with my best friend, and my best friend's my wife. Who could ask for anything more?
John Lennon (1940-1980, British Rock Musician)

16   Do let him read the papers. But not while you accusingly tiptoe around the room, or perch much like a silent bird of prey on the edge of your most uncomfortable chair. (He will read them anyway, and he should read them, so let him choose his own good time.) Don't make a big exit. Just go. But kiss him quickly, before you go, otherwise he might think you are angry; he is used to suspecting he is doing something wrong.
Marlene Dietrich (1904-1992, German-born American Film Actor)

17   Husbands are awkward things to deal with; even keeping them in hot water will not make them tender.
Mary Buckley

18   When a man brings his wife flowers for no reason, there's a reason.
Molly Mcgee

19   A husband is a guy who tells you when you've got on too much lipstick and helps you with your girdle when your hips stick.
Ogden Nash (1902-1971, American Humorous Poet)

20   The husbands of very beautiful women belong to the criminal classes.
Oscar Wilde (1856-1900, British Author, Wit)

21   They are horribly tedious when they are good husbands, and abominably conceited when they are not.
Oscar Wilde (1856-1900, British Author, Wit)

22   The bitterest creature under heaven is the wife who discovers that her husband's bravery is only bravado, that his strength is only a uniform, that his power is but a gun in the hands of a fool.
Pearl S. Buck (1892-1973, American Novelist)

23   His purity was too great, his aspiration too high for this poor, miserable world! His great soul is now only enjoying that for which it was worthy!
Queen Victoria (1819-1901, Queen of Great Britain)

24 In marriage, a man becomes slack and selfish, and undergoes a fatty degeneration of his moral being.
Robert Louis Stevenson (1850-1895, Scottish Essayist, Poet, Novelist)

25 From the moment I liberated Brigitte, the moment I showed her how to be truly herself, our marriage was all downhill.
Roger Vadim (1928-, French Film Director)

26 Some pray to marry the man they love, my prayer will somewhat vary; I humbly pray to Heaven above that I love the man I marry.
Rose Pastor Stokes

27 The best way to get husbands to do something is to suggest that perhaps they are too old to do it.
Shirley Maclaine (1934-, American Actress)

28 To catch a husband is an art; to hold him is a job.
Simone De Beauvoir (1908-1986, French Novelist, Essayist)

29 A little in drink, but at all times your faithful husband.
Sir Richard Steele (1672-1729, British Dramatist, Essayist, Editor)

30 No man worth his salt, no man of spirit and spine, no man for whom I could have any respect, could rejoice in the identification of Tallulah's husband. It's tough enough to be bogged down in a legend. It would be even tougher to marry one.
Tallulah Bankhead (1903-1968, American Actress)

31 Though bachelors be the strongest stakes, married men are the best binders, in the hedge of the commonwealth.
Thomas Fuller (1608-1661, British Clergyman, Author)

32 Those men are most apt to be obsequious and conciliating abroad, who are under the discipline of shrews at home.
Washington Irving (1783-1859, American Author)

33 You know I won't turn over a new leaf I am so obstinate, but then I am no less obstinate in being your affectionate Husband.
William Hogarth (1697-1764, British Painter, Engraver)

34 Husbands are like fires. They go out when unattended.
Zsa Zsa Gabor (1918-, Hungarian-born American Actress)

HYGIENE

1 Bath twice a day to be really clean, once a day to be passably clean, once a week to avoid being a public menace.
Anthony Burgess (1917-1993, British Writer, Critic)

2 Man does not live by soap alone; and hygiene, or even health, is not much good unless you can take a healthy view of it -- or, better still, feel a healthy indifference to it.
Gilbert K. Chesterton (1874-1936, British Author)

3 Hygiene is the corruption of medicine by morality. It is impossible to find a hygienist who does not debase his theory of the healthful with a theory of the virtuous. The true aim of medicine is not to make men virtuous; it is to safeguard and rescue them from the consequences of their vices.
H. L. Mencken (1880-1956, American Editor, Author, Critic, Humorist)

4 Hygiene is two thirds of health.
Lebanese Proverb

HYPOCRISY

1 The wicked work harder to preach hell than the righteous do to get to heaven.
American Proverb

2 With people of limited ability modesty is merely honesty. But with those who possess great talent it is hypocrisy.
Arthur Schopenhauer (1788-1860, German Philosopher)

3 Clean your finger before you point at my spots.
Benjamin Franklin (1706-1790, American Scientist, Publisher, Diplomat)

4 No habit or quality is more easily acquired than hypocrisy, nor any thing sooner learned than to deny the sentiments of our hearts and the principle we act from: but the seeds of every passion are innate to us, and nobody comes into the world without them.
Bernard Mandeville (1670-1733, Dutch-born British Author, Physician)

5 And why do you look at the speck that is in your brother's eye, but do not notice the log that is in your own eye? [Matthew 7:3]
Bible (Sacred Scriptures of Christians and Judaism)

6 With affection beaming in one eye, and calculation shining out of the other.
Charles Dickens (1812-1870, British Novelist)

7 When you see a great deal of religion displayed in his shop window, you may depend on it, that he keeps a very small stock of it within.
Charles Haddon Spurgeon (1834-1892, British Baptist Preacher)

8 If we divine a discrepancy between a man's words and his character, the whole impression of him becomes broken and painful; he revolts the imagination by his lack of unity, and even the good in him is hardly accepted.
Charles Horton Cooley (1864-1929, American Sociologist)

9 Hypocrisy in anything whatever may deceive the cleverest and most penetrating man, but the least wide-awake of children recognizes it, and is revolted by it, however ingeniously it may be disguised.
Count Leo Tolstoy (1828-1910, Russian Novelist, Philosopher)

10 Often a noble face hides filthy ways.
Euripides (480-406 BC, Greek Tragic Poet)

11 Hypocrisy is the homage that vice pays to virtue.
François de La Rochefoucauld (1613-1680, French classical writer)

12 Never to talk to ones self is a form of hypocrisy.
Fredrich

13 We ought to see far enough into a hypocrite to see even his sincerity.
Gilbert K. Chesterton (1874-1936, British Author)

14 What makes it so plausible to assume that hypocrisy is the vice of vices is that integrity can indeed exist under the cover of all other vices except this one. Only crime and the criminal, it is true, confront us with the perplexity of radical evil; but only the hypocrite is really rotten to the core.
Hannah Arendt (1906-1975, German-born American Political Philosopher)

15 Man is the only animal that learns by being hypocritical. He pretends to be polite and then, eventually, he becomes polite.
Jean Kerr (1923-, American Author, Playwright)

16 For neither man nor angel can discern hypocrisy, the only evil that walks invisible, except to God alone.
John Milton (1608-1674, British Poet)

17 There are two sorts of hypocrites; ones that are deceived with their outward morality and external religion; and the others; those that are deceived with false discoveries and elevation; which often cry down works, and men's own righteousness, and talk much of free grace; but at the same time make righteousness of their discoveries, and of their humiliation, and exalt themselves to heaven with them.
Jonathan Edwards (1703-1758, British Theologian, Metaphysician)

18 Keep thy smooth words and juggling homilies for those who know thee not.
Lord Byron (1788-1824, British Poet)

19 And the wild regrets, and the bloody sweats, none knew so well as I: for he who lives more lives than one more deaths than one must die.
Oscar Wilde (1856-1900, British Author, Wit)

20 The value of an idea has nothing whatever to do with the sincerity of the man who expresses it.
Oscar Wilde (1856-1900, British Author, Wit)

21 How clever you are, my dear! You never mean a single word you say.
Oscar Wilde (1856-1900, British Author, Wit)

22 All humans are hypocrites; the biggest hypocrite of all is the one who claims to detest hypocrisy.
Peter Wastholm

23 Better to be known as a sinner than a hypocrite.
Proverb

24 At the entrance of a second person, hypocrisy begins.
Ralph Waldo Emerson (1803-1882, American Poet, Essayist)

25 The only thing worse than a liar is a liar that's also a hypocrite!
Tennessee Williams (1914-1983, American Dramatist)

26 A favorite has no friend!
Thomas Gray (1716-1771, British Poet)

27 It is impossible to calculate the moral mischief, if I may so express it, that mental lying has produced in society. When a man has so far corrupted and prostituted the chastity of his mind as to subscribe his professional belief to things he does not believe he has prepared himself for the commission of every other crime.
Thomas Paine (1737-1809, Anglo-American Political Theorist, Writer)

28 Hypocrisy is the most difficult and nerve-racking vice that any man can pursue; it needs an unceasing vigilance and a rare detachment of spirit. It cannot, like adultery or gluttony, be practiced at spare moments; it is a whole-time job.
W. Somerset Maugham (1874-1965, British Novelist, Playwright)

29 A hypocrite despises those whom he deceives, but has no respect for himself. He would make a dupe of himself too, if he could.
William Hazlitt (1778-1830, British Essayist)

30 The only vice which cannot be forgiven is hypocrisy. The repentance of a hypocrite is itself hypocrisy.
William Hazlitt (1778-1830, British Essayist)

IDEALS AND IDEALISM

1 We for a certainty are not the first have sat in taverns while the tempest hurled their hopeful plans to emptiness, and cursed whatever brute and blackguard made the world.
A. E. Housman (1859-1936, British Poet, Classical Scholar)

2 Instead of killing and dying in order to produce the being that we are not, we have to live and let live in order to create what we are.
Albert Camus (1913-1960, French Existential Writer)

3 A man gazing on the stars is proverbially at the mercy of the puddles in the road.
Alexander Smith (1830-1867, Scottish Poet, Author)

4 Our ideals are our better selves.
Amos Bronson Alcott (1799-1888, American Educator, Social Reformer)

5   It's really a wonder that I haven't dropped all my ideals because they seem so absurd and impossible to carry out. Yet, I keep them, because in spite of everything I still believe that people are really good at heart. I simply can't build up my hopes on a foundation consisting of confusion, misery, and death. I see the world gradually being turned into a wilderness, I hear the ever- approaching thunder, which will destroy us too, I can feel the sufferings of millions and yet, if I look up into the heavens, I think that it will all come right, that this cruelty too will end, and that peace and tranquility will return again.
Anne Frank (1929-1945, German Jewish Refugee, Diarist)

6   I keep my ideals, because in spite of everything I still believe that people are really good at heart.
Anne Frank (1929-1945, German Jewish Refugee, Diarist)

7   There is no force so democratic as the force of an ideal.
Calvin Coolidge (1872-1933, Thirtieth President of the USA)

8   I am an idealist. I don't know where I'm going but I'm on my way.
Carl Sandburg (1878-1967, American Poet)

9   Ideals are like the stars: we never reach them, but like the mariners of the sea, we chart our course by them.
Carl Schurz (1829-1906, German-born American Senator)

10   The idealist's program of political or economic reform may be impracticable, absurd, demonstrably ridiculous; but it can never be successfully opposed merely by pointing out that this is the case. A negative opposition cannot be wholly effectual: there must be a competing idealism; something must be offered that is not only less objectionable but more desirable.
Charles Horton Cooley (1864-1929, American Sociologist)

11   Why should we strive, with cynic frown, to knock their fairy castles down?
Eliza Cook (1818-1889, British Poet)

12   When one paints an ideal, one does not need to limit one's imagination.
Ellen Key (1849-1926, Swedish Author, Feminist)

13   Idealists are foolish enough to throw caution to the winds. They have advanced mankind and have enriched the world.
Emma Goldman (1869-1940, American Anarchist)

14   What we need most, is not so much to realize the ideal as to idealize the real.
Francis Herbert Hedge (1846-1924, British Philosopher)

15   The idealist is incorrigible: if he is thrown out of his heaven he makes an ideal of his hell.
Friedrich Nietzsche (1844-1900, German Philosopher)

16   If you are going to build something in the air it is always better to build castles than houses of cards.
Georg C. Lichtenberg (1742-1799, German Physicist, Satirist)

17   An idealist is one who, on noticing that a rose smells better than a cabbage, concludes that it is also more nourishing.
H. L. Mencken (1880-1956, American Editor, Author, Critic, Humorist)

18   You should never have your best trousers on when you turn out to fight for freedom and truth.
Henrik Ibsen (1828-1906, Norwegian Dramatist)

19   Don't use that foreign word "ideals." We have that excellent native word "lies."
Henrik Ibsen (1828-1906, Norwegian Dramatist)

20   An idealist is a person who helps other people to be prosperous.
Henry Ford (1863-1947, American Industrialist, Founder of Ford Motor Company)

21   Words without actions are the assassins of idealism.
Herbert Clark Hoover (1874-1964, American - 31st American President)

22   Idealist: a cynic in the making.
Irving Layton (1912-, Canadian Poet)

23   Some day the soft Ideal that we wooed confronts us fiercely, foe-beset, pursued, and cries reproachful: "Was it then my praise, and not myself was loved? Prove now thy truth; I claim of thee the promise of thy youth."
James Russell Lowell (1819-1891, American Poet, Critic, Editor)

24   The true ideal is not opposed to the real but lies in it; and blessed are the eyes that find it.
James Russell Lowell (1819-1891, American Poet, Critic, Editor)

25   The ideal, without doubt, varies, but its enemies, alas, are always the same.
Jean Rostand (1894-1977, French Biologist, Writer)

26   Idealism increases in direct proportion to one's distance from the problem.
John Galsworthy (1867-1933, British Novelist, Playwright)

27   Our ideals, like pictures, are made from lights and shadows.
Joseph Joubert (1754-1824, French Moralist)

28   Ideals are the worlds masters.
Josiah Gilbert Holland (1819-1881, American Author)

29   It is the style of idealism to console itself for the loss of something old with the ability to gape at something new.
Karl Kraus (1874-1936, Austrian Satirist)

30   When your dreams tire, they go underground and out of kindness that's where they stay.
Libby Houston (1941-, British Poet)

31   When they come downstairs from their Ivory Towers, idealists are very apt to walk straight into the gutter.
Logan Pearsall Smith (1865-1946, Anglo-American Essayist, Aphorist)

32   The idealist walks on tiptoe, the materialist on his heels.
Malcolm De Chazal (1902-1981, French Writer)

33 Saddle your dreams before you ride em.
Mary Webb (1881-1927, British Novelist)

34 Idealism is the despot of thought, just as politics is the despot of will.
Mikhail Bakunin (1814-1876, Russian Political Theorist)

35 The enemy of idealism is zealotry.
Neil Kinnock (1942-, British Labor Politician)

36 Many have dreamed up republics and principalities that have never in truth been known to exist; the gulf between how one should live and how one does live is so wide that a man who neglects what is actually done for what should be done learns the way to self-destruction rather than self-preservation.
Niccolo Machiavelli (1469-1527, Italian Author, Statesman)

37 Man is born a predestined idealist, for he is born to act. To act is to affirm the worth of an end, and to persist in affirming the worth of an end is to make an ideal.
Oliver Wendell Holmes (1809-1894, American Author, Wit, Poet)

38 A map of the world that does not include Utopia is not worth even glancing at, for it leaves out the one country at which Humanity is always landing.
Oscar Wilde (1856-1900, British Author, Wit)

39 A perfect human being: Man in search of his ideal of perfection. Nothing less.
Pir Vilayat Khan (1916-, Western Philosopher Teacher, Master, Author)

40 Our salvation is in striving to achieve what we know we'll never achieve.
Ryszard Kapuscinski (1932, Polish Report and Foreign Correspondent)

41 An idealist believes the short run doesn't count. A cynic believes the long run doesn't matter. A realist believes that what is done or left undone in the short run determines the long run.
Sidney J. Harris (1917-, American Journalist)

42 The attainment of an ideal is often the beginning of a disillusion.
Stanley Baldwin (1867-1947, British Conservative Politician, Prime Minister)

43 Some men can live up to their loftiest ideals without ever going higher than a basement.
Theodore Roosevelt (1858-1919, Twenty-sixth President of the USA)

44 The actual well seen is ideal.
Thomas Carlyle (1795-1881, Scottish Philosopher, Author)

45 Nearly all the Escapists in the long past have managed their own budget and their social relations so unsuccessfully that I wouldn't want them for my landlords, or my bankers, or my neighbors. They were valuable, like powerful stimulants, only when they were left out of the social and industrial routine.
Willa Cather (1876-1947, American Author)

46 Idealism is fine, but as it approaches reality the cost becomes prohibitive.
William F. Buckley (1925-, American Writer)

47 The further limits of our being plunge, it seems to me, into an altogether other dimension of existence from the sensible and merely "understandable" world. Name it the mystical region, or the supernatural region, whichever you choose. So far as our ideal impulses originate in this region (and most of them do originate in it, for we find them possessing us in a way for which we cannot articulately account), we belong to it in a more intimate sense than that in which we belong to the visible world, for we belong in the most intimate sense wherever our ideals belong.
William James (1842-1910, American Psychologist, Professor, Author)

48 No folly is more costly than the folly of intolerant idealism.
Winston Churchill (1874-1965, British Statesman, Prime Minister)

IDEAS

1 Mere words are cheap and plenty enough, but ideas that rouse and set multitudes thinking come as gold for the mines.
A. Owen Penny

2 Never hesitate to steal a good idea.
Al Neuharth (American publisher, Founder, USA Today)

3 Nothing is more dangerous than an idea, when you only have one.
Alain Chartier (1385-1435, French Writer)

4 They come into being not through demonstration but through revelation, through the medium of powerful personalities.
Albert Einstein (1879-1955, German-born American Physicist)

5 Think for thyself one good idea, but known to be thine own, is better than a thousand gleaned from fields by others sown.
Alexander Wilson

6 In Texas, years ago, almost all of the oil came from surface operations. Then someone got the idea that there were greater sources of supply deeper down. A well was drilled five thousand feet deep. The result? A gusher. Too many of us operate on the surface. We never go deep enough to find supernatural resources. The result is, we never operate at our best. More time and investment is involved to go deep but a gusher will pay off.
Alfred A. Montapert (American Author)

7 Human life is driven forward by its dim apprehension of notions too general for its existing language.
Alfred North Whitehead (1861-1947, British Mathematician, Philosopher)

8 The vitality of thought is in adventure. Ideas won't keep. Something must be done about them. When the idea is new, its custodians have fervor, live for it, and if need be, die for it.
Alfred North Whitehead (1861-1947, British Mathematician, Philosopher)

9 It is not always by plugging away at a difficulty and sticking to it that one overcomes it; often it is by working on the one next to it. Some things and some people have to be approached obliquely, at an angle.
Andre Gide (1869-1951, French Author)

10 A pile of rocks ceases to be a rock when somebody contemplates it with the idea of a cathedral in mind.
Antoine De Saint-Exupery (1900-1944, French Aviator, Writer)

11 Ideas are a capital that bears interest only in the hands of talent.
Antoine Rivarol (1753-1801, French Journalist, Epigrammatist)

12 Eureka! I've got it.
Archimedes (287-212 BC, Greek Mathematician)

13 Ideas not coupled with action never become bigger than the brain cells they occupied.
Arnold H. Glasgow

14 Every revolutionary idea seems to evoke three stages of reaction. They may be summed up by the phrases: (1) It's completely impossible. (2) It's possible, but it's not worth doing. (3) I said it was a good idea all along.
Arthur C. Clarke (1917-, British Science Fiction Writer)

15 An idea is the only level which moves the world.
Arthur F. Corey

16 The greatest achievements of the human mind are generally received with distrust.
Arthur Schopenhauer (1788-1860, German Philosopher)

17 If you have the same ideas as everybody else but have them one week earlier than everyone else then you will be hailed as a visionary. But if you have them five years earlier you will be named a lunatic.
Barry Jones

18 He was distinguished for ignorance; for he had only one idea, and that was wrong.
Benjamin Disraeli (1804-1881, British Statesman, Prime Minister)

19 Take the obvious, add a cupful of brains, a generous pinch of imagination, a bucketful of courage and daring, stir well and bring to a boil.
Bernard M. Baruch (1870-1965, American Financier)

20 Go out and buy yourself a five-cent pencil and a ten-cent notebook and begin to write down some million-dollar ideas for yourself.
Bob Grinde

21 Great ideas need landing gear as well as wings.
C. O. Jackson

22 Ideas move fast when their time comes.
Carolyn Heilbrun (1926-, American Author, Educator)

23 If you want to kill any idea in the world today, get a committee working on it.
Charles F. Kettering (1876-1958, American Engineer, Inventor)

24 Men who accomplish great things in the industrial world are the ones who have faith in the money producing power of ideas.
Charles Fillmore (American Co-founder of Unity School of Christianity)

25 It is the nature of thought to find its way into action.
Christian Nevell Bovee (1820-1904, American Author, Lawyer)

26 Not the one who has many ideas, but the one who has a single conviction may become a great person.
Cotvos

27 The ideas I stand for are not mine. I borrowed them from Socrates. I swiped them from Chesterfield. I stole them from Jesus. And I put them in a book. If you don't like their rules, whose would you use?
Dale Carnegie (1888-1955, American Author, Trainer)

28 People will accept your ideas much more readily if you tell them Benjamin Franklin said it first.
David H Comins

29 The ideas dictate everything, you have to be true to that or you're dead.
David Lynch (1946-, American Director, Screenwriter)

30 Do not follow the ideas of others, but learn to listen to the voice within yourself. Your body and mind will become clear and you will realize the unity of all things.
Dogen

31 An idea that is not dangerous is unworthy of being called an idea at all.
Don Marquis (1878-1937, American Humorist, Journalist)

32 An idea is not responsible for the people who believe in it.
Don Marquis (1878-1937, American Humorist, Journalist)

33 So long as new ideas are created, sales will continue to reach new highs.
Dorothea Brande (American Success Writer)

34 Good ideas are a dime a dozen, bad ones are free.
Doug Horton

35 Getting an idea should be like sitting down on a pin. It should make you jump up and do something.
E. L. Simpson

36 Everything begins with an idea.
Earl Nightingale (1921-1989, American Radio Announcer, Author, Motivator, Speaker)

37 Ideas are fatal to caste.
Edward M. Forster (1879-1970, British Novelist, Essayist)

38 The idea that is not dangerous is not worthy of being called an idea at all.
Elbert Hubbard (1859-1915, American Author, Publisher)

39 It doesn't matter how new an idea is: what matters is how new it becomes.
Elias Canetti (1905-, Austrian Novelist, Philosopher)

40 A great idea is usually original to more than one discoverer. Great ideas come when the world needs them. Great ideas surround the world's ignorance and press for admission.
Elizabeth Stuart Phelps (1844-1911, American Writer)

41 Ideas are the roots of creation.
Ernest Dimnet (1866-1954, French Clergyman)

42 People find ideas a bore because they do not distinguish between live ones and stuffed ones on a shelf.
Ezra Pound (1885-1972, American Poet, Critic)

43 In every great time there is some one idea at work which is more powerful than any other, and which shapes the events of the time and determines their ultimate issues.
Francis Bacon (1561-1626, British Philosopher, Essayist, Statesman)

44 Neither man or nation can exist without a sublime idea.
Fyodor Dostoevski (1821-1881, Russian Novelist)

45 Ideas are refined and multiplied in the commerce of minds. In their splendor, images effect a very simple communion of souls.
Gaston Bachelard (1884-1962, French Scientist, Philosopher, Literary Theorist)

46 Ideas are invented only as correctives to the past. Through repeated rectification of this kind one may hope to disengage an idea that is valid.
Gaston Bachelard (1884-1962, French Scientist, Philosopher, Literary Theorist)

47 Ideas too are a life and a world.
Georg C. Lichtenberg (1742-1799, German Physicist, Satirist)

48 I tell you that as long as I can conceive something better than myself I cannot be easy unless I am striving to bring it into existence or clearing the way for it.
George Bernard Shaw (1856-1950, Irish-born British Dramatist)

49 It is useless to send armies against ideas.
George Brandes (1842-1927, Swedish Author)

50 Harold, like the rest of us, had many impressions which saved him the trouble of distinct ideas.
George Eliot (1819-1880, British Novelist)

51 The simple joy of taking an idea into one's own hands and giving it proper form, that's exciting.
George Nelson

52 If a man had as many ideas during the day as he does when he has insomnia, he would make a fortune.
Griff Niblack

53 We like to test things... no matter how good an idea sounds, test it first.
Henry Block (American Businessman, Founder of H&R Block)

54 Ideas are, in truth, force.
Henry James (1843-1916, American Author)

55 We are not to make the ideas of contentment and aspiration quarrel, for God made them fast friends. A man may aspire, and yet be quite content until it is time to raise; and both flying and resting are but parts of one contentment. The very fruit of the gospel is aspiration. It is to the heart what spring is to the earth, making every root, and bud, and bough desire to be more. -
Henry Ward Beecher (1813-1887, American Preacher, Orator, Writer)

56 Don't worry about people stealing your ideas. If your ideas are any good, you'll have to ram them down people's throats.
Howard Aiken (1900-1973, American Inventor)

57 Little words hurt big ideas.
Howard W. Newton

58 Good ideas and innovations must be driven into existence by courageous patience.
Hyman G. Rickover (1900-1986, Naval Engineering Officer)

59 You look at any giant corporation, and I mean the biggies, and they all started with a guy with an idea, doing it well.
Irvine Robbins (American Businessman, Co-Founder of Baskin-Robbins Ice Cream)

60 It first appeared like a crazy idea. It turned out he had a great idea.
J. Richard Munro (American Businessman, CEO of Time, Inc.)

61 A single idea, if it is right, saves us the labor of an infinity of experiences.
Jacques Maritain (1882-1973, French Philosopher)

62 Ideas control the world.
James A. Garfield (1831-1881, Twentieth President of the USA)

63 There is nothing in the world more powerful than an idea. No weapon can destroy it; no power can conquer it except the power of another idea.
James R. Smith

64 To love an idea is to love it a little more than one should.
Jean Rostand (1894-1977, French Biologist, Writer)

65 Labor gives birth to ideas.
Jim Rohn (American Businessman, Author, Speaker, Philosopher)

66 Ideas can be life-changing. Sometimes all you need to open the door is just one more good idea.
Jim Rohn (American Businessman, Author, Speaker, Philosopher)

67 Lots of people know a good thing the minute the other fellow sees it first.
Job E. Hodges

68 Whenever I hear people talking about liberal ideas, I am always astounded that men should love to fool themselves with empty sounds. An idea should never be liberal; it must be vigorous, positive, and without loose ends so that it may fulfill its divine mission and be productive. The proper place for liberality is in the realm of the emotions.
Johann Wolfgang Von Goethe (1749-1832, German Poet, Dramatist, Novelist)

69 Daring ideas are like chessmen moved forward. They may be beaten, but they may start a winning game.
Johann Wolfgang Von Goethe (1749-1832, German Poet, Dramatist, Novelist)

70 A good idea plus capable men cannot fail; it is better than money in the bank.
John Berry

71 Ideas are the factors that lift civilization. They create revolutions. There is more dynamite in an idea than in many bombs.
John H. Vincent

72 The public interest is best served by the free exchange of ideas.
John Kane

73 It is ideas, not vested interests, which are dangerous for good or evil.
John Maynard Keynes (1883-1946, British Economist)

74 The difficulty lies, not in the new ideas, but in escaping from the old ones, which ramify, for those brought up as most of us have been, into every corner of our minds.
John Maynard Keynes (1883-1946, British Economist)

75 The ideas of economists and political philosophers, both when they are right and when they are wrong, are more powerful than is commonly understood. Indeed the world is ruled by little else. Practical men, who believe themselves to be quite exempt from any intellectual influence, are usually the slaves of some defunct economist.
John Maynard Keynes (1883-1946, British Economist)

76 The point, simply, is that we are doing more rediscovering these days than discovering coming anew upon truths that ignorant people refused to examine, over the centuries, because the wise people who held custody of the fundamental truths of nature were unpopular.
John Williamson

77 An idea is a putting truth in check-mate.
Jose Ortega Y Gasset (1883-1955, Spanish Essayist, Philosopher)

78 Hang ideas! They are tramps, vagabonds, knocking at the back-door of your mind, each taking a little of your substance, each carrying away some crumb of that belief in a few simple notions you must cling to if you want to live decently and would like to die easy!
Joseph Conrad (1857-1924, Polish-born British Novelist)

79 Nothing dies harder than a bad idea.
Julie Cameron (American Author of "The Artist's Way")

80 I'm not impressed with the power of a corporate president. I am impressed with the power of ideas.
Ken Mason (American Businessman, President of Quaker Oats)

81 Ideas that enter the mind under fire remain there securely and for ever.
Leon Trotsky (1879-1940, Russian Revolutionary)

82 Get your ideas on paper and study them. Do not let them go to waste!
Les Brown (1945-, American Speaker, Author, Trainer, Motivator Lecturer)

83 The best way to have a good idea is to have a lot of ideas.
Linus Pauling (1901-1994, American Chemist, 2 Time Nobel Winner)

84 A powerful idea communicates some of its strength to him who challenges it.
Marcel Proust (1871-1922, French Novelist)

85 When an idea reaches critical mass there is no stopping the shift its presence will induce.
Marianne Williamson (1952-, American Author, Lecturer on Spirituality)

86 A crank is someone with a new idea -- until it catches on.
Mark Twain (1835-1910, American Humorist, Writer)

87 There are more ideas on earth than intellectuals imagine. And these ideas are more active, stronger, more resistant, more passionate than "politicians" think. We have to be there at the birth of ideas, the bursting outward of their force: not in books expressing them, but in events manifesting this force, in struggles carried on around ideas, for or against them. Ideas do not rule the world. But it is because the world has ideas... that it is not passively ruled by those who are its leaders or those who would like to teach it, once and for all, what it must think.
Michel Foucault (1926-1984, French Essayist, Philosopher)

88 Ideas are powerful things, requiring not a studious contemplation but an action, even if it is only an inner action. Their acquisition obligates each man in some way to change his life, even if it is only his inner life. They demand to be stood for. They dictate where a man must concentrate his vision. They determine his moral and intellectual priorities. They provide him with allies and make him enemies. In short, ideas impose an interest in their ultimate fate which goes far beyond the realm of the merely reasonable.
Midge Decter (1927-, American Author, Editor, Social Critic)

89 The idea is in my head to put it down is nothing.
Milton Avery (1893-1965, American Painter)

90 Long is the road from conception to completion.
MoliFre (1622-1673, French Playwright)

91 We are governed not by armies, but by ideas.
Mona Caird

92 Man's fear of ideas is probably the greatest dike holding back human knowledge and happiness.
Morris L. Ernst (1888-18?, American Lawyer, Statesman, Author)

93 All achievements, all earned riches, have their beginning in an idea.
Napoleon Hill (1883-1970, American Speaker, Motivational Writer, "Think and Grow Rich")

94 Ideas... they have the power...
Napoleon Hill (1883-1970, American Speaker, Motivational Writer, "Think and Grow Rich")

95 Many ideas grow better when transplanted into another mind than in the one where they sprung up.
Oliver Wendell Holmes (1809-1894, American Author, Wit, Poet)

96 A new and valid idea is worth more than a regiment and fewer men can furnish the former than command the latter.
Oliver Wendell Holmes (1809-1894, American Author, Wit, Poet)

97 A mind once stretched by a new idea never regains its original dimensions.
Oliver Wendell Holmes (1809-1894, American Author, Wit, Poet)

98 Man's mind, stretched by a new idea, never goes back to its original dimensions.
Oliver Wendell Holmes (1809-1894, American Author, Wit, Poet)

99 But how shall I get ideas? "Keep your wits open! Observe! Observe! Study! Study! But above all, Think! Think! And when a noble image is indelibly impressed upon the mind -- Act!
Orison Swett Marden (1850-1924, American Author, Founder of Success Magazine)

100 There is no adequate defense, except stupidity, against the impact of a new idea.
P. W. Bridgman (1882-1961, American Professor, Philosopher)

101 An idea is a point of departure and no more. As soon as you elaborate it, it becomes transformed by thought.
Pablo Picasso (1881-1973, Spanish Artist)

102 It's very good for an idea to be commonplace. The important thing is that a new idea should develop out of what is already there so that it soon becomes an old acquaintance. Old acquaintances aren't by any means always welcome, but at least one can't be mistaken as to who or what they are.
Penelope Fitzgerald (1916-, British Author)

103 If you pray for only one thing, .let it be for an idea.
Percy Sutton (American Businessman, President of Inner City Broadcasting)

104 If you want to get across an idea, wrap it up in a person.
Ralph Bunche

105 It is a lesson which all history teaches wise men, to put trust in ideas, and not in circumstances.
Ralph Waldo Emerson (1803-1882, American Poet, Essayist)

106 Ideas must work through the brains and the arms of good and brave men, or they are no better than dreams.
Ralph Waldo Emerson (1803-1882, American Poet, Essayist)

107 We are prisoners of ideas.
Ralph Waldo Emerson (1803-1882, American Poet, Essayist)

108 There is no prosperity, trade, art, city, or great material wealth of any kind, but if you trace it home, you will find it rooted in a thought of some individual man. --
Ralph Waldo Emerson (1803-1882, American Poet, Essayist)

109 You have to hatch ideas -- and then hitch them.
Ray D. Everson

110 Very simple ideas lie within the reach only of complex minds
Remy De Gourmont (1858-1915, French Novelist, Philosopher, Poet, Playwright)

111 An idea is never given to you without you being given the power to make it reality. You must, nevertheless, suffer for it.
Richard Bach (1936-, American Author)

112 The difference between people and ideas is... only superficial.
Richard Rorty (1931-, American Philosopher)

113 Brain cells create ideas. Stress kills brain cells. Stress is not a good idea.
Richard Saunders

114 An idea is a feat of association, and the height of it is a good metaphor.
Robert Frost (1875-1963, American Poet)

115 Our greatest lack is not money for any undertaking, but rather ideas, If the ideas are good, cash will somehow flow to where it is needed.
Robert H. Schuller (1926-, American Minister (Crystal Cathedral), Author, Social Leader)

116 Many ideas are good for a limited time -- not forever.
Robert Townsend (American Businessman, President of Avis)

117 Once I thought ideas were exceptions not the rule. That is not so. Ideas are so plentiful that they ride by on air. You've only to reach out and snatch one...
Rod Mckeun

118 It's easy to come up with new ideas; the hard part is letting go of what worked for you two years ago, but will soon be out-of-date.
Roger Von Oech

119 Every new idea is an impossibility until it is born.
Ron Brown (Secretary of Commerce)

120 Such as take lodgings in a head that's to be let unfurnished.
Samuel Butler (1612-1680, British Poet, Satirist)

121 I had a monumental idea this morning, but I didn't like it.
Samuel Goldwyn (1882-1974, American Film Producer, Founder, MGM)

122 The wise only possess ideas; the greater part of mankind are possessed by them.
Samuel Taylor Coleridge (1772-1834, British Poet, Critic, Philosopher)

123 There are well-dressed foolish ideas, just as there are will-dressed fools.
Sebastien-Roch Nicolas De Chamfort (1741-1794, French Writer, Journalist, Playwright)

124 A man is not necessarily intelligent because he has plenty of ideas, any more than he is a good general because he has plenty of soldiers.
Sebastien-Roch Nicolas De Chamfort (1741-1794, French Writer, Journalist, Playwright)

125 Sometimes the best, and only effective, way to kill an idea is to put it into practice.
Sidney J. Harris (1917-, American Journalist)

126 The human mind treats a new idea the way the body treats a strange protein; it rejects it.
Sir Peter Medawar (1915-1987, British Immunologist)

127 The most important thing in science is not so much to obtain new facts as to discover new ways of thinking about them.
Sir William Bragg (1862-1942-, Australian Physicist, 1915 Nobel Prize Laureate in Physics)

128 Concepts, like individuals, have their histories and are just as incapable of withstanding the ravages of time as are individuals. But in and through all this they retain a kind of homesickness for the scenes of their childhood.
Soren Kierkegaard (1813-1855, Danish Philosopher, Writer)

129 Not just in commerce but in the world of ideas too our age is putting on a veritable clearance sale. Everything can be had so dirt cheap that one begins to wander whether in the end anyone will want to make a bid.
Soren Kierkegaard (1813-1855, Danish Philosopher, Writer)

130 A new idea is like a child. It's easier to conceive than to deliver.
Ted Koysis

131 Great ideas originate in the muscles.
Thomas A. Edison (1847-1931, American Inventor, Entrepreneur, Founder of GE)

132 The value of an idea lies in the using of it.
Thomas A. Edison (1847-1931, American Inventor, Entrepreneur, Founder of GE)

133 To have a great idea, have a lot of them.
Thomas A. Edison (1847-1931, American Inventor, Entrepreneur, Founder of GE)

134 Ideas lose themselves as quickly as quail, and one must wing them the minute they rise out of the grass, or they are gone.
Thomas F. Kennedy

135 If you are possessed by an idea, you find it expressed everywhere, you even smell it.
Thomas Mann (1875-1955, German Author, Critic)

136 Great people talk about ideas. Small people talk about other people.
Tobias S. Gibson

137 When patterns are broken, new worlds can emerge.
Tuli Kupferberg

138 There is one thing stronger than all the armies in the world, and that is an idea whose time has come.
Victor Hugo (1802-1885, French Poet, Dramatist, Novelist)

139 Greater than the tread of mighty armies is an idea whose time has come.
Victor Hugo (1802-1885, French Poet, Dramatist, Novelist)

140 An idea, to be suggestive, must come to the individual with the force of revelation.
William James (1842-1910, American Psychologist, Professor, Author)

141 A new idea is first condemned as ridiculous and then dismissed as trivial, until finally, it becomes what everybody knows.
William James (1842-1910, American Psychologist, Professor, Author)

142 The thinker dies, but his thoughts are beyond the reach of destruction. Men are mortal, but ideas are immortal.
William Lippmann

143 What you need is an idea.
William P. Lear

144 The ideas of a time are like the clothes of a season: they are as arbitrary, as much imposed by some superior will which is seldom explicit. They are utilitarian and political, the instruments of smooth-running government.
Wyndham Lewis (1882-1957, British Author, Painter)

145 An idea discovered is much better possessed.
Young

IDENTITY

1 Trying to define yourself is like trying to bite your own teeth.
Alan W. Watts (1915-1973, British-born American Philosopher, Author)

2 I is another.
Arthur Rimbaud (1854-1891, French Poet)

3 I'm not Jack Nicholson. I'm not Brando. But I do mumble.
Benicio Del Toro (Born 1967, Puerto Rico, Actor, Director, Writer)

4 There comes a point in many people's lives when they can no longer play the role they have chosen for themselves. When that happens, we are like actors finding that someone has changed the play.
Brian Moore (1921-, Irish Novelist)

5 I'm Chevy Chase, and you're not.
Chevy Chase (1943-, American Actor)

6 Man may be defined as the animal that can say "I," that can be aware of himself as a separate entity.
Erich Fromm (1900-1980, American Psychologist)

7 The real meditation is... the meditation on one's identity. Ah, voila une chose!! You try it. You try finding out why you're you and not somebody else. And who in the blazes are you anyhow? Ah, voila une chose!
Ezra Pound (1885-1972, American Poet, Critic)

8 I believe that man is in the last resort so free a being that his right to be what he believes himself to be cannot be contested.
Georg C. Lichtenberg (1742-1799, German Physicist, Satirist)

9 The Beatles exist apart from my Self. I am not really Beatle George. Beatle George is like a suit or shirt that I once wore on occasion and until the end of my life people may see that shirt and mistake it for me.
George Harrison (1943-, British-born American Musician, Guitarist, Singer, Actor, Film and record)

10 The minute you or anybody else knows what you are you are not it, you are what you or anybody else knows you are and as everything in living is made up of finding out what you are it is extraordinarily difficult really not to know what you are and yet to be that thing.
Gertrude Stein (1874-1946, American Author)

11 An identity is questioned only when it is menaced, as when the mighty begin to fall, or when the wretched begin to rise, or when the stranger enters the gates, never, thereafter, to be a stranger. Identity would seem to be the garment with which one covers the nakedness of the self: in which case, it is best that the garment be loose, a little like the robes of the desert, through which one's nakedness can always be felt, and, sometimes, discerned. This trust in one's nakedness is all that gives one the power to change one's robes.
James Baldwin (1924-1987, American Author)

12 An identity would seem to be arrived at by the way in which the person faces and uses his experience.
James Baldwin (1924-1987, American Author)

13 It is always the same: once you are liberated, you are forced to ask who you are.
Jean Baudrillard (French Postmodern Philosopher, Writer)

14 Identity is a bag and a gag. Yet it exists for me with all the force of a fatal disease. Obviously I am here, a mind and a body. To say there's no proof my body exists would be arty and specious and if my mind is more ephemeral, less provable, the solution of being a writer with solid (touchable, tearable, burnable) books is as close as anyone has come to a perfect answer.
Judith Rossner (1935-, American Author)

15 I know you are, but what am I? [As Pee-Wee Herman]
Paul Reubens (1952-, American Actor, Comedian, Writer)

16 Sir, a man may be so much of everything, that he is nothing of anything.
Samuel Johnson (1709-1784, British Author)

IDEOLOGY

1 Whoever today speaks of human existence in terms of power, efficiency, and "historical tasks" is an actual or potential assassin.
Albert Camus (1913-1960, French Existential Writer)

2 Methods of thought which claim to give the lead to our world in the name of revolution have become, in reality, ideologies of consent and not of rebellion.
Albert Camus (1913-1960, French Existential Writer)

3 It is possible to lead astray an entire generation, to strike it blind, to drive it insane, to direct it towards a false goal. Napoleon proved this.
Alexander Herzen (1812-1870, Russian Journalist, Political Thinker)

4 Our blight is ideologies -- they are the long-expected Antichrist!
Carl Jung (1875-1961, Swiss Psychiatrist)

5 There cannot be peaceful coexistence in the ideological realm. Peaceful coexistence corrupts.
Jiang Qing (1914-1991, Chinese Politician)

6 Ideologies have no heart of their own. They're the whores and angels of our striving selves.
John Le Carre

7 Art and ideology often interact on each other; but the plain fact is that both spring from a common source. Both draw on human experience to explain mankind to itself; both attempt, in very different ways, to assemble coherence from seemingly unrelated phenomena; both stand guard for us against chaos.
Kenneth Tynan (1927-1980, British Critic)

8 Now different races and nationalities cherish different ideals of society that stink in each other's nostrils with an offensiveness beyond the power of any but the most monstrous private deed.
Rebecca West (1892-1983, British Author)

9 If you take away ideology, you are left with a case by case ethics which in practice ends up as me first, me only, and in rampant greed.
Richard A. Nelson

10 What persuades men and women to mistake each other from time to time for gods or vermin is ideology. One can understand well enough how human beings may struggle and murder for good material reasons -- reasons connected, for instance, with their physical survival. It is much harder to grasp how they may come to do so in the name of something as apparently abstract as ideas. Yet ideas are what men and women live by, and will occasionally die for.
Terry Eagleton (1943-, British Critic)

11 There are no more ideologies in the authentic sense of false consciousness, only advertisements for the world through its duplication and the provocative lie which does not seek belief but commands silence.
Theodor W. Adorno (1903-1969, German Philosopher, Sociologist, Music Critic)

12 Everything ideological possesses meaning: it represents, depicts, or stands for something lying outside itself. In other words, it is a sign. Without signs there is no ideology.
V. N. Volosinov

IDIOTS

1 It takes 50000 nuts to put a car together, but only one to scatter them all over the road.
Darryl Somers

2 Why is it that wherever I go, the resident idiot heads straight for me?
Gwynn Thomas

3 In the first place God made idiots. This was for practice. Then he made School Boards.
Mark Twain (1835-1910, American Humorist, Writer)

IDLENESS

1 Idleness is a constant sin, and labor is a duty. Idleness is the devil's home for temptation and for unprofitable, distracting musings; while labor profit others and ourselves.
Anne Baxter (1923-1985, American Actress)

2 You've got to make haste while it's still light of day. My godmother used to say, "I don't want to rust out, I just want to work out." If you stand still long enough, people will throw dirt on you."
Ben Vereen

3 Sloth makes all things difficult, but industry, all things easy. He that rises late must trot all day, and shall scarce overtake his business at night, while laziness travels so slowly that poverty soon overtakes him.
Benjamin Franklin (1706-1790, American Scientist, Publisher, Diplomat)

4 Sloth, like rust, consumes faster than labor wears, while the used key is always bright.
Benjamin Franklin (1706-1790, American Scientist, Publisher, Diplomat)

5 Trouble springs from idleness, and grievous toil from needless ease.
Benjamin Franklin (1706-1790, American Scientist, Publisher, Diplomat)

6 The harvest truly is plenteous, but the laborers are few. [Matthew 9:37]
Bible (Sacred Scriptures of Christians and Judaism)

7 Idleness is only a coarse name for my infinite capacity for living in the present.
Cyril Connolly (1903-1974, British Critic)

8 Go to the ant, thou sluggard, learn to live, and by her busy ways, reform thy own.
Elizabeth Smart

9 An idle brain is the devil's workshop.
English Proverb

10 There is nothing worse than an idle hour, with no occupation offering. People who have many such hours are simply animals waiting docilely for death. We all come to that state soon or late. It is the curse of senility.
H. L. Mencken (1880-1956, American Editor, Author, Critic, Humorist)

11 Idleness among children, as among men, is the root of all evil, and leads to no other evil more certain than ill temper.
Hannah More (1745-1833, British Writer, Reformer, Philanthropist)

12 To have done anything just for money is to have been truly idle.
Henry David Thoreau (1817-1862, American Essayist, Poet, Naturalist)

13 'Tis the voice of the sluggard; I heard him complain, you have waked me too soon, I must slumber again.
Isaac Watts (1674-1748, British hymn-writer)

14 It is better to have loafed and lost than never to have loafed at all.
James Thurber (1894-1961, American Humorist, Illustrator)

15 Idleness is many gathered miseries in one name.
Jean Paul

16 Idleness is an inlet to disorder, and makes way for licentiousness. People who have nothing to do are quickly tired of their own company.
Jeremy Collier (1650-1726, British Clergyman, Conjuror)

17 It is impossible to enjoy idling thoroughly unless one has plenty of work to do.
Jerome K. Jerome (1859-1927, British Humorous Writer, Novelist, Playwright)

18 Idleness is the stupidity of the body, and stupidity is the idleness of the mind.
Johann G. Seume (1763-1810, German Theologist)

19 Democracy divides people into workers and loafers. It makes no provision for those who have no time to work.
Karl Kraus (1874-1936, Austrian Satirist)

20 Just as iron rusts from disuse, even so does inaction spoil the intellect.
Leonardo Da Vinci (1452-1519, Italian Inventor, Architect, Painter, Scientist, Sculptor)

21 Purity of mind and idleness are incompatible.
Mahatma Gandhi (1869-1948, Indian Political, Spiritual Leader)

22 The way to be nothing is to do nothing.
Nathaniel Howe

23 He that is doing nothing is seldom in need of helpers.
Proverb

24 The hardest work of all is to do nothing.
Proverb

25 That man is idle who can do something better.
Ralph Waldo Emerson (1803-1882, American Poet, Essayist)

26 Idleness is an appendix to nobility.
Robert Burton (1576-1640, British Clergyman, Scholar)

27 A faculty for idleness implies a catholic appetite and a strong sense of personal identity.
Robert Louis Stevenson (1850-1895, Scottish Essayist, Poet, Novelist)

28 Perhaps man is the only being that can properly be called idle.
Samuel Johnson (1709-1784, British Author)

29 As peace is the end of war, so to be idle is the ultimate purpose of the busy.
Samuel Johnson (1709-1784, British Author)

30 I never remember feeling tired by work, though idleness exhausts me completely.
Sherlock Holmes (Fictional Detective (Sir Conan Doyle))

31 It is not the hours we put in on the job, it is what we put into the hours that counts.
Sidney Madwed (American Speaker, Consultant, Author, Poet)

32 You must have been warned against letting the golden hours slip by. Yes, but some of them are golden only because we let them slip.
Sir James M. Barrie (1860-1937, British Playwright)

33 The insupportable labor of doing nothing.
Sir Richard Steele (1672-1729, British Dramatist, Essayist, Editor)

34 Far from idleness being the root of all evil, it is rather the only true good.
Soren Kierkegaard (1813-1855, Danish Philosopher, Writer)

35 A man is not idle because he is absorbed in thought. There is visible labor and there is invisible labor.
Victor Hugo (1802-1885, French Poet, Dramatist, Novelist)

36 Yet it is in our idleness, in our dreams, that the submerged truth sometimes comes to the top.
Virginia Woolf (1882-1941, British Novelist, Essayist)

37 Shun idleness is the rust that attaches itself to the most brilliant metals.
Voltaire (1694-1778, French Historian, Writer)

38 Expect poison from standing water.
William Blake (1757-1827, British Poet, Painter)

39 The life of ease is a difficult pursuit.
William Cowper (1731-1800, British Poet)

IDOLS

1 Even the people we most admire often feel inadequate.
Andrew Matthews (American Artist, Cartoonist, Author)

2 The savage bows down to idols of wood and stone: the civilized man to idols of flesh and blood.
George Bernard Shaw (1856-1950, Irish-born British Dramatist)

3 The idol is the measure of the worshipper.
James Russell Lowell (1819-1891, American Poet, Critic, Editor)

4 Idolatry is in a man's own thought, not in the opinion of another.
John Selden (1584-1654, British Jurist, Statesman)

5 When men have gone so far as to talk as though their idols have come to life, it is time that someone broke them.
Richard H. Tawney (1880-1962, British Educator)

6 Whatever a man seeks, honors, or exalts more than God, this is the god of his idolatry.
William B. Ullathorne

7 'Tis mad idolatry To make the service greater than the god.
William Shakespeare (1564-1616, British Poet, Playwright, Actor)

8 Rapine, avarice, expense, This is idolatry; and these we adore; Plain living and high thinking are no more.
William Wordsworth (1770-1850, British Poet)

IGNORANCE

1 Most ignorance is evincible ignorance. We don't know because we don't want to know.
Aldous Huxley (1894-1963, British Author)

2 A child-like man is not a man whose development has been arrested; on the contrary, he is a man who has given himself a chance of continuing to develop long after most adults have muffled themselves in the cocoon of middle-aged habit and convention.
Aldous Huxley (1894-1963, British Author)

3 You must not enthrone ignorance just because there is much of it.
American Proverb

4 To be ignorant of one's ignorance is the malady of the ignorant.
Amos Bronson Alcott (1799-1888, American Educator, Social Reformer)

5 A person is never happy except at the price of some ignorance.
Anatole France (1844-1924, French Writer)

6 A man profits more by the sight of an idiot than by the orations of the learned.
Arabian Proverb

7 It is harder to conceal ignorance than to acquire knowledge.
Arnold H. Glasgow

8 The greatest pride, or the greatest despondency, is the greatest ignorance of one's self.
Baruch (Benedict de) Spinoza (1632-1677, Dutch Philosopher and Theologian)

9 To be conscience that you are ignorant is a great step to knowledge.
Benjamin Disraeli (1804-1881, British Statesman, Prime Minister)

10 Being ignorant is not so much a shame as being unwilling to learn.
Benjamin Franklin (1706-1790, American Scientist, Publisher, Diplomat)

11 He was so learned that he could name a horse in nine languages; so ignorant that he bought a cow to ride on.
Benjamin Franklin (1706-1790, American Scientist, Publisher, Diplomat)

12 A learned blockhead is a greater blockhead than an ignorant one.
Benjamin Franklin (1706-1790, American Scientist, Publisher, Diplomat)

13 Men are born ignorant, not stupid; they are made stupid by education.
Bertrand Russell (1872-1970, British Philosopher, Mathematician, Essayist)

14 The sage awakes to light in the night of all creatures. That which the world calls day is the night of ignorance to the wise.
Bhagavad Gita (400 BC, Sanskrit Poem Incorporated Into the Mahabharata)

15 The opposite of love is not hate, the opposite of love is ignorance.
Brian Hwang

16 I do not pretend to know where many ignorant men are sure -- that is all that agnosticism means.
Clarence Darrow (1857-1938, American Lawyer)

17 I am an agnostic; I do not pretend to know what many ignorant men are sure of.
Clarence Darrow (1857-1938, American Lawyer)

18 Ignorance is the night of the mind, but a night without moon or star.
Confucius (551-479 BC, Chinese Ethical Teacher, Philosopher)

19 If you think education is expensive, try ignorance.
Derek Bok (American academic)

20 Naivete in grownups is often charming; but when coupled with vanity it is indistinguishable from stupidity.
Eric Hoffer (1902-1983, American Author, Philosopher)

21 Unintelligent people always look for a scapegoat.
Ernest Bevin (1881-1951, British Statesman)

22 Ignorance of one's misfortunes is clear gain.
Euripides (480-406 BC, Greek Tragic Poet)

23 The reason there's so much ignorance is that those who have it are so eager to share it.
Frank A. Clark

24 Ignorance is never out of style. It was in fashion yesterday, it is the rage today and it will set the pace tomorrow.
Frank Dane

25 Ignorance doesn't kill you, but it makes you sweat a lot.
Haitian Proverb

26 Ignorance is like the itch -- the less you have of it the better off you are.
Harry Mendelson (1855-1937, American Financier, Philanthropist, Statesman)

27 There is one principle that can keep a man in everlasting ignorance. That is contempt prior to investigation.
Herbert Spencer (1820-1903, British Philosopher)

28 Ignorance breeds monsters to fill up the vacancies of the soul that are unoccupied by the verities of knowledge.
Horace Mann (1796-1859, American Educator)

29 Ignorance is no excuse, it's the real thing.
Irene Peter

30 Nothing is more terrible than to see ignorance in action.
Johann Wolfgang Von Goethe (1749-1832, German Poet, Dramatist, Novelist)

31 Ignorance and inconsideration are the two great causes of the ruin of mankind.
John Tillotson (1630-1694, British Theologian - Archbishop of Canterbury)

32 I am not ashamed to confess I am ignorant of what I do not know.
Marcus T. Cicero (106-43 BC, Great Roman Orator, Politician)

33 When I was fourteen, my father was so ignorant I could hardly stand to have him around. When I got to be twenty-one, I was astonished at how much he had learned in seven years.
Mark Twain (1835-1910, American Humorist, Writer)

34 I would rather have my ignorance than another man's knowledge, because I have so much of it.
Mark Twain (1835-1910, American Humorist, Writer)

35 Nothing in the world is more dangerous than sincere ignorance and conscientious stupidity.
Martin Luther King Jr. (1929-1968, American Black Leader, Nobel Prize Winner, 1964)

36 The fact is that we all seem capable of living, because at some time or other we have taken refuge in a lie, in blindness, in enthusiasm, in optimism, in some conviction, in pessimism or something of the sort. He has never taken refuge in anything. He is absolutely incapable of lying. He has nothing to take refuge in, no shelter. It's as if he were naked and everyone else had clothes on.
Milena Jesenska

37 Ignorance is a voluntary misfortune.
Nicholas Ling

38 Ignorance is like a delicate fruit; touch it, and the bloom is gone.
Oscar Wilde (1856-1900, British Author, Wit)

39 There's a sucker born every minute.
P.T. Barnum (1810-1891, American Showman, Entertainer, Circus Builder)

40 What you don't know can't hurt you .
Proverb

41 Better to ask a question than to remain ignorant.
Proverb

42 Better to be ignorant of a matter than half know it.
Publilius Syrus (1st Century BC, Roman Writer)

43 Ignorance is not innocence, but sin.
Robert Browning (1812-1889, British Poet)

44 The greater the ignorance the greater the dogmatism.
Sir William Osler (1849-1919, Canadian Physician)

45 Have the courage to be ignorant of a great number of things, in order to avoid the calamity of being ignorant of everything.
Sydney Smith (1771-1845, British Writer, Clergyman)

46 I do not believe in the collective wisdom of individual ignorance.
Thomas Carlyle (1795-1881, Scottish Philosopher, Author)

47 Where ignorance is bliss, 'Tis folly to be wise.
Thomas Gray (1716-1771, British Poet)

48 Ignorance is preferable to error; and he is less remote from the truth who believes nothing, than he who believes what is wrong.
Thomas Jefferson (1743-1826, Third President of the USA)

49 Ignorance is bold and knowledge reserved.
Thucydides (460-400 BC, Greek Historian of Athens)

50 The highest form of ignorance is when you reject something you don't know anything about.
Wayne Dyer (1940-, American Psychotherapist, Author, Lecturer)

51 Everybody is ignorant -- only on different subjects.
Will Rogers (1879-1935, American Humorist, Actor)

52 There are many who talk on from ignorance rather than from knowledge, and who find the former an inexhaustible fund of conversation.
William Hazlitt (1778-1830, British Essayist)

53 There is no darkness, but ignorance.
William Shakespeare (1564-1616, British Poet, Playwright, Actor)

ILLITERACY

1 The illiterate of the future are not those that cannot read or write. They are those that can not learn, unlearn, relearn.
Alvin Toffler (1928-, American Author)

2 There is no such thing as a functional illiterate.
Kelvin Throop III

ILLNESS

1 If you be sick, your own thoughts make you sick
Ben Johnson (1573-1637, British Dramatist, Poet)

2 To be sick is to enjoy monarchical prerogatives.
Charles Lamb (1775-1834, British Essayist, Critic)

3 To be too conscious is an illness. A real thorough going illness.
Fyodor Dostoevski (1821-1881, Russian Novelist)

4 Oh, the blues ain't nothing but a good woman feeling bad.
Georgia White

5 There are two kinds of people; those who are always well and those who are always sick. Most of the evils of the world come from the first sort and most of the achievement from the second.
Louis Dudek

6 Illness is the doctor to whom we pay most heed; to kindness, to knowledge we make promise only; pain we obey.
Marcel Proust (1871-1922, French Novelist)

7 For every ailment under the sun, There is a remedy, or there is none, If there be one, try to find it; If there be none, never mind it.
Mother Goose

8 The modern sympathy with invalids is morbid. Illness of any kind is hardly a thing to be encouraged in others.
Oscar Wilde (1856-1900, British Author, Wit)

9 I reckon being ill as one of the great pleasures of life, provided one is not too ill and is not obliged to work till one is better.
Samuel Butler (1612-1680, British Poet, Satirist)

10 The most important thing when ill, is to never lose heart.
Vladimir Ilyich Lenin (1870-1924, Russian Revolutionary Leader)

ILLUSION

1 People who have realized that this is a dream imagine that it is easy to wake up, and are angry with those who continue sleeping, not considering that the whole world that environs them does not permit them to wake. Life proceeds as a series of optical illusions, artificial needs and imaginary sensations.
Alexander Herzen (1812-1870, Russian Journalist, Political Thinker)

2 Nothing is more sad than the death of an illusion.
Arthur Koestler (1905-1983, Hungarian Born British Writer)

3 A hallucination is a fact, not an error; what is erroneous is a judgment based upon it.
Bertrand Russell (1872-1970, British Philosopher, Mathematician, Essayist)

4 A pleasant illusion is better than a harsh reality.
Christian Nevell Bovee (1820-1904, American Author, Lawyer)

5 We must select the Illusion which appeals to our temperament and embrace it with passion, if we want to be happy.
Cyril Connolly (1903-1974, British Critic)

6 What difference is there, do you think, between those in Plato's cave who can only marvel at the shadows and images of various objects, provided they are content and don't know what they miss, and the philosopher who has emerged from the cave and sees the real things?
Desiderius Erasmus (1466-1536, Dutch Humanist)

7 Half the work that is done in this world is to make things appear what they are not.
E. R. Beadle

8 We always think every other man's job is easier than our own. The better he does it, the easier it looks.
Eden Phillpotts (1862-1960, Indian-born British Novelist)

9 For me, it is as though at every moment the actual world had completely lost its actuality. As though there was nothing there; as though there were no foundations for anything or as though it escaped us. Only one thing, however, is vividly present: the constant tearing of the veil of appearances; the constant destruction of everything in construction. Nothing holds together, everything falls apart.
Eugene Ionesco (1912-, Romanian-born French Playwright)

10 For what we call illusions are often, in truth, a wider vision of past and present realities --a willing movement of a man's soul with the larger sweep of the world's forces --a movement towards a more assured end than the chances of a single life.
George Eliot (1819-1880, British Novelist)

11 Oh, how powerfully the magnet of illusion attracts.
Gutzkow

12 Better a dish of illusion and a hearty appetite for life, than a feast of reality and indigestion therewith.
Harry A. Overstreet (American Psychologist)

13 Therefore trust to thy heart, and to what the world calls illusions.
Henry Wadsworth Longfellow (1819-1892, American Poet)

14 It appears to me that almost any man may like the spider spin from his own inwards his own airy citadel.
John Keats (1795-1821, British Poet)

15 It is respectable to have no illusions, and safe, and profitable and dull.
Joseph Conrad (1857-1924, Polish-born British Novelist)

16 Artists use frauds to make human beings seem more wonderful than they really are. Dancers show us human beings who move much more gracefully than human beings really move. Films and books and plays show us people talking much more entertainingly than people.
Kurt Vonnegut Jr. (1922-, American Novelist)

17 It isn't safe to sit in judgment upon another person's illusion when you are not on the inside. While you are thinking it is a dream, he may be knowing it is a planet.
Mark Twain (1835-1910, American Humorist, Writer)

18 Pray look better, Sir... those things yonder are no giants, but windmills.
Miguel De Cervantes (1547-1616, Spanish Novelist, Dramatist, Poet)

19 The one person who has more illusions than the dreamer is the man of action.
Oscar Wilde (1856-1900, British Author, Wit)

20 Pleasure can be supported by an illusion; but happiness rests upon truth.
Sebastien-Roch Nicolas De Chamfort (1741-1794, French Writer, Journalist, Playwright)

21 The impression forces itself upon one that men measure by false standards, that everyone seeks power, success, riches for himself, and admires others who attain them, while undervaluing the truly precious thing in life.
Sigmund Freud (1856-1939, Austrian Physician - Founder of Psychoanalysis)

22 Disillusion is a natural stage that follows the holding of an illusion.
Susan Shaughnessy

23 What seems to be, is, to those to whom it seems to be, and is productive of the most dreadful consequences to those to whom it seems to be, even of torments, despair, eternal death.
William Blake (1757-1827, British Poet, Painter)

24 The fundamental delusion of humanity is to suppose that I am here and you are out there.
Yasutani Roshi

IMAGE

1 Isn't life a series of images that change as they repeat themselves?
Andy Warhol (1930-, American Artist, Filmmaker)

2 The visual is sorely undervalued in modern scholarship. Art history has attained only a fraction of the conceptual sophistication of literary criticism. Drunk with self-love, criticism has hugely overestimated the centrality of language to western culture. It has failed to see the electrifying sign language of images.
Camille Paglia (1947-, American Author, Critic, Educator)

3 The Image is more than an idea. It is a vortex or cluster of fused ideas and is endowed with energy.
Ezra Pound (1885-1972, American Poet, Critic)

4 We operate with nothing but things which do not exist, with lines, planes, bodies, atoms, divisible time, divisible space -- how should explanation even be possible when we first make everything into an image, into our own image!
Friedrich Nietzsche (1844-1900, German Philosopher)

5 The reign of imagagology begins where history ends.
Milan Kundera (1929-, Czech Author, Critic)

6 Metaphors are much more tenacious than facts.
Paul De Man (1919-1983, Belgian-born American Literary Critic)

7 Nowadays people's visual imagination is so much more sophisticated, so much more developed, particularly in young people, that now you can make an image which just slightly suggests something, they can make of it what they will.
Robert Doisneau (1912-, French Photographer)

8 We are all hungry and thirsty for concrete images. Abstract art will have been good for one thing: to restore its exact virginity to figurative art.
Salvador Dali (1904-1989, Spanish Painter)

9 Industrial societies turn their citizens into image-junkies; it is the most irresistible form of mental pollution. Poignant longings for beauty, for an end to probing below the surface, for a redemption and celebration of the body of the world. Ultimately, having an experience becomes identical with taking a photograph of it.
Susan Sontag (1933-, American Essayist)

10 Logicians may reason about abstractions. But the great mass of men must have images. The strong tendency of the multitude in all ages and nations to idolatry can be explained on no other principle.
Thomas B. Macaulay (1800-1859, American Essayist and Historian)

11 For such an advanced civilization as ours to be without images that are adequate to it is as serious a defect as being without memory.
Werner Herzog (1942-, German Film Director)

IMAGINATION

1 The most evident difference springs from the important part which is played in man by a relatively strong power of imagination and by the capacity to think, aided as it is by language and other symbolically devices.
Albert Einstein (1879-1955, German-born American Physicist)

2 Imagination is more important than knowledge. For knowledge is limited to all we now know and understand, while imagination embraces the entire world, and all there ever will be to know and understand.
Albert Einstein (1879-1955, German-born American Physicist)

3 In that way imagination and intelligence enter into our existence in the part of servants of the primary instincts.
Albert Einstein (1879-1955, German-born American Physicist)

4 Your imagination is your preview of life's coming attractions.
Albert Einstein (1879-1955, German-born American Physicist)

5 To know is nothing at all; to imagine is everything.
Albert Einstein (1879-1955, German-born American Physicist)

6 Imagination is everything. It is the preview of life's coming attractions.
Albert Einstein (1879-1955, German-born American Physicist)

7 You must first clearly see a thing in your mind before you can do it.
Alex Morrison

8 To reduce the imagination to a state of slavery --even though it would mean the elimination of what is commonly called happiness --is to betray all sense of absolute justice within oneself. Imagination alone offers me some intimation of what can be.
Andre Breton (1989-1966, French Surrealist)

9 Death is the tyrant of the imagination.
Barry Cornwall

10 The Chinese pianist Liu Chi Kung was imprisoned for seven years during the Cultural Revolution, during which time he had no access to a piano. When he returned to giving concerts again after he was released, his playing was better than ever. Asked how this was possible since he had not practice for seven years, he replied: "I did practice, every day. I rehearsed every piece I had ever played, note by note, in my mind."
Bernie Zilbergeld

11 I think my securities far outweigh my insecurities. I am not nearly as afraid of myself and my imagination as I used to be.
Billy Connelly

12 Imagination decides everything.
Blaise Pascal (1623-1662, French Scientist, Religious Philosopher)

13 Imagination disposes of everything; it creates beauty, justice, and happiness, which is everything in this world.
Blaise Pascal (1623-1662, French Scientist, Religious Philosopher)

14 All the works of man have their origin in creative fantasy. What right have we then to depreciate imagination.
Carl Jung (1875-1961, Swiss Psychiatrist)

15 Without this playing with fantasy no creative work has ever yet come to birth. The debt we owe to the play of the imagination is incalculable.
Carl Jung (1875-1961, Swiss Psychiatrist)

16 It is not that the child lives in a world of imagination, but that the child within us survives and starts into life only at rare moments of recollection, which makes us believe, and it is not true, that, as children, we were imaginative?
Cesare Pavese (1908-1950, Italian Poet, Novelist, Translator)

17 Peak performers develop powerful mental images of the behavior that will lead to the desired results. They see in their mind's eye the result they want, and the actions leading to it.
Charles A. Garfield (American Peak Performance Expert, Researcher, Trainer)

18 Our imagination is the only limit to what we can hope to have in the future.
Charles F. Kettering (1876-1958, American Engineer, Inventor)

19 The opportunities of man are limited only by his imagination. But so few have imagination that there are ten thousand fiddlers to one composer.
Charles F. Kettering (1876-1958, American Engineer, Inventor)

20 The imaginations which people have of one another are the solid facts of society.
Charles Horton Cooley (1864-1929, American Sociologist)

21 Understand that you, yourself, are no more than the composite picture of all your thoughts and actions. In your relationships with others, remember the basic and critically important rule: If you want to be loved, be lovable. If you want respect, set a respectable example!
Denis Waitley (1933-, American Author, Speaker, Trainer, Peak Performance Expert)

22 You have all the reason in the world to achieve your grandest dreams. Imagination plus innovation equals realization.
Denis Waitley (1933-, American Author, Speaker, Trainer, Peak Performance Expert)

23 We are what and where we are because we have first imagined it.
Donald Curtis

24 By going over your day in imagination before you begin it, you can begin acting successfully at any moment.
Dorothea Brande (American Success Writer)

25 Act as if you have already achieved your goal and it is yours.
Dr. Robert Anthony (American educator)

26 Nevertheless, the consuming hunger of the uncritical mind for what it imagines to be certainty or finality impels it to feast upon shadows in the prevailing famine of substance.
E. T. Bell

27 It will be found, in fact, that the ingenious are always fanciful, and the truly imaginative never otherwise than analytic.
Edgar Allan Poe (1809-1845, American Poet, Critic, short-story Writer)

28 When the imagination and will power are in conflict, are antagonistic, it is always the imagination which wins, without any exception.
Emile CouT (1857-1926, French Pharmacist, Hypnotist, Pioneer)

29 It is more than likely that the brain itself is, in origin and development, only a sort of great clot of genital fluid held in suspense or reserved. This hypothesis would explain the enormous content of the brain as a maker or presenter of images.
Ezra Pound (1885-1972, American Poet, Critic)

30 What you see is what you get.
Flip Wilson (1933-, American Actor, Comedian)

31 An idea is salvation by imagination.
Frank Lloyd Wright (1869-1959, American Architect)

32 Man is an imagining being.
Gaston Bachelard (1884-1962, French Scientist, Philosopher, Literary Theorist)

33 The bridges that you cross before you come to them are over rivers that aren't there.
Gene Brown

34 People can die of mere imagination.
Geoffrey Chaucer (1340-1400, British Poet)

35 Imagination is the beginning of creation. You imagine what you desire; you will what you imagine; and at last you create what you will.
George Bernard Shaw (1856-1950, Irish-born British Dramatist)

36 The most dire disaster in love is the death of imagination.
George Meredith (1828-1909, British Author)

37 I have discovered that people with money have no imagination, and people with imagination have no money.
George Weiss Rainbow (1940-, British Eccentric)

38 When you think something, you think in picture. You don't think a thought in words. You think a picture that expresses your thought. Working with this picture will produce it into your experience.
Grace Speare

39 It is impossible to imagine the universe run by a wise, just and omnipotent God, but it is quite easy to imagine it run by a board of gods. If such a board actually exists it operates precisely like the board of a corporation that is losing money.
H. L. Mencken (1880-1956, American Editor, Author, Critic, Humorist)

40 Hold a picture of yourself long and steadily enough in your mind's eye and you will be drawn toward it. Picture yourself vividly as winning and that alone will contribute immeasurably to success. Great living starts with a picture, held in your imagination, of what you would like to do or be.
Harry Emerson Fosdick (1878-1969, American Minister)

41 I do not know how to distinguish between our waking life and a dream. Are we not always living the life that we imagine we are?
Henry David Thoreau (1817-1862, American Essayist, Poet, Naturalist)

42 It is usually the imagination that is wounded first, rather than the heart; it being much more sensitive.
Henry David Thoreau (1817-1862, American Essayist, Poet, Naturalist)

43 Imagination is the voice of daring. If there is anything Godlike about God it is that. He dared to imagine everything.
Henry Miller (1891-1980, American Author)

44 The soul without imagination is what an observatory would be without a telescope.
Henry Ward Beecher (1813-1887, American Preacher, Orator, Writer)

45 Image creates desire. You will what you imagine.
J. G. Gallimore

46 I never hit a shot, not even in practice, without having a very sharp, in-focus picture of it in my head. First I see the ball where I want it to finish, nice and white and sitting up high on the bright green grass. Then the scene quickly changes, and I see the ball going there: its path, trajectory, and shape, even its behavior on landing. Then there is a sort of fade-out, and the next scene shows me making the kind of swing that will turn the previous images into reality.
Jack Nicklaus (1940-, American Golfer)

47 There is nothing more frightful than imagination without taste.
Johann Wolfgang Von Goethe (1749-1832, German Poet, Dramatist, Novelist)

48 The human imagination... has great difficulty in living strictly within the confines of a materialist practice or philosophy. It dreams, like a dog in its basket, of hares in the open.
John Berger (1926-, British Actor, Critic)

49 My imagination is a monastery and I am its monk.
John Keats (1795-1821, British Poet)

50 We have been endowed with the capacity and the power to create desirable pictures within and to find them automatically in the outer world of our environment.
John Mcdonald

51 Imaginary evils soon become real one by indulging our reflections on them.
John Ruskin (1819-1900, British Critic, Social Theorist)

52 The imagination is never governed, it is always the ruling and divine power.
John Ruskin (1819-1900, British Critic, Social Theorist)

53 It is eminently a weariable faculty, eminently delicate, and incapable of bearing fatigue; so that if we give it too many objects at a time to employ itself upon, or very grand ones for a long time together, it fails under the effort, becomes jaded, exactly as the limbs do by bodily fatigue, and incapable of answering any farther appeal till it has had rest.
John Ruskin (1819-1900, British Critic, Social Theorist)

54 An unimaginative person can neither be reverent or kind.
John Ruskin (1819-1900, British Critic, Social Theorist)

55 Only in men's imagination does every truth find an effective and undeniable existence. Imagination, not invention, is the supreme master of art as of life.
Joseph Conrad (1857-1924, Polish-born British Novelist)

56 One who has imagination without learning has wings without feet.
Joseph Joubert (1754-1824, French Moralist)

57 Imagination is the eye of the soul.
Joseph Joubert (1754-1824, French Moralist)

58 Imagination is the one weapon in the war against reality.
Jules de Gaultier

59 Anything one man can imagine, other men can make real.
Jules Verne (1828-1905, French Writer)

60 We are what we imagine ourselves to be.
Kurt Vonnegut Jr. (1922-, American Novelist)

61 Imagination is the highest kite one can fly.
Lauren Bacall (1924-, American Actress)

62 It takes as much imagination to create debt as to create income.
Leonard Orr

63 Live out of your imagination instead of out of your memory.
Les Brown (1945-, American Speaker, Author, Trainer, Motivator Lecturer)

64 Fortunately, somewhere between chance and mystery lies imagination, the only thing that protects our freedom, despite the fact that people keep trying to reduce it or kill it off altogether.
Luis Bunuel (1900-1983, Spanish Film Director)

65 The mind must see visual achievement of the purpose before action is initiated.
Mack R. Douglas

66 Sentiment is the ripened fruit of fantasy.
Madame Belazy

67 The genius of Man in our time has gone into jet-propulsion, atom-splitting, penicillin-curing, etc. There is none over for works of imagination; of spiritual insight or mystical enlightenment. I asked for bread and was given a tranquilizer. It is important to recognize that in our time man has not written one word, thought one thought, put two notes or two bricks together, splashed color on to canvas or concrete into space, in a manner which will be of any conceivable imaginative interest to posterity.
Malcolm Muggeridge (1903-1990, British Broadcaster)

68 Often it is just lack of imagination that keeps a man from suffering very much.
Marcel Proust (1871-1922, French Novelist)

69 When you stop having dreams and ideals -- well, you might as well stop altogether.
Marian Anderson (1902-1993, American Contralto Concert and Opera Singer)

70 You cannot depend on your judgments when your imagination is out of focus.
Mark Twain (1835-1910, American Humorist, Writer)

71 How delightful are the pleasures of the imagination! In those delectable moments, the whole world is ours; not a single creature resists us, we devastate the world, we repopulate it with new objects which, in turn, we immolate. The means to every crime is ours, and we employ them all, we multiply the horror a hundredfold.
Marquis De Sade (1740-1814, French Author)

72 The imagination is the spur of delights... all depends upon it, it is the mainspring of everything; now, is it not by means of the imagination one knows joy? Is it not of the imagination that the sharpest pleasures arise?
Marquis De Sade (1740-1814, French Author)

73 The imagination equips us to perceive reality when it is not fully materialized.
Mary Caroline Richards

74 For imagination sets the goal "picture" which our automatic mechanism works on. We act, or fail to act, not because of "will," as is so commonly believed, but because of imagination.
Maxwell Maltz (American Plastic Surgeon, Author of "Psycho-Cybernetics")

75 Thus man of all creatures is more than a creature, he is also a creator. Man alone can direct his success mechanism by the use of imagination, or imaging ability.
Maxwell Maltz (American Plastic Surgeon, Author of "Psycho-Cybernetics")

76 Begin to imagine what the desirable outcome would be like. Go over these mental pictures and delineate details and refinements. Play them over and over to yourself.
Maxwell Maltz (American Plastic Surgeon, Author of "Psycho-Cybernetics")

77 Study the situation thoroughly, go over in your imagination the various courses of action possible to you and the consequences which can and may follow from each course. Pick out the course which gives the most promise and go ahead.
Maxwell Maltz (American Plastic Surgeon, Author of "Psycho-Cybernetics")

78 When you see a thing clearly in your mind, your creative "success mechanism" within you takes over and does the job much better than you could do it by conscious effort or "willpower."
Maxwell Maltz (American Plastic Surgeon, Author of "Psycho-Cybernetics")

79 The man who has no imagination has no wings.
Muhammad Ali (1942-, American Boxer)

80 Imagination rules the world.
Napoleon Bonaparte (1769-1821, French General, Emperor)

81 The human race is governed by its imagination.
Napoleon Bonaparte (1769-1821, French General, Emperor)

82 First comes thought; then organization of that thought, into ideas and plans; then transformation of those plans into reality. The beginning, as you will observe, is in your imagination.
Napoleon Hill (1883-1970, American Speaker, Motivational Writer, "Think and Grow Rich")

83 Our minds become magnetized with the dominating thoughts we hold in our minds and these magnets attract to us the forces, the people, the circumstances of life which harmonize with the nature of our dominating thoughts.
Napoleon Hill (1883-1970, American Speaker, Motivational Writer, "Think and Grow Rich")

84 All the breaks you need in life wait within your imagination, Imagination is the workshop of your mind, capable of turning mind energy into accomplishment and wealth.
Napoleon Hill (1883-1970, American Speaker, Motivational Writer, "Think and Grow Rich")

85 Capability means imagination...
Napoleon Hill (1883-1970, American Speaker, Motivational Writer, "Think and Grow Rich")

86 The imagination is literally the workshop wherein are fashioned all plans created by man.
Napoleon Hill (1883-1970, American Speaker, Motivational Writer, "Think and Grow Rich")

87 Before I put a sketch on paper, the whole idea is worked out mentally. In my mind I change the construction, make improvements, and even operate the device. Without ever having drawn a sketch I can give the measurements of all parts to workmen, and when completed all these parts will fit, just as certainly as though I had made the actual drawings. It is immaterial to me whether I run my machine in my mind or test it in my shop. The inventions I have conceived in this way have always worked. In thirty years there has not been a single exception. My first electric motor, the vacuum wireless light, my turbine engine and many other devices have all been developed in exactly this way.
Nikola Tesla (1856-1943, Croatian Physicist and Electrical Engineer)

88 Imagination is a quality given a man to compensate him for what he is not, and a sense of humor was provided to console him for what he is.
Oscar Wilde (1856-1900, British Author, Wit)

89 People often get their imagination's mixed up with their memories.
P.K. Shaw

90 Everything you can imagine is real.
Pablo Picasso (1881-1973, Spanish Artist)

91 Some people have just enough imagination to spoil their judgment.
Paul Mallory

92 Imagination grows by exercise, and contrary to common belief, is more powerful in the mature than in the young.
Paul Mccartney (1942-, British Pop Star, Composer, Songwriter, Member of "Beatles")

93 The great instrument of moral good is the imagination.
Percy Bysshe Shelley (1792-1822, British Poet)

94 Soft focus is an important skill that can effect us metaphorically. In other words, the way we see the future has everything to do with how well we can look up and see the expanded horizon before us.
Peter Kline (American Peak Performance Expert)

95 First have being in your mind. Make real in your mind then bring that being into reality. The genius is he who sees what is not yet and causes it to come to be.
Peter Nivio Zarlenga (American Businessman, Founder of Blockbuster Videos)

96 If a child is to keep alive his inborn sense of wonder without any such gift from the fairies, he needs the companionship of at least one adult who can share it, rediscovering with him the joy, excitement, and mystery of the world we live in.
Rachel Carson (1907-1964, American Marine Biologist, Author)

97 Reason can answer questions, but imagination has to ask them.
Ralph Gerard

98 The quality of the imagination is to flow and not to freeze.
Ralph Waldo Emerson (1803-1882, American Poet, Essayist)

99 We live by our imagination, our admiration s, and our sentiments.
Ralph Waldo Emerson (1803-1882, American Poet, Essayist)

100 Science does not know its debt to imagination.
Ralph Waldo Emerson (1803-1882, American Poet, Essayist)

101 What is the imagination? Only an arm or weapon of the interior energy; only the precursor of the reason.
Ralph Waldo Emerson (1803-1882, American Poet, Essayist)

102 There are no days in life so memorable as those which vibrate to some stroke of the imagination.
Ralph Waldo Emerson (1803-1882, American Poet, Essayist)

103 Imagination is not a talent of some people but is the health of everyone.
Ralph Waldo Emerson (1803-1882, American Poet, Essayist)

104 To fly as fast as thought, to anywhere that is." "He said, you must begin by knowing that you have already arrived."
Richard Bach (1936-, American Author)

105 The way we imagine ourselves to appear to another person is an essential element in our conception of ourselves. In other words, I am not what I think I am, and I am not what you think I am. I am what I think you think I am.
Robert Bierstedt

106 Make every thought, every fact, that comes into your mind pay you a profit. Make it work and produce for you. Think of things not as they are but as they might be. Don't merely dream -- but create!
Robert Collier (American Writer, Publisher)

107 Pictures help you to form the mental mold...
Robert Collier (American Writer, Publisher)

108 See the things you want as already yours. Think of them as yours, as belonging to you, as already in your possession.
Robert Collier (American Writer, Publisher)

109 Visualize this thing that you want, see it, feel it, believe in it. Make your mental blue print, and begin to build.
Robert Collier (American Writer, Publisher)

110 The great successful men of the world have used their imaginations... they think ahead and create their mental picture, and the go to work materializing that picture in all its details, filling in here, adding a little there, altering this a bit and that a bit, but steadily building -- steadily building.
Robert Collier (American Writer, Publisher)

111 Let your imagination release your imprisoned possibilities.
Robert H. Schuller (1926-, American Minister (Crystal Cathedral), Author, Social Leader)

112 The entrepreneur is essentially a visualizer and an actualizer. He can visualize something, and when visualizes it he sees exactly how to make it happen.
Robert L Schwartz

113 Imagination... its limits are only those of the mind itself.
Rod Serling (1924-1975, American Television Script-writer)

114 Were it not for imagination a man would be as happy in arms of a chambermaid as of a duchess.
Samuel Johnson (1709-1784, British Author)

115 If you close your eyes, you could just as well imagine me to be vintage Ali MacGraw, circa 1968.
Sandra Bernhard (1955, American Actress)

116 Imagination gallops; judgment merely walks.
Saying

117 Imagination is always the fabric of social life and the dynamic of history. The influence of real needs and compulsions, of real interests and materials, is indirect because the crowd is never conscious of it.
Simone Weil (1910-1943, French Philosopher, Mystic)

118 Imagination and fiction make up more than three quarters of our life.
Simone Weil (1910-1943, French Philosopher, Mystic)

119 A man may imagine things that are false, but he can only understand things that are true, for if the things be false, the apprehension of them is not understanding.
Sir Isaac Newton (1642-1727, British Scientist, Mathematician)

120 We are told never to cross a bridge till we come to it, but this world is owned by men who have "crossed bridges" in their imagination far ahead of the crowd.
Speakers Library

121 I noticed an almost universal trait among Super Achievers, and it was what I call Sensory Goal Vision. These people knew what they wanted out of life, and they could sense it multidimensionally before they ever had it. They could not only see it, but also taste it, smell it, and imagine the sounds and emotions associated with it. They pre-lived it before they had it. And the sharp, sensory vision became a powerful driving force in their lives.
Stephen Devore

122 Live out of your imagination, not your history.
Stephen R. Covey (American Speaker, Trainer, Author of "The 7 Habits of Highly Effective People")

123 Perhaps in a book review it is not out of place to note that the safety of the state depends on cultivating the imagination.
Stephen Vizinczey (1933-, Hungarian Novelist, Critic)

124 By visualizing your goals, you can get your subconscious to work toward making these mental pictures come true.
Success Magazine (American Business Magazine)

125 Not our logical faculty, but our imaginative one is king over us. I might say, priest and prophet to lead us to heaven-ward, or magician and wizard to lead us hellward.
Thomas Carlyle (1795-1881, Scottish Philosopher, Author)

126 Imagination is a poor matter when it has to part company with understanding.
Thomas Carlyle (1795-1881, Scottish Philosopher, Author)

127 Celebrate what you want to see more of.
Thomas J. Peters (1942-, American Management Consultant, Author, Trainer)

128 We can gradually grow into any condition we desire, provided we first make ourselves in habitual mental attitude the person who corresponds to those conditions.
Thomas Troward

129 My imagination makes me human and makes me a fool; it gives me all the world and exiles me from it.
Ursula K. Le Guin (1929-, American Author)

130 Imagination, the supreme delight of the immortal and the immature, should be limited. In order to enjoy life, we should not enjoy it too much.
Vladimir Nabokov (1899-1977, Russian-born American Novelist, Poet)

131 I believe that there never was a creator of a philosophical system who did not confess at the end of his life that he had wasted his time. It must be admitted that the inventors of the mechanical arts have been much more useful to men that the inventors of syllogisms. He who imagined a ship towers considerably above him who imagined innate ideas.
Voltaire (1694-1778, French Historian, Writer)

132 To regard the imagination as metaphysics is to think of it as part of life, and to think of it as part of life is to realize the extent of artifice. We live in the mind.
Wallace Stevens (1879-1955, American Poet)

133 The imagination is man's power over nature.
Wallace Stevens (1879-1955, American Poet)

134 If you can imagine it, you can achieve it; if you can dream it, you can become it.
William A. Ward (1921-,)

135 To me this world is all one continued vision of fancy or imagination, and I feel flattered when I am told so. What is it sets Homer, Virgil and Milton in so high a rank of art? Why is the Bible more entertaining and instructive than any other book? Is it not because they are addressed to the imagination, which is spiritual sensation, and but immediately to the understanding or reason?
William Blake (1757-1827, British Poet, Painter)

136 What is now proved was only once imagined.
William Blake (1757-1827, British Poet, Painter)

137 If you want a quality, act as if you already had it. Try the "as if" technique.
William James (1842-1910, American Psychologist, Professor, Author)

IMITATION

1 We forfeit three-quarters of ourselves in order to be like other people.
Arthur Schopenhauer (1788-1860, German Philosopher)

2 Man is an idiot. He doesn't know how to do anything without copying, without imitating, without plagiarizing, without aping. It might even have been that man invented generation by coitus after seeing the grasshopper copulate.
Augusto Roa Bastos (1917-, Paraguayan Novelist)

3 To equal a predecessor, one must have twice they worth.
Baltasar Gracian (1601-1658, Spanish Philosopher, Writer)

4 Everything that irritates us about others can lead us to an understanding of ourselves.
Carl Jung (1875-1961, Swiss Psychiatrist)

5 Imitation belittles.
Christian Nevell Bovee (1820-1904, American Author, Lawyer)

6 It is well to respect the leader. Learn from him. Observe him. Study him. But don't worship him. Believe you can surpass. Believe you can go beyond. Those who harbor the second-best attitude are invariably second-best doers.
David J. Schwartz (American Trainer, Author of "The Magic of Thinking Big")

7 When people are free to do as they please, they usually imitate each other.
Eric Hoffer (1902-1983, American Author, Philosopher)

8 One who imitates what is bad always goes beyond his model; while one who imitates what is good always comes up short of it.
Francesco Guicciardini (1483-1540, Italian Historian)

9 The only good imitations are those that poke fun at bad originals.
François de La Rochefoucauld (1613-1680, French classical writer)

10 There is only one kind of love, but there are a thousand imitations.
François de La Rochefoucauld (1613-1680, French classical writer)

11 I have found some of the best reasons I ever had for remaining at the bottom simply by looking at the men at the top.
Frank Moore Colby (1865-1925, American Editor, Essayist)

12 Imitation is the sincerest form of television.
Fred Allen (American Businessman, Chairman of Pitney-Bowes)

13 To do the opposite of something is also a form of imitation, namely an imitation of its opposite.
Georg C. Lichtenberg (1742-1799, German Physicist, Satirist)

14 Nature is commonplace. Imitation is more interesting.
Gertrude Stein (1874-1946, American Author)

15 You may imitate, but never counterfeit.
Honore De Balzac (1799-1850, French Novelist)

16 Imitation, if it is not forgery, is a fine thing. It stems from a generous impulse, and a realistic sense of what can and cannot be done.
James Fenton (1949-, British Poet, Critic)

17 An original artist is unable to copy. So he has only to copy in order to be original.
Jean Cocteau (1889-1963, French Author, Filmmaker)

18 Posterity weaves no garlands for imitators.
Johann Friedrich Von Schiller (1759-1805, German Dramatist, Poet, Historian)

19 Man's natural character is to imitate; that of the sensitive man is to resemble as closely as possible the person whom he loves. It is only by imitating the vices of others that I have earned my misfortunes.
Marquis De Sade (1740-1814, French Author)

20 Men nearly always follow the tracks made by others and proceed in their affairs by imitation, even though they cannot entirely keep to the tracks of others or emulate the prowess of their models. So a prudent man should always follow in the footsteps of great men and imitate those who have been outstanding. If his own prowess fails to compare with theirs, at least it has an air of greatness about it. He should behave like those archers who, if they are skilful, when the target seems too distant, know the capabilities of their bow and aim a good deal higher than their objective, not in order to shoot so high but so that by aiming high they can reach the target.
Niccolo Machiavelli (1469-1527, Italian Author, Statesman)

21 To copy others is necessary, but to copy oneself is pathetic.
Pablo Picasso (1881-1973, Spanish Artist)

22 Imitation is suicide.
Ralph Waldo Emerson (1803-1882, American Poet, Essayist)

23 Those who do not want to imitate anything, produce nothing.
Salvador Dali (1904-1989, Spanish Painter)

24 No man was ever great by imitation.
Samuel Johnson (1709-1784, British Author)

25 Almost all absurdity of conduct arises from the imitation of those who we cannot resemble.
Samuel Johnson (1709-1784, British Author)

26 Whatever is well said by another, is mine.
Seneca (4 BC-65 AD, Spanish-born Roman Statesman, philosopher)

27 Simplicity of all things is the hardest to be copy.
Sir Richard Steele (1672-1729, British Dramatist, Essayist, Editor)

28 Artistic genius is an expansion of monkey imitativeness.
W. Winwood Reade (1838-1875, American Writer)

29 To be as good as our fathers we must be better, imitation is not discipleship
Wendell Phillips (1811-1884, American Reformer, Orator)

IMMIGRATION

1 Alien. An American sovereign in his probationary state.
Ambrose Bierce (1842-1914, American Author, Editor, Journalist, "The Devil's Dictionary")

2 Without comprehension, the immigrant would forever remain shut -- a stranger in America. Until America can release the heart as well as train the hand of the immigrant, he would forever remain driven back upon himself, corroded by the very richness of the unused gifts within his soul.
Anzia Yezierska (1885-1970, Polish Writer)

3 There is nothing less to our credit than our neglect of the foreigner and his children, unless it be the arrogance most of us betray when we set out to "Americanize" him.
Charles Horton Cooley (1864-1929, American Sociologist)

4 Keep, ancient lands, your storied pomp!" cries she with silent lips. "Give me your tired, your poor, your huddled masses yearning to breathe free, the wretched refuse of your teeming shore. Send these, the homeless, tempest-tossed, to me; I lift my lamp beside the golden door."
Emma Lazarus

5 It almost seems that nobody can hate America as much as native Americans. America needs new immigrants to love and cherish it.
Eric Hoffer (1902-1983, American Author, Philosopher)

6 The making of an American begins at the point where he himself rejects all other ties, any other history, and himself adopts the vesture of his adopted land.
James Baldwin (1924-1987, American Author)

7 The proposition that Muslims are welcome in Britain if, and only if, they stop behaving like Muslims is a doctrine which is incompatible with the principles that guide a free society.
Roy Hattersley (1932-, British Statesman)

8 Every immigrant who comes here should be required within five years to learn English or leave the country.
Theodore Roosevelt (1858-1919, Twenty-sixth President of the USA)

9 The great social adventure of America is no longer the conquest of the wilderness but the absorption of fifty different peoples.
Walter Lippmann (1889-1974, American Journalist)

IMMORTALITY

1 The belief in immortality has always seemed cowardly to me. When very young I learned that all things die, and all that we wish of good must be won on this earth or not at all.
Anne Smedley (1894-1950, American Author, Lecturer)

2 We feel and know that we are eternal.
Baruch (Benedict de) Spinoza (1632-1677, Dutch Philosopher and Theologian)

3 Now this is eternal life: that they may know you, the only true God, and Jesus Christ whom thou has sent. [Jesus -- John 17:3]
Bible (Sacred Scriptures of Christians and Judaism)

4 For them that think death's honesty won't fall upon them naturally life sometimes must get lonely.
Bob Dylan (1941-, American Musician, Singer, Songwriter)

5 Every idea is endowed of itself with immortal life, like a human being. All created form, even that which is created by man, is immortal. For form is independent of matter: molecules do not constitute form.
Charles Baudelaire (1821-1867, French Poet)

6 Deathlessness should be arrived at in a... haphazard fashion. Loving fame as much as any man, we shall carve our initials in the shell of a tortoise and turn him loose in a peat bog.
E(lwyn) B(rooks) White (1899-1985, American Author, Editor)

7 If there is a God, man's immortality is certain. If not, Immortality would not be worth having.
Edgar Sheffield Brightman

8 Perhaps nature is our best assurance of immortality.
Eleanor Roosevelt (1884-1962, American First Lady, Columnist, Lecturer, Humanitarian)

9 Man, as long as he lives, is immortal. One minute before his death he shall be immortal. But one minute later, God wins.
Elie Wiesel (1928-, Rumanian-born American Writer)

10 All things by immortal power. Near of far, to each other linked are, that thou canst not stir a flower without troubling of a star.
Francis Thompson (1859-1907, British Poet)

11 Immortality is the genius to move others long after you yourself have stopped moving.
Frank Rooney

12 Immortality is what nature possesses without effort and without anybody's assistance, and immortality is what the mortals must therefore try to achieve if they want to live up to the world into which they were born, to live up to the things which surround them and to whose company they are admitted for a short while.
Hannah Arendt (1906-1975, German-born American Political Philosopher)

13 Immortal mortals, mortal immortals, one living the others death and dying the others life.
Heraclitus (535-475 BC, Greek Philosopher)

14 The only thing wrong with immortality is that it tends to go on forever.
Herb Caen

15 He had decided to live forever or die in the attempt.
Joseph Heller (1923-, American Author)

16 The self-existent Lord pierced the senses to turn outward. Thus we look to the world outside and see not the Self within us. A sage withdrew his senses from the world of change and, seeking immortality, looked within and beheld the deathless self.
Katha Upanishad (Ancient Hindu Scripture)

17 It has been said that the immortality of the soul is a "grand peut-"tre" --but still it is a grand one. Everybody clings to it --the stupidest, and dullest, and wickedest of human bipeds is still persuaded that he is immortal.
Lord Byron (1788-1824, British Poet)

18 To achieve great things we must live as though we were never going to die.
Marquis De Vauvenargues (1715-1747, French Moralist)

19 Films and gramophone records, music, books and buildings show clearly how vigorously a man's life and work go on after his "death," whether we feel it or not, whether we are aware of the individual names or not. There is no such thing as death according to our view!
Martin Bormann (1900-1945, German Nazi Leader)

20 I have good hope that there is something after death.
Plato (427-347 BC, Greek Philosopher)

21 Higher than the question of our duration is the question of our deserving. Immortality will come to such as are fit for it, and he would be a great soul in future must be a great soul now.
Ralph Waldo Emerson (1803-1882, American Poet, Essayist)

22 To himself everyone is an immortal. He may know that he is going to die, but he can never know that he is dead.
Samuel Butler (1612-1680, British Poet, Satirist)

23 The first requisite for immortality is death.
Stanislaw J. Lec (1909-, Polish Writer)

24 Millions long for immortality who do not know what to do with themselves on a rainy Sunday afternoon.
Susan Ertz

25 The best argument I know for an immortal life is the existence of a man who deserves one.
William James (1842-1910, American Psychologist, Professor, Author)

26 But thy eternal summer shall not fade.
William Shakespeare (1564-1616, British Poet, Playwright, Actor)

27 I don't want to achieve immortality through my work. I want to achieve it through not dying.
Woody Allen (1935-, American Director, Screenwriter, Actor, Comedian)

IMPARTIALITY

1 Impartial. Unable to perceive any promise of personal advantage from espousing either side of a controversy.
Ambrose Bierce (1842-1914, American Author, Editor, Journalist, "The Devil's Dictionary")

2 Man is always partial and is quite right to be. Even impartiality is partial.
Georg C. Lichtenberg (1742-1799, German Physicist, Satirist)

3 Our impartiality is kept for abstract merit and demerit, which none of us ever saw.
George Eliot (1819-1880, British Novelist)

4 What people call impartiality may simply mean indifference, and what people call partiality may simply mean mental activity.
Gilbert K. Chesterton (1874-1936, British Author)

5 If we keep an open mind, too much is likely to fall into it.
Natalie Clifford Barney (1876-1972, American-born French Author)

6 Balance is the enemy of art.
Richard Eyre

IMPORTANCE

1 The main things which seem to me important on their own account, and not merely as a means to other account, and not merely as a means to other things, are knowledge, art instinctive happiness, and relations of friendship or affection.
Bertrand Russell (1872-1970, British Philosopher, Mathematician, Essayist)

2 The things which are most important don't always scream the loudest.
Bob Hawke

3 If people concentrated on the really important things in life, there'd be a shortage of fishing poles.
Doug Larson

4 The simple lack of her is more to me than others presence.
Edward Thomas

5 Each shot is important.
Gary Player (Born 1969, American Golfer)

6 Things which matter most must never be at the mercy of things which matter least.
Johann Wolfgang Von Goethe (1749-1832, German Poet, Dramatist, Novelist)

7 People who matter are most aware that everyone else does, too.
Malcolm S. Forbes (1919-1990, American Publisher, Businessman)

8 Every human being is trying to say something to others. Trying to cry out I am alive, notice me! Speak to me! Confirm that I am important, that I matter!!
Marion D. Hanks

9 My importance to the world is relatively small. On the other hand, my importance to myself is tremendous. I am all I have to work with, to play with, to suffer and to enjoy. It is not the eyes of others that I am wary of, but of my own. I do not intend to let myself down more than I can possibly help, and I find that the fewer illusions I have about myself or the world around me, the better company I am for myself.
Noel Coward (1899-1973, British Writer)

10 Half of the harm that is done in this world is due to people who want to feel important. They don't mean to do harm. But the harm does not interest them.
T. S. Eliot (1888-1965, American-born British Poet, Critic)

11 You are important enough to ask and you are blessed enough to receive back.
Wayne Dyer (1940-, American Psychotherapist, Author, Lecturer)

12 Much Ado About Nothing,
William Shakespeare (1564-1616, British Poet, Playwright, Actor)

IMPOSSIBILITY

1 There is nothing impossible to him who will try.
Alexander The Great (352-323 BC, Alexander III, Ancient Macedonian King)

2 If you can't, you must. If you must, you can.
Anthony Robbins (1960-, American Author, Speaker, Peak Performance Expert / Consultant)

3 Attempt the impossible in order to improve your work.
Bette Davis (1908-1989, American Actress, Producer)

4 Scientists have proven that it's impossible to long-jump 30 feet, but I don't listen to that kind of talk. Thoughts like that have a way of sinking into your feet.
Carl Lewis (1961-, American Track Athlete)

5 All parents believe their children can do the impossible. They thought it the minute we were born, and no matter how hard we've tried to prove them wrong, they all think it about us now. And the really annoying thing is, they're probably right.
Cathy Guisewite

6 Impossibilities are merely things which we have not yet learned.
Charles W. Chesnutt

7 Something which we think is impossible now is not impossible in another decade.
Constance Baker Motley (First Black American Woman Federal Judge)

8 With love and patience, nothing is impossible.
Daisaku Ikeda

9 The Wright brothers flew through the smoke screen of impossibility.
Dorothea Brande (American Success Writer)

10 You must do the thing that you think you cannot do.
Eleanor Roosevelt (1884-1962, American First Lady, Columnist, Lecturer, Humanitarian)

11 When anyone tells me I can't do anything. I'm just not listening any more.
Florence Griffith Joyner (1959-, American Track Athlete)

12 Nothing is impossible to the man who will.
Gabriel Riqueti Mirabeau (1749-1791, French Revolutionary Politician, Orator)

13 The Difficult is that which can be done immediately; the Impossible that which takes a little longer.
George Santayana (1863-1952, American Philosopher, Poet)

14 All limits are self imposed.
Icarus

15 The impossible is often the untried.
Jim Goodwin

16 To the timid soul, nothing is possible.
John Bach (American   Basketball Coach)

17 If someone says can't, that shows you what to do.
John Cage (1912-1992, American Composer)

18 Nothing is impossible to a willing heart.
John Heywood (1497-1580, British Dramatist, Proverb Collection)

19 Most of the things worth doing in the world had been declared impossible before they were done.
Louis D. Brandeis (1856-1941, American Judge)

20 Apparently there is nothing that cannot happen today.
Mark Twain (1835-1910, American Humorist, Writer)

21 The only lack or limitation is in your own mind.
N. H. Moos

22 Impossible is a word only to be found in the dictionary of fools.
Napoleon Bonaparte (1769-1821, French General, Emperor)

23 All who have accomplished great things have had a great aim, have fixed their gaze on a goal which was high, one which sometimes seemed impossible.
Orison Swett Marden (1850-1924, American Author, Founder of Success Magazine)

24 Man can believe the impossible, but man can never believe the improbable.
Oscar Wilde (1856-1900, British Author, Wit)

25 Every man is an impossibility until he is born.
Ralph Waldo Emerson (1803-1882, American Poet, Essayist)

26 It is difficult to say what is impossible, for the dream of yesterday is the hope of today and the reality of tomorrow.
Robert H. Goddard (1882-1945, Physicist, Rocketry Pioneer)

27 The only place where your dream becomes impossible is in your own thinking.
Robert H. Schuller (1926-, American Minister (Crystal Cathedral), Author, Social Leader)

28 Impossible situations can become possible miracles.
Robert H. Schuller (1926-, American Minister (Crystal Cathedral), Author, Social Leader)

29 Today's accomplishments were yesterday's impossibilities.
Robert H. Schuller (1926-, American Minister (Crystal Cathedral), Author, Social Leader)

30 To the timid and hesitating everything is impossible because it seems so.
Sir Walter Scott (1771-1832, British Novelist, Poet)

31 Start by doing what's necessary, then what's possible and suddenly you are doing the impossible.
St. Francis of Assisi (1181-1226, Italian Preacher, Founder of the Franciscan Orde)

32 It is not a lucky word, this name "impossible"; no good comes of those who have it so often in their mouths.
Thomas Carlyle (1795-1881, Scottish Philosopher, Author)

33 It's kind of fun to do the impossible.
Walt Disney (1901-1966, American Artist, Film Producer)

34 Nothing is impossible for the man who doesn't have to do it himself.
Weiler

IMPROVEMENT

1 If you improve or tinker with something long enough, eventually it will break or malfunction.
Arthur Bloch

2 Where we cannot invent, we may at least improve.
Charles Caleb Colton (1780-1832, British Sportsman Writer)

3 Much of the wisdom of one age, is the folly of the next.
Charles Simmons

4 Acorns were good until bread was found.
Francis Bacon (1561-1626, British Philosopher, Essayist, Statesman)

5 As long as I can conceive something better than myself I cannot be easy unless I am striving to bring it into existence or clearing the way for it.
George Bernard Shaw (1856-1950, Irish-born British Dramatist)

6 The best performance improvement is the transition from the nonworking state to the working state.
John Ousterhout

7 Judge of thine improvement, not by what thou speakest or writest, but by the firmness of thy mind, and the government of thy passions and affections.
Thomas Fuller (1608-1661, British Clergyman, Author)

8   Things will get better -- despite our efforts to improve them.
    Will Rogers (1879-1935, American Humorist, Actor)

9   Undoubtedly a man is to labor to better his condition, but first to better himself.
    William Ellery Channing (1780-1842, American Unitarian Minister, Author)

IMPUDENCE

1   Impudence is the worst of all human diseases.
    Euripides (480-406 BC, Greek Tragic Poet)

IMPULSE

1   The most decisive actions of our life -- I mean those that are most likely to decide the whole course of our future -- are, more often than not, unconsidered.
    Andre Gide (1869-1951, French Author)

2   The awful daring of a moment's surrender which an age of prudence can never retract.
    T. S. Eliot (1888-1965, American-born British Poet, Critic)

INACTION

1   The sleeping fox catches no poultry.
    Benjamin Franklin (1706-1790, American Scientist, Publisher, Diplomat)

2   How long will they kill our prophets while we stand aside and look?
    Bob Marley (1954-, Jamaican-born American Musician, Song Writer)

3   Oh, I'm not going to do anything to them. The thought that I might will be enough to keep them going.
    Chris Bowkett

4   Man who stand on hill with mouth open will wait long time for roast duck to drop in.
    Confucius (551-479 BC, Chinese Ethical Teacher, Philosopher)

5   If you stand still long enough, you'll get stuck
    David Hasslehoff

6   A sedentary life is the real sin against the Holy Spirit. Only those thoughts that come by walking have any value.
    Friedrich Nietzsche (1844-1900, German Philosopher)

7   It's better to waste one's youth than to do nothing with it at all.
    Georges Courteline

8   One of the best lessons children learn through video games is standing still will get them killed quicker than anything else.
    Jinx Milea

9   You won't skid if you stay in a rut.
    Kin Hubbard (1868-1930, American Humorist, Journalist)

10 Just as there is no loss of basic energy in the universe, so no thought or action is without its effects, present or ultimate, seen or unseen, felt or unfelt.
    Norman Cousins (1915-1990, American Editor, Humanitarian, Author)

11 Many are called but few get up.
    Oliver Herford (1863-1935, American Author, Illustrator)

12 Nothing else so destroys the power to stand alone as the habit of leaning upon others. If you lean, you will never be strong or original. Stand alone or bury your ambition to be somebody in the world.
    Orison Swett Marden (1850-1924, American Author, Founder of Success Magazine)

13 To do nothing at all is the most difficult thing in the world, the most difficult and the most intellectual.
    Oscar Wilde (1856-1900, British Author, Wit)

14 To sit back hoping that someday, some way, someone will make things right is to go on feeding the crocodile, hoping he will eat you last -- but eat you he will.
    Ronald Reagan (1911-, Fortieth President of the USA, Actor)

15 Solve it. Solve it quickly, solve it right or wrong. If you solve it wrong, it will come back and slap you in the face, and then you can solve it right. Lying dead in the water and doing nothing is a comfortable alternative because it is without risk, but it is an absolutely fatal way to manage a business.
    Thomas J. Watson (18?-1956, American Businessman, Founder of IBM)

16 There's as much risk in doing nothing as in doing something.
    Trammell Crow

17 Sitting quietly, doing nothing, spring comes and the grass grows by itself.
    Zen Saying

INCOME

1   I'm living so far beyond my income that we may almost be said to be living apart.
    E.E. (Edward. E.) Cummings (1894-1962, American Poet)

2   There is nothing more demoralizing than a small but adequate income.
    Edmund Wilson (1895-1972, American Writer, Critic)

3   First secure an independent income, then practice virtue.
    Greek Proverb

4   A large income is the best recipe for happiness I ever heard of.
    Jane Austen (1775-1817, British Novelist)

5   There are few sorrows, however poignant, in which a good income is of no avail.
    Robert Frost (1875-1963, American Poet)

INCONSISTENCY

1. No author ever drew a character consistent to human nature, but he was forced to ascribe to it many inconsistencies.
Edward G. Bulwer-Lytton (1803-1873, British Novelist, Poet)

2. Mutability of temper and inconsistency with ourselves is the greatest weakness of human nature.
Joseph Addison (1672-1719, British Essayist, Poet, Statesman)

INCREDULITY

1. The curse of man, and the cause of nearly all his woe, is his stupendous capacity for believing the incredible.
H. L. Mencken (1880-1956, American Editor, Author, Critic, Humorist)

2. Incredulity robs us of many pleasures, and gives us nothing in return.
James Russell Lowell (1819-1891, American Poet, Critic, Editor)

3. Incredulity is the wisdom of the fool.
Josh Billings (1815-1885, American Humorist, Lecturer)

INDECISION

1. We know what happens to people who stay in the middle of the road. They get run over.
Aneurin Bevan (1897-1960, British Labor Politician)

2. I used to be indecisive; now I'm not sure.
Graffiti

3. Indecision is debilitating; it feeds upon itself; it is, one might almost say, habit-forming. Not only that, but it is contagious; it transmits itself to others.
H. A. Hopf

4. To do nothing is also a good remedy.
Hippocrates (Ancient Greek Physician)

5. He who hesitates is sometimes saved.
James Thurber (1894-1961, American Humorist, Illustrator)

6. You need an infinite stretch of time ahead of you to start to think, infinite energy to make the smallest decision. The world is getting denser. The immense number of useless projects is bewildering. Too many things have to be put in to balance up an uncertain scale. You can't disappear anymore. You die in a state of total indecision.
Jean Baudrillard (French Postmodern Philosopher, Writer)

7. He has conferred on the practice of vacillation the aura of statesmanship.
Kenneth Baker (American Professor)

8. The risk of a wrong decision is preferable to the terror of indecision.
Maimonides (1135-1204, Spanish-born Jewish Philosopher)

9. Perhaps, on the whole, embarrassment and perplexity are a kind of natural accompaniment to life and movement; and it is better to be driven out of your senses with thinking which of two things you ought to do than to do nothing whatever, and be utterly uninteresting to all the world.
Margaret Oliphant (1828-1897, British Novelist, Historian)

10. It is human nature to stand in the middle of a thing.
Marianne Moore (1887-1972, American Poet)

11. I must have a prodigious quantity of mind; it takes me as much as a week, sometimes, to make it up.
Mark Twain (1835-1910, American Humorist, Writer)

12. The human heart is like a ship on a stormy sea driven about by winds blowing from all four corners of heaven.
Martin Luther (1483-1546, German Leader of the Protestant Reformation)

13. Once I make up my mind, I'm full of indecision.
Oscar Levant (1906-1972, American Pianist, Actor)

14. Once he makes up his mind, he's full of indecision. [On Dwight D. Eisenhower]
Oscar Levant (1906-1972, American Pianist, Actor)

15. Don't stand shivering upon the bank; plunge in at once, and have it over.
Sam Slick

16. Neither have they hearts to stay, nor wit enough to run away.
Samuel Butler (1612-1680, British Poet, Satirist)

17. Most men ebb and flow in wretchedness between the fear of death and the hardship of life; they are unwilling to live, and yet they do not know how to die.
Seneca (4 BC-65 AD, Spanish-born Roman Statesman, philosopher)

18. In a minute there is time for decisions and revisions which a minute will reverse.
T. S. Eliot (1888-1965, American-born British Poet, Critic)

19. There is no more miserable human being than one in whom nothing is habitual but indecision, and for whom the lighting of every cigar, the drinking of every cup, the time of rising and going to bed every day, and the beginning of every bit of work, are subjects of express volitional deliberation.
William James (1842-1910, American Psychologist, Professor, Author)

INDEPENDENCE

1. I am lord of myself, accountable to none.
Benjamin Franklin (1706-1790, American Scientist, Publisher, Diplomat)

2. Without moral and intellectual independence, there is no anchor for national independence.
David Ben-Gurion (1886-1973, Polish-born Israeli Statesman, Prime Minister)

3   The man who goes alone can start today; but he who travels with another must wait till that other is ready, and it may be a long time before they get off.
Henry David Thoreau (1817-1862, American Essayist, Poet, Naturalist)

4   In the word of no master am I bound to believe.
Horace (65-8 BC, Italian Poet)

5   I equally dislike the favor of the public with the love of a woman -- they are both a cloying treacle to the wings of independence.
John Keats (1795-1821, British Poet)

6   It's easy to be independent when you've got money. But to be independent when you haven't got a thing -- that's the Lord's test.
Mahalia Jackson (1911-1972, American Gospel Singer)

7   Our treatment of both older people and children reflects the value we place on independence and autonomy. We do our best to make our children independent from birth. We leave them all alone in rooms with the lights out and tell them, "Go to sleep by yourselves." And the old people we respect most are the ones who will fight for their independence, who would sooner starve to death than ask for help.
Margaret Mead (1901-1978, American Anthropologist)

8   Independence I have long considered as the grand blessing of life, the basis of every virtue; and independence I will ever secure by contracting my wants, though I were to live on a barren heath.
Mary Wollstonecraft (1759-1797, British Feminist Writer)

9   Nature never said to me: Do not be poor; still less did she say: Be rich; her cry to me was always: Be independent.
Sebastien-Roch Nicolas De Chamfort (1741-1794, French Writer, Journalist, Playwright)

10   The price for independence is often isolation and solitude.
Steve Schmidt

11   The beauty of independence, departure, actions that rely on themselves.
Walt Whitman (1819-1892, American Poet)

12   No one can build his security upon the nobleness of another person.
Willa Cather (1876-1947, American Author)

INDIFFERENCE

1   Lukewarmness I account a sin, as great in love as in religion.
Abraham Cowley (1618-1667, British Poet)

2   Only one enemy is worse than despair: indifference. In every area of human creativity, indifference is the enemy; indifference of evil is worse than evil, because it is also sterile.
Elie Wiesel (1928-, Rumanian-born American Writer)

3   The opposite of love is not hate, it's indifference. The opposite of art is not ugliness, it's indifference. The opposite of faith is not heresy, it's indifference. And the opposite of life is not death, it's indifference.
Elie Wiesel (1928-, Rumanian-born American Writer)

4   Pain has its reasons, pleasure is totally indifferent.
Francis Picabia (1878-1953, French Painter, Poet)

5   Nothing can contribute more to peace of soul than the lack of any opinion whatever.
Georg C. Lichtenberg (1742-1799, German Physicist, Satirist)

6   The worst sin towards our fellow creatures is not to hate them, but to be indifferent to them; that's the essence of inhumanity.
George Bernard Shaw (1856-1950, Irish-born British Dramatist)

7   The worst sin... is... to be indifferent.
George Bernard Shaw (1856-1950, Irish-born British Dramatist)

8   Men are accomplices to that which leaves them indifferent.
George Steiner (1929-, French-born American Critic, Novelist)

9   Wherever the citizen becomes indifferent to his fellows, so will the husband be to his wife, and the father of a family toward the members of his household.
Karl Wilhelm Von Humboldt (1767-1835, German Statesman, Philologist)

10   It means nothing to me. I have no opinion about it, and I don't care.
Pablo Picasso (1881-1973, Spanish Artist)

11   A different world cannot be built by indifferent people.
Peter Marshall (1902-1949, American Presbyterian Clergyman)

12   I have protracted my work till most of those whom I wished to please have sunk into the grave, and success and miscarriage are empty sounds: I therefore dismiss it with frigid tranquillity, having little to fear or hope from censure or from praise.
Samuel Johnson (1709-1784, British Author)

INDIVIDUALITY

1   More and more, when faced with the world of men, the only reaction is one of individualism. Man alone is an end unto himself. Everything one tries to do for the common good ends in failure.
Albert Camus (1913-1960, French Existential Writer)

2   Each makes this cosmos and its construction the pivot of his emotional life, in order to find in this way peace and security which he can not find in the narrow whirlpool of personal experience.
Albert Einstein (1879-1955, German-born American Physicist)

3 Writers write to influence their readers, their preachers, their auditors, but always, at bottom, to be more themselves.
Aldous Huxley (1894-1963, British Author)

4 Those who talk about individuality the most are the ones who most object to deviation, and in a few years it may be the other way around. Some day everybody will just think what they want to think, and then everybody will probably be thinking alike; that
Andy Warhol (1930-, American Artist, Filmmaker)

5 The definition of the individual was: a multitude of one million divided by one million.
Arthur Koestler (1905-1983, Hungarian Born British Writer)

6 No one can transcend their own individuality.
Arthur Schopenhauer (1788-1860, German Philosopher)

7 Every single one of us can do things that no one else can do -- can love things that no one else can love. We are like violins. We can be used for doorstops, or we can make music. You know what to do.
Barbara Sher (American Author of "I Could Do Anything If I Only Knew What It Was")

8 The trouble with the sacred Individual is that he has no significance, except as he can acquire it from others, from the social whole.
Bernard Devoto (1897-1955, American Writer, Critic, Historian)

9 Never follow the crowd.
Bernard M. Baruch (1870-1965, American Financier)

10 Resistance to the organized mass can be effected only by the man who is as well organized in his individuality as the mass itself.
Carl Jung (1875-1961, Swiss Psychiatrist)

11 The shoe that fits one person pinches another; there is no recipe for living that suits all cases.
Carl Jung (1875-1961, Swiss Psychiatrist)

12 It is said that if Noah's ark had to be built by a company; they would not have laid the keel yet; and it may be so. What is many men's business is nobody's business. The greatest things are accomplished by individual men.
Charles Haddon Spurgeon (1834-1892, British Baptist Preacher)

13 Each man must have his "I"; it is more necessary to him than bread; and if he does not find scope for it within the existing institutions he will be likely to make trouble.
Charles Horton Cooley (1864-1929, American Sociologist)

14 Follow your own star!
Dante (Alighieri) (1265-1321, Italian Philosopher, Poet)

15 It is the individual only who is timeless. Societies, cultures, and civilizations --past and present --are often incomprehensible to outsiders, but the individual's hungers, anxieties, dreams, and preoccupations have remained unchanged through the millennia.
Eric Hoffer (1902-1983, American Author, Philosopher)

16 We would worry less about what others think of us if we realized how seldom they do.
Ethel Barrett (Missionary)

17 Be yourself, who else is better qualified?
Frank J. Giblin

18 Individuality is either the mark of genius or the reverse. Mediocrity finds safety in standardization.
Frederick E. Crane

19 Every man must get to Heaven his own way.
Frederick The Great (Frederick II) (1712-1786, Born in Berlin, King of Prussia (1740-1786))

20 You have your way. I have my way. As for the right way, the correct way, and the only way, it does not exist.
Friedrich Nietzsche (1844-1900, German Philosopher)

21 What is wanted -- whether this is admitted or not -- is nothing less than a fundamental remolding, indeed weakening and abolition of the individual: one never tires of enumerating and indicating all that is evil and inimical, prodigal, costly, extravagant in the form individual existence has assumed hitherto, one hopes to manage more cheaply, more safely, more equitably, more uniformly if there exist only large bodies and their members.
Friedrich Nietzsche (1844-1900, German Philosopher)

22 In each individual the spirit is made flesh, in each one the whole of creation suffers, in each one a Savior is crucified.
Hermann Hesse (1877-1962, German-born Swiss Novelist, Poet)

23 The great challenge which faces us is to assure that, in our society of big-ness, we do not strangle the voice of creativity, that the rules of the game do not come to overshadow its purpose, that the grand orchestration of society leaves ample room for the man who marches to the music of another drummer.
Hubert H. Humphrey (1911-1978, American Democratic Politician, Vice President)

24 The work of the individual still remains the spark that moves mankind forward.
Igor Sikorsky

25 Individuality is the aim of political liberty. By leaving to the citizen as much freedom of action and of being, as comports with order and the rights of others, the institutions render him truly a freeman. He is left to pursue his means of happiness in his own manner.
James F. Cooper (1789-1851, American Novelist)

26 The nail that sticks up will be hammered down.
Japanese Proverb

27 Your labor only may be sold, your soul must not.
John Ruskin (1819-1900, British Critic, Social Theorist)

28 What ever crushes individuality is despotism, no matter what name it is called.
John Stuart Mill (1806-1873, British Philosopher, Economist)

29 That so few now dare to be eccentric, marks the chief danger of the time.
John Stuart Mill (1806-1873, British Philosopher, Economist)

30 But society has now fairly got the better of individuality; and the danger which threatens human nature is not the excess, but the deficiency, of personal Impulses and preferences.
John Stuart Mill (1806-1873, British Philosopher, Economist)

31 The privilege of a lifetime is being who you are.
Joseph Campell

32 In bourgeois society capital is independent and has individuality, while the living person is dependent and has no individuality.
Karl Marx (1818-1883, German Political Theorist, Social Philosopher)

33 Except in a few well-publicized instances (enough to lend credence to the iconography painted on the walls of the media), the rigorous practice of rugged individualism usually leads to poverty, ostracism and disgrace. The rugged individualist is too often mistaken for the misfit, the maverick, the spoilsport, the sore thumb.
Lewis H. Lapham (1935-, American Essayist, Editor)

34 The individual, man as a man, man as a brain, if you like, interests me more than what he makes, because I've noticed that most artists only repeat themselves.
Marcel Duchamp (1887-1968, French Artist)

35 Be content to be what you are, and prefer nothing to it, and do not fear or wish for your last day.
Marcus Valerius Martial (40-104, Latin poet and epigrammatist)

36 A gesture cannot be regarded as the expression of an individual, as his creation (because no individual is capable of creating a fully original gesture, belonging to nobody else), nor can it even be regarded as that person's instrument; on the contrary, it is gestures that use us as their instruments, as their bearers and incarnations.
Milan Kundera (1929-, Czech Author, Critic)

37 Comrades! We must abolish the cult of the individual decisively, once and for all.
Nikita Khrushchev (1894-1971, Soviet Premier)

38 My great mistake, the fault for which I can't forgive myself, is that one day I ceased my obstinate pursuit of my own individuality.
Oscar Wilde (1856-1900, British Author, Wit)

39 My mother said to me, "If you become a soldier, you'll be a general; if you become a monk you'll end up as the pope." Instead, I became a painter and wound up as Picasso. --Pablo Picasso Never permit a dichotomy to rule your life, a dichotomy in which you hate what you do so you can have pleasure in your spare time. Look for a situation in which your work will give you as much happiness as your spare time.
Pablo Picasso (1881-1973, Spanish Artist)

40 Losing faith in your own singularity is the start of wisdom, I suppose; also the first announcement of death.
Peter Conrad (1948-, Australian Critic, Author)

41 There used to be a real me, but I had it surgically removed.
Peter Seller (British Actor)

42 If I am not for myself, who will be for me? If I am not for others, what am I? And if not now, when?
Rabbi Hillel (30 BC-9 AD, Jewish Rabbi, Teacher)

43 A man must consider what a rich realm he abdicates when he becomes a conformist.
Ralph Waldo Emerson (1803-1882, American Poet, Essayist)

44 Our expenses are all for conformity.
Ralph Waldo Emerson (1803-1882, American Poet, Essayist)

45 Each man must grant himself the emotions that he needs and the morality that suits him.
Remy De Gourmont (1858-1915, French Novelist, Philosopher, Poet, Playwright)

46 The best things and best people rise out of their separateness; I'm against a homogenized society because I want the cream to rise.
Robert Frost (1875-1963, American Poet)

47 The greatest enemy of individual freedom is the individual himself.
Saul Alinsky (1909-1972, American Radical Activist)

48 A happy life is one which is in accordance with its own nature.
Seneca (4 BC-65 AD, Spanish-born Roman Statesman, philosopher)

49 Do not wish to be anything but what you are, and try to be that perfectly.
St. Francis De Sales (1567-1622, Roman Catholic Bishop, Writer)

50 Pin your faith to no ones sleeves, haven't you two eyes of your own.
Thomas Carlyle (1795-1881, Scottish Philosopher, Author)

51 No one should part with their individuality and become that of another.
William Ellery Channing (1780-1842, American Unitarian Minister, Author)

52 America is not anything if it consists of each of us. It is something only if it consists of all of us.
Woodrow T. Wilson (1856-1924, Twenty-eighth President of the USA)

53 Everything without tells the individual that he is nothing; everything within persuades him that he is everything.
X. Doudan

INDOLENCE

1   There are men here and there to whom the whole of life is like an after-dinner hour with a cigar; easy, pleasant, empty, perhaps enlivened by some fable of strife to be forgotten -- before the end is told -- even if there happens to be any end to it.
Joseph Conrad (1857-1924, Polish-born British Novelist)

2   I look upon indolence as a sort of suicide; for the man is effectually destroyed, though the appetites of the brute may survive.
Lord Chesterfield (1694-1773, British Statesman, Author)

3   Indolence is a delightful but distressing state; we must be doing something to be happy. Action is no less necessary than thought to the instinctive tendencies of the human frame.
Mahatma Gandhi (1869-1948, Indian Political, Spiritual Leader)

4   The present generation, wearied by its chimerical efforts, relapses into complete indolence. Its condition is that of a man who has only fallen asleep towards morning: first of all come great dreams, then a feeling of laziness, and finally a witty or clever excuse for remaining in bed.
Soren Kierkegaard (1813-1855, Danish Philosopher, Writer)

5   Prostration is our natural position. A worm-like movement from a spot of sunlight to a spot of shade, and back, is the type of movement that is natural to men.
Wyndham Lewis (1882-1957, British Author, Painter)

INDUSTRY

1   It is an axiom, enforced by all the experience of the ages, that they who rule industrially will rule politically.
Aneurin Bevan (1897-1960, British Labor Politician)

2   The reality is that zero defects in products plus zero pollution plus zero risk on the job is equivalent to maximum growth of government plus zero economic growth plus runaway inflation.
Dixie Lee Ray (1914-1994, American Educator, Governor, Zoologist)

3   The great cry that rises from all our manufacturing cities, louder than the furnace blast, is all in very deed for this -- that we manufacture everything there except men.
John Ruskin (1819-1900, British Critic, Social Theorist)

4   Colonial system, public debts, heavy taxes, protection, commercial wars, etc., these offshoots of the period of manufacture swell to gigantic proportions during the period of infancy of large-scale industry. The birth of the latter is celebrated by a vast, Hero-like slaughter of the innocents.
Karl Marx (1818-1883, German Political Theorist, Social Philosopher)

5   We have created an industrial order geared to automatism, where feeble-mindedness, native or acquired, is necessary for docile productivity in the factory; and where a pervasive neurosis is the final gift of the meaningless life that issues forth at the other end.
Lewis Mumford (1895-1990, American Social Philosopher)

6   It has been my fate in a long life of production to be credited chiefly with the equivocal virtue of industry, a quality so excellent in morals, so little satisfactory in art.
Margaret Oliphant (1828-1897, British Novelist, Historian)

7   In an industrial society which confuses work and productivity, the necessity of producing has always been an enemy of the desire to create.
Raoul Vaneigem (1934-, Belgian Situationist Philosopher)

8   Industry has operated against the artisan in favor of the idler, and also in favor of capital and against labor. Any mechanical invention whatsoever has been more harmful to humanity than a century of war.
Remy De Gourmont (1858-1915, French Novelist, Philosopher, Poet, Playwright)

INEQUALITY

1   However energetically society in general may strive to make all the citizens equal and alike, the personal pride of each individual will always make him try to escape from the common level, and he will form some inequality somewhere to his own profit.
Alexis De Tocqueville (1805-1859, French Social Philosopher)

2   We accept and welcome... as conditions to which we must accommodate ourselves, great inequality of environment; the concentration of business, industrial and commercial, in the hands of a few; and the law of competition between these, as being not only beneficial, but essential for the future progress of the race.
Andrew Carnegie (1835-1919, American Industrialist, Philanthropist)

3   Two nations between whom there is no intercourse and no sympathy; who are as ignorant of each other's habits, thoughts, and feelings, as if they were dwellers in different zones, or inhabitants of different planets. The rich and the poor.
Benjamin Disraeli (1804-1881, British Statesman, Prime Minister)

4   The rich man in his castle, the poor man at his gate, God made them, high or lowly, and ordered their estate.
Cecil F. Alexander

5   No amount of artificial reinforcement can offset the natural inequalities of human individuals.
Henry P. Fairchild (American Sociologist)

6   The only inequalities that matter begin in the mind. It is not income levels but differences in mental equipment that keep people apart, breed feelings of inferiority.
Jacquetta Hawkes

755

7 The very existence of government at all, infers inequality. The citizen who is preferred to office becomes the superior to those who are not, so long as he is the repository of power, and the child inherits the wealth of the parent as a controlling law of society.
James F. Cooper (1789-1851, American Novelist)

8 When Adam delved and Eve span, who was then the gentleman?
John Ball (12th Century, British Priest, Social Agitator)

9 People differ in capacity, skill, health, strength; and unequal fortune is a necessary result of unequal condition. Such inequality is far from being disadvantageous either to individuals or to the community.
Leo XIII (1810-1903, Pope from 1878 to 1903)

10 My grandma (rest her soul) used to say, "There were but two families in the world, have-much and have-little."
Miguel De Cervantes (1547-1616, Spanish Novelist, Dramatist, Poet)

11 I never could believe that Providence had sent a few men into the world, ready booted and spurred to ride, and millions ready saddled and bridled to be ridden.
Richard Rumbold (1622-1685, British Rebel)

12 So far is it from being true that men are naturally equal, that no two people can be half an hour together, but one shall acquire an evident superiority over the other.
Samuel Johnson (1709-1784, British Author)

13 There is no good in living in a society where you are merely the equal of everybody else. The true pleasure of life is to live with your inferiors.
William M. Thackeray (1811-1863, Indian-born British Novelist)

INERTIA

1 Fix'd like a plan on his peculiar spot, to draw nutrition, propagate, and rot.
Alexander Pope (1688-1744, British Poet, Critic, Translator)

2 You must take the first step. The first steps will take some effort, maybe pain. But after that, everything that has to be done is real-life movement.
Ben Stein (American Professor, Writer)

3 All that is necessary to break the spell of inertia and frustration is this: Act as if it were impossible to fail. That is the talisman, the formula, the command of right-about-face which turns us from failure towards success.
Dorothea Brande (American Success Writer)

4 Once in motion, a pattern tends to stay in motion.
J. G. Gallimore

5 The first step is the hardest.
Marie De Vichy-Chamrond

6 Create a definite plan for carrying out your desire and begin at once, whether you ready or not, to put this plan into action.
Napoleon Hill (1883-1970, American Speaker, Motivational Writer, "Think and Grow Rich")

7 The great thing is the start -- to see an opportunity for service, and to start doing it, even though in the beginning you serve but a single customer -- and him for nothing.
Robert Collier (American Writer, Publisher)

8 Once you're moving you can keep moving.
Ronald Alan Weiss

9 Nothing happens, nobody comes, nobody goes, it's awful.
Samuel Beckett (1906-1989, Irish Dramatist, Novelist)

10 Every body continues in its state of rest, or of uniform motion in a right line, unless it is compelled to change that state by forces impressed upon it.
Sir Isaac Newton (1642-1727, British Scientist, Mathematician)

11 That's why many fail -- because they don't get started -- they don't go. They don't overcome inertia. They don't begin.
W. Clement Stone (1902-, American Businessman, Author)

12 The natural law of inertia: Matter will remain at rest or continue in uniform motion in the same straight line unless acted upon by some external force.
W. Clement Stone (1902-, American Businessman, Author)

13 Lest he should wander irretrievably from the right path, he stands still.
William Hazlitt (1778-1830, British Essayist)

INFALLIBILITY

1 We like security: we like the pope to be infallible in matters of faith, and grave doctors to be so in moral questions so that we can feel reassured.
Blaise Pascal (1623-1662, French Scientist, Religious Philosopher)

2 From a worldly point of view, there is no mistake so great as that of being always right.
Samuel Butler (1612-1680, British Poet, Satirist)

3 We are none of us infallible -- not even the youngest of us.
William Hepworth Thompson

INFATUATION

1 One does not kill oneself for love of a woman, but because love -- any love -- reveals us in our nakedness, our misery, our vulnerability, our nothingness.
Cesare Pavese (1908-1950, Italian Poet, Novelist, Translator)

2 I know I am but summer to your heart, and not the full four seasons of the year.
Edna St. Vincent Millay (1892-1950, American Poet)

3   I understand by this passion the union of desire, friendship, and tenderness, which is inflamed by a single female, which prefers her to the rest of her sex, and which seeks her possession as the supreme or the sole happiness of our being.
Edward Gibbon (1737-1794, British Historian)

4   There aren't many irritations to match the condescension which a woman metes out to a man who she believes has loved her vainly for the past umpteen years.
Edward Hoagland (1932-, American Novelist, Essayist)

5   Strange, that some of us, with quick alternate vision, see beyond our infatuations, and even while we rave on the heights, behold the wide plain where our persistent self pauses and awaits us.
George Eliot (1819-1880, British Novelist)

6   Take me to you, imprison me, for I, except you enthrall me, never shall be free, nor ever chaste, except you ravish me.
John Donne (1572-1632, British Metaphysical Poet)

7   Infatuation is when you think that he's as sexy as Robert Redford, as smart as Henry Kissinger, as noble as Ralph Nader, as funny as Woody Allen, and as athletic as Jimmy Conners. Love is when you realize that he's as sexy as Woody Allen, as smart as Jimmy Conners, as funny as Ralph Nader, as athletic as Henry Kissinger, and nothing like Robert Redford--but you'll take him anyway.
Judith Viorst (1935-, American Poet, Journalist)

8   Men who care passionately for women attach themselves at least as much to the temple and to the accessories of the cult as to their goddess herself.
Marguerite Yourcenar (1903-1987, French Novelist)

9   Nay, but Jack, such eyes! such eyes! so innocently wild! so bashfully irresolute! Not a glance but speaks and kindles some thought of love! Then, Jack, her cheeks! her cheeks, Jack! so deeply blushing at the insinuations of her tell-tale eyes! Then, Jack, her lips! O, Jack, lips smiling at their own discretion! and, if not smiling, more sweetly pouting -- more lovely in sullenness! Then, Jack, her neck! O, Jack, Jack!
Richard Brinsley Sheridan (1751-1816, Anglo-Irish Dramatist)

10 Can it be that chance has made me one of those women so immersed in one man that, whether they are barren or not, they carry with them to the grave the shriveled innocence of an old maid?
Sidonie Gabrielle Colette (1873-1954, French Author)

11 It is best to love wisely, no doubt: but to love foolishly is better than not to be able to love at all.
William M. Thackeray (1811-1863, Indian-born British Novelist)

12 I stalk about her door like a strange soul upon the Stygian banks staying for wattage.
William Shakespeare (1564-1616, British Poet, Playwright, Actor)

INFERIORITY

1   An inferiority complex would be a blessing, if only the right people had it.
Alan Reed

2   The feeling of inferiority rules the mental life and can be clearly recognized in the sense of incompleteness and unfulfillment, and in the uninterrupted struggle both of individuals and humanity.
Alfred Adler (1870-1937, Austrian Psychiatrist)

3   To be human means to feel inferior.
Alfred Adler (1870-1937, Austrian Psychiatrist)

4   The greater the feeling of inferiority that has been experienced, the more powerful is the urge to conquest and the more violent the emotional agitation.
Alfred Adler (1870-1937, Austrian Psychiatrist)

5   Exaggerated sensitiveness is an expression of the feeling of inferiority.
Alfred Adler (1870-1937, Austrian Psychiatrist)

6   We must interpret a bad temper as a sign of inferiority.
Alfred Adler (1870-1937, Austrian Psychiatrist)

7   Nobody can make you feel inferior without your consent.
Eleanor Roosevelt (1884-1962, American First Lady, Columnist, Lecturer, Humanitarian)

8   It is part of a poor spirit to undervalue himself and blush.
George Herbert (1593-1632, British Metaphysical Poet)

9   Let a man once overcome his selfish terror at his own infinitude, and his infinitude is, in one sense, overcome.
George Santayana (1863-1952, American Philosopher, Poet)

10 No man likes to have his intelligence or good faith questioned, especially if he has doubts about it himself.
Henry Brooks Adams (1838 - 1918, American Historian)

11 One often has need of one, inferior to himself.
Jean De La Fontaine (1621-1695, French Poet)

12 Rancor is an outpouring of a feeling of inferiority.
Jose Ortega Y Gasset (1883-1955, Spanish Essayist, Philosopher)

13 Inferiority is what you enjoy in your best friends.
Lord Chesterfield (1694-1773, British Statesman, Author)

14 You have no idea what a poor opinion I have of myself; and how little I deserve it.
W. S. Gilbert (1836-1911, British Librettist)

INFIDELITY

1   Men and women are not born inconstant: they are made so by their early amorous experiences.
Andre Maurois (1885-1967, French Writer)

2 Every man wants a woman to appeal to his better side, his nobler instincts and his higher nature -- and another woman to help him forget them.
Helen Rowland (1875-1950, American Journalist)

3 The hood-winked husband shows his anger, and the word jealous is flung in his face. Jealous husband equals betrayed husband. And there are women who look upon jealousy as synonymous with impotence, so that the betrayed husband can only shut his eyes, powerless in the face of such accusations.
J. August Strindberg (1849-1912, Swedish Dramatist, Novelist, Poet)

4 A woman one loves rarely suffices for all our needs, so we deceive her with another whom we do not love.
Marcel Proust (1871-1922, French Novelist)

5 No lover, if he be of good faith, and sincere, will deny he would prefer to see his mistress dead than unfaithful.
Marquis De Sade (1740-1814, French Author)

6 Those who are faithful know only the trivial side of love: it is the faithless who know love's tragedies.
Oscar Wilde (1856-1900, British Author, Wit)

7 You may build castles in the air, and fume, and fret, and grow thin and lean, and pale and ugly, if you please. But I tell you, no man worth having is true to his wife, or can be true to his wife, or ever was, or will be so.
Sir John Vanbrugh (1664-1726, British Playwright and Baroque architect)

INFINITY

1 If any philosopher had been asked for a definition of infinity, he might have produced some unintelligible rigmarole, but he would certainly not have been able to give a definition that had any meaning at all.
Bertrand Russell (1872-1970, British Philosopher, Mathematician, Essayist)

2 Offer unto me that which is very dear to thee -- which thou holdest most covetable. Infinite are the results of such an offering.
Bhagavad Gita (400 BC, Sanskrit Poem Incorporated Into the Mahabharata)

3 There is no more steely barb than that of the Infinite.
Charles Baudelaire (1821-1867, French Poet)

4 I mistrust the satisfaction which makes a display of the possession of Infinity; that is called fatuity in philosophic terms.
Edgar Quinet (1803-1875, French Poet, Historian, Politician)

5 While many people are trying to be in tune with infinite, what they really are is in tune with the indefinite.
Eric Butterworth

6 The poetic notion of infinity is far greater than that which is sponsored by any creed.
Joseph Brodsky (1940-, Russian-born American Poet, Critic)

7 Seek the Infinite, for that alone is Joy unlimited, imperishable, unfailing, self-sustaining, unconditioned, timeless. When you have this joy, human life becomes a paradise; the light, the grace, the power, the perfections of that which is highest in your inner consciousness, appear in your everyday life.
Swami Omkarananda (1929-, Indian Mystic, Spiritual Teacher)

8 This moment exhibits infinite space, but there is a space also wherein all moments are infinitely exhibited, and the everlasting duration of infinite space is another region and room of joys.
Thomas Traherne (1636-1674, British Clergyman, Poet, Mystic)

9 Whenever we encounter the Infinite in man, however imperfectly understood, we treat it with respect. Whether in the synagogue, the mosque, the pagoda, or the wigwam, there is a hideous aspect which we execrate and a sublime aspect which we venerate. So great a subject for spiritual contemplation, such measureless dreaming -- the echo of God on the human wall!
Victor Hugo (1802-1885, French Poet, Dramatist, Novelist)

INFLATION

1 Someone said that inflation is like jumping off the top of the Empire State Building. The sensation is great as long as you keep on going.
David H. Scott

2 Remember when $25, 000 was a success? Now it is a garbage collector.
Frank Dane

3 What this country needs is a good five cent cigar.
Franklin Pierce Adams (1881 - 1960, American Journalist, Humorist)

4 There are plenty of good five cent cigars in the country. The trouble is they cost a quarter.
Franklin Pierce Adams (1881 - 1960, American Journalist, Humorist)

5 I wasn't affected by inflation, I had nothing to inflate.
Gerald Barzan

6 The best way to destroy the capitalist system is to debauch the currency. By a continuing process of inflation governments can confiscate, secretly and unobserved, an important part of the wealth of their citizens.
John Maynard Keynes (1883-1946, British Economist)

7 In spite of the cost of living, it's still popular.
Kathleen Norris (1880-1966, American Novelist)

8 Having a little inflation is like being a little pregnant.
Leon Henderson

9 Government is the only institution that can take a valuable commodity like paper, and make it worthless by applying ink.
Ludwig Van Moses

10 One good thing can be said for inflation: without it there would be no football.
Marty Ragaway

11 Imagine believing in the control of inflation by curbing the money supply! That is like deciding to stop your dog fouling the sidewalk by plugging up its rear end. It is highly unlikely to succeed, but if it does it kills the hound.
Michael D. Stephens

12 Inflation is one form of taxation that can be imposed without legislation.
Milton Friedman (1912-, American Economist)

13 Next to inflation, majority rule is the most ingenious scheme ever contrived by government. Most people have never dared to question the basic morality or logic in the assumption that the majority should have power over the minority. A majority of the people in the South once believed in black slavery. Did that make it moral? A lynch mob is majority rule stripped of its fancy trappings and its facade of respectability. In a community where homosexuals outnumber heterosexuals, should the majority have the right to outlaw sex between married partners of the opposite sex? In a community where atheists outnumber non- atheists, should the majority have the right to outlaw the practice of religion? ... a dictatorship allows only a small number of people to interfere with the rights of others, a democracy makes it possible for great numbers of people to impose their will on others -- through the force of government. Is an act of aggression more right if carried out by the majority than by a dictator? Since approximately half the eligible voters vote this means that approximately 75% of the people are ruled by 25% of the people.
Robert J. Ringer (American Writer)

14 Inflation is the crabgrass in your savings.
Robert Orben (1927-, American Editor, Writer, Humorist)

15 Inflation is determined by money supply growth.
Roger Bootle

16 Inflation is as violent as a mugger, as frightening as an armed robber and as deadly as a hit man.
Ronald Reagan (1911-, Fortieth President of the USA, Actor)

17 Nowadays, a penny saved is ridiculous!
Shelby Friedman

18 Bankers know that history is inflationary and that money is the last thing a wise man will hoard.
William J. Durant (1885-1981, American Historian, Essayist)

INFLUENCE

1 At the same time, as social beings, we are moved in the relations with our fellow beings by such feelings as sympathy, pride, hate, need for power, pity, and so on.
Albert Einstein (1879-1955, German-born American Physicist)

2 Those who sleep with dogs gets up with fleas.
American Proverb

3 Influence is like a savings account. The less you use it, the more you've got.
Andrew Young (1932-, Civil Rights Activist, Protestant Minister, Public Official)

4 Give me a child and I'll shape him into anything.
B. F. Skinner (1904-1990, American Psychologist)

5 See that no one puts a stumbling block, or an occasion to fall in his brothers way.
Bible (Sacred Scriptures of Christians and Judaism)

6 The least movement is of importance to all nature. The entire ocean is affected by a pebble.
Blaise Pascal (1623-1662, French Scientist, Religious Philosopher)

7 There is no power on earth that can neutralize the influence of a high, simple and useful life.
Booker T. Washington (1856-1915, American Black Leader and Educator)

8 Every one comes between men's souls and God, either as a brick wall or as a bridge. Either you are leading men to God or you are driving them away.
Canon Lindsay Dewar

9 Nothing has a stronger influence psychologically on their environment and especially on their children than the unlived life of the parent.
Carl Jung (1875-1961, Swiss Psychiatrist)

10 A true measure of your worth includes all the benefits others have gained from your success.
Cullen Hightower

11 He who influences the thought of his times influences the times that follow.
Elbert Hubbard (1859-1915, American Author, Publisher)

12 It would be difficult to exaggerate the degree to which we are influenced by those we influence.
Eric Hoffer (1902-1983, American Author, Philosopher)

13 Some wisdom you must learn from one who's wise.
Euripides (480-406 BC, Greek Tragic Poet)

14 People will sit up and take notice of you if you will sit up and take notice of what makes them sit up and take notice.
Frank Romer

15 Blessed is the influence of one true, loving human soul on another.
George Eliot (1819-1880, British Novelist)

16 In our society a man is known by the company he owns.
Gerald F. Lieberman (American Writer)

17 What little Jack does not learn, big John will never.
German Proverb

18 Every life is a profession of faith, and exercises an inevitable and silent influence.
Henri Frederic Amiel (1821-1881, Swiss Philosopher, Poet, Critic)

¹⁹ We perceive and are affected by changes too subtle to be described.
Henry David Thoreau (1817-1862, American Essayist, Poet, Naturalist)

²⁰ Let no man imagine that he has no influence. Whoever he may be, and where ever he may be placed, the man who thinks becomes a light and a power.
Henry George (1839-1897, American Social Reformer, Economist)

²¹ He is greatest whose strength carries up the most hearts by the attraction of his own.
Henry Ward Beecher (1813-1887, American Preacher, Orator, Writer)

²² What a mother sings to the cradle goes all the way down to the coffin.
Henry Ward Beecher (1813-1887, American Preacher, Orator, Writer)

²³ The humblest individual exerts some influence, either for good or evil, upon others.
Henry Ward Beecher (1813-1887, American Preacher, Orator, Writer)

²⁴ The influence of individual character extends from generation to generation.
Iain Macleod (1913-1970, British Statesman)

²⁵ The person who lives with cripples will soon learn to limp.
Italian Proverb

²⁶ The words that a father speaks to his children in the privacy of home are not heard by the world, but, as in whispering galleries, they are clearly heard at the end, and by posterity.
Jean Paul Richter (1763-1825, German Novelist)

²⁷ Get around people who have something of value to share with you. Their impact will continue to have a significant effect on your life long they have departed.
Jim Rohn (American Businessman, Author, Speaker, Philosopher)

²⁸ There are only about a half dozen things that make 80% of the difference in any area of our lives.
Jim Rohn (American Businessman, Author, Speaker, Philosopher)

²⁹ Influence: What you think you have until you try to use it.
Joan Welsh

³⁰ We are like chameleons, we take our hue and the color of our moral character, from those who are around us.
John Locke (1632-1704, British Philosopher)

³¹ One concept corrupts and confuses the others. I am not speaking of the Evil whose limited sphere is ethics; I am speaking of the infinite.
Jorge Luis Borges (1899-1986, Argentinean Author)

³² Power lasts ten years; influence not more than a hundred.
Korean Proverb

³³ A community is like the ones who govern it.
Marcus T. Cicero (106-43 BC, Great Roman Orator, Politician)

³⁴ The influential man is the successful man, whether he be rich or poor.
Orison Swett Marden (1850-1924, American Author, Founder of Success Magazine)

³⁵ The best efforts of a fine person is felt after we have left their presence.
Ralph Waldo Emerson (1803-1882, American Poet, Essayist)

³⁶ Who shall set a limit to the influence of a human being?
Ralph Waldo Emerson (1803-1882, American Poet, Essayist)

³⁷ Every thought which genius and piety throw into the world alters the world.
Ralph Waldo Emerson (1803-1882, American Poet, Essayist)

³⁸ The secret of my influence has always been that it remained secret.
Salvador Dali (1904-1989, Spanish Painter)

³⁹ Let him that would move the world, first move himself.
Socrates (469-399 BC, Greek Philosopher of Athens)

⁴⁰ People exercise an unconscious selection in being influenced.
T. S. Eliot (1888-1965, American-born British Poet, Critic)

⁴¹ It is a strange trade that of advocacy. Your intellect, your highest heavenly gift is hung up in the shop window like a loaded pistol for sale.
Thomas Carlyle (1795-1881, Scottish Philosopher, Author)

⁴² We live in a world which is full of misery and ignorance, and the plain duty of each and all of us is to try to make the little corner he can influence somewhat less miserable and somewhat less ignorant than it was before he entered it.
Thomas H. Huxley (1825-1895, British Biologist, Educator)

⁴³ Be not angry that you cannot make another what you wish them to be; since you cannot make yourself what you wish to be.
Thomas p Kempis (1379-1471, German Monk, Mystic, Religious Writer)

⁴⁴ It's easy to make a buck. It's a lot tougher to make a difference.
Tom Brokaw (1940-, American TV Personality, Editor)

⁴⁵ Socrates had a student named Plato, Plato had a student named Aristotle, and Aristotle had a student named Alexander the Great.
Tom Morris

INFORMATION

¹ With so much information now online, it is exceptionally easy to simply dive in and drown.
Alfred Glossbrenner

2 We aren't in an information age, we are in an entertainment age.
Anthony Robbins (1960-, American Author, Speaker, Peak Performance Expert / Consultant)

3 Information's pretty thin stuff unless mixed with experience.
Clarence Day (1874-1935, American Essayist)

4 Imagine being able to sit at your desk and with a few keystrokes on your computer-being able to access almost any information you need from a storehouse of the world's published knowledge.
Dialog Brochure

5 There's a compelling reason to master information and news. Clearly there will be better job and financial opportunities. Other high stakes will be missed by people if they don't master and connect information.
Everette Dennis

6 Information networks straddle the world. Nothing remains concealed. But the sheer volume of information dissolves the information. We are unable to take it all in.
Gunther Grass (1927-, German Author)

7 What information consumes is rather obvious: it consumes the attention of its recipients. Hence, a wealth of information creates a poverty of attention and a need to allocate that attention efficiently among the overabundance of information sources that might consume it.
Herbert Simon

8 Information can tell us everything. It has all the answers. But they are answers to questions we have not asked, and which doubtless don't even arise.
Jean Baudrillard (French Postmodern Philosopher, Writer)

9 Knowledge in the form of an informational commodity indispensable to productive power is already, and will continue to be, a major --perhaps the major --stake in the worldwide competition for power. It is conceivable that the nation-states will one day fight for control of information, just as they battled in the past for control over territory, and afterwards for control over access to and exploitation of raw materials and cheap labor.
Jean Frantois Lyotard (1924-, French Philosopher)

10 Among all the world's races, some obscure Bedouin tribes possibly apart, Americans are the most prone to misinformation. This is not the consequence of any special preference for mendacity, although at the higher levels of their public administration that tendency is impressive. It is rather that so much of what they themselves believe is wrong.
John Kenneth Galbraith (1908-, American Economist)

11 We have for the first time an economy based on a key resource [Information] that is not only renewable, but self-generating. Running out of it is not a problem, but drowning in it is.
John Naisbitt (American Trend Analyst, Futurist, Author)

12 If you were designing the sort of information-processing system a brain is, it would be extremely impractical to store memories permanently in their original form. You need mechanisms for transforming and recording them; for "chunking" information into categories . Is your memory a phonograph record on which the information is stored in localized grooves to be replayed on demand? Is so, it's a very bizarre record, for the songs are different every time they're played. Human memory is more like the village storyteller; it doesn't passively store facts but weaves them into a good (coherent, plausible) story, which is recreated with each telling.
Judith Hooper Teresi

13 Not having the information you need when you need it leaves you wanting. Not knowing where to look for that information leaves you powerless. In a society where information is king, none of us can afford that.
Lois Horowitz (American Librarian)

14 The more the data banks record about each one of us, the less we exist.
Marshall Mcluhan (1911-1980, Canadian Communications Theorist)

15 The idea that information can be stored in a changing world without an overwhelming depreciation of its value is false. It is scarcely less false than the more plausible claim that after a war we may take our existing weapons, fill their barrels with information.
Norbert Wiener (1894-1964, American Mathematician, Educator, Founder of Cybernetics)

16 Private information is practically the source of every large modern fortune.
Oscar Wilde (1856-1900, British Author, Wit)

17 Information storage has to take place at the unconscious level.
Paul G. Thomas

18 Even though these technological advances originally sought to control information and bring order to the office, in many instances they have done just the opposite. The electronic office promised to reduce paper work and lessen work loads, but it has, in fact, generated more information that must sill be printed and -even more challenging-be assimilated. Since computers entered office systems, paper utilization has increased six-fold.
Peter D. Moore

19 Information is recorded in vast interconnecting networks. Each idea or image has hundreds, perhaps thousands, of associations and is connected to numerous other points in the mental network.
Peter Russell

20 Information is the oxygen of the modern age. It seeps through the walls topped by barbed wire, it wafts across the electrified borders.
Ronald Reagan (1911-, Fortieth President of the USA, Actor)

21 Where is the wisdom we have lost in knowledge? Where is the knowledge we have lost in information.
T. S. Eliot (1888-1965, American-born British Poet, Critic)

22 The original root of the word "information" is the Latin word informare, which means to fashion, shape, or create, to give form to. Information is an idea that has been given a form, such as the spoken or written word. It is a means of representing an image or thought so that it can be communicated from one mind to another rather than worrying about all the information afloat in the world, we must ask ourselves what matters to us, what do we want to know. It's having ideas and learning to deal with issues that is important, not accumulating lots and lots of data.
Theordore Roszak

23 Information is the currency of democracy.
Thomas Jefferson (1743-1826, Third President of the USA)

24 When action grows unprofitable, gather information; when information grows unprofitable, sleep.
Ursula K. Le Guin (1929-, American Author)

25 Information is a negotiator's greatest weapon.
Victor Kiam (American Businessman, CEO of Remington)

INGRATITUDE

1 Nothing more detestable does the earth produce than an ungrateful man.
Decimus Magnus Ausonius (310-395, Latin Poet, Man of Letters)

2 Too great a hurry to discharge an obligation is a kind of ingratitude.
François de La Rochefoucauld (1613-1680, French classical writer)

3 Ingratitude is treason to mankind.
James Thomson (1700-1748, Scottish Poet)

4 One ungrateful man does an injury to all who stand in need of aid.
Publilius Syrus (1st Century BC, Roman Writer)

5 That's the trouble with directors. Always biting the hand that lays the golden egg.
Samuel Goldwyn (1882-1974, American Film Producer, Founder, MGM)

6 We think that we suffer from ingratitude, while in reality we suffer from self-love.
Walter Savage Landor (1775-1864, British Poet, Essayist)

INHERITANCE

1 But thousands die without or this or that, die, and endow a college, or a cat: To some, indeed, Heaven grants the happier fate, T'enrich a bastard, or a son they hate.
Alexander Pope (1688-1744, British Poet, Critic, Translator)

2 Die and endow a college or a cat.
Alexander Pope (1688-1744, British Poet, Critic, Translator)

3 I would as soon leave my son a curse as the almighty dollar.
Andrew Carnegie (1835-1919, American Industrialist, Philanthropist)

4 A person can receive nothing except it be given him from heaven.
Bible (Sacred Scriptures of Christians and Judaism)

5 One does not jump, and spring, and shout hurrah! at hearing one has got a fortune, one begins to consider responsibilities, and to ponder business; on a base of steady satisfaction rise certain grave cares, and we contain ourselves, and brood over our bliss with a solemn brow.
Charlotte Bronte (1816-1855, British Novelist)

6 Nothing succeeds like ones own successor.
Clarence H. Hincks

7 We pay for the mistakes of our ancestors, and it seems only fair that they should leave us the money to pay with.
Don Marquis (1878-1937, American Humorist, Journalist)

8 In this choice of inheritance we have given to our frame of polity the image of a relation in blood; binding up the constitution of our country with our dearest domestic ties; adopting our fundamental laws into the bosom of our family affections; keeping inseparable and cherishing with the warmth of all their combined and mutually reflected charities, our state, our hearths, our sepulchres, and our altars.
Edmund Burke (1729-1797, British Political Writer, Statesman)

9 If you want to really know what your friends and family think of you die broke, and then see who shows up for the funeral.
Gregory Nunn (1955-, American Golfer)

10 To inherit property is not to be born -- it is to be still-born, rather.
Henry David Thoreau (1817-1862, American Essayist, Poet, Naturalist)

11 There are only two lasting bequests we can hope to give our children. One of these is roots, the other, wings.
Hodding Carter

12 To kill a relative of whom you are tired is something. But to inherit his property afterwards, that is genuine pleasure.
Honore De Balzac (1799-1850, French Novelist)

13 The weak shall inherit the earth, but not the mineral rights.
J. Paul Getty (1892-1976, American Oil Tycoon, Billionaire)

14 Never say you know a man until you have divided an inheritance with him.
Johann Kaspar Lavater (1741-1801, Swiss Theologian, Mystic)

15 Say not you know another entirely till you have divided an inheritance with him.
Johann Kaspar Lavater (1741-1801, Swiss Theologian, Mystic)

16 My sword I give to him that shall succeed me in my pilgrimage, and my courage and skill to him that can get it.
John Bunyan (1628-1688, British Author)

17 All heiresses are beautiful.
John Dryden (1631-1700, British Poet, Dramatist, Critic)

18 An infinitude of tenderness is the chief gift and inheritance of all truly great men.
John Ruskin (1819-1900, British Critic, Social Theorist)

19 A third heir seldom enjoys what has been dishonestly acquired.
Juvenal (Decimus Junius Juvenalis) (55-130, Roman Satirical Poet)

20 It's going to be fun to watch and see how long the meek can keep the earth after they inherit it.
Kin Hubbard (1868-1930, American Humorist, Journalist)

21 Lifestyles and sex roles are passed from parents to children as inexorably as blue eyes or small feet.
Letty Cottin Pogrebin (1939-, American Journalist, Author)

22 For pleasures past I do not grieve, nor perils gathering near; My greatest grief is that I leave nothing that claims a tear.
Lord Byron (1788-1824, British Poet)

23 The way to be immortal (I mean not to die at all) is to have me for your heir. I recommend you to put me in your will and you will see that (as long as I live at least) you will never even catch cold.
Lord Byron (1788-1824, British Poet)

24 People don't have fortunes left them in that style nowadays; men have to work and women to marry for money. It's a dreadfully unjust world.
Louisa May Alcott (1832-1888, American Author)

25 I have also seen children successfully surmounting the effects of an evil inheritance. That is due to purity being an inherent attribute of the soul.
Mahatma Gandhi (1869-1948, Indian Political, Spiritual Leader)

26 You give me nothing during your life, but you promise to provide for me at your death. If you are not a fool, you know what I wish for!
Marcus Valerius Martial (40-104, Latin poet and epigrammatist)

27 The weeping of an heir is laughter in disguise.
Michel Eyquem De Montaigne (1533-1592, French Philosopher, Essayist)

28 There is a strange charm in the thoughts of a good legacy, or the hopes of an estate, which wondrously removes or at least alleviates the sorrow that men would otherwise feel for the death of friends.
Miguel De Cervantes (1547-1616, Spanish Novelist, Dramatist, Poet)

29 Men sooner forget the death of their father than the loss of their patrimony.
Niccolo Machiavelli (1469-1527, Italian Author, Statesman)

30 The best inheritance a parent can give his children is a few minutes of his time each day.
Orlando A. Battista

31 Those in supreme power always suspect and hate their next heir.
Publius Cornelius Tacitus (55-117 AD, Roman Historian)

32 Of course, money will do after its kind, and will steadily work to unspiritualize and unchurch the people to whom it was bequeathed.
Ralph Waldo Emerson (1803-1882, American Poet, Essayist)

33 Sometimes the poorest man leaves his children the richest inheritance.
Ruth E. Renkel

34 It is the fate of the great ones of this earth, to be appreciated only after they are gone.
Saying

35 You may not be able to leave your children a great inheritance, but day by day, you may be weaving coats for them which they will wear for all eternity.
Theodore L. Cuyler (1822-1909, American Pastor, Author)

36 The patient is not likely to recover who makes the doctor his heir.
Thomas Fuller (1608-1661, British Clergyman, Author)

37 A man cannot leave a better legacy to the world than a well-educated family.
Thomas Scott

38 The are of will-making chiefly consists in baffling the importunity of expectation.
William Hazlitt (1778-1830, British Essayist)

39 I would rather make my name than inherit it.
William M. Thackeray (1811-1863, Indian-born British Novelist)

40 No legacy is so rich as honestly.
William Shakespeare (1564-1616, British Poet, Playwright, Actor)

41 He who comes for the inheritance is often made to pay for the funeral.
Yiddish Proverb

INHIBITION

1 How very seldom do you encounter in the world a man of great abilities, acquirements, experience, who will unmask his mind, unbutton his brains, and pour forth in careless and picturesque phrase all the results of his studies and observation; his knowledge of men, books, and nature. On the contrary, if a man has by any chance an original idea, he hoards it as if it were old gold; and rather avoids the subject with which he is most conversant, from fear that you may appropriate his best thoughts.
Benjamin Disraeli (1804-1881, British Statesman, Prime Minister)

2 Yet if a woman never lets herself go, how will she ever know how far she might have got? If she never takes off her high-heeled shoes, how will she ever know how far she could walk or how fast she could run?
Germaine Greer (1939-, Australian Feminist Writer)

3 My defenses were so great. The cocky rock and roll hero who knows all the answers was actually a terrified guy who didn't know how to cry. Simple.
John Lennon (1940-1980, British Rock Musician)

INJURY

1 To live is to hurt others, and through others, to hurt oneself. Cruel earth! How can we manage not to touch anything? To find what ultimate exile?
Albert Camus (1913-1960, French Existential Writer)

2 It's a fact that it is much more comfortable to be in the position of the person who has been offended than to be the unfortunate cause of it.
Barbara Walters (1931-, American TV Personality)

3 Everyone suffers wrongs for which there is no remedy.
Edgar Watson Howe (1853-1937, American Journalist, Author)

4 There are some cases in which the sense of injury breeds -- not the will to inflict injuries and climb over them as a ladder, but -- a hatred of all injury.
George Eliot (1819-1880, British Novelist)

5 Young men soon give, and soon forget, affronts; old age is slow in both.
Joseph Addison (1672-1719, British Essayist, Poet, Statesman)

6 Children show scars like medals. Lovers use them as secrets to reveal. A scar is what happens when the word is made flesh.
Leonard Cohen (1934-, Canadian-born American Musician, Songwriter, Singer)

7 There is nothing that people bear more impatiently, or forgive less, than contempt: and an injury is much sooner forgotten than an insult.
Lord Chesterfield (1694-1773, British Statesman, Author)

8 No one likes having offended another person; hence everyone feels so much better if the other person doesn't show he's been offended. Nobody likes being confronted by a wounded spaniel. Remember that. It is much easier patiently -- and tolerantly -- to avoid the person you have injured than to approach him as a friend. You need courage for that.
Ludwig Wittgenstein (1889-1951, Austrian Philosopher)

9 Reject your sense of injury and the injury itself disappears.
Marcus Aurelius (121-80 AD, Roman Emperor, Philosopher)

10 The troubles of the young are soon over; they leave no external mark. If you wound the tree in its youth the bark will quickly cover the gash; but when the tree is very old, peeling the bark off, and looking carefully, you will see the scar there still. All that is buried is not dead.
Olive Schreiner

11 Where there is injury let me sow pardon.
St. Francis of Assisi (1181-1226, Italian Preacher, Founder of the Franciscan Orde)

12 An honest man speaks the truth, though it may give offence; a vain man, in order that it may.
William Hazlitt (1778-1830, British Essayist)

13 Kindnesses are easily forgotten; but injuries! -- what worthy man does not keep those in mind?
William M. Thackeray (1811-1863, Indian-born British Novelist)

INJUSTICE

1 Children will still die unjustly even in a perfect society. Even by his greatest effort, man can only propose to diminish, arithmetically, the sufferings of the world.
Albert Camus (1913-1960, French Existential Writer)

2 If thou suffer injustice, console thyself; the true unhappiness is in doing it.
Democritus (460-370 BC, Greek Philosopher)

3 Progress is the injustice each generation commits with regard to its predecessors.
E. M. Cioran (1911-, Rumanian-born French Philosopher)

4 Undeservedly you will atone for the sins of your fathers.
Horace (65-8 BC, Italian Poet)

5 One had better die fighting against injustice than die like a dog or a rat in a trap.
Ida B. Wells

6 When one has been threatened with a great injustice, one accepts a smaller as a favor.
Jane Welsh Carlyle (1801-1866, British Diarist)

7 As long as justice and injustice have not terminated their ever renewing fight for ascendancy in the affairs of mankind, human beings must be willing, when need is, to do battle for the one against the other.
John Stuart Mill (1806-1873, British Philosopher, Economist)

8 Since when do you have to agree with people to defend them from injustice?
Lillian Hellman (1905-1984, American Playwright)

9 The 8 Equities: Physical, Spiritual, Psychological, Intellectual, Emotional, Financial, Social and Family
Michael Vance (American Creativity Expert, Lecturer)

10 It is from numberless diverse acts of courage and belief that human history is shaped. Each time a man stands up for an ideal, or acts to improve the lot of others, or strikes out against injustice, he sends forth a tiny ripple of hope, and crossing each other from a million different centers of energy and daring those ripples build a current which can sweep down the mightiest walls of oppression and injustice.
Robert F. Kennedy (1925-1968, American Attorney General, Senator)

11 We have so many people who can't see a fat man standing beside a thin one without coming to the conclusion that the fat man got that way by taking advantage of the thin one!
Ronald Reagan (1911-, Fortieth President of the USA, Actor)

12 Justice is my being allowed to do whatever I like. Injustice is whatever prevents my doing so.
Samuel Butler (1612-1680, British Poet, Satirist)

13 A hurtful act is the transference to others of the degradation which we bear in ourselves.
Simone Weil (1910-1943, French Philosopher, Mystic)

14 I tremble for my country when I reflect that God is just; that his justice cannot sleep forever.
Thomas Jefferson (1743-1826, Third President of the USA)

INNOCENCE

1 The innocent is the person who explains nothing.
Albert Camus (1913-1960, French Existential Writer)

2 It is well for the heart to be naive and the mind not to be.
Anatole France (1844-1924, French Writer)

3 Innocence most often is a good fortune and not a virtue.
Anatole France (1844-1924, French Writer)

4 Innocence is like polished armor; it adorns and defends.
Bishop Robert South (1634-1716, British Clergyman)

5 I know we're not saints or virgins or lunatics; we know all the lust and lavatory jokes, and most of the dirty people; we can catch buses and count our change and cross the roads and talk real sentences. But our innocence goes awfully deep, and our discreditable secret is that we don't know anything at all, and our horrid inner secret is that we don't care that we don't.
Dylan Thomas (1914-1953, Welsh Poet)

6 She looked as though butter wouldn't melt in her mouth --or anywhere else.
Else Lanchester (1902-1986, British-born American Actor)

7 All things truly wicked start from an innocence.
Ernest Hemingway (1898-1961, American Writer)

8 Those who are incapable of committing great crimes do not readily suspect them in others.
François de La Rochefoucauld (1613-1680, French classical writer)

9 Prudishness is pretense of innocence without innocence. Women have to remain prudish as long as men are sentimental, dense, and evil enough to demand of them eternal innocence and lack of education. For innocence is the only thing which can ennoble lack of education.
Friedrich Schlegel (1772-1829, German Philosopher, Critic, Writer)

10 The greenhorn is the ultimate victor in everything; it is he that gets the most out of life.
Gilbert K. Chesterton (1874-1936, British Author)

11 Innocence always calls mutely for protection when we would be so much wiser to guard ourselves against it: innocence is like a dumb leper who has lost his bell, wandering the world, meaning no harm.
Graham Greene (1904-1991, British Novelist)

12 Innocent as a dove you will harm no one, but wise as a serpent no one will harm you.
Haug

13 He is armed without who is innocent within, be this thy screen, and this thy wall of brass.
Horace (65-8 BC, Italian Poet)

14 People who shut their eyes to reality simply invite their own destruction, and anyone who insists on remaining in a state of innocence long after that innocence is dead turns himself into a monster.
James Baldwin (1924-1987, American Author)

15 There is no aphrodisiac like innocence.
Jean Baudrillard (French Postmodern Philosopher, Writer)

16 Now my innocence begins to weigh me down.
Jean Racine (1639-1699, French Dramatist)

17 The essential self is innocent, and when it tastes its own innocence knows that it lives for ever.
John Updike (1932-, American Novelist, Critic)

18 Only the old are innocent. That is what the Victorians understood, and the Christians. Original sin is a property of the young. The old grow beyond corruption very quickly.
Malcolm Bradbury (1932-, British Author)

19 Children, I grant, should be innocent; but when the epithet is applied to men, or women, it is but a civil term for weakness.
Mary Wollstonecraft (1759-1797, British Feminist Writer)

20 It's innocence when it charms us, ignorance when it doesn't.
Mignon McLaughlin (1915?-, American Author, Editor)

21 Nothing looks so like innocence as an indiscretion.
Oscar Wilde (1856-1900, British Author, Wit)

22 To vice, innocence must always seem only a superior kind of chicanery.
Ouida (1838-1908, British Writer)

23 If you would live innocently, seek solitude.
Publilius Syrus (1st Century BC, Roman Writer)

24 No man ever looks at the world with pristine eyes. He sees it edited by a definite set of customs and institutions and ways of thinking.
Ruth Benedict (1887-1948, American Anthropologist)

25 One threatens the innocent who spares the guilty.
Sir Edward Coke (1552-1634, British Jurist)

26 Certainly Adam in Paradise had not more sweet and curious apprehensions of the world, than I when I was a child.
Thomas Traherne (1636-1674, British Clergyman, Poet, Mystic)

27 I am to be broken. I am to be derided all my life. I am to be cast up and down among these men and women, with their twitching faces, with their lying tongues, like a cork on a rough sea. Like a ribbon of weed I am flung far every time the door opens.
Virginia Woolf (1882-1941, British Novelist, Essayist)

28 Every harlot was a virgin once.
William Blake (1757-1827, British Poet, Painter)

INNOVATION

1 Anyone who has invented a better mousetrap, or the contemporary equivalent, can expect to be harassed by strangers demanding that you read their unpublished manuscripts or undergo the humiliation of public speaking, usually on remote Midwestern campuses.
Barbara Ehrenreich (1941-, American Author, Columnist)

2 Innovation! One cannot be forever innovating. I want to create classics.
Coco Chanel (1883-1971, French Couturier)

3 To innovate is not to reform.
Edmund Burke (1729-1797, British Political Writer, Statesman)

4 Innovators are inevitably controversial.
Eva Le Gallienne

5 You let me throw the bricks through the front window. You go in at the back and take the swag.
Ezra Pound (1885-1972, American Poet, Critic)

6 As the births of living creatures, at first, are ill-shapen: so are all Innovations, which are the births of time.
Francis Bacon (1561-1626, British Philosopher, Essayist, Statesman)

7 Pure innovation is more gross than error.
George Chapman (1557-1634, British Dramatist, Translator, Poet)

8 No one asks you to throw Mozart out of the window. Keep Mozart. Cherish him. Keep Moses too, and Buddha and Lao Tzu and Christ. Keep them in your heart. But make room for the others, the coming ones, the ones who are already scratching on the window-panes.
Henry Miller (1891-1980, American Author)

9 An important scientific innovation rarely makes its way by gradually winning over and converting its opponents. What does happen is that its opponents gradually die out, and that the growing generation is familiarized with the ideas from the beginning.
Max Planck (1858-1947, German Theoretical Physicist)

10 Innovation is the creation of the new or the re-arranging of the old in a new way.
Michael Vance (American Creativity Expert, Lecturer)

11 INNOVATION is the specific tool of entrepreneurs, the means by which they exploit change as an opportunity for a different business or a different service. It is capable of being presented as a discipline, capable of being learned, capable of being practiced. Entrepreneurs need to search purposefully for the sources of innovation, the changes and their symptoms that indicate opportunities for successful innovation. And they need to know and to apply the principles of successful innovation.
Peter F. Drucker (1909-, American Management Consultant, Author)

12 Sometimes when you innovate, you make mistakes. It is best to admit them quickly, and get on with improving your other innovations.
Steve Jobs (1955-, American Businessman, Founder of Apple Computers)

13 CREATIVITY is thinking up new things. INNOVATION is doing new things.
Theodore Levitt

14 Most new things are not good, and die an early death; but those which push themselves forward and by slow degrees force themselves on the attention of mankind are the unconscious productions of human wisdom, and must have honest consideration, and must not be made the subject of unreasoning prejudice.
Thomas Brackett Reed (1839-1902, American Republican Politician)

15 Great innovations should not be forced on slender majorities.
Thomas Jefferson (1743-1826, Third President of the USA)

16 The INNOVATION point is the pivotal moment when talented and motivated people seek the opportunity to act on their ideas and dreams.
W. Arthur Porter

17 One of the greatest pains to human nature is the pain of a new idea.
Walter Bagehot (1826-1877, British Economist, Critic)

18 INNOVATION is the process of turning ideas into manufacturable and marketable form.
Watts Humprey

INSANITY

1 For virtue's self may too much zeal be had; the worst of madmen is a saint run mad.
Alexander Pope (1688-1744, British Poet, Critic, Translator)

2 I saw the best minds of my generation destroyed by madness, starving hysterical naked.
Allen Ginsberg (1926-, American Poet)

3 There is in every madman a misunderstood genius whose idea, shining in his head, frightened people, and for whom delirium was the only solution to the strangulation that life had prepared for him.
Antonin Artaud (1896-1948, French Theater Producer, Actor, Theorist)

4 No excellent soul is exempt from a mixture of madness.
Aristotle (384-322 BC, Greek Philosopher)

5 Better mad with the rest of the world than wise alone.
Baltasar Gracian (1601-1658, Spanish Philosopher, Writer)

6 I'm a nut, but not just a nut.
Bill Murray (1950-, American Comedian, Actor, Writer)

7 Insanity is doing the same thing in the same way and expecting a different outcome.
Chinese Proverb

8 You want to hear about insanity? I was found running naked through the jungles in Mexico. At the Mexico City airport, I decided I was in the middle of a movie and walked out on the wing on takeoff. My body... my liver... okay, my brain... went.
Dennis Hopper (1936-, American Actor, Director)

9 I doubt if a single individual could be found from the whole of mankind free from some form of insanity. The only difference is one of degree. A man who sees a gourd and takes it for his wife is called insane because this happens to very few people.
Desiderius Erasmus (1466-1536, Dutch Humanist)

10 I became insane, with long intervals of horrible sanity.
Edgar Allan Poe (1809-1845, American Poet, Critic, short-story Writer)

11 Insanity in individuals is something rare -- but in groups, parties, nations, and epochs it is the rule.
Friedrich Nietzsche (1844-1900, German Philosopher)

12 I teach that all men are mad.
Horace (65-8 BC, Italian Poet)

13 You must always be puzzled by mental illness. The thing I would dread most, if I became mentally ill, would be your adopting a common sense attitude; that you could take it for granted that I was deluded.
Ludwig Wittgenstein (1889-1951, Austrian Philosopher)

14 When we remember that we are all mad, the mysteries disappear and life stands explained.
Mark Twain (1835-1910, American Humorist, Writer)

15 The way it is now, the asylums can hold the sane people but if we tried to shut up the insane we would run out of building materials.
Mark Twain (1835-1910, American Humorist, Writer)

16 Let us consider that we are all partially insane. It will explain us to each other; it will unriddle many riddles; it will make clear and simple many things which are involved in haunting and harassing difficulties and obscurities now.
Mark Twain (1835-1910, American Humorist, Writer)

17 The great proof of madness is the disproportion of one's designs to one's means.
Napoleon Bonaparte (1769-1821, French General, Emperor)

18 Insanity destroys reason, but not wit.
Nathaniel Emmons

19 Insanity is often the logic of an accurate mind overtasked.
Oliver Wendell Holmes (1809-1894, American Author, Wit, Poet)

20 There's a fine line between genius and insanity. I have erased this line.
Oscar Levant (1906-1972, American Pianist, Actor)

21 If you commit a big crime then you are crazy, and the more heinous the crime the crazier you must be. Therefore you are not responsible, and nothing is your fault.
Peggy Noonan (1950-, American Author, Presidential Speechwriter)

22 Whom God wishes to destroy, he first makes mad.
Proverb

23 Everyone is more or less mad on one point.
Rudyard Kipling (1865-1936, British Author of Prose, Verse)

24 We are all born mad. Some remain so.
Samuel Beckett (1906-1989, Irish Dramatist, Novelist)

25 Insanity is hereditary. You get it from your children.
Samuel Levenson

26 A man should not strive to eliminate his complexes, but to get into accord with them; they are legitimately what directs his conduct in the world.
Sigmund Freud (1856-1939, Austrian Physician - Founder of Psychoanalysis)

27 Where does one go from a world of insanity? Somewhere on the other side of despair.
T. S. Eliot (1888-1965, American-born British Poet, Critic)

28 What is madness but nobility of soul. At odds with circumstance?
Theodore Roethke (1908-1963, American Poet)

29 I may be crazy but it keeps me from going insane.
Waylon Jennings

30 There is no insanity so devastating in man's life as utter sanity.
William Allen White (1868-1944, American Editor, Writer)

[31] Man disavows, and Deity disowns me: hell might afford my miseries a shelter; therefore hell keeps her ever-hungry mouths all bolted against me.
William Cowper (1731-1800, British Poet)

[32] Though this be madness, yet there is method in it. [Hamlet]
William Shakespeare (1564-1616, British Poet, Playwright, Actor)

[33] All of us are crazy in one way or another.
Yiddish Proverb

INSECTS

[1] That is your trick, your bit of filthy magic: invisibility, and the anaesthetic power to deaden my attention in your direction.
D. H. Lawrence (1885-1930, British Author)

[2] a man thinks he amounts to a great deal but to a flea or a mosquito a human being is merely something good to eat
Don Marquis (1878-1937, American Humorist, Journalist)

[3] Butterflies... not quite birds, as they were not quite flowers, mysterious and fascinating as are all indeterminate creatures.
Elizabeth Goudge

[4] His Labor is a Chant -- his Idleness -- a Tune -- oh, for a Bee's experience of Clovers, and of Noon!
Emily Dickinson (1830-1886, American Poet)

[5] Of what use, however, is a general certainty that an insect will not walk with his head hindmost, when what you need to know is the play of inward stimulus that sends him hither and thither in a network of possible paths?
George Eliot (1819-1880, British Novelist)

[6] As a thinker and planner the ant is the equal of any savage race of men; as a self-educated specialist in several arts she is the superior of any savage race of men; and in one or two high mental qualities she is above the reach of any man, savage or civilized!
Mark Twain (1835-1910, American Humorist, Writer)

[7] After the planet becomes theirs, many millions of years will have to pass before a beetle particularly loved by God, at the end of its calculations will find written on a sheet of paper in letters of fire that energy is equal to the mass multiplied by the square of the velocity of light. The new kings of the world will live tranquilly for a long time, confining themselves to devouring each other and being parasites among each other on a cottage industry scale.
Primo Levi (1919-1987, Italian Chemist, Author)

[8] The butterfly's attractiveness derives not only from colors and symmetry: deeper motives contribute to it. We would not think them so beautiful if they did not fly, or if they flew straight and briskly like bees, or if they stung, or above all if they did not enact the perturbing mystery of metamorphosis: the latter assumes in our eyes the value of a badly decoded message, a symbol, a sign.
Primo Levi (1919-1987, Italian Chemist, Author)

[9] Long after the bomb falls and you and your good deeds are gone, cockroaches will still be here, prowling the streets like armored cars.
Tama Janowitz

[10] The mortal enemies of man are not his fellows of another continent or race; they are the aspects of the physical world which limit or challenge his control, the disease germs that attack him and his domesticated plants and animals, and the insects that carry many of these germs as well as working notable direct injury. This is not the age of man, however great his superiority in size and intelligence; it is literally the age of insects.
W. C. Allee

[11] Now what sort of man or woman or monster would stroke a centipede I have ever seen? "And here is my good big centipede!" If such a man exists, I say kill him without more ado. He is a traitor to the human race.
William S. Burroughs (1914-1997, American Writer)

INSECURITY

[1] I'm insecure about everything, because... I'm never going to look in the mirror and see this blond, blue-eyed girl. That is my idea of what I'd like to look like.
Cher (1946-, American Actress, Director, Singer)

[2] In a world we find terrifying, we ratify that which doesn't threaten us.
David Mamet (1947-, American Playwright)

[3] Probably the only place where a man can feel really secure is in a maximum security prison, except for the imminent threat of release.
Germaine Greer (1939-, Australian Feminist Writer)

[4] The man who looks for security, even in the mind, is like a man who would chop off his limbs in order to have artificial ones which will give him no pain or trouble.
Henry Miller (1891-1980, American Author)

[5] A man who has nothing which he cares about more than he does about his personal safety is a miserable creature who has no chance of being free, unless made and kept so by the existing of better men than himself.
John Stuart Mill (1806-1873, British Philosopher, Economist)

[6] I'm hostile to men, I'm hostile to women, I'm hostile to cats, to poor cockroaches, I'm afraid of horses.
Norman Mailer (1923-, American Author)

[7] Men are afraid to rock the boat in which they hope to drift safely through life's currents, when, actually, the boat is stuck on a sandbar. They would be better off to rock the boat and try to shake it loose, or, better still, jump in the water and swim for the shore.
Thomas Szasz (1920-, American Psychiatrist)

INSENSITIVITY

1. It's what you do, unthinking, that makes the quick tear start; The tear may be forgotten -- but the hurt stays in the heart.
Ella Higginson (1862-1940, American Writer, Journalist)

2. We may have civilized bodies and yet barbarous souls. We are blind to the real sights of this world; deaf to its voice; and dead to its death. And not till we know, that one grief outweighs ten thousand joys will we become what Christianity is striving to make us.
Herman Melville (1819-1891, American Author)

3. My doctor told me to stop having intimate dinners for four unless there are three other people.
Orson Welles (1915-1985, American Film Maker)

INSIGHTS

1. Hamming's Motto: The purpose of computing is insight, not numbers.
Hamming

2. A moment's insight is sometimes worth a life's experience.
Oliver Wendell Holmes (1809-1894, American Author, Wit, Poet)

3. Nothing is more terrible than activity without insight.
Thomas Carlyle (1795-1881, Scottish Philosopher, Author)

INSIGNIFICANCE

1. There is hardly any one so insignificant that he does not seem imposing to some one at some time.
Charles Horton Cooley (1864-1929, American Sociologist)

2. We are merely the stars tennis-balls, struck and bandied which way please them.
John Webster (1580-1625, British Dramatist)

3. No man is much regarded by the rest of the world. He that considers how little he dwells upon the condition of others, will learn how little the attention of others is attracted by himself. While we see multitudes passing before us, of whom perhaps not one appears to deserve our notice or excites our sympathy, we should remember, that we likewise are lost in the same throng, that the eye which happens to glance upon us is turned in a moment on him that follows us, and that the utmost which we can reasonably hope or fear is to fill a vacant hour with prattle, and be forgotten.
Samuel Johnson (1709-1784, British Author)

INSOMNIA

1. Impossible to spend sleepless nights and accomplish anything: if, in my youth, my parents had not financed my insomnias, I should surely have killed myself.
E. M. Cioran (1911-, Rumanian-born French Philosopher)

2. The last refuge of the insomniac is a sense of superiority to the sleeping world.
Leonard Cohen (1934-, Canadian-born American Musician, Songwriter, Singer)

3. O sleep, O gentle sleep, nature's soft nurse, how have I frightened thee, that thou no more wilt weigh my eye-lids down and steep my senses in forgetfulness?
William Shakespeare (1564-1616, British Poet, Playwright, Actor)

INSPIRATION

1. Inspiration may be a form of super-consciousness, or perhaps of subconsciousness -- I wouldn't know. But I am sure it is the antithesis of self-consciousness.
Aaron Copland

2. You beat your Pate, and fancy Wit will come: Knock as you please, there's no body at home.
Alexander Pope (1688-1744, British Poet, Critic, Translator)

3. To the artist is sometimes granted a sudden, transient insight which serves in this matter for experience. A flash, and where previously the brain held a dead fact, the soul grasps a living truth! At moments we are all artists.
Arnold Bennett (1867-1931, British Novelist)

4. Had it not been for you, I should have remained what I was when we first met, a prejudiced, narrow-minded being, with contracted sympathies and false knowledge, wasting my life on obsolete trifles, and utterly insensible to the privilege of living in this wondrous age of change and progress.
Benjamin Disraeli (1804-1881, British Statesman, Prime Minister)

5. The inspiration of the almighty gives man understanding.
Bible (Sacred Scriptures of Christians and Judaism)

6. My sole inspiration is a telephone call from a director.
Cole Porter (1893-1964, American Composer, Lyricist)

7. The greatest inspiration is often born of desperation.
Comer Cotrell (American Businessman, Founder of Pro-Line Corporation)

8. Most of us who turn to any subject we love remember some morning or evening hour when we got on a high stool to reach down an untried volume, or sat with parted lips listening to a new talker, or for very lack of books began to listen to the voices within, as the first traceable beginning of our love.
George Eliot (1819-1880, British Novelist)

9 Write while the heat is in you. The writer who postpones the recording of his thoughts uses an iron which has cooled to burn a hole with. He cannot inflame the minds of his audience.
Henry David Thoreau (1817-1862, American Essayist, Poet, Naturalist)

10 I didn't have to think up so much as a comma or a semicolon; it was all given, straight from the celestial recording room. Weary, I would beg for a break, an intermission, time enough, let's say, to go to the toilet or take a breath of fresh air on the balcony. Nothing doing!
Henry Miller (1891-1980, American Author)

11 Without inspiration the best powers of the mind remain dormant, they is a fuel in us which needs to be ignited with sparks.
Johann Gottfried Von Herder (1744-1803, German Critic and Poet)

12 There never was a great soul that did not have some divine inspiration.
Marcus T. Cicero (106-43 BC, Great Roman Orator, Politician)

13 The artist is a receptacle for emotions that come from all over the place: from the sky, from the earth, from a scrap of paper, from a passing shape, from a spider's web.
Pablo Picasso (1881-1973, Spanish Artist)

14 The torpid artist seeks inspiration at any cost, by virtue or by vice, by friend or by fiend, by prayer or by wine.
Ralph Waldo Emerson (1803-1882, American Poet, Essayist)

15 When you do not know what you are doing and what you are doing is the best -- that is inspiration.
Robert Bresson (1907-, French Film Director)

16 Stung by the splendor of a sudden thought.
Robert Browning (1812-1889, British Poet)

17 Invention flags, his brain goes muddy, and black despair succeeds brown study.
William Congreve (1670-1729, British Dramatist)

18 Here is the secret of inspiration: Tell yourself that thousands and tens of thousands of people, not very intelligent and certainly no more intelligent than the rest of us, have mastered problems as difficult as those that now baffle you.
William Feather (1888-18, American Writer, Businessman)

19 Out of the closets and into the museums, libraries, architectural monuments, concert halls, bookstores, recording studios and film studios of the world. Everything belongs to the inspired and dedicated thief... Words, colors, light, sounds, stone, wood, bronze belong to the living artist. They belong to anyone who can use them. Loot the Louver! A bas I Originality, the sterile and assertive ego that imprisons us as it creates. Vive le sol -- pure, shameless, total. We are not responsible. Steal anything in sight.
William S. Burroughs (1914-1997, American Writer)

INSTINCT

1 If men as individuals surrender to the call of their elementary instincts, avoiding pain and seeking satisfaction only for their own selves, the result for them all taken together must be a state of insecurity, of fear, and of promiscuous misery.
Albert Einstein (1879-1955, German-born American Physicist)

2 Instinct is untaught ability.
Alexander Bain (1845-1928, Scottish Philosopher and Psychologist)

3 The active part of man consists of powerful instincts, some of which are gentle and continuous; others violent and short; some baser, some nobler, and all necessary.
Francis W. Newman

4 Instinct. When the house burns one forgets even lunch. Yes, but one eats it later in the ashes.
Friedrich Nietzsche (1844-1900, German Philosopher)

5 An absolute can only be given in an intuition, while all the rest has to do with analysis. We call intuition here the sympathy by which one is transported into the interior of an object in order to coincide with what there is unique and consequently inexpressible in it. Analysis, on the contrary, is the operation which reduces the object to elements already known.
Henri L. Bergson (1859-1941, French Philosopher)

6 What is peculiar in the life of a man consists not in his obedience, but his opposition, to his instincts. In one direction or another he strives to live a supernatural life.
Henry David Thoreau (1817-1862, American Essayist, Poet, Naturalist)

7 Intuition and concepts constitute... the elements of all our knowledge, so that neither concepts without an intuition in some way corresponding to them, nor intuition without concepts, can yield knowledge.
Immanuel Kant (1724-1804, German Philosopher)

8 It is the rooted instinct in men to admire what is better and more beautiful than themselves.
James Russell Lowell (1819-1891, American Poet, Critic, Editor)

9 There is not, in my opinion, anything more mysterious in nature than this instinct in animals, which thus rise above reason, and yet fall infinitely short of it.
Joseph Addison (1672-1719, British Essayist, Poet, Statesman)

10 Instinct is the nose of the mind.
Madame de Girardin

11 A goose flies by a chart which the Royal Geographical Society could not mend.
Oliver Wendell Holmes (1809-1894, American Author, Wit, Poet)

12 A few strong instincts and a few plain rules suffice us.
Ralph Waldo Emerson (1803-1882, American Poet, Essayist)

13 The natural man has only two primal passions, to get and to beget.
Sir William Osler (1849-1919, Canadian Physician)

14 Instinct is action taken in pursuance of a purpose, but without conscious perception of what the purpose is.
Van Hartmann

INSTITUTIONS

1 Power is not of a man. Wealth does not center in the person of the wealthy. Celebrity is not inherent in any personality. To be celebrated, to be wealthy, to have power requires access to major institutions.
C. Wright Mills (1916-1962, American Sociologist)

2 Institutions -- government, churches, industries, and the like -- have properly no other function than to contribute to human freedom; and in so far as they fail, on the whole, to perform this function, they are wrong and need reconstruction.
Charles Horton Cooley (1864-1929, American Sociologist)

3 Why has mankind had such a craving to be imposed upon? Why this lust after imposing creeds, imposing deeds, imposing buildings, imposing language, imposing works of art? The thing becomes an imposition and a weariness at last. Give us things that are alive and flexible, which won't last too long and become an obstruction and a weariness. Even Michelangelo becomes at last a lump and a burden and a bore. It is so hard to see past him.
D. H. Lawrence (1885-1930, British Author)

4 Every institution not only carries within it the seeds of its own dissolution, but prepares the way for its most hated rival.
Dean William R. Inge (1860-1954, Dean of St Paul's, London)

5 What are all political and social institutions, but always a religion, which in realizing itself, becomes incarnate in the world?
Edgar Quinet (1803-1875, French Poet, Historian, Politician)

6 The more rational an institution is the less it suffers by making concessions to others.
George Santayana (1863-1952, American Philosopher, Poet)

7 The way in which men cling to old institutions after the life has departed out of them, and out of themselves, reminds me of those monkeys which cling by their tails -- aye, whose tails contract about the limbs, even the dead limbs, of the forest, and they hang suspended beyond the hunter's reach long after they are dead. It is of no use to argue with such men. They have not an apprehensive intellect, but merely, as it were a prehensile tail.
Henry David Thoreau (1817-1862, American Essayist, Poet, Naturalist)

8 Wherever a man goes, men will pursue him and paw him with their dirty institutions, and, if they can, constrain him to belong to their desperate odd-fellow society.
Henry David Thoreau (1817-1862, American Essayist, Poet, Naturalist)

9 If you're treated a certain way you become a certain kind of person. If certain things are described to you as being real they're real for you whether they're real or not.
James Baldwin (1924-1987, American Author)

10 In any great organization it is far, far safer to be wrong with the majority than to be right alone.
John Kenneth Galbraith (1908-, American Economist)

11 Whether lawyer, politician or executive, the American who knows what's good for his career seeks an institutional rather than an individual identity. He becomes the man from NBC or IBM. The institutional imprint furnishes him with pension, meaning, proofs of existence. A man without a company name is a man without a country.
Lewis H. Lapham (1935-, American Essayist, Editor)

12 Monarchies, aristocracies, and religions are all based upon that large defect in your race -- the individual's distrust of his neighbor, and his desire, for safety's or comfort's sake, to stand well in his neighbor's eye. These institutions will always remain, and always flourish, and always oppress you, affront you, and degrade you, because you will always be and remain slaves of minorities. There was never a country where the majority of the people were in their secret hearts loyal to any of these institutions.
Mark Twain (1835-1910, American Humorist, Writer)

13 An institution is the lengthened shadow of one man.
Ralph Waldo Emerson (1803-1882, American Poet, Essayist)

14 The whole history of civilization is strewn with creeds and institutions which were invaluable at first, and deadly afterwards.
Walter Bagehot (1826-1877, British Economist, Critic)

15 What is a wife and what is a harlot? What is a church and what is a theatre? are they two and not one? Can they exist separate? Are not religion and politics the same thing? Brotherhood is religion. O demonstrations of reason dividing families in cruelty and pride!
William Blake (1757-1827, British Poet, Painter)

INSULTS

1 I am not going to spend any time whatsoever in attacking the Foreign Secretary. If we complain about the tune, there is no reason to attack the monkey when the organ grinder is present.
Aneurin Bevan (1897-1960, British Labor Politician)

2 Write your injuries in dust, your benefits in marble.
Benjamin Franklin (1706-1790, American Scientist, Publisher, Diplomat)

3 Never insult an alligator until you've crossed the river.
Cordell Hull (1871-1955, American Statesman)

4   Calumny is only the noise of madmen.
    Diogenes of Sinope (410-320 BC, Cynic Philosopher)

5   It is not he who gives abuse that affronts, but the view that we take of it as insulting; so that when one provokes you it is your own opinion which is provoking.
    Epictetus (50-120, Stoic Philosopher)

6   By indignities men come to dignities.
    Francis Bacon (1561-1626, British Philosopher, Essayist, Statesman)

7   Insults are the arguments employed by those who are in the wrong.
    Jean Jacques Rousseau (1712-1778, Swiss Political Philosopher, Educationist, Essayist)

8   He who puts up with insult invites injury.
    Jewish Proverb

9   Young people soon give, and forget insults, but old age is slow in both.
    Joseph Addison (1672-1719, British Essayist, Poet, Statesman)

10 You will find that silence or very gentle words are the most exquisite revenge for insult.
    Judge Hall

11 The slight that can be conveyed in a glance, in a gracious smile, in a wave of the hand, is often the knee plus ultra of art. What insult is so keen or so keenly felt, as the polite insult which it is impossible to resent?
    Julia Kavanagh

12 Oppression is more easily endured than insult.
    Junius (1769-1771, Anonymous British Letter Writer)

13 A graceful taunt is worth a thousand insults.
    Louis Nizer (1902-1904, British Born American Lawyer, Writer)

14 No one can be as calculatedly rude as the British, which amazes Americans, who do not understand studied insult and can only offer abuse as a substitute.
    Paul Gallico

15 Even rabbits insult an dead lion.
    Proverb

16 Little enemies and little wounds must not be despised.
    Proverb

17 Daily life is governed by an economic system in which the production and consumption of insults tends to balance out.
    Raoul Vaneigem (1934-, Belgian Situationist Philosopher)

18 Whenever anyone has offended me, I try to raise my soul so high that the offense cannot reach it.
    Rene Descartes (1596-1650, French Philosopher, Scientist)

19 If you can't ignore an insult, top it; if you can't top it, laugh it off; and if you can't laugh it off, it's probably deserved.
    Russell Lynes (1910-, American Editor, Critic)

20 The only gracious way to accept an insult is to ignore it; if you can't ignore it, top it; if you can't top it, laugh at it; if you can't laugh at it, it's probably deserved.
    Russell Lynes (1910-, American Editor, Critic)

21 Never offend people with style when you can offend them with substance.
    Sam Brown

22 It is often better not to see an insult than to avenge it.
    Seneca (4 BC-65 AD, Spanish-born Roman Statesman, philosopher)

23 The best way to procure insults is to submit to them.
    William Hazlitt (1778-1830, British Essayist)

24 People think that they just want movies like Pretty Woman, when really they -- at least the ones that I know personally -- have been waiting for something that doesn't completely insult them.
    Winona Ryder (Born 1971, American Actress)

INSURANCE

1   Insurance is like marriage. You pay, pay, pay, and you never get anything back.
    Al Bundy (American TV Character, Married with Children)

2   Insurance: An ingenious modern game of chance in which the player is permitted to enjoy the comfortable conviction that he is beating the man who keeps the table.
    Ambrose Bierce (1842-1914, American Author, Editor, Journalist, "The Devil's Dictionary")

3   You don't need to pray to God any more when there are storms in the sky, but you do have to be insured.
    Bertolt Brecht (1898-1956, German Dramatist, Poet)

4   For almost seventy years the life insurance industry has been a smug sacred cow feeding the public a steady line of sacred bull.
    Ralph Nader (1934-, American Lawyer, Consumer Activist)

5   The chief beneficiary of life insurance policies for young, single people is the life insurance agent.
    Wes Smith

INSURANCE AGENTS

1   I detest life-insurance agents: they always argue that I shall some day die, which is not so.
    Stephen B. Leacock (1869-1944, Canadian Humorist, Economist)

INTEGRITY

1   A man can do only what a man can do. But if he does that each day he can sleep at night and do it again the next day.
    Albert Schweitzer (1875-1965, German Born Medical Missionary, Theologian, Musician, and Philosopher)

2   A building has integrity just like a man. And just as seldom.
    Ayn Rand (1905-1982, Russian Writer, Philosopher)

3 In all things preserve integrity; and the consciousness of thine own uprightness will alleviate the toil of business, soften the hardness of ill-success and disappointments, and give thee an humble confidence before God, when the ingratitude of man, or the iniquity of the times may rob thee of other rewards.
Barbara Paley

4 The glue that holds all relationships together -- including the relationship between the leader and the led is trust, and trust is based on integrity.
Brian Tracy (American Trainer, Speaker, Author, Businessman)

5 If humanity does not opt for integrity we are through completely. It is absolutely touch and go. Each one of us could make the difference.
Buckminster Fuller (American Engineer, Inventor, Designer, Architect "Geodesic Dome")

6 Integrity is the essence of everything successful.
Buckminster Fuller (American Engineer, Inventor, Designer, Architect "Geodesic Dome")

7 I ever will profess myself the greatest friend to those whose actions best correspond with their doctrine; which, I am sorry to say, is too seldom the case amongst those nations who pretend most to civilization.
Captain J. G. Stedman (1744-1797, British Soldier, Author, Artist)

8 Nothing more completely baffles one who is full of tricks and duplicity than straight forward and simple integrity in another.
Charles Caleb Colton (1780-1832, British Sportsman Writer)

9 Integrity is the first step to true greatness. Men love to praise, but are slow to practice it. To maintain it in high places costs self-denial; in all places it is liable to opposition, but its end is glorious, and the universe will yet do it homage.
Charles Simmons

10 A task becomes a duty from the moment you suspect it to be an essential part of that integrity which alone entitles a man to assume responsibility.
Dag Hammarskjold (1905-1961, Swedish Statesman, Secretary-general of U.N.)

11 Losers make promises they often break. Winners make commitments they always keep.
Denis Waitley (1933-, American Author, Speaker, Trainer, Peak Performance Expert)

12 A life lived with integrity -- even if it lacks the trappings of fame and fortune is a shinning star in whose light others may follow in the years to come.
Denis Waitley (1933-, American Author, Speaker, Trainer, Peak Performance Expert)

13 You must consider the bottom line, but make it integrity before profits.
Denis Waitley (1933-, American Author, Speaker, Trainer, Peak Performance Expert)

14 Integrity is what we do, what we say, and what we say we do.
Don Galer

15 Can one preach at home inequality of races and nations and advocate abroad good-will towards all men?
Dorothy Thompson

16 Integrity simple means not violating one's own identity.
Erich Fromm (1900-1980, American Psychologist)

17 Be right, and then be easy to live with, if possible, but in that order.
Ezra Taft Benson (1899-1994, American Government Official and Religious Leader)

18 If you believe in unlimited quality and act in all your business dealings with total integrity, the rest will take care of itself.
Frank Perdue (American Businessman, Founder Perdue Chicken)

19 In great matters men show themselves as they wish to be seen; in small matters, as they are.
Gamaliel Bradford (1863-1932, American Poet, Biographer)

20 Keep true, never be ashamed of doing right; decide on what you think is right and stick to it.
George Eliot (1819-1880, British Novelist)

21 No man should advocate a course in private that he's ashamed to admit in public.
George Mcgovern (1922-, American Democratic Politician)

22 The laboring man has not leisure for a true integrity day by day.
Henry David Thoreau (1817-1862, American Essayist, Poet, Naturalist)

23 I will never again go to people under false pretenses even if it is to give them the Holy Bible. I will never again sell anything, even if I have to starve. I am going home now and I will sit down and really write about people.
Henry Miller (1891-1980, American Author)

24 He who is upright in his way of life and free from sin.
Horace (65-8 BC, Italian Poet)

25 The person who is slowest in making a promise is most faithful in its performance.
Jean Jacques Rousseau (1712-1778, Swiss Political Philosopher, Educationist, Essayist)

26 Do the next thing.
John Wanamaker (1838-1922, American Merchant)

27 You can t, in sound morals, condemn a man for taking care of his own integrity. It is his clear duty. And least of all can you condemn an artist pursuing, however humbly and imperfectly, a creative aim. In that interior world where his thought and his emotions go seeking for the experience of imagined adventures, there are no policemen, no law, no pressure of circumstance or dread of opinion to keep him within bounds. Who then is going to say Nay to his temptations if not his conscience?
Joseph Conrad (1857-1924, Polish-born British Novelist)

28 The integrity of men is to be measured by their conduct, not by their professions.
Junius (1769-1771, Anonymous British Letter Writer)

29 Integrity is praised and then left out in the cold.
Juvenal (Decimus Junius Juvenalis) (55-130, Roman Satirical Poet)

30 Honor your commitments with integrity.
Les Brown (1945-, American Speaker, Author, Trainer, Motivator Lecturer)

31 A man should be upright, not be kept upright.
Marcus Aurelius (121-80 AD, Roman Emperor, Philosopher)

32 If it is not right do not do it; if it is not true do not say it.
Marcus Aurelius (121-80 AD, Roman Emperor, Philosopher)

33 I cannot and will not recant anything, for to go against conscience is neither right nor safe. Here I stand, I can do no other, so help me God. Amen.
Martin Luther (1483-1546, German Leader of the Protestant Reformation)

34 Integrity: A name is the blueprint of the thing we call character. You ask, What's in a name? I answer, Just about everything you do.
Morris Mandel

35 There is always room for those who can be relied upon to delivery the goods when they say they will.
Napoleon Hill (1883-1970, American Speaker, Motivational Writer, "Think and Grow Rich")

36 Live with integrity, respect the rights of other people, and follow your own bliss.
Nathaniel Branden (American Expert on Self-esteem, Author, Psychologist)

37 Integrity is not a 90 percent thing, not a 95 percent thing; either you have it or you don't.
Peter Scotese

38 It is part of a good man to do great and noble deeds, though he risk everything.
Plutarch (46-120 AD, Greek Essayist, Biographer)

39 It is his nature, not his standing, that makes the good man.
Publilius Syrus (1st Century BC, Roman Writer)

40 In failing circumstances no one can be relied on to keep their integrity.
Ralph Waldo Emerson (1803-1882, American Poet, Essayist)

41 Nothing is at last sacred but the integrity of your own mind.
Ralph Waldo Emerson (1803-1882, American Poet, Essayist)

42 Integrity without knowledge is weak and useless, and knowledge without integrity is dangerous and dreadful.
Samuel Johnson (1709-1784, British Author)

43 He that doth not as other men do, but endeavoureth that which ought to be done, shall thereby rather incur peril than preservation; for who so laboreth to be sincerely perfect and good shall necessarily perish, living among men that are generally evil.
Sir Walter Raleigh (1552-1618, British Courtier, Navigator, Writer)

44 Blessed is the servant who loves his brother as much when he is sick and useless as when he is well and an be of service to him. And blessed is he who loves his brother as well when he is afar off as when he is by his side, and who would say nothing behind his back he might not, in love, say before his face.
St. Francis of Assisi (1181-1226, Italian Preacher, Founder of the Franciscan Orde)

45 There is no alleviation for the sufferings of mankind except veracity of thought and of action, and the resolute facing of the world as it is when the garment of make-believe by which pious hands have hidden its uglier features is stripped off.
Thomas H. Huxley (1825-1895, British Biologist, Educator)

46 It is necessary to the happiness of man that he be mentally faithful to himself. Infidelity does not consist in believing, or in disbelieving; it consists in professing to believe what he does not believe.
Thomas Paine (1737-1809, Anglo-American Political Theorist, Writer)

47 Your life works to the degree you keep your agreements.
Werner Erhard (American Entrepreneur, Scientologist)

48 Man is a make-believe animal -- he is never so truly himself as when he is acting a part.
William Hazlitt (1778-1830, British Essayist)

49 There is nothing more likely to drive a man mad, than the being unable to get rid of the idea of the distinction between right and wrong, and an obstinate, constitutional preference of the true to the agreeable.
William Hazlitt (1778-1830, British Essayist)

INTELLIGENCE AND INTELLECTUALS

1 A highbrow is the kind of person who looks at a sausage and thinks of Picasso.
A. P. Herbert (1890-1971, British Author, Politician)

2 Intelligence appears to be the thing that enables a man to get along without education. Education enables a man to get along without the use of his intelligence.
Albert Edward Wiggam

3 We should take care not to make the intellect our god: it has, of course, powerful muscles, but no personality.
Albert Einstein (1879-1955, German-born American Physicist)

4 The true sign of intelligence is not knowledge but imagination.
Albert Einstein (1879-1955, German-born American Physicist)

5 Intellectuals solve problems; geniuses prevent them.
Albert Einstein (1879-1955, German-born American Physicist)

6 Science and art are only too often a superior kind of dope, possessing this advantage over booze and morphia: that they can be indulged in with a good conscience and with the conviction that, in the process of indulging, one is leading the "higher life."
Aldous Huxley (1894-1963, British Author)

7 Man is an intelligence, not served by, but in servitude to his organs.
Aldous Huxley (1894-1963, British Author)

8 Intelligence is quickness to apprehend as distinct form ability, which is capacity to act wisely on the thing apprehended.
Alfred North Whitehead (1861-1947, British Mathematician, Philosopher)

9 The intellect is weak; it has no power except over what is as weak as itself.
Al-Nuri

10 Undernourished, intelligence becomes like the bloated belly of a starving child: swollen, filled with nothing the body can use.
Andrea Dworkin (1946-, American Feminist Critic)

11 Unless one is a genius, it is best to aim at being intelligible.
Anthony Hope (1863-1933, British Writer)

12 It has yet to be proven that intelligence has any survival value.
Arthur C. Clarke (1917-, British Science Fiction Writer)

13 Nature shows that with the growth of intelligence comes increased capacity for pain, and it is only with the highest degree of intelligence that suffering reaches its supreme point.
Arthur Schopenhauer (1788-1860, German Philosopher)

14 The more unintelligent a man is, the less mysterious existence seems to him.
Arthur Schopenhauer (1788-1860, German Philosopher)

15 The trouble with the world is that the stupid are cocksure and the intelligent full of doubt.
Bertrand Russell (1872-1970, British Philosopher, Mathematician, Essayist)

16 A highbrow is a person educated beyond his intelligence.
Brander Matthews (1852-1929, American Writer)

17 I was street smart, but unfortunately the street was Rodeo Drive.
Carrie Fisher (1956-, American Actress, Novelist)

18 My great religion is a belief in the blood, the flesh, as being wiser than the intellect. We can go wrong in our minds. But what our blood feels and believes and says, is always true. The intellect is only a bit and a bridle.
D. H. Lawrence (1885-1930, British Author)

19 Intellectual brilliance is no guarantee against being dead wrong.
David Fasold

20 Ask a wise man to dinner and he'll upset everyone by his gloomy silence or tiresome questions. Invite him to a dance and you'll have a camel prancing about. Haul him off to a public entertainment and his face will be enough to spoil the people's entertainment.
Desiderius Erasmus (1466-1536, Dutch Humanist)

21 To label me an intellectual is a misunderstanding of what that is.
Dick Cavett

22 There is nobody so irritating as somebody with less intelligence and more sense than we have.
Don Herold

23 An intellectual is a man who takes more words than necessary to tell more than he knows.
Dwight D. Eisenhower (1890-1969, Thirty-fourth President of the USA)

24 Never be lucid, never state, if you would be regarded great.
Dylan Thomas (1914-1953, Welsh Poet)

25 Intellectual sodomy, which comes from the refusal to be simple about plain matters, is as gross and abundant today as sexual perversion and they are nowise different from one another.
Edward Dahlberg (1900-1977, American Author, Critic)

26 Many highly intelligent people are poor thinkers. Many people of average intelligence are skilled thinkers. The power of a car is separate from the way the car is driven.
Edward De Bono (Born 1933, Maltan-Born American Psychologist and Writer)

27 Intelligence is not to make no mistakes, But quickly to see how to make them good.
Elbert Hubbard (1859-1915, American Author, Publisher)

28 The good are so harsh to the clever, the clever so rude to the good!
Elizabeth Wordsworth

29 Reason is man's faculty for grasping the world by thought, in contradiction to intelligence, which is man's ability to manipulate the world with the help of thought. Reason is man's instrument for arriving at the truth, intelligence is man's instrument for manipulating the world more successfully; the former is essentially human, the latter belongs to the animal part of man.
Erich Fromm (1900-1980, American Psychologist)

30 The only chance for victory over the brainwash is the right of every man to have his ideas judged one at a time. You never get clarity as long as you have these packaged words, as long as a word is used by twenty-five people in twenty-five different ways. That seems to me to be the first fight, if there is going to be any intellect left.
Ezra Pound (1885-1972, American Poet, Critic)

31 The intellect is a very nice whirligig toy, but how people take it seriously is more than I can understand.
Ezra Pound (1885-1972, American Poet, Critic)

32 God has placed no limits to the exercise of the intellect he has given us, on this side of the grave.
Francis Bacon (1561-1626, British Philosopher, Essayist, Statesman)

33 It's easier to be wise for others than for ourselves.
François de La Rochefoucauld (1613-1680, French classical writer)

34 I hate intellectuals. They are from the top down. I am from the bottom up.
Frank Lloyd Wright (1869-1959, American Architect)

35 The difference between a smart man and a wise man is that a smart man knows what to say, a wise man knows whether or not to say it.
Frank M. Garafola

36 Clever people seem not to feel the natural pleasure of bewilderment, and are always answering questions when the chief relish of a life is to go on asking them.
Frank Moore Colby (1865-1925, American Editor, Essayist)

37 It's good to be clever, but not to show it.
French Proverb

38 She was short on intellect, but long on shape.
George Ade (1866-1944, American Humorist, Playwright)

39 Only those who know the supremacy of the intellectual life can understand the grief of one who falls from that serene activity into the absorbing soul-wasting struggle with worldly annoyances.
George Eliot (1819-1880, British Novelist)

40 The intellectual is different from the ordinary man, but only in certain sections of his personality, and even then not all the time.
George Orwell (1903-1950, British Author, "Animal Farm")

41 Merely having an open mind is nothing; the object of opening the mind, as of opening the mouth, is to shut it again on something solid.
Gilbert K. Chesterton (1874-1936, British Author)

42 A large section of the intelligentsia seems wholly devoid of intelligence.
Gilbert K. Chesterton (1874-1936, British Author)

43 People generally treat me like I'm very intelligent and really, I'm much less intelligent than she is. Scully is insanely intelligent.
Gillian Anderson (Born 1968, American Actress)

44 Intelligence is that faculty of mind, by which order is perceived in a situation previously considered disordered.
Haneef Fatmi

45 Clever people will recognize and tolerate nothing but cleverness.
Henri Frederic Amiel (1821-1881, Swiss Philosopher, Poet, Critic)

46 Truly great madness can not be achieved without significant intelligence.
Henrik Tikkanen

47 We need only travel enough to give our intellects an airing.
Henry David Thoreau (1817-1862, American Essayist, Poet, Naturalist)

48 To me, being an intellectual doesn't mean knowing about intellectual issues; it means taking pleasure in them.
Jacob Bronowski (1908-1974, British Scientist, Author)

49 Intelligence: I was asked tonight why I refuse to have truck with intellectuals after business hours. But of course I won t. 1. I am not an intellectual. Two minutes talk with Aldous Huxley, William Glock, or any of the New Statesman crowd would expose me utterly. 2. I am too tired after my day's work to man the intellectual palisade. 3. When my work is finished I want to eat, drink, smoke, and relax. 4. I don't know very much, but what I do know I know better than anybody, and I don't want to argue about it. I know what I think about an actor or an actress, and am not interested in what anybody else thinks. My mind is not a bed to be made and re-made.
James Agate (1877-1947) British Author, Critic)

50 People who are smart get into Mensa. People who are really smart look around and leave.
James Randi

51 It is not the insurrections of ignorance that are dangerous, but the revolts of the intelligence.
James Russell Lowell (1819-1891, American Poet, Critic, Editor)

52 You don't need intelligence to have luck, but you do need luck to have intelligence.
Jewish Proverb

53 The intelligent man finds almost everything ridiculous, the sensible man hardly anything.
Johann Wolfgang Von Goethe (1749-1832, German Poet, Dramatist, Novelist)

54 Clever people are always the best conversations lexicon.
Johann Wolfgang Von Goethe (1749-1832, German Poet, Dramatist, Novelist)

55 Nothing mattered except states of mind, chiefly our own.
John Maynard Keynes (1883-1946, British Economist)

56 On a level plain, simple mounds look like hills; and the insipid flatness of our present bourgeoisie is to be measured by the altitude of its "great intellects."
Karl Marx (1818-1883, German Political Theorist, Social Philosopher)

57 I was taught that the human brain was the crowning glory of evolution so far, but I think it's a very poor scheme for survival.
Kurt Vonnegut Jr. (1922-, American Novelist)

58 The best intelligence test is what we do with our leisure.
Laurence J. Peter

59 Intellectuals can tell themselves anything, sell themselves any bill of goods, which is why they were so often patsies for the ruling classes in nineteenth-century France and England, or twentieth- century Russia and America.
Lillian Hellman (1905-1984, American Playwright)

60 The intellectual is a middle-class product; if he is not born into the class he must soon insert himself into it, in order to exist. He is the fine nervous flower of the bourgeoisie.
Louise Bogan (1897-1970, American Poet, Critic)

61 Never stay up on the barren heights of cleverness, but come down into the green valleys of silliness.
Ludwig Wittgenstein (1889-1951, Austrian Philosopher)

62 The level of the development of a country is determined, in considerable part, by the level of development of its people's intelligence.
Luis Albert Machado

63 Our intellect is not the most subtle, the most powerful, the most appropriate, instrument for revealing the truth. It is life that, little by little, example by example, permits us to see that what is most important to our heart, or to our mind, is learned not by reasoning but through other agencies. Then it is that the intellect, observing their superiority, abdicates its control to them upon reasoned grounds and agrees to become their collaborator and lackey.
Marcel Proust (1871-1922, French Novelist)

64 The fact that man knows right from wrong proves his intellectual superiority to the other creatures; but the fact that he can do wrong proves his moral inferiority to any creatures that cannot.
Mark Twain (1835-1910, American Humorist, Writer)

65 The sign of an intelligent people is their ability to control emotions by the application of reason.
Marya Mannes (1904-1990, American Writer)

66 The work of an intellectual is not to mould the political will of others; it is, through the analyses that he does in his own field, to re-examine evidence and assumptions, to shake up habitual ways of working and thinking, to dissipate conventional familiarities, to re-evaluate rules and institutions and to participate in the formation of a political will (where he has his role as citizen to play).
Michel Foucault (1926-1984, French Essayist, Philosopher)

67 I think, therefore I am is the statement of an intellectual who underrates toothaches.
Milan Kundera (1929-, Czech Author, Critic)

68 There are three kinds of intelligence: one kind understands things for itself, the other appreciates what others can understand, the third understands neither for itself nor through others. This first kind is excellent, the second good, and the third kind useless.
Niccolo Machiavelli (1469-1527, Italian Author, Statesman)

69 The intellectual tradition is one of servility to power, and if I didn't betray it I'd be ashamed of myself.
Noam Chomsky (1928-, American Linguist, Political Activist)

70 And still they gazed, and still the wonder grew, that one small head could carry all he knew.
Oliver Goldsmith (1728-1774, Anglo-Irish Author, Poet, Playwright)

71 The intellect is not a serious thing, and never has been. It is an instrument on which one plays, that is all.
Oscar Wilde (1856-1900, British Author, Wit)

72 Nowadays to be intelligible is to be found out.
Oscar Wilde (1856-1900, British Author, Wit)

73 The true knowledge or science which exists nowhere but in the mind itself, has no other entity at all besides intelligibility; and therefore whatsoever is clearly intelligible, is absolutely true.
Ralph J. Cudworth (1617-1688, British Theologian, Philosopher)

74 If intellection and knowledge were mere passion from without, or the bare reception of extraneous and adventitious forms, then no reason could be given at all why a mirror or looking- glass should not understand; whereas it cannot so much as sensibly perceive those images which it receives and reflects to us.
Ralph J. Cudworth (1617-1688, British Theologian, Philosopher)

75 A sage is the instructor of a hundred ages.
Ralph Waldo Emerson (1803-1882, American Poet, Essayist)

76 We lie in the lap of immense intelligence.
Ralph Waldo Emerson (1803-1882, American Poet, Essayist)

77 One definition of man is "an intelligence served by organs."
Ralph Waldo Emerson (1803-1882, American Poet, Essayist)

78 Intellect annuls fate. So far as a man thinks, he is free.
Ralph Waldo Emerson (1803-1882, American Poet, Essayist)

79 If a man's eye is on the Eternal, his intellect will grow.
Ralph Waldo Emerson (1803-1882, American Poet, Essayist)

80 If we listened to our intellect, we'd never have a love affair. We'd never have a friendship. We'd never go into business, because we'd be cynical. Well, that's nonsense. You've got to jump off cliffs all the time and build your wings on the way down.
Ray Bradbury (1920-, American Science Fiction Writer)

81 To be wholly devoted to some intellectual exercise is to have succeeded in life.
Robert Louis Stevenson (1850-1895, Scottish Essayist, Poet, Novelist)

82 Once something becomes discernible, or understandable, we no longer need to repeat it. We can destroy it.
Robert Wilson (1941-, American Theater Director, Designer)

83 A person of intellect without energy added to it, is a failure.
Sebastien-Roch Nicolas De Chamfort (1741-1794, French Writer, Journalist, Playwright)

84 The woman who thinks she is intelligent demands equal rights with men. A woman who is intelligent does not.
Sidonie Gabrielle Colette (1873-1954, French Author)

85 Whatever debases the intelligence degrades the entire human being.
Simone Weil (1910-1943, French Philosopher, Mystic)

86 The role of the intelligence --that part of us which affirms and denies and formulates opinions is merely to submit.
Simone Weil (1910-1943, French Philosopher, Mystic)

87 Half of being smart is knowing what you are dumb about.
Solomon Short

88 Intelligence, in diapers, is invisible. And when it matures, out the window it flies. We have to pounce on it earlier.
Stanislaw J. Lec (1909-, Polish Writer)

89 It is not clear that intelligence has any long-term survival value.
Stephen Hawking (1942-, British Theoretical Physicist)

90 Intelligence is really a kind of taste: taste in ideas.
Susan Sontag (1933-, American Essayist)

91 I've been called many things, but never an intellectual.
Tallulah Bankhead (1903-1968, American Actress)

92 He is far too intelligent to become really cerebral.
Ursula K. Le Guin (1929-, American Author)

93 There's always something suspect about an intellectual on the winning side.
Vaclav Havel (1936-, Czech Playwright, President)

94 There can be no two opinions as to what a highbrow is. He is the man or woman of thoroughbred intelligence who rides his mind at a gallop across country in pursuit of an idea.
Virginia Woolf (1882-1941, British Novelist, Essayist)

95 Whenever the cause of the people is entrusted to professors, it is lost.
Vladimir Ilyich Lenin (1870-1924, Russian Revolutionary Leader)

96 To the man-in-the-street, who, I'm sorry to say, is a keen observer of life. The word "Intellectual" suggests straight away. A man who's untrue to his wife.
W. H. Auden (1907-1973, Anglo-American Poet)

97 If we look into ourselves we discover propensities which declare that our intellects have arisen from a lower form; could our minds be made visible we should find them tailed.
W. Winwood Reade (1838-1875, American Writer)

98 It is the mind that makes the body rich; and as the sun breaks through the darkest clouds, so honor peereth in the meanest habit."
William Shakespeare (1564-1616, British Poet, Playwright, Actor)

99 I've never been an intellectual but I have this look.
Woody Allen (1935-, American Director, Screenwriter, Actor, Comedian)

100 A sort of war of revenge on the intellect is what, for some reason, thrives in the contemporary social atmosphere.
Wyndham Lewis (1882-1957, British Author, Painter)

INTENTIONS

1 The greatest events occur without intention playing any part in them; chance makes good mistakes and undoes the most carefully planned undertaking. The world's greatest events are not produced, they happen.
Georg C. Lichtenberg (1742-1799, German Physicist, Satirist)

2 Hell is paved with good intentions, not with bad ones. All men mean well.
George Bernard Shaw (1856-1950, Irish-born British Dramatist)

3 His designs were strictly honorable, as the phrase is; that is, to rob a lady of her fortune by way of marriage.
Henry Fielding (1707-1754, British Novelist, Dramatist)

4 I am sure of nothing so little as my own intentions.
Lord Byron (1788-1824, British Poet)

5 No one would remember the Good Samaritan if he only had good intentions. He had money as well.
Margaret Thatcher (1925-, British Stateswoman, Prime Minister (1979-90))

6 Would that well-thinking people should be replaced by thinking ones.
Natalie Clifford Barney (1876-1972, American-born French Author)

7 What is the quality of your intent?
Thurgood Marshall (1908-1993, American Judge)

8 Moral of the Work. In war: resolution. In defeat: defiance. In victory: magnanimity. In peace: goodwill.
Winston Churchill (1874-1965, British Statesman, Prime Minister)

INTEREST

1 Interest makes some people blind, and others quick-sighted.
Francis Beaumont (1584-1616, British Dramatist)

2 The virtues and vices are all put in motion by interest.
François de La Rochefoucauld (1613-1680, French classical writer)

3 A man's interest in the world is only an overflow from his interest in himself.
George Bernard Shaw (1856-1950, Irish-born British Dramatist)

4   There are no uninteresting things, there are only uninterested people.
Gilbert K. Chesterton (1874-1936, British Author)

5   If I seem to give a damn, please tell me. I would hate to be giving the wrong impression.
Haythum R. Khalid (Born 1972, British-born Egyptian Author, Critic)

6   I don't believe in principle, but I do in interest.
James Russell Lowell (1819-1891, American Poet, Critic, Editor)

7   No use to shout at them to pay attention. If the situations, the materials, the problems before the child do not interest him, his attention will slip off to what does interest him, and no amount of exhortation of threats will bring it back.
John Holt (1908-1967, Australian Politician, Prime Minister)

8   Only free peoples can hold their purpose and their honor steady to a common end and prefer the interest of mankind to any narrow interest of their own.
Woodrow T. Wilson (1856-1924, Twenty-eighth President of the USA)

INTERNALIZATION

1   Internalization. This occurs when you've exploited impact, when you've molded the standard material to your needs and made it yours, when you've made your new skills strong through hard use. All of a sudden these new concepts stopped churning within you, and a new reality is born: You and the concepts are one. They have literally become you. You have become them.
Tom Hopkins (American Sales Trainer, Speaker, Author)

INTERNET

1   The ides of surfing the net -- I don't know who called it that -- it's more like slogging through the net.
Al Di Guido

2   Information on the Internet is subject to the same rules and regulations as conversation at a bar.
George Lundberg (American Editor)

3   The difference between e-mail and regular mail is that computers handle e-mail, and computers never decide to come to work one day and shoot all the other computers.
Jamais Cascio

4   In Cyberspace, the 1st Amendment is a local ordinance.
John Perry Barlow (1947-, American Musician, Lyricist for the "Grateful Dead")

INTERVENTION

1   Americans think of themselves collectively as a huge rescue squad on twenty-four-hour call to any spot on the globe where dispute and conflict may erupt.
Eldridge Cleaver (1935-, American Black Leader, Writer)

2   Mutual respect implies discretion and reserve even in love itself; it means preserving as much liberty as possible to those whose life we share. We must distrust our instinct of intervention, for the desire to make one's own will prevail is often disguised under the mask of solicitude.
Henri Frederic Amiel (1821-1881, Swiss Philosopher, Poet, Critic)

3   Those who in quarrels interpose, must often wipe a bloody nose.
John Gay (1688-1732, British Playwright, Poet)

4   All of Western tradition, from the late bloom of the British Empire right through the early doom of Vietnam, dictates that you do something spectacular and irreversible whenever you find yourself in or whenever you impose yourself upon a wholly unfamiliar situation belonging to somebody else. Frequently it's your soul or your honor or your manhood, or democracy itself, at stake.
June Jordan (1939-, American Poet, Civil Rights Activist)

5   If everybody minded their own business," the Duchess said in a hoarse growl, "the world would go round a deal faster than it does."
Lewis Carroll (1832-1898, British Writer, Mathematician)

6   Everything intercepts us from ourselves.
Ralph Waldo Emerson (1803-1882, American Poet, Essayist)

7   We best avoid wars by taking even physical action to stop small ones.
Sir Anthony Eden (1897-1977, British Statesman and Prime Minister (1955--7))

8   I am not willing to risk the lives of German soldiers for countries whose names we cannot spell properly.
Volker Rnhe

9   Most of the trouble in this world has been caused by folks who can't mind their own business, because they have no business of their own to mind, any more than a smallpox virus has.
William S. Burroughs (1914-1997, American Writer)

INTERVIEWS

1   Never try to look into both eyes at the same time. Switch your gaze from one eye to the other. That signals warmth and sincerity.
Dorothy Sarnoff

2   If, Sir, I possessed the power of conveying unlimited sexual attraction through the potency of my voice, I would not be reduced to accepting a miserable pittance from the BBC for interviewing a faded female in a damp basement.
Gilbert Harding

3 My opposition [To Interviews] lies in the fact that offhand answers have little value or grace of expression, and that such oral give and take helps to perpetuate the decline of the English language.
James Thurber (1894-1961, American Humorist, Illustrator)

4 It rots a writer's brain, it cretinises you. You say the same thing again and again, and when you do that happily you're well on the way to being a cretin. Or a politician.
John Updike (1932-, American Novelist, Critic)

5 The best interviews -- like the best biographies -- should sing the strangeness and variety of the human race.
Lynn Barber

6 Questions are never indiscreet. Answers sometimes are.
Oscar Wilde (1856-1900, British Author, Wit)

7 It is not every question that deserves an answer.
Publilius Syrus (1st Century BC, Roman Writer)

8 I'm notorious for giving a bad interview. I'm an actor and I can't help but feel I'm boring when I'm on as myself.
Rock Hudson

9 The politician being interviewed clearly takes a great deal of trouble to imagine an ending to his sentence: and if he stopped short? His entire policy would be jeopardized!
Roland Barthes (1915-1980, French Semiologist)

10 The media no longer ask those who know something to share that knowledge with the public. Instead they ask those who know nothing to represent the ignorance of the public and, in so doing, to legitimate it.
Serge Daney (1944-1992, French Film Critic)

INTIMACY

1 Intimacies between women go backwards, beginning with revelations and ending up in small talk without loss of esteem.
Elizabeth Bowen (1899-1973, Anglo-Irish Novelist)

2 If ever a man and his wife, or a man and his mistress, who pass nights as well as days together, absolutely lay aside all good breeding, their intimacy will soon degenerate into a coarse familiarity, infallibly productive of contempt or disgust.
Lord Chesterfield (1694-1773, British Statesman, Author)

3 To really know someone is to have loved and hated him in turn.
Marcel Jouhandeau

4 The many faces of intimacy: the Victorians could experience it through correspondence, but not through cohabitation; contemporary men and women can experience it through fornication, but not through friendship.
Thomas Szasz (1920-, American Psychiatrist)

5 If one could be friendly with women, what a pleasure -- the relationship so secret and private compared with relations with men. Why not write about it truthfully?
Virginia Woolf (1882-1941, British Novelist, Essayist)

6 What people don't realize is that intimacy has its conventions as well as ordinary social intercourse. There are three cardinal rules -- don't take somebody else's boyfriend unless you've been specifically invited to do so, don't take a drink without being asked, and keep a scrupulous accounting in financial matters.
W. H. Auden (1907-1973, Anglo-American Poet)

INTOLERANCE

1 Intolerance is evidence of impotence.
Aleister Crowley (1875-1947, British Occultist)

2 Intolerance is the "Do Not Touch" sign on something that cannot bear touching. We do not mind having our hair ruffled, but we will not tolerate any familiarity with the toupee which covers our baldness.
Eric Hoffer (1902-1983, American Author, Philosopher)

3 Intolerance is a form of egotism, and to condemn egotism intolerantly is to share it.
George Santayana (1863-1952, American Philosopher, Poet)

4 Nothing dies so hard, or rallies so often as intolerance.
Henry Ward Beecher (1813-1887, American Preacher, Orator, Writer)

5 The greatest problem in the world today is intolerance. Everyone is so intolerant of each other.
Princess of Wales Diana (1961-1997, Wife of Charles, Prince of Wales)

6 If Woody Allen were a Muslim, he'd be dead by now.
Salman Rushdie (1948-, Indian-born British Author)

7 Intolerance has been the curse of every age and state.
Samuel Davies (1723-1761, American Protestant clergyman, Educator)

8 Intolerance respecting other people's religion is toleration itself in comparison with intolerance respecting other people's art.
Wallace Stevens (1879-1955, American Poet)

INTROSPECTION

1 What is interesting about self-analysis is that it leads nowhere -- it is an art form in itself.
Anita Brookner (1938-, British Novelist, Art Historian)

2 The man whose whole activity is diverted to inner meditation becomes insensible to all his surroundings. If he loves, it is not to give himself, to blend in fecund union with another being, but to meditate on his love. His passions are mere appearances, being sterile. They are dissipated in futile imaginings, producing nothing external to themselves.
Emile Durkheim (1858-1917, French Sociologist)

3 One receives as reward for much ennui, despondency, boredom --such as a solitude without friends, books, duties, passions must bring with it --those quarter-hours of profoundest contemplation within oneself and nature. He who completely entrenches himself against boredom also entrenches himself against himself: he will never get to drink the strongest refreshing draught from his own innermost fountain.
Friedrich Nietzsche (1844-1900, German Philosopher)

4 The terrible fluidity of self-revelation.
Henry James (1843-1916, American Author)

5 The mind can weave itself warmly in the cocoon of its own thoughts, and dwell a hermit anywhere.
James Russell Lowell (1819-1891, American Poet, Critic, Editor)

6 Self-revelation is a cruel process. The real picture, the real "you" never emerges. Looking for it is as bewildering as trying to know how you really look. Ten different mirrors show you ten different faces.
Shashi Deshpande (1938-, Indian Author)

7 But when the self speaks to the self, who is speaking? The entombed soul, the spirit driven in, in, in to the central catacomb; the self that took the veil and left the world -- a coward perhaps, yet somehow beautiful, as it flits with its lantern restlessly up and down the dark corridors.
Virginia Woolf (1882-1941, British Novelist, Essayist)

INTUITION

1 The only real valuable thing is intuition.
Albert Einstein (1879-1955, German-born American Physicist)

2 Intuition comes very close to clairvoyance; it appears to be the extrasensory perception of reality.
Alexis Carrel (1873-1944, French Biologist)

3 Often you have to rely on intuition.
Bill Gates (1955-, American Computer Engineer, Businessman, Founder of Microsoft)

4 The mind can assert anything and pretend it has proved it. My beliefs I test on my body, on my intuitional consciousness, and when I get a response there, then I accept.
D. H. Lawrence (1885-1930, British Author)

5 It is always with excitement that I wake up in the morning wondering what my intuition will toss up to me, like gifts from the sea. I work with it and rely on it. It's my partner.
Dr. Jonas Salk (1914-1995, Virologist, Discovered The First Vaccine Against Poliomyelitis)

6 Trust your hunches. They're usually based on facts filed away just below the conscious level.
Dr. Joyce Brothers (1927-, American Psychologist, Television and Radio Personality)

7 Cease trying to work everything out with your minds. It will get you nowhere. Live by intuition and inspiration and let your whole life be Revelation.
Eileen Caddy (American Spiritual Writer)

8 Intuition is a spiritual faculty and does not explain, but simply points the way.
Florence Scovel Shinn (American Artist, Metaphysics Teacher, Author)

9 A woman uses her intelligence to find reasons to support her intuition.
Gilbert K. Chesterton (1874-1936, British Author)

10 The struggle of the male to learn to listen to and respect his own intuitive, inner prompting is the greatest challenge of all. His conditioning has been so powerful that it has all but destroyed his ability to be self-aware.
Herb Goldberg

11 Intuition is the clear concept of the whole at once.
Johann Kaspar Lavater (1741-1801, Swiss Theologian, Mystic)

12 Intuition becomes increasingly valuable in the new information society precisely because there is so much data.
John Naisbitt (American Trend Analyst, Futurist, Author)

13 There is no instinct like that of the heart.
Lord Byron (1788-1824, British Poet)

14 Good instincts usually tell you what to do before your head has figured it out.
Michael Burke

15 Follow your instincts. That's where true wisdom manifests itself.
Oprah Winfrey (1954-, American TV Personality, Producer, Actress, Author)

16 I have a woman's instinct and it's always a good one.
Princess of Wales Diana (1961-1997, Wife of Charles, Prince of Wales)

17 If the single man plant himself indomitably on his instincts, and there abide, the huge world will come round to him.
Ralph Waldo Emerson (1803-1882, American Poet, Essayist)

18 Never ignore a gut feeling, but never believe that it's enough
Robert Heller (American Business Writer, Editor of Management Today)

INVENTION AND INVENTOR

1 Discovery consists of seeing what everybody has seen and thinking what nobody has thought.
Albert Gyorgyi

2 Great discoveries and improvements invariably involve the cooperation of many minds. I may be given credit for having blazed the trail, but when I look at the subsequent developments I feel the credit is due to others rather than to myself.
Alexander Graham Bell (1847-1922, British-born American Inventor of Telephone)

3 We can invent only with memory.
Alphonse Karr

4 We owe to the Middle Ages the two worst inventions of humanity -- gunpowder and romantic love.
Andre Maurois (1885-1967, French Writer)

5 Today every invention is received with a cry of triumph which soon turns into a cry of fear.
Bertolt Brecht (1898-1956, German Dramatist, Poet)

6 An inventor is simply a person who doesn't take his education too seriously. You see, from the time a person is six years old until he graduates form college he has to take three or four examinations a year. If he flunks once, he is out. But an inventor is almost always failing. He tries and fails maybe a thousand times. It he succeeds once then he's in. These two things are diametrically opposite. We often say that the biggest job we have is to teach a newly hired employee how to fail intelligently. We have to train him to experiment over and over and to keep on trying and failing until he learns what will work.
Charles F. Kettering (1876-1958, American Engineer, Inventor)

7 Everything that can be invented has been invented. .
Charles H. Duell (Commissioner, U.S. Office of Patents, 1899)

8 The right of an inventor to his invention is no monopoly; in any other sense than a man's house is a monopoly.
Daniel Webster (1782-1852, American Lawyer, Statesman)

9 That is what we are supposed to do when we are at our best --make it all up --but make it up so truly that later it will happen that way.
Ernest Hemingway (1898-1961, American Writer)

10 A new gadget that lasts only five minutes is worth more than an immortal work that bores everyone.
Francis Picabia (1878-1953, French Painter, Poet)

11 Fear is a great inventor.
French Proverb

12 If you build a better mousetrap, you will catch better mice.
George Gobel

13 The march of invention has clothed mankind with powers of which a century ago the boldest imagination could not have dreamt.
Henry George (1839-1897, American Social Reformer, Economist)

14 The coming of the printing press must have seemed as if it would turn the world upside down in the way it spread and, above all, democratized knowledge. Provide you could pay and read, what was on the shelves in the new bookshops was yours for the taking. The speed with which printing presses and their operators fanned out across Europe is extraordinary. From the single Mainz press of 1457, it took only twenty-three years to establish presses in 110 towns: 50 in Italy, 30 in Germany, 9 in France, 8 in Spain, 8 in Holland, 4 in England, and so on.
James E. Burke (American Businessman, Chairman of Johnson & Johnson)

15 Invention is the talent of youth, as judgment is of age.
Jonathan Swift (1667-1745, Anglo-Irish Satirist)

16 Interest is the spur of the people, but glory that of great souls. Invention is the talent of youth, and judgment of age.
Jonathan Swift (1667-1745, Anglo-Irish Satirist)

17 I don't mind occasionally having to reinvent a wheel; I don't even mind using someone's reinvented wheel occasionally. But it helps a lot if it is symmetric, contains no fewer than ten sides, and has the axle centered. I do tire of trapezoidal wheels with offset axles.
Joseph Newcomer

18 This is the patent age of new inventions for killing bodies, and for saving souls. All propagated with the best intentions.
Lord Byron (1788-1824, British Poet)

19 The guns and bombs, the rockets and the warships, all are symbols of human failure.
Lyndon B. Johnson (1908-1973, Thirty-sixth President of the USA)

20 Accident is the name of the greatest of all inventors.
Mark Twain (1835-1910, American Humorist, Writer)

21 It is only the unimaginative who ever invents. The true artist is known by the use he makes of what he annexes.
Oscar Wilde (1856-1900, British Author, Wit)

22 Man is a shrewd inventor, and is ever taking the hint of a new machine from his own structure, adapting some secret of his own anatomy in iron, wood, and leather, to some required function in the work of the world.
Ralph Waldo Emerson (1803-1882, American Poet, Essayist)

23 In my own time there have been inventions of this sort, transparent windows tubes for diffusing warmth equally through all parts of a building short-hand, which has been carried to such a perfection that a writer can keep pace with the most rapid speaker. But the inventing of such things is drudgery for the lowest slaves; philosophy lies deeper. It is not her office to teach men how to use their hands. The object of her lessons is to form the soul.
Seneca (4 BC-65 AD, Spanish-born Roman Statesman, philosopher)

24 Invention strictly speaking, is little more than a new combination of those images which have been previously gathered and deposited in the memory; nothing can come from nothing.
Sir Joshua Reynolds (1723-1792, British Artist, Critic)

25 I am proud of the fact that I never invented weapons to kill.
Thomas A. Edison (1847-1931, American Inventor, Entrepreneur, Founder of GE)

26 Anything that won't sell, I don't want to invent. Its sale is proof of utility, and utility is success.
Thomas A. Edison (1847-1931, American Inventor, Entrepreneur, Founder of GE)

27 The real use of gunpowder is to make all men tall.
Thomas Carlyle (1795-1881, Scottish Philosopher, Author)

28 Inventions have long since reached their limit, and I see no hope for further development.
Ursula K. Le Guin (1929-, American Author)

INVESTMENTS

1 Never invest your money in anything that eats or needs repairing.
Billy Rose (1899-1966, American Composer of Popular Music)

2 It's not the bulls and bears you need to avoid -- it's the bum steers.
Chuck Hillis

3 Sometimes your best investments are the ones you don't make.
Donald Trump (1946-, 45th President of the United States of America)

4 'Tis money that begets money.
English Proverb

5 Spend not on hopes.
George Herbert (1593-1632, British Metaphysical Poet)

6 Gambling with cards or dice or stocks is all one thing. It's getting money without giving an equivalent for it.
Henry Ward Beecher (1813-1887, American Preacher, Orator, Writer)

7 I do not regard a broker as a member of the human race.
Honore De Balzac (1799-1850, French Novelist)

8 The social object of skilled investment should be to defeat the dark forces of time and ignorance which envelope our future.
John Maynard Keynes (1883-1946, British Economist)

9 Money itself isn't lost or made, it's simply transferred from one perception to another. This painting here. I bought it 10 years ago for 60 thousand dollars. I could sell it today for 600. The illusion has become real and the more real it becomes, the more desperately they want it.
Oliver Stone (1946-, American Director, Writer, Producer)

10 With an evening coat and a white tie, anybody, even a stock broker, can gain a reputation for being civilized.
Oscar Wilde (1856-1900, British Author, Wit)

11 Our favorite holding period is forever.
Warren Buffett (1930-, American Investment Entrepreneur)

INVOLVEMENT

1 America I'm putting my queer shoulder to the wheel.
Allen Ginsberg (1926-, American Poet)

2 None of us liveth to himself, and no man dieth to himself. [Romans 14:7]
Bible (Sacred Scriptures of Christians and Judaism)

3 I ask you to join in a re-United States. We need to empower our people so they can take more responsibility for their own lives in a world that is ever smaller, where everyone counts. We need a new spirit of community, a sense that we are all in this together, or the American Dream will continue to wither. Our destiny is bound up with the destiny of every other American.
Bill Clinton (1946-, Forty-second President of the USA)

4 The kind of relatedness to the world may be noble or trivial, but even being related to the basest kind of pattern is immensely preferable to being alone.
Erich Fromm (1900-1980, American Psychologist)

5 To say yes, you have to sweat and roll up your sleeves and plunge both hands into life up to the elbows. It's easy to say no, even if it means dying.
Jean Anouilh (1910-1987, French Playwright)

6 One must either take an interest in the human situation or else parade before the void.
Jean Rostand (1894-1977, French Biologist, Writer)

7 The gap between the committed and the indifferent is a Sahara whose faint trails, followed by the mind's eye only, fade out in sand.
Nadine Gordimer (1923-, South African Author)

8 I recommend limiting one's involvement in other people's lives to a pleasantly scant minimum. This may seem too stoical a position in these madly passionate times, but madly passionate people rarely make good on their madly passionate promises.
Quentin Crisp (1908-, British Author)

9 It is easy to talk of sitting at home contented, when others are seeing or making shows. But not to have been where it is supposed, and seldom supposed falsely, that all would go if they could; to be able to say nothing when everyone is talking; to have no opinion when everyone is judging; to hear exclamations of rapture without power to depress; to listen to falsehoods without right to contradict, is, after all, a state of temporary inferiority, in which the mind is rather hardened by stubbornness, than supported by fortitude. If the world be worth winning let us enjoy it, if it is to be despised let us despise it by conviction. But the world is not to be despised but as it is compared with something better.
Samuel Johnson (1709-1784, British Author)

IQ TEST

1 If the aborigine drafted an IQ test, all of Western civilization would presumably flunk it.
Stanley Garn

IRONY

1 Humor brings insight and tolerance. Irony brings a deeper and less friendly understanding.
Agnes Repplier (1858-1950, American Author, Social Critic)

2 Irony is the gaiety of reflection and the joy of wisdom.
Anatole France (1844-1924, French Writer)

3 Irony is an insult conveyed in the form of a compliment.
Edwin P. Whipple (1819-1886, American Essayist)

4 Irony is the form of paradox. Paradox is what is good and great at the same time.
Friedrich Schlegel (1772-1829, German Philosopher, Critic, Writer)

5 A taste for irony has kept more hearts from breaking than a sense of humor for it takes irony to appreciate the joke which is on oneself.
Jessamyn West (1903-1984, American Author)

6 Irony is jesting behind hidden gravity.
John Weiss

7 Sentimental irony is a dog that bays at the moon while pissing on graves.
Karl Kraus (1874-1936, Austrian Satirist)

8 Irony is a disciplinarian feared only by those who do not know it, but cherished by those who do. He who does not understand irony and has no ear for its whispering lacks of what might called the absolute beginning of the personal life. He lacks what at moments is indispensable for the personal life, lacks both the regeneration and rejuvenation, the cleaning baptism of irony that redeems the soul from having its life in finitude though living boldly and energetically in finitude.
Soren Kierkegaard (1813-1855, Danish Philosopher, Writer)

9 Jesus wept; Voltaire smiled. From that divine tear and from that human smile is derived the grace of present civilization.
Victor Hugo (1802-1885, French Poet, Dramatist, Novelist)

IRREVERENCE

1 Impiety. Your irreverence toward my deity.
Ambrose Bierce (1842-1914, American Author, Editor, Journalist, "The Devil's Dictionary")

2 Conventionality is not morality. Self-righteousness is not religion. To attack the first is not to assail the last. To pluck the mask from the face of the Pharisee is not to lift an impious hand to the Crown of Thorns.
Charlotte Bronte (1816-1855, British Novelist)

3 True irreverence is disrespect for another man's god.
Mark Twain (1835-1910, American Humorist, Writer)

4 In America few people will trust you unless you are irreverent.
Norman Mailer (1923-, American Author)

ISOLATION

1 Not only does democracy make every man forget his ancestors, but also clouds their view of their descendants and isolates them from their contemporaries. Each man is for ever thrown back on himself alone, and there is danger that he may be shut up in the solitude of his own heart.
Alexis De Tocqueville (1805-1859, French Social Philosopher)

2 Life's an awfully lonesome affair. You come into the world alone and you go out of the world alone yet it seems to me you are more alone while living than even going and coming.
Emily Carr (1871-1945, Canadian Artist)

3 It isn't the oceans which cut us off from the world -- it's the American way of looking at things.
Henry Miller (1891-1980, American Author)

4 National isolation breeds national neurosis.
Hubert H. Humphrey (1911-1978, American Democratic Politician, Vice President)

5 I am greatly pleased with the public, authentic isolation in which we two, you and I, now find ourselves. It is wholly in accord with our attitude and our principles.
Karl Marx (1818-1883, German Political Theorist, Social Philosopher)

6 We allow our ignorance to prevail upon us and make us think we can survive alone, alone in patches, alone in groups, alone in races, even alone in genders.
Maya Angelou (1928-, African-American poet, Writer, Performer)

7 We're born alone, we live alone, we die alone. Only through our love and friendship can we create the illusion for the moment that we're not alone.
Orson Welles (1915-1985, American Film Maker)

8 We're all of us sentenced to solitary confinement inside our own skins, for life!
Tennessee Williams (1914-1983, American Dramatist)

JARGON

1 Jargon is the verbal sleight of hand that makes the old hat seem newly fashionable; it gives an air of novelty and specious profundity to ideas that, if stated directly, would seem superficial, stale, frivolous, or false. The line between serious and spurious scholarship is an easy one to blur, with jargon on your side.
David Lehman (1948-, American Poet, Editor, Critic)

2 Psychobabble is... a set of repetitive verbal formalities that kills off the very spontaneity, candor, and understanding it pretends to promote. It's an idiom that reduces psychological insight to a collection of standardized observations, that provides a frozen lexicon to deal with an infinite variety of problems.
Richard D. Rosen

JAZZ

1 Jazz is the big brother of the blues. If a guy's playing blues like we play, he's in high school. When he starts playing jazz it's like going on to college, to a school of higher learning.
B. B. King (1925-, American Blues Singer, Guitarist)

2 Jazz music is an intensified feeling of nonchalance.
Françoise Sagan (1935-2004, French novelist, playwright)

3 The further jazz moves away from the stark blue continuum and the collective realities of Afro- American and American life, the more it moves into academic concert-hall lifelessness, which can be replicated by any middle class showing off its music lessons.
Imamu Amiri Baraka Jones

4 It seems to me monstrous that anyone should believe that the jazz rhythm expresses America. Jazz rhythm expresses the primitive savage. ·
Isadora Duncan (1878-1927, American Dancer)

5 There's more bad music in jazz than any other form. Maybe that's because the audience doesn't really know what's happening.
Pat Metheny

6 What kills me is that everybody thinks I like jazz.
Samuel L. Jackson (1948-, American Actor)

7 Something was still there, that something that distinguishes an artist from a performer: the revealing of self. Here I be. Not for long, but here I be. In sensing her mortality, we sensed our own.
Studs Terkel (1912-, American Interviewer, Actor and Writer)

JEALOUSY

1 Always remember, Peggy, it's matrimonial suicide to be jealous when you have a really good reason.
Clare Boothe Luce (1903-1987, American Diplomat, Writer)

2 The heart of the jealous knows the best and most satisfying love, that of the other's bed, where the rival perfects the lover's imperfections.
Djuna Barnes (1892-1982, American Author, Poet, Columnist)

3 Jealousy is no more than feeling alone against smiling enemies.
Elizabeth Bowen (1899-1973, Anglo-Irish Novelist)

4 Jealousy is indeed a poor medium to secure love, but it is a secure medium to destroy one's self-respect. For jealous people, like dope-fiends, stoop to the lowest level and in the end inspire only disgust and loathing.
Emma Goldman (1869-1940, American Anarchist)

5 Jealousy is all the fun you think they had...
Erica Jong (1942-, American Author)

6 In jealousy there is more of self-love than love.
François de La Rochefoucauld (1613-1680, French classical writer)

7 Live on doubts; it becomes madness or stops entirely as soon as we pass from doubt to certainty.
François de La Rochefoucauld (1613-1680, French classical writer)

8 Jealously is always born with love but it does not die with it.
François de La Rochefoucauld (1613-1680, French classical writer)

9 Jealousy contains more of self-love than of love.
François de La Rochefoucauld (1613-1680, French classical writer)

10 To jealousy, nothing is more frightful than laughter.
Françoise Sagan (1935-2004, French novelist, playwright)

11 Never waste jealousy on a real man: it is the imaginary man that supplants us all in the long run.
George Bernard Shaw (1856-1950, Irish-born British Dramatist)

12 There is a sort of jealousy which needs very little fire; it is hardly a passion, but a blight bred in the cloudy, damp despondency of uneasy egoism.
George Eliot (1819-1880, British Novelist)

13 Jealousy is never satisfied with anything short of an omniscience that would detect the subtlest fold of the heart.
George Eliot (1819-1880, British Novelist)

14 Jealousy is love bed of burning snarl.
George Meredith (1828-1909, British Author)

15 Jealousy, that dragon which slays love under the pretence of keeping it alive.
Havelock Ellis (1859-1939, British Psychologist)

16 Potter is jealous of potter, and craftsman of craftsman; and the poor have a grudge against the poor, and the poet against the poet.
Hesiod (8th Century BC, Greek Poet)

17 I've never been jealous. Not even when my dad finished the fifth grade a year before I did.
Jeff Foxworthy (American Comedian)

18 The jealous are possessed by a mad devil and a dull spirit at the same time.
Johann Kaspar Lavater (1741-1801, Swiss Theologian, Mystic)

19 Jealousy is the jaundice of the soul.
John Dryden (1631-1700, British Poet, Dramatist, Critic)

20 The disease of jealously is so malignant that is converts all it takes into its own nourishment.
Joseph Addison (1672-1719, British Essayist, Poet, Statesman)

21 Who surpasses or subdues mankind, must look down on the hate of those below.
Lord Byron (1788-1824, British Poet)

22 The "Green-eyed Monster" causes much woe, but the absence of this ugly serpent argues the presence of a corpse whose name is Eros.
Minna Antrim (1861-18?, American Epigrammist)

23 Plain women are always jealous of their husbands. Beautiful women never are. They are always so occupied with being jealous of other women's husbands.
Oscar Wilde (1856-1900, British Author, Wit)

24 My wife's jealousy is getting ridiculous. The other day she looked at my calendar and wanted to know who May was.
Rodney Dangerfield (American Comedian, Actor)

25 Jealousy is not at all low, but it catches us humbled and bowed down, at first sight.
Sidonie Gabrielle Colette (1873-1954, French Author)

26 There is never jealousy where there is not strong regard.
Washington Irving (1783-1859, American Author)

27 I had rather be a toad, and live upon the vapor of a dungeon than keep a corner in the thing I love for others uses.
William Shakespeare (1564-1616, British Poet, Playwright, Actor)

JEST

1 Many a true word is spoken in jest.
English Proverb

2 Jesting is often only indigence of intellect.
Jean De La Bruyere (1645-1696, French Writer)

3 The jest loses its point when he who makes it is the first to laugh.
Johann Friedrich Von Schiller (1759-1805, German Dramatist, Poet, Historian)

4 Jests that give pains are no jests.
Miguel De Cervantes (1547-1616, Spanish Novelist, Dramatist, Poet)

5 Judge of a jest when you have done laughing.
William Lloyd

JESUS CHRIST

1 Thou has conquered, O pale Galilean.
A. C. Swinburne (1837-1909, British Poet)

2 Christianity takes for granted the absence of any self-help and offers a power which is nothing less than the power of God.
A. W. Tozer (Deceased 1963, American Preacher)

3 We believe that the history of the world is but the history of His influence and that the center of the whole universe is the cross of Calvary.
Alexander Maclaren (1826-1910, British Preacher)

4 Somewhere in the bible it say Jesus hair was like lamb's wool, I say. Well, say Shug, if he came to any of these churches we talking bout he'd have to have it conked before anybody paid him any attention. The last thing niggers want to think about they God is that his hair kinky.
Alice Walker (1944-, American Author, Critic)

5 The name of Jesus is as ointment poured forth; It nourishes, and illumines, and stills the anguish of the soul.
Angelus Silesius

6 The men who followed Him were unique in their generation. They turned the world upside down because their hearts had been turned right side up. The world has never been the same.
Billy Graham (1918-, American Evangelist)

7 No man ever loved like Jesus. He taught the blind to see and the dumb to speak. He died on the cross to save us. He bore our sins. And now God says, "Because He did, I can forgive you."
Billy Graham (1918-, American Evangelist)

8 Jesus is the God whom we can approach without pride and before whom we can humble ourselves without despair.
Blaise Pascal (1623-1662, French Scientist, Religious Philosopher)

9   Jesus was a brilliant Jewish stand-up comedian, a phenomenal improviser. His parables are great one-liners.
Camille Paglia (1947-, American Author, Critic, Educator)

10   Jesus Christ turns life right-side-up, and heaven outside-in.
Carl F. H. Henry

11   The Christian is not one who has gone all the way with Christ. None of us has. The Christian is one who has found the right road.
Charles L. Allen

12   The greatest thing about any civilization is the human person, and the greatest thing about this person is the possibility of his encounter with the person of Jesus Christ.
Charles Malik

13   Jesus says, "I love you just the way you are. And I love you too much to let you stay the way you are."
Chris Lyons

14   The Lord has turned all our sunsets into sunrise.
Clement of Alexandria (150-220, Church Father)

15   I wouldn't put it past God to arrange a virgin birth if He wanted, but I very much doubt if He would.
David Jenkins (1925-, British Ecclesiastic, Bishop of Durham)

16   All that I am I owe to Jesus Christ, revealed to me in His divine Book.
David Livingstone (1813-1873, British Missionary, Explorer)

17   The blood of Jesus Christ can cover a multitude of sins, it seems to me.
Denis Diderot (1713-1784, French Philosopher)

18   By a Carpenter mankind was made, and only by that Carpenter can mankind be remade.
Desiderius Erasmus (1466-1536, Dutch Humanist)

19   Let us pardon him his hope of a vain apocalypse, and of a second coming in great triumph upon the clouds of heaven. Perhaps these were the errors of others rather than his own; and if it be true that he himself shared the general illusion, what matters it, since his dream rendered him strong against death, and sustained him in a struggle to which he might otherwise have been unequal?
Ernest Renan (1823-1892, French Writer, Critic, Scholar)

20   Never has any one been less a priest than Jesus, never a greater enemy of forms, which stifle religion under the pretext of protecting it. By this we are all his disciples and his successors; by this he has laid the eternal foundation-stone of true religion; and if religion is essential to humanity, he has by this deserved the Divine rank the world has accorded him.
Ernest Renan (1823-1892, French Writer, Critic, Scholar)

21   A heroic figure... not wholly to blame for the religion that's been foisted on him.
Ezra Pound (1885-1972, American Poet, Critic)

22   Two thousand years ago there was One here on this earth who lived the grandest life that ever has been lived yet--a life that every thinking man, with deeper or shallower meaning, has agreed to call divine.
Frederick W. Robertson

23   The word "Christianity" is already a misunderstanding -- in reality there has been only one Christian, and he died on the Cross.
Friedrich Nietzsche (1844-1900, German Philosopher)

24   The most pressing question on the problem of faith is whether a man as a civilized being... can believe in the divinity of the Son of God, Jesus Christ, for therein rests the whole of our faith.
Fyodor Dostoevski (1821-1881, Russian Novelist)

25   To become Christ-like is the only thing in the whole world worth caring for, the thing before which every ambition of man is folly and all lower achievement vain.
Henry Drummond (1786-1860, British Banker, Politician, Religious Leader)

26   I thank God for the honesty and virility of Jesus religion which makes us face the facts and calls us to take a man's part in the real battle of life.
Henry Van Dyke (1852-1933, American Protestant Clergyman, Poet and Writer)

27   He comes into the world God knows how, walks on the water, gets out of his grave and goes up off the Hill of Howth. What drivel is this?
James Joyce (1882-1941, Irish Author)

28   I love to hear my Lord spoken of, and wherever I have seen the print of His shoe in the earth, there have I coveted to put mine also.
John Bunyan (1628-1688, British Author)

29   Each eye can have its vision separately; but when we are looking at anything... our vision, which in itself is divided, joins up and unites in order to give itself as a whole to the object that is put before it.
John Calvin (1509-1564, French Protestant Reformer)

30   No one else holds or has held the place in the heart of the world which Jesus holds. Other gods have been as devoutly worshipped; no other man has been so devoutly loved.
John Knox (1505-1572, Scottish Historian, Reformer)

31   Jesus was all right, but his disciples were thick and ordinary. It's them twisting it that ruins it for me.
John Lennon (1940-1980, British Rock Musician)

32   We're more popular than Jesus Christ now. I don't know which will go first; rock and roll or Christianity.
John Lennon (1940-1980, British Rock Musician)

33   Only Christ could have conceived Christ.
Joseph Parker

34   A lot of people say to me, "Why did you kill Christ?" "I dunno... it was one of those parties, got out of hand, you know." "We killed him because he didn't want to become a doctor, that's why we killed him."
Lenny Bruce (1925-1966, American Comedian)

35 None speak of the bravery, the might, or the intellect of Jesus; but the devil is always imagined as a being of acute intellect, political cunning, and the fiercest courage. These universal and instinctive tendencies of the human mind reveal much.
Lydia M. Child (1802-1880, American Abolitionist, Writer, Editor)

36 A man who was completely innocent, offered himself as a sacrifice for the good of others, including his enemies, and became the ransom of the world. It was a perfect act.
Mahatma Gandhi (1869-1948, Indian Political, Spiritual Leader)

37 You should point to the whole man Jesus and say, "That is God."
Martin Luther (1483-1546, German Leader of the Protestant Reformation)

38 In every pang that rends the heart the Man of Sorrows has a part.
Michael Bruce

39 Jesus was the first socialist, the first to seek a better life for mankind.
Mikhail Gorbachev (1931-, Soviet Statesman and President of USSR (1988-91))

40 There is but one love of Jesus, as there is but one person in the poor -- Jesus. We take vows of chastity to love Christ with undivided love; to be able to love him with undivided love we take a vow of poverty which frees us from all material possessions, and with that freedom we can love him with undivided love, and from this vow of undivided love we surrender ourselves totally to him in the person who takes his place.
Mother Teresa (1910-1997, Albanian-born Roman Catholic Missionary)

41 I believe in person to person. Every person is Christ for me, and since there is only one Jesus, that person is the one person in the world at that moment.
Mother Teresa (1910-1997, Albanian-born Roman Catholic Missionary)

42 Alexander, Caesar, Charlemagne, and myself founded empires; but what foundation did we rest the creations of our genius? Upon force. Jesus Christ founded an empire upon love; and at this hour millions of men would die for Him.
Napoleon Bonaparte (1769-1821, French General, Emperor)

43 The Galilean is not a favorite of mine. So far from owing him any thanks for his favor, I cannot avoid confessing that I owe a secret grudge to his carpentership.
Percy Bysshe Shelley (1792-1822, British Poet)

44 Jesus Christ, the condescension of divinity, and the exaltation of humanity.
Phillips Brooks (1835-1893, American Minister, Poet)

45 Jesus Christ is God's everything for man's total need.
Richard Halverson

46 Every time that I think of the crucifixion of Christ, I commit the sin of envy.
Simone Weil (1910-1943, French Philosopher, Mystic)

47 Jesus whom I know as my Redeemer cannot be less than God.
St. Athanasius (293-373, Bishop of Alexandria)

48 Above all the grace and the gifts that Christ gives to his beloved is that of overcoming self.
St. Francis of Assisi (1181-1226, Italian Preacher, Founder of the Franciscan Orde)

49 I am pretty sure that we err in treating these sayings as paradoxes. It would be nearer the truth to say that it is life itself which is paradoxical and that the sayings of Jesus are simply a recognition of that fact.
Thomas Taylor

50 Jesus promised His disciples three things: that they would be entirely fearless, absurdly happy, and that they would get into trouble.
W. Russell Maltby

51 Thinking as I do that the Creator of this world is a very cruel being, and being a worshipper of Christ, I cannot help saying: "the Son, O how unlike the Father!" First God Almighty comes with a thump on the head. Then Jesus Christ comes with a balm to heal it.
William Blake (1757-1827, British Poet, Painter)

52 God speaks to me not through the thunder and the earthquake, nor through the ocean and the stars, but through the Son of Man, and speaks in a language adapted to my imperfect sight and hearing.
William Lyon Phelps

JOB

1 We may not be able to offer long-term employment, but we should try to offer long-term employability.
Brian Corby (American Business Executive, Chairman of Prudential Insurance)

2 If two men on a job agree all the time, then one is useless. If they disagree all the time, then both are useless.
Darryl F. Zanuck

3 It's a job -- someone's gotta do it. The reality is, Jennifer and I can do our job well because we truly are friends. But when the day's over, she goes home to her boyfriend and I go home to a magazine. [On what it's like kissing sex symbol Jennifer Aniston]
David Schwimmer (1966-, American Actor, Director)

4 The biggest mistake that you can make is to believe that you are working for somebody else. Job security is gone. The driving force of a career must come from the individual. Remember: Jobs are owned by the company, you own your career!
Earl Nightingale (1921-1989, American Radio Announcer, Author, Motivator, Speaker)

5 Our job is not to set things right but to see them right.
Eric Butterworth

6 There is no indispensable man.
Franklin D. Roosevelt (1882-1945, Thirty-second President of the USA)

7 The tougher the job, the greater the reward.
George Allen (American Football Coach)

8 We've entered an era when very good, competent people aren't getting jobs. One remedy is to stand out, to self-promote. If you do, you're going to get the nod over some co-worker.
Jeffrey P. Davidson (American Marketing Consultant)

9 Work harder on yourself than you do on your job.
Jim Rohn (American Businessman, Author, Speaker, Philosopher)

10 I couldn't get any jobs, and when that happens, you get so humble it's disgusting. I didn't feel like a man anymore -- I felt really creepy. I was bumping into walls and saying, "Excuse me."
Joe Pesci (1943-, American Actor)

11 Make yourself indispensable, and you will move up. Act as though you are indispensable, and you will move out.
Jules Ormont

12 The trouble with the rat race is that even if you win you're still a rat.
Lily Tomlin (1939-, American Comedienne)

13 Man's biggest mistake is to believe that he's working for someone else.
Nashua Cavalier

14 I've met a few people who had to change their jobs in order to change their lives, but I've met many more people who merely had to change their motive to service in order to change their lives.
Peace Pilgrim (1908-1981, American Peace Activist)

15 If you're not a white male, consider sales seriously. Most employers, regardless of how sexist or racist they may be, will pay for any sales they can get. And they care little for the color or gender of the person who brings that business to the firm. Most will be glad to get the business even if it comes from a green, bisexual Martian.
Ramona E.F. Arnett (American Business Executive, President of Ramona Enterprises)

16 There's no scarcity of opportunity to make a living at what you love. There is only a scarcity of resolve to make it happen.
Wayne Dyer (1940-, American Psychotherapist, Author, Lecturer)

JOKES AND JOKERS

1 Witticism. A sharp and clever remark, usually quoted and seldom noted; what the Philistine is pleased to call a "joke."
Ambrose Bierce (1842-1914, American Author, Editor, Journalist, "The Devil's Dictionary")

2 Times change. The farmer's daughter now tells jokes about the traveling salesman.
Carey Williams

3 I remain just one thing, and one thing only -- and that is a clown. It places me on a far higher plane than any politician.
Charlie Chaplin (1889-1977, British Comic Actor, Filmmaker)

4 Prithee don't screw your wit beyond the compass of good manners.
Colley Cibber (1671-1757, British Actor-Manager, Playwright)

5 Being a funny person does an awful lot of things to you. You feel that you mustn't get serious with people. They don't expect it from you, and they don't want to see it. You're not entitled to be serious, you're a clown, and they only want you to make them laugh.
Fanny Brice (1891-1951, American Entertainer)

6 In polite society one laughs at all the jokes, including the ones one has heard before.
Frank Dane

7 The funniest line in English is "Get it?" When you say that, everyone chortles.
Garrison Keillor (1942-, American Humorous Writer, Radio Performer)

8 If all else fails, the character of a man can be recognized by nothing so surely as by a jest which he takes badly.
Georg C. Lichtenberg (1742-1799, German Physicist, Satirist)

9 Suppose the world were only one of God's jokes, would you work any the less to make it a good joke instead of a bad one?
George Bernard Shaw (1856-1950, Irish-born British Dramatist)

10 My way of joking is to tell the truth. It's the funniest joke in the world.
George Bernard Shaw (1856-1950, Irish-born British Dramatist)

11 A dirty joke is a sort of mental rebellion.
George Orwell (1903-1950, British Author, "Animal Farm")

12 The old idea that the joke was not good enough for the company has been superseded by the new aristocratic idea that the company was not worthy of the joke. They have introduced an almost insane individualism into that one form of intercourse which is specially and uproariously communal. They have made even levities into secrets. They have made laughter lonelier than tears.
Gilbert K. Chesterton (1874-1936, British Author)

13 His hilarity was like a scream from a crevasse.
Graham Greene (1904-1991, British Novelist)

14 If you've heard this story before, don't stop me, because I'd like to hear it again.
Groucho Marx (1895-1977, American Comic Actor)

15 All human race would be wits. And millions miss, for one that hits.
Jonathan Swift (1667-1745, Anglo-Irish Satirist)

16 All womankind, from the highest to the lowest love jokes; the difficulty is to know how they choose to have them cut; and there is no knowing that, but by trying, as we do with our artillery in the field, by raising or letting down their breeches, till we hit the mark.
Laurence Sterne (1713-1768, British Author)

17 'Tis no extravagant arithmetic to say, that for every ten jokes, thou hast got an hundred enemies; and till thou hast gone on, and raised a swarm of wasps about thine ears, and art half stung to death by them, thou wilt never be convinced it is so.
Laurence Sterne (1713-1768, British Author)

18 Jokes are grievances.
Marshall Mcluhan (1911-1980, Canadian Communications Theorist)

19 My life has been one great big joke, a dance that's walked a song that's spoke, I laugh so hard I almost choke when I think about myself.
Maya Angelou (1928-, African-American poet, Writer, Performer)

20 A pun does not commonly justify a blow in return. But if a blow were given for such cause, and death ensued, the jury would be judges both of the facts and of the pun, and might, if the latter were of an aggravated character, return a verdict of justifiable homicide.
Oliver Wendell Holmes (1809-1894, American Author, Wit, Poet)

21 I gleaned jests at home from obsolete farces.
Samuel Johnson (1709-1784, British Author)

22 Alas, poor Yorick! I knew him, Horatio: a fellow of infinite jest, of most excellent fancy. Where be your jibes now, your gambols, your songs, your flashes of merriment that were wont to set the table on a roar?
William Shakespeare (1564-1616, British Poet, Playwright, Actor)

23 He jests at scars that never felt a wound.
William Shakespeare (1564-1616, British Poet, Playwright, Actor)

JOURNALISM AND JOURNALISTS

1 Freedom of the press is limited to those who own one.
A. J. Liebling (1904-1963, American Journalist)

2 In America journalism is apt to be regarded as an extension of history: in Britain, as an extension of conversation.
Anthony Sampson

3 Journalists are like dogs, when ever anything moves they begin to bark.
Arthur Schopenhauer (1788-1860, German Philosopher)

4 The lowest form of popular culture -- lack of information, misinformation, misinformation, and a contempt for the truth or the reality of most people's lives -- has overrun real journalism. Today, ordinary Americans are being stuffed with garbage.
Carl Bernstein (1944-, American Journalist, writer)

5 The man must have a rare recipe for melancholy, who can be dull in Fleet Street.
Charles Lamb (1775-1834, British Essayist, Critic)

6 Evidently there are plenty of people in journalism who have neither got what they liked nor quite grown to like what they get. They write pieces they do not much enjoy writing, for papers they totally despise, and the sad process ends by ruining their style and disintegrating their personality, two developments which in a writer cannot be separate, since his personality and style must progress or deteriorate together, like a married couple in a country where death is the only permissible divorce.
Claud Cockburn (1904-1981, British Author, Journalist)

7 Journalism could be described as turning one's enemies into money.
Craig Brown

8 Literature is the art of writing something that will be read twice; journalism what will be grasped at once.
Cyril Connolly (1903-1974, British Critic)

9 We need not be theologians to see that we have shifted responsibility for making the world interesting from God to the newspaperman.
Daniel J. Boorstin (1914-, American Historian)

10 I get up in the morning with an idea for a three-volume novel and by nightfall it's a paragraph in my column.
Don Marquis (1878-1937, American Humorist, Journalist)

11 We now demand the light artillery of the intellect; we need the curt, the condensed, the pointed, the readily diffused -- in place of the verbose, the detailed, the voluminous, the inaccessible. On the other hand, the lightness of the artillery should not degenerate into pop-gunnery -- by which term we may designate the character of the greater portion of the newspaper press -- their sole legitimate object being the discussion of ephemeral matters in an ephemeral manner.
Edgar Allan Poe (1809-1845, American Poet, Critic, short-story Writer)

12 Journalism is organized gossip.
Edward Eggleston (American Writer, Historian)

13 Personal columnists are jackals and no jackal has been known to live on grass once he had learned about meat -- no matter who killed the meat for him.
Ernest Hemingway (1898-1961, American Writer)

14 If, for instance, they have heard something from the postman, they attribute it to "a semi- official statement"; if they have fallen into conversation with a stranger at a bar, they can conscientiously describe him as "a source that has hitherto proved unimpeachable." It is only when the journalist is reporting a whim of his own, and one to which he attaches minor importance, that he defines it as the opinion of "well-informed circles."
Evelyn Waugh (1903-1966, British Novelist)

15 Journalism is the entertainment business.
Frank Herbert (1920-1986, American Writer)

16 Most rock journalism is people who can't write, interviewing people who can't talk, for people who can't read.
Frank Zappa (1940-, American Rock Musician)

17 Opinionated writing is always the most difficult... simply because it involves retaining in the cold morning-after crystal of the printed word the burning flow of molten feeling.
Gavin Lyall

18 The journalists have constructed for themselves a little wooden chapel, which they also call the Temple of Fame, in which they put up and take down portraits all day long and make such a hammering you can't hear yourself speak.
Georg C. Lichtenberg (1742-1799, German Physicist, Satirist)

19 It was when "reporters" became "journalists" and when "objectivity" gave way to "searching for truth," that an aura of distrust and fear arose around the New Journalist.
Georgie Anne Geyer

20 Journalists belong in the gutter because that is where the ruling classes throw their guilty secrets.
Gerald Priestland

21 Journalism consists largely in saying "Lord James is dead" to people who never knew Lord James was alive.
Gilbert K. Chesterton (1874-1936, British Author)

22 Journalism is popular, but it is popular mainly as fiction. Life is one world, and life seen in the newspapers another.
Gilbert K. Chesterton (1874-1936, British Author)

23 People accuse journalism of being too personal; but to me it has always seemed far too impersonal. It is charged with tearing away the veils from private life; but it seems to me to be always dropping diaphanous but blinding veils between men and men. The Yellow Press is abused for exposing facts which are private; I wish the Yellow Press did anything so valuable. It is exactly the decisive individual touches that it never gives; and a proof of this is that after one has met a man a million times in the newspapers it is always a complete shock and reversal to meet him in real life.
Gilbert K. Chesterton (1874-1936, British Author)

24 A petty reason perhaps why novelists more and more try to keep a distance from journalists is that novelists are trying to write the truth and journalists are trying to write fiction.
Graham Greene (1904-1991, British Novelist)

25 In journalism it is simpler to sound off than it is to find out. It is more elegant to pontificate than it is to sweat.
Harold Evans

26 Write the news as if your very life depended on it. It does!
Heywood Broun (1888-1939, American Journalist, Novelist)

27 Journalism will kill you, but it will keep you alive while you're at it.
Horace Greeley (1811-1872, American Newspaper Editor)

28 You cannot hope to bribe or twist (thank God!) the British journalist. But, seeing what the man will do unbribed, there's no occasion to.
Humbert Wolfe (1885-1940, British Poet)

29 Gonzo journalism is a style of "reporting" based on William Faulkner's idea that the best fiction is far more true than any kind of journalism -- and the best journalists have always known this. True gonzo reporting needs the talents of a master journalist, the eye of an artist/photographer and the heavy balls of an actor. Because the writer must be a participant in the scene, while he's writing it -- or at least taping it, or even sketching it. Or all three. Probably the closest analogy to the ideal would be a film director/producer who writes his own scripts, does his own camera work and somehow manages to film himself in action, as the protagonist or at least a main character.
Hunter S. Thompson (1939-, American Journalist)

30 If I'd written all the truth I knew for the past ten years, about 600 people -- including me -- would be rotting in prison cells from Rio to Seattle today. Absolute truth is a very rare and dangerous commodity in the context of professional journalism.
Hunter S. Thompson (1939-, American Journalist)

31 I find I journalize too tediously. Let me try to abbreviate.
James Boswell (1740-1795, British Writer, Journalist)

32 Europe has a press that stresses opinions; America a press, radio, and television that emphasize news.
James Reston (1909-1995, Dutch Born American Journalist)

33 The dominant and most deep-dyed trait of the journalist is his timorousness. Where the novelist fearlessly plunges into the water of self-exposure, the journalist stands trembling on the shore in his beach robe. The journalist confines himself to the clean, gentlemanly work of exposing the grieves and shames of others.
Janet Malcolm (1934-, American Author)

34 Every journalist who is not too stupid or too full of himself to notice what is going on knows that what he does is morally indefensible. He is a kind of confidence man, preying on people's vanity, ignorance, or loneliness, gaining their trust and betraying them without remorse.
Janet Malcolm (1934-, American Author)

35 Every journalist owes tribute to the evil one.
Jean De La Fontaine (1621-1695, French Poet)

36 If the reporter has killed our imagination with his truth, he threatens our life with his lies.
Karl Kraus (1874-1936, Austrian Satirist)

37 Journalist: a person without any ideas but with an ability to express them; a writer whose skill is improved by a deadline: the more time he has, the worse he writes.
Karl Kraus (1874-1936, Austrian Satirist)

38 What a squalid and irresponsible little profession it is. Nothing prepares you for how bad Fleet Street really is until it craps on you from a great height.
Ken Livingstone

39 More than illness or death, the American journalist fears standing alone against the whim of his owners or the prejudices of his audience. Deprive William Safire of the insignia of the New York Times, and he would have a hard time selling his truths to a weekly broadsheet in suburban Duluth.
Lewis H. Lapham (1935-, American Essayist, Editor)

40 A professional whose job it is to explain to others what it personally does not understand.
Lord Northcliffe

41 Journalism over here is not only an obsession but a drawback that cannot be overrated. Politicians are frightened of the press, and in the same way as bull-fighting has a brutalizing effect upon Spain (of which she is unconscious), headlines of murder, rape, and rubbish, excite and demoralize the American public.
Margot Asquith (1864-1945, British Socialite)

42 Journalism without a moral position is impossible. Every journalist is a moralist. It's absolutely unavoidable. A journalist is someone who looks at the world and the way it works, someone who takes a close look at things every day and reports what she sees, someone who represents the world, the event, for others. She cannot do her work without judging what she sees.
Marguerite Duras (1914-, French Author, Filmmaker)

43 I see journalists as the manual workers, the laborers of the word. Journalism can only be literature when it is passionate.
Marguerite Duras (1914-, French Author, Filmmaker)

44 In the real world, nothing happens at the right place at the right time. It is the job of journalists and historians to correct that.
Mark Twain (1835-1910, American Humorist, Writer)

45 The real news is bad news.
Marshall Mcluhan (1911-1980, Canadian Communications Theorist)

46 Journalism is literature in a hurry.
Matthew Arnold (1822-1888, British Poet, Critic)

47 If you can't get a job as a pianist in a brothel you become a royal reporter.
Max Hastings

48 If a person is not talented enough to be a novelist, not smart enough to be a lawyer, and his hands are too shaky to perform operations, he becomes a journalist.
Norman Mailer (1923-, American Author)

49 Bad manners make a journalist.
Oscar Wilde (1856-1900, British Author, Wit)

50 It was a fatal day when the public discovered that the pen is mightier than the paving-stone, and can be made as offensive as the brickbat. They at once sought for the journalist, found him, developed him, and made him their industrious and well-paid servant. It is greatly to be regretted, for both their sakes.
Oscar Wilde (1856-1900, British Author, Wit)

51 There is much to be said in favor of modern journalism. By giving us the opinions of the uneducated, it keeps us in touch with the ignorance of the community. By carefully chronicling the current events of contemporary life, it shows us of what very little importance such events really are. By invariably discussing the unnecessary, it makes us understand what things are requisite for culture, and what are not.
Oscar Wilde (1856-1900, British Author, Wit)

52 A journalist is a person who has mistaken their calling.
Otto Von Bismarck (1815-1898, Prussian Statesman, Prime Minister)

53 I am a journalist and, under the modern journalist's code of Olympian objectivity (and total purity of motive), I am absolved of responsibility. We journalists don't have to step on roaches. All we have to do is turn on the kitchen light and watch the critters scurry.
P. J. O'Rourke (1947-, American Journalist)

54 Now he is a statesman, when what he really wants is to be what most reporters are, adult delinquents.
Peggy Noonan (1950-, American Author, Presidential Speechwriter)

55 I think there ought to be a club in which preachers and journalists could come together and have the sentimentalism of the one matched with the cynicism of the other. That ought to bring them pretty close to the truth.
Reinhold Niebuhr (1892-1971, American Theologian, Historian)

56 He types his labored column -- weary drudge! Senile fudge and solemn: spare, editor, to condemn these dry leaves of his autumn.
Robertson Davies (1913-, Canadian Novelist, Journalist)

57 Our job is like a baker's work -- his rolls are tasty as long as they're fresh; after two days they're stale; after a week, they're covered with mould and fit only to be thrown out.
Ryszard Kapuscinski (1932, Polish Report and Foreign Correspondent)

58 I still believe that if your aim is to change the world, journalism is a more immediate short- term weapon.
Tom Stoppard (1937-, Czech Playwright)

59 The facts fairly and honestly presented; truth will take care of itself.
William Allen White (1868-1944, American Editor, Writer)

60 I hate journalists. There is nothing in them but tittering jeering emptiness. They have all made what Dante calls the Great Refusal. The shallowest people on the ridge of the earth.
William Butler Yeats (1865-1939, Irish Poet, Playwright.)

61 The press is like the air, a chartered libertine.
William Pitt (1759-1806, British Statesman)

JOY

1   Happy is the person who not only sings, but feels God's eye is on the sparrow, and knows He watches over me. To be simply ensconced in God is true joy.
    Alfred A. Montapert (American Author)

2   A leaf fluttered in through the window this morning, as if supported by the rays of the sun, a bird settled on the fire escape, joy in the task of coffee, joy accompanied me as I walked...
    Anais Nin (1914-1977, French-born American Novelist, Dancer)

3   I have no greater joy then to hear that my children walk in truth. [John 4]
    Bible (Sacred Scriptures of Christians and Judaism)

4   Rejoice in the Lord always; again I will say, rejoice! [Philippians 4:4]
    Bible (Sacred Scriptures of Christians and Judaism)

5   I sometimes wander whether all pleasures are not substitutes for joy.
    C. S. Lewis (1898-1963, British Academic, Writer, Christian Apologist)

6   The joys we expect are not so bright, nor the troubles so dark as we fancy they will be.
    Charles Reade (1814-1884, British Novelist, Dramatist)

7   One joy scatters a hundred grieves.
    Chinese Proverb

8   Tranquil pleasures last the longest; we are not fitted to bear the burden of great joys.
    Christian Nevell Bovee (1820-1904, American Author, Lawyer)

9   I know the joy of fishes in the river through my own joy, as I go walking along the same river.
    Chuang Tzu (369-286 BC, Chinese Philosopher)

10 With coarse rice to eat, with water to drink, and my bent arm for a pillow -- I have still joy in the midst of all these things.
    Confucius (551-479 BC, Chinese Ethical Teacher, Philosopher)

11 Joy runs deeper than despair
    Corrie Ten Boom (Dutch Evangelist)

12 Joy is a subtle elf; I think one's happiest when he forgets himself.
    Cyril Tourneur

13 Joy is the feeling of grinning on the inside.
    Dr. Melba Colgrove (American Physician)

14 For one mother, joy is the quiet pleasure found in gently rubbing shampoo into her young child's hair. For another woman it's taking a long walk alone, while for yet another it's reviling in a much -- anticipated vacation.
    Eileen Stukane

15 Joy is free, unrestrained passion
    Eileen Stukane

16 One can endure sorrow alone, but it takes two to be glad.
    Elbert Hubbard (1859-1915, American Author, Publisher)

17 'Tis so much joy! 'Tis so much joy! If I should fail, what poverty! And yet, as poor as I Have ventured all upon a throw; Have gained! Yes! Hesitated so this side the victory!
    Emily Dickinson (1830-1886, American Poet)

18 All human joys are swift of wing, For heaven doth so allot it; That when you get an easy thing, You find you haven't got it.
    Eugene Field (1850-1895, American Writer)

19 The joy in life is to be used for a purpose. I want to be used up when I die.
    George Bernard Shaw (1856-1950, Irish-born British Dramatist)

20 Great joy, especially after a sudden change of circumstances, is apt to be silent, and dwells rather in the heart than on the tongue.
    Henry Fielding (1707-1754, British Novelist, Dramatist)

21 In this world, full often, our joys are only the tender shadows which our sorrows cast.
    Henry Ward Beecher (1813-1887, American Preacher, Orator, Writer)

22 Joys are our wings, sorrows our spurs.
    Jean Paul

23 Unexplained joy is always so keen that... it seems to hold enough to reconcile one to the inevitable.
    Jessie B. Fremont

24 The walls we build around us to keep sadness out also keeps out the joy.
    Jim Rohn (American Businessman, Author, Speaker, Philosopher)

25 For present joys are more to flesh and blood than a dull prospect of a distant good.
    John Dryden (1631-1700, British Poet, Dramatist, Critic)

26 The joy is that we can take back our bodies, reclaim our health, and restore ourselves to balance. We can take power over what and how we eat. We can rejuvenate and recharge ourselves, bringing healing to the wounds we carry inside us, and bringing to fuller life the wonderful person that each of us can be.
    John Robbins (American Health Expert, Author, Founder of Earthsave)

27 The primary joy of life is acceptance, approval, the sense of appreciation and companionship of our human comrades. Many men do not understand that the need for fellowship is really as deep as the need for food, and so they go through life accepting many substitutes for genuine, warm, simple.
    Joshua Loth Liebman

28 Joys divided are increased.
    Josiah Gilbert Holland (1819-1881, American Author)

29 What joy can the years bring half so sweet as the unhappiness they've taken away?
    Logan Pearsall Smith (1865-1946, Anglo-American Essayist, Aphorist)

30 Joy, has no cost.
Marianne Williamson (1952-, American Author, Lecturer on Spirituality)

31 Occasionally in life there are those moments of unutterable fulfillment which cannot be completely explained by those symbols called words. Their meanings can only be articulated by the inaudible language of the heart.
Martin Luther King Jr. (1929-1968, American Black Leader, Nobel Prize Winner, 1964)

32 The most profound joy has more of gravity than of gaiety in it.
Michel Eyquem De Montaigne (1533-1592, French Philosopher, Essayist)

33 Joy is a net of love by which you can catch souls. A joyful heart is the inevitable result of a heart burning with love
Mother Teresa (1910-1997, Albanian-born Roman Catholic Missionary)

34 Real joy comes not from ease or riches or from the praise of men, but from doing something worthwhile.
Pierre Coneille

35 Joy has this in common with pain, that it robs people of reason.
Platen

36 We ask God to forgive us for our evil thoughts and evil temper, but rarely, if ever ask Him to forgive us for our sadness.
R. W. Dale (Late 19th Century British Reverend)

37 We French found it and called it joie de vivre -- the joy of living.
Renee Repound

38 Joy is not in things, it is in us.
Richard Wagner (1813-1883, German Poet, Essayist, Composer)

39 Oh the wild joys of living! The leaping from rock to rock ... the cool silver shock of the plunge in a pool's living waters.
Robert Browning (1812-1889, British Poet)

40 Joy, rather than happiness, is the goal of life, for joy is the emotion which accompanies our fulfilling our natures as human beings. It is based on the experience of one's identity as a being of worth and dignity.
Rollo May (American Psychologist)

41 The surest mark of a Christian is not faith, or even love, but joy.
Samuel M. Shoemaker

42 Those who bring sunshine into the lives of others, cannot keep it from themselves.
Sir James M. Barrie (1860-1937, British Playwright)

43 When you were born, you cried and everybody else was happy. The only question that matters is this: When you die, will YOU be happy when everybody else is crying?
Tony Campolo (American Sociologist, Theologian)

44 He who binds to himself a joy doth the winged life destroy. But he who kisses the joy as it flies lives in Eternity's sunrise.
William Blake (1757-1827, British Poet, Painter)

45 Uncertainty and expectation are the joys of life.
William Congreve (1670-1729, British Dramatist)

JUDAISM AND JEWS

1 Being a Jew, one learns to believe in the reality of cruelty and one learns to recognize indifference to human suffering as a fact.
Andrea Dworkin (1946-, American Feminist Critic)

2 You can never betray the people who are dead, so you go on being a public Jew; the dead can't answer slurs, but I'm here. I would love to think that Jesus wants me for a sunbeam, but he doesn't.
Anita Brookner (1938-, British Novelist, Art Historian)

3 Is discord going to show itself while we are still fighting, is the Jew once again worth less than another? Oh, it is sad, very sad, that once more, for the umpteenth time, the old truth is confirmed: "What one Christian does is his own responsibility, what one Jew does is thrown back at all Jews.
Anne Frank (1929-1945, German Jewish Refugee, Diarist)

4 I marvel at the resilience of the Jewish people. Their best characteristic is their desire to remember. No other people has such an obsession with memory.
Elie Wiesel (1928-, Rumanian-born American Writer)

5 We found nothing grand in the history of the Jews nor in the morals inculcated in the Pentateuch. I know of no other books that so fully teach the subjection and degradation of woman.
Elizabeth Cady Stanton (1815-1902, American Social Reformer and Women's Suffrage Leader)

6 The Jews generally give value. They make you pay; but they deliver the goods. In my experience the men who want something for nothing are invariably Christians.
George Bernard Shaw (1856-1950, Irish-born British Dramatist)

7 The sons of Judah have to choose that God may again choose them. The divine principle of our race is action, choice, resolved memory.
George Eliot (1819-1880, British Novelist)

8 Pessimism is a luxury that a Jew can never allow himself.
Golda Meir (1898-1978, Prime Minister of Israel, 1969-74)

9 Who hates the Jews more than the Jew?
Henry Miller (1891-1980, American Author)

10 I determine who is a Jew.
Karl Lueger

11 From the outset, the Christian was the theorizing Jew, the Jew is therefore the practical Christian, and the practical Christian has become a Jew again.
Karl Marx (1818-1883, German Political Theorist, Social Philosopher)

12 Now a Jew, in the dictionary, is one who is descended from the ancient tribes of Judea, or one who is regarded as descended from that tribe. That's what it says in the dictionary; but you and I know what a Jew is -- One Who Killed Our Lord. And although there should be a statute of limitations for that crime, it seems that those who neither have the actions nor the gait of Christians, pagan or not, will bust us out, unrelenting dues, for another deuce.
Lenny Bruce (1925-1966, American Comedian)

13 Being a Jew is like walking in the wind or swimming: you are touched at all points and conscious everywhere.
Lionel Trilling (1905-1975, American Critic)

14 The Jew is neither a newcomer nor an alien in this country or on this continent; his Americanism is as original and ancient as that of any race or people with the exception of the American Indian and other aborigines. He came in the caravels of Columbus, and he knocked at the gates of New Amsterdam only thirty-five years after the Pilgrim Fathers stepped ashore on Plymouth Rock.
Oscar Solomon Straus

15 A Jewish man with parents alive is a fifteen-year-old boy, and will remain a fifteen-year-old boy until they die!
Philip Roth (1933-, American Novelist)

16 A Jew without Jews, without Judaism, without Zionism, without Jewishness, without a temple or an army or even a pistol, a Jew clearly without a home, just the object itself, like a glass or an apple.
Philip Roth (1933-, American Novelist)

17 That the Jews assumed a right exclusively to the benefits of God will be a lasting witness against them and the same will it be against Christians.
William Blake (1757-1827, British Poet, Painter)

JUDGMENT AND JUDGES

1 If we could first know where we are, and whither we are tending, we could then better judge what to do, and how to do it.
Abraham Lincoln (1809-1865, Sixteenth President of the USA)

2 There are few things wholly evil or wholly good. Almost everything, especially of government policy, is an inseparable compound of the two, so that our best judgment of the preponderance between them is continually demanded.
Abraham Lincoln (1809-1865, Sixteenth President of the USA)

3 There's no need to hang about waiting for the last judgment. It takes place every day.
Albert Camus (1913-1960, French Existential Writer)

4 It is with our judgments as with our watches: no two go just alike, yet each believes his own.
Alexander Pope (1688-1744, British Poet, Critic, Translator)

5 One out of four people in this country is mentally imbalanced. Think of your three closest friends. If they seem okay, then you're the one.
Ann Landers (1918-, American Advice Columnist)

6 Make no judgments where you have no compassion. .
Anne Mccaffrey

7 Don't judge men's wealth or godliness by their Sunday appearance.
Benjamin Franklin (1706-1790, American Scientist, Publisher, Diplomat)

8 Judge not according to appearance, but judge righteous judgment.
Bible (Sacred Scriptures of Christians and Judaism)

9 But let judgment run down as waters, and righteousness as a mighty stream.
Bible (Sacred Scriptures of Christians and Judaism)

10 Give me six lines written by the most honorable person alive, and I shall find enough in them to condemn them to the gallows.
Cardinal De Richelieu (1585-1642, French Statesman)

11 We are ashamed to seem evasive in the presence of a straightforward man, cowardly in the presence of a brave one, gross in the eyes of a refined one, and so on. We always imagine, and in imagining share, the judgments of the other mind.
Charles Horton Cooley (1864-1929, American Sociologist)

12 Never judge someone by who he's in love with; judge him by his friends. People fall in love with the most appalling people. Take a cool, appraising glance at his pals.
Cynthia Heimel

13 Hesitancy in judgment is the only true mark of the thinker.
Dagobert D. Runes (1902-1982, American Philosophical Writer)

14 Do not condemn the judgment of another because it differs from your own. You may both be wrong.
Dandemis

15 Let us remember, when we are inclined to be disheartened, that the private soldier is a poor judge of the fortunes of a great battle.
Dean William R. Inge (1860-1954, Dean of St Paul's, London)

16 I have a thing with the camera. The lens is unconditional. It doesn't judge you.
Debra Winger (1955-, American Actress)

17 Listening to both sides does not necessarily bring about a correct judgment.
Donald Rumsfeld

18 We should be lenient in our judgment, because often the mistakes of others would have been ours had we had the opportunity to make them.
Dr. Alsaker

19 The average man's judgment is so poor, he runs a risk every time he uses it.
Edgar Watson Howe (1853-1937, American Journalist, Author)

20 How easy it is to judge rightly after one sees what evil comes from judging wrongly!
Elizabeth Gaskell (1810-1865, British Novelist)

21 Judges don't age. Time decorates them.
Enid Bagnold (1889-1981, British Novelist, Playwright)

22 We find it hard to apply the knowledge of ourselves to our judgment of others. The fact that we are never of one kind, that we never love without reservations and never hate with all our being cannot prevent us from seeing others as wholly black or white.
Eric Hoffer (1902-1983, American Author, Philosopher)

23 It is a purely relative matter where one draws the plimsoll-line of condemnation, and if you find the whole of humanity falls below it you have simply made a mistake and drawn it too high. And are probably below it yourself.
Frances Partridge

24 Everyone complains of the badness of his memory, but nobody of his judgment.
François de La Rochefoucauld (1613-1680, French classical writer)

25 My guiding principle is this: Guilt is never to be doubted.
Franz Kafka (1883-1924, German Novelist, Short-Story Writer)

26 Judgments, value judgments concerning life, for or against, can in the last resort never be true: they possess value only as symptoms, they come into consideration only as symptoms -- in themselves such judgments are stupidities.
Friedrich Nietzsche (1844-1900, German Philosopher)

27 A judgment about life has no meaning except the truth of the one who speaks last, and the mind is at ease only at the moment when everyone is shouting at once and no one can hear a thing.
Georges Bataille (1897-1962, French Novelist, Critic)

28 Do not mind anything that anyone tells you about anyone else. Judge everyone and everything for yourself.
Henry James (1843-1916, American Author)

29 We judge ourselves by what we feel capable of doing, while others judge us by what we have already done.
Henry Wadsworth Longfellow (1819-1892, American Poet)

30 We judge others by their behavior. We judge ourselves by our intentions.
Ian Percy

31 People from a planet without flowers would think we must be mad with joy the whole time to have such things about us.
Iris Murdoch (1919-, British Novelist, Philosopher)

32 Human nature is so well disposed towards those who are in interesting situations, that a young person, who either marries or dies, is sure of being kindly spoken of.
Jane Austen (1775-1817, British Novelist)

33 Do not judge, and you will never be mistaken.
Jean Jacques Rousseau (1712-1778, Swiss Political Philosopher, Educationist, Essayist)

34 To say of men that they are bad is to say they are worse than we think we are, or worse than the ideal man whose image we have built up on the basis of a certain few.
Jean Rostand (1894-1977, French Biologist, Writer)

35 In the last analysis sound judgment will prevail.
Joseph Cannon

36 Remember, when the judgment's weak, the prejudice is strong.
K. O'Hara

37 One is never more on trial than in the moment of excessive good fortune.
Lew Wallace (1827-1905, American Writer, Soldier)

38 A judge is not supposed to know anything about the facts of life until they have been presented in evidence and explained to him at least three times.
Lord Chief Justice Parker

39 But men never violate the laws of God without suffering the consequences, sooner or later.
Lydia M. Child (1802-1880, American Abolitionist, Writer, Editor)

40 If you are pained by external things, it is not they that disturb you, but your own judgment of them. And it is in your power to wipe out that judgment now.
Marcus Aurelius (121-80 AD, Roman Emperor, Philosopher)

41 When one cannot appraise out of one's own experience, the temptation to blunder is minimized, but even when one can, appraisal seems chiefly useful as appraisal of the appraiser.
Marianne Moore (1887-1972, American Poet)

42 You can't depend on your judgment when your imagination is out of focus.
Mark Twain (1835-1910, American Humorist, Writer)

43 I have tried to make all my acts and commercial moves the result of definite consideration and sound judgment. There were never any great ventures or risks. I practiced honest, slow-growing business methods, and tried to back them with energy and good system.
Marshall Field (1834-1906, American Merchant)

44 We need very strong ears to hear ourselves judged frankly, and because there are few who can endure frank criticism without being stung by it, those who venture to criticize us perform a remarkable act of friendship, for to undertake to wound or offend a man for his own good is to have a healthy love for him.
Michel Eyquem De Montaigne (1533-1592, French Philosopher, Essayist)

45 It is a common seen by experience that excellent memories do often accompany weak judgments.
Michel Eyquem De Montaigne (1533-1592, French Philosopher, Essayist)

46 The judges of normality are present everywhere. We are in the society of the teacher-judge, the doctor-judge, the educator-judge, the "social worker" -judge.
Michel Foucault (1926-1984, French Essayist, Philosopher)

47   If you judge people, you have no time to love them.
Mother Teresa (1910-1997, Albanian-born Roman Catholic Missionary)

48   No accurate thinker will judge another person by that which the other person's enemies say about him.
Napoleon Hill (1883-1970, American Speaker, Motivational Writer, "Think and Grow Rich")

49   Don't judge any man until you have walked two moons in his moccasins.
Native American Proverb

50   Men in general judge more by the sense of sight than by the sense of touch, because everyone can see, but only a few can test by feeling. Everyone sees what you seem to be, few know what you really are, and those few do not dare take a stand against the general opinion.
Niccolo Machiavelli (1469-1527, Italian Author, Statesman)

51   Men in general judge more from appearances than from reality. All men have eyes, but few have the gift of penetration.
Niccolo Machiavelli (1469-1527, Italian Author, Statesman)

52   Men are more apt to be mistaken in their generalizations than in their particular observations.
Niccolo Machiavelli (1469-1527, Italian Author, Statesman)

53   Rule # 1 -- "Use your good judgment in all situations." There will be no additional rules.
Nordstrom Employee Manual (American Retail Department Stores)

54   People see themselves as the center of the universe and judge everything as it relates to them.
Peace Pilgrim (1908-1981, American Peace Activist)

55   A hasty judgment is a first step to recantation.
Publilius Syrus (1st Century BC, Roman Writer)

56   In our judgment of human transactions, the law of optics is reversed, we see most dimly the objects which are close around us.
Richard Whately (1787-1863, British Prelate, Writer)

57   When you meet a man, you judge him by his clothes; when you leave, you judge him by his heart.
Russian Proverb

58   It took me a long time not to judge myself through someone else's eyes.
Sally Field (American actress)

59   A Judge may be a farmer; but he is not to geld his own pigs. A Judge may play a little at cards for his own amusement; but he is not to play at marbles, or chuck farthing in the Piazza.
Samuel Johnson (1709-1784, British Author)

60   If you would judge, understand.
Seneca (4 BC-65 AD, Spanish-born Roman Statesman, philosopher)

61   If you judge, investigate.
Seneca (4 BC-65 AD, Spanish-born Roman Statesman, philosopher)

62   Great Spirit, help me never to judge another until I have walked in his moccasins.
Sioux Indian Prayer

63   Men of ill judgment ignore the good that lies within their hands, till they have lost it.
Sophocles (495-406 BC, Greek Tragic Poet)

64   Outward judgment often fails, inward judgment never.
Theodore Parker (1810-1860, American Minister)

65   For all right judgment of any man or things it is useful, nay, essential, to see his good qualities before pronouncing on his bad.
Thomas Carlyle (1795-1881, Scottish Philosopher, Author)

66   Foolish men imagine that because judgment for an evil thing is delayed, there is no justice; but only accident here below. Judgment for an evil thing is many times delayed some day or two, some century or two, but it is sure as life, it is sure as death.
Thomas Carlyle (1795-1881, Scottish Philosopher, Author)

67   A man is not good or bad for one action.
Thomas Fuller (1608-1661, British Clergyman, Author)

68   It is no little wisdom for a man to keep himself in silence and in good peace when evil words are spoken to him, and to turn his heart to God and not to be troubled with man's judgment.
Thomas p Kempis (1379-1471, German Monk, Mystic, Religious Writer)

69   I followed his argument with the blank uneasiness which one might feel in the presence of a logical lunatic.
Victor Serge

70   Be curious, not judgmental.
Walt Whitman (1819-1892, American Poet)

71   Rabbi Zusya said that on the Day of Judgment, God would ask him, not why he had not been Moses, but why he had not been Zusya.
Walter Kaufmann (1921-1980, American Philosopher)

72   We are more casual about qualifying the people we allow to act as advocates in the courtroom than we are about licensing electricians.
Warren E. Burger

73   When you judge another, you do not define them, you define yourself.
Wayne Dyer (1940-, American Psychotherapist, Author, Lecturer)

74   To sit in judgment of those things which you perceive to be wrong or imperfect is to be one more person who is part of judgment, evil or imperfection.
Wayne Dyer (1940-, American Psychotherapist, Author, Lecturer)

75   Real magic in relationships means an absence of judgment of others.
Wayne Dyer (1940-, American Psychotherapist, Author, Lecturer)

⁷⁶ Less judgment than wit is more sail than ballast.
William Penn (1644-1718, British Religious Leader, Founder of Pennsylvania)

⁷⁷ Speak of me as I am. Nothing extenuate, nor set down aught in malice.
William Shakespeare (1564-1616, British Poet, Playwright, Actor)

⁷⁸ My salad days, when I was green in judgment.
William Shakespeare (1564-1616, British Poet, Playwright, Actor)

⁷⁹ One cool judgment is worth a thousand hasty counsels. The thing to do is to supply light and not heat.
Woodrow T. Wilson (1856-1924, Twenty-eighth President of the USA)

JURIES

¹ The stupidity of one brain multiplied by twelve.
Elbert Hubbard (1859-1915, American Author, Publisher)

² Our civilization has decided that determining the guilt or innocence of men is a thing too important to be trusted to trained men. When it wants a library catalogued, or the solar system discovered, or any trifle of that kind, it uses up its specialists. But when it wishes anything done which is really serious, it collects twelve of the ordinary men standing round. The same thing was done, if I remember right, by the Founder of Christianity.
Gilbert K. Chesterton (1874-1936, British Author)

³ The penalty for laughing in a courtroom is six months in jail; if it were not for this penalty, the jury would never hear the evidence.
H. L. Mencken (1880-1956, American Editor, Author, Critic, Humorist)

⁴ I'm no idealist to believe firmly in the integrity of our courts and in the jury system -- that is no ideal to me, it is a living, working reality. Gentlemen, a court is no better than each man of you sitting before me on this jury. A court is only as sound as its jury, and a jury is only as sound as the men who make it up.
Harper Lee (1926-, American Author)

⁵ A jury is composed of twelve men of average ignorance.
Herbert Spencer (1820-1903, British Philosopher)

⁶ Write that down," the King said to the jury, and the jury eagerly wrote down all three dates on their slates, and then added them up, and reduced the answer to shillings and pence.
Lewis Carroll (1832-1898, British Writer, Mathematician)

⁷ A fox should not be of the jury at a goose's trial.
Thomas Fuller (1608-1661, British Clergyman, Author)

⁸ The jury, passing on the prisoner's life, may have in the sworn twelve a thief or two guiltier than him they try.
William Shakespeare (1564-1616, British Poet, Playwright, Actor)

JUSTICE

¹ The probability that we may fail in the struggle ought not to deter us from the support of a cause we believe to be just.
Abraham Lincoln (1809-1865, Sixteenth President of the USA)

² Justice is better than chivalry if we cannot have both.
Alice Stone Blackwell (1857-1950, American suffrage Writer and Journalist)

³ The virtue of justice consists in moderation, as regulated by wisdom.
Aristotle (384-322 BC, Greek Philosopher)

⁴ Justice is truth in action.
Benjamin Disraeli (1804-1881, British Statesman, Prime Minister)

⁵ There is no such thing as justice, in or out of court.
Clarence Darrow (1857-1938, American Lawyer)

⁶ Reconciliation should be accompanied by justice, otherwise it will not last. While we all hope for peace it shouldn't be peace at any cost but peace based on principle, on justice.
Corazon Aquino (President of the Philippines)

⁷ Justice is always violent to the party offending, for every man is innocent in his own eyes.
Daniel Defoe (1661-1731, British Author)

⁸ Sentences are like sharp nails, which force truth upon our memories.
Denis Diderot (1713-1784, French Philosopher)

⁹ The essence of justice is mercy.
Edwin Hubbel Chapin (1814-1880, American Author, Clergyman)

¹⁰ You don't have many suspects who are innocent of a crime. That's contradictory. If a person is innocent of a crime, then he is not a suspect.
Edwin Meese

¹¹ There is no such thing as justice in the abstract; it is merely a compact between men
Epicurus (341-270 BC, Greek Philosopher)

¹² Every story has three sides. Yours, mine and the facts.
Foster M. Russell

¹³ Next to religion, let your care be to promote justice.
Francis Bacon (1561-1626, British Philosopher, Essayist, Statesman)

¹⁴ Law and justice are not always the same. When they aren't, destroying the law may be the first step toward changing it.
Gloria Steinem (1934-, American Feminist Writer, Editor)

¹⁵ Injustice is relatively easy to bear what stings is justice.
H. L. Mencken (1880-1956, American Editor, Author, Critic, Humorist)

¹⁶ The court is most merciful when the accused is most rich.
Hebrew Proverb

17 A good and faithful judge ever prefers the honorable to the expedient.
Horace (65-8 BC, Italian Poet)

18 Justice is incidental to law and order.
J. Edgar Hoover (1895-1972, American Public Servant)

19 Every offense is avenged on earth.
Johann Wolfgang Von Goethe (1749-1832, German Poet, Dramatist, Novelist)

20 A judge who cannot punish, in the end associates themselves with the criminal.
Johann Wolfgang Von Goethe (1749-1832, German Poet, Dramatist, Novelist)

21 The injustice done to an individual is sometimes of service to the public.
Junius (1769-1771, Anonymous British Letter Writer)

22 In the halls of justice, the only justice is in the halls.
Lenny Bruce (1925-1966, American Comedian)

23 Justice is a concept. Muscle is the reality.
Linda Blandford

24 True liberty can exist only when justice is equally administered to all.
Lord Mansfield (1867-1915, British Artist, Author)

25 The foundation of justice is good faith.
Marcus T. Cicero (106-43 BC, Great Roman Orator, Politician)

26 Justice consists of doing no one injury, decency in giving no one offense.
Marcus T. Cicero (106-43 BC, Great Roman Orator, Politician)

27 Never pray for justice, because you might get some.
Margaret Atwood (1939-, Canadian Novelist, Poet, Critic)

28 Justice is a temporary thing that must at last come to an end; but the conscience is eternal and will never die.
Martin Luther (1483-1546, German Leader of the Protestant Reformation)

29 Injustice anywhere is a threat to justice everywhere.
Martin Luther King Jr. (1929-1968, American Black Leader, Nobel Prize Winner, 1964)

30 Our judgments judge us, and nothing reveals us, exposes our weaknesses, more ingeniously than the attitude of pronouncing upon our fellows.
Paul Valery (1871-1945, French Poet, Essayist)

31 They do injury to the good who spares the bad.
Publilius Syrus (1st Century BC, Roman Writer)

32 He who spares the bad injures the good.
Publilius Syrus (1st Century BC, Roman Writer)

33 The sad duty of politics is to establish justice in a sinful world.
Reinhold Niebuhr (1892-1971, American Theologian, Historian)

34 Justice should remove the bandage from her eyes long enough to distinguish between the vicious and the unfortunate.
Robert Green Ingersoll (1833-1899, American Orator, Lawyer)

35 Let justice be done through the heavens fall.
Roman Maxim

36 We leave unmolested those who set the fire to the house, and prosecute those who sound the alarm.
Sebastien-Roch Nicolas De Chamfort (1741-1794, French Writer, Journalist, Playwright)

37 May be is very well, but Must is the master. It is my duty to show justice without recompense.
Seneca (4 BC-65 AD, Spanish-born Roman Statesman, philosopher)

38 Nothing is to be preferred before justice.
Socrates (469-399 BC, Greek Philosopher of Athens)

39 How unfair the fate which ordains that those who have the least should be always adding to the treasury of the wealthy.
Terence (185-159 BC, Roman Writer of Comedies)

40 I am unjust, but I can strive for justice. My life's unkind, but I can vote for kindness. I, the unloving, say life should be lovely. I, that am blind, cry out against my blindness.
Vachel Lindsay (1878-1931, American Poet)

41 A man's vanity tells him what is honor, a man's conscience what is justice.
Walter Savage Landor (1775-1864, British Poet, Essayist)

42 The right to be let alone is indeed the beginning of all freedom.
William O. Douglas (1898-1980, American Supreme Court Justice)

43 Time is the justice that examines all offenders. [As You Like It]
William Shakespeare (1564-1616, British Poet, Playwright, Actor)

44 The whole history of the world is summed up in the fact that, when nations are strong, they are not always just, and when they wish to be just, they are no longer strong.
Winston Churchill (1874-1965, British Statesman, Prime Minister

TABLE OF CONTENTS

802

Printed in Great Britain
by Amazon

14672400R00459